WEBSTER'S
Student Dictionary

WEBSTER'S
Student Dictionary

Edited by P. H. Collin

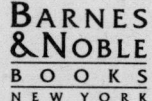
BARNES
&NOBLE
BOOKS
NEW YORK

Contents

About This Dictionary

This entirely revised dictionary lists the words most commonly used in English, giving definitions and in many cases examples of use. Grammar notes are given in many entries – irregular plurals for nouns, comparatives and superlatives for adjectives, past forms for verbs. Where a word is commonly used with a preposition, that preposition is given in bold letters.

To make the dictionary as compact as possible, many derived words are listed under the main headwords and do not appear separately: so *package* is to be found under *pack*, *secrecy* under *secret*, etc.

Abbreviations Used in the Dictionary

adj.	adjective	*inter.*	interjection
adv.	adverb	*n.*	noun
approx.	approximately	*pl.*	plural
Brit.	British	*prep.*	preposition
def.	definite	*sl.*	slang
e.g.	for example	*s.o.*	someone
esp.	especially	*sth.*	something
indef.	indefinite	*usu.*	usually
inf.	informal	*v.*	verb

Pronunciation

The following signs are used to show the pronunciation of words in the dictionary.

Where there are several pronunciations that are current only the most common are indicated, -r is never pronounced at the end of words, but when a word ending in -r is followed by a vowel the -r can be pronounced.

Words are also marked with a sign (') to show where the strong beat should be placed, but this is only a guide; the pronunciation of a word can change depending on the position of the word in a sentence.

æ	back	ə	afraid	ð	then	p	penny
ɑː	farm	əʊ	boat	dʒ	just	r	round
ɒ	top	əʊə	lower	f	fog	s	some
aɪ	pipe	ɜː	word	g	go	ʃ	short
aʊ	how	iː	heap	h	hand	t	too
aɪə	fire	ɪ	hit	j	yes	tʃ	chop
aʊə	flower	ɪə	hear	k	catch	θ	thing
ɔː	bought	uː	school	χ	loch	v	voice
ɔɪ	toy	ʊ	book	l	last	w	was
e	fed	ʌ	but	m	mix	z	zoo
eə	hair	b	back	n	nut	ʒ	treasure
eɪ	take	d	dog	ŋ	sing		

Alphabet

These are the letters of the English alphabet, showing their pronunciation.

Aa	eɪ	**Hh**	eɪtʃ	**Oo**	əʊ	**Vv**	viː
Bb	biː	**Ii**	aɪ	**Pp**	piː	**Ww**	dʌbljuː
Cc	siː	**Jj**	dʒeɪ	**Qq**	kjuː	**Xx**	eks
Dd	diː	**Kk**	keɪ	**Rr**	ɑː	**Yy**	waɪ
Ee	iː	**Ll**	el	**Ss**	es	**Zz**	zee
Ff	ef	**Mm**	em	**Tt**	tiː		
Gg	dʒiː	**Nn**	en	**Uu**	juː		

Aa

a, an [*stressed* eɪ, æn; *unstressed* ə, ən] (a *before words beginning with a consonant, and before words beginning with* **u** *pronounced* juː; **an** *before* **a, e, i, o** *or* **u** *and before* **h** *where* **h** *is not pronounced*) *indefinite article* (a) one; **give me a stamp and an envelope.** (b) not a particular one; **he has a big nose.** (c) for each one/in each one; **thirty miles an hour.** (d) a certain; **I know a Dr. Smith.**

A1 [eɪ'wʌn] in very good condition.

aard•vark ['ɑːdvɑːk] *n.* ant-eating animal of South America.

AB ['eɪ'biː] *n.* able seaman.

a•back [ə'bæk] *adv.* **taken aback** = surprised, usu. unpleasantly.

ab•a•cus ['æbəkəs] *n.* (*pl.* **-ses, -ci**) device for counting, made of small beads which slide along rods in a frame.

a•baft [ə'bɑːft] *adv.* (*of ships*) at/toward the stern; aft.

a•a•lo•ne [æbə'ləʊnɪ] *n.* type of Pacific shellfish.

a•ban•don [ə'bændən] *v.* (a) to leave. (b) to give up. **a•ban•don•ment,** *n.* giving up.

a•base [ə'beɪs] *v.* (a) (*formal*) to lower the rank, esteem or position of (s.o.); **to a. oneself** = to grovel/to apologize. (b) to humiliate.

a•bashed [ə'bæʃt] *adj.* ashamed.

a•bate [ə'beɪt] *v.* to become less strong. **a•bate•ment,** *n.* reduction (in amount, force, etc.); **a. in taxes** = reduction in taxes.

ab•at•toir ['æbətwɑː] *n.* slaughterhouse/place where animals are killed for meat.

ab•bess ['æbes] *n.* (*pl.* **-es**) woman in charge of nuns in a convent.

ab•bey ['æbɪ] *n.* Christian religious establishment with living quarters, etc., grouped around a church.

ab•bot ['æbət] *n.* man in charge of monks in an abbey.

ab•bre•vi•ate [ə'briːvɪeɪt] *v.* to shorten (words, names, etc.). **ab•bre•vi•a•tion** [əbriːvɪ'eɪʃn] *n.* group of letters representing a larger word.

ABC [eɪbiː'siː] *n.* the alphabet.

ab•di•cate ['æbdɪkeɪt] *v.* to give up the throne. **ab•di•ca•tion** [æbdɪ'keɪʃn] *n.* giving up (of a throne).

ab•do•men ['æbdəmen] *n.* lower part of the body, containing the stomach, bowels, etc. **ab•dom•i•nal** [æb'dɒmɪnl] *adj.* referring to the abdomen.

ab•duct [æb'dʌkt] *v.* to remove or carry off (s.o.) by force. **ab•duc•tion,** *n.* removal (of s.o.) by force. **ab•duc•tor,** *n.* person who abducts s.o.

a•beam [ə'biːm] *adv.* (*of ships*) side by side.

ab•er•ra•tion [æbə'reɪʃn] *n.* (a) change from what is usual. (b) sudden attack of forgetfulness; **mental a.** = slight confusion. **ab•er•rant** [ə'berənt] *adj.* abnormal/not usual.

a•bet [ə'bet] *v.* (**abetted**) to aid and a. s.o. = to be s.o.'s accomplice in a crime. **a•bet•tor,** *n.* person who abets s.o.

a•bey•ance [ə'beɪəns] *n.* suspension (of a law, etc.); **in a.** = not being applied.

ab•hor [əb'hɔː] *v.* to feel hatred/horror for (sth). **ab•hor•rent** [əb'hɒrənt] *adj.* disgusting/which makes you shudder. **ab•hor•rence,** *n.* horror/great dislike.

a•bide [ə'baɪd] *v.* (a) to stick to/to follow; **to a. by a promise** = to stand by what you have promised. (b) (*only with negative*) to like; **I can't a. the smell of garlic. a•bid•ing,** *adj.* which stays/remains.

a•bil•i•ty [ə'bɪlɪtɪ] *n.* power to do sth; capability; **to the best of my a.** = as best I can.

ab in•i•ti•o [æbɪ'nɪʃɪəʊ] *adj.* (course) which starts from the beginning.

ab•ject ['æbdʒekt] *adj.* (a) very miserable. (b) cowardly/extremely humble. **ab•ject•ly,** *adv.* in a miserable/humble way.

ab•jure [æb'dʒʊə] *v.* to swear not to do sth.

æ back, ɑː farm, ɒ top, aɪ pipe, aʊ how, aɪə fire, aʊə flower, ɔː bought, ɔɪ toy, e fed, eə hair, eɪ take, ə afraid, əʊ boat, ʊə lower, vː word, iː heap, ɪ hit, ɪə hear, uː school, ʊ book, ʌ but, b back, d dog, ð then, dʒ just, f fog, g go, h hand, j yes, k catch, l last, m mix, n nut, ŋ sing, p penny, r round, s some, ʃ short, t too, tʃ chop, θ thing, v voice, w was, z zoo, ʒ treasure

ab•la•tion [æ'bleɪʃn] *n.* operation to remove an organ.

a•blaze [ə'bleɪz] *adv.* in flames.

a•ble ['eɪbl] *adj.* having the ability (**to do sth**). **a. seaman** = experienced seaman. **a•ble•ism**, *n.* bias against disabled people. **a•bly** ['eɪblɪ] *adv.* very efficiently.

ab•iu•tions [ə'bluːʃənz] *n. pl.* (*formal*) washing (face/hands, etc.).

ab•nor•mal [æb'nɔːml] *adj.* not normal. **ab•nor•mal•ly,** *adv.* not normally/unusually. **ab•nor•mal•i•ty** [æbnɔː'mælɪtɪ] *n.* (*pl.* **abnormalities**) being abnormal; unusualness/peculiarity.

a•board [ə'bɔːd] *adv. & prep.* on/in (a ship/aircraft/train/bus).

a•bode [ə'bəʊd] *n.* (*formal*) home; **of no fixed a.** = with no permanent address; **right of a.** = the right to live in a country.

a•bol•ish [ə'bolɪʃ] *v.* to cancel/to remove. **ab•o•li•tion** [æbə'lɪʃn] *n.* act of abolishing. **ab•o•li•tion•ist**, *n.* person who is in favor of abolition (esp. of slavery/capital punishment).

a•bom•i•na•ble [ə'bomɪnəbl] *adj.* horrible/disgusting; **the a. snowman** = yeti. **a•bom•i•na•bly,** *adv.* in a horrible way. **a•bom•i•nate** [ə'bomɪneɪt] *v.* to dislike intensely. **a•bom•i•na•tion** [əbomɪ'neɪʃn] *n.* unpleasant/disgusting thing.

ab•o•rig•i•ne [æbə'rɪdʒɪnɪ] *n.* member of a race which was living in a country before the country was settled: original inhabitant. **ab•o•rig•i•nal.** 1. *adj.* referring to aborigines. 2. *n.* aborigine.

a•bor•tion [ə'bɔːʃn] *n.* (deliberate) termination of a pregnancy. **a•bort,** *v.* (a) to cause an abortion to (s.o.). (b) to stop (a project) taking place. **a•bor•tion•ist**, *n.* person who carries out an illegal abortion. **a•bor•tive,** *adj.* (plan) which fails.

ABO sys•tem [eɪbiː'əʊ] *n.* system of classifying blood by the letters A, B and O.

a•bound [ə'baʊnd] *v.* (**in**) to be full of.

a•bout [ə'baʊt] *adv. & prep.* (a) in various places; **clothes lying a. on the floor; there's a lot of flu a.** (b) concerning; **tell me a. your book; what do you want to speak to me a.? how a. a cup of tea?** = would you like a cup of tea? (c) (*in the army*) round; **a. turn** = facing the opposite direction. (d) approximately; **a. three feet deep; at a. four o'clock.** (e) on the point (of doing sth); **just a. to go out.** (f) in the process of doing sth; **while you're a. it, can you mail this letter?**

a•bove [ə'bʌv] *adv. & prep.* (a) higher than; **a. the clouds; the temperature was a. 40°.** (b) louder than; **I can't hear you a. the noise.** (c) they're living a. their means = more extravagantly than they can afford. (d) earlier on (in a book); higher up (on a page). **a•bove•board,** *adj.* open/honest; not corrupt.

ab•ra•ca•dab•ra [æbrəkə'dæbrə] *n.* traditional magic spell.

a•brade [æ'breɪd] *v.* to scrape off (a surface).

a•bra•sion [ə'breɪʒn] *n.* scraping off (of the skin). **a•bra•sive** [ə'breɪzɪv] 1. *adj.* (a) grinding (substance). (b) sharp/rude (manner, comment). 2. *n.* rough substance for smoothing a surface.

a•breast [ə'brest] *adv.* in a row; level (with sth); **walking three a.** = three people side by side; **to keep a. of/with sth** = to keep up with the latest developments.

a•bridged [ə'brɪdʒd] *adj.* shortened. **a•bridg•ment**, *n.* shortened version (of a long book).

a•broad [ə'brɔːd] *adv.* in or to another country.

ab•ro•gate ['æbrəgeɪt] *v.* (*formal*) to end (a law, a treaty). **ab•ro•ga•tion** [æbrə'geɪʃn] *n.* ending (of a treaty).

ab•rupt [ə'brʌpt] *adj.* sudden (departure); brusque (way of speaking). **ab•rupt•ly,** *adv.* suddenly; brusquely. **ab•rupt•ness,** *n.* suddenness; brusqueness.

ab•scess ['æbses] *n.* (*pl.* **-es**) collection of pus in the body.

ab•scond [æb'skond] *v.* to run away.

ab•seil ['æbseɪl] *v.* to come down a cliff or wall by means of a fixed rope coiled around one's body.

ab•sence ['æbsəns] *n.* (a) not being there; **she was sentenced in her a.** (b) lack; **in the a. of a map we had to ask our way. ab•sent** 1. *adj.* ['æbsənt] not present. 2. *v.* [əb'sent] **to a. oneself** = to stay away (**from** class/a meeting) deliberately. **ab•sen•tee** [æbsən'tiː] *n.* person who is absent; **a. landlord** = landlord/owner who does not live near the property owned and takes no interest in it. **ab•sen•tee•ism**, *n.* deliberately staying away from work. **ab•sent-mind•ed,** *adj.* forgetful. **ab•sent-mind•ed•ly,** *adv.* forgetfully. **ab•sent-mind•ed•ness,** *n.* being often forgetful.

ab•so•lute ['æbsəluːt] *adj.* complete; **the president assumed a. power** = became a dictator. **ab•so•lute•ly,** *adv.* totally. **ab•so•lut•ism**, *n.* political theory that governments should have absolute power.

ab•so•lu•tion [æbsə'luːʃn] *n.* blessing by a priest to forgive sin.

ab•solve [əb'zolv] *v.* to remove blame for a sin from (s.o.); to release (s.o.) from a promise.

ab•sorb [əb'zɔːb] v. (a) to soak up (liquid); to deaden (a shock); to accept (a stranger/outside body) into a group. (b) **absorbed in** = completely busy with; **it's an absorbing story** = it holds your attention. **ab•sorb•ent**, adj. which absorbs. **ab•sorb•er**, n. **shock a.** = part of a car which softens the shock of a bump to the passengers. **ab•sorp•tion** [əb-'zɔːpʃn] n. act of absorbing.

ab•stain [əb'steɪn] v. (**from**) not to do sth deliberately; **Mr. Smith abstained** = refused to vote. **ab•stain•er**, n. person who does not drink alcohol.

ab•ste•mi•ous [əb'stiːmɪəs] adj. not drinking (or eating) too much. **ab•ste•mi•ous•ness**, n. not drinking (or eating) too much.

ab•sten•tion [əb'stenʃn] n. refusal to do sth; **several abstentions** = several people did not vote.

ab•sti•nence ['æbstɪnəns] n. not drinking/eating to excess; **total a.** = not drinking any alcohol.

ab•stract 1. adj ['æbstrækt] not concrete; (painting) which does not reproduce sth recognizable. 2. n. ['æbstrækt] (a) quality of not being concrete; **in the a.** = without mentioning specific cases. (b) abstract picture. (c) summary. 3. v. [əb'strækt] (a) to remove; to steal. (b) to summarize. **ab•stract•ed**, adj vague/dreamy; thoughtful. **ab•strac•tion**, n. (a) removing; stealing. (b) vague idea.

ab•struse [əb'struːs] adj. very difficult to understand.

ab•surd [əb'sɜːd] adj. very odd; ridiculous. **ab•surd•i•ty**, n. fact of being absurd. **ab•surd•ly**, adv. ridiculously.

a•bun•dant [ə'bʌndənt] adj. in large quantities. **a•bun•dance**, n. large quantity. **a•bun•dant•ly**, adv. plentifully; very much.

a•buse 1. n. [ə'bjuːs] (a) wrong use/bad use. (b) evil. (c) rude words/insults; **term of a.** = rude/insulting word. (d) very bad treatment (often sexual, of a person, such as a child). 2. v. [ə'bjuːz] (a) to put to wrong use; **he abused my confidence** = he took advantage of my confidence. (b) to insult. (c) to mistreat; to make bad use of. **a•bu•sive** [ə'bjuːsɪv] adj. insulting.

a•but [ə'bʌt] v. (**abutted**) (formal) **to a. on a property** = to be next to a property.

a•bys•mal [ə'bɪzml] adj. extremely large; **the weather was a.** = very bad. **a•bys•mal•ly**, adv. extremely badly.

a•byss [ə'bɪs] n. (pl. -es) very deep hole; very deep part of the sea.

Ac symbol for actinium.

AC abbrev. for alternating current.

A/C = account.

a•ca•cia [ə'keɪʃə] n. common tropical tree which produces gum.

ac•a•dem•ic [ækə'demɪk] 1. adj. (a) abstract (idea, question). (b) relating to study at a school, college, or university; **a. staff** = teaching staff at school, college, or university. 2. student/teacher at a college or university. **ac•a•dem•i•cal•ly**, adv. referring to academic matters/to teaching at a school, college, or university. **ac•a•de•mi•cian** [ækædə-'mɪʃn] n. member of an academy. **a•cad•e•my** [ə'kædəmɪ] n. (a) school giving specialized instruction or training. **military a.** = training school for officers in the armed forces. **a. of music** = school for musicians. (b) society for the promotion of literature/art/science.

ac•cede [ək'siːd] v. (a) **to a. to the throne** = to become king or queen. (b) (formal) to agree (**to**).

ac•cel•er•ate [æk'seləreɪt] v. (to cause to) go faster. **ac•cel•er•a•tion** [ækselə'reɪʃn] n. going faster. **ac•cel•er•a•tor** [æk'seləreɪtə] n. pedal (in a car) which allows more fuel into the engine, and increases speed.

ac•cent ['æksənt] n. (a) way of pronouncing; **an Irish a.** (b) small sign over a letter to show that it is pronounced differently. (c) stress. **ac•cen•tor**, n. small brown singing bird. **ac•cen•tu•ate** [ək'sentjʊeɪt] v. to stress/to make more obvious. **ac•cen•tu•a•tion** [əksentjʊ'eɪʃn] n. stressing.

ac•cept [ək'sept] v. (a) to take (thing which is offered). (b) to agree (to do sth). (c) **accepted custom** = sth which is usually done. **ac•cept•a•bil•i•ty**, n. being acceptable. **ac•cept•a•ble**, adj. which you can easily accept. **ac•cept•ance**, n. (a) receiving (of thing offered). (b) agreement (to do sth).

ac•cess ['ækses] 1. n. way of getting to person/place; **a. road** = road leading off a main road to buildings; **to have easy a. to** = to be able to get sth easily. 2. v. to call up information which is stored in a computer. **ac•ces•si•ble** [ək'sesɪbl] adj. able to be reached easily. **ac•ces•si•bil•i•ty** [əksesɪ-'bɪlɪtɪ] n. being accessible.

ac•ces•sion [ək'seʃn] n. **a.** (**to the throne**) = be-

æ back, aː farm, ɒ top, aɪ pipe, aʊ how, aɪə fire, aʊə flower, ɔː bought, ɔɪ toy, e fed, eə hair, eɪ take, ə afraid, əʊ boat, əʊə lower, ɜː word, iː heap, ɪ hit, ɪə hear, uː school, ʊ book, ʌ but, b back, d dog, ð then, dʒ just, f fog, g go, h hand, j yes, k catch, l last, m mix, n nut, ŋ sing, p penny, r round, s some, ʃ short, t too, tʃ chop, θ thing, v voice, w was, z zoo, ʒ treasure

coming king or queen. **ac•ces•sion**, *n.* sth. added; **a. to a library** = new books added to a library.

ac•ces•so•ry [ək'sesərɪ] 1. *n.* (a) piece of minor equipment which is added to main items; **a. bag** = bag for carrying extra items to attach to a camera. (b) nonessential items of clothing (handbag, gloves, hat, etc.). (c) **charged with being an a. to the crime** = with helping to commit the crime. 2. *adj.* nonessential.

ac•ci•dent ['æksɪdənt] *n.* thing which happens by chance, often with unfortunate results; **I discovered the documents by a.; fatal a.** = accident where s.o. is killed. **ac•ci•den•tal** [æksɪ'dentl] 1. *adj.* by accident; not on purpose. 2. *n. (in music)* additional sharp, flat or natural. **ac•ci•den•tal•ly**, *adv.* by accident; not on purpose. **ac•ci•dent-prone**, *adj.* (of a person) likely to have a lot of accidents.

ac•claim [ə'kleɪm] 1. *n.* great shout of praise. 2. *v.* to greet with a shout of praise. **ac•cla•ma•tion** [æklə'meɪʃn] *n.* act of acclaiming.

ac•cli•mate [ə'klaɪmət] *v.* to make (sth/s.o.) used to a new climate or a new way of living. **ac•cli•ma•tion** [əklaɪ'meɪʃn] *n.* becoming acclimated.

ac•co•lade ['ækʊleɪd] *n.* sign of praise or approval.

ac•com•mo•date [ə'kɒmədeɪt] *v.* (a) to adapt; to supply (s.o.) with sth. (b) to provide lodging for (s.o.). **ac•com•mo•dat•ing**, *adj.* helpful; giving satisfaction; always ready to help. **ac•com•mo•da•tion** [əkɒmə-'deɪʃn] *n.* (a) place to live/to sleep; **all the a. in the town have been booked.** (b) agreement/compromise. (c) adjustment.

ac•com•pa•ny [ə'kʌmpnɪ] *v.* (a) to go with; **sauce to a. the fish** = to be served with the fish. (b) to play (usu. the piano) while s.o. sings or plays another instrument. **ac•com•pa•ni•ment**, *n.* (a) thing which accompanies. (b) music played to accompany a soloist. **ac•com•pa•nist**, *n.* person who accompanies a soloist.

ac•com•plice [ə'kʌmplɪs] *n.* person who helps another person commit a crime.

ac•com•plish [ə'kʌmplɪʃ] *v.* to finish/to carry out (a plan, etc.). **ac•com•plished**, *adj.* gifted/talented; skilled. **ac•com•plish•ment**, *n.* (a) finishing (of a task). (b) **accomplishments** = talents.

ac•cord [ə'kɔːd] *n.* (a) agreement; **with one a.** = all together/in agreement. (b) **of your own a.** = spontaneously/with no prompting. **ac•cord•ance**, *n.* agreement; **in a. with your instructions** = following your instructions. **ac•cord•ing•ly**, *adv.* in accordance; corre-

spondingly. **ac•cord•ing to**, *adv.* (a) as s.o. says or writes; as stated by s.o. (b) by/in relation to; **separate the children into groups a. to their ages.**

ac•cor•di•on [ə'kɔːdɪən] *n.* **(piano) a.** = musical instrument with a bellows and a keyboard. **ac•cor•di•on•ist**, *n.* person who plays an accordion.

ac•cost [ə'kɒst] *v.* to go to/to come up to (s.o.) and speak to him/her.

ac•count [ə'kaʊnt] 1. *n.* (a) story/description; **by all accounts** = according to what everyone said. (b) statement of money; **bank a.** = money deposited in a bank; **checking a.** = account from which you can draw money without giving notice; **savings a.** = account where you leave money for some time and on which interest is paid; **to pay money on a.** = to pay part of the total bill in advance; **expense a.** = money which an employee of a business is allowed to spend on entertainment and personal expenses which are paid for by the business. (c) statement or record showing the financial position of a business. (d) **he turned the accident to a.** = he was able to profit from the accident. (e) **he was called to a.** = he was asked to explain; **she gave a good a. of herself** = she came out of the game/examination, etc., very well. (f) **to take sth into a.** = to make allowances for sth. (g) **on a. of** = because of; **I was worried on her a.** = I was afraid sth might happen to her; **on no a.** = not under any circumstances. 2. *v.* **to a. for sth** = to explain. **ac•count•a•bil•i•ty** [əkaʊntə'bɪlɪtɪ] *n.* being accountable **(for** sth). **ac•count•a•ble**, *adj.* responsible. **ac•count•an•cy**, *n.* principles/profession of being an accountant. **ac•count•ant**, *n.* person who deals with the accounts (of a business). **ac•count•ing**, *n.* accountancy.

ac•cou•ter•ments [ə'kuːtrəmənts] *n. pl.* (usu. bulky or complicated) equipment which is carried.

ac•cred•it [ə'kredɪt] *v.* to authorize.

ac•cre•tion [ə'kriːʃn] *n.* increase in size by gradual additions.

ac•crue [ə'kruː] *v.* to increase by addition. **ac•cru•al**, *n.* increase made by addition.

acct. *abbrev. for* account.

ac•cu•mu•late [ə'kjuːmjʊleɪt] *v.* to pile up. **ac•cu•mu•la•tion** [əkjuːmjʊ'leɪʃn] *n.* act of accumulating; pile/heap. **ac•cu•mu•la•tor** [ə'kjuːmjʊleɪtə] *n.* a person or thing which accumulates.

ac•cu•rate ['ækjʊrət] *adj.* completely correct. **ac•cu•ra•cy**, *n.* being accurate; complete correctness. **ac•cu•rate•ly**, *adv.* completely correctly.

ac•cuse [ə'kju:z] *v.* to say that s.o. has done sth wrong; **the police accused him of stealing the car. ac•cu•sa•tion** [ækju'zeɪʃn] *n.* saying that s.o. has done sth wrong. **ac•cu•sa•tive** [ə'kju:zətɪv] *adj. & n. (in grammar)* (case) which shows the object of a verb. **ac•cused,** *n.* person who has been accused of a crime. **ac•cus•er,** *n.* person who accuses s.o. **ac•cus•ing,** *adj.* **in an a. tone** = as if accusing. **ac•cus•ing•ly,** *adv.* as if accusing.

ac•cus•tom [ə'kʌstəm] *v.* to make (s.o.) used (to sth).

ace [eɪs] *n.* (a) playing card which shows only one spot; **the a. of diamonds.** (b) person who is very brilliant at doing sth; **an a. pilot.** (c) *(in tennis)* shot which your opponent cannot return.

ac•er•bate ['æsəbeɪt] *v.* to make worse.

a•cer•bi•ty [ə'sɜːbɪti] *n. (formal)* sharpness (of flavor/character).

ac•e•tate ['æsɪteɪt] *n.* type of synthetic fiber.

a•ce•tic [ə'si:tɪk] *adj.* referring to vinegar.

ac•e•tone ['æsɪtəʊn] *n.* colorless liquid, used to dissolve solids.

a•cet•y•lene [ə'setɪli:n] *n.* gas which burns with a very bright light.

ache [eɪk] 1. *n.* pain; *(see* **toothache, head-ache,** *etc.).* 2. *v.* to hurt. **ach•ing,** *adj.* which hurts.

a•chieve [ə'tʃi:v] *v.* to succeed in doing (sth); to reach (a goal). **a•chieve•ment,** *n.* what you achieve; successful undertaking/exploit.

A•chil•les' heel [ə'kɪli:z'hi:l] *n.* weak spot. **A•chil•les' tendon,** *n.* tendon at the back of the ankle.

ach•ro•mat•ic [ækrəʊ'mætɪk] *adj.* without color.

ac•id ['æsɪd] 1. *n.* usually liquid chemical substance which contains hydrogen, corrodes some metals, and turns litmus paper red; **the a. test** = test which will show the true value of s.o. or sth. 2. *adj.* bitter/unpleasant. **a•cid•i•fy,** *v.* to make substances acid. **a•cid•i•ty** [ə'sɪdɪti] *n.* (a) acid contents. (b) bitterness. **ac•id rain,** *n.* rain with a high level of acidity, caused by pollution.

ac•knowl•edge [ək'nɒlɪdʒ] *v.* (a) to admit (that sth is true). (b) to reply to say you have received (a letter). **ac•knowl•edg•ment,** *n.* admission (that sth is true); reply stating that you have received sth; **my letter has not had any a.** = no one has replied to it; *(in a book)* **ac-knowledgments** = the list of people the author wants to thank for help.

ac•me ['ækmɪ] *n.* highest point.

ac•ne ['æknɪ] *n.* skin disease, with spots on the face/neck, etc.

ac•o•lyte ['ækəlaɪt] *n.* person who helps a priest during religious ceremonies.

ac•o•nite ['ækənaɪt] *n.* small spring flower which is poisonous.

a•corn ['eɪkɔ:n] *n.* fruit of an oak tree.

a•cous•tic [ə'ku:stɪk] 1. *adj.* referring to sound; **a. coupler** = device for linking a computer to a telephone handset, allowing data to be transmitted; **a. guitar** = ordinary guitar (as opposed to an electric guitar). 2. *n.* **acoustics** = (i) study of sound; (ii) ability to carry sound without distortion.

ac•quaint [ə'kweɪnt] *v.* (a) to inform. (b) **to be acquainted with** = to know. **ac•quaint•ance,** *n.* (a) knowing; **to make the a. of** = to get to know. (b) person you know (slightly).

ac•qui•esce [ækwɪ'es] *v. (formal)* to agree. **ac•qui•es•cence,** *n.* agreement. **ac•qui•es•cent,** *adj.* in agreement.

ac•quire [ə'kwaɪə] *v.* to get into your possession; **acquired immune deficiency syndrome (AIDS)** = condition, caused by the human immunodeficiency virus (HIV), in which the body's immune system breaks down, making the patient susceptible to any infection. **ac•qui•si•tion** [ækwɪ'zɪʃn] *n.* (a) act of acquiring. (b) thing you have acquired. **ac•quis•i•tive** [ə'kwɪzɪtɪv] *adj.* always ready to acquire things. **ac•quis•i•tive•ness,** *n.* love of acquiring things.

ac•quit [ə'kwɪt] *v.* **(acquitted)** (a) to decide that someone is innocent. (b) **he acquitted himself well** = he did well. **ac•quit•tal,** *n.* decision that a person is innocent.

a•cre ['eɪkə] *n.* unit for measuring the area of land (43,560 square feet or 4047 square meters). **a•cre•age** ['eɪkrɪdʒ] *n.* area in acres.

ac•rid ['ækrɪd] *adj.* bitter/pungent (smell).

ac•ri•mo•ni•ous [ækrɪ'məʊnɪəs] *adj.* bitter (argument). **ac•ri•mo•ny** ['ækrɪmənɪ] *n.* bitterness (of argument).

ac•ro•bat ['ækrəbæt] *n.* person who does spectacular physical exercises. **ac•ro•bat•ic** [ækrə'bætɪk] *adj.* referring to spectacular exercises. **ac•ro•bat•ics,** *n. pl.* spectacular physical exercises.

æ back, ɑ: farm, ɒ: top, aɪ pipe, aʊ how, aɪə fire, aʊə flower, ɔ: bought, ɔɪ toy, e fed, eəhair, eɪ take, ə afraid, əʊ boat, əʊə lower, ɜ: word, i: heap, ɪ hit, ɪə hear, u: school, ʊ book, ʌ but, b back, d dog, ð then, dʒ just, f frog, g go, h hand, j yes, k catch, l last, m mix, n nut, ŋ sing, p penny, r round, s some, ʃ short, t too, tʃ chop, θ thing, v voice, w was, z zoo, ʒ treasure

ac•ro•nym ['ækrənɪm] *n.* word (like NATO) formed from the initials of other words.

a•crop•o•lis [æ'krɒpəlɪs] *n.* castle protecting a town in ancient Greece.

a•cross [ə'krɒs] *adv. & prep.* (a) from one side to the other; **it is twelve inches a.** (b) on the other side; **a. the street.** (c) **I came/ran a. this** = I found it. **across-the-board,** *adj.* which applies to everyone or everyone.

a•cros•tic [ə'krɒstɪk] *n.* poem/puzzle in which the first letters of each line form a word.

a•cryl•ic [ə'krɪlɪk] *adj. & n.* (material/paint) made from acid.

act [ækt] 1. *n.* (a) thing which is done; **we caught him in the a.** = as he was doing it; **a. of God** = natural disaster which cannot be prevented. (b) large section of a play. 2. *v.* (a) to play (a part in a play). (b) to do sth; **to a. on behalf of** = represent; **to a. as** = do the work of. (c) to behave. (d) to take effect/to work. **act•ing.** 1. *adj.* **a. president** = person who is taking the place of the president. 2. *n.* profession of an actor. **ac•tion** ['ækʃn] *n.* (a) doing; **out of a.** = not working. (b) thing done. (c) **the a. of the play** = what happens in it. (d) mechanism (of a gun, watch, etc.). (e) lawsuit; **an a. for libel.** (f) warfare; **killed in a.** = on the battlefield. **ac•tion•a•ble,** *adj.* (sth) for which s.o. could bring a lawsuit against you. **ac•ti•vate** ['æktɪveɪt] *v.* to put into action. **ac•tive** ['æktɪv] *adj.* vigorous/agile; (volcano) which still erupts; **on a. duty** = serving full-time military duty. **ac•tive•ly,** *adv.* in an active way. **ac•tiv•ist,** *n.* person who actively supports a political policy. **ac•tiv•i•ty** [æk'tɪvɪtɪ] *n.* (a) movement/being active. (b) occupation. **ac•tor, actress** ['æktə, 'æktrəs] *n.* (*pl.* **-es**) person who acts in the theater/motion pictures/on television.

ac•tin•i•um [æk'tɪnɪəm] *n.* (*element:* Ac) radioactive metal.

ac•tu•al ['æktjʊəl] *adj.* real; **in a. fact** = really. **ac•tu•al•i•ty** [æktjʊ'ælɪtɪ] *n.* reality. **ac•tu•al•ly,** *adv.* really.

ac•tu•ary ['æktjʊərɪ] *n.* person who calculates insurance rates. **ac•tu•ar•i•al** [æktjʊ'eərɪəl] *adj.* referring to insurance rates.

ac•tu•ate ['æktjʊeɪt] *v.* to set in motion/to start off.

a•cu•i•ty [ə'kjuːɪtɪ] *n.* sharpness (of sight).

a•cu•men ['ækjuːmən] *n.* ability to make shrewd decisions.

ac•u•punc•ture ['ækjʊpʌŋktʃə] *n.* way of healing and curing by placing the tips of needles in the skin. **ac•u•punc•tur•ist,** *n.* doctor who practices acupuncture.

a•cute [ə'kjuːt] *adj.* (a) very sharp (angle). (b) sudden serious (illness/pain). (c) perceptive.

a•cute•ly, *adv.* very sharply (aware).
a•cute•ness, *n.* sharpness (of pain); seriousness (of illness); clearness (of hearing).

ad [æd] *n. inf.* advertisement.

A.D. ['eɪ'diː] *abbreviation for* Anno Domini (*Latin for* in the year of our Lord) (*used to show dates after the birth of Christ*) **A.D.** 923.

ad•age ['ædɪdʒ] *n.* wise old saying.

a•da•gio [ə'dɑːdʒɪəʊ] *n.* slow piece of music.

Ad•am ['ædəm] *n. inf.* **I don't know him from A.** = I have no idea who he is; **A.'s apple** = lump in the front of a person's neck.

ad•a•mant ['ædəmənt] *adj.* fixed in your opinion/intentions.

a•dapt [ə'dæpt] *v.* to change (sth) so that it fits; to make (sth) more suitable. **a•dapt•a•bil•i•ty** [ədæptə'bɪlɪtɪ] *n.* ease of adapting yourself to new circumstances. **a•dapt•a•ble,** *adj.* able to (be) adapt(ed) easily. **ad•ap•ta•tion** [ædæp'teɪʃn] *n.* written work which is adapted from another. **a•dapt•er, adaptor,** *n.* electric plug which allows several plugs to be fitted to the same socket; small disk which allows a record with a large central hole to be fitted on a turntable.

add [æd] *v.* (a) to join (sth to sth else). (b) to say/to write sth more. (c) to make a total. **ad•den•dum** [ə'dendəm] *n.* (*pl.* **addenda**) piece added, as at the end of a book. **add up,** *v.* to make a total of (figures); **these figures don't add up** = the total given is incorrect.

ADD ['eɪ'diː'diː] *abbrev. for* attention deficit disorder.

ad•der ['ædə] *n.* viper.

ad•dict ['ædɪkt] *n.* person who cannot stop from doing sth (usu. which is harmful); **drug a.** = person who cannot stop taking a drug; **TV a.** = person who is always watching television. **ad•dict•ed** [ə'dɪktɪd] *adj.* (to) (person) who cannot stop (taking a drug). **ad•dic•tion** [ə'dɪkʃn] *n.* **drug a.** = inability to stop taking a drug. **ad•dic•tive,** *adj.* which causes addiction.

ad•di•tion [ə'dɪʃn] *n.* (a) act of adding; **in a.** = added to this; also. (b) thing added. **ad•di•tion•al,** *adj.* further. **ad•di•tive** ['ædɪtɪv] *n.* substance, usu. chemical, which is added.

ad•dled ['ædld] *adj.* (a) confused. (b) rotten (egg).

ad•dress [ə'dres] 1. *n.* (*pl.* **-es**) (a) number of house, name of street, town, county, etc., where a person lives/where an office is situated; **a. book** = book containing a list of addresses. (b) formal speech. 2. *v.* (a) to write the name and address of the person/the business to whom sth is being sent. (b) to speak to (s.o.). (c) (*in golf*) to aim at the ball.

ad•dress•ee [ædre'si:] *n.* person to whom a letter is addressed.

ad•duce [ə'dju:s] *v.* (*formal*) to bring added proof (of sth).

ad•e•noids ['ædənɔɪdz] *n. pl.* small growths in the back of the throat. **ad•e•noi•dal** [ædɪ-'nɔɪdl] *adj.* referring to the adenoids.

a•dept ['ædept] *adj. & n.* (person who is) clever (at doing sth).

ad•e•quate ['ædɪkwət] *adj.* (large) enough. **ad•e•quate•ly**, *adv.* enough.

ad•here [əd'hɪə] *v.* to stick (**to**). **ad•her•ence**, *n.* sticking/attachment. **ad•her•ent**, *n.* person who belongs to (a society, etc.).

ad•he•sion [əd'hi:ʒn] *n.* attachment/sticking; ability to stick. **ad•he•sive** [əd'hi:zɪv] 1. *adj.* which sticks; **a. tape** = tape coated on one side with a substance which sticks. 2. *n.* glue.

ad hoc [æd'hɒk] *adj.* which applies to a particular case.

a•dieu [ə'dju:] *n.* (*poetic*) goodbye.

ad in•fi•ni•tum [ædɪnfɪ'naɪtəm] *adv.* for ever.

ad•i•pose ['ædɪpəus] *adj.* fatty (tissue).

ad•ja•cent [ə'dʒeɪsənt] *adj.* (**to**) next to/touching/side by side.

ad•jec•tive ['ædʒəktɪv] *n.* word used to describe a noun. **ad•jec•ti•val** [ædʒek'taɪvl] *adj.* used like an adjective. **ad•jec•ti•val•ly**, *adv.* like an adjective.

ad•join [ə'dʒɔɪn] *v.* to be next to sth/to touch sth.

ad•journ [ə'dʒɜ:n] *v.* to put off (a meeting) to a later date; **let's a. to the bar** = let's stop talking here and continue in the bar. **ad•journ•ment**, *n.* putting off (a meeting) to a later date.

ad•ju•di•cate [ə'dʒu:dɪkeɪt] *v.* to give a decision (in a dispute); to be the judge (in a competition). **ad•ju•di•ca•tion** [ədʒu:dɪ'keɪʃn] *n.* decision (in a dispute); judging (of a competition). **ad•ju•di•ca•tor** [ə'dʒu:dɪkeɪtə] *n.* judge.

ad•junct ['ædʒʌŋkt] *n.* thing additional (**to** sth).

ad•just [ə'dʒʌst] *v.* to put right by making a slight change. **ad•just•a•ble**, *adj.* which can be changed slightly. **ad•just•er, adjustor** *n.* person who calculates the extent of losses in an insurance claim. **ad•just•ment**, *n.* slight change made (**to** a mechanism).

ad•ju•tant ['ædʒətənt] *n.* military officer who assists in administration.

ad-lib ['æd'lɪb] *v.* (**ad-libbed**) *inf.* to speak without a script.

ad•min•is•ter [əd'mɪnɪstə] *v.* to govern/to rule (a country/an office); to run (a business/an estate); **to a. an oath to s.o.** = to make s.o. swear an oath. **ad•min•is•tra•tion** [ədmɪnɪ'streɪʃn] *n.* ruling (of a country); the government. **ad•min•is•tra•tive**, *adj.* which administers; referring to administration. **ad•min•is•tra•tor**, *n.* person who administers.

ad•mi•ra•ble ['ædmərəbl] *adj. see* **admire**.

ad•mi•ral ['ædmərəl] *n.* highest-ranking officer in the navy; **red a.** = type of red and black butterfly. **ad•mi•ral•ty**, *n.* court or laws that deal with maritime affairs. **the Admiralty**, *n.* British government department dealing with the navy.

ad•mire [əd'maɪə] *v.* to look at (sth) with pleasure. **ad•mi•ra•ble** ['ædmərəbl] *adj.* remarkable; excellent. **ad•mi•ra•bly**, *adv.* remarkably; excellently. **ad•mi•ra•tion** [ædmə'reɪʃn] *n.* feeling of pride/pleasure. **ad•mir•er** [əd'maɪərə] *n.* person who admires. **ad•mir•ing**, *adj.* (look) showing admiration. **ad•mir•ing•ly**, *adv.* in an admiring way.

ad•mis•sion [əd'mɪʃn] *n.* (a) being allowed to enter; **no a.** = no one can enter. (b) saying that sth is true. **ad•mis•si•ble** [əd'mɪsɪbl] *adj.* (evidence) that can be admitted.

ad•mit [əd'mɪt] *v.* (**admitted**) (a) to allow to enter. (b) to say that sth is true. (c) to accept (evidence/idea, etc.). **ad•mit•tance**, *n.* entrance. **ad•mit•ted•ly**, *adv.* according to general opinion.

ad•mix•ture [æd'mɪkstʃə] *n.* thing which is added to make a mixture.

ad•mon•ish [əd'mɒnɪʃ] *v.* to scold s.o./to tell s.o. off. **ad•mo•ni•tion** [ædmə'nɪʃn] *n.* scolding.

ad nau•se•am [æd'nɔ:zɪəm] *adv.* until one is sick of it.

a•do [ə'du:] *n.* **without any more a.** = without any more fuss.

a•do•be [ə'dəubɪ] *n.* bricks made from clay dried in the sun.

ad•o•les•cence [ædə'lesns] *n.* period between childhood and being an adult. **ad•o•les•cent**, *adj. & n.* (referring to) a young person between child and adult.

æ back, a: farm, ɒ: top, aɪ pipe, aʊ how, aɪə fire, aʊə flower, ɔ: bought, ɔɪ toy, e fed, eəhair, eɪ take, ə afraid, əʊ boat, əʊə lower, v: word, i: heap, ɪ hit, ɪə hear, u: school, ʊ book, ʌ but, b back, d dog, ð then, dʒ just, f fog, g go, h hand, j yes, k catch, l last, m mix, n nut, ŋ sing, p penny, r round, s some, ʃ short, t too, tʃ chop, θ thing, v voice, w was, z zoo, ʒ treasure

a•dopt [ə'dɒpt] v. (a) to take (s.o.) legally as your son or daughter. (b) to follow/to take up (a line of argument); to put on (an air). (c) to prescribe (a book) for use in class. **a•dop•tion** [ə'dɒpʃn] n. (a) legal taking of a child as your own. (b) prescribing (of a book) for use in class. **a•dop•tive**, adj. who has (been) adopted.

a•dore [ə'dɔ:] v. to love very strongly. **a•dor•a•ble**, adj. pretty/lovely. **ad•o•ra•tion** [ædə'reɪʃn] n. strong love/worship. **a•dor•er**, n. person who adores.

a•dorn [ə'dɔ:n] v. to cover with ornaments/to decorate. **a•dorn•ment**, n. adorning; ornament.

ad•re•nal [ə'dri:nəl] adj. referring to the kidneys. **a•dren•a•line** [ə'drenəlɪn] n. secretion which is produced by a gland when s.o. is excited/afraid.

a•drift [ə'drɪft] adv. **to cast a boat a.** = to let a boat float without control; **to cut yourself a.** = to separate yourself.

a•droit [ə'drɔɪt] adj. skillful/clever (with your hands). **a•droit•ly**, adv. smartly.

ad•sorb [æd'zɔ:b] v. to form a thin film on the surface of sth.

ad•u•la•tion [ædjʊ'leɪʃn] n. wild praise/excessive flattery.

a•dult ['ædʌlt, ə'dʌlt] adj. & n. grown-up (person); fully grown (animal).

a•dul•ter•ate [ə'dʌltəreɪt] v. to water down; to add sth of inferior quality to (a substance).

a•dul•ter•er, **a•dul•ter•ess** [ə'dʌltərə, ə'dʌltərəs] n. person who commits adultery. **a•dul•ter•ous**, adj. referring to adultery. **a•dul•ter•y**, n. (of married person) having sexual intercourse with s.o. to whom he/she is not married.

ad va•lo•rem [ædvə'lɔ:rəm] adj. (tax) calculated on the value of the thing being taxed.

ad•vance [əd'vɑ:ns] 1. n. (a) forward movement: **a. guard** = troops sent ahead of the main force. (b) **in a.** = early; beforehand. (c) **to make advances to** = to try to attract. (d) payment made early. 2. v. (a) to go forward. (b) to put forward; **he advanced me ten dollars** = he gave me ten dollars as an early payment. **ad•vanced**, adj. (a) (subject) which is studied after several years' initial study; **a. student** = student who has studied for several years. (b) **the season is well a.** = the season is coming to an end; **in an a. state of decay** = very decayed. **ad•vance•ment**, n. progress (of science, etc.).

ad•van•tage [əd'vɑ:ntɪdʒ] n. useful thing which will help you to be successful; **to take a. of** = to profit from; **to take a. of s.o.** = to use or cheat for your own benefit; **her dress shows off** her figure to a. = makes her figure look perfect. **ad•van•ta•geous** [ædvən'teɪdʒəs] adj. profitable/useful.

ad•vent ['ædvent] n. (a) coming; arrival. (b) **Advent** = church season before Christmas.

ad•ven•ti•tious [ædven'tɪʃəs] adj. (root) which develops from a plant's stem and not from another root.

ad•ven•ture [əd'ventʃə] n. new, exciting and dangerous experience. **ad•ven•tur•er**, n. person who aims to make a fortune by taking risks. **ad•ven•tur•ous**, adj. bold (person); exciting (life). **ad•ven•tur•ous•ly**, adv. boldly. **ad•ven•tur•ous•ness**, n. being adventurous.

ad•verb ['ædvɜ:b] n. word used to describe a verb/an adjective/another adverb. **ad•ver•bi•al** [əd'vɜ:bɪəl] adj. used as an adverb. **ad•ver•bi•al•ly**, adv. like an adverb.

ad•ver•sar•y ['ædvəsrɪ] n. person you are fighting against.

ad•verse ['ædvɜ:s] adj. (a) contrary (winds). (b) bad; unfavorable (conditions). **ad•verse•ly**, adv. badly. **ad•ver•si•ty** [əd'vɜ:sɪtɪ] n. difficulty.

ad•vert [æd'vɜ:t] v. (formal) to refer to.

ad•ver•tise ['ædvətaɪz] v. to show that sth is for sale/to publicize sth; **she advertised for a new secretary** = put an advertisement in the paper asking people to apply for the job; **there's no need to a. the fact** = there's no need to tell everyone the secret. **ad•ver•tise•ment** [əd'vɜ:tɪsmənt] n. announcement that sth is for sale/is wanted. **ad•ver•tis•er**, n. person who advertises. **ad•ver•tis•ing**, n. action of announcing the sale of sth; business of describing goods for sale; **a. agency** = company which designs and places advertisements. **ad•ver•to•ri•al** [ˌædvə'tɔːrɪəl] n. advertisement in the style of an editorial.

ad•vice [əd'vaɪs] n. (a) suggestion as to what should be done; **a piece of a.** (b) official notification.

ad•vise [əd'vaɪz] v. to suggest what should be done. **ad•vis•a•bil•i•ty**, n. being recommended. **ad•vis•a•ble**, adj. which you would recommend. **ad•vis•ed•ly**, adv. after a lot of thought; deliberately. **ad•vis•er, advisor**, n. person who gives advice. **ad•vi•so•ry**, adj. **in an a. capacity** = as an adviser.

ad•vo•ca•cy ['ædvəkəsɪ] n. pleading for; support for.

ad•vo•cate 1. n. ['ædvəkət] (a) person who pleads for a cause. (b) lawyer who pleads in certain courts. 2. ['ædvəkeɪt] v. to recommend/to plead.

adz [ædz] *n.* ax with the blade at right angles to the handle.

ae•gis ['iːdʒɪs] *n.* (*formal*) **under the a. of** = supported/patronized by.

ae•o•li•an [iːˈəʊlɪən] *adj.* caused by the wind.

ae•on ['iːɒn] *n. see* **eon.**

aer•ate [eəˈreɪt] *v.* to fill sth with air or gas.

aer•i•al ['eərɪəl] 1. *adj.* referring to the air. 2. *n.* device for sending or receiving radio or TV signals.

aer•ie ['iːrɪ] *n.* nest of an eagle; high and inaccessible house.

aer•o•bat•ics [eərəˈbætɪks] *n. pl.* trick flying (as a display).

aer•o•bic [eəˈrəʊbɪk] *adj.* needing oxygen to take place or to exist. **aer•o•bics,** *n. pl.* exercises to improve the body's use of oxygen.

aer•o•drome ['eərədrəʊm] *n. Brit* small airfield.

aer•o•dy•nam•ics [eərədaɪˈnæmɪks] *n.* science of movement of flying bodies in the air.

aer•o•nau•ti•cal [eərəˈnɔːtɪkl] *adj.* referring to aircraft flying. **aer•o•nau•tics,** *n.* science of flying aircraft.

aer•o•pha•gia [eərəʊˈfeɪdʒɪə] *n.* habit of swallowing air.

aer•o•plane ['eərəpleɪn] *n. Brit.* airplane.

aer•o•sol ['eərəsɒl] *n.* canister filled under pressure, which sends out a spray when the button is pushed.

aer•o•space ['eərəʊspeɪs] *n.* the space around the earth, including the atmosphere.

aes•thete ['iːsθiːt] *n.* person who appreciates beauty in art. **aes•thet•ic** [iːsˈθetɪk] *adj.* pleasing from an artistic point of view. **aes•thet•i•cal•ly,** *adv.* from an artistic point of view.

a•far [əˈfɑː] *adv.* **from a.** = from a long way away.

af•fa•ble ['æfəbl] *adj.* pleasant/courteous. **af•fa•bil•i•ty** [æfəˈbɪlɪtɪ] *n.* pleasantness/courtesy. **af•fa•bly,** *adv.* in a pleasant/friendly way.

af•fair [əˈfeə] *n.* (a) business; **that's my a.** = it's my business and not yours; **his affairs** = his business. (b) **he's having an a. with her** = he's her lover. (c) **the present state of affairs** = how things are at present.

af•fect [əˈfekt] *v.* (a) to pretend/to put on. (b) to touch/to change sth. **af•fec•ta•tion** [æfekˈteɪʃn] *n.* pretense. **af•fect•ed,** *adj.* pretended/put on. **af•fect•ing,** *adj.* touching/which makes you feel emotion.

af•fec•tion [əˈfekʃn] *n.* liking/love.
af•fec•tion•ate, *adj.* showing love or fondness for s.o. **af•fect•ive dis•or•der,** *n.* any mental disorder, e.g. depression, characterized by abnormal moods. **af•fec•tion•ate•ly,** *adv.* in a loving way.

af•fi•da•vit [æfɪˈdeɪvɪt] *n.* written sworn statement.

af•fil•i•ate [əˈfɪlɪeɪt] *v.* to link (a small group to a larger one). **af•fil•i•a•tion** [əfɪlɪˈeɪʃn] *n.* **political a.** = political link.

af•fin•i•ty [əˈfɪnɪtɪ] *n.* (*pl.* **affinities**) closeness/similarity of character; strong attraction. **affinity card,** *n.* card that gives a discount to members of a club, college, etc. when used to buy goods.

af•firm [əˈfɜːm] *v.* (a) to state. (b) to make a statement (in court, but not under oath). **af•fir•ma•tion** [æfəˈmeɪʃn] *n.* statement. **af•firm•a•tive** [əˈfɜːmətɪv] 1. *adj.* agreeing. 2. *n.* **the answer is in the a.** = the answer is yes. **af•firm•a•tive•ly,** *adj.* **she answered a.** = she answered yes. **affirmative ac•tion,** *n.* policy to counter discrimination, esp. in employment, by providing special opportunities for women and minorities.

af•fix [əˈfɪks] *v.* (*formal*) to attach.

af•flict [əˈflɪkt] *v.* to torture/to torment. **af•flic•tion** [əˈflɪkʃn] *n.* torment; cause of distress.

af•flu•ence ['æfluəns] *n.* wealth. **af•flu•ent,** *adj.* rich; **a. society** = society where most people have enough money.

af•ford [əˈfɔːd] *v.* to have enough money to pay for (sth).

af•for•est•a•tion [æfɒrɪˈsteɪʃn] *n.* planting trees to make a forest.

af•fray [əˈfreɪ] *n.* (*formal*) fight between several people in public.

af•front [əˈfrʌnt] 1. *n.* offense. 2. *v.* to insult.

a•field [əˈfiːld] *adv.* **to go far a.** = to go a long way.

a•fire [əˈfaɪə] *adj.* on fire.

a•flame [əˈfleɪm] *adj.* (*formal*) on fire.

af•la•tox•in [æfləˈtɒksɪn] *n.* poison substance which forms on seeds and nuts.

a•float [əˈfləʊt] *adv.* floating.

a•foot [əˈfʊt] *adv.* **there's a plan a.** = a plan is being prepared; **there's sth a.** = sth is being plotted.

a•fore•said [əˈfɔːsed] *adj.* (*formal*) which has been mentioned before.

a•fore•thought [əˈfɔːθɔːt] *adj.* (*formal*) **with**

æ back, ɑː farm, ɒ top, aɪ pipe, aʊ how, aɪə fire, aʊə flower, ɔː bought, ɔɪ toy, e fed, eəhair, eɪ take, ə afraid, əʊ boat, əʊə lower, ɜː word, iː heap, ɪ hit, ɪə hear, uː school, ʊ book, ʌ but, b back, d dog, ð then, dʒ just, f fog, g go, h hand, j yes, k catch, l last, m mix, n nut, ŋ sing, p penny, r round, s some, ʃ short, t too, tʃ chop, θ thing, v voice, w was, z zoo, ʒ treasure

malice a. = having planned the crime beforehand.

a•fraid [əˈfreɪd] *adj.* (a) frightened (by); **she's a. of the dark.** (b) sorry to have to say; **I'm a. she's ill.**

a•fresh [əˈfreʃ] *adv.* (all over) again.

Af•ri•can [ˈæfrɪkən] *adj. & n.* (person) from Africa; **A. violet** = small houseplant with blue or pink flowers.

Afro- [ˈæfrəʊ] *prefix meaning* African/between Africa and another country.

Af•ro [ˈæfrəʊ] *adj. & n.* **A. (hairstyle)** = type of bouffant hairstyle.

aft [ɑːft] *adv.* at/toward the back of a ship.

af•ter [ˈɑːftə] 1. *adv.* next/later. 2. *prep.* next to/following; **the police are a. you** = the police are looking for you; **what's he a.?** = what does he want? **a. you** = please go first. 3. *conj.* following the time when. **af•ter•birth,** *n.* placenta which comes out of the womb after the birth of young. **af•ter•care,** *n.* care for people after an operation, etc. **aftereffects,** *n. pl.* effects that follow on sth. **af•ter•glow,** *n.* glow in the sky after the sun has set. **af•ter-hours,** *adj.* open for business after the usual or legal time for closing. **af•ter•math,** *n.* what takes place after a catastrophe. **af•ter•noon,** *n.* part of the day between 12 noon and evening. **af•ter•shave,** *n.* **a. (lotion)** = lotion for soothing the face after shaving. **af•ter•shock,** *n.* lighter earth tremor felt after a major earthquake. **af•ter•thought,** *n.* thing which you think of later. **af•ter•ward, afterwards,** *adv.* after that; next/later.

Ag *symbol for* silver.

a•gain [əˈɡeɪn, əˈɡen] *adv.* once more; **once a.** = another time; **a. and a.** = several times; **now and a.** = sometimes; *inf.* **come a.?** = could you repeat that?

a•gainst [əˈɡenst] *prep.* (a) touching. (b) contrary to (rules, etc.); **he's a. lending her any more money** = he's opposed to lending her money.

ag•a•ric [əˈɡærɪk] *n.* type of fungus.

ag•ate [ˈæɡət] *n.* semi-precious stone, usu. with bands of different colors.

age [eɪdʒ] 1. *n.* (a) number of years you have lived; **under a.** = below the legal age (to do sth). (b) period; **the Stone A.** (c) **for ages** = for a very long time. 2. *v.* to become old. **aged** 1. *adj.* [eɪdʒd] **a. 74** = 74 years old. 2. [ˈeɪdʒɪd] (a) *adj.* very old. (b) *n.* **the a.** = old people. **age•ism,** *n.* bias against the elderly. **age•less,** *adj.* which does not grow old or look old.

a•gen•cy [ˈeɪdʒənsɪ] *n.* (a) office which represents a larger company/which works on behalf of another company; **we are the a. for Ford cars** = we are the distributors for Ford cars. (b) means.

a•gen•da [əˈdʒendə] *n.* list of things to be discussed at a meeting.

a•gent [ˈeɪdʒənt] *n.* (a) person who represents s.o. else; **secret a.** = spy. (b) substance which has an effect on another; **a. provocateur** = person who provokes people to commit crimes, esp. crimes against the state.

ag•glom•er•a•tion [əɡlɒməˈreɪʃn] *n.* a jumbled mass or collection.

ag•gran•dize•ment [əˈɡrændɪzmənt] *n.* making larger/more powerful.

ag•gra•vate [ˈæɡrəveɪt] *v.* to make worse. **ag•gra•va•ting,** *adj. inf.* annoying. **ag•gra•va•tion** [æɡrəˈveɪʃn] *n.* worsening (of a quarrel); *inf.* annoyance.

ag•gre•gate [ˈæɡrɪɡət] *n.* (a) total; **in the a.** = as a total. (b) mixture of sand, gravel, etc., with cement.

ag•gres•sion [əˈɡreʃn] *n.* hostility; attacking; **act of a.** = attack. **ag•gres•sive** [əˈɡresɪv] *adj.* hostile; attacking. **ag•gres•sive•ly,** *adv.* violently. **ag•gres•sive•ness,** *n.* being aggressive. **ag•gres•sor,** *n.* attacker.

ag•grieved [əˈɡriːvd] *adj.* upset; hurt.

a•ghast [əˈɡɑːst] *adj.* horrified.

ag•ile [ˈædʒaɪl] *adj.* lightfooted; (animal/person) who can climb/swing/run, etc., very easily. **a•gil•i•ty** [əˈdʒɪlɪtɪ] *n.* being agile.

a•gi•o [ˈædʒɪəʊ] *n.* charge made for converting money to another currency.

ag•i•tate [ˈædʒɪteɪt] *v.* to stir up public opinion **(for/against** sth). **ag•i•ta•tion** [ædʒɪˈteɪʃn] *n.* (a) worry. (b) **political a.** = political unrest. **ag•i•ta•tor** [ˈædʒɪteɪtə] *n.* person who stirs up political unrest.

ag•nos•tic [æɡˈnɒstɪk] *adj. & n.* (person) who believes that nothing can be known about God. **ag•nos•ti•cism,** *n.* belief that nothing can be known about God.

a•go [əˈɡəʊ] *adv.* in the past; **three years a.**

a•gog [əˈɡɒɡ] *adj.* **all a.** = very eager.

ag•o•nize [ˈæɡənaɪz] *v.* to worry **(over** a decision). **a•go•nized,** *adj.* as if in pain/in agony. **a•go•niz•ing,** *adj.* (a) very sharp (pain). (b) upsetting, painful (decision).

ag•o•ny [ˈæɡənɪ] *n.* extreme pain/extreme discomfort; **a. column** = letters and advice about personal problems in a newspaper.

ag•o•ra•pho•bi•a [æɡərəˈfəʊbɪə] *n.* irrational fear of public places or open spaces.

a•grar•i•an [əˈɡreərɪən] *adj.* dealing with the land.

a•gree [əˈɡriː] *v.* (a) **(with)** to say that you think the same way as (s.o.). (b) **(to)** to say yes to (a suggestion). (c) **eggs don't a. with me** = make me feel ill. **a•gree•a•ble**, *adj.* (a) pleasant. (b) in agreement; **are you a. to this?** = do you agree? **a•gree•a•bly**, *adv.* pleasantly. **a•gree•ment**, *n.* act of saying yes; **to be in a. with** = to agree with.

ag•ri•cul•ture [ˈægrɪkʌltʃə] *n.* use of the land for growing crops/raising animals, etc. **ag•ri•cul•tur•al** [ægrɪˈkʌltʃərəl] *adj.* referring to agriculture. **ag•ri•busi•ness**, *n.* farming and making products for farmers, seen as a business.

a•gron•o•my [əˈgrɒnəmɪ] *n.* study of agriculture.

a•ground [əˈgraʊnd] *adv.* no longer afloat; **the ship went a.**

a•head [əˈhed] *adv.* in front; in advance (of a time); **full speed a.** = go forward as fast as possible.

a•hoy [əˈhɔɪ] *inter. used by sailors in order to call a ship.*

AI *abbreviation for* (a) artificial insemination. (b) artificial intelligence.

aid [eɪd] 1. *n.* (a) help; **first a.** = help to injured/sick people; **first-a. kit** = box with bandages/medicines, etc.; **in a. of the Red Cross** = to help the Red Cross. (b) instrument to help; **a hearing a.** 2. *v.* to help.

aide [eɪd] *n.* assistant (of a president, etc.).

aide-de-camp [eɪddəˈkɒŋ] *n.* (*pl.* **aides-**) officer who assists a senior officer.

AIDS [eɪdz] = acquired immune deficiency syndrome.

ail [eɪl] *v.* (*old*) to be ill. **ail•ing** [ˈeɪlɪŋ] *adj.* sick. **ail•ment** [ˈeɪlmənt] *n.* A minor illness.

ai•ler•on [ˈeɪlərɒn] *n.* flap on the edge of an aircraft's wing.

aim [eɪm] 1. *n.* target; what you are trying to do; **he took a.** = he pointed his gun at the target. 2. *v.* (a) to plan/to intend to do. (b) to point (**at**). **aim•less**, *adj.*, **aim•less•ly**, *adv.* with no particular plan.

air [ˈeə] 1. *n.* (a) mixture of gases which we breathe, and which surrounds the earth; **travel by a.** = in an aircraft; **in the a.** = not yet decided; **on the a.** = speaking live on TV/on radio. (b) little tune. (c) appearance/feeling. 2. *v.* to freshen (a room, clothes, etc.) by giving more air. **air base**, *n.* military airfield. **air bed**, *n.* inflatable plastic/rubber mattress. **air•borne**, *adj.* carried in the air. **air brake**, *n.* (a) movable part on an aircraft to slow it down. (b) brake (on trucks) which works by compressed air. **air-con•di•tioned**, *adj.*

cooled by an air conditioner. **air con•di•tion•er**, *n.* machine which keeps a room at the right temperature. **air con•di•tion•ing**, *n.* cooling of the air by an air conditioner. **air-cooled**, *adj.* (engine) cooled by air, not by water. **air•craft**, *n.* (*pl.* **aircraft**) machine which flies. **air•craft car•ri•er**, *n.* large warship which carries aircraft and has a long deck for landing and taking off. **air•crew**, *n.* the crew of an aircraft. **air•field**, *n.* small landing field for aircraft. **air force**, *n.* military air defense branch of a country's armed forces. **air•freight**. 1. *n.* shipping goods by air. 2. *v.* to ship goods by air. **air•gun**, *n.* gun which shoots pellets using compressed air. **air•i•ly**, *adv.* in an airy way. **air•less**, *adj.* with no air or wind; stuffy. **air let•ter**, *n.* very light piece of writing paper which, when folded and stuck down, becomes its own envelope. **air•lift**. 1. *n.* transport of emergency supplies/people by air. 2. *v.* to transport emergency supplies/people by air. **air•line**, *n.* company which runs passenger or cargo air services. **air lock**, *n.* blockage in the flow of a liquid in a pipe (caused by air). **air•mail**, *n. & adv.* (mail) sent by air. **air•man**, *n.* (*pl.* **-men**) man serving in an air force. **air mat•tress**, *n.* mattress which can be inflated. **Air Miles**, *n. pl.* points awarded to buyers of certain products that can be used to purchase airline tickets. **air•plane**, *n.* machine that flies. **air pock•et**, *n.* sudden turbulence in air. **air•port**, *n.* commercial installation where passenger and cargo planes land and take off. **air raid**, *n.* attack by military aircraft. **air•ship**, *n.* large inflated balloon driven by an engine. **air•sick**, *adj.* sick because of traveling by air. **air•sick•ness**, *n.* feeling of being airsick. **airspeed**, *n.* speed of an aircraft in the air. **air•strip**, *n.* small runway where planes can land and take off. **air•tight**, *adj.* not letting in any air. **air traf•fic con•trol**, *n.* control of the movement of aircraft by people on the ground. **air•way**, *n.* passage (such as the throat) through which air passes in the body. **air•wor•thi•ness**, *n.* safety of an aircraft for use. **air•y**, *adj.* (-ier, -iest) (a) full of air. (b) vague (promise). **air•y-fair•y**, *adj.* impractical (plan).

aisle [aɪl] *n.* passageway; side part in a church parallel to the nave.

æ back, aː farm, ɒ top, aɪ pipe, aʊ how, aiə fire, aʊə flower, ɔː bought, ɔɪ toy, e fed, eəhair, eɪ take, ə afraid, əʊ boat, əʊə lower, vː word, iː heap, ɪ hit, ɪə hear, uː school, ʊ book, ʌ but, b back, d dog, ð then, dʒ just, f fog, g go, h hand, j yes, k catch, l last, m mix, n nut, ŋ sing, p penny, r round, s some, ʃ short, t too, tʃ chop, θ thing, v voice, w was, z zoo, ʒ treasure

a•jar [ə'dʒɑ:] adj. (of door/window) slightly open.

aka [eɪkeɪ'eɪ] = also known as.

a•kim•bo [ə'kɪmbəu] adv. **with her arms a.** = with her hands on her hips.

a•kin [ə'kɪn] adj. similar (**to**).

Al symbol for aluminum.

al•a•bas•ter ['æləbɑːstə] n. smooth white stone.

à la carte [ælæ'kɑːt] adv. & adj. (meal) made of several dishes ordered separately from a menu.

a•lac•ri•ty [ə'lækrɪtɪ] n. speed.

à la mode [ælæ'məud] adv. served with ice cream.

a•larm [ə'lɑːm] 1. n. thing which gives a loud warning; **false a.** = warning signal which is false; **fire a.** = bell which rings when a fire breaks out; **a. (clock)** = clock which rings at a certain time. 2. v. to warn (s.o.); to frighten (s.o.). **a•larm•ist,** adj. & n. (person) who is unnecessarily worried by sth.

a•las [ə'læs] inter. showing sadness.

al•ba•tross ['ælbətrɒs] n. (pl. **-es**) very large white sea bird.

al•be•do [æl'biːdəu] n. ability to reflect light.

al•be•it [ɔːl'biːɪt] conj. (formal) although.

al•bi•no [æl'biːnəu] n. animal or person born with pale skin, white hair, and pink eyes.

al•bum ['ælbəm] n. (a) large book for sticking things in. (b) long-playing record.

al•bu•men ['ælbjumən] n. white part of an egg.

al•che•my ['ælkəmɪ] n. medieval chemistry, aimed at converting metals to gold. **al•che•mist,** n. person who studied alchemy.

al•co•hol ['ælkəhɒl] n. intoxicating liquid distilled from a fermented mixture. **al•co•hol•ic** [ælkə'hɒlɪk] 1. adj. referring to alcohol. 2. n. person who is addicted to drinking alcohol. **al•co•hol•ism,** n. addiction to drinking alcohol. **al•co•pop** ['ælkəu,pɒp] n. inf. alcoholic drink that resembles a soft drink.

al•cove ['ælkəuv] n. small recess in a wall.

al•der ['ɔːldə] n. tree which often grows near water.

ale [eɪl] n. type of beer.

a•lert [ə'lɜːt] 1. adj. watchful; lively. 2. n. **to be on the a.** = to be watchful/to watch out for sth; **he gave the a.** = he gave a warning signal. 3. v. **to a. s.o. to** = to warn s.o. of. **a•lert•ness,** n. watchfulness; promptness (in doing sth).

al•fal•fa [æl'fælfə] n. cloverlike plant used as fodder.

al•fres•co [æl'freskəu] adj. & adv. in the open air; **an a. meal.**

al•gae ['ældʒiː] n. pl. tiny water plants with no stems or leaves.

al•ge•bra ['ældʒɪbrə] n. branch of mathematics where numbers are replaced by letters. **al•ge•bra•ic** [ældʒɪ'breɪk] adj. referring to algebra.

al•go•rithm ['ælgərɪðm] n. plan for working out a complicated calculation.

a•li•as ['eɪlɪəs] 1. adv. otherwise known as. 2. n. (pl. **-es**) assumed name.

al•i•bi ['ælɪbaɪ] n. proof that you were somewhere else when a crime was committed.

al•ien ['eɪlɪən] 1. adj. foreign (**to**). 2. n. foreigner.

al•ien•ate ['eɪlɪəneɪt] v. to turn away/to repel. **al•ien•a•tion** [eɪlɪə'neɪʃn] n. turning away/repelling.

a•light [ə'laɪt] 1. v. (formal) **to a. from** = to get off (a train/bus, etc.). 2. adj. on fire.

a•lign [ə'laɪn] v. to put (yourself/sth) in line; to put (yourself) on the same side as. **a•lign•ment,** n. row (of objects); putting (countries) on the same side.

a•like [ə'laɪk] adv. almost the same.

al•i•men•ta•ry [ælɪ'mentərɪ] adj. which feeds; **a. canal** = tube by which food goes into the stomach, and passes through the body.

al•i•mo•ny ['ælɪmənɪ] n. money paid regularly by a person to that person's former spouse.

a•live [ə'laɪv] adj. (a) living/not dead. (b) **a. to** = aware of. (c) lively.

al•ka•li ['ælkəlaɪ] n. substance which will neutralize an acid, and which turns litmus paper blue. **al•ka•line,** adj. not acid.

all [ɔːl] 1. adj. & pron. (a) everything; everyone; **a. the children; a. of us prefer beer.** (b) (in tennis) **fifteen a.** = fifteen points each. (c) **once (and) for a.** = for the last time; **not at a.** = certainly not; **a. but** = nearly. 2. adv. completely; **dressed a. in blue; a. at once/a. of a sudden** = suddenly; inf. **not a. there** = mad. **all in,** adj. inf. worn out. **all-night,** adj. which goes on for the whole night. **all-out,** adj. complete (strike); **we must make an a.-out effort** = we must do everything. **all right** [ɔːl'raɪt] adj. (a) fine; well. (b) yes, I will. **all-a•round, all-round,** adj. general; **a.-around athlete** = person who is good at all sorts of sports. **all-star,** adj. with many stars appearing. **all-time,** adj. (greatest level, etc.) ever.

Al•lah ['ælæ] n. Muslim name for God.

al•lay [ə'leɪ] v. to calm (fear/anger).

al•le•ga•tion [ælɪ'geɪʃn] n. suggestion as if it were fact. **al•lege** [ə'ledʒ] v. to suggest (as a fact that). **al•leged,** adj. suggested. **al•leg•ed•ly** [ə'ledʒɪdlɪ] adv. as is alleged.

al•le•giance [ə'liːdʒəns] n. faithfulness; **they**

swore a. to the President = they swore to obey him.

al•le•go•ry ['ælɪgərɪ] *n*. piece of writing where the characters represent abstract qualities or defects. **al•le•gor•i•cal** [ælɪ'gɒrɪkl] *adj*. referring to allegory.

al•le•gro [ə'legrəʊ] *adv. & adj. (in music)* played quite fast.

al•ler•gy ['ælədʒɪ] *n*. illness caused by a reaction to irritant substances. **al•ler•gen**, *n*. substance (such as pollen) which produces an allergic reaction. **al•ler•gic** [ə'lɜːdʒɪk] *adj*. reacting badly against; **I am a. to grass pollen; she is a. to jazz** = dislikes it intensely.

al•le•vi•ate [ə'liːvɪeɪt] *v*. to lessen/to soften. **al•le•vi•a•tion** [əliːvɪ'eɪʃn] *n*. lessening.

al•ley ['ælɪ] *n*. (a) very narrow street. (b) **bowling a.** = long narrow area for bowling or playing bowls.

al•li•ance [ə'laɪəns] *n*. link between two groups or countries.

al•lied ['ælaɪd] *adj*. (a) linked by an alliance; **the a. powers** = western countries linked against communist states. (b) linked.

al•li•ga•tor ['ælɪgeɪtə] *n*. large flesh-eating reptile living in tropical rivers.

al•lit•er•a•tion [əlɪtə'reɪʃn] *n*. use of repeated consonants at the beginning of words in poetry.

al•lo•cate ['æləkeɪt] *v*. to give (sth) as a share (for a particular purpose. **al•lo•ca•tion** [ælə'keɪʃn] *n*. division/giving as a share; amount allocated.

al•lot [ə'lɒt] *v*. **(allotted)** to share out between several people. **al•lot•ment**, *n*. sharing out.

al•low [ə'laʊ] *v*. (a) **to a. s.o. to do sth** = to let (s.o. do sth). (b) to give; **we will a. you six weeks to pay**. **al•low•a•ble**, *adj*. which is permitted; **a. expenses** = expenses which are allowed against tax. **al•low•ance**, *n*. (a) money paid regularly. (b) **to make allowances for** = take into account.

al•loy ['ælɔɪ] 1. *n*. mixture of two or more metals. 2. *v*. to mix (metals).

all•spice ['ɔːlspaɪs] *n*. small round tropical seed used as a spice.

al•lude [ə'luːd] *v*. **to a. to sth** = to refer to sth indirectly or briefly.

al•lure [ə'ljʊə] *v*. to attract. **al•lur•ing**, *adj*. attractive.

al•lu•sion [ə'luːʒn] *n*. slight reference. **al•lu•sive**, *adj*. which makes reference to sth.

al•lu•vi•al [ə'luːvɪəl] *adj*. (soil/land) which has been deposited by rivers. **al•lu•vi•um**, *n*. soil which has been deposited by a river.

al•ly 1. *n*. ['ælaɪ] person/country who is on the same side as you in a quarrel or war. 2. *v*. [ə'laɪ] **to a. oneself to** = to join forces with/to support.

al•ma ma•ter [ælmə'meɪtə] *n*. school or college which s.o. has attended.

al•ma•nac ['ɔːlmənæk] *n*. calendar which also contains advice or information.

al•might•y [ɔːl'maɪtɪ] 1. *adj. inf.* very powerful; **an a. row** = a very loud noise. 2. *n*. **the A.** = God.

al•mond ['ɑːmənd] *n*. nut from a tree of the peach family.

al•mon•er ['ɑːmənə] *n*. *(old)* person who distributes alms for a church, royal family, etc.

al•most ['ɔːlməʊst] *adv*. nearly; not quite.

alms [ɑːmz] *n. pl. (old)* gift to old/sick/poor people. **alms•hous•es**, *n. pl.* houses formerly built as homes for the poor.

al•oe ['æləʊ] *n*. desert plant with thick leaves and bitter juice.

a•loft [ə'lɒft] *adv. (formal)* high up (in the air).

a•lone [ə'ləʊn] *adj. & adv.* with no one else.

a•long [ə'lɒŋ] 1. *prep*. **a. the road** = from one end of the road to the other; for some distance down the road. 2. *adv*. **come a. with me** = come with me; **all a.** = from the beginning; **they don't get a. very well together** = they do not agree. **a•long•side,** *adv. & prep.* beside.

a•loof [ə'luːf] *adv. & adj.* coldly/unfriendly; **they kept a.** = they did not mix with others. **a•loof•ness**, *n*. cold and haughty.

al•o•pe•ci•a [æləʊ'piːsɪə] *n*. baldness.

a•loud [ə'laʊd] *adv*. loud enough to be heard; in a loud voice.

alp [ælp] *n*. mountain or mountain meadow in Switzerland.

al•pac•a [æl'pækə] *n*. wool from a llama.

al•pha ['ælfə] *n*. first letter of the Greek alphabet.

al•pha•bet ['ælfəbet] *n*. letters used to write words, laid out in a set order (A, B, C, etc.). **al•pha•bet•i•cal** [ælfə'betɪkl] *adj*. **in a. order** = in order based on the first letter of each word. **al•pha•bet•i•cal•ly**, *adv*. in alphabetical order.

al•pine ['ælpaɪn] *adj. & n.* referring to high mountains; (plant) which grows on high mountains. **al•pin•ist** *n*. person who climbs mountains.

al•read•y [ɔːl'redɪ] *adv*. by now.

---

al•right [ɔːl'raɪt] *adj. & inter. inf.* = **all right.**

al•sa•tian [æl'seɪʃn] *n.* large dog (of German origin) often used as a guard dog.

al•so ['ɔːlsəu] *adv.* as well/at the same time.

al•tar ['ɒltə] *n.* table in church/temple for religious ceremonies.

al•ter ['ɒltə] *v.* to change. **al•ter•a•tion** [ɒltə-'reɪʃn] *n.* change.

al•ter•ca•tion [ɔːltə'keɪʃn] *n. (formal)* argument.

al•ter•nate 1. *adj.* [ɔːl'tɜːnət] every other/missing one each time. 2. *v.* ['ɔːltəneɪt] to put (sth) in place of sth else, and then switch them around. **al•ter•nate•ly** [ɔːl'tɜːnətlɪ] *adv.* in turns; one first and then the other. **al•ter•nat•ing**, *adj.* (electric current) which flows one way and then the other. **al•ter•na•tive** [ɔːl'tɜːnətɪv] *n. & adj.* thing in place of sth else. **al•ter•na•tive•ly**, *adv.* on the other hand. **al•ter•na•tor** ['ɔːltəneɪtə] *n.* device which produces alternating current.

al•though [ɔːl'ðəu] *conj.* in spite of the fact that.

al•tim•e•ter ['æltɪmiːtə] *n.* instrument for measuring altitude.

al•ti•tude ['æltɪtjuːd] *n.* height (measured above the level of the sea).

al•to ['æltəu] *n. (pl.* **-os**) (man with a) high-pitched voice; (woman with a) low-pitched voice.

al•to•geth•er [ɔːltə'geðə] *adv.* considering everything together.

al•tru•ism ['æltruːɪzəm] *n.* being unselfish. **al•tru•is•tic**, *adj.* unselfish.

a•lum ['æləm] *n.* natural mineral salt.

a•lu•mi•num [ə'luːmɪnəm], *Brit.* **a•lu•min•i•um** [ælju'mɪnjəm] *n. (element:* Al) light white metal.

a•lum•nus [ə'lʌmnəs] *n. (pl.* **alumni** [ə-'lʌmnaɪ]) graduate (of a college/university).

al•ways ['ɔːlweɪz] *adv.* every time/all the time.

a•lys•sum ['ælɪsəm] *n.* low garden plant with small white flowers.

Alz•heim•er's dis•ease ['æltseɪməz dɪ'ziːz] *n.* condition where a patient becomes prematurely senile.

am [æm] *v. see* **be.**

a.m. ['eɪ'em] *adv.* in the morning.

a•mal•gam [ə'mælgəm] *n. (formal)* mixture of substances. **a•mal•ga•mate** [ə'mælgəmeɪt] *v.* to mix together/to link up. **a•mal•ga•ma•tion** [əmælgə'meɪʃn] *n.* amalgamating; things amalgamated.

a•man•u•en•sis [æmænju:'ensɪs] *n.* person who writes for s.o. else.

am•a•ryl•lis [æmə'rɪlɪs] *n.* lily.

a•mass [ə'mæs] *v.* to pile up (a fortune).

am•a•teur ['æmətɜː] *n. & adj.* (person) who is not paid to do sth; (person) who does sth because he likes doing it. **am•a•teur•ish**, *adj.* not very well done.

am•a•to•ry ['æmətərɪ] *adj.* referring to love.

a•maze [ə'meɪz] *v.* to surprise. **a•mazed**, *adj.* surprised. **a•maze•ment**, *n.* surprise. **a•maz•ing**, *adj.* very surprising.

am•bas•sa•dor, am•bas•sa•dress [æm-'bæsədə, -dres] *n.* person who represents a country in another country.

am•ber ['æmbə] *n.* yellow or orange translucent stone made of fossilized resin.

am•ber•gris ['æmbəgrɪ] *n.* substance from sperm whales, used in making perfume.

am•bi•dex•trous [æmbɪ'dekstrəs] *adj.* (person) who can use either right or left hand equally well.

am•bi•ence ['æmbɪəns] *n.* surroundings. **am•bi•ent**, *adj.* which surrounds; **a. temperature** = temperature of the air around sth.

am•big•u•ous [æm'bɪgjuəs] *adj.* which has two possible meanings. **am•bi•gu•i•ty** [æmbɪ'gjuːɪtɪ] *n.* state of having two possible meanings; vagueness.

am•bit ['æmbɪt] *n.* general area covered by sth.

am•bi•tion [æm'bɪʃn] *n.* desire to improve your status in the world. **am•bi•tious**, *adj.* wanting to be successful; (project) which aims very high.

am•biv•a•lent [æm'bɪvələnt] *adj.* undecided/with two points of view.

am•ble ['æmbl] *v.* **he was ambling along** = walking slowly along.

am•bro•sia [æm'brəuzɪə] *n.* delectable food.

am•bu•lance ['æmbjuləns] *n.* vehicle for taking sick people to a hospital.

am•bush ['æmbuʃ] 1. *n. (pl.* **-es**) surprise attack. 2. *v.* to attack by surprise.

a•me•ba [ə'miːbə] *n. (pl.* **amebas, amebae** [-biː]) tiny organism consisting of a single cell.

a•mel•io•rate [ə'miːljəreɪt] *v. (formal)* to make better. **a•mel•io•ra•tion** [əmiːljə-'reɪʃn] *n.* becoming better.

a•men [ɑː'men, eɪ'men] *inter.* word (meaning let this be so) which is used at the end of Christian prayers; **I say a. to that** = I agree entirely.

a•me•na•ble [ə'miːnəbl] *adj.* docile/easy-going; **a. to new ideas** = willing to accept new ideas.

a•mend [ə'mend] *v.* to change (for the better). **a•mend•ment**, *n.* change, esp. suggested change to a proposal. **a•mends** *n.* **to make a. for something** = to compensate for an injury, etc.

a•men•i•ty [ə'miːnɪtɪ] *n.* (a) pleasantness (of a place). (b) pleasant or agreeable feature.

A•mer•i•can [ə'merɪkən] 1. *adj.* referring to

America; **A. plan** = full board (in a hotel). 2. *n.* person from the United States.

am•e•thyst ['æməθɪst] *n.* purple precious stone.

a•mi•a•ble ['eɪmɪəbl] *adj.* pleasant. **a•mi•a•bil•i•ty** [eɪmɪə'bɪlɪtɪ] *n.* being amiable. **a•mi•a•bly**, *adv.* pleasantly.

am•i•ca•ble ['æmɪkəbl] *adj.* friendly. **am•i•ca•bly**, *adv.* in a friendly way.

a•mid(st) [ə'mɪd(st)] *prep.* in the middle of. **a•mid•ships**, *adv. & prep.* in the middle of a ship.

a•mi•no ac•id [ə'miːnəʊ 'æsɪd] *n.* acid found in protein, necessary for growth.

a•miss [ə'mɪs] *adv. & adj.* **don't take it a.** = don't be annoyed; **something is a.** = has gone wrong.

am•i•ty ['æmɪtɪ] *n.* friendship.

am•me•ter ['æmɪtə] *n.* device for measuring electricity in amperes.

am•mo•nia [ə'məʊnɪə] *n.* gas made of hydrogen and nitrogen, which has a strong smell.

am•mo•nite ['æmənaɪt] *n.* fossil shell like that of a large snail.

am•mu•ni•tion [æmju'nɪʃn] *n.* (*no pl.*) bullets/shells, etc., for using in warfare/hunting, etc.

am•ne•sia [æm'niːzɪə] *n.* medical state when you forget everything.

am•nes•ty ['æmnəstɪ] 1. *n.* pardon (to criminals). 2. *v.* to offer (criminals) a pardon.

am•ni•ot•ic flu•id ['æmnɪɒtɪk 'fluːɪd] *n.* liquid surrounding a baby in the womb.

a•moe•ba [ə'miːbə] *n.* (*pl.* **amebas, amoebae** [ə-'miːbiː]) *see* **ameba**.

a•mok [ə'mɒk] *adv.* **to run a.** = to run wild killing people.

a•mong(st) [ə'mʌŋ(st)] *prep.* (a) in the middle of. (b) out of.

a•mor•al [eɪ'mɒrəl] *adj.* with no sense of values/of morality.

am•o•rous ['æmərəs] *adj.* tending to fall in love; showing (sexual) love.

a•mor•phous [ə'mɔːfəs] *adj.* having no particular shape.

am•or•tize ['æmɔːtaɪz] *v.* to write off (a debt).

a•mount [ə'maʊnt] 1. *n.* (a) quantity. (b) sum (of money). 2. *v.* to add up (to); **it amounts to the same thing** = it means the same.

a•mour pro•pre [æmuː 'prɒpr] *n.* respect for oneself.

amp, am•pere [æmp, 'æmpeə] *n.* quantity of electricity flowing in a current.

am•per•sand ['æmpəsænd] *n.* printing sign (&) meaning 'and.'

am•phet•a•mine [æm'fetəmiːn] *n.* drug which stimulates.

am•phib•i•an [æm'fɪbɪən] *n.* (a) animal which lives both in water and on land. (b) (military) vehicle that moves in water and on land. **am•phib•i•ous**, *adj.* which lives/travels in water and on land.

am•phi•the•a•ter, am•phi•the•a•tre ['æmfɪθɪətə] *n.* (a) Greek or Roman circular theater. (b) lecture hall with rows of seats rising in tiers.

am•pho•ra ['æmfərə] *n.* Greek or Roman wine jar.

am•ple ['æmpl] *adj.* (a) large. (b) enough/sufficient. **am•ply**, *adv.* in large enough quantity.

am•pli•fy ['æmplɪfaɪ] *v.* (a) to make (a sound, etc.) louder. (b) to develop (sth) in more detail. **am•pli•fi•ca•tion** [æmplɪfɪ'keɪʃn] *n.* development; making louder. **am•pli•fi•er**, *n.* machine which amplifies a sound.

am•pule, am•poule ['æmpuːl] *n.* small container containing liquid for injections.

am•pu•tate ['æmpjuteɪt] *v.* to cut off (a limb). **am•pu•ta•tion** [æmpju'teɪʃn] *n.* cutting off.

a•muck [ə'mʌk] *adv. see* **amok**

am•u•let ['æmjulet] *n.* lucky charm.

a•muse [ə'mjuːz] *v.* to give (s.o.) pleasure; **to a. yourself** = to spend time happily. **a•muse•ment**, *n.* pleasure; **a•muse•ment park**, outdoor area with games, rides, and entertainment. **a•mus•ing**, *adj.* which makes you laugh.

an [æn, ən] *see* **a**.

an•a•bol•ic ster•oids ['ænə'bɒlɪk 'sterɔɪdz] *n.* chemical substances which make the body create more tissue.

a•nach•ro•nism [ə'nækrənɪzəm] *n.* thing which is out of keeping with the period. **a•nach•ro•nis•tic** [ənækrə'nɪstɪk] *adj.* which is not in keeping with the period.

an•a•con•da [ænə'kɒndə] *n.* very large snake.

a•nae•mi•a [ə'niːmɪə] *n. see* **anemia**.

an•aer•o•bic [æneə'rəʊbɪk] *adj.* not needing oxygen to take place.

an•aes•thet•ic [ænəs'θetɪk] *n. see* **anesthetic**.

an•a•gram ['ænəgræm] *n.* word or phrase containing the letters of another word or phrase jumbled up (e.g. *Cathy* and *yacht*).

a•nal ['eɪnl] *adj.* referring to the anus.

æ back, ɑː farm, ɒ top, aɪ pipe, aʊ how, aɪə fire, ɔː bought, ɔɪ toy, e fed, eəhair, eɪ take, ə afraid, əʊ boat, aʊə lower, vː word, iː heap, ɪ hit, ɪə hear, uː school, ʊ book, ʌ but, b back, d dog, ð then, dʒ just, f fog, g go, h hand, j yes, k catch, l last, m mix, n nut, ŋ sing, p penny, r round, s some, ʃ short, t too, tʃ chop, θ thing, v voice, w was, z zoo, ʒ treasure

an•al•ge•sic [ænəl'dʒiːzɪk] *adj. & n.* (drug) which relieves pain. **an•al•ge•si•a,** *n.* absence of pain.

a•nal•o•gous [ə'næləgəs] *adj.* similar/parallel. **an•a•log** ['ænɒg] *adj.* (computer) working on a more or less continuous signal. **a•nal•o•gy** [ə'næləʤɪ] *n.* similarity/parallel.

an•a•lyze ['ænəlaɪz] *v.* to examine (sth) closely to see how it is formed. **a•nal•y•sis** [ə'nælɪsɪs] *n.* (*pl.* **analyses** [ə'nælɪsiːz]) close examination. **an•a•lyst** ['ænəlɪst] *n.* (a) person who carries out analyses. (b) psychoanalyst. **an•a•lyt•i•cal** [ænə'lɪtɪkl] *adj.* which examines closely in detail.

an•ar•chy ['ænəkɪ] *n.* total lack of order or government. **an•ar•chic** [ə'nɑːkɪk] *adj.* lacking in order. **an•ar•chist,** *n.* person who believes in anarchy.

a•nath•e•ma [ə'næθəmə] *n.* curse; **it's a. to him** = he dislikes it intensely.

a•nat•o•my [ə'nætəmɪ] *n.* structure (esp. of a body). **an•a•tom•i•cal** [ænə'tɒmɪkl] *adj.* relating to the structure of the body.

an•ces•tor ['ænsestə] *n.* member of your family many generations ago. **an•ces•tral** [æn'sestrəl] *adj.* **a. home** = home of a family for many generations. **an•ces•try** ['ænsestrɪ] *n.* origin (of a family).

an•chor ['æŋkə] 1. *n.* (a) heavy metal hook dropped to the bottom of the sea to hold a ship in one place; **they dropped a. in the bay; the ship was at a.** (b) thing which holds secure/which gives security. 2. *v.* to drop anchor; hold (a ship) with an anchor. **an•chor•age,** *n.* place where ships can anchor safely. **an•chor•man, anchorwoman,** *n.* main presenter on a TV news program.

an•cho•vy ['æntʃəvɪ, æn'tʃəʊvɪ] *n.* small fish with a strong taste.

an•cient ['eɪnʃənt] *adj.* very old.

an•cil•lar•y [æn'sɪlərɪ] *adj.* secondary.

and [ænd, ənd] *conj.* *showing connection between two things;* **try a. sing** = try to sing.

an•dan•te [æn'dæntɪ] *adv. & adj.* (*in music*) played quite slowly.

and•i•ron ['ændaɪən] *n.* metal stand to hold logs in a hearth.

an•droid ['ændrɔɪd] *adj.* shaped like a human being.

an•drol•o•gy [æn'drɒləʤɪ] *n.* study of diseases of men, esp. of the reproductive system.

an•ec•dote ['ænɪkdəʊt] *n.* short humorous story told by s.o.

a•ne•mi•a [ə'niːmɪə] *n.* illness caused by lack or red cells in the blood. **a•ne•mic** [ə'niːmɪk] *adj.* looking pale; suffering from anemia.

an•e•mom•e•ter [ænɪ'mɒmɪtə] *n.* instrument for measuring wind. **a•nem•o•graph,** *n.* instrument which records wind force on paper.

a•nem•o•ne [ə'nemənɪ] *n.* small flower; **sea a.** = animal which looks like a flower, living in the sea.

an•er•oid ['ænərɔɪd] *adj.* **a. barometer** = barometer which measures atmospheric pressure by the movement of a vacuum box.

an•es•thet•ic [ænɪs'θetɪk] *n.* substance which makes you lose consciousness; **local a.** = substance which numbs part of the body. **an•es•the•sia** [ænɪs'θiːzɪə] *n.* loss of consciousness from being given an anesthetic. **an•es•the•tist** [ə'niːsθətɪst] *n.* doctor who gives anesthetics. **an•es•the•tize** [ə'niːsθətaɪz] *v.* to give (s.o.) an anesthetic.

an•eu•rysm, an•eu•rism ['ænjʊrɪzəm] *n.* swelling of an artery.

a•new [ə'njuː] *adv.* (*formal*) again.

an•gel ['eɪndʒl] *n.* heavenly being with wings; *inf.* kind person. **an•gel•ic** [æn'dʒelɪk] *adj.* looking innocent/like an angel.

an•gel•i•ca [æn'dʒelɪkə] *n.* sweet-smelling plant of which the green stalks are preserved in sugar and used in desserts.

an•ge•lus ['ændʒeləs] *n.* service said in Roman Catholic churches, esp. at the sunset.

an•ger ['æŋgə] 1. *n.* great annoyance. 2. *v.* to make (s.o.) annoyed.

an•gi•na [æn'dʒaɪnə] *n.* pains in the chest.

an•gle ['æŋgl] 1. *n.* (a) corner; **right a.** = angle of 90°; **acute a.** = angle of less than 90°; **obtuse a.** = angle of more than 90°. (b) point of view. 2. *v.* (a) to kick a ball/to shoot at an angle and not straight. (b) **to a. for a raise** = to try to get an increase in salary by dropping hints. **an•gler,** *n.* person who fishes with a hook and line. **an•gling,** *n.* fishing with a hook and line.

An•gli•can ['æŋglɪkən] *adj. & n.* (person) belonging to the Church of England or a church affiliated with it.

An•gli•cism ['æŋglɪsɪzəm] *n.* way of saying sth which is English or influenced by English.

Anglo- ['æŋgləʊ] *prefix meaning* English/between England and another country. **an•glo•phile,** *n.* person who likes England. **an•glo•phobe,** *n.* person who hates England.

an•go•ra [æŋ'gɔːrə] *n. & adj.* (animal) with thick very soft wool; **a. cat; a. rabbit; a. jumper.**

an•gos•tu•ra [æŋgo'stuːrə] *n.* bitter substance used to flavor drinks.

an•gry ['æŋgrɪ] *adj.* (**-ier, -iest**) very annoyed. **an•gri•ly,** *adv.* in an angry way.

ang•strom ['æŋstrɒm] *n.* unit of measurement of wavelengths.

an•guish ['æŋgwɪʃ] *n.* great suffering. **an•guished,** *adj.* showing great suffering.

an•gu•lar ['æŋgjulə] *adj. (of rock)* sharp/with sharp angles; *(of person)* with prominent bones.

an•i•line ['ænɪliːn] *n.* liquid produced from coal, used to make paint and plastics.

an•i•mal ['ænɪml] *n.* living creature which is not a plant.

an•i•mate ['ænɪmeɪt] *v.* (a) to make lively. (b) to draw on a film a series of cartoon figures, each with slightly different poses, so that when the film is projected the figures appear to move; **animated cartoon. an•i•ma•tion** [ænɪ'meɪʃn] *n.* (a) liveliness/vivacity. (b) act of making an animated cartoon.

an•i•mos•i•ty, an•i•mus [ænɪ'mɒsɪtɪ, 'ænɪməs] *n.* unfriendly attitude/hostility **(to- ward).**

an•i•on [æ'naɪən] *n.* negative ion.

an•i•seed ['ænɪsiːd] *n.* plant whose seeds are used to flavor sweets and drinks.

an•kle ['æŋkl] *n.* part of your body joining the foot to the leg; **a. socks** = short socks which stop just above the ankles; **a.-deep** = up to one's ankles.

an•nals ['ænlz] *n. pl.* written yearly account of events/discoveries, etc., which have taken place.

an•neal [ə'niːl] *v.* to strengthen (sth) by heating and cooling.

an•nex [ə'neks] 1. *v.* to join (one country to an- other). 2. *n.* (a) building attached to another building. (b) document attached to another document. **an•nex•a•tion** [ænek'seɪʃn] *n.* joining of one country to another.

an•ni•hi•late [ə'naɪəleɪt] *v.* to destroy com- pletely. **an•ni•hi•la•tion** [ənaɪə'leɪʃn] *n.* complete destruction.

an•ni•ver•sa•ry [ænɪ'vɜːsərɪ] *n.* day which falls on the same date as an important event in the past.

an•no•tate ['ænəteɪt] *v.* to make notes on (sth); to add notes to (a book). **an•no•ta•tion,** *n.* adding of notes; note added.

an•nounce [ə'naʊns] *v.* to tell publicly. **an•nounce•ment,** *n.* public statement. **an•nounc•er,** *n.* person on radio or TV who announces programs, reads the news, etc.

an•noy [ə'nɔɪ] *v.* to make (s.o.) angry.

an•noy•ance, *n.* state of being annoyed. **an•noyed,** *adj.* angry; irritated.

an•nu•al ['ænjuəl] 1. *adj.* which happens once a year. 2. *n.* plant that lives for one year only; book which comes out in a new edition each year. **an•nu•al•ized,** *adj.* shown on an an- nual basis. **an•nu•al•ly,** *adv.* every year.

an•nu•i•ty [ə'njuɪtɪ] *n.* sum of money which is paid annually.

an•nul [ə'nʌl] *v.* **(annulled)** to end/to cancel. **an•nul•ment,** *n.* cancellation.

an•nu•lar ['ænjuːlə] *adj.* shaped like a ring.

an•ode ['ænəʊd] *n.* positive electric terminal. **an•o•dize,** *v.* to cover (metal) with a film by using it in electrolysis.

an•o•dyne ['ænədaɪn] *adj. & n.* (medicine) which makes pain less strong; (thing) which stops you worrying.

a•noint [ə'nɔɪnt] *v.* to put oil on (a person) as part of a religious ceremony.

a•nom•a•ly [ə'nɒməlɪ] *n.* thing which is un- usual/which does not fit into the normal pat- tern. **a•nom•a•lous,** *adj.* abnormal/strange.

a•non [ə'nɒn] *adv.* soon.

a•non. = anonymous.

a•non•y•mous [ə'nɒnɪməs] *adj.* (person) who does not give his/her name; **a. letter** = a letter with no signature. **an•o•nym•i•ty** [ænə- 'nɪmɪtɪ] *n.* hiding of your name. **a•non•y•mous•ly,** *adv.* without giving your name.

a•noph•e•les [æ'ɔfeliːz] *n.* mosquito which transmits malaria.

a•o•rak ['ænəræk] *n.* waterproof jacket with a hood.

a•o•rex•i•a ner•vo•sa [ænə'reksɪə nɜː- 'vəʊsə] *n.* condition where you refuse to eat because of worry that you may become fat.

an•oth•er [ə'nʌðə] *adj. & pron.* (a) (one) more. (b) a different one. (c) **one a.** = each other.

an•swer ['ɑːnsə] 1. *n.* reply. 2. *v.* to reply; **to a. back** = reply rudely. **an•swer•a•ble,** *adj.* re- sponsible **(for** something **to** a person). **an•swer•ing,** *adj.* in answer; **a. machine** = machine having a recorded message on the telephone which answers automatically for s.o. who is out.

ant [ænt] *n.* small insect living in large commu- nities. **ant•eat•er,** *n.* animal which eats ants. **ant•hill,** *n.* mound of earth containing an ants' nest.

an•tag•o•nize [æn'tægənaɪz] *v.* to arouse s.o.'s hostility. **an•tag•o•nism,** *n.* hostil-

---

æ back, ɑː farm, ɒ top, aɪ pipe, aʊ how, aɪə fire, aʊə flower, ɔː bought, ɔɪ toy, e fed, eə hair, eɪ take, ə afraid, əʊ boat, əʊə lower, vː word, iː heap, ɪ hit, ɪə hear, uː school, ʊ book, ʌ but, b back, d dog, ð then, dʒ just, f fog, g go, h hand, j yes, k catch, l last, m mix, n nut, ŋ sing, p penny, r round, s some, ʃ short, t too, tʃ chop, θ thing, v voice, w was, z zoo, ʒ treasure

ity/opposition. **an•tag•o•nist,** *n.* opponent. **an•tag•o•nis•tic** [æntægə'nɪstɪk] *adj.* hostile.

ant•arc•tic [æn'tɑːktɪk] *adj. & n.* (referring to) the area around the South Pole. **Ant•arc•ti•ca,** *n.* region around the South Pole.

an•te [' æntɪ] *n.* money gambled by a player at the beginning of a game of poker.

ante- [' æntɪ] *prefix meaning* before.

an•te•ced•ent [æntɪ'siːdənt] *n.* earlier form of sth; thing which comes before.

an•te•date ['æntɪdeɪt] *v.* to put an earlier date on (a check); to happen earlier.

an•te•di•lu•vi•an [æntɪdɪ'luːvɪən] *adj.* very ancient.

an•te•lope ['æntɪləʊp] *n.* type of deer found in Africa.

an•te•na•tal [æntɪ'neɪtl] *adj.* before birth; **a. clinic** = clinic for pregnant women.

an•ten•na [æn'tenə] *n.* (a) (*pl.* **-ae** [æn'teniː]) feeler/sensitive apparatus for sensing. (b) (*pl.* **-as**) aerial.

an•te•ri•or [æn'tɪərɪə] *adj.* which comes earlier.

an•te•room ['æntɪruːm] *n.* small room leading to a larger room.

ant•hel•min•tic [ænθel'mɪntɪk] *adj. & n.* (substance) to remove worms.

an•them ['ænθəm] *n.* choral music (for a special occasion); **national a.** = official music of a country, played to honor the state.

an•ther ['ænθə] *n.* tip of a stamen which carries pollen.

an•thol•o•gy [æn'θɒlədʒɪ] *n.* collection of poems/stories, etc., by various people in one book. **an•thol•o•gize,** *v.* to put (a poem) into an anthology.

an•thra•cite ['ænθrəsaɪt] *n.* hard coal which gives off a lot of heat but not much smoke or flame.

an•thrax ['ænθræks] *n.* serious disease of cattle, which can be caught by people.

an•thro•poid ['ænθrəpɔɪd] *adj. & n.* (ape) which is like a human being.

an•thro•pol•o•gy [ænθrə'pɒlədʒɪ] *n.* study of human beings. **an•thro•po•log•i•cal** [ænθrəpə'lɒdʒɪkl] *adj.* referring to the study of human beings. **an•thro•pol•o•gist** [ænθrə'pɒlədʒɪst] *n.* scientist who studies human beings.

an•thro•po•mor•phic [ænθrəpə'mɔːfɪk] *adj.* (religion, etc.) which gives gods, animals, etc., the form of human beings.

anti- [' æntɪ] *prefix meaning* against; **anti-tank gun; anti-malaria tablet; anti-inflationary measures. anti-se•mit•ic,** *adj.* against Jews.

an•ti•bi•ot•ic [æntɪbaɪ'ɒtɪk] *adj. & n.* (drug) which kills bacteria.

an•ti•bod•y ['æntɪbɒdɪ] *n.* chemical substance built up in the body to fight a particular disease.

an•tic•i•pate [æn'tɪsɪpeɪt] *v.* (a) to act because you see sth is about to happen. (b) to expect sth to happen. **an•tic•i•pa•tion** [æntɪsɪ'peɪʃn] *n.* expectation that sth will happen. **an•tic•i•pa•to•ry,** *adj.* which anticipates.

an•ti•cli•max [æntɪ'klaɪmæks] *n.* (*pl.* **-es**) feeling of being let down when sth exciting does not happen.

an•tics ['æntɪks] *n. pl.* playing around; fooling.

an•ti•cy•clone [æntɪ'saɪkləʊn] *n.* area of high atmospheric pressure.

an•ti•dote ['æntɪdəʊt] *n.* (**to**) thing which counteracts the effects of a poison.

an•ti•freeze ['æntɪfriːz] *n.* liquid put in the radiator of a car to prevent it freezing in cold weather.

an•ti•gen ['æntɪdʒən] *n.* substance which produces antibodies.

an•ti•his•ta•mine [æntɪ'hɪstəmiːn] *n.* medicine which prevents allergies.

an•ti•mo•ny ['æntɪmənɪ] *n.* (*element*: Sb) white metal used to make alloys.

an•ti•ox•i•dant [æntɪ'ɒksɪdənt] *n.* (a) any substance that slows deterioration by oxidation of a material. (b) any substance, e.g. vitamin E, that inhibits oxidation in the body.

an•tip•a•thy [æn'tɪpəθɪ] *n.* (**to**) feeling of not liking s.o./sth.

an•ti•per•spi•rant [æntɪ'pɜːspɪrənt] *n.* spray which stops you perspiring.

an•ti•phon ['æntɪfɒn] *n.* (religious) chant for two sets of singers, each singing in turn. **an•tiph•o•nal,** *adj.* (sung) like an antiphon.

an•tip•o•des [æn'tɪpədiːz] *n. pl.* two places which are on opposite sides of the earth from one another **an•tip•o•de•an** [æntɪpə'diːən] *adj.* from the antipodes.

an•ti•py•ret•ic [æntɪpaɪə'retɪk] *adj. & n.* (substance) which reduces fever.

an•ti•quar•y [æn'tɪkwərɪ] *n.* person who collects, studies, or sells antiques. **an•ti•quar•i•an** [æntɪ'kweərɪən] *adj.* **a. bookseller** = bookseller who sells old books.

an•ti•quat•ed ['æntɪkweɪtɪd] *adj.* old (and decrepit).

an•tique [æn'tiːk] 1. *adj.* very old (and valuable). 2. *n.* old and valuable object; **a. shop** = shop which sells old objects.

an•tiq•ui•ty [æn'tɪkwɪtɪ] *n.* ancient times.

an•ti•sep•tic [æntɪ'septɪk] *adj. & n.* (substance) which prevents a wound becoming septic.

an•ti•so•cial [æntɪ'səʊʃl] *adj.* disliking society; bad for society.

an•ti•stat•ic [æntɪ'stætɪk] *adj.* which stops the effect of static electricity.

an•tith•e•sis [æn'tɪθəsɪs] *n.* (*pl.* **-theses**) [-θəsiːz] opposite.

an•ti•tox•in [æntɪ'tɒksɪn] *n.* substance which counteracts the effects of a toxin. **an•ti•tox•ic,** *adj.* which counteracts a toxin.

an•ti•ven•in [æntɪ'veniːn] *n.* substance which counteracts snake bites.

an•ti•vi•ral [æntɪ'vaɪrəl] *adj. & n.* (drug) which inhibits the growth of viruses.

an•ti•viv•i•sec•tion•ist [æntɪvɪvɪ'sekʃənɪst] *n.* person who is opposed to using live animals for experiments.

ant•ler ['æntlə] *n.* horn (on deer).

an•to•nym ['æntənɪm] *n.* word which means the opposite of another word.

a•nus ['eɪnəs] *n.* (*pl.* **-es**) hole through which animals produce waste matter from the bowels.

an•vil ['ænvɪl] *n.* (a) block on which a blacksmith beats hot metal. (b) one of the ossicles in the ear.

anx•i•e•ty [æŋ'zaɪətɪ] *n.* (*a*) great worry (**about**). (b) eagerness (**to**). **anx•ious** ['æŋkʃəs] *adj.* (a) very worried. (b) eager (**to**). **anx•ious•ly,** *adv.* worriedly.

an•y ['enɪ] 1. *adj. & pron.* (a) it does not matter which. (b) some; **have you a. sugar? I haven't got a.; he hasn't a. money.** 2. *adv.* **I can't go a. further** = I can go no further.

an•y•bod•y ['enɪbɒdɪ] *pron.* (a) it does not matter who. (b) some person; **hardly a.** = very few.

an•y•how ['enɪhaʊ] 1. *adv.* carelessly. 2. *conj.* = **an•y•way.**

an•y•one ['enɪwʌn] *pron.* = **an•y•bod•y.**

an•y•thing ['enɪθɪŋ] *pron.* (a) it does not matter what; **hardly a.** = almost nothing. (c) *inf.* **like a.** = very strongly; **raining like a.** = pouring down.

an•y•way ['enɪweɪ] *adv. & conj.* in any case.

an•y•where ['enɪweə] *prep.* (a) it does not matter where. (b) somewhere; **can you see it a.?**

a•or•ta [eɪ'ɔːtə] *n.* (*pl.* **-as, -ae**) main artery taking blood from the heart.

a•pace [ə'peɪs] *adv.* (*formal*) fast.

a•part [ə'pɑːt] *adv.* (a) separated. (b) separate; **the watch came a.** = fell to pieces; **can you tell them a.?** = can you say which is which? (c) **a. from** = except.

a•part•heid [ə'pɑːtaɪt] *n.* (formerly) policy in South Africa of racial segregation.

a•part•ment [ə'pɑːtmənt] *n.* set of rooms in a building, usu. on one floor, as a separate living unit.

ap•a•thy ['æpəθɪ] *n.* lack of interest. **ap•a•thet•ic** [æpə'θetɪk] *adj.* uninterested.

ape [eɪp] 1. *n.* large manlike monkey with no tail. 2. *v.* to imitate (s.o.).

a•per•i•ent [ə'pɪərɪənt] *adj. & n.* substance which makes the bowels work.

a•pe•ri•tif [ə'perɪtiːf] *n.* drink taken before a meal to give you an appetite.

ap•er•ture ['æpətʃə] *n.* hole; opening.

a•pex ['eɪpeks] *n.* (*pl.* **apexes, apices**) top (of a triangle).

a•pha•sia [ə'feɪzjə] *n.* being unable to speak, caused by brain damage.

a•phid, a•phis ['eɪfɪd, 'eɪfɪs, 'æfɪs] *n.* (*pl.* **aphids, aphides**) small insect which sucks the sap from plants.

aph•o•rism ['æfərɪzəm] *n.* short wise saying.

aph•ro•dis•i•ac [æfrə'dɪzɪæk] *n. & adj.* (substance) which increases sexual desire.

a•pi•ar•y ['eɪpɪərɪ] *n.* place where bees are kept. **a•pi•a•rist,** *n.* (*formal*) beekeeper.

a•pi•cul•ture ['æpɪkʌltʃə] *n.* keeping of bees (for honey).

a•piece [ə'piːs] *adv.* each.

a•plomb [ə'plɒm] *n.* calmness/self-confidence.

a•poc•a•lyp•tic [əpɒkə'lɪptɪk] *adj.* which prophesies doom. **A•poc•a•lypse,** *n.* last book of the New Testament, prophesying doom.

a•poc•ry•phal [ə'pɒkrɪfl] *adj.* probably untrue. **A•poc•ry•pha,** *npl.* collection of texts of the Old Testament which are not accepted as genuine.

ap•o•gee ['æpədʒiː] *n.* highest point (in the orbit of a planet/in the career of a diplomat, politician, etc.).

a•pol•o•get•ic [əpɒlə'dʒetɪk] *adj.* making excuses; saying you are sorry. **a•pol•o•get•i•cal•ly,** *adv.* in an apologetic way. **a•pol•o•gist,** *n.* person who writes or speaks on behalf of a cause. **a•pol•o•gize** [ə'pɒlədʒaɪz] *v.* to say you are sorry. **a•pol•o•gy,** *n.* saying you are sorry; **my apologies for being late** = I'm sorry I'm late.

ap•o•plex•y ['æpəpleksɪ] *n.* sudden inability to move caused by a stroke. **ap•o•plec•tic** [æpə'plektɪk] *adj.* (a) referring to apoplexy. (b) red-faced.

æ back, ɑː farm, ɒ top, aɪ pipe, aʊ how, aɪə fire, aʊə flower, ɔː bought, ɔɪ toy, e fed, eəhair, eɪ take, ə afraid, əʊ boat, əʊə lower, ɜː word, iː heap, ɪ hit, ɪə hear, uː school, ʊ book, ʌ but, b back, d dog, ð then, dʒ just, f fog, g go, h hand, j yes, k catch, l last, m mix, n nut, ŋ sing, p penny, r round, s some, ʃ short, t too, tʃ chop, θ thing, v voice, w was, z zoo, ʒ treasure

a•pos•ta•sy [æ'pɒstəsɪ] *n.* abandoning a religious belief.

a•pos•tle [ə'pɒsl] *n.* one of the twelve men who were the original disciples of Jesus; **a. spoon** = small spoon with the figure of an apostle on the end of the handle. **a•pos•tate** [ə'pɒsteit] *n.* person who has given up his/her beliefs. **ap•os•tol•ic** [æpəs'tɒlɪk] *adj.* of the apostles.

a pos•te•ri•o•ri [eɪpɒsteri'ɔːrɪ] *adj.* based on observed facts.

a•pos•tro•phe [ə'pɒstrəfɪ] *n.* printing sign (') which shows either that a letter has been left out (**weren't**) or with **s** to show possession (**a boy's coat, the girls' team**).

a•poth•e•o•sis [æpɒθɪ'əʊsɪs] *n.* making s.o. into a god.

ap•pall, ap•pal [ə'pɔːl] *v.* to frighten/to make horrified. **ap•pal•ling,** *adj.* horrible/frightening. **ap•pall•ing•ly,** *adv.* frighteningly.

ap•pa•rat•us [æpə'reɪtəs] *n.* (*no pl.*) equipment (for doing scientific tests, etc.

ap•par•el [ə'pærəl] *n.* (*formal*) clothes.

ap•par•ent [ə'pærənt] *adj.* which seems. **ap•par•ent•ly,** *adv.* as it seems.

ap•pa•ri•tion [æpə'rɪʃn] *n.* ghost; thing which seems strange.

ap•peal [ə'piːl] 1. *n.* (a) asking for (help, etc.). (b) request to the law courts to reconsider a verdict. (c) attraction; **sex a.** = physical attraction. 2. *v.* (a) to ask **for.** (b) **to a. to** = (i) to ask (s.o.) to judge; (ii) to attract. **ap•peal•ing,** *adj.* attractive; as if asking for help. **ap•pel•lant,** *n.* person who appeals.

ap•pear [ə'pɪə] *v.* (a) to come into sight. (b) to be present (**at**). (c) to act (**in** a play). (d) to seem. **ap•pear•ance,** *n.* (a) how a thing or person looks. (b) being present; **to put in an a.** = to be present.

ap•pease [ə'piːz] *v.* to try to avoid/to soothe. **ap•pease•ment,** *n.* policy of avoiding conflict.

ap•pel•la•tion [æpə'leɪʃn] *n.* (*formal*) name.

ap•pend [ə'pend] *v.* to attach/to join. **ap•pend•age,** *n.* thing attached.

ap•pen•dix [ə'pendɪks] *n.* (a) (*pl.* **appendixes, appendices** [ə'pendɪsiːz]) small tube attached to main intestine. (b) section at the back of a book giving information which is additional to the text. **ap•pen•dec•to•my** [æpen'dektəmɪ] *n.* operation to remove an appendix. **ap•pen•di•ci•tis** [əpendɪ'saɪtɪs] *n.* illness caused by inflammation of the appendix.

ap•per•tain [æpə'teɪn] *v.* (*formal*) to be relevant.

ap•pe•tite ['æpɪtaɪt] *n.* desire to eat, etc. **ap•pe•tiz•er,** *n.* snack taken with drinks before the main meal. **ap•pe•tiz•ing,** *adj.* which makes you want to eat.

ap•plaud [ə'plɔːd] *v.* to clap or cheer to show you appreciate sth. **ap•plause,** *n.* clapping and cheering.

ap•ple ['æpl] *n.* common hard fruit, growing on a tree; tree which bears this fruit.

ap•plet ['æplɪt] *n.* computer program that runs within a page on the Internet.

ap•pli•ance [ə'plaɪəns] *n.* machine/device.

ap•pli•qué [ə'pliːkeɪ] *n.* decoration made by sewing shaped pieces of cloth on to a larger piece.

ap•ply [ə'plaɪ] *v.* (a) to put (sth) on sth. (b) to be relevant. (c) to ask s.o. **for** sth (esp. a job). (d) **to a. yourself** = to work hard. **ap•pli•ca•ble** [ə'plɪkəbl] *adj.* which refers to. **ap•pli•cant** ['æplɪkənt] *n.* person who applies for a job; candidate. **ap•pli•ca•tion** [æplɪ'keɪʃn] *n.* (a) action of putting something on something; **for external a. only** = only to be used on the skin. (b) asking for (a job, etc.); **a. form** = form to be filled in when applying. **ap•plied,** *adj.* (science) which is put to practical use.

ap•point [ə'pɔɪnt] *v.* to give (s.o.) a job (**as**). **ap•point•ed,** *adj.* (a) arranged/stated. (b) equipped/furnished. **ap•point•ment,** *n.* (a) being given a job. (b) meeting time which has been agreed. (c) **appointments** = furniture and equipment.

ap•por•tion [ə'pɔːʃn] *v.* (*formal*) to divide up/to share out.

ap•po•site ['æpəzɪt] *adj.* fitting/appropriate (remark). **ap•po•si•tion,** *n.* putting a word next to another; **noun in a.** = noun used as an adjective to describe another noun.

ap•praise [ə'preɪz] *v.* to judge the value of (sth). **ap•prais•al,** *n.* evaluation.

ap•pre•ci•ate [ə'priːʃɪeɪt] *v.* (a) to feel the value of (sth). (b) to increase in value. **ap•pre•ci•a•ble,** *adj.* which can be felt. **ap•pre•ci•a•bly,** *adv.* in a way which could be felt. **ap•pre•ci•a•tion** [əpriːʃɪ'eɪʃn] *n.* (a) estimation (of the value of sth). (b) increase in value. **ap•pre•cia•tive** [ə'priːʃjətɪv] *adj.* praising.

ap•pre•hend [æprɪ'hend] *v.* to arrest (a criminal). **ap•pre•hen•sion** [æprɪ'henʃn] *n.* fear. **ap•pre•hen•sive,** *adj.* afraid/nervous. **ap•pre•hen•sive•ly,** *adv.* nervously.

ap•pren•tice [ə'prentɪs] *n.* youth who works with a skilled man to learn from him. **ap•pren•tice•ship,** *n.* time you spend as an apprentice.

ap•prise [ə'praɪz] *v.* (*formal*) to inform (s.o. **of** sth).

ap•proach [ə'prəʊtʃ] 1. *n.* (*pl.* **-es**) (a) way of

dealing (with a problem). (b) **he made approaches to her to join his company** = he contacted her to ask her to join his company. (c) way into. 2. *v.* (a) to go near. (b) to deal with (a question). **ap•proach•a•ble**, *adj.* easy to talk to. **ap•proach•ing**, *adj.* which is coming closer.

ap•pro•ba•tion [æprə'beɪʃn] *n.* (*formal*) approval.

ap•pro•pri•ate 1. *adj.* [ə'prəʊprɪət] suitable/which fits. 2. *v.* [ə'prəʊprɪeɪt] to seize (sth which belongs to s.o. else). **ap•pro•pri•a•tion** [əprəʊprɪ'eɪʃn] *n.* (a) seizure. (b) money voted to a budget.

ap•prove [ə'pruːv] *v.* to express agreement with (sth); to allow; **to a. of sth** = to be in agreement with sth. **ap•prov•al**, *n.* allowing (sth); **on a.** = on trial. **ap•prov•ing**, *adj.* which shows agreement. **ap•prov•ing•ly**, *adv.* showing agreement.

ap•prox•i•mate 1. *adj.* [ə'prɒksɪmət] rough (calculation). 2. *v.* [ə'prɒksɪmeɪt] to be nearly correct. **ap•prox•i•mate•ly**, *adv.* roughly. **ap•prox•i•ma•tion** [əprɒksɪ'meɪʃn] *n.* rough estimate.

ap•pur•te•nance [ə'pɜːtənəns] *n.* (*formal*) thing which is connected to or belongs to sth else.

APR = annual percentage rate.

ap•ri•cot ['eɪprɪkɒt] *n.* yellow fruit with large stone, grown in warm countries; tree which bears apricots.

A•pril ['eɪprəl] *n.* 4th month of the year. **April Fool**, *n.* person who is tricked on April 1st. **April Fool's Day**, *n.* April 1st/day when people are tricked.

a pri•o•ri [eɪpraɪ'ɔːrɪ] *adj.* based on theory or assumptions.

a•pron ['eɪprən] *n.* (a) piece of cloth, worn over clothes to protect them when working. (b) area in an airport where aircraft are parked.

ap•ro•pos [æprə'pəʊ] *adv.* referring to.

apse [æps] *n.* rounded end of a church.

apt [æpt] *adj.* (a) expression which fits well. (b) likely (to). **ap•ti•tude**, *n.* ability; **a. test** = test to see if you are fitted for a job. **apt•ly**, *adv.* fittingly. **apt•ness**, *n.* fitness (of an expression).

aq•ua•lung ['ækwəlʌŋ] *n.* skindiver's portable oxygen equipment.

aq•ua•ma•rine [ækwəmə'riːn] 1. *adj.* dark blue-green. 2. *n.* semi-precious blue stone.

aq•ua•plane ['ækwəpleɪn] *v.* (*of car*) to slide along the wet surface of a road.

a•quar•i•um [ə'kweərɪəm] *n.* (a) tank for keeping fish. (b) exhibition where fish are displayed.

A•quar•i•us [ə'kweərɪəs] *n.* one of the signs of the Zodiac, shaped like a man carrying water.

a•quat•ic [æ'kwætɪk] *adj.* which lives in water; **a. plants.**

aq•ua•tint ['ækwətɪnt] *n.* print which has been shaded to look like a drawing.

aq•ue•duct ['ækwɪdʌkt] *n.* channel which takes water over land.

a•que•ous ['ækwɪəs] *adj.* containing water.

aq•ui•fer ['ækwɪfə] *n.* layer of porous rock in which water gathers.

aq•ui•line ['ækwɪlaɪn] *adj.* hooked (nose).

Ar *symbol for* argon.

Ar•ab ['ærəb] 1. *adj.* referring to Arabia. 2. *n.* Muslim person living in Arabia or some other Near Eastern countries. **A•ra•bi•an** [ə'reɪbɪən] *adj.* referring to Arabia. **Ar•a•bic** ['ærəbɪk] 1. *n.* language spoken by Arabs. 2. *adj.* **arabic numerals** = signs for numbers written 1, 2, 3, 4, etc. **a•ra•bis**, *n.* small garden plant, with little white flowers.

ar•a•besque [ærə'besk] *n.* complicated design of leaves/flowers.

ar•a•ble ['ærəbl] *adj. & n.* (land) which is good for growing crops.

a•rach•nid [ə'ræknɪd] *n.* type of animal with eight legs, such as a spider.

ar•bi•trage ['ɑːbɪtreɪdʒ] *n.* buying shares in a company which is likely to be taken over, so as to sell them later at a profit. **ar•bi•tra•geur**, *n.* person whose business is arbitrage.

ar•bi•trate ['ɑːbɪtreɪt] *v.* to judge between two parties in a quarrel. **ar•bi•ter**, *n.* person who decides (usu. on questions of fashion). **ar•bi•trar•i•ly**, *adv.* at random. **ar•bi•trar•y**, *adj.* (decision) taken at random. **ar•bi•tra•tion** [ɑːbɪ'treɪʃn] *n.* judgement in a dispute. **ar•bi•tra•tor** ['ɑːbɪtreɪtə] *n.* person who judges a dispute.

ar•bo•re•al [ɑː'bɔːrɪəl] *adj.* living in trees.

ar•bo•re•tum [ɑːbə'riːtəm] *n.* collection of trees grown for study.

ar•bor, *Brit.* **ar•bour** ['ɑːbə] *n.* shady place where trees are trained to form a shelter.

arc [ɑːk] *n.* (a) part of a circle. (b) electric spark jumping between two points. **arc lamp, arc light**, *n.* very bright light. **arc weld•ing**, *n.* welding by an electric arc.

æ back, ɑː farm, ɒ top, aɪ pipe, aʊ how, aɪə fire, aʊə flower, ɔː bought, ɔɪ toy, e fed, eə hair, eɪ take, ə afraid, əʊ boat, əʊə lower, ɜː word, iː heap, ɪ hit, ɪə hear, uː school, ʊ book, ʌ but, b back, d dog, ð then, dʒ just, f fog, g go, h hand, j yes, k catch, l last, m mix, n nut, ŋ sing, p penny, r round, s some, ʃ short, t too, tʃ chop, θ thing, v voice, w was, z zoo, ʒ treasure

ar•cade [ɑ:'keɪd] *n.* covered area with an arched roof; **shopping a.** = row of stores covered by a roof.

ar•cane [ɑ:'keɪn] *adj.* mysterious/secret.

arch [ɑ:tʃ] 1. *n.* (*pl.* **-es**) (a) vault/rounded structure forming a roof, or top of a door. (b) **triumphal a.** = large construction with a rounded vault over a carriageway, usu. built to celebrate a victory. (c) rounded part under the foot. 2. *v.* to make (sth) round. 3. *adj.* wicked and playful. **arch•ed,** *adj.* made with an arch. **arch•way,** *n.* passage/entrance with an arch.

arch- [ɑ:tʃ] *prefix meaning* greatest; **arch-enemy.**

ar•chae•ol•o•gy, ar•che•ol•o•gy [ɑ:kɪ'ɒlədʒɪ] *n.* study of ancient civilization. **ar•chae•o•log•i•cal** [ɑ:krə'lɒdʒɪkl] *adj.* referring to archaeology. **ar•chae•ol•o•gist** [ɑ:kɪ'ɒlədʒɪst] *n.* person who studies archaeology.

ar•cha•ic [ɑ:'keɪɪk] *adj.* very ancient.

arch•an•gel ['ɑ:keɪndʒl] *n.* highest rank of angel.

arch•bish•op [ɑ:tʃ'bɪʃəp] *n.* very important bishop/leader of bishops.

arch•er ['ɑ:tʃə] *n.* person who shoots with a bow and arrow. **ar•cher•y,** *n.* sport of shooting arrows at a target.

ar•che•type ['ɑ:kɪtaɪp] *n.* original version from which other versions can be copied. **ar•che•typ•al,** *adj.* original; perfect (example).

ar•chi•pel•a•go [ɑ:kɪ'peləgəʊ] *n.* (*pl.* **-os, -oes**) group of islands.

ar•chi•tect ['ɑ:kɪtekt] *n.* person who designs buildings. **ar•chi•tec•ture,** *n.* design of buildings. **ar•chi•tec•tur•al,** *adj.* referring to architecture.

ar•chi•trave ['ɑ:tʃɪtreɪv] *n.* molding around a door or window.

ar•chives ['ɑ:kaɪvz] *n. pl.* collection of documents, esp. public or historical records. **ar•chi•vist** ['ɑ:kɪvɪst] *n.* librarian who looks after archives.

arc•tic ['ɑ:ktɪk] *adj. & n.* (referring to) the area around the North Pole; extremely cold (weather).

ar•dent ['ɑ:dənt] *adj.* very strenuous; keen. **ar•dent•ly,** *adj.* strenuously/fiercely.

ar•dor, *Brit.* **ar•dour** ['ɑ:də] *n.* violence (of emotions).

ar•du•ous ['ɑ:djʊəs] *adj.* very difficult/hard (task). **ar•du•ous•ly,** *adv.* with great difficulty.

are [ɑ:] *v. see* **be.**

ar•e•a ['eərɪə] *n.* (a) space; measure of the surface of sth. (b) region. (c) **ar•e•a code,** *n.*

number which you dial in addition to the telephone number to call a particular town or country. (d) general subject.

a•re•ca [ə'ri:kə] *n.* type of tropical nut.

a•re•na [ə'ri:nə] *n.* space where sports and fights take place.

Ar•gen•tine, Ar•gen•tin•i•an ['ɑ:dʒəntaɪn, ɑ:dʒən'tɪnjən] 1. *adj.* referring to Argentina. 2. *n.* person from Argentina.

ar•gon ['ɑ:gɒn] *n.* (element: Ar) inert gas.

ar•gue ['ɑ:gju:] *v.* to discuss without agreeing; to quarrel. **ar•gu•a•ble,** *adj.* which is open to discussion. **ar•gu•ment,** *n.* (a) quarrel/discussion without agreement. (b) reasoning. **ar•gu•men•ta•tive** [ɑ:gju'mentətɪv] *adj.* (person) who likes to quarrel.

a•ri•a ['ɑ:rɪə] *n.* long solo song in opera.

ar•id ['ærɪd] *adj.* very dry. **a•rid•i•ty** [ə'rɪdɪtɪ] *n.* extreme dryness.

Ar•ies ['eəri:z] *n.* one of the signs of the Zodiac, shaped like a ram.

a•rise [ə'raɪz] *v.* (**arose; arisen**) (a) to appear; to start. (b) to result **from.**

a•ris•to•crat ['ærɪstəkræt] *n.* person who is born into the aristocracy. **ar•is•toc•ra•cy** [ærɪ'stɒkrəsɪ] *n.* top rank (by birth) of society. **a•ris•to•crat•ic** [ærɪstə'krætɪk] *adj.* referring to the aristocracy; superior (attitude).

a•rith•me•tic [ə'rɪθmetɪk] *n.* calculations with figures. **ar•ith•met•i•cal** [ærɪθ'metɪkl] *adj.* referring to arithmetic.

arm [ɑ:m] 1. *n.* (a) part of the body between the hand and shoulder; **a. in a.** = with their arms linked. (b) thing shaped like an arm; piece at the side of a chair to rest your arms on. (c) narrow stretch of water running inland. (d) **arms** = weapons; **up in arms about** = very angry/furious. 2. *v.* to equip with weapons. **ar•ma•ments,** *n. pl.* heavy weapons/war equipment. **arm•band,** *n.* piece of cloth worn around your arm. **arm•chair,** *n.* chair with arms. **armed,** *adj.* equipped with weapons; **the a. forces** = the army, navy and air force of a country. **arm•ful,** *n.* load carried in your arms. **arm•hole,** *n.* hole in a piece of clothing through which you put your arms. **ar•mor,** *Brit.* **ar•mour** *n.* (a) metal protective clothes for medieval soldiers. (b) thick protecting material covering ships or tanks. **armored,** *adj.* protected by metal; **a. car** = military car made of thick metal which carries a small gun. **armor-plat•ed,** *adj.* protected by thick metal plates. **ar•mor•y,** *n.* place where weapons are kept; arsenal. **arm•pit,** *n.* part of your body under where your arm joins the shoulder. **arm•rest,** *n.* thing which you rest your arm on. **ar•my,** *n.* all the soldiers of a country.

ar•ma•da [ɑːˈmɑːdə] *n.* fleet of warships.

ar•ma•dil•lo [ɑːməˈdrɪləʊ] *n.* small South American animal covered with a flexible shell.

ar•ma•ged•don [ɑːməˈgedən] *n.* great final battle.

ar•ma•ture [ˈɑːmətjə] *n.* moving part of an electric motor; coil in a dynamo.

ar•mi•stice [ˈɑːmɪstɪs] *n.* decision to stop fighting temporarily.

a•ro•ma [əˈrəʊmə] *n.* (pleasant) smell (of coffee/wine, etc.). **ar•o•mat•ic** [ærəˈmætɪk] *adj.* (herb) with a strong pleasant smell.

a•rose [əˈrəʊz] *v. see* **arise.**

a•round [əˈraʊnd] 1. *adv.* (a) surrounding a place, person, or thing, in a circle. (b) in an indefinite place. (c) on all sides; **he looked a. him; she handed around the letters; is there enough cake to go around?** 2. *prep.* (a) surrounding. (b) approximately.

a•rouse [əˈraʊz] *v.* (a) to wake. (b) to excite (emotion).

ar•peg•gi•o [ɑːˈpedʒɪəʊ] *n.* (*pl.* **-os**) chord with the notes played one after the other and not all together.

ar•range [əˈreɪndʒ] *v.* (a) to put in order. (b) to adapt (a piece of music). (c) to organize. **ar•range•ment,** *n.* (a) way in which something is laid out. (b) organizing. (c) agreement.

ar•rant [ˈærənt] *adj.* complete, unmitigated.

ar•ray [əˈreɪ] 1. *n.* display. 2. *v.* (a) to set out in order. (b) (*formal*) to dress (in fine costume).

ar•rears [əˈrɪəz] *n.* **to be in a.** = to be late (in doing sth).

ar•rest [əˈrest] 1. *n.* being held (by the police) on a charge; **he's under a.; cardiac a.** = stoppage of the heart. 2. *v.* to hold (s.o.) for breaking the law. **ar•rest•ing,** *adj.* which attracts the attention.

ar•rive [əˈraɪv] *v.* to reach a place; (*of baby*) to be born. **ar•ri•val,** *n.* (a) reaching a place. (b) person who has arrived.

ar•ro•gant [ˈærəgənt] *adj.* very proud. **ar•ro•gance,** *n.* being very proud; thinking that you are superior. **ar•ro•gant•ly,** *adv.* proudly.

ar•row [ˈærəʊ] *n.* (a) long stick with a sharp point which is shot by a bow. (b) sign showing the way to a place. **ar•row•root,** *n.* flour made from the root of a tropical American plant.

arse [ɑːs] *n.* (*vulgar*) buttocks.

ar•se•nal [ˈɑːsənl] *n.* store of weapons.

ar•se•nic [ˈɑːsnɪk] *n.* (*element:* As) powerful poison.

ar•son [ˈɑːsn] *n.* criminal act of setting fire to a property. **ar•son•ist,** *n.* person who sets fire to property.

art [ɑːt] *n.* painting, drawing, sculpture and music; **a. gallery** = museum of paintings, sculptures, etc.; **arts subjects** = subjects (such as languages, history, etc.) which are not sciences. **art•ful,** *adj.* clever; up to the latest tricks. **art•ful•ly,** *adv.* cleverly. **art•less,** *adj.* natural/not forced; naive.

ar•te•fact [ˈɑːtɪfækt] *n. see* **artifact.**

ar•te•ri•o•scle•ro•sis [ɑːtɪərɪəʊsklə'rəʊsɪs] *n.* hardening of the arteries (esp. in old age).

ar•ter•y [ˈɑːtərɪ] *n.* (a) tube that blood flows through from the heart to other parts of the body. (b) important road. **ar•te•ri•al** [ɑː-ˈtɪərɪəl] *adj.* referring to an artery.

ar•te•sian [ɑːˈtiːʒn] *adj.* **a. well** = well drilled in the ground which does not require a pump to make the water rise.

ar•thri•tis [ɑːˈθraɪtɪs] *n.* illness where joints become swollen and stiff. **ar•thrit•ic** [ɑːˈθrɪtɪk] *adj.* stiff from arthritis.

ar•thro•de•sis [ɑːθrəʊˈdiːsɪs] *n.* operation to fix a hip joint so that it does not move. **ar•thro•plas•ty** [ˈɑːθrəʊplæstɪ] *n.* operation to replace a hip joint with an artificial one. **ar•thro•pod,** *n.* animal with a body formed of joined sections, such as a spider.

ar•ti•choke [ˈɑːtɪtʃəʊk] *n.* (a) (**globe**) **a.** = green vegetable like the flower of a thistle. (b) (**Jerusalem**) **a.** = root vegetable.

ar•ti•cle [ˈɑːtɪkl] *n.* (a) clause (in agreement). (b) piece of writing in a newspaper, etc. (c) thing/object. (d) part of speech; **"the" is a definite a.; "a" is an indefinite a.**

ar•tic•u•late 1. *v.* [ɑːˈtɪkjʊleɪt] (a) to speak (a word). (b) to join. 2. *adj.* [ɑːˈtɪkjʊlət] clear-speaking. **ar•tic•u•la•tion** [ɑːtɪkjuˈleɪʃn] *n.* (*Med.*) joint.

ar•ti•fice, *n.* trick. **ar•tif•i•cer,** *n.* skilled craftsman.

ar•ti•fact [ˈɑːtɪfækt] *n.* object (usu. a tool) made by a human being.

ar•ti•fi•cial [ɑːtɪˈfɪʃl] *adj.* which is an imitation/not the real thing; **a. respiration** = reviving s.o. who is nearly dead. **ar•ti•fi•ci•al•i•ty,** *n.* falseness/not being sincere. **ar•ti•fi•cial•ly,** *adv.* unnaturally.

ar•til•ler•y [ɑːˈtɪlərɪ] *n.* section of the army concerned with guns; **the a.** = the guns.

æ back, aː farm, ɒ top, aɪ pipe, aʊ how, aie fire, aʊə flower, ɔː bought, ɔɪ toy, e fed, eəhair, eɪ take, ə afraid, əʊ boat, əʊə lower, vː word, iː heap, ɪ hit, ɪə hear, uː school, ʊ book, ʌ but, b back, d dog, ð then, dʒ just, f fog, g go, h hand, j yes, k catch, l last, m mix, n nut, ŋ sing, p penny, r round, s some, ʃ short, t too, tʃ chop, θ thing, v voice, w was, z zoo, ʒ treasure

ar•til•ler•y•man, n. (pl. -men) soldier working with guns.

ar•ti•san [ɑːtɪ'zæn] n. skilled workman/craftsman.

art•ist ['ɑːtɪst] n. person who draws, paints, or plays music. ar•tis•tic [ɑː'tɪstɪk] adj. (person) who has a feeling or skill for art; (thing) which looks good because it is made by an artistic person. ar•tis•ti•cal•ly, adv. with art. art•ist•ry ['ɑːtɪstrɪ] n. skill in art.

ar•tiste [ɑː'tiːst] n. performer in a theater (esp. dancer/acrobat).

art•y ['ɑːtɪ] adj. inf. pretending to be artistic.

ar•um ['eərəm] n. lily with a tall white flower.

as [æz, əz] conj. (a) like. (b) because. (c) at the same time that. (d) doing the job of; acting the part of. (e) in a certain way. (f) as for = referring to/concerning. (g) as from = starting from. (h) as if/as though = like/seeming. (i) as long as = on condition that. (j) as soon as = immediately. (k) as to = referring to. (l) as well as = in addition to.

As symbol for arsenic.

ASAP [ereser'piː] = as soon as possible.

as•bes•tos [æs'bestəs] n. mineral substance which is fireproof. as•bes•to•sis [æsbes-'təʊsɪs] n. lung disease caused by breathing in particles of asbestos.

as•cend [ə'send] v. (formal) to go up. as•cend•an•cy, n. influence. as•cend•ant, n. rising; in the a. = becoming powerful/popular. as•cen•sion [ə'senʃn], as•cent [ə'sent] n. going up.

as•cer•tain [æsə'teɪn] v. (formal) to check/to find out (the facts). as•cer•tain•a•ble, adj. which can be checked.

as•cet•ic [ə'setɪk] 1. adj. (way of life) where you do not allow yourself any comfort or pleasure. 2. n. religious person who does not allow himself any pleasures. as•cet•i•cism, n. belief in an ascetic way of life.

ASCII ['æski] American Standard Code for Information Interchange.

a•scor•bic [ə'skɔːbɪk] adj. a. acid = vitamin C occurring in oranges, vegetables, etc.

as•cot ['æskət] n. type of scarf worn around the neck.

as•cribe [æ'skraɪb] v. (formal) to attribute (sth to s.o.). a•scrib•a•ble, adj. which can be ascribed.

a•sep•tic [ə'septɪk] adj. sterilized/with no infection.

a•sex•u•al ['eɪseksjuəl] adj. not involving sex.

ash [æʃ] n. (pl. ashes) (a) common tree in northern countries; wood of this tree. (b) dust left after something has burned. (c) ashes = remains of a person's body after cremation. ash•can, n. container for putting ashes or

trash in. ash•en ['æʃən] adj. very pale.

ash•tray, n. small bowl for putting ash from cigarettes, etc.

a•shamed [ə'ʃeɪmd] adj. sorry because of sth wrong.

ash•lar ['æʃlə] n. (no pl.) building stones cut square.

a•shore [ə'ʃɔː] adv. on land.

A•sian ['eɪʒn] adj. & n. (person) from Asia. A•si•at•ic [eɪsɪ'ætɪk] adj. referring to Asia.

a•side [ə'saɪd] 1. adv. to one side; a. from = apart from. 2. n. words spoken in a play which the other characters are not supposed to hear.

as•i•nine ['æsɪnaɪn] adj. stupid.

ask [ɑːsk] v. (a) to put a question (about); to a. after s.o. = to inquire about s.o.'s health. (b) to a. for = to request/to want (sth) to be given to you. (c) to invite (s.o. to a party, etc.). ask•ing, n. it's yours for the a. = you only have to ask for it and you will get it.

a•skance [ə'skɑːns] adv. to look at sth/s.o. a. = to be suspicious of.

a•skew [ə'skjuː] adv. not straight.

a•slant [ə'slɑːnt] adv. sloping.

a•sleep [ə'sliːp] adj. sleeping.

asp [æsp] n. small poisonous snake.

as•par•a•gus [ə'spærəgəs] n. cultivated plant of which you eat the new shoots as a vegetable.

as•pect ['æspekt] n. (a) direction which a house faces. (b) side; way of looking at sth.

as•pen ['æspn] n. small tree with leaves which tremble in the wind.

as•per•i•ty [æ'sperɪtɪ] n. sharpness.

as•per•sions [ə'spɜːʃnz] n. pl. bad comments (on s.o.).

as•phalt ['æsfælt] 1. n. mixture of tar and sand which is used for surfacing roads. 2. v. to cover with asphalt.

as•phyx•i•ate [əs'fɪksɪeɪt] v. to stifle/to kill (s.o.) by preventing them from breathing. as•phyx•i•a, asphyxiation [əsfɪksɪ'eɪʃn] n. being unable to breathe.

as•pic ['æspɪk] n. jelly made from meat, fish, poultry, or vegetable juices.

as•pi•dis•tra [æspɪ'dɪstrə] n. type of indoor plant.

as•pi•rate ['æspɪrət] adj. & n. (sound) which has to be breathed (as "h" in "horse").

as•pire [ə'spaɪə] v. (to) to have the ambition to do sth. as•pir•ant ['æspərənt] n. person who aspires to do sth. as•pi•ra•tion [æspɪ'reɪʃn] n. ambition. as•pir•ing, adj. ambitious/hopeful.

as•pi•rin ['æspɪrɪn] n. (tablet of) common drug taken to stop headaches/colds, etc.

ass [æs] n. (pl. -es) (a) donkey. (b) stupid person. (c) Sl. buttocks.

as•sail•ant [əˈseɪlənt] *n.* person who attacks (s.o.).

as•sas•si•nate [əˈsæsɪneɪt] *v.* to kill (s.o.) for political reasons. **as•sas•sin,** *n.* person who kills for political reasons. **as•sas•si•na•tion** [əsæsɪˈneɪʃn] *n.* political murder.

as•sault [əˈsɔːlt] 1. *n.* attack. 2. *v.* to attack.

as•say [əˈseɪ] 1. *n.* test to see how pure metal is. 2. *v.* to test (metal) to see how pure it is.

as•se•gai [ˈæsəgaɪ] *n.* native spear from Southern Africa.

as•sem•ble [əˈsembl] *v.* to get together; to put together. **as•sem•bly,** *n.* (a) meeting. (b) putting together; **a. line** = continuous moving line in a factory, where machines, etc., are put together.

as•sent [əˈsent] 1. *n.* agreement. 2. *v.* to agree (to).

as•sert [əˈsɜːt] *v.* to state firmly; **to a. yourself** = take a firm position. **as•ser•tion** [əˈsɜːʃn] *n.* statement (of rights). **as•ser•tive,** *adj.* forceful.

as•sess [əˈses] *v.* (a) to calculate the amount of damages/of tax which should be paid. (b) to value. (c) to estimate. **as•sess•ment,** *n.* (a) calculation of damages/of tax. (b) calculation of value. (c) estimate. **as•ses•sor,** *n.* person who assesses.

as•set [ˈæset] *n.* (a) valuable thing which belongs to you. (b) *pl.* **assets** = anything owned which can be sold to pay debts.

as•sid•u•ous [əˈsɪdjuəs] *adj.* regular and very careful. **as•si•du•i•ty** [æsɪˈdjuːɪtɪ] *n.* regularity of work. **as•sid•u•ous•ly,** *adv.* regularly and very carefully; without fail.

as•sign [əˈsaɪn] *v.* (a) to appoint (s.o. **to do** sth). (b) to transfer sth **to** s.o. **as•sig•na•tion** [æsɪgˈneɪʃn] *n.* (a) transfer (of property). (b) lovers' meeting. **as•sign•ment,** *n.* (a) delegation (of a task to s.o.). (b) work which you have been told to do.

as•sim•i•late [əˈsɪmɪleɪt] *v.* to digest (food); to learn and understand (facts). **as•sim•i•la•tion** [əsɪmɪˈleɪʃn] *n.* act of assimilating food or information.

as•sist [əˈsɪst] *v.* to help (s.o.). **as•sis•tance,** *n.* help. **as•sis•tant.** 1. *n.* person who helps. 2. *adj.* deputy.

as•siz•es [əˈsaɪzɪz] *n. pl.* (*old*) local courts held in various parts of England and Wales at regular intervals (now the Crown Courts).

as•so•ci•ate 1. *v.* [əˈsəʊsɪeɪt] (**with**) to link

(with s.o.)/to be linked (to s.o./sth). 2. *n.* [əˈsəʊsɪət] person who is linked to s.o. **as•so•ci•a•tion** [əsəʊsɪˈeɪʃn] *n.* group/society.

as•so•nance [ˈæsənəns] *n.* rhyme using vowels only.

as•sort•ed [əˈsɔːtɪd] *adj.* (a) matched. (b) mixed. **as•sort•ment,** *n.* collection/mixture.

as•suage [əˈsweɪdʒ] *v.* (*formal*) to calm/to soothe.

as•sume [əˈsjuːm] *v.* (a) to take (power, responsibility) upon yourself. (b) to suppose. **as•sumed,** *adj.* false. **as•sump•tion** [əˈsʌmpʃn] *n.* (a) taking up (of office). (b) belief that sth is true, even if it has not been proved.

as•sure [əˈʃʊə] *v.* (a) to make safe/certain. (b) to state/to affirm. **as•sur•ance,** *n.* (a) promise. (b) calm; feeling of certainty. **as•sured** *adj.* certain. **as•sur•ed•ly** [əˈʃʊərədlɪ] *adv.* certainly.

as•ter [ˈæstə] *n.* garden plant with star-shaped flowers.

as•ter•isk [ˈæstərɪsk] *n.* sign (*) to indicate some special mention.

a•stern [əˈstɜːn] *adv.* behind a ship; (*of ship*) **to go a.** = to go backward.

as•ter•oid [ˈæstərɔɪd] *n.* very small planet.

asth•ma [ˈæsmə] *n.* wheezing, usu. caused by allergy. **asth•mat•ic** [æsˈmætɪk] *adj. & n.* (person) who suffers from asthma.

a•stig•ma•tism [əˈstɪgmətɪzəm] *n.* condition of the eyes where the image focuses correctly at one angle but not at another. **as•tig•mat•ic** [æstɪgˈmætɪk] *adj.* referring to astigmatism.

as•ton•ish [əˈstɒnɪʃ] *v.* to surprise. **as•ton•ish•ing,** *adj.* surprising. **as•ton•ish•ing•ly,** *adv.* surprisingly. **as•ton•ish•ment,** *n.* surprise.

as•tound [əˈstaʊnd] *v.* to surprise completely. **as•tound•ing,** *adj.* very surprising.

as•tra•khan [æstrəˈkæn] *n.* dark fur from the skin of black lambs.

as•tral [ˈæstrəl] *adj.* referring to stars.

a•stray [əˈstreɪ] *adv.* lost; **to go a.** = get lost; **to lead a.** = to lead into bad habits.

a•stride [əˈstraɪd] *adv. & prep.* with your legs on either side (of).

as•trin•gent [əˈstrɪndʒənt] 1. *adj.* harsh/severe (comments, etc.). 2. *n.* medicine/cosmetic for closing pores, etc. **as•trin•gen•cy,** *n.* being astringent.

as•trol•o•gy [əˈstrɒlədʒɪ] *n.* art of foretelling

æ back, aː farm, ɒ top, aɪ pipe, aʊ how, aɪə fire, aʊə flower, ɔː bought, ɔɪ toy, e fed, eəhair, eɪ take, ə afraid, əʊ boat, əʊə lower, vː word, iː heap, ɪ hit, ɪə hear, uː school, ʊ book, ʌ but, b back, d dog, ð then, dʒ just, f fog, g go, h hand, j yes, k catch, l last, m mix, n nut, ŋ sing, p penny, r round, s some, ʃ short, t too, tʃ chop, θ thing, v voice, w was, z zoo, ʒ treasure

events from the stars and planets.
as•trol•o•ger, *n.* person who gives advice
based on reading the position of the stars.
as•tro•log•i•cal [æstrə'lɒdʒɪkl] *adj.* referring to astrology.
as•tro•naut ['æstrənɔːt] *n.* person who travels
in a spacecraft.
as•tron•o•my [ə'strɒnəmɪ] *n.* science of
studying the stars, the sun and the universe.
as•tron•o•mer, *n.* person who studies astronomy. **as•tro•nom•i•cal** [æstrə'nɒmɪkl]
adj. (a) referring to astronomy. (b) *inf.* very
large. **as•tro•nom•i•cal•ly,** *adv.* (a) using
astronomy. (b) *inf.* enormously.
as•tro•phys•ics [æstrəʊ'fɪzɪks] *n.* study of the
physics of the universe.
as•tute [ə'stjuːt] *adj.* clever/wise. **as•tute•ly,**
adv. cleverly. **as•tute•ness,** *n.* being astute.
a•sun•der [ə'sʌndə] *adv.* (*old*) apart.
a•sy•lum [ə'saɪləm] *n.* (a) place of refuge; **political a.** = permission to stay in a country
when one is politically undesirable in one's
own. (b) (*old*) mental hospital.
a•sym•me•try [ə'sɪmətrɪ] *n.* lack of symmetry. **a•sym•met•ri•cal** [æsɪ'metrɪkl] *adj.*
not symmetrical.
at [æt, ət] *prep.* (a) (*showing time or place*) **at the
office; at night.** (b) (*showing speed or rate*) **at
100 miles an hour; at fifty cents a pound.** (c)
(*showing cause*) **she laughed at my old coat.** (d)
busy; **at work.** (e) **at first** = at the beginning; **at
once** = immediately.
at•a•rax•i•a [ætə'ræksɪə] *n.* excessive calmness.
at•a•vis•tic [ætə'vɪstɪk] *adj.* reverting to the
characteristics of one's ancestors.
a•tax•i•a [æ'tæksɪə] *n.* being unable to coordinate the use of muscles.
ate [et] *v. see* **eat.**
a•the•ism ['eɪθɪzəm] *n.* believing there is no
god. **a•the•ist,** *n.* person who believes there
is no god. **a•the•is•tic** [eɪθɪ'ɪstɪk] *adj.* referring to atheism.
ath•lete ['æθliːt] *n.* person who takes part in a
sport, in particular, running, jumping, throwing; **athlete's foot** = skin infection on the feet.
ath•let•ic [æθ'letɪk] *adj.* referring to sport.
ath•let•ics, *n.* organized sports where you
run, jump or throw.
At•lan•tic [ət'læntɪk] *n.* **the A. (Ocean)** =
ocean separating Europe and Africa from
North and South America.
at•las ['ætləs] *n.* (*pl.* **-es**) book of maps.
at•mos•phere ['ætməsfɪə] *n.* (a) air which
surrounds the earth. (b) general feeling (at a
party, etc.). **at•mos•pher•ic** [ætməs'ferɪk]
adj. referring to the atmosphere.
at•mos•pher•ics, *n. pl.* electric distur-

bances which interfere with radio or TV
signals.
at•oll ['ætɒl] *n.* tropical coral island.
at•om ['ætəm] *n.* (a) basic particle of matter.
(b) very small thing. **a•tom•ic** [ə'tɒmɪk] *adj.*
referring to physical atoms; **a. bomb** = bomb
which uses nuclear energy; **a. number** = number of protons in one atom of a chemical element; **a. weight** = ratio of the mass of an atom
of an element to the mass of carbon 12.
at•om•ize ['ætəmaɪz] *v.* to reduce to very
fine particles. **at•om•iz•er,** *n.* device for at-
omizing, esp. a spray for scent.
a•ton•al [,eɪtəʊnəl] *adj.* without any tones.
a•tone [ə'təʊn] *v.* to make amends (**for**).
a•tone•ment, *n.* making amends (**for** a sin).
a•tri•um ['ætrɪəm] *n.* (a) central court of a
large building, usu. with a glass roof. (b) one
of the chambers of the heart.
a•tro•cious [ə'trəʊʃəs] *adj.* (a) very wicked.
(b) very bad. **a•tro•cious•ly,** *adv.* very badly.
a•troc•i•ty [ə'trɒsɪtɪ] *n.* very wicked deed.
at•ro•phy ['ætrəfɪ] **1.** *n.* wasting away (of a
limb). **2.** *v.* to waste away.
at•tach [ə'tætʃ] *v.* to fasten. **at•ta•ché** [ə-
'tæʃeɪ] *n.* specialized member of the staff of an
embassy. **attaché case,** *n.* small case for carrying papers. **at•tach•ment,** *n.* (a) device
which is attached to something else. (b)
affection.
at•tack [ə'tæk] **1.** *n.* (a) starting to fight. (b)
sudden start of a disease. **2.** *v.* to start fighting
(s.o.). **at•tack•er,** *n.* person who attacks.
at•tain [ə'teɪn] *v.* to reach (an age, an ambition). **at•tain•a•ble,** *adj.* which can be
reached. **at•tain•ment,** *n.* (a) reaching. (b)
attainments = talents/intellectual capacities.
at•tain•der [ə'teɪndə] *n.* loss of a person's
civil rights as a result of having been convicted
of a felony or treason and sentenced to death.
at•tempt [ə'tempt] **1.** *n.* try. **2.** *v.* to try.
at•tend [ə'tend] *v.* (a) **to a. to s.o.** = to look
after s.o. (b) to be present at. **at•tend•ance,**
n. being present. **at•tend•ant,** *n.* (a) person
who waits on or goes with another person. (b)
person who is on duty (in a public restroom,
etc.).
at•ten•tion [ə'tenʃn] *n.* (a) careful thought
about sth.; **a. deficit disorder** = condition, esp.
of children, characterized by a short concentration span and hyperactivity. (b) (*of soldiers*) **to stand at a.** = to stand straight with
heels together. **at•ten•tive** [ə'tentɪv] *adj.* (a)
paying attention; careful. (b) taking care of
(s.o.). **at•ten•tive•ly,** *adv.* with attention.
at•ten•u•ate [ə'tenjʊeɪt] *v.* (*formal*) to make
thinner/weaker; **attenuating circumstances** =
circumstances which reduce the blame at-

tached to a crime. **at•ten•u•a•tion,** *n.* becoming weaker.

at•test [ə'test] *v.* (*formal*) (**to**) to say that sth is true.

at•tic ['ætɪk] *n.* room under the roof of a house.

at•tire [ə'taɪə] *n.* (*no pl.*) (*formal*) clothing. **at•tired,** *adj.* (**in**) wearing.

at•ti•tude ['ætɪtjuːd] *n.* (a) way of standing/sitting, etc. (b) way of thinking.

at•tor•ney [ə'tɜːnɪ] *n.* (a) lawyer. (b) **power of a.** = power to act on behalf of s.o. else.

at•tract [ə'trækt] *v.* to make (sth) come towards you. **at•trac•tion** [ə'trækʃn] *n.* (a) pull. (b) ability to attract (s.o.)/to make (s.o.) interested. (c) thing which attracts people. **at•trac•tive,** *adj.* pleasant-looking. **at•trac•tive•ly,** *adv.* in an attractive way.

at•trib•ute 1. *n.* ['ætrɪbjuːt] (a) quality. (b) symbol. 2. *v.* [ə'trɪbjuːt] **to a. sth to s.o.** = to say that sth belongs to s.o. **at•trib•ut•a•ble** [ə-'trɪbjʊtəbl] *adj.* which can be attributed to s.o.

at•tri•tion [ə'trɪʃn] *n.* wearing down; **war of a.** = war to be won by wearing down your enemy's forces.

at•tuned to [ə'tjuːnd tu] *adj.* aware of (latest fashions, etc.).

Au *symbol for* gold.

au•ber•gine ['əʊbəʒiːn] *n.* eggplant.

au•brie•tia [ɔː'briːʃə] *n.* low growing plant with bright purple flowers.

au•burn ['ɔːbən] *adj.* reddish chestnut-colored (hair).

auc•tion ['ɔːkʃn] 1. *n.* sale where the item is sold to the highest bidder. 2. *v.* to sell (sth) to the highest bidder. **auc•tion•eer** [ɔːkʃə'nɪə] *n.* person who is in charge of an auction. **auc•tion off,** *v.* to sell (sth) by auction to get rid of it. **auction gal•ler•y,** *n.* place where auctions are carried out.

au•da•cious [ɔː'deɪʃəs] *adj.* very daring. **au•da•cious•ly,** *adv.* daringly. **au•dac•i•ty** [ɔː'dæsɪtɪ] *n.* daring.

au•di•ble ['ɔːdɪbl] *adj.* which can be heard. **au•di•bil•i•ty** [ɔːdɪ'bɪlɪtɪ] *n.* capacity for being heard. **au•di•bly** ['ɔːdɪblɪ] *adv.* in an audible way.

au•di•ence ['ɔːdɪəns] *n.* (a) people listening to a concert/watching a movie or play, etc. (b) (*formal*) hearing.

au•di•o book ['ɔːdɪəʊ bʊk] *n.* tape or compact disk of a recording of the reading aloud of a book.

au•di•o-vis•u•al [ɔːdɪəʊ'vɪzjʊəl] *adj.* refer-ring to a method of teaching using tapes, records, films, etc.

au•dit ['ɔːdɪt] 1. *n.* official checking of accounts. 2. *v.* to check (the accounts of a company). **au•di•tor,** *n.* expert accountant who checks the accounts of a company, etc.

au•di•tion [ɔː'dɪʃn] 1. *n.* testing of the suitability of actors/dancers, etc., for a job. 2. *v.* (a) to test the suitability of (an actor/dancer, etc., for a job). (b) (*of actor*) **to a. for a part** = to go to a test for a part.

au•di•to•ri•um [ɔːdɪ'tɔːrɪəm] *n.* huge hall for meetings/concerts, etc.

au fait [əʊ'feɪ] *adj.* (*French*) familiar (**with**).

auf Wie•der•seh•en [aʊf'viːdəzeɪn] (*German*) goodbye.

au•ger ['ɔːgə] *n.* tool for boring holes.

aug•ment [ɔːg'ment] *v.* to increase. **aug•men•ta•tion** [ɔːgmen'teɪʃn] *n.* increase.

au•gur ['ɔːgə] *v.* to be a sign for the future.

au•gust [ɔː'gʌst] *adj.* solemn and dignified.

Au•gust ['ɔːgəst] *n.* 8th month of the year.

auk [ɔːk] *n.* large black and white sea bird.

aunt [ɑːnt] *n.* sister of your mother or father; wife of an uncle.

au pair [əʊ'peə] *adj.* & *n.* (*pl.* **au pairs**) **she is going to France as an au pair (girl)** = she is going to live with a French family to do light housework (and learn French).

au•ra ['ɔːrə] *n.* general feeling surrounding a person/a place.

au•ral ['ɔːrəl] *adj.* using the ear. **au•ral•ly,** *adv.* by listening.

au re•voir [əʊrə'vwɑːr] (*French*) goodbye.

au•ri•cle ['ɒrɪkl] *n.* (a) outside part of the ear. (b) space in the heart which fills with blood and then pumps it into the ventricles.

au•ro•ra [ə'rɔːrə] *n.* **a. borealis** = the Northern lights/bright lights seen in the sky in the far North.

aus•cul•ta•tion [ɔːskəl'teɪʃn] *n.* listening to the chest of a patient, using a stethoscope.

aus•pic•es ['ɔːspɪsɪz] *n. pl.* (a) forecast/signs of the future. (b) patronage; **under the a. of** = subsidized/organized by. **aus•pi•cious** [ɔː-'spɪʃəs] *adj.* favorable/lucky. **aus•pi•cious•ly,** *adv.* favorably.

Aus•sie ['ɒzɪ] *n.* & *adj. inf.* Australian.

aus•tere [ɔː'stɪə] *adj.* cold/severe; without luxury. **aus•ter•i•ty** [ɔː'sterɪtɪ] *n.* absence of luxury.

Aus•tral•ian [ɒs'treɪlɪən] 1. *adj.* referring to

æ back, ɑː farm, ɒ top, aɪ pipe, aʊ how, aɪə fire, aʊə flower, ɔː bought, ɔɪ toy, e fed, eəhair, eɪ take, ə afraid, əʊ boat, əʊə lower, vː word, iː heap, ɪ hit, ɪə hear, uː school, ʊ book, ʌ but, b back, d dog, ð then, dʒ just, f fog, g go, h hand, j yes, k catch, l last, m mix, n nut, ŋ sing, p penny, r round, s some, ʃ short, t too, tʃ chop, θ thing, v voice, w was, z zoo, ʒ treasure

Australia. 2. *n.* person from Australia.
Aus•tral•a•sian, *adj.* referring to
Australasia (the part of the Southern Hemisphere including Australia, New Zealand, and
the Pacific Islands.
Aus•tri•an ['ɒstrɪən] 1. *adj.* referring to Austria. 2. *n.* person from Austria.
au•tar•chy ['ɔːtɑːkɪ] *n.* self rule, situation
where a state rules itself.
au•tar•ky ['ɔːtɑːkɪ] *n.* self-sufficiency.
au•then•tic [ɔːˈθentɪk] *adj.* real; genuine.
au•then•ti•cate [ɔːˈθentɪkeɪt] *v.* to swear
that sth is true. **au•then•tic•i•ty** [ɔːθen-
ˈtɪsɪtɪ] *n.* being authentic.
au•thor ['ɔːθə] *n.* person who writes books, etc.
au•thor•ship, *n.* identity of the author.
au•thor•i•ty [ɔːˈθɒrɪtɪ] *n.* (a) power. (b) permission. (c) source. (d) ruling committee or
group. (e) expert. **au•thor•i•tar•i•an**
[ɔːθɒrɪˈteərɪən] *adj.* exercising strict control.
au•thor•i•ta•tive [ɔːˈθɒrɪtətɪv] *adj.* (a)
commanding. (b) which sounds as if it is correct. **au•thor•i•ta•tive•ly**, *adv.* in an authoritative way.
au•thor•ize ['ɔːθəraɪz] *v.* to give (s.o.) permission. **au•thor•i•za•tion** [ɔːθəraɪˈzeɪʃn] *n.*
permission.
au•tis•tic [ɔːˈtɪstɪk] *adj.* suffering from autism.
au•tism, *n.* mental illness which makes you
withdrawn and unable to communicate.
auto- ['ɔːtəu] *prefix meaning* self; **automatic;
automobile.**
au•to•bi•og•ra•phy [ɔːtəbaɪˈɒɡrəfɪ] *n.* life
story of a person written by himself/herself.
au•to•bi•o•graph•i•cal [ɔːtəbaɪəˈɡræfɪkl]
adj. referring to the life of the writer.
au•toc•ra•cy [ɔːˈtɒkrəsɪ] *n.* system of government by one person. **au•to•crat** ['ɔːtəkræt]
n. dictator/person who does not allow anyone
else to rule him. **au•to•crat•ic** [ɔːtəˈkrætɪk]
adj. ruled by one person.
au•to•crat•i•cal•ly, *adv.* like a dictator.
au•tog•a•my [ɔːˈtɒɡəmɪ] *n.* self-fertilization.
au•to•graph ['ɔːtəɡrɑːf] 1. *n.* signature (of a
famous person). 2. *v.* **to a. a book for s.o.** = to
write your signature in it.
au•to•mat•ed *adj.* controlled by automation.
a. teller machine = machine that automatically
dispenses cash when a plastic card is inserted
and certain buttons are pushed.
au•to•mat•ic [ɔːtəˈmætɪk] *adj. & n.* (device)
which works by itself. **au•to•mat•i•cal•ly**,
adv. working by itself. **au•to•ma•tion** [ɔːtə-
ˈmeɪʃn] *n.* installation of machinery to make a
process more automatic. **au•tom•a•ton** [ɔː-
ˈtɒmətən] *n.* (*pl.* -**ta**) doll which moves with a
motor inside it; person who acts like a robot.
au•to•mo•bile ['ɔːtəməbiːl] *n.* car.

au•to•mo•tive [ɔːtəˈməʊtɪv] *adj.* referring
to cars.
au•ton•o•my [ɔːˈtɒnəmɪ] *n.* self-government.
au•ton•o•mous, *adj.* (region) which governs itself.
au•top•sy ['ɔːtɒpsɪ] *n.* cutting up of a dead
body to discover the cause of death.
au•to•sug•ges•tion [ɔːtəusəˈdʒestʃən] *n.*
state where a person makes himself/herself believe sth. about himself/herself.
au•tumn ['ɔːtəm] *n.* season of the year when
the leaves fall off the trees. **au•tum•nal** [ɔː-
ˈtʌmnl] *adj.* referring to autumn.
aux•il•ia•ry [ɔːɡˈzɪlɪərɪ] 1. *n.* (a) helper. (b)
verb which is used to form part of another
verb. 2. *adj.* (person/machine) which helps.
a•vail [əˈveɪl] 1. *v.* **to a. oneself of** = to use. 2. *n.*
of no a. = no use. **a•vail•a•bil•i•ty** [əveɪlə-
ˈbɪlɪtɪ] *n.* being available. **a•vail•a•ble**, *adj.*
ready to be used; which can be obtained.
av•a•lanche ['ævəlɑːnʃ] *n.* fall of snow down a
mountainside.
a•vant-garde [ævɒŋˈɡɑːd] *adj.* experimental
(music/drama).
av•a•rice ['ævərɪs] *n.* state of not wanting to
spend money. **av•a•ri•cious** [ævəˈrɪʃəs] *adj.*
wanting to hoard money and not spend it.
a•venge [əˈvendʒ] *v.* to pay s.o. back for (a
crime). **a•veng•er**, *n.* person who pays back
a crime.
av•e•nue ['ævənjuː] *n.* (a) wide, tree-lined,
road in a city. (b) two parallel rows of trees. (c)
way of approaching a problem.
a•ver [əˈvɜː] *v.* (*formal*) to state.
av•er•age ['ævərɪdʒ] 1. *n.* (a) figure arrived at
when a total is divided by the number of
figures added. (b) **on a.** = as a general rule. 2.
adj. general; ordinary. 3. *v.* to work out as an
average.
a•verse [əˈvɜːs] *adj.* **he is a. to hard work** = he
dislikes it. **a•ver•sion** [əˈvɜːʃn] *n.* (a) (**to**) dislike. (b) **my pet a.** = thing I dislike most.
a•vert [əˈvɜːt] *v.* (a) to turn away (one's eyes).
(b) to prevent (a disaster).
a•vi•ar•y ['eɪvɪərɪ] *n.* building for keeping
birds in.
a•vi•a•tion [eɪvɪˈeɪʃn] *n.* art/technology of
flying (aircraft). **a•vi•a•tor** ['eɪvɪeɪtə] *n.* airplane pilot.
av•id ['ævɪd] *adj.* eager/enthusiastic. **av•id•ly**,
adv. eagerly.
av•o•ca•do (pear) [ævəˈkɑːdəu ('peə)] *n.* (*pl.*
-os) green tropical fruit with a large stone in
the middle, eaten as a vegetable.
av•o•cet ['ævəset] *n.* white wader with a long
bill which is curved upwards.
a•void [əˈvɔɪd] *v.* (a) to try not to do (sth). (b)
to keep away from. **a•void•a•ble**, *adj.*

which you could have avoided. **a•void•ance,** *n.* act of avoiding.

av•oir•du•pois [ævədə'pɔɪz] *n.* system of weights based on ounces, pounds, etc.

a•vow•al [ə'vauəl] *n.* (*formal*) admission. **a•vowed** [ə'vaud] *adj.* stated; admitted.

a•vun•cu•lar [ə'vʌŋkjulə] *adj.* like an uncle.

a•wait [ə'weɪt] *v.* to wait for.

a•wake [ə'weɪk] 1. *v.* (**awoke; awoken**) (a) to wake (s.o.) up. (b) to become aware of. 2. *adj.* not sleeping.

a•wak•en [ə'weɪkn] *v.* to wake/to arouse. **a•wak•en•ing,** *n.* **a rude a.** = a disturbing realization.

a•ward [ə'wɔːd] 1. *n.* (a) prize. (b) decision which settles a dispute. 2. *v.* to give (a prize, etc.).

a•ware [ə'weə] *adj.* knowing. **a•ware•ness,** *n.* state of being aware.

a•wash [ə'wɒʃ] *adj.* covered with a liquid.

a•way [ə'weɪ] *adv.* (a) not here/far; **a. game** = at another team's field. (b) **the birds were singing a.** = they were going on singing; **right a.** = immediately.

awe [ɔː] *n.* fear/terror. **awe-in•spir•ing, awesome,** *adj.* frightening. **awe-struck,** *adj.* frightened/full of terror. **aw•ful** ['ɔːfl] *adj.* (a) (*old*) very frightening. (b) very bad/very strong; unpleasant. **aw•ful•ly,** *adv.* *inf.* very.

a•while [ə'waɪl] *adv.* for a short time.

awk•ward ['ɔːkwəd] *adj.* (a) difficult. (b) em-

barrassing. (c) clumsy. **awk•ward•ly,** *adv.* with difficulty; inconveniently. **awk•ward•ness,** *n.* (a) embarrassment. (b) difficulty.

awl [ɔːl] *n.* tool used for making small holes.

awn•ing ['ɔːnɪŋ] *n.* canvas roof stretched out to protect from the sun or rain.

a•woke, a•wok•en [ə'wəuk, ə'wəukn] *v. see* **awake.**

AWOL ['eɪwɒl] = absent without leave.

a•wry [ə'raɪ] *adv.* not straight.

ax, axe [æks] 1. *n.* instrument with a sharp metal head for chopping wood; **to have an a. to grind** = a particular point of view to put across. 2. *v.* to reduce (expenditure); to fire (staff).

ax•il ['æksɪl] *n.* place where a leaf joins a stem.

ax•i•om ['æksɪəm] *n.* well-known saying/obviously true statement. **ax•i•o•mat•ic** [æksɪə'mætɪk] *adj.* obvious; well-known.

ax•is ['æksɪs] *n.* (*pl.* **axes** ['æksiːz]) imaginary line through center of a sphere.

ax•le ['æksl] *n.* rod going through the middle of a wheel.

a•ya•tol•lah [aɪə'tɒlə] *n.* Muslim leader.

aye [aɪ] *n.* yes; **the ayes have it** = more people have voted yes than no.

a•zal•ea [ə'zeɪlɪə] *n.* small shrub with showy scented flowers.

azo ['eɪzəu] *n.* **a. dyes** = dyes added to food to give it a better color.

az•ure ['eɪʒə] *adj.* blue like the sky.

æ back, aː farm, ɒ top, aɪ pipe, au how, aie fire, auə flower, ɔː bought, ɔɪ toy, e fed, eə hair, eɪ take, ə afraid, əu boat, əuə lower, vː word, iː heap, ɪ hit, ɪə hear, uː school, u book, ʌ but, b back, d dog, ð then, dʒ just, f fog, g go, h hand, j yes, k catch, l last, m mix, n nut, ŋ sing, p penny, r round, s some, ʃ short, t too, tʃ chop, θ thing, v voice, w was, z zoo, ʒ treasure

Bb

Ba *symbol for* barium.

BA [biːˈeɪ] Bachelor of Arts.

bab•ble [ˈbæbl] 1. *n.* (a) trickling sound (of water). (b) chatter. 2. *v.* (a) to make a trickling sound. (b) to chatter.

babe [beɪb] *n.* (*formal*) baby.

ba•bel [ˈbeɪbl] *n.* loud noise of talking.

ba•boon [bəˈbuːn] *n.* large African monkey.

ba•by [ˈbeɪbɪ] *n.* (a) very young child; **to have a b.** = to give birth to a baby; **the b. of the family** = the youngest of the children. (b) small animal. (c) small object; **b. grand (piano)**. **baby carriage**, *n.* small carriage in which you can push a baby. **baby car•ri•er**, *n.* canvas cot with handles for carrying a baby. **ba•by•ish**, *adj.* like a baby. **ba•by-sit**, *v.* (**baby-sat**) to look after children while their parents are out. **ba•by-sit•ter**, *n.* person who baby-sits.

bach•e•lor [ˈbætʃələ] *n.* (a) unmarried man; **b. pad** = small apartment for a single person; **b. girl** = unmarried woman. (b) holder of a bachelor's degree from a university, having completed a four-year course of study.

ba•cil•lus [bəˈsɪləs] *n.* (*pl.* **bacilli** [bæˈsɪlaɪ]) type of bacterium.

back [bæk] 1. (a) part of the body down the spine between the neck and buttocks; **he did it behind my b.** = without my knowing; **I was glad to see the b. of him** = I was glad to see him go; **to put s.o.'s b. up** = to annoy s.o.; **we've broken the b. of the work** = we have done most of the work. (b) opposite part/side to the front; **he knows Chicago like the b. of his hand** = very well; **I have an idea at the b. of my mind** = I have the beginnings of an idea; **b. to front** = the wrong way round. (c) sportsman who plays in a defensive position in football/hockey, etc. 2. *adj.* (a) referring to the rear; **he's had to take a b. seat** = he's had to take a less prominent position; **b. seat driver** = passenger in a car who offers the driver unwanted advice. (b) in arrears; **b. pay** = pay which is owed to s.o. 3. *adv.* (a) to the rear; **stand b.** = move backward; **please sit b., I can't see** = please lean backward in your chair. (b) in return; **I'll call you b.** = I'll phone you again; **as soon as I get b. to the office** = as soon as I return to the office. (c) ago; **a few years b.** 4. *v.* (a) to (make sth) go backward; **can you b. the**

car into the garage? **he backed away from the fire.** (b) to support (with money). (c) to gamble on (a horse). (d) (*of wind*) to blow in another direction. **back•ache**, *n.* pain in the back. **back bench•er**, *n.* any member of a legislature. **back•bit•ing**, *n.* sharp criticism. **back•bone**, *n.* spine/column of bones forming the main support of the back. **back•break•ing**, *adj.* very hard (work). **back•date**, *v.* to put an earlier date than true on (a check). **back down**, *v.* to retreat from your former position. **back•drop**, *n.* (*in theater*) painted sheet at the back of the stage. **back•er**, *n.* person who supports sth with money; person who gambles money on horse racing. **back•fire**, *v.* (*of a car*) to make a small bang, due to misfiring of the ignition; (*of a plan*) to go wrong with unfortunate consequences for the planner. **back•gam•mon**, *n.* game like checkers played on a special board. **back•ground**, *n.* the back part of a painting against which the foreground stands out; **he comes from a working class b.** = his family is working class; **b. music** = music played quietly in a movie or in a restaurant. **back•hand**, *adj. & n.* (tennis/table tennis shot) played with the back of the racket/paddle. **back•hand•ed**, *adj.* (compliment) that could be taken also as an insult. **back•hand•er**, *n.* blow/shot with the back of the hand. **back•ing**, *n.* (a) material used on the back of sth to strengthen it. (b) musical accompaniment to a singer or instrument. (c) (financial) support. (d) reversing (of a car). **back•lash**, *n.* reverse effect (of a political or social move); **white b.** = reaction among white people against measures taken to protect black people. **back•less**, *adj.* (dress, etc.) with no back. **back•log**, *n.* work not done/bills not paid. **back num•ber**, *n.* old copy of a magazine or newspaper. **back out**, *v.* to decide not to continue (with a project). **back•pack**, *n.* bag carried on a walker's back. **back•pack•er**, *n.* person who goes backpacking. **back•pack•ing**, *n.* going for a long walk, carrying your clothes, food, tent, etc., in a backpack. **back•ped•al**, *v.* (**-pedaled**) (a) to pedal backwards. (b) to reverse your opinions. **back•side**, *n. inf.* buttocks.

back•slid•ing, n. going back to a bad habit after having reformed. **back•space,** n. moving a cursor back one space on a computer monitor. **back•stage,** adv. & adj. in the parts of a theater where the audience can't go; behind the scenes/hidden from view. **back•stairs,** n. stairs (for servants) in the back part of a large house. **back•stroke,** n. style of swimming on your back. **back talk,** n. replying rudely. **back•track,** v. to change your opinion. **back up,** v. (a) to support (s.o.). (b) to make a copy of a computer file, for security reasons. (c) to reverse a car. **back•up (copy)** n. copy of a computer file or disk. **back•ward,** adj. (a) slow/retarded (child); (country) which is not industrially advanced. (b) **b. in paying bills** = slow in paying. **back•ward•ness,** n. being backward. **back•ward, backwards,** adv. in reverse/toward the rear; **he knows the song b.** = extremely well. **back•wa•ter,** n. (a) small slow-moving branch of a river. (b) quiet/old-fashioned place. **back•woods,** n. pl. forest; **they live in the b.** = they live far from other houses. **back•woods•man,** n. (pl. -men) person who lives in the forest. **back•yard,** n. small, usu. grassy area behind a house.

ba•con ['beɪkn] n. pork which has been salted or smoked; inf. **it saved his b.** = it got him out of the difficult situation.

bac•te•ri•um [bæk'tɪərɪəm] n. (pl. **bacteria**) microscopic organism which produces germs or decay. **bac•te•ri•al, bacteriological** [bæktɪərɪə'lɒdʒɪkl] adj. referring to bacteria; **b. warfare** = method of conducting war by using bacteria to kill the enemy. **bac•ter•i•ol•o•gist** [bæktɪərɪ'ɒlədʒɪst] n. scientist who specializes in bacteriology. **bac•te•ri•ol•o•gy,** n. study of bacteria.

bad [bæd] 1. adj. (**worse, worst**) (a) not good; **b. meat; b. driver.** (b) wicked. (c) unpleasant; **b. news; she's in a b. temper.** (d) serious; **b. accident.** (e) diseased; injured; **b. leg.** 2. n. (a) s.o. which is bad; **I'm $50 to the b.** = I have lost/wasted $50. **bad•die, baddy,** n. inf. villain. **bad•lands,** n. land which cannot be cultivated. **bad•ly,** adv. (**worse, worst**) (a) not well (done). (b) seriously (wounded). (c) very much; **he b. needs a shave.**

bade [bæd] v. see **bid.**

badge [bædʒ] n. small sign worn to show that you belong to a group, or simply as a decoration.

badg•er ['bædʒə] 1. n. wild animal with striped black and white head which lives underground and comes out at night. 2. v. to bother (s.o.); **he badgered me into helping him.**

bad•i•nage [bædɪ'nɑːʒ] n. light teasing talk.

bad•min•ton ['bædmɪntən] n. game for two or four people, played with rackets and a shuttlecock.

baf•fle ['bæfl] 1. n. shield (to cut out noise). 2. v. (a) to puzzle. (b) to frustrate. **baf•fle•ment,** n. being baffled.

bag [bæg] 1. n. (a) thing made of paper/cloth/plastic which you can carry things in; **shopping b.** = large bag for carrying shopping; inf. **bags of money** = lots of money. (b) **bags under the eyes** = puffy layer of skin beneath the eyes showing that you are ill or tired. (c) inf. **it's in the b.** = the deal is agreed. (d) animals killed while hunting. (e) inf. **old b.** = dirty old woman. 2. v. (**bagged**) to catch (an animal when hunting). **bag•gy,** adj. (**-ier, -iest**) (of clothes) too big/hanging in folds.

bag•asse [bæ'gæs] n. residue left after crushing sugar cane.

bag•a•telle [bægə'tel] n. (a) game where small metal balls are sent round a board. (b) unimportant thing.

bag•gage ['bægɪdʒ] n. (no pl.) luggage.

bag•pipes ['bægpaɪps] n. pl. musical instrument made of an air sack attached to pipes.

bail [beɪl] n. (a) money paid to a court as security for a prisoner's temporary release; **he was released on b. of $5000.** (b) small piece of wood resting on the top of stumps in cricket. **bail•er,** n. scoop for removing water from a boat. **bail out,** v. (a) to scoop water out of (a boat); to help (s.o.) who is in financial difficulties. (b) to jump out of a crashing aircraft with the help of a parachute. (c) to pay money to let a prisoner out temporarily between hearings.

Bai•ley bridge ['beɪlɪ'brɪdʒ] n. prefabricated bridge which is supported by boats.

bail•iff ['beɪlɪf] n. court official who can seize property in payment of debts. (b) landowner's agent on an estate.

bairn ['beən] n. (in Scotland) child.

bait [beɪt] 1. n. fly, worm, etc., used to at-

æ back, ɑː farm, ɒ top, aɪ pipe, aʊ how, aɪə fire, aʊə flower, ɔː bought, ɔɪ toy, e fed, eə hair, eɪ take, ə afraid, əʊ boat, əʊə lower, vː word, iː heap, ɪ hit, ɪə hear, uː school, ʊ book, ʌ but, b back, d dog, ð then, dʒ just, f fog, g go, h hand, j yes, k catch, l last, m mix, n nut, ŋ sing, p penny, r round, s some, ʃ short, t too, tʃ chop, θ thing, v voice, w was, z zoo, ʒ treasure

tract fish or animals. 2. *v.* to attach bait to (a hook or trap).

baize [beɪz] *n.* green cloth made of wool.

bake [beɪk] *v.* to cook (in an oven). **bake•house,** *n.* building with ovens for baking. **bak•er,** *n.* person who makes bread and cakes; **baker's dozen** = thirteen. **bak•er•y,** *n.* place where baked goods are sold. **bak•ing.** *n.* cooking (in an oven); **b. dish** = fireproof dish which can be put in the oven; **b. sheet** = flat sheet of metal for baking cookies, biscuits, etc. on. **bak•ing pow•der,** *n.* powder which when added to a cake mix helps it to rise.

bal•a•cla•va [bælə'klɑːvə] *n.* **b. (helmet)** = knitted woolen helmet covering the whole head and neck, with a round opening for the face.

bal•a•lai•ka [bælə'laɪkə] *n.* Russian stringed instrument like a small guitar.

bal•ance ['bæləns] 1. *n.* (a) machine which weighs; **the result hangs in the b.** = you cannot tell which way the result will turn out. (b) staying steady; **to keep/to lose one's b.; the b. of power** = the division of power between countries. (c) what remains after all payments have been made; **we have a b. of $25 in the bank; b. of payments** = difference between money obtained from exports and money paid for imports by a country; **b. sheet** = statement drawn up at the end of a year showing the financial situation of a company. 2. *v.* (a) to remain in one position without falling. (b) to make (sth) stand without falling. (c) to counteract the effect of (sth). (d) **to make the accounts b.** = to make the total of income and expenditure cancel each other out. **bal•anced,** *adj.* level; sensible.

bal•co•ny ['bælkənɪ] *n.* (a) small terrace jutting out from an upper floor. (b) upper terrace of seats in a theater/auditorium, etc.

bald [bɔːld] *adj.* (a) with no hair. (b) not elaborate; **a b. statement of fact. bald•ing,** *adj.* becoming bald. **bald•ly,** *adv.* plainly; drily. **bald•ness,** *n.* lack of hair.

bal•der•dash ['bɔːldədæʃ] *n.* nonsense.

bale [beɪl] 1. *n.* large bundle. 2. *v.* **to b. hay** = to make hay into large bundles.

bale•ful ['beɪlful] *adj.* threatening/unpleasant; **a b. look. bale•ful•ly,** *adv.* in a baleful way.

balk [bɔːk] *v.* (a) to prevent s.o. from doing sth. (b) **to b. at sth** = to refuse to do sth.

ball [bɔːl] *n.* (a) round object for playing games; **keep the b. rolling** = keep everything moving; **I'll start the b. rolling** = I'll start things off; **he's on the b.** = he knows his job very well/he is up to date; **they won't play b.** = they won't cooperate with us. (b) thing with a round shape; **a b. of wool.** (c) formal dance. (d) game like (baseball) played with a ball. **b. park** = area set aside for playing baseball. **ball-and-**

sock•et, *adj.* (joint) where a ball at the end of one rod/bone fits a socket at the end of another. **ball bear•ing,** *n.* bearing using a ring of little steel balls; one of these steel balls. **ball boy, ball girl,** *n.* boy or girl who picks up the balls during a tennis match. **ball cock,** *n.* mechanism with a valve operated by a floating ball (for filling tanks/cisterns). **ball•point,** *adj.* **b. pen** = pen with a tiny ball which is automatically coated with ink from a tube. **ball•room,** *n.* large room for formal dances; **b. dancing** = formal dancing.

bal•lad ['bæləd] *n.* romantic popular song or poem telling a story. **bal•lade,** *n.* form of poetry, with a repeated refrain.

bal•last ['bæləst] *n.* (a) material carried in ship/balloon to give extra weight. (b) stones used to bed down railroad ties.

bal•let ['bæleɪ] *n.* (a) dancing as a spectacle for public performance; **b. dancer.** (b) piece danced for performance; **the ballet "Swan Lake."** (c) company which performs ballets. **bal•le•ri•na** [bælə'riːnə] *n.* woman ballet dancer.

bal•lis•tics [bə'lɪstɪks] *n.* science of shooting bullets or shells.

bal•loon [bə'luːn] *n.* large round object which is inflated; **hot-air b.** = large passenger-carrying balloon inflated with hot air. **bal•loon•ing,** *n.* sport of racing large passenger-carrying balloons.

bal•lot ['bælət] 1. *n.* voting by pieces of paper; **a secret b.** = election where the votes of individual voters are not disclosed; **absentee b.** = election where voters can mail in their votes; **b. box** = sealed box for putting ballot papers in. 2. *v.* to vote by pieces of paper. **bal•lot-rig•ging,** *n.* illegal arrangement of votes in a ballot, so that one side wins.

bal•ly•hoo [bælɪ'huː] *n.* energetic publicity/advertising (during an election campaign, etc.).

balm•y ['bɑːmɪ] *adj.* fragrant/soft (air/breeze).

bal•sa ['bɔːlsə] *n.* very light wood (used for making models).

bal•sam ['bɔːlsəm] *n.* fragrant flowering plant.

bal•us•trade [bælə'streɪd] *n.* stone fence made of small carved pillars along the edge of a terrace/balcony, etc. **bal•us•ter** ['bæləstə] *n.* small pillar.

bam•boo [bæm'buː] *n.* tropical plant which provides tall, strong, jointed canes; **b. shoots** = young shoots of bamboo which can be eaten.

bam•boo•zle [bæm'buːzl] *v.* to trick/to puzzle (s.o.).

ban [bæn] 1. *n.* law/instruction which forbids sth; **a b. on smoking in public places.** 2. *v.* **(banned)** to forbid (sth).

ba•nal [bə'nɑːl] *adj.* ordinary/trivial. **ban•al•i•ty** [bə'nælɪtɪ] *n.* ordinariness.

ba•nan•a [bə'nɑːnə] n. long yellow tropical fruit; **b. republic** = corrupt central American state.

band [bænd] 1. n. (a) thin loop of material for tying things together. (b) group of frequencies in radio transmission. (c) group of people. (d) group of musicians, esp. playing brass and percussion instruments. 2. v. to form a group. **band•mas•ter,** n. leader of a brass band. **bands•man,** n. (pl. **bandsmen**) musician playing in a band. **band•stand,** n. small stage (in public gardens) for outdoor concerts. **band•wag•on,** n. **to jump on the b.** = to join a popular movement/to start to do sth which is already proving popular.

band•age ['bændɪdʒ] 1. n. piece of cloth to tie around a wound/around a twisted ankle, etc. 2. v. to tie a cloth around a wound.

ban•dan•na [bæn'dænə] n. large silk hand-kerchief.

ban•deau ['bændəu] n. ribbon to tie back the hair.

ban•dit ['bændɪt] n. robber/brigand.

ban•dy ['bændɪ] 1. adj. **he has b. legs** = when he stands with feet together, his knees do not touch. 2. v. (**bandied**) **to b. about** = to shout/write (words to several people).

bane [beɪn] n. **it's the b. of my life** = it's what an-noys me most.

bang [bæŋ] 1. n. (a) loud noise; **supersonic b.** = loud noise made when an aircraft goes faster than the speed of sound. (b) sharp blow. (c) hair cut straight across the forehead. 2. v. to make a bang (by hitting sth). 3. inter. showing noise of an explosion; **the gun suddenly went b.; b. in the middle** = right in the middle. **bang•er,** n. Brit. inf. sausage. **bang•ing,** n. noise of repeated bangs.

ban•gle ['bæŋgl] n. bracelet made of metal or rigid material.

ban•ish ['bænɪʃ] v. to send (s.o.) away/to exile (s.o.); to get rid of (sth).

ban•is•ters ['bænɪstəz] n. pl. set of vertical rods with a handrail along the side of stairs.

ban•jo ['bændʒəu] n. stringed instrument with a round body.

bank [bæŋk] 1. n. (a) long pile or mound of earth/sand/snow, etc. (b) edge of a river or canal. (c) row (of lights). (d) institution for keeping or lending money; **b. charges** = charges made by a bank for its services; **b. holi-day** = public holiday when the banks are closed. 2. v. (a) to pile up in a long mound; **the snow banked up along the road** = the wind blew

the snow into banks. (b) (of plane) to roll to one side. (c) to put money into a bank; to use a bank; **where do you b.?** = which bank do you use? (d) **I'm banking on taking two weeks off next month** = I'm counting on/relying on tak-ing two weeks off. **bank•er,** n. person who directs a bank. **bank•ing,** n. the profession of being a banker. **bank note,** n. paper money issued by a bank. **bank•roll,** v. inf. to pay for (a project). **bank•rupt,** adj. & n. (per-son) whose debts exceed his assets and who has been declared incapable of meeting his debts; **he has been declared b. bank•rupt•cy,** n. state of being bankrupt.

bank•sia ['bæŋksɪə] n. Australian shrub with yellow flowers.

ban•ner ['bænə] n. (a) long flag; **b. headlines** = very large headlines in a newspaper. (b) large piece of material with a slogan written on it, carried in a procession or protest march.

banns [bænz] n. pl. official statement in church of intention to marry.

ban•quet ['bæŋkwɪt] n. large formal dinner. **ban•quet•ing hall,** n. large room where banquets are held.

ban•tam ['bæntəm] n. breed of very small chickens. **ban•tam•weight,** n. light weight in boxing between flyweight and featherweight.

ban•ter ['bæntə] n. sarcastic teasing com-ments. **ban•ter•ing,** adj. (tone of voice) used when making light sarcastic comments.

ban•yan ['bænjæn] n. tropical tree with roots which come down from the branches.

ba•o•bab ['bæəubæb] n. very large tropical tree, found in Africa.

bap•tize [bæp'taɪz] v. to admit s.o. to the church and give them a Christian name. **bap•tism** ['bæptɪzəm] n. church ceremony where s.o. is given a Christian name. **bap•tis•mal** [bæp'tɪzml] adj. referring to baptism.

bar [bɑː] 1. n. (a) long piece (of metal/chocolate, etc.). (b) obstacle; **harbor b.** = ridge of sand at the entrance to a harbor; **color b.** = objection to persons because of the color of their skin. (c) place where drinks are served; **snack b./sandwich b.** = counter/shop where food/drinks are served. (e) officially recog-nized lawyers; legal profession. (f) division (in music). (g) unit of atmospheric pressure. 2. v. (**barred**) to block (a road); to stop (s.o. **from** doing sth). 3. prep. **b. none** = with no excep-

---

æ back, ɑː farm, ɒ top, aɪ pipe, aʊ how, aɪə fire, aʊə flower, ɔː bought, ɔɪ toy, ə fed, eə hair, eɪ take, ə afraid, əʊ boat, əʊə lower, ɜː word, iː heap, ɪ hit, ɪə hear, uː school, ʊ book, ʌ but, b back, d dog, ð then, dʒ just, f fog, g go, h hand, j yes, k catch, l last, m mix, n nut, ŋ sing, p penny, r round, s some, ʃ short, t too, tʃ chop, θ thing, v voice, w was, z zoo, ʒ treasure

tions. **bar code,** n. system of lines printed on a product which can be read by a computer.

bar•ring, prep. excepting.

barb [bɑːb] n. small tooth (on a fish-hook or arrow). **barbed,** adj. with sharp points; **b. comment** = sharp critical comment; **b. wire** = wire (for fences) with sharp spikes.

bar•bar•i•an [bɑːˈbeərɪən] n. wild/uncivilized person. **bar•bar•ic** [bɑːˈbærɪk] adj. cruel/uncivilized. **bar•bar•i•ty** [bɑːˈbærɪtɪ] n. cruelty. **bar•ba•rous** [ˈbɑːbərəs] adj. cruel/uncivilized.

bar•be•cue [ˈbɑːbɪkjuː] 1. n. (a) charcoal fire/grill for cooking food outdoors. (b) meal cooked on a barbecue. 2. v. to cook on a barbecue.

bar•ber [ˈbɑːbə] n. man who cuts men's hair.

bar•bi•tu•rate [bɑːˈbɪtjʊrət] n. drug which makes you sleep.

bard [bɑːd] n. (formal) poet.

bare [beə] 1. adj. (a) naked/not covered with clothes or leaves. (b) just enough; **a b. living** = just enough to live on; **b. necessities** = absolutely essential items for existence; **elected with a b. majority** = with a very small majority. 2. v. to strip naked; **he bared his soul** = he told all his innermost thoughts. **bare•back,** adj. & adv. riding a horse with no saddle. **bare•faced,** adj. crude/cynical (lie). **bare•foot,** adv. with no shoes on. **bare•foot•ed,** adj. with no shoes on. **bare•head•ed,** adv. & adj. with no hat on. **bare•ly,** adv. hardly/scarcely; **I b. had enough money to pay the bill. bare•ness,** n. nakedness.

bar•gain [ˈbɑːgɪn] 1. n. (a) thing bought; sale agreed; **to strike a b.** = to agree on a sale; **he drives a hard b.** = he is a tough negotiator. (b) thing bought more cheaply than it usually is; **into the b.** = as well as everything else; **b. basement** = part of a store where cheap items are sold; 2. v. (a) to negotiate a sale; **I got more than I bargained for** = more than I expected. (b) to haggle. **bar•gain•ing,** n. discussion about prices/wages, etc.: **collective b.** = discussion between management and unions to fix new salaries for union members.

barge [bɑːdʒ] 1. n. large flat-bottomed cargo boat on inland waters. 2. v. to bump heavily (into). **barge•man** (pl -men) n. man in charge of a barge. **barge pole,** n. long pole for moving a barge along.

bar•i•tone [ˈbærɪtəʊn] adj. & n. (singer with a) voice between tenor and bass.

bar•i•um [ˈbeərɪəm] n. (element: Ba) white soft metal; **b. cocktail** = liquid which you drink before having your stomach X-rayed, which will show up clearly on the X-ray.

bark [bɑːk] 1. n. (a) outer part of a tree. (b) loud noise made by dog; **his b. is worse than his bite** = he is not as terrifying as he sounds. 2. v. (a) **he barked his shin on the rock** = he scraped the skin off his shin. (b) to make a loud call like a dog; **to b. up the wrong tree** = to get the wrong idea. **bark•er,** n. person who calls out to advertise sth in the street. **bark•ing,** n. continuous calls of dogs.

bar•ley [ˈbɑːlɪ] n. cereal crop; **pearl b.** = grains of barley used in cooking; **b. sugar** = candy made of boiled sugar.

bar•maid [ˈbɑːmeɪd] n. woman who serves drinks in a bar. **bar•man** [ˈbɑːmən] n. (pl. -men) bartender.

barm•y [ˈbɑːmɪ] adj. (-ier, -iest) inf. mad.

barn [bɑːn] n. large farm building for storing grain or hay. **barn•yard,** n. yard in a farm.

bar•na•cle [ˈbɑːnəkl] n. (a) small shellfish which clings to the bottoms of ships/to submerged wooden posts, etc. (b) **b. goose** = common northern goose.

bar•ney [ˈbɑːnɪ] n. sl. argument.

ba•rom•e•ter [bəˈrɒmɪtə] n. instrument for measuring atmospheric pressure, and therefore for forecasting the weather. **bar•o•met•ric** [bærəˈmetrɪk] adj. referring to a barometer; **b. pressure.**

bar•on [ˈbærən] n. lowest rank of hereditary peers, now also title of life peers. **bar•on•ess,** n. wife of a baron; title of a life peeress. **bar•on•et,** n. hereditary knight. **ba•ro•ni•al** [bəˈrəʊnɪəl] adj. large/sumptuous (castle).

ba•roque [bəˈrɒk] adj. in the ornate style of architecture of the late 17th and 18th centuries.

bar•racks [] n. buildings where military personnel are housed.

bar•ra•cu•da [bærəˈkjuːdə] n. large tropical fish.

bar•rage [ˈbærɑːʒ] n. (a) dam across a river, etc. (b) rapid fire (of guns/questions).

bar•rel [ˈbærəl] n. (a) large wooden container (for wine/oil/fish/oysters, etc.); **he's got me over a b.** = in a very awkward situation. (b) firing tube (on a gun). (c) **b. organ** = machine for making music when a handle is turned.

bar•ren [ˈbærən] adj. unproductive (land); (woman/animal) who cannot have young; (tree) which does not produce fruit. **bar•ren•ness,** n. being barren.

bar•ri•cade [bærɪˈkeɪd] 1. n. makeshift heap of cars/rubbish, etc., made to block a street. 2. v. to block (a street/a door).

bar•ri•er [ˈbærɪə] n. thing which stops you moving forward.

bar•ris•ter [ˈbærɪstə] n. Brit. lawyer who is allowed to speak in court.

bar•row ['bærəʊ] *n.* (a) small wheeled truck which is pushed by hand. (b) mound of earth piled over a prehistoric tomb.

bar•tend•er ['bɑːtendə] *n.* man who serves drinks in a bar.

bar•ter ['bɑːtə] 1. *n.* exchange (of one product for another). 2. *v.* to exchange (one product for another).

ba•salt ['bæsɔːlt] *n.* black volcanic rock.

base [beɪs] 1. *n.* (a) bottom part. (b) military camp; **air force b.** (c) substance which is the main part of a mixture. (d) chemical compound which reacts with an acid to form a salt. 2. *v.* **to b. sth on** = to use sth as a base. 3. *adj.* low/cheap; **b. metal** = not a precious metal.

base•ball ['beɪsbɔːl] *n.* team game played with a bat and ball. **base•board,** *n.* decorative board running along the bottom edge of a wall in a room. **base•less,** *adj.* (accusation) without any basis in fact. **base•ment,** *n.* floor beneath the ground floor.

bash [bæʃ] 1. *n.* (*pl.* **-es**) **a b. on the head** = you bumped your head. 2. *v.* to hit (sth) hard.

bash•ful ['bæʃful] *adj.* shy/modest. **bash•ful•ly,** *adv.* shyly. **bash•ful•ness,** *n.* being bashful.

ba•sic ['beɪsɪk] *adj.* elementary; **b. vocabulary** = most commonly used words. **ba•si•cal•ly,** *adv.* at bottom. **ba•sics** *pl. n.* simple and important facts; **to get back to b.** = to consider the basic points again.

BASIC ['beɪsɪk] Beginners All-purpose Symbolic Instruction Code.

bas•il ['bæzl] *n.* type of scented herb.

ba•sil•i•ca [bə'zɪlɪkə] *n.* (a) large rectangular church. (b) large catholic church.

ba•sin ['beɪsn] *n.* large bowl; **wash b.** = bowl in a bathroom with faucets giving running water for washing the hands.

ba•sis ['beɪsɪs] *n.* (*pl.* **bases**) (scientific) reason.

bask [bɑːsk] *v.* to lie (in the sun/in glory).

bas•ket ['bɑːskɪt] *n.* container made of woven straw/cane, etc.; **b. chair** = chair made of woven cane. **bas•ket•ball** ['bɑːskɪtbɔːl] *n.* team game where you try to throw a ball into a small net high up. **bas•ket•work,** *n.* making of baskets; objects made of woven straw/cane, etc.

bas-re•lief ['bæsrɪliːf] *n.* type of carving in stone where the figures stand out against (but are joined to) the background.

bass 1. [bæs] *n.* type of edible freshwater fish. 2.

[beɪs] *adj. & n.* (*pl.* **-es**) low/deep voice or music; **double b.** = instrument like a very large cello; **b. guitar/trombone** = large guitar/trombone tuned to play low notes; **b. clef** = sign in music showing that the notes are lower.

bas•set ['bæsɪt] *n.* **b. (hound)** = breed of dog with short legs and long ears.

bas•soon [bə'suːn] *n.* low-pitched wind instrument. **bas•soon•ist,** *n.* person who plays a bassoon.

bas•tard ['bɑːstəd] *adj. & n.* (person) not born of married parents; (thing) which is not pure; *inf.* hateful person/thing.

baste [beɪst] *v.* (a) to sew (material) loosely. (b) to spread juices over (meat which is cooking).

bas•tion ['bæstɪən] *n.* fortified part/stronghold.

bat [bæt] 1. *n.* (a) small mammal which flies by night and hangs upside down to rest. (b) instrument for hitting a ball (in some games). 2. *v.* (**batted**) (a) to be one of the two batsmen (in baseball, cricket, etc.); (*of a baseball/cricket team, etc.*) to have the turn to bat. (b) **she never batted an eyelid** = she did not show any surprise. **bats•man,** *n.* (*pl.* **-men**) person (esp. in cricket) who is batting.

batch [bætʃ] *n.* (*pl.* **-es**) quantity of bread/cakes baked at one time; group of letters/goods taken together.

bat•ed ['beɪtɪd] *adj.* **with b. breath** = holding your breath.

bath [bɑːθ] 1. *n.* (a) water used for washing all the body. (b) container for such water; container full of a liquid; **will you run my b. for me?** = will you fill the bath tub with water for me? (c) act of washing all the body; **to take a b.** (d) **public baths** = large (public) building with a swimming pool. 2. *v.* to wash (s.o./yourself) all over; **he is bathing the baby. bath mat,** *n.* small mat to step on as you get out of the bath. **bath oil,** *n.* scented oil to put in a bath. **bath•robe,** *n.* loose coatlike garment worn before or after a bath or for relaxing in. **bath•room,** *n.* room with a toilet, wash basin and usu. a bathtub or shower. **bath salts,** *n. pl.* scented crystals to put in a bath. **bath towel,** *n.* very large towel for drying yourself after a bath. **bath•tub,** *n.* tub/container for washing all the body.

bathe [beɪð] 1. *n.* swim. 2. *v.* (a) to swim. (b) to wash (a wound) carefully. (c) to take a bath. **bath•er,** *n.* person who is swimming. **bath•ing,** *n.* swimming (in the sea, river or a

---

æ **back,** ɑː **farm,** ɒ **top,** aɪ **pipe,** aʊ **how,** aɪə **fire,** aʊə **flower,** ɔː **bought,** ɔɪ **toy,** e **fed,** eəhair, eɪ **take,** ə **afraid,** əʊ **boat,** əʊə **lower,** ɜː **word,** iː **heap,** ɪ **hit,** ɪə **hear,** uː **school,** ʊ **book,** ʌ **but,** b **back,** d **dog,** ð **then,** dʒ **just,** f **fog,** g **go,** h **hand,** j **yes,** k **catch,** l **last,** m **mix,** n **nut,** ŋ **sing,** p **penny,** r **round,** s **some,** ʃ **short,** t **too,** tʃ **chop,** θ **thing,** v **voice,** w **was,** z **zoo,** ʒ **treasure**

pool); **b. suit** = piece of clothing worn when swimming.

ba•thos ['beɪθɒs] *n.* sudden drop from a serious subject to a trivial one.

bath•y•sphere ['bæθɪsfɪə] *n.* round pressurized cabin for exploring deep parts of the sea. **bath•y•scaph**, *n.* type of small submarine, used for underwater research.

ba•tik [bæ'tiːk] *n.* type of cloth, colored in patterns by dyeing it with wax designs on it.

ba•ton ['bætn] *n.* stick (of orchestra conductor or police officer).

ba•tra•chi•an [bə'treɪkɪən] *n.* amphibian, such as a toad.

bat•tal•ion [bə'tælɪən] *n.* part of the army often commanded by a lieutenant-colonel.

bat•ten ['bætn] 1. *n.* thin strip of wood. 2. *v.* (*on ship*) **to b. down the hatches** = to close down the hatch covers before a storm.

bat•ter ['bætə] 1. *n.* thin liquid mixture of flour/eggs/milk, for making pancakes, etc. 2. *v.* to hit hard and continuously. **bat•tered**, *adj.* which has been hit hard; **b. babies/wives** = babies/wives who have been constantly ill-treated. **bat•ter•ing ram**, *n.* long beam used to break down castle gates.

bat•ter•y ['bætərɪ] *n.* (a) group of artillery guns. (b) container with a cell or several cells charged with electricity. (c) **assault and b.** = criminal charge of attacking s.o. with violence. **bat•ter•y-pow•ered** *adj.* worked by an electric battery.

bat•tle ['bætl] 1. *n.* important fight between large enemy forces; **a b. royal** = a great struggle. 2. *v.* to fight (**against**). **bat•tle•ax**, **battleaxe**, *n. inf.* large fierce woman. **bat•tle•field**, *n.* site of a battle. **bat•tle•front**, *n.* line along which fighting is taking place. **bat•tle•ments**, *n. pl.* top part of a castle wall, with a walk for soldiers. **bat•tle•ship**, *n.* very large warship.

bat•ty ['bætɪ] *adj. inf.* mad.

bau•ble ['bɔːbl] *n.* (*formal*) cheap piece of jewelery.

baud rate ['bɔːdreɪt] *n.* number of signal changes transmitted per second.

baulk [bɔːlk] *v. see* **balk**.

baux•ite ['bɔːksaɪt] *n.* mineral from which aluminum is produced.

bawd•y ['bɔːdɪ] *adj.* rude/coarse.

bawl [bɔːl] *v.* to shout loudly. **bawl out**, *v.* to criticize (s.o.).

bay [beɪ] 1. *n.* (a) fragrant shrub whose leaves are used in cooking. (b) large rounded inlet in a coast; **the B. of Biscay**. (c) arch of a bridge; section of a church between pillars; **b. window** = window which projects from an outside wall. (d) **parking b.** = place marked for park-

ing; **loading b.** = place where trucks can be parked with a high platform for loading. (e) light brown horse. (f) **to keep attackers at b.** = to keep them away. 2. *v.* (*of hunting dog*) to bark.

bay•o•net ['beɪənət] *n.* sharp blade attached to the end of a rifle.

ba•zaar [bə'zɑː] *n.* (a) oriental market. (b) market selling goods for charity.

ba•zoo•ka [bə'zuːkə] *n.* small anti-tank gun.

b. & b. = bed and breakfast.

BBC [biːbiːˈsiː] British Broadcasting Corporation.

B.C. ['biːˈsiː] *abbrev. for* before Christ; **Julius Caesar died in 44 B.C.**

be [biː] *v.* (**I am, you are, he is, we/they are; I/he was, we/you/they were; he has been**) 1. (a) (*describing a person or thing*) **the house is big.** (b) to add up to; **two and three are five.** (c) to exist/to live; **where are we? there he is; how are you today? tomorrow is Friday.** (d) to feel; **I am cold; they are hungry.** (e) to go; **have you ever been to New York? the police had been into every room.** (f) (*showing time*) **it is four o'clock.** (g) (*showing future*) **he is to see the doctor tomorrow.** 2. (*used to make part of verbs*) **I am coming; he has been waiting for hours;** (*passive use*) **he was killed by a train.** **be•ing.** 1. *adj.* **for the time b.** = temporarily/for now. 2. *n.* (a) existence; **the association came into b. in 1946.** (b) **human b.** = person.

beach [biːtʃ] 1. *n.* (*pl.* **-es**) stretch of sand/pebbles by the side of the sea. 2. *v.* to bring (a boat) on to the beach. **beach•comb•er**, *n.* person who collects things thrown up on the beach by the sea. **beach•head**, *n.* small area occupied by troops at the beginning of an invasion from the sea. **beach•wear**, *n.* (*no pl.*) clothes to wear on the beach.

bea•con ['biːkən] *n.* light (used as a signal); **radio b.** = radio transmitter which guides aircraft into an airport.

bead [biːd] *n.* (a) small ornament with a hole so that it can be threaded. (b) small drop of liquid. **bead•ing**, *n.* thin strip of wood (usu. carved in a pattern) used to decorate. **bead•y**, *adj.* **b. eyed** = with eyes small and bright like beads.

bea•gle ['biːgl] *n.* breed of dog used for hunting.

beak [biːk] *n.* hard covering of a bird's mouth.

beak•er ['biːkə] *n.* metal/plastic cup, usu. with no handle; glass container used in scientific experiments.

beam [biːm] 1. (a) large block of wood used in building. (b) ray (of light/sound); **radio b.** = wavelength for radio transmission. (c) width of a ship; *inf.* **he's broad in the b.** = rather fat. 2. *v.* (a) to send out rays. (b) to smile.

beam•ing, *adj.* radiant (sunshine/smile/face).

bean [bi:n] *n.* (a) vegetable with edible seeds (and pods); *inf.* **full of beans** = full of vigor. (b) **coffee beans** = fruit of the coffee plant which, when roasted and ground, are used to make coffee.

bear ['beə] 1. *n.* (a) large furry wild animal; **polar b.** = large white bear living in Arctic regions; **teddy b.** = toy bear. (b) person who believes the stock market prices will fall. 2. *v.* **(bore; has borne)** (a) to carry; **this tree has borne fruit every year; the deposit bears interest at 5%.** (b) to stand/to put up with; **I can't b. noise.** (c) to support; **will this branch b. my weight?** (d) to turn; **b. right at the crossroads.** (e) to aim; **the enemy brought their guns to b. on our ship. bear•a•ble,** *adj.* which you can put up with. **bear down on,** *v.* to advance heavily toward (s.o.). **bear•er,** *n.* person who carries sth. **bear•ing,** *n.* (a) **ball bearings** = set of small balls around an axle to spread the weight evenly and make the wheel turn smoothly. (b) **to get your bearings** = to find out where you are; **to lose your bearings** = to lose all idea of where you are. (c) **stately b.** = stately way of standing/walking. **bear out,** *v.* to confirm. **bear•skin,** *n.* tall fur hat worn by a soldier in some armies. **bear up,** *v.* to survive cheerfully. **bear with,** *v.* to endure patiently.

beard ['biəd] *n.* hair on the lower part of a man's face; whiskers on a mussel/oyster, etc. **beard•ed,** *adj.* with a beard. **beard•less,** *adj.* with no beard.

beast [bi:st] *n.* (a) wild animal; **b. of burden** = donkey/horse, etc., trained to carry loads. (b) nasty, difficult, or unpleasant person. **beast•li•ness,** *n.* nastiness/unpleasantness (of person). **beast•ly,** *adj.* nasty; unpleasant.

beat [bi:t] 1. *n.* (a) regular sound; **heart b.** (b) regular measure in music. (c) area regularly patrolled by a policeman. 2. *v.* **(beat; has beaten)** (a) to hit hard several times. (b) to chase (birds); **we b. a hasty retreat** = we went away very quickly; **don't b. about the bush** = get to the point quickly; *Sl.* **b. it!** = go away! (c) to defeat. (d) to do better than (a record). (e) to stir (eggs, etc.) vigorously. **beat back,** *v.* to push back. **beat down,** *v.* (a) to flatten. (b) **I beat down his price** = I reduced the price he was asking by haggling; **he beat me down** = he made me reduce my price. (c) (*of the sun*) to strike hard on. **beat•en,** *adj.* off the b. track

= away from other houses. **beat•er,** *n.* (a) person who drives birds towards the people who will shoot them. (b) machine for beating eggs. **beat•ing,** *n.* act of hitting. **beat up,** *v.* (a) to whip (cream). (b) to attack (s.o.).

be•at•i•fy [bi:'ætɪfaɪ] *v.* to declare (s.o.) blessed (as the first step to declaring s.o. a saint). **be•at•i•fi•ca•tion** [bi:ætɪfɪ'keɪʃn] *n.* declaring s.o. blessed.

Beau•fort scale ['bəufət'skeɪl] *n.* scale for measuring wind strengths.

beau•ti•ful ['bju:tɪful] *adj.* very pleasing to look at. **beau•ti•cian,** *n.* person who makes people beautiful (by applying makeup, etc.). **beau•ti•ful•ly,** *adv.* in a very pleasing way. **beau•ti•fy,** *v.* to make sth beautiful. **beau•ty,** *n.* state of being beautiful; **b. salon** = establishment specializing in women's appearance; **b. spot** = dark spot, usu. on the face.

bea•ver ['bi:və] *n.* small American mammal which lives in water and makes dams with trees which it gnaws down.

be•calmed [bi:'ka:md] *adj.* (*of a sailing ship*) not able to move because there is no wind.

be•came [bɪ'keɪm] *v. see* **be•come.**

be•cause [bɪ'kɒz] *conj.* for the reason that; owing to the fact that. **because of,** *prep.* on account of.

beck [bek] *n.* (a) (*in northern England*) mountain stream. (b) **he is always at her b. and call** = he always does exactly what she wants him to do.

beck•on ['bekən] *v.* to make a sign (**to** s.o.) to come.

be•come [bɪ'kʌm] *v.* **(became; has become)** to change into sth different; **what became of him?** = what happened to him? **be•com•ing,** *adj.* **her dress is very b.** = her dress suits her very well.

bec•que•rel ['bekərel] *n.* SI unit of radiation.

bed [bed] 1. *n.* (a) piece of furniture for sleeping on; **double b.** = bed for two people; **single b.** = bed for one person; **to go to b.** = to lie down in bed to sleep for the night; **he took to his b.** = he was ill and had to stay in bed; **to make the b.** = to straighten the bedclothes after getting out of bed. (b) bottom (of a river/lake); **oyster b.** = collection of oysters at the bottom of the sea; **watercress b.** = mass of watercress growing in a river. (c) area of garden kept for plants. 2. *v.* **(bedded) b. down** = to give (horses) fresh straw. **bed•clothes,** *n. pl.* sheets/blankets, etc., on a bed. **bed•cov•er,** *n.* cloth which

---

æ back, a: farm, ɒ: top, aɪ pipe, aʊ how, aɪe fire, aʊə flower, ɔ: bought, ɔɪ toy, e fed, eəhair, eɪ take, ə afraid, əʊ boat, əʊə lower, v: word, i: heap, ɪ hit, ɪə hear, u: school, ʊ book, ʌ but, b back, d dog, ð then, dʒ just, f fog, g go, h hand, j yes, k catch, l last, m mix, n nut, ŋ sing, p penny, r round, s some, ʃ short, t too, tʃ chop, θ thing, v voice, w was, z zoo, ʒ treasure

covers a bed during the daytime. **bed•ding,** *n.* (a) bedclothes (mattress/pillows, etc.); straw (for horses). (b) **bedding plants** = plants suitable for putting into flower beds. **bed•fel•low,** *n.* person who sleeps in the same bed; person who is associated with s.o. **bed jack•et,** *n.* warm jacket worn in bed. **bed•pan,** *n.* bowl for passing waste water into when lying in bed. **bed•rid•den,** *adj.* forced to stay in bed because of illness. **bed•rock,** *n.* bottom rock beneath various mineral seams. **bed•room,** *n.* room for sleeping in. **bed•side,** *n.* side of a bed; **b. manner** = attitude of a doctor to his sick patient. **bed•sore,** *n.* sore which is caused by lying in bed for long periods. **bed•spread,** *n.* decorative cloth to put over a bed. **bed•stead,** *n.* solid frame of a bed. **bed•time,** *n.* time to go to bed; **it's past your b.** = it's later than the time you usually go to bed.

be•dev•iled [bɪ'devld] *adj.* surrounded (with difficulties).

bed•lam ['bedləm] *n.* loud noise; chaos.

be•drag•gled [bɪ'drægld] *adj.* wet and dirty.

bee [biː] *n.* small insect which makes honey. **bee•eat•er,** *n.* small tropical bird, which eats insects such as bees. **beehive,** *n.* box in which a colony of bees lives. **bee•keep•er,** *n.* person who keeps bees. **bee•keep•ing,** *n.* keeping of bees (for honey). **bee•line,** *n.* straight line; **he made a b. for the drinks** = he went straight to the drinks. **bees•wax,** *n.* wax produced by bees, used as a polish.

beech [biːtʃ] *n.* (*pl.* **-es**) large northern tree; wood of this tree.

beef [biːf] 1. *n.* (a) meat from a bull or cow; **corned b.** = beef which has been salted. (b) *inf.* grumble. 2. *v. inf.* to grumble (**about**). **beef•burg•er** ['biːfbɜːgə] *n.* hamburger. **beef•y,** *adj.* (**-ier, -iest**) muscular.

beep [biːp] 1. *n.* short high sound made by an electronic device, such as a computer. 2. *v.* to make a short high-pitched sound. **beep•er,** *n.* small radio receiver that emits a beep (or vibrates) when signaled in order to call the person carrying it.

beer [bɪə] *n.* alcoholic drink made from malt, flavored with hops; a glass of this drink. **beer•y,** *adj.* referring to beer.

beet [biːt] *n.* (a) **sugar b.** root vegetable grown for processing into sugar. (b) beetroot. **beet•root,** *n.* dark red root vegetable.

bee•tle ['biːtl] *n.* small winged insect with a hard cover over its wings.

beet•ling ['biːtlɪŋ] *adj.* (cliff) which is high and looks threatening.

be•fall [bɪ'fɔːl] *v.* (**befell; has befallen**) (*formal*) to happen (to).

be•fit [bɪ'fɪt] *v.* (*formal*) (**befitted**) to suit.

be•fore [bɪ'fɔː] *adv., prep. & conj.* (a) in front (of). (b) earlier (than). **be•fore•hand,** *adv.* in advance.

be•friend [bɪ'frend] *v.* to be friendly to and help (s.o.).

beg [beg] *v.* (**begged**) (a) to ask for money. (b) to ask; **to b. a favor of s.o.** = to ask s.o. a favor; **I b. your pardon** = excuse me. **beg•gar,** *n.* person who asks for money; *inf.* **lucky beggar!** = what a lucky person! **beg•gar•ly,** *adj.* small/poor (wage). **beg•ging,** *n.* asking for money; **it's going b.** = no one wants it.

be•get [bɪ'get] *v.* (**beget; begot; has begotten**) (*old*) to give birth to; to produce.

be•gin [bɪ'gɪn] *v.* (**began; has begun**) to start; **b. again** = start from the beginning. **be•gin•ner,** *n.* person who is starting to do sth. **be•gin•ning,** *n.* first part/start; **at the b.** = to start with.

be•go•nia [bɪ'gəʊnɪə] *n.* pot plant with large bright flowers.

be•grudge [bɪ'grʌdʒ] *v.* to feel resentment because of sth s.o. has or does; **I don't b. him his money.**

be•guile [bɪ'gaɪl] *v.* to make (time) pass quickly and pleasantly.

be•half [bɪ'hɑːf] *n.* (a) **I am speaking on b. of the association** = I am speaking to get support for the association. (b) **acting on my b.** = acting for me. (c) **don't worry on my b.** = do not worry about me.

be•have [bɪ'heɪv] *v.* to act; **b. yourself** = be good. **be•haved,** *adj.* **well-behaved child** = polite/quiet child; **badly-behaved child** = child who is rude/dirty/noisy. **be•hav•ior,** *Brit.* **be•hav•iour,** *n.* conduct/way of acting. **be•hav•ior•al,** *adj.* concerning the behavior of human beings.

be•head [bɪ'hed] *v.* to cut off a head.

be•hind [bɪ'haɪnd] 1. *adv.* (a) after; **he stayed b.** = he stayed at the place everyone started from. (b) late; **I am b. with my work.** 2. *prep.* (a) at the back of; **what is really b. it all?** = what is the real cause of it all? **I'm b. you completely** = I'm in full support. (b) late/retarded (by comparison with s.o. else); less advanced than (s.o.). 3. *n. inf.* buttocks. **be•hind•hand,** *adv.* late.

be•hold [bɪ'həʊld] *v.* (**beheld**) (*formal*) to see. **be•hold•er,** *n.* person who sees.

be•hold•en [bɪ'həʊldən] *adj.* (*formal*) grateful (**to** s.o. for sth).

be•hoove [bɪ'həʊv] *v.* to be fitting.

beige [beɪʒ] *adj.* pale fawn color.

be•lat•ed [bɪ'leɪtɪd] *adj.* late. **be•lat•ed•ly,** *adv.* late.

be•lay [bɪ'leɪ] *v.* to attach a rope.

belch [beltʃ] 1. *n.* (*pl.* **-es**) noise made when

bringing up gas from the stomach. 2. *v.* (a) to make a noise by bringing up gas from the stomach through the mouth. (b) to pour **out** (smoke, flames).

be•lea•guered [bɪ'liːgəd] *adj.* in a difficult position; surrounded by enemies.

bel•fry ['belfrɪ] *n.* tower for bells.

Bel•gian ['beldʒən] 1. *adj.* referring to Belgium. 2. *n.* person from Belgium.

be•lie [bɪ'laɪ] *v.* (*formal*) to hide/to show (sth) wrongly.

be•lieve [bɪ'liːv] *v.* to feel sure of (sth), without any proof; **I b. so** = I think that is correct; **to b. in sth** = to believe that sth exists. **be•lief,** *n.* feeling sure of sth. **be•liev•a•ble,** *adj.* which one can believe. **be•liev•er,** *n.* person who believes in sth, esp. God.

be•lit•tle [bɪ'lɪtl] *v.* to make (sth) seem small or unimportant.

bell [bel] *n.* metal cup-shaped object which makes a ringing sound when hit; mechanism to make a ringing sound; **that rings a b.** = that reminds me of something. **bell•boy, bell-hop,** *n.* messenger boy employed in a hotel. **bell push,** *n.* button which rings a bell when pushed. **bell tow•er,** *n.* tower for bells.

bel•la•don•na [belə'dɒnə] *n.* deadly night-shade, a poisonous plant.

belle [bel] *n.* beautiful woman.

bel•li•cose ['belɪkəus] *adj.* (*formal*) warlike.

bel•lig•er•ent [bə'lɪdʒərənt] 1. *adj.* warlike. 2. *n.* country fighting a war. **bel•lig•er•en•cy,** *n.* being belligerent.

bel•low ['beləu] 1. *n.* loud cry (of bull/angry person). 2. *v.* to make a loud cry.

bel•lows ['beləuz] *n. pl.* apparatus for blowing air into a fire to make it burn brightly.

bel•ly ['belɪ] *n.* (*pl.* -ies) *inf.* abdomen. **bel•ly•ache.** 1. *n.* pain in the stomach. 2. *v. inf.* to complain bitterly (**about** sth). **bel•ly flop,** *n. inf.* **to do a b.** = to fall flat on to the water instead of diving into it. **bel•ly•ful,** *n. inf.* **I've had a b. of his complaints** = I've had as many of his complaints as I can stand.

be•long [bɪ'lɒŋ] *v.* (a) **to b. to s.o.** = to be s.o.'s property. (b) **to be to a club** = to be a member (of a club). **be•long•ings,** *n. pl.* personal property.

be•lov•ed [bɪ'lʌvɪd] 1. *adj.* whom s.o. loves. 2. *n.* person who is loved by s.o.

be•low [bɪ'ləu] 1. *adv.* lower down. 2. *prep.* lower than; **the temperature never goes b. 25°.**

belt [belt] 1. *n.* (a) strap which goes around your waist; **seat b.** = belt in a car or aircraft which holds you safely in place. (b) zone; **green b.** = area around a town having woods/parks where building is not permitted. 2. *v. inf.* **they were belting out a song** = singing a song very loudly.

be•moan [bɪ'məun] *v.* (*formal*) to complain about (sth).

be•mused [bɪ'mjuːzd] *adj.* bewildered/puzzled.

bench [bentʃ] *n.* (*pl.* -es) (a) long hard seat (for several people). (b) **the b.** = judge or judges who try cases in court. (c) table (for working). **bench mark,** *n.* standard against which something can be tested.

bend [bend] 1. *n.* (a) curve; **S-bend** = double curve in a pipe; *inf.* **around the b.** = quite mad. (b) **the bends** = illness in divers caused by coming up from a deep dive too quickly. 2. *v.* (**bent**) to make (a straight object) curved; to curve. **bend down,** *v.* to stoop.

be•neath [bɪ'niːθ] 1. *adv.* underneath/below. 2. *prep.* under; **he thinks it is b. him** = he thinks it is too unimportant for him to deal with.

ben•e•dic•tion [benɪ'dɪkʃn] *n.* blessing (in church).

ben•e•fac•tor, benefactress ['benɪfæktə, 'benɪfæktrəs] *n.* person who gives s.o./a society money.

be•nef•i•cent [bɪ'nefɪsənt] *adj.* (*formal*) (person) who does good.

ben•e•fi•cial [benɪ'fɪʃl] *adj.* which does good; useful.

ben•e•fi•ci•ar•y [benɪ'fɪʃərɪ] *n.* (*pl.* -ies) person who inherits sth from a person who has died.

ben•e•fit ['benɪfɪt] 1. *n.* (a) profit/advantage. (b) payment; **unemployment b.** = payment (by the state) to unemployed people; **maternity b.** = payment to a woman who has had a baby. 2. *v.* to be of profit.

be•nev•o•lence [bə'nevələns] *n.* goodness/charity. **be•nev•o•lent,** *adj.* good/charitable. **be•nev•o•lent•ly,** *adv.* in a benevolent way.

be•night•ed [bɪ'naɪtəd] *adj.* uneducated.

be•nign [bɪ'naɪn] *adj.* (a) pleasant (person). (b) non-malignant (growth).

bent [bent] 1. *adj.* (a) curved. (b) **he is b. on becoming a sailor** = he is very eager to become a sailor. (c) *Sl.* dishonest. 2. *n.* **she has a natural b. to be a doctor** = she has an instinct to become a doctor. 3. *v. see also* **bend.**

æ back, aː farm, ɒ top, aɪ pipe, aʊ how, aɪə fire, aʊə flower, ɔː bought, ɔɪ toy, e fed, eə hair, eɪ take, ə afraid, əʊ boat, əʊə lower, vː word, iː heap, ɪ hit, ɪə hear, uː school, ʊ book, ʌ but, b back, d dog, ð then, dʒ just, f fog, g go, h hand, j yes, k catch, l last, m mix, n nut, ŋ sing, p penny, r round, s some, ʃ short, t too, tʃ chop, θ thing, v voice, w was, z zoo, ʒ treasure

ben•zene ['benziːn] *n.* liquid obtained from coal, which is used as a fuel and causes cancer. **ben•zine** ['benziːn] *n.* liquid mixture obtained from petroleum, and used for cleaning.

be•queath [bɪ'kwiːð] *v.* to leave (property/money) **to** s.o. when you die. **be•quest** [bɪ'kwest] *n.* property left to s.o.

ber•ber•is ['bɜːbərɪs] *n.* plant with small red berries, grown for decoration.

be•reaved [bɪ'riːvd] *n.* **the b.** = (i) widow/widower; (ii) family of a person who has died. **be•reave•ment,** *n.* loss of member of the family through death.

be•ret ['bereɪ] *n.* round cloth or felt cap with no peak.

ber•i•ber•i [berɪ'berɪ] *n.* tropical disease of the nervous system.

ber•ry ['berɪ] *n.* (*pl.* **-ies**) fruit of a shrub.

ber•serk [bə'zɜːk] *adj.* **to go b.** = to go wild/mad.

berth [bɜːθ] 1. *n.* (a) place where a ship ties up to a quay or dock; **to give sth a wide b.** = to avoid sth at all costs. (b) bed (in a ship/train). 2. *v.* to tie up (a ship).

ber•yl ['berɪl] *n.* type of precious stone.

be•seech [bɪ'siːtʃ] *v.* (**beseeched/besought** [bɪ'sɔːt]) (*formal*) to ask (s.o. to do sth).

be•set [bɪ'set] *v.* (**beset**) to surround, causing problems. **be•set•ting sin,** *n.* defect which is always present.

be•side [bɪ'saɪd] *prep.* at the side of; **b. the point** = nothing to do with the subject.

be•sides [bɪ'saɪdz] 1. *prep.* other than. 2. *adv.* also/in any case.

be•siege [bɪ'siːdʒ] *v.* (*of troops/newspaper reporters*) to surround.

be•sought [bɪ'sɔːt] *v. see* **be•seech.**

best [best] (*superlative of* **good** *and* **well**) 1. *adj. & n.* very good; better than anyone/anything else; **b. man** = friend of the bridegroom who helps him at a wedding; **the b. of it is that** = the most interesting/funniest part of the story is that; **do your b.** = do as well as you can; **for the b. part of an hour** = for almost a whole hour; **to the b. of my knowledge** = as far as I know. 2. *adv.* in a way which is better than anyone else; **best-dressed** = wearing the most fashionable clothes. **best•sel•ler,** *n.* book/article that sells in very large numbers.

bes•tial ['bestjəl] *adj.* like a beast. **bes•ti•al•i•ty** [bestɪ'ælɪtɪ] *n.* being bestial.

be•stir [bɪ'stɜː] *v.* (*formal*) **to b. yourself** = to get the energy to do sth.

be•stow [bɪ'stəʊ] *v.* (*formal*) to give.

bet [bet] 1. *n.* money put down as a pledge when you try to forecast the result of a race, etc., and which you lose if you guess wrongly. 2. *v.* (**bet**) to offer to pay money if what you think

will happen does not happen; **I b. you he's going to be late** = I am quite sure. **bet•tor, better,** *n.* person who bets. **bet•ting,** *n.* placing of bets; **b. parlor** = place where you can bet money on horse races.

be•ta ['biːtə] *n.* second letter of the Greek alphabet. **be•ta block•er** *n.* drug which reduces the heart's activity.

be•take [bɪ'teɪk] *v.* (**betook**) (*formal*) to take.

be•tel ['biːtl] *n.* type of tropical nut.

bête noire [bet'nwɑː] *n.* thing which you dislike particularly.

be•tide [bɪ'taɪd] *v.* (*formal*) to happen to (s.o.).

be•tray [bɪ'treɪ] *v.* to reveal a secret about s.o. to his enemies. **be•tray•al,** *n.* giving s.o. up to his enemies.

be•troth [bɪ'trəʊð] *v.* (*formal*) to engage s.o. to marry. **be•troth•al,** *n.* act of betrothing s.o.

bet•ter ['betə] (*comp. of* **good** *and* **well**) 1. *adj.* superior; of higher quality; less ill; finer (weather). 2. *adv.* **I'm feeling b.** = I'm feeling less ill; **he thought b. of it** = he decided not to do what he had planned; **you'd b. be going** = it's time you went; **he's b. off where he is** = he's in a better position where he is. 3. *v.* **to b. oneself/one's position** = to improve one's position.

be•tween [bɪ'twiːn] *prep.* with things on both sides; **b. you and me** = privately; **in b.** = in the middle of.

be•twixt [bɪ'twɪkst] *prep* (*old*) between.

bev•el ['bevl] 1. *n.* angled edge of a flat surface. 2. *v.* (**beveled, bevelled**) to give a flat surface an angled edge.

bev•er•age ['bevərɪdʒ] *n.* drink.

bev•y ['bevɪ] *n.* (*pl.* **-ies**) group (esp. of girls).

be•wail [bɪ'weɪl] *v.* (*formal*) to complain about (sth).

be•ware [bɪ'weə] *v.* **to b. of** = to watch out for.

be•wil•der [bɪ'wɪldə] *v.* to puzzle. **be•wil•der•ment,** *n.* puzzle/surprise.

be•witch [bɪ'wɪtʃ] *v.* to charm/to cast a spell on. **be•witch•ing,** *adj.* charming (girl).

be•yond [bɪ'jɒnd] 1. *adv.* further than; on the other side of; **it's b. a joke** = it's no longer funny.

bi•an•nu•al [baɪ'ænjuəl] *adj.* which happens twice a year. **bi•an•nu•al•ly,** *adv.* twice a year.

bi•as ['baɪəs] *n.* (a) **to cut material on the b.** = slantwise/diagonally. (b) slant/strong opinion in one direction. **bi•ased,** *adj.* showing strong opinion in one direction/prejudiced.

bib [bɪb] *n.* small cloth tied under a baby's chin.

bi•ble ['baɪbl] *n.* (a) book of Christian or Jewish scriptures. (b) important book of reference. **bib•li•cal** ['bɪblɪkl] *adj.* referring to the bible.

bib•li•og•ra•phy [bɪblɪ'ɒɡrəfɪ] *n.* list of

books/articles referring to a special subject. **bib•li•og•ra•pher**, *n.* person who writes a bibliography. **bib•li•o•graph•i•cal** [bɪblɪəˈgræfɪkl] *adj.* (details) referring to a particular subject. **bib•li•o•phile** [ˈbɪblɪəufaɪl] *n.* person who loves books.

bib•u•lous [ˈbɪbjuːləs] *adj.* fond of drinking.

bi•cam•er•al•ism [baɪˈkæmərəlɪzm] *n.* system of government where there are two legislative parts or branches.

bi•car•bo•nate [baɪˈkɑːbənət] *n.* **b. of soda** = chemical used as a medicine for stomach pains or as an ingredient in cooking.

bi•cen•ten•ar•y [baɪsenˈtiːnərɪ] *n.* anniversary of 200 years. **bi•cen•ten•ni•al** [baɪsenˈtenɪəl] *adj.* referring to a bicentenary.

bi•ceps [ˈbaɪseps] *n.* large muscle in the top part of the arm.

bick•er [ˈbɪkə] *v.* to quarrel.

bi•coast•al [baɪˈkəustl] *adj.* referring to both the east and west coasts of the U.S.

bi•cy•cle [ˈbaɪsɪkl] 1. *n.* two-wheeled vehicle driven by pedals. 2. *v.* to ride on a bicycle.

bid [bɪd] 1. *n.* offer/attempt; **he made a b. for power** = he tried to seize power; **takeover b.** = attempt to take over a company. 2. *v.* (a) (**bid/bade** [bæd]; **has bidden**) to wish; **he bade me farewell.** (b) (**bid; has bid**) to make an offer at an auction. **bidder**, *n.* person who makes an offer at an auction. **bid•ding**, *n.* (a) command; **I did it at his b.** = I did it because he told me to do it. (b) offers made at an auction.

bide [baɪd] *v.* **to b. your time** = to wait for the right moment.

bi•det [ˈbiːdeɪ] *n.* low washbasin for washing the genitals.

bi•en•ni•al [baɪˈenjəl] *adj. & n.* (plant) which flowers in its second year; (event) which occurs every two years. **bi•en•ni•al•ly**, *adv.* every two years.

bier [ˈbɪə] *n.* table/hearse for carrying a coffin.

biff [bɪf] 1. *n. inf.* hit. 2. *v. inf.* to hit.

bi•fo•cal [baɪˈfəukl] *adj. & n.* **b. glasses/bifocals** = glasses with two types of lens in each frame, one for reading and one for long distance.

bi•fur•cate [ˈbaɪfəkeɪt] *v.* to split. **bi•fur•ca•tion** [baɪfəˈkeɪʃn] *n.* splitting (of a road).

big [bɪg] 1. *adj.* (**bigger, biggest**) large; **b. game** = large animals (lions, etc.) which are hunted for sport. 2. *adv.* **to talk b.** = to pretend to be important. **big•head**, *n. inf.* person who is

proud of himself and shows off. **big•wig**, *n.* important person in an official position.

big•a•my [ˈbɪgəmɪ] *n.* action of illegally marrying a second wife/husband, when the first is still alive and has not been divorced. **big•a•mist**, *n.* person who is illegally married to two people at the same time. **big•a•mous**, *adj.* **b. marriage** = illegal marriage when you are already married to s.o. else.

bight [baɪt] *n.* (a) loop of a rope. (b) wide curved bay.

big•ot [ˈbɪgət] *n.* person with a narrow-minded attitude to religion/politics; fanatic. **big•ot•ed**, *adj.* with very unbending ideas about religion/politics, etc. **big•ot•ry**, *n.* narrow-minded attitude to religion/politics, etc.

bike [baɪk] *n. inf.* bicycle.

bi•ki•ni [bɪˈkiːnɪ] *n.* brief two-piece bathing suit for women.

bi•lat•er•al [baɪˈlætərəl] *adj.* on two sides; **b. agreement** = agreement between two sides.

bil•ber•ry [ˈbɪlbərɪ] *n.* small edible blue berry growing in northern mountains; plant which bears these berries.

bile [baɪl] *n.* bitter fluid produced by the liver to digest fat.

bilge [bɪldʒ] *n.* dirty water (in a ship's hull); *inf.* nonsense.

bi•lin•gual [baɪˈlɪŋgwəl] *adj.* using two languages; (person) who can speak two languages equally fluently.

bil•ious [ˈbɪlɪəs] *adj.* sick. **bil•ious•ness**, *n.* feeling sick.

bilk [bɪlk] *v.* to cheat (s.o.) **of** sth.

bill [bɪl] *n.* (a) hard covering of a bird's mouth. (b) note showing the amount of money you have to pay. (c) draft of a proposed law or act. (d) bank note. (e) poster (showing what is on at a theater); **that will fill the b.** = will be very suitable. (f) **b. of fare** = menu. **bill•board**, *n.* large wooden panel for posters. **bill•fold**, *n.* wallet for paper money, etc. **bill•hook**, *n.* large hooked knife, used for cutting small branches.

bil•la•bong [ˈbɪləbɒŋ] *n.* (*in Australia*) loop in a river where there is no current.

bil•let [ˈbɪlɪt] 1. *n.* lodgings (for soldiers). 2. *v.* to lodge (soldiers).

bil•liards [ˈbɪljədz] *n.* game involving hitting balls with a long rod on a smooth green-covered table. **bil•liard ball, billiard table**, *n.* ball/table used in the game of billiards.

æ back, ɑː farm, ɒ top, aɪ pipe, au how, aiə fire, auə flower, ɔː bought, ɔɪ toy, e fed, eəhair, eɪ take, ə afraid, əu boat, əuə lower, vː word, iː heap, ɪ hit, ɪə hear, uː school, u book, ʌ but, b back, d dog, ð then, dʒ just, f fog, g go, h hand, j yes, k catch, l last, m mix, n nut, ŋ sing, p penny, r round, s some, ʃ short, t too, tʃ chop, θ thing, v voice, w was, z zoo, ʒ treasure

bil•lion ['bɪljən] *n. U.S.* one thousand millions; *Brit.* (formerly) one million millions; **billions of letters** = a great many letters.

bil•low ['bɪləʊ] 1. *n.* large wave. 2. *v.* to move in large waves.

bil•ly goat ['bɪlɪgəʊt] *n.* male goat.

bim•bo ['bɪmbəʊ] *n. Sl.* attractive young girl.

bi•month•ly [baɪ'mʌnθlɪ] 1. *adj.* every two months; twice a month. 2. *n.* bimonthly magazine.

bin [bɪn] *n.* storage box.

bi•na•ry ['baɪnərɪ] *adj.* in twos; **b. system** = where numbers are shown by the figures 1 and 0 only.

bind [baɪnd] *v.* (**bound** [baʊnd]) (a) to tie. (b) to cover (a book). (c) to oblige (s.o.) to do sth.; **to b. (s.o.) over** = to make s.o. legally obligated to do sth. **bind•er,** *n.* (a) bookbinder. (b) stiff cover for holding and protecting loose sheets of paper/magazines. **bind•er•y,** *n.* factory which binds books. **bind•ing,** 1. *adj.* **this contract is b. on both parties** = both parties have to do what it says. 2. *n.* outside cover of a book. **bind•weed,** *n.* type of climbing weed.

binge [bɪndʒ] *n. inf.* wild drunken party.

bin•go ['bɪŋgəʊ] *n.* game (played in public) where the aim is to cover up all the numbers on a card as they are called out.

bin•na•cle ['bɪnəkl] *n.* box containing the compass on a ship.

bin•oc•u•lar [bɪ'nɒkjʊlə] 1. *adj.* **b. vision** = ability to see the same object with two eyes, and therefore to judge distance. 2. *n. pl.* **binoculars** = double glasses for seeing long distances.

bi•no•mi•al [baɪ'nəʊmɪəl] *adj.* (theory) based on two figures; **b. classification** = way of classifying plants and animals, using two Latin names.

bi•o•chem•is•try [baɪəʊ'kemɪstrɪ] *n.* science of the chemical constituents of animals or plants. **bi•o•chem•i•cal,** *adj.* referring to biochemistry. **bi•o•chem•ist,** *n.* person who studies the chemical composition of animals or plants.

bi•o•de•grad•a•ble [baɪəʊdɪ'greɪdəbl] *adj.* which decomposes naturally to form harmless material.

bi•o•eth•ics [baɪəʊ'eθɪks] *n.* the study of the moral issues arising from biological and medical research.

bi•og•ra•phy [baɪ'ɒgrəfɪ] *n.* story of the life of s.o. **bi•og•ra•pher,** *n.* person who writes a biography. **bi•o•graph•i•cal** [baɪə'græfɪkl] *adj.* referring to a biography.

bi•ol•o•gy [baɪ'ɒlədʒɪ] *n.* study of living things. **bi•o•log•i•cal** [baɪə'lɒdʒɪkl] *adj.* referring to living things; **b. warfare** = war in

which germs are used. **bi•ol•o•gist,** *n.* person who studies biology.

bi•o•mass ['baɪəʊmæs] *n.* all living organisms in a certain place.

bi•o•me•chan•ics [baɪəʊmɪ'kænɪks] *n.* the study of the mechanics of the movement/structure of living organisms.

bi•on•ic [baɪ'ɒnɪk] *adj.* with powers reinforced by electronic devices.

bi•o•phys•ics [baɪəʊ'fɪzɪks] *n.* science of the physics of living things.

bi•op•sy ['baɪɒpsɪ] *n.* operation to remove a growth/a piece of tissue.

bi•o•rhythms ['baɪəʊrɪðmz] *n. pl.* cycles of activity which are said to recur regularly in each person's life.

bi•par•tite [baɪ'pɑːtaɪt] *adj.* with two sides taking part.

bi•ped ['baɪped] *n.* animal with two legs.

bi•plane ['baɪpleɪn] *n.* aircraft with two sets of wings, one above the other.

birch [bɜːtʃ] 1. *n.* (*pl.* **-es**) **silver b.** = common northern tree with white bark. 2. *v.* to beat with a bundle of twigs.

bird [bɜːd] *n.* (a) animal with wings and feathers. (b) *inf.* person. **bird's-eye view,** *n.* view from high up looking down. **bird watch•er,** *n.* person who studies birds. **bird watch•ing,** *n.* study of birds.

bi•ret•ta [bɪ'retə] *n.* small cap worn by a Catholic priest.

birth [bɜːθ] *n.* being born; **he is French by b.** = he has French nationality because his parents are French; **b. certificate** = official document showing date and place of s.o.'s birth; **b. control** = method of preventing pregnancy; **b. rate** = average number of children born per thousand population; **to give b. to** = to have (a child)/to produce (young). **birth•day,** *n.* date on which you were born; **in his b. suit** = naked/with no clothes on. **birth•mark,** *n.* mark on the skin which is there from birth. **birth•place,** *n.* place where s.o. was born/sth was invented. **birth•right,** *n.* right which you inherit at birth.

bis•cuit ['bɪskɪt] *n.* small soft cake or bread. **water biscuits** = biscuits made of flour and water.

bi•sect [baɪ'sekt] *v.* to cut into two equal parts.

bi•sex•u•al [baɪ'seksjʊəl] *adj.* who is attracted to both sexes.

bish•op ['bɪʃəp] *n.* (a) church leader in charge of a diocese. (b) piece in chess shaped like a bishop's hat. **bish•op•ric,** *n.* post of bishop.

bis•muth ['bɪzməθ] *n.* (*element:* Bi) white metal used in medicine.

bi•son ['baɪsn] *n.* (*pl.* **bison**) large wild ox or cow.

bis•tro ['bi:strəʊ] *n.* (*pl.* **-os**) small restaurant/café.

bit [bɪt] *n.* (a) small piece; **a b. longer** = a little while longer; **the chair has fallen to bits** = has come apart; **she's thrilled to bits** = very pleased; **he is a b. of a nuisance** = he is rather a nuisance; **b. by b.** = in stages; **not a b. of use** = of no use at all; **he's every b. as ugly as you said** = just as ugly; **b. part** = small part (in a play). (b) piece of metal for making holes which is placed in a drill. (c) piece of metal going through a horse's mouth to which the reins are attached. (d) small piece of information (in a computer) represented by 0 or 1. **bit•map** ['bɪt mæp] *n.* image created on a visual display unit where the number of bits per pixel determines the number of possible colors. (e) *v. see* also **bite**.

bitch [bɪtʃ] 1. *n.* (*pl.* **-es**) (a) female dog. (b) *inf.* unpleasant woman. 2. *v. inf.* to complain.

bite [baɪt] 1. *v.* (**bit; has bitten**) to cut with teeth; **he bit my head off** = he spoke angrily to me. 2. *n.* (a) mouthful. (b) place where you have been bitten. **bit•ing**, *adj.* sharp (wind); piercing (cold); sharp (remark).

bit•ten ['bɪtn] *v. see* **bite**.

bit•ter ['bɪtə] *adj.* (a) not sweet; sour. (b) resentful/cruel; **to the b. end** = right to the very end. (c) very cold. **bit•ter•ly**, *adv.* sharply/resentfully. **bit•ter•ness**, *n.* resentment.

bit•tern ['bɪtən] *n.* marsh bird which makes a booming call.

bi•tu•men ['bɪtjumən] *n.* black substance, like tar. **bi•tu•mi•nous** [bɪ'tjuːmɪnəs] *adj.* referring to bitumen.

bi•valve ['baɪvælv] *n.* shellfish with two shells hinged together.

biv•ou•ac ['bɪvuæk] *v.* (**bivouacked**) to camp out in the open without a tent.

bi•zarre [bɪ'zɑː] *adj.* very strange.

blab [blæb] *v.* (**blabbed**) *inf.* to talk too much/to gossip.

black [blæk] 1. *adj.* (**-er, -est**) (a) of a very dark color, the opposite of white; **b. coffee** = coffee without milk or cream; **b. ice** = dangerous layer of thin ice on a road; **b. box** = device which stores information about an aircraft's flight; **b. market** = selling illegally, at high prices, products which are not normally available. (b) bad; **b. deeds** = evil deeds. 2. *n.* (a) very dark color, opposite to white; **to be in the b.** = to have money in a bank account. (b) member of a dark-skinned race of people originating in Africa. **black•ball**, *v.* to vote against (s.o.) joining a club. **black•ber•ry**, *n.* common wild fruit, growing on long prickly stems. **black•bird**, *n.* common northern bird, the male of which has black feathers and yellow beak. **black•board**, *n.* board on the wall which can be written on. **black cur•rant**, *n.* common black soft fruit grown in the garden. **black•en**, *v.* to make black. **black fly**, *n.* small black aphis. **black•guard** ['blægɑːd] *n.* scoundrel/wicked person. **black•head**, *n.* blocked pore which shows up as a black dot on the skin. **black•ish**, *adj.* rather black. **black•list**. 1. *n.* list of undesirable things or people. 2. *v.* to put (s.o.) on a list of undesirable people. **black•mail**. 1. *v.* to make s.o. pay money by threatening to reveal some unpleasant or shameful detail about them. 2. *n.* act of blackmailing. **black•mail•er**, *n.* person who blackmails. **Black Ma•ri•a**, *n. Sl.* patrol wagon. **black•ness**, *n.* total darkness. **black out**, *v.* (a) to wipe off/to suppress. (b) to faint/to lose consciousness. (c) to cut off the electricity. **black•out**, *n.* (a) loss of consciousness. (b) sudden stoppage of electricity supply. **black•smith**, *n.* man who makes horseshoes, gates, etc., out of metal. **black•thorn**, *n.* wild prickly bush, with white flowers.

blad•der ['blædə] *n.* (a) bag in the body where urine is stored. (b) bag inside a ball which is inflated.

blade [bleɪd] *n.* (a) cutting part of knife, etc. (b) thin leaf of grass. (c) one arm of a propeller. (d) flat part at the end of an oar.

blame [bleɪm] 1. *n.* criticism of s.o. for having done sth; **to get the b. for** = to be said to be responsible for. 2. *v.* **to b. s.o. for sth** = to say that sth was caused by s.o.; **he is to b. for the accident** = he is responsible for the accident; **I don't b. you** = I think you were quite right. **blame•less**, *adj.* Pure or innocent. **blame•wor•thy**, *adj.* (person) who can rightly be blamed.

blanch [blɑːntʃ] *v.* (a) to put quickly into boiling water. (b) to turn white.

blanc•mange [blə'mɒnʒ] *n.* dessert like a cream jelly flavored with chocolate/strawberry, etc.

bland [blænd] *adj.* smooth/not striking; (food) without much flavor. **bland•ly**, *adv.* in a smooth casual way. **bland•ness**, *n.* smoothness; lack of any striking features.

æ back, aː farm, ɒ top, aɪ pipe, aʊ how, aɪə fire, aʊə flower, ɔː bought, ɔɪ toy, e fed, eəhair, eɪ take, ə afraid, əʊ boat, əʊə lower, vː word, iː heap, ɪ hit, ɪə hear, uː school, ʊ book, ʌ but, b back, d dog, ð then, dʒ just, f fog, g go, h hand, j yes, k catch, l last, m mix, n nut, ŋ sing, p penny, r round, s some, ʃ short, t too, tʃ chop, θ thing, v voice, w was, z zoo, ʒ treasure

blan•dish•ments ['blændɪʃmənts] *n. pl.* attractive flattery.

blank [blæŋk] 1. *adj.* (**-er, -est**) (a) (paper, etc.) with nothing on it; **b. check** = check where the figures are not written in; **b. verse** = poetry which does not rhyme; **he looked b.** = he looked lost/surprised. (b) **b. cartridge** = with no bullet in it. 2. *n.* (a) white space (with nothing printed on it); **my mind is a b.** = I cannot remember anything; **he drew a b.** = he failed to make any progress. (b) cartridge with no bullet in it. **blank•ly**, *adv.* with vacant expression.

blan•ket ['blæŋkɪt] 1. *n.* woolen bed covering; **electric b.** = electrically heated pad to warm a bed; **b. order** = order which covers many items. 2. *v.* to cover (with fog, etc.).

blare ['bleə] 1. *n.* loud noise. 2. *v.* to make a loud noise.

blar•ney ['blɑːnɪ] *n.* talk which is intended to trick.

bla•sé ['blɑːzeɪ] *adj.* with a couldn't-care-less attitude.

blas•pheme [blæs'fiːm] *v.* to swear; to talk without respect for God. **blas•phem•er**, *n.* person who swears. **blas•phe•mous** ['blæsfəməs] *adj.* showing no respect for religion; antireligious (talk). **blas•phe•my**, *n.* disrespect for religion; swearing.

blast [blɑːst] 1. *n.* (a) sharp blowing of wind. (b) short whistle. (c) **going full b.** = working at full power. (d) explosion; shock wave from an explosion. 2. *v.* (a) to blow up. (b) to ruin. **blast fur•nace**, *n.* furnace used to make steel. **blast off**, *v. (of rocket)* to take off. **blast-off**, *n.* departure of a rocket.

bla•tant ['bleɪtənt] *adj.* obvious/unmistakable. **bla•tant•ly**, *adv.* obviously/unmistakably.

blath•er [missing] *n.* silly talk.

blaze [bleɪz] 1. *n.* (a) fierce fire; **she worked like blazes** = she worked extremely hard. (b) white mark made by cutting away the bark of a tree; white mark on the forehead of an animal. 2. *v.* (a) to burn fiercely. (b) **to b. a trail** = to mark a path by cutting the bark on trees/to be the first to do something. **blaz•ing**, *adj.* fiery.

blaz•er ['bleɪzə] *n.* jacket with metal buttons, originally worn with a badge to show membership of a club/school.

bla•zon ['bleɪzn] 1. *n.* coat of arms. 2. *v.* to proclaim (sth).

bleach [bliːtʃ] 1. *n.* substance which takes the color out of something. 2. *v.* to take the color out of sth. **bleach•ers**, *n. pl.* raised tiers of seats at a sports stadium.

bleak [bliːk] *adj.* (**-er, -est**) cold/inhospitable. **bleak•ly**, *adv.* in a cold/inhospitable way.

blear•y ['blɪərɪ] *adj.* watery/dim (eyes). **blear•y-eyed**, *adj.* with watery eyes.

bleat [bliːt] 1. *n.* noise made by a sheep or goat. 2. *v.* (a) to make a noise like a goat/sheep. (b) to complain; **what is he bleating about?** = what does he keep complaining about?

bleed [bliːd] 1. *n.* **a nose b.** = loss of blood from the nose. 2. *v.* (**bled**) to lose blood; **my heart bleeds for you** = I am very sorry for you.

bleep [bliːp] 1. *n.* small noise made by a radio/a radar screen. 2. *v. (of a radio)* to make a small noise. **bleep•er**, *n.* machine which makes a bleep.

blem•ish ['blemɪʃ] 1. *n.* (*pl.* **-es**) imperfection/mark. 2. *v.* to spoil.

blench [blenʃ] *v.* to tremble with fear.

blend [blend] 1. *n.* mixture (of coffee/tea/tobacco). 2. *v.* to mix. **blend•er**, *n.* machine for mixing food.

bless [bles] *v.* to make sacred; to bring happiness/wealth to (s.o.); *inf.* **b. you!** = *phrase said when someone sneezes.* **bless•ed** ['blesɪd] *adj.* (a) protected by God. (b) *inf.* cursed/annoying. **bless•ing**, *n.* (a) thing which is useful/which brings happiness; **it's a b. in disguise** = it doesn't look like it, but it is very useful. (b) short prayer, esp. before or after a meal.

bleth•er ['bleðə] *n. see* **blath•er.**

blew [bluː] *v. see* **blow.**

blight [blaɪt] 1. *n.* fungoid disease (attacking vegetables/leaves, etc.). 2. *v.* to spoil/to ruin.

blimp [blɪmp] *n.* small airship.

blind [blaɪnd] 1. *n.* (a) covering (over a window); **Venetian b.** = blind made of many horizontal flat strips of wood or plastic. (b) **the b.** = people who cannot see. 2. *adj.* not able to see; **to turn a b. eye to sth** = pretend not to notice; **b. alley** = (i) alley with no way out; (ii) position with no prospect of progress; **b. spot** = (i) part of the road which a motorist cannot see; (ii) thing which s.o. is incapable of understanding. 3. *v.* to prevent s.o. from seeing; to make s.o. blind. 4. *adv.* **flying b.** = flying an aircraft, using the instruments only. **blind•fold**, 1. *n.* bandage put over s.o.'s eyes to prevent him from seeing. 2. *v.* to put a bandage over s.o.'s eyes. **blind•ly**, *adv.* without being able to see. **blind•ness**, *n.* not being able to see.

blink [blɪŋk] 1. *n. inf.* **on the b.** = not working properly. 2. *v.* to close your eyelids very quickly. **blink•ers**, *n.* shades put on a horse's eyes to prevent it from looking sideways.

blip [blɪp] *n.* small dot of light on a radar screen.

bliss [blɪs] *n.* great happiness. **bliss•ful**, *adj.* extremely happy. **bliss•ful•ly**, *adv.* happily.

blis•ter ['blɪstə] 1. *n.* bump on the skin (with

water underneath) made by rubbing; **b. pack** =
type of container, where the product is covered by a stiff plastic bubble. 2. *v.* to make
bumps on the surface (of sth).

blithe•ly ['blaɪðlɪ] *adv.* in a happy carefree way.

blith•er•ing ['blɪðərɪŋ] *adj. inf.* carrying on or
talking foolishly.

blitz [blɪts] 1. *n. (pl.* **-es)** (a) bombing (of a
town). (b) *inf.* **b. on sth** = sudden campaign to
clear sth up. 2. *v.* to bomb.

bliz•zard ['blɪzəd] *n.* heavy snowstorm with
strong winds.

bloat•ed ['bləʊtɪd] *adj.* full; too fat.

bloat•er ['bləʊtə] *n.* dried salt herring.

blob [blɒb] *n.* large spot.

bloc [blɒk] *n. (political)* group; **b. vote** = vote by
a group voting together.

block [blɒk] 1. *n.* (a) piece/lump (of stone or
wood). (b) large building; **he lives two blocks
away** = there are two crossroads between here
and his house. (c) **b. capitals/letters** = capital
letters. (d) **b. and tackle** = arrangement of pulleys and ropes for lifting heavy objects. 2. *v.* to
prevent sth going past; **the truck blocked the
road for hours. block•ade** [blɒ'keɪd] 1. *n.* preventing supplies being brought into a place. 2.
v. to prevent supplies being brought into a
place. **block•age,** *n.* blocking. **block up,** *v.*
to stop (a hole), to fill (a pipe).

bloke [bləʊk] *n. Brit. inf.* man.

blond, blonde [blɒnd] *adj. & n.* (man/woman)
with fair hair.

blood [blʌd] *n.* red liquid in the body; **b. group**
= type of blood a person has; **b. donor** = person who gives blood to be used in operations;
b. pressure = pressure at which the heart
pumps blood; **b. transfusion** = giving blood to
a sick person. **it makes my b. boil** = it makes
me very angry; **his b. ran cold** = he was scared.
blood bank, *n.* place where blood is stored
until it is needed for transfusions.
blood•bath, *n.* massacre.
blood•cur•dling, *adj.* very frightening.
blood•hound, *n.* dog trained to follow
tracks. **blood•less,** *adj.* with no blood; **b.
revolution** = revolution where no one was
killed. **blood•shed,** *n.* killing. **blood•shot,**
adj. red (eyes). **blood•sports,** *n. pl.* sports
which involve killing animals. **blood•stain,**
n. stain caused by blood. **blood•stained,**
adj. stained with blood. **blood•stock,** *n.* race
horses. **blood•stream,** *n.* flow of blood
through the body. **blood•suck•er,** *n.* animal

which sucks your blood. **blood test,** *n.* test to
show the condition of the blood.
blood•thirst•y, *adj.* cruel/liking gory details.
blood ves•sel, *n.* vein/artery which carries
blood. **blood•y,** *adj.* **(-ier, -iest)** (a) covered
with blood; where much blood has been shed;
(b) *Brit. Sl.* awful. **blood•y-mind•ed,** *adj.
inf.* awkward/uncooperative.

bloom [bluːm] 1. *n.* (a) flower; **the apple trees
are in full b.** = all the apple flowers are out. (b)
velvety skin (of a peach); dust (on skin of a
grape). (c) **b. of youth** = healthy glow of a
young person. (d) layer of algae on the surface
of the water. 2. *v.* to flower/to flourish.
bloo•mers *inf.* wide knickers.

blos•som ['blɒsəm] 1. *n.* flower (on trees). 2. *v.*
to flower.

blot [blɒt] 1. *n.* dirty spot; drop (of ink on
paper). 2. *v.* **(blotted)** to drop a spot (of ink) on
sth; to dry the ink on a letter. **blot•ter,** *n.* pad
of blotting paper. **blot•ting pa•per,** *n.*
thick absorbent paper for drying ink. **blot•to**
['blɒtəʊ] *adj. inf.* drunk.

blotch [blɒtʃ] *n.* large patch of color.
blotch•y, *adj.* (face) with patches of red.

blouse [blaʊz] *n.* (woman's) shirt.

blow [bləʊ] 1. *n.* knock/punch. 2. *v.* **(blew** [bluː]**;
has blown)** to make air move; (*of air*) to move;
it's blowing hard = there is a strong wind; **he
blew his nose** = he cleared his nose by blowing
down it into a handkerchief; **to b. a fuse** = to
burn out a fuse by overloading it. **blow
away,** *v.* to move (sth) away by blowing.
blow down, *v.* to fall down/to make (sth) fall
down by blowing. **blow dry,** *v.* **(blow drying)**
to dry (s.o.'s hair) with a blower. **blow-dry,**
n. act of drying hair with a blower. **blow•er,**
n. device which blows. **blow•fly,** *n.* large
blue-green fly that is attracted by meat.
blow•gun, *n.* pipe through which poison arrows can be blown. **blow off,** *v.* to go off/to
make (sth) go off by blowing. **blow out,** *v.* to
go out/to make (sth) go out by blowing.
blow•out, *n.* (a) *inf.* huge meal. (b) bursting
(of a tire). **blow over,** *v.* (*of storm*) to end; to
knock (sth) down by blowing. **blow•torch,**
n. device with a strong gas flame used in met-
alworking. **blow up,** *v.* (a) to explode. (b) to
destroy by explosives. (c) to fill (sth) with air.
(d) to enlarge (a photograph). **blow•y,** *adj.*
windy.

blowz•y ['blaʊzɪ] *adj.* common, redfaced
(woman).

æ back, ɑ: farm, ɒ: top, aɪ pipe, aʊ how, aiə fire, aʊə flower, ɔ: bought, ɔɪ toy, e fed, eəhair, eɪ take, ə
afraid, əʊ boat, əʊə lower, v: word, i: heap, ɪ hit, ɪə hear, u: school, ʊ book, ʌ but, b back, d dog, ð then,
dʒ just, f fog, g go, h hand, j yes, k catch, l last, m mix, n nut, ŋ sing, p penny, r round, s some, ʃ short, t
too, tʃ chop, θ thing, v voice, w was, z zoo, ʒ treasure

blub•ber ['blʌbə] 1. *n.* fat (of a whale/seal). 2. *v.* to cry noisily.

bludg•eon ['blʌdʒən] 1. *n.* large stick for hitting people. 2. *v.* to beat (s.o.) with a stick.

blue [bluː] 1. *adj.* (-er, -est) (a) colored like the sky; **b. baby** = baby with blue skin caused by heart disease; **once in a b. moon** = very seldom. (b) pornographic; **b. movies.** (c) sad. 2. *n.* (a) color like that of the sky; **out of the b.** = as a complete surprise. (b) **blues** = Afro-American folk music, the basis of jazz. **blue•bell,** *n.* common blue wild flower/wild hyacinth. **blue be•ret** *n. inf.* soldier of a United Nations peacekeeping force. **blue•ber•ry,** *n.* small blue berry; plant which bears this berry. **blue•bot•tle,** *n.* large blue-green fly that is attracted to meat. **blue chip (share),** *n.* share in a safe company. **blue col•lar work•er,** *n.* manual laborer. **blue-eyed,** *adj.* with blue eyes; **blue-eyed boy** = favorite. **Blue laws,** *n.* laws which regulate what can be done on a Sunday. **blue jeans,** *n.* pants or trousers, usu. made of blue denim, worn for work or casual wear. **blue-pen•cil,** *v.* (-pen-ciled, -pencilled) to change or correct. **blue•print,** *n.* detailed plan. **blu•ish,** *adj.* rather blue.

bluff [blʌf] 1. *n.* (a) steep rocky hill. (b) trick; **to call s.o.'s b.** = to claim (successfully) that s.o. is tricking/is lying. 2. *adj.* down-to-earth/straightforward (person). 3. *v.* to trick/to pretend. **bluff•ly,** *adv.* in a straightforward way. **bluff•ness,** *n.* being blunt/straightforward.

blun•der ['blʌndə] 1. *n.* mistake. 2. *v.* (a) to make a mistake. (b) **to b. into** = to bump into. **blun•der•ing,** *adj.* clumsy.

blunt [blʌnt] 1. *adj.* (a) not sharp. (b) straightforward/frank/almost rude. 2. *v.* to make blunt. **blunt•ly,** *adv.* frankly/almost rudely. **blunt•ness,** *n.* being blunt.

blur [blɜː] 1. *n.* indistinct picture. 2. *v.* (blurred) to make indistinct.

blurb [blɜːb] *n.* piece of publicity describing sth. as a book.

blurt [blɜːt] *v.* to let out (a secret).

blush [blʌʃ] 1. *n.* (*pl.* -es) red shade (on skin). 2. *v.* to go red (with embarrassment).

blus•ter ['blʌstə] 1. *n.* swaggering talk; attitude of defiance. 2. *v.* to swagger/to show off. **blus•ter•y,** *adj.* strong (wind/gale).

bo•a ['bəʊə] *n.* **b. constrictor** = large tropical snake which kills animals by wrapping itself round them and squeezing them; **feather b.** = type of scarf made of feathery material.

boar [bɔː] *n.* male pig, usu. wild.

board [bɔːd] 1. *n.* (a) large flat piece of wood, etc.; **ironing b.** = narrow table for ironing. (b) food; **full b.** = room and all meals (in a hotel). (c) group of people in charge of a business. (d) **to go on b.** = to go on to a ship/into an aircraft. 2. *v.* (a) to go on to a (ship/bus), into (an aircraft). **board•er,** *n.* person who receives regular meals and usu. lodging for a fixed rate. **board•ing,** *adj.* (a) **b. card** = card which allows you to go into an aircraft. (b) **b. house** = house where you pay a fixed rate for regular meals and lodging. **b. school** = school where the children receive food and lodging during the term. **board•room,** *n.* room where a board of directors meets. **board up,** *v.* to cover (windows/doors) with boards for protection.

boast [bəʊst] 1. *n.* act of boasting. 2. *v.* (a) (of/about) to talk about how clever/strong/handsome, etc., you are. (b) to possess (sth), and be proud. **boast•er,** *n.* person who is always boasting. **boast•ful,** *adj.* very proud; always boasting.

boat [bəʊt] *n.* (small) ship; **b. train** = train which connects with a boat; **we're all in the same b.** = we're all in equal circumstances. **boat•er,** *n.* flat straw hat. **boat•house,** *n.* shed for storing boats. **boat•ing,** *n.* rowing (for pleasure). **boat•man,** *n.* (*pl.* -men) man in charge of boats. **boat•swain** ['bəʊsn] *n.* (*at sea*) man in charge of the boats and sails.

bob [bɒb] 1. *n.* (a) little curtsy. (b) hair tied in a knot. 2. *v.* (bobbed) to move quickly up and down.

bob•bin ['bɒbɪn] *n.* small reel for holding thread (for a sewing machine/a spinning wheel).

bob•ble [bɒbl] *n.* little fluffy ball used for decoration.

bob•by ['bɒbɪ] *n. Brit.* policeman. **bob•by-pin,** *n.* flat type of hairpin. **bob•by-socks,** *n. pl.* girls' ankle socks.

bob•sled, bobsleigh ['bɒbsleɪ] *n.* sled with two runners, used for racing.

bode [bəʊd] *v.* **it bodes ill** = it promises to bring ruin.

bod•ice ['bɒdɪs] *n.* top part (of a dress).

bod•kin ['bɒdkɪn] *n.* large thick needle used for threading tape or elastic.

bod•y ['bɒdɪ] *n.* (*pl.* -ies) (a) main structure of an animal or person; main part of an animal or person not including the head and limbs; **dead b.** = corpse. (b) group of people. (c) main part (of a building/a car, etc.). (d) strength (of wine). **bod•i•ly.** 1. *adj.* of the body; **to cause s.o. grievous b. harm** = to attack s.o. and beat him up. 2. *adv.* **they carried him out b.** = they lifted him up and carried him. **bod•y•guard,** *n.* person or group of people who guards s.o. **bod•y•work,** *n.* outer covering of a car.

bog [bɒg] 1. *n*. area of marshland. 2. *v*. **(bogged) to get bogged down** = to get stuck (in mud); **the discussion got bogged down in details** = they got stuck in details. **bog•gy**, *adj*. marshy.

bo•gey ['bəʊgɪ] *n*. (a) (*also* **bogeyman**) thing which frightens children. (b) (*in golf*) normal number of strokes which a player should take to play a hole.

bog•gle ['bɒgl] *v*. to be reluctant (**at** = to do sth); **the mind boggles** = it is impossible to imagine.

bo•gus ['bəʊgəs] *adj*. false.

bo•he•mi•an [bəʊ'hiːmɪən] *adj. & n*. (person) living a wild/unconventional life.

boil [bɔɪl] 1. *n*. (a) swelling in the body full of pus. (b) **bring the water to a b.** = make the water boil. 2. *v*. (a) to heat (a liquid) until it bubbles. (b) to cook in boiling water; **hard-boiled egg** = egg which has been cooked until it is solid (usu. eaten cold). **boil away**, *v*. to evaporate (through boiling). **boil down**, *v*. (a) to evaporate (through boiling); to reduce (a piece of writing). (b) to be reduced to; **it all boils down to whether he will resign willingly or not** = the main question is, will he resign willingly or not. **boil•er**, *n*. large metal container for boiling water; large metal container and arrangement of tubes for supplying heat or power. **boil•ing**. 1. *n*. action of heating a liquid until it bubbles; **212°F (100°C) is the b. point of water**. 2. *adj*. (liquid) which is boiling or very hot; **it is b. in this room** = it is very hot. 3. *adv*. **b. hot** = very hot. **boil over**, *v*. to rise in a pan when boiling, and run over the sides.

bois•ter•ous ['bɔɪstrəs] *adj*. noisy/violent (crowd/wind/sea, etc.). **bois•ter•ous•ly**, *adv*. in a boisterous way. **bois•ter•ous•ness**, *n*. noise/violence.

bold [bəʊld] *adj*. (-er, -est) (a) strongly marked (color/outline). (b) daring/brave. **bold•ly**, *adv*. bravely/defiantly. **bold•ness**, *n*. daring/bravery.

bole [bəʊl] *n*. tree trunk.

bo•le•ro *n*. (a) [bə'leərəʊ] type of Spanish dance. (b) ['bɒlərəʊ] short sleeveless jacket worn by women.

boll [bɒl] *n*. seed head of the cotton plant.

bol•lard ['bɒlɑːd] *n*. low post on a wharf quay for attaching a ship's rope.

bol•ster ['bəʊlstə] 1. *n*. long pillow going right across a bed. 2. *v*. (*also* **to bolster up**) to support or uphold; **to b. s.o. spirits** = to make s.o. feel better.

bolt [bəʊlt] 1. *n*. (a) flash of lightning with thunder; **it came as a b. from the blue** = it came as a complete surprise. (b) metal rod which slides into a hole to secure a door. (c) metal rod with a screw which fastens with a nut. (d) **to make a b. for** = to rush toward. 2. *v*. (a) to run fast/to escape; **the horse bolted** = the horse got out of control. (b) to eat quickly and with big mouthfuls. (c) to fasten (a door) with a bolt. (d) to fasten with a bolt and nut. 3. *adv*. **sitting b. upright** = sitting straight upright.

bomb [bɒm] 1. *n*. (a) large explosive weapon, often dropped from an aircraft; **b. disposal** = removing the fuse from an unexploded bomb. (b) *inf*. complete failure. 2. *v*. (a) to drop bombs on. (b) to fail completely. **bom•bard** [bɒm'bɑːd] *v*. to attack (repeatedly). **bom•bard•ment**, *n*. attack (with bombs/shells/questions). **bomb•er**, *n*. special aircraft for dropping bombs. **bomb•shell**, *n*. great (usu. unpleasant) surprise.

bom•bast•ic [bɒm'bæstɪk] *adj*. flowery/boasting (way of speaking).

bo•na fide ['bəʊnə'faɪdɪ] 1. *adj*. made in good faith; **a bona fide offer**. 2. *n*. **the police are checking on his bona fides** = they are checking that he is speaking the truth.

bo•nan•za [bə'nænzə] *n*. great wealth (discovered suddenly).

bond [bɒnd] 1. *n*. (a) link; joining together. (b) paper showing that money has been lent to the government; (c) **in b.** (goods held) in a customs warehouse until taxes or duties are paid. 2. *v*. to link/to join (with glue). **bond•age**, *n*. slavery. **bond•ed ware•house**, *n*. warehouse containing goods in bond.

bone [bəʊn] 1. *n*. one of the solid white pieces which make up the framework of the body; **b. dry** = completely dry; **I've got a b. to pick with you** = I want to complain about sth which you've done. 2. *v*. to take the bones out of (meat, fish). **bone•less**, *adj*. with no bones. **bon•y**, *adj*. with big bones; with many bones.

bon•fire ['bɒnfaɪə] *n*. outdoor fire for burning leaves, etc. or as a celebration.

bon•go ['bɒŋgəʊ] *n*. small drum, tapped with the hand.

bon•kers ['bɒŋkəz] *adj. Sl*. mad.

bon•net ['bɒnɪt] *n*. (a) child's/woman's hat, with a brim framing the face. (b) *Brit*. hinged cover for the front part of a car.

bon•ny ['bɒnɪ] *adj*. (-ier, -iest) good-looking and healthy.

æ back, ɑː farm, ɒ top, aɪ pipe, aʊ how, aɪə fire, aʊə flower, ɔː bought, ɔɪ toy, e fed, eə hair, eɪ take, ə afraid, əʊ boat, əʊə lower, ɜː word, iː heap, ɪ hit, ɪə hear, uː school, ʊ book, ʌ but, b back, d dog, ð then, dʒ just, f fog, g go, h hand, j yes, k catch, l last, m mix, n nut, ŋ sing, p penny, r round, s some, ʃ short, t too, tʃ chop, θ thing, v voice, w was, z zoo, ʒ treasure

bon•sai ['bɒnsaɪ] *n.* (art of growing) trees in small pots, pruned so that they remain small.

bo•nus ['bəʊnəs] *n.* (*pl.* -es) extra money.

boo [buː] 1. *inter.* call to show disapproval or to surprise. 2. *v.* to show disapproval by saying "boo."

boob [buːb] *n. Sl.* (a) stupid, silly person. (b) breast.

boo•by ['buːbɪ] *n.* silly person. **boo•by prize,** *n.* (silly) prize given to the last person in a competition. **boo•by trap.** *n.* trap to catch s.o. unawares. **boob•y-trap,** *v.* (**boobytrapped**) to set a trap (in a place).

book [bʊk] 1. *n.* (a) printed pages attached together with a cover. (b) **exercise b.** = book of blank pages with lines for writing on; **check b.** = book of blank checks; (c) script (of musical). (d) **b. of tickets** = several tickets fastened together and sold as a unit; **b. of matches** = matches fastened together in a cardboard holder. 2. *v.* (a) to reserve (a place/seat/table) on plane/in theater/in restaurant. (b) **he was booked for speeding** = the police have made a charge against him for speeding. **book•a•ble,** *adj.* which can be reserved in advance. **book•bind•er,** *n.* person who puts covers on printed sheets to make a book. **book•bind•ing,** *n.* art of binding books. **book•case,** *n.* cabinet/set of shelves for keeping books. **book•ie,** *n. inf.* person who collects bets before a race. **book in,** *v.* to register (at a hotel). **book•ing,** *n.* (a) reservation (of seats/places); **b. office** = office (at railway station, theater, etc.) where you can book seats in advance. (b) arrangement (for actor, etc.) to appear at a theater. **book•ish,** *adj.* learned/studious. **book•keep•er,** *n.* person who keeps systematic records of money transactions. **book•keep•ing,** *n.* skill or work of being a bookkeeper. **book•let,** *n.* small book with only a few pages. **book•lov•er,** *n.* person who loves (and collects) books. **book•mak•er,** *n.* person who collects bets before a race. **book•mark•(er),** *n.* (a) long, narrow, piece of card/cloth/leather used to keep your place in a book. (b) a marker put on a site on the Internet so that the computer user can find the site again easily and quickly. **book•mo•bile** ['bʊkməbiːl] *n.* traveling library. **book•sell•er,** *n.* person who sells books. **book•shelf,** *n.* shelf for keeping books. **book•shop,** *n.* bookstore. **book•stall, bookstand,** *n.* stand or stall selling books, usu. outdoors. **book•store,** *n.* store selling books. **book up,** *v.* to reserve. **book•worm,** *n.* person who reads many books.

bool•e•an *adj.* referring to a system of sym-

bolic logic that is used in computer programming.

boom [buːm] 1. *n.* (a) floating barrier across a harbor. (b) long rod attached to the lower edge of a sail; long rod (for holding a microphone over speakers' heads). (c) low muffled sound. (d) sudden increase (in value/sales/general prosperity). 2. *v.* (a) to make a low muffled sound. (b) to increase suddenly/to become more prosperous.

boo•mer•ang ['buːməræŋ] 1. *n.* curved piece of wood which, when thrown, comes back to the thrower. 2. *v.* to backfire/to rebound.

boon [buːn] 1. *n.* advantage/blessing. 2. *adj.* **b. companion** = great friend.

boor [bɔː, 'bʊə] *n.* rough/uncouth man. **boor•ish,** *adj.* rude/uncouth.

boost [buːst] 1. *n.* help/publicity. 2. *v.* (a) to help/to promote. (b) to increase (voltage in electricity cable). **boost•er,** *n.* (a) apparatus for increasing voltage. (b) **b. rocket** = rocket which helps keep up the speed of the main rocket; **b. shot** = injection which keeps up the protection given by a former injection.

boot [buːt] 1. *n.* (a) footwear which goes above the ankle. (b) *Brit.* back part of a car (where the luggage can be put). 2. *v.* (a) to kick. (b) (*computers*) to carry out a set of instructions automatically. **boot camp,** *n. Sl.* (a) basic training camp in the U.S. Marine Corps/Navy. (b) prison for juvenile offenders with a military-style regime. **boot•ee,** *n.* small knitted boot for babies. **boot•la•ces,** *n. pl.* very long laces for boots. **boot•leg,** *adj.* illegal (whisky, etc.). **boot•leg•ger,** *n.* person who makes/transports illegal spirits.

booth [buːð] *n.* (a) stall for display of goods at a market/fair/exhibition. (b) small enclosed space for a specific use by one person.

boo•ty ['buːtɪ] *n.* treasure captured in a war.

booze [buːz] 1. *n. inf.* alcoholic drink. 2. *inf.* to drink (alcohol). **booz•er,** *n. inf.* person who drinks a lot.

bo•rac•ic [bə'ræsɪk] *adj.* chemical substance used in ointments.

bo•rax ['bɔːræks] *n.* white powder used in making glass and as an antiseptic.

Bor•deaux mix•ture ['bɔːdəʊ'mɪkstʃə] *n.* sulfur spray, used on plants.

bor•der ['bɔːdə] 1. *n.* frontier/edge; **flower b.** = edging of flowers along a flower bed. 2. *v.* **France borders on Germany** = France touches Germany; **it is a movie which borders on the indecent** = which is almost indecent. **bor•der•ing,** *adj.* close to. **bord•er•line,** *n.* line between two surfaces; **b. case** = case which is on the dividing line (between two types).

bore [bɔː] 1. *n.* (a) width of a tube. (b) person/thing which is dull and tiresome. **what a b.** = what a nuisance. (c) wave in a river caused by the tide. 2. *v.* (a) to make (a hole). (b) to tire (s.o.) by being dull. **I'm bored stiff** = very bored. (c) *see also* **bear**. **bore•dom**, *n.* being bored. **bor•ing**, *adj.* which makes you lose interest completely.

born [bɔːn] *adj.* **he was b. in 1962** = his birth took place in 1962; **she's a b. actress** = she has always had a gift for acting; **I wasn't b. yesterday** = I'm not as stupid as you think.

borne [bɔːn] *v. see* **bear**.

bo•ron ['bɔːrɒn] *n.* (*element:* B) brown powder which resists high temperatures and is used to make borax.

bor•ough ['bʌrə] *n.* incorporated municipality which is smaller than a city, in some U.S. states.

bor•row ['bɒrəʊ] *v.* to take (sth) for a short time with the owner's permission; to take (money) from a bank, etc., for a time, usu. paying interest on it. **bor•row•er**, *n.* person who borrows (money, etc.). **bor•row•ing**, *n.* (a) act of borrowing money. (b) money borrowed.

bor•zoi [bɔːˈzɔɪ] *n.* breed of long-haired hound.

bos•om ['bʊzəm] *n.* breast; **b. friend** = close friend.

boss [bɒs] 1. *n.* (*pl.* **-es**) *inf.* (a) person who is in charge. (b) round knob. 2. *v. inf.* to command/to give orders; **she bosses him around** = she is always telling him what to do. **boss•i•ness**, *n.* being bossy. **boss•y**, *adj.* (**-ier, -iest**) (person) always giving orders.

bo•sun ['bəʊsn] *n.* (*at sea*) man in charge of the boats and sails.

bot•a•ny ['bɒtənɪ] *n.* study of plants. **bo•tan•i•cal** [bəˈtænɪkl] *adj.* relating to plants; **b. gardens** = gardens scientifically arranged to show different species of plants. **bot•a•nist** ['bɒtənɪst] *n.* person who studies plants.

botch [bɒtʃ] *v.* to ruin/to make a mess of (a job).

both [bəʊθ] 1. *adj. & pron.* two persons/objects together. 2. *adv.* at the same time.

both•er ['bɒðə] 1. *n.* worry/annoyance. 2. *v.* (a) to annoy (s.o.). (b) to take trouble (**to do** sth). **both•ered**, *adj.* worried/embarrassed.

bot•tle ['bɒtl] 1. *n.* tall glass/plastic container for liquids; **hot water b.** = container for hot water which is used for warming a part of the body. 2. *v.* to put/pour (sth) into a bottle.

bot•tle-feed•ing, *n.* feeding of babies by a bottle, not at the breast. **bot•tle•neck**, *n.* (a) narrow part of a bottle. (b) place where traffic or progress is hindered. **bot•tle up**, *v.* (a) to hold back (one's feelings). (b) to hinder, as traffic. **bot•tling**, *n.* putting into bottles.

bot•tom ['bɒtəm] 1. *n.* (a) lowest part; base; **prices have touched rock b.** = they are at their lowest; **he finished at the b. of the class** = he had the worst marks. (b) buttocks. 2. *adj.* lowest. **bot•tom•less**, *adj.* with no bottom. **bot•tom•ry**, *n.* mortgage on a ship.

bot•u•lism ['bɒtjʊlɪzəm] *n.* illness caused by bacteria in food.

bou•clé ['buːkleɪ] *n.* wool with many loops in it.

bou•doir ['buːdwɑː] *n.* small private room for a woman.

bouf•fant ['buːfɒŋ] *adj.* fluffy (hairstyle).

bou•gain•vil•le•a [buːgənˈvɪlɪə] *n.* tropical climbing plant with purple or pink flowers.

bough [baʊ] *n.* large branch.

bought [bɔːt] *v. see* **buy**.

boul•der ['bəʊldə] *n.* large rock.

boul•e•vard ['buːləvɑːd] *n.* wide road.

bounce [baʊns] 1. *n.* (a) springiness; **the bed has a lot of b. in it.** (b) **he's got a lot of b.** = he is full of energy. 2. *v.* (a) to spring up and down; to make (sth) spring up and down; **the ball bounced down the stairs.** (b) *inf.* **his check bounced** = there was not enough money in the account to pay the sum on the check. **bounc•er**, *n.* person who throws undesirable customers out of a restaurant/club, etc. **bounc•ing**, *adj.* (ball) which bounces; **b. baby** = healthy-looking baby. **bounc•y**, *adj.* (a) which bounces well. (b) (person) who is full of energy.

bound [baʊnd] 1. *n.* leap. 2. *adj.* (a) **b. for South America** = leaving for/on the way to South America; **homeward b.** = on the way home. (b) tied up. (c) obliged. (d) very likely; **they are b. to be late.** (e) *see also* **bind**. 3. *v.* to leap. **bound•en**, *adj.* **b. duty** = obligation. **bound•less**, *adj.* without any limits. **bounds**, *n.* limits/edges; **out of b.** = (place) where people are not allowed to go.

bound•a•ry ['baʊndrɪ] *n.* frontier/outer limit of sth.

boun•ty ['baʊntɪ] *n.* (a) giving (as of money); generosity. (b) money given as a reward or in excess of usual wages. **boun•ti•ful**, *adj.* generous.

æ back, ɑː farm, ɒ top, aɪ pipe, aʊ how, aɪə fire, aʊə flower, ɔː bought, ɔɪ toy, e fed, eə hair, eɪ take, ə afraid, əʊ boat, əʊə lower, ɜː word, iː heap, ɪ hit, ɪə hear, uː school, ʊ book, ʌ but, b back, d dog, ð then, dʒ just, f fog, g go, h hand, j yes, k catch, l last, m mix, n nut, ŋ sing, p penny, r round, s some, ʃ short, t too, tʃ chop, θ thing, v voice, w was, z zoo, ʒ treasure

bou•quet [bʊ'keɪ] *n.* artistically arranged bunch of flowers.

bour•bon ['bɜːbən] *n.* corn whisky.

bour•geois ['bʊəʒwɑː] *adj. & n.* middle-class (person). **bour•geoi•sie** [bʊəʒwɑ'ziː] *n.* the middle class.

bout [baʊt] *n.* (a) sports contest. (b) attack (of illness).

bou•tique [buːˈtiːk] *n.* small store selling fashionable clothes/perfume, etc.; small clothing department in a large store.

bo•vine ['bəʊvaɪn] *adj.* referring to cows and bulls; **b. spongiform encephalopathy** = fatal disease of the nervous system in cattle, caused by an abnormal prion protein in the brain.

bow¹ ['bəʊ] *n.* (a) long piece of wood with taut string joining both ends, used for shooting arrows. (b) wooden rod with hair stretched taut between its ends, used for playing a violin or other stringed instrument. (c) ribbon/tie knotted to look like a butterfly. **bow•leg•ged,** *adj.* with legs which curve apart at the knee. **bow tie,** *n.* short necktie tied in a bow. **bow win•dow,** *n.* window projecting out from the wall in a curve.

bow² [baʊ] **1.** *n.* (a) salute made by bending the body forward. (b) (*usu.* **bows**) front part of a ship. (c) rower who sits nearest the bow of a rowing boat. **2.** *v.* to bend forward. **bow•sprit,** *n.* horizontal mast going forward from the bows of a ship.

bowd•ler•ize ['baʊdlǝraɪz] *v.* to cut indecent parts from (a book).

bow•els (*sometimes* **bowel**) ['baʊǝlz] *n.* intestines; **in the b. of the earth** = deep underground.

bow•er ['baʊǝ] *n.* shelter covered by trees or plants.

bowl [bəʊl] **1.** *n.* (a) wide container (of china/plastic, etc.). (b) wooden ball for playing game of bowls. (c) **bowls** = game where wooden balls are rolled to try to get nearest to small target ball. **2.** *v.* (a) to throw a ball, esp. in cricket. (b) to roll a bowl (in a game of bowls). **bowl•er,** *n.* (a) person who plays bowls. (b) (*in cricket*) person who throws the ball to the opposing batsman. (c) **b. (hat)** = black round-topped man's hat. **bowl•ing,** *n.* (a) game of bowls; **b. green** = level grassy area for playing bowls. (b) game of knocking down wooden pins with a large ball; **b. alley** = establishment for bowling. **bowl over,** *v.* to knock down/to surprise.

box [bɒks] **1.** *n.* (*pl.* **-es**) (a) container with a lid; **mailbox** = box in the street for mailing letters. (b) evergreen tree, with very small leaves; hard wood from this tree. (c) small balcony room in a theater; cubicle for a horse; place where a witness gives evidence in court. (d) smack (on the ear). **2.** *v.* (a) **to b. s.o.'s ears** = to smack s.o. on the ears. (b) to fight an opponent in the boxing ring. **box•er,** *n.* (a) man who practices the sport of boxing. (b) breed of large dog with short hair. **box•ing,** *n.* sport of fighting with gloves in a ring; *Brit.* **B. Day** = day after Christmas Day, December 26. **box of•fice,** *n.* office in a theater where you buy tickets.

boy [bɔɪ] *n.* male child; **old b.** = old friend/old man/former pupil of a school. **boy•friend,** *n.* young male friend. **boy•hood,** *n.* youth/time of life when you are a boy. **boy•ish,** *adj.* like a boy. **Boy Scouts,** *n.* social/educational organization for boys.

boy•cott ['bɔɪkɒt] **1.** *n.* act of boycotting. **2.** *v.* to refuse to have anything to do with s.o./sth.

bra [brɑː] *n. inf.* brassiere/woman's undergarment for supporting the breasts.

brace [breɪs] **1.** *n.* (a) support; (*on teeth*) metal clamp to make teeth grow straight. (b) *Brit.* **braces** = elastic straps over the shoulders to hold up trousers. (c) pair; **a b. of grouse** = two grouse. (d) tool for holding a bit to drill holes. **2.** *v.* to support/to strengthen; **he braced himself for the ordeal** = he stiffened his muscles to prepare himself for the ordeal. **brac•ing,** *adj.* invigorating/healthy (climate).

brace•let ['breɪslǝt] *n.* ornamental chain/band worn round the wrist.

brack•en ['brækǝn] *n.* wild fern growing often in open country.

brack•et ['brækɪt] **1.** *n.* (a) support (for shelf, etc., against a wall). (b) printing symbol showing that sth is separated from the rest of the text. (c) (administrative) group; **the middle-income b. 2.** *v.* (a) to put (words) into brackets. (b) to link; **his name was bracketed with that of the mayor.**

brack•ish ['brækɪʃ] *adj.* salty/undrinkable water.

bract [brækt] *n.* part of a plant which is shaped like a leaf but can be colored like a flower.

brad [bræd] *n.* small nail with a flat head.

brad•awl ['brædɔːl] *n.* boring tool for making holes (esp. in leather).

brag [bræg] *v.* (**bragged**) to boast.

Brah•min ['brɑːmɪn] *n.* (a) highest-ranking Hindu; (b) very important person.

braid [breɪd] **1.** *n.* plaited decoration. **2.** *v.* to plait (hair) with ribbon.

braille [breɪl] *n.* system of raised dots on paper for the blind to read by touch.

brain [breɪn] **1.** *n.* nervous center of the head which thinks and directs the body; **use your b.** = think hard; **she's got brains** = she's intelligent; *inf.* **b. drain** = departure of highly intelligent people to other countries in order to work for higher salaries. **2.** *v.* to knock s.o. out by hitting him on the head. **brain•child,** *n.* original idea/plan thought up by s.o. **brain•i•ness,** *n.* intelligence. **brain•less,** *adj.* idiotic/stupid. **brain•pow•er,** *n.* intelligence/ability to think or reason. **brain•storm,** *n.* sudden mad idea. **brain•wash,** *v.* to indoctrinate (s.o.)/to make s.o. think in a totally different manner from before. **brain wave,** *n.* brilliant idea. **brain•y,** *adj.* (-ier, -iest) *inf.* intelligent.

braise [breɪz] *v.* to cook (meat/vegetables) in a covered pot with very little liquid.

brake [breɪk] 1. *n.* mechanism for stopping a car/bicycle, etc.; **hand b.** = brake operated by a hand lever. 2. *v.* to stop/to slow down by applying the brakes. **brak•ing,** *n.* putting on the brakes; **b. distance** = distance a car travels after the brakes are applied before it comes to a halt.

bram•ble ['bræmbl] *n.* wild blackberry.

bran [bræn] *n.* skins of wheat seeds which are separated from the flour.

branch [brɑːntʃ] 1. *n.* (*pl.* -es) (a) limb of a tree. (b) offshoot; **b. of a river; b. line** = minor railroad line. (c) office (of a bank, etc.); store (of a chain of stores). 2. *v.* **to b. out** = to spread out/to diversify.

brand [brænd] 1. *n.* (a) identification mark made (on cattle) by a hot iron. (b) named product made by one manufacturer. 2. *v.* (a) to mark (cattle) with a hot iron. (b) **he was branded as a thief** = he was called a thief. **brand•ed,** *adj.* (a) marked (cattle, etc.). (b) (goods) with a brand name. **brand name,** *n.* name applied to one product. **brand-new,** *adj.* completely new.

brand•ish ['brændɪʃ] *v.* to wave (sth) about.

bran•dy ['brændɪ] *n.* strong alcohol distilled from wine; glass of this alcohol.

brash [bræʃ] *adj.* vulgar, pushy.

brass [brɑːs] *n.* (a) yellow metal made from copper and zinc; **top b.** = directors/high-ranking officers; **to get down to b. tacks** = to discuss the basic problem. (b) musical instruments made of brass; **a b. band.** (c) *inf.* money. (d) something, as ornamental hardware, made of brass. **brass-rub•bing,** *n.* reproduction of a brass plate by covering it with paper and rubbing with wax. **brass•y,** *adj.* (a) (noise) like that of brass instruments. (b) rude, loud-mouthed (person).

bras•si•cas ['bræsɪkəz] *n. pl.* plants of the cabbage family.

bras•siere ['bræzɪə] *n.* woman's undergarment for supporting the breasts.

brat [bræt] *n.* rude child.

bra•va•do [brə'vɑːdəʊ] *n.* reckless bravery.

brave [breɪv] 1. *adj.* (-er, -est) not afraid; courageous. 2. *v.* to defy. 3. *n.* male American Indian warrior. **brave•ly,** *adv.* with courage. **brav•er•y,** *n.* courage.

bra•vo [brɑː'vəʊ] *inter. showing approval.*

brawl [brɔːl] 1. *n.* wild fight. 2. *v.* to fight wildly. **brawl•er,** *n.* person who is fighting wildly.

brawn [brɔːn] *n.* (a) muscle power. (b) flesh of a boar, esp. boiled and pickled. **brawn•y,** *adj,* muscular/strong.

bray [breɪ] *v.* to make a loud call like a donkey.

bra•zen ['breɪzn] 1. *adj.* (a) like brass/made of brass. (b) shameless. 2. *v.* **he brazened it out** = he impudently got through the awkward situation.

bra•zier ['breɪzɪə] *n.* metal basket for burning coal.

Bra•zil•i•an [brə'zɪlɪən] 1. *adj.* referring to Brazil. 2. *n.* person from Brazil.

breach [briːtʃ] 1. *n.* (*pl.* -es) (a) crack (in a defense/dam). (b) breaking (of a law/promise); **b. of the peace** = disorderly behavior; **b. of faith** = going back on what has been promised; **b. of promise** = refusing to marry s.o. after having promised to do so. 2. *v.* to split; to make a crack in (a wall).

bread [bred] *n.* (*no pl.*) food made from flour, water and yeast baked in an oven; **wholemeal b.** = bread made from flour which contains the whole grain; **bread-and-butter letter** = letter written to say thank you for hospitality; **b. box** = metal/plastic container for keeping bread fresh. **bread•crumbs,** *n. pl.* bread broken up into very small pieces. **bread•win•ner,** *n.* person who earns money to feed the family.

breadth [bredθ] *n.* (a) measurement of how broad or wide sth is. (b) wideness (of views).

break [breɪk] 1. *n.* (a) split/crack (where two parts have broken). (b) quarrel. (c) **b. in the weather** = change in the weather. (d) rest period; **coffee b.** = period where you stop work for a cup of coffee; **morning b.** = short period of play during the morning at school. (e) **he had a lucky b.** = his bad luck changed. (f) **at b. of day** = at dawn. (g) series of shots in billiards or pool. 2. *v.* (**broke; has broken**) (a) to fall to pieces/to smash (sth) into pieces; **my watch is broken** = my watch has stopped working; **it**

æ back, a: farm, ɒ: top, aɪ pipe, aʊ how, aɪe fire, aʊə flower, ɔ: bought, ɔɪ toy, e fed, eəhair, eɪ take, ə afraid, əʊ boat, əʊə lower, v: word, i: heap, ɪ hit, ɪə hear, u: school, ʊ book, ʌ but, b back, d dog, ð then, dʒ just, f fog, g go, h hand, j yes, k catch, l last, m mix, n nut, ŋ sing, p penny, r round, s some, ʃ short, t too, tʃ chop, θ thing, v voice, w was, z zoo, ʒ treasure

broke her heart = she was extremely upset; **he broke the record for the high jump** = did better than anyone had ever done before. (b) **we are breaking even** = we are not making a loss or a profit. (c) not to keep (a promise/a rule). (d) **the storm broke** = storm suddenly started; **the day was breaking** = daylight was coming. (e) (*of boy's voice*) to become deeper as the boy grows older. (f) to cushion (a fall). (g) (*of wave*) to grow tall and crash down. **break•a•ble**, *adj.* which can easily be broken. **break•a•bles**, *n. pl.* fragile objects (glasses/cups, etc.). **break•a•ges**, *n. pl.* breaking (of glass, etc.); things which have been broken. **break away**, *v.* to escape/to be detached (**from**). **break•a•way**, *adj.* which has become detached; **the b. nationalist party** = the nationalist party which has split off from a larger party. **break down**, *v.* (a) to smash (sth). (b) to collapse; to go wrong. (c) to list (items). **break•down**, *n.* (a) collapse; **nervous b.** = state where you become severely depressed. (b) list under various headings. (c) **we had a b. on the highway** = our car stopped working; **b. lane** = lane for cars which do not work. **break•er**, *n.* big wave which is breaking. **break•fast** ['brekfəst] 1. *n.* first meal of the day; food eaten at this meal; **continental b.** = breakfast of bread and coffee; 2. *v.* to eat the first meal of the day; **break in**, *v.* (a) to enter forcibly. (b) to interrupt. (c) to train (a horse). **break-in**, *n.* burglary. **break•ing**, *n.* (a) action of smashing/falling to pieces. (b) **b. and entering** = crime of breaking into s.o.'s property. **break in•to**, *v.* to enter forcibly. **break loose**, *v.* to escape. **break•neck**, *adj.* **at b. speed** = extremely fast. **break off**, *v.* (a) to split away/to crack; to remove (sth) by breaking. (b) to stop; **they have broken off negotiations. break o•pen**, *v.* to smash (in order to open). **break out**, *v.* (a) to start; **war has broken out.** (b) to escape; **three prisoners broke out from prison. break•out**, *n.* escape. **break through**, *v.* to smash in order to go through. **break•through**, *n.* sudden success or new development. **break up**, *v.* (a) to smash to pieces. **break it up!** = stop fighting; **they had a quarrel and broke up** = did not work/live together any more. (b) to come to an end; **the meeting broke up at noon. break•up**, *n.* coming to pieces/an end. **break•wa•ter**, *n.* wall/fence going into the sea to prevent waves from battering the coast.

bream [bri:m] *n.* (*pl.* **bream**) type of fat edible fish.

breast [brest] *n.* (a) one of two milk-giving organs in a woman's body; **b. feeding** = feeding a child with milk from the breast. (b) chest/front part of the top of the body; **b. pocket** = pocket on the front of a jacket; **b. stroke** = swimming stroke where both arms stretch out together and are brought back to the chest.

breath [breθ] *n.* air which goes into and out of the body; **out of b./gasping for b.** = having difficulty in breathing; **don't waste your b. on them** = don't waste time talking to them; **it took my b. away** = I was completely astonished; **he muttered under his b.** = quietly; **a b. of wind** = a slight breeze. **breath•a•lyz•er**, *n.* instrument for testing if a driver has drunk too much alcohol. **breath•less**, *adj.* out of breath/panting. **breath•less•ly**, *adv.* in a rush/without taking time to breathe. **breath•tak•ing**, *adj.* so exciting/beautiful that it takes your breath away.

breathe [bri:ð] *v.* to suck air in or out through the nose or mouth; **b. deeply** = take in lots of air; **don't b. a word about it!** = don't say anything about it. **breath•er**, *n.* rest period; **I'm going out for a b.** = I'm going out to get some fresh air. **breath•ing**, *n.* act of taking air in and out of the body; **b. apparatus** = mask, etc., which allows you to breathe when in gas/smoke, etc.; **b. space** = rest period.

bred [bred] *v. see* **breed.**

breech [bri:tʃ] *n.* (*pl.* **-es**) (a) back part of a gun where the ammunition is loaded. (b) **b. birth, breech delivery** = birth in which the baby's feet or buttocks appear first. (c) **breeches** = trousers which come down to below the knees; **breeches buoy** = device, like a canvas seat, used to rescue people at sea.

breed [bri:d] 1. *n.* particular race of animal. 2. *v.* (**bred**) to produce young animals/plants; **I was born and bred in the country** = I was born and grew up in the country; **well-bred person** = s.o. who is polite/who has been well educated. **breed•er**, *n.* (a) person who breeds (animals). (b) (**fast**) **b. reactor** = nuclear machine which makes a surplus of nuclear material. **breed•ing**, *n.* (a) production of animals. (b) training in good manners.

breeze [bri:z] 1. *n.* slight wind; **a stiff breeze** = quite a strong wind. 2. *v.* **he breezed into the restaurant** = he rushed in looking very pleased with himself. **breez•i•ly**, *adv.* in a happy-go-lucky way. **breez•y**, *adj.* (a) windy. (b) happy-go-lucky.

breth•ren ['breðren] *n. pl.* (*religious*) brothers.

breve [bri:v] *n.* long note in music.

bre•vi•ar•y ['bri:vjərɪ] *n.* book of Roman Catholic prayers.

brev•i•ty ['brevɪtɪ] *n.* conciseness/shortness.

brew [bru:] 1. *n.* liquid which has been brewed. 2. *v.* (a) to make (beer/coffee/tea). (b) **there's trouble brewing** = there is trouble coming. **brew•er**, *n.* person who makes beer; **brewer's yeast** = yeast used in brewing beer, and taken

in tablet form as a source of vitamin B.
brew•er•y, *n.* place where beer is made.
bri•ar ['braɪə] *n. see* **bri•er.**
bribe [braɪb] 1. *n.* money given illegally to s.o.
to get sth done. 2. *v.* to give (s.o.) money illegally to get sth done. **brib•er•y**, *n.* act of
bribing.
bric-à-brac ['brɪkəbræk] *n.* (*no pl.*) ornaments
or furniture of little value.
brick [brɪk] *n.* block of baked clay, used for
building; **he dropped a b.** = he made an unfortunate remark by mistake. **brick•lay•er**, *n.*
person who builds with bricks. **brick up**, *v.* to
fill in (window/doorway) with bricks.
brick•work, *n.* bricks built up into a wall.
brick•yard, *n.* place where bricks are made,
sold, or kept.
bride [braɪd] *n.* woman who is about to get
married or who has just got married. **brid•al**,
adj. referring to a wedding. **bride•groom**, *n.*
man who is about to get married or who has
just got married. **brides•maid**, *n.* woman
who is the bride's attendant at a wedding.
bridge [brɪdʒ] 1. *n.* (a) construction to take a
road/railroad across a river/road/railroad
line. (b) top part of a ship where a captain
stands. (c) top of the nose. (d) (*in a violin*) support for the strings. (e) type of card game for
four people. 2. *v.* to put a bridge across (a
river, etc.). **bridge•head**, *n.* preliminary position held by attackers who have attacked
across water. **bridge loan**, *n.* short-term
loan, esp. one to help s.o. buy a house before
he has sold his old one.
bri•dle ['braɪdl] 1. *n.* headstraps (for a horse).
2. *v.* (a) to hold back (a horse). (b) to take
offense. **bri•dle path**, *n.* path for
horseriders.
brief [briːf] 1. *adj.* short. 2. *n.* (a) papers concerning a legal case. (b) instructions. (c) **briefs**
= underpants. 3. *v.* to give a case to (a lawyer);
to give (s.o.) information/instructions.
brief•case, *n.* small case for carrying papers.
brief•ing, *n.* conference where information
is given. **brief•ly**, *adv.* shortly/speaking for a
short time.
bri•er [braɪə] *n.* prickly wild bush, esp. a rose.
bri•gade [brɪ'geɪd] *n.* (a) army group, smaller
than a division. (b) **fire b.** = group of people
whose job is to fight fires. **brig•a•dier**
[brɪgə'dɪə] *n.* army officer in charge of a brigade; rank in the army above colonel.
brig•and ['brɪgənd] *n.* robber.

bright [braɪt] *adj.* (-er, -est) (a) shining very
strongly/having a very vivid color; **to look on
the b. side of things** = to be optimistic. (b) intelligent. **bright•en**, *v.* (a) to make bright. (b)
she brightened up when she saw him = she became more cheerful; **the weather is brightening
up** = it is getting nicer. **bright•ly**, *adv.* (a)
with a strong light. (b) in an intelligent/cheerful tone of voice. **bright•ness**, *n.* strength (of
light); intelligence (of person).
brill [brɪl] *n.* (*pl.* **brill**) type of flat white edible
sea fish.
bril•liant ['brɪljənt] 1. *adj.* (a) very shiny. (b)
very clever. 2. *n.* gem, esp. a diamond.
bril•liance, *n.* brightness; intelligence.
brim [brɪm] 1. *n.* edge. 2. *v.* (**brimmed**) **the glass
was brimming over with wine** = the glass was
overflowing. **brim•ful**, *adj.* very full/full to
overflowing.
brin•dled ['brɪndld] *adj.* (*of animals*) brown
with streaks of another color.
brine [braɪn] *n.* salt water.
bring [brɪŋ] *v.* (**brought** [brɔːt]; **has brought**) to
take (sth/s.o.) to this place. **bring about**, *v.*
to cause/to make (sth) happen. **bring along**,
v. to bring with you. **bring back**, *v.* to return
(here); **that picture brings it all back to me** =
makes me remember it all. **bring down**, *v.* to
make (sth/s.o.) fall down; to lower (sth).
bring forward, *v.* **to bring forward the date
of the meeting** = to arrange an earlier date for
it. **bring in**, *v.* to make (sth/s.o.) come in.
bring off, *v.* to succeed in; **he brought it off** =
he did it successfully. **bring on**, *v.* to produce/to make grow; **you've brought it on yourself** = it's your own fault. **bring out**, *v.* to
make (sth/s.o.) come out; **to b. out a new book**
= to publish a new book; **to b. out the color** =
to make the color more noticeable/more effective. **bring a•round** or **round**, *v.* (a) to take
(sth) to s.o.'s house. (b) to revive (s.o.) who is
unconscious. **bring up**, *v.* (a) to raise (a subject). (b) to vomit. (c) to educate in manners.
brink [brɪŋk] *n.* edge (of cliff); **on the b. of a nervous breakdown** = very close to having a nervous breakdown.
brin•y ['braɪnɪ] *adj.* salty; *inf.* **the b.** = the sea.
brisk [brɪsk] *adj.* (-er, -est) rapid. **brisk•ly**, *adv.*
rapidly.
bris•ket ['brɪskɪt] *n.* beef from the breast of an
animal.
bris•ling ['brɪzlɪŋ] *n.* small sea fish, like a sardine.

æ **back**, a: **farm**, ɒ: **top**, aɪ **pipe**, aʊ **how**, aɪə **fire**, aʊə **flower**, ɔ: **bought**, ɔɪ **toy**, e **fed**, eə **hair**, eɪ **take**, ə
afraid, əʊ **boat**, əʊə **lower**, vː **word**, iː **heap**, ɪ **hit**, ɪə **hear**, uː **school**, ʊ **book**, ʌ **but**, b **back**, d **dog**, ð **then**,
dʒ **just**, f **fog**, g **go**, h **hand**, j **yes**, k **catch**, l **last**, m **mix**, n **nut**, ŋ **sing**, p **penny**, r **round**, s **some**, ʃ **short**, t
too, tʃ **chop**, θ **thing**, v **voice**, w **was**, z **zoo**, ʒ **treasure**

bris•tle ['brɪsl] 1. *n.* short stiff hair (on ani-mal/brush). 2. *v.* (a) to take offense. (b) **to b. with** = to be full of/covered with; **to bristle with excitement. brist•ly,** *adj.* covered with short stiff hair.

Brit•ish ['brɪtɪʃ] *adj. & n.* referring to Great Britain; **the B.** = the people of Great Britain. **the B. Isles** = group of islands off the north coast of Europe, including England, Wales, Scotland, Ireland, and many smaller islands. **Brit,** *n. Sl.* a Briton. **Brit•on** ['brɪtn] *n.* per-son from Great Britain.

brit•tle ['brɪtl] *adj.* which breaks easily. **brit•tle•ness,** *n.* fragility.

broach [brəʊtʃ] *v.* (a) to open (a cask of wine, etc.). (b) to start talking about (a problem).

broad [brɔːd] *adj.* (**-er, -est**) very wide; **in b. day-light** = in full daylight; **a b. Scottish accent** = a strong accent; **b. beans** = type of beans with large flat seeds. **broad•cast.** 1. *n.* radio/tele-vision program; 2. *v.* (**broadcast**) (a) to sow (by throwing seed by hand). (b) to send out by radio/television; **they b. an appeal to the peo-ple.** (c) to tell everyone (the news); **don't b. the fact** = keep it a secret. 3. *adv.* (sowing) by throwing the seed by hand. 4. *adj.* sent by radio/television. **broad•cast•er,** *n.* person who speaks on the radio/television. **broad•en,** *v.* to make wider; **travel broadens the mind** = travel makes your knowledge/in-terest more extensive. **broad•loom,** *adj.* (carpet) woven in a very wide strip. **broad•ly,** *adv.* **b. speaking** = in a general way. **broad•mind•ed,** *adj.* tolerant; not easily taking offense. **broad-shoul•der•ed,** *adj.* with wide shoulders. **broad•side,** *n.* (a) firing of all the guns on one side of a ship. (b) sharp written or spoken criticism.

bro•cade [brə'keɪd] *n.* thick cloth with a raised pattern.

broc•co•li ['brɒkəlɪ] *n.* (*pl.* **broccoli**) cabbagelike vegetable of which the flowerheads are eaten.

bro•chure ['brəʊʃə] *n.* small book; small pub-licity pamphlet.

brogue [brəʊg] *n.* (a) heavy shoe with pat-terned leather top. (b) accent (usu. Irish).

broil [brɔɪl] *v.* to grill. **broil•er,** *n.* chicken spe-cially bred for roasting.

broke [brəʊk] *adj. inf.* **to be flat b.** = to have no money; *see also* **break.**

bro•ken ['brəʊkən] *adj.* (a) in pieces; **a b. home** = home where the parents have separated. (b) spoken with a foreign accent and with many mistakes. (c) *see also* **break. bro•ken-down,** *adj.* not working. **bro•ken-heart•ed,** *adj.* very upset/sad.

bro•ker ['brəʊkə] *n.* person who deals in stocks/insurance. **bro•ker•age,** *n.* fee charged by a broker for his work.

bro•mide ['brəʊmaɪd] *n.* (a) chemical used to make a calming medicine. (b) photographic paper.

bron•chi•al ['brɒŋkɪəl] *adj.* referring to the re-spiratory tubes; **b. asthma** = asthma in the lungs. **bron•chi,** *n. pl.* air passages leading into the lungs. **bron•chi•tis** [brɒŋ'kaɪtɪs] *n.* disease of the respiratory tubes.

bronze [brɒnz] *n.* metal made from copper and tin; **B. Age** = prehistoric period when weapons of bronze were used. **bronzed,** *adj.* tanned/sunburned.

brooch [brəʊtʃ] *n.* ornament to pin on to cloth-ing.

brood [bruːd] 1. *n.* group of chicks/small chil-dren. 2. *v.* to have gloomy thoughts; **she's brooding sth.** = she is thinking about some-thing. **brood•y,** *adj.* (a) (hen) preparing to sit on a clutch of eggs. (b) (person) who has gloomy thoughts.

brook [brʊk] 1. *n.* small stream. 2. *v.* to allow/to accept.

broom [bruːm] *n.* (a) shrub with yellow flow-ers. (b) brush with long handle for sweeping the floor. **broom•stick,** *n.* long handle of a broom.

bros. [brɒs] *abbreviation for* brothers.

broth [brɒθ] *n.* light soup; **Scotch b.** = thick soup with barley, vegetables and lamb.

broth•el ['brɒθl] *n.* house of prostitutes.

broth•er ['brʌðə] *n.* (a) male child of the same parents as another child. (b) man belonging to a monastic order. **broth•er•hood,** *n.* frater-nity; companionship (between men). **broth•er-in-law,** *n.* (*pl.* **brothers-in-law**) brother of your husband or wife; husband of your sister; husband of the sister of your husband or wife. **broth•er•ly,** *adj.* as of brothers.

brought [brɔːt] *v. see* bring.

brow [braʊ] *n.* (a) forehead/top part of the face above the eyes. (b) line of hair above each eye. (c) rounded top of a hill. **brow•beat,** *v.* (**browbeat; has browbeaten**) to intimidate (s.o.).

brown [braʊn] 1. *adj.* (**-er, -est**) colored like the color of wood or soil. 2. *n.* color of wood or soil. 3. *v.* to become brown; to make brown. **brown•field** *adj. & n.* (urban site) that has previously been built on. **Brown•ie,** *n.* (a) girl in the junior section of the Girl Scouts. (b) chocolate cookie. **brown•ish,** *adj.* rather brown.

browse [braʊz] *v.* (a) (*of animal*) to wander about eating grass. (b) (*of person*) to wander round a store. looking at goods for sale.

brows•er, *n.* person who is browsing in a store.

bru•cel•lo•sis [brəsel'əʊsɪs] *n.* disease caught from drinking infected milk.

bruise [bruːz] 1. *n.* mark made on the skin by a blow. 2. *v.* to get/to make marks on the skin from a blow. **bruis•er**, *n.* bully; fighter.

brunch [brʌntʃ] *n.* large meal (as a combination of breakfast and lunch) taken in the middle of the morning.

bru•nette [bruː'net] *adj. & n.* (woman) with brown hair.

brunt [brʌnt] *n.* **to bear the b. of** = to suffer most from.

brush [brʌʃ] 1. *n.* (*pl.* **-es**) (a) instrument with a handle and hair/wire/nylon bristles for painting or cleaning. (b) scrub land. (c) cleaning with a brush. (d) short argument/fight with an opponent. (e) piece of carbon which makes an electric contact. (f) tail (of a fox). 2. *v.* (a) to clean with a brush. (b) to go past sth touching it gently. **brush aside,** *v.* to reject. **brush away,** *v.* to clear away with a brush. **brush down,** *v.* to brush (sth) vigorously. **brush off,** *v.* to clean (sth) off with a brush. **brush-off,** *n. inf.* **to give s.o. the b.-off** = to send s.o. away without listening or agreeing to what they want. **brush up,** *v.* (a) to make (yourself) smart. (b) to improve (your knowledge of). **brush•wood,** *n.* low undergrowth.

brusque [bruːsk] *adj.* abrupt/impolite. **brusque•ly,** *adv.* rudely.

Brus•sels sprouts ['brʌslz'sprauts] *n. pl.* vegetable like tiny cabbages.

brute [bruːt] *n.* (a) animal. (b) rude/violent person; **to use b. force** = to use rough methods. **bru•tal,** *adj.* violent. **brut•al•i•ty** [bruː-'tælɪtɪ] *n.* violent action. **bru•tal•ize,** *v.* to beat (s.o.). **bru•tal•ly,** *adv.* in a brutal way. **brut•ish,** *adj.* rude/violent.

bry•o•ny ['braɪənɪ] *n.* type of climbing plant with poisonous berries.

BS [biːes'siː] Bachelor of Science.

BSE [biːes'iː] *abbrev. for* bovine spongiform encephalopathy.

bub•ble ['bʌbl] 1. *n.* small amount of air trapped in liquid. 2. *v.* to make bubbles. **bub•bly.** 1. *adj.* with bubbles. 2. *n. inf.* champagne.

bu•bon•ic plague [bjuː'bɒnɪk 'pleɪg] *n.* fatal disease, transmitted by rats.

buck [bʌk] 1. *n.* (a) male deer/rabbit. (b) *inf.* dollar. (c) *inf.* **to pass the b.** = to hand responsibility on to s.o. else. 2. *v.* (*of horse*) to jump in the air (with rounded back). **buck•teeth,** *n. pl.* teeth which stick out in front. **buck up,** *v. inf.* to make (s.o.) feel more lively.

buck•et ['bʌkɪt] *n.* round container with an open top and a handle. **buck•et•ful,** *n.* quantity contained in a bucket. **buck•et seat,** *n.* rounded seat (in a car).

buck•le ['bʌkl] 1. *n.* metal fastener for attaching a belt/strap/shoe. 2. *v.* (a) to attach (sth) with a metal clasp. (b) to bend/to collapse.

buck•ram ['bʌkrəm] *n.* thick cloth for covering books.

buck•wheat ['bʌkwiːt] *n.* dark grain, giving a brown flour.

bu•col•ic [bjuː'kɒlɪk] *adj.* referring to the countryside.

bud [bʌd] 1. *n.* (a) point on a plant where a new shoot is appearing; flower not yet opened; **the roses are in b.** = the flowers are ready to open. (b) buddy. 2. *v.* (**budded**) (a) to make buds. (b) to graft a bud. **bud•ding,** *adj.* (flower) not yet open; **b. concert pianist** = person who hopes to be a concert pianist.

Bud•dhism ['bʊdɪzəm] *n.* religion following the teaching of Buddha. **Bud•dhist,** *adj. & n.* (person) who follows the teaching of Buddha.

bud•dle•ia ['bʌdlɪə] *n.* garden shrub with long purple flowers.

bud•dy ['bʌdɪ] *n. inf.* friend.

budge [bʌdʒ] *v.* to move.

budg•er•i•gar ['bʌdʒərɪgaː] *n.* blue or green tropical bird like a small parrot.

budg•et ['bʌdʒɪt] 1. *n.* list of proposed expenditure. 2. *v.* **to b. for** = to plan how to spend money on sth.

budg•ie ['bʌdʒɪ] *n. inf.* budgerigar.

buff [bʌf] 1. (a) *adj. & n.* (of a) pale yellowy-brown color. (b) *n. inf.* enthusiast. 2. *v.* to polish/to shine.

buf•fa•lo ['bʌfələʊ] *n.* (*pl.* **-oes/-o**) large wild ox or cow (in America and parts of Africa and Asia).

buff•er ['bʌfə] *n.* shock-absorbing pad; **b. state** = small country between two larger states, which may be antagonistic to each other; **b. zone** = area between two areas of fighting.

buf•fet[1] ['bʊfeɪ] *n.* (a) counter or snack bar (in railroad station, etc.) where light meals or refreshments are sold; **b. car** = railroad car containing a buffet. (b) self-service meal. (c) sideboard.

buf•fet[2] ['bʌfɪt] *v.* to bang/to jolt.

æ back, aː farm, ɒ top, aɪ pipe, aʊ how, aɪe fire, aʊə flower, ɔː bought, ɔɪ toy, e fed, eəhair, eɪ take, ə afraid, əʊ boat, aʊə lower, vː word, iː heap, ɪ hit, ɪə hear, uː school, ʊ book, ʌ but, b back, d dog, ð then, dʒ just, f fog, g go, h hand, j yes, k catch, l last, m mix, n nut, ŋ sing, p penny, r round, s some, ʃ short, t too, tʃ chop, θ thing, v voice, w was, z zoo, ʒ treasure

buf•foon [bə'fuːn] *n.* fool/clown.
buf•foon•er•y, *n.* foolish action.

bug [bʌg] 1. *n.* (a) small insect which sucks. (b) any small insect. (c) *inf.* germ. (d) hidden microphone. (e) defect in a computer program. 2. *v.* (**bugged**) (a) to install a hidden microphone in (a room). (b) *inf.* **what's bugging you?** = what's bothering you? **bug•bear,** *n.* thing which you hate.

bu•gle ['bjuːgl] *n.* military trumpet. **bu•gler,** *n.* person who blows a bugle.

build [bɪld] 1. *n.* size/shape (of person). 2. *v.* (**built** [bɪlt]; **has built**) to construct; to make by putting pieces together. **build•er,** *n.* person who constructs houses, etc. **build•ing,** *n.* (a) constructing; **b. land** = land for construction of houses. (b) construction; house/office block. **build up,** *v.* to construct/to create/to increase. **built-in,** *adj.* (cupboards, etc.) which are constructed as part of a building. **built-up,** *adj.* **built-up area** = area of a town where there are many buildings.

bulb [bʌlb] *n.* (a) fleshy underground stem of a plant, which produces leaves and flowers in spring. (b) glass globe full of gas which produces light when an electric current passes through it. **bul•bous,** *adj.* fat and rounded.

bulge [bʌldʒ] 1. *n.* swelling. 2. *v.* to swell out (**with**).

bu•lim•i•a [bʊ'limiə] *n.* disease where you have a craving to eat and force yourself to vomit.

bulk [bʌlk] 1. *n.* large quantity; size; **in b.** = in large quantities; **b. purchase** = purchase in large quantities; **the b. of our sales** = most of our sales. 2. *v.* **to b. large** = to be important; to take up a lot of room. **bulk•head,** *n.* dividing wall in a ship or aircraft. **bulk•i•ness,** *n.* being bulky. **bulk•y,** *adj.* (**-ier, -iest**) very large/taking up an inconvenient amount of room.

bull [bʊl] *n.* (a) male ox. (b) male of certain species. (c) person who believes the stock market prices will rise. (d) official pronouncement by the pope. (e) *Sl.* foolish or exaggerated talk; nonsense. **bull•dog,** *n.* breed of squat, flatfaced dogs. **bull•doze,** *v.* (a) to knock down/to clear using a bulldozer. (b) to force; **he bulldozed his proposal through the committee** = forced them to agree to it. **bull•doz•er,** *n.* large tractor with a shovel in front for moving earth. **bull•fight,** *n.* entertainment in Spain, where a man fights a bull. **bull•fight•er,** *n.* man who fights bulls. **bull•finch,** *n.* small finch with red breast. **bull•frog,** *n.* large frog. **bul•lock,** *n.* castrated bull. **bull•ring,** *n.* arena where bullfights take place. **bull's-eye,** *n.* center point of a target.

bul•let ['bʊlɪt] *n.* piece of metal fired from a revolver or small gun. **bul•let•proof,** *adj.* (jacket/window) specially made so that bullets cannot pierce it.

bul•le•tin ['bʊlɪtɪn] *n.* piece of information; report on a situation.

bul•lion ['bʊljən] *n.* gold or silver bars.

bul•ly ['bʊlɪ] 1. *n.* person who frightens people who are weaker than he is; = thugs. 2. *v.* to intimidate (s.o.). **bul•ly beef,** *n. inf.* corned beef.

bul•rush ['bʊlrʌʃ] *n.* (*pl.* **-es**) tall reed with a brown furry head.

bul•wark ['bʊlwək] *n.* side of a ship which rises higher than the deck.

bum [bʌm] 1. *n.* tramp; person who loafs about doing nothing. 2. *v.* (**bummed**) *inf.* **to b. off s.o.** = to live at s.o.'s expense.

bum•ble ['bʌmbl] *v.* to move/do things in a clumsy way. **bum•ble•bee,** *n.* large furry bee.

bump [bʌmp] 1. *n.* (a) slight shock from hitting sth lightly. (b) small bulge on the body (from being hit). 2. *v.* to hit sth (lightly); **I bumped into him at the station** = I met him by chance. **bump off,** *v. inf.* to murder. **bump•y,** *adj.* (**-ier, -iest**) uneven (path/flight).

bump•er ['bʌmpə] *n.* (a) something very large; **a b. crop.** (b) metal or rubber strip at front and rear of a car to protect it when it is hit.

bump•tious ['bʌmpʃəs] *adj.* (person) full of his own importance.

bun [bʌn] *n.* (a) small cake; (b) hair wound round in a knot at the back of the head.

bunch [bʌntʃ] 1. *n.* (*pl.* **-es**) (a) cluster (of things) tied together; (b) group of people. 2. *v.* to gather together in a group.

bun•dle ['bʌndl] 1. *n.* parcel (of papers, etc.); group of nerves. 2. *v.* to tie (several things) together.

bung [bʌŋ] 1. *n.* stopper; thing which stops up a hole (in a cask). 2. *v.* to block/to stop up a hole.

bun•ga•low ['bʌŋgələʊ] *n.* house with only a ground floor.

bun•gle ['bʌŋgl] *v.* to do (sth) badly. **bun•gler,** *n.* person who has done a job badly.

bun•ion ['bʌnjən] *n.* painful swelling at the base of the big toe.

bunk [bʌŋk] *n.* (a) bed attached to a wall; **b. beds** = two beds, one on top of the other. (b) *inf.* nonsense.

bun•ker ['bʌŋkə] *n.* (a) storage area or bin for coal, as on a ship. (b) sandy pit on a golf course. (c) fortified gun emplacement.

bun•ny ['bʌnɪ] *n.* pet name for a rabbit.

bunt•ing ['bʌntɪŋ] *n.* (a) type of small singing bird. (b) (*no pl.*) strings of small flags.

bu•oy [bɔɪ] 1. *n.* floating marker showing a channel (in a river/at the entrance to a harbor). 2. *v.* **to b. s.o. up** = to cheer s.o. up.

buoy•an•cy, *n.* ability to float; **buoy•ant,** *adj.* (a) which can float easily. (b) full of vigor.

bur•ble ['bɜːbl] 1. *n.* low murmur. 2. *v.* to murmur softly.

bur•den ['bɜːdn] 1. *n.* (a) heavy load; sth which is hard to do/to bear; **beast of b.** = animal (like a donkey) used to carry loads; **to make s.o.'s life a b.** = to make things difficult for s.o. (b) theme music of a song. 2. *v.* to load.

bu•reau ['bjuərəu] *n.* (*pl.* **bureaus, bureaux** ['bjuərəuz]) (a) office; **information b.** = office which collects and hands out information. (b) (*old*) desk; (c) chest of drawers.

bu•reauc•ra•cy [bjuə'rɒkrəsɪ] *n.* rule by civil servants. **bu•reau•crat** ['bjuərəkræt] *n.* civil servant. **bu•reau•crat•ic** [bjuərə'krætɪk] *adj.* referring to the civil service.

bur•geon ['bɜːdʒn] *v.* to begin to grow.

burgh ['bʌrə] *n.* (*Scotland*) chartered town.

bur•glar ['bɜːglə] *n.* person who enters a house to steal; **b. alarm** = electric alarm which rings if a burglar attempts to enter the house. **bur•gla•ry,** *n.* robbery committed by a burglar. **bur•gle,** *v.* to steal from (a house).

bur•gun•dy ['bɜːgəndɪ] *n.* type of French red wine.

bur•i•al ['berɪəl] *n.* act of burying (a dead body); **b. ground** = cemetery.

bur•lap ['bɜːlæp] *n.* thick canvas.

bur•lesque [bɜː'lesk] 1. *adj. & n.* light satirical (play). 2. *v.* to satirize.

bur•ly ['bɜːlɪ] *adj.* (-**ier, -iest**) strong/solid (man).

Bur•mese [bɜː'miːz] 1. *adj.* coming from Burma. 2. *n.* (a) person from Burma. (b) language spoken in Burma.

burn [bɜːn] 1. *n.* (a) place (on the body) which has been burned. (b) (*in Scotland*) stream. 2. *v.* (**burned/burnt; has burned/burnt**) (a) to destroy by fire; **he got his fingers burned** = he suffered a loss/he did not do at all as well as he expected; **he's burned his bridges** = he can't go back now. (b) to use as a fuel. **burn down,** *v.* to destroy by fire. **burn•er,** *n.* apparatus for burning. **burn out,** *v.* **the fire has burned itself out** = the fire has gone out because there was nothing left to burn. **burned,** *adj.* which has gone black with fire.

bur•nish ['bɜːnɪʃ] *v.* to make (sth) shine by rubbing.

burp [bɜːp] 1. *n.* noise made when bringing up gas from the stomach through the mouth. 2. *v.* to make a burp.

burr [bɜː] *n.* (a) prickly part of a plant, containing seeds, which clings to clothes, etc. (b) country accent with a strongly pronounced "r." (c) rough edge to a piece of cut metal.

bur•row ['bʌrəu] 1. *n.* hole in the ground where rabbits live. 2. *v.* to make a long hole underground.

bur•sar ['bɜːsə] *n.* person in charge of the finances of a school/college/university. **bur•sa•ry,** *n.* scholarship/money given to a student to help him pay for his studies.

burst [bɜːst] 1. *n.* (a) sudden explosion; **b. of gunfire; b. of laughter.** (b) sudden attack; **b. of speed.** 2. *v.* (**burst; has burst**) to explode/to break open; **she b. into the room** = she rushed into the room; **the boy b. into tears** = he started to cry; **he was bursting to tell everyone the secret** = he was eagerly waiting to tell the secret. **burst o•pen,** *v.* to (make sth) come open with a bang. **burst out,** *v.* to shout out; **he burst out laughing.**

bur•y ['berɪ] *v.* to put (sth) into a hole in the ground.

bus [bʌs] 1. *n.* (*pl.* **-es**) motor vehicle for carrying passengers; **school b.** = bus which takes children to school. 2. *v.* (**bussed**) to take (children) to school in a different part of the town in order to mix racial groups. **bus driv•er,** *n.* person who drives a bus; **a busman's holiday** = spending your spare time doing sth similar to your normal job. **bus•sing,** *n.* action of sending children to school in a different part of the town in order to mix racial groups. **bus stop,** *n.* place where a bus stops regularly to let people on or off.

bus•by ['bʌzbɪ] *n.* tall fur hat worn by some soldiers.

bush [buʃ] *n.* (*pl.* **-es**) (a) plant which is smaller than a tree. (b) **the b.** = wild uncultivated land (in Africa/Australia); **b. fire** = fire in wild uncultivated land; **b. pilot** = pilot of a plane flying in the bush. **bushed,** *adj. inf.* tired out. **bush•man,** *n.* (*pl.* **-men**) native of the African bush. **bush•y,** *adj.* growing thickly.

bush•el ['buʃl] *n.* measure for grain (= 8 gallons).

busi•ness ['bɪznəs] *n.* (*pl.* **-es**) (a) affair; **it's none of your b.** = it has nothing to do with you. (b) commercial work; **to do b. with s.o.** = to trade with s.o.; **do you think he means b.?** = do you think he is serious? (c) commercial or in-

dustrial organization. **busi•ness•like,** *adj.*
practical/serious. **busi•ness•man, businesswoman,** *n.* (*pl.* **-men/-women**) person
who works in a business.

bust [bʌst] 1. *n.* (a) sculpture of head and shoulders. (b) measurement round a woman's
breasts. 2. *adj. inf.* broken. 3. *v.* **(busted/bust)**
inf. to break.

bus•tard ['bʌstəd] *n.* large brown bird, which
runs fast.

bus•tle ['bʌsl] 1. *n.* (a) pad at the back of a
dress (in Victorian times). (b) rushing around.
2. *v.* to rush around.

bus•y ['bɪzɪ] *adj.* (**-ier, -iest**) occupied with
doing sth; **he is b. fixing the lawnmower; b.
street** = street with lots of pedestrians and
traffic. **bus•i•ly,** *adv.* in a busy way.
bus•y•bod•y, *n.* person who interferes in
other people's affairs.

but [bʌt] *conj., adv. & prep.* (suggesting the op-
posite/a reservation) **he is tall b. his sister is
short; nothing b.** = only; **b. for his letter, we
would not have known he was here** = if it had
not been for his letter.

bu•tane ['bjuːteɪn] *n.* gas (often used for cooking or heating).

butch [butʃ] *adj. Sl.* (of woman) very masculine.

butch•er ['butʃə] 1. *n.* person who prepares
and sells meat. 2. *v.* (a) to kill in cold blood. (b)
to ruin by doing badly; **they butchered the
play. shop, butcher's shop,** *n.* store which
sells meat and poultry. **butch•er•y,** *n.* mas-
sacre/brutal killing.

but•ler ['bʌtlə] *n.* main male servant in a large
house.

butt [bʌt] 1. *n.* (a) large barrel for keeping a liquid. (b) end of a cigarette. (c) shoulder end of a
rifle. (d) place where you practice shooting.
(e) person who is often teased. (f) push (with
the head). (g) *inf.* buttocks. 2. *v.* (a) to push
(s.o.) with your head. (b) **to b. in** = to interrupt
a conversation.

but•ter ['bʌtə] 1. *n.* solid yellow fat made from
cream. 2. *v.* to spread butter on (sth); **to b. s.o.
up** = to flatter s.o. **but•ter•cup,** *n.* common
bright yellow wild flower.
but•ter•fin•gers, *n.* person who can't
catch/who drops things. **but•ter•fly,** *n.* insect with brightly colored wings.
but•ter•milk, *n.* thin milk left after butter
has been churned. **but•ter•scotch,** *n.* sweet
made from butter and sugar.

but•tock(s) ['bʌtək(s)] *n.* fleshy part of the
body which you sit on.

but•ton ['bʌtn] 1. *n.* small object stitched to
clothes for attaching one part of clothing to

another; small round object which you press
to make a machine work; **b. mushroom** = small
round mushroom which is not fully grown. 2.
v. to close or attach with buttons.
but•ton•hole. 1. *n.* hole for putting a button through. 2. *v.* **to b. s.o.** = to trap s.o. and
talk to him at length.

but•tress ['bʌtrəs] 1. *n.* (*pl.* **-es**) supporting pillar (reinforcing a wall). 2. *v.* to support.

bux•om ['bʌksəm] *adj.* plump and attractive
(woman).

buy [baɪ] 1. *v.* (**bought** [bɔːt] **has bought**) to get
by paying money. 2. *n.* thing which you have
bought/which you might buy; **a good b.** = a
bargain. **buy•er,** *n.* person who buys, esp.
person who buys stock for a large store. **buy
out,** *v.* to buy a partner's share in a business.

buzz [bʌz] 1. *n.* (a) (*pl.* **-es**) noise like a bee. (b)
inf. telephone call; **give me a b. tomorrow.** 2. *v.*
(a) to make a noise like a bee. (b) (*of aircraft*)
to fly low and close to (sth, as a house or another aircraft). **buzz•er,** *n.* device which
makes a buzzing noise. **buzz off,** *v. inf.* to go
away. **buzz word,** *n.* word which is frequently used.

buz•zard ['bʌzəd] *n.* kind of bird of prey.

by [baɪ] 1. *prep.* (a) near. (b) before; **by ten
o'clock.** (c) using; **by airmail; by car.** (d) painting **by Rembrandt** = which Rembrandt
painted; **play by Shakespeare** = which Shakespeare wrote. (e) **by yourself** = alone. (f) **by the
dozen** = a dozen at a time. 2. *adv.* (a) near; **put
some money by for a rainy day** = put money to
one side/save money. (b) past; **he drove by
without stopping. by•gone.** 1. *adj.* past/for-
mer. 2. *n.* thing which comes from the past; **let
bygones be bygones** = forget past insults.
by•law, *n.* law which is passed by a municipal council. **by•pass.** 1. *n.* (a) road which
goes around a town. (b) **heart b.** = operation
to insert a tube to go around a diseased part of
an artery. 2. *v.* to go around (a town), avoiding the center; to avoid (sth) by going around
it. **by-prod•uct,** *n.* secondary product made
as a result of manufacturing something else.
by-road, *n.* small local road. **by•stand•er,**
n. person standing near the scene of action.
by•way, *n.* small path/road. **by•word,** *n.*
(for) famous or common saying or phrase.

bye [baɪ] *n.* (a) right to pass to the next round of
a sporting tournament without having to
play. (b) (*in cricket*) run scored without the
batsman having hit the ball.

bye(-bye) [baɪ(baɪ)] *inter. used when leaving
someone.*

byte [baɪt] *n.* series of bits processed by a computer as one piece.

Cc

C *symbol for* carbon.

Ca *symbol for* calcium.

cab [kæb] *n.* taxi. **cab•driv•er,** *n.* person who drives a taxi.

ca•bal [kæ'bɑːl] *n.* small group of politicians who plot in secret.

cab•a•ret ['kæbəreɪ] *n.* entertainment given in a restaurant or club.

cab•bage ['kæbɪdʒ] *n.* green leafy vegetable; **c. white** = common type of white butterfly.

cab•in ['kæbɪn] *n.* (a) small room on a ship. (b) small hut. (c) interior of an aircraft; **c. crew** = air hostesses and stewards.

cab•i•net ['kæbɪnət] *n.* (a) piece of furniture with shelves. (b) central committee of advisers or ministers in a government; **cab•i•net•mak•er,** *n.* woodworker who makes furniture.

ca•ble ['keɪbl] 1. *n.* (a) thick rope/wire; **c. railway** = railway where railroad cars are pulled up a steep hill by a cable. (b) telegraph wire for sending messages underwater. (c) message sent by underwater cable. (d) **c. TV** = television sent by cable. 2. *v.* to send a message to (s.o.) by cable. **ca•ble•car,** *n.* cabin on a cable railway. **ca•ble•gram,** *n.* telegram sent by cable.

ca•boo•dle [kə'buːdl] *n. inf.* **the whole c.** = everything.

ca•ca•o [kə'kɑːəʊ] *n.* tropical tree, of which the seeds provide cocoa and chocolate.

cache [kæʃ] *n.* hidden store.

ca•chet ['kæʃeɪ] *n.* special mark.

cack•le ['kækl] 1. *n.* noise made by hens; *Sl.* **cut the c.** = stop chattering. 2. *v.* to chatter.

ca•coph•o•ny [kə'kɒfənɪ] *n.* loud unpleasant mixture of sounds. **ca•coph•o•nous,** *adj.* unpleasantly noisy.

cac•tus ['kæktəs] *n.* (*pl.* **cacti** ['kæktaɪ], **cactuses, cactus**) prickly plant which grows in the desert.

cad [kæd] *n.* (*old*) unpleasant/dishonest person. **cad•dish,** *adj.* like a cad.

ca•dav•er [kə'dɑːvə] *n.* corpse. **ca•dav•er•ous,** *adj.* looking like a corpse.

CAD/CAM = computer-assisted design/computer-assisted manufacture.

cad•die ['kædɪ] 1. *n.* person who carries the clubs for a golfer. 2. *v.* to act as a caddie (**for s.o.**).

cad•dis fly ['kædɪsflaɪ] *n.* insect living near water.

cad•dy ['kædɪ] *n.* (*pl.* **caddies**) box for keeping tea in.

ca•dence ['keɪdəns] *n.* rhythm (of music/poetry).

ca•den•za [kə'denzə] *n.* flowery piece for a solo instrument in the middle of concerto/symphony, etc.

ca•det [kə'det] *n.* young person training for the armed forces.

cadge [kædʒ] *v.* to scrounge/to try to get (sth) without having to pay for it. **cadg•er,** *n.* person who cadges.

cad•mi•um ['kædmɪəm] *n.* (*element:* Cd) gray metal which can be poisonous to human beings.

ca•dre ['kɑːdə] *n.* (a) small group of expert people in a political party or the military. (b) active specialist working in a cadre.

cae•cum ['siːkəm] *see* **ce•cum.**

cae•sar•e•an [sɪ'zeərɪən] *n.* **c. (section)** = operation on a pregnant woman to deliver her baby through the wall of the womb.

ca•fé ['kæfeɪ] *n.* (a) small restaurant. (b) bar or nightclub.

caf•e•te•ri•a [kæfɪ'tɪərɪə] *n.* self-service restaurant.

caf•feine ['kæfiːn] *n.* stimulating substance in coffee, tea, and cola drinks

caf•tan ['kæftæn] *n.* long Arab-style gown.

cage [keɪdʒ] 1. *n.* enclosure of wire or with metal bars for keeping birds or animals. 2. *v.* to put in a cage.

cag•ey ['keɪdʒɪ] *adj.* (**cagier, cagiest**) secretive/unwilling to reveal sth. **cag•i•ly,** *adv.* in a cagey way. **cag•i•ness,** *n.* being cagey.

æ back, ɑː farm, ɒ top, aɪ pipe, aʊ how, aɪc fire, aʊə flower, ɔː bought, ɔɪ toy, e fed, eəhair, eɪ take, ə afraid, əʊ boat, əʊə lower, vː word, iː heap, ɪ hit, ɪə hear, uː school, ʊ book, ʌ but, b back, d dog, ð then, dʒ just, f fog, g go, h hand, j yes, k catch, l last, m mix, n nut, ŋ sing, p penny, r round, s some, ʃ short, t too, tʃ chop, θ thing, v voice, w was, z zoo, ʒ treasure

ca•hoots [kə'huːts] n. inf. **to be in c. with s.o.** = to work with s.o., against another person.

cairn [keən] n. heap of stones to mark an important spot.

cais•son [kə'suːn] n. watertight enclosure, as in a dry dock.

ca•jole [kə'dʒəʊl] v. to persuade by flattering. **ca•jol•er•y**, n. act of flattering.

cake [keɪk] 1. n. (a) cooked food made of eggs, flour and sugar, usu. eaten cold; Sl. **it's a piece of c.** = it is very easy; **you can't have your c. and eat it** = you can't benefit from two quite opposite things. (b) block of soap. 2. v. to form a dry crust.

cal•a•mine ['kæləmaɪn] n. **c. lotion** = pink liquid put on skin to soothe and stop itching.

ca•lam•i•ty [kə'læmɪtɪ] n. disaster. **ca•lam•i•tous**, adj. very unfortunate/disastrous.

cal•car•e•ous [kæl'keərɪəs] adj. (soil) containing chalk.

cal•ce•o•lar•i•a [kælsɪəʊ'leərɪə] n. house plant, with colored boat-shaped flowers.

cal•cin•ate ['kælsɪneɪt] v. to burn to ashes.

cal•ci•um ['kælsɪəm] n. (a) (element: Ca) gray metal which forms bones. (b) white substance found in water, lime, etc. **cal•ci•fy**, v. to turn (sth) into calcium.

cal•cu•late ['kælkjʊleɪt] v. to work out (a sum); to estimate (quite accurately); **calculated insult** = deliberate insult. **cal•cu•la•ble**, adj. which can be calculated. **cal•cu•lat•ing**, adj. (person) who plans clever schemes. **cal•cu•la•tion** [kælkjʊ'leɪʃn] n. act of calculating; sum which has been calculated. **cal•cu•la•tor**, n. electronic machine for doing sums. **cal•cu•lus**, n. (a) mathematical way of calculating. (b) stone formed inside the body.

cal•dron ['kɔːldrən] n. see **caul•dron**.

cal•en•dar ['kælendə] n. sheet showing the days and months of a year; **c. month, c. year** = month/year as shown on a calendar.

ca•len•du•la [kə'lendjuːlə] n. yellow flower, the marigold.

calf [kɑːf] n. (pl. **calves** [kɑːvz]) (a) young cow/bull; young (of elephant, etc.). (b) leather (from cow's skin). (c) fleshy back part of the leg between the ankle and the knee.

cal•i•ber, Brit. **cal•i•bre** ['kælɪbə] n. (a) interior diameter of a gun. (b) standing/intellectual ability. **cal•i•brate**, v. to mark/to correct degrees on (a thermometer)/to mark units on (a scale). **cal•i•bra•tion**, n. marking of degrees; degree marked.

cal•i•co ['kælɪkəʊ] n. thick cotton cloth.

cal•i•pers, callipers ['kælɪpəz] n. pl. instru-

ment for measuring the diameter of sth. round (like a pipe).

call [kɔːl] n. (a) shout/cry; song of a bird; **I want a c. at 7 o'clock** = I want to be waked at 7 o'clock; **on c.** = available for duty. (b) conversation on the telephone. (c) visit. (d) need; **there's no c. for alarm.** 2. v. (a) to shout; **c. me at 7 o'clock** = wake me at 7 o'clock. (b) to telephone. (c) to give (s.o.) a name. (d) to visit. **call back,** v. (a) to telephone in reply; to telephone again. (b) to come back to visit again. **call•box,** n. street telephone or signal box for calling the police or fire department. **call•boy,** n. (a) young man in a theater who tells performers when it is time for them to go on stage. (b) young man in a hotel who runs messages; bellhop. **call•er,** n. (a) person who comes to visit. (b) person who telephones. **call for,** v. (a) **he called for help** = he shouted to ask for help. (b) **to c. for s.o.** = to go to s.o.'s house to pick them up. (c) to need/to require. **call girl,** n. prostitute who can be called by telephone. **call in,** v. to call (s.o.) to make them come in; **they called in the police. call•ing,** n. vocation; job. **call off,** v. to cancel. **call on,** v. (a) to visit. (b) to appeal to (s.o.). **call out,** v. (a) to shout. (b) to ask (police/military) to come to help. **call sign,** n. letters/words which identify a radio station. **call up,** v. (a) to telephone. (b) to order (s.o.) to join the military. **call-up,** n. order to join the military.

cal•lig•ra•phy [kə'lɪgrəfɪ] n. art of fine handwriting. **cal•li•graph•ic** [kælɪ'græfɪk] adj. referring to calligraphy.

cal•li•pers ['kælɪpəz] see **cal•i•pers**.

cal•lis•then•ics [kælɪs'θenɪks] n. exercises which are supposed to make the body strong and beautiful.

cal•lous ['kæləs] adj. hard/unfeeling. **cal•lous•ly,** adv. cruelly. **cal•lous•ness,** n. cruelty.

cal•low ['kæləʊ] adj. young and inexperienced.

cal•lus ['kæləs] n. (pl. **-es**) hard patch on the skin.

calm [kɑːm] 1. adj. (**-er, -est**) quiet/not rough. 2. n. period of quiet. 3. v. to become/to make quiet. **calm•ly,** adv. quietly. **calm•ness,** n. period of quiet.

cal•o•rie ['kælərɪ] n. measure of heat/of energy-giving value of food. **cal•o•rif•ic** [kælə-'rɪfɪk] adj. referring to heat.

cal•um•ny ['kæləmnɪ] n. lie/false statement. **ca•lum•ni•ate** [kə'lʌmnɪeɪt] v. to tell lies about (s.o.).

calve [kɑːv] 1. v. to give birth to a calf. 2. n. pl. see **calf**.

ca•lyp•so [kə'lɪpsəʊ] n. type of topical song sung in the West Indies.

ca•lyx ['kælɪks] *n.* (*pl.* **-es**) outer covering of a flower bud.

cam [kæm] *n.* ring on a camshaft, which makes pistons move up and down.

ca•ma•ra•de•rie [kæmə'rædərɪ] *n.* friendship among comrades, esp. in the armed forces.

cam•ber ['kæmbə] *n.* bend/curve (in a surface); way in which the road slopes. **cam•bered**, *adj.* sloping/rounded (surface).

cam•bric ['kæmbrɪk] *n.* thin cotton cloth.

cam•cord•er ['kæmkɔːdə] *n.* portable cine-camera which records pictures for video.

came [keɪm] *v. see* **come**.

cam•el ['kæml] *n.* desert animal with one or two humps, used for riding. **cam•el's hair** (*also* **cam•el•hair**, *n.* thick pale brown wool, used for making coats, etc.

ca•mel•lia [kə'miːlɪə] *n.* evergreen bush with pink or white flowers.

cam•e•o ['kæmɪəʊ] *n.* (a) small stone with a design of a head which stands out against a darker background. (b) small but sharply defined part in a play/film.

cam•er•a ['kæmərə] *n.* (a) machine for taking photographs or pictures to be shown on a screen. (b) **in c.** = in closed session/in secret. **cam•er•a•man**, *n.* (*pl.* **-men**) man who operates a movie or television-camera.

cam•o•mile ['kæməmaɪl] *n.* fragrant plant, of which the dried leaves are used for making hot drinks.

cam•ou•flage ['kæməflɑːʒ] 1. *n.* hiding (sth) by means of coloring, so that it is difficult to see it against the background. 2. *v.* to hide (sth) so that it is difficult to see it against the background.

camp [kæmp] 1. *n.* place where people live in tents or cabins in the open temporarily; **c. bed** = folding bed; **c. fire** = fire round which campers sit at night. 2. *v.* (a) to live or sleep in a tent temporarily. (b) **to c. it up** = to put on an affected style. 3. *adj.* in an affected (often playful) style. **camp•er**, *n.* (a) small van equipped with beds, tables, cooking facilities, etc. (b) person who lives in a tent or camper. **camp•ing**, *n.* going on vacation with a tent or camper. **camp•site**, *n.* area specially laid out for tents and campers.

cam•paign [kæm'peɪn] 1. *n.* (a) organized military movement. (b) organized method of working; **a sales c.** 2. *v.* (a) to take part in a war. (b) (**for**) to work in an organized fashion to achieve an end. **cam•paign•er**, *n.* person who campaigns.

cam•pa•nol•o•gy [kæmpə'nɒlədʒɪ] *n.* study of ringing church bells.

cam•pan•u•la [kæm'pænjuːlə] *n.* the bell flower, with blue bell-shaped flowers.

cam•phor ['kæmfə] *n.* strong-smelling substance which comes from certain trees; **c. balls** = small white balls impregnated with camphor which prevent moths from attacking clothes. **cam•pho•rat•ed**, *adj.* impregnated with camphor.

cam•pi•on ['kæmpjən] *n.* wild plant with small pink flowers.

cam•pus ['kæmpəs] *n.* (*pl.* **-es**) land on which a school/college/university is built.

cam•shaft ['kæmʃɑːft] *n.* shaft with projecting rings which open and close pistons in turn.

can [kæn] 1. *n.* (a) metal box for liquids, esp. for preserving food or drink. (b) **watering c.** = bucket with a long spout for watering plants. 2. *v.* (a) (**I/he can;** *neg.* **cannot;** *short form* **can't;** *past* **I/he could;** *neg.* **could not;** *short form* **couldn't**) able to do sth/knowing how to do sth. (b) (**canned**) to put (fruit/vegetables, etc.) into cans to preserve them. **canned**, *adj.* in a metal box; **c. music** = recorded music. **can•ner•y**, *n.* canning factory.

Can•a•da goose [kænədə'guːs] *n.* large wild goose, with black neck and white chin, originally native of N. America.

Ca•na•di•an [kə'neɪdjən] 1. *adj.* referring to Canada. 2. *n.* person from Canada.

ca•nal [kə'næl] *n.* (a) artificial waterway. (b) passage in the body.

can•a•pé ['kænəpeɪ] *n.* small cocktail snack.

ca•nar•y [kə'neərɪ] *n.* small yellow singing bird.

can•can ['kænkæn] *n.* French cabaret dance, where the dancers kick their legs in the air.

can•cel ['kænsl] *v.* (**canceled, cancelled**) (a) to stop (sth which had been planned). (b) to mark a postage stamp with a rubber stamp. **can•cel•la•tion** [kænsə'leɪʃn] *n.* act of canceling; seat/ticket which is on sale because a purchaser cannot use it. **can•cel out**, *v.* to balance (sth) and so remove its force.

can•cer ['kænsə] *n.* (a) disease of the blood or tissue. (b) **Cancer** = one of the signs of the Zodiac, shaped like a crab; **Tropic of C.** = imaginary line 23° 28′ north of the equator. **can•cer•ous**, *adj.* referring to cancer.

æ back, ɑː farm, ɒ top, aɪ pipe, aʊ how, aɪə fire, aʊə flower, ɔ bought, ɔɪ toy, e fed, eəhair, eɪ take, ə afraid, əʊ boat, əʊə lower, vː word, iː heap, ɪ hit, ɪə hear, uː school, ʊ book, ʌ but, b back, d dog, ð then, dʒ just, f fog, g go, h hand, j yes, k catch, l last, m mix, n nut, ŋ sing, p penny, r round, s some, ʃ short, t too, tʃ chop, θ thing, v voice, w was, z zoo, ʒ treasure

can•de•la•bra [kændɪ'lɑ:brə] *n. pl.* branched candlesticks; chandeliers.

can•did ['kændɪd] *adj.* frank/open. **can•did•ly**, *adv.* in a candid way.

can•di•date ['kændɪdət] *n.* person seeking election; person who has entered a competition/an examination. **can•di•da•cy**, *n.* act of standing as a candidate.

can•died ['kændɪd] *adj.* dried and sugared; **c. peel** = dried orange/lemon peel.

can•dle ['kændl] *n.* stick of wax with a wick in the center; **to burn the c. at both ends** = to work hard during the day and enjoy yourself late into the night. **can•dle•light**, *n.* light from a candle. **can•dle•lit**, *adj.* lit by candles. **can•dle•stick**, *n.* holder for a candle. **can•dle•wick**, *n.* cotton material for bedcovers, with patterns of tufts.

can•dor, *Brit.* **can•dour** ['kændə] *n.* frankness/openness.

can•dy ['kændɪ] *n.* something sweet to eat. **can•dy-striped**, *adj.* with stripes of color on a white background like certain fabrics. **can•dy•tuft**, *n.* plant with pink or blue flowers.

cane [keɪn] 1. *n.* (a) stem (esp. of jointed plants like bamboo). (b) walking stick (cut from such plants). 2. *v.* to hit with a cane. **can•ing**, *n.* beating with a cane.

ca•nine ['keɪnaɪn] 1. *adj.* referring to dogs. 2. *n.* **c. (tooth)** = round pointed tooth.

can•is•ter ['kænɪstə] *n.* round metal box.

can•ker ['kæŋkə] *n.* disease/sore which eats into flesh/into wood of trees.

can•na ['kænæ] *n.* tropical plant, with large leaves and red or orange flowers.

can•na•bis ['kænəbɪs] *n.* plant, parts of which can be smoked to give a pleasant feeling of relaxation.

can•nel•o•ni [kæne'ləʊnɪ] *n.* type of pasta, like small pancakes with a meat or spinach filling.

can•ni•bal ['kænɪbl] *n.* person who eats people. **can•ni•bal•ism**, *n.* custom of eating people. **can•ni•bal•ize**, *v.* to take pieces of old machinery to repair another machine.

can•non ['kænən] 1. *n.* (a) large gun; gun in an aircraft. (b) (*in billiards*) hitting of one ball off the other two. 2. *v.* to bounce off (another ball/the cushion); to bump (**into** sth). **can•non•ball**, *n.* large metal ball fired by a cannon.

can•not ['kænət] *v. see* **can.**

can•ny ['kænɪ] *adj.* (**-ier, -iest**) wise/clever. **can•ni•ly**, *adv.* cleverly.

ca•noe [kə'nu:] 1. *n.* boat propelled by one or more people with paddles. 2. *v.* (**canoed**) to travel in a canoe. **ca•noe•ing**, *n.* sport of

going in a canoe. **ca•noe•ist**, *n.* person who paddles a canoe.

can•on ['kænən] *n.* (a) religious rule or instructions; **c. law** = the church's laws. (b) clergyman attached to a cathedral. **ca•non•i•cal**, *adj.* referring to a canon. **can•on•i•za•tion**, *n.* declaring s.o. a saint. **can•on•ize**, *v.* to declare (s.o.) a saint.

can•o•py ['kænəpɪ] *n.* small roof over a platform/balcony, etc.

cant [kænt] *n.* (a) hypocrisy/insincere language. (b) jargon/language of a certain group of people.

can't [kɑ:nt] *v. see* **can.**

can•ta•loupe ['kæntəlu:p] *n.* type of melon with pink flesh.

can•tan•ker•ous [kæn'tæŋkrəs] *adj.* bad-tempered. **can•tan•ker•ous•ness**, *n.* continual bad temper.

can•ta•ta [kæn'tɑ:tə] *n.* musical piece for several voices and orchestra (usu. on a religious theme).

can•teen [kæn'ti:n] *n.* (a) self-service restaurant, as on a military base. (b) portable container for water.

can•ter ['kæntə] 1. *n.* gentle gallop. 2. *v.* to go at a canter.

can•ti•cle ['kæntɪkl] *n.* religious song.

can•ti•le•ver ['kæntɪli:və] *n.* projecting support which holds up a balcony/a bridge. **can•ti•le•vered**, *adj.* held up by a cantilever.

can•to ['kæntəʊ] *n.* (*pl.* **-os**) long section of an epic poem.

can•ton ['kæntɒn] *n.* administrative division of Switzerland.

can•vas ['kænvəs] *n.* (*pl.* **-es**) thick cloth (for making tents/sails, or for painting on); a painting on canvas.

can•vass ['kænvəs] *v.* to try to persuade people to vote for s.o./to buy sth. **can•vass•er**, *n.* person who canvasses. **can•vas•sing**, *n.* going from door to door to persuade people to vote.

can•yon ['kænjən] *n.* large valley with perpendicular sides.

cap [kæp] 1. *n.* (a) hat with a peak; **c. and gown** = hat and robes worn by graduates of a school/college/university. (b) top/cover (of a bottle, pen, etc.). (c) small piece of paper with gunpowder. 2. *v.* (**capped**) (a) to top with a cap; to fix a cover on (a pipe) to stop it leaking. (b) to surpass/to do better than.

ca•pa•ble ['keɪpəbl] *adj.* competent/able. **ca•pa•bil•i•ty** [keɪpə'bɪlɪtɪ] *n.* ability. **ca•pa•bly** ['keɪpəblɪ] *adv.* competently/efficiently.

ca•pac•i•ty [kə'pæsɪtɪ] *n.* (a) amount which a

container can hold; **seating c.** = number of seats (in a bus/theater, etc.). (b) **engine c.** = power of an engine. (c) ability to do something. (d) position; **in his c. as manager. ca•pac•i•tor**, *n.* device for storing an electric charge. **ca•pa•cious** [kə'peɪʃəs] *n.* very large/which contains a lot.

cape [keɪp] *n.* (a) long cloak. (b) headland jutting into the sea.

ca•per ['keɪpə] 1. *n.* (a) jumping/leaping. (b) small bitter seed used in cooking. (c) *inf.* trick. 2. *v.* **to c. about** = to jump/to leap.

cap•il•lar•y [kə'pɪlərɪ] *adj. & n.* very thin (tube); very thin blood vessel; **c. attraction** = physical phenomenon where water is drawn up in a thin tube.

cap•i•tal ['kæpɪtl] 1. *n.* (a) decorated stone on the top of a column. (b) large letter. (c) main city of a country/a state, etc. (d) money which is invested. (e) **c. punishment** = execution/legal killing of a criminal. 2. *adj.* (a) very important. (b) *inf.* very good. **cap•i•tal•ism**, *n.* economic system based on ownership of resources by individuals or companies and not by the state. **cap•i•tal•ist**, *adj. & n.* (person) who supports the theory of capitalism; businessman. **cap•i•tal•i•za•tion** [kæpɪtəlaɪ'zeɪʃn] *n.* amount of capital invested in a company. **cap•i•tal•ize** ['kæpɪtəlaɪz] *v.* (a) to invest capital in a company. (b) **to c. on** = to take advantage of (sth).

cap•i•ta•tion [kæpɪ'teɪʃn] *n.* tax or payment accrued uniformly on each individual.

Cap•i•tol ['kæpɪtəl] *n.* building where the U.S. Congress meets; **on C. Hill** = in the U.S. Congress.

ca•pit•u•late [kə'pɪtjuleɪt] *v.* to give in/to surrender. **ca•pit•u•la•tion** [kəpɪtju'leɪʃn] *n.* surrendering.

ca•pon ['keɪpɒn] *n.* fat castrated chicken.

cap•pu•ci•no [kæpu:'tʃi:nəʊ] *n.* frothy Italian coffee, with milk and sometimes chocolate.

ca•price [kə'pri:s] *n.* whim/sudden fancy. **ca•pri•cious** [kə'prɪʃəs] *adj.* whimsical/prone to change your mind. **ca•pri•cious•ness**, *n.* tendency to change your mind suddenly.

Cap•ri•corn ['kæprɪkɔːn] *n.* one of the signs of the Zodiac, shaped like a goat; **Tropic of C.** = imaginary line 23° 28 south of the equator.

cap•si•cum ['kæpsɪkəm] *n.* green pepper (plant).

cap•size [kæp'saɪz] *v.* (*of boats*) to turn over.

cap•stan ['kæpstən] *n.* machine which turns to haul in a rope or anchor.

cap•sule ['kæpsjuːl] *n.* enclosed case; small case for a dose of medicine which melts when swallowed; **space c.** = living compartment in a spacecraft.

cap•tain ['kæptɪn] 1. *n.* (a) officer in charge of a ship or aircraft. (b) rank in the army, airforce, etc. above lieutenant; rank in the navy above commander. (c) leader of sports team. 2. *v.* to lead (an expedition/a team). **cap•tain•cy**, *n.* (a) rank of captain (in the military). (b) post of leader of a sports team.

cap•tion ['kæpʃn] *n.* phrase printed beneath a picture.

cap•tious ['kæpʃəs] *adj.* continually finding fault.

cap•ti•vate ['kæptɪveɪt] *v.* to charm/to seduce.

cap•tive ['kæptɪv] 1. *n.* prisoner. 2. *adj.* **held c.** = held as a prisoner. **cap•tiv•i•ty** [kæp'tɪvɪtɪ] *n.* imprisonment. **cap•tor**, *n.* person who captures s.o. **cap•ture** ['kæptʃə] 1. *n.* taking of s.o./sth captive. 2. *v.* (a) to take (s.o./sth) captive. (b) **they have captured 10% of the market** = they have taken 10% of the possible sales.

cap•y•ba•ra [kæpɪ'bɑːrə] *n.* very large rodent, native of S. America.

car [kɑː] *n.* (a) private motor vehicle; *Brit.* **c. park** = parking lot. (b) railroad car. **car pool**, *n.* group of people who each take turns in driving all their children to school, etc. **car•port**, *n.* shelter for a car. **car•sick**, *adj.* feeling ill when traveling by motor vehicle. **car wash**, *n.* place where cars are washed automatically.

ca•rafe [kə'ræf] *n.* glass jug for serving wine.

car•a•mel ['kærəmel] *n.* (a) sweet made with sugar and butter. (b) burned sugar; **c. custard** = pudding of egg custard topped with browned sugar. **car•a•mel•ize**, *v.* to heat sugar until it becomes brown.

car•a•pace ['kærəpeɪs] *n.* outside shell (of an animal).

car•at ['kærət] *n.* (a) *see* **karat.** (b) weight of a diamond.

car•a•van ['kærəvæn] *n.* (*a*) group of vehicles/animals traveling together (esp. across a desert). (b) *Brit.* van with beds, table, washing facilities, etc., which can be towed by a car.

car•a•way ['kærəweɪ] *n.* spicy seed used to flavor cakes and biscuits.

car•ba•mate ['kɑːbəmeɪt] *n.* type of pesticide.

car•bine ['kɑːbaɪn] *n.* type of light rifle.

car•bo•hy•drate [kɑ:bəʊ'haɪdreɪt] *n.* chemical substance containing carbon, hydrogen and oxygen, and derived from sugar; **she eats too many carbohydrates** = too much fattening food.

car•bol•ic [kɑ:'bɒlɪk] *adj.* referring to an acid used to disinfect; **c. soap.**

car•bon ['kɑ:bən] *n.* (*element:* C) substance found in charcoal, soot, diamonds; **c. dioxide** = colorless gas (CO_2) forming a small part of the atmosphere; **c. monoxide** = colorless poisonous gas (CO) present in car exhaust fumes; **c. paper** = paper with black substance on one side, used to make copies, as in typing; **c. copy** = identical copy. **car•bo•nate**, *n.* salt of carbonic acid. **car•bon•ic** [kɑ:'bɒnɪk] *adj.* referring to carbon; **c. acid** = acid formed when carbon dioxide is dissolved in water. **car•bon•if•er•ous** [kɑ:bə'nɪfərəs] *adj.* coal-bearing. **car•bon•ize** ['kɑ:bənaɪz] *v.* to make into carbon by burning.

car•bo•run•dum [kɑ:bə'rʌndəm] *n.* hard substance used for polishing or sharpening.

car•boy ['kɑ:bɔɪ] *n.* very large glass bottle for containing corrosive liquids.

car•bun•cle ['kɑ:bʌŋkl] *n.* (a) red precious stone. (b) large inflamed spot on the skin.

car•bu•re•tor [kɑ:bə'retə] *n.* device in a car for changing liquid fuel into vapor.

car•case/car•cass ['kɑ:kəs] *n.* (a) body of a dead animal ready for the butcher; bones left after you have eaten a cooked bird. (b) body (of a person).

car•cin•o•gen [kɑ:'sɪnədʒən] *n.* substance which causes cancer.

car•ci•no•ma [kɑ:sɪ'nəʊmə] *n.* cancer.

card [kɑ:d] 1. *n.* (a) small rectangle of stiff paper for writing on. (b) rectangle of stiff paper with a design on it, used for playing games; **playing cards** = ordinary cards, marked in four designs (diamonds, hearts, clubs, spades); **c. games** = games using packs of special cards; **they were playing cards** = they were playing games of cards. (c) (**calling/business**) **c.** = small piece of stiff paper with your name and address printed on it; **credit c.** = plastic card which allows you to buy goods without paying for them immediately; 2. *v.* to comb (raw wool). **card•board**, *n.* thick card, used for packing. **card in•dex.** 1. *n.* series of small cards classified into alphabetical or numerical order. 2. *v.* to classify (sth) on to small filing cards. **card•sharpe**, *n.* person who cheats at cards to win money.

car•di•ac ['kɑ:dɪæk] *adj.* referring to the heart; **c. arrest** = heart attack.

car•di•gan ['kɑ:dɪgən] *n.* woolen jacket which buttons at the front.

car•di•nal ['kɑ:dɪnl] 1. *adj.* (a) very important (rule, etc.). (b) **c. numbers** = numbers which show quantity (1, 2, 3, etc.). 2. *n.* (a) high dignitary of the Catholic church. (b) bright red North American bird.

car•di•o•gram ['kɑ:dɪəgræm] *n.* chart showing heart beats. **car•di•o•graph**, *n.* machine for recording heart beats in the form of cardiograms. **car•di•ol•o•gy** [kɑ:dɪ'ɒlədʒɪ] *n.* study of the heart and its diseases. **car•di•ol•o•gist**, *n.* doctor specializing in cardiology. **car•di•o•vas•cu•lar**, *adj.* referring to the heart and the blood circulation system.

care ['keə] 1. *n.* (a) worry. (b) looking after s.o./sth; **to take c.** = to watch out/to be careful; **in the c. of** = being looked after by; 2. *v.* (a) to worry; **I don't c. if I never see you again.** (b) to like; **would you c. for a cake?** (c) **to c. for** = to look after. **care•free**, *adj.* without any worries. **care•ful**, *adj.* cautious/taking care. **care•ful•ly**, *adv.* with care. **care•less**, *adj.* not paying attention/not taking care. **care•less•ly**, *adv.* in a careless way. **care•less•ness**, *n.* being careless. **care•tak•er**, *n.* (a) person who looks after a building; (government) which runs a country temporarily (until a permanent one is elected). (b) person who looks after another person. **care•worn**, *adj* tired because of worries.

ca•reen [kə'ri:n] *v.* (a) to tilt (a boat) over, so as to clean the bottom. (b) *inf.* to go along very fast.

ca•reer [kə'rɪə] 1. *n.* (a) life of professional work. (b) forward rush. 2. *v.* to rush forward out of control. **ca•reer•ist**, *adj. & n.* (person) only aiming at advancing his career.

ca•ress [kə'res] 1. *n.* (*pl.* **-es**) gentle touch. 2. *v.* to stroke gently.

car•et ['kærɪt] *n.* mark (∧) used to show that sth is missing.

car•go ['kɑ:gəʊ] *n.* (*pl.* **-oes, gos**) goods carried (esp. on a ship).

car•i•bou ['kærɪbu:] *n.* (*pl.* **caribou**) reindeer of North America.

car•i•ca•ture ['kærɪkətjʊə] 1. *n.* amusing drawing which satirizes by emphasizing s.o.'s particular features. 2. *v.* to satirize by emphasizing s.o.'s bad features.

car•ies ['keəri:z] *n.* (*pl.* **caries**) decayed place in a tooth.

car•il•lon ['kærɪlon] *n.* set of bells, usu. in a tower, on which tunes can be played.

car•min•a•tive ['kɑ:mɪnətɪv] *n.* medicine which relieves indigestion.

car•mine ['kɑ:mɪn] *adj. & n.* bright red (color).

car•nage ['kɑ:nɪdʒ] *n.* bloodshed/massacre/killing.

car•nal ['kɑ:nl] *adj.* referring to the body; sensual.

car•na•tion [kɑːˈneɪʃn] *n.* strongly scented flower often worn in a buttonhole.

car•net [ˈkɑːneɪ] *n.* customs permit to take a car from one country to another at no charge.

car•ni•val [ˈkɑːnɪvl] *n.* festival often with dancing and eating in the open air.

car•ni•vore [ˈkɑːnɪvɔː] *n.* animal which eats flesh. **car•niv•o•rous** [kɑːˈnɪvərəs] *adj.* flesh-eating.

car•ol [ˈkærəl] 1. *n.* special song sung at a particular time of the year; **Christmas c.** 2. *v.* (**caroled**) to sing Christmas carols. **car•ol•er,** *n.* person singing Christmas carols.

ca•rot•id [kæˈrɒtɪd] *n.* artery in the neck.

ca•rouse [kəˈraʊz] *v.* to drink alcohol and enjoy yourself. **ca•rous•al,** *n.* (*formal*) drunken party.

car•ou•sel [kæruːˈsel] *n.* (a) circular conveyor belt which distributes luggage. (b) merry-go-round.

carp [kɑːp] 1. *n.* (*pl.* **carp**) fat edible fish often bred in captivity for eating. 2. *v.* to keep on finding fault with things.

car•pel [ˈkɑːpəl] *n.* female part of a flower.

car•pen•ter [ˈkɑːpəntə] *n.* person who works with wood, esp. in building. **car•pen•try,** *n.* art of working with wood.

car•pet [ˈkɑːpɪt] 1. *n.* woven or knotted covering for the floor; *inf.* **to call on the c.** = to criticize s.o. 2. *v.* to cover (as) with a carpet. **car•pet•bag•ger,** *n.* politician who tries to make his fortune in a part of the country which is not his home. **car•pet•ing,** *n.* covering with a carpet; wide piece of carpet. **car•pet sweep•er,** *n.* device which cleans carpets by means of rotating brushes.

car•riage [ˈkærɪdʒ] *n.* (a) action of carrying goods. (b) open vehicle pulled by a horse. (c) way of walking. (d) movable part on a typewriter which goes from side to side. (e) small, light vehicle in which you can push a baby.

car•ri•er [ˈkærɪə] *n.* (a) thing/person who carries; **c. pigeon** = pigeon specially trained for carrying messages; (b) person who carries the germ of a disease without suffering and can infect others with it. (c) **aircraft c.** = ship which carries aircraft.

car•ri•on [ˈkærɪən] *n.* (*no pl.*) rotting meat. **car•ri•on crow,** *n.* type of large black crow.

car•rot [ˈkærət] *n.* bright orange root vegetable.

car•ry [ˈkærɪ] *v.* (a) to lift (sth) up and move it from one place to another. (b) to win (a vote).

(c) (*of sound*) to be heard at a distance. (d) to keep (in a store). **car•ry a•long,** *v.* to carry (sth) which cannot prevent it. **car•ry a•way,** *v.* (a) to take away/to demolish. (b) **to get carried away** = to get overcome with emotion/excitement. **car•ry for•ward,** *v.* (*in bookkeeping*) to take (a sum) on to the next page or column. **carry off,** *v.* (a) to win/to take away; **to carry off first prize.** (b) **he carried it off very well** = he got through a potentially embarrassing situation very well. **carry on,** *v.* (a) to continue/to go on. (b) *inf.* to be very angry; make a fuss. **carry out,** *v.* to do (sth) successfully. **carry through,** *v.* to bring (sth) to a finish.

cart [kɑːt] 1. *n.* vehicle pulled by a horse; **to put the c. before the horse** = not to put first things first. 2. *v.* to carry (sth heavy). **car•ter,** *n.* person or company which transports goods. **cart horse,** *n.* large strong horse. **cart•load,** *n.* quantity carried in a cart. **cart•wheel,** *n.* (a) wheel of a cart. (b) **to turn cartwheels** = to turn over and over sideways on your outstretched hands and feet.

carte blanche [kɑːtˈblɒnʃ] *n.* **to have c. b. to do sth** = to be able to do whatever you want.

car•tel [kɑːˈtel] *n.* group of companies which try to fix the price of sth.

car•ti•lage [ˈkɑːtɪlɪdʒ] *n.* strong flexible material which acts as a cushion in joints in the body. **car•ti•lag•i•nous** [kɑːtɪˈlædʒɪnəs] *adj.* made of cartilage.

car•tog•ra•pher [kɑːˈtɒgrəfə] *n.* person who draws maps. **car•to•graph•ic,** *adj.* referring to maps. **car•tog•ra•phy,** *n.* science of drawing maps.

car•ton [ˈkɑːtən] *n.* cardboard box.

car•toon [kɑːˈtuːn] *n.* (a) funny drawing in a newspaper, magazine, etc. (b) movie made of moving drawings. (c) sketch for a painting. **car•toon•ist,** *n.* person who draws cartoons.

car•tridge [ˈkɑːtrɪdʒ] *n.* (a) tube packed with gunpowder and a bullet for firing from a gun. (b) film/recording tape enclosed in a plastic case which fits directly into the camera/tape recorder; tube of ink which fits into a pen. (c) part of a record player which holds the stylus.

carve [kɑːv] *v.* (a) to cut (meat) up. (b) to cut (stone/wood) to make a shape. **car•ver,** *n.* (a) person who carves. (b) carving knife. **carv•ing,** *n.* (a) cutting up cooked meat; **c. knife** = large sharp knife for cutting meat. (b)

æ back, ɑː farm, ɒ top, aɪ pipe, aʊ how, aɪə fire, aʊə flower, ɔː bought, ɔɪ toy, e fed, eəhair, eɪ take, ə afraid, əʊ boat, əʊə lower, ɜː word, iː heap, ɪ hit, ɪə hear, uː school, ʊ book, ʌ but, b back, d dog, ð then, dʒ just, f fog, g go, h hand, j yes, k catch, l last, m mix, n nut, ŋ sing, p penny, r round, s some, ʃ short, t too, tʃ chop, θ thing, v voice, w was, z zoo, ʒ treasure

art of cutting stone/wood into shapes. (c) an object which has been made by carving.

car•y•at•id [kær'jætɪd] *n.* statue of a female figure, which acts as a column holding up a roof.

cas•cade [kæs'keɪd] 1. *n.* (artificial) waterfall. 2. *v.* to fall in large quantities.

case [keɪs] 1. *n.* (a) box (of goods). (b) protective box or covering. (c) suitcase. (d) way in which sth happens; example; **in any c.** = anyway; **in c. of fire** = if fire breaks out; **just in c.** = to guard against a possible emergency. (e) sick person; **c. history** = details of a patient's past history, progress, etc. (f) legal affair. 2. *v.* to put (sth) in a case.

ca•sein [keɪ'siːɪn] *n.* protein found in milk.

case•ment ['keɪsmənt] *n.* window that opens on hinges; frame around such a window.

cash [kæʃ] 1. *n.* money (in coins and notes); **c. crop** = crop grown for sale; **c. register** = machine which shows the amount to be paid and has a drawer for keeping money. 2. *v.* to change (a check) into cash; **to c. in on** = to make a lot of money by profiting from sth. **cash and car•ry**, *adj* selling items for cash only and no delivery. **cash•back**, *n.* service in which customers paying for goods by debit card can draw cash. **cash flow**, *n.* rate at which money comes into and is paid out of a business.

cash•ew [kə'ʃuː] *n.* small sweetish nut, often eaten salted.

cash•ier [kə'ʃiːə] 1. *n.* person who deals with money. 2. *v.* to expel (an officer) from the armed forces.

cash•mere ['kæʃmɪə] *adj. & n.* (made of) fine soft goat's wool.

cas•ing ['keɪsɪŋ] *n.* hard covering which protects something. `

ca•si•no [kə'siːnəʊ] *n.* (*pl.* **-os**) building where you can gamble.

cask [kɑːsk] *n.* large barrel.

cas•ket ['kɑːskɪt] *n.* (a) ornamental box (for jewels). (b) coffin.

cas•sa•ta [kə'sɑːtə] *n.* Italian ice cream with dried fruit in it.

cas•se•role ['kæsərəʊl] *n.* (a) oven-proof covered dish. (b) food cooked in a covered dish in the oven.

cas•sette [kə'set] *n.* (a) magnetic tape in a plastic case which can fit directly into a playing or recording machine; **c. player** = machine for playing cassettes; **c. recorder** = machine for recording and playing back cassettes. (b) film in a plastic case which fits directly into a camera.

cas•sock ['kæsək] *n.* long, usu. black, gown worn by priests, choirboys, etc.

cast [kɑːst] 1. *n.* (a) throwing (of a fishing line). (b) plaster shape made from a mold. (c) list of

actors in a play/movie; all the actors in a play/movie. (d) **c. of mind** = way of thinking. (e) squint (in an eye). 2. *v.* (**cast**) (a) to throw. (b) to mold metal/plaster. (c) to choose actors for a play/movie. 3. *adj.* which has been cast in a mold; **a cast-iron alibi** = a perfect alibi. **cast a•bout for,** *v.* to look for. **cast a•drift,** *v.* to abandon (a boat/a family). **cast a•side,** *v.* to throw away. **cast a•way,** *v.* to throw away; **cast away on a desert island** = shipwrecked on a desert island. **cast•a•way,** *n.* person who has been shipwrecked. **cast down,** *v.* to throw down; **they were cast down** = they were miserable. **cast•ing.** 1. *n.* (a) molding of a shape/thing which has been molded. (b) choosing of actors. 2. *adj.* **c. vote** = vote which decides when the other votes are equal. **cast off,** *v.* (a) to calculate roughly the number of pages in (a book), before it is printed. (b) to untie the ropes holding a boat. (c) (*in knitting*) to finish stitches. **cast•off cloth•ing,** *n.,* **cast•offs,** *n. pl.* clothes which have been thrown away. **cast on,** *v.* to put (stitches) on to the needles when knitting.

cas•ta•nets [kæstə'nets] *n. pl.* hollow clappers made of wood which are held in the hand and clicked in time to music by Spanish dancers.

caste [kɑːst] *n.* hereditary class (in Indian society).

cas•ti•gate ['kæstɪgeɪt] *v.* (*formal*) to punish/to beat s.o. as a punishment; to criticize s.o. sharply.

cas•tle ['kɑːsl] *n.* (a) large fortified building. (b) piece in chess which looks like a castle.

cast•or/cast•er ['kɑːstə] *n.* (a) container with holes in the lid for sprinkling sugar, pepper, etc. (b) wheel screwed on to the leg of a chair. **cas•tor oil,** *n.* oil from a palm which is used as a laxative.

cas•trate [kæ'streɪt] *v.* to remove the testicles from (a male animal). **cas•tra•tion** [kæ'streɪʃn] *n.* act of castrating.

cas•u•al ['kæʒjʊəl] *adj.* (a) not formal. (b) not serious. **cas•u•al•ly,** *adv.* by chance; in an informal way. **cas•u•al•ness,** *n.* being casual.

cas•u•al•ty ['kæʒjʊəltɪ] *n.* person injured or killed in a battle/an accident; person or thing destroyed or damaged.

cas•u•ist•ry ['kæʒjuːɪstrɪ] *n.* debating problems in very fine detail.

cat [kæt] *n.* (a) furry domestic pet, which purrs and has a long tail; wild animal of the same family as the domestic cat; *inf.* **he let the c. out of the bag** = he revealed the secret; **c. burglar** = burglar who climbs walls or drainpipes to enter a house. (b) *inf.* woman who makes spiteful remarks. **cat•call,** *n.* whistle/hoot (to show displeasure). **cat•fish,** *n.* (*pl.* **catfish**) large ugly freshwater fish with whiskers. **cat•gut**, *n.* gut used as thread. **cat•nap**, *n.* short nap. **cat•nip**, *n.* plant much liked by cats. **cat•walk**, *n.* open metal gangway running along the outside of a ship/building.

ca•tab•o•lism [kæ'tæbɒlɪzm] *n.* breaking down of complex substances into simple chemicals.

cat•a•clysm ['kætəklɪzm] *n.* disaster. **cat•a•clys•mic** [kætə'klɪzmɪk] *adj.* disastrous.

cat•a•combs ['kætəkuːmz] *n. pl.* underground rooms (used in ancient times for burying the dead).

cat•a•lep•sy ['kætəlepsɪ] *n.* state where s.o. becomes unconscious and stiff. **cat•a•lep•tic**, *adj.* referring to catalepsy.

cat•a•log, catalogue ['kætəlɒg] 1. *n.* list of things for sale/in a library/in a museum. 2. *v.* to make a list of books in a library/of treasures in a museum/of things for sale. **cat•a•log•er**, *n.* person who specializes in the making of catalogs.

ca•tal•y•sis [kə'tælɪsɪs] *n.* chemical reaction which is helped by a substance which does not itself change. **cat•a•lyst** ['kætəlɪst] *n.* chemical substance which helps to produce a chemical reaction; anything which helps sth to take place. **cat•a•lyt•ic**, *adj.* referring to catalysis; **c. converter** = device attached to the exhaust pipe of a car to reduce carbon monoxide.

cat•a•ma•ran [kætəmə'ræn] *n.* boat with two parallel hulls.

cat•a•pult ['kætəpʌlt] 1. *n. Brit.* slingshot. **c. launching gear** = mechanism on an aircraft carrier for sending an aircraft into the air. 2. *v.* to send (an aircraft, etc.) into the air; to put (s.o.) into a new job quickly.

cat•a•ract ['kætərækt] *n.* (a) waterfall on a river. (b) film which grows over the eye and eventually prevents you from seeing.

ca•tarrh [kə'tɑː] *n.* type of cold caused by inflammation of the nose and bronchial tubes. **ca•tarrh•al** [kə'tɑːrəl] *adj.* referring to catarrh.

ca•tas•tro•phe [kə'tæstrəfɪ] *n.* disaster. **cat•a•stroph•ic** [kætə'strɒfɪk] *adj.* disastrous.

cat•a•ton•ic [kætə'tɒnɪk] *adj.* (condition) where a patient is either violent or stays without moving at all.

catch [kætʃ] 1. *n.* (*pl.* **-es**) (a) things which have been caught; **we had a good c.** = we caught a lot

of fish; **he's/she's a good c.** = he/she is a good prospective husband/worker. (b) action of catching (a ball, etc.). (c) awkwardness/hitch; **there must be a c. to it** = there must be something wrong with it/there must be a trap; **c. 22** = vicious circle which cannot be escaped from. 2. *v.* (**caught**) (a) to grab hold of (sth) which is moving; **I didn't c. what you said** = I was not able to hear. (b) to get (a disease). (c) to find (s.o.) by surprise. **catch•ing**, *adj.* (disease) which can be caught/which is infectious. **catch•ment area**, *n.* (a) land from which a river gets its water. (b) area served by a government agency, hospital, etc. **catch on**, *v.* (a) to understand. (b) to become fashionable. **catch phrase**, *n.* popular phrase, usu. associated with an entertainer or advertisement. **catch up**, *v.* to move faster than s.o. so as to draw level with. **catch•word**, *n.* popular phrase. **catch•y**, *adj.* (tune) which is easy to remember.

cat•e•chize ['kætɪkaɪz] *v.* to ask questions. **cat•e•chism** ['kætɪkɪzəm] *n.* book of religious instruction; religious classes.

cat•e•go•ry ['kætɪgərɪ] *n.* classification of things/people. **cat•e•gor•ic(al)** [kætɪ'gɒrɪk(l)] *adj.* straightforward/definite. **cat•e•gor•i•cal•ly**, *adv.* definitely.

ca•ter ['keɪtə] *v.* to supply food and drink (at a party, etc.). **ca•ter•er**, *n.* person who supplies food. **cater for**, *v.* to provide for. **ca•ter•ing**, *n.* supplying of food.

cat•er•pil•lar ['kætəpɪlə] *n.* insect larva which turns into a moth or butterfly; **c. track** = endless metal belt running round a pair of wheels (on a tank, etc.); **c. tractor** = tractor which runs on caterpillar tracks.

cat•er•waul ['kætəwɔːl] *v.* to howl (like cats at night).

ca•the•dral [kə'θiːdrəl] *n.* large church which is the seat of a bishop.

cath•er•ine wheel ['kæθrɪnwiːl] *n.* firework which spins around and around.

cath•e•ter ['kæθɪtə] *n.* very thin tube which can be inserted into the body to remove fluid.

cath•ode ['kæθəʊd] *n.* negative electric pole; **c. ray tube** = tube (as in a television set) where a stream of electrons hits a screen.

cath•o•lic ['kæθlɪk] 1. *adj.* (a) wide/general (taste). (b) **Catholic** referring to the Roman Catholic Church. 2. *n.* **Catholic** = s.o. who is a member of the Roman Catholic Church.

æ back, ɑ: farm, ɒ: top, aɪ pipe, aʊ how, aɪə fire, aʊə flower, ɔ: bought, ɔɪ toy, e fed, eəhair, eɪ take, ə afraid, əʊ boat, əʊə lower, vː word, iː heap, ɪ hit, ɪə hear, uː school, ʊ book, ʌ but, b back, d dog, ð then, dʒ just, f fog, g go, h hand, j yes, k catch, l last, m mix, n nut, ŋ sing, p penny, r round, s some, ʃ short, t too, tʃ chop, θ thing, v voice, w was, z zoo, ʒ treasure

ca•thol•i•cism [kə'θɒlɪsɪzəm] *n.* beliefs of the Roman Catholic church.

cat•kin ['kætkɪn] *n.* flower of a willow or hazel tree.

cat•sup ['kætsəp] *n. see* **ketchup.**

cat•tle ['kætl] *n. pl.* animals of the cow family (such as bulls, calves, oxen, etc.).

cat•ty ['kætɪ] *adj.* (**-ier, -iest**) nasty/sharp-tongued (woman).

cau•cus ['kɔ:kəs] *n.* (*pl.* **-es**) group of party leaders who plan electoral strategy and choose candidates.

caught [kɔ:t] *v. see* **catch.**

caul•dron, caldron ['kɔ:ldrən] *n.* large deep pan for cooking.

cau•li•flow•er ['kɒlɪflauə] *n.* cabbagelike vegetable with a large white flower head which is eaten; **c. ear** = permanently swollen ear, found in boxers.

caulk ['kɔ:k] *v.* to fill the cracks in a boat's hull to make it watertight.

cause [kɔ:z] 1. *n.* (a) thing which makes sth happen; **he died from natural causes** = he died naturally, and was not killed in an accident or murdered. (b) reason for doing sth. (c) area of interest/principle/charity to which s.o. gives support. 2. *v.* to make (sth) happen. **cause cé•lèbre,** *n.* famous court case. **caus•al,** *adj.* referring to a cause.

cause•way ['kɔ:zweɪ] *n.* road/path built up on a bank above marshy ground or water.

caus•tic ['kɔ:stɪk] *adj.* (a) burning; **c. soda** = chemical used for cleaning. (b) sharp (wit). **caus•ti•cal•ly,** *adv.* in a sharp/witty way.

cau•ter•ize ['kɔ:təraɪz] *v.* to burn (a wound) to stop infection. **cau•ter•i•za•tion** [kɔ:tərar'zeɪʃn] *n.* cauterizing.

cau•tion ['kɔ:ʃn] 1. *n.* care/precaution. 2. *v.* to warn. **cau•tion•ar•y,** *adj.* which warns. **cau•tious,** *adj.* careful/prudent. **cau•tious•ly,** *adv.* in a cautious way. **cau•tious•ness,** *n.* being cautious.

cav•al•cade ['kævəlkeɪd] *n.* procession (usu. of horseriders/cars).

cav•a•lier [kævə'lɪə] *adj.* high-handed/with no respect for other people or customs.

cav•al•ry ['kævəlrɪ] *n.* soldiers on horseback.

cave [keɪv] 1. *n.* large underground hole in rock or earth; **c. bears** = prehistoric bears which lived in caves; **c. paintings** = paintings on walls of caves done by cavemen. 2. *v.* **to c. in** = to collapse. **cave•man,** *n.* (*pl.* **-men**) primitive person who lived in caves.

ca•ve•at ['kævɪæt] *n.* warning (esp. against doing sth); **c. emptor** = let the buyer beware.

cav•ern ['kævən] *n.* very large cave. **cav•ern•ous,** *adj.* like a cavern.

cav•i•ar(e) ['kævɪɑ:] *n.* very expensive delicacy consisting of the eggs of a sturgeon.

cav•il ['kævɪl] *v.* (**cavilled**) **to c. at sth** = to object to sth.

cav•i•ty ['kævɪtɪ] *n.* hole; **c. wall** = wall made of two rows of bricks with a gap in between.

ca•vort [kə'vɔ:t] *v.* to behave in an excited, merry way.

caw [kɔ:] *v.* to make a croaking sound like a crow.

cay•enne ['keɪen] *n.* type of hot red pepper.

cay•man ['keɪmən] *n.* alligator.

CB ['si:'bi:] *abbrev. for* citizens' band.

cc ['si:si:] *abbrev. for* cubic centimeter.

Cd *symbol for* cadmium.

CD ['si:'di:] *abbrev. for* compact disk.

CD-ROM ['si:di:'rɒm] *abbrev. for* compact disk read-only memory; compact disk that can be read by a computer.

cease [si:s] *v.* to stop. **cease•fire,** *n.* agreement to stop shooting (in a war). **cease•less,** *adj.* without stopping. **cease•less•ly,** *adv.* without stopping.

ce•cum ['si:kəm] *n.* wide part of the large intestine.

ce•dar ['si:də] *n.* large evergreen tree, with sweet-smelling wood; wood from this tree. **ce•dar•wood,** *n.* wood from a cedar.

cede [si:d] *v.* to pass (property/land) **to** s.o. else.

ce•dil•la [sɪ'dɪlə] *n.* accent placed under the letter "c," showing that it is pronounced "s."

cei•lidh ['keɪlɪ] *n.* (*in Scotland, Ireland*) party with performances of songs and dances.

ceil•ing ['si:lɪŋ] *n.* (a) inside roof over a room. (b) upper limit.

cel•an•dine ['seləndaɪn] *n.* small wild plant with yellow flowers.

cel•e•brate ['selɪbreɪt] *v.* (a) to remember a special day with parties and feasts. (b) to perform (a mass). **cel•e•brant,** *n.* priest who celebrates mass. **cel•e•brat•ed,** *adj.* very famous. **cel•e•bra•tion** [selɪ'breɪʃn] *n.* festivity. **ce•leb•ri•ty** [sə'lebrɪtɪ] *n.* (a) famous person. (b) being famous.

ce•ler•i•ac [sɪ'lerɪæk] *n.* vegetable with a thick root tasting like celery.

ce•ler•i•ty [sə'lerɪtɪ] *n.* speed.

cel•er•y ['selərɪ] *n.* white- or green-stemmed plant, eaten as a vegetable, esp. raw.

ce•les•tial [sə'lestjəl] *adj.* (*formal*) heavenly/referring to the sky.

cel•i•bate ['selɪbət] *adj.* not married, esp. because of religious vows. **cel•i•ba•cy,** *n.* state of being celibate.

cell [sel] *n.* (a) room in a prison/in a monastery; (b) basic unit of an organism. (c) basic political group. (d) part of an electric battery. **cel•lu•lar,** *adj.* made up of many small cells.

cel•lu•li•tis, *n.* inflammation of tissue under the skin.

cel•lar ['selə] *n.* underground room or rooms beneath a house.

cel•lo ['tʃeləu] *n.* large stringed musical instrument, smaller than a double bass. **cel•list**, *n.* person who plays the cello.

cel•lo•phane ['seləfeɪn] *n.* trademark for transparent flexible sheet for wrapping or covering.

cel•lu•lose ['seljuləus] *n.* chemical substance found in plants, used for making paper and paint.

Cel•si•us ['selsɪəs] *adj. & n.* (scale for) measuring temperature, where the boiling point of water is 100°, and the freezing point 0°.

Celt [kelt] *n.* descendant of a European people now found in Scotland, Ireland, Wales, Brittany, etc. **Celt•ic**, *adj.* referring to ancient or modern Celts.

ce•ment [sɪ'ment] 1. *n.* (a) powder made from limestone heated with clay, which when mixed with water dries hard. (b) mortar. (c) strong glue. 2. *v.* (a) to stick together with cement. (b) to strengthen/to make close. **ce•ment mix•er**, *n.* machine for mixing cement.

cem•e•ter•y ['semətrɪ] *n.* burial ground.

ce•no•taph ['senətɑːf] *n.* war memorial; empty tomb.

cen•ser ['sensə] *n.* (*in church*) metal receptacle on a chain for burning incense.

cen•sor ['sensə] 1. *n.* official who inspects letters/newspaper articles/plays/books, etc., to see if they can be sent or published. 2. *v.* to forbid the publication of (sth) because it may be obscene or may reveal secrets. **cen•so•ri•ous** [sen'sɔːrɪəs] *adj.* critical/which criticizes. **cen•sor•ship**, *n.* office of censor; act of censoring.

cen•sure ['senʃə] 1. *n.* condemnation/criticism. 2. *v.* to condemn/to criticize (s.o.).

cen•sus ['sensəs] *n.* (*pl.* **-es**) official counting of the population of a country.

cent [sent] *n.* small coin/one-hundredth part of a dollar.

cen•taur ['sentɔː] *n.* mythical animal, half man, half horse.

cen•ten•ar•y [sen'tiːnərɪ] *n.* hundredth anniversary. **cen•te•nar•i•an** [sentɪ'neərɪən] *n.* person who is 100 years old or more. **cen•ten•ni•al** [sen'tenjəl] *adj.* referring to a centenary.

cen•ti•grade ['sentɪgreɪd] *adj. & n.* Celsius.

cen•ti•li•ter, *Brit.* **cen•ti•li•tre** ['sentɪliːtə] *n.* liquid measure, one hundredth part of a liter.

cen•ti•me•ter, *Brit.* **cen•ti•me•tre** ['sentɪmiːtə] *n.* measure of length, one hundredth part of a meter.

cen•ti•pede ['sentɪpiːd] *n.* creeping animal with a large number of legs.

cen•ter, *Brit.* **cen•tre** ['sentə] 1. *n.* (a) middle; **c. party** = political party in the center, neither right nor left. (b) large building containing several different units. (c) player who plays in the middle of the field. 2. *v.* (a) to place in the center. (b) to put the main emphasis (**on**). **cen•tral**, *adj.* in the middle; **c. heating** = heating for a whole building which comes from one heating apparatus. **cen•tral•i•za•tion** [sentrəlar'zeɪʃn] *n.* act of centralizing. **cen•tral•ize**, *v.* to put under the control of a central system. **cen•tral•ly**, *adv.* in the middle.

cen•trif•u•gal [sentrɪ'fjuːgl] *adj.* which tends to go away from the center.

cen•trip•e•tal [sentrɪ'piːtl] *adj.* which tends to go toward the center.

cen•tu•ry ['sentʃərɪ] *n.* hundred years.

ce•ram•ic [sə'ræmɪk] *adj.* made of pottery. **ce•ram•ics**, *n.* art of working in pottery.

ce•re•al ['sɪərɪəl] *n.* (a) grain crop such as wheat, barley, corn, etc. (b) (**breakfast**) **c.** = grain foods eaten with sugar and milk for breakfast.

cer•e•bel•lum [serɪ'beləm] *n.* back part of the brain, which governs balance.

ce•re•bral ['serɪbrəl] *adj.* (a) referring to the brain. (b) intellectual (rather than emotional). **c. palsy** = disorder of the brain which affects control of the voluntary muscles. **ce•re•brum**, *n.* main part of the brain.

cer•e•mo•ny ['serɪmənɪ] *n.* official occasion; solemn behavior on an official occasion; **don't stand on c.** = be informal. **cer•e•mo•ni•al** [serɪ'məunɪəl] 1. *n.* way of conducting a ceremony. 2. *adj.* referring to a ceremony. **cer•e•mo•ni•al•ly**, *adv.* with ceremony. **cer•e•mo•ni•ous**, *adj.* with a lot of ceremony. **cer•e•mo•ni•ous•ly**, *adv.* with a lot of ceremony.

ce•rise [sə'riːz] *n.* bright cherry pink color.

cer•tain ['sɜːtn] *adj.* (a) sure. (b) particular. **cer•tain•ly**, *adv.* of course. **cer•tain•ty**, *n.* (a) being certain. (b) sure/certain thing.

cer•tif•i•cate [sɜː'tɪfɪkət] *n.* official document

æ back, ɑː farm, ɒ top, aɪ pipe, aʊ how, aɪə fire, aʊə flower, ɔː bought, ɔɪ toy, e fed, eəhair, eɪ take, ə afraid, əʊ boat, əʊə lower, vː word, iː heap, ɪ hit, ɪə hear, uː school, ʊ book, ʌ but, b back, d dog, ð then, dʒ just, f fog, g go, h hand, j yes, k catch, l last, m mix, n nut, ŋ sing, p penny, r round, s some, ʃ short, t too, tʃ chop, θ thing, v voice, w was, z zoo, ʒ treasure

which proves/shows sth. **cer•ti•fi•a•ble** [sɜːtɪˈfaɪəbl] *adj.* (person) who should be declared insane; (thing) which should be certified. **cer•ti•fi•ca•tion** [sɜːtɪfɪˈkeɪʃn] *n.* act of certifying. **cer•ti•fy** [ˈsɜːtɪfaɪ] *v.* to write a certificate; to put in writing an official declaration; to declare (s.o.) insane.

cer•ti•tude [ˈsɜːtɪtjuːd] *n.* certainty.

cer•vix [ˈsɜːvɪks] *n.* (*pl.* **-es**) neck, esp. the neck of the womb. **cer•vi•cal**, *adj.* referring to the cervix.

ces•sa•tion [seˈseɪʃn] *n.* stopping.

ces•sion [ˈseʃn] *n.* ceding.

cess•pool, cesspit [ˈsesprt, ˈsespuːl] *n.* underground tank for collecting sewage.

cf. *abbrev for* confer, meaning to compare.

CFS [siːefˈes] *abbrev. for* chronic fatigue syndrome.

cg *abbrev for* centigram.

chafe [tʃeɪf] *v.* (a) to rub/to wear out by rubbing. (b) to become irritated/annoyed. **chaf•ing dish,** *n.* dish which keeps food hot.

chaff [tʃɑːf] *n.* (a) dried corn stalks left after the grain is extracted. (b) good-humored teasing.

chaf•finch [ˈtʃæfɪntʃ] *n.* common pink-breasted finch.

cha•grin [ˈʃægrɪn] *n.* annoyance/sadness.

chain [tʃeɪn] 1. *n.* (a) series of rings joined together; **c. reaction** = events/chemical reactions which build up rapidly. (b) row (of mountains). (c) **c. store** = group of stores belonging to the same company. 2. *v.* to attach with a chain. **chain•saw,** *n.* saw where the teeth are set in a continuous chain driven by a motor. **chain-smoke,** *v.* to smoke (cigarettes) one after the other. **chain-smok•er,** *n.* person who chain-smokes.

chair [ˈtʃeə] 1. *n.* (a) piece of furniture for one person to sit on. (b) position of chairman at a meeting; position of professor at a university; **in the c.** = in position of authority. 2. *v.* to be in charge of (a meeting). **chair•lift,** *n.* chairs on a cable which take skiers up a mountain. **chair•man,** *n.* (*pl.* **-men**) person who is in charge of a meeting; head of a company. **chair•man•ship,** *n.* position of chairman; art of being a chairman. **chair•per•son,** *n.* person who is in charge of a meeting. **chair•wom•an,** *n.* (*pl.* **-women**) woman who is in charge of a meeting.

chaise longue [ʃeɪzˈlɒŋ] *n.* chair with a long seat.

chal•ced•o•ny [kælˈsedənɪ] *n.* whitish stone, a variety of quartz.

cha•let [ˈʃæleɪ] *n.* small (vacation) house, usu. made of wood.

chal•ice [ˈtʃælɪs] *n.* metal cup in which wine is offered at a communion service.

chalk [tʃɔːk] 1. *n.* (a) soft white rock. (b) stick of white or colored material for writing on a blackboard. 2. *v.* to mark or write with chalk. **chalk up,** *v.* to mark (a score/a victory). **chalk•y,** *adj.* white like chalk; gritty like chalk.

chal•lenge [ˈtʃæləndʒ] 1. *n.* invitation to fight/struggle; **to take up the c.** = accept the invitation to fight. 2. *v.* to ask (s.o.) to fight; to ask (s.o.) to prove that they are right. **chal•leng•er,** *n.* person who challenges. **chal•leng•ing,** *adj.* provocative.

cham•ber [ˈtʃeɪmbə] *n.* (a) room/hall. **c. of commerce** = official group of businessmen in a town; **judge's chambers** = office of a judge. (b) space in a piece of machinery, esp. one of the spaces for cartridges in a revolver. (c) space in an organ, such as the heart. (d) **c. music** = music for a few instruments, originally played in a small room. **cham•ber•maid,** *n.* woman who cleans rooms in a hotel. **cham•ber pot,** *n.* pot in which you can urinate, and which is usu. kept in the bedroom.

cha•me•le•on [kəˈmiːlɪən] *n.* lizard which changes its color according to its natural surroundings.

cham•fer [ˈʃæmfə] *v.* to bevel the edge of (sth).

cham•my cloth [ˈʃæmɪleðə] *n.* very soft leather used for washing windows, etc.

cham•ois, *n.* (a) [ˈʃæmwɑː] mountain goat. (b) [ˈʃæmɪ] very soft leather.

champ [tʃæmp] 1. *n. inf.* champion. 2. *v.* to chew hard and noisily; **c. at the bit** = to be impatient to go.

cham•pagne [ʃæmˈpeɪn] *n.* sparkling French white wine.

cham•pi•on [ˈtʃæmpɪən] 1. *n.* best person/animal in a particular competition. 2. *v.* to support (a cause) strenuously. **cham•pi•on•ship,** *n.* (a) support of a cause. (b) contest to determine who is the champion.

chance [tʃɑːns] 1. *n.* (a) luck; **games of c.** = games where you gamble on the possibility of winning; **to take chances** = to take risks. (b) possibility/opportunity. 2. *v.* (a) to happen unexpectedly. (b) to risk. **chanc•y,** *adj. inf.* risky.

chan•cel [ˈtʃɑːnsl] *n.* part of a church near the altar where a choir sits.

chan•cel•ler•y [ˈtʃɑːnsələrɪ] *n.* office of a chancellor; office attached to an embassy.

chan•cel•lor [ˈtʃɑːnsələ] *n.* (a) government minister; (*in Germany/Austria*) = Prime Minister; **C. of the Exchequer** = British finance minister. (b) chief administrative head of a university.

Chan•ce•ry ['tʃɑːnsərɪ] *n.* one of the divisions of the British High Court.

chan•de•lier [ʃændə'lɪə] *n.* lighting device hanging from the ceiling with several branches for holding lights.

chan•dler ['tʃɑːndlə] *n.* person who deals in food and other supplies for ships.

change [tʃeɪndʒ] 1. *n.* (a) difference from what was before; **c. of clothes** = new set of clothes to wear; **to ring the changes** = (i) to ring peals of bells; (ii) to try several alternatives to see which works best. (b) money given back when you pay a larger amount than the price asked; **(small) c.** = money in coins. 2. *v.* (a) to make (sth) different; to become different. (b) to put on different clothes; **changing room** = room where you can change clothes. (c) **(for)** to give sth in place of sth else; **to c. (trains)** = get off one train to catch another. **change•a•bil•i•ty** [tʃeɪndʒə'bɪlɪtɪ] *n.* being changeable. **change•a•ble,** *adj.* which changes often/is likely to change. **change•less,** *adj.* which never changes. **change•ling,** *n.* baby supposed to have been substituted for another by fairies.

chan•nel ['tʃænl] 1. *n.* (a) piece of water connecting two seas. (b) bed (of a stream); ditch/gutter along which liquid can flow. (c) means/ways; **channels of communication** = ways of communicating. (d) frequency band for radio or TV. 2. *v.* **(channeled, channelled)** to direct/to persuade to take a certain direction.

chant [tʃɑːnt] 1. *n.* regular singing of a repeated phrase; monotonous song. 2. *v.* to sing to a regular beat.

chant•ey ['ʃæntɪ] *n* song sung by sailors; **sea c.**

cha•os ['keɪɒs] *n.* confusion. **cha•ot•ic** [keɪ'ɒtɪk] *adj.* confused/disorderly.

chap [tʃæp] 1. *n. inf.* man. 2. *v.* to crack (skin). **chaps,** *n. pl.* wide leggings worn by cowboys.

chap•el ['tʃæpl] *n.* (a) small church; part of a large church with a separate altar. (b) local branch of a union (in the printing and publishing industry).

chap•er•on(e) ['ʃæpərəʊn] 1. *n.* (a) older woman who goes around with a young girl on social visits. (b) older person who is with or supervises young people at social gatherings. 2. *v.* to act as a chaperon.

chap•lain ['tʃæplɪn] *n.* priest (attached to a private individual or in the armed forces). **chap•lain•cy,** *n.* position of chaplain.

chapped [tʃæpt] *adj.* (of skin) cracked (with cold).

chap•ter ['tʃæptə] *n.* (a) division of a book. (b) group of priests who administer a cathedral.

char [tʃɑː] 1. *n.* (a) small freshwater fish. (b) *Brit. inf.* charwoman. 2. *v.* **(charred)** (a) *Brit. inf.* to do housework for s.o.. (b) to burn black.

char•ac•ter ['kærəktə] *n.* (a) central being of a person which makes him/her an individual who is different from all others. (b) person in a play/novel. (c) odd person. (d) letter/symbol used in writing or printing. **char•ac•ter•is•tic** [kærəktə'rɪstɪk] 1. *adj.* special/typical. 2. *n.* special/typical feature. **char•ac•ter•is•ti•cal•ly,** *adv.* typically. **char•ac•ter•i•za•tion** [kærəktərai'zeɪʃn] *n.* indication of character. **char•ac•ter•ize** ['kærəktəraɪz] *v.* to be a typical feature of (sth). **char•ac•ter•less,** *adj.* ordinary/with no special features.

cha•rade [ʃə'rɑːd] *n.* (a) game where spectators have to guess a word from a scene acted by others. (b) action which has no meaning/which is simply a pretense.

char•coal ['tʃɑːkəʊl] *n.* black material formed by partly burned wood; **c. gray** = dark, dull gray color.

chard [tʃɑːd] *n.* (*pl.* **chard**) green vegetable like spinach.

charge [tʃɑːdʒ] 1. *n.* (a) money to be paid; **free of c.** (b) care (of s.o./sth). (c) accusation (of an offense). (d) attack (by soldiers running forward). (e) amount of gunpowder in a cartridge/bomb. (f) amount of electric current. 2. *v.* (a) to make (s.o.) pay **for** sth. (b) **(with)** to accuse (of an offense). (c) to put a cartridge in (a gun); to put electricity into (a battery). (d) to attack (by running forward). **charge•a•ble,** *adj.* which can be charged. **charg•er,** *n.* (a) battle horse. (b) device for putting electricity into a car battery.

char•gé d'af•faires [ʃɑːʒeɪdæ'feə] *n.* deputy of an ambassador; an official who takes the place of an ambassador.

char•i•ot ['tʃærɪət] *n.* two-wheeled vehicle pulled by horses. **char•i•ot•eer** [tʃærɪə'tɪə] *n.* person who drives a chariot.

cha•ris•ma [kə'rɪzmə] *n.* personal appeal. **char•is•mat•ic** [kærɪz'mætɪk] *adj.* which appeals to the people.

char•i•ty ['tʃærɪtɪ] *n.* (a) organization which collects money to help the poor or support some cause; giving of money to the poor. (b)

æ back, aː farm, ɒ top, aɪ pipe, aʊ how, aɪe fire, aʊə flower, ɔː bought, ɔɪ toy, e fed, eəhair, eɪ take, ə afraid, əʊ boat, əʊə lower, vː word, iː heap, ɪ hit, ɪə hear, uː school, ʊ book, ʌ but, b back, d dog, ð then, dʒ just, f fog, g go, h hand, j yes, k catch, l last, m mix, n nut, ŋ sing, p penny, r round, s some, ʃ short, t too, tʃ chop, θ thing, v voice, w was, z zoo, ʒ treasure

kindness (to the poor/the oppressed).—
char•i•ta•ble, *adj.* (a) which refers to a
charity. (b) kind/not critical. **char•i•ta•bly,**
adv. in a charitable way.

char•la•dy ['tʃɑːleɪdɪ] *n. Brit.* charwoman.

char•la•tan ['ʃɑːlətən] *n.* person who pretends
to be an expert, but really is not.

char•lotte ['ʃɑːlɒt] *n.* pudding with fruit and
wafers on the outside.

charm [tʃɑːm] 1. *n.* (a) supposedly magic object;
c. bracelet = bracelet hung with little ornaments. (b) attractiveness. 2. *v.* (a) to be-
witch/to put under a spell; **he has a charmed
life** = he is very lucky. (b) to attract (s.o.)/to
make (s.o.) pleased. **charm•er,** *n.* person
who charms. **charm•ing,** *adj.* attractive.

chart [tʃɑːt] 1. *n.* (a) map of the sea, a river or
lake. (b) diagram showing statistics; **the charts**
= the list of most popular records. 2. *v.* (a) to
make a map of (the sea, a river or lake). (b) to
make a diagram of; to show (information) in a
diagram.

char•ter ['tʃɑːtə] 1. *n.* (a) aircraft hired for a
particular flight. (b) legal document giving
rights or privileges to (a town/a university). 2.
v. to hire (an aircraft or boat).

char•wom•an ['tʃɑːwʊmən] *n. Brit.* (*pl.*
-women) woman who does housework for s.o.

char•y ['tʃeərɪ] *adj.* reluctant to do sth; cautious.

chase [tʃeɪs] 1. *n.* hunt; **wild goose c.** = useless
search. 2. *v.* to run after (s.o.) to try to catch
them. **chas•er,** *n.* alcoholic drink such as
beer, drunk after another, stronger, alcoholic
drink.

chasm ['kæzəm] *n.* huge crack in the ground.

chas•sis ['ʃæsɪ] *n.* (*pl.* **chassis** ['ʃæsɪz]) metal
framework of a car; undercarriage of an aircraft.

chaste [tʃeɪst] *adj.* (sexually) pure. **chas•ti•ty**
['tʃæstɪtɪ] *n.* being chaste.

chas•ten ['tʃeɪsn] *v.* to reprimand; to make
(s.o.) less proud. **chas•tened,** *adj.* meek/less
proud.

chas•tise [tʃæ'staɪz] *v.* (*formal*) to punish.
chas•tise•ment, *n.* punishing.

chas•u•ble ['tʃæzjʊbl] *n.* long sleeveless coat
worn by priests at ceremonies.

chat [tʃæt] 1. *n.* casual friendly talk. 2. *v.* (**chat-
ted**) to talk in a casual and friendly way; *inf.* **to
c. s.o. up** = to get into conversation/to flirt
with. **chat•ty,** *adj.* (person) who likes to chat;
(letter) full of unimportant news.

chat•tel ['tʃætl] *n.* object which you possess.

chat•ter ['tʃætə] 1. *n.* quick talking. 2. *v.* to talk
quickly and not seriously; **his teeth were chattering** = were rattling because of cold.

chat•ter•box, *n.* person who cannot stop
talking.

chauf•feur ['ʃəʊfə] *n.* person who is paid to
drive a car for s.o. else.

chau•vin•ism ['ʃəʊvɪnɪzəm] *n.* excessive pride
in your native country. **chau•vin•ist,** *n.* person who is excessively proud of his/her native
country; **male c.** = man who feels that men are
superior to women. **chau•vin•is•tic** [ʃəʊvɪ-
'nɪstɪk] *adj.* nationalistic.

cheap [tʃiːp] *adj.* (**-er, -est**) (a) not costing a lot
of money; **on the c.** = in the cheapest possible
way. (b) low/sly (joke, etc.). **cheap•en,** *v.* to
reduce the value of (sth). **cheap•ly,** *adv.* not
expensively/for a low price. **cheap•ness,** *n.*
low cost.

cheat [tʃiːt] 1. *n.* person who tricks s.o. so that
he loses. 2. *v.* (a) to trick (s.o.) so that he loses.
(b) to try to win by trickery.

check [tʃek] 1. *n.* (a) making sure; examina-
tion/test. (b) sudden halt. (c) (*in chess*) state
where your opponent has to move to protect
his king. (d) pattern of squares in different
colors. (e) ticket. (f) bill (in a restaurant). (g)
note to a bank asking them to pay money
from one account to another; **c. book** = book
of blank checks; **blank c.** = check which has no
details filled. 2. *v.* (*a*) to make sure; to examine. (b) to bring (s.o.) to a halt. (c) (*in chess*) to
put the opponent's king in danger. (d) to hold
back. (e) to mark with a sign to show that sth
is correct. **checked,** *adj.* with a squared pattern. **check•ers,** *n.* game for two people
played with counters on a board marked with
sixty-four alternately colored squares. **check
in,** *v.* (a) to register when you arrive at a
hotel/at an airport/at work. (b) to hand in
(luggage) for safe keeping. **check•list,** *n.* list
which is used for checking. **check•mate,** (*in
chess*) 1. *n.* position where the king cannot
move. 2. *v.* to put your opponent's king in a
position from which he cannot escape. **check
out,** *v.* (a) to leave a hotel; to take (luggage)
out of safe keeping. (b) to verify/to see if sth is
correct. **check•out,** *n.* cash register in a supermarket. **check o•ver,** *v.* to look over sth
to make sure it is all there/all in working
order. **check•room,** *n.* place where you
leave your coat in a restaurant, theater, etc.
check up on, *v.* to verify/to see if sth is correct. **check•up,** *n.* complete medical examination; general examination (of a car).

check•ers ['tʃəkəz] *n. pl.* squares in a pattern.
check•ered, *adj.* (a) laid out in a pattern of
squares; **c. flag** = flag used to show the end of
a motor race. (b) varied/with good and bad
parts.

cheek [tʃiːk] 1. *n.* (a) fat side of the face on either
side of the nose and below the eye. (b) *inf.*

rudeness. (c) *Sl.* buttock. 2. *v. inf.* to be rude to (s.o.). **cheek•i•ly**, *adv.* in a cheeky way. **cheek•i•ness**, *n.* being cheeky. **cheek•y**, *adj.* (-ier, -iest) rude.

cheep [tʃiːp] 1. *n.* little cry, like that made by a baby bird. 2. *v.* to make a little cry.

cheer ['tʃɪə] 1. *n.* (a) shout of praise or encouragement. **cheers!** = (*when drinking*) here's to you; 2. *v.* (a) to shout encouragement. (b) to comfort; to make happier. (c) **to c. up** = to make or become happier; **c. up!** = don't be miserable. **cheer•ful**, *adj.* happy. **cheer•ful•ly**, *adv.* in a cheerful way. **cheer•ful•ness**, *n.* being cheerful. **cheer•i•ly**, *adv.* in a cheery way. **cheer•ing**, *n.* cheers of encouragement. **cheer•i•o**, *inter. Brit. inf.* goodbye. **cheer•lead•er**, *n.* person who directs the cheering of a crowd. **cheer•less**, *adj.* gloomy/sad. **cheer•y**, *adj.* happy.

cheese [tʃiːz] *n.* solid food made from milk. **cheese•burg•er**, *n.* hamburger with melted cheese on top. **cheese•cake**, *n.* cake of sweet pastry and cream cheese, sometimes with fruit. **cheese•cloth**, *n.* thin cotton cloth such as cheeses are wrapped in. **chees•y**, *adj. inf.* smelling of cheese.

chee•tah ['tʃiːtə] *n.* large animal like a leopard, which can run very fast.

chef [ʃef] *n.* (chief) cook (in a restaurant). **chef d'œu•vre**, *n.* masterpiece.

chem•i•cal ['kemɪkl] 1. *adj.* referring to chemistry. 2. *n.* substance (either natural or man-made) which is formed by reactions between elements. **chem•i•cal•ly**, *adj.* by a chemical process. **chem•ist**, *n.* person who specializes in chemistry. **chem•is•try**, *n.* science of chemical substances, elements, compounds, and their reactions.

che•mo•ther•a•py ['kiːməʊ'θerəpɪ] *n.* using chemical drugs to fight disease.

che•nille [ʃə'niːl] *n.* soft cotton cloth, with a tufted surface.

cheque [tʃek] *n. see* **check.**

cher•ish ['tʃerɪʃ] *v.* to love/to treat kindly; to nourish (a hope).

che•root [ʃə'ruːt] *n.* long thin cigar with both ends open.

cher•ry ['tʃerɪ] *n.* small summer fruit, growing on a long stalk; **c. (tree)** = tree which bears cherries.

cher•ub ['tʃərəb] *n.* small fat childlike angel; child who looks like an angel. **che•ru•bic** [tʃə'ruːbɪk] *adj.* round and innocent (face).

cher•vil ['tʃɜːvɪl] *n.* herb used to flavor soups.

chess [tʃes] *n.* (*no pl.*) game for two people played on a board with sixteen pieces on each side. **chess•board**, *n.* black and white squared board you play chess on. **chess•men**, *n. pl.* pieces used in chess.

chest [tʃest] *n.* (a) piece of furniture, like a large box; **c. of drawers** = piece of furniture with several drawers for keeping clothes in. (b) top front part of the body, where the heart and lungs are; **to get sth off your c.** = to speak frankly about sth which is worrying you.

ches•ter•field ['tʃestəfiːld] *n.* sofa with soft back and arms.

chest•nut ['tʃesnʌt] *n.* (a) bright red-brown nut; large tree which grows these nuts; wood of this tree. (b) red-brown color. (c) red-brown horse. (d) *inf.* old joke; cliché.

chev•ron ['ʃevrən] *n.* sign shaped like a V.

chew [tʃuː] *v.* to make (sth) soft with your teeth. **chew•ing gum**, *n.* sweet gum which you chew but do not swallow. **chew•y**, *adj.* which can be chewed for a long time.

chi•an•ti [ki'æntɪ] *n.* Italian red wine.

chic [ʃiːk] *adj.* elegant; **radical c.** = fashionable left-wing opinions or people who hold them.

chi•cane [ʃɪ'keɪn] 1. *n.* trickery. 2. *v* to deceive by trickery. **chi•can•er•y**, *n.* trickery.

chick [tʃɪk] *n.* baby bird, esp. hen. **chick•pea**, *n.* type of yellow pea. **chick•weed**, *n.* common weed with small yellow flowers.

chick•en ['tʃɪkɪn] 1. *n.* young farmyard bird, esp. young hen; meat from a (young) hen. 2. *v. inf.* **to c. out** = to back out of a fight/argument because you are afraid. **chick•en•feed**, *n.* not much money/profit. **chick•en-liv•ered**, *adj.* scared/frightened. **chick•en•pox**, *n.* disease (usu. of children) which gives red itchy spots.

chic•o•ry ['tʃɪkərɪ] *n.* vegetable of which the leaves are used for salads, and the roots are dried and ground to mix with coffee to make it bitter.

chide [tʃaɪd] *v.* (**chided/chid; was chided**) (*formal*) to criticize.

chief [tʃiːf] 1. *adj.* most important; **commander-in-chief** = commander above all other officers. 2. *n.* leader. **chief•ly**, *adv.* mainly. **chief•tain** ['tʃiːftən] *n.* leader of a tribe.

chiff•chaff ['tʃɪftʃæf] *n.* European warbler.

chif•fon ['ʃɪfɒn] *n.* type of very thin material.

æ back, aː farm, ɒ top, aɪ pipe, aʊ how, aɪə fire, aʊə flower, ɔː bought, ɔɪ toy, e fed, eəhair, eɪ take, ə afraid, əʊ boat, əʊə lower, vː word, iː heap, ɪ hit, ɪə hear, uː school, ʊ book, ʌ but, b back, d dog, ð then, dʒ just, f fog, g go, h hand, j yes, k catch, l last, m mix, n nut, ŋ sing, p penny, r round, s some, ʃ short, t too, tʃ chop, θ thing, v voice, w was, z zoo, ʒ treasure

chi•gnon ['ʃiːnjɒn] *n.* hair tied together in a knot at the back of the head.

chi•hua•hua [tʃɪˈwɑːwɑː] *n.* breed of very small dog.

chil•blain ['tʃɪlbleɪn] *n.* painful swelling on hands, feet, etc., caused by the cold.

child [tʃaɪld] *n. (pl.* **children** ['tʃɪldrən]) young boy or girl; **it's child's play** = it's very easy. **child•birth,** *n.* act of giving birth to a child. **child•hood,** *n.* state of being a child; time when you are a child. **child•ish,** *adj.* like a child; silly/foolish. **child•ish•ly,** *adv.* in a childish way. **child•ish•ness,** *n.* being childish. **child•less,** *adj.* with no children. **child•like,** *adj.* innocent like a child.

Chil•e•an ['tʃɪlɪən] 1. *adj.* referring to Chile. 2. *n.* person from Chile.

chil•i, chilli ['tʃɪlɪ] *n.* dried seed pod of the pepper plant, used to make very hot sauces.

chill [tʃɪl] 1. *n.* (a) coldness in the air. (b) illness caused by cold. 2. *v.* to cool. **chill•i•ness,** *n.* coldness. **chill•y,** *adj.* cold; not very welcoming.

chime [tʃaɪm] 1. *n.* ringing of bells. 2. *v. (of bells)* to ring. **chime in,** *v. inf.* to enter a conversation.

chim•ney ['tʃɪmnɪ] *n.* tall tube or brick column for taking smoke away from a fire. **chim•ney pot,** *n. Brit.* round top to a chimney on a house. **chim•ney stack,** *n.* tall chimney rising above the roof of a factory; group of chimneys on the roof of a house. **chim•ney sweep,** *n.* person who cleans chimneys.

chim•pan•zee, *inf.* **chimp** [tʃɪmpænˈziː, tʃɪmp] *n.* type of intelligent ape from Africa.

chin [tʃɪn] *n.* front part of the bottom jaw.

chi•na ['tʃaɪnə] *n. (no pl.)* porcelain; cups, plates, etc. made of fine white clay. **c. clay** = fine white clay, used for making china.

chin•chil•la [tʃɪnˈtʃɪlə] *n.* gray fur from a small American animal.

chine [tʃaɪn] *v.* to cut the rib bones from the backbone of (a joint of meat).

Chi•nese [tʃaɪˈniːz] 1. *adj.* referring to China. **C. lantern** = garden plant, whose seed pods form bright red balls. 2. *n.* (a) *(pl.* **Chinese**) person from China. (b) language spoken in China.

chink [tʃɪŋk] 1. *n.* (a) little crack. (b) noise of chinking. 2. *v.* to make a noise by knocking glasses/metal objects together.

chintz [tʃɪnts] *n.* thick cotton cloth with bright flower patterns, used for upholstery.

chip [tʃɪp] 1. *n.* (a) little piece of wood/stone, etc.; **to have a c. on your shoulder** = to be permanently indignant about sth where you feel you have been treated unfairly. (b) long piece

of potato fried in oil. (c) small, usu. thin, piece of food; **chocolate chips** = small pieces of chocolate. (d) **silicon c.** = small piece of silicon, able to store data, used in computers. 2. *v.* **(chipped)** to break off a small piece of. **chip•board,** *n.* thick board made of small chips of wood glued together, and used in building. **chip in,** *v.* (a) to contribute. (b) to interrupt. **chip off,** *v.* to break off.

chip•munk ['tʃɪpmʌŋk] *n.* small North American animal, like a striped squirrel.

chi•po•la•ta [tʃɪpəˈlɑːtə] *n.* long thin sausage.

chi•rop•o•dist [kɪˈrɒpədɪst] *n.* person who specializes in chiropody. **chi•rop•o•dy,** *n.* treatment of feet.

chi•ro•prac•tor ['kaɪrəpræktə] *n.* person who heals by massage and manipulation of joints.

chirp [tʃɜːp] 1. *n.* sharp short call of birds/grasshoppers. 2. *v. (of birds/grasshoppers)* to call. **chirp•y,** *adj. inf.* bright and cheerful.

chis•el ['tʃɪzl] 1. *n.* metal tool for cutting small pieces of wood/stone, when hit with a hammer. 2. *v.* **(chiseled, chiselled)** (a) to cut wood/stone with a chisel. (b) *Sl.* to swindle.

chit [tʃɪt] *n.* (a) note/small invoice. (b) young girl.

chit•chat ['tʃɪttʃæt] *n.* gossip/talk.

chit•ter•lings ['tʃɪtəlɪŋz] *n. pl.* pig's intestines prepared as food.

chiv•al•rous ['ʃɪvəlrəs] *adj.* courteous/very polite. **chiv•al•ry,** *n.* politeness/courtesy.

chives [tʃaɪvz] *n. pl.* onionlike plant with small green leaves.

chlo•rine ['klɔːriːn] *n. (element:* Cl) greenish gas used to disinfect swimming pools, etc. **chlo•ride** ['klɔːraɪd] *n.* compound of chlorine with another substance. **chlo•ri•nate** ['klɔːrɪneɪt] *v.* to disinfect with chlorine. **chlo•ri•na•tion** [klɔrɪˈneɪʃn] *n.* disinfecting with chlorine.

chlo•ro•fluor•o•car•bon [klɔːrəʊfluˈɔːrəʊˈkɑːbən] *n.* compound of chlorine fluorine, used in aerosols, which remains in the upper atmosphere and contributes to the greenhouse effect.

chlo•ro•form ['klɒrəfɔːm] 1. *n.* chemical, whose vapor when breathed makes you unconscious. 2. *v.* to make unconscious with chloroform.

chlo•ro•phyll ['klɒrəfɪl] *n.* substance which makes plants green.

chock [tʃɒk] *n.* small block of wood which prevents wheels turning. **chock-a-block, chock-full,** *adj.* completely full.

choc•o•late ['tʃɒklət] *n.* (a) food made from cacao tree seeds; **plain c.** = bitter chocolate; **milk c.** = sweet chocolate made with milk; **hot c.** = hot drink made of powdered chocolate.

(b) small sweet made from chocolate. (c) dark brown color.

choice [tʃɔɪs] *n.* thing which you choose; **I haven't any c.** = I have to do it; **c. peaches** = peaches which have been specially selected.

choir ['kwaɪə] *n.* (a) group of people singing together. (b) part of the church where the choir sits. **choir•boy**, *n.* boy who sings in a church choir. **choir•mast•er**, *n.* person who conducts and rehearses a choir.

choke [tʃəuk] 1. *n.* (a) blockage in the throat. (b) (*in a car engine*) valve which increases the flow of air to the engine; knob on the dashboard which activates this valve. (c) central inedible part of a globe artichoke. 2. *v.* (a) to block (a pipe, etc.). (b) to stop breathing because you have swallowed sth. **choke back,** *v.* to hold back (tears). **chok•er**, *n.* piece of ribbon, etc., worn tightly round the neck. **chok•ing**, *adj.* stifling.

chol•er•a ['kɒlerə] *n.* serious infectious disease causing severe diarrhea.

cho•les•ter•ol [kɒ'lesterɒl] *n.* substance in fats and eggs, also produced by the liver, which deposits fat in the arteries.

chomp [tʃɒmp] *v.* to chew noisily.

choose [tʃuːz] *v.* (**chose; chosen**) to decide to take (sth)/to do one particular thing. **choos•ing**, *n.* act of making a choice. **choos•y**, *adj.* difficult to please.

chop [tʃɒp] 1. *n.* (a) piece of meat with a rib bone. (b) jaw, esp. in animals. 2. *v.* (**chopped**) to cut into small pieces with an ax/a knife. **chop down**, *v.* to cut down (a tree) with an ax. **chop off**, *v.* to cut off. **chop•per**, *n.* (a) ax for cutting meat. (b) *inf.* helicopter. **chop•py**, *adj.* quite rough (sea). **chop su•ey**, *n.* Chinese dish of fried meat and bean sprouts. **chop up**, *v.* to cut up into little bits.

chop•sticks ['tʃɒpstɪks] *n. pl.* long sticks used by oriental people for eating food.

cho•ral ['kɔːrəl] *adj.* referring to a choir.

cho•rale [kɒ'rɑːl] *n.* piece of music for a choir, based on a hymn.

chord [kɔːd] *n.* (a) several notes played together in harmony. (b) line which joins two points on the circumference of a circle.

chore [tʃɔː] *n.* piece of routine work, esp. housework.

cho•re•og•ra•phy [kɒrɪ'ɒɡrəfɪ] *n.* art of working out the steps for a ballet. **cho•re•og•ra•pher**, *n.* person who works out the steps for a ballet.

chor•is•ter ['kɒrɪstə] *n.* person who sings in a choir.

chor•tle ['tʃɔːtl] *v.* to chuckle loudly.

cho•rus ['kɔːrəs] 1. *n.* (a) group of people who sing or dance together. (b) part of a song which is repeated by everyone together. 2. *v.* to say sth all together. **chor•us-girl**, *n.* girl who appears as a member of a chorus in a variety show.

chose [tʃəuz], **cho•sen** ['tʃəuzən] *v. see* **choose.**

chough [tʃʌf] *n.* large black bird with a red bill.

chow [tʃau] *n.* (a) type of Chinese dog with thick fur. (b) *inf.* food.

chow•der ['tʃaudə] *n.* fish soup.

chris•ten ['krɪsn] *v.* (a) to give a name to (a baby) in church; to give a name to (a ship/a bell, etc.) at a ceremony. (b) to use (sth) for the first time. **chris•ten•ing**, *n.* ceremony in church where a baby is given a name.

Chris•tian ['krɪstʃən] 1. *n.* person who believes in Christianity. 2. *adj.* referring to Christianity; **C. name** = first name given at a ceremony in church. **Chris•ti•an•i•ty** [krɪstɪ'ænɪtɪ] *n.* religion based on the doctrine preached by Jesus Christ and followed by Christians ever since.

Christ•mas ['krɪsməs] *n.* Christian holiday on December 25th; **C. Day** = December 25th; **Father C.** = Santa Claus. **Christ•mas•sy**, *adj.* like Christmas.

chro•mat•ic [krə'mætɪk] *adj.* referring to colors or to a musical scale.

chrome [krəum] *n.* chromium; **c. yellow** = bright yellow. **chro•mi•um** ['krəumɪəm] *n.* (*element:* Cr) hard shiny metal which does not rust.

chro•mo•some ['krəuməsəum] *n.* one of several elements which form a biological cell, and which carries the genes.

chron•ic ['krɒnɪk] *adj.* continual/repeating (illness, etc.); *inf.* very bad. **chron•i•cal•ly**, *adv.* very badly.

chron•ic fa•tigue syn•drome *n.* (= myalgic encephalomyelitis/postviral syndrome) long-lasting condition, sometimes occurring after a viral infection, characterized by muscular pain, weakness, and exhaustion.

chron•i•cle ['krɒnɪkl] 1. *n.* record of things which take place; news story. 2. *v.* to write the history of (events) in the order in which they took place. **chron•i•cler**, *n.* person who writes a chronicle.

æ **back,** ɑː **farm,** ɒ **top,** aɪ **pipe,** au **how,** aɪə **fire,** auə **flower,** ɔː **bought,** ɔɪ **toy,** e **fed,** eəhair, eɪ **take,** ə **afraid,** əu **boat,** auə **lower,** vː **word,** iː **heap,** ɪ **hit,** ɪə **hear,** uː **school,** u **book,** ʌ **but,** b **back,** d **dog,** ð **then,** dʒ **just,** f **fog,** g **go,** h **hand,** j **yes,** k **catch,** l **last,** m **mix,** n **nut,** ŋ **sing,** p **penny,** r **round,** s **some,** ʃ **short,** t **too,** tʃ **chop,** θ **thing,** v **voice,** w **was,** z **zoo,** ʒ **treasure**

chro•nol•o•gy [krɒ'nɒlədʒɪ] *n.* statement of the order in which things happened. **chron•o•log•i•cal** [krɒnə'lɒdʒɪkl] *adj.* in order of when the events happened. **chron•o•log•i•cal•ly,** *adv.* in chronological order.

chro•nom•e•ter [krə'nɒmɪtə] *n.* very accurate watch (as used for timing races).

chrys•a•lis ['krɪsəlɪs] *n.* (*pl.* **-es**) hard-cased stage through which a caterpillar passes before turning into a butterfly or moth.

chry•san•the•mum [krɪ'sænθəməm] *n.* bright-colored autumn flower.

chub [tʃʌb] *n.* (*pl.* **chub**) fat river fish.

chub•by ['tʃʌbɪ] *adj.* (**-ier, -est**) quite plump.

chuck [tʃʌk] 1. *n.* (a) part of a drill which holds the bit. (b) type of beef steak. 2. *v. inf.* to throw.

chuck•le ['tʃʌkl] 1. *n.* quiet laugh. 2. *v.* to give a quiet laugh.

chug [tʃʌg] *v.* (**chugged**) to make a regular puffing noise like a steam engine.

chuk•ka ['tʃʌkə] *n.* period of play in a polo match.

chum [tʃʌm] *n. inf.* friend. **chum•my,** *adj.* friendly.

chump [tʃʌmp] *n.* silly fool.

chunk [tʃʌŋk] *n.* large thick piece. **chunk•y,** *adj.* made of large pieces.

church [tʃɜːtʃ] *n.* (*pl.* **-es**) (a) large building for Christian religious ceremonies. (b) group of Christians together. **church•go•er,** *n.* person who goes to church (regularly). **church•ward•en,** *n.* senior member of a parish. **church•yard,** *n.* cemetery round a church.

churl•ish ['tʃɜːlɪʃ] *adj.* rude. **churl•ish•ly,** *adv.* rudely. **churl•ish•ness,** *n.* rudeness.

churn [tʃɜːn] 1. *n.* large metal container for milk; container in which cream is churned. 2. *v.* to turn cream to make butter. **churn out,** *v. inf.* to produce in a series. **churn up,** *v.* to mix/stir up.

chute [ʃuːt] *n.* (a) slide into water (in a swimming pool). (b) slide for sending things to a lower level.

chut•ney ['tʃʌtnɪ] *n.* highly-flavored sauce usu. made with tomatoes, onions, vinegar and spices.

CIA [siːaɪ'eɪ] *abbreviation for* Central Intelligence Agency.

CID [siːaɪ'diː] *abbreviation for* Criminal Investigation Department of Scotland Yard.

ci•der ['saɪdə] *n.* alcoholic drink made from fermented apple juice.

c.i.f. [siːaɪ'ef] *abbrev for* cost, insurance, freight.

ci•gar [sɪ'gɑː] *n.* tight roll of tobacco leaves which you can light and smoke.

cig•a•rette [sɪgə'ret] *n.* chopped tobacco rolled in very thin paper which you can light and smoke. **cigarette case,** *n.* special case for holding cigarettes. **cigarette end,** *n.* end of a cigarette which has been smoked. **cig•ar•ette hold•er,** *n.* holder for putting cigarettes in to smoke.

cinch [sɪntʃ] *n. inf.* (a) thing which is very easy to do. (b) sth. which is certain to work.

cin•ders ['sɪndəz] *n. pl.* lumps of coarse ash left after coal has been burned.

cine- [sɪnɪ] *prefix* referring to motion pictures.

cin•e•ma ['sɪnəmə] *n.* (a) theater for showing motion pictures. (b) art of making motion pictures.

cin•e•ra•ri•a [sɪnə'reərɪə] *n.* houseplant with blue, pink, or purple flowers.

cin•na•mon ['sɪnəmən] *n.* spice made from the bark of a tropical tree.

ci•pher ['saɪfə] *n.* (a) code/secret message. (b) monogram/initials of a name linked together artistically. (c) zero; person of no importance.

cir•ca ['sɜːkə] *prep.* (used of dates) about.

cir•cle ['sɜːkl] 1. *n.* (a) line forming a round shape. (b) row of seats in a theater. (c) group of people/society. 2. *v.* (a) to go around in a ring. (b) to draw a circle around (sth).

cir•cuit ['sɜːkɪt] *n.* (a) trip around sth. (b) area visited by a judge who travels from court to court. (c) path of electricity; **printed c. board** = flat card with metal tracks printed on it to form an electric circuit; **short c.** = fault (caused by crossed wires, etc.) when electricity follows a shorter path than usual; **closed c. television** = private television operating over a short area by cable. **cir•cu•i•tous** [sə'kjuːɪtəs] *adj.* roundabout (way).

cir•cu•lar ['sɜːkjulə] *adj. & n.* (sth) round in shape; publicity leaflet given out to many people. **cir•cu•lar•ize,** *v.* to send circulars to (people).

cir•cu•late ['sɜːkjuleɪt] *v.* (a) to distribute/to pass around. (b) to move around. **cir•cu•la•tion** [sɜːkju'leɪʃn] *n.* (a) act of circulating; **bank notes in c.** = notes which are in use. (b) movement of blood around the body. (c) number of copies of a newspaper, etc., which are sold. **cir•cu•la•to•ry,** *adj.* referring to circulation of the blood.

cir•cum•cise ['sɜːkəmsaɪz] *v.* to remove the foreskin of (a male person). **cir•cum•ci•sion** [sɜːkəm'sɪʒn] *n.* act of removing the foreskin.

cir•cum•fer•ence [sə'kʌmfərəns] *n.* (distance around) the edge of a circle.

cir•cum•lo•cu•tion [sɜːkəmlə'kjuːʃn] *n.* roundabout way of saying sth.

cir•cum•nav•i•gate [sɜːkəm'nævɪgeɪt] *v.* (*formal*) to sail around (the world).

cir•cum•nav•i•ga•tion [sɜːkəmnævɪ-ˈgeɪʃn] *n.* sailing around the world.

cir•cum•scribe [sɜːkəmˈskraɪb] *v. (formal)* to draw a line around sth; to set limits to sth. **cir•cum•scrip•tion** [sɜːkəmˈskrɪpʃən] *n.* limiting; a limited area.

cir•cum•spect [ˈsɜːkəmspekt] *adj.* very careful.

cir•cum•stan•ces [ˈsɜːkəmstənsɪz] *n. pl.* (a) way in which something took place; **under the c.** = as things have turned out like this/as it happens. (b) state of one's finances. **cir•cum•stan•tial** [sɜːkəmˈstænʃl] *adj.* giving details; **c. evidence** = evidence which suggests sth but does not offer firm proof. **cir•cum•stan•ti•ate**, *v.* to give details to prove (sth).

cir•cum•vent [sɜːkəmˈvent] *v.* to avoid. **cir•cum•ven•tion**, *n.* avoidance.

cir•cus [ˈsɜːkəs] *n. (pl. -es)* traveling show, often given under a large tent, with animals, clowns, etc.

cir•rho•sis [sɪˈrəʊsɪs] *n.* disease of the liver caused esp. by alcohol.

cir•rus [ˈsɪrəs] *n.* small very high fleecy cloud.

CIS [siːaɪˈes] *abbrev. for* Commonwealth of Independent States.

cis•tern [ˈsɪstən] *n.* water tank.

cit•a•del [ˈsɪtədəl] *n.* fort guarding a town.

cite [saɪt] *v.* (a) to quote (a reference, a person) as proof. (b) to call (s.o.) to appear in court. **ci•ta•tion** [saɪˈteɪʃn] *n.* (a) official document recognizing an act of bravery. (b) quotation of sth as a reference or proof. (c) summons to appear in court.

cit•i•zen [ˈsɪtɪzn] *n.* (a) inhabitant of a town. (b) person with full rights as an inhabitant of a country; **citizen's arrest** = arrest of a suspected criminal by an ordinary citizen; **citizens' band** = private radio, mainly used by drivers of road vehicles. **cit•i•zen•ship**, *n.* state of being a citizen.

cit•ric [ˈsɪtrɪk] *adj.* **c. acid** = acid found in citrus fruit. **cit•rus** [ˈsɪtrəs] *n.* **c. fruit** = fruit such as oranges, lemons or grapefruit.

cit•y [ˈsɪtɪ] *n.* (a) very large town. (b) *(U.S.)* incorporated municipality with a charter from the state.

civ•et [ˈsɪvɪt] *n.* wild cat, which provides a substance used in making perfume.

civ•ic [ˈsɪvɪk] *adj.* referring to a city; **c. center** = social/sports center run by a city; **c. authorities** = leaders of a city. **civ•ics,** *n.* study of municipal affairs.

civ•il [ˈsɪvl] *adj.* (a) belonging to the general public, not to the military; **c. service** = the government bureaucracy; **c. servant** = person who works in a government department. (b) referring to the ordinary citizen; **c. rights** = the rights of a citizen; **c. rights movement** = campaign to ensure that all citizens have equal rights; **c. war** = war between groups in the same country; **c. defense** = defense by ordinary citizens, not the military; **c. law** = law referring to the private matters, rather than criminal or military matters. **c. action** = court action brought by one citizen against another; **c. engineer** = person who designs roads, bridges, etc. (c) polite. **ci•vil•ian** [sɪˈvɪljən] *adj. & n.* (person) not belonging to the armed forces; private citizen. **ci•vil•i•ty,** *n.* politeness. **civ•il•ly,** *adv.* politely.

civ•i•lize [ˈsɪvɪlaɪz] *v.* (a) to educate (primitive people) to a higher level of society. (b) to make (s.o.) less rude/uncouth. **civ•i•li•za•tion** [sɪvɪlaɪˈzeɪʃn] *n.* regular civilized way of conducting society; making s.o. civilized.

civ•vy *(usu.* [ˈsɪvɪ] **civ•vies),** *n. pl. inf.* civilian clothes.

CJD [siːdʒeɪˈdiː] *abbrev. for* Creutzfeldt-Jakob Disease.

Cl *symbol for* chlorine.

clad [klæd] *adj.* covered. **clad•ding,** *n.* material used for the outside covering of walls.

claim [kleɪm] **1.** *n.* *(a*) demand. (b) statement/assertion. **2.** *v.* (a) to demand as one's right. (b) to state/to assert (without any proof). (c) to say you own (sth) which has been left/lost. **claim•ant,** *n.* person who claims a right.

clair•voy•ant [kleəˈvɔɪənt] *n.* person who can see in his mind things which are happening elsewhere/who can foretell the future. **clair•voy•ance,** *n.* act of communicating with spirits/of foretelling the future.

clam [klæm] *n.* large shellfish with a hinged shell.

clam•ber [ˈklæmbə] *v.* to climb with difficulty.

clam•my [ˈklæmɪ] *adj. (-ier, -iest)* damp and cold; humid (weather). **clam•mi•ness,** *n.* being clammy.

clam•or, *Brit.* **cla•mour** [ˈklæmə] **1.** *n.* shouting. **2.** *v.* to shout/to demand loudly. **clam•or•ous,** *adj.* noisy/shouting.

clamp [klæmp] **1.** *n.* metal pieces which are

æ back, a: farm, ɒ: top, aɪ pipe, aʊ how, aɪə fire, aʊə flower, ɔ: bought, ɔɪ toy, e fed, eəhair, eɪ take, ə afraid, əʊ boat, əʊə lower, ɜ: word, iː heap, ɪ hit, ɪə hear, uː school, ʊ book, ʌ but, b back, d dog, ð then, dʒ just, f fog, g go, h hand, j yes, k catch, l last, m mix, n nut, ŋ sing, p penny, r round, s some, ʃ short, t too, tʃ chop, θ thing, v voice, w was, z zoo, ʒ treasure

screwed tightly to hold sth together. 2. *v.* (a) to hold tight with a clamp. (b) **to c. down on** = to stop (petty crime, etc.). **clamp•down**, *n.* **(on)** severe action to stop sth.

clan [klæn] *n.* Scottish family tribe. **clan•nish**, *adj.* loyal to the clan; supporting your own group. **clan•nish•ness**, *n.* being clannish. **clans•man**, *n.* (*pl.* -**smen**) member of a clan.

clan•des•tine [klæn'destɪn] *adj.* secret/undercover.

clang [klæŋ] 1. *n.* loud noise of metal ringing. 2. *v.* to make a loud ringing noise.

clank [klæŋk] 1. *n.* noise of metal hitting metal. 2. *v.* to make a noise of metal hitting other metal.

clap [klæp] 1. *n.* (a) beating of hands against each other to show pleasure. (b) friendly tap (with the hand). (c) loud noise (of thunder). (d) *Sl.* gonorrhea. 2. *v.* (**clapped**) (a) to beat your hands together to show you are pleased. (b) to give (s.o.) a friendly tap with the hand. (c) to put (s.o. in jail) suddenly. **clap•per**, *n.* swinging metal piece inside a bell which strikes the bell. **clap•board**, *n.* black board with a striped hinged section at the top, used in film-making to indicate the start of a scene. **clap•ping**, *n.* applause.

clap•trap ['klæptræp] *n. inf.* nonsense.

clar•et ['klærət] *n.* red Bordeaux wine.

clar•i•fy ['klærɪfaɪ] *v.* (a) to make clear. (b) to heat (butter, etc.) until it becomes transparent. **clar•i•fi•ca•tion** [klærɪfɪ'keɪʃn] *n.* making clear/explanation.

clar•i•net [klærɪ'net] *n.* wind instrument in the woodwind group. **clar•i•net•ist**, *n.* person who plays a clarinet.

clar•i•on ['klærɪən] *n.* trumpet; **c. call** = loud clear call.

clar•i•ty ['klærɪtɪ] *n.* clearness.

clash [klæʃ] 1. *n.* (*pl.* -**es**) (a) loud noise of things hitting each other. (b) battle/conflict; shock of two colors seen side by side. 2. *v.* (a) to bang together making a loud noise. (b) not to agree/to be in conflict. (c) to fight.

clasp [klɑːsp] 1. *n.* (a) device for holding sth shut. (b) brooch. (c) act of holding in your hand. 2. *v.* to hold (sth) tight. **clasp•knife**, *n.* (*pl.* -**knives**) pocket knife which folds.

class [klɑːs] 1. *n.* (*pl.* -**es**) (a) group of people with the same position in society; **middle c.** = class of professional people/bourgeoisie; **working c.** = class of people who do mainly manual labor; **upper c.** = the rich/the aristocracy. (b) group of people (usu. children) who study together. (c) category/group into which things are classified; **first c.** = very good; **to travel first c.** = in the most expensive seats; **tourist c./economy c.** = less expensive seats on aircraft and ships. 2. *v.* to put (sth) in a cate-

gory. **class ac•tion**, *n.* legal action taken by one or more individuals representing the interests of a large group, e.g. smokers. **clas•si•fi•a•ble**, *adj.* which can be classified. **clas•si•fi•ca•tion** [klæsɪfɪ'keɪʃn] *n.* way of ordering things into categories. **clas•si•fy** ['klæsɪfaɪ] *v.* to arrange things into groups; **classified information** = information which is officially secret. **class•less**, *adj.* with no division into social classes. **class•room**, *n.* room in which a class is taught. **class•y**, *adj.* (-**ier**, -**iest**) *inf.* chic/expensive-looking.

clas•sic ['klæsɪk] 1. *n.* (a) great book/play/piece of music/writer/composer, etc. (b) **the classics** = Ancient Greek and Roman literature, culture, etc. 2. *adj.* (a) (style) which is elegant and based on that of Greek or Roman architecture/literature, etc. (b) typical. **clas•si•cal**, *adj.* (a) referring to the classics. (b) serious (music). **clas•si•cist**, *n.* person who studies the classics.

clat•ter ['klætə] 1. *n.* noise of things hitting together. 2. *v.* to make a noise.

clause [klɔːz] *n.* (a) paragraph in a treaty or legal document. (b) part of a sentence; **main c.** = the central part of a sentence; **subordinate clauses** = clauses which depend on the main clause.

claus•tro•pho•bi•a [klɒstrə'fəʊbɪə] *n.* terror of being shut inside a closed place. **claus•tro•pho•bic**, *adj.* referring to claustrophobia.

clav•i•chord ['klævɪkɔːd] *n.* old musical instrument like a small piano, with a very quiet sound.

clav•i•cle ['klævɪkl] *n.* collarbone.

claw [klɔː] 1. *n.* (a) nail (of animal/bird). (b) pincer/part of a crab or lobster which pinches. 2. *v.* to scratch with a claw. **claw ham•mer**, *n.* hammer with the back of the head curved and split for removing nails.

clay [kleɪ] *n.* stiff soil found in river valleys; stiff earth used for making bricks or china. **clay•ey**, *adj.* containing clay. **clay•more**, *n.* sword used in Scotland.

clean [kliːn] 1. *adj.* (-**er**, -**est**) not dirty; **c. break** = complete break; **to come c.** = to confess (to a crime, etc.). 2. *adv.* completely. 3. *v.* to remove dirt. **clean•er**, *n.* person/thing which removes dirt; **vacuum c.** = machine for sucking up dirt; (**dry**) **cleaner's** = store where clothes can be taken to be cleaned; **oven c.** = strong substance for cleaning dirty ovens. **clean•ing**, *n.* removing dirt. **clean•li•ness**, **cleanness** ['klenlɪnəs, 'kliːnnəs] *n.* state of being clean. **clean•ly**, *adv.* in a clean way. **clean•shav•en**, *adj.* with no beard or mustache.

cleanse [klenz] *v.* to make very clean; **cleansing cream** = cream for cleansing the skin. **cleans•er**, *n.* material which removes dirt.

clear ['klɪə] 1. *adj.* (-er, -est) (a) pure; transparent. (b) with nothing in the way. (c) easily understood. (d) complete. (e) free (of). 2. *adv.* in a clear way. 3. *v.* (a) to remove (obstacles); **to c. the table** = to remove dirty dishes and cutlery; **to c. one's throat** = to cough slightly to get ready for speaking. (b) to make clear/pure; to become clear/pure. (c) to show that s.o. is innocent. (d) not to hit. **clear•ance**, *n.* (a) act of removing obstacles; act of removing plants from land; **c. sale** = sale where all the goods are reduced in price to clear them from the shelves. (b) space for sth to pass through. **clear a•way**, *v.* to remove (sth) which is in the way; to remove (dirty dishes) from a table. **clear-cut**, *adj.* definite/distinct. **clear-head•ed**, *adj.* clever/with a sharp understanding. **clear•ing**, *n.* (a) act of removing obstacles. (b) area in a wood where the trees have been cut down. **clear•ly**, *adv.* (a) in a way which is easily understood or heard. (b) obviously. **clear•ness**, *n.* being clear. **clear off**, *v.* (a) to pay off (one's debts). (b) to run away. **clear out**, *v.* (a) to empty by throwing out. (b) to go away. **clear up**, *v.* (a) to make clear/pure. (b) to become brighter.

cleat [kliːt] *n.* wooden/metal device for attaching ropes on ships.

cleave [kliːv] *v.* (**clove/cleft; has cloven/cleft**) (*old*) (a) to split. (b) to cling (to). **cleav•age** ['kliːvɪdʒ] *n.* space between the breasts. **cleav•er** ['kliːvə] *n.* large ax used by butchers.

clef [klef] *n.* sign at the beginning of a piece of music which shows whether it is bass or treble.

cleft [kleft] *adj. & n.* split; **c. palate** = split roof of the mouth.

clem•a•tis [klə'meɪtɪs] *n.* climbing garden plant with large purple or pink flowers.

clem•ent ['klemənt] *adj.* (*formal*) kind/soft (weather). **clem•en•cy**, *n.* mercy (to a criminal).

clem•en•tine ['klemənti:n] *n.* small sweet orange with a skin which is easily removed.

clench [klentʃ] *v.* to close tightly.

clere•sto•ry ['klɪəstɔːrɪ] *n.* high row of windows in a medieval church.

cler•gy ['klɜːdʒɪ] *n.* persons ordained to perform religious services. **cler•gy•man**, *n.* (*pl.* -men) member of the clergy, as a priest or minister.

cler•ic ['klerɪk] *n.* (*formal*) clergyman. **cler•i•cal** ['klerɪkl] *adj.* (a) referring to a clerk. (b) referring to clergy; **c. collar** = stiff white collar fastening at the back, worn by some members of the clergy.

cler•i•hew ['klerɪ'hjuː] *n.* short four-lined humorous poem.

clerk [klɜːk] *n.* (a) person who works in an office; (b) official in charge of records, as for a town, court, etc. (c) salesperson in a store.

clev•er ['klevə] *adj.* intelligent/able to learn quickly; **c. with one's hands** = good at making things. **clev•er•ly**, *adv.* in a clever way. **clev•er•ness**, *n.* being clever.

cli•ché ['kliːʃeɪ] *n.* saying/phrase which is frequently used.

click [klɪk] 1. *n.* short sharp sound. 2. *v.* (a) to make a short sharp sound; **to c. one's heels** = to bring the heels of one's boots together to make a noise. (b) to be surprisingly successful; **it suddenly clicked** = it was suddenly understood. (c) to press and release a button on a mouse linked to a computer in order to select a function.

cli•ent ['klaɪənt] *n.* person with whom you do business/to whom you give a service. **cli•en•tele** [kliːɒn'tel] *n.* all the customers (of a business).

cliff [klɪf] *n.* high rock face, usu. by the sea. **cliff•hang•er**, *n.* suspense story; situation where one does not know what will happen.

cli•mac•ter•ic [klaɪ'mæktərɪk] *n.* critical point in life, when changes take place in your body.

cli•mate ['klaɪmət] *n.* general weather conditions. **cli•mat•ic** [klaɪ'mætɪk] *adj.* referring to climate. **cli•ma•tol•o•gy** [klaɪmə'tɒlədʒɪ] *n.* study of climate.

cli•max ['klaɪmæks] *n.* (*pl.* -es) peak/greatest amount/highest point. **cli•mac•tic** [klaɪ'mæktɪk] *adj.* referring to a climax.

climb [klaɪm] 1. *n.* act of going up; place where you go up. 2. *v.* to go up. **climb down**, *v.* to come down a mountain/a ladder. **climb•er**, *n.* person who climbs; plant which climbs. **climb•ing**, *n.* sport of climbing mountains.

clime [klaɪm] *n.* (*formal*) country.

clinch [klɪntʃ] 1. *n.* (*pl.* -es) (a) (*in boxing*) a position where both boxers hold on to each other. (b) *inf.* close embrace. 2. *v.* (a) (*in boxing*) to hold tight to the other boxer. (b) to settle (a deal).

cling [klɪŋ] *v.* (**clung**) to hold tight **to** (sth).

æ back, aː farm, ɒ top, aɪ pipe, aʊ how, aɪe fire, aʊə flower, ɔː bought, ɔɪ toy, e fed, eəhair, eɪ take, ə afraid, əʊ boat, əʊə lower, ɜː word, iː heap, ɪ hit, ɪə hear, uː school, ʊ book, ʌ but, b back, d dog, ð then, dʒ just, f fog, g go, h hand, j yes, k catch, l last, m mix, n nut, ŋ sing, p penny, r round, s some, ʃ short, t too, tʃ chop, θ thing, v voice, w was, z zoo, ʒ treasure

clin•ic ['klɪnɪk] *n.* specialized medical office or hospital. **clin•i•cal,** *adj.* involving direct observation and treatment of patients as opposed to experimentation and research. **c. thermometer** = thermometer for taking a person's temperature; **to take a c. view of something** = to look at it coolly. **clin•i•cal•ly,** *adv.* in a clinical way. **cli•ni•cian,** *n.* doctor who treats patients directly, as in a hospital.

clink [klɪŋk] 1. *n.* (a) noise of glasses/metal objects hitting each other. (b) *Sl.* prison. 2. *v. (of glasses/metal objects)* to make a noise (when hitting together).

clink•er ['klɪŋkə] *n.* hard waste material after coal has been burned.

clip [klɪp] 1. *n.* (a) piece of bent wire for attaching papers, etc., together. (b) *inf.* sharp blow; smack. (c) *inf.* **at a good c.** = quite fast. 2. *v.* **(clipped)** (a) to attach (papers) together. (b) to cut with scissors or shears. **clip•per,** *n. (old)* fast sailing vessel, used mainly for carrying tea. **clip•pers,** *n. pl.* small scissors; instrument with a movable blade for cutting hair. **clip•ping,** *n.* small piece cut out of a newspaper, cut off a hedge, etc.

clique [kliːk] *n.* small select group of people. **cli•quey, cliquish,** *adj.* like a clique.

clit•o•ris ['klɪtərɪs] *n.* small erectile part (in female genitals).

cloak [kləʊk] 1. *n.* long outer coat with no sleeves. 2. *v.* to cover/to hide as if with a cloak. **cloak•room,** *n.* place where you leave your coat in a restaurant/theater, etc.

clob•ber ['klɒbə] *v. sl.* to hit hard, esp. many times.

cloche [klɒʃ] *n.* (a) a type of close-fitting women's hat. (b) small glass or polythene tent used in gardening for covering young plants.

clock [klɒk] 1. *n.* machine for telling the time; **alarm c.** = clock which rings a bell to wake you up; **to work right around the c.** = to work all day long. 2. *v.* **to c. in/out,** = to record your time of arrival or departure at work. **clock•wise,** *adv.* in the same direction as the hands of a clock. **clock•work,** *n. (no pl.)* machine which works on a spring which is wound up with a key; **like c.** = smoothly.

clod [klɒd] *n.* large lump of earth.

clog [klɒg] 1. *n.* wooden shoe. 2. *v.* **(clogged)** to block.

cloi•son•né ['klwæzɒneɪ] *n.* type of enamel decoration, where the sections of enamel are separated by little ridges of metal.

clois•ter ['klɔɪstə] *n. (in a monastery)* covered walk round a courtyard. **clois•tered,** *adj.* shut up (as in a monastery).

clone [kləʊn] *n.* plant/animal which is grown from a piece of another plant/animal, and not from a seed.

close¹ [kləʊs] 1. *adj.* **(-er, -est)** (a) very near **(to);** **to keep a c. watch on someone** = to watch someone attentively; **c. election** = election where the winner is separated from the loser by only a small number of votes. (b) shut. (c) stuffy. (d) very friendly. 2. *adv.* near; **she is c. to forty. close-fist•ed,** *adj.* miserly. **close-fit•ting,** *adj.* tight (dress). **close•ly,** *adv.* (a) attentively. (b) tightly. **close•ness,** *n.* (a) nearness. (b) stuffiness. **close-up,** *n.* photograph taken at very close range.

close² [kləʊz] 1. *n.* end. 2. *v.* (a) to shut. (b) to end (an argument/a debate). **closed,** *adj.* shut; **c. shop** = system whereby a factory or business can only employ members of a certain labor union. **close down,** *v.* to shut a factory or business, etc., (permanently); to stop transmitting radio/TV programs. **close in,** *v.* (a) **the days are closing in** = the period of daylight is becoming shorter. (b) **to close in on s.o.** = to run s.o. to earth/to come close to s.o. one is chasing. **clos•ing,** 1. *adj.* final; **c. bid** = last bid at an auction. 2. *n.* shutting (of a store, etc.); **c. time** = time when a store, etc., closes. **clo•sure** ['kləʊʒə] *n.* shutting.

clos•et ['klɒzɪt] 1. *n.* (a) small, private room. (b) small room or cupboard, as for clothes, linens, etc. 2. *v.* to shut oneself up **with** s.o.

clot [klɒt] 1. *n.* lump of solidified blood, etc. 2. *v.* **(clotted)** to form lumps; **clotted cream** = cream which has been heated until it solidifies.

cloth [klɒθ] *n.* (a) piece of woven material. (b) woven material.

clothe [kləʊð] *v.* to dress. **clothes** [kləʊðz] *n. pl.* things you wear; **c. brush** = brush for cleaning clothes; **c. line** = long rope for hanging wet clothes to dry; **c. horse** = wooden or metal frame for hanging clothes to air or dry; **c. pin** = small plastic or wooden clip for attaching wet clothes to a clothes line. **cloth•ing** [kləʊðɪŋ] *n. (no pl.)* clothes.

cloud [klaʊd] 1. *n.* mass of vapor/smoke (in the air); **under a c.** = (a) gloomy; (b) unpopular with the authorities. 2. *v.* to hide with a cloud. **cloud•burst,** *n.* sudden downpour of rain. **cloud-capped,** *adj.* (mountain) topped with clouds. **cloud•i•ness,** *n.* being cloudy. **cloud•less,** *adj.* (sky) with no clouds. **cloud•y,** *adj.* **(-ier, -iest)** covered with clouds; not clear/not transparent.

clout [klaʊt] 1. *n.* (a) blow (with the fist). (b) *inf.* power/influence. 2. *v.* to give (s.o.) a blow with the fist.

clove [kləʊv] *n.* (a) spice formed by small dried flower buds of a tropical tree. (b) piece of garlic. **clove hitch,** *n.* type of knot.

clo•ven ['kləʊvn] *adj.* split.

clo•ver ['kləʊvə] *n.* common weed, used as fodder for cattle; **to be in c.** = to live very comfortably; **c. leaf intersection** = crossroads formed by two highways and their linking roads, which when seen from above looks like the leaf of clover.

clown [klaʊn] 1. *n.* (a) man who makes people laugh in a circus. (b) stupid fool. 2. *v.* (**about, around**) to play the fool.

cloy [klɔɪ] *v.* to be sickly sweet.

club [klʌb] 1. *n.* (a) large stick; **golf c.** = long stick with which you hit the ball when playing golf. (b) one of the four suits in a pack of cards. (c) group of people who allow others to join them (usu. on payment of a fee); **golf c.; drama c.** 2. *v.* (**clubbed**) (a) to hit with a club. (b) to unite; join **together**. **club•foot**, *n.* deformed foot. **club•house**, *n.* house where members of a club meet.

cluck [klʌk] *v.* (*of hen*) to make a low noise in the throat.

clue [kluː] *n.* information which helps you solve a mystery/puzzle; **I haven't a c.** = I do not know at all. **clue•less**, *adj. inf.* stupid.

clump [klʌmp] 1. *n.* group of shrubs, trees, etc. 2. *v.* to move making a dull noise.

clum•sy ['klʌmzɪ] *adj.* (-**ier**, -**iest**) not graceful; frequently breaking things. **clum•si•ly**, *adv.* in a clumsy way. **clum•si•ness**, *n.* being clumsy.

clung [klʌŋ] *v. see* **cling**.

clunk [klʌŋk] *n.* noise of heavy metal objects hitting each other.

clus•ter ['klʌstə] 1. *n.* group of small objects together. 2. *v.* to group (**together**).

clutch [klʌtʃ] 1. *n.* (*pl.* -**es**) (a) several eggs laid together in a nest. (b) clasp; **into his clutches** = into his hands. (c) mechanism for changing the gears in a car; pedal which works the clutch; **to let in the c.** = to make the gears connect; **to let out the c.** = to disengage the engine from the gears. 2. *v.* to grab.

clut•ter ['klʌtə] 1. *n.* mass of things left lying about. 2. *v.* to fill (a room) with a mass of things.

cm *abbrev. for* centimeter.

co- [kəʊ] *prefix meaning* together.

co. [kəʊ, 'kʌmpənɪ] *abbrev. for* company.

Co *symbol for* cobalt.

CO ['siː'əʊ] commanding officer.

c/o *abbrev. for* care of.

coach [kəʊtʃ] 1. *n.* (*pl.* -**es**) (a) large bus for long distance traveling. (b) passenger car (on a train). (c) person who trains sportsmen, etc. 2.

v. (a) to train (sportsmen). (b) to give private lessons to.

co•ag•u•late [kəʊ'ægjuleɪt] *v.* to form into lumps/to cake. **co•ag•u•la•tion** [kəʊægjuˈleɪʃn] *n.* forming into lumps/caking.

coal [kəʊl] *n.* black mineral used as fuel; **coal-fired boiler** = boiler which is heated by coal. **coal•field**, *n.* area of coal underground. **coal•mine**, *n.* mine where coal is dug. **coal•min•er**, *n.* person who mines coal. **coal scut•tle**, *n.* metal receptacle for keeping and carrying coal.

co•a•lesce [kəʊə'les] *v.* to join together. **co•a•les•cence**, *n.* joining together.

co•a•li•tion [kəʊə'lɪʃn] *n.* joining together; combination of political parties forming a government.

coarse [kɔːs] *adj.* (-**er**, -**est**) (a) not fine/rough (laugh, etc.). (b) rude. **coarse•ly**, *adv.* in a coarse way. **coars•en**, *v.* to make coarse. **coarse•ness**, *n.* being coarse.

coast [kəʊst] 1. *n.* land by the sea; **from c. to c.** = across an area of land from one sea to another. 2. *v.* (a) to ride a vehicle without using the engine or the pedals. (b) to sail along the coast. **coast•al**, *adj.* referring to the coast. **coast•er**, *n.* (a) ship which sails from port to port along the coast. (b) flat dish or small mat for standing a bottle/glass on. **coast guard**, *n.* member of a government organization which patrols a country's coast (watching out for wrecks/smugglers, etc.). **coast•line**, *n.* line of the coast.

coat [kəʊt] 1. *n.* (a) long piece of outdoor clothing which covers the top part of the body. (b) fur of an animal. (c) layer (of paint, etc.). (d) **c. of arms** = symbolic design on the shield of a family/town, etc. 2. *v.* to cover (sth) with a layer. **coat hang•er**, *n.* piece of wood/wire/plastic on which you hang clothes. **coat hook**, *n.* hook (on a wall/door) for hanging a coat. **coat•ing**, *n.* covering (of paint, etc.). **coat•rack**, *n.* pole where several coats can be hung.

coax [kəʊks] *v.* to persuade (s.o.) to do sth.

co•ax•i•al [kəʊˈæksɪəl] *adj.* **c. cable** = electric cable where several wires are laid parallel to each other.

cob [kɒb] *n.* (a) seed head (of corn); (b) male swan. (c) short horse.

co•balt ['kəʊbɔːlt] *n.* (*element:* Co) white metal; blue color obtained from the metal.

cob•ble ['kɒbl] *v.* to put things **together**

roughly. **cobbled,** *adj.* covered with cobble-stones. **cob•ble•(stone),** *n.* rounded stone formerly used for paving streets.

cob•bler ['kɒblə] *n.* person who mends shoes.

co•bra ['kɒbrə] *n.* large poisonous tropical snake.

cob•web ['kɒbweb] *n.* net of fine thread made by a spider.

co•caine [kə'keɪn] *n.* painkilling drug, also used as a stimulant.

coc•cus ['kɒkəs] *n.* (*pl.* **cocci**) ball-shaped bacterium.

coc•cyx ['kɒksɪks] *n.* (*pl.* **-es**) small bone at the end of the spine.

coch•i•neal [kɒtʃɪ'niːl] *n.* red coloring used in cooking.

coch•le•a ['kɒtʃlɪə] *n.* spiral tube in the inner ear.

cock [kɒk] **1.** *n.* (a) male bird (esp. a domestic chicken); rooster. (b) tap. (c) hammer on a gun which fires the cartridge. **2.** *v.* (a) to prick up (your ears). (b) to put (your head) to one side. (c) to set (a gun) ready for firing. **cock-a-doo•dle doo!** *inter. showing* the noise made by a cock. **cock•crow,** *n.* early morning.

cock•ade [kɒ'keɪd] *n.* rosette of ribbons worn on a hat.

cock•a•too [kɒkə'tuː] *n.* type of large parrot.

cock•chaf•er ['kɒktʃeɪfə] *n.* large beetle.

cock•er ['kɒkə] *n.* type of spaniel.

cock•er•el ['kɒkrəl] *n.* young cock.

cock-eyed ['kɒkaɪd] *adj. inf.* stupid/odd (idea).

cock•le ['kɒkl] **1.** *n.* small edible shellfish with a double shell. **2.** *v.* (*of paper*) to curl up/wrinkle.

cock•ney ['kɒknɪ] *adj. & n.* (person) who comes from the east part of London; way of speaking of a person from the east part of London.

cock•pit ['kɒkpɪt] *n.* place where the pilot sits in an aircraft or boat.

cock•roach ['kɒkrəʊtʃ] *n.* (*pl.* **-es**) large brown or black beetle.

cock•sure [kɒk'ʃʊə] *adj.* very sure/self-confident.

cock•tail ['kɒkteɪl] *n.* mixed alcoholic drink; **c. lounge** = lounge or room where drinks are served in a hotel, restaurant, etc. **fruit c./shrimp c.** = mixture of fruit/shrimp in salad; **Molotov c.** = grenade made of a bottle of fuel and a fuse which you light before throwing.

cock•y ['kɒkɪ] *adj.* unpleasantly proud and conceited.

co•coa ['kəʊkəʊ] *n.* (*no pl.*) brown powder ground from the seeds of the cacao tree, used for making a drink; drink made from this.

co•co•nut ['kəʊkənʌt] *n.* large nut from a palm tree; **c. matting** = rough matting made from the outer fibers of a coconut.

co•coon [kə'kuːn] **1.** *n.* protective case of thread made by a larva before it turns into a moth or butterfly. **2.** *v.* to wrap (sth) up for protection (**in**).

cod [kɒd] *n.* (*pl.* **cod**) large sea fish; **c. liver oil** = oil from the livers of cod.

c.o.d. [siːəʊ'diː] *abbreviation for* cash on delivery.

co•da ['kəʊdə] *n.* last part of a piece of music.

cod•dle ['kɒdl] *v.* (a) to spoil/to pamper (s.o.). (b) to cook (eggs) in warm, but not boiling, water.

code [kəʊd] **1.** *n.* (a) set of laws/of rules of behavior; (b) secret signs agreed in advance for sending messages; **the Morse c.** = series of dots and dashes used for sending telegraphic messages; **c. word** = secret agreed word. **2.** *v.* to write (a message) in code.

co•deine ['kəʊdiːn] *n.* drug used to relieve pain and produce sleep.

co•dex ['kəʊdeks] *n.* very ancient manuscript of the Bible.

codg•er ['kɒdʒə] *n. inf.* man.

cod•i•cil ['kəʊdɪsɪl] *n.* additional clause to a will.

cod•i•fy ['kəʊdɪfaɪ] *v.* to write (rules of conduct/laws) as a code. **cod•i•fi•ca•tion** [kəʊdɪfɪ'keɪʃn] *n.* act of codifying.

co-di•rect•or [kəʊdaɪ'rektə] *n.* one of two or more directors.

cod•ling ['kɒdlɪŋ] *n.* small apple used for cooking; **c. moth,** moth whose larvae feed on apples.

co-ed•u•ca•tion•al [kəʊedju'keɪʃənl] *adj.* (school) where boys and girls are taught together. **co-ed.** **1.** *adj.* co-educational. **2.** *n.* girl who goes to a co-educational school.

co•ef•fi•cient [kəʊɪ'fɪʃənt] *n.* factor in mathematics.

coe•la•canth ['siːləkænθ] *n.* prehistoric type of fish which is not extinct.

coel•i•ac ['siːlɪæk] *adj.* referring to the abdomen.

co•erce [kəʊ'ɜːs] *v.* to force. **co•er•cion** [kəʊ'ɜːʃn] *n.* force. **co•er•cive,** *adj.* using force.

co•e•val [kəʊ'iːvəl] *adj.* belonging to the same generation.

co•ex•ist [kəʊɪg'zɪst] *v.* to exist/to live together. **co•ex•ist•ence,** *n.* living together; **peaceful c.** = where countries with different types of government exist side by side in peace. **co•ex•ist•ent,** *adj.* living at the same time (as sth else).

cof•fee ['kɒfɪ] *n.* (a) seeds of a tropical plant, roasted and ground to make a drink. (b) drink made from these beans; **instant c.** = powdered extract of coffee which makes a drink when hot water is poured on it; **c. table** = low table for putting cups/glasses, etc., on; **c. table book** = large colorful art book. **cof•fee shop,** *n.* small restaurant (often in a hotel) serving light meals and snacks.

cof•fers ['kɒfəz] *n. pl.* money chests. **cof•fer dam,** *n.* watertight wall which allows work to be done on the bed of a river or the sea.

cof•fin ['kɒfɪn] *n.* long wooden box in which a dead person is buried or cremated.

cog [kɒg] *n.* tooth (on a toothed wheel). **cog rail•way,** *n.* railway with engines driven by a toothed wheel connecting with a central toothed rail. **cog•wheel,** *n.* wheel with teeth round the edge which fit into the teeth on another wheel and make it turn.

co•gent ['kəʊdʒənt] *adj.* valid (argument); powerful (reason). **co•gen•cy,** *n.* being cogent.

cog•i•tate ['kɒdʒɪteɪt] *v.* to ponder/to think deeply. **cog•i•ta•tion** [kɒdʒɪ'teɪʃn] *n.* deep thought.

co•gnac ['kɒnjæk] *n.* French brandy.

cog•nate ['kɒgneɪt] *adj.* (*formal*) with the same origin.

cog•ni•zance ['kɒgnɪzəns] *n.* knowledge (of a fact). **cog•ni•zant,** *adj.* (**of**) knowing/being aware.

co•gno•scen•ti [kɒnjə'ʃentɪ] *n. pl.* specialists in the arts.

co•hab•it [kəʊ'hæbɪt] *v.* to live together as man and wife, esp. when not married.

co•here [kəʊ'hɪə] *v.* to hold together; to form a whole. **co•her•ence,** *n.* being coherent. **co•her•ent,** *adj.* clear/logical (ideas). **co•her•ent•ly,** *adv.* clearly/logically. **co•he•sion** [kəʊ'hiːʒn] *n.* sticking together. **co•he•sive** [kəʊ'hiːsɪv] *adj.* which stick together.

co•hort ['kəʊhɔːt] *n.* division of a Roman army; large group of people.

coif•fure [kwɑː'fjʊə] *n.* hairstyle. **coif•feur** [kwɑ'fɜː] *n.* hairdresser.

coil [kɔɪl] 1. *n.* (a) roll (of rope); one loop (in sth coiled). (b) **electric c.** = wire wrapped round a shaft which conducts electricity. (c) contraceptive device. 2. *v.* to roll up; to make loops.

coin [kɔɪn] 1. *n.* piece of metal money. 2. *v.* (a) to strike/to produce (metal money). (b) to invent (a new word). **coin•age,** *n.* (a) system of money (of a country). (b) new word.

co•in•cide [kəʊɪn'saɪd] *v.* to happen (by chance) at the same time as sth else. **co•in•ci•dence** [kəʊ'ɪnsɪdəns] *n.* two things

which happen at the same time by chance. **co•in•ci•den•tal** [kəʊɪnsɪ'dentl] *adj.* happening by coincidence.

coir ['kɔɪə] *n.* coconut fiber.

co•i•tion, coitus [kəʊ'ɪʃn, 'kəʊɪtəs] *n.* (*formal*) act of sexual intercourse.

coke [kəʊk] *n.* (a) (*no pl.*) fuel processed from coal, which gives a very fierce heat. (b) *inf.* Coca-Cola/trademark for a type of soft drink. (c) *inf.* cocaine.

col [kɒl] *n.* high pass between mountains.

col•an•der ['kɒləndə] *n.* bowl with holes in it for draining water from pasta, fruit, or vegetables.

cold [kəʊld] 1. *adj.* (**-er, -est**) (a) not hot; **he got c. feet** = he was not brave enough to continue; **c. chisel** = hard steel chisel; **c. war** = fight for power between countries without actually using weapons. (b) unfriendly (reception, manner). 2. *n.* (a) state of being cold; **left out in the c.** = left on one side. (b) infectious illness when you sneeze and cough; **to catch a c.** **cold-blood•ed,** *adj.* (a) (animal such as fish) with blood whose temperature varies with its surroundings. (b) with no feelings. **cold•ly,** *adv.* in an unfriendly way. **cold•ness,** *n.* state of being cold. **cold-shoul•der,** *v.* to be deliberately unfriendly to (s.o.).

cole•slaw ['kəʊlslɔː] *n.* cabbage salad.

col•ic ['kɒlɪk] *n.* severe pain in the abdomen. **co•li•tis** [kə'laɪtɪs] *n.* inflammation of the colon.

col•lab•o•rate [kə'læbəreɪt] *v.* to work together. **col•lab•o•ra•tion** [kəlæbə'reɪʃn] *n.* collaborating. **col•lab•o•ra•tor,** *n.* person who collaborates.

col•lage [kɒ'lɑːʒ] *n.* picture made from pieces of paper, etc., which are stuck on to a backing.

col•la•gen ['kɒlədʒən] *n.* fibers which form tissue.

col•lapse [kə'læps] 1. *n.* falling down/ruin. 2. *v.* to fall down suddenly. **col•laps•i•ble,** *adj.* which can be folded up.

col•lar ['kɒlə] 1. *n.* part of clothing which goes around the neck. 2. *v. inf.* to grab/to catch (s.o.). **col•lar•bone,** *n.* bone from the top of the ribs to the shoulder blade.

col•late [kə'leɪt] *v.* to compare texts, etc. **col•la•tion** [kə'leɪʃn] *n.* (a) (*formal*) light cold lunch. (b) comparison of texts. **col•la•tor,** *n.* someone who compares texts. **col•lat•er•al** [kə'lætərəl] *adj. & n.* parallel; (se-

---

æ **back,** a: **farm,** ɒ: **top,** aɪ **pipe,** aʊ **how,** aɪə **fire,** aʊə **flower,** ɔ: **bought,** ɔɪ **toy,** e **fed,** eəhair, eɪ **take,** ə **afraid,** əʊ **boat,** əʊə **lower,** v: **word,** i: **heap,** ɪ **hit,** ɪə **hear,** u: **school,** ʊ **book,** ʌ **but,** b **back,** d **dog,** ð **then,** dʒ **just,** f **fog,** g **go,** h **hand,** j **yes,** k **catch,** l **last,** m **mix,** n **nut,** ŋ **sing,** p **penny,** r **round,** s **some,** ʃ **short,** t **too,** tʃ **chop,** θ **thing,** v **voice,** w **was,** z **zoo,** ʒ **treasure**

curity) which is used as an additional guarantee.

col•league ['kɒliːg] *n.* person who works with you.

col•lect 1. ['kɒlɪkt] *n.* short prayer used on a particular day. 2. [kə'lekt] *v.* (a) to fetch and bring together. (b) to gather money for charity. (c) **to call c.** = to ask the person you are phoning to pay for the call. **col•lect•ed,** *adj.* calm/not flustered. **col•lec•tion,** *n.* (a) group of objects brought together. (b) gathering of money; money which has been gathered; **to take a c. for sth. col•lec•tive,** *adj.* brought together; **c. farm** = farm where everything belongs to and is run by the workers on behalf of the state; **c. bargaining** = negotiations for new salaries carried out between union and management. **col•lec•tive•ly,** *adv.* all together. **col•lec•tor,** *n.* person who collects; **ticket c.** = person who takes tickets from railroad passengers, etc.

col•leen [kɒ'liːn] *n.* (in Ireland) girl.

col•lege ['kɒlɪdʒ] *n.* institution of higher education which gives degrees for specialized study. **col•le•giate** [kə'liːdʒɪət] *adj.* belonging to/referring to a college.

col•lide [kə'laɪd] *v.* **to c. with** = to bump into.

col•lie ['kɒlɪ] *n.* type of sheepdog.

col•li•sion [kə'lɪʒən] *n.* bumping into sth.

col•lo•ca•tion [kɒlə'keɪʃn] *n.* (*formal*) group.

col•loid ['kɒlɔɪd] *n.* viscous liquid.

col•lo•qui•al [kə'ləʊkwɪəl] *adj.* as is commonly spoken; conversational. **col•lo•qui•al•ism,** *n.* colloquial expression. **col•lo•qui•al•ly,** *adv.* as in conversational speech.

col•lu•sion [kə'luːʒn] *n.* secret illegal agreement.

co•lon ['kəʊlən] *n.* (a) large part of the intestines. (b) punctuation sign (:) to show a break in a sentence.

colo•nel ['kɜːnl] *n.* military officer above lieutenant-colonel.

col•on•nade [kɒlə'neɪd] *n.* row of columns.

col•o•ny ['kɒlənɪ] *n.* (a) territory ruled by another country. (b) group of animals/humans living together. **co•lo•ni•al** [kə'ləʊnɪəl] *adj.* referring to a colony. **co•lo•ni•al•ism,** *n.* exploitation of colonies. **co•lo•ni•al•ist,** *n.* person who advocates colonialism. **col•o•nist** ['kɒlənɪst] *n.* person sent from the home country to settle in a colony. **col•o•ni•za•tion** [kɒlənaɪ'zeɪʒn] *n.* act of making a colony out of a territory. **col•o•nize,** *v.* to occupy (land) and make it a colony. **col•o•phon** ['kɒlɒfən] *n.* printed device which identifies a publisher or printer.

col•or *Brit.* **col•our** ['kʌlə] 1. *n.* (a) shade/tint which an object has in light; **c. TV** = not black and white; **c. scheme** = arrangement of colors (as in the furnishing of a room); (b) shade (of a person's skin); **c. bar** = bar to s.o. because of the color of his/her skin. (c) paint; **water colors** = paints which have to be mixed with water. (d) **color(s)** = flag; **with flying colors** = with great success; **in his true colors** = as he really is. 2. *v.* to paint with color; to make (sth) colored. **col•or•ant,** *n.* coloring material. **col•or•a•tion;** *n.* coloring. **col•or-blind,** *adj.* unable to distinguish some colors (usu. red and green). **col•or-blind•ness,** *n.* being color-blind. **col•ored,** (a) *adj.* (illustration) in color. (b) *adj. & n.* (person) whose skin is not white. **col•or•ful,** *adj.* brightly colored; picturesque/full of local color. **col•or•ing,** *n.* way in which sth is colored; substance which gives color to sth (such as food). **color•less,** *adj.* pale/uninteresting.

Col•o•ra•do bee•tle [kɒlərɑːdəʊ'biːtl] *n.* striped beetle which attacks potato plants.

co•los•sal [kə'lɒsl] *adj.* (a) very large/huge. (b) splendid. **co•los•sal•ly,** *adv.* greatly/enormously. **co•los•sus,** *n.* (*pl.* **-es**) huge statue; huge man.

co•los•to•my [kɒ'lɒstəmɪ] *n.* operation to attach a colon to an artificial hole in the belly.

col•our ['kʌlə] *n.&v. Brit. see* **col•or.**

colt [kəʊlt] *n.* young male horse. **colts•foot,** *n.* wild plant with small yellow flowers.

col•ter ['kəʊltə] *n.* blade of a plow.

co•lum•bine ['kɒləmbaɪn] *n.* garden plant with delicate pink or blue flowers.

col•umn ['kɒləm] *n.* (a) tall pillar. (b) thing which is round and long; **spinal c.** = backbone; **steering c.** = shaft with a wheel on top for steering an aircraft/a car. (c) line of soldiers; **fifth c.** = subversive elements working behind the enemy lines to weaken the morale of the population. (d) long thin block of printing on a page; regular article in a newspaper. **col•um•nist** ['kɒləmɪst] *n.* journalist who writes regularly for a paper.

co•ma ['kəʊmə] *n.* state of unconsciousness. **com•a•tose** ['kəʊmətəʊs] *adj.* (a) in a coma. (b) sleepy/half awake.

comb [kəʊm] 1. *n.* (a) long-toothed instrument for disentangling hair. (b) red crest on the head of a bird (such as a cock). (c) honeycomb. 2. *v.* (a) to disentangle (hair). (b) to search (an area).

com•bat ['kɒmbæt] 1. *n.* fighting. 2. *v.* to fight. **com•bat•ant** ['kɒmbətənt] *adj. & n.* (person) who takes part in a fight. **com•bat•ive,** *adj.* quarrelsome/argumentative.

com•bine 1. *n.* ['kɒmbaɪn] (a) financial/commercial group. (b) **c. (harvester)** = large machine for cutting and threshing grain. 2. *v.* [kəm'baɪn] to join together. **com•bi•na•tion** [kɒmbɪ'neɪʃn] *n.* (a) several things joined together. (b) series of numbers which open a lock; **a c. lock.** (c) long one-piece winter underwear.

com•bus•tion [kəm'bʌstʃən] *n.* burning. **com•bus•ti•ble** [kəm'bʌstɪbl] *adj. & n.* (substance) which can easily catch fire and burn.

come [kʌm] *v.* **(came; has come)** (a) to arrive here; **c. and see us; c. up to my room.** (b) to happen; **how does the door c. to be open?** *inf.* **how c.?** = why/how did it happen? (c) to add up to; **it comes to $5; c. to that** = by the way/while we are talking of that. (d) **to c.** = in the future. **come a•cross**, *v.* to find. **come af•ter**, *v.* to follow. **come a•long**, *v.* to arrive. **come back**, *v.* to return. **come•back**, *n.* (a) retort. (b) return (of a singer/sportsman) after retirement. **come by**, *v.* to obtain. **come down**, *v.* to descend. **come•down**, *n.* humiliation. **come into**, *v.* (a) to enter. (b) to inherit (money). **come off**, *v.* (a) to fall off. (b) to result; **he came off badly** = the result was bad for him. **come on**, *v.* (a) to hurry. (b) to arrive. **come out**, *v.* (a) to move outside. (b) (*of photograph, etc.*) to result/to show. (c) **to c. out (on strike)** = to strike. **come o•ver**, *v.* (a) to cross. (b) to start to feel; **what has c. over him?** = what is the matter with him? **com•er**, *n.* person who comes; **late comers; all comers.** **come a•round**, *v.* (a) to visit. (b) to recover from unconsciousness. (c) to change one's way of thinking; to agree with s.o. else. **come to**, *v.* to recover (from unconsciousness). **come•up•pance**, *n. inf.* **he got his c.** = he was punished. **com•ing**, 1. *adj.* approaching. 2. *n.* arrival; **comings and goings.**

com•e•dy ['kɒmədɪ] *n.* play or movie which makes you laugh; funny aspect (of an event). **co•me•di•an** [kə'miːdɪən] *n.* man who tells jokes to make people laugh. **co•me•di•enne** [kəmiːdɪ'en] *n.* woman who tells jokes to make people laugh.

come•ly ['kʌmlɪ] *adj.* attractive (woman).

co•mes•ti•bles [kʌ'mestɪbəlz] *n. pl.* (*formal*) food.

com•et ['kɒmɪt] *n.* body which moves visibly through space with a bright tail.

com•fort ['kʌmfət] 1. *n.* (a) thing which helps to relive suffering. (b) ease of living; **c. station**

= public toilet. 2. *v.* to relieve the suffering of (s.o. who is miserable, etc.). **com•fort•a•ble**, *adj.* soft/relaxing, giving ease. **com•fort•a•bly**, *adv.* in a soft/relaxing way; **c. off** = having plenty of money. **com•fort•er**, *n.* (a) person who comforts. (b) long woolen scarf. (c) bed covering made of a large bag full of feathers. **com•fort•ing**, *adj.* consoling. **com•fort•less**, *adj.* harsh/hard. **com•fy**, *adj.* (-ier, -iest) *inf.* comfortable.

com•frey ['kʌmfrɪ] *n.* herb, used both medicinally and also to make compost.

com•ic ['kɒmɪk] 1. *adj.* funny, amusing. 2. *n.* (a) person who tells jokes to make people laugh. (b) (*usu.* **comics**) children's paper with cartoon stories. **com•i•cal**, *adj.* funny. **com•i•cal•ly**, *adv.* in a funny way.

com•ma ['kɒmə] *n.* punctuation mark (,) showing a break in a sentence around a clause; **inverted commas** (" ") = quotation marks

com•mand [kə'mɑːnd] 1. *n.* (a) order; **c. performance** = play, motion picture, etc. put on at the command of a monarch. **second-in-c.** = officer/person directly under the main commander/director; **in c. of** = in charge of. (b) knowledge (of a language). 2. *v.* (a) to order. (b) to be in charge of. (c) to demand (a price). **com•man•dant** [kɒmən'dænt] *n.* officer in charge of a military base, etc. **com•man•deer** [kɒmən'dɪə] *v.* to order that (sth) should be given over to the armed forces. **com•mand•er** [kə'mɑːndə] *n.* officer in charge of a military unit/ship); rank in the navy below captain. **com•mand•ing**, *adj.* in command. **com•mand•ment**, *n.* rule; **the Ten Commandments** = rules given by God to Moses. **com•man•do**, *n.* (*pl.* -os) group troops specially trained to raid inside enemy territory; member of such a group.

com•mem•o•rate [kə'meməreɪt] *v.* to celebrate (the memory of something/a special occasion, etc.). **com•mem•o•ra•tion** [kəmemə'reɪʃn] *n.* commemorating. **com•mem•o•ra•tive** [kə'memərətɪv] *adj.* which commemorates.

com•mence [kə'mens] *v.* (*formal*) to begin. **com•mence•ment**, *n.* (a) beginning. (b) day when degrees are awarded at a school, college, or university.

com•mend [kə'mend] *v.* (*formal*) to praise. **com•mend•a•ble**, *adj.* praiseworthy. **com•mend•a•bly**, *adv.* in a praiseworthy way. **com•men•da•tion** [kɒmen'deɪʃn] *n.* official praise. **com•mend•a•to•ry** [kə-'mendətrɪ] *adj.* which praises.

com•men•su•rate [kə'mensjurət] *adj.* **c. with** = in proportion to.

com•ment ['kɒment] 1. *n.* remark/what you feel about something; **no c.** = I refuse to discuss the matter. 2. *v.* to make remarks (**on**). **com•men•tar•y**, *n.* (a) remarks about a book, etc. (b) spoken report on a sports event. **com•men•ta•tor**, *n.* person who reports on events on the radio or television.

com•merce ['kɒmɜːs] *n.* business transactions; **chamber of c.** = association of businessmen. **com•mer•cial** [kə'mɜːʃl] 1. *adj.* dealing with business; **c. vehicle** = vehicle used for business purposes. 2. *n.* piece of publicity of television. **com•mer•cial•i•za•tion** [kəmɜːʃəlaɪ'zeɪʃn] *n.* making sth into a business proposition. **com•mer•cial•ize**, *v.* to make into a business proposition. **com•mer•cial•ly**, *adv.* in a commercial way.

com•mis•er•ate [kə'mɪzəreɪt] *v.* to sympathize (**with** s.o.). **com•mis•er•a•tion** [kəmɪzə'reɪʃn] *n.* sympathizing.

com•mis•sar [kɒmɪ'sɑː] *n.* political leader (in a communist state).

com•mis•sar•i•at [kɒmɪ'seərɪət] *n.* department (esp. in the army) dealing with the supply of food.

com•mis•sion [kə'mɪʃn] 1. *n.* (a) group of people which investigates problems of national importance. (b) document naming someone an officer. (c) order for sth to be made/to be used; **out of c.** = not in working order. (d) percentage of sales value given to a salesperson. 2. *v.* (a) to authorize (s.o.) to be an officer/to authorize (an artist/architect, etc.) to do a piece of work; to put (a ship) into commission. (b) to authorize (a piece of work) to be done. **com•mis•sion•aire** [kəmɪʃə-'neə] *n. Brit.* doorkeeper (in a hotel/office building). **com•mis•sion•er** [kə'mɪʃnə] *n.* (a) representative of authority; **c. of police** = highest-ranking police officer; (b) member of a commission.

com•mit [kə'mɪt] *v.* (**committed**) (a) to carry out (a crime). (b) to put in official custody; **to c. to prison** = to send to prison. (c) **to c. oneself** = to promise to do sth. **com•mit•ted**, *adj.* firmly believing in (sth). **com•mit•ment**, *n.* (a) promise. (b) agreement to do sth. (c) promise to pay money. **com•mit•tal**, *n.* act of committing.

com•mit•tee [kə'mɪtɪ] *n.* official group of people who organize or discuss on behalf of a larger body; **to be on a c.** = to be a member of it.

com•mode [kə'məʊd] *n.* (a) chest of drawers. (b) chair with a chamberpot in the seat.

com•mo•di•ous [kə'məʊdɪəs] *adj.* spacious/large (room/house, etc.).

com•mod•i•ty [kə'mɒdɪtɪ] *n.* merchandise; thing sold; **basic commodities** = basic foodstuffs and raw materials.

com•mo•dore ['kɒmədɔː] *n.* (a) rank in the navy above captain. (b) person who directs a yacht club.

com•mon ['kɒmən] 1. *adj.* (**-er**, **-est**) (a) belonging to everyone/to the public in general; **it is c. knowledge** = everyone knows it. (b) belonging to two or more people; **we have two things in c.**; **C. Market** (formerly) = European Union. (c) ordinary/which happens frequently. (d) vulgar/of the lower class. 2. *n.* land which belongs to a community. **com•mon•er**, *n.* ordinary citizen/not a noble. **com•mon law**, *n.* law which is derived from decisions of courts, rather than from statutes; **c.-l. wife** = woman who lives with a man as his wife, without being married to him. **com•mon•ly**, *adv.* frequently. **com•mon•place**, *adj. & n.* (thing) which happens frequently. **com•mons**, *n.* **the (House of) C.** = the lower (elected) house of the British parliament. **com•mon•sense**, *n.* ordinary good sense. **com•mon•wealth**, *n.* republic; group of states; **the (British) C.** = association of countries, most of which were formerly colonies of Britain but are now independent; **C. of Independent States** = association of countries that were formerly part of the Soviet Union.

com•mo•tion [kə'məʊʃən] *n.* confusion/trouble.

com•mune 1. *n.* ['kɒmjuːn] group of people who work together sharing everything. 2. *v.* [kə'mjuːn] to be in touch (**with** s.o./sth) in spirit. **com•mu•nal** [kə'mjuːnəl] *adj.* (property) held in common/belonging to several people. **com•mu•nal•ly**, *adv.* done by several people together.

com•mu•ni•cate [kə'mjuːnɪkeɪt] *v.* (**with**) to pass information to s.o./to be in touch with s.o. **com•mu•ni•ca•ble**, *adj.* which can be passed on to s.o. **com•mu•ni•cant**, *n.* person who takes Holy Communion. **com•mu•ni•ca•tion** [kəmjuːnɪ'keɪʃn] *n.* act of communicating/passing of information. **com•mu•ni•ca•tive** [kə'mjuːnɪkətɪv] *adj.* talkative; (person) who is willing to give information. **com•mun•ion**, *n.* (a) fellowship with s.o.; (b) **Holy C.** = central Christian religious ceremony, celebrating the Last Supper. **com•mu•ni•qué** [kə'mjuːnɪkeɪ] *n.* official news item given to the press.

com•mu•nism ['kɒmjʊnɪzəm] *n.* political

doctrine whereby the state owns all industry and land. **com•mu•nist.** 1. *adj.* referring to communism. 2. *n.* (a) person who believes in communism. (b) member of the Communist Party.

com•mu•ni•ty [kə'mjuːnɪtɪ] *n.* (a) group of people living in one place; **an urban c.** = a town and its inhabitants; **c. center** = sports/arts center belonging to a town; **the European Economic C.,** *n.* organization linking several European countries for purposes of trade. **religious c.** = group of monks or nuns. (b) the population as a whole. (c) group of organisms living in an area.

com•mute [kə'mjuːt] *v.* (a) to reduce (a legal penalty). (b) to travel to work every day for some distance. **com•mut•a•ble,** *adj.* which can be commuted. **com•mu•ta•tion** [kɒmju'teɪʃn] *n.* act of commuting a sentence. **com•mut•er,** *n.* person who travels to work every day for some distance; **c. train** = train for commuters.

com•pact 1. *n.* ['kɒmpækt] (a) agreement. (b) small box for carrying face powder. (c) small car. 2. *adj* [kəm'pækt] small; tight/close together. 3. *v.* to make (sth) compact. **com•pact disk,** *n.* metal recording disk, which can hold a larger amount of music than a plastic record, and which is read by a laser in a special player. **com•pact•ly,** *adv.* tightly/close together.

com•pan•ion [kəm'pænjən] *n.* (a) person who travels or lives with s.o. (b) handbook; **travel companion** = travel handbook. **com•pan•ion•a•ble,** *adj.* friendly. **com•pan•ion•ship,** *n.* friendship. **com•pan•ion•way,** *n.* stairway on a ship.

com•pa•ny ['kʌmpənɪ] *n.* (a) being together with other people; **he is good c.** = he is an entertaining companion; **to part c.** = to split up; **to get into bad c.** = to get in with bad companions. (b) group of soldiers within a battalion; crew of a ship. (c) **theatrical c.** = group of actors who play together. (d) (*usu. written Co. in names*) commercial or industrial company.

com•pare [kəm'peə] *v.* to put two things side by side to see how they differ; **he compared our bread to a lump of concrete** = he said it was like a lump of concrete; **his work doesn't c. very well with his brother's** = is not as good as his brother's. **com•pa•ra•bil•i•ty** [kɒmpərə-'bɪlɪtɪ] *n.* being comparable. **com•pa•ra•ble** ['kɒmprəbl] *adj.* which can

be compared. **com•par•a•tive** [kəm-'pærətɪv] 1. *adj.* relative. 2. *n.* form of an adjective/adverb showing an increase in level; **"better" and "more stupidly" are the comparatives of "good" and "stupidly."** **com•par•a•tive•ly,** *adv.* more or less; relatively. **com•par•i•son,** *n.* act of comparing; **there is no c.** = you cannot compare them, one is so much better than the other.

com•part•ment [kəm'pɑːtmənt] *n.* division inside a box; separate section in a railroad car/in a ship.

com•pass ['kʌmpəs] *n.* (*pl.* -es) (a) device which indicates the north by means of a needle. (b) **a pair of compasses** = instrument for drawing a circle. (c) scope/range.

com•pas•sion [kəm'pæʃn] *n.* pity; **to have c. on s.o.** = to take pity on s.o. **com•pas•sion•ate,** *adj.* merciful/pitying. **com•pas•sion fa•tigue,** *n.* indifference towards a humanitarian crisis/disaster due to previous overexposure to such situations.

com•pat•i•ble [kəm'pætəbl] *adj.* able to fit with sth. **com•pat•i•bil•i•ty** [kəmpætə-'bɪlɪtɪ] *n.* ability to fit together.

com•pa•tri•ot [kəm'pætrɪət] *n.* person who comes from the same country.

com•pel [kəm'pel] *v.* (**compelled**) to force. **com•pel•ling,** *adj.* which forces; very exciting (story/film).

com•pen•di•um [kəm'pendɪəm] *n.* collection (of paper/notes/games).

com•pen•sate ['kɒmpenseɪt] *v.* to pay (s.o.) for damage done; to pay for a loss. **com•pen•sa•tion** [kɒmpen'seɪʃn] *n.* payment for damage. **com•pen•sa•to•ry,** *adj.* which compensates.

com•pete [kəm'piːt] *v.* to try to beat others in a race/a game/a business.

com•pe•tent ['kɒmpɪtənt] *adj.* able (to do sth)/capable (of doing sth); efficient. **com•pe•tence,** *n.* (a) capability/efficiency. (b) professional responsibilities; **the case is outside the c. of this court. com•pe•tent•ly,** *adv.* in a capable/efficient way.

com•pe•ti•tion [kɒmpə'tɪʃn] *n.* (a) game where several teams or people try to win. (b) commercial rivalry/trying to sell more than another company. **com•pet•i•tive** [kəm-'petɪtɪv] *adj.* (person) who likes entering competitions; (sport) which is based on competitions; (prices) which aim to compete with those of rival companies. **com•pet•i•tor,** *n.*

æ back, ɑ: farm, ɒ: top, aɪ pipe, aʊ how, aɪə fire, aʊə flower, ɔ: bought, ɔɪ toy, e fed, eəhair, eɪ take, ə afraid, əʊ boat, əʊə lower, vː word, iː heap, ɪ hit, ɪə hear, uː school, ʊ book, ʌ but, b back, d dog, ð then, dʒ just, f fog, g go, h hand, j yes, k catch, l last, m mix, n nut, ŋ sing, p penny, r round, s some, ʃ short, t too, tʃ chop, θ thing, v voice, w was, z zoo, ʒ treasure

person who goes in for a competition; rival company.

com•pile [kəm'paɪl] *v.* to draw up (a list); to make a collection (of poetry); to write (a dictionary). **com•pi•la•tion** [kɒmpɪ'leɪʃn] *n.* act of compiling; work which has been compiled. **com•pil•er** [kəm'paɪlə] *n.* (a) person who compiles. (b) computer program which converts coded data to a machine-readable program.

com•pla•cent [kəm'pleɪsnt] *adj.* self-satisfied. **com•pla•cen•cy**, *n.* being complacent. **com•pla•cent•ly**, *adv.* in a complacent way.

com•plain [kəm'pleɪn] *v.* to grumble because sth is wrong. **com•plaint,** *n.* (a) grumble/statement that sth is wrong. (b) illness.

com•plai•sant [kəm'pleɪznt] *adj.* eager to please.

com•ple•ment 1. *n.* ['kɒmplɪmənt] (a) number of people needed to fill sth. (b) thing which adds to or fits in with sth else. 2. *v.* [kɒmplɪ'ment] to complete/to fit in (with sth). **com•ple•men•ta•ry** [kɒmplɪ'mentərɪ] *adj.* which fills/completes sth.

com•plete [kəm'pliːt] 1. *adj.* (a) full/whole. (b) finished. 2. *v.* (a) to finish. (b) to fill in (a form). **com•plete•ly,** *adv.* wholly. **com•plete•ness,** *n.* fullness (of success). **com•ple•tion** [kəm'pliːʃn] *n.* finishing; finish; **c. of a contract** = signing of a contract.

com•plex ['kɒmpleks] 1. *adj.* complicated. 2. *n. (pl.* **-es)** (a) series of buildings. (b) repressed emotions/obsessions; **inferiority c.** = feeling that you are inferior; **Œdipus c.** = feeling of hatred for one's father and love for one's mother. **com•plex•i•ty** [kəm'pleksɪtɪ] *n.* complicated nature.

com•plex•ion [kəm'plekʃn] *n.* color of the skin on your face; general way things are.

com•pli•cate ['kɒmplɪkeɪt] *v.* to make things complicated. **com•pli•cat•ed,** *adj.* with many small details/difficult to understand. **com•pli•ca•tion** [kɒmplɪ'keɪʃn] *n.* being complicated; second illness which makes the first illness worse.

com•plic•i•ty [kəm'plɪsɪtɪ] *n.* being an accomplice to a crime.

com•pli•ment 1. *n.* ['kɒmplɪmənt] praise; **send him my compliments** = send him my good wishes. 2. *v.* ['kɒmplɪment] to praise. **com•pli•men•ta•ry** [kɒmplɪ'mentərɪ] *adj.* which praises; **c. ticket** = free ticket.

com•pline ['kɒmplɪn] *n.* last service of the day.

com•ply [kəm'plaɪ] *v.* **(with)** to observe (a rule); to obey (an order). **com•pli•ance,** *n.* agreement to do sth. **com•pli•ant,** *adj.* (person) who agrees to do sth/who obeys the rules.

com•po•nent [kəm'pəʊnənt] *adj. & n.* (piece) which forms part of sth.

com•pose [kəm'pəʊz] *v.* (a) to make up (music); to write (a letter/a poem). (b) **c. yourself** = to be calm. **com•posed,** *adj.* calm/unflustered. **com•pos•er,** *n.* person who writes music. **com•pos•ite** ['kɒmpəzɪt] *adj.* made of several different parts. **com•po•si•tion** [kɒmpə'zɪʃn] *n.* (a) way in which sth is formed. (b) piece of music/poem/long essay. (c) mixture of several things. **com•pos•i•tor** [kəm'pɒzɪtə] *n.* person who sets type for printing. **com•po•sure** [kəm'pəʊʒə] *n.* calmness. **com•pos men•tis** ['kɒmpɒs'mentɪs] *adj.* sane.

com•post ['kɒmpɒst] *n.* rotted vegetable matter used as a fertilizer.

com•pound 1. *adj.* ['kɒmpaʊnd] made up of several parts; **c. fracture** = fracture where the broken bone pierces the skin; **c. interest** = interest calculated on the total sum including the previous year's interest. 2. *n.* ['kɒmpaʊnd] (a) chemical made up of two or more elements. (b) yard enclosed by a fence. 3. *v.* [kəm'paʊnd] (a) to come to an agreement with people to whom you owe money. (b) to increase/to aggravate (a crime/a feeling).

com•pre•hend [kɒmprɪ'hend] *v.* (a) to understand. (b) to include. **com•pre•hen•si•ble,** *adj.* which can be understood/understandable. **com•pre•hen•sion,** *n.* understanding. **com•pre•hen•sive,** *adj.* which includes everything; **com•pre•hen•sive•ness,** *n.* wide range (of knowledge, etc.).

com•press 1. *n.* ['kɒmpres] pad of material put on a bruise/sore. 2. *v.* [kəm'pres] to squeeze into a small space; **compressed air** = air under pressure. **com•pres•sor,** *n.* machine which compresses air/gas, etc.

com•prise [kəm'praɪz] *v.* to be formed of.

com•pro•mise ['kɒmprəmaɪz] 1. *n.* agreement of two opposing points of view, where each side gives way to some extent. 2. *v.* (a) to come to an agreement by giving way. (b) to embarrass/to put in a difficult position. **com•pro•mis•ing,** *adj.* embarrassing.

comp•trol•ler [kən'trəʊlə] *n. (old)* person who controls the finances in an establishment.

com•pul•sion [kəm'pʌlʃn] *n.* force/urge. **com•pul•sive,** *adj.* (person) who cannot stop himself doing sth; **a c. smoker. com•pul•so•ry,** *adj.* which you are forced to do.

com•punc•tion [kəm'pʌŋkʃn] *n.* remorse/regret.

com•pute [kəm'pjuːt] *v.* to calculate. **com•pu•ta•tion** [kɒmpjuˈteɪʃn] *n.* calculation. **com•put•er,** *n.* electronic machine which calculates and keeps information automatically; **c. fraud** = fraud committed by using a computer. **com•pu•ter-as•sist•ed,** *adj.* helped by using a computer; **c.-a. design.** **com•put•er•i•za•tion,** *n.* act of computerizing. **com•put•er•ize,** *v.* (a) to process by computer. (b) to equip (a business, etc.) with a computer.

com•rade ['kɒmreɪd] *n.* friend/companion; fellow member of a socialist or communist party. **com•rade•ship,** *n.* fellowship/friendliness.

con [kɒn] 1. *n.* (a) *inf.* deception; **c. man** = trickster. (b) argument against. 2. *v.* (**conned**) *inf.* to deceive/to trick (s.o.).

con•cat•e•na•tion [kɒnkætɪ'neɪʃən] *n.* chain of events.

con•cave [kɒn'keɪv] *adj.* (surface) which is hollowed in the middle like a spoon.

con•ceal [kən'siːl] *v.* to hide. **con•cealed,** *adj.* hidden; **c. entrance** = entrance which is difficult to see. **con•ceal•ment,** *n.* hiding.

con•cede [kən'siːd] *v.* (a) to admit (that you are wrong). (b) to admit that you have lost.

con•ceit [kən'siːt] *n.* high opinion of oneself. **con•ceit•ed,** *adj.* (person) who thinks too much of himself.

con•ceive [kən'siːv] *v.* (a) to become pregnant. (b) to think up (an idea). **con•ceiv•a•ble,** *adj.* which can be imagined. **con•ceiv•a•bly,** *adv.* in a conceivable way.

con•cen•trate ['kɒnsəntreɪt] 1. *n.* concentrated substance. 2. *v.* (a) (**on**) to pay great attention to (sth). (b) to put (all one's resources) together in one place. **con•cen•trat•ed,** *adj.* very strong (juice after water has been extracted). **con•cen•tra•tion** [kɒnsən'treɪʃn] *n.* (a) attentiveness. (b) putting all your resources into one area. (c) **c. camp** = camp where many political prisoners are held in captivity.

con•cen•tric [kən'sentrɪk] *adj.* (circles) inside each other, each with the same central point.

con•cept ['kɒnsept] *n.* idea/philosophical notion. **con•cep•tion** [kən'sepʃn] *n.* (a) becoming pregnant. (b) idea. **con•cep•tu•al,** *adj.* referring to concepts. **con•cep•tu•al•ize,** *v.* to form a concept of (sth).

con•cern [kən'sɜːn] 1. *n.* (a) worry. (b) interest; **it is no c. of yours** = it is none of your business. (c) company/business; **a big industrial c.** 2. *v.* (a) to deal with; **this concerns you** = is about

you; **that does not c. him** = it has nothing to do with him; **as far as money is concerned** = with reference to money. (b) **to be concerned (about)** = to worry (about). **con•cern•ing,** *prep.* about/referring to.

con•cert ['kɒnsət] *n.* program of music played in public. **con•cert•ed** [kən'sɜːtɪd] *adj.* (effort/attack) done or planned jointly. **concert hall,** *n.* large hall for giving concerts.

con•cer•ti•na [kɒnsə'tiːnə] 1. *n.* portable musical instrument with bellows and a set of keys at either end. 2. *v.* to become crushed/crumpled.

con•cer•to [kən'tʃeətəʊ] *n.* (*pl.* **-os**) piece of music for a solo instrument and orchestra, or for a small group of instruments.

con•ces•sion [kən'seʃn] *n.* act of conceding/of admitting sth; **to make a c.** = to change what you planned to fit in with s.o. else's wishes.

conch [kɒntʃ] *n.* (*pl.* **-es**) type of sea shell, like a large snail shell. **con•chol•o•gy** [kɒŋ-'kɒlədʒɪ] *n.* study of shells.

con•cil•i•ate [kən'sɪlɪeɪt] *v.* to win over (s.o.) who was previously unfriendly; to reconcile. **con•cil•i•a•tion** [kənsɪlɪ'eɪʃn] *n.* act of conciliating. **con•cil•i•a•tor** [kən'sɪlɪeɪtə] *n.* person who tries to reconcile people of opposing views. **con•cil•i•a•to•ry** [kən'sɪlɪətrɪ] *adj.* which is aimed at conciliating.

con•cise [kən'saɪs] *adj.* short; meaning a lot, but using few words. **con•cise•ly,** *adv.* in a concise way. **con•cise•ness, concision** [kən'sɪʒn] *n.* briefness.

con•clave ['kɒŋkleɪv] *n.* religious assembly, esp. meeting of cardinals to elect a pope.

con•clude [kən'kluːd] *v.* (a) to come to an end. (b) to deduce/to come to an opinion. (c) to arrange (a treaty). **con•clud•ing,** *adj.* final. **con•clu•sion** [kən'kluːʒn] *n.* (a) end. (b) opinion reached by reasoning. **con•clu•sive,** *adj.* decisive/which offers firm proof. **con•clu•sive•ly,** *adv.* in a decisive way.

con•coct [kən'kɒkt] *v.* (a) to make (a dish of food). (b) to make up/to invent (a story). **con•coc•tion,** *n.* curious mixture of food or drink.

con•com•i•tant [kən'kɒmɪtənt] *adj.* (*formal*) which accompanies/goes with.

con•cord ['kɒŋkɔːd] *n.* harmony/peace.

con•cord•ance [kən'kɔːdəns] *n.* alphabetical list of words used in a book.

æ back, a: farm, ɒ: top, aɪ pipe, aʊ how, aɪə fire, aʊə flower, ɔ: bought, ɔɪ toy, e fed, eəhair, eɪ take, ə afraid, əʊ boat, əʊə lower, ʌː word, iː heap, ɪ hit, ɪə hear, uː school, ʊ book, ʌ but, b back, d dog, ð then, dʒ just, f fog, g go, h hand, j yes, k catch, l last, m mix, n nut, ŋ sing, p penny, r round, s some, ʃ short, t too, tʃ chop, θ thing, v voice, w was, z zoo, ʒ treasure

con•cor•dat [kɒnˈkɔːdæt] *n.* agreement (between church and state).

con•course [ˈkɒŋkɔːs] *n.* (a) crowd/mass of people. (b) large open space inside a railroad station/concert hall, etc.

con•crete [ˈkɒnkriːt] 1. *adj.* real/firm. 2. *adj. & n.* (made of) hard stonelike substance made by mixing sand, gravel, cement and water. **con•crete mix•er,** *n.* machine for mixing concrete. **con•cre•tion** [kɒnˈkriːʃn] *n.* mass of things which have solidified together.

con•cu•bine [ˈkɒŋkjubaɪn] *n.* woman who lives with a man as his second wife, but who is not married to him.

con•cur [kənˈkɜː] *v.* (**concurred**) to agree. **con•cur•rence** [kənˈkʌrəns] *n.* agreement. **con•cur•rent** [kənˈkʌrənt] *adj.* which happen at the same time. **con•cur•rent•ly,** *adv.* happening at the same time.

con•cus•sion [kənˈkʌʃn] *n.* shock to the brain caused by being hit on the head. **con•cussed,** *adj.* in a state of concussion.

con•demn [kənˈdem] *v.* to blame; to sentence (a criminal); to declare (buildings) to be unfit to use or live in. **con•dem•na•tion** [kɒndemˈneɪʃn] *n.* blame.

con•dense [kənˈdens] *v.* (a) to reduce the size of (sth); **condensed milk** = milk which has been concentrated and sweetened. (b) (*of steam*) to form drops of water. **con•den•sa•tion** [kɒndenˈseɪʃn] *n.* act of condensing; steam which has formed into a film on a cold surface. **con•dens•er,** *n.* part of a machine which turns gas into liquid.

con•de•scend [kɒndɪˈsend] *v.* to speak/to act as if you are superior to s.o. else. **con•de•scend•ing,** *adj.* unpleasantly superior (voice/smile, etc.). **con•de•scen•sion,** *n.* acting with a feeling of superiority.

con•di•ment [ˈkɒndɪmənt] *n.* seasoning for food, such as salt, pepper, mustard.

con•di•tion [kənˈdɪʃn] 1. *n.* (a) state. (b) term (of a bargain); **on c. that** = provided that. (c) bad state; **a heart c.** = a weak heart. 2. *v.* (a) to put into good condition. (b) to make (s.o.) used to sth.; **conditioned reflex** = reaction to a stimulus which has been repeated many times. **con•di•tion•al,** *adj. & n.* provided that certain things happen; part of a verb which shows this; "**I would come**" **is a conditional form of "to come."** **con•di•tion•al•ly,** *adv.* under certain conditions. **con•di•tion•er,** *n.* lotion which puts sth (esp. hair) into good condition.

con•dole [kənˈdəʊl] *v.* **to c. with s.o.** = to express your regrets for some tragedy which has happened. **con•do•lences,** *n. pl.* expressions of regret (at the death of s.o.).

con•dom [ˈkɒndəm] *n.* rubber contraceptive sheath.

con•do•min•i•um [kɒndəˈmɪnɪəm] *n.* (a) joint ownership or rule. (b) building held in joint ownership.

con•done [kənˈdəʊn] *v.* to excuse/forgive (a crime, etc.).

con•dor [ˈkɒndɔː] *n.* large South American vulture.

con•du•cive [kənˈdjuːsɪv] *adj.* favorable (**to**).

con•duct 1. *n.* [ˈkɒndʌkt] way of behaving. 2. *v.* [kənˈdʌkt] (a) to lead/to guide/to control (a business, an orchestra); **conducted tour** = tour led by a guide. (b) to allow (electricity/heat) to pass through. (c) **to c. yourself** = to behave. **con•duc•tion** [kənˈdʌkʃn] *n.* passing of heat/electricity. **con•duc•tiv•i•ty** [kɒndʌkˈtɪvɪtɪ] *n.* ability to conduct electricity or heat. **con•duc•tor,** *n.* (a) substance (such as metal) which conducts heat/electricity. (b) person who directs an orchestra. (c) **bus c.** = person who collects money from the passengers on a bus, train, etc. **con•duc•tress,** *n.* (*pl.* **-es**) woman who is a conductor.

con•duit [ˈkɒndɪt] *n.* tube along which liquids can be passed.

cone [kəʊn] *n.* geometrical figure, round at the base, rising to a point; **ice cream c.** = cone-shaped biscuit for holding ice cream; **pine c.** = fruit of a pine tree; **nose c.** = pointed end of a rocket. **cone-shaped,** *adj.* shaped like a cone.

con•fab [ˈkɒnfæb] *n. inf.* chat/discussion.

con•fec•tion [kənˈfekʃən] *n.* food made of a mixture of sweet things. **con•fec•tion•er•y** [kənˈfekʃənrɪ] *n.* sweets and cakes. **con•fec•tion•er's,** *n.* shop selling candy and cakes.

con•fed•er•ate [kənˈfedərət] *n.* person who has joined with others (usu. to do a crime). **con•fed•er•a•cy,** *n.* joining together. **con•fed•er•a•tion** [kənfedəˈreɪʃn] *n.* group (of states/labor unions, etc.).

con•fer [kənˈfɜː] *v.* (**conferred**) (a) to discuss. (b) **to c. an honor on s.o.** = to award s.o. an honor. **con•fer•ence** [ˈkɒnfərəns] *n.* discussion; meeting of a group/society.

con•fess [kənˈfes] *v.* to admit that you have done sth wrong. **con•fes•sion** [kənˈfeʃn] *n.* admission of fault; **to make your c.** = to admit your sins to a priest. **con•fes•sion•al,** *n.* small private box in a church where a priest hears confessions. **con•fes•sor,** *n.* priest who hears confessions.

con•fet•ti [kənˈfetɪ] *n.* small pieces of colored paper thrown over the bride and bridegroom after a wedding.

con•fi•dant, confidante [kɒnfrˈdænt] *n.* man/woman you tell secrets to.

con•fide [kənˈfaɪd] *v.* **to c. in s.o.** = to tell s.o. a secret. **con•fi•dence** [ˈkɒnfɪdəns] *n.* (a) feeling sure. (b) secrecy; **in c.** = as a secret. (c) **c. trick** = trick whereby a trickster gains s.o.'s confidence to steal money from him. **con•fi•dent,** *adj.* sure (of yourself). **con•fi•dent•ly,** *adv.* in a sure way. **con•fi•den•tial** [kɒnfrˈdenʃl] *adj.* secret/private; (secretary) entrusted with confidential matters. **con•fi•den•ti•al•i•ty,** *n.* being secret/private. **con•fi•den•tial•ly,** *adv.* in a confidential way.

con•fig•u•ra•tion [kənfɪgəˈreɪʃn] *n.* (a) (*formal*) shape. (b) way in which computer hardware or software are planned.

con•fine [kənˈfaɪn] *v.* to restrict/to shut up; **confined to bed** = forced to stay in bed. **con•fine•ment,** *n.* (a) imprisonment. (b) period when a woman gives birth to a baby.

con•firm [kənˈfɜːm] *v.* (a) to make definite/to make sure. (b) **to be confirmed** = to be made a full member of a church. **con•fir•ma•tion** [kɒnfəˈmeɪʃn] *n.* (a) making sure. (b) ceremony in which s.o. is made a full member of the church. **con•firm•a•to•ry,** *adj.* which confirms. **con•firmed,** *adj.* permanent; **he is a c. bachelor** = he will never get married.

con•fis•cate [ˈkɒnfɪskeɪt] *v.* to take away s.o.'s possessions as a punishment. **con•fis•ca•tion** [kɒnfɪsˈkeɪʃn] *n.* act of confiscating.

con•fla•gra•tion [kɒnfləˈgreɪʃn] *n.* (*formal*) big fire.

con•flate [kənˈfleɪt] *v.* to put together.

con•flict 1. *n.* [ˈkɒnflɪkt] battle/fight. 2. *v.* [kənˈflɪkt] to clash/to contradict.

con•flu•ence [ˈkɒnfluəns] *n.* (*formal*) place where two rivers join together.

con•form [kənˈfɔːm] *v.* to fit in (**to** a pattern); to act in the same way as other people. **con•form•ist,** *n.* person who conforms. **con•form•i•ty,** *n.* conforming.

con•found [kənˈfaʊnd] *v.* to confuse/to bother.

con•front [kənˈfrʌnt] *v.* to face up to (a danger); **to c. s.o. with** = to bring s.o. face to face with. **con•fron•ta•tion** [kɒnfrʌnˈteɪʃn] *n.* bringing face to face; meeting between opposing sides.

con•fuse [kənˈfjuːz] *v.* to mix/to muddle. **con•fused,** *adj.* mixed-up/muddled.

con•fus•ed•ly [kənˈfjuːzɪdlɪ] *adv.* in a muddled way. **con•fus•ing,** *adj.* muddling. **con•fu•sion** [kənˈfjuːʒn] *n.* muddle/disorder.

con•fute [kənˈfjuːt] *v.* (*formal*) to prove (sth) wrong. **con•fu•ta•tion** [kɒnfjuːˈteɪʃn] *n.* proving wrong.

con•geal [kənˈdʒiːl] *v.* to set solid; to become solid (as of dried blood).

con•gen•ial [kənˈdʒiːnɪəl] *adj.* sympathetic/friendly.

con•gen•i•tal [kənˈdʒenɪtl] *adj.* (illness/defect) present in a person since birth. **con•gen•i•tal•ly,** *adv.* from birth.

con•ger eel [ˈkɒŋgə iːl] *n.* very large type of eel.

con•gest•ed [kənˈdʒestɪd] *adj.* blocked/crowded. **con•ges•tion** [kənˈdʒeʃtʃn] *n.* blocking (of streets); filling (of the lungs) with liquid.

con•glom•er•a•tion [kənglɒməˈreɪʃn] *n.* mass of things heaped together. **con•glom•er•ate** [kənˈglɒmərət] *n.* (a) rock made of small pieces fused together. (b) many subsidiary companies linked together.

Con•go•lese [kɒŋgəˈliːz] *adj.* & *n.* (person) from the Congo.

con•grat•u•late [kənˈgrætjuleɪt] *v.* to give (s.o.) good wishes on a special occasion; to praise (s.o.) for some achievement. **con•grat•u•la•tions** [kəngrætjuˈleɪʃnz] *n.* good wishes. **con•grat•u•la•to•ry** [kənˈgrætjulətrɪ] *adj.* which gives good wishes.

con•gre•gate [ˈkɒŋgrɪgeɪt] *v.* to gather together. **con•gre•ga•tion** [kɒŋgrɪˈgeɪʃn] *n.* people gathered together; people meeting together in a church.

con•gress [ˈkɒŋgres] *n.* meeting of a group of people; **Congress** = the elected legislative body of the United States. **con•gres•sion•al,** *adj.* referring to the U.S. Congress. **con•gress•man, congresswoman,** *n.* (*pl.* -men -women) member of the Congress of the United States.

con•gru•ent [ˈkɒŋgruənt] *adj.* which fit together.

con•i•cal [ˈkɒnɪkl] *adj.* shaped like a cone.

co•ni•fer [ˈkɒnɪfə] *n.* tree which bears cones. **con•if•er•ous** [kəˈnɪfərəs] *adj.* referring to conifers.

con•jec•ture [kənˈdʒektʃə] 1. *n.* guess. 2. *v.* to guess. **con•jec•tur•al,** *adj.* possible/which has been guessed at.

con•ju•gal ['kɒndʒʊgl] *adj.* referring to marriage.

con•ju•gate ['kɒndʒʊgeɪt] *v.* to show the different parts of (a verb). **con•ju•ga•tion** [kɒndʒʊ'geɪʃn] *n.* way in which a verb changes according to tense and person.

con•junc•tion [kən'dʒʌŋkʃn] *n.* word which links different parts of a sentence; **in c. with** = together with.

con•junc•ti•vi•tis [kəndʒʌŋktɪ'vaɪtɪs] *n.* inflammation of the eyes.

con•junc•ture [kən'dʒʌŋktʃə] *n.* circumstances.

con•jure ['kʌnʒə] *v.* (a) to do tricks with cards/rabbits, etc. (b) to call **up** (a spirit/a picture). **con•jur•er, conjuror,** *n.* person who does tricks. **con•jur•ing,** *n.* magic tricks.

conk [kɒŋk] *n. Sl.* head. **conk out,** *v. inf.* to stop working.

con•nect [kə'nekt] *v.* to join/to link; **this train connects with the 3:06** = this train arrives in time for you to get off it and catch the 3:06; **they are connected to the Williams family** = they are related to them. **con•nect•ed,** *adj.* joined/linked; **well c.** = with influential friends and relations. **con•nec•tion,** *Brit.* **connexion,** *n.* join/link; **in c. with your visit** = with reference to/concerning your visit; **there is a connection to Chicago** = there is a train which connects with this one for Chicago; **he has connections in the theater** = he has friends/relations in the theater.

conn•ing tow•er ['kɒnɪŋtaʊə] *n.* highest part of a submarine.

con•nive [kə'naɪv] *v.* **to c. at sth** = to allow it to take place. **con•niv•ance,** *n.* conniving (at sth).

con•nois•seur [kɒnə'sɜː] *n.* expert/person who knows a lot (about sth).

con•note [kə'nəʊt] *v.* to imply sth in addition. **con•no•ta•tion,** *n.* additional meaning.

con•nu•bi•al [kə'njuːbɪəl] *adj. (formal)* referring to marriage.

con•quer ['kɒŋkə] *v.* to defeat by force. **con•quer•ing,** *adj.* triumphant/victorious. **con•quer•or,** *n.* person who leads the invasion of a country; state which captures another country. **con•quest** ['kɒŋkwest] *n.* (a) capturing. (b) thing/country which has been captured.

con•san•guin•i•ty [kɒnsæn'gwɪnɪtɪ] *n. (formal)* connection by blood.

con•science ['kɒnʃəns] *n.* feeling which tells you if you have done right or wrong. **con•sci-ence-strick•en,** *adj.* ashamed. **con•sci•en•tious** [kɒnʃɪ'enʃəs] *adj.* who works carefully and well; **c. objector** = person who refuses to join the armed forces because he feels war is wrong. **con•sci•en•tious•ly,** *adv.* in a conscientious way.

con•scious ['kɒnʃəs] *adj.* aware of things around you; **a c. decision** = a deliberate decision. **con•scious•ly,** *adv.* in a conscious way. **con•scious•ness,** *n.* being conscious; **to lose c.** = to become unconscious.

con•script 1. *n.* ['kɒnskrɪpt] person who has been ordered to join the armed forces. 2. *v.* [kən'skrɪpt] to order (people) to join the armed forces. **con•scrip•tion** [kən'skrɪpʃn] *n.* legal obligation to join the armed forces.

con•se•crate ['kɒnsɪkreɪt] *v.* to bless (a new church/a ruler); to devote (one's life **to** sth). **con•se•cra•tion** [kɒnsɪ'kreɪʃn] *n.* blessing; devoting (of your life).

con•sec•u•tive [kən'sekjʊtɪv] *adj.* following one after the other. **con•sec•u•tive•ly,** *adv.* in order.

con•sen•sus [kən'sensəs] *n.* generally agreed opinion.

con•sent [kən'sent] 1. *n.* agreement. 2. *v.* to agree (**to** sth).

con•se•quence ['kɒnsɪkwəns] *n.* (a) result. (b) importance; **it is of no c.** = it does not matter. **con•se•quent,** *adj.* **c. on** = resulting from. **con•se•quen•tial** [kɒnsɪ'kwenʃl] *adj.* resulting. **con•se•quent•ly,** *adv.* because of this/for this reason.

con•serve [kən'sɜːv] *v.* to save. **con•serv•an•cy,** *n.* body which controls a river, etc. **con•ser•va•tion** [kɒnsə'veɪʃn] *n.* preservation/saving (of energy, natural resources, old buildings, etc.). **con•ser•va•tion•ist,** *n.* person who is interested in conservation. **con•serv•a•tism,** *n.* (a) being conservative. (b) *(in politics)* policies of the Conservative party. **con•serv•a•tive** [kən'sɜːvətɪv] *adj.* (a) not wanting to change; **C. party** = political party in Great Britain which does not want to change the existing system of government, and which does not favor state control of industry; **a C.** = member of the Conservative Party. (b) **at a c. estimate** = at the lowest/most moderate estimate. **con•serv•a•tive•ly,** *adv.* moderately. **con•serv•a•to•ry,** *n.* (a) room with large windows, where you keep tropical flowers and plants. (b) *also* **con•ser•va•toire** [kən'sɜːvətwɑːr] academy of music, art, etc.

con•sid•er [kən'sɪdə] *v.* to think deeply about (sth). **con•sid•er•a•ble,** *adj.* quite large. **con•sid•er•a•bly,** *adv.* to a great extent. **con•sid•er•ate,** *adj.* full of feeling/understanding toward s.o. **con•sid•er•ate•ly,** *adv.* thoughtfully. **con•sid•er•a•tion** [kənsɪdə'reɪʃn] *n.* (a) being thought about. (b) small sum of money. **con•sid•er•ing,** *prep.* when you think of/taking into account.

con•sign [kən'saɪn] *v.* to give (goods) into s.o.'s care. **con•sign•ee,** *n.* (*formal*) person who receives goods from s.o. **con•sign•ment,** *n.* (a) sending of goods. (b) goods which have been sent. **con•sign•or,** *n.* person who consigns goods to s.o.

con•sist [kən'sɪst] *v.* (a) (**in**) to have as a basis. (b) (**of**) to be made up of. **con•sist•en•cy,** *n.* (a) being the same throughout. (b) thickness (of a paste, etc.). **con•sist•ent,** *adj.* which does not contradict; always the same/unchanging. **con•sist•ent•ly,** *adv.* always/permanently.

con•sis•to•ry [kən'sɪstəri:] *n.* meeting of the Pope and cardinals at which a decision is taken.

con•sole 1. *n.* ['kɒnsəʊl] (a) flat table with the keyboard (of an organ/telex machine, etc.). (b) cabinet for a TV set. 2. *v.* [kən'səʊl] to comfort (s.o.) after a loss. **con•so•la•tion** [kɒnsə'leɪʃn] *n.* comfort; **c. prize** = prize given to s.o. who did not win, but who tried hard.

con•sol•i•date [kən'sɒlɪdeɪt] *v.* to make firm/solid. **con•sol•i•da•tion** [kənsɒlɪ'deɪʃn] *n.* making firm.

con•som•mé [kən'sɒmeɪ] *n.* thin clear soup.

con•so•nant ['kɒnsənənt] 1. *n.* (letter representing) a sound which is not a vowel. 2. *adj.* which agrees with.

con•sort 1. *n.* ['kɒnsɔ:t] husband or wife (of a queen or king). 2. *v.* [kən'sɔ:t] to go around with s.o.

con•sor•ti•um [kən'sɔ:tɪəm] *n.* (*pl.* -tia) group of companies who work together.

con•spic•u•ous [kən'spɪkjʊəs] *adj.* very obvious; **he was c. by his absence** = everyone noticed that he was not there. **con•spic•u•ous•ly,** *adv.* very obviously.

con•spire [kən'spaɪə] *v.* to plot (**to** do sth). **con•spir•a•cy** [kən'spɪrəsɪ] *n.* plot. **con•spir•a•tor,** *n.* plotter. **con•spir•a•to•ri•al** [kənspɪrə'tɔ:rɪəl] *adj.* like s.o. who is plotting.

con•sta•ble ['kʌnstəbl] *n.* (a) a peace officer in a town, rural area, etc. (b) *Brit.* police officer. **con•stab•u•lar•y** [kən'stæbjʊlərɪ] *n.* constables of a district.

con•stant ['kɒnstənt] *adj.* (a) not changing or stopping. (b) faithful. **con•stan•cy,** *n.* faithfulness. **con•stant•ly,** *adv.* all the time.

con•stel•la•tion [kɒnstə'leɪʃn] *n.* group of stars forming a pattern in the sky.

con•ster•na•tion [kɒnstə'neɪʃn] *n.* shock/surprise.

con•sti•pat•ed ['kɒnstɪpeɪtɪd] *adj.* unable to empty the bowels regularly. **con•sti•pa•tion** [kɒnstɪ'peɪʃn] *n.* slow working of the bowels.

con•stit•u•ent [kən'stɪtjʊənt] 1. *adj.* (part) which makes up a whole. 2. *n.* (a) part which goes to make up a whole. (b) voter who lives in a district served by a particular elected official. **con•stit•u•en•cy,** *n.* district of voters served by a particular elected official.

con•sti•tute ['kɒnstɪtju:t] *v.* to make up; to establish. **con•sti•tu•tion** [kɒnstɪ'tju:ʃn] *n.* (a) bodily health. (b) laws and principles which form the basis of a country's organization. **con•sti•tu•tion•al.** 1. *adj.* referring to the legal basis of a state; (monarchy) where the power is held by an elected government. 2. *n.* short walk which is supposed to be good for the health. **con•sti•tu•tion•al•ly,** *adv.* according to the constitution.

con•strain [kən'streɪn] *v.* to force. **con•straint,** *n.* force.

con•strict [kən'strɪkt] *v.* to squeeze/to strangle. **con•stric•tion** [kən'strɪkʃn] *n.* constricting.

con•struct [kən'strʌkt] *v.* to build. **con•struc•tion** [kən'strʌkʃn] *n.* (a) act of building; way in which sth is made up. (b) thing which has been built. **con•struc•tive,** *adj.* which aims at improving. **con•struc•tive•ly,** *adv.* in a constructive way. **con•struct•or,** *n.* person who constructs.

con•strue [kən'stru:] *v.* to take to mean.

con•sul ['kɒnsəl] *n.* country's representative abroad, particularly looking after the business interests and personal affairs of its citizens. **con•su•lar** ['kɒnsjʊlə] *adj.* referring to a consul. **con•su•late,** *n.* house/offices of a consul.

con•sult [kən'sʌlt] *v.* to ask for advice. **con•sult•ant,** *n.* specialist who gives advice, esp. medical specialist attached to a hospital. **con•sul•ta•tion** [kɒnsʌl'teɪʃn] *n.* act of consulting. **con•sul•ta•tive** [kən'sʌltətɪv] *adj.* which gives advice. **con•sult•ing,** *n.* asking for advice.

con•sume [kən'sju:m] *v.* (a) to eat or drink. (b) to use up. **con•sum•a•bles,** *n.* (a) consumer

---

æ **back,** ɑ: **farm,** ɒ: **top,** aɪ **pipe,** aʊ **how,** aɪə **fire,** aʊə **flower,** ɔ: **bought,** ɔɪ **toy,** e **fed,** eə **hair,** eɪ **take,** ə **afraid,** əʊ **boat,** əʊə **lower,** v: **word,** i: **heap,** ɪ **hit,** ɪə **hear,** u: **school,** ʊ **book,** ʌ **but,** b **back,** d **dog,** ð **then,** dʒ **just,** f **fog,** g **go,** h **hand,** j **yes,** k **catch,** l **last,** m **mix,** n **nut,** ŋ **sing,** p **penny,** r **round,** s **some,** ʃ **short,** t **too,** tʃ **chop,** θ **thing,** v **voice,** w **was,** z **zoo,** ʒ **treasure**

goods. (b) (*computers*) paper, ribbons, etc., which are used in peripherals. **con•sum•er**, *n.* person who uses goods or eats food; **c. goods** = goods which are bought by ordinary members of the public (and not by industry). **con•sum•er•ism**, *n.* fighting for the rights of the consumer.

con•sum•mate 1. *adj.* [kən'sʌmɪt] perfect (artist, etc.). 2. *v.* ['kɒnsəmeɪt] to complete; **to c. a marriage** = to have sexual intercourse for the first time after marriage. **con•sum•ma•tion** [kɒnsə'meɪʃn] *n.* completion; end.

con•sump•tion [kən'sʌmpʃn] *n.* (a) act of consuming; quantity consumed. (b) (*old*) tuberculosis. **con•sump•tive**, *adj.* looking as though one is suffering from tuberculosis.

cont. *abbrev for* continued.

con•tact ['kɒntækt] 1. *n.* (a) touch; **c. lenses** = tiny lenses worn on the eyeballs, replacing glasses. (b) person whom you know/whom you have contacted. 2. *v.* to get into communication with (s.o.).

con•ta•gion [kən'teɪdʒn] *n.* passing on of a disease by touching. **con•ta•gious** [kən'teɪdʒəs] *adj.* (disease) which is transmitted by touching.

con•tain [kən'teɪn] *v.* (a) to hold/to have inside. (b) to hold back/to restrain (an attack, anger). **con•tain•er**, *n.* (a) box/bottle, etc., which holds sth else. (b) large case for easy loading on a ship, truck, etc. **con•tain•er•i•za•tion**, *n.* using containers for shipping goods. **con•tain•ment**, *n.* holding back (an enemy).

con•tam•i•nate [kən'tæmɪneɪt] *v.* to make bad/dirty. **con•tam•i•nant**, *n.* substance which contaminates. **con•tam•i•na•tion** [kəntæmɪ'neɪʃn] *n.* act of contaminating.

con•tem•plate ['kɒntempleɪt] *v.* (a) to look at (sth) intently. (b) to plan to do sth. **con•tem•pla•tion** [kɒntem'pleɪʃn] *n.* meditation/deep thought. **con•tem•pla•tive** [kən'templətɪv] *adj.* which meditates.

con•tem•po•rar•y [kən'tempɹərɪ] *adj. & n.* (a) (**with**) (person) who lives at the same time or is (about) the same age as another; (thing) which dates back to the same period as another thing. (b) modern/up-to-date. **con•tem•po•ra•ne•ous** [kəntempə-'reɪnɪəs] *adj.* of the same date/period.

con•tempt [kən'tempt] *n.* feeling of hatred/disrespect for s.o.; **c. of court** = conduct which a judge rules is offensive to a court. **con•tempt•i•ble**, *adj.* which deserves contempt. **con•temp•tu•ous**, *adj.* scornful (**of**).

con•tend [kən'tend] *v.* (a) (**with**) to fight. (b) to

state/to believe. **con•tend•er**, *n.* person who challenges s.o. to a fight; person who fights.

con•tent 1. *adj.* [kən'tent] (**with**) satisfied/happy. 2. *n.* (a) [kən'tent] satisfaction; **to your heart's c.** = as much as you like. (b) ['kɒntent] thing which is contained/which is in a container; **table of contents** = list of chapters/sections in a book; **the contents of the letter** = what was written in it; **mineral c. of water** = percentage of minerals in water. 3. *v.* [kən'tent] to satisfy. **con•tent•ed**, *adj.* satisfied/happy. **con•tent•ed•ly**, *adv.* in a contented way. **con•tent•ed•ness, contentment**, *n.* being contented.

con•ten•tion [kən'tenʃn] *n.* (a) dispute; **bone of c.** = source of argument. (b) statement/belief. **con•ten•tious** [kən'tenʃəs] *adj.* (person) who likes arguments; (problem) which is a frequent source of dispute.

con•ter•mi•nous [kəʊ'tɜːmɪnəs] *adj.* which has the same boundaries as sth. else.

con•test 1. *n.* ['kɒntest] fight; competition. 2. *v.* [kən'test] (a) to fight (an election). (b) to query; argue that (a will) is invalid. **con•test•ant**, *n.* competitor/person who enters a contest.

con•text ['kɒntekst] *n.* phrase in which a word occurs, which helps show its meaning; **out of c.** = without the surrounding text. **con•tex•tu•al** [kən'tekstjʊəl] *adj.* referring to a context.

con•tig•u•ous [kən'tɪgjʊəs] *adj.* (*formal*) next to/touching. **con•ti•gu•i•ty** [kɒntɪ'gjuːɪtɪ] *n.* being contiguous.

con•ti•nent ['kɒntɪnənt] 1. *n.* large mass of land; **on the C.** = in Europe. 2. *adj.* able to control the passing of urine or excreta. **con•ti•nen•tal** [kɒntɪ'nentl] *adj.* (a) referring to a continent. (b) referring to Europe (excluding the British Isles); **a Continental** = a European (but not an inhabitant of the British Isles); **c. breakfast** = coffee and rolls or bread; **c. climate** = climate with hot dry summers and very cold winters, found in the central parts of continents; **c. quilt** = a duvet, a bag stuffed with feathers, used as the only covering for a bed.

con•tin•gent [kən'tɪndʒənt] 1. *adj.* which depends on sth. 2. *n.* group of soldiers, etc. **con•tin•gen•cy**, *n.* emergency.

con•tin•ue [kən'tɪnjuː] *v.* to go on doing sth. **con•tin•u•al**, *adj.* which goes on all the time without stopping. **con•tin•u•al•ly**, *adv.* very frequently; all the time. **con•tin•u•a•tion** [kəntɪnjuˈeɪʃn] *n.* (a) (*also* **con•tin•u•ance**) going on without stopping. (b) extension/thing which has been continued. **con•ti•nu•i•ty** [kɒntɪ'njuːɪtɪ] *n.* state of continuing without a break; **c. girl** = girl who ensures that each scene in a motion picture follows on smoothly. **con•tin•u•ous** [kən'tɪnjʊəs] *adj.* with no break. **con•tin•u•ous•ly,** *adv.* one after the other with no break in between. **con•tin•u•um,** *n.* thing which continues.

con•tort [kən'tɔːt] *v.* to twist unnaturally. **con•tor•tion** [kən'tɔːʃn] *n.* twisting unnaturally. **con•tor•tion•ist,** *n.* person in a show who twists his body into odd shapes.

con•tour ['kɒntʊə] *n.* shape of the outline of sth; **c. (line)** = line on a map drawn through points at the same height above sea level.

con•tra ['kɒntræ] *prep.* against.

con•tra•band ['kɒntrəbænd] *n.* (*no pl.*) goods on which customs duty has not been paid.

con•tra•cep•tion [kɒntrə'sepʃn] *n.* prevention of pregnancy. **con•tra•cep•tive,** *adj. & n.* (thing) which prevents pregnancy.

con•tract 1. *n.* ['kɒntrækt] legal agreement. 2. *v.* [kən'trækt] (a) to get smaller; to make smaller; to tighten. (b) to sign an agreement to do some work. (c) to catch (a disease). **con•trac•tion** [kən'trækʃn] *n.* shortening; shrinking. **con•trac•tor,** *n.* person who does work according to a signed agreement. **con•trac•tu•al,** *adj.* according to a contract.

con•tra•dict [kɒntrə'dɪkt] *v.* to deny what s.o. else says. **con•tra•dic•tion** [kɒntrə'dɪkʃn] *n.* saying the opposite. **con•tra•dic•to•ry,** *adj.* which says the opposite.

con•tral•to [kən'træltəʊ] *n.* (*pl.* -os) (woman with a) low-pitched singing voice.

con•trap•tion [kən'træpʃn] *n.* machine/device.

con•tra•pun•tal [kɒntrə'pʌntl] *adj.* using counterpoint.

con•trar•y ['kɒntrərɪ] 1. *adj.* (a) opposite; **c. winds** = winds blowing in the opposite direction to the one you want. (b) [kən'treərɪ] rude; always doing the opposite of what you want. 2. *n.* **the c.** = the opposite; **on the c.** = quite the opposite; **to the c.** = stating sth different/opposite. 3. *adv.* in an opposite way (**to**). **con•trar•i•ly,** *adv.* in a contrary way. **con•trar•i•ness** [kən'treərɪnəs] *n.* always doing the opposite of what people want/awkwardness (of a child).

con•trast 1. *n.* ['kɒntrɑːst] sharp difference. 2. *v.* [kən'trɑːst] to show up the difference between.

con•tra•vene [kɒntrə'viːn] *v.* to break the law/the regulations. **con•tra•ven•tion** [kɒntrə'venʃn] *n.* breaking of a law.

con•trib•ute [kən'trɪbjuːt] *v.* (a) to help with; **to c. to** = write articles for (a newspaper, etc.). (b) to give money (**to** a charity). **con•tri•bu•tion** [kɒntrɪ'bjuːʃn] *n.* (a) article submitted to a newspaper. (b) money, etc., given to help sth. **con•trib•u•tor** [kən'trɪbjutə] *n.* a person who contributes. **con•trib•u•to•ry,** *adj.* which helps; **c. factors** = factors which have helped produce the situation.

con•trite ['kɒntraɪt] *adj.* (person) who is sorry. **con•tri•tion** [kən'trɪʃn] *n.* regret.

con•trive [kən'traɪv] *v.* to manage; to plan. **con•triv•ance,** *n.* machine/device. **con•trived,** *adj.* artificial/not natural.

con•trol [kən'trəʊl] 1. *n.* (a) authority/power; keeping in order; **under c.** = in order; **birth c.** = limiting of the number of babies born. (b) **the controls** = the gears/levers, etc., for directing a machine. (c) standard with which the results of an experiment can be compared. 2. *v.* (**controlled**) (a) to direct. (b) to limit/to regulate. **con•trol•la•ble,** *adj.* which can be controlled. **con•trol•ler,** *n.* person who controls. **con•trol tow•er,** *n.* high building at an airport, which houses the radio operators who direct planes on landing or takeoff.

con•tro•ver•sy [kən'trɒvəsɪ] *n.* violent discussion. **con•tro•ver•sial** [kɒntrə'vɜːʃl] *adj.* (subject) which provokes violent discussions. **con•tro•vert,** *v.* (*formal*) to deny. **con•tro•vert•i•ble,** *adj.* which can be denied.

con•tu•ma•cious [kɒntju'meɪʃəs] *adj.* (*formal*) persistently disobedient.

con•tu•me•ly ['kɒntjumlɪ] *n.* (*formal*) rudeness/insults.

con•tu•sion [kən'tjuːʒn] *n.* (*formal*) bruise.

co•nun•drum [kə'nʌndrəm] *n.* riddle.

con•ur•ba•tion [kɒnə'beɪʃn] *n.* very large spread of a built-up area.

con•va•lesce [kɒnvə'les] *v.* to recover after an illness/an operation. **con•va•les•cence,** *n.* period when you are convalescing. **con•va•les•cent,** *adj. & n.* (person) who is convalescing; **c. home** = rest home for people who are convalescing.

con•vec•tion [kən'vekʃn] *n.* upward movement of heat in air/liquid. **con•vec•tor,** *n.* heater which warms the air moving through it.

æ back, aː farm, ɒ top, aɪ pipe, aʊ how, aɪe fire, aʊe flower, ɔː bought, ɔɪ toy, e fed, eəhair, eɪ take, ə afraid, əʊ boat, əʊe lower, vː word, iː heap, ɪ hit, ɪə hear, uː school, ʊ book, ʌ but, b back, d dog, ð then, dʒ just, f fog, g go, h hand, j yes, k catch, l last, m mix, n nut, ŋ sing, p penny, r round, s some, ʃ short, t too, tʃ chop, θ thing, v voice, w was, z zoo, ʒ treasure

con•vene [kən'viːn] *v.* to call together (a meeting). **con•ve•nor,** *n.* person who convenes.

con•ven•ience [kən'viːnɪəns] *n.* (a) suitableness; **at your earliest c.** = as soon as it suits you. (b) public toilet. (c) **all modern conveniences** = all modern comforts (in a house). (d) **c. foods** = dishes which are easy/quick to prepare. **con•ven•ient,** *adj.* suitable; practical. **con•ven•ient•ly,** *adv.* handily.

con•vent ['kɒnvənt] *n.* religious house for women.

con•ven•tion [kən'venʃn] *n.* (a) custom/usual way of doing things. (b) contract. (c) congress/general meeting of an association/political party. **con•ven•tion•al,** *adj.* ordinary/usual; **c. weapons** = ordinary (not nuclear) weapons. **con•ven•tion•al•ly,** *adv.* in a conventional/ordinary/usual way.

con•verge [kən'vɜːdʒ] *v.* to come together at a certain place. **con•ver•gence,** *n.* meeting. **con•ver•gent,** *adj.* meeting at a certain point.

con•ver•sant [kən'vɜːsənt] *adj.* familiar (**with** a subject).

con•verse 1. *n.* ['kɒnvɜːs] the opposite. 2. *v.* [kən'vɜːs] to talk. **con•ver•sa•tion** [kɒnvə-'seɪʃn] *n.* talk. **con•ver•sa•tion•al,** *adj.* in conversation. **con•ver•sa•tion•al•ist,** *n.* person who converses well. **con•verse•ly,** *adv.* in the opposite way.

con•ver•sion [kən'vɜːʃn] *n.* (a) changing (of one thing into another). (b) turning of a person to another religion.

con•vert 1. *n.* ['kɒnvɜːt] person who has changed religion. 2. *v.* [kən'vɜːt] (a) to turn (s.o.) from one religion to another. (b) to change. **con•vert•er,** *n.* machine which converts. **con•vert•i•bil•i•ty** [kənvɜːtɪ'bɪlɪtɪ] *n.* easiness of change of one currency to another. **con•vert•i•ble** [kən'vɜːtəbl] 1. *adj.* which can easily be changed (esp. of a currency). 2. *n.* car with a roof which folds back.

con•vex ['kɒnveks] *adj.* (surface) which is rounded outward like the back of a spoon.

con•vey [kən'veɪ] *v.* to transport/to carry; to give (greetings, etc.). **con•vey•ance,** *n.* (a) transporting. (b) means of transport. (c) transfer of property from one owner to another. **con•vey•anc•ing,** *n.* transferring of property. **con•vey•or,** *n.* person who transports/thing which transports; **c. belt** = long moving surface used in a factory to move products through the production processes.

con•vict 1. *n.* ['kɒnvɪkt] criminal who has been sentenced to prison. 2. *v.* [kən'vɪkt] to find (s.o.) guilty; to sentence (a criminal) to prison. **con•vic•tion** [kən'vɪkʃn] *n.* (a) being found guilty. (b) firm belief.

con•vince [kən'vɪns] *v.* **to c. s.o. of sth** = to persuade/to make (s.o.) believe sth. **con•vinc•ing,** *adj.* (argument) which convinces. **con•vinc•ing•ly,** *adv.* in a convincing way.

con•viv•i•al [kən'vɪvɪəl] *adj.* lively/jolly. **con•viv•i•al•i•ty** [kənvɪvɪ'ælɪtɪ] *n.* liveliness.

con•voke [kən'vəuk] *v.* to call (a meeting). **con•vo•ca•tion** [kɒnvə'keɪʃn] *n.* (a) calling of a meeting. (b) meeting of a church assembly/university.

con•vo•lut•ed ['kɒnvəluːtɪd] *adj.* (a) twisted. (b) very complicated (story, etc.). **con•vo•lu•tion** [kɒnvə'luːʃn] *n.* twisting; complication.

con•vol•vu•lus [kən'vɒlvjʊləs] *n.* common climbing weed.

con•voy ['kɒnvɔɪ] 1. *n.* group of ships/trucks traveling together in line under protection. 2. *v.* to escort/to protect (esp. a line of merchant ships).

con•vulse [kən'vʌls] *v.* to make (sth/s.o.) shake. **con•vul•sions,** *n. pl.* violent shaking of the body; violent spasms which make the body twitch. **con•vul•sive,** *adj.* which causes violent shaking.

coo [kuː] *v.* to make soft noises (like a pigeon). **coo•ing,** *n.* noise made by a pigeon.

cook [kʊk] 1. *n.* person who prepares food by heating it. 2. *v.* (a) to prepare (food) by heating. (b) (*of food*) to be prepared; **dinner is cooking.** (c) *sl.* **to c. the books** = to falsify the entries in account books. **cook•book,** *n.* book of recipes. **cook•er,** *n.* stove or receptacle for cooking. **cook•er•y,** *n.* (*no pl.*) art of cooking; **c. book** = cookbook. **cook•ie,** *n.* small, sweet cake which is baked. **cook•ing,** *n.* action of preparing food, usu. by heating; **c. apple** = apple for cooking.

cool [kuːl] 1. *adj.* (**-er, -est**) (a) quite cold. (b) calm. (c) unfriendly (reception). 2. *n.* (a) state of being cool; place where it is cool; **in the c. of the evening.** (b) *Sl.* calmness; **she lost her c.** = she lost her temper. 3. *v.* to make cool; to become cool. **cool•ant,** *n.* substance (usu. water) used to keep engines cool. **cool down,** *v.* (a) to become cool. (b) to become calm. **cool•er,** *n.* (a) thing/machine which cools. (b) *Sl.* prison. **cool•ing.** 1. *adj.* refreshing (drink, etc.). 2. *n.* action of becoming cool. **cool•ly,** *adv.* in a cool/calm way. **cool•ness,** *n.* (a) being cool. (b) calmness. (c) unfriendliness (of a reception, etc.). **cool off,** *v.* to become cooler.

coo•lie ['kuːlɪ] *n.* workman/porter (in the Far East).

coop [ku:p] 1. *n.* cage for chickens. 2. *v.* **to be cooped up** = to be shut up inside.

co-op ['kəʊɒp] *n. inf.* cooperative store, apartment building, etc.

coop•er ['ku:pə] *n.* person who makes barrels.

co•op•er•ate [kəʊ'ɒpəreɪt] *v.* to work with s.o. **co•op•er•a•tion** [kəʊɒpə'reɪʃn] *n.* working together. **co•op•er•a•tive** [kəʊ'ɒprətɪv] 1. *adj. & n.* (store, etc.) which works on a profit-sharing basis. 2. *adj.* willing to work with s.o.

co-opt [kəʊ'ɒpt] *v.* to elect (s.o.) to join a committee by votes from those who are already members. **co-op•tion**, *n.* act of co-opting.

co-or•di•nate 1. *n.* [kəʊ'ɔ:dɪnət] (a) set of figures which fix a point on a map/graph. (b) **co-ordinates** = matching outer clothes for women. 2. *v.* [kəʊ'ɔ:dɪneɪt] to make things work together/fit in with each other. **co-or•di•na•tion** [kəʊɔ:dɪ'neɪʃn] *n.* co-ordinating. **co-or•di•nat•or**, *n.* person who co-ordinates.

coot [ku:t] *n.* black water bird with a white forehead.

co-own•er•ship [kəʊ'əʊnəʃɪp] *n.* ownership by several people or groups.

cop [kɒp] *n. inf.* police officer.

cope [kəʊp] 1. *n.* long colored cloak worn by a priest. 2. *v.* to deal with.

co•pi•lot ['kəʊpaɪlət] *n.* pilot who is second in command to the captain of an aircraft.

cop•ing ['kəʊpɪŋ] *n.* **c. stone** = top stone on a wall, which protects the wall from the weather.

co•pi•ous ['kəʊpɪəs] *adj.* plentiful/in good supply. **co•pi•ous•ly**, *adv.* in large quantities.

cop•per ['kɒpə] *n.* (a) (*element:* Cu) reddish metal which turns green when exposed to air. (b) large container or pan made of copper. (c) *inf.* policeman. (d) small coin made of copper or other brown metal. **cop•per•plate**, *n.* old-fashioned neat round handwriting.

cop•pice, copse ['kɒpɪs, kɒps] *n.* wood of young trees.

cop•ra ['kɒprə] *n.* dried coconut kernel used to make oil.

cop•u•late ['kɒpjʊleɪt] *v.* to have sexual intercourse. **cop•u•la•tion** [kɒpjʊ'leɪʃn] *n.* sexual intercourse.

cop•y ['kɒpɪ] 1. *n.* (a) an imitation/reproduction. (b) book; newspaper. (c) material to be used in a newspaper article/in an advertise-ment, etc. 2. *v.* to imitate/to make a reproduction of (sth). **cop•y•ed•it,** *v.* to correct (what s.o. has written before it is printed. **cop•y•ed•i•tor,** *n.* person who copyedits. **cop•i•er,** *n.* machine which makes copies. **cop•y•ing,** *n.* imitation. **cop•y•right,** *n.* right to publish a book/put on a play, etc., and not to have it copied without permission; **under c.** = protected by the laws of copyright. **cop•y•writ•er,** *n.* person who writes copy for advertisements.

co•quette [kɒ'ket] *n.* woman who flirts. **co•quet•tish,** *adj.* flirtatious. **co•quet•ry** ['kɒketrɪ] *n.* being coquettish.

cor•a•cle ['kɒrəkl] *n.* light round boat, covered with animal skin.

cor•al ['kɒrəl] *n.* (a) rocklike substance formed of the skeletons of tiny animals in the sea.

cor an•glais ['kɔ:'ɒŋgleɪ] *n.* bass oboe.

cor•bel ['kɔ:bl] *n.* piece of stone or wood which juts out from a wall and supports sth (usu. a roof beam).

cord [kɔ:d] *n.* (a) string/thin rope. (b) stringlike part of the body; **spinal c.** (c) *inf.* **cords** = corduroy trousers.

cor•dial ['kɔ:dɪəl] 1. *adj.* friendly. 2. *n.* sweet, aromatic alcoholic drink; liquer. **cor•dial•i•ty** [kɔ:dɪ'ælɪtɪ] *n.* friendliness. **cor•dial•ly,** *adv.* in a cordial way.

cord•ite ['kɔ:daɪt] *n.* type of explosive.

cor•don ['kɔ:dən] 1. *n.* (a) barrier to prevent s.o. escaping; line of police/soldiers surrounding a point. (b) fruit tree grown as a single stem, with side shoots cut back. 2. *v.* **to c. off a street** = to put up a cordon across a street. **cor•don bleu** [kɔ:dɒŋ'blɜ:] *adj.* top quality (cooking).

cor•du•roy ['kɔ:djʊrɔɪ] *n.* velvetlike cloth with ribs.

core [kɔ:] 1. *n.* central part; **rotten to the c.** = rotten right through; **to take a c. sample** = to cut a long round sample of rock with a drill. 2. *v.* to scoop out the core of (an apple, etc.).

co-re•spond•ent [kəʊrɪ'spɒndənt] *n.* person cited in a divorce case.

cor•gi ['kɔ:gɪ] *n.* breed of small dogs, with short hair and pointed faces.

co•ri•an•der [kɒrɪ'ændə] *n.* small plant, whose seeds and leaves are used for flavoring.

cork [kɔ:k] 1. *n.* (a) (material made from) very light bark of a type of oak tree; **c. oak** = oak tree with very light bark. (b) stopper which closes wine bottles. 2. *v.* to put a cork into (a

---

æ back, a: farm, ɒ: top, aɪ pipe, aʊ how, aɪə fire, aʊə flower, ɔ: bought, ɔɪ toy, e fed, eəhair, eɪ take, ə afraid, əʊ boat, əʊə lower, ɜ: word, i: heap, ɪ hit, ɪə hear, u: school, ʊ book, ʌ but, b back, d dog, ð then, dʒ just, f fog, g go, h hand, j yes, k catch, l last, m mix, n nut, ŋ sing, p penny, r round, s some, ʃ short, t too, tʃ chop, θ thing, v voice, w was, z zoo, ʒ treasure

bottle). **cork•age,** *n.* charge made by a restaurant for uncorking a customer's own wine bottle. **corked,** *adj.* (wine) which has an unpleasant taste because of a rotting cork. **cork•screw,** *n.* special screwing device for taking corks out of bottles.

corm [kɔːm] *n.* fat root which can be planted like a bulb.

cor•mo•rant ['kɔːmərənt] *n.* large dark seabird which eats fish.

corn [kɔːn] *n.* (a) cereal crops. (b) tall plant having spiky ears which contain rows of kernels; **sweet c.** = corn grown for human consumption; **c. cob** = core of corn with many rows of kernels. (c) painful hard growth (on a foot). **corn•crake,** *n.* small bird which lives in cornfields. **corn•field,** *n.* field in which corn is grown. **corn•flakes,** *n. pl.* breakfast cereal of crisp pieces of toasted corn. **corn•flow•er,** *n.* blue flower growing in corn fields. **corn•starch,** *n.* powdery starch made from corn, used in cooking. **corn•y,** *adj.* (**-ier, -iest**) *inf.* old/out-of-date (joke).

cor•ne•a ['kɔːnɪə] *n.* transparent covering of the eyeball. **cor•ne•al,** *adj.* referring to the cornea.

corned [kɔːnd] *adj.* salted/preserved (beef).

cor•ner ['kɔːnə] 1. *n.* angle made by two flat surfaces joining; **she has turned the c.** = she is beginning to recover from an illness. 2. *v.* (a) to turn a corner. (b) to monopolize (a market). (c) to drive (s.o.) into a corner. **cor•ner•stone,** *n.* (a) stone at the bottom of a corner of a building which records the start of building. (b) strong foundation/basis.

cor•net ['kɔːnɪt] *n.* (a) cone-shaped piece of paper for holding candy, nuts, etc. (b) trumpetlike brass musical instrument.

cor•nice ['kɔːnɪs] *n.* decorated molding around a ceiling/around the eaves (of a building).

cor•nu•co•pi•a [kɔːnjuˈkəʊpɪə] *n.* (*formal*) horn overflowing with fruit and flowers, the symbol of rich harvest.

co•rol•la [kəˈrɒlə] *n.* petals near the center of a flower.

cor•ol•lar•y [kəˈrɒlərɪ] *n.* natural result/thing which follows naturally.

co•ro•na [kəˈrəʊnə] *n.* ring of light; ring of light visible when the sun is totally eclipsed.

cor•o•nar•y ['kɒrənrɪ] *adj.* referring to the arteries to the heart; **c. thrombosis,** *inf.* **a c.** = heart attack caused by blocking of an artery.

cor•o•na•tion [kɒrəˈneɪʃn] *n.* crowning (of a king/queen/emperor).

cor•o•ner ['kɒrənə] *n.* public official who investigates sudden or accidental deaths.

cor•o•net ['kɒrənət] *n.* small crown.

cor•po•ral ['kɔːprəl] 1. *adj.* referring to the body; **c. punishment** = beating/whipping/caning. 2. *n.* non-commissioned rank in the army below sergeant.

cor•po•rate ['kɔːpərət] *adj.* forming a body; **c. culture** = ethos of a company that is reflected in the behavior of its employees; **c. plan** = overall plan for a whole company. **cor•po•ra•tion** [kɔːpəˈreɪʃn] *n.* (a) town council. (b) large company. (c) *inf.* large stomach.

corps [kɔː] *n.* (*pl.* **corps** [kɔːz]) military or organized group.

corpse [kɔːps] *n.* dead body.

cor•pu•lent ['kɔːpjʊlənt] *adj.* fat. **cor•pu•lence,** *n.* fatness.

cor•pus ['kɔːpəs] *n.* all the works (of an author).

cor•pus•cle ['kɔːpʌsl] *n.* red or white cell in blood.

cor•ral [kɒˈrɑːl] 1. *n.* fence to enclose cattle. 2. *v.* to enclose (cattle).

cor•rect [kəˈrekt] 1. *adj.* accurate/right/true. 2. *v.* to show the mistakes in (sth); to remove the mistakes from (sth). **cor•rec•tion** [kəˈrekʃn] *n.* making correct. **cor•rec•tive,** *adj.* & *n.* (thing) which corrects. **cor•rect•ly,** *adv.* accurately. **cor•rect•ness,** *n.* accuracy (of answer, etc.); rightness (of clothes).

cor•re•late ['kɒrəleɪt] *v.* to correspond to/to be linked to. **cor•re•la•tion** [kɒrəˈleɪʃn] *n.* correspondence/link.

cor•re•spond [kɒrɪˈspɒnd] *v.* (a) (**to**) to fit in with; to match. (b) to write letters; to exchange letters (**with** s.o.). **cor•re•spond•ence,** *n.* (a) matching. (b) exchange of letters; letters which have come; **c. course** = course of study taken at home with lessons sent by mail. **cor•re•spond•ent,** *n.* person who writes letters; journalist who writes articles for newspapers on particular subjects. **cor•res•pond•ing,** *adj.* which fits/matches. **cor•re•spond•ing•ly,** *adv.* in a similar way.

cor•ri•dor ['kɒrɪdɔː] *n.* long, narrow passage.

cor•ri•gen•da [kɒrɪˈdʒendə] *pl. n.* corrections (in a text).

cor•rob•o•rate [kəˈrɒbəreɪt] *v.* to confirm (a statement). **cor•rob•o•ra•tion** [kərɒbəˈreɪʃn] *n.* confirmation of a statement. **cor•rob•o•ra•to•ry,** *adj.* which corroborates.

cor•rode [kəˈrəʊd] *v.* to rot (metal); to rust. **cor•ro•sion** [kəˈrəʊʒn] *n.* rusting/eating away (of metal). **cor•ro•sive** [kəˈrəʊsɪv] *adj.* & *n.* (substance) which eats away metal.

cor•ru•gat•ed ['kɒrəgeɪtɪd] *adj.* bent into waves; **c. paper.**

cor•rupt [kəˈrʌpt] 1. *adj.* not honest; (judge,

etc.) who takes bribes. 2. *v.* to make dishonest/to bribe. **cor•rupt•i•bil•i•ty** [kərʌptə-'bɪlɪtɪ] *n.* being corruptible. **cor•rupt•i•ble**, *adj.* (person) who can be bribed. **cor•rup•tion** [kə'rʌpʃn] *n.* dishonesty/bribery.

cor•sage [kɔ:'sɑ:ʒ] *n.* flowers worn on the front of a dress.

cor•set ['kɔ:sɪt] *n.* tight underwear worn by women to support their bodies.

cor•tege [kɔ:'teɪʒ] *n.* (*formal*) procession at a funeral.

cor•tex ['kɔ:teks] *n.* outer covering of part of the body, esp. the brain.

cor•ti•sone ['kɔ:tɪzəʊn] *n.* hormone medicine used against skin allergies/arthritis, etc.

cor•vette [kɔ:'vet] *n.* small naval gunboat.

co•sine ['kəʊsaɪn] *n.* (*in mathematics*) ratio between the length of a side forming an acute angle to that of the hypotenuse in a right-angled triangle.

cos•met•ic [kɒz'metɪk] *adj. & n.* (substance) used in beautifying the face/in improving the look of sth.; **c. surgery** = surgery to improve someone's appearance.

cos•mic ['kɒzmɪk] *adj.* referring to the universe. **cos•mo•naut**, *n.* Soviet astronaut. **cos•mos**, *n.* (*formal*) the universe.

cos•mo•pol•i•tan [kɒzmə'pɒlɪtən] *adj.* (a) made up of people from different parts of the world. (b) at ease in different cities/with people of different nationalities.

cos•set ['kɒsɪt] *v.* to spoil (s.o.) with comfort.

cost [kɒst] 1. *n.* amount which you have to pay for sth; **at all costs** = at no matter what price; **c. of living** = money paid for food, clothing, housing, etc., shown as a monthly index figure. 2. *v.* (a) (**cost**) to have a price of. (b) (**costed**) to calculate the price for (sth). **cost•ing**, *n.* calculation of a selling price. **cost•li•ness**, *n.* expensiveness. **cost•ly**, *adj.* (**-ier, -iest**) expensive.

co-star ['kəʊstɑ:] 1. *n.* famous actor/actress starring in a motion picture, play, etc. with other famous actors/actresses. 2. *v.* (**co-starred**) to act in a motion picture, play, etc. as a co-star.

cos•tume ['kɒstjuːm] *n.* (a) set of clothes; **c. jewelery** = cheap imitation jewelery. (b) set of clothes worn in a motion picture, play, etc.

co•sy ['kəʊzɪ] 1. *adj.* (**-ier, -iest**) warm and comfortable. 2. *n.* cover (for a teapot, etc.).

co•si•ly, *adv.* comfortably/warmly. **co•si•ness**, *n.* being cosy.

cot [kɒt] *n.* child's bed with sides.

cot•tage ['kɒtɪdʒ] *n.* little house in the country; **c. cheese** = soft white cheese made from curds; **c. industry** = handicrafts made in people's houses. **cot•tag•er**, *n.* person who lives or vacations in a cottage.

cot•ter pin ['kɒtəpɪn] *n.* pin with a split end, used to hold parts of a machine together.

cot•ton ['kɒtn] 1. *n.* (a) fiber from the downy seed heads of a tropical plant. (b) cloth made of this fiber. (c) thread (for sewing). 2. *v. inf.* **to c. to** = to take a liking to. **cot•ton can•dy**, *n.* molten sugar spun to make a fluffy mass, eaten as a sweet. **cot•ton bat•ting**, *n.* fluffy thin layers or pads of cotton, used for wiping wounds, applying ointment, filling quilts, etc.

cot•y•le•don [kɒtɪ'liːdən] *n.* first leaf on a seedling.

couch [kaʊtʃ] *n.* (*pl.* **-es**) sofa/low bed. **couch grass** [kuːtʃ] *n.* weedlike grass which spreads from underground roots.

cou•chette [kuː'ʃet] *n.* folding bed in a train.

cou•gar ['kuːgə] *n.* large brown American wild cat.

cough [kɒf] 1. *n.* sending air out of the lungs suddenly because of an irritation in the throat; **c. drop** = medicated sweet sucked to relieve irritation in the throat. 2. *v.* to send air out of the lungs suddenly because of irritation; *Sl.* **to c. up** = to pay. **cough•ing**, *n.* series of coughs.

could, couldn't [kʊd, 'kʊdnt] *v. see* **can.**

cou•lomb ['kuːlɒm] *n.* unit of the quantity of electricity passed in one second over a given point by a current of one ampere.

coul•ter ['kuːltə] *n. see* **colter**

coun•cil ['kaʊnsl] *n.* elected or appointed committee, esp. one which acts as an administrative, legislative, or advisory group in a town, city, etc. **coun•cil•lor**, *n.* elected member of a council.

coun•sel ['kaʊnsl] 1. *n.* (a) advice. (b) lawyer. **coun•sel•ing**, *n.* giving advice. **coun•se•lor, counsellor**, *n.* adviser.

count [kaʊnt] 1. *n.* (a) action of counting/adding figures; **to lose c.** = to have no longer any idea of what the total is. (b) accusation. (c) lower rank of noble. 2. *v.* (a) to add up a total. (b) to say numbers in order. (c) to rely (**on**). (d) to be important. **count down**, *v.* to count backwards (9, 8, 7, 6, etc.). **count•down**, *n.*

æ back, a: farm, ɒ: top, aɪ pipe, aʊ how, aɪə fire, aʊə flower, ɔ: bought, ɔɪ toy, e fed, eəhair, eɪ take, ə afraid, əʊ boat, ʊə lower, v: word, iː heap, ɪ hit, ɪə hear, u: school, ʊ book, ʌ but, b back, d dog, ð then, dʒ just, f fog, g go, h hand, j yes, k catch, l last, m mix, n nut, ŋ sing, p penny, r round, s some, ʃ short, t too, tʃ chop, θ thing, v voice, w was, z zoo, ʒ treasure

counting backwards. **count•ing,** *n.* action of adding up a total. **count•less,** *adj.* which cannot be counted/numerous.

coun•te•nance ['kaʊntnəns] 1. *n.* (*formal*) face. 2. *v.* (*formal*) to approve of (s.o.'s action).

coun•ter ['kaʊntə] 1. *n.* (a) machine which counts. (b) small round disk used in games. (c) long flat surface in a store for displaying goods, or in a bank for placing money. 2. *adj.*, *adv. & prefix.* opposite (**to**). 3. *v.* (a) to stop/to block. (b) to reply with an opposing response. **coun•ter•act,** *v.* to neutralize/to stop the effects of (sth). **coun•ter-at•tack.** 1. *n.* attack in return/attack against s.o. who has just attacked you. 2. *v.* to attack in return. **coun•ter•bal•ance,** *v.* to compensate for a force in one direction by going in the opposite direction. **coun•ter•blast,** *n.* strong written or spoken reply to an attack. **coun•ter•charge,** *n.* accusation against s.o. who has just accused you. **coun•ter•claim,** *n.* claim made in response to another claim. **coun•ter•clock•wise,** *adj. & adv.* in the opposite direction to the hands of a clock. **coun•ter-dem•on•stra•tion,** *n.* rival/opposed demonstration in reply to a demonstration. **coun•ter-es•pi•o•nage,** *n.* secret service working against spies. **coun•ter•feit** ['kaʊntəfɪt] 1. *adj.* false/forged (money). 2. *v.* to forge/to make false money. **coun•ter•foil,** *n.* slip of paper which you retain after giving s.o. a check/an invoice, etc. **coun•ter•mand,** *v.* to say that (an order) should not be carried out. **coun•ter•meas•ure,** *n.* way of stopping the effects of sth. **coun•ter•pane,** *n.* bedcover. **coun•ter•part,** *n.* person who has a similar job/is in a similar situation; parallel thing. **coun•ter•point,** *n.* combination of melodies in a piece of music. **coun•ter•poise,** *n.* heavy weight which counterbalances. **coun•ter-pro•duc•tive,** *adj.* which produces a contrary effect to the one intended. **Coun•ter Ref•or•ma•tion,** *n.* movement in the Catholic church in the 16th century, a response to the Protestant Reformation. **coun•ter-rev•o•lu•tion,** *n.* revolt against a revolution. **coun•ter-rev•o•lu•tion•ar•y,** *adj. & n.* (person who is) in revolt against a revolution. **coun•ter•sign,** *v.* to sign (a document) which s.o. else has signed, in order to authorize it. **coun•ter•sink,** *v.* (countersank; countersunk) to make a hole for the head of (a nail or screw) to fit into so that it is level with the surface.

coun•try ['kʌntrɪ] *n.* (a) political or geographical unit of land. (b) region. (c) not town; to live in the c. **coun•tri•fied,** *adj.* like the country. **coun•try•man,** *n.* (*pl.* -men) person who comes from the same country as you. **coun•try•side,** *n.* the country/the land (excluding towns and cities).

coun•ty ['kaʊntɪ] *n.* (a) largest local administrative district of a U.S. state. (b) the people who live in a county.

coup [kuː] *n.* (*pl.* **coups** [kuːz]) (a) coup d'état. (b) successful move. **coup d'état** [kuːdeɪ'tɑː] *n.* armed overthrow of a government.

coupe ['kuːpeɪ] *n.* car with two doors and a fixed roof.

cou•ple ['kʌpl] 1. *n.* pair/two things/two people together; two people together, esp. a man and woman; a husband and wife; **a c. of** = (i) two; (ii) a few. 2. *v.* to link together. **cou•plet,** *n.* two lines of poetry which rhyme. **cou•pling,** *n.* metal links for joining two pieces of machinery/two wagons together.

cou•pon ['kuːpɒn] *n.* piece of paper which acts in place of money/in place of a ticket.

cour•age ['kʌrɪdʒ] *n.* (*no pl.*) bravery. **cou•ra•geous** [kə'reɪdʒəs] *adj.* brave. **cou•ra•geous•ly,** *adv.* bravely.

cour•i•er ['kʊrɪə] *n.* (a) person who carries messages; (b) guide for a person/persons traveling, who takes care of hotel reservations, luggage, etc.

course [kɔːs] 1. *n.* (a) passing of time; **in the c. of** =during; **in due c.** = eventually. (b) road; direction. (c) **of c.** = naturally; **as a matter of c.** = in the usual way. (d) series of lessons; book/series of books for studying. (e) series of treatments for an illness. (f) dish of food for a meal. (g) track (for racing). (h) **golf c.** = area of land specially designed for playing golf. (i) line of bricks (in a wall). 2. *v.* to flow fast.

court [kɔːt] 1. *n.* (a) legal proceeding where a judge (and jury) try criminals. (b) group of people living around a king or queen. (c) area where a game of tennis/squash, etc., is played. 2. *v.* (a) to try to persuade (a woman) to marry you. (b) to look for; to try to win (praise, etc.); to risk (disaster). **cour•te•ous** ['kɜːtjəs] *adj.* very polite. **cour•te•ous•ly,** *adv.* politely. **cour•te•sy** ['kɜːtəsɪ] *n.* politeness; **by c. of** = with the kind permission of; **c. car** = free car waiting for hotel guests at an airport. **cour•ti•er** ['kɔːtjə] *n.* member of a royal court. **court-mar•tial** [kɔːt'mɑːʃl] 1. *n.* trial of a soldier by other soldiers. 2. *v.* (**court-martialed, court-martialled**) to try (a soldier). **court•room,** *n.* room where a trial is held. **court•ship,** *n.* courting a woman. **court•yard,** *n.* square yard surrounded by buildings.

cous•in ['kʌzn] *n.* son or daughter of an uncle or aunt.

cou•tu•ri•er [kuː'tjʊrɪeɪ] *n.* dress-designer.

cove [kəʊv] *n.* small bay.

cov•en ['kʌvn] *n.* group of witches.

cov•e•nant ['kʌvənənt] 1. *n.* contract/agreement. 2. *v.* to agree by contract.

Cov•en•try ['kɒvəntrɪ] *n.* **to send s.o. to C.** = to refuse to speak to s.o.

cov•er ['kʌvə] 1. *n.* (a) thing which is put over sth to protect it; **under c. of night** = under the protection of the dark. (b) lid. (c) (cardboard) binding of a book; outer pages of a magazine. (d) shelter; **to take c.** 2. *v.* (a) to put sth over (sth) to protect it. (b) to travel (a certain distance). (c) to point a gun at. (d) to be enough to pay for. (e) to deal with. (f) to protect with insurance. (g) to be a reporter at (an event). **cov•er•age,** *n.* amount of space/time devoted to an event in a newspaper/on TV. **cov•er•ing.** 1. *n.* thing which covers. 2. *adj.* **c. letter** = explanatory letter sent with a form/with another letter, etc. **cov•er•mount,** *n.* gift attached to the cover of a magazine. **cov•er up,** *v.* to hide completely. **cov•er-up,** *n.* hiding (of a scandal).

cov•er•let ['kʌvələt] *n.* cover for a bed.

co•vert ['kʌvət] *adj.* (*formal*) hidden/secret.

cov•et ['kʌvɪt] *v.* to want (sth which belongs to s.o. else). **cov•et•ous,** *adj.* wanting sth which belongs to s.o. else.

cov•ey ['kʌvɪ] *n.* group (of partridges).

cow [kaʊ] 1. *n.* (a) female animal of the bull family kept to give milk. (b) female of certain animals, e.g. the elephant. 2. *v.* to frighten. **cow•boy,** *n.* man who drives herds of cattle. **cow•hand, cowherd, cowman,** *n.* man who looks after cattle. **cow flop,** *n.* round flat cake of cow dung. **cow•shed,** *n.* shed for cows. **cow•slip,** *n.* common yellow wild flower.

cow•ard ['kaʊəd] *n.* person who is not brave. **cow•ard•ice,** *n.* lack of bravery. **cow•ard•ly,** *adj.* not brave.

cow•er ['kaʊə] *v.* to crouch down because of fear.

cowl [kaʊl] *n.* hood (for a monk's habit); cover for a chimney. **cowl•ing,** *n.* cover for an airplane engine, airplane part, etc.

cow•rie ['kaʊrɪ] *n.* colorful seashell.

cox [kɒks] 1. *n.* (*pl.* **-es**) person who steers a rowing boat. 2. *v.* to steer a rowing boat.

cox•swain ['kɒksn] *n.* (a) sailor in charge of a

ship's boat. (b) person who steers a rowing boat. **cox•wain•less,** *adj.* coxless.

coy [kɔɪ] *adj.* timid; shy. **coy•ly,** *adv.* in a coy way. **coy•ness,** *n.* being coy.

coy•o•te [kɔɪ'əʊtɪ] *n.* small American wolf.

coy•pu ['kɔɪpuː] *n.* small animal like a beaver.

CPU [siːpiː'juː] central processing unit.

crab [kræb] *n.* edible ten-footed crustacean with large pincers, which walks sideways; **c. apple** = bitter wild or cultivated apple. **crabbed,** *adj.* (a) bad-tempered. (b) (handwriting) which is difficult to read. **crab•by,** *adj. inf.* bad-tempered.

crack [kræk] 1. *n.* (a) sharp dry sound. (b) sharp blow. (c) thin break; split; **at c. of dawn** = at daybreak. (d) *inf.* **to have a c. at sth** = to try to do sth. (e) *Sl.* strong form of cocaine. 2. *adj. inf.* first-class. 3. *v.* (a) to make a sharp sound. (b) to make a thin split in (sth). (c) **to c. jokes** = to tell jokes. (d) *inf.* **get cracking!** = start (working, etc.). (e) to decipher (a code). **crack down on,** *v. inf.* to campaign against. **crack•er,** *n.* (a) small firework which makes a bang. (b) paper tube which makes a little explosion when it is pulled. (c) dry unsweetened biscuit. **crack•ers,** *adj. inf.* mad. **crack•pot,** *adj. & n. inf.* mad (person). **crack up,** *v. inf.* (a) to praise (sth) extravagantly. (b) to collapse.

crack•le ['krækl] 1. *n.* small explosive sounds. 2. *v.* to make little explosive sounds. **crack•ling,** *n.* hard cooked pork skin.

cra•dle ['kreɪdl] 1. *n.* (a) baby's bed which can be rocked. (b) support (for a piece of machinery). (c) starting point (for civilization, etc.). 2. *v.* to rock (in your arms).

craft [krɑːft] *n.* (a) artistry; skill; **crafts** = types of work done by hand. (b) ship. (c) cunning; slyness. **craft•i•ly,** *adv.* cunningly. **craft•i•ness,** *n.* cunning; slyness. **crafts•man,** *n.* (*pl.* **-men**) artist; person who is expert in using his hands. **crafts•man•ship,** *n.* skill of a craftsman. **craft•y,** *adj.* (**-ier, -iest**) sly.

crag [kræg] *n.* steep rock cliff. **crag•gy,** *adj.* rough (rock or person's face).

cram [kræm] *v.* (**crammed**) (a) to squeeze (**into**). (b) to learn facts hurriedly before an examination.

cramp [kræmp] 1. *n.* sudden pain where the muscles tighten up and cannot be relaxed. 2. *v.* to hinder; to squeeze tight. **cram•pon,** *n.*

æ back, ɑː farm, ɒ top, aɪ pipe, aʊ how, aiə fire, aʊə flower, ɔː bought, ɔɪ toy, e fed, eə hair, eɪ take, ə afraid, əʊ boat, əʊə lower, vː word, iː heap, ɪ hit, ɪə hear, uː school, ʊ book, ʌ but, b back, d dog, ð then, dʒ just, f fog, g go, h hand, j yes, k catch, l last, m mix, n nut, ŋ sing, p penny, r round, s some, ʃ short, t too, tʃ chop, θ thing, v voice, w was, z zoo, ʒ treasure metal hook/spike attached to boots for climbing in ice and snow.

cran•ber•ry ['krænbərɪ] *n.* wild red edible berry.

crane [kreɪn] 1. *n.* (a) tall metal construction for lifting heavy weights. (b) long-legged tropical bird. 2. *v.* to stretch (one's neck). **crane•fly,** *n.* common insect with long legs.

cra•ni•um ['kreɪnɪəm] *n.* bones covering the top part of the skull. **cra•ni•al,** *adj.* referring to the cranium; **c. nerves** = the nerves which link the brain with the head and neck.

crank [kræŋk] 1. *n.* (a) shaft with a right-angled bend, used for transmitting motion. (b) very odd person; irritable person. 2. *v.* to turn or lift with a crank. **crank•shaft,** *n.* rod which is turned by a crank. **crank•y,** *adj.* odd/bizarre/irritable (person).

cran•ny ['krænɪ] *n.* small crack/small gap.

crap [kræp] *n. sl.* shit/trash. **craps** [kræps] *n.* game played with two dice.

crash [kræʃ] 1. *n.* (*pl.* -es) (a) loud noise. (b) accident; **c. helmet** = helmet worn by motorcyclists to protect them in case of a crash. (c) financial collapse. (d) complete breakdown of a computer. 2. *v.* (a) to explode; to make a great noise. (b) to be damaged/destroyed in an accident; **to c. into** = to hit in an accident. (c) to collapse financially. (d) (*of a computer*) to ‑break down completely. 3. *adj.* urgent; **a c. course** = very rapid course. **crash-land,** *v.* to land heavily, without using the undercarriage, so that the aircraft is damaged. **crash-land•ing,** *n.* act of landing heavily.

crass [kræs] *adj.* (a) rude/coarse. (b) obviously materialistic.

crate [kreɪt] 1. *n.* large rough wooden box. 2. *v.* to put into a crate.

cra•ter ['kreɪtə] *n.* hole at the top of a volcano; hole made by a bomb.

cra•vat [krə'væt] *n.* type of scarf worn by men knotted round the neck in place of a tie.

crave [kreɪv] *v.* to want (sth) very much. **crav•ing,** *n.* strong desire (**for**).

cra•ven ['kreɪvn] *adj.* cowardly.

crawl [krɔːl] 1. *n.* (a) creeping on hands and knees. (b) fast swimming stroke with arms going overarm. (c) very slow progress. 2. *v.* (a) to move around on hands and knees. (b) to creep along slowly. (c) to be covered (**with** creeping things).

cray•fish ['kreɪfɪʃ] *n.* (*pl.* crayfish) kind of fresh-water crustacean like a small lobster.

cray•on ['kreɪɒn] *n.* stick of colored material for drawing.

craze [kreɪz] *n.* mania (**for** sth). **cra•zi•ly,** *adv.* madly. **cra•zi•ness,** *n.* madness. **cra•zy,** *adj.* (-ier, -iest) mad.

creak [kriːk] 1. *n.* squeaky cracking noise. 2. *v.* to make a squeaky cracking noise. **creak•y,** *adj.* which makes a creaking noise.

cream [kriːm] 1. *n.* (a) rich fatty part of milk; **c. cheese** = rich soft cheese; **the c. of the undergraduates** = the top few. (b) smooth paste; **face c.** 2. *adj.* colored like cream; very pale fawn. 3. *v.* to whip into a smooth paste. **cream•er•y,** *n.* dairy. **cream•y,** *adj.* (-ier, -iest) smooth; full of cream.

crease [kriːs] 1. *n.* fold made by ironing; fold made accidentally. 2. *v.* (a) to iron a fold into (sth). (b) to make folds accidentally in (sth).

cre•ate [krɪ'eɪt] *v.* (a) to make; to invent. (b) *inf.* to make a disturbance/a fuss. **cre•a•tion** [krɪ'eɪʃn] *n.* thing which has been made. **cre•a•tive,** *adj.* full of ideas; always making sth. **cre•a•tiv•i•ty** [krɪeɪ'tɪvɪtɪ] *n.* aptitude for creating. **cre•a•tor,** *n.* person who makes/invents sth.

crea•ture ['kriːtʃə] *n.* animal; person.

crèche [kreʃ] *n.* model scene representing the birth of Jesus Christ, including a stable with figures, usu. displayed at Christmas.

cre•dence ['kriːdəns] *n.* belief (that sth is correct/true).

cre•den•tials [krɪ'denʃəlz] *n. pl.* papers which prove your identity or rank so that people can trust you.

cred•i•ble ['kredɪbl] *adj.* which can be believed. **cred•i•bil•i•ty** [kredɪ'bɪlɪtɪ] *n.* ability to be believed; **he suffers from a c. gap** = people do not believe him. **cred•i•bly,** *adv.* reliably.

cred•it ['kredɪt] 1. *n.* (a) merit; recognition of quality; **it does you c.** = you are to be praised for it; **he's a c. to the school** = he has made the school proud of him. (b) belief; faith. (c) time given to pay; **c. card** = card which allows you to buy goods without having to pay immediately; **on c.** = without paying immediately. (d) side of an account showing money in hand or which is owed to you; (e) **credits** = list of actors'/directors' names which appear at the beginning or end of ‑a motion picture/TV program. 2. *v.* (**credited**) (a) **to c. s.o. with** = to attribute a quality, etc., to. s.o. (b) to believe. (c) to promise to pay (s.o.); to pay money into (an account). **cred•it•a•ble,** *adj.* honorable (deed). **cred•it•a•bly,** *adv.* honorably. **cred•i•tor,** *n.* person who is owed money.

cred•u•lous ['kredjʊləs] *adj.* (person) who believes anything easily. **cre•du•li•ty** [krɪ'djuːlɪtɪ], **cred•u•lous•ness,** *n.* belief/trust. **cred•u•lous•ly,** *adv.* in a credulous way.

creed [kriːd] *n.* statement of what you believe; **the Apostles' C.** = the statement of Christian faith.

creek [kriːk] *n.* small stream.

creel [kriːl] *n.* basket to put fish in.

creep [kriːp] 1. *n.* (a) *inf.* sly, unpleasant person. (b) **he gives me the creeps** = he makes me shudder. 2. *v.* (**crept** [krept]) (a) to move around stealthily. (b) **creeping plant** = plant which spreads close to the ground/which climbs up a wall. **creep•er,** *n.* plant which climbs over walls. **creep•y,** *adj.* (**-ier, -iest**) *inf.* which makes you shudder. **creep•y-crawl•y** *n. inf.* insect.

cre•mate [krɪ'meɪt] *v.* to burn (a dead body). **cre•ma•tion,** *n.* burning of a dead body. **cre•ma•to•ri•um** [kremə'tɔːrɪəm] *n.* (*pl.* -ia) place where bodies are burned.

cren•el•at•ed, crenellated ['krənəleɪtɪd] *adj.* (castle wall) with openings to shoot through.

cre•ole ['kriːəʊl] *adj. & n.* (person) of mixed West Indian and European descent.

cre•o•sote ['krɪəsəʊt] 1. *n.* dark brown liquid, used for protecting wood from rotting. 2. *v.* to paint with creosote.

crepe [kreɪp] *n.* (a) **c. paper** = slightly crinkly colored paper; (b) **c. soles** = thick wrinkled rubber soles for shoes.

crept [krept] *v. see* **creep.**

cre•scen•do [krɪ'ʃendəʊ] *n.* (*pl.* -os) increasing noise (esp. in music).

cres•cent ['kresnt] *n.* (a) curved shape, like a new moon. (b) street which forms a semicircle.

cress [kres] *n.* (*no pl.*) small green salad plant, usu. eaten with seedlings of mustard.

crest [krest] *n.* (a) top (of hills/waves). (b) plumes/fleshy growth on the head of a bird. (c) coat of arms. **crest•fal•len,** *adj.* discouraged/depressed.

cre•tin ['kretɪn] *n.* person who is mentally weak; *inf.* very stupid person. **cre•tin•ous,** *adj.* very stupid.

Creutz•feldt-Ja•kob Dis•ease ['krɔɪtsfəlt 'jɑːkɒp] *n.* fatal disease of the nervous system, caused by an abnormal prion protein in the brain, characterized by progressive dementia and loss of physical co-ordination.

cre•vasse [krɪ'væs] *n.* deep crack in a glacier.

crev•ice ['krevɪs] *n.* small crack in a rock/wall.

crew [kruː] *n.* (a) people who work a boat/aircraft/bus, etc. (b) gang. **crew•cut,** *n.* very short haircut.

crib [krɪb] 1. *n.* (a) manger/box for food for horses or cows. (b) baby's bed. (c) word-for-word translation/list of answers to help a bad student with homework. (d) **c.**

death = sudden unexplained death of a sleeping baby, possibly caused by overheating. 2. *v.* (**cribbed**) to copy.

crib•bage ['krɪbɪdʒ] *n.* card game where the points are marked by pegs on a special board.

crick [krɪk] 1. *n.* **c. in the neck** = sprain/pulled muscle in the neck. 2. *v.* to pull a muscle in (one's neck).

crick•et ['krɪkɪt] *n.* (a) small jumping insect, like a grasshopper. (b) game played between two teams of eleven players using bats, hard balls and wickets as targets, played esp. in Great Britain and Commonwealth countries. *inf.* **it isn't c.** = it is not fair. **crick•et•er,** *n.* person who plays cricket.

crime [kraɪm] *n.* illegal act. **crim•i•nal** ['krɪmɪnl] 1. *adj.* referring to an illegal act. 2. *n.* person who commits a crime. **crim•i•nal•ly,** *adv.* so bad as to be against the law. **crim•i•nol•o•gy** [krɪmɪ'nɒlədʒɪ] *n.* study of crime.

crimp [krɪmp] *v.* to press into waves or folds.

crim•son ['krɪmzn] *adj. & n.* deep red color.

cringe [krɪndʒ] *v.* (a) to bend to avoid a blow. (b) to be excessively humble.

crin•kle ['krɪŋkl] *v.* to fold making many small creases. **crin•kly,** *adj.* (**-ier, -iest**) with many creases/curls.

crin•o•line ['krɪnəliːn] *n.* (*old*) very wide skirt.

crip•ple ['krɪpl] 1. *n.* person who is disabled or lame. 2. *v.* (a) to make (s.o.) disabled. (b) to prevent (a machine/a factory) from working.

cri•sis ['kraɪsɪs] *n.* (*pl.* crises ['kraɪsiːz]) critical moment; turning point.

crisp [krɪsp] 1. *adj.* (**-er, -est**) dry and brittle; sharp/cold (air); crunchy (lettuce). 2. *n.* piece of food that is thin and crisp. **crisp•ness,** *n.* being crisp. **crisp•y,** *adj.* very crisp.

criss-cross ['krɪskrɒs] 1. *adj.* with lines crossing in two directions. 2. *v.* to go backward and forward in different directions.

cri•te•ri•on [kraɪ'tɪərɪən] *n.* (*pl.* criteria) standard by which things are judged.

crit•ic ['krɪtɪk] *n.* (a) person who examines sth and comments on it, esp. person who writes comments on new plays and motion pictures for a newspaper. (b) person who comments unfavorably on sth/who finds fault with sth. **crit•i•cal,** *adj.* (a) dangerous (situation); extremely urgent/important (decision); very serious (medical condition). (b) unfavorable (comment). **crit•i•cal•ly,** *adv.* in a critical way. **crit•i•cism** ['krɪtɪsɪzəm] *n.* (a) com-

---

æ back, ɑ: farm, ɒ: top, aɪ pipe, aʊ how, aɪə fire, aʊə flower, ɔ: bought, ɔɪ toy, e fed, eəhair, eɪ take, ə afraid, əʊ boat, əʊə lower, v: word, iː heap, ɪ hit, ɪə hear, uː school, ʊ book, ʌ but, b back, d dog, ð then, dʒ just, f fog, g go, h hand, j yes, k catch, l last, m mix, n nut, ŋ sing, p penny, r round, s some, ʃ short, t too, tʃ chop, θ thing, v voice, w was, z zoo, ʒ treasure

ment; **literary c.** = comment on a work of literature. (b) unfavorable comment. **crit•i•cize,** *v.* to comment unfavorably on (sth). **cri•tique** [krɪ'tiːk] *n.* piece of careful literary criticism.

croak [krəʊk] 1. *n.* hoarse noise (like that made by frogs). 2. *v.* to make a hoarse sound. **croak•y,** *adj.* (**-ier, -iest**) hoarse (voice).

cro•chet ['krəʊʃeɪ] 1. *n.* type of knitting using one needle with a hook at the end. 2. *v.* (**crocheted** ['krəʊʃeɪd]; **crocheting** ['krəʊʃeɪŋ]) to make (sth) using a hooked needle. **cro•chet-hook,** *n.* hooked needle for crocheting.

crock [krɒk] *n.* rough earthenware pot. **crock•er•y,** *n.* (*no pl.*) rough pottery tableware.

croc•o•dile ['krɒkədaɪl] *n.* large meat-eating reptile living in rivers in Africa; **she wept c. tears** = she pretended to cry when she was not in any way sad.

cro•cus ['krəʊkəs] *n.* (*pl.* **-es**) purple, yellow or white spring flower.

croft [krɒft] *n.* (*in Scotland*) small farm held by a tenant. **croft•er,** *n.* farmer who holds a croft.

crois•sant ['krwæsɒŋ] *n.* rolled pastry, made in the shape of a crescent.

crone [krəʊn] *n.* ugly old witch.

cro•ny ['krəʊnɪ] *n.* old friend.

crook [krʊk] *n.* (a) bend. (b) long stick with a bent top; (c) *inf.* criminal. **crook•ed** ['krʊkɪd] *adj.* (a) bent. (b) dishonest. **crook•ed•ly,** *adv.* in a bent way; not straight.

croon [kruːn] *v.* to sing in a low voice. **croon•er,** *n.* person who croons.

crop [krɒp] 1. *n.* (a) vegetables/grain, etc., grown for food. (b) part of a bird's throat shaped like a bag. (c) small whip used by a rider. (d) short haircut. 2. *v.* (**cropped**) (a) to cut (a hedge/s.o.'s hair) short. (b) (*of sheep*) to eat (grass) so that it is very short. **crop•per,** *n. inf.* **he came a c.** = (i) he fell badly; (ii) his plans did not succeed. **crop up,** *v.* to occur.

cro•quet ['krəʊkeɪ] *n.* lawn game played with hoops, balls and mallets.

cro•quette [krə'ket] *n.* small ball of mashed potato, covered with breadcrumbs and fried.

cro•sier ['krəʊzɪə] *n.* staff (like a crook) carried by a bishop.

cross [krɒs] 1. *n.* (a) shape with two lines cutting across each other at right angles. (b) shape of a vertical line, with another cutting across it at right angles, forming the symbol of the Christian church; wooden construction of this shape; **the Red C.** = international rescue

and medical organization. (c) thing which is hard to bear. (d) mixture of two breeds; mixture of two different things. 2. *v.* (a) **to c. oneself** = to make a sign of the cross on oneself. (b) to go across; to place across; **crossed line** = telephone connection where you can hear other people talking. (d) to breed (two animals/plants) together. 3. *adj.* (a) opposed/contrary; **they are at c. purposes** = they are in disagreement; **to talk at c. purposes** = to misunderstand what each other is saying. (b) bad-tempered/angry. **cross•bar,** *n.* beam which goes across a space. **cross•bill,** *n.* type of bird, with a bill of which the top part crosses over the bottom. **cross•breed,** *n.* animal produced by crossing two animals of different breeds. **cross•check,** *v.* to check again to make sure. **cross-coun•try,** *adj.* & *n.* (race) across fields and along roads, not on a track. **cross-ex•am•i•na•tion,** *n.* searching questioning by an opposing lawyer. **cross-ex•am•ine,** *v.* to ask (s.o.) searching questions. **cross•eyed,** *adj.* (person) whose eyes do not face forward; (person) with a squint. **cross-fer•ti•lize,** *v.* to fertilize (one plant) with another variety. **cross•fire,** *n.* gunfire from two directions, so that the fire crosses. **cross-grained,** *adj.* bad-tempered. **cross•ing,** *n.* (a) act of going across. (b) place where you cross; **pedestrian c.** = crosswalk. **cross•legged,** *adj.* & *adv.* with one ankle over the other. **cross•ly,** *adv.* in an angry way. **cross off, cross out,** *v.* to draw a line through (sth written). **cross•o•ver,** 1. *n.* book/play/recording, etc. that is transposed into a different genre. 2. *adj.* (a) (book/play/recording, etc.) existing in more than one genre. (b) (author/performer, etc.) working in more than one genre. (c) (writing/art/music, etc.) combining two or more styles. **cross-ques•tion,** *v.* to cross-examine. **cross-ques•tion•ing,** *n.* cross-examining. **cross-ref•er•ence,** *n.* line in a reference book telling you to look in another section for further information. **cross•roads,** *n. pl.* place where two roads cross. **cross-sec•tion,** *n.* (a) diagram as if a cut had been made across sth. (b) sample. **cross•walk,** *n.* pedestrian crossing. **cross•wind,** *n.* wind blowing across a road, etc. **cross•wise,** *adv.* in the shape of a cross. **cross•word,** *n.* puzzle where small squares have to be filled with letters forming words to which clues are given.

crosse [krɒs] *n.* stick with a net, used in playing lacrosse.

crotch [krɒtʃ] *n.* (*pl.* **-es**) place where the two legs fork.

crotch•et ['krɒtʃɪt] *n.* note in music lasting two quavers or half as long as a minim.

crotch•et•y, *adj.* (a) bad-tempered. (b) odd/slightly mad; capricious.

crouch [kraʊtʃ] *v.* to bend down low.

croup [kruːp] *n.* (a) infection in the throat, which makes children cough noisily. (b) rear part of a horse.

croup•i•er ['kruːpɪə] *n.* person who is in charge of a gaming table.

crow [krəʊ] 1. *n.* large common black bird; **as the c. flies** = in a straight line. 2. *v.* (a) (*of a cockerel*) to call. (b) **to c. over s.o.** = to exclaim happily because you have beaten s.o. **crow•bar,** *n.* large metal lever for opening boxes. **crow's-feet,** *n.* little wrinkles at the outer corners of the eyes. **crow's nest,** *n.* platform on top of a mast for a lookout.

crowd [kraʊd] 1. *n.* mass of people. 2. *v.* to group together.

crown [kraʊn] 1. *n.* (a) gold and jeweled headdress for a king/queen, etc. (b) symbol of monarchy; (c) top (of the head, a tooth, etc.). (d) type of coin. 2. *v.* (a) to make (s.o.) king/queen/emperor, etc. by placing a crown on his head. (b) to be a splendid end to (sth). (c) *inf.* to hit (s.o.) on the head. (d) to reward. (e) to put a false top on (a tooth). **Crown Prince,** *n.* eldest son of a monarch, who will inherit the throne.

cru•cial ['kruːʃl] *adj.* extremely important/critical. **cru•cial•ly,** *adv.* vitally/critically.

cru•ci•ble ['kruːsɪbl] *n.* small pot used for heating substances in chemical experiments.

cru•ci•fix ['kruːsɪfɪks] *n.* (*pl.* **-es**) statue representing Jesus Christ on the cross. **cru•ci•fix•ion** [kruːsɪ'fɪkʃn] *n.* killing by nailing to a cross. **cru•ci•fy,** *v.* to kill (s.o.) by nailing to a cross.

crude [kruːd] 1. *adj.* (**-er, -est**) (a) unpurified; unrefined (oil). (b) rude/ill-mannered. 2. *n.* unrefined oil. **crude•ly,** *adv.* in a crude way. **crude•ness, crudity,** *n.* being crude.

cru•el ['kruəl] *adj.* (**crueler, cruelest**) which causes pain/suffering. **cru•el•ly,** *adv.* savagely/unkindly. **cru•el•ty,** *n.* being cruel.

cru•et ['kruɪt] *n.* set of containers for salt, pepper, mustard, etc.

cruise [kruːz] 1. *n.* long pleasure voyage in a ship calling at different ports. 2. *v.* (a) to go about steadily (in a boat) visiting places. (b) to travel at an even speed. **cruis•er,** *n.* large warship, smaller than a battleship; **cabin c.** = motor boat with a cabin for living in.

crumb [krʌm] *n.* small piece (of bread, etc.).

crum•ble ['krʌmbl] 1. *n.* dessert made of fruit covered with a mixture of flour, shortening and sugar. 2. *v.* to break into small pieces. **crum•bly,** *adj.* which easily falls to pieces.

crum•my ['krʌmɪ] *adj.* (**-ier, -iest**) *inf.* rotten/no good.

crum•pet ['krʌmpɪt] *n.* thick round batter cake, served toasted with butter.

crum•ple ['krʌmpl] *v.* to crush/to screw up into a ball. **crum•ple zones,** *pl. n.* areas at the front and rear of a vehicle that absorb some of the impact of a crash by crumpling.

crunch [krʌntʃ] 1. *n.* (*pl.* **-es**) (a) sound of sth crisp being crushed. (b) *inf.* crisis point; **when it comes to the c.** 2. *v.* to crush (sth crisp); to chew (sth hard). **crunch•y,** *adj.* hard and crisp.

crup•per ['krʌpə] *n.* piece of leather which fastens around a horse's tail to keep the saddle in place.

cru•sade [kruː'seɪd] 1. *n.* (a) medieval campaign by Christians against Muslims who occupied the Holy Land. (b) campaign. 2. *v.* to campaign/to fight (**against** or **for**). **cru•sad•er,** *n.* person who goes on a crusade.

crush [krʌʃ] 1. *n.* (a) drink made of fruit juice. (b) mass of people squeezed together. (c) infatuation. 2. *v.* to squash.

crust [krʌst] *n.* hard exterior (of bread/cake/the earth, etc.). **crust•y,** *adj.* (**-ier, -iest**) (bread) with a hard crust.

crus•ta•cean [krʌ'steɪʃn] *n.* one of many types of animals with hard shells, mainly living in the sea, such as lobsters, crabs, etc.

crutch [krʌtʃ] *n.* (*pl.* **-es**) (a) lame person's long stick which goes under the armpit. (b) (*old*) crotch.

crux [krʌks] *n.* central point of a problem; **the c. of the matter.**

cry [kraɪ] 1. (a) act of making tears. (b) shout; exclamation (esp. of pain). (c) call (of a bird/animal). 2. *v.* (a) to make tears. (b) (*also* **cry out**) to shout; to exclaim (in pain). **cry•ing,** *adj.* scandalous/which needs putting right.

cry•o•gen•ics [kraɪəʊ'dʒenɪks] *n.* study of very low temperatures.

crypt [krɪpt] *n.* cellar under a church.

cryp•tic ['krɪptɪk] *adj.* secret; mysterious.

crypto- ['krɪptəʊ] *prefix* hidden.

æ back, ɑː farm, ɒ top, aɪ pipe, aʊ how, aɪə fire, aʊə flower, ɔː bought, ɔɪ toy, e fed, eəhair, eɪ take, ə afraid, əʊ boat, əʊə lower, ʌː word, iː heap, ɪ hit, ɪə hear, uː school, ʊ book, ʌ but, b back, d dog, ð then, dʒ just, f fog, g go, h hand, j yes, k catch, l last, m mix, n nut, ŋ sing, p penny, r round, s some, ʃ short, t too, tʃ chop, θ thing, v voice, w was, z zoo, ʒ treasure

cryp•to•gam ['krɪptəgæm] *n.* plant (like moss) which has no flowers.

cryp•to•gram ['krɪptəgræm] *n.* message written in a secret language; coded message. **cryp•tog•ra•phy**, *n.* study of codes.

crys•tal ['krɪstl] *n.* (a) chemical formation of regular-shaped solids. (b) very clear bright glass. **crys•tal•line**, *adj.* shaped like a crystal; clear as a crystal. **crys•tal•li•za•tion** [krɪstəlaɪ'zeɪʃn] *n.* formation of crystals. **crys•tal•lize** ['krɪstəlaɪz] *v.* (a) to form crystals. (b) to preserve fruit in sugar. (c) to take shape. **crys•tal•log•ra•phy** [krɪstə'lɒɡrəfɪ] *n.* study of crystals.

Cu *symbol for* copper.

cub [kʌb] *n.* (a) young animal (esp. bear/fox). (b) **C. Scout** = boy in the younger section of the Boy Scouts.

Cu•ban ['kjuːbn] 1. *adj.* referring to Cuba. 2. *n.* person from Cuba.

cub•by-hole ['kʌbɪhəʊl] *n.* small dark cupboard/hiding place.

cube [kjuːb] 1. *n.* (a) geometric solid shape where all six sides are square and join each other at right angles. (b) the result where a number is multiplied by itself twice; **c. root** = number which when multiplied by itself twice produces a given number. 2. *v.* (a) to multiply (a number) by itself twice. (b) **cubed sugar** = sugar in square lumps. **cu•bic**, *adj.* solid; **c. capacity** = capacity to hold something; **c. centimeter** = (i) cube where each side measures one centimeter; (ii) the volume of this size.

cu•bi•cle ['kjuːbɪkl] *n.* small room (in a dormitory); small space (in an office); changing room (in a store, etc.).

cub•ism ['kjuːbɪzəm] *n.* art movement where geometric shapes predominate. **cub•ist**, *adj. & n.* (painter) using geometric shapes.

cuck•oo ['kuku:] 1. *n.* common summer bird, which lays its eggs in other birds' nests. 2. *adj. inf.* stupid. **cuck•oo clock**, *n.* clock where a small bird makes a noise like a cuckoo to call the time.

cu•cum•ber ['kjuːkʌmbə] *n.* long vegetable used in salads or for pickling.

cud [kʌd] *n.* food chewed a second time.

cud•dle ['kʌdl] 1. *n.* a hug. 2. *v.* to hug and kiss (s.o.). **cud•dle•some, cuddly**, *adj.* warm and soft.

cudg•el ['kʌdʒl] 1. *n.* large stick for hitting people with; **to take up the cudgels for** = to go to defend s.o. 2. *v.* (**cudgelled**) **to c. one's brains** = to think hard.

cue [kjuː] *n.* (a) (*in a play*) the line which indicates that you speak or act next; **to take your c. from s.o.** = to follow s.o. closely/to do as s.o. does. (b) long stick for playing billiards/pool.

cuff [kʌf] 1. *n.* (a) end of the sleeve round the wrist; **speaking off the c./an off the c. speech** = speech made without any notes; impromptu speech. (b) folded part at the bottom of each leg of a pair of trousers. (c) smack (with an open hand). 2. *v.* to give (s.o.) a smack. **cuff-links**, *n. pl.* fasteners for attaching shirt cuffs.

cui•rass [kwiː'ræs] *n.* armor for the top part of the body.

cui•sine [kwɪ'ziːn] *n.* style of cooking.

cul-de-sac ['kʌldəsæk] *n.* small street open at only one end.

cu•li•nar•y ['kʌlɪnərɪ] *adj.* referring to cooking.

cull [kʌl] *v.* to kill (some animals in a herd) when there are too many of them.

cul•let ['kʌlɪt] *n.* broken glass for recycling.

cul•mi•nate ['kʌlmɪneɪt] *v.* to reach a climax/to end (**in**). **cul•mi•na•tion** [kʌlmɪ-'neɪʃn] *n.* final point/grand ending.

cu•lottes [kjuː'lɒts] *n. pl.* woman's wide shorts, like a split skirt.

cul•pa•ble ['kʌlpəbl] *adj.* guilty. **cul•pa•bil•i•ty** [kʌlpə'bɪlɪtɪ] *n.* guilt.

cul•prit ['kʌlprɪt] *n.* person who has done something wrong.

cult [kʌlt] *n.* religious or semi-religious worship; **c. hero** = person worshipped by a group of admirers.

cul•ti•vate ['kʌltɪveɪt] *v.* (a) to dig and water (the land) to grow plants; to grow (plants). (b) to do everything to win (s.o.'s friendship). **cul•ti•vat•ed**, *adj.* (person) who has been educated/who is civilized. **cul•ti•va•tion** [kʌltɪ'veɪʃn] *n.* (a) act of cultivating. (b) education. **cul•ti•va•tor**, *n.* (a) farmer/person who cultivates. (b) small motor-powered plow.

cul•ture ['kʌltʃə] *n.* (a) cultivation of plants/pearls. (b) growing (of germs in a laboratory). (c) civilization. **cul•tur•al**, *adj.* referring to culture. **cul•tured**, *adj.* (a) civilized; well educated (person). (b) (pearl) which has been artificially grown.

cul•vert ['kʌlvət] *n.* drain which goes under a road in a pipe.

cum•ber•some ['kʌmbəsəm] *adj.* large and heavy.

cum•in ['kʌmɪn] *n.* herb whose seeds are used for flavoring.

cum•mer•bund ['kʌməbʌnd] *n.* type of decorative belt, usu. worn by men with formal clothes.

cu•mu•la•tive ['kjuːmjʊlətɪv] *adj.* which accumulates; which grows by adding new parts.

cu•mu•lus ['kjuːmjʊləs] *n.* type of large white cloud; rounded masses of clouds.

cu•ne•i•form ['kju:nɪfɔ:m] *adj. & n.* type of ancient writing done on wet clay with a stick.

cun•ning ['kʌnɪŋ] 1. *n.* (a) cleverness. (b) trickery. 2. *adj.* (a) clever. (b) tricky/sly.

cup [kʌp] 1. *n.* (a) bowl with a handle for drinking coffee or tea, etc. (b) silver goblet or vase given as a prize in sporting events/competitions, etc.; **c. final** = final match for a championship. 2. *v.* (**cupped**) to put (hands) in the shape of a cup. **cup•ful**, *n.* quantity held by a cup.

cup•board ['kʌbəd] *n.* large piece of furniture with shelves and doors; alcove in a wall with shelves and doors.

cu•pid•i•ty [kju:'pɪdɪtɪ] *n.* greed; desire for sth.

cu•po•la ['kju:pələ] *n.* small dome.

cur [kɜ:] *n.* dirty dog.

cu•ra•re [kjʊə'rɑːri] *n.* S. American poison, now used to relax the muscles.

cu•rate ['kjʊərət] *n.* minor priest who helps the parish priest. **cu•ra•cy**, *n.* post of curate.

cu•ra•tor [kjʊ'reɪtə] *n.* person in charge of a museum.

curb [kɜ:b] 1. *n.* (a) stone edging to a pavement/path. (b) thing which holds you back. 2. *v.* to control; to hold back.

curd [kɜ:d] *n.* solid food made from sour milk. **cur•dle** ['kɜ:dl] *v.* to (cause to) go sour.

cure ['kjuə] 1. *n.* (a) making better. (b) remedy. 2. *v.* (a) to make better. (b) to preserve (fish/pork, etc.) by salting/smoking, etc.; to preserve (skins) to make leather. **cur•a•ble**, *adj.* (disease) which can be cured. **cur•a•tive**, *adj.* which can cure.

cu•ret•tage [kjure'tɑː:ʒ] *n.* scraping of the inside of part of the body. **cu•rette**, *n.* surgical instrument for scraping.

cur•few ['kɜ:fjuː] *n.* period when no one is allowed on the streets.

cu•rie ['kjuərɪ] *n.* unit of measurement of radioactivity.

cu•ri•o ['kjʊərɪəʊ] *n.* (*pl.* -os) old/rare object.

cu•ri•os•i•ty [kjʊərɪ'ɒsɪtɪ] *n.* (a) desire for knowledge. (b) odd/rare object. **cu•ri•ous** ['kjʊərɪəs] *adj.* (a) wanting to know. (b) odd/peculiar. **cu•ri•ous•ly**, *adv.* oddly.

curl [kɜ:l] 1. *n.* lock of wavy twisted hair. 2. *v.* (a) to make (hair) wave/twist. (b) to grow in waves/twists naturally. **curl•er**, *n.* small tube for wrapping hair round to make it curl. **curl•ing**, *n.* team game where heavy weights are slid across ice towards a target. **curl up**, *v.*

to roll up into a ball. **curl•y**, *adj.* (-ier, -iest) with natural waves, twists.

cur•lew ['kɜ:ljuː] *n.* brown wading bird with a long curved beak.

cur•rant ['kʌrənt] *n.* (a) small black or red soft fruit; bush of this fruit. (b) small dried grape.

cur•ren•cy ['kʌrənsɪ] *n.* (a) (system of) money; **hard c.** = money which can be easily exchanged internationally. (b) being well known; **to gain c.** = to become more frequently heard.

cur•rent ['kʌrənt] 1. *n.* flow of water/air/electricity. 2. *adj.* of the present time; frequent; **c. affairs** = things which are happening at the present moment. **cur•rent•ly**, *adv.* at the present time.

cur•ric•u•lum [kə'rɪkjʊləm] *n.* list of subjects studied in a school, etc. **c. vitae** ['viːtɪ] = summary of biographical details, esp. details of education and work experience.

cur•ry ['kʌrɪ] 1. *n.* hot spice; dish made with hot spice; **c. powder.** 2. *v.* (a) to cook with hot spices. (b) to brush down (a horse). (c) **to c. favor with s.o.** = to try to make s.o. favor you. **cur•ry•comb**, *n.* stiff brush for brushing a horse.

curse [kɜ:s] 1. *n.* (a) evil magic spell. (b) swear word. (c) calamity/evil. (d) *inf.* **the c.** = woman's menstrual periods. 2. *v.* (a) to cast an evil spell on (s.o.). (b) to swear.

cur•sive ['kɜ:sɪv] *adj.* (writing) with the letters joined together.

cur•sor ['kɜ:sə] *n.* spot of light which moves round a computer screen, showing where work is being done.

cur•so•ry ['kɜ:sərɪ] *adj.* rapid/superficial (inspection/glance). **cur•so•ri•ly**, *adv.* rapidly.

curt [kɜ:t] *adj.* (-er, -est) abrupt. **curt•ly**, *adv.* abruptly. **curt•ness**, *n.* being curt.

cur•tail [kɜ:'teɪl] *v.* to shorten; to reduce. **cur•tail•ment**, *n.* act of curtailing.

cur•tain ['kɜ:tn] 1. *n.* long piece of material hanging by hooks from a pole, covering a window or cutting off the stage in a theater. 2. *v.* (*also* **c. off**) to hide/to cover with a curtain. **cur•tain-call**, *n.* calling of an actor to take a bow after the end of a performance. **cur•tain-rod**, *n.* rod on which a curtain is hung.

curt•sy ['kɜ:tsɪ] 1. *n.* respectful movement made by women/girls, by bending the knees

---

æ back, a: farm, ɒ: top, aɪ pipe, aʊ how, aiə fire, aʊə flower, ɔ: bought, ɔɪ toy, e fed, eəhair, eɪ take, ə afraid, əʊ boat, əʊə lower, ɜ: word, iː heap, ɪ hit, ɪə hear, uː school, ʊ book, ʌ but, b back, d dog, ð then, dʒ just, f fog, g go, h hand, j yes, k catch, l last, m mix, n nut, ŋ sing, p penny, r round, s some, ʃ short, t too, tʃ chop, θ thing, v voice, w was, z zoo, ʒ treasure

and putting one foot forward. 2. *v.* **to c. to s.o.** = to make a curtsy to s.o.

curve [kɜːv] 1. *n.* rounded shape like a semi-circle. 2. *v.* to make a rounded shape. **cur•va•ceous** [kɜːˈveɪʃəs] *adj.* (girl) with a rounded figure. **cur•va•ture** [ˈkɜːvətʃə] *n.* bending of something into a curve; **c. of the spine** = abnormal bending of the spine. **curved,** *adj.* rounded.

cush•ion [ˈkʊʃn] 1. *n.* bag filled with feathers, etc., for sitting/leaning on. 2. *v.* to soften (a blow).

cush•y [ˈkʊʃɪ] *adj.* (**-ier, -iest**) *inf.* easy (job).

cusp [kʌsp] *n.* point where two curves meet.

cus•pi•dor [ˈkʌspɪˈdɔː] *n.* bowl into which one can spit.

cuss•ed [ˈkʌsɪd] *adj. inf.* awkward and contrary. **cuss•ed•ness** [ˈkʌsɪdnəs] *n. inf.* being cussed.

cus•tard [ˈkʌstəd] *n.* sweet dessert made with eggs, milk and flavoring, baked or boiled.

cus•to•dy [ˈkʌstədɪ] *n.* keeping. **cus•to•di•an** [kʌˈstəʊdɪən] *n.* person who keeps sth safe; guardian of an ancient monument, etc.

cus•tom [ˈkʌstəm] *n.* (a) habit. (b) patronizing a business establishment. **custom-built/custom-made** = made to special order. **cus•tom•ar•i•ly,** *adv.* usually. **cus•tom•ar•y,** *adj.* habitual. **cus•tom•er,** *n.* client/person who patronizes a business establishment. **cus•tom•ize,** *v.* to convert (car) to a customer's special and peculiar requirements. **cus•toms,** *n.* tax on goods imported into a country.

cut [kʌt] 1. *n.* (a) reduction (in salary); breaking off (electricity supply). (b) opening made with a sharp blade; small wound. (c) **short c.** = way which is shorter than usual. (d) way in which a suit/jacket, etc., is made. (e) piece/slice of meat. (f) *inf.* share (of profits, etc.). 2. (**cut**) (a) to make an opening (using a sharp blade); to wound (with a knife); to shorten; to reduce. (b) to divide (a pack of playing cards) in half. (c) not to look at (s.o.) whom you know. (d) to miss (a lecture). 3. *adj.* which has been cut. **cut down,** *v.* to chop down (a tree); to reduce (an amount). **cut in,** *v.* to interrupt a conversation; to move in quickly in front of another car in traffic. **cut off,** *v.* to disconnect (electricity supply); to remove; to stop (s.o.) reaching a place. **cut out,** *v.* (a) to stop (eating sth, etc.). (b) to remove a small piece by cutting it from a large piece (of paper, etc.); **he is not cut out for the army** = he does not fit in with/is not suitable for the army. **cut-rate,** *adj.* cheap. **cut•ter,** *n.* (a) person who cuts. (b) machine which cuts. (c) small, fast boat. **cut•throat,**

adj. vicious/intense. **cut•ting,** 1. *adj.* which cuts; sharply critical (remark). 2. *n.* (a) small piece of paper cut out of a newspaper. (b) little piece of a plant which will take root if stuck in dirt or the ground. **cut up,** *v.* to make into small pieces by cutting; *inf.* **cut up** = very upset.

cu•ta•ne•ous [kjuːˈteɪnɪəs] *adj.* referring to the skin.

cute [kjuːt] *adj. inf.* nice. **cute•ness,** *n.* niceness.

cu•ti•cle [ˈkjuːtɪkl] *n.* skin round a fingernail or toenail.

cut•lass [ˈkʌtləs] *n.* short sword, used in the navy and in cavalry.

cut•ler•y [ˈkʌtlərɪ] *n.* (*no pl.*) knives, forks and spoons.

cut•let [ˈkʌtlət] *n.* (a) thin slice of meat (usu. with the rib bone attached). (b) fried patty made with meat, etc.

cut•tle•fish [ˈkʌtlfɪʃ] *n.* animal (like a squid) which lives in the sea and squirts ink when attacked.

CV [siːˈviː] *n.* curriculum vitae.

cwt *abbrev for* hundredweight.

cy•a•nide [ˈsaɪənaɪd] *n.* strong poison.

cyber- [ˈsaɪbə] *prefix meaning* computer; **cybercafé; cyberspace.**

cy•ber•ca•fé [ˈsaɪbəkæfeɪ] *n.* café with computers offering customers access to the Internet.

cy•ber•net•ics [saɪbəˈnetɪks] *n.* science of the communication of information.

cy•ber•space [ˈsaɪbəspeɪs] *n.* a three-dimensional representation of information stored in a computer/computer network.

cy•cla•men [ˈsɪkləmən] *n.* common indoor plant with pink flowers which grow from a corm.

cy•cle [ˈsaɪkl] 1. *n.* (a) period during which sth returns. (b) series of songs or poems. (c) bicycle. 2. *v.* to go on a bicycle. **cy•clic, cyclical** [ˈsɪklɪk(l)] *adj.* occuring in cycles. **cy•cling,** *n.* riding a bicycle as a sport. **cy•clist,** *n.* person who rides a bicycle.

cy•clone [ˈsaɪkləʊn] *n.* tropical storm.

cy•clo•styled [ˈsaɪkləʊstaɪld] *adj.* (copy) produced from a stencil.

cy•clo•tron [ˈsaɪkləʊtrɒn] *n.* machine which accelerates the spiral movement of particles, used in nuclear processes.

cyg•net [ˈsɪgnət] *n.* baby swan.

cyl•in•der [ˈsɪlɪndə] *n.* shape like a tube; part of an engine, of this shape, in which a piston moves. **cy•lin•dri•cal** [sɪˈlɪndrɪkl] *adj.* tube-shaped.

cym•bals [ˈsɪmbəlz] *n. pl.* pair of round metal plates which are banged together to make a loud noise in music.

cyn•ic ['sınık] *n.* person who mocks/who doubts that anything is good. **cyn•i•cal,** *adj.* referring to a cynic. **cyn•i•cal•ly,** *adv.* in a cynical, mocking way. **cyn•i•cism** ['sınısızəm] *n.* being cynical.

cy•no•sure ['saınəsjυə] *n.* center of attraction.

cy•press ['saıprəs] *n.* (*pl.* **-es**) tall slim evergreen tree.

Cyp•ri•ot ['sıprıət] 1. *adj.* referring to Cyprus. 2. *n.* person from Cyprus.

cyst [sıst] *n.* small growth on or inside the body. **cys•ti•tis** [sıs'taıtıs] *n.* inflammation of the bladder. **cys•tos•co•py,** *n.* operation to examine the bladder by means of a very small telescope on the end of a tube.

cy•tol•o•gy [saı'tɒlədʒı] *n.* study of cells.

Czech [tʃek] 1. *adj.* referring to the Czech Republic. 2. *n.* (a) person from the Czech Republic. (b) language spoken in the Czech Republic.

æ back, a: farm, ɒ: top, aı pipe, aυ how, aıe fire, aυə flower, ɔ: bought, ɔı toy, e fed, eəhair, eı take, ə afraid, əυ boat, əυə lower, v: word, i: heap, ı hit, ıə hear, u: school, υ book, ʌ but, b back, d dog, ð then, dʒ just, f fog, g go, h hand, j yes, k catch, l last, m mix, n nut, ŋ sing, p penny, r round, s some, ʃ short, t too, tʃ chop, θ thing, v voice, w was, z zoo, ʒ treasure

Dd

dab [dæb] 1. *n.* (a) light tap. (b) small flat fish. (c) small quantity. 2. *v.* (**dabbed**) to give (sth) a light tap; **to d. (sth) on** = to apply (paint, etc.) by pressing lightly.

dab•ble ['dæbl] *v.* to paddle (in water); **he dabbles in politics** = he does a little political work.

dab•chick ['dæbtʃɪk] *n.* common small dark waterbird with a red forehead.

dace [deɪs] *n.* (*pl.* **dace**) small edible freshwater fish.

dachs•hund ['dækshʊnd] *n.* breed of long low dog (originally from Germany).

dac•tyl ['dæktɪl] *n.* measure (one long and two short syllables) used in poetry.

dad [dæd], **dad•dy** ['dædɪ] *n. inf.* father. **dad•dy-long-legs,** *n.* insect with very long legs.

da•do ['deɪdəʊ] *n.* (*pl.* **-os**) lower part of a wall, which is paneled or painted differently from the upper part.

daf•fo•dil ['dæfədɪl] *n.* spring flower in shades of yellow, with a trumpet-shaped center.

daft [dɑːft] *adj. inf.* silly.

dag•ger ['dægə] *n.* short knife; **to look daggers at** = to look at angrily.

da•guerre•o•type [də'gerɪəʊtaɪp] *n.* photographic process, where the image is captured on silver-coated plate.

dahl•ia ['deɪlɪə] *n.* autumn garden flower (produced from a bulbous root).

Dail [dɔɪl] *n.* lower house of the Irish Parliament.

dai•ly ['deɪlɪ] 1. *adj.* every day. 2. *adv.* **twice d.** = two times a day. 3. *n.* newspaper published every weekday.

dain•ty ['deɪntɪ] *adj.* (**-ier, -iest**) delicate; small. **dain•ti•ly,** *adv.* delicately.

dair•y ['deərɪ] *n.* place where milk, cream and butter are processed or sold; **d. produce** = milk, butter, cream and cheese. **d. farm** = farm which produces milk. **dair•y•man,** *n* (*pl.* **-men**) man who looks after dairy cows.

da•is ['deɪɪs] *n.* low platform (in large hall).

dai•sy ['deɪzɪ] *n.* small pink and white summer flower; **d. wheel printer** = typewriter/computer printer, where the characters are on the ends of spokes of a wheel.

dale [deɪl] *n.* (*in north of England*) valley.

dal•ly ['dælɪ] *v.* to idle; to spend time doing nothing. **dal•li•ance,** *n.* (*old*) idling.

dal•ma•tian [dæl'meɪʃn] *n.* large white dog with black spots.

dam [dæm] 1. *n.* (a) wall (of earth or concrete) blocking a river, etc. (b) female mammal which is a mother. 2. *v.* (**dammed**) to block (a river) by building a wall across it.

dam•age ['dæmɪdʒ] 1. *n.* (a) harm (done to things, not to people). (b) **damages** = payment ordered by a court to a victim. (c) *inf.* total of a bill. 2. *v.* to spoil or harm (sth).

dam•ask ['dæməsk] *n.* kind of patterned material, used esp. for tablecloths, etc. **dam•a•scene,** *adj.* (steel) decorated with patterns of silver or gold.

dame [deɪm] *n.* (a) *inf.* woman. (b) *Brit.* title given to women (*equivalent to* Sir *for men*).

damn [dæm] 1. *n.* curse. 2. *v.* to condemn; to curse; to criticize. 3. *inter. inf.* expressing annoyance. **dam•na•ble,** *adj.* cursed. **dam•na•tion** [dæm'neɪʃn] *n.* state of being eternally condemned. **damned,** *adj. inf.* very annoying. **damn•ing,** *adj.* which shows that sth is wrong.

damp [dæmp] 1. *n.* wetness. 2. *adj.* (**-er, -est**) rather wet. 3. *v.* to wet; to reduce (enthusiasm). **damp•en,** *v.* to damp. **damp•er,** *n.* (a) plate at the back of a fireplace which regulates the draft. (b) soft pad which touches a piano string to soften the tone. **damp•ness,** *n.* state of being wet. **damp-proof,** *adj.* resistant to wet.

dam•sel ['dæmzl] *n.* (*old*) girl.

dam•son ['dæmzən] *n.* small purple plum; tree which bears this fruit.

dance [dɑːns] 1. *n* (a) way of moving to music. (b) evening entertainment where people dance. 2. *v.* (a) to move (in time to music). (b) to jump up and down (with excitement). **danc•er,** *n.* person who dances; **ballet d.** = person who dances in ballet.

dan•de•li•on ['dændɪlaɪən] *n.* wild plant with yellow flowers and bitter sap.

dan•druff ['dændrʌf] *n.* small pieces of dry skin (in the hair).

dan•dy ['dændɪ] *n.* man who is too interested in clothes. **dan•di•fied,** *adj.* like a dandy.

Dane [deɪn] *n.* person from Denmark; **Great D.** = breed of very large short-haired dog.

dan•ger ['deɪndʒə] *n.* risk; possibility of harm or death; **in d.** = at risk; **out of d./off the d. list** = no longer likely to die. **dan•ger•ous,** *adj.* which can cause injury or death. **dan•ger•ous•ly,** *adv.* in a dangerous way.

dan•gle ['dæŋgl] *v.* to (cause to) hang limply.

Dan•ish ['deɪnɪʃ] 1. *adj.* referring to Denmark; **D. pastry** = sweet pastry cake with jam or fruit folded in it. 2. *n.* language spoken in Denmark.

dank [dæŋk] *adj.* cold and damp.

daph•ne ['dæfnɪ] *n.* small shrub with pink flowers which appear very early in the spring.

dap•per ['dæpə] *adj.* smart/elegant.

dap•pled ['dæpld] *adj.* covered with patches of light and dark color.

dare ['deə] 1. *n.* act of daring s.o. to do sth. 2. *v.* (a) to be brave enough (to do sth); **I d. say** = perhaps/probably. (b) to challenge (s.o.) to do sth by suggesting it is cowardly not to do it. **dare•dev•il,** *adj. & n.* (person) full of reckless bravery. **dar•ing.** 1. *adj.* brave but foolish. 2. *n.* foolish bravery.

dark [dɑːk] 1. *adj.* (**-er, -est**) (a) with little or no light. (b) not a light color; **d. horse** = person/thing which succeeds though not expected to do so; **D. Ages** = period between the end of the Roman civilization in Northern Europe and the Middle Ages. (c) gloomy. 2. *n.* (a) absence of light. (b) **to keep s.o. in the d.** = to keep sth a secret from s.o. **dark•en,** *v.* to become dark. **dark•ly,** *adv.* in a gloomy way. **dark•ness,** *n.* absence of light. **dark•room,** *n.* room with a special light, in which you can develop and print films.

dar•ling ['dɑːlɪŋ] *n. & adj.* (person) loved; lovable.

darn [dɑːn] 1. *v.* to mend (holes in clothes). 2. *n.* place where clothes have been mended. **darn•ing,** *n.* action of mending; clothes which are waiting to be mended.

dart [dɑːt] 1. *n.* (a) light arrow with a sharp point. (b) small heavy arrow with feathers (for playing a game with); **darts** = games where two teams throw small heavy arrows at a round target. (c) small tuck sewn into a garment to make it fit. (d) quick rush. 2. *v.* to run fast. **dart•board,** *n.* round target at which darts are thrown.

dash [dæʃ] 1. *n.* (*pl.* **-es**) (a) small amount. (b) little line. (c) sudden rush. 2. *v.* (a) to rush. (b) to smash (sth). **dash•board,** *n.* instrument panel in a car. **dash•ing,** *adj.* very smart and energetic (person).

das•tard•ly ['dɑːstədlɪ] *adj.* cowardly and unpleasant.

da•ta ['deɪtə] *n.* statistical information; **d. bank** = store of information in a computer; **d. protection** = keeping information or computer records safely, so that they cannot be copied. *see also* **da•tum. da•ta•base,** *n.* data stored in a computer, which can be used to provide information of various kinds. **da•ta pro•cess•ing,** *n.* analysis of statistical information using a computer.

date [deɪt] 1. *n.* (a) number of a day, month or year; **up to d.** = recent; **he is bringing the book up to d.** = he is revising the book to put in the most recent information; **out of d.** = not modern; **the book is three years out of d.** (b) agreed meeting time. (c) fruit of a date palm. 2. *v.* (a) to write the number of the day on (sth). (b) to give the date of (an antique, etc.). (c) to agree to meet (s.o. of the opposite sex) at a particular time. (c) **this house dates from 1600** = this house has existed since 1600. (d) to seem old-fashioned. **dat•a•ble,** *adj.* which can be dated. **dat•ed,** *adj.* old-fashioned. **date•less,** *adj.* with no date. **date•line,** *n.* heading (with date and place) of a report from a foreign correspondent. **date line,** *n.* line of longitude (in the Pacific Ocean) which indicates the change in date from east to west. **date palm,** *n.* palm tree which provides small, very sweet brown fruit.

da•tive ['deɪtɪv] *adj. & n.* (*in grammar*) (case) showing giving.

da•tum ['deɪtəm] *n.* (*pl.* **data**) piece of information.

daub [dɔːb] 1. *n.* (a) smear. (b) *inf.* bad painting. 2. *v.* to smear with paint/with mud, etc.

daugh•ter ['dɔːtə] *n.* female child (of a parent). **daugh•ter-in-law,** *n.* (*pl.* **daughters-in-law**) son's wife.

daunt [dɔːnt] *v.* to discourage. **not daunted** = not frightened. **daunt•less,** *adj.* fearless.

dav•en•port ['dævənpɔːt] *n.* (a) sofa. (b) small writing desk.

da•vit ['dævɪt] *n.* (*on a ship*) small crane for lowering the lifeboats into the sea.

daw•dle ['dɔːdl] *v.* to walk slowly and aimlessly.

æ back, aː farm, ɒ top, aɪ pipe, aʊ how, aɪe fire, aʊe flower, ɔː bought, ɔɪ toy, e fed, eəhair, eɪ take, ə afraid, əʊ boat, əʊə lower, vː word, iː heap, ɪ hit, ɪə hear, uː school, ʊ book, ʌ but, b back, d dog, ð then, dʒ just, f fog, g go, h hand, j yes, k catch, l last, m mix, n nut, ŋ sing, p penny, r round, s some, ʃ short, t too, tʃ chop, θ thing, v voice, w was, z zoo, ʒ treasure

dawn [dɔ:n] 1. *n.* (a) beginning of day, when the sun rises. (b) beginning (of civilization). 2. *v.* (a) (*of day*) to begin. (b) **it dawned on him that** = he began to realize that.

day [deɪ] *n.* (a) period of time lasting 24 hours. (b) period of time from morning to night. (c) light. (d) **two apples a d.** = every day. (e) **one d./some d.** = sometime in the future. (f) period (in the past). **day•break,** *n.* early morning when the sun is about to rise. **day care cen•ter,** *n.* place where elderly or disabled people can meet and be looked after or where young children can be cared for during the day. **day•dream.** 1. *n.* dream which you have during the day when you are not asleep. 2. *v.* to think about other things; not to concentrate. **day•light,** *n.* light of day; **d. saving time** = system of advancing the clocks in summer to take advantage of the longer daylight period. **day•time,** *n.* **in the d.** = during the day.

daze [deɪz] 1. *n.* state of not being mentally alert. 2. *v.* to stun (s.o.).

daz•zle ['dæzl] *v.* to blind (temporarily). **daz•zling,** *adj.* very bright (light).

db, dB *abbrev. for* decibel.

D & C *abbrev. for* dilation and curettage.

DC *abbrev. for* direct current.

DDT [di:di:'ti:] *n.* insecticide, highly damaging to the environment.

dea•con ['di:kən] *n.* minor priest. **dea•con•ess,** *n.* woman who can direct services (in some Protestant churches).

dead [ded] 1. *adj.* (a) not alive; (telephone line, etc.) not working. (b) complete (silence, etc.). (c) no longer used. 2. *n.* (a) **the d.** =dead people. (b) **in the d. of night** = in the middle of the night. 3. *adv.* (a) completely. (b) exactly. **dead•beat,** *n. sl.* person who does not pay his debts. **dead•en,** *v.* to make (a sound) quieter; to make (a blow) soft. **dead end,** *n.* (street/way) leading nowhere. **dead heat,** *n.* race where two contestants come in equal first. **dead let•ter,** *n.* (a) letter which cannot be delivered. (b) law which is no longer obeyed. **dead•line,** *n.* date by which sth has to be done. **dead•li•ness,** *n.* being deadly. **dead•lock.** 1. *n.* state where two sides cannot agree. 2. *v.* to (cause to) be unable to agree. **dead•ly,** *adj.* (**-ier, -iest**) so strong as to kill; **d. nightshade** = very poisonous plant. **dead•pan,** *adj.* not showing any emotion.

deaf [def] 1. *adj.* (**-er, -est**) unable to hear; having difficulty in hearing. 2. *n.* **the d.** = people who cannot hear. **deaf•en,** *v.* to make deaf (by a loud noise). **deaf•en•ing,** *adj.* so loud as to make you deaf. **deaf•ness,** *n.* state of being deaf.

deal [di:l] 1. *n.* (a) large quantity; **a good d. better** = much better. (b) handing out (playing cards). (c) (business) affair. (d) wood from a pine tree. 2. *v.* (**dealt** [delt]) (a) to hand out. (b) **to d. with** = to organize to solve a problem. (c) **to d. in** = to buy and sell. **deal•er,** *n.* person who buys and sells. **deal•er•ship,** *n.* business of a dealer. **deal•ings,** *n. pl.* business/affairs.

dean [di:n] *n.* person in charge of lecturers or priests. **dean•er•y,** *n.* position or house of a dean (in a cathedral).

dear ['dɪə] *adj.* (**-er, -est**) (a) well liked; loved. (b) (*addressing someone at the beginning of a letter*) **D. Mr. Smith; D. Sir.** (c) expensive. 2. *inter.* **oh d.!** = how annoying! **dear•ly,** *adv.* tenderly; very much.

dearth [dɜ:θ] *n.* scarcity.

death [deθ] *n.* act of dying. **d. duty** = tax paid on money left by dead person; **d. mask** = plaster mask made of s.o.'s face, after death; **d. rate** = number of people who die (as a percentage of the population). **death•bed,** *n.* bed on which s.o. is dying. **death•less,** *adj.* which will live for ever. **death•ly,** *adv.* as if dead. **death•trap,** *n.* dangerous place. **death watch bee•tle,** *n.* beetle which bores holes in wood and makes a clicking sound.

deb [deb] *n. inf.* debutante.

de•ba•cle [deɪ'bɑːkl] *n.* (a) sudden defeat/collapse. (b) breakup of ice on a river in spring.

de•bar [dɪ'bɑː] *v.* (**debarred**) **to d. s.o. from sth** = to forbid s.o. to do sth.

de•base [dɪ'beɪs] *v.* to degrade; to reduce the value of (sth, esp. the value of the metal in coinage). **de•base•ment,** *n.* act of debasing.

de•bate [dɪ'beɪt] 1. *n.* formal discussion. 2. *v.* to discuss. **de•bat•a•ble,** *adj.* not absolutely certain.

de•bauched [dɪ'bɔːtʃt] *adj.* (person) who spends his time in wild living and enjoys immoral pleasures. **de•bauch•er•y,** *n.* wild living.

de•ben•ture [dɪ'bentʃə] *n.* document showing that a company agrees to repay a debt, and to pay a fixed interest on it, the money being secured on the company's assets.

de•bil•i•tate [dɪ'bɪlɪteɪt] *v.* to make weak. **de•bil•i•ty,** *n.* Weakness.

deb•it ['debɪt] 1. *n.* (money) which is owed; **on the d. side** = against (a proposal). 2. *v.* to deduct money from (an account). **deb•it card,** *n.* card that allows customers to pay for goods by deducting money from their bank accounts via an electronic link through telephone networks.

deb•o•nair [debə'neə] *adj.* carefree/relaxed (air).

de•brief ['di:'bri:f] *v.* to ask (s.o.) questions to obtain information about a mission which he has just completed. **de•brief•ing,** *n.* obtaining information about a mission by questioning the person who carried it out.

de•bris ['debri:] *n.* pieces (of a demolished building/crashed aircraft, etc.).

debt [det] *n.* money owed to s.o.; **he is in d.** = he owes money. **debt•or,** *n.* person who owes money.

de•bug [di:'bʌg] *v.* (**debugged**) to remove bugs from (sth); to correct errors in a computer program.

de•bunk [di'bʌŋk] *v. inf.* to disprove.

de•but ['deɪbju:] *n.* first appearance (of an artist/actor, etc.). **deb•u•tante,** *n.* girl who goes into adult society for the first time.

deca- ['dekə] *prefix meaning* ten.

dec•ade ['dekeɪd] *n.* period of ten years.

dec•a•dence ['dekədəns] *n.* decline in moral values. **dec•a•dent,** *adj.* declining in moral values.

de•caf•fein•at•ed [di:'kæfɪneɪtɪd] *adj.* (coffee) which has had the caffeine removed.

de•cal ['di:kæl] *n.* sticker/piece of plastic or paper with a pattern or slogan which you can stick to a surface as a decoration.

de•camp [di:'kæmp] *v. inf.* to go away.

de•cant [dɪ'kænt] *v.* to pour (liquid, esp. wine) from a bottle into another container. **de•cant•er,** *n.* glass bottle which wine is poured into before serving.

de•cap•i•tate [dɪ'kæpɪteɪt] *v.* to cut off the head of (s.o.). **de•cap•i•ta•tion** [dɪkæpɪ-'teɪʃn] *n.* act of cutting off a head.

de•car•bon•ize [de'kɑ:bənaɪz] *v.* to remove carbon deposits from (a gas engine).

de•cath•lon [dɪ'kæθlən] *n.* sporting competition where each athlete competes in ten different types of sport.

de•cay [dɪ'keɪ] 1. *n.* falling into ruin; rotting. 2. *v.* to fall into ruin; to rot.

de•cease [dɪ'si:s] *n.* (*formal*) death. **de•ceased,** *n.* dead person.

de•ceit [dɪ'si:t] *n.* trickery. **de•ceit•ful,** *adj.* tricking. **de•ceit•ful•ly,** *adv.* in a deceitful way. **de•ceive** [dɪ'si:v] *v.* to trick; to make (s.o.) believe sth which is not true.

de•cel•er•ate [di:'seləreɪt] *v.* to (make sth) go slower. **de•cel•er•a•tion** [di:selə'reɪʃn] *n.* going slower.

De•cem•ber [dɪ'sembə] *n.* 12th month of the year.

de•cent ['di:sənt] *adj.* (a) honest. (b) quite good. **de•cen•cy,** *n.* honor; good morals. **de•cent•ly,** *adv.* in a decent way.

de•cen•tral•ize [di:'sentrəlaɪz] *v.* to move (authority/offices) from the center. **de•cen•tral•i•za•tion** [di:sentrəlaɪ'zeɪʃn] *n.* act of decentralizing.

de•cep•tion [dɪ'sepʃn] *n.* fraud; making s.o. believe sth which is not true. **de•cep•tive,** *adj.* not as it looks. **de•cep•tive•ly,** *adv.* in a way which deceives.

dec•i•bel ['desɪbel] *n.* unit of measurement of noise.

de•cide [dɪ'saɪd] *v.* to make up your mind (to do sth). **de•cid•ed,** *adj.* (a) firm (tone, manner). (b) certain/obvious (difference, etc.). **de•cid•ed•ly,** *adv.* (a) in a firm manner. (b) certainly.

de•cid•u•ous [dɪ'sɪdjʊəs] *adj.* (tree) which loses its leaves in winter.

dec•i•mal ['desɪml] 1. *adj.* (system of mathematics) based on the number 10; **d. point** = dot indicating the division between units and parts which are less than one unit (such as 2.05). 2. *n.* figure expressed on the base of 10. **dec•i•mal•ize,** *v.* to change to decimals. **dec•i•mate,** *v.* to remove one out of ten of; to cut down/to remove/to kill in large numbers.

de•ci•pher [dɪ'saɪfə] *v.* to make out (sth badly written, or written in code). **de•ci•pher•ment,** *n.* act of deciphering.

de•ci•sion [dɪ'sɪʒn] *n.* making up your mind; ability to make up your mind. **de•ci•sive** [dɪ-'saɪsɪv] *adj.* firm (voice); (contest, etc.) which brings about a result. **de•ci•sive•ly,** *adv.* in a decisive way; firmly.

deck [dek] *n.* (a) floor (of ship/bus). **flight deck** = (i) control cabin (of plane); (ii) flat surface on an aircraft carrier where aircraft land and take off. (b) pack (of playing cards). (c) apparatus for playing records, tapes, cassettes. **deck•chair,** *n.* collapsible canvas chair (for sitting in the sun). **decked,** *adj.* decorated/covered with.

deck•le-edged [dekl'edʒd] *adj.* (paper) with a ragged edge.

de•claim [dɪ'kleɪm] *v.* to recite in a loud voice. **de•clam•a•to•ry** [dɪ'klæmətərɪ] *adj.* as if in a loud voice.

de•clare [dɪ'kleə] *v.* (a) to state (officially). (b)

æ back, a: farm, ɒ: top, aɪ pipe, aʊ how, aɪə fire, aʊə flower, ɔ: bought, ɔɪ toy, e fed, eəhair, eɪ take, ə afraid, əʊ boat, əʊə lower, ɜ: word, i: heap, ɪ hit, ɪə hear, u: school, ʊ book, ʌ but, b back, d dog, ð then, dʒ just, f fog, g go, h hand, j yes, k catch, l last, m mix, n nut, ŋ sing, p penny, r round, s some, ʃ short, t too, tʃ chop, θ thing, v voice, w was, z zoo, ʒ treasure

(*at customs*) to say what (dutiable goods) one has. (c) (*at cards*) to say which suit is trumps.

dec•la•ra•tion [deklə'reɪʃn] *n.* (official) statement.

de•cline [dɪ'klaɪn] 1. *n.* downward trend. 2. *v.* (a) to refuse (an invitation). (b) to become weaker. (c) (*in grammar*) to show the different cases of (a word). **de•clen•sion,** *n.* form of the different cases of a word.

de•cliv•i•ty [dɪ'klɪvɪtɪ] *n.* slope downwards.

de•code [di:'kəʊd] *v.* to translate (a message) out of code. **de•cod•er,** *n.* person who decodes.

de•col•late ['dekəleɪt] *v.* to separate copies. **de•col•la•tor,** *n.* machine which separates copies (of computer printouts).

de•com•pose [di:kəm'pəʊz] *v.* to rot. **de•com•po•si•tion** [di:kɒmpə'zɪʃn] *n.* act of rotting.

de•com•pres•sion [di:kəm'preʃn] *n.* reducing the pressure in sth; **d. chamber** = room where divers stay to get used gradually to normal pressures after working in very deep water.

de•con•ges•tant [di:kən'dʒestənt] *n.* medicine which unblocks, esp. a blocked nose.

de•con•tam•i•nate [di:kən'tæmɪneɪt] *v.* to remove infection/radioactivity from (sth). **de•con•tam•i•na•tion** [di:kəntæmɪ'neɪʃn] *n.* act of decontaminating.

de•con•trol [di:kən'trəʊl] *v.* to remove controls from sth.

de•cor ['deɪkɔ:] *n.* (a) scenery (for a play). (b) interior decoration (of a room).

dec•o•rate ['dekəreɪt] *v.* (a) to paint (a building); to put new wallpaper in (a room); to put up flags/lights (to celebrate an occasion). (b) to award (s.o.) a medal. **dec•o•ra•tions** [dekə'reɪʃnz] *n.pl.* (a) flags/lights, etc., used to celebrate an occasion. (b) medals. **dec•o•ra•tive** ['dekərətɪv] *adj.* pleasant to look at; serving as a decoration. **dec•o•ra•tive•ly,** *adv.* in a decorative way. **dec•o•ra•tor,** *n.* person who paints houses; **interior d.** = person who designs ways of decorating the inside of buildings.

de•co•rum [dɪ'kɔ:rʌm] *n.* being decorous. **dec•o•rous** ['dekərəs] *adj.* very well-behaved.

de•coy 1. *n.* ['di:kɔɪ] object to attract and trap sth. 2. *v.* [dɪ'kɔɪ] to attract and trap (sth/s.o.).

de•crease 1. *n.* ['di:kri:s] fall; lessening. 2. *v.* [di:'kri:s] to fall; to become less.

de•cree [dɪ'kri:] 1. *n.* official legal order, as of a government, church, etc. 2. *v.* to state as a legal order.

de•crep•it [dɪ'krepɪt] *adj.* falling to pieces; old and feeble (person). **de•crep•i•tude,** *n.* being decrepit.

de•cry [dɪ'kraɪ] *v.* to say that (sth) is bad.

ded•i•cate ['dedɪkeɪt] *v.* to place (a church) under the patronage of a saint; to write a book for/to offer a book to (s.o.); to spend (all your life) on sth. **ded•i•cat•ed,** *adj.* (computer/program) reserved for a particular task. **ded•i•ca•tion** [dedɪ'keɪʃn] *n.* (a) devotion. (b) inscription at the beginning of a book showing to whom it is dedicated.

de•duce [dɪ'dju:s] *v.* to conclude (from examining evidence).

de•duct [dɪ'dʌkt] *v.* to remove (from a sum of money). **de•duct•i•ble,** *adj.* which can be deducted. **de•duc•tion** [dɪ'dʌkʃn] *n.* (a) thing which is deduced; conclusion. (b) thing which is deducted; sum of money which is taken away.

deed [di:d] *n.* (a) (noble) act. (b) legal document; **the deeds of a house** = papers showing who owns the house.

deem [di:m] *v.* (*formal*) to consider.

deep [di:p] 1. *adj.* (-er, -est) (a) which goes down a long way. (b) rich/dark (color). (c) low-pitched/bass (voice). 2. *adv.* a long way down. 3. *n.* **the d.** = the sea. **deep•en,** *v.* to go further down; to become deeper; to make (sth) deeper. **deep-freeze,** *n.* refrigerator for freezing food and keeping it frozen. **deep-fried,** *adj.* cooked in deep oil. **deep•ly,** *adv.* profoundly; very much. **deep-root•ed,** *adj.* which goes down a long way. **deep-seat•ed,** *adj.* solid/firm.

deer [dɪə] *n.* (*pl.* deer) wild animal which runs fast, and of which the male usually has horns. **deer•hound,** *n.* large fast-running dog, bred for chasing deer. **deer•stalk•er,** *n.* round tweed hat, with small peaks at the front and back.

de•face [dɪ'feɪs] *v.* to spoil the surface of (sth); to write on (a wall); to mutilate (a statue). **de•face•ment,** *n.* act of defacing.

de fac•to [di:'fæktəʊ] *adj.* existing in fact/real.

def•a•ma•tion [defə'meɪʃn] *n.* **d. of character** = saying bad things about s.o. **de•fam•a•to•ry** [dɪ'fæmətrɪ] *adj.* which says bad things about s.o. **de•fame,** [dɪ'feɪm] *v.* to say bad things about s.o.

de•fault [dɪ'fɔ:lt] 1. *n.* (a) failing to carry out the terms of a contract. (b) (*computers*) set way of working; **d. drive** = the drive which is set to be accessed first. 2. *v.* to fail to carry out the terms of a contract. **de•fault•er,** *n.* person who defaults.

de•feat [dɪ'fi:t] 1. *n.* loss (of fight/vote). 2. *v.* to beat (s.o. in a fight/vote). **de•feat•ism,** *n.* feeling sure that you will lose. **de•feat•ist,** *adj.* sure that you will lose.

def•e•cate ['defəkeɪt] *v.* to pass waste matter from the bowels.

de•fect 1. *n.* ['diːfekt] fault. 2. *v.* [dɪ'fekt] to leave the armed forces/your country, to go over to the enemy side. **de•fec•tion,** *n.* going over to the side of the enemy. **de•fec•tive,** *adj.* faulty. **de•fec•tor,** *n.* person who defects.

de•fend [dɪ'fend] *v.* (a) to protect (from attack). (b) to speak on behalf of (an accused person). **de•fend•ant,** *n.* person who is accused of doing sth illegal/person who is sued in a civil law suit. **de•fend•er,** *n.* person who defends.

de•fense, *Brit.* **de•fence** [dɪ'fens] *n.* (a) protection. (b) **the d.** = lawyers who speak on behalf of an accused person. **de•fense•less,** *adj.* unprotected. **de•fen•si•bil•i•ty,** *n.* being defensible. **de•fen•si•ble,** *adj.* which can be defended. **de•fen•sive.** 1. *adj.* which protects. 2. *n.* **on the d.** = feeling one has to justify oneself. **de•fen•sive•ly,** *adv.* in a defensive way.

de•fer [dɪ'fɜː] *v.* (**deferred**) (a) to put off/to put back. (b) **to d. to s.o./to s.o.'s opinion** = to accept the advice of s.o. who knows better. **def•er•ence** ['defərəns] *n.* respect. **def•er•en•tial,** *adj.* respectful. **de•fer•ment,** *n.* postponement.

de•fi•ance [dɪ'faɪəns] *n.* acting against (law/authority). **de•fi•ant,** *adj.* very proud and antagonistic.

de•fib•ril•la•tor [diː'fɪbrɪleɪtə] *n.* machine which stimulates a weak heart by giving it electric shocks.

de•fi•cien•cy [dɪ'fɪʃənsɪ] *n.* lack. **de•fi•cient,** *adj.* (**in**) lacking (sth). **mentally deficient** = below normal intelligence.

def•i•cit ['defɪsɪt] *n.* amount by which expenditure is larger than receipts (in a company's/a country's accounts).

de•file 1. *n.* ['diːfaɪl] narrow pass between mountains. 2. *v.* [dɪ'faɪl] to dirty/to pollute. **de•file•ment,** *n.* act of polluting.

de•fine [dɪ'faɪn] *v.* (a) to explain clearly/to give the meaning of. (b) to state the boundary of. **de•fin•a•ble,** *adj.* which can be defined. **def•i•nite** ['defɪnət] *adj.* very clear; **d. article** = "the" (*as opposed to the indefinite article,* "a" *or* "an"). **def•i•nite•ly,** *adv.* certainly. **def•i•ni•tion** [defɪ'nɪʃn] *n.* (a) clear explanation (of a word). (b) clearness (of a picture).

de•fin•i•tive [dɪ'fɪnɪtɪv] *adj.* final/which cannot be improved.

de•flate [dɪ'fleɪt] *v.* (a) to let the air out of (a tire). (b) to reduce inflation in (the economy). **de•fla•tion** [dɪ'fleɪʃn] *n.* reducing inflation. **de•fla•tion•ar•y,** *adj.* which leads to deflation.

de•flect [dɪ'flekt] *v.* to turn aside (an arrow/a bullet, etc.). **de•flec•tion,** *n.* act of deflecting.

de•fo•li•ate [diː'fəʊlɪeɪt] *v.* to remove the leaves of (a tree, etc.). **de•fo•li•a•tion,** *n.* act of defoliating. **de•fo•li•ant,** *n.* chemical used to defoliate.

de•for•est•a•tion [diːfores'teɪʃn] *n.* removal of trees from an area of land.

de•formed [dɪ'fɔːmd] *adj.* badly shaped. **de•for•ma•tion** [defɔː'meɪʃn] *n.* spoiling the shape of sth. **de•form•i•ty,** *n.* badly shaped part of the body.

de•fraud [dɪ'frɔːd] *v.* to cheat.

de•fray [dɪ'freɪ] *v.* to pay (costs).

de•freeze [diː'friːz] *v.* to thaw (frozen food).

de•frock [diː'frɒk] *v.* to remove (a priest) from holy orders.

de•frost [diː'frɒst] *v.* to melt the ice or frost from (as the inside of a refrigerator). **de•frost•er,** *n.* blower in a car or truck which prevents the windows fogging up.

deft [deft] *adj.* (**-er, -est**) very agile/clever (with your hands). **deft•ly,** *adv.* in a deft way. **deft•ness,** *n.* being deft.

de•funct [dɪ'fʌŋkt] *adj.* dead (person); (law) which is no longer applied.

de•fuse [diː'fjuːz] *v.* to take the fuse out of (a bomb) so that it cannot explode; to make (a situation) less tense.

de•fy [dɪ'faɪ] *v.* (a) to refuse to obey (law). (b) to challenge (s.o. **to** sth).

de•gen•er•ate 1. *adj.* [dɪ'dʒenərət] which has degenerated/become depraved. 2. *v.* [dɪ'dʒenəreɪt] (a) to become depraved. (b) to get worse. **de•gen•er•a•cy,** *n.* being degenerate. **de•gen•er•a•tion** [dɪdʒenə'reɪʃn] *n.* becoming degenerate; becoming worse.

de•grade [dɪ'greɪd] *v.* (a) to humiliate (s.o.); to make (s.o.) like an animal. (b) to make (a chemical compound) simpler. **de•grad•a•ble,** *adj.* which can be degraded. **deg•ra•da•tion** [degrə'deɪʃn] *n.* becoming like an animal. **de•grad•ing,** *adj.* lowering; which humiliates/which makes a person like an animal.

æ back, ɑ: farm, ɒ: top, aɪ pipe, aʊ how, aɪə fire, aʊə flower, ɔ: bought, ɔɪ toy, e fed, eəhair, eɪ take, ə afraid, əʊ boat, əʊə lower, ɜː word, iː heap, ɪ hit, ɪə hear, uː school, ʊ book, ʌ but, b back, d dog, ð then, dʒ just, f fog, g go, h hand, j yes, k catch, l last, m mix, n nut, ŋ sing, p penny, r round, s some, ʃ short, t too, tʃ chop, θ thing, v voice, w was, z zoo, ʒ treasure

de•gree [dɪ'griː] n. (a) division of an angle or scale. (b) level; amount; **to a certain d.** = to some extent. (c) diploma (of a university).

de•his•cence [diː'hɪsəns] n. bursting of a seed pod.

de•hu•mid•i•fi•er [diːhjuː'mɪdɪfaɪə] n. device which removes humidity from the air.

de•hy•drate [diː'haɪ'dreɪt] v. to remove water from (sth). **de•hy•dra•tion,** n. becoming dehydrated.

de-ice [diː'aɪs] v. to remove the ice from (sth). **de-ic•er,** n. thing which de-ices.

de•i•fy ['deɪɪfaɪ] v. to make (sth/s.o.) into a god. **de•i•fi•ca•tion** [deɪɪfɪ'keɪʃn] n. making into a god.

deign [deɪn] v. to condescend (**to** to sth).

de•i•ty ['deɪtɪ] n. god.

dé•jà vu [dɪʒæ'vuː] adv. feeling that you have already seen sth before.

de•ject•ed [dɪ'dʒektɪd] adj. depressed/unhappy. **de•ject•ed•ly,** adv. in a gloomy way. **de•jec•tion** [dɪ'dʒekʃn] n. gloom/depression.

de ju•re [diː'jʊərɪ] adv. correct according to the law.

de•lay [dɪ'leɪ] 1. n. time during which one is late. 2. v. (a) to make late. (b) to wait; to put (sth) off until later.

de•lec•ta•ble [dɪ'lektəbl] adj. very pleasant; very attractive. **de•lec•ta•tion** [dɪlek'teɪʃn] n. pleasure/enjoyment.

del•e•gate 1. n. ['delɪgət] person who represents others at a meeting. 2. v. ['delɪgeɪt] to pass (authority/responsibility) on to a subordinate. **del•e•ga•tion** [delɪ'geɪʃn] n. (a) group of representatives. (b) passing of authority to a subordinate.

de•lete [dɪ'liːt] v. to cross out (a word/text). **de•le•tion** [dɪ'liːʃn] n. word/phrase which has been crossed out.

del•e•te•ri•ous [dɪlɪ'tɪərɪəs] adj. (formal) harmful.

de•lib•er•ate 1. adj. [dɪ'lɪbərət] (a) done on purpose. (b) slow and thoughtful (speech/manner). 2. v. [dɪ'lɪbəreɪt] to debate/to discuss. **de•lib•er•ate•ly,** adv. (a) on purpose. (b) slowly and thoughtfully. **de•lib•er•a•tion** [dɪlɪbə'reɪʃn] n. (a) thought; consideration. (b) **the deliberations of a meeting** = the debate/discussion.

del•i•ca•cy ['delɪkəsɪ] n. (a) sensitivity. (b) state of being delicate. (c) rare thing to eat. **del•i•cate,** adj. (a) easily damaged; very thin. (b) liable to get illnesses. (c) very fine. **del•i•cate•ly,** adv. with care.

del•i•ca•tes•sen [delɪkə'tesn] n. store selling cold meat, salads, cheeses, etc.

de•li•cious [dɪ'lɪʃəs] adj. which tastes very good. **de•li•cious•ly,** adv. in a delicious way.

de•light [dɪ'laɪt] 1. n. pleasure. 2. v. to take pleasure (**in**). **de•light•ed,** adj. very pleased. **de•light•ful,** adj. very pleasant.

de•lin•e•ate [dɪ'lɪnɪeɪt] v. (formal) to draw. **de•lin•e•a•tion** [dɪlɪnɪ'eɪʃn] n. (formal) drawing.

de•lin•quen•cy [dɪ'lɪŋkwənsɪ] n. minor crime; **juvenile d.** = crimes committed by young people. **de•lin•quent,** adj. & n. criminal, esp. one who is young.

de•lir•i•ous [dɪ'lɪrɪəs] adj. mad with fever/with happiness. **de•lir•i•um,** n. madness caused by fever; great excitement.

de•liv•er [dɪ'lɪvə] v. (a) to bring (sth) to s.o. (b) to make (a speech). (c) to help the mother give birth to (a baby). **de•liv•er•ance,** n. (formal) rescue. **de•liv•er•y,** n. (a) bringing sth to s.o. (b) birth (of a child).

dell [del] n. small hollow filled with trees.

del•phin•i•um [del'fɪnɪəm] n. garden plant with tall blue flowers.

del•ta ['deltə] n. (a) land around the mouth of a river made of mud brought by the river. (b) fourth letter of the Greek alphabet. **d. wing aircraft** = with wings forming a triangle.

de•lude [dɪ'luːd] v. to make (s.o.) believe sth which is wrong. **de•lu•sion** [dɪ'luːʒn] n. wrong belief.

del•uge ['deljuːdʒ] 1. n. flood. 2. v. to flood (**with**).

de luxe [dɪ'lʌks] adj. very expensive; of very high quality.

delve [delv] v. to dig (**into** the past/archives, etc.).

dem•a•gogue ['deməgɒg] n. politician who appeals to the crowd for support. **dem•a•gogu•er•y,** n. appealing for support from the crowd as a means of obtaining political power.

de•mand [dɪ'mɑːnd] 1. n. asking for sth; **it is in d.** = many people want it. 2. v. to ask insistently for sth. **de•mand•ing,** adj. (job) which takes up much time and energy.

de•mar•ca•tion [diːmɑː'keɪʃn] n. showing of boundaries.

dé•marche ['deɪmɑː] n. official, often diplomatic, approach to another party.

de•mean [dɪ'miːn] v **to d. yourself** = to make yourself appear undignified or contemptible.

de•mean•or [dɪ'miːnə] n. behavior/manner.

de•ment•ed [dɪ'mentɪd] adj. mad. **de•men•tia** [dɪ'menʃə] n. (formal) madness.

de•mer•it [diː'merɪt] n. fault; unattractive point.

demi- ['demɪ] prefix meaning half.

dem•i•john ['demɪdʒɒn] n. large bottle for alcoholic drink.

de•mil•i•ta•rized [diː'mɪlɪtəraɪzd] adj. (zone) which no longer has armed forces in it.

de•mise [dɪ'maɪz] n. (formal) death.

dem•o ['deməʊ] n. inf. demonstration.

de•mo•bi•lize [diː'məʊbɪlaɪz] v. to release (s.o.) from the armed forces. **de•mo•bi•li•za•tion** [diːməʊbɪlaɪ'zeɪʃn] n. being demobilized.

de•moc•ra•cy [dɪ'mɒkrəsɪ] n. system of government by freely elected representatives of the people. **dem•o•crat** ['deməkræt] n. (a) person who believes in democracy. (b) **Democrat** = member of one of the two main political parties in the U.S. **dem•o•crat•ic** [demə'krætɪk] adj. referring to democracy. **dem•o•crat•i•cal•ly**, adv. in a democratic way.

dem•o•graph•ic [demə'græfɪk] adj. referring to demography. **de•mog•ra•phy** [dɪ'mɒgrəfɪ] n. study of population figures.

de•mol•ish [dɪ'mɒlɪʃ] v. to knock down. **dem•o•li•tion** [demə'lɪʃn] n. knocking down.

de•mon ['diːmən] n. devil. **de•mo•ni•a•cal** [diːmə'naɪəkl], **de•mon•ic** [diː'mɒnɪk] adj. like a devil.

dem•on•strate ['demənstreɪt] v. (a) to show. (b) to form a crowd to protest (**against** sth). **de•mon•stra•ble**, adj. which can be demonstrated. **dem•on•stra•tion** [demən'streɪʃn] n. (a) showing. (b) march to protest against sth; crowd which is protesting against sth. **dem•on•stra•tor**, n. person who marches/who forms part of a crowd to protest against sth; person who shows how to do sth. **de•mon•stra•tive** [dɪ'mɒnstrətɪv] adj (person) who shows his feelings openly.

de•mor•al•ize [dɪ'mɒrəlaɪz] v. to lower the morale/confidence of (s.o.). **de•mor•al•i•za•tion** [dɪmɒrəlaɪ'zeɪʃn] n. lowering of morale. **de•mor•al•ized**, adj. doubtful that you can win.

de•mote [diː'məʊt] v. to give (s.o.) a less important job. **de•mo•tion**, n. act of demoting.

de•mur [dɪ'mɜː] v. (**demurred**) to d. at = to object to sth.

de•mure [dɪ'mjʊə] adj. quiet and serious (girl). **de•mure•ly**, adv. in a demure way.

de•mur•rage [diː'mʌrɪdʒ] n. payment for keeping a ship in dock when unloading.

den [den] n. (a) place to hide away in. (b) inf. small room where you can hide away to work.

de•na•tion•al•ize [diː'næʃnəlaɪz] v. to put (a nationalized industry) into private ownership. **de•na•tion•al•i•za•tion** [dɪnæʃnlaɪ'zeɪʃn] n. act of denationalizing.

den•dro•chro•nol•o•gy [dendrəʊkrə'nɒlədʒɪ] n. finding the age of wood by the study of the tree rings.

den•gue ['deŋg] n. tropical fever.

de•ni•al [dɪ'naɪəl] n. statement that sth is not true.

den•i•grate ['denɪgreɪt] v. to say that (an action) is worse than it is.

den•im ['denɪm] n. thick cotton cloth; **denims** = clothes made of this cloth.

den•i•zen ['denɪzən] n. (formal) inhabitant of a particular place.

de•nom•i•na•tion [dɪnɒmɪ'neɪʃn] n. (a) unit of money (on a bank note/coin). (b) religious sect; church. **de•nom•i•na•tion•al**, adj. belonging to a particular sect. **de•nom•i•na•tor** [dɪ'nɒmɪneɪtə] n. figure beneath the line in a fraction.

de•note [dɪ'nəʊt] v. to mean.

de•noue•ment, dénouement [deɪ'nuːmɒŋ] n. ending (of a plot).

de•nounce [dɪ'naʊns] v. to blame/to accuse (s.o./sth) openly.

dense [dens] adj. (-er, -est) (a) very thick; crowded together. (b) stupid. **dense•ly**, adv. thickly. **dense•ness**, n. being dense. **den•si•ty**, n. (a) physical degree of mass per unit of volume. (b) **high d. of population** = many people per unit of area.

dent [dent] 1. n. slight hollow (as made by a blow). 2. v. to make a slight hollow in (sth).

den•tist ['dentɪst] n. person who looks after teeth. **den•tal**, adj. referring to teeth; **d. floss** = thin thread for cleaning between teeth. **den•ti•frice**, n. toothpaste. **den•tis•try**, n. work of a dentist. **den•ti•tion**, n. arrangement of a person's teeth. **den•tures** ['dentʃəz] n.pl. false teeth.

de•nude [dɪ'njuːd] v. to make (sth) bare; to remove all the covering from (sth).

de•nun•ci•a•tion [dɪnʌnsɪ'eɪʃn] n. public accusation/blame.

de•ny [dɪ'naɪ] v. to state that (sth) is not correct; to prevent (s.o.) having sth; **to d. oneself** = not to eat/drink, etc., very much.

de•o•dor•ant [dɪ'əʊdərənt] n. preparation which removes unpleasant smells.

æ back, ɑː farm, ɒ top, aɪ pipe, aʊ how, aɪə fire, aʊə flower, ɔː bought, ɔɪ toy, e fed, eəhair, eɪ take, ə afraid, əʊ boat, əʊə lower, ɜː word, iː heap, ɪ hit, ɪə hear, uː school, ʊ book, ʌ but, b back, d dog, ð then, dʒ just, f fog, g go, h hand, j yes, k catch, l last, m mix, n nut, ŋ sing, p penny, r round, s some, ʃ short, t too, tʃ chop, θ thing, v voice, w was, z zoo, ʒ treasure

de•o•dor•ize, *v.* to remove unpleasant smells from (sth).

de•ox•y•ri•bo•nu•cle•ic ac•id [diːˌɒksɪraɪbəʊnjuˈkleɪɪkˈæsɪd] *n.* DNA, the basic genetic material in a cell.

de•part [dɪˈpɑːt] *v.* to go away. **de•part•ed.** *n.* **the d.** = the dead. **de•par•ture** [dɪˈpɑːtʃə] *n.* leaving. **d. lounge** = large waiting room at an airport for passengers about to leave.

de•part•ment [dɪˈpɑːtmənt] *n.* section of a large organization; **d. store** = large store with many different sections. **dé•parte•ment,** *n.* administrative division of France. **de•part•men•tal** [dɪpɑːtˈmentl] *adj.* referring to a department.

de•pend [dɪˈpend] *v.* (a) **(on)** to be decided according to sth. (b) to rely **(on** sth). **de•pend•a•ble,** *adj.* that can be relied on. **de•pend•ant,** *n.* member of family supported by another. **de•pend•ence,** *n.* being dependent. **de•pend•en•cy,** *n.* country which is ruled by another. **de•pend•ent,** *adj.* (a) supported by s.o. else; relying on s.o. else. (a) addicted to (a drug).

de•pict [dɪˈpɪkt] *v.* (*formal*) to show. **de•pic•tion,** *n.* showing.

de•pil•a•to•ry [dɪˈpɪlətrɪ] *adj. & n.* (substance) which removes hair from the body.

de•plete [dɪˈpliːt] *v.* to run down/to use up (stores).

de•plore [dɪˈplɔː] *v.* to be extremely sorry that sth has happened; to dislike (an action/an attitude). **de•plor•a•ble,** *adj.* very bad (behavior).

de•ploy [dɪˈplɔɪ] *v.* to spread out (soldiers, etc.) for action. **de•ploy•ment,** *n.* act of deploying.

de•pop•u•late [diːˈpɒpjuleɪt] *v.* to reduce the number of people living in an area. **de•pop•u•la•tion** [diːpɒpjuˈleɪʃn] *n.* act of being depopulated.

de•port [dɪˈpɔːt] *v.* to expel (s.o.) from a country. **de•por•ta•tion** [diːpɔːˈteɪʃn] *n.* expulsion (of a foreigner). **de•port•ment,** *n.* way of walking/sitting.

de•pose [dɪˈpəʊz] *v.* (a) to force (s.o.) to leave his position; to force (a king, etc.) to give up his throne. (b) to state (in court). **dep•o•si•tion** [depəˈzɪʃn] *n.* (a) forcing s.o. to leave his position. (b) statement (by a witness).

de•pos•it [dɪˈpɒzɪt] 1. *n.* (a) money placed (in a bank); money given to secure sth you want to buy. (b) mineral layer (in the ground); sediment/chemical left at the bottom of a container. 2. *v.* to put (money) in a bank. **de•pos•i•tar•y,** *n.* person who receives something which is deposited for safe keeping.

de•pos•i•tor, *n.* person with money in a bank. **de•pos•i•to•ry,** *n.* place for storing furniture, etc.

de•pot [ˈdepəʊ] *n.* central warehouse; central garage; central place for assembling military personnel.

de•praved [dɪˈpreɪvd] *adj.* corrupted/wicked. **de•prav•i•ty** [dɪˈprævɪtɪ] *n.* state of living a wicked life.

dep•re•cate [ˈdeprəkeɪt] *v.* to disapprove of (sth).

de•pre•ci•ate [dɪˈpriːʃɪeɪt] *v.* to lose value. **de•pre•ci•a•tion** [dɪprɪʃɪˈeɪʃn] *n.* regular loss in value. **de•pre•ci•a•to•ry,** *adj.* which depreciates.

dep•re•da•tion [deprəˈdeɪʃn] *n.* attack/ruining.

de•press [dɪˈpres] *v.* (a) to make miserable. (b) to push down (a button). **de•pressed,** *adj.* miserable. **de•press•ing,** *adj.* gloomy. **de•pres•sion** [dɪˈpreʃn] *n.* (a) miserable feeling. (b) low pressure area bringing bad weather. (c) economic crisis. (d) hollow (in the ground). **de•pres•sive,** *adj.* which makes s.o. depressed.

de•prive [dɪˈpraɪv] *v.* **to d. s.o. of sth** = to take sth away from s.o. **dep•ri•va•tion** [deprɪˈveɪʃn] *n.* being deprived of sth. **de•prived,** *adj.* (person) who has not enjoyed any of society's benefits.

dept. = department.

depth [depθ] *n.* (a) how deep sth is; distance downwards; **he's out of his d.** = (i) the water is too deep for him; (ii) it is too difficult for him to understand. (b) very deep point. **depth charge,** *n.* type of bomb dropped into the sea which explodes deep beneath the surface.

dep•u•ta•tion [depjuˈteɪʃn] *n.* group of people who speak on behalf of others. **de•pute** *v.* [dɪˈpjuːt] to give responsibility **(to** s.o.). **dep•u•tize** [ˈdepjutaɪz] *v.* to stand in **(for** s.o.). **dep•u•ty** [ˈdepjutɪ] *n.* person who can take the place of another person.

de•rail [dɪˈreɪl] *v.* to make (a train) leave the rails. **de•rail•ment,** *n.* leaving the rails. **de•rail•leur** [dɪˈreɪljə] *n.* bicycle gear system, where the chain goes round a movable sprocket.

de•ranged [dɪˈreɪnʒd] *adj.* mad.

der•by [ˈdɜːrbɪ] *n.* (a) sporting contest. (b) bowler hat.

de•reg•u•late [dɪˈregjuleɪt] *v.* to remove government restrictions from an industry. **de•reg•u•la•tion,** *n.* removal of official restrictions.

der•e•lict [ˈderəlɪkt] 1. *n.* tramp. 2. *adj.* ruined and abandoned. **der•e•lic•tion** [derəˈlɪkʃən] *n.* neglecting (to do your duty).

de•ride [dɪˈraɪd] v. to laugh at (s.o.). **de•ri•sion** [dɪˈrɪʒn] n. mockery. **de•ri•sive** [dɪˈraɪsɪv] adj. mocking (laughter). **de•ri•so•ry** [dɪˈraɪzərɪ] adj. laughably small (amount).

de ri•gueur [dərɪˈgɜ:ə] adv. obligatory.

de•rive [dɪˈraɪv] v. to come originally (**from** sth). **der•i•va•tion** [derɪˈveɪʃn] n. origin (of a word). **de•riv•a•tive** [dɪˈrɪvətɪv] n. thing which is derived.

der•ma•ti•tis [dɜːməˈtaɪtɪs] n. disease of the skin. **der•ma•tol•o•gist** [dɜːməˈtɒlədʒɪst] n. person who studies dermatology. **der•ma•tol•o•gy**, n. study of skin diseases.

de•rog•a•to•ry [dɪˈrɒgətrɪ] adj. showing contempt.

der•rick [ˈderɪk] n. large metal construction (like a crane); **oil d.** = metal frame which holds the drilling equipment for an oil well.

de•sal•i•nate [diːˈsælɪneɪt] v. to remove salt (from sea water).

des•cant [ˈdeskænt] n. musical part which is played/sung much higher than the rest.

de•scend [dɪˈsend] v. (a) to go down (a staircase, etc.). (b) **to d. from s.o.** = to have s.o. as an ancestor. (c) **to d. upon** = to attack; inf. to visit unexpectedly. **de•scend•ant**, n. person whose family goes back to a certain ancestor. **de•scent**, n. (a) going down. (b) **he is of Irish descent** = his family was Irish.

de•scribe [dɪˈskraɪb] v. to say what (sth/s.o.) is like. **de•scrip•tion** [dɪˈskrɪpʃn] n. picture in words of what sth is like. **de•scrip•tive**, adj. which says what sth is like.

des•e•crate [ˈdesɪkreɪt] v. to use (a church/a grave) in a disrespectful way. **des•e•cra•tion**, n. act of desecrating.

de•seg•re•gate [dɪˈsegrəgeɪt] v. to end the segregation of (a group of people, or institution). **de•seg•re•ga•tion**, n. action of desegregating.

des•ert 1. adj. & n. [ˈdezət] very dry, usu. sandy (place). 2. v. [dɪˈzɜːt] to leave the armed forces without permission; to leave (s.o.) all by himself. **de•sert•ed**, adj. abandoned; with no inhabitants. **de•sert•er**, n. person who leaves the armed forces without permission. **de•ser•tion**, n. act of deserting. **de•serts** [dɪˈzɜːts] n. pl. (formal) **just d.** = rightful reward.

de•serve [dɪˈzɜːv] v. to merit (sth). **de•serv•ed•ly** [dɪˈzɜːvɪdlɪ] adv. in a way

which is right. **de•serv•ing**, adj. which ought to be supported/helped.

des•ic•cate [ˈdesɪkeɪt] v. to dry.

de•sign [dɪˈzaɪn] 1. n. plan; drawing of sth, before it is constructed; **to have designs on** = to plan to attack/take (sth). 2. v. to plan (sth). **de•sign•er**, n. artist who plans sth. **de•sign•ing**, adj. crafty (person).

des•ig•nate [ˈdezɪgneɪt] 1. v. to appoint (s.o.) to a post. 2. suffix showing person who has been appointed but has not started work; **the ambassador-designate. des•ig•na•tion**, n. act of designating.

de•sire [dɪˈzaɪə] 1. n. want. 2. v. to want. **de•sir•a•bil•i•ty**, n. being desirable. **de•sir•a•ble**, adj. which a lot of people want. **de•sir•ous**, adj. (of) wanting.

de•sist [dɪˈzɪst] v. (formal) (**from**) to stop doing (sth).

desk [desk] n. table for writing. **desk•top pub•lish•ing**, n. creating finished printed documents using a computer and a special program.

des•o•late [ˈdesələt] adj. bleak inhospitable (place). **des•o•la•tion** [desəˈleɪʃn] n. bleakness; ruin (of a place).

de•spair [dɪˈspeə] 1. n. hopelessness. 2. v. **he despaired of being rescued** = he had given up all hope of being rescued.

des•per•ate [ˈdesprət] adj. (a) hopeless. (b) wild (through being in despair). **des•per•ate•ly**, adv. urgently; wildly. **des•per•a•tion** [despəˈreɪʃn] n. hopelessness.

des•pi•ca•ble [dɪˈspɪkəbl] adj. worthless/which you can look down on.

de•spise [dɪˈspaɪz] v. to look down on (s.o.)/to think (s.o.) is not worth much.

de•spite [dɪˈspaɪt] prep. in spite of.

de•spoil [dɪˈspɔɪl] v. to ruin, to plunder.

de•spond•en•cy [dɪˈspɒndənsɪ] n. discouragement. **de•spond•ent**, adj. discouraged.

des•pot [ˈdespɒt] n. tyrant/dictator. **des•pot•ic** [dɪˈspɒtɪk] adj. like a dictator. **des•pot•ism** n. tyranny/dictatorship.

des•sert [dɪˈzɜːt] n. sweet course (in a meal). **dessert spoon**, n. spoon for eating dessert.

des•ti•na•tion [destɪˈneɪʃn] n. place a person/vehicle is going to. **des•tine** [ˈdestɪn] v. to aim (s.o.) **for** a certain position. **des•ti•ny**, n. what may happen in the future.

des•ti•tute [ˈdestɪtjuːt] adj. with no money or

æ back, a: farm, ɒ: top, aɪ pipe, aʊ how, aɪe fire, aʊə flower, ɔ: bought, ɔɪ toy, e fed, eəhair, eɪ take, ə afraid, əʊ boat, əʊə lower, ɜ: word, i: heap, ɪ hit, ɪə hear, u: school, ʊ book, ʌ but, b back, d dog, ð then, dʒ just, f fog, g go, h hand, j yes, k catch, l last, m mix, n nut, ŋ sing, p penny, r round, s some, ʃ short, t too, tʃ chop, θ thing, v voice, w was, z zoo, ʒ treasure

belongings. **des•ti•tu•tion** [destɪ'tjuːʃn] n. being destitute.

de•stroy [dɪ'strɔɪ] v. to remove/to kill/to ruin completely. **de•stroy•er,** n. medium-sized naval ship.

de•struc•tion [dɪ'strʌkʃn] n. complete ruining. **de•struc•tive** [dɪ'strʌktɪv] adj. which destroys. **de•struc•tive•ness,** n. tendency to destroy things.

des•ul•to•ry ['dezəltrɪ] adj. haphazard/with no connecting links.

de•tach [dɪ'tætʃ] v. to separate; **detached house** = house which is not attached to another. **de•tach•a•ble,** adj. which you can separate. **de•tach•ment,** n. (a) indifference; lack of immediate interest. (b) small group of military personnel, etc.

de•tail ['diːteɪl] 1. n. small item. 2. v. (a) to list all the small items. (b) **to d. s.o. to do sth** = to give a task or duty to s.o.

de•tain [dɪ'teɪn] v. (a) to keep (s.o. in prison). (b) to hold (s.o.) back; to stop (s.o.) from leaving. **de•tain•ee** [diːteɪ'niː] n. person held in prison.

de•tect [dɪ'tekt] v. to discover; to notice. **de•tec•tion** [dɪ'tekʃn] n. discovery. **de•tec•tive,** n. police officer who investigates crimes. **de•tec•tor,** n. instrument which discovers sth.

dé•tente, detente [deɪ'tɑːnt] n. friendly atmosphere between two formerly hostile countries.

de•ten•tion [dɪ'tenʃn] n. imprisonment; keeping s.o. from leaving; **d. home** = place where young criminals are imprisoned for a short time.

de•ter [dɪ'tɜː] v. (**deterred**) to discourage (s.o. **from** doing sth).

de•ter•gent [dɪ'tɜːdʒənt] n. chemical used instead of soap for washing clothes or dishes.

de•te•ri•o•rate [dɪ'tɪərɪəreɪt] v. to go bad; to get worse. **de•te•ri•o•ra•tion** [dɪtɪərɪə-'reɪʃn] n. worsening.

de•ter•mine [dɪ'tɜːmɪn] v. (a) to fix (a date, etc.). (b) to decide finally (**to**). **de•ter•mi•nant,** n. thing which determines. **de•ter•mi•na•tion** [dɪtɜːmɪ'neɪʃn] n. firm intention. **de•ter•mined,** adj. resolved (**to**).

de•ter•rent [dɪ'terənt] n. thing which discourages; **nuclear d.** = nuclear weapon which it is hoped will discourage the enemy from attacking.

de•test [dɪ'test] v. to dislike intensely. **de•test•a•ble,** adj. very unpleasant. **de•tes•ta•tion** [diːtes'teɪʃn] n. strong dislike.

det•o•nate ['detəneɪt] v. to set off (an explo-

sive). **det•o•na•tion** [detə'neɪʃn] n. explosion. **det•o•na•tor,** n. small explosive charge which will set off a large explosion.

de•tour ['diːtʊə] n. roundabout road taken to avoid an obstacle/to see sth not on the direct route.

de•tract [dɪ'trækt] v. (**from**) to remove part of sth/to make sth less important. **de•trac•tor,** n. person who criticizes sth.

det•ri•ment ['detrɪmənt] n. hurt; damage; **to the d. of** = damaging to. **det•ri•men•tal** [detrɪ'mentl] adj. which damages.

de•tri•tus [diː'trɪtəs] n. debris which is formed by the weathering of rock; any waste matter.

deuce [djuːs] n. (a) score in tennis when both players are at 40 points. (b) score of two (in cards).

deu•te•ri•um [djuː'tɪərɪəm] n. heavy form of hydrogen.

Deutsch•mark ['dɔɪtʃmɑːk] n. currency used in Germany.

de•val•ue [diː'væljuː] v. to reduce value of (a currency) in relationship to that of other countries. **de•val•u•a•tion** [diːvæljuː'eɪʃn] n. reducing the international value of currency.

dev•as•tate ['devəsteɪt] v. to wreck/to lay waste (countryside). **dev•as•tat•ing,** adj overwhelming. **dev•as•ta•tion** [devə'steɪʃn] n. widespread damage.

de•vel•op [dɪ'veləp] v. (a) to use to good purpose. (b) to expand. (c) to start (a disease, etc.). (d) to produce and fix (a photograph) from film. (e) to grow. **de•vel•op•er,** n. (a) liquid for developing photographs. (b) person who builds property. **de•vel•op•ing,** adj. growing; **d. countries** = countries which are becoming industrialized. **de•vel•op•ment,** n. (a) growth. (b) **developments** = what will happen.

de•vi•ate ['diːvɪeɪt] v. to swerve/to turn away (from a direct line). **de•vi•a•tion** [diːvɪ'eɪʃn] n. moving away from a direct or normal line. **de•vi•ance,** n. deviation from normal human behavior. **de•vi•ant,** adj. & n. (person) who deviates from normal human behavior.

de•vice [dɪ'vaɪs] n. (a) small (useful) machine. (b) **left to his own devices** = left to do whatever he wanted. (c) emblem (on a coat of arms).

dev•il ['devl] n. (a) evil spirit; inf. **what the devil?** = what on earth? **d.'s advocate** = person who argues the opposite point of view, in order to oppose a widely held opinion. (b) inf. person; **lucky d.!** **dev•il•ish,** adj. referring to the devil. **dev•iled,** adj. cooked in a spicy sauce. **dev•il•ment, devilry,** n. wicked behavior.

de•vi•ous ['diːvɪəs] adj. not straightforward; roundabout. **de•vi•ous•ly,** adv. in a devious way. **de•vi•ous•ness,** *n.* not being straight-forward.

de•vise [dɪˈvaɪz] *v.* to think up; to invent.

de•void [dɪˈvɔɪd] *adj.* empty (of).

dev•o•lu•tion [diːvəˈljuːʃn] *n.* removing of power from the center. **de•volve** [dɪˈvɒlv] *v.* to pass on (responsibility, duty, etc.).

de•vote [dɪˈvəʊt] *v.* **to d. time to sth** = to spend time on sth. **de•vot•ed,** *adj.* (person) who spends all his time on sth. **dev•o•tee** [devəˈtiː] *n.* **(of)** person who is very enthusiastic about sth. **de•vo•tion** [dɪˈvəʊʃn] *n.* (religious) attachment; **devotions** = prayers. **de•vo•tion•al,** *adj.* religious.

de•vour [dɪˈvaʊə] *v.* (*formal*) to eat (greedily).

de•vout [dɪˈvaʊt] *adj.* pious; deeply concerned with religion.

dew [djuː] *n.* water which forms at night on objects in the open air. **dew•drop,** *n.* drop of dew. **dew claw,** *n.* small claw on the side of a dog's foot. **dew•lap,** *n.* skin which hangs in folds on the throat. **dew•y,** *adj.* covered in dew. **dew•y-eyed,** *adj.* innocent and sentimental.

dex•ter•i•ty [dekˈsterətɪ] *n.* skill (with hands). **dex•trous** [ˈdekstrəs] *adj.* clever (with one's hands).

dex•trose [ˈdekstrəʊz] *n.* sweet substance found naturally.

dhow [daʊ] *n.* Arab sailing boat.

di•a•be•tes [daɪəˈbiːtiːz] *n.* (*no pl.*) illness where the sugar content of the blood rises because of lack of insulin. **di•a•be•tic** [daɪəˈbetɪk] 1. *adj.* referring to diabetes; **d. food** = food with a low sugar content which can be eaten by people suffering from diabetes. 2. *n.* person suffering from diabetes.

di•a•bol•ic(al) [daɪəˈbɒlɪk(l)] *adj.* referring to the devil; evil.

di•a•crit•ic [daɪəˈkrɪtɪk] *n.* sign written above a character to show pronunciation.

di•a•dem [ˈdaɪədem] *n.* crown.

di•ag•nose [daɪəgˈnəʊz] *v.* to identify (an illness). **di•ag•no•sis,** *n.* (*pl.* -ses) identification (of an illness). **di•ag•nos•tic** [daɪəgˈnɒstɪk] *adj.* referring to diagnosis. **di•ag•nos•tics,** *pl. n.* test to find faults in computer hardware/software.

di•ag•o•nal [daɪˈægənl] *adj. & n.* (line) going from one corner to another slantwise. **di•ag•o•nal•ly,** *adv.* slantwise.

di•a•gram [ˈdaɪəgræm] *n.* sketch/plan.

di•a•gram•mat•ic [daɪəgrəˈmætɪk] *adj.* in the form of a diagram.

di•al [ˈdaɪəl] 1. *n.* round face (of a clock/meter/telephone). 2. *v.* (**dialed**) to make a telephone call; **to call the police you must dial 911. di•a•ling,** *n.* making a call on the telephone; **d. tone** = sound on the telephone which shows that you can dial.

di•a•lect [ˈdaɪəlekt] *n.* variety of a language spoken in a particular area. **di•a•lec•tal,** *adj.* referring to a dialect.

di•a•lec•tic [daɪəˈlektɪk] *n.* reasoned investigation of philosophical truth.

di•a•logue [ˈdaɪəlɒg] *n.* conversation between two people/two groups.

di•al•y•sis [daɪˈælɪsɪs] *n.* cleaning of the blood by passing it through a filter.

di•am•e•ter [daɪˈæmɪtə] *n.* distance across the center of a circle. **di•a•met•ri•cal•ly** [daɪəˈmetrɪklɪ] *adv.* **d. opposed to** = completely against/opposite.

dia•mond [ˈdaɪəmənd] *n.* (a) very hard transparent precious stone; **d. wedding** = 60th wedding anniversary. (b) one of the four suits in a pack of cards.

di•an•thus [daɪˈænθəs] *n.* Latin name for carnations or pinks.

dia•per [ˈdaɪəpə] *n.* cloth or absorbent fabric used to cover a baby's bottom.

di•aph•a•nous [daɪˈæfənəs] *adj.* (cloth) which is so thin that you can see through it.

di•a•phragm [ˈdaɪəfræm] *n.* (a) thin sheet which vibrates with noise. (b) thin wall of muscle separating the chest and the abdomen.

di•ar•rhe•a, di•ar•rhoe•a [daɪəˈrɪə] *n.* illness of the intestines where your bowel movements are very fluid.

di•a•ry [ˈdaɪərɪ] *n.* (a) description of what has happened in your life day by day; **he has kept a d. for years.** (b) small book in which you write notes/appointments for each day of the week. **di•a•rist,** *n.* person who writes a diary.

di•a•stase [ˈdaɪəsteɪz] *n.* enzyme which breaks down starch and converts it to sugar.

di•as•to•le [daɪəˈstəʊl] *n.* phase in the beating of the heart when the heart swells and fills with blood.

di•a•tom [ˈdaɪətəm] *n.* type of microscopic sea creature.

di•a•tribe [ˈdaɪətraɪb] *n.* violent spoken or written criticism.

dib•ble [ˈdɪbl] *n.* tool used to make holes in the ground for planting.

æ back, aː farm, ɒ top, aɪ pipe, aʊ how, aɪə fire, aʊə flower, ɔː bought, ɔɪ toy, e fed, eəhair, eɪ take, ə afraid, əʊ boat, əʊə lower, vː word, iː heap, ɪ hit, ɪə hear, uː school, ʊ book, ʌ but, b back, d dog, ð then, dʒ just, f fog, g go, h hand, j yes, k catch, l last, m mix, n nut, ŋ sing, p penny, r round, s some, ʃ short, t too, tʃ chop, θ thing, v voice, w was, z zoo, ʒ treasure

dice [daɪs] 1. *n.* (*pl.* **dice**) small cube with one to six dots on each face (for games). 2. *v.* (a) to cut up (vegetables, etc.) into very small cubes. (b) to gamble. **dic•ey**, *adj. inf.* dangerous/difficult.

di•chot•o•my [daɪ'kɒtəmɪ] *n.* splitting into two (usu. contradictory) parts.

dick•ens ['dɪkɪnz] *n. inf.* **what the d.?** = what on earth?

dick•er ['dɪkə] *v. inf.* **to d. about** = to barter or bargain.

dick•y ['dɪkɪ] *n. inf.* false shirt front.

di•cot•y•le•don [daɪkɒtɪ'liːdən] *n.* plant whose seedlings have two fleshy leaves.

dic•tate [dɪk'teɪt] *v.* (a) to say (sth) to s.o. who writes down your words. (b) to tell s.o. what to do. **dic•ta•tion** [dɪk'teɪʃn] *n.* act of dictating (sth to be written down). **dic•ta•tor**, *n.* person who rules a country alone. **dic•ta•to•ri•al** [dɪktə'tɔːrɪəl] *adj.* like a dictator. **dic•ta•tor•ship**, *n.* rule of a country by one person.

dic•tion ['dɪkʃn] *n.* way of speaking.

dic•tion•ar•y ['dɪkʃənrɪ] *n.* (a) book which lists words in alphabetical order, giving their meanings or translations. (b) list of correctly spelled words in a spelling check program.

dic•tum ['dɪktəm] *n.* (*pl.* **-ta**) saying (made by a notable person).

did [dɪd] *v. see* **do.**

di•dac•tic [daɪ'dæktɪk] *adj.* which teaches.

did•dle ['dɪdl] *v. inf.* to trick/to cheat.

die [daɪ] 1. *n.* metal stamp for making coins. 2. *v.* to stop living; *inf.* **I'm dying to read his book** = I am very eager to read his book; **I'm dying for a cup of coffee** = I'd love a cup of coffee; **the sound died away** = became fainter; **the wind died down** = became less strong; **the old customs are dying out** = not being continued. **die•cast**, *adj.* cast from metal in a mold. **die•hard**, *adj. & n. inf.* very reactionary (person).

diel•drin [daɪ'eldrɪn] *n.* powerful insecticide.

di•er•e•sis [daɪ'ɪərɪsɪs] *n.* (*pl.* **-ses**) two dots (¨) put over a vowel to show that it is pronounced separately from another.

die•sel ['diːzl] *n.* **d. engine** = engine which runs on thicker fuel than gas; **d. oil** = oil used in diesel engines.

di•et ['daɪət] 1. *n.* (a) kind of food you eat; **to be on a d.** = to eat only one sort of food/to eat less. (b) (*in some countries*) parliament. 2. *v.* to eat less food/only one sort of food. **di•e•tar•y**, *adj.* referring to a diet. **di•et•er**, *n.* person who is on a diet. **di•e•tet•ics**, *n.* study of food and its nutritional value. **di•e•ti•cian** [daɪə'tɪʃn] *n.* person who specializes in the study of diets.

dif•fer ['dɪfə] *v.* **to d. from** = not to be the same as; **I beg to d.** = I must disagree.

dif•fer•ence ['dɪfrəns] *n.* way in which two things are not the same; **it doesn't make any d.** = it does not change the situation. **dif•fer•ent**, *adj.* not the same; **that is quite a d. thing** = it is not at all the same. **dif•fer•en•tial** [dɪfə'renʃl] 1. *adj.* showing up the difference; **d. equation.** 2. *n.* (a) part of the axle of a car which allows wheels to turn at different speeds at corners. (b) difference in rate, amount, etc. **dif•fer•en•ti•ate**, *v.* to make/to tell the difference (**between**). **dif•fer•en•ti•a•tion**, *n.* act of differentiating. **dif•fer•ent•ly**, *adv.* not in the same way.

dif•fi•cult ['dɪfɪkʌlt] *adj.* not easy. **dif•fi•cul•ty**, *n.* thing which is not easy; **she got into difficulties when swimming** = she was in danger of drowning; **he is in financial difficulties** = he has problems to do with money.

dif•fi•dence ['dɪfɪdəns] *n.* being diffident. **dif•fi•dent**, *adj.* shy; lacking confidence. **dif•fi•dent•ly**, *adv.* shyly.

dif•fract [dɪ'frækt] *v.* to split light into its different colors. **dif•frac•tion** [dɪ'frækʃn] *n.* splitting up of light into its different colors.

dif•fuse 1. *adj.* [dɪ'fjuːs] vague/unclear; **d. lighting** = soft lighting, not giving any sharp shadows. 2. *v.* [dɪ'fjuːz] to spread out; to send out; **diffused lighting** = soft lighting, not giving any sharp shadows. **dif•fu•sion**, *n.* act of diffusing.

dig [dɪg] 1. *n.* (a) poke; **he gave me a d. in the ribs** = he nudged me with his elbow. (b) satirical attack. (c) archaeological excavation. 2. *v.* (**dug; has dug**) to make a hole in the ground; **we dug up an old bottle in the garden** = we found the bottle when digging. **dig•ger**, *n.* person/machine that digs. **dig•ging**, *n.* action of making a hole in the ground. **dig in**, *v. inf.* to start eating. **digs**, *n. pl. inf.* living quarters.

di•gest 1. *n.* ['daɪdʒest] summary. 2. *v.* [daɪ'dʒest] (a) to turn (food) into energy in the stomach and intestine; **I cannot d. my dinner** = I am feeling unwell after my dinner. (b) to ponder over (a piece of information). **di•gest•i•ble**, *adj.* which can be digested. **di•ges•tion**, *n.* action of turning food into energy. **di•ges•tive**, *adj.* which helps you to digest.

dig•it ['dɪdʒɪt] *n.* (a) single figure (from 0 to 9). (b) finger or toe. **dig•it•al**, *adj.* which involves figures; **d. watch** = watch where the time is shown by figures (such as 11:52); **d. camera** = camera that produces pictures that can be saved, viewed, and printed on a computer; **d. computer** = computer which works on a varied signal; **d. television** = television transmitted as digital rather than analog signals; **d. video** = video in digital rather than analog form; **d. video disk** = computer disk that contains large amounts of digitized audio and video information. **dig•i•tize**, *v.* to convert information to digital form.

dig•i•tal•in, digitalis [dɪdʒɪ'teɪlɪn, -ɪs] *n.* drugs made from foxgloves.

dig•ni•fied ['dɪgnɪfaɪd] *adj.* solemn/important-looking. **dig•ni•fy**, *v.* to honor (s.o.) with a title; to give dignity to (s.o.). **dig•ni•tar•y**, *n.* important person. **dig•ni•ty**, *n.* solemn/serious way of behaving; **it is beneath his d. to clean his own shoes** = he is too proud to clean them.

di•gress [daɪ'gres] *v.* to wander away from the subject when speaking. **di•gres•sion**, *n.* speech/writing which does not deal with the subject.

di•hed•ral [daɪ'hiːdrəl] *n.* angle at which an aircraft's wing varies from the horizontal.

dike, dyke [daɪk] *n.* (a) long wall of earth to keep out water. (b) long ditch.

dik•tat ['dɪktæt] *n.* official command.

di•lap•i•dat•ed [dɪ'læpɪdeɪtɪd] *adj.* falling into ruin. **di•lap•i•da•tion**, *n.* being in ruins.

di•late [daɪ'leɪt] *v.* to make (eyes) grow larger; (*of the eyes*) to grow larger. **di•late up•on**, *v.* to talk at length about. **dil•a•ta•tion** [dɪlə'teɪʃn], **di•la•tion** [daɪ'leɪʃn] *n.* act of dilating. **di•la•tor**, *n.* drug used to make a part of the body (such as the eyes) grow larger.

dil•a•to•ry ['dɪlətərɪ] *adj.* slow (to act). **dil•a•to•ri•ness**, *n.* slowness.

di•lem•ma [dɪ'lemə] *n.* serious problem, where a choice has to be made between several bad alternatives; **in a d.** = not knowing which course of action to follow.

dil•et•tante [dɪlɪ'tæntɪ] *n.* person who is interested in a subject, but not very seriously.

dil•i•gence ['dɪlɪdʒəns] *n.* hard work/taking care. **dil•i•gent**, *adj.* hard-working.

dill [dɪl] *n.* herb used for flavoring fish and pickles.

dil•ly-dal•ly ['dɪlɪ'dælɪ] *v.* to hang back; to loiter.

di•lute [daɪ'ljuːt] 1. *v.* to add water to (another liquid) to make it weaker. 2. *adj.* with water added. **di•lu•tion**, *n.* act of diluting.

dim [dɪm] 1. *adj.* (**dimmer, dimmest**) (a) weak (light); **I have a d. recollection of it** = I can remember it vaguely. (b) rather stupid. 2. *v.* (**dimmed**) to turn down (a light); **the house lights dimmed** = the lights in the theater were turned down (as the play started). **dim•ly**, *adv.* vaguely; unclearly. **dim•mer**, *n.* light switch which dims a light. **dim•ness**, *n.* weakness (of light); vagueness (of memory).

dime [daɪm] *n. U.S.* ten cent coin.

di•men•sion [dɪ'menʃn] *n.* measurement (in figures). **di•men•sion•al**, *adj.* **two-dimensional** = having two dimensions, flat; **three-dimensional** = having three dimensions/in the round.

di•min•ish [dɪ'mɪnɪʃ] *v.* to make (sth) smaller; to become smaller. **dim•i•nu•tion** [dɪmɪ'njuːʃn] *n.* becoming smaller. **di•min•u•tive** [dɪ'mɪnjutɪv] 1. *adj.* very small. 2. *n.* word used to show that sth is small; **"Kate" is a d. of "Catherine".**

di•min•u•en•do [dɪmɪnju'endəu] *n.* (*in music*) decreasing noise.

dim•ple ['dɪmpl] *n.* small hollow (in cheeks/in babies' fat elbows). **dim•pled**, *adj.* with dimples.

din [dɪn] 1. *n.* loud noise. 2. *v.* (**dinned**) to force (a piece of information **into** s.o.'s head) by frequently repeating it.

dine [daɪn] *v.* to have dinner. **din•er**, *n.* (a) person eating dinner. (b) dining car. (c) small restaurant selling hot food. **din•ing car**, *n.* restaurant car (on a train). **din•ing room**, *n.* room where people usually eat.

ding-dong ['dɪŋdɒŋ] *n.* sound made by a bell.

din•ghy ['dɪŋgɪ] *n.* small boat.

din•go ['dɪŋgəu] *n.* Australian wild dog.

din•gy ['dɪndʒɪ] *adj.* (**-ier, -iest**) dirty. **din•gi•ness**, *n.* dirt.

din•ner ['dɪnə] *n.* main meal (usu. the evening meal); **d. table** = table (where people eat); **d. party** = dinner to which guests are invited; **d. jacket** = formal (usu. black) jacket worn for dinner with a black bow tie.

di•no•saur ['daɪnəsɔː] *n.* large prehistoric reptile.

dint [dɪnt] *n.* **by d. of** = through; by means of.

di•o•cese ['daɪəsɪs] *n.* area under the charge of a bishop. **di•oc•e•san** [daɪ'ɒsɪzn] *adj.* referring to a diocese.

di•ox•ide [daɪ'ɒksaɪd] *n.* oxide with two parts of oxygen to one part of another substance.

dip [dɪp] 1. *n.* (a) quick covering with liquid. (b)

æ **back,** aː **farm,** ɒ **top,** aɪ **pipe,** aʊ **how,** aɪə **fire,** aʊə **flower,** ɔː **bought,** ɔɪ **toy,** e **fed,** eəhair, eɪ **take,** ə **afraid,** əʊ **boat,** əʊə **lower,** vː **word,** iː **heap,** ɪ **hit,** ɪə **hear,** uː **school,** ʊ **book,** ʌ **but,** b **back,** d **dog,** ð **then,** dʒ **just,** f **fog,** g **go,** h **hand,** j **yes,** k **catch,** l **last,** m **mix,** n **nut,** ŋ **sing,** p **penny,** r **round,** s **some,** ʃ **short,** t **too,** tʃ **chop,** θ **thing,** v **voice,** w **was,** z **zoo,** ʒ **treasure**

sudden drop (of a road/of land). (c) soft mixture into which crackers, raw vegetables, etc. can be dipped as cocktail snacks. (d) short bathe/swim. (e) **sheep d.** = place where sheep are dipped in pesticide to kill ticks. 2. *v.* (**dipped**) (a) to put (sth) quickly **into** a liquid. (b) to dive. (c) **to d. a flag** = to lower a flag. (d) **to d. into a book** = to read a few lines here and there. **dip•per**, *n.* small brown bird which dives into water. **dip•stick**, *n.* rod (in the engine of a car) which shows the level of oil in the engine.

diph•the•ri•a [dɪf'θɪərɪə] *n.* (*no pl.*) serious infectious disease of babies.

diph•thong ['dɪfθɒŋ] *n.* two vowel sounds which are pronounced together.

di•plo•ma [dɪ'pləʊmə] *n.* certificate showing that you have passed an examination.

di•plo•ma•cy [dɪ'pləʊməsɪ] *n.* art of negotiating between different parties, esp. between different countries. **dip•lo•mat** #ɪpləmæt] *n.* person (such as an ambassador) who represents his country abroad. **dip•lo•mat•ic** [dɪplə'mætɪk] *adj.* (a) representing one's country. (b) careful not to give offense. **dip•lo•mat•i•cal•ly**, *adv.* in a diplomatic way. **dip•lo•ma•tist** [dɪ'pləʊmətɪst] *n.* diplomat.

dip•so•ma•ni•a [dɪpsə'meɪnɪə] *n.* habitual drinking of alcohol. **dip•so•ma•ni•ac**, *n.* person who wants to drink alcohol all the time.

dire ['daɪə] *adj.* very serious; **d. necessity** = urgent necessity.

di•rect [daɪ'rekt/dɪ'rekt] 1. *v.* (a) to aim toward a point. (b) to tell (s.o.) to do sth; to manage/organize (a motion picture, play, etc.). 2. *adj.* straight; **d. hit** = hit on the target; **there is a d. flight to Paris** = the plane does not stop between here and Paris. 3. *adv.* straight; without stopping. **d. debit**, *n.* arrangement made by a bank account holder for the regular (usu. monthly) payment of any amount demanded by a specified party. **di•rec•tion** [daɪ'rekʃn] *n.* (a) point to which you are going/at which you are aiming. (b) instruction. (c) guiding (of the making of a motion picture). **di•rec•tion•al**, *adj.* going in one direction. **di•rec•tive**, *n.* official instruction. **di•rect•ly**. 1. *adv.* immediately; straight. 2. *conj.* **I will write the letter d. I get home** = as soon as I get home. **di•rect•ness**, *n.* frankness (of a reply). **di•rec•tor** [daɪ'rektə] *n.* (a) person who is appointed by the shareholders to help run a company; **managing d.** = person who is in charge of a company. (b) person in charge of making a motion picture/a play. **di•rec•to•rate**, *n.* group of directors. **di•rec•tor•ship**, *n.* position of director.

di•rec•to•ry, *n.* list of people/businesses showing their telephone numbers and addresses; book giving lists of people/businesses with their addresses and telephone numbers; **classified d.** = telephone directory where companies are classified into various groups.

dirge [dɜːdʒ] *n.* funeral song.

dir•i•gi•ble [dɪ'rɪdʒɪbl] *n.* large airship which can be steered.

dirk [dɜːk] *n.* short dagger.

dirn•dl ['dɜːndl] *n.* wide skirt gathered tight at the waist.

dirt [dɜːt] *n.* mud; earth; filth; **d. cheap** = extremely cheap. **dirt•i•ness**, *n.* being dirty/not being clean. **dirt•y**. 1. *adj.* (-**ier**, -**iest**) (a) not clean; covered with dirt. (b) **d. trick** = low/unpleasant trick. 2. *v.* to cover with dirt.

dis, diss [dɪs] *v. Sl.* to treat with contempt/disrespect.

dis•a•bil•i•ty [dɪsə'bɪlɪtɪ] *n.* physical handicap. **dis•a•bled** [dɪs'eɪbld] 1. *adj.* physically handicapped. 2. *n.* **the d.** = physically handicapped people.

dis•a•buse [dɪsə'bjuːz] *v.* to make (s.o.) see that he was wrong.

dis•ad•van•tage [dɪsəd'vɑːntɪdʒ] *n.* handicap; drawback; lack of advantage. **dis•ad•van•taged**, *adj.* handicapped. **dis•ad•van•ta•geous** [dɪsædvɑːn'teɪdʒəs] *adj.* which does not give an advantage; unfavorable.

dis•af•fect•ed [dɪsə'fektɪd] *adj.* discontented/rebellious.

dis•a•gree [dɪsə'griː] *v.* not to agree; **cabbage disagrees with me** = makes me feel ill. **dis•a•gree•a•ble**, *adj.* unpleasant. **dis•a•gree•ment**, *n.* lack of agreement.

dis•al•low [dɪsə'laʊ] *v.* to refuse to accept; **the team's second goal was disallowed** = was not counted.

dis•ap•pear [dɪsə'pɪə] *v.* to vanish. **dis•ap•pear•ance**, *n.* vanishing.

dis•ap•point [dɪsə'pɔɪnt] *v.* to let (s.o.) down; not to turn out as expected. **dis•ap•point•ing**, *adj.* unsatisfactory; not coming up to expectations. **dis•ap•point•ment**, *n.* sadness because what was expected did not take place.

dis•ap•prove [dɪsə'pruːv] *v.* not to approve (of sth). **dis•ap•prov•al, disapprobation** [dɪsæprəʊ'beɪʃn] *n.* lack of approval. **dis•ap•prov•ing•ly**, *adv.* in a way which shows you do not approve.

dis•arm [dɪs'ɑːm] *v.* to remove weapons from (s.o.). **dis•ar•ma•ment**, *n.* abolition of weapons by a country. **dis•arm•ing**, *adj.*

charming (manner) which prevents people from criticizing.

dis•ar•range [dɪsə'reɪndʒ] v. to put (sth) into disorder.

dis•ar•ray [dɪsə'reɪ] n. lack of order.

dis•as•ter [dɪ'zɑːstə] n. catastrophe; very bad accident; **air d.** = crash of an aircraft killing many people. **dis•as•trous**, adj. very bad/catastrophic. **dis•as•trous•ly**, adv. very badly.

dis•band [dɪs'bænd] v. to send (soldiers) back home; to split up (a group of soldiers/musicians, etc.).

dis•bar [dɪs'bɑː] v. (**disbarred**) (formal) to remove (a lawyer) from the legal profession.

dis•be•lief [dɪsbɪ'liːf] n. lack of belief. **dis•be•liev•er**, n. person who does not believe.

dis•bud [dɪs'bʌd] v. (**disbudded**) to remove some of the buds from (a plant).

dis•burse [dɪs'bɜːs] v. to pay out (money).

disc [dɪsk] n. round flat object, esp. a record for playing on a record-player; **slipped d.** = painful condition where one of the cushioning discs in the spine has become displaced; **d. brakes** = round, flat brakes in a car. **d. harrow** = type of harrow, formed of a series of circular metal blades; **d. jockey** = person who plays records on the radio/in a club, etc.

dis•card 1. n. ['dɪskɑːd] thing which has been discarded. 2. v. [dɪs'kɑːd] to put (sth) aside; to reject.

dis•cern [dɪ'sɜːn] v. to see/to make out. **dis•cern•i•ble**, adj. which can be seen. **dis•cern•ing**, adj. (person) who has good judgement. **dis•cern•ment**, n. ability to judge correctly.

dis•charge 1. n. ['dɪstʃɑːdʒ] (a) liquid (coming out of a pipe, etc.); pus (coming out of a wound). (b) payment (of a debt). (c) release (of a prisoner). 2. v. [dɪs'tʃɑːdʒ] (a) to unload (a cargo); to let off (a gun). (b) to send (s.o.) away; **he was discharged from the hospital** = he was allowed to go home because he was better. (c) to release (a prisoner). (d) to pay (a debt).

dis•ci•ple [dɪ'saɪpl] n. follower (of a religious leader).

dis•ci•pline ['dɪsɪplɪn] 1. n. keeping people under control. 2. v. to control/to punish (s.o.). **dis•ci•pli•nar•i•an** [dɪsɪplɪ'neərɪən] n. person who believes in strict discipline. **dis•ci•pli•nar•y** [dɪsɪ'plɪnərɪ] adj. (action) which keeps s.o. under control.

dis•claim [dɪs'kleɪm] v. not to admit/to deny; **he disclaims all knowledge of the payment** = he says he knows nothing about the payment. **dis•claim•er**, n. statement in which you disclaim all knowledge of sth.

dis•close [dɪs'kləʊz] v. to reveal (a secret). **dis•clo•sure** [dɪs'kləʊʒə] n. revealing (of a secret).

dis•co ['dɪskəʊ] n. (pl. -os) inf. discotheque; place where people dance to recorded music; dancing to pop/rock music.

dis•col•or, Brit. **dis•col•our** [dɪs'kʌlə] v. to change the color of (sth). **dis•col•or•a•tion** [dɪskʌlə'reɪʃn] n. change of color.

dis•com•fort [dɪs'kʌmfət] n. lack of comfort.

dis•con•cert [dɪskən'sɜːt] v. to surprise/to embarrass. **dis•con•cert•ing**, adj. worrying/surprising.

dis•con•nect [dɪskə'nekt] v. to undo (two things which are connected); **they disconnected the refrigerator** = they unplugged the refrigerator. **dis•con•nect•ed**, adj. disjointed; with no links.

dis•con•so•late [dɪs'kɒnsələt] adj. very sad. **dis•con•so•late•ly**, adv. very sadly.

dis•con•tent [dɪskən'tent] n. state of not being satisfied. **dis•con•tent•ed**, adj. not satisfied.

dis•con•tin•ue [dɪskən'tɪnjuː] v. not to continue to do/produce (sth). **dis•con•ti•nu•i•ty** [dɪskɒntɪ'njuɪtɪ] n. being discontinuous. **dis•con•tin•u•ous**, adj. which stops and starts; intermittent.

dis•cord ['dɪskɔːd] n. lack of agreement. **dis•cord•ant** [dɪs'kɔːdənt] adj. (a) not in agreement. (b) out of harmony.

dis•co•theque ['dɪskətek] n. place where people dance to recorded music.

dis•count 1. n. ['dɪskaʊnt] percentage less than the normal price; **d. store** = shop where goods are cheaper than elsewhere. 2. v. [dɪs'kaʊnt] (a) not to pay any attention to (sth). (b) to put a discount on (a price).

dis•cour•age [dɪs'kʌrɪdʒ] v. not to encourage; **to d. s.o. from doing sth** = to stop s.o. doing sth. **dis•cour•age•ment**, n. being discouraged; thing which stops you doing sth. **dis•cour•ag•ing**, adj. not encouraging.

dis•course 1. n. ['dɪskɔːs] (formal) talk/speech. 2. v. [dɪs'kɔːs] (formal) to speak.

dis•cour•te•ous [dɪs'kɜːtɪəs] adj. rude. **dis•cour•te•ous•ly**, adv. rudely. **dis•cour•te•sy**, n. rudeness.

æ back, ɑː farm, ɒ top, aɪ pipe, aʊ how, aɪə fire, aʊə flower, ɔː bought, ɔɪ toy, e fed, eə hair, eɪ take, ə afraid, əʊ boat, əʊə lower, ɜː word, iː heap, ɪ hit, ɪə hear, uː school, ʊ book, ʌ but, b back, d dog, ð then, dʒ just, f fog, g go, h hand, j yes, k catch, l last, m mix, n nut, ŋ sing, p penny, r round, s some, ʃ short, t too, tʃ chop, θ thing, v voice, w was, z zoo, ʒ treasure

dis•cov•er [dɪsˈkʌvə] *v.* to find (sth new).
dis•cov•er•er, *n.* person who finds sth.
dis•cov•er•y, *n.* act of finding sth new.

dis•cred•it [dɪsˈkredɪt] 1. *n.* doubt/lack of belief (in s.o.). 2. *v.* to make people doubt (s.o./sth); **he has been discredited** = no one believes him any more. **dis•cred•it•a•ble,** *adj.* not honorable (conduct). **dis•cred•it•a•bly,** *adv.* dishonorably.

dis•creet [dɪsˈkriːt] *adj.* quiet; not allowing anyone to notice. **dis•creet•ly,** *adv.* quietly; without anyone noticing.

dis•crep•an•cy [dɪsˈkrepənsɪ] *n.* lack of agreement (between figures/accounts).

dis•crete [dɪsˈkriːt] *adj.* separate/not connected.

dis•cre•tion [dɪsˈkreʃn] *n.* wisdom/good sense; **I leave it to your d.** = I leave it for you to decide. **dis•cre•tion•ar•y,** *adj.* (powers) used at s.o.'s discretion.

dis•crim•i•nate [dɪsˈkrɪmɪneɪt] *v.* to distinguish; **to d. between** = to treat (two things) differently; **to d. against** = to prefer (one thing to another). **dis•crim•i•nat•ing,** *adj.* able to distinguish/judge. **dis•crim•i•na•tion** [dɪskrɪmɪˈneɪʃn] *n.* (a) judgment; **a person of d.** = of good taste. (b) preference (for or against sth); **racial d.** = preference for or against a race.

dis•cur•sive [dɪsˈkɜːsɪv] *adj.* not succinct/not to the point.

dis•cus [ˈdɪskəs] *n.* (*pl.* **-es**) flat round disk which is thrown as a sport.

dis•cuss [dɪsˈkʌs] *v.* to talk about (a problem). **dis•cus•sion** [dɪsˈkʌʃn] *n.* talking about (a problem); **the question under d.** = the problem we are talking about.

dis•dain [dɪsˈdeɪn] 1. *n.* looking down; feeling that s.o./sth is inferior. 2. *v.* to look down on (sth); to refuse to do (sth) because it is beneath you. **dis•dain•ful,** *adj.* superior (air). **dis•dain•ful•ly,** *adv.* with a superior air.

dis•ease [dɪˈziːz] *n.* serious illness (of animals, plants, etc.). **dis•eased,** *adj.* sick.

dis•em•bark [dɪsɪmˈbɑːk] *v.* to get off a ship. **dis•em•bar•ka•tion** [dɪsembɑːˈkeɪʃn] *n.* getting off a ship.

dis•em•bod•ied [dɪsɪmˈbɒdɪd] *adj.* not connected to a body.

dis•em•bow•el [dɪsɪmˈbaʊəl] *v.* to remove the intestines from (s.o.).

dis•en•chant•ed [dɪsɪnˈtʃɑːntɪd] *adj.* (**with**) feeling that sth has not turned out as well as expected. **dis•en•chant•ment,** *n.* feeling that sth has not turned out as well as expected.

dis•en•fran•chise [dɪsɪnˈfræntʃaɪz] *v.* see **dis•fran•chise.**

dis•en•gage [dɪsɪnˈɡeɪdʒ] *v.* (a) to break off; the troops disengaged = the troops broke off the fighting. (b) to separate (the gears of a car).

dis•en•tan•gle [dɪsɪnˈtæŋɡl] *v.* to untie (knotted string, etc.).

dis•fa•vor, *Brit.* **dis•fa•vour** [dɪsˈfeɪvə] *n.* shame; lack of favor; **the senator fell into d.** = he was disgraced; **the minister incurred the king's d.** = he fell into disgrace with the king.

dis•fig•ure [dɪsˈfɪɡə] *v.* to make ugly. **dis•fig•ure•ment,** *n.* act of disfiguring.

dis•fran•chise [dɪsˈfræntʃaɪz] *v.* to remove the right to vote from (s.o.). **dis•fran•chise•ment,** *n.* removal of the right to vote.

dis•gorge [dɪsˈɡɔːdʒ] *v.* (a) to pour out. (b) to give up (things which have been stolen).

dis•grace [dɪsˈɡreɪs] 1. *n.* shame; being out of favor with s.o.; **the mayor fell into d.** = he was out of favor. 2. *v.* to bring shame on. **dis•grace•ful,** *adj.* which you should be ashamed of. **dis•grace•ful•ly,** *adv.* in a disgraceful way.

dis•grun•tled [dɪsˈɡrʌntld] *adj.* annoyed/discontented.

dis•guise [dɪsˈɡaɪz] 1. *n.* costume, wig, etc., to make a person look like s.o. else; **in d.** = dressed to look like s.o. else. 2. *v.* to dress so as to look like s.o. else; to make (sth) look/sound different; **there is no disguising the fact** = you cannot hide the fact.

dis•gust [dɪsˈɡʌst] 1. *n.* (**at**) strong dislike; feeling sick/very discontented. 2. *v.* to make (s.o.) feel sick. **dis•gust•ing,** *adj.* which makes you feel sick.

dish [dɪʃ] 1. *n.* (*pl.* **-es**) (a) large plate (for serving food); (b) part of a meal; (plate of) prepared food. 2. *v. inf.* **he is dishing out the food** = he is serving the meal; **they are dishing out tickets** = they are handing out tickets. **dish•cloth,** *n.* cloth for washing dishes. **dish•wash•er,** *n.* machine for washing dishes. **dish•wa•ter,** *n.* water which has been used for washing dishes.

dis•har•mo•ny [dɪsˈhɑːmənɪ] *n.* not being in agreement/in harmony.

dis•heart•en [dɪsˈhɑːtn] *v.* to discourage. **dis•heart•en•ing,** *adj.* discouraging.

di•shev•elled [dɪˈʃevəld] *adj.* untidy (appearance)/uncombed (hair).

dis•hon•est [dɪsˈɒnɪst] *adj.* not honest. **dis•hon•est•ly,** *adv.* not honestly; illegally. **dis•hon•es•ty,** *n.* lack of honesty.

dis•hon•or, *Brit.* **dis•hon•our** [dɪsˈɒnə] 1. *n.* lack of honor. 2. *v.* (a) to treat rudely. (b) not to honor; **dishonored check** = check which the bank will not pay. **dis•hon•or•a•ble,** *adj.* not honorable; shameful.

dis•hon•or•a•bly, *adv.* in a dishonorable way.

dis•il•lu•sion [dɪsɪ'luːʒn] *n.* feeling of being let down/that sth has not turned out as you expected. **dis•il•lu•sion•ed,** *adj.* feeling that sth has not turned out as expected. **dis•il•lu•sion•ment,** *n.* feeling of being let down/that sth has not turned out as expected.

dis•in•cen•tive [dɪsɪn'sentɪv] *n.* thing which discourages; **the low salary is a d. to work** = the salary does not encourage people to work.

dis•in•clin•ed [dɪsɪn'klaɪnd] *adj.* not inclined; **she is feeling d. to go to work today** = she does not want to go to work today. **dis•in•cli•na•tion** [dɪsɪnklɪ'neɪʃn] *n.* not wanting to do sth.

dis•in•fect [dɪsɪn'fekt] *v.* to remove/to prevent infection. **dis•in•fect•ant,** *n.* chemical liquid for fighting infection.

dis•in•for•ma•tion [dɪsɪnfə'meɪʃən] *n.* false information to confuse an enemy.

dis•in•gen•u•ous [dɪsɪn'dʒenjuəs] *adj.* false; lacking frankness; pretending to be naive.

dis•in•her•it [dɪsɪn'herɪt] *v.* to change your will so that s.o. will no longer inherit your money when you die.

dis•in•te•grate [dɪs'ɪntɪgreɪt] *v.* to fall to pieces. **dis•in•te•gra•tion** [dɪsɪntɪ'greɪʃn] *n.* falling to pieces.

dis•in•ter [dɪsɪn'tɜː] *v.* (**disinterred**) to dig up (sth) which has been buried.

dis•in•ter•est•ed [dɪs'ɪntrəstɪd] *adj.* not in favor of one side or the other; **he is a totally d. observer** = he is an impartial observer. **dis•in•ter•est•ed•ness,** *n.* being disinterested.

dis•joint•ed [dɪs'dʒɔɪntɪd] *adj.* without any links; unconnected.

disk [dɪsk] *n.* any round flat object, especially a piece of magnetized plastic used in computers to record information; **floppy d.** = small disk which can be inserted and removed from a computer; **hard d.** = disk with a large capacity, which is permanently fixed in a computer. **disk•ette,** *n.* small floppy disk. **disk drive,** *n.* device which spins a disk in a computer and controls the access of information.

dis•like [dɪs'laɪk] 1. *n.* lack of liking; **to take a d. to** = to start to hate. 2. *v.* not to like; **I don't d. honey** = I like honey.

dis•lo•cate ['dɪsləkeɪt] *v.* (a) to put (an arm/leg, etc.) out of joint. (b) to disorganize. **dis•lo•ca•tion** [dɪslə'keɪʃn] *n.* (a) disorgani-

zation. (b) putting an arm/leg, etc., out of joint.

dis•lodge [dɪs'lɒdʒ] *v.* to detach/to remove.

dis•loy•al [dɪs'lɔɪəl] *adj.* not loyal. **dis•loy•al•ty,** *n.* being disloyal.

dis•mal ['dɪzməl] *adj.* miserable. **dis•mal•ly,** *adv.* miserably; (to fail a test) very badly.

dis•man•tle [dɪs'mæntl] *v.* to take to pieces.

dis•may [dɪs'meɪ] 1. *n.* horror/consternation. 2. *v.* to strike (s.o.) with horror.

dis•mem•ber [dɪs'membə] *v.* to cut up (a body) into parts; to take apart.

dis•miss [dɪs'mɪs] *v.* (a) to send (s.o.) away. (b) to remove (s.o.) from a job. (c) to refuse or disregard. **dis•miss•al,** *n.* removal from a job.

dis•mount [dɪs'maʊnt] *v.* to get off a horse/bicycle, etc.

dis•o•bey [dɪsə'beɪ] *v.* to refuse to obey. **dis•o•be•di•ence** [dɪsə'biːdɪəns] *n.* lack of obedience. **dis•o•be•di•ent,** *adj.* not obedient.

dis•or•der [dɪs'ɔːdə] *n.* (a) lack of order; untidiness. (b) riot; disturbance. (c) illness. **dis•or•der•ly,** *adj.* wild (crowd).

dis•or•gan•ize [dɪs'ɔːgənaɪz] *v.* to put (sth) out of its usual order.

dis•o•ri•en•tate [dɪs'ɔːrɪənteɪt] *v.* to make (s.o.) lose their sense of direction; to confuse (s.o.). **dis•o•ri•en•ta•tion,** *n.* feeling lost.

dis•own [dɪs'əʊn] *v.* to refuse to acknowledge (sth) is yours.

dis•par•age [dɪs'pærɪdʒ] *v.* to say that sth is bad. **dis•par•age•ment,** *n.* act of disparaging. **dis•par•ag•ing,** *adj.* critical; saying that sth is bad.

dis•pa•rate ['dɪspərət] *adj.* varied/different. **dis•par•i•ty** [dɪs'pærɪtɪ] *n.* difference.

dis•pas•sion•ate [dɪs'pæʃnət] *adj.* calm and without emotion. **dis•pas•sion•ate•ly,** *adv.* calmly.

dis•patch [dɪs'pætʃ] 1. *n.* (*pl.* **-es**) (a) sending. (b) speed (of doing sth). (c) message. 2. *v.* (a) to send. (b) to finish quickly. (c) to kill off.

dis•pel [dɪs'pel] *v.* (**dispelled**) to clear away.

dis•pense [dɪs'pens] *v.* (a) to distribute. (b) to prepare and sell (medicine). (c) **to d. with** = to do without. **dis•pen•sa•ble,** *adj.* which can be dispensed with. **dis•pen•sa•ry,** *n.* place where medicines, etc. are dispensed. **dis•pen•sa•tion** [dɪspən'seɪʃn] *n.* permission not to follow a rule, etc. **dis•pens•er,** *n.* automatic machine/box with a hole to allow one object to come out at a time.

æ back, aː farm, ɒ top, aɪ pipe, aʊ how, aɪə fire, aʊə flower, ɔː bought, ɔɪ toy, ə fed, eəhair, eɪ take, ə afraid, əʊ boat, əʊə lower, vː word, iː heap, ɪ hit, ɪə hear, uː school, ʊ book, ʌ but, b back, d dog, ð then, dʒ just, f fog, g go, h hand, j yes, k catch, l last, m mix, n nut, ŋ sing, p penny, r round, s some, ʃ short, t too, tʃ chop, θ thing, v voice, w was, z zoo, ʒ treasure

dis•perse [dɪs'pɜːs] *v.* to clear away; to scatter in different directions. **dis•per•sal, dispersion,** *n.* act of dispersing.

dis•pir•it•ed [dɪ'spɪrɪtɪd] *adj.* sad/discouraged; feeling disappointed.

dis•place [dɪs'pleɪs] *v.* to move (sth) from its usual place; **displaced persons** = refugees who have fled from their home lands. **dis•place•ment,** *n.* moving (of sth); amount of water removed by a ship, (hence) the volume of the ship.

dis•play [dɪs'pleɪ] 1. *n.* show/exhibition; **d. screen** = screen on which data is displayed. **d. unit** = special stand for showing goods for sale. 2. *v.* to put (sth) on show.

dis•please [dɪs'pliːz] *v.* not to please. **dis•pleas•ure** [dɪs'pleʒə] *n.* annoyance.

dis•port [dɪs'pɔːt] *v.* (*formal*) **to d. oneself** = to amuse oneself.

dis•pose [dɪs'pəuz] *v.* **to d. of sth** = to get rid of sth. **dis•pos•a•ble,** *adj.* which can be thrown away after use; **d. income** = amount of income left after personal taxes have been deducted. **dis•pos•al,** *n.* (a) machine attached to a sink which grinds up waste. (b) **I am at your d.** = you can ask me to do anything you wish. **dis•posed,** *adj.* **he is well d. towards us** = he favors us. **dis•po•si•tion** [dɪspə'zɪʃn] *n.* (a) character. (b) act of passing property to another person.

dis•pos•sess [dɪspə'zes] *v.* **to d. s.o. of** = to remove possessions from s.o.

dis•pro•por•tion [dɪsprə'pɔːʃn] *n.* being out of proportion. **dis•pro•por•tion•ate,** *adj.* unusual; out of proportion. **dis•pro•por•tion•ate•ly,** *adv.* in a disproportionate way.

dis•prove [dɪs'pruːv] *v.* to prove (sth) is wrong.

dis•pute [dɪs'pjuːt] 1. *n.* argument. 2. *v.* to argue that (sth) is incorrect. **dis•put•a•ble,** *adj.* which can be disputed. **dis•pu•tant,** *n.* person who disputes. **dis•pu•ta•tion,** *n.* (*formal*) argument.

dis•qual•i•fy [dɪs'kwɒlɪfaɪ] *v.* to rule that (s.o.) is incapable of doing sth/not qualified to do sth. **dis•qual•i•fi•ca•tion** [dɪskwɒlɪfɪ'keɪʃn] *n.* rule that s.o. is disqualified.

dis•qui•et [dɪs'kwaɪət] *n.* worry. **dis•qui•et•ing,** *adj.* which makes you worried.

dis•qui•si•tion [dɪskwɪ'zɪʃn] *n.* (*formal*) long, formal speech.

dis•re•gard [dɪsrɪ'gɑːd] 1. *n.* (for) indifference (to sth); lack of worry (about sth). 2. *v.* to take no notice of.

dis•re•pair [dɪsrɪ'peə] *n.* **in d.** = needing to be repaired.

dis•re•pute [dɪsrɪ'pjuːt] *n.* bad reputation.

dis•rep•u•ta•ble [dɪs'repjutəbl] *adj.* with a bad reputation; **he is a d. character** = a wicked person.

dis•re•spect [dɪsrɪ'spekt] *n.* lack of respect. **dis•re•spect•ful,** *adj.* lacking respect; rude.

dis•robe [dɪs'rəub] *v.* (*formal*) to undress.

dis•rupt [dɪs'rʌpt] *v.* to break up/to interrupt (a meeting). **dis•rup•tion** [dɪs'rʌpʃn] *n.* breaking up; interruption (of a meeting). **dis•rup•tive,** *adj.* which disrupts.

dis•sat•is•fac•tion [dɪssætɪs'fækʃn] *n.* lack of satisfaction. **dis•sat•is•fied** [dɪs'sætɪsfaɪd] *adj.* not satisfied.

dis•sect [dɪ'sekt] *v.* to cut up (a dead body/plant) in order to examine the inside. **dis•sec•tion,** *n.* cutting up (a body or plant).

dis•sem•ble [dɪ'sembl] *v.* (*formal*) to hide one's feelings.

dis•sem•i•nate [dɪ'semɪneɪt] *v.* to spread (news) around. **dis•sem•i•na•tion,** *n.* act of spreading news around.

dis•sen•sion [dɪ'senʃn] *n.* lack of agreement. **dis•sent** [dɪ'sent] 1. *n.* lack of agreement. 2. *v.* **to d. from** = not to agree with. **dis•sent•er,** *n.* person who does not agree (esp. with the established church).

dis•ser•ta•tion [dɪsə'teɪʃn] *n.* short (university) thesis.

dis•serv•ice [dɪs'sɜːvɪs] *n.* unintentional harm; **you do yourself a d.** = you are harming your reputation.

dis•si•dent ['dɪsɪdənt] *adj. & n.* (person) who does not agree with the opinion of his political party/with the state, etc. **dis•si•dence,** *n.* disagreement (with the state).

dis•sim•i•lar [dɪ'sɪmɪlə] *adj.* not the same; **they are not d.** = they are quite alike.

dis•sim•u•late [dɪ'sɪmjuleɪt] *v.* (*formal*) to hide one's feelings. **dis•sim•u•la•tion,** *n.* (*formal*) hiding one's feelings.

dis•si•pate ['dɪsɪpeɪt] *v.* to clear away; to get rid of. **dis•si•pa•tion** [dɪsɪ'peɪʃn] *n.* throwing away (a fortune); wild living.

dis•so•ci•ate [dɪ'səusɪeɪt] *v.* **to d. yourself from** = to say that you have nothing to do with. **dis•so•ci•a•tion,** *n.* act of dissociating oneself.

dis•so•lute ['dɪsəljuːt] *adj.* depraved; undisciplined.

dis•solve [dɪ'zɒlv] *v.* (a) to make (a solid substance) become part of a liquid; to become part of a liquid. (b) to bring to an end. **dis•so•lu•tion,** *n.* act of dissolving a government organization, partnership, etc. **dis•sol•vent,** *n.* substance which can dissolve other substances.

dis•so•nant ['dɪsənənt] *adj.* out of harmony.

dis•suade [dɪ'sweɪd] *v.* **to d. s.o. from sth** = to

persuade s.o. not to do sth. **dis•sua•sion,** *n.* persuading s.o. not to do sth.

dis•tal ['dɪstəl] *adj.* away from the center of the body.

dis•tance ['dɪstəns] 1. *n.* space from one point to another; **in the d.** = quite a long way away. 2. *v.* **to d. yourself from** = to put yourself at a distance from. **dis•tant,** *adj.* far away; **he is a d. relative** = he is related to me, but not of my close family. **dis•tant•ly,** *adv.* in a distant way.

dis•taste [dɪs'teɪst] *n.* dislike. **dis•taste•ful,** *adj.* unpleasant.

dis•tem•per [dɪs'tempə] 1. *n.* (a) water color paint for walls. (b) sickness of dogs, cats, and horses. 2. *v.* to put distemper on (a wall).

dis•tend [dɪs'tend] *v.* to swell. **dis•ten•sion,** *n.* swelling.

dis•til [dɪ'stɪl] *v.* **(distilled)** to make pure water/alcohol by heating and collecting the vapor; **distilled water** = pure water. **dis•til•la•tion,** *n.* act of distilling (water/alcohol). **dis•till•er,** *n.* person who distils alcohol. **dis•till•er•y,** *n.* factory for distilling alcohol.

dis•tinct [dɪ'stɪŋkt] *adj.* (a) separate. (b) clear. **dis•tinc•tion** [dɪ'stɪŋkʃn] *n.* (a) difference. (b) special excellence. **dis•tinc•tive,** *adj.* very noticeable; particular to one thing; which makes one thing different from others. **dis•tinct•ly,** *adv.* clearly. **dis•tinct•ness,** *n.* being distinct.

dis•tin•guish [dɪ'stɪŋgwɪʃ] *v.* (a) to see clearly; to make out (detail). (b) to see a difference (**between** two things). (c) **he distinguished himself** = he made himself noticed. **dis•tin•guish•a•ble,** *adj.* which can be distinguished. **dis•tin•guished,** *adj.* important/well-known (writer/painter, etc.).

dis•tort [dɪ'stɔːt] *v.* to twist; to give a false impression of. **dis•tor•tion** [dɪ'stɔːʃn] *n.* twisting; giving a false impression.

dis•tract [dɪ'strækt] *v.* to attract attention from. **dis•tract•ed,** *adj.* wild (with worry/grief). **dis•trac•tion** [dɪ'strækʃn] *n.* (a) amusement. (b) worry; **he loved her to d.** = he was wild about her.

dis•train [dɪs'treɪn] *v.* to seize goods to pay for debts.

dis•traught [dɪs'trɔːt] *adj.* wild (with worry/grief, etc.).

dis•tress [dɪ'stres] 1. *n.* (a) great sorrow/pain. (b) difficulty; trouble; **d. signal** = signal sent out by ship/aircraft in trouble. 2. *v.* to make (s.o.) very sad. **dis•tress•ing,** *adj.* very sad; worrying.

dis•trib•ute [dɪ'strɪbjuːt] *v.* to give to several people; **we d. Japanese cars** = we are the agents for Japanese cars. **dis•tri•bu•tion** [dɪstrɪ-'bjuːʃn] *n.* giving to several people. **dis•tri•bu•tive** [dɪ'strɪbjutɪv] *adj.* which distributes. **dis•trib•u•tor,** *n.* (a) company which sells goods for another (usu. overseas) company. (b) (*in a car engine*) mechanism which passes the electric spark to each sparking plug in turn.

dis•trict ['dɪstrɪkt] *n.* area/region; **d. attorney** = government official who acts as a lawyer in prosecuting cases for the government or the people in a certain region.

dis•trust [dɪs'trʌst] 1. *n.* lack of trust. 2. *v.* to have no trust in.

dis•turb [dɪ'stɜːb] *v.* to bother/to worry (s.o.); to interrupt (s.o.). **dis•tur•bance,** *n.* (a) noise. (b) public disorder. **dis•turb•ing,** *adj.* worrying.

dis•u•nit•ed [dɪsju:'naɪtəd] *adj.* no longer united.

dis•use [dɪs'juːs] *n.* **to fall into d.** = not to be used any more. **dis•used** ['dɪsju:zd] *adj.* not used.

ditch [dɪtʃ] 1. *n.* long trench for taking away water. 2. *v.* (a) to make a ditch. (b) (*of aircraft*) to come down in the sea. (c) *inf.* to abandon; **he ditched his car and walked** = he left his car by the side of the road.

dith•er ['dɪðə] 1. *n.* **all of a d.** = very agitated. 2. *v.* not to be able to make up one's mind.

dit•to ['dɪtəʊ] *n.* the same thing; printer's sign (.) meaning that the same thing is to be repeated.

dit•ty ['dɪtɪ] *n.* little song.

di•u•ret•ic [daɪju'retɪk] *adj. & n.* (substance) which makes you produce more urine.

di•ur•nal [daɪ'ɜːnəl] *adj.* (*poetic*) daily.

di•van [dɪ'væn] *n.* low couch; bed with a solid base and no back or ends.

dive [daɪv] 1. *n.* (a) plunge downward head first. (b) *inf.* disreputable bar/club. 2. *v.* (**dived,** **dove** [dəʊv]) to plunge head first. **div•er,** *n.* person who works underwater. **div•ing board,** *n.* plank at swimming pool from which people dive. **div•ing suit,** *n.* heavy suit for divers working at great depths.

di•verge [daɪ'vɜːdʒ] *v.* to split; to go in different ways. **di•ver•gence,** *n.*

æ back, aː farm, ɒ top, aɪ pipe, aʊ how, aɪə fire, aʊə flower, ɔː bought, ɔɪ toy, e fed, eəhair, eɪ take, ə afraid, əʊ boat, əʊə lower, ɜː word, iː heap, ɪ hit, ɪə hear, u: school, ʊ book, ʌ but, b back, d dog, ð then, dʒ just, f fog, g go, h hand, j yes, k catch, l last, m mix, n nut, ŋ sing, p penny, r round, s some, ʃ short, t too, tʃ chop, θ thing, v voice, w was, z zoo, ʒ treasure

split/difference. **di•ver•gent,** *adj.* which split/which are different. **di•verg•ing,** *adj.* splitting; **d. opinions** = opinions which are quite different.

di•verse [daɪ'vɜːs] *adj.* varied. **di•ver•si•fi•ca•tion** [daɪvɜːsɪfɪ'keɪʃn] *n.* act of diversifying. **di•ver•si•fy,** *v.* to vary; to do other sorts of work. **di•ver•si•ty,** *n.* great variety.

di•ver•sion [daɪ'vɜːʃn] *n.* (a) sending traffic another way. (b) amusement. (c) **to create a d.** = to do sth to distract s.o.'s attention from another thing which you do not want him to see. **di•vert,** *v.* (a) to send traffic another way. (b) to amuse. (c) **I am trying to d. his attention** = to distract his attention.

di•vest [daɪ'vest] *v.* (*formal*) **to d. s.o. of sth** = to take sth away from s.o.

di•vide [dɪ'vaɪd] *v.* (a) to cut into parts. (b) to calculate how many of one number there are in another. **di•vid•ers,** *n. pl.* pair of compasses for measuring.

div•i•dend ['dɪvɪdend] *n.* part of profits shared out among shareholders.

di•vine [dɪ'vaɪn] 1. *adj.* referring to God. 2. *v.* to predict the future; to search for hidden sources of water. 3. *n.* (*formal*) learned priest. **div•i•na•tion** [dɪvɪ'neɪʃn] *n.* predicting what will happen in the future. **di•vin•er,** *n.* person who finds hidden sources of water. **di•vin•i•ty** [dɪ'vɪnɪtɪ] *n.* god; state of being a god.

di•vi•sion [dɪ'vɪʒn] *n.* (a) splitting up into parts; calculation of how many of one number there are in another; **long d.** = working out of a complicated division (such as 2,894 divided by 19) on paper. (b) important part (of army/company). **di•vi•sion•al,** *adj.* referring to a division. **di•vis•i•ble** [dɪ'vɪzəbl] *adj.* which can be divided. **di•vi•sive,** *adj.* which produces quarrels. **di•vi•sor** [dɪ'vaɪzə] *n.* number which divides another.

di•vorce [dɪ'vɔːs] 1. *n.* legal separation of husband and wife leaving each free to remarry. 2. *v.* (a) to separate (two ideas, etc.). (b) to break off a marriage legally. **di•vor•cee** [dɪvɔː'siː] *n.* person who is divorced.

div•ot ['dɪvət] *n.* small piece of turf.

di•vulge [daɪ'vʌldʒ] *v.* to reveal (a secret).

diz•zy ['dɪzɪ] *adj.* (-ier, -iest) feeling that everything is spinning around; **I feel d.** = my head is turning; **d. heights** = such great heights that they make your head turn. **diz•zi•ly,** *adv.* in a dizzy way. **diz•zi•ness,** *n.* feeling that everything is turning around you.

DJ ['diːdʒeɪ] *abbrev. for* disc jockey.

DNA [diːen'eɪ] *abbrev. for* deoxyribonucleic acid; **DNA fin•ger•print•ing, DNA pro•fi•ling** *see* genetic fingerprinting.

do [duː] 1. *n.* (*pl.* **dos**) party; social gathering. 2. *v.* (**did; done**) (a) to work at (sth); to make/to complete (sth); **I'm doing my hair** = I am combing my hair; **she was doing the laundry; he hasn't done the dishes; can you do today's crossword? well done!** = congratulations, you have worked/run, etc., well! (b) **the potatoes aren't done yet** = aren't cooked yet; **the meat is done to a turn** = the meat is well cooked; *inf.* **I feel done in** = I am tired out. (c) to be satisfactory; **will this color do?** we will have to make do with **paper plates** = we will have to accept paper plates because there is no alternative. (d) to go (at a certain speed). (e) (*used in negatives, questions and answers*) **it doesn't matter; we didn't laugh; do you live in town?—yes, I do; but your parents don't live there, do they?—no, they do not.** (f) (*takes the place of another verb*) **can you swim as fast as he does? he speaks French better than I do; she arrived before we did.** (g) (*telling someone not to do something*) **don't throw that paper away!** (h) **how do you do?** = hello! (i) (*to emphasize*) **why don't you work?—I do work! why didn't she tell you?—she did tell me! do a•way,** *v.* **to do away with sth** = to abolish sth; **to do away with s.o.** = to murder s.o. **do for,** *v. inf.* to kill/to destroy. **do-good•er,** *n.* (*pl.* **do-gooders**) *inf.* person who tries to help others, but in an ineffectual or officious way. **do in,** *v. inf.* to kill. **do•ing,** *n.* (a) **it takes some d.** = it is quite difficult to do. (b) *inf.* **doings** = things. **do-it-your•self,** *n.* repairing/building/painting by yourself, without employing a professional. **do up,** *v.* (a) to fasten. (b) to renovate; **they bought an old cottage and did it up. do with,** *v.* (a) *inf.* to need; **I could do with a drink.** (b) to concern; **it is nothing to do with me** = it is not my business; **it is to do with the new book** = it concerns/it is about the new book; **what have you done with my hat?** = where have you put my hat? **do with•out,** *v.* to manage without.

doc•ile ['dəusaɪl] *adj.* quiet/not aggressive. **do•cil•i•ty** [dʊ'sɪlɪtɪ] *n.* being docile.

dock [dɒk] 1. *n.* (a) artificial harbor; **the docks** = the whole harbor; **dry d.** = dock where the water is pumped out to allow repairs to be done to a ship. (b) box in a court of law, where the prisoner sits. (c) wild plant with very large leaves. 2. *v.* (a) to put a ship into harbor; (*of ship*) to arrive in harbor. (b) to link two spacecraft together in space. (c) to cut off/to remove. **dock•er,** *n.* man who works in the docks. **dock•yard,** *n.* place where ships are built.

dock•et ['dɒkɪt] 1. *n.* list of cases to be tried in a court of law. 2. *v.* to enter in a docket.

doc•tor ['dɒktə] 1. *n.* (*shortened in names to* **Dr.**) person who looks after people's health; learned person with the highest degree from a university. 2. *v.* (a) to look after (a patient/a sick animal). (b) to change figures in (accounts). **doc•tor•al,** *adj.* referring to a doctorate. **doc•tor•ate** ['dɒktərət] *n.* highest degree from a university.

doc•trine ['dɒktrɪn] *n.* statement of what a group of people believe. **doc•tri•naire** [dɒktrɪ'neə] *adj.* very dogmatic. **doc•tri•nal** [dɒk'traɪnl] *adj.* referring to a doctrine.

doc•u•ment ['dɒkjumənt] *n.* paper with writing on it. **doc•u•men•ta•ry** [dɒkju-'mentərɪ] 1. *n.* factual film about a real subject. 2. *adj.* referring to documents. **doc•u•men•ta•tion,** *n.* all the documents which refer to sth.

dod•der ['dɒdə] *v.* to walk uncertainly/to totter. **dod•der•y,** *adj.* old and trembly.

dodge [dɒdʒ] 1. *n.* trick. 2. *v.* to avoid/to get out of the way. **dodg•ems,** *n. pl.* ride at an amusement park where small electric cars are driven around and bump into each other.

do•do ['dəʊdəʊ] *n.* large extinct bird.

doe ['dəʊ] *n.* female (deer/rabbit).

doff [dɒf] *v.* to take off (one's hat/clothes).

dog [dɒg] 1. *n.* (a) carnivorous animal which barks, often kept as a pet; **let sleeping dogs lie** = not to disturb the existing state of affairs. (b) male fox. (c) **the dogs** = dog races; **to go to the dogs** = to go to ruin. (d) **d. days** = very hot period in late summer. 2. *v.* (**dogged**) **to d. s.o.'s footsteps** = to follow s.o. **dog-col•lar,** *n.* (a) leather band to go around a dog's neck. (b) *sl.* white collar worn by members of the clergy. **dog-eared,** *adj.* (book) with its pages bent or torn. **dog-fish,** *n.* huss/small white sea fish. **dog•ged** ['dɒgɪd] *adj.* not giving in easily. **dog•ged•ly,** *adv.* in a dogged way. **dog•house,** *n.* kennel; *inf.* **in the d.** = in disgrace. **dog rose,** *n.* wild pink rose. **dog-tired,** *adj.* worn out. **dog•watch,** *n.* (*in the navy*) one of two watches in the evening. **dog•wood,** *n.* shrub with bright red stems.

dog•ger•el ['dɒgərəl] *n.* bad poetry.

dog•ma ['dɒgmə] *n.* official belief. **dog•mat•ic** [dɒg'mætɪk] *adj.* insistent that what you say is right. **dog•mat•i•cal•ly,** *adv.* in a dogmatic way. **dog•ma•tism,** *n.* insistence that you are right. **dog•ma•tize,** *v.* to insist that you are right.

doi•ly ['dɔɪlɪ] *n.* decorated paper/lace mat to put under a cake on a plate.

dol•drums ['dɒldrəmz] *n. pl.* **in the d.** = in a gloomy, depressed mood.

dole [dəʊl] 1. *n.* money given by the government to people without work; **on the d.** = unemployed and receiving government payments. 2. *v.* **to d. out** = to hand out.

dole•ful ['dəʊlful] *adj.* gloomy. **dole•ful•ly,** *adv.* gloomily.

doll [dɒl] *n.* toy which looks like a baby. **dolled up,** *adj. inf.* very smartly dressed. **dol•ly,** *n.* (a) *inf.* doll. (b) wheeled platform for a TV camera/for moving heavy loads.

dol•lar ['dɒlə] *n.* unit of money used in the United States and certain other countries.

dol•lop ['dɒləp] *n. inf.* large lump (of sth soft).

dol•men ['dɒlmən] *n.* prehistoric tomb with a flat stone supported by uprights.

dol•phin ['dɒlfɪn] *n.* mammal like a small whale living in the sea.

do•main [də'meɪn] *n.* (a) area controlled by s.o. (b) area of knowledge.

dome [dəʊm] *n.* semi-spherical roof. **domed,** *adj.* with a dome.

Domes•day Book ['du:mzdeɪ bʊk] *n.* record of land and population in England, made for William I in 1086.

do•mes•tic [də'mestɪk] *adj.* (a) referring to the home; **d. animals** = animals kept by humans for wool/milk/meat, etc. (b) **d. flights** = flights inside a country. **do•mes•ti•cat•ed** [də-'mestɪkeɪtɪd] *adj.* (animal) trained to live in the house. **do•mes•tic•i•ty** [dəʊme'stɪsɪtɪ] *n.* life at home.

dom•i•cile ['dɒmɪsaɪl] *n.* (*formal*) place where s.o. lives. **dom•i•cil•i•ary,** *adj.* which takes place in the home. **dom•i•ciled,** *adj.* (*formal*) living; resident.

dom•i•nant ['dɒmɪnənt] *adj.* most important; supreme; commanding. **dom•i•nance,** *n.* being dominant. **dom•i•nate** ['dɒmɪneɪt] *v.* (a) to rule. (b) to be very obvious. **dom•i•nat•ing,** *adj.* ruling; over-shadowing. **dom•i•na•tion** [dɒmɪ-'neɪʃn] *n.* act of dominating. **dom•i•neer** [dɒmɪ'nɪə] *v.* to rule (s.o.); **a domineering wife** = a wife who rules her husband.

do•min•ion [də'mɪnjən] *n.* (a) self-governing state in the British Commonwealth. (b) rule (over a territory).

dom•i•no ['dɒmɪnəʊ] *n.* (*pl.* **-oes**) one of a set of small flat blocks, each divided into two sec-

---

æ **back,** a: **farm,** ɒ: **top,** aɪ **pipe,** aʊ **how,** aɪə **fire,** aʊə **flower,** ɔ: **bought,** ɔɪ **toy,** ə **fed,** eəhair, eɪ **take,** ə **afraid,** əʊ **boat,** əʊə **lower,** v: **word,** i: **heap,** ɪ **hit,** ɪə **hear,** u: **school,** ʊ **book,** ʌ **but,** b **back,** d **dog,** ð **then,** dʒ **just,** f **fog,** g **go,** h **hand,** j **yes,** k **catch,** l **last,** m **mix,** n **nut,** ŋ **sing,** p **penny,** r **round,** s **some,** ʃ **short,** t **too,** tʃ **chop,** θ **thing,** v **voice,** w **was,** z **zoo,** ʒ **treasure**

tions, with up to six dots in each section; **d. theory** = theory that if one event occurs, others will inevitably follow.

don [dɒn] 1. *n.* head, tutor, or fellow of a college at Oxford or Cambridge University. 2. *v.* **(donned)** to put on (a piece of clothing). **don•nish**, *adj.* like a don.

do•nate [dəʊ'neɪt] *v.* to give. **do•na•tion** [dəʊ'neɪʃn] *n.* gift.

done [dʌn] *v. see* **do.**

don•key ['dɒŋkɪ] *n.* farm animal like a small horse but with long ears; *inf.* **I haven't seen him for donkey's years** = I have not seen him for a long time; **d. work** = hard dull work.

do•nor ['dəʊnə] *n.* person who gives; **blood d.** = person who gives blood for blood transfusions.

doo•dle ['duːdl] *v.* to make meaningless drawings/patterns on paper.

doom [duːm] 1. *n.* (a) fate. (b) unhappy ending/ruin. 2. *v.* to condemn (s.o./sth). **Dooms•day**, *n.* end of the world.

door [dɔː] *n.* barrier of wood/metal, etc., which closes an entrance; **front d.** = main door of a house; **back d.** = door at the back of a house; **he lives two doors down the street** = he lives two houses away. **door•keep•er**, *n.* person who is on guard at a main door. **door•knob**, *n.* handle or knob for opening/shutting a door. **door•man**, *n.* (*pl.* -men) person who is in attendance at a door (of a restaurant/hotel, etc.). **door•mat**, *n.* mat or carpet in front of a door. **door•step**, *n.* block of stone/wood, etc., forming the base of a doorway. **door•way**, *n.* space filled by a door.

dope [dəʊp] *n.* (a) *inf.* drug. (b) strong glue/varnish for making models. (c) *inf.* information. (d) *inf.* stupid fool. **dope•y**, *adj. inf.* stupid/silly.

dor•mant ['dɔːmənt] *adj.* sleeping; **d. account** = bank account which is not used; **d. plant** = plant which is not growing because it is winter; **d. volcano** = volcano which is not erupting, but which is not extinct.

dor•mer ['dɔːmə] *n.* **d. (window)** = window with a small gable roof jutting out from a sloping roof.

dor•mi•to•ry ['dɔːmɪtrɪ] *n.* (a) long room full of beds. (b) building which has many bedrooms and provides living quarters for students, etc.

dor•mouse ['dɔːmaʊs] *n.* (*pl.* **dormice**) small mouselike animal.

dor•sal ['dɔːsl] *adj.* (muscle/fin) on the back of an animal.

DOS [dɒs] disk operating system.

dose [dəʊs] 1. *n.* (a) quantity of medicine. (b) *inf.* attack of a disease. (c) *Sl.* attack of venereal disease. 2. *v.* to give (s.o.) medicine. **dos•age**, *n.* amount of medicine to be given.

dos•si•er ['dɒsɪə] *n.* collection of relevant papers.

dot [dɒt] 1. *n.* small round spot; **he arrived at three o'clock on the d.** = exactly at three o'clock. 2. *v.* **(dotted)** to mark with small spots; **dotted line** = line made up of small spots; **the hillside is dotted with houses** = there are houses here and there on the hillside. **dot-ma•trix print•er**, *n.* computer printer which forms letters from many small dots. **dot•ty**, *adj.* (-ier, -iest) *inf.* slightly mad.

dote [dəʊt] *v.* **to d. on s.o.** = to be very fond of s.o. **dot•age**, *n.* feebleness of mind from old age.

dot•ter•el ['dɒtərəl] *n.* type of field bird.

dot•tle ['dɒtl] *n.* mass of unburned tobacco at the bottom of a pipe.

dou•ble ['dʌbl] 1. *adj.* (a) with two parts; **d. bed** = bed for two people; **d. chin** = chin with a second fold of flesh beneath. (b) twice as big; **a d. whisky** = two measures of whisky; **it takes d. the time** = twice as long; **it is d. the distance** = twice as far. 2. *adv.* **I am seeing d.** = I can see two things when there is only one there. 3. *n.* (a) **on the d.** = at a run. (b) **he is my d.** = he and I look exactly alike. (c) **men's/women's/mixed doubles** = tennis matches for two men or two women or one man and one woman on each side. 4. *v.* (a) to multiply by two. (b) **he doubled back** = he turned around and came back along the same way. (c) **she was doubled up in pain** = was bent forward. **dou•ble-bar•rel•led**, *adj.* (a) (gun) with two barrels. (b) having two purposes. **dou•ble bass**, *n.* very large stringed musical instrument. **dou•ble-breast•ed**, *adj.* (jacket) which overlaps in front. **dou•ble-cross**, *v.* to trick (s.o.) when he thinks that you are working on his side. **dou•ble-cross•er**, *n.* trickster/cheat. **dou•ble deal•ing**, *n.* trickery. **dou•ble-deck•er**, *n.* (a) bus with an upper as well as a lower deck. (b) *inf.* sandwich made with three slices of bread. **dou•ble den•si•ty**, *adj. & n.* (computer disk) having twice the standard storage capacity. **dou•ble Dutch**, *n. inf.* nonsense. **dou•ble-edged**, *adj.* (a) with two sharp edges. (b) which has two quite different meanings. **dou•ble glaz•ing**, *n.* two panes of glass in windows, which insulate. **dou•ble he•lix**, *n.* structure of DNA molecules, comprising two parallel helical chains with a common axis. **dou•ble-joint•ed**, *adj.* with very flexible joints. very flexibly. **dou•ble-park**, *v.* to park alongside a car which is already parked at the side of the street. **dou•ble-park•ing**, *n.* parking alongside a car which is already parked at the side of the street. **dou•ble-quick,** *adj. & adv.* extremely fast. **dou•ble take,** *n.* second reaction which comes after a first. **dou•ble-talk,** *n.* words which mean sth quite different from what they seem. **dou•bly,** *adv.* twice.

dou•blet ['dʌblət] *n.* (a) tight-fitting jacket. (b) word of the same origin as another word.

doubt [daut] 1. *n.* not being sure; **to have doubts about** = not to be sure; **no d.** = of course/certainly; **in d.** = uncertain. 2. *v.* not to be sure of. **doubt•ful,** *adj.* uncertain. **doubt•ful•ly,** *adv.* hestitatingly. **doubt•less,** *adv.* certainly.

douche [duːʃ] *n.* spray of water to clean part of the body.

dough [dəu] *n.* (a) uncooked mixture of water and flour for making bread, etc. (b) *Sl.* money. **dough•nut,** *n.* small round or ring-shaped cake cooked by frying in oil. **dough•y,** *adj.* soft and wet (like uncooked dough).

dough•ty ['dauti] *adj.* (*poetic*) brave.

dour ['duə] *adj.* gloomy/silent. **dour•ly,** *adv.* gloomily.

douse [daus] *v.* to throw water on (sth).

dove [dʌv] *n.* (a) white domesticated pigeon. (b) politician who is in favor of negotiating for peace. (c) [dəuv] *v. see* **dive. dove•tail,** *v.* (a) to join (wood) together with a V-shaped joint. (b) to fit in neatly. **dove•cote,** *n.* house for doves.

dow•a•ger ['dauədʒə] *n.* widow of a nobleman who has kept her title and property.

dow•dy ['daudɪ] *adj.* (**-ier, -iest**) badly-dressed (person); dull/unfashionable (clothes). **dow•di•ly,** *adv.* in a dowdy way.

dow•el ['dauəl] *n.* round wooden peg like a nail for attaching pieces of wood together. **dow•el•ling,** *n.* **a piece of d.** = a long round stick of wood from which dowels can be cut.

dow•er ['dauə] *n.* share of property which belongs to a widow.

down [daun] 1. *adv., adj. & prep.* (a) toward the bottom; **he fell d.** = fell to the ground; **d. with examinations!** = let's do away with examinations; **he tried to go up the d. escalator** = the one which was going downward. (b) at the bottom; **she is d. with influenza** = she has gone to bed with influenza; *inf.* **d. under** = in Australia and New Zealand; **inflation is d. again** = inflation is lower again. 2. *n.* (a) soft feathers

(of a duck). (b) **the downs** = rounded chalk hills in the south of England. 3. *v.* to swallow quickly. **down-and-out,** *n.* tramp/person with no money who lives in the street. **down-at-heel,** *adj.* looking worn/shabby (clothes). **down•cast,** *adj.* gloomy/depressed. **down•fall,** *n.* collapse/ruin. **down•grade,** *v.* to reduce the status of (s.o.). **down•heart•ed,** *adj.* depressed/gloomy. **down•hill,** *adv.* toward the bottom (of a hill). **down•load,** *v.* to load data/program into a computer. **down pay•ment,** *n.* part of a total cost paid in advance. **down•pour,** *n.* heavy fall of rain. **down•right.** 1. *adj.* complete/distinct. 2. *adv.* completely/distinctly. **down•shift•ing,** *n.* changing to a less busy/materialistic lifestyle, usu. by moving house and job. **down•side,** *n.* negative/pessimistic view. **down•size,** *v.* (a) to make smaller. (b) to reduce a company's costs by reducing the size of its workforce. **down•stage,** *adv.* toward the front of a stage. **down•stairs,** *adv. & n.* on/to a lower, esp. the ground, floor. **down•stream,** *adj. & adv.* toward the mouth of a river. **down-to-earth,** *adj.* straightforward/matter-of-fact (way of speaking, etc.). **down•town,** *adv. & n.* (in/to the) central business district of a town. **down•trod•den,** *adj.* oppressed/badly treated. **down•ward,** *adj.* (movement) toward the bottom. **down•ward, downwards,** *adv.* toward the bottom. **down•y,** *adj.* covered with down/with soft feathers.

Down•ing Street ['daunɪŋstriːt] *n.* residence of the British Prime Minister; *inf.* the British government.

Down's syn•drome ['daunz'sɪndrəum] *n.* congenital defect, where the patient has slanting eyes, a wide flat face, and has difficulty in speaking.

dow•ry ['dauri] *n.* money or goods which a bride brings to her husband.

dowse [dauz] *v.* to look for water using a forked twig which moves above water. **dows•er,** *n.* person who dowses.

doy•en ['dɔiən] *n.* senior member of a group.

doze [dəuz] 1. *n.* short sleep. 2. *v.* to be half asleep; **he dozed off** = he went into a light sleep. **doz•y,** *adj.* sleepy.

doz•en ['dʌzn] *n.* twelve; **half a d. apples** = six apples; **dozens of people/times** = many people/times.

æ back, ɑː farm, ɒ top, aɪ pipe, au how, aiə fire, auə flower, ɔː bought, ɔi toy, e fed, eə hair, eɪ take, ə afraid, əu boat, əuə lower, vː word, iː heap, ɪ hit, ɪə hear, uː school, u book, ʌ but, b back, d dog, ð then, dʒ just, f fog, g go, h hand, j yes, k catch, l last, m mix, n nut, ŋ sing, p penny, r round, s some, ʃ short, t too, tʃ chop, θ thing, v voice, w was, z zoo, ʒ treasure

Dr. ['dɒktə] *abbreviation for* Doctor.
drab [dræb] *adj.* lacking bright colors; brown, gray.
drach•ma ['drækmə] *n.* unit of money used in Greece.
dra•co•ni•an [drə'kəunɪən] *adj.* very severe/harsh (law, etc.).
draft [drɑːft] 1. *n.* (a) rough plan (of a document). (b) obligatory military service. (c) order for money to be paid by a bank. (*also Brit.* **draught**) (d) pulling; **d. horse** = horse trained to pull heavy loads; **beer on d./d. beer** = beer which is pumped out of a barrel, by hand. (e) mouthful/swallow. (f) amount of a ship's bottom which is under water; **boat with a shallow draft** = boat which does not go very deep into the water. (g) breeze (in a room). 2. *v.* (a) to draw up a rough plan of. (b) to call (s.o.) for service; **drafts•man,** *Brit.* **draughtsman** ['drɑːftsmən] *n.* (*pl.* **-men**) person who draws plans. **drafts•man•ship,** *Brit.* **draughtsmanship** *n.* skill at drawing. **draft•y,** *Brit.* **draughty** *adj.* (-**ier, -iest**) full of breezes.
drag [dræg] 1. *n.* (a) long uphill climb; *Sl.* **what a d.!** = how boring! (b) *Sl.* wearing of women's clothes by a man; **he was in d.** (c) *inf.* one puff on a cigarette. 2. *v.* (**dragged**) (a) to pull sth heavy along. (b) to hang back/to stay behind; to go slowly. (c) to pull a net along the bottom of (a lake) to try to find sth. **drag•net,** *n.* net used to drag a lake; full search for criminals. **drag on,** *v.* to continue slowly. **drag out,** *v.* to pull out; to make (a story) last a long time.
drag•on ['drægən] *n.* mythological animal which breathes fire. **drag•on•fly,** *n.* common insect with brilliant transparent wings. **dragon mar•ket,** *n. inf.* an emerging market on the Pacific rim, e.g. Malaysia.
dra•goon [drə'guːn] 1. *n.* (*old*) soldier on horseback. 2. *v.* to force.
drain [dreɪn] 1. *n.* (a) pipe for carrying waste water; *inf.* **it's like pouring money down the d.** = it is a waste of money. (b) **d. on resources** = gradual loss of money; **brain d.** = movement of professional people to work for other companies or overseas for better pay. 2. *v.* (a) to remove (a liquid). (b) to drink the contents of (a glass). **drain•age,** *n.* system of pipes for taking away waste water. **drain•ing,** *n.* removal of excess liquid; **d. board** = sloping surface next to a sink for draining water off dishes. **drain•pipe,** *n.* pipe which takes away waste water.
drake [dreɪk] *n.* male duck.
dram [dræm] *n.* small drink (of spirits).
dra•ma ['drɑːmə] *n.* (a) serious theatrical performance; **d. department** = department which deals with plays. (b) series of serious events.
dra•mat•ic [drə'mætɪk] *adj.* (a) referring to

drama. (b) surprising; giving a shock.
dra•mat•i•cal•ly, *adv.* very surprisingly.
dra•mat•ics, *n. pl.* putting on plays.
dram•a•tist ['dræmətɪst] *n.* person who writes plays. **dram•a•ti•za•tion,** [dræmətaɪ'zeɪʃn] *n.* adaptation (of a novel) for the stage/for TV. **dram•a•tize** ['dræmətaɪz] *v.* (a) to adapt (a novel) for the stage/for TV. (b) to make (sth) seem much more dramatic than it really is.
drank [dræŋk] *v. see* **drink.**
drape [dreɪp] 1. *n.* **drapes** = long curtains. 2. *v.* to hang (clothes) around sth.
dra•per•y ['dreɪpərɪ] *n.* (a) (*usu.* **draperies**) long curtains. (b) cloth which is hung or falls in long, loose folds.
dras•tic ['dræstɪk] *adj.* severe/sudden. **dras•ti•cal•ly,** *adv.* suddenly.
draught [drɑːft] *n. Brit. see also* **draft.** **draughts** = game played with black and white counters on a board with black and white squares.
draw [drɔː] 1. *n.* (a) lottery. (b) attraction. (c) **he is quick on the d.** = he pulls out his gun and shoots quickly. (d) game where neither side wins. 2. *v.* (**drew, drawn**) (a) to make a picture with a pen or pencil. (b) to pull; **he drew the curtains** = he opened/closed the curtains; **to d. lots** = take a piece of paper/stick, etc., from a bundle, the person taking the marked paper/stick being the one selected; **he drew a blank** = he was unsuccessful in his search. (c) to move (sth) closer, etc. (d) not to have a winner in a game; **the match was drawn** = neither side won. (e) to collect liquid; **to d. blood** = to cut s.o. so that they bleed. (f) to take (money) from an account. **draw a•side,** *v.* to take (s.o.)/to move to one side. **draw back,** *v.* **he drew back the curtains** = he opened the curtains; **she drew back** = she moved backward.
draw•back, *n.* inconvenient thing; obstacle.
draw•bridge, *n.* bridge which can be raised or lowered to give access across water.
draw•er, *n.* sliding compartment in a desk or cupboard which you open by pulling on a handle; **chest of drawers** = piece of bedroom furniture made of several sliding compartments. **draw•ing,** *n.* picture done with pen or pencil; **d. board** = large board used by designers, on which paper is laid for drawing on; **it was back to the d. board** = he had to start the project all over again. **draw•ing room,** *n.* sitting room; room for sitting and talking in, but not eating. **drawn,** *adj.* looking tired. **draw out,** *v.* to pull (sth) out; to make (sth) last a long time. **draw•string,** *n.* string which, when pulled, closes a bag. **draw up,** *v.* to make (a plan, etc.).

drawl [drɔːl] 1. *n.* slow way of speaking. 2. *v.* to speak slowly, dragging the words.

drawn [drɔːn] *v. see* **draw.**

dray [dreɪ] *n.* low flat truck or cart for carrying barrels.

dread [dred] 1. *n.* great fear. 2. *v.* to fear greatly. **dread•ful,** *adj.* awful. **dread•ful•ly,** *adv.* awfully/extremely.

dream [driːm] 1. *n.* (a) things which you think you see happening when you are asleep. (b) lovely thing. 2. *v.* (**he dreamed/he dreamt** [dremt]) to think you see things happening while you are asleep; **I wouldn't d. of wearing pink socks** = I wouldn't ever think of wearing pink socks. **dream•er,** *n.* person who thinks a lot/who is out of touch with practical things. **dream•i•ly,** *adv.* as in a dream. **dream•less,** *adj.* without dreams. **dream tick•et,** *n.* partnership, usu. of two election candidates, thought to be perfect. **dream up,** *v.* to invent. **dream•y,** *adj.* like a dream.

drear•y ['drɪərɪ] *adj.* (-ier, -iest) sad/gloomy; not interesting. **drear•i•ly,** *adv.* sadly/gloomily. **drear•i•ness,** *n.* being dreary; dreary appearance.

dredge [dredʒ] *v.* (a) to scrape the bottom of (a river or lake) to remove sand or mud. (b) to sprinkle (a cake) with sugar, etc. **dredg•er,** *n.* (a) machine for removing sand or mud from the bottom of a river or lake; boat with such a machine in it. (b) container with holes in the top for sprinkling (sugar, etc.).

dregs [dregz] *n. pl.* sediment at the bottom of a bottle; rubbish.

drench [drentʃ] *v.* to soak; **drenched** = wet through.

dress [dres] 1. *n.* (*pl.* **-es**) (a) piece of woman's/girl's clothing, covering more or less all the body. (b) special clothes; **d. rehearsal** = rehearsal where the actors wear their costumes; **d. circle** = first balcony of seats above the orchestra in a theater; **d. coat** = man's formal black coat. 2. *v.* (a) to put on clothes. (b) to clean (a wound)/to put a bandage on (a wound). (c) to arrange a display in (a store window). (d) to prepare (meat or fowl) for cooking. **dress down,** *v.* to criticize. **dress•er,** *n.* (a) person in a theater who helps the actors with their costumes; **window d.** = person who arranges displays in store windows. (b) piece of kitchen furniture with open shelves above and cupboards below. **dress•ing,** *n.* (a) putting on clothes; **d. room**

= room for getting dressed, esp. room where an actor puts on his costume; **d. gown** = long robe worn over pyjamas or nightdress; **d. table** = bedroom table with mirrors. (b) sauce (for salad); **French d.** = sauce made of oil and vinegar. (c) bandage (for a wound). **dress•mak•er,** *n.* person who makes women's clothes. **dress•mak•ing,** *n.* making of women's clothes by hand. **dress up,** *v.* to put on a costume. **dress•y,** *adj.* very showily dressed; showy (clothes).

dres•sage ['dresɑːʒ] *n.* training of a horse which shows how obedient it is.

drew [druː] *v. see* **draw.**

drib•ble ['drɪbl] *v.* (a) to let drops of liquid run out of your mouth. (b) to move a ball by little amounts along as you are walking or running.

drib•lets, dribs and drabs ['drɪbləts, 'drɪbzən'dræbz] *n. pl.* little bits; **in dribs and drabs** = a little at a time.

dri•er ['draɪə] *n.* = **dry•er.**

drift [drɪft] 1. *n.* (a) general direction; **I got the general d. of his argument** = I understood the general sense of his argument. (b) pile of snow blown by the wind. (c) **North Atlantic D.** = current which crosses the North Atlantic. 2. *v.* (a) to let yourself move. (b) (*of snow*) to pile up. **drift•er,** *n.* person with no set plan in life/person who moves aimlessly from job to job. **drift•wood,** *n.* (*no pl.*) wood which floats and blows on to the shore.

drill [drɪl] 1. *n.* (a) machine for making holes (in wood/metal, etc.); **pneumatic d.** = machine driven by compressed air for making holes in roads. (b) military practice in marching, etc.; *inf.* **fire d.** = practice in reaching the life boats on a ship/practice in evacuating a building in case of fire. (c) small furrow in the ground in which you sow seeds. (d) thick cotton cloth. 2. *v.* (a) to make holes; **he is drilling for oil** = he is making holes in the ground in the hope of finding oil. (b) to do military practice.

dri•ly ['draɪlɪ] *adv.* = **dry•ly.**

drink [drɪŋk] 1. *n.* liquid which you swallow; alcohol; **soft drinks** = non-alcoholic drinks; **he has a d. problem** = he suffers from alcoholism; **he was much the worse for d.** = he was drunk. 2. *v.* (**drank; has drunk**) to swallow (liquid); **he was drinking at the bar** = he was drinking alcohol at the bar; **she doesn't d.** = she never drinks alcohol; **let's d. to the success of the expedition** = let us raise our glasses and wish it success. **drink•a•ble,** *adj.* nice to drink. **drink•er,** *n.* person who drinks (too much alcohol).

æ back, ɑː farm, ɒ top, aɪ pipe, aʊ how, aɪə fire, aʊə flower, ɔː bought, ɔɪ toy, e fed, eəhair, eɪ take, ə afraid, əʊ boat, əʊə lower, vː word, iː heap, ɪ hit, ɪə hear, uː school, ʊ book, ʌ but, b back, d dog, ð then, dʒ just, f fog, g go, h hand, j yes, k catch, l last, m mix, n nut, ŋ sing, p penny, r round, s some, ʃ short, t too, tʃ chop, θ thing, v voice, w was, z zoo, ʒ treasure

drink•ing, *n.* action of swallowing liquid; consumption of alcohol; alcoholism; **d. water** = water which is safe to drink.

drip [drɪp] 1. *n.* (a) small drop of water. (b) (*in a hospital*) **intravenous d.** = device which allows liquid to drip regularly into the bloodstream of a patient. 2. *v.* (**dripped**) to fall in drops; **the faucet is dripping** = drops of water are coming out of the faucet which has not been turned off tightly enough; **drip-dry shirt** = shirt which does not crease if hung to dry while wet. **drip•pings,** *n.* fat left in a pan after roasting meat.

drive [draɪv] 1. *n.* (a) ride in a motor vehicle. (b) way in which a car is propelled or guided; **car with front-wheel d.** = car where the engine is connected directly to the front wheels; **car with right-hand d.** = car where the driver sits on the right-hand side. (c) device in a computer which spins a disk. (d) short private road leading to a house. (e) stroke (in golf or cricket) where the ball is hit hard and far. (f) energy. (g) campaign (to collect money for charity). 2. *v.* (**drove; has driven**) (a) to make a motor vehicle travel in a certain direction; **I will d. you to the airport** = I will take you to the airport in my car. (b) to force/to push; **he was driven to it** = he was forced to do it; **she drives a hard bargain** = she is a very tough businesswoman; **the pressure of work was driving her frantic** = making her become frantic. (c) (*in golf, etc.*) to hit the ball hard and far. **drive a•long,** *v.* to ride along a road in a motor vehicle. **drive at,** *v.* **what is he driving at?** = what is he trying to say? **drive a•way,** *v.* (a) to force (sth/s.o.) to go away. (b) to ride away in a motor vehicle. **drive back,** *v.* (a) to force back. (b) to go/to come back in a motor vehicle. **drive in,** *v.* to go in by car; **drive-in movie theater/restaurant** = movie theater/restaurant where you can drive in in a car and watch a motion picture or eat while still sitting in the car. **drive on,** *v.* to continue one's journey. **driv•er,** *n.* person who drives (a motor vehicle); **driver's license** = permit which allows you to drive. **drive•way,** *n.* short private road leading to a house. **driv•ing.** 1. *adj.* (rain/snow) blown by the wind. 2. *n.* action of driving a motor vehicle; **d. test** = test taken before you can have a driving license; **d. school** = school where you learn to drive; **d. wheel** = wheel which moves a part of the machinery (in a machine)/steering wheel (in a car/truck, etc.).

driv•el ['drɪvl] *n.* nonsense.

driv•en ['drɪvn] *v. see* **drive.**

driz•zle ['drɪzl] 1. *n.* thin continuous rain. 2. *v.* to rain in a thin mist. **driz•zly,** *adj.* (weather) where it is raining in thin mist.

drogue [drəʊg] *n.* (*a*) funnel-shaped object, made of cloth, used to pull behind an aircraft for target practice. (b) parachute used as a brake.

droll [drəʊl] *adj.* funny in an odd way.

drom•e•dar•y ['drɒmədərɪ] *n.* camel with only one hump.

drone [drəʊn] 1. *n.* (a) male bee. (b) lazy person. (c) buzz (of an insect/an engine); monotonous noise. 2. *v.* to buzz; to talk slowly and in a monotonous voice.

drool [druːl] *v.* (a) to slobber. (b) *inf.* to show excessive pleasure about something.

droop [druːp] *v.* to hang down; **his spirits drooped** = he was feeling miserable.

drop [drɒp] 1. *n.* (a) tiny quantity of liquid which falls; **the doctor has given me some drops for my eyes** = liquid to be put in the eyes in small quantities. (b) small round jewel; small round candy. (c) fall. (d) jumping by a group of people with parachutes. 2. *v.* (**dropped**) to fall; to let (sth) fall; **she dropped a stitch** = she let a stitch slip in her knitting; *inf.* **d. me a line when you are in Paris** = send me a short letter when you are in Paris; **shall I d. you at your door?** = shall I drive you back and leave you at your door? **he has dropped the idea of going to live in Greece** = he has given up the idea; **the whole project has been dropped** = has been stopped; **d. it** = stop talking about it. **drop in,** *v.* to call on s.o. **drop-kick,** *n.* kick in football where you drop the ball to the ground and kick it as it is falling. **drop•let,** *n.* little drop. **drop off,** *v.* to fall off; **he dropped off** = he fell asleep. **drop out,** *v.* to stop competing; **he has dropped out** = he has given up his studies/has stopped living conventionally. **drop-out,** *n.* person who has stopped studying/stopped living conventionally. **drop•per,** *n.* glass tube for putting drops in eyes, etc. **drop•pings,** *n. pl.* solid waste matter from birds/animals.

drop•sy ['drɒpsɪ] *n.* disease where liquid forms in parts of the body. **drop•si•cal,** *adj.* suffering from dropsy.

dross [drɒs] *n.* worthless matter; refuse.

drought [draʊt] *n.* long period when there is no rain/when the land is dry.

drove [drəʊv] 1. *n.* large number (of people/animals). 2. *v. see* **drive.**

drown [draʊn] *v.* (a) to die by being unable to breathe in water. (b) to flood (a field). (c) to cover up (a noise).

drowse [draʊz] *v.* to be half asleep. **drow•si•ly,** *adv.* sleepily. **drow•si•ness,** *n.* feeling of wanting to go to sleep. **drow•sy,** *adj.* sleepy.

drub•bing ['drʌbɪŋ] *n.* beating.

drudge [drʌdʒ] *n.* person who does hard/boring work. **drudg•er•y,** *n.* hard/boring work.

drug [drʌg] 1. *n.* (a) medicine. (b) substance which affects the nerves, and which can be habit forming. 2. *v.* (**drugged**) to give a drug to (s.o.); **his coffee had been drugged** = s.o. had put a drug in his coffee. **drug•gist,** *n.* person who makes or sells medicines. **drug•store,** *n.* store having a druggist and usu. selling cosmetics, medical supplies, and a variety of other items.

dru•id ['druːɪd] *n.* priest of the old Celtic religion.

drum [drʌm] 1. *n.* (a) large round percussion instrument, covered with tightly stretched material and played with a stick; **d. major** = head of a military band. (b) large barrel; cylindrical container. 2. *v.* (**drummed**) (a) to bang on a drum; to tap your fingers quickly on a surface. (b) **to d. up support** = to encourage people vigorously to give their support. (c) **to d. sth into s.o.** = to make s.o. learn sth by constantly repeating it. **drum•mer,** *n.* person who plays the drums. **drum•stick,** *n.* (a) wooden stick for playing a drum. (b) lower part of a leg (of a cooked chicken/turkey, etc.).

drunk [drʌŋk] 1. *adj.* excited/incapable because of drinking alcohol. 2. *n.* person who is drunk. **drunk•ard,** *n.* person who is often drunk. **drunk•en,** *adj.* referring to an excess of alcohol. **drunk•en•ly,** *adv.* in a drunken way. **drunk•en•ness,** *n.* (habit of) being drunk.

drupe [druːp] *n.* fruit with a large stone (like a peach).

dry [draɪ] 1. *adj.* (**drier, driest**) (a) not wet; **he only had d. bread to eat** = bread with no butter or jam; **d. land** = solid land; **at the end of the play there wasn't a d. eye in the house** = the play made all the audience cry. (b) (*of wine*) not sweet. (c) (area) where alcohol is forbidden. (d) uninteresting/boring (book). (e) **d. sense of humor** = where you make jokes without seeming to know they are funny. 2. *v.* to stop being wet; to wipe (sth) until it is dry. **dry-clean,** *v.* to clean (clothes) with chemicals. **dry-clean•er's,** *n.* business establishment where clothes are dry-cleaned. **dry•er,** *n.* machine for drying; **spin d.** = machine which dries wet clothes by spinning them around very fast. **dry-goods store,** *n.* store which sells fabric and related merchandise, as opposed to groceries or hardware. **dry ice,** *n.*

solid carbon dioxide, used to produce very cold temperatures. **dry•ing,** *n.* action of making something dry; **I'll do the d.** = I'll dry the dishes. **dry•ly,** *adv.* in a sharp, sarcastic way. **dry•ness,** *n.* state of being dry. **dry out,** *v.* to make (sth) dry. **dry rot,** *n.* disease in wood which makes the wood powdery. **dry run,** *n.* practice. **dry up,** *v.* to stop flowing; **he dried up in the middle of his speech** = he stopped talking and could not continue.

dry•ad ['draɪæd] *n.* mythological wood goddess.

du•al ['djuəl] *adj.* double; in a pair; **he has d. nationality** = he is a citizen of two countries; **du•al•i•ty** [djuːˈælɪtɪ] *n.* being dual.

dub [dʌb] *v.* (**dubbed**) (a) to make (s.o.) a knight. (b) to add a dialogue to (a motion picture) in another language from the original.

dub•bin ['dʌbɪn] *n.* type of thick oil for making leather soft and waterproof.

du•bi•ous ['djuːbɪəs] *adj.* (a) doubtful/vague; suspicious. (b) hesitant. **du•bi•ous•ly,** *adv.* doubtfully. **du•bi•e•ty** [djuːˈbaɪətɪ], **du•bi•ous•ness,** *n.* doubt.

duch•ess ['dʌtʃes] *n.* wife/widow of a duke. **duch•y,** *n.* land ruled by a duke.

duck [dʌk] 1. *n.* (a) common water bird; female of this bird; meat of this bird used a food; **lame d.** = elected official who has lost an election but continues in office until his/her successor takes over. (b) strong cotton cloth. 2. *v.* (a) to lower your head quickly (to avoid hitting sth). (b) to push (s.o.) under water. (c) to avoid (an unpleasant job). **duck•boards,** *n. pl.* boards placed as a path across wet ground. **duck•ling,** *n.* baby duck. **duck•weed,** *n.* green weed which floats on the surface of ponds.

duct [dʌkt] *n.* tube for carrying air/liquid, etc.

duc•tile ['dʌktaɪl] *adj.* (metal) which can be pulled to form thin wires.

dud [dʌd] *n. inf.* failure; (shell) which will not explode.

dude [djuːd] *n.* dandy; visitor to a ranch.

dudg•eon ['dʌdʒən] *n.* **to leave in high d.** = to leave feeling very indignant.

due [djuː] 1. *adj.* (a) expected; **when is the baby d.?** = when is the baby expected to be born? (b) (money which is) owed. (c) just/deserved. (d) **d. to** = caused by. (e) **in d. course** = subsequently. 2. *adv.* **the plane flew d. west** = straight in a westerly direction. 3. *n.* what is

æ back, ɑː farm, ɒ top, aɪ pipe, aʊ how, aɪə fire, aʊə flower, ɔː bought, ɔɪ toy, e fed, eəhair, eɪ take, ə afraid, əʊ boat, əʊə lower, ɜː word, iː heap, ɪ hit, ɪə hear, uː school, ʊ book, ʌ but, b back, d dog, ð then, dʒ just, f fog, g go, h hand, j yes, k catch, l last, m mix, n nut, ŋ sing, p penny, r round, s some, ʃ short, t too, tʃ chop, θ thing, v voice, w was, z zoo, ʒ treasure

owed/deserved; **to give s.o. his d.** = to be fair to s.o.

du•el ['djʊəl] *n.* fight between two people (with swords/guns). **du•el•ist**, *n.* person who fights a duel.

du•en•na [djuː'enə] *n.* elderly Spanish lady, who acts as chaperone.

du•et [dju'et] *n.* piece of music played/sung by two people.

duf•fel, duffle ['dʌfl] *n.* **d. coat** = thick coat (often with a hood) fastened with toggles; **d. bag** = large bag, usu. canvas, which is closed by a string.

dug [dʌg] *v. see* **dig. dug•out**, *n.* hole in the ground, made as a shelter for soldiers; **d. canoe** = boat made from a tree trunk which has been hollowed out.

duke [djuːk] *n.* highest rank of nobleman.

dul•cet ['dʌlsɪt] *adj.* (voice, etc.) which sounds pleasant.

dul•ci•mer ['dʌlsɪmə] *n.* musical instrument with strings hit with little hammers.

dull [dʌl] *adj.* (**duller, dullest**) (a) not exciting/not interesting. (b) gloomy (weather). (c) not sharp (sound). (d) not bright; gloomy (color). (e) rather stupid. **dull•ard**, *n.* stupid person. **dull•ness**, *n.* (a) lack of excitement. (b) gloominess (of color/weather). (c) boredom. (d) slowness; stupidity. **dul•ly**, *adv.* in a dull way.

du•ly ['djuːlɪ] *adv.* properly; as you should.

dumb [dʌm] *adj.* (a) unable to speak. (b) stupid. **dumb•bell** ['dʌmbel] *n.* bar with weights on each end used by weightlifters. **dumb down**, *v.* to make sth, such as a TV program, less mentally challenging. **dumb•found** [dʌm'faʊnd] *v.* to surprise/to flabbergast; **I am dumbfounded at the news** = I am astonished by the news. **dumb•ly**, *adv.* silently/without saying anything.

dum•dum ['dʌmdʌm] *n.* soft-nosed bullet which flattens out when it hits its target.

dum•my ['dʌmɪ] *n.* (a) false thing; (b) stupid person; (c) model of a human figure used to show clothes (in a store or store window).

dump [dʌmp] 1. *n.* place to put garbage and other refuse; **what a d.!** = what an awful place. 2. *v.* (a) to put (sth) heavily on the ground. (b) to throw away; to get rid of. (c) to sell (surplus goods) at a very cheap price (usu. overseas).

dump•ling ['dʌmplɪŋ] *n.* small ball of dough served in stew; **apple dumplings** = apples baked in dough.

dumps [dʌmps] *n. pl. inf.* **down in the d.** = miserable.

dump•y ['dʌmpɪ] *adj.* short and squat.

dun [dʌn] 1. *n.* (a) debt collector. (b) demand to

be paid. 2. *adj.* dull brown color. 3. *v.* (**dunned**) to demand that (a debtor) pay you.

dunce [dʌns] *n.* stupid person.

dune [djuːn] *n.* **sand dunes** = grass-covered sandy ridges by the seashore.

dung [dʌŋ] *n.* solid waste matter (of animals).

dun•ga•rees [dʌŋgə'riːz] *n. pl.* overalls/working clothes, usu. of thick blue cloth.

dun•geon ['dʌndʒən] *n.* dark and unpleasant underground prison.

dunk [dʌŋk] *v.* to dip (bread, etc.) into a liquid.

dun•lin ['dʌnlɪn] *n.* small shore bird.

dun•no [də'nəʊ] *v. inf.* = (**I**) **don't know.**

du•o ['djuːəʊ] *n.* two people (usu. two performers).

du•o•dec•i•mal [djuːəʊ'desɪml] *adj.* (system of calculating) based on the number 12.

du•o•de•num [djuːəʊ'diːnəm] *n.* part of the intestine immediately below the stomach. **du•o•de•nal**, *adj.* referring to the duodenum.

dupe [djuːp] 1. *n.* person who has been tricked. 2. *v.* to trick (s.o.).

du•plex ['djuːpleks] *n.* (*pl.* -es) two-family house; **d. apartment** = apartment with rooms on two floors.

du•pli•cate 1. *n. & adj.* ['djuːplɪkət] copy/double. 2. *v.* ['djuːplɪkeɪt] to make a copy (of a letter, etc.); **you are just duplicating his work** = you are simply doing his work all over again. **du•pli•cat•ing**, *n.* action of making a copy. **du•pli•ca•tion** [djuːplɪ'keɪʃn] *n.* copying; repetition. **du•pli•ca•tor**, *n.* machine which makes copies of documents.

du•plic•i•ty [djuː'plɪsɪtɪ] *n.* dishonesty; tricking s.o.

du•ra•ble ['djʊərəbl] *adj.* which lasts/which does not wear away. **du•ra•bil•i•ty** [djʊərə-'bɪlɪtɪ] *n.* ability to last/not wear out. **du•ra•bly**, *adv.* in a durable way.

du•ra•tion [djuː'reɪʃn] *n.* period of time for which sth lasts.

du•ress [dju'res] *n.* force/illegal threats used to make s.o. do sth.

dur•ing ['djʊərɪŋ] *prep.* for the time sth lasts.

du•rum ['djuərəm] *n.* hard wheat, used for making pasta.

dusk [dʌsk] *n.* twilight/period in the evening just before it gets dark. **dusk•y**, *adj.* dark-skinned.

dust [dʌst] 1. *n.* thin layer of dry dirt. 2. *v.* (a) to remove dust from (sth). (b) to sprinkle (sugar) on a cake. **dust bowl**, *n.* area where the dry surface soil has been blown away. **dust cov•er**, *n.* dust jacket. **dust•er**, *n.* cloth for removing dust; **feather d.** = brush made of feathers for removing dust. **dust•ing**, *n.* (a) removing of dust. (b) sprinkling (of snow, sugar, etc.). **dust jack•et,** *n.* paper cover around a book. **dust•pan,** *n.* small wide shovel with a handle, for sweeping dirt into. **dust•y,** *adj.* (**-ier, -iest**) covered with dust.

Dutch [dʌtʃ] 1. *adj.* referring to the Netherlands; **D. courage** = courage which comes from being drunk; **D. treat** = party where each person pays his share. 2. *n.* (a) language spoken in the Netherlands. (b) **the Dutch** = the people of the Netherlands. (c) **to go d.** = to split the expenses. **Dutch•man, Dutchwoman,** (*pl.* **-men, -women**) man/woman from the Netherlands.

du•ty ['djuːtɪ] *n.* (a) what one has to do; service; **to be on d. all day; d. officer** = officer who is in charge at a particular time. (b) money which has to be paid; **d. free shop** = shop at an airport/on a boat where goods can be bought free of local tax. **du•ti•a•ble,** *adj.* (goods) on which a customs duty must be paid. **dut•i•ful,** *adj.* (person) who does what they should do. **dut•i•ful•ly,** *adv.* as one should.

du•vet ['duːveɪ] *n.* bag stuffed with feathers, used as the only covering for a bed.

DVD ['diːviːˈdiː] *abbrev. for* digital video disk.

dwarf [dwɔːf] 1. *n.* person who is much smaller than normal; variety of plant or animal which is smaller than usual; 2. *v.* to make (sth) appear small.

dwell [dwel] *v.* (**dwelt/dwelled**) to live. **dwell•er,** *n. & suffix* person who lives (in a place). **dwell•ing,** *n.* house. **dwell on,** *v.* to refer at length to (a subject).

dwin•dle ['dwɪndl] *v.* to get less. **dwin•dling,** *adj.* which is getting less.

dye [daɪ] 1. *n.* color used to stain cloth; 2. *v.* to stain with a color. **dye•ing,** *n.* staining (of cloth).

dy•ing ['daɪɪŋ] *adj.* about to die.

dyke [daɪk] *n. see* **dike.**

dy•na•mic [daɪˈnæmɪk] *adj.* energetic/forceful (person). **dy•nam•ics,** *n. pl.* study of objects in movement.

dy•na•mite ['daɪnəmaɪt] 1. *n.* high explosive. 2. *v.* to blow up with dynamite.

dy•na•mo ['daɪnəməʊ] *n.* (*pl.* **-os**) small electricity generator.

dy•nas•ty ['dɪnəstɪ] *n.* several generations of one family, esp. a family of rulers.

dys•en•ter•y ['dɪsəntrɪ] *n.* disease of the intestines.

dys•func•tion [dɪsˈfʌŋkʃən] *n.* (a) abnormal functioning of an organ. (b) abnormal functioning/breakdown of a family/relationship/groups, etc. **dys•func•tion•al,** *adj.* functioning abnormally.

dys•lex•i•a [dɪsˈleksɪə] *n.* being dyslexic. **dys•lex•ic,** *adj.* (person) who has great difficulty in reading and writing.

dys•pep•sia [dɪsˈpepsɪə] *n.* inability to digest food properly. **dys•pep•tic,** *adj.* unable to digest food properly.

dys•tro•phy ['dɪstrəfɪ] *n.* **muscular d.** = disease causing gradual weakening of the muscles. **dys•troph•ic** [dɪsˈtrɒfɪk] *adj.* (lake) with acid peaty water.

æ back, aː farm, ɒ top, aɪ pipe, aʊ how, aiə fire, aʊə flower, ɔː bought, ɔɪ toy, e fed, eəhair, eɪ take, ə afraid, əʊ boat, əʊə lower, vː word, iː heap, ɪ hit, ɪə hear, uː school, ʊ book, ʌ but, b back, d dog, ð then, dʒ just, f fog, g go, h hand, j yes, k catch, l last, m mix, n nut, ŋ sing, p penny, r round, s some, ʃ short, t too, tʃ chop, θ thing, v voice, w was, z zoo, ʒ treasure

Ee

each [iːtʃ] 1. *adj.* every. 2. *pron.* every person; everything. 3. **e. other** = both of two people or things; **we write to e. other.**

ea•ger ['iːgə] *adj.* very willing to do sth. **ea•ger•ly,** *adv.* in an eager way. **ea•ger•ness,** *n.* being eager.

ea•gle ['iːgl] *n.* large bird of prey. **ea•gle-eyed,** *adj.* (person) who can see very clearly/who notices small details.

ear ['ɪə] *n.* (a) part of the head, used for hearing; **middle e.** = space inside the head beyond the eardrum; **inner e.** = space inside the head, beyond the middle ear, which controls balance and hearing. (b) sense of hearing; sense of correct tone. (c) **e. of corn** = head of the corn plant, with rows of kernels. **ear•ache** ['ɪəreɪk] *n.* pain in an ear. **ear•drum,** *n.* tight skin inside the ear which resonates to sound waves and so allows you to hear. **ear•lobe,** *n.* lobe on an ear. **ear•mark,** *v.* to reserve (sth such as money) for a special purpose. **ear•phone,** *n.* part of a pair of headphones which fits over one ear. **ear•ring,** *n.* ring attached to the earlobe as an ornament. **ear•shot,** *n.* **within e./out of e.** = near enough to be heard/too far away to be heard.

earl [ɜːl] *n.* high-ranking nobleman.

ear•ly ['ɜːlɪ] (-ier, -iest) 1. *adv.* before the proper time; at the beginning of a period of time; **the train left five minutes e.; e. in the afternoon.** 2. *adj.* which happens at the beginning of a period of time; which happens before the usual time; **at an e. date** = soon.

earn [ɜːn] *v.* to be paid money for working. **earn•ings** ['ɜːnɪŋz] *n. pl.* amount of money earned; salary/wages.

ear•nest ['ɜːnɪst] 1. *adj.* serious. 2. *n.* (a) money paid as a guarantee. (b) **in e.** = seriously/really. **ear•nest•ly,** *adv.* seriously. **ear•nest•ness,** *n.* being earnest.

earth [ɜːθ] *n.* (a) planet on which we live; *inf.* **why on e. did you say that?** = whatever made you say that? (b) soil. **to run s.o. to e.** = to find s.o. after a difficult search. **earth•en** ['ɜːθən] *adj.* made of clay. **earth•en•ware,** *n. & adj.* (pottery) made of clay. **earth•ly,** *adj. inf.* **of no e. use** = of no possible use. **earth•quake,** *n.* shaking of the earth caused by a fault or un-

derground volcanic activity. **earth-shat•ter•ing,** *adj. inf.* momentous or upsetting (news). **earth•works,** *n. pl.* walls of earth built as defenses. **earth•worm,** *n.* worm/small animal which looks like a very small snake and lives in earth. **earth•y,** *adj.* (-ier, -iest) coarse/rude (humor).

ear•wig ['ɪəwɪg] *n.* small insect with curved pincers on its tail.

ease [iːz] 1. *n.* absence of difficulty; **ill at e.** = nervous/uncomfortable. 2. *v.* (a) to make less painful. (b) to make easy. (c) to make less tight. **ease off,** *v.* to become less. **ease up,** *v.* to slow down.

ea•sel ['iːzl] *n.* vertical frame on legs (to support a blackboard/painting, etc.).

ease•ment ['iːzmənt] *n.* right to use a path across someone else's property.

e•ast [iːst] 1. *n.* one of the points of the compass, the direction of the rising sun; the eastern part of a country; **the Far E.** = countries to the east of India; **the Middle E.** = countries to the east of Egypt and west of Pakistan; **the Near E.** = countries at the eastern end of the Mediterranean. 2. *adj.* of the east; **E. coast** = eastern part of the United States, on the Atlantic Ocean. 3. *adv.* toward the east. **east•bound,** *adj.* going toward the east. **east•er•ly,** *adj.* (a) **e. wind** = wind from the east. (b) toward the east. **east•ern,** *adj.* of the east. **east•ern•most,** *adj.* furthest east. **east•ward.** 1. *adj.* toward the east. 2. *adv.* (*also* **eastwards**) toward the east.

Eas•ter ['iːstə] *n.* Christian festival (in March or April); **E. Sunday** = Sunday celebrating Christ's rising from the dead; **E. egg** = chocolate or sugar egg eaten at Easter.

eas•y ['iːzɪ] (-ier, -iest) 1. *adj.* not difficult; **the house is an e. walk from the station** = is conveniently close to the station; **my boss is very e. to get along with** = not difficult to work for. 2. *adv.* **to take things e.** = to rest/to do only light work; **e. now!** = be careful/don't get excited! **go e. on/with the jam!** = don't take too much of it. **eas•i•ly,** *adv.* without difficulty. **eas•i•ness,** *n.* state of being easy/of not being difficult. **eas•y chair,** *n.* large comfortable armchair. **eas•y-go•ing,** *adj.* (person who is) easy to get on with/not very critical.

eat [iːt] v. (**ate** [et]; **has eaten**) to chew and swallow (food); **eating apple** = apple to be eaten raw, rather than cooked; **I had him eating out of my hand** = he did everything I told him to do; **he had to e. his words** = to take back what he had said. **eat•a•ble**, adj. edible. **eat•a•bles**, n. pl. things to eat. **eat away**, v. (of acid) to corrode. **eat•er**, n. person who eats. **eat in•to**, v. to reduce gradually. **eat up**, v. to finish eating all of sth; inf. **car that eats up gas** = car that uses a lot of gas.

eau de Co•logne [əʊdəkəˈləʊn] n. liquid with a light scent.

eaves [iːvz] n. pl. edge of a roof overhanging the wall. **eaves•drop**, v. (**eavesdropped**) to listen to a conversation which you are not supposed to hear. **eaves•drop•per**, n. person who eavesdrops.

ebb [eb] 1. n. (of tide) going down. 2. v. (of tide) to go down.

Eb•o•la vi•rus [iːˈbəʊlə] n. virus causing a serious contagious disease characterized by internal bleeding and fever.

eb•on•y [ˈebənɪ] n. black tropical wood.

e•bul•lient [ɪˈbʌljənt] adj. very excited/full of life. **e•bul•lience**, n. high spirits.

EC [ˈiːsiː] n. European Community.

ec•cen•tric [ɪkˈsentrɪk] adj. odd (person). **ec•cen•tri•cal•ly**, adv. in an eccentric way. **ec•cen•tric•i•ty** [eksenˈtrɪsɪtɪ] n. being eccentric.

ec•cle•si•as•ti•cal [ɪkliːzɪˈæstɪkl] adj. belonging to the church.

ECG [ˈiːsiːˈdʒiː] n. electrocardiogram.

ech•e•lon [ˈeʃəlɒn] n. (a) arrangement of separate things in steps, and not in a straight line. (b) group of people at a certain level in an organization.

ech•o [ˈekəʊ] 1. n. (pl. **echoes**) repeated sound reverberating in a cave, etc. 2. v. (of sound) to repeat.

éclair [eɪˈkleə] n. long cake made of pastry, filled with cream and covered with chocolate.

ec•lec•tic [ɪˈklektɪk] adj. taking ideas, etc., from several different sources.

e•clipse [ɪˈklɪps] 1. n. temporary disappearance of (part of) the sun or moon, because another body passes across them. 2. v. (a) to hide (another planet) by passing in front of it. (b) to be more brilliant/successful than s.o.

eco- [ˈiːkəʊ] prefix meaning ecology/ecological; **ecocentric; ecotourism.**

e•co•cen•tric [iːkəʊˈsentrɪk] adj. concerned for the environment; e.g. ecocentric planning.

e•co•friend•ly [ˈiːkəʊfrendlɪ] adj. having a positive (or negligible negative) impact on the environment.

E. coli [iːˈkəʊlaɪ] n. abbrev. for Escherichia coli.

e•col•o•gy [ɪˈkɒlədʒɪ] n. study of the relationship between plants and animals and their environment. **ec•o•log•i•cal** [iːkəˈlɒdʒɪkl] adj. referring to ecology. **e•col•o•gist**, n. person who studies ecology.

e•con•o•my [ɪˈkɒnəmɪ] n. (a) saving (of money or resources); e. **pack** = cheaper packet of goods. (b) way in which a country makes money; financial state of a country. **ec•o•nom•ic** [iːkəˈnɒmɪk] adj. referring to economy. **ec•o•nom•i•cal**, adj. which saves money or resources. **ec•o•nom•i•cal•ly**, adv. without waste. **ec•o•nom•ics**, n. (a) study of the finance of industry/of a country. (b) financial structure. **e•con•o•mist** [ɪˈkɒnəmɪst] n. person who specializes in the study of finance. **e•con•o•mize**, v. to e. (on) = to save/avoid waste.

e•co•ter•ror•ist [ˈiːkəʊterərɪst] n. person who uses violence in an attempt to further environmentalist goals.

e•co•tour•ism [ˈiːkəʊtʊərɪzəm] n. tourism that has a positive (or negligible negative) impact on the environment.

ec•ru [eɪˈkruː] n. pale fawn color.

ec•sta•sy [ˈekstəsɪ] n. great happiness. **ec•stat•ic** [ɪkˈstætɪk] adj. very happy. **ec•stat•i•cal•ly**, adv. extremely happy.

ECT [iːsiːˈtiː] n. electroconvulsive therapy.

ec•to•plasm [ˈektəʊplæzəm] n. substance said to come from the body of a person in a trance.

ECU [ˈekjuː] n. European Currency Unit.

ec•u•men•i•cal [iːkjuːˈmenɪkl] adj. referring to Christian unity/concerned with joining together all Christian groups.

ec•ze•ma [ˈeksɪmə] n. skin disease which causes itchy red spots.

ed•dy [ˈedɪ] 1. n. small swirl of water (in a stream). 2. v. to swirl around.

e•del•weiss [ˈeɪdəlveɪs] n. alpine plant with white flowers.

e•de•ma [ɪˈdiːmə] n. excess liquid gathering in tissues, causing a swelling.

edge [edʒ] 1. n. (a) (sharp) side of flat object;

æ back, aː farm, ɒ top, aɪ pipe, aʊ how, aɪə fire, aʊə flower, ɔː bought, ɔɪ toy, e fed, eə hair, eɪ take, ə afraid, əʊ boat, əʊə lower, vː word, iː heap, ɪ hit, ɪə hear, uː school, ʊ book, ʌ but, b back, d dog, ð then, dʒ just, f fog, g go, h hand, j yes, k catch, l last, m mix, n nut, ŋ sing, p penny, r round, s some, ʃ short, t too, tʃ chop, θ thing, v voice, w was, z zoo, ʒ treasure

the scraping noise set my teeth on e. = made me shudder; **on e.** = nervous/jumpy. (b) sharpened side of a knife/ax, etc. (c) point at the outside of sth; **a house at the e. of the forest. 2.** *v.* (a) to creep sideways. (b) to put along the edge; **a dress edged with silk. edge•wise, edgeways,** *adv.* sideways. **edg•ing,** *n.* material used to edge with. **edg•y,** *adj.* nervous/jumpy.

ed•i•ble ['edɪbl] *adj.* which can be safely eaten.

e•dict ['iːdɪkt] *n.* official order.

ed•i•fice ['edɪfɪs] *n.* large building.

ed•i•fy ['edɪfaɪ] *v.* (*formal*) to instruct and improve (s.o.). **ed•i•fi•ca•tion** [edɪfɪ'keɪʃn] *n.* instruction and improvement.

ed•it ['edɪt] *v.* to make notes on (a text); to change (a text) to make it more acceptable; to prepare (a text) for publication; to cut up (motion-picture film/tape) and stick it together in correct order to make it ready to be shown/played. **e•di•tion** [ɪ'dɪʃn] *n.* (a) number of books/papers printed at the same time; **first e.** = copy of the first printing of a book. (b) form in which a book is published. **ed•i•tor,** *n.* (a) person who makes notes on a text/who prepares a text for publication. (b) director or head of a newspaper or a department of a newspaper; **the sports e.** (c) device for editing. **ed•i•to•ri•al** [edɪ'tɔːrɪəl] 1. *adj.* referring to editors/to editing. 2. *n.* leading article written by the editor of a newspaper.

ed•u•cate ['edjukeɪt] *v.* to teach/to instruct (s.o.); **an educated person** = person who is cultivated. **ed•u•ca•tion** [edju'keɪʃn] *n.* (system of) teaching/being taught; **adult e.** = teaching of adults. **ed•u•ca•tion•al,** *adj.* referring to education/teaching/schools; **e. publisher** = publisher who produces school books. **ed•u•ca•tion•ist,** *n.* person who specializes in the study of teaching methods.

ed•u•tain•ment [edju'teɪnmənt] *n.* communication of educational material in an entertaining manner.

Ed•ward•i•an [ed'wɔːdjən] *adj.* referring to the time of Edward VII of England (1901–1910).

eel [iːl] *n.* long thin fish like a snake.

ee•rie ['ɪərɪ] *adj.* (**eerier, eeriest**) frightening/weird. **ee•ri•ly,** *adv.* in an eerie way. **ee•ri•ness,** *n.* being eerie.

ef•face [ɪ'feɪs] *v.* to rub out. **ef•face•ment,** *n.* rubbing out.

ef•fect [ɪ'fekt] 1. *n.* (a) result/influence; **this rule takes e./comes into e. on November 1st** = starts to be applied. (b) meaning; **words to that e.** = words with that meaning. (c) (*in theater/motion pictures/on radio*) **sound effects** = artificial or reproduced sounds (such as thunder, horses, creaking doors). 2. *v.* to pro-

duce/to carry out. **ef•fec•tive,** *adj.* (a) which produces a (good) result. (b) which takes effect; **a rule e. on November 1st. ef•fec•tive•ly,** *adv.* in a way which produces a good result. **ef•fec•tu•al,** *adj.* (*formal*) which produces the intended effect. **ef•fec•tu•al•ly,** *adv.* in an effectual way. **ef•fec•tu•ate,** *v.* to carry out (sth) effectively.

ef•fem•i•nate [ɪ'femɪnət] *adj.* (*of man*) behaving in a feminine way. **ef•fem•i•na•cy,** *n.* being effeminate.

ef•fer•vesce [efə'ves] *v.* (*of liquid*) to make bubbles giving off gas. **ef•fer•ves•cence,** *n.* bubbles in liquid; act of making bubbles. **ef•fer•ves•cent,** *adj.* which bubbles.

ef•fete [e'fiːt] *adj.* weak/with no strength left.

ef•fi•ca•cious [efɪ'keɪʃəs] *adj.* (medicine, etc.) which produces the correct result. **ef•fi•ca•cy** ['efɪkəsɪ] *n.* being effective; power to produce the correct result.

ef•fi•cien•cy [ɪ'fɪʃənsɪ] *n.* ability to produce the required result. **ef•fi•cient,** *adj.* able to work well/to produce the required result. **ef•fi•cient•ly,** *adv.* in an efficient way.

ef•fi•gy ['efɪdʒɪ] *n.* statue/model of s.o.

ef•flu•ent ['efluənt] *n.* sewage; liquid waste (from a factory). **ef•flu•vi•um,** *n.* hidden liquid which has a strong unpleasant smell.

ef•fort ['efət] *n.* use of physical energy. **ef•fort•less,** *adj.* without apparently using any energy.

ef•fron•ter•y [ɪ'frʌntərɪ] *n.* rudeness.

ef•fu•sive [ɪ'fjuːsɪv] *adj.* too enthusiastic (in thanks). **ef•fu•sive•ly,** *adv.* very enthusiastically.

e.g. [iː'dʒiː] *abbreviation for* exempli gratia, *meaning* for example.

e•gal•i•tar•i•an [ɪgælɪ'teərɪən] *adj. & n.* (person) who believes in equality for everyone.

egg [eg] 1. *n.* (a) ovum produced by a female animal. (b) hard-shelled cell, produced by a bird, esp. that of a hen. 2. *v.* **to e. s.o. on** = to encourage s.o. to do sth. **egg•cup,** *n.* holder for a boiled egg. **egg•head,** *n. inf.* intellectual. **egg•plant,** *n.* aubergine/purple fruit eaten as vegetable. **egg•shell,** *n.* shell around an egg; **e. paint** = paint with a slightly shiny matt finish. **egg•tim•er,** *n.* device for timing how long an egg is boiled.

e•go ['iːgəʊ] *n.* yourself; high opinion of yourself; **e. trip** = action which boosts your opinion of yourself. **e•go•cen•tric** [egəʊ'sentrɪk] *adj.* thinking only about yourself. **e•go•ism** ['egəʊɪzəm] *n.* thinking about oneself. **e•go•ist,** *n.* person who only thinks of himself/herself. **e•go•tism** ['egəʊtɪzəm] *n.* talking only about oneself. **e•go•tist,** *n.* person

who only talks about himself/herself.
e•go•tis•tic(al) [egəu'tɪstɪk(l)] *adj.* conceited.

e•gre•gious [ɪ'griːdʒəs] *adv.* very bad; shocking.

e•gret ['iːgrət] *n.* type of heron with beautiful white tail feathers.

E•gyp•tian [ɪ'dʒɪpʃn] 1. *adj.* referring to Egypt. 2. *n.* person from Egypt.

eh [eɪ] *inter.* showing surprise/inquiry.

ei•der ['aɪdə] *n.* type of duck. **ei•der•down** ['aɪdədaun] *n.* bed covering made of a large bag full of feathers.

eight [eɪt] (a) number 8. **he is e. (years old); come to see us at e. (o'clock).** (b) eight people (the crew of a rowing boat). **eight•een,** number 18; **the e. hundreds** = the years between 1800 and 1899. **eight•eenth, 18th,** *adj. & n.* referring to eighteen; **the e. century** = period from 1700 to 1799. **eighth, 8th,** *adj. & n.* referring to eight. **eight•i•eth, 80th,** *adj. & n.* referring to eighty. **eight•y,** number 80.

Eire ['ɛərə] *n.* Irish Republic.

ei•ther ['aɪðə, 'iːðə] 1. *adj. & pron.* (a) one or the other; **I don't believe e. of you.** (b) both; **there are trees on e. side of our house.** 2. *conj. & adv.* (*showing choice*) **e. you come here or I will come to you;** (*emphatic*) **he isn't French and he isn't American e.**

e•jac•u•late [ɪ'dʒækjuleɪt] *v.* (a) (*formal*) to exclaim/to say (sth) suddenly. (b) (*of male*) to produce sperm. **e•jac•u•la•tion** [ɪdʒækju-'leɪʃn] *n.* act of ejaculating; sperm which has been ejaculated.

e•ject [ɪ'dʒekt] *v.* to throw out. **ejection/ejector seat,** *n.* seat in an aircraft which throws the pilot out in an emergency.

eke [iːk] *v.* **to e. out** = to economize (savings)/to try not to use up (resources).

e•lab•o•rate 1. *adj.* [ɪ'læbərət] very detailed, very complicated. 2. *v.* [ɪ'læbəreɪt] to go into details. **e•lab•o•ra•tion** [ɪlæbʊ'reɪʃn] *n.* being elaborate; detailed explanation. **e•lab•o•rate•ly,** *adv.* in a complicated/detailed way.

e•land ['iːlənd] *n.* large S. African antelope.

e•lapse [ɪ'læps] *v.* (*of time*) to pass.

e•las•tic [ɪ'læstɪk] 1. *adj.* which stretches and contracts; not rigid. 2. *n.* rubber band. **e•las•tic•i•ty** [ɪlæ'stɪsɪtɪ] *n.* ability to stretch.

e•lat•ed [ɪ'leɪtɪd] *adj.* very excited and pleased.

e•la•tion [ɪ'leɪʃn] *n.* feeling of excitement and pleasure.

el•bow ['elbəu] *n.* joint in the arm. **el•bow•room,** *n.* space to move about.

eld•er ['eldə] 1. *adj.* older (person); **e. statesman** = statesman who is older (and wiser) than others. 2. *n.* (a) older person. (b) common tree with white flowers and bunches of small purple berries. **eld•er•ber•ry,** *n.* (a) elder tree. (b) fruit of an elder. **eld•er•ly,** *adj.* quite old. **eld•est,** *adj.* oldest (of a group).

El Do•ra•do [eldɒ'rɑːdəu] *n.* legendary country of gold.

e•lect [ɪ'lekt] 1. *v.* (a) to choose by voting. (b) **to e. to do sth** = to choose to do sth. 2. *suffix* showing person who has been elected to a post, but who has not taken it up officially; **the mayor-elect. e•lec•tion** [ɪ'lekʃn] *n.* process of choosing by voting; **general e.** = regularly scheduled election for local, state, or national office. **e•lec•tion•eer•ing,** *n.* working for an election campaign. **e•lec•tive,** *adj.* which can be chosen. **e•lec•tor,** *n.* person who is qualified to vote in an election. **e•lec•tor•al,** *adj.* referring to an election; **e. college** = group of people elected to elect s.o. (such as a president). **e•lec•tor•ate,** *n.* all the people in a country who are qualified to vote.

e•lec•tric [ɪ'lektrɪk] *adj.* (a) generating/worked by electricity. (b) **the atmosphere was e.** = full of excitement. **e•lec•tri•cal,** *adj.* referring to electricity. **e•lec•tri•cal•ly,** *adj.* by electricity. **e•lec•tric chair,** *n.* chair used to execute criminals by passing a strong electric current through their bodies. **e•lec•tri•cian** [elek'trɪʃn] *n.* person who installs or works on electrical wiring or equipment. **e•lec•tric•i•ty** [elek'trɪsɪtɪ] *n.* form of energy used for power. **e•lec•tri•fi•ca•tion** [ɪlektrɪfɪ'keɪʃn] *n.* changing to an electric source of power. **e•lec•tri•fy** [ɪ'lektrɪfaɪ] *v.* (a) to convert to an electric source of power. (b) to startle and excite. **e•lec•tro•car•di•o•gram,** *n.* chart made by an electrocardiograph. **e•lec•tro•car•di•o•graph,** *n.* device for recording the electric impulses made by a beating heart. **e•lec•tro•con•vul•sive ther•a•py,** *n.* treatment of mental disorders by giving the patient small electric shocks. **e•lec•tro•cute,** *v.* to kill by electricity. **e•lec•tro•cu•tion** [ɪlektrə'kjuːʃn] *n.* killing by electricity. **e•lec•trode,** *n.* rod which

---

æ back, ɑː farm, ɒ top, aɪ pipe, aʊ how, aiə fire, aʊə flower, ɔː bought, ɔɪ toy, e fed, eəhair, eɪ take, ə afraid, əu boat, əuə lower, vː word, iː heap, ɪ hit, ɪə hear, uː school, u book, ʌ but, b back, d dog, ð then, dʒ just, f fog, g go, h hand, j yes, k catch, l last, m mix, n nut, ŋ sing, p penny, r round, s some, ʃ short, t too, tʃ chop, θ thing, v voice, w was, z zoo, ʒ treasure

leads the electric current into or out of a cell.
e•lec•tro•en•ceph•a•lo•gram, *n.* chart made by an electroencephalograph.
e•lec•tro•en•ceph•a•lo•graph, *n.* device for recording the electric impulses made by the brain. **e•lec•trol•y•sis** [ɪlek'trɒlɪsɪs] *n.* (a) separation of the parts of a compound liquid by passing an electric current through it. (b) removal of unwanted hair by electric current. **e•lec•tro•lyte** [ɪ'lektrəlaɪt] *n.* chemical solution which can be broken into its parts by electrolysis. **e•lec•tro•mag•net**, *n.* magnet made of material wound with a coil of wire with an electric current passing through it. **e•lec•tro•mag•net•ic**, *adj.* made by an electromagnet. **e•lec•tro•mo•tive**, *adj.* (force) which produces an electric current. **e•lec•tron**, *n.* basic particle in an atom. **e•lec•tron•ic** [ɪlek'trɒnɪk] *adj.* referring to electrons or electronics. **e•lec•tron•ic mail**, *n.* system of sending messages from one computer to another, using telephone lines. **e•lec•tron•i•cal•ly**, *adv.* in an electronic way. **e•lec•tron•ic or•gan•iz•er**, *n. see* **personal organizer. e•lec•tron•ics**, *n.* science of conduction of electrons; industry which makes TV sets/radios/calculators, etc. **e•lec•tro•plate**, *v.* to coat (a metal, usu. copper), with a thin layer of silver by means of electrolysis.

el•ee•mos•y•nar•y [eli:məu'saɪnəri] *adj.* referring to charity.

el•e•gant ['elɪgənt] *adj.* well dressed; very fashionable. **el•e•gance**, *n.* being elegant. **el•e•gant•ly**, *adv.* fashionably.

el•e•gy ['elədʒɪ] *n.* sad poem about s.o. who is dead. **el•e•gi•ac** [elɪ'dʒaɪək] *adj.* sad and regretful.

el•e•ment ['elɪmənt] *n.* (a) basic chemical substance. (b) basic part (of sth). (c) natural environment; **he's in his e. when he's talking about gardening.** (d) **the elements** = bad weather (wind/rain, etc.). (e) wire which heats in an electric heater/stove, etc. **el•e•men•ta•ry** [elɪ'mentrɪ] *adj.* basic/simple; **e. mathematics. el•e•men•ta•ry school**, *n.* school which includes the first through the sixth or eighth grades.

el•e•phant ['elɪfənt] *n.* very large African or Indian animal, with a trunk and tusks; **white e.** = expensive but useless thing. **el•e•phan•ti•a•sis** [elɪfən'taɪəsɪs] *n.* tropical disease where parts of the body become huge. **el•e•phan•tine** [elɪ'fæntaɪn] *adj.* very large, heavy and difficult to move.

el•e•vate ['elɪveɪt] *v.* to raise up. **el•e•va•tion** [elɪ'veɪʃn] *n.* (a) raising. (b)

(drawing of) one side of a building. (c) height (above sea-level). **el•e•va•tor**, *n.* (a) device for lifting people or goods from one floor of a building to another; **grain e.** = large building for hoisting and storing grain. (b) part of the tail of an aircraft.

e•lev•en [ɪ'levn] *adj. & n.* (a) number 11; **he arrived at e. (o'clock); he is e. (years old).** (b) eleven people (as in a sports team). **e•lev•enth, 11th,** *adj. & n.* referring to eleven; **at the e. hour** = at the last minute; **the e. century** = period from 1000 to 1099.

elf [elf] *n.* (*pl.* **elves** [elvz]) small, usu. male, supernatural being. **elf•in**, *adj.* referring to elves.

e•lic•it [ɪ'lɪsɪt] *v.* to obtain (information) (**from** s.o.).

e•lide [ɪ'laɪd] *v.* to omit a sound when speaking. **e•li•sion** [ɪ'lɪʒn] *n.* omitting of a sound.

el•i•gi•ble ['elɪdʒɪbl] *adj.* able to be chosen (for sth); **e. bachelor** = man who has all the qualifications (esp. money) to be married. **el•i•gi•bil•i•ty** [elɪdʒə'bɪlɪtɪ] *n.* being eligible.

e•lim•i•nate [ɪ'lɪmɪneɪt] *v.* (a) to remove (waste, etc.). (b) to exclude (s.o.) after a test. **e•lim•i•na•tion** [ɪlɪmɪ'neɪʃn] *n.* act of eliminating. **e•lim•i•na•tor**, *n.* game, etc., which decides who is eliminated.

e•lite [ei'li:t] *n.* group of privileged people/the best people. **e•lit•ism**, *n.* rule by an elite.

e•lix•ir [ɪ'lɪksə] *n.* medicine which people imagine will cure everything.

E•liz•a•be•than [elɪzə'bi:θən] *adj.* referring to the time of Elizabeth I of England (1558–1603).

elk [elk] *n.* (*pl.* **elk**) large European deer with flat antlers.

el•lipse [ɪ'lɪps] *n.* oval shape. **el•lip•sis**, *n.* absence of a word which is needed to complete the meaning of a phrase. **el•lip•tic(al)**, *adj.* (a) oval. (b) difficult to understand because of a missing word or phrase.

elm [elm] *n.* large deciduous tree; **Dutch e. disease** = disease which kills elms.

el•o•cu•tion [elə'kju:ʃn] *n.* clear and elegant way of speaking.

e•lon•gate ['i:lɒŋgeɪt] *v.* to stretch out to make longer. **e•long•a•tion** [i:lɒŋ'geɪʃn] *n.* act of elongating.

e•lope [ɪ'ləup] *v.* to run away from home to get married (**with** s.o.). **e•lope•ment**, *n.* act of eloping.

el•o•quence ['eləkwəns] *n.* art of speaking well. **el•o•quent**, *adj.* good and persuasive (speech). **el•o•quent•ly**, *adv.* in an eloquent way.

else [els] *adv.* (a) otherwise; **you had better pay,**

or e. = or I will force you to pay. (b) other; **anyone e.** = any other person; **nobody e.** = no other person; **anything e.** = any other thing; **nowhere e.** = no other place; **somewhere e./someplace e.** = in some other place. **else•where,** *adv.* somewhere else; in other places.

e•lu•ci•date [ɪ'luːsɪdeɪt] *v.* to make clear/to make easy to understand. **e•lu•ci•da•tion** [ɪluːsɪ'deɪʃn] *n.* making clear.

e•lude [ɪ'luːd] *v.* to escape/to avoid (capture). **e•lu•sion,** *n.* act of eluding. **e•lu•sive** [ɪ'luːsɪv] *adj.* difficult to find.

el•ver ['elvə] *n.* baby eel.

em [em] *n.* space in printing equal to the width of the letter "m".

e•ma•ci•at•ed [ɪ'meɪsɪeɪtɪd] *adj.* extremely thin. **e•ma•ci•a•tion,** *n.* being emaciated.

e•mail ['iːmeɪl] *n. see* **e•lec•tron•ic mail.**

em•a•nate ['emɪneɪt] *v.* to come **from.** **em•a•na•tion,** *n.* thing which comes.

e•man•ci•pate [ɪ'mænsɪpeɪt] *v.* to make (s.o.) free. **e•man•ci•pa•tion** [ɪmænsɪ'peɪʃn] *n.* setting free.

e•mas•cu•late [ɪ'mæskjuleɪt] *v.* to make feeble. **e•mas•cu•la•tion** [ɪmæskju'leɪʃn] *n.* making feeble.

em•balm [ɪm'bɑːm] *v.* to treat (a dead body) with chemicals to prevent it from decaying.

em•bank•ment [ɪm'bæŋkmənt] *n.* artificial bank (along a river); road along such a bank.

em•bar•go [ɪm'bɑːgəʊ] 1. *n. (pl.* -oes) official prohibition (**on** goods/traffic/information). 2. *v.* to prohibit (sth) officially.

em•bark [ɪm'bɑːk] *v.* 1. to go on board a ship; **the passengers embarked at New York.** 2. **to e. on sth** = to start doing sth. **em•bar•ka•tion** [embɑː'keɪʃn] *n.* act of going on board a ship or aircraft.

em•bar•rass [ɪm'bærəs] *v.* to make (s.o.) feel uncomfortable (by rudeness/indecency, etc.). **em•bar•rass•ment,** *n.* act of making s.o. feel uncomfortable.

em•bas•sy ['embəsɪ] *n.* home or offices of an ambassador.

em•bat•tled [ɪm'bætld] *adj.* under attack; constantly criticized.

em•bed [ɪm'bed] *v.* (**embedded**) to fix (sth) into a mass of concrete/flesh, etc.

em•bel•lish [ɪm'belɪʃ] *v.* to decorate/to make beautiful. **em•bel•lish•ments,** *n. pl.* decorations/beautiful improvements.

em•bers ['embəz] *n. pl.* pieces of wood/coal which are red hot.

em•bez•zle [ɪm'bezl] *v.* to steal (money which you are looking after for s.o.). **em•bez•zle•ment,** *n.* act of embezzling. **em•bez•zler,** *n.* person who embezzles.

em•bit•tered [ɪm'bɪtəd] *adj. (of person)* made angry and sad (by disappointment/envy).

em•blem ['embləm] *n.* design which is adopted as the characteristic of a country/team/town, etc. **em•blem•at•ic** [emblə'mætɪk] *adj.* which acts as an emblem.

em•bod•y [ɪm'bɒdɪ] *v.* to show (an idea) in a physical form. **em•bod•i•ment,** *n.* physical expression of an idea.

em•bo•lism ['embəlɪzəm] *n.* blocking of a blood vessel by a blood clot or a bubble of air.

em•boss [ɪm'bɒs] *v.* to raise (a design) above a flat surface; **embossed letterhead** = address pressed on writing paper so that it stands above the surface.

em•brace [ɪm'breɪs] *v.* (a) to hold and kiss (s.o.) as a gesture of affection. (b) to become a convert to (a belief).

em•bro•ca•tion [embrə'keɪʃn] *n.* liquid which you rub into parts of the body which are stiff.

em•broi•der [ɪm'brɔɪdə] *v.* to make artistic patterns by sewing with colored threads. **em•broi•der•y,** *n.* art of sewing flower designs/patterns.

em•broil [em'brɔɪl] *v.* to involve (s.o.) in a quarrel.

em•bry•o ['embrɪəʊ] *n. (pl.* -os) earliest state of a living organism; rudimentary idea. **em•bry•ol•o•gy,** *n.* study of embryos. **em•bry•on•ic** [embrɪ'ɒnɪk] *adj.* original/in a very early state.

e•mend [iː'mend] *v.* to change/to make correct. **e•men•da•tion** [iːmen'deɪʃn] *n.* change/correction.

em•er•ald ['emrəld] *adj. & n.* green precious stone; color of this stone.

e•merge [ɪ'mɜːdʒ] *v.* to come out (**from** inside sth); to become apparent/known. **e•mer•gence,** *n.* act of emerging. **e•mer•gent,** *adj.* **e. nations** = countries which are slowly becoming economically independent.

e•mer•gen•cy [ɪ'mɜːdʒənsɪ] *n.* dangerous state where decisions have to be made quickly (such as fire/accident/breakdown of law and order); **state of e.** = when normal administra-

---

æ back, ɑː farm, ɒ top, aɪ pipe, aʊ how, aɪə fire, aʊə flower, ɔː bought, ɔɪ toy, e fed, eə hair, eɪ take, ə afraid, əʊ boat, əʊə lower, vː word, iː heap, ɪ hit, ɪə hear, uː school, ʊ book, ʌ but, b back, d dog, ð then, dʒ just, f fog, g go, h hand, j yes, k catch, l last, m mix, n nut, ŋ sing, p penny, r round, s some, ʃ short, t too, tʃ chop, θ thing, v voice, w was, z zoo, ʒ treasure

tive processes are taken over by the police or armed forces; **e. exit** = door used when a fire breaks out; **e. operation** = operation carried out at short notice because the patient is seriously ill; **e. services** = the police, fire and ambulance services.

e•mer•i•tus [ɪ'merɪtəs] *adj.* (professor) who has retired but keeps his title.

em•er•y ['eməri] *n.* fine crystals used for polishing. **em•er•y board,** *n.* thin stick of cardboard covered with fine crystals, used for filing fingernails. **em•er•y pa•per,** *n.* fine sandpaper.

e•met•ic [ɪ'metɪk] *n.* substance which makes you vomit.

em•i•grate ['emɪɡreɪt] *v.* to leave a country to live in another. **em•i•grant,** *n.* person who emigrates. **em•i•gra•tion** [emɪ'ɡreɪʃn] *n.* act of leaving a country to live in another. **em•i•gré** ['emɪɡreɪ] *n.* person who has emigrated for political reasons.

em•i•nence ['emɪnəns] *n.* high place; high rank. **em•i•nent** ['emɪnənt] *adj.* very highly respected because of position or work. **em•i•nent•ly,** *adv.* remarkably; particularly.

e•mir ['emɪə] *n.* Muslim ruler. **e•mir•ate,** *n.* country ruled by an emir.

em•is•sar•y ['emɪsəri] *n.* person sent to negotiate on s.o.'s behalf.

e•mit [ɪ'mɪt] *v.* (**emitted**) to send out (a sound/smoke, etc.). **e•mis•sion,** *n.* act of emitting; thing emitted.

e•mol•lient [ɪ'mɒlɪənt] *adj. & n.* (substance) which softens.

e•mol•u•ment [ɪ'mɒljʊmənt] *n.* (*formal*) payment/salary.

e•mo•tion [ɪ'məʊʃn] *n.* (strong) feeling. **e•mo•tion•al,** *adj.* showing emotion. **e•mo•tion•al•ly,** *adv.* in an emotional way. **e•mo•tive,** *adj.* which is likely to cause strong feeling.

em•pan•el [ɪm'pænəl] *v. see* **impanel.**

em•pa•thy ['empəθɪ] *n.* being able to share the feelings of another person, by imagining yourself as that person.

em•per•or ['emprə] *n.* ruler of an empire.

em•pha•size ['emfəsaɪz] *v.* to stress the importance of (sth). **em•pha•sis** ['emfəsɪs] *n.* stress (usu. in speech). **em•phat•ic** [ɪm-'fætɪk] *adj.* using emphasis. **em•phat•i•cal•ly,** *adv.* in a forceful way.

em•pire ['empaɪə] *n.* large number of territories ruled by a central government.

em•pir•i•cal [em'pɪrɪkl] *adj.* based on practical experiment and not on theory.

em•place•ment [ɪm'pleɪsmənt] *n.* place where guns are set.

em•ploy [ɪm'plɔɪ] *v.* (a) to give (s.o.) regular work. (b) to use. **em•ploy•ee** [emplɔɪ'iː] *n.* person who is employed. **em•ploy•er,** *n.* person who gives work to people and pays them. **em•ploy•ment,** *n.* regular paid work.

em•po•ri•um [ɪm'pɔːrɪəm] *n.* large store, usu. selling a large variety of merchandise.

em•pow•er [ɪm'paʊə] *v.* to give (s.o.) the authority to do sth.

em•press ['emprəs] *n.* woman ruler of an empire; wife/widow of an emperor.

emp•ty ['emtɪ] 1. *adj.* with nothing inside. 2. *n.* thing, usu. bottle, which has nothing in it. 3. *v.* to make (sth) empty; to remove (the contents) from sth. **emp•ti•ness,** *n.* being empty. **emp•ty-hand•ed,** *adj.* with no results; having received nothing.

EMS [iːem'es] *n.* European Monetary System.

e•mu ['iːmjuː] *n.* large Australian bird which cannot fly.

em•u•late ['emjʊleɪt] *v.* to try to do as well as or better than (s.o.). **em•u•la•tion** [emjʊ-'leɪʃn] *n.* act of emulating.

e•mul•sion [ɪ'mʌlʃn] *n.* mixture of two liquids which do not unite completely, such as oil and water. **e•mul•si•fi•er,** *n.* thing which emulsifies. **e•mul•si•fy,** *v.* to make into an emulsion.

en [en] *n.* space in printing equal to the width of the letter "n".

en•a•ble [ɪ'neɪbl] *v.* to make it possible for s.o. to do sth.

en•act [ɪ'nækt] *v.* to make (a law). **en•act•ment,** *n.* making (of a law).

e•nam•el [ɪ'næml] 1. *n.* (a) very hard covering of color. (b) hard colored coating fixed to metal by heating. (c) hard coating on the teeth. 2. *v.* (**enameled**) to cover with very hard color.

en•am•oured [ɪ'næməd] *adj.* **I'm not e. of her hair style** = I don't like it very much.

en bloc [ɒn'blɒk] *adv.* French. all together as a group.

en•camped [ɪn'kæmpd] *adj.* in a camp. **en•camp•ment,** *n.* large camp.

en•cap•su•late [ɪn'kæpsjʊleɪt] *v.* to put in a capsule; to put in a shortened form.

en•case [ɪn'keɪs] *v.* to surround as if in a case.

en•chant [ɪn'tʃɑːnt] *v.* to charm. **en•chant•ing,** *adj.* very beautiful/magical. **en•chant•ment,** *n.* magic spell.

en•cir•cle [ɪn'sɜːkl] *v.* to surround completely.

en•clave ['enkleɪv] *n.* small group/small area completely surrounded by another quite different and larger group/mass.

en•close [ɪn'kləʊz] *v.* to put (an object) inside sth; **I am enclosing a bill with my letter. en•clo•sure** [ɪn'kləʊʒə] *n.* (a) fenced area for keeping animals. (b) paper enclosed with a letter in an envelope.

en•code [en'kəud] v. to put data/a message into code.

en•co•mi•um [ɪn'kəumɪəm] n. (formal) praise.

en•com•pass [ɪn'kʌmpəs] v. to surround.

en•core ['ɒŋkɔ:] 1. n. (a) calling (by the audience) for a performer to repeat a song, a piece of music. (b) song/piece of music repeated at the request of the audience. 2. v. to call for a song, etc., to be repeated.

en•coun•ter [ɪn'kauntə] 1. n. (a) meeting. (b) short conflict. 2. v. to meet.

en•cour•age [ɪn'kʌrɪdʒ] v. to give (s.o.) the confidence to do sth. **en•cour•age•ment,** n. giving s.o. the confidence to do sth. **en•cour•ag•ing,** adj. which encourages.

en•croach [ɪn'krəutʃ] v. to e. on = to occupy space belonging to s.o. else. **en•croach•ment,** n. act of encroaching.

en•crust [ɪn'krʌst] v. see incrust.

en•cum•ber [ɪn'kʌmbə] v. (formal) to weigh down (s.o.) with sth. **en•cum•brance,** n. thing which encumbers.

en•cyc•li•cal [ɪn'sɪklɪkl] n. solemn letter from the Pope.

en•cy•clo•pe•di•a, encyclopaedia [ɪnsaɪklə'pi:dɪə] n. reference book which gives facts about things/people/events, etc. **en•cy•clo•pe•dic, encyclopaedic,** adj. like an encyclopedia.

end [end] 1. n. (a) final part; inf. no e. of = very many; to go off the deep e. = to act in an irrational way; to be at a loose e. = to have nothing to do; to make ends meet = to have enough money to live on. (b) final part of a period of time. (c) aim; to this e. = in order to do this. 2. v. to finish. **end•game,** n. way of playing the last moves in chess game. **end•ing,** n. way a story, etc., finishes. **end•less,** adj. with no apparent end. **end•less•ly,** adv. with no apparent end. **end•pa•pers,** n. pages (usually left blank) at the beginning and end of a book. **end•ways, endwise,** adv. with the end first.

en•dan•ger [ɪn'deɪndʒə] v. to put in danger.

en•dear [ɪn'dɪə] v. to e. s.o. to s.o. = to make s.o. loved by s.o. **en•dear•ment,** n. term of e. = word showing that you love.

en•deav•or, Brit. en•deav•our [ɪn'devə] 1. n. (formal) attempt. 2. v. (formal) to try hard.

en•dem•ic [en'demɪk] adj. (disease) which is often found in a particular place.

en•dive ['endɪv] n. salad vegetable with curly leaves.

en•do•car•di•um [endəu'kɑ:dɪəm] n. membrane lining the heart.

en•do•crine ['endəkraɪn] adj. e. gland = gland which makes hormones and passes them directly into the bloodstream without using ducts.

en•dorse [ɪn'dɔ:s] v. to show approval; to e. a check = to sign it on the back to show it is yours. **en•dorse•ment,** n. approval.

en•dow [ɪn'dau] v. (a) to give a regular income to (a school/hospital, etc.). (b) endowed with = having (naturally) certain qualities. **en•dow•ment,** n. (a) giving of money (to a school, etc.) to provide a regular income. (b) e. insurance = type of insurance policy where a sum of money is paid to the insured person on a certain date, or to his heirs if he dies.

en•dure [ɪn'djuə] v. (a) to suffer. (b) to stay/to last. **en•dur•a•ble,** adj. which can be endured. **en•dur•ance,** n. ability to suffer hardship; e. test = test of a machine/person to see if it/he works well under bad conditions.

en•e•ma ['enɪmə] n. liquid medicine put into the rectum with a syringe.

en•e•my ['enəmɪ] n. opponent (in war).

en•er•gy ['enədʒɪ] n. force/strength; atomic e. = power from atomic energy. **en•er•get•ic** [enə'dʒetɪk] adj. having or using energy; lively. **en•er•get•i•cal•ly,** adv. having or using much force. **en•er•gize,** v. to make (sth) vigorous.

en•er•vate ['enəveɪt] v. to make (s.o.) lazy/sluggish.

en•fee•ble [ɪn'fi:bl] v. to make (s.o.) feeble.

en•fold [ɪn'fəuld] v. to wrap (sth) up in sth.

en•force [ɪn'fɔ:s] v. to make sure (a law) is obeyed. **en•force•a•ble,** adj. which can be enforced. **en•force•ment,** n. act of enforcing.

en•fran•chise [ɪn'fræntʃaɪz] v. to give (s.o.) the right to vote in elections.

en•gage [ɪn'geɪdʒ] v. (a) to attach together (legally); to employ (new staff). (b) to make parts of a machine fit into each other; e. first gear = put your car into first gear. (c) to be occupied (in doing sth). (d) to attack (the enemy). **en•gaged,** adj. (a) having officially stated one's intention to marry. (b) busy; occupied. **en•gage•ment,** n. (a) appointment. (b) statement of intention to marry; e. ring = ring given by man to woman when they agree to

---

æ back, a: farm, ɒ: top, aɪ pipe, au how, aiə fire, auə flower, ɔ: bought, ɔɪ toy, e fed, eəhair, eɪ take, ə afraid, əu boat, əuə lower, v: word, i: heap, ɪ hit, ɪə hear, u: school, u book, ʌ but, b back, d dog, ð then, dʒ just, f fog, g go, h hand, j yes, k catch, l last, m mix, n nut, ŋ sing, p penny, r round, s some, ʃ short, t too, tʃ chop, θ thing, v voice, w was, z zoo, ʒ treasure

marry. (c) battle. **en•gag•ing,** *adj.* charming.

en•gen•der [ɪn'dʒendə] *v.* (*formal*) to produce.

en•gine ['endʒɪn] *n.* (a) machine/large motor which produces power. (b) locomotive/vehicle for pulling trains. **en•gined,** *adj.* with an engine; **single-e. aircraft. en•gi•neer** [endʒɪ-'nɪə] 1. *n.* (a) person who looks after technical equipment, esp. engines. (b) (*in the armed forces*) person who specializes in construction of bridges/defenses, etc.; **civil e.** = person who specializes in construction of roads/bridges, etc. (c) person who drives a locomotive. 2. *v.* to arrange (sth) by plotting. **en•gi•neer•ing,** *n.* science/study of technical equipment; **civil e.** = science of construction (esp. of roads/bridges, etc.).

Eng•lish ['ɪŋglɪʃ] 1. *adj.* referring to England; **I think he is E. although he speaks with an American accent. 2.** *n.* (a) **the E.** = the people of England. (b) language spoken in the United States, England, Australia, and many other countries; **can you speak E.? what is that in E.? Eng•lish•man, Englishwoman,** *n.* (*pl.* -men, -women) person from England.

en•grave [ɪn'greɪv] *v.* to cut (a pattern/a letter) on to a hard surface. **en•grav•er,** *n.* artist who engraves. **en•grav•ing,** *n.* picture printed from an engraved plate.

en•gross [ɪn'grəus] *v.* to take up all the attention of.

en•grossed [ɪn'grəust] *adj.* **e. in** = very interested/busy in.

en•gulf [ɪn'gʌlf] *v.* to swallow up.

en•hance [ɪn'hɑːns] *v.* to increase (beauty/value). **en•hance•ment,** *n.* increase (in value, etc.).

e•nig•ma [ɪ'nɪgmə] *n.* mystery/puzzle. **en•ig•mat•ic** [enɪg'mætɪk] *adj.* difficult to explain/difficult to understand.

en•join [ɪn'dʒɔɪn] *v.* (*formal*) to command.

en•joy [ɪn'dʒɔɪ] *v.* to take pleasure in (sth); **to e. yourself** = to have a good time. **en•joy•a•ble,** *adj.* pleasing. **en•joy•ment,** *n.* pleasure.

en•large [ɪn'lɑːdʒ] *v.* (a) to make bigger. (b) **to e. upon** = to give more details about. **en•large•ment,** *n.* bigger photograph (than the original negative). **en•larg•er,** *n.* device for enlarging photographs.

en•light•en [ɪn'laɪtn] *v.* **to e. s.o. on/about sth** = to give s.o. a clear picture of sth. **en•light•ened,** *adj.* free of prejudice; holding approved ideas. **en•light•en•ment,** *n.* knowledge/absence of ignorance; **the Enlightenment** = period in the 18th century when many scientific discoveries were made.

en•list [ɪn'lɪst] *v.* (a) to join the armed forces. (b) **to e. s.o.'s help** = to get help from s.o. **en•list•ment,** *n.* joining the armed forces.

en•liv•en [ɪn'laɪvn] *v.* to make more lively.

en masse [ɒn'mæs] *adv.* all together in a crowd.

en•mi•ty ['enmɪtɪ] *n.* hatred **toward** s.o.

en•no•ble [ɪ'nəubl] *v.* (a) to make more excellent, dignified, or respected. (b) to make (s.o.) a peer.

e•nor•mous [ɪ'nɔːməs] *adj.* very large. **e•nor•mi•ty,** *n.* seriousness (of a crime). **e•nor•mous•ly,** *adv.* very much.

e•nough [ɪ'nʌf] 1. *adj.* sufficient; as much as is needed; **have you got e. money?** 2. *n.* sufficient quantity; **have you had e. to eat?** 3. *adv.* sufficiently; **it is not light e. to take pictures.**

en•quire [ɪŋ'kwaɪə] *v. see* **inquire. en•quir•y,** *n. see* **inquiry.**

en•rage [ɪn'reɪdʒ] *v.* to make (s.o.) very annoyed.

en•rap•ture [ɪn'ræptʃə] *v.* to charm (s.o.).

en•rich [ɪn'rɪtʃ] *v.* to make richer. **en•rich•ment,** *n.* making richer.

en•roll, enrol [ɪn'rəul] *v.* (**enrolled**) to admit (new members/new students); **he enrolled in a cooking class. en•roll•ment, enrolment,** *n.* action of admitting new members/students; list of all new students.

en route [ɒn'ruːt] *adv.* on the way.

en•sconced [ɪn'skɒnst] *adj.* firmly settled.

en•sem•ble [ɒn'sɒmbl] *n.* (a) group (of musicians/singers). (b) set of women's clothes which match. (c) group of things which fit together.

en•shrine [ɪn'ʃraɪn] *v.* to enclose as if in a shrine.

en•sign ['ensaɪn] *n.* (a) national flag used by a ship. (b) junior naval officer.

en•slave [ɪn'sleɪv] *v.* to make a slave of (s.o.).

en•snare [ɪn'snɛə] *v.* to catch in a trap.

en•sue [ɪn'sjuː] *v.* to follow. **en•su•ing,** *adj.* which follows.

en suite [ɒŋ'swiːt] *adv.* joined in a series.

en•sure [ɪn'ʃuə] *v.* to make sure of.

en•tail [ɪn'teɪl] *v.* to involve/to include.

en•tan•gle [ɪn'tæŋgl] *v.* to be caught up in (**in** string/bushes/problems). **en•tan•gle•ment,** *n.* state of being entangled.

en•tente [ɒn'tɒnt] *n.* peaceful agreement (between countries).

en•ter ['entə] *v.* (a) to go in/to come in. (b) to write down (a name, etc.). (c) to type information on a keyboard, and put it into a computer system. (d) to put your name on a list as a competitor. **en•ter into,** *v.* to take part in (an agreement).

en•ter•i•tis [entə'raɪtɪs] *n.* infection of the intestines. en•ter•ic [en'terɪk] *adj.* referring to the intestines.

en•ter•prise ['entəpraɪz] *n.* (a) new plan/adventure. (b) ability to plan. (c) method of working in business; **private e.** = business companies which are not state-owned. en•ter•pris•ing, *adj.* with initiative.

en•ter•tain [entə'teɪn] *v.* (a) to amuse. (b) to offer (s.o.) a meal. (c) to consider (a suggestion/an idea). en•ter•tain•er, *n.* person/performer who entertains. en•ter•tain•ing, *adj.* amusing. en•ter•tain•ment, *n.* (a) amusement. (b) hospitality.

en•thral•ling [ɪn'θrɔːlɪŋ] *adj.* extremely interesting.

en•throne [ɪn'θrəʊn] *v.* to put (s.o.) on a throne.

en•thu•si•asm [ɪn'θjuːzɪæzəm] *n.* great interest. en•thuse [ɪn'θjuːz] *v. inf.* to show great interest (over sth). en•thu•si•ast, *n.* person who shows great interest in sth. en•thu•si•as•tic [ɪnθjuːzɪ'æstɪk] *adj.* showing great interest; **he was very e. about my book.** en•thu•si•as•ti•cal•ly, *adv.* with enthusiasm.

en•tice [ɪn'taɪs] *v.* to attract/to tempt. en•tice•ment, *n.* act of enticing; thing which entices.

en•tire [ɪn'taɪə] *adj.* whole. en•tire•ly, *adv.* wholly; **I e. agree with you.** en•tire•ty [ɪn-'taɪərətɪ] *n.* being whole; **he translated the book in its e.** = completely.

en•ti•tle [ɪn'taɪtl] *v.* (a) to give the right to; **he is entitled to two weeks' vacation a year.** (b) to give a title to; **a book entitled** *War and Peace.* en•ti•tle•ment, *n.* right to have.

en•ti•ty ['entɪtɪ] *n.* thing which exists as a separate unit.

en•tomb [ɪn'tuːm] *v.* to bury.

en•to•mol•o•gy [entə'mɒlədʒɪ] *n.* study of insects. en•to•mo•log•i•cal [entəmə-'lɒdʒɪkl] *adj.* referring to entomology. en•to•mol•o•gist [entə'mɒlədʒɪst] *n.* person who studies insects.

en•tou•rage [ɒntuː'rɑːʒ] *n.* group of people (secretaries/assistants/advisers, etc.) surrounding an important person.

en•trails ['entreɪlz] *n. pl.* intestines of an animal.

en•trance¹ ['entrəns] *n.* (act of) going in; (door for) going in; **main e.** = main doorway.

en•trance² [ɪn'trɑːns] *v.* to bewitch. en•tranc•ing, *adj.* very attractive/beautiful.

en•trant ['entrənt] *n.* person who enters a race/a competition.

en•treat [ɪn'triːt] *v.* to plead. en•treat•ing, *adj.* pleading. en•treat•ing•ly, *adv.* pleadingly. en•treat•y, *n.* plea.

en•trée ['ɒntreɪ] *n.* (a) freedom to go in. (b) small dish served before the main dish (in a formal meal).

en•trench [ɪn'trenʃ] *v.* to dig trenches/to dig in. en•trenched, *adj.* **firmly e.** = firmly established.

en•tre•pre•neur [ɒntrəprə'nɜː] *n.* (a) person who directs a company and speculates commercially. (b) contractor who acts as a middleman. en•tre•pre•neur•i•al [ɒntrəprə'nɜːrɪəl] *adj.* speculative.

en•trust [ɪn'trʌst] *v.* **to e. sth to s.o./to e. s.o. with sth** = to give s.o. the responsibility for sth.

en•try ['entrɪ] *n.* (a) going in. (b) written information in a reference book/accounts ledger/computer system.

en•twine [ɪn'twaɪn] *v.* to twist around.

e•nu•mer•ate [ɪ'njuːməreɪt] *v.* to mention one by one/to make a list of. e•nu•mer•a•tion, *n.* list; act of enumerating.

e•nun•ci•ate [ɪ'nʌnsɪeɪt] *v.* to speak (words) clearly. e•nun•ci•a•tion [ɪnʌnsɪ'eɪʃn] *n.* clear pronunciation.

en•vel•op [ɪn'veləp] *v.* to cover/to surround with a covering. en•vel•ope ['envələʊp] *n.* paper covering for sending letters.

en•vi•ron•ment [ɪn'vaɪərənmənt] *n.* surroundings (in which you live). en•vi•ron•men•tal [ɪnvaɪərən'mentl] *adj.* which refers to the surroundings of sth; **e. audit** = assessment of a company's impact on the environment, esp. in relation to pollution reduction targets; **E. Protection Agency** = official U.S. government agency which oversees protection of the environment and pollution control. en•vi•ron•men•tal•ist, *n.* person concerned with conservation of the environment. en•vi•rons [ɪn'vaɪərənz] *n. pl.* area surrounding a place.

en•vis•age [ɪn'vɪzɪdʒ] *v.* to foresee; to plan (sth) which may take place.

en•voy ['envɔɪ] *n.* person sent officially (by a country)/high-ranking diplomat.

en•vy ['envɪ] 1. *n.* feeling of wishing to have sth which s.o. else has/of wanting to be or do sth

---

æ back, ɑː farm, ɒ top, aɪ pipe, aʊ how, aɪə fire, aʊə flower, ɔː bought, ɔɪ toy, e fed, eə hair, eɪ take, ə afraid, əʊ boat, əʊə lower, vː word, iː heap, ɪ hit, ɪə hear, uː school, ʊ book, ʌ but, b back, d dog, ð then, dʒ just, f fog, g go, h hand, j yes, k catch, l last, m mix, n nut, ŋ sing, p penny, r round, s some, ʃ short, t too, tʃ chop, θ thing, v voice, w was, z zoo, ʒ treasure

else. **2.** *v.* **to e. s.o. sth** = to wish to have sth belonging to s.o.; to be unhappy because you want to be like s.o. else. **en•vi•a•ble**, *adj.* which one can envy. **en•vi•ous**, *adj.* feeling envy.

en•zyme ['enzaɪm] *n.* substance which can make other substances change (as in digestion).

e•on ['iːən] *n.* very long time.

ep•au•let, epaulette ['epəlet] *n.* decorative strip on the shoulder of a uniform.

e•phem•er•al [ɪ'fiːmərəl] *adj.* which disappears quickly/does not last long. **e•phem•er•a**, *n. pl.* printed papers (like tickets) which are thrown away after use.

ep•ic ['epɪk] **1.** *n.* long story/poem/motion picture. **2.** *adj.* long and difficult.

ep•i•cen•ter ['epɪsentə] *n.* point on the surface of the earth which an earthquake reaches first.

ep•i•cure ['epɪkjʊə] *n.* person who is fond of, and knows a lot about, food. **e•pi•cu•re•an** [epɪkju'riːən] *adj. & n.* (referring to) an epicure.

ep•i•dem•ic [epɪ'demɪk] *n.* wave of disease which affects a lot of people.

ep•i•der•mis [epɪ'dɜːmɪs] *n.* outer layer of skin.

ep•i•du•ral [epɪ'djʊərəl] *adj.* (anaesthetic) given in the spine.

ep•i•glot•tis [epɪ'glotɪs] *n.* cartilage at the back of the throat which prevents food from being taken into the windpipe.

ep•i•gram ['epɪgræm] *n.* short, witty saying. **ep•i•gram•mat•ic** [epɪgrə'mætɪk] *adj.* witty, like an epigram. **ep•i•graph**, *n.* text used to illustrate sth. (as at the end of a book).

ep•i•lep•sy ['epɪlepsɪ] *n.* disease usu. characterized by convulsive fits. **ep•i•lep•tic** [epɪ'leptɪk] **1.** *adj.* referring to epilepsy. **2.** *n.* person who suffers from epilepsy.

ep•i•logue, epilog ['epɪlog] *n.* short text at the end of a longer work.

E•piph•a•ny [ɪ'pɪfənɪ] *n.* Christian festival on January 6th, celebrating the visit of the Kings to the Christ child.

e•pis•co•pal [ɪ'pɪskəpl] *adj.* referring to bishops; (church) which has bishops. **e•pis•co•pa•lian** [ɪpɪskə'peɪlɪən] *adj. & n.* (member) of an episcopal church.

ep•i•sode ['epɪsəʊd] *n.* (a) short piece of action in longer story. (b) short period (in your life).

e•pis•te•mol•o•gy [epɪstə'molədʒɪ] *n.* study of knowledge.

e•pis•tle [ɪ'pɪsl] *n.* (*formal*) long letter.

ep•i•taph ['epɪtɑːf] *n.* writing on a gravestone.

ep•i•thet ['epɪθet] *n.* special name describing s.o.; **William I has the e. of "the Conqueror."**

e•pit•o•me [ɪ'pɪtəmɪ] *n.* person who shows a particular quality very strongly. **e•pit•o•mize,** *v.* to show (a quality) very strongly.

ep•och ['iːpɒk] *n.* major period of time. **ep•och-mak•ing**, *adj.* very important historically.

eq•ua•ble ['ekwəbl] *adj.* calm/not easily upset.

e•qual ['iːkwəl] **1.** *v.* (**equaled, equalled**) to be exactly the same as/to add up to; **two plus two equals four. 2.** *adj.* (a) exactly the same as/level with something; **all things being e.** = having considered everything carefully. (b) **he wasn't e. to the task** = he wasn't strong enough/brave enough to do it. **3.** *n.* person who is on the same level as s.o. else. **e•qual•i•ty** [ɪ'kwolɪtɪ] *n.* state of being equal. **e•qual•ize** ['iːkwəlaɪz] *v.* to make equal; to score and make the points of both teams the same. **e•qual•iz•er,** *n.* goal, etc., which makes the score equal. **e•qual•ly,** *adv.* in exactly the same way.

e•qua•nim•i•ty [ekwə'nɪmɪtɪ] *n.* not getting flustered/calmness.

e•quate [ɪ'kweɪt] *v.* to see (two things) as equal. **e•qua•tion** [ɪ'kweɪʒn] *n.* mathematical or chemical formula showing two parts are equal.

e•qua•tor [ɪ'kweɪtə] *n.* imaginary line around the circumference of the earth which is the same distance from the North and South Poles. **e•qua•tor•i•al** [ekwə'tɔːrɪəl] *adj.* referring to the equator.

eq•uer•ry ['ekwərɪ] *n.* man who is in attendance on a king/queen.

e•ques•tri•an [ɪ'kwestrɪən] *adj. & n.* (person) riding on a horse.

e•qui•dis•tant [iːkwɪ'dɪstənt] *adj.* at an equal distance from sth.

e•qui•lat•er•al [iːkwɪ'lætərəl] *adj.* (triangle) with all sides of the same length.

e•qui•lib•ri•um [iːkwɪ'lɪbrɪəm] *n.* state of being perfectly balanced.

e•quine ['ekwaɪn] *adj.* referring to horses.

e•qui•nox ['iːkwɪnɒks] *n.* time of the year when the day and night are of equal length. **e•qui•noc•tial** [iːkwɪ'nɒkʃl] *adj.* referring to an equinox.

e•quip [ɪ'kwɪp] *v.* (**equipped**) to provide (sth/s.o.) **with** arms/machinery/furniture; **well equipped** = with all the arms/machinery, etc., which are thought necessary. **e•quip•ment,** *n.* things which are provided to equip sth.

eq•ui•ty ['ekwɪtɪ] *n.* (a) quality of being fair, just. (b) value of a property in addition to what is owed on it as a mortgage, etc. **eq•ui•ta•ble,** *adj.* fair/just. **eq•ui•ta•bly,** *adv.* in an equitable way.

e•quiv•a•lent [ɪ'kwɪvələnt] *adj. & n.* (thing) of the same value/same strength (as sth). e•quiv•a•lence, *n.* being equivalent.

e•quiv•o•cate [ɪ'kwɪvəkeɪt] *v.* to mislead/to give an ambiguous answer. e•quiv•o•cal, *adj.* uncertain/ambiguous. e•quiv•o•cal•ly, *adv.* in an equivocal way. e•quiv•o•ca•tion, *n.* ambiguous reply.

e•ra ['ɪərə] *n.* long period of history; **the Victorian e.**

e•rad•i•cate [ɪ'rædɪkeɪt] *v.* to wipe out/to destroy completely. e•rad•i•ca•tion [ɪrædɪ'keɪʃn] *n.* wiping out.

e•rase [ɪ'reɪz] *v.* to rub out (writing)/to remove (recorded material) from a tape; to remove data on a disk. e•ras•er, *n.* piece of rubber for removing pencil/pen/chalk marks. e•ra•sure [ɪ'reɪʒə] *n.* place where a piece of writing has been erased.

ere [ɛːə] *prep.* (*poetic*) before.

e•rect [ɪ'rekt] 1. *adj.* straight upright. 2. *v.* to put up a building, tent, etc. e•rec•tile, *adj.* (tissue) which can become erect. e•rec•tion, *n.* (a) action of putting up; thing which has been erected. (b) state where the penis becomes erect.

erg [ɜːg] *n.* unit of measurement of work.

er•go•nom•ics [ɜːgə'nɒmɪks] *n.* study of people at work and their working environment.

er•got ['ɜːgɒt] *n.* poisonous disease of rye.

er•i•ca ['erɪkə] *n.* heather.

er•mine ['ɜːmɪn] *n.* white fur (from the winter coat of a stoat).

e•rode [ɪ'rəʊd] *v.* to wear away. e•ro•sion [ɪ'rəʊʒn] *n.* act of wearing away.

e•rog•e•nous [ɪ'rɒdʒənəs] *adj.* very sensitive sexually.

e•rot•ic [ɪ'rɒtɪk] *adj.* strongly sexual. e•rot•i•cism, *n.* erotic quality.

err [ɜː] *v.* to make a mistake/to be at fault.

er•rand ['erənd] *n.* being sent out (esp. to buy sth); **to run errands for s.o.**

er•rant ['erənt] *adj.* (knight) wandering in search of adventure.

er•rat•ic [ɪ'rætɪk] *adj.* irregular/wild. er•rat•i•cal•ly, *adv.* in a wild manner.

er•ra•tum [ɪ'rɑːtəm] *n.* (*pl.* **errata**) mistake in a printed book.

er•ror ['erə] *n.* mistake; **in e.** = by mistake. er•ro•ne•ous [ɪ'rəʊnɪəs] *adj.* wrong. er•ro•ne•ous•ly, *adv.* by mistake.

er•satz ['eəzæts] *adj.* artificial; imitated.

erst•while [ɜːstwaɪl] *adj.* former.

e•ruc•ta•tion [erʌk'teɪʃn] *n.* (*formal*) belching.

er•u•dite ['erjuːdaɪt] *adj.* learned. er•u•di•tion [erjuː'dɪʃn] *n.* learning/knowledge.

e•rupt [ɪ'rʌpt] *v.* (*of volcano*) to throw out lava, ash, etc.; (*of person*) to become angry suddenly. e•rup•tion, *n.* (a) (*of volcano*) throwing out of lava/ash. (b) appearance of a rash on the skin.

er•y•sip•e•las [erɪ'sɪpələs] *n.* red rash on the skin.

es•ca•late ['eskəleɪt] *v.* to get worse/more violent; to increase steadily. es•ca•la•tion [eskə'leɪʃn] *n.* getting worse/bigger. es•ca•la•tor, *n.* moving stairs.

es•ca•lope [eskæ'lɒp] *n.* thin slice of meat, esp. veal.

es•ca•pade ['eskəpeɪd] *n.* wild act.

es•cape [ɪ'skeɪp] 1. *n.* (a) action of getting away from prison/from an awkward situation; **we had a narrow e.** = we were almost killed; **e. clause** = part of a contract which allows one party to avoid the obligations of the contract. (b) key/program which controls the actions of a computer. 2. *v.* (a) to get away (**from prison/from** an awkward situation); **he escaped through the window.** (b) to avoid/to miss; **his name escapes me** = I cannot remember his name. es•cap•ee [eskeɪ'piː] *n.* person who has escaped from prison. es•cape•ment, *n.* device in a watch or clock which regulates the movement. es•cap•ism, *n.* retreat from reality. es•cap•ist *adj. & n.* (person) who retreats from reality.

es•carp•ment [ɪ'skɑːpmənt] *n.* steep slope.

es•chew [es'tʃuː] *v.* (*formal*) to avoid.

es•cort 1. *n.* ['eskɔːt] person or group of people accompanying s.o. 2. *v.* [es'kɔːt] to accompany (s.o.).

Es•ki•mo ['eskɪməʊ] *n. & adj.* (*pl.* **-o** *or* **-os**) one of a people living in the north of Canada and Greenland.

e•soph•a•gus [ə'sɒfəgəs] *n.* part of the throat down which food passes from the mouth to the stomach.

es•o•ter•ic [ɪsəʊ'terɪk] *adj.* understood by very few people; difficult to understand.

es•pa•drille [espə'driːj, -drɪl] *n.* canvas rope-soled shoe.

es•pal•ier [ɪ'spælɪə] *n.* artificial shape of a

æ back, ɑː farm, ɒ top, aɪ pipe, aʊ how, aie fire, aʊə flower, ɔː bought, ɔɪ toy, e fed, eəhair, eɪ take, ə afraid, əʊ boat, əʊə lower, ɜː word, iː heap, ɪ hit, ɪə hear, uː school, ʊ book, ʌ but, b back, d dog, ð then, dʒ just, f fog, g go, h hand, j yes, k catch, l last, m mix, n nut, ŋ sing, p penny, r round, s some, ʃ short, t too, tʃ chop, θ thing, v voice, w was, z zoo, ʒ treasure

fruit tree, with a central stem and branches which form the shape of a ladder.

es•par•to [es'pɑːtəʊ] *n.* type of grass.

es•pe•cial [e'speʃl] *adj.* particular. **es•pe•cial•ly,** *adv.* particularly/very.

es•pi•o•nage ['espɪɑnɑːʒ] *n.* spying; **industrial e.** = spying on a rival company to try to find out trade secrets.

es•pla•nade ['espləneɪd] *n.* level place (along a seashore) where people can walk.

es•pouse [es'paʊz] *v.* (*formal*) to support (a cause).

es•pres•so [ɪ'spresəʊ] *n.* coffee made by forcing boiling water through ground coffee.

es•prit de corps [espriːdə'kɔː] *n.* feeling of loyalty to a group (usually a military unit).

es•py [ɪ'spaɪ] *v.* (*old*) to see.

Esq. [es'kwaɪə] *abbreviation for* esquire (*very polite form of address written after man's name on envelope*) George Martin, Esq.

es•say. 1. *n.* ['eseɪ] piece of prose writing on a particular subject. **2.** *v.* [e'seɪ] (*formal*) to attempt. **es•say•ist,** *n.* person who writes essays.

es•sence ['esəns] *n.* pure extract taken from sth; central part (of an argument). **es•sen•tial** [ɪ'senʃl] *adj. & n.* (thing) which is very important/indispensable; **the bare essentials** = the things which are absolutely necessary. **es•sen•tial•ly,** *adv.* basically/for the most important part.

es•tab•lish [ɪ'stæblɪʃ] *v.* (a) to set up/to create. (b) to show sth to be true. **es•tab•lish•ment,** *n.* (a) creation/setting up. (b) sth established, as a business, household, organization, etc. (c) **the E.** = (small) group of people in positions of authority or influence.

es•tate [ɪ'steɪt] *n.* (a) large area of land belonging to one person. (b) property owned by a person at the time of death.

es•teem [ɪ'stiːm] **1.** *n.* respect; **to hold s.o. in (high) e.** = to respect s.o. (very much). **2.** *v.* (*formal*) to consider; **I esteem it an honor.** **es•teemed,** *adj.* highly respected. **es•ti•ma•ble,** *adj.* which can be respected.

es•ter ['estə] *n.* compound of an acid and an alcohol.

es•ti•mate 1. *n.* ['estɪmət] calculation which shows the worth/cost/number of sth; price quoted by a supplier; **rough e.** = an approximate calculation. **2.** *v.* ['estɪmeɪt] to calculate (approximately) the cost/the number, etc., of sth; to calculate a price (before supplying the item). **es•ti•ma•tion** [estɪ'meɪʃn] *n.* calculation of how much sth is worth; judgment of how valuable a person is.

es•ter ['estə] *n.* compound of an acid and an alcohol.

es•trange [ɪ'streɪndʒ] *v.* to make unfriendly. **es•trange•ment,** *n.* becoming estranged.

es•tro•gen [estrədʒen] *n.* female hormone, controlling bodily changes in the reproductive cycle.

es•tu•ar•y ['estjʊərɪ] *n.* wide part of a river where the sea comes in at high tide.

etc. [et'setərə] *abbreviation for* et cetera *meaning* and so on/and the others. **et•cet•er•as** [et'setərəz] *n. pl.* other things.

etch [etʃ] *v.* to engrave on metal with acid. **etch•ing,** *n.* picture reproduced from a metal plate which has been engraved with acid.

e•ter•ni•ty [ɪ'tɜːnɪtɪ] *n.* never-ending period of time; *inf.* **it will take an e.** = it will take a very long time. **e•ter•nal,** *adj.* everlasting. **e•ter•nal•ly,** *adv.* for ever; *inf.* all the time.

e•ther ['iːθə] *n.* very volatile liquid which burns easily and is used as an anesthetic.

e•the•re•al [ɪ'θɪərɪəl] *adj.* very light like a fairy.

eth•ics ['eθɪks] *n.* moral principles. **eth•i•cal,** *adj.* morally right; **e. investment** = investment in companies considered ethical by the investor.

eth•nic ['eθnɪk] *adj.* relating to a particular race; **e. minority** = minority of a different racial origin than that of the majority. **eth•nog•ra•phy,** *n.* writing about different races. **eth•no•log•i•cal** [eθnə'lɒdʒɪkl] *adj.* referring to ethnology. **eth•nol•o•gist** [eθ'nɒlədʒɪst] *n.* person who studies ethnology. **eth•nol•o•gy** [eθ'nɒlədʒɪ] *n.* study of the customs of different races.

e•thos ['iːθɒs] *n.* beliefs or characteristics (esp. of a group of people).

eth•yl ['eθɪl] *n.* liquid formed from ether and alcohol, used to add to gasoline.

et•i•quette ['etɪket] *n.* correct way of behaving in society; **professional e.** = the rules of behavior of a particular group of professional people.

et•y•mol•o•gy [etɪ'mɒlədʒɪ] *n.* way in which a word and its meaning have developed historically. **et•y•mo•log•i•cal** [etɪmə'lɒdʒɪkl] *adj.* referring to etymology.

EU [iː'juː] *abbrev. for* European Union.

eu•ca•lyp•tus [juːkə'lɪptəs] *n.* evergreen tree which gives a strong-smelling oil used to treat colds.

eu•char•ist ['juːkərɪst] *n.* Christian ceremony of taking consecrated bread and wine. **eu•char•is•tic** [juːkə'rɪstɪk] *adj.* referring to the eucharist.

eu•gen•ics [juː'dʒenɪks] *n.* science of breeding strong human beings.

eu•lo•gy ['juːlədʒɪ] *n.* (*formal*) speech or writing praising s.o. **eu•lo•gize,** v. to praise (s.o.) strongly. **eu•lo•gis•tic** [juːlə'dʒɪstɪk] adj. which eulogizes.

eu•nuch ['juːnək] n. castrated man, usu. a servant.

eu•phe•mism ['juːfəmɪzəm] n. word or phrase used in place of a more offensive or unpleasant word. **eu•phe•mis•tic** [juːfə'mɪstɪk] adj. referring to euphemism. **eu•phe•mis•ti•cal•ly,** adv. as a euphemism.

eu•pho•ni•um [juː'fəʊnɪəm] n. large brass wind instrument.

eu•pho•ny ['juːfəni] n. pleasant sound.

eu•pho•ri•a [juː'fɔːrɪə] n. extreme happiness. **eu•phor•ic** [juː'fɒrɪk] adj. very happy.

eu•re•ka [juː'riːkə] interj. meaning a discovery has been made.

eu•ro ['jʊərəʊ] n. unit of money used in those EU countries who are participating in European Monetary Union.

Euro- ['jʊərəʊ] prefix referring to Europe; **Eurocurrency, Eurodollar.**

Eu•ro•pe•an [jʊərə'piːən] adj. & n. (person) from Europe; **the E. Union** = group of European countries forming a single market and having some common social, monetary, foreign, and security policies; **the E. Parliament** = the parliament to which members (MEPs) are elected from each country of the EU; **the E. monetary system** = system of controlled exchange rates between some member states of the EU; **E. Currency Unit** = accounting unit of E. Monetary System; **E. Monetary Union** = currency union of those EU countries who choose to participate.

Eu•sta•chian [juː'steɪʃn] adj. **E. tube** = tube which connects the middle ear to the throat.

eu•tha•na•sia [juːθə'neɪzɪə] n. painless killing of s.o./sth (as a sick animal) to put them out of their misery.

eu•troph•ic [juː'trɒfɪk] adj. (lake) which is rich in nutrients.

e•vac•u•ate [ɪ'vækjʊeɪt] v. (a) to make (people) leave a dangerous place; to remove (troops) from a place; to remove people from (a place). (b) to empty (the bowels). **e•vac•u•a•tion** [ɪvækjʊ'eɪʃn] n. (a) leaving a dangerous place. (b) emptying of the bowels. **e•vac•u•ee** [ɪvækjʊ'iː] n. person who has been evacuated.

e•vade [ɪ'veɪd] v. to avoid.

e•val•u•ate [ɪ'væljʊeɪt] v. to calculate value.

e•val•u•a•tion [ɪvælju'eɪʃn] n. act of calculating.

ev•a•nes•cent [ɪvə'nesənt] adj. (formal) which fades quickly.

e•van•gel•i•cal [iːvæn'dʒelɪkl] adj. referring to certain Protestant churches and their teaching of the Bible. **e•van•ge•list** [ɪ'vændʒəlɪst] n. (a) one of the four men who wrote the Gospels. (b) preacher.

e•vap•o•rate [ɪ'væpəreɪt] v. (a) to turn liquid into vapor. (b) to disappear. **e•vap•o•ra•tion** [ɪvæpə'reɪʃn] n. process of turning liquid into vapor. **e•vap•o•rat•ed,** adj. **e. milk** = milk which has been reduced in volume by evaporation.

e•va•sion [ɪ'veɪʒn] n. avoiding (a direct answer). **e•va•sive** [ɪ'veɪsɪv] adj. which tries to avoid. **e•va•sive•ly,** adv. trying to avoid a direct answer. **e•va•sive•ness,** n. trying to avoid a direct answer.

eve [iːv] n. night before; short time before; **on the e. of our departure** = just before we were due to leave; **Christmas E.** = December 24th/day before Christmas; **New Year's E.** = December 31st.

e•ven ['iːvn] 1. adj. (a) flat/level. (b) regular; **a man of very e. temper** = who never gets very excited. (c) equal (in a competition); **to get e. with s.o.** = try to have revenge on s.o.; **the company is just breaking e.** = it is making no profit, but no loss either. (d) **e. number** = number which can be divided by 2. 2. v. (a) to flatten/to smooth (sth). (b) to make equal; **to e. things up** = to make things equal. 3. adv. not only; **he doesn't e. like strawberries** = most people like strawberries, but he doesn't; **e. worse** = worse than before; **e. so** = however/if you consider everything; **e. now** = right at this minute. **e•ven•ly,** adv. (a) in a level way. (b) equally; **they are e. matched** = they are equals (in competition). **e•ven•ness,** n. being even.

eve•ning ['iːvnɪŋ] n. late part of the day, as night falls; **this e.** = today in the evening. **eve•ning-dress,** n. clothes worn to special occasions in the evening (long dress for women, black clothes and black or white bow tie for men).

e•ven•song ['iːvnsɒŋ] n. Anglican church service held in the evening.

e•vent [ɪ'vent] n. (a) happening; **happy e.** = birth of a child; **in the course of events** = as things turned out; **in the e. of his refusing** = if he should refuse. (b) result; **in any e.** = whatever happens; **at all events** = in any case. (c) sporting competition; **field events** = jumping and throwing competitions; **track events** = running and hurdling. **e•vent•ful**, *adj.* exciting/full of unexpected happenings.

e•ven•tide [iːvnˈtaɪd] *n.* (*old*) evening.

e•ven•tu•al [ɪˈventjʊəl] *adj.* final. **e•ven•tu•al•i•ty** [ɪventjuˈælɪtɪ] *n.* thing which might happen; **in that e.** = if that should happen. **e•ven•tu•al•ly**, *adv.* in the end.

ev•er [ˈevə] *adv.* (a) at any time; **I hardly e. see her** = almost never see her; **louder than e.** = louder than before. (b) always; **e. since then** = from that time onward; **they lived happily e. after** = always, from then on; **I will love you for e. and e.** = always. (c) *inf.* **e. so** = extremely. (d) (*emphatic*) **what e. is the matter?** = what on earth is the matter? **what e. is it for?** = what can it be used for? **ev•er•more**, *adv.* always. **ev•er•green** [ˈevəɡriːn] 1. *adj.* (plant) which keeps its leaves all winter. 2. *n.* tree which keeps its leaves all winter. **ev•er•last•ing** [evəˈlɑːstɪŋ] *adj.* going on for ever.

eve•ry [ˈevrɪ] *adj.* each; all (taken separately); **e. other day** = each alternate day. **eve•ry•bod•y**, *pron.* all people. **eve•ry•day**, *adj.* ordinary/very common. **eve•ry•one**, *pron.* everybody. **eve•ry•thing**. *pron.* all things. **eve•ry•where**, *adv.* in all places.

e•vict [ɪˈvɪkt] *v.* to put (s.o.) out of his/her home. **e•vic•tion** [ɪˈvɪkʃn] *n.* act of putting s.o. out of his/her home.

ev•i•dence [ˈevɪdəns] *n.* (a) traces (of crime). (b) written or spoken report (at a trial); **the criminal turned State's e.** = gave information to the court which proved that his accomplices were guilty. (c) **in e.** = visible. **ev•i•dent**, *adj.* obvious. **ev•i•dent•ly**, *adv.* obviously; presumably.

e•vil [ˈiːvl] 1. *adj.* very wicked. 2. *n.* wickedness; injustice.

e•vince [ɪˈvɪns] *v.* (*formal*) to show (a certain quality/feeling).

e•voke [ɪˈvəʊk] *v.* to call up (an image). **ev•o•ca•tion** [ɪvəʊˈkeɪʃn] *n.* act of evoking. **e•voc•a•tive** [ɪˈvɒkətɪv] *adj.* which calls up a sensation in the mind of the onlooker or reader.

e•volve [ɪˈvɒlv] *v.* (a) to work out gradually (a scientific theory/a way of working). (b) to develop (gradually). **ev•o•lu•tion** [iːvəˈluːʃn] *n.* gradual development; **the theory of e.** = theory that human beings and other living organisms developed gradually from primitive forms of life. **ev•o•lu•tion•ar•y**, *adj.* referring to evolution.

ewe [juː] *n.* female sheep.

ew•er [ˈjuːə] *n.* large jug.

ex- [eks] *prefix meaning* (a) former; who used to be; **my ex-girlfriend.** (b) out of; **export.**

ex•ac•er•bate [ɪɡˈzæsəbeɪt] *v.* (*formal*) to make worse/more painful. **ex•ac•er•ba•tion** [ɪɡzæsəˈbeɪʃn] *n.* making worse.

ex•act [ɪɡˈzækt] 1. *adj.* precise. 2. *v.* to force (sth) **from** s.o. **ex•act•ing**, *adj.* (person) who demands a lot (of effort). **ex•ac•tion**, *n.* (*formal*) demand (for money). **ex•ac•ti•tude**, *n.* precision. **ex•act•ly**, *adv.* precisely; **e.!** = that's right.

ex•ag•ger•ate [ɪɡˈzædʒəreɪt] *v.* to make things seem larger/worse/better than they really are. **ex•ag•ger•a•tion** [ɪɡzædʒəˈreɪʃn] *n.* (statement, etc.) making things seem larger/worse/better; **without e.** = quite truthfully.

ex•al•ted [ɪɡˈzɔːltɪd] *adj.* in a high position in authority; very happy. **ex•al•ta•tion** [eɡzəlˈteɪʃn] *n.* exalted feeling.

ex•am•ine [ɪɡˈzæmɪn] *v.* to inspect (sth) to see if it is correct; to test (a student); to ask (a witness) questions. **ex•am** [ɪɡˈzæm] *n. inf.* written or spoken test. **ex•am•i•na•tion** [ɪɡzæmɪˈneɪʃn] *n.* inspection; written or spoken test. **ex•am•in•ee** [ɪɡzæmɪˈniː] *n.* person being tested. **ex•am•in•er** [ɪɡˈzæmɪnə] *n.* person who inspects or tests.

ex•am•ple [ɪɡˈzɑːmpl] *n.* case selected to show sth; **to set an e.** = to act well, so that others may copy you; **to make an e. of s.o.** = to punish s.o. so that others will learn not to do what he did; **for e.** = to name one thing out of many.

ex•as•per•ate [ɪɡˈzɑːspəreɪt] *v.* to make (s.o.) furious. **ex•as•per•a•tion** [ɪɡzɑːspəˈreɪʃn] *n.* fury.

ex•ca•vate [ˈekskəveɪt] *v.* to dig (a hole in the ground); to carry out an archaeological investigation of (a place). **ex•ca•va•tion** [ekskəˈveɪʃn] *n.* large hole; archaeological investigation. **ex•ca•va•tor**, *n.* machine for making holes in the ground.

ex•ceed [ɪkˈsiːd] *v.* to go beyond (a limit). **ex•ceed•ing•ly**, *adv.* very.

ex•cel [ɪkˈsel] *v.* (**excelled**) to be very good (**at** sth). **ex•cel•lence** [ˈeksələns] *n.* very good quality. **Ex•cel•len•cy**, *n.* title given to high officials, as ambassadors and Roman Catholic bishops. **ex•cel•lent**, *adj.* very good.

ex•cept [ɪkˈsept] 1. *prep. & conj.* not including; other than; **all went well e. that James was sick** = apart from the fact that. 2. *v.* not to include (sth). **ex•cep•tion** [ɪkˈsepʃn] *n.* thing not included; **he took e. to what she said** = he was annoyed at what she said. **ex•cep•tion•a•ble**, *adj.* not to be approved of. **ex•cep•tion•al**, *adj.* outstanding. **ex•cep•tion•al•ly,** *adv.* particularly.

ex•cerpt ['eksɜ:pt] 1. *n.* small part (of a larger piece of music/writing). 2. *v.* to make an excerpt.

ex•cess [ɪk'ses] *n.* (a) too much (of sth); **in e. of** = more than; **to e.** = too much; **e. baggage** = more baggage than one is allowed to carry. (b) action or behavior which is worse than is normally acceptable. **ex•ces•sive,** *adj.* more than is normal. **ex•ces•sive•ly,** *adv.* too much.

ex•change [ɪks'tʃeɪndʒ] 1. *n.* giving of one thing for another; **foreign e.** = exchange of the money of one country for that of another; **rate** = rate at which one money is given for another; **telephone e.** = central place or station where telephone calls are linked; **stock e.** = place where stocks and shares are bought and sold. 2. *v.* to swap/to give (sth) **for** sth else; **they exchanged addresses** = each of them gave the other his address. **ex•change•a•ble,** *adj.* which can be exchanged.

ex•cheq•uer [eks'tʃekə] *n.* British government department dealing with public money.

ex•cise 1. *n.* ['eksaɪz] tax on certain goods (as alcohol or tobacco). 2. *v.* [ɪk'saɪz] to cut out. **ex•ci•sion** [ɪk'sɪʒn] *n.* cutting out.

ex•cite [ɪk'saɪt] *v.* to arouse (s.o./sth); to make (s.o.) very emotional; **he was excited at/by the thought of going on vacation. ex•cit•a•bil•i•ty** [ɪksaɪtə'bɪlɪti] *n.* ease with which you are made very excited. **ex•cit•a•ble** [ɪk'saɪtəbl] *adj.* easily excited. **ex•cite•ment,** *n.* state of being excited. **ex•cit•ing,** *adj.* which makes s.o. excited.

ex•claim [ɪk'skleɪm] *v.* to say (sth) loudly and suddenly. **ex•cla•ma•tion** [ekskla'meɪʃn] *n.* shouting out; **exclamation mark** = written sign (!) to show exclamation.

ex•clude [ɪk'sklu:d] *v.* to shut out (s.o./sth **from** somewhere). **ex•clud•ing,** *prep.* without; other than; not including. **ex•clu•sion** [ɪk'sklu:ʒn] *n.* act of shutting out. **ex•clu•sive.** 1. *adj.* (a) very select; not open to everyone. (b) **e. right** = right to do sth which no one else is allowed to do. 2. *adv.* not including. **ex•clu•sive•ly,** *adv.* solely/only.

ex•com•mu•ni•cate [ekskə'mju:nɪkeɪt] *v.* to expel from membership in a church; refuse communion to (a member of a church). **ex•com•mu•ni•ca•tion** [ekskəmju:nɪ'keɪʃn] *n.* being excommunicated.

ex•cre•ment ['ekskrəmənt] *n.* solid waste matter produced by the body.

ex•cres•cence [ɪk'skresns] *n.* ugly growth/lump.

ex•crete [ɪk'skri:t] *v.* to produce (waste matter). **ex•cre•ta,** *n. pl.* (*formal*) waste matter produced by the body.

ex•cru•ci•at•ing [ɪk'skru:ʃɪeɪtɪŋ] *adj.* very painful.

ex•cul•pate ['ekskʌlpeɪt] *v.* (*formal*) to remove blame from (s.o.).

ex•cur•sion [ɪk'skɜ:ʃn] *n.* short pleasure trip; **e. ticket** = special round-trip ticket at a reduced rate.

ex•cuse 1. *n.* [ɪk'skju:s] reason; apology. 2. *v.* [ɪk'skju:z] to pardon (s.o.); to allow (s.o.) not to do sth; **e. me** = I am sorry. **ex•cus•a•ble,** *adj.* which can be pardoned. **ex•cus•a•bly,** *adv.* in an excusable way.

ex•e•crate ['eksɪkreɪt] *v.* (*formal*) to curse/to hate (s.o.). **ex•e•cra•ble,** *adj.* extremely bad. **ex•e•cra•bly,** *adv.* extremely badly.

ex•e•cute ['eksɪkju:t] *v.* to carry out (an official order), esp. to kill s.o. who has been condemned to death. **ex•ec•u•tant** [eg-'zekjutənt] *n.* performer (of a piece of music). **ex•e•cu•tion** [eksɪ'kju:ʃn] *n.* carrying out (of plan); legal killing of person sentenced to death. **ex•e•cu•tion•er** [eksɪ'kju:ʃənə] *n.* official who executes people. **ex•ec•u•tive** [ɪg'zekjutɪv] 1. *adj.* responsible for carrying out plans, laws, official policies, etc.; which puts things into practice; **e. committee** = committee which runs the business, etc. 2. *n.* (a) person in business who makes decisions/plans, etc. (b) **Chief E.** = person having executive power in a government; **the Chief E. in the United States is the president. ex•ec•u•tor** [ɪg'zekjutə] *n.* person who sees that a dead person's will is carried out. **ex•ec•u•trix** [ɪg'zekjutrɪks] *n.* woman who sees that a dead person's will is carried out.

ex•e•ge•sis [eksɪ'dʒi:sɪs] *n.* commentary (on the Bible).

ex•em•pla•ry [ɪg'zemplərɪ] *adj.* which serves as an example. **ex•em•plar,** *n.* perfect example. **ex•em•pli•fy,** *v.* to show as an example.

ex•empt [ɪg'zempt] 1. *adj.* not forced to obey (law, etc.). 2. *v.* to free (s.o.) **from** having to obey a rule or law/**from** doing sth. **ex•emp•tion** [ɪg'zempʃn] *n.* (**from**) ruling that s.o. does not have to do sth.

ex•er•cise ['eksəsaɪz] 1. *n.* use of physical or

æ back, ɑ: farm, ɒ: top, aɪ pipe, aʊ how, aɪə fire, aʊə flower, ɔ: bought, ɔɪ toy, ə fed, eəhair, eɪ take, ə afraid, əʊ boat, əʊə lower, ʌ: word, i: heap, ɪ hit, ɪə hear, u: school, ʊ book, ʌ but, b back, d dog, ð then, dʒ just, f fog, g go, h hand, j yes, k catch, l last, m mix, n nut, ŋ sing, p penny, r round, s some, ʃ short, t too, tʃ chop, θ thing, v voice, w was, z zoo, ʒ treasure

mental powers; **e. book** = book for writing out work at school. 2. *v.* (a) to make (an animal) take exercise. (b) to use (power); **he exercised his right of veto.**

ex•ert [ɪg'zɜ:t] *v.* to use (force/pressure, etc.). **ex•er•tion** [ɪg'zɜ:ʃn] *n.* effort.

ex gra•ti•a [eks'greɪʃə] *adj.* (payment) made as a present, with no obligation implied.

ex•hale [eks'heɪl] *v.* (*formal*) to breathe out.

ex•haust [ɪg'zɔ:st] 1. *n.* escape (of steam/gas); **e. (pipe)** = pipe in a car which carries away fumes from the engine. 2. *v.* to wear out; to finish. **ex•haust•ed,** *adj.* (a) tired out. (b) completely used up. **ex•haus•tion** [ɪg-'zɔ:stʃn] *n.* state of being very tired. **ex•haus•tive,** *adj.* very thorough. **ex•haus•tive•ly,** *adv.* thoroughly.

ex•hib•it [ɪg'zɪbɪt] 1. *n.* object displayed (in court/at an exhibition). 2. *v.* to display. **ex•hi•bi•tion** [eksɪ'bɪʃn] *n.* display of works of art, flowers, etc.). **ex•hi•bi•tion•ist,** *n.* person who acts in a strange way so that people will look at him. **ex•hib•i•tor,** *n.* person who displays sth at an exhibition.

ex•hil•a•rate [ɪg'zɪləreɪt] *v.* to make extremely happy. **ex•hil•ar•at•ing,** *adj.* which makes you full of energy. **ex•hil•a•ra•tion** [ɪgzɪlə'reɪʃn] *n.* extreme happiness.

ex•hort [ɪg'zɔ:t] *v.* (*formal*) to urge/to encourage (s.o. to do sth). **ex•hor•ta•tion** [ɪgzɔ:-'teɪʃn] *n.* encouragement.

ex•hume [ɪg'zju:m] *v.* to dig up (a dead person who has been buried). **ex•hu•ma•tion** [eksju'meɪʃn] *n.* act of digging up a dead body which has been buried.

ex•i•gent ['egzɪdʒənt] *adj.* (*formal*) very urgent. **ex•i•gen•cy** [eg'zɪdʒənsɪ] *n.* (*formal*) urgent need.

ex•ig•u•ous [eg'zɪgjʊəs] *adj.* very small.

ex•ile ['egzaɪl] 1. *n.* (a) banishment (from one's native country); **he went into e.** (b) person who is banished. 2. *v.* to send (s.o.) away from his native country as a punishment.

ex•ist [ɪg'zɪst] *v.* to live/to be. **ex•ist•ence,** *n.* life/being. **ex•ist•ent, existing,** *adj.* actual/which is present at this moment.

ex•it ['egzɪt, 'eksɪt] 1. *n.* way out; going out; **he made his e. by the window** = he went out by the window; **emergency e.** = door used in emergency; **fire e.** = door used in case of fire. 2. *v.* (*in a play*) goes out; **e. Mr. Smith.**

ex lib•ris [eks'li:brɪs] *n.* printed label stuck in a book to show who it belongs to.

ex•o•crine ['eksəʊkri:n] *adj.* (gland) with ducts.

ex•o•dus ['eksədəs] *n.* departure/leaving (usu. of a crowd).

ex of•fi•ci•o [eksɒ'fɪʃɪəʊ] *adv. & adj.* because of your position.

ex•on•er•ate [ɪg'zɒnəreɪt] *v.* to state that no blame should be attached to (s.o.). **ex•on•er•a•tion** [ɪgzɒnə'reɪʃn] *n.* statement that no blame is attached to s.o.

ex•or•bi•tant [ɪg'zɔ:bɪtənt] *adj.* very high (price).

ex•or•cise, exorcize ['egzɔ:saɪz] *v.* to drive (a devil/a ghost) from a place. **ex•or•cism** ['egzɔ:sɪzəm] *n.* driving away a devil/a ghost. **ex•or•cist,** *n.* person who exorcises.

ex•ot•ic [ɪg'zɒtɪk] *adj.* unusual; referring to a tropical place; from a foreign place. **ex•ot•i•cal•ly,** *adv.* in an exotic way.

ex•pand [ɪk'spænd] *v.* to increase in size/to become larger.

ex•panse [ɪk'spæns] *n.* wide extent. **ex•pan•sion** [ɪk'spænʃn] *n.* increase in size. **ex•pan•sive,** *adj.* (person) who talks freely. **ex•pan•sive•ness,** *n.* being expansive.

ex•pa•ti•ate [ɪk'speɪʃɪeɪt] *v.* (*formal*) to talk at great length **on** sth.

ex•pa•tri•ate 1. *n.* [ɪk'spætrɪət] person who is not living in his native country. 2. *v.* [ɪk-'spætrɪeɪt] to send (s.o.) away from his native country.

ex•pect [ɪk'spekt] *v.* to think/to hope/to assume sth is going to happen; **I e. she is tired; he expects me to do all the housework; is it going to rain?—I e. so; we're expecting visitors** = we are waiting for visitors to arrive; **she's expecting** = she is pregnant. **ex•pect•an•cy,** *n.* hope; **life e.** = number of years a person will probably live. **ex•pect•ant,** *adj.* expecting; **e. mother** = pregnant woman. **ex•pect•ant•ly,** *adv.* hopefully. **ex•pec•ta•tion** [ekspek'teɪʃn] *n.* hope.

ex•pec•to•rant [ɪk'spektərənt] *n.* cough medicine which makes you cough up phlegm. **ex•pec•to•rate,** *v.* (*formal*) to cough up phlegm.

ex•pe•di•en•cy [ɪk'spi:dɪənsɪ] *n.* most simple/straightforward way of doing sth. **ex•pe•di•ent.** 1. *n.* simple way of doing sth. 2. *adj.* simple/straightforward.

ex•pe•dite ['ekspɪdaɪt] *v.* to make sth happen faster. **ex•pe•di•tion** [ekspɪ'dɪʃn] *n.* (a) rapidity. (b) journey of exploration; **to go on an e. to the North Pole. ex•pe•di•tion•ar•y,** *adj.* (army) which is on a journey. **ex•pe•di•tious,** *adj.* prompt/rapid. **ex•pe•di•tious•ly,** *adv.* rapidly.

ex•pel [ɪk'spel] *v.* (**expelled**) to throw (s.o.) out; to send (s.o.) away.

ex•pend•a•ble [ɪk'spendəbl] *adj.* which is not

worth keeping after it has been used; **he is e.** = he can be fired/left behind/killed.

ex•pend•i•ture [ɪkˈspendɪtʃə] *n.* amount spent.

ex•pense [ɪkˈspens] *n.* amount of money spent; **e. account** = money which a businessman is allowed to spend on entertainment and personal expenses which are paid for by his firm; **they had a good laugh at his e.** = they laughed at him. **ex•pen•sive**, *adj.* which costs a lot of money.

ex•pe•ri•ence [ɪkˈspɪərɪəns] **1.** *n.* thing lived through; wisdom gained by living through various situations; **I have no e. of traveling in the desert. 2.** *v.* to live through (sth). **ex•pe•ri•enced**, *adj.* wise from plenty of practice.

ex•per•i•ment [ɪkˈsperɪmənt] **1.** *n.* scientific test. **2.** *v.* to carry out a scientific test. **ex•per•i•men•tal** [ɪksperɪˈmentl] *adj.* used as part of a test. **ex•per•i•men•tal•ly,** *adv.* as an experiment. **ex•per•i•men•ta•tion,** *n.* carrying out of experiments.

ex•pert [ˈekspɜːt] **1.** *adj.* referring to s.o. who knows a great deal about a subject; **e. system** = computer program which has been devised for a particular purpose. **2.** *n.* person who knows a great deal about a subject. **ex•per•tise** [ekspəˈtiːz] *n.* specialist knowledge.

ex•pi•ate [ˈekspɪeɪt] *v.* *(formal)* to make amends for (a crime). **ex•pi•a•tion** [ekspɪˈeɪʃn] *n.* making amends.

ex•pire [ɪkˈspaɪə] *v.* (a) to come to an end. (b) *(formal)* to die. **ex•pi•ra•tion, expiry,** *n.* coming to an end; **the e. date of a ticket.**

ex•plain [ɪkˈspleɪn] *v.* to give reasons for (sth); to make (sth) clear. **ex•pla•na•tion** [eksplə-ˈneɪʃn] *n.* reason for sth. **ex•plan•a•to•ry** [ɪkˈsplænətərɪ] *adj.* which gives reasons; which makes clear.

ex•ple•tive [ɪkˈspliːtɪv] *n.* swear word.

ex•pli•ca•ble [ɪkˈsplɪkəbl] *adj.* which can be explained.

ex•plic•it [ekˈsplɪsɪt] *adj.* straightforward/clear. **ex•plic•it•ly,** *adv.* clearly.

ex•plode [ɪkˈspləʊd] *v.* (a) *(of bombs, etc.)* to go off/to blow up. (b) to make (bombs) go off; to discredit (a theory).

ex•ploit 1. *n.* [ˈeksplɔɪt] great/daring achievement. **2.** *v.* [ɪkˈsplɔɪt] to take commercial advantage of (sth); **to e. mineral resources. ex•ploi•ta•tion** [eksplɔɪˈteɪʃn] *n.* taking advantage.

ex•plore [ɪkˈsplɔː] *v.* to investigate/to travel and discover · (esp. unknown lands). **ex•plo•ra•tion** [eksplɔˈreɪʃn] *n.* investigation (of unknown lands). **ex•plor•a•to•ry** [ɪkˈsplɔrətərɪ] *adj.* tentative/preliminary. **ex•plor•er,** *n.* person who explores unknown lands.

ex•plo•sion [ɪkˈspləʊʒn] *n.* blowing up (of bombs/oil tanks, etc.); **population e.** = rapid increase in population. **ex•plo•sive** [ɪk-ˈspləʊsɪv] **1.** *adj.* liable to blow up. **2.** *n.* material (like gunpowder) which can blow up.

ex•po•nent [ɪkˈspəʊnənt] *n.* person who practices a certain belief/a certain art. **ex•po•nen•tial** [ekspəˈnenʃəl] *adj.* growing in proportion to the original number (i.e. growing faster as numbers increase).

ex•port 1. *n.* [ˈekspɔːt] goods sent to a foreign country for sale. **2.** *v.* [ɪkˈspɔːt] to send (goods) to a foreign country for sale. **ex•port•er,** *n.* person or company which sells goods to foreign countries.

ex•pose [ɪkˈspəʊz] *v.* (a) to show. (b) to let light go onto photographic film or plate. (c) to reveal (a scandal). **exposed,** *adj.* (a) open; **in a very e. position** = not sheltered from the wind. (b) **e. film** = where the pictures have been taken but not developed. **ex•po•si•tion** [ekspəˈzɪʃn] *n.* detailed explanation. **ex•po•sure** [ɪkˈspəʊʒə] *n.* (a) state of not being sheltered from cold/danger, etc. (b) time and amount of light needed for a picture to be taken on film; **e. meter** = device for calculating the exposure for a photograph. (c) revealing (of corruption, etc.). (d) direction in which (a house) faces.

ex•pos•é [ɪkˈspəʊzeɪ] *n.* newspaper/magazine report revealing corruption/wrongdoing, etc.

ex•pos•tu•late [ɪkˈspɒstjuleɪt] *v.* *(formal)* to protest/to reason **(with** s.o.). **ex•pos•tu•la•tion** [ˈɪkspɒstjuˈleɪʃn] *n.* protest.

ex•pound [ɪkˈspaʊnd] *v.* to explain in detail.

ex•press [ɪkˈspres] **1.** *adj.* done on purpose; **I did it with the e. intention of embarrassing him. 2.** *adj. & n.* rapid (train/postal service). **3.** *v.* (a) to put into words; **I expressed myself badly** = I did not make clear what I wanted to say. (b) to put into symbols; **to e. a fraction in decimals. ex•pres•sion** [ɪkˈspreʃn] *n.* (a) way of showing feeling on the face. (b) phrase. **ex•pres•sive,** *adj.* showing feeling. **ex•press•ly,** *adv.* on purpose.

æ back, aː farm, ɒ top, aɪ pipe, aʊ how, aiə fire, aʊə flower, ɔː bought, ɔɪ toy, e fed, eəhair, eɪ take, ə afraid, əʊ boat, əʊə lower, vː word, iː heap, ɪ hit, ɪə hear, uː school, ʊ book, ʌ but, b back, d dog, ð then, dʒ just, f fog, g go, h hand, j yes, k catch, l last, m mix, n nut, ŋ sing, p penny, r round, s some, ʃ short, t too, tʃ chop, θ thing, v voice, w was, z zoo, ʒ treasure

ex•press•way, n. fast road with few points of access or exit.

ex•pro•pri•ate [ɪk'sprəuprɪeɪt] v. (of the state/a local authority) to take away (property) from a private owner. **ex•pro•pri•a•tion** [ɪksprəuprɪ'eɪʃn] n. taking of property away from a private owner.

ex•pul•sion [ɪk'spʌlʃn] n. act of being thrown out/sent away.

ex•punge [ek'spʌndʒ] v. (formal) to wipe out/to cross out.

ex•pur•gate ['ekspəgeɪt] v. to remove rude/offensive expressions from (a book). **ex•pur•ga•tion** [ekspə'geɪʃn] n. act of expurgating.

ex•quis•ite [ɪk'skwɪzɪt] adj. very finely made/very refined. **ex•quis•ite•ly,** adv. finely.

ex•ser•vice•man [eks'sɜːvɪsmən] n. (pl. -men) man who used to be a member of the armed forces.

ex•tant [ɪk'stænt] adj. still in existence.

ex•tem•po•re [ɪk'stempərɪ] adv. & adj. without notes; **he spoke for ten minutes e.; an e. speech. ex•tem•po•rize,** v. to speak without preparation/without notes.

ex•tend [ɪk'stend] v. (a) to stretch out; **extended family** = family group which includes various relatives. (b) to make longer. **ex•tend•a•ble, extensible,** adj. which can be extended. **ex•ten•sion,** n. (a) act of extending; thing added on. (b) subsidiary telephone in a home/office. **ex•ten•sive,** adj. very widespread; very vast. **ex•ten•sive•ly,** adv. very greatly/widely. **ex•ten•sor,** n. muscle which makes a joint become straight.

ex•tent [ɪk'stent] n. degree; size; range; area.

ex•ten•u•at•ing [ɪk'stenjueɪtɪŋ] adj. which lessens or explains a crime; **e. circumstances. ex•ten•u•a•tion** [ɪkstenju'eɪʃn] n. lessening (of the seriousness of a crime).

ex•te•ri•or [ɪk'stɪərɪə] 1. adj. outside. 2. n. outside; **the e. of a house.**

ex•ter•mi•nate [ɪk'stɜːmɪneɪt] v. to kill (large number of living things). **ex•ter•mi•na•tion** [ɪkstɜːmɪ'neɪʃn] n. act of killing (large numbers).

ex•ter•nal [ɪk'stɜːnl] adj. outside; **medicine for e. use only** = which must not be drunk or eaten. **ex•ter•nal•ly,** adv. outside.

ex•tinct [ɪk'stɪŋkt] adj. (volcano) which no longer erupts; (species) which has died out. **ex•tinc•tion** [ɪk'stɪŋkʃn] n. putting out (of a fire); dying out (of a species).

ex•tin•guish [ɪk'stɪŋgwɪʃ] v. to put out (a fire). **ex•tin•guish•er,** n. **fire e.** = apparatus for putting out fires.

ex•tir•pate ['ekstɜːpeɪt] v. (formal) to destroy completely.

ex•tol [ɪk'stəul] v. (extolled) (formal) to praise very highly.

ex•tort [ɪk'stɔːt] v. to get (money) from s.o. by threats. **ex•tor•tion** [ɪk'stɔːʃn] n. getting money from s.o. by threats. **ex•tor•tion•ate,** adj. excessive (demands); very high (price).

ex•tra ['ekstrə] 1. adj. more than normal; additional. 2. adv. (a) more than usual; **e. strong string.** (b) in addition; **the service charge is e. 3.** n. (a) person (not a star) appearing in crowd scenes in a motion picture. (b) sth more than usual. 4. **extra-** prefix meaning outside; **extracurricular** = outside the curriculum; **extramarital** = outside marriage; **extrasensory** = (perception) by other means than the five senses; **extraterritorial** = outside the territory.

ex•tract 1. n. ['ekstrækt] thing reduced from sth larger; **meat e.** = substance concentrated from meat. 2. v. [ɪk'strækt] to pull (sth) out; to produce (sth). **ex•trac•tion** [ɪk'strækʃn] n. (a) pulling out (of a tooth); production (of coal, etc.). (b) origin; **he is of French e.** = his family originally was French.

ex•tra•dite ['ekstrədaɪt] v. to bring back (a criminal) to his own state or country for trial (by agreement with the state or country where he was arrested). **ex•tra•dit•a•ble,** adj. (crime) for which you can be extradited. **ex•tra•di•tion** [ekstrə'dɪʃn] n. return of a criminal to his own state or country.

ex•tra•ne•ous [ɪk'streɪnɪəs] adj. not directly connected with sth.

ex•traor•di•nar•y [ɪk'strɔːdnrɪ] adj. marvelous; quite different from everything else; strange/unusual. **ex•traor•di•nar•i•ly,** adv. in an extraordinary way.

ex•trap•o•late [ɪk'stræpəleɪt] v. to calculate (sth unknown) on the basis of available information. **ex•trap•o•la•tion** [ɪkstræpə'leɪʃn] n. calculating sth unknown on the basis of available information.

ex•tra•va•gance [ɪk'strævəgəns] n. excessive expense and luxury. **ex•trav•a•gant,** adj. (a) (person) who spends a lot of money. (b) expensive and luxurious. **ex•trav•a•gant•ly,** adv. in an extravagant way. **ex•trav•a•gan•za** [ɪkstrævə'gænzə] n. expensive and luxurious party/show/motion picture.

ex•treme [ɪk'striːm] 1. adj. very great; excessive; **at the e. end** = at the outermost end. 2. n. **to go to extremes** = to do everything in an excessive way. **ex•treme•ly,** adv. very; excessively. **ex•trem•ist,** n. person who has extreme views (usu. about politics).

ex•trem•i•ty [ɪk'stremɪtɪ] *n.* end point; **the extremities** = the hands and feet.

ex•tri•cate ['ekstrɪkeɪt] *v.* to get (s.o.) out of a difficult situation.

ex•tro•vert ['ekstrəvɜːt] *n.* person who is very outgoing and active. **ex•tro•vert•ed** *adj.* referring to an extrovert.

ex•trude [ɪk'struːd] *v.* to squeeze out under pressure. **ex•tru•sion** [ɪk'struːʒn] *n.* squeezing (of metal) under pressure.

ex•u•ber•ance [ɪg'zjuːbərəns] *n.* wild enthusiasm. **ex•u•ber•ant,** *adj.* wildly enthusiastic.

ex•ude [ɪg'zjuːd] *v.* to send out/to give off (a smell/a feeling) in all directions; **he exudes self-confidence.**

ex•ult [ɪg'zʌlt] *v.* to rejoice/to be glad; **he exulted over his victory** = he showed great pleasure at winning. **ex•ult•ant,** *adj.* full of triumph. **ex•ul•ta•tion,** *n.* great rejoicing.

eye [aɪ] 1. *n.* (a) part of the head, used for seeing; **keep your eyes open!** = watch out! **to set/clap eyes on sth** = to see sth (suddenly); **it catches the e.** = it is very noticeable; **to keep an e. on** = to guard; **they don't see e. to e.** = they do not agree. (b) *inf.* **private e.** = private detective. (c) small hole in a needle for passing the thread through; small loop for attaching a hook; bud on a potato through which sprouts grow. 2. *v.* to look at (s.o./sth) carefully.

eye•ball, *n.* ball of the eye; *inf.* **I'm up to my eyeballs in work** = I have masses of work to do. **eye•bath,** *n.* small cup for bathing the eye. **eye•brow,** *n.* small arch of hair above the eye. **eye•ful,** *n. inf.* good look at sth. **eye•glas•ses,** *n. pl.* pair of glass lenses in a frame, for correcting poor vision. **eye•lash,** *n.* one of the hairs growing round the rim of the eye. **eye•let,** *n.* small hole (as in a shoe, for passing the lace through). **eye•lid,** *n.* skin that covers and uncovers the eye. **eye•lin•er,** *n.* cosmetic substance for drawing a line around the eye. **eye-o•pen•er,** *n.* thing which surprises you. **eye•piece,** *n.* lens at the end of a telescope through which you look. **eye•shade,** *n.* shade worn on the forehead for keeping bright light out of the eyes. **eye•shad•ow,** *n.* cosmetic substance for coloring the eyelids. **eye•sight,** *n.* (*no pl.*) ability to see; **his e. is failing** = he can see less well. **eye•sore,** *n.* thing which is hideous/unpleasant to look at. **eye•strain,** *n.* (*no pl.*) tiredness of the eyes. **eye•tooth,** *n.* (*pl.* -teeth) canine. **eye•wash,** *n.* (*no pl.*) liquid for bathing the eyes; *inf.* **it's all e.** = it is nonsense. **eye•wit•ness,** *n.* person who has seen sth happen.

ey•rie ['ɪərɪ] *n. see* **aerie.**

æ back, ɑ: farm, ɒ: top, aɪ pipe, aʊ how, aie fire, aʊə flower, ɔ: bought, ɔɪ toy, e fed, eəhair, eɪ take, ə afraid, əʊ boat, əʊə lower, vː word, iː heap, ɪ hit, ɪə hear, uː school, ʊ book, ʌ but, b back, d dog, ð then, dʒ just, f fog, g go, h hand, j yes, k catch, l last, m mix, n nut, ŋ sing, p penny, r round, s some, ʃ short, t too, tʃ chop, θ thing, v voice, w was, z zoo, ʒ treasure

Ff

F *symbol for* fluorine.

fa•ble ['feɪbl] *n.* moral story usu. about animals, making them seem like human beings.

fab•ric ['fæbrɪk] *n.* (a) material. (b) basic structure (of society). **fab•ri•cate** ['fæbrɪkeɪt] *v.* to invent (an untrue story); to forge (a paper). **fab•ri•ca•tion** [fæbrɪ'keɪʃn] *n.* invention.

fab•u•lous ['fæbjuləs] *adj.* (a) imaginary, as in a fable. (b) *inf.* marvelous/wonderful. **fab•u•lous•ly**, *adv. inf.* wonderfully.

fa•cade [fə'sɑːd] *n.* front of a large building; outward appearance which is intended to give a false impression.

face [feɪs] 1. *n.* (a) front part of the head; **f. to f.** = talking and looking at each other; **to make a f.** = to make a rude expression; **to lose f.** = to feel humiliated. (b) front of an object. 2. *v.* (a) to put a facing/an outward covering on (sth). (b) to turn your head toward; **the house faces east** = the house looks toward the east; **to f. up to** = to accept bravely. **face•cloth**, *n.* washcloth. **face•less**, *adj.* threateningly anonymous. **face•lift**, *n.* operation to remove wrinkles from your face. **face pack**, *n.* cream which is left on the face to improve the skin. **face val•ue**, *n.* value written on a banknote/stock/bond; **to take sth at f. v.** = to assume that the first/obvious meaning is the correct one. **fac•ing**, *n.* material covering the surface of a building/the edges of a garment.

fac•et ['fæsɪt] *n.* (a) one of the flat sides on a cut gem. (b) aspect (of a problem, etc.).

fa•ce•tious [fə'siːʃəs] *adj.* funny/joking (in an offensive way). **fa•ce•tious•ly**, *adv.* not seriously/in a joking way. **fa•ce•tious•ness**, *n.* being facetious.

fa•cial ['feɪʃl] 1. *adj.* referring to a face. 2. *n.* beauty treatment to make your face more beautiful.

fac•ile ['fæsaɪl] *adj.* done too easily. **fa•cil•i•ty** [fə'sɪlɪtɪ] *n.* (a) ease/absence of difficulty. (b) sth, as a building or equipment, which can be used for a specific purpose; **hospital facilities, sports facilities. fa•cil•i•tate**, *v.* to make (sth) easy.

fac•sim•i•le [fæk'sɪmɪlɪ] *n.* (a) perfect reproduction; perfect copy. (b) fax.

fact ['fækt] *n.* thing that is true; **in f./as a matter of f.** = really/actually.

fac•tion ['fækʃn] *n.* group of people linked together in opposition to a leader/a government. **fac•tion•al**, *adj.* referring to factions.

fac•tor ['fæktə] *n.* (a) one of the numbers which produce a given number when multiplied. (b) thing which is influential/important. (c) person who buys the debts of a company at a discount and then tries to reclaim the full amount from the debtor.

fac•to•ry ['fæktrɪ] *n.* building where things are made; **f. ship** = ship which freezes or cans fish which are caught by smaller fishing boats.

fac•to•tum [fæk'təutəm] *n.* person who does all types of work.

fac•tu•al ['fæktjuəl] *adj.* containing facts. **fac•tu•al•ly**, *adv.* in a factual way.

fac•ul•ty ['fækəltɪ] *n.* (a) special ability. (b) teaching staff (of a school/university/college, etc.).

fad [fæd] *n.* strange temporary mania. **fad•dist**, *n.* person who follows a fad. **fad••dy**, *adj. inf.* (person) who has odd likes and dislikes about food.

fade [feɪd] *v.* to lose color, brightness or strength; **to make (sth)** lose color.

fag [fæg] 1. *n.* (a) *Sl.* cigarette. (b) *Sl.* male homosexual. 2. *v.* to tire by working hard; exhaust; *Sl.* **fagged out** = tired out.

fag•ot ['fægət] *n.* bundle of sticks for lighting a fire.

Fahr•en•heit ['færənheɪt] *adj.* (scale for) measuring heat where the boiling point of water is 212° and the freezing point 32°.

fa•ience [faɪ'ɑːns] *n.* thick glazed earthenware.

fail [feɪl] 1. *v.* (a) to be unsuccessful in doing sth. (b) to grow weaker. (c) not to pass (a candidate) in an examination. 2. *n.* **without f.** = certainly. **fail•ing**. 1. *n.* weakness/bad point. 2. *prep.* **f. that** = if that does not work. **fail-safe**, *adj.* (machine) made so that if anything goes wrong it will stop working and therefore not be dangerous. **fail•ure** ['feɪljə] *n.* (a) breakdown/stoppage; **heart f.** = dangerous condition when the heart has stopped beating; **power f.** = breakdown in the supply of electricity. (b) thing which did not work out satisfactorily.

faint [feɪnt] 1. *adj.* (a) not clear; difficult to see or hear; weak. 2. *v.* to lose consciousness for a short time. **faint•heart•ed**, *adj.* timid. **faint•ly**, *adv.* weakly. **faint•ness**, *n.* being faint.

fair [feə] 1. *n.* (a) group of sideshows/amusements/food booths, etc., set up in one place for a short time. (b) market for selling and advertising goods. 2. *adj.* (**-er, -est**) (a) light-colored (skin, hair). (b) honest/correct. (c) not bad. (d) (*of weather*) dry and warm. **fair•ground**, *n.* place in the open air where a fair is held. **fair•ly**, *adv.* (a) quite/not completely. (b) justly/correctly. **fair•ness**, *n.* (a) light coloring. (b) honesty/correctness. **fair•way**, *n.* (a) part of a golf course where the grass is kept cut. (b) navigable channel.

fair•y ['feərɪ] *n.* (a) small supernatural creature who is able to work magic; **f. story** = fairytale. (b) *Sl.* male homosexual. **fair•y•land**, *n.* land where fairies are supposed to live. **fair•y•tale**, *n.* story about fairies/princesses/giants, etc.

faith [feɪθ] *n.* belief/trust; **f. healer** = person who heals by prayer; **in good f.** = honorably, even though wrongly. **faith•ful**, *adj.* (a) trusting/loyal. (b) completely correct. **faith•ful•ness**, *n.* being faithful. **faith•ful•ly**, *adv.* loyally. **faith•less**, *adj.* disloyal.

fake [feɪk] 1. *n.* imitation/forgery; not the real thing. 2. *v.* to make an imitation of (sth).

fa•kir ['feɪkɪə] *n.* Indian holy man.

fal•con ['fɔːlkən] *n.* small bird of prey, sometimes trained to catch other birds in sport. **fal•con•ry**, *n.* sport of hunting with falcons.

fall [fɔːl] 1. *n.* (a) drop/collapse. (b) the autumn. (c) **falls** = waterfall. (d) **f. from power** = loss of a powerful position. 2. *v.* (**fell; has fallen**) to drop down. **fall back**, *v.* to retreat/to go back. **fall back on**, *v.* to use (sth) which was kept as a reserve. **fall down**, *v.* to drop to the ground. **fall•en**, *adj.* dropped. **fall for**, *v.* (a) to fall in love with (s.o.). (b) to be tricked by (sth). **fall in**, *v.* (*in the military*) to stand in line. **fall in with**, *v.* to join with (s.o.); to agree with (an idea). **fall off**, *v.* to become less. **fall out**, *v.* (a) to drop. (b) to have an argument. **fall•out**, *n.* radioactive dust from a nuclear explosion. **fall through**, *v.* to fail. **fall to**, *v.* to start to do sth (esp. eat or work).

fal•la•cy ['fæləsɪ] *n.* false argument; error. **fal•la•cious** [fə'leɪʃəs] *adj.* wrong.

fal•li•bil•i•ty [fælɪ'bɪlɪtɪ] *n.* being fallible. **fal•li•ble** ['fælɪbl] *adj.* (person) who can make a mistake.

Fal•lo•pi•an [fə'ləʊpɪən] *adj.* **F. tube** = tube in a woman from an ovary to the womb.

fal•low ['fæləʊ] *adj.* (land) which is purposely not used for crops for a time so that it can regain its goodness. **fallow deer**, *n.* small deer with white spots.

false [fɔːls] *adj.* (**-er, -est**) (a) not true. (b) not real; **f. teeth** = artificial teeth; **f. alarm** = signal for an emergency when there isn't one. **false•hood**, *n.* lie. **false•ly**, *adv.* in a false way. **false mem•o•ry syn•drome**, *n.* supposed syndrome in which a person in psychotherapy is mistakenly convinced that he/she has recovered a repressed memory of childhood trauma. **false•ness**, *n.* being false. **fal•si•fi•ca•tion**, *n.* act of falsifying. **fal•si•fy**, *v.* to change (sth) thus making it invalid.

fal•set•to [fɒl'setəʊ] *n.* unnaturally high voice (used by a man singing).

fal•ter ['fɔːltə] *v.* to move or speak hesitantly.

fame [feɪm] *n.* being well known. **famed**, *adj.* well known.

fa•mil•iar [fə'mɪljə] *adj.* (a) heard or seen before; well known; **I am f. with that type of machine** = I know that type of machine. (b) very informal/(too) friendly. **fa•mil•iar•i•ty** [fəmɪlɪ'ærɪtɪ] *n.* (a) (**with**) good knowledge of s.o./sth. (b) excessively informal way of speaking to s.o. **fa•mil•iar•i•za•tion** [fəmɪljəraɪ'zeɪʃn] *n.* act of familiarizing. **fa•mil•iar•ize** [fə'mɪljəraɪz] *v.* **to f. yourself with sth** = to become informed about sth. **fa•mil•iar•ly**, *adv.* in a familiar way.

fam•i•ly ['fæmɪlɪ] *n.* (a) group of people who are closely related, esp. mother, father and their children; **f. planning** = birth control; **f. tree** = table of the family going back over many generations. (b) group of animals/plants, etc., which are closely related.

fam•ine ['fæmɪn] *n.* very serious lack/shortage of food. **fam•ished**, *adj. inf.* very hungry.

fa•mous ['feɪməs] *adj.* well known.

fan [fæn] 1. *n.* (a) object/machine for moving air, to make things cooler or warmer; **f. belt** = loop of rubber which turns a fan to cool the engine of a car. (b) passionate admirer. 2. *v.* (**fanned**) to make the air move. **fan club**, *n.* organized group of admirers (of an actor, singer, athlete, etc.). **fan mail**, *n.* admiring letters received by an actor, etc. **fan out,** *v.* to spread out (like a fan).

fa•nat•ic [fə'nætɪk] *adj. & n.* (person) who is madly enthusiastic about sth, esp. religion. **fa•nat•i•cal,** *adj.* too enthusiastic. **fa•nat•i•cal•ly,** *adv.* in a fanatical way. **fa•nat•i•cism,** *n.* being fanatical.

fan•ci•er ['fænsɪə] *n.* person who has an interest (in a certain type of plant or animal); **pigeon f.** = person who breeds and races pigeons.

fan•cy ['fænsɪ] 1. *n.* (a) imagination. (b) desire; **it took his f.** = made him want it. 2. *adj.* pretty/decorated. 3. *v.* (a) to imagine/to believe. (b) to like/to want to have; *inf.* **I think she fancies you** = she is attracted to you. **fancy dress,** *n.* unusual costume (worn to a party). **fan•ci•ful,** *adj.* imaginative.

fan•fare ['fænfeə] *n.* piece of music played on trumpets to signal the entrance of an important person/the start of a show.

fang [fæŋ] *n.* animal's long tooth.

fan•light ['fænlaɪt] *n.* small window over a door or a large window.

fan•ta•sy ['fæntəsɪ] *n.* invented story/not a true story. **fan•ta•size,** *v.* to imagine/to dream. **fan•tas•tic** [fæn'tæstɪk] *adj.* (a) strange/like a dream. (b) *inf.* wonderful/amazing. **fan•tas•ti•cal•ly,** *adv.* in a fantastic way.

far [fɑː] **(farther/further; farthest/furthest)** 1. *adv.* (a) a long way away/not near; **so f.** = up to now. (b) much; **by f. the best.** 2. *adj.* distant/not near. **far•a•way,** *adj.* distant/remote. **far-fetched,** *adj.* difficult to believe. **far-reach•ing,** *adj.* which has important results. **far-sight•ed,** *adj.* looking to the future.

far•ad ['færæd] *n.* unit of electrical capacity.

farce [fɑːs] *n.* comedy based on slapstick and ridiculous situations; absurd situation. **far•ci•cal,** *adj.* absurd.

fare [feə] 1. *n.* (a) price to be paid for a journey; **roundtrip f.** = fare from one place to another and back again. (b) passenger in a bus/taxi. (c) food. 2. *v.* to get on; to do (well/badly). **fare•well** [feə'wel] *inter. & n.* (*formal*) goodbye.

far•i•na•ceous [færɪ'neɪʃəs] *adj.* made of flour.

farm [fɑːm] 1. *n.* land used for growing crops and keeping animals. 2. *v.* to look after a farm; to grow crops/to keep animals for sale. **farm•er,** *n.* person who looks after a farm. **farm•house,** *n.* house where the farmer and his family live. **farm•ing,** *n.* job of looking after a farm/growing crops/keeping animals for sale. **farm out,** *v.* to hand over

(work/child, etc.) to another person. **farm•stead,** *n.* farm and all its buildings. **farm•yard,** *n.* space outside a farmhouse, usu. surrounded by farm buildings or a wall.

far•ra•go [fə'rɑːgəʊ] *n.* tangled, confused mass.

far•ri•er ['færɪə] *n.* blacksmith who shoes horses.

far•row ['færəʊ] *v.* to have a litter of piglets.

fart [fɑːt] 1. *n.* (*vulgar*) noise made when passing gas from the intestines through the anus. 2. *v.* (*vulgar*) to make a fart.

far•ther ['fɑːðə] *adj. & adv.* to a greater distance; more distant. **far•thest** ['fɑːðəst] *adj. & adv.* to the greatest distance; most distant.

fas•ci•cle ['fæsɪkl] *n.* section of a large book, which is published in sections.

fas•ci•nate ['fæsɪneɪt] *v.* to attract/to charm. **fas•ci•nat•ing,** *adj.* attractive/very interesting. **fas•ci•na•tion** [fæsɪ'neɪʃn] *n.* attraction/charm. **fas•ci•na•tor,** *n.* person who fascinates.

fas•cism ['fæʃɪzəm] *n.* extreme right-wing political movement. **fas•cist,** *adj. & n.* (person) supporting fascism.

fash•ion ['fæʃn] 1. *n.* (a) manner/way; **after/in a f.** = not very well. (b) most admired style at a particular moment. 2. *v.* to make. **fash•ion•a•ble,** *adj.* in fashion. **fash•ion•a•bly,** *adv.* (dressed) in a fashionable way.

fast [fɑːst] 1. *adj. & adv.* (**-er, -est**) (a) quick; **my watch is five minutes f.** = my watch shows a time five minutes later than it really is; **f. film** = film which requires very short exposure times; **f. food** = food which is prepared and served quickly. (b) tightly fixed; **f. colors** = colors in fabric which do not run when washed; **to make sth f.** = to attach sth tightly. (c) **f. asleep** = soundly sleeping. 2. *n.* period when you stop eating. 3. *v.* to stop eating (for a time).

fast•en ['fɑːsn] *v.* to fix tightly. **fast•en•er,** *n.* device which fastens/attaches. **fast•en•ing,** *n.* thing which fastens.

fas•tid•i•ous [fæ'stɪdɪəs] *adj.* hard to please; easily shocked. **fas•tid•i•ous•ly,** *adv.* in a fastidious way. **fas•tid•i•ous•ness,** *n.* being fastidious.

fast•ness ['fɑːsnəs] *n.* (*pl.* **-es**) secure place; stronghold (as in the mountains).

fat [fæt] 1. *adj.* (**fatter, fattest**) (a) big and round; overweight; *inf.* **a f. lot of good** = very little good. (b) thick. (c) full of grease. 2. *n.* (a) grease/white layer on an animal's body under the skin. (b) **cooking f.** = refined oil (either vegetable or animal) used in frying, etc. **fat•ness,** *n.* being fat.

fate [feɪt] *n.* destiny; thing that is certain to happen as we think it has been decided by a power beyond human control. **fa•tal,** *adj.* deadly/causing death. **fa•tal•ism,** *n.* accepting fate. **fa•tal•ist,** *n.* person who accepts what happens, knowing that it is usually bad and cannot be avoided. **fa•tal•is•tic** [feɪtə-'lɪstɪk] *adj.* like a fatalist. **fa•tal•i•ties** [fə-'tælɪtɪz] *n. pl.* deaths. **fa•tal•ly,** *adv.* causing death. **fat•ed,** *adj.* destined/condemned by fate. **fate•ful,** *adj.* (decision, etc.) important for its serious consequences in the future.

fa•ther ['fɑːðə] 1. *n.* (a) male parent; **f. figure** = older man who is consulted for advice. (b) originator. (c) title given to a priest. 2. *v.* to be the father of. **fa•ther-in-law,** *n.* (*pl.* **fathers-in-law**) father of your wife or husband. **fa•ther•land,** *n.* native country. **fa•ther•less,** *adj.* with no father. **fa•ther•ly,** *adj.* like a father.

fath•om ['fæðəm] 1. *n.* measure of depth of water (6 feet or 1.8 meters). 2. *v.* to find the meaning or truth of.

fa•tigue [fə'tiːg] 1. *n.* (a) tiredness; **metal f.** = wearing out of metal used in a construction, causing weak points. (b) (*also* **fatigue duty**) cleaning duty in the military; **fatigues** = uniform worn when doing this. 2. *v.* to tire (s.o.) out.

fat•ten ['fætn] *v.* to make fat. **fat•ten•ing,** *adj.* (foods) which make you fat. **fat•ty,** *adj.* (food/tissue) which has a lot of fat in it.

fat•u•ous ['fætjuəs] *adj.* stupid/silly. **fat•u•ous•ly,** *adv.* in a fatuous way. **fat•u•ous•ness, fatuity** [fə'tjuːɪtɪ] *n.* being fatuous.

fau•cet ['fɔːsɪt] *n.* apparatus with a twisting knob and a valve which, when you turn it, allows liquid to come out of a pipe/container; tap.

fault [fɔːlt] 1. *n.* (a) mistake; **she's at f.** = has made a mistake. (b) imperfection/thing which is not as it should be. (c) (*in geology*) break in a rock layer where a section of rock slips down and another section rises. (d) (*in tennis*) error in serving. 2. *v.* to criticize/to find (sth) wrong. **fault•i•ness,** *n.* being faulty. **fault•less,** *adj.* perfect. **fault•less•ly,** *adv.* perfectly. **fault•y,** *adj.* (-ier, -iest) with mistakes or imperfections.

faun [fɔːn] *n.* mythical creature, like a man with goat's legs and horns.

fau•na ['fɔːnə] *n.* wild animals (of an area).

faux pas [fəʊ'pɑː] *n.* piece of embarrassing behavior.

fa•vor, *Brit.* **fa•vour** ['feɪvə] 1. *n.* (a) friendly act/kindness. (b) support for one group/one person at the expense of others; **out of f.** = disliked; **the score is 3-2 in his f.** = he is leading 3-2. (c) preference/liking; **to be in f. of** = to prefer. (d) ribbon/badge (worn by a supporter). 2. *v.* (a) to like/to prefer. (b) to make things easy for (s.o.). **fa•vor•a•ble** ['feɪvrəbl] *adj.* helpful/kind; good (impression). **fa•vor•a•bly,** *adv.* in a favorable way. **fa•vored,** *adj.* preferred/liked. **fa•vor•ite.** 1. *adj.* preferred/most liked. 2. *n.* (a) most liked thing/person. (b) horse, team, etc., which most people think will win. **fa•vor•it•ism,** *n.* prejudice/preference for one thing/person.

fawn [fɔːn] 1. *n.* young deer. 2. *adj.* brownish cream color. 3. *v.* **to f. on s.o.** = to try to get s.o.'s favor by doing everything they ask.

fax [fæks]. 1. *n.* (*pl.* **faxes**) copy of a text or image sent by telephone. 2. *v.* to send an image by telephone.

FBI [efbiː'aɪ] *n.* Federal Bureau of Investigation.

Fe *symbol for* iron.

fear ['fɪə] 1. *n.* terror/worry/feeling of being afraid. 2. *v.* to be afraid of (sth). **fear•ful,** *adj.* terrible. **fear•ful•ly,** *adv.* terribly/very. **fear•less,** *adj.* with no feeling of terror. **fear•less•ly,** *adv.* not feeling afraid. **fear•some,** *adj.* frightening.

fea•si•ble ['fiːzəbl] *adj.* (a) which can be done. (b) likely/probable. **fea•si•bil•i•ty** [fiːzə-'bɪlɪtɪ] *n.* ability to be done; **f. study** = study to see if sth can be done. **fea•si•bly,** *adv.* possibly.

feast [fiːst] 1. *n.* (a) special religious day when we remember a saint or special event. (b) very large meal. 2. *v.* (a) to eat expensive food. (b) to eat a very large meal.

feat [fiːt] *n.* unusually difficult act.

feath•er ['feðə] 1. *n.* one of many growths which form the covering of a bird's body; **light as a f.** = very light. 2. *v.* (a) **to f. one's nest** = to make a lot of money (usu. fraudulently). (b) to make the blade of an oar skim fast across the surface of the water. **feather-brained,** *adj.* silly and forgetful. **feath•ered,** *adj.* with feathers. **feath•er•weight,** *n.* weight in boxing between bantamweight and lightweight. **feath•er•y,** *adj.* light/delicate (like a feather).

fea•ture ['fiːtʃə] 1. *n.* (a) special part of the face

æ back, aː farm, ɒ top, aɪ pipe, aʊ how, aie fire, aʊə flower, ɔː bought, ɔɪ toy, e fed, eəhair, eɪ take, ə afraid, əʊ boat, əʊə lower, vː word, iː heap, ɪ hit, ɪə hear, uː school, ʊ book, ʌ but, b back, d dog, ð then, dʒ just, f fog, g go, h hand, j yes, k catch, l last, m mix, n nut, ŋ sing, p penny, r round, s some, ʃ short, t too, tʃ chop, θ thing, v voice, w was, z zoo, ʒ treasure

(such as nose/mouth, etc.); important aspect of sth. (b) important item in a news program or article; important article on a special subject. (c) **f. film** = main motion picture in a program. 2. *v.* (a) to have as the main actor/as the main subject, esp. on TV, or in a motion picture or newspaper. (b) to play an important part. **fea•ture•less**, *adj.* with no striking features.

Feb•ru•ar•y ['februərɪ] *n.* 2nd month of the year.

fe•ces ['fiːsɪz] *n. pl.* (*formal*) solid waste matter from the body. **fe•cal**, *adj.* referring to feces.

feck•less ['fekləs] *adj.* (person) who has no sense of responsibility/who is incompetent.

fe•cund ['fekənd] *adj.* fertile/fruitful. **fe•cun•di•ty** [fɪ'kʌndɪtɪ] *n.* being fecund.

fed [fed] *v. see* **feed. fed up**, *adj. inf.* bored/tired (**with**).

fed•er•a•tion [fedə'reɪʃn] *n.* group of states or societies which have joined together. **fed•er•al** ['fedərəl] *adj.* referring to a system where a group of semi-independent states exist under a central government. **fed•er•ate** ['fedəreɪt] *v.* to join (states) together in a federation.

fee [fiː] *n.* money paid for professional services, to schools, etc.

fee•ble ['fiːbl] *adj.* (**-er, -est**) weak. **fee•ble-mind•ed**, *adj.* of low intelligence. **fee•ble•ness**, *n.* weakness. **fee•bly**, *adv.* weakly.

feed [fiːd] 1. *n.* (a) food given to animals. (b) *inf.* meal; **morning f.** = morning meal given to babies. (c) means of putting material into a machine; device for feeding material into a machine. 2. *v.* (**fed**) (a) to give food to (s.o./sth). (b) (*esp. of animals*) to eat. (c) to put (**in**). **feed•back**, *n.* (a) return of a signal in an electronic circuit causing a high-pitched noise. (b) information/details about sth which has been done. **feed•er**, *n.* s.o./sth that gives food; **sheet f.** = device on a printer for inserting single sheets of paper. **feed•ing**, *adj.* giving food; **f. bottle** = bottle used for giving milk, etc., to a baby. **feed•lot**, *n.* fenced area of land where livestock are fattened.

feel [fiːl] 1. *n.* touch, esp. with the fingers. 2. *v.* (**felt**) (a) to touch, esp. with your fingers; **the knife felt cold; to f. one's way** = act cautiously until one has more experience. (b) to have a feeling/sensation; **he feels it would be unwise** = he thinks it would be unwise; **do you f. like a cup of coffee?** = would you like a cup of coffee? **to f. up to doing sth** = to feel strong enough to do it. **feel•er**, *n.* antenna/long part on an insect's head with which it touches; **to put out a f.** = to explore sth/to see if sth is ac-

ceptable. **feel•ing**, *n.* (a) sense of touch. (b) thing felt inside/emotion.

feet [fiːt] *n. pl. see* **foot.**

feign [feɪn] *v.* (*formal*) to pretend.

feint [feɪnt] 1. *n.* false attack; move to confuse your opponent. 2. *v.* to make a move to confuse your opponent.

feist•y ['feɪstɪ] *adj.* aggressive.

fe•lic•i•ty [fə'lɪsɪtɪ] *n.* (*formal*) happiness. **fe•lic•i•tous**, *adj.* well chosen (words).

fe•line ['fiːlaɪn] 1. *adj.* referring to a cat; like a cat. 2. *n.* member of the cat family.

fell [fel] 1. *n.* (*England*) high moorland. 2. *adj.* (*old*) cruel; **at one f. swoop** = swiftly. 3. *v.* to cut down (a tree); to knock (s.o.) down; *see also* **fall.**

fel•low ['feləʊ] *n.* (a) man. (b) person who is in the same group; **f. workers.** (c) member of a learned society. **fel•low•ship**, *n.* (a) friendly feeling. (b) group of people with similar interests.

fel•on ['felən] *n.* criminal. **fel•o•ny**, *n.* serious crime.

felt [felt] 1. *n.* thick, matted material made of wool; **f. tipped pen** = pen of which the writing end is made of hard felt. 2. *v.* to cover (sth) with felt; *see also* **feel. felt-tip**, *n.* felt tipped pen.

fe•male ['fiːmeɪl] 1. *adj.* (a) referring to women/girls. (b) referring to the sex which has young. 2. *n.* (a) *inf.* woman/girl. (b) animal/insect/bird which gives birth to young or lays eggs; flower which produces seeds.

fem•i•nine ['femənɪn] *adj.* (a) belonging to a woman, like a woman. (b) (*in grammar*) referring to words which have a particular form to indicate the female gender. **fem•i•nin•i•ty** [femɪ'nɪnətɪ] *n.* womanliness; female qualities. **fem•i•nism** ['femɪnɪzəm] *n.* being a feminist. **fem•i•nist**, *n.* person (usu. woman) who actively supports the right of women to equal status with men.

fem•o•ral ['fiːmərəl] *adj.* referring to the femur.

fe•mur ['fiːmə] *n.* thigh bone.

fen [fen] *n.* large area of marsh.

fence [fens] 1. *n.* (a) barrier, usu. of wood or wire, used to keep people or animals in or out of a place; **to sit on the f.** = to avoid giving a definite answer to a question. (b) *Sl.* person who takes stolen goods to resell them. 2. *v.* (a) **to f. in/off** = to surround with a fence. (b) to fight with swords as a sport. **fenc•er**, *n.* person who fences. **fenc•ing**, *n.* (a) material making up a fence. (b) sport of fighting with swords.

fend [fend] *v.* (a) **to f. off** = to push away. (b) **to f. for yourself** = to look after yourself.

fend•er ['fendə] *n.* (a) low guard around a fireplace to stop coal or wood falling out into the room. (b) rope mat/rubber tire, etc., hung against the side of a boat to protect it from bumps. (c) strip of metal over the wheels of a car, bicycle, or other vehicle to protect against mud or water; mudguard.

feng shui ['fʌŋ 'ʃweɪ] *n.* Chinese art of deciding the optimum location and design of a building/room, etc. so that it is in harmony with energies believed to flow around the earth.

fen•nel ['fenl] *n.* herb with a smell like aniseed.

fe•ral ['fɪərəl] *adj.* (animal) which is wild (having once been domesticated).

fer•ment 1. *n.* ['fɜːmənt] upset/agitation. 2. *v.* [fə'ment] to change by fermentation. **fer•men•ta•tion** [fɜːmen'teɪʃn] *n.* chemical change brought about in liquids, usu. leading to the production of alcohol.

fern [fɜːn] *n.* green plant often with feathery leaves which does not have flowers or seeds.

fe•ro•cious [fə'rəʊʃəs] *adj.* fierce/angry. **fe•ro•cious•ly,** *adv.* in a ferocious way. **fe•roc•i•ty** [fə'rɒsɪtɪ] *n.* fierceness.

fer•ret ['ferɪt] 1. *n.* small weasellike animal half-tamed and used to drive rabbits or rats from holes. 2. *v.* **to f. out** = to find out by endless searching.

Fer•ris wheel ['ferɪswiːl] *n.* large vertical wheel with seats, at an amusement park or fair.

fer•ro•con•crete [ferəʊ'kɒŋkriːt] *n.* concrete reinforced with steel bars.

fer•rous ['ferəs] *adj.* containing iron.

fer•rule ['feruːl] *n.* metal cap on the end of an umbrella or stick.

fer•ry ['ferɪ] 1. *n.* (a) (*also* **ferryboat**) boat which carries goods or people back and forth across a stretch of water. (b) place where a boat crosses a stretch of water. 2. *v.* to take (s.o.) across in a boat; **the bus ferried people to and from the station** = took them back and forth. **fer•ry•man,** *n.* (*pl.* **-men**) man in charge of a ferry.

fer•tile ['fɜːtl, *Brit.* 'fɜːtaɪl] *adj.* rich enough to produce crops; (*of female*) able to produce young; **she has a f. imagination** = she is very imaginative/she can imagine things very easily. **fer•til•i•ty** [fə'tɪlətɪ] *n.* ability to produce crops or young. **fer•ti•li•za•tion** [fɜːtɪlaɪ'zeɪʃn] *n.* the act of fertilizing. **fer•ti•lize** ['fɜːtɪlaɪz] *v.* (a) to join male and female cells together, so that a new animal/plant will be made. (b) to spread fertilizer on. **fer•ti•liz•er,** *n.* chemical or manure spread

over the ground to make it richer and more able to produce crops.

fer•vor, *Brit.* **fer•vour** ['fɜːvə] *n.* passion. **fer•vent, fervid,** *adj.* passionate. **fer•vent•ly,** *adv.* in a fervent way.

fes•cue ['feskjuː] *n.* grass grown in meadows.

fes•ter ['festə] *v.* (*of wound*) to become bad and produce pus.

fes•ti•val ['festɪvl] *n.* (a) religious celebration which comes at the same time each year. (b) artistic celebration/entertainment which is put on at regular intervals; **arts f., music f. fes•tive,** *adj.* happy; fit for a celebration. **fes•tiv•i•ty** [fe'stɪvɪtɪ] *n.* celebration.

fes•toon [fe'stuːn] 1. *n.* long chain of hanging decorations. 2. *v.* to hang with decorations.

fetch [fetʃ] *v.* (a) to go and bring (s.o./sth) back. (b) to be sold at (a certain price). **fetch•ing,** *adj.* attractive/pretty. **fetch up,** *v. inf.* to arrive/to end up (in a certain place).

fete, fête [feɪt] 1. *n.* public celebration/entertainment, often held outdoors. 2. *v.* to celebrate or honor with a fete.

fet•id ['fiːtɪd] *adj.* bad-smelling (water/breath).

fet•ish ['fetɪʃ] *n.* (a) object worshipped by s.o. (b) obsession.

fet•lock ['fetlɒk] *n.* back part of a horse's leg just above the hoof.

fet•ter ['fetə] *v.* to chain (a prisoner). **fet•ters,** *n. pl.* chains.

fet•tle ['fetl] *n.* **in fine f.** = in very good condition.

fe•tus, *Brit.* **foe•tus** ['fiːtəs] *n.* unborn child/reptile/bird, etc., which is developing from an embryo. **fe•tal,** *adj.* referring to a fetus.

feud [fjuːd] 1. *n.* bitter quarrel. 2. *v.* to quarrel bitterly all the time.

feu•dal ['fjuːdl] *adj.* **f. system** = medieval system of holding land in return for services to an overlord or king. **feu•dal•ism,** *n.* feudal system.

fe•ver ['fiːvə] *n.* (a) state when the body's temperature is higher than normal. (b) **f. (pitch)** = great excitement. **fe•ver•ish,** *adj.* suffering from a fever. **fe•ver•ish•ly,** *adv.* excitedly; impatiently.

few [fjuː] *adj. & n.* (a) (**-er, -est**) not many. (b) **a f.** = some/several.

fey [feɪ] *adj.* otherworldly, supernatural.

fez [fez] *n.* round hat worn in some Muslim countries.

æ back, aː farm, ɒ top, aɪ pipe, aʊ how, aɪə fire, aʊə flower, ɔː bought, ɔɪ toy, e fed, eəhair, eɪ take, ə afraid, əʊ boat, əʊə lower, vː word, iː heap, ɪ hit, ɪə hear, uː school, ʊ book, ʌ but, b back, d dog, ð then, dʒ just, f fog, g go, h hand, j yes, k catch, l last, m mix, n nut, ŋ sing, p penny, r round, s some, ʃ short, t too, tʃ chop, θ thing, v voice, w was, z zoo, ʒ treasure

fi•an•cé, fi•an•cée [fɪ'ɒnseɪ] *n.* man/woman who is engaged to be married.

fi•as•co [fɪ'æskəʊ] *n.* (*pl.* **-os**) total failure.

fib [fɪb] 1. *n.* lie. 2. *v.* (**fibbed**) to tell lies. **fib•ber,** *n.* person who tells lies.

fi•ber, *Brit.* **fi•bre** ['faɪbə] *n.* small thread of material. (b) **moral f.** = strength of moral feelings. **fi•ber•glass,** *n.* (a) glass fiber wool used as insulation. (b) strong material made of woven threads of glass; plastic containing threads of glass. **fi•ber op•tics,** *n.* use of thin strands of material through which light can be passed, in order to convey messages or images over long distances. **fi•broid,** *adj.* (growth, etc.) made of fibers. **fi•bro•my•al•gi•a,** *n.* any of several rheumatoid disorders characterized by pain, tenderness and stiffness of the muscles, fatigue, and headaches. **fi•bro•my•o•si•tis,** *n.* fibromyalgia. **fi•brous,** *adj.* made of fibers.

fib•u•la ['fɪbjʊlə] *n.* thin bone between the knee and the ankle behind the tibia.

fick•le ['fɪkl] *adj.* changeable/not steady. **fick•le•ness,** *n.* being fickle.

fic•tion ['fɪkʃn] *n.* (a) story that is not true. (b) novels. **fic•tion•al** *adj.* (character) who exists in fiction. **fic•ti•tious** [fɪk'tɪʃəs] *adj.* untrue/not real.

fid•dle ['fɪdl] 1. *n. inf.* (a) violin. (b) dishonest/illegal dealings. 2. *v. inf.* (a) to play the fiddle. (b) to play idly with sth. **fid•dler,** *n. inf.* violin player. **fid•dle•sticks,** *n. inf.* nonsense.

fi•del•i•ty [fɪ'delɪtɪ] *n.* faithfulness/accuracy (of a reproduction).

fidg•et ['fɪdʒɪt] 1. *n.* person who cannot stay still. 2. *v.* to move restlessly. **fidg•et•y,** *adj.* restless.

field [fiːld] 1. *n.* (a) piece of cultivated land surrounded by fences or hedges. (b) large surface/area; **f. day** = busy and exciting time. (c) piece of ground for playing games; **f. events** = jumping and throwing competitions. (d) special area of study. (e) area of influence (of a magnet/of gravity/of a charged particle). 2. *v.* (*in baseball, cricket*) (a) to stop (a ball hit by s.o. at bat). (b) to be part of the side which is not batting. **field•er,** *n.* (*in baseball, cricket*) member of the side which is not batting. **field glas•ses,** *n. pl.* binoculars. **field hock•ey,** *n.* team game played on grass with long curved sticks and a hard ball. **field mar•shal,** *n.* highest rank in the British and certain other armies. **field•mouse,** *n.* (*pl.* **-mice**) small mouse living in fields and meadows. **field•work,** *n.* scientific research done outside, and not in a laboratory.

field•work•er, *n.* person engaged in fieldwork.

fiend [fiːnd] *n.* devil; monster; *inf.* addict; **dope f.** = dope addict. **fiend•ish,** *adj.* devilish; very cruel.

fierce ['fɪəs] *adj.* ferocious/angry; which will attack anything; very violent or strong; **f. winds.** **fierce•ly,** *adv.* strongly and angrily. **fierce•ness,** *n.* violence; intensity.

fier•y ['faɪərɪ] *adj.* burning/full of fire; angry.

fi•es•ta [fɪ'estə] *n.* Spanish festival.

fife [faɪf] *n.* small metal flute played in military bands.

fif•teen [fɪf'tiːn] *n.* (a) number 15. (b) group of fifteen people (as in a sports team). **fif•teenth, 15th,** *adj. & n.* referring to fifteen.

fifth, 5th [fɪfθ] *adj. & n.* referring to five. **Fifth A•mend•ment,** *n.* the Amendment to the Constitution of the United States which allows citizens not to give evidence in court which might incriminate themselves. **fifth col•umn,** *n.* enemy sympathizers inside a country under attack.

fif•ty ['fɪftɪ] *number* 50; **f.-f.** = each paying half of the cost. **fif•ti•eth, 50th,** *adj.* referring to fifty.

fig [fɪg] *n.* juicy sweet fruit of the fig tree.

fight [faɪt] 1. *n.* struggle/battle; boxing match. 2. *v.* (**fought**) to struggle with (s.o./sth). **fight•er,** *n.* (a) person who fights. (b) fast attacking aircraft. **fight•ing,** *n.* action of struggling with s.o.

fig•ment ['fɪgmənt] *n.* **f. of the imagination** = thing which has been imagined.

fig•ure ['fɪgə, *Am.* 'fɪgjə] 1. *n.* (a) written number (such as 28). (b) geometric shape such as a triangle or circle; drawing/diagram in a book. (c) shape of a person. (d) **f. of speech** = colorful expression used to illustrate a meaning. (e) pattern of movement (in skating/dancing). 2. *v.* (a) **to f. out** = to try to understand; *inf.* **that figures** = that makes sense. (b) to appear (in a novel, etc.). **fig•ur•a•tive** ['fɪgjurətɪv] *adj.* (usage of a word) which is not the literal meaning. **fig•ur•a•tive•ly,** *adv.* in a figurative way. **fig•ure•head,** *n.* (a) wooden figure carved on the front of a ship. (b) person who seems important but who has no real power. **fig•ur•ine** ['fɪgjuriːn] *n.* small figure (in china/wood, etc.).

fil•a•ment ['fɪləmənt] *n.* thin wire (in an electric bulb).

fil•bert ['fɪlbət] *n.* type of hazel nut.

filch [fɪltʃ] *v.* to steal.

file [faɪl] 1. *n.* (a) metal tool used for smoothing rough surfaces. (b) holder for papers and documents. (c) section of data on a computer; **f.**

server = central unit of a computer network that allows other computers access to files. (d) line of people; **in single f.** = one behind the other. 2. v. (a) to smooth (a surface) with a file. (b) to put (papers) away in a folder or case. (c) to walk in a line. **fil•ing cab•i•net,** *n.* box with drawers for putting files in. **fil•ings,** *n. pl.* small pieces of metal which come away when metal is filed smooth.

fil•i•al ['fɪlɪəl] *adj. (formal)* referring to a son or daughter.

fil•i•bus•ter ['fɪlɪbʌstə] 1. *n.* attempt to prevent a law being passed by speaking for a very long time in the debate. 2. v. to delay the passing of a law by speaking for a very long time in the debate.

fil•i•gree ['fɪlɪgriː] *n.* very decorative ornamental work done in precious metals.

Fil•i•pi•no [fɪlɪ'piːnəu] *adj. & n. (pl. -os)* (person) from the Philippines.

fill [fɪl] v. to put as much as possible into (sth)/to make (sth) full; to become full; to drill a hole in (a bad tooth) and fill it up with metal, etc.; to find s.o. to do (a job). **fill•er,** *n.* material used to fill holes and cracks in walls/woodwork, etc. **fill in,** v. (a) to fill a hole. (b) to complete the blank spaces in (a form/document). (c) *inf.* **to f. s.o. in on** = to tell/to inform (s.o.). **fill•ing,** *n.* thing that fills up sth else. **fill•ing sta•tion,** place where you can buy fuel and oil. **fill out,** v. (a) to write everything that is asked for on (a form). (b) to get fatter. **fill up,** v. to fill (sth) until it is completely full; to become completely full.

fil•let ['fɪlɪt] 1. *n.* good cut of meat or fish from which all the bones have been removed. 2. v. to remove the bones from (a fish).

fil•lip ['fɪlɪp] *n.* sharp stroke.

fil•ly ['fɪlɪ] *n.* young female horse.

film [fɪlm] 1. *n.* (a) motion picture. (b) roll of coated plastic put in a camera and used for taking photographs or pictures to be shown on a screen. (c) thin covering (of dust, etc.). 2. v. to take pictures of (sth) with a motion-picture camera. **film star,** *n.* well-known motion-picture actor or actress. **film•strip,** *n.* strip of film with several still pictures which are projected one after the other. **film•y,** *adj.* very thin/almost transparent.

fil•ter ['fɪltə] 1. *n.* (a) device/material for straining liquids or air, stopping any solids from passing through. (b) glass on a camera which allows only certain colors or intensities of light to pass through. 2. v. (a) to pass through

a filter. (b) to move gradually and quietly. (c) **to f. through/down** = to go/come slowly through or down. **fil•ter pa•per,** *n.* paper used for filtering liquids. **fil•ter-tip cig•a•rettes,** *n. pl.* cigarettes with a filter at the mouth end.

filth [fɪlθ] *n.* dirt; obscene words/books, etc. **filth•y,** *adj.* (-ier, -iest) (a) very dirty. (b) obscene. **filth•i•ly,** *adv.* in a filthy way. **filth•i•ness,** *n.* being filthy; filthy things.

fil•trate ['fɪltreɪt] *n.* liquid which has been filtered. **fil•tra•tion,** *n.* action of filtering.

fin [fɪn] *n.* (a) thin limb on the body of a fish which it moves to swim. (b) piece shaped in a similar way on a bomb, rocket or aircraft.

fi•na•gle [fɪ'neɪgl] v. *inf.* to work dishonestly; to get (sth) dishonestly.

fi•nal ['faɪnl] 1. *adj.* coming at the end; last; **the decision is f.** = cannot be changed. 2. *n.* (a) last competition in a contest between several teams or competitors. (b) **finals** = last examinations at the end of a school/college/university course. **fi•nal•ist,** *n.* person taking part in the final competition. **fi•nal•i•ty** [faɪ'nælɪtɪ] *n.* state of being at the end. **fi•nal•i•za•tion** [faɪnəlaɪ'zeɪʃn] *n.* act of finalizing. **fi•nal•ize** ['faɪnəlaɪz] v. to finish making plans for sth. **fi•nal•ly,** *adv.* at last; in the last place.

fi•na•le [fɪ'nɑːlɪ] *n.* last part of a piece of music/of a show.

fi•nance ['faɪnæns] 1. *n.* money, esp. belonging to the public or to a company. 2. v. to provide money for. **fi•nan•cial** [fɪ'nænʃl] *adj.* concerning finance. **fi•nan•cial•ly,** *adv.* regarding finance. **fin•an•cier** [fɪ'nænsɪə] *n.* person who deals with money on a large scale.

finch [fɪntʃ] *n.* (pl. -es) small seed-eating bird.

find [faɪnd] 1 *n.* good thing which you have discovered. 2. v. (**found**) to discover (sth hidden or lost); **to be found** = to exist; **to f. out** = to discover; to learn; **to f. s.o. out** = to discover the true nature, character, or identity of s.o.; **it has been found that** = it is a known fact that. **find•er,** *n.* person who finds. **find•ings,** *n. pl.* facts discovered/recommendations.

fine [faɪn] 1. *n.* money to be paid as a punishment for doing wrong. 2. *adj.* (-er, -est) (a) pure. (b) lovely/good. (c) (*of weather*) good; with no precipitation. (d) very thin; very small. 3. *inter.* **f.!** = all right/agreed. 4. v. (a) to make (sth) fine. (b) to punish by making s.o. pay a fine. **fine art,** *n.* painting/sculpture, etc.

æ back, aː farm, ɒ top, aɪ pipe, au how, aiə fire, auə flower, ɔː bought, ɔɪ toy, e fed, eəhair, eɪ take, ə afraid, əu boat, əuə lower, vː word, iː heap, ɪ hit, ɪə hear, uː school, u book, ʌ but, b back, d dog, ð then, dʒ just, f fog, g go, h hand, j yes, k catch, l last, m mix, n nut, ŋ sing, p penny, r round, s some, ʃ short, t too, tʃ chop, θ thing, v voice, w was, z zoo, ʒ treasure

fine•ly, *adv.* delicately/thinly/beautifully. **fin•er•y,** *n.* fine clothes.

fi•nesse [fɪ'nes] *n.* skill (in dealing with awkward situations).

fin•ger ['fɪŋgə] 1. *n.* (a) one of the five parts at the end of a hand, usu. other than the thumb; **to keep your fingers crossed** = to hope that sth will happen as you want it; **to put your f. on sth** = to identify it. (b) part of a glove into which a finger goes. (c) thing shaped like a finger. 2. *v.* to touch with the fingers. **fin•ger•ing,** *n.* use of the fingers when playing a musical instrument. **fin•ger•nail,** *n.* thin horny substance which grows at the end of the fingers. **fin•ger•print,** *n.* mark left by the end of the fingers. **fin•ger•stall,** *n.* cover put over a finger which has been hurt. **fin•ger•tip,** *n.* end of the finger; **she has the information at her fingertips** = she has the information close at hand or at her disposal.

fin•i•al ['fɪnɪəl] *n.* decoration on a gable.

fin•ick•y ['fɪnɪkɪ] *adj.* (*also* **finical**) *inf.* (a) awkward and detailed (work). (b) fussy (person) who dislikes things, esp. certain types of food; **f. eater.**

fin•ish ['fɪnɪʃ] 1. *n.* (a) end. (b) way in which sth is completed; appearance of sth when it is finished. 2. *v.* to end. **finish off,** *v.* (a) to complete or use all of sth. (b) to kill. **finish up,** *v.* (a) to end up. (b) to finish completely. **finish with,** *v.* **to f. with s.o.** = to stop being friendly with s.o.; **to f. with sth** = to need sth no longer.

fi•nite ['faɪnaɪt] *adj.* with an end/with a limit; **f. verb** = verb which indicates a tense.

Finn [fɪn] *n.* person from Finland. **Finn•ish** ['fɪnɪʃ] 1. *adj.* referring to Finland. 2. *n.* language spoken in Finland.

fiord ['fɪɔːd] *n.* fjord.

fir [fɜː] *n.* **f. (tree)** = evergreen tree with needle-shaped leaves.

fire ['faɪə] 1. *n.* (a) thing that is burning; **to catch f.** = to start burning because of sth else which is in flames; **to set f. to sth** = to make sth start burning. (b) great enthusiasm or excitement. (c) shooting of guns. 2. *v.* (a) to make (sth) burn. (b) to make (s.o.) excited. (c) to bake/to heat. (d) to shoot (a gun); **f. away** = ask your question. (e) to dismiss (s.o.) from a job. **fire a•larm,** *n.* bell/siren which gives warning that a fire has started. **fire•arm,** *n.* any gun held in the hand. **fire•brand,** *n.* agitator. **fire•break,** *n.* strip of land which has been cleared of trees, to prevent forest fires from spreading. **fire bri•gade,** *n.* people whose job is to put out fires. **fire•damp,** *n.* explosive gas in a mine. **fire en•gine,** *n.* vehicle used by the fire brigade to carry pumps/hoses/ladders, etc., to put out fires.

fire es•cape, *n.* stairs/ladder which can be used by people to get out of buildings on fire. **fire ex•tin•guish•er,** *n.* portable cylinder filled with chemicals or foam to put out a small fire. **fire•fight,** *n.* military skirmish involving light weapons. **fire•fly,** *n.* type of insect which glows at night. **fire•guard,** *n.* metal screen put in front of a fireplace. **fire•light,** *n.* light from a fire. **fire•man,** *n.* (*pl.* **-men**) (a) man whose job it is to put out fires. (b) man who keeps the fire burning in a furnace/a steam train. **fire•place,** *n.* place where a fire is lit indoors. **fire•proof,** *adj.* which will not burn. **fire•side,** *n.* area around a fireplace in a room. **fire sta•tion,** *n.* center where fire engines are based. **fire•ward•en,** *n.* person in charge of putting out fires, as in a forest. **fire•wood,** *n.* (*no pl.*) wood for making fires. **fire•work** (*usu.* **fireworks**) *n.* small container holding chemicals which will sparkle or explode when lit.

firm [fɜːm] 1. *n.* business/company. 2. *adj.* solid/fixed/strong. 3. *adv.* **to stand f.** = to refuse to change your mind. **firm•ly,** *adv.* in a strong way.

fir•ma•ment ['fɜːməmənt] *n.* (*formal*) sky.

first [fɜːst] 1. *adj. & adv.* (*as a number can be written* **1st**) (a) at the beginning/coming before everything else; **at f.** = at the beginning. (b) for the first time. (c) in a first class seat. 2. *n.* thing/person coming before everything else; **in f.** = in first gear. **first aid,** *n.* help given to a person who is hurt before a doctor or ambulance arrives. **First A•mend•ment,** *n.* the Amendment to the Constitution of the United States which grants citizens freedom of speech. **first class.** 1. *adj.* excellent; highest; most expensive. 2. *adv.* (travel) with the most expensive seats. **first day cov•er,** *n.* special stamped envelope canceled on the first day of issue of the stamp on it. **first floor,** *n.* (a) story above the ground floor in a building. (b) ground floor. **first•hand,** *adj. & adv.* direct from the original source. **First La•dy,** *n.* wife of the President of the United States. **first•ly,** *adv.* to start with. **first mate,** *n.* second-in-command of a merchant ship. **first night,** *n.* evening when a play is performed for the first time. **first-rate,** *adj.* excellent.

firth [fɜːθ] *n.* (*in Scotland*) long arm of the sea.

fis•cal ['fɪskl] *adj.* referring to tax/government revenue.

fish [fɪʃ] 1. *n.* (*pl.* **fish,** *occasionally* **fishes**) cold-blooded animal with fins and scales, that lives in water; **he's like a f. out of water** = awkward, because he feels he is not in his usual surroundings. 2. *v.* (a) to try to catch fish; *inf.* **to f. out** = to take out. (b) to try to get (infor-

mation). **fish•bone,** *n.* bone in a fish.
fish•cake, *n.* round cake of fish and potato
mixed together. **fish•er•man,** *n.* (*pl.* **-men**)
man who catches fish, either as his job or for
sport. **fish•er•y,** *n.* business of catching fish.
fish stick, *n.* frozen finger-shaped piece of
fish covered in breadcrumbs. **fish-hook,** *n.*
metal hook at the end of a line which catches
in the mouth of the fish. **fish•ing,** *n.* catching
fish. **fish•ing boat,** *n.* boat used for fishing.
fish•ing rod, *n.* long piece of wood to which
is attached the line and hook. **fish•ing
tack•le,** *n.* all the equipment used by a
fisherman. **fish•y,** *adj.* (a) like a fish. (b) *inf.*
suspicious/odd (story, etc.).

fis•sion ['fɪʃn] *n.* breaking up of sth into parts;
nuclear f. = breaking up of an atom in an explosion.

fis•sure ['fɪʃə] *n.* crack/split, esp. in a rock or in
the ground.

fist [fɪst] *n.* tightly closed hand. **fist•ful,** *n.*
amount you can hold in your fist.
fist•i•cuffs, *n. pl.* (*old*) fighting.

fit [fɪt] 1. *n.* sudden sharp attack of illness, etc.;
by fits and starts = at odd moments/with continual stoppages. 2. *adj.* (**fitter, fittest**) (a)
right/suitable. (b) capable. (c) healthy. 3. *v.*
(**fitted**) (a) to be the right size for. (b) to put in
the right place. (c) to make suitable for.
fit•ful, *adj.* irregular. **fit•ful•ly,** *adv.* irregularly. **fit in,** *v.* (a) to be suitable/to match
(with). (b) to find room/time for (s.o./sth).
fit•ment, *n.* furniture/equipment which is
fixed in a room. **fit•ness,** *n.* being fit. **fit
out, fit up,** *v.* to provide all the equip-
ment/clothing necessary for. **fit•ted,** *adj.*
suitable/right; which has been made to fit.
fit•ter, *n.* (a) skilled mechanic who adjusts
machines and their parts. (b) person who
makes sure clothes fit. **fit•ting.** 1. *adj.* suit-
able/right. 2. *n.* (a) action of making sth fit/of
trying on a new piece of clothing; **f. room** =
small room in a store where you can try on
clothes before you buy them. (b) thing which
is fixed in a building but which could be removed.

five [faɪv] *n.* number 5. **fiv•er,** *n. inf.* five dollar
bill.

fix [fɪks] 1. *n.* (*pl.* **-es**) (a) difficult position. (b)
Sl. injection of a drug such as heroin. 2. *v.* (a)
to fasten/to attach. (b) to arrange. (c) to
make/to prepare (a drink/meal, etc.). (d) to
pass (a photographic plate) through a liquid

to stop the image changing. (e) to mend.
fix•at•ed, *adj.* obsessed. **fix•a•tion** [fɪk-
'seɪʃn] *n.* obsession. **fix•a•tive** ['fɪksətɪv] *n.*
substance which fixes the colors on a painting.
fixed, *adj.* (a) attached firmly. (b) (price, etc.)
arranged or agreed upon. **fix•ed•ly**
['fɪksɪdlɪ] *adv.* with eyes fixed on s.o. **fix•er,**
n. person who can arrange sth. **fix•i•ty,** *n.*
state of being fixed. **fix•ture** ['fɪkstʃə] *n.* object permanently fixed in a house (like a sink,
toilet, radiator). **fix up,** *v.* to arrange.

fizz [fɪz] 1. *n.* sound like a lot of bubbles. 2. *v.* to
bubble up. **fizz•y,** *adj.* bubbly.

fiz•zle out ['fɪzl'aut] *v. inf.* to come to noth-
ing/not to work.

fjord ['fjɔːd] *n.* long arm of the sea among
mountains in Norway.

flab•ber•gast ['flæbəgɑːst] *v.* to amaze.

flab•by ['flæbɪ] *adj.* (**-ier, -iest**) (person) who is
soft and fat. **flab,** *n. inf.* soft excess flesh.
flab•bi•ness, *n.* being flabby.

flac•cid ['flæksɪd] *adj.* hanging loosely.

flag [flæg] 1. *n.* (a) piece of material with the
emblem of a country/club, etc., on it. (b) large
paving stone. (c) iris/marsh plant with long fat
leaves and purple flowers. (d) mark inserted in
a computer text. 2. *v.* (**flagged**) (a) to grow
tired. (b) **to f. down** = to wave to make (a cab)
stop. (c) to insert a mark in a computer file.
flag•pole, flagstaff, *n.* tall pole on which
large flags are flown. **flag•ship,** *n.* ship on
which a high-ranking naval officer (as an ad-
miral) sails, and which therefore flies his special flag. **flag•stone,** *n.* large flat stone used
for making pavements/floors.

flag•el•late ['flædʒəleɪt] *v.* (*formal*) to whip.
flag•el•la•tion [flædʒə'leɪʃn] *n.* (*formal*)
whipping.

flag•on ['flægən] *n.* large round container for
liquids.

fla•grant ['fleɪgrənt] *adj.* (crime) which is obvious. **fla•grance,** *n.* being flagrant.
fla•grant•ly, *adv.* in a flagrant way.

flail [fleɪl] 1. *n.* implement for threshing grain.
2. *v.* to wave (your arms) about.

flair ['fleə] *n.* natural ability (**for** sth).

flak [flæk] *n.* (*no pl.*) gun fire against aircraft;
sharp criticism.

flake [fleɪk] 1. *n.* tiny, thin piece. 2. *v.* **to f.
off/away** = to fall off in little pieces; *Sl.* **to f.
out** = to collapse with tiredness. **flak•y,** *adj.* in
thin pieces.

flam•boy•ant [flæm'bɔɪənt] *adj.* brightly col-

æ **back,** ɑː **farm,** ɒ **top,** aɪ **pipe,** aʊ **how,** aɪə **fire,** aʊə **flower,** ɔː **bought,** ɔɪ **toy,** e **fed,** eə **hair,** eɪ **take,** ə
afraid, əʊ **boat,** əʊə **lower,** ɜː **word,** iː **heap,** ɪ **hit,** ɪə **hear,** uː **school,** ʊ **book,** ʌ **but,** b **back,** d **dog,** ð **then,**
dʒ **just,** f **fog,** g **go,** h **hand,** j **yes,** k **catch,** l **last,** m **mix,** n **nut,** ŋ **sing,** p **penny,** r **round,** s **some,** ʃ **short,** t
too, tʃ **chop,** θ **thing,** v **voice,** w **was,** z **zoo,** ʒ **treasure**

ored; too bright. **flam•boy•ance,** *n.* being flamboyant. **flam•boy•ant•ly,** *adv.* in a flamboyant way.

flame [fleɪm] 1. *n.* (a) bright tongue of fire. (b) *inf.* abusive electronic mail. 2. *v. inf.* to send abusive electronic mail. **flame•proof, flame-resistant,** *adj.* specially treated so that it will not catch fire or melt. **flam•ing,** *adj.* in flames.

fla•min•go [fləˈmɪŋɡəʊ] *n.* (*pl.* -os) water bird with long legs and neck, often with pink feathers.

flam•ma•ble [ˈflæməbl] *adj.* easily set on fire/inflammable.

flan [flæn] *n.* open tart; sweet baked custard.

flange [flændʒ] *n.* rim/edge which sticks out on a pipe or wheel.

flank [flæŋk] 1. *n.* side (esp. of an animal, an army). 2. *v.* to be at the side of (sth).

flan•nel [ˈflænl] *n.* warm woolen material; **flannels** = flannel trousers. **flan•nel•et, flannelette,** *n.* warm cotton material, which feels like flannel.

flap [flæp] 1. *n.* (a) hinged part (which hangs down). (b) *inf.* excitement and worry. (c) movement like that of a bird's wing. 2. *v.* (**flapped**) to move up and down like a bird's wing. **flap•jack,** *n.* pancake.

flare [ˈfleə] 1. *n.* (a) device which gives a sudden blaze of light (esp. as a signal). (b) widening bottom part (of a skirt/of trousers). 2. *v.* (a) to burn brightly. (b) (*of a skirt/trousers*) to widen gradually. **flare up,** *v.* (a) to blaze suddenly. (b) to get angry.

flash [flæʃ] 1. *n.* (*pl.* -es) (a) short sudden burst of light or emotion; **in a f.** = very quickly. (b) apparatus for taking photographs in the dark. (c) short item of news. 2. *v.* (a) to light up quickly and suddenly. (b) to show (sth) quickly. (c) **to f. by/past** = to move/to pass by quickly. **flash•back,** *n.* scene in a motion picture, novel, etc., showing what happened at an earlier date. **flash•bulb,** *n.* photographic light bulb which makes a short burst of light when you take a photograph. **flash•cube,** *n.* square block of four flash bulbs. **flash•er,** *n. inf.* man who exposes his private parts. **flash•gun,** *n.* photographic device for holding a flashbulb. **flash•i•ly,** *adv.* in a flashy way. **flash•i•ness,** *n.* being flashy. **flash•ing,** *n.* metal strip which covers a joint in a roof. **flash•light,** *n.* portable electric light which you can hold in your hand. **flash•point,** *n.* temperature at which gas or gasoline vapor will ignite/moment at which a revolution will break out. **flash•y,** *adj.* showy and bright but of poor quality.

flask [flɑːsk] *n.* (small) bottle or other container for liquids.

flat [flæt] 1. *adj. & adv.* (**flatter, flattest**) (a) level/smooth; punctured (tire); **f. rate** = fixed charge which never changes. (b) (*of drink*) no longer sparkling. (c) (*of battery*) no longer producing electricity. (d) (*of music*) below the correct pitch. (e) definite (refusal). (f) **to go f. out** = as fast as you can go; **f. broke** = with no money at all. 2. *n.* (a) place which is level; **f. racing** = horse racing on a level course, not over jumps. (b) flat tire. (c) (*esp. Brit.*) accommodation made up of a set of rooms, usu. on one floor, in a building containing several such groups of rooms. (d) note in music which is a semitone lower. **flat•fish,** *n.* type of fish with a flattened body. **flat•ly,** *adv.* definitely. **flat•ten,** *v.* to make flat. **flat•worm,** *n.* worm with a flat body.

flat•ter [ˈflætə] *v.* (a) to praise (s.o.) insincerely. (b) to make (s.o.) feel honored. (c) **to f. yourself** = to deceive yourself/to persuade yourself that sth is true, when it is not. **flat•ter•er,** *n.* person who flatters. **flat•ter•y,** *n.* insincere praise.

flat•u•lence [ˈflætjʊləns] *n.* gas in the intestine. **flat•u•lent,** *adj.* suffering from flatulence.

flaunt [flɔːnt] *v.* to display (sth) in a vulgar way to attract attention.

flau•tist [ˈflɔːtɪst] *n.* flutist.

fla•vor, *Brit.* **fla•vour** [ˈfleɪvə] 1. *n.* taste. 2. *v.* to add spices and seasoning in cooking; to add a flavor to (sth). **fla•vor•ing,** *n.* substance added to food to give a particular taste.

flaw [flɔː] 1. *n.* fault/mistake; defect. 2. *v.* to spoil. **flaw•less,** *adj.* perfect.

flax [flæks] *n.* (*no pl.*) plant used for making linen cloth. **flax•en-haired,** *adj.* fair-haired.

flay [fleɪ] *v.* (a) to strip the skin off (an animal). (b) to criticize (s.o.) harshly.

flea [fliː] *n.* tiny blood-sucking insect that jumps. **flea bite,** *n.* place where a flea has bitten. **flea mar•ket,** *n.* market for secondhand goods.

fleck [flek] 1. *n.* small spot. 2. *v.* to mark (sth) with spots.

fled [fled] *v. see* **flee.**

fledg•ling [ˈfledʒlɪŋ] *n.* small bird ready to fly from the nest.

flee [fliː] *v.* (**fled**) to run away (**from**).

fleece [fliːs] 1. *n.* wool of a sheep. 2. *v. Sl.* to cheat (s.o.) and take their money. **fleec•y,** *adj.* made of fleece; covered with fleece; looking like fleece.

fleet [fliːt] 1. *n.* (a) group of ships belonging together. (b) collection of vehicles. 2. *adj.* rapid (footsteps). **fleet•ing** ['fli:tɪŋ] *adj.* short and quick. **fleet•ing•ly,** *adv.* rapidly.

flesh [fleʃ] *n.* (a) soft part of the body covering the bones; **in the f.** = in reality (not on TV or in photographs); **a f. wound** = one which is not too deep; **his own f. and blood** = his relations/his family. (b) soft part of a fruit. **flesh•y,** *adj.* fat/plump.

fleur-de-lys [flɜ:də'li:s] *n.* lily design, formerly the emblem of France.

flew [flu:] *v. see* **fly.**

flex [fleks] 1. *n.* flexible insulated cable for carrying electricity. 2. *v.* to bend. **flex•i•bil•i•ty** [fleksɪ'bɪlɪtɪ] *n.* ability to bend easily/to adapt to new circumstances. **flex•i•ble,** *adj.* (a) easy to bend. (b) adaptable. **flex•i•bly,** *adv.* in a flexible way. **flex•time, flexitime,** *n.* system where workers can start and stop their day's work at various times.

flib•ber•ti•gib•bet ['flɪbətɪdʒɪbɪt] *n.* silly, empty-headed person.

flick [flɪk] 1. *n.* little sharp blow/tap. 2. *v.* (a) to hit lightly. (b) to move sth with a light, quick movement.

flick•er ['flɪkə] 1. *n.* trembling/quivering. 2. *v.* to tremble/to quiver; to burn unsteadily.

fli•er ['flaɪə] *n. see* **fly.**

flight [flaɪt] *n.* (a) journey through the air; flying. (b) group of birds/aircraft flying together. (c) **f. of stairs** = group of stairs in one direction. (d) running away; **to put to f.** = to chase away; **to take f.** = to run away. **flight deck,** *n.* (a) flat surface on an aircraft carrier on which aircraft land and take off. (b) section at the front of a large aircraft where the pilots sit. **flight•less,** *adj.* (bird) which cannot fly. **flight re•cord•er,** *n.* box carried on a plane where details of the flight are recorded automatically. **flight•y** ['flaɪtɪ] *adj.* silly and empty-headed.

flim•sy ['flɪmzɪ] *adj.* (*of material*) light and thin; poorly made; poor (excuse). **flim•si•ly,** *adv.* in a flimsy way. **flim•si•ness,** *n.* being flimsy.

flinch [flɪntʃ] *v.* to move back in pain/fear.

fling [flɪŋ] 1. *n.* (a) lively dance (esp. as done in Scotland). (b) period of letting off one's high spirits. 2. *v.* (**flung**) to throw wildly.

flint [flɪnt] *n.* (a) very hard type of rock which makes sparks when struck. (b) small piece of metal which makes a spark to light a cigarette lighter. **flint•y,** *adj.* hard/severe (look).

flip [flɪp] *v.* (**flipped**) to hit lightly; **to f. over** = to

turn over quickly. **flip flops,** *n. pl.* rubber sandals held on by a strap between the toes. **flip side,** *n.* second side of a record.

flip•pant ['flɪpənt] *adj.* joking about things which should be taken seriously. **flip•pant•ly,** *adv.* in a flippant way.

flip•per ['flɪpə] *n.* (a) limb of a sea animal used for swimming. (b) long flat piece of rubber which you can attach to your foot to help you swim faster.

flirt [flɜ:t] 1. *n.* person, esp. woman, who flirts. 2. *v.* to play at attracting people of the opposite sex for amusement. **flir•ta•tion** [flɜ:'teɪʃn] *n.* brief love affair. **flir•ta•tious,** *adj.* (person) who flirts a lot.

flit [flɪt] 1. *n.* light, quick movement. 2. *v.* (**flitted**) to move lightly and quickly.

flitch [flɪtʃ] *n.* (*pl.* **-es**) side of bacon.

float [fləʊt] 1. *n.* (a) piece of cork, etc., attached to a fishing line which will float on the surface of the water. (b) decorated vehicle in a parade. 2. *v.* to (make sth) lie on the top of a liquid; to start up (a company) by selling shares in it; to let (a currency) find its own exchange rate internationally and not fix it at a certain amount. **float•ing,** *adj.* resting on the surface of a liquid.

flock [flɒk] 1. *n.* (a) group of similar animals together, esp. sheep/goats/birds. (b) waste cotton. 2. *v.* to move in a group; **to f. together** = to come together in a group.

floe [fləʊ] *n.* large sheet of ice floating on the sea.

flog [flɒg] *v.* (**flogged**) (a) to beat hard, usu. with a whip. (b) *Sl.* to sell.

flood [flʌd] 1. *n.* large amount of water over land which is usu. dry. (b) large amount of (tears/letters, etc.). 2. *v.* to cover with water; **they flooded in** = came in large numbers. **flood•gate,** *n.* part of a lock/sluice/dam in a river, which can be opened or shut and which helps control the flow of the water. **flood•light.** 1. *n.* powerful light often used for lighting the outside of a building or a sports playing field at night. 2. *v.* (**floodlit**) to light with floodlights.

floor [flɔ:] 1. *n.* (a) part of a room on which you walk. (b) story/one level of rooms in a building. (c) part of an assembly room where people discuss; **to take the f.** = to start speaking in a discussion. 2. *v.* (a) to knock to the ground. (b) to amaze and puzzle (s.o.). **floor•board,** *n.* long flat piece of wood used for making wooden floors. **floor•cloth,** *n.* cloth for

æ back, a: farm, ɒ: top, aɪ pipe, aʊ how, aɪə fire, aʊə flower, ɔ: bought, ɔɪ toy, e fed, eəhair, eɪ take, ə afraid, əʊ boat, əʊə lower, ʌ: word, i: heap, ɪ hit, ɪə hear, u: school, ʊ book, ʌ but, b back, d dog, ð then, dʒ just, f fog, g go, h hand, j yes, k catch, l last, m mix, n nut, ŋ sing, p penny, r round, s some, ʃ short, t too, tʃ chop, θ thing, v voice, w was, z zoo, ʒ treasure

washing floors. **floor•show,** *n.* nightclub entertainment.

flop [flɒp] 1. *n.* (a) *inf.* failure. (b) movement of sth falling limply. 2. *v.* (**flopped**) (a) to fall/to sit/to lie limply or heavily. (b) *inf.* to fail. **flop•py,** *adj.* which hangs limply; **f. disk** = disk used in a computer.

flo•ra ['flɔːrə] *n.* wild plants (of an area). **flo•ral,** *adj.* referring to flowers.

flo•ret ['flɒrɪt] *n.* little flower which is part of a flowerhead.

flo•ri•bun•da [flɒrɪ'bʌndə] *n.* type of rose with many small flowers.

flor•id ['flɒrɪd] *adj.* red (face).

flor•in ['flɒrɪn] *n.* (*old*) British coin worth two shillings.

flo•rist ['flɒrɪst] *n.* person who sells flowers.

floss [flɒs] *n.* waste silk threads; **dental f.** = thin thread for pulling between the teeth to remove pieces of food.

flo•ta•tion [fləʊ'teɪʃn] *n.* starting of a new company by selling shares in it.

flo•til•la [flə'tɪlə] *n.* small group of boats.

flot•sam ['flɒtsəm] *n.* (*no pl.*) trash or refuse floating in the water.

flounce [flaʊns] 1. *n.* border of ruffled cloth (attached to a skirt, etc.). 2. *v.* **to f. out** = to go out of a room showing your impatience and annoyance. **flounced,** *adj.* with flounces.

floun•der ['flaʊndə] 1. *n.* common edible flat fish. 2. *v.* (*also* **flounder about**) to move (in water) with difficulty; to be uncertain of an answer to a question.

flour ['flaʊə] *n.* grain crushed to powder, used for making bread/cakes, etc. **flour•mill,** *n.* place where grain is ground into flour. **flour•y,** *adj.* like flour.

flour•ish ['flʌrɪʃ] 1. *n.* (*pl.* **-es**) (a) wide movement of the arm in the air. (b) large curve in handwriting. (c) fanfare (of trumpets). 2. *v.* (a) to grow well. (b) to wave (sth) in the air.

flout [flaʊt] *v.* to scorn/to disregard (sth).

flow [fləʊ] 1. *n.* movement of liquid/air, etc. 2. *v.* to move along smoothly. **flow•chart,** *n.* diagram showing the stages in a process.

flow•er ['flaʊə] 1. *n.* colorful part of a plant which produces the seed. 2. *v.* to make flowers. **flow•er•bed,** *n.* part of a garden where flowers are grown. **flow•er•pot,** *n.* container to grow plants in. **flow•er•y,** *adj.* (a) (*also* **flowered**) decorated with a pattern of flowers. (b) ornate (style).

flown [fləʊn] *v. see* **fly.**

flu [fluː] *n.* influenza/common illness like a bad cold, often with a high temperature.

fluc•tu•ate ['flʌktjʊeɪt] *v.* to move backward and forward/up and down. **fluc•tu•a•tion** [flʌktju'eɪʃn] *n.* movement backward and forward/up and down.

flue [fluː] *n.* pipe leading to a chimney.

flu•en•cy ['fluːənsɪ] *n.* ease of speaking. **flu•ent,** *adj.* able to speak easily. **flu•ent•ly,** *adv.* easily.

fluff [flʌf] 1. *n.* soft pieces of wool or hair. 2. *v. inf.* to do (sth) badly. **fluff•i•ness,** *n.* being fluffy. **fluff•y,** *adj.* like fluff; covered with fluff.

flu•id ['fluːɪd] 1. *n.* liquid. 2. *adj.* (situation/movement) which is not settled; changing. **flu•id•i•ty** [fluː'ɪdɪtɪ] *n.* being fluid.

fluke [fluːk] *n.* (a) *inf.* chance/lucky event. (b) one of the two flat parts of a whale's tail/of an anchor. (c) type of flatworm.

flum•mox ['flʌməks] *v. inf.* to confuse (s.o.).

flung [flʌŋ] *v. see* **fling.**

flunk [flʌŋk] *v. inf.* to fail (an examination/a candidate).

flun•ky, flunkey ['flʌŋkɪ] *n.* (a) person who fawns on s.o. and tries to please. (b) servant.

fluo•res•cence [fluə'resns] *n.* ability to send out a glow of light when an electric current is applied. **fluo•res•cent,** *adj.* giving off light when electric current is applied.

fluor•ine ['fluəriːn] *n.* (*element:* F) pale yellow-green gas. **fluor•i•da•tion** [fluərai'deɪʃn] *n.* adding fluoride to water (to prevent tooth decay). **fluor•ide** ['fluəraɪd] *n.* compound of fluorine; **f. toothpaste** = toothpaste with small amount of fluoride added in order to prevent tooth decay.

flur•ry ['flʌrɪ] *n.* (a) hurried excitement. (b) sudden small amount of snow, rain or wind.

flush [flʌʃ] 1. *n.* (*pl.* **-es**) (a) redness of the face. (b) rush of water. (c) (*at cards*) hand with all the cards of the same suit. 2. *v.* (a) to go red in the face. (b) **to f. out** = to drive out of hiding. (c) **to f. a toilet** = to wash it out by moving a handle which makes water rush through. 3. *adj.* (a) **f. with** = level with. (b) *inf.* having plenty of money to spend.

flust•er ['flʌstə] 1. *n.* nervous worry. 2. *v.* to worry/to confuse (s.o.).

flute [fluːt] *n.* (a) wind instrument played by blowing across a small hole at the end of a pipe. (b) long rounded groove. **flut•ed,** *adj.* decorated with grooves or scallops. **flut•ist,** *n.* person who plays the flute.

flut•ter ['flʌtə] 1. *n.* light movement, esp. of wings. 2. *v.* (a) to move (wings, etc.) quickly and lightly. (b) to move softly and quickly.

flu•vi•al ['fluːvɪəl] *adj.* referring to rivers.

flux [flʌks] *n.* (a) constant change. (b) substance used in soldering.

fly [flaɪ] 1. *n.* (*pl.* **flies**) (a) small insect with two wings; **f. fishing** = sport of fishing with an imitation fly as bait. (b) strip of material sewn along one edge, which covers a zipper, buttons, or other fastening on the front of trousers. 2. *v.* (**flew; has flown**) (a) to move through the air. (b) to move fast. (c) to put up (a flag). **fly•blown**, *adj.* rotten (meat). **fly•by**, *n.* flight of aircraft over a certain spot to celebrate sth. **fly-by-night**, *n. inf.* unreliable company. **fly•catch•er**, *n.* bird which catches flies. **fli•er, flyer**, *n.* (a) person who pilots an aircraft. (b) paper advertising sth. **fly•ing club**, *n.* club for people interested in flying aircraft. **fly•ing fish**, *n.* fish which jumps out of the water as it moves. **fly•ing sau•cer**, *n.* unidentified flying object which people claim to see and which they think comes from another planet. **fly•ing squad**, *n.* group of policemen who arrive quickly at the scene of a crime. **fly•ing start**, *n.* good beginning to a race/a new job, etc. **fly•leaf**, *n.* blank leaf of paper at the beginning and end of a book. **fly•past**, *n.* flyby. **fly•weight**, *n.* lightest category of boxer. **fly•wheel**, *n.* large heavy wheel which turns, keeping an engine working at a steady pace.

foal [fəʊl] *n.* young horse.

foam [fəʊm] 1. *n.* mass of small bubbles; **f. rubber** = rubber in blocks with many little holes in it, used for chair cushions, etc. 2. *v.* to make froth. **foam•y**, *adj.* covered with foam.

fob [fɒb] 1. *n.* little ornament attached to a watch-chain. 2. *v.* (**fobbed**) **to f. s.o. off with sth** = to deceive s.o. into accepting sth which they don't really want.

fo'c'sle ['fəʊksl] *n.* front part of a ship where the crew lives.

fo•cus ['fəʊkəs] 1. *n.* (a) (*pl.* **foci** ['fəʊsaɪ] point where rays of light from an object meet; **in f.** = clearly visible; **out of f.** = blurred/not clear. (b) center of attention. 2. *v.* to adjust so as to be able to see clearly. **fo•cal**, *adj.* referring to a focus.

fod•der ['fɒdə] *n.* food for cows/sheep, etc.

foe [fəʊ] *n.* (*formal*) enemy/opponent.

foe•tus ['fiːtəs] *n. see* **fe•tus**.

fog [fɒg] *n.* thick mist through which it is difficult to see. **fog•gi•ness**, *n.* being foggy. **fog•gy**, *adj.* misty. **fog•horn**, *n.* horn which makes a deep, loud sound, used in fog as a warning to ships. **fog light**, *n.* headlight on a car, used in fog.

fo•gy, fogey ['fəʊgɪ] *n.* **old f.** = reactionary old man.

foi•ble ['fɔɪbl] *n.* slight flaw in character; weakness.

foil [fɔɪl] 1. *n.* (a) thin metal sheet; **tin f./aluminum f.** = foil used for wrapping food before cooking or for storage. (b) long thin sword with a button on the end used in the sport of fencing. (c) person who contrasts sharply with another and so makes the other's qualities stand out. 2. *v.* to defeat; to prevent (a plot) being put into effect.

foist [fɔɪst] *v.* **to f. sth on s.o.** = to force s.o. to accept sth which they don't want.

fold [fəʊld] 1. *n.* (a) small enclosure for sheep. (b) crease (in paper/cloth, etc.) 2. *v.* (a) to bend (sth) so that one part is on top of another. (b) **to f. your arms** = to bend your arms together in front of your chest. **fold•er**, *n.* cardboard envelope for holding papers. **fold•ing**, *adj.* able to be folded. **fold up**, *v.* (a) to bend (sth) over to make smaller than before. (b) *inf.* to finish/to end.

fo•li•age ['fəʊlɪɪdʒ] *n.* leaves on a tree or plant. **fo•li•ar**, *adj.* referring to leaves.

fo•li•o ['fəʊlɪəʊ] *n.* (a) very large size of book. (b) page number.

folk [fəʊk] *n. pl.* people; **my f.** = my family. **folk dance**, *n.* traditional dance. **folk•lore**, *n.* traditional stories and beliefs. **folk•song**, *n.* traditional song.

fol•li•cle ['fɒlɪkl] *n.* small hole (in the skin) out of which a hair grows.

fol•low ['fɒləʊ] *v.* (a) to go after/to come after; to continue along (a road). (b) to act in accordance with (a rule). (c) to understand. **fol•low•er**, *n.* supporter. **fol•low•ing**, *adj.* which follows; next. **follow up**, *v.* to investigate/to research (sth) further.

fol•ly ['fɒlɪ] *n.* silly behavior.

fo•ment [fə'ment] *v.* (*formal*) to stir up (trouble). **fo•men•ta•tion** [fəʊmen'teɪʃn] *n.* act of stirring up trouble.

fond [fɒnd] *adj.* loving; **I am f. of music** = I like music. **fond•ly**, *adv.* in a fond way. **fond•ness**, *n.* liking/love.

fon•dle ['fɒndl] *v.* to stroke lovingly.

fon•due ['fɒndjuː] *n.* dish of melted cheese into which pieces of bread are dipped, or of hot oil into which pieces of meat are dipped, or of chocolate into which pieces of fruit are dipped.

font [fɒnt] *n.* (a) basin holding holy water for baptism in a church. (b) set of type of one particular size and design.

æ back, ɑː farm, ɒ top, aɪ pipe, aʊ how, aɪə fire, aʊə flower, ɔː bought, ɔɪ toy, e fed, eəhair, eɪ take, ə afraid, əʊ boat, əʊə lower, ɜː word, iː heap, ɪ hit, ɪə hear, uː school, ʊ book, ʌ but, b back, d dog, ð then, dʒ just, f fog, g go, h hand, j yes, k catch, l last, m mix, n nut, ŋ sing, p penny, r round, s some, ʃ short, t too, tʃ chop, θ thing, v voice, w was, z zoo, ʒ treasure

fon•ta•nel, fon•ta•nelle [fɒntə'nel] *n.* soft membrane between the pieces of the skull of a baby.

food [fuːd] *n.* substances eaten by people and animals or taken in by plants; **f. poisoning** = illness caused by sth eaten. **food•stuff**, *n.* thing that can be eaten.

fool [fuːl] 1. *n.* idiot/stupid person. 2. *v.* (a) **to f. around** = to play around in a silly way. (b) to trick (s.o.). **fool•har•dy**, *adj.* brave, but taking unnecessary risks. **fool•ish**, *adj.* silly/stupid. **fool•ish•ly**, *adv.* stupidly. **fool•ish•ness**, *n.* silliness/stupidity. **fool•proof**, *adj.* so simple that even an idiot could use it safely; which cannot fail. **fools•cap** ['fuːlskæp] *n.* large size of writing paper.

foot [fʊt] 1. *n.* (*pl.* **feet**) (a) end part of the leg on which you stand; **on f.** = walking; **under f.** = on the ground; *inf.* **to put your f. in it** = to say sth embarrassing; **to put your f. down** = to be firm/not to give in. (b) base/end of sth. (c) measure of length (= 12 inches or 30.5 cm); **three feet wide.** 2. *v.* (a) **to f. it** = to walk. (b) **to f. the bill** = to pay the bill. **foot-and-mouth dis•ease**, *n.* disease of cows. **foot•age**, *n.* (*no pl.*) length or amount of motion picture which has been exposed. **foot•ball** *n.* (a) game played between two teams with a ball which is kicked; (b) ball used in the game of football. **foot•brake**, *n.* brake (on a machine or car) operated by the foot. **foot•bridge**, *n.* small bridge for people to walk across. **foot•fall**, *n.* footstep. **foot•hills**, *n. pl.* lower slopes. **foot•hold**, *n.* (a) place where you can put your foot when climbing. (b) small position on which you can build. **foot•ing**, *n.* (a) safe place for your feet. (b) **to put things on a firm f.** = to base things firmly. **foot•lights**, *n. pl.* row of lights along the front of the stage in a theater. **foot•loose**, *adj.* free to go anywhere; with no ties. **foot•man**, *n.* (*pl.* **-men**) male servant. **foot•note**, *n.* explanation at the bottom of a page, referring to sth on the page. **foot•path**, *n.* path for walkers. **foot•print**, *n.* mark left by the foot on the ground. **foot sol•dier**, *n.* soldier who travels on foot. **foot•sore**, *adj.* (person) with feet which hurt. **foot•step**, *n.* sound of a foot touching the ground. **foot•stool**, *n.* small stool which supports the feet. **foot•wear**, *n.* (*no pl.*) boots and shoes. **foot•work**, *n.* (*no pl.*) way of using your feet (esp. in sports).

foot•ling ['fuːtlɪŋ] *adj.* silly/insignificant.

for [fɔː] 1. *prep.* (a) in exchange. (b) in support of. (c) used as. (d) because of. (e) in the direction of; **the train f. Chicago.** (f) toward; **my love f. you.** (g) over a distance of/over a length of time; **f. miles; f. a month.** (h) as a present to; belonging to; **a letter f. you.** (i) in the place of; **can you write this letter f. me?** (j) with the purpose of; **to go f. a walk; run f. the bus** = to catch the bus. (k) **f. all that** = in spite of everything; **as f.** = regarding; **f. sale** = able to be bought; **f. example** = to name one thing out of many; **f. ever/f. good** = always; **f. the most part** = usually. 2. *conj.* because.

for•age ['fɒrɪdʒ] 1. *n.* food for horses and cattle. 2. *v.* (a) to search for food/supplies. (b) to rummage/to look **for** sth.

for•ay ['fɒreɪ] *n.* sudden attack.

for•bade [fə'bæd] *v. see* **for•bid.**

for•bear•ance [fɔː'beərəns] *n.* patience. **for•bear•ing,** *adj.* patient/long-suffering.

for•bid [fə'bɪd] *v.* (**forbade** [fə'bæd]; **forbidden**) to tell (s.o.) not to do sth. **for•bid•ding,** *adj.* sinister/looking dangerous.

force [fɔːs] 1. *n.* (a) strength/power; **in f.** = (i) in large numbers; (ii) (law which is) operating/working. (b) organized group of people; **police f; the armed forces** = navy, army and air force. 2. *v.* (a) to move by using strength. (b) to compel/to make (s.o.) do sth. (c) to make (plants) grow faster/earlier than normal. **force back**, *v.* to push sth back very hard. **forced**, *adj.* (a) compelled; **f. landing** = quick landing of an aircraft because sth is wrong. (b) artificial/not real. **force-feed**, *v.* (**force-fed**) to feed (s.o. on hunger strike) by force. **force•ful**, *adj.* strong/powerful. **force•ful•ly**, *adv.* in a forceful way. **force•ful•ness**, *n.* being forceful. **force majeure**, *n.* thing which happens (such as a war) which cannot be controlled by parties to a contract. **force•meat**, *n.* minced meat used as stuffing (for turkeys, etc.).

for•ceps ['fɔːseps] *n.* (*no pl.*) pincers used by doctors in surgery.

for•ci•ble ['fɔːsɪbl] *adj.* done by/with force. **for•ci•bly**, *adv.* using force.

ford [fɔːd] 1. *n.* shallow part of a river where you can cross by going through the water. 2. *v.* to cross a river by going through a shallow part. **ford•a•ble**, *adj.* (river) which can be forded.

fore [fɔː] 1. *n.* front part of a ship; **f. and aft** = front and back of a ship. **to come to the f.** = to become prominent. 2. *adj.* front/before (*used as a prefix in words such as* **forearm, foresee**). **fore•arm**. 1. *n.* ['fɔːrɑːm] part of the arm between the hand and the elbow. 2. *v.* [fɔː'ɑːm] to get ready (as for a fight) beforehand. **fore•bears**, *n. pl.* (*old*) ancestors. **fore•bod•ing** [fɔː'bəʊdɪŋ] *n.* feeling that sth evil will take place. **fore•cast.** 1. *n.* description of what will happen in the future. 2. *v.*

(forecast) to say what will happen in the future. **fore•cast•er**, *n.* person who says what will happen in the future, esp. concerning the weather. **fore•cas•tle** ['fəʊksl] *n.* front part of a ship where the crew live. **fore•close** [fɔː-'kləʊz] *v.* to take away property because the owner cannot pay back money which he has borrowed on its security. **fore•clo•sure**, *n.* act of foreclosing. **fore•court**, *n.* courtyard in front of a building. **fore•fa•ther**, *n.* ancestor. **fore•fin•ger**, *n.* index finger/first finger next to the thumb. **fore•foot**, *n.* front foot (of an animal). **fore•front**, *n.* **to be in the f. of a campaign** = to be one of the leaders. **fore•go** [fɔː'gəʊ] *v.* (**forewent, has foregone**) to do without. **fore•go•ing**, *adj.* which has gone before. **fore•gone**, *adj.* decided in advance; **it was a f. conclusion** = everyone knew. **fore•ground**, *n.* part of a picture/scene nearest the viewer. **fore•hand**, *adj.* (*in tennis*) (stroke) played with the palm of the hand facing forward. **fore•head** ['fɒrɪd, 'fɔːhed] *n.* part of the head between the eyes and the hair. **fore•knowl•edge**, *n.* knowledge in advance. **fore•land**, *n.* headland. **fore•leg**, *n.* front leg of an animal. **fore•man**, *n.* (*pl.* **-men**) (a) (*in a factory*) workman in charge of several others. (b) **f. of a jury** = spokesperson for the jury. **fore•most**, *adj. & adv.* first/chief; **first and f.** = first of all. **fore•noon**, *n.* morning. **fore•paw**, *n.* front paw. **fore•run•ner**, *n.* person/thing coming before another more important one. **fore•see** [fɔː'siː] *v.* (**foresaw; has foreseen**) to feel in advance that sth will happen. **fore•see•a•ble**, *adj.* which can be foreseen. **fore•shad•ow** [fɔː'ʃædəʊ] *v.* to be a sign of (sth to come). **fore•shore**, *n.* part of a beach which is covered by the sea at each high tide. **fore•sight**, *n.* ability to see what will probably happen in the future; ability to plan for emergencies. **fore•skin**, *n.* loose skin covering the end of the penis. **fore•stall** [fɔː'stɔːl] *v.* to anticipate/to stop (s.o. doing sth). **fore•taste**, *n.* small bit of sth that will be had later on. **fore•tell** [fɔː'tel] *v.* (**foretold**) to predict/to say what will happen in the future. **fore•thought**, *n.* thinking ahead. **fore•warned**, *adj.* warned in advance. **fore•word**, *n.* short section at the beginning of a book introducing it to the reader.

for•eign ['fɒrən] *adj.* (a) not belonging to your own country. (b) strange; **f. exchange** = ex-

changing the money of one country for money of another; **f. to s.o.'s nature** = very strange for s.o. to do it. (c) **f. body** = thing from outside which lodges in your body. **for•eign•er**, *n.* person who does not belong to your country.

fo•ren•sic [fə'rensɪk] *adj.* referring to or used in courts of law or public discussion and debate; **f. medicine** = use of medicine for purposes of the law, as in solving crimes involving death.

for•est ['fɒrɪst] *n.* large area covered with trees. **for•est•er, forest ranger**, *n.* person whose job it is to look after a forest. **for•est•ry**, *n.* job of looking after a forest and its trees; science of growing and maintaining forests.

for•ev•er [fə'revə] *adv.* always.

for•ex ['fɒreks] *n. abbrev. for* foreign exchange.

for•feit ['fɔːfɪt] 1. *n.* thing taken/lost as a punishment. 2. *v.* to lose (sth), esp. as a punishment. **for•fei•ture** ['fɔːfɪtʃə] *n.* act of forfeiting.

for•gath•er [fɔː'gæðə] *v.* (*formal*) to gather together.

for•gave [fə'geɪv] *v. see* **for•give**.

forge [fɔːdʒ] 1. *n.* blacksmith's workshop where he makes horseshoes and other iron objects. 2. *v.* (a) to work (metal) in a forge. (b) to copy (sth) illegally. (c) **to f. ahead** = to go forward quickly. **forged**, *adj.* copied illegally. **forg•er**, *n.* person who copies sth illegally. **for•ger•y**, *n.* (a) making an illegal copy. (b) illegal copy.

for•get [fə'get] *v.* (**forgot; has forgotten**) not (to be able) to remember; to leave (sth) behind. **for•get•ful**, *adj.* often unable to remember. **for•get•ful•ness**, *n.* being forgetful. **for•get-me-not**, *n.* small blue-flowered plant.

for•give [fə'gɪv] *v.* (**forgave** [fə'geɪv]; **has forgiven**) to pardon/to stop being angry with (s.o.). **for•giv•a•ble**, *adj.* able to be pardoned/understandable. **for•give•ness**, *n.* pardon(ing).

for•go [fɔː'gəʊ] *v.* (**forwent, has forgone**) to do without.

for•got [fə'gɒt] *v. see* **for•get**.

fork [fɔːk] 1. *n.* (a) object with a handle at one end and sharp points at the other, used for picking things up. (b) place where a branch leaves a tree trunk. (c) place where two roads split. 2. *v.* (a) (*of a road*) to split into two parts. (b) *inf.* **to f. out** = to pay for sth, usu. unwillingly. **forked**, *adj.* divided into two. **fork•lift**

truck, *n.* motor vehicle which can lift heavy loads on metal arms.

for•lorn [fə'lɔːn] *adj.* left alone and feeling sad; **f. hope** = very slight hope. **for•lorn•ly,** *adv.* sadly.

form [fɔːm] 1. *n.* (a) shape. (b) paper with blank spaces for you to fill in. (c) condition of an athlete/racing animal; **he's in good f.** = he's in a good mood/he's very amusing. (d) structure/style of a piece of writing/a piece of music. (e) school class, esp. in a private school. (f) custom/behavior. (g) frame in which type is placed for printing. 2. *v.* (a) to shape; to take shape. (b) to be produced. (c) to organize; **they formed a club. for•ma•tion** [fɔːˈmeɪʃn] *n.* shaping/forming of sth. **for•ma•tive** [ˈfɔːmətɪv] *adj.* referring to the early years of life when a person's character is being formed.

for•mal [ˈfɔːml] *adj.* (a) ceremonial/done according to certain rules. (b) regular; clearly written (agreement). **for•mal•i•ty** [fɔːˈmælɪtɪ] *n.* thing which has to be done to conform with the rules but which does not mean much. **for•mal•i•za•tion,** *n.* making formal. **for•mal•ize,** *v.* to make (an agreement) formal/regular. **for•mal•ly,** *adv.* according to rules/ceremonially.

form•al•de•hyde [fɔːˈmældɪhaɪd] *n.* gas used in solution to make formalin. **for•ma•lin,** *n.* solution used as a disinfectant and preservative.

for•mat [ˈfɔːmæt] 1. *n.* (a) shape/size (in which sth is made). (b) dimensions of a page/book. 2. *v.* **(formatted)** to arrange text on a computer, so that it is ready for final printing; to prepare a computer disk so that it is ready to receive data.

form•er [ˈfɔːmə] *adj.* (a) earlier. (b) first thing mentioned (of two). **for•mer•ly,** *adv.* at an earlier time.

for•mic [ˈfɔːmɪk] *adj.* **f. acid** = acid found in the sting of ants.

For•mi•ca [fɔːˈmaɪkə] *n.* trademark for a hard plastic.

for•mi•da•ble [ˈfɔːmɪdəbl] *adj.* frighteningly difficult; very impressive (person).

for•mu•la [ˈfɔːmjʊlə] *n.* (pl. **-ae** [-iː]) (a) statement, usu. of a scientific fact and often by means of symbols. (b) milky food for babies. **for•mu•late,** *v.* (a) to express (sth) as a formula. (b) to express (an idea) clearly. **for•mu•la•tion,** *n.* expressing clearly.

for•ni•cate [ˈfɔːnɪkeɪt] *v.* to have sexual intercourse (when not married). **for•ni•ca•tion,** *n.* act of fornicating.

for•sake [fɔːˈseɪk] *v.* (**forsook; has forsaken**) to leave behind. **for•sak•en,** *adj.* abandoned/deserted.

for•swear [fɔːˈsweə] *v.* (*formal*) to swear not to do (sth).

for•syth•i•a [fɔːˈsaɪθɪə] *n.* common garden shrub with yellow flowers.

fort [fɔːt] *n.* strong building which can be defended against enemy attacks; **to hold the f.** = to be in charge while s.o. is away.

for•te [ˈfɔːtɪ] 1. *n.* (a) loud piece of music. (b) particular ability. 2. *adv.* played loudly.

forth [fɔːθ] *adv.* (*formal*) forward; **back and f.** = backward and forward; **and so f.** = and so on. **forth•com•ing,** *adj.* (a) soon to appear. (b) *inf.* friendly/full of information. **forth•right,** *adj.* direct/blunt (way of speaking). **forth•with,** *adv.* immediately.

for•ti•fy [ˈfɔːtɪfaɪ] *v.* to make strong; **fortified wine** = wine (like sherry/port) with extra alcohol added. **for•ti•fi•ca•tion** [fɔːtɪfɪˈkeɪʃn] *n.* (a) making strong. (b) **fortifications** = walls/towers built to defend a city.

for•tis•si•mo [fɔːˈtɪsɪməʊ] *adv.* very loudly (in music).

for•ti•tude [ˈfɔːtɪtjuːd] *n.* strength of mind/bravery, esp. when in pain.

fort•night [ˈfɔːtnaɪt] *n.* two weeks. **fort•night•ly,** *adj. & adv.* once every two weeks.

for•tress [ˈfɔːtrəs] *n.* (pl. **-es**) strong building/castle.

for•tu•i•tous [fɔːˈtjuːɪtəs] *adj.* accidental/happening by chance. **for•tu•i•tous•ly,** *adv.* by chance/accidentally.

for•tune [ˈfɔːtjuːn] *n.* (a) luck/chance. (b) what will happen in the future. (c) large amount of money. **for•tu•nate** [ˈfɔːtʃənət] *adj.* lucky. **for•tu•nate•ly,** *adv.* by good luck. **for•tune-tel•ler,** *n.* person who says what will happen in the future by looking at cards or lines on your hand.

for•ty [ˈfɔːtɪ] *n.* number 40; *inf.* **f. winks** = short sleep in the daytime. **for•ti•eth, 40th,** *adj. & n.* referring to 40.

fo•rum [ˈfɔːrəm] *n.* (a) place where matters of general interest can be discussed. (b) public discussion.

for•ward [ˈfɔːwəd] 1. *adj.* (a) toward the front. (b) advanced/well ahead. (c) too confident. 2. *adv.* (a) **from that day f.** = from then on. (b) to the front; **to look f. to sth** = to wait for sth with pleasure. 3. *n.* (*in sports*) player in an attacking/front position. 4. *v.* (a) to send on (a letter) to another address. (b) to help (sth) progress. **for•ward-look•ing,** *adj.* thinking ahead/dealing with the future optimistically. **for•ward, forwards,** *adv.* to the front.

fos•sil [ˈfɒsl] *n.* remains of an animal/plant left in a rock; *inf.* elderly old-fashioned person. **fos•sil•i•za•tion,** *n.* becoming fossilized.

fos•sil•iz•ed ['fɒsɪlaɪzd] *adj.* turned into a rock.

fos•ter ['fɒstə] *v.* (a) to bring up (a child who is not your own). (b) to encourage (an idea, etc.). **fos•ter-child,** *n.* (*pl.* **-children**) child brought up by parents who are not his own. **fos•ter home,** *n.* family/home where a foster-child is brought up. **fos•ter-moth•er,** *n.* mother who fosters a child. **fos•ter-par•ents,** *n. pl.* parents who foster a child.

fought [fɔːt] *v. see* **fight.**

foul [faʊl] 1. *adj.* (**-er, -est**) (a) bad/dirty/unpleasant (taste, language, air, etc.). (b) against the rules of a game. (c) **f. play** = murder. (d) **to fall/run f. of** = to get into trouble with. 2. *n.* action against the rules of the game. 3. *v.* (a) to make dirty. (b) to do sth against the rules of the game. (c) **the boat fouled its anchor** = its anchor got stuck in weeds, etc.; *inf.* **to f. sth up** = to make a mess of sth/to create a problem. **foul•ly,** *adv.* in a foul way. **foul•mouthed,** *adj.* with foul language. **foul•ness,** *n.* being foul.

found [faʊnd] *v.* (a) to establish/to begin (sth). (b) to base (a story, etc.). (c) to melt (metal); to make (sth) out of molten metal; *see also* **find.** **foun•da•tion** [faʊn'deɪʃn] *n.* (a) establishing/beginning. (b) base below ground on which a building is laid; **f. stone** = cornerstone. (c) organization which provides money for certain projects. (d) colored cream put on the face under powder. **found•er.** 1. *n.* person who establishes/begins sth. 2. *v.* (*of a boat, scheme*) to collapse/to sink. **found•ling,** *n.* baby abandoned by its parents and found by s.o. else. **found•ry,** *n.* works where things are made from molten metal, etc.

fount [faʊnt] *n.* (*old*) fountain.

foun•tain ['faʊntɪn] *n.* jet of water in a street or garden; **f. pen** = pen which you can fill up with ink.

four [fɔː] *n.* (*a*) number 4; **on all fours** = on hands and knees. (b) four people (in a rowing boat). **four-by-four,** *n.* motor vehicle with four-wheel drive. **four•fold,** *adv. & adj.* four times as much. **four•post•er (bed),** *n.* bed with a tall post at each corner and curtains. **four•some,** *n.* (a) activity/game played by four people. (b) group of four people. **four•teen,** *n.* number 14. **four•teenth, 14th,** *adj.* referring to fourteen. **fourth, 4th.** 1. *adj.* referring to four. 2. *n.* quarter.

four-wheel drive, *n.* system powering all four wheels of a motor vehicle.

fowl [faʊl] *n.* (*pl.* **fowl**) domestic birds kept for food or eggs (chickens, ducks, turkeys and geese); **wild f.** = game birds which are shot for sport. **fowl•ing piece,** *n.* gun for shooting wild fowl.

fox [fɒks] 1. *n.* wild animal with reddish fur and a bushy tail. 2. *v.* to puzzle/to trick. **fox cub,** *n.* young fox. **fox•glove,** *n.* tall purple and white flower found in woods. **fox•hound,** *n.* dog used for hunting foxes. **fox•hunt•ing,** *n.* chasing foxes to catch and kill them, usu. with dogs. **fox ter•ri•er,** *n.* type of small dog. **fox•trot,** *n.* type of ballroom dance. **fox•y,** *adj.* crafty/cunning.

foy•er ['fɔɪeɪ] *n.* large entrance hall at the front of a hotel/theater/apartment house or in a house or apartment.

fra•cas ['fræka:] *n.* noisy disturbance.

frac•tion ['frækʃn] *n.* (a) very small piece/amount. (b) (*in mathematics*) less than a whole number. **frac•tion•al,** *adj.* very small. **frac•tion•al•ly,** *adv.* by a very small amount.

frac•tious ['frækʃəs] *adj.* bad-tempered/crying (child). **frac•tious•ness,** *n.* being fractious.

frac•ture ['fræktʃə] 1. *n.* break (esp. in bones); **simple f.** = clean break of a bone; **compound f.** = one where the broken bone has pierced the skin. 2. *v.* to break (a bone).

frag•ile ['frædʒaɪl] *adj.* easily broken/delicate. **fra•gil•i•ty** [frə'dʒɪlɪtɪ] *n.* being easily broken.

frag•ment 1. *n.* ['frægmənt] small piece. 2. *v.* [fræg'ment] to break into small pieces. **frag•men•tar•y,** *adj.* in pieces/not complete. **frag•men•ta•tion,** *n.* breaking into small pieces.

fra•grance ['freɪgrəns] *n.* pleasant smell. **fra•grant,** *adj.* sweet-smelling.

frail [freɪl] *adj.* weak. **frail•ty,** *n.* weakness.

frame [freɪm] 1. *n.* (a) supporting structure of a building/ship/aircraft/bicycle/glasses, etc.; **f. house** = wooden house. (b) bone structure of a person/animal; **f. of mind** = temper/mood. (c) border of wood/metal/plastic around a picture/mirror/window. (d) one picture in a length of motion-picture film. (e) glass box for protecting young plants in a garden. 2. *v.* (a) to put into words. (b) to put a border around (sth). (c) *inf.* to make (an innocent person) appear guilty. **frame-up,** *n. inf.* arrangement

---

æ back, ɑ: farm, ɒ top, aɪ pipe, aʊ how, aɪə fire, aʊə flower, ɔ: bought, ɔɪ toy, e fed, eəhair, eɪ take, ə afraid, əʊ boat, əʊə lower, v: word, i: heap, ɪ hit, ɪə hear, u: school, ʊ book, ʌ but, b back, d dog, ð then, dʒ just, f fog, g go, h hand, j yes, k catch, l last, m mix, n nut, ŋ sing, p penny, r round, s some, ʃ short, t too, tʃ chop, θ thing, v voice, w was, z zoo, ʒ treasure

whereby an innocent person is framed.
frame•work, *n.* (a) structure supporting a
building, etc. (b) basis of a plan.

franc [fræŋk] *n.* unit of money in France, Belgium and Switzerland.

fran•chise ['fræntʃaɪz] 1. *n.* (a) right to vote.
(b) permit to sell a company's products in a
certain region/to trade using a well-known
brand name. 2. *v.* to license a product to others who will sell it and pay a fee for its use.
fran•chi•see, *n.* person who runs a business
under franchise. **fran•chis•or,** *n.* person
who licenses s.o. to operate a franchise.

Franco- ['fræŋkəʊ] *prefix meaning* between
France and another country.

frank [fræŋk] 1. *adj.* plain-speaking; (person)
who says what he thinks. 2. *v.* to stamp (a letter) on a special machine. **frank•ly,** *adv.*
speaking truthfully. **frank•ness,** *n.* saying
what you think.

frank•furt•er ['fræŋkfɜːtə] *n.* long spiced sausage, which is boiled and sometimes eaten
with a roll.

frank•in•cense ['fræŋkɪnsens] *n.* gum from a
tree, burned as incense.

fran•tic ['fræntɪk] *adj.* worried and wildly excited. **fran•ti•cal•ly,** *adv.* in an excited and
worried way.

fra•ter•nal [frə'tɜːnl] *adj.* brotherly.
fra•ter•nal•ly, *adv.* in a fraternal way.
fra•ter•ni•ty, *n.* (a) society of men with similar interests. (b) student association for men
at a college or university. (c) brotherly feeling.
frat•er•ni•za•tion [frætənar'zeɪʃn] *n.* act of
fraternizing. **frat•er•nize** ['frætənaɪz] *v.* to
become friendly (with s.o.).

frat•ri•cide ['frætrɪsaɪd] *n.* murder of your
brother.

fraud [frɔːd] *n.* (a) (piece of) dishonesty. (b) person pretending to be sth he is not; thing that is
not what you expect. **fraud•u•lence,** *n.* dishonesty. **fraud•u•lent,** *adj.* dishonest.

fraught [frɔːt] *adj.* (a) (with) full of (problems,
danger). (b) *inf.* full of anxiety; worrying (situation).

fray [freɪ] 1. *n.* fight; **ready for the f.** = ready to
fight/ready to take part in the action. 2. *v.* (*of
material*) to become worn/to unravel so that
threads are loose.

fraz•zle ['fræzl] *n.* state of exhaustion.

freak [friːk] *n.* (a) unusual type of person/animal/plant. (b) extraordinary change in the
weather. (c) person who is fanatic about sth.
freak•ish, *adj.* unusual/extraordinary. **freak
out,** *v. inf.* to become very excited (as because
of the effect of drugs).

freck•le ['frekl] *n.* small brown mark on the
skin, often caused by the sun. **freck•led,** *adj.*
covered in freckles.

free [friː] 1. *adj.* (**freer, freest**) (a) not imprisoned/not tied down. (b) not occupied. (c) not
costing any money. (d) able to do what you
want; **to be f. with sth** = to give sth away generously. (e) **to be f. from/of sth** = to be without
sth (usu. unpleasant). 2. *v.* (a) to get (a person)
out of prison. (b) to release from a difficult situation. **free•dom,** *n.* state of being free; **f. of
speech** = ability to say what you like.
free-for-all, *n.* general fight/general argument among several people. **free•hand,** *adj.*
& *adv.* (drawing) drawn without the help of
rulers/compasses, etc. **free•hold,** *n. & adj.*
right to own a property for ever.
free•hold•er, *n.* person who owns a freehold property. **free•lance.** 1. *adj. & n.* independent (worker), not employed by one
particular company. 2. *adv.* (to work) independently. 3. *v.* to work independently.
free•load•er, *n. inf.* person who lives on
money/gifts, etc. which he gets from other
people. **free•ly,** *adv.* in a frank manner/without being tied. **Free•ma•son,** *n.* member of
a secret society. **free•ma•son•ry,** *n.* brotherhood/fraternity. **free-range,** *adj.* (hens)
kept in the open, not in boxes. **free style,** *n.*
(*in sport*) any style; (*in swimming*) any stroke,
usu. crawl. **free trade,** *n.* system of trade
agreements between countries where goods
are imported and exported free of tax.
free•ware, *n.* computer software that is distributed to users without charge. **free•way,**
n. fast highway with few points of access or
exit. **free•wheel** [friː'wiːl] *v.* to go along on a
bicycle without pedaling. **free will,** *n.* ability
to decide for yourself.

free•si•a ['friːʒə] *n.* scented flower grown from
a bulb.

freeze [friːz] 1. *n.* (a) period of frost. (b) **wage
f./price f.** = period of standstill in wages or
prices. 2. *v.* (**froze; has frozen**) (a) to change
from liquid to solid because of the cold. (b) to
become very cold. (c) to stay very still. (d) to
store (food) at below freezing point. (e) to
keep prices or wages at the present level. (f) to
prevent the owner from collecting, using or
selling (assets). **freez•er,** *n.* deep-freeze/refrigerator for freezing food and keeping it
frozen. **freez•ing point,** *n.* temperature at
which a liquid becomes solid.

freight [freɪt] 1. *n.* (a) transport of goods by air,
sea or land. (b) goods transported; **f. train** =
train used for transporting goods; **f. car** = car
which carries goods not passengers. 2. *v.* to
transport (goods). **freight•er,** *n.* aircraft/ship which carries goods.
freight•train, *n.* train of freight cars.

French [frentʃ] 1. *adj.* referring to France; **F.
window** = door made of glass usu. opening on

to a garden; **F. dressing** = salad dressing made of oil and vinegar; **F. fries/F. fried potatoes** = long pieces of potato fried in oil; **to take F. leave** = to go away without permission; **F. horn** = brass instrument with a coiled tube. 2. *n.* (a) language spoken in France and some other countries. (b) **the F.** = the people of France. **French•man, Frenchwoman,** *n.* (*pl.* **-men, -women**) person from France. **French pol•ish,** *v.* to polish (wood) with a resin polish.

fre•net•ic [frə'netɪk] *adj.* wildly excited.

fren•zy ['frenzɪ] *n.* wild excitement. **fren•zied,** *adj.* wildly excited. **fren•zied•ly,** *adv.* in a frenzied way.

fre•quent 1. *adj.* ['friːkwənt] happening often/often seen. 2. *v.* [frɪ'kwent] go go (somewhere) very often. **fre•quen•cy,** *n.* (a) rate at which sth happens. (b) number of vibrations per second made by a radio wave. **fre•quent•ly,** *adv.* often.

fres•co ['freskəu] *n.* (*pl.* **-oes**) painting done on wet plaster on a wall.

fresh [freʃ] *adj.* (**-er, -est**) (a) new/not used; **f. air** = open air. (b) recent (news); newly-made (cakes). (c) not canned or frozen. (d) quite strong (wind). (e) healthy-looking. (f) rude; impudent. **fresh•en,** *v.* to become/to make fresh. **fresh•man,** *n.* (*pl.* **-men**) new student in his/her first year at a school, college or university. **fresh•ly,** *adv.* newly/recently. **fresh•ness,** *n.* being fresh. **fresh wa•ter,** *n.* water in rivers or lakes. **fresh•wa•ter,** *adj.* referring to river or lake water, not salt water.

fret [fret] 1. *n.* raised metal strip crossing the neck of a guitar against which you press the strings. 2. *v.* (**fretted**) to worry/be unhappy. **fret•ful,** *adj.* crying and unhappy (child). **fret•ful•ly,** *adv.* in a fretful way.

fret•work ['fretwɜːk] *n.* patterns in wood cut with a very fine saw. **fret•saw,** *n.* fine saw used for cutting patterns in wood.

Freud•i•an ['frɔɪdɪən] *adj.* referring to Freud and his theories of psychoanalysis; **a F. slip** = a mistake in speaking which seems to show your real feelings, when you are trying to hide them.

fri•a•ble ['fraɪəbl] *adj.* (earth) which can be crumbled easily.

fri•ar ['fraɪə] *n.* member of a Christian religious order.

fric•as•see ['frɪkæseɪ] *n.* dish of pieces of meat cooked in a rich sauce.

fric•tion ['frɪkʃn] *n.* (a) rubbing one thing against another. (b) disagreement between two or more people.

Fri•day ['fraɪdeɪ] *n.* fifth day of the week/day between Thursday and Saturday; **Good F.** = the Friday before Easter Day.

fridge [frɪdʒ] *n. inf.* refrigerator.

fried [fraɪd] *v. see* **fry.**

friend [frend] *n.* person whom you know well and like; supporter (of a cause); **the Society of Friends** = religious society, also called the Quakers. **friend•less,** *adj.* having no friends. **friend•li•ness,** *n.* friendly feeling. **friend•ly,** *adj.* like a friend/kind/helpful. **friend•ship,** *n.* state of being friends.

frieze [friːz] *n.* decorative border around the top of walls, pillars, etc.

frig•ate ['frɪgət] *n.* small fast-moving naval ship.

fright [fraɪt] *n.* (a) fear. (b) *inf.* awful-looking person. **fright•ful,** *adj. inf.* terrible/awful. **fright•ful•ly,** *adv. inf.* extremely/terribly/very. **fright•ful•ness,** *n.* unpleasantness.

fright•en ['fraɪtn] *v.* to make (s.o.) afraid. **fright•en•ed,** *adj.* afraid/scared (**of**). **fright•en•ing,** *adj.* causing fear.

frig•id ['frɪdʒɪd] *adj.* (a) very cold/icy. (b) unfriendly/not showing any warm feelings; (woman) not interested in sex. **fri•gid•i•ty** [frɪ'dʒɪdɪtɪ] *n.* (a) great cold. (b) coldness of feelings, esp. lack of interest in sex. **fri•gid•ly,** *adv.* in a cold way.

frill [frɪl] *n.* (a) piece of material gathered together and sewn onto a dress, etc. (b) **frills** = unnecessary ornaments. **frilled,** *adj.* with frills. **frill•y,** *adj.* with many frills.

fringe [frɪndʒ] *n.* (a) hair lying over the forehead. (b) edging of material consisting of loose threads hanging down (on a shawl/dress/carpet, etc.). (c) outer edge of an area; **f. benefits** = extra benefits on top of a salary (such as a free car, etc.).

frip•per•y ['frɪpərɪ] *n.* useless ornament.

frisk [frɪsk] *v.* (a) to jump (**about**). (b) to search (s.o.) by running your hands over him to see if he is carrying a weapon. **frisk•i•ly,** *adv.* in a frisky way. **frisk•i•ness,** *n.* feeling full of life. **frisk•y,** *adj.* lively.

frit•il•lar•y [frɪ'tɪlərɪ] *n.* type of small butterfly.

frit•ter ['frɪtə] 1. *n.* piece of meat/fruit/vegetable dipped in a mixture of flour, egg and milk

---

æ back, aː farm, ɒː top, aɪ pipe, aʊ how, aɪə fire, aʊə flower, ɔː bought, ɔɪ toy, e fed, eəhair, eɪ take, ə afraid, əʊ boat, əʊə lower, ɜː word, iː heap, ɪ hit, ɪə hear, uː school, ʊ book, ʌ but, b back, d dog, ð then, dʒ just, f fog, g go, h hand, j yes, k catch, l last, m mix, n nut, ŋ sing, p penny, r round, s some, ʃ short, t too, tʃ chop, θ thing, v voice, w was, z zoo, ʒ treasure

and fried. 2. *v.* **f. away** = to waste (time, money).

friv•o•lous ['frɪvələs] *adj.* silly/not serious. **friv•o•lous•ly,** *adv.* in a frivolous way. **friv•o•lous•ness, fri•vol•i•ty** [frɪ'vɒlɪtɪ] *n.* silliness/lack of seriousness.

friz•zle ['frɪzl] *v. inf.* (a) (*of hair*) to be very tightly curled. (b) to fry in hot fat.

friz•zy ['frɪzɪ] *adj. inf.* tightly curled (hair). **frizz,** *v. inf.* to put (hair) into tight curls.

fro [frəʊ] *adv.* **to and f.** = backward and forward.

frock [frɒk] *n.* (a) dress/piece of female clothing covering more or less all the body. (b) long robe worn by monks or priests.

frog [frɒg] *n.* (a) small tailless reptile which lives on both land and water; **to have a f. in your throat** = to feel you have sth in your throat which stops you speaking clearly. (b) decorated fastening on a uniform. **frog•man,** *n.* (*pl.* -men) underwater diver.

frol•ic ['frɒlɪk] 1. *n.* happy game/party. 2. *v.* (**frolicked**) to play happily.

from [frɒm] *prep.* (a) (*showing movement away*) **the plane f. Paris.** (b) (*showing where something started*) **f. beginning to end; f. time to time** = sometimes. (c) (*showing difference*) **I can't tell butter f. margarine.** (d) sent by; **a letter f. Peter.** (e) because of; **he died f. pneumonia.** (f) according to; **f. what I heard.**

frond [frɒnd] *n.* large leaf of a fern or palm tree.

front [frʌnt] 1. *n.* (a) part which faces forward; most prominent part; **in f. of** = before. (b) land which runs along a road, street, shoreline, etc. (c) line of an army nearest the enemy in battle. (d) (*of weather*) line separating cold and warm masses of air. (e) business used to hide an illegal activity. 2. *adj.* foremost/first (seat, door, etc.). 3. *v.* to face (**on to**). **front•age** ['frʌntɪdʒ] *n.* (a) length of a property along a road, street, etc. (b) land between a building and a road, street, body of water, etc. **fron•tal,** *adj.* of/in the front; belonging to the front.

fron•tier ['frʌntɪə] *n.* (a) boundary line between two countries or states. (b) **frontiers** = the outermost limit of human knowledge.

fron•tis•piece ['frʌntɪspiːs] *n.* picture opposite the title page of a book.

frost [frɒst] *n.* (a) weather when the temperature is below the freezing point of water. (b) white covering on the ground/trees, etc., when the temperature is below freezing. **frost•bite,** *n.* damage to a part of the body due to cold. **frost•bit•ten,** *adj.* attacked by frostbite. **frost•ed,** *adj.* (a) covered in frost; damaged by frost. (b) (glass) which has a rough surface through which it is difficult to see. (c) (cake) covered with frosting.

frost•i•ly, *adv.* coldly/in an unfriendly way. **frost•ing,** *n.* icing on a cake. **frost•y,** *adj.* (a) very cold; covered with frost. (b) cold/unfriendly (manner).

froth [frɒθ] 1. *n.* mass of bubbles on top of a liquid. 2. *v.* to have masses of bubbles. **froth•y,** *adj.* having bubbles on top.

frown [fraʊn] 1. *n.* pulling down the eyebrows as a sign of anger/puzzlement, etc. 2. *v.* to pull down the eyebrows; **to f. on** (sth) = to disapprove of sth.

frowz•y ['fraʊzɪ] *adj.* untidy and dirty.

froze [frəʊz] *v. see* **freeze.**

fro•zen ['frəʊzn] *adj.* (a) very cold. (b) at a temperature below freezing point; **f. food** = food stored at a temperature below freezing point; *see also* **freeze.**

fru•gal ['fruːgl] *adj.* spending/costing very little money. **fru•gal•i•ty** [fruː'gælɪtɪ] *n.* being frugal. **fru•gal•ly,** *adv.* in a frugal way.

fruit [fruːt] 1. *n.* (a) (*pl. usu.* fruit) part of a plant which contains the seeds and which is often eaten; **f. salad** = pieces of fresh fruit mixed and served cold. (b) product (of hard work). 2. *v.* to carry/to produce edible parts. **fruit•cake,** *n.* cake with a lot of dried fruit in it. **fruit•ful,** *adj.* (work) which produces good results. **fruit•ful•ly,** *adv.* in a fruitful way. **fru•i•tion** [fruː'ɪʃn] *n.* to come to f. = to be accomplished with good results. **fruit•less,** *adj.* producing no results. **fruit•less•ly,** *adv.* in a fruitless way. **fruit•y,** *adj.* (a) tasting of fruit. (b) *inf.* deep and tuneful (voice).

frump [frʌmp] *n.* person, usu. a woman, who wears old-fashioned clothes. **frump•ish,** *adj.* (wearing) out-of-date clothes.

frus•trate [frʌ'streɪt] *v.* to prevent (s.o.) doing what he/she wants to do. **frus•tra•tion** [frʌ-'streɪʃn] *n.* feeling of anger and impatience when stopped from doing what you want.

fry [fraɪ] 1. *n.* (*pl.* fry) baby fish; **small f.** = unimportant people. 2. *v.* to cook in oil/fat. **fry•ing pan,** *n.* shallow, open pan used for frying; **to jump out of the f. p. into the fire** = to go from one difficult situation to sth worse.

ft *abbreviation for* **foot.**

fuch•sia ['fjuːʃə] *n.* garden plant with colorful hanging flowers.

fud•dle ['fʌdl] *v.* to make (s.o.) feel hazy and confused.

fud•dy-dud•dy ['fʌdɪdʌdɪ] *n. inf.* old-fashioned person.

fudge [fʌdʒ] 1. *n.* soft candy made from butter, sugar and milk. 2. *v.* to avoid dealing with sth; **to f. the issue** = to avoid making a decision on an issue.

fuel ['fjʊəl] 1. *n.* substance (coal/gas/oil/wood, etc.) which can be burned to give heat/power;

to add f. to the fire = to make matters worse. 2. *v.* (**fueled, fuelled**) to provide fuel for.

fug [fʌg] *n. inf.* stuffy/hot atmosphere. **fug•gi•ness**, *n.* being fuggy. **fug•gy**, *adj.* stuffy/hot.

fu•gi•tive ['fjuːdʒətɪv] *n. & adj.* (person) who is running away.

fugue [fjuːg] *n.* piece of music where a tune is repeated in several patterns.

ful•crum ['fʊlkrəm] *n.* point on which a lever rests/on which a seesaw balances.

ful•fill, fulfil [fʊl'fɪl] *v.* (**fulfilled**) to complete (sth) satisfactorily. **ful•fill•ment**, *n.* satisfactory ending.

full [fʊl] 1. *adj.* (**-er, -est**) (a) containing as much as possible; **f. up** = with no more room; **I'm f. (up)** = I have eaten as much as I can; **f. skirt** = wide skirt made from lots of material. (b) all; as many (as possible). (c) complete; **f. year** = one complete year. (d) round and plump (face); **f. moon** = moon when completely round. 2. *n.* **in f.** = completely/entirely. **full back**, *n.* (*in games*) defensive player near the goal. **full•blood•ed**, *adj.* (a) vigorous (argument). (b) (*of horses*) strongly typical. **full-blown**, *adj.* (a) (*of a flower*) wide open. (b) **he is a f.-b. doctor** = he has passed all his examinations and is qualified. **full-fledged**, *adj.* experienced/qualified. **full-grown**, *adj.* adult. **full-length**, *adj.* (a) from head to toe. (b) long (story/motion picture). **full•ness**, *n.* (a) state of containing as much as possible. (b) state when all is completed. **full-scale**, *adj.* complete/total. **full-time**, *adj. & adv.* all the time. **ful•ly**, *adv.* completely/entirely.

ful•mar ['fʊlmɑː] *n.* gray and white northern seabird.

ful•mi•nate ['fʌlmɪneɪt] *v.* (*formal*) to protest angrily. **ful•min•a•tions** [fʌlmɪ'neɪʃnz] *n. pl.* angry protests.

ful•some ['fʊlsəm] *adj.* excessive/too much.

fu•ma•role ['fjuːmərəʊl] *n.* hole in the side of a volcano through which smoke escapes.

fum•ble ['fʌmbl] *v.* (**with**) to touch/to feel clumsily. **fum•bling**, *adj.* clumsy.

fume [fjuːm] 1. *n. pl.* **fumes** = smoke/gas. 2. *v.* to be angry.

fu•mi•gate ['fjuːmɪgeɪt] *v.* to clean (a room) by smoking out germs and insects. **fu•mi•ga•tion** [fjuːmɪ'geɪʃn] *n.* smoking out germs/insects.

fun [fʌn] *n.* amusement/pleasure; **to make f. of/to poke f. at** = to laugh at/to mock; **for f./in**

f. = not seriously/as a joke. **fun fair,** *n.* amusement park.

func•tion ['fʌŋkʃn] 1. *n.* (a) job/duty. (b) gathering of people; party. 2. *v.* (a) to work. (b) to serve (**as**). **func•tion•al**, *adj.* useful but not decorative. **func•tion•al•ly**, *adv.* in a functional way. **func•tion•ar•y**, *n.* official. **function key**, *n.* key on a computer keyboard which activates a set of instructions.

fund [fʌnd] 1. *n.* (a) sum of money set aside for a special purpose. (b) collection. 2. *v.* to provide money for (a special purpose).

fun•da•men•tal [fʌndə'mentl] *adj.* basic/essential. **fun•da•men•tal•ly**, *adv.* basically.

fu•ner•al ['fjuːnərəl] *n.* ceremony where a dead person is buried/cremated. **fu•ner•ar•y**, *adj.* used in a funeral. **fu•ne•re•al** [fjuː'nɪərɪəl] *adj.* sad and gloomy.

fun•gus ['fʌŋgəs] *n.* (*pl.* **fungi** ['fʌŋgaɪ]) plant which has no green leaves or flowers and which frequently lives on other plants. **fun•gi•cide** ['fʌndʒɪsaɪd] *n.* chemical which kills fungus. **fun•gi•cid•al**, *adj.* which kills fungus. **fun•goid**, *adj.* like a fungus.

fu•nic•u•lar [fə'nɪkjulə] *n.* **f.** (**railway**) = railway where cars held by cables travel up a slope.

funk [fʌŋk] 1. *n. inf.* (a) fear. (b) **to be in a f.** = be depressed/in low spirits. 2. *v. inf.* to be afraid to do sth.

fun•nel ['fʌnl] 1. *n.* (a) tube with a wide mouth and narrow bottom used when pouring liquids from one container into another. (b) chimney on a ship from which the smoke comes. 2. (**funneled, funnelled**) *v.* to pass through a funnel/through a narrow space.

fun•ny ['fʌnɪ] *adj.* (a) which makes people laugh. (b) odd/unusual; **I feel f.** = I feel ill. **fun•ni•ly**, *adv.* oddly. **fun•ny bone**, *n. inf.* part of the elbow which hurts sharply if it is hit.

fur [fɜː] 1. *n.* (a) soft coat of an animal. (b) coating like fur, as a deposit in kettles/water pipes, etc., or on the tongue when sick. 2. *v.* (**furred**) to become covered with a coating like fur. **fur•ry**, *adj.* covered with fur.

fur•bish ['fɜːbɪʃ] *v.* to polish/to clean.

fu•ri•ous ['fjʊərɪəs] *adj.* very angry. **fu•ri•ous•ly**, *adv.* in a furious way.

furl [fɜːl] *v.* to roll up and tie securely.

fur•long ['fɜːlɒŋ] *n.* measure of length (= 220 yards).

æ **back**, ɑː **farm**, ɒ: **top**, aɪ **pipe**, aʊ **how**, aɪə **fire**, aʊə **flower**, ɔː **bought**, ɔɪ **toy**, e **fed**, eə **hair**, eɪ **take**, ə **afraid**, əʊ **boat**, əʊə **lower**, ʌː **word**, iː **heap**, ɪ **hit**, ɪə **hear**, uː **school**, ʊ **book**, ʌ **but**, b **back**, d **dog**, ð **then**, dʒ **just**, f **fog**, g **go**, h **hand**, j **yes**, k **catch**, l **last**, m **mix**, n **nut**, ŋ **sing**, p **penny**, r **round**, s **some**, ʃ **short**, t **too**, tʃ **chop**, θ **thing**, v **voice**, w **was**, z **zoo**, ʒ **treasure**

fur•lough ['fɜːləʊ] *n.* leave of absence (esp. from the armed forces).

fur•nace ['fɜːnəs] *n.* large structure with a chamber which can be heated to a very high temperature for heating a building, producing steam, etc.

fur•nish ['fɜːnɪʃ] *v.* (a) to provide with chairs/tables, etc.; **furnished apartment** = rented apartment where the furniture is provided by the owner. (b) to supply (**with**). **fur•nish•ings,** *n. pl.* fittings in a house.

fur•ni•ture ['fɜːnɪtʃə] *n.* (*no pl.*) tables/chairs/cupboards/beds, etc.; **a piece of f.** = one article of furniture.

fu•ror [fjuːˈrɔː], *Brit.* **fu•ro•re** [fjuːˈrɔːrɪ] *n.* outburst of anger/excitement.

fur•ri•er ['fʌrɪə] *n.* person who sells fur coats, etc.

fur•row ['fʌrəʊ] 1. *n.* long groove cut in the earth by a plow. 2. *v.* to make furrows in (the land, etc.).

fur•ther ['fɜːðə] 1. *adv. & adj.* (a) farther/to a greater distance/more distant. (b) additional; **f. delays.** 2. *v.* to advance (a plan). **fur•ther•ance,** *n.* advancing (of a plan). **fur•ther•more** [fɜːðəˈmɔː] *adv.* also/in addition. **fur•ther•most** ['fɜːðəməʊst] *adj.* most distant. **fur•thest,** *adj. & adv.* to the greatest distance/most distant.

fur•tive ['fɜːtɪv] *adj.* secret; as if hiding something. **fur•tive•ly,** *adv.* in a furtive way. **fur•tive•ness,** *n.* being furtive.

fu•ry ['fjʊərɪ] *n.* fierce anger.

furze [fɜːz] *n.* gorse.

fuse [fjuːz] 1. *n.* (a) length of string attached to a bomb which burns slowly when lit. (b) small piece of wire in an electrical circuit which melts and breaks if the circuit is overloaded, and so prevents further damage; **to blow a f.** = to overload the electric circuit and make the fuse break. 2. *v.* **to f. together** = to join together (wires/companies, etc.). **fuse•box,** *n.* box where the fuses are kept.

fu•se•lage ['fjuːzəlɑːʒ] *n.* body of an aircraft.

fu•sil•lade [fjuːzɪˈleɪd] *n.* rapid gunfire.

fu•sion ['fjuːʒn] *n.* (a) melting together of two pieces of metal. (b) joining together of two different things.

fuss [fʌs] 1. *n.* agitated complaints about little things that do not matter; **to make a f. about sth** = to complain at length about sth unimportant; **to make a f. of s.o.** = to pay great attention to s.o. 2. *v.* to be agitated; to show unnecessary care and attention (**over** little things). **fuss•i•ly,** *adv.* in a fussy way. **fuss•i•ness,** *n.* being fussy. **fuss•y,** *adj.* (a) unnecessarily careful and demanding about little things. (b) disliking lots of things.

fus•ty ['fʌstɪ] *adj.* smelling of dampness. **fus•ti•ness,** *n.* being fusty.

fu•tile ['fjuːtaɪl, *Am.* 'fjuːtl] *adj.* useless. **fu•til•i•ty** [fjuːˈtɪlɪtɪ] *n.* uselessness.

fu•ture ['fjuːtʃə] 1. *n.* time which has not yet happened; **in the f.** = from now on. 2. *adj.* coming/not yet happened. **fu•tures,** *n.* trade in something, such as foreign currency or commodities, for delivery at a later date. **fu•tur•is•tic** [fjuːtʃəˈrɪstɪk] *adj.* oddly modern (art).

fuzz [fʌz] *n.* (a) fluffy hair or other matter. (b) *Sl.* **the f.** = the police. **fuzz•i•ness,** *n.* being fuzzy. **fuzz•y,** *adj.* (a) fluffy and curly. (b) not clear/blurred. **fuz•zy log•ic** 1. *n.* logic that accommodates and describes imprecise reasoning and uncertainty in a way that can be processed by a computer. 2. *adj.* (computer program/system) able to process data formulated by fuzzy logic.

Gg

g *abbrev. for* gram.

gab [gæb] *n. inf.* talk/chat; **the gift of g.** = talent for speaking.

gab•ar•dine ['gæbədi:n] *n.* closely woven cotton, wool, or other material, used for making clothes.

gab•ble ['gæbl] 1. *n.* loud, unintelligible talk. 2. *v.* to speak very quickly.

ga•ble ['geɪbl] *n.* triangular upper part of a wall at the end of a roof. **ga•bled,** *adj.* with gables.

gad [gæd] *v.* **(gadded) to g. about** = to be constantly out and about. **gad•a•bout,** *n.* person who is always out and about. **gad•fly,** *n.* fly which attacks cows; irritating person.

gadg•et ['gædʒɪt] *n.* useful machine/tool. **gadg•et•ry,** *n.* lots of gadgets.

Gael•ic ['geɪlɪk, *in Scotland* 'gælɪk] *n.* language of Scots, Manx and Irish Celts.

gaff [gæf] 1. *n.* stick with iron hook for catching large fish. 2. *v.* to catch with a gaff.

gaffe [gæf] *n.* blunder; indiscreet act or remark.

gaf•fer ['gæfə] *n. inf.* old man.

gag [gæg] 1. *n.* (a) soft object put into or tied round the mouth to stop s.o. speaking. (b) joke. 2. *v.* **(gagged)** (a) to bind (s.o.) round the mouth; **to g. the press** = to impose censorship. (b) to retch/to choke.

ga•ga ['ga:ga:] *adj. inf.* senile/stupid.

gag•gle ['gægl] *n.* flock (of geese).

gai•e•ty ['geɪətɪ] *n.* happiness/cheerfulness. **gai•ly** ['geɪlɪ] *adv.* happily.

gain [geɪn] 1. *n.* increase of possessions; profit. 2. *v.* (a) to obtain/to get; **to g. the upper hand** = to get control. (b) **the clock gains five minutes a day** = it moves five minutes ahead of the correct time in every twenty-four hours. (c) **to g. on s.o./sth** = to get closer to a person or thing you are chasing. **gain•ful,** *adj.* which earns money; **g. employment. gain•ful•ly,** *adv.* **g. employed** = doing work which earns money.

gain•say [geɪn'seɪ] *v.* **(gainsaid)** *(formal)* to deny (sth).

gait [geɪt] *n.* manner of walking.

gait•er ['geɪtə] *n.* covering of cloth or leather worn over the leg below the knee.

gal. *abbrev. for* gallon.

ga•la ['ga:lə] *n.* festive occasion.

gal•ax•y ['gæləksɪ] *n.* collection of stars, found singly and in groups and clusters. **ga•lac•tic** [gə'læktɪk] *adj.* belonging to a galaxy.

gale [geɪl] *n.* very strong wind.

ga•le•na [gə'li:nə] *n.* natural form of lead sulfide.

gall [gɔ:l] 1. *n.* (a) bile/bitter liquid produced by the liver to digest fat. (b) growth produced by insects on trees, esp. the oak. (c) painful swelling/blister (esp. on horses). (d) *inf.* rudeness/impudence. 2. *v.* to annoy/to humiliate. **gall•ing,** *adj.* humiliating; annoying. **gall-blad•der,** *n.* bag in the body where bile is stored. **gall•stone,** *n.* small stonelike substance which sometimes forms in the gall-bladder.

gal•lant ['gælənt] *adj.* (a) brave/chivalrous. (b) very polite towards women. **gal•lant•ly,** *adv.* in a gallant way. **gal•lant•ry** ['gæləntrɪ] *n.* bravery.

gal•le•on ['gælɪən] *n.* large Spanish warship in the 16th century.

gal•ler•y ['gælərɪ] *n.* (a) room in which pictures are hung, often for sale. (b) store selling pictures/antiques, etc. (c) *(in a church/hall, etc.)* balcony which runs around part of the main hall; *(in a theater)* highest rows of usu. cheapest seats; **to play to the g.** = to appeal to the public; **minstrels' g.** = balcony above the end of a castle dining hall from where musicians entertained the diners. (d) **shooting g.** = long, narrow room at one end of which is a target for shooting.

gal•ley ['gælɪ] *n.* (a) low, flat, single-decked ship, rowed by slaves. (b) ship's kitchen. (c) *(in printing)* rectangular tray which holds type. **galley proof,** *n.* proof printed on long sheets of paper.

Gal•lic ['gælɪk] *adj.* French. **gall•i•cism**

['gælɪsɪzəm] *n.* French word or phrase adopted into another language.

gal•li•vant ['gælɪvænt] *v. inf.* to be always out and about looking for amusement.

gal•lon ['gælən] *n.* liquid measure equal to 4 quarts or 4.5 liters.

gal•lop ['gæləp] 1. *n.* (a) fastest pace of a horse running with all feet off the ground in each stride. (b) fast ride on a horse. 2. *v.* to run/to go fast; **galloping inflation** = rapidly rising inflation.

gal•lows ['gæləuz] *n.* structure on which criminals are hanged.

Gal•lup poll ['gæləp'pəul] *n.* test of public opinion on an important topic, esp. of how a representative sample of the public will vote, in order to forecast an election result.

ga•lore [gə'lɔ:] *adv.* (*always after the noun*) plenty; **apples g.**

ga•losh•es [gə'lɒʃɪz] *n. pl.* plastic/rubber shoes worn over other shoes to protect them.

ga•lumph [gə'lʌmf] *v. inf.* to walk about heavily.

gal•va•nize ['gælvənaɪz] *v.* (a) **galvanized iron** = iron coated with zinc to protect it from rust. (b) to rouse by shock into action. **gal•va•ni•za•tion** [gælvənaɪ'zeɪʃn] *n.* process of galvanizing. **gal•va•nom•e•ter** [gælvə'nɒmɪtə] *n.* instrument for measuring small electric currents.

gam•bit ['gæmbɪt] *n.* (a) (*in chess*) opening move whereby a player sacrifices a minor piece in order to take a major one later. (b) opening move in some action.

gam•ble ['gæmbl] 1. *n.* risk taken in the hope of getting good results. **it's a bit of a g.** = you can't be sure it will succeed. 2. *v.* to risk (money) on cards or sporting results; **to g. on sth happening** = to act in the hope that it will happen. **gam•bler,** *n.* person who gambles. **gam•bling,** *n.* risking money; betting **on** sth.

gam•bol ['gæmbl] *v.* (**gamboled, gambolled**) to run, leap, or jump in play.

game [geɪm] 1. *n.* (a) contest played according to rules and decided by skill, strength or luck; **a g. of tennis/chess; to play the g.** = to act honorably; **so that's his little g.** = now we know what his plans are. (b) (*in tennis/bridge, etc.*) single round. (c) wild animals and birds (deer, rabbits, pheasants, etc.) hunted for sport or food; **g. soup** = soup made from game; **big g.** = large wild animals (lions/elephants, etc.) shot for sport. 2. *adj.* (a) willing/courageous. (b) lame (leg). **game•keep•er,** *n.* person employed to breed and look after game. **game•ly,** *adv.* bravely. **game•ness,** *n.* being game. **games•man•ship,** *n.* (*no pl.*) the art of winning by devious means, such as

distracting your opponent. **gam•ing,** *n.* gambling.

gam•ete ['gæmi:t] *n.* plant or animal cell which can link with another to reproduce.

gam•ma ['gæmə] *n.* third letter of the Greek alphabet. **gam•ma glob•u•lin,** *n.* protein found in blood plasma. **gamma rays** *n. pl.* rays of short wavelength sent out by radioactive substances.

gam•mon ['gæmən] *n.* smoked or cured ham.

gam•ut ['gæmət] *n.* (a) whole range of musical notes. (b) whole range or scope.

gan•der ['gændə] *n.* male goose.

gang [gæŋ] 1. *n.* band of people acting or going about together. 2. *v.* **to g. together** = to join together; **to g. up on (s.o.)** = to take sides with one or more people against s.o. **gang•plank,** *n.* long piece of wood giving access to a boat from the shore. **gang•ster,** *n.* member of a gang of violent criminals. **gang•way,** *n.* (a) passageway. (b) bridge from the shore to a ship.

gan•gling ['gæŋglɪŋ] *adj.* tall (person) with long arms and legs.

gan•gli•on ['gæŋglɪən] *n.* (a) nucleus of nerves in the central nervous system. (b) small lump on a tendon.

gan•grene ['gæŋgri:n] *n.* rotting of body tissue, caused by a blockage of the blood supply. **gan•gre•nous** ['gæŋgrɪnəs] *adj.* affected by gangrene.

gan•net ['gænɪt] *n.* large white sea bird.

gan•try ['gæntrɪ] *n.* metal bridge for carrying lights/a crane, etc.

gap [gæp] *n.* (a) space/hole in a hedge/wall, etc. (b) gorge or pass (between mountains). (c) space/difference; **age g.** = difference in age; **generation g.** = difference in years between one generation and another, often resulting in intolerance between them.

gape [geɪp] *v.* to open your mouth wide. **gap•ing,** *adj.* wide open.

ga•rage ['gærɪdʒ, 'gærɑ:ʒ] 1. *n.* (a) building for storing motor vehicles; **g. sale** = private sale of unwanted household goods (held in the garage or yard of a house). (b) station/place where motor vehicles are repaired and serviced. 2. *v.* to put (a vehicle) into a garage.

garb [gɑ:b] *n.* (*no pl.*) (*formal*) clothing. **garbed,** *adj.* dressed (**in**).

gar•bage ['gɑ:bɪdʒ] *n.* refuse/trash; **g. can** = container for refuse/trash.

gar•ble ['gɑ:bl] *v.* to select certain items from speeches in order to give an unfair or malicious representation; to distort/confuse.

gar•den ['gɑ:dn] 1. *n.* piece of ground used for growing flowers, fruit, or vegetables; **g. center** = place where plants, seeds and garden tools are sold. 2. *v.* to look after a garden.

gar•den•er, *n.* person who looks after a garden. **gar•den•ing,** *n.* looking after a garden.

gar•de•nia [gɑ:'di:nɪə] *n.* shrub with fragrant white or yellow flowers.

gar•gan•tu•an [gɑ:'gæntjʊən] *adj.* huge/enormous.

gar•gle ['gɑ:gl] 1. *n.* antiseptic liquid used for washing the throat. 2. *v.* to wash the throat by holding antiseptic liquid in it and breathing out at the same time.

gar•goyle ['gɑ:gɔɪl] *n.* water spout on a medieval building, carved like a grotesque head.

gar•ish ['geərɪʃ] *adj.* bright/showy/over-decorated. **gar•ish•ly,** *adv.* very brightly.

gar•land ['gɑ:lənd] 1. *n.* (a) circle of flowers or leaves worn as a decoration. (b) decoration made of linked paper/ribbon, etc. 2. *v.* to hang with garlands.

gar•lic ['gɑ:lɪk] *n.* plant whose bulb has a strong smell and taste, used as a flavoring. **gar•lick•y,** *adj.* tasting/smelling of garlic.

gar•ment ['gɑ:mənt] *n.* article of clothing.

gar•ner ['gɑ:nə] *v.* (*formal*) to collect and store.

gar•net ['gɑ:nɪt] *n.* semi-precious dark red stone.

gar•nish ['gɑ:nɪʃ] 1. *n.* thing used to decorate food. 2. *v.* to decorate (esp. food).

gar•ret ['gærət] *n.* attic room immediately under the roof of a house.

gar•ri•son ['gærɪsn] 1. *n.* (a) troops stationed in a fortress/town, etc., in order to defend it. (b) fortress. 2. *v.* to place troops on garrison duty in (a town).

gar•rotte [gə'rɒt] *v.* to strangle (s.o.) with a cord.

gar•ru•lous ['gærjʊləs] *adj.* talkative. **gar•ru•lous•ly,** *adv.* in a garrulous way. **gar•ru•lous•ness, garrulity** [gæ'ru:lɪtɪ] *n.* being garrulous.

gar•ter ['gɑ:tə] *n.* band worn above or below the knee to keep a stocking or sock up; **Order of the Garter** = highest order of English knighthood.

gas [gæs] 1. *n.* (a) chemical substance like air, which is completely fluid and has no definite shape or volume. (b) substance, produced from coal or extracted naturally from the ground, which is used for cooking or heating; **to cook by g.; g. stove** = stove which uses gas; **natural g.** = gas which is extracted from the earth. (c) substance used as an anesthetic while having a tooth removed, etc. (d) gasoline, *inf.* **to step on the g.** = to accelerate. (e) *inf.*

unimportant talk. 2. *v.* (**gassed**) (a) to poison (s.o.) by making them breathe gas. (b) *inf.* to talk about nothing in particular. **gas•e•ous** ['gæsjəs] *adj.* referring to gas. **gas•mask,** *n.* mask used as protection against poison gases.

gas•o•line, *n.* inflammable liquid produced from petroleum and used as a fuel to drive motor vehicles. **gas•om•e•ter** [gæ'sɒmɪtə] *n.* large container in which gas is stored in a laboratory. **gas sta•tion,** *n.* place where you can buy gasoline. **gas•sy,** *adj.* full of gas/full of bubbles. **gas•works,** *n.* place where gas is manufactured.

gash [gæʃ] 1. *n.* long deep cut/wound. 2. *v.* to make a gash.

gas•ket ['gæskɪt] *n.* piece of thin material used to seal two parts of an engine to prevent air/gas, etc., from escaping.

gasp [gɑ:sp] 1. *n.* sharp intake of breath. 2. *v.* to struggle to breathe/to catch your breath in surprise.

gas•tric ['gæstrɪk] *adj.* referring to the stomach. **gas•trec•to•my,** *n.* operation to remove the stomach. **gas•tro•en•ter•i•tis** [gæstrəʊentə'raɪtɪs] *n.* illness of the stomach and intestines. **gas•tro•nome** ['gæstrənəʊm] *n.* expert on food and drink. **gas•tro•nom•ic** [gæstrə'nɒmɪk] *adj.* referring to food and drink. **gas•tron•o•my** [gæs'trɒnəmɪ] *n.* art of cooking.

gate [geɪt] *n.* (a) barrier, usu. made of wood or iron, closing an opening in a wall/fence, etc. (b) number of people who watch a match/sports competition; money paid by spectators at a match, etc. **gate•crash,** *v.* to go uninvited to (a party). **gate•crash•er,** *n.* uninvited guest. **gate-legged ta•ble,** *n.* table with hinged legs which fold like a gate. **gate•post,** *n.* post to which a gate is attached by hinges. **gate•way,** *n.* (a) gap in a wall/fence, etc., where a gate can be fitted. (b) hardware/software connecting different computer networks.

ga•teau ['gætəʊ] *n.* (*pl.* **gateaux** ['gætəʊz]) large decorated cake.

gath•er ['gæðə] *v.* (a) to bring together/to collect. (b) to gain (speed). (c) to understand; **I g. that you are coming.** (d) to pull (material) into folds by means of tiny stitches. **gath•er•ing.** 1. *n.* (a) group of people who have come together. (b) swelling with pus. 2. *adj.* imminent; **a g. storm. gather up,** *v.* to bring (things) together and pick them up.

æ back, ɑ: farm, ɒ: top, aɪ pipe, aʊ how, aɪe fire, aʊə flower, ɔ: bought, ɔɪ toy, e fed, eəhair, eɪ take, ə afraid, əʊ boat, əʊə lower, v: word, i: heap, ɪ hit, ɪə hear, u: school, ʊ book, ʌ but, b back, d dog, ð then, dʒ just, f fog, g go, h hand, j yes, k catch, l last, m mix, n nut, ŋ sing, p penny, r round, s some, ʃ short, t too, tʃ chop, θ thing, v voice, w was, z zoo, ʒ treasure

gauche [gəʊʃ] *adj.* clumsy/tactless.

gau•cho ['gaʊtʃəʊ] *n.* South American herdsman.

gaud•y ['gɔːdɪ] *adj.* (**-ier, -iest**) too brightly colored; showy; lacking in taste. **gaud•i•ly,** *adv.* showily. **gaud•i•ness,** *n.* being gaudy.

gauge [geɪdʒ] 1. *n.* (a) standard measure of width/thickness, etc. (b) distance between rails on a railroad track. (c) instrument measuring depth/pressure, etc. 2. *v.* (a) to measure exactly. (b) to estimate/to guess.

gaunt [gɔːnt] *adj.* lean/haggard. **gaunt•ness,** *n.* being gaunt.

gaunt•let ['gɔːntlət] *n.* strong glove with long wrist cover, for driving, fencing, etc.; **to throw down/take up the g.** = to issue/accept a challenge; **to run the g.** = to go through a difficult time.

gauss [gaʊs] *n.* unit for measuring the strength of a magnetic field.

gauze [gɔːz] *n.* thin/transparent material. **gauz•y,** *adj.* thin (material).

gave [geɪv] *v. see* **give.**

gav•el ['gævl] *n.* auctioneer's or chairman's hammer.

gawk•y ['gɔːkɪ] *adj.* (**-ier, -iest**) awkward/ungainly. **gawk•i•ness,** *n.* being gawky.

gawp [gɔːp] *v. inf.* to stare rudely (**at**).

gay [geɪ] 1. *adj.* (**-er, -est**) happy; full of fun. 2. *adj. & n. inf.* homosexual. **gay•ness,** *n.* being gay.

gaze [geɪz] 1. *n.* intent look. 2. *v.* to look steadily for a long time.

ga•ze•bo [gə'ziːbəʊ] *n.* small summerhouse.

ga•zelle [gə'zel] *n.* kind of antelope.

ga•zette [gə'zet] *n.* official newspaper, giving details of public appointments, etc. **gaz•et•teer** [gæzə'tɪə] *n.* geographical dictionary.

GDP [dʒiːdiː'piː] *n.* gross domestic product.

gear ['gɪə] 1. *n.* (a) equipment; **landing g.** = undercarriage of an aircraft. (b) *inf.* clothing. (c) **gears** = arrangement of toothed wheels, levers, etc., connecting an engine/pedals, etc., with wheels; **in g.** = with the gears connected. 2. *v.* **to g. sth to** = to fit/to match. **gear•box,** *n.* casing for gears in cars. **gear•shift,** *n.* handle by which the gears are changed in a car. **gear•wheel,** *n.* toothed wheel connecting with another wheel of different diameter to change the power ratio of the engine.

geck•o ['gekəʊ] *n.* (*pl.* **-os**) small tropical lizard.

gee [dʒiː] *inter. showing surprise.*

geese [giːs] *n. pl. see* **goose.**

gee•zer ['giːzə] *n. Sl.* (old) man.

Gei•ger count•er ['gaɪgəkaʊntə] *n.* device for detecting and recording radioactivity.

gei•sha ['geɪʃə] *n.* Japanese hostess and dancing girl.

gel [dʒel] *n.* substance like a jelly. **gel•a•tin(e)** ['dʒelətiːn] *n.* substance obtained after stewing skin, bones, etc., and used to make jellies. **ge•lat•i•nous** [dʒə'lætɪnəs] *adj.* like jelly.

geld [geld] *v.* to castrate. **geld•ing** ['geldɪŋ] *n.* castrated animal, esp. horse.

gel•ig•nite ['dʒelɪgnaɪt] *n.* nitroglycerine explosive.

gem [dʒem] *n.* precious stone. **gem•ol•o•gy** [dʒe'mɒlədʒɪ] *n.* the science of gems.

Gem•i•ni ['dʒemɪnaɪ] *n.* one of the signs of the zodiac, shaped like twins.

gen•der ['dʒendə] *n.* grammatical classification of objects roughly corresponding to the two sexes and absence of sex, masculine, feminine, and neuter.

gene [dʒiːn] *n.* part of a chromosome which carries characteristics transmitted by the parent; **g. bank** = gene library; **g. library** = collection of cloned genes representing the entire genetic material of an organism; **g. pool** = all the genes present in a population; **g. therapy** = modification/replacement of defective genes in order to prevent hereditary diseases.

ge•ne•a•log•i•cal [dʒiːnɪə'lɒdʒɪkl] *adj.* referring to genealogy. **ge•ne•al•o•gist** [dʒiːnɪ'ælədʒɪst] *n.* person who studies genealogy. **ge•ne•al•o•gy,** *n.* study of family descent through the generations.

gen•er•a ['dʒenərə] *n. see* **ge•nus.**

gen•er•al ['dʒenrəl] 1. *adj.* completely or approximately universal; including or affecting all or nearly all parts; **g. anesthetic** = anesthetic which makes the patient lose consciousness; **g. election** = local, state, or national election in which the whole country is involved; **in g.** = as a rule. 2. *n.* superior military officer. **gen•er•al•is•si•mo** [dʒenrə-'lɪsɪməʊ] *n.* commander-in-chief of the armed forces in some countries. **gen•er•al•i•ty** [dʒenə'rælɪtɪ] *n.* being general; **generalities** = general subjects (for a conversation). **gen•er•al•i•za•tion** [dʒenrəlaɪ'zeɪʃn] *n.* general statement. **gen•er•al•ize** ['dʒenrəlaɪz] *v.* to try to express sth as a general notion. **gen•er•al•ly** ['dʒenrəlɪ] *adv.* as a rule. **gen•er•al prac•ti•tion•er,** *n.* doctor who treats all illnesses/family doctor. **gen•er•al-pur•pose,** *adj.* serving many purposes.

gen•er•ate ['dʒenəreɪt] *v.* to bring into existence; to produce. **gen•er•a•tion** [dʒenə-'reɪʃn] *n.* (a) bringing into existence. (b) all people born about the same time; **g. gap** = age difference between one generation and another, often resulting in intolerance between them. (c) period of years separating parents and children. (d) members of a family born about the same time. **gen•er•a•tor** ['dʒenəreɪtə] *n.* apparatus for producing electricity by gas, etc.

ge•ner•ic [dʒə'nerɪk] *adj.* referring to a genus/group/type. **ge•ner•i•cal•ly,** *adv.* in a generic way.

gen•er•ous ['dʒenərəs] *adj.* (a) g. **with sth** = willing to give sth. (b) large; **a g. helping.** **gen•er•os•i•ty** [dʒenə'rɒsɪtɪ] *n.* willingness to give (money, etc.). **gen•er•ous•ly,** *adv.* in a generous way.

gen•e•sis ['dʒenəsɪs] *n.* origin/beginning.

ge•net•ics [dʒə'netɪks] *n.* study of heredity. **ge•net•ic,** *adj.* referring to genes/to genetics. **ge•net•i•cal•ly,** *adv.* in a genetic way. **ge•net•ic en•gi•neer•ing,** *n.* modification/replacement of genes in order to produce an organism with desired characteristics, e.g. pest-resistant plants. **ge•net•ic fin•ger•print•ing, genetic profiling,** *n.* analysis of DNA in a sample of body tissue in order to identify an individual, e.g. in forensic medicine.

ge•ni•al ['dʒiːnɪəl] *adj.* cheerful/kindly. **gen•ial•ly,** *adv.* cheerfully.

ge•nie ['dʒiːniː] *n.* in the Arabian Nights, a magic slave who appears from a bottle or lamp.

gen•i•tal ['dʒenɪtl] 1. *adj.* referring to the sex organs. 2. *n.pl.* **genitals** = external sex organs.

gen•i•tive ['dʒenɪtɪv] *adj. & n.* (*in grammar*) g. (**case**) = form of a word showing possession.

gen•ius ['dʒiːnɪəs] *n.* (*pl.* **-es**) (a) person with very great intelligence. (b) very great intelligence. (c) g. **for** = ability to do sth easily.

gen•o•cide ['dʒenəsaɪd] *n.* mass killing of a race.

gen•re ['ʒɑːnrə] *n.* particular type (of art, etc.).

gent [dʒent] *n. inf.* gentleman.

gen•teel [dʒen'tiːl] *adj.* refined, often excessively so. **gen•teel•ly,** *adv.* in a genteel way. **gen•til•i•ty** [dʒen'tɪlɪtɪ] *n.* refinement (of manners).

gen•tian ['dʒenʃn] *n.* small blue alpine flower.

gen•tile ['dʒentaɪl] *n.* person not of Jewish race.

gen•tle ['dʒentl] *adj.* (-er, -est) mild/tender/soft. **gent•le•folk,** *n. pl.* (*old*) people of good breeding. **gent•le•man** ['dʒentlmən]

n. (*pl.* **-men**) (a) man of good breeding and manners; **g.'s agreement** = agreement which is not written down. (b) (*polite way of referring to men*) **Well, gentlemen, shall we begin?** **gen•tle•man•ly,** *adj.* like a gentleman. **gen•tle•ness,** *n.* softness/carefulness. **gent•ly** ['dʒentlɪ] *adv.* softly/carefully.

gen•try ['dʒentrɪ] *n.* people of high class and breeding.

gen•u•flect ['dʒenjuflekt] *v.* to bend the knee, esp. in worship. **gen•u•flec•tion,** *n.* bending the knee.

gen•u•ine ['dʒenjuɪn] *adj.* authentic/true. **gen•u•ine•ly,** *adv.* truly. **gen•u•ine•ness,** *n.* being genuine.

ge•nus ['dʒiːnəs] *n.* (*pl.* **genera** ['dʒenərə]) group of animals/plants which have common characteristics, and are distinct from all other groups.

ge•o•cen•tric [dʒiːəʊ'sentrɪk] *adj.* (astronomy, etc.) using the earth as the starting point when measuring distances.

ge•od•e•sy [dʒɪ'ɒdɪsɪ] *n.* science of measurement of the earth. **ge•o•des•ic** [dʒɪəʊ'diːsɪk] *adj.* referring to geodesy; **g. dome** = dome made of set of polygons.

ge•og•ra•phy [dʒɪ'ɒgrəfɪ] *n.* science of the earth's surface/form/physical features/climate, etc. **ge•og•ra•pher** [dʒɪ'ɒgrəfə] *n.* person who studies geography. **ge•o•graph•ic(al)** [dʒɪə'græfɪk(l)] *adj.* referring to geography. **ge•o•graph•i•cal•ly,** *adv.* in a geographical way.

ge•ol•o•gy [dʒɪ'ɒlədʒɪ] *n.* science of the earth's crust, esp. rock formations. **ge•o•log•i•cal** [dʒɪə'lɒdʒɪkl] *adj.* referring to geology. **ge•o•log•i•cal•ly.** *adv.* in a geological way. **ge•ol•o•gist** [dʒɪ'ɒlədʒɪst] *n.* person who studies geology.

ge•om•e•try [dʒɪ'ɒmətrɪ] *n.* mathematical science of properties and relations of lines/surfaces/solids, etc., in space. **ge•o•met•ric(al)** [dʒɪə'metrɪk(l)] *adj.* referring to geometry; **a g. design** = design of lines/curves, etc. **ge•o•met•ri•cal•ly,** *adv.* in a geometrical way.

ge•o•phys•ics [dʒiːəʊ'fɪzɪks] *n.* study of the physical properties of the earth. **ge•o•phys•i•cist,** *n.* person who studies geophysics.

geor•gette [dʒɔː'dʒet] *n.* thin silk cloth.

Geor•gian ['dʒɔːdʒɪən] *adj.* referring to the

reigns of George I to IV of England (1714–1830).

ge•o•sta•tion•ar•y or•bit [dʒiːˈsteɪʃənrɪˈɔːbɪt] n. orbit of a satellite that remains over the same point on the earth's surface.

ge•o•ther•mal [dʒiːəʊˈθɜːməl] adj. (energy) derived from the earth's heat.

ge•ra•ni•um [dʒəˈreɪniəm] n. perennial plant with white, pink or red flowers.

ger•bil [ˈdʒɜːbl] n. small desert rat which jumps, kept as a pet.

ger•i•at•rics [dʒerɪˈætrɪks] n. branch of medical science dealing with old age and its diseases. **ger•i•at•ric**, adj. for old people. **ger•i•a•tri•cian** [dʒerɪəˈtrɪʃn] n. doctor specializing in geriatrics.

germ [dʒɜːm] n. (a) portion of organism capable of developing into a new one; **wheat g.** (b) micro-organism, often causing disease. **ger•mi•cid•al**, adj. which kills germs. **ger•mi•cide**, n. substance which kills germs. **germ war•fare**, n. war fought using germs as a weapon.

Ger•man [ˈdʒɜːmən] adj. referring to Germany; **G. measles** = mild disease which gives a red rash and which can affect the development of an unborn child if caught by a pregnant woman; **G. shepherd** = large dog often used as a guard dog. 2. n. (a) person from Germany. (b) language spoken in Germany, Austria and parts of Switzerland. **Ger•man•ic** [dʒɜːˈmænɪk] adj. referring to the Germans. **Ger•man•o**, prefix meaning between Germany and another country.

ger•mane [dʒɜːˈmeɪn] adj. relevant.

ger•mi•nate [ˈdʒɜːmɪneɪt] v. (of seeds) to begin to grow/to sprout. **ger•mi•na•tion** [dʒɜːmɪˈneɪʃn] n. beginning of plant growth from a seed.

ger•on•tol•o•gy [dʒerɒnˈtɒlədʒɪ] n. scientific study of old age and its problems, illnesses, etc.

ger•ry•man•der [ˈdʒerɪmændə] v. to alter the boundaries of voting districts in order to improve the chances of a political party in an election.

ger•und [ˈdʒerʌnd] n. noun formed from the -ing form of a verb.

ges•ta•tion [dʒeˈsteɪʃn] n. period between conception and birth.

ges•tic•u•late [dʒeˈstɪkjʊleɪt] v. to make expressive signs with the hands and arms. **ges•tic•u•la•tion** [dʒestɪkjuˈleɪʃn] n. sign with arms or hands.

ges•ture [ˈdʒestʃə] 1. n. (a) movement of limb or body, esp. hands, to give an expression of feeling. (b) action which expresses some positive feeling; **token g.** = small action which symbolizes feelings. 2. v. to make a movement to express a feeling.

get [get] v. (got; has got or has gotten) (a) to obtain. (b) to receive. (c) **to have/have got** = to possess. (d) go for and bring back. (e) inf. to understand; **you've got it!** = you've found the right answer/you understand correctly. (f) to cause to happen; to make (s.o.) do sth; **he got his shoes mended; she got the policeman to show her the way.** (g) **to have got to** = to be obliged to. (h) to arrive at; **to g. home early.** (i) inf. to start; **let's get going** = let's start now. (j) to catch (a disease). (k) to become; **he's getting too old for the job.** (l) to be doing sth; **she's getting dressed. get a•bout,** v. (a) to go from place to place. (b) to be rumored. **get a•cross,** v. (a) to cross (a road). (b) to make (sth) understood. **get a•long,** v. (a) to manage. (b) to be on friendly terms (with s.o.). **get at,** v. (a) to reach. (b) to suggest; **what are you getting at? get a•way,** v. to manage to go away; to escape; **he got away with it** = he wasn't found out. **get•a•way,** n. escape; **g. car** = car used to escape in. **get back,** v. (a) to return. (b) to recover (sth). **get by,** v. (a) to pass. (b) inf. to manage. **get down,** v. (a) to descend. (b) to bring down. (c) to depress; to make (s.o.) gloomy. (d) to make (sth) be written. (e) **to get down to some hard work** = to start to work hard. **get in,** v. (a) to go inside (a car, etc.). (b) to be elected. **get in•to,** v. (a) to go inside (a car, etc.). (b) **to g. i. trouble** = to be in a difficult situation. **get off,** v. (a) to come down from. (b) **he got off lightly** = he received a light punishment. **get on,** v. (a) to mount (a bicycle, etc.). (b) to age; **he is getting on** = he is past middle age. (c) **to g. o. with s.o.** = to be friendly with s.o.; **get out,** v. (a) to bring out/to go out; **get out!** = leave the room. (b) **I've gotten out of the habit of eating chocolates** = I don't eat chocolates any more. (c) **to get out of (doing) sth** = to avoid doing sth. **get o•ver,** v. (a) to overcome (a difficulty). (b) to recover from (an illness). (c) to climb over. **get a•round/round,** v. (a) to go around (a corner). (b) to flatter (s.o.). (c) **to g. a. to (doing) sth** = to find time to do (sth). **get through,** v. (a) to pass (a test). (b) **to g. t. to s.o.** = to manage to get in contact with s.o. (by telephone). **get-to•geth•er,** n. inf. meeting. **get up,** v. to rise (from sitting or lying position); to get out of bed. **get-up,** n. odd clothes.

gey•ser [ˈgiːzə] n. hot spring of water.

ghast•ly [ˈgɑːstlɪ] adj. (-ier, -iest) horrible/frightful. **ghast•li•ness,** n. being ghastly.

gher•kin [ˈgɜːkɪn] n. small vegetable of the cucumber family, used for pickling.

ghet•to ['getəu] *n.* (*pl.* **-os**) area in a city where deprived people live.

ghost [gəust] 1. *n.* (a) spirit of a dead person; **g. story** = story about ghosts which aims at frightening the reader. (b) **the Holy G.** = third person of the Christian Trinity. (c) ghost writer. (d) **a g. of a smile** = very slight smile. 2. *v.* to write (book/article/speech, etc.) for s.o. else who then takes the credit. **ghost•ly,** *adj.* like a ghost. **ghost writ•er,** *n.* person who writes a book for s.o. else who then takes the credit.

ghoul [gu:l] *n.* evil ghost which haunts graves. **ghoul•ish** ['gu:lɪʃ] *adj.* weird/bloodthirsty.

gi•ant ['dʒaɪənt] 1. *n.* (a) (*in fairy tales and myths*) huge human being. (b) abnormally tall person, animal or plant. (c) very powerful industrial organization. (d) extremely able or important person. 2. *adj.* very large. **gi•ant•ess** ['dʒaɪən'tes] *n.* (*pl.* **-es**) female giant.

gib•ber ['dʒɪbə] *v.* to speak very fast, without any meaning. **gib•ber•ish** ['dʒɪbrɪʃ] *n.* (*no pl.*) fast unintelligible speech.

gib•bet ['dʒɪbɪt] *n.* gallows/structure on which criminals were hanged.

gib•bon ['gɪbən] *n.* long-armed ape.

gibe [dʒaɪb] 1. *n.* sarcastic remark. 2. *v.* to jeer/to mock.

gib•lets ['dʒɪbləts] *n. pl.* liver/heart, etc., of poultry, removed before the bird is cooked.

gid•dy ['gɪdɪ] *adj.* (**-ier, -iest**) dizzy; feeling as if everything is spinning round. **gid•di•ly,** *adv.* in a giddy way. **gid•di•ness,** *n.* dizzy feeling.

gift [gɪft] *n.* (a) present/thing given; **g. certificate** = certificate given as a present, which allows the person who receives it to buy sth at a store. (b) talent; **she has a g. for music. gift•ed,** *adj.* talented. **gift-wrap,** *v.* (**gift-wrapped**) to wrap (sth) in colored paper to give as a present.

gig [gɪg] *n.* (a) light carriage on two wheels. (b) *inf.* performance by popular musicians.

giga- ['gɪgə] *prefix* one thousand million.

gi•gan•tic [dʒaɪ'gæntɪk] *adj.* huge/colossal.

gig•gle ['gɪgl] 1. *n.* little nervous laugh; **to have a fit of the giggles** = to be unable to stop giggling. 2. *v.* to laugh little nervous laughs.

gig•o•lo ['dʒɪgələu] *n.* (*pl.* **-os**) man who is paid by a woman to be her lover.

gild [gɪld] *v.* to cover with a thin layer of gold.

gill [dʒɪl] *n.* liquid measure equal to a quarter of a pint (140 ml).

gills [gɪlz] *n. pl.* (a) breathing organs in fish and other aquatic creatures. (b) thin vertical folds on the underside of mushrooms.

gilt [gɪlt] 1. *adj.* covered with a thin layer of gold. 2. *n.* (a) young female pig. (b) gilt-edged security. **gilt-edged,** *adj.* (investment) which will not lose its value.

gim•bals ['gɪmbəlz] *n. pl.* device (of several rings balanced inside each other) to keep a compass level at sea.

gim•crack ['dʒɪmkræk] *adj.* cheap and badly made.

gim•let ['gɪmlət] *n.* small tool used for boring holes.

gim•mick ['gɪmɪk] *n.* device adopted for the purpose of attracting attention or publicity.

gin [dʒɪn] *n.* (a) colorless alcoholic drink flavored with juniper; glass of this drink. (b) trap for catching wild animals and game. (c) machine for cleaning raw cotton.

gin•ger ['dʒɪndʒə] 1. *n.* plant with a hot-tasting root used in cooking and medicine. 2. *adj.* (hair) of reddish color. **gin•ger•bread,** *n.* cake made with molasses and flavored with ginger. **gin•ger ale, ginger beer,** *n.* fizzy ginger-flavored drink. **gin•ger•ly,** 1. *adj.* cautious. 2. *adv.* delicately/with caution. **ginger up,** *v.* to stimulate/to enliven.

ging•ham ['gɪŋəm] *n.* checked cotton cloth.

gin•gi•vi•tis [dʒɪndʒɪ'vaɪtɪs] *n.* swelling and bleeding of the gums.

gink•go ['gɪŋgəu] *n.* Chinese tree, which is similar to trees which flourished millions of years ago.

gip•sy ['dʒɪpsɪ] *n. see* **gyp•sy.**

gi•raffe [dʒɪ'rɑ:f] *n.* African animal with a very long neck and spotted skin.

gird [gɜ:d] *v.* (*formal*) (**girded/girt**) to tie a belt round (sth).

gird•er ['gɜ:də] *n.* iron/steel beam used as a support.

gir•dle ['gɜ:dl] *n.* (a) belt/sash. (b) corset. (c) **pelvic g.** = bones around the hips supporting the lower limbs.

girl [gɜ:l] *n.* female child; young woman. **girl•friend,** *n.* female companion (esp. of a man). **girl•hood,** *n.* period when you are a girl (before becoming a woman). **girl•ie,** *adj. inf.* **g. magazine** = one with photographs of naked young women. **girl•ish,** *adj.* like a young girl.

girt [gɜ:t] *v. see* **gird.**

æ **back,** ɑ: **farm,** ɒ **top,** aɪ **pipe,** aʊ **how,** aɪə **fire,** aʊə **flower,** ɔ: **bought,** ɔɪ **toy,** e **fed,** eəhair, eɪ **take,** ə **afraid,** əʊ **boat,** əʊə **lower,** v: **word,** i: **heap,** ɪ **hit,** ɪə **hear,** u: **school,** ʊ **book,** ʌ **but,** b **back,** d **dog,** ð **then,** dʒ **just,** f **fog,** g **go,** h **hand,** j **yes,** k **catch,** l **last,** m **mix,** n **nut,** ŋ **sing,** p **penny,** r **round,** s **some,** ʃ **short,** t **too,** tʃ **chop,** θ **thing,** v **voice,** w **was,** z **zoo,** ʒ **treasure**

girth [gɜ:θ] n. (a) circumference/distance round sth. (b) band of leather or cloth tied round the body of a horse to secure the saddle.

gist [dʒɪst] n. real point of a matter; basic essentials.

give [gɪv] 1. v. (gave; has given) (a) to hand (sth) **to** s.o.; to transfer (sth) **to** s.o. (b) to utter (a cry). (c) to collapse; to bend. 2. n. (a) suppleness; **the plank hasn't enough g.** (b) **g. and take** = agreement between two people/parties to make concessions. **give away,** v. (a) to hand over (sth) without asking for anything in return. (b) to betray/to tell (a secret). (c) to give (a bride) to the bridegroom. **give back,** v. to return. **give in,** v. to surrender/to yield. **giv•en,** adj. (a) **she is g. to crying** = she cries frequently. (b) particular/which has been identified. (c) **g. name** = first name/Christian name. **give off,** v. to let out gas. **give out,** v. (a) to distribute. (b) inf. to fail. (c) to make known. **give o•ver,** v. inf. to stop. **giv•er,** n. person who gives. **give up,** v. to stop (doing sth); **I give up!** = I cannot think of the answer; **the murderer gave himself up** = surrendered to the police. **give way,** v. (a) to allow s.o. to go first. (b) to yield; to bend; to collapse.

giz•zard [ˈgɪzəd] n. second stomach of a bird, where its food is ground up into tiny pieces.

gla•brous [ˈglæbrəs] adj. smooth, with no hair.

gla•cé [ˈglæseɪ] adj. (cherries) preserved in sugar.

gla•cier [ˈglæsɪə] n. mass of ice which moves slowly down from a mountain. **gla•cial** [ˈgleɪʃl] adj. (a) referring to ice. (b) very cold; without emotion. **gla•ci•a•tion** [gleɪsɪˈeɪʃn] n. effect of ice on rocks.

glad [glæd] adj. pleased/happy. **glad•den,** v. to make glad. **glad•ly,** adv. happily. **glad•ness,** n. happiness.

glade [gleɪd] n. (formal) clear open space in the midst of trees.

glad•i•a•tor [ˈglædɪeɪtə] n. man who fought in an arena (in ancient Rome). **glad•i•a•to•ri•al** [glædɪəˈtɔːrɪəl] adj. referring to gladiators.

glad•i•o•lus [glædɪˈəʊləs] n. (pl. gladioli [glædɪˈəʊlaɪ]) tall garden plant with sword-shaped leaves and bright flower spikes.

glair [gleːə] n. white of egg, used as a glaze.

glam•or, Brit. **glam•our** [ˈglæmə] n. (a) magic/enchantment. (b) outward charm/attractiveness (of a woman). **glam•or•ize,** v. to make (sth) appear more appealing than it really is. **glam•or•ous,** adj. attractive/enchanting.

glance [glɑːns] 1. n. quick look. 2. v. (a) to look briefly. (b) to slide off an object instead of striking it fully. **glan•cing,** adj. sliding off to the side; not straight.

gland [glænd] n. organ of the body which produces a liquid which controls bodily changes, such as growth. **glan•du•lar** [ˈglændjʊlə] adj. referring to glands; **g. fever** = severe illness which affects the glands.

glare [ˈgleə] 1. n. (a) strong/fierce light. (b) fierce/fixed look. 2. v. (a) to shine too brightly. (b) to look angrily at s.o. **glar•ing,** adj. **g. mistake** = very obvious mistake.

glas•nost [ˈglæznɒst] n. openness, freedom of information.

glass [glɑːs] n. (a) substance made from sand and soda or potash, usu. transparent, used for making windows, etc. (b) open container made of glass used esp. for drinking; contents of such a glass. (c) mirror; **looking g.; stained g.** = colored glass used frequently in the windows of a church. **glass blow•er,** n. person who blows and shapes molten glass into bottles, etc. **glas•ses,** n. pl. eyeglasses. **glass•ware,** n. (no pl.) articles made of glass. **glass wool,** n. soft substance, made from glass fiber, used as an insulating material in buildings. **glass•y,** adj. (a) resembling glass. (b) dull/unseeing; **a g. stare.**

glau•co•ma [glɔːˈkəʊmə] n. disease of the eyes which can cause blindness.

glaze [gleɪz] 1. n. shiny surface (on pottery). 2. v. (a) to fit with glass; to put glass in (a window). (b) to cover with a shiny coating. **gla•zier** [ˈgleɪzɪə] n. person whose trade is to fit glass in windows. **glaz•ing,** n. fitting with windows; **double g.** = windows with two sheets of glass a small distance apart, which help insulation.

gleam [gliːm] 1. n. (a) short-lived weak light. (b) faint/temporary show of some quality. 2. v. to shine.

glean [gliːn] v. to collect (grain) left after the harvest; to gather or discover (news/information, etc.). **glean•er,** n. person who gleans. **glean•ings,** n. pl. things obtained by gleaning.

glee [gliː] n. (a) short song sung by several singers. (b) joy/gaiety. **glee•ful,** adj. joyful. **glee•ful•ly,** adv. happily.

glen [glen] n. narrow valley.

glib [glɪb] adj. fluent but insincere way of speaking. **glib•ly,** adv. smoothly and insincerely.

glide [glaɪd] 1. n. smooth movement. 2. v. to move smoothly. **glid•er,** n. small aircraft without an engine that relies on wind currents for propulsion. **glid•ing,** n. sport of flying gliders.

glim•mer [ˈglɪmə] 1. n. (a) feeble light. (b) tiny

quantity; faint/temporary show of (interest, etc.). 2. *v.* to shine feebly/intermittently.

glimpse [glɪmps] 1. *n.* quick/passing sight. 2. *v.* to catch sight of (sth).

glint [glɪnt] 1. *n.* flash/glitter/sparkle. 2. *v.* to flash/to glitter (like metal).

glis•ten ['glɪsn] *v.* (*of something wet*) to shine/to sparkle.

glit•ter ['glɪtə] 1. *n.* bright light/sparkle. 2. *v.* to shine brightly/to sparkle.

gloam•ing ['gləumɪŋ] *n.* twilight.

gloat [gləut] *v.* **to g. over** = to take pleasure in (s.o.'s misfortune); to look at (sth) greedily.

globe [gləub] *n.* (a) **the g.** = the earth. (b) ball with a map of the world on it. (c) round object; glass shade which covers an electric light bulb; **g. artichoke** = tall green thistlelike plant of which you eat parts of the flower head. **glob•al**, *adj.* world-wide. **glob•al•ly**, *adv.* all over the world. **glob•al po•si•tion•ing sys•tem**, *n.* navigation system that can give the location on the earth of a device when it transmits and receives signals from satellites. **glob•al warm•ing**, *n.* increase in the temperature of the earth's atmosphere, thought to be caused by the greenhouse effect. **globe•trot•ter**, *n.* tourist who travels all over the world.

glob•ule ['glɒbjuːl] *n.* small round object (such as a drop of water). **glob•u•lar**, *adj.* shaped like a globe. **glob•u•lin**, *n.* protein found in blood, which contains antibodies.

glock•en•spiel ['glɒknspiːl] *n.* musical instrument like a xylophone with metal bars.

gloom [gluːm] *n.* (a) darkness. (b) despair/melancholy. **gloom•i•ly**, *adv.* in a gloomy way. **gloom•y**, *adj.* (**-ier, -iest**) melancholy; pessimistic.

glo•ry ['glɔːrɪ] 1. *n.* (a) fame/renown. (b) magnificent sight. 2. *v.* **to g. in** = to get great pleasure from/to pride oneself on. **glo•ri•fi•ca•tion** [glɔːrɪfɪ'keɪʃn] *n.* transforming into sth more splendid. **glo•ri•fy**, *v.* to make glorious/to transform into sth more splendid. **glo•ri•ous** ['glɔːrɪəs] *adj.* splendid. **glo•ri•ous•ly**, *adv.* in a glorious way. **glo•ry•hole**, *n.* cupboard/room where you can keep junk.

gloss [glɒs] 1. *n.* (a) shine on a surface; showy appearance; **g. paint** = paint which is shiny when dry. (b) comment about a text. 2. *v.* **to g. over** = to try to hide (a mistake, etc.). **gloss•i•ness**, *n.* being glossy. **gloss•y**, *adj.*

& *n.* (**-ier, -iest**) **g. magazines/glossies** = colorful, expensive magazines printed on shiny paper.

glos•sa•ry ['glɒsərɪ] *n.* short explanation of meanings of words, usu. found at the end of a book.

glot•tis ['glɒtɪs] *n.* space in the vocal cords, which makes sound when opened or closed. **glot•tal**, *adj.* referring to the glottis; **g. stop** = type of clicking sound made by closing the glottis.

glove [glʌv] *n.* article of clothing worn on the hand; **to handle s.o. with kid gloves** = to deal gently with s.o.; **hand in g. with s.o.** = closely associated with s.o.; **g. compartment** = small cupboard on the dashboard of a car, in which you can put small items. **gloved**, *adj.* wearing gloves.

glow [gləu] 1. *n.* (a) brightness/warmth. (b) blush/bloom. 2. *v.* to shine; to show warm color. **glow•ing**, *adj.* shining/warm. **glow-worm**, *n.* female beetle which gives off a green light in the dark.

glow•er ['glauə] *v.* to frown.

glox•in•i•a [glɒk'sɪnɪə] *n.* type of pot plant with large trumpet-shaped flowers.

glu•cose ['gluːkəuz] *n.* natural sugar found in fruit.

glue [gluː] 1. *n.* substance which will stick things together. 2. *v.* to stick together. **glue•y**, *adj.* sticky.

glum [glʌm] *adj.* (**glummer, glummest**) sullen; looking dejected/miserable.

glut [glʌt] 1. *n.* too much of (sth); supply exceeding demand. 2. *v.* **to be glutted (with)** = to have too much.

glu•ten ['gluːtən] *n.* protein left when starch is removed from flour. **glu•ti•nous** ['gluːtɪnəs] *adj.* sticky.

glut•ton ['glʌtn] *n.* (a) person who eats too much. (b) person with great enthusiasm **for** sth. **glut•ton•ous**, *adj.* referring to overeating. **glut•ton•y**, *n.* eating too much.

glyc•er•in, glycerine ['glɪsərɪn] *n.* colorless, sweet liquid (used in medicines/in explosives, etc.).

gm *abbrev. for* gram.

GMT [dʒiːem'tiː] *abbreviation for* Greenwich Mean Time.

gnarled [nɑːld] *adj.* twisted/rugged; covered with hard lumps.

gnash [næʃ] *v.* to grind (the teeth).

æ back, aː farm, ɒ: top, aɪ pipe, au how, aiə fire, auə flower, ɔ: bought, ɔɪ toy, e fed, eəhair, eɪ take, ə afraid, əu boat, əuə lower, ɜː word, iː heap, ɪ hit, ɪə hear, uː school, u book, ʌ but, b back, d dog, ð then, dʒ just, f fog, g go, h hand, j yes, k catch, l last, m mix, n nut, ŋ sing, p penny, r round, s some, ʃ short, t too, tʃ chop, θ thing, v voice, w was, z zoo, ʒ treasure

gnat [næt] *n.* small, two-winged fly which stings.

gnaw [nɔ:] *v.* to chew.

gneiss [naɪs] *n.* type of hard rock.

gnome [nəʊm] *n.* dwarf/mischievous ugly little man (in fairy stories). **gno•mic,** *adj.* concise and clever (saying).

GNP [dʒi:en'pi:] *n.* gross national product.

gnu [nu:] *n.* large South African antelope.

go [gəʊ] 1. *n.* (a) act of moving; *inf.* **he's always on the g.** = always moving about. (b) *inf.* energy; **she's full of g.** (c) attempt/try. (d) **to try and make a g. of it** = to try to make the business successful. 2. *v.* (**went; has gone**) (a) to move from one place to another; to travel. (b) to work; **my car won't g.** (c) to leave; **from the word g.** = from the start. (d) **to be going to do sth** = to intend to do sth; to be about to do sth. (e) to fit; **it's too big to g. into the box.** (f) to become; **she went pale.** (g) to make a noise; **the guns went bang.** (h) to have a certain tune/certain words; **how does the song g.?** (i) to fail; **the brakes went. go a•bout,** *v.* (a) to try to do sth/to plan how to do sth. (b) *(of sailing boat)* to turn to sail in another direction. (c) to move around. **go a•head,** *v.* to start to do sth. **go-a•head.** 1. *n.* permission to start. 2. *adj.* enterprising; active. **go a•long with,** *v.* to agree with (s.o./sth). **go back,** *v.* to return. **go back on,** *v.* not to keep (a promise). **go-be•tween,** *n.* person who carries messages from one person to another. **go-cart,** *n.* flat wooden frame with four wheels for children to play with. **go down,** *v.* (a) to descend. (b) **to go down well** = to be accepted. **go for,** *v.* (a) to apply for. (b) to like. (c) to be sold. (d) to attack. **go-get•ter,** *n. inf.* energetic, ambitious person. **go-go danc•er,** *n. inf.* person who performs an energetic (and usu. erotic) dance in a nightclub. **go in,** *v.* to enter; **the sun's gone in** = is hidden by clouds. **go in for,** *v.* (a) to approve of. (b) to do or like to do (sth); **to g. i. f. fishing. go•ing.** 1. *adj.* (a) working. (b) **g. rate** = usual rate/current rate. 2. *v.* **do it while the g. is good** = while you have the chance. (b) **goings-on** = unusual things which are happening. **go in•to,** *v.* (a) to enter. (b) *(in math)* to divide. (c) to examine. **go-kart,** *n.* flat frame with four wheels and an engine, used as a small racing car. **go-kart•ing,** *n.* racing in go-karts. **go off,** *v.* (a) to explode. (b) to turn out; happen. **go on,** *v.* (a) to continue. (b) *(showing disbelief)* *inf.* **go on!** = I don't believe you! (c) to happen; **what's going on here?** (d) **to go on about sth** = to talk all the time; to nag. **go out,** *v.* (a) to leave. (b) to stop operating; **the electricity went off. go out with,** *v.* to go to parties/the theater, etc. with (s.o. of the opposite sex). **go a•round,** *v.* (a) to be enough for all. (b) to visit. **go un•der,** *v.* (a) to drown. (b) to be ruined. **go up,** *v.* to rise; **to g. u. in flames** = to burn. **go with,** *v.* to match/to fit with. **go with•out,** *v.* not to have.

goad [gəʊd] 1. *n.* long stick for driving cattle. 2. *v.* **to g. s.o. into doing sth** = to urge/to drive s.o. on by annoying him/her.

goal [gəʊl] *n.* (a) object of effort/ambition; aim. (b) two posts between which a ball has to be driven to score a point in a game. (c) points won (in football/hockey, etc.). **goal•keep•er,** *inf.* **goal•ie,** *n.* player who defends the goal. **goal•mouth,** *n.* area just in front of the goal. **goal•post,** *n.* one of the two posts between which a ball is driven to score a goal.

goat [gəʊt] *n.* domestic animal with horns and a beard; **to separate the sheep from the goats** = to divide the good from the bad; *inf.* **to get s.o.'s g.** = to annoy s.o. **goat•ee** [gəʊ'ti:] *n.* small beard, like that of a goat.

gob [gɒb] *n. Sl.* 1. mouth; **shut your g.!** = stop talking! 2. *v. Sl.* to spit.

gob•bet ['gɒbɪt] *n.* large lump (of fat).

gob•ble ['gɒbl] *v.* (a) to eat quickly and greedily. (b) to make a noise like a turkey. **gob•ble•de•gook** ['gɒbldɪgu:k] *n. inf.* meaningless official/technical language.

gob•let ['gɒblət] *n.* metal or glass drinking cup without handles.

gob•lin ['gɒblɪn] *n.* *(in fairy stories)* mischievous ugly little man.

god [gɒd] *n.* (a) deity; superhuman power. (b) **God** = creator and ruler of the Universe, according to Christian/Jewish/Muslim, etc., belief. (c) thing which is worshipped. **god•child,** *n.* (*pl.* **-children**) child who was sponsored at baptism. **god-daugh•ter,** *n.* girl who was sponsored at baptism. **god•dess,** *n.* female god. **god•fa•ther,** *n.* man who sponsors a child at baptism; *inf.* head of a mafia group. **god-fear•ing,** *adj.* sincerely religious. **god•for•sak•en,** *adj.* bad/awful. **god•like,** *adj.* like a god. **god•li•ness,** *n.* being godly. **god•ly,** *adj.* holy. **god•moth•er,** *n.* woman who sponsors a child at baptism. **god•par•ents,** *n. pl.* people who sponsor a child at baptism. **god•send,** *n.* blessing. **god•son,** *n.* boy who was sponsored at baptism.

go•down ['gəʊdaʊn] *n.* warehouse (in the Far East).

gog•gle ['gɒgl] *v.* to stare (at). **gog•gles,** *n. pl.* protective glasses against dust and glare.

goi•ter, *Brit.* **goi•tre** ['gɔɪtə] *n.* disease in which the thyroid gland in the neck swells up.

gold [gəʊld] 1. *n.* (a) (*element:* Au) precious yellow metal. (b) medal made of gold (won in a sports competition). 2. *adj.* made of gold; **g. leaf** = thin covering of gold; **g. plate** = dishes made of gold. **gold•crest**, *n.* very small bird, with an orange crest on its head. **gold-dig•ger**, *n.* (a) person who digs for gold. (b) *inf.* woman who marries a man for his money. **gold•en**, *adj.* made of gold; gold-colored; **g. opportunity** = wonderful chance; **g. rule** = very important rule; **g. wedding** = fiftieth anniversary of marriage; **g. handshake** = sum of money or other benefit given to an employee, usu. older, as an incentive to retire earlier than planned. **gold•field**, *n.* land where gold is mined. **gold•finch**, *n.* brightly colored song bird. **gold•fish**, *n.* (*pl.* goldfish) small orange fish kept in ponds/bowls. **gold•mine**, *n.* mine which produces gold; very profitable business. **gold rec•ord**, *n.* award given to a singer whose record has sold one million copies. **gold•smith**, *n.* person who works in gold.

golf [gɒlf] *n.* game for two people, or two couples, where a small hard ball is struck with long-handled clubs into a series of holes, the object being to use as few strokes as possible. **golf club**, *n.* (a) wooden- or metal-headed stick for striking the golf ball. (b) group of people who play golf, and allow others to join them on payment of a fee; clubhouse where golfers meet. **golf course**, *n.* ground on which golf is played. **golf•er**, *n.* person who plays golf.

go•nad ['gəʊnæd] *n.* gland which produces gametes.

gon•do•la ['gɒndələ] *n.* (a) boat used on the canals in Venice. (b) basket/passenger compartment hanging underneath a balloon. **gon•do•lier** [gɒndə'lɪə] *n.* man who pushes a gondola, using a pole.

gone [gɒn] *v. see* **go. gon•er** ['gɒnə] *n. inf.* dying person; dead person.

gong [gɒŋ] *n.* metal disk with a turned rim which gives a resonant sound when struck, used esp. to call people to meals.

gon•na ['gɒnə] *v. Sl.* = going to.

gon•or•rhe•a, *Brit.* **gon•or•rhoe•a** [gɒnə'riːə] *n.* type of venereal disease.

goo [guː] *n. inf.* (*no pl.*) sticky stuff. **goo•ey**, *adj. inf.* sticky.

good [gʊd] 1. *adj.* (**better, best**) (a) having the right qualities/satisfactory; **did you have a g. time?** = did you enjoy yourself? (b) able; **he is g. at French.** (c) right/proper; **it is a g. idea.** (d) morally excellent/virtuous; **he is a g. man.** (e) well behaved/not troublesome. (f) efficient/suitable/competent; **he was as g. as his word** = he did what he said he would do. (g) **g. morning! g. afternoon! g. evening!** *interjections used when meeting or leaving someone in the morning, afternoon or evening.* (h) valid/sound/thorough. (i) not less than; **she waited a g. half-hour.** (j) a lot of; **a g. many people; a g. deal of money.** (k) **as g. as** = practically/almost. 2. *n.* (a) **the g.** = virtuous people. (b) profit/advantage; **what g. will it do him? to do g.** = to act kindly; **for g.** = permanently/forever; **he is up to no g.** = he is acting in a suspicious manner. (c) **goods** = movable property. **good•bye** [gʊd'baɪ] *n. & inter. used when leaving someone.* **good-for-noth•ing**, *n.* useless, lazy person. **Good Fri•day**, *n.* Friday before Easter Day. **good-hu•mored**, *adj.* pleasant; in a happy mood. **good•ies**, *n. pl.* good things/money/treasure. **good•ish**, *adj.* quite good. **good-look•ing**, *adj.* handsome/pretty. **good-na•tured**, *adj.* kindly/pleasant. **good•ness**, *n.* virtue/kindness/generosity. **good•night**, *n. & inter. used when leaving someone late at night.* **good•will**, *n.* (a) kindly feeling toward a person. (b) good reputation of a business. **good•y-good•y**, *adj. inf.* (person) who is too good.

goof [guːf] 1. *n. Sl.* stupid person. 2. *v.* to make a stupid mistake. **goof•y**, *adj. inf.* stupid.

goon [guːn] *n.* silly fool.

goos•an•der [guː'sændə] *n.* type of wild duck.

goose [guːs] *n.* (*pl.* geese) (a) web-footed water bird, larger than a duck. (b) *inf.* silly person. **goose•ber•ry** ['guːzbrɪ] *n.* small edible green fruit; bush which bears this fruit. **goose•flesh**, *n.*, **goose-pim•ples**, *n.pl.* mass of small bumps on the skin caused by fear/by cold, etc. **goose-step.** 1. *n.* way of marching without bending the knees. 2. *v.* (**goosestepped**) to march without bending the knees.

go•pher ['gəʊfə] *n.* North American rodent which lives in burrows.

gore [gɔː] 1. *n.* (a) (*formal*) blood which has thickened after coming from a wound. (b) section of a skirt, shaped like a triangle. 2. *v.* to pierce with a horn. **gored**, *adj.* (skirt) with a gore.

æ back, ɑː farm, ɒ top, aɪ pipe, aʊ how, aɪə fire, aʊə flower, ɔː bought, ɔɪ toy, e fed, eəhair, eɪ take, ə afraid, əʊ boat, əʊə lower, vː word, iː heap, ɪ hit, ɪə hear, uː school, ʊ book, ʌ but, b back, d dog, ð then, dʒ just, f fog, g go, h hand, j yes, k catch, l last, m mix, n nut, ŋ sing, p penny, r round, s some, ʃ short, t too, tʃ chop, θ thing, v voice, w was, z zoo, ʒ treasure

gorge [gɔːdʒ] 1. *n.* narrow opening between hills. 2. *v.* to eat greedily; **he gorged himself on chocolates.**

gor•geous ['gɔːdʒəs] *adj.* magnificent/splendid; richly colored. **gor•geous•ly,** *adv.* splendidly.

gor•gon ['gɔːgən] *n.* mean, ugly woman.

go•ril•la [gə'rɪlə] *n.* large, powerful African ape.

gor•mand•ize ['gɔːməndaɪz] *v.* to eat far too much.

gorse [gɔːs] *n.* prickly yellow-flowered shrub.

gor•y ['gɔːrɪ] *adj.* (**-ier, -iest**) covered in blood.

gosh [gɒʃ] *inter. showing* surprise.

gos•hawk ['gɒshɔːk] *n.* type of trained hawk.

gos•ling ['gɒzlɪŋ] *n.* baby goose.

gos•pel ['gɒspl] *n.* record of Christ's life in the books of the four evangelists; **it's the g. truth** = it's absolutely true.

gos•sa•mer ['gɒsəmə] *n.* (a) very fine cobweb. (b) very fine material.

gos•sip ['gɒsɪp] 1. *n.* (a) idle talk, esp. about other people; **g. column** = section in a paper which gives news about the private lives of famous people. (b) person who spreads rumors. 2. *v.* to talk idly; to spread rumors. **gos•sip•y,** *adj.* full of gossip.

got [gɒt] *v.* (a) *see* **get.** (b) **to have g. to do sth** = to be obliged/to have to do sth.

goth•ic ['gɒθɪk] *adj.* style of architecture with pointed arches used in Western Europe in 12th–16th centuries.

got•ta ['gɒtə] *v. Sl.* = (have) got to.

got•ten ['gɒtn] *v. see* **get.**

gouache [gu'ɑːʃ] *n.* kind of thick watercolor paint.

gouge [gaʊdʒ] 1. *n.* kind of chisel used in carpentry. 2. *v.* to scoop out.

gou•lash ['guːlæʃ] *n.* Hungarian stew flavored with paprika.

gourd ['gʊəd] *n.* dried fruit of a climbing plant, used as a bowl.

gour•mand ['gʊəmənd] *n.* person who eats too much.

gour•met ['gʊəmeɪ] *n.* connoisseur of food and wine.

gout [gaʊt] *n.* painful inflammation of the joints, esp. the big toe. **gout•y,** *adj.* afflicted with gout.

gov•ern ['gʌvən] 1. *v.* (a) to rule with authority. (b) to influence/to determine. **gov•ern•ance,** *n.* (*formal*) way of governing. **gov•ern•ess,** *n.* female teacher, usu. in a private household. **gov•ern•ment** ['gʌvənmənt] *n.* group of people ruling a country. **gov•ern•men•tal** [gʌvən'mentl] *adj.* referring to a government. **gov•er•nor,**

n. head of a state government in the United States.

gown [gaʊn] *n.* (a) (*formal*) dress. (b) long official robe (worn by a judge/person with a degree, etc.). (c) **dressing-g.** = long coat worn over night clothes.

G.P. ['dʒiː'piː] *abbreviation for* general practitioner; family doctor.

G.P.O. [dʒiː.piː'əʊ] *abbreviation for* General Post Office.

GPS [dʒiː.piː'es] *abbrev. for* global positioning system.

grab [græb] 1. *n.* sudden seizing with the hands; **to make a g. for** = to try to seize. 2. *v.* (**grabbed**) to seize.

grace [greɪs] 1. *n.* (a) pleasing quality/attractiveness; **with good g.** = with a show of willingness. (b) short prayer of thanksgiving before or after a meal. (c) act of mercy; pardon from all sin. (d) favor shown by granting a delay; **ten days' g.** 2. *v.* to honor. **grace•ful,** *adj.* moving with ease. **grace•ful•ly,** *adv.* moving easily. **grace•ful•ness,** *n.* ease of movement. **grace•less,** *adj.* with no grace. **grace note,** *n.* note in music which need not be played, but which adds to the attraction of the piece. **gra•cious** ['greɪʃəs] *adj.* kind/agreeable; elegant (way of living); **good g.!** = how surprising! **gra•cious•ly,** *adv.* kindly. **gra•cious•ness,** *n.* being gracious.

grade [greɪd] 1. *n.* (a) degree/level/rank; **to make the g.** = to succeed. (b) mark in an exam. (c) class (in school). 2. *v.* to arrange in grades/to sort out. **gra•da•tion** [grə'deɪʃn] *n.* series of steps, passing from one level to another. **grade cross•ing,** *n.* place where a railroad track crosses a road, etc. at the same level.

gra•di•ent ['greɪdɪənt] *n.* amount of slope in a road, railroad, etc.

grad•u•al ['grædjuəl] *adj.* slow/progressive. **grad•u•al•ly,** *adv.* little by little.

grad•u•ate 1. *n.* ['grædjuət] person who has obtained a degree; **g. of Yale University.** 2. *v.* ['grædjueɪt] (a) to obtain a degree (**from** a university). (b) to arrange in gradations. (c) to mark in a scale; **graduated measuring glass** = one with quantities marked on it. **grad•u•a•tion** [grædju'eɪʃn] *n.* (a) obtaining a degree. (b) act of marking a scale.

graf•fi•ti [grə'fiːtɪ] *n. pl.* unofficial drawings or writing on walls.

graft [grɑːft] 1. *n.* (a) shoot of a plant inserted into another plant from which it receives sap and of which it becomes part. (b) (*in surgery*) piece of transplanted living tissue. (c) *Sl.* bribery; bribe. 2. *v.* to insert (part of a plant) into another plant so that it can grow; to attach (skin, etc.) to other parts of the body.

Grail [greɪl] *n*. **the Holy G.** = precious object (the cup used at the Last Supper) which was sought by medieval knights.

grain [greɪn] *n*. (a) seed of cereal. (b) small particle of sand/gold, etc. (c) texture of particles (in stone); lines of fibers in wood/material; **it goes against the g.** = it goes against natural instincts. (d) measurement of weight. **grain•y**, *adj.* (wood) with a strongly marked grain.

gram [græm] *n*. measurement of weight, one thousandth part of a kilogram.

gram•mar ['græmə] *n.* (a) art and science of a language; rules of the forms of words and their relationship in a language. (b) book which explains/teaches the rules of a language. **gram•mar•i•an** [grə'mɛərɪən] *n.* specialist in the study of grammar. **gram•mar school**, *n.* elementary school. **gram•mat•i•cal** [grə'mætɪkl] *adj.* conforming to the rules of grammar. **gram•mat•i•cal•ly**, *adv.* according to the rules of grammar.

gram•pus ['græmpəs] *n.* sea animal similar to a dolphin.

gra•na•ry ['grænərɪ] *n.* storehouse for grain.

grand [grænd] 1. *adj.* (-er, -est) (a) important/imposing. (b) final. (c) conducted with solemnity. (d) very good. 2. *n.* (a) *inf.* grand piano. (b) *Sl.* thousand dollars. **gran•dad**, *n. inf.* grandfather. **grand•child**, *n.* (*pl.* -children) child of a son or daughter. **grand•daugh•ter**, *n.* daughter of a son or daughter. **gran•dee** [græn'diː] *n.* proud aristocrat (usu. Spanish). **gran•deur** ['grændʒə] *n.* splendor/majesty. **grand•fa•ther**, *n.* father of a mother or father; **g. clock** = tall clock standing on the floor. **gran•dil•o•quence** [græn'dɪləkwəns] *n.* pompous/wordy speech. **gran•dil•o•quent**, *adj.* speaking in a pompous way. **gran•di•ose** ['grændɪəʊs] *adj.* very splendid. **grand•ly**, *adv.* in a grand way. **grand•ma** ['grænmɑː] *n. inf.* grandmother. **grand•mas•ter**, *n.* chessplayer of international quality. **grand•moth•er**, *n.* mother of a mother or father. **grand•ness**, *n.* being grand. **grand•pa** ['grænpɑː] *n. inf.* grandfather. **grand•par•ents**, *n. pl.* parents of a mother or father. **grand pi•a•no**, *n.* large horizontal piano. **Grand Prix** [grɒŋ'priː] *n.* motor/motorcycle race. **grand•son**, *n.* son of a son or daughter. **grand•stand**, *n.* building with a sloping bank of seats for spectators at a racetrack or sports stadium.

grange [greɪndʒ] *n.* farm with its buildings.

gran•ite ['grænɪt] *n.* hard light-gray stone used for building.

gran•ny ['grænɪ] *n. inf.* grandmother; **g. knot** = insecure type of reef knot.

grant [grɑːnt] 1. *n.* financial aid. 2. *v.* (a) to agree/to give consent; **to take sth for granted** = not to appreciate it any more. (b) to agree; **I g. you it is a difficult job** = I admit that it is difficult. **grant•ed**, *adj.* admitted/understood.

gran•u•late ['grænjuleɪt] *v.* to form into grains. **gran•u•lar**, *adj.* containing grains; like grains. **gran•ule**, *n.* very small particle.

grape [greɪp] *n.* small green or purple fruit growing in clusters on a vine, eaten as fruit or made into wine. **grape•fruit**, *n.* (*pl.* grapefruit) large round yellow citrus fruit. **grape•vine**, *n.* climbing plant on which grapes grow. **I heard it on the g.** = I learned the news by gossip/unofficially.

graph [grɑːf] *n.* mathematical diagram/curve. **graph•ic** ['græfɪk] *adj.* (a) referring to graphs/diagrams/signs, etc. (c) vivid (description). **graph•i•cal**, *adj.* referring to graphs/diagrams/signs, etc. **graph•i•cal•ly**, *adv.* (a) using graphs/diagrams/signs, etc. (b) in a graphic way. **graph•i•cal us•er in•ter•face (GUI)**, *n.* means by which a user interacts with a computer that involves graphics, e.g. by using a mouse to select options on screen. **graph•ics**, *n.* pictures/charts on a printed document or on a computer screen. **graph pa•per**, *n.* paper with small squares for drawing graphs on.

graph•ite ['græfaɪt] *n.* naturally occurring form of carbon; lead (as used in a pencil).

graph•ol•o•gy [græ'fɒlədʒɪ] *n.* science of discovering s.o.'s character from handwriting. **graph•ol•o•gist**, *n.* person who practices graphology.

grap•nel ['græpnl] *n.* small anchor with several hooks.

grap•ple ['græpl] *v.* to wrestle/to fight (**with**). **grap•pling i•ron**, *n.* grapnel.

grasp [grɑːsp] 1. *n.* (a) tight hold/grip. (b) understanding. 2. *v.* (a) to seize; to grab tightly. (b) to understand. **grasp at**, *v.* to try to grab. **grasp•ing**, *adj.* (person) who is eager to get more things.

grass [grɑːs] 1. *n.* (a) low green plant of which the thin leaves and stalks are eaten by cattle, etc.; **don't let the g. grow under your feet** =

æ back, ɑː farm, ɒ top, aɪ pipe, aʊ how, aɪə fire, aʊə flower, ɔː bought, ɔɪ toy, e fed, eəhair, eɪ take, ə afraid, əʊ boat, aʊə lower, ɜː word, iː heap, ɪ hit, ɪə hear, uː school, ʊ book, ʌ but, b back, d dog, ð then, dʒ just, f fog, g go, h hand, j yes, k catch, l last, m mix, n nut, ŋ sing, p penny, r round, s some, ʃ short, t too, tʃ chop, θ thing, v voice, w was, z zoo, ʒ treasure

waste no time in doing sth. (b) plant of a species related to grass (including bamboo, etc.). (c) lawn/piece of ground covered with grass. (d) *Sl.* marijuana. 2. *v.* **to g. over** = to cover with grass. **grass•hop•per,** *n.* green jumping insect with long back legs. **grass•land,** *n.* prairie or pasture. **grass•roots,** *n. pl.* ordinary members of a political party/a labor union; common people; **g. reaction** = reaction by the ordinary members (of a party, etc.). **grass-snake,** *n.* common snake. **grass•wid•ow,** *n.* wife whose husband has temporarily gone away. **grass•wid•ow•er,** *n.* husband whose wife has temporarily gone away. **grass•y,** *adj.* covered with growing grass.

grate [greɪt] 1. *n.* metal frame for holding wood, coal, etc. when burning in a fireplace, etc. 2. *v.* (a) to reduce to small bits by rubbing on a rough surface. (b) to make a noise like two rough surfaces rubbing together. (c) to have an irritating effect upon. **grat•er,** *n.* instrument for grating cheese, etc. **grat•ing,** 1. *n.* grille; framework of wooden or metal bars. 2. *adj.* **a g. sound** = an irritating sound as of the rubbing together of rough surfaces.

grate•ful ['greɪtfʊl] *adj.* thankful. **grate•ful•ly,** *adv.* thankfully.

grat•i•fy ['grætɪfaɪ] *v.* (a) to satisfy/to delight. (b) to please. **grat•i•fi•ca•tion** [grætɪfɪ-'keɪʃn] *n.* satisfaction. **gra•ti•fy•ing,** *adj.* pleasing/satisfying.

grat•in ['grætæn] *n.* dish cooked with a crust, often of cheese, on top.

grat•is ['grɑːtɪs] *adv.* free/without charge.

grat•i•tude ['grætɪtjuːd] *n.* appreciation.

gra•tu•i•ty [grə'tjuːɪtɪ] *n.* present of money given in return for services in excess of the cost of the services. **gra•tu•i•tous,** *adj.* unasked for; undeserved.

grave [greɪv] 1. *n.* tomb/hole in the ground to put a dead body in; burial place; **to have one foot in the g.** = to be very near to death. 2. *adj.* (-er, -est) serious/solemn. **grave•dig•ger,** *n.* man who digs graves. **grave•stone,** *n.* memorial stone placed on a grave. **grave•yard,** *n.* cemetery/place where people are buried.

grav•el ['grævl] *n.* mixture of sand and small stones.

grav•en ['greɪvn] *adj.* (*old*) carved.

grav•i•tate ['grævɪteɪt] *v.* to move (**towards** sth). **grav•i•ta•tion** [grævɪ'teɪʃn] *n.* force of the earth's center which attracts and causes objects to fall to the ground if dropped.

grav•i•ty ['grævɪtɪ] *n.* (a) seriousness. (b) weight; **specific g.** = density of a substance divided by the density of water. (c) force attract-

ing all objects to the earth's center, causing objects to fall to the ground if dropped.

gra•vy ['greɪvɪ] *n.* (*no pl.*) (a) juices that drip from meat during cooking. (b) brown sauce served with meat. **gravy boat,** *n.* small dish for serving gravy.

gray [greɪ] (*also* **grey**) 1. *adj.* (-er, -est) of a color between black and white; **g. matter** = active part of the brain; *inf.* intelligence. 2. *n.* color between black and white. **gray-haired,** *adj.* with gray hair. **gray•ish,** *adj.* rather gray. **gray•lag,** *n.* common European wild goose.

gray•ling ['greɪlɪŋ] *n.* (a) type of brown butterfly. (b) gray fish.

graze [greɪz] 1. *n.* slight surface wound/scratch. 2. *v.* (a) to feed on growing grass. (b) to wound slightly in passing. **graz•ing,** *n.* pasture.

grease [griːs] 1. *n.* (a) melted animal fat. (b) oily/fatty substance. 2. *v.* (a) to cover/to coat with oil/fat, etc. (b) *inf.* **to g. s.o.'s palm** = to bribe s.o. **grease•gun,** *n.* device for putting grease into machines. **grease•paint,** *n.* make-up used by actors. **greas•y,** *adj.* smeared with grease; oily.

great [greɪt] 1. *adj.* (-er, -est) (a) large/big. (b) extreme. (c) distinguished/grand. (d) remarkable. (e) *inf.* wonderful. **great-aunt,** *n.* aunt of a father or mother. **Great Dane,** *n.* breed of very large dog. **great-grand•chil•dren,** *n. pl.* grandchildren of a son or daughter. **great-grand•daugh•ter,** *n.* granddaughter of a son or daughter. **great-grand•fa•ther,** *n.* grandfather of a father or mother. **great-grand•moth•er,** *n.* grandmother of a father or mother. **great-grand•par•ents,** *n. pl.* grandparents of a father or mother. **great-grand•son,** *n.* grandson of a son or daughter. **great•ly,** *adv.* very much. **great•ness,** *n.* remarkable ability. **great-un•cle,** *n.* uncle of a father or mother.

grebe [griːb] *n.* type of diving bird with a long neck.

Gre•cian ['griːʃn] *adj.* referring to ancient Greece.

greed [griːd] *n.* too great appetite; desire for more than is necessary. **greed•i•ly,** *adv.* with great appetite. **greed•i•ness,** *n.* being greedy. **greed•y,** *adj.* (-ier, -iest) wanting too much food, etc.; **g. for** = always wanting (power, etc.).

Greek [griːk] 1. *adj.* referring to Greece. 2. *n.* (a) person from Greece. (b) language spoken in Greece.

green [griːn] 1. *adj.* (-er, -est) (a) of a color like grass; **g. light** = light which shows you can go ahead; **g. with envy** = very envious. (b) immature/gullible. (c) referring to a concern about the environment; **g. party** = political party concerned with environmental issues. 2. *n.* (a) color like that of grass. (b) piece of public land covered with grass. (c) piece of land covered with smooth grass on which you can play certain games. **green•back**, *n. inf.* dollar bill. **green belt**, *n.* area of countryside around a town where building is prohibited. **green card**, *n.* work permit given by the U.S. government to s.o. who is going to live in the United States. **green•er•y**, *n.* vegetation. **green•finch**, *n.* bird with yellow and green plumage. **green•fly**, *n.* (*pl.* **greenfly**) small green aphid. **green•gage**, *n.* kind of green plum. **green•gro•cer**, *n.* person who sells fruit and vegetables. **green•horn**, *n.* inexperienced person. **green•house**, *n.* shelter made of glass and wood or metal for cultivation of delicate plants; **g. effect** = warming effect on the atmosphere, caused by carbon dioxide in the upper atmosphere. **green•ish**, *adj.* rather green. **green mail**, *n.* buying shares in a company, threatening to take the company over, then selling the shares at a profit. **green•room**, *n.* room where actors can rest when they are off-stage. **greens**, *n. pl. inf.* cooked green vegetables. **green•stick frac•ture**, *n.* fracture of a long bone in a child, where the bone bends, but does not break. **green thumb**, *n.* skill in gardening.

greet [griːt] *v.* to salute/to welcome. **greet•ing**, *n.* reception/way of welcoming s.o. **greet•ings**, *n. pl.* good wishes.

gre•gar•i•ous [grɪˈgeərɪəs] *adj.* fond of company/sociable.

grem•lin [ˈgremlɪn] *n.* imaginary imp, supposed to be responsible for faults in machinery.

gre•nade [grɪˈneɪd] *n.* small bomb thrown by hand.

gren•a•dine [grenəˈdiːn] *n.* red drink, made from pomegranate juice.

grew [gruː] *v. see* **grow**.

grey [greɪ] *adj. & n. see* **gray. greyhound**, *n.* slender, long-legged, swift dog, often used for racing.

grid [grɪd] *n.* (a) grating/frame of spaced parallel bars. (b) system of numbered squares on a map. (c) electricity supply system over a large area. **grid•dle**, *n.* flat frying pan or other surface for cooking pancakes, bacon, etc. **grid•dle•cake**, *n.* pancake. **grid•i•ron**, *n.*

(a) metal frame for cooking food over an open fire. (b) football field.

grief [griːf] *n.* deep sorrow; **to come to g.** = to meet with disaster. **grief-strick•en**, *adj.* very sad.

griev•ance [ˈgriːvəns] *n.* real or imagined grounds for complaint; **to air one's grievances** = to tell about one's complaints.

grieve [griːv] *v.* to feel sad (**for**); **it grieves me** = it makes me sad. **grieve o•ver**, *v.* to mourn; to feel sad because of (sth). **griev•ous**, *adj.* severe; **g. bodily harm** = severe injury to s.o.

grif•fin [ˈgrɪfɪn] *n.* imaginary animal with a lion's head and eagle's wings.

grif•fon [ˈgrɪfən] *n.* (a) type of small terrier. (b) type of vulture.

grill [grɪl] 1. *n.* (a) metal frame for cooking food over a direct source of heat. (b) (*also* **grillroom**) restaurant where most food is cooked on a grill. (c) **mixed g.** = collection of grilled food. (d) framework of metal/wooden bars. 2. *v.* (a) to cook over a grill. (b) *inf.* to interrogate (s.o.)/to ask (s.o.) searching questions.

grille [grɪl] *n.* grating; frame of spaced parallel bars; **radiator g.** = parallel bars in front of a radiator on a car.

grilse [grɪls] *n.* young salmon, returning to the river from the sea for the first time.

grim [grɪm] *adj.* (**grimmer, grimmest**) (a) sinister/severe. (b) bad/gloomy. **grim•ly**, *adv.* tenaciously; with determination. **grim•ness**, *n.* being grim.

grim•ace [grɪˈmeɪs] 1. *n.* twisted expression on the face. 2. *v.* to make a grimace.

grime [graɪm] *n.* ingrained dirt. **grim•i•ness**, *n.* being grimy. **grim•y**, *adj.* dirty.

grin [grɪn] 1. *n.* wide smile. 2. *v.* (**grinned**) to smile broadly; **to g. and bear it** = to accept things bravely.

grind [graɪnd] 1. *n.* boring/monotonous work; **the daily g.** = repetitive work to be done every day. 2. *v.* (**ground**) (a) to reduce to small pieces by crushing; **to g. corn/coffee**. (b) to mince; **ground beef** = minced beef. (c) to rub surfaces together; **to g. your teeth** = to rub together the upper and lower teeth, usu. in anger; **to g. to a halt** = to stop. (d) to sharpen (a tool)/to smooth (sth rough); **to have an ax to g.** = to have a particular interest or point of view which makes your judgment biased. **grind•er**, *n.* machine or device for grinding; **coffee g. grind•stone**, *n.* stone which turns

---

to sharpen knives; **to keep one's nose to the g.** = to keep working very hard.

grin•go ['grɪŋgəʊ] *n. inf. (esp. in Mexico)* foreigner, usu. American.

grip [grɪp] 1. *n.* (a) firm hold; **to come to grips with** = to deal with; **to keep a g. on** = to remain in control of. (b) *(old)* small bag for carrying clothes, etc. when traveling. 2. *v.* **(gripped)** (a) to seize. (b) to hold (attention). **grip•ping**, *adj.* holding the attention.

gripe [graɪp] *v.* to moan/to complain **about** sth.

gris•ly ['grɪzlɪ] *adj.* **(ier, -iest)** causing horror/dread.

grist [grɪst] *n. inf.* **g. for/to the mill** = it's all useful/it all helps.

gris•tle ['grɪsl] *n.* tough, whitish, flexible tissue in meat. **gris•tly**, *adj.* full of pieces of gristle.

grit [grɪt] 1. *n.* (a) small particles of stone/sand, as in water, food, etc. (b) *inf.* courage. (c) **grits** = type of porridge made of corn or wheat. 2. *v.* **(gritted)** (a) to make a scratchy sound: (b) **to g. your teeth** = to clench your teeth together, usu. in fear/determination. **grit•ti•ness**, *n.* being gritty. **grit•ty**, *adj.* full of grit.

griz•zled ['grɪzld] *adj.* with gray or partly gray hair. **griz•zly** ['grɪzlɪ] 1. *adj.* gray or grayish. 2. *n.* **g. (bear)** = large, fierce North American bear.

groan [grəʊn] 1. *n.* deep sound expressing pain/grief/disapproval. 2. *v.* (a) to moan deeply. (b) **to g. under a weight** = to be heavily laden.

groats [grəʊts] *n. pl.* crushed oats.

gro•cer ['grəʊsə] *n.* person who sells canned foods, butter, sugar, eggs, etc., and miscellaneous household supplies. **gro•cer•ies**, *n. pl.* items on sale in a grocery. **gro•cer•y, grocery store**, *n.* grocer's store.

grog [grɒg] *n.* drink of spirits and water. **grog•gi•ly**, *adv.* unsteadily. **grog•gy**, *adj.* unsteady.

groin [grɔɪn] *n.* (a) hollow where the thigh joins the belly. (b) place where two vaults join. **groined**, *adj.* (roof) with joined vaults.

groom [gru:m] 1. *n.* (a) person who looks after horses. (b) bridegroom/new husband. 2. *v.* to look after/to make smart; **well-groomed** = smart and well-dressed.

groove [gru:v] *n.* (a) channel/hollow. (b) routine; **to get into a g.** = to be stuck in a routine. **groov•y**, *adj. Sl.* fine/fashionable.

grope [grəʊp] *v.* to feel with your hands as if you were blind.

gros•beak ['grəʊsbi:k] *n.* small bird with a large beak.

gross [grəʊs] 1. *n. (pl.* **gross)** twelve dozen, 144. 2. *adj.* **(-er, -est)** (a) bloated; horribly fat. (b) great/excessive; **g. injustice.** (c) total; **g. weight** = combined weight of container and contents; **g. income** = total income before deductions and allowances are made. **gross•ly**, *adv.* greatly.

gro•tesque [grə'tesk] *adj.* outrageous/fantastic; strange and ugly.

grot•to ['grɒtəʊ] *n. (pl.* **-oes)** picturesque cave; room decorated to resemble a cave.

grot•ty ['grɒtɪ] *adj. inf.* dirty.

grouch [graʊtʃ] 1. *n. inf.* grumble. 2. *v. inf.* to grumble. **grouch•y**, *adj. inf.* grumpy.

ground [graʊnd] 1. *n.* (a) soil/earth. (b) surface of the earth; **to go to g.** = to hide away. (c) area of land; **to stand one's g.** = to maintain one's position/authority; **to lose g.** = to become less successful; **to break new g.** = to be the first to start a project; **to get (sth) off the g.** = to start (sth) successfully/to get (a project) going. (d) large area of land set aside for a particular purpose; **picnic g.** (e) **grounds** = land surrounding a large house. (f) reason; **grounds for complaint.** (g) **coffee grounds** = small pieces of ground coffee beans left after the coffee has been made. 2. *v.* (a) to base. (b) to run (a boat) on to the land. (c) to keep (aircraft/pilot) on the ground. (d) *see also* **grind. ground•less**, *adj.* without reason. **ground•nut**, *n.* peanut. **ground rule**, *n.* basic rule of procedure. **grounds•keep•er**, *n.* person who looks after an area of land, as a park, gardens, golfcourse, etc. **ground•speed**, *n.* the speed of an aircraft over the ground. **ground•swell**, *n. (no pl.)* large slow-moving waves. **ground•work**, *n.* basic work/preliminary work.

group [gru:p] 1. *n.* (a) number of people or animals gathered close together. (b) classification; **blood g.; age g.** (c) small number of people playing music together. 2. *v.* **to g. (together)** = to form into groups. **group•er**, *n.* large tropical sea fish, used as food. **group•ie**, *n. Sl.* girl follower of a rock group, celebrity, etc. **group prac•tice**, *n.* several doctors who share patients between them and usu. work from the same offices. **group•ware**, *n.* computer software that allows many users to share files, etc. and to exchange electronic mail.

grouse [graʊs] 1. *n.* (a) *(pl.* **grouse)** reddish/black bird shot for sport and food. (b) *inf.* grumble. 2. *v. inf.* to grumble (**about** sth).

grout [graʊt] *v.* to fill the spaces between tiles on a floor or wall with cement. **grout•ing**, *n.* cement used to fill spaces between tiles.

grove [grəʊv] *n.* small group of trees.

grov•el ['grɒvl] *v.* **(groveled, grovelled)** to humble yourself; to lie with your face on the ground.

grow [grəʊ] 1. *v.* (**grew** [gru:], **has grown**) (a) to develop/to exist as a living plant. (b) to increase in size/height. (c) to become/to evolve gradually. (d) to cultivate; **she grows roses**. **grow•er**, *n.* (a) person who cultivates. (b) plant that grows in a specified way; **a slow g. grow•ing**, *adj.* getting bigger. **grown**, *adj.* developed to full size. **grown-up**, *adj. & n.* adult. **grow on**, *v. inf.* to become accepted; **this picture grows on you** = you gradually come to like it. **grow out of**, *v.* to become bigger/older (so that clothes no longer fit, etc.). **growth**, *n.* (a) development; increase in height/size. (b) lump of tissue in the body. **growth rate**, *n.* speed with which sth grows. **grow up**, *v.* to become adult.

growl [graʊl] 1. *n.* sound made in the throat expressing anger, like that made by dogs. 2. *v.* to murmur angrily.

grown [grəʊn] *v. see* **grow**.

grub [grʌb] 1. *n.* (a) larva of an insect; short worm which grows into an insect. (b) *Sl.* food. 2. *v.* (**grubbed**) to dig. **grub•bi•ness**, *n.* dirty appearance. **grub•by**, *adj.* (**-ier, -iest**) dirty.

grudge [grʌdʒ] 1. *n.* feeling of resentment/ill will (**against** s.o.). 2. *v.* to be unwilling to give (s.o. sth). **grudg•ing**, *adj.* reluctant.

gruel [ˈgruəl] *n.* thin porridge.

gruel•ing [ˈgruəlɪŋ] *adj.* exhausting/tiring; very difficult.

grue•some [ˈgru:səm] *adj.* causing horror/dread.

gruff [grʌf] *adj.* (**-er, -est**) (a) deep/rough (voice). (b) stern (manner). **gruff•ly**, *adv.* in a gruff way. **gruff•ness**, *n.* being gruff.

grum•ble [ˈgrʌmbl] 1. *n.* moan/complaint. 2. *v.* to complain (**about** sth). **grum•bler**, *n.* person who complains.

grump•y [ˈgrʌmpɪ] *adj.* (**-ier, -iest**) bad-tempered. **grump•i•ly**, *adv.* in a bad-tempered manner. **grump•i•ness**, *n.* being grumpy.

grunt [grʌnt] 1. *n.* low sound, like that made by pigs. 2. *v.* to make a low snorting sound.

gua•no [ˈgwɑːnəʊ] *n.* (*no pl.*) droppings of sea-birds.

guar•an•tee [gærənˈtiː] 1. *n.* (a) legal document promising that a machine will work for a certain time; **the car is still under g.** (b) person who receives a guarantee. (c) thing that assures a certain result. 2. *v.* to give assurance (**that** sth will happen). **guar•an•teed**, *adj.*

assured. **guar•an•tor** [gærənˈtɔː] *n.* person who makes or gives a guarantee.

guard [gɑːd] 1. *n.* (a) watch/looking out; **to be on g.** = to be watchful; **to be on your g.** = to be prepared against attack/surprise, etc.; **to be caught off g.** = to be taken unawares. (b) soldier/police officer who protects s.o./a building; **g. of honor** (*also* **honor guard**) = group of soldiers acting as a ceremonial escort to an important person. (c) device to prevent injury or accident. 2. *v.* (a) to defend/to protect; to watch (prisoners) carefully so that they cannot escape; **closely guarded secret** = secret which is carefully kept secret. (b) to be careful. **guard•ed**, *adj.* careful/noncommittal (reply). **guard•i•an**, *n.* keeper/protector responsible for the upbringing of a child. **guard•i•an•ship**, *n.* protection. **guard•room**, *n.* room used as a prison. **guards•man**, *n.* (*pl.* **-men**) members of the National Guard.

gua•va [ˈgwɑːvə] *n.* orange-colored tropical fruit.

guel•der rose [ˈgeldəˈrəʊʊz] *n.* garden shrub with white pompom flowers.

gue•ril•la, guerrilla [gəˈrɪlə] *n.* person (not a regular soldier) engaged in unofficial fighting; group of these soldiers.

guern•sey [ˈgɜːnzɪ] *n.* (a) breed of cow, which gives rich milk. (b) heavy knitted shirt.

guess [ges] 1. *n.* rough estimate; **it is anybody's g.** = no one really knows. 2. *v.* (a) to estimate. (b) to think. **guess•ti•mate**, *n. inf.* rough calculation. **guess•work**, *n.* process of guessing.

guest [gest] *n.* (a) person entertained at another's house; **paying g.** = lodger/boarder; **g. artist/g. conductor** = person who is invited to play with/to conduct an orchestra. (b) person staying in a hotel. **guest•house**, *n.* house where guests are lodged.

guff [gʌf] *n. inf.* words which mean nothing.

guf•faw [gəˈfɔː] 1. *n.* loud/coarse laugh. 2. *v.* to laugh loudly.

GUI [dʒiːjuːˈaɪ] *abbrev. for* graphical user interface.

guide [gaɪd] 1. *n.* (a) person who shows the way/who describes buildings/works of art, etc., as you see them. (b) indication. (c) book of helpful advice. 2. *v.* to conduct/to lead; **guided tour** = tour where the tourists are led by a guide; **guided missile** = missile which is led to the target by a controlling device. **guid•ance**, *n.* advice. **guide•book**, *n.*

æ back, ɑː farm, ɒ top, aɪ pipe, aʊ how, aɪə fire, aʊə flower, ɔː bought, ɔɪ toy, e fed, eəhair, eɪ take, ə afraid, əʊ boat, əʊə lower, ɜː word, iː heap, ɪ hit, ɪə hear, uː school, ʊ book, ʌ but, b back, d dog, ð then, dʒ just, f fog, g go, h hand, j yes, k catch, l last, m mix, n nut, ŋ sing, p penny, r round, s some, ʃ short, t too, tʃ chop, θ thing, v voice, w was, z zoo, ʒ treasure

book of helpful advice/information. **guide dog,** n. dog which is specially trained to lead a blind person. **guide•lines,** n. pl. advice how to proceed. **guid•ing,** adj. directing.

guild [gɪld] n. association of people with similar interests or goals.

guile [gaɪl] n. treachery/cunning/trickery. **guile•less,** adj. honest/straightforward.

guil•le•mot ['gɪlɪmɒt] n. black and white sea bird.

guil•lo•tine ['gɪlətiːn] 1. n. (a) machine with a sharp blade for beheading criminals. (b) machine with a sharp blade for cutting paper. 2. v. (a) to cut the head off (s.o.) with a guillotine. (b) to cut (paper) with a guillotine.

guilt [gɪlt] n. having committed a crime; being aware that you have committed a crime. **guilt•i•ly,** adv. showing that you know you have done wrong. **guilt•less,** adj. innocent. **guilt•y,** adj. (-ier, -iest) blameworthy/criminal; having done wrong.

guin•ea fowl ['gɪnɪfaʊl] n. small black bird with white spots, used for food.

guin•ea pig ['gɪnɪpɪg] n. (a) small furry animal with no tail, often kept as a pet. (b) person/animal used in a scientific experiment.

guise [gaɪz] n. (formal) appearance; **in the g. of** = pretending to be.

gui•tar [gɪ'tɑː] n. stringed musical instrument played with the fingers; **electric g.** = guitar which is connected to an amplifier. **gui•tar•ist,** n. person who plays a guitar.

gulch [gʌltʃ] n. gully.

gulf [gʌlf] n. (a) area of ocean or sea partly surrounded by land. (b) wide difference (**between** points of view). **Gulf Stream,** n. warm current which crosses the Atlantic from West to East.

Gulf War syn•drome, n. supposed condition characterized by debilitating symptoms, experienced by soldiers following the Persian Gulf War (1991).

gull [gʌl] n. long-winged, web-footed sea bird.

gul•let ['gʌlɪt] n. food tube from the mouth to the stomach; esophagus.

gul•li•ble ['gʌlɪbl] adj. easily taken in/ready to believe anything. **gul•li•bil•i•ty** [gʌlɪ'bɪlɪtɪ] n. being gullible.

gul•ly ['gʌlɪ] n. small ravine/channel, usu. cut by a stream.

gulp [gʌlp] 1. n. quick swallow. 2. v. (also **to gulp down**) to swallow hastily.

gum [gʌm] 1. n. (a) sticky substance produced by some trees. (b) thin glue. (c) flesh in which the teeth are set. (d) (**chewing**) **g.** = sweet sticky substance you chew but do not swallow. 2. v. (**gummed**) to stick together; **gummed label** = label with dry glue, which sticks if moistened.

gum•boil, n. small abcess on a gum. **gum•boot,** n. rubber boot. **gum•drop,** n. type of candy. **gum•shoe,** n. Sl. private detective. **gum tree,** n. eucalyptus tree.

gump•tion ['gʌmpʃn] n. enterprising spirit/resourcefulness.

gun [gʌn] 1. n. weapon which uses an explosive force to send out a bullet; **starting g.** = weapon used to make a bang to start a race; **grease g.** = instrument for injecting a small amount of grease into a part of an engine; **to stick to one's guns** = to maintain one's position; **to jump the g.** = to start doing sth before you should. 2. v. (**gunned**) (a) to shoot at. (b) **to be gunning for s.o.** = to be trying to attack s.o. **gun•boat,** n. small ship carrying heavy guns. **gun car•riage,** n. vehicle which carries a heavy gun. **gun•dog,** n. dog trained to accompany hunters shooting birds. **gun•fire,** n. firing of a gun. **gun•man,** n. (pl. -men) armed robber. **gun•ner,** n. soldier in the artillery; person who fires a gun. **gun•ner•y,** n. management of large guns. **gun met•al,** n. dark gray metal, made of copper, tin, lead and zinc. **gun•pow•der,** n. explosive substance. **gun•room,** n. room where you keep sporting guns. **gun run•ner,** n. person who brings guns into a country illegally. **gun run•ning,** n. illegal importing of guns. **gun•shot,** n. bullet from a gun; sound made by a gun being fired. **gun•smith,** n. manufacturer of guns. **gun•wale** ['gʌnl] n. upper edge of ship's side.

gung-ho [gʌŋ'həʊ] adj. inf. wildly enthusiastic.

gun•ny ['gʌnɪ] n. thick material for making sacks.

gup•py ['gʌpɪ] n. small tropical fish often kept as a pet.

gur•gle ['gɜːgl] 1. n. bubbling sound. 2. v. to make a bubbling sound.

gu•ru ['guːruː] n. notable thinker who has many disciples.

gush [gʌʃ] 1. n. sudden stream/sudden rush of liquid. 2. v. (a) to flow heavily. (b) to speak effusively; to praise too much. **gush•er,** n. oil well where the oil comes out so strongly that it does not need to be pumped. **gush•ing,** adj. praising/talking extravagantly.

gus•set ['gʌsɪt] n. triangle of cloth inserted in an article of clothing to make it larger. **gus•set•ed,** adj. with gussets.

gust [gʌst] 1. n. sudden violent rush of wind or rain. 2. v. to blow in gusts. **gust•i•ly,** adv. in gusts. **gust•y,** adj. windy.

gus•to ['gʌstəʊ] n. (no pl.) zest/enthusiasm.

gut [gʌt] 1. n. (a) lower part of the intestine; inf. **g. reaction** = natural/instinctive reaction; inf. **I hate his guts** = I dislike him a lot. (b) inf. **guts** = courage. (c) material made from the intestines of animals and used for violin and tennis racket strings. 2. *v.* (**gutted**) (a) to take out the internal organs of (animal/fish). (b) to remove/to destroy (the contents of sth); **the house was gutted by fire. guts•y,** *adj. inf.* brave.

gut•ta-per•cha [gʌtə'pɜːʃə] *n.* soft rubbery substance from Malaya.

gut•ter ['gʌtə] 1. *n.* shallow trough below the eaves of a house or at the side of a street to carry away rainwater. 2. *v.* (*of a candle*) to flicker so that the molten wax runs down the side. **gut•ter•ing,** *n.* (*no pl.*) curved metal or plastic used to make gutters. **gut•ter•snipe,** *n.* dirty child, living in the poor part of a town.

gut•tur•al ['gʌtərəl] *adj.* produced in the throat. **gut•tur•al•ly,** *adv.* spoken in the throat.

guy [gaɪ] *n.* (a) man/fellow. (b) rope.

guz•zle ['gʌzl] *v.* to eat or drink greedily. **guz•zler,** *n.* person who eats greedily.

gym [dʒɪm], **gym•na•si•um** [dʒɪm'neɪzɪəm] *n.* room or building for indoor athletic events and exercise. **gym•nast** ['dʒɪmnæst] *n.* expert in gymnastics. **gym•nas•tic** [dʒɪm-'næstɪk] *adj.* referring to gymnastics. **gym•nas•tics,** *n.* exercises on wall bars/wooden horse, etc., to help develop muscles and physical coordination.

gym•kha•na [dʒɪm'kɑːnə] *n.* competition for horse riding and racing; display of driving sports cars on a special course.

gyn•e•col•o•gy [gaɪnə'kɒlədʒɪ] *n.* study of the diseases of women's reproductive system. **gy•ne•col•o•gist,** *n.* doctor specializing in diseases of women's reproductive system. **gyn•e•co•log•i•cal** [gaɪnəkə'lɒdʒɪkl] *adj.* referring to women's diseases.

gyp•soph•i•la [dʒɪp'sɒfɪlə] *n.* garden plant with masses of small white flowers.

gyp•sum ['dʒɪpsəm] *n.* sulfate of lime.

gyp•sy ['dʒɪpsɪ] *n.* member of a wandering race.

gy•rate [dʒaɪ'reɪt] *v.* to turn round; to move rhythmically. **gy•ra•tion** [dʒaɪ'reɪʃn] *n.* circular movement. **gy•ra•to•ry** [dʒaɪ'reɪtərɪ] *adj.* turning round in a circle.

gyro- ['dʒaɪrəʊ] *prefix meaning* revolving; **gyro-compass** = compass which uses a gyroscope to avoid the shock of movement. **gy•ro•scope** ['dʒaɪrəskəʊp] *n.* spinning wheel mounted so that it can rotate on any axis. **gy•ro•scop•ic** [dʒaɪrə'skɒpɪk] *adj.* rapidly spinning.

æ back, aː farm, ɒ top, aɪ pipe, aʊ how, aiə fire, aʊə flower, ɔː bought, ɔɪ toy, e fed, eəhair, eɪ take, ə afraid, əʊ boat, əʊə lower, vː word, iː heap, ɪ hit, ɪə hear, uː school, ʊ book, ʌ but, b back, d dog, ð then, dʒ just, f fog, g go, h hand, j yes, k catch, l last, m mix, n nut, ŋ sing, p penny, r round, s some, ʃ short, t too, tʃ chop, θ thing, v voice, w was, z zoo, ʒ treasure

Hh

H *symbol for* hydrogen.

ha [hɑː] (a) *inter. showing surprise.* (b) *abbrev. for* hectare.

ha•be•as cor•pus ['heɪbɪəs 'kɔːpəs] *n.* order to bring a prisoner to answer a charge in court.

hab•er•dash•er•y ['hæbədæʃrɪ] *n.* store/department selling men's shirts, ties, etc.

hab•it ['hæbɪt] *n.* (a) custom; regular way of doing sth; **from force of h.** = because it is sth you ordinarily do. (b) dress; **riding h.** = special dress for horse riding. **hab•it-form•ing,** *adj.* (drug) which you can become addicted to. **ha•bit•u•al** [hə'bɪtjʊəl] *adj.* regular/normal. **ha•bit•u•al•ly,** *adv.* ordinarily/in the usual way. **ha•bit•u•ate,** *v.* to accustom (s.o.) to doing sth. **ha•bit•u•é** [hæ'bɪtjʊeɪ] *n.* regular client/visitor.

hab•i•tat ['hæbɪtæt] *n.* place where a certain animal or plant is usually found.

hab•i•ta•tion [hæbɪ'teɪʃn] *n.* place/building where s.o. lives; **not fit for h.** = not fit to live in. **hab•it•a•ble** ['hæbɪtəbl] *adj.* fit to live in.

hack [hæk] 1. *n.* (a) horse which is hired. (b) writer, artist, etc. who sacrifices his/her talent, training, integrity to work solely for money doing dull, unimaginative work. (c) *Sl.* second-rate writer. 2. (a) *v.* to chop roughly. (b) to enter a computer system illegally, using a modem. **hack•er,** *n.* person who hacks into a computer system. **hack•ing,** *adj.* dry and unpleasant (cough).

hack•les ['hæklz] *n. pl.* neck feathers (on a cock); hairs on the neck (of a dog); **to raise s.o.'s h.** = to make s.o. annoyed.

hack•ney ['hæknɪ] *n.* **h. coach** = taxi. **hack•neyed** ['hæknɪd] *adj.* (phrase) which is often used.

hack•saw ['hæksɔː] *n.* saw for cutting metal, which has a narrow blade attached to a frame.

had [hæd] *v. see* **ha•ve.**

had•dock ['hædək] *n.* (*pl.* **haddock**) common white sea fish.

Ha•des ['heɪdiːz] *n.* hell.

haft [hɑːft] *n.* handle (of a knife, etc.).

hag [hæg] *n.* witch; ugly old woman.

hag•gard ['hægəd] *adj.* thin/tired (face).

hag•gis ['hægɪs] *n.* Scottish food, made of sheep's heart, liver, etc., cooked with oatmeal in a bag.

hag•gle ['hægl] *v.* (**over**) to discuss a price to try to reduce it.

hag•i•og•ra•phy ['hægɪɒgrəfɪ] *n.* writing about saints.

ha-ha ['hɑːhɑː] 1. *inter. to show that you are amused.* 2. *n.* fence put at the bottom of a ditch.

hai•ku ['haɪkuː] *n.* very short Japanese poem.

hail [heɪl] 1. *n.* (a) small pieces of ice which fall like frozen rain. (b) small missiles which fall; **a h. of bullets.** (c) call. 2. *v.* (a) to fall as small pieces of ice; to fall in small pieces. (b) to call out to (s.o.); to wave to (a taxi) to stop. (c) to come **from. hail•stone,** *n.* small piece of ice falling from the sky. **hail•storm,** *n.* storm when hailstones fall from the sky.

hair ['heə] *n.* (a) single long thread growing on the body of a human or animal. (b) mass of hairs growing on the head; *inf.* **to let your h. down** = to relax/become less formal. **hair•brush,** *n.* special brush for keeping your hair neat. **hair•cut,** *n.* making your hair shorter by cutting. **hair•do,** *n. inf.* style of a woman's hair. **hair•dress•er,** *n.* person who cuts/dyes/styles hair. **hair•dres•ser's,** *n.* business where people can have their hair cut and styled. **hair•dress•ing,** *n.* cutting/dyeing/styling hair. **hair•less,** *adj.* with no hair. **hair•line,** *n.* (a) line where the hair meets the forehead. (b) very thin line/crack. **hair•net,** *n.* light net worn over the hair to keep it in place. **hair•piece,** *n.* small wig; piece of false hair. **hair•pin,** *n.* bent piece of wire used to keep hair in place; **h. turn** = very sharp turn, as on a mountain road. **hair-rais•ing,** *adj.* frightening. **hair•spring,** *n.* spiral spring in a watch. **hair•style,** *n.* way of dressing/cutting, etc., the hair. **hair•y,** *adj.* (-ier, -iest) (a) covered with hairs. (b) *Sl.* frighteningly dangerous.

hake [heɪk] *n.* (*pl.* **hake**) common small white sea fish.

hal•cy•on ['hælsɪən] *adj.* calm/beautiful (weather); carefree (days).

hale [heɪl] *adj.* **h. and hearty** = very healthy.

half [hɑːf] 1. *n.* (*pl.* **halves** [hɑːvs]) one of two equal parts; **first h.** = first part of a sports match; **to go halves** = each pays half. 2. *adj.* being divided into two equal parts; **h. an hour** = 30 minutes. 3. *adv.* partly/not fully; **h. as tall** = smaller by half, 50 per cent of the size. **half-and-half,** *adv.* in two equal quantities. **half-back,** *n.* defense player in football/rugby, etc. **half-baked,** *adj. inf.* (plan) which has not been well thought out. **half-breed,** *n.* person/animal with parents of different races. **half-broth•er,** *n.* brother who has one parent the same as you. **half-caste,** *n.* person with parents of two different races. **half-cocked,** *adj.* **to go off h.-c.** (or **at half cock**) = to behave or have happen hastily or without enough planning. **half-doz•en,** *n.* six. **half-emp•ty,** *adj.* partly empty/not completely empty. **half-fare,** *n.* fare reduced by half. **half-full,** *adj.* partly full/not completely full. **half-heart•ed,** *adj.* lacking conviction/enthusiasm. **half-hour•ly,** *adj. & adv.* every thirty minutes. **half-life,** *n.* time taken for a substance to lose half its radioactivity. **half-mast,** *n.* **the flags are at h.-m.** = the flags are flying halfway up the flagpole as a sign of mourning. **half-nel•son,** *n.* hold in wrestling, where one wrestler twists the arm of his opponent below his back. **half-o•pen,** *adj.* partly open/not completely open. **half•pen•ny** ['heɪpnɪ] *n.* (*pl.* **-pennies** = *coins,* **-pence** = *price*) (*old*) British coin worth half a penny. **half-sis•ter,** *n.* sister who has one parent the same as you. **half-tim•bered,** *adj.* (house) whose walls are made of wooden beams with brick or plaster walls between. **half-time,** *n.* short rest in the middle of a game. **half-tone,** *n.* photograph reproduced by means of dots of varying sizes. **half-track,** *n.* vehicle driven by caterpillar tracks behind and by ordinary wheels in front. **half-vol•ley,** *n.* (*in tennis*) hitting the ball just after it has bounced. **half•way,** *adv.* in the middle of a distance or length; **to meet s.o. h.** = to compromise with s.o. **half•wit,** *n.* idiot. **half-wit•ted,** *adj.* stupid. **half-year,** *n.* six months. **half-year•ly,** *adj. & adv.* (taking place) every six months.

hal•i•but ['hælɪbʌt] *n.* (*pl.* **halibut**) large white flatfish living in the sea.

hal•i•to•sis [hælɪ'təʊsɪs] *n.* bad-smelling breath.

hall [hɔːl] *n.* (a) large room or building for public meetings; large building where students live in a college or university. (b) **(entrance) h.** = room or passage through which you enter a house or building.

hal•le•lu•jah [hælɪ'luːjə] *inter. meaning* praise to God.

hall•mark ['hɔːlmɑːk] *n.* mark put on gold and silver to show that it has the correct purity. **hall•marked,** *adj.* (silver spoon, etc.) with a hallmark stamped on it.

hal•lo [hə'ləʊ] *inter. showing a greeting.*

hal•loo [hə'luː] 1. *n.* call to dogs when hunting. 2. *v.* to shout halloo.

hal•low ['hæləʊ] *v.* to bless (sth)/to declare (sth) holy; **hallowed ground** = ground (near a church) which has been blessed. **Hal•low•een, Hallowe'en** [hæləʊ'iːn] *n.* the evening of October 31st, the eve of All Saints' Day, when witches and ghosts are said to roam about.

hal•lu•ci•na•tion [həluːsɪ'neɪʃn] *n.* seeing things which are not there; thing seen when you hallucinate. **hal•lu•ci•nate** [hə'luːsɪneɪt] *v.* to see things which are not there. **hal•lu•ci•na•to•ry** [hə'luːsɪnətrɪ] *adj.* (drug) which causes hallucinations. **hal•lu•ci•no•gen** [hə'luːsɪnədʒən] *n.* substance which gives you hallucinations. **hal•lu•ci•no•gen•ic,** *adj.* which causes hallucinations.

ha•lo ['heɪləʊ] *n.* (*pl.* **-oes**) glow of light (around the moon/around the head of a saint).

hal•o•gen ['hælədʒən] *n.* one of a group of chemical elements (including chlorine/fluorine/iodine).

halt [hɔːlt] 1. *n.* complete stop; **to come to a h.** = to stop; **to call a h. to** = to bring to a stop. 2. *v.* to stop. **halt•ing,** *adj.* hesitant.

halt•er ['hɔːltə] *n.* rope put around animal's neck to lead it; **h. top** = woman's top with a piece of material going around the back of the neck, leaving the arms and back bare.

halve [hɑːv] *v.* (a) to divide into two equal parts. (b) to reduce by half. **halves,** *n. pl. see* **half.**

hal•yard ['hæljəd] *n.* rope used to pull up a flag/sail.

ham [hæm] 1. *n.* (a) salted or smoked meat from a pig's leg. (b) *inf.* bad actor. (c) *inf.* amateur radio operator working from home. 2. *v.* (**hammed**) to act badly. **ham-hand•ed,** *adj.* clumsy.

ham•burg•er ['hæmbɜːgə] *n.* flat cake of

æ back, ɑː farm, ɒ top, aɪ pipe, aʊ how, aɪə fire, aʊə flower, ɔː bought, ɔɪ toy, e fed, eəhair, eɪ take, ə afraid, əʊ boat, əʊə lower, ɜː word, iː heap, ɪ hit, ɪə hear, uː school, ʊ book, ʌ but, b back, d dog, ð then, dʒ just, f fog, g go, h hand, j yes, k catch, l last, m mix, n nut, ŋ sing, p penny, r round, s some, ʃ short, t too, tʃ chop, θ thing, v voice, w was, z zoo, ʒ treasure

ground beef, cooked and eaten as a sandwich in a roll.
ham•let ['hæmlət] n. small village.
ham•mer ['hæmə] 1. n. (a) heavy metal tool for knocking nails into wood/pins into the ground, etc. (b) object which hits sth as part of a machine. (c) metal ball which is thrown in sporting contests. 2. v. to hit hard, as with a hammer. **hammer out,** v. (a) to make (sth) flat with a hammer. (b) **to h. out an agreement** = to come to an agreement after long difficult discussions. **hammer toe,** n. deformed toe which bends downwards.
ham•mock ['hæmək] n. hanging bed made of a strong cloth or net.
ham•per ['hæmpə] 1. n. large basket. 2. v. to stop/to hinder/to get in the way.
ham•ster ['hæmstə] n. small rodent, often kept as a pet.
ham•string ['hæmstrɪŋ] n. tendon behind the knee. **ham•strung,** adj. powerless; unable to do anything.
hand [hænd] 1. n. (a) part of the body at the end of each arm; **to have a h. in sth** = to help to make sth happen; **to give a h./lend a h. with** = to help with; **at h.** = near; **in h.** = in reserve; **on h.** = readily available; **out of h.** = uncontrollable. (b) workman; sailor; **an old h.** = very experienced person. (c) cards which have been dealt to you in a game. (d) one of the pointers on a clock or dial. (e) round of applause. (f) unit of measurement of the height of a horse. 2. v. to pass (sth) **to** s.o. by hand. **hand•bag,** n. woman's bag for carrying money, cosmetics, and other belongings. **hand•bill,** n. small announcement or advertisement given out by hand. **hand•book,** n. book which gives instructions or information. **hand•brake,** n. lever in a vehicle which works the brakes. **hand•clap,** n. clapping of the hands. **hand•cuff,** v. to attach (s.o.'s hands) with handcuffs. **handc•uffs,** n. pl. metal rings linked by a chain for attaching a prisoner's hands together. **hand•ful,** n. as much as you can hold in your hand; small number; person who is difficult to control. **hand•gun,** n. small gun which is carried in the hand. **hand•i•cap.** 1. n. (a) physical/mental disability; thing which puts you at a disadvantage. (b) penalty imposed in a race or competition on opponents who have exceptional ability to make it harder for them to win. 2. v. (**handicapped**) to put at a disadvantage; **the mentally handicapped** = people with a disability of the mind. **hand•i•cap•per,** n. person who calculates the handicaps in a race or competition. **hand•i•craft,** n. work done by hand; **handicrafts** = artistic work done by hand (such as knitting/pottery, etc.).

hand•i•ly, adv. in a handy way. **hand in,** v. to give in by hand. **hand•i•work,** n. work done by a particular person. **hand•ker•chief** ['hæŋkətʃiːf] n. square piece of cloth or paper for wiping your nose. **hand•made,** adj. made by hand, not by machine. **hand on,** v. to pass on. **hand out,** v. to distribute. **hand•out,** n. (a) money which is given out to people. (b) printed information sheet given out to people. **hand o•ver,** v. to give (sth) to s.o. **hand•picked,** adj. carefully selected. **hand•rail,** n. bar which you hold on to (next to a staircase, escalator, etc.). **hand a•round,** v. to pass around by hand. **hand•shake,** n. greeting when you grasp hands. **hand•spring,** n. gymnastic exercise where you turn a somersault on your hands and land on your feet. **hand•stand,** n. **to do a h.** = to balance on the palms of your hands with your feet in the air. **hand•writ•ing,** n. writing done by hand. **hand•writ•ten,** adj. written by hand, not typed or printed. **hand•y,** adj. (**-ier, -iest**) useful; in a convenient place. **hand•y•man,** n. (pl. **-men**) person who can do any sort of work, esp. repairs in the house.

han•dle ['hændl] 1. n. part of an object which you hold in the hand; inf. **to fly off the h.** = to lose your temper. 2. v. (a) to move, touch, feel, etc. with the hand or hands. (b) to deal with (sth); **handling charge** = charge which has to be paid to s.o. who has delivered or dealt with sth. **han•dle•bar(s),** n. (pl.) bar on the front of a bicycle or motorcycle which steers the front wheel.

hand•some ['hænsəm] adj. (a) good-looking. (b) fine/large (profit). **hand•some•ly,** adv. elegantly; generously.

hang [hæŋ] 1. n. (a) way in which sth hangs/drops/falls; inf. **to get the h. of sth** = to understand how sth works. (b) inf. **he doesn't give a h.** = he doesn't worry about it at all. 2. v. (**hung**) (a) to attach/to be attached above the ground to a nail or by a string/chain, etc. (b) to stick (wallpaper) on a wall. (c) (**hanged**) to kill (s.o.) by tying a rope round his neck and suspending him off the ground. **hang a•bout, hang around,** v. inf. to wait/to wander aimlessly in a certain place. **hang back,** v. to stay behind the others. **hang•dog,** adj. inf. sheepish (expression). **hang down,** v. to hang in a long piece. **hang•er,** n. object for hanging sth; **coat h.** = piece of wood/plastic/metal which is placed inside a coat to hang it up. **hang•er-on,** n. (pl. **hangers-on**) person who stays near s.o. in the hope of getting money or food. **hang glid•er,** n. huge kite used in hang gliding. **hang glid•ing,** n. sport of floating through the air by hanging on to a huge kite made of a metal frame covered with plastic. **hang•ing**, *n.* carpet/tapestry which is hung on a wall as decoration. **hang•man**, *n. (pl.* **-men)** executioner who kills people by hanging them. **hang•nail**, *n.* torn skin at the root of a fingernail. **hang on**, *v.* (a) **to h. on to sth** = to clutch (sth)/to keep (sth). (b) *inf.* to wait. **hang out**, *v. inf.* to live (in a place). **hang•o•ver**, *n.* (a) unpleasant effects of having drunk too much alcohol. **hang up**, *v.* to hang (sth) on a hook; to replace (a telephone receiver). **hang-up**, *n. (pl.* **hang-ups)** *Sl.* thing which worries you and prevents you from acting normally.

hang•ar ['hæŋə] *n.* large shed for keeping aircraft in.

hank [hæŋk] *n.* wool coiled into a loose loop.

hank•er ['hæŋkə] *v.* **to h. after/for** = to want (very much). **hank•er•ing**, *n.* desire.

han•ky ['hæŋkɪ] *n. inf.* handkerchief.

han•ky•pan•ky [hæŋkɪ'pæŋkɪ] *n. inf.* trouble/bad behavior; trickery.

hap•haz•ard [hæp'hæzəd] *adj.* done at random/unplanned. **hap•haz•ard•ly**, *adv.* at random; without any plan.

hap•less ['hæpləs] *adj. (formal)* unfortunate/unlucky.

hap•pen ['hæpn] *v.* (a) to take place; **what has happened to him?** = (i) what is he doing now? (ii) what harm has come to him? (b) to take place by chance. **hap•pen•ing**, *n.* event/thing which takes place. **hap•pen•stance**, *n.* **by h.** = by a coincidence.

hap•py ['hæpɪ] *adj.* **(-ier, -iest)** glad/full of joy. **hap•pi•ly**, *adv.* joyfully/gladly. **hap•pi•ness**, *n.* joy/gladness. **hap•py-go-luck•y**, *adj.* easy-going/carefree.

ha•ra-ki•ri [hærə'kɪrɪ] *n.* Japanese form of suicide.

ha•rangue [hə'ræŋ] 1. *n.* long loud, often scolding, speech. 2. *v.* to deliver a harangue to (s.o.).

ha•rass [hə'ræs] *v.* to bother/to worry (s.o.). **ha•rass•ment**, *n.* bothering/worrying; many small attacks on an enemy.

har•bin•ger ['hɑːbɪndʒə] *n. (formal)* thing which shows that sth else is approaching.

har•bor, *Brit.* **har•bour** ['hɑːbə] 1. *n.* port/safe place where ships can tie up to load

or unload. 2. *v.* (a) to continue to have (a grudge) **against** s.o. (b) to protect (a criminal).

hard [hɑːd] 1. *adj.* **(-er, -est)** (a) firm/not soft. (b) **h. currency** = one which does not lose its value compared to other currencies. (c) difficult; **h. times/h. luck** = bad luck; **h. labor** = punishment involving difficult manual work. (d) strict/severe. (e) *(of water)* containing calcium, which makes it difficult to form a lather. (f) strong (drink); (drug) which makes you become addicted; **h. drinker** = person who drinks a lot of alcohol. 2. *adv.* (a) strongly. (b) with difficulty. **hard-and-fast,** *adj.* strict/absolute (rule). **hard•back,** *n.* hardcover. **hard•board,** *n.* artificial board made of small shreds of wood stuck together. **hard-boiled,** *adj.* (a) (egg) which has been boiled until the white and yolk are set solid. (b) (person) without much feeling/who is not easily shocked. **hard by,** *adv.* close. **hard-core.** 1. *n.* central part (of a group) which is totally loyal and dedicated. 2. *adj.* totally loyal and dedicated. **hard•cov•er,** *n.* book with a stiff cover. **hard disk,** *n.* solid disk, fixed in a computer. **hard•en,** *v.* to make hard; **hardened criminal** = regular/permanent criminal. **hard•en off,** *v.* to bring (tender plants) into the open air. **hard hat,** *n.* protective helmet worn by construction workers, etc. **hard-head•ed,** *adj.* practical/sensible. **hard-heart•ed,** *adj.* cruel. **hard•lin•er,** *n.* person who is very antagonistic/stern towards s.o./an enemy, etc. **hard•ly,** *adv.* almost not. **hard•ness,** *n.* being solid/hard/not soft; difficulty; strictness. **hard of hear•ing,** *adj.* (person) who is quite deaf. **hard sell,** *n.* strenuous efforts to sell sth. **hard•ship,** *n.* suffering caused by lack of sth. **hard up,** *adj. inf.* with no money. **hard•ware,** *n. (no pl.)* (a) tools, nails, cutlery, and other metal articles; **h. store** = store selling pans/hammers/nails/paint, etc.; **military h.** = guns, tanks, and other military equipment. (b) physical parts/machinery of a computer. **hard-wear•ing,** *adj.* which does not wear out easily. **hard•wood,** *n.* wood which comes from deciduous trees. **hard•work•ing,** *adj.* (person) who works hard. **har•dy,** *adj.* **(-ier, -iest)** which can survive in difficult conditions; (plant) which can stay out of doors all the year round.

hare [heə] *n.* common field mammal, like a large rabbit. **hare-brained,** *adj.* mad/sense-

---

æ back, ɑ: farm, ɒ: top, aɪ pipe, aʊ how, aɪə fire, aʊə flower, ɔː bought, ɔɪ toy, e fed, eəhair, eɪ take, ə afraid, əʊ boat, əʊə lower, vː word, iː heap, ɪ hit, ɪə hear, uː school, ʊ book, ʌ but, b back, d dog, ð then, dʒ just, f fog, g go, h hand, j yes, k catch, l last, m mix, n nut, ŋ sing, p penny, r round, s some, ʃ short, t too, tʃ chop, θ thing, v voice, w was, z zoo, ʒ treasure

less (plan). **hare•bell,** *n.* wild flower shaped like a little blue bell. **hare•lip,** *n.* split in the upper lip from birth.

har•em [hɑːˈriːm] *n.* women in a Muslim household; women's quarters in a Muslim house.

har•i•cot [ˈhærɪkəʊ] *n.* **h. (bean)** = dry white bean eaten cooked.

hark [hɑːk] 1. *old inter. meaning* listen. 2. *v.* **to h. back to** = to go back to (a subject talked about earlier).

har•le•quin [ˈhɑːlɪkwɪn] *n.* character in old pantomime, wearing a mask and a suit of diamond-patterned cloth.

har•lot [ˈhɑːlət] *n.* (*formal*) prostitute.

harm [hɑːm] 1. *n.* damage. 2. *v.* to damage/to hurt. **harm•ful,** *adj.* which hurts/which causes damage. **harm•less,** *adj.* which causes no damage/which does not hurt.

har•mo•ny [ˈhɑːmənɪ] *n.* (a) musical sounds which do not clash. agreeable effect (of music/color, etc.). (b) general agreement. **har•mon•ic** [hɑːˈmɒnɪk]. 1. *adj.* referring to harmony. 2. *n.* higher note which is heard when a note is played. **har•mon•i•ca** [hɑːˈmɒnɪkə] *n.* mouth organ. **har•mo•ni•ous** [hɑːˈməʊnɪəs] *adj.* (sounds) which are in agreement/which sound well together. **har•mo•ni•ous•ly,** *adv.* in a harmonious way. **har•mo•ni•um** [hɑːˈməʊnɪəm] *n.* musical instrument like an organ where the sound comes from air pumped through reeds. **har•mo•ni•za•tion,** [hɑːmənaɪˈzeɪʃn] *n.* act of harmonizing. **har•mo•nize,** *v.* (a) to be in or bring to agreement. (b) to form chords out of the main tune of a piece of music.

har•ness [ˈhɑːnəs] 1. *n.* (a) leather straps which attach a horse to a cart; **he is still in h.** = he is still working. (b) straps for attaching a parachute to s.o.; straps which have a leash attached to control a small child. 2. *v.* (a) to attach (a horse) to a cart. (b) to use (natural resources/atomic power, etc.) for making energy.

harp [hɑːp] 1. *n.* large upright musical instrument, with many strings which are plucked with the fingers. 2. *v.* **to h. on** = keep talking about. **harp•ist,** *n.* person who plays a harp.

har•poon [hɑːˈpuːn] 1. *n.* long barbed spear used to kill whales. 2. *v.* to kill (a whale) with a harpoon.

harp•si•chord [ˈhɑːpsɪkɔːd] *n.* old musical instrument, like a piano, but with strings which are plucked.

har•py [ˈhɑːpɪ] *n.* (a) cruel mythical monster, with a woman's body and an eagle's claws. (b) cruel person (esp. woman).

har•ri•er [ˈhærɪə] *n.* (a) dog who hunts hares. (b) long-distance runner. (c) type of falcon.

har•row [ˈhærəʊ] 1. *n.* large rake pulled by a tractor for breaking up heavy soil. 2. *v.* to break up soil with a harrow. **har•row•ing,** *adj.* very disturbing, causing mental pain.

har•ry [ˈhærɪ] *v.* to bother/to worry (s.o.) by continual attacks.

harsh [hɑːʃ] *adj.* (-er, -est) (a) cruel/sharp (punishment, etc.). (b) rough/unpleasant (voice, etc.). **harsh•ly,** *adv.* in a harsh way. **harsh•ness,** *n.* cruelty/roughness.

hart [hɑːt] *n.* male deer.

har•um-scar•um [heərəmˈskeərəm] *adj. & n.* wild (young person).

har•vest [ˈhɑːvɪst] 1. *n.* (a) cutting/picking of ripe crops. (b) period of the year when crops are picked. 2. *v.* to cut/to pick ripe crops. **har•vest•er,** *n.* person/machine which cuts crops.

has [hæz] *v. see* **ha•ve. has-been** [ˈhæzbiːn] *n.* (*pl.* **has-beens**) *inf.* person/thing no longer as well known/important as before.

hash [hæʃ] 1. *n.* (a) minced or chopped meat; *inf.* **he made a h. of it** = he did it badly. (b) *inf.* hashish. (c) **h. (mark)** = printed sign (#) used in computers as an indicator. 2. *v.* to mince or chop (meat, etc.); **h. brown potatoes** = fried grated or chopped potatoes.

hash•ish [ˈhæʃɪʃ] *n.* hemp used as a drug.

hasp [hɑːsp] *n.* metal bar, which closes a door or lid by fitting over a loop which is locked with a padlock.

has•sle [ˈhæsl] 1. *n. inf.* bother/struggle to do sth. 2. *v. inf.* to struggle/to argue.

has•sock [ˈhæsək] *n.* cushion for the feet or for kneeling on in a church.

haste [heɪst] *n.* speed; **to make h.** = to hurry up. **has•ten** [ˈheɪsn] *v.* to make (sth) go faster/come faster; to hurry up. **hast•i•ly,** *adv.* rapidly. **hast•i•ness,** *n.* being hasty. **hast•y,** *adj.* (-ier, -iest) rapid and with not enough preparation.

hat [hæt] *n.* piece of clothing worn on the head; **keep it under your h.** = keep it secret; **h. trick** = three goals, etc., scored by the same person in the same game. **hat•band,** *n.* piece of ribbon which goes round a hat. **hat•less,** *adj.* not wearing a hat.

hatch [hætʃ] 1. *n.* opening in a ship's deck; opening in the floor or wall of an aircraft. 2. *v.* (a) to warm (eggs) until baby birds appear; (*of a baby bird*) to break out of the egg; to plan (a plot). (b) to indicate shade in a sketch by drawing parallel lines close together. **hatch•back,** *n.* type of car with a sloping back and a large rear door which opens upwards. **hatch•er•y,** *n.* place where eggs are kept until they develop into young. **hatch•way,** *n.* opening in a ship's deck.

hatch•et ['hætʃɪt] *n.* small ax; *inf.* **to bury the h.** = to make peace; *Sl.* **h. man** = person brought into a company to fire some of the staff. **hatchet-faced,** *adj.* (person) with a grim pointed face.

hate [heɪt] 1. *n.* great dislike. 2. *v.* to dislike intensely. **hate•ful,** *adj.* horrible/unpleasant. **ha•tred,** *n.* great dislike.

hat•ter ['hætə] *n.* person who makes hats.

haugh•ty ['hɔːtɪ] *adj.* (-ier, -iest) very proud. **haugh•ti•ly,** *adv.* in a very proud manner. **haugh•ti•ness,** *n.* being haughty.

haul [hɔːl] 1. *n.* (a) catch (of fish); **the burglars made a good h.** = they stole a lot of valuable property. (b) distance traveled. 2. *v.* to pull with difficulty. **haul•age,** *n.* moving of things. **haul•er,** *n.* person or company who moves goods or things; **trash h.**

haulm [hɔːm] *n.* stems of peas/beans/potatoes.

haunch [hɔːnʃ] *n.* thigh and loin (of an animal); **the dog was sitting on its haunches** = sitting in a squatting position.

haunt [hɔːnt] 1. *n.* place where s.o. goes frequently. 2. *v.* to go to (a place) frequently; (*of ghosts*) to appear in (a place). **haunt•ed,** *adj.* (house) where a ghost appears.

ha•ve [hæv] *v.* (**I have, he has; I had, he had**) (a) (*also* have got) to possess. **the house has (got) no telephone.** (b) to take (a meal/a bath). (c) to play; **will you h. a game of tennis?** (d) to get (sth) done. (f) (*making the past tense of verbs*) **h. you finished your work?** (g) (*showing compulsion to do something*) **you will h. to sing that song again; you had better say nothing. have got,** *v.* **to have got to do sth** = to be obliged/to have to do sth. **have had,** *v. inf.* **he's had it** = he is finished/he has missed an opportunity. **have on,** *v.* (a) to be wearing. (b) to have arranged or be occupied with; **have you anything on for tonight?** (c) *inf.* to trick (s.o.); **they're having you on. have it out,** *v.* to settle a quarrel with s.o.

ha•ven ['heɪvn] *n.* safe port; safe place; **tax h.** = country where taxes are low.

hav•er•sack ['hævəsæk] *n.* bag carried on the back.

hav•oc ['hævək] *n.* damage; **to play h. with** = do a lot of damage to.

haw [hɔː] *n.* small red berry on the hawthorn. **haw•finch,** *n.* largest European finch.

hawk [hɔːk] 1. *n.* (a) bird of prey; **she has eyes like a h.** = she has very good eyesight/notices every detail. (b) person who is in favor of military attacks on an enemy/who is prepared to take a hard line in international relations. 2. *v.* (a) to sell goods from door to door. (b) to clear your throat. **hawk•er,** *n.* person who sells things from place to place.

hawse [ɔːz] *n.* bow of a ship, with holes for the anchor cable. **haw•ser** ['hɔːzə] *n.* thick rope for attaching a boat to a mooring.

haw•thorn ['hɔːθɔːn] *n.* common hedge shrub with white flowers and red berries.

hay [heɪ] *n.* long dried grass used as forage; **to make h. while the sun shines** = to enjoy yourself/to make money while you can. **hay•fe•ver,** *n.* running nose/eyes, etc., caused by an allergy to pollen or dust. **hay•field,** *n.* field of grass which will be cut to make hay. **hay•seed,** *n. inf.* unsophisticated country person. **hay•stack,** *n.* pile of hay, usu. cone shaped, stored outdoors. **hay•wire,** *adj. inf.* **he's gone h.** = he's gone mad.

haz•ard ['hæzəd] 1. *n.* (a) risk. (b) rough ground (on a golf course). 2. *v.* to risk; **he hazarded a guess** = he made a rough guess. **haz•ard•ous,** *adj.* dangerous/risky.

haze [heɪz] *n.* light mist. **ha•zi•ly,** *adv.* vaguely. **ha•zi•ness,** *n.* being hazy. **ha•zy,** *adj.* (-ier, -iest) (a) misty. (b) vague.

ha•zel ['heɪzl] 1. *n.* tree which bears small nuts. 2. *adj. & n.* light brown (color). **hazel nut,** *n.* nut from a hazel tree.

he [hiː] (a) *pronoun referring to a male person or animal;* **he is my father.** (b) *prefix meaning male;* **he-goat. he-man,** *n.* (*pl.* **he-men**) strong/virile man.

He *symbol for* helium.

head [hed] 1. *n.* (a) part of the body with brain, eyes, ears, mouth, etc., attached to the rest of the body by the neck; **the horse won by a h.** = by the length of a head; **h. over heels** = with the head first; **to fall h. over heels down the stairs.** (b) brain; **a good h. for figures.** (c) top; leafy part (of a cabbage); foam (on the top of a glass of beer). (d) first one (of a group/a procession). (e) most important person; **h. waiter.** (f) **heads** *n. pl.* = top side of a coin; **to play heads or tails** = to spin a coin and try to guess which side will be on top. (g) part of a machine which records/picks up data (as on a tape recorder/computer). (h) (*no pl.*) number of animals; **fifty h. of sheep.** 2. *v.* (a) to be first/to lead. (b) to go **toward.** (c) (*soccer*) to hit (a ball) with your head. **head•ache,** *n.* (a) pain

---

æ back, ɑː farm, ɒ top, aɪ pipe, aʊ how, aɪə fire, aʊə flower, ɔː bought, ɔɪ toy, e fed, eəhair, eɪ take, ə afraid, əʊ boat, əʊə lower, ɜː word, iː heap, ɪ hit, ɪə hear, uː school, ʊ book, ʌ but, b back, d dog, ð then, dʒ just, f fog, g go, h hand, j yes, k catch, l last, m mix, n nut, ŋ sing, p penny, r round, s some, ʃ short, t too, tʃ chop, θ thing, v voice, w was, z zoo, ʒ treasure

in the head. (b) complicated problem. **head•board,** *n.* board/panel at the top of a bed. **head•dress,** *n.* ornamental covering for the head. **head•er,** *n.* (a) dive. (b) (*soccer*) hitting a ball with the head. **head first,** *adv.* with one's head first. **head•gear,** *n.* hat or cap. **head•hunt,** *v.* to look for candidates for important jobs. **head•hunt•er,** *n.* (a) member of a tribe which cuts off the heads of enemies and collects them. (b) *inf.* person who tries to find suitably qualified candidates for important jobs. **head•ing,** *n.* words at the top of a text. **head•lamp,** *n.* headlight. **head•land,** *n.* (a) promontory. (b) land at the edge of a field, where the tractor turns. **head•less,** *adj.* with no head. **head•light,** *n.* main light on the front of a car/bicycle, etc. **head•line,** *n.* words in large capitals in a newspaper; **news headlines** = short summary of the main items of news on TV/radio. **head•line rate,** *n.* rate of inflation/interest/taxation, etc. before adjustment to allow for distorting factors. **head•long,** *adj. & adv.* rushing/non-stop; with your head first. **head•mas•ter,** *n.* man in charge of a private school. **head•mis•tress,** *n.* woman in charge of a private school. **head off,** *v.* to prevent (sth) from taking place. **head-on,** *adj. & adv.* with the front; head first. **head•phones,** *n. pl.* apparatus for listening to radio/records, etc., which fits over your ears. **head•quar•ters,** *n. pl.* main offices (of a military force/company). **head•rest,** *n.* cushion/part of a seat for leaning your head on. **head•room,** *n.* space to pass upright. **head•scarf,** *n.* (*pl.* **-scarves**) square piece of cloth worn by women to cover their hair. **head•set,** *n.* apparatus for listening to radio/records, etc., which fits over your ears with a band across the top of your head. **head•ship,** *n.* position of headmaster/headmistress. **head•stone,** *n.* gravestone. **head•strong,** *adj.* obstinate/self-willed. **head•way,** *n.* progress/movement forward. **head•wind,** *n.* wind blowing in your face. **head•word,** *n.* main word in a dictionary. **head•y,** *adj.* (**-ier, -iest**) (drink) which is likely to make you drunk; (news) which is likely to make you excited.

heal [hiːl] *v.* to make (a person/a wound) become healthy; to become healthy. **heal•ing,** *n.* making healthy.

health [helθ] *n.* (a) state of the body where there is no sickness; **h. foods** = natural foods (such as yogurt/nuts, etc.) which are good for your health. (b) general state of the body. **health•i•ly,** *adv.* in a healthy way. **health•i•ness** *n.* being healthy. **health•y,** *adj.* (a) full of good health/not ill. (b) which gives good health. (c) strong (dislike, etc.).

heap [hiːp] 1. *n.* large pile; *inf.* **heaps** = lots. 2. *v.* to put in a pile.

hear ['hɪə] *v.* (**heard** [hɜːʳd]) to sense sounds by the ear; to listen to (sth); **he's never heard of it** = does not know about it; **he won't h. of it** = he will not allow it. **hear•er,** *n.* person who hears. **hear hear!** *inter. used to show agreement.* **hear•ing,** *n.* (a) ability to hear; **h. aid** = small device for improving the hearing of s.o. who is nearly deaf; **h. dog** = dog that is specially trained to alert deaf people to sounds, e.g. alarms. (b) listening to s.o. (c) court case. **hear•say,** *n.* what people say, rather than what is true.

heard [hɜːd] *v. see* **hear.**

hearse [hɜːs] *n.* vehicle for carrying a coffin.

heart [hɑːt] *n.* (a) organ in an animal which pumps blood round the body; **h. attack** = severe illness when the heart stops temporarily; **h. failure** = dangerous condition when the heart has stopped beating; **to learn by h.** = learn by memory so that you can repeat it. (b) center of the emotions; **with all my h.** = with great emotion. (c) center (of a town/forest). (d) courage; **to lose h.** = to become discouraged; **to take h.** = to be encouraged. (e) **hearts** = one of the four suits of playing cards. **heart•beat,** *n.* sound of the heart pumping blood. **heart-break•ing** *adj.* which makes you very sad/upset. **heart-bro•ken,** *adj.* extremely sad/disappointed. **heart•burn,** *n.* burning feeling in the chest and stomach after eating indigestible food. **heart•en,** *v.* to encourage. **heart•felt,** *adj.* sincere. **heart•i•ly,** *adv.* vigorously; warmly. **heart•i•ness,** *n.* being hearty. **heart•land,** *n.* central part of a country. **heart•less,** *adj.* cruel. **heart•less•ly,** *adv.* in a heartless way. **heart-rend•ing,** *adj.* pitiful. **heart•strings,** *n. pl.* deepest feelings (of pity/love, etc.). **heart-throb,** *n.* popular film-star, etc. **heart-to-heart,** *adj.* earnest private (conversation). **heart•warm•ing,** *adj.* which encourages/pleases. **heart•y,** *adj.* (**-ier, -iest**) vigorous/strong; large (meal/appetite).

hearth [hɑːθ] *n.* floor of a fireplace; fireplace. **hearth•rug,** *n.* small rug placed in front of a fireplace.

heat [hiːt] 1. *n.* (a) great warmth. (b) qualifying round in a competition; **dead h.** = race where two competitors reach the finish line at the same time. (c) (*of female animal*) **in h.** = sexually excited. 2. *v.* to warm to a higher temperature; **heated discussion** = discussion where people become quite angry. **heat•ed•ly,** *adv.*

angrily. **heat•er**, *n.* apparatus for warming. **heat•ing**, *n.* making sth warm; means of heating; **central h.** = heating system for a whole building from one source. **heat•wave**, *n.* period of very hot weather.

heath [hi:θ] *n.* (a) area of wild country covered with low shrubs. (b) heather.

heath•en ['hi:ðn] *adj. & n.* (person) who is not a Christian; (person) who is not a member of any important religious group.

heath•er ['heðə] *n.* wild plant with small purple or white bell-shaped flowers, which grows on moors and mountains in England and Scotland.

heave [hi:v] 1. *n.* hard pull. 2. *v.* (**heaved**) (a) to pull hard. (b) (**hove**) **to h. to** = to stop a ship; **to h. in sight** = to appear. (c) *inf.* to throw. (d) to breathe noisily.

heav•en ['hevn] *n.* paradise/place where God and the angels live; **the heavens** = the sky; **good heavens!** = how surprising! **heav•en•ly**, *adj.* (a) belonging to heaven. (b) *inf.* beautiful; very fine. **heav•en-sent**, *adj.* coming at an opportune time; lucky.

heav•y ['hevɪ] *adj.* (**-ier, -iest**) (a) weighing a lot; (meal) which is very filling and indigestible. (b) strong/great. (c) rough (sea). (d) full (schedule, etc.). (e) **h. drinker** = person who drinks a lot of alcohol. **heav•i•ly**, *adv.* (a) as if weighing a lot. (b) greatly; **h. underlined** = with thick lines put underneath. (c) (to sleep) soundly. **heav•i•ness**, *n.* being heavy. **heav•y-du•ty**, *adj.* (machine, etc.) specially made for rough work. **heav•y in•dus•try**, *n.* industry which makes large products (like steel/ships/cars, etc.). **heav•y wa•ter**, *n.* water containing deuterium in place of hydrogen. **heav•y•weight**, *n.* heaviest category of boxer.

He•brew ['hi:bru:] *n.* (a) member of Jewish people living in ancient Palestine. (b) language of the Jews.

heck•le ['hekl] *v.* to call out; to interrupt a public speaker. **heck•ler**, *n.* person who interrupts a speaker at a meeting. **heck•ling**, *n.* interrupting a speaker.

hect-, hecto- ['hekt(əʊ)] *prefix meaning* one hundred. **hec•to•li•ter**, *n.* one hundred liters.

hec•tare ['hektɑ:] *n.* (measure of) area of 10,000 square meters (approx. 2.4 acres).

hec•tic ['hektɪk] *adj.* very busy/active. **hec•ti•cal•ly**, *adv.* in a hectic way.

hec•tor ['hektə] *v.* to bully/to intimidate. **hec•tor•ing**, *adj.* bullying (tone of voice).

hedge [hedʒ] 1. *n.* (a) screen/fence made of growing shrubs. (b) protection (**against**). 2. *v.* (a) to surround with a hedge. (b) to avoid answering a question. (c) **to h. your bets** = to arrange things so that you will be protected against losing. **hedge•hog**, *n.* small mammal covered with prickles. **hedge•row**, *n.* row of shrubs forming a hedge. **hedge spar•row**, *n.* common sparrow found in the country.

he•don•ist ['hi:dənɪst] *n.* person who lives for pleasure. **he•don•is•tic**, *adj.* like a hedonist.

heed [hi:d] 1. *n.* **to take h. of/to pay h. to** = to pay attention to. 2. *v.* to pay attention to. **heed•less**, *adj.* careless/imprudent; without paying attention. **heed•less•ly**, *adv.* in a heedless way.

heel [hi:l] 1. *n.* (a) back part of the foot; back part of a sock/stocking into which the heel of the foot goes; **to take to one's heels** = to run away. (b) raised block under the back of a shoe. (c) *Sl.* unpleasant person. 2. *v.* to put a new heel on (a shoe). (b) (*of a ship*) **to h. over** = to lean to one side.

heft•y ['heftɪ] *adj.* (**-ier, -iest**) large/strong.

he•gem•o•ny [hɪ'gemənɪ] *n.* leadership by one country.

heif•er ['hefə] *n.* young cow.

height [haɪt] *n.* (a) measurement of how tall or high sth is. (b) highest point. **height•en**, *v.* to increase/to make more noticeable.

hei•nous ['heɪnəs] *adj.* wicked (crime).

heir, heiress ['eə, eə'res] *n.* person who is going to inherit money, etc., from s.o. **heir•loom**, *n.* valuable object which has belonged to a family for years.

held [held] *v. see* **hold.**

hel•i•cal ['helɪkl] *adj. see* **he•lix.**

hel•i•cop•ter ['helɪkɒptə] *n.* type of aircraft with revolving blades on top, enabling it to take off vertically. **hel•i•pad**, *n.* small marked area where a helicopter may land. **hel•i•port**, *n.* place where helicopters land and take off.

he•li•o•graph ['hi:lɪəgrɑːf] *n.* apparatus for signaling, using mirrors which flash in the sun.

he•li•o•trope ['hi:lɪətrəʊp] *n. & adj.* plant with purple flowers; purple (color).

æ back, ɑ: farm, ɒ: top, aɪ pipe, aʊ how, aɪə fire, aʊə flower, ɔ: bought, ɔɪ toy, e fed, eəhair, eɪ take, ə afraid, əʊ boat, əʊə lower, v: word, i: heap, ɪ hit, ɪə hear, u: school, ʊ book, ʌ but, b back, d dog, ð then, dʒ just, f fog, g go, h hand, j yes, k catch, l last, m mix, n nut, ŋ sing, p penny, r round, s some, ʃ short, t too, tʃ chop, θ thing, v voice, w was, z zoo, ʒ treasure

he•li•um ['hiːlɪəm] n. (element: He) light gas which does not burn.

he•lix ['hiːlɪks] n. spiral shape. **hel•i•cal** ['helɪkl] adj. spiral.

hell [hel] n. (a) place where devils live and wicked people are punished after death. (b) inf. **a h. of a noise** = a very loud noise; **one h. of a party** = a very good party; **to give s.o. h.** = to make life difficult for s.o.; Sl. **what the h.?** = what on earth? **hell-bent on**, adj. inf. very determined to do sth. **hell•ish**, adj. like hell; inf. unbearable.

hel•le•bore ['helɪbɔ:] n. winter plant with greenish white flowers.

Hel•len•ic [he'lenɪk] adj. referring to Greece.

hel•lo [hə'ləu] inter. showing a greeting.

helm [helm] n. wheel or handle connecting to the rudder of a ship; **at the h.** = in charge. **helms•man**, n. (pl. -men) person who is steering a ship.

hel•met ['helmət] n. metal or plastic hat used as a protection; **crash h.** = helmet worn by motorcyclists.

help [help] 1. n. (a) aid/assistance. (b) person who helps. 2. v. (a) to aid (s.o.)/to come to s.o.'s assistance. (b) **to h. yourself** = to serve yourself; inf. **to h. yourself to** = to take without asking; steal. (c) **can't h. doing sth** = can't stop (doing sth)/can't avoid (sth). **help•er**, n. person who helps. **help•ful**, adj. (person) who helps; (thing) which is useful. **help•ful•ly**, adv. in a helpful way. **help•ful•ness**, n. being helpful. **help•ing**. 1. adj. which helps. 2. n. serving/portion (of food). **help•less**, adj. weak/unable to help yourself. **help•less•ly**, adv. unable to help. **help•less•ness**, n. being helpless. **help•mate**, n. helper. **help out**, v. to come to (s.o.'s) assistance in an emergency.

hel•ter-skel•ter ['heltə'skeltə] adv. in a confused rush.

hem [hem] 1. n. sewn edge on a piece of cloth/a skirt/tablecloth/handkerchief, etc. 2. v. (**hemmed**) (a) to sew a hem. (b) **to h. in** = to enclose. (c) **to h. and haw** = to have difficulty in making up your mind. **hem•line**, n. bottom edge of a dress/skirt, etc. **hem•stitch**. 1. n. stitch used in a hem. 2. v. to sew a hem using a hemstitch.

he•ma•tite ['hiːmətaɪt] n. iron ore.

hemi- ['hemɪ] prefix half. **hem•i•ple•gi•a**, n. paralysis affecting one side of the body.

hem•i•sphere ['hemɪsfɪə] n. half a sphere, esp. half of the earth's globe; **northern h./southern h.** = parts of the earth north and south of the equator. **hem•i•spher•i•cal** [hemɪ'sferɪkl] adj. shaped like half a sphere.

hem•lock ['hemlɒk] n. (a) common poisonous plant. (b) type of American evergreen tree.

he•mo•glo•bin [hiːmə'gləubɪn] n. substance in red blood cells which contains iron and carries oxygen.

he•mo•phil•i•a [hiːmə'fɪlɪə] n. hereditary disease, esp. in males, which prevents blood from clotting. **he•mo•phil•i•ac**, n. person suffering from hemophilia.

hem•or•rhage ['hemərɪdʒ] 1. n. loss of much blood, usu. internally. 2. v. to suffer a hemorrhage.

hem•or•rhoids ['hemərɔɪdz] n. pl. small swollen veins at the anus.

hemp [hemp] n. tropical plant, which gives rough fibers for making sacks/ropes, etc., and which also provides a drug. **hemp•en**, adj. (formal) made of hemp.

hen [hen] n. (a) female chicken. (b) female bird; inf. **h. party** = party for women only. **hen•house**, n. place for keeping chickens in. **hen•pecked**, adj. (husband) whose wife nags him continuously and tells him what to do.

hence [hens] adv. (a) from this time; **five years h.** (b) for this reason. **hence•forth, henceforward**, adv. from now on.

hench•man ['hentʃmən] n. (pl. -men) helper/accomplice (of a criminal).

hen•na ['henə] n. red dye used to color hair. **hen•naed** ['henəd] adj. (hair) colored with henna.

hep•a•ti•tis [hepə'taɪtɪs] n. disease of the liver.

hep•ta•gon ['heptəgən] n. geometrical figure with seven sides. **hep•tag•o•nal** [hep'tægənl] adj. seven-sided.

her [hɜ:] 1. pronoun referring to a female; object form of she; **have you seen her?** 2. adj. belonging to a female; **have you seen her brother?**

her•ald ['herəld] 1. n. messenger sent to announce sth. 2. v. to be a sign that sth is approaching; to announce. **he•ral•dic** [he'rældɪk] adj. referring to heraldry. **her•ald•ry** ['herəldrɪ] n. study of coats of arms.

herb [hɜ:b] n. tasty or pungent plant used in cooking or as a medicine. **her•ba•ceous border** [hɜ:'beɪʃəs 'bɔ:də] n. flowerbed planted with flowers which sprout up again every year. **herb•age**, n. grass or other green plants. **herb•al**, adj. containing/using herbs. **herb•al•ist**, n. person who sells herbs as medicines. **her•bar•i•um**, n. collection of dried plants arranged systematically. **herb•i•cide**, n. substance which kills weeds. **her•biv•ore** ['hɜ:bɪvɔ:] n. animal which eats plants. **her•biv•o•rous** [hɜː'bɪvərəs] *adj.* (animal) which eats plants.

her•cu•le•an [hɜːkjuː'liːən] *adj.* showing great strength; (task) which needs great effort.

herd [hɜːd] 1. *n.* group of animals; **h. instinct** = tendency of people to do what others do. 2. *v.* to form/to make into a group. **herds•man**, *n.* (*pl.* **-men**) man who looks after a herd of cows, etc.

here ['hɪə] *adv.* to/in this place. **here•a•bouts**, *adv.* around about here/in this area. **here•af•ter**, *adv.* from this time on. **here•by**, *adv.* (*formal*) in this way. **here•to**, *adv.* to this. **here•with** [hɪə'wɪθ] *adv.* with this.

he•red•i•ty [hɪ'redɪtɪ] *n.* passing on of characteristics from parent to child. **her•e•dit•a•ment**, *n.* property which can be inherited. **he•red•i•tar•y**, *adj.* which is passed on from parent to child.

her•e•sy ['herəsɪ] *n.* heretical belief. **her•e•tic**, *n.* person who does not hold generally accepted religious beliefs. **he•ret•i•cal** [hə'retɪkl] *adj.* (belief) which is not generally accepted/which is condemned by the church.

her•it•age ['herɪtɪdʒ] *n.* thing which is passed on from one generation to the next.

her•maph•ro•dite [hɜː'mæfrədaɪt] *n.* animal/plant which is both male and female.

her•met•ic [hɜː'metɪk] *adj.* sealed; airtight. **her•met•i•cal•ly**, *adv.* (sealed) tightly so that no air can get in.

her•mit ['hɜːmɪt] *n.* person who lives alone and refuses to see other people; **h. crab** = small crab which lives in empty sea shells. **her•mit•age**, *n.* place where a hermit lives; secluded place.

her•ni•a ['hɜːnɪə] *n.* condition where part of the bowel has pushed through a weak place in the wall of the abdomen.

he•ro, heroine ['hɪərəʊ, 'herəʊɪn] *n.* (*pl.* **-oes**) person who does brave deeds; main character in a book/motion picture, etc. **he•ro•ic** [hɪ'rəʊɪk] *adj.* brave/like a hero. **he•ro•i•cal•ly**, *adv.* like a hero. **her•o•ism** ['herəʊɪzəm] *n.* bravery.

her•o•in ['herəʊɪn] *n.* drug made from poppies.

her•on ['herən] *n.* common water bird with long legs and neck.

her•pes ['hɜːpiːz] *n.* disease which gives blisters on the skin.

her•ring ['herɪŋ] *n.* common sea fish; **red h.** = distraction/false lead. **herring-bone**, *adj.* (pattern) in a zigzag. **herring gull**, *n.* common large gray and white gull.

hers [hɜːz] *adj.* belonging to her. **her•self** [hɜː-'self] *pronoun referring to a female subject;* **she was washing h.; all by h.; she wrote to me h.**

hertz [hɜːts] *n.* (*no pl.*) standard unit of frequency of radio waves.

hes•i•tate ['hezɪteɪt] *v.* to stop for a moment; to be unable to decide. **hes•i•tance, hesi•tancy**, *n.* being hesitant. **hes•i•tant**, *adj.* doubtful/undecided. **hes•i•tant•ly**, *adv.* in a hesitant way. **hes•i•ta•tion** [hezɪ'teɪʃn] *n.* indecision/doubt.

hes•sian ['hesɪən] *n.* rough cloth like burlap.

het•er•o•ge•ne•ous [hetərəʊ'dʒiːnjəs] *adj.* of varied sorts.

het•er•o•sex•u•al [hetərəʊ'seksjʊəl] *adj. & n.* (person) who is attracted to people of the opposite sex.

het up ['het 'ʌp] *adj. inf.* excited; anxious.

heu•ris•tic [hjuː'rɪstɪk] *adj.* which stimulates interest or investigation.

hew [hjuː] *v.* (**hewn**) to carve/to cut.

hex•a•gon ['heksəgən] *n.* geometrical figure with six sides. **hex•a•gon•al** [hek'sægənl] *adj.* six-sided.

hex•am•e•ter [hek'sæmɪtə] *n.* line of poetry with six beats.

hey [heɪ] *inter. showing a greeting/surprise.*

hey•day ['heɪdeɪ] *n.* period of greatest glory/success/power.

Hg *symbol for* mercury.

hi [haɪ] *inter. showing a greeting.*

hi•a•tus [haɪ'eɪtəs] *n.* (*pl.* **-uses**) gap/interruption.

hi•ber•nate ['haɪbəneɪt] *v.* (*of animals*) to sleep during the winter. **hi•ber•na•tion** [haɪbə'neɪʃn] *n.* spending the winter asleep.

hi•bis•cus [hɪ'bɪskəs] *n.* tropical shrub with large trumpet-shaped flowers.

hic•cup, hiccough ['hɪkʌp] 1. *n.* repeated spasm in the throat like a small cough. 2. *v.* (**hiccuped, hiccupped**) to make a loud noise because of a hiccup.

hick [hɪk] *n. inf.* stupid person from the country.

hick•o•ry ['hɪkərɪ] *n.* North American tree like a walnut.

hid, hidden [hɪd, 'hɪdn] *v. see* **hide.**

hide [haɪd] 1. *n.* leather; whole skin of an animal. 2. *v.* (**hid, has hidden**) to be out of sight; to

---

æ back, ɑː farm, ɒ top, aɪ pipe, aʊ how, aɪə fire, aʊə flower, ɔː bought, ɔɪ toy, e fed, eəhair, eɪ take, ə afraid, əʊ boat, əʊə lower, ɜː word, iː heap, ɪ hit, ɪə hear, uː school, ʊ book, ʌ but, b back, d dog, ð then, dʒ just, f fog, g go, h hand, j yes, k catch, l lull, m mix, n nut, ŋ sing, p penny, r round, s some, ʃ short, t too, tʃ chop, θ thing, v voice, w was, z zoo, ʒ treasure

put (a thing) somewhere so that no one can see it. **hide-and-seek,** *n.* children's game, where some hide and the others try to find them. **hide•bound,** *adj.* unwilling to change ideas/narrow-minded. **hide-out,** *n.* secret place where you cannot be found. **hid•ing,** *n.* (a) putting yourself/sth out of sight. (b) *inf.* beating/whipping.

hid•e•ous ['hɪdɪəs] *adj.* horribly ugly. **hid•e•ous•ly,** *adv.* in a hideous way. **hid•e•ous•ness,** *n.* being hideous.

hi•er•ar•chy ['haɪərɑːkɪ] *n.* arrangement in a system of ranks/grades. **hi•er•ar•chi•cal** [haɪə'rɑːkɪkl] *adj.* arranged in a set system of ranks.

hi•er•o•glyph•ics [haɪərəʊ'glɪfɪks] *n. pl.* system of picture writing used by the ancient Egyptians. **hi•er•o•glyph,** *n.* symbol used in hieroglyphics.

hi-fi ['haɪ'faɪ] *adj. & n. inf.* high fidelity radio/stereo (equipment).

hig•gle•dy-pig•gle•dy [hɪgldɪ'pɪgldɪ] *adv.* in disorder/all over the place.

high [haɪ] 1. *adj.* (-er, -est) (a) going far above; tall. (b) great (rank, price, etc.); **h. fidelity** = (radio equipment) which gives excellent reproduction of sound. (c) shrill (note). (d) (*of meat*) going rotten. (e) main; most important. (f) powerful (explosive). (g) *inf.* influenced by drugs. 2. *adv.* (-er, -est) (a) far above. (b) to a great degree. 3. *n.* (a) high-pressure zone in the atmosphere. (b) **an all-time h.** = the highest point ever reached. (c) *inf.* state of intoxication produced by a drug, etc. **high•ball,** *n.* whiskey and soda. **high•brow,** *adj. & n.* intellectual (person). **high chair,** *n.* small chair with very long legs for a baby to sit in to eat. **High Church,** *adj. & n.* (part of the Anglican Church) which regards ritual as very important. **high-fa•lu•tin,** *adj. inf.* which sounds/looks imposing. **high-fi•del•i•ty,** *adj.* which produces sound of a very high quality. **high fli•er, high flyer,** *n.* extravagant, as in goals, ideas, or tastes. **high-hand•ed,** *adj.* (action) done without considering other people. **high•land,** *adj.* coming from the highlands/from a mountain region. **High•land•er,** *n.* person who lives in the Highlands of Scotland. **High•lands,** *n. pl.* mountain region, esp. in northern Scotland. **high•light.** 1. *n.* most interesting event. 2. *v.* to accentuate/to draw attention to. **high•ly,** *adv.* very/greatly. **high-mind•ed,** *adj.* noble/very serious. **high•ness,** *n.* (a) being high/being above other things. (b) title given to princes, etc. **high-pitched,** *adj.* sharp/shrill (sound); steep (roof). **high-pow•ered,** *adj.* very powerful (en-

gine). **high priest,** *n.* most important priest. **high-rise,** *adj.* (building) with many floors. **high school,** *n.* school attended after elementary school or junior high school which includes the ninth or tenth grade through twelfth grade. **high seas,** *n. pl.* the oceans. **high sea•son,** *n.* most popular season for vacation travel. **high-speed,** *adj.* which goes/works very fast. **high-spirit•ed,** *adj.* lively. **high spot,** *n.* most enjoyable part of an entertainment. **high-strung,** *adj.* very emotional/excitable. **high tea,** *n.* (*in North of England and Scotland*) large meal of tea, cold meat, cakes, etc., eaten in the early evening. **high•wa•ter mark,** *n.* highest point (reached by the tide/by sth advancing). **high•way,** *n.* main road. **high•way•man,** *n.* (*pl.* -men) person who attacked travelers and robbed them.

hi•jack ['haɪdʒæk] *v.* to take control of (an aircraft/a train, etc.) with passengers on board, by threatening the pilot/driver. **hi•jack•er,** *n.* person who hijacks.

hike [haɪk] 1. *n.* (a) strenuous walk. (b) increase (in price, etc.). 2. *v.* (a) to go for a strenuous walk. (b) to increase (prices, etc.). **hik•er,** *n.* person who goes for long walks. **hik•ing,** *n.* walking as a relaxation.

hi•lar•i•ous [hɪ'leərɪəs] *adj.* very funny/very happy. **hi•lar•i•ous•ly,** *adv.* in a very funny way. **hi•lar•i•ty** [hɪ'lærɪtɪ] *n.* great laughter.

hill [hɪl] *n.* rise in the land, lower than a mountain. **hill•bil•ly,** *n.* person who lives in a remote area. **h. music** = country style music. **hill•ock,** *n.* little hill. **hill•side,** *n.* side of a hill. **hill•y,** *adj.* (-ier, -iest) (region) with many hills.

hilt [hɪlt] *n.* protective shield on the handle of a sword; **to the h.** = totally.

him [hɪm] *pronoun referring to a male; object form of* he; **have you seen h.?** **him•self** [hɪm-'self] *pronoun referring to a male subject;* **he was washing h.; he is all by h.; he wrote to me h.**

hind [haɪnd] 1. *n.* female red deer. 2. *adj.* **h. legs** = back legs (of an animal).

hind•er ['hɪndə] *v.* to prevent (s.o.) from doing sth. **hin•drance,** *n.* obstacle.

hind•most ['haɪndməʊst] *adj.* furthest back.

hind•sight ['haɪndsaɪt] *n.* knowing facts about an event in the past which could have been useful if they had been known at the time.

Hin•du ['hɪnduː] *adj. & n.* (person) following the main religion of India. **Hin•di,** *n.* language spoken in the central part of India.

hinge [hɪndʒ] 1. *n.* (a) metal bracket on which a door/a window hangs and opens. (b) small piece of gummed paper for sticking stamps into a stamp album. 2. *v.* to center/to depend (on). **hinged,** *adj.* with hinges.

hint [hɪnt] 1. *n.* (a) hidden suggestion/clue. (b) sign. (c) **hints** = helpful advice. 2. *v.* to suggest/to insinuate.

hin•ter•land ['hɪntəlænd] *n.* area inland from a sea port/around a large town.

hip [hɪp] *n.* (a) projecting bone where the legs join the body; wide part of the body where the legs join it. (b) fruit of a wild rose. (c) **h. h. hooray!** = *words used to give a cheer.* **hipped,** *adj.* (roof) which breaks at an angle.

hip•pie ['hɪpɪ] *n. inf.* person who lives/dresses in a different way from the majority of people in society.

hip•po•pot•a•mus, *inf.* **hip•po** [hɪpə'pɒtəməs, 'hɪpəʊ] *n.* (*pl.* **-muses, -mi** [-maɪ]; **-os**) very large African animal living in water and mud.

hire ['haɪə] 1. *n.* renting (of a car, etc.) usu. for a short time. 2. *v.* to rent (a car, etc.); to engage the services of (s.o.); **to h. out** = to offer one's services for a fee. **hire•ling,** *n.* person who is hired to do a job. **hir•er,** *n.* person who hires.

hir•sute ['hɜːsjuːt] *adj.* covered with hair.

his [hɪz] *adj.* (a) belonging to a male. (b) belonging to him; **a friend of h.**

His•pa•no [hɪs'pɑːnəʊ] *prefix meaning* between Spain and another country. **His•pan•ic,** *n.* person living in the United States who is of Spanish or Latin American descent.

hiss [hɪs] 1. *n.* whistling sound like an "s," made by snakes/by gas escaping, etc.; similar sound made to show you do not like sth. 2. *v.* to make a hissing sound.

his•ta•mine ['hɪstəmiːn] *n.* substance which causes an allergy.

his•tol•o•gy [hɪ'stɒlədʒɪ] *n.* science of body cells. **his•tol•o•gist,** *n.* person who specializes in histology.

his•to•ry ['hɪstərɪ] *n.* (a) study of the past; story of what happened in the past. (b) **natural h.** = study of animals and plants. **his•to•ri•an** [hɪ'stɔːrɪən] *n.* person who studies or writes about the past. **his•tor•ic** [hɪ'stɒrɪk] *adj.* (event) which is so important that it will be remembered. **his•tor•i•cal,** *adj.* referring to history; **h. novel** = novel set in the past. **his•tor•i•cal•ly,** *adv.* as in the past. **his•tri•on•ic** [hɪstrɪ'ɒnɪk] *adj.* referring to acting. **his•tri•on•ics,** *n. pl.* dramatic behavior.

hit [hɪt] 1. *n.* (a) blow; **he scored three hits** = he

hit the target three times. (b) song/play, etc. which is very popular. 2. *v.* (**hit; has hit**) (a) to knock against; to touch (sth) hard. (b) to affect (badly). **hit back,** *v.* to defend yourself against attack. **hit-man,** *n.* (*pl.* **-men**) person employed to kill/to hurt s.o. **hit off,** *v. inf.* **to hit it off with s.o.** = to get on well with s.o. **hit-or-miss,** *adj.* erratic/careless. **hit out,** *v.* (**at**) to try to attack (s.o.). **hit on,** *v.* to discover; **to h. o. a new restaurant.**

hitch [hɪtʃ] 1. *n.* awkward delay/unexpected stoppage. 2. *v.* (a) to pull **up.** (b) to hitch-hike. (c) to attach with a rope; *inf.* **to get hitched** = to get married. **hitch-hike,** *v.* to get a free ride in s.o.'s car, stopping the car by pointing your thumb. **hitch-hik•er,** *n.* person who hitch-hikes.

hith•er ['hɪðə] *adv.* (*formal*) to this place; **h. and thither** = all over the place; **h. and yon** = from here to another, farther, place. **hith•er•to,** *adv.* up till now.

HIV ['eɪtʃaɪ'viː] *n.* human immunodeficiency virus.

hive [haɪv] *n.* (a) box in which bees make their nest. (b) **hives** = sore red patches on the skin, usu. on the face.

hoard [hɔːd] 1. *n.* mass/store (of money/food, etc.) which has been collected. 2. *v.* to collect and store (money/food, etc.). **hoard•er,** *n.* person who buys food when supplies are low. **hoard•ing,** *n.* (a) buying food, etc., when supplies are low. (b) temporary fence made of rough planks.

hoar•frost ['hɔːfrɒst] *n.* white frost which covers trees/plants, etc.

hoarse [hɔːs] *adj.* rough (voice). **hoarse•ly,** *adv.* in a hoarse voice. **hoarse•ness,** *n.* roughness/harshness (of voice).

hoar•y ['hɔːrɪ] *adj.* (**-ier, -iest**) (a) (*formal*) white-haired. (b) *inf.* very old (joke).

hoax [həʊks] 1. *n.* trick. 2. *v.* to trick/to deceive. **hoax•er,** *n.* person who hoaxes.

hob [hɒb] *n.* shelf or ledge where a kettle or food can be put by the side of a fire for warmth.

hob•ble ['hɒbl] *v.* (a) to attach the legs of (a horse) so that it cannot move easily. (b) to walk with difficulty.

hob•by ['hɒbɪ] *n.* pastime; thing done as a relaxation. **hob•by•horse,** *n.* subject which s.o. always talks about.

hob•gob•lin [hɒb'gɒblɪn] *n.* goblin.

hob•nail ['hɒbneɪl] *n.* large nail used to protect

æ back, aː farm, ɒ top, aɪ pipe, aʊ how, aɪə fire, aʊə flower, ɔː bought, ɔɪ toy, e fed, eə hair, eɪ take, ə afraid, əʊ boat, əʊə lower, vː word, iː heap, ɪ hit, ɪə hear, uː school, ʊ book, ʌ but, b back, d dog, ð then, dʒ just, f fog, g go, h hand, j yes, k catch, l last, m mix, n nut, ŋ sing, p penny, r round, s some, ʃ short, t too, tʃ chop, θ thing, v voice, w was, z zoo, ʒ treasure

the soles of boots. **hob•nailed,** *adj.* (boots) with large metal nails.

hob•nob ['hɒbnɒb] *v.* **(hobnobbed)** *inf.* to be on friendly terms (**with** s.o. important).

ho•bo ['həʊbəʊ] *n.* person with no home or money.

hock [hɒk] *n.* (a) middle joint of an animal's leg; lower part of a leg of an animal used for food. (b) German white wine. (c) *Sl.* **in h.** = pawned.

hock•ey ['hɒkɪ] *n.* (a) team game played on grass with long curved sticks and a hard ball. (b) ice hockey.

ho•cus-po•cus ['həʊkəs'pəʊkəs] *n.* (a) meaningless words (used by magicians). (b) trickery.

hod [hɒd] *n.* (a) wooden container on the end of a pole, used by builders for carrying bricks. (b) metal container for coal.

hoe [həʊ] 1. *n.* garden tool with a blade on the end of a long handle. 2. *v.* to take out weeds/to loosen the soil with a hoe.

hog [hɒg] 1. *n.* domestic pig, raised for market; *inf.* **to go (the) whole h.** = to do sth completely. 2. *v.* **(hogged)** to monopolize.

hogs•head ['hɒgzhed] *n.* (a) large barrel. (b) liquid measure of about 63 gallons.

hoi pol•loi [hɔɪpə'lɔɪ] *n.* the ordinary people.

hoist [hɔɪst] 1. *n.* apparatus for lifting; goods lift. 2. *v.* to lift up.

hoi•ty-toi•ty ['hɔɪtɪ'tɔɪtɪ] *adj. inf.* snobbish; superior (air).

hold [həʊld] 1. *n.* (a) grip. (b) influence/power. (c) part of a ship/aircraft where cargo is carried. 2. *v.* **(held)** (a) to have in your hand, etc. (b) to contain. (c) to make (sth) take place. (d) to keep in (one's breath, a liquid). (e) to stay. (f) **to h. office** = to have a post (in a government). **hold back,** *v.* to keep back; not to go forward. **hold down,** *v.* to keep (sth) down; to work hard to keep (a job). **hold•er,** *n.* person or thing which holds. **hold forth,** *v.* to talk at great length. **hold•ing,** *n.* number of shares which you own; **h. company** = company formed to control shares in other companies. **hold off,** *v.* not to act. **hold on,** *v.* (a) to cling on to/to take a grip on (sth). (b) to wait. **hold out,** *v.* (a) to offer. (b) to last. **hold o•ver,** *v.* to postpone (sth). **hold up,** *v.* (a) to raise. (b) to support. (c) to hinder/to delay. (d) to attack and rob. **hold-up,** *n.* (a) delay; breakdown. (b) armed attack. **hold with,** *v. inf.* to accept/to agree with/approve of.

hole [həʊl] 1. *n.* opening/space. 2. *v.* (a) to make a hole in. (b) (in *golf*) to send (the ball) into the hole. **hole up,** *v. inf.* to hide away.

hol•i•day ['hɒlɪdeɪ] 1. *n.* period when you do not work, esp. a day when business is legally suspended to celebrate sth or to honor s.o. 2. *v.* (*esp. Brit.*) to go on vacation.

ho•li•ness ['həʊlɪnəs] *n. see* **ho•ly.**

ho•lis•tic [hɒ'lɪstɪk] *adj.* (attitude) which considers many sides to a problem; (medical treatment) which deals with the environment of the patient as well as the illness itself.

hol•ler ['hɒlə] *v. inf.* to shout.

hol•low ['hɒləʊ] 1. *n.* low-lying land; small depression in a flat surface. 2. *adj.* empty/with nothing inside; meaningless (success). 3. *v.* **to h. out** = to make (sth) hollow.

hol•ly ['hɒlɪ] *n.* very prickly evergreen bush with red berries.

hol•ly•hock ['hɒlɪhɒk] *n.* common garden flower which produces very tall spikes of blossom.

holm oak ['hɒlməʊk] *n.* evergreen oak found in temperate climates.

hol•o•caust ['hɒləkɔːst] *n.* destruction by fire.

hol•o•graph ['hɒləgrɑːf] *n.* letter, etc., written by hand by the person whose signature it bears. **hol•o•gram,** *n.* three-dimensional picture produced by lasers. **hol•og•ra•phy,** *n.* science of making holograms.

hol•ster ['həʊlstə] *n.* leather pouch for carrying a revolver.

ho•ly ['həʊlɪ] *adj.* (**-ier, -iest**) sacred (place); very pious (person); **h. orders** = being a priest. **ho•li•ness,** *n.* being holy; **his H.** = title given to the Pope. **Ho•ly Week,** *n.* the week which ends with Easter Sunday.

hom•age ['hɒmɪdʒ] *n.* (a) respect; **to pay h. to s.o.** = to show s.o. signs of respect. (b) (*formal*) duty/service (to a feudal lord).

home [həʊm] 1. *n.* (a) place where you live/place where you come from originally. (b) (*in sports*) **at h.** = playing on one's own sports field, etc. (c) house where people are looked after. 2. *adv.* to/at the place where you live; **to strike h.** = to hit the target. 3. *adj.* (a) referring to the place where you live. (b) not foreign; domestic. (c) (*in sports*) referring to the local team/the local sports field, etc.; (match) played by the local team on their own field, etc. 4. *v.* **to h. in on** = to go to a target. **home-grown,** *adj.* (vegetables) grown in the garden, not bought; (industry) which is developed in a country, and not imported. **home•land,** *n.* land which is the home of a people/one's native country. **home•less,** *adj.* with nowhere to live. **home•li•ness,** *n.* being homely. **home•ly,** *adj.* (a) simple; not ostentatious. (b) plain/ugly (person). **home-made,** *adj.* made at home/not bought. **home page,** *n.* page on the Internet that introduces a website and details its contents. **home run,** *n.* (*in baseball*) run made by a batter who touches all the bases. **home•sick,** *adj.* unhappy because of wanting to go home. **home•sick•ness,** *n.* feeling of being homesick. **home•stead,** *n.* house and its land and buildings. **home•ward,** *adj. & adv.* going toward home. **home•ward, homewards,** *adv.* toward home. **home•work,** *n.* work which children take from school to be done at home in the evening. **hom•ing,** *adj.* **h. pigeon** = pigeon trained to return to the place where it usually lives; **h. device** = device (on a missile) which guides it to the target.

hom•i•cide ['hɒmɪsaɪd] *n.* murder. **hom•i•cid•al** [hɒmɪ'saɪdl] *adj.* likely to murder.

hom•i•ly ['hɒmɪlɪ] *n.* sermon/talk, esp. one dealing with morality.

ho•me•op•a•thy [həʊmɪ'ɒpəθɪ] *n.* method of curing sick people by accustoming them to very small quantities of drugs which would normally make them ill. **ho•me•o•path** ['həʊmjəpæθ] *n.* doctor who practices homeopathy. **hom•e•o•path•ic,** *adj.* referring to homeopathy.

ho•mo•ge•ne•ous [hɒməʊ'dʒiːnɪəs] *adj.* of the same sort/quality (as other things). **ho•mo•ge•ne•i•ty** [hɒməʊdʒə'niːətɪ] *n.* being homogeneous.

ho•mog•e•nize [hə'mɒdʒənaɪz] *v.* to mix various parts until they become a single whole, to the cream mix the cream into milk. **ho•mog•e•ni•za•tion** [həmɒdʒənaɪ-'zeɪʃn] *n.* treatment of milk so that the cream does not separate.

hom•o•nym ['hɒmənɪm] *n.* word which is spelled and pronounced the same as another word but has a different meaning.

ho•mo•phone ['hɒməfəʊn] *n.* word which is pronounced the same as another, but has a different meaning and usu. spelling.

ho•mo•sex•u•al [həʊməʊ'seksjʊəl] *adj. & n.* (person) who is attracted to persons of the same sex as himself/herself. **ho•mo•sex•u•al•i•ty** [həʊməʊseksjʊ'ælɪtɪ] *n.* being homosexual.

hone [həʊn] *v.* to smooth/to sharpen (a blade).

hon•est ['ɒnɪst] *adj.* truthful; not cheating or stealing. **hon•est•ly,** *adv.* truthfully. **hon•es•ty,** *n.* (a) truthfulness. (b) garden flower with silvery seed cases, used as a winter decoration.

hon•ey ['hʌnɪ] *n.* sweet substance produced by bees. **honey-bee,** *n.* type of bee which makes honey. **hon•ey•comb,** *n.* construction of wax cells in which bees store honey; pattern of six-sided shapes like bees' cells. **hon•ey•combed,** *adj.* full of little holes. **hon•ey•dew,** *n.* type of melon which has green flesh. **hon•eyed,** *adj.* sweet/flattering (words). **hon•ey•moon.** 1. *n.* trip or vacation taken by a husband and wife immediately after their wedding. 2. *v.* to go on a honeymoon. **hon•ey•suck•le,** *n.* common climbing plant with scented yellow and pink flowers.

honk ['hɒŋk] 1. *n.* noise made by a goose/by a car horn. 2. *v.* to make a noise like a goose/a car horn.

hon•o•rar•i•um [ɒnə'reərɪəm] *n.* money paid to s.o. for work which is usually done free.

hon•or•ar•y ['ɒnərɪ] *adj.* given as a mark of respect or honor.

hon•or, *Brit.* **hon•our** ['ɒnə] 1. *n.* (a) self-respect. (b) mark of respect; title given as a mark of respect. (c) **honors course** = university course which involves independent research. (d) title given to a judge. 2. *v.* (a) to respect; to give a title/medal to (s.o.) as a mark of respect. (b) to pay (a bill); (*of a bank*) to pay (a check). **hon•or•a•ble,** *adj.* that can be respected. **hon•or•a•bly,** *adv.* in a way which you can respect.

hooch [huːtʃ] *n. Sl.* alcoholic drink.

hood [hʊd] *n.* (a) loose covering for the head, attached to a coat. (b) folding roof on a car or baby carriage. (c) lid covering the engine of a car. (d) *Sl.* gangster. **hood•ed,** *adj.* wearing a hood.

hood•lum ['huːdləm] *n.* thug/gangster.

hood•wink ['hʊdwɪŋk] *v.* to trick.

hoof [huːf] *n.* (*pl.* **hooves**) hard part of the foot of a horse, etc. **hoofed,** *adj.* (animal) which has hooves.

hoo-ha ['huːhɑː] *n. inf.* fuss/bother.

hook [hʊk] 1. *n.* (a) bent piece of metal used for holding or pulling, etc.; **to get s.o. off the h.** = to release s.o. from a difficult situation; **by h. or by crook** = by any means available; **h. and eye** = small hook and loop for fastening clothing. (b) very small, bent piece of metal used for catching fish. (c) (*in boxing*) blow/stroke made with the arm bent. 2. *v.* (a) to hang on a hook; to attach with a hook. (b) to catch (a fish) with a hook. **hooked,** *adj.* (a) shaped like a hook. (b) caught with/on a hook. (c) *inf.* **h. on** = very interested in (a book, etc.); addicted to (drugs). **hook•er,** *n. inf.* prostitute.

æ **back,** ɑː **farm,** ɒ: **top,** aɪ **pipe,** aʊ **how,** aɪə **fire,** aʊə **flower,** ɔ: **bought,** ɔɪ **toy,** e **fed,** eəhair, eɪ **take,** ə **afraid,** əʊ **boat,** əʊə **lower,** vː **word,** iː **heap,** ɪ **hit,** ɪə **hear,** uː **school,** ʊ **book,** ʌ **but,** b **back,** d **dog,** ð **then,** dʒ **just,** f **fog,** g **go,** h **hand,** j **yes,** k **catch,** l **last,** m **mix,** n **nut,** ŋ **sing,** p **penny,** r **round,** s **some,** ʃ **short,** t **too,** tʃ **chop,** θ **thing,** v **voice,** w **was,** z **zoo,** ʒ **treasure**

hook-up, n. radio or TV link. **hook•worm,** n. type of parasitic worm.

hook•ah ['hʊkə] n. tobacco pipe where the smoke is cooled by being passed through water.

hook•y, hookey ['hʊkɪ] n. **to play h.** = to avoid going to school.

hoo•li•gan ['huːlɪgən] n. rowdy wild person. **hoo•li•gan•ism,** n. wild behavior.

hoop [huːp] n. large ring of wood or metal. **hoop-la,** n. excitement; bustle.

hoo•poe ['huːpuː] n. large cream-colored bird with a crest.

hoo•ray [hʊ'reɪ] inter. showing great pleasure/excitement.

hoot [huːt] 1. n. call of an owl; **hoots of laughter** = sound like an owl call, made when you are laughing. 2. v. (of an owl) to call; **to h. with laughter** = laugh hilariously.

Hoo•ver ['huːvə] n. trademark for a type of vacuum cleaner.

hop [hɒp] 1. n. (a) little jump. (b) short flight (in a plane). (c) bitter fruit used in making beer; climbing plant which bears this fruit. 2. v. (**hopped**) to jump on one leg; (of birds) to jump with both feet together.

hope [həʊp] 1. n. expectation/wanting sth to happen. 2. v. to expect that sth will happen; to want sth to happen. **hope•ful,** adj. full of hope/confident; giving hope; **h. signs. hope•ful•ly,** adv. (a) confidently. (b) **h. the rain will stop** = let's hope/I hope it will stop. **hope•less,** adj. with no hope; **he's h. at chess** = he plays very badly. **hope•less•ly,** adv. with no hope. **hope•less•ness,** n. being hopeless.

hop•per ['hɒpə] n. very large funnel for channeling loose material (like sand/corn, etc.).

hop•sack•ing ['hɒpsækɪŋ] (also **hopsack**) n. thick rough material.

hop•scotch ['hɒpskɒtʃ] n. children's game in which you hop over marked squares on the ground.

horde [hɔːd] n. crowd/mass.

ho•ri•zon [hə'raɪzn] n. (a) line where the earth seems to meet the sky. (b) layer of soil.

hor•i•zon•tal [hɒrɪ'zɒntl] adj. lying flat/not upright. **hor•i•zon•tal•ly,** adv. lying flat.

hor•mone ['hɔːməʊn] n. substance produced by glands in the body, which causes various physical reactions. **hor•mo•nal,** adj. referring to hormones.

horn [hɔːn] n. (a) hard bony growth on the head of some animals. (b) feeler on a snail's head. (c) brass musical instrument shaped like an animal's horn. (d) instrument on a car, etc., which makes a loud warning noise. **horned,** adj. with horns. **horn in (on),** v. inf. to join

(a meeting) uninvited. **horn•pipe,** n. vigorous dance danced by sailors. **horn•rimmed,** adj. (glasses) with tortoiseshell or tortoise-shell-like frames. **horn•y,** adj. hard/rough (hands).

horn•beam ['hɔːnbiːm] n. common hedgerow tree.

hor•net ['hɔːnɪt] n. large red wasp.

ho•rol•o•gy [hɒ'rɒlədʒɪ] n. study of time and clocks.

hor•o•scope ['hɒrəskəʊp] n. description of a person's character/forecasting of what will happen to a person in the future, based on the position of the stars when he or she was born.

hor•ren•dous [hɒ'rendəs] adj. horrible; dreadful.

hor•ri•ble ['hɒrəbl] adj. terrible/frightening. **hor•ri•bly,** adv. frighteningly/badly. **hor•rid** ['hɒrɪd] adj. offensive/unpleasant. **hor•ri•fic** [hə'rɪfɪk] adj. frightening/shocking. **hor•ri•fi•cal•ly,** adv. in a horrific way. **hor•ri•fy** ['hɒrɪfaɪ] v. to make (s.o.) very frightened/to shock (s.o.).

hor•ror ['hɒrə] n. terror/feeling of being very frightened; **h. film** = film which aims to frighten the audience. **horror-struck, horror-stricken,** adj. very frightened.

hors-d'œu•vre [ɔː'dɜːv] n. pl. cold food served at the beginning of a meal.

horse [hɔːs] 1. n. (a) large animal with hooves, which is used for riding or pulling vehicles; **h. racing** = racing of horses; **dark h.** = person you know nothing about and who may win; inf. **straight from the horse's mouth** = from a very reliable source. (b) apparatus made of wood over which you jump in gymnastics. (c) **clothes h.** = wooden frame used for drying clothes. 2. v. **to h. around** = to play roughly. **horse•back,** n. **on h.** = riding on a horse. **horse-chest•nut,** n. type of large tree; shiny inedible nut of this tree. **horse•fly,** n. large fly which bites animals. **horse•hair,** n. hair from the mane or tail of a horse, used for padding furniture. **horse laugh,** n. loud unpleasant laugh. **horse•man,** n. (pl. **-men**) person riding a horse; person skilled at riding horses. **horse•play,** n. rough play. **horse•pow•er,** n. unit formerly used when calculating the power of a car engine. **horse•rad•ish,** n. plant with a large root used to make a sharp sauce. **horse sense,** n. inf. commonsense. **horse•shoe,** n. curved metal strip nailed to the hooves of horses. **horse•tail,** n. common leafless weed. **horse trad•ing,** n. bargaining between parties before coming to an agreement. **horse•wom•an,** n. (pl. **-women**) woman riding a horse; woman skilled at riding horses.

hors•y, *adj.* (a) looking like a horse. (b) interested in horses.

hor•ti•cul•ture ['hɔːtɪkʌltʃə] *n.* science of gardening. **hor•ti•cul•tur•al** [hɔːtɪ'kʌltʃərəl] *adj.* referring to horticulture. **hor•ti•cul•tur•ist,** *n.* person who specializes in gardening.

hose [həuz] 1. *n.* (a) long, flexible tube for carrying liquid, esp. water. (b) stockings/socks; **panty h.** = tights/stockings and briefs in one piece. 2. *v.* (*also* **hose down**) to spray with water, etc., from a hose. **ho•sier•y** ['həuzjərɪ] *n.* knitted pieces of clothing (esp. stockings/socks).

hos•pice ['hɒspɪs] *n.* place where poor or terminally ill people can live.

hos•pi•ta•ble [hɒ'spɪtəbl] *adj.* welcoming. **hos•pi•ta•bly,** *adv.* in a welcoming way. **hos•pi•tal•i•ty** [hɒspɪ'tælɪtɪ] *n.* welcome to visitors; giving visitors food, drink, etc.

hos•pi•tal ['hɒspɪtl] *n.* place where sick people are treated. **hos•pi•tal•ize,** *v.* to put (s.o.) in a hospital.

host [həust] 1. *n.* (a) man who invites guests. (b) hotel keeper. (c) animal/plant on which other animals/plants live. (d) large number. (e) (*in church*) consecrated bread. 2. *v.* to be the host at (a dinner reception/a conference/TV show). **host•ess,** *n.* woman who invites guests.

hos•ta ['hɒstæ] *n.* common garden plant which grows in shade.

hos•tage ['hɒstɪdʒ] *n.* person kept prisoner until the demands of the captor are met.

hos•tel ['hɒstl] *n.* (a) building providing rooms for homeless families/students, etc. (b) **youth h.** = building where young hikers, etc. may stay the night cheaply.

hos•tile ['hɒstl] *adj.* referring to an enemy; unfriendly. **hos•til•i•ty** [hɒ'stɪlɪtɪ] *n.* (a) dislike (of a plan)/opposition (to a plan). (b) **hostilities** = warfare.

hot [hɒt] *adj.* (**hotter, hottest**) (a) very warm; *inf.* **to get into h. water** = to get into trouble; **to make things h. for s.o.** = make life unbearable. (b) highly spiced. (c) very strong; **h. line** = direct telephone link between heads of state; **he's in the h. seat** = his job involves him in awkward decisions. (d) *inf.* very recent (news); (goods) which have just been stolen. **hot air,** *n. inf.* useless excited talk. **hot•bed,** *n.* place where sth unpleasant breeds rapidly. **hot-blood•ed,** *adj.* (person) with a violent temper. **hot-desk•ing,** *n.* office system in which employees do not have their own desks but may work at any unoccupied desk. **hot dog,** *n.* hot frankfurter eaten in a long roll with mustard, pickles, etc. **hot•foot,** *adv.* running fast. **hot•head,** *n.* impetuous person. **hot•house,** *n.* heated greenhouse. **hot link,** *n.* word/phrase in a computer hypertext document that provides an active link to relevant information, which can be displayed by selecting the word/phrase. **hotplate,** *n.* piece of metal heated usu. by electricity, used to heat food. **hot-tem•pered,** *adj.* (person) with a violent temper. **hot-wa•ter bot•tle,** *n.* container filled with hot water which is used to warm a part of the body.

ho•tel [həu'tel] *n.* building where you can buy food and drink, and rent a room for the night. **ho•te•lier** [həu'telɪə] *n.* person who runs a hotel.

hound [haund] 1. *n.* large hunting dog. 2. *v.* to chase (s.o.)/to victimize (s.o.).

hour ['auə] *n.* (a) period of time lasting sixty minutes; *inf.* **they took hours to do it** = a very long time. (b) particular point in time; **on the h.** = at nine o'clock, ten o'clock, etc. exactly. **hour•glass,** *n.* timing device made of two glass containers joined by a narrow tube, through which sand falls. **hour•ly,** *adj. & adv.* every hour.

house 1. *n.* [haus, *pl.* 'hauzɪz] (a) building in which people live; *inf.* **like a h. on fire** = very fast; quickly. (b) dynasty/royal family. (c) commercial establishment; business. (d) audience (at a play); members (of a legislative or other deliberative body). (e) **drinks are on the h.** = drinks offered free by the owner of a restaurant, bar, etc. 2. *v.* [hauz] to provide accommodation for (s.o./sth). **house ar•rest,** *n.* **under h. arrest** = not allowed to leave one's house which is being guarded by the police. **house•boat,** *n.* large boat which is used for living in. **house•bound,** *adj.* not able to leave the house. **house•break•er,** *n.* burglar/person who breaks into a house to steal. **house•break•ing,** *n.* breaking into a house to steal. **house•coat,** *n.* light coat/dressing gown worn by women in the house. **house•hold,** *n.* family/people who live together in the same house; **h. word** = saying which everybody uses. **house•hold•er,** *n.* head of a family/person who owns/who is in charge of a house. **house•keep•er,** *n.* woman employed to look after and direct the

---

æ back, aː farm, ɒ top, aɪ pipe, au how, aie fire, auə flower, ɔː bought, ɔɪ toy, e fed, eəhair, eɪ take, ə afraid, əu boat, əuə lower, vː word, iː heap, ɪ hit, ɪə hear, uː school, u book, ʌ but, b back, d dog, ð then, dʒ just, f fog, g go, h hand, j yes, k catch, l last, m mix, n nut, ŋ sing, p penny, r round, s some, ʃ short, t too, tʃ chop, θ thing, v voice, w was, z zoo, ʒ treasure

management of a house. **house•keep•ing,** *n.* looking after a house; **h. money** = money set aside for paying food/heating, etc., in a house. **house•maid,** *n.* girl employed to do housework. **house•mas•ter, housemistress,** *n.* person in charge of a dormitory in a private school. **House of Com•mons,** *n.* lower house of the British Parliament. **House of Lords,** *n.* upper house of the British Parliament. **House of Rep•re•sen•ta•tives,** *n.* lower house of the U.S. Congress. **house phy•si•cian,** *n.* doctor working and usu. living in a hospital, hotel, or other public institution. **house plant,** *n.* plant which is kept in the house. **house sur•geon,** *n.* doctor working and usu. living in a hospital. **house-trained,** *adj.* (animal) trained not to pass excreta in the house. **house•warm•ing,** *n.* party to celebrate moving into a new house. **house•wife,** *n.* (*pl.* -wives) woman who spends her time looking after a house and usu. has no outside work. **house•work,** *n.* general cleaning work in a house. **hous•ing** [ˈhaʊzɪŋ] *n.* (a) providing accommodation for people; **h. development** = area of houses or apartments built at one time. (b) covering for part of a machine.

hove [həʊv] *v. see* **heave.**

hov•el [ˈhɒvl] *n.* small dirty house.

hov•er [ˈhɒvə] *v.* (a) to fly/to hang in the air without moving forward. (b) to hang (**around** s.o.). **hov•er•craft,** *n.* vehicle which moves over water or land on a cushion of air. **hov•er•fly,** *n.* small insect which hovers.

how [haʊ] *adv.* (a) in what way/to what extent; **h. are you?** (b) the means of; **tell me h. to do it.** (c) (*showing surprise*) **h. green the trees are! how do you do?** *inter. showing greeting.* **how•ev•er** [haʊˈevə] *adv.* (a) to whatever extent. (b) in spite of this.

how•dah [ˈhaʊdɑː] *n.* seat on an elephant's back.

how•itz•er [ˈhaʊɪtsə] *n.* short gun which fires shells high into the air.

howl [haʊl] 1. *n.* loud wail. 2. *v.* to make a loud wailing noise. **howl down,** *v.* to stop (s.o.) making a speech by shouting at him. **howl•er,** *n. inf.* bad mistake. **howl•ing,** *n.* loud wailing.

hoy•den [ˈhɔɪdn] *n.* boisterous girl. **hoy•den•ish,** *adj.* like a hoyden.

HQ [ˈeɪtʃˈkjuː] *n.* headquarters.

HTML [eɪtʃtiːemˈel] *abbrev. for* hypertext markup language.

hub [hʌb] *n.* (a) center of a wheel where it is connected to the axle. (b) center of activity/business. **hub cap,** *n.* metal plate covering the center of a car wheel.

hub•ble-bub•ble [ˈhʌblbʌbl] *n. inf.* hookah.

hub•bub [ˈhʌbʌb] *n.* confused sound of voices.

hud•dle [ˈhʌdl] 1. *n.* **to go into a h.** = to meet together to discuss sth in secret. 2. *v.* to crowd together.

hue [hjuː] *n.* (a) color. (b) **h. and cry** = public protest of anger/alarm.

huff [hʌf] *n.* **in a h.** = in a bad temper. **huff•y,** *adj. inf.* bad-tempered.

hug [hʌg] 1. *n.* throwing your arms round s.o. 2. *v.* (**hugged**) (a) to throw your arms around (s.o.). (b) to keep close to (sth).

huge [hjuːdʒ] *adj.* very large/enormous. **huge•ly,** *adv. inf.* enormously.

hug•ger-mug•ger [ˈhʌgəmʌgə] *adj. inf.* (a) secret. (b) confused; messy.

hulk [hʌlk] *n.* (a) rotten old ship which is no longer used for sailing. (b) large and clumsy thing/person. **hulk•ing,** *adj.* big and awkward.

hull [hʌl] 1. *n.* (a) main body of a ship. (b) pea or bean pod. 2. *v.* to take (peas) out of their pods.

hul•la•ba•loo [hʌləbəˈluː] *n.* loud disorderly noise or excitement.

hul•lo [həˈləʊ] *inter. showing a greeting.*

hum [hʌm] 1. *n.* low buzzing noise. 2. *v.* (**hummed**) (a) to make a continual low buzzing noise. (b) to sing the tune of a song without using the words. **hum•ming•bird,** *n.* very small brightly colored tropical bird which hovers.

hu•man [ˈhjuːmən] 1. *adj.* referring to people; **a h. being** = a person; **h. immunodeficiency virus (HIV)** = virus which causes AIDS, transmitted through sexual intercourse/blood; **h. nature** = general characteristics of people. 2. *n.* person. **hu•mane** [hjuːˈmeɪn] *adj.* kind/gentle. **hu•mane•ly,** *adv.* kindly/gently. **hu•man•ism** [ˈhjuːmənɪzəm] *n.* concern with human beings rather than with religions. **hu•man•ist,** *n.* person who believes in humanism. **hu•man•is•tic,** *adj.* referring to humanism. **hu•man•i•tar•i•an** [hjuːmænɪˈteərɪən] *adj.* kind toward other humans. **hu•man•i•ty** [hjuːˈmænɪtɪ] *n.* (a) all people. (b) great kindness. (c) **the humanities** = arts subjects (not sciences). **hu•man•i•za•tion,** *n.* act of humanizing. **hu•man•ize,** *v.* to make (more) human. **hu•man•kind,** *n.* people, seen as a biological group. **hu•man•ly,** *adv.* **we will do everything h. possible** = all we can.

hum•ble [ˈhʌmbl] 1. *adj.* (-er, -est) modest/not proud; **to eat h. pie** = to admit you were wrong. 2. *v.* to make (s.o.) less proud/less important. **hum•ble•ness,** *n.* being humble.

hum•bug ['hʌmbʌg] *n.* (a) confidence trick. (b) person who tricks s.o./who pretends to be sth which he is not.

hum•ding•er [hʌm'dɪŋə] *n. inf.* wonderful/remarkable person/thing.

hum•drum ['hʌmdrʌm] *adj.* dull/ordinary.

hu•mer•us ['hjuːmərəs] *n.* bone in the top part of the arm.

hu•mid ['hjuːmɪd] *adj.* damp. **hu•mid•i•fi•er** [hjuː'mɪdɪfaɪə] *n.* machine which dampens the air (in a house). **hu•mid•i•ty** [hjuː'mɪdɪtɪ] *n.* dampness.

hu•mil•i•ate [hjuː'mɪlɪeɪt] *v.* to make (s.o.) feel unimportant/humble/ashamed. **hu•mil•i•a•tion** [hjuːmɪlɪ'eɪʃn] *n.* making s.o. feel unimportant/humble/ashamed. **hu•mil•i•ty** [hjuː'mɪlɪtɪ] *n.* humbleness/being humble.

hum•mock ['hʌmək] *n.* low rise in the ground.

hu•mor, *Brit.* **hu•mour** ['hjuːmə] 1. *n.* (a) seeing the funny aspects of sth. (b) general feeling/mood. 2. *v.* to do what s.o. wants in order to keep him happy. **hu•mor•ist,** *n.* person who makes jokes; writer of funny stories or articles. **hu•mor•ous,** *adj.* funny/amusing. **hu•mor•ous•ly,** *adv.* in a humorous way.

hump [hʌmp] 1. *n.* lump on the back; small rounded bump in the ground. 2. *v. inf.* to carry (on your shoulder). **hump•backed,** *adj.* (person) with a hump.

hu•mus ['hjuːməs] *n.* good soil made rich with decayed animal or vegetable matter.

hunch [hʌntʃ] 1. *n. inf.* feeling that sth is going to happen. 2. *v.* to bend low. **hunch•back,** *n.* person with a hunched back.

hun•dred ['hʌndrəd] *n.* number 100; **hundreds of** = very many. **hun•dred•fold,** *adv.* a hundred times. **hun•dredth, 100th,** *adj.* referring to a hundred. **hun•dred•weight,** *n.* weight of 100 pounds (approx. 45.359 kilos).

hung [hʌŋ] *v. see* **hang; h. jury** = jury which cannot reach a majority decision. **hung o•ver,** *adj. inf.* feeling ill after drinking too much alcohol. **hung up,** *adj. inf.* suffering from an emotional disturbance.

Hun•gar•i•an [hʌŋ'geərɪən] 1. *adj.* referring to Hungary. 2. *n.* (a) person from Hungary. (b) language spoken in Hungary.

hun•ger ['hʌŋgə] *n.* wanting/needing to eat. **hun•ger strike,** *n.* refusing to eat to force s.o. to do sth. **hun•gri•ly,** *adv.* in a hungry way. **hun•gry,** *adj.* feeling hunger.

hunk [hʌŋk] *n.* large rough piece (of bread/cheese).

hunt [hʌnt] 1. *n.* (a) chasing of wild animals for sport; group of people who meet regularly to chase wild animals, esp. foxes. (b) search (**for** s.o.). 2. *v.* (a) to look **for** (s.o./sth). **hunt down,** *v.* to track (a person/an animal) and catch them. **hunt•er,** *n.* person who chases wild animals; horse used in hunting; **bargain h.** = person who is looking for bargains in stores, etc. **hunt•ing,** *n.* (a) chasing wild animals. (b) looking for sth. **hunt•ing ground,** *n.* place where wild animals are often found. **hunts•man,** *n.* (*pl.* **-men**) man who hunts wild animals; man who looks after a pack of hunting hounds.

hur•dle ['hɜːdl] *n.* (a) small fence which has to be jumped over in a race. (b) difficulty; obstacle. **hurd•ler,** *n.* person who takes part in races with hurdles.

hur•dy-gur•dy ['hɜːdɪ'gɜːdɪ] *n.* machine which produces music if a handle is turned.

hurl [hɜːl] *v.* to throw hard. **hurl•ing,** *n.* game similar to hockey, traditionally played in Ireland.

hurl•y-burl•y ['hɜːlɪ'bɜːlɪ] *n.* rough activity.

hur•rah, hurray [hʊ'rɑː, hʊ'reɪ] *inter. showing great pleasure/excitement.*

hur•ri•cane ['hʌrɪkən] *n.* violent tropical storm, esp. in the West Indies; **h. lamp** = lamp with a glass shield around the flame.

hur•ry ['hʌrɪ] 1. *n.* rush. 2. *v.* (*also* **hurry up**) (a) to go fast. (b) to make (s.o.) go faster. **hur•ried,** *adj.* quick/rushed. **hur•ried•ly,** *adv.* quickly.

hurt [hɜːt] 1. *n.* pain. 2. *v.* (**hurt**) to give (s.o.) pain/to make (s.o.) sad. **hurt•ful,** *adj.* which is painful to the feelings/which makes s.o. sad.

hur•tle ['hɜːtl] *v.* to move quickly/to rush dangerously.

hus•band ['hʌzbənd] 1. *n.* man who is married to a certain woman. 2. *v.* (*formal*) to look after carefully/not waste (your resources). **hus•band•ry,** *n.* farming; **animal h.** = rearing of animals on a farm.

hush [hʌʃ] 1. *n.* quiet. 2. *v.* to make quiet. **hush-hush,** *adj. inf.* secret. **hush mon•ey,** *n.* money paid to s.o. to stop them from revealing a secret. **hush up,** *v.* to suppress (a scandal).

husk [hʌsk] 1. *n.* hard outside covering of a seed. 2. *v.* to take the husk off (a seed).

husk•y ['hʌskɪ] 1. *adj.* (**-ier, -iest**) rough/hoarse (voice). 2. *n.* dog which pulls sleds in the Arctic. **husk•i•ly**, *adv.* in a husky voice. **husk•i•ness**, *n.* hoarseness of the voice.

hus•sar ['hʌzɑː] *n.* soldier on horseback.

hus•sy ['hʌsɪ] *n.* **brazen h.** = wicked girl/woman.

hust•ings ['hʌstɪŋz] *n.* **on the h.** = on an election campaign trail.

hus•tle ['hʌsl] 1. *n.* rush/violent activity. 2. *v.* to push/to hurry (roughly). **hus•tler,** *n.* person who gets things going/who hurries business along.

hut [hʌt] *n.* small rough house, usu. made of wood.

hutch [hʌtʃ] *n.* enclosure for rabbits.

hy•a•cinth ['haɪəsɪnθ] *n.* strongly-scented spring flower grown from a bulb.

hy•brid ['haɪbrɪd] *adj. & n.* (plant/animal, etc.) produced from two different species.

hy•da•tid ['haɪdætɪd] *adj.* (cyst) caused by a tapeworm.

hy•dran•gea [haɪ'dreɪndʒə] *n.* garden shrub with large blue, white, or pink flowers.

hy•drant ['haɪdrənt] *n.* water pipe in a street to which a hose can be attached; **fire h.** = one to which firemen can attach fire hoses.

hy•drate ['haɪdreɪt] *n.* chemical compound with water.

hy•drau•lic [haɪ'drɔːlɪk] *adj.* worked by fluid. **hy•drau•li•cal•ly,** *adv.* using hydraulic force. **hy•drau•lics,** *n.* study of fluids used mechanically.

hy•dro ['haɪdrəʊ] *n.* (*pl.* **-os**) *inf.* hydroelectric power.

hydro- ['haɪdrəʊ] *prefix meaning* water.

hy•dro•car•bon [haɪdrəʊ'kɑːbən] *n.* organic compound of hydrogen and carbon.

hy•dro•chlo•ric [haɪdrəʊ'klɒrɪk] *adj.* (acid) made of hydrogen and chlorine.

hy•dro•e•lec•tric [haɪdrəʊɪ'lektrɪk] *adj.* referring to hydroelectricity. **hy•dro•e•lec•tric•i•ty** [haɪdrəʊelek-'trɪsɪtɪ] *n.* electricity produced by water power.

hy•dro•foil ['haɪdrəfɔɪl] *n.* boat which skims over the water on thin legs.

hy•dro•gen ['haɪdrədʒən] *n.* (*element:* H) common gas which combines with oxygen to form water; **h. bomb** = extremely powerful nuclear bomb.

hy•drog•ra•pher [haɪ'drɒɡrəfə] *n.* person who makes maps of the ocean/sea or ocean/sea bed.

hy•drol•y•sis [haɪ'drɒlɪsɪs] *n.* decomposition of a chemical substance by water.

hy•drom•e•ter [haɪ'drɒmɪtə] *n.* device for measuring the relative density of water.

hy•dro•pho•bi•a ['haɪdrəfəʊbɪə] *n.* (a) ra-

bies. (b) fear of water (usu. a symptom of rabies).

hy•dro•plane ['haɪdrəpleɪn] *n.* powerful flat-bottomed motorboat which skims over the surface of the water.

hy•dro•pon•ics [haɪdrə'pɒnɪks] *n.* science of growing plants in water, without using soil.

hy•dro•stat•ic [haɪdrəʊ'stætɪk] *adj.* referring to fluids at rest.

hy•dro•ther•a•py [haɪdrə'θerəpɪ] *n.* treatment of sick people with water.

hy•e•na [haɪ'iːnə] *n.* fierce doglike African animal.

hy•giene ['haɪdʒiːn] *n.* keeping clean and free of germs. **hy•gi•en•ic** [haɪ'dʒiːnɪk] *adj.* (which keeps) clean and free of germs. **hy•gi•en•i•cal•ly,** *adv.* in a hygienic way. **hy•gien•ist,** person who specializes in (esp. dental) hygiene.

hy•grom•e•ter [haɪ'grɒmɪtə] *n.* instrument for measuring humidity.

hy•men ['haɪmen] *n.* thin tissue which covers the entrance to the vagina of a girl who has never had sexual intercourse.

hymn [hɪm] *n.* religious song. **hym•nal** ['hɪmnl], **hymn-book,** *n.* book of hymns.

hype [haɪp] 1. *n. inf.* excessive publicity. 2. *v.* to publicize (a product) excessively.

hyper- ['haɪpə] *prefix meaning* to a great degree; **hyperactive** = very active.

hy•per•bo•la [haɪ'pɜːbələ] *n.* type of curve. **hy•per•bol•ic** [haɪpə'bɒlɪk] *adj.* referring to a hyperbola.

hy•per•bo•le [haɪ'pɜːbəlɪ] *n.* exaggerated comparison. **hy•per•bol•i•cal** [haɪpə-'bɒlɪkl] *adj.* referring to hyperbole.

hy•per•crit•i•cal [haɪpə'krɪtɪkl] *adj.* extremely critical.

hy•per•me•di•a ['haɪpəmiːdɪə] *n. pl.* computer software/hardware that provides active links to relevant items of text, graphics, video, and sound, which can be accessed by selecting a particular word/phrase/image, etc.

hy•per•sen•si•tive [haɪpə'sensɪtɪv] *adj.* very easily offended.

hy•per•ten•sion [haɪpə'tenʃn] *n.* very high blood pressure.

hy•per•text ['haɪpətekst] *n.* computer software/hardware that allows the creation and use of active links to relevant information, which can be displayed by selecting a particular image/word/phrase; **h. markup language** = text description language, consisting of markers embedded in the text to control document structure and active links, used in electronic publishing, esp. on the Internet.

hy•phen ['haɪfn] *n.* short line (-) which joins two words or separates one word into parts. **hy•phen•ate,** *v.* to join (words) with a hyphen or separate (one word) into parts with a hyphen. **hy•phen•a•tion** [haɪfə'neɪʃn] *n.* act of hyphenating.

hyp•no•sis [hɪp'nəʊsɪs] *n.* putting s.o. into a trance, so that they obey your orders; **under h.** = while in a trance. **hyp•not•ic** [hɪp'nɒtɪk] *adj.* referring to hypnosis. **hyp•not•i•cal•ly**, *adv.* in a hypnotic way. **hyp•no•tism** ['hɪpnətɪzəm] *n.* use of hypnosis as a medical process or for amusement. **hyp•no•tist**, *n.* person who practices hypnosis. **hyp•no•tize**, *v.* to put (s.o.) into a trance.

hy•po ['haɪpəʊ] *n.* substance used for fixing the picture when developing a photograph.

hypo- ['haɪpəʊ] *prefix meaning* under/below.

hy•po•caust ['haɪpəʊkɔːst] *n.* ancient Roman heating system, where hot air flowed under a raised floor.

hy•po•chon•dri•a [haɪpə'kɒndrɪə] *n.* being permanently worried about your health. **hy•po•chon•dri•ac**, *n.* person who is always worried about his/her health.

hy•poc•ri•sy [hɪ'pɒkrəsɪ] *n.* pretending to be the opposite of what you really are/to feel the opposite of what you really feel. **hyp•o•crite** ['hɪpəkrɪt] *n.* hypocritical person. **hyp•o•crit•i•cal** [hɪpə'krɪtɪkl] *adj.* referring to hypocrisy.

hy•po•der•mic [haɪpə'dɜːmɪk] *adj.* **h. syringe/needle** = medical instrument used for injections just below the surface of the skin.

hy•po•ten•sion [haɪpəʊ'tenʃn] *n.* very low blood pressure.

hy•pot•e•nuse [haɪ'pɒtənjuːz] *n.* longest side of a right-angled triangle.

hy•po•ther•mi•a [haɪpə'θɜːmɪə] *n.* state where the temperature of the body is abnormally low.

hy•poth•e•sis [haɪ'pɒθəsɪs] *n.* (*pl.* **-theses** [-θəsiːz]) suggestion that sth is true, though without proof. **hy•po•thet•i•cal** [haɪpə'θetɪkl] *adj.* suggested as true, but not necessarily so. **hy•po•thet•i•cal•ly**, *adv.* in a hypothetical way.

hys•ter•ec•to•my [hɪstə'rektəmɪ] *n.* surgical operation to remove a woman's womb.

hys•te•ri•a [hɪ'stɪərɪə] *n.* nervous excitement leading to wild fits of laughing or crying. **hys•ter•i•cal** [hɪ'sterɪkl] *adj.* suffering from hysteria; laughing/crying in a wild manner. **hys•ter•i•cal•ly**, *adv.* in an uncontrollable way. **hys•ter•ics**, *n. pl.* attack of hysteria.

æ back, ɑː farm, ɒ top, aɪ pipe, aʊ how, aiə fire, aʊə flower, ɔː bought, ɔɪ toy, e fed, eə hair, eɪ take, ə afraid, əʊ boat, əʊə lower, ɜː word, iː heap, ɪ hit, ɪə hear, uː school, ʊ book, ʌ but, b back, d dog, ð then, dʒ just, f fog, g go, h hand, j yes, k catch, l last, m mix, n nut, ŋ sing, p penny, r round, s some, ʃ short, t too, tʃ chop, θ thing, v voice, w was, z zoo, ʒ treasure

Ii

I, i [aɪ] **to dot one's i's and cross one's t's** = to be very careful to settle the final details.

I [aɪ] *pronoun referring to the speaker.*

I *symbol for* iodine

i•amb ['aɪæmb] *n.* Greek poetic measure, formed of a short and a long syllable. **i•am•bic,** *adj.* referring to iambs.

I•be•ri•an [aɪ'biːərɪən] *adj.* referring to Spain and Portugal.

i•bex ['aɪbeks] *n.* (*pl.* **ibex(es))** mountain goat with large curved horns.

i•bid, ibidem ['ɪbɪd(em)] *adv.* in the same book/chapter/page.

i•bis ['aɪbɪs] *n.* tropical water bird with long legs and a curved bill.

ice [aɪs] 1. *n.* (a) frozen water; **to break the i.** = to bring an embarrassing silence to an end; **to keep sth on i.** = not do anything about it for the moment. (b) **dry i.** = frozen carbon dioxide. 2. *v.* (a) to cool with ice. (b) to freeze. (c) to cover with sugar icing. **Ice age,** *n.* geological period when parts of the world were covered with ice. **ice ax,** *n.* ax used by mountaineers to cut footholds in ice. **ice•berg,** *n.* large floating mass of ice at sea; **tip of the i.** = small part of sth (usu. unpleasant) which makes you eventually discover the rest. **ice•box,** *n.* (a) box containing ice to keep food or drink cool. (b) (*old*) refrigerator. **ice-break•er,** *n.* boat specially strengthened to break up ice in shipping lanes. **ice cream,** *n.* frozen dessert made of cream and flavoring. **ice•field,** *n.* large area of ice floating on the sea. **ice•floe,** *n.* sheet of ice floating in the sea. **ice hock•ey,** *n.* form of hockey played on ice. **ice•house,** *n.* house for storing ice during the summer. **Ice•land•er,** *n.* person from Iceland. **Ice•lan•dic.** 1. *adj.* referring to Iceland. 2. *n.* language spoken in Iceland. **ice skate,** *n.* shoe with a sharp blade for skating on ice. **ice-skate,** *v.* to move on ice skates. **i•ci•cle,** *n.* long hanging piece of ice formed by dripping water in cold weather. **i•ci•ly,** *adv.* in a cold/unfriendly way. **i•ci•ness,** *n.* bitter coldness (of weather/of greeting). **ic•ing,** *n.* sugar topping for a cake or cookie, etc. **i•cy,** *adj.* (**-ier, -iest**) (a) covered with ice. (b) very cold/unwelcoming.

ich•neu•mon fly [ɪk'njuːmən 'flaɪ] *n.* insect, whose larvae live on other insects.

i•con ['aɪkən] *n.* (a) picture of Christ or a saint in the Eastern Christian church. (b) little pictorial symbol on a computer screen. **i•con•o•clast** [aɪ'kɒnəklæst] *n.* person who attacks beliefs which are held by many people. **i•con•o•clas•tic** [aɪkɒnə'klæstɪk] *adj.* which attacks beliefs which are held by many people. **i•co•nog•ra•phy,** *n.* the study of icons; the study of pictures of a particular subject.

id [ɪd] *n.* the basic unconscious drives in a person.

I'd [aɪd] *short for* **I would/I had/I should.**

i•de•a [aɪ'dɪə] *n.* thought/plan in the mind; **I had no i.** = I did not know.

i•de•al [aɪ'dɪəl] 1. *n.* summit of perfection; **person of high ideals** = person who has high standards of perfection. 2. *adj.* perfect; very suitable. **i•de•al•ism,** *n.* aiming at achieving an ideal. **i•de•al•ist,** *n.* person who aims at achieving an ideal; impractical person. **i•de•al•is•tic** [aɪdrə'lɪstɪk] *adj.* aiming at an ideal; too perfect. **i•de•al•ize,** *v.* to make (s.o./sth) seem perfect. **i•de•al•ly,** *adv.* if everything were perfect.

i•den•ti•fy [aɪ'dentɪfaɪ] *v.* (a) to say who s.o. is/what sth is. (b) to state that sth belongs to you. (c) **to i. with** = to feel you have the same characteristics as (s.o.); to have a feeling of sympathy for (s.o./sth). **i•den•ti•cal,** *adj.* (**with/to**) exactly the same as. **i•den•ti•cal•ly,** *adv.* in exactly the same way. **i•den•ti•fi•a•ble,** *adj.* which can be identified. **i•den•ti•fi•ca•tion** [aɪdentɪfɪ'keɪʃn] *n.* saying who s.o. is/who sth belongs to. **i•den•ti•kit,** *n.* trademark for a method of making a portrait of a criminal using pieces of photographs or drawings of different faces to form a composite picture. **i•den•ti•ty,** *n.* (a) who s.o. is; **i. card** = card which identifies the holder, usu. showing a photograph of the holder, with the name, date of birth and other details. (b) being the same/being identical.

id•e•o•gram ['ɪdɪəugræm] *n.* picture/character which represents a word.

i•de•ol•o•gy [aɪdɪ'ɒlədʒɪ] *n.* theory of life based on political or economic philosophy rather than religious belief. **i•de•o•log•i•cal** [aɪdɪə'lɒdʒɪkl] adj. referring to ideology.

ides [aɪdz] npl. in the Latin calendar, the 15th of some months and the 13th of others.

id•i•o•cy ['ɪdɪəsɪ] n. see **id•i•ot**.

id•i•om ['ɪdɪəm] n. (a) characteristic way of speaking/of writing. (b) particular expression where the words do not have their literal meaning. **id•i•o•mat•ic** [ɪdɪə'mætɪk] adj. referring to a particular way of speaking.

id•i•o•syn•cra•sy [ɪdɪəʊ'sɪŋkrəsɪ] n. particular way of behaving. **id•i•o•syn•crat•ic** [ɪdɪəʊsɪŋ'krætɪk] adj. odd/peculiar; particular to one person.

id•i•ot ['ɪdɪət] n. (a) mentally deficient person. (b) person who is stupid. **id•i•o•cy**, n. stupidity. **id•i•ot•ic** [ɪdɪ'ɒtɪk] adj. stupid. **id•i•ot•i•cal•ly**, adv. in a stupid way.

i•dle ['aɪdl] 1. adj. (**idler, idlest**) (a) lazy. (b) not working. (c) aimless/not worthwhile. 2. v. (a) to spend time doing nothing. (b) (of an engine) to run gently. **i•dle•ness**, n. laziness. **i•dler**, n. person who idles. **i•dly**, adv. (a) lazily. (b) without being involved.

i•dol ['aɪdl] n. (a) statue of a god. (b) favorite person. (c) star performer (who is worshipped by fans). **i•dol•a•ter**, n. person who worships idols. **i•dol•a•try** [aɪ'dɒlətrɪ] n. worship of idols. **i•dol•ize**, v. to worship.

i•dyll ['ɪdɪl] n. pleasant/happy scene. **i•dyl•lic** [ɪ'dɪlɪk] adj. pleasant/happy (in a romantic way). **i•dyl•li•cal•ly**, adv. in an idyllic way.

i.e. ['aɪ'iː] abbrev. for id est, meaning that is.

if [ɪf] 1. conj. (a) (showing what might happen) **if it rains the ground gets wet.** (b) (showing supposition) **if only to please her.** (c) (exclamation) **if only I had known!** (d) whether; **do you know if the plane is late?** (e) although; **he is nice, if rather lazy.** (f) at any time when. 2. n. inf. undecided question.

ig•loo ['ɪgluː] n. dome-shaped shelter built by Eskimos out of blocks of snow.

ig•ne•ous ['ɪgnɪəs] adj. (rock) which was originally formed from solidified lava.

ig•nite [ɪg'naɪt] v. to set fire to; to catch fire. **ig•ni•tion** [ɪg'nɪʃn] n. (in a car) electrical device which makes the spark which fires the fuel; **i. key** = key used to switch on the ignition.

ig•no•ble [ɪg'nəʊbl] adj. (formal) unworthy.

ig•no•min•y ['ɪgnəmɪnɪ] n. shame/disgrace. **ig•no•min•i•ous** [ɪgnə'mɪnɪəs] adj. shame-

ful. **ig•no•min•i•ous•ly**, adv. in an ignominious way.

ig•nore [ɪg'nɔː] v. not notice (on purpose). **ig•no•ra•mus** [ɪgnə'reɪməs] n. (pl. -es) person who is stupid/who knows nothing. **ig•no•rance** ['ɪgnərəns] n. not knowing. **ig•no•rant** ['ɪgnərənt] adj. not knowing/stupid. **ig•no•rant•ly**, adv. stupidly.

i•gua•na [ɪgjʊ'ɑːnə] kind of large tropical lizard.

il•e•um ['Rɪləm] n. long part of the small intestine.

il•i•um ['ɪlɪəm] n. top part of the hip bone.

ilk [ɪlk] n. inf. sort/type.

ill [ɪl] 1. adj. (**worse, worst**) (a) sick; not well. (b) bad. 2. n. bad thing. 3. adv. badly. **ill-ad•vised**, adj. not recommended. **ill-bred**, adj. badly brought up; with bad manners. **ill-fat•ed**, adj. fated to fail. **ill-feel•ing**, n. resentment; dislike. **ill-got•ten**, adj. illegally acquired. **ill-man•nered**, adj. badly behaved/with bad manners/rude. **ill•ness**, n. sickness. **ill-starred**, adj. fated to fail. **ill-treat**, v. to treat (animals/children) badly. **ill will**, n. **to bear s.o. ill will** = to want sth bad to happen to s.o.

I'll [aɪl] short for **I will/I shall.**

il•le•gal [ɪ'liːgl] adj. against the law. **il•le•gal•i•ty**, n. being illegal. **il•le•gal•ly**, adv. against the law.

il•leg•i•ble [ɪ'ledʒɪbl] adj. (writing) which cannot be read. **il•leg•i•bil•i•ty**, n. being illegible. **il•leg•i•bly**, adv. in an illegible way.

il•le•git•i•mate [ɪlɪ'dʒɪtəmət] adj. (a) (person) born of unmarried parents. (b) against the law. **il•le•git•i•mate•ly**, adv. in an illegitimate way. **il•le•git•i•ma•cy**, n. being illegitimate.

il•lic•it [ɪ'lɪsɪt] adj. against the law/illegal. **il•lic•it•ly**, adv. in an illicit way.

il•lit•er•a•cy [ɪ'lɪtərəsɪ] n. inability to read and write. **il•lit•er•ate**, adj. & n. (person) who cannot read or write.

il•log•i•cal [ɪ'lɒdʒɪkl] adj. not sensible/not reasonable. **il•log•i•cal•ly**, adv. in an illogical way. **il•log•i•cal•i•ty** [ɪlɒdʒɪ'kælɪtɪ] n. being illogical.

il•lu•mi•nate [ɪ'luːmɪneɪt] v. (a) to light up. (b) to draw colored initials/pictures in a manuscript. **il•lu•mi•nat•ing**, adj. which throws light on (a subject).

æ back, ɑː farm, ɒ top, aɪ pipe, aʊ how, aɪə fire, aʊə flower, ɔː bought, ɔɪ toy, e fed, eəhair, eɪ take, ə afraid, əʊ boat, əʊə lower, ɜː word, iː heap, ɪ hit, ɪə hear, uː school, ʊ book, ʌ but, b back, d dog, ð then, dʒ just, f fog, g go, h hand, j yes, k catch, l last, m mix, n nut, ŋ sing, p penny, r round, s some, ʃ short, t too, tʃ chop, θ thing, v voice, w was, z zoo, ʒ treasure

il•lu•mi•na•tion [ɪluːmɪ'neɪʃn] *n.* (a) decoration using usu. colored lights. (b) colored initial illustration in a manuscript.

il•lu•sion [ɪ'luːʒn] *n.* impression which is not true; **optical i.** = thing which appears different from what it really is because the eye is being deceived. **il•lu•sion•ist,** *n.* person who entertains with optical illusions. **il•lu•sive,** *adj.* false. **il•lu•so•ry,** *adj.* which is an illusion.

il•lus•trate ['ɪləstreɪt] *v.* (a) to add pictures to. (b) to give/to be an example . of. **il•lus•tra•tion** [ɪlə'streɪʃn] *n.* (a) picture (in a book). (b) example. **il•lus•tra•tive** ['ɪləstrətɪv] *adj.* which illustrates/which is an example. **il•lus•tra•tor** ['ɪləstreɪtə] *n.* person who draws the pictures for a book.

il•lus•tri•ous [ɪ'lʌstrɪəs] *adj.* very famous.

I'm [aɪm] *short for* **I am.**

im•age ['ɪmɪdʒ] *n.* (a) portrait/statue; *inf.* **he's the spitting i. of his father** = he looks exactly like his father. (b) idea which other people have of a person/a company. (c) picture produced by a lens/seen in a mirror. (d) comparison/symbol used esp. in poetry. **im•age•ry,** *n.* using comparison/symbols (in writing) as a way of making people imagine things.

im•ag•ine [ɪ'mædʒɪn] *v.* to picture (sth) in your mind. **im•ag•i•na•ble,** *adj.* which you can imagine. **im•ag•i•nar•y,** *adj.* false/not real. **im•ag•i•na•tion** [ɪmædʒɪ'neɪʃn] *n.* ability to picture things in your mind. **im•ag•i•na•tive** [ɪ'mædʒɪnətɪv] *adj.* (artist) with a strong imagination; (drawing/poem) which shows a lot of imagination. **im•ag•i•na•tive•ly,** *adv.* in an imaginative way.

i•ma•go [ɪ'mɑːgəʊ] *n.* final form of an insect (such as a butterfly) after the larval and pupal stages.

i•mam ['ɪmæm] *n.* Muslim priest.

im•bal•ance [ɪm'bæləns] *n.* lack of balance.

im•be•cile ['ɪmbəsiːl] *n.* (a) mentally deficient person. (b) stupid person. **im•be•cil•i•ty** [ɪmbə'sɪlɪtɪ] *n.* being mentally deficient.

im•bibe [ɪm'baɪb] *v.* (*formal*) to drink.

im•bri•cat•ed ['ɪmbrɪkeɪtɪd] *adj.* overlapping.

im•bro•glio [ɪm'brəʊljəʊ] *n.* (*pl.* -os) complicated dispute/situation.

im•bue [ɪm'bjuː] *v.* (*formal*) to fill with a feeling.

IMF [aɪem'ef] *abbrev. for* International Monetary Fund.

im•i•tate ['ɪmɪteɪt] *v.* to copy/to do like (s.o.). **im•i•ta•tion** [ɪmɪ'teɪʃn] *n.* copy; act of imitating. **im•i•ta•tive** ['ɪmɪtətɪv] *adj.* which copies. **im•i•ta•tor** ['ɪmɪteɪtə] *n.* person who copies.

im•mac•u•late [ɪ'mækjʊlət] *adj.* extremely clean/tidy. **im•mac•u•la•cy,** *n.* being immaculate. **im•mac•u•late•ly,** *adv.* extremely tidily.

im•ma•nent ['ɪmənənt] *adj.* existing as an inherent part.

im•ma•te•ri•al [ɪmə'tɪərɪəl] *adj.* not important.

im•ma•ture [ɪmə'tʃʊə] *adj.* not mature/not fully grown/not fully developed. **im•ma•tur•i•ty,** *n.* not being mature.

im•meas•ur•a•ble [ɪ'meʒrəbl] *adj.* which cannot be measured/very large. **im•meas•ur•a•bly,** *adv.* enormously.

im•me•di•ate [ɪ'miːdjət] *adj.* (a) close/nearest. (b) very soon. **im•me•di•a•cy,** *n.* being immediate. **im•me•di•ate•ly,** *adv. & conj.* without delay; at once.

im•me•mo•ri•al [ɪmə'mɔːrɪəl] *adj.* **from time i.** = from very ancient times.

im•mense [ɪ'mens] *adj.* huge/very wide/enormous. **im•mense•ly,** *adv.* very much. **im•men•si•ty,** *n.* vastness/huge size.

im•merse [ɪ'mɜːs] *v.* to plunge (sth) in a liquid. **im•mer•sion** [ɪ'mɜːʃn] *n.* plunging (into a liquid); **i. heater** (*also* **immersion coil**) = small electrical device immersed in liquid, as water, to heat it.

im•mi•grate ['ɪmɪgreɪt] *v.* to come to settle in a country. **im•mi•grant,** *n.* person who comes to a country to settle. **im•mi•gra•tion** [ɪmɪ'greɪʃn] *n.* settling in a new country; **i. office** = office dealing with immigrants; **i. controls** = restrictions placed by a country on the numbers of immigrants.

im•mi•nent ['ɪmɪnənt] *adj.* which is about to happen. **im•mi•nence,** *n.* being about to happen.

im•mo•bile [ɪ'məʊbaɪl] *adj.* without moving; unable to move. **im•mo•bil•i•ty** [ɪmə'bɪlɪtɪ] *n.* state of not moving. **im•mo•bi•li•za•tion** [ɪməʊbɪlaɪ'zeɪʃn] *n.* stopping sth moving. **im•mo•bi•lize** [ɪ'məʊbɪlaɪz] *v.* to stop (sth) moving.

im•mod•er•ate [ɪ'mɒdərət] *adj.* extravagant/not moderate. **im•mod•er•ate•ly,** *adv.* in an immoderate way.

im•mod•est [ɪ'mɒdɪst] *adj.* not modest.

im•mo•late ['ɪməʊleɪt] *v.* (*poetic*) to sacrifice.

im•mor•al [ɪ'mɒrəl] *adj.* not concerned with the principles of good behavior. **im•mo•ral•i•ty** [ɪmə'rælɪtɪ] *n.* lack of morality. **im•mor•al•ly,** *adv.* in an immoral way.

im•mor•tal [ɪ'mɔːtl] 1. *adj.* like a god; who never dies. 2. *n.* god. **im•mor•tal•i•ty** [ɪmɔː-'tælɪtɪ] *n.* being immortal/never dying.

im•mor•tal•ize [ɪ'mɔːtəlaɪz] v. to make (s.o.) be remembered forever.

im•mov•a•ble [ɪ'muːvəbl] adj. which cannot be moved. **im•mov•a•bly**, adv. in an immovable way.

im•mune [ɪ'mjuːn] adj. (to) (person) who cannot catch a disease. **im•mu•ni•ty**, n. (a) protection (**against** a disease). (b) protection against arrest; **diplomatic i.** = protection of diplomats against being arrested. **im•mu•ni•za•tion** [ɪmjunaɪ'zeɪʃn] n. giving protection against a disease. **im•mu•nize** ['ɪmjunaɪz] v. to give protection **against** a disease. **im•mu•nol•o•gy**, n. study of immunity.

im•mure [ɪ'mjʊə] v. to shut (s.o.) in prison.

im•mu•ta•ble [ɪ'mjuːtəbl] adj. (formal) which cannot be changed/which does not change. **im•mu•ta•bil•i•ty**, n. being immutable. **im•mu•ta•bly**, adv. in an immutable way.

imp [ɪmp] n. little devil; mischievous child.

im•pact ['ɪmpækt] n. forceful shock/effect. **im•pact•ed** [ɪm'pæktɪd] adj. (tooth) which is stuck in the jawbone and cannot grow.

im•pair [ɪm'peə] v. to harm. **im•pair•ment**, n. harm.

im•pal•a [ɪm'pɑːlə] n. large African antelope.

im•pale [ɪm'peɪl] v. to jab a sharp object through (s.o.'s body).

im•pal•pa•ble [ɪm'pælpəbl] adj. (formal) which cannot be touched.

im•pan•el [ɪm'pænəl] v. to choose (a jury).

im•part [ɪm'pɑːt] v. (formal) to pass on/to communicate (sth to s.o.).

im•par•tial [ɪm'pɑːʃl] adj. not biased. **im•par•ti•al•i•ty**, n. being impartial. **im•par•tial•ly**, adv. in an impartial way.

im•pas•sa•ble [ɪm'pɑːsəbl] adj. which you cannot go through or across.

im•passe ['æmpæs] n. deadlock/state where two sides cannot agree.

im•pas•sioned [ɪm'pæʃnd] adj. very deeply felt/excited (speech).

im•pas•sive [ɪm'pæsɪv] adj. expressionless. **im•pas•sive•ly**, adv. in an impassive way.

im•pa•tient [ɪm'peɪʃnt] adj. (a) (**with**) not patient; unable to wait for sth. (b) in a hurry (to do sth). **im•pa•tience**, n. lack of patience. **im•pa•tient•ly**, adv. in a hurried way/not patiently.

im•peach [ɪm'piːtʃ] v. to charge (a public official) with improper conduct or a crime while in office. **im•peach•ment**, n. act of impeaching.

im•pec•ca•ble [ɪm'pekəbl] adj. perfect/perfectly correct. **im•pec•ca•bly**, adv. perfectly.

im•pe•cu•ni•ous [ɪmpɪ'kjuːnɪəs] adj. (formal) with no money.

im•pede [ɪm'piːd] v. to get in the way of (sth); to prevent (sth) happening. **im•ped•ance** [ɪm'piːdəns] n. resistance to an electric current. **im•ped•i•ment** [ɪm'pedɪmənt] n. obstacle; **speech i.** = stammer, etc., which prevents you speaking clearly. **im•ped•i•men•ta**, n. pl. heavy/awkward baggage or equipment.

im•pel [ɪm'pel] v. (**impelled**) to push/to force.

im•pend•ing [ɪm'pendɪŋ] adj. imminent/about to happen.

im•pen•e•tra•ble [ɪm'penɪtrəbl] adj. which you cannot go through or into. **im•pen•e•tra•bil•i•ty**, n. being impenetrable.

im•pen•i•tent [ɪm'penɪtənt] adj. not penitent/not sorry for having done sth wrong.

im•per•a•tive [ɪm'perətɪv] adj. (a) urgent/obligatory. (b) (in grammar) **i. verb** = verb used as a command.

im•per•cep•ti•ble [ɪmpə'septɪbl] adj. which you can hardly notice. **im•per•cep•ti•bly**, adv. scarcely noticeably.

im•per•fect [ɪm'pɜːfɪkt] adj. not perfect/not complete. **im•per•fec•tion** [ɪmpə'fekʃn] n. flaw.

im•pe•ri•al [ɪm'pɪərɪəl] adj. (a) referring to an empire. (b) (weights/measures) conforming to standards used in the United Kingdom and the British Commonwealth. **im•pe•ri•al•ism**, n. belief in the good of building an empire. **im•pe•ri•al•ist. 1.** n. person who builds an empire. **2.** adj. (also **imperialistic**) referring to imperialism.

im•per•il [ɪm'perɪl] v. (**imperiled**) (formal) to put in danger.

im•pe•ri•ous [ɪm'pɪərɪəs] adj. arrogant (way of behaving/giving orders). **im•pe•ri•ous•ly**, adv. in an imperious way.

im•per•ma•nent [ɪm'pɜːmənənt] adj. not permanent/not lasting.

im•per•me•a•ble [ɪm'pɜːmɪəbl] adj. which liquids cannot go through.

im•per•son•al [ɪm'pɜːsnl] adj. (a) without a personal touch. (b) (verb) used without a person or thing as the subject.

æ back, aː farm, ɒ top, aɪ pipe, aʊ how, aiə fire, aʊə flower, ɔː bought, ɔɪ toy, e fed, eəhair, eɪ take, ə afraid, əʊ boat, əʊə lower, vː word, iː heap, ɪ hit, ɪə hear, uː school, ʊ book, ʌ but, b back, d dog, ð then, dʒ just, f fog, g go, h hand, j yes, k catch, l last, m mix, n nut, ŋ sing, p penny, r round, s some, ʃ short, t too, tʃ chop, θ thing, v voice, w was, z zoo, ʒ treasure

im•per•son•al•ly, *adv.* in an impersonal way.

im•per•son•ate [ɪm'pɜːsəneɪt] *v.* to imitate (s.o.)/to disguise yourself as (s.o.). **im•per•son•a•tion**, *n.* act of impersonating. **im•per•son•a•tor**, *n.* person who impersonates.

im•per•ti•nence [ɪm'pɜːtɪnəns] *n.* rudeness/insolence. **im•per•ti•nent**, *adj.* rude/insolent. **im•per•ti•nent•ly**, *adv.* in an impertinent way.

im•per•turb•a•ble [ɪmpə'tɜːbəbl] *adj.* calm. **im•per•turb•a•bil•i•ty**, *n.* being imperturbable. **im•per•turb•a•bly**, *adv.* calmly.

im•per•vi•ous [ɪm'pɜːvɪəs] *adj.* **(to)** which liquids cannot go through.

im•pe•ti•go [ɪmpɪ'taɪɡəʊ] *n.* contagious disease of the skin (esp. in children).

im•pet•u•ous [ɪm'petjʊəs] *adj.* thoughtless/hasty (act); (person) who rushes to do sth without thinking. **im•pet•u•os•i•ty** [ɪmpetjʊ'ɒsɪtɪ] *n.* rushing to do sth without thinking. **im•pet•u•ous•ly** [ɪm'petjʊəslɪ] *adv.* without thinking.

im•pe•tus ['ɪmpətəs] *n.* (*pl.* **-es**) movement forward/stimulus.

im•pinge [ɪm'pɪndʒ] *v.* **(on)** to affect.

im•pi•ous ['ɪmpɪəs] *adj.* not pious/not religious. **im•pi•e•ty** [ɪm'paɪətɪ] *n.* being impious.

imp•ish ['ɪmpɪʃ] *adj.* like an imp.

im•plac•a•ble [ɪm'plækəbl] *adj.* who/which cannot be satisfied. **im•plac•a•bly**, *adv.* in an implacable way.

im•plant [ɪm'plɑːnt] 1. *n.* tissue which has been implanted. 2. *v.* to fix (sth) in deeply.

im•plau•si•ble [ɪm'plɔːzəbl] *adj.* not likely to be true.

im•ple•ment 1. *n.* ['ɪmplɪmənt] tool/instrument. 2. *v.* ['ɪmplɪment] to put into effect. **im•ple•men•ta•tion** [ɪmplɪmən'teɪʃn] *n.* putting into effect.

im•pli•cate ['ɪmplɪkeɪt] *v.* **to i. s.o. in sth** = to suggest that s.o. was connected with sth. **im•pli•ca•tion** [ɪmplɪ'keɪʃn] *n.* (a) suggestion (that s.o. is connected with a crime). (b) thing which is implied.

im•plic•it [ɪm'plɪsɪt] *adj.* which is not definitely said, but is suggested. **im•plic•it•ly**, *adv.* without questioning.

im•plore [ɪm'plɔː] *v.* to beg (s.o. to do sth).

im•ply [ɪm'plaɪ] *v.* to suggest.

im•po•lite [ɪmpə'laɪt] *adj.* rude/not polite. **im•po•lite•ly**, *adv.* rudely. **im•po•lite•ness**, *n.* lack of politeness.

im•pol•i•tic [ɪm'pɒlɪtɪk] *adj.* (*formal*) not wise.

im•pon•der•a•bles [ɪm'pɒndrəblz] *n. pl.* things whose importance you cannot easily calculate.

im•port. 1. *n.* ['ɪmpɔːt] (a) **imports** = goods which are brought into a country; **i. duty** = tax paid on goods brought into a country. (b) (*formal*) meaning (of words). 2. *v.* [ɪm'pɔːt] to bring goods into a country. **im•por•ta•tion** [ɪmpɔː'teɪʃn] *n.* act of importing; goods imported. **im•port•er** [ɪm'pɔːtə] *n.* person or country which imports.

im•por•tance [ɪm'pɔːtns] *n.* seriousness/serious effect/influence. **im•por•tant**, *adj.* (a) serious/with a serious effect/which matters a great deal. (b) with great influence/holding an influential position. **im•por•tant•ly**, *adv.* seriously/with a serious effect.

im•por•tune [ɪm'pɔːtjuːn] *v.* (*formal*) to pester/to bother (s.o.). **im•por•tu•nate** [ɪm'pɔːtjʊnət] *adj.* pestering/bothering.

im•pose [ɪm'pəʊz] *v.* (a) to inflict. (b) **to i. on** = cause trouble/inconvenience. **im•pos•ing**, *adj.* grand/solemn. **im•po•si•tion** [ɪmpə'zɪʃn] *n.* (a) laying down (of duties/conditions/obligations). (b) taking advantage (of s.o.).

im•pos•si•ble [ɪm'pɒsɪbl] *adj.* (a) which cannot be done. (b) awkward/difficult (person/situation). **im•pos•si•bil•i•ty**, *n.* being impossible. **im•pos•si•bly**, *adv.* in an impossible way; *inf.* greatly.

im•pos•tor [ɪm'pɒstə] *n.* person who pretends to be s.o. else. **im•pos•ture** [ɪm'pɒstʃə] *n.* pretending to be s.o. else.

im•po•tence ['ɪmpətəns] *n.* (a) lack of strength. (b) (*of man*) inability to have sexual intercourse. **im•po•tent**, *adj.* (a) weak. (b) (*of man*) unable to have sexual intercourse. **im•po•tent•ly**, *adv.* without being able to act.

im•pound [ɪm'paʊnd] *v.* to take (sth) away and put it in a safe place.

im•pov•er•ish [ɪm'pɒvərɪʃ] *v.* to make poor. **im•pov•er•ish•ment**, *n.* making poor.

im•prac•ti•ca•ble [ɪm'præktɪkəbl] *adj.* (plan) which cannot work; (road) which cannot be used.

im•prac•ti•cal [ɪm'præktɪkl] *adj.* (plan) which is not easy to put into practice; (person) who is not good at doing things with his/her hands.

im•pre•ca•tion [ɪmprɪ'keɪʃn] *n.* (*formal*) oath/curse.

im•pre•cise [ɪmprɪ'saɪs] *adj.* not precise/not accurate. **im•pre•ci•sion**, *n.* lack of precision.

im•preg•na•ble [ɪm'pregnəbl] *adj.* (fortress) which cannot be captured. **im•preg•na•bil•i•ty**, *n.* being impregnable.

im•preg•nate ['ɪmpregneɪt] v. (a) to soak (**with** sth). (b) to make pregnant. **im•preg•na•tion**, n. act of impregnating.

im•pre•sa•ri•o [ɪmprɪ'sɑːrɪəʊ] n. (pl. **-os**) person who organizes concerts and operas.

im•press [ɪm'pres] v. (a) to make (s.o.) admire/respect s.o./sth. (b) **to i. sth on s.o.** = to make s.o. understand. (c) to stamp (a pattern on sth). **im•pres•sion** [ɪm'preʃn] n. (a) effect on s.o.'s mind. (b) imitation of how s.o. talks/behaves. (c) mark (of a pattern). (d) printing (of a book). **im•pres•sion•a•ble**, adj. (person) who is easily influenced (by others). **im•pres•sion•ism**, n. art movement where painters tried to convey an impression of reality, in particular of light. **im•pres•sion•ist**. 1. adj. referring to impressionism. 2. n. painter in the impressionist movement. **im•pres•sion•is•tic** [ɪmpreʃə'nɪstɪk] adj. vague/sketchy. **im•pres•sive** [ɪm'presɪv] adj. which commands respect. **im•pres•sive•ly**, adv. in an impressive way.

im•pri•ma•tur [ɪmprɪ'mɑːtə] n. official permission to print a book.

im•print. 1. n. ['ɪmprɪnt] (a) mark made by sth pressed down. (b) name of publishing company printed in its books. 2. v. [ɪm'prɪnt] to stamp/to mark.

im•pris•on [ɪm'prɪzn] v. to put/to keep in prison. **im•pris•on•ment**, n. putting/keeping in prison.

im•prob•a•ble [ɪm'prɒbəbl] adj. not probable; unlikely. **im•prob•a•bil•i•ty**, n. lack of probability. **im•prob•a•bly**, adv. not likely.

im•promp•tu [ɪm'prɒmptjuː] adj. & adv. without any rehearsal or practice.

im•prop•er [ɪm'prɒpə] adj. (a) rude. (b) (word) used in a wrong way. **im•prop•er•ly**, adv. (a) not correctly. (b) (word which is used) wrongly. **im•pro•pri•e•ty** [ɪmprə'praɪətɪ] n. being improper; improper action.

im•prove [ɪm'pruːv] v. to make/to get better. **im•prove•ment**, n. thing which makes better/is better.

im•prov•i•dent [ɪm'prɒvɪdənt] adj. (person) who spends too much money or who does not plan for the future. **im•prov•i•dence**, n. being improvident. **im•prov•i•dent•ly**, adv. not thinking about saving for the future.

im•pro•vise ['ɪmprəvaɪz] v. to do/to make (sth) without preparation.

im•prov•i•sa•tion [ɪmprəvaɪ'zeɪʃn] n. making sth without any preparation.

im•pru•dent [ɪm'pruːdənt] adj. careless/not prudent. **im•pru•dent•ly**, adv. in an imprudent way.

im•pu•dent ['ɪmpjʊdənt] adj. rude/insolent. **im•pu•dence**, n. rudeness/insolence. **im•pu•dent•ly**, adv. rudely/insolently.

im•pugn [ɪm'pjuːn] v. (formal) to attack (s.o.'s character/the truth of a statement).

im•pulse ['ɪmpʌls] n. (a) shock (which makes sth move/work). (b) sudden feeling/decision; **i. buying** = buying goods on the basis of a sudden decision. **im•pul•sive** [ɪm'pʌlsɪv] adj. acting on a sudden decision/without thinking. **im•pul•sive•ly**, adv. in an impulsive way. **im•pul•sive•ness**, n. being impulsive.

im•pu•ni•ty [ɪm'pjuːnɪtɪ] n. **with i.** = without risk of punishment.

im•pure [ɪm'pjʊə] adj. not pure. **im•pu•ri•ties** [ɪm'pjʊərɪtɪz] n. pl. substances which make sth impure.

im•pute [ɪm'pjuːt] v. to attribute (sth **to** s.o.); to say that (sth) is caused by (s.o./sth). **im•pu•ta•tion**, n. saying that s.o. is at fault.

in [ɪn] 1. prep. & adv. (a) (showing place) **in Russia; in bed**. (b) (showing time) **in autumn; in January; long skirts are in** = fashionable. (c) **one in ten** = one out of ten. (d) (showing state) **dressed in pink; in public**; inf. **all in** = tired out. 2. n. **the ins and outs** = the intricate details. 3. adj. inf. fashionable. **in-box**, n. file/basket for incoming letters, messages, etc. **in for**, adv. **to be in for sth** = to be about to get sth. **in on**, adv. **to be in on (a secret)** = to know a secret.

in. abbreviation for **inch**.

in•a•bil•i•ty [ɪnə'bɪlɪtɪ] n. being unable (**to**).

in•ac•ces•si•ble [ɪnək'sesɪbl] adj. impossible to reach.

in•ac•cu•rate [ɪn'ækjʊrət] adj. not exact/not accurate. **in•ac•cu•rate•ly**, adv. not accurately. **in•ac•cu•ra•cy**, n. not being exact; lack of accuracy.

in•ac•tive [ɪn'æktɪv] adj. not active/not doing anything. **in•ac•tion, inactivity** [ɪnæk'tɪvɪtɪ] n. lack of action/doing nothing.

in•ad•e•quate [ɪn'ædɪkwət] adj. (a) not enough/insufficient. (b) not competent enough. **in•ad•e•qua•cy**, n. being inadequate. **in•ad•e•quate•ly**, adv. not enough; insufficiently.

in•ad•mis•si•ble [ɪnəd'mɪsəbl] adj. (evidence) not allowed to be presented in a court.

æ back, ɑː farm, ɒ top, aɪ pipe, aʊ how, aɪə fire, aʊə flower, ɔː bought, ɔɪ toy, e fed, eəhair, eɪ take, ə afraid, əʊ boat, əʊə lower, vː word, iː heap, ɪ hit, ɪə hear, uː school, ʊ book, ʌ but, b back, d dog, ð then, dʒ just, f fog, g go, h hand, j yes, k catch, l last, m mix, n nut, ŋ sing, p penny, r round, s some, ʃ short, t too, tʃ chop, θ thing, v voice, w was, z zoo, ʒ treasure

in•ad•vert•ent [ɪnəd'vɜːtənt] *adj.* said/done by mistake, not on purpose. **in•ad•vert•ence,** *n.* being inadvertent; thing done inadvertently. **in•ad•vert•ent•ly,** *adv.* by mistake.

in•ad•vis•a•ble [ɪnəd'vaɪzəbl] *adj.* unwise/not recommended.

in•al•ien•a•ble [ɪn'eɪljənəbl] *adj.* (formal) which cannot be taken away or refused.

in•ane [ɪ'neɪn] *adj.* stupid. **in•an•i•ty** [ɪn'ænɪti] *n.* being stupid.

in•an•i•mate [ɪn'ænɪmət] *adj.* not alive.

in•ap•pli•ca•ble [ɪnə'plɪkəbl] *adj.* unsuitable/which does not apply (to).

in•ap•pro•pri•ate [ɪnə'prəuprɪət] *adj.* (to) not appropriate/not suitable/not fitting the circumstances.

in•ap•ti•tude [ɪn'æptɪtjuːd] *n.* (for) unsuitableness; lack of ability.

in•ar•tic•u•late [ɪnɑː'tɪkjʊlət] *adj.* (a) not speaking clearly. (b) unable to speak.

in•ar•tis•tic [ɪnɑː'tɪstɪk] *adj.* not artistic; not concerned with the arts.

in•as•much as [ɪnəz'mʌtʃæz] *conj.* (formal) seeing that/owing to the fact that.

in•at•ten•tive [ɪnə'tentɪv] *adj.* not paying attention/not attentive. **in•at•ten•tion,** *n.* not paying attention.

in•au•di•ble [ɪn'ɔːdɪbl] *adj.* which cannot be heard. **in•au•di•bly,** *adv.* so quietly that it cannot be heard.

in•au•gu•rate [ɪn'ɔːgjʊreɪt] *v.* to swear in (a new president); to open officially (a new building/a festival, etc. **in•au•gu•ral,** *adj.* (speech) given at an opening ceremony; first (use); opening (ceremony). **in•au•gu•ra•tion** [ɪnɔːgjʊ'reɪʃn] *n.* swearing in (of a new president); official opening.

in•aus•pi•cious [ɪnɔː'spɪʃəs] *adj.* unlucky/not giving hope for the future.

in•board ['ɪbɔːd] *adj.* inside a boat.

in•born ['ɪnbɔːn] *adj.* (feelings/ideas) which a person has had since birth.

in•bred ['ɪnbred] *adj.* (feelings/ideas) which a person has had since a very young age. **in•breed•ing,** *n.* breeding between closely related persons/animals, etc.

Inc. [ɪn'kɔːpəreɪtɪd] *short for* incorporated.

in•cal•cu•la•ble [ɪn'kælkjʊləbl] *adj.* which cannot be calculated/so large that it cannot be measured.

in cam•er•a [ɪn'kæmərə] *adv.* in secret; not in public.

in•can•des•cent [ɪnkæn'desnt] *adj.* which burns with a very bright light. **in•can•des•cence,** *n.* very bright light.

in•can•ta•tion [ɪnkæn'teɪʃn] *n.* magic words.

in•ca•pa•ble [ɪn'keɪpəbl] *adj.* (a) (of) not able. (b) not capable; not competent. **in•ca•pa•bil•i•ty** [ɪnkeɪpə'bɪlɪti] *n.* incompetence/not being capable.

in•ca•pac•i•ty [ɪnkə'pæsɪti] *n.* lack of strength/ability to do sth. **in•ca•pac•i•tate,** *v.* to make (s.o.) unable to do sth.

in•car•cer•ate [ɪn'kɑːsəreɪt] *v.* (formal) to put/to keep in prison. **in•car•cer•a•tion** [ɪnkɑːsə'reɪʃn] *n.* putting/keeping in prison.

in•car•nate [ɪn'kɑːnət] *adj.* in human form. **in•car•na•tion** [ɪnkɑː'neɪʃn] *n.* appearance in human form.

in•cau•tious [ɪn'kɔːʃəs] *adj.* not prudent. **in•cau•tious•ly,** *adv.* rashly.

in•cen•di•ar•y [ɪn'sendjərɪ] 1. *adj.* which causes fire. 2. *n.* (a) bomb which causes fire. (b) person who sets fire to buildings.

in•cense. 1. *n.* ['ɪnsens] spice powder which when burned gives a strong smell. 2. *v.* [ɪn'sens] to make (s.o.) angry.

in•cen•tive [ɪn'sentɪv] *n.* thing which encourages, as extra money paid when production is increased.

in•cep•tion [ɪn'sepʃn] *n.* beginning.

in•ces•sant [ɪn'sesnt] *adj.* unceasing/continuous.

in•cest ['ɪnsest] *n.* sexual intercourse with a close member of the family. **in•ces•tu•ous** [ɪn'sestjuəs] *adj.* referring to incest.

inch [ɪnʃ] 1. *n.* (pl. -es) measure of length (= 1/12 of a foot or 2.54 cm). 2. *v.* to go (slowly).

in•cho•ate [ɪn'kəueɪt] *adj.* (formal) not fully developed.

in•ci•dent ['ɪnsɪdənt] *n.* (a) minor happening. (b) (usu. violent) action/disturbance. **in•ci•dence,** *n.* rate. **in•ci•den•tal** [ɪnsɪ'dentl] *adj. & n.* (thing) which happens in connection with sth else, but forming an unimportant part; subsidiary; **i. music** = background music which accompanies a motion picture. **in•ci•den•tal•ly,** *adv.* by the way. **in•ci•den•tals,** *n. pl.* minor expenses.

in•cin•er•ate [ɪn'sɪnəreɪt] *v.* to destroy by burning. **in•cin•er•a•tion** [ɪnsɪnə'reɪʃn] *n.* destruction by burning. **in•cin•er•a•tor,** *n.* furnace for burning trash.

in•cip•i•ent [ɪn'sɪpɪənt] *adj.* which is beginning/coming.

in•cise [ɪn'saɪz] *v.* to make a cut in (esp. a stone). **in•ci•sion** [ɪn'sɪʒn] *n.* cut. **in•ci•sive** [ɪn'saɪsɪv] *adj.* sharp/cutting. **in•ci•sive•ly,** *adv.* sharply. **in•ci•sor** [ɪn'saɪzə] *n.* sharp front tooth for cutting.

in•cite [ɪn'saɪt] *v.* to encourage (s.o. **to** do sth). **in•cite•ment,** *n.* encouragement (**to**).

in•ci•vil•i•ty [ɪnsɪ'vɪlɪti] *n.* (formal) rudeness.

in•clem•ent [ɪn'klemənt] *adj.* (formal) (of weather) bad.

in•cline 1. *n.* ['ɪnklaɪn] slope. 2. *v.* [ɪn'klaɪn] (a) to slope. (b) to encourage or dispose (s.o.) to do sth. (c) to tend. (d) to bend/to bow. **in•cli•na•tion** [ɪnklɪ'neɪʃn] *n.* (a) (angle of) slope. (b) slight bow (of the head). (c) tendency. **in•clined** *adj.* (a) sloping. (b) likely (**to do sth**).

in•clude [ɪn'kluːd] *v.* to count (s.o./sth) along with others. **in•clu•sion** [ɪn'kluːʒn] *n.* counting s.o./sth in among others. **in•clu•sive**, *adj.* which includes everything; **from Monday to Friday i.** = including both Monday and Friday; **i. language** = language that does not use words/phrases that might be seen as excluding certain groups of people, esp. non-sexist language.

in•cog•ni•to [ɪnkɒg'niːtəʊ] *adv. & n.* **to travel i.** = under a false name or identity.

in•co•her•ent [ɪnkəʊ'hɪərənt] *adj.* not coherent; not linked; which does not make sense. **in•co•her•ence**, *n.* being incoherent. **in•co•her•ent•ly**, *adv.* not in a coherent way; in a way which does not make sense.

in•come ['ɪŋkʌm] *n.* money which you receive; **i. tax** = tax on income; **unearned i.** = income from investments/rents.

in•com•ing ['ɪnkʌmɪŋ] 1. *adj.* which is arriving/coming in; **i. calls** = telephone calls received. 2. *n. pl.* **incomings** = revenue.

in•com•mode [ɪnkɒ'məʊd] *v.* (*formal*) to inconvenience (s.o.).

in•com•mu•ni•ca•do [ɪnkəmjuːnɪ'kɑːdəʊ] *adv.* not allowed to see or write to any person.

in•com•pa•ra•ble [ɪn'kɒmprəbl] *adj.* which cannot be compared to anything else. **in•com•pa•ra•bly**, *adv.* vastly; so much that it cannot be compared.

in•com•pat•i•ble [ɪnkəm'pætɪbl] *adj.* (**with**) which cannot live/work/fit together. **in•com•pat•i•bil•i•ty** [ɪnkəmpætə'bɪlɪti] *n.* being incompatible (**with**).

in•com•pe•tent [ɪn'kɒmpɪtənt] *adj.* not good at doing sth/not competent. **in•com•pe•tence**, *n.* lack of competence. **in•com•pe•tent•ly**, *adv.* in an incompetent way.

in•com•plete [ɪnkəm'pliːt] *adj.* not complete/not finished. **in•com•plete•ly**, *adv.* not completely.

in•com•pre•hen•si•ble [ɪnkɒmprɪ'hensɪbl] *adj.* which cannot be understood. **in•com•pre•hen•sion**, *n.* lack of understanding.

in•con•ceiv•a•ble [ɪnkən'siːvəbl] *adj.* which cannot be imagined.

in•con•clu•sive [ɪnkən'kluːsɪv] *adj.* not final; without a definite result. **in•con•clu•sive•ly**, *adv.* in an inconclusive way.

in•con•gru•ous [ɪn'kɒŋgrʊəs] *adj.* which does not fit with the rest; which seems out of place. **in•con•gru•i•ty**, *n.* being out of place.

in•con•se•quen•tial [ɪnkɒnsɪ'kwenʃl] *adj.* not of any importance.

in•con•sid•er•a•ble [ɪnkən'sɪdərəbl] *adj.* small.

in•con•sid•er•ate [ɪnkən'sɪdərət] *adj.* not thinking of other people. **in•con•sid•er•ate•ly**, *adv.* not thinking about other people.

in•con•sist•ent [ɪnkən'sɪstənt] *adj.* (a) which does not follow/which contradicts. (b) (person) who changes his/her mind frequently. **in•con•sist•en•cy**, *n.* lack of consistency.

in•con•sol•a•ble [ɪnkən'səʊləbl] *adj.* (person) who cannot be comforted.

in•con•spic•u•ous [ɪnkən'spɪkjʊəs] *adj.* not very noticeable. **in•con•spic•u•ous•ly**, *adv.* without being noticed.

in•con•stant [ɪn'kɒnstənt] *adj.* (*formal*) not constant; unfaithful. **in•con•stan•cy**, *n.* lack of constancy.

in•con•test•a•ble [ɪnkən'testəbl] *adj.* which cannot be argued with.

in•con•ti•nent [ɪn'kɒntɪnənt] *adj.* unable to control your bladder or bowels. **in•con•ti•nence**, *n.* being incontinent.

in•con•tro•vert•i•ble [ɪnkɒntrə'vɜːtəbl] *adj.* (fact) with which you must agree; which cannot be disputed.

in•con•ven•ience [ɪnkən'viːnɪəns] 1. *n.* which causes difficulty, awkwardness or bother. 2. *v.* to bother (s.o.). **in•con•ven•ient**, *adj.* awkward; not handy. **in•con•ven•ient•ly**, *adv.* awkwardly.

in•cor•po•rate [ɪn'kɔːpəreɪt] *v.* (a) to bring into one main part. (b) to form an official body. (c) to form a corporation. **in•cor•po•ra•tion** [ɪnkɔːpə'reɪʃn] *n.* act of incorporating.

in•cor•rect [ɪnkə'rekt] *adj.* not correct/false. **in•cor•rect•ly**, *adv.* wrongly/falsely.

in•cor•ri•gi•ble [ɪn'kɒrɪdʒəbl] *adj.* (person) who cannot be corrected/improved.

in•cor•ri•gi•bly, *adv.* in an incorrigible way.

in•cor•rupt•i•ble [ɪnkə'rʌptəbl] *adj.* (person) who cannot be corrupted/be persuaded to behave dishonestly. **in•cor•rupt•i•bil•i•ty** [ɪnkərʌptɪ'bɪlɪtɪ] *n.* being incorruptible.

in•crease 1. *n.* ['ɪnkriːs] growth/expansion; rise (in salary). 2. *v.* [ɪn'kriːs] to rise/to grow/to expand. **in•creas•ing,** *adj.* growing. **in•creas•ing•ly,** *adv.* more and more.

in•cred•i•ble [ɪn'kredɪbl] *adj.* which it is difficult to believe. **in•cred•i•bly,** *adv.* unbelievably.

in•cred•u•lous [ɪn'kredjuləs] *adj.* (person) who does not believe. **in•cre•du•li•ty** [ɪnkrə'djuːlɪtɪ] *n.* lack of belief. **in•cred•u•lous•ly,** *adv.* as if you do not believe.

in•cre•ment ['ɪnkrəmənt] *n.* regular automatic addition (to salary). **in•cre•men•tal** [ɪnkrɪ'mentl] *adj.* referring to increments.

in•crim•i•nate [ɪn'krɪmɪneɪt] *v.* to show that (s.o.) took part in a crime, etc. **in•crim•i•nat•ing,** *adj.* which shows that s.o. took part in a crime. **in•crim•i•na•to•ry** [ɪn'krɪmɪnətərɪ] *adj.* which incriminates.

in•crust [ɪn'krʌst] *v.* to cover with a hard covering. **in•crus•ta•tion,** *n.* layer (of dirt, etc.) incrusted on a surface.

in•cu•bate ['ɪnkjubeɪt] *v.* to keep (eggs) warm until they hatch; to have (the germs of a disease) in your body. **in•cu•ba•tion** [ɪnkju'beɪʃn] *n.* keeping eggs warm until they hatch; **i. period** = period during which a disease develops in your body. **in•cu•ba•tor,** *n.* warm box in which eggs are kept until they hatch; sterilized receptacle for keeping very small babies in until they are strong.

in•cu•bus ['ɪnkjubəs] *n.* nightmare; problem which causes great worry.

in•cul•cate ['ɪnkʌlkeɪt] *v.* (*formal*) to fix (ideas, etc.) in the mind of a person.

in•cum•bent [ɪn'kʌmbənt] 1. *n.* person who holds an office, position, etc. at the present time. 2. *adj.* (*formal*) **it is i. on you** = it is your responsibility. **in•cum•ben•cy,** *n.* period when s.o. holds an office, position, etc.

in•cur [ɪn'kɜː] *v.* (**incurred**) to run (a risk); to be liable to; to bring (sth) on yourself.

in•cur•a•ble [ɪn'kjuərəbl] *adj.* which cannot be made better. **in•cur•a•bly,** *adv.* in a way which cannot be made better.

in•cu•ri•ous [ɪn'kjuərɪəs] *adj.* not curious/not showing any curiosity.

in•cur•sion [ɪn'kɜːʃn] *n.* movement into sth; attack on sth.

in•debt•ed [ɪn'detɪd] *adj.* owing sth **to** s.o. **in•debt•ed•ness,** *n.* being indebted.

in•de•cent [ɪn'diːsnt] *adj.* not decent/rude/offensive. **in•de•cen•cy,** *n.* being indecent. **in•de•cent•ly,** *adv.* not decently; in a way which shocks.

in•de•ci•pher•a•ble [ɪndɪ'saɪfrəbl] *adj.* (writing/message) that cannot be read/understood.

in•de•ci•sion [ɪndɪ'sɪʒn] *n.* (state of) not being able to decide; hesitating. **in•de•ci•sive** [ɪndɪ'saɪsɪv] *adj.* without a positive result; which/who cannot decide anything.

in•dec•o•rous [ɪn'dekərəs] *adj.* (*formal*) slightly improper.

in•deed [ɪn'diːd] *adv.* (a) really/truly. (b) in fact. (c) *inter. meaning* really! **i. not!** = of course not!

in•de•fat•i•ga•ble [ɪndɪ'fætɪgəbl] *adj.* tireless/who cannot be tired out. **in•de•fat•i•ga•bly,** *adv.* tirelessly.

in•de•fen•si•ble [ɪndɪ'fensɪbl] *adj.* which cannot be defended/excused.

in•de•fin•a•ble [ɪndɪ'faɪnəbl] *adj.* which cannot be defined/explained.

in•def•i•nite [ɪn'defɪnɪt] *adj.* vague; not definite; **i. article** = "a"/"an" (*as opposed to the definite article* "the"). **in•def•i•nite•ly,** *adv.* for an indefinite period.

in•del•i•ble [ɪn'delɪbl] *adj.* which cannot be rubbed out. **in•del•i•bly,** *adv.* permanently (marked).

in•del•i•cate [ɪn'delɪkət] *adj.* rude/not polite. **in•del•i•ca•cy,** *n.* being indelicate.

in•dem•ni•fy [ɪn'demnɪfaɪ] *v.* to pay (s.o.) for damage. **in•dem•ni•ty,** *n.* (a) payment (for loss/damage). (b) guarantee (of payment) against loss/damage.

in•dent [ɪn'dent] *v.* to start a line several spaces in from the left-hand margin. **in•den•ta•tion** [ɪnden'teɪʃn] *n.* inward cut along an edge. **in•dent•ed,** *adj.* with a jagged edge.

in•den•ture [ɪn'dentʃə] *n.* contract by which a person is apprenticed to a master craftsman.

in•de•pend•ent [ɪndɪ'pendənt] *adj.* free/not ruled by anyone else; not needing/not relying on anyone else; (candidate) not belonging to a political party. **in•de•pend•ence,** *n.* freedom; not needing/not relying on anyone else. **in•de•pend•ent•ly,** *adv.* freely; separately.

in•de•scrib•a•ble [ɪndɪ'skraɪbəbl] *adj.* which cannot be described. **in•de•scrib•a•bly,** *adv.* in a way which cannot be described.

in•de•struct•i•ble [ɪndɪ'strʌktəbl] *adj.* which cannot be destroyed.

in•de•ter•mi•na•ble [ɪndɪ'tɜ:mɪnəbl] *adj.* which cannot be decided/solved.

in•de•ter•mi•nate [ɪndɪ'tɜ:mɪnət] *adj.* vague/not precise.

in•dex ['ɪndeks] 1. *n.* (*pl.* **-dexes, -dices** [-dɪsi:z]) (a) **i. (finger)** = first finger (next to the thumb). (b) classified list (showing the contents/references in a book). (c) **cost of living i.** = regular government statistics which show the rises and falls in the cost of living. 2. *v.* (a) to write an index for (a book). (b) to relate (wages, taxes, pensions, etc.) to the cost of living index. **in•dex•er**, *n.* person who compiles indexes. **in•dex•ing**, *n.* (a) (*also* **indexation**) relating sth to the cost of living index. (b) compiling of an index.

In•di•an ['ɪndjən] 1. *adj.* referring to India; referring to the indigenous people of North and South America; **in I. file** = in line/one behind the other; **I. summer** = period of hot weather in autumn. 2. *n.* (a) person from India. (b) member of one of the indigenous tribes of North and South America.

in•di•a rub•ber [ɪndjə'rʌbə] *n.* rubber eraser for rubbing out pencil marks.

in•di•cate ['ɪndɪkeɪt] *v.* to show/to point out. **in•di•ca•tion** [ɪndɪ'keɪʃn] *n.* sign/pointer. **in•dic•a•tive** [ɪn'dɪkətɪv] *adj.* (a) typical/which indicates. (b) (tense of a verb) which shows that the action actually took place/is taking place. **in•di•ca•tor**, *n.* (a) thing which indicates.

in•dict [ɪn'daɪt] *v.* to accuse (s.o.) of a crime. **in•dict•a•ble**, *adj.* (offense) which you can be charged with. **in•dict•ment** [ɪn'daɪtmənt] *n.* detailed accusation.

in•dif•fer•ent [ɪn'dɪfrənt] *adj.* (a) not caring; not interested. (b) ordinary/mediocre; not special. **in•dif•fer•ence**, *n.* lack of interest. **in•dif•fer•ent•ly**, *adv.* (a) not bothering. (b) in a mediocre way.

in•dig•e•nous [ɪn'dɪdʒənəs] *adj.* (**to**) which is born in/belongs to (a place).

in•di•gent ['ɪndɪdʒənt] *adj.* (*formal*) very poor. **in•di•gence**, *n.* great poverty.

in•di•ges•tion [ɪndɪ'dʒestʃn] *n.* not being able to digest food; pain caused when the body is unable to digest food. **in•di•gest•i•ble**, *adj.* which cannot be digested; which causes pain because the body cannot digest it.

in•dig•nant [ɪn'dɪgnənt] *adj.* feeling offended/angry. **in•dig•nant•ly**, *adv.* in an indignant way. **in•dig•na•tion** [ɪndɪg'neɪʃn] *n.* being indignant.

in•dig•ni•ty [ɪn'dɪgnɪtɪ] *n.* injury to s.o.'s dignity.

in•di•go ['ɪndɪgəʊ] *n.* blue dye; deep blue color.

in•di•rect [ɪndɪ'rekt, ɪndaɪ'rekt] *adj.* (a) not direct/oblique; (tax) added to the price of goods before they are sold and not paid directly to the government. (b) (discourse) reporting what s.o. has said but not in his exact words. **in•di•rect•ly**, *adv.* not directly.

in•dis•creet [ɪndɪ'skri:t] *adj.* revealing/not discreet. **in•dis•cre•tion** [ɪndɪ'skreʃn] *n.* (a) lack of discretion/being careless about what you do or say. (b) doing sth careless.

in•dis•crim•i•nate [ɪndɪ'skrɪmənət] *adj.* widespread/not selective. **in•dis•crim•i•nate•ly**, *adv.* (a) in every direction. (b) without selecting/without choosing.

in•dis•pen•sa•ble [ɪndɪ'spensəbl] *adj.* which you cannot do without.

in•dis•posed [ɪndɪ'spəʊzd] *adj.* (a) slightly ill. (b) unwilling. **in•dis•po•si•tion** [ɪndɪspə'zɪʃn] *n.* (a) slight illness. (b) unwillingness.

in•dis•put•a•ble [ɪndɪ'spju:təbl] *adj.* which cannot be argued over. **in•dis•put•a•bly**, *adv.* certainly.

in•dis•sol•u•ble [ɪndɪ'sɒljʊbl] *adj.* which cannot be destroyed/dissolved.

in•dis•tinct [ɪndɪ'stɪŋkt] *adj.* vague/unclear. **in•dis•tinct•ly**, *adv.* vaguely/unclearly.

in•dis•tin•guish•a•ble [ɪndɪ'stɪŋgwɪʃəbl] *adj.* which cannot be told apart **from** sth.

in•di•vid•u•al [ɪndɪ'vɪdjʊəl] 1. *n.* (a) single person. (b) *inf.* person. 2. *adj.* (a) single. (b) belonging to a particular person. (c) for one person. **in•di•vid•u•al•ist**, *n.* person who emphasizes that he is unique and not a member of a group. **in•di•vid•u•al•is•tic**, *adj.* like an individualist. **in•di•vid•u•al•i•ty** [ɪndɪvɪdju'ælɪtɪ] *n.* quality which makes each person different from all others. **in•di•vid•u•al•ly**, *adv.* singly/as a single person.

in•di•vis•i•ble [ɪndɪ'vɪzəbl] *adj.* which cannot be divided/separated. **in•di•vis•i•bly**, *adv.* in a way which prevents it being divided/separated.

in•doc•tri•nate [ɪn'dɒktrɪneɪt] *v.* to teach (s.o.), esp. political ideas.

æ **back**, ɑ: **farm**, ɒ: **top**, aɪ **pipe**, aʊ **how**, aɪə **fire**, aʊə **flower**, ɔ: **bought**, ɔɪ **toy**, e **fed**, eə**hair**, eɪ **take**, ə **afraid**, əʊ **boat**, əʊə **lower**, ɜ: **word**, i: **heap**, ɪ **hit**, ɪə **hear**, u: **school**, ʊ **book**, ʌ **but**, b **back**, d **dog**, ð **then**, dʒ **just**, f **fog**, g **go**, h **hand**, j **yes**, k **catch**, l **last**, m **mix**, n **nut**, ŋ **sing**, p **penny**, r **round**, s **some**, ʃ **short**, t **too**, tʃ **chop**, θ **thing**, v **voice**, w **was**, z **zoo**, ʒ **treasure**

in•doc•tri•na•tion [ɪndɒktrɪˈneɪʃn] *n.* teaching s.o., esp. political ideas.

in•do•lence [ˈɪndələns] *n.* laziness. **in•do•lent,** *adj.* lazy.

in•dom•i•ta•ble [ɪnˈdɒmɪtəbl] *adj.* which cannot be overcome.

in•door [ˈɪndɔː] *adj.* done/found inside a building. **in•doors** [ɪnˈdɔːz] *adv.* inside a building.

in•du•bi•ta•ble [ɪnˈdjuːbɪtəbl] *adj.* which cannot be doubted. **in•du•bi•ta•bly,** *adv.* certainly/definitely.

in•duce [ɪnˈdjuːs] *v.* (a) to persuade (s.o.) to do sth. (b) to provoke (sth)/to make (sth) happen; to make (a birth) happen. **in•duce•ment,** *n.* thing which helps persuade you to do sth.

in•duct [ɪnˈdʌkt] *v.* to place (s.o.) in an office, position, etc. **in•duc•tion** [ɪnˈdʌkʃn] *n.* (a) formal entry of a person into a new job, office, position, etc. (b) creation of electricity in an object by placing it near a magnet or near sth which is electrically charged. **in•duc•tive,** *adj.* (reasoning) based on known facts.

in•dulge [ɪnˈdʌldʒ] *v.* (a) to spoil (s.o.). (b) (in) to give way to (sth enjoyable). **in•dul•gence,** *n.* being indulgent; indulgent action. **in•dul•gent,** *adj.* kind/soft; too generous. **in•dul•gent•ly,** *adv.* kindly; too generously.

in•dus•try [ˈɪndəstrɪ] *n.* (a) all manufacturing processes. (b) hard work/steady work. **in•dus•tri•al** [ɪnˈdʌstrɪəl] *adj.* referring to manufacturing work. **in•dus•tri•al•ist,** *n.* owner/director of a factory. **in•dus•tri•al•i•za•tion** [ɪndʌstrɪəlaɪˈzeɪʃn] *n.* changing of a society from agricultural to industrial. **in•dus•tri•al•ize** [ɪnˈdʌstrɪəlaɪz] *v.* to create industries (where there were none before). **in•dus•tri•al•ly,** *adv.* (made) by industry. **in•dus•tri•ous,** *adj.* (person) who works steadily and hard. **in•dus•tri•ous•ly,** *adv.* in an industrious way.

in•e•bri•ate [ɪˈniːbrɪət] *adj.* (*formal*) (person) who is often drunk. **in•e•bri•at•ed,** *adj.* drunk. **in•e•bri•a•tion,** *n.* drunken state.

in•ed•i•ble [ɪnˈedɪbl] *adj.* which you cannot eat.

in•ed•u•ca•ble [ɪnˈedjʊkəbl] *adj.* (person) who cannot be educated.

in•ef•fa•ble [ɪnˈefəbl] *adj.* (*formal*) so wonderful that it cannot be properly described.

in•ef•fec•tive [ɪnɪˈfektɪv] *adj.* which does not have any effect.

in•ef•fec•tu•al [ɪnɪˈfektjʊəl] *adj.* (attempt) which is unsuccessful; (person) who is weak/incapable of asserting his authority.

in•ef•fi•cient [ɪnɪˈfɪʃnt] *adj.* not efficient; not competent. **in•ef•fi•cien•cy,** *n.* incompe-

tence/lack of efficiency. **in•ef•fi•cient•ly,** *adv.* in an inefficient way.

in•el•e•gant [ɪnˈelɪgənt] *adj.* not elegant.

in•el•i•gi•ble [ɪnˈelɪdʒəbl] *adj.* (person) who is not qualified (**for** sth, **to** do sth).

in•ept [ɪnˈept] *adj.* stupid (remark); incapable (person). **in•ept•i•tude,** *n.* stupidity/silliness; being unable to do sth.

in•e•qual•i•ty [ɪnɪˈkwɒlɪtɪ] *n.* lack of equality.

in•eq•ui•ta•ble [ɪnˈekwɪtəbl] *adj.* unjust/not fair.

in•e•rad•i•ca•ble [ɪnɪˈrædɪkəbl] *adj.* which cannot be eradicated/removed. •

in•ert [ɪˈnɜːt] *adj.* unmoving; (gas) which does not react with other substances. **in•er•tia** [ɪˈnɜːʃə] *n.* (a) lack of motion in a body. (b) continuous movement of a body, unless checked by a force. (c) laziness.

in•es•cap•a•ble [ɪnɪˈskeɪpəbl] *adj.* which you cannot avoid.

in•es•sen•tial [ɪnɪˈsenʃl] *adj. & n.* (thing) which is not absolutely necessary.

in•es•ti•ma•ble [ɪnˈestɪməbl] *adj.* which cannot be estimated/calculated.

in•ev•i•ta•ble [ɪnˈevɪtəbl] *adj.* which cannot be avoided. **in•ev•i•ta•bil•i•ty** [ɪnevɪtəˈbɪlɪtɪ] *n.* being inevitable. **in•ev•i•ta•bly,** *adv.* of course; with certainty.

in•ex•act [ɪnɪgˈzækt] *adj.* not exact/not correct. **in•ex•act•i•tude,** *n.* error.

in•ex•cus•a•ble [ɪnɪkˈskjuːzəbl] *adj.* which cannot be excused/forgiven. **in•ex•cus•a•bly,** *adv.* in an inexcusable way.

in•ex•haust•i•ble [ɪnɪgˈzɔːstəbl] *adj.* which cannot be used up.

in•ex•o•ra•ble [ɪnˈeksərəbl] *adj.* which cannot be changed/influenced.

in•ex•pe•di•ent [ɪnɪkˈspiːdɪənt] *adj.* (action) which is not expedient.

in•ex•pen•sive [ɪnɪkˈspensɪv] *adj.* cheap/not expensive.

in•ex•pe•ri•ence [ɪnɪkˈspɪərɪəns] *n.* lack of experience. **in•ex•pe•ri•enced,** *adj.* with no experience/lacking experience.

in•ex•pert [ɪnˈekspɜːt] *adj.* (at) not expert/not skilled.

in•ex•pli•ca•ble [ɪnɪkˈsplɪkəbl] *adj.* which cannot be explained. **in•ex•pli•ca•bly,** *adv.* in a way which cannot be explained.

in•ex•press•i•ble [ɪnɪkˈspresɪbl] *adj.* which cannot be expressed in words.

in ex•tre•mis [ɪneksˈtriːmɪs] *adv.* at the very end; (*of person*) when near to death.

in•ex•tri•ca•ble [ɪneksˈtrɪkəbl] *adj.* which you cannot get out of. **in•ex•tri•ca•bly,** *adv.* in an inextricable way.

in•fal•li•ble [ɪn'fæləbl] *adj.* always correct/true; (person) who never makes mistakes. in•fal•li•bil•i•ty [ɪnfælɪ'bɪlɪtɪ] *n.* being infallible. in•fal•li•bly, *adv.* unfailingly/always.

in•fa•mous ['ɪnfəməs] *adj.* very wicked (person/action). in•fa•my, *n.* (*formal*) great wickedness.

in•fant ['ɪnfənt] *n.* young child. in•fan•cy, *n.* young childhood. in•fan•ti•cide [ɪn-'fæntɪsaɪd] *n.* killing of a baby. in•fan•tile ['ɪnfəntaɪl] *adj.* referring to a small child; childish.

in•fan•try ['ɪnfəntrɪ] *n.* section of an army which fights on foot.

in•fat•u•at•ed [ɪn'fætjueɪtɪd] *adj.* mad (about); wildly in love (**with**). in•fat•u•a•tion [ɪnfætju'eɪʃn] *n.* blind love for someone.

in•fect [ɪn'fekt] *v.* to make diseased. in•fec•tion, *n.* (a) making diseased. (b) disease which spreads. in•fec•tious, *adj.* (disease) which can be passed from one person to another.

in•fer [ɪn'fɜ:] *v.* (**inferred**) (a) to deduce (**from**). (b) to imply/to hint. in•fer•ence ['ɪnfərəns] *n.* conclusion/deduction.

in•fe•ri•or [ɪn'fɪərɪə] 1. *adj.* not as good. 2. *n.* person of a lower rank/subordinate. in•fe•ri•or•i•ty [ɪnfɪərɪ'ɒrɪtɪ] *n.* state of being not as good as s.o. else; i. **complex** = exaggerated idea that one is not as good as others.

in•fer•nal [ɪn'fɜ:nl] *adj. inf.* like hell/hellish. in•fer•nal•ly, *adv. inf.* extremely.

in•fer•no [ɪn'fɜ:nəu] *n.* (**-os**) blaze of fire.

in•fer•tile [ɪn'fɜ:tl] *adj.* not fertile/not capable of having young; (land) which is not rich enough to produce crops. in•fer•til•i•ty [ɪnfə'tɪlɪtɪ] *n.* being unable to bear young.

in•fest [ɪn'fest] *v.* to cover/to swarm over in large numbers. in•fes•ta•tion [ɪnfes'teɪʃn] *n.* being covered with pests.

in•fi•del ['ɪnfɪdəl] *n.* person who is opposed to a religion, esp. Christianity.

in•fi•del•i•ty [ɪnfɪ'delɪtɪ] *n.* being unfaithful.

in•fight•ing ['ɪnfaɪtɪŋ] *n.* bitter argument between members of a group.

in•fil•trate ['ɪnfɪltreɪt] *v.* to enter (a political or other group) secretly. in•fil•tra•tion [ɪnfɪl'treɪʃn] *n.* act of infiltrating. in•fil•tra•tor ['ɪnfɪltreɪtə] *n.* person who infiltrates.

in•fi•nite ['ɪnfɪnət] *adj.* endless/with no end. in•fi•nite•ly, *adv.* completely; much more. in•fin•i•tes•i•mal [ɪnfɪnɪ'tesɪml] *adj.* tiny/microscopic. in•fin•i•tive [ɪn'fɪnɪtɪv] *adj. & n.* form of the verb using "to". in•fin•i•ty, *n.* never-ending space.

in•firm [ɪn'fɜ:m] *adj.* sick/weak (person). in•fir•ma•ry, *n.* (a) hospital. (b) place in a factory or school for the care of the sick or injured. in•fir•mi•ty, *n.* physical weakness.

in•flame [ɪn'fleɪm] *v.* (a) (*formal*) to make violent. (b) to cause inflammation in. in•flam•ma•ble [ɪn'flæməbl] *adj.* which catches fire easily. in•flam•ma•tion [ɪnflə-'meɪʃn] *n.* swelling/redness caused by infection. in•flam•ma•to•ry [ɪn'flæmətərɪ] *adj.* (speech) which makes people behave violently.

in•flate [ɪn'fleɪt] *v.* to blow up (balloon/tire); to increase (prices, etc.) artificially. in•flat•a•ble, *adj.* which can be blown up. in•fla•tion [ɪn'fleɪʃn] *n.* economic state where prices and wages are rising to keep pace with each other. in•fla•tion•ar•y, *adj.* (policy) which tends to increase inflation.

in•flect [ɪn'flekt] *v.* to change the ending of (a word, e.g. when used in the plural). in•flec•tion, *Brit.* in•flex•ion, *n.* ending of a word which changes to indicate the plural, the gender, etc.

in•flex•i•ble [ɪn'fleksəbl] *adj.* which cannot be bent/altered; (person) who cannot be persuaded to change his mind. in•flex•i•bil•i•ty [ɪnfleksɪ'bɪlɪtɪ] *n.* not being able to bend/to adapt. in•flex•i•bly, *adv.* in an unbending way.

in•flict [ɪn'flɪkt] *v.* to i. **pain/damage on** = to cause pain/damage to; to i. **oneself on s.o.** = force s.o. to accept one's presence. in•flic•tion [ɪn'flɪkʃn] *n.* (act of) inflicting.

in•flo•res•cence [ɪnflɒ'resəns] *n.* group of flowers arranged on one stem.

in•flow ['ɪnfləu] *n.* flowing in.

in•flu•ence ['ɪnfluəns] 1. *n.* (**on**) ability to make s.o./sth change; effect on others. 2. *v.* to make (s.o./sth) change. in•flu•en•tial [ɪnflu'enʃl] *adj.* so powerful as to cause change; having an effect on others.

in•flu•en•za [ɪnflu'enzə] *n.* virus disease like a bad cold with a high temperature.

in•flux ['ɪnflʌks] *n.* (*pl.* **-es**) entry (of a crowd or group of people).

æ back, a: farm, ɒ: top, aɪ pipe, aʊ how, aɪə fire, aʊə flower, ɔ: bought, ɔɪ toy, e fed, eəhair, eɪ take, ə afraid, əʊ boat, əʊə lower, v: word, i: heap, ɪ hit, ɪə hear, u: school, ʊ book, ʌ but, b back, d dog, ð then, dʒ just, f fog, g go, h hand, j yes, k catch, l last, m mix, n nut, ŋ sing, p penny, r round, s some, ʃ short, t too, tʃ chop, θ thing, v voice, w was, z zoo, ʒ treasure

in•fo•mer•cial [ɪnfə'mɜːʃəl] *n.* an extended TV advertisement in an informative style.

in•form [ɪn'fɔːm] *v.* to tell officially; to give details; **to i. against s.o.** = to tell (the police, etc.) about s.o. **in•form•ant,** *n.* person who passes on information/who gives details. **in•for•mat•ics,** *n.* study of information processing. **in•for•ma•tion** [ɪnfə'meɪʃn] *n.* details/knowledge; **i. superhighway** = high-speed global computer network (the Internet); **i. technology** = technology of the communication and storage of information by computers. **in•for•ma•tive** [ɪn'fɔːmətɪv] *adj.* which tells you a lot/which conveys much detailed information. **in•formed,** *adj.* up-to-date/reliable. **in•form•er,** *n.* person who informs against his accomplices.

in•for•mal [ɪn'fɔːml] *adj.* not formal/relaxed; not following any rules; not official. **in•for•mal•ly,** *adv.* not formally/unofficially. **in•for•mal•i•ty** [ɪnfɔː'mælɪtɪ] *n.* lack of any special ceremony.

in•fo•tain•ment [ɪnfə'teɪnmənt] *n.* TV program presenting information, esp. news, in an entertaining style.

in•fra dig ['ɪnfrə'dɪg] *adv. inf.* beneath one's dignity.

in•fra-red [ɪnfrə'red] *adj.* (heat rays) which are invisible and have a longer wave-length than visible red heat rays.

in•fra•struc•ture ['ɪnfrəstrʌktʃə] *n.* basic structure; supporting framework.

in•fre•quent [ɪn'friːkwənt] *adj.* not frequent; not happening very often. **in•fre•quen•cy,** *n.* lack of frequency. **in•fre•quent•ly,** *adv.* not very often/not frequently.

in•fringe [ɪn'frɪndʒ] *v.* to break (a law). **in•fringe•ment,** *n.* breaking (**of** a law).

in•fu•ri•ate [ɪn'fjʊərɪeɪt] *v.* to make furious.

in•fuse [ɪn'fjuːz] *v.* to pour hot water (on tea leaves, etc.) to make a drink. **in•fu•sion** [ɪn'fjuːʒn] *n.* drink made by pouring hot water on dried leaves, etc.

in•gen•ious [ɪn'dʒiːnɪəs] *adj.* very clever (device/person). **in•ge•nu•i•ty** [ɪndʒə'njuːɪtɪ] *n.* cleverness/skill in inventing new techniques.

in•gé•nue [ænʒeɪnjuː] *n.* supposedly simple girl.

in•gen•u•ous [ɪn'dʒenjʊəs] *adj.* naive/innocent; lacking experience. **in•gen•u•ous•ness,** *n.* being ingenuous.

in•gest [ɪn'dʒest] *v.* (*formal*) to take into the body (as food).

in•gle•nook ['ɪŋgəlnʊk] *n.* seat at the side of a very large fireplace.

in•glo•ri•ous [ɪn'glɔːrɪəs] *adj.* (*formal*) dishonorable/not glorious.

in•got ['ɪŋgət] *n.* bar (of gold, etc.).

in•grained ['ɪngreɪnd] *adj.* fixed.

in•gra•ti•ate [ɪn'greɪʃɪeɪt] *v.* **to i. oneself with s.o.** = make oneself liked by s.o. **in•gra•ti•at•ing,** *adj.* which will help you worm your way into s.o.'s favor.

in•grat•i•tude [ɪn'grætɪtjuːd] *n.* lack of gratitude; not being grateful.

in•gre•di•ent [ɪn'griːdɪənt] *n.* substance which is a component of sth.

in•gress ['ɪngres] *n.* (*formal*) entry.

in•grow•ing ['ɪngrəʊɪŋ] *adj.* (toenail) which grows into the flesh.

in•hab•it [ɪn'hæbɪt] *v.* to live in. **in•hab•it•a•ble,** *adj.* (place) which can be lived in. **in•hab•it•ant,** *n.* person who lives in a place.

in•hale [ɪn'heɪl] *v.* to draw (sth) into the lungs when breathing. **in•hal•ant, inhalation,** *n.* medicine which has to be inhaled. **in•hal•er,** *n.* device which makes a vapor which has to be inhaled.

in•her•ent [ɪn'hɪərənt] *adj.* natural/inborn. **in•her•ent•ly,** *adv.* naturally.

in•her•it [ɪn'herɪt] *v.* (a) to take over (money, etc.) from a person who has died; to have (characteristics) passed on from a parent. (b) to take over (a client/a problem) from a predecessor. **in•her•it•ance,** *n.* money/goods which you receive on the death of s.o. **in•her•i•tor,** *n.* person who inherits.

in•hib•it [ɪn'hɪbɪt] *v.* to restrain (s.o.) **from** doing sth. **in•hi•bi•tion** [ɪnhɪ'bɪʃn] *n.* thing which prevents you from expressing yourself freely/from letting yourself go. **in•hib•i•to•ry,** *adj.* which inhibits.

in•hos•pi•ta•ble [ɪnhɒ'spɪtəbl] *adj.* not welcoming.

in-house [ɪn'haʊs] *adj. & adv.* inside an office or factory.

in•hu•man [ɪn'hjuːmən] *adj.* not human; savage/brutal. **in•hu•mane** [ɪnhjuː'meɪn] *adj.* not humane; showing great cruelty. **in•hu•man•i•ty** [ɪnhjuː'mænɪtɪ] *n.* great cruelty. **in•hu•man•ly,** *adv.* savagely/brutally.

in•im•i•cal [ɪ'nɪmɪkl] *adj.* (*formal*) unfriendly.

in•im•i•ta•ble [ɪ'nɪmɪtəbl] *adj.* which cannot be imitated.

in•iq•ui•tous [ɪ'nɪkwɪtəs] *adj.* (*formal*) wicked. **in•iq•ui•ty,** *n.* wickedness.

in•i•tial [ɪ'nɪʃl] 1. *adj.* first. 2. *n.* **initials** = first letters (of name). 3. *v.* (**initialed, initialled**) to write your initials on (a document) to show you have read and approved it. **in•i•tial•ly,** *adv.* in the first place/at the beginning.

in•i•ti•ate [ɪ'nɪʃɪeɪt] *v.* (a) to start (sth). (b) to introduce (s.o.) **into** a secret society; to show (s.o.) the basic information about sth.

in•i•ti•a•tion [ɪnɪʃɪˈeɪʃn] *n.* introduction to a secret society. **in•i•ti•a•tive** [ɪˈnɪʃɪətɪv] *n.* decision to start sth; ability to decide. **in•i•ti•a•tor,** *n.* person who starts (a project).

in•ject [ɪnˈdʒekt] *v.* to pump a liquid into (sth/s.o.) under pressure; to put (sth new) into. **in•jec•tion,** *n.* act of injecting; liquid which has been injected.

in•ju•di•cious [ɪndʒuːˈdɪʃəs] *adj.* (*formal*) unwise.

in•junc•tion [ɪnˈdʒʌŋkʃn] *n.* (a) order (by a court) preventing s.o. from doing sth. (b) instruction; command.

in•jure [ˈɪndʒə] *v.* to hurt/to wound; **the injured party** = the party in a court case who has been offended. **the injured,** *n. pl.* people who have been wounded. **in•ju•ri•ous** [ɪnˈdʒuːərɪəs] *adj.* which can injure. **in•ju•ry,** *n.* hurt/wound.

in•jus•tice [ɪnˈdʒʌstɪs] *n.* lack of justice; not being fair.

ink [ɪŋk] 1. *n.* liquid for writing with a pen. 2. *v.* to write with a pen and ink; to mark with ink. **ink pad,** *n.* pad of cloth soaked in ink for inking date stamps, etc. **ink•well,** *n.* container to put ink in. **ink•y,** *adj.* (black) like ink; covered with ink.

ink•ling [ˈɪŋklɪŋ] *n.* suspicion/idea.

in•laid [ɪnˈleɪd] *v. see* **in•lay.**

in•land [ˈɪnlænd] *adj. & adv.* (to/of) the interior of a country.

in-laws [ˈɪnlɔːz] *n. pl. inf.* parents related to you by marriage.

in•lay [ɪnˈleɪ] 1. *n.* thing which is inlaid. 2. *v.* (**inlaid**) to insert small pieces of stone/wood/metal in (a surface) to create a pattern.

in•let [ˈɪnlet] *n.* small channel of water between islands or extending from a large body of water.

in-line skate [ɪnlaɪn ˈskeɪt] *n.* type of roller-skate in which all four wheels are set in a straight line.

in•mate [ˈɪnmeɪt] *n.* resident (of a house); person living in a hospital/prison, etc.

in•most [ˈɪnməʊst] *adj.* deepest (thoughts, etc.).

inn [ɪn] *n.* small hotel. **inn•keep•er,** *n.* person who runs an inn.

in•nards [ˈɪnədz] *n. pl. inf.* intestines; inside workings (of a machine).

in•nate [ɪˈneɪt] *adj.* inborn/natural.

in•ner [ˈɪnə] *adj.* inside; **i. room** = room leading off another room; **i. tube** = light tube containing air inside a tire; **i. ear** = space inside the head, beyond the middle ear, which controls balance and hearing. **in•ner•most,** *adj.* furthest inside.

in•ning [ˈɪnɪŋz] *n.* (*in baseball*) time when a team has a chance to score, until three batters are put out.

in•no•cent [ˈɪnəsnt] *adj.* not guilty; lacking experience/knowledge. **in•no•cence,** *n.* lack of guilt. **in•no•cent•ly,** *adv.* in a way which shows lack of experience/knowledge.

in•noc•u•ous [ɪˈnɒkjʊəs] *adj.* inoffensive/harmless.

in•no•vate [ˈɪnəveɪt] *v.* to introduce changes/new methods. **in•no•va•tion** [ɪnəˈveɪʃn] *n.* invention which is new; change (in doing sth). **in•no•va•tive** [ˈɪnəveɪtɪv] *adj.* which breaks new ground/which changes everything. **in•no•va•tor,** *n.* person who introduces changes.

in•nu•en•do [ɪnjuˈendəʊ] *n.* (*pl.* -**oes**) remark which suggests criticism.

in•nu•mer•a•ble [ɪˈnjuːmərəbl] *adj.* countless/which cannot be counted.

in•oc•u•late [ɪˈnɒkjuleɪt] *v.* **to i. s.o. against** = to prevent s.o. catching a disease by injecting him/her with a vaccine. **in•oc•u•la•tion** [ɪnɒkjuˈleɪʃn] *n.* injection to stop you catching a disease.

in•of•fen•sive [ɪnəˈfensɪv] *adj.* mild/harmless.

in•op•er•a•ble [ɪnˈɒprəbl] *adj.* which cannot be operated on.

in•op•er•a•tive [ɪnˈɒprətɪv] *adj.* which is not in operation/which is not working.

in•op•por•tune [ɪnˈɒpətjuːn] *adj.* awkward/badly timed.

in•or•di•nate [ɪnˈɔːdɪnət] *adj.* excessive. **in•or•di•nate•ly,** *adv.* excessively.

in•or•gan•ic [ɪnɔːˈɡænɪk] *adj.* not relating to living organisms; **i. chemistry** = chemistry dealing with substances which are not organic.

in-pa•tient [ˈɪnˈpeɪʃnt] *n.* patient who stays in a hospital.

in•put [ˈɪnput] *n.* (a) electric current put into an apparatus. (b) data/information fed into a computer.

in•quest [ˈɪŋkwest] *n.* legal inquiry into a death.

in•quire [ɪŋˈkwaɪə] *v.* (a) to ask questions (**about** sth). (b) to conduct an official investi-

---

æ **back,** aː **farm,** ɒ **top,** aɪ **pipe,** aʊ **how,** aɪə **fire,** aʊə **flower,** ɔː **bought,** ɔɪ **toy,** e **fed,** eə **hair,** eɪ **take,** ə **afraid,** əʊ **boat,** əʊə **lower,** vː **word,** iː **heap,** ɪ **hit,** ɪə **hear,** uː **school,** ʊ **book,** ʌ **but,** b **back,** d **dog,** ð **then,** dʒ **just,** f **fog,** ɡ **go,** h **hand,** j **yes,** k **catch,** l **last,** m **mix,** n **nut,** ŋ **sing,** p **penny,** r **round,** s **some,** ʃ **short,** t **too,** tʃ **chop,** θ **thing,** v **voice,** w **was,** z **zoo,** ʒ **treasure**

gation (**into**). **in•quir•er**, *n*. person who inquires. **in•quir•ing**, *adj*. interested in finding out information. **in•quir•ing•ly**, *adv*. in a questioning way. **in•quir•y**, *n*. (a) formal investigation (**into**). (b) question.

in•qui•si•tion [ɪŋkwɪˈzɪʃn] *n*. (a) asking very thorough questions, usu. using threats or force. (b) (*old*) Catholic tribunal for discovering heretics. **in•quis•i•tor** [ɪŋˈkwɪzɪtə] *n*. person who asks very thorough questions.

in•quis•i•tive [ɪŋˈkwɪzətɪv] *adj*. curious/asking questions. **in•quis•i•tive•ly**, *adv*. curiously/inquiringly. **in•quis•i•tive•ness**, *n*. being inquisitive.

in•roads [ˈɪnrəʊdz] *n. pl*. **to make i. into sth** = to use up a large quantity of sth.

in•rush [ˈɪnrʌʃ] *n*. sudden quick pouring in of sth.

in•sa•lu•bri•ous [ɪnsəˈluːbrɪəs] *adj*. not healthy.

in•sane [ɪnˈseɪn] *adj*. mad. **in•sane•ly**, *adv*. madly. **in•san•i•ty** [ɪnˈsænɪtɪ] *n*. madness.

in•san•i•tar•y [ɪnˈsænɪtərɪ] *adj*. not clean/not hygienic.

in•sa•tia•ble [ɪnˈseɪʃəbl] *adj*. which cannot be satisfied. **in•sa•tia•bly**, *adv*. in a way which cannot be satisfied.

in•scribe [ɪnˈskraɪb] *v*. to write (officially) (in a book/on a stone). **in•scrip•tion** [ɪnˈskrɪpʃn] *n*. writing inscribed on a stone, etc.

in•scru•ta•ble [ɪnˈskruːtəbl] *adj*. mysterious/which you cannot understand.

in•sect [ˈɪnsekt] *n*. small six-legged animal with a body in three parts. **in•sec•ti•cide** [ɪnˈsektɪsaɪd] *n*. liquid/powder which kills insects. **in•sec•tiv•o•rous** [ɪnsekˈtɪvərəs] *adj*. (animal) which eats insects.

in•se•cure [ɪnsɪˈkjʊə] *adj*. not safe; wobbly/not firmly fixed. **in•se•cure•ly**, *adv*. not firmly. **in•se•cu•ri•ty**, *n*. feeling of not being safe.

in•sem•i•nate [ɪnˈsemɪneɪt] *v*. to introduce male seed into (a female). **in•sem•i•na•tion** [ɪnsemɪˈneɪʃn] *n*. **artificial i.** = introduction of sperm from a male into a female by a doctor or veterinarian.

in•sen•sate [ɪnˈsenseɪt] *adj*. without any feeling.

in•sen•si•ble [ɪnˈsensəbl] *adj*. (a) not conscious. (b) with no feeling. (c) very small (change); imperceptible.

in•sen•si•tive [ɪnˈsensɪtɪv] *adj*. not sensitive. **in•sen•si•tiv•i•ty** [ɪnsensɪˈtɪvɪtɪ] *n*. lack of sensitivity/lack of awareness of how other people feel.

in•sep•a•ra•ble [ɪnˈseprəbl] *adj*. which cannot be separated; (of people) always together.

in•sert. 1. *n*. [ˈɪnsɜːt] thing which is put in. **2.** *v*.

[ɪnˈsɜːt] to put (sth) in. **in•ser•tion** [ɪnˈsɜːʃn] *n*. act of putting sth in; thing which is put in.

in•set [ˈɪnset] *n*. small piece which is put into sth larger.

in•shore [ɪnˈʃɔː] *adj. & adv*. near or toward a coast.

in•side [ɪnˈsaɪd] **1.** *n*. inner part; **i. out** = with the inner part facing outward; **to know i. out** = to know very well. **2.** *adj*. (a) indoors; which is in the interior. (b) (information) known only to people working in a certain organization. **3.** *adv*. (a) to/in the interior. (b) *inf*. in prison. **4.** *prep*. (a) to/in the interior of (sth). (b) within; **i. three hours** = in less than three hours. **in•sid•er**, *n*. person who works in an organization and therefore knows secret information; **i. trading** = illegal buying or selling of shares by people who have secret information about a company.

in•sid•i•ous [ɪnˈsɪdɪəs] *adj*. quietly treacherous; working secretly to do harm. **in•sid•i•ous•ly**, *adv*. quietly and dangerously. **in•sid•i•ous•ness**, *n*. being insidious.

in•sight [ˈɪnsaɪt] *n*. (a) clear thought. (b) deep knowledge; clear understanding.

in•sig•ni•a [ɪnˈsɪgnɪə] *n*. badge or other symbol of office or honor.

in•sig•nif•i•cant [ɪnsɪgˈnɪfɪkənt] *adj*. unimportant. **in•sig•nif•i•cance**, *n*. being insignificant.

in•sin•cere [ɪnsɪnˈsɪə] *adj*. not sincere/false. **in•sin•cer•i•ty** [ɪnsɪnˈserɪtɪ] *n*. lack of sincerity.

in•sin•u•ate [ɪnˈsɪnjʊeɪt] *v*. (a) to suggest (by dropping hints); **to i. oneself** = work one's way gradually (**into** a favorable position). **in•sin•u•a•tion** [ɪnsɪnjʊˈeɪʃn] *n*. (usu. cruel) hint/suggestion.

in•sip•id [ɪnˈsɪpɪd] *adj*. watery/not strong; with no flavor/no excitement. **in•sip•id•i•ty** [ɪnsɪˈpɪdɪtɪ] *n*. being insipid.

in•sist [ɪnˈsɪst] *v*. **to i. on sth being done** = to state firmly that sth should be done. **in•sist•ence**, *n*. firm demands. **in•sist•ent**, *adj*. demanding firmly. **in•sist•ent•ly**, *adv*. in a way which demands attention.

in si•tu [ɪnˈsiːtjuː] *adv*. on the site; in its original place.

in•sole [ˈɪnsəʊl] *n*. soft pad which you put inside a shoe to make it more comfortable or fit better.

in•so•lent [ˈɪnsələnt] *adj*. rude. **in•so•lence**, *n*. rudeness. **in•so•lent•ly**, *adv*. rudely.

in•sol•u•ble [ɪnˈsɒljʊbl] *adj*. (a) (substance) which will not dissolve, usu. in water. (b) (problem) which cannot be solved.

in•sol•u•bil•i•ty [ɪnsɒljuˈbɪlɪtɪ] n. inability (of a chemical) to dissolve.

in•sol•vent [ɪnˈsɒlvənt] adj. bankrupt/unable to pay one's debts. **in•sol•ven•cy**, n. being insolvent.

in•som•ni•a [ɪnˈsɒmnɪə] n. chronic inability to sleep. **in•som•ni•ac**, n. person who suffers from insomnia.

in•sou•ci•ant [ɪnˈsuːsjənt] adj. not caring about anything. **in•sou•ci•ance**, n. being insouciant.

in•spect [ɪnˈspekt] v. to examine closely. **in•spec•tion** [ɪnˈspekʃn] n. examining sth closely. **in•spec•tor**, n. (a) person, esp. an official, who inspects. (b) officer in the police force, usu. ranking next below a superintendent. **in•spec•tor•ate**, n. all inspectors taken as a group.

in•spire [ɪnˈspaɪə] v. to make (s.o.) feel a certain sensation. **in•spi•ra•tion** [ɪnspɪˈreɪʃn] n. (a) sudden urge to write poems/to compose music, etc. (b) sudden good idea.

in•sta•bil•i•ty [ɪnstəˈbɪlɪtɪ] n. lack of stability/not being steady.

in•stall [ɪnˈstɔːl] v. to put (a person into a job/a machine into position for operation. **in•stal•la•tion** [ɪnstəˈleɪʃn] n. (a) putting (a machine in position for operation). (b) group of machines which have been put in position for operation.

in•stall•ment [ɪnˈstɔːlmənt] n. part (of sth which is being delivered in parts); regular payment (of part of a total sum owed); **i. plan** = system where you buy sth by paying in installments.

in•stance [ˈɪnstəns] 1. n. example/case; **for i.** = as an example. 2. v. to give as an example.

in•stant [ˈɪnstənt] 1. n. moment/second. 2. adj. immediate; **i. coffee** = coffee powder to which you add hot water to make coffee rapidly. **in•stan•ta•ne•ous** [ɪnstənˈteɪnɪəs] adj. immediate. **in•stan•ta•ne•ous•ly**, adv. immediately. **in•stant•ly**, adv. straight away/immediately.

in•stead [ɪnˈsted] adv. in the place of/rather than (sth).

in•step [ˈɪnstep] n. arched part of a foot.

in•sti•gate [ˈɪnstɪgeɪt] v. to provoke/to start (sth). **in•sti•ga•tion** [ɪnstɪˈgeɪʃn] n. suggestion. **in•sti•ga•tor**, n. person who stirs up trouble/who provokes action.

in•still, instil [ɪnˈstɪl] v. to put (an idea, etc.) into s.o.'s mind gradually.

in•stinct [ˈɪnstɪŋkt] n. feeling/ability for doing sth which you have from birth and have not learned. **in•stinc•tive** [ɪnˈstɪŋktɪv] adj. natural/inborn (reaction). **in•stinc•tive•ly**, adv. because of a natural impulse.

in•sti•tute [ˈɪnstɪtjuːt] 1. n. (a) organization set up for a purpose. (b) building which houses such an organization. 2. v. to set up/to start. **in•sti•tu•tion** [ɪnstɪˈtjuːʃn] n. (a) setting up (of an organization). (b) organization/society set up for a purpose. (c) permanent feature; longstanding custom. **in•sti•tu•tion•al**, adj. referring to an institution. **in•sti•tu•tion•al•ize**, v. to make (sth) into an institution; to put (s.o.) into an institution (such as an old people's home, etc.).

in•struct [ɪnˈstrʌkt] v. (a) to teach. (b) to give information or orders to. **in•struc•tion** [ɪnˈstrʌkʃn] n. (a) teaching. (b) **instructions** = orders; indication of how sth is to be used. **in•struc•tive**, adj. which teaches. **in•struc•tor, instructress**, n. teacher.

in•stru•ment [ˈɪnstrumənt] n. (a) piece of equipment. (b) formal legal document, as a contract. (c) **musical i.** = device which is blown/hit/plucked, etc., to make a musical note. **in•stru•men•tal** [ɪnstrʊˈmentl] adj. (a) responsible/playing an important role (in getting sth done). (b) referring to a musical instrument. **in•stru•men•tal•ist**, n. person who plays a musical instrument.

in•sub•or•di•nate [ɪnsəˈbɔːdɪnət] adj. unruly; not obeying orders. **in•sub•or•di•na•tion** [ɪnsəbɔːdɪˈneɪʃn] n. not obeying orders.

in•sub•stan•tial [ɪnsəbˈstænʃl] adj. not substantial/not solid.

in•suf•fer•a•ble [ɪnˈsʌfrəbl] adj. intolerable/which you cannot bear. **in•suf•fer•a•bly**, adv. intolerably.

in•suf•fi•cient [ɪnsəˈfɪʃnt] adj. not sufficient/not enough. **in•suf•fi•cien•cy**, n. lack. **in•suf•fi•cient•ly**, adv. not enough.

in•su•lar [ˈɪnsjʊlə] adj. (a) referring to an island. (b) narrow-minded. **in•su•lar•i•ty** [ɪnsjʊˈlærɪtɪ] n. prejudice/narrowness of opinions.

in•su•late [ˈɪnsjʊleɪt] v. to cover so as to prevent heat/electricity/sound escaping or entering. **in•su•la•tion** [ɪnsjʊˈleɪʃn] n. act of insulating; material which insulates.

æ back, a: farm, ɒ: top, aɪ pipe, aʊ how, aɪe fire, aʊə flower, ɔ: bought, ɔɪ toy, e fed, eəhair, eɪ take, ə afraid, əʊ boat, əʊə lower, v: word, i: heap, ɪ hit, ɪə hear, u: school, ʊ book, ʌ but, b back, d dog, ð then, dʒ just, f fog, g go, h hand, j yes, k catch, l last, m mix, n nut, ŋ sing, p penny, r round, s some, ʃ short, t too, tʃ chop, θ thing, v voice, w was, z zoo, ʒ treasure

in•su•la•tor ['ɪnsjʊleɪtə] n. material/device which insulates.

in•su•lin ['ɪnsjʊlɪn] n. hormone which regulates the use of sugar by the body, and is used to treat diabetes.

in•sult. 1. n. ['ɪnsʌlt] rude word said to or about a person. 2. v. [ɪn'sʌlt] to say rude things about (s.o.). in•sult•ing, adj. rude.

in•su•per•a•ble [ɪn'sjuːprəbl] adj. which cannot be overcome.

in•sup•port•a•ble [ɪnsə'pɔːtəbl] adj. unbearable/which cannot be borne.

in•sure [ɪn'ʃʊə] v. to agree with a company that if you pay them a regular sum, they will compensate you for loss or damage to property or persons; to i. a diamond ring for $5000. in•sur•ance, n. agreement with a company by which you are paid compensation for loss or damage in return for regular payments of money; i. policy = document with the details of an insurance; i. broker/agent = person who arranges an insurance; life i. = insurance paying a sum of money when s.o. dies. in•sur•er, n. person/company which insures.

in•sur•gent [ɪn'sɜːdʒənt] adj. & n. (person) in a state of revolt.

in•sur•mount•a•ble [ɪnsə'maʊntəbl] adj. which cannot be overcome.

in•sur•rec•tion [ɪnsə'rekʃn] n. uprising/revolution.

in•tact [ɪn'tækt] adj. in one piece/not broken.

in•tagl•io [ɪn'tɑːlɪəʊ] n. design cut into a surface (as of a precious stone).

in•take ['ɪnteɪk] n. thing which is taken in.

in•tan•gi•ble [ɪn'tændʒəbl] adj. which cannot be touched/which cannot be defined.

in•te•gral ['ɪntɪɡrəl] adj. forming (part of) a whole. in•te•ger ['ɪntɪdʒə] n. whole number (not a fraction). in•te•grate ['ɪntɪɡreɪt] v. to link to form a whole; to make (people) full members of society by giving them equal opportunities, treatment, etc.; integrated circuit = electronic circuit on a microchip. in•te•gra•tion [ɪntɪ'ɡreɪʃn] n. (act of) integrating.

in•teg•ri•ty [ɪn'tegrɪtɪ] n. honesty.

in•teg•u•ment [ɪn'tegjʊmənt] n. (formal) skin.

in•tel•lect ['ɪntəlekt] n. ability to think or reason; brainpower. in•tel•lec•tu•al [ɪntə'lektjʊəl] 1. adj. referring to the intellect; good at using the brain. 2. n. person who believes that brainpower is very important/who uses his brain to make a living. in•tel•lec•tu•al•ly, adv. referring to intelligence.

in•tel•li•gence [ɪn'telɪdʒəns] n. (a) quickness of understanding/mental ability; i. quotient = number showing how intelligent you are compared to others. (b) secret information.

in•tel•li•gent, adj. clever/mentally able. in•tel•li•gent•ly, adv. in an intelligent way. in•tel•li•gent•si•a [ɪntelɪ'dʒensɪə] n. intellectual class of society.

in•tel•li•gi•ble [ɪn'telɪdʒəbl] adj. which can be understood. in•tel•li•gi•bil•i•ty [ɪntelɪgə'bɪlɪtɪ] n. being intelligible.

in•tem•per•ate [ɪn'temprət] adj. wild/not moderate.

in•tend [ɪn'tend] v. to plan to do (sth)/to mean.

in•tense [ɪn'tens] adj. (-er, -est) very strong/vigorous (action); extremely serious (person). in•tense•ly, adv. strongly. in•ten•si•fi•ca•tion, n. becoming stronger. in•ten•si•fy, v. to grow stronger/to make (sth) stronger. in•ten•si•ty, n. strength/violence (of sth). in•ten•sive, adj. very concentrated; i. care unit = section of a hospital dealing with seriously ill patients who need a lot of attention. in•ten•sive•ly, adv. very strongly.

in•tent [ɪn'tent] 1. adj. determined/absorbed. 2. n. with i. to defraud = with the aim of deceiving; to/for all intents and purposes = virtually/in nearly every way. in•tent•ly, adv. fixedly.

in•ten•tion [ɪn'tenʃn] n. aim. in•ten•tion•al, adj. done on purpose. in•ten•tion•al•ly, adv. on purpose.

in•ter [ɪn'tɜː] v. (interred) (formal) to bury.

inter- ['ɪntə-] prefix meaning between.

in•ter•act [ɪntə'rækt] v. to have an effect on each other. in•ter•ac•tion [ɪntər'ækʃn] n. effect of two things on each other. in•ter•ac•tive, adj. (computer program) which allows the user to communicate with the computer.

in•ter a•li•a [ɪntə'ɑːlɪə] among other things.

in•ter•breed [ɪntə'briːd] v. (interbred) to breed (with an adult of another strain).

in•ter•cede [ɪntə'siːd] v. to plead; to make an appeal. in•ter•ces•sion [ɪntə'seʃn] n. pleading (on behalf of s.o.).

in•ter•cept [ɪntə'sept] v. to stop (sth) as it is passing. in•ter•cep•tion [ɪntə'sepʃn] n. stopping (of sth which is passing). in•ter•cep•tor, n. person/aircraft which intercepts.

in•ter•change ['ɪntətʃeɪndʒ] 1. n. (a) exchange (of ideas). (b) large road intersection where highways cross. 2. v. to exchange one thing for another. in•ter•change•a•ble [ɪntə'tʃeɪndʒəbl] adj. which can be substituted for each other.

in•ter•cit•y [ɪntə'sɪtɪ] adj. (train/plane) between two cities.

in•ter•com ['ɪntəkɒm] n. radio for speaking

to people over a short distance (as within a house).

in•ter•con•nect•ed [ɪntəkə'nektɪd] *adj.* which connect with each other.

in•ter•con•ti•nen•tal [ɪntəkɒntɪ'nentl] *adj.* from one continent to another.

in•ter•course ['ɪntəkɔːs] *n.* (a) reproductive act between a male and a female. (b) (*formal*) communication between people.

in•ter•dict ['ɪntədɪkt] *n.* (*formal*) order forbidding sth.

in•ter•est ['ɪntrəst] 1. *n.* (a) percentage return on investment; percentage payable on a loan. (b) financial share. (c) particular attention. (d) thing which you pay attention to. (e) advantage. 2. *v.* to attract s.o.'s attention. in•ter•est•ed, *adj.* with a personal (usu. financial) interest in sth. in•ter•est•ing, *adj.* which attracts attention.

in•ter•face ['ɪntəfeɪs] *n.* area where two different systems meet and interact.

in•ter•fere [ɪntə'fɪə] *v.* (a) to meddle/to get involved (**in/with**). (b) to affect the reception of radio/TV programs. in•ter•fer•ence, *n.* (a) involvement/meddling. (b) noise which affects radio/TV programs. in•ter•fer•on, *n.* protein which fights a virus.

in•ter•im ['ɪntərɪm] *adj. & n.* (report) given halfway through an investigation; **in the i.** = meanwhile.

in•ter•i•or [ɪn'tɪərɪə] *adj. & n.* inner part (of a building/car).

in•ter•ject [ɪntə'dʒekt] *v.* to make a sudden exclamation. in•ter•jec•tion [ɪntə'dʒekʃn] *n.* exclamation; word used to show surprise.

in•ter•lace [ɪntə'leɪs] *v.* to weave together.

in•ter•lard [ɪntə'lɑːd] *v.* to insert comments into (a text).

in•ter•leave [ɪntə'liːv] *v.* to put (sth) between the pages of a book.

in•ter•lock [ɪntə'lɒk] *v.* to fit together.

in•ter•loc•u•tor [ɪntə'lɒkjutə] *n.* person who speaks to s.o. else.

in•ter•lop•er ['ɪntələupə] *n.* person who comes in/who intrudes.

in•ter•lude ['ɪntəluːd] *n.* quiet time between two lively periods; rest period between parts of a performance.

in•ter•mar•ry [ɪntə'mærɪ] *v.* to marry within the same family group. in•ter•mar•riage, *n.* act of intermarrying.

in•ter•me•di•ar•y [ɪntə'miːdjərɪ] *adj. & n.*

(person) who goes between two others/who acts as messenger.

in•ter•me•di•ate [ɪntə'miːdjət] *adj.* halfway between two extremes.

in•ter•ment [ɪn'tɜːmənt] *n.* (*formal*) burial.

in•ter•mez•zo [ɪntə'metzəʊ] *n.* (*pl.* -os) short piece (of music) linking two other pieces.

in•ter•mi•na•ble [ɪn'tɜːmɪnəbl] *adj.* never-ending. in•ter•mi•na•bly, *adv.* without coming to an end.

in•ter•min•gle [ɪntə'mɪŋgl] *v.* to mix together.

in•ter•mis•sion [ɪntə'mɪʃn] *n.* (a) interval (in a play/motion picture/concert). (b) **without i.** = without a break/without stopping.

in•ter•mit•tent [ɪntə'mɪtənt] *adj.* which takes place from time to time. in•ter•mit•tent•ly, *adv.* (taking place) from time to time/on and off.

in•tern. 1. *n.* ['ɪntɜːn] recently graduated doctor who works in a hospital under supervision. 2. *v.* [ɪn'tɜːn] to put (prisoners) in a prison without trial, esp. during a war. in•tern•ee [ɪntɜː'niː] *n.* prisoner who has been interned. in•tern•ment, *n.* putting prisoners in a prison or camp without trial.

in•ter•nal [ɪn'tɜːnl] *adj.* inside; **i. combustion engine** = engine in which the fuel is burned inside a closed space (as in the cylinders in a car engine). in•ter•nal•ly, *adv.* inside.

in•ter•na•tion•al [ɪntə'næʃnl] *adj.* between countries. in•ter•na•tion•al•ly, *adv.* (done) between countries.

in•ter•ne•cine [ɪntə'niːsaɪn] *adj.* (*formal*) (two things) which destroy each other.

In•ter•net ['ɪntənet] *n.* informally organized global computer network that links individual computers and computer networks and thereby transfers at high speed information, usu. located on World Wide Web sites, and services, e.g. electronic mail.

in•ter•node ['ɪntənəʊd] *n.* space between two joints in a plant. in•ter•nod•al *adj.* between joints.

in•ter•phone ['ɪntəfəʊn] *n.* telephone used to communicate between rooms or parts of a building or ship.

in•ter•plan•e•tar•y [ɪntə'plænətɪ] *adj.* between planets.

in•ter•play ['ɪntəpleɪ] *n.* reaction between two forces.

In•ter•pol ['ɪntəpɒl] *n.* international police system.

æ back, aː farm, ɒ: top, aɪ pipe, aʊ how, aɪə fire, aʊə flower, ɔː bought, ɔɪ toy, e fed, eəhair, eɪ take, ə afraid, əʊ boat, əʊə lower, ɜː word, iː heap, ɪ hit, ɪə hear, uː school, ʊ book, ʌ but, b back, d dog, ð then, dʒ just, f fog, g go, h hand, j yes, k catch, l last, m mix, n nut, ŋ sing, p penny, r round, s some, ʃ short, t too, tʃ chop, θ thing, v voice, w was, z zoo, ʒ treasure

in•ter•po•late [ɪn'tɜːpəleɪt] v. to add (words) in between others. **in•ter•po•la•tion** [ɪntɜːpə'leɪʃn] n. adding of words between existing words in a text; word(s) thus added.

in•ter•pose ['ɪntəpəʊz] v. to place (sth) in between.

in•ter•pret [ɪn'tɜːprɪt] v. (a) to explain (sth) to s.o. who does not understand. (b) to translate aloud what is spoken from one language into another. **in•ter•pre•ta•tion** [ɪntɜːprɪ'teɪʃn] n. (a) meaning. (b) translating aloud from one language to another. **in•ter•pret•er**, n. person who translates aloud from one language to another.

in•ter•reg•num [ɪntə'regnəm] n. period between the reigns of successive kings; period of inactivity between one management and another.

in•ter•re•lat•ed [ɪntərɪ'leɪtɪd] adj. (several things) which are related.

in•ter•ro•gate [ɪn'terəgeɪt] v. to question severely. **in•ter•ro•ga•tion** [ɪntere'geɪʃn] n. severe questioning (of a prisoner). **in•ter•rog•a•tive** [ɪntə'rɒgətɪv] adj. & n. questioning; **i. pronoun** = pronoun which asks a question; **i. sentence** = sentence which asks a question. **in•ter•ro•ga•tor** [ɪn'terəgeɪtə] n. person who questions (a prisoner) closely.

in•ter•rupt [ɪntə'rʌpt] v. to break into (a speech); to stop (sth) continuing. **in•ter•rup•tion** [ɪntə'rʌpʃn] n. (act of) interrupting; thing which interrupts.

in•ter•sect [ɪntə'sekt] v. to cut across; to cut across (each other). **in•ter•sec•tion**, n. place where lines, roads, etc. cut across each other.

in•ter•sperse [ɪntə'spɜːs] v. to scatter.

in•ter•state [ɪntə'steɪt] adj. between two states.

in•ter•stel•lar [ɪntə'stelə] adj. between stars.

in•ter•stice [ɪn'tɜːstɪs] n. small space in between other things.

in•ter•twine [ɪntə'twaɪn] v. to twist (things) together; to be twisted together.

in•ter•val ['ɪntəvl] n. period/gap (between two points/between two acts in a play); (in music) difference in pitch.

in•ter•vene [ɪntə'viːn] v. to come/to arrive in between. **in•ter•ven•tion** [ɪntə'venʃn] n. coming between; entry into sth.

in•ter•view ['ɪntəvjuː] 1. n. (a) discussion (on radio/TV/in the newspaper) between an important or interesting person and a journalist. (b) questioning (by one or more people) of a person applying for a job. 2. v. (a) to ask (a famous/interesting person) questions in order to publish or air the answers publicly. (b) to ask questions of (a person applying for a job). **in•ter•view•ee** [ɪntəvjuː'iː] n. person who is

being/who is going to be interviewed. **in•ter•view•er**, n. person who asks the questions at an interview.

in•ter•weave [ɪntə'wiːv] v. (interwove; interwoven) to weave/to bind together.

in•tes•tate [ɪn'testeɪt] adj. not having made a will.

in•tes•tine [ɪn'testɪn] n. long tube in the body through which food passes from the stomach to the anus. **in•tes•ti•nal**, adj. referring to the intestine.

in•ti•mate. 1. adj. ['ɪntɪmət] (a) very close (friend); detailed (knowledge). (b) sexual (relationship). 2. n. ['ɪntɪmət] close friend. 3. v. ['ɪntɪmeɪt] to announce; to suggest. **in•ti•ma•cy**, n. close relationship (with s.o.). **in•ti•mate•ly**, adv. closely. **in•ti•ma•tion** [ɪntɪ'meɪʃn] n. suggestion.

in•tim•i•date [ɪn'tɪmɪdeɪt] v. to frighten (s.o.) by threats. **in•tim•i•dat•ing**, adj. frightening. **in•tim•i•da•tion** [ɪntɪmɪ'deɪʃn] n. frightening by threats.

in•to ['ɪntu] prep. (a) (movement) toward the inside. (b) so as to become; to develop as; **the tadpole changed i. a frog; he burst i. tears.** (c) dividing; **four i. three won't go.**

in•tol•er•a•ble [ɪn'tɒlərəbl] adj. which you cannot bear. **in•tol•er•a•bly**, adv. unbearably.

in•tol•er•ant [ɪn'tɒlərənt] adj. (person) who cannot bear people with different ideas from his own. **in•tol•er•ance**, n. not accepting other people's points of view.

in•to•na•tion [ɪntə'neɪʃn] n. rise or fall of the voice (in speech or singing).

in•tone [ɪn'təʊn] v. to recite (psalms, etc.) in a singing voice.

in•tox•i•cate [ɪn'tɒksɪkeɪt] v. to make (s.o.) drunk. **in•tox•i•cant**, n. substance which intoxicates. **in•tox•i•cat•ing**, adj. which makes you drunk; exciting. **in•tox•i•ca•tion** [ɪntɒksɪ'keɪʃn] n. drunkenness.

intra- ['ɪntrə-] prefix meaning within.

in•trac•ta•ble [ɪn'træktəbl] adj. very difficult to deal with; (problem) which is impossible to solve.

in•tran•si•gent [ɪn'trænsɪdʒənt] adj. firm; obstinate/not shifting your position/not changing your mind. **in•tran•si•gence**, n. firmness/being obstinate.

in transit [ɪn'trænzɪt] adv. (goods) which are being transported.

in•tran•si•tive [ɪn'trænsɪtɪv] adj. (verb) which has no object.

in•tra•u•ter•ine [ɪntrə'juːtəriːn] adj. inside the uterus; **i. device** = contraceptive device which is placed inside a woman's uterus.

in•tra•ve•nous [ɪntrə'viːnəs] *adj.* (injection) made into a vein.

in•trep•id [ɪn'trepɪd] *adj.* fearless/very brave. **in•tre•pid•i•ty** [ɪntrə'pɪdɪtɪ] *n.* being intrepid.

in•tri•cate ['ɪntrɪkət] *adj.* very complicated; made of many different parts. **in•tri•ca•cy**, *n.* complexity. **in•tri•cate•ly**, *adv.* in an intricate way.

in•trigue [ɪn'triːg] 1. *n.* secret plot. 2. *v.* (a) to plot. (b) to make (s.o.) interested.

in•trin•sic [ɪn'trɪnzɪk] *adj.* forming a basic part of sth. **in•trin•si•cal•ly**, *adv.* basically.

in•tro•duce [ɪntrə'djuːs] *v.* (a) to present (s.o.) to another person/to people who did not know him/her previously. (b) to announce (a TV/radio program, etc.). (c) to make (sth) go in; to bring (sth) in. **in•tro•duc•tion** [ɪntrə'dʌkʃn] *n.* (a) act of presenting sth; thing which presents sth. (b) making s.o. known to another person/to people who did not know him/her previously. (c) piece at the beginning of a book which explains the rest of the book. (d) elementary book about a subject; **an i. to art history. in•tro•duc•to•ry**, *adj.* (words) which introduce; **i. offer** = offer of a new product at a special low price.

in•troit ['ɪntrɔɪt] *n.* music sung at the beginning of a church service.

in•tro•spec•tive [ɪntrə'spektɪv] *adj.* inward-looking; thinking a lot about yourself. **in•tro•spec•tion** [ɪntrə'spekʃn] *n.* looking inward at yourself.

in•tro•vert ['ɪntrəvɜːt] *n.* person who thinks mainly about himself/herself. **in•tro•vert•ed**, *adj.* (person) who thinks mainly about himself/herself.

in•trude [ɪn'truːd] *v.* to enter where you are not wanted. **in•trud•er**, *n.* person who has intruded; **in•tru•sion** [ɪn'truːʒn] *n.* act of intruding. **in•tru•sive** [ɪn'truːsɪv] *adj.* unwanted.

in•tu•i•tion [ɪntjuː'ɪʃn] *n.* thinking of sth/knowing sth naturally without it being explained. **in•tu•i•tive** [ɪn'tjuːɪtɪv] *adj.* based on intuition. **in•tu•i•tive•ly**, *adv.* in an intuitive way.

In•u•it ['ɪnjuːɪt] *n.* Eskimos.

in•un•date ['ɪnʌndeɪt] *v.* to flood. **in•un•da•tion** [ɪnʌn'deɪʃn] *n.* flood.

in•ure [ɪn'jʊə] *v.* (*formal*) to accustom to sth unpleasant.

in•vade [ɪn'veɪd] *v.* to attack and enter (a country) with an army. **in•vad•er**, *n.* person who enters a country with an army.

in•val•id 1. *adj. & n.* ['ɪnvəlɪd] sick/disabled (person); **i. chair** = small vehicle for one disabled person. 2. *adj.* [ɪn'vælɪd] not valid/not legal. **in•val•i•da•tion** [ɪnvælɪ'deɪʃn] *n.* making invalid. **in•val•i•date** [ɪn'vælɪdeɪt] *v.* to make (sth) invalid; to nullify. **in•va•lid•i•ty**, *n.* being an invalid; lack of validity.

in•val•u•a•ble [ɪn'væljuəbl] *adj.* extremely valuable.

in•var•i•a•ble [ɪn'veərɪəbl] *adj.* always the same/not changing. **in•var•i•a•bly**, *adv.* always.

in•va•sion [ɪn'veɪʒn] *n.* (a) entering a country with armed forces. (b) **i. of privacy** = illegal entering of a person's home in a way which intrudes on his private life.

in•vec•tive [ɪn'vektɪv] *n.* insulting speech/abuse.

in•veigh [ɪn'veɪ] *v.* (*formal*) to speak violently (**against** sth).

in•vei•gle [ɪn'veɪgl] *v.* to trick (s.o.) **into** doing sth.

in•vent [ɪn'vent] *v.* to create (a new process/new machine); to think up (an excuse). **in•ven•tion** [ɪn'venʃn] *n.* (a) creation of new process/new machine). (b) new machine. **in•ven•tive**, *adj.* creative. **in•ven•tive•ness**, *n.* ability to invent. **in•ven•tor**, *n.* person who invents new processes/new machines.

in•ven•to•ry ['ɪnvəntrɪ] *n.* list (of contents of a house, etc.); stock (in a store/business/warehouse).

in•verse ['ɪnvɜːs] *adj. & n.* opposite/contrary. **in•ver•sion** [ɪn'vɜːʃn] *n.* turning sth around in a contrary way. **in•vert** [ɪn'vɜːt] *v.* to turn (sth) upside down/back to front.

in•ver•te•brate [ɪn'vɜːtɪbreɪt] *adj. & n.* (animal) without a backbone.

in•vest [ɪn'vest] *v.* to put (money) into savings/property, etc., so that it will increase in value. **in•vest•ment**, *n.* money placed so that it will increase in value. **in•ves•tor**, *n.* person who puts money into savings or property.

in•ves•ti•gate [ɪn'vestɪgeɪt] *v.* to study/to examine. **in•ves•ti•ga•tion** [ɪn'vestɪ'geɪʃn] *n.* examination. **in•ves•ti•ga•tor**, *n.* detective; person who investigates.

in•ves•ti•ture [ɪn'vestɪtʃə] *n.* ceremony where

æ back, ɑː farm, ɒ top, aɪ pipe, aʊ how, aɪə fire, aʊə flower, ɔː bought, ɔɪ toy, e fed, eəhair, eɪ take, ə afraid, əʊ boat, əʊə lower, ɜː word, iː heap, ɪ hit, ɪə hear, uː school, ʊ book, ʌ but, b back, d dog, ð then, dʒ just, f fog, g go, h hand, j yes, k catch, l last, m mix, n nut, ŋ sing, p penny, r round, s some, ʃ short, t too, tʃ chop, θ thing, v voice, w was, z zoo, ʒ treasure

s.o. is given a medal/where s.o. is installed in office.

in•vet•er•ate [ɪn'vetərət] *adj.* obstinate/hardened; firmly established (as by habit); **i. liar.**

in•vid•i•ous [ɪn'vɪdɪəs] *adj.* which is likely to offend people unreasonably.

in•vig•or•ate [ɪn'vɪgəreɪt] *v.* to make strong/vigorous; to make (s.o.) feel livelier.

in•vin•ci•ble [ɪn'vɪnsəbl] *adj.* which cannot be defeated. **in•vin•ci•bil•i•ty** [ɪnvɪnsə'bɪlɪtɪ] *n.* being unbeatable.

in•vi•o•la•ble [ɪn'vaɪələbl] *adj.* which cannot be violated. **in•vi•o•la•bil•i•ty** [ɪnvaɪələ'bɪlɪtɪ] *n.* being inviolable.

in•vis•i•ble [ɪn'vɪzəbl] *adj.* which cannot be seen. **in•vis•i•bil•i•ty** [ɪnvɪzə'bɪlɪtɪ] *n.* not being able to be seen.

in•vite [ɪn'vaɪt] *v.* (a) to ask (s.o.) to do sth. (b) to ask for (comments, etc.). **in•vi•ta•tion** [ɪnvɪ'teɪʃn] *n.* asking (s.o. to do sth). **in•vit•ing,** *adj.* attractive.

in vi•tro [ɪn'viːtrəʊ] *adj.* (experiment) which is carried out in a laboratory.

in•vo•ca•tion [ɪnvə'keɪʃn] *n. (formal)* calling on s.o. for help/support.

in•voice ['ɪnvɔɪs] 1. *n.* note sent to ask for payment for services or goods. 2. *v.* to send a note asking for payment for services or goods. **in•voic•ing,** *n.* sending of an invoice.

in•voke [ɪn'vəʊk] *v.* to call on (s.o./sth) for help/support.

in•vol•un•tar•y [ɪn'vɒləntrɪ] *adj.* not voluntary/not willingly done. **in•vol•un•tar•i•ly,** *adv.* not willingly.

in•volve [ɪn'vɒlv] *v.* (a) to bring (s.o./sth) into (a dispute/a scheme). (b) to make necessary. **in•volved,** *adj.* intricate/complicated. **in•volve•ment,** *n.* contact/collaboration.

in•vul•ner•a•ble [ɪn'vʌlnərəbl] *adj.* which cannot be successfully attacked.

in•ward ['ɪnwəd] *adj.* on/to the inside. **in•ward•ly,** *adv.* on the inside. **in•ward, inwards,** *adv.* toward the inside.

i•o•dine ['aɪədiːn] *n. (element:* I) substance which is used in solution, e.g. as a disinfectant. **i•o•dize,** *v.* to fill with iodine.

i•on ['aɪən] *n.* atom with an electric charge. **i•on•ize,** *v.* to produce ions; to become ions. **i•on•o•sphere** [aɪ'ɒnəsfɪə] *n.* part of the atmosphere surrounding the earth which reflects radio waves back to earth.

i•o•ta [aɪ'əʊtə] *n.* very small piece.

IOU [aɪəʊ'juː] *n.* paper promising that you will pay back money which you have borrowed.

ip•e•cac [ɪpɪkækjuː'ɑːnə] *n.* drug made from the root of a plant, used as an emetic and also as cough medicine.

ip•so fac•to ['ɪpsəʊ'fæktəʊ] *adv.* because of this fact.

IQ ['aɪ'kjuː] *abbrev. for* intelligence quotient.

IRA ['aɪɑː'eɪ] *abbrev. for* Irish Republican Army; Individual Retirement Account.

I•ra•ni•an [ɪ'reɪnjən] 1. *adj.* referring to Iran. 2. *n.* person from Iran.

I•ra•qi [ɪ'rɑːkɪ] 1. *adj.* referring to Iraq. 2. *n.* (*pl.* **-is**) person from Iraq.

i•ras•ci•ble [ɪ'ræsɪbl] *adj.* easily becoming angry. **i•ras•ci•bil•i•ty** [ɪræsɪ'bɪlɪtɪ] *n.* being irascible.

ire ['aɪə] *n. (formal)* anger. **i•rate** [aɪ'reɪt] *adj.* very angry.

ir•i•des•cent [ɪrɪ'desnt] *adj.* with changing/shimmering colors. **ir•i•des•cence,** *n.* being iridescent.

i•ris ['aɪərɪs] *n. (pl.* **-es**) (a) plant with tall flat leaves and usu. yellow or purple flowers. (b) part of the eye which is colored.

I•rish ['aɪərɪʃ] 1. *adj.* referring to Ireland. 2. *n.* (a) Celtic language spoken in parts of Ireland. (b) **the I.** = people from Ireland. **I•rish•man, Irishwoman,** *n. (pl.* **-men, -women**) person from Ireland.

irk [ɜːk] *v.* to annoy/to bother. **irk•some** ['ɜːksəm] *adj.* annoying/bothersome.

i•ron ['aɪən] 1. *n. & adj. (element:* Fe) (a) common gray metal which can be made into a magnet; **i. ore** = iron in its natural state. (b) electric household instrument for smoothing the creases from clothes. (c) **in irons** = imprisoned with iron chains around one's ankles. (d) golf club with a metal head. 2. *v.* to press (cloth) with an iron; **to i. out** = to sort out (a problem/difficulty). **I•ron Age,** *n.* period when human beings first used iron. **I•ron Cur•tain,** *n.* imaginary border formerly existing between Communist countries in Eastern Europe and non-communist Western Europe. **i•ron•ing,** *n.* (a) pressing clothes with an electric iron. (b) clothes which need pressing. **i•ron•ing board,** *n.* high narrow table used for ironing clothes. **iron lung,** *n.* machine which encloses a patient's body, and in which pressure is increased and reduced, formerly used to make the patient breathe. **i•ron•work,** *n.* (decorative) locks/handles/gates, etc., made of iron. **i•ron•works,** *n.* factory which produces iron.

i•ro•ny ['aɪərənɪ] *n.* (a) way of referring to sth where you say the opposite of what you mean. (b) quality of happening at the wrong moment, as if deliberately planned. **i•ron•ic(al)** [aɪ'rɒnɪk(l)] *adj.* mocking/slightly funny. **i•ron•i•cal•ly,** *adv.* in a mocking way.

ir•ra•di•ate [ɪ'reɪdɪeɪt] *v. (of heat/light/rays)*

to shine on (sth). **ir•ra•di•a•tion** [ɪreɪdɪ'eɪʃn] *n.* act of irradiating.

ir•ra•tion•al [ɪ'ræʃnl] *adj.* not rational/not sensible/against common-sense. **ir•ra•tion•al•ly**, *adv.* in an irrational way.

ir•rec•on•cil•a•ble [ɪrekən'saɪləbl] *adj.* which cannot be made to agree.

ir•re•cov•er•a•ble [ɪrɪ'kʌvərəbl] *adj.* which cannot be recovered.

ir•re•deem•a•ble [ɪrɪ'diːməbl] *adj.* (loss) which cannot be made good; (pledge) which cannot be redeemed.

ir•re•duc•i•ble [ɪrɪ'djuːsəbl] *adj.* which cannot be reduced.

ir•ref•u•ta•ble [ɪrɪ'fjuːtəbl] *adj.* (argument) which cannot be disproved.

ir•reg•u•lar [ɪ'regjulə] 1. *adj.* (a) not regular; not level; not happening at the same time. (b) not according to the rules; (verb) which has forms which do not fit the usual patterns of grammar. 2. *n. pl.* **irregulars** = soldiers who do not form part of a regular army. **ir•reg•u•lar•i•ty** [ɪregju'lærɪtɪ] *n.* thing which goes against the rules/the law. **ir•reg•u•lar•ly**, *adv.* not regularly.

ir•rel•e•vant [ɪ'reləvənt] *adj.* **(to)** not relevant/which has no connection to the subject. **ir•rel•e•vance**, *n.* having no connection with the subject.

ir•re•li•gious [ɪrɪ'lɪdʒəs] *adj.* not religious; not showing respect for religion.

ir•rep•a•ra•ble [ɪ'repərbl] *adj.* which cannot be repaired. **ir•rep•a•ra•bly**, *adv.* in a way which cannot be repaired.

ir•re•place•a•ble [ɪrɪ'pleɪsəbl] *adj.* which cannot be replaced; (thing) for which there is no substitute.

ir•re•press•i•ble [ɪrɪ'presəbl] *adj.* which cannot be held back.

ir•re•proach•a•ble [ɪrɪ'prəʊtʃəbl] *adj.* perfect/which cannot be criticized.

ir•re•sist•i•ble [ɪrɪ'zɪstəbl] *adj.* which cannot be resisted; which you cannot help accepting.

ir•res•o•lute [ɪ'rezəluːt] *adj.* undecided; (person) who hesitates/cannot decide. **ir•res•o•lute•ly**, *adv.* not knowing what to do. **ir•res•o•lu•tion**, *n.* being irresolute.

ir•re•spec•tive [ɪrɪ'spektɪv] *prep.* taking no account (**of**).

ir•re•spon•si•ble [ɪrɪ'spɒnsəbl] *adj.* wild/senseless; not responsible. **ir•re•spon•si•bly**, *adv.* with no sense of responsibility.

ir•re•triev•a•ble [ɪrɪ'triːvəbl] *adj.* which cannot be found again. **ir•re•triev•a•bly**, *adv.* hopelessly.

ir•rev•er•ent [ɪ'revrənt] *adj.* not serious; disrespectful. **ir•rev•er•ence**, *n.* being irreverent. **ir•rev•er•ent•ly**, *adv.* not in a serious way; disrespectfully.

ir•re•vers•i•ble [ɪrɪ'vɜːsəbl] *adj.* (decision) which cannot be changed.

ir•rev•o•ca•ble [ɪ'revəkəbl] *adj.* (decision) which cannot be changed.

ir•ri•gate ['ɪrɪgeɪt] *v.* (a) to water (land) by using canals and pumps. (b) to wash (a wound) with a flow of water. **ir•ri•ga•tion** [ɪrɪ'geɪʃn] *n.* watering of fields (by using canals and pumps).

ir•ri•tate ['ɪrɪteɪt] *v.* (a) to annoy. (b) to cause to burn, swell, or hurt. **ir•ri•ta•bil•i•ty** [ɪrɪtə'bɪlɪtɪ] *n.* being irritable. **ir•ri•ta•ble** ['ɪrɪtəbl] *adj.* easily annoyed. **ir•ri•ta•bly**, *adv.* in a bad-tempered way. **ir•ri•tant**, *n.* thing which irritates. **ir•ri•tat•ing**, *adj.* which irritates. **ir•ri•ta•tion** [ɪrɪ'teɪʃn] *n.* annoyance/burning, swollen, or painful condition; thing which causes this.

ir•rupt [ɪ'rʌpt] *v.* (*formal*) to appear/to come in suddenly. **ir•rup•tion** [ɪ'rʌpʃn] *n.* sudden appearance.

is [ɪz] *v. see* **be**.

Is•lam ['ɪzlæm] *n.* religion of the Muslims. **Is•lam•ic** [ɪz'læmɪk] *adj.* referring to Islam.

is•land ['aɪlənd] *n.* piece of land entirely surrounded by water; **traffic i.** = small raised piece of pavement in the center of the road where pedestrians can safely stand. **is•land•er**, *n.* person who lives on an island. **isle** [aɪl] *n.* island. **is•let**, *n.* small island.

is•n't ['ɪznt] *v. short for* **is not**.

i•so•bar ['aɪsəʊbɑː] *n.* line on a weather map showing places of equal barometric pressure.

i•so•late ['aɪsəleɪt] *v.* (a) to put (sth/s.o.) in a place alone; **isolated attack** = single attack, not repeated. (b) to separate (a chemical) substance from a compound. **i•so•la•tion** [aɪsə'leɪʃn] *n.* cutting off from communication with other people; **i. ward** = place in a hospital for people suffering from dangerous diseases. **i•so•la•tion•ism**, *n.* policy of not communicating with other countries. **i•so•la•tion•ist**, *n.* person who advocates isolationism.

i•so•mer ['aɪsɒmə] *n.* chemical compound

with the same molecular formula as another, but with a different arrangement of atoms.

i•so•met•ric [aɪsəu'metrɪk] *adj.* (exercises) using muscles acting against each other or a fixed object.

i•sos•ce•les [aɪ'sɒsɪliːz] *adj.* **i. triangle** = triangle with two sides of the same length.

i•so•therm ['aɪsəuθɜːm] *n.* line on a weather map showing places with equal temperatures.

i•so•ton•ic [aɪsəu'tɒnɪk] *adj.* (drink) formulated to replenish fluid and salts lost by the body during exercise.

i•so•tope ['aɪsətəup] *n.* one of two or more forms of a chemical element which have atoms which are chemically similar but with different atomic weights.

Is•rae•li [ɪz'reɪlɪ] 1. *adj.* referring to Israel. 2. *n.* (*pl.* **-is**) person from Israel.

is•sue ['ɪʃuː] 1. *n.* (a) result. (b) problem; **to make an i. of** = have a big discussion about; **the point at i.** = the question which is being discussed; **to take i. with** = disagree with. (c) publication (of a book); putting on sale (new stamps); putting into circulation (new coins/bank notes); giving out (of uniforms/official permits, etc.). (d) one copy of a newspaper or magazine. (e) (*old*) children. 2. *v.* (a) to come out. (b) to put (new stamps) on sale; to publish (books); to put (new bank notes) into circulation; to give out/to hand out (uniforms/official permits, etc.).

isth•mus ['ɪsməs] *n.* (*pl.* **-es**) narrow piece of land connecting two larger pieces of land.

it [ɪt] *pronoun referring to a thing.* (a) (*standing in the place of thing just mentioned*) **put it down;** **it's here.** (b) (*referring to nothing in particular*) **it's raining;** *inf.* **you're for it** = you are going to be in trouble.

IT ['aɪ'tiː] *abbrev. for* information technology.

I•tal•ian [ɪ'tæljən] 1. *adj.* referring to Italy. 2. *n.* (a) person from Italy. (b) language spoken in Italy.

i•tal•ic [ɪ'tælɪk] *adj. & n.* sloping (letter); *this is printed in italics.* **i•tal•i•cize** [ɪ'tælɪsaɪz] *v.* to print in italics.

itch [ɪtʃ] 1. *n.* (*pl.* **-es**) tickling sensation. 2. *v.* to tickle; to be very eager (to do sth). **itch•ing,** *n.* tickling sensation. **itch•y,** *adj.* making you feel you want to scratch.

i•tem ['aɪtəm] *n.* thing (in a list); **news items** = separate pieces of news on a news program. **i•tem•ize,** *v.* to make a detailed list of (things).

i•tin•er•ar•y [ɪ'tɪnərərɪ] *n.* route; list of places to be visited on a tour. **i•tin•er•ant,** *adj.* wandering/traveling.

its [ɪts] *adj.* belonging to a thing/to it.

it's [ɪts] *short for* **it is/it has.**

it•self [ɪt'self] *pronoun referring to a thing/to it.* (a) (*referring to an object*) **all by i.; the dog has hurt i.** (b) (*for emphasis*) **the television i.**

IUD [aɪjuː'diː] *abbrev. for* intrauterine device.

I've [aɪv] *short for* **I have.**

i•vo•ry ['aɪvərɪ] *adj. & n.* (made of) whitish substance from an elephant's tusk; **i. tower** = imaginary place where a person can avoid contact with the everyday world.

i•vy ['aɪvɪ] *n.* evergreen plant which climbs up walls and trees.

Jj

jab [dʒæb] 1. *n.* (a) sharp blow. (b) thrust with a pointed object; **j. with a needle.** 2. *v.* (**jabbed**) to poke firmly (as with a pointed object).

jab•ber ['dʒæbə] 1. *n.* quick, indistinct talk. 2. *v.* to speak quickly and indistinctly.

jac•a•ran•da [dʒækæ'rændə] *n.* tropical tree with scented pale purple flowers.

jack [dʒæk] *n.* (a) instrument for raising a heavy object (esp. a motor vehicle). (b) (*in playing cards*) the card between the queen and the ten. (c) male of certain mammals. (d) (*at bowls*) small white ball for players to aim at. **jack•boot,** *n.* high military boot. **jack•boot•ed,** *adj.* wearing jackboots. **jack•ham•mer,** *n.* power drill held in the hand. **jack-in-the-box,** *n.* box from which a toy figure springs up when the lid is opened. **jack-knife,** 1. *n.* (*pl.* **-knives**) type of large folding knife. 2. *v.* (*of vehicle pulling a trailer*) to fold in half in an accident. **jack-of-all-trades,** *n.* person who is reasonably good at a large number of jobs. **jack up,** *v.* (a) to raise with a jack. (b) *inf.* to raise (profits or prices).

jack•al ['dʒækl] *n.* wild dog, which feeds chiefly on dead flesh.

jack•ass ['dʒækæs] *n.* male donkey.

jack•daw ['dʒækdɔː] *n.* type of small crow.

jack•et ['dʒækɪt] *n.* (a) short coat. (b) outer casing or covering; loose paper cover for a book. (c) skin (of a potato). **jack•et•ed,** *adj.* with a jacket.

jack•pot ['dʒækpɒt] *n.* **to win/to hit the j.** = to win a high prize in a lottery/to enjoy particular success in sth.

Jac•o•be•an [dʒækə'biːən] *adj.* referring to the time of James I of England (1601–1625).

Jac•o•bite ['dʒækəbaɪt] *adj. & n.* (person) who supported James II of England or his descendants in exile.

jade [dʒeɪd] *n.* hard, usu. green, precious stone. **jade-green,** *adj.* of the bluish-green color of jade.

jad•ed ['dʒeɪdɪd] *adj.* worn out/tired.

jag [dʒæg] *n. Sl.* time of overindulgence or unrestraint in some activity.

jag•ged ['dʒægɪd] *adj.* with an irregular, rough, spiky edge.

jag•uar ['dʒægjuə] *n.* large wild cat of Central and South America.

jail [dʒeɪl] 1. *n.* prison. 2. *v.* to put (s.o.) in prison. **jail•bird,** *n.* person who has been sent to prison often. **jail•er,** *n.* person who guards prisoners in jail.

ja•lop•y [dʒə'lɒpɪ] *n. inf.* dilapidated old car.

jam [dʒæm] 1. *n.* (a) stoppage/blockage caused by too many things in too small a space. (b) *inf.* **in a j.** = in a difficult situation. (c) sweet food made by boiling together fruit, sugar, etc. 2. *v.* (**jammed**) (a) (*of machine*) to stop/to stick so that it cannot move. (b) to crowd/to force (things) into a small space. (c) to make (a radio broadcast) impossible to understand by broadcasting noise on the same wavelength. **jam•ming,** *n.* making a radio broadcast impossible to understand. **jam-packed,** *adj. inf.* packed full. **jam ses•sion,** *n.* impromptu jazz concert.

Ja•mai•can [dʒə'meɪkən] 1. *adj.* referring to Jamaica. 2. *n.* person from Jamaica.

jamb [dʒæm] *n.* side post of a door or window.

jam•bo•ree [dʒæmbə'riː] *n.* large meeting (esp. of Scouts); big festival/party.

jan•gle ['dʒæŋgl] 1. *n.* harsh clanging noise. 2. *v.* (a) to make a harsh clanging noise. (b) to disturb/to irritate (the nerves).

jan•i•tor ['dʒænɪtə] *n.* caretaker, esp. in a school or college.

Jan•u•ar•y ['dʒænjuərɪ] *n.* 1st month of the year.

Jap•a•nese [dʒæpə'niːz] 1. *adj.* referring to Japan. 2. *n.* (a) (*pl.* **Japanese**) person from Japan. (b) language spoken in Japan.

ja•pon•i•ca [dʒə'pɒnɪkə] *n.* flowering quince bush.

jar [dʒɑː] 1. *n.* container for food, etc., often of glass and usu. cylindrical; **a j. of jam.** 2. *v.* (**jarred**) (a) to make a harsh/unpleasant sound. (b) to bump/to shake. (c) to affect suddenly and unpleasantly; **to j. on s.o.'s nerves.**

jar•di•nière [ʒɑ:dɪnɪ'ɜ:] *n.* ornamental container for plants.

jar•gon ['dʒɑ:gən] *n.* special form of language used by a trade/profession or particular group of people.

jas•mine ['dʒæzmɪn] *n.* shrub with sweet-smelling white or yellow flowers.

jas•per ['dʒæspə] *n.* colored quartz.

jaun•dice ['dʒɔ:ndɪs] *n.* sickness which makes the skin turn yellow, due to a disorder of the liver or bile. **jaun•diced,** *adj.* (a) suffering from jaundice. (b) miserable/dispirited; envious; resentful.

jaunt [dʒɔ:nt] *n.* short excursion.

jaun•ty ['dʒɔ:ntɪ] *adj.* (**-ier, -iest**) cheerful/lively. **jaun•ti•ly,** *adv.* cheerfully. **jaun•ti•ness,** *n.* lively manner.

jave•lin ['dʒævlɪn] *n.* long spear used in battle or in sport.

jaw [dʒɔ:] 1. *n.* (a) arrangement of bones which allow the mouth to open and shut. (b) **jaws** = two parts of a tool which grip. 2. *v. inf.* to talk (too much). **jaw•bone,** *n.* one of the two bones forming a jaw.

jay [dʒeɪ] *n.* brightly colored bird of the crow family. **jay•walk•er,** *n.* pedestrian who does not take care/pays no attention to traffic rules or signals when crossing the street. **jay•walk•ing,** *n.* being a jaywalker.

jazz [dʒæz] *n.* type of music with strong rhythm, originally played by American blacks. **jazz up,** *v. inf.* to make bright/attractive. **jazz•y,** *adj.* bright (color).

jeal•ous ['dʒeləs] *adj.* (**of**) feeling sorrow/anger because you want sth which belongs to s.o. else. **jeal•ous•ly,** *adv.* in a jealous way. **jeal•ous•y,** *n.* jealous feeling.

jeans [dʒi:nz] *n. pl. see* **blue jeans.**

jeep [dʒi:p] *n.* trademark for a strongly built vehicle used for traveling over rough ground.

jeer ['dʒɪə] 1. *n.* mocking/laughing in a mean, rude way. 2. *v.* (**at**) to mock/to laugh at (s.o.) in a mean, rude way.

Je•ho•vah [dʒɪ'həʊvə] *n.* God of Israel.

je•june [dʒɪ'dʒu:n] *adj.* naive.

jell [dʒel] *v.* (*of liquid*) to become a jelly. (b) (*of plan*) to become definite. **jel•ly** ['dʒelɪ] *n.* (a) type of jam made of fruit juice boiled with sugar. (b) semi-solid substance like this. **jel•lied** ['dʒelɪd] *adj.* cooked/preserved in a jelly. **jel•ly bean,** *n.* colored candy shaped like a bean, which has a hard covering and a jellylike center. **jel•ly•fish,** *n.* sea creature with jellylike body. **jel•ly roll,** *n.* type of thin

sponge cake rolled up with cream or jam as a filling.

jen•ny ['dʒenɪ] *n.* female donkey or bird.

jeop•ard•ize ['dʒepədaɪz] *v.* to put in danger/at risk. **jeop•ard•y** ['dʒepədɪ] *n.* danger/risk.

jer•e•mi•ad [dʒerɪ'maɪəd] *n.* (*formal*) long complaint about your problems.

jerk [dʒɜ:k] 1. *n.* (a) sudden uneven movement; sharp pull. (b) *Sl.* stupid person. 2. *v.* to make a sudden movement; to pull sharply. **jerk•i•ly,** *adv.* with an abrupt/sudden movement. **jerk•i•ness,** *n.* being jerky. **jerk•y,** *adj.* abrupt/sudden.

jer•kin ['dʒɜ:kɪn] *n.* short coat with no sleeves.

jer•ry-build•er ['dʒerɪbɪldə] *n.* person who builds cheap, poorly constructed, buildings. **jer•ry-built,** *adj.* (building) which is cheaply built.

jer•sey ['dʒɜ:zɪ] *n.* (a) close-fitting warm upper garment. (b) **j.** (**cloth**) = type of loosely woven, usu. woolen, cloth. (c) type of cow.

jest [dʒest] 1. *n.* joke; thing done/said for amusement only. 2. *v.* to make jokes. **jest•er,** *n.* person who plays jokes, esp. someone employed to do this at a royal court.

jet [dʒet] 1. *n.* (a) type of black mineral which can be highly polished; **j. black** = very black. (b) long narrow spray of liquid or gas. (c) opening to allow gas to escape. (d) jet-propelled aircraft; **j. lag** = tiredness felt by travelers who fly by jet across time zones; **j. set** = wealthy people who frequently travel by jet. 2. *v.* (**jetted**) *inf.* to travel by jet. **jet en•gine,** *n.* engine which is propelled by a jet. **jet-pro•pelled,** *adj.* pushed forward by a backward movement of jets of gas. **jet pro•pul•sion,** *n.* being jet-propelled. **jet•stream,** *n.* (a) wind in the upper atmosphere. (b) stream of gases coming from a jet engine.

jet•sam ['dʒetsəm] *n.* (*no pl.*) things which have been thrown into the water from a boat.

jet•ti•son ['dʒetɪzn] *v.* to throw out (unwanted things) from a ship/balloon, etc.

jet•ty ['dʒetɪ] *n.* wall built into water, where boats can tie up.

Jew [dʒu:] *n.* person descended from the Hebrews of ancient Palestine. **Jew•ess,** *n.* Jewish woman. **Jew•ish,** *adj.* referring to Jews. **Jew•ry,** *n.* the Jews.

jew•el ['dʒuəl] *n.* (a) precious stone. (b) ornament to be worn, made from precious stones and/or precious metals, or of imitation stones. **jew•eled,** *adj.* covered with jewels. **jew•el•er,** *n.* person who makes/sells jewelry. **jew•el•ry,** *n.* ornaments to be worn, made of precious stones/metals.

jib [dʒɪb] *n.* (a) triangular sail in front of a boat. (b) arm of a crane.

jibe¹ [dʒaɪb] *n. & v. see* **gibe.**

jibe² *v.* to agree; to be in harmony; **your information jibes with mine** = it agrees with mine.

jif•fy ['dʒɪfɪ] *n. inf.* very short time.

jig [dʒɪg] 1. *n.* (a) type of fast lively dance; music for this dance. (b) instrument for guiding a tool and holding the material being worked on. 2. *v.* (**jigged**) to jump up and down; to move about jerkily. **jig•ger,** *n.* (a) small insect which lives in sand. (b) measure for serving alcohol. **jig•saw,** *n.* (a) type of saw with very fine blade for cutting out shapes. (b) **j. (puzzle)** = puzzle of irregularly shaped pieces of wood/cardboard which when fitted together form a picture.

jig•gle ['dʒɪgl] *v. inf.* to move rapidly/nervously.

jilt [dʒɪlt] *v.* to (encourage and then) reject (a lover).

jim•my ['dʒɪmɪ] *n.* flat iron bar with a curved end, used by burglars to open doors or windows.

jin•gle ['dʒɪŋgl] 1. *n.* (a) sound made by small pieces of metal knocking together. (b) verse with a very simple rhyme and/or rhythm; catchy tune advertising a product. 2. *v.* to make a tinkling sound (like pieces of metal).

jin•go•ism ['dʒɪŋgəʊɪzəm] *n.* excessive love for your country and hatred for others. **jin•go•is•tic** [dʒɪŋgəʊ'ɪstɪk] *adj.* full of jingoism.

jinks [dʒɪŋks] *n. pl.* **high j.** = lively activity; noisy fun.

jinx [dʒɪŋks] *n.* (*pl.* **-es**) *inf.* bad luck.

jit•ters ['dʒɪtəz] *n. pl.* **to have the j.** = to be (unnecessarily) nervous/flustered. **jit•ter•y,** *adj.* nervous/flustered.

jive [dʒaɪv] 1. *n.* type of fast rhythmic dance; music for this dance. 2. *v.* to dance to jive music.

job [dʒɒb] *n.* (a) piece of work; **to do a good j.** = to do sth well; **odd jobs** = pieces of work, esp. repairs in the house. (b) difficult task. (c) position in employment; **to be out of a j.** = to be unemployed. (d) *inf.* crime, esp. a theft. **job•ber,** *n.* wholesaler. **job•less,** 1. *adj.* with no job. 2. *n.* **the j.** = people who have no jobs. **job lot,** *n.* group of miscellaneous items sold together.

jock•ey ['dʒɒkɪ] 1. *n.* person who rides horses in races. 2. *v.* **to j. for position** = to try to improve your position, esp. by cheating or trickery. **jock•strap** ['dʒɒkstræp] *n.* support for genitals, worn, esp. by men participating in sports.

jo•cose [dʒə'kəʊs] *adj.* humorous. **joc•u•lar** ['dʒɒkjʊlə] *adj.* good humored; treating things as a joke. **joc•u•lar•i•ty** [dʒɒkjʊ'lærɪtɪ] *n.* good humor. **joc•u•lar•ly,** *adv.* in a joking way.

joc•und ['dʒɒkənd] *adj.* (*formal*) cheerful.

jodh•purs ['dʒɒdpəz] *n. pl.* special trousers for horse riding which are narrow below the knee.

jo•ey ['dʒəʊɪ] *n.* (*in Australia*) *inf.* young kangaroo.

jog [dʒɒg] 1. *n.* (a) rather slow pace. (b) light blow, esp. from the elbow. 2. *v.* (**jogged**) (a) to move at a steady, but rather slow pace. (b) to run at an easy pace, esp. for exercise. (c) to shake/to push lightly; **it jogged his memory** = it made him remember. **jog•ger,** *n.* person who jogs for exercise. **jog•ging,** *n.* running at an easy pace for exercise. **jog•trot,** *n.* rather slow, easy pace.

jog•gle ['dʒɒgl] *v. inf.* to move rapidly/nervously.

john [dʒɒn] *n. Sl.* toilet.

join [dʒɔɪn] 1. *n.* place/line where two things come together. 2. *v.* (a) to come together/to be united; to bring together. (b) to (meet and) go along with; to meet and do sth together; **to j. forces** = to do sth by combined effort. (c) to become a member of (a club). **join•er,** *n.* person who constructs things from wood, esp. furniture and woodwork in a house. **join•er•y,** *n.* joiner's trade. **join in,** *v.* to take part. **join up,** *v.* to become a member of the armed forces.

joint [dʒɔɪnt] 1. *n.* (a) (place where) two or more pieces are attached, esp. in building or carpentry. (b) place where bones come together, allowing movement; **out of j.** = dislocated. (c) large piece of meat, esp. for roasting. (d) *inf.* low-class night club or gambling den. (e) *Sl.* cigarette containing marijuana. 2. *v.* (a) to cut up (a chicken, etc.) into pieces. (b) to provide with joints. 3. *adj.* together/combined; shared by two or more; **j. account** = bank account shared by two people; **j. author** = author who writes a book with another. **joint•ed,** *adj.* having joints. **joint•ly,** *adv.* together; by combined effort.

joist [dʒɔɪst] *n.* beam which supports a ceiling or floorboards.

joke [dʒəʊk] 1. *n.* thing said or done for amusement, to cause laughter; **practical j.** = action which makes s.o. uncomfortable for the amusement of others. 2. *v.* to tell or make jokes; to say or do sth for amusement; **I was only joking** = I did not mean it seriously. **jok•er,** *n.* (a) person who jokes. (b) extra card in a pack used as a bonus in certain games. **jok•ing•ly,** *adv.* in a joking way.

jol•ly ['dʒɒlɪ] 1. *adj.* (-ier, -iest) merry/happy. 2. *adv.* (*esp. Brit.*) *inf.* very. 3. *v. inf.* **to j. s.o. along** = to encourage s.o. by keeping him happy. **jol•li•fi•ca•tion** [dʒɒlɪfɪ'keɪʃn] *n.* enjoyment/being jolly. **jol•li•ty,** *n.* gaiety.

jolt [dʒəʊlt] 1. *n.* abrupt shake/shock; violent jerk. 2. *v.* (a) to move with a jumping movement. (b) to push/to shake abruptly. (c) to give a sudden shock to.

jon•quil ['dʒɒŋkwɪl] *n.* narcissus.

joss stick ['dʒɒsstɪk] *n.* stick with incense painted on it, which burns slowly giving off a pleasant smell.

jos•tle ['dʒɒsl] *v.* to push/to bump (esp. with the elbows).

jot [dʒɒt] 1. *n.* very small amount. 2. *v.* (**jotted**) **to j. sth down** = to make (quick) notes. **jot•ter,** *n.* small pad of paper for making notes. **jot•tings,** *n. pl.* (random) notes.

joule [dʒuːl] *n.* standard unit of work and energy.

jour•nal ['dʒɜːnl] *n.* (a) diary. (b) periodical, esp. on a learned subject. (c) book for recording each day's business. **jour•nal•ese** [dʒɜːnə'liːz] *n.* style used by bad journalists. **jour•nal•ism** ['dʒɜːnəlɪzəm] *n.* profession of writing for newspapers or periodicals. **jour•nal•ist,** *n.* person who writes for newspapers or periodicals.

jour•ney ['dʒɜːnɪ] *n.* (a) long trip. (b) long distance traveled; **it's two days' j. from here.** 2. *v.* (*formal*) to make a long trip. **jour•ney•man,** *n.* (*pl.* **-men**) craftsman who works for s.o.

joust [dʒaʊst] *v.* to fight with spears on horseback (as an entertainment).

jo•vi•al ['dʒəʊvɪəl] *adj.* good-humored/merry. **jo•vi•al•i•ty** [dʒəʊvɪ'ælɪtɪ] *n.* good humor. **jo•vi•al•ly,** *adv.* in a jovial way.

jowl [dʒaʊl] *n.* jaw/cheek; **cheek by j.** = very close together.

joy [dʒɔɪ] *n.* (cause of) very great happiness. **joy•ful,** *adj.* very happy. **joy•ful•ly,** *adv.* very happily. **joy•less,** *adj.* very sad. **joy•ous,** *adj.* very happy. **joy•ride,** *n.* excursion for pleasure, esp. in a stolen car. **joy•stick,** *n.* (a) rod which controls the movements of an aircraft. (b) device with a movable arm, which moves a cursor on a computer monitor.

JP ['dʒeɪ'piː] *abbreviation for* Justice of the Peace.

ju•bi•lant ['dʒuːbɪlənt] *adj.* full of happiness/triumph. **ju•bi•lant•ly,** *adv.* triumphantly. **ju•bi•la•tion** [dʒuːbɪ'leɪʃn] *n.* great happiness/triumph.

ju•bi•lee ['dʒuːbɪliː] *n.* (celebration of the) anniversary of an important event; **silver/golden/diamond j.** = celebration 25/50/60 or 75 years after an event took place.

Ju•da•ism ['dʒuːdeɪɪzəm] *n.* religion of the Jews.

Ju•das tree ['dʒuːdəstriː] *n.* ornamental tree with pink flowers.

judge [dʒʌdʒ] 1. *n.* (a) public official authorized to make decisions in a court of law. (b) person who decides which is the best entry in a competition. (c) person with good judgment; **he's a good j. of character.** 2. *v.* (a) to make decisions in a court of law/competition, etc. (b) to have as your opinion; to estimate. **judg•ment, judgement,** *n.* (a) making a decision. (b) sentence of a court; legal decision. (c) ability to see things clearly/to make good decisions; **against my better j.** = although I felt it was not the right thing to do.

ju•di•cial [dʒuː'dɪʃl] *adj.* referring to a legal process/to a court of law. **ju•di•ca•ture** ['dʒuːdɪkətʃə] *n.* (a) judicial system. (b) judiciary. **ju•di•cial•ly,** *adv.* legally. **ju•di•ci•ar•y** [dʒuː'dɪʃərɪ] *n.* judges as a group. **ju•di•cious,** *adj.* based on/having good judgment. **ju•di•cious•ly,** *adv.* exhibiting or using good judgment.

ju•do ['dʒuːdəʊ] *n.* modern form of Japanese wrestling.

jug [dʒʌg] *n.* (a) container with a handle, used for pouring liquids. (b) *Sl.* jail. **jugged hare,** *n.* stew made of wild rabbit soaked in wine and cooked slowly.

jug•ger•naut ['dʒʌgənɔːt] *n.* overpowering force to which people sacrifice themselves.

jug•gle ['dʒʌgl] *v.* (a) to throw and catch several objects, so that most of them are in the air at the same time. (b) to change things around, esp. in order to deceive. **jug•gler,** *n.* person who juggles.

jug•u•lar ['dʒʌgjʊlə] *n. & adj.* **j. (vein)** = main vein in the neck.

juice [dʒuːs] *n.* (a) liquid from fruit/vegetables/meat, etc; **to stew in your own j.** = to suffer the consequences of your own mistakes. (b) *inf.* fuel; electricity. **juic•i•ness,** *n.* state of being full of juice. **juic•y,** *adj.* full of juice.

ju•jit•su [dʒuː'dʒɪtsuː] *n.* traditional Japanese unarmed combat.

ju•ju ['dʒuːdʒuː] *n.* African magic charm.

ju•jube ['dʒuːdʒuːb] *n.* type of soft candy.

juke•box ['dʒuːkbɒks] *n.* coin-operated record-playing machine.

ju•lep ['dʒuːləp] *n.* drink made of alcohol and water, usu. with a mint flavor.

Ju•ly [dʒʊ'laɪ] *n.* 7th month of the year. **Jul•ian cal•en•dar,** *n.* calendar instituted by Julius Caesar, slightly longer than the present-day calendar.

jum•ble ['dʒʌmbl] 1. *n.* mixture/confusion. 2. *v.* (**up**) to mix; to confuse.

jum•bo ['dʒʌmbəʊ] *n.* (*pl.* **-os**) anything very large, esp. a very large aircraft holding several hundred people.

jump [dʒʌmp] 1. *n.* (a) leap (in the air); (*in sports*) **long j./high j.** = competition to see how far/how high you can leap. (b) sudden movement. (c) (*in sports*) obstacle to be jumped over. 2. *v.* (a) to move suddenly, esp. upward. (b) to move by jumping; **to j. over the stream.** (c) to make a sudden movement, esp. from some emotion; **to j. to conclusions** = to make a decision too quickly; **to j. the gun** = to begin before your turn/before the correct time. **jump at,** *v.* to seize (an opportunity) eagerly. **jump•er,** *n.* (a) person who jumps. (b) article of clothing, esp. a one-piece sleeveless dress. **jumper (cable),** *n.* cable which allows two car batteries to be connected to help a car to start. **jump jet,** *n.* aircraft which can take off vertically. **jump rope,** *n.* rope which you jump over as it turns. **jump suit,** *n.* one-piece suit, with trousers attached to the shirt. **jump•y,** *adj.* (**-ier, -iest**) *inf.* nervous; excited.

junc•tion ['dʒʌŋkʃn] *n.* joining (place), esp. of railroad lines/roads; **j. box** = box where several electric wires join.

junc•ture ['dʒʌŋktʃə] *n.* (*formal*) point in time.

June [dʒuːn] *n.* 6th month of the year.

jun•gle ['dʒʌŋgl] *n.* (a) almost impassable tropical forest. (b) confused mass; place or circumstances where progress is difficult; **concrete j.** = area of tall impersonal buildings.

jun•ior ['dʒuːnɪə] 1. *adj.* (a) younger; **John Smith, Jr.** = son of John Smith Senior. (b) for younger children. (c) lower in rank. 2. *n.* (a) person who is younger/lower in rank. (b) third-year student in a school or college, next below a senior.

ju•ni•per ['dʒuːnɪpə] *n.* shrub with evergreen leaves and dark berries, used as flavoring for gin.

junk [dʒʌŋk] *n.* (a) large Chinese sailing boat. (b) useless articles/articles to be thrown away; **j. bonds** = bonds giving a high interest, based on the security of a company which is the target of a takeover bid. (c) (*inferior*) second-hand goods. (d) *Sl.* drugs, esp. heroin. **junk food,** *n.* commercially prepared food with little nutritional value. **junk•ie,** *n. Sl.* drug addict. **junk store,** *n.* store selling junk.

jun•ket ['dʒʌŋkɪt] 1. *n.* (a) sweet dessert made of curdled milk. (b) feast/celebration. (c) pleasure trip made by an official at public expense. 2. *v.* to have a celebration, esp. by eating and drinking.

jun•ta ['dʒʌntə] *n.* group of soldiers who seize power and rule a country.

ju•ris•dic•tion [dʒʊərɪs'dɪkʃn] *n.* (legal) power.

ju•ris•pru•dence [dʒʊərɪs'pruːdəns] *n.* study of the law.

ju•rist ['dʒʊərɪst] *n.* person who specializes in law.

ju•ry ['dʒʊərɪ] *n.* (a) group of citizens sworn to decide a verdict on the strength of evidence in a court of law. (b) group of judges in a competition. **ju•ror, juryman,** *n.* (*pl.* **-men**) member of a jury. **ju•ry•box** *n.* place where the jury sits.

just [dʒʌst] 1. *adj.* showing no favor; true/correct. 2. *adv.* (a) exactly; very nearly/almost; **j. by the door; it's j. about ready** = almost ready; **that's j. it** = that is exactly the problem. (b) (*used to indicate the immediate past or future*) **he's j. arrived; I'm j. going.** (c) only; **we're j. good friends.** (d) **j. now** = (i) at the present moment. (ii) a short time ago. (e) **j. as** = (i) exactly when; (ii) exactly in the manner that. **just•ly,** *adv.* fairly; with justice. **just•ness,** *n.* fairness.

jus•tice ['dʒʌstɪs] *n.* (a) quality of being fair; **to do j. to** = to treat (sth) as it deserves; **the portrait doesn't do her j.** = it is not a good likeness. (b) **to bring to j.** = to bring legal proceedings against. (c) (*esp. as title*) judge/magistrate. **Justice of the Peace,** *n.* local public official authorized to carry out some judicial duties (as performing civil marriages, trying minor cases).

jus•ti•fy ['dʒʌstɪfaɪ] *v.* (a) to show that sth is fair/to prove that sth is right. (b) to adjust the

---

æ back, ɑ: farm, ɒ top, aɪ pipe, aʊ how, aɪə fire, aʊə flower, ɔ: bought, ɔɪ toy, e fed, eə hair, eɪ take, ə afraid, əʊ boat, əʊə lower, ɜ: word, i: heap, ɪ hit, ɪə hear, u: school, ʊ book, ʌ but, b back, d dog, ð then, dʒ just, f fog, g go, h hand, j yes, k catch, l last, m mix, n nut, ŋ sing, p penny, r round, s some, ʃ short, t too, tʃ chop, θ thing, v voice, w was, z zoo, ʒ treasure

space between characters in lines of text so that the right margin of the page is even. **jus•ti•fi•a•ble,** *adj.* which can be justified. **jus•ti•fi•a•bly,** *adv.* in a way which can be justified. **jus•ti•fi•ca•tion** [dʒʌstɪfɪ'keɪʃn] *n.* (a) reason which shows that sth is fair. (b) making a right margin of a page of text even.

jut [dʒʌt] *v.* **(jutted) to j. (out)** = to stick out, usu. horizontally.

jute [dʒuːt] *n.* fiber of plants used for making sacks, etc.

ju•ve•nile ['dʒuːvənaɪl] 1. *adj.* of/for young people; **j. delinquent** = young person who is a criminal. 2. *n.* young person. **ju•ve•nil•i•a** [dʒuːvə'nɪlɪə] *n.* works written when a child.

jux•ta•pose [dʒʌkstə'pəʊz] *v.* to place side by side/very close together. **jux•ta•po•si•tion** [dʒʌkstəpə'zɪʃn] *n.* being side by side/very close together.

Kk

K 1. *symbol for* potassium. 2. *abbrev. for* one thousand.

ka•bob [kɪ'bɒb] *n.* small cubes of meat grilled on a skewer.

kaf•tan ['kæftæn] *n. see* **caftan**.

kale [keɪl] *n.* (*no pl.*) type of cabbage with wrinkled leaves.

ka•lei•do•scope [kə'laɪdəskəʊp] *n.* tube with mirrors which reflect small pieces of colored glass and make patterns which can be seen through a viewer. **ka•lei•do•scop•ic** [kəlaɪdə'skɒpɪk] *adj.* like a kaleidoscope/with bright changing colors; frequently changing.

ka•mi•ka•ze ['kæmɪkɑːzɪ] *n. & adj.* suicidally daring (air attack).

kan•ga•roo [kæŋgə'ruː] *n.* large Australian animal, which carries its young in a pouch; **k. court** = illegal court set up by terrorists/strikers, etc., to judge one of their members.

ka•o•lin ['keɪəlɪn] *n.* fine white clay, used for making porcelain, and sometimes in medicine.

ka•pok ['keɪpɒk] *n.* kind of cotton wool, used for stuffing pillows, cushions, life jackets, etc.

ka•put [kə'pʊt] *adj. inf.* finished; broken.

kar•at ['kærət] *n.* measure of purity of gold; **18-k gold.**

ka•ra•te [kə'rɑːtɪ] *n.* Japanese style of fighting, where you hit with the side of the hand.

kar•ma ['kɑːmə] *n.* in Buddhism, the way in which a person acts which will affect his future life.

kay•ak ['kaɪæk] *n.* (a) Eskimo canoe, covered with sealskins. (b) small canoe with a narrow opening for the canoeist.

ke•bab [kɪ'bæb] *n. see* **ka•bob**.

ked•ger•ee [kedʒə'riː] *n.* spicy mixture of rice, fish and eggs.

keel [kiːl] 1. *n.* lowest timber in a ship, on which the framework is built; **on an even k.** = stable/steady. 2. *v.* **to k. over** = to fall over.

keen [kiːn] 1. *adj.* (**-er, -est**) (a) (**on**) eager/willing. (b) sharp. (c) sensitive/acute (sense). 2. *v.* to wail/to cry (because s.o. has died).

keen•ly, *adv.* sharply. **keen•ness**, *n.* being keen.

keep [kiːp] 1. *n.* (a) central tower/strongest part of a castle. (b) maintenance; **she doesn't earn her k.** = she doesn't earn enough money to pay for her food and lodging. (c) *inf.* **for keeps** = for ever. 2. *v.* (**kept** [kept]) (a) to continue to have/to possess. (b) to continue; **he kept running.** (c) to pay regard to (a promise, etc.). (d) to own/to manage (animals). (e) to maintain. (f) to support financially. (g) to have for sale/in stock. (h) to detain/to restrain. (i) to conceal. (j) to reserve. (k) to prevent (s.o. **from** doing sth). (l) to remain; **let's k. in touch** = we mustn't lose contact with each other; **she kept him company** = she stayed with him. (m) **to k. a diary** = to write notes every day about what you have done. (n) to continue to stay in good condition; **raspberries don't k.** = go rotten quickly. **keep•er**, *n.* (a) person in charge of animals in a zoo. (b) fruit which stays in good condition for a long time. **keep•ing**, *n.* (a) custody. (b) **in k. with** = in harmony with. **keep in with**, *v.* to stay on friendly terms with (s.o.). **keep on**, *v.* to continue (to do sth); **he kept on running. keep•sake**, *n.* memento; thing kept to remind you of the giver. **keep up**, *v.* to continue. **keep up with**, *v.* (a) to keep yourself informed about. (b) to go forward at the same pace; **to k. u. w. the Joneses** = to try to maintain the same social level as your neighbors.

keg [keg] *n.* small barrel; **k. beer** = beer kept in pressurized metal kegs.

kelp [kelp] *n.* large seaweed.

kel•vin ['kelvɪn] *n.* standard unit of temperature.

ken [ken] *n.* knowledge; **beyond our k.** = out of our normal range of knowledge.

ken•nel ['kenl] 1. *n.* shelter for a dog; **kennels** = place where dogs can be left when their owners go away/where dogs are bred. 2. *v.* (**kenneled, kennelled**) to keep in a kennel.

kent•ledge ['kentlɪdʒ] *n.* iron used as ballast.

Ken•yan ['kenjən] 1. *adj.* referring to Kenya. 2. *n.* person from Kenya.

kept [kept] *v. see* **keep.**

ker•chief ['kɜːtʃɪf] *n.* large square scarf worn over your head.

ker•nel ['kɜːnl] *n.* (a) softer part inside the hard shell of a nut. (b) essential part/center.

ker•o•sene ['kerəsiːn] *n.* thin oil for lamps/heaters, etc.

kes•trel ['kestrəl] *n.* type of small falcon.

ketch [ketʃ] *n.* (*pl.* **-es**) two-masted sailboat.

ketch•up ['ketʃəp] *n.* sauce made from tomatoes and spices.

ket•tle ['ketl] *n.* metal container, with a lid and a spout, used for boiling water; **a fine k. of fish** = an awkward state of affairs. **ket•tle•drum,** *n.* large drum with a round bottom.

key [kiː] 1. *n.* (a) piece of metal for turning locks. (b) solution/explanation. (c) system of musical notes related to each other. (d) part of a piano/flute/typewriter/computer, etc., which you press down to make the instrument work. (e) seed case, shaped like a key. 2. *adj.* most important (thing/person). 3. *v.* (a) to link to/to make suitable for. (b) to type (words/figures) on a keyboard. **key•board.** 1. *n.* set of keys on a piano/typewriter/computer, etc. 2. *v.* to input data into a computer, using a keyboard. **keyed up,** *adj.* nervous/tense (before an examination/a battle, etc.). **key•hole,** *n.* hole in a lock into which a key is put. **key•note,** *n.* (a) dominating musical note. (b) main theme in a speech; **k. speech** = main speech (at a conference). **key•pad,** *n.* small set of keys on a computer; **numeric k.** = set of numbered keys on a computer keyboard, used for various functions. **key ring,** *n.* ring for carrying several keys together. **key•stone,** *n.* central supporting block of stone or brick in an arch; important idea on which everything else is based. **key•word,** *n.* (a) word that is the key to a code. (b) word that describes the content of a document and is used in computerized information retrieval. (c) significant or meaningful word, e.g. a password.

kg *abbrev. for* kilogram.

khak•i ['kɑːkɪ] *adj. & n.* dull yellow-brown (color); the color of soldiers' uniforms.

kib•butz [kɪ'bʊts] *n.* (*pl.* **-tzim** [-'tsiːm]) farming settlement in Israel.

ki•bosh ['kaɪbɒʃ] *n. Sl.* **to put the k. on sth** = to stop sth happening.

kick [kɪk] 1. *n.* (a) blow with the foot. (b) *inf.* thrill/excitement; **he did it for kicks** = to give himself a thrill. 2. *v.* to strike with the foot. **kick•back,** *n.* (a) recoil (of a gun). (b) *Sl.* bribe/illegal commission paid to s.o. who helps a business deal. **kick off,** *v.* to start a game of football. **kick-off,** *n.* start (of a football game). **kick start•(er),** *n.* pedal to start a motorcycle engine. **kick up,** *v. inf.* to make (a fuss/a row).

kid [kɪd] 1. *n.* (a) young goat. (b) *inf.* child. 2. *v.* (**kidded**) *inf.* to make (s.o.) believe sth that is not true; **I'm only kidding** = I don't mean it; **no kidding?** = is it really true? **kid•dy,** *n. inf.* child.

kid•nap ['kɪdnæp] *v.* (**kidnapped**) to steal (a child); to carry (a person) off by force illegally. **kid•nap•per,** *n.* person who kidnaps. **kid•nap•ping,** *n.* carrying away of a person by force.

kid•ney ['kɪdnɪ] *n.* one of a pair of organs in animals that extract impurities from the blood; this organ used as food; **k. bean** = type of bean with reddish seeds.

kill [kɪl] 1. *n.* putting an animal to death for sport. 2. *v.* to put to death; to make (s.o./an animal/a plant) die; **to k. time** = to spend time doing very little while waiting for sth; **to k. two birds with one stone** = to get two successful results from one action; *inf.* **my feet are killing me** = my feet hurt. **kill•er,** *n.* person who kills; **k. whale** = medium-sized black and white carnivorous whale. **kill•ing.** 1. *adj. inf.* very funny. 2. *n.* (a) putting to death. (b) large profit (on the stock market). **kill•joy,** *n.* person who stops others enjoying themselves. **kill off,** *v.* to get rid of (sth) by killing.

kiln [kɪln] *n.* oven for baking pottery or bricks.

ki•lo ['kiːləʊ] 1. *prefix meaning* one thousand. 2. *n.* (*pl.* **-os**) kilogram.

kil•o•byte ['kɪləʊbaɪt] *n.* storage unit of computer data equal to 1,024 bytes.

kil•o•cy•cle ['kɪləʊsaɪkl] *n.* one thousand cycles as a frequency of radio waves.

kil•o•gram ['kɪləʊgræm] *n.* one thousand grams.

kil•o•hertz ['kɪləʊhɜːts] *n.* one thousand hertz.

kil•o•me•ter, *Brit.* **kil•o•me•tre** [kɪ'lɒmɪtə] *n.* one thousand meters.

kil•o•volt ['kɪləʊvɒlt] *n.* one thousand volts.

kil•o•watt ['kɪləwɒt] *n.* one thousand watts.

kilt [kɪlt] *n.* pleated skirt, usu. of tartan cloth, worn by men in Scotland, and also by women. **kilt•ed,** ['kɪltɪd] *adj.* wearing a kilt.

ki•mo•no [kɪ'məʊnəʊ] *n.* (*pl.* **-os**) long, loose robe worn by Japanese women.

kin [kɪn] *n.* next of k. = nearest relative(s); *see also* **kith.**

kind [kaɪnd] 1. *n.* type/variety; **two of a k.** = two the same; **it's nothing of the k.** = not at all true; **payment in k.** = payment in goods or natural produce, not in money; *inf.* **k. of sorry** = rather sorry. 2. *adj.* (**-er, -est**) amiable/thoughtful;

friendly/thinking of others. **kind-heart•ed,** *adj.* thoughtful about other people. **kind•li•ness,** *n.* being kindly. **kind•ly,** *adj. & adv.* thoughtful/pleasant; in a thoughtful/pleasant way; **she doesn't take k. to** = she doesn't like; **k. shut the door** = please shut the door. **kind•ness,** *n.* being kind.

kin•der•gar•ten ['kɪndəgɑːtn] *n.* school for very young children.

kin•dle ['kɪndl] *v.* to make a fire; to catch fire. **kin•dling,** *n.* (*no pl.*) small pieces of wood used to start a fire.

kin•dred ['kɪndrɪd] *adj.* similar; **k. spirit** = person with whom you have sth in common.

ki•net•ic [kɪ'netɪk] *adj.* produced by moving; (energy) which a body has in motion.

king [kɪŋ] *n.* (a) male sovereign or hereditary ruler of a country. (b) main piece in chess; (*in cards*) card following the queen. **king•cup,** *n.* large buttercup. **king•dom,** *n.* (a) land ruled over by a king. (b) part of the world of nature. (c) **until k. come** = until the end of the world. **king•fish•er,** *n.* small brilliant blue bird that dives for fish. **king•ly,** *adj.* like a king. **king•pin,** *n.* central bolt; central person in an organization. **king-size(d),** *adj.* very large.

kink [kɪŋk] 1. *n.* (a) knot/twist in a length of cord, wire or rope. (b) peculiar mental state. 2. *v.* to make a kink in (sth). **kink•y,** *adj. Sl.* sexually odd/peculiar.

kin•ship ['kɪnʃɪp] *n.* family relationship. **kin•folk, kinsfolk,** *n. pl.* relatives. **kins•man, kinswoman,** *n.* (*pl.* **-men, -women**) relative.

ki•osk ['kiːɒsk] *n.* small outdoor structure for the sale of newspapers/candy, etc.

kip•per ['kɪpə] *n.* split smoked herring. **kip•pered,** *adj.* smoked (fish).

kirsch [kiːəʃ] *n.* cherry brandy.

kiss [kɪs] 1. *n.* (*pl.* **-es**) touching with the lips; **she blew him a k.** = signaled to send him a kiss from a distance; **k. of life** = resuscitation by breathing into a person's mouth; **k. of death** = act which ruins (a business, etc.). 2. *v.* to touch with the lips. **kiss•er,** *n. Sl.* mouth.

kit [kɪt] *n.* (a) equipment, supplies, etc. packed for a specific purpose; **first aid k.** = supplies for the emergency treatment of injuries. (b) box containing pieces which can be put together to make a model/a piece of furniture, etc. **kit•bag,** *n.* small bag for carrying a soldier's clothes and equipment.

kitch•en ['kɪtʃɪn] *n.* room in which food is cooked. **kitch•en•ette,** *n.* very small kitchen. **kit•chen gar•den,** *n.* fruit and vegetable plot in a garden.

kite [kaɪt] *n.* (a) bird of the hawk family. (b) toy made of light wood and paper or cloth which is flown in a strong wind on the end of a string.

kith [kɪθ] *n.* **k. and kin** = friends and relatives.

kitsch [kɪtʃ] *n.* lack of artistic taste; tasteless artistic production.

kit•ten ['kɪtn] *n.* young cat. **kit•ten•ish,** *adj.* playful/like a kitten.

kit•ti•wake ['kɪtɪweɪk] *n.* type of gull.

kit•ty ['kɪtɪ] *n.* joint fund shared by a number of people for a common purpose.

ki•wi ['kiːwiː] *n.* non-flying bird, native of New Zealand. **ki•wi fruit,** *n.* small tropical fruit, with a hairy skin and green flesh.

Kleen•ex ['kliːneks] *n.* (*pl.* **-es**) trademark for a paper handkerchief.

klep•to•ma•ni•a [kleptə'meɪnɪə] *n.* irresistible tendency to steal. **klep•to•ma•ni•ac,** *n.* person who cannot stop stealing.

km *abbrev. for* kilometer.

knack [næk] *n.* talent/ability.

knack•er ['nækə] *n.* person who buys and kills useless horses.

knap•sack ['næpsæk] *n.* canvas/leather bag carried on the back.

knave [neɪv] *n.* (a) (*old*) trickster. (b) (*in cards*) jack/card between the ten and the queen.

knead [niːd] *v.* to press with the hands.

knee [niː] *n.* joint between your thigh and lower leg; **she was sitting on his k.** = sitting on his thighs. **knee•cap.** 1. *n.* bone in front of the knee. 2. *v.* to punish (s.o.) by shooting him in the kneecap. **knee-deep,** *adj.* up to the knees (in).

kneel [niːl] *v.* (**knelt** [nelt] or **kneeled**) to go on your knees. **kneel down,** *v.* to go down on your knees. **kneel•er,** *n.* hard cushion for kneeling on.

knell [nel] *n.* (*formal*) sound of a bell, rung at a solemn ceremony such as a funeral.

knelt [nelt] *v. see* **kneel.**

knew [njuː] *v. see* **know.**

knick•er•bock•ers ['nɪkəbɒkəz] *n. pl.* loose-fitting trousers which are gathered at the knees. **knick•ers** ['nɪkəz] *n. pl.* undergarment worn by a woman or girl on the lower part of the body.

knick-knack ['nɪknæk] *n.* small/light article; trinket.

æ **back,** ɑː **farm,** ɒ **top,** aɪ **pipe,** aʊ **how,** aɪə **fire,** aʊə **flower,** ɔː **bought,** ɔɪ **toy,** e **fed,** eə **hair,** eɪ **take,** ə **afraid,** əʊ **boat,** əʊə **lower,** ɜː **word,** iː **heap,** ɪ **hit,** ɪə **hear,** uː **school,** ʊ **book,** ʌ **but,** b **back,** d **dog,** ð **then,** dʒ **just,** f **fog,** g **go,** h **hand,** j **yes,** k **catch,** l **last,** m **mix,** n **nut,** ŋ **sing,** p **penny,** r **round,** s **some,** ʃ **short,** t **too,** tʃ **chop,** θ **thing,** v **voice,** w **was,** z **zoo,** ʒ **treasure**

knife [naɪf] 1. *n*. (*pl.* **knives** [naɪvz]) cutting blade with a sharpened edge fixed into a handle. 2. *v*. (**knifed**) to stab (s.o.) with a knife.

knight [naɪt] 1. *n*. (a) man honored by a monarch for personal merit or services to his country (and taking the title **Sir**). (b) (*in medieval times*) brave soldier often devoted to the service of a lady. (c) piece in a chess set with a horse's head. 2. *v*. to make (s.o.) a knight. **knight•hood**, *n*. title of knight.

knit [nɪt] *v*. (a) (**knitted** or **knit**) to make (a garment) out of wool, etc., by linking two threads together with the aid of two long needles; **to k. one's brows** = to frown. (b) (**knit**) (*of broken bone*) to join together again. **knit•ter**, *n*. person who knits. **knit•ting**, *n*. woolen garment which is in the process of being made. **knit•ting ma•chine**, *n*. machine for knitting. **knit•ting nee•dle**, *n*. long needle for knitting. **knit•wear**, *n*. knitted garments.

knives [naɪvz] *n. see* **knife.**

knob [nɒb] *n*. (a) rounded bump; round lump. (b) round handle of door/drawer. **knob•by**, *adj*. bumpy; covered with knobs.

knock [nɒk] 1. *n*. sharp blow; sound of a sharp blow. 2. *v*. (a) to strike (sth) with a hard blow; **he knocked on/at the door** = hit the door with his knuckles to call attention. (b) *inf*. to criticize. (c) (*of car engine*) to make a regular/sharp noise because of misfiring. **knock a•bout**, *v*. (a) to drift aimlessly. (b) **to knock (s.o.) about** = to beat (s.o.). **knock back**, *v. inf*. to swallow quickly. **knock down**, *v*. (a) to hit (s.o./sth) to the ground. (b) to sell (an item) at an auction to a purchaser. **knock-down**, *adj*. very low (price). **knock•er**, *n*. knob or ring hinged to a door which can be struck against it to call attention. **knock•ing**, *n*. series of sharp blows; noise made by an engine which is misfiring. **knock-kneed**, *adj*. having knees that touch each other when walking. **knock off**, *v*. (a) to hit (sth) so that it falls off. (b) *inf*. **he knocked off work at 4:30** = he stopped working at 4:30. (c) **the dealer knocked $100 off the price of the car** = he reduced the price of the car by $100. **knock out**, *v*. to hit (s.o.) so hard that he loses consciousness. **knock•out**, *n*. hitting s.o. so hard that he loses consciousness.

knoll [nɒl] *n*. small hill.

knot [nɒt] 1. *n*. (a) looping the ends of string/rope, etc., and fastening them together; small group (of people). (b) hard round place in a piece of wood where a branch used to join it. (c) measurement by which a ship's/an aircraft's speed is calculated (= one nautical mile per hour). (c) type of small shore bird. 2. *v*. (**knotted**) to tie in a knot. **knot•ty**, *adj*. (**-ier, -iest**) difficult (problem).

know [nəʊ] 1. *n*. **to be in the k.** = to be well informed about sth which is not generally known. 2. *v*. (**knew** [njuː]; **has known**) (a) to have in your mind because of learning or experience; **do you k. French?** = do you speak French? (b) to recognize (s.o.). (c) to be acquainted with; **I k. him by sight/by name.** (d) **to k. what it is like to** = to have personal experience of; **to k. your own mind** = to be clear and firm in your views. **know-all**, *n*. know-it-all. **know-how**, *n. inf*. knowledge about how sth is made/is done. **know•ing**, *adj*. understanding; having knowledge. **know•ing•ly**, *adv*. deliberately. **know-it-all**, *n*. person who claims to know everything. **knowl•edge** [ˈnɒlɪdʒ] *n*. (a) what s.o. knows. (b) what is generally known. **knowl•edge•a•ble, knowledgable** *adj*. (person) who knows a lot about sth. **know of**, *v*. to be aware of.

knuck•le [ˈnʌkl] *n*. (a) finger joint. (b) (*on an animal*) joint on the leg (esp. when used as food). **knuckle down**, *v*. to apply yourself seriously to work. **knuck•le under**, *v*. to give in/to submit.

KO *abbrev. for* knock out.

ko•a•la [kəʊˈɑːlə] *n*. **k. (bear)** = small Australian animal which carries its young in a pouch and lives in trees.

kohl [kəʊl] *n*. powder used to make eyelids darker.

kohl•ra•bi [kəʊlˈrɑːbiː] *n*. vegetable with a thick purplish stem which is eaten.

kook•a•bur•ra [ˈkʊkəbʌrə] *n*. large Australian kingfisher.

kop [kɒp] *n*. (*in South Africa*) small hill.

Ko•ran [kɒˈrɑːn] *n*. holy book of the Muslims.

Ko•re•an [kəˈrɪən] 1. *adj*. referring to Korea. 2. *n*. (a) person from Korea. (b) language spoken in Korea.

ko•sher [ˈkəʊʃə] *adj*. (food) prepared according to Jewish law.

kow•tow [kaʊˈtaʊ] *v*. to show great respect (to).

kraal [krɑl] *n*. (*in South Africa*) village with a fence round it.

krill [krɪl] *n*. (*pl.* **krill**) minute shrimps living in the sea.

kryp•ton [ˈkrɪptɒn] *n*. (*element:* Kr) rare gas.

ku•dos [ˈkjuːdɒs] *n*. glory/renown.

ku•du [ˈkuːduː] *n*. small African antelope.

kum•quat [ˈkʌmkwɒt] *n*. very small orange.

kung fu [kuːŋˈfuː] *n*. Chinese style of fighting.

Ll

lab [læb] *n. short for* **laboratory.**

la•bel ['leɪbl] 1. *n.* (a) piece of paper/card, etc., attached to sth to indicate price/contents/name/address, etc. (b) name under which sth is generally known. 2. *v.* (**labeled, labelled**) (a) to put a label on. (b) to name/to describe.

la•bi•al ['leɪbɪəl] *adj.* referring to the lips.

lab•o•ra•to•ry [lə'bɒrətrɪ, *Am.* 'læbrətɔːrɪ] *n.* place where scientific experiments/research are carried out.

la•bo•ri•ous [lə'bɔːrɪəs] *adj.* (a) involving a great deal of work. (b) (style) showing signs of effort. **la•bo•ri•ous•ly,** *adv.* in a laborious way.

la•bor, *Brit.* **la•bour** ['leɪbə] 1. *n.* (a) (hard) work. (b) workers/the workforce. (c) (pains of) childbirth. 2. *v.* (a) to work (hard). (b) **to l. under a delusion** = to have a (persistently) wrong impression; **to l. the point** = to argue/to discuss sth too long. **la•bored,** *adj.* (a) (*of style*) heavy/clumsy. (b) (*of breathing*) heavy/difficult. **la•bor•er,** *n.* person who does heavy manual work. **la•bor-sav•ing,** *adj.* (*of machine/gadget*) which lessens work. **la•bor un•ion,** *n.* organization which groups together workers from similar industries to represent them in bargaining for wages, benefits, etc. with employers. **la•bor un•ion•ist,** *n.* member of a labor union.

lab•ra•dor ['læbrədɔː] *n.* type of large dog, usu. black or yellow.

la•bur•num [lə'bɜːnəm] *n.* tree with bright yellow flowers and poisonous seeds in pods.

lab•y•rinth ['læbɪrɪnθ] *n.* maze; place where it is difficult to find your way about. **lab•y•rin•thine** [læbə'rɪnθaɪn] *adj.* like a labyrinth.

lace [leɪs] 1. *n.* (a) thin strip of material for tying up a shoe, etc. (b) decorative cloth with open patterns of threads. 2. *v.* (a) to tie with a lace. (b) to pour a little alcohol into (sth).

lac•er•ate ['læsəreɪt] *v.* (*formal*) to wound/to tear (flesh). **lac•er•a•tion** [læsə'reɪʃn] *n.* tearing; place where flesh has been torn.

lach•ry•mose ['lækrɪməʊs] *adj.* (*formal*) (person) who tends to cry. **lach•ry•mal,** *adj.* (gland) which produces tears.

lack [læk] 1. *n.* not having sth. 2. *v.* not to have (enough of) sth. **lack•ing,** *adj.* not enough/without.

lack•a•dai•si•cal [lækə'deɪzɪkl] *adj.* not showing any vigor/any enthusiasm.

lack•ey ['lækɪ] *n.* servant who obeys without questioning.

lack•lus•ter ['læklʌstə] *adj.* dull/not brilliant.

la•con•ic [lə'kɒnɪk] *adv.* using few words. **la•con•i•cal•ly,** *adv.* in a laconic way.

lac•quer ['lækə] 1. *n.* type of hard shiny varnish/paint, often used on metals. 2. *v.* to coat with lacquer.

la•crosse [lə'krɒs] *n.* team game played with a ball and a curved stick with a net at the end.

lac•tic ['læktɪk] *adj.* referring to milk. **lac•ta•tion** [læk'teɪʃn] *n.* (*of female*) production of milk. **lac•tose,** *n.* sugar occurring in milk. **lac•to-veg•e•tar•i•an,** *n.* vegetarian who eats dairy products and eggs.

la•cu•na [lə'kjuːnə] *n.* (*pl.* **-ae**) gap/space.

la•cus•trine ['lækuːstriːn] *adj.* referring to lakes.

lac•y ['leɪsɪ] *adj.* (**-ier, -iest**) like lace; made of a network of fine threads.

lad [læd], **lad•die** ['lædɪ] *n. inf.* boy; young man.

lad•der ['lædə] *n.* object made of horizontal bars between two uprights, used for climbing.

lad•en ['leɪdn] *adj.* (**with**) carrying a (heavy) load; (*of ship*) containing a cargo. **lad•ing,** *n.* (a) loading of ships. (b) cargo.

la•dle ['leɪdl] 1. *n.* large deep spoon for serving soup, etc. 2. *v.* (*also* **ladle out**) to serve with a ladle.

la•dy ['leɪdɪ] *n.* (a) woman, esp. of high social standing or with good manners. (b) (*as title*) *Brit.* **Lady** = feminine equivalent of Lord; title

---

of wife or sometimes daughter of a peer; title of wife of a knight or baronet. (c) **Our Lady** = the Virgin Mary. **la•dy•bug, ladybird,** *n.* type of small beetle, usu. red with black spots. **la•dy•kill•er,** *n. inf.* man who is attractive to women. **la•dy•like,** *adj.* well-mannered/polite (as a lady should be). **la•dy•ship,** *n.* (*form of address to a titled lady*) **Your Ladyship.**

lag [læg] 1. *n.* (*in time*) space/interval, esp. between two parts of an event. 2. *v.* (**lagged**) (a) to go/fall/be behind. (b) to cover (a heating appliance, pipes, etc.) to prevent heat loss or to prevent freezing. **lag•gard** ['lægəd] *n.* person who is behind the others. **lag•ging,** *n.* material for wrapping around pipes.

la•ger ['lɑːgə] *n.* type of light beer.

la•goon [lə'guːn] *n.* area of sea water almost completely surrounded by land, esp. by a coral island.

laid [leɪd] *v. see* **lay. laid-back,** *adj. inf.* unhurried/relaxed.

lain [leɪn] *v. see* **lie.**

lair ['leə] *n.* resting place of a wild animal.

laird ['leəd] *n.* (*in Scotland*) owner of a country estate.

lais•sez-faire [leseɪ'feə] *adj.* (economy) where the government does not interfere on principle.

la•i•ty ['leɪɪtɪ] *n.* people who have not been trained as priests.

lake [leɪk] *n.* (a) (large) inland stretch of water. (b) type of reddish dye.

lam [læm] *v. inf.* to hit.

la•ma ['lɑːmə] *n.* Buddhist priest, esp. in Tibet. **la•ma•ser•y,** *n.* monastery for lamas.

lamb [læm] 1. *n.* (a) young sheep. (b) flesh of sheep used as food. 2. *v.* to give birth to a lamb. **lamb•ing** ['læmɪŋ] *n.* giving birth to lambs. **lambs•wool,** *n.* (*no pl.*) very soft wool.

lam•baste, lambast [læm'beɪst] *v.* to criticize (s.o.) sharply.

lame [leɪm] 1. *adj.* (-er, -est) (a) unable to walk properly. (b) weak/unsatisfactory. 2. *v.* to injure (s.o.) so that he cannot walk properly. **lame duck,** *n.* person/company in difficulties and having to rely on outside support. **lame•ly,** *adv.* in a weak way. **lame•ness,** *n.* being lame.

la•mé ['lɑːmeɪ] *n.* cloth with gold or silver threads.

la•mel•la [læ'melə] *n.* (*pl.* **-ae**) thin scale.

la•ment [lə'ment] 1. *n.* (a) song/music for mourning. (b) expression of grief; complaint. 2. *v.* to be very sad about (the death of s.o.). **lam•en•ta•ble** ['læməntəbl] *adj.* very bad. **lam•en•ta•bly,** *adv.* very badly.

lam•en•ta•tion [læmən'teɪʃn] *n.* expression of great sorrow.

lam•i•nat•ed ['læmɪneɪtɪd] *adj.* (a) formed in thin layers. (b) covered with a thin layer of plastic. **lam•i•na•tion** [læmɪ'neɪʃn] *n.* process of covering with a thin plastic film.

lamp [læmp] *n.* object which produces light. **lamp•light,** *n.* light from a lamp. **lamp•post,** *n.* large post which holds a street lamp. **lamp•shade,** *n.* (decorative) cover to put over a lamp.

lam•poon [læm'puːn] 1. *n.* writing which makes s.o. seem ridiculous. 2. *v.* to ridicule (s.o.) in writing.

lam•prey ['læmprɪ] *n.* edible fish, like an eel.

lance [lɑːns] 1. *n.* type of long spear. 2. *v.* to cut (a wound/an abscess, etc.) with a lancet. **lance cor•po•ral,** *n.* (*in the U.S. Marine Corps*) enlisted person above a private first class and below a corporal. **lanc•er,** *n.* soldier in a regiment which used to be armed with lances. **lan•cet,** *n.* (a) pointed two-edged surgical knife. (b) tall thin pointed window.

land [lænd] 1. *n.* (a) solid part of the earth's surface. (b) earth/soil. (c) country. (d) farm areas as distinguished from urban areas. 2. *v.* (a) to come to land; to bring to land. (b) to bring a fish out of water and onto the land; to obtain (a good job). (c) to give/to deal (a blow). (d) **to l. (up) in** = to arrive/to reach. **land•ed,** *adj.* owning land. **land•fall,** *n.* seeing land for the first time from sea or air. **land•fill,** *n.* disposing of refuse in holes in the ground. **land•ing,** *n.* (a) (*esp. of aircraft*) touching land; **l. gear** = wheels on which an aircraft lands. (b) space at the top of a flight of stairs. **land•ing net,** *n.* net at the end of a long pole, for taking fish out of water. **land•ing stage,** *n.* (floating) platform where passengers can leave boats. **land•la•dy,** *n.* (a) woman from whom you rent a house/room, etc. (b) woman who runs a hotel or inn, etc. **land•locked,** *n.* (sea/harbor) surrounded by land. **land•lord,** *n.* (a) man from whom you rent a house/room, etc. (b) man who runs a hotel or inn, etc. **land•lub•ber,** *n. inf.* person who is not used to going on ships. **land•mark,** *n.* (a) object on land which you can see easily, esp. one used by ships to find out their position. (b) outstanding/important event, etc. **landmine,** *n.* mine hidden in the ground. **land•own•er,** *n.* person who owns land. **land•scape** ['lændskeɪp] 1. *n.* (a) scenery/appearance of the countryside; **l. gardening** = making a garden more beautiful by making artificial lakes, hills, planting trees, etc. (b) painting of a country scene. 2. *v.* to improve (a garden) by creating small hills/lakes, planting trees, etc. **land•scape gar•den•er,** *n.* person who designs the layout of large gardens/pieces of land.

land•slide, *n.* (a) slipping of large amounts of earth, etc., down a hillside. (b) overwhelming event, esp. an electoral victory in which one party is totally defeated. **land•ward,** *adj. & adv.* toward the land. **land•wards,** *adv.* toward the land.

lan•dau ['lændɔ:] *n.* horse-drawn carriage with a folding top.

lane [leɪn] *n.* (a) narrow road, often in the country. (b) way/road for traffic, usu. in a particular direction; **shipping lanes** = routes followed by ships; **bus l.** = part of a road where only buses may drive.

lan•guage ['læŋgwɪdʒ] *n.* (a) way of speaking of a country/a group of people; **l. laboratory** = room with tape recorders where students can study foreign languages. (b) way of speaking; **bad l.** = swearing. (c) human speech. (d) means of communication, esp. signs, letters and other symbols used to instruct a computer.

lan•guid ['læŋgwɪd] *adj.* slow-moving/lacking energy. **lan•guid•ly,** *adv.* lazily. **lan•guish** ['læŋgwɪʃ] *v.* to become weak/ill, often because of sorrow. **lan•guor** ['læŋgə] *n.* (a) lack of energy. (b) tender emotional mood. **lan•guor•ous,** *adj.* slow-moving/lazy.

lank [læŋk] *adj.* (a) (*of hair*) straight/dull/lifeless. (b) (*of person*) thin/drooping. **lank•i•ness,** *n.* being lanky. **lank•y,** *adj.* (-ier, iest) tall/thin/awkward (person).

lan•o•lin ['lænəlɪn] *n.* fat from sheep's wool used in skin creams.

lan•tern ['læntən] *n.* lamp with a covering to protect it, which can be carried in the hand.

lan•yard ['lænjəd] *n.* string worn around your neck or shoulder with a whistle, etc., on it.

lap [læp] 1. *n.* (a) your body from waist to knees, when you are sitting; **in the l. of luxury** = in great luxury. (b) one complete circuit (of a racecourse). 2. *v.* (**lapped**) (a) (*of animal*) to drink with the tongue. (b) (**up**) to take in greedily. (c) (*of waves*) to wash against (the shore/the edge of sth). (d) to go so fast that you are a whole lap ahead of (another competitor). (e) to fold (sth) so that it overlaps. **lap dog,** *n.* small pet dog. **lap•top,** *n.* small computer which can be held on the lap.

la•pel [lə'pel] *n.* part of collar of coat, etc., which folds back.

lap•i•dar•y ['læpɪdərɪ] *adj.* (a) referring to stones (esp. precious stones). (b) very short and precise (statement).

lap•is laz•u•li [læpɪs'læzjulaɪ] *n.* bright blue stone.

lapse [læps] 1. *n.* (a) failure to do sth properly. (b) interval of time, esp. when sth does not take place. 2. *v.* (a) to fail/to cease to do sth. (b) to cease to be valid. (c) to fall **into** a lower/less active state.

lap•wing ['læpwɪŋ] *n.* bird found in fields.

lar•board ['lɑ:bəd] *n.* (*old*) port side (of ship).

lar•ce•ny ['lɑ:snɪ] *n.* crime of stealing.

larch [lɑ:tʃ] *n.* (*pl.* -es) cone-bearing tree which loses its leaves in winter.

lard [lɑ:d] 1. *n.* melted down pig fat used in cooking. 2. *v.* to cover (meat) with bacon or lard; to fill (a speech) with quotations, etc.

lard•er ['lɑ:də] *n.* room/cupboard for storing food.

large [lɑ:dʒ] *adj.* (-er, -est) (a) (very) big. (b) **at l.** = (i) free/not imprisoned; (ii) in general. **large•ly,** *adv.* mostly/for the most part. **large-scale,** *adj.* in a large way/involving large numbers of people or large sums of money.

lar•gess, largesse [lɑ:'dʒes] *n.* generous giving of gifts or money.

lar•go ['lɑ:gəʊ] *adv. & n.* (piece of music) which is played slowly.

lar•i•at ['lærɪət] *n.* lasso.

lark [lɑ:k] 1. *n.* (a) bird which sings and flies high in the sky. (b) *inf.* prank; joke. 2. *v. inf.* to have fun/play jokes. **lark•spur,** *n.* plant with tall spikes of flowers.

lar•rup ['lærəp] *v. inf.* to beat (s.o.) up.

lar•va ['lɑ:və] *n.* (*pl.* -vae [-vi:]) early stage of development of an insect, different in form from the adult.

lar•ynx ['lærɪŋks] *n.* (*pl.* -es) upper part of the windpipe, where sounds are made by the voice. **lar•yn•gi•tis** [lærɪn'dʒaɪtɪs] *n.* inflammation of the larynx causing a sore throat.

la•sa•gne [læ'zænə] *n.* type of pasta which is made of wide flat strips.

las•civ•i•ous [lə'sɪvɪəs] *adj.* full of sexual desire. **las•civ•i•ous•ly,** *adv.* in a lascivious way. **las•civ•i•ous•ness,** *n.* being lascivious.

la•ser ['leɪzə] *n.* instrument which produces a highly concentrated beam of light; **l. printer** = printer that uses a laser beam to produce

---

æ back, ɑ: farm, ɒ: top, aɪ pipe, aʊ how, aiə fire, aʊə flower, ɔ: bought, ɔɪ toy, e fed, eəhair, eɪ take, ə afraid, əʊ boat, əʊə lower, v: word, i: heap, ɪ hit, ɪə hear, u: school, ʊ book, ʌ but, b back, d dog, ð then, dʒ just, f fog, g go, h hand, j yes, k catch, l last, m mix, n nut, ŋ sing, p penny, r round, s some, ʃ short, t too, tʃ chop, θ thing, v voice, w was, z zoo, ʒ treasure

high-quality print; **l. treatment** = medical treatment using a laser beam.

lash [læ∫] 1. n. (pl. **-es**) (a) stroke with a whip. (b) flexible part of a whip. (c) eyelash. 2. v. (a) to beat (sth) wth a whip. (b) to make a movement like beating with a whip. (c) to fasten/to tie down tightly with rope/string. **lash•ing,** n. (a) whipping. (b) tying/binding with rope, etc. **lash out,** v. **to l. o. at** = to become (unexpectedly) very angry at/to try to hit.

lass [læs], **las•sie** ['læsɪ] n. (pl. **-es**) inf. girl; young woman.

Las•sa fe•ver ['læsə'fi:və] n. fatal viral disease which originated in Africa.

las•si•tude ['læsɪtju:d] n. (formal) tiredness.

las•so [lə'su:] 1. n. (pl. **-os**) rope with looped end for catching horses/cattle, etc. 2. v. to catch (animals) with a lasso.

last [lɑːst] 1. adj. (a) placed/coming at the end (of a list/line/period of time); **l. thing at night** = at the very end of the day; **l. but one** = the one before the end one; **l. but not least** = at the end of a list, but not because it is the least important; **the l. straw** = last of a series of events etc. which leads to a loss of patience, tolerance, etc.; **the l. word in hats** = the very latest fashion; **the l. person I would want to go on vacation with** = the most unlikely person. (b) most recent; **l. Monday; l. week.** 2. n. (a) shape on which a shoe is made or repaired. (b) final thing/period/sight; **at (long) l.** = in the end/after a long time; **to the l.** = till the very end. 3. adv. (a) at the end. (b) most recently. 4. v. to continue (to exist); to remain in good condition. **last•ing,** adj. which continues for a long time. **last•ly,** adv. at the end/finally. **Last Sup•per,** n. last meal take by Christ with his disciples.

latch [læt∫] 1. n. (pl. **-es**) fastening for a door, etc., consisting of a small bar which fits into a catch. 2. v. (a) to close with a latch. (b) inf. **to l. on to sth** = to seize/to obtain. **latch•key,** n. key for a front door; **l. child** = child who has a key to the house and lets himself in when he comes home from school because both parents are at work.

late [leɪt] 1. adj. (**-er, -est**) (a) at a time after that decided/intended; **the train is ten minutes l.** (b) at/toward the end of a period of time. (c) at/toward/past the end of a season. (d) **latest** = last/most recent. (e) (formal) referring to s.o. who has died; **my l. father.** 2. adv. (**-er, -est**) (a) after the appointed time. (b) after a certain time. **late•com•er,** n. person who arrives after others/after the appointed time. **late•ly,** adv. during recent days/weeks. **late•ness,** n. being late.

la•tent ['leɪtənt] adj. present but not developed.

lat•er•al ['lætərəl] adj. referring to the side; (fin) on the side of a fish's body. **lat•er•al•ly,** adv. toward the side.

lat•er•ite ['lætərɑɪt] n. hard clay, like rock.

la•tex ['leɪteks] n. milky juice from a rubber tree.

lath [lɑːθ] n. narrow thin strip of wood.

lathe [leɪð] n. machine for holding and turning wood/metal, so that it can be shaped.

lath•er ['lɑːðə] 1. n. (a) mass of (soap) bubbles. (b) (esp. on horse) frothy sweat; **to be in a l.** = be upset/flustered. 2. v. (a) to make (sth) form a lather; to form a lather. (b) to cover with lather.

Lat•in ['lætɪn] 1. n. (a) language formerly spoken by the Romans. (b) person from Italy, Spain, Portugal or South America. 2. adj. (a) referring to the language of ancient Rome. (b) referring to Italy, Spain, Portugal and South America; **L. America** = countries in South and Central America where Spanish or Portuguese is spoken.

lat•i•tude ['lætɪtjuːd] n. (a) breadth of view/tolerance/scope. (b) position on the earth's surface measured in degrees north or south of the equator; **northern latitudes** = in areas north of the equator.

la•trine [lə'triːn] n. lavatory in a military camp or prison.

lat•te ['lætɛɪ, 'lɑːtɛɪ] n. coffee made with hot milk.

lat•ter ['lætə] 1. adj. (a) second thing mentioned (of two). (b) recent; of the final part/period. **lat•ter•ly,** adv. recently.

lat•tice ['lætɪs] n. pattern (of pieces of wood in a fence, etc.) made of crisscross diagonal lines; **l. window** = window with small panes and lead frames forming a crisscross pattern.

laud [lɔːd] v. (formal) to praise. **laud•a•ble,** adj. worthy of praise. **laud•a•bly,** adv. in a laudable way. **laud•a•to•ry,** adj. containing praise.

lau•da•num ['lɔːdnəm] n. opium in alcohol, used as a sedative.

laugh [lɑːf] 1. n. sound made to express amusement/happiness; **to do sth for a l.** = to do it for amusement only/as a joke. 2. v. (a) to make sounds which express amusement/happiness; **to l. up one's sleeve** = to laugh secretly. (b) **to l. at** = to make fun of. **laugh•a•ble,** adj. only worth laughing at; ridiculous. **laugh•ing gas,** n. gas which makes you laugh when you breathe it, used esp. by dentists as an anesthetic. **laugh•ing stock,** n. person whom everyone makes fun of. **laugh•ter,** n. (sound/act of) laughing.

launch [lɔːnt∫] 1. n. (pl. **-es**) (a) type of small motor boat. (b) act of launching (boat/rocket/new project, etc.). 2. v. (a) to put (a boat/ship) into the water, esp. for the first time. (b) to send off (a rocket into the air). (c) to give (sth/s.o.) a start. **launch•ing pad,** *n.* starting platform for a rocket, etc.

laun•dry ['lɔːndrɪ] *n.* (a) place where clothes/sheets, etc., are washed. (b) clothes/sheets, etc. for washing, or which have been washed. **laun•der,** *v.* (a) to wash clothes. (b) *inf.* to pass (illegal profits, etc.) into the conventional banking system. **laun•der•ette, laundrette** ['lɔːndret] *n.* laundry with coin-operated washing machines for public use. **Laun•dro•mat** ['lɔːndrəmæt] *n.* trademark for a launderette. **laun•dress,** *n.* woman who washes laundry.

lau•re•ate ['lɔːrɪət] *n.* person who has been awarded a prize; **Poet L.** = leading poet who is asked to write commemorative verse for special occasions.

lau•rel ['lɒrəl] *n.* tree with smooth shiny evergreen leaves; **to rest on your laurels** = to enjoy your past success, without trying to gain more.

la•va ['lɑːvə] *n.* molten material flowing from a volcano which becomes solid when it cools.

lav•a•to•ry ['lævətrɪ] *n.* (a) small room with facilities for washing the hands and face and a toilet. (b) toilet.

lav•en•der ['lævɪndə] *n.* (a) plant with sweet-smelling bluish-purple flowers. (b) bluish-purple color.

lav•ish ['lævɪʃ] 1. *adj.* (a) generous/ample (helping of food, etc.). (b) extravagant/over-generous. 2. *v.* (**on** s.o.) to give (over-)generously. **lav•ish•ly,** *adv.* in a lavish way. **lav•ish•ness,** *n.* being lavish.

law [lɔː] *n.* (a) rules by which a country is governed and the people controlled. (b) rule/controlling force; **to lay down the l.** = to state sth in a dogmatic way. (c) process of upholding the rules of a country. **law-a•bid•ing,** *adj.* obeying the law. **law•court,** *n.* court where cases are heard and justice is administered. **law•ful,** *adj.* according to law/legal. **law•ful•ly,** *adv.* in a lawful way. **law•less,** *adj.* wild/uncivilized; paying no attention to law. **law•less•ness,** *n.* being lawless. **law•suit,** *n.* legal case. **law•yer,** *n.* person who has studied law and can advise people on legal matters.

lawn [lɔːn] *n.* (a) (area of) short grass in a garden; **l. tennis** = tennis played on grass. (b) very fine cotton material. **lawn•mow•er,** *n.* machine for cutting grass.

lax [læks] *adj.* (**-er, -est**) loose/not rigid. **lax•a•tive,** *adj. & n.* (substance) which helps to loosen the bowels. **lax•i•ty, laxness,** *n.* being loose/not being rigid.

lay [leɪ] 1. *adj.* (a) (person) who is not trained as a priest. (b) not belonging to a profession or specialization. 2. *n.* (*old*) short narrative poem. 3. *v.* (**laid**) (a) to place/to put, often in a horizontal position. (b) to place in the right position; **to l. a carpet.** (c) (*of bird*) to produce (an egg). (d) to make (a bet). (e) to set/to place dishes, etc. on (a table); **l. the table for three.** (f) to set (a trap/a scene). (g) *see also* **lie. lay a•side, lay by,** *v.* to put (sth) away for future use. **lay down,** *v.* to put (sth) down/to give (sth) up. **lay•er.** 1. *n.* (a) (horizontal) thickness of sth. (b) shoot which is layered. 2. *v.* to make a new plant by attaching a shoot to the ground so that it takes root. **lay fig•ure,** *n.* large doll used by artists as a model. **lay in,** *v.* to store for future use. **lay in•to,** *v. inf.* to attack/to hit (s.o.). **lay•man,** *n.* (*pl.* **-men**) person who does not belong to a particular profession or specialization. **lay off,** *v.* (a) to dismiss (workers) temporarily. (b) *inf.* to stop doing sth. **lay-off,** *n.* temporary dismissal from work. **lay on,** *v.* to put on. **lay out,** *v.* (a) to place in an orderly way, esp. on a table, etc. (b) to make a design for (a garden/a book, etc.). (c) to spend (money). (d) to prepare (a corpse) for burial. **lay•out,** *n.* design, esp. of a garden/a book. **lay up,** *v.* (a) to store (away). (b) **to be laid up** = to be ill in bed.

lay•ette [leɪ'et] *n.* clothes for a new-born baby.

la•zy ['leɪzɪ] *adj.* (**-ier, -iest**) not wanting to do any work. **laze,** *v.* to do nothing or very little. **la•zi•ly,** *adv.* in a lazy way. **la•zi•ness,** *n.* being lazy. **la•zy•bones,** *n. inf.* person who does not like work/who does nothing.

lb [paʊnd] *abbrev. for* pound (in weight).

LCD *abbrev. for* liquid crystal display.

lea [liː] *n.* field used for pasture; meadow.

leach [liːtʃ] *v.* to remove a substance from soil, etc., by passing water through it.

lead[1] [led] *n.* (a) (*element:* Pb) heavy soft bluish-gray metal. (b) weight at the end of a rope, used for measuring the depth of water. (c) writing part of a pencil. **lead•en** ['ledn] *adj.* of/like lead; **l. sky** = dull gray sky.

lead[2] [liːd] 1. *n.* (a) front position/first action; **to go into the l./to take the l.** (b) (*in cards*) right to play first. (c) leash to keep a dog in control. (d) electric wire, etc., which joins an appliance to its source of power. (e) (actor who plays a) main role. (f) amount by which one is ahead. 2. v. (**led** [led]) (a) to go/to be ahead; to show the way; to go toward. (b) to be the first/to have the most important place. (c) to make (sth) have; to have; **it led me to think she was lying** = made me think. (d) to be at the head of/to direct. (e) (*in cards*) to play as first card; to play first. (f) to go in a particular direction. **lead•er** ['liːdə] n. (a) person who manages/directs others. (b) chief player, esp. of the violin, in an orchestra. **lead•er•ship**, n. being the person who manages/directs others. **lead•ing**, adj. which leads; most important; **l. article** = main article in a newspaper, giving views on topics of current interest; **l. lady/man** = actress/actor taking the main role; **l. question** = question which is worded in order to get a particular answer. **lead on**, v. to go ahead, so that others will follow; to encourage (s.o.) to go on, esp. to do sth stupid. **lead time**, n. time between placing an order and receiving the goods. **lead up to**, v. to prepare the way for sth (in conversation).

leaf [liːf] 1. n. (*pl.* **leaves** [liːvz]) (a) flat, usu. green, part of a plant, growing from a stem or branch; **trees in l.** = with leaves. (b) sheet of paper forming two pages of a book; **to turn over a new l.** = to change your ways/to try to improve. (c) flat folding part (of a table). (d) very thin sheet of metal, etc. 2. v. **to l. through the pages of a book** = to turn them over rapidly without reading. **leaf•let**, n. sheet of paper, often folded, giving information as an advertisement. **leaf mold**, n. compost made of rotted leaves. **leaf•y**, adj. covered with leaves.

league [liːg] 1. n. (a) group joined together for some purpose; **in l. with s.o.** = working with s.o. against s.o. else. (b) association of sports clubs which play against each other. (c) (*old*) measure of distance (about 3 miles). 2. v. to join together/to form a group for a particular purpose.

leak [liːk] 1. n. (a) hole through which liquid/gas, etc., can escape or enter; **the canoe sprang a l.** = got a hole. (b) escape of secret information. 2. v. (a) (*of liquid/gas, etc.*) to flow away/to escape. (b) (*of container*) to allow liquid/gas, etc., to escape or enter. (c) to pass on (secret information). **leak•age**, n. (a) action of leaking. (b) amount of liquid, etc., which has escaped. **leak•y**, adj. which leaks.

lean [liːn] 1. adj. (-er, -est) (a) thin/with little flesh. (b) (*of meat*) with little fat. (c) poor/unproductive. 2. n. meat with little fat. 3. v. (**leaned**, (*esp. Brit.*) **lent** [lent]) (a) to support (yourself/sth) (**on** sth/s.o.). (b) to stand/to be in

a position at an angle. (c) to have a tendency **toward. lean•ing**, n. tendency **toward**/interest in. **lean•ness**, n. being thin. **lean o•ver**, v. to bend (in a particular direction); **to l. o. backward to help** = make every effort to help. **lean-to**, n. (small) building supported against the wall of a larger building.

leap [liːp] 1. n. (a) jump. (b) upward/forward movement; **to advance by leaps and bounds** = to make rapid progress; **l. in the dark** = action where you are unsure of the consequences. 2. v. (**leaped/leapt** [lept]) (a) to jump. (b) to rise suddenly. **leap at**, v. to seize/to accept eagerly. **leap•frog**. 1. n. game in which one person jumps over the bent back of another. 2. v. (**leapfrogged**) to jump over s.o.'s bent back. **leap year**, n. every fourth year, in which February has 29 days.

learn [lɜːn] v. (**learned/learnt** [lɜːnd/lɜːnt]) (a) to gain knowledge of (sth)/of how to do (sth). (b) to hear (news, etc.). **learn•ed** ['lɜːnɪd] adj. (a) (person) who has much knowledge. (b) (journal) for specialists. **learn•er**, n. person who is learning. **learn•ing**, n. (a) gaining knowledge of sth/of how to do sth. (b) great study/knowledge.

lease [liːs] 1. n. renting of a building/piece of land, etc., for a specified period; **it's given him a new l. on life** = it's made him want to make a fresh start/to live more fully. 2. v. (a) (*also* **lease out**) to take/to give on a lease. (b) to hold on a lease. **lease•hold**. 1. n. (holding of) property on a lease. 2. adj. held on a lease. **lease•hold•er**, n. person who holds a property on a lease.

leash [liːʃ] n. (*pl.* -**es**) strap/cord to keep a dog in control.

least [liːst] 1. adj. & n. (of) the smallest/most unimportant (amount). 2. adv. in the smallest way.

leath•er ['leðə] n. skin of certain animals, used to make shoes/bags, etc. **leath•er•jack•et**, n. grub of a fly. **leath•er•y**, adj. (tough) like leather.

leave [liːv] 1. n. (a) permission. (b) time off; permission to be away. (c) **to take l. of** = to say goodbye to; **to take l. of one's senses** = to become quite mad. 2. v. (**left** [left]) (a) to go away (from). (b) to allow to remain behind/to forget to take; **l. me alone** = don't pester me; **l. it to me** = let me deal with it. (c) to abandon. (d) to give (sth) **to** s.o. in your will. (e) to have at the time of one's death. **leave behind**, v. to forget to take (s.o./sth) with you. **leave off**, v. to stop. **leave out**, v. to forget/to omit (sth).

leav•en ['levn] 1. n. substance which causes a dough to rise; thing which causes a change for the better. 2. v. to add leaven to (dough); to cause a change.

Leb•a•nese [lebə'niːz] 1. *adj.* referring to Lebanon. 2. *n.* (*pl.* **Lebanese**) person from Lebanon.

lech•er ['letʃə] *n.* man who frequently indulges in sex. **lech•er•ous,** *adj.* indulging in sex. **lech•er•y,** *n.* indulgence in sex.

lec•tern ['lektən] *n.* stand with a sloping surface on which you can put a book/papers, etc., from which you are going to read aloud in public.

lec•ture ['lektʃə] 1. *n.* (a) talk, esp. to students or other group of people on a particular subject. (b) (long) scolding. 2. *v.* to give a lecture (**on** sth). **lec•tur•er,** *n.* (a) person who gives a talk on a particular subject. (b) teacher in a university or college below an assistant professor. **lec•ture•ship,** *n.* position as a lecturer.

led [led] *v. see* **lead²**.

ledge [ledʒ] *n.* flat (narrow) part which sticks out from a cliff or building.

ledg•er ['ledʒə] *n.* book in which accounts are kept. **led•ger line,** *n.* leger line.

lee [liː] *n.* side of a ship sheltered from the wind; **l. shore** = shore toward which the wind is blowing. **lee•ward,** *adj., adv. & n.* (side of a ship) sheltered from the wind. **lee•way,** *n.* extra time/extra space.

leech [liːtʃ] *n.* (*pl.* **-es**) (a) type of worm which sucks blood. (b) (*old inf.*) doctor.

leek [liːk] *n.* vegetable related to the onion, with white stem and long green leaves.

leer ['lɪə] 1. *n.* nasty sideways look, often expressing sexual desire. 2. *v.* to look with a leer (**at** s.o.).

lees [liːz] *n. pl.* sediment left at the bottom of a wine bottle, etc.

left [left] 1. *n.* (a) side of the body which normally has the weaker hand. (b) left hand/fist. (c) (*in politics*) group/policy having liberal or radical views. 2. *adj.* (a) of/on the side of the body which normally has the weaker hand; **l. bank** = bank of a river, etc., on your left when facing down stream. (b) of the left (in politics). 3. *adv.* on/to the left. 4. *see also* **leave**. **left-handed,** *adj.* using the left hand more than the right. **left•ist,** *adj. & n.* (person) who is on the left politically. **left•o•vers,** *n. pl.* what is not used, esp. food which has not been eaten. **left-wing,** *adj.* politically on the left. **left-wing•er,** *n.* person who is on the left politically.

leg [leg] 1. *n.* (a) part of the body on which a person or animal walks; **to be on one's last legs** = to be almost exhausted; **to give s.o. a l. up** = to help him to climb to a higher position; **to pull s.o.'s l.** = to joke by telling him sth untrue. (b) leg of an animal used for food. (c) part of a garment which covers the leg. (d) part of a piece of furniture which supports. (e) section of a race/journey. 2. *v. inf.* **to l. it** = to walk. **leg•ged** [legd, 'legɪd] *suffix meaning* with legs; **four-legged animal. leg•gings,** *n. pl.* thick coverings for the lower legs. **leg•gy,** *adj.* with long legs. **leg•less,** *adj.* without any legs. **leg-pull,** *n. inf.* hoax. **leg warm•ers,** *n. pl.* knitted garments for the legs, like like long socks with no feet.

leg•a•cy ['legəsɪ] *n.* what is left to a person (after s.o.'s death). **leg•a•tee** [legə'tiː] *n.* person who receives a legacy.

le•gal ['liːgl] *adj.* (a) in accordance with/obeying the law; **l. aid** = free legal representation given to people without enough money to pay lawyers' fees; **l. tender** = money which must legally be accepted if you give it in payment. (b) referring to (the processes of the) law. **le•gal•is•tic** [liːgə'lɪstɪk] *adj.* too concerned with the law. **le•gal•i•ty** [lɪ'gælɪtɪ] *n.* being allowed by law. **le•gal•ize,** *v.* to authorize (sth) by law. **le•gal•ly,** *adv.* in accordance with the law.

leg•ate ['legət] *n.* official envoy (from the Pope). **le•ga•tion** [lɪ'geɪʃn] *n.* group of officials who represent their government in a foreign country; building where they live and work.

leg•end ['ledʒənd] *n.* (a) story from the past which may not be based on fact. (b) key to symbols used on a map. **leg•end•ar•y,** *adj.* referring to a legend.

leg•er•de•main [ledʒədə'meɪn] *n.* trickery; conjuring.

leg•er line ['ledʒə'laɪn] *n.* small line on a musical score, written above or below the normal five lines.

leg•i•ble ['ledʒɪbl] *adj.* clear/able to be (easily) read. **leg•i•bil•i•ty** [ledʒɪ'bɪlɪtɪ] *n.* being easily read. **leg•i•bly,** *adv.* in a legible way.

le•gion ['liːdʒən] *n.* (a) division of an army. (b) association/body, esp. of soldiers; **the Foreign L.** = private army, organized by France, which serves overseas. (c) very large number. **le•gion•naire,** *n.* member of a legion, such as the Foreign Legion; **legionnaires' disease** =

æ back, ɑː farm, ɒ top, aɪ pipe, aʊ how, aɪə fire, aʊə flower, ɔː bought, ɔɪ toy, e fed, eəhair, eɪ take, ə afraid, əʊ boat, aʊə lower, ɜː word, iː heap, ɪ hit, ɪə hear, uː school, ʊ book, ʌ but, b back, d dog, ð then, dʒ just, f fog, g go, h hand, j yes, k catch, l last, m mix, n nut, ŋ sing, p penny, r round, s some, ʃ short, t too, tʃ chop, θ thing, v voice, w was, z zoo, ʒ treasure

disease, similar to pneumonia, caused by bacteria in air-conditioning systems.

leg•is•late ['ledʒɪsleɪt] v. to make laws. **leg•is•la•tion** [ledʒɪ'sleɪʃn] n. (making of) laws. **leg•is•la•tive** ['ledʒɪslətɪv] adj. referring to laws/law-making. **leg•is•la•tor** n. person who makes laws. **leg•is•la•ture** ['ledʒɪslətʃə] n. law-making body.

le•git•i•ma•cy [lɪ'dʒɪtɪməsɪ] n. being in accordance with the law. **le•git•i•mate**, adj. (a) legal/lawful; (child) born to married parents. (b) reasonable/justifiable. **le•git•i•mate•ly**, adv. in accordance with the law; correctly. **le•git•i•mize**, v. to make legitimate.

leg•ume ['legjuːm] n. plant (like a pea or bean) which has seeds in pods. **le•gu•mi•nous** [le-'gjuːmɪnəs] adj. (plant) which has seeds in pods.

lei•sure ['leʒə] n. time free to do what you want; **at your l.** = when there is an opportunity/without hurry; **l. pursuits** = pastimes. **lei•sured**, adj. having plenty of leisure; **l. classes** = people who do not need to work to earn money. **lei•sure•ly**, adj. without hurry.

leit•mo•tiv ['laɪtməʊtiːf] n. theme (in music) which reappears and which shows a special feeling/state.

lem•ming ['lemɪŋ] n. small Scandinavian mammal which travels in groups and is said to fall blindly over cliffs into the sea.

lem•on ['lemən] n. pale yellow sour-tasting fruit; tree which bears such fruit. **lem•on•ade** [lemə'neɪd] n. drink made with lemon juice, water, and sometimes, sugar.

le•mur ['liːmə] n. monkeylike animal with a long tail.

lend [lend] v. (**lent**) (a) to give (sth to s.o.) for a certain period of time; **will you l. me your book for a day or two?** (b) to give/to contribute (to); **to l. a hand** = to help; **to lend itself to** = to be suitable for. **lend•er**, n. person who lends (money). **lend•ing li•brar•y**, n. section of a library from which books may be taken away for a time.

length [leŋθ] n. (a) measurement of how long sth is from end to end; **he won the race by a l.** = by the length of a horse/man/boat, etc. (b) piece of sth of a particular length; **a l. of rope.** (c) being long; **a stay of some l.** = quite a long stay; **at l.** = (i) at last; (ii) for a long time. (d) **to go to great lengths** = to make great efforts. **length•en**, v. to make/to become longer. **length•i•ly**, adv. for a long time/at length. **length•i•ness**, n. being long. **length•wise, lengthways**, adv. along the length/along the longest side. **length•y**, adj. (-ier, -iest) (very) long.

le•ni•en•cy, lenience ['liːnjəns(ɪ)] n. being merciful/not being strict. **le•ni•ent**, adj. showing mercy/not strict or severe. **le•ni•ent•ly**, adv. in a lenient way.

lens [lenz] n. (pl. -es) (a) piece of glass/plastic, etc., curved so as to cause light rays to join or spread out, and used in glasses/telescopes/cameras, etc. (b) part of the eye. (c) **contact l.** = small lens worn on the eyeball to help you to see.

lent [lent] v. see lend.

Lent [lent] n. (in the Christian church) period before Easter when many Christians eat less/give up some luxury. **Lent•en**, adj. referring to Lent.

len•til ['lentl] n. small round dried seed used as food.

Le•o ['liːəʊ] n. one of the signs of the Zodiac, shaped like a lion. **le•o•nine** ['liːəʊnaɪn] adj. referring to a lion.

leop•ard ['lepəd] n. large spotted animal of the cat family. **leop•ard•ess**, n. female leopard.

le•o•tard ['lɪəʊtɑːd] n. skintight one-piece costume worn by ballet dancers.

lep•er ['lepə] n. person who has leprosy. **lep•ro•sy**, n. serious infectious skin disease which slowly destroys flesh and nerves. **lep•rous**, adj. like leprosy.

lep•i•dop•ter•a [lepɪ'dɒptərə] n. pl. group of insects, including butterflies and moths.

lep•re•chaun ['leprəkɔːn] n. (in Irish folklore) wicked little elf.

les•bi•an ['lezbɪən] adj. & n. (woman) who is sexually attracted to other women. **les•bi•an•ism**, n. state of being lesbian.

le•sion ['liːʒn] n. wound; change in body tissue.

less [les] 1. adj. & n. (of a) smaller quantity/size/value. 2. prep. minus/with a certain amount taken away. 3. adv. in a smaller amount/to a smaller degree. **less•en**, v. to make (sth) become less; to reduce. **less•er**, adj. smaller.

les•see [le'siː] n. person who holds a lease/who pays rent. **les•sor** [le'sɔː] n. person who gives a lease/who receives rent.

les•son ['lesn] n. (a) period of time in school, etc., during which you are taught. (b) means by which you learn; **he's learned his l.** = he is wiser; **to teach s.o. a l.** = to make s.o. wiser/to punish s.o. (c) part of the Bible which is read in church.

lest [lest] conj. (a) (formal) in order to avoid. (b) for fear that.

let [let] 1. v. (**let**) (a) to permit/to allow. (b) to lend (a house, etc.) for a period of time in return for money. 2. v. (showing command/suggestion) **let's hurry; don't let's start yet.** 3. n. inf. period of lease of a property. **let a•lone**, *adv.* not to mention. **let down,** *v.* (a) to take down/to lower. (b) to fail to help/to disappoint. **let•down,** *n.* disappointment. **let go,** *v.* (a) to lose hold (**of** sth). (b) to allow (s.o.) to leave. **let in,** *v.* (a) to allow to come in. (b) **to let yourself in for** = to allow yourself to get involved in (a difficult situation). **let off,** *v.* (a) to make (a gun, etc.) fire. (b) **to let s.o. off** = not to punish s.o. after all. **let on,** *v. inf.* to tell a secret. **let out,** *v.* (a) to allow to go out/to escape. (b) to lend for a period of time in return for money. (c) to make (a garment, etc.) wider. **let up,** *v.* to stop/to become less. **let-up,** *n.* stopping/slackening.

le•thal ['liːθəl] *adj.* deadly/causing death.

leth•ar•gy ['leθədʒɪ] *n.* (feeling of) unwillingness to do anything; lack of energy. **le•thar•gic** [ləˈθɑːdʒɪk] *adj.* feeling/appearing unwilling to do anything; lacking energy.

let's [lets] *short for* **let us.**

let•ter ['letə] 1. *n.* (a) written/printed symbol representing a sound of speech; **to the l.** = to the last detail. (b) piece of writing sent from one person/organization to another to pass on information. (c) **letters** = literary learning. 2. *v.* to mark with letters. **let•ter•head,** *n.* printed heading on writing paper. **let•ter•ing,** *n.* (a) writing letters. (b) letters in an inscription, etc. **let•ter•press,** *n.* method of printing using metal letters.

let•tuce ['letɪs] *n.* green vegetable whose leaves are often used in salads.

leu•ko•cyte ['ljuːkəʊsaɪt] *n.* white blood cell.

leu•ke•mi•a [luːˈkiːmɪə] *n.* serious, often fatal, illness, which increases the white cells in the blood.

lev•ee ['levɪ] *n.* embankment built along the bank of a river which is liable to flood.

lev•el ['levl] 1. *n.* (a) flat/horizontal position; **on the l.** = (i) in a flat position; (ii) *inf.* straight/honest. (b) position in relation to height and depth; position on a scale/in a list. (c) instrument for testing whether sth is horizontal or not. 2. *adj.* (a) flat/even/horizontal. (b) (**with**) at the same level as. (c) calm/even; *inf.* **to do one's l. best** = one's very best. 3. *v.* (**leveled, levelled**) (a) to make/to become level; **they leveled the house to the ground** = they destroyed it completely. (b) to point/to aim (an accusation) **at** s.o. **lev•el-head•ed,** *adj.* calm/able to act sensibly. **level with,** *v. inf.* to speak frankly.

lev•er ['liːvə] 1. *n.* instrument such as a bar which helps to raise a heavy object, or to move part of a machine, etc. 2. *v.* to move with a lever. **lev•er•age,** *n.* (a) force of a lever. (b) influence which you can use to reach your aims. **lev•er•aged buy•out,** *n.* buying a company, using the company's assets as security for the money borrowed to buy it.

lev•er•et ['levrət] *n.* young hare.

le•vi•a•than [lɪˈvaɪəθən] *n.* huge powerful monster or machine.

lev•i•tate ['levɪteɪt] *v.* (*of person/heavy body*) to rise into the air. **lev•i•ta•tion** [levɪˈteɪʃn] *n.* rising into the air.

lev•i•ty ['levɪtɪ] *n.* disrespectful way of considering serious things.

le•vy ['levɪ] 1. *n.* (a) demand for/collection of (a tax/a number of soldiers). (b) tax/number of soldiers (which has been collected). 2. *v.* to demand/to collect (a tax/a number of soldiers).

lewd [luːd] *adj.* (**-er, -est**) indecent/rude. **lewd•ly,** *adv.* in a lewd way. **lewd•ness,** *n.* lewd action.

lex•i•con ['leksɪkən] *n.* dictionary. **lex•i•cog•ra•phy** [leksɪˈkɒgrəfɪ] *n.* writing of dictionaries. **lex•i•cog•ra•pher,** *n.* person who writes dictionaries.

ley [leɪ] *n.* lea.

li•a•ble ['laɪəbl] *adj.* (a) (legally) responsible (**for** sth). (b) apt/likely (**to** do sth). **li•a•bil•i•ty** [laɪəˈbɪlɪtɪ] *n.* (a) debt; obligation; **he couldn't meet his liabilities** = he couldn't pay his debts. (b) disadvantage; handicap.

li•ai•son [lɪˈeɪzɒn] *n.* joining/relationship/connection; **l. officer** = person responsible for dealings with another group. **li•aise,** *v.* to join with others, esp. for discussion (**with s.o.**).

li•ar ['laɪə] *n.* person who tells lies.

lib [lɪb] *n. inf. short for* **liberation.**

li•ba•tion [laɪˈbeɪʃn] *n.* (*formal*) drink offered to a god.

li•bel ['laɪbl] 1. *n.* untrue statement(s) in writing, damaging to s.o.'s character. 2. *v.* (**libeled, libelled**) to damage s.o.'s character in writing. **li•bel•ous,** *adj.* (writing) which libels s.o.

lib•er•al ['lɪbrəl] 1. *adj.* (a) wide in views/meaning, etc. (b) ample/generous. (c) (*in politics*) having views/policies based on freedom of individuals, democratic reform, etc. 2. *n.* (*in politics*) person having liberal views; **Liberal** = member or supporter of a liberal party or policy. **lib•er•al•ism,** *n.* (*in politics*) liberal views/policies. **lib•er•al•i•ty** [lɪbəˈrælɪtɪ] *n.* (a) being open-minded. (b) generos-

---

æ **back,** ɑː **farm,** ɒ: **top,** aɪ **pipe,** aʊ **how,** aɪə **fire,** aʊə **flower,** ɔː **bought,** ɔɪ **toy,** e **fed,** eəhair, eɪ **take,** ə **afraid,** əʊ **boat,** aʊə **lower,** ʌː **word,** iː **heap,** ɪ **hit,** ɪə **hear,** uː **school,** ʊ **book,** ʌ **but,** b **back,** d **dog,** ð **then,** dʒ **just,** f **fog,** g **go,** h **hand,** j **yes,** k **catch,** l **last,** m **mix,** n **nut,** ŋ **sing,** p **penny,** r **round,** s **some,** ʃ **short,** t **too,** tʃ **chop,** θ **thing,** v **voice,** w **was,** z **zoo,** ʒ **treasure**

ity. **lib•er•al•i•za•tion** [lɪbərəlaɪ'zeɪʒn] *n.* act of liberalizing. **lib•er•al•ize** ['lɪbərəlaɪz] *v.* to make (laws, etc.) more liberal; to become more liberal. **lib•er•al•ly**, *adv.* in a liberal way.

lib•er•ate ['lɪbəreɪt] *v.* to set/to make (s.o./sth) free (**from** sth). **lib•er•a•tion** [lɪbə'reɪʃn] *n.* setting free. **lib•er•a•tor**, *n.* person who sets s.o. free. **lib•er•tar•i•an** [lɪbə'teərɪən] *n.* person who believes in freedom of thought and action. **lib•er•tine** ['lɪbəti:n] *n.* man who is sexually immoral. **lib•er•ty** ['lɪbətɪ] *n.* freedom; **at l.** = free/not in captivity; **to take liberties** = to do sth without permission; **to take liberties with sth/s.o.** = to treat sth./s.o. too familiarly.

li•bi•do [lɪ'bi:dəu] *n.* (*pl.* **-os**) sexual urge. **li•bid•i•nous**, *adj.* full of sexual urge.

Li•bra ['li:brə] *n.* one of the signs of the zodiac, shaped like a pair of scales.

li•brar•y ['laɪbrərɪ] *n.* (a) place where books are stored (to be read/borrowed/consulted). (b) collection of books. **li•brar•i•an** [laɪ'breərɪən] *n.* person who works in a library. **li•brar•i•an•ship**, *n.* art of being a librarian.

li•bret•to [lɪ'bretəu] *n.* (*pl.* **-os**) words of an opera. **li•bret•tist**, *n.* person who writes a libretto.

Lib•y•an ['lɪbjən] 1. *adj.* referring to Libya. 2. *n.* person from Libya.

lice [laɪs] *n. pl. see* **louse**.

li•cense ['laɪsəns] 1. *n.* (a) (document giving) official permission to have/to do sth. (b) freedom, esp. when used too much or wrongly. (c) **poetic l.** = use of language in poetry which would not be acceptable in prose. 2. *v.* to give (s.o.) official permission to do sth. **li•cen•see** [laɪsən'si:] *n.* holder of a license. **li•cen•ti•ate** [laɪ'senʃɪət] *n.* person who has been licensed to practice a profession. **li•cen•tious** [laɪ'senʃəs] *adj.* indulging in sex or other pleasures beyond what is normally permitted. **li•cen•tious•ness**, *n.* excessive indulgence in sex.

li•chen ['laɪkən] *n.* flat gray/yellow/green plant which grows on stones or on other plants.

lic•it ['lɪsɪt] *adj.* legal.

lick [lɪk] 1. *n.* (a) stroke with the tongue. (b) *inf.* speed. (c) *inf.* **a l. and a promise** = a quick job of doing something. 2. *v.* (a) to taste/to stroke with the tongue; **to l. s.o.'s boots** = to behave very humbly toward s.o. to gain favor; **to l. into shape** = to put into proper form, as through hard work or discipline. (b) to beat/to hit. (c) *inf.* to defeat (in a game). **lick•ing**, *n.* (a) stroking with the tongue. (b) beating. (c) *inf.* defeat.

lic•o•rice ['lɪkərɪs] *n.* black substance from the root of a plant, used in medicine and in candy and liquor.

lid [lɪd] *n.* (a) covering for a container, often with a handle. (b) eyelid/covering of the eye.

lie [laɪ] 1. *n.* (a) statement which is not true; **to give the l. to** = to prove (sth) is wrong. (b) position/direction in which sth is situated. 2. *v.* (a) (**lied, lying**) to say something which is not true. (b) (**lay, lying, has lain**) to be in a horizontal position; **he lay dead on the ground.** (c) to be. **lie down**, *v.* to put yourself in a horizontal position (**on** sth); **they won't take that lying down** = they won't accept it without protest. **lie low**, *v.* to hide.

lie•der ['li:də] *n.* German romantic song.

liege [li:dʒ] *n.* (*old*) lord (to whom people give service).

li•en ['lɪən] *n.* legal right to take and hold s.o.'s goods until a debt is paid.

lieu [lju:] *n.* **in l. of** = instead of.

lieu•ten•ant [lu:'tenənt] *n.* rank in the armed forces (*in the army below* captain, *in the navy below* lieutenant-commander); **l.-colonel** = rank in the army below colonel; **l.-commander** = rank in the navy below commander.

life [laɪf] *n.* (*pl.* **lives** [laɪvz]) (a) state of being alive; **run for your lives** = as fast as you can; **I can't for the l. of me understand** = I can't understand at all; **not on your l.** = not under any circumstances. (b) liveliness/energy. (c) living things; **is there l. on Mars?** (d) (length of) time you are alive; **in early l.** = when he was a child; **l. insurance** = insurance paid if you die; **l. imprisonment** = imprisonment for the rest of your life. (e) story of s.o.'s life. **life•belt**, *n.* cork-filled ring to keep s.o. afloat. **life•boat**, *n.* boat used to rescue people at sea. **life cy•cle**, *n.* life of an animal/plant through various stages. **life•guard**, *n.* person who rescues people who get into difficulties while swimming. **life jack•et**, *n.* buoyant jacket to keep s.o. afloat. **life•less**, *adj.* (a) not alive. (b) not lively. **life•like**, *adj.* (*of a picture, etc.*) looking like the real person/thing. **life•line**, *n.* rope thrown to a drowning person; help given to s.o. in difficulties. **life•long**, *adj.* lasting your whole life. **life pre•serv•er**, *n.* lifebelt/life jacket. **lif•er**, *n.* person who is serving a sentence of life imprisonment. **life-sav•ing**, *n.* rescuing people from drowning. **life-size(d)**, *adj.* (statue/painting, etc.) which is the same size as the real thing or person. **life•style**, *n.* way in which s.o. or a group of people live their daily lives; **life•style busi•ness**, *n.* small business primarily run to allow the owner to pursue personal interests rather than to maximize profits. **life•time,** *n.* time when you are alive; **the chance of a l.** = the best chance you are ever likely to get.

lift [lɪft] 1. *n.* (a) (act of) raising. (b) ride in a car. (c) *Brit.* elevator; **ski l.** = device to take skiers to the top of a ski slope. 2. *v.* (a) to raise (to a higher position). (b) to take plants or tubers out of the ground. (c) to take away/to remove (a ban). (d) *inf.* to steal. (e) (*of fog/clouds*) to rise. **lift-off,** *n.* vertical take-off of a space rocket.

lig•a•ment ['lɪɡəmənt] *n.* tough tissue which holds bones together.

li•ga•ture ['lɪɡətʃʊə] *n.* thread used for tying in surgical operations; link between two printed letters.

light [laɪt] 1. *n.* (a) brightness which allows you to see; **don't stand in my l.** = between me and the source of light. (b) bulb/object which gives light. (c) **in l. of what he said** = in consideration of it; **to throw l. on sth** = make it clearer; **to come to l.** = be discovered. (d) appearance/aspect. (e) means of making a cigarette, etc., catch fire. (f) *pl.* **lights** = (i) lungs of certain animals used as food; (ii) traffic lights. 2. *v.* (**lit**) (a) to make (sth) start to burn. (b) to give light to. 3. *adj.* (**-er, -est**) (a) having a lot of light, allowing you to see well. (b) pale (color). (c) not heavy; **she's a l. sleeper** = wakens easily. (d) not serious; **to make l. of** = to treat as unimportant. 4. *adv.* (to travel) with little luggage. **light•en,** *v.* (a) to make lighter/not so dark. (b) to make lighter/not so heavy. **light•er,** *n.* (a) small instrument for making cigarettes, etc., burn. (b) boat used for loading other boats. **light•er•man,** *n.* (*pl.* **-men**) man who works on a lighter. **light-fin•gered,** *adj.* (person) who is likely to steal. **light-head•ed,** *adj.* dizzy; feeling excited. **light-heart•ed,** *adj.* cheerful/without a care. **light heav•y•weight,** *n.* weight in boxing between middleweight and heavyweight. **light•house,** *n.* tall building containing a light to guide ships. **light•ly,** *adv.* in a light way; **l. dressed** = wearing thin clothes; **to get off l.** = with little or no punishment. **light•ness,** *n.* being light. **light pen,** *n.* pen with a tip which is sensitive to light, and which can "read" lines or images and transfer them to a computer. **light•ship,** *n.* ship which carries a large light, acting as a floating lighthouse. **light up,** *v.* (a) to give light to (sth). (b) to become bright. (c) to start to smoke a cigar, cigarette, or pipe. **light•weight.** 1. *n.* (a)

weight in boxing between featherweight and welterweight. (b) person without much influence. 2. *adj.* (a) light (clothes). (b) not very influential/important. **light year,** *n.* distance traveled by light during one year (about six trillion miles).

light•ning ['laɪtnɪŋ] 1. *n.* flash of electricity in the sky, followed by thunder; **like l.** = very fast; **l. rod** = rod for carrying a lightning charge straight to the ground to prevent damage to buildings. 2. *adj.* extremely fast.

lig•nite ['lɪɡnaɪt] *n.* brown coal.

like [laɪk] 1. *adj.* (nearly) the same/similar. 2. *prep.* in the same way as/the same as/similar to; **I feel l. some chocolate** = I would like to eat some chocolate. 3. *n.* similar thing(s). 4. *adv.* **l. as not** = probably. 5. *conj.* in the same way as. 6. *v.* (a) to have pleasant feelings about. (b) to desire/to want. **like•a•ble,** *adj.* pleasant. **like•li•hood,** *n.* probability. **like•ly.** 1. *adj.* (**-ier, -iest**) (a) probable. (b) suitable (for)/apt (to). 2. *adv.* probably; **not l.!** = certainly not. **like-mind•ed,** *adj.* (person) who has the same opinions. **lik•en** ['laɪkən] *v.* **to l. sth to sth** = to compare, by showing how one thing is similar to another. **like•ness,** *n.* thing which looks like s.o./sth. **likes,** *n. pl.* (a) **l. and dislikes** = things you like and don't like. (b) *inf.* **the l. of him** = people like him. **like•wise,** *adv.* (a) in the same way. (b) similarly/the same. **lik•ing,** *n.* pleasant feeling towards s.o./fondness for s.o./sth.

li•lac ['laɪlək] *n.* (a) tree with clusters of (pale) purple or white flowers. (b) pale purple color.

lil•li•pu•tian [lɪlɪ'pjuːʃn] *adj.* very small.

lilt [lɪlt] 1. *n.* song/way of speaking with a light well-marked rhythm. 2. *v.* to sing/to play a tune with a light well-marked rhythm. **lilt•ing,** *adj.* (song) which has a lilt.

lil•y ['lɪlɪ] *n.* type of white flower which grows from a bulb. **lil•y-of-the-val•ley,** *n.* spring plant with small white flowers growing in clusters.

li•ma bean ['liːməbiːn] *n.* bean with flat pale seeds.

limb [lɪm] *n.* (a) leg/arm/wing. (b) branch of a tree; **out on a l.** = in a difficult/exposed situation.

lim•ber ['lɪmbə] *v.* **to l. up** = to do exercises to warm your muscles before taking part in a sporting contest.

lim•bo ['lɪmbəʊ] *n.* (a) place between heaven and hell, where unbaptized people are said to

---

æ back, aː farm, ɒ top, aɪ pipe, aʊ how, aɪə fire, aʊə flower, ɔː bought, ɔɪ toy, e fed, eəhair, eɪ take, ə afraid, əʊ boat, əʊə lower, vː word, iː heap, ɪ hit, ɪə hear, uː school, ʊ book, ʌ but, b back, d dog, ð then, dʒ just, f fog, g go, h hand, j yes, k catch, l last, m mix, n nut, ŋ sing, p penny, r round, s some, ʃ short, t too, tʃ chop, θ thing, v voice, w was, z zoo, ʒ treasure

go when they die. (b) position of not being accepted or rejected; being halfway between two stages. (c) **l. dancing** = West Indian dance where the dancer bends his body backwards parallel to the floor to pass under a horizontal bar.

lime [laɪm] *n.* (a) white substance containing calcium, used in making cement. (b) small yellowish-green tropical fruit like a lemon; tree which bears such fruit. (c) northern deciduous tree with smooth leaves and yellowish flowers. **lime green,** *adj. & n.* green color of lime. **lime•light,** *n.* attention/publicity. **lime•stone,** *n.* light-colored stone containing calcium.

lim•er•ick ['lɪmərɪk] *n.* type of amusing five-line poem.

lim•it ['lɪmɪt] 1. *n.* furthest point/extent; boundary; end (beyond which you cannot go); *inf.* **that's the l.** = too much. 2. *v.* to put a limit on/to keep within limits; not to allow (sth) to go beyond a certain point. **lim•i•ta•tion** [lɪmɪ'teɪʃn] *n.* (a) act of limiting. (b) thing which stops you going further; **to know your limitations** = to know what you are capable of doing.

limn *v.* (a) to draw or describe sth. (b) to highlight sth, esp. with bright colors.

lim•ou•sine [lɪmə'ziːn] *n.* large luxurious car, with a partition between the driver and the passenger.

limp [lɪmp] 1. *n.* way of walking unevenly. 2. *v.* to walk with an uneven step. 3. *adj.* without stiffness/soft; without energy. **limp•ly,** *adv.* in a limp way. **limp•ness,** *n.* being limp.

lim•pet ['lɪmpɪt] *n.* cone-shaped shellfish which clings to rocks.

lim•pid ['lɪmpɪd] *adj.* clear. **lim•pid•i•ty** [lɪm'pɪdɪtɪ] *n.* (*formal*) being clear.

linch•pin ['lɪnʃpɪn] *n.* (a) pin which goes through an axle to hold a wheel on. (b) very important person/piece of machinery.

lin•dane ['lɪndeɪn] *n.* powerful insecticide.

lin•den ['lɪndən] *n.* (*formal*) lime tree.

line [laɪn] 1. *n.* (a) (long) thin mark; **to draw the l. at** = to stop short of/not to do. (b) long wire/cord. (c) **telephone l.** = cable along which telephone messages are sent; **the l.'s bad** = it is difficult to make out what s.o. is saying; **crossed l.** = two telephone conversations which intermingle by error. (d) row of people/cars/words, etc.; *inf.* **to drop s.o. a l.** = to send a short letter; **l. printer** = computer printer which prints each line separately. (e) number of people or things waiting one behind the other for sth. (f) tracks on which trains run. (g) shipping/air company. (h) sequence of ancestors/descendants. (i) **lines** = shape/outline; general design. (j) direction;

method; course of action; **in l. with** = according to/following (a decision); **to take a hard l.** = to be aggressive/not to weaken in any way. (k) type of work/goods. 2. *v.* (a) to put lines on. (b) to form a line along the edge of a street, etc. (c) to put a layer of material inside (a piece of clothing); **to l. one's pockets** = to make money (usu. dishonestly). **lin•e•age** ['lɪnɪdʒ] *n.* line of descendants (from an ancestor). **lin•e•al** ['lɪnɪəl] *adj.* (descendant) in direct line. **lin•e•a•ments,** *n. pl.* outline of the face/features. **lin•e•ar** ['lɪnɪə] *adj.* referring to lines/to length. **line•man,** *n.* (*pl.* -men) man who installs or repairs electric/telephone/railroad lines. **lin•er,** *n.* (a) thing used for lining. (b) large passenger ship. **line up,** *v.* to form a line. **line-up,** *n.* row/list of people. **lin•ing,** *n.* layer of material inside sth.

lin•en ['lɪnɪn] *n.* (a) cloth made from flax. (b) **(household) l.** = sheets/pillowcases/tablecloths, etc.; **to wash your dirty l. in public** = tell shameful personal secrets.

ling [lɪŋ] *n.* (a) type of small edible fish. (b) heather.

lin•ger ['lɪŋgə] *v.* (a) to wait/to remain/to stay longer than necessary/expected. (b) (*of sick person*) to remain alive.

lin•ge•rie ['lænʒərɪ] *n.* women's underwear.

lin•go ['lɪŋgəʊ] *n. Sl.* language.

lin•gua fran•ca [lɪŋgwə'fræŋkə] *n.* language used by speakers of various languages as a common means of communication.

lin•gual ['lɪŋgwəl] *adj.* referring to the tongue.

lin•guist ['lɪŋgwɪst] *n.* (a) person who knows foreign languages well. (b) person who studies linguistics. **lin•guis•tic** [lɪŋ'gwɪstɪk] *adj.* (a) referring to language(s). (b) referring to the science of language. **lin•guis•tics,** *n.* science of language.

lin•i•ment ['lɪnɪmənt] *n.* oily substance which you rub on the skin to lessen pains.

link [lɪŋk] 1. *n.* (a) ring which forms part of a chain. (b) thing which connects two parts. 2. *v.* to join. **link•age,** *n.* act of linking.

links [lɪŋks] *n. pl.* golf course.

lin•net ['lɪnɪt] *n.* small singing bird.

li•no•cut ['laɪnəʊkʌt] *n.* design printed from a block of linoleum which has been cut into a pattern. **li•no•le•um** [lɪ'nəʊlɪəm] *n.* hard smooth floor covering.

lin•seed ['lɪnsiːd] *n.* seed of flax.

lint [lɪnt] *n.* soft cloth used for putting on wounds.

lin•tel ['lɪntl] *n.* piece of wood/stone over a door or window.

li•on ['laɪən] *n.* large wild animal of the cat family, the male of which has a long mane; **the l.'s share** = the biggest part. **li•on•ess,** *n.* female lion. **li•on•ize,** *v.* to treat (s.o.) as very important.

lip [lɪp] *n.* (a) one of two fleshy parts round the outside of the mouth; **to keep a stiff upper l.** = not to show emotion in time of trouble; **to smack one's lips over** = to express great enjoyment of. (b) *Sl.* impudence/rudeness. (c) edge of a bowl/cup, etc. **lipped,** *adj.* with lips. **lip•read,** *v.* **(lipread** ['lɪpred]) *(of a deaf person)* to follow speech by watching the movements of the lips of the person speaking. **lip serv•ice,** *n.* **to pay l. s. to sth** = to give a false impression of respecting/obeying sth. **lip•stick,** *n.* (stick of) substance for coloring the lips.

lip•id ['lɪpɪd] *n.* fatty substance in the tissue in human bodies.

liq•ue•fy ['lɪkwɪfaɪ] *v.* to become liquid; to make (sth) become liquid. **liq•ue•fac•tion** [lɪkwɪ'fækʃn] *n.* making/becoming liquid.

li•queur [lɪ'kɜː] *n.* strong alcoholic drink.

liq•uid ['lɪkwɪd] 1. *n.* substance which flows easily like water, and which is neither a gas nor a solid. 2. *adj.* (a) which is neither gas nor solid, and which flows easily; **l. crystal display** = display panel, where the figures appear black. (b) *(of assets, etc.)* able to be changed easily into cash. (c) *(of sounds)* pure/clear. **liq•ui•date,** *v.* (a) *(of a company)* to settle accounts by selling assets to pay off debts. (b) to pay (a debt). (c) *inf.* to kill. **liq•ui•da•tion** [lɪkwɪ'deɪʃn] *n.* the settling of accounts by selling assets to pay off debts. **liq•ui•da•tor,** *n.* person authorized to liquidate assets. **liq•uid•i•ty** [lɪ'kwɪdɪtɪ] *n.* *(in finance)* being able to change assets into cash. **liq•uid•ize,** *v.* to reduce fruit to liquid. **liq•uid•iz•er,** *n.* machine which liquidizes.

liq•uor ['lɪkə] *n.* (a) alcoholic drink. (b) liquid produced in cooking.

liq•uo•rice ['lɪkərɪs] *n.* see **lic•o•rice.**

li•ra ['lɪrə] *n.* unit of money used in Italy.

lisle [laɪl] *n.* fine cotton (used to make shirts, stockings, etc.).

lisp [lɪsp] 1. *n.* speech defect in which "s" is pronounced as "th". 2. *v.* to speak with a lisp.

lis•som ['lɪsəm] *adj.* lithe/supple.

list [lɪst] 1. *n.* (a) number of items written/spoken one after another; **wine l.** = list of wines available in a restaurant; **to be on the danger l.** = to be dangerously ill; **l. price** = price of sth as shown in a catalog. (b) *(of ship)* leaning to one side. (c) **to enter the lists** = to become involved

in sth, as a candidate in an election. 2. *v.* (a) to say/to write (a number of items) one after the other. (b) *(of ship)* to lean over to one side.

lis•ten ['lɪsn] *v.* to pay attention (**to** s.o./sth) in order to hear. **lis•ten•er,** *n.* person who listens.

lis•te•ri•a [lɪs'tiːərɪə] *n.* bacteria found in some foods and in domestic animals, which can cause infections such as meningitis.

list•less ['lɪstləs] *adj.* (feeling) dull, without interest or energy. **list•less•ly,** *adv.* in a way which shows lack of interest. **list•less•ness,** *n.* lack of interest/energy.

lit [lɪt] *v.* see **light.**

lit•a•ny ['lɪtənɪ] *n.* form of prayer with repeated responses, used in churches.

li•tchi ['laɪtʃɪ] *n.* small Chinese fruit, with a red skin and large stone.

li•ter, *Brit.* **li•tre** ['liːtə] *n.* measurement for liquids (almost 2 pints).

lit•er•a•cy ['lɪtərəsɪ] *n.* ability to read and write. **lit•er•al** 1. *adj.* keeping to the exact meaning of the original words. 2. *n.* typesetting mistake. **lit•er•al•ly,** *adv.* in a literal way; *(to emphasize)* his eyes were l. **popping out of his head. lit•er•al•ness,** *n.* being literal. **lit•er•ar•y,** *adj.* referring to literature. **lit•er•ate** ['lɪtərət] *adj.* (a) able to read and write. (b) well educated, esp. in literary subjects. **lit•er•a•ti** [lɪtə'rɑːtiː] *n. pl.* literary people. **lit•er•a•ture** ['lɪtrɪtʃə] *n.* (a) books/writing, esp. novels, poetry, drama, biography, etc. (b) what has been written on a particular subject. (c) written information about sth.

lithe [laɪð] *adj.* supple/bending easily.

lith•o•graph ['lɪθəɡrɑːf] 1. *n.* painting/drawing, etc., reproduced by lithography. 2. *v.* to print by lithography. **lith•o•graph•ic** [lɪθə'ɡræfɪk] *adj.* of lithography. **lith•og•ra•phy** [lɪ'θɒɡrəfɪ] *n.* method of printing using oil and ink on a flat surface such as a stone/a sheet of metal, etc.

lit•i•gate ['lɪtɪɡeɪt] *v.* to go to law; to bring a lawsuit against s.o. **lit•i•gant,** *n.* person involved in a lawsuit. **lit•i•ga•tion** [lɪtɪ'ɡeɪʃn] *n.* (a) bringing a lawsuit against s.o. (b) lawsuit. **li•ti•gious** [lɪ'tɪdʒəs] *adj.* always ready to go to law.

lit•mus ['lɪtməs] *n.* blue substance which is turned red by an acid and back to blue by an alkali. **lit•mus pa•per,** *n.* paper containing litmus, used to test for acids and alkalis.

æ back, ɑː farm, ɒ top, aɪ pipe, aʊ how, aɪə fire, aʊə flower, ɔː bought, ɔɪ toy, e fed, eəhair, eɪ take, ə afraid, əʊ boat, əʊə lower, ɜː word, iː heap, ɪ hit, ɪə hear, uː school, ʊ book, ʌ but, b back, d dog, ð then, dʒ just, f fog, g go, h hand, j yes, k catch, l last, m mix, n nut, ŋ sing, p penny, r round, s some, ʃ short, t too, tʃ chop, θ thing, v voice, w was, z zoo, ʒ treasure

li•tre ['li:tə] *n. see* **li•ter.**

lit•ter ['lɪtə] 1. *n.* (a) paper, etc. left on streets. (b) stretcher/bed on which a person is carried. (c) bedding of straw, etc., for animals. (d) (*of animals*) group of young born at one time. 2. *v.* (a) to drop paper, etc. about. (b) (*of animals*) to produce young.

lit•tle ['lɪtl] 1. *adj.* (**less, least**) (a) small; **his l. sister** = his younger sister. (b) **a l.** = small amount of. (c) not much. 2. *n.* small amount; **l. by l.** = gradually. 3. *adv.* (a) (by) a small amount; **I see him very l.** = not very often. (b) **he l. thought he would win** = he had no idea that he would win.

lit•to•ral ['lɪtərəl] *adj. & n.* (referring to the) coast.

lit•ur•gy ['lɪtədʒɪ] *n.* form of public service in church. **li•tur•gi•cal** [lɪ'tɜːdʒɪkl] *adj.* referring to liturgy.

live. 1. *adj.* [laɪv] (a) in a living state. (b) burning. (c) (*of broadcast*) not recorded. (d) carrying an electric current; (ammunition) which has not been exploded; *inf.* **l. wire** = very lively and energetic person. 2. *v.* [lɪv] (a) to be alive/to have life; **l. and let l.** = be tolerant. (b) to have your (place of) residence. (c) to lead a certain type of life; **he lives in style;** *inf.* **to l. it up** = to lead a life of wild parties, etc. (d) **to l. on** = to get food/money, etc., from. **live down,** *v.* to cause (a disgrace) to be forgotten; **he'll never l. it down** = it will never be forgotten. **live in,** *v.* to live in the building where you work. **live•li•hood** ['laɪvlɪhʊd] *n.* (way of getting) your means of living. **live•li•ness** ['laɪvlɪnəs] *n.* being lively. **live•long** ['lɪvlɒŋ] *adj.* (*formal*) **the l. day** = all the day. **live•ly** ['laɪvlɪ] *adj.* (**-ier, -iest**) bright/wide-awake/(very) active. **liv•en,** *v.* to make lively. **live•stock** ['laɪvstɒk] *n.* animals kept on a farm. **liv•ing** ['lɪvɪŋ] 1. *adj.* alive. 2. *n.* (a) (way of) life. (b) means of subsistence. (c) **the l.** = people who are alive. **liv•ing room,** *n.* room in a house for general use.

liv•er ['lɪvə] *n.* organ in the lower part of the body which helps the digestion by producing bile; animal's liver used as food. **liv•er•ish,** *adj.* feeling rather sick and unwell; irritable.

liv•er•y ['lɪvrɪ] *n.* (a) special clothing of a group of servants/of an organization. (b) care of horses for payment; **l. stable** = place where horses may be looked after and may also be hired. **liv•er•ied,** *adj.* wearing a livery.

liv•id ['lɪvɪd] *adj.* (a) of the dark gray color of lead. (b) extremely angry.

liz•ard ['lɪzəd] *n.* type of reptile with four legs and scales.

lla•ma ['lɑːmə] *n.* thick-haired camellike animal found in South America.

lo [ləʊ] *inter.* (*old*) look!

load [ləʊd] 1. *n.* (a) heavy object(s) which have to be carried. (b) (*on vehicle*) what has to be/what is being transported. (c) amount of material transported. (d) amount of power carried by an electric circuit. (e) thing which is difficult to bear; **that's a l. off my mind** = I feel much less worried. (f) *inf.* **loads of** = plenty/lots. 2. *v.* (a) to put (esp. sth heavy) **into/on to.** (b) to put ammunition into (a gun)/to put film into (a camera); to put a disk program into a computer. (c) **to l. s.o. with** = to give large quantities to. **load•ed,** *adj.* (a) *inf.* having a lot of money. (b) **l. question** = question which is worded in such a way so as to trap the person who answers. (c) (dice) which has a secret weight in it. **load•er,** *n.* person who loads.

loaf [ləʊf] 1. *n.* (*pl.* **loaves** [ləʊvz]) (large) piece of bread baked separately. 2. *v.* to wander about/to waste time doing nothing. **loaf•er,** *n.* (a) person who does nothing all day. (b) light casual shoe with no laces.

loam [ləʊm] *n.* fertile soil which crumbles easily. **loam•y,** *adj.* crumbly fertile (soil).

loan [ləʊn] 1. *n.* (a) lending. (b) thing lent (esp. a sum of money from a bank). 2. *v.* to lend.

loath [ləʊθ] *adj.* very unwilling.

loathe [ləʊð] *v.* to hate very much. **loath•ing,** *n.* feeling of hate/disgust (**for**). **loath•some,** *adj.* disgusting/horrible.

lob [lɒb] 1. *n.* ball which is hit high into the air. 2. *v.* (**lobbed**) to throw/hit (a ball) slowly in a high curve.

lob•by ['lɒbɪ] 1. *n.* entrance hall/corridor. 2. *v.* to try to influence (s.o.) (esp. in order to get a bill through a legislature).

lobe [ləʊb] *n.* (a) lower curved part of the ear. (b) division of the lungs/brain/liver, etc. **lo•bar,** *adj.* referring to a lobe. **lo•bot•o•my** [lə'bɒtəmɪ] *n.* operation to remove a lobe.

lo•bel•ia [lɒ'biːlɪə] *n.* low plant with blue flowers.

lob•ster ['lɒbstə] *n.* shellfish with a long body, two large claws, and eight legs, used as food. **lob•ster pot,** *n.* cage left in the sea to catch lobsters.

lo•cal ['ləʊkl] 1. *adj.* referring to a place/district; near at hand; **l. anesthetic** = which numbs a particular area of the body. 2. *n.* person who lives in a district, esp. the district where you live. **lo•cale** [ləʊ'kɑːl] *n.* place where sth takes place. **lo•cal•i•ty** [ləʊ'kælɪtɪ] *n.* area/district. **lo•cal•ize** ['ləʊkəklaɪz] *v.* to set in a particular place; to be confined to a particular area. **lo•cal•ly,** *adv.* in the (same) district. **lo•cate** [ləʊ'keɪt] *v.* (a) to find (the position of). (b) **to be located** = to be in a particular position. **lo•ca•tion** [ləʊ'keɪʃn] *n.* (a) finding the position of sth. (b) place/position. (c) **on l.** = (filming) which takes place in a real setting, not in a studio.

loch [lɒk] *n.* (*in Scotland*) lake; arm of the sea.

lock [lɒk] 1. *n.* (a) device for closing a door/container, etc., by means of a key; **under l. and key** = shut up securely. (b) part in a gun by which it is fired; **l., stock, and barrel** = (everything) all together. (c) section of a canal/river with barriers which can be opened or closed to control the flow of water, thus allowing boats to move up or down to different levels. (d) bundle of hair hanging together. 2. *v.* (a) to close (a door/a box, etc.) with a key. (b) to fix/to become fixed in a certain position. **lock•a•ble**, *adj.* which can be locked. **lock•er**, *n.* small compartment for personal belongings which you can close with a key; **l. room** = room in a sports stadium where players change and leave their clothes in lockers. **lock•jaw**, *n.* disease where your jaws become closed tight together. **lock•nut**, *n.* second nut, used to keep the first nut in place. **lock out**, *v.* to prevent (s.o.) from going in by locking the door. **lock•out**, *n.* industrial dispute in which employees are kept out of the factory until they agree to certain terms. **lock•smith**, *n.* person who makes/repairs locks. **lock up**, *v.* (a) to close (a building) by locking doors. (b) to keep (a person/thing) inside by locking doors, etc. **lock•up**, *n.* prison cell.

lock•et ['lɒkɪt] *n.* small ornamental case to hold a picture/lock of hair, etc., worn round the neck.

lo•co•mo•tive [ləʊkə'məʊtɪv] 1. *adj.* referring to movement. 2. *n.* engine of a train. **lo•co•mo•tion**, *n.* (power of) movement.

lo•cus ['ləʊkəs] *n.* (*pl.* **loci** ['ləʊsaɪ]) point, line, curve, etc., in a technical diagram.

lo•cust ['ləʊkəst] *n.* insect, like a large grasshopper, which destroys crops.

lode [ləʊd] *n.* vein of metal ore. **lode•star**, *n.* pole star. **lode•stone**, *n.* magnetic iron ore.

lodge [lɒdʒ] 1. *n.* (a) small house, cabin, etc. used temporarily, as during vacations or hunting season. (b) small house or cottage on an estate or in a park, where a caretaker, gardener, etc. lives. (c) (meeting place for a) group of freemasons, etc. (d) home of beavers. 2. *v.* (a) to rent a room (in a boarding house). (b) to be/to remain. (c) (*formal*) to make/to place (a complaint). **lodg•er**, *n.* person who

rents a room. **lodg•ing**, *n.* (a) accommodation. (b) **lodgings** = rented rooms.

lo•ess ['ləʊəs] *n.* yellow powdery earth found in China, North America, etc.

loft [lɒft] *n.* (a) top part of a house immediately under the roof; attic. (b) upper level in a church, etc. used for a special purpose. (c) **hay l.** = top part of a barn used for storing hay.

loft•y ['lɒftɪ] *adj.* (**-ier, -iest**) (a) very high. (b) arrogant/proud. **loft•i•ly**, *adv.* in a proud way.

log [lɒg] 1. *n.* (a) thick piece of a tree trunk/large branch; **to sleep like a l.** = very soundly; **as easy as falling off a l.** = very easy. (b) device for calculating the speed of a ship. (c) daily detailed record of speed/position/happenings, esp. on a ship. (d) *short for* **log•a•rithm.** 2. *v.* (**logged**) (a) to write down details of (sth which has happened) in a logbook. (b) to cover a (distance)/to spend (time). **log•book**, *n.* (*on ship, etc.*) book with record of a journey. **log•ging**, *n.* cutting trees for timber.

lo•gan•ber•ry ['ləʊgənberɪ] *n.* soft fruit, a cross between a blackberry and a raspberry.

log•a•rithm ['lɒgərɪðm] *n.* one of a set of numbers listed in such a way as to help with calculations by adding and subtracting instead of multiplying and dividing. **log•a•rith•mic** [lɒgə'rɪθmɪk] *adj.* referring to logarithms.

log•ger•heads ['lɒgəhedz] *n.* **to be at l.** = to quarrel or disagree with s.o.

log•gia ['lɒdʒɪə] *n.* covered gallery which is open on one side.

log•ic ['lɒdʒɪk] *n.* science of reasoning; power of reasoning clearly. **log•i•cal**, *adj.* (a) clearly reasoned. (b) (*of person*) able to reason clearly. **log•i•cal•ly**, *adv.* in a logical/reasonable way.

lo•gis•tics [lɒ'dʒɪstɪks] *n.* organization of the movement of supplies/people, etc.

lo•go ['lɒgəʊ] *n.* (*pl.* **-os**) symbol/design used by a company to identify its products.

loin [lɔɪn] *n.* (a) (meat from the) back of an animal. (b) **loins** = part of the body between the hips. **loin•cloth**, *n.* long cloth wrapped round the hips.

loi•ter ['lɔɪtə] *v.* to wander about slowly/aimlessly; to stand about. **loi•ter•er**, *n.* person who wanders/who is standing about.

loll [lɒl] *v.* (a) to sit/stand/lie in a lazy way. (b) (*of tongue*) to hang out.

æ **back,** a: **farm,** ɒ: **top,** aɪ **pipe,** aʊ **how,** aɪə **fire,** aʊə **flower,** ɔ: **bought,** ɔɪ **toy,** e **fed,** eəhair, eɪ **take,** ə **afraid,** əʊ **boat,** əʊə **lower,** v: **word,** i: **heap,** ɪ **hit,** ɪə **hear,** u: **school,** ʊ **book,** ʌ **but,** b **back,** d **dog,** ð **then,** dʒ **just,** f **fog,** g **go,** h **hand,** j **yes,** k **catch,** l **last,** m **mix,** n **nut,** ŋ **sing,** p **penny,** r **round,** s **some,** ʃ **short,** t **too,** tʃ **chop,** θ **thing,** v **voice,** w **was,** z **zoo,** ʒ **treasure**

lol•li•pop ['lɒlɪpɒp] *n.* candy on the end of a stick.

lol•lop ['lɒləp] *v. inf.* to walk with long clumsy steps.

lone [ləʊn] *adj.* alone; lonely; **l. wolf** = person who likes to be alone. **lone•ly,** *adj.* (a) with few or no people. (b) feeling sad because of being alone. **lone•li•ness,** *n.* being alone; feeling sad because you are alone. **lon•er,** *n.* person who prefers to be alone. **lone•some,** *adj.* lonely/sad because of being alone.

long [lɒŋ] 1. *adj.* (-er, -est) (a) measured in space from end to end; not short. (b) measured in time; **they stayed for a l. time. 2.** *adv.* for a long time; **all night l.** = for the whole night. (b) **as l. as** = while/since. (c) **so/as l. as** = provided that. 3. *n.* long time; **before l.** = in a short time; **for l.** = for a long time. 4. *v.* **to l. for** = to want very much. **long-dis•tance,** *adj.* (a) (*in sport*) (race) run between two places which are far apart. (b) (telephone call) made over a long distance. **long•hand,** *n.* ordinary writing (not shorthand). **long•horn,** *n.* type of cow with long horns. **long•ing,** *n.* great desire (**for** sth). **long johns,** *n. pl. inf.* long underpants. **long-lived,** *adj.* (person) who lives for a long time. **long-play•ing,** *adj.* (record) which plays for about 20 minutes each side. **long-range,** *adj.* which covers a long distance. **long•shore•man,** *n.* (*pl.* -men) person who works at a port, loading or unloading ships. **long shot,** *n.* attempt which has little chance of being successful. **long-sight•ed,** *adj.* able to see things at a distance more clearly than things which are close. **long•stand•ing,** *adj.* which has been arranged some time before. **long-suf•fer•ing,** *adj.* patient/tolerating much. **long-term,** *adj.* lasting/planned to last for a long time. **long-wind•ed,** *adj.* (person) who talks too much in a boring way; (talk) which lasts too long.

lon•gev•i•ty [lɒn'dʒevɪtɪ] *n.* very long life.

lon•gi•tude ['lɒndʒɪtjuːd] *n.* position on the earth's surface measured in degrees east or west of an imaginary line running through Greenwich, England. **lon•gi•tu•di•nal,** *adj.* which runs lengthwise. **lon•gi•tu•di•nal•ly,** *adv.* from end to end.

loo•fah ['luːfə] *n.* type of sponge, made from a dried pod.

look [lʊk] 1. *n.* (a) turning your eyes (often quickly) to see sth. (b) search (**for** sth). (c) appearance; the way sth/s.o. appears. (d) **good looks** = beauty/pleasing personal appearance. 2. *v.* (a) (**at**) to make efforts to see. (b) to stare at; **he looked me straight in the face.** (c) to seem/to have the appearance of; **he looks ill;**

she looks the part = looks right for the job. **look af•ter,** *v.* to take care of. **look a•head,** *v.* to make plans for the future. **look•a•like,** *n. inf.* person who looks like s.o. else. **look at,** *v.* to make efforts to see/to examine/to consider. **look back,** *v.* (a) to turn around to see what is behind you. (b) to recall the past. **look back on,** *v.* to think about (sth) in the past. **look down,** *v.* **to look down on s.o./to look down your nose at s.o./sth** = to think you are better than s.o./to regard with disdain. **look•er-on,** *n.* (*pl.* lookers-on) person who is watching (without taking part). **look for,** *v.* to try to find. **look for•ward,** *v.* (**to**) to think about (sth) in the future (usu. with pleasure). **look in (on),** *v. inf.* to visit (s.o.) briefly. **look•ing glass,** *n.* mirror. **look in•to,** *v.* to examine/to find out about. **look on,** *v.* (a) to watch without taking part. (b) to consider/to think of sth as. **look out,** *v.* (a) (**on**) to have a view toward. (b) (**for**) to keep looking in order to find. (c) (**for**) to be careful of. **look•out,** *n.* (a) place from which you can see what is happening. (b) careful attention. (c) affair; **that's his l.** = he must deal with it himself. (d) person who watches. **look o•ver,** *v.* to examine. **look a•round,** *v.* (a) to turn to see behind you. (b) to examine all of a place. **look through,** *v.* (a) to examine the whole of (sth) (often quickly). (b) to pretend not to see. **look to,** *v.* (a) to expect (help) from. (b) (*formal*) to take care of. **look up,** *v.* (a) to turn your eyes in an upward direction. (b) to get better. (c) to try to find (sth) in a reference book, etc. (d) to get in contact with. **look up to,** *v.* to consider with respect/admiration.

loom [luːm] 1. *n.* machine on which cloth is woven. 2. *v.* to appear/to come into sight (gradually).

loon [luː] *n.* grebe.

loon•y ['luːnɪ] *adj. & n. inf.* mad (person). **loon•y bin,** *n. inf.* lunatic asylum.

loop [luːp] 1. *n.* (a) curve formed by a piece of thread/ribbon, etc. which crosses over itself. (b) thing of this shape. 2. *v.* to make a loop/loops; (*of aircraft*) **to l. the loop** = to fly in a complete circle vertically, turning upside down at the top. **loop•hole,** *n.* (a) narrow hole in a wall for shooting through. (b) means of escape/of avoiding (a law).

loose [luːs] 1. *adj.* (-er, -est) (a) not (fully) attached/not fixed; **to be at l. ends** = to have nothing special to do. (b) not tight. (c) with pieces separated. (d) **l. change** = money in coins only. (e) (translation) which is not very exact. (f) of doubtful morals. 2. *v.* to make (sth) become untied/to let (sth) go. 3. *adv.* not tightly. **loose•ly,** *adv.* (a) not tightly. (b) in an inexact way. **loose•leaf**, *adj.* (book) of which the pages can be removed and replaced. **loos•en**, *v.* to make (sth) less tight. **loose•ness**, *n.* being loose.

loot [luːt] 1. *n.* (a) things which have been taken. (b) *Sl.* money. 2. *v.* to steal. **loot•er**, *n.* person who steals (esp. from stores during a riot).

lop [lɒp] *v.* (**lopped**) to cut off (esp. tree branches).

lope [ləʊp] 1. *n.* running with long strides. 2. *v.* to run with long (slow) strides.

lop-eared ['lɒpɪəd] *adj.* (rabbit) with drooping ears.

lop•sid•ed [lɒp'saɪdɪd] *adj.* with one side larger/lower/heavier than the other.

lo•qua•cious [lɒ'kweɪʃəs] *adj.* (person) who talks a lot/too much. **lo•quac•i•ty** [lɒ-'kwæsɪtɪ], **loquaciousness**, *n.* talking too much.

lord [lɔːd] 1. *n.* (a) nobleman/ruler. (b) *Brit.* title for certain peers; **House of Lords** = upper chamber of the British Parliament. (c) **the Lord** = Jesus Christ. (d) *Brit.* title for men in certain positions (such as bishops/judges, etc.). (e) expression of surprise/shock; **Good Lord!** 2. *v.* **to l. it over s.o.** = to behave as if you are superior. **lord•li•ness**, *n.* (a) nobility. (b) pride. **lord•ly**, *adj.* (a) referring to the nobility. (b) proud/arrogant. **lord•ship**, *n. Brit.* (*form of address to a lord*) **Your Lordship.**

lore [lɔː] *n.* (*no pl.*) traditional beliefs and knowledge.

lor•gnette [lɔː'njet] *n.* glasses which you hold in front of your eyes with a handle.

lose [luːz] *v.* (**lost** [lɒst]) (a) to stop having/owning (sth); **she lost her gloves** = did not know where they were; **they lost sight of it** = could no longer see it; **that joke was lost on him** = he did not understand it. (b) to fail to win. (c) to cause the loss of. (d) **to get lost/to l. your way** = to be/become unable to find the way to where you were going; *Sl.* **get lost!** = go away! (e) **to l. weight** = to become lighter. (f) (*of clock/watch*) to become/to go slow. **los•er**, *n.* person who does not win; **he's a bad l.** = behaves badly when he loses a game. **lost** [lɒst] *adj.* which has been lost; **to give sth up for l.** = have no hope of ever having it again; **he looks l.** = looks bewildered.

loss [lɒs] *n.* (*pl.* -es) (a) no longer having sth. (b) thing/amount which you no longer have; **they sold it at a l.** = for less than they paid for it. (c) **to be at a l. what to do** = not to know what to

do. **loss lead•er**, *n.* article which is sold at a loss to attract customers.

lost [lɒst] *v. see* **lose.**

lot [lɒt] *n.* (a) *inf.* **a lot (of)/lots (of)** = a large amount/number (of); **I've seen quite a l. of him lately** = seen him many times. (b) **the l.** = everything. (c) set of things (for selling); thing/group of things together offered at an auction sale. (d) piece of land; **parking l.** = place where cars can be parked. (e) fate/fortune. (f) **to draw lots** = to decide sth by taking pieces of paper from a box/throwing dice, etc.

loth [ləʊθ] *adj.* loath.

lo•tion ['ləʊʃn] *n.* liquid used to soothe/to soften/to heal the skin.

lot•ter•y ['lɒtrɪ] *n.* game of chance in which tickets are sold with prizes given for certain numbers.

lo•tus ['ləʊtəs] *n.* tropical water plant, with large flowers.

loud [laʊd] 1. *adj.* (-er, -est) (a) having a sound which is (too) easily heard. (b) (*of colors, etc.*) too striking/showy. 2. *adv.* in a way which is easily heard. **loud•ly**, *adv.* in a way which is easily heard. **loud-mouthed**, *adj.* talking indiscreetly or in a way which is too easily heard. **loud•ness**, *n.* being (too) easily heard. **loud•speak•er**, *n.* part of a radio, etc., which allows sound to be heard.

lounge [laʊndʒ] 1. *n.* (a) room for sitting in. (b) bar in a hotel; **departure l.** = room at an airport where passengers wait to board their planes. (c) sitting around doing nothing or very little. 2. *v.* to sit/to lie doing nothing or very little. **loung•er**, *n.* person who lounges.

louse [laʊs] *n.* (*pl.* lice [laɪs]) small insect which lives on human and animal bodies. **lous•y** ['laʊzɪ] *adj.* (a) covered with lice. (b) *inf.* horrible/unfair.

lout [laʊt] *n.* loutish person. **lout•ish**, *adj.* awkward/rude/ill-mannered.

lou•ver, *Brit.* **lou•vre** ['luːvə] *n.* sloping wooden strips in a frame which overlap and only allow some light to enter. **lou•vered**, *adj.* with louvers.

love [lʌv] 1. *n.* (a) great liking/respect for s.o./sth; **to do sth for the l. of it** = without looking for profit; **it can't be had for l. nor money** = not at all/by any means; **there's no l. lost between them** = they hate each other. (b) great liking/passion for s.o., esp. strong sexual feeling toward s.o.; **to be in l./to fall in l. with s.o.; to make l. (to s.o.)** = have sexual intercourse with; **l. story** = one about sexual love; **l. affair** = (often short) sexual relationship. (c) person whom you love. (d) *inf.* form of address, esp. to a woman or child. (e) (*in tennis, etc.*) score of zero. 2. *v.* (a) to have strong feelings of affection for. (b) to have great liking/passion, esp. strong sexual feelings for (s.o.). (c) to like very much. **lov•a•ble**, *adj.* pleasant/easy to love. **love•bird**, *n.* budgerigar. **love-child**, *n.* illegitimate child. **love•less**, *adj.* without love. **love•li•ness**, *n.* being very attractive. **love•lorn**, *adj.* sad because you love s.o. who does not love you. **love•ly**, *adj.* (**-ier, -iest**) (a) beautiful. (b) *inf.* very pleasant. **lov•er**, *n.* (a) person (esp. a man) who is in love. (b) person who loves (sth). **love•sick**, *adj.* unhappy because of being in love. **lov•ing**, *adj.* affectionate/showing love. **lov•ing•ly**, *adv.* in a loving way.

low [ləu] 1. *adj.* (**-er, -est**) (a) at/near/toward the bottom; in a position below (others); **l. voice** = not easily heard. (b) coarse/mean; inferior. (c) feeling depressed/ill, etc. 2. *adv.* in a low direction/way/position; **to lie l.** = to keep hidden; **supplies are running l.** = are becoming scarce. 3. *n.* (a) low-pressure zone in the atmosphere, bringing bad weather. (b) **sales are at an all-time l.** = the lowest point ever. 4. *v.* to make a sound like a cow. **low•brow**, *adj. & n.* (person) without intellectual interests. **low•down**. 1. *adj.* mean/bad/to be despised. 2. *n. inf.* **to give the lowdown (on sth)** = the details (esp. confidential). **low•er.** 1. *adj.* further down; **l. deck** = deck under another deck; **l. case** = small (letter), not a capital; **l. house** = more important of two parts of a parliament. 2. *v.* (a) to make (sth) reach a position further down; **l. your voice** = speak more quietly. (b) **to l. yourself (so far as to)** = to do sth of which you should be ashamed. **low fre•quen•cy**, *n.* radio frequency which is low and can be heard. **low-grade**, *adj.* of poor quality. **low-key**, *adj.* quiet/without excitement. **low•land**, *adj.* coming from a low-lying region. **low•lands**, *n. pl.* low-lying region. **low•li•ness**, *n.* being lowly. **low•ly**, *adj.* (**-ier, -iest**) humble/modest. **low-ly•ing**, *adj.* (region) which is at a low altitude/almost at sea level.

low•er•ing ['lauərɪŋ] *adj.* gloomy/threatening(-looking).

loy•al ['lɔɪəl] *adj.* (**to**) faithful/supporting (s.o./sth). **loy•al•ist**, *n.* person who is loyal. **loy•al•ly**, *adv.* in a loyal way. **loy•al•ty**, *n.* being faithful.

loz•enge ['lɒzɪndʒ] *n.* (a) diamond shape (esp. as used in heraldry). (b) flavored medicine tablet.

LP [el'pi:] *abbreviation for* long-playing record.
Ltd. ['lɪmɪtɪd] *short for* limited.

lu•bri•cate ['lu:brɪkeɪt] *v.* to cover (sth) with oil or grease to make it run smoothly. **lu•bri•cant**, *adj. & n.* (substance) which makes sth run smoothly. **lu•bri•ca•tion** [lu:brɪ'keɪʃn] *n.* covering with oil or grease.

lu•cerne [lu'sɜ:n] *n.* plant like clover used as fodder for cattle.

lu•cid ['lu:sɪd] *adj.* (a) clear/easily understood. (b) able to think clearly. **lu•cid•i•ty** [lu:'sɪdɪtɪ] *n.* being clear. **lu•cid•ly**, *adv.* in a lucid way.

luck [lʌk] *n.* (a) chance/fortune; **as l. would have it** = as it happened; **to be down on your l.** = have bad luck. (b) good fortune; **to be out of l.** = have bad luck. **luck•i•ly**, *adv.* by good fortune. **luck•less**, *adj.* with no luck/unlucky. **luck•y**, *adj.* (**-ier, -iest**) (a) having good fortune/success. (b) having good fortune associated with it; **13's my l. number.**

lu•cre ['lu:kə] *n. inf.* money. **lu•cra•tive** ['lu:krətɪv] *adj.* bringing in (much) money/profit.

lu•di•crous ['lu:dɪkrəs] *adj.* causing laughter; ridiculous.

luff [lʌf] *v.* to sail toward the wind.

lug [lʌg] 1. *n.* small projecting piece for carrying sth or for attaching sth to it. 2. *v.* (**lugged**) to pull (sth heavy) along.

lug•gage ['lʌgɪdʒ] *n.* (*no pl.*) suitcases/bags, etc., for carrying your belongings when traveling; **l. rack** = space for bags, etc., above seats in a train, etc.

lug•ger ['lʌgə] *n.* small sailboat.

lu•gu•bri•ous [lə'gu:brɪəs] *adj.* very miserable/mournful. **lu•gu•bri•ous•ly**, *adv.* in a lugubrious way.

luke•warm ['lu:kwɔ:m] *adj.* (a) slightly warm, but not hot. (b) without enthusiasm.

lull [lʌl] 1. *n.* quiet(er)/calm(er) interval. 2. *v.* to make calmer/to soothe. **lull•a•by** ['lʌləbaɪ] *n.* song/piece of music designed to make a child sleep.

lum•ba•go [lʌm'beɪgəu] *n.* pain in the lower part of the back. **lum•bar** ['lʌmbə] *adj.* referring to the lower part of the back.

lum•ber ['lʌmbə] 1. *n.* (a) wood which has been cut. (b) old articles which are not in use at the moment; junk. 2. *v.* (a) *inf.* (**with**) to give (s.o.) things he doesn't really want. (b) to move with a slow heavy step/pace. **lum•ber•jack**, *n.* person who cuts down trees. **lum•ber jack•et**, *n.* short thick working coat.

lu•men ['lu:mɪn] *n.* unit of measurement of light.

lu•mi•nous ['lu:mɪnəs] *adj.* giving out light (in

the dark). **lu•mi•nar•y**, *n.* learned person. **lu•mi•nes•cence**, *n.* sending out light without heat. **lu•mi•nos•i•ty** [luːmɪ'nɒsɪtɪ] *n.* being luminous.

lump [lʌmp] 1. *n.* (a) (often shapeless) mass; **l. of sugar** = solid cube of sugar; **l. sum** = money (paid) in one amount/not divided up. (b) swelling on the body. (c) *inf.* heavy, clumsy person. 2. *v.* (a) **to l. together** = to put together in one place/in one group. (b) *inf.* **he can l. it** = he'll just have to tolerate it. **lump•y**, *adj.* (-ier, -iest) having solid parts.

lu•na•cy ['luːnəsɪ] *n.* madness. **lu•na•tic**, *adj. & n.* mad (person).

lu•nar ['luːnə] *adj.* referring to the moon; **l. month** = period from one new moon to the next.

lunch [lʌnʃ] 1. *n.* (*pl.* -es) midday meal. 2. *v.* (*formal*) to have lunch. **lunch•eon** ['lʌnʃən] *n.* (*formal*) midday meal; **l. meat** = canned sausage or meat loaf. **lunch hour, lunchtime**, *n.* period when the midday meal is usually eaten.

lung [lʌŋ] *n.* one of two organs in the chest, with which you breathe. **lung fish**, *n.* type of fish which breathes through lungs.

lunge [lʌndʒ] 1. *n.* sudden forward movement. 2. *v.* to make a sudden movement forward.

lu•pine ['luːpaɪn] 1. *n.* garden flower with tall flower spikes. 2. *adj.* referring to a wolf.

lurch [lɜːtʃ] 1. *n.* (*pl.* -es) (a) sudden (unsteady) movement. (b) *inf.* **to leave in the l.** = to leave/fail in time of trouble or crisis. 2. *v.* to move with a sudden unsteady movement. **lurch•er**, *n.* dog used to retrieve game.

lure ['ljʊə] 1. *n.* (a) small object used to attract fish, etc., in order to catch them. (b) thing which traps/attracts. 2. *v.* to attract, esp. into sth bad.

lu•rid ['ljʊərɪd] *adj.* (a) which glows in an unpleasant sinister way. (b) (*of book/motion picture*) sensational/meant to shock. **lu•rid•ly**, *adv.* in a lurid way. **lu•rid•ness**, *n.* being lurid.

lurk [lɜːk] *v.* to hide/to remain hidden.

lus•cious ['lʌʃəs] *adj.* good to taste.

lush [lʌʃ] 1. *adj.* (plants) growing thickly/richly. 2. *n. Sl.* drunkard. **lush•ness**, *n.* being lush.

lust [lʌst] 1. *n.* (a) strong sexual desire. (b) great desire for sth. 2. *v.* **to l.** (**after**) = to have a great desire for. **lust•ful**, *adj.* full of sexual desire.

lus•ter, *Brit.* **lus•tre** ['lʌstə] *n.* shine/brilliance. **lus•trous**, *adj.* brilliant.

lust•y ['lʌstɪ] *adj.* (-ier, -iest) strong/healthy. **lust•i•ly**, *adv.* strongly. **lust•i•ness**, *n.* great strength/health.

lute [luːt] *n.* old stringed musical instrument played like a guitar.

lux•u•ri•ance [lʌg'ʒuːrɪəns] *n.* great quantity/abundance. **lux•u•ri•ant**, *adj.* growing abundantly. **lux•u•ri•ant•ly**, *adv.* in a luxuriant way. **lux•u•ri•ate**, *v.* to enjoy freely/to laze happily.

lux•u•ry ['lʌkʃərɪ] *n.* (a) great comfort. (b) thing which is pleasant to have but not necessary. **lux•u•ri•ous** [lʌg'ʒuːrɪəs] *adj.* very comfortable; very expensive. **lux•u•ri•ous•ly**, *adv.* in a luxurious way. **lux•u•ri•ous•ness**, *n.* being comfortable/expensive.

lye [laɪ] *n.* water mixed with ashes, used for washing.

ly•ing ['laɪɪŋ] *v. see* **lie**.

lymph [lɪmf] *n.* liquid found in animal tissues. **lym•phat•ic** [lɪm'fætɪk] *adj.* referring to lymph.

lynch [lɪnʃ] *v.* (*of a mob*) to kill (s.o.) without trial (esp. by hanging).

lynx [lɪŋks] *n.* (*pl.* -es) spotted short-tailed animal of the cat family. **lynx-eyed**, *adj.* with very good eyesight.

lyre ['laɪə] *n.* old stringed musical instrument. **lyre•bird**, *n.* tropical bird with tail feathers shaped like a lyre.

lyr•ic ['lɪrɪk] *adj. & n.* (a) (poem, etc.) concerned with feeling. (b) (poem, etc.) intended to be sung. **lyr•i•cal**, *adj.* (a) (poem) using suitable language to express feelings. (b) *inf.* eager/enthusiastic. **lyr•i•cal•ly**, *adv.* in a lyrical way. **lyr•i•cism** ['lɪrɪsɪzəm] *n.* quality of a poem which expresses feelings. **lyr•i•cist**, *n.* person who writes the words of a song. **lyr•ics**, *n. pl.* words of a song.

æ back, aː farm, ɒ: top, aɪ pipe, aʊ how, aɪə fire, aʊə flower, ɔ: bought, ɔɪ toy, e fed, eəhair, eɪ take, ə afraid, əʊ boat, əʊə lower, vː word, iː heap, ɪ hit, ɪə hear, uː school, ʊ book, ʌ but, b back, d dog, ð then, dʒ just, f fog, g go, h hand, j yes, k catch, l last, m mix, n nut, ŋ sing, p penny, r round, s some, ʃ short, t too, tʃ chop, θ thing, v voice, w was, z zoo, ʒ treasure

Mm

m *abbrev. for* meter; mile.

ma [mɑ:] *n. inf.* mother.

ma'am [mɑ:m] *n.* 1. madam. 2. term used to address the Queen of England.

mac [mæk] *n. inf.* raincoat.

ma•ca•bre [mə'kɑ:br] *adj.* causing horror; gruesome.

mac•ad•am [mə'kædəm] *n.* road surface made of small pieces of broken stone. **mac•ad•am•ized,** *adj.* covered with macadam.

mac•a•ro•ni [mækə'rəʊnɪ] *n.* food made of short thick tubes of flour paste.

mac•a•roon [mækə'ru:n] *n.* small sweet almond biscuit.

ma•caw [mə'kɔ:] *n.* brightly colored South American parrot.

mace [meɪs] *n.* (a) heavy bar of wood/metal used in ceremonies to symbolize authority. (b) spice made from the outside of a nutmeg.

mac•er•ate ['mæsəreɪt] *v.* to soak in a liquid until soft.

Mach (num•ber) ['mæk('nʌmbə)] *n.* figure showing the speed of supersonic aircraft in relation to the speed of sound; **at M. one** = at the speed of sound.

ma•chet•e [mə'tʃetɪ] *n.* jungle knife used in South America.

Mach•i•a•vel•li•an [mækɪə'velɪən] *adj.* sly/clever (in political plotting).

mach•i•na•tion [mækɪ'neɪʃn] *n.* plot.

ma•chine [mə'ʃi:n] 1. *n.* (a) device in which power from a motor drives wheels/gears, etc. (b) organization; **political machine.** 2. *v.* to make/to shape with a machine. **ma•chine gun,** *n.* gun which automatically fires many bullets one after the other. **ma•chin•er•y,** *n.* (*no pl.*) mechanism; (working parts of) machines. **machine tools,** *n. pl.* tools operated by a motor and used to shape metal/wood, etc. **ma•chin•ing,** *n.* working with a machine. **ma•chin•ist,** *n.* person who works machinery, esp. machine tools.

ma•chis•mo [mə'kɪzməʊ] *n.* exaggerated sense of male pride. **ma•cho** ['mætʃəʊ] *adj.* (man) who is aggressively male.

mack•er•el ['mækrəl] *n.* (*pl.* **mackerel**) common sea fish.

mack•in•tosh ['mækɪntɒʃ] *n.* raincoat.

ma•cra•mé [mə'krɑ:meɪ] *n.* (*no pl.*) knotted string articles.

macro- ['mækrəʊ] *prefix meaning* very large/covering a wide area.

mac•ro•bi•ot•ic [mækrəʊbaɪ'ɒtɪk] *adj.* referring to a health-giving diet of cereals/vegetables, etc.

mac•ro•cosm ['mækrəʊkɒzəm] *n.* large complete system; the universe.

mad [mæd] *adj.* (**madder, maddest**) (a) not sane; wild/silly; *inf.* **like m.** = (i) very fast; (ii) very enthusiastically; **he's m. with/at you** = angry with you. (b) very enthusiastic (**about** s.o./sth). (c) (dog or other animal) suffering from rabies. **mad•cap,** *adj. & n.* wild (person). **mad cow dis•ease,** *n. inf.* bovine spongiform encephalopathy. **mad•den,** *v.* to make mad; to exasperate/to annoy. **mad•den•ing,** *adj.* exasperating. **mad•house,** *n.* place which is full of noise and people rushing about. **mad•ly,** *adv.* like a madman. **mad•man,** *n.* (*pl.* **-men**) lunatic; **he drove like a m.** = he drove very fast/furiously. **mad•ness,** *n.* being mad; lunacy. **mad•wom•an,** *n.* (*pl.* **-women**) female lunatic.

mad•am ['mædəm] *n.* (a) formal way of addressing a woman. (b) woman who keeps a brothel.

mad•der ['mædə] *n.* plant which gives a red dye.

made [meɪd] *v. see* **make.**

ma•dei•ra [mə'dɪərə] *n.* sweet dessert wine.

ma•don•na [mə'dɒnə] *n.* (picture/statue of) the Virgin Mary.

mad•ri•gal ['mædrɪgl] *n.* group song popular in the sixteenth and seventeenth centuries.

mael•strom ['meɪlstrɒm] *n.* violent whirlpool in the sea; violent confusion.

maes•tro ['maɪstrəʊ] *n.* (*pl.* **-os**) *inf.* musical genius; conductor.

ma•fi•a ['mæfɪə] *n.* secret (Italian) organization dealing in crime.

mag•a•zine [mægə'zi:n] *n.* (a) (illustrated) paper which appears at regular intervals. (b) radio/TV program made up from various items on the same theme, broadcast regularly. (c) box containing ammunition/film/slides which clips on to a gun/a camera/projector.

(d) room/building used as a store for explosives.

ma•gen•ta [mə'dʒentə] n. & adj. dark red-purple (color).

mag•got ['mægət] n. white grub (of a bluebottle) which lives in rotting meat. **mag•got•y**, adj. full of maggots.

Ma•gi ['meɪdʒaɪ] n. pl. wise men who brought gifts to the infant Christ.

mag•ic ['mædʒɪk] 1. n. spells/conjuring tricks, etc., which do not appear to follow normal scientific rules; **as if by m.** = suddenly/from nowhere; **black m.** = evil spells designed to harm people. 2. adj. enchanted. **mag•i•cal**, adj. produced by magic; fairylike. **mag•i•cal•ly**, adv. by magic. **mag•ic bul•let**, n. inf. any drug that targets diseased tissue without producing adverse side effects. **ma•gi•cian** [mə'dʒɪʃn] n. wizard/conjuror.

mag•is•te•ri•al [mædʒɪ'stɪərɪəl] adj. with an air of authority. **mag•is•te•ri•al•ly**, adv. in a commanding way.

mag•is•trate ['mædʒɪstreɪt] n. judge in a minor court.

mag•ma ['mɑgmə] n. (a) molten rock under the earth's crust. (b) paste.

Mag•na Car•ta ['mægnə 'kɑːtə] n. charter, signed by King John of England in 1215, which gave basic rights to some subjects.

mag•nan•i•mous [mæg'nænɪməs] adj. very generous. **mag•na•nim•i•ty** [mægnə'nɪmɪtɪ] n. great generosity. **mag•nan•i•mous•ly**, adv. in a magnanimous way.

mag•nate ['mægneɪt] n. important businessman.

mag•ne•si•um [mæg'niːzɪəm] n. (element: Mg) metal which burns with a brilliant white light. **mag•ne•sia**, n. white powder made from magnesium, used in medicines.

mag•net ['mægnət] n. thing which attracts, esp. a metal object which attracts iron and steel and points roughly north and south when suspended. **mag•net•ic** [mæg'netɪk] adj. having a power of attraction; **m. pole/m. north** = the point to which the needle of a compass points; **m. field** = area around a magnet which is under its influence; **m. mine** = floating bomb which is attracted to the metal hull of a passing ship; **m. tape** = plastic tape for recording music/information, etc. **mag•net•i•cal•ly**, adv. by a magnet. **mag•net•ism** ['mægnətɪzəm] n. (a) natural

attractive power of magnets. (b) personal power of attraction. **mag•net•ize**, v. to make (a piece of metal) into a magnet.

mag•ne•to [mæg'niːtəʊ] n. (pl. -os) device in an engine which produces electricity used for ignition.

mag•nif•i•cent [mæg'nɪfɪsnt] adj. very fine/splendid/very luxurious. **mag•nif•i•cence**, n. splendor/luxury. **mag•nif•i•cent•ly**, adv. in a magnificent way.

mag•ni•fy ['mægnɪfaɪ] v. to make (something) appear larger; **magnifying glass** = lens which makes small objects appear larger. **mag•ni•fi•ca•tion** [mægnɪfɪ'keɪʃn] n. making something appear larger; degree to which things appear larger. **mag•ni•fi•er**, n. thing which magnifies.

mag•ni•tude ['mægnɪtjuːd] n. size; (of stars) brightness.

mag•no•lia [mæg'nəʊlɪə] n. large tree with huge flowers.

mag•num ['mægnəm] n. very large bottle (of wine, esp. champagne).

mag•pie ['mægpaɪ] n. common large black and white bird.

ma•ha•ra•jah [mɑːhə'rɑːdʒə] n. Indian prince. **ma•ha•ra•ni** [mɑːhə'rɑːniː] n. Indian princess.

ma•hat•ma [mə'hætmə] n. (in India) title given to a holy man.

mah•jong [mɑː'dʒɒŋ] n. Chinese game played with small counters.

ma•hog•a•ny [mə'hɒgənɪ] n. dark wood used for making furniture.

maid [meɪd] n. female servant; **old m.** = middle-aged unmarried woman. **maid•en**. 1. n. (formal) unmarried girl/woman. 2. adj. (a) unmarried (woman); **m. aunt** = unmarried aunt; **m. name** = surname of a woman before she is married. (b) first; **m. voyage/flight** = first voyage of a new ship/of a new aircraft. **maid•en•hair**, n. type of fern. **maid•en•hood**, n. (formal) being a maiden. **maid•en•ly**, adj. (formal) like a maiden.

mail [meɪl] 1. n. (a) letters delivered. (b) postal service; **m. order** = ordering and buying by mail. (c) **chain m.** = type of armor made of small interlocking metal rings. 2. v. to send (sth) by the postal service. **mail•bag**, n. large canvas bag for carrying mail. **mail•box**, n. box where letters are deposited to be picked up and delivered by the postal service.

æ back, ɑː farm, ɒ top, aɪ pipe, aʊ how, aɪə fire, aʊə flower, ɔː bought, ɔɪ toy, e fed, eəhair, eɪ take, ə afraid, əʊ boat, əʊə lower, ɜː word, iː heap, ɪ hit, ɪə hear, uː school, ʊ book, ʌ but, b back, d dog, ð then, dʒ just, f fog, g go, h hand, j yes, k catch, l last, m mix, n nut, ŋ sing, p penny, r round, s some, ʃ short, t too, tʃ chop, θ thing, v voice, w was, z zoo, ʒ treasure

mail•ing list, *n.* list of names and addresses of people to whom information can be sent. **mail car•ri•er,** *n.* person employed to deliver mail.

maim [meɪm] *v.* to wound; to make lame.

main [meɪn] 1. *n.* (a) *(formal)* **with might and m.** = with all your strength or power. (b) **in the m.** = generally speaking. (c) central pipe for distributing water/gas, etc. 2. *adj.* most important. **main•land** ['meɪnlənd] *n.* large solid mass of land. **main•ly,** *adv.* mostly/in a very important way. **main•mast,** *n.* most important mast on a ship. **main•sail** ['meɪnsl] *n.* most important sail on a ship. **main•spring,** *n.* (a) central spring of a watch. (b) most important force which makes you do sth. **main•stay,** *n.* principal support. **main•stream,** *n.* most important trend or dominating force.

main•tain [meɪn'teɪn] *v.* (a) to keep (order); to keep (doing sth). (b) to keep sth in working order. (c) to state/to assert. **main•te•nance,** *n.* (a) keeping. (b) money for upkeep.

mai•son•ette [meɪzə'net] *n.* apartment on two floors.

maî•tre d' [metrə'diː], **maître d'hôtel** ['metrəd əu'tel] *n.* head waiter.

maize [meɪz] *n.* corn.

maj•es•ty ['mædʒəstɪ] *n.* (a) greatness. (b) form of address to a King or Queen. **ma•jes•tic** [mə'dʒestɪk] *adj.* grand/stately. **ma•jes•ti•cal•ly,** *adv.* grandly.

ma•jor ['meɪdʒə] 1. *n.* (a) *(in the armed forces)* officer above a captain. (b) *(formal)* legally adult person. 2. *adj.* (a) bigger; more important; **the m. part of the work** = most of the work. (b) musical key where there are semitones between the third and fourth, and between the seventh and eighth notes. 3. *v.* to specialize in a subject as an undergraduate. **ma•jor•do•mo,** *n.* chief servant in a large house. **ma•jor•ette** [meɪdʒə'ret] *n.* girl or woman who leads a marching band. **ma•jor-gen•er•al,** *n.* *(in the armed forces)* army officer below a lieutenant-general. **ma•jor•i•ty** [mə'dʒɒrɪtɪ] *n.* (a) larger part. (b) larger number of voters. (c) legally adult age.

make [meɪk] 1. *n.* (a) brand; country of origin (of an object). (b) *inf.* **he's on the m.** = all he wants to do is to make money. 2. *v.* **(made)** (a) to prepare; to do; to construct; **to m. the beds** = to put the beds in proper order after they have been slept in. (b) to earn; **I m. $200 a week.** (c) to add up to; to score. (d) to cause (s.o.) to be; **he made himself comfortable.** (e) to force (s.o.) to do sth; **make a•way with,** *v.* to remove (sth)/to make (sth) disappear.

make-be•lieve, *n.* pretending/believing sth is true when it is not. **make do,** *v.* **(with)** to put up with (sth)/to use (sth) even if it is not suitable. **make for,** *v.* to aim; to go toward. **make good,** *v.* (a) to put (sth) right. (b) to carry out (a promise). (c) to become successful. **make of,** *v.* to consider; **what do you make of it?** = what do you think of it? **make off with,** *v.* to run away with (sth)/to steal (sth). **make out,** *v.* (a) to draw up (a list); to write (a check). (b) to distinguish/to see properly. (c) to assert/to maintain. (d) *inf.* to succeed. **make o•ver,** *v.* to transfer. **make•o•ver,** *n.* complete restyling, esp. of a person's clothes/hair, etc. **mak•er,** *n.* person who makes sth. **make•shift,** *adj. & n.* (thing) used temporarily in place of sth else. **make up,** *v.* (a) to complete/to fill up; **I can't make up my mind** = I can't decide; **to make up for lost time** = to act specially quickly. (b) to put lipstick/powder, etc., on your face. (c) to invent. (d) **to make it up to s.o.** = to compensate s.o. for sth lost/damaged, etc. **make-up,** *n.* (a) composition. (b) character. (c) lipstick/cream/powder, etc., used to beautify your face. **make•weight,** *n.* small quantity added to make up the weight of sth. **mak•ing,** *n.* formation; **it was 3 years in the m.** = it took 3 years to make; **it has the makings of** = it may develop into.

ma•lac•ca [mæl'ækə] *n.* tropical cane used to make walking sticks.

mal•a•chite ['mæləkaɪt] *n.* green stone.

mal•ad•just•ed [mælə'dʒʌstɪd] *adj.* (person) who does not fit into society. **mal•ad•just•ment,** *n.* being maladjusted.

mal•ad•min•is•tra•tion [mælədmɪnɪ'streɪʃn] *n.* incompetent administration.

mal•a•droit [mælə'drɔɪt] *adj. (formal)* clumsy.

mal•a•dy ['mælədɪ] *n. (formal)* illness.

ma•laise [mæ'leɪz] *n. (formal)* awkward feeling; slight sickness.

mal•a•prop•ism ['mæləprɒpɪzəm] *n.* incorrect use of a word which sounds similar to the correct one.

ma•lar•i•a [mə'leərɪə] *n.* tropical fever caused by a parasite carried by mosquitoes. **ma•lar•i•al,** *adj.* referring to malaria.

Ma•lay•sian [mə'leɪʒn] 1. *adj.* referring to Malaysia. 2. *n.* person from Malaysia. **Ma•lay,** *n. & adj.* (person) from Malaysia; language spoken in Malaysia.

mal•con•tent ['mælkəntent] *n. (formal)* dissatisfied person.

male [meɪl] 1. *adj.* (a) referring to men/boys. (b) referring to the sex which fertilizes eggs produced by females. 2. *n.* (a) man/boy. (b) animal/insect of the sex which does not give birth to offspring.

mal•e•fac•tor ['mælɪfæktə] *n.* (*formal*) criminal.

ma•lev•o•lence [mə'levələns] *n.* (*formal*) ill-will; desire to hurt others. **ma•lev•o•lent**, *adj.* wishing (s.o.) ill.

mal•fea•sance [mæl'fiːzəns] *n.* (*formal*) an unlawful act.

mal•for•ma•tion [mælfɔː'meɪʃn] *n.* being wrongly shaped/badly formed. **mal•formed**, *adj.* bady formed/shaped.

mal•func•tion [mæl'fʌŋkʃn] 1. *n.* bad/incorrect working (of a machine/of the heart, etc.). 2. *v.* to work badly.

mal•ice ['mælɪs] *n.* unfriendly feelings; **out of m.** = to be spiteful. **ma•li•cious** [mə'lɪʃəs] *adj.* wicked/intentionally spiteful; wanting to hurt others. **ma•li•cious•ly**, *adv.* in a malicious way.

ma•lign [mə'laɪn] *v.* to say bad things about (s.o.); **he has been much maligned** = people have criticized him a lot. **ma•lig•nan•cy** [mə'lɪgnənsɪ] *n.* being malignant. **ma•lig•nant** [mə'lɪgnənt] *adj.* (a) wishing harm to someone. (b) likely to be fatal. **ma•lig•ni•ty**, *n.* malignant feeling.

ma•lin•ger [mə'lɪŋgə] *v.* to pretend to be ill (to avoid work). **ma•lin•ger•er**, *n.* person who pretends to be ill.

mall [mɔːl] *n.* shopping complex with many different kinds of retail stores and usu. restaurants and other businesses.

mal•lard ['mælɑːd] *n.* common wild duck.

mal•le•a•ble ['mælɪəbl] *adj.* soft/which can be molded into shape. **mal•le•a•bil•i•ty**, *n.* being malleable.

mal•let ['mælɪt] *n.* large wooden hammer.

mal•low ['mæləʊ] *n.* wild flower growing in marshy ground.

mal•nu•tri•tion [mælnjuː'trɪʃn] *n.* lack of enough good food.

mal•o•dor•ous [mæl'əʊdərəs] *adj.* (*formal*) which smells bad.

mal•prac•tice [mæl'præktɪs] *n.* improper or illegal conduct by a professional, as a doctor or lawyer.

malt [mɔːlt] *n.* grain which has been prepared for making beer or whisky by being allowed to sprout and then dried. **malt•ed**, *adj.* tasting of malt.

Mal•tese [mɒl'tiːz] *adj. & n.* (person) from Malta.

mal•treat [mæl'triːt] *v.* to treat (s.o.) badly. **mal•treat•ment**, *n.* rough treatment.

ma•ma [mə'mɑː] *n.* child's name for mother.

mam•ba ['mæmbə] *n.* poisonous African snake.

mam•bo ['mæmbəʊ] *n.* South American dance.

mam•ma [mə'mɑː] *n.* = **ma•ma**.

mam•mal ['mæml] *n.* type of animal which gives birth to live young and suckles them with milk. **mam•ma•li•an** [mə'meɪlɪən] *adj.* referring to mammals. **mam•ma•ry**, *adj.* referring to the breast.

mam•mon ['mæmən] *n.* wealth regarded as evil and the object of greedy pursuit.

mam•moth ['mæməθ] 1. *n.* very large prehistoric hairy elephant. 2. *adj.* huge.

man [mæn] 1. *n.* (*pl.* **men**) (a) adult male human being. (b) person; **the m. in the street** = the ordinary citizen; **no man's land** = land between two armies which belongs to neither side. (c) husband. (d) servant; ordinary soldier/worker. (e) piece (in chess, etc.). 2. *v.* (**manned**) to provide with men; to be the workforce for (a machine/an office, etc.). **man-eat•er**, *n.* animal which eats people. **man-eat•ing**, *adj.* (animal) which eats people. **man•ful•ly**, *adv.* like a man; in a strong/forceful way. **man•han•dle**, *v.* (a) to move (something large and heavy) by hand. (b) to handle someone roughly. **man•hole**, *n.* hole in the road or pavement through which you go down into the sewers, etc. **man•hood**, *n.* (*no pl.*) state of being an adult male. **man-hour**, *n.* work done by one person in one hour. **man•hunt**, *n.* search (for a criminal). **man•kind** [mæn'kaɪnd] *n.* (*no pl.*) the human race. **man•li•ness**, *n.* virility/male characteristics. **man•ly**, *adj.* virile/with very strong male features; brave. **man-made**, *adj.* artificial (material, etc.). **man•nish**, *adj.* (woman) who looks/dresses like a man. **man•pow•er**, *n.* work force/number of workers. **man-of-war**, *n.* (a) (*old*) battleship. (b) **Portuguese man-of-war** = type of very large jellyfish. **man•serv•ant**, *n.* male servant. **man-sized**, *adj.* very large. **man•slaugh•ter**, *n.* killing s.o. without intending to do so.

man•a•cle ['mænəkl] 1. *n.* one of two steel rings connected by a chain, which attach the wrists of a prisoner together. 2. *v.* to attach (a prisoner's) wrists together.

æ back, ɑː farm, ɒ: top, aɪ pipe, aʊ how, aɪə fire, aʊə flower, ɔː bought, ɔɪ toy, e fed, eəhair, eɪ take, ə afraid, əʊ boat, əʊə lower, vː word, iː heap, ɪ hit, ɪə hear, uː school, ʊ book, ʌ but, b back, d dog, ð then, dʒ just, f fog, g go, h hand, j yes, k catch, l last, m mix, n nut, ŋ sing, p penny, r round, s some, ʃ short, t too, tʃ chop, θ thing, v voice, w was, z zoo, ʒ treasure

man•age ['mænɪdʒ] v. (a) to direct. (b) to arrange to do sth; to succeed in doing sth; **can she m. all by herself?** = can she cope/can she do the work all by herself? **man•age•a•ble,** adj. which can be managed/directed. **man•age•ment,** n. (a) handling of (a tool); directing (of work). (b) group of people who direct workers; **under new m.** = with a new owner/manager. **man•ag•er,** n. (a) head of a department in a company. (b) person who manages/directs; director of a theater; organizer of a sports team/singer, etc.; person who runs a store. **man•ag•er•ess** [mænɪdʒə'res] n. (pl. -es) woman who runs a store. **man•a•ge•ri•al** [mænə'dʒɪərɪəl] adj. referring to a manager; **discussions at m. level** = discussions among managers. **man•ag•ing di•rec•tor,** n. overall director of a company.

man•a•tee [mænə'ti:] n. large plant-eating sea mammal.

man•da•mus [mæn'deɪməs] n. order from a higher court to a lower court.

man•da•rin ['mændərɪn] n. (a) small orange with a soft easily-peeled skin. (b) important member of a group. (c) **Mandarin** = principal form of the Chinese language.

man•date ['mændeɪt] n. power given to a person to act on behalf of s.o. else; **the government has a m. from the people to cut taxes** = people approved of the plan to cut taxes when they voted for the government. **man•dat•ed,** adj. (territory) which is entrusted to a country to administer. **man•da•to•ry** ['mændətərɪ] adj. obligatory/compulsory.

man•di•ble ['mændɪbl] n. lower jawbone (of birds/insects, etc.).

man•do•lin ['mændəlɪn] n. stringed instrument like a small guitar.

man•drel ['mændrəl] n. the turning central shaft of a lathe.

man•drill ['mændrɪl] n. large baboon.

mane [meɪn] n. long hair on neck of a lion or horse; long untidy hair.

ma•neu•ver [mə'nu:və] n. & v. 1. n. (a) action of moving sth. (b) **maneuvers** = military exercises. 2. v. (a) to move (sth) heavy/awkward. (b) to work to put yourself in a good position. **ma•neu•ver•a•bil•i•ty** [mənu:vrə'bɪlɪtɪ] n. ability to be easily maneuvered. **ma•neu•ver•a•ble,** adj. which can be maneuvered/moved.

man•ga•nese ['mæŋgəni:z] n. (element: Mn) gray metal.

mange [meɪndʒ] n. disease of the skin of animals, which makes the hair fall out. **man•gy,** adj. dirty/diseased.

man•ger ['meɪndʒə] n. box for food for horses/cows, etc.

man•gle ['mæŋgl] 1. n. device with rollers for squeezing the water out of clothes. 2. v. (a) to squeeze water out of (clothes) by passing them through a mangle. (b) to tear; to chop up; to mess up.

man•go ['mæŋgəʊ] n. (pl. -oes) large tropical fruit with a big stone.

man•grove ['mæŋgrəʊv] n. kind of tropical tree growing in wet areas.

ma•ni•a ['meɪnɪə] n. madness; exaggerated passion (for sth). **ma•ni•ac,** n. mad person. **ma•ni•a•cal** [mə'naɪəkl] adj. mad. **man•ic** ['mænɪk] adj. referring to mania.

man•i•cure ['mænɪkjʊə] 1. n. treatment for the hands; **to have a m.** = to have your hands cleaned and nails trimmed. 2. v. to care for the hands. **manicure set,** n. small box or bag with scissors/nail file, etc. **man•i•cur•ist,** n. person who gives treatment to people's hands.

man•i•fest ['mænɪfest] 1. adj. (formal) obvious/plain to see. 2. n. list of goods in a shipment. 3. v. (formal) to appear/to show. **man•i•fes•ta•tion** [mænɪfe'steɪʃn] n. appearance. **man•i•fest•ly,** adv. (formal) obviously. **man•i•fes•to** [mænɪ'festəʊ] n. (pl. -oes) program of action outlined by a political party.

man•i•fold ['mænɪfəʊld] 1. adj. (formal) of varying sorts. 2. n. **exhaust m.** = tubes of an exhaust pipe of a car.

man•i•kin ['mænɪkɪn] n. very small man.

ma•nil•a [mə'nɪlə] n. (also **Manila paper**) thick brown paper (used for envelopes).

man•i•oc ['mænɪɒk] n. tropical plant from which a flour is made.

ma•nip•u•late [mə'nɪpjʊleɪt] v. to handle; to falsify (accounts) to make them seem more profitable. **ma•nip•u•la•tion** [mənɪpjʊ'leɪʃn] n. handling (of machinery); falsification (of accounts). **ma•nip•u•la•tor,** n. person who manipulates.

man•na ['mænə] n. unexpected help/food.

man•ne•quin ['mænɪkɪn] n. person or dummy wearing clothes to show them to possible buyers.

man•ner ['mænə] n. (a) way of behaving/acting; (b) **manners** = way of acting in public. (c) sort; **in a m. of speaking** = in a sort of way. **man•nered,** adj. full of mannerisms. **man•ner•ism,** n. characteristic way of acting/of doing sth. **man•ner•ly,** adj. well-behaved.

ma•nœu•vre [mə'nu:və] n. Brit. see **ma•neu•ver.**

ma•nom•e•ter [mæ'nɒmɪtə] n. instrument for measuring pressure.

man•or ['mænə] n. main house on a country estate, etc.; **m. house** = country house.

man•sard ['mænsɑːd] *n.* **m. (roof)** = roof where the top part slopes more gently than the bottom.

man•sion ['mænʃən] *n.* very large private house.

man•tel ['mæntl] (*also* **mantelpiece** ['mæntlpiːs]) *n.* shelf above a fireplace.

man•tis ['mæntɪs] *n.* **praying m.** = large tropical insect.

man•tle ['mæntl] *n.* (a) cloak. (b) gauze cover for a gas or kerosene lamp.

man•u•al ['mænjʊəl] 1. *adj.* done by hand. 2. *n.* (a) book of instructions. (b) car where the gears are changed by hand. (c) keyboard of an organ. **man•u•al•ly,** *adv.* (done) by hand.

man•u•fac•ture [mænjuˈfæktʃə] 1. *n.* making of a commercially produced product. 2. *v.* to make (products) commercially. **man•u•fac•tur•er,** *n.* person/company producing commercial products.

ma•nure [məˈnjʊə] 1. *n.* dung of animals used as a fertilizer on land. 2. *v.* to spread manure on (land).

man•u•script ['mænjuskrɪpt] *adj. & n.* (document/novel/poem) written by hand or typed, etc., but not printed.

Manx [mæŋks] *adj. & n.* (person, etc.) from the Isle of Man.

man•y ['menɪ] *adj. & n.* (**more, most**) great number; **a good m. prisoners** = quite a large number; **m. a time** = often.

Ma•o•ri ['maʊrɪ] 1. *adj.* referring to the original natives of New Zealand. 2. *n.* (a) language spoken by the native race of New Zealand. (b) member of the native race of New Zealand.

map [mæp] 1. *n.* diagram of an area showing features and places and their relative positions and sizes; **street m.** = diagram showing streets with their names; **physical m.** = diagram showing mountains/rivers, etc.; **political m.** = diagram showing the borders of countries/administrative districts, etc. 2. *v.* (**mapped**) to draw a diagram of (an area); **to m. out a route** = to plan a journey in advance. **map•ping,** *n.* art of making maps.

ma•ple ['meɪpl] *n.* northern tree, with sweet sap; **m. sugar/m. syrup** = sugar/syrup made from the sap of the maple tree.

mar [mɑː] *v.* (**marred**) to spoil.

mar•a•bou ['mærəbuː] *n.* large stork, with a heavy bill.

ma•rac•as [məˈrækəs] *n. pl.* percussion instrument, formed of a pair of gourds with dried seeds inside them.

mar•a•schi•no [mærəˈskiːnəʊ] *n.* (*pl.* **-os**) cherry used to make liqueur in desserts, cocktails, etc.

mar•a•thon ['mærəθən] *n.* long distance race; (sth) which lasts a long time.

ma•raud [məˈrɔːd] *v.* to raid; to go about looking for plunder. **ma•raud•er,** *n.* person who raids. **ma•raud•ing,** *adj.* (person) who raids.

mar•ble ['mɑːbl] *n.* (a) very hard type of limestone which can be brilliantly polished. (b) small glass ball for playing with. **mar•bled,** *adj.* with streaks of different colors.

March [mɑːtʃ] *n.* 3rd month of the year.

march [mɑːtʃ] 1. *n.* (*pl.* **-es**) (a) military walking in step; **quick m.** = rapid walking pace; **slow m.** = slow walking pace. (b) **protest m.** = mass of people walking in a line to protest about sth. (c) music for marching. (d) progress/advance of time/events. 2. *v.* (a) to walk in step; **the police marched him off to prison** = removed him quickly to prison. (b) to walk quickly and purposefully. (c) to walk in a protest march. **march•er,** *n.* person who marches.

mare ['meə] *n.* female horse; **mare's tails** = thin wispy clouds showing a change in the weather; **mare's nest** = discovery which turns out to be useless.

mar•ga•rine [mɑːdʒəˈriːn] *n.* mixture of animal or vegetable fat which is used instead of butter.

mar•gin ['mɑːdʒɪn] *n.* (a) edge/border (of a page). (b) extra space/time; **leave a m. for error** = allow extra space/time in case you have made a mistake in your calculations; **safety m.** = space/time left to allow for safety. (c) money received which is more than money paid. **mar•gin•al,** *adj.* (a) (note) in a margin. (b) slight. **mar•gin•al•ly,** *adv.* slightly.

mar•gue•rite [mɑːgəˈriːt] *n.* common large white daisy.

mar•i•gold ['mærɪgəʊld] *n.* common garden plant with yellow flowers.

ma•ri•jua•na [mærɪˈhwɑːnə] *n.* drug made from hemp.

ma•ri•na [məˈriːnə] *n.* harbor for yachts/motor boats, etc.

mar•i•nade [mærɪˈneɪd] 1. *n.* mixture of wine and herbs, etc., in which meat or fish is soaked before cooking. 2. *v.* (*also* **marinate**) to soak (meat or fish) in a mixture of wine and herbs.

ma•rine [məˈriːn] 1. *adj.* referring to the sea. 2. *n.* (a) **the merchant m.** = the merchant ships of

---

æ back, ɑː farm, ɒ top, aɪ pipe, aʊ how, aɪə fire, aʊə flower, ɔː bought, ɔɪ toy, e fed, eəhair, eɪ take, ə afraid, əʊ boat, əʊə lower, ɜː word, iː heap, ɪ hit, ɪə hear, uː school, ʊ book, ʌ but, b back, d dog, ð then, dʒ just, f fog, g go, h hand, j yes, k catch, l last, m mix, n nut, ŋ sing, p penny, r round, s some, ʃ short, t too, tʃ chop, θ thing, v voice, w was, z zoo, ʒ treasure

a country. (b) soldier serving on a ship. (c) **Marine.** member of the U.S. Marine Corps. **Marine Corps,** n. branch of the U.S. armed forces used for combat on land, air, and sea.
mar•i•ner ['mærɪnə] n. sailor.

mar•i•on•ette [mærɪə'net] n. string puppet.

mar•i•tal ['mærɪtl̩] adj. referring to marriage.

mar•i•time ['mærɪtaɪm] adj. referring to the sea.

mar•jo•ram ['mɑːdʒərəm] n. common herb used as flavoring.

mark [mɑːk] 1. n. (a) spot/stain; thing which can be seen. (b) target; **wide of the m.** = far from correct. (c) sign; **punctuation m.** = printing sign (such as period/comma, etc.). (d) rating given to a student to show level or quality of performance. (e) starting line in a race; **on your marks** = get ready at your places. (f) line indicating a point reached. (g) unit of money in Germany. 2. v. (a) to make a sign on (sth). (b) to correct and give a rating to. (c) **to m. time** = (i) to march on one spot; (ii) to stay in one place/not to advance. **mark down,** v. to lower the price of (sth). **marked,** adj. obvious/noticeable; **a m. man** = man who has been selected by the enemy as a probable target. **mark•ed•ly** ['mɑːkɪdlɪ] adv. obviously. **mark•er,** n. thing which marks; person who notes the scores in a competition, etc.; **m. buoy** = buoy used to indicate a dangerous spot. **mark•ing,** n. (a) making marks. (b) **markings** = spots/stripes, etc., on a bird or animal. (c) correcting (exercises/homework, etc). **mark out,** v. to indicate the boundaries of (a land); to select. **marks•man,** n. (pl. **-men**) person who shoots well. **marks•man•ship,** n. ability to shoot well. **mark up,** v. to increase the price of (sth). **mark-up,** n. amount added to the cost price to give the selling price.

mar•ket ['mɑːkɪt] 1. n. (a) place where produce is sold outdoors, usu. from booths. (b) sale; **on the m.** = for sale. (c) place where a product is required/could be sold; need for a product; **m. research** = examination of the possible sales of a product before it is launched; **the Common M.** = the European Economic Community; **black m.** = illegal selling at high prices. 2. v. to sell (products). **mar•ket•a•ble,** adj. which can be sold easily. **mar•ket•ing,** n. selling techniques (publicity/packaging, etc.) for a product. **mar•ket•place,** n. place where a market is held/where goods are sold.

marl [mɑːl] n. soil which is a mixture of clay and lime.

mar•line•spike ['mɑːlɪnspaɪk] n. pointed hook, used for unraveling rope.

mar•ma•lade ['mɑːməleɪd] n. jam made from oranges/lemons or grapefruit.

mar•mo•set [mɑːmə'zet] n. small South and Central American monkey.

mar•mot ['mɑːmət] n. small burrowing animal.

ma•roon [mə'ruːn] 1. adj. & n. deep purple red (color). 2. v. to abandon in an awkward place.

mar•quee [mɑː'kiː] n. rooflike top over an entrance, esp. to a theater.

mar•que•try ['mɑːkətrɪ] n. (making) patterns on the surface of wood with inlaid pieces of different-colored wood or ivory.

mar•ram grass ['mærəm'grɑːs] n. type of grass used to stabilize sand dunes.

mar•riage ['mærɪdʒ] n. (a) state of being legally joined as husband and wife. (b) ceremony of being married. **mar•riage•a•ble,** adj. suitable to become married.

mar•row ['mærəʊ] n. (a) soft interior of bones. (b) large green vegetable growing on a creeping plant. **mar•row•fat pea,** n. type of pea with large seeds.

mar•ry ['mærɪ] v. (a) to make (two people) husband and wife. (b) to become married to (s.o.). **mar•ried,** adj. joined as husband and wife; **m. name** = name taken by a woman when she gets married.

mar•sa•la [mɑː'sɑːlə] n. sweet Italian wine.

marsh [mɑːʃ] n. (pl. **-es**) wet/swampy land; **m. marigold** = common yellow flower growing in marshes; **m. mallow** = common pink flower growing in marshes. **marsh•mal•low,** n. soft and sticky white or pink candy. **marsh•y,** adj. (**-ier, -iest**) swampy/wet (land).

mar•shal ['mɑːʃl] 1. n. (a) very high-ranking military officer in certain armies. (b) organizer (of a race/a show). (c) police or fire chief. 2. v. (**marshaled**) to set or arrange in order.

mar•su•pi•al [mɑː'suːpɪəl] adj. & n. (animal) which carries its young in a pouch.

mart [mɑːt] n. market.

mar•tel•lo tow•er [mɑː'teləʊ'taʊə] n. round fort, built by the sea in the 19th century.

mar•ten ['mɑːtɪn] n. small wild flesh-eating animal like a weasel.

mar•tial ['mɑːʃl] adj. referring to war; **m. music** = marches played by military bands; **m. law** = maintenance of law by the military instead of the police; **m. arts** = oriental fighting techniques using swords/sticks, etc.

Mar•tian ['mɑːʃn] n. being which is said to inhabit the planet Mars.

mar•tin ['mɑːtɪn] n. small dark bird similar to a swallow.

mar•ti•net [mɑːtɪ'net] n. very strict person.

mar•tin•gale ['mɑːtɪŋgeɪl] n. strap to hold a horse's head down.

mar•ti•ni [mɑː'tiːnɪ] n. drink made of gin/vodka and vermouth.

mar•tyr ['mɑːtə] 1. *n.* person killed because of his religious beliefs; **a m. to** = suffering a lot from. 2. *v.* to kill (s.o.) for their religious beliefs. **mar•tyr•dom**, *n.* death for one's beliefs.

mar•vel ['mɑːvl] 1. *n.* object of wonder. 2. *v.* (**marveled, marvelled**) to show wonder/surprise (**at** s.o./sth). **mar•vel•ous**, *adj.* wonderful/amazing.

Marx•ism ['mɑːksɪzəm] *n.* political theory of the philosopher Marx, on which communism is based. **Marx•ist**, *adj. & n.* (person) who follows Marxism.

mar•zi•pan ['mɑːzɪpæn] *n.* paste made from almonds, used for making sweets or covering cakes.

mas•car•a [mæ'skɑːrə] *n.* liquid/paste for making eyelashes dark.

mas•cot ['mæskət] *n.* object/animal which brings good luck.

mas•cu•line ['mæskjʊlɪn] *adj.* (a) male/manly. (b) (*in grammar*) referring to words which have a particular form to indicate the male gender. **mas•cu•lin•ist, mas•cu•list**, *n.* person (usu. man) who actively supports the rights of males. **mas•cu•lin•i•ty** [mæskjʊ-'lɪnɪtɪ] *n.* manliness.

ma•ser ['meɪzə] *n.* device which amplifies microwaves.

mash [mæʃ] 1. *n.* (a) mixture of things crushed together. (b) food mixture for horses. (c) mixture used as the base for making beer. 2. *v.* to crush (sth) into a paste. **mash•er**, *n.* device for crushing. **mash•ie**, *n.* type of heavy metal golf club.

mask [mɑːsk] 1. *n.* covering to disguise/to protect the face. 2. *v.* to cover up/to hide. **masked**, *adj.* wearing a mask. **mask•ing tape**, *n.* tape used to cover an area which is not being painted.

mas•och•ist ['mæsəkɪst] *n.* person who enjoys being hurt. **mas•och•ism**, *n.* enjoyment at being hurt. **mas•och•is•tic**, *adj.* referring to masochism.

ma•son ['meɪsn] *n.* (a) person who builds with stone. (b) member of a secret society of freemasons. **ma•son•ic** [mə'sɒnɪk] *adj.* referring to freemasons. **ma•son•ry** ['meɪsnrɪ] *n.* art of building with stone; large stones in a building.

mas•quer•ade [mɑːskə'reɪd] 1. *n.* (a) dance/party where people wear masks. (b) pretense/hiding of the truth. 2. *v.* (**as**) to pretend to be (s.o.).

mass [mæs] 1. *n.* (*pl.* **-es**) (a) Catholic communion service; **high m.** = mass with full ceremony; **low m.** = mass without ceremony; **Requiem M.** = (music for) a mass for the dead. (b) (*in physics*) solid body. (c) (*in physics*) amount of matter in a body. (d) large number/large quantity; **m. murderer** = killer of a large number of people; **m. meeting** = meeting of a lot of people; **m. production** = production of a large number of products; **m. media** = means of communicating (TV/radio/newspapers) which reach a large number of people. (e) **the masses** = the common people. 2. *v.* to group together into a mass. **mass-pro•duce**, *v.* to produce a large number of (products) at the same time.

mas•sa•cre ['mæsəkə] 1. *n.* killing of a lot of people/animals. 2. *v.* to kill a lot of people/animals.

mas•sage ['mæsɑːʒ] 1. *n.* rubbing of the body to relieve pain or to reduce weight. 2. *v.* to rub (s.o.'s body) to relieve pain or to reduce weight. **mas•seur** [mæ'sɜː] *n.* man who massages. **mas•seuse** [mæ'sɜːz] *n.* woman who massages.

mas•sive ['mæsɪv] *adj.* very large. **mas•sive•ly**, *adv.* very much. **mas•sive•ness**, *n.* being massive.

mast [mɑːst] *n.* (a) tall pole on a ship to carry the sails. (b) tall metal construction to carry an aerial. (c) (*no pl.*) seeds of beech/oak, etc., trees.

mas•tec•to•my [mæ'stektəmɪ] *n.* operation to remove a breast.

mas•ter ['mɑːstə] 1. *n.* (a) person in control; captain (of a merchant ship). (b) person with a second degree from a university. (c) skilled person; **an old m.** = painting by a great painter of the past. 2. *adj.* controlling; **m. key** = main key; **m. switch** = switch which controls all other switches; **m. bedroom** = main bedroom. 3. *v.* to become skilled at (sth); to gain control of (sth). **master-at-arms**, *n.* (*in the navy*) petty officer in charge of small arms and discipline. **mas•ter•ful**, *adj.* commanding/like a commander. **mas•ter•ful•ly**, *adv.* in a commanding way. **mas•ter•ly**, *adj.* clever; like an expert. **mas•ter•mind**. 1. *n.* very clever person. 2. *v.* to be the brains behind (a plan). **mas•ter•piece**, *n.* very fine painting/book/piece of music, etc. **mas•ter•stroke**, *n.* very clever action.

æ **back,** aː **farm,** ɒ **top,** aɪ **pipe,** aʊ **how,** aɪə **fire,** aʊə **flower,** ɔː **bought,** ɔɪ **toy,** e **fed,** eə **hair,** eɪ **take,** ə **afraid,** əʊ **boat,** əʊə **lower,** vː **word,** iː **heap,** ɪ **hit,** ɪə **hear,** uː **school,** ʊ **book,** ʌ **but,** b **back,** d **dog,** ð **then,** dʒ **just,** f **fog,** g **go,** h **hand,** j **yes,** k **catch,** l **last,** m **mix,** n **nut,** ŋ **sing,** p **penny,** r **round,** s **some,** ʃ **short,** t **too,** tʃ **chop,** θ **thing,** v **voice,** w **was,** z **zoo,** ʒ **treasure**

mas•ter•y, *n.* control over s.o.; complete understanding of a subject; great skill at a game.

mas•tic ['mæstɪk] *n.* gum from certain trees.

mas•ti•cate ['mæstɪkeɪt] *v.* (*formal*) to chew. **mas•ti•ca•tion** [mæstɪ'keɪʃn] *n.* chewing.

mas•tiff ['mæstɪf] *n.* large fierce breed of dog.

mas•toid ['mæstɔɪd] *n.* bone just behind the ear.

mas•tur•bate ['mæstəbeɪt] *v.* to rub the sex organs to excite them. **mas•tur•ba•tion** [mæstə'beɪʃn] *n.* exciting the sex organs by rubbing.

mat [mæt] *n.* (a) small piece of carpet/woven straw, etc. used as a floor covering; **bath m.** = small carpet to step on to when getting out of a bath. (b) small piece of cloth/wood/glass put under a plate on a table. **mat•ted,** *adj.* stuck together (like a mat). **mat•ting,** *n.* (material for making) large mats; **coconut m.** = floor covering made from coconut fibers.

mat•a•dor ['mætædɔ:] *n.* bullfighter who fights on foot.

match [mætʃ] 1. *n.* (*pl.* -es) (a) equal (person/thing); **they are a good m.** = they go well together. (b) game. (c) small piece of wood/cardboard with a chemical tip which lights when rubbed against a rough surface. (d) marriage. 2. *v.* (a) to be equal to. (b) to fit/to go with. **match•board,** *n.* tongue-and-groove board, with a projecting tongue along one edge and a corresponding groove along the other. **match•box,** *n.* small box containing matches. **match•less,** *adj.* with no equal. **match•mak•er,** *n.* person who arranges a marriage. **match•stick,** *n.* stick of wood forming a match. **match•wood,** *n.* small pieces of wood.

mate [meɪt] 1. *n.* (a) one of a pair of animals; husband or wife. (b) *inf.* friend/companion. (c) fellow worker. (d) workman's helper; assistant. (e) (*on merchant ship*) officer below a captain. (f) (*in chess*) position where the king cannot move, and the game ends. 2. *v.* (a) (*of animals*) to breed. (b) (*in chess*) to put (your opponent's king) in a position from which he cannot escape.

ma•te•ri•al [mə'tɪərɪəl] 1. *n.* (a) substance which can be used for making sth. (b) useful implements; **writing materials** = pens/pencils/ink/paper, etc. (c) cloth. (d) subject matter/notes (for a book, etc.). 2. *adj.* (a) referring to physical things. (b) important. **ma•te•ri•al•ism,** *n.* interest only in physical things/belief that only physical things are important. **ma•te•ri•al•ist,** *n.* person who believes in materialism. **ma•te•ri•al•is•tic,** *adj.* referring to materialism. **ma•te•ri•al•ize,** *v.* to become real/to ap-

pear. **ma•te•ri•al•ly,** *adv.* greatly/noticeably.

ma•ter•nal [mə'tɜ:nl] *adj.* referring to a mother; **m. grandfather** = father of your mother. **ma•ter•nal•ly,** *adv.* like a mother. **ma•ter•ni•ty,** *n.* becoming a mother; giving birth; **m. leave** = paid leave from a job while you are having a baby.

math•e•mat•ics [mæθə'mætɪks] *n.* science of numbers and measurements. **math•e•mat•i•cal,** *adj.* referring to mathematics. **math•e•mat•i•cal•ly,** *adv.* by mathematics. **math•e•ma•ti•cian** [mæθəmə'tɪʃn] *n.* expert at mathematics. **math,** *n. inf.* mathematics.

ma•tin•ée ['mætɪneɪ] *n.* afternoon performance of a play or motion picture.

mat•ins ['mætɪnz] *n. pl.* prayers said in the morning.

ma•tri•arch ['meɪtrɪɑːk] *n.* woman who leads a family/a group. **ma•tri•ar•chal** [meɪtrɪ'ɑːkl] *adj.* referring to a matriarch; (society) where women rule families. **ma•tri•ar•chy,** *n.* matriarchal society.

mat•ri•cide ['mætrɪsaɪd] *n.* murder of one's mother.

ma•tric•u•late [mə'trɪkjuleɪt] *v.* to enroll in a college or university. **ma•tric•u•la•tion** [mətrɪkju'leɪʃn] *n.* act of matriculating.

mat•ri•mo•ny ['mætrɪmənɪ] *n.* state of being married. **mat•ri•mo•ni•al** [mætrɪ'məunɪəl] *adj.* referring to marriage.

ma•trix ['meɪtrɪks] *n.* (*pl.* -trices [-trɪsiːz] -trixes) (a) plan/pattern from which copies are made. (b) mathematical arrangement of figures in a series of columns.

ma•tron ['meɪtrən] *n.* (a) woman who guards or has charge of inmates of a prison, hospital, or other institution. (b) middle-aged married woman. **ma•tron•ly,** *adj.* like a matron.

matte, matt [mæt] *adj.* dull/not shiny.

mat•ter ['mætə] 1. *n.* (a) substance/material. (b) thing/business; **that's quite another m.** = that's quite different. (c) problem. 2. *v.* to be important. **matter-of-fact,** *adj.* practical.

mat•tock ['mætək] *n.* type of pickax with a wide blade, used for breaking up soil.

mat•tress ['mætrəs] *n.* (*pl.* -es) thick, soft part of a bed made of a canvas case with various fillings.

ma•ture [mə'tjuə] 1. *adj.* ripe; older; reasonable/adult (attitude). 2. *v.* to ripen. **mat•u•ra•tion,** *n.* becoming mature. **ma•tu•ri•ty,** *n.* ripeness/readiness.

maud•lin ['mɔːdlɪn] *adj.* weeping/silly through drink.

maul [mɔːl] *v.* to attack/handle roughly.

maul•stick, *n.* stick used by a painter to hold his hand steady.

maun•der ['mɔːndə] *v.* to mumble disconnected phrases.

Maun•dy Thurs•day ['mɔːndɪ'θɜːzdɪ] *n.* Thursday before Easter Sunday.

mau•so•le•um [mɔːzə'lɪəm] *n.* important burial building.

mauve [məʊv] *adj. & n.* light pinkish-purple (color).

mav•er•ick ['mævərɪk] *n.* (a) animal which has not been branded and is running loose. (b) person who does not fit into the usual pattern.

maw [mɔː] *n.* (*of animal*) large mouth; stomach.

mawk•ish ['mɔːkɪʃ] *adj.* silly/falsely sentimental.

max•il•la [mæk'sɪlə] *n.* upper jawbone. **max•il•lar•y,** *adj.* referring to the upper jaw.

max•im ['mæksɪm] *n.* wise saying.

max•i•mum ['mæksɪməm] *adj. & n.* greatest possible (number/amount); **at m.** = at most. **max•i•mize** ['mæksɪmaɪz] *v.* to make as large as possible.

May [meɪ] *n.* 5th month of the year; **M. Day** = May 1st. **May•day,** *n.* international distress signal. **may•fly,** *n.* small fly which appears in summer. **May•pole,** *n.* tall pole around which people dance on the first of May.

may [meɪ] *v.* (**might**) (a) *used with other verbs to mean* it is possible; **you might have left it on the train** = perhaps you left it on the train. (b) *used with other verbs to mean* it is allowed. **may•be,** *adv.* perhaps; **maybe not** = possibly not.

may•hem ['meɪhem] *n.* wild confusion.

may•on•naise [meɪə'neɪz] *n.* cream sauce made with egg yolks and oil.

may•or ['meə] *n.* elected leader of a town. **may•or•ess** ['meəres] *n.* wife of a mayor; woman mayor.

maze [meɪz] *n.* network of puzzling paths in which you can get lost.

Mb megabyte.

me [miː] *pron. referring to the speaker.*

ME ['em'iː] *abbrev. for* myalgic encephalomyelitis; *see* **chronic fatigue syndrome**.

mead [miːd] *n.* alcoholic drink made from honey.

mead•ow ['medəʊ] *n.* large green field. **mead•ow•sweet,** *n.* common wild plant with many little white flowers.

mea•ger, *Brit.* **mea•gre** ['miːgə] *adj.* (a) scanty/few. (b) thin. **mea•ger•ness,** *n.* small amount.

meal [miːl] *n.* (a) food taken at a sitting. (b) coarse flour. **meal•time,** *n.* time when you usually eat. **meal•y,** *adj.* floury. **meal•y-mouthed,** *adj.* not straightforward; (person) who tries not to offend and so doesn't say what he thinks.

mean [miːn] 1. *n.* (a) middle; average; middle point between two extremes. (b) **means** = way/method of doing sth; **by no means** = not at all; **by all means** = certainly. (c) **means** = money/resources; **it's beyond my means** = it's too expensive for me. 2. *adj.* (-er, -est) (a) average/middle. (b) miserable/low; **m. trick** = unkind trick. (c) miserly. (d) *Sl.* very good. 3. *v.* (**meant** [ment]) (a) to intend; **he means well** = he has good intentions; **do you m. Richard?** = are you talking about Richard?; **you are meant to** = you are supposed to. (b) to signify/to show. **mean•ing.** 1. *n.* signification. 2. *adj.* significant. **mean•ing•ful,** *adj.* full of meaning/significant. **mean•ing•ful•ly,** *adv.* significantly. **mean•ing•less,** *adj.* not signifying anything. **mean•ly,** *adv.* poorly. **mean•ness,** *n.* miserliness; dislike of sharing things/of spending money. **mean•spir•it•ed,** *adj.* sly/unpleasant.

me•an•der [mɪ'ændə] 1. *n.* bend in a river. 2. *v.* to wind/to wander about. **me•an•der•ing,** *adj.* wandering/very winding (path).

meant [ment] *v. see* **me•an.**

mean•time ['miːntaɪm] 1. *n.* **in the m.** = between two events. 2. *adv.* during this time.

mean•while ['miːnwaɪl] *adv.* during this time.

mea•sles ['miːzlz] *n.* children's disease which gives you a red rash; **German m.** = mild disease which gives a red rash and which can affect an unborn child if caught by a pregnant woman. **mea•sly,** *adj. inf.* miserable/small.

meas•ure ['meʒə] 1. *n.* (a) quantity; size; **made to m.** = made specially to fit. (b) unit for showing the size/quantity of sth. (c) thing for showing the size/quantity of sth; small metal cup; long tape with inches/centimeters marked on it. (d) action; **as a precautionary m.** = as a precaution. (e) seam/layer of coal. (f) plan of a new law/a bill. (g) time (in music); rhythm (in poetry). 2. *v.* to be of a certain size/length/quantity, etc.; to find out the length/quantity of (sth). **meas•ur•a•ble,** *adj.* which can be measured. **meas•ured,**

æ back, aː farm, ɒ top, aɪ pipe, aʊ how, aɪə fire, aʊə flower, ɔː bought, ɔɪ toy, e fed, eə hair, eɪ take, ə afraid, əʊ boat, əʊə lower, vː word, iː heap, ɪ hit, ɪə hear, uː school, ʊ book, ʌ but, b back, d dog, ð then, dʒ just, f fog, g go, h hand, j yes, k catch, l last, m mix, n nut, ŋ sing, p penny, r round, s some, ʃ short, t too, tʃ chop, θ thing, v voice, w was, z zoo, ʒ treasure

adj. regular; **with m. steps** = in a slow and stately way. **meas•ure•less,** *adj.* so large that it cannot be measured. **meas•ure•ment,** *n.* (a) finding out the size/length/quantity of sth. (b) quantity/size, etc., found out when you measure. **measure up to,** *v.* to be able to do (a difficult job). **meas•ur•ing,** *n.* finding out the size/length/quantity of sth; **m. tape** = long tape with inches/centimeters marked on it; **m. cup** = cup with quantities marked on it by lines.

meat [miːt] *n.* flesh of an animal which is eaten. **meat•ball,** *n.* minced meat rolled into a ball and cooked. **meat•y,** *adj.* (a) with a lot of meat. (b) with a lot of details/information.

mec•ca ['mekə] *n.* place which attracts a large number of people.

me•chan•ic [mɪ'kænɪk] *n.* person who works on engines. **me•chan•i•cal,** *adj.* referring to a machine. **me•chan•i•cal•ly,** *adv.* by machine; like a machine; automatically. **me•chan•ics,** *n.* (a) the study of force and power. (b) the study of machines. (c) way in which sth works. **mech•an•ism** ['mekənɪzəm] *n.* (a) working parts (of a machine). (b) way in which sth works. **mech•a•ni•za•tion** [mekənaɪ'zeɪʃn] *n.* introduction of machines to take the place of manual labor. **mech•a•nize** ['mekənaɪz] *v.* to introduce machines in place of manual labor. **mech•a•nized,** *adj.* (soldiers/military unit) equipped with armored vehicles.

mech•a•tron•ics [mekə'tronɪks] *n.* combination of mechanics and electronics in manufacturing processes.

med•al ['medl] *n.* metal disk, usu. attached to a ribbon, made to commemorate an important occasion; **gold/silver/bronze m.** = medal for first/second/third place in competitions. **me•dal•lion** [mɪ'dæljən] *n.* large medal. **med•al•list** ['medəlɪst] *n.* person who has won a medal in a sports competition, etc.

med•dle ['medl] *v.* (**in/with**) to interfere; to get involved with. **med•dler,** *n.* person who likes to meddle. **med•dle•some,** *adj.* (person) who interferes. **med•dling.** 1. *n.* interfering. 2. *adj.* (person) who is always interfering.

me•di•a ['miːdɪə] *n. pl.* (a) means of communicating information; **the (mass) m.** = newspapers/TV/radio, etc. (b) *see also* **me•di•um.**

me•di•ae•val [medɪ'iːvl] *adj.* *see* **me•di•e•val.**

me•di•an ['miːdɪən] *adj. & n.* (point) which is in the middle/(line) which goes through the middle. **me•di•al,** *adj.* in the middle.

me•di•ate ['miːdɪeɪt] *v.* to intervene/to try to bring peace between two opponents.

me•di•a•tion [miːdɪ'eɪʃn] *n.* attempt to make two opponents agree. **me•di•a•tor,** *n.* person who tries to make two opponents agree.

med•i•cal ['medɪkl] 1. *adj.* referring to the study of disease; **the m. profession** = all doctors. 2. *n. inf.* examination of the body by a doctor. **med•ic,** *n. inf.* doctor. **med•i•cal•ly,** *adv.* in a medical way. **me•dic•a•ment,** *n.* (*formal*) medicine. **med•i•cate,** *v.* to add a medicine to (sth). **med•i•ca•tion,** *n.* drug.

med•i•cine ['medsɪn] *n.* (a) study of disease, ill health and their cure. (b) liquid/powder/pill taken to cure an illness; **m. ball** = large heavy ball used for physical exercises; **m. chest** = cupboard for keeping medicines in. **me•dic•i•nal** [me'dɪsɪnl] *adj.* used to treat an illness. **me•dic•i•nal•ly,** *adv.* (used) as a medicine. **med•i•cine man,** *n.* witch doctor.

me•di•e•val [medɪ'iːvl] *adj.* referring to the Middle Ages.

me•di•o•cre [miːdɪ'əʊkə] *adj.* ordinary/not good or bad. **me•di•oc•ri•ty** [miːdɪ'ɒkrɪtɪ] *n.* (a) not being good or bad/ordinariness. (b) very ordinary person with no special talents.

med•i•tate ['medɪteɪt] *v.* (**on/about**) to think deeply about (sth). **med•i•ta•tion** [medɪ'teɪʃn] *n.* long deep (often religious) thought. **med•i•ta•tive,** *adj.* thoughtful.

me•di•um ['miːdɪəm] 1. *adj.* middle/average. 2. *n.* (*pl.* **media/mediums**) (a) middle point; **happy m.** = compromise. (b) type of paint used by an artist. (c) means of doing sth/of communicating sth. (d) person who thinks the spirits of dead people can talk through him/her.

med•lar ['medlə] *n.* fruit like a brown apple; tree which bears this fruit.

med•ley ['medlɪ] *n.* mixture.

me•dul•la ['medjulə] *n.* bone marrow; the soft inner part of any organ.

meek [miːk] *adj.* (**-er, -est**) quiet/humble. **meek•ly,** *adv.* quietly/humbly. **meek•ness,** *n.* quietness/humility.

meer•schaum ['mɪəʃəm] *n.* white substance, used to make tobacco pipes.

meet [miːt] 1. *n.* gathering, as of huntsmen or swimmers/runners for a competition. 2. *v.* (**met**) (a) to come together. (b) to become acquainted with s.o.; **we have already met** = we know each other already. (c) to satisfy (needs). **meet•ing,** *n.* (a) coming together. (b) group of people who meet for a special purpose. **meet with,** *v.* (a) to find/to come up against; to have (an accident). (b) to have a meeting.

mega- ['megə] *prefix meaning* (a) very large. (b) one million.

meg•a•byte ['megəbaɪt] n. unit of storage for a computer, equal to 1,048,576 bytes.

meg•a•cy•cle ['megəsaɪkl], **meg•a•hertz** ['megəhɜːts] n. frequency of radio waves of one million cycles per second.

meg•a•lith ['megəlɪθ] n. huge stone set up by prehistoric people.

meg•a•lo•ma•ni•a [megələ'meɪnɪə] n. mad belief that you are more important/more powerful than you really are. **meg•a•lo•ma•ni•ac**, n. person suffering from megalomania.

meg•a•phone ['megəfəʊn] n. metal trumpet which makes the voice sound louder.

meg•a•ton ['megətʌn] n. force of an explosion equal to the force produced by exploding one million tons of TNT.

mei•o•sis [miː'əʊsɪs] n. splitting of cells.

mel•an•chol•y ['melənkəlɪ] 1. n. great sadness. 2. adj. very sad. **mel•an•cho•li•a**, [melən'kəʊlɪə] n. (formal) melancholy state. **mel•an•chol•ic** [melən'kɒlɪk] adj. very sad.

mel•a•nin ['melənɪn] n. pigment which colors the hair and skin. **mel•a•no•ma**, n. cancer caused by sunlight.

mel•lee ['meleɪ] n. crowd of struggling people.

mel•lif•lu•ous [me'lɪflʊəs] adj. soothing/pleasant (sound).

mel•low ['meləʊ] 1. adj. ripe (fruit); (wine) which has matured; soft/rich (voice); calm and relaxed (older person). 2. v. to grow ripe/to mature; to become soft/rich; **he has mellowed** = he is much less angry/unpleasant than he used to be. **mel•low•ness**, n. ripeness/maturity.

mel•o•dra•ma ['melədrɑːmə] n. extremely exciting but badly-written play which emphasizes violently alternating passions. **mel•o•dra•mat•ic** [melədrə'mætɪk] adj. arousing violent emotions. **me•lo•dra•mat•i•cal•ly**, adv. in a melodramatic way.

mel•o•dy ['melədɪ] n. tune. **me•lod•ic** [mɪ'lɒdɪk] adj. referring to tunes. **me•lo•di•ous** [mə'ləʊdɪəs] adj. tuneful. **me•lo•di•ous•ly**, adv. in a tuneful way.

mel•on ['melən] n. large round fruit of a creeping plant; **waterm.** = very large type of melon with red flesh and black seeds.

melt [melt] v. to change from solid to liquid by heating; **to m. down scrap metal** = to heat it and make it into blocks so that it can be used again; **my heart melted at the sight of the pup-**

pies = became softened/less angry. **melt•ing point**, n. temperature at which a solid becomes liquid. **melt•ing pot**, n. (a) pot in which metals can be melted. (b) place where people of different origins come to live together.

mem•ber ['membə] n. (a) person who belongs to a group, organization, etc. (b) limb on a human body. **mem•ber•ship**, n. (a) belonging to a group, organization, etc.; **m. card** = card which shows you belong (to a club/party). (b) all the members of a group, organization, etc.

mem•brane ['membreɪn] n. thin layer of tissue in the body.

me•men•to [mə'mentəʊ] n. (pl. -os, -oes) thing kept to remind you of sth; souvenir.

mem•o ['meməʊ] n. (pl. -os) note/short message between people working in the same organization; **m. pad** = pad of paper for writing short notes.

mem•oir ['memwɑː] n. usu. **memoirs** = written account of what you can remember of your life.

mem•o•ran•dum [memə'rændəm] n. (pl. -dums, -da) note/short message.

mem•o•ry ['memərɪ] n. (a) ability to remember; **he recited the poem from m.; if my m. serves me right** = if I can remember it correctly. (b) what you remember; **in m. of** = to remind us of. (c) capacity for storing information (in a computer). **mem•o•ra•ble**, adj. which you cannot forget/very striking. **me•mo•ri•al** [mɪ'mɔːrɪəl] 1. adj. which reminds you of sth/s.o.; **m. service** = church service to remember someone who has died. 2. n. monument to remind you of sth/s.o. **mem•o•rize**, v. to learn (sth) by heart.

men [men] n. pl. see **man**.

men•ace ['menəs] 1. n. threat; bad thing; **that child's a m.** = very naughty. 2. v. to threaten; **menacing clouds** = clouds which threaten to bring rain. **men•ac•ing•ly**, adv. in a threatening way.

mé•nage [me'nɑːʒ] n. household.

me•nag•er•ie [mɪ'nædʒərɪ] n. small zoo; collection of more or less wild animals.

mend [mend] 1. n. (a) place where a piece of clothing has been repaired. (b) inf. **on the m.** = getting better. 2. v. to repair; to be repaired. **mend•er**, n. person who mends.

æ back, ɑː farm, ɒ top, aɪ pipe, aʊ how, aɪə fire, aʊə flower, ɔː bought, ɔɪ toy, e fed, eəhair, eɪ take, ə afraid, əʊ boat, əʊə lower, ɜː word, iː heap, ɪ hit, ɪə hear, uː school, ʊ book, ʌ but, b back, d dog, ð then, dʒ just, f fog, g go, h hand, j yes, k catch, l last, m mix, n nut, ŋ sing, p penny, r round, s some, ʃ short, t too, tʃ chop, θ thing, v voice, w was, z zoo, ʒ treasure

mend•ing, *n.* (a) repairing. (b) clothes which need repairing.

men•dac•i•ty [men'dæsɪtɪ] *n.* (*formal*) telling lies. **men•da•cious** [men'deɪʃəs] *adj.* not truthful.

men•di•cant ['mendɪkənt] *adj.* (person) who begs.

men•folk ['menfəʊk] *n. pl.* all the men (in a family/group, etc.).

men•hir ['menhɪə] *n.* tall standing stone, erected by prehistoric people.

me•ni•al ['miːnɪəl] *adj.* low; badly paid.

Mé•nière's dis•ease ['meɪnɪeəzdɪ'siːz] *n.* disease of the middle ear, causing dizziness.

men•in•gi•tis [menɪn'dʒaɪtɪs] *n.* inflammation of the membrane covering the brain.

me•nis•cus [me'nɪskəs] *n.* curved surface of a drop of water.

men•o•pause ['menəpɔːz] *n.* period of life (around the age of 50) when women become no longer capable of bearing children; **male m.** = difficult period in a man's life (around the age of 50).

men•stru•ate ['menstruːeɪt] *v.* (*of women*) to lose blood through the vagina at regular periods. **men•stru•al,** *adj.* referring to the regular monthly loss of blood through the vagina. **men•stru•a•tion** [menstruː'eɪʃn] *n.* monthly loss of blood through the vagina.

men•su•ra•tion [mensjʊə'reɪʃn] *n.* study of measurement.

men's wear, menswear ['menzweə] *n.* (*no pl.*) clothes for men.

men•tal ['mentl] *adj.* referring to the mind; **m. arithmetic** = calculations done in the head; **m. age** = way of showing the development of a person's mind, by expressing it as the age at which such development is normal; **m. hospital** = hospital for those who suffer from illnesses of the mind. **men•tal•i•ty** [men'tælɪtɪ] *n.* (a) mental power. (b) way of thinking which is typical of s.o./of a group. **men•tal•ly,** *adv.* concerning the brain; **m. defective** = well below normal intelligence.

men•thol ['menθɒl] *n.* white substance which tastes strongly of mint. **men•tho•lat•ed,** *adj.* treated with menthol; with menthol added.

men•tion ['menʃn] 1. *n.* reference to sth. 2. *v.* to refer to (sth); **not to m.** = not forgetting/as well as.

men•tor ['mentɔː] *n.* (*formal*) person who teaches/helps another (younger) person.

men•u ['menjuː] *n.* (a) list of food available in a restaurant. (b) list of options available on a computer program.

me•ow, miaow [miː'aʊ] 1. *n.* call of a cat. 2. *v.* to call like a cat.

mer•can•tile ['mɜːkəntaɪl] *adj.* referring to commerce.

mer•ce•nar•y ['mɜːsənərɪ] 1. *adj.* (person) who is interested only in money. 2. *n.* person who serves foreigners as a soldier for money.

mer•cer•ize ['mɜːsəraɪz] *v.* to make (cotton cloth) shiny.

mer•chant ['mɜːtʃənt] *n.* businessman; person who buys and sells; **m. marine** = commercial ships of a country; **m. seaman** = seaman in the merchant marine. **mer•chan•dise,** 1. *n.* goods for sale. 2. *v.* to sell (goods) by wide and varied advertising. **mer•chant•man, merchant ship,** *n.* (*pl.* -men) commercial ship.

mer•cu•ry ['mɜːkjərɪ] *n.* (*element:* Hg) liquid metal used in thermometers/barometers, etc. **mer•cu•ri•al** [mɜː'kjʊərɪəl] *adj.* (person) whose temper changes frequently.

mer•cy ['mɜːsɪ] *n.* (a) compassion/pity; kindness toward unfortunate people; **to have m. on** = to forgive/not to want to punish/harm s.o.; **m. killing** = euthanasia, killing of s.o. who is very ill or in pain; (b) sth to be grateful for. **mer•ci•ful,** *adj.* (person) who forgives/who is kind. **mer•ci•ful•ly,** *adv.* thankfully; in a forgiving/kindly way. **mer•ci•less,** *adj.* harsh/cruel. **mer•ci•less•ly,** *adv.* without mercy. **mer•ci•less•ness,** *n.* lack of pity; hardness (of character).

mere ['mɪə] 1. *n.* (*old*) small lake. 2. *adj.* simply/only; **he's a m. boy** = only a boy; **the m. sight of grass makes me sneeze** = simply the sight of grass makes me sneeze. **mere•ly,** *adv.* only/simply.

mer•e•tri•cious [merɪ'trɪʃəs] *adj.* showy and cheap.

mer•gan•ser [mɜː'gænzə] *n.* type of large duck, with a crest.

merge [mɜːdʒ] *v.* to join together (**with sth**). **merg•er,** *n.* amalgamation/joining of two companies.

me•rid•i•an [mə'rɪdɪən] *n.* imaginary line drawn from the North Pole to the South Pole; **the Greenwich m.** = line passing through Greenwich, England, from which longitude is calculated.

me•ringue [mə'ræŋ] *n.* sweet baked dessert made of egg whites and sugar.

me•ri•no [mə'riːnəʊ] *n.* (*pl.* -os) type of long-haired sheep/fine woolen material.

mer•it ['merɪt] 1. *n.* value/quality/excellence; **to go into the merits of** = to examine the good and bad points of. 2. *v.* to be worthy of/to deserve (sth). **mer•i•to•ri•ous** [merɪ'tɔːrɪəs] *adj.* (*formal*) which is valuable/which should be rewarded.

mer•maid ['mɜːmeɪd] *n.* mythical creature,

half woman and half fish. **mer•man,** *n.* mythical creature, half man and half fish.

mer•ry ['merɪ] *adj.* (**-ier, -iest**) happy; **to make m.** = to have a good time; **the more the merrier** = the more there are the happier everything is. **mer•ri•ly,** *adv.* happily. **mer•ri•ment,** *n.* fun. **mer•ry-go-round,** *n.* platform that revolves, with wooden horses, etc., in an amusement park, etc. **mer•ry•mak•er,** *n.* person who is enjoying himself. **mer•ry•mak•ing,** *n.* festivity/celebration.

mesh [meʃ] 1. *n.* (*pl.* **-es**) space between the threads of a net. 2. *v.* (*of a cogwheel*) to link together with another toothed wheel.

mes•mer•ize ['mezməraɪz] *v.* to hypnotize.

mess [mes] 1. *n.* (*pl.* **-es**) (a) dirt; disorder/confusion; **they made a m. of the repair job** = they did the repair job badly. (b) group of soldiers/sailors, etc. who eat together; room where officers eat and sleep. 2. *v.* (**with**) to eat together. **mess a•bout,** *v.* (a) to spend your spare time doing sth. (b) to waste time. **mess•i•ly,** *adv.* in a messy way. **mess up,** *v. inf.* (a) to dirty. (b) to ruin/to spoil. **mess•y,** *adj.* (**-ier, -iest**) dirty; disorderly.

mes•sage ['mesɪdʒ] *n.* news/information sent; *inf.* **he got the m.** = he understood. **mes•sen•ger,** *n.* person who brings a message.

mes•si•ah [mɪ'saɪə] *n.* (a) person whom the Jews expect will come to free them. (b) Jesus Christ. **mes•si•an•ic** [mesɪ'ænɪk] *adj.* referring to the Messiah.

Messrs. ['mesəz] *n. used formally as plural of* Mr.

met [met] *v. see* **meet.**

meta- ['metə] *prefix meaning* change.

me•tab•o•lism [me'tæbəlɪzəm] *n.* processes by which plants and animals use food to create energy. **met•a•bol•ic** [metə'bɒlɪk] *adj.* referring to metabolism.

met•a•car•pus ['metə'kɑːpəs] *n.* the bones in the hand.

met•al ['metl] *n.* usu. solid mineral substance which can conduct heat and electricity. **me•tal•lic** [mə'tælɪk] *adj.* referring to metal. **met•al•lur•gist** [me'tælədʒɪst] *n.* person who studies metals. **met•al•lur•gy** [me'tælədʒɪ] *n.* study of metals. **met•al•work,** *n.* making things with metal; pieces of metal made into a construction/a work of art.

met•a•mor•pho•sis [metə'mɔːfəsɪs] *n.* (*pl.* **-phoses** [-fəsiːz]) change, esp. an insect's

change of form. **met•a•mor•phose** [metə'mɔːfəʊz] *v.* to change from one state to another.

met•a•phor ['metəfə] *n.* way of describing sth by suggesting it has the properties of sth else. **met•a•phor•i•cal** [metə'fɒrɪkl] *adj.* like a metaphor. **met•a•phor•i•cal•ly,** *adv.* in a metaphorical way.

met•a•phys•ics [metə'fɪzɪks] *n.* philosophical study of truth/knowledge/existence, etc. **met•a•phys•i•cal,** *adj.* referring to metaphysics.

met•a•tar•sus [metə'tɑːsəs] *n.* the bones in the foot.

me•tath•e•sis [me'tæθəsɪs] *n.* change of sounds in a word, where letters are transposed.

mete out ['miːt'aʊt] *v.* to give (punishment).

me•te•or ['miːtɪə] *n.* small object which flashes through space and shines brightly as it burns up on entering the earth's atmosphere. **me•te•or•ic** [miːtɪ'ɒrɪk] *adj.* like a meteor/very rapid. **me•te•or•ite** ['miːtɪəraɪt] *n.* lump of rock/iron which falls to earth from space.

me•te•or•ol•o•gy [miːtɪə'rɒlədʒɪ] *n.* study of climate and weather. **me•te•or•o•log•i•cal** [miːtɪərə'lɒdʒɪkl] *adj.* referring to the climate and weather; **m. station** = research station which notes weather conditions. **me•te•or•ol•o•gist** [miːtɪə'rɒlədʒɪst] *n.* person who studies climate and weather.

me•ter, *Brit.* **me•tre** ['miːtə] 1. *n.* (a) device for counting how much time/water/gas, etc., has been used; **parking m.** = device into which you put money to pay for parking. (b) standard measurement of length (approximately 39.4 inches). (c) regular rhythm in poetry. 2. *v.* to count by a meter. **met•ric** ['metrɪk] *adj.* (a) referring to meter as a measurement; **the m. system** = system of measurement based on meters, liters, etc. (b) referring to meter as rhythm. **met•ri•cal,** *adj.* (poem) written in a regular rhythm. **met•ri•cate** ['metrɪkeɪt] *v.* to express in meters/centimeters, etc. **met•ri•ca•tion** [metrɪ'keɪʃn] *n.* changing of a measuring system to the metric system.

meth•ane ['miːθeɪn] *n.* colorless gas, which easily catches fire and is found naturally in the ground.

meth•a•nol ['meθənɒl] *n.* methyl alcohol.

meth•od ['meθəd] *n.* (a) way of doing sth. (b)

æ back, ɑ: farm, ɒ: top, aɪ pipe, aʊ how, aɪe fire, aʊə flower, ɔ: bought, ɔɪ toy, e fed, eəhair, eɪ take, ə afraid, əʊ boat, əʊə lower, v: word, i: heap, ɪ hit, ɪə hear, u: school, ʊ book, ʌ but, b back, d dog, ð then, dʒ just, f fog, g go, h hand, j yes, k catch, l last, m mix, n nut, ŋ sing, p penny, r round, s some, ʃ short, t too, tʃ chop, θ thing, v voice, w was, z zoo, ʒ treasure

well-organized system. **me•thod•i•cal** [mɪˈθɒdɪkl] *adj.* ordered/regulated. **me•thod•i•cal•ly,** *adv.* in a well-organized way. **Meth•od•ist,** *n. & adj.* (person) following the teaching of John Wesley. **meth•od•ol•o•gy,** *n.* methods used in a certain process or study.

meth•yl [meθɪl] *n.* **m. alcohol** = poisonous alcohol found in wood. **meth•yl•at•ed spir•its** [ˈmeθɪleɪtɪdˈspɪrɪts] *n.* alcohol used for lighting or heating.

me•tic•u•lous [meˈtɪkjuləs] *adj.* attentive to detail (**about** doing sth). **me•tic•u•lous•ly,** *adv.* carefully/paying attention to details. **me•tic•u•lous•ness,** *n.* being meticulous.

me•tier [ˈmetɪeɪ] *n.* profession; occupation one is good at.

me•tre [ˈmiːtə] *n. & v. Brit. see* **me•ter.**

met•ro•nome [ˈmetrənəum] *n.* device which beats time regularly, used when practicing/playing music.

me•trop•o•lis [məˈtrɒpəlɪs] *n.* (*pl.* **-es**) large capital city. **met•ro•pol•i•tan** [metrəˈpɒlɪtən] 1. *adj.* referring to a large capital city. 2. *n.* chief bishop in the Orthodox Church.

met•tle [ˈmetl] *n.* vigor/strength of character (of a person); **to put s.o. on his m.** = to make s.o. try to do his best. **met•tle•some,** *adj.* (*formal*) vigorous/active.

mew [mjuː] 1. *n.* soft cry which a cat makes. 2. *v.* to make a soft cry like a cat.

mews [mjuːz] *n.* (*esp. Brit.*) (a) row of former stables or garages converted into houses. (b) stables.

Mex•i•can [ˈmeksɪkən] 1. *adj.* referring to Mexico. 2. *n.* person from Mexico.

mez•za•nine [ˈmetsəniːn] *n.* floor between the ground floor and the first floor.

mez•zo-so•pran•o [ˈmetsəusəˈprɑːnəu] *n.* singer or voice lower in pitch than a soprano.

mez•zo•tint [ˈmedzəutɪnt] *n.* print made from a plate which has rough and smooth areas.

Mg *symbol for* magnesium.

mg *abbrev. for* milligram.

mi•aow [miːˈau] *see* **me•ow.**

mi•as•ma [mɪˈæzmə] *n.* unpleasant/poisonous air.

mi•ca [ˈmaɪkə] *n.* type of mineral which splits into thin glittering layers.

mice [maɪs] *n. pl. see* **mouse.**

Mich•ael•mas [ˈmɪkəlməs] *n.* (*esp. Brit.*) 29th September; **M. daisy** = common autumn garden flower.

micro- [ˈmaɪkrəu] 1. *prefix meaning* (a) very small. (b) one millionth. 2. *n.* microcomputer.

mi•crobe [ˈmaɪkrəub] *n.* germ; tiny living organism.

mi•cro•chip [ˈmaɪkrəutʃɪp] *n.* small piece of silicon used in electronics.

mi•cro•com•pu•ter [maɪkrəukʌmˈpjuːtə] *n.* small computer for office or personal use.

mi•cro•cli•mate [ˈmaɪkrəuˈklaɪmət] *n.* climate of a small area.

mi•cro•cosm [ˈmaɪkrəkɒzəm] *n.* miniature version.

mi•cro•fiche [ˈmaɪkrəfiːʃ] *n.* index card made of microfilms.

mi•cro•film [ˈmaɪkrəfɪlm] 1. *n.* film on which sth is photographed in very small scale. 2. *v.* to make a very small-scale photograph of.

mi•cro•me•ter [maɪˈkrɒmɪtə] *n.* instrument for measuring very small distances.

mi•cron [ˈmaɪkrɒn] *n.* one millionth of a meter.

mi•cro•or•gan•ism [maɪkrəuˈɒgənɪzm] *n.* tiny living organism.

mi•cro•phone [ˈmaɪkrəfəun] *n.* apparatus for capturing sound and passing it to a loudspeaker or recording apparatus.

mi•cro•proc•es•sor [maɪkrəuˈprəusesə] *n.* small central processing unit using microchips.

mi•cro•scope [ˈmaɪkrəskəup] *n.* apparatus which enlarges things which are very small. **mi•cro•scop•ic** [maɪkrəˈskɒpɪk] *adj.* so small as to be visible only through a microscope.

mi•cro•wave [ˈmaɪkrəweɪv] *n.* very short electric wave; **m. oven** = small oven which cooks very rapidly using microwaves.

mid- [mɪd] *prefix meaning* middle. **mid•day,** *n.* twelve o'clock noon. **mid•land,** *adj. & n.* (referring to the) central part of a country; **the Midlands** = the central part of England. **mid•night,** *n.* twelve o'clock at night. **mid•riff,** *n.* front part of the body above the waist and below the chest. **mid•ship•man,** *n.* (*pl.* **-men**) student trainee officer in the U.S. Navy. **midst,** *n.* middle; **in our m.** = among us. **mid•stream,** *n.* middle part of a river. **mid•sum•mer,** *n.* middle of the summer. **mid•way,** *adv.* half-way. **Mid•west,** *n.* central northern part of the United States. **mid•win•ter,** *n.* middle of the winter.

mid•den [ˈmɪdn] *n.* heap of dung.

mid•dle [ˈmɪdl] 1. *adj.* in the center; half-way between two things; **m. sized** = neither big nor small; **m. class** = professional class (between the upper class and the lower class); **the M. Ages** = historical period between the Dark Ages and the Renaissance (about 1000 to 1500). 2. *n.* (a) center; central point. (b) waistline. **mid•dle-aged,** *adj.* not young and not old (between 40 and 60 years of age). **Mid•dle East,** *n.* area between Egypt and

Pakistan. **Mid•dle East•ern,** *adj.* referring to the Middle East. **mid•dle•man,** *n.* (*pl.* -men) businessman who buys from one source to sell to another. **mid•dle-of-the-road,** *adj.* center/moderate (politics). **mid•dle•weight,** *n.* weight in boxing between welterweight and light heavyweight. **mid•dling,** *adj.* neither good nor bad; not very large or small.

midge [mɪdʒ] *n.* small stinging flying insect.

mid•get ['mɪdʒɪt] *n.* very small person or thing.

mid•wife ['mɪdwaɪf] *n.* (*pl.* -wives ['-waɪvz]) person (usu. a woman) trained to help deliver a baby. **mid•wife•ry** ['mɪdwɪfrɪ] *n.* work of helping deliver babies.

mien [miːn] *n.* way in which a person behaves or looks.

miff [mɪf] *v. inf.* to offend/to annoy (s.o.).

might [maɪt] 1. *v. see* **may.** 2. *n.* force/strength. **might•y.** 1. *adj.* (-ier, -iest) (a) strong. (b) great; *inf.* **you're in a m. hurry** = you are very impatient. 2. *adv. inf.* very. **might•i•ly,** *adv.* greatly.

mi•gnon•ette [mɪnjə'net] *n.* scented garden plant.

mi•graine ['miːgreɪn] *n.* recurrent very bad headache.

mi•grate [maɪ'greɪt] *v.* to move from one place to another with the seasons. **mi•grant** ['maɪgrənt] *adj. & n.* (bird) which moves from one place to another with the seasons; (worker) who moves from one job to another or from one country to another. **mi•gra•tion** [maɪ'greɪʃn] *n.* movement of birds from one country to another. **mi•gra•to•ry** ['maɪgrətərɪ] *adj.* referring to migration.

mike [maɪk] *n. inf.* microphone.

milch [mɪltʃ] *adj.* **m. cow** = cow kept for milk.

mild [maɪld] *adj.* (-er, -est) (a) soft/not severe (punishment). (b) not harsh (weather). (c) not strong/powerful. **mild•ly,** *adj.* softly/kindly; **to put it m.** = not to say anything rude. **mild•ness,** *n.* kindness/softness; warmness (of winter weather).

mil•dew ['mɪldjuː] 1. *n.* powdery fungus on plants/paper/leather, etc. 2. *v.* to become covered with mildew. **mil•dewed,** *adj.* covered with mildew.

mile [maɪl] *n.* measure of length (1,760 yards/1.61 kilometers); *inf.* **miles of string** = very long piece of string; **it's miles too big** =

much too big. **mile•age,** *n.* (a) distance traveled in miles; **car with a low m.** = car which has not traveled as much as is normal. (b) *inf.* **to get a lot of m. out of** = to gain benefit from. **mil•er,** *n.* person who runs in a 1 mile race. **mile•stone,** *n.* stone showing distance in miles; important point (history, etc.).

mi•lieu ['miːljɜː] *n.* surroundings/environment.

mil•i•tant ['mɪlɪtənt] *adj. & n.* (person) who supports a policy of violence; (person) who is very active in supporting a cause/a political party. **mil•i•tan•cy,** *n.* activity/vigor (in supporting a political party/a cause).

mil•i•tar•y ['mɪlɪtrɪ] 1. *adj.* referring to the army or armed forces. 2. *n.* **the m.** = the armed forces. **mil•i•ta•rism,** *n.* belief in the use of the military to solve political problems. **mil•i•ta•rist,** *n.* person who believes in militarism. **mil•i•ta•ris•tic,** *adj.* believing that the military should be used to solve political problems. **mil•i•tate,** *v.* to work actively (against). **mi•li•tia** [mɪ'lɪʃə] *n.* emergency military force made of ordinary citizens rather than professional soldiers.

milk [mɪlk] 1. *n.* white liquid produced by female mammals for feeding their young, esp. the milk produced by cows; **m. shake** = milk mixed with flavoring and ice cream; **m. choco-late** = pale brown chocolate (flavored with milk); **m. teeth** = first set of teeth produced by a child. 2. *v.* (a) to take the milk from (an animal). (b) to get all the money from (s.o.). **milk•er,** *n.* (a) person who milks. (b) **good m.** = cow which produces a lot of milk. **milk•ing,** *n.* taking milk from a cow; **m. ma-chine** = machine which milks cows automatically. **milk•man,** *n.* (*pl.* -men) person who delivers the milk to houses each morning. **milk•y,** *adj.* (-ier, -iest) tasting like milk; cloudy like milk; containing milk; **the M. Way** = luminous band in the night sky composed of many stars.

mill [mɪl] 1. *n.* (a) machine for grinding corn into flour; building which contains such a machine; *inf.* **he's been through the m.** = he has suffered a great deal. (b) small instrument for grinding. (c) large factory. 2. *v.* (a) to grind (corn, etc.). (b) to put vertical lines around the edge of a coin. **mill a•bout, mill around,** *v.* to move in various directions. **mill•er,** *n.* man who runs a flour mill. **mill•pond,** *n.* water dammed to provide power for a watermill. **mill•stone,** *n.* (a) large grooved stone used

---

æ back, ɑː farm, ɒ top, aɪ pipe, aʊ how, aɪə fire, aʊə flower, ɔː bought, ɔɪ toy, e fed, eəhair, eɪ take, ə afraid, əʊ boat, əʊə lower, ɜː word, iː heap, ɪ hit, ɪə hear, uː school, ʊ book, ʌ but, b back, d dog, ð then, dʒ just, f fog, g go, h hand, j yes, k catch, l last, m mix, n nut, ŋ sing, p penny, r round, s some, ʃ short, t too, tʃ chop, θ thing, v voice, w was, z zoo, ʒ treasure

to grind corn, etc. (b) great obstacle which causes trouble.

mil•len•ni•um [mɪˈlenɪəm] n. (pl. -ia) (a) period of a thousand years; m. bug = problems with computer software/hardware caused by the change in date to the year 2000. (b) period of great happiness.

mil•le•pede [ˈmɪlɪpiːd] n. millipede.

mil•let [ˈmɪlɪt] n. grain used for food.

milli- [ˈmɪlɪ] prefix meaning one thousandth.

mil•li•bar [ˈmɪlɪbɑ:] n. unit of atmospheric pressure.

mil•li•gram [ˈmɪlɪɡræm] n. one thousandth of a gram.

mil•li•me•ter [ˈmɪlɪmiːtə], Brit. mil•li•me•tre n. one thousandth of a meter.

mil•li•ner [ˈmɪlɪnə] n. person who makes/sells women's hats. mil•li•ner•y, n. hats and ribbons.

mil•lion [ˈmɪljən] number 1,000,000. mil•lion•aire [mɪljəˈneə] n. person who has more than a million dollars. mil•lionth, 1,000,000th, 1. adj. referring to a million. 2. n. one of a million parts.

mil•li•pede [ˈmɪlɪpiːd] n. small creeping animal with a large number of legs.

milt [mɪlt] n. sperm from a male fish.

mime [maɪm] 1. n. (a) actor who does not speak, but conveys a story/emotions through gesture. (b) gesture used to convey a story/emotions. (c) story conveyed by gestures. 2. v. to convey a story/emotions through gesture.

mim•ic [ˈmɪmɪk] 1. n. person who imitates. 2. v. (mimicked) to imitate. mim•ic•ry, n. imitation.

mi•mo•sa [mɪˈməʊzə] n. semi-tropical tree with yellow, scented flowers.

min•a•ret [mɪnəˈret] n. tower attached to a mosque.

mince [mɪns] 1. n. meat which has been ground up into very small pieces. 2. v. (a) to grind up (meat/vegetables) until they are in very small pieces; he didn't m. his words = he said what he had to say in a straightforward way. (b) to m. along = to walk along in a very affected manner, taking small steps. mince•meat, n. mixture of apples, spices, dried fruit, etc.; to make m. out of = to defeat/destroy completely. mince pie, n. small pie filled with mincemeat, often eaten at Christmas. minc•er, n. machine for grinding up meat, etc. minc•ing, adj. (a) affected (way of walking). (b) m. machine = mincer.

mind [maɪnd] 1. n. power of thinking; memory; keep him in m. = remember him; to make up your m. = to decide what to do; I'm in two minds about going = I can't decide whether to go or not; I've a good m. to do it myself = I would very much like to do it myself; he's changed his m. twice already = he has changed his decision/his point of view; what do you have in m.? = what are you thinking of? state of m. = general opinion/mood/feeling; he's got sth on his m. = he is worried about sth; try to take her m. off the subject = try to stop her thinking about the subject; not in his right m. = mad. 2. v. (a) to be careful about. (b) to bother about/to be busy about; m. your own business = don't interfere in my affairs; never m. = don't bother/don't worry. (c) to object to/to be annoyed by; would you m. shutting the door? = please shut the door; I wouldn't m. a cup of tea = I would rather like a cup of tea. (d) to look after (sth) while the owner is away. mind-bog•gling, adj. inf. very surprising. mind•ed, adj. interested (in doing sth); commercially m. = businesslike. mind•ful, adj. remembering/thinking of sth. mind•less, adj. without thinking/stupid. mind read•er, n. person who seems to be able to guess what s.o. else is thinking.

mine [maɪn] 1. n. (a) deep hole in the ground for digging out minerals; he is a m. of information = he is full of information. (b) explosive device which is planted underground or underwater. 2. v. (a) to excavate/to dig for minerals. (b) to plant mines underground or under water. 3. pron. belonging to me; he's a friend of m. = one of my friends. mine•field, n. area of land/sea full of mines. mine•lay•er, n. ship which specializes in planting mines under water. min•er, n. person who works in a mine; m.'s lamp = special lamp worn by a miner on his helmet. mine•sweep•er, n. ship which specializes in removing mines placed under water by the enemy. mine•work•er, n. worker in a mine. min•ing, n. (a) action of extracting minerals. (b) placing mines underground or under water.

min•er•al [ˈmɪnrəl] adj. & n. (non-living substance) which is extracted from the earth; m. water = (i) water from a spring; (ii) non-alcoholic fizzy drink; m. rights = permission to dig out minerals. min•er•al•o•gist [mɪnəˈrælədʒɪst] n. scientist who studies minerals. min•er•al•o•gy, n. study of minerals.

min•e•stro•ne [mɪnɪˈstrəʊnɪ] n. type of vegetable soup.

min•gle [ˈmɪŋɡl] v. to mix.

min•gy [ˈmɪndʒɪ] adj. inf. mean/not generous (with money, etc.).

min•i [ˈmɪnɪ] 1. n. miniskirt. 2. adj. & prefix. very small. min•i•bus, n. small bus holding about twelve people. min•i•com [ˈmɪnɪkɒm] *n.* machine enabling deaf people to send and receive typed messages by telephone. **min•i•com•put•er,** *n.* small computer, but larger than a micro. **min•i•mar•ket,** *n.* small self-service store. **min•i•skirt,** *n.* very short skirt.

min•i•a•ture ['mɪnɪtʃə] 1. *n.* very small model/portrait/painting. 2. *adj.* very small. **min•i•a•tur•ize,** *v.* to produce a very small version of (sth).

min•im ['mɪnɪm] *n.* note in music lasting half as long as a semibreve.

min•i•mum ['mɪnɪməm] *adj. & n. (pl.* **-mums,** **-ma)** smallest possible (quantity). **min•i•mal,** *adj.* smallest possible. **min•i•mize,** *v.* to reduce to the smallest amount; to make (sth) seem very small.

min•ion ['mɪnjən] *n.* low-grade assistant (who flatters his boss).

min•is•ter ['mɪnɪstə] 1. *n.* (a) member of a government in charge of a department. (b) Protestant members of the clergy. 2. *v.* **to m. to s.o.'s needs** = to look after s.o./to take care of s.o. **min•is•te•ri•al** [mɪnɪ'stɪərɪəl] *adj.* referring to a government minister. **min•is•tra•tion** [mɪnɪ'streɪʃn] *n.* care/aid, as given by a priest. **min•is•try,** *n.* (a) government department; offices of a government department. (b) work of a member of the clergy.

mink [mɪŋk] *n.* (a) small animal whose fur is very valuable; **m. farm** = farm where these animals are reared. (b) *inf.* mink coat.

min•now ['mɪnəʊ] *n.* small freshwater fish.

mi•nor ['maɪnə] 1. *adj.* (a) lesser; less important; **Asia M.** = Turkey. (b) (musical key) where there are semitones between the second and third, and between the fifth and sixth notes. 2. *n.* young person under the legal age, usu. 18. **mi•nor•i•ty** [maɪ'nɒrɪtɪ] *n.* (a) number/quantity less than half of a total; **the men are in the m.** = there are more women than men. (b) period when a person is less than the legal age, usu. 18 years old.

min•strel ['mɪnstrəl] *n. (old)* traveling singer or musician. (b) one of a group of performers made up to look like black people.

mint [mɪnt] 1. *n.* (a) factory where coins are made; **in m. condition** = perfect/exactly as when it was made; *inf.* **a m. (of money)** = a great deal of money. (b) common herb used as flavoring. (c) small white candy tasting of peppermint. 2. *v.* to make coins.

min•u•et [mɪnju'et] *n.* slow stately dance.

mi•nus ['maɪnəs] 1. *prep.* less; *inf.* **he came m. his wife** = without his wife. 2. *n.* sign (–) meaning less; **m. 10 degrees (–10°).**

mi•nus•cule ['mɪnəskjuːl] *adj.* very small.

mi•nute¹ ['mɪnɪt] *n.* (a) one sixtieth part of an hour or of a degree in an angle; **ten minutes past three** = 3:10; **five minutes to four** = 3:55; **m. hand** = long hand on watch or clock; **m. steak** = thin slice of beef which can be cooked quickly. (b) very short space of time; **he'll be here any m. now** = any time now. (c) **minutes** = notes of what is said at a meeting. **min•ut•ed,** *adj.* put in the minutes of a meeting.

mi•nute² [maɪ'njuːt] *adj.* very small. **mi•nute•ly** [maɪ'njuːtlɪ] *adv.* in great detail. **mi•nute•ness** [maɪ'njuːtnəs] *n.* very small size. **mi•nu•ti•ae** [mɪ'njuːʃɪiː] *n. pl.* very small details.

minx [mɪŋks] *n.* naughty girl.

mir•a•cle ['mɪrəkl] *n.* marvelous thing which happens apparently by the power of God; very wonderful happening. **mi•rac•u•lous** [mɪ'rækjʊləs] *adj.* wonderful/inexplicable. **mi•rac•u•lous•ly,** *adv.* wonderfully/inexplicably.

mi•rage ['mɪrɑːʒ] *n.* imaginary image caused by heat (such as water and palm trees seen in a desert).

mire ['maɪə] *n. (formal)* muddy place; mud.

mir•ror ['mɪrə] 1. *n.* glass backed by metal which reflects an image; **rear-view m.** = mirror inside a car which enables the driver to see what is behind without turning his head; **m. image** = exact copy, but reversed as in a mirror. 2. *v.* to reflect as in a mirror.

mirth [mɜːθ] *n. (formal)* gaiety/happiness.

mis- [mɪs] *prefix meaning* wrongly.

mis•ad•ven•ture [mɪsəd'ventʃə] *n.* unlucky accident.

mis•an•thrope, misanthropist ['mɪzənθrəʊp, mɪ'zænθrəpɪst] *n.* person who dislikes the human race. **mis•an•throp•ic** [mɪzən'θrɒpɪk] *adj.* (person) who dislikes the human race. **mis•an•thro•py** [mɪ'zænθrəpɪ] *n.* dislike of the human race.

mis•ap•ply [mɪsə'plaɪ] *v.* to use (sth) wrongly.

mis•ap•pre•hend [mɪsæprɪ'hend] *v.* not to understand. **mis•ap•pre•hen•sion** [mɪsæprɪ'henʃən] *n.* not understanding; **laboring under a m.** = not understanding the situation correctly.

mis•ap•pro•pri•ate [mɪsə'prəʊprɪeɪt] *v.* to

æ back, ɑː farm, ɒ top, aɪ pipe, aʊ how, aɪə fire, aʊə flower, ɔː bought, ɔɪ toy, e fed, eəhair, eɪ take, ə afraid, əʊ boat, əʊə lower, vː word, iː heap, ɪ hit, ɪə hear, uː school, ʊ book, ʌ but, b back, d dog, ð then, dʒ just, f fog, g go, h hand, j yes, k catch, l last, m mix, n nut, ŋ sing, p penny, r round, s some, ʃ short, t too, tʃ chop, θ thing, v voice, w was, z zoo, ʒ treasure

use (public money) for your own purposes. **mis•ap•pro•pri•a•tion** [mɪsəprəʊprɪ'eɪʃn] *n.* using public money for your own purposes.

mis•be•have [mɪsbɪ'heɪv] *v.* to act badly/to behave badly. **mis•be•hav•ior,** *n.* bad behavior.

mis•cal•cu•late [mɪs'kælkjʊleɪt] *v.* to calculate wrongly. **mis•cal•cu•la•tion** [mɪskælkjʊ'leɪʃn] *n.* mistake in calculating.

mis•car•ry [mɪs'kærɪ] *v.* (a) (*of plan*) to go wrong. (b) to produce a baby which is not sufficiently developed to live. **mis•car•riage** ['mɪskærɪdʒ] *n.* (a) failure (of a scheme); **m. of justice** = wrong decision by a court. (b) loss of a baby during pregnancy.

mis•cast [mɪs'kɑːst] *v.* (**miscast**) to cast (an actor/actress) in a part which is unsuitable.

mis•cel•la•ne•ous [mɪsə'leɪnɪəs] *adj.* varied/mixed. **mis•cel•la•ny** [mɪ'selənɪ] *n.* collection of varied things (usu. varied pieces of writing).

mis•chance ['mɪs'tʃɑːns] *n.* (*formal*) bad luck.

mis•chief ['mɪstʃɪf] *n.* bad behavior/bad action; **they mean m.** = they are intending to do damage; **to make m.** = to make trouble/to make two people angry with each other; **the boy is always getting into m.** = he's always doing something naughty. **mis•chief-mak•er,** *n.* person who tries to start trouble. **mis•chie•vous** ['mɪstʃɪvəs] *adj.* wicked/naughty. **mis•chie•vous•ly,** *adv.* in a mischevous way. **mis•chie•vous•ness,** *n.* tendency to cause trouble.

mis•con•cep•tion [mɪskən'sepʃən] *n.* mistaken idea.

mis•con•duct [mɪs'kɒndʌkt] *n.* bad conduct/bad behavior; **professional m.** = behavior which is not acceptable in a member of a profession.

mis•con•strue [mɪskən'struː] *v.* not to understand. **mis•con•struc•tion** [mɪskən'strʌkʃn] *n.* wrong interpretation of an action.

mis•count [mɪs'kaʊnt] *v.* to count wrongly.

mis•cre•ant ['mɪskrɪənt] *n.* wicked person/criminal.

mis•deed [mɪs'diːd] *n.* wicked action.

mis•de•mean•or [mɪsdɪ'miːnə], *Brit.* **mis•de•mean•our** *n.* (not very serious) unlawful act.

mis•di•rect [mɪsdaɪ'rekt] *v.* to give wrong directions to.

mi•ser ['maɪzə] *n.* person who hoards money and refuses to spend it. **mi•ser•li•ness,** *n.* dislike of spending money. **mi•ser•ly,** *adj.* not wanting to spend money.

mis•er•a•ble ['mɪzrəbl] *adj.* sad/unhappy; awful/bad/unpleasant (weather); very low (salary). **mis•er•a•bly,** *adv.* sadly/unhappily.

mis•er•i•cord [mɪ'zerɪkɔːd] *n.* seat in a medieval church which folds back to show carving on its underside.

mis•er•y ['mɪzərɪ] *n.* sadness; suffering; **her life was sheer m.** = was very unhappy; **to put a dog out of its m.** = to kill a dog because it is in pain; **to put s.o. out of his m.** = to tell s.o. the result/not to keep s.o. waiting any longer.

mis•fire [mɪs'faɪə] *v.* not to fire properly; **the car engine is misfiring** = is not igniting the fuel at the right time; **his plan misfired** = went wrong.

mis•fit ['mɪsfɪt] *n.* person who does not fit in with a group/fit into society.

mis•for•tune [mɪs'fɔːtjuːn] *n.* bad luck.

mis•giv•ing [mɪs'gɪvɪŋ] *n.* doubt/fear.

mis•guid•ed [mɪs'gaɪdɪd] *adj.* badly advised; wrongly judged; foolish.

mis•hap ['mɪshæp] *n.* slight accident.

mish•mash ['mɪʃmæʃ] *n.* disorderly collection; jumble.

mis•in•form [mɪsɪn'fɔːm] *v.* to give (s.o.) wrong information.

mis•in•ter•pret [mɪsɪn'tɜːprɪt] *v.* to interpret wrongly, not to understand correctly. **mis•in•ter•pre•ta•tion** [mɪsɪntɜːprɪ'teɪʃn] *n.* wrong interpretation; misunderstanding.

mis•judge [mɪs'dʒʌdʒ] *v.* to judge wrongly; to form a wrong opinion about (s.o./sth).

mis•lay [mɪs'leɪ] *v.* (**mislaid**) to put (sth) down and not to remember where you have put it.

mis•lead [mɪs'liːd] *v.* (**misled**) to give (s.o.) wrong information/to make (s.o.) make a mistake. **mis•lead•ing,** *adj.* wrong/erroneous; likely to cause a mistake.

mis•man•age [mɪs'mænɪdʒ] *v.* to manage wrongly/badly. **mis•man•age•ment,** *n.* bad management.

mis•match [mɪs'mætʃ] 1. *n.* bad match. 2. *v.* to match (two opponents) badly.

mis•no•mer [mɪs'nəʊmə] *n.* wrong name/wrong term.

mi•sog•y•nist [mɪ'sɒdʒɪnɪst] *n.* man who dislikes women. **mi•sog•y•ny,** *n.* hatred of women.

mis•place [mɪs'pleɪs] *v.* to put in the wrong place.

mis•print ['mɪsprɪnt] *n.* error in printing.

mis•pro•nounce [mɪsprə'naʊns] *v.* to pronounce wrongly. **mis•pro•nun•ci•a•tion** [mɪsprənʌnsɪ'eɪʃn] *n.* pronouncing wrongly.

mis•quote [mɪs'kwəʊt] *v.* to quote wrongly/incorrectly. **mis•quo•ta•tion** [mɪskwəʊ'teɪʃn] *n.* incorrect quotation.

mis•read [mɪs'riːd] *v.* (**misread** [mɪs'red]) to

read wrongly; to make a mistake when reading.

mis•rep•re•sent [mɪsreprɪ'zent] v. to show (sth) wrongly; to give a wrong idea of (sth); to distort (facts). **mis•rep•re•sen•ta•tion** [mɪsreprɪzen'teɪʃn] n. distortion of what s.o. said or wrote.

mis•rule [mɪs'ruːl] 1. n. bad rule/bad government. 2. v. to rule badly.

miss [mɪs] 1. n. (pl. **-es**) (a) failure to hit. (b) title of unmarried woman; **Miss Jones**. (c) title used to address/call s.o., as a waitress, etc. 2. v. (a) not to hit/see, etc.; **you didn't m. much** = there wasn't much to see/the performance was not very good. (b) **he just missed being killed** = he was very nearly killed. (c) to regret the absence of (s.o./sth). **miss•ing**, adj. absent/lost; stolen. **miss out on**, v. inf. not to enjoy (sth) because of being absent.

mis•sal ['mɪsl] n. book containing the text of the Catholic mass and other prayers.

mis•shap•en [mɪs'ʃeɪpn] adj. deformed/oddly shaped.

mis•sile ['mɪsl] n. (a) weapon which is thrown. (b) explosive rocket which can be guided to its target.

mis•sion ['mɪʃn] n. (a) aim/purpose for which s.o. is sent; **her m. in life is to help orphans** = her calling/her chosen task. (b) house/office of a missionary. (c) group of people sent somewhere with a particular aim. (d) embassy or consulate. **mis•sion•ar•y** ['mɪʃənrɪ] adj. & n. (person) whose duty is to try to convert people to his religion. **mis•sion state•ment**, n. formal statement of the objectives of a company/organization.

mis•sive ['mɪsɪv] n. (formal) letter.

mis•spell [mɪs'spel] v. (**mispelled/mispelt**) to spell wrongly. **mis•spell•ing**, n. spelling mistake.

mis•spent ['mɪsspent] adj. (youth) which has been wasted.

mis•state•ment [mɪs'steɪtmənt] n. wrong statement of facts.

mist [mɪst] 1. n. thin fog/haze. 2. v. to get covered with mist; **to m. up** = to become covered with condensation. **mist•i•ness**, n. being misty. **mist•y**, adj. (**-ier, iest**) (a) full of mist. (b) vague (memory).

mis•take [mɪs'teɪk] 1. n. error; wrong action. 2. v. (**mistook; mistaken**) (a) to understand (sth) wrongly. (b) **to m. s.o. for s.o.** = to assume

(s.o.) is s.o. else. **mis•tak•en**, adj. wrong. **mis•tak•en•ly**, adv. by mistake/in error.

mis•ter ['mɪstə] n. inf. form of address to a man.

mis•time [mɪs'taɪm] v. to choose the wrong time/an inconvenient time to do something.

mis•tle•toe ['mɪzltəu] n. parasitic plant which grows on oaks or apple trees, used as a Christmas decoration.

mis•took [mɪs'tʊk] v. see **mis•take**.

mis•treat•ment [mɪs'triːtmənt] n. bad treatment (of prisoners, etc.).

mis•tress ['mɪstrəs] n. (pl. **-es**) (a) woman in charge/who employs/teaches; **she's her own m.** = she is independent. (b) woman who has a sexual relationship with a man without being married to him.

mis•trust [mɪs'trʌst] 1. n. wariness/lack of trust. 2. v. not to trust (s.o.)/to be doubtful about (s.o.). **mis•trust•ful**, adj. not trusting.

mis•un•der•stand [mɪsʌndə'stænd] v. (**misunderstood**) not to understand. **mis•un•der•stand•ing**, n. wrong understanding/disagreement.

mis•use 1. n. [mɪs'juːs] wrong use. 2. v. [mɪs'juːz] to use (sth) in a wrong way; to treat (s.o.) badly.

mite [maɪt] n. (a) very small child. (b) very small creature like a spider, living in stale food.

mi•ter, Brit. **mi•tre** ['maɪtə] n. (a) hat worn by bishops and archbishops. (b) (in woodwork) type of sloping joint/sloping edge. **mi•tred**, adj. sloping (joint/edge).

mit•i•gate ['mɪtɪgeɪt] v. to make (a crime) less serious. **mit•i•ga•tion** [mɪtɪ'geɪʃn] n. making less serious.

mi•to•sis [maɪ'təusɪs] n. cell division.

mi•tre ['maɪtə] n. Brit. see **mi•ter**.

mitt, mitten [mɪt, 'mɪtn] n. (a) glove without separate fingers, esp. a glove to wash with or to hold hot dishes with. (b) glove which leaves the fingers bare.

mix [mɪks] 1. n. (pl. **-es**) blend/mingling of several things. 2. v. to blend/to mingle. **mixed**, adj. made up of different things put together; **a m. marriage** = marriage between two people of different races; (in tennis) **m. doubles** = doubles match where a man and woman play against another man and woman; **I have very m. feelings about the project** = in some ways I am for it and in others I am against it; **it's a m. blessing** = in some ways it is a good thing, but

æ back, ɑː farm, ɒ top, aɪ pipe, aʊ how, aɪə fire, aʊə flower, ɔː bought, ɔɪ toy, e fed, eəhair, eɪ take, ə afraid, əʊ boat, əʊə lower, ɜː word, iː heap, ɪ hit, ɪə hear, uː school, ʊ book, ʌ but, b back, d dog, ð then, dʒ just, f fog, g go, h hand, j yes, k catch, l last, m mix, n nut, ŋ sing, p penny, r round, s some, ʃ short, t too, tʃ chop, θ thing, v voice, w was, z zoo, ʒ treasure

in others it is not. **mix•er,** *n.* (a) machine for mixing. (b) person who fits in well with other people. **mix•ture** ['mɪkstʃə] *n.* blend/mingling together; **cough m.** = liquid medicine to cure a cough. **mix up,** *v.* (a) to confuse; **I always mix him up with his brother** = I always think he is his brother. (b) to involve. (c) **the speaker got all mixed up** = he got confused/lost his notes. **mix-up,** *n. inf.* confusion.

miz•zen•mast ['mɪzənmɑːst] *n.* mast nearest the stern of a ship. **miz•zen,** *n.* sail on a mizzenmast.

ml *abbrev. for* milliliter.

mm *abbrev. for* millimeter.

Mn *symbol for* manganese.

Mo *symbol for* molybdenum.

mne•mon•ic [nɪˈmɒnɪk] *adj. & n.* (rhyme) which helps you to remember certain facts.

moan [məʊn] **1.** *n.* (a) low groan. (b) general complaint. **2.** *v.* (a) to make a low groan. (b) to complain (**about** sth). **moan•er,** *n. inf.* person who complains.

moat [məʊt] *n.* wide ditch with water in it, surrounding a castle/old house. **moat•ed,** *adj.* with a moat.

mob [mɒb] **1.** *n.* (a) crowd of unruly people. (b) *inf.* criminal gang. **2.** *v.* (**mobbed**) to surround in a wild crowd. **mob•ster,** *n. inf.* member of a criminal gang.

mo•bile ['məʊbaɪl, *Am.* 'məʊbl] **1.** *adj.* which can move; **he is not very m.** = he can't walk easily. **2.** *n.* artistic creation using pieces of metal/paper, etc., which when hung up can move. **mo•bile phone,** *n.* portable telephone that operates on radio signals. **mo•bil•i•ty** [məʊˈbɪlɪtɪ] *n.* ability to move. **mo•bi•li•za•tion** [məʊbɪlaɪˈzeɪʃn] *n.* grouping of people together (esp. to join the armed forces). **mo•bi•lize** ['məʊbɪlaɪz] *v.* to group (people) together (esp. to join the armed forces).

moc•ca•sins ['mɒkəsɪnz] *n. pl.* soft leather shoes.

mo•cha ['mɒkə] *n.* (a) type of coffee from Arabia. (b) coffee and chocolate flavoring.

mock [mɒk] **1.** *adj.* false/imitation. **2.** *v.* to laugh at (s.o./sth). **mock•er•y,** *n.* (a) laughing at (s.o./sth). (b) thing which is only a bad imitation. **mock•ing,** *adj. & n.* laughing at (s.o./sth). **mock•ing•bird,** *n.* bird from the southern United States which imitates the song of other birds. **mock-up,** *n.* scale model of a new product for testing purposes.

mod [mɒd] *adj. inf. short for* **mod•ern.**

mode [məʊd] *n.* way (of doing sth). **mod•al,** *adj. & n.* (verb such as **can, must,** etc.) which is used with other verbs, and not alone.

mod•el ['mɒdl] **1.** *n. & adj.* (a) small-scale copy. (b) thing which you can take as a perfect example to be copied; **artist's m.** = person whose job is to sit while an artist draws pictures of him/her. (c) person whose job is to wear new clothes to show them to customers. (d) style of car, etc., produced in a particular period. **2.** *v.* (**modeled, modelled**) (a) to make a model; to make shapes (of clay); **modeling clay** = special clay for sculpture. (b) **he modeled his way of walking on that of his father** = he imitated his father's way. (c) to wear (new clothes) to show to customers.

mo•dem ['məʊdem] *n.* device for sending data by telephone, linking a computer to the telephone lines.

mod•er•ate **1.** *adj. & n.* ['mɒdərət] (a) not excessive; middling. (b) (person) without a violent political bias. **2.** *v.* ['mɒdəreɪt] to diminish/to make less strong. **mod•er•ate•ly,** *adv.* quite/not excessively. **mod•er•a•tion** [mɒdəˈreɪʃn] *n.* not an excessive use; calming down. **mod•er•a•tor,** *n.* chairman of a church meeting, public discussion, etc.

mod•ern ['mɒdən] *adj.* of the present day; not ancient; **m. languages** = languages which are spoken today. **mod•ern•ism,** *n.* 20th-century rejection of former traditions in architecture/literature, etc. and in favor of new ideas/methods. **mo•der•ni•ty** [məˈdɜːnɪtɪ] *n.* being modern. **mod•ern•i•za•tion** [mɒdənaɪˈzeɪʃn] *n.* act of modernizing. **mod•ern•ize** ['mɒdənaɪz] *v.* to make modern; to renovate.

mod•est ['mɒdɪst] *adj.* (a) not boasting. (b) not demanding/not excessive. **mod•est•ly,** *adv.* in a modest way. **mod•es•ty,** *n.* (a) not being boastful. (b) not being excessive/demanding.

mod•i•cum ['mɒdɪkəm] *n.* small quantity.

mod•i•fy ['mɒdɪfaɪ] *v.* (a) to change/to alter (sth) to fit a different use. (b) to reduce. **mod•i•fi•ca•tion** [mɒdɪfɪˈkeɪʃn] *n.* change. **mod•i•fi•er,** *n.* thing which modifies; word which qualifies another word.

mod•ish ['məʊdɪʃ] *adj.* fashionable.

mod•u•late ['mɒdjʊleɪt] *v.* to change the pitch of a note/a musical key. **mod•u•la•tion** [mɒdjuˈleɪʃn] *n.* change of pitch.

mod•ule ['mɒdjuːl] *n.* section of a larger combination; **lunar m.** = section of a spacecraft which lands on the moon. **mod•u•lar,** *adj.* made of various modules.

mo•dus op•e•ran•di ['məʊdəsɒpəˈrændɪ] *n.* way of working.

mo•dus vi•ven•di ['məʊdəsvɪˈvendɪ] *n.* informal way of working together.

mo•gul ['məʊgəl] *n.* bump on a ski slope.

mo•hair ['məʊheə] *n.* very soft wool from a type of goat.

moist [mɔɪst] *adj.* (-er, -est) slightly wet/damp. **mois•ten** ['mɔɪsn] *v.* to make moist. **moist•ness,** *n.* being moist. **mois•ture** ['mɔɪstʃə] *n.* slight wetness. **mois•tur•iz•er** ['mɔɪstʃəraɪzə] *n.* cream which makes the skin softer. **mois•tur•iz•ing,** *adj.* (cream) which makes the skin softer.

mo•lar ['məʊlə] *n.* large back tooth used for grinding food.

mo•las•ses [mə'læsɪz] *n.* thick black raw syrup removed from unrefined sugar.

mold, *Brit.* **mould** [məʊld] 1. *n.* (a) soft earth; **leaf m.** = soft earth formed from dead leaves. (b) hollow shape into which a liquid is poured, so that when the liquid becomes hard it takes that shape; **jelly m.** = shape for making jelly. (c) grayish powdery fungus. 2. *v.* to shape (sth). **mold•er.** 1. *n.* person who molds. 2. *v.* to rot away. **mold•i•ness,** *n.* being moldy/rotten. **mold•ing,** *n.* thing which has been molded. **mold•y,** *adj.* rotten/covered with mold.

mole [məʊl] *n.* (a) small black mammal which lives underground. (b) small dark spot on the skin. (c) *inf.* member of an organization who is in the pay of the opponent/enemy. (d) stone jetty/pier used as a breakwater. (e) standard measurement of the amount of a substance. **mole•hill,** *n.* little heap of earth pushed up by a mole; **to make a mountain out of a m.** = to make a fuss about sth which is really trivial. **mole•skin,** *n.* skin of a mole used for making clothes.

mol•e•cule ['mɒlɪkjuːl] *n.* smallest unit into which a substance can be divided. **mo•lec•u•lar** [mə'lekjʊlə] *adj.* referring to molecules: **m. weight** = mass of one molecule of a substance compared to that of one atom of carbon.

mo•lest [mə'lest] *v.* to attack/to beat (s.o.). **mo•les•ta•tion** [mɒlɪs'teɪʃn] *n.* (*formal*) act of molesting.

mol•li•fy ['mɒlɪfaɪ] *v.* to make (s.o.) feel less annoyed. **mol•li•fi•ca•tion** [mɒlɪfɪ'keɪʃn] *n.* act of mollifying.

mol•lusk ['mɒləsk], **mol•lusc** *n.* animal with no backbone, but usu. with a shell (such as snails/oysters, etc.).

mol•ly•cod•dle ['mɒlɪkɒdl] *v.* to spoil (s.o.)/to treat (s.o.) too softly.

Mo•lo•tov cock•tail ['mɒlətɒf'kɒkteɪl] *n.* handmade bomb, made of a bottle filled with flammable liquid, with a short wick.

molt *Brit.* **moult** [məʊlt] *v.* to lose feathers/fur. **mol•ten** ['məʊltən] *adj.* not solid; melted.

mo•lyb•de•num [mɒ'lɪbdənəm] *n.* (*element:* Mo) whitish metal.

mo•ment ['məʊmənt] *n.* (a) very short space of time; **at any m.** = very soon; **at the m.** = just now; **for the m.** = for the time being. (b) importance. **mo•men•tar•i•ly,** *adv.* for a short space of time. **mo•men•tar•y,** *adj.* shortlived/passing. **mo•men•tous** [mə'mentəs] *adj.* very important.

mo•men•tum [mə'mentəm] *n.* impetus; movement forward; **to gain/to lose m.** = to progress faster/slower.

mon•arch ['mɒnək] *n.* king or queen; ruler. **mon•ar•chi•c(al)** [mə'nɑːkɪk(l)] *adj.* referring to a monarchy. **mon•ar•chist** ['mɒnəkɪst] *n.* supporter of a monarchy. **mon•ar•chy** ['mɒnəkɪ] *n.* system of government with a hereditary ruler such as a king or queen.

mon•as•ter•y ['mɒnəstrɪ] *n.* group of buildings where monks live. **mo•nas•tic** [mɒ'næstɪk] *adj.* referring to a monastery/to monks.

Mon•day ['mʌndɪ] *n.* first day of the week/day between Sunday and Tuesday.

mon•e•tar•y ['mʌnɪtərɪ] *adj.* referring to money or currency. **mon•e•ta•rism,** *n.* belief that inflation can be checked by reducing the amount of money available in the economy. **mon•e•ta•rist,** *n.* person who believes in monetarism.

mon•ey ['mʌnɪ] *n.* coins or notes which are used for buying and selling; **to come into m.** = to inherit money; **we were offered our m. back** = a refund of what we had already paid; **we ran out of m.** = we had no money left. **money box,** *n.* box that can be locked and in which you can keep money. **mon•eyed,** *adj.* rich. **mon•ey•lend•er,** *n.* person who lends money. **mon•ey or•der,** *n.* order for passing money from one person to another via the post office.

mon•gol ['mɒŋgəl] *adj. & n.* (person) born with mongolism. **mon•gol•ism** *n.* defect in a person from birth, of which the symptoms are slanting eyes, flattened skull and low intelligence.

mon•goose ['mɒŋguːs] *n.* small tropical mammal which kills snakes.

æ back, ɑ: farm, ɒ: top, aɪ pipe, aʊ how, aɪə fire, aʊə flower, ɔ: bought, ɔɪ toy, e fed, eəhair, eɪ take, ə afraid, əʊ boat, əʊə lower, v: word, i: heap, ɪ hit, ɪə hear, u: school, ʊ book, ʌ but, b back, d dog, ð then, dʒ just, f fog, g go, h hand, j yes, k catch, l last, m mix, n nut, ŋ sing, p penny, r round, s some, ʃ short, t too, tʃ chop, θ thing, v voice, w was, z zoo, ʒ treasure

mon•grel ['mʌŋgrəl] *adj. & n.* not pure-bred (dog)/(dog) of mixed breeds.

mon•i•tor ['mɒnɪtə] 1. *n.* (a) person who watches/surveys the progress of sth. (b) student (in a school) who has a particular duty to perform. (c) apparatus for checking the progress of sth, esp. the screen of a computer or a small television screen in a television studio. 2. *v.* to check/to survey (the progress of sth).

monk [mʌŋk] *n.* man who is a member of a religious group and lives in a monastery. **monk•ish**, *adj.* like a monk.

mon•key ['mʌŋkɪ] 1. *n.* usu. a tropical mammal which resembles a human being, but which normally has a tail; **m. nut** = peanut; **m. puzzle tree** = type of tropical pine tree with spiky branches; **m. wrench** = large spanner with an adjustable grip. 2. *inf.* **to m. about** = to play/to mess around.

mon•o ['mɒnəʊ] 1. *prefix meaning* single. 2. *n. & adj.* not stereophonic; (machine/record) which reproduces sound through a single channel.

mon•o•chrome ['mɒnəkrəʊm] *adj. & n.* (in a) single color, usu. black and white.

mon•o•cle ['mɒnəkl] *n.* eye glass/single lens worn to correct sight.

mo•noc•u•lar [mɒ'nɒkjuːlə] *adj.* (vision) as with one eye, with no sense of depth.

mo•nog•a•my [mə'nɒgəmɪ] *n.* system of marriage to one person at a time. **mo•nog•a•mous**, *adj.* (marriage) to one husband or wife.

mon•o•gram ['mɒnəgræm] *n.* design based on the initials of your name. **mon•o•grammed**, *adj.* with your initials on it.

mon•o•graph ['mɒnəgrɑːf] *n.* short book about a specialized subject.

mon•o•lith ['mɒnəlɪθ] *n.* single standing stone. **mon•o•lith•ic** [mɒnə'lɪθɪk] *adj.* solid/heavy; changeless.

mon•o•logue, monolog ['mɒnəlɒg] *n.* long speech by one actor alone on the stage.

mon•o•ma•ni•a [mɒnə'meɪnɪə] *n.* mania about a single thing.

mo•no•nu•cle•o•sis [mɒnənjuːklɪ'əʊsɪs] *n.* glandular fever.

mon•o•phon•ic [mɒnə'fɒnɪk] *adj.* not stereophonic; (record) with sound coming from a single channel.

mon•o•plane ['mɒnəpleɪn] *n.* plane with one pair of wings.

mo•nop•o•ly [mə'nɒpəlɪ] *n.* system where one person or company supplies all needs in one area without any competition. **mo•nop•o•li•za•tion** [mənɒpəlaɪ'zeɪʃn] *n.* creating of a monopoly. **mo•nop•o•lize** [mə'nɒpəlaɪz] *v.* to create a monopoly; to use

(sth) entirely for yourself; **to m. the conversation** = to do all the talking and not let anyone else speak.

mon•o•rail ['mɒnəreɪl] *n.* train which runs on a single rail.

mon•o•syl•la•ble ['mɒnəsɪləbl] *n.* word which only has one syllable. **mon•o•syl•lab•ic** [mɒnəsɪ'læbɪk] *adj.* (word) with only one syllable; (conversation) using only monosyllables.

mon•o•the•ism [mɒnəʊ'θiːɪzəm] *n.* belief that there is only one god.

mon•o•tone ['mɒnətəʊn] *n.* flat/level tone of voice. **mo•not•o•nous** [mə'nɒtənəs] *adj.* not varied/not changing/boring. **mo•not•o•nous•ly**, *adv.* in a monotonous way. **mo•not•o•ny**, *n.* lack of variety.

mon•ox•ide [mə'nɒksaɪd] *n.* chemical compound containing one atom of oxygen.

mon•sig•nor [mɒn'siːnə] *n.* title given to an important priest in the Roman Catholic church.

mon•soon [mɒn'suːn] *n.* (a) season of wind and rain in the tropics. (b) wind blowing in the Indian Ocean.

mon•ster ['mɒnstə] 1. *n.* (a) horrible/strange creature. (b) very large and terrifying animal/thing. (c) cruel/wicked person. 2. *adj.* very large. **mon•stros•i•ty** [mɒn'strɒsɪtɪ] *n.* horrible/strange/ugly thing. **mon•strous** ['mɒnstrəs] *adj.* huge/ugly/horrible.

mon•tage [mɒn'tɑːʒ] *n.* picture/piece of music, etc., made of several items brought together; action of putting several items together to make a picture/piece of music, etc.

month [mʌnθ] *n.* one of the twelve periods which form a year. **month•ly**. 1. *adj. & adv.* occurring every month. 2. *n.* magazine which appears each month.

mon•u•ment ['mɒnjumənt] *n.* (a) (to s.o.) stone/building/statue, etc., erected in memory of s.o. who is dead. (b) building which is very old. **mon•u•men•tal** [mɒnju'mentl] *adj.* (a) very large. (b) referring to a monument.

moo [muː] 1. *n.* sound made by a cow. 2. *v.* to make a sound like a cow.

mooch [muːtʃ] *v.* **(about)** to go about aimlessly.

mood [muːd] *n.* (a) general feeling. (b) bad temper. (c) group of forms of a verb which indicates a fact, a possibility or a condition. **mood•i•ly**, *adv.* in a moody way. **mood•i•ness**, *n.* gloomy feeling; quick change from good to bad temper. **mood•y**, *adj.* **(-ier, -iest)** often gloomy/often bad-tempered; changing quickly from good to bad temper.

moon [muːn] *n.* satellite which travels around a planet, esp. the one which travels around the earth each month and shines with reflected light from the sun; **once in a blue m.** = very rarely. **moon•beam,** *n.* ray of light from the moon. **moon•light** 1. *n.* light from the moon. 2. *v.* to work at a second job after one's regular job. **moon•light•er,** *n.* person who works at a second job after his regular job. **moon•light•ing,** *n. inf.* working at a second job (usu. in the evening) after your regular job. **moon•lit,** *adj.* lit by light from the moon. **moon•shine,** *n. inf.* (a) nonsense. (b) illegal alcohol. **moon•stone,** *n.* semi-precious stone with a white shine.

moor ['mʊə, mɔː] 1. *n.* uncultivated land covered with low shrubs. 2. *v.* to attach (a boat) to a dock, etc. **moor•ing,** *n.* (a) action of attaching a boat. (b) **moorings** = place where a boat is moored; ropes, etc., used to moor a boat.

moose [muːs] *n.* (*pl.* **moose**) American elk.

moot [muːt] 1. *adj.* **m. point** = question which is open to discussion. 2. *v.* to raise (a question/a suggestion).

mop [mɒp] 1. *n.* brush for washing floors with a head made of soft string or foam rubber; **m. of hair** = long and untidy hair. 2. *v.* (**mopped**) (a) to wash the floor, using a mop. (b) to wipe. **mop up,** *v.* (a) to clear up (liquid) using a mop. (b) to clear up (pockets of resistance).

mope [məʊp] *v.* to be miserable/gloomy.

mo•ped ['məʊped] *n.* two-wheeled vehicle with a low-powered motor.

mo•quette [mɒ'ket] *n.* thick cloth for covering chairs, etc.

mo•raine [mə'reɪn] *n.* heap of gravel, etc., left by a glacier.

mor•al ['mɒrəl] 1. *adj.* (a) referring to right and wrong in human behavior. (b) referring to good human behavior; **m. support** = encouragement without active help. 2. *n.* lesson to be drawn from a story. 3. **morals** = personal character and way of behaving. **mor•al•ist,** *n.* person who criticizes low moral standards. **mo•ral•i•ty** [mə'rælɪtɪ] *n.* correct way of behaving; sense of moral standards. **mor•al•ize** ['mɒrəlaɪz] *v.* to draw a lesson from a story or event. **mor•al•ly,** *adv.* according to correct human behavior.

mo•rale [mə'rɑːl] *n.* feeling of confidence.

mo•rass [mə'ræs] *n.* (*pl.* **-es**) (a) deep swamp/marsh. (b) mass of things which prevent any progress.

mor•a•to•ri•um [mɒrə'tɔːrɪəm] *n.* (*pl.* **-ia,** **-iums**) temporary ban.

mo•ray eel [mɒreɪ'iːl] *n.* type of large eel.

mor•bid ['mɔːbɪd] *adj.* (a) interested in death/unpleasant things. (b) connected with disease. **mor•bid•i•ty** [mɔː'bɪdɪtɪ] *n.* sickly interest in death/unpleasant things. **mor•bid•ly,** *adv.* in a morbid way.

mor•dant ['mɔːdənt] *adj.* (*formal*) cruel (sarcasm).

more [mɔː] 1. *adj.* extra/additional. 2. *n.* extra/additional amount. 3. *adv.* (a) additionally/to a larger extent. (b) (*forming comparative*) **she is m. intelligent than her brother.** (c) **not any m.** = no longer; **m. or less** = approximately/practically. **more•o•ver** [mɔː'rəʊvə] *adv.* besides; in addition.

mor•ga•nat•ic [mɔːgə'nætɪk] *adj.* **m. marriage** = marriage of a king or queen to s.o. of lower rank who does not take their title.

morgue [mɔːg] *n.* building where dead bodies are kept before burial.

mor•i•bund ['mɒrɪbʌnd] *adj.* dying; going out of existence.

Mor•mon ['mɔːmən] *adj. & n.* (member) of a Christian sect, founded in the United States in 1830.

mor•nay ['mɔːneɪ] *adj.* cooked with a cheese sauce.

morn•ing ['mɔːnɪŋ] *n.* early part of the day, before 12 noon; **4 in the m.** = 4 a.m.; **the m. train** = the train which leaves every morning.

mo•roc•co [mə'rɒkəʊ] *n.* fine soft leather.

mo•ron ['mɔːrɒn] *n.* (a) adult with the intelligence of a child. (b) stupid person. **mo•ron•ic** [mə'rɒnɪk] *adj.* stupid.

mo•rose [mə'rəʊs] *adj.* gloomy and bad-tempered. **mo•rose•ly,** *adv.* in a morose way. **mo•rose•ness,** *n.* being morose.

mor•phine, morphia ['mɔːfiːn, 'mɔːfɪə] *n.* drug which kills pain and makes you go to sleep.

morph•ing ['mɔːfɪŋ] *n.* computer graphics technique in which one image is gradually changed into another, used esp. in films.

mor•phol•o•gy [mɔː'fɒlədʒɪ] *n.* (a) study of the way in which words change in the plural, or according to gender or conjugation. (b) study of the forms of plants or animals. **mor•pho•log•i•cal** [mɔːfə'lɒdʒɪkl] *adj.* referring to morphology.

mor•ris ['mɒrɪs] *n.* **m. dance** = old English dance, danced by men in white clothes with bells on their legs.

mor•row ['mɒrəʊ] *n.* (*old*) next day.

æ back, aː farm, ɒ top, aɪ pipe, aʊ how, aɪə fire, aʊə flower, ɔː bought, ɔɪ toy, e fed, eəhair, eɪ take, ə afraid, əʊ boat, əʊə lower, vː word, iː heap, ɪ hit, ɪə hear, uː school, ʊ book, ʌ but, b back, d dog, ð then, dʒ just, f fog, g go, h hand, j yes, k catch, l last, m mix, n nut, ŋ sing, p penny, r round, s some, ʃ short, t too, tʃ chop, θ thing, v voice, w was, z zoo, ʒ treasure

Morse code [mɔːsˈkəʊd] n. system of dots and dashes for sending messages.

mor•sel [ˈmɔːsl] n. small piece.

mor•tal [ˈmɔːtl] 1. adj. (a) causing death; **m. enemy** = deadly enemy. (b) referring to the body; **m. remains** = corpse. 2. n. human being. **mor•tal•i•ty** [mɔːˈtælɪtɪ] n. (a) human state. (b) **m. rate** = number of deaths (as a percentage of population). **mor•tal•ly**, adv. so as to cause death.

mor•tar [ˈmɔːtə] n. (a) cement mixture for holding together bricks or stones when building. (b) bowl for crushing things with a pestle. (c) short cannon. **mor•tar•board**, n. black cap with a square top worn at academic ceremonies, as by people receiving or giving university degrees.

mort•gage [ˈmɔːgɪdʒ] 1. n. agreement whereby s.o. lends money on the security of a property; money lent on the security of property; **second m.** = further loan obtained on a property which is already mortgaged. 2. v. to give (a property) as security for a loan. **mort•ga•gee** [mɔːgɪˈdʒiː] n. person who loans money on mortgage. **mort•ga•gor**, **mortgager** [mɔːgɪˈdʒɔː] n. person who borrows money on a mortgage.

mor•tice [ˈmɔːtɪs] n. see **mor•tise**.

mor•ti•cian [mɔːˈtɪʃn] n. undertaker.

mor•ti•fy [ˈmɔːtɪfaɪ] v. to humiliate. **mor•ti•fi•ca•tion** [mɔːtɪfɪˈkeɪʃn] n. feeling of shame/humiliation.

mor•tise [ˈmɔːtɪs] n. hole cut in the end of a piece of wood into which another piece (a tenon) fits to form a joint; **m. lock** = lock which is fitted into a door.

mor•tu•ar•y [ˈmɔːtjʊərɪ] n. place where dead bodies are kept before burial.

mo•sa•ic [məˈzeɪɪk] n. tiny pieces of colored stone stuck to a wall or floor in patterns.

Mos•lem [ˈmɒzləm] adj. & n. = **Mus•lim**.

mosque [mɒsk] n. religious building for Muslims.

mos•qui•to [məsˈkiːtəʊ] n. (pl. -oes) small flying insect which sucks blood; **m. net** = thin net spread over a bed to prevent mosquitoes biting at night.

moss [mɒs] n. (pl. -es) primitive green plant growing in compact low clumps on the ground or on stones. **moss•y**, adj. covered with moss.

most [məʊst] 1. adj. the largest number/largest quantity (of sth). 2. n. the largest number/largest quantity; **to make the m. of** = get as much profit/value from sth as possible. 3. adv. to the largest extent. (a) (forming superlative) **the m. intelligent child**. (b) (intensive) very. **most•ly**, adv. in most cases/most often.

mo•tel [məʊˈtel] n. hotel for people traveling by car where there is a parking space for every room.

mo•tet [məʊˈtet] n. music for a small group of unaccompanied singers.

moth [mɒθ] n. flying insect with large wings like a butterfly, but flying mainly at night; **clothes m.** = type of moth of which the grub eats wool or fur. **moth•ball**, v. inf. to store (a ship, etc.) in working order for future use. **moth•balls**, n. pl. balls of a chemical substance put among clothes to keep moths away; **in m.** = stored for future use. **moth-eat•en**, adj. full of holes made by moths; old and decrepit.

moth•er [ˈmʌðə] 1. n. female parent; **m. country** = country where you or your ancestors were born; **m. tongue** = first language a child speaks; **M. Superior** = woman head of a religious community. 2. v. to look after (s.o.) very attentively. **moth•er•hood**, n. being a mother. **moth•er-in-law**, n. (pl. **mothers-in-law**) mother of your wife or husband; **mother-in-law plant** = type of house plant with a few tall stiff vertical leaves. **moth•er•less**, adj. with no mother. **moth•er•ly**, adj. maternal/like a mother. **moth•er-of-pearl**, n. shiny substance found on the inside of oyster shells.

mo•tif [məʊˈtiːf] n. distinctive repeating pattern in a design/in a piece of music.

mo•tion [ˈməʊʃn] 1. n. (a) movement/act of moving; **in m.** = moving. (b) gesture/movement; **to go through the motions** = to do sth for the sake of appearances, without believing in it. (c) proposal which is to be put to the vote (at a meeting); **to second a m.** = to support the person who proposed the motion. 2. v. to make a gesture. **mo•tion•less**, adj. still/not moving. **mo•tion pic•ture**, n. moving picture shown on a screen.

mo•tive [ˈməʊtɪv] 1. n. reason for doing sth. 2. adj. which makes sth move. **mo•ti•vate** [ˈməʊtɪveɪt] v. to make (s.o.) do sth; to encourage (s.o.) to do sth; **highly motivated** = eager. **mo•ti•va•tion** [məʊtɪˈveɪʃn] n. reason for doing sth/encouragement to do sth.

mot•ley [ˈmɒtlɪ] adj. varied; of varied sorts of colors.

mo•tor [ˈməʊtə] 1. n. (a) machine which causes motion; engine. (b) car. 2. v. to travel in a car. 3. adj. (a) operated by a motor. (b) (nerve) which links the brain to the muscles, so causing motion; **m. neuron disease** = disease of the nerves which control the muscles. **mo•tor•bike**, n. inf. motorcycle. **mo•tor•boat**, n. small boat with a motor. **mo•tor•cade**, n. official procession of cars. **mo•tor•cy•cle**, n. two-wheeled vehicle powered by a motor. **mo•tor•cy•clist,** *n.* person riding a motorcycle. **mo•tor•ing,** *n.* traveling in a car. **mo•tor•ist,** *n.* driver of a car. **mo•tor•ize,** *v.* to provide (sth) with an engine; to equip (s.o.) with motor transport.

mot•tled ['mɒtld] *adj.* spotted with different colors.

mot•to ['mɒtəʊ] *n.* (*pl.* -oes, -os) short phrase which is used to sum up an attitude.

mould [məʊld] *n., v. Brit. see* **mold.**

moult [məʊlt] *v. Brit. see* **molt.**

mound [maʊnd] *n.* small heap/hill.

mount [maʊnt] 1. *n.* (a) (*usu. in names*) mountain. (b) cardboard frame for a picture. (c) horse/donkey, etc., on which a rider sits. 2. *v.* (a) to climb on to (sth); to rise; **mounted police** = police on horseback. (b) to stand on or put on guard to protect sth. (c) to set (sth) in a cardboard frame/in a metal ring/brooch, etc. (d) to organize (an expedition). **Moun•tie,** *n. inf.* member of the Royal Canadian Mounted Police. **mount up,** *v.* to rise/to increase.

moun•tain ['maʊntn] *n.* (a) very high land; **m. sheep** = sheep which are specially bred to live on mountains; **m. ash** = common northern tree with red berries. (b) large amount; **m. of work** = large quantity of work. **moun•tain•eer** [maʊntə'nɪə] *n.* person who climbs mountains for pleasure. **moun•tain•eer•ing,** *n.* climbing of mountains as a sport. **moun•tain•ous,** *adj.* (area) full of mountains; very high (waves).

moun•te•bank ['maʊntɪbæŋk] *n.* person who persuades people to pay money by talking cleverly.

mourn [mɔːn] *v.* to regret (sth). **mourn•er,** *n.* person who grieves s.o. has died; **the mourners** = people attending a funeral. **mourn•ful,** *adj.* very sad. **mourn•ful•ly,** *adv.* in a very sad way. **mourn•ing,** *n.* (a) period of time when one grieves over the death of a relative or friend. (b) dark clothes worn as a mark of respect for someone who has died.

mouse [maʊs] *n.* (*pl.* **mice** [maɪs]) (a) small rodent with a long tail, often living in houses. (b) device which is held in the hand and moved across a flat surface, used to control a cursor on a computer monitor. **mouse•hole,** *n.* small hole in which mice live. **mous•er,** *n.* **the cat is a good m.** = good at catching mice. **mouse•trap,** *n.* trap for catching mice. **mous•y,** *adj.* (a) small and insignificant (person). (b) brownish-gray (color).

mous•sa•ka ['muːsækæ] *n.* Greek dish, made of eggplant and minced meat.

mousse [muːs] *n.* light food made of whipped eggs, cream and flavoring.

mous•tache ['mʌstæʃ] *n. see* **mus•tache.**

mouth 1. *n.* [maʊθ] (a) part of the head through which you take in food and drink and through which you speak. (b) wide entrance; **m. of a river** = place where a river enters the sea. 2. *v.* [maʊð] to move the mouth as if speaking, without making any sound; to speak without being heard. **mouth•ful,** *n.* (a) quantity contained in the mouth. (b) *inf.* complicated word/phrase. **mouth•or•gan,** *n.* small musical instrument played by blowing, with a series of small valves giving different notes. **mouth•piece,** *n.* (a) part of a musical instrument which goes into the mouth. (b) person who speaks on behalf of s.o. **mouth•wash,** *n.* antiseptic solution for cleaning the inside of the mouth. **mouth-wa•ter•ing,** *adj.* very delicious.

move [muːv] 1. *n.* (a) action of changing place; movement; **get a m. on!** = hurry up; *inf.* **we must make a m.** = we must act. (b) movement (of a piece in chess); **what's the next m.?** = what do we have to do next? (c) changing of place of residence. 2. *v.* (a) to change the position (of sth); to change position; **don't m.!** = stand still! *inf.* **we must be moving** = we must leave. (b) to leave one place to go to live in another. (c) to change the feelings of (s.o.). (d) to propose (a motion in a debate). **mov•a•ble, move•able** *adj.* which can be moved. **move a•bout,** *v.* to change (sth) from one place to another. **move a•way,** *v.* to change to another place further away; to change (sth) to a position further away; **we are moving away from San Francisco** = we are leaving San Francisco to live in another town. **move back,** *v.* (a) to go backward; to change (sth) to a place further back. (b) to return to a previous place. **move for•ward,** *v.* to go forward; to make (s.o.) go to a place further forward. **move in,** *v.* to settle with furniture in a new house. **move•ment,** *n.* (a) action of changing position/of not being still. (b) mechanism (of a clock). (c) main part of a large piece of music. (d) group of people working toward a certain aim. **move off,** *v.* to go away. **move on,** *v.* to go forward; to make (s.o.) go forward. **mov•er,** *n.* person who moves furniture from one house to another. **mov•ie,** *n.*

æ back, ɑː farm, ɒ top, aɪ pipe, aʊ how, aɪə fire, aʊə flower, ɔː bought, ɔɪ toy, e fed, eəhair, eɪ take, ə afraid, əʊ boat, əʊə lower, ɜː word, iː heap, ɪ hit, ɪə hear, uː school, ʊ book, ʌ but, b back, d dog, ð then, dʒ just, f fog, g go, h hand, j yes, k catch, l last, m mix, n nut, ŋ sing, p penny, r round, s some, ʃ short, t too, tʃ chop, θ thing, v voice, w was, z zoo, ʒ treasure

motion picture. **mov•ing**, *adj.* (a) which changes position/which is not still; **m. stair-case** = escalator. (b) which affects your feelings.

mow [məu] *v.* (**has mown**) to cut (grass). **mow down**, *v.* to kill/to slaughter. **mow•er**, *n.* (a) person who cuts grass. (b) machine which cuts grass; lawnmower.

mpg *abbrev. for* miles per gallon.

mph *abbrev. for* miles per hour.

Mr. ['mɪstə] *n.* title given to a man.

Mrs. ['mɪsɪz] *n.* title given to a married woman.

Ms. [mʌz, mɪz] *n.* title given to a woman (married or unmarried).

much [mʌtʃ] 1. *adj.* a lot of. 2. *adv.* (**more/most**) to a great extent/very; *inf.* **it's a bit m.!** = it's quite unreasonable! **m. to my amazement** = to my great surprise. 3. *n.* a lot; *inf.* **not up to m.** = relatively inactive.

muck [mʌk] 1. *n.* dirt; manure. 2. *v.* **to m. out a stable** = to clean a stable; *inf.* **to m. about with** = to play about with; *inf.* **to m. up** = to ruin. **muck•rak•ing**, *n.* discovering and publishing scandalous stories about famous people. **muck•y**, *adj.* (**-ier, -iest**) dirty; covered with muck.

mu•cus ['mjuːkəs] *n.* shiny substance which coats the inside of cavities of the body. **mu•cous**, *adj.* referring to mucus; **m. mem-brane** = wet membrane which lines inside passages of the body.

mud [mʌd] *n.* very wet earth. **mud•di•ness**, *n.* being muddy. **mud•dy**, 1. *adj.* (**-ier, -iest**) full of mud; covered with mud. 2. *v.* to put mud on sth; **to m. the waters** = to stir up trouble/confusion. **mud•flap**, *n.* flap hanging behind the wheel of a car to prevent mud and water being splashed. **mud•flats**, *n. pl.* flat muddy land covered by the sea at high tide. **mud•guard**, *n.* strip of metal over the wheel on a bicycle to stop mud and water being splashed. **mud•pack**, *n.* paste put on the face to improve the texture of the skin. **mud•sling•ing**, *n.* insults.

mud•dle ['mʌdl] 1. *n.* confusion/mixture. 2. *v.* to confuse/to mix up. **mud•dle•head•ed**, *adj.* confused. **muddle through**, *v.* to get through one's business/to succeed in a muddled way.

mues•li ['mjuːzlɪ] *n.* breakfast food of flakes of cereal/dried fruit, etc., eaten with milk or yogurt.

mu•ez•zin [muːˈezɪn] *n.* person who calls Muslims to prayer.

muff [mʌf] 1. *n.* warm covering for a particular part of the body, esp. the hands. 2. *v.* to do (sth) badly.

muf•fin ['mʌfɪn] *n.* small round cake, usu. eaten with butter.

muf•fle ['mʌfl] *v.* (a) to wrap up in clothes. (b) to deaden (a loud noise). **muf•fler**, *n.* (a) long scarf. (b) silencer (on car exhaust).

muf•ti ['mʌftɪ] *n. inf.* **in m.** = in civilian clothes; not in uniform.

mug [mʌg] 1. *n.* (a) large glass/cup with a handle. (b) *inf.* face. 2. *v.* (**mugged**) to attack and rob (in the street). **mug•ger**, *n.* person who attacks and robs s.o. in the street. **mug•ging**, *n.* robbery with violence (in the street). **mug shot**, *n. inf.* photograph of s.o.'s face.

mug•gy ['mʌgɪ] *adj. inf.* warm and wet (weather).

mu•lat•to [mjuːˈlætəu] *n.* (*pl.* **-oes**) person of mixed Negro and White race.

mul•ber•ry ['mʌlbərɪ] *n.* soft purple fruit; tree which bears this fruit.

mulch [mʌltʃ] 1. *n.* (*pl.* **-es**) covering of manure/rotten leaves, etc., spread on the ground to improve the soil. 2. *v.* to spread mulch on (the ground).

mulct [mʌlkt] *v.* to take money away from (s.o.).

mule [mjuːl] *n.* (a) hybrid between a donkey and a horse; obstinate person. (b) light shoe with an open heel. **mu•le•teer** [mjuːlə'tɪə] *n.* person who drives mules carrying loads. **mul•ish**, *adj.* obstinate/difficult to deal with.

mull [mʌl] *v.* to heat (wine) with spices/sugar, etc. **mull o•ver**, *v.* to ponder/to think about (sth).

mul•lah ['mʊlə] *n.* Muslim religious thinker.

mul•let ['mʌlɪt] *n.* small sea fish.

mul•li•ga•taw•ny [mʌlɪgə'tɔːnɪ] *n.* hot soup made with curry.

mul•lion ['mʌljən] *n.* vertical (wooden/metal) bar between panes of glass in a window.

multi- ['mʌltɪ] *prefix meaning* many.

mul•ti•col•ored ['mʌltɪkʌləd] *adj.* with many colors.

mul•ti•far•i•ous [mʌltɪ'feərɪəs] *adj.* very varied/in many different types.

mul•ti•lat•er•al [mʌltɪ'lætərəl] *adj.* between more than two partners.

mul•ti•me•di•a [mʌltɪ'miːdɪə] *adj.* (a) (teaching method/advertising campaign, etc.) using several media. (b) (computer hardware/software) using data in several media, e.g. graphics/sound/text.

mul•ti•mil•lion•aire [mʌltɪmɪljə'neə] *n.* person who has several million dollars.

mul•ti•na•tion•al [mʌltɪ'næʃnl] *adj. & n.* (company) which operates in several different countries.

mul•ti•ple ['mʌltɪpl] 1. *adj.* many/repeated; **m. sclerosis** = disease of the nervous system, which gets progressively worse. 2. *n.* (a) number which contains another number several times exactly. (b) repeated groups of the same number of sth; **sold in multiples of five** = you can buy five, ten, fifteen, etc. **mul•ti•pli•ca•tion** [mʌltɪplɪ'keɪʃn] *n.* action of multiplying; **m. sign** () = sign used to show that numbers are to be multiplied; **m. tables** = lists of figures to learn by heart how each number is multiplied. **mul•ti•plic•i•ty** [mʌltɪ'plɪsɪtɪ] *n.* vast and varied mass. **mul•ti•ply** ['mʌltɪplaɪ] *v.* (a) to calculate the sum of several numbers repeated a stated number of times. (b) to increase in number.

mul•ti•ra•cial [mʌltɪ'reɪʃl] *adj.* (society) whose members come from various races.

mul•ti•sto•ry ['mʌltɪstɔːrɪ] *adj.* (building) with many stories.

mul•ti•tude ['mʌltɪtjuːd] *n.* great number/crowd. **mul•ti•tu•di•nous** [mʌltɪ'tjuːdɪnəs] *adj.* in very large numbers.

mum [mʌm] *adj.* silent; **he kept m.** = he didn't say a word.

mum•ble ['mʌmbl] 1. *n.* speech which you can't understand because it is indistinct. 2. *v.* to speak indistinctly.

mum•bo-jum•bo [mʌmbəʊ'dʒʌmbəʊ] *n.* nonsense/meaningless talk.

mum•mer ['mʌmə] *n.* member of a group acting in a traditional Christmas play.

mum•my ['mʌmɪ] *n.* corpse preserved with ointments and bandages as in ancient Egypt. **mum•mi•fy,** *v.* to preserve (a dead body) in a perfect state.

mumps [mʌmps] *n.* infectious illness with swelling on either side of the neck.

munch [mʌnʃ] *v.* to chew (sth crisp or dry) with large regular movements of the jaws.

Mun•chau•sen's syn•drome ['mʌntʃəʊzən] *n.* psychiatric condition in which s.o. feigns illness/injury to get medical treatment; **M. s. by proxy** = psychiatric condition in which s.o. inflicts injury on or claims illness in others in order to get medical treatment for that person.

mun•dane [mʌn'deɪn] *adj.* ordinary.

mu•nic•i•pal [mjuː'nɪsɪpl] *adj.* referring to a town; **m. park** = park which belongs to a town. **mu•nic•i•pal•i•ty** [mjuːnɪsɪ'pælɪtɪ] *n.* self-governing city or town.

mu•nif•i•cence [mjuː'nɪfɪsns] *n.* (*formal*) great generosity. **mu•nif•i•cent,** *adj.* (*formal*) extremely generous.

mu•ni•tions [mjuː'nɪʃnz] *n. pl.* weapons and ammunition.

mu•ral ['mjʊərəl] 1. *adj.* referring to walls. 2. *n.* painting on a wall.

mur•der ['mɜːdə] 1. *n.* (a) illegal killing of s.o. (b) *inf.* awful or unpleasant thing. 2. *v.* (a) to kill (s.o.) illegally. (b) *inf.* to ruin (a song) by singing it badly. **mur•der•er,** *n.* person who has committed a murder. **mur•der•ess** ['mɜːdrəs] *n.* woman who has committed a murder. **mur•der•ous** ['mɜːdərəs] *adj.* likely to kill.

murk [mɜːk] *n.* (*formal*) darkness/gloominess. **murk•i•ness,** *n.* being dark/gloomy. **murk•y** ['mɜːkɪ] *adj.* (-ier, -iest) dark/gloomy (water).

mur•mur ['mɜːmə] 1. *n.* low whisper of voices/low sound. 2. *v.* to speak in a low voice; to complain in a low voice. **mur•mur•ing,** *n.* (a) speaking in a low voice. (b) **murmurings** = grumblings/complaints.

mus•cat ['mʌskət] *n.* type of sweet grape; wine made from this grape.

mus•ca•tel [mʌskə'tel] *n.* type of sweet black grape, usually dried.

mus•cle ['mʌsl] 1. *n.* springlike parts of the body which allow the limbs to move. 2. *v. inf.* **to m. in on sth** = to push yourself forward to take part in sth which is organized by s.o. else. **mus•cu•lar** ['mʌskjulə] *adj.* referring to muscles; **m. dystrophy** = disease causing gradual weakening of the muscles.

muse [mjuːz] 1. *n.* (*formal*) goddess who inspires poets, musicians, etc. 2. *v.* to think deeply; to daydream.

mu•se•um [mjuː'zɪəm] *n.* building in which a collection of valuable or rare objects are put on display permanently.

mush [mʌʃ] *n.* soft half-liquid mess. **mush•i•ness,** *n.* being mushy. **mush•y,** *adj.* (a) soft and partly liquid. (b) *inf.* very sentimental.

mush•room ['mʌʃruːm] 1. *n.* edible round white fungus. 2. *v.* to spring up rapidly.

mu•sic ['mjuːzɪk] *n.* sounds made by playing instruments or singing; **to face the m.** = to face sth unpleasant. **mu•si•cal.** 1. *adj.* referring to music; (person) who likes music/plays music a lot; **m. chairs** = (i) game where people try to sit on chairs when the music stops, with one chair and one person less each time; (ii) *inf.* continual movement from office to office/from job to job. 2. *n.* (*also* **musical comedy**) play with

---

æ back, a: farm, ɒ: top, aɪ pipe, aʊ how, aɪə fire, aʊə flower, ɔ: bought, ɔɪ toy, e fed, eəhair, eɪ take, ə afraid, əʊ boat, əʊə lower, v: word, i: heap, ɪ hit, ɪə hear, u: school, ʊ book, ʌ but, b back, d dog, ð then, dʒ just, f fog, g go, h hand, j yes, k catch, l last, m mix, n nut, ŋ sing, p penny, r round, s some, ʃ short, t too, tʃ chop, θ thing, v voice, w was, z zoo, ʒ treasure

songs and popular music. **mu•sic box,** *n.* small box with a clockwork motor which plays a tune when the box is opened. **mu•si•cal•ly,** *adv.* in a musical way. **music hall,** *n.* theater specializing in variety shows. **mu•si•cian** [mjuːˈzɪʃn] *n.* person who plays music professionaly/skillfully. **mu•si•col•o•gy** [mjuːzɪˈkɒlədʒɪ] *n.* academic study of music. **mu•si•col•o•gist,** *n.* specialist in the study of music.

musk [mʌsk] *n.* perfume obtained from glands of a deer. **musk ox,** *n.* large wild ox, found in North America. **musk•rat,** *n.* North American water rat with fine fur. **musk rose,** *n.* old-fashioned scented rose. **musk•y,** *adj.* with a smell like musk.

mus•keg [ˈmʌskeg] *n.* (*in northern North America*) marsh.

mus•ket [ˈmʌskɪt] *n.* early portable gun with a long barrel. **mus•ket•eer,** *n.* soldier who was armed with a musket.

Mus•lim [ˈmʊzlɪm] *adj. & n.* (person) following the religion of the prophet Mohammed.

mus•lin [ˈmʌzlɪn] *n.* very fine thin cotton cloth.

muss [mʌs] *v. inf.* to disorder or ruffle (hair, etc.).

mus•sel [ˈmʌsl] *n.* mollusk with a dark blue shell, whose soft parts can be eaten.

must [mʌst] 1. *v.* (a) *used with verbs to mean* it is necessary. (b) *used with verbs to mean* it is probable; **it m. be the doctor** = it cannot be anyone else. 2. *n.* (a) *inf.* very necessary thing. (b) grape juice.

mus•tache, moustache [ˈmʌstæʃ] *n.* hair grown on the upper lip.

mus•tang [ˈmʌstæŋ] *n.* wild horse of the American plains.

mus•tard [ˈmʌstəd] *n.* (a) sharp-tasting yellow powder made from crushed seeds; paste made from this powder; **m. gas** = poisonous gas which burns the skin; **m. yellow** = dull yellow color. (b) plant whose seeds make mustard powder.

mus•ter [ˈmʌstə] 1. *n.* gathering; parade and inspection of soldiers, etc.; **to pass m.** = to be acceptable. 2. *v.* to gather together.

mus•ty [ˈmʌstɪ] *adj.* (**-ier, -iest**) smelling damp/rotten/stale; smelling old. **mus•ti•ness,** *n.* rotten/stale smell.

mu•tate [mjuːˈteɪt] *v.* to change genetically. **mu•ta•bil•i•ty** [mjuːtəˈbɪlɪtɪ] *n.* being mutable. **mu•ta•ble,** *adj.* which is likely to change/which can be changed. **mu•tant** [ˈmjuːtənt] *n.* animal/plant which has changed genetically. **mu•ta•tion** [mjuːˈteɪʃn] *n.* genetic change.

mute [mjuːt] 1. *adj.* (a) silent/dumb (person). (b) (letter) which is not pronounced. 2. *n.* (a) person who cannot speak/who is dumb; **deaf m.** = person who cannot hear or speak. (b) device used to soften the sound of a musical instrument. 3. *v.* to soften the sound of (a musical instrument). **mute•ly,** *adv.* silently.

mu•ti•late [ˈmjuːtɪleɪt] *v.* to cut off a limb/an ear, etc., from (s.o.); to damage (an object). **mu•ti•la•tion** [mjuːtɪˈleɪʃn] *n.* loss of a limb; great damage.

mu•ti•ny [ˈmjuːtɪnɪ] 1. *n.* uprising, esp. of soldiers/sailors, etc., against the orders of their officers. 2. *v.* to refuse to carry out orders/to rise up against officers. **mu•ti•neer** [mjuːtɪˈnɪə] *n.* person who mutinies. **mu•ti•nous** [ˈmjuːtɪnəs] *adj.* likely to mutiny/rebellious. **mu•ti•nous•ly,** *adv.* in a mutinous way.

mutt [mʌt] *n. Sl.* (a) idiot/stupid person. (b) dog.

mut•ter [ˈmʌtə] 1. *n.* low indistinct way of speaking. 2. *v.* to mumble/to speak in a low and indistinct voice. **mut•ter•ing,** *n.* speaking indistinctly.

mut•ton [ˈmʌtn] *n.* meat of a sheep.

mu•tu•al [ˈmjuːtjʊəl] *adj.* felt/done by two people to each other; between two people; belonging to two people; **our m. friend** = the friend of both of us; **by m. consent** = with the agreement of both parties. **mu•tu•al•ly,** *adv.* to two people; by two people.

Mu•zak [ˈmjuːzæk] *n.* trademark for system of playing recorded music in public places.

muz•zle [ˈmʌzl] 1. *n.* (a) nose of an animal. (b) device placed round the mouth of a dog to prevent it biting. (c) mouth of a gun. 2. *v.* to put a muzzle on the mouth of (a dog) to prevent it biting; **to m. the press** = to stop newspapers from printing what they want.

muz•zy [ˈmʌzɪ] *adj. inf.* dizzy/in a daze. **muz•zi•ness,** *n.* feeling muzzy.

my [maɪ] *adj.* belonging to me.

my•al•gi•a [maɪˈældʒɪə] *n.* muscle pain. **my•al•gic en•ceph•a•lo•my•e•li•tis (ME)** [maɪˈældʒɪk enˈsefələʊmaɪˈlaɪtɪs] *n. see* **chronic fatigue syndrome.**

my•col•o•gy [maɪˈkɒlədʒɪ] *n.* study of fungi. **my•co•log•i•cal** [maɪkəˈlɒdʒɪkl] *adj.* referring to mycology.

my•e•li•tis [maɪəˈlaɪtɪs] *n.* inflammation of the spinal cord.

my•nah (bird) [ˈmaɪnə(bɜːd)] *n.* black tropical bird which can be taught to talk.

my•o•pi•a [maɪˈəʊpɪə] *n.* short-sightedness/not being able to see things which are far away. **my•op•ic** [maɪˈɒpɪk] *adj.* short-sighted.

myr•i•ad ['mɪrɪəd] (*formal*) 1. *n.* very large number. 2. *adj.* very many.

myrrh [mɜː] *n.* sweet-smelling resin used to make incense, etc.

myr•tle ['mɜːtl] *n.* evergreen plant with scented flowers.

my•self [maɪ'self] *pronoun referring to* me. **all by m.** = on my own.

mys•ter•y ['mɪstrɪ] *n.* thing which cannot be explained; state of not being able to be explained. **mys•te•ri•ous** [mɪ'stɪərɪəs] *adj.* secret/which cannot be explained. **mys•te•ri•ous•ly**, *adv.* secretly/in a way which cannot be explained.

mys•tic ['mɪstɪk] 1. *n.* person who attempts to make contact with God through prayer/meditation, etc. 2. *adj.* in contact with God. **mys•ti•cal**, *adj.* in contact with God by some process which cannot be understood. **mys•ti•cism** ['mɪstɪsɪzəm] *n.* religion based on attempts to contact God by prayer and meditation.

mys•ti•fy ['mɪstɪfaɪ] *v.* to puzzle/to bewilder. **mys•ti•fi•ca•tion** [mɪstɪfɪ'keɪʃn] *n.* puzzle/bewilderment.

mys•tique [mɪ'stiːk] *n.* mysterious atmosphere about a person or thing.

myth [mɪθ] *n.* (a) ancient folk story about gods. (b) untrue, but commonly held, notion. **myth•i•cal,** *adj.* (a) referring to ancient tales of gods. (b) untrue/not existing. **myth•o•log•i•cal** [mɪθə'lɒdʒɪkl] *adj.* referring to mythology. **my•thol•o•gy** [mɪ'θɒlədʒɪ] *n.* study of myths; ancient folk stories from a particular source.

myx•o•ma•to•sis [mɪksəmə'təʊsɪs] *n.* fatal disease of rabbits.

æ back, aː farm, ɒ top, aɪ pipe, aʊ how, aie fire, aʊə flower, ɔː bought, ɔɪ toy, e fed, eəhair, eɪ take, ə afraid, əʊ boat, əʊə lower, vː word, iː heap, ɪ hit, ɪə hear, uː school, ʊ book, ʌ but, b back, d dog, ð then, dʒ just, f fog, g go, h hand, j yes, k catch, l last, m mix, n nut, ŋ sing, p penny, r round, s some, ʃ short, t too, tʃ chop, θ thing, v voice, w was, z zoo, ʒ treasure

Nn

N *symbol for* nitrogen.

Na *symbol for* sodium.

nab [næb] *v.* (**nabbed**) (a) *inf.* to snatch/to pull away (sth) suddenly/to steal. (b) *inf.* to catch (s.o.) in the act/to pounce on (s.o.).

na•dir ['neɪdɪə] *n.* lowest point.

nag [næg] 1. *n. inf.* horse. 2. *v.* (**nagged**) to try to persuade (s.o.) by saying the same thing again and again/to criticize without seeming to stop. **nag•ging**, *adj.* persistent (pain, etc.).

nai•ad ['naɪæd] *n.* goddess living in a stream.

nail [neɪl] 1. *n.* (a) hard covering at the ends of fingers and toes; **n. scissors** = curved scissors for cutting nails. (b) small metal spike with a pointed end, used to hold things together; **hard as nails** = very tough; *inf.* **to hit the n. on the head** = to make an accurate judgment/to give the right answer. 2. *v.* to attach with nails.

na•ive [naɪ'iːv] *adj.* inexperienced and innocent. **na•ive•ly**, *adv.* in a naive way. **na•ive•té, naivety**, *n.* being naive.

na•ked ['neɪkɪd] *adj.* with no clothes on; with no covering; **n. flame** = flame with no protective shield; **invisible to the n. eye** = which can only be seen using a telescope/microscope. **na•ked•ly**, *adv.* with no covering. **na•ked•ness**, *n.* being naked.

nam•by-pam•by ['næmbɪpæmbɪ] *adj.* weak and silly.

name [neɪm] 1. *n.* (a) title/word which you use to call people/things; **Christian n./first n.** = particular name given to someone as a child; **he put his n. down to join the club** = he applied to join; **to call s.o. names** = to insult s.o. (b) **in n. only** = according to the name used, but not really in fact. (c) **to have a bad n.** = a bad reputation; **to make a n. for oneself** = to become famous or successful. 2. *v.* (a) to call by a name; to give a name to. (b) to specify; **to n. the day** = to fix the date for a wedding. (c) to appoint s.o. to a post. **name•less**, *adj.* with no name; (word/name) not to be used because of disgust or in order to remain anonymous. **name•ly**, *adv.* that is to say. **name•sake**, *n.* person with the same name as another.

nan•a [næn, 'nænə] *n.* child's name for grandmother.

nan•ny ['nænɪ] *n.* (a) nurse paid to look after children in their own home. (b) **n. goat** = female goat.

nano- ['nænəʊ] *prefix meaning* one billionth; **nanometer; nanosecond.**

na•no•me•ter ['nænəʊmiːtə] *n.* one billionth of a meter.

na•no•sec•ond ['nænəʊsekənd] *n.* one billionth of a second.

na•no•tech•nol•o•gy [nænəʊtek'nɒlədʒɪ] *n.* technology used to manufacture/manipulate objects with dimensions of less than 100 nanometers.

nap [næp] 1. *n.* (a) short sleep. (b) raised surface of cloth, such as velvet. 2. *v.* to sleep for a short time; **to catch s.o. napping** = to find s.o. off guard.

na•palm ['neɪpɑːm] *n.* inflammable substance used in incendiary bombs.

nape [neɪp] *n.* back of the neck.

naph•tha ['næfθə] *n.* oil derived from coal/petroleum, used to light fires/clean clothes, etc. **naph•tha•lene** ['næfθəliːn] *n.* strong-smelling white chemical used to make mothballs.

nap•kin ['næpkɪn] *n.* square piece of cloth or paper used to protect clothes and wipe your mouth at mealtimes.

nar•cis•sus [nɑː'sɪsəs] *n.* (*pl.* -issus, issuses, -issi [-ɪsaɪ]) white flower similar to a daffodil. **nar•cis•sism**, *n.* great love for your own appearance. **nar•cis•sis•tic** [nɑːsɪ'sɪstɪk] *adj.* loving your own appearance.

nar•cot•ic [nɑː'kɒtɪk] *adj. & n.* (substance) which can make you feel sleepy or become unconscious; **narcotics squad** = police department dealing with drug offenses.

nar•rate [nə'reɪt] *v.* to write/to speak about events; to tell (a story). **nar•ra•tion** [nə'reɪʃn] *n.* speaking/writing about events. **nar•ra•tive** ['nærətɪv] 1. *n.* what is actually written or told. 2. *adj.* describing events which took place. **nar•ra•tor** [nə'reɪtə] *n.* person who gives an actual account; person who reads a story.

nar•row ['nærəʊ] 1. *adj.* (a) not wide; **n. escape** = escape at the last minute from an awkward or dangerous situation. (b) **n. majority** = very small margin of votes. (c) restricted (opinions). 2. *v.* to make/to become less wide; to

make/to become smaller. **nar•row•ly,** *adv.*
nearly/only just. **nar•row-mind•ed,** *adj.*
not capable of seeing many points of view/not
tolerant. **nar•row•ness,** *n.* being narrow.
nar•rows, *n. pl.* narrow stretch of water.

nar•whal ['nɑ:wəl] *n.* type of whale which lives
in the Arctic and has a long tusk.

nar•y ['neɪrɪ] *adj.* (*old*) not one.

na•sal ['neɪzl] *adj.* referring to the nose; spoken
as if through the nose. **na•sal•ly,** *adv.* in a
nasal way.

nas•tur•tium [nə'stɜ:ʃəm] *n.* creeping plant
with large orange or yellow flowers.

nas•ty ['nɑ:stɪ] *adj.* (-ier, -iest) unpleasant/dis-
agreeable; **to turn n.** = to become hostile/un-
friendly/unpleasant. **nas•ti•ly,** *adv.* in a
nasty way. **nas•ti•ness,** *n.* being nasty; nasty
happening.

na•tal ['neɪtl] *adj.* referring to birth.

na•tion ['neɪʃn] *n.* people of a particular country. **na•tion•al** ['næʃnl] 1. *adj.* belonging to
the people of a particular country. 2. *n.* person
of a particular country. **Na•tion•al Guard,**
n. part of the U.S. army made up of military
forces from each state, used in time of war or
national emergency. **na•tion•al•ism**
['næʃnəlɪzəm] *n.* feeling of pride in one's nation; desire for independence for a country.
na•tion•al•ist, *n.* person who supports nationalism. **na•tion•al•is•tic,** *adj.* referring
to nationalism. **na•tion•al•i•ty** [næʃə-
'nælɪtɪ] *n.* citizenship of a country.
na•tion•al•i•za•tion [næʃnəlaɪ'zeɪʃn] *n.*
conversion of private industries to ownership
by the national government. **na•tion•al•ize**
['næʃnəlaɪz] *v.* to put (a private industry)
under central government ownership and control. **na•tion•al•ly,** *adv.* in a national way;
(done) all over the nation. **na•tion•al park,**
n. area of land run by the national government
for public use, where building/tourism, etc.
are controlled. **na•tion•wide** ['neɪʃnwaɪd]
adj. all over the country.

na•tive ['neɪtɪv] 1. *n.* (a) person born in a particular country. (b) uncivilized original inhabitant. (c) plant/animal which originally comes
from a particular country. 2. *adj.* (a) natural;
(qualities) with which a person is born. (b) un-
altered/undeveloped. (c) belonging to those
born in a country. (d) **n. to** = (plant/animal)
which originally comes from a certain country.

na•tiv•i•ty [nə'tɪvɪtɪ] *n.* birth, esp. that of

Jesus Christ; **n. play** = play describing the
events surrounding the birth of Jesus Christ.

nat•ter ['nætə] 1. *n. inf.* friendly informal con-
versation/chat. 2. *v. inf.* to have a friendly informal chat.

nat•ty ['nætɪ] *adj.* (-ier, -iest) smart/tidy (personal appearance).

nat•u•ral ['nætʃrəl] 1. *adj.* (a) based on inner
knowledge or instinct; not learned. (b) nor-
mal/not artificial. (c) not surprising/not unexpected. (d) dealing with (the study of) nature;
n. gas = gas which is found in the earth. (e) (*in
music*) (note) which is neither sharp nor flat. 2.
n. person who is naturally suitable for a job/a
part in a play, etc. **nat•u•ral his•to•ry,** *n.*
(also **natural science**) study of nature.
nat•u•ral•ism, *n.* (*in art/literature*) showing
things as they really are. **nat•u•ral•ist,** *n.*
person who studies animals or plants.
nat•u•ral•is•tic, *adj.* (art, etc.) which shows
things as they really are.
nat•ur•al•i•za•tion [nætʃərəlaɪ'zeɪʃn] *n.*
act of naturalizing; being naturalized.
nat•ur•al•ize ['nætʃərəlaɪz] *v.* (a) to introduce (a plant or animal) into another country.
(b) to let cultivated plants become wild. (c) to
grant (s.o.) citizenship of a country other than
that in which he was born. **nat•u•ral•ly**
['nætʃrəlɪ] *adv.* (a) in a natural/unstudied way.
(b) as you would expect/of course.
nat•u•ral•ness, *n.* being natural.

na•ture ['neɪtʃə] *n.* (a) character (of a per-
son/thing/animal); **human n.** = attitudes and
behavior which are typical of human beings.
(b) kind/class (of thing). (c) world of plants
and animals; **the laws of n.** = what happens in
the world of plants and animals. **-natured,**
suffix showing a characteristic; **good-natured.**
na•tur•ist, *n.* nudist.

naught [nɔ:t] *n.* zero/nothing; the symbol 0; **to
come to n.** = to be unsuccessful/fail.

naugh•ty ['nɔ:tɪ] *adj.* (-ier, -iest) bad/disobedi-
ent (child). **naugh•ti•ly,** *adv.* wickedly.
naugh•ti•ness, *n.* wickedness/bad behavior.

nau•se•a ['nɔ:zɪə] *n.* feeling of sickness/of extreme dislike. **nau•se•ate,** *v.* to make (s.o.)
loathe/dislike very much. **nau•se•at•ing,**
adj. horrible/which makes you sick.
nau•seous, *adj.* (a) which nauseates. (b) feeling unwell.

nau•ti•cal ['nɔ:tɪkl] *adj.* referring to ships, sailing and boating; **n. mile** = measure of length at sea (2025 yards or 1.85 kilometers).

nau•ti•lus [nɔː'tɪləs] *n.* large type of shell fish.

na•val ['neɪvl] *adj.* referring to ships and esp. to a navy; **n. engagement** = battle at sea; **n. base** = port for warships; **n. college** = establishment for training naval officers.

nave [neɪv] *n.* main part of a church.

na•vel ['neɪvl] *n.* small hollow in the middle of your stomach where the umbilical cord was attached; **n. orange** = large seedless orange with a small hollow at the bottom.

nav•i•gate ['nævɪgeɪt] *v.* to guide/to steer (a ship or aircraft). **nav•i•ga•bil•i•ty** [nævɪgə'bɪlɪtɪ] *n.* being navigable. **nav•i•ga•ble**, *adj.* (a) steerable/seaworthy. (b) (river) deep enough for ships to sail in it. **nav•i•ga•tion** [nævɪ'geɪʃn] *n.* guiding/steering a ship/an aircraft along a certain course. **nav•i•ga•tor** ['nævɪgeɪtə] *n.* person who guides/steers a ship or an aircraft.

na•vy ['neɪvɪ] 1. *n.* all a country's warships and crews. 2. *adj. & n.* **n. (blue)** = dark blue.

nay [neɪ] *adv.* (*old*) no.

N.B. [en'biː] *short for* nota bene, *meaning* please note.

NCO [ensiː'əʊ] *n.* non-commissioned officer.

neap [niːp] *n.* **n. tide** = tide which does not rise or fall very much, midway between the spring tides.

Ne•a•pol•i•tan [nɪə'pɒlɪtən] *adj.* referring to Naples; **N. ice cream** = ice cream made of layers of different colors and flavors.

near ['nɪə] (**-er, -est**) 1. *adv.* close/at only a little distance in space or time. 2. *prep.* close by (an object); not far away in time. 3. *adj.* **n. relations** = closest relations; **n. miss** = (i) sth which is not quite successful; (ii) narrow escape. 4. *v.* to draw near to/to approach. **near•by.** 1. *adj.* which is situated close by. 2. *adv.* close by. **Near East**, *n.* countries at the eastern end of the Mediterranean. **near•ly**, *adv.* (a) almost. (b) closely; **not n. big enough** = far too small. **near•ness**, *n.* closeness. **near•sight•ed**, *adj.* short-sighted/only able to see clearly things which are near.

neat [niːt] *adj.* (**-er,-est**) (a) tidy/clean. (b) (alcohol) with no water added. (c) apt/precise (words). (d) skillful/well handled. **neat•ly**, *adv.* in a neat way. **neat•ness**, *n.* tidy/clean appearance.

neb•u•la ['nebjulə] *n.* (*pl.* **-ae** [-liː], **-as**) cloud of dust in space which shines like a star at night. **neb•u•lous** ['nebjuləs] *adj.* vague.

nec•es•sar•y ['nesəsərɪ] 1. *n.* what is essential/what must be done. 2. *adj.* essential/which cannot be avoided. **nec•es•sar•i•ly** [nesə-'serəlɪ] *adv.* in an unavoidable way; **taking the**

train isn't n. more expensive than the bus = it can be cheaper. **ne•ces•si•tate** [nɪ'sesɪteɪt] *v.* to make essential/to compel. **ne•ces•si•tous**, *adj.* (*formal*) poor. **ne•ces•si•ty**, *n.* (a) need/compulsion. (b) absolutely essential thing.

neck [nek] 1. *n.* (a) part of the body connecting the head to the shoulders; *inf.* **to be up to your n. in work** = have a lot of work to do; **to breathe down s.o.'s n.** = to watch s.o. very closely/to follow close behind s.o.; **to win by a n.** = win a race by a very short distance; **to finish n. and n.** = to be equal winners; *inf.* **a pain in the n.** = a troublesome person/thing; **to save your n.** = escape hanging/punishment; *inf.* **to get it in the n.** = to be severely criticized; *inf.* **to stick your n. out** = take a chance/to be asking for trouble. (b) narrow passage leading to a wider area; *inf.* **in this n. of the woods** = this part of the world. (c) part of a garment which goes around your neck. (d) part of an animal eaten as food. 2. *v. inf.* to fondle/caress. **neck•lace**, *n.* string of beads/pearls, etc., worn around the neck. **neck•let**, *n.* ornament worn tightly around the neck. **neck•line**, *n.* edge of a dress, etc., around the neck. **neck•tie**, *n.* band of material worn around the neck and tied in front with a knot.

nec•ro•man•cy ['nekrəmænsɪ] *n.* art of black magic/of predicting the future by speaking to the dead. **nec•ro•man•cer**, *n.* person who practices necromancy.

ne•crop•o•lis [ne'krɒpəlɪs] *n.* large ancient cemetery.

nec•tar ['nektə] *n.* (a) sweet substance produced by flowers. (b) any extremely pleasant drink.

nec•tar•ine ['nektəriːn] *n.* fruit like a peach with a smooth skin.

nee, née [neɪ] *adj.* with the maiden name of; **Mrs. Smith, n. Taylor.**

need [niːd] 1. *n.* (a) what is necessary. (b) **in n. of** = requiring. (c) time of difficulty/poverty; **a friend in n. is a friend indeed** = a person who helps you when you are in difficulties is a real friend. 2. *v.* to be necessary/to be required. **need•ful**, *adj.* (*old*) necessary. **need•less**, *adj.* unnecessary/not called for. **needs.** 1. *n. pl.* actual requirements. 2. *adv.* **if n. be** = if it has to be done. **need•y**, *adj.* (**-ier, -iest**) in need of/requiring help or food.

nee•dle ['nɪːdl] 1. *n.* (a) thin metal/plastic/wooden tool with a sharp point at one end; **it's like looking for a n. in a haystack** = it's a hopeless task. (b) **hypodermic n.** = needle used for injections. (c) hand/pointer (on a dial); **compass n.** = the indicator on the dial of a compass. (d) leaf of a pine tree. 2. *v.* to irritate/to provoke (s.o.). **nee•dle•wom•an**, *n.*

woman who is good at sewing.
nee•dle•work, *n.* sewing done with needle
and thread.

ne'er-do-well ['neədu:wel] *n.* person who is
good for nothing.

ne•far•i•ous [nɪ'feərɪəs] *adj.* (*formal*) very
wicked.

ne•gate [nɪ'geɪt] *v.* to oppose/to cancel out
(sth). **ne•ga•tion** [nɪ'geɪʃn] *n.* what is canceled out/negated. **neg•a•tive** ['negətɪv] 1. *n.*
(a) reply indicating no. (b) reverse image of a
photograph. (c) one of the terminals in a battery. 2. *adj.* (a) meaning no; showing opposi-
tion/refusal.   (b)   without   good/positive
qualities. (c) minus/less than zero. 3. *v.* to con-
tradict/to   oppose   (sth).   **neg•a•tive
eq•ui•ty,** *n.* state of owning a property valued at less than what is owed on it as a mortgage. **neg•a•tive•ly,** *adv.* in a way which
suggests opposition.

ne•glect [nɪ'glekt] 1. *n.* disregard/lack of care
or attention. 2. *v.* (a) to fail to look after/to fail
to maintain. (b) to omit to do (sth which
should be done). **ne•glect•ed,** *adj.* not
looked after. **ne•glect•ful,** *adj.* **to be n. of** =
to forget about. **neg•li•gence** ['neglɪdʒəns]
n. absence of proper care and attention.
neg•li•gent, *adj.* not giving proper care and
attention.   **neg•li•gi•ble,**   *adj.*   not
significant/not worth regarding.

neg•li•gee, negligé ['neglɪʒeɪ] *n.* woman's
light dressing gown.

ne•go•ti•ate [nɪ'gəʊsɪeɪt] *v.* (a) to discuss so
as to make an agreement with s.o. (b) to make
a financial arrangement. (c) to overcome an
obstacle/difficulty.   **ne•go•ti•a•ble**   [nɪ-
'gəʊsɪəbl] *adj.* which can be negotiated.
ne•go•ti•a•tion [nɪgəʊsɪ'eɪʃn] *n.* discuss-
ing/arranging   by   discussion.
ne•go•ti•a•tor [nɪ'gəʊsɪeɪtə] *n.* person who
discusses to try to reach an agreement.

Ne•gro ['ni:grəʊ, 'ni:grəs] *adj. & n.* (*pl.* **-oes**)
member of a dark-skinned race of people originating in Africa. **Ne•groid,** *adj.* having the
characteristics of Negroes.

neigh [neɪ] 1. *n.* sound made by a horse. 2. *v.* to
make a sound like a horse.

neigh•bor ['neɪbə], *Brit.* **neigh•bour** *n.* (a)
person   who   lives   in   a   nearby
house/road/country. (b) person sitting beside
you. **neigh•bor•hood,** *n.* (a) district and its
people. (b) **in the n. of** = around/near to (in
space or amount). **neigh•bor•ing,** *adj.* next

to each other. **neigh•bor•ly,** *adj.* in a
friendly/helpful way.

nei•ther ['naɪðə, 'ni:ðə] 1. *adv. & conj.* **n. ... nor**
= not one ... and not the other. 2. *adj. & pron.*
not either of two things or persons.

nel•son ['nelsən] *n.* (*in wrestling*) way of holding the opponent, with the arms under his
armpits and the hands on the back of his neck.

nem. con. ['nem'kɔn] *adv.* with no one voting
against.

nem•e•sis ['nemɪsɪs] *n.* (*no pl.*) just punishment from which you cannot escape.

neo- ['ni:əʊ] *prefix meaning* new.

ne•o•lith•ic [ni:əʊ'lɪθɪk] *adj.* belonging to the
late Stone Age.

ne•ol•o•gism   [nɪ'ɒlədʒɪzəm]   *n.*
newly-invented word.

ne•on ['ni:ɒn] *n.* (*element:* Ne) colorless gas
often used in tubes to make illuminated signs.

ne•o•phyte ['ni:əʊfaɪt] *n.* beginner; person
who is learning.

neph•ew ['nefju:] *n.* son of your brother or sister.

ne•phri•tis [nef'raɪtɪs] *n.* kidney disease.

nep•o•tism ['nepətɪzəm] *n.* giving members of
your family jobs for which they are not necessarily qualified.

nerve [nɜ:v] 1. *n.* (a) one of many thin threads
forming part of the body's system for conveying messages to and from the brain; **in a state
of nerves** = in a tense/anxious state; **to get on
s.o.'s nerves** = to irritate/annoy s.o. (b) cour-
age/confidence; *inf.* **he's got n.** = he's bold/im-
pudent/rude; **to have the n. to** = to be so rude
as to. (c) **to strain every n.** = to make tremen-
dous efforts. 2. *v.* **to n. yourself** = to summon
up strength/confidence.   **nerve-rack•ing,**
adj. disturbing. **nerv•ous,** *adj.* (a) **the n. system** = the pattern of nerve fibers in the body;
n. breakdown = physical and mental collapse
caused by worry. (b) timid/easily dis-
turbed/easily upset. **nerv•ous•ly,** *adv.* in a
worried/frightened way. **nerv•ous•ness,** *n.*
being nervous. **nerv•y,** *adj. inf.* boldly impu-
dent/rude.

nest [nest] 1. *n.* (a) place built by birds to lay
their eggs; **to feather your n.** = to make a lot of
money (usu. fraudulently). (b) hiding
place/collecting place for people or animals.
(c) **n. of tables** = tables of different sizes fitting
under each other. 2. *v.* (*of birds*) to build a
nest. **nest egg,** *n.* investment/money put

æ **back,** a: **farm,** ɒ: **top,** aɪ **pipe,** aʊ **how,** aɪə **fire,** aʊə **flower,** ɔ: **bought,** ɔɪ **toy,** e **fed,** eəhair, eɪ **take,** ə
afraid, əʊ **boat,** əʊə **lower,** v: **word,** i: **heap,** ɪ **hit,** ɪə **hear,** u: **school,** ʊ **book,** ʌ **but,** b **back,** d **dog,** ð **then,**
dʒ **just,** f **fog,** g **go,** h **hand,** j **yes,** k **catch,** l **last,** m **mix,** n **nut,** ŋ **sing,** p **penny,** r **round,** s **some,** ʃ **short,** t
too, tʃ **chop,** θ **thing,** v **voice,** w **was,** z **zoo,** ʒ **treasure**

aside for future use. **nest•ling** ['neslɪŋ] *n.* small bird not yet ready to leave the nest.

nes•tle ['nesl] *v.* (a) to settle down comfortably. (b) to have close and loving contact.

net [net] 1. *n.* loosely woven material; piece of this material used for fishing/catching/fencing, etc. 2. *v.* (**netted**) (a) to catch in a net. (b) to make a true profit; **to n. a big profit** = to make a lot of money. 3. *adj.* (price/weight) left after taking away the weight of the container/the tax paid, etc.; **n. profit** = actual gain after expenses have been paid; **n. weight** = true weight without the wrappings. **net•ting,** *n.* material made of string/wire loosely woven into a regular pattern of holes. **net•work,** *n.* interconnecting system (of railroads, etc.); radio/TV system; interconnected computer system.

Net [net] *n. inf.* **the Net** = the Internet.

neth•er ['neðə] *adj.* (*formal*) lower; **n. regions** = bottom part. **neth•er•most,** *adj.* lowest.

net•i•quette ['netɪket] *n.* Internet etiquette.

ne•tsu•ke ['netskɪ] *n.* carved ivory toggle, formerly used in Japan.

net•tle ['netl] 1. *n.* (**stinging**) **n.** = weed with stinging leaves. 2. *v.* to anger/to irritate. **net•tle•rash,** *n.* skin rash caused by an allergy.

neu•ral ['njʊrəl] *adj.* referring to nerves. **neu•ral•gia** [njuˈrældʒə] *n.* nerve pains in the face or head. **neu•ral•gic,** *adj.* referring to neuralgia. **neu•ri•tis** [njuˈraɪtɪs] *n.* inflammation of nerves. **neu•ro•bi•ol•o•gy,** *n.* study of the biology of the nervous system. **neu•ro•log•i•cal** [njurəˈlɒdʒɪkl] *adj.* referring to neurology. **neu•rol•o•gist** [njuˈrɒlədʒɪst] *n.* person who studies the nervous system. **neu•rol•o•gy** [njuˈrɒlədʒɪ] *n.* study of the body's nervous system. **neu•ron,** *n.* cell in the nerve system which passes on impulses. **neu•ro•sis** [njuˈrəʊsɪs] *n.* (*pl.* **-oses** [-əʊsiːz]) mental illness caused by a nervous disorder. **neu•rot•ic** [njuˈrɒtɪk] *adj.* unbalanced (behavior). **neu•rot•ic•al•ly,** *adv.* in an unbalanced way.

neu•ter ['njuːtə] 1. *adj.* (*in grammar*) not having a masculine or feminine gender. 2. *v.* to castrate. **neu•tral.** 1. *adj.* (a) not favoring or supporting either side in a dispute. (b) not having a distinctive color. (c) neither acid or alkali. 2. *n.* (a) citizen of a neutral country. (b) **the car is in n.** = not in gear. **neu•tral•i•ty** [njuˈtrælɪtɪ] *n.* being uncommitted/neutral; not taking sides. **neu•tral•i•za•tion** [njuːtrəlaɪˈzeɪʃn] *n.* act of neutralizing. **neu•tral•ize** ['njuːtrəlaɪz] *v.* to cancel out by using an opposite. **neu•tral•ly,** *adv.* in a neutral way. **neu•tron,** *n.* basic particle with no

electric charge; **n. bomb** = nuclear bomb which kills people but does little damage to buildings.

nev•er ['nevə] *adv.* (a) not ever/not at any time. (b) (*for emphasis*) not at all. (c) (*exclamation of surprise*) surely not; **well I n.!** how surprising! **nev•er-end•ing,** *adj.* which does not stop. **nev•er•more,** *adv.* (*formal*) not any more. **nev•er•the•less** [nevəðəˈles] *adv.* despite all that/all the same. **nev•er-to-be-for•got•ten,** *adj.* memorable.

new [njuː] *adj.* (**-er, -est**) (a) completely different/not thought of before/not met before. (b) changed/different. (c) fresh/unused; **to turn over a n. leaf** = become better/start again. (d) most recent; **n. moon** = moon when it is a thin crescent. (e) just bought/just acquired. **new•born,** *adj.* just born. **new•com•er,** *n.* person who has just come to an area. **new•fan•gled,** *adj.* newly invented. **new•ly,** *adv.* most recently; **newlyweds** = people who have just gotten married. **new•ness,** *n.* being recent/fresh; not having been used. **news** [njuːz] *n.* spoken or written information about events; **it's in the n.** = it is of topical interest; **to break the n. to s.o.** = to tell s.o. bad/unwelcome news; **no n. is good n.** = the absence of bad news means things may be going well. **news•cast•er,** *n.* person who reads the news on television. **news flash,** *n.* short news item. **news•group,** *n.* Internet service that enables users to exchange electronic mail on a common theme. **news•let•ter,** *n.* printed sheet giving news to members of a church/club, etc. **news•man,** *n.* (*pl.* **-men**) journalist. **news•pa•per,** *n.* daily/weekly paper containing information and news. **news•print,** *n.* paper for printing newspapers and magazines. **news•reel,** *n.* short motion picture about current events. **news•wor•thy,** *adj.* (events) worth recording/mentioning in papers or on television. **news•y,** *adj. inf.* full of news. **New World,** *n.* North and South America. **new year,** *n.* the year which has just started; period just after 1st January. **New Year's Day,** *n.* January 1st. **New Year's Eve,** *n.* December 31st.

new•el ['njuːəl] *n.* post at the top or bottom of stairs, to which the banisters are attached.

newt [njuːt] *n.* small, lizardlike animal which can live either in or out of water.

new•ton ['njuːtən] *n.* standard measurement of force.

next [nekst] 1. *adj.* (a) (*of time/sequence*) coming after. (b) (*of place*) closest to/nearest; **she lives n. door** = in the house/apartment next to this one. 2. *adv.* coming after in place/time; **what n.?** = what other amazing or absurd things can we expect? **it costs n. to nothing** = it costs very little. 3. *n.* person/thing following; **the week after n.** = not the next week but the following one. **next-door,** *adj.* living next door. **next of kin,** *n.* (*no pl.*) nearest relative(s).

nex•us ['neksəs] *n.* link/connecting point for ideas, organizations, etc.

Ni *symbol for* nickel.

nib [nɪb] *n.* pointed writing end of a pen.

nib•ble ['nɪbl] 1. *n.* bite/very small amount eaten. 2. *v.* to take very small, cautious bites. **nib•ble a•way,** *v.* to remove gradually/in little pieces.

nice [naɪs] *adj.* (**-er, -est**) (a) generally pleasant. (b) precise; subtle. **nice-look•ing,** *adj.* pretty/pleasant to look at. **nice•ly,** *adv.* in a satisfactory/good manner. **nice•ness,** *n.* quality of being agreeable. **ni•ce•ty,** *n.* fine/exact detail.

niche [niːʃ] *n.* (a) hollow in a wall or pillar to put a statue/vase/decoration in; **to find your n./to find a n. for yourself** = to find a completely satisfying or suitable role/job. (b) special place in a market.

nick [nɪk] 1. *n.* small dent/notch (usu. to mark a place); *inf.* **in the n. of time** = just in time. 2. *v.* to make a small notch/cut.

nick•el ['nɪkl] 1. *n.* (a) (*element:* Ni) silver-colored metal. (b) 5-cent coin. 2. *v.* (**nickeled, nickelled**) to coat with nickel.

nick•name ['nɪkneɪm] 1. *n.* abbreviated or pet name. 2. *v.* to give (s.o.) a nickname.

nic•o•tine ['nɪkətiːn] *n.* poisonous brown liquid obtained from tobacco.

niece [niːs] *n.* daughter of your brother or sister.

nif•ty ['nɪftɪ] *adj. inf.* (a) attractive/fashionable. (b) very good; excellent (idea).

Ni•ge•ri•an [naɪˈdʒɪərɪən] 1. *adj.* referring to Nigeria. 2. *n.* person who comes from Nigeria.

nig•gard•ly ['nɪgədlɪ] *adj.* mean; very small (amount).

nig•gle ['nɪgl] *v.* to be fussy about relatively unimportant details. **nig•gling,** *adj.* unimportant/insignificant.

nigh [naɪ] *adv.* (*formal*) near.

night [naɪt] *n.* last part of each day; period of darkness from sunset to sunrise; **last n.** = yesterday after dark; **the first n.** = the official opening performance of a play or entertainment; **n. out** = evening spent outside the home. **night•cap,** (a) (*old*) cap worn in bed. (b) bed-time drink. **night•clothes,** *n. pl.* clothes worn in bed. **night•club,** *n.* club only open at night. **night•dress,** *n.* nightgown. **night•fall,** *n.* time when night starts. **night•gown,** *n.* gown worn by women in bed. **night•ie,** *n. inf.* nightgown. **night•in•gale,** *n.* small brown singing bird. **night•jar,** *n.* dark-colored bird which flies by night. **night•life,** *n.* entertainment which takes place in a town at night. **night•light,** *n.* small dim light left burning at night. **night•ly,** *adv.* every night. **night•mare,** *n.* (a) vivid frightening dream. (b) horrible event. **night•mar•ish,** *adj.* vividly frightening. **night school,** *n.* school which has classes for adults in the evening. **night•shade,** *n.* poisonous plant. **night•shirt,** *n.* long shirt worn in bed. **night soil,** *n.* human excreta, used as manure. **night•time,** *n.* period of night; **nighttime flight** = flight during the hours of darkness. **night•watch•man,** *n.* (*pl.* -men) man who guards a building at night.

ni•hil•ism ['naɪhɪlɪzəm] *n.* belief that nothing which exists is good. **ni•hil•ist,** *n.* person who believes in nihilism.

nil [nɪl] *n.* nothing/zero.

nim•ble ['nɪmbl] *adj.* (**-er, -est**) agile/fast-moving; physically fit and alert. **nim•bly,** *adv.* in an expert way.

nim•bus ['nɪmbəs] *n.* (a) dark raincloud. (b) shining halo.

nin•com•poop ['nɪnkəmpuːp] *n.* silly person/fool.

nine [naɪn] *n.* number 9; **n. times out of ten** = in most cases; *inf.* **dressed to the nines** = wearing your most elaborate clothes; **possession is n. tenths of the law** = it is easy to claim ownership of something which is already in your possession. **nine•pins,** *n. pl.* skittles. **nine•teen,** *n.* number 19; **the n. hundreds** = the years after 1900. **nine•teenth, 19th,** *adj. & n.* referring to nineteen; **the n. century** = period from 1800 to 1899. **nine•ti•eth, 90th,** *adj. & n.* referring to ninety. **nine•ty,** *n.* number 90; **she's in her nineties** = she is between 90 and 99 years old. **ninth, 9th,** *adj. & n.* referring to nine; **the n. century** = period from 800 to 899.

nin•ny ['nɪnɪ] *n.* idiot.

nip [nɪp] 1. *n.* (a) small amount of alcohol. (b) short sharp bite/pinch; **a n. in the air** = a sud-

---

æ **back,** ɑː **farm,** ɒ **top,** aɪ **pipe,** aʊ **how,** aɪə **fire,** aʊə **flower,** ɔː **bought,** ɔɪ **toy,** e **fed,** eə **hair,** eɪ **take,** ə **afraid,** əʊ **boat,** əʊə **lower,** ɜː **word,** iː **heap,** ɪ **hit,** ɪə **hear,** uː **school,** ʊ **book,** ʌ **but,** b **back,** d **dog,** ð **then,** dʒ **just,** f **fog,** g **go,** h **hand,** j **yes,** k **catch,** l **last,** m **mix,** n **nut,** ŋ **sing,** p **penny,** r **round,** s **some,** ʃ **short,** t **too,** tʃ **chop,** θ **thing,** v **voice,** w **was,** z **zoo,** ʒ **treasure**

den/sharp burst of cold weather. 2. *v.* (**nipped**). to bite/to pinch sharply or suddenly. **nip•per**, *n. inf.* (a) small child. (b) **nippers** = pincers. **nip•py**, *adj. inf.* (a) sharp-tasting. (b) cold.

nip•ple ['nɪpl] *n.* (a) small projection on the tip of a breast from which, in females, the mother's milk comes. (b) short piece of pipe with threads at both ends, used for coupling two parts.

nir•va•na [nɪə'vɑːnə] *n.* (*for Buddhists*) happy state after death when the dead person's soul joins the divine soul.

Nis•sen hut ['nɪsən'hʌt] *n.* shed with a semi-circular roof of corrugated iron and a concrete floor.

nit [nɪt] *n.* egg of a louse. **nit-pick•ing**, *n. inf.* petty criticism/finding small faults to criticize. **nit•wit**, *n. inf.* idiot.

ni•tro•gen ['naɪtrədʒən] *n.* (*element:* N) gas which makes up four-fifths of the atmosphere. **ni•tro•gly•cer•ine**, *n.* liquid explosive. **ni•trate**, *n.* salt of nitric acid. **ni•tric ac•id**, *n.* acid containing nitrogen. **ni•trous**, *adj.* containing nitrogen.

nit•ty-grit•ty [nɪtɪ'grɪtɪ] *n. inf.* basic details (of a matter).

nm *abbrev. for* nanometer.

no. *abbrev. for* number.

no [nəu] 1. *n. & adv.* showing the negative/opposite of yes; **the noes have it** = most people have voted no. 2. *adj.* none of/not any of; **it's n. distance** = not at all far/a very short distance away; **it's n. joke** = not funny but serious; **n. admission** = entrance not allowed; *inf.* **n. way** = certainly not. 3. *adv.* not/not at all; **n. sooner said than done** = it will be done immediately.

no•ble ['nəubl] 1. *n.* person of high rank by title or birth. 2. *adj.* (**-er, -est**) of high rank/dignified; worthy or praise/splendid. **no•bil•i•ty** [nə'bɪlɪtɪ] *n.* (a) titled members of society/the aristocracy. (b) high-mindedness. **no•ble•man,** *n.* (*pl.* **-men**) noble. **no•ble-mind•ed•ness,** *n.* high-mindedness/worthy thoughts. **no•ble•ness,** *n.* being noble; nobility. **no•ble•wom•an,** *n.* (*pl.* **-women**) woman of high rank. **no•bly,** *adv.* in a noble fashion/heroically.

no•bod•y ['nəubədɪ] 1. *n.* person of no importance. 2. *pron.* no one/no person.

noc•tur•nal [nɒk'tɜːnl] *adj.* referring to the night; (animals which are) most active at night. **noc•turne** ['nɒktɜːn] *n.* painting/piece of music conveying a feeling of night.

nod [nɒd] 1. *n.* forward movement of the head as a greeting/as a sign of agreement. 2. *v.* (**nodded**) to show agreement/to give permission/to

agree by a forward movement of the head; **to n. off** = to fall asleep; **nodding acquaintance** = (i) person you know only slightly; (ii) slight knowledge.

node [nəud] *n.* (a) place where leaves grow from a plant's stem. (b) knob on a root/branch/human joint. (c) point where curves cross. **nod•al**, *adj.* central/at the point where lines meet. **nod•ule** ['nɒdjuːl] *n.* small node.

No•el [nəu'el] *n.* Christmas.

nog [nɒg] *n.* **egg n.** = drink made of alcohol and raw eggs. **nog•gin**, *n.* small quantity of alcohol.

noise [nɔɪz] 1. *n.* loud (usu. unpleasant) sound. 2. *v.* **to n. sth about/abroad** = to make sth public/to spread the news. **noise•less**, *adj.* without any sound. **noise•less•ly**, *adv.* in a silent way. **nois•i•ly**, *adv.* in a noisy/loud way. **nois•y**, *adj.* (**-ier, -iest**) making a lot of noise; loud.

no•mad ['nəumæd] *adj. & n.* (member) of a wandering tribe with no fixed home. **no•mad•ic** [nəu'mædɪk] *adj.* not staying in one place/traveling.

no man's land ['nəumænzlænd] *n.* territory between two armies which belongs to neither side.

nom de plume [nɒmdə'pluːm] *n.* name used by an author in place of his own.

no•men•cla•ture [nə'menklətʃə] *n.* (*formal*) system of naming.

nom•i•nal ['nɒmɪnl] *adj.* (a) referring to names. (b) in name rather than in fact; **n. fee** = very small amount of money/token payment. **nom•i•nal•ly**, *adv.* in name rather than in fact.

nom•i•nate ['nɒmɪneɪt] *v. tr.* to name/to propose. **nom•i•na•tion** [nɒmɪ'neɪʃn] *n.* act of nominating; suggested name. **nom•i•na•tor**, *n.* person who nominates. **nom•i•nee** [nɒmɪ'niːi] *n.* person who is nominated.

nom•i•na•tive ['nɒmɪnətɪv] *n.* form of a noun when it is the subject of a verb.

non- [nɒn] *prefix meaning* not/the opposite.

non•a•ge•nar•i•an [nɒnədʒə'neərɪən] *adj. & n.* (person) who is between 90 and 99 years old.

non•ag•gres•sion [nɒnə'greʃn] *n.* agreement not to engage in war.

non•al•co•hol•ic [nɒnælkə'hɒlɪk] *adj.* not intoxicating/not containing alcohol.

non•a•ligned [nɒnə'laɪnd] *adj.* (country) which is not linked to a large and powerful bloc of countries. **non•a•lign•ment**, *n.* policy of being nonaligned.

non•cha•lant ['nɒnʃələnt] *adj.* casual/unexcited. **non•cha•lance,** *n.* being calm/unmoved. **non•cha•lant•ly,** *adv.* in a nonchalant way.

non•com•bat•ant [nɒn'kʌmbətənt] *adj. & n.* (person) who does not fight; doctor/priest, etc., attached to an army.

non•com•mis•sioned [nɒnkə'mɪʃnd] *adj.* **noncommissioned officer** = soldier of a lower rank than a commissioned officer.

non•com•mit•tal [nɒnkə'mɪtl] *adj.* not favoring a definite course of action/not agreeing with either side in an argument.

non com•pos men•tis [nɒnkɒmpɒs'mentɪs] *adj.* mad.

non•con•form•ist [nɒnkən'fɔːmɪst] *adj. & n.* (person) who does not act in the same way as most people. **non•con•form•i•ty,** *n.* being nonconformist.

non•de•script ['nɒndɪskrɪpt] *adj.* very ordinary/without individual qualities.

none [nʌn] 1. *pron.* (a) not any (**of**). (b) no person/no one. 2. *adv.* (*used with* **the** *and comparative or* **too**) not at all; **n. too good; n. the worse for the accident.**

non•en•ti•ty [nɒ'nentɪtɪ] *n.* person of no importance.

none•the•less [nʌnθə'les] *adv.* nevertheless.

non•e•vent [nɒnɪ'vent] *n.* happening which was expected to be important but which turns out not to be so.

non•ex•ist•ent [nɒnɪg'zɪstənt] *adj.* not having any existence in fact/not real.

non•fic•tion ['nɒnfɪkʃn] *n.* (*no pl.*) books which are not fiction/which are factual.

non•in•ter•ven•tion [nɒnɪntə'venʃən] *n.* act of not interfering.

non•pay•ment [nɒn'peɪmənt] *n.* failing to pay what is due.

non•plussed, nonplused [nɒn'plʌst] *adj.* puzzled/confused.

non•prof•it-mak•ing [nɒn'prɒfɪtmeɪkɪŋ] *adj.* (organization such as a charity) which is not allowed to make a profit.

non•re•fund•a•ble [nɒnrɪ'fʌndəbl] *adj.* which will not be refunded.

non•res•i•dent [nɒn'rezɪdənt] *adj. & n.* (person) not living in/not staying very long in a place.

non•re•turn•a•ble [nɒnrɪ'tɜːnəbl] *adj.* (bottle) on which there is no deposit and which the manufacturers do not want back.

non•sense ['nɒnsəns] *n.* foolish ideas/ridiculous behavior. **non•sen•si•cal** [nɒn'sensɪkl] *adj.* absurd.

non se•qui•tur [nɒn'sekwɪtə] *n.* phrase which does not follow logically from what has gone before; conclusion drawn incorrectly from the evidence.

non•skid [nɒn'skɪd] *adj.* which prevents skidding.

non•smok•er ['nɒnsməʊkə] *n.* (a) person who does not smoke. (b) place where smoking is not allowed. **non•smok•ing,** *adj.* where smoking is not allowed.

non•start•er [nɒn'stɑːtə] *n. inf.* project/plan which never materializes.

non•stick ['nɒnstɪk] *adj.* (pan) covered with a substance which prevents food from sticking when cooking.

non•stop ['nɒnstɒp] 1. *adj.* not stopping/traveling directly from point of departure to the end of the journey. 2. *adv.* ceaselessly/without stopping.

non•un•ion [nɒn'juːnɪən] *adj.* not belonging to a union.

non•vi•o•lence [nɒn'vaɪələns] *n.* absence of physical violence/of aggression.

noo•dles ['nuːdlz] *n. pl.* strips of paste for cooking. **noo•dle,** *n. sl.* fool.

nook [nʊk] *n.* small hiding place; **in every n. and cranny** = in every little hole and corner.

noon [nuːn] *n.* midday. **noon•day,** *n.* **the n. sun** = the sun at noon.

no one ['nəʊwʌn] *pron.* nobody/no person.

noose [nuːs] *n.* rope knotted to form a loop which can be tightened by pulling.

nor [nɔː] *conj.* (a) (*usu. followed by verb then subject*) not either/and not. (b) **neither...n.** = not one...and not the other.

Nor•dic ['nɔːdɪk] *adj.* referring to Scandinavia.

norm [nɔːm] *n.* normal/standard pattern.

nor•mal ['nɔːml] *adj.* usual/regular/expected. **nor•mal•i•ty** [nɔː'mælɪtɪ] *n.* being normal/not having unusual features. **nor•mal•ly,** *adv.* in the usual way.

Nor•man ['nɔːmən] *adj. & n.* (person) from Normandy; (architecture, etc.) developed in England after the conquest by the Normans in 1066.

Norse [nɔːs] 1. *adj.* referring to ancient Scandinavia. 2. *n.* ancient Scandinavian language. **Norse•man,** *n.* (*pl.* **-men**) person from ancient Scandinavia.

north [nɔːθ] 1. *n.* one of the points of the compass, the direction to the right when you are facing the setting sun. 2. *adv.* toward the north; 3. *adj.* referring to the north. **n. wind** =

wind which blows from the north.
north•bound, *adj.* going toward the north.
north•east, *n.* direction half-way between
east and north. **north•east•er•ly,** *adj.* to-
ward/from the northeast. **north•east•ern,**
adj. referring to the northeast. **north•er•ly**
['nɔːðəlɪ] *adj. & n.* in/to/from the north; (wind)
from the north. **north•ern** ['nɔːðn] *adj.* referring to the north. **north•ern•er,** *n.* person
who lives in/comes from the north.
north•ward. 1. *adj.* toward the north. 2.
adv. (*also* **northwards**) toward the north.
north•ern•most, *adj.* furthest north.
north•west, *n.* direction half-way between
west and north. **north•west•er•ly,** *adj.* to-
ward/from the northwest. **north•west•ern,**
adj. referring to the northwest.

Nor•we•gian [nɔːˈwiːdʒən] 1. *adj.* referring to
Norway. 2. *n.* (a) person from Norway. (b)
language spoken in Norway.

nose [nəʊz] 1. *n.* (a) part of the face used for
breathing in air and smelling; **as plain as the n.
on your face** = very obvious; **to speak through
your n.** = speak as if your nose is blocked; *inf.* **I
paid through the n. for it** = I paid far too much
for it; **I did it under his very n.** = did it right in
front of him but he didn't notice; **to poke your
n. into** = to interfere unasked; **to cut off your n.
to spite your face** = to do sth when you are
angry which in fact harms you; **follow your n.**
= go straight on; **to keep s.o.'s n. to the grind-
stone** = to make s.o. work hard all the time; **to
look down your n. at s.o.** = to regard s.o. as inferior; **to turn up your n. at sth** = to reject sth as
not good enough. (b) good sense of smell; **a
good n. for** = an instinct for finding sth. (c)
front end of a vehicle. 2. *v.* (a) to discover by
smell. (b) *inf.* to detect/to discover. (c) (*of
boat*) to go in gently. **nose a•bout, nose
around,** *v.* to look/to search around.
nose•bag, *n.* bag of food hung around an
animal's neck. **nose•bleed,** *n.* flow of blood
from the nose. **nose cone,** *n.* round pointed
part at the top of a rocket. **nose•dive.** 1. *n.*
steep downward dive of an aircraft. 2. *v.* to
dive down steeply. **nose•gay,** *n.* small bunch
of flowers. **nos•y, nosey,** *adj.* (**-ier, -iest**) *inf.*
curious/interested in the affairs of other people; **N. Parker** = very inquisitive person.
nos•i•ly, *adv.* in a nosy way.

nosh [nɒʃ] *n. Sl.* snack.

nos•tal•gia [nɒˈstældʒɪə] *n.* longing for/senti-
mental recollection of the past. **nos•tal•gic,**
adj.   encouraging   nostalgia.
nos•tal•gi•cal•ly, *adv.* in a nostalgic way.

nos•tril ['nɒstrɪl] *n.* one of the two holes in the
nose to admit air and smells.

nos•trum ['nɒstrəm] *n.* quack medicine.

not [nɒt] *adv.* (a) (*used with verbs to make the
action negative; short form* **n't**) **he will not
come/he won't come.** (b) (*used to make negative
words/phrases/sentences*) **I think not** = I don't
think so. (c) (*providing emphasis by a form of
contrast*) **not yours but mine.** (d) (*used to show
the opposite*) **not a few** = many; **not too well** =
badly; **not sorry to leave** = glad to leave; **not
without reason** = with good reason.

no•ta be•ne ['nəʊtə'beneɪ] note well, pay attention to this.

no•ta•ble ['nəʊtəbl] 1. *adj.* worth noticing;
large. 2. *n.* important person. **no•ta•bil•i•ty**
[nəʊtəˈbɪlɪtɪ] *n.* (a) being important. (b) nota-
ble/important person. **no•ta•bly,** *adv.*
significantly/particularly.

no•ta•ry (public) ['nəʊtərɪ('pʌblɪk)] *n.* person who has authority to see that legal documents are correctly written and who witnesses
their signing.

no•ta•tion [nəʊˈteɪʃn] *n.* system of symbols
used to show notes in music/to show mathematical signs.

notch [nɒtʃ] 1. *n.* (*pl.* **-es**) small cut (usu.
V-shaped) used to mark/to record. 2. *v.* (a) to
mark with notches. (b) to score (a goal/a victory).

note [nəʊt] 1. *n.* (a) music sound. (b) written
sign which indicates a musical sound. (c) key
on a piano, etc.; **to strike the right n.** = to play
the correct note/to provide the appropriate
tone/atmosphere/words in a particular situation. (d) very short letter; very brief writ-
ten/printed document. (e) bank note/piece of
paper money. (f) notice/attention/importance;
of n. = important; **to take n. of** = to pay attention to/to be aware of. (g) indication. 2. *v.* (a)
to write down. (b) to pay attention to.
note•book, *n.* book in which you write
notes. **note•book com•pu•ter,** *n.* portable
computer that is smaller than a laptop but bigger than a palmtop. **not•ed,** *adj.* fa-
mous/well-known. **note•pad,** *n.* pad of
paper for notes. **note•pa•per,** *n.* writing
paper for letters. **note•wor•thy,** *adj.* deserving attention.

noth•ing ['nʌθɪŋ] 1. *n.* (a) not anything; **to say
n. about** = to keep silent about; **there's n. in it** =
no truth in it; **to make sth out of n.** = to exaggerate sth; *inf.* **n. doing!** = I refuse; **to get sth for
n.** = get sth free; **to think n. of it** = make it seem
easy; **to have n. to do with** = not to associate
with/not to become involved in; **it's n. to do
with you** = not your concern; **to come to n.** = be
unsuccessful. (b) (*used with an adj. following*)
not anything. (c) (*used as a comparison/to suggest something inferior*) **that's n. to what I saw.**
2. *adv.* in no way/not at all. **noth•ing•ness,**
n. void/nothing at all.

no•tice ['nəʊtɪs] 1. *n.* (a) advance information/warning; warning to leave one's job. (b) **to take n. of** = to pay attention to. (c) written account/announcement; written information. (d) review in a newspaper. 2. *v.* to pay attention to. **no•tice•a•ble,** *adj.* easily seen. **no•tice•a•bly,** *adv.* in a noticeable way.

no•ti•fy ['nəʊtɪfaɪ] *v.* to announce/to declare/to advise/to inform. **no•ti•fi•ca•tion** [nəʊtɪfɪ'keɪʃn] *n.* formal information.

no•tion ['nəʊʃn] *n.* (a) vague awareness/idea/thought. (b) **notions** = small personal items, as buttons/thread/ribbons, etc. **no•tion•al,** *adj.* vague but assumed to be correct. **no•tion•al•ly,** *adv.* in a notional way.

no•to•ri•ous [nəʊ'tɔːrɪəs] *adj.* well known (usu. for doing sth bad). **no•to•ri•e•ty** [nəʊtə'raɪətɪ] *n.* bad/unfavorable reputation. **no•to•ri•ous•ly,** *adv.* unfavorably significant.

not•with•stand•ing [nɒtwɪθ'stændɪŋ] (*formal*) 1. *prep.* despite. 2. *adv.* all the same/anyway.

nou•gat ['nuːgɑː] *n.* type of white candy made with nuts, honey and egg whites.

nought [nɔːt] *n.* naught.

noun [naʊn] *n.* word used as a name of a person or thing.

nour•ish ['nʌrɪʃ] *v.* (a) to provide (sth) with food so that it will grow. (b) to keep alive (ideas/feelings). **nour•ish•ing,** *adj.* providing nourishment. **nour•ish•ment,** *n.* food which enables plants/animals to grow.

nous [naʊs] *n. inf.* common sense/ordinary intelligent reaction.

no•va ['nəʊvə] *n.* star which suddenly becomes much brighter and then fades away.

nov•el ['nɒvl] 1. *n.* long fictional story in the form of a book. 2. *adj.* new/original. **nov•el•ette** [nɒvə'let] *n.* short novel. **nov•el•ist** ['nɒvəlɪst] *n.* person who writes novels. **nov•el•ty,** *n.* (a) new/original thing. (b) small/unusual toy or trinket. (c) newness.

No•vem•ber [nə'vembə] *n.* 11th month of the year.

nov•ice ['nɒvɪs] *n.* (a) beginner; inexperienced person. (b) person who is intending to join a religious order but who has not yet taken the vows. **no•vi•ti•ate,** *n.* state of being a novice in a religious order.

now [naʊ] 1. *adv.* (a) at this moment. (b) immediately/beginning from this time. (c) **just n.** = in the immediate past. (d) (*when relating events*) then/next/by that time. 2. *inter.* showing warning/criticism; **n. then!** 3. *conj.* as a result of/since. 4. *n.* this time; the present time. **now•a•days** ['naʊədeɪz] *adv.* at the present day/in these modern times.

no•where ['nəʊweə] *adv.* not in/at/to any place; **n. near completion** = far from being finished; **I got n.** = I was totally unsuccessful in what I was trying to do.

nox•ious ['nɒkʃəs] *adj.* unpleasant/harmful.

noz•zle ['nɒzl] *n.* special fitting at the end of a pipe or hose for controlling what comes out.

ns *abbrev. for* nanosecond.

nth [enθ] *adj.* to a very great extent.

nu•ance ['njuːɑːns] *n.* shade of meaning or color.

nub [nʌb] *n.* central point.

nu•bile ['njuːbaɪl] *adj.* (*of a young woman*) very attractive physically.

nu•cle•us ['njuːklɪəs] *n.* (*pl.* **-lei**) (a) vital central part around which things collect. (b) central part of an atom. **nu•cle•ar,** *adj.* concerned with/belonging to a nucleus, esp. of an atom; **n. energy** = energy produced by nuclear power; **n. family** = family group consisting of the parents and children. **n. reactor** = device for producing atomic energy; **n. power** = power from atomic energy; **n. submarine** = driven by nuclear power. **nu•cle•on•ics** [njuːklɪ'ɒnɪks] *n.* study of the application of nuclear energy.

nude [njuːd] 1. *n.* (a) naked person. (b) **in the n.** = naked. 2. *adj.* naked/bare. **nud•ism,** *n.* belief in the physical and mental advantages of going about naked. **nud•ist,** *n.* person who believes in going about naked; **n. colony** = club/camp for those who wish to go about naked. **nu•di•ty,** *n.* not wearing any clothes/nakedness.

nudge [nʌdʒ] 1. *n.* slight push/prod with the elbow to attract attention. 2. *v.* to attract attention, usu. by pushing with the elbow.

nu•ga•to•ry ['njuːgətrɪ] *adj.* (*formal*) worthless; useless.

nug•get ['nʌgɪt] *n.* lump of gold in its natural state; **n. of information** = piece of useful information.

nui•sance ['njuːsns] *n.* annoying or disagreeable person/thing; **public n.** = action which bothers other people in such a way as to be against the law.

null [nʌl] *adj.* without significance/canceled

æ back, ɑː farm, ɒ top, aɪ pipe, aʊ how, aɪə fire, aʊə flower, ɔː bought, ɔɪ toy, e fed, eəhair, eɪ take, ə afraid, əʊ boat, əʊə lower, vː word, iː heap, ɪ hit, ɪə hear, uː school, ʊ book, ʌ but, b back, d dog, ð then, dʒ just, f fog, g go, h hand, j yes, k catch, l last, m mix, n nut, ŋ sing, p penny, r round, s some, ʃ short, t too, tʃ chop, θ thing, v voice, w was, z zoo, ʒ treasure

out; **n. and void** = no longer valid. **nul•li•fy,** *v.* to cancel out/to make invalid. **nul•li•ty,** *n.* nothingness/thing that is null.

numb [nʌm] 1. *adj.* without feeling or sensation/unable to move. 2. *v.* to make incapable of movement or feeling. **numb•ly,** *adv.* not moving because of being numb. **numb•ness,** *n.* having no feeling or sensation/being incapable of action. **numb•skull,** *n. inf.* stupid person.

num•ber ['nʌmbə] 1. *n.* (a) name of a figure; total of objects or persons; **one of their n.** = one of them; *inf.* **to take care of n. one** = to look after yourself/your own interests. (b) **numbers** = many in quantity. (c) (*in grammar*) term indicating whether a noun is singular or plural. (d) copy of a periodical/a song/a piece of played music; **back n.** = thing which is out of date; *inf.* **his number's up** = he's dying. 2. *v.* (a) to count/to include among/to total; **his days are numbered** = he hasn't much time to live. (b) to put a number/figure on. **num•ber•less,** *adj.* which cannot be counted.

nu•mer•al ['nju:mərəl] *n.* actual sign representing a number. **nu•mer•ate** ['nju:mərət] *adj.* able to calculate mathematically. **nu•mer•a•tion** [nju:mə'reɪʃn] *n.* calculation. **nu•mer•a•tor,** *n.* figure above the line in a fraction. **nu•mer•ic key•pad,** *n.* set of numbered keys on a computer keyboard. **nu•mer•i•cal** [nju:'merɪkl] *adj.* referring to numbers; **in n. order** = in order of numbers. **nu•mer•i•cal•ly,** *adv.* by/in number. **nu•mer•ous** ['nju:mərəs] *adj.* many/a lot of.

nu•mis•mat•ics [nju:mɪz'mætɪks] *n.* study of coins. **nu•mis•ma•tist** [nju:'mɪzmətɪst] *n.* person who collects/studies coins.

nun [nʌn] *n.* woman who is a member of a religious order living in a separate community or convent. **nun•like,** *adj.* very calm/good/restrained. **nun•ner•y,** *n.* convent/community where nuns live.

nun•ci•o ['nʌnsɪəʊ] *n.* ambassador sent by the Pope to a foreign country.

nup•tial ['nʌpʃl] *adj.* (*formal*) referring to marriage/wedding ceremonies. **nup•tials,** *n. pl.* wedding.

nurse [nɜ:s] 1. *n.* (a) person trained and employed to look after the sick; **night n.** = nurse who is on duty at night. (b) woman employed to look after children. 2. *v.* (a) to look after (a sick person). (b) to look after very carefully. (c) to think about/to ponder over. (d) to hold close. **nurse•maid,** *n.* woman or girl who is paid to look after children. **nurs•er•y,** *n.* (a) room/building where babies or young children are looked after; **n. school** = school for very young children; **n. rhyme** = little poem telling a simple story told or sung to young children. (b) place where young plants are grown. **nurs•er•y•man,** *n.* (*pl.* -men) man who owns or manages a nursery for plants. **nurs•ing.** 1. *adj.* (person) who nurses/looks after; **n. mother** = mother who breast-feeds her baby; **n. staff** = hospital nurses; **n. home** = small (*usu.* private) hospital. 2. *n.* profession of looking after the sick.

nur•ture ['nɜ:tʃə] *v.* (*formal*) to protect and bring up carefully.

nut [nʌt] 1. *n.* (a) fruit with an edible center inside a hard shell; **to crack nuts** = to open the shells to get at the edible centers; *inf.* **a tough n. to crack** = a hard person/a difficult problem. (b) small metal ring used for tightening a bolt; **wing n.** = nut with two projecting pieces for turning. (c) *inf.* head; **he's off his n.** = he's mad. (d) *inf.* **nuts about** = very keen on/enthusiastic about. (e) small lump (of butter). 2. *v.* **to go nutting** = to gather nuts. **nut case,** *n. inf.* mad person. **nut•crack•ers,** *n. pl.* pincers for cracking nuts. **nut•hatch,** *n.* small gray and brown bird which climbs up tree trunks. **nut•meg,** *n.* seed of a tropical tree, used as a spice. **nut•shell,** *n.* hard outside covering of a nut; **in a n.** = giving all the important details as briefly as possible. **nut•ty,** *adj.* (a) tasting of/full of nuts. (b) *inf.* crazy/very enthusiastic (**about** s.o./sth).

nu•tri•ment ['nju:trɪmənt] *n.* thing which nourishes. **nu•tri•ent,** *adj. & n.* (food) which feeds/nourishes. **nu•tri•tion** [nju:'trɪʃn] *n.* giving/receiving of nourishment. **nu•tri•tious** [nju:'trɪʃəs] *adj.* nourishing/providing food which is necessary for growth. **nu•tri•tive** ['nju:trətɪv] 1. *n.* food which is necessary for growth. 2. *adj.* providing food/nourishment.

nuz•zle ['nʌzl] *v.* to press the nose up to/to snuggle up to.

ny•lon ['naɪlɒn] *n.* very tough synthetic material. **ny•lons,** *n. pl.* women's stockings.

nymph [nɪmf] *n.* (a) young girl; minor goddess. (b) young insect, esp. young dragonfly. **nymph•et,** *n.* sexually desirable young girl. **nym•pho•ma•ni•a** [nɪmfə'meɪnɪə] *n.* (*in woman*) uncontrollably strong sexual desire. **nym•pho•ma•ni•ac,** *n.* woman who has uncontrollable sexual desires.

Oo

O, o [əʊ] zero/nothing.

O *symbol for* oxygen.

oaf [əʊf] *n.* stupid/clumsy/unfeeling person. **oaf•ish**, *adj.* like an oaf.

oak [əʊk] *n.* type of large deciduous tree; wood of this tree. **oak gall**, *n.* (*also* **oak apple**) round growth on oak trees caused by an insect. **oak•en**, *adj.* (*formal*) made of oak.

oa•kum ['əʊkəm] *n.* (*no pl.*) loose pieces of old rope formerly used for stuffing into the seams of wooden ships.

oar [ɔ:] *n.* long pole with a flat end, used for moving a boat along; *inf.* **to put in one's o.** = to interfere. **oar•lock**, *n.* metal support for oars. **oars•man**, *n.* (*pl.* **-men**) person who rows a boat. **oars•man•ship**, *n.* being skilled at rowing.

o•a•sis [əʊ'eɪsɪs] *n.* (*pl.* **-ses** [-si:z]) (a) place in the desert with water, where plants grow. (b) place which is pleasantly different from its surroundings.

oat•cake ['əʊtkeɪk] *n.* dry biscuit made of oatmeal.

oath [əʊθ] *n.* (a) swearing that you are telling the truth. (b) promise. (c) swear word.

oat•meal ['əʊtmi:l] *n.* coarse flour made from oats.

oats [əʊts] *n. pl.* cereal plant whose grain is used as food; **to sow one's wild o.** = behave in a very free and unruly way when young.

ob•bli•ga•to [ɒblɪ'gɑ:təʊ] *n.* (*pl.* **-os, -ti**) (*in music*) important accompanying part played by a solo instrument.

ob•du•rate ['ɒbdjʊrət] *adj.* stubborn/unyielding/unmoving. **ob•du•ra•cy**, *n.* being obdurate.

o•be•di•ence [ə'bi:dɪəns] *n.* being obedient. **o•be•di•ent**, *adj.* (person) who does what he is told to do. **o•be•di•ent•ly**, *adv.* in an obedient way.

o•bei•sance [əʊ'beɪsəns] *n.* sign of respect, such as a bow or curtsey.

ob•e•lisk ['ɒbəlɪsk] *n.* four-sided pillar which becomes narrower towards the top.

o•bese [ə'bi:s] *adj.* very fat. **o•be•si•ty** [ə'bi:sɪtɪ] *n.* being obese.

o•bey [ə'beɪ] *v.* to do what you are told to do (by s.o.).

ob•fus•cate ['ɒbfʌskeɪt] *v.* (*formal*) to make (sth) difficult to understand.

o•bit•u•ar•y [ə'bɪtjʊərɪ] *n.* written report of s.o.'s death, usu. with details of his life; **o. column** = part of a newspaper which gives obituaries.

ob•ject 1. *n.* ['ɒbdʒekt] (a) thing; **o. lesson** = thing which makes a course of action very clear. (b) aim; target/purpose. (c) person/thing to which feeling, etc., is directed. (d) (*in grammar*) noun/pronoun, etc., which follows directly from a verb or preposition. (e) **money is no o.** = is no obstacle/problem. 2. *v.* [əb'dʒekt] (**to**) to refuse to agree; to express unwillingness towards/disapproval (of). **ob•jec•tion** [ɒb'dʒekʃn] *n.* act of objecting; reason against. **ob•jec•tion•a•ble**, (a) *adj.* causing disapproval. (b) (*esp. of person*) very unpleasant. **ob•jec•tive** [ɒb'dʒektɪv] 1. *adj.* (a) (*in grammar*) referring to the object. (b) referring to the external world. (c) considering matters from a general viewpoint and not just your own. 2. *n.* (a) aim/object in view. (b) lens in a microscope which is nearest to the object being examined. **ob•jec•tive•ly**, *adv.* in an objective way/without being influenced by your own feelings. **ob•jec•tiv•i•ty**, *n.* being objective. **ob•jec•tor**, *n.* person who objects; **conscientious o.** = person who refuses to join the armed forces because he feels war is wrong.

ob•jet d'art [ɒbdʒeɪ'dɑ:] *n.* ornament.

ob•late ['ɒbleɪt] *n.* person who has vowed to do religious work.

o•blige [ə'blaɪdʒ] *v.* (a) to make (s.o.) feel it is their duty to do sth. (b) to force (s.o.) to do sth. (c) to be useful/helpful to (s.o.). (d) **to be obliged to s.o.** = to owe s.o. gratitude.

æ back, ɑ: farm, ɒ: top, aɪ pipe, aʊ how, aɪə fire, aʊə flower, ɔ: bought, ɔɪ toy, e fed, eə hair, eɪ take, ə afraid, əʊ boat, əʊə lower, ɜ: word, i: heap, ɪ hit, ɪə hear, u: school, ʊ book, ʌ but, b back, d dog, ð then, dʒ just, f fog, g go, h hand, j yes, k catch, l last, m mix, n nut, ŋ sing, p penny, r round, s some, ʃ short, t too, tʃ chop, θ thing, v voice, w was, z zoo, ʒ treasure

ob•li•gate ['ɒblɪgeɪt] *v.* to oblige.
ob•li•ga•tion [ɒblɪ'geɪʃn] *n.* (a) duty; legal bond. (b) duty to be grateful; **under an o. to s.o.** = morally obliged to help s.o.
ob•li•ga•to•ry [ə'blɪgətərɪ] *adj.* necessary according to rules or laws. **o•blig•ing,** *adj.* ready to help. **o•blig•ing•ly,** *adv.* in an obliging way.

o•blique [ə'bliːk] *adj.* (a) at a slant; **o. angle** = angle which is not a right angle. (b) from the side; not direct. **o•blique•ly,** *adv.* in an oblique way.

ob•lit•er•ate [ə'blɪtəreɪt] *v.* to wipe out/to destroy. **ob•lit•er•a•tion** [əblɪtə'reɪʃn] *n.* act of obliterating; being obliterated.

ob•liv•i•on [ə'blɪvɪən] *n.* forgetting totally; being completely forgotten. **ob•liv•i•ous,** *adj.* forgetful/unaware.

ob•long ['ɒblɒŋ] *n. & adj.* (referring to a) rectangular shape with two pairs of equal sides, one pair being longer than the other.

ob•lo•quy ['ɒbləkwɪ] *n.* (*formal*) criticism.

ob•nox•ious [ɒb'nɒkʃəs] *adj.* very unpleasant/offensive.

o•boe ['əʊbəʊ] *n.* high-pitched woodwind instrument. **o•bo•ist,** *n.* person who plays the oboe.

ob•scene [ɒb'siːn] *adj.* offending moral standards/sensitive feelings; indecent. **ob•scene•ly,** *adj.* in an obscene way. **ob•scen•i•ty** [ɒb'senɪtɪ] *n.* (a) being obscene. (b) obscene word.

ob•scure [əb'skjuə] 1. *adj.* (a) (*of place*) dark/gloomy. (b) not clear. (c) not well-known. 2. *v.* to hide, esp. by covering. **ob•scure•ly,** *adv.* in an obscure way. **ob•scu•ri•ty,** *n.* being obscure.

ob•se•qui•ous [əb'siːkwɪəs] *adj.* too humble; showing too much respect for/obedience to (s.o.). **ob•se•quies** ['ɒbsɪkwɪz] *n. pl.* funeral ceremonies. **ob•se•qui•ous•ly,** *adv.* in an obsequious way. **ob•se•qui•ous•ness,** *n.* being obsequious.

ob•serve [əb'zɜːv] *v.* (a) to follow/to obey (a law/rule/custom). (b) to watch/to look (at). (c) to notice. (d) to remark/to note. **ob•serv•ance,** *n.* (act of) observing. **ob•serv•ant,** *adj.* noticing (many details). **ob•ser•va•tion** [ɒbzə'veɪʃn] *n.* (a) (act of) observing; **under o.** = being carefully watched. (b) calculation of position of a ship. (c) remark. **ob•serv•a•to•ry,** *n.* place from which stars and planets can be watched. **ob•serv•er,** *n.* person who attends a meeting and watches (esp. without taking part).

ob•sess [ɒb'ses] *v.* to fill s.o.'s thoughts. **ob•ses•sion** [əb'seʃn] *n.* idea/subject which fills your mind constantly. **ob•ses•sive,** *adj.*

caused by an obsession. **ob•ses•sive•ly,** *adv.* in an obsessive way.

ob•sid•i•an [ɒb'sɪdɪən] *n.* hard glasslike volcanic rock.

ob•so•lete ['ɒbsəliːt] *adj.* (word, custom) no longer in general use. **ob•so•les•cence,** *n.* being obsolescent. **ob•so•les•cent** [ɒbsə'lesənt] *adj.* going out of use/out of fashion.

ob•sta•cle ['ɒbstəkl] *n.* thing which is in the way/which prevents progress. **obstacle race,** *n.* race in which various obstacles have to be passed.

ob•stet•ric(al) [ɒb'stetrɪk(l)] *adj.* referring to obstetrics or childbirth. **ob•ste•tri•cian** [ɒbstə'trɪʃn] *n.* doctor who specializes in obstetrics. **ob•stet•rics,** *n.* branch of medicine dealing with childbirth.

ob•sti•nate ['ɒbstɪnət] *adj.* (a) sticking to your opinion/course of action, etc. against all arguments. (b) which will not go away. **ob•sti•na•cy,** *n.* being obstinate. **ob•sti•nate•ly,** *adv.* in an obstinate way.

ob•strep•er•ous [ɒb'strepərəs] *adj.* behaving in an uncontrolled/wild/loud way.

ob•struct [əb'strʌkt] *v.* to get in the way of (sth); to prevent/to hinder the progress of (sth). **ob•struc•tion** [ɒb'strʌkʃn] *n.* (a) act of obstructing. (b) thing which gets in the way. **ob•struc•tive,** *adj.* which obstructs; which aims to cause an obstruction.

ob•tain [ɒb'teɪn] *v.* (a) to get. (b) to exist as a rule. **ob•tain•a•ble,** *adj.* which can be obtained.

ob•trude [əb'truːd] *v.* (*formal*) to come/to put in the way; to form an obstacle. **ob•tru•sion** [əb'truːʒn] *n.* (a) (act of) obtruding. (b) thing which is in the way. **ob•tru•sive** [əb'truːsɪv] *adj.* (thing) which sticks out/which is in the way.

ob•tuse [əb'tjuːs] *adj.* (a) stupid/dull (person). (b) **o. angle** = angle of between 90° and 180°. **ob•tuse•ly,** *adv.* in an obtuse way. **ob•tuse•ness,** *n.* being obtuse.

ob•verse ['ɒbvɜːs] *n.* side of a coin with the head on it/the main side of a coin.

ob•vi•ate ['ɒbvɪeɪt] *v.* to avoid/to get round.

ob•vi•ous ['ɒbvɪəs] *adj.* clear; easily seen/easily noticed. **ob•vi•ous•ly,** *adv.* in an obvious way/clearly. **ob•vi•ous•ness,** *n.* being obvious.

oc•a•ri•na [ɒkə'riːnə] *n.* wind instrument, made of a small pot, with holes to be covered by the fingers.

oc•ca•sion [ə'keɪʒn] 1. *n.* (a) thing which causes sth else. (b) (time of a) happening; **on o.** = from time to time. (c) special event. 2. *v.* to cause (sth) to happen. **oc•ca•sion•al,** *adj.* happening now and then/not often.

oc•ca•sion•al•ly, *adv.* sometimes/not often.

Oc•ci•dent ['ɒksɪdənt] *n. (formal)* the West; Western countries. **oc•ci•den•tal** [ɒksɪ'dentl] *adj.* referring to the Occident.

oc•ci•put ['ɒksɪpʌt] *n.* back of the head. **oc•cip•i•tal** [ɒk'sɪpɪtəl] *adj.* referring to the back of the head.

oc•clude [ɒ'kluːd] *v. (formal)* to shut up. **oc•clu•sion,** *n.* (a) movement of warm air upward, caused by the arrival of colder air. (b) blockage in a blood vessel.

oc•cult ['ɒkʌlt] *adj. & n.* (referring to the) supernatural; magic.

oc•cu•py ['ɒkjupaɪ] *v.* (a) to fill/to take up (space or time). (b) to take/to have possession of. (c) to take possession and remain in control of. (d) to give work/activity to. **oc•cu•pan•cy,** *n.* being occupied. **oc•cu•pant,** *n.* person who occupies a place/who is in a certain seat. **oc•cu•pa•tion** [ɒkju'peɪʃn] *n.* (a) (act of) occupying; being occupied. (b) job/position/employment. **oc•cu•pa•tion•al,** *adj.* referring to an occupation; **o. therapy** = treating sick people by encouraging them to do special activities. **oc•cu•pi•er,** *n.* person who lives in (a house).

oc•cur [ə'kɜː] *v.* **(occurred)** (a) to take place/to happen. (b) **(to)** to come into one's thoughts. (c) to be (found). **oc•cur•rence** [ə'kʌrəns] *n.* happening.

o•cean ['əʊʃn] *n.* large expanse of sea surrounding the land masses of the earth; a part of this sea. **o•ce•an•ic** [əʊsɪ'ænɪk] *adj.* referring to the ocean. **o•cea•nog•ra•phy** [əʊʃə-'nɒgrəfɪ] *n.* study of the sea.

oc•e•lot ['ɒsɪlɒt] *n.* leopardlike animal found in Central and South America.

o•cher, ochre ['əʊkə] *n.* yellow/red natural material used for coloring; dull yellow color.

o'clock [ə'klɒk] *adv. phrase used with numbers meaning the exact hour;* **at six o'clock; the six o'clock train.**

oc•ta•gon ['ɒktəgən] *n.* geometrical figure with eight sides. **oc•tag•o•nal** [ɒk'tægənl] *adj.* eight-sided.

oc•tane ['ɒkteɪn] *n.* **o. number/o. rating** = number given to types of gasoline to indicate their quality.

oc•tave ['ɒkteɪv] *n. (in music)* space between the first and last notes of an eight-note scale.

oc•ta•vo [ɒk'teɪvəʊ] *n.* size of a book, when a sheet of paper is folded to make sixteen pages.

oc•tet [ɒk'tet] *n.* group of eight people, esp. musicians; piece of music for such a group.

Oc•to•ber [ɒk'təʊbə] *n.* 10th month of the year.

oc•to•ge•nar•i•an [ɒktədʒə'neərɪən] *adj. & n.* (person) who is between 80 and 89 years old.

oc•to•pus ['ɒktəpəs] *n.* (*pl.* **-es, -pi**) sea animal with eight arms.

oc•u•lar ['ɒkjulə] *adj.* referring to the eyes/to sight. **oc•u•list,** *n.* doctor who specializes in care of the eyes.

odd [ɒd] *adj.* (**-er, -est**) (a) (number) which cannot be divided exactly by two. (b) approximately/a little more than. (c) occasional; referring to various individual things/items; *(in an auction)* **o. lots** = groups of different items for sale. (d) referring to a member of a set or pair, when separated from the rest. (e) strange/peculiar. **odd•ball,** *n. inf.* eccentric person. **odd•i•ty,** *n.* (a) being odd. (b) odd thing/person. **odd•ly,** *adv.* in an odd way; for odd reasons. **odd•ments,** *n. pl.* bits and pieces; items left over. **odd•ness,** *n.* being odd. **odds,** *n. pl.* (a) difference between the amount which has been bet and the amount to be won; **o. of 10 to 1.** (b) more than an equal chance; **the o. are against it. (c)** to be at **o. with s.o.** = to quarrel constantly. (d) **o. and ends** = bits and pieces.

ode [əʊd] *n.* long poem often addressed to a person or thing.

o•di•ous ['əʊdɪəs] *adj.* hateful/horrible. **o•di•ous•ly,** *adv.* in an odious way. **o•di•ous•ness,** *n.* being odious. **o•di•um,** *n.* great unpopularity/hatred.

o•dom•e•ter [əʊ'dɒmɪtə] *n.* device for measuring the distance a vehicle travels.

o•don•tol•o•gy [ɒdɒn'tɒlədʒɪ] *n.* study of teeth.

o•dor, *Brit.* **o•dour** ['əʊdə] *n.* (a) scent/smell. (b) **to be in good/bad o. with** = to be in/out of favor with. **o•dor•ous,** *adj.* with a strong scent. **o•dor•less,** *adj.* without any smell.

od•ys•sey ['ɒdɪsɪ] *n.* long voyage of adventure.

oe•de•ma [ɪ'diːmə] *n. see* **edema.**

Oed•i•pus com•plex ['iːdɪpəs'kɒmpleks] *n.* feeling (in a man) of hatred for his father and love for his mother.

of [ɒv] *prep.* (a) belonging to/connected with.

æ back, aː farm, ɒ top, aɪ pipe, aʊ how, aɪə fire, aʊə flower, ɔː bought, ɔɪ toy, e fed, eəhair, eɪ take, ə afraid, əʊ boat, əʊə lower, vː word, iː heap, ɪ hit, ɪə hear, uː school, ʊ book, ʌ but, b back, d dog, ð then, dʒ just, f fog, g go, h hand, j yes, k catch, l last, m mix, n nut, ŋ sing, p penny, r round, s some, ʃ short, t too, tʃ chop, θ thing, v voice, w was, z zoo, ʒ treasure

(b) being a part/a quantity. (c) (who/which) is; **a child of ten.** (d) by/from; **south of the border; made of wool.** (e) about/concerning.

off [ɒf] 1. *adv.* (a) away (from); **they're o.** = they've started running; **day o.** = day away from work. (b) not on; **the deal is o.** = has been canceled. (c) no longer fresh. (d) **well/badly o.** = having plenty/not enough (money). (e) **right/straight o.** = immediately; **on and o.** = from time to time. (f) (*with verbs*) completely; **to finish o.** 2. *prep.* (a) (away) from. (b) (*at sea*) a certain distance from. (c) branching from. (d) disliking/not wanting (food). 3. *adj.* away; not on; **o. day** = one on which you are less successful; **o. season** = less busy season. **off•beat,** *adj. inf.* rather odd/unusual. **off chance,** *n.* slight possibility. **off-col•or,** *adj.* not well. **off•hand,** *adv. & adj.* (a) without preparation/without thinking carefully. (b) (*also* **offhanded**) rude/without courtesy. **off•hand•ed•ly,** *adv.* rudely. **off-line,** *adj.* (computer) which is not connected to a network or to a main system. **off-load,** *v.* (**on to**) to pass a load to sth/s.o. else. **off-peak,** *adj.* away from the busiest/most used times. **off-put•ting,** *adj. inf.* causing (mild) annoyance. **off-road,** *adj.* (vehicle) designed for use on rough terrain. **off-sea•son,** *adj. & n.* (period, usually winter) when prices are lower because fewer people travel. **off•set.** 1. *n.* [ˈɒfset] method of printing from a plate to a rubber surface and then to paper. 2. *v.* [ɒfˈset] (**offset**) to balance (one thing) against another. **off•shoot** [ˈɒfʃuːt] *n.* small side shoot of a plant; thing which branches from sth else. **off•shore,** *adj.* (away) from/at a distance from the shore. **off•spring** [ˈɒfsprɪŋ] *n.* child; young (of an animal). **off•stage,** *adv. & adj.* not on the stage/unseen by the audience.

of•fal [ˈɒfl] *n.* internal organs (heart, etc.) of animals, used as food.

of•fense [əˈfens] *n.* (a) state of offending; being offended; **to take o. at** = to be offended by. (b) crime; (act of) offending (esp. against a law). **of•fend** [əˈfend] *v.* to be/to go against (the law/opinions/wishes/feelings). **of•fend•er,** *n.* person who offends (esp. **against** a law). **of•fen•sive.** 1. *adj.* (a) which is unpleasant. (b) (*in military*) which is used in an attack. 2. *n.* (military) attack; **to take the o.** = to start the attack. **of•fen•sive•ly,** *adv.* in an offensive way. **of•fen•sive•ness,** *n.* being offensive.

of•fer [ˈɒfə] 1. *n.* (act of) indicating that you will do/give sth; thing which is offered; **special o.** = goods which are put on sale at a reduced price. 2. *v.* (a) to say/to indicate that you will do/give (sth). (b) to make/to express (an opinion, etc.). **of•fer•ing,** *n.* thing which is offered. **of•fer•to•ry,** *n.* (a) offering of wine and bread in the communion service. (b) collection of money taken while the wine and bread are being offered.

of•fice [ˈɒfɪs] *n.* (a) room/building where business or professional activity is carried out; **doctor's o.** = room where a doctor sees patients. (b) position/function. (c) (*esp. in titles*) organization; government department. (d) help/services. **of•fi•cer,** *n.* (a) person who holds an official position. (b) person who holds one of the commissioned ranks in the armed forces, etc. (c) **police o.** = policeman. **of•fi•cial** [əˈfɪʃl] 1. *adj.* referring to an organization which is recognized by a government, etc. 2. *n.* person holding a recognized position. **of•fi•cial•dom,** *n.* bureaucracy. **of•fi•cial•ese,** *n. inf.* clumsy language used by bureaucrats. **of•fi•cial•ly,** *adv.* in an official way. **of•fi•ci•ate** [əˈfɪʃɪeɪt] *v.* (a) (*of clergy*) (**at**) to perform a religious ceremony. (b) to act as chairman, etc. **of•fi•cious,** *adj.* too ready to interfere or to offer help. **of•fi•cious•ly,** *adv.* in an officious way. **of•fi•cious•ness,** *n.* being officious.

off•ing [ˈɒfɪŋ] *n.* **in the o.** = coming/available soon.

of•ten [ˈɒfn] *adv.* many times; in many instances. **of•ten•times,** *adv.* often.

o•gee [ˈəʊdʒiː] *n.* S-shaped curve in architecture; an arch with two S-shaped curves, joining at a point.

o•gle [ˈəʊgl] *v.* to leer/look at (s.o.) with sexual desire.

o•gre [ˈəʊgə] *n.* cruel giant who eats human beings; cruel terrifying person.

oh [əʊ] *inter. expressing surprise/shock.*

ohm [əʊm] *n.* standard measure of electrical resistance.

oil [ɔɪl] 1. *n.* (a) thick smooth-running liquid of various kinds (used in cooking/heating/engineering/painting). (b) liquid found mainly underground and used to produce power. (c) picture painted with oil paints. 2. *v.* to put oil on/in (esp. to make a machine run more smoothly); **to o. the wheels** = to help to make things run more smoothly; *inf.* **well-oiled** = rather drunk. **oil-bear•ing,** *adj.* (rocks, etc.) which contain oil. **oil field,** *n.* area where oil is found. **oil•i•ness,** *n.* being oily. **oil rig,** *n.* structure for drilling for oil. **oil•skin(s),** *n.* (clothing of) material made waterproof with oil. **oil slick,** *n.* thin covering of oil on the surface of the sea. **oil tank•er,** *n.* large ship/large truck for carrying oil. **oil•y,** *adj.* (**-ier, -iest**) (a) like oil; covered with oil. (b) (*of manner*) too smooth and pleasant; insincere.

oint•ment [ˈɔɪntmənt] *n.* smooth healing or soothing substance spread on the skin.

OK, okay [əʊˈkeɪ] *inf. inter. & adj.* all right. 2. *n.* sign of approval. 3. *v.* to give a sign of approval to.

o•ka•pi [ɒˈkɑːpiː] *n.* African animal, like a large black horse, with white stripes on its rear legs.

o•kra [ˈɒkrə] *n.* tropical plant with edible green pods.

old [ould] *adj.* (**-er, -est**) (a) having great age; **o. wives' tale** = belief based on tradition rather than on fact. (b) having been in use for a long time. (c) being of a particular age. (d) having been in a certain state/having been done for a long time. (e) former. (f) term showing vagueness/affection/disrespect, etc.; *inf.* **the o. man** = boss/husband/father. **old-boy net•work,** *n.* system where men who were at school together or are members of a particular profession or group help each other get ahead in business, politics, etc. **old•en,** *adj.* (*formal*) old (times). **old-fash•ioned,** *adj.* not in fashion; out of date. **old•ie,** *n. inf.* old-fashioned/out of date thing. **old•ish,** *adj.* rather old. **old maid,** *n.* older woman who has never married. **old-time,** *adj.* not of the present/done in an old-fashioned way. **old tim•er,** *n.* s.o. who has been doing sth or been a member of sth for a long time. **Old World,** *n.* Europe, Asia and Africa.

o•le•ag•i•nous [ɒliˈæʒɪnəs] *adj.* (*formal*) oily.

o•le•an•der [ɒliˈændə] *n.* tropical shrub with pink flowers.

ol•fac•to•ry [ɒlˈfæktərɪ] *adj.* (*formal*) referring to the sense of smell.

ol•i•gar•chy [ˈɒlɪɡɑːkɪ] *n.* (country with a) government by a few powerful people.

ol•ive [ˈɒlɪv] *n.* (a) small black or green fruit which produces oil and is used as food; tree which bears this fruit; **o. branch** = sign of peace. (b) **o. (green)** = dull green color of unripe olives; **o. skin** = yellowish skin.

O•lym•pic [əˈlɪmpɪk] *adj. & n.* **the O. Games/the Olympics** = international athletic competition held every four years. **O•lym•pi•ad,** *n.* major international sporting competition. **O•lym•pi•an,** *adj.* like a god; majestic.

om•buds•man [ˈɒmbədzmən] *n.* (*pl.* **-men**) official who investigates complaints by members of the public against a government department or official.

o•me•ga [ˈəʊmɪɡə] *n.* last letter of the Greek alphabet.

om•e•let, om•e•lette [ˈɒmlət] *n.* cooked egg mixture often with mushrooms, vegetables, cheese, etc. folded inside.

o•men [ˈəʊmən] *n.* thing giving an indication of the future. **om•i•nous** [ˈɒmɪnəs] *adj.* threatening bad results. **om•i•nous•ly,** *adv.* in an ominous way.

o•mit [əˈmɪt] *v.* (**omitted**) (a) to leave out. (b) (**to**) not to do sth. **o•mis•sion** [əˈmɪʃn] *n.* (a) act of omitting. (b) thing omitted.

om•ni•bus [ˈɒmnɪbəs] 1. *n.* (*old*) bus. 2. *n. & adj.* (book) which includes several books all together.

om•ni•di•rec•tion•al [ɒmnɪdaɪˈrekʃənəl] *adj.* (aerial which can capture signals) from any direction.

om•nip•o•tence [ɒmˈnɪpətəns] *n.* quality of being all-powerful. **om•nip•o•tent,** *adj.* all-powerful.

om•ni•pres•ent [ˈɒmnɪprezənt] *adj.* which is everywhere.

om•nis•cient [ɒmˈnɪsɪənt] *adj.* (person) who knows everything. **om•nis•cience,** *n.* knowing everything.

om•niv•o•rous [ɒmˈnɪvərəs] *adj.* eating everything; (animal) which eats both plants and other animals.

on [ɒn] 1. *prep.* (a) touching the top/outer surface of sth. (b) in/at. (c) with; **have you any money on you?** (d) belonging to/a member of; **on the staff.** (e) indicating a means of moving; **on foot.** (f) engaged in; **on business.** (g) from/by; **to live on a small income.** (h) (*indicating a time*) **on Sundays; on application** = when you apply; **on sale** = for sale; (i) approximately; **just on a year ago.** (j) because of; **to congratulate s.o. on his success.** (k) about/concerning; **a book on whales.** (l) toward/against; **an attack on s.o.** (m) *inf.* paid by; **the drinks are on me.** (n) (*as a bet*) **to put $5 on a horse** = to bet $5 that the horse will win. 2. *adv.* (a) in action; open; **the light is on.** (b) happening; **what's on for tonight?** (c) being worn; **put your shoes on** (d) (in a) continuing (way); **they worked on.** (e) (*indicating passing of time*) **later on.** (f) **on and off** = not continuously/with breaks in between; **on and on** = without stopping.

on•a•ger [ˈɒnədʒə] *n.* wild Asian donkey.

once [wʌns] 1. *adv.* (a) for one time. (b) at all/ever. (c) at a (particular) time in the past. (d) **at o.** = (i) immediately; (ii) at the same time. 2. *conj.* as soon as. **once-o•ver,** *n. inf.* quick examination.

æ back, ɑː farm, ɒ top, aɪ pipe, aʊ how, aɪə fire, aʊə flower, ɔː bought, ɔɪ toy, e fed, eəhair, eɪ take, ə afraid, əʊ boat, əʊə lower, vː word, iː heap, ɪ hit, ɪə hear, uː school, ʊ book, ʌ but, b back, d dog, ð then, dʒ just, f fog, g go, h hand, j yes, k catch, l last, m mix, n nut, ŋ sing, p penny, r round, s some, ʃ short, t too, tʃ chop, θ thing, v voice, w was, z zoo, ʒ treasure

on•com•ing ['ɒnkʌmɪŋ] *adj.* coming toward you.

one [wʌn] 1. *n.* number 1. (a) first number; *inf.* **look after number o.** = look after yourself first. (b) single unit in quantity or number. (c) *inf.* **a quick o.** = a quick drink. 2. *adj.* (a) single (example of). (b) the only. (c) the same; **all of o. mind.** 3. *pron.* (a) thing/person indicated. (b) example of a type. 4. *indefinite adj.* (on) a certain; **o. night.** 5. *indefinite pron.* (a) (*pl.* **some/any**) an example of sth. (b) (*formal*) anyone/an indefinite person. **one-armed ban•dit,** *n.* gambling machine worked by a handle. **one-horse town,** *n. inf.* small town where very little happens. **one-leg•ged** ['wʌn'legɪd] *adj.* with only one leg. **one-night stand,** *n.* performance (of a play/of a show) for one night only. **one•self,** *pronoun referring to a person as an indefinite subject.* **one-sid•ed,** *adj.* treating or giving justice to one side only. **one•time,** *adj.* former. **one-track mind,** *n.* mind which concentrates on one thing at a time. **one-up•man•ship,** *n.* art of putting yourself at an advantage over others. **one-way,** *adj.* (street) for traffic in one direction only; (ticket) for one direction only.

on•er•ous ['ɒnərəs] *adj.* causing much (tiring) effort.

on•ion ['ʌnjən] *n.* strong-smelling vegetable with a round white bulb.

on-line ['ɒnlaɪn] *adv. & adj.* linked directly to a computer.

on•look•er ['ɒnlʊkə] *n.* person who watches.

on•ly ['əʊnlɪ] 1. *adj.* (the) single/(the) one without any others. 2. *adv.* (a) and not anyone/anything else. (b) as recently as. (c) **if o.** = expressing a strong wish/desire; **o. too** = very. 3. *conj.* but.

on•o•mas•tics [ɒnə'mæstɪks] *n.* study of names.

on•o•mat•o•poe•ia [ɒnəmætə'piːə] *n.* making/using words which imitate a sound. **on•o•mat•o•poe•ic,** *adj.* using onomatopoeia.

on•rush ['ɒnrʌʃ] *n.* rushing in/on.

on•set ['ɒnset] *n.* beginning (of an attack, etc.)

on•slaught ['ɒnslɔːt] *n.* sudden severe attack.

on•to ['ɒntuː] *prep.* to a position on sth.

on•tol•o•gy [ɒn'tɒlədʒɪ] *n.* study of reality. **on•to•log•i•cal** [ɒntə'lɒdʒɪkl] *adj.* referring to reality.

o•nus ['əʊnəs] *n.* responsibility (for a difficult task)

on•ward ['ɒnwəd] 1. *adj.* forward. 2. *adv.* (*also* **on•wards**) forward.

on•yx ['ɒnɪks] *n.* (*pl.* **-es**) multicolored precious stone.

oo•dles ['uːdlz] *n. pl. inf.* lots (**of**).

ooh [uː] *inter. showing surprise/shock.*

ooze [uːz] 1. *n.* slimy mud. 2. *v.* to flow slowly and gently.

o•pac•i•ty [ə'pæsɪtɪ] *n.* state of being opaque.

o•pal ['əʊpl] *n.* semi-precious stone with varied or changing colors. **o•pal•es•cence,** *n.* being opalescent. **o•pal•es•cent,** *adj.* shining like an opal.

o•paque [əʊ'peɪk] *adj.* which you cannot see through.

O•PEC ['əʊpek] *n.* (= Organization of Petroleum Exporting Countries) group of countries who produce and export oil.

o•pen ['əʊpn] 1. *adj.* (a) not closed. (b) which you can enter. (c) without limits. (d) **o. to** = without protection (from sth). (e) ready to accept/to be accepted. (f) with no attempt (being made) to hide sth. (g) with space between the parts. (h) with no fixed idea(s)/conditions. (i) (competition) without restrictions. 2. *v.* (a) to become open. (b) to start (up)/to set going. (c) to have an exit (**on to**). 3. *n.* unlimited area outdoors. **o•pen-air,** *adj.* not in a building. **o•pen-end•ed,** *adj.* with no definite end. **o•pen•er,** *n.* device for opening sth. **o•pen•hand•ed,** *adj.* generous. **open-heart,** *adj.* (surgery) with the chest cut open to expose the heart. **o•pen•ing.** 1. *n.* (a) act of opening. (b) beginning. (c) place where sth opens. (d) opportunity, such as a job vacancy. 2. *adj.* which opens. **o•pen let•ter,** *n.* letter published as an article in a newspaper and not sent to the addressee. **o•pen•ly,** *adv.* in an open way. **open-mind,** *n.* to **have an o. m.** = not to have a fixed opinion on sth. **o•pen•ness,** *n.* quality of being open. **open out,** *v.* to open (fully); to spread out widely. **open up,** *v.* (a) to open (completely). (b) to begin. **o•pen•work,** *n.* pattern (on a shoe, etc.) with holes in it.

o•pe•ra ['ɒprə] *n.* (a) dramatic performance with music, in which the words are partly or wholly sung. (b) company which performs operas. **op•er•a glass•es,** *n. pl.* small binoculars for looking at performers on the stage. **op•er•a house,** *n.* theater in which opera is performed. **op•er•at•ic** [ɒpə'rætɪk] *adj.* of/like/for opera. **op•er•et•ta** [ɒpə'retə] *n.* opera with a light-hearted story in which some of the words are spoken.

op•er•ate ['ɒpəreɪt] 1. *v.* (a) to act. (b) to (cause to) work. (c) **to o. on a patient** = to treat a patient by cutting open the body. **op•er•a•ble** ['ɒpərəbl] *adj.* which can be operated on. **op•er•a•tion** [ɒpə'reɪʃn] *n.* (a) (act of) operating; being operated on; **to come**

into o. = begin to be applied. **op•er•a•tion•al**, *adj.* referring to the working of sth. (b) ready for use. **op•er•a•tive** ['ɒpərətɪv] 1. *adj.* in operation. 2. *n.* worker, esp. one who operates a machine, etc. **op•er•a•tor** ['ɒpəreɪtə] *n.* (a) person who works instruments, etc. (b) person who carries things out/organizes things; *inf.* smart o. = clever businessman.

oph•thal•mic [ɒf'θælmɪk] *adj.* referring to (the medical treatment of) the eye. **oph•thal•mol•o•gist** [ɒfθæl'mɒlədʒɪst] *n.* doctor who specializes in diseases of the eye. **oph•thal•mol•o•gy**, *n.* study of the eye.

o•pi•ate ['əʊpɪət] *n.* drug which puts you to sleep.

o•pin•ion [ə'pɪnjən] *n.* (a) (of) what a person thinks/feels about sth; **public o.** = what people think/feel about sth. (b) view; piece of (usu. expert) advice. **o•pin•ion•at•ed**, *adj.* (person) with rigid opinions/who thinks he is always right.

o•pi•um ['əʊpɪəm] *n.* drug which puts you to sleep, made from a type of poppy.

o•pos•sum [ə'pɒsəm] *n.* small North American animal which carries its young in a pouch.

op•po•nent [ə'pəʊnənt] *n.* person/group which is against you.

op•por•tune ['ɒpətjuːn] *adj.* coming (by chance) at the right time. **op•por•tune•ly**, *adv.* in an opportune way; at the right time. **op•por•tun•ism**, *n.* being an opportunist. **op•por•tun•ist**, *n.* person who takes advantage of opportunities, esp. at the expense of others. **op•por•tu•ni•ty** [ɒpə'tjuːnɪtɪ] *n.* chance/circumstances which allow you to do sth.

op•pose [ə'pəʊz] *v.* to act against (s.o./sth); to try to prevent. **op•posed to**, *adj.* (a) against. (b) in contrast.

op•po•site ['ɒpəzɪt] 1. *adj.* (a) facing. (b) at/in/toward the other side of sth; **o. number** = person who is in a similar position in another organization. (c) belonging to a completely different type/position. 2. *n.* thing which is completely different. 3. *prep.* in an opposite position to. **op•po•si•tion** [ɒpə'zɪʃn] *n.* (a) (act of) opposing. (b) (*esp. in politics*) the party/group which opposes the party/group in power. (c) rivalry.

op•press [ə'pres] *v.* (a) to cause to suffer, esp. by harsh rule. (b) to cause depression/sadness in. **op•pres•sion** [ə'preʃn] *n.* (act of) op-

pressing; being oppressed. **op•pres•sive**, *adj.* oppressing. **op•pres•sive•ly**, *adv.* in an oppressive way. **op•pres•sive•ness**, *n.* being oppressive. **op•pres•sor**, *n.* person who oppresses.

op•pro•bri•um [ə'prəʊbrɪəm] *n.* (*formal*) disgrace; (cause of) strong disapproval. **op•pro•bri•ous**, *adj.* disgraceful; rude.

opt [ɒpt] *v.* (for) to decide (in favor of). **opt out**, *v.* (of) to decide not to (take part).

op•ti•cal ['ɒptɪkl] *adj.* referring to the eyes/to the eyesight; referring to optics. **op•tic**, *adj.* referring to the eye/to sight. **op•ti•cal•ly**, *adv.* referring to optics. **op•ti•cian** [ɒp'tɪʃn] *n.* person who prescribes/makes/sells glasses or contact lenses, etc. **op•tics**, *n.* science of light; **fiber o.** = use of fine threads of glass to transmit light signals.

op•ti•mal ['ɒptɪməl] *adj.* best.

op•ti•mism ['ɒptɪmɪzəm] *n.* belief that everything is as good as it can be/will work out for the best; confident/cheerful attitude. **op•ti•mist** ['ɒptɪmɪst] *n.* person who believes everything will work out for the best. **op•ti•mis•tic** [ɒptɪ'mɪstɪk] *adj.* feeling that everything will work out for the best; giving cause for optimism. **op•ti•mis•ti•cal•ly**, *adv.* in an optimistic way.

op•ti•mum ['ɒptɪməm] 1. *n.* best way. 2. *adj.* best.

op•tion ['ɒpʃn] *n.* (a) choice/alternative possibility. (b) **o. on sth** = opportunity to buy/sell sth within a certain time or at a certain price. **op•tion•al**, *adj.* which may or may not be chosen.

op•tom•e•trist [ɒp'tɒmətrɪst] *n.* optician. **op•tom•e•try**, *n.* science of eyesight.

op•u•lence ['ɒpjʊləns] *n.* being opulent. **op•u•lent**, *adj.* rich/luxurious/splendid. **op•u•lent•ly**, *adv.* in an opulent way.

o•pus ['əʊpəs] *n.* (*pl.* -es *or* opera) (a) piece of music which is given a number. (b) large work of art.

or [ɔː] *conj.* (a) the opposite/the alternative/the other (possibility). (b) approximately. (c) **or (else)** = if not.

or•a•cle ['ɒrəkl] *n.* (a) (*in ancient Greece*) place where the gods answered questions about the future; person who answered questions about the future. (b) very wise and knowing person. **o•rac•u•lar** [ɒ'rækjʊlə] *adj.* referring to an oracle.

o•ral ['ɔːrl] 1. *adj.* (a) by speaking. (b) taken by

æ back, ɑː farm, ɒ top, aɪ pipe, aʊ how, aɪə fire, aʊə flower, ɔː bought, ɔɪ toy, e fed, eəhair, eɪ take, ə afraid, əʊ boat, əʊə lower, ɜː word, iː heap, ɪ hit, ɪə hear, uː school, ʊ book, ʌ but, b back, d dog, ð then, dʒ just, f fog, g go, h hand, j yes, k catch, l last, m mix, n nut, ŋ sing, p penny, r round, s some, ʃ short, t too, tʃ chop, θ thing, v voice, w was, z zoo, ʒ treasure

the mouth. 2. *n.* examination where you answer questions by speaking. **o•ral•ly,** *adv.* (a) in/by speech. (b) by the mouth.

or•ange ['ɒrɪndʒ] 1. *n.* usu. sweet citrus fruit, reddish yellow when ripe; tree which bears this fruit. 2. *adj. & n.* color of an orange. **or•ange•ade** [ɒrɪndʒ'eɪd] *n.* orange-flavored drink.

o•rang•u•tang [ərænjuː'tæŋ] *n.* large red ape found in southeast Asia.

o•ra•tion [ə'reɪʃn] *n.* (*formal*) speech. **or•a•tor** ['ɒrətə] *n.* person who is able to speak forcefully and persuasively to large numbers of people; person making a speech. **or•a•tor•i•cal** [ɒrə'tɒrɪkl] *adj.* full of eloquence. **or•a•to•ry** ['ɒrətərɪ] *n.* (a) eloquent/forceful public speaking. (b) private chapel.

or•a•to•ri•o [ɒrə'tɔːrɪəʊ] *n.* (*pl.* -os) piece of music for orchestra, choir and soloists, often telling a religious story.

orb [ɔːb] *n.* (a) spherical object (such as a planet or an eyeball). (b) ornamental globe with a cross on top used by a king as a symbol of state power.

or•bit ['ɔːbɪt] 1. *n.* (a) curved track (of an object moving through space). (b) extent of influence. 2. *v.* to move in an orbit around sth.

or•chard ['ɔːtʃəd] *n.* field with fruit trees.

or•ches•tra [ˈɔːkəstrə] *n.* (a) large group of musicians who play together. (b) part of a theater, usu. next to the stage, where the musicians sit; **o. seats** = seats in a theater very close to where the orchestra sits. **or•ches•tral** [ɔː-'kestrəl] *adj.* referring to an orchestra. **or•ches•trate** ['ɔːkɪstreɪt] *v.* (a) to arrange (a piece of music) for an orchestra. (b) to organize (a demonstration, etc.). **or•ches•tra•tion** [ɔːkɪ'streɪʃn] *n.* (act of) orchestrating; being orchestrated.

or•chid, orchis ['ɔːkɪd, 'ɔːkɪs] *n.* flowering plant with showy flowers.

or•dain [ɔː'deɪn] *v.* (a) to make (s.o.) a priest/a clergyman in a formal ceremony. (b) (*formal*) to order/to command (that sth be done).

or•deal [ɔː'diːl] *n.* painful test of strength/courage; difficult period.

or•der ['ɔːdə] 1. *n.* (a) command/demand that sth should be done. (b) obeying of rules or laws without unrest or violence. (c) demand/request for goods from a customer; goods supplied to a customer; *inf.* **a tall o.** = a difficult task. (d) organization of items in succession. (e) good/correct arrangement; **in o.** = correct/valid; **out of o.** = not working. (f) rules for an assembly/meeting. (g) organization of monks/priests, etc.; **in holy orders** = being a priest. (h) organization of knighthood; group of people to whom a certain honor has been given. (i) type/kind/classification/rank. (j) paper which authorizes the transfer of money. (k) **in o. to/that** = so that/for the purpose of. 2. *v.* (a) to command/to demand/to say (that sth should be done). (b) to demand/to request (goods/services, etc.). (c) to arrange/to put in order. **or•der•li•ness** ['ɔːdəlɪnəs] *n.* (a) being in good order/tidiness. (b) being quiet/being orderly. **or•der•ly.** 1. *adj.* (a) in good order; tidy or well-arranged. (b) well-behaved. 2. *n.* person whose duty it is to carry out routine tasks (in a hospital or in the armed services).

or•di•nal ['ɔːdɪnl] *n. & adj.* (referring to a) number indicating the position in a series.

or•di•nance ['ɔːdɪnəns] *n.* laws/rule made by an authority.

or•di•nar•y ['ɔːdnrɪ] *adj.* normal/not unusual; typical of its class/not having any special characteristics; **out of the o.** = extraordinary. **or•di•nar•i•ly,** *adv.* in the usual way/usually.

or•di•na•tion [ɔːdɪ'neɪʃn] *n.* (act/ceremony of) ordaining s.o. as a priest.

ord•nance ['ɔːdnəns] *n.* (a) heavy guns. (b) (government department dealing with) military supplies.

ore [ɔː] *n.* material found in the earth from which metals are obtained.

o•reg•a•no [ɒrɪ'gɑːnəʊ] *n.* spicy herb used in cooking.

or•gan ['ɔːgən] *n.* (a) part of the body with a special function. (b) periodical which gives the views of a group/of an organization. (c) musical instrument with keyboard(s) and many pipes through which air is pumped to make a sound. **or•gan•ic** [ɔː'gænɪk] *adj.* (a) referring to an organ/to organs. (b) referring to living things; **o. chemistry** = concerned with carbon compounds; **o. farming** = using only natural fertilizers. **or•gan•i•cal•ly** [ɔː'gænɪklɪ] *adv.* in an organic way. **or•gan•ism** ['ɒːgənɪzəm] *n.* living thing. **or•gan•ist,** *n.* person who plays the organ. **or•gan•i•za•tion** [ɔːgənaɪ-'zeɪʃn] *n.* (a) (act of) arranging; being arranged. (b) organized group or institution. **or•gan•ize** ['ɔːgənaɪz] *v.* to arrange/to put into a special form of order; to put into good order. **or•gan•iz•er,** *n.* person who arranges things.

or•gan•dy, organdie [ɔː'gændɪ] *n.* very thin stiff cotton cloth.

or•gan•o•phos•phate [ɔːgænəʊ'fɒsfeɪt] *n.* any organic pesticide containing phosphorus.

or•gasm ['ɔːgæzəm] *n.* climax of sexual excitement.

or•gy ['ɔːdʒɪ] *n.* uncontrolled indulgence in drinking/dancing; uncontrolled state or activity.

o•ri•el ['ɔːrɪəl] n. o. window = upstairs window which projects from the wall.

o•ri•ent ['ɔːrɪənt] 1. n. the O. = the East/Eastern countries. 2. v. to put in a certain direction. o•ri•en•tal [ɔːrɪ'entl] 1. adj. referring to the Orient. 2. n. person from the Orient. o•ri•en•tal•ist, n. person who studies the East. o•ri•en•tate ['ɔːrɪənteɪt] v. to put in a certain direction. o•ri•en•ta•tion [ɔːrɪən'teɪʃn] n. (act of) orientating/putting in a certain position/direction. o•ri•en•teer•ing [ɔːrɪən'tiːərɪŋ] n. sport of finding your way across country by means of maps and compasses.

or•i•fice ['ɒrɪfɪs] n. (formal) hole/opening.

o•ri•ga•mi [ɒrɪ'gɑːmɪ] n. (no pl.) art of folding colored paper to make shapes.

or•i•gin ['ɒrɪdʒɪn] n. beginning/root; where sth/s.o. comes from. o•rig•i•nal [ə'rɪdʒɪnl] 1. adj. (a) from its beginning(s); from earliest times. (b) new/different; created for the first time/not a copy. (c) showing ideas not based on those of other people. 2. n. (a) thing from which other things are copied/translated, etc. (b) unusual person. o•rig•i•nal•i•ty [ɒrɪdʒɪ'nælɪtɪ] n. (a) being original/new/different. (b) ability to create sth which has never been done before. o•rig•i•nal•ly, adv. (a) in an original way. (b) at or from the beginning. o•rig•i•nate [ə'rɪdʒɪneɪt] v. (a) to bring into existence for the first time. (b) to begin/to have its beginning. o•rig•i•na•tion [ərɪdʒɪ'neɪʃn] n. act of originating. o•rig•i•na•tor, n. person who originates.

o•ri•ole ['ɒrɪəl] n. bird with black and yellow feathers.

or•mo•lu ['ɔːməluː] n. (no pl.) decorations made of bronze covered with gold leaf.

or•na•ment. 1. n. ['ɔːnəmənt] thing used as decoration. 2. v. ['ɔːnəment] to decorate/to help to make more beautiful. or•na•men•tal [ɔːnə'mentl] adj. acting as an ornament; being pretty rather than useful. or•na•men•ta•tion [ɔːnəmən'teɪʃn] n. act of ornamenting; group of ornaments.

or•nate [ɔː'neɪt] adj. having (too) much ornament.

or•ner•y ['ɔːnərɪ] adj. inf. bad-tempered.

or•ni•thol•o•gy [ɔːnɪ'θɒlədʒɪ] n. study of birds. or•ni•tho•log•i•cal [ɔːnɪθə'lɒdʒɪkl] adj. referring to ornithology.

or•ni•thol•o•gist [ɒnɪ'θɒlədʒɪst] n. person who studies birds.

o•ro•tund ['ɒrətʌnd] adj. pompous (speech or writing).

or•phan ['ɔːfn] 1. n. child who has no parents. 2. v. to make (s.o.) an orphan. or•phan•age ['ɔːfənɪdʒ] n. home where orphans are looked after.

or•rer•y ['ɒrərɪ] n. mechanical model of the solar system.

or•ris root ['ɒrɪs'ruːt] n. perfume from the dried roots of a type of iris.

or•tho•don•tics [ɔːθə'dɒntɪks] n. treatment to correct badly formed teeth.

or•tho•dox ['ɔːθədɒks] adj. (a) holding the generally accepted beliefs of a religion/a philosophy, etc. (b) (Jews) who observe traditional practices very strictly; the O. Church = the Christian Church of Eastern Europe. or•tho•dox•y, n. being orthodox.

or•thog•ra•phy [ɔː'θɒgrəfɪ] n. (correct) spelling. or•tho•graph•i•cal [ɔːθə'græfɪkl] adj. referring to orthography.

or•tho•pe•dic, orthopaedic [ɔːθə'piːdɪk] adj. referring to diseases and deformities of bones. or•tho•pe•dics, orthopaedics, n. branch of medicine dealing with bones, etc. or•tho•pe•dist, orthopaedist, n. doctor who specializes in orthopaedics.

or•thop•tics [ɔː'θɒptɪks] n. correction of squints.

o•ryx [ɒrɪks] n. large rare Arabian antelope.

os•cil•late ['ɒsɪleɪt] v. to swing from one side to the other. os•cil•la•tion [ɒsɪ'leɪʃn] n. (act of) oscillating. os•cil•lo•scope [ɒ'sɪləskəʊp] n. device which shows oscillations on a screen.

o•sier ['əʊzɪə] n. type of willow tree whose branches are used to make baskets/furniture, etc.

os•mo•sis [ɒz'məʊsɪs] n. movement of liquid into another liquid through the porous walls of a container.

os•prey ['ɒsprɪ] n. large bird of prey which eats fish.

os•si•cle ['ɒsɪkəl] n. small bone in the middle ear.

os•si•fy ['ɒsɪfaɪ] v. to make into bone; to make rigid. os•si•fi•ca•tion [ɒsɪfɪ'keɪʃn] n. act of ossifying.

os•ten•si•ble [ɒ'stensɪbl] adj. which shows on the surface; which is meant to seem real. os•ten•si•bly, adv. seemingly.

æ back, ɑː farm, ɒ top, aɪ pipe, aʊ how, aɪə fire, aʊə flower, ɔː bought, ɔɪ toy, e fed, eəhair, eɪ take, ə afraid, əʊ boat, əʊə lower, vː word, iː heap, ɪ hit, ɪə hear, uː school, ʊ book, ʌ but, b back, d dog, ð then, dʒ just, f fog, g go, h hand, j yes, k catch, l last, m mix, n nut, ŋ sing, p penny, r round, s some, ʃ short, t too, tʃ chop, θ thing, v voice, w was, z zoo, ʒ treasure

os•ten•ta•tious [ɒsten'teɪʃəs] *adj.* showy/aiming to impress. **os•ten•ta•tion,** *n.* showing off in a luxurious way which is intended to impress. **os•ten•ta•tious•ly,** *adv.* in an ostentatious way.

os•te•o•ar•thri•tis [ɒstɪəvɑː'θraɪtɪs] *n.* painful disease of the joints.

os•te•o•path ['ɒstəpæθ] *n.* doctor who treats diseases of the bones and muscles by moving or massaging the patient's limbs. **os•te•o•path•ic** [ɒstɪə'pæθɪk] *adj.* referring to osteopathy. **os•te•op•a•thy** [ɒstɪ'ɒpəθɪ] *n.* school of medicine that emphasizes treatment of diseases of the bones and muscles by moving or massaging limbs.

os•tra•cism ['ɒstrəsɪzəm] *n.* being cut off from a group/from society. **os•tra•cize** ['ɒstrəsaɪz] *v.* to force/to keep (s.o.) out of a group.

os•trich ['ɒstrɪtʃ] *n.* (*pl.* **-es**) large, fast-running, flightless bird found in Africa.

oth•er ['ʌðə] **1.** *adj.* (a) different/not the one already mentioned/not the same. (b) second of two; **every o. week** = every second week. (c) (*expressing a vague idea*) **the o. day** = a day or two ago. **2.** *pron.* (a) different person/different thing. (b) (*used to contrast two things or groups*) **one after the o. 3.** *adv.* **o. than** = apart from. **oth•er•wise,** *adv.* (a) in a different way/situation. (b) in other respects. (c) if not/or else. **oth•er•world•ly,** *adj.* (person) who is not interested in material things/who is vague and impractical.

o•ti•ose ['əʊtɪəʊs] *adj.* (*formal*) superfluous/unwanted.

o•ti•tis [əʊ'taɪtɪs] *n.* inflammation of the ear.

ot•ter ['ɒtə] *n.* fish-eating mammal with webbed feet living mainly in rivers.

ot•to•man ['ɒtəmən] *n.* low padded seat.

ouch [aʊtʃ] *inter.* showing reaction to pain.

ought [ɔːt] *v.* (*past tense:* **ought to have**) *used with other verbs* (a) (*expressing duty or obligation*) **you o. to go** = it is your duty to go. (b) (*expressing something which is vaguely desirable*) **you o. to hear that concert.** (c) (*expressing something which is probable*) **that horse o. to win.**

ounce [aʊns] *n.* measure of weight (=1/16 of a pound).

our ['aʊə] *adj.* belonging to us. **ours** ['aʊəz] *pron.* thing(s)/person(s) belonging to us. **our•selves** [aʊə'selvz] *pron. referring to the subject* we.

oust [aʊst] *v.* to force s.o. to leave a place/position.

out [aʊt] **1.** *adv.* (a) not in (a building, etc.). (b) away from the starting point (of sth). (c) (in a direction) away from the inside/from the starting point. (d) having appeared/become known; **her book is just o.** = has just been published. (e) **o. loud** = so that it can be heard. (f) not in the right position/state; **o. of practice** = not having had enough practice. (g) (*of fire/light*) no longer burning; (*of hairstyle/dress*) no longer fashionable. (h) finished; having reached the end. **2.** *n.* **to know the ins and outs of** = to know sth in all its details.

out-and-out, *adj. & adv.* complete(ly)/total(ly). **out•back,** *n.* (*in Australia*) area(s) away from centers of population. **out•bid,** *v.* (**outbid**) (*at auction*) to bid a higher sum than (s.o.). **out•board,** *adj.* (engine) which is attached to the outside of a boat. **out•break,** *n.* sudden occurrence of an illness or unrest. **out•build•ings,** *n. pl.* buildings standing apart from the main building. **out•burst,** *n.* sudden display of (violent) emotion. **out•cast,** *n. & adj.* (person who has been) rejected by/driven away from a society or a group. **out•class,** *v.* to be much better than. **out•come,** *n.* result. **out•crop,** *n.* rock which sticks out of the surface of the ground. **out•cry,** *n.* loud protest from a number of people. **out•dat•ed,** *adj.* old-fashioned. **out•do,** *v.* (**outdid; outdone**) to do better than. **out•door,** *adj.* in the open air. **out•doors,** *adv. & n.* (in/to) the open air. **out•er,** *adj.* farther out; on the outside; beyond the limits; **o. space** = space beyond the earth's atmosphere. **out•er•most,** *adj.* farthest out. **out•fit,** *n.* (a) set of equipment needed for a particular purpose. (b) set of clothing. (c) *inf.* organization. **out•fit•ter,** *n.* supplier of outfits. **out•flank,** *v.* to go by the side of (an enemy). **out•flow,** *n.* quantity which flows out. **out•go•ing,** *adj.* (a) which is going out. (b) open/lively (personality). **out•grow,** *v.* (**outgrew; outgrown**) to grow too big for (clothes); to leave behind as one grows up. **out•ing,** *n.* trip, usu. for pleasure. **out•land•ish,** *adj.* strange/different from the usual. **out•last,** *v.* to live/to last longer than. **out•law. 1.** *n.* person who is a fugitive from the law. **2.** *v.* to declare illegal or outside the law. **out•lay,** *n.* expenditure. **out•let,** *n.* (a) means by which sth can escape. (b) place where sth can be sold or distributed. **out•line. 1.** *n.* line showing the outer edge(s) of sth; broad description without much detail. **2.** *v.* to make a broad description of (a plan, etc.). **out•live,** *v.* to live longer than. **out•look,** *n.* view from a building/of the world/of the future. **out•ly•ing,** *adj.* away from the center/from the main part. **out•ma•neu•ver, out•man•œu•vre,** *v.* to beat s.o. by acting/working more cleverly. **out•mod•ed,** *adj.* old-fashioned.

out•num•ber, v. to be greater in number than. **out of,** prep. (a) outside of; away from; **o. of your mind** = mad. (b) from; **one o. of ten.** (c) made from. (d) no longer having; **o. of print** = with no printed copies left; **o. of stock** = with no stock left. **out-of-date,** adj. (a) no longer in fashion (b) no longer valid. **out-of-pock•et,** adj. having paid expenses personally. **out-of-the-way,** adj. (a) very far from the center. (b) unusual/extraordinary. **out•pa•tient,** n. person who is treated at a hospital without staying overnight. **out•post,** n. small group of soldiers in a distant part of an occupied territory. **out•pour•ing,** n. sth that flows out. **out•put,** n. amount which a firm/machine/person produces; information produced by a computer. **out•rank,** v. to be of a higher rank than (s.o.). **out•rid•er** ['autraidə] n. guard on a motorcycle or horse, riding beside a car/carriage in a procession. **out•rig•ger,** n. long piece with a float at the end, which is attached to the side of a boat to make it more stable. **out•right** ['autrait] adv. & adj. (a) complete(ly); all at once. (b) straight out/without pretending. **out•set** ['autset] n. beginning. **out•shine** [aut'ʃain] v. (outshone) to do much better than (s.o.). **out•side** [aut'said] 1. n. (a) outer surface (of sth); what is beyond the outer surface/edge of sth. (b) **at the o.** = at the most. 2. adj. (a) on the outer surface. (b) the most (possible). (c) from the outside/from another group, etc. 3. adv. & prep. beyond the outer surface/edge of (sth). **out•sid•er,** n. (a) person who does not belong to a group, etc. (b) s.o./sth which is not expected to win. **out•size** ['autsaiz] n. & adj. (of) size which is larger than the normal or usual range. **out•skirts** ['autskɜːts] n. pl. outer edges of a town, etc. **out•smart** [aut'smɑːt] v. to trick (s.o.) by being cleverer. **out•spo•ken** [aut'spəukən] adj. speaking (too) frankly. **out•stand•ing** [aut'stændɪŋ] adj. (a) excellent; of unusual quality; of very high standard. (b) not yet fulfilled/incomplete. **out•stand•ing•ly,** adv. to an outstanding degree. **out•stay** [aut'stei] v. to stay longer than. **out•stretched,** adj. (arm, etc.) which is stretched out. **out•strip,** v. (outstripped) to run past (s.o.); to do better than (s.o.). **out to,** adj. trying to/aiming for. **out box,** n. receptacle for correspondence which is to be sent out. **out•vote** [aut'vəut] v. to defeat by having more votes than. **out•ward** ['autwəd] adj. & adv. (a) toward the outside; away from the center or starting point. (b) on the outside. **out•ward•ly,** adv. (appearing) on the outside. **out•ward, outwards,** adv. toward the outside. **out•weigh** [aut'wei] v. to be more important than (sth). **out•wit** [aut'wit] v. (outwitted) to trick (s.o.) by being cleverer.

out•rage ['autreidʒ] 1. n. offense; vigorous attack (esp. against moral standards). 2. v. to shock/to be a cause of moral indignation. **out•ra•geous** [aut'reidʒəs] adj. causing (moral) indignation/shock/offense. **out•ra•geous•ly,** adv. in an outrageous way.

ou•tré ['uːtrei] adj. strange/weird.

ou•zel ['uːzl] n. type of diving bird.

o•va ['əuvə] n. pl. see **o•vum.**

o•val ['əuvl] n. & adj. (of) a long rounded shape; egg-shaped(d).

o•va•ry ['əuvəri] n. one of the two organs of a female mammal in which eggs are produced. **o•var•i•an** [əu'veəriən] adj. referring to ovaries.

o•va•tion [ə'veiʃn] n. great applause.

ov•en ['ʌvn] n. enclosed box which can be heated for cooking/for baking pottery, etc. **ov•en•ware,** n. (no pl.) dishes which can be put in a hot oven.

o•ver ['əuvə] 1. prep. (a) on the top (surface) of. (b) higher than. (c) across/to the other side of. (d) from the top of. (e) on the other/on the far side of. (f) everywhere in. (g) during. (h) more than. (i) better than. (j) about. 2. adv. (a) in all parts of (sth). (b) repeatedly. (c) above the top of (sth). (d) downward from a previous vertical position. (e) into another position; **please turn o.** = turn the page. (f) to the other side of. (g) more/higher in number. (h) in excess/left behind. (i) past/finished. (j) prefix meaning too (much); **overexcited; overtired. o•ver•arm,** adv. with the arm higher than the shoulder. **o•ver•awe** [əuvə'ɔː] v. to frighten. **o•ver•bal•ance,** v. to (cause to) lose balance. **o•ver•bear•ing,** adj. trying to dominate others. **o•ver•blown,** adj. (rose) which has almost finished flowering; (claim) which is excessive. **o•ver•board,** adv. into the water from the edge of a ship, etc.; inf. **to go o. for** = to be enthusiastic about. **o•ver•book,** v. to book more places than there are rooms/seats. **o•ver•charge,** v. to charge too much for sth. **o•ver•coat,** n.

æ back, a: farm, ɒ: top, ai pipe, au how, aiə fire, auə flower, ɔ: bought, ɔi toy, e fed, eəhair, ei take, ə afraid, əu boat, ɔuə lower, vː word, iː heap, ɪ hit, ɪə hear, uː school, ʊ book, ʌ but, b back, d dog, ð then, dʒ just, f fog, g go, h hand, j yes, k catch, l last, m mix, n nut, ŋ sing, p penny, r round, s some, ʃ short, t too, tʃ chop, θ thing, v voice, w was, z zoo, ʒ treasure

(full-length) coat for outdoor wear. **o•ver•crowd•ed**, *adj.* containing too many people/animals, etc. **o•ver•do**, *v.* (**overdid; overdone**) (a) to do too much; to exaggerate. (b) to cook too much. **o•ver•dose**, *n.* too large a dose (of a drug). **o•ver•draft**, *n.* amount by which a bank account is overdrawn. **o•ver•draw**, *v.* (**overdrew; overdrawn**) to take out money (from a bank account) when there is no money there. **o•ver•drive**, *n.* mechanism in a car which gives an extra gear above the top gear. **o•ver•due**, *adj.* (debt) which has not been paid at the correct time; (book) which should have been returned to the library; (visit) which should have been made; (plane, etc.) which is late. **o•ver•eat**, *v.* (**overate; overeaten**) to eat too much. **o•ver•eat•ing**, *n.* eating too much. **o•ver•es•ti•mate**, *v.* to estimate too much; to think (sth) is larger than it is. **o•ver•ex•posed**, *adj.* (film) which has been exposed too much. **o•ver•fed**, *adj.* given too much to eat. **o•ver•flow**. 1. *v.* (a) to flow over the top. (b) to occupy greater space. 2. *n.* (a) liquid which has overflowed. (b) pipe to catch overflowing liquid. (c) amount or number which will not fit a given space. **o•ver•grown**, *adj.* covered (**with** plants, etc.). **o•ver•hang•ing**, *adj.* which juts out over. **o•ver•haul**. 1. [əʊvə'hɔːl] *v.* (a) to examine carefully, repairing where necessary. (b) to overtake (another ship). 2. *n.* ['əʊvəhɔːl] (act of) overhauling. **o•ver•head**. 1. *adv.* above. 2. *adj.* above; **o. projector** = projector which projects a picture from a flat surface onto a screen. 3. *n.* general expenses incurred by a business as a whole, such as salaries/heating/rent, etc. **o•ver•heat**, *v.* to heat too much. **o•ver•joyed**, *adj.* very happy. **o•ver•kill**, *n.* excess of weapons/excessive strength for what is required. **o•ver•land**, *adv. & adj.* by land. **o•ver•lap**. 1. *v.* (**overlapped**) to cover a section of (sth). 2. *n.* amount by which sth overlaps. **o•ver•leaf**, *adv.* on the other side of a page. **o•ver•load**, *v.* to put too heavy a load on (sth). **o•ver•look**, *v.* (a) not to notice. (b) to pretend not to notice; to pay no attention to. (c) to look out on to. **o•ver•lord**, *n.* person in supreme command. **o•ver•ly**, *adv.* too much. **o•ver•man**, *v.* (**overmanned**) to have more workers than are needed for the job. **o•ver•much**, *adv.* too much. **o•ver•pass**, *n.* road which crosses over the top of another road. **o•ver•pay**, *v.* (**overpaid**) to pay (s.o.) too much. **o•ver•pay•ment**, *n.* paying too much. **o•ver•play**, *v.* **to o. your hand** = to attempt (to gain) too much in negotiations.

o•ver•pow•er, *v.* to gain control of (s.o.) by force. **o•ver•pow•er•ing**, *adv.* very strong. **o•ver•pro•duc•tion**, *n.* excess production. **o•ver•rate**, *v.* to estimate/to value (sth) higher than it is. **o•ver•reach**, *v.* **to o. yourself** = to go too far (and fail in what you are trying to do). **o•ver•re•act**, *v.* to react very violently. **o•ver•ride**, *v.* (**overrode; overridden**) (a) to pay no attention to (an order, etc.). (b) to be more important than other things. **o•ver•ripe**, *adj.* too ripe. **o•ver•rule**, *v.* to rule/to order against. **o•ver•run**, *v.* (**overran; overrun**) (a) to go into/to attack all parts of. (b) to continue beyond (a time limit). **o•ver•seas**, *adv. & adj.* across the sea. **o•ver•see**, *v.* (**oversaw; overseen**) to manage/supervise. **o•ver•seer**, *n.* person who supervises other people at work. **o•ver•shad•ow**, *v.* to hide/to make less conspicuous by greater brilliance. **o•ver•shoes**, *n. pl.* rubber/plastic shoes worn over ordinary shoes to protect them. **o•ver•shoot**, *v.* (**overshot**) to go beyond a natural stopping place. **o•ver•sight**, *n.* not doing sth because of forgetfulness/not noticing. **o•ver•sleep**, *v.* (**overslept; has overslept**) to sleep longer than you meant to. **o•ver•spend**, *n.* (**overspent**) to spend more than you should. **o•ver•state**, *v.* to state too strongly/with too much detail. **o•ver•state•ment**, *n.* act of overstating; what is overstated. **o•ver•stay**, *v.* **to o. your welcome** = to stay for such a long time that you are no longer welcome. **o•ver•step**, *v.* (**overstepped**) to go further than you ought to. **o•ver•stuffed**, *adj.* well padded (sofa). **o•ver•sub•scribed**, *adj.* which more people applied for than there were available. **o•ver•take**, *v.* (**overtook; overtaken**) to reach and go past (s.o. ahead of you); to pass (another car) which is going more slowly than you. **o•ver•tax**, *v.* to demand too much tax from; **to o. one's strength** = to do more than one is physically capable of. **o•ver-the-coun•ter**, *adj* (securities) not listed on a main Stock Exchange. **o•ver•throw**. 1. *n.* removal (of a government/dictator) from power. 2. *v.* (**overthrew; overthrown**) to defeat. **o•ver•time**. 1. *n.* (a) time worked beyond normal working hours. (b) money paid for working beyond normal hours. 2. *adv.* beyond normal hours. **o•ver•turn** [əʊvə'tɜːn] *v.* to (cause to) fall over/to turn upside down. **o•ver•view**, *n.* general view (of a subject). **o•ver•ween•ing** [əʊvə'wiːnɪŋ] *adj.* excessive/arrogant (pride). **o•ver•weight** [əʊvə'weɪt] *adj.* too heavy. **o•ver•whelm** [əʊvə-

'welm] v. (a) to conquer (completely). (b) **overwhelmed with work** = having more work than you can do. **o•ver•whelm•ing,** adj. enormous; greater than all others. **o•ver•work** [əʊvə'wɜːk] 1. n. too much work. 2. v. to (cause to) work too hard. **o•ver•wrought** [əʊvə'rɔːt] adj. very agitated/under a lot of stress.

o•ver•all ['əʊvəɔːl] 1. adj. covering; taking in all aspects. 2. n. **overalls** = one-piece suit worn to protect the other clothes.

o•ver•cast [əʊvə'kaːst] adj. (of sky) heavy/dull/cloudy.

o•ver•come [əʊvə'kʌm] v. (**overcame; has overcome**) to gain victory over (an enemy/a problem/an emotion).

o•ver•hear [əʊvə'hiə] v. (**overheard** [əʊvə'hɜːd]) to hear accidentally (what you are not meant to hear).

o•ver•night [əʊvə'naɪt] 1. adv. until morning. 2. adj. for the night.

o•vert [əʊ'vɜːt] adj. open/not hidden.

o•ver•tones ['əʊvətəʊns] n. pl. suggestion of sth which is different from the general content.

o•ver•ture ['əʊvətʃə] n. (a) (short) piece of music played at the beginning of an opera/concert, etc. (b) **to make overtures to s.o.** = to try to begin a conversation/negotiations with s.o.

o•vi•duct ['ɒvɪdʌkt] n. tube through which ova are passed to the womb.

o•vip•a•rous [ɒ'vɪpərəs] adj. which lays eggs.

o•void ['əʊvɔɪd] adj. shaped like an egg.

o•vum ['əʊvəm] n. (pl. **ova** ['əʊvə]) female egg which can develop inside the mother's body when fertilized. **ov•u•late** ['ɒvjuleɪt] v. to produce female eggs. **ov•u•la•tion,** n. producing female eggs. **ov•ule,** n. part of a plant where the seeds develop.

ow [aʊ] inter. showing pain.

owe [əʊ] v. (a) to be obliged; to be due to pay (s.o.). (b) **to o. sth to** = to have sth because of (s.o./sth). **ow•ing to,** prep. because of.

owl [aʊl] n. bird of prey which is mainly active at night. **owl•ish,** adj. like an owl.

own [əʊn] 1. v. (a) to have/to possess. (b) to recognize as belonging to you. (c) to admit; to say that sth is true. (d) inf. **to o. up to sth** = to admit/to say that you have done sth wrong. 2. adj. belonging to yourself (alone). 3. n. (a) **my o./his o.** = mine/his; **of your o.** = belonging to you; **to come into your o.** = to have the success which you deserve; **to hold your o.** = to remain firm against some threat. (b) **on your o.** = alone/by yourself. **own•er,** n. person who owns. **own•er•ship,** n. state of owning.

ox [ɒks] n. (pl. **oxen**) (a) large animal of the cow family. (b) castrated bull. **ox•bow,** n. bend of a river where the current no longer runs. **ox•eye,** n. daisy with large flowers. **ox•tail,** n. tail of the ox used as food.

ox•a•lis [ɒk'sælɪs] n. type of flower, which produces a poisonous substance.

ox•ide ['ɒksaɪd] n. chemical compound of oxygen. **ox•i•da•tion** [ɒksɪ'deɪʃn] n. act of oxidizing. **ox•i•dize** ['ɒksɪdaɪz] v. to (cause to) combine with oxygen.

ox•y•a•cet•y•lene [ɒksɪə'setɪliːn] n. & adj. (referring to a) mixture of oxygen and acetylene.

ox•y•gen ['ɒksɪdʒən] n. (element: O) gas which forms part of the earth's atmosphere and is essential for plant and animal life.

o•yez ['ɒ'jez] int. hear this.

oys•ter ['ɔɪstə] n. type of double-shelled shellfish highly valued as food; **o. bed** = part of the sea floor where oysters are found. **oy•ster•catch•er,** n. common black and white bird which lives on the seashore.

oz abbrev. for ounce.

o•zone ['əʊzəʊn] n. (a) harmful form of oxygen; **o. hole** = gap which forms in the ozone layer, allowing harmful radiation from the sun to reach the earth; **o. layer** = layer of ozone in the stratosphere, formed by the action of sunlight on oxygen, which acts as protection against harmful rays from the sun. (b) inf. refreshing pure air.

æ back, aː farm, ɒ top, aɪ pipe, aʊ how, aie fire, aʊə flower, ɔː bought, ɔɪ toy, e fed, eəhair, eɪ take, ə afraid, əʊ boat, əʊə lower, vː word, iː heap, ɪ hit, ɪə hear, uː school, ʊ book, ʌ but, b back, d dog, ð then, dʒ just, f fog, g go, h hand, j yes, k catch, l last, m mix, n nut, ŋ sing, p penny, r round, s some, ʃ short, t too, tʃ chop, θ thing, v voice, w was, z zoo, ʒ treasure

Pp

P *symbol for* phosphorus.

pa [pɑː] *n. inf. child's name for* father.

p.a. *abbrev. for* per annum.

pace [peɪs] 1. *n.* (a) stride/step; distance covered by one step. (b) speed; **to keep p. with** = keep up with; (*of a runner*) **to set the p.** = to decide how fast a race should be run. 2. *v.* (a) to walk; to measure by walking. (b) to set the pace for (a runner, etc.). **pace•mak•er,** *n.* (a) runner who sets the pace in a race; person who runs alongside a runner to encourage him to run faster. (b) electric device which makes heartbeats regular.

pach•y•derm ['pækɪdɜːm] *n.* animal with a thick skin (such as an elephant).

pac•i•fy ['pæsɪfaɪ] *v.* to calm. **pa•cif•ic** [pə-'sɪfɪk] *adj.* peaceful/calm. **pa•cif•i•cal•ly,** *adv.* in a pacific way. **pac•i•fi•ca•tion** [pæsɪfɪ'keɪʃn] *n.* calming (of people in revolt). **pac•i•fi•er** ['pæsɪfaɪə] *n.* rubber nipple (for babies). **pac•i•fism,** *n.* opposition to war. **pac•i•fist,** *n.* person who believes in pacifism.

pack [pæk] 1. *n.* (a) bundle of things. (b) bag carried on the back, as when hiking. (c) group of animals/people. (d) articles put in a box for selling. (e) **face p.** = cream which is spread on your face and left on it for a time to clean the skin. (f) **ice p.** = bag of ice placed on the forehead to cure a headache, etc. 2. *v.* (a) to put (things) in order in a case/box. (b) to squeeze (many things) into a small area. **pack•age.** 1. *n.* (a) bundle of things/parcel. (b) **p. deal** = deal where several items are offered at the same time; **p. tour** = tour which is organized and paid for in advance. 2. *v.* to wrap/to present (goods) in an attractive way. **pack•ag•ing,** *n.* wrapping of goods in an attractive way. **pack•er,** *n.* person who packs goods. **pack•et,** *n.* small parcel; small box. **pack ice,** *n.* mass of ice covering the sea. **pack•ing,** *n.* (a) putting things into containers; **p. case** = special wooden box for packing goods (esp. for transport). (b) material used to protect goods which are being packed. (c) **to send s.o. p.** = to send s.o. away. **pack off,** *v.* to send (s.o.) away. **pack up,** *v.* to put things away (before closing a store/before leaving a place).

pact [pækt] *n.* agreement/treaty.

pad [pæd] 1. *n.* (a) soft part under the feet of some animals; soft protective cushion. (b) (*in sports*) protective guards for the leg; **knee p.** (c) set of sheets of paper lightly attached. (d) **launching p.** = area from which a rocket is launched. (e) *Sl.* room/apartment. 2. *v.* (**padded**) (a) to soften (sth hard) by using soft material; to walk about softly. (b) to make (a speech/an article) longer by inserting irrelevant material. **pad•ding,** *n.* (a) words added to pad a speech or article. (b) soft material used to make cushions, etc.

pad•dle ['pædl] 1. *n.* (a) short oar used to propel a canoe. (b) round bat used in table tennis. (c) device with a knob, used for moving a cursor on a computer screen. 2. *v.* (a) to make (a boat) move forward using a paddle. (b) to move the hands or feet in very shallow water. **pad•dle steam•er,** *n.* boat driven by large wheels on either side. **pad•dle wheel,** *n.* wheel on a paddle steamer.

pad•dock ['pædək] *n.* small field for horses.

pad•dy ['pædɪ] *n.* (*also* **paddy field**) field where rice is grown.

pad•lock ['pædlɒk] 1. *n.* small portable lock with a hook which can be unlocked and twisted to pass through a ring to lock a gate/a box, etc. 2. *v.* to lock with a padlock.

pa•dre ['pɑːdrɪ] *n.* priest or chaplain.

pae•an ['piːən] *n.* (*formal*) great song praising s.o.

pa•gan ['peɪgn] *adj. & n.* (person) who does not believe in one of the established religions; (person) who is not a Christian.

page [peɪdʒ] 1. *n.* (a) one of the sides of a sheet of paper in a book or magazine. (b) messenger boy in a hotel. (c) small boy who accompanies the bride at a wedding. 2. *v.* to call (s.o.) over a loudspeaker in a hotel, etc. **page•boy,** *n.* (a) (*old*) boy attendant on a medieval lord. (b) **p. hairstyle** = woman's hair cut quite short and straight.

pag•eant ['pædʒənt] *n.* grand display of people in costume. **pag•eant•ry,** *n.* grand ceremonies where people wear showy costumes.

pag•i•nate ['pædʒɪneɪt] *v.* to number the

pages in a book. **pag•i•na•tion** [pædʒɪ-'neɪʃn] n. act of paginating.

pa•go•da [pə'gəʊdə] n. tall tower made of several stories, found in the Far East.

paid [peɪd] v. see **pay**.

pail [peɪl] n. bucket.

pain [peɪn] 1. n. (a) sensation of being hurt. (b) **to take pains with sth/to do sth** = to take care. (c) **on p. of death** = at the risk of being sentenced to death. 2. v. to hurt. **pained**, adj. sad/sorrowful (expression). **pain•ful**, adj. which hurts. **pain•ful•ly**, adv. in a painful way. **pain•kil•ler**, n. painkilling drug. **pain•kil•ling**, adj. (drug) which stops part of your body hurting. **pain•less**, adj. which does not hurt. **pain•less•ly**, adv. in a painless way. **pain•stak•ing**, adj. careful/well-done (work).

paint [peɪnt] 1. n. liquid in various colors used to color. 2. v. (a) to cover with color. (b) to make a picture of (s.o./sth). **paint•er**, n. (a) person who paints pictures. (b) person who paints houses/cars, etc. **paint•ing**, n. (a) making pictures. (b) painted picture. **paint•work**, n. (no pl.) painted surfaces (doors/windows, etc.).

pair ['peə] 1. n. (a) two things taken together; two people. (b) two things joined together to make one. 2. v. (a) to join together in twos. (b) to mate.

pais•ley ['peɪzlɪ] n. pattern on textiles, of curved shapes.

pa•ja•mas [pə'dʒɑːməz] n. pl. light shirt and trousers worn in bed.

Pak•i•sta•ni [pækɪ'stɑːnɪ] 1. adj. referring to Pakistan. 2. n. person from Pakistan.

pal [pæl] n. inf. friend.

pal•ace ['pæləs] n. large building where a king/queen/president, etc., lives.

pal•an•quin ['pælənkwɪn] n. seat with a roof, carried by bearers.

pal•ate ['pælət] n. top part of the inside of the mouth. **pal•at•a•ble**, adj. nice to eat/tasting good.

pa•la•tial [pə'leɪʃl] adj. magnificent/like a palace.

pa•lav•er [pə'lɑːvə] n. inf. idle talk; chatter.

pale [peɪl] 1. adj. (-er, -est) light-colored. 2. n. **beyond the p.** = doing things which are not acceptable in society. 3. v. (a) to lose color; to become light. (b) to become less important. **pale•ness**, n. light color.

pa•le•o•gra•phy [pælɪ'ɒgrəfɪ] n. study of ancient writing.

pa•le•o•lith•ic [pælɪəʊ'lɪθɪk] adj. referring to the early part of the Stone Age.

pa•le•on•tol•o•gy [pælɪɒn'tɒlədʒɪ] n. study of fossils.

Pal•es•tin•i•an [pælɪ'stɪnɪən] adj. & n. (person) from Palestine.

pal•ette ['pælət] n. (a) flat board on which an artist mixes colors; **p. knife** = long flat knife with a rounded end. (b) range of colors available, esp. on a computer graphics program.

pal•i•mo•ny ['pælɪmənɪ] n. alimony paid to a friend when parting after years of life together.

pal•in•drome ['pælɪndrəʊm] n. word or phrase which is spelled the same backward and forward.

pal•ing(s) ['peɪlɪŋ(z)], **pal•i•sade** [pælɪ'seɪd] n. fence made of pointed pieces of wood.

pall [pɔːl] 1. n. (a) (formal) thick layer (of smoke). (b) cloth put over a coffin. 2. v. to become less interesting. **pall•bear•er**, n. person who walks beside a coffin in a funeral procession.

pal•let ['pælɪt] n. (a) flat platform on which goods can be stacked and moved from place to place. (b) straw-filled mattress.

pal•liasse ['pælɪæs] n. straw-filled mattress.

pal•li•ate ['pælɪeɪt] v. to try to reduce (a vice/pain); to cover up (a mistake). **pal•li•a•tive** ['pælɪətɪv] adj. & n. (thing) which reduces pain.

pal•lid ['pælɪd] adj. pale (face).

pal•lor ['pælə] n. paleness (of face).

palm [pɑːm] n. (a) soft inside surface of your hand. (b) tall tropical tree with long leaves at the top. **palm•cord•er** ['pɑːmkɔːdə] n. camcorder that is small enough to hold in the palm of the hand. **palm•ist**, n. person who tells the future by palmistry. **palm•is•try**, n. telling what will happen to you in the future from the lines in the palm of your hand. **palm off**, v. inf. (on) to give (sth bad) to s.o. without his knowing. **Palm Sun•day**, n. Sunday before Easter Sunday. **palm•top** ['pɑːmtɒp] n. portable computer that is small enough to hold in the palm of the hand, smaller than a notebook computer, and used esp. as a personal organizer. **palm•y**, adj. (-ier, -iest) pleasant; prosperous.

pal•pa•ble ['pælpəbl] adj. which can be felt/which can be easily seen. **pal•pa•bly**,

---

æ back, ɑː farm, ɒ top, aɪ pipe, aʊ how, aɪə fire, aʊə flower, ɔː bought, ɔɪ toy, e fed, eə hair, eɪ take, ə afraid, əʊ boat, əʊə lower, ɜː word, iː heap, ɪ hit, ɪə hear, uː school, ʊ book, ʌ but, b back, d dog, ð then, dʒ just, f fog, g go, h hand, j yes, k catch, l last, m mix, n nut, ŋ sing, p penny, r round, s some, ʃ short, t too, tʃ chop, θ thing, v voice, w was, z zoo, ʒ treasure

adv. in a palpable way. **pal•pa•tion** [pæl-'peɪʃn] *n.* examination of part of the body by feeling it with the hand.

pal•pi•tate ['pælpɪteɪt] *v.* to beat very quickly. **pal•pi•ta•tions** [pælpɪ'teɪʃnz] *n. pl.* rapid beating of the heart.

pal•sy ['pɒlzɪ] *n.* (a) paralysis. (b) trembling (of the hands, etc.). **pal•sied,** *adj.* with trembling limbs.

pal•try ['pɔːltrɪ] *adj.* (**-ier, -iest**) insignificant.

pal•u•dism ['pæljuːdɪzm] *n.* (*old*) malaria.

pam•pas ['pæmpəs] *n. pl.* grass-covered plains in South America; **p. grass** = type of tall ornamental grass.

pam•per ['pæmpə] *v.* to spoil (a child/a dog) by giving them too much food/by treating them too well.

pam•phlet ['pæmflət] *n.* small book with only a few pages, which is not bound with a hard cover. **pam•phlet•eer** [pæmflə'tɪə] *n.* person who writes political pamplets.

pan- [pæn] *prefix meaning* over a wide area; **pan-American** = including North America, South America and Central America.

pan [pæn] 1. *n.* (a) metal cooking container with a handle. (b) metal dish; one of the dishes on a pair of scales. 2. (**panned**) (a) to move a camera sideways to take in a wider view. (b) *inf.* to criticize. (c) **to p. for gold** = to sift mud in a stream, hoping to find gold in it. **pan•cake** ['pænkeɪk] *n.* thin soft flat cake made of flour, milk, eggs, etc. **pan out,** *v. inf.* to turn out/to succeed.

pan•a•ce•a [pænə'siːə] *n.* thing which cures everything/which solves every problem.

pa•nache [pə'næʃ] *n.* showy way of doing things.

pan•a•ma [pænə'mɑː] *n.* hat made of fine straw.

pan•a•tel•la [pænə'telə] *n.* long thin cigar.

pan•chro•mat•ic [pænkrə'mætɪk] *adj.* (film) which is sensitive to all colors.

pan•cre•as ['pæŋkrɪəs] *n.* (*pl.* **-es**) gland which produces insulin, and also a liquid which helps digest food.

pan•da ['pændə] *n.* (**giant**) **p.** = large black and white Chinese animal.

pan•dem•ic [pæn'demɪk] *adj.* (disease) which occurs over the whole world/over a large area.

pan•de•mo•ni•um [pændɪ'məunɪəm] *n.* great uproar and confusion.

pan•der ['pændə] *v.* to give in (**to** low tastes).

pane [peɪn] *n.* sheet of glass (in a window, etc.).

pan•e•gyr•ic [pænɪ'dʒɪrɪk] *n.* (*formal*) speech in praise of s.o.

pan•el ['pænl] 1. *n.* (a) flat surface which is higher/lower/thicker, etc., than the rest of the surface. (b) section of different-colored material. (c) group of people who answer questions/who judge a competition. 2. *v.* (**paneled, panelled**) to cover with sheets of wood. **panel game,** *n.* game (on radio/TV) where a group of people answer questions/guess answers, etc. **pan•el•ing, panelling,** *n.* sheets of wood used to cover walls, etc. **pan•el•ist,** *n.* member of a panel answering questions/judging a competition.

pang [pæŋ] *n.* sudden sharp pain.

pan•ic ['pænɪk] 1. *n.* terror/fright. 2. *v.* (**panicked**) to become frightened. **pan•ic-strick•en,** *adj.* wild with fright. **pan•ick•y,** *adj.* likely to panic.

pan•i•cle ['pænɪkl] *n.* cluster of flowers which hangs down.

pan•nier ['pænɪə] *n.* one of a pair of bags carried on the side of an animal or a bicycle.

pan•o•ply ['pænəplɪ] *n.* fine show/grand display of costume, etc.

pan•o•ram•a [pænə'rɑːmə] *n.* wide expanse of landscape. **pan•o•ram•ic** [pænə'ræmɪk] *adj.* wide.

pan•sy ['pænzɪ] *n.* (a) small multicolored garden flower. (b) *inf.* effeminate man.

pant [pænt] *v.* to breathe fast.

pan•the•ism ['pænθɪɪzəm] *n.* belief that God and the universe are one and the same; worship of many gods.

pan•ther ['pænθə] *n.* large black leopard.

pant•ies ['pæntɪz] *n. inf.* women's brief undergarment worn on the lower part of the body.

pan•tile ['pæntaɪl] *n.* curved tile for a roof.

pan•to•graph ['pæntəgrɑːf] *n.* metal frame on the roof of an electric locomotive which rises to touch an overhead electric wire to pick up electricity.

pan•to•mime ['pæntəmaɪm] *n.* theatrical entertainment presented without words, using only gestures and other body movements.

pan•try ['pæntrɪ] *n.* cool cupboard or room for keeping food in.

pants [pænts] *n. pl.* (a) *inf.* brief undergarment worn on the lower part of the body. (b) *inf.* trousers.

pan•ty•hose ['pæntɪ'həuz] *n. pl.* women's tights.

pap [pæp] *n.* soft food for invalids.

pa•pa [pə'pɑː] *n. child's name for* father.

pa•pa•cy ['peɪpəsɪ] *n.* position of pope. **pa•pal,** *adj.* referring to the pope.

pa•pa•ya [pə'pæjə], **pa•paw** ['pɔːpɔː] *n.* yellow fruit from a tropical tree.

pa•per ['peɪpə] 1. *n.* (a) thin material made from rags or wood pulp, used for printing/writing, etc. (b) sheet of paper. (c) newspaper. (d) scientific/learned article. 2. *v.* to cover (the walls of a room) with paper. **pa•per•back,** *n.* book with a paper cover.

pa•per boy, *n.* boy who delivers newspapers to houses. **pa•per clip,** *n.* piece of bent wire for holding pieces of paper together. **pa•per•knife,** *n.* (*pl.* **-knives**) long knife for cutting paper (esp. for opening envelopes). **pa•per•weight,** *n.* heavy block put on papers to prevent them from being blown away. **pa•per•work,** *n.* office work. **pa•per•y,** *adj.* thin like paper.

pa•pier-mâ•ché [pæpɪeɪ'mæʃeɪ] *n.* mixture of wet paper, used to make models, etc.

pa•pist ['peɪpɪst] *n.* (*rude*) Roman Catholic.

pa•poose [pə'puːs] *n.* North American Indian baby.

pap•ri•ka ['pæprɪkə] *n.* red spice made from powdered sweet peppers.

pa•py•rus [pə'paɪrəs] *n.* reed growing in the Middle East, used by the ancient Egyptians to make a type of paper.

par [pɑː] *n.* (a) equal level; **to be on a p. with** = to be equal to. (b) **to buy shares at p.** = at their original price or at face value. (c) (*in golf*) number of strokes usu. needed to hit the ball into the hole; **below p.** = not very well.

par•a•ble ['pærəbl] *n.* usu. religious story with a moral.

pa•rab•o•la [pə'ræbələ] *n.* curve like the path of an object which is thrown into the air and comes down again. **par•a•bol•ic** [pærə'bɒlɪk] *adj.* referring to a parabola.

par•a•chute ['pærəʃuːt] 1. *n.* large piece of thin material shaped like an umbrella, with cords and a harness attached, which allows you to float down safely from an aircraft. 2. *v.* to jump from an aircraft with a parachute. **par•a•chut•ist,** *n.* person who jumps regularly with a parachute.

pa•rade [pə'reɪd] 1. *n.* (a) military display/march; **p. ground** = square area on a military camp where parades are held. (b) series of bands/decorated cars, etc., passing in a street; **fashion p.** = display of new clothes by models. 2. *v.* to march past in ordered lines.

par•a•digm ['pærədaɪm] *n.* example to be copied.

par•a•dise ['pærədaɪs] *n.* ideal place where good people are supposed to live after death; any beautiful place.

par•a•dox ['pærədɒks] *n.* thing which appears to contradict itself but may really be true. **par•a•dox•i•cal** [pærə'dɒksɪkl] *adj.* contradictory. **par•a•dox•i•cal•ly,** *adv.* in a paradoxical way.

par•af•fin ['pærəfɪn] *n. Brit. see* **kerosene. p.** wax = solid white substance used for making candles.

par•a•gon ['pærəgən] *n.* perfect model (of virtue, etc.).

par•a•graph ['pærəgrɑːf] *n.* section of several lines of prose, usu. starting with a short blank space at the beginning of a new line.

par•a•keet [pærə'kiːt] *n.* kind of small tropical parrot.

par•a•le•gal [pærə'liːgl] *n.* person who is not a lawyer, but who assists lawyers in legal matters.

par•al•lax ['pærəlæks] *n.* difference in the position of an object when it is seen from different points.

par•al•lel ['pærələl] 1. *adj.* (a) (**to/with**) (lines) which are side by side and remain the same distance apart without ever touching. (b) similar. 2. *n.* (a) geometrical line which runs parallel to another. (b) line running around the globe from east to west parallel to the equator. (c) closely similar situation; thing which can be compared. 3. *v.* to be similar to. **par•al•lel•o•gram** [pærə'leləgræm] *n.* four-sided figure where each side is parallel to the one opposite.

par•a•lyze, *Brit.* **par•a•lyse** ['pærəlaɪz] *v.* to make unable to move. **pa•ral•y•sis** [pə'ræləsɪs] *n.* being unable to move. **par•a•lyt•ic** [pærə'lɪtɪk] 1. *adj.* unable to move. 2. *n.* paralyzed person.

par•a•med•i•cal [pærə'medɪkl] *adj.* helping in medical treatment. **par•a•med•ic,** *n. inf.* person who is not a doctor, but who helps give medical treatment.

pa•ram•e•ter [pə'ræmɪtə] *n.* figure which shows the upper or lower level of some expected result; data which defines the limits of sth.

par•a•mil•i•tar•y [pærə'mɪlətrɪ] *adj.* organized in the same way as the army, but not a part of it.

par•a•mount ['pærəmaʊnt] *adj.* extreme/supreme.

par•a•mour ['pærəmuːə] *n.* (*old*) lover; mistress.

par•a•noi•a [pærə'nɔɪə] *n.* type of mental disease where you feel that everyone is against you. **par•a•noi•ac,** *adj. & n.* (person) who suffers from paranoia. **par•a•noid,** *adj. & n.* (person) suffering from paranoia.

par•a•pet ['pærəpet] *n.* small wall at the edge of a ledge/bridge, etc.

æ back, ɑː farm, ɒ top, aɪ pipe, aʊ how, aɪə fire, aʊə flower, ɔː bought, ɔɪ toy, e fed, eəhair, eɪ take, ə afraid, əʊ boat, əʊə lower, vː word, iː heap, ɪ hit, ɪə hear, uː school, ʊ book, ʌ but, b back, d dog, ð then, dʒ just, f fog, g go, h hand, j yes, k catch, l last, m mix, n nut, ŋ sing, p penny, r round, s some, ʃ short, t too, tʃ chop, θ thing, v voice, w was, z zoo, ʒ treasure

par•a•pher•na•lia [pærəfə'neɪlɪə] *n. (no pl.)* mass of bits and pieces; equipment.

par•a•phrase ['pærəfreɪz] 1. *n.* writing which repeats sth in different words. 2. *v.* to repeat (what s.o. has said or written) using different words.

par•a•ple•gi•a [pærə'pli:dʒə] *n.* paralysis of the legs and lower part of the body. **par•a•ple•gic,** *adj. & n.* (person) who suffers from paraplegia.

par•a•psy•chol•o•gy [pærəsai'kɒlədʒi] *n.* study of unexplained psychological phenomena.

par•a•quat ['pærəkwæt] *n.* dangerous weedkiller.

par•a•site ['pærəsaɪt] *n.* animal/plant which lives on other animals or plants; person who does no useful work. **par•a•sit•ic** [pærə'sɪtɪk] *adj.* which lives off others.

par•a•sol ['pærəsɒl] *n.* light umbrella to keep off the rays of the sun.

par•a•stat•al [pɑrə'steɪtl] *adj. & n.* (organization) owned by the state.

par•a•troop•er ['pærətru:pə] *n.* soldier who is a parachutist. **par•a•troops,** *n. pl.* paratroopers.

par•a•ty•phoid [pærə'taɪfɔɪd] *n.* fever which is similar to typhoid, but less dangerous.

par•boil ['pɑ:bɔɪl] *v.* to half-cook (food) in boiling water.

par•cel ['pɑ:sl] 1. *n.* (a) sth wrapped up; package. (b) small area of land. 2. *v.* (**parceled, parcelled**) to wrap and tie (something) up to send. **parcel out,** *v.* to divide up between several people.

parch [pɑ:tʃ] *v.* to dry.

parch•ment ['pɑ:tʃmənt] *n.* (a) skins of animals which have been treated and which can be used for writing on. (b) fine quality yellowish paper.

par•don ['pɑ:dn] 1. *n.* (a) forgiveness. (b) freeing s.o. from prison or from punishment. 2. *v.* (a) to forgive. (b) to allow (s.o.) to leave prison; to release from punishment. **par•don•a•ble,** *adj.* which can be excused. **par•don•a•bly,** *adv.* in a way which can be excused.

pare ['peə] *v.* to cut the skin/peel (off a fruit/vegetable, etc.); to cut back (expenses). **par•ings,** *n. pl.* pieces of skin cut off a fruit/vegetable, etc.

par•ent ['peərənt] *n.* father or mother; (organization) which rules another. **par•ent•age,** *n.* origin. **pa•ren•tal** [pə'rentl] *adj.* referring to parents. **par•ent•hood,** *n.* being a parent.

pa•ren•the•sis [pə'renθəsɪs] *n.* (*pl.* **-ses** [-si:z]) (a) phrase in the middle of a sentence which is placed in brackets or between dashes. (b) **parentheses** = (round) brackets.

par•en•thet•ic(al) [pærən'θetɪk(l)] *adj.* which is not part of a main sentence.

par•get•ing ['pɑ:dʒetɪŋ] *n.* decorated plaster on the outside of a house.

pa•ri•ah [pə'raɪə] *n.* person who is thrown out by civilized society.

pa•ri•e•tal [pə'raɪətl] *adj.* referring to the walls of cavities in the body.

pa•ri pas•su [pærɪ 'pæsu:] *adv.* equally/with equal shares.

par•ish ['pærɪʃ] *n.* (*pl.* **-es**) (a) administrative area around a church and under the care of a clergyman. (b) county. **par•ish•ion•er** [pə'rɪʃənə] *n.* person who lives in or belongs to a parish.

par•i•ty ['pærɪtɪ] *n.* equality.

park [pɑ:k] 1. *n.* open public place usu. with grass and trees; **business p.** = area with buildings specially built for businesses; **national p.** = large area of countryside kept in a natural state. 2. *v.* to leave (one's car) in a particular place; **no parking** = don't leave your car here; **parking meter** = device into which you put money to pay for parking; **parking lot** = place where cars can be left temporarily.

par•ka ['pɑ:kə] *n.* warm jacket with a hood.

Par•kin•son's dis•ease ['pɑ:kɪnsənzdɪ'zi:z] *n.* progressive disease, which affects the parts of the brain which control movement.

par•lance ['pɑ:ləns] *n.* (*formal*) way of speaking.

par•ley ['pɑ:lɪ] 1. *n.* discussion between enemies with a view to agreeing to peace terms. 2. *v.* to discuss peace terms with an enemy.

par•lia•ment ['pɑ:ləmənt] *n.* group of elected representatives who vote the laws of a country. **par•lia•men•tar•i•an** [pɑ:ləmən'teərɪən] *n. Brit.* (experienced and knowledgable) member of a parliament. **par•lia•men•ta•ry** [pɑ:lə'mentərɪ] *adj.* referring to parliament.

par•lor, *Brit.* **par•lour** ['pɑ:lə] *n.* (a) sitting room. (b) **beauty p.** = place where women can have their hair done and their faces made up.

par•lous ['pɑ:ləs] *adj.* bad/dangerous (state).

pa•ro•chi•al [pə'rəukɪəl] *adj.* (a) referring to a parish. (b) restricted (view); narrow-minded (person).

par•o•dy ['pærədɪ] 1. *n.* imitation in order to make fun of s.o./sth. 2. *v.* to imitate in order to make fun.

pa•role [pə'rəul] 1. *n.* **prisoner on p.** = prisoner let out of prison before the end of his sentence on condition that he behaves well. 2. *v.* to let (a prisoner) out of prison on condition that he behaves well.

par•ox•ysm ['pærəksɪzəm] *n.* wild fit (of anger, etc.).

par•quet ['pɑːkeɪ] *n.* flooring of small wooden blocks.

par•ri•cide ['pærɪsaɪd] *n.* murder of your own parent or other close relative; person who kills his parent or other close relative.

par•rot ['pærət] *n.* colorful tropical bird with a large curved beak.

par•ry ['pærɪ] *v.* to prevent (a blow) from hitting you.

parse [pɑːz] *v.* to describe the grammatical function of each word in a sentence.

par•sec ['pɑːsek] *n.* unit of measurement in astronomy (3.26 light years).

par•si•mo•ny ['pɑːsɪmənɪ] *n.* (*formal*) miserliness. **par•si•mo•ni•ous** [pɑːsɪ'məʊnɪəs] *adj.* miserly. **par•si•mo•ni•ous•ly,** *adv.* in a parsimonious way.

pars•ley ['pɑːslɪ] *n.* green herb used in cooking.

pars•nip ['pɑːsnɪp] *n.* vegetable with a long white edible root.

par•son ['pɑːsn] *n.* clergyman, esp. in a Protestant Church. **par•son•age,** *n.* house of a parson.

part [pɑːt] 1. *n.* (a) piece/bit; **in p.** = not completely; **spare parts** = replacement pieces (for a machine); **parts of speech** = types of words according to usage (noun/verb, etc.). (b) role; **take p. in** = to be active in. (c) **for my p.** = as far as I am concerned. (d) separation in the hair. 2. *adv.* not entirely; **part white.** 3. *v.* to separate. **part•ing,** *n.* leaving. **part•ly,** *adv.* not entirely. **part-time,** *adj. & adv.* not for the whole working day. **part with,** *v.* to give away.

par•take [pɑː'teɪk] *v.* (**partook; partaken**) (*formal*) (**of**) to eat (food).

par•terre ['pɑːteə] *n.* formal arrangement of flowerbeds.

par•tial ['pɑːʃl] *adj.* (a) (**to**) biased/with a liking for. (b) not complete. **par•ti•al•i•ty** [pɑːʃɪ'ælɪtɪ] *n.* strong bias **for. par•tial•ly,** *adv.* (a) in a biased way. (b) not completely.

par•tic•i•pate [pɑː'tɪsɪpeɪt] *v.* to take part **in** (sth). **par•tic•i•pant,** *n.* person who participates. **par•tic•i•pa•tion** [pɑːtɪsɪ'peɪʃn] *n.* taking part in sth. **par•tic•i•pa•to•ry,** *adj.* in which you participate.

par•ti•ci•ple ['pɑːtɪsɪpl] *n.* part of a verb, used either to form compound tenses or as an adjective or noun. **par•ti•cip•i•al** [pɑːtɪ'sɪpɪəl] *adj.* referring to a participle.

par•ti•cle ['pɑːtɪkl] *n.* very small piece; minor part of speech.

par•ti•col•ored, *Brit.* **par•ti•col•oured** ['pɑːtɪkʌləd] *adj.* with one part in one color, and the other part in another.

par•tic•u•lar [pə'tɪkjulə] 1. *adj.* (a) special; referring to one thing or person; **in p.** = as a special point. (b) fussy. 2. *n.* detail. **par•tic•u•lar•i•ty** [pɑːtɪkju'lærɪtɪ] *n.* particular quality. **par•tic•u•lar•ize** [pɑːtɪkjulə'raɪz] *v.* to list details. **par•tic•u•lar•ly,** *adv.* specially.

par•ti•san [pɑːtɪ'zæn] *adj. & n.* (a) (person) who strongly supports a certain point of view. (b) (guerrilla) fighting against an army which has occupied his country. **par•ti•san•ship,** *n.* being a partisan.

par•ti•tion [pɑː'tɪʃn] 1. *n.* (a) division into parts. (b) thin wall between two spaces, esp. splitting a large room into two. 2. *v.* to divide (by means of a partition).

part•ner ['pɑːtnə] *n.* (a) person who has a part share in a business. (b) person who plays/dances with s.o. **part•ner•ship,** *n.* business association between two or more people where the risks and profits are shared.

par•tridge ['pɑːtrɪdʒ] *n.* large brown and gray bird, shot for sport and food.

par•tu•ri•tion [pɑːtju'rɪʃn] *n.* giving birth.

par•ty ['pɑːtɪ] *n.* (a) enjoyable meeting of several people on invitation. (b) group of people. (c) person involved (esp. in legal matters); **third p.** = third person, in addition to the two principal people involved. (d) **p. line** = a shared telephone line. (e) (**political**) **p.** = official group of people with the same political ideas; **p. line** = official doctrine.

pas•chal ['pæskəl] *adj.* referring to passover or Easter.

pass [pɑːs] 1. *n.* (*pl.* **-es**) (a) lower area between two mountain peaks. (b) (*in football/hockey, etc.*) moving the ball/puck to another player. (c) acceptance at an examination. (d) bus/train season ticket; permit to go in or out. (e) **to make a p. at s.o.** = to try to start a sexual relationship with s.o. 2. *v.* (a) to go past. (b) to move (sth) **to** s.o. (c) to get through (an examination/inspection). (d) to vote by a majority for (a motion). (e) **to p. comments** = to make comments. (f) **to p. water** = to urinate. **pass•a•ble,** *adj.* fairly good. **pass•a•bly,** *adv.* fairly well. **pas•sage** ['pæsɪdʒ] *n.* (a) corridor. (b) section of a text. (c) **sea p.** = journey by sea. **pas•sage•way,** *n.* corridor. **pass a•way,** *v.* to die. **pass•book,** *n.* book which records how much money you put in or take out of your savings account in a bank. **pas•sen•ger** ['pæsɪndʒə] *n.* traveler (in a vehicle). **pass•er•by** [pɑːsə'baɪ] *n.* (*pl.* **passersby**) person who is walking past. **pass for**, *v.* to be thought to be. **pass•ing**, *adj.* (a) not permanent. (b) which is going past. **pass key**, *n.* main key which opens several doors. **pass off**, *v.* **to pass oneself off as** = to pretend to be. **pass on**, *v.* to die. **pass out**, *v. inf.* to faint. **pass o•ver**, *v.* (a) to go past above. (b) **to pass s.o. over for promotion** = to miss s.o. who should have been promoted. **Pass•o•ver** ['pɑːsəuvə] *n.* Jewish festival which celebrates the freeing of the Jews from captivity in Egypt. **pass•port**, *n.* official document allowing you to pass from one country to another. **pass up**, *v. inf.* not to take (an opportunity). **pass•word**, *n.* secret word which you say to go past a guard or to access a computer file.

pass•é ['pæseɪ] *adj.* old-fashioned.

pas•sim ['pæsɪm] *adv.* throughout.

pas•sion ['pæʃn] *n.* violent emotion/enthusiasm. **pas•sion•ate,** *adj.* violently emotional. **pas•sion•ate•ly,** *adv.* violently. **pas•sion•flow•er,** *n.* climbing plant with green and purple flowers. **pas•sion•fruit,** *n.* (*no pl.*) edible tropical fruit.

pas•sive ['pæsɪv] *adj.* (a) not resisting; which allows things to happen; **p. resistance** = resisting (the police, etc.) by refusing to obey orders but not using violence. (b) (verb) which shows that the subject is being acted upon. **pas•sive•ly,** *adv.* not offering any resistance/not doing anything positive. **pas•sive•ness,** *n.* being passive. **pas•siv•i•ty** [pə'sɪvɪtɪ] *n.* being passive.

past [pɑːst] 1. *adj.* (time) which has gone by. 2. *n.* time which has gone by. 3. *prep.* after; beyond. **past mas•ter,** *n.* expert.

pas•ta ['pæstə] *n.* (*pl.* **pasta**). food of Italian origin made of flour and water, such as spaghetti/macaroni, etc.

paste [peɪst] 1. *n.* (a) thin glue, usu. made of flour and water. (b) soft substance. (c) imitation jewel. 2. *v.* to glue (paper, etc.). **paste•board,** *n.* cardboard.

pas•tel ['pæstl] *n.* (a) colored crayon like chalk; **p. colors** = soft, light shades. (b) picture done with colored crayons like chalk.

pas•tern ['pæstɜːn] *n.* part of a horse's foot above the hoof.

pas•teur•ize ['pɑːstʃəraɪz] *v.* to kill the germs in (milk) by heating. **pas•teur•i•za•tion** [pɑːstʃərər'zeɪʃn] *n.* action of pasteurizing.

pas•tiche [pæ'stiːʃ] *n.* poem/piece of music, etc., which is a deliberate imitation of the style of another artist.

pas•tille ['pæstl] *n.* small candy made of fruit-flavored jelly.

pas•time ['pɑːstaɪm] *n.* hobby/way of passing your spare time.

pas•tor ['pɑːstə] *n.* clergyman. **pas•to•ral,** *adj.* (a) referring to shepherds. (b) referring to the country or rustic life.

pas•try ['peɪstrɪ] *n.* (a) paste made of flour, fat and water which is used to make pies, etc. (b) cooked pie crust. (c) **pastries** = sweet cakes made of pastry filled with cream/fruit, etc.

pas•ture ['pɑːstʃə] 1. *n.* grassy area where cows and sheep can graze. 2. *v.* to put (cows and sheep) to graze. **pas•tur•age,** *n.* (*no pl.*) land used for pasturing.

pas•ty ['peɪstɪ] *adj.* white (face).

pat [pæt] 1. *n.* (a) light hit; **a p. on the back** = praise. (b) small piece (of butter). 2. *v.* (**patted**) to give (s.o./sth) a pat. 3. *adj. & adv.* (answer) given promptly.

patch [pætʃ] 1. *n.* (*pl.* **-es**) (a) small piece of material used for covering up holes. (b) small area. 2. *v.* to repair by attaching a piece of material over a hole. **patch•i•ly,** *adv.* in a patchy way. **patch•i•ness,** *n.* being patchy. **patch up,** *v.* to end (a quarrel). **patch•work,** *n.* small pieces of material sewn together in patterns. **patch•y,** *adj.* in small areas; not the same all through.

pate [peɪt] *n.* (*old*) head.

pâ•té ['pæteɪ] *n.* paste made of cooked meat or fish finely minced.

pa•tel•la [pə'telə] *n.* (*formal*) kneecap.

pat•ent ['peɪtənt] 1. *n.* (*also* ['pætnt]) official confirmation that you have the right to make or sell a new invention. 2. *adj.* (a) covered by an official patent; **p. medicine** = medicine made under a trade name by one company. (b) **p. leather** = extremely shiny leather. (c) obvious. 3. *v.* to obtain a patent for. **pat•ent•ee** [peɪtən'tiː] *n.* person who has obtained a patent. **pat•ent•ly,** *adv.* obviously/clearly.

pa•ter•ni•ty [pə'tɜːnɪtɪ] *n.* being a father. **pa•ter•nal,** *adj.* referring to a father; like a father; **my p. grandfather** = my father's father. **pa•ter•nal•ism,** *n.* paternalistic way of ruling a country/a company. **pa•ter•nal•is•tic** [pətɜːnə'lɪstɪk] *adj.* (way of ruling/of managing) which is kindly but does not give enough freedom or responsibility to individuals. **pa•ter•nal•ly,** *adv.* in a paternal way.

path [pɑːθ] *n.* (a) narrow way for walking/cycling, etc. (b) way in which sth moves. **path•way,** *n.* track for walking along.

pa•thet•ic [pə'θetɪk] *adj.* which makes you

feel pity or contempt. **pa•thet•i•cal•ly,** *adv.* in a pathetic way.

path•o•gen ['pæθədʒən] *n.* germ which causes a disease. **path•o•gen•ic,** *adj.* which causes a disease.

pa•thol•o•gy [pə'θɒlədʒɪ] *n.* study of disease. **path•o•log•i•cal** [pæθə'lɒdʒɪkl] *adj.* (a) referring to pathology. (b) caused by mental or physical disease. (c) unhealthy (interest). **pa•thol•o•gist** [pə'θɒlədʒɪst] *n.* doctor specializing in the study of disease; doctor who examines dead bodies to discover the cause of death.

pa•thos ['peɪθɒs] *n.* quality in sth which makes you feel pity.

pa•tience ['peɪʃns] *n.* (a) being patient. (b) card game for one person. **pa•tient.** 1. *adj.* (a) (person) who can wait for a long time/who remains calm/who doesn't lose his temper. (b) careful/painstaking. 2. *n.* person who is in a hospital or being treated by a doctor/dentist, etc. **pa•tient•ly,** *adv.* calmly.

pat•i•na ['pætɪnə] *n.* green sheen on old bronze objects; shine on old wooden furniture, etc.

pat•i•o ['pætɪəʊ] *n.* (*pl.* -os) paved area outside a house for sitting or eating.

pa•tis•se•rie [pə'tiːsərɪ] *n.* store selling cakes and pastries, esp. French cakes and pastries.

pat•ois ['pætwɑː] *n.* dialect spoken in a small area.

pa•tri•arch ['peɪtrɪɑːk] *n.* (a) bishop/high dignitary of an Eastern church. (b) respected old man. **pa•tri•ar•chal,** *adj.* referring to a patriarch.

pa•tri•cian [pə'trɪʃn] *adj. & n.* (referring to an) aristocrat.

pat•ri•cide ['pætrɪsaɪd] *n.* murder of your own father; person who kills his father.

pat•ri•mo•ny ['pætrɪmənɪ] *n.* inheritance/property which has been passed from father to son for generations.

pa•tri•ot ['peɪtrɪət] *n.* person who fights for/who is proud of his country. **pa•tri•ot•ic** [pætrɪ'ɒtɪk] *adj.* proud of your country; willing to fight for your country. **pa•tri•ot•i•cal•ly,** *adv.* in a patriotic way. **pa•tri•ot•ism** ['peɪtrɪətɪzəm] *n.* pride in your country.

pa•trol [pə'trəʊl] 1. *n.* (a) keeping guard by walking or driving up and down. (b) group of people keeping guard; **p. car** = police car which drives up and down the streets. (c)

group of Boy Scouts or Girl Scouts. 2. *v.* (**patrolled**) to keep guard by walking or driving up and down. **pa•trol•man,** *n.* (*pl.* -men) police officer. **pa•trol wag•on,** *n.* police van used to transport prisoners.

pa•tron ['peɪtrən] *n.* (a) person who protects or supports s.o./sth; **p. saint** = saint who is believed to protect a special group of people. (b) regular customer (of a store); person who goes regularly to the theater. **pa•tron•age** ['pætrənɪdʒ] *n.* giving support/encouragement (to an artist, etc.). **pa•tron•ess,** *n.* woman patron. **pa•tron•ize** ['pætrənaɪz] *v.* (a) to support/to encourage (an artist, etc.). (b) to act in a condescending way to (s.o.). (c) to go regularly to (a store/theater). **pa•tron•iz•ing,** *adj.* condescending; (tone) which makes s.o. feel inferior.

pat•ro•nym•ic [pætrə'nɪmɪk] *n.* name which is derived from the name of a father.

pat•ten ['pætən] *n.* wooden clog with high sole and heel.

pat•ter ['pætə] 1. *n.* (a) soft repeated tapping noise. (b) rapid talk by a magician/salesman/trickster to distract attention from what he is really doing. 2. *v.* to make a soft repeated tapping noise.

pat•tern ['pætən] *n.* (a) model/example which you should copy; paper which shows how to cut out cloth to make a piece of clothing; **knitting p.** = instructions on how to knit sth. (b) design of repeated lines/pictures, etc. **pat•terned,** *adj.* with a repeated design.

pat•ty ['pætɪ] *n.* small round piece of food, as meat or candy; **hamburger p., peppermint p.**

pau•ci•ty ['pɔːsɪtɪ] *n.* (*formal*) small number/too little (**of** sth).

paunch [pɔːnʃ] *n.* (*pl.* -es) fat stomach.

pau•per ['pɔːpə] *n.* poor person.

pause [pɔːz] 1. *n.* short stop in work, etc. 2. *v.* to stop doing sth for a short time.

pave [peɪv] *v.* to cover (a road/path, etc.) with a hard surface; **to p. the way** = to prepare the way. **pave•ment,** *n.* (a) sidewalk. (b) hard road surface. **pav•ing stone,** *n.* large flat stone slab used for making paths/courtyards, etc.

pa•vil•ion [pə'vɪljən] *n.* (a) usu. open building in a park, public garden, etc. for an exhibition, entertainment, etc.

paw [pɔː] 1. *n.* (a) hairy foot of an animal with claws. (b) *inf.* hand. 2. *v.* to tap with a paw/hands, etc.; *inf.* to fondle.

æ back, ɑː farm, ɒ top, aɪ pipe, aʊ how, aɪə fire, aʊə flower, ɔː bought, ɔɪ toy, e fed, eəhair, eɪ take, ə afraid, əʊ boat, əʊə lower, ɜː word, iː heap, ɪ hit, ɪə hear, uː school, ʊ book, ʌ but, b back, d dog, ð then, dʒ just, f fog, g go, h hand, j yes, k catch, l last, m mix, n nut, ŋ sing, p penny, r round, s some, ʃ short, t too, tʃ chop, θ thing, v voice, w was, z zoo, ʒ treasure

pawl [pɔ:l] *n.* metal piece which catches in the teeth of a ratchet wheel.

pawn [pɔ:n] 1. *n.* (a) smallest piece on the chessboard. (b) person used by s.o. more powerful. (c) sth left in exchange for money which has been borrowed. 2. *v.* to leave (an object) in exchange for borrowing money (which you claim back when the money is repaid). **pawn•brok•er,** *n.* person who lends money in exchange for valuables left with him. **pawn•shop,** *n.* shop where goods can be pawned.

pay [peɪ] 1. *n.* wages/salary; **in the p. of** = paid by. 2. *v.* (**paid**) (a) to give money for sth. (b) to be worthwhile. (c) to suffer punishment **for.** (d) to make (a visit/a call). (e) to make/to show (attention, etc.). **pay•a•ble,** *adj.* which must be paid. **pay back,** *v.* (a) to return money to (s.o.). (b) to get your revenge on (s.o.). **pay•check,** *n.* salary payment. **pay•ee,** *n.* person who receives money. **pay•er,** *n.* person who pays money. **pay•load,** *n.* load carried by an aircraft or rocket. **pay•mas•ter,** *n.* officer who pays soldiers. **pay•ment,** *n.* giving money for sth. **pay off,** *v.* (a) to remove (a debt) by paying the money owed. (b) *inf.* to be successful. **pay•off,** *n. inf.* (a) reward. (b) final success. **pay•o•la,** *n.* bribery. **pay out,** *v.* (a) to give money to s.o. (b) to unroll a rope. **pay•roll,** *n.* list of people who receive wages. **pay up,** *v.* to pay what you owe.

Pb *symbol for* lead.

PC *abbrev. for* 1. ['pi:'si:] personal computer. 2. [pi:'si:] politically correct.

PCB [pi:si:'bi:] printed circuit board.

pea [pi:] *n.* climbing plant of which the round green seeds are eaten as vegetables; **sweet peas** = plant of the pea family grown for its scented flowers. **pea green,** *adj.* bright green. **pea jack•et,** *n.* double-breasted wool jacket, often worn by sailors.

peace [pi:s] *n.* (a) state of not being at war. (b) calm/quiet. **peace•a•ble,** *adj.* liking peace; not quarrelsome. **peace•a•bly,** *adv.* calmly/without quarreling. **peace div•i•dend,** *n.* extra public money available when defense spending is cut after a conflict/war, etc. **peace•ful,** *adj.* (a) calm. (b) liking peace; **p. coexistence** = living side by side without making war. **peace•ful•ly,** *adv.* (a) calmly. (b) without making war. **peace•ful•ness,** *n.* being peaceful. **peace•keep•ing,** *n.* maintaining of peace, esp. the enforcement of a cessation of hostilities by an international body, e.g. a UN peacekeeping force. **peace•mak•er,** *n.* person who tries to bring about peace.

peach [pi:tʃ] 1. *n.* (*pl.* **-es**) (a) sweet fruit, with a large stone and velvety skin; tree which bears peaches. (b) pinkish-yellow color. 2. *v. inf.* **to p. on s.o.** = to inform (the police) about s.o.

pea•cock ['pi:kɒk], **pea•hen** [pi:'hen] *n.* (a) large bird, of which the cock has a huge tail with brilliant blue and green feathers. (b) type of brown butterfly with round purple spots.

peak [pi:k] 1. *n.* (a) top of a mountain. (b) highest point; **p. period** = period of the day when most electricity is used/when most traffic is on the roads, etc. (c) front part of a cap which juts out. 2. *v.* to reach a high point. **peaked,** *adj.* (a) (cap) with a peak. (b) looking ill. **peak•y,** *adj.* peaked; sickly.

peal [pi:l] 1. *n.* (a) set of bells of different sizes; sound of bells ringing. (b) loud reverberating noise. 2. *v.* (a) to ring a peal of bells. (b) (*of thunder*) to roll/to make a loud noise.

pea•nut ['pi:nʌt] *n.* (a) nut which grows in the ground in pods like a pea; **p. butter** = paste made from crushed peanuts. (b) *inf.* **peanuts** = very little money.

pear ['peə] *n.* elongated fruit with one end fatter than the other; tree which bears pears. **pear-shaped,** *adj.* shaped like a pear.

pearl [pɜ:l] *n.* precious round white gem formed inside an oyster; **p. barley** = barley grains which have been rolled until they are shaped like pearls. **pearl div•er,** *n.* person who dives to the bottom of the sea to look for oysters with pearls in them. **pearl•y,** *adj.* shiny like a pearl.

peas•ant ['pezənt] *n.* farm laborer or small farmer living in a backward region. **peas•ant•ry,** *n.* (*no pl.*) peasants (seen as a class in society).

peat [pi:t] *n.* decayed vegetable matter cut out of a bog and used as fuel or in gardening. **peat•y,** *adj.* smelling/tasting like peat.

peb•ble ['pebl] *n.* small round stone. **peb•bly,** *adj.* covered with pebbles.

pe•can ['pi:kæn] *n.* nut from a tree which grows in the south United States.

pec•ca•dil•lo [pekə'dɪləu] *n.* (*pl.* **-oes, -os**) (*formal*) slight error/fault.

pec•ca•ry ['pekərɪ] *n.* wild South American pig.

peck [pek] 1. *n.* (a) bite with a bird's beak. (b) *inf.* little kiss. (c) *(old)* measurement of quantity of grain. 2. *v.* (a) to bite with a beak; **pecking order** = unwritten order of importance of people in a firm/office, etc. (b) *inf.* to give (s.o.) a little kiss.

pec•tin ['pektɪn] *n.* jellylike substance in fruit which helps jam to set hard.

pec•to•ral ['pektərəl] 1. *adj.* (*formal*) referring to the chest; **p. cross** = cross worn by a priest around the neck. 2. *n.* muscle in the chest.

pec•u•late ['pekjuleɪt] *v.* (*formal*) to embezzle

money. **pec•u•la•tion** [pekju'leɪʃn] *n.* embezzlement.

pe•cu•liar [pɪ'kju:ljə] *adj.* (a) odd/strange. (b) belonging to one particular place or person. **pe•cu•li•ar•i•ty,** *n.* being peculiar; strange feature/detail which stands out. **pe•cu•liar•ly,** *adv.* oddly/strangely.

pe•cu•ni•ar•y [pɪ'kju:njərɪ] *adj.* referring to money.

ped•a•gog•i•cal [pedə'gɒdʒɪkl] *adj.* referring to teaching. **ped•a•gogue** ['pedəgɒg] *n.* pedantic person, esp. a teacher.

ped•al ['pedl] 1. *n.* lever worked by your foot. 2. *v.* (**pedaled, pedalled**) to make (a bicycle) go by pushing on the pedals.

ped•ant ['pedənt] *n.* pedantic person. **pe•dan•tic** [pɪ'dæntɪk] *adj.* paying too much attention to detail/showing off knowledge. **pe•dan•ti•cal•ly,** *adv.* in a pedantic way. **ped•ant•ry** ['pedəntrɪ] *n.* being pedantic.

ped•dle ['pedl] *v.* to go from house to house trying to sell sth. **ped•dler,** *n.* person who goes from house to house trying to sell sth.

ped•er•ast ['pedəræst] *n.* person who practices pederasty. **ped•er•as•ty,** *n.* homosexual relations with boys.

ped•es•tal ['pedɪstl] *n.* base (for a statue).

pe•des•tri•an [pə'destrɪən] 1. *n.* person who goes on foot; **p. crossing** = place where pedestrians can cross a road; **p. mall** = street or group of streets closed to traffic so that people can walk about freely. 2. *adj.* (a) referring to pedestrians. (b) heavy/unimaginative.

pe•di•a•tri•cian [pi:dɪə'trɪʃn] *n.* doctor who specializes in pediatrics. **pe•di•at•ric** [pi:dSIætrik] *adj.* referring to the medical care of children. **pe•di•at•rics** [pi:dɪ'ætrɪks] *n.* science of treatment of children's diseases.

ped•i•cure ['pedɪkjuə] *n.* looking after the feet.

ped•i•gree ['pedɪgri:] *n.* table of ancestors of a person/animal; **p. animal** = animal with a certificate showing it is pure bred.

ped•i•ment ['pedɪmənt] *n.* triangular part at the top of the front of a classical building.

ped•lar ['pedlə] *n.* peddler.

pe•dom•e•ter [pe'dɒmɪtə] *n.* instrument which measures how far you have walked.

pe•dun•cle [pə'dʌŋkl] *n.* stalk of an inflorescence.

pee [pi:] 1. *n. inf.* (a) waste water from the body. (b) passing waste water from the body. 2. *v. inf.* to pass waste water from the body.

peek [pi:k] 1. *n. inf.* quick look. 2. *v. inf.* to look **at** sth quickly.

peel [pi:l] 1. *n.* outer skin of a fruit, etc. 2. *v.* (a) to take the outer skin off (a fruit/a vegetable). (b) to come off in layers. **peel•er,** *n.* special instrument for peeling vegetables. **peel•ings,** *n. pl.* bits of skin from vegetables. **peel off,** *v.* (a) (*of peel/paint*) to come off. (b) *inf.* to take off (clothes).

peep [pi:p] 1. *n.* (a) short/quick look. (b) cheep. 2. *v.* to look quickly and secretly. **peep•hole,** *n.* small hole in a door which you can look through to see who is outside.

peer ['pɪə] 1. *n.* (a) member of the nobility. (b) person of the same rank/class as another; **p. group** = group of people of equal (social) status. 2. *v.* to look at sth hard when you cannot see very well. **peer•age,** *n.* (*no pl.*) all nobles, taken as a group. **peer•ess,** *n.* woman peer. **peer•less,** *adj.* excellent/which has no equal.

peeved [pi:vd] *adj. inf.* annoyed/bothered. **peev•ish,** *adj.* bad-tempered/complaining. **peev•ish•ly,** *adv.* in a peevish way. **peev•ish•ness,** *n.* being peevish.

pee•wit ['pi:wɪt] *n.* lapwing.

peg [peg] 1. *n.* small wooden or metal stake/pin. 2. *v.* (**pegged**) (a) to attach with a peg. (b) to hold (prices, etc.) stable.

pe•jo•ra•tive [pə'dʒɒrətɪv] *adj.* disapproving/showing that you feel sth is bad.

Pe•king•ese, Pekinese [pɪkɪ'ni:z] *n.* breed of low flat-faced dogs.

pe•lag•ic [pə'lædʒɪk] *adj.* referring to the top and middle layers of the sea.

pel•ar•go•ni•um [pelɑ:'gəʊnɪəm] *n.* flowering plant, the geranium.

pel•i•can ['pelɪkən] *n.* large white water bird, with a pouch under its beak in which it keeps the fish it has caught.

pel•let ['pelɪt] *n.* (a) small ball, as of medicine or food. (b) small lead ball, used in shotguns.

pel•li•cle ['pelɪkl] *n.* thin layer of skin.

pell-mell [pel'mel] *adv.* in disorder.

pel•lu•cid [pə'lu:sɪd] *adj.* very transparent.

pel•met ['pelmɪt] *n.* decorative strip of wood/cloth, etc., over a window which hides the curtain fittings.

pelt [pelt] 1. *n.* (a) skin of an animal with fur on it. (b) **at full p.** = going fast. 2. *v.* (a) **to p. s.o. with** = to fling things at s.o. (b) **the rain was pelting down** = pouring down.

pel•vis ['pelvɪs] *n.* (*pl.* -es) bones in the lower

æ back, a: farm, ɒ: top, aɪ pipe, aʊ how, aɪe fire, aʊə flower, ɔ: bought, ɔɪ toy, e fed, eəhair, eɪ take, ə afraid, əʊ boat, əʊə lower, v: word, i: heap, ɪ hit, ɪə hear, u: school, ʊ book, ʌ but, b back, d dog, ð then, dʒ just, f fog, g go, h hand, j yes, k catch, l last, m mix, n nut, ŋ sing, p penny, r round, s some, ʃ short, t too, tʃ chop, θ thing, v voice, w was, z zoo, ʒ treasure

part of the body forming the hips. **pel•vic,** *adj.* referring to the pelvis.

pem•mi•can ['pemɪkən] *n.* dried meat, used by explorers as rations.

pen [pen] 1. *n.* (a) small fenced area for sheep. (b) writing instrument using ink; **p. name** = name used by a writer which is not his own; **p. pal** = person whom you have never met, but with whom you exchange letters. (c) female swan. 2. *v.* (**penned**) (a) to enclose (sheep) in a pen. (b) to write with a pen.

pe•nal ['piːnl] *adj.* referring to a legal punishment; **p. system** = system of punishments relating to various crimes. **pe•nal•i•za•tion** [piːnəlaɪ'zeɪʃn] *n.* act of penalizing. **pe•nal•ize,** *v.* to punish. **pen•al•ty** ['penəltɪ] *n.* (a) punishment. (b) punishment in sport. (c) disadvantages.

pen•ance ['penəns] *n.* punishment which a person accepts to make amends for a sin.

pence [pens] *n. Brit. see* **pen•ny.**

pen•chant ['pɑːŋʃɑːŋ] *n.* liking (**for** sth).

pen•cil ['pensl] 1. *n.* instrument for writing, made of wood with a graphite center. 2. *v.* (**penciled, pencilled**) to write with a pencil. **pen•cil sharp•en•er,** *n.* instrument for sharpening pencils.

pend•ant ['pendənt] *n.* ornament which hangs from a chain worn around the neck. **pend•ent,** *adj.* hanging.

pend•ing ['pendɪŋ] *adj. & prep.* awaiting; until.

pen•du•lum ['pendjʊləm] *n.* weight on the end of a rod or chain which swings from side to side, such as that which makes a clock work. **pen•du•lous,** *adj.* which hangs down heavily.

pen•e•trate ['penɪtreɪt] *v.* go into/through. **pen•e•tra•bil•i•ty** [penɪtrə'bɪlɪtɪ] *n.* ability to be penetrated. **pen•e•tra•ble,** *adj.* which can be penetrated. **pen•e•trat•ing,** *adj.* deep/searching (look); very profound (questions). **pen•e•tra•tion** [penɪ'treɪʃn] *n.* (a) getting into sth. (b) deep understanding.

pen•guin ['peŋgwɪn] *n.* Antarctic bird which swims well but cannot fly.

pen•i•cil•lin [penɪ'sɪlɪn] *n.* substance made from a mold, used to kill bacteria.

pen•in•su•la [pə'nɪnsjʊlə] *n.* large piece of land jutting into the sea. **pen•in•su•lar,** *adj.* referring to a peninsula.

pe•nis ['piːnɪs] *n.* (*pl.* **-es**) part of the male body used for urinating and for sexual intercourse.

pen•i•tent ['penɪtənt] *adj. & n.* (person) who is sorry for having done sth wrong. **pen•i•tence,** *n.* being penitent. **pen•i•ten•tial** [penɪ'tenʃl] *adj.* referring to

penance. **pen•i•ten•tia•ry** [penɪ'tenʃərɪ] *n.* prison.

pen•knife ['pennaɪf] *n.* (*pl.* **-knives** [-naɪvz]) small folding pocket knife.

pen•nant ['penənt] *n.* long thin flag.

pen•non ['penən] *n.* small forked flag.

pen•ny ['penɪ] *n.* (*pl.* **pennies**; *Brit.* **pennies** or **pence**) small coin (the smallest unit in some currencies); (*in Britain*) one hundredth part of a pound. **pen•ni•less,** *adj.* with no money.

pe•nol•o•gy [piː'nɒlədʒɪ] *n.* study of punishment and crime.

pen•sion ['penʃn] 1. *n.* money paid regularly to s.o. who has retired from work/to a widow, etc. 2. *v.* **to p. s.o. off** = to make s.o. stop working and live on a pension. **pen•sion•a•ble,** *adj.* (person) who has the right to have a pension; (job) which gives you the right to have a pension; (age) at which a pension begins to be paid. **pen•sion•er,** *n.* person who gets a pension.

pen•sive ['pensɪv] *adj.* thoughtful. **pen•sive•ly,** *adv.* thoughtfully. **pen•sive•ness,** *n.* being pensive.

pent [pent] *adj.* **pent-up emotions** = emotions which are repressed.

pen•ta•gon ['pentəgən] *n.* (a) geometrical figure with five sides. (b) **the Pentagon** = the U.S. Defense Department. **pen•tag•o•nal** [pen'tægənl] *adj.* five-sided.

pen•tam•e•ter [pen'tæmɪtə] *n.* line of poetry with five beats.

pen•tath•lon [pen'tæθlən] *n.* athletic competition where competitors have to compete in five different sports.

pent•house ['penthaʊs] *n.* apartment on the top of a high building.

pe•nul•ti•mate [pe'nʌltɪmət] *adj.* next to last.

pe•num•bra [pe'nʌmbrə] *n.* edge of a shadow where only part of the light is cut off.

pen•u•ry ['penjʊrɪ] *n.* (*formal*) (a) extreme poverty. (b) great lack. **pe•nu•ri•ous** [pɪ'njʊərɪəs] *adj.* very poor.

pe•o•ny ['pɪənɪ] *n.* perennial summer flower with large scented flowerheads.

peo•ple ['piːpl] 1. *n.* (a) (*pl.*) persons; human beings. (b) citizens (of a town or country). 2. *v.* to fill with people.

pep [pep] 1. *n. inf.* vigor; **p. talk** = talk designed to encourage people to work hard/to win a match, etc. 2. *v. inf.* **to p. up** = to make livelier and more active.

pep•per ['pepə] 1. *n.* (a) sharp spice used in cooking. (b) green or red fruit used as a vegetable. 2. *v.* (**with**) to sprinkle/to throw (things) at. **pep•per•corn,** *n.* dried seed of pepper. **pep•per•mill,** *n.* small grinder used for grinding peppercorns. **pep•per•mint**, *n.* (a) common plant with a sharp mint flavor. (b) candy flavored with peppermint. **pep•per•y**, *adj.* (a) (soup, etc.) with too much pepper in it. (b) very easily angered.

pep•tic ['peptɪk] *adj.* referring to the digestive system; **p. ulcer** = ulcer in the stomach.

per [pɜː] *prep.* (a) out of; **ten p. thousand.** (b) in; **sixty miles p. hour.** (c) for; **p. annum** = in each year; **p. capita** = for each person.

per•am•bu•late [pə'ræmbjʊleɪt] *v.* (*formal*) to walk about slowly. **per•am•bu•la•tion**, *n.* slow walk. **per•am•bu•la•tor**, *n.* (*formal*) baby carriage.

per•ceive [pə'siːv] *v.* to notice through the senses; to become aware of. **per•cep•ti•ble** [pə'septɪbl] *adj.* which can be seen/heard/smelled, etc. **per•cep•ti•bly**, *adv.* noticeably. **per•cep•tion** [pə'sepʃn] *n.* ability to notice. **per•cep•tive**, *adj.* acute; able to notice quickly. **per•cep•tive•ly**, *adv.* in a perceptive way. **per•cep•tive•ness, perceptivity,** *n.* being perceptive.

per•cent [pə'sent] *adv. & n.* out of each hundred. **per•cent•age** [pə'sentɪdʒ] *n.* proportion shown as part of a hundred. **per•cen•tile** [pə'sentaɪl] *n.* one of a hundred equal groups into which a large number can be divided.

perch [pɜːtʃ] 1. *n.* (a) (*pl.* -es) branch/ledge on which a bird can sit. (b) (*pl.* perch) type of freshwater fish. 2. *v.* to sit on a perch; to be set in a high place.

per•chance [pə'tʃɑːns] *adv.* (*old*) perhaps.

per•cip•i•ent [pə'sɪpɪənt] *adj.* perceptive/able to notice quickly. **per•cip•i•ence**, *n.* being percipient.

per•co•late ['pɜːkəleɪt] *v.* to filter (through). **per•co•la•tion** [pɜːkə'leɪʃn] *n.* filtering. **per•co•la•tor**, *n.* coffee pot where the water boils up and filters through coffee.

per•cus•sion [pə'kʌʃn] *n.* action of hitting together; **p. instruments** = musical instruments which are hit (drums/triangles, etc.); **p. cap** = piece of paper with a small amount of explosive powder which explodes when hit.

per•e•gri•na•tions [perɪgrɪ'neɪʃnz] *n. pl.* (*formal*) traveling/wandering.

per•e•grine ['perɪgrɪn] *n.* type of falcon.

per•emp•to•ry [pə'remptərɪ] *adj.* abrupt (tone)/curt (refusal). **per•emp•to•ri•ly**, *adv.* in a peremptory way.

per•en•ni•al [pə'renɪəl] 1. *adj.* which continues from year to year. 2. *n.* plant which flowers every year without needing to be sown again. **per•en•ni•al•ly**, *adv.* always.

pe•re•stroi•ka [perɪ'strɔɪkə] *n.* reconstruction (of the Russian economy).

per•fect 1. *adj.* ['pɜːfɪkt] (a) without any mistakes/flaws. (b) total (stranger). (c) **p. (tense)** = past tense of a verb which shows that the action has been completed. 2. *v.* [pə'fekt] to make perfect. **per•fec•tion** [pə'fekʃn] *n.* state of being perfect; **to p.** = perfectly. **per•fec•tion•ist**, *n.* person who insists that perfection is possible/that everything has to be perfect. **per•fect•ly** ['pɜːfɪktlɪ] *adv.* completely.

per•fi•dy ['pɜːfɪdɪ] *n.* (*formal*) treachery. **per•fid•i•ous** [pə'fɪdɪəs] *adj.* (*formal*) treacherous.

per•fo•rate ['pɜːfəreɪt] *v.* to make a hole in/to pierce. **per•fo•ra•tion** [pɜːfə'reɪʃn] *n.* (a) action of making a hole. (b) small hole.

per•force [pə'fɔːs] *adv.* (*old*) because it is necessary.

per•form [pə'fɔːm] *v.* (a) to carry out an action. (b) to act in public. **per•for•mance**, *n.* (a) working of a machine; action of a sportsman. (b) public show. **per•form•er**, *n.* person who gives a public show.

per•fume 1. *n.* ['pɜːfjuːm] (a) pleasant smell. (b) liquid scent. 2. *v.* [pə'fjuːm] (a) to give a pleasant smell to (sth). (b) to pour perfume on. **per•fum•er•y**, *n.* shop which makes and sells perfumes.

per•func•to•ry [pə'fʌŋktərɪ] *adj.* rapid and superficial. **per•func•to•ri•ly**, *adv.* in a perfunctory way.

per•go•la ['pɜːgələ] *n.* framework of wood over which climbing plants can be trained.

per•haps [pə'hæps] *adv.* possibly/maybe.

per•i•car•di•um [perɪ'kɑːdɪəm] *n.* membrane round the heart. **per•i•car•di•tis**, *n.* inflammation of the pericardium.

per•i•he•li•on [perɪ'hiːlɪɒn] *n.* point where a planet is nearest to the sun.

per•il ['perəl] *n.* great danger. **per•il•ous**, *adj.* very dangerous. **per•il•ous•ly**, *adv.* in a perilous way.

pe•rim•e•ter [pə'rɪmɪtə] *n.* outside line around an enclosed area.

pe•ri•od ['pɪərɪəd] *n.* (a) length of time; **p. furniture** = antique furniture from a certain time; **p. piece** = piece of antique furniture, etc. (b)

æ back, ɑː farm, ɒ top, aɪ pipe, aʊ how, aɪə fire, aʊə flower, ɔː bought, ɔɪ toy, e fed, eəhair, eɪ take, ə afraid, əʊ boat, əʊə lower, ɜː word, iː heap, ɪ hit, ɪə hear, uː school, ʊ book, ʌ but, b back, d dog, ð then, dʒ just, f fog, g go, h hand, j yes, k catch, l last, m mix, n nut, ŋ sing, p penny, r round, s some, ʃ short, t too, tʃ chop, θ thing, v voice, w was, z zoo, ʒ treasure

class time in a school. (c) punctuation mark (.) used in writing to mark the end of a sentence. (d) regular monthly flow of blood from a woman's womb. **pe•ri•od•ic** [pi:rɪ'ɒdɪk] *adj.* repeated after a regular length of time; **p. table** = list of chemical elements arranged in order of their atomic numbers. **pe•ri•od•i•cal.** 1. *adj.* periodic; repeated after a regular length of time. 2. *n.* magazine which appears regularly. **pe•ri•od•i•cal•ly,** *adv.* from time to time.

per•i•pa•tet•ic [perɪpə'tetɪk] *adj.* (person) who wanders from place to place.

pe•riph•er•y [pə'rɪfərɪ] *n.* edge. **pe•riph•er•al,** 1. *adj.* minor/not very important. 2. *n.* peripherals = items of hardware (such as printers) which are attached to a computer.

pe•riph•ra•sis [pə'rɪfrəsɪs] *n.* (*pl.* -ses) way of saying sth which is not straightforward. **per•i•phras•tic** [perɪ'fræstɪk] *adj.* not straightforward (expression).

per•i•scope ['perɪskəup] *n.* long tube with mirrors which allows s.o. in a submerged submarine to look above the surface of the water.

per•ish ['perɪʃ] *v.* (a) (*formal*) to die. (b) to rot. **per•ish•a•ble,** *adj.* (food) which can go bad easily; **perishables** = perishable food.

per•i•stal•sis [perɪ'stælsɪs] *n.* regular movement of the muscles in the intestine.

per•i•to•ni•tis [perɪtə'naɪtɪs] *n.* inflammation of the lining of the abdomen.

per•i•wig ['perɪwɪg] *n.* large wig, worn in the 17th and 18th centuries.

per•i•win•kle ['perɪwɪŋkl] *n.* (a) small creeping plant with blue flowers. (b) edible snail which lives in salt water.

per•jure ['pɜːdʒə] *v.* **to p. yourself** = to tell lies in a court of law when you have sworn to tell the truth. **per•jur•er,** *n.* person who has committed perjury. **per•ju•ry,** *n.* crime of perjuring yourself.

perk [pɜːk] 1. *v.* **to p. up** = to become more alert/more interested. 2. *n. inf.* valuable extras which are given to you by your employer in addition to your salary. **perk•y,** *adj. inf.* lively/interested.

perm [pɜːm] 1. *n. inf.* curls or a wave put into your hair artificially. 2. *v. inf.* to put a wave or curl into (s.o.'s hair).

per•ma•cul•ture ['pɜːməkʌltʃə] *n.* agriculture/power generation, etc. that does not deplete natural resources or cause pollution.

per•ma•frost ['pɜːməfrɒst] *n.* (*no pl.*) soil in the Arctic which remains permanently frozen, even in summer.

per•ma•nent ['pɜːmənənt] *adj.* lasting forever/supposed to last for ever. **per•ma•nence, permanency,** *n.* state of

being permanent. **per•ma•nent•ly,** *adv.* always.

per•man•ga•nate [pə'mæŋgəneɪt] *n.* salt containing manganese; **p. of potash** = dark purple crystals used for disinfecting.

per•me•ate ['pɜːmɪeɪt] *v.* to filter; to spread right through. **per•me•a•bil•i•ty** [pɜːmɪə'bɪlɪtɪ] *n.* being permeable. **per•me•a•ble,** *adj.* which lets liquid pass through. **per•me•a•tion** [pɜːmɪ'eɪʃn] *n.* act of permeating.

per•mis•si•ble [pə'mɪsəbl] *adj.* which can be allowed. **per•mis•sion** [pə'mɪʃn] *n.* freedom which you are given to do sth. **per•mis•sive** [pə'mɪsɪv] *adj.* free; allowing many things to be done which formerly were not allowed. **per•mis•sive•ness,** *n.* being permissive.

per•mit 1. *n.* ['pɜːmɪt] paper which allows you to do sth. 2. *v.* [pə'mɪt] (**permitted**) to allow.

per•mu•ta•tion [pɜːmju:'teɪʃn] *n.* grouping of several items together in varied combinations; combination of various items in a different order.

per•ni•cious [pə'nɪʃəs] *adj.* harmful/evil.

per•nick•et•y [pə'nɪkətɪ] *adj. inf.* very fussy.

per•o•ra•tion [perə'reɪʃn] *n.* (*formal*) very long speech.

per•ox•ide [pə'rɒksaɪd] *n.* chemical used for bleaching hair or killing germs.

per•pen•dic•u•lar [pɜːpən'dɪkjulə] *adj. & n.* (line) standing vertically/at right angles to a base; style of late medieval English church architecture. **per•pen•dic•u•lar•ly,** *adv.* in a perpendicular way.

per•pe•trate ['pɜːpɪtreɪt] *v.* (*formal*) to commit (a crime). **per•pe•tra•tion** [pɜːpɪ'treɪʃn] *n.* act of perpetrating. **per•pe•tra•tor,** *n.* person who commits (a crime).

per•pet•u•al [pə'petjuəl] *adj.* continuous/without any end. **per•pet•u•al•ly,** *adv.* always. **per•pet•u•ate,** *v.* to make (sth) continue forever. **per•pe•tu•i•ty** [pɜːpɪ'tju:ɪtɪ] *n.* (*formal*) **in p.** = forever/without any end.

per•plex [pə'pleks] *v.* to confuse/to puzzle. **per•plex•i•ty,** *n.* bewilderment/puzzled state.

per•qui•site ['pɜːkwɪzɪt] *n.* (*formal*) valuable extra which is given to you by your employer in addition to your salary.

per•ry ['perɪ] *n.* alcoholic drink made from fermented pear juice.

per se [pɜː'seɪ] *adv.* in itself.

per•se•cute ['pɜːsɪkju:t] *v.* to torment/to treat cruelly. **per•se•cu•tion** [pɜːsɪ'kju:ʃn] *n.* relentless killing (because of religious beliefs); **p. complex** = mental disease where you feel that everyone is persecuting you. **per•se•cu•tor** ['pɜːsɪkjuːtə] *n.* person who persecutes.

per•se•vere [pɜːsɪ'vɪə] *v.* (**with/in**) to continue doing sth (in spite of obstacles). **per•se•ver•ance,** *n.* act of persevering.

Per•sian ['pɜːʃn] 1. *adj.* referring to Persia. 2. *n.* (a) person from Persia. (b) cat with long silky fur.

per•si•flage [pɜːsɪ'flɑːʒ] *n.* (*formal*) frivolous talk.

per•sist [pə'sɪst] *v.* (**in**) to continue doing sth (in spite of obstacles); to continue to exist. **per•sist•ence,** *n.* obstinacy; refusal to stop doing sth. **per•sist•ent,** *adj.* continual. **per•sist•ent•ly,** *adv.* in a persistent way. **per•sist•ent veg•e•ta•tive state,** *n.* irreversible medical condition, caused by brain damage, in which consciousness is absent.

per•son ['pɜːsn] *n.* (a) human being; **she appeared in p.** = appeared herself. (b) (*in grammar*) one of the three forms of verbs or pronouns which indicate who the speaker is; **first p.** = I or we; **second p.** = you; **third p.** = he, she, it, they. **per•so•na** [pɜː'səʊnə] *n.* a person's character as seen by others. **per•son•a•ble,** *adj.* attractive/good-looking/having a pleasant character. **per•son•age,** *n.* important person. **per•son•al,** *adj.* (a) referring to a person; (letter) addressed so that you and no one else may open it; **p. computer** = small computer used by a person at home; **p. organizer** (= electronic organizer) = computer used as a diary that is small enough to carry in a pocket. (b) rude (remarks). (c) (*in grammar*) **p. pronoun** = pronoun which refers to s.o., such as "I", "he", "she", etc. **per•son•al•i•ty** [pɜːsə'nælɪtɪ] *n.* (a) character. (b) famous person; **p. cult** = publicity given to a political leader or other famous person, making him into a kind of god. **per•son•al•ized,** *adj.* with your name or initials printed on it. **per•son•al•ly,** *adv.* (a) from your own point of view. (b) in person. (c) **don't take it p.** = don't think it was meant to criticize you. **per•so•na non gra•ta** [pɜː'səʊnənɒn'grɑːtə] *n.* person (esp. a diplomat) who is not acceptable to a foreign country. **per•son•i•fi•ca•tion** [pəsɒnɪfɪ'keɪʃn] *n.* good example of an abstract quality in a person. **per•son•i•fy** [pə'sɒnɪfaɪ] *v.* to be a good example of. **per•son•nel** [pɜːsə'nel] *n.* staff/people employed by a company; **p. manager** = manager who looks after

pay/sick leave/administration, etc., for all the staff.

per•spec•tive [pə'spektɪv] *n.* (a) (*in art*) way of drawing objects/scenes, so that they appear to have depth or distance; **to put things in p.** = to show things in an objective way. (b) way of looking at sth.

Per•spex ['pɜːspeks] *n.* trademark for a type of tough clear plastic.

per•spi•ca•cious [pɜːspɪ'keɪʃəs] *adj.* (person) who understands clearly. **per•spi•cac•i•ty** [pɜːspɪ'kæsɪtɪ] *n.* clearness of understanding.

per•spi•cu•i•ty [pɜːspɪ'kjuːɪtɪ] *n.* clearness of expression. **per•spic•u•ous** [pə'spɪkjuəs] *adj.* clearly expressed.

per•spire [pə'spaɪə] *v.* to sweat. **per•spi•ra•tion** [pɜːspə'reɪʃn] *n.* sweat.

per•suade [pə'sweɪd] *v.* to get s.o. to do what you want by explaining or pleading. **per•sua•sion** [pə'sweɪʒn] *n.* (a) act of persuading. (b) firm (usu. religious) belief. **per•sua•sive** [pə'sweɪzɪv] *adj.* which persuades. **per•sua•sive•ly,** *adv.* in a persuasive way. **per•sua•sive•ness,** *n.* being persuasive.

pert [pɜːt] *adj.* lively; spirited.

per•tain [pə'teɪn] *v.* (*formal*) to be relevant.

per•ti•na•cious [pɜːtɪ'neɪʃəs] *adj.* obstinate. **per•ti•nac•i•ty** [pɜːtɪ'næsɪtɪ] *n.* obstinateness/stubbornness.

per•ti•nent ['pɜːtɪnənt] *adj.* relevant; to the point. **per•ti•nence,** *n.* being pertinent. **per•ti•nent•ly,** *adv.* in a pertinent way.

per•turb [pə'tɜːb] *v.* to make (s.o.) anxious. **per•tur•ba•tion** [pɜːtə'beɪʃn] *n.* anxiety/bother.

pe•ruse [pə'ruːz] *v.* (*formal*) to read carefully. **pe•rus•al,** *n.* reading.

Per•u•vi•an [pə'ruːvɪən] 1. *adj.* referring to Peru. 2. *n.* person from Peru.

per•vade [pə'veɪd] *v.* to spread everywhere. **per•va•sive** [pə'veɪsɪv] *adj.* penetrating. **per•va•sive•ness,** *n.* penetrating everywhere.

per•verse [pə'vɜːs] *adj.* obstinately awkward; continuing to do sth even if it is wrong. **per•verse•ly,** *adv.* in an obstinate way. **per•verse•ness,** *n.* contrariness. **per•ver•sion** [pə'vɜːʃn] *n.* corruption (of s.o. to do sth evil). **per•ver•si•ty,** *n.* being perverse. **per•vert.** 1. *n.* ['pɜːvɜːt] person who commits unnatural sexual acts. 2. *v.* [pə'vɜːt]

(a) to corrupt (s.o.) to do evil. (b) to misinterpret; distort the meaning of.

per•vi•ous ['pɜːvɪəs] *adj.* (membrane) which allows liquid to pass through.

pe•se•ta [pe'seɪtə] *n.* unit of currency used in Spain.

pe•so ['peɪzəʊ] *n.* unit of currency used in many S. American countries.

pes•sa•ry ['pesərɪ] *n.* contraceptive device placed in the vagina.

pes•si•mism ['pesɪmɪzəm] *n.* belief that only bad things will happen. **pes•si•mist** ['pesɪmɪst] *n.* pessimistic person. **pes•si•mis•tic** [pesɪ'mɪstɪk] *adj.* gloomy/believing that only bad things will happen. **pes•si•mis•ti•cal•ly,** *adv.* gloomily.

pest [pest] *n.* (a) troublesome plant, animal, or often an insect. (b) *inf.* person who annoys. **pes•ter,** *v.* to bother (s.o.). **pes•ti•cide** ['pestɪsaɪd] *n.* poison to kill pests.

pes•ti•lence ['pestɪləns] *n.* (*formal*) plague/disease. **pes•ti•len•tial** [pestɪ'lenʃl] *adj.* like a plague/very unpleasant.

pes•tle ['pesl] *n.* round-headed heavy tool for crushing things in a bowl.

pet [pet] 1. *n.* animal kept in the home to give pleasure. 2. *adj.* (a) favorite; **p. name** = special name given to s.o. you are fond of. (b) tame (animal). 3. *v.* (**petted**) to caress/to fondle.

pet•al ['petl] *n.* one of several colorful leaflike parts of a flower.

pe•tard [pə'tɑːd] *n.* (*formal*) **to be hoist with/by your own p.** = to be caught in a trap which you have set for s.o. else.

pe•ter ['piːtə] *v.* **to p. out** = to come to an end/to fade away.

pe•tite [pə'tiːt] *adj.* (*of a woman*) small and dainty.

pe•tit four [pətɪ'fʊə] *n.* small fancy cake or biscuit eaten at parties.

pe•ti•tion [pə'tɪʃn] 1. *n.* (a) official request (often signed by many people). (b) legal request. 2. *v.* to ask (s.o.) for sth/to make an official request. **pe•ti•tion•er,** *n.* person who makes a petition.

pet•rel ['petrəl] *n.* sea bird which flies long distances.

pet•ri•fy ['petrɪfaɪ] *v.* (a) to turn to stone. (b) to strike (s.o.) still with fear. **pet•ri•fac•tion, petrification,** *n.* act of petrifying.

pet•ro•chem•i•cal [petrəʊ'kemɪkl] *adj. & n.* (chemical) produced from petroleum or natural gas.

pet•ro•dol•lar [petrəʊ'dɒlə] *n.* dollar which is earned by a country selling oil.

pet•rol ['petrəl] *n.* *Brit.* gasoline. **pe•tro•le•um** [pə'trəʊlɪəm] *n.* raw mineral oil (from the earth); **p. products** = substances (like gasoline/plastics, etc.) which are made from petroleum. **pe•trol•o•gy,** *n.* study of rocks.

pet•ti•coat ['petɪkəʊt] *n.* piece of women's underwear/light skirt worn under another skirt.

pet•ti•fog•ging ['petɪfɒgɪŋ] *adj.* (a) dealing with small useless details. (b) dishonest (lawyer).

pet•ty ['petɪ] *adj.* (a) insignificant/unimportant; **p. cash** = small amounts of cash (in an office); **p. officer** = non-commissioned officer in the U.S. Navy. (b) with a narrow point of view. **pet•ti•ness,** *n.* (a) unimportance. (b) narrowness of outlook.

pet•u•lant ['petjulənt] *adj.* irritable/bad-tempered. **pet•u•lance,** *n.* irritability. **pet•u•lant•ly,** *adv.* in a petulant way.

pe•tu•nia [pɪ'tjuːnɪə] *n.* common summer garden flower.

pew [pjuː] *n.* long bench seat in a church; *inf.* **take a p.** = sit down.

pew•ter ['pjuːtə] *n.* alloy, usu. a mixture of tin and lead, used for making mugs/plates, etc.

pH [piː'eɪtʃ] *n.* **pH factor** = measurement of how much acidity or alkalinity there is (in the soil, etc.).

pha•lanx ['fælæŋks] *n.* (a) tight mass of people (esp. marching forward). (b) bone in a finger or toe.

phal•lus ['fæləs] *n.* (*pl.* **-es**) (*formal*) penis in erection. **phal•lic,** *adj.* referring to a phallus; **p. symbol** = thing which resembles a penis, and is taken to symbolize male sex.

phan•tasm ['fæntæzəm] *n.* seeing sth in the imagination/seeing ghosts. **phan•tas•ma•go•ri•a** [fæntæzmə'gɒrɪə] *n.* mass of ghostly shapes.

phan•tom ['fæntəm] *n.* ghost.

phar•i•sa•ic(al) [færɪ'seɪɪk(l)] *adj.* self-righteously good; hypocritical.

phar•ma•ceu•ti•cal [fɑːmə'sjuːtɪkl] *adj.* referring to medicines. **phar•ma•cist** ['fɑːməsɪst] *n.* person who makes and sells medicines. **phar•ma•col•o•gy** [fɑːmə'kɒlədʒɪ] *n.* study of medicines. **phar•ma•co•pe•ia, pharmacopoeia** [fɑːməkə'piːə] *n.* collection of drugs; book which lists drugs. **phar•ma•cy,** *n.* study of medicines; place which makes and sells medicines.

phar•ynx ['færɪŋks] *n.* (*pl.* **-es**) passage at the back of the nose leading to the esophagus. **phar•yn•gi•tis** [færɪn'dʒaɪtɪs] *n.* inflammation of the pharynx.

phase [feɪz] 1. *n.* period; stage in development of sth. 2. *v.* **to p. in/out** = to introduce/to remove gradually.

pheas•ant ['fezənt] *n.* large bright-colored bird with a long tail, shot for sport and food.

phe•no•bar•bi•tal [fiːnəʊ'bɑːbɪtəʊn] *n.* drug which makes the patient sleep.

phe•nol ['fiːnɒl] *n.* carbon derivative, used in medicine.

phe•nom•e•non [fe'nɒmɪnɒn] *n.* (*pl.* **-mena**) thing which happens naturally; esp. remarkable thing/happening. **phe•nom•e•nal,** *adj.* remarkable. **phe•nom•e•nal•ly,** *adv.* remarkably.

phi•al ['faɪl] *n.* (*formal*) small bottle.

phi•lan•der•er [fɪ'lændərə] *n.* man who flirts with women.

phi•lan•thro•py [fɪ'lænθrəpɪ] *n.* love of/caring for human beings, shown esp. by giving money to charity. **phil•an•throp•ic** [fɪlən'θrɒpɪk] *adj.* kind (towards human beings). **phi•lan•thro•pist** [fɪ'lænθrəpɪst] *n.* person who is philanthropic.

phi•lat•e•ly [fɪ'lætəlɪ] *n.* stamp collecting. **phil•a•tel•ic** [fɪlə'telɪk] *adj.* referring to stamp collecting. **phi•lat•e•list,** *n.* person who studies or collects stamps.

-phile [faɪl] *suffix meaning* (person) who likes; **Francophile** = person who likes the French.

phil•har•mon•ic [fɪlɑː'mɒnɪk] *adj.* liking music (used in names of orchestras/concert halls, etc.).

phi•lis•tine ['fɪlɪstaɪn] *adj. & n.* (person) who is unsympathetic to the arts.

phil•o•den•dron [fɪlə'dendrən] *n.* tropical climbing plant, often used as a house plant.

phi•lol•o•gy [fɪ'lɒlədʒɪ] *n.* study of (the history of) language. **phil•o•log•i•cal** [fɪlə'lɒdʒɪkl] *adj.* referring to philology. **phi•lol•o•gist** [fɪ'lɒlədʒɪst] *n.* expert in philology.

phi•los•o•phy [fɪ'lɒsəfɪ] *n.* study of the meaning of human existence; study of the methods and limits of human knowledge; general way of thinking. **phi•los•o•pher,** *n.* person who studies the meaning of human existence. **phil•o•soph•i•cal** [fɪlə'sɒfɪkl] *adj.* (a) thoughtful; calm. (b) referring to philosophy. **phil•o•soph•i•cal•ly,** *adv.* thoughtfully; calmly. **phi•los•o•phize,** *v.* to think seriously (like a philosopher).

phil•ter ['fɪltə] *n.* (*old*) magic potion to make s.o. fall in love.

phle•bi•tis [flɪ'baɪtɪs] *n.* inflammation of a vein.

phlegm [flem] *n.* (a) slimy substance in the throat, etc., when you have a cold. (b) calmness. **phleg•mat•ic** [fleg'mætɪk] *adj.* calm/not easily annoyed. **phleg•mat•i•cal•ly,** *adv.* in a phlegmatic way.

phlox [flɒks] *n.* (*pl.* **phlox**) common perennial flower.

-phobe [fəʊb] *suffix meaning* (person) who does not like; **xenophobe** = person who dislikes foreigners.

pho•bi•a ['fəʊbɪə] *n.* abnormal terror/hatred of something.

phoe•nix ['fiːnɪks] *n.* mythical bird, said to die by burning and reappear from its ashes.

phone [fəʊn] 1. *n.* telephone. 2. *v.* to call (s.o.) by telephone. **phone book,** *n.* book which lists people's names, addresses and phone numbers. **phone booth,** *n.* small booth containing a public telephone.

pho•net•ic [fə'netɪk] 1. *adj.* referring to spoken sounds. 2. *n. pl.* **phonetics** = (i) study of sounds of a language; (ii) written signs which indicate sounds. **pho•net•i•cal•ly,** *adv.* using phonetics; (language spoken) in a way which closely follows the written letters. **pho•ne•ti•cian** [fəʊnə'tɪʃn] *n.* person who studies phonetics. **phon•ics** ['fɒnɪks] *n.* method of teaching reading, using letters as guides to pronunciation. **pho•nol•o•gy** [fə'nɒlədʒɪ] *n.* study of sounds of speech.

phon(e)y ['fəʊnɪ] 1. *adj.* (**-ier, -iest**) *inf.* false. 2. *n. inf.* person who pretends to be richer/more famous, etc., than he really is.

pho•no•graph ['fəʊnəɡrɑːf] *n.* machine on which records are played.

phos•phate ['fɒsfeɪt] *n.* chemical compound containing phosphorus, often used as a fertilizer.

phos•pho•res•cence [fɒsfə'resns] *n.* ability to shine in the dark after being exposed to light. **phos•pho•res•cent,** *adj.* which shines in the dark after being exposed to light. **phos•pho•rus** ['fɒsfərəs] *n.* (*element:* P) poisonous yellow substance which shines in the dark.

pho•to ['fəʊtəʊ] 1. *n.* (*pl.* **-os**) *inf.* photograph. 2. **photo-** *prefix meaning* (i) light; (ii) photograph. **pho•to•chem•i•cal,** *adj.* (chemical reaction) which is caused by light. **pho•to•cop•y** ['fəʊtəʊkɒpɪ] 1. *n.* copy (of a document) made by photographing it. 2. *v.* to copy (sth) photographically and make a print of it. **pho•to•cop•i•er,** *n.* machine which

---

æ back, ɑː farm, ɒ top, aɪ pipe, aʊ how, aɪə fire, aʊə flower, ɔː bought, ɔɪ toy, e fed, eəhair, eɪ take, ə afraid, əʊ boat, əʊə lower, vː word, iː heap, ɪ hit, ɪə hear, uː school, ʊ book, ʌ but, b back, d dog, ð then, dʒ just, f fog, g go, h hand, j yes, k catch, l last, m mix, n nut, ŋ sing, p penny, r round, s some, ʃ short, t too, tʃ chop, θ thing, v voice, w was, z zoo, ʒ treasure

takes photocopies. **pho•to•e•lec•tric** [fəutəuɪ'lektrɪk] adj. referring to electricity controlled by light; **p. cell** = cell which converts light into electricity or which operates a machine when a beam of light is broken. **pho•to fin•ish** ['fəutəufɪnɪʃ] n. very close end of a race when a photograph is used to decide who is the winner. **pho•to•gen•ic** [fəutəu'dʒiːnɪk] adj. (person) who looks well in photographs. **pho•to•graph** ['fəutəgrɑːf] 1. n. picture taken by a camera by means of exposing sensitive film to light. 2. v. to take a picture with a camera. **pho•tog•ra•pher** [fə'tɒgrəfə] n. person who takes photographs. **pho•to•graph•ic** [fəutəu'græfɪk] adj. referring to photography; **p. memory** = ability to remember things in exact detail, as if seen. **pho•tog•ra•phy** [fə'tɒgrəfɪ] n. (art of) taking pictures on sensitive film with a camera. **pho•to•gra•vure**, n. engraving of a photograph. **Pho•to•stat** ['fəutəustæt] 1. n. trademark for a type of photographic copy. 2. v. (**photostated, photostatted**) to make a photographic copy of. **pho•to•syn•the•sis**, n. process by which plants use sunlight to form carbohydrates.

phrase [freɪz] 1. n. (a) expression; short sentence; group of words taken together; **p. book** = book of translations of common expressions. (b) group of notes in a piece of music. 2. v. to express/to word (a sentence, etc.). **phras•al** ['freɪzl] adj. referring to a phrase; (verb) making a phrase. **phra•se•ol•o•gy** [freɪzɪ'ɒlədʒɪ] n. way of expressing sth; choice of words and phrases.

phre•nol•o•gy [fre'nɒlədʒɪ] n. study of the outside shape of the skull.

phut [fʌt] adv. inf. **to go p.** = to stop working.

phys•i•cal ['fɪzɪkl] adj. (a) referring to matter/energy, etc.; **p. geography** = study of rocks and earth, etc.; **p. chemistry** = study of chemical substances. (b) referring to the human body; **p. exercise** = exercise of the body. **phys•i•cal•ly**, adv. referring to the body or to the laws of nature.

phy•si•cian [fɪ'zɪʃn] n. doctor.

phys•ics ['fɪzɪks] n. study of matter/energy, etc. **phys•i•cist** ['fɪzɪsɪst] n. person who studies physics.

phys•i•og•no•my [fɪzɪ'ɒnəmɪ] n. human face.

phys•i•ol•o•gy [fɪzɪ'ɒlədʒɪ] n. study of the way in which living things work. **phys•i•o•log•i•cal** [fɪzɪə'lɒdʒɪkl] adj referring to physiology. **phys•i•ol•o•gist**, n. person who studies physiology.

phys•i•o•ther•a•py [fɪzɪəu'θerəpɪ] n. treatment of an illness, pain, etc., by exercise or rubbing. **phys•i•o•ther•a•pist**, n. person who practices physiotherapy.

phy•sique [fɪ'ziːk] n. shape of a person's body.

pi [paɪ] n. letter of the Greek alphabet (), symbolizing the quantity 3.14159, which is used to calculate the circumference of a circle from a known radius.

pi•a•no ['pjænəu] n. (pl. **-os**) musical instrument with keys which makes notes by striking wires with hammers; **grand p.** = large piano with horizontal wires. **player p.** = piano which plays music mechanically from a reel of perforated paper. **pi•an•ist** ['pɪənɪst] n. person who plays the piano. **pi•an•o•forte** ['pjænəufɔːtɪ] n. (old) piano.

pi•az•za [pɪ'ætsə] n. Italian square, often surrounded by arcades.

pi•broch ['piːbrɒk] n. mournful bagpipe music.

pi•ca ['paɪkə] n. measure of type.

pic•a•resque [pɪkə'resk] adj. fancifully romantic (story).

pic•ca•lil•li [pɪkə'lɪlɪ] n. pickle made of vegetables, such as cauliflower, onions, etc., in a mustard sauce.

pic•co•lo ['pɪkələu] n. (pl. **-os**) small wind instrument, like a little flute.

pick [pɪk] 1. n. (a) heavy tool (for breaking hard ground/concrete, etc.) with a long handle and a curved metal bar with pointed ends. (b) selected group; **to take your p.** = choose which one you want. 2. v. (a) to break up (hard ground/concrete, etc.) with a pick. (b) to remove things with your fingers/with a pointed tool; to clean the inside of (your nose) with your fingers. (c) to eat very daintily and without any appetite. (d) to choose. (e) to collect (ripe fruit); to cut (flowers). (f) to open (a lock) with a piece of wire. (g) to steal from (s.o.'s pocket). (h) **to p. s.o.'s brains** = to ask for ideas/information. **pick•ax, pickaxe**, n. pick. **pick•er**, n. person who picks. **pick•ings**, n. pl. bits and pieces left which people can pick up. **pick-me-up**, n. inf. alcoholic drink that makes s.o. feel better. **pick off**, v. to defeat/kill (an enemy) one by one. **pick on**, v. to select (s.o.) as a target for criticism/for bullying. **pick out**, v. to select/to choose. **pick•pock•et**, n. person who steals things from people's pockets. **pick up**, v. (a) to take (sth) which is on the ground. (b) to learn (a language, etc.) unsystematically. (c) to give (s.o.) a lift in a car; (of a bus) to take (passengers) on board; (of police) to arrest/to take to a police station; to start an acquaintanceship with (s.o.) by chance. (d) to get stronger. **pick•up**, n. (a) inf. person who has been picked up. (b) needle and arm of a record player. (c) light van with an open back.

pick•et ['pɪkɪt] 1. *n.* (a) guard. (b) pointed stake. (c) striking workman/union official who stands at the entrance to a factory to try to prevent other workmen from going to work; **p. line** = line of pickets preventing other workmen going to work. 2. *v.* to post strikers at the entrance of a factory to try to prevent workers going to work.

pick•le ['pɪkl] 1. *n.* (a) vegetables preserved in vinegar, etc. (b) *inf.* difficult or embarassing situation. 2. *v.* to preserve (vegetables, etc.) in vinegar. **pick•led,** *adj. inf.* drunk.

pic•nic ['pɪknɪk] 1. *n.* (a) pleasure trip with a meal eaten outdoors. 2. *v.* (**picknicked**) to eat a picnic. **pic•nick•er,** *n.* person who goes on a picnic.

pic•to•ri•al [pɪk'tɔːrɪəl] *adj.* referring to pictures.

pic•ture ['pɪktʃə] 1. *n.* (a) painting/drawing, etc.; *inf.* **to give s.o. the p.** = to tell them all the relevant details. (b) image (on a TV screen, etc.). 2. *v.* to imagine. **pic•tur•esque** [pɪktʃə'resk] *adj.* which would make a good picture; very artistic.

pid•dle ['pɪdl] *v. inf.* (*child's language*) to urinate. **pid•dling,** *adj. inf.* very small.

pidg•in ['pɪdʒɪn] *n.* simple language made from several languages, used as a lingua franca; **p. (English)** = simplified form of English used in the Far East.

pie [paɪ] *n.* cooked dish, usu. of pastry with a filling of meat or fruit; **p. in the sky** = unattainable ideal. **pie chart,** *n.* diagram shaped like a circle with segments showing how sth is divided up. **pie-eyed,** *adj. inf.* drunk.

pie•bald ['paɪbɔːld] *adj.* (horse) with black and white patches.

piece [piːs] 1. *n.* (a) small part/bit; **he went to pieces** = he lost control of himself/had a nervous breakdown. (b) short composition in music. (c) one of the figures used in chess, but not usu. a pawn. (d) gun. 2. *v.* **to p. together** = to join separate parts together. **piece•meal,** *adv.* in bits; a bit at a time; separately. **piece•work,** *n.* work for which you are paid by the amount of work done and not by the hour.

pièce de ré•sis•tance [pɪesdəreɪsɪs'tɑ̃s] *n.* main item.

pied [paɪd] *adj.* having two colors, usu. black and white.

pied-à-terre [pjeɪdæ'teə] *n.* small apartment/house which you use to live in from time to time when visiting a place.

pier ['pɪə] *n.* (a) construction going out into the water, used as a landing place for ships. (b) pillar (of a bridge).

pierce ['pɪəs] *v.* to make a hole. **pierc•ing,** *adj.* very loud, shrill (cry); very sharp/severe (cold or wind).

pi•e•ty ['paɪətɪ] *n.* being pious; great respect for religion.

pif•fle [pɪfl] *n. inf.* nonsense.

pig [pɪg] *n.* (a) farm animal which gives pork/bacon, etc.; various wild species of this animal. (b) *inf.* dirty/greedy person. (c) large block of metal; **p. iron** = iron in rough molded blocks. (d) *Sl.* policeman. **pig•ger•y,** *n.* place where pigs are kept. **pig•gy,** *n.* child's name for a pig. **pig•gy•back,** *n. adj. & adv.* carrying s.o. on your back with his arms round your neck. **pig•gy•bank,** *n.* child's savings bank, usu. in the shape of a pig. **pig•head•ed,** *adj. inf.* obstinate. **pig•let,** *n.* little pig. **pig•meat,** *n.* meat from a pig. **pig•skin,** *n.* leather made from the skin of a pig. **pig•sty,** *n.* shed where pigs are kept. **pig•tail,** *n.* hair hanging down in a plait at the back of the head.

pi•geon ['pɪdʒn] *n.* common grayish bird. **pi•geon•hole.** 1. *n.* small space used for filing papers/letters, etc. 2. *v.* (a) to file letters/papers, etc. (often as the best way to forget them). (b) to put (s.o./sth) into a particular category. **pi•geon-toed,** *adj.* with the feet turned inwards, towards each other.

pig•ment ['pɪgmənt] 1. *n.* coloring matter. 2. *v.* to color with pigment. **pig•men•ta•tion** [pɪgmən'teɪʃn] *n.* coloring of the skin.

Pig•my ['pɪgmɪ] *n. see* **Pygmy.**

pike [paɪk] *n.* (a) (*pl.* **pike**) large ferocious freshwater fish. (b) (*old*) weapon, like a spear with a broad blade.

pi•laf, pilaff ['pɪlæf] *n.* Indian dish of meat with savory rice.

pi•las•ter [pɪ'læstə] *n.* rectangular column, usu. attached to a wall.

pi•lau ['pɪlaʊ] *n. see* **pi•laf.**

pil•chard ['pɪltʃəd] *n.* small fish similar to a herring.

pile [paɪl] 1. *n.* (a) heap; *inf.* **he's made a p. in real estate** = a lot of money. (b) large stake/concrete shaft driven into the earth to provide a foundation. (c) thickness of tufts of wool in a carpet. (d) **piles** = hemorrhoids. 2. *v.* **to p. (up)** = to heap up. **pile driv•er,** *n.* machine for

---

æ back, ɑː farm, ɒ top, aɪ pipe, aʊ how, aɪə fire, aʊə flower, ɔː bought, ɔɪ toy, e fed, eə hair, eɪ take, ə afraid, əʊ boat, aʊə lower, vː word, iː heap, ɪ hit, ɪə hear, uː school, ʊ book, ʌ but, b back, d dog, ð then, dʒ just, f fog, g go, h hand, j yes, k catch, l last, m mix, n nut, ŋ sing, p penny, r round, s some, ʃ short, t too, tʃ chop, θ thing, v voice, w was, z zoo, ʒ treasure

forcing piles into the earth. **pile•up**, *n*. series of cars which have smashed into each other.

pil•fer ['pɪlfə] *v*. to steal small objects or small amounts of money. **pil•fer•er**, *n*. person who pilfers. **pil•fer•age, pilfering**, *n*. stealing small objects or amounts of money.

pil•grim ['pɪlgrɪm] *n*. person who goes to visit a holy place. **pil•grim•age**, *n*. journey to visit a holy place/a famous place.

pill [pɪl] *n*. small round tablet of medicine; *inf*. **she's on the p.** = she takes contraceptive tablets. **pill•box**, *n*. (a) round box for pills. (b) concrete shelter for a small gun.

pil•age ['pɪlɪdʒ] 1. *n*. plundering by soldiers. 2. *v*. (*of soldiers*) to plunder/to steal goods (from a captured town, etc.).

pil•lar ['pɪlə] *n*. (a) column. (b) strong supporter.

pil•lion ['pɪljən] *n*. rear saddle for a passenger on a motorcycle.

pil•lo•ry ['pɪlərɪ] 1. *n*. (*old*) wooden stand with holes for the head and hands, where criminals were placed so that the public could throw things at them. 2. *v*. to make (s.o.) appear ridiculous or foolish in public.

pil•low ['pɪləʊ] *n*. bag full of soft material which you put your head on in bed. **pil•low•case, pillowslip**, *n*. cloth bag to cover a pillow with.

pi•lot ['paɪlət] 1. *n*. (a) person who guides ships into harbor or through dangerous channels. (b) person who flies an aircraft. (c) **p. light** = small gas light on a stove/water-heater, etc., from which the main gas jets are lit. 2. *v*. (a) to guide (a ship). (b) to fly (an aircraft).

pi•mien•to [pɪmɪ'entəʊ], **pi•men•to** *n*. (*pl*. -os) green or red fruit with a hot spicy taste used as a vegetable.

pimp [pɪmp] 1. *n*. man who organizes and makes money from prostitutes. 2. *v*. to work as a pimp.

pim•per•nel ['pɪmpənel] *n*. wild plant with small red flowers.

pim•ple ['pɪmpl] *n*. small bump on the surface of the skin. **pim•ply**, *adj*. covered with pimples.

pin [pɪn] 1. *n*. (a) small sharp metal stick with a round head, used for attaching clothes/papers, etc., together; **safety p.** = type of bent pin where the sharp point is held by a metal shield; **pins and needles** = prickling feeling in your hand or foot after it has been numb for a time. (b) blunt wooden or metal bolt used for fastening things together. 2. *v*. (**pinned**) (a) to attach with a pin; **to p. s.o. down** = to get him to say what he really thinks/to make his mind up. (b) to hold fast. **pin•ball**, *n*. table game where a ball has to be rolled into holes. **pin•cush•ion**, *n*. round pad in which you

can stick pins. **pin mon•ey**, *n*. *inf*. small amount of money for buying extra items. **pin•point**, *v*. to indicate exactly. **pin•prick**, *n*. slight annoyance. **pin•stripe**, *n*. dark cloth with a very thin white line in it. **pin•up**, *n*. *inf*. photograph of a pretty girl which you can pin up on a wall.

pin•a•fore ['pɪnəfɔː] *n*. apron worn to cover a dress.

pince-nez ['pænsneɪ] *n. pl.* glasses which clip onto your nose.

pin•cers ['pɪnsəz] *n. pl.* (a) (**pair of**) **p.** = scissor-shaped tool for holding sth tight. (b) claws of a crab/lobster.

pinch [pɪnʃ] 1. *n*. (*pl*. -es) (a) squeezing tightly/nipping between finger and thumb; **in a p.** = if really necessary; **to feel the p.** = find you have less money than you need. (b) small quantity of sth held between finger and thumb. 2. *v*. (a) to squeeze tightly, using the finger and thumb. (b) to hold tight and hurt. (c) *inf*. to steal. (d) *Sl.* to arrest.

pine [paɪn] 1. *n*. type of evergreen tree; wood from a pine tree. 2. *v*. (**to**) waste away (because you want sth). **pine•ap•ple** ['paɪnæpl] *n*. large tropical fruit, shaped like a pine cone with stiff prickly leaves on top. **pine cone**, *n*. fruit of a pine tree. **pine wood**, *n*. wood of pine trees. **pin•e•al gland**, *n*. small gland, shaped like a pine cone, found in the brain.

ping [pɪŋ] 1. *n*. noise made when a small bell/a glass, etc., is hit. 2. *v*. to make a ping.

ping pong ['pɪŋpɒŋ] *n*. *inf*. table tennis.

pin•ion ['pɪnjən] *n*. (a) large outer feather on a bird's wing. (b) toothed wheel or cogwheel. 2. *v*. to tie up (s.o.'s arms) tightly.

pink [pɪŋk] 1. *adj. & n*. (color) like pale red or flesh color. 2. *n*. (a) scented garden flower like a small carnation. (b) **in the p.** = very well/prosperous. **pink•ing shears**, *n. pl.* large scissors used by dressmakers, which give a zigzag edge to a cut.

pin•na•cle ['pɪnəkl] *n*. topmost point (of a pointed rock, of s.o.'s career); tall, thin stone spire or tower.

pint [paɪnt] *n*. liquid measure (= 16 ounces or 0.473 liter).

pi•o•neer [paɪə'nɪə] 1. *n*. person who is among the first to try to do sth/who is the first to explore/settle in a new land. 2. *v*. to be first to do (sth).

pi•ous ['paɪəs] *adj*. showing great respect for religion. **pi•ous•ly**, *adv*. in a pious way.

pip [pɪp] *n*. (a) small seed. (b) star on the shoulder showing an officer's rank in the British army.

pipe [paɪp] 1. *n*. (a) tube. (b) instrument for smoking tobacco. (c) thin metal flute; **the pipes** = bagpipes. 2. *v*. to send (water/gas, etc.)

along a pipe; **piped music** = recorded music played continuously (in a restaurant, etc.). **pipe down**, *v. inf.* to stop talking. **pipe dream**, *n.* plan which is impossible to carry out. **pipe•line**, *n.* very large tube for carrying oil/natural gas, etc., over long distances; **in the p.** = being worked on/on the way. **pip•er**, *n.* person who plays the bagpipes. **pipe up**, *v. inf.* to start talking (esp. in a high-pitched voice). **pip•ing**. 1. *n.* (a) collection of tubes; section of metal tube. (b) decoration like white tubes on a cake/on a dress. 2. *adv.* **p. hot** = extremely hot.

pi•pette [pɪˈpet] *n.* thin glass measuring tube used in laboratories.

pip•it [ˈpɪpɪt] *n.* small singing bird.

pip•pin [ˈpɪpɪn] *n.* type of sweet apple.

pi•quant [ˈpiːkənt] *adj.* nice sharp (flavor); pleasantly interesting/amusing. **pi•quan•cy**, *n.* being piquant. **pi•quant•ly**, *adv.* in a piquant way.

pique [piːk] 1. *n.* resentment/annoyance. 2. *v.* (a) to make (s.o.) resentful. (b) to arouse s.o.'s curiosity.

pi•qué [ˈpikei] *n.* cotton material with ribs.

pi•ra•nha [pɪˈrɑːnə] *n.* small tropical fish which attacks animals, including man.

pi•rate [ˈpaɪərət] 1. *n.* (a) robber (esp. at sea). (b) person who copies a patented invention or a copyrighted work. **p. radio** = illegal radio station. 2. *v.* to publish books/make recordings which are copied from those of another publisher without having the right to do so. **pi•ra•cy**, *n.* robbery (at sea); illegal publishing of books/making of records. **pi•rat•i•cal** [paɪˈrætɪkl] *adj.* referring to a pirate.

pir•ou•ette [pɪruˈet] 1. *n.* spinning around on one foot when dancing. 2. *v.* to spin around on one foot.

pis•ca•to•ri•al [pɪskəˈtɔːriəl] *adj.* referring to fishing.

Pis•ces [ˈpaɪsiːz] *n.* one of the signs of the zodiac, shaped like fish.

pis•ci•cul•ture [pɪsɪˈkʌltʃə] *n.* raising fish for food.

piss [pɪs] 1. *n. inf. & vulgar* (a) waste water from the body. (b) passing waste water from the body. 2. *v. inf. & vulgar* to pass waste water from the body.

pis•tach•i•o [pɪˈstæʃɪəu] *n.* (*pl.* -os) small green tropical nut.

piste [piːst] *n.* track for skiing.

pis•til [ˈpɪstɪl] *n.* female part of a flower, which produces seeds.

pis•tol [ˈpɪstl] *n.* small gun which is held in the hand.

pis•ton [ˈpɪstn] *n.* (*in an engine*) metal disk which moves up and down in a cylinder; **p. rod** = rod which is attached to a piston and which drives other parts of the engine.

pit [pɪt] 1. *n.* (a) deep, dark hole in the ground. (b) coalmine. (c) hole in the floor of a garage (for inspecting the underside of a car); (*at car races*) place where the cars are inspected and repaired. (d) stone of some fruit. 2. *v.* (**pitted**) (a) to try (your strength) **against.** (b) to take the stone out of (a fruit). (c) to mark with a hole.

pitch [pɪtʃ] 1. *n.* (*pl.* -es) (a) black substance which comes from tar and is used for waterproofing boats/roofs, etc. (b) level of tone in music. (c) height (of anger/of excitement). (d) angle of a sloping roof. (e) **sales p.** = smooth talk, aimed at selling sth. 2. *v.* (a) to put up (a tent). (b) to throw (a ball). (c) to set the level of a musical tone. (d) (*of boat*) to rock with the front and back going up and down. **pitch-black, pitch dark**, *adj.* very black; very dark. **pitch•blende**, *n.* mineral which produces radium. **pitched**, *adj.* **p. battle** = battle fought on a selected piece of ground; fierce argument. **pitch•er** [ˈpɪtʃə] *n.* (a) large container for liquids, usu. with a handle. (b) person who pitches a ball. **pitch•fork**, *n.* large fork for moving bales of hay. **pitch in•to**, *v.* to attack. **pitch pine**, *n.* type of pine which produces strong resin.

pit•fall [ˈpɪtfɔːl] *n.* trap/danger.

pith [pɪθ] *n.* (a) soft part in the center of a plant stem; soft white stuff under the skin of a lemon/an orange, etc. (b) important part (of an argument). **pith•i•ly**, *adv.* in a pithy way. **pith•y**, *adj.* (-ier, -iest) (a) (wood) with a soft center. (b) concise; full of serious meaning.

pi•ton [ˈpiːtɒn] *n.* metal peg used in rock-climbing.

pit•tance [ˈpɪtns] *n.* low wage.

pit•ter-pat•ter [ˈpɪtəpætə] *n.* series of small sounds.

pi•tu•i•tar•y [pɪˈtjuːɪtrɪ] *adj.* **p. gland** = gland in the brain which produces hormones which control the development and function of the body.

pit•y [ˈpɪtɪ] 1. *n.* feeling of sympathy for s.o. unfortunate; **to take p. on s.o.** = to be sorry for s.o. 2. *v.* to feel sympathy for (s.o.).

æ back, ɑː farm, ɒ top, aɪ pipe, aʊ how, aɪə fire, aʊə flower, ɔː bought, ɔɪ toy, e fed, eəhair, eɪ take, ə afraid, əʊ boat, əʊə lower, ɜː word, iː heap, ɪ hit, ɪə hear, uː school, ʊ book, ʌ but, b back, d dog, ð then, dʒ just, f fog, g go, h hand, j yes, k catch, l last, m mix, n nut, ŋ sing, p penny, r round, s some, ʃ short, t too, tʃ chop, θ thing, v voice, w was, z zoo, ʒ treasure

pit•e•ous ['pɪtɪəs], **pit•i•a•ble**, *adj.* which deserves pity. **pit•i•ful**, *adj.* (a) deserving pity; sad. (b) inadequate. **pit•i•ful•ly**, *adv.* in a pitiful way. **pit•i•less**, *adj.* showing no pity.

piv•ot ['pɪvət] 1. *n.* point on which sth turns. 2. *v.* to turn **on** a point; to depend **on** sth. **piv•ot•al**, *adj.* of great importance.

pix•el ['pɪksəl] *n.* tiny element of color or light on a TV screen or computer monitor. **pix•e•la•tion**, *n.* (a) appearance of the squares of color that make up a digitized image when the image is displayed at low resolution. (b) covering of a video image with a grid of colored squares, usu. to conceal s.o.'s identity.

pix•ie ['pɪksɪ] *n.* small fairy.

piz•za ['piːtsə] *n.* Italian dish, consisting of a flat round piece of dough cooked with tomatoes, onions, etc., on top. **piz•ze•ri•a, *n.* restaurant which sells pizzas.

piz•zi•ca•to [pɪtsɪ'kɑːtəʊ] *n. & adv.* (music) played by plucking the strings instead of using the bow.

plac•ard ['plækɑːd] 1. *n.* poster. 2. *v.* to stick posters up.

pla•cate [plə'keɪt] *v.* to calm (s.o.); to make (s.o.) less angry. **pla•ca•to•ry**, *adv.* which placates.

place [pleɪs] 1. *n.* (a) location/spot. (b) house/home. (c) open area. (d) set position; **to take p.** = to happen/to be held. (e) rank (in a series); **in the first p.** = first of all. (f) job. (g) one of the first three positions in a horse race. 2. *v.* (a) to put. (b) to give (an order). (c) to put in a set position. (d) to remember who s.o. is. **place•mat**, *n.* mat which a person's plate is put on. **place•ment**, *n.* placing s.o. in a job. **place set•ting**, *n.* set of knife/fork/spoon, etc. for one person.

pla•ce•bo [plə'siːbəʊ] *n.* (*pl.* -os) harmless substance given to a patient instead of a drug to make him believe he is receiving treatment.

pla•cen•ta [plə'sentə] *n.* tissue in the womb which nourishes the unborn baby.

plac•id ['plæsɪd] *adj.* (-er, -est) calm. **pla•cid•i•ty** [plə'sɪdɪtɪ] *n.* calmness. **plac•id•ly**, *adv.* calmly.

plack•et ['plækɪt] *n.* opening with buttons at the waist of a skirt.

pla•gia•rism ['pleɪdʒərɪzəm] *n.* copying what s.o. else has written. **pla•gia•rist**, *n.* author who copies the work of s.o. else. **pla•gia•rize**, *v.* to copy the work of (another author).

plague [pleɪg] 1. *n.* (a) fatal infectious disease transmitted by fleas from rats. (b) great quantity of pests. 2. *v.* to annoy/to bother (s.o.).

plaice [pleɪs] *n.* (*pl.* **plaice**) common flat sea fish.

plaid [plæd] *n.* (a) (*in Scotland*) long piece of (tartan) cloth. (b) pattern of differently colored stripes that cross over each other; cloth with this pattern.

plain [pleɪn] 1. *adj.* (-er, -est) (a) obvious/easy to understand. (b) simple/uncomplicated. (c) not pretty. 2. *n.* large flat area of country. **plain•clothes**, *n. pl.* ordinary/everyday clothes (not uniform). **plain•ly**, *adv.* (a) obviously. (b) simply. **plain•ness**, *n.* (a) clearness. (b) simpleness. **plain•song**, *n.* medieval music for church services. **plain-spo•ken**, *adj.* (person) who speaks in a straightforward way.

plain•tiff ['pleɪntɪf] *n.* person who starts a legal action against s.o. else.

plain•tive ['pleɪntɪv] *adj.* sad.

plait [plæt] 1. *n.* (hair/wool, etc.) with three strands woven into a long rope. 2. *v.* to weave hair, etc., to form a plait.

plan [plæn] 1. *n.* (a) scheme; **according to p.** = as we had intended. (b) drawing of the way sth is to be built or constructed. (c) map of streets. 2. *v.* (**planned**) (a) to draw up a scheme to construct sth. (b) to scheme/to propose to do sth. **plan•ner**, *n.* person who draws up schemes; **town p.** = person who designs how a town should develop. **plan•ning**, *n.* making plans; **family p.** = decision by parents on how many children to have.

plane [pleɪn] 1. *n.* (a) flat surface. (b) aircraft. (c) tool for smoothing wood. (d) tree often grown in towns, of which bark comes off in large pieces. 2. *adj.* level/flat. 3. *v.* to smooth (wood) flat with a plane.

plan•et ['plænɪt] *n.* body which revolves around a star, esp. around the sun. **plan•e•tar•i•um** [plænɪ'teərɪəm] *n.* domed building in which you sit and watch as pictures of the stars are projected against the ceiling. **plan•e•tar•y** ['plænɪtrɪ] *adj.* referring to the planets.

plan•gent ['plændʒənt] *adj.* sad resonant (music).

plank [plæŋk] *n.* (a) long flat piece of wood used in building. (b) proposal in a political program. **plank•ing**, *n.* series of planks.

plank•ton ['plæŋktn] *n.* tiny organisms living in the sea.

plant [plɑːnt] 1. *n.* (a) thing which grows in the ground, is usu. green, and cannot move from one place to another. (b) factory. (c) machinery. 2. *v.* (a) to put (a plant) into the ground. (b) to put in a special position. (c) to put (sth) secretly; to put (stolen goods) secretly **on** s.o., in order to make it look as if he stole them. **plan•ta•tion** [plɑːn'teɪʃn] *n.* (a) area of trees specially planted. (b) tropical estate growing a particular crop. **plant•er,** *n.* (a) person in charge of a plantation. (b) decorative container to hold plants in pots.

plan•tain ['plæntɪn] *n.* (a) common weed. (b) tropical fruit.

plaque [plæk] *n.* (a) decorative plate hung on a wall; stone/metal/earthenware plate with an inscription. (b) deposit which forms on the teeth.

plas•ma ['plæzmə] *n.* liquid part of blood.

plas•ter ['plɑːstə] 1. *n.* (a) mixture of fine sand and lime which when mixed with water is used for covering walls of houses. (b) white paste, used to make molds/to make coverings to hold broken arms and legs in place. (c) **sticking p.** = adhesive cloth/tape used for holding bandages in place/for covering small wounds. 2. *v.* (a) to cover with plaster. (b) to cover thickly as if with plaster. **plas•ter cast,** *n.* (a) block of plaster put round a broken leg, etc. (b) mold made by covering sth with plaster. (c) copy of a statue made in plaster. **plas•tered,** *adj. Sl.* drunk. **plas•ter•er,** *n.* person who covers walls with plaster.

plas•tic ['plæstɪk] 1. *n.* artificial substance, which can be molded into any shape; **p. bomb** = explosive material which can be molded in the hand. 2. *adj.* soft/pliable; **p. surgery** = operation to replace damaged skin or to improve s.o.'s appearance. **plas•tic•i•ty** [plæs'tɪsɪtɪ] *n.* state of being plastic.

plate [pleɪt] 1. *n.* (a) thin flat sheet of metal/glass, etc. (b) flat dish for putting food on. (c) dishes made of gold or silver. (d) thin layer of gold/silver on a less precious metal; objects made of this. (e) book illustration on shiny paper. (f) piece of plastic with false teeth attached which fits into your mouth. 2. *v.* to cover with a thin layer of gold or silver. **plate•ful,** *n.* quantity held by a plate. **plate glass,** *n.* glass in very large sheets.

pla•teau ['plætəʊ] *n.* (*pl.* **-eaus, -eaux** [-əʊz]) high flat area of land.

plate•let ['pleɪtlət] *n.* small cell in the blood which helps blood to clot.

plat•en ['plætən] *n.* roller around which the paper goes in a typewriter.

plat•form ['plætfɔːm] *n.* (a) raised floor space for speakers in a hall. (b) raised pavement by the side of the rails in a railroad station so that passengers can get on and off trains easily. (c) proposals put forward by the leaders of a political party before an election. (d) computer system that requires unique versions of software.

plat•i•num ['plætɪnəm] *n.* (*element:* Pt) rare light-colored precious metal; **p. blonde** = woman with silvery blonde hair.

plat•i•tude ['plætɪtjuːd] *n.* ordinary saying, esp. one which the speaker thinks is very important.

pla•ton•ic [plə'tɒnɪk] *adj.* (love between man and woman) which is not sexual.

pla•toon [plə'tuːn] *n.* small group of soldiers/part of a company.

plat•ter ['plætə] *n.* large serving plate.

plat•y•pus ['plætɪpəs] *n.* (*pl.* **-es**) Australian mammal which lays eggs.

plau•dits ['plɔːdɪts] *n. pl.* applause.

plau•si•ble ['plɔːzɪbl] *adj.* which sounds as though it is correct when it often is not. **plau•si•bly,** *adv.* in a plausible way. **plau•si•bil•i•ty** [plɔːzɪ'bɪlɪtɪ] *n.* being plausible.

play [pleɪ] 1. *n.* (a) way of amusing yourself; sport. (b) theatrical performance; script of a theatrical performance. (c) freedom to move. 2. *v.* (a) to amuse yourself/to pass the time in a pleasant way. (b) to take part in a game. (c) to perform on a musical instrument. (d) to act a part in a theatrical performance. (e) to let a fish which has been caught on a hook swim until it is tired and can easily be landed. (f) to make (a record player) work. **play at,** *v.* (a) to work in a slack way. (b) (*of children*) to pretend to be. **play back,** *v.* to listen to (sth) which you have just recorded on tape. **play•boy,** *n.* rich man who spends his time amusing himself rather than working. **play down,** *v.* to make (sth) seem less important. **play•er,** *n.* person who plays. **play•fel•low,** *n.* playmate. **play•ful,** *adj.* liking to play. **play•ful•ly,** *adv.* in a playful way. **play•ful•ness,** *n.* being playful. **play•ground,** *n.* area, esp. around school buildings, where children can play. **play•group,** *n.* group of small children who play together under supervision. **play•house,** *n.* theater. **play•ing card,** *n.* one of a set of fifty-two cards, marked in four designs, used for playing various games. **play•ing field,** *n.* area of grass where sports can be played. **play•mate,** *n.* child another child plays with. **play off,** *v.* **to p. s.o. off against s.o.** = to try to benefit by making two people oppose each other. **play on,** *v.* to take

---

æ **back,** ɑː **farm,** ɒ **top,** aɪ **pipe,** aʊ **how,** aɪə **fire,** aʊə **flower,** ɔː **bought,** ɔɪ **toy,** e **fed,** eəhair, eɪ **take,** ə **afraid,** əʊ **boat,** əʊə **lower,** vː **word,** iː **heap,** ɪ **hit,** ɪə **hear,** uː **school,** ʊ **book,** ʌ **but,** b **back,** d **dog,** ð **then,** dʒ **just,** f **fog,** g **go,** h **hand,** j **yes,** k **catch,** l **last,** m **mix,** n **nut,** ŋ **sing,** p **penny,** r **round,** s **some,** ʃ **short,** t **too,** tʃ **chop,** θ **thing,** v **voice,** w **was,** z **zoo,** ʒ **treasure**

advantage by exciting (s.o.'s sympathy). **play•pen,** *n.* type of enclosed space in which babies can be left to play safely. **play•thing,** *n.* toy. **play•time,** *n.* time in nursery school when children can play. **play up,** *v. inf.* to make stand out. **play•wright,** *n.* person who writes plays.

pla•za ['plɑːzə] *n.* open area in a town.

plea [pliː] *n.* (a) answer to a charge in court; **p. bargaining** = arrangement where an accused person pleads guilty to some charges so as to be let off others. (b) (*formal*) request. (c) excuse.

plead [pliːd] *v.* (a) to answer a charge in a law court. (b) to give as an excuse. (c) to **p. with s.o.** = to try to change s.o.'s mind by asking again and again.

pleas•ant ['pleznt] *adj.* (-er, -est) agreeable/which pleases. **pleas•ant•ly,** *adv.* in a pleasant way. **pleas•ant•ry,** *n.* joke; pleasant remark.

please [pliːz] *v.* (a) to make (s.o.) happy/satisfied; **p. yourself** = do as you like. (b) *polite expression after an order or request, meaning* if you would like. **pleased,** *adj.* happy; satisified. **pleas•ing,** *adj.* which pleases. **pleas•ur•a•ble** ['pleʒərəbl] *adj.* pleasant. **pleas•ure** ['pleʒə] *n.* amusement/happiness.

pleat [pliːt] 1. *n.* vertical fold (in a skirt, etc.). 2. *v.* to iron vertical folds in.

pleb•i•scite ['plebɪsɪt] *n.* general vote by the inhabitants of a country on an important issue.

ple•be•ian [pliːˈbiːən] 1. *n.* a member of the common people; ordinary person. 2. *adj.* common/ordinary; of the working class. **plebs,** *n. pl. inf.* the common people.

plec•trum ['plektrəm] *n.* small stick for plucking the strings of a guitar, etc.

pledge [pledʒ] 1. *n.* (a) object given to the lender when borrowing money, and which will be returned to the borrower when the money is paid back. (b) promise. 2. *v.* (a) to give (sth) as a pledge when borrowing money. (b) to promise.

ple•na•ry ['pliːnərɪ] *adj.* complete; **p. session** = session of a conference where all the delegates meet together.

plen•i•po•ten•ti•ar•y [plenɪpəˈtenʃərɪ] *adj. & n.* (person) who has full powers to act on behalf of his country.

plen•te•ous ['plentɪəs] *adj.* (*formal*) more than enough.

plen•ty ['plentɪ] *n.* large quantity. **plen•ti•ful,** *adj.* abundant; in large quantities.

ple•num ['pliːnəm] *n.* general meeting.

ple•o•nasm ['plɪənæzəm] *n.* use of more words than necessary.

ple•o•nas•tic [plɪəˈnæstɪk] *adj.* (expression) where some words are superfluous.

pleth•o•ra ['pleθərə] *n.* (*formal*) too many (of).

pleu•ra ['plʊərə] *n.* membrane covering the lungs. **pleu•ri•sy,** *n.* disease of the membrane covering the lungs.

plex•us ['pleksəs] *n.* network of nerves.

pli•a•ble ['plaɪəbl], **pli•ant** ['plaɪənt] *adj.* which can be bent easily; (person) who can be easily persuaded. **pli•a•bil•i•ty, pliancy,** *n.* being pliable/pliant.

pli•ers ['plaɪəz] *n. pl.* **(pair of) p.** = tool shaped like scissors for pinching, twisting or cutting wire.

plight [plaɪt] 1. *n.* bad state. 2. *v.* (*formal*) to promise.

Plim•soll line ['plɪmsɒllaɪn] *n.* line along the side of a ship which shows the level of the water when the ship is loaded.

plinth [plɪnθ] *n.* pedestal on which a statue stands.

plod [plɒd] *v.* (**plodded**) (a) to walk heavily. (b) to work steadily. **plod•der,** *n.* person who works steadily but rather slowly.

plop [plɒp] 1. *n.* noise made by a stone falling into water. 2. *v.* (**plopped**) to make a noise like a stone falling into water.

plot [plɒt] 1. *n.* (a) small area of land for building/for growing vegetables, etc. (b) basic story of a book/play/motion picture. (c) wicked plan. 2. *v.* (**plotted**) (a) to mark on a map; to draw a graph. (b) to draw up a wicked plan. **plot•ter,** *n.* person who plots.

plough [plaʊ] *n. & v. Brit. see* **plow.**

plov•er ['plʌvə] *n.* type of wading bird (found in fields and moors).

plow, *Brit.* **plough** [plaʊ] 1. *n.* (a) farm machine for turning over soil. (b) **snow p.** = machine like a tractor with a large blade in front, used for clearing snow from streets, etc. 2. *v.* (a) to turn over the soil. (b) to work slowly. **plow back,** *v.* to invest (profits) back in a business. **plow•man,** *n.* (*pl.* -men) farm worker who drives a plow. **plow•share,** *n.* blade of a plow.

ploy [plɔɪ] *n.* clever trick.

pluck [plʌk] 1. *n.* courage. 2. *v.* (a) to pull out feathers or eyebrows. (b) to pick (flowers, etc.). (c) to pull and release the strings of a guitar to make a sound; **to p. up one's courage** = to get ready to face a danger. **pluck•i•ly,** *adv.* in a plucky way. **pluck•y,** *adj.* (-ier, -iest) brave.

plug [plʌg] 1. *n.* (a) disk which covers a hole, esp. the hole for waste water in a bath/sink, etc. (b) device with pins which go into the holes in an electric socket, and allow the current to pass through; (*in a car*) **spark p.** = device which passes electric sparks to ignite the fuel mixture. (c) *inf.* piece of publicity. (d) piece of tobacco which you chew. 2. *v.* (**plugged**) (a) to block up (a hole). (b) *inf.* to publicize. (c) *inf.* to shoot. **plug a•way**, *v. inf.* to work hard (**at**). **plug in**, *v.* to push an electric plug into a socket.

plum [plʌm] *n.* (a) gold, red or purple fruit with a smooth skin and a large stone; tree which bears this fruit; **p. pudding** = rich boiled fruit pudding, usu. eaten at Christmas. (b) deep purple color.

plum•age ['pluːmɪdʒ] *n.* feathers on a bird.

plumb [plʌm] 1. *adj.* straight; vertical. 2. *n.* lead weight for testing if sth is straight. 3. *v.* (a) to measure (the depth of water) by using a plumb line. (b) to understand or solve sth. (c) to fix the plumbing in (a house). 4. *adv.* (a) exactly (in the middle). (b) *inf.* completely. **plumb•er**, *n.* person who installs and repairs water pipes, etc. **plumb•ing**, *n.* system of water pipes in a house. **plumb line**, *n.* rope with a weight on the end, dropped over the side from a ship to find how deep the water is or held beside a wall to see if it is vertical.

plume [pluːm] *n.* tall feather (worn in a hat, etc.); tall column of smoke. **plumed**, *adj.* with a plume.

plum•met ['plʌmɪt] *v.* to fall sharply.

plump [plʌmp] 1. *adj.* (**-er, -est**) fat and tender; round fat (person). 2. *v.* (a) to **p. up** = to shake (squashed cushions) until they are fat. (b) to throw or put down with force. **plump•ness**, *n.* fatness.

plun•der ['plʌndə] 1. *n.* booty/goods seized, esp. in war. 2. *v.* to seize goods by force.

plunge [plʌndʒ] 1. *n.* dive; to **take the p.** = suddenly decide to do sth. 2. *v.* to dive deeply; to throw yourself into. **plung•er**, *n.* (a) device which goes up and down in a cylinder. (b) handle with a soft rubber head, for clearing blocked pipes by suction.

plu•per•fect [pluːˈpɜːfɪkt] *adj. & n.* (tense) showing sth which took place before a time in the past.

plu•ral ['plʊərəl] *adj. & n.* (*in grammar*) form of a word showing more than one. **plu•ral•ism**, *n.* system in a country or society where groups which have different ethnic, cultural, religious, etc. backgrounds are allowed to exist. **plu•ral•i•ty** [plʊəˈrælɪtɪ] *n.* majority.

plus [plʌs] 1. *prep.* in addition to. 2. *adj. & n.* (a) sign (+) meaning more than. (b) *inf.* favorable

sign. **plus-fours**, *n. pl.* baggy golfing trousers, attached at the calf.

plush [plʌʃ] 1. *n.* soft-pile cloth for furnishings. 2. *adj.* (**-er, -est**) *inf.* luxurious.

plu•to•crat ['pluːtəkræt] *n.* person who is very rich and powerful. **plu•toc•ra•cy** [pluːˈtɒkrəsɪ] *n.* government by the very rich.

plu•to•ni•um [pluːˈtəʊnɪəm] *n.* (*element:* Pu) radioactive substance, used to produce nuclear power.

ply [plaɪ] 1. *n.* (a) thickness of wood in plywood. (b) strand of wool. 2. *v.* (a) to go backward and forward. (b) **to p. s.o. with** = to force s.o. to eat/drink sth. **ply•wood**, *n.* sheet made of several thin sheets of wood stuck together.

p.m. [piːˈem] *adv.* in the afternoon/after midday.

pneu•mat•ic [njuːˈmætɪk] *adj.* driven by compressed air. **pneu•mat•i•cal•ly**, *adv.* using compressed air.

pneu•mo•nia [njuːˈməʊnɪə] *n.* illness caused by inflammation of the lungs.

PO ['piːˈəʊ] *n.* post office.

poach [pəʊtʃ] *v.* (a) to cook (eggs without their shells/fish, etc.) in gently boiling water. (b) to catch game illegally. **poach•er**, *n.* person who catches game illegally.

pock•et ['pɒkɪt] 1. *n.* (a) small bag attached to the inside of a coat/trousers, etc., for holding money/keys, etc.; **p. dictionary** = small dictionary which you can keep in your pocket; **p. money** = money given each week to a child to spend as he pleases. (b) **to be in p.** = to have made a profit; **to be out of p.** = to have lost money. (c) hole with a small bag at each corner and side of a billiard table. (d) small patch/small group in a certain place. 2. *v.* (a) to put in your pocket. (b) to send (a billiard ball) into a pocket. **pock•et•book**, *n.* woman's purse. **pock•et•ful**, *n.* amount contained in a pocket.

pock•marked ['pɒkmɑːkt] *adj.* covered with round scars.

pod [pɒd] *n.* long case in which peas/beans, etc., are formed.

podg•y ['pɒdʒɪ] *adj. inf.* (**-ier, -iest**) fat.

po•di•um ['pəʊdɪəm] *n.* raised platform (for winning sportsmen/orchestral conductors, etc., to stand on).

po•em ['pəʊɪm] *n.* piece of writing, in a particular rhythm, often with lines of a regular length which rhyme. **po•et, poetess,** *n.* person who writes poems. **po•et•ic(al)** [pəʊ-

---

æ back, aː farm, ɒ top, aɪ pipe, aʊ how, aɪə fire, aʊə flower, ɔː bought, ɔɪ toy, e fed, eəhair, eɪ take, ə afraid, əʊ boat, əʊə lower, ɜː word, iː heap, ɪ hit, ɪə hear, uː school, ʊ book, ʌ but, b back, d dog, ð then, dʒ just, f fog, g go, h hand, j yes, k catch, l last, m mix, n nut, ŋ sing, p penny, r round, s some, ʃ short, t too, tʃ chop, θ thing, v voice, w was, z zoo, ʒ treasure

'etɪk(l)] *adj.* referring to poetry;
imaginative/rhythmic (as in a poem).
po•et•i•cal•ly, *adv.* in a poetic way.
po•et•ry ['pəʊətrɪ] *n.* writing of poems;
poems taken as a type of literature.

po•grom ['pɒgrəm] *n.* official persecu-
tion/massacre (esp. of Jews).

poign•ant ['pɔɪnjənt] *adj.* moving/sad
(thought). **poign•an•cy,** *n.* sadness.
poign•ant•ly, *adv.* sadly/in a way which
moves you to sadness.

poin•set•ti•a [pɔɪn'setɪə] *n.* plant with large
green leaves, turning red at the top, used as a
Christmas decoration.

point [pɔɪnt] 1. *n.* (a) sharp end (of a pin, etc.).
(b) dot; **decimal p.** = dot used to indicate the
division between units and decimals (such as
3.25). (c) place/spot; **p. of no return** = place
where you can only go on and not go back. (d)
reason/purpose. (e) meaning/argument. (f)
specific time; **on the p. of** = just about to. (g)
headland. (h) mark in games or competitions;
mark on a scale. (i) (*in an engine*) electrical
contacts. 2. *v.* (a) to aim (a gun/your finger) **at**
s.o./sth. (b) to sharpen to a point. (c) to fill the
spaces in between bricks with mortar.
point-blank, *adj. & adv.* (a) at very close
range. (b) sharply/directly. **point•ed,** *adj.* (a)
with a sharp end. (b) obviously unfriendly (remark). **point•ed•ly,** *adv.* in an unfriendly
way. **point•er,** *n.* (a) dog which is trained to
point out game with its nose. (b) arrow/rod
which points. **point•less,** *adj.* meaningless.
point•less•ly, *adv.* meaninglessly. **point
out,** *v.* to indicate/to show. **point up,** *v.* to
make (sth) seem even more obvious.

poise [pɔɪz] 1. *n.* balance/graceful way of holding your head or of standing upright. 2. *v.* to
balance. **poised,** *adj.* ready (**to kill/for** action).

poi•son ['pɔɪzn] 1. *n.* substance which kills or
makes you ill if it is swallowed or if it gets into
the bloodstream. 2. *v.* to kill with poison.
poi•son•er, *n.* person who poisons.
poi•son•ous, *adj.* which can kill or harm
with poison.

poke [pəʊk] *v.* (a) to push with your finger/with
a stick. (b) **to p. about/around** = to search.
pok•er, *n.* (a) long metal rod for stirring up a
fire. (b) card game in which the players gamble. **pok•er face,** *n.* expression which shows
no emotion. **po•ker•faced,** *adj.* showing no
emotion.

pok•y ['pəʊkɪ] *adj.* (**-ier, -iest**) *inf.*
cramped/small (room).

po•lar ['pəʊlə] *adj.* referring to the
North/South Poles. **po•lar bear,** *n.* white
bear which lives in the Arctic. **po•lar•ize**

['pəʊləraɪz] *v.* to divide into two opposite
groups. **po•lar•i•za•tion** [pəʊləraɪ'zeɪʃn] *n.*
attraction around two opposite poles; division
into main groups.

pol•der ['pɒldə] *n.* land which has been re-
claimed from the sea.

pole [pəʊl] *n.* (a) one of the points at each end
of the earth's axis. (b) one of the two opposing
ends of a magnet; **they are poles apart** = they
are very different/they will never come to an
agreement. (c) long wooden/metal rod; **p.
vaulting** = sport where you have to jump over
a high bar with the help of a long pole. (d) **Pole**
= person from Poland. **pole•ax, poleaxe.** 1.
n. (*old*) large ax used in battle. 2. *v.* to knock
(s.o.) down. **pole star,** *n.* star which appears
to be near to the North Pole.

pole•cat ['pəʊlkæt] *n.* small wild flesh-eating
animal, like a weasel.

po•lem•ic [pə'lemɪk] *n.* argument/attack on
s.o.'s views. **po•lem•i•cal,** *adj.* controver-
sial/likely to start an argument.

po•lice [pə'liːs] 1. *n.* group of people who keep
law and order in a country; **p. force** = group of
police in a certain area; **p. station** = local office
of a police force. 2. *v.* to keep law and order in
(a town, etc.). **po•lice•man, police-
woman,** *n.* (*pl.* **-men, -women**) member of the
police. **po•lice of•fi•cer,** *n.* policeman/po-
licewoman. **po•lice state,** *n.* country which
is terrorized by the police.

pol•i•cy ['pɒlɪsɪ] *n.* (a) way of acting. (b) written agreement with an insurance company.

po•li•o•my•e•li•tis [pəʊlɪəʊmaɪə'laɪtɪs] *inf.*
po•li•o ['pəʊlɪəʊ] *n.* disease of the nerves in
the spinal cord, sometimes causing paralysis.

pol•ish ['pɒlɪʃ] 1. *n.* (*pl.* **-es**) (a) shiny surface.
(b) rubbing to make sth shiny. (c) substance
used to make things shiny. 2. *v.* to rub (sth) to
make it shiny. **pol•ished,** *adj.* (a) shiny. (b)
made perfect by practice. (c) polite (manners).
pol•ish•er, *n.* machine which polishes.
pol•ish off, *v.* to finish off (a job) quickly/to
eat (a meal) quickly. **pol•ish up,** *v. inf.* to improve.

Po•lish ['pəʊlɪʃ] 1. *adj.* referring to Poland. 2. *n.*
language spoken in Poland.

Pol•it•bu•ro [pɒ'lɪtbjuːrəʊ] *n.* central committee of a communist party.

po•lite [pə'laɪt] *adj.* (**-er, -est**) not rude; courte-
ous. **po•lite•ly,** *adv.* courteously; in a
well-mannered way. **po•lite•ness,** *n.* good
manners.

pol•i•tics ['pɒlɪtɪks] *n.* study of how to govern
a country. **pol•i•tic** ['pɒlɪtɪk] *adj.* wise/care-
ful. **po•lit•i•cal** [pə'lɪtɪkl] *adj.* referring to
government/party politics; **p. party** = organized group of people who believe in one par-

ticular method of ruling a country. **po•lit•i•cal•ly,** *adv.* as far as politics are concerned. **po•lit•i•cal•ly cor•rect,** *adj.* referring to language or actions chosen to avoid giving offense or showing prejudice, esp. concerning race and gender. **pol•i•ti•cian** [pɒlɪ'tɪʃn] *n.* person who works in politics, esp. a member of parliament.

pol•ka ['pɒlkə] *n.* type of lively dance; **p. dots** = small round dots (as a pattern on cloth).

poll [pəʊl] 1. *n.* (a) vote/voting. (b) number of votes. (c) **public opinion p.** = questioning of a sample group of people to guess at the views of the whole population on a question. 2. *v.* (a) to vote. (b) to get a number of votes in an election. (c) to cut the horns off (a cow). **poll•ing,** *n.* voting; elections; **p. booth** = small booth in which each voter writes his vote; **p. place** = place where you vote in an election. **poll tax,** *n.* tax which is levied equally on each person.

pol•lard ['pɒləd] *v.* to cut the branches of (a tree) back to the main trunk.

pol•len ['pɒln] *n.* usu. yellow powder in flowers which fertilizes them; **p. count** = number showing the amount of pollen in the air (which can cause hayfever). **pol•li•nate** ['pɒlɪneɪt] *v.* to fertilize with pollen. **pol•li•na•tion** [pɒlɪ'neɪʃn] *n.* fertilizing with pollen.

pol•lute [pə'luːt] *v.* to make dirty. **pol•lu•tant,** *n.* substance which pollutes. **pol•lut•er,** *n.* person or company which pollutes. **pol•lu•tion** [pə'luːʃn] *n.* making dirty.

po•lo ['pəʊləʊ] *n.* (a) ball game in which the two teams ride on ponies; **water p.** = ball game played by two teams in the water. (b) **p. shirt** = pullover sports shirt, usu. with short sleeves.

pol•ter•geist ['pɒltəgaɪst] *n.* ghost which knocks things over/makes loud sounds, etc.

poly- ['pɒlɪ] *prefix meaning* several.

pol•y•an•thus [pɒlɪ'ænθəs] *n.* common garden flower, like a primrose with a large flower head.

pol•y•chrome ['pɒlɪkrəʊm] *adj.* with several colors.

pol•y•es•ter [pɒlɪ'estə] *n.* type of synthetic fiber used esp. in clothing.

po•lyg•a•my [pə'lɪgəmɪ] *n.* custom of having several wives at the same time. **po•lyg•a•mist,** *n.* man with several wives. **po•lyg•a•mous,** *adj.* referring to polygamy.

pol•y•glot ['pɒlɪglɒt] *adj. & n.* (person) who speaks several languages; (dictionary, etc.) written in several languages.

pol•y•gon ['pɒlɪgən] *n.* geometrical figure with many sides. **po•lyg•o•nal** [pə'lɪgənl] *adj.* with many sides.

pol•y•mer ['pɒlɪmə] *n.* chemical compound whose molecule is made of several single similar molecules. **po•lym•er•i•za•tion,** *n.* act of polymerizing. **po•lym•er•ize,** *v.* to make/to become a polymer.

pol•yp ['pɒlɪp] *n.* (a) small primitive water animal shaped like a tube. (b) growth inside the human body.

pol•y•sty•rene [pɒlɪ'staɪriːn] *n.* light plastic used as a heat insulator or as packing material.

pol•y•syl•la•ble ['pɒlɪsɪləbl] *n.* word with several syllables. **pol•y•syl•lab•ic** [pɒlɪsɪ'læbɪk] *adj.* (word) with several syllables.

pol•y•tech•nic [pɒlɪ'teknɪk] *n.* educational establishment giving degrees, esp. in technical subjects.

pol•y•the•ism [pɒlɪ'θiːɪzm] *n.* belief in the existence of many gods.

pol•y•thene ['pɒlɪθiːn] *n.* type of almost transparent plastic used in thin sheets.

pol•y•un•sat•u•rat•ed [pɒlɪʌn'sætjʊreɪtɪd] *adj.* (fat) which does not form cholesterol in the blood.

pol•y•u•re•thane [pɒlɪ'jʊərɪθeɪn] *n.* type of plastic used in paints.

po•man•der [pə'mændə] *n.* (box containing) dried scented herbs; **p. ball** = dried orange with cloves stuck into it.

pome•gran•ate ['pɒmɪgrænɪt] *n.* tropical fruit with red flesh and many seeds.

pom•mel ['pɒml] *n.* high front part of a saddle.

pomp [pɒmp] *n.* splendid ceremony. **pom•pos•i•ty** [pɒm'pɒsɪtɪ] *n.* being pompous. **pomp•ous** ['pɒmpəs] *adj.* very solemn/too dignified.

pom•pom ['pɒmpɒm] *n.* small tufted ball of wool worn as an ornament on a hat, etc.

pon•cho ['pɒnʃəʊ] *n.* (*pl.* **-os**) cloak made of a single large piece of material, with a hole in the center for your head.

pond [pɒnd] *n.* small lake.

pon•der ['pɒndə] *v.* to think deeply. **pon•der•ous,** *adj.* very heavy and slow-moving. **pon•der•ous•ly,** *adv.* in a ponderous way.

æ back, ɑː farm, ɒ top, aɪ pipe, aʊ how, aɪə fire, aʊə flower, ɔː bought, ɔɪ toy, e fed, eəhair, eɪ take, ə afraid, əʊ boat, əʊə lower, vː word, iː heap, ɪ hit, ɪə hear, uː school, ʊ book, ʌ but, b back, d dog, ð then, dʒ just, f fog, g go, h hand, j yes, k catch, l last, m mix, n nut, ŋ sing, p penny, r round, s some, ʃ short, t too, tʃ chop, θ thing, v voice, w was, z zoo, ʒ treasure

pon•tiff ['pɒntɪf] *n.* the Pope. **pon•tif•i•cal** [pɒn'tɪfɪkl] *adj.* referring to the Pope. **pon•tif•i•cate** [pɒn'tɪfɪkeɪt] *v.* to speak/to write in a pompous way.

pon•toon [pɒn'tuːn] *n.* boat used to support a floating temporary bridge; **p. bridge** = one built on pontoons.

po•ny ['pəʊnɪ] *n.* small horse. **pony tail,** *n.* hairstyle where the hair is tied at the back and falls loosely.

poo•dle ['puːdl] *n.* type of curly-haired dog, usu. clipped.

poof [puːf] *n. Sl. (rude)* homosexual.

pooh-pooh [puː'puː] *v. inf.* to ridicule (an idea).

pool [puːl] **1.** *n.* (a) small lake. (b) area of water or other liquid. (c) **swimming p.** = enclosed tank of water for swimming. (d) common supply of money/food, etc., for a group of people. (e) group where people share facilities; **car p.** = arrangement where several people share cars; **typing p.** = group of typists working for several departments. (f) (*in sports*) system of gambling where you have to forecast the results of a game or match. (g) game similar to billiards. **2.** *v.* to group (resources) together. **pool•room,** *n.* public place where you can play pool.

poop [puːp] *n.* high raised stern of a ship.

poor ['pʊə, pɔː] *adj.* (**-er, -est**) (a) having little or no money; **p. in** = with very little (of sth). (b) not very good. **poor•ly. 1.** *adv.* (a) in quite a bad way. (b) without money. **2.** *adj.* ill. **poor•ness,** *n.* bad quality.

pop [pɒp] **1.** *n.* (a) noise like a cork coming out of a bottle. (b) *inf.* father. (c) *inf.* popular song. (d) *inf.* nonalcoholic sweet drink. **2.** *v.* (**popped**) (a) to make a pop. (b) *inf.* to go quickly. (c) to put quickly. (d) to ask (a question) quickly. **3.** *adj. inf.* popular. **pop•corn,** *n.* sweet corn which has been heated until it bursts. **pop•gun,** *n.* toy gun which makes a pop.

Pope [pəʊp] *n.* the head of the Roman Catholic Church.

pop•lar ['pɒplə] *n.* common tall and slender tree.

pop•lin ['pɒplɪn] *n.* strong cotton cloth used for making shirts.

pop•py ['pɒpɪ] *n.* common flower, red when wild.

pop•u•lace ['pɒpjʊləs] *n.* ordinary people.

pop•u•lar ['pɒpjʊlə] *adj.* (a) referring to the ordinary people. (b) liked by a lot of people. **pop•u•lar•i•ty** [pɒpjʊ'lærɪtɪ] *n.* being popular. **pop•u•lar•i•za•tion** [pɒpjʊlərəɪ'zeɪʃn] *n.* act of popularizing. **pop•u•lar•ize** ['pɒpjʊləraɪz] *v.* to make (sth) under-

stood/liked by a lot of people. **pop•u•lar•ly,** *adv.* generally; by most people.

pop•u•late ['pɒpjʊleɪt] *v.* to put people to live in (a place). **pop•u•la•tion** [pɒpjʊ'leɪʃn] *n.* number of people who live in a place. **pop•u•lous** ['pɒpjʊləs] *adj.* thickly populated.

por•bea•gle ['pɔːbiːgl] *n.* type of shark.

por•ce•lain ['pɔːslɪn] *n.* fine china.

porch [pɔːtʃ] *n.* (*pl.* **-es**) shelter over a doorway.

por•cine ['pɔːsaɪn] *adj.* like a pig.

por•cu•pine ['pɔːkjʊpaɪn] *n.* rodent with long sharp spikes covering its body.

pore [pɔː] **1.** *n.* small hole in the skin through which sweat passes. **2.** *v.* **to p. over** = to look at (a book, etc.) very closely.

pork [pɔːk] *n.* (*no pl.*) meat from a pig. **pork•er,** *n. inf.* pig.

por•nog•ra•phy [pɔː'nɒgrəfɪ] *n.* pornographic motion pictures/books/art. **porn** [pɔːn] *n. inf.* pornography; **hard/soft p.** = extremely indecent/less indecent pornographic material. **por•no•graph•ic** [pɔːnə'græfɪk] *adj.* (book, etc.) which deals with sex in an indecent way.

po•rous ['pɔːrəs] *adj.* (solid) which allows liquid to pass through. **po•ros•i•ty** [pɔː'rɒsɪtɪ] *n.* being porous.

por•phy•ry ['pɔːfɪrɪ] *n.* type of stone with crystals in it.

por•poise ['pɔːpəs] *n.* large sea mammal which tends to swim in groups.

por•ridge ['pɒrɪdʒ] *n.* (*no pl.*) oatmeal cooked in water.

port [pɔːt] *n.* (a) harbor. (b) town with a harbor. (c) left side (when looking forward on board a ship/aircraft). (d) strong sweet wine from Portugal. (e) opening in a ship's side for a gun. (f) opening in a computer for plugging in an attachment.

port•a•ble ['pɔːtəbl] **1.** *adj.* which can be carried. **2.** *n.* machine, such as a small computer, which can be carried.

por•tage ['pɔː'tɑːʒ] *n.* transporting a boat across country.

por•tal ['pɔːtl] *n.* imposing entrance.

port•cul•lis [pɔː'tkʌlɪs] *n.* (*pl.* **-es**) gate which was dropped to close the entrance to a medieval castle.

por•tend [pɔː'tend] *v.* (*formal*) to warn (that sth unpleasant is going to happen).

por•tent ['pɔːtənt] *n.* (*formal*) warning (that sth unpleasant is going to happen). **por•ten•tous** [pɔː'tentəs] *adj.* important/significant; warning that sth unpleasant is going to happen.

por•ter ['pɔːtə] *n.* (a) person who carries luggage for travelers. (b) doorkeeper (in a hotel).

(c) person who does general work in a restaurant, store, etc. **por•ter•age**, *n.* charge for carrying sth. **por•ter•house (steak)**, *n.* piece of best quality steak.

port•fo•li•o [pɔːt'fəʊlɪəʊ] *n.* (*pl.* **-os**) (a) large cardboard case for carrying paintings, etc. (b) collection of shares. (c) (*in government*) office of minister or cabinet member.

port•hole ['pɔːthəʊl] *n.* round window in the side of a ship.

por•ti•co ['pɔːtɪkəʊ] *n.* (*pl.* **-oes, -os**) roof supported by columns forming a porch in front of the entrance to a building.

por•tion ['pɔːʃn] 1. *n.* (a) part. (b) serving of food. 2. *v.* **to p. out** = to share out.

port•ly ['pɔːtlɪ] *adj.* (**-ier, -iest**) rather fat.

port•man•teau [pɔːt'mæntəʊ] *n.* trunk for carrying clothes.

por•trait ['pɔːtreɪt] *n.* painting/photograph of a person. **por•trai•ture** ['pɔːtrətʃə] *n.* art of painting portraits. **por•tray** [pɔː'treɪ] *v.* to paint/to describe (a scene or a person). **por•tray•al**, *n.* painting; description of a scene or person.

Por•tu•guese [pɔːtju'giːz] 1. *adj.* referring to Portugal; **P. man-of-war** = type of very large jelly fish. 2. *n.* (a) person from Portugal. (b) language spoken in Portugal.

pose [pəʊz] 1. *n.* (a) way of standing/sitting. (b) way of behaving which is just a pretense. 2. *v.* (a) **to p. for s.o.** = to stand/to sit still while s.o. paints/photographs you. (b) to pretend to be. (c) to set (a problem); to put (a question). **pos•er**, *n. inf.* difficult question. **po•seur** [pəʊ'zɜː] *n.* person who behaves in a false way.

posh [pɒʃ] *adj.* (**-er, -est**) inf. very smart.

po•si•tion [pə'zɪʃn] 1. *n.* (a) way of standing/sitting. (b) place. (c) job. 2. *v.* to place.

pos•i•tive ['pɒzɪtɪv] 1. *adj.* (a) meaning yes. (b) certain; sure/convinced. (c) registering the existence of sth. (d) plus/more than zero. 2. *n.* (a) photograph printed from a negative, where the light and dark appear as they are in nature. (b) one of the terminals in a battery. **pos•i•tive•ly**, *adv.* absolutely. **pos•i•tron**, *n.* positive electron.

pos•se ['pɒsɪ] *n.* group of armed men/police.

pos•sess [pə'zes] *v.* (a) to own. (b) to occupy s.o.'s mind; **what posssessed him?** = why did he do it? **pos•ses•sion** [pə'zeʃn] *n.* (a) ownership. (b) thing you own. **pos•ses•sive**, *adj.* (a) (*in grammar*) (word) which indicates possession. (b) (person) who treats another person as if he owns him. **pos•ses•sive•ly**, *adv.* in a possessive way. **pos•ses•sor**, *n.* owner.

pos•si•ble ['pɒsɪbl] *adj.* (a) which can happen. (b) likely. **pos•si•bil•i•ty** [pɒsɪ'bɪlɪtɪ] *n.* (a) chance; being likely. (b) **the plan has possibilities** = may well work. **pos•si•bly**, *adv.* (a) which may happen. (b) perhaps.

pos•sum ['pɒsəm] *n. inf.* **to play p.** = to pretend to sleep/to be dead so as to trick an opponent.

post [pəʊst] 1. *n.* (a) wooden/concrete stake fixed in the ground. (b) place where a sentry is on duty. (c) job/position. (d) small settlement far from civilization. (e) (*esp. Brit.*) mail; letters, etc., sent by mail. 2. *v.* (a) to send (s.o.) on duty. (b) (*esp. Brit.*) to send (a letter, etc.) by mail; **to keep s.o. posted** = to keep s.o. informed. (c) to stick up (a notice). **post•age**, *n.* payment for sending a letter by mail; **p. stamp** = piece of paper which you buy and stick on a letter, etc., to pay for it to be sent to its destination. **post•al**, *adj.* referring to the post office. **post•card**, *n.* card (sometimes with a picture) which you send through the mail. **post•er**, *n.* large notice stuck up on a wall, etc.; large picture/advertisement stuck on a wall. **post•haste**, *adv.* very fast. **post•man**, *n.* (*pl.* **-men**) person who delivers letters to houses. **post•mark**. 1. *n.* mark stamped on a letter to show when it was mailed. 2. *v.* to stamp (a letter) with a postmark. **post•mas•ter, postmistress**, *n.* (a) person in charge of a post office. (b) person in charge of electronic mail at a site. **post of•fice**, *n.* (a) building where mail is received/stamps sold, etc. (b) government organization which runs the postal services. **post•paid**, *adj.* (reply) with postage paid by the sender.

post- [pəʊst] *prefix meaning* later than/after. **post•date**, *v.* to put a date on (a check) which is later than the day on which you actually write it. **post•grad•u•ate**, *n.* person who has a first degree from a college or university and who is studying for a further degree. **post•hu•mous** ['pɒstjuməs] *adj.* after death. **post•hu•mous•ly**, *adv.* after death. **post•mod•ern**, *adj.* (architecture/literature, etc.) rejecting modernism, esp. by mixing styles or by drawing attention to generic conventions. **post mor•tem** [pəʊst'mɔːtəm] *adj. & n.* (examination) to find out the cause of death. **post•na•tal**, *adj.* referring to the time just after the birth of a child. **post•pone**

[pəs'pəʊn] v. to put off until later. **post•pone•ment,** n. putting off until later. **post•pran•di•al,** adj. after dinner. **post•script,** n. additional note at the end of a letter. **post•vi•ral syn•drome.** n. see **chronic fatigue syndrome. post•war,** adj. referring to the period after the war.

pos•te•ri•or [pɒ'stɪərɪə] n. behind/buttocks. **pos•ter•i•ty** [pɒ'sterɪtɪ] n. generations which will follow.

pos•tern ['pɒstən] n. (old) back door or gate.

pos•tu•late ['pɒstjʊleɪt] 1. n. basis upon which sth is postulated. 2. v. to suppose (that sth is true). **pos•tu•lant,** n. person who is a candidate to join a religious order.

pos•ture ['pɒstʃə] 1. n. way of sitting/standing, etc. 2. v. to take up a particular position for effect.

po•sy ['pəʊzɪ] 1. n. small bunch of flowers.

pot [pɒt] 1. n. (a) container made of glass or clay. (b) inf. **to go to p.** = to become ruined/useless. (c) Sl. marijuana. 2. v. (**potted**) to put in a pot. **pot•bel•ly,** n. inf. fat stomach. **pot•boil•er,** n. worthless novel written rapidly for money. **potbound,** adj. (of plant) with roots too large for the pot. **pot•hole,** n. (a) hole in rock worn away by water. (b) hole in a road surface. **pot•luck,** n. **to take p.** = to take whatever comes, with no possibility of choice. **pot•sherd,** n. piece of broken pot. **pot•shot,** n. inf. **to take a p. at s.o.** = to try to shoot s.o. without aiming properly. **pot•ted,** adj. preserved in a pot. **pot•ting shed,** n. shed in a garden where you put plants in pots.

po•ta•ble ['pɒtəbl] adj. which can be drunk safely.

pot•ash ['pɒtæʃ] n. potassium salts.

po•tas•si•um [pə'tæsɪəm] n. (element: K) light white metallic substance.

po•ta•to [pə'teɪtəʊ] n. (pl. -oes) common vegetable, formed under the soil; **sweet p.** = yam.

po•teen [pɒ'tiːn] n. illegal distilled whiskey.

po•ten•cy ['pəʊtənsɪ] n. strength. **po•tent,** adj. strong.

po•ten•tate ['pəʊtənteɪt] n. Eastern ruler.

po•ten•tial [pə'tenʃl] 1. adj. possible. 2. n. (a) possibility of developing into sth valuable. (b) (in physics) electrical property which governs the flow of an electric charge. **po•ten•ti•al•i•ty,** n. being potential. **po•ten•tial•ly,** adv. possibly. **po•ten•ti•om•e•ter,** n. instrument for measuring differences in electrical potential.

po•tion ['pəʊʃn] n. liquid mixture to make you sleep, etc.

pot•pour•ri [pəʊpuː'riː] n. (a) dried flowers/herbs kept in a bowl to scent a room. (b) general mixture of bits and pieces.

pot•ter ['pɒtə] 1. n. person who makes pots out of clay. 2. v. (esp. Brit.) **to p. about** = to putter around. **pot•ter•y,** n. (a) potter's workshop. (b) pots; articles made of clay, earthenware.

pot•ty ['pɒtɪ] inf. 1. n. child's toilet. 2. adj. (-ier, -iest) (esp. Brit.) mad.

pouch [paʊtʃ] n. (pl. -es) (a) small bag for carrying coins/ammunition, etc. (b) bag in the skin in front of some marsupials where the young live and grow for some time after birth.

poul•tice ['pəʊltɪs] 1. n. hot wet dressing put on a wound. 2. v. to dress (a wound) with a poultice.

poul•try ['pəʊltrɪ] n. (no pl.) common farm birds such as ducks/hens, reared for eggs or to be eaten.

pounce [paʊns] 1. n. act of pouncing. 2. v. to jump (**on** sth).

pound [paʊnd] 1. n. (a) measure of weight (= approx. 16 ounces or 0.45 kilogram). (b) standard unit of money in Great Britain and several other countries. (c) place where stray animals or illegally-parked cars are put. 2. v. (a) to smash into little pieces; to hit hard. (b) to run heavily. (c) (of heart) to beat fast. **pound•age** ['paʊndɪdʒ] n. rate charged for each pound.

pour [pɔː] v. (a) to flow out/down. (b) to transfer liquid from one container to another.

pout [paʊt] 1. n. (a) sulky expression where the lips stick out. (b) type of fish. 2. v. to make a sulky expression with the lips.

pov•er•ty ['pɒvətɪ] n. being poor; **a p. of** = a lack of.

pow•der ['paʊdə] 1. n. very fine dry grains (like flour); (**face**) **p.** = scented flourlike substance for putting on the face; **p. room** = women's toilet. 2. v. to put powder on. **pow•dered,** adj. covered with powder. **pow•der•y,** adj. fine/like powder.

pow•er ['paʊə] n. (a) strength. (b) ability. (c) driving force; **p. pack** = portable source of electricity. (d) (in mathematics) number of times a number is multiplied by itself. (e) (in physics) strength of a lens. (f) (also **power base**) political/social strength (of a person/a group). (g) political control. **pow•er•boat,** n. boat which has a powerful engine, used for racing. **power down,** v. to shut down (a computer) in stages, finishing by switching off the power. **power drill,** n. powerful electric drill. **pow•ered,** adj. driven/worked. **pow•er•ful,** adj. very strong. **pow•er•less,** adj. unable to do anything. **power sta•tion, pow•er plant,** n. works where electricity is produced. **pow•er steer•ing,** n. steering (in a car) which is powered by the engine. **power up,** *v.* to switch on the power to sth, esp. a computer.

pow•wow ['pauwau] *n. inf.* meeting to discuss some problem.

PR [pi:'ɑ:] *n.* public relations; proportional representation.

prac•ti•ca•ble ['præktɪkəbl] *adj.* which can be done/which can be put into practice. **prac•ti•ca•bil•i•ty** [præktɪkə'bɪlɪtɪ] *n.* ability to be put into practice.

prac•ti•cal ['præktɪkl] *adj.* interested in practice/action rather than ideas; referring to practice rather than theory; **p. joke** = trick played on s.o. to make other people laugh. **prac•ti•cal•i•ty,** *n.* way in which sth works in practice. **prac•ti•cal•ly,** *adv.* (a) in practice. (b) almost.

prac•tice ['præktɪs] 1. *n.* (a) actual application; **to put sth into p.** = to apply sth/to use sth. (b) habit. (c) repeated exercise; **out of p.** = not capable because of lack of exercise. (d) business of a doctor/dentist/lawyer. (e) **practices** = ways of doing things. 2. *v.* (a) to put sth into practice. (b) to do repeated exercises. (c) to carry on a job as a doctor or lawyer. **prac•ticed,** *adj.* skilled.

prac•ti•tion•er [præk'tɪʃənə] *n.* doctor; **general p.** = doctor who treats all patients/all illnesses.

prag•mat•ic [præg'mætɪk] *adj.* dealing with fact/practical matters, not concerned with theory. **prag•mat•i•cal•ly,** *adv.* in a pragmatic way. **prag•ma•tism** ['prægmətɪzəm] *n.* pragmatic approach (to a problem). **prag•ma•tist,** *n.* person who is pragmatic.

prai•rie ['preərɪ] *n.* grass-covered plain in North America; **p. dog** = small North American mammal, living in burrows; **p. oyster** = mixture of raw egg, tomato juice and spices, taken to cure a hangover.

praise [preɪz] 1. *n.* admiration/expression of approval. 2. *v.* to express strong approval of (s.o./sth). **praise•wor•thy,** *adj.* which should be praised.

pra•line ['prɑ:li:n] *n.* candy made of crushed nuts and honey.

pram [præm] *n. Brit. inf.* baby carriage.

prance [prɑ:ns] *v.* to jump about/to move lightly.

prank [præŋk] *n.* trick.

prat•tle ['prætl] 1. *n.* chatter. 2. *v.* to chatter in a childish way.

prawn [prɔ:n] *n.* shellfish like a large shrimp.

prax•is ['præksɪs] *n.* practice.

pray [preɪ] *v.* to speak to God; to ask God for sth; *(formal)* **p. be seated** = please sit down. **prayer,** *n.* act of speaking to God; request.

pre- [prɪ] *prefix meaning* before.

preach [pri:tʃ] *v.* (a) to give a sermon in church. (b) to recommend/to advise; to give moral advice. **preach•er,** *n.* person who gives a sermon.

pre•am•ble [pri:'æmbl] *n.* introduction/remarks at the beginning (of a speech/treaty, etc.).

pre•ar•range [pri:ə'reɪndʒ] *v.* to arrange in advance.

pre•car•i•ous [prɪ'keərɪəs] *adj.* likely to fall; uncertain. **pre•car•i•ous•ly,** *adv.* unsafely.

pre•cau•tion [prɪ'kɔ:ʃn] *n.* care taken in advance (to avoid sth unpleasant). **pre•cau•tion•ar•y,** *adj.* (measure) taken to avoid sth unpleasant.

pre•cede [prɪ'si:d] *v.* to take place before (sth). **prec•e•dence** ['presɪdəns] *n.* **to take p. over** = to go before/to be more important than. **prec•e•dent** ['presɪdənt] *n.* thing which has happened before, and which can be a guide as to what should be done. **pre•ced•ing** [prɪ'si:dɪŋ] *adj.* which comes before.

pre•cen•tor [prɪ'sentɔ:] *n.* person in charge of leading a church choir or the congregation in singing.

pre•cept ['pri:sept] *n.* command; guiding rule.

pre•cinct ['pri:sɪŋkt] *n.* area surrounded by a wall; administrative district of a town or city.

pre•cious ['preʃəs] *adj.* worth a lot of money; of great value.

prec•i•pice ['presɪpɪs] *n.* high cliff (not usu. near the sea). **pre•cip•i•tous** [prɪ'sɪpɪtəs] *adj.* very steep.

pre•cip•i•tate 1. *n.* [prɪ'sɪpɪtət] chemical substance which settles at the bottom of a liquid. 2. *v.* [prɪ'sɪpɪteɪt] (a) to make sth happen suddenly. (b) to settle at the bottom of a liquid. 3. *adj.* [prɪ'sɪpɪtət] rushed/hurried. **pre•cip•i•tate•ly,** *adv.* in a rushed way. **pre•cip•i•ta•tion** [prɪsɪpɪ'teɪʃn] *n.* (a) *(formal)* great hurry. (b) quantity of rain/snow, etc., which falls on a certain place.

pré•cis ['preɪsɪ] 1. *n.* (*pl.* **précis** ['preɪsi:z]) summary of the main points of a text. 2. *v.* to summarize.

pre•cise [prɪ'saɪs] *adj.* (a) exact. (b) careful. **pre•cise•ly,** *adv.* (a) exactly. (b) in a careful way. **pre•ci•sion** [prɪ'sɪʒn] *n.* accuracy.

æ back, ɑ: farm, ɒ: top, aɪ pipe, au how, aiə fire, auə flower, ɔ: bought, ɔɪ toy, e fed, eəhair, eɪ take, ə afraid, əu boat, əuə lower, v: word, i: heap, ɪ hit, ɪə hear, u: school, u book, ʌ but, b back, d dog, ð then, dʒ just, f fog, g go, h hand, j yes, k catch, l last, m mix, n nut, ŋ sing, p penny, r round, s some, ʃ short, t too, tʃ chop, θ thing, v voice, w was, z zoo, ʒ treasure

pre•clude [prɪˈkluːd] *v.* to prevent.

pre•co•cious [prɪˈkəʊʃəs] *adj.* (child) who is surprisingly advanced for his/her age. **pre•co•cious•ly,** *adv.* in a precocious way. **pre•co•cious•ness, precocity** [prɪˈkɒsɪtɪ] *n.* being precocious.

pre•con•ceive [priːkənˈsiːv] *v.* to have an idea or belief from the beginning/before sth starts. **pre•con•cep•tion** [priːkənˈsepʃn] *n.* preconceived idea.

pre•con•di•tion [priːkənˈdɪʃn] *n.* condition which is set in advance.

pre•cur•sor [prɪˈkɜːsə] *n.* thing which leads to an invention/person who goes in advance. **pre•cur•so•ry,** *adj.* which is in advance.

pre•date [ˈpriːdeɪt] *v.* to come before in date.

pred•a•tor [ˈpredətə] *n.* animal which lives by eating other animals. **pred•a•to•ry,** *adj.* (animal) which eats other animals; (person) who lives off other people.

pre•de•cease [priːdɪˈsiːs] *v.* (*formal*) to die before (s.o.). **pred•e•ces•sor** [ˈpriːdɪsesə] *n.* person who has held the same job, etc., before you.

pre•des•tine [priːˈdestɪn] *v.* to decide the fate of (s.o.) in advance. **pre•des•ti•na•tion** [priːdestɪˈneɪʃn] *n.* being predestined.

pre•de•ter•mine [priːdɪˈtɜːmɪn] *v.* to decide in advance.

pre•dic•a•ment [prɪˈdɪkəmənt] *n.* troubles/difficult situation.

pred•i•cate 1. *n.* [ˈpredɪkət] (*in grammar*) statement about the subject. 2. *v.* [ˈpredɪkeɪt] (*formal*) to base a supposition on (sth).

pred•i•ca•tive [prɪˈdɪkətɪv] *adj.* (adjective, etc.) which makes a statement about a noun.

pre•dict [prɪˈdɪkt] *v.* to foretell/to tell in advance what will happen. **pre•dict•a•ble,** *adj.* which could be predicted. **pre•dict•a•bly,** *adv.* in a way which could have been predicted. **pre•dic•tion** [prɪˈdɪkʃn] *n.* foretelling.

pre•di•lec•tion [priːdɪˈlekʃn] *n.* liking/preference.

pre•dis•pose [priːdɪˈspəʊz] *v.* to make (s.o.) favor sth in advance. **pre•dis•po•si•tion** [priːdɪspəˈzɪʃn] *n.* being predisposed.

pre•dom•i•nate [prɪˈdɒmɪneɪt] *v.* to be bigger/stronger/more numerous. **pre•dom•i•nance,** *n.* being predominant. **pre•dom•i•nant** [prɪˈdɒmɪnənt] *adj.* most striking/obvious. **pre•dom•i•nant•ly,** *adv* in a predominant way.

pre•em•i•nent, pre-eminent [priːˈemɪnənt] *adj.* excellent/much better than everything else. **pre•em•i•nence, pre-eminence,** *n.* being preeminent.

pre•empt, pre-empt [priːˈempt] *v.* to get an advantage by doing sth before anyone else. **pre•emp•tion, pre-emption,** *n.* act of preempting. **pre•emp•tive, pre-emptive,** *adj.* which gains an advantage by acting before anyone else.

preen [priːn] *v.* (*of bird*) to smooth its feathers; **to p. yourself** = to smarten yourself up; **to p. yourself on sth** = to congratulate yourself.

pre•fab•ri•cat•ed [priːˈfæbrɪkeɪtɪd] *adj.* built in advance; (house) built out of pieces which are assembled on the site. **pre•fab** [ˈpriːfæb] *n. inf.* prefabricated house. **pre•fab•ri•ca•tion** [priːfæbrɪˈkeɪʃn] *n.* building in advance.

pref•ace [ˈprefəs] 1. *n.* piece written (usu. by the author) to introduce a book. 2. *v.* to say/to write sth as an introduction. **pref•a•to•ry** [ˈprefətrɪ] *adj.* which acts as a preface.

pre•fect [ˈpriːfekt] *n.* high official, as the administrative head of one of the departments of France.

pre•fer [prɪˈfɜː] *v.* (**preferred**) (a) **to p. sth to sth** = to like (to do) sth better than sth else. (b) (*formal*) to promote (s.o.). **pref•er•a•ble** [ˈprefrəbl] *adj.* which you would prefer. **pref•er•a•bly,** *adv.* if possible. **pref•er•ence** [ˈprefrəns] *n.* liking for one thing more than another. **pref•er•en•tial** [prefəˈrenʃl] *adj.* showing one thing is preferred to another. **pre•fer•ment** [prɪˈfɜːmənt] *n.* promotion to a more important post.

pre•fix [ˈpriːfɪks] 1. *n.* (*pl.* -es) part of a word put in front of another. 2. *v.* to put some word in front of another/to preface.

preg•nan•cy [ˈpregnənsɪ] *n.* state of being pregnant; **p. test** = test to see if a woman is pregnant. **preg•nant,** *adj.* carrying an unborn child; **p. pause** = pause while everyone waits for sth to happen/for s.o. to speak.

pre•hen•sile [priːˈhensaɪl] *adj.* which can grasp/hold on to sth.

pre•his•to•ry [priːˈhɪstərɪ] *n.* time before written history. **pre•his•to•ri•an** [priːhɪˈstɔːrɪən] *n.* person who specializes in the study of prehistory. **pre•his•tor•ic** [priːhɪˈstɒrɪk] *adj.* belonging to prehistory.

pre•judge [priːˈdʒʌdʒ] *v.* to judge (sth) without hearing all the facts.

prej•u•dice [ˈpredʒədɪs] 1. *n.* (usu. unjust) feeling against s.o.. 2. *v.* (a) to make (s.o.) unfriendly toward s.o./sth. (b) to harm. **prej•u•diced,** *adj.* unfairly biased (**against** s.o.). **prej•u•di•cial** [predʒuˈdɪʃl] *adj.* which might be damaging.

prel•ate [ˈprelət] *n.* person of high rank in a church.

pre•lim•i•nar•y [prɪˈlɪmɪnərɪ] *adj.* which

goes before. **pre•lim•i•nar•ies**, *n. pl.* things which have to be done before sth can take place.

prel•ude ['prelju:d] *n.* thing (esp. piece of music) which introduces sth more important; short piece of music on one theme.

pre•mar•i•tal [prɪ'mærɪtəl] *adj.* before marriage.

pre•ma•ture [premə'tjʊə] *adj.* which happens before the right time; (baby) born less than nine months after conception. **pre•ma•ture•ly**, *adv.* before the right time.

pre•med•i•tate [pri:'medɪteɪt] *v.* to think over/to plan in advance. **pre•med•i•ta•tion** [pri:medɪ'teɪʃn] *n.* planning in advance.

pre•mier ['premɪə] 1. *n.* prime minister. 2. *adj.* first/most important. **pre•mière** ['premɪeə] *n.* first performance of a motion picture/play, etc. **pre•mier•ship**, *n.* being prime minister; time when s.o. is prime minister.

prem•ise ['premɪs] *n.* (*pl.* **-es**) statement which is the basis for reasoning.

prem•is•es ['premɪsɪz] *n. pl.* building and land around it.

pre•mi•um ['pri:mɪəm] *n.* (a) annual amount paid for an insurance policy. (b) **at a p.** = scarce, and therefore valuable; **to put a p. on sth** = to show that sth is useful/valuable. (c) bonus.

pre•mo•lar [pri:'məʊlə] *n.* tooth between the canines and the molars.

pre•mo•ni•tion [premə'nɪʃn] *n.* feeling that sth is going to happen. **pre•mon•i•to•ry** [prɪ'mɒnɪtrɪ] *adj.* warning (sign).

pre•na•tal [pri:'neɪtl] *adj.* referring to the time before the birth of a child.

pre•oc•cu•pa•tion [pri:ɒkju'peɪʃn] *n.* only thinking about one thing. **pre•oc•cu•pied**, *adj.* thinking only about one thing; worried. **pre•oc•cu•py**, *v.* to make (s.o.) think about only one thing and worry about it.

prep [prep] *adj. inf.* (a) used in preparing for sth. (b) **p. school** = preparatory school.

pre•pare [prɪ'peə] *v.* to get ready. **prep•a•ra•tion** [prepə'reɪʃn] *n.* (a) getting ready. (b) substance which has been mixed. **pre•par•a•to•ry** [prɪ'pærətrɪ] *adj.* which prepares; **p. school** = private or parochial school that prepares students for college. **pre•pared**, *adj.* ready (to).

pre•pay ['pri:peɪ] *v.* (prepaid) to pay in advance. **pre•pay•ment**, *n.* paying in advance.

pre•pon•der•ate [prɪ'pɒndəreɪt] *v.* (*formal*) to be in a majority. **pre•pon•der•ance** [prɪ'pɒndərəns] *n.* large number. **pre•pon•der•ant**, *adj.* in a majority.

prep•o•si•tion [prepə'zɪʃn] *n.* word which is used with a noun/pronoun to show how it is linked to another word.

pre•pos•sess•ing [pri:pə'zesɪŋ] *adj.* pleasant.

pre•pos•ter•ous [prɪ'pɒstərəs] *adj.* silly/absurd.

pre•pro•grammed; preprogramed [pri:-'prəʊgræmd] *adj.* which has been programmed beforehand.

pre•req•ui•site [pri:'rekwɪzɪt] *n.* thing which you must have before you can do sth.

pre•rog•a•tive [prɪ'rɒgətɪv] *n.* privilege belonging to one person or group.

presby•o•pi•a [prezbɪ'əʊpɪə] *n.* gradual failing sight (in an old person).

pres•by•ter•y ['prezbɪtərɪ] *n.* (a) Roman Catholic priest's house. (b) court of a church made of ministers and important laymen. **Pres•by•te•ri•an** [prezbɪ'ti:ərɪən] *adj. & n.* (member) of a Protestant church, ruled by a group of laymen.

pre•scient ['presɪənt] *adj.* (*formal*) (person) who can tell what is likely to take place in the future. **pre•science**, *n.* being prescient.

pre•scribe [prɪ'skraɪb] *v.* to order (sth) to be done; to tell s.o. to use (sth). **pre•scrip•tion** [prɪ'skrɪpʃn] *n.* paper on which a doctor has written out instructions for the preparation and use of a medicine to be taken by the patient. **pre•scrip•tive**, *adj.* which prescribes.

pres•ence ['prezns] *n.* (a) being present. (b) **p. of mind** = sense/calmness; ability to act quickly. (c) impressive appearance/way of acting (on the stage).

pre•sent 1. *adj.* ['preznt] (a) being at the place/at the time. (b) being here now. (c) (*in grammar*) (tense) which describes what is happening now. 2. *n.* ['preznt] *n.* (a) at the time we are in now; **at p.** = now. (b) gift. 3. *v.* [prɪ'zent] (a) to give. (b) to put on (a play/show). (c) to introduce (s.o. into society/an artist to the audience). (d) **to p. oneself** = to arrive/to come. **pre•sent•a•ble** [prɪ'zentəbl] *adj.* (person) who is suitable to appear in company. **pres•en•ta•tion** [prezən'teɪʃn] *n.* act of giving. **pres•ent-day**, *adj.* modern. **pres•ent•ly**, *adv.* (a) soon. (b) now.

æ back, a: farm, ɒ: top, aɪ pipe, aʊ how, aie fire, aʊə flower, ɔ: bought, ɔɪ toy, e fed, eəhair, eɪ take, ə afraid, əʊ boat, əʊə lower, ɜ: word, i: heap, ɪ hit, ɪə hear, u: school, ʊ book, ʌ but, b back, d dog, ð then, dʒ just, f fog, g go, h hand, j yes, k catch, l last, m mix, n nut, ŋ sing, p penny, r round, s some, ʃ short, t too, tʃ chop, θ thing, v voice, w was, z zoo, ʒ treasure

pre•sen•ti•ment [prɪ'zentɪmənt] *n.* feeling that sth unpleasant will soon happen.

pre•serve [prɪ'zɜːv] 1. *n.* (a) place where game/fish, etc., are protected so that they can be killed for sport. (b) **preserves** = jam/pickles, etc. 2. *v.* (a) (*formal*) to keep/to protect. (b) to treat (food) so that it keeps for a long time. **pres•er•va•tion** [prezə'veɪʃn] *n.* protecting. **pres•erv•a•tive** [prɪ'zɜːvətɪv] *n.* substance used to make food keep/to stop food from going bad. **pre•serv•er,** *n.* person/thing that preserves; *see also* **life preserver.** **pre•serv•ing pan,** *n.* very large pan for making preserves.

pre•side [prɪ'zaɪd] *v.* to sit at the head of the table (at a meeting). **pres•i•den•cy** ['prezɪdnsɪ] *n.* job of president. **pres•i•dent** ['prezɪdənt] *n.* head of a republic; chief member of a club; head of a business firm. **pres•i•den•tial** [prezɪ'denʃl] *adj.* referring to a president. **pre•sid•i•um** [prɪ'sɪdɪəm] *n.* ruling committee (in a communist country).

press [pres] 1. *n.* (*pl.* **-es**) (a) machine which squeezes. (b) **printing p.** = machine for printing books/newspapers, etc. (c) newspapers and magazines taken as a whole. (d) crowd. 2. *v.* (a) to push down; to push against; to squeeze. (b) to iron the creases from (clothes). (c) to force (s.o.) to do sth. (d) **to p. on/forward** = to continue/to go ahead. **pressed,** *adj.* **I'm p. for time** = I haven't much time; **I'd be hard p. to do it** = I would find it difficult. **press con•fer•ence,** *n.* interview given by a famous person to several journalists. **press clip•ping,** *n.* piece cut out from a newspaper with an article which is relevant to s.o/sth. **press gang.** 1. *n.* (*old*) group of people who forced men to join the navy or army. 2. *v.* to force (s.o.) **into** doing sth. **press•ing.** 1. *adj.* urgent. 2. *n.* record/series of records. **pres•sure** ['preʃə] *n.* (a) act of squeezing/pushing down; **to put p. on s.o. to do sth** = to try to force s.o. to do sth. (b) force pushing down/moving/being heavy, etc.; **blood p.** = force with which the blood is driven through the body; **p. group** = group of people who try to influence the government, etc. (c) stress. **pres•sure cook•er,** *n.* type of saucepan with a tight-fitting lid, which cooks food rapidly under pressure. **pres•sur•i•za•tion** [preʃərər'zeɪʃn] *n.* keeping an aircraft cabin at a constant atmospheric pressure. **pres•sur•ize,** *v.* to put under pressure. **pres•su•rized,** *adj.* (aircraft cabin) kept at a constant atmospheric pressure.

pres•tige [pre'stiːʒ] *n.* admiration aroused by s.o. because of rank or qualifications or job. **pres•tig•ious** [pre'stɪdʒəs] *adj.* which brings prestige.

pres•to ['prestəʊ] *adv.* (*in music*) rapidly; **p.!** = word used by magicians when carrying out magic tricks.

pre•stressed ['priː'strest] *adj.* which has been stressed in advance.

pre•sume [prɪ'zjuːm] *v.* (a) to suppose/to assume. (b) (**to**) to take the liberty of doing sth. (c) (*formal*) **to p. (up)on s.o.'s good nature** = to take unfair advantage of s.o.'s kindness. **pre•sum•a•bly,** *adv.* probably; as you would expect. **pre•sump•tion** [prɪ'zʌmpʃn] *n.* (a) thing which is assumed to be true. (b) rudeness. **pre•sump•tive,** *adj.* which is presumed to be true; **heir p.** = heir (to a throne) who may be displaced by the birth of s.o. with a better right. **pre•sump•tu•ous** [prɪ'zʌmptjʊəs] *adj.* rude/bold. **pre•sump•tu•ous•ly,** *adv.* in a presumptuous way.

pre•sup•pose [priːsə'pəʊz] *v.* to assume in advance (that sth is true/that certain conditions are met). **pre•sup•po•si•tion** [priːsəpə'zɪʃn] *n.* thing which is assumed in advance.

pre•tax ['priːtæks] *adj.* before tax is paid.

pre•teen ['priːtiːn] *adj. & n.* (boy/girl) just under the age of 13.

pre•tend [prɪ'tend] *v.* (a) to make believe so as to deceive s.o. (b) (**to**) to be bold enough to claim. **pre•tense,** *Brit.* **pre•tence** [prɪ'tens] *n.* making believe. **pre•tend•er,** *n.* person who has (false) claims to sth, usu. person who claims to be king. **pre•ten•sion** [prɪ'tenʃn] *n.* claim. **pre•ten•tious** [prɪ'tenʃəs] *adj.* very showy; claiming to be more important than you are. **pre•ten•tious•ness,** *n.* being pretentious.

pre•ter•nat•u•ral [priːtə'nætʃrəl] *adj.* supernatural; extraordinary.

pre•text ['priːtekst] *n.* excuse.

pret•ty ['prɪtɪ] 1. *adj.* (**-ier, -iest**) pleasant to look at; attractive. 2. *adv. inf.* quite. **pret•ti•ly,** *adv.* daintily. **pret•ti•ness,** *n.* attractiveness/pleasantness.

pret•zel ['pretsəl] *n.* hard salty biscuit, made in the shape of a knot.

pre•vail [prɪ'veɪl] *v.* (*formal*) (a) **to p. upon** = to persuade. (b) to be usual/common. **pre•vail•ing,** *adj.* usual/common; **p. wind** = wind which usually blows from a certain direction. **prev•a•lence** ['prevələns] *n.* being widespread. **prev•a•lent,** *adj.* widespread.

pre•var•i•cate [prɪ'værɪkeɪt] *v.* (*formal*) to try not to tell the truth. **pre•var•i•ca•tion** [prɪværɪ'keɪʃn] *n.* act of prevaricating; lie. **pre•var•i•ca•tor,** *n.* person who prevaricates.

pre•vent [prɪ'vent] *v.* to stop (sth) from happening; **to p. s.o. from** = to stop (s.o.) from doing sth. **pre•vent•a•ble**, *adj.* which could be prevented. **pre•ven•tion** [prɪ'venʃn] *n.* preventing. **pre•ven•ta•tive, preventive** [prɪ'vent(ə)tɪv] *adj.* which prevents.

pre•view ['pri:vju:] *n.* showing of a motion picture/an exhibition, etc., before it is open to the general public.

pre•vi•ous ['pri:vɪəs] 1. *adj.* former, earlier. 2. *adv.* **p. to** = before. **pre•vi•ous•ly**, *adv.* before.

pre•war ['pri:wɔ:] *adj. & adv.* existing/happening before a war.

prey [preɪ] 1. *n.* animal eaten by another; **birds of p.** = birds which eat other birds/animals. 2. *v.* **to p. (up)on** = to attack animals and eat them; **sth is preying on his mind** = sth is worrying him.

price [praɪs] 1. *n.* quantity of money which has to be paid to buy sth; **at a p.** = if you are willing to pay a lot. 2. *v.* to give (sth) a price. **price•less**, *adj.* (a) extremely valuable. (b) very funny (joke). **pric•ey**, *adj. inf.* expensive.

prick [prɪk] 1. *n.* pain caused by sth sharp. 2. *v.* (a) to jab with sth sharp; to make small holes in (sth). (b) **to p. up your ears** = to listen attentively. **prick•le**, *n.* thorn/sharp point (on a plant/hedgehog, etc.). **prick•li•ness**, *n.* being prickly. **prick•ly**, *adj.* covered with prickles; **p. pear** = type of cactus; **p. heat** = skin rash caused by hot climate.

pride [praɪd] 1. *n.* (a) pleasure in your own abilities/achievements/possessions. (b) very high opinions of yourself. (c) group of lions. 2. **to p. oneself on** = to be extremely proud of.

priest [pri:st] *n.* person who has been ordained to serve God/to interpret the wishes of God/to carry out formal religious duties; **parish p.** = priest who is in charge of a parish. **priest•ess**, *n.* female priest. **priest•hood**, *n.* job of being a priest. **priest•ly**, *adj.* referring to priests.

prig [prɪg] *n.* very moral and conceited person. **prig•gish**, *adj.* very moral and conceited. **prig•gish•ness**, *n.* being priggish.

prim [prɪm] *adj.* (**primmer, primmest**) very correct/unbending. **prim•ly**, *adj.* in a prim way. **prim•ness**, *n.* being prim.

pri•ma bal•ler•i•na [pri:məbælə'ri:nə] *n.* leading woman dancer in a ballet company. **pri•ma don•na** [pri:mə'dɒnə] *n.* leading woman singer in opera; person who is conceited and liable to outbursts of emotion.

pri•ma•cy ['praɪməsɪ] *n.* being in first place, being most important.

pri•ma fa•cie [praɪmə'feɪʃɪ] *adv. & adj.* based on what seems right at first sight.

pri•mal ['praɪml] *adj.* (*formal*) primeval.

pri•ma•ry ['praɪmərɪ] 1. *adj.* basic; **p. colors** = basic colors (red, yellow and blue) which go to make up all the other colors; **p. election** = first election to choose a candidate to represent a political party in a main election; **p. school** = school for small children (up to the age of nine or ten). 2. *n.* primary election. **pri•ma•ri•ly**, *adv.* mainly/mostly.

pri•mate *n.* (a) ['praɪmət] leading bishop. (b) ['praɪmeɪt] **the primates** = members of the highest level of mammals (apes, human beings, etc.).

prime [praɪm] 1. *adj.* (a) most important. (b) of best quality. (c) **p. number** = number (such as 2, 5, 11, etc.) which can only be divided by itself or by 1. 2. *n.* period when you are at your best. 3. *v.* (a) to get (sth) prepared; to give (wood/metal) a first coat of special paint, before giving the top coat. (b) to put water into (a water pump)/oil into (a machine) so as to start it working. (c) to give (s.o.) information or instruct beforehand. **prime min•is•ter**, *n.* head of the government in Britain and other countries. **prim•er**, *n.* (a) special paint to cover an unpainted surface. (b) elementary textbook.

pri•me•val [praɪ'mi:vl] *adj.* referring to the period at the beginning of the world.

prim•i•tive ['prɪmɪtɪv] *adj.* (a) referring to very early/prehistoric times. (b) rough/crude.

pri•mo•gen•i•ture [praɪməu'dʒenɪtʃə] *n.* rule by which the eldest son is the heir.

pri•mor•di•al [praɪ'mɔ:djəl] *adj.* (*formal*) which existed at the beginning (a long time ago).

prim•rose ['prɪmrəuz] *n.* small pale yellow wild spring flower.

prim•u•la ['prɪmjulə] *n.* garden flower, like a primrose, but with many colors.

prince [prɪns] *n.* son of a king; male ruler of a small state; male member of a royal family. **prince•ly**, *adj.* like a prince; large (sum of money/salary). **prin•cess**, *n.* daughter of a king; female member of a royal family; female ruler of a small state; wife of a prince.

prin•ci•pal ['prɪnsɪpl] 1. *adj.* main/most important. 2. *n.* (a) head (of a primary or secondary school); main actor (in a play). (b) money on which interest is paid/capital which has

---

æ **back**, a: **farm**, ɒ: **top**, aɪ **pipe**, aʊ **how**, aɪə **fire**, aʊə **flower**, ɔ: **bought**, ɔɪ **toy**, e **fed**, eəhair, eɪ **take**, ə **afraid**, əʊ **boat**, əʊə **lower**, v: **word**, i: **heap**, ɪ **hit**, ɪə **hear**, u: **school**, ʊ **book**, ʌ **but**, b **back**, d **dog**, ð **then**, dʒ **just**, f **fog**, g **go**, h **hand**, j **yes**, k **catch**, l **last**, m **mix**, n **nut**, ŋ **sing**, p **penny**, r **round**, s **some**, ʃ **short**, t **too**, tʃ **chop**, θ **thing**, v **voice**, w **was**, z **zoo**, ʒ **treasure**

been invested. **prin•ci•pal•i•ty** [prɪnsɪ-'pælɪtɪ] *n.* land ruled by a prince. **prin•ci•pal•ly,** *adv.* mainly.

prin•ci•ple ['prɪnsɪpl] *n.* (a) law/general rule; **in p.** = in agreement with the general rule. (b) personal sense of truth; **on p.** = because of what you believe.

print [prɪnt] 1. *n.* (a) mark made on sth; *see also* **footprint, fingerprint.** (b) letters printed on a page; **the small p.** = conditions on a contract, usu. written in very small letters. (c) picture which has been printed; photograph which has been reproduced on paper; cloth with a design printed on it. 2. *v.* (a) to mark letters on paper by a machine. (b) to write capital letters or letters which are not joined together. (c) to reproduce a photograph/pattern, etc. **print•ed cir•cuit,** *n.* electronic circuit where the connections are printed on a board; **p.c. board** = flat board on which metal strips are printed to form a circuit. **print•er,** *n.* (a) person who prints books/newspapers, etc. (b) machine which prints automatically. **print•ing,** *n.* art of printing books/newspapers, etc.; **p. press** = machine which prints books, etc. **print•out,** *n.* printed information from a computer.

pri•on ['priːɒn] *n.* protein found in the brain, an abnormal form of which causes such diseases as bovine spongiform encephalopathy (BSE), Creutzfeldt-Jakob Disease (CJD), and scrapie.

pri•or ['praɪə] 1. *adj. & adv.* before; previous; **p. to** = before. 2. *n.* male head of a priory. **pri•or•ess,** *n.* woman head of a priory. **pri•or•i•ty** [praɪ'ɒrɪtɪ] *n.* (a) right to be first. (b) thing which has to be done first. **pri•o•ry** ['praɪərɪ] *n.* building where monks or nuns live.

prise [praɪz] *v.* to prize.

prism ['prɪzəm] *n.* glass block usu. with a triangular cross-section, which splits white light up into the colors of the rainbow. **pris•mat•ic** [prɪz'mætɪk] *adj.* referring to a prism.

pris•on ['prɪzn] *n.* place where people are kept by law after they have been found guilty of a crime. **pris•on•er,** *n.* person who is in prison; **p. of war** = soldier/airman, etc., who has been captured by the enemy.

pris•sy ['prɪsɪ] *adj.* (-ier, -iest) unpleasantly proud of being good.

pris•tine ['prɪstiːn] *adj. (formal)* fresh/unspoilt.

pri•vate ['praɪvət] 1. *adj.* (a) belonging to one person, not to everyone; **p. means** = personal income from investments; **p. parts** = sex organs; **p. eye** = detective employed by an ordinary person. (b) belonging to certain people, but not to the state or the general public; **p. showing** = preview of an exhibition for certain

invited guests. 2. *n.* (a) **in p.** = being away from other people. (b) ordinary soldier of the lowest rank. (c) **privates** = private body parts.

pri•va•cy ['prɪvəsɪ] *n.* being away from other people. **pri•va•teer,** *n.* armed ship which belongs to a private individual. **pri•vate•ly,** *adv.* (a) in private. (b) (owned) by private individuals. **pri•va•ti•za•tion** [praɪvətaɪ'zeɪʃn] *n.* act of privatizing. **pri•va•tize** ['praɪvətaɪz] *v.* to return (a nationalized industry) to private ownership.

pri•va•tion [praɪ'veɪʃn] *n.* lack of money/food, etc.

priv•et ['prɪvɪt] *n.* common shrub, used for garden hedges.

priv•i•lege ['prɪvɪlɪdʒ] *n.* favor/right granted to some people but not to everyone. **priv•i•leged,** *adj.* having a privilege.

priv•y ['prɪvɪ] 1. *adj. (formal)* **to be p. to a secret** = to know the details of a secret. 2. *n. inf.* rough toilet outside a house. **priv•y coun•cil,** *n.* group of important people who advise a king or queen.

prize [praɪz] 1. *n.* (a) money or object given to a winner. (b) ship captured in war. 2. *v.* (a) to value. (b) *(also prise)* to life or pull with the help of a lever. **prize•fight,** *n.* boxing match where the winner wins money. **prize•fight•er,** *n.* boxer.

pro [prəʊ] 1. *prefix meaning* in favor of. 2. *n.* (a) **pros and cons of a case** = arguments for and against it. (b) *inf.* professional sportsman/actor, etc.

prob•a•ble ['prɒbəbl] *adj.* likely. **prob•a•bil•i•ty** [prɒbə'bɪlɪtɪ] *n.* likelihood. **prob•a•bly,** *adv.* likely.

pro•bate ['prəʊbeɪt] *n.* proving in law that a document (esp. a will) is valid.

pro•ba•tion [prə'beɪʃn] *n.* (a) period when s.o. is being tested. (b) period when a criminal is supervised instead of being put in prison; **p. officer** = official who looks after prisoners on probation. **pro•ba•tion•ar•y,** *adj.* (period) when s.o. is being tested. **pro•ba•tion•er,** *n.* criminal who is on probation.

probe [prəʊb] 1. *n.* (a) instrument used by doctors to examine wounds, etc. (b) thorough investigation. (c) **space p.** = spacecraft sent into space for scientific purposes. 2. *v.* to examine (sth) deeply.

pro•bi•ty ['prəʊbɪtɪ] *n. (formal)* total honesty.

prob•lem ['prɒbləm] *n.* thing which is difficult to solve. **prob•lem•at•ic(al)** [prɒblə-'mætɪk(l)] *adj.* doubtful; likely to cause a problem.

pro•bos•cis [prəʊ'bɒsɪs] *n. (pl. -es)* long sucking tube coming from the head of an animal (such as the trunk of an elephant/the sting of a mosquito).

pro•ceed [prə'si:d] v. to continue/to go further. **pro•ce•dur•al** [prə'si:dʒərəl] adj. referring to procedure. **pro•ce•dure** [prə'si:dʒə] n. (a) way in which sth ought to be carried out. (b) medical treatment. **pro•ceed a•gainst**, v. to start a lawsuit against (s.o.). **pro•ceed•ings**, n. pl. report of what takes place at a meeting. **pro•ceeds** ['prəusi:dz] n. pl. money which you receive when you sell sth.

proc•ess ['prəuses] 1. n. (pl. -es) (a) method of making sth. (b) **in the p. (of)** = while doing sth. 2. v. (a) to make manufactured goods using raw materials; **processed cheese** = cheese which has been treated so that it will keep for a long time. (b) to prepare (figures) for a computer; to sort out (information). **pro•cess•ing**, n. treating raw materials; sorting out information. **pro•ces•sion** [prə'seʃn] n. group of people marching (with a band, etc.) in line. **pro•ces•sion•al**, adj. referring to a procession. **proc•es•sor**, n. machine/person who processes; computer device which processes information.

pro•claim [prə'kleɪm] v. to state officially and in public. **proc•la•ma•tion** [prɒklə'meɪʃn] n. official public statement.

pro•cliv•i•ty [prə'klɪvɪtɪ] n. (formal) tendency.

pro•cras•ti•nate [prəu'kræstɪneɪt] (formal) v. to delay/to put sth off until later. **pro•cras•ti•na•tion** [prəkræstɪ'neɪʃn] n. delaying/putting off.

pro•cre•ate ['prəukrieɪt] v. (formal) to produce (young). **pro•cre•a•tion**, n. act of procreating.

proc•tor ['prɒktə] n. university official who watches over students during examinations.

pro•cure [prə'kjuə] v. (formal) (a) to obtain. (b) to provide (girls) for sex. **pro•cur•a•ble**, adj. which can be obtained. **pro•cure•ment**, n. obtaining.

prod [prɒd] 1. n. poke; **give him a p.** = nudge him/try to get him to act. 2. v. (**prodded**) to poke with a finger/stick, etc.

prod•i•gal ['prɒdɪgl] adj. wasteful; (person) who spends a lot. **prod•i•gal•i•ty** [prɒdɪ'gælɪtɪ] n. being prodigal. **prod•i•gal•ly**, adv. wastefully.

prod•i•gy ['prɒdɪdʒɪ] n. remarkable person or thing. **pro•di•gious** [prə'dɪdʒəs] adj. remarkable/enormous. **pro•di•gious•ly**, adv. remarkably/enormously.

pro•duce 1. n. ['prɒdju:s] things grown on the land. 2. v. [prə'dju:s] (a) to bring out. (b) to make/to manufacture. (c) to put on (a play/a motion picture). (d) to yield (crops, etc.). **pro•duc•er** [prə'dju:sə] n. (a) person who puts on a play/a motion picture. (b) person/country which makes/grows sth.

prod•uct ['prɒdʌkt] n. (a) thing which is manufactured/produced; **p. placement** = advertising method in which a product is used or displayed in a TV program or a film. (b) result. (c) (in mathematics) result of multiplying two numbers. **pro•duc•tion** [prə'dʌkʃn] n. (a) manufacturing. (b) putting on a play/motion picture. **pro•duc•tive** [prə'dʌktɪv] adj. which produces. **pro•duc•tiv•i•ty** [prɒdʌk'tɪvɪtɪ] n. rate of output/of production (in a factory).

pro•fane [prə'feɪn] adj. not religious; blasphemous. **pro•fane•ly**, adv. in a profane way. **pro•fan•i•ty** [prə'fænɪtɪ] n. rudeness; swearing/blasphemy.

pro•fess [prə'fes] v. to declare. **pro•fessed**, adj. declared. **pro•fess•ed•ly** [prə'fesɪdlɪ] adv. openly. **pro•fes•sion** [prə'feʃn] n. (a) work which needs special training/skill/knowledge. (b) declaration (of belief in sth). **pro•fes•sion•al**. 1. adj. (a) referring to a profession; expert; **p. athlete** = athlete who is paid to play. 2. n. (a) expert. (b) athlete who is paid to play. **pro•fes•sion•al•ism**, n. (a) expertise/skill. (b) being a professional athlete. **pro•fes•sion•al•ly**, adv. in a professional way. **pro•fes•sor**, n. (a) chief teacher in a subject at a college/university. (b) teacher of music/art, etc. **pro•fes•so•ri•al** [prɒfə'sɔ:rɪəl] adj. referring to a professor. **pro•fes•sor•ship**, n. position of professor at a college/university.

prof•fer ['prɒfə] v. (formal) to offer.

pro•fi•cient [prə'fɪʃnt] adj. (at) very capable (of doing sth). **pro•fi•cien•cy**, n. skill in doing sth. **pro•fi•cient•ly**, adv. in a capable way.

pro•file ['prəufaɪl] n. (a) view of s.o.'s head from the side; **to maintain a low p.** = to be quiet/unobtrusive. (b) short biography/description of a famous person (in a newspaper).

prof•it ['prɒfɪt] 1. n. money gained; **p. margin** = percentage of money gained against money paid out. 2. v. to gain. **prof•it•a•bil•i•ty**

æ back, a: farm, ɒ: top, aɪ pipe, aʊ how, aɪə fire, aʊə flower, ɔ: bought, ɔɪ toy, e fed, eəhair, eɪ take, ə afraid, əʊ boat, əʊə lower, v: word, i: heap, ɪ hit, ɪə hear, u: school, ʊ book, ʌ but, b back, d dog, ð then, dʒ just, f fog, g go, h hand, j yes, k catch, l last, m mix, n nut, ŋ sing, p penny, r round, s some, ʃ short, t too, tʃ chop, θ thing, v voice, w was, z zoo, ʒ treasure

[prɒfɪtə'bɪlɪtɪ] *n.* ability to produce a profit. **prof•it•a•ble** ['prɒfɪtəbl] *adj.* likely to produce a profit. **prof•it•a•bly,** *adv.* at a profit. **prof•it•eer** [prɒfɪ'tɪə] 1. *n.* person who makes too much profit. 2. *v.* to make too much profit. **prof•it•eer•ing,** *n.* making too much profit.

prof•li•gate ['prɒflɪgət] *adj. & n.* (*formal*) (person) who is very extravagant/who leads a wild life. **prof•li•ga•cy** ['prɒflɪgəsɪ] *n.* extravagance/spending money wildly.

pro•for•ma [prəu'fɔːmə] *adj. & n.* (invoice) sent asking the purchaser to pay in advance.

pro•found [prə'faund] *adj.* very serious/very deep (understanding/thought). **pro•found•ly,** *adv.* extremely. **pro•fun•di•ty** [prə'fʌndɪtɪ] *n.* depth (of thought or understanding).

pro•fuse [prə'fjuːs] *adj.* abundant/excessive. **pro•fuse•ly,** *adv.* excessively/too much. **pro•fuse•ness,** *n.* being . profuse. **pro•fu•sion** [prə'fjuːʒn] *n.* very large quantity.

prog•e•ny ['prɒdʒənɪ] *n.* (*no pl.*) (*formal*) children/offspring. **pro•gen•i•tor** [prəu'dʒenɪtə] *n.* ancestor; animal/plant from which others are descended.

pro•ges•ter•one [prəu'dʒestərəun] *n.* hormone which stops women ovulating, and helps the uterus in the first stages of pregnancy.

prog•na•thous [prɒg'neɪθəs] *adj.* with a lower jaw which is longer than the upper.

prog•nos•ti•cate [prɒg'nɒstɪkeɪt] *v.* (*formal*) to foretell. **prog•no•sis** [prɒg'nəusɪs] *n.* forecast. **prog•nos•ti•ca•tion,** *n.* (*formal*) forecast.

pro•gram ['prəugrəm], *Brit.* **pro•gramme** ['prəugræm] 1. *n.* (a) list of items in an entertainment. (b) show/item on TV or radio. 2. *v.* (**-mmed, -med**) to arrange shows on TV/radio. **pro•gram** ['prəugræm] 1. *n.* instructions given to a computer. 2. *v.* to give instructions to (a computer); **programming language** = system of signs and words used to program a computer. **pro•gram•mable, programable,** *adj.* (device) which can be programmed. **pro•gram•mer, programer,** *n.* (a) person who arranges shows on TV/radio. (b) person who programs a computer.

pro•gress 1. *n.* ['prəugres] (*pl.* **-es**) movement forward; **work in p.** = work which is being done. 2. *v.* [prə'gres] to advance. **pro•gres•sion** [prə'greʃn] *n.* advance/movement forward. **pro•gres•sive,** *adj.* (a) (movement) in stages. (b) advanced (ideas). **pro•gres•sive•ly,** *adv.* by stages.

pro•hib•it [prə'hɪbɪt] *v.* to forbid. **pro•hi•bi•tion** [prəuhɪ'brɪʃn] *n.* forbidding (esp. the sale of alcohol). **pro•hib•i•tive** [prə'hɪbɪtɪv] *adj.* (price) which is so high that you cannot pay it.

pro•ject 1. *n.* ['prɒdʒekt] (a) plan. (b) work planned by students on their own. 2. *v.* [prə'dʒekt] (a) to plan. (b) to throw (a picture on a screen). **pro•jec•tile** [prə'dʒektaɪl] *n.* thing which is thrown/shot. **pro•jecting,** *adj.* sticking/jutting/standing out. **pro•jec•tion,** *n.* (a) thing planned/forecast. (b) (*in geography*) picture of the shape of the earth on a flat surface. (c) thing which stands/sticks out. (d) action of projecting a picture on a screen. **pro•jec•tion•ist,** *n.* person who operates a projector in a movie theater. **pro•jec•tor,** *n.* apparatus for throwing pictures on a screen.

pro•lapse ['prəulæps] *n.* state where an organ in the body moves out of place.

pro•le•gom•e•na [prəule'gomɪnə] *pl. n.* (*formal*) introduction.

pro•le•tar•i•at [prəulɪ'teərɪət] *n.* working class. **pro•le•tar•i•an,** *adj. & n.* (member) of the working class.

pro•lif•ic [prə'lɪfɪk] *adj.* producing many children; very productive. **pro•lif•i•cal•ly,** *adv.* in a prolific way. **pro•lif•er•ate** [prə'lɪfəreɪt] *v.* to produce shoots/young, etc., rapidly. **pro•lif•er•a•tion** [prəlɪfə'reɪʃn] *n.* rapid spread.

pro•lix ['prəulɪks] *adj.* (*formal*) long-winded/using too many words. **pro•lix•i•ty** [prəu'lɪksitɪ] *n.* being prolix.

pro•logue, prolog ['prəulɒg] *n.* piece spoken as the introduction of a play or poem; preliminary section in a book.

pro•long [prə'lɒŋ] *v.* to lengthen. **pro•lon•ga•tion** [prəulɒŋ'geɪʃn] *n.* lengthening. **pro•longed,** *adj.* lasting for a long time.

prom•e•nade [prɒmə'nɑːd] 1. *n.* area where you can walk; (*on a ship*) **p. deck** = deck where passengers can stroll about. 2. *v.* to walk about. **prom** [prɒm] *n.* formal dance at a school or college at the end of a school year; **p. concerts/the proms** = promenade concerts. **prom•e•nad•er,** *n.* person who promenades.

prom•i•nence ['prɒmɪnəns] *n.* (a) standing out; thing which stands out. (b) fame. **prom•i•nent,** *adj.* (a) standing out/easily seen. (b) famous. **prom•i•nent•ly,** *adv.* so as to be easily seen.

pro•mis•cu•ous [prə'mɪskjuəs] *adj.* (person) who does not prefer one thing to another, esp. who has sexual relations with many people. **prom•is•cu•i•ty** [prɒmɪ'skjuːɪtɪ] *n.* having sexual relations with many people. **pro•mis•cu•ous•ly,** *adv.* in a promiscuous way.

prom•ise ['promɪs] 1. *n.* (a) act of promising that you will definitely do sth. (b) **to show p.** = to make people feel that you will do well in the future. 2. *v.* (a) to give your word that you will definitely do sth. (b) to show signs of what may happen in the future. **prom•is•ing,** *adj.* (person) who is likely to succeed.

prom•is•so•ry ['promɪsərɪ] *adj.* (note) in which you promise to pay s.o. money on a certain date.

prom•on•to•ry ['promantərɪ] *n.* piece of land jutting out into the sea.

pro•mote [prə'məʊt] *v.* (a) to give (s.o.) a better job. (b) to advertise. (c) to encourage. **pro•mot•er,** *n.* person who promotes; person who organizes a boxing match, etc. **pro•mo•tion** [prə'məʊʃn] *n.* (a) advancement to a better job. (b) advertising (a new product). **pro•mo•tion•al,** *adj.* (material) used in advertising.

prompt [prompt] 1. *adj.* (**-er, -est**) done at once; quick/rapid. 2. *v.* (a) to suggest to (s.o.) that he should do sth. (b) to tell an actor words which he has forgotten. 3. *n.* message to a computer user, telling him to do sth. **prompt•er,** *n.* person who prompts an actor. **promp•ti•tude,** *n.* being prompt. **prompt•ly,** *adv.* immediately; rapidly. **prompt•ness,** *n.* quickness.

prom•ul•gate ['promʌlgeɪt] *v.* (*formal*) to make (a law) known to the public. **prom•ul•ga•tion** [proml'geɪʃn] *n.* (*formal*) announcement of a law.

prone [prəʊn] *adj.* (a) (lying) flat. (b) likely (**to**).

prong [proŋ] *n.* one of the sharp points of a fork; point of an attack. **pronged,** *adj.* with prongs.

pro•noun ['prəʊnaʊn] *n.* (*in grammar*) word which stands in place of a noun.

pro•nounce [prə'naʊns] *v.* (a) to speak a series of sounds which form a word; to speak clearly. (b) to declare in a formal way. **pro•nounced,** *adj.* noticeable. **pro•nounce•ment,** *n.* official/formal statement. **pro•nun•ci•a•tion** [prənʌnsɪ'eɪʃn] *n.* way of pronouncing words.

pron•to ['prontəʊ] *adv. inf.* immediately.

proof [pruːf] 1. *n.* (a) thing which proves/which shows that sth is true. (b) percentage of alcohol in a drink. (c) test sheet of printing which has to be corrected by the author before the book can be produced; copy of a photograph/lithograph, etc., for the artist to examine to see if it is acceptable. 2. *adj.* (**against**) safe from/not affected by. 3. *v.* to paint with a protective coat. **proof•read,** *v.* to read and correct proofs.

-proof [pruːf] *suffix* safe against/protected against.

prop [prop] 1. *n.* (a) support; stick which holds sth up. (b) **props** = articles used in the production of a play/motion picture. 2. *v.* (**propped**) to support.

prop•a•gan•da [propə'gændə] *n.* spreading of (frequently false) political ideas. **prop•a•gan•dist,** *n.* person who spreads political ideas.

prop•a•gate ['propəgeɪt] *v.* (a) to make (new plants) by sowing seed/taking cuttings. (b) to spread (ideas). **prop•a•ga•tion** [propə'geɪʃn] *n.* act of propagating. **prop•a•ga•tor,** *n.* small glass-covered box for growing new plants.

pro•pane ['prəʊpeɪn] *n.* colorless gas used for heating and cooking.

pro•pel [prə'pel] *v.* (**propelled**) to send forward. **pro•pel•lant,** *n.* fuel used to propel. **pro•pel•ler,** *n.* mechanism with blades which turns rapidly to drive boats and aircraft.

pro•pen•si•ty [prə'pensɪtɪ] *n.* (*formal*) tendency/leaning.

prop•er ['propə] *adj.* (a) right. (b) thorough (cleaning, etc.). (c) (*in grammar*) **p. noun** = noun which is a name of a person/a country, etc. (d) very correct. (e) (thing) itself exactly. **prop•er•ly,** *adv.* (a) rightly/correctly. (b) thoroughly.

prop•er•ty ['propətɪ] *n.* (a) thing which belongs to s.o. (b) building or buildings. (c) **properties** = articles used in the production of a play/motion picture; **p. man** = person responsible for all the articles used in a play/motion picture. (d) quality.

proph•e•cy ['profəsɪ] *n.* act of prophesying; thing prophesied. **proph•e•sy** ['profɪsaɪ] *v.* to foretell what will happen in the future. **proph•et** ['profɪt] *n.* person who foretells what will happen; religious leader. **proph•et•ess,** *n.* woman prophet. **proph•et•ic(al)** [prə'fetɪk(l)] *adj.* which is like a prophecy. **pro•phet•i•cal•ly,** *adv.* in a prophetic way.

æ back, ɑː farm, ɒ top, aɪ pipe, aʊ how, aɪə fire, aʊə flower, ɔː bought, ɔɪ toy, e fed, eəhair, eɪ take, ə afraid, əʊ boat, əʊə lower, ɜː word, iː heap, ɪ hit, ɪə hear, uː school, ʊ book, ʌ but, b back, d dog, ð then, dʒ just, f fog, g go, h hand, j yes, k catch, l last, m mix, n nut, ŋ sing, p penny, r round, s some, ʃ short, t too, tʃ chop, θ thing, v voice, w was, z zoo, ʒ treasure

pro•phy•lax•is [prɒfɪ'læksɪs] n. prevention of a disease. **pro•phy•lac•tic** [prɒfɪ'læktɪk] adj. & n. (substance) which prevents disease.

pro•pin•qui•ty [prɒ'pɪŋkwɪtɪ] n. (formal) closeness/nearness.

pro•pi•ti•ate [prə'pɪʃɪeɪt] v. (formal) to appease/to make (s.o.) less angry. **pro•pi•ti•a•tion** [prəpɪʃɪ'eɪʃn] n. act of appeasing. **pro•pi•ti•a•to•ry** [prə'pɪʃɪətərɪ] adj. which tries to appease/to make less angry. **pro•pi•tious** [prə'pɪʃəs] adj. favorable. **pro•pi•tious•ly,** adv. in a propitious way.

pro•po•nent [prɒ'pəʊnənt] n. person who proposes sth.

pro•por•tion [prə'pɔːʃn] n. (a) part (of a total). (b) relationship between a part and a total; **in p.** = in the right amount. (c) **proportions** = the relative height/length (of a building/picture, etc.). **pro•por•tion•al,** adj. which is directly related; **p. representation** = system of voting where the votes cast for each party determine the number of seats each party has in a legislative body. **pro•por•tion•al•ly,** adv. in proportion. **pro•por•tion•ate,** adj. which is in proportion. **pro•por•tion•ate•ly,** adv. in proportion.

pro•pose [prə'pəʊz] v. (a) to suggest/to make a suggestion. (b) **to p. to s.o.** = to ask s.o. to marry you. **pro•pos•al,** n. (a) suggestion/thing which is suggested. (b) asking s.o. to marry you. **pro•pos•er,** n. person who proposes (a motion). **prop•o•si•tion** [prɒpə'zɪʃn] n. (a) thing which has been proposed. (b) **tough p.** = problem which is difficult to solve.

pro•pound [prə'paʊnd] v. (formal) to put forward (an idea).

pro•pri•e•tor [prə'praɪətə] n. owner. **pro•pri•e•tar•y** [prə'praɪətrɪ] adj. (a) referring to a proprietor. (b) **p. medicine** = medicine which is sold under a brand name and manufactured by a particular company. **pro•pri•e•tress,** n. woman proprietor. **pro•pri•e•to•ri•al,** adj. like a proprietor.

pro•pri•e•ty [prə'praɪətɪ] n. decency; good behavior.

pro•pul•sion [prə'pʌlʃn] n. moving forward.

pro ra•ta [prəʊ'rɑːtə] adv. & adj. in proportion.

pro•sa•ic [prə'zeɪɪk] adj. ordinary; not poetic; rather dull. **pro•sa•i•cal•ly,** adv. in a prosaic way.

pro•sce•ni•um [prə'siːnɪəm] n. part of a stage in a theater which sticks out beyond the curtain; **p. arch** = arch above the front part of a stage in a theater.

pro•scribe [prəʊ'skraɪb] v. (formal) to forbid

by law. **pro•scrip•tion** [prɒs'krɪpʃn] n. (formal) act of proscribing.

prose [prəʊz] n. writing which is not in verse. **pros•y,** adj. wordy/dull in style.

pros•e•cute ['prɒsɪkjuːt] v. to bring (s.o.) to court to answer a charge. **pros•e•cu•tion** [prɒsɪ'kjuːʃn] n. (a) court case against s.o. (b) people who have accused s.o. of a crime in a court. **pros•e•cut•ing at•tor•ney,** n. public official who accuses a criminal in a law court on behalf of the state. **pros•e•cu•tor** ['prɒsɪkjuːtə] n. person who prosecutes.

pros•e•lyte ['prɒsɪlaɪt] n. person recently converted to a religion. **pros•e•lyt•ize,** v. to try to convert (people) to a religion.

pros•o•dy ['prɒsədɪ] n. rules of writing poetry.

pros•pect 1. n. ['prɒspekt] (a) view. (b) **to have sth in p.** = to expect sth to happen. (c) **prospects** = future possibilities. (d) person who may become a customer. 2. v. [prə'spekt] to search (a land for minerals). **pro•spec•tive,** adj. which may happen in the future. **pros•pec•tor,** n. person who searches for minerals. **pro•spec•tus** [prə'spektəs] n. paper giving information about sth in the hope of attracting clients/customers.

pros•per ['prɒspə] v. to succeed; to become rich. **pros•per•i•ty** [prɒsperɪtɪ] n. being rich. **pros•per•ous** ['prɒspərəs] adj. wealthy/rich.

pros•tate ['prɒsteɪt] n. gland around the bladder in men.

pros•the•sis ['prɒsθəsɪs] n. (pl. -ses) (formal) artificial leg/arm, etc.

pros•ti•tute ['prɒstɪtjuːt] 1. n. person who receives money for sexual intercourse. 2. v. to use (your talents) in a low/unworthy way. **pros•ti•tu•tion** [prɒstɪ'tjuːʃn] n. offering sexual intercourse for payment.

pros•trate 1. adj. ['prɒstreɪt] (lying) flat. 2. v. [prə'streɪt] **to p. oneself before s.o.** = to fall down (in front of s.o. as a mark of respect, fear, etc.); **he was prostrated by malaria** = he had to stay lying down. **pros•tra•tion** [prɒ'streɪʃn] n. lying down/falling down in front of s.o.

pro•tag•o•nist [prə'tægənɪst] n. main character in a play/book, etc.; leader of one side in a conflict.

pro•te•an ['prəʊtɪən] adj. which changes easily.

pro•tect [prə'tekt] v. to defend against attack; to shield against dirt/germs, etc. **pro•tec•tion** [prə'tekʃn] n. (a) shelter. (b) defense. **pro•tec•tive,** adj. which protects. **pro•tec•tive•ly,** adv. in a protective way. **pro•tec•tor,** n. person/thing which protects. **pro•tec•tor•ate,** n. country which is protected (and usu. controlled) by another country.

pro•té•gé ['prɒtezeɪ] *n.* person (usu. young) who is supported in work with money or advice by s.o. else.

pro•tein ['prəʊtiːn] *n.* compound which is an essential part of living cells; one of the elements in food which is necessary to keep the human body working properly.

pro tem•po•re, pro tem [prəʊ'tempɒreɪ, 'prəʊ'tem] *adv.* temporarily.

pro•test 1. *n.* ['prəʊtest] statement that you object or disapprove; **p. march** = march in procession to show that you protest against sth. 2. *v.* [prə'test] (a) to object/to raise a violent objection (**against**). (b) to state solemnly. **Prot•es•tant** ['prɒtɪstənt] *adj. & n.* (member) of a Western Christian church which is not part of the Roman Catholic Church. **Prot•es•tant•ism**, *n.* beliefs of the Protestant church. **prot•es•ta•tion** [prɒtɪ'steɪʃn] *n.* violent statement of protest.

pro•to•col ['prəʊtəkɒl] *n.* (a) correct (diplomatic) behavior. (b) draft agreement.

pro•ton ['prəʊtɒn] *n.* nucleus of a hydrogen atom, found in all atoms.

pro•to•plasm ['prəʊtəplæzəm] *n.* basic jellylike substance in all living matter.

pro•to•type ['prəʊtətaɪp] *n.* first model of a new machine, etc.

pro•to•zo•a [prəʊtəʊ'zəʊə] *n. pl.* simplest types of living creatures.

pro•tract•ed [prə'træktɪd] *adj.* very lengthy. **pro•trac•tion,** *n.* being protracted. **pro•trac•tor,** *n.* semicircular device, used for measuring angles in geometry.

pro•trude [prə'truːd] *v.* to stick out. **pro•tru•sion,** *n.* thing which protrudes.

pro•tu•ber•ance [prə'tjuːbərəns] *n.* bump/swelling. **pro•tu•ber•ant,** *adj.* which swells outwards.

proud [praʊd] *adj.* (**of**) full of pride; thinking a lot of yourself/of sth belonging to you; *inf.* **he did us p.** = he treated us generously. **proud•ly,** *adv.* with pride; with great satisfaction.

prove [pruːv] *v.* (a) to demonstrate that sth is right. (b) to turn out. **prov•a•ble,** *adj.* which can be proved. **prov•en** [prəʊvn] *adj.* which has been shown to be right.

prov•e•nance ['prɒvənəns] *n.* (*formal*) origin. **prov•en•der** ['prɒvəndə] *n.* (*no pl.*) (*formal*) food.

pro•verb ['prɒvɜːb] *n.* saying which has a moral/which teaches you sth. **pro•ver•bi•al** [prə'vɜːbɪəl] *adj.* mentioned in a proverb; well-known. **pro•ver•bi•al•ly,** *adv.* in a proverbial way.

pro•vide [prə'vaɪd] *v.* (a) to supply; **to p. for** = earn enough to feed and clothe. (b) to take care of. **pro•vid•er,** *n.* person who provides. **pro•vid•ed that, providing,** *conj.* on condition that.

prov•i•dence ['prɒvɪdəns] *n.* (lucky) fate. **prov•i•dent,** *adj.* careful to think about the future and keep money/supplies for use in time of need. **prov•i•den•tial** [prɒvɪ'denʃl] *adj.* lucky. **prov•i•den•tial•ly,** *adv.* luckily.

prov•ince ['prɒvɪns] *n.* (a) large administrative division of a country; **the provinces** = parts of a country away from the capital. (b) area of knowledge; area of responsbility. **pro•vin•cial** [prə'vɪnʃl] 1. *adj.* referring to a province/to the provinces; narrow-minded/not very worldly. 2. *n.* person from the provinces.

pro•vi•sion [prə'vɪʒn] 1. *n.* (a) thing that is provided; **to make p. for** = to see that sth is allowed for in the future. (b) *pl.* **provisions** = food. (e) condition in a document. 2. *v.* to stock up with food. **pro•vi•sion•al,** *adj.* temporary; conditional. **pro•vi•sion•al•ly,** *adv.* temporarily.

pro•vi•so [prə'vaɪzəʊ] *n.* (*pl.* **-os**) condition.

pro•voke [prə'vəʊk] *v.* (a) to incite (s.o.) to do sth violent. (b) to make (a reaction) start. **prov•o•ca•tion** [prɒvə'keɪʃn] *n.* action of provoking. **pro•voc•a•tive** [prɒ'vɒkatɪv] *adj.* likely to provoke a violent response. **pro•voc•a•tive•ly,** *adv.* in a provocative way. **pro•vok•ing,** *adj.* annoying.

pro•vost ['prɒvəst] *n.* (a) administrative official at a college/university. (b) **p. marshal** = head of a group of military police in the army/navy.

prow [praʊ] *n.* front end of a ship.

prow•ess ['praʊes] *n.* (*formal*) skill.

prowl [praʊl] 1. *n.* **on the p.** = creeping about. 2. *v.* to creep about quietly. **prowl•er,** *n.* person who creeps about, esp. a burglar.

prox•i•mate ['prɒksɪmət] *adj.* (*formal*) nearest/closest. **prox•im•i•ty** [prɒk'sɪmɪtɪ] *n.* closeness.

prox•y ['prɒksɪ] *n.* (a) document giving s.o. the power to act/to vote on your behalf. (b) person who acts/votes on your behalf.

Pro•zac ['prəuzæk] *n.* trademark for type of antidepressant drug.

prude [pru:d] *n.* prudish person. **prud•er•y, prudishness,** *n.* state of being prudish. **prud•ish,** *adj.* with strict principles and easily shocked.

pru•dence ['pru:dns] *n.* great care/caution. **pru•dent,** *adj.* very careful/very cautious. **pru•den•tial** [pru:'denʃl] *adj.* (*formal*) showing prudence. **pru•dent•ly,** *adv.* in a prudent way.

prune [pru:n] 1. *n.* dried plum. 2. *v.* to cut branches off (a tree); to cut back (a tree/shrub) to keep it in good shape or to encourage it to produce flowers; to cut back (expenditure, etc.); to cut out (parts of a book, etc.).

pru•ri•ent ['pruəriənt] *adj.* which causes indecent thoughts. **pru•ri•ence,** *n.* being prurient.

prus•sic ac•id ['prʌsɪk 'æsɪd] *n.* type of poisonous acid.

pry [praɪ] *v.* (a) to look inquisitively into sth. (b) to lift open or move with a lever.

P.S. [pi:'es] *short for* post scriptum, additional note at the end of a letter.

psalm [sɑːm] *n.* religious song from the Bible. **psalm•ist,** *n.* person who wrote the psalms. **psal•ter** ['sɔːltə] *n.* book of psalms with music, for use in church.

pse•phol•o•gy [se'fɒlədʒɪ] *n.* study of elections/voting patterns and opinion polls of voters. **pse•phol•o•gist,** *n.* person who specializes in psephology.

pseud [sju:d] *n. inf.* person who is not really as he pretends to be.

pseudo- ['sju:dəu] *prefix meaning* false.

pseu•do•nym ['sju:dənɪm] *n.* false/invented name. **pseu•don•y•mous** [sju:'dɒnɪməs] *adj.* (writer) using a pseudonym.

psit•ta•co•sis [psɪtə'kəusɪs] *n.* serious disease, caught by people from birds.

pso•ri•a•sis [sɔː'raɪəsɪs] *n.* itching disease which causes red patches on the skin.

psych•e•del•ic [saɪkə'delɪk] *adj.* so full of bright moving colors that you become hallucinated.

psy•chi•a•try [saɪ'kaɪətrɪ] *n.* study of mental disease. **psy•chi•at•ric** [saɪkɪ'ætrɪk] *adj.* referring to psychiatry. **psy•chi•a•trist** [saɪ'kaɪətrɪst] *n.* person who studies and treats mental disease.

psy•chic ['saɪkɪk] *adj. & n.* (person) in contact with supernatural forces. **psy•chi•cal,** *adj.* in contact with supernatural forces.

psy•cho•a•nal•y•sis [saɪkəuə'næləsɪs] *n.* treatment of mental disorder by discussion. **psy•cho•an•a•lyze,** *Brit.* **psy•cho•a•nal•yse,** *v.* to treat (s.o.) by psy-

choanalysis. **psy•cho•an•a•lyst** [saɪkəu'ænəlɪst] *n.* person who treats patients by psychoanalysis.

psy•chol•o•gy [saɪ'kɒlədʒɪ] *n.* study of the human mind. **psy•cho•log•i•cal** [saɪkə'lɒdʒɪkl] *adj.* referring to psychology. **psy•cho•log•i•cal•ly,** *adv.* mentally. **psy•chol•o•gist** [saɪ'kɒlədʒɪst] *n.* person who studies the human mind.

psy•cho•neu•ro•im•mu•nol•o•gy ['saɪkəunjuərəuɪmju'nɒlədʃɪ] *n.* study of the impact of psychology on the immune system.

psy•cho•path ['saɪkəpæθ] *n.* psychopathic criminal. **psy•cho•path•ic** [saɪkə'pæθɪk] *adj.* mentally unstable in a dangerous way.

psy•cho•sis [saɪ'kəusɪs] *n.* (*pl.* **-oses** [-əusiːz]) mental illness which changes the patient's personality. **psy•chot•ic** [saɪ'kɒtɪk] *adj. & n.* (person) suffering from a psychosis.

psy•cho•so•mat•ic [saɪkəusə'mætɪk] *adj.* (physical illness) created by a mental state.

psy•cho•ther•a•py [saɪkəu'θerəpɪ] *n.* treatment of mental disorder by psychological means.

Pt *symbol for* platinum.

PTA Parent Teacher Association.

ptar•mi•gan ['tɑːmɪgən] *n.* type of mountain bird.

pter•o•dac•tyl [terəu'dæktɪl] *n.* prehistoric flying dinosaur.

P.T.O. [pi:ti:'əu] *short for* please turn over (a page, etc.).

Pu *symbol for* plutonium.

pub [pʌb] *n. inf.* bar/tavern.

pu•ber•ty ['pju:bətɪ] *n.* period of adolescence when a person becomes sexually mature.

pu•bic ['pju:bɪk] *adj.* referring to the area around the sexual organs.

pub•lic ['pʌblɪk] 1. *adj.* (a) referring to the people in general; **p. holiday** = holiday for everyone. (b) **p. school** = (i) (*in the United States*) primary or secondary school supported by state and local funds; (ii) (*in Britain*) private fee-paying school which is not part of the state system. 2. *n.* people in general; **in p.** = in the open; in front of everyone. **pub•li•ca•tion** [pʌblɪ'keɪʃn] *n.* (a) making public/publishing. (b) book/paper which has been published. **pub•li•cist** ['pʌblɪsɪst] *n.* person who attracts people's attention to a product. **pub•lic•i•ty** [pʌb'lɪsɪtɪ] *n.* advertising; attracting people's attention to a product. **pub•li•cize,** *v.* to attract people's attention to sth/to make publicity for sth. **pub•lic•ly,** *adv.* in public. **pub•lic re•la•tions,** *n.* maintaining good relations between an organization and the public. **pub•lic ser•vice,** *n.* working for the government; all government

agencies and their personnel.
pub•lic-spir•it•ed, *adj.* (person) who acts energetically for the good of the community.
pub•lish ['pʌblɪʃ] *v.* to make publicly known; to bring out (a book/newspaper) for sale. **pub•lish•er**, *n.* person who produces books/newspapers for sale. **pub•lish•ing**, *n.* producing books/newspapers for sale; **p. house** = company which publishes books.
puce [pjuːs] *adj.* dark purplish red.
puck [pʌk] *n.* small disk which is hit in ice hockey.
puck•er ['pʌkə] 1. *n.* wrinkle/fold. 2. *v.* to wrinkle (your brow).
puck•ish ['pʌkɪʃ] *adj.* mischievous/full of playful tricks.
pud•ding ['pʊdɪŋ] *n.* (a) sweet/dessert. (b) sweet food which has been cooked or boiled.
pud•dle ['pʌdl] *n.* small pool of water (e.g. one left after rain).
pudg•y ['pʌdʒɪ] *adj.* soft and fat.
pu•er•ile ['pjʊəraɪl] *adj.* childish/stupid. **pu•er•il•i•ty** [pjʊə'rɪlɪtɪ] *n.* being puerile.
puff [pʌf] 1. *n.* (a) small breath. (b) **powder p.** = light pad for powdering the skin. (c) **p. pastry** = light sort of pastry. 2. *v.* to blow. **puff•ball**, *n.* type of round white fungus. **puff•i•ness**, *n.* being puffy. **puff•y**, *adj.* swollen (face).
puf•fin ['pʌfɪn] *n.* black and white bird with a large colored beak, living near the sea.
pug [pʌg] *n.* type of small dog, with a flat face. **pug•nosed**, *adj.* with a flattened nose.
pu•gi•list ['pjuːdʒɪlɪst] *n.* (*formal*) fighter/boxer. **pu•gi•lism**, *n.* (*formal*) boxing.
pug•na•cious [pʌg'neɪʃəs] (*formal*) *adj.* (person) who likes fighting; quarrelsome. **pug•na•cious•ly**, *adv.* in a pugnacious way. **pug•nac•i•ty** [pʌg'næsɪtɪ] *n.* being pugnacious.
puis•ne ['pjuːnɪ] *adj.* lower in rank.
pu•is•sance ['pwiːsɑːns] *n.* power; strength.
puke [pjuːk] *v. inf.* to vomit.
puk•ka ['pʌkə] *adj. inf.* real; of good quality.
pul•chri•tude ['pʌlkrɪtjuːd] *n.* (*formal*) beauty.
pule [pjuːl] *v.* (*of children*) to wail/to whimper.
pull [pʊl] 1. *n.* (a) act of dragging/moving sth toward you. (b) *inf.* influence. (c) handle (which has to be pulled). (d) deep inhaling (of a cigarette). 2. *v.* (a) to move (sth) by dragging; to move (sth) toward you. (b) to strain (a muscle). **pull down**, *v.* to bring (sth) down by

pulling. **pull in**, *v.* to reach a place. **pull off**, *v.* (a) to take off (a piece of clothing/a handle, etc.) by pulling. (b) *inf.* to succeed in doing (sth). (c) to drive off a road and stop. **pull out**, *v.* (a) to bring (sth) out by pulling. (b) to drive away from the side of the road; to drive towards the middle of the road. **pull through**, *v.* to recover from an illness. **pull to•geth•er**, *v.* **he pulled himself together** = he became calmer/he controlled his emotions. **pull up**, *v.* (a) to stop (in a vehicle). (b) to raise by pulling.
pul•let ['pʊlɪt] *n.* young chicken.
pul•ley ['pʊlɪ] *n.* apparatus for lifting heavy weights with a grooved wheel around which a rope runs.
pull•man ['pʊlmən] *n.* sleeping car (on a train).
pull•o•ver ['pʊləʊvə] *n.* piece of clothing made of wool, etc., covering the top part of the body and which you pull on over your head.
pul•mo•nar•y ['pʌlmənrɪ] *adj.* referring to the lungs.
pulp [pʌlp] 1. *n.* squashy mass. 2. *v.* to crush to a pulp. **pulp•y**, *adj.* in a pulp.
pul•pit ['pʊlpɪt] *n.* enclosed platform in a church where the priest preaches.
pul•sar ['pʌlsə] *n.* invisible star which sends out radio signals.
pulse [pʌls] *n.* 1. (a) regular beat of the heart. (b) dried seed of peas/beans. 2. *v.* to pulsate. **pul•sate** [pʌl'seɪt] *v.* to throb regularly. **pul•sa•tion** [pʌl'seɪʃn] *n.* regular throbbing.
pul•ver•ize ['pʌlvəraɪz] *v.* to crush to powder. **pul•ver•i•za•tion** [pʌlvərar'zeɪʃn] *n.* crushing to powder.
pu•ma ['pjuːmə] *n.* large wild American cat.
pum•ice (stone) ['pʌmɪs('stəʊn)] *n.* block of light gray porous lava used for rubbing stains off your skin.
pum•mel ['pʌml] *v.* (**pummeled, pummelled**) to hit s.o. with many blows.
pump [pʌmp] 1. *n.* (a) machine for forcing liquids or air. (b) low-cut shoe for women. 2. *v.* (a) to force (liquid/air) with a pump. (b) *inf.* to ask (s.o.) searching questions.
pump•kin ['pʌmpkɪn] *n.* large round orange-colored vegetable.
pun [pʌn] 1. *n.* play with words of different meanings. 2. *v.* (**punned**) to make puns. **pun•ster**, *n.* a person who is always making puns.
punch [pʌntʃ] 1. *n.* (*pl.* **-es**) (a) blow with the fist; **p. line** = last sentence of a story/joke

---

æ back, ɑ: farm, ɒ: top, aɪ pipe, aʊ how, aɪe fire, aʊə flower, ɔ: bought, ɔɪ toy, e fed, eəhair, eɪ take, ə afraid, əʊ boat, əʊə lower, vː word, iː heap, ɪ hit, ɪə hear, uː school, ʊ book, ʌ but, b back, d dog, ð then, dʒ just, f fog, g go, h hand, j yes, k catch, l last, m mix, n nut, ŋ sing, p penny, r round, s some, ʃ short, t too, tʃ chop, θ thing, v voice, w was, z zoo, ʒ treasure

which gives the point. (b) metal tool for making holes. (c) drink made of wine or spirits and spices. 2. *v.* (a) to hit (s.o.) with your fist. (b) to make holes in (sth) with a punch. **Punch and Ju•dy,** *n.* form of children's puppet show, with traditional characters. **punch bowl,** *n.* bowl for mixing wine and spices to make punch. **punch-drunk,** *adj.* suffering from brain damage from being punched on the head too often. **punch-out,** *n. inf.* fight.

punc•til•i•ous [pʌŋk'tɪlɪəs] *adj.* attentive to detail/extremely fussy. **punc•til•i•ous•ly,** *adv.* in a punctilious way. **punc•til•i•ous•ness,** *n.* being punctilious.

punc•tu•al ['pʌŋktjʊəl] *adj.* on time. **punc•tu•al•i•ty** [pʌŋktjuˈælɪtɪ] *n.* being on time/never being late. **punc•tu•al•ly,** *adv.* on time.

punc•tu•ate ['pʌŋktjueɪt] *v.* (a) to split a sentence using punctuation marks. (b) to interrupt. **punc•tu•a•tion** [pʌŋktjuˈeɪʃn] *n.* splitting of a sentence using punctuation marks; **p. marks** = signs used in writing (such as period, comma, dash) to show how a sentence is split up.

punc•ture ['pʌŋktʃə] 1. *n.* hole in a tire; very small hole. 2. *v.* to make a small hole in (sth).

pun•dit ['pʌndɪt] *n.* expert (esp. in political matters).

pun•gent ['pʌndʒənt] *adj.* sharp (taste, smell); sarcastic (comment). **pun•gen•cy,** *n.* being pungent. **pun•gent•ly,** *adv.* in a pungent way.

pun•ish ['pʌnɪʃ] *v.* to make (s.o.) suffer because of sth he has done. **pun•ish•a•ble,** *adj.* (offense) for which you can be punished. **pun•ish•ment,** *n.* treatment given to punish s.o. **pu•ni•tive** ['pjuːnətɪv] *adj.* which aims to punish.

punk [pʌŋk] 1. *n. inf.* (a) young hoodlum. (b) follower of punk rock. 2. *adj. inf.* bad/inferior. **punk rock,** *n.* loud music played by people wearing outrageous costumes.

punt [pʌnt] 1. *n.* (a) long flat-bottomed boat, propelled with a pole. (b) (*Ireland*) monetary unit. 2. *v.* (a) to push (a punt) with a pole. (b) to kick a ball which is in the air. (c) to bet on a horse race. **punt•er,** *n.* (a) person who gambles, esp. on horseraces. (b) person who pushes a punt along with a pole.

pu•ny ['pjuːnɪ] *adj.* (-ier, -iest) weak/feeble; very small.

pup [pʌp] 1. *n.* young of certain animals, esp. young dog; **p. tent** = small tent made of two sloping sides and a horizontal pole. 2. *v.* (**pupped**) to have pups.

pu•pa ['pjuːpə] *n.* (*pl.* **-pae** [-piː], **-as**) resting period in the life of an insect when it is changing from a grub/caterpillar to a butterfly/beetle. **pu•pal,** *adj.* referring to a pupa. **pu•pate** [pjuːˈpeɪt] *v.* (*of caterpillar*) to turn into a pupa.

pu•pil ['pjuːpl] *n.* (a) child at a school; person learning from a teacher. (b) hole in the central part of the eye, through which the light passes.

pup•pet ['pʌpɪt] *n.* doll which moves and which is used to give a performance; **p. show** = performance given using puppets; **p. state** = country controlled by another country. **pup•pet•eer** [pʌpɪ'tɪə] *n.* person who gives a performance using puppets.

pup•py ['pʌpɪ] *n.* young dog.

pur•blind ['pɜːblaɪnd] *adj.* partly blind.

pur•chase ['pɜːtʃəs] 1. *n.* (a) thing bought. (b) ability to grip/ability to lift sth by using a lever. 2. *v.* to buy; **purchasing power** = quantity that can be bought with a certain amount of money. **pur•chas•er,** *n.* person who buys sth.

pur•dah ['pɜːdə] *n.* seclusion of women (in Eastern countries).

pure ['pjʊə] *adj.* (-er, -est) (a) very clean; not mixed with other things. (b) innocent; with no faults. **pure•ly,** *adv.* only/solely.

pu•rée ['pjʊəreɪ] 1. *n.* semi-liquid pulp (of a vegetable/fruit). 2. *v.* to make (sth) into a purée.

pur•ga•to•ry ['pɜːgətrɪ] *n.* place where you suffer temporarily after death; (place of) suffering.

purge [pɜːdʒ] 1. *n.* (a) medicine which clears the bowels. (b) removal of political opponents. 2. *v.* (a) to clear out (waste matter). (b) to remove (political opponents). **pur•ga•tive** ['pɜːgətɪv] *adj. & n.* (medicine) which clears the bowels.

pu•ri•fy ['pjʊərɪfaɪ] *v.* to clean/to make pure. **pu•ri•fi•ca•tion** [pjʊərɪfɪ'keɪʃn] *n.* making pure. **pu•ri•fi•er,** *n.* machine that purifies. **pur•ist** ['pjʊərɪst] *n.* person who insists on everything being done in the correct way. **pu•ri•ty,** *n.* being pure/absolutely clean.

pu•ri•tan ['pjʊərɪtən] *n.* puritanical person. **pu•ri•tan•i•cal** [pjʊərɪ'tænɪkl] *adj.* very strict concerning morals.

purl [pɜːl] *v.* to knit putting your needle into the back of the loop.

pur•lieus ['pɜːljuːz] *pl. n.* (*formal*) surroundings; neighborhood.

pur•loin [pɜːˈlɔɪn] *v.* (*formal*) to steal.

pur•ple ['pɜːpl] *adj. & n.* reddish-blue (color). **pur•plish,** *adj.* quite purple.

pur•port [pɜːˈpɔːt] (*formal*) 1. *n.* meaning. 2. *v.* to mean.

pur•pose ['pɜːpəs] *n.* aim/plan; use; **on p.** = according to what was planned; intentionally.

pur•pose•ful, *adj.* intentional; with an aim in view; (person) with set aims. **pur•pose•ful•ly,** *adv.* in a purposeful way. **pur•pose•ful•ness,** *n.* being purposeful. **pur•pose•ly,** *adv.* on purpose/intentionally.

purr [pɜː] 1. *n.* (a) noise made by a cat when pleased. (b) low noise made by a powerful engine. 2. *v.* (a) (*of cat*) to make a noise to show pleasure. (b) (*of engine*) to make a low noise.

purse [pɜːs] 1. *n.* (a) small bag for carrying money. (b) handbag. 2. **to p. your lips** = to pinch/to press your lips together to show you are displeased. **purs•er,** *n.* officer on a ship who deals with the money, supplies and the passengers' accommodation.

pur•sue [pə'sjuː] *v.* (a) to chase (s.o./sth). (b) to continue to do (sth). **pur•su•ance,** *n.* (*formal*) carrying out of (duty, plan, etc.). **pur•su•ant to,** *adv.* relating to. **pur•su•er,** *n.* person who chases s.o. **pur•suit** [pə'sjuːt] *n.* (a) chase; **in p. of** = looking for. (b) (*formal*) career/occupation.

pu•ru•lent ['pjʊərʊlənt] *adj.* (*formal*) full of pus.

pur•vey [pɜː'veɪ] *v.* (*formal*) to supply (goods). **pur•vey•or,** *n.* person who supplies goods.

pur•view ['pɜːvjuː] *n.* general scope of a document.

pus [pʌs] *n.* yellowish liquid which gathers in infected wounds/spots.

push [pʊʃ] 1. *n.* (-es) (a) act of pressing sth so that it moves away from you. (b) energy; *inf.* determination to do well. 2. *v.* (a) to press; to move (sth) by pressing. (b) *inf.* **I am pushed for time** = I haven't much time to spare. (c) *Sl.* to sell (drugs) illegally. **push but•ton,** *n.* switch which is operated by pushing. **push•er,** *n. Sl.* person who sells drugs illegally. **push•ful,** *adj.* ambitious; eager to get what you want. **push off,** *v. inf.* to get going/to start a journey. **push•o•ver,** *n. inf.* easy task; person who is easily influenced. **push-up,** *n.* exercise where you lie flat on the floor and push yourself up with your hands. **push•y,** *adj. inf.* wanting to succeed/ambitious.

pu•sil•lan•i•mous [pjuːsɪ'lænɪməs] *adj.* (*formal*) timid/afraid. **pu•sil•la•nim•i•ty** [pjuːsɪlə'nɪmɪtɪ] *n.* being pusillanimous.

puss [pʊs], **pus•sy** ['pʊsɪ], **pus•sy•cat** ['pʊsɪkæt] *n.* familiar words for a cat. **pus•sy•foot,** *v. inf.* **to p. about** = to dither/to be undecided.

pus•tule ['pʌstjuːl] *n.* blister/spot (on the skin).

put [pʊt] *v.* (**put; putting**) (a) to place; *inf.* **to stay p.** = to stay where you are. (b) to express in words. (c) to estimate **at.** (d) **to p. a stop to** = to stop. (e) (*in sports*) to throw (the shot). **put a•cross,** *v.* to explain (sth) in a convincing way. **put a•way,** *v.* to clear (things) away. **put back,** *v.* to place (sth) where it was before. **put by,** *v.* to save. **put down,** *v.* (a) to place at a lower level/on the ground. (b) to land an aircraft. (c) to note. (d) to kill (a sick animal). (e) **to p. your foot down** = to be very strict/firm. **put in,** *v.* (a) to place inside. (b) **he p. in three hour's work** = he worked for three hours. (c) **to p. in for a job** = to apply. **put off,** *v.* (a) to delay. (b) to upset or repel. **put on,** *v.* (a) to place. (b) to get dressed in (a piece of clothing). (c) to switch on (a light, etc.). (d) to add (weight). **put out,** *v.* (a) to place outside. (b) to stretch out (one's hand, etc.). (c) to switch off (a light, etc.). (d) *inf.* **to be p. out** = to be annoyed. (e) (*of ships*) **to p. out to sea** = to leave harbor. **put up,** *v.* (a) to fix upright; to build. (b) to raise. (c) to offer. (d) to find a place for (s.o.) to sleep. (e) **to p. up with s.o./sth** = to accept s.o./sth, even if they are unpleasant/noisy, etc. (f) **to p. s.o. up to sth** = to encourage s.o. to do sth. **put-up•on,** *adj.* forced to do sth unpleasant.

pu•ta•tive ['pjuːtətɪv] *adj.* (*formal*) **the p. author** = the person who is supposed to be the author.

pu•tre•fy ['pjuːtrɪfaɪ] *v.* to rot. **pu•tre•fac•tion** [pjuːtrɪ'fækʃn] *n.* rotting. **pu•tres•cent,** *adj.* which is rotting. **pu•trid,** *adj.* rotten; smelling rotten.

putsch [pʊtʃ] *n.* armed overthrow of a government.

putt [pʌt] 1. *n.* short shot (on a green) in golf. 2. *v.* to hit a short shot in golf. **put•ter.** 1. *n.* golf club for putting. 2. *v.* **to p. around** = not to do anything in particular/to do little jobs here and there.

put•tee ['pʌtɪ] *n.* long piece of cloth wound round the leg to act as protection.

put•ty ['pʌtɪ] *n.* soft substance which hardens after a time, used esp. for sealing the glass in windows.

puz•zle ['pʌzl] 1. *n.* (a) problem; thing which is difficult to solve. (b) game where you have to solve a problem. 2. *v.* to perplex/to mystify; to be a problem. **puz•zle•ment,** *n.* being puz-

---

æ back, ɑː farm, ɒ top, aɪ pipe, aʊ how, aɪə fire, aʊə flower, ɔː bought, ɔɪ toy, e fed, eəhair, eɪ take, ə afraid, əʊ boat, əʊə lower, ɜː word, iː heap, ɪ hit, ɪə hear, uː school, ʊ book, ʌ but, b back, d dog, ð then, dʒ just, f fog, g go, h hand, j yes, k catch, l last, m mix, n nut, ŋ sing, p penny, r round, s some, ʃ short, t too, tʃ chop, θ thing, v voice, w was, z zoo, ʒ treasure

zled. **puzz•ling,** *adj.* which does not make sense/which is a problem.

PVC [piːviːˈsiː] *n.* type of plastic.

PVS [piːviːˈes] *abbrev. for* persistent vegetative state.

pyg•my [ˈpɪgmɪ] *adj. & n.* (type of animal) which is smaller than normal; very short (person).

py•ja•mas [pɪˈdʒɑːməz] *n. pl. Brit.* pajamas.

py•lon [ˈpaɪlən] *n.* tall metal tower for carrying electric cables.

py•or•rhe•a [paɪəˈrɪə] *n.* infection of the gums around the teeth.

pyr•a•mid [ˈpɪrəmɪd] *n.* shape with a square base and four sides rising to meet at a point. **py•ram•i•dal** [pɪˈræmɪdl] *adj.* shaped like a pyramid.

pyre [ˈpaɪə] *n.* ceremonial fire; **funeral p.** = pile on which a dead body is cremated.

py•re•thrum [paɪˈriːθrəm] *n.* insecticide made from a flower.

py•ri•tes [paɪˈraɪtiːz] *n.* yellowish chemical substance containing a metal.

py•ro•ma•ni•ac [paɪrəʊˈmeɪnɪæk] *n.* person who sets fire to buildings.

py•ro•tech•nics [paɪrəʊˈtekniks] *n. pl.* science of fireworks. **py•ro•tech•nic(al),** *adj.* referring to fireworks.

Pyr•rhic vic•to•ry [ˈpɪrɪk ˈvɪktrɪ] *n.* victory which costs the victor too much effort/too many losses.

py•thon [ˈpaɪθn] *n.* large snake which kills its prey by crushing.

pyx [pɪks] *n.* box in church where consecrated bread and wine are kept.

Qq

qua [kweɪ] *adv.* acting or functioning as.

quack [kwæk] 1. *n.* (a) sound made by a duck. (b) *inf.* unqualified doctor. 2. *v.* to make a noise like a duck.

quad [kwɒd] *n. inf.* quadrangle. **quad•ran•gle** ['kwɒdræŋgl] *n.* open square surrounded by buildings (in a school/college).

quad•rant ['kwɒdrənt] *n.* (a) quarter of a circle. (b) instrument used for measuring angles.

quad•ra•phon•ic [kwɒdrə'fɒnɪk] *adj.* (sound) which is reproduced through four loudspeakers.

quad•rat•ic [kwɒd'rætɪk] *adj.* (equation) involving the square of the unknown quantity.

quad•ren•ni•al [kwɒd'renɪəl] *adj.* happening every four years.

quad•ri•lat•er•al [kwɒdrɪ'lætərəl] *adj. & n.* (shape) with four sides.

quad•ru•ped ['kwɒdrʊped] *n.* animal with four legs.

quad•ru•ple [kwɒ'drʊpl] *v.* to multiply four times. **quad•ru•plets** ['kwɒdrʊplets] *n. pl.* four babies born at the same birth. **quad•ru•pli•cate** [kwɒ'druːplɪkət] *n.* **in q.** = in four copies. **quads** [kwɒdz] *n. pl. inf.* quadruplets.

quaff [kwɒf] *v.* to drink with large gulps.

quag•mire ['kwɒgmaɪə] *n.* bog/area of dangerous marsh.

quail [kweɪl] 1. *n.* small game bird. 2. *v.* to shrink back in fear; to shudder (**at** sth).

quaint [kweɪnt] *adj.* (-er, -est) picturesque/oddly old-fashioned. **quaint•ly,** *adv.* in a quaint way. **quaint•ness,** *n.* old-fashioned oddness.

quake [kweɪk] 1. *n. inf.* earthquake. 2. *v.* to shake (with fear/cold). **Quak•er,** *n. inf.* member of a Christian religious society, known as the Society of Friends.

qual•i•fy ['kwɒlɪfaɪ] *v.* (a) **to q. as** = to study for and obtain a license or permit which allows you to do a certain type of work. (b) **to q. for** = to pass a test/a section of a competition and so proceed to the next step. (c) to modify; to attach conditions. **qual•i•fi•ca•tion** [kwɒlɪfɪ'keɪʃn] *n.* (a) knowledge, skill, or other proof that shows you have the necessary requirements for a job, position, etc. (b) modification/condition which limits. **qual•i•fi•er,** *n.* person who qualifies.

qual•i•ty ['kwɒlɪtɪ] *n.* (a) worth. (b) characteristic. **qual•i•ta•tive,** *adj.* referring to quality.

qualm [kwɑːm] *n.* feeling of guilt/worry.

quan•da•ry ['kwɒndrɪ] *n.* puzzle/problem; **in a q.** = puzzled/not knowing what to do.

quan•ti•fy ['kwɒntɪfaɪ] *v.* to calculate in quantities/in amounts. **quan•ti•fi•a•ble,** *adj.* which can be quantified.

quan•ti•ty ['kwɒntɪtɪ] *n.* amount; **an unknown q.** = person/thing you know nothing about. **quan•ti•ta•tive,** *adj.* referring to quantity.

quan•tum ['kwɒntəm] *n.* **q. theory** = theory in physics that energy exists in fixed amounts.

quar•an•tine ['kwɒrəntiːn] 1. *n.* period of time when an animal/a person/thing (usu. coming from another country) has to be kept apart to avoid the risk of passing on disease. 2. *v.* to put (s.o./an animal/sth) in quarantine.

quark [kwɑːk] *n.* smallest particle.

quar•rel ['kwɒrəl] 1. *n.* argument; **to pick a q. with s.o.** = to start an argument. 2. *v.* (**quarreled, quarrelled**) to argue (**about/over** sth). **quar•rel•ing,** *n.* arguments. **quar•rel•some,** *adj.* argumentative/often getting into quarrels.

quar•ry ['kwɒrɪ] 1. *n.* (a) place where stone, etc., is dug out of the ground. (b) animal which is being hunted; person/thing which is being looked for. 2. *v.* to dig (stone) out of the ground.

quart [kwɔːt] *n.* measure of liquid (= 2 pints).

quar•ter ['kwɔːtə] 1. *n.* (a) one of four parts. (b) period of fifteen minutes before or after the hour. (c) period of three months. (d) area. (e) **quarters** = accommodation for people in the armed forces. (f) 25 cent coin. 2. *v.* (a) to cut into four equal parts. (b) to place (soldiers) in lodgings. **quarter day,** *n.* day which marks the beginning of a three month period for accounting purposes. **quar•ter•deck,** *n.* top deck of a ship near the stern. **quar•ter•fi•nal,** *n.* (*in sport*) one of four

---

æ back, aː farm, ɒ top, aɪ pipe, aʊ how, aie fire, aʊə flower, ɔː bought, ɔɪ toy, e fed, eəhair, eɪ take, ə afraid, əʊ boat, əʊə lower, vː word, iː heap, ɪ hit, ɪə hear, uː school, ʊ book, ʌ but, b back, d dog, ð then, dʒ just, f fog, g go, h hand, j yes, k catch, l last, m mix, n nut, ŋ sing, p penny, r round, s some, ʃ short, t too, tʃ chop, θ thing, v voice, w was, z zoo, ʒ treasure

matches in a competition, the winners of which go into the semi-finals. **quar•ter•ly,** *adj., adv. & n.* (magazine) which appears every three months. **quar•ter•mas•ter,** *n.* (*Military*) officer in charge of clothing, equipment, quarters, etc.

quar•tet(te) [kwɔːˈtet] *n.* (a) four people. (b) four musicians playing together. (c) piece of music for four musicians.

quar•to [ˈkwɔːtəʊ] *adj. & n.* size of paper one quarter of a standard sheet.

quartz [kwɔːts] *n.* hard crystalline mineral, used for making watches because of its very regular vibrations.

qua•sar [ˈkweɪsɑː] *n.* distant star which gives off intense radiation.

quash [kwɒʃ] *v.* to annul (a legal sentence).

quasi- [ˈkweɪzaɪ] *prefix meaning* almost.

quat•rain [ˈkwɒtreɪn] *n.* stanza of poetry with four lines.

qua•ver [ˈkweɪvə] 1. *n.* tremble (in the voice). 2. *v.* to tremble (of voice). **qua•ver•ing,** *adj.* trembling (voice).

quay [kiː] *n.* stone wharf/place where ships tie up to load or unload.

quea•sy [ˈkwiːzɪ] *adj.* feeling sick. **quea•si•ness,** *n.* being queasy.

queen [kwiːn] *n.* (a) wife of a king; woman ruler of a country; **q. mother** = mother of a king or queen who is the widow of a king. (b) (*at cards*) card between the jack and the king. (c) important piece in chess. (d) **q. ant/bee** = leading ant/bee in a colony. (e) the best/the most perfect woman. (f) *Sl.* male homosexual. **queen•ly,** *adj.* like a queen.

queer [ˈkwɪə] 1. *adj.* (-er, -est) (a) odd/strange. (b) *Sl. adj. & n.* homosexual. (c) ill. 2. *v.* to make sth go wrong. **queer•ness,** *n.* strangeness/oddness.

quell [kwel] *v.* to calm (a riot); to hold back (your feelings).

quench [kwenʃ] *v.* **to q. your thirst** = to have a drink.

quern [kwɜːn] *n.* mill for grinding flour by hand.

quer•u•lous [ˈkwerjuləs] *adj.* bad-tempered/peevish; always complaining. **quer•u•lous•ly,** *adv.* in a querulous way. **quer•u•lous•ness,** *n.* being querulous.

que•ry [ˈkwɪərɪ] 1. *n.* (a) question. (b) question mark. 2. *v.* to doubt whether sth is true; to ask a question.

quest [kwest] *n.* (*formal*) search.

ques•tion [ˈkwestʃn] 1. *n.* (a) sentence which requires an answer; **q. mark** = sign (?) which shows that a question is being asked. (b) problem; **the human rights q.** (c) matter; **the matter in q.** = which is being discussed; **it's out of the q.** = it's unthinkable. 2. *v.* (a) to ask (s.o.) ques-

tions. (b) to doubt. **ques•tion•a•ble,** *adj.* doubtful. **ques•tion•er,** *n.* person who asks questions. **ques•tion•naire** [kwestʃənˈneə] *n.* printed list of questions given to people to answer.

queue [kjuː] (*esp. Brit.*) 1. *n.* line of people/cars, etc., waiting one behind the other for sth. 2. *v.* (*also* **queue up**) to form a queue.

quib•ble [ˈkwɪbl] 1. *n.* argument about details; petty objection. 2. *v.* to argue about details. **quib•bler,** *n.* person who argues about details.

quiche [kiːʃ] *n.* open tart with a filling of eggs/meat/vegetables, etc.

quick [kwɪk] 1. *adj.* (-er, -est) (a) fast/rapid. (b) **she has a q. temper** = she loses her temper easily. 2. *n.* live flesh (esp. flesh around fingernails/toenails); **he was cut to the q.** = he was very hurt. **quick-act•ing,** *adj.* (medicine) which takes effect rapidly. **quick•en,** *v.* (a) to make (sth) go faster. (b) to stimulate. **quick•ie,** *n. inf.* (a) quick drink/question, etc. (b) quick divorce. **quick•lime,** *n.* lime. **quick•ly,** *adv.* rapidly. **quick•ness,** *n.* being quick. **quick•sand,** *n.* dangerous area of soft sand where you can sink in easily. **quick•sil•ver,** *n.* mercury. **quick•step,** *n.* dance with quick steps. **quick-tem•pered,** *adj.* (person) who loses his temper easily. **quick-wit•ted,** *adj.* intelligent (person)/(person) who understands quickly.

quid [kwɪd] *n.* lump of chewing tobacco.

quid pro quo [kwɪdprəʊˈkwəʊ] *n.* something done in return for something else.

qui•es•cent [kwaɪˈesnt] *adj.* (*formal*) calm. **qui•es•cence,** *n.* calmness.

qui•et [ˈkwaɪət] 1. *n.* absence of noise; calm/tranquility. 2. *adj.* (-er, -est) (a) calm/making no noise. (b) simple; **q. color scheme** = where the colors aren't bright. 3. *v.* to calm; to stop (s.o.) being noisy. **qui•et•ly,** *adv.* without making any noise. **qui•et•ness,** *n.* calm/tranquility. **qui•e•tude,** *n.* (*formal*) quietness.

quill [kwɪl] *n.* long feather (formerly used as a pen).

quilt [kwɪlt] *n.* padded cover for a bed. **quilt•ed,** *adj.* made with a pad sewn between two layers of cloth.

quince [kwɪns] *n.* hard fruit used for making jelly; tree producing this fruit.

qui•nine [ˈkwɪniːn] *n.* drug made from the bark of a tropical tree, used to treat malaria.

quin•quen•ni•al [kwɪnˈkwenɪəl] *adj.* happening every five years.

quins [kwɪnz] *n. pl. inf.* quintuplets.

quin•sy [ˈkwɪnzɪ] *n.* (*old*) infection of the tonsils.

quin•tes•sence [kwɪn'tesns] *n.* essential part (of sth); perfect example. **quin•tes•sen•tial** [kwinti'senʃl] *adj.* which is a perfect example.

quin•tet(te) [kwɪn'tet] *n.* (a) group of five musicians playing together. (b) piece of music for five musicians.

quin•tu•ple ['kwɪntjupl] *v.* to multiply five times. **quin•tup•lets,** *n. pl.* five babies born at the same birth.

quip [kwɪp] 1. *n.* joke/clever remark. 2. *v.* (**quipped**) to make a joke/a clever remark.

quire ['kwaɪə] *n.* 24 or 25 sheets of paper.

quirk [kwɜːk] *n.* oddity/strange event.

quis•ling ['kwɪzlɪŋ] *n.* person who betrays his country by helping the enemy who is occupying it.

quit [kwɪt] *v.* (**quit/quitted**) (a) *inf.* to leave (a job/house, etc.). (b) *inf.* to stop. **quits,** *adj.* **to be q.** = to be equal. **quit•tance,** *n.* (*formal*) receipt. **quit•ter,** *n. inf.* person who gives up easily.

quite [kwaɪt] *adv.* (a) completely. (b) fairly/relatively; **q. a few** = several.

quiv•er ['kwɪvə] 1. *n.* (a) tremor/slight shake. (b) holder for arrows. 2. *v.* to tremble.

quix•ot•ic [kwɪk'sɒtɪk] *adj.* strange/impractical (person). **quix•ot•i•cal•ly,** *adv.* in a quixotic way.

quiz [kwɪz] 1. *n.* (*pl.* **quizzes**) series of questions; **q. show** = TV/radio program where people are asked questions. 2. *v.* (**quizzed**) to ask (s.o.) questions. **quizmaster,** *n.* person who asks the questions in a TV/radio quiz.

quiz•zi•cal ['kwɪzɪkl] *adj.* odd.

quoin [kɔɪn] *n.* block of stone making a corner of a building.

quoit [kwɔɪt] *n.* large ring used in a game to throw over pegs.

quo•rum ['kwɔːrəm] *n.* number of people who have to be present to make a vote valid.

quo•ta ['kwəʊtə] *n.* fixed amount of goods which can be supplied/share; fixed number.

quote [kwəʊt] 1. *n.* (a) passage quoted; quotation. (b) estimate. (c) *inf.* **quotes** = quotation marks. 2. *v.* (a) to repeat a number (as a reference); to repeat a text of an author; **can I q. you?** = can I repeat what you have said? (b) to indicate the beginning of a quotation (when speaking). (c) to give an estimate **for** work to be done. **quot•a•ble,** *adj.* which can be quoted; suitable to be quotable. **quo•ta•tion** [kwəʊ'teɪʃn] *n.* (a) passage quoted. (b) estimate. (c) **q. mark** = punctuation mark (" ") used to indicate what s.o. has said.

quoth [kwəʊθ] *v.* (*old*) said.

quo•tient ['kwəʊʃnt] *n.* result when one number is divided by another.

q.v. [kjuː'viː] *abbreviation for* quod vide, *meaning* which see.

qwert•y ['kwɜːtɪ] *n.* normal English keyboard for a typewriter or computer.

æ back, aː farm, ɒː top, aɪ pipe, aʊ how, aie fire, aʊə flower, ɔː bought, ɔɪ toy, e fed, eəhair, eɪ take, ə afraid, əʊ boat, əʊə lower, vː word, iː heap, ɪ hit, ɪə hear, uː school, ʊ book, ʌ but, b back, d dog, ð then, dʒ just, f fog, g go, h hand, j yes, k catch, l last, m mix, n nut, ŋ sing, p penny, r round, s some, ʃ short, t too, tʃ chop, θ thing, v voice, w was, z zoo, ʒ treasure

Rr

R [ɑː] **the three Rs** = basic subjects in primary school (reading, writing, arithmetic).

Ra *symbol for* radium.

rab•bi ['ræbaɪ] *n.* Jewish priest. **rab•bin•i•cal** [rə'bɪnɪkl] *adj.* referring to a rabbi.

rab•bit ['ræbɪt] *n.* common wild animal with long ears and short tail which lives in burrows.

rab•ble ['ræbl] *n.* crowd/unruly mass of people.

rab•id ['ræbɪd] *adj.* (a) suffering from rabies. (b) wild/fanatic. **rab•id•i•ty** [rə'bɪdɪtɪ] *n.* being rabid. **ra•bies** ['reɪbiːz] *n.* hydrophobia.

rac•coon [rə'kuːn] *n.* type of small North American flesh-eating wild animal.

race [reɪs] 1. *n.* (a) competition to see who is the fastest; **to run a r.** (b) rush of water in a narrow channel. (c) group of human beings with similar physical characteristics; **r. relations** = relations between different racial groups in the same country. (d) species/breed of plant/animal, etc. 2. *v.* (a) to run/to drive, etc., to see who is the fastest. (b) to go very fast. **race•course,** *n.* grassy track where horse races are run. **race•horse,** *n.* horse specially bred and trained to run in races. **rac•er,** *n.* (a) person who is running in a race. (b) special bicycle/car for racing. **race•track,** *n.* track, usu. grassy, where horse races are run. **ra•cial** ['reɪʃl] *adj.* referring to race; **r. discrimination/prejudice** = discrimination/prejudice against s.o. because of race. **ra•cial•ism,** *n.* racism. **ra•cial•ist,** *adj. & n.* racist. **ra•cial•ly,** *adv.* in a racial way. **rac•ing,** *n.* competitions to see who is fastest. **rac•ism,** *n.* prejudice against a group of people because of their race. **rac•ist,** *adj. & n.* (person) who treats s.o. differently because of race. **rac•y,** *adj.* (**-ier, -iest**) vigorous (style of writing).

ra•ceme [rə'siːm] *n.* flowers growing along a stem.

rack [ræk] 1. *n.* (a) frame to hold things (such as letters/hats); **roof r.** = grid attached to the roof of a car for carrying luggage. (b) **to go to r. and ruin** = to become dilapidated. (c) **r. of lamb** = rib section of lamb, formed of a series of chops, roasted. 2. *v.* (a) **to r. your brains** = to think very hard. (b) to cause pain (to). (c) to draw (wine, beer) off the dregs. **rack and pin•ion,** *n.* toothed wheel which connects with a toothed bar to drive a machine (esp. a cog railway) forward. **rack rail•way,** *n.* cog railway.

rack•et ['rækɪt] 1. *n.* (a) instrument made of a light frame with tight strings across it, used for hitting the ball in tennis, squash and badminton. (b) *inf.* loud noise. (c) *inf.* illegal profit-making deal. **rack•et•eer** [rəkɪ'tɪə] *n.* swindler/gangster. **rack•et•eer•ing,** *n.* crime of running a racket. **rack•et•y,** *adj.* (car) which makes a lot of noise.

rac•on•teur [rækɒn'tɜː] *n.* person who is good at telling stories.

rac•quet ['rækɪt] *n.* (sports) racket.

ra•dar ['reɪdɑː] *n.* system by which you can detect objects and judge their position by sending radio signals to them which are reflected back as dots on a small screen.

ra•di•ate ['reɪdɪeɪt] *v.* to send out/to give off (rays/heat); to spread out (from a central point). **ra•di•al,** *adj.* which spreads out from a central point; (tire) with grooves which give a better grip of the road surface. **ra•di•ance,** *n.* brightness. **ra•di•ant,** *adj.* bright (smile); (heat) which radiates. **ra•di•ant•ly,** *adv.* in a radiant way. **ra•di•a•tion** [reɪdɪ'eɪʃn] *n.* sending out/giving off (rays, heat). **ra•di•a•tor** ['reɪdɪeɪtə] *n.* (a) heating device in which steam or hot water passes through a series of coils or pipes. (b) water-filled metal panel for cooling a car engine.

rad•i•cal ['rædɪkl] 1. *adj.* thorough/complete; basic (difference); **r. party** = a party which believes in the necessity of making great changes in the system of running a country. 2. *n.* member of a radical party. **rad•i•cal•ly,** *adv.* in a radical way.

rad•i•cle ['rædɪkl] *n.* small root (on a pea or bean).

ra•di•o ['reɪdɪəʊ] 1. *n.* (*pl.* **-os**) system for sending out/receiving messages using atmospheric waves; apparatus which sends out/receives messages using atmospheric waves. 2. *v.* to send (a message) using a radio. **ra•di•o•ac•tive** [reɪdɪəʊ'æktɪv] *adj.* (substance) which gives off harmful radiation through the breaking up of its atoms.

ra•di•o•ac•tiv•i•ty [reɪdɪəvæk'tɪvɪtɪ] *n.* giving off of harmful radiation due to the breaking up of atoms. **ra•di•o•car•bon,** *n.* radioactive form of carbon; **r. dating** = calculating the age of sth. by measuring the amount of radiocarbon that has decayed. **ra•di•og•ra•pher** [reɪdɪ'ɒɡrəfə] *n.* person who takes X-rays. **ra•di•og•ra•phy,** *n.* making X-rays. **ra•di•o•i•so•tope,** *n.* radioactive isotope, used in radiation treatment. **ra•di•ol•o•gist,** *n.* person who studies X-rays. **ra•di•ol•o•gy** [reɪdɪ'ɒlədʒɪ] *n.* science of X-rays and their use in medicine. **ra•di•o•tel•e•phone,** *n.* long-distance telephone (from a ship) which uses radio. **ra•di•o•ther•a•py** *n.* use of X-rays to treat disease.

rad•ish ['rædɪʃ] *n.* small red root vegetable, eaten raw.

ra•di•um ['reɪdɪəm] *n.* (*element:* Ra) radioactive metal used in treating cancer.

ra•di•us ['reɪdɪəs] *n.* (*pl.* **radii** ['reɪdɪaɪ], **radiuses**) (a) distance from the center of a circle to the circumference. (b) one of the two bones in the lower part of the arm.

ra•don ['reɪdɒn] *n.* (*element:* Rn) natural radioactive gas occurring in certain types of soil and construction materials.

raf•fi•a ['ræfɪə] *n.* (*no pl.*) strips from a palm leaf used to make baskets, etc.

raff•ish ['ræfɪʃ] *adj.* vulgar and showy; rather disreputable. **raff•ish•ness,** *n.* being raffish.

raf•fle ['ræfl] 1. *n.* lottery where you buy a numbered ticket in the hope of winning a prize. 2. *v.* to offer (a prize) for a lottery.

raft [rɑːft] *n.* flat boat made of pieces of wood/logs tied together.

raft•er ['rɑːftə] *n.* sloping beam which holds up a roof.

rag [ræɡ] 1. *n.* (a) piece of torn cloth; **dressed in rags** = wearing old, torn clothes; *inf.* **the r. trade/business** = clothing or fashion industry. (b) *inf.* newspaper, esp. one thought of with contempt. (c) piece of ragtime music. 2. *v.* (**ragged** [ræɡd]) to play jokes on (s.o.). **rag•bag,** *n.* collection of mismatched items. **rag•a•muf•fin,** *n.* dirty child wearing ragged clothes. **rag doll,** *n.* doll made of bits of cloth. **rag•ged** ['ræɡɪd] *adj.* (a) torn; uneven (edge). (b) (person) wearing rags. **rag rug,** *n.* rug made of strips of torn cloth sewn together. **rag•time,** *n.* music written with a strongly syncopated rhythm.

rage [reɪdʒ] 1. *n.* violent anger; *inf.* **all the r.** = very fashionable. 2. *v.* to be violently angry; to be violent.

rag•lan ['ræɡlən] *n.* style of coat where the sleeves continue straight to the collar, with no seam on the shoulder.

ra•gout ['ræɡuː] *n.* meat and vegetable stew.

raid [reɪd] 1. *n.* sudden attack. 2. *v.* to make a sudden attack on/a sudden visit to. **raid•er,** *n.* person who takes part in a raid.

rail [reɪl] 1. *n.* (a) bar of wood/metal (in a fence, etc.). (b) **rails** = metal bars along which trains run; live r. = rail which conducts electricity for electric trains. (c) railroad; **by r.** = on a train. (d) small bird which lives near water. 2. *v.* **to r. against** = to speak violently against. **rail•head,** *n.* end of a railroad line. **rail•ing,** *n. pl.* fence made of rails. **rail•ler•y,** *n.* making fun of s.o. **rail•road.** 1. *n.* track with two metal rails along which trains run; train system of a country. 2. *v. inf.* to force (sth) hurriedly. **rail•way,** *n.* railroad, esp. one which runs for a short distance.

rai•ment ['reɪmənt] *n.* clothing.

rain [reɪn] 1. *n.* water falling from clouds in drops. 2. *v.* to fall like rain. **rain•bow,** *n.* colored arc which appears in the sky when the sun's light falls on rain. **rain check,** *n.* agreement to have/to do sth later; **I'll take a r. check on that** = I'll not accept your offer now, but I will take it up again later. **rain•coat,** *n.* waterproof coat. **rain•drop,** *n.* drop of rain. **rain•fall,** *n.* amount of rain which falls in a certain place over a certain period. **rain for•est,** *n.* thick, lush tropical jungle where it rains frequently. **rain•wa•ter,** *n.* water which has fallen as rain. **rain•y,** *adj.* (-ier, -iest) with a lot of rain.

raise [reɪz] 1. *n.* increase in salary. 2. *v.* (a) to lift; to make (sth) higher. (b) to bring up (a subject) for discussion. (c) to rear (animals/a family). (d) to collect; **to r. money.**

rai•sin ['reɪzn] *n.* dried grape.

rai•son d'ê•tre [reɪzɒn'detr] *n.* reason for the existence of sth.

raj [rɑːdʒ] *n.* **the r.** = British rule in India. **ra•jah** ['rɑːdʒə] *n.* Indian ruler.

rake [reɪk] 1. *n.* (a) tool with a long handle and bent metal teeth, used for smoothing earth/for gathering fallen leaves, etc. (b) immoral man. (c) angle of slope. 2. *v.* (a) to smooth/to gather using a rake. (b) to slope. **rake-off,** *n. inf.* illegal payment paid as a commission. **rake up,**

æ back, aː farm, ɒ top, aɪ pipe, aʊ how, aɪə fire, aʊə flower, ɔ: bought, ɔɪ toy, e fed, eəhair, eɪ take, ə afraid, əʊ boat, əʊə lower, vː word, ɪ: heap, ɪ hit, ɪə hear, uː school, ʊ book, ʌ but, b back, d dog, ð then, dʒ just, f fog, ɡ go, h hand, j yes, k catch, l last, m mix, n nut, ŋ sing, p penny, r round, s some, ʃ short, t too, tʃ chop, θ thing, v voice, w was, z zoo, ʒ treasure

v. to start talking again about (sth which had been forgotten). **rak•ish,** *adj.* (that) worn at a slant/tilted sideways.

ral•ly ['rælɪ] 1. *n.* (a) gathering of members of a group/association/political party. (b) car competition where cars have to cross difficult country in a certain time. (c) return to strength (of s.o. who is ill). (d) long series of shots in tennis. 2. *v.* (a) to gather together. (b) to recover (temporarily) from an illness/a setback.

ram [ræm] 1. *n.* (a) male sheep. (b) heavy machine for pressing down hard. 2. *v.* **(rammed)** (a) to batter sth down hard. (b) to hit (another ship/car, etc.,) hard.

RAM [ræm] *n.* random access memory, memory in a computer which allows access to data.

Ram•a•dan [ræmə'dæn] *n.* 9th month of the year, when Muslims fast.

ram•ble ['ræmbl] 1. *n.* walk for pleasure in the country. 2. *v.* (a) to go for a walk. (b) to talk on and on in a confused way. **ram•bler,** *n.* (a) person who goes for walks in the country. (b) type of rose which climbs. **ram•bling,** *adj.* (a) confused (speech). (b) (house) which is full of rooms and corridors.

ram•bu•tan [ræmbu'tæn] *n.* small reddish fruit found in S.E. Asia.

ram•e•kin ['ræməkɪn] *n.* small dish for baking food in an oven; food cooked in this way.

ram•i•fi•ca•tion [ræmɪfɪ'keɪʃn] *n.* (a) part of a large complicated system. (b) consequence; result.

ramp [ræmp] *n.* slightly sloping surface joining two different levels.

ram•page [ræm'peɪdʒ] 1. *n.* **to go on the r.** = to go about breaking things/creating disorder. 2. *v.* to rush about creating disorder.

ramp•ant ['ræmpənt] *adj.* which is widespread and uncontrollable, as crime.

ram•part ['ræmpɑːt] *n.* defensive wall.

ram•rod ['ræmrɒd] *n.* **to stand stiff as a r.** = to stand very straight.

ram•shack•le ['ræmʃækl] *adj.* dilapidated/falling to pieces.

ran [ræn] *v. see* **run.**

ranch [rɑːntʃ] *n.* farm where horses or cattle are reared. **ranch•er,** *n.* person who owns/runs a ranch.

ran•cid ['rænsɪd] *adj.* bad/stale (butter). **ran•cid•i•ty,** *n.* being rancid.

ran•cor, *Brit.* **ran•cour** ['ræŋkə] *n.* bitterness/dislike. **ran•cor•ous,** *adj.* bitter/hateful.

rand [rɒnt] *n.* money used in South Africa.

ran•dom ['rændəm] *adj. & n.* done aimlessly/without any planning; **at r.** = aimlessly/with no selection; **r. sample** = sample for testing taken without any selection. **ran•dom•ness,** *n.* being random.

rand•y ['rændɪ] *adj.* **(-ier, -iest)** eager to have sexual intercourse. **rand•i•ness,** *n.* being randy.

rang [ræn] *v. see* **ring.**

range [reɪndʒ] 1. *n.* (a) series (of buildings/mountains) in line. (b) large open pasture; **free-range hens** = chickens which are allowed to run about in fields. (c) choice/series (of colors, etc.). (d) distance which a shell/bullet can reach; distance which an aircraft can fly without refueling; distance that you can see/hear. (e) large kitchen stove which has cooking surfaces and an oven. 2. *v.* to spread/to vary. **range find•er,** *n.* device (on a gun/camera) for calculating the distance of an object. **rang•er,** *n.* person who looks after a forest or park. **rang•y,** *adj.* with long legs.

rank [ræŋk] 1. *n.* (a) row of soldiers. (b) **ranks** = ordinary soldiers; **he rose from the ranks** = from being an ordinary soldier he became an officer; **the r. and file** = ordinary people. (c) position in society/in the armed forces. 2. *v.* to classify/to be classified in order of importance. 3. *adj.* **(-er, -est)** (a) (plants) which grow luxuriantly. (b) complete/total. (c) with an unpleasant smell. **rank•ness,** *n.* being rank.

ran•kle ['ræŋkl] *v.* to cause bitterness.

ran•sack ['rænsæk] *v.* to search/to turn over (a room) to find sth.

ran•som ['rænsəm] 1. *n.* payment asked for before a hostage is set free; **to hold s.o. for r.** = to demand payment before s.o. is set free. 2. *v.* to pay a ransom for (s.o.).

rant [rænt] *v.* to declaim/to shout violently.

rap [ræp] 1. *n.* (a) tap/sharp blow; *inf.* **to take the r.** = to accept responsibility. (b) form of West Indian music where the singer improvises. 2. *v.* **(rapped)** (a) to tap/to give a sharp blow. (b) to sing rap music.

ra•pa•cious [rə'peɪʃəs] *adj.* greedy. **ra•pac•i•ty** [rə'pæsɪtɪ] *n.* greed.

rape [reɪp] 1. *n.* (a) act of having sexual intercourse with s.o. against their will. (b) vegetable with yellow flowers, whose seeds are used to produce oil. 2. *v.* to have sexual intercourse with (s.o.) against their will. **rap•ist,** *n.* person who rapes s.o.

rap•id ['ræpɪd] 1. *adj.* fast. 2. *n. pl.* **rapids** = place where a river runs fast over boulders and down a steep slope. **ra•pid•i•ty** [rə'pɪdɪtɪ] *n.* speed. **rap•id•ly,** *adv.* fast.

ra•pi•er ['reɪpɪə] *n.* long, thin sword for thrusting.

rap•port [ræ'pɔː] *n.* understanding/close link.

rap•proche•ment [ræ'prɒʃmɒŋ] *n.* becoming closer (of former enemies).

rapt [ræpt] *adj.* **with r. attention** = very attentively. **rapt•ly,** *adv.* attentively.

rap•tor ['ræptə] *n.* bird of prey.

rap•ture ['ræptʃə] n. delight; **to go into raptures over** = to be delighted by. **rap•tur•ous,** adj. excited and delighted (applause, etc.). **rap•tur•ous•ly,** adv. in a rapturous way.

rare [reə] adj. (-er, -est) (a) very unusual. (b) (meat) which is very lightly cooked. **rare•ly,** adv. hardly ever. **rar•e•fied** ['reərɪfaɪd] adj. (air) which is not very dense. **rar•i•ty,** n. (a) (also **rareness**) uncommonness. (b) rare object.

rare•bit ['reəbɪt] n. Welsh r. = cooked cheese on toast.

rar•ing ['reərɪŋ] adj. inf. **r. to go** = eager to go.

ras•cal ['rɑːskəl] n. naughty person/child. **ras•cal•ly,** adj. naughty.

rash [ræʃ] 1. n. red area/red spots on the skin; **heat r.** = spots caused by hot weather. 2. adj. (-er, -est) not cautious/thoughtless; done without thinking. **rash•ly,** adv. without thinking. **rash•ness,** n. being rash/acting rashly.

rash•er ['ræʃə] n. slice (of bacon or ham).

rasp [rɑːsp] 1. n. rough metal file used for smoothing surfaces. 2. v. to make a grating noise.

rasp•ber•ry ['rɑːzbrɪ] n. (a) common red soft fruit growing on tall canes; bush which bears this fruit. (b) inf. rude noise made with the mouth to show derision.

Ras•ta•far•i•an [ræstə'feərɪən] adj. & n. (member) of a West Indian sect.

rat [ræt] 1. n. (a) common gray rodent, living in cellars/sewers/on ships. (b) sly unpleasant person. 2. v. (**ratted**) (a) to hunt rats. (b) inf. (**on**) to go back on a promise/to betray (s.o.). **rat race,** n. competition for success in the business world. **rat•ty,** adj. inf. annoyed/short-tempered.

rat•a•fi•a [rætə'fɪə] n. sweet liqueur flavored with almonds.

rat•chet (wheel) ['rætʃət('wiːl)] n. wheel with teeth and a catch to prevent it from turning backward.

rate [reɪt] 1. n. (a) number expressed as a proportion of one quantity to another; **birth r./death r.** = number of births/deaths per 1000 of population. (b) frequency at which sth is done/level of cost (as compared to a previous level). (c) speed. (d) **first r.** = very good; **second r.** = rather bad. (e) **at any r.** = in any case. 2. v. to value. **rat•ing,** n. (a) valuing. (b) TV **ratings** = comparative estimates of audiences for competing TV shows.

rath•er ['rɑːðə] adv. (a) relatively/quite. (b) (used with **would** to show preference) **I'd r. stay** = I would prefer to stay; **I'd r. not** = I would prefer not to. (c) **r. than** = in preference to.

rat•i•fy ['rætɪfaɪ] v. to approve (a treaty) officially. **rat•i•fi•ca•tion** [rætɪfɪ'keɪʃn] n. official approval.

ra•tio ['reɪʃɪəʊ] n. (pl. -os) proportion.

ra•ti•oc•i•nate [rætɪ'ɒsɪneɪt] v. to think coherently.

ra•tion ['ræʃn] 1. n. amount of food/supplies allowed. 2. v. to allow only a certain amount of food/supplies. **ra•tion•ing,** n. allowing only a certain amount of food/supplies.

ra•tion•al ['ræʃənl] adj. reasonable/based on reason. **ra•tion•ale** [ræʃə'nɑːl] n. set of reasons which are the basis of a system/of a series of actions. **ra•tion•al•i•ty,** n. being rational. **ra•tion•al•i•za•tion** [ræʃnəlaɪ'zeɪʃn] n. act of rationalizing. **ra•tion•al•ize** [ræʃnə'laɪz] v. to find a reason for usu. unreasonable actions. **ra•tion•al•ly,** adv. based on reason.

rat•tan [rə'tæn] n. tropical cane, used to make furniture.

rat•tle ['rætl] 1. n. (a) (wooden) instrument which makes a loud repeated noise. (b) repeated clattering noise. 2. v. (a) to make a repeated clattering noise. (b) inf. to worry/to upset. **rat•tle off,** v. inf. to speak rapidly. **rat•tle•snake,** n. American poisonous snake which makes a rattling noise with its tail. **rat•tling,** adj. inf. very good.

rau•cous ['rɔːkəs] adj. rough/hoarse (cough/cry). **rau•cous•ly,** adv. in a raucous way. **rau•cous•ness,** n. being raucous.

raun•chy ['rɔːntʃɪ] adj. (-ier, -iest) coarse/openly obscene.

rav•age ['rævɪdʒ] v. to devastate/to ruin (a town, etc.). **rav•ages,** n. pl. damage.

rave [reɪv] v. (a) to be wildly mad. (b) inf. to be fanatical (**about** sth). **rav•ing,** adj. wild (madman). **rav•ings,** n. pl. wild mad talk.

rav•el ['rævl] v. (a) to disentangle (sth which is twisted). (b) to tangle/to make sth knotted and twisted.

rav•en ['reɪvn] n. large black bird of the crow family.

rav•en•ous ['rævənəs] adj. very hungry. **rav•en•ous•ly,** adv. extremely (hungry).

ra•vine [rə'viːn] n. deep narrow valley.

ra•vi•o•li [rævɪ'əʊlɪ] n. Italian dish of small pasta squares filled with a meat stuffing.

rav•ish ['rævɪʃ] v. (a) to steal by force. (b) to en-

æ back, ɑː farm, ɒ top, aɪ pipe, aʊ how, aɪə fire, aʊə flower, ɔː bought, ɔɪ toy, e fed, eəhair, eɪ take, ə afraid, əʊ boat, əʊə lower, ɜː word, iː heap, ɪ hit, ɪə hear, uː school, ʊ book, ʌ but, b back, d dog, ð then, dʒ just, f fog, g go, h hand, j yes, k catch, l last, m mix, n nut, ŋ sing, p penny, r round, s some, ʃ short, t too, tʃ chop, θ thing, v voice, w was, z zoo, ʒ treasure

chant. **rav•ish•ing,** *adj.* very beautiful/very delightful.

raw [rɔː] 1. *adj.* (**-er, -est**) (a) uncooked. (b) basic/untreated (sewage/data); untrained (recruits). (c) cold and damp (weather). (d) **r. deal** = bad/unfair treatment. (e) exposed/sensitive; **to touch a r. nerve** = to touch a sensitive spot. 2. *n.* (a) sensitive spot. (b) wild natural state. **raw•hide,** *n.* leather which has not been tanned. **raw•ness,** *n.* being raw.

ray [reɪ] *n.* (a) beam of light/heat; small quantity (of hope); **X-rays** = rays which go through the soft tissue, and allow the bones and organs in the body to be photographed. (b) large, flat sea fish.

ray•on ['reɪɒn] *n.* synthetic fiber resembling silk.

raze [reɪz] *v.* **to r. to the ground** = to demolish completely.

ra•zor ['reɪzə] *n.* instrument with a very sharp blade for removing hair. **ra•zor•bill,** *n.* type of black and white sea bird. **razor-sharp,** extremely sharp (blade/mind, etc.).

razz•ma•tazz ['ræzmətæz] *n. inf.* energetic, showy display or activity.

Rd. *short for* road.

re [riː] *prep.* concerning.

re- [riː] *prefix meaning* again.

reach [riːtʃ] 1. *n.* (*pl.* **-es**) (a) distance you can travel easily; distance you can stretch out your hand. (b) continuous section, as of a river. 2. *v.* (a) to stretch out. (b) to arrive at. (c) to come to (an agreement). **reach•a•ble,** *adj.* which can be reached.

re•act [rɪ'ækt] *v.* to do/to say sth in reply to words or an action; **to r. against** = show opposition to; **acids r. with metals** = change their chemical composition. **re•ac•tion** [rɪ'ækʃn] *n.* act of reacting; thing done/said in reply; **what was his r.?** = what did he say/do? **re•ac•tion•ar•y,** *adj. & n.* (person) who is opposed to any political change/to any reforms. **re•ac•ti•vate,** *v.* to make (sth) work again. **re•ac•tive,** *adj.* which is active chemically. **re•ac•tor,** *n.* device for producing atomic energy.

read [riːd] 1. *n. inf.* looking at and understanding writtten or printed words. 2. *v.* (**read, has read** [red]) (a) to look at and understand written words; to speak aloud words which are written; **to r. between the lines** = to understand a hidden meaning which is not immediately apparent. (b) to interpret; **to r. s.o.'s palm** = to interpret the lines on a hand as indications of what will happen in the future. **read•a•bil•i•ty,** *n.* being readable. **read•a•ble,** *adj.* (a) legible/which can be read. (b) (story) which is a pleasure to read. **read•er,** *n.* (a) person who reads. (b) profes-

sor's assistant who helps grade exams, etc. (c) school book to help children to read. (d) apparatus for reading microfilms. (e) person who reads manuscripts/proofs to check them. **read•ing,** *n.* (a) act of looking at and understanding printed words. (b) interpretation. **read•ing room,** *n.* room (in a library) set aside for reading.

re•ad•dress [riːə'dres] *v.* to put another address on (an envelope/package).

re•ad•just [riːə'dʒʌst] *v.* to adjust again; to put back to the original position. **re•ad•just•ment,** *n.* act of readjusting.

read•y ['redɪ] *adj.* (**-ier, -iest**) (a) prepared (**to**). (b) fit to be used. (c) quick/rapid; **he has a r. answer to everything** = he always has an answer. (d) **r. cash** = cash which is immediately available. **read•i•ly,** *adv.* willingly. **read•i•ness,** *n.* willingness; **to hold sth in r.** = to keep sth ready for use. **ready-cooked,** *adj.* (food) which has been cooked in advance. **read•y•made, ready-to-wear,** *adj.* (clothes) which are made by mass production, to fit any person of a certain size.

re•a•gent [rɪ'eɪdʒnt] *n.* substance used in a chemical reaction.

re•al [rɪəl] *adj.* (a) true/not imitation; (sth) which exists. (b) **r. estate** = land or buildings which are bought or sold. **re•al•ism,** *n.* (a) facing facts/accepting life as it is. (b) showing things (in writing/painting) as they really are. **re•al•ist,** *n.* (a) artist/writer who shows things as they really are. (b) person who accepts life as it really is, and doesn't idealize it. **re•al•is•tic** [rɪə'lɪstɪk] *adj.* (a) which looks as if it is real. (b) accepting life as it really is. **re•al•is•ti•cal•ly,** *adv.* in a realistic way. **re•al•i•ty** [rɪ'ælɪtɪ] *n.* what is real/not imaginary. **re•al•ly,** *adv.* truly. **re•al time,** *n.* action of a computer which takes place at the same time as the problem it is solving.

re•a•lign [riːə'laɪn] *v.* to set in a new direction; to set in a new group. **re•a•lign•ment,** *n.* change in a series of alliances between countries or political parties.

re•al•ize ['rɪəlaɪz] *v.* (a) to come to understand clearly. (b) to sell property for (money). (c) to make real; to make (sth) come true. **re•al•i•za•tion** [rɪəlaɪ'zeɪʃn] *n.* (a) gradual understanding. (b) conversion of property into money. (c) carrying out of a plan.

realm [relm] *n.* (a) kingdom. (b) general area.

Re•al•po•li•tik [reɪ'ælpɒlɪtɪk] *n.* politics based on real situations, not on moral principles.

re•al•tor ['rɪəltə] *n.* person who arranges the sale of houses and land. **re•al•ty,** *n.* real estate.

ream [riːm] *n.* (a) 500 sheets of paper. (b) **reams** = very large quantity (of paper).

re•an•i•mate [rɪ'ænɪmeɪt] *v.* to bring back to life.

reap [riːp] *v.* to harvest (corn, etc.). **reap•er,** *n.* person/machine which harvests corn, etc.

re•ap•pear [riːə'pɪə] *v.* to appear again. **re•ap•pear•ance,** *n.* second appearance.

re•ap•prais•al [riːə'preɪzl] *n.* fresh examination of sth to see if your former opinion was correct.

rear ['rɪə] 1. *n.* back part; **to bring up the r.** = march behind. 2. *adj.* at the back; **r. view mirror** = mirror in a car in which you can see what is behind you without turning around. 3. *v.* (a) to breed/to raise (animals). (b) to lift (part of the body). (c) (*of horse, etc.*) to stand up on its back legs. **rear ad•mi•ral,** *n.* high-ranking naval officer (below vice-admiral). **rear guard,** *n.* soldiers defending the back part of an army. **rear•most,** *adj.* farthest at the back.

re•arm [rɪ'ɑːm] *v.* to arm/to stock up with weapons again. **re•ar•ma•ment** [rɪ'ɑːməmənt] *n.* arming again.

re•ar•range [riːə'reɪnʒ] *v.* to arrange again. **re•ar•range•ment,** *n.* new arrangement.

rea•son ['riːzn] 1. *n.* (a) cause/explanation for why sth happens. (b) power of thought; commonsense. 2. *v.* (a) to think/to plan carefully and logically. (b) **to r. with s.o.** = to try to calm s.o./to make s.o. change his mind. **rea•son•a•ble,** *adj.* (a) not extravagant/moderate. (b) sensible. **rea•son•a•bly,** *adv.* in a reasonable way. **rea•son•ing,** *n.* putting your mind to use; **I don't follow your r.** = I can't see how you reached this conclusion.

re•as•sem•ble [riːə'sembl] *v.* (a) to put back together. (b) to gather together again.

re•as•sure [riːə'ʃuə] *v.* to calm (s.o.)/to make (s.o.) less afraid/less doubtful. **re•as•sur•ance,** *n.* act of reassuring.

re•bate ['riːbeɪt] *n.* (a) reduction in the amount of money which should be paid; money which is returned to the person who paid it. (b) groove cut into a piece of wood to hold the tongue on another piece.

reb•el 1. *n.* ['rebəl] person who fights against the government/against the person in charge. 2. *v.* [rɪ'bel] (**rebelled**) to fight (**against** s.o./sth). **re•bel•lion** [rɪ'beljən] *n.* revolt/fight against the government/against authority. **re•bel•lious** [rɪ'beliəs] *adj.* fighting against the government/against authority.

re•boot [riː'buːt] *v.* to restart (a computer).

re•bound 1. *n.* ['riːbaʊnd] bouncing back; **on the r.** = (i) as it bounces back; (ii) while still shocked by a dissappointment. 2. *v.* [riː'baʊnd] to bounce back.

re•buff [rɪ'bʌf] 1. *n.* refusal. 2. *v.* to refuse.

re•build [riː'bɪld] *v.* (**rebuilt**) to build again.

re•buke [rɪ'bjuːk] (*formal*) 1. *n.* blame/reproof. 2. *v.* to blame/to scold.

re•bus ['riːbuːs] *n.* trick, where pictures are used to represent words.

re•but [rɪ'bʌt] *v.* (**rebutted**) to reject/to disprove (an argument). **re•but•tal,** *n.* act of rebutting.

re•cal•ci•trant [rɪ'kælsɪtrənt] *adj.* (*formal*) difficult/disobedient. **re•cal•ci•trance,** *n.* being recalcitrant.

re•call [rɪ'kɔːl] 1. *n.* calling back. 2. *v.* (a) to call/to summon back (an ambassador/defective cars). (b) to remember.

re•cant [rɪ'kænt] *v.* to admit that your former beliefs were wrong. **re•can•ta•tion** [rɪkæn-'teɪʃn] *n.* act of recanting.

re•ca•pit•u•late [riːkə'pɪtjuleɪt] *inf.* **re•cap** ['riːkæp] *v.* to repeat the main points of an argument. **re•ca•pit•u•la•tion** [riːkəpɪtju-'leɪʃn] *inf.* **re•cap,** *n.* repeating the main points.

re•cap•ture [riː'kæptʃə] 1. *n.* act of recapturing. 2. *v.* to catch again (an escaped prisoner); to take again (a seat in an election).

re•cast [riː'kɑːst] *v.* to make again; to write (a statement) again in a different way.

recd. *abbrev. for* received.

re•cede [rɪ'siːd] *v.* to go away/to retreat. **re•ced•ing,** *adj.* (forehead) which slopes backward; (hair) which begins to disappear from the front of the forehead.

re•ceipt [rɪ'siːt] *n.* (a) receiving; **on r. of** = when you receive. (b) paper showing that you have paid/that you have received sth. (c) **receipts** = money taken in a business.

re•ceive [rɪ'siːv] *v.* (a) to get sth which has been sent; *inf.* **he was on the receiving end of a lot of criticism** = he had to suffer a lot of criticism. (b) to greet/to welcome; to entertain. **re•ceiv•er,** *n.* (a) person who accepts stolen goods. (b) person put in charge of a bankrupt company or person. (c) part of a telephone which you can lift and listen to. (d) part of a radio which receives broadcast programs.

æ back, ɑː farm, ɒ top, aɪ pipe, aʊ how, aɪə fire, aʊə flower, ɔː bought, ɔɪ toy, e fed, eə hair, eɪ take, ə afraid, əʊ boat, əʊə lower, ɜː word, iː heap, ɪ hit, ɪə hear, uː school, ʊ book, ʌ but, b back, d dog, ð then, dʒ just, f fog, g go, h hand, j yes, k catch, l last, m mix, n nut, ŋ sing, p penny, r round, s some, ʃ short, t too, tʃ chop, θ thing, v voice, w was, z zoo, ʒ treasure

re•cent ['ri:sənt] *adj.* which took place not very long ago. **re•cent•ly**, *adv.* not long ago/only a short time ago.

re•cep•ta•cle [rɪ'septəkl] *n.* container.

re•cep•tion [rɪ'sepʃn] *n.* (a) welcome. (b) (*in a hotel*) desk where you check in. (c) big party held to welcome special guests. (d) quality of sound of a radio/TV broadcast. **re•cep•tion•ist**, *n.* person in a hotel/doctor's office, etc., who meets visitors and answers the telephone. **re•cep•tive**, *adj.* eager to take in new ideas. **re•cep•tive•ness, re•ceptivity** [risep'tiviti] *n.* being receptive. **re•cep•tor**, *n.* cell at the end of a nerve, which receives impulses.

re•cess [rɪ'ses] *n.* (*pl.* **-es**) (a) alcove/part of the wall of a room which is set back. (b) temporary stopping of usual business or activity, as of a legislature. (c) recreation period at school. (d) inaccessible part. **re•cessed**, *adj.* set back. **re•ces•sive**, *adj.* (*of genes*) not likely to predominate.

re•ces•sion [rɪ'seʃn] *n.* collapse of world economy/of trade.

re•cher•ché [rə'ʃeəʃeɪ] *adj.* chosen with care.

re•cid•i•vist [rə'sɪdɪvɪst] *n.* hardened criminal/person who commits a crime repeatedly.

rec•i•pe ['resɪpɪ] *n.* (a) instructions for cooking. (b) effective way to do sth; **it's a r. for disaster** = it's bound to lead to disaster.

re•cip•i•ent [rɪ'sɪpɪənt] *n.* person who receives.

re•cip•ro•cate [rɪ'sɪprəkeɪt] *v.* to do the same thing in return. **re•cip•ro•cal.** 1. *adj.* mutual; **r. trade agreement** = agreement on two-way trade between countries. 2. *n.* (*in math*) quantity produced when 1 is divided by a figure. **re•cip•ro•cal•ly**, *adv.* in a reciprocal way. **rec•i•proc•i•ty** [resɪ'prɒsɪtɪ] *n.* mutual interchange between countries, states or groups.

re•cite [rɪ'saɪt] *v.* to speak (verse, etc.) aloud in public. **re•cit•al**, *n.* reciting in public sth which has been written. (b) performance of music by one or a few musicians. **rec•i•ta•tion** [resɪ'teɪʃn] *n.* thing recited from memory; recital. **rec•i•ta•tive** [resɪtə'ti:v] *n.* (*in an opera*) speech sung in a rhythmic way.

reck•less ['rekləs] *adj.* foolish/rash/not thinking. **reck•less•ly**, *adv.* in a reckless way. **reck•less•ness**, *n.* foolishness/rashness.

reck•on ['rekn] *v.* (a) to calculate/to estimate; (b) to think. (c) **to r. on** = to count on/to depend on. (d) **to r. with** = to have to deal with. **reck•on•er**, *n.* book with tables to help calculations. **reck•on•ing**, *n.* calculation; **day of r.** = time when you have to pay for your mistakes.

re•claim [rɪ'kleɪm] *v.* to make (useless land) fit for use; to take back (land) from the sea. **rec•la•ma•tion** [reklə'meɪʃn] *n.* reclaiming (of land).

re•cline [rɪ'klaɪn] *v.* to lie back.

rec•luse [rɪ'klu:s] *n.* person who lives alone and hidden away.

rec•og•nize ['rekəgnaɪz] *v.* (a) to know (s.o./sth) because you have seen him/it before. (b) to admit (a mistake). (c) to admit (the value of sth). (d) **to r. a government** = to accept that a new government is the legal authority in a country; **to r. a union** = to agree that a union can officially represent workers in a factory. **rec•og•ni•tion** [rekəg'nɪʃn] *n.* recognizing; **he's changed beyond all r.** = so much that you can't recognize him. **rec•og•niz•a•ble** [rekəg'naɪzəbl] *adj.* which can be recognized. **rec•og•ni•zance** [rɪ'kɒgnɪzəns] *n.* money given as a pledge to a court that s.o. will obey the conditions laid down by the court.

re•coil 1. *n.* ['ri:kɔɪl] sudden movement backward of a gun when it is fired. 2. *v.* [rɪ'kɔɪl] to move backward suddenly; to shrink back from sth unpleasant.

rec•ol•lect [rekə'lekt] *v.* to remember. **rec•ol•lec•tion** [rekə'lekʃn] *n.* remembering.

rec•om•mend [rekə'mend] *v.* (a) to advise s.o. to do sth. (b) to praise (sth/s.o.). **rec•om•men•da•tion** [rekəmen'deɪʃn] *n.* (a) advice. (b) praise; thing which is in your favor.

rec•om•pense ['rekəmpens] 1. *n.* payment for sth done/for the time lost, etc. 2. *v.* to pay s.o. for sth done/for time lost, etc.

rec•on•cile ['rekənsaɪl] *v.* (a) to make two enemies become friendly. (b) **to reconcile oneself to** = to accept. (c) to make (two accounts/statements) agree. **rec•on•cil•i•a•tion** [rekənsɪlɪ'eɪʃn] *n.* bringing together of two enemies, so that they become friends; making two accounts/statements agree.

rec•on•dite [rɪ'kɒndaɪt] *adj.* (*formal*) obscure (information).

re•con•di•tion [rɪkən'dɪʃn] *v.* to overhaul thoroughly.

re•con•nais•sance [rɪ'kɒnɪsns] *n.* survey of land for military information.

re•con•noi•ter, *Brit.* **re•con•noi•tre** [rekə'nɔɪtə] *v.* to make a survey to get information/to make a reconnaissance.

re•con•sid•er [ri:kən'sɪdə] *v.* to think over again.

re•con•sti•tute [rɪ'kɒnstɪtjut] *v.* to form (sth) again as it was before.

re•con•struct [riːkən'strʌkt] v. (a) to build
again. (b) to work out how (a crime) must
have been committed. **re•con•struc•tion,**
n. act of reconstructing; thing reconstructed.

re•con•vene [riːkən'viːn] v. to meet again.

re•cord 1. n. ['rekɔːd] (a) report of sth which
has happened; **he is on r. as saying** = he is accurately reported as saying; **she spoke off the r.** =
in private/what she said is not to be made public. (b) note/written account. (c) flat plastic
disk on which sound is fixed by a recording instrument. (d) description of s.o.'s past career.
(e) sporting achievement which is better than
any other; **at r. speed** = very fast. 2. v. ['rɪ'kɔːd]
(a) to report; to make a note. (b) to fix sound
on a plastic disk or tape.
rec•ord-break•ing, adj. which breaks records. **re•cord•er** [rɪ'kɔːdə] n. (a) person
whose job is to take notes and keep records.
(b) instrument which records. (c) wooden
flute held forward when played.
re•cord•ing, n. (a) act of fixing sounds on
tape/on disk. (b) music/speech which has been
recorded. **re•cord•ist,** n. person who records sounds on tape or disk. **rec•ord
play•er,** n. machine for playing back
music/speech, etc., from a record.

re•count 1. n. ['riːkaunt] counting votes again
(when the result is very close). 2. v. (a) [rɪ-
'kaunt] to tell (a story). (b) [riː'kaunt] to count
again.

re•coup [rɪ'kuːp] v. **to r. your losses** = to get
back money which you have lost.

re•course [rɪ'kɔːs] n. **to have r. to sth** = to use
sth in an emergency.

re•cov•er [rɪ'kʌvə] v. (a) to get back (sth
which has been stolen/lost). (b) (**from**) to get
well again after an illness. (c) (**from**) to get
over (a shock). (d) [riː'kʌvə] to put a new cover
(on a chair). **re•cov•er•a•ble,** adj. which
can be gotten back. **re•cov•ered
mem•o•ry,** n. apparent recollection, usu. by
s.o. in psychotherapy, of an alleged childhood
trauma, the memory of which had previously
been suppressed. **re•cov•er•y,** n. (a) getting
back (stolen property). (b) getting well again.
(c) return to good condition.

rec•re•a•tion [rekrɪ'eɪʃn] n. pleasant occupation for your spare time. **rec•re•a•tion•al,**
adj. referring to recreation.

re•crim•i•nate [rɪ'krɪmɪneɪt] v. to accuse
(s.o.) who has accused you.
re•crim•i•na•tion [rɪkrɪmɪ'neɪʃn] n. accu-

sation made by s.o. who is accused.
re•crim•i•na•to•ry [rɪ'krɪmɪnətrɪ] adj. (remarks) which accuse s.o.

re•cru•des•cence [riːkruː'desəns] n. (formal)
breaking out again (of a disease).

re•cruit [rɪ'kruːt] 1. n. new soldier; new member of a club, etc. 2. v. to encourage (s.o.) to
join the armed forces/a club, etc.
re•cruit•ment, n. encouraging people to
join the armed forces/a club, etc.

rec•tal ['rektəl] adj. referring to the rectum.

rec•tan•gle ['rektæŋgl] n. four-sided shape
with right angles and two sets of opposite and
equal sides. **rec•tan•gu•lar** [rek'tæŋgjulə]
adj. like a rectangle.

rec•ti•fy ['rektɪfaɪ] v. to correct/to make right.
rec•ti•fi•a•ble, adj. which can be corrected.
rec•ti•fi•ca•tion [rektɪfɪ'keɪʃn] n. correction.

rec•ti•lin•e•ar [rektɪ'lɪnɪə] adj. with straight
lines.

rec•ti•tude ['rektɪtjuːd] n. (esp. moral) correctness.

rec•to ['rektəu] n. right/main side (of a piece of
paper, page of a book, etc.).

rec•tor ['rektə] n. (a) priest in charge of a parish. (b) head of certain schools/colleges/uni-
versities. **rec•to•ry,** n. house of a rector.

rec•tum ['rektəm] n. lower part of the intestine, leading to the anus.

re•cum•bent [rɪ'kʌmbənt] adj. (formal) lying
down.

re•cu•per•ate [rɪ'kjuːpəreɪt] v. to recover/to
get better after an illness or a loss.
re•cu•per•a•tion [rɪkjuːpə'reɪʃn] n. getting
better. **re•cu•per•a•tive,** adj. which helps
recuperation.

re•cur [rɪ'kɜː] v. (**recurred**) to happen again.
re•cur•rence [rɪ'kʌrəns] n. reappear-
ance/happening again. **re•cur•rent** [rɪ-
'kʌrənt], **re•cur•ring** [rɪ'kɜːrɪŋ] adj. (a)
which happens again. (b) (decimal figure)
which is repeated for ever.

rec•u•sant ['rekjuzənt] adj. & n. (old) (person)
who refuses to comply, esp. one who refused
to accept the Anglican Church in England.

re•cy•cle [riː'saɪkl] v. to process (waste material) so that it can be used again.

red [red] adj. & n. (**redder, reddest**) (color) like
blood or fire; inf. see **r.** = to be in debt; **r. to
be in the r.** = to be in debt; **r. carpet** = official
welcome; **r. tape** = official rules which stop
you doing sth quickly; **r. herring** = false

track/sth which leads you away from the main problem; *inf.* **the Reds** = the Communists.
red-blood•ed, *adj.* strong, vigorous.
red•breast, *n.* robin. **Red Cres•cent,** *n.* organization similar to the Red Cross, working in Muslim countries. **Red Cross,** *n.* international organization which cares for the sick and injured, and also organizes relief work.
red cur•rant, *n.* common red soft fruit growing in small clusters; bush which bears this fruit. **red•den,** *v.* to turn red/to blush.
red•dish, *adj.* rather red. **red flag,** *n.* flag of the communist party. **red-hand•ed,** *adj.* **they caught him red-handed** = as he was committing a crime. **red•head,** *n.* person with red hair. **red-hot,** *adj.* (*of metal*) very hot. **Red In•dian,** *n.* (*rude*) North American Indian. **red-let•ter day,** *n.* very special day. **red•ness,** *n.* being red. **red•shank,** *n.* large sandpiper. **red•start,** *n.* small singing bird with red feathers beneath the tail. **red•wood,** *n.* type of very tall coniferous tree growing on the west coast of North America.
re•dec•o•rate [riː'dekəreɪt] *v.* to decorate/to paint again.
re•deem [rɪ'diːm] *v.* (a) to buy back (sth which you have pledged to borrow money); to pay off (a debt). (b) to compensate. (c) to save from sin. **Re•deem•er,** *n.* Jesus Christ. **re•deem•ing,** *adj.* which compensates. **re•demp•tion** [rɪ'dempʃn] *n.* (a) payment of a debt. (b) being saved from sin.
re•de•ploy [riːdɪ'plɔɪ] *v.* to move (workers/soldiers) from one place to another. **re•de•ploy•ment,** *n.* act of redeploying.
re•di•rect [riːdaɪ'rekt] *v.* to change the direction or movement of.
red•o•lent ['redələnt] *adj.* which smells (of sth); which reminds you (of sth). **red•o•lence,** *n.* being redolent.
re•dou•ble [riː'dʌbl] *v.* **to r. your efforts** = to try even harder.
re•doubt [rɪ'daʊt] *n.* small fort. **re•doubt•a•ble** [rɪ'daʊtəbl] *adj.* formidable/bold.
re•dound [rɪ'daʊnd] *v.* (*formal*) **it will r. to your credit** = will make you more admired.
re•dress [rɪ'dres] 1. *n.* compensation done to make up for something wrong. 2. *v.* to correct/to compensate/to repair; **to r. a wrong** = to make things right again.
re•duce [rɪ'djuːs] *v.* (a) to make smaller/lower; **to r. s.o. to the ranks** = to punish an officer by making him an ordinary soldier; **to r. one's weight** = to get thinner. (b) to force (s.o.) to do sth humiliating. **re•duc•i•ble,** *adj.* which

can be reduced. **re•duc•tion** [rɪ'dʌkʃn] *n.* lowering (of price/speed/standards).
re•dun•dant [rɪ'dʌndənt] *adj.* more than necessary; excess. **re•dun•dan•cy,** *n.* state of being redundant.
re•du•pli•cate [rɪ'djuplɪkeɪt] *v.* to repeat (sth).
re•ech•o, re-echo [riː'ekəʊ] *v.* to echo again.
reed [riːd] *n.* (a) marsh plant with tall stem. (b) part of a wind instrument which vibrates to make a note. **reed•i•ness,** *n.* being reedy. **reed•y,** *adj.* (a) high-pitched (voice). (b) (marsh) which is full of reeds.
reef [riːf] 1. *n.* (a) ridge of rock in the sea. (b) **r. knot** = type of flat knot which does not come undone easily. 2. *v.* to reduce the size of (a sail) by rolling part of it up. **reef•er,** *n.* (a) sailor's short coat. (b) *Sl.* marijuana cigarette.
reek [riːk] 1. *n.* strong smell. 2. *v.* to smell strongly (of).
reel [riːl] 1. *n.* (a) spool for winding thread/string/film around. (b) lively Scottish dance. 2. *v.* (a) to wind around a reel. (b) **to r. off** = to quote at length. (c) to stagger.
re•el•ect [riːɪ'lekt] *v.* to elect again. **re•e•lec•tion** [riːɪ'lekʃn] *n.* being reelected.
re•em•ploy [riːem'plɔɪ] *v.* to employ (s.o.) again.
re•en•ter [riː'entə] *v.* to enter again. **re•en•try** [riː'entrɪ] *n.* entering again.
ref [ref] *n. inf.* (*in sports*) referee.
re•fec•to•ry [rɪ'fektərɪ] *n.* dining hall (in a school, etc.); **r. table** = long narrow dining table.
re•fer to [rɪ'fɜː] *v.* (**referred**) (a) to mention. (b) to look into sth for information. (c) to pass (a problem) to s.o. to decide. (d) to tell (s.o.) to see s.o. else. **ref•er•ee** [refə'riː] 1. *n.* (*in sports*) person who sees that the game is played according to the rules/who judges between two sides. 2. *v.* to act as a referee in a sports match. **ref•er•ence** ['refrəns] *n.* (a) (to) mention; **with r. to** = concerning/about. (b) direction for further information; **r. book** = book (such as dictionary/encyclopedia) where you can look up information; **r. library** = library of reference books. (c) statement about s.o.'s character, etc. **re•fer•ral** [rɪ'fɜːrl] *n.* act of referring.
ref•er•en•dum [refə'rendəm] *n.* (*pl.* -da/-dums) vote by all the people of a country or state on a proposed or current law to let them decide.
re•fill 1. *n.* ['riːfɪl] container with a fresh quantity of liquid/ink, etc.; another drink. 2. *v.* [riː'fɪl] to fill again.
re•fine [rɪ'faɪn] *v.* to make better/more pure. **re•fined,** *adj.* very elegant/polite.

re•fine•ment, *n.* (a) elegance. (b) improvement. **re•fin•er,** *n.* business/person that refines. **re•fin•er•y,** *n.* factory where sth is refined.

re•fit 1. *n.* ['ri:fit] repairs (to a ship). 2. *v.* [ri:'fit] (**refitted**) to repair (a ship).

re•flate [ri:'fleɪt] *v.* to stimulate (an economy which has previously been deflated). **re•fla•tion** [ri:'fleɪʃn] *n.* action of stimulating a deflated economy. **re•fla•tion•ar•y,** *adj.* likely to cause reflation.

re•flect [rɪ'flekt] *v.* (a) to send back (light/heat/an image). (b) to think back into the past/to ponder. (c) **to r. on** = to be a criticism of. **re•flec•tion,** *Brit.* **re•flex•ion** [rɪ-'flekʃn] *n.* (a) sending back of light/heat; reflected image (in a mirror). (b) thought; **on r.** = on thinking more about it. (c) criticism. **re•flec•tive,** *adj.* thoughtful. **re•flec•tor,** *n.* apparatus which reflects.

re•flex ['ri:fleks] 1. *n.* (*pl.* **-es**) automatic action/instinctive response. 2. *adj.* (a) which is automatic; **r. action** = action done instinctively. (b) which returns as a reflection; **r. camera** = camera where the picture is reflected from the lens to the viewfinder exactly as it will appear on the photograph; **r. angle** = angle of more than 180°. **re•flex•ive** [rɪ-'fleksɪv] *adj.* (*in grammar*) verb or pronoun which refers back to the subject.

re•float [ri:'fləʊt] *v.* to float again (a ship which has gone aground).

re•flux ['ri:flʌks] *n.* flowing back.

re•form [rɪ'fɔːm] 1. *n.* improving/improvement. 2. *v.* (a) to correct/to improve. (b) to become good/to stop committing crime or doing wrong. **ref•or•ma•tion** [refə'meɪʃn] *n.* act of reforming; **the Reformation** = religious movement in sixteenth century Europe which brought about the creation of the Protestant churches. **re•form•a•to•ry** [rɪ'fɔːmətrɪ] *n.* type of prison school where young criminals are sent in the hope that they will be reformed. **re•form•er,** *n.* person who tries to improve (a system).

re•fract [rɪ'frækt] *v.* to bend (rays of light, etc.) as they pass through the surface of water. **re•frac•tion** [rɪ'frækʃn] *n.* bending of light as it goes from one substance to another (such as into water). **re•frac•tive,** *adj.* producing refraction. **re•frac•tor,** *n.* object/substance which refracts.

re•frac•to•ry [rɪ'fræktərɪ] *adj.* difficult/disobedient.

re•frain [rɪ'freɪn] 1. *n.* chorus which is repeated after each section of a song or poem. 2. *v.* **to r. from** = to keep from doing sth.

re•fresh [rɪ'freʃ] *v.* to make fresh again; to make less tired; **let me r. your memory** = help you to remember sth which you seem to have forgotten. **re•fresh•er (course),** *n.* lessons which bring your knowledge of sth up to date. **re•fresh•ing,** *adj.* (a) which refreshes. (b) new and invigorating. **re•fresh•ment,** *n.* **refreshments** = food and drink.

re•frig•er•a•tor [rɪ'frɪdʒəreɪtə] *n.* box or room for keeping things (esp. food) cold by ice or mechanical means. **re•frig•er•ant,** *n.* substance used to make other substances very cold. **re•frig•er•at•ed,** *adj.* kept cold. **re•frig•er•a•tion** [rɪfrɪdʒə'reɪʃn] *n.* keeping things cold.

re•fu•el [ri:'fjʊəl] *v.* (**refueled, refuelled**) to put more fuel into (a ship/plane/car, etc.).

ref•uge ['refju:dʒ] *n.* place to hide/to shelter; **to take r.** = to shelter. **ref•u•gee** [refju'dʒi:] *n.* person who has been driven out of his own country and needs shelter; **political r.** = person who has left his country for political reasons.

re•fund 1. *n.* ['ri:fʌnd] repayment of money. 2. *v.* [rɪ'fʌnd] to pay back (money).

re•fur•bish [rɪ'fɜːbɪʃ] *v.* to polish up again.

ref•use 1. *n.* ['refju:s] things to be thrown out; garbage; rubbish. 2. *v.* [rɪ'fju:z] (a) to say that you do not accept/that you will not do sth. (b) not to give s.o. (permission). **re•fus•al** [rɪ-'fju:zl] *n.* (a) saying no; **to meet with a flat r.** = to be refused completely. (b) **to give s.o. first r. of sth** = to let them have first choice of buying sth.

re•fute [rɪ'fju:t] *v.* to prove that (sth) is wrong. **ref•u•ta•tion** [refju'teɪʃn] *n.* proof that sth is wrong.

re•gain [ri:'geɪn] *v.* to get back.

re•gal ['ri:gl] *adj.* referring to a king/queen; royal. **re•ga•li•a** [rɪ'geɪlɪə] *n.* *pl.* robes/crown, etc., worn by a king/queen/mayor. **re•gal•ly,** *adv.* like a king/queen.

re•gale [rɪ'geɪl] *v.* to entertain.

re•gard [rɪ'gɑːd] 1. *n.* (a) concern. (b) esteem. (c) **regards** = best wishes. 2. *v.* (a) to consider. (b) **as regards** = concerning. **re•gard•ing,** *prep.* concerning. **re•gard•less,** *adj.* paying no attention to; **carry on r.** = carry on in spite of everything.

re•gat•ta [rɪˈgætə] n. series of boat races (for either yachts or rowboats).

re•gen•er•ate [rɪˈdʒenəreɪt] v. to start up again. **re•gen•er•a•tion** [rɪdʒenəˈreɪʃn] n. growing again/starting again.

re•gent [ˈriːdʒənt] n. person who rules in place of a king or queen. **re•gen•cy,** n. period when a regent is ruling.

reg•gae [ˈregeɪ] n. type of West Indian music.

reg•i•cide [ˈredʒɪsaɪd] n. person who kills a king.

re•gime [reˈʒiːm] n. system of government/administration.

reg•i•men [ˈredʒɪmən] n. planned course of action to improve your health.

reg•i•ment [ˈredʒɪmənt] 1. n. group of soldiers, usu. commanded by a colonel or lieutenant-colonel. 2. v. to keep (s.o.) under strict discipline. **reg•i•men•tal** [redʒɪˈmentl] adj. belonging to a regiment. **reg•i•men•tals,** n. pl. military uniform of a certain regiment. **reg•i•men•ta•tion** [redʒɪmenˈteɪʃn] n. very strict discipline.

re•gion [ˈriːdʒən] n. area; **the metropolitan r.** = area around a city; **in the r. of $10,000** = about $10,000. **re•gion•al,** adj. referring to a region.

reg•is•ter [ˈredʒɪstə] 1. n. (a) list (of names). (b) range of notes covered by a voice/a musical instrument. (c) **cash r.** = device which records sales/money taken in a store. (d) (in printing) fitting of several printing plates in such a way that various colors correspond exactly on the paper. (e) level of language (such as formal/colloquial, etc.). 2. v. (a) to write (a name) officially in a list; **to r. at a hotel** = to write your name and address when you arrive at the hotel. (b) to record (a temperature, etc.). **reg•is•tered,** adj. which has been officially recorded. **reg•is•trar** [ˈredʒɪstrɑː] n. person who keeps official records; person who keeps the records of a school/college/university. **reg•is•tra•tion** [redʒɪˈstreɪʃn] n. (a) act of registering. (b) official document proving that sth has been registered; **car registration. reg•is•try** [ˈredʒɪstrɪ] n. place where official records are kept.

re•gress [rɪˈgres] v. to go back to an earlier, and usu. worse, condition. **re•gres•sion,** n. going back. **re•gres•sive,** adj. which regresses.

re•gret [rɪˈgret] 1. n. sorrow; **much to my r.** = I am very sorry. 2. v. (**regretted**) to be sorry that sth has happened. **re•gret•ful,** adj. sorry/sad. **re•gret•ful•ly,** adv. sadly. **re•gret•ta•ble,** adj. which must be regret-

ted. **re•gret•ta•bly,** adv. in a regrettable way.

reg•u•lar [ˈregjulə] 1. adj. (a) habitual/done at the same time each day. (b) usual/ordinary. (c) **r. army** = permanent, professional army; **r. officer** = professional officer. (d) (in grammar) **r. verb** = verb which has no unusual parts. 2. n. (a) inf. customer who always shops in a particular store/who always drinks in a certain bar, etc. (b) professional soldier. **reg•u•lar•i•ty** [regjuˈlærɪtɪ] n. being regular. **reg•u•lar•i•za•tion** [regjulərɑɪˈzeɪʃn] n. act of regularizing. **reg•u•lar•ize** [ˈregjulərɑɪz] v. to make legal. **reg•u•lar•ly,** adv. in a regular way. **reg•u•late** [ˈregjuleɪt] v. to adjust (a machine) so that it works regularly. **reg•u•la•tion** [regjuˈleɪʃn] n. act of regulating; rule. **reg•u•la•tor,** n. person/instrument which regulates a machine.

re•gur•gi•tate [rɪˈgɜːdʒɪteɪt] v. (formal) to spout out (food which has already been swallowed/information which has already been learned). **re•gur•gi•ta•tion** [rɪgəːdʒɪˈteɪʃn] n. act of regurgitating.

re•ha•bil•i•tate [riːhəˈbɪlɪteɪt] v. to train (a disabled person/an ex-prisoner, etc.) to lead a normal life and fit into society. **re•ha•bil•i•ta•tion** [riːhəbɪlɪˈteɪʃn] n. act of rehabilitating.

re•hash 1. n. [ˈriːhæʃ] thing rehashed. 2. v. [riːˈhæʃ] to bring out (an old story/book, etc.) in more or less the same form as before.

re•hearse [rɪˈhɜːs] v. to practice (a play/a concert, etc.) before a public performance. **re•hears•al** [rɪˈhɜːsəl] n. practice of a play/concert, etc., before a public performance; **dress r.** = last rehearsal of a play, etc., when everyone is in costume.

re•house [riːˈhaʊz] v. to put (s.o.) into a new house or apartment.

reign [reɪn] 1. n. period when a king/queen/emperor rules; **r. of terror** = period when law and order have broken down. 2. v. to rule.

re•im•burse [riːɪmˈbɜːs] v. to pay (s.o.) back the money he has spent. **re•im•burse•ment,** n. act of reimbursing; money reimbursed.

rein [reɪn] 1. n. strap which controls a horse; **to keep on a tight r.** = under strict control. 2. v. to **r. in** = to pull on the reins to control (a horse).

re•in•car•nate [riːɪnˈkɑːneɪt] v. (formal) to make (the soul of a dead person) be born again in another body. **re•in•car•na•tion** [riːɪnkɑːˈneɪʃn] n. survival of a person's soul born again in another body after death.

rein•deer [ˈreɪndɪə] n. (pl. **reindeer**) type of deer which lives in the Arctic.

re•in•force [riːɪnˈfɔːs] v. to strengthen/to consolidate; **reinforced concrete** = concrete

strengthened with metal rods.
re•in•force•ment, *n.* (a) act of reinforcing.
(b) **reinforcements** = new soldiers to support others already fighting.

re•in•state [riːn'steɪt] *v.* to put back into a former position or condition. **re•in•state•ment,** *n.* putting back into a former position or condition.

re•in•sure [riːɪn'ʃuə] *v.* to spread the risk of insurance, by insuring part of the risk with another insurer.

re•in•vest [riːɪn'vest] *v.* to invest again.

re•it•er•ate [riː'ɪtəreɪt] *v.* to repeat. **re•it•er•a•tion** [riːɪtə'reɪʃn] *n.* repetition.

re•ject 1. *n.* ['riːdʒekt] thing which has been thrown away as not satisfactory; **rejects** = substandard goods sold at a reduced price. 2. *v.* [rɪ'dʒekt] to refuse to accept (sth); to throw (sth) away as not satisfactory. **re•jec•tion** [rɪ'dʒekʃn] *n.* refusal.

re•jig•ger [riː'dʒɪg] *v.* **(rejiggered)** *inf.* to arrange in a different way.

re•joice [rɪ'dʒɔɪs] *v.* to be very happy. **re•joic•ing,** *n.* great happiness.

re•join [rɪ'dʒɔɪn] *v.* (a) to join again. (b) (*formal*) to reply. **re•join•der,** *n.* (*formal*) reply.

re•ju•ve•nate [rɪ'dʒuːvəneɪt] *v.* to make (s.o.) young again; to give (sth) new strength. **re•ju•ve•na•tion** [rɪdʒuːvə'neɪʃn] *n.* act of rejuvenating.

re•kin•dle [riː'kɪndl] *v.* to light again.

re•lapse [rɪ'læps] 1. *n.* becoming ill again (after a temporary improvement); getting back into old bad habits. 2. *v.* to become ill again; to get back into old bad habits.

re•late [rɪ'leɪt] *v.* (a) to tell (a story). (b) to connect (two things). (c) to have a successful relationship (**with** s.o.). **re•lat•ed,** *adj.* (a) linked. (b) belonging to the same family. **re•la•tion** [rɪ'leɪʃn] *n.* (a) story. (b) linking/links (between two things); **public relations** = maintaining good connections with the public, esp. to put across a point of view/to publicize a product. (c) member of a family. **re•la•tion•ship,** *n.* link/connection; being related.

rel•a•tive ['relətɪv] 1. *n.* person who is related to s.o.; member of a family. 2. *adj.* (a) which is compared to sth; **their r. poverty** = their poverty compared with really wealthy people or with the wealth they used to have. (b) (*in grammar*) **r. pronoun** = pronoun (such as "who" and "which") which connects two

clauses. **rel•a•tive•ly,** *adv.* comparatively/more or less. **rel•a•tiv•i•ty** [relə'tɪvɪti] *n.* (*in physics*) relationship between objects and time and speed.

re•lax [rɪ'læks] *v.* (a) to slacken/to decrease tension; to make less strict. (b) to rest from work. **re•lax•a•tion** [riːlæk'seɪʃn] *n.* (a) slackening of a rule, etc. (b) rest. **re•laxed,** *adj. inf.* happy/not upset.

re•lay 1. *n.* ['riːleɪ] (a) shift of people working. (b) **r. race** = running race by teams in which one runner passes a baton to another who then runs on. 2. *v.* [rɪ'leɪ] to pass on (a message); to pass on (a TV/radio broadcast) through a relay station. **re•lay sta•tion,** *n.* transmitting station which receives signals from a main transmitter and broadcasts them further.

re•lease [rɪ'liːs] 1. *n.* (a) setting free. (b) new record/piece of information which is made public. 2. *v.* (a) to set free. (b) to make public.

rel•e•gate ['relɪgeɪt] *v.* to put into a worse position. **rel•e•ga•tion** [relɪ'geɪʃn] *n.* moving into a worse position.

re•lent [rɪ'lent] *v.* to change your mind about a strict decision you have taken/to be less strict. **re•lent•less,** *adj.* pitiless. **re•lent•less•ly,** *adv.* with no pity.

rel•e•vant ['relɪvənt] *adj.* which relates/has to do with sth being spoken of. **rel•e•vance,** *n.* being relevant.

re•li•a•ble [rɪ'laɪəbl] *adj.* which can be relied on/which can be trusted. **re•li•a•bly,** *adv.* in a way which can be trusted. **re•li•a•bil•i•ty** [rɪlaɪə'bɪlɪti] *n.* being reliable. **re•li•ance,** *n.* trust/confidence. **re•li•ant,** *adj.* which relies on sth.

rel•ic ['relɪk] *n.* object which has been left over from the past; holy remains (such as the bones of a saint). **rel•ict,** *n.* (*formal*) widow.

re•lief [rɪ'liːf] *n.* (a) reducing pain/tension. (b) help; **r. fund** = money collected to help victims of a disaster. (c) person/thing that takes over from another. **a r. nurse.** (d) carving in which the details of design stand out; **in r.** = standing out/prominent; **r. map** = map where mountains are drawn so that an impression of height is given. **re•lieve** [rɪ'liːv] *v.* (a) to reduce (pain/tension); **to r. oneself** = to urinate or defecate. (b) to help. (c) to take over from (s.o.). (d) to remove a weight from (s.o.).

re•li•gion [rɪ'lɪdʒən] *n.* belief in gods or in one God; system of worship. **re•li•gious,** *adj.* re-

---

æ **back,** ɑː **farm,** ɒ **top,** aɪ **pipe,** aʊ **how,** aɪə **fire,** aʊə **flower,** ɔː **bought,** ɔɪ **toy,** e **fed,** eə **hair,** eɪ **take,** ə **afraid,** əʊ **boat,** əʊə **lower,** ɜː **word,** iː **heap,** ɪ **hit,** ɪə **hear,** uː **school,** ʊ **book,** ʌ **but,** b **back,** d **dog,** ð **then,** dʒ **just,** f **fog,** g **go,** h **hand,** j **yes,** k **catch,** l **last,** m **mix,** n **nut,** ŋ **sing,** p **penny,** r **round,** s **some,** ʃ **short,** t **too,** tʃ **chop,** θ **thing,** v **voice,** w **was,** z **zoo,** ʒ **treasure**

ferring to religion. **re•li•gious•ly,** *adv.* regularly/at a fixed time of day.

re•lin•quish [rɪ'lɪŋkwɪʃ] *v.* (*formal*) to leave/to let go.

rel•i•quar•y ['relɪkwerɪ] *n.* container for holy relics.

rel•ish ['relɪʃ] 1. *n.* (*pl.* **-es**) (a) seasoning/flavor; spicy pickles/spicy sauce. (b) enjoyment. 2. *v.* to enjoy.

re•lo•cate [ri:lə'keɪt] *v.* to set (offices) in a new location; move to another place. **re•lo•ca•tion** [rɪlə'keɪʃn] *n.* act of relocating.

re•luc•tant [rɪ'lʌktənt] *adj.* not eager/not willing. **re•luc•tant•ly,** *adv.* not willingly. **re•luc•tance,** *n.* lack or eagerness.

re•ly [rɪ'laɪ] *v.* (**on**) to trust.

re•main [rɪ'meɪn] *v.* (a) to stay. (b) **it remains to be seen** = we will see in due course. **re•main•der.** 1. *n.* (a) what is left over. (b) **remainders** = books which are sold off cheaply. 2. *v.* to sell off (new books) cheaply. **re•mains,** *n. pl.* (a) dead body. (b) things left over/left behind.

re•mand [rɪ'mɑːnd] *v.* to order (a prisoner) back into custody to appear at a later hearing of a trial when more evidence will be produced.

re•mark [rɪ'mɑːk] 1. *n.* comment/observation. 2. *v.* to notice/to comment. **re•mark•a•ble,** *adj.* unusual/which you might comment on. **re•mark•a•bly,** *adv.* unusually.

rem•e•dy ['remədɪ] 1. *n.* thing which may cure. 2. *v.* to make (sth) better/to put (sth) right. **re•me•di•al** [rɪ'miːdɪəl] *adj.* which cures/which makes sth better; **r. reading** = class of special instruction for students who are weak in reading.

re•mem•ber [rɪ'membə] *v.* (a) to call back into your mind (sth which you have seen/read/heard, etc., before). (b) to send good wishes to s.o. (c) **he remembered me in his will** = he left me sth in his will. **re•mem•brance,** *n.* memory.

re•mind [rɪ'maɪnd] *v.* **to r. s.o. of sth** = to make (s.o.) remember sth. **re•mind•er,** *n.* thing which reminds you of sth.

rem•i•nis•cence [remɪ'nɪsəns] *n.* memory of sth from the past. **rem•i•nisce** [remɪ'nɪs] *v.* to talk about memories of the past. **rem•i•nis•cent,** *adj.* which reminds you of the past.

re•miss [rɪ'mɪs] *adj.* careless.

re•mis•sion [rɪ'mɪʃn] *n.* pardon (for your sins).

re•mit 1. *n.* ['riːmɪt] orders; area of responsibility. 2. *v.* [rɪ'mɪt] (**remitted**) (a) to pardon (sins).

(b) to send (money). **re•mit•tance,** *n.* sending money; money which is sent.

rem•nant ['remnənt] *n.* piece/quantity left over.

re•mon•strate ['remənstreɪt] *v.* to protest **against** sth. **re•mon•strance** [rɪ'mɒnstrəns] *n.* act of remonstrating.

re•morse [rɪ'mɔːs] *n.* regret about sth wicked which you have done. **re•morse•ful,** *adj.* full of remorse. **re•morse•less,** *adj.* pitiless/cruel. **re•morse•less•ly,** *adv.* in a remorseless way.

re•mote [rɪ'məut] *adj.* (**-er, -est**) (a) distant; **r. control** = (a) control (of a model plane, etc.) by radio signals. (b) device used to control the operation of sth, as a TV, from a distance. (c) slight (possibility). (d) uncommunicative (person). **re•mote•ly,** *adv.* distantly. **re•mote•ness,** *n.* being remote.

re•mold ['riːməuld] *v.* to mold again.

re•mount [riː'maunt] *v.* to get back on to (a horse/bicycle, etc.).

re•move [rɪ'muːv] 1. *n.* step or grade; **one r. from** = one grade up/down from. 2. *v.* (a) to take away. (b) to dismiss (s.o.) from a job. **re•mov•a•ble,** *adj.* which can be removed. **re•mov•al,** *n.* changing of location, as of a business. **re•mov•er,** *n.* thing which removes; **paint r.** = liquid which removes old paint.

re•mu•ner•ate [rɪ'mjuːnəreɪt] *v.* (*formal*) to pay (s.o.). **re•mu•ner•a•tion** [rɪmjuːnə'reɪʃn] *n.* payment. **re•mu•ner•a•tive** [rɪ'mjuːnərətɪv] *adj.* well paid.

ren•ais•sance [re'neɪsəns] *n.* rebirth/starting again; **the Renaissance** = artistic movement in late medieval Europe based on a renewal of interest in the Greek and Roman civilizations.

re•nal ['riːnl] *adj.* referring to the kidneys.

re•nas•cent [rɪ'neɪsənt] *adj.* which is rising again.

rend [rend] *v.* (**rent**) to tear.

rend•er ['rendə] *v.* (a) to give (back); to send in (an account). (b) to translate. (c) **to r. (down)** = to melt (fat). (d) to cover (a wall) with a coating of plaster. (e) to make (s.o.) be (speechless, etc.). **rend•er•ing,** *n.* translation; performance (of a song, etc.).

ren•dez•vous ['rɒndeɪvuː] 1. *n.* meeting place/appointment; meeting. 2. *v.* (**rendezvoused** ['rɒndeɪvuːd]) to arrange to meet.

ren•di•tion [ren'dɪʃn] *n.* performance (of a song, etc.).

ren•e•gade ['renɪgeɪd] *adj. & n.* (person) who gives up a faith/a belief to adopt another; (person) who leaves one group to join another.

re•nege [rɪ'neɪg] *v.* **to r. on** = to fail to do sth which you had promised to do.

re•new [rɪ'njuː] v. to start again; to replace (sth old) with sth new. **re•new•a•ble**, adj. which can be renewed. **re•new•al**, n. act of renewing.

ren•net ['renɪt] n. substance which when added to milk makes it curdle and so form cheese.

re•nounce [rɪ'naʊns] v. to give up officially. **re•nounce•ment**, n. act of renouncing.

ren•o•vate ['renəveɪt] v. to make (sth) like new. **ren•o•va•tion** [renə'veɪʃn] n. making like new. **ren•o•va•tor**, n. person/machine that renovates.

re•nown [rɪ'naʊn] n. fame. **re•nowned**, adj. famous (for sth).

rent [rent] 1. n. (a) money paid for the use of an apartment/house/office, etc. (b) tear/slit (in cloth). 2. v. (a) to pay money to live in (a house/apartment, etc.). (b) to give use of (a house/apartment, etc.) for money. (c) see also **rend. ren•tal**, n. rent/money paid to live in a room/apartment/office, etc.

re•nun•ci•a•tion [rɪnʌnsɪ'eɪʃn] n. giving up/renouncing of a claim.

re•o•pen [riː'əʊpən] v. (a) to open again. (b) to start to investigate a case again.

re•or•gan•ize [riː'ɔːgənaɪz] v. to organize in a new way. **re•or•gan•i•za•tion** [riːɔːgənaɪ'zeɪʃn] n. act of reorganizing.

re•or•i•ent [rɪ'ɔːrɪənteɪt] v. to set (s.o.) in another direction.

rep [rep] n. inf. (a) traveling salesman. (b) repertory theater. (c) strong corded material used in upholstery.

re•paid [riː'peɪd] v. see **re•pay.**

re•pair [rɪ'peə] 1. n. (a) mending. (b) **to be in a good state of r./in good r.** = to be in good condition. 2. v. (a) to mend. (b) (old) to go. **re•pair•er**, n. person who mends. **re•pair•a•ble**, adj. which can be mended. **rep•a•ra•tion** [repə'reɪʃn] n. thing/money which makes up for a wrong.

rep•ar•tee [repɑː'tiː] n. series of witty answers in a conversation.

re•past [rɪ'pɑːst] n. (formal) meal.

re•pa•tri•ate [riː'pætrɪeɪt] v. to bring/to send (s.o.) back to their home country. **re•pa•tri•a•tion** [riːpætrɪ'eɪʃn] n. act of repatriating.

re•pay [riː'peɪ] v. (repaid) to pay back. **re•pay•a•ble**, adj. which can be repaid. **re•pay•ment**, n. paying back.

re•peal [rɪ'piːl] 1. n. abolition of a law, so that it is no longer valid. 2. v. to do away with (a law).

re•peat [rɪ'piːt] 1. n. & adj. performance which is repeated. 2. v. to say/to do (sth) again. **re•peat•a•ble**, adj. which can be repeated. **re•peat•ed•ly** [rɪ'piːtɪdlɪ] adv. over and over again. **re•peat•er**, n. old pocket watch which rings the hours; gun which can fire several times without being reloaded.

re•pel [rɪ'pel] v. (repelled) (a) to drive back (an attack). (b) to disgust/to be so unpleasant that you drive people away. **re•pel•ling**, adj. disgusting. **re•pel•lent**, adj. & n. (thing) which drives away/which repels; insect r. = spray which keeps insects away.

re•pent [rɪ'pent] v. to be very sorry. **re•pent•ance**, n. great regret. **re•pent•ant**, adj. full of repentance.

re•per•cus•sion [rɪpɜː'kʌʃn] n. result/effect.

rep•er•toire ['repətwɑː] n. works which s.o. can play/sing by heart; works which a theater company has ready for performance.

rep•er•to•ry ['repətrɪ] n. (a) r. theater = theater with a permanent group of actors who present a series of plays, changing them at regular intervals. (b) store (of information/stories, etc.).

rep•e•ti•tion [repɪ'tɪʃn] n. act of repeating; thing which is repeated. **rep•e•ti•tious, repetitive** [rɪ'petɪtɪv] adj. which repeats sth too frequently.

re•place [riː'pleɪs] v. (a) to put (sth) back in place. (b) to put (sth) in place of sth else. **re•place•a•ble**, adj. which can be replaced. **re•place•ment**, n. (a) putting back; replacing sth with sth else. (b) thing which is used to replace; **r. parts** = spare parts (of an engine) used to replace parts which have worn out.

re•play ['riːpleɪ] n. (a) (in sports) second match between teams, competitors, etc. (b) **instant r.** = section of a sporting event which is shown again on TV at a slower speed, so that the action can be appreciated.

re•plen•ish [rɪ'plenɪʃ] v. to fill up again. **re•plen•ish•ment**, n. act of replenishing; thing which replenishes.

re•plete [rɪ'pliːt] adj. (formal) full and satisfied.

rep•li•ca ['replɪkə] n. exact copy.

re•ply [rɪ'plaɪ] 1. n. answer. 2. v. to answer.

re•port [rɪ'pɔːt] 1. n. (a) description/story of what has happened. (b) comments by teachers on a child's progress in school; comments by a

---

æ back, ɑː farm, ɒ top, aɪ pipe, aʊ how, aɪə fire, aʊə flower, ɔː bought, ɔɪ toy, e fed, eəhair, eɪ take, ə afraid, əʊ boat, əʊə lower, vː word, iː heap, ɪ hit, ɪə hear, uː school, ʊ book, ʌ but, b back, d dog, ð then, dʒ just, f fog, g go, h hand, j yes, k catch, l last, m mix, n nut, ŋ sing, p penny, r round, s some, ʃ short, t too, tʃ chop, θ thing, v voice, w was, z zoo, ʒ treasure

commission on a problem. (c) explosion. 2. *v.* (a) to write a description of what happened; **you must r. the burglary to the police** = give them the details. (b) to make a complaint about (s.o.). (c) to present oneself officially; **to r. for work.** (d) **to r. to** = be responsible to. **re•port•age** [repɔː'tɑːʒ] *n.* reporting of news (esp. for a magazine or TV). **re•port•ed•ly,** *adv.* according to what has been reported. **re•port•er,** *n.* journalist who writes articles for a newspaper on events.

re•pose [rɪ'pəuz] 1. *n.* (*formal*) calm/resting. 2. *v.* (*formal*) (a) to rest. (b) to place (trust) in s.o.

re•pos•i•to•ry [rɪ'pɒzɪtrɪ] *n.* store (of information, etc.).

re•pos•sess [riːpə'zes] *v.* to take back (goods) when the purchaser cannot pay the payments.

re•pous•sé [rə'puːseɪ] *adj. & n.* (metalwork) which is hammered into relief from the back.

rep•re•hend [riprɪ'hend] *v.* to criticize. **rep•re•hen•si•ble** *adj.* which can be criticized. **rep•re•hen•si•bly,** *adv.* in a reprehensible way.

rep•re•sent [reprɪ'zent] *v.* (a) to mean/to show. (b) to speak on behalf of (s.o./a group of people). (c) to sell goods on behalf of (s.o.). **rep•re•sen•ta•tion** [reprɪzen'teɪʃn] *n.* (a) being represented. (b) **representations** = complaints/protests. **rep•re•sen•ta•tive** [reprɪ'zentətɪv] 1. *adj.* typical. 2. *n.* person who represents; traveling salesman; member of the lower house of the U.S. Congress; **the House of Representatives.**

re•press [rɪ'pres] *v.* to keep down/to control. **re•pressed,** *adj.* kept under strict control. **re•pres•sion** [rɪ'preʃn] *n.* keeping under control. **re•pres•sive,** *adj.* severe/sharp.

re•prieve [rɪ'priːv] 1. *n.* pardon given to a prisoner. 2. *v.* to pardon.

rep•ri•mand ['reprɪmɑːnd] 1. *n.* severe rebuke. 2. *v.* to criticize (s.o.) severely.

re•print 1. *n.* ['riːprɪnt] book which has been printed again. 2. *v.* [riː'prɪnt] to print (a book) again.

re•pris•al [rɪ'praɪzl] *n.* punishment of people in revenge for sth.

re•pro ['riːprəu] *n.* (*also* **reproproof**) proof which is photographed to make a printing film.

re•proach [rɪ'prəutʃ] 1. *n.* (a) thing which is a disgrace. (b) **beyond r.** = blameless. (c) rebuke. 2. *v.* **to r. s.o. with sth** = to blame s.o. for sth. **re•proach•ful,** *adj.* which blames. **re•proach•ful•ly,** *adv.* in a reproachful way.

rep•ro•bate ['reprəbeɪt] *n.* wicked person/scoundrel.

re•pro•duce [riːprə'djuːs] *v.* (a) to copy. (b) to produce young. **re•pro•duc•tion** [riːprə-'dʌkʃən] *n.* (a) copy (of a painting, etc.); **the r. is bad on this recording** = the quality of the sound is bad. (b) production of young. **re•pro•duc•tive,** *adj.* (organs) which produce young.

re•proof [rɪ'pruːf] *n.* (*formal*) blame/criticism. **re•prove** [rɪ'pruːv] *v.* (*formal*) to criticize/to blame (someone). **re•prov•ing,** *adj.* criticizing.

rep•tile ['reptaɪl] *n.* cold-blooded animal which lays eggs and is covered with scales. **rep•til•i•an** [rep'tɪlɪən] *adj.* like a reptile.

re•pub•lic [rɪ'pʌblɪk] *n.* system of government where final authority is given to all citizens entitled to vote and is carried out by representatives elected directly or indirectly by these citizens. **re•pub•li•can,** *adj. & n.* referring to a republic; (supporter) of a republic. **Re•pub•li•can,** *adj. & n.* (member) of one of the two main political parties in the United States. **re•pub•li•can•ism,** *n.* belief in the republic as a means of government.

re•pu•di•ate [rɪ'pjuːdɪeɪt] *v.* to reject/to refuse to accept. **re•pu•di•a•tion** [rɪpjuːdɪ-'eɪʃn] *n.* rejection.

re•pug•nant [rɪ'pʌgnənt] *adj.* unpleasant/nasty. **re•pug•nance,** *n.* feeling of distaste/dislike.

re•pulse [rɪ'pʌls] *v.* to push back. **re•pul•sion** [rɪ'pʌlʃn] *n.* (a) act of repulsing. (b) feeling of dislike/distaste. **re•pul•sive,** *adj.* unpleasant/nasty.

re•pute [rɪ'pjuːt] *n.* reputation/general opinion; **of good r. re•pu•ta•ble** ['repjutəbl] *adj.* well thought of/with a good reputation. **rep•u•ta•tion** [repju'teɪʃn] *n.* general opinion (of s.o.); **I only know her by r.** = I have never met her, but I know what people think of her. **re•put•ed** [rɪ'pjuːtɪd] *adj.* supposed. **re•put•ed•ly** [rɪ'pjuːtɪdlɪ] *adv.* according to most people.

re•quest [rɪ'kwest] 1. *n.* asking/demand; **on r.** = if asked for. 2. *v.* to ask/to demand politely.

req•ui•em ['rekwɪəm] *v.* mass for the dead; music to be sung at a requiem.

re•quire [rɪ'kwaɪə] *v.* (a) to demand/to request. (b) to need. **re•quire•ment,** *n.* what is needed.

req•ui•si•tion [rekwɪ'zɪʃn] 1. *n.* official order. 2. *v.* to demand/to order that sth should be handed over; to demand and take (supplies) for an army; to order (supplies) for a school. **req•ui•site** ['rekwɪzɪt] *adj. & n.* (thing) which is necessary. etc.

rere•dos ['rɪədɒs] *n.* carved screen behind an altar.

re•run ['ri:rʌn] *n.* second showing of a program or motion picture on TV.

re•sale [ri:'seɪl] *n.* selling to s.o. goods which you have bought.

re•scind [rɪ'sɪnd] *v.* to annul/to cancel (a law).

res•cue ['reskju:] 1. *n.* saving; **r. squad** = group of people who are going to save s.o. 2. *v.* to save. **res•cu•er**, *n.* person who rescues or tries to rescue.

re•search [rɪ'sɜ:tʃ] 1. *n.* scientific study/trying to find out facts. 2. *v.* to study/to try to find out facts. **re•search•er**, *n.* person who researches.

re•sem•ble [rɪ'zembl] *v.* to be similar to. **re•sem•blance**, *n.* looking like s.o.

re•sent [rɪ'zent] *v.* to feel annoyed at a real or imaginary injury. **re•sent•ful**, *adj.* annoyed. **re•sent•ful•ly**, *adv.* in a resentful way. **re•sent•ment**, *n.* annoyance.

re•serve [rɪ'zɜ:v] 1. *n.* (a) quantity kept back for future special use; **in r.** = waiting to be used. (b) (*in sports*) extra player; **reserves** = part-time troops kept to help the regular army if necessary. (c) area of land set aside for a particular purpose; **nature r.** = area where animals and vegetation are protected. (d) shyness; not speaking openly. (e) (*at an auction*) price which an item must reach before the owner will allow it to be sold. 2. *v.* to keep back for a special use; to book (a seat/a table). **res•er•va•tion** [rezə'veɪʃn] *n.* (a) booking (of a seat/table). (b) doubt. (c) area of land set aside for a particular purpose; area set aside by the U.S. government for North American Indians to live. **re•served**, *adj.* (a) booked. (b) shy; (person) who does not speak openly. **re•serv•ist** ['rezə:vist] *n.* part-time soldier who is a member of the army reserves.

res•er•voir ['rezəvwɑ:] *n.* (a) large (usu. artificial) lake where water is kept for pumping to a town or city. (b) container for storing liquids); mass (of information/facts) which can be used if necessary.

re•side [rɪ'zaɪd] *v.* (*formal*) to live/to have a house. **res•i•dence** ['rezɪdəns] *n.* (a) place where you live. (b) act of living in a place; **r. hall** = building with rooms where students live. **res•i•den•cy**, *n.* act of residing. **res•i•dent** ['rezɪdənt] 1. *adj.* living permanently in a place. 2. *n.* person who lives in a place. **res•i•den•tial** [rezɪ'denʃl] *adj.* (part of a town) with houses rather than stores or factories.

res•i•due ['rezɪdju:] *n.* what is left over. **re•sid•u•al** [re'zɪdjʊəl] *adj.* remaining. **re•sid•u•ar•y**, *adj.* (*formal*) residual (part of an estate).

re•sign [rɪ'zaɪn] *v.* (a) to give up a job or position. (b) **to r. yourself to** = to accept. **res•ig•na•tion** [rezɪg'neɪʃn] *n.* (a) giving up a job; **he tendered/handed in his r.** = he resigned. (b) acceptance that sth has to happen. **re•signed**, *adj.* accepting that sth has to happen. **re•sign•ed•ly** [rɪ'zaɪnɪdlɪ] *adv.* patiently/calmly/without complaining.

re•sil•ient [rɪ'sɪlɪənt] *adj.* (material) which easily returns to its original shape (after being crushed); (person) who is strong/able to recover easily from a blow. **re•sil•ience**, *n.* being resilient.

res•in ['rezɪn] *n.* sticky sap, esp. from pine trees. **res•in•ous**, *adj.* like resin; made of resin.

re•sist [rɪ'zɪst] *v.* to oppose/not to give in to (sth). **re•sist•ance**, *n.* (a) opposition/fight against sth; **r. movement** = movement of ordinary people against an invader of a country; **he took the line of least r.** = he did it the easiest way. (b) (*in physics*) force which opposes sth; ability not to conduct electricity/heat, etc. **re•sist•ant**, *adj.* which resists. **re•sis•tiv•i•ty**, *n.* ability to resist the flow of an electric current. **re•sis•tor**, *n.* device which increases the resistance to an electric current/which prevents a current from flowing.

re•skill [ri:'skɪl] *v.* to train (a workforce/worker) in new skills.

res•o•lute ['rezəlu:t] *adj.* determined/having made up your mind. **res•o•lute•ly**, *adv.* in a resolute way. **res•o•lu•tion** [rezə'lu:ʃn] *n.* (a) decision reached at a meeting; proposal to be decided at a meeting. (b) (*also* **resoluteness**) determination (to do sth)/strength of character. (c) solving (of a problem). (d) splitting up into separate parts. (e) clearness of a computer image (calculated as the number of pixels per unit of area).

re•solve [rɪ'zɒlv] 1. *n.* determination (to do sth). 2. *v.* (a) to decide to do sth. (b) to solve (a problem). (c) to split up into separate parts.

res•o•nant ['rezənənt] *adj.* which sounds/rings/echoes loudly. **res•o•nance**, *n.* deep loud ringing tone.

re•sort [rɪ'zɔ:t] 1. *n.* (a) place where people go on vacations. (b) **as a last r.** = when everything

æ back, ɑ: farm, ɒ: top, aɪ pipe, aʊ how, aɪe fire, aʊə flower, ɔ: bought, ɔɪ toy, e fed, eəhair, eɪ take, ə afraid, əʊ boat, əʊə lower, v: word, i: heap, ɪ hit, ɪə hear, u: school, ʊ book, ʌ but, b back, d dog, ð then, dʒ just, f fog, g go, h hand, j yes, k catch, l last, m mix, n nut, ŋ sing, p penny, r round, s some, ʃ short, t too, tʃ chop, θ thing, v voice, w was, z zoo, ʒ treasure

else fails. 2. v. **to r. to** = to use sth in a difficult situation/when everything else has failed.

re•sound [rɪ'zaʊnd] v. to make a loud, echoing, deep noise. **re•sound•ing**, adj. great/complete; **r. success.**

re•source [rɪ'sɔːs] n. source of supply for what is needed/used; **natural resources** = minerals/oil/trees; **left to one's own resources** = left to look after oneself. **re•source•ful**, adj. good at looking after yourself/at dealing with problems. **re•source•ful•ly**, adv. in a resourceful way. **re•source•ful•ness**, n. being resourceful.

re•spect [rɪ'spekt] 1. n. (a) admiration/regard. (b) concern/detail; **with r. to** = concerning; **in some respects** = in some ways. (c) **respects** = polite good wishes. 2. v. (a) to admire/to honor (s.o.). (b) to pay attention to (sth). **re•spect•a•bil•i•ty** [rɪspektə'brlɪtɪ] n. being respectable. **re•spect•a•ble** [rɪ'spektəbl] adj. (a) proper/worthy of respect. (b) quite large/fairly large. **re•spect•a•bly**, adv. properly. **re•spect•er**, n. person who respects others. **re•spect•ful**, adj. full of respect. **re•spect•ful•ly**, adv. showing respect. **re•spect•ing**, prep. concerning. **re•spec•tive**, adj. referring to each one separately. **re•spec•tive•ly**, adv. referring to each one separately.

re•spire [res'paɪə] v. (formal) to breathe. **res•pi•ra•tion** [respɪ'reɪʃn] n. breathing in of air; **to give s.o. artificial r.** = to force s.o. (who is almost dead from drowning) to breathe. **res•pi•ra•tor** ['respɪreɪtə] n. device which helps you to breathe, esp. a mask worn as protection against gas, smoke, etc. **res•pi•ra•to•ry**, adj. referring to breathing.

res•pite ['respaɪt] n. rest; **without r.** = without stopping.

re•splend•ent [rɪ'splendənt] adj. very splendid.

re•spond [rɪ'spɒnd] v. to reply/to react (to); **he responded to treatment** = he began to get better. **re•spond•ent**, n. defendant in a law suit, esp. in a divorce case. **re•sponse**, n. (a) answer. (b) reply made by the congregation to the clergyman in a church service. **re•spon•si•bil•i•ty** [rɪspɒnsɪ'bɪlɪtɪ] n. (a) being responsible; **he has taken on a lot of r.** = he has agreed to be responsible for many things. (b) thing which you are responsible for. **re•spon•si•ble**, adj. (a) (for) causing. (b) (person) taking decisions for sth/directing sth. (c) **r. to s.o.** = being under the authority of s.o. who expects you to carry out the work well. (d) trustworthy (person). (e) **r. position** = job where decisions have to be made. **re•spon•si•bly**, adv. in a responsible way.

re•spon•sive, adj. (person) who reacts quickly/who shows sympathy. **re•spon•sive•ness**, n. sensitivity.

rest [rest] 1. n. (a) sleep/calm state; **to set s.o.'s mind at r.** = to calm s.o.'s worries. (b) stop; **the wagon came to r. at the bottom of the hill** = stopped moving. (c) (in music) short break between notes. (d) support; **arm r.** = part of a chair which you put your arms on; **head r.** = cushion to support your head (usu. attached to a seat in a car). (e) **the r.** = remains/what is left over/other people. 2. v. (a) to sleep/to be calm. (b) to make (sth) be calm. (c) **to let the matter r.** = not to deal with the problem any more. **rest•ful**, adj. calm/which makes you feel calm. **rest•less**, adj. agitated; always on the move. **rest•less•ly**, adv. in a restless way. **rest•less•ness**, n. being restless. **rest•room, rest room** n. room having a sink and toilet, for use by the public or employees, as in a restaurant, store, etc.

res•tau•rant ['restrɒnt] n. place where you can buy a meal; **self-service r.** = where you serve yourself. **res•tau•ra•teur** [restəræ'tɜː] n. person who runs a restaurant.

res•ti•tu•tion [restɪ'tjuːʃn] n. compensation/paying back.

res•tive ['restɪv] adv. nervous/agitated. **res•tive•ness**, n. agitation.

re•store [rɪs'tɔː] v. (a) to give back. (b) to repair/to make (sth) new again. **res•to•ra•tion** [restə'reɪʃn] n. (a) giving back. (b) reparing sth/making sth look like new again. **re•stor•a•tive** [rɪ'stɒrətɪv] adj. & n. (medicine) which makes you stronger. **re•stor•er**, n. person who restores old paintings, etc.

re•strain [rɪ'streɪn] v. to hold back; to prevent/to try and stop. **re•strained**, adj. controlled/calm. **re•straint**, n. control; **with great r.** = without losing your temper; **lack of r.** = (excessive) freedom.

re•strict [rɪ'strɪkt] v. to limit. **re•strict•ed**, adj. limited; **r. area** = area where only certain people are allowed. **re•stric•tion** [rɪ'strɪkʃn] n. limitation. **re•stric•tive**, adj. which restricts/limits.

re•sult [rɪ'zʌlt] 1. n. (a) thing which happens because of sth; outcome. (b) score (in a game); grades (in an exam). 2. v. **to r. from** = to happen because of sth which has been done; **to r. in** = to produce as an effect. **re•sult•ant**, adj. which results.

re•su•me [rɪ'zjuːm] v. to start again after an interruption. **re•sump•tion** [rɪ'zʌmpʃn] n. starting again.

ré•su•mé ['rezuːmeɪ] n. (a) short summing up of the main points. (b) summary of biographical details, esp. details of education and work experience, used in applying for a job.

re•sur•face [riːˈsɜːfəs] *v.* (a) to put a new surface (on a road). (b) to reappear on the surface.

re•sur•gent [rɪˈsɜːdʒənt] *adj.* which is rising again/becoming more powerful again. **re•sur•gence,** *n.* reappearance/rising again.

res•ur•rect [rezəˈrekt] *v.* to bring back to use; to start up again. **res•ur•rec•tion** [rezəˈrekʃn] *n.* bringing back to life.

re•sus•ci•tate [rɪˈsʌsɪteɪt] *v.* to bring (someone who is almost dead) back to life. **re•sus•ci•ta•tion** [rɪsʌsɪˈteɪʃn] *n.* bringing back to life.

re•tail [ˈriːteɪl] 1. *n.* selling small quantities of goods to an ordinary customer; **r. outlet** = shop which sells goods direct to the customer. 2. *v.* (a) to sell (goods) direct to customers who will not sell them again; **to r. at** = to sell for (a certain price). (b) to pass on (gossip). **re•tail•er,** *n.* owner of a store which sells goods to consumers.

re•tain [rɪˈteɪn] *v.* to keep; **to r. a lawyer to act for you** = to agree with a lawyer that he will act for you (and usu. to pay him in advance); **retaining wall** = wall which holds back a mass of earth/the water in a reservoir, etc. **re•tain•er,** *n.* (a) money paid in advance to s.o. for work he will do later. (b) (old) servant.

re•tal•i•ate [rɪˈtælɪeɪt] *v.* to hit back/to attack (s.o.) in revenge. **re•tal•i•a•tion** [rɪtælɪˈeɪʃn] *n.* **in r. for** = as a reprisal for. **re•tal•i•a•to•ry** [rɪˈtælɪətrɪ] *adj.* (measures) taken in retaliation.

re•tard [rɪˈtɑːd] *v.* to make slow/to delay the progress of. **re•tar•da•tion** [rɪtɑːˈdeɪʃn] *n.* act of retarding. **re•tard•ed,** *adj.* mentally slower than s.o. of the same age. **re•tard•ed•ness,** *n.* being retarded.

retch [retʃ] *v.* to have spasms in the throat as if you were about to vomit.

re•ten•tion [rɪˈtenʃn] *n.* keeping/holding. **re•ten•tive,** *adj.* (memory) which retains well.

re•think [riːˈθɪŋk] 1. *n. inf.* second thought about a problem. 2. *v.* (**rethought**) to think again/to reconsider.

ret•i•cent [ˈretɪsənt] *adj.* uncommunicative/not willing to talk about sth. **ret•i•cence,** *n.* unwillingness to talk.

ret•i•na [ˈretɪnə] *n.* layer on the inside of the surface of the eye, which is sensitive to light.

ret•i•nue [ˈretɪnjuː] *n.* group of people following an important person.

re•tire [rɪˈtaɪə] *v.* (a) to stop work (and usu. draw a pension); to make (s.o.) stop work (and draw a pension). (b) to go away into a place by yourself. (c) **to r. to bed for the night** = to go to bed. **re•tire•ment,** *n.* (a) act of retiring from work. (b) period of life when you are retired. **re•tir•ing,** *adj.* quiet and reserved (person).

re•tort [rɪˈtɔːt] 1. *n.* (a) sharp reply. (b) glass bottle with a long, thin bent neck used for distilling. 2. *v.* to reply sharply.

re•touch [riːˈtʌtʃ] *v.* to improve (a picture/a photograph) by adding or removing lines by hand.

re•trace [riːˈtreɪs] *v.* to go back to the origins of (sth); **to r. one's steps** = go back over the same path again.

re•tract [rɪˈtrækt] *v.* to pull back; to withdraw (sth said). **re•tract•a•ble,** *adj.* (undercarriage of a plane) which folds up into the body of the plane. **re•trac•tion** [rɪˈtrækʃn] *n.* pulling back; folding up. **re•trac•tor,** *n.* surgical instrument used to hold back the flesh during an operation.

re•tread 1. *n.* [ˈriːtred] tire which has had its surface renewed. 2. *v.* [riːˈtred] to renew the surface of a tire.

re•treat [rɪˈtriːt] 1. *n.* (a) withdrawing of an army from a battle. (b) quiet place. (c) period of calm meditation (in a religious establishment). 2. *v.* to withdraw from a battle.

re•trench [rɪˈtrentʃ] *v.* to economize/to cut back on expenditure. **re•trench•ment,** *n.* reduction of expenditure.

re•tri•al [riːˈtraɪəl] *n.* second trial.

ret•ri•bu•tion [retrɪˈbjuːʃn] *n.* well-deserved punishment. **re•trib•u•tive** [rɪˈtrɪbjuːtɪv] *adj.* acting as a punishment.

re•trieve [rɪˈtriːv] *v.* to get back (sth) which was lost; to bring back (sth). **re•triev•a•ble,** *adj.* which can be retrieved. **re•triev•al,** *n.* getting back; **r. system** = system (in a catalog/in a computer program) to allow information to be retrieved. **re•triev•er,** *n.* type of dog trained to fetch birds which have been shot.

ret•ro•ac•tive [retrəʊˈæktɪv] *adj.* which takes effect from a time in the past; **r. to last April** = which takes effect from last April.

ret•ro•grade [ˈretrəɡreɪd] *adj.* backward.

ret•ro•gress [retrəʊˈɡres] *v.* to move backward. **ret•ro•gres•sion**, *n.* moving back-ward.

ret•ro•rock•et ['retrəʊrɒkɪt] *n.* rocket which slows down a space vehicle/a plane.

ret•ro•spect ['retrəspekt] *n.* **in r.** = when you look back. **ret•ro•spec•tive** [retrə'spektɪv] *adj. & n.* which looks back on past events; (ex-hibition) of works of art covering the whole career of an artist.

re•trous•sé [rə'truːseɪ] *adj.* turned up (nose).

ret•si•na [re'tsiːnə] *n.* Greek wine flavored with resin.

re•turn [rɪ'tɜːn] 1. *n.* (a) going back/coming back; **on my r. home** = when I got back home; **r. ticket** = ticket which allows you to go to one place and come back; **many happy returns of the day** = best wishes for a happy birthday; **by r. mail** = by the next mail service back. (b) profit/income from money invested. (c) send-ing back. (d) report of results of an election; **tax r.** = official statement of income, etc., to a government agency. (e) (*in tennis, etc.*) send-ing back of a ball. (f) **r. match** = match played between two teams who have played each other recently. (g) key on a computer key-board which shows that data has been com-pletely entered. 2. *v.* (a) to come back/to go back. (b) to give back/to send back. (c) to elect (s.o.) to a legislative body, etc. **re•turn•a•ble**, *adj.* which can be returned.

re•un•ion [riː'juːnɪən] *n.* meeting of people who have not met for a long time. **re•u•nite** [riːjuː'naɪt] *v.* to join (two things) together again.

re•us•a•ble [riː'juːzəbl] *adj.* which can be used again.

rev [rev] 1. *n. inf.* revolution. 2. *v.* (**revved**) *inf.* (*also* **rev up**) to make (a car engine) go quickly while the car is standing still.

Rev. ['revrənd] *abbrev. for* Reverend.

re•val•ue [riː'væljuː] *v.* to value again (usu. at a higher value). **re•val•u•a•tion** [riːvæljuː'eɪʃn] *n.* revaluing/recalculating the value.

re•vamp [riː'væmp] *v. inf.* to improve the ap-pearance of (sth which is slightly old-fashioned).

re•veal [rɪ'viːl] *v.* to show (sth) which was hid-den. **rev•e•la•tion** [revə'leɪʃn] *n.* surprise.

rev•eil•le [rɪ'vælɪ] *n.* (*in the military*) signal to soldiers to get up in the morning.

rev•el ['revəl] 1. *n.* **revels** = merrymak-ing/happy celebrations. 2. *v.* (**reveled, revelled**) to take delight (in); to have a happy time. **rev•el•er**, *Brit.* **rev•el•ler**, *n.* person who is celebrating. **rev•el•ry**, *n.* celebration.

re•venge [rɪ'venʒ] 1. *n.* action to harm s.o. in return for harm he has caused you. 2. *v.* to harm s.o. in return for harm he has caused you. **re•venge•ful**, *adj.* wanting revenge.

rev•e•nue ['revənjuː] *n.* money which is re-ceived; taxes which a government receives.

re•ver•ber•ate [rɪ'vɜːbəreɪt] *v.* to echo/to ring out loudly in an echo. **re•ver•ber•a•tion** [rɪvɜːbə'reɪʃn] *n.* echoing.

re•vere [rɪ'vɪə] *v.* to worship/to respect (s.o.) very highly. **rev•er•ence** ['revrəns] *n.* (a) great respect. (b) bow (as a mark of respect). **rev•er•end**, *adj.* (a) worthy of respect. (b) **Reverend** = title given to members of the clergy or religious orders; **Reverend Mother** = title given to the head of a convent. **rev•er•ent**, *adj.* showing respect. **rev•er•en•tial**, *adj.* extremely respectful. **rev•er•ent•ly**, *adv.* in a reverent way.

rev•er•ie ['revərɪ] *n.* daydream.

re•vers [rɪ'vɪə] *n.* edge of a coat collar, etc., which is turned back to form the lapel.

re•ver•sal [rɪ'vɜːsəl] *n.* change to sth opposite; **r. of fortune** = bad luck.

re•verse [rɪ'vɜːs] 1. *adj.* opposite; **in r. order** = backward. 2. *n.* (a) the opposite. (b) gear of a car which makes you go backward. (c) defeat (in battle). 3. *v.* (a) to do the opposite; to make a car go backward; (*on the phone*) **to r. the charges** = to ask the person you are calling to pay for the call. (b) to change a decision to the opposite. **re•vers•i•ble**, *adj.* cloth/coat which can be worn with either side out. **re•ver•sion** [rɪ'vɜːʃn] *n.* return to an original state/to an original owner or his heirs. **re•ver•sion•ar•y**, *adj.* (property) which passes to the original owner or his heirs on the death of the existing one.

re•vert [rɪ'vɜːt] *v.* to go back/to come back (**to**); **to r. to type** = to go back to an original state; **to r. to a subject** = to start talking about the sub-ject again.

re•vet•ment [rɪ'vetmənt] *n.* stone facing to a wall.

re•view [rɪ'vjuː] 1. *n.* (a) written opinion of a book/play/motion picture, etc. (b) magazine which contains articles about new books/mo-tion pictures/plays. (c) general examination. (d) general inspection of soldiers/naval ves-sels, etc. 2. *v.* (a) to write your opinion of (a book/play/motion picture, etc.). (b) to inspect (soldiers/naval vessels). (c) to consider gener-ally. **re•view•er**, *n.* person who writes opin-ions of books/play/motion pictures.

re•vile [rɪ'vaɪl] *v.* (*formal*) to insult; to criticize sharply.

re•vise [rɪ'vaɪz] *v.* (a) to read/to study a lesson again. (b) to correct/to change. **re•vi•sion** [rɪ'vɪʒən] *n.* act of revising; thing revised. **re•vi•sion•ism**, *n.* revising the original pure concept (of a political movement, esp. com-munism).

re•vive [rɪ'vaɪv] *v.* to come back/to bring back

to life again. **re•viv•al**, *n.* bringing back to life; renewal of interest in sth. **re•viv•al•ist**, *n.* person who leads a religious revival.

re•voke [rɪ'vəʊk] *v.* to cancel. **rev•o•ca•tion** [revɒ'keɪʃn] *n.* act of revoking.

re•volt [rɪ'vəʊlt] 1. *n.* uprising against authority. 2. *v.* (a) to rise up **against** authority. (b) to disgust. **re•volt•ing**, *adj.* (a) in revolt. (b) disgusting/which makes you feel ill.

rev•o•lu•tion [revə'lu:ʃn] *n.* (a) rotation/turning around a central point. (b) uprising against a government. **rev•o•lu•tion•ar•y**. 1. *adj.* (a) aiming to change things completely/very new. (b) referring to a political revolution. 2. *n.* person who takes part in an uprising against a government. **rev•o•lu•tion•ize**, *v.* to change completely.

re•volve [rɪ'vɒlv] *v.* (a) to turn around. (b) to be centered on. **re•volv•er**, *n.* small hand gun with a cartridge chamber which turns after each shot is fired. **re•volv•ing**, *adj.* which turns around.

re•vue [rɪ'vju:] *n.* stage show with satirical sketches/songs, etc.

re•vul•sion [rɪ'vʌlʃn] *n.* (*formal*) disgust.

re•ward [rɪ'wɔːd] 1. *n.* money/present given to s.o. as a prize or for information or the return of sth. 2. *v.* to give (s.o.) money/a present as a prize or for giving information or returning sth. **re•ward•ing**, *adj.* which gives moral satisfaction.

re•write ['riːraɪt] 1. *n. inf.* act of rewriting. 2. *v.* (**rewrote, rewritten**) to write (sth) again in different words.

Rh *abbrev. for* Rh factor.

rhap•so•dy ['ræpsədɪ] *n.* poetry/music/song showing great excitement/passion. **rhap•sod•i•cal** [ræp'sɒdɪkl] *adj.* excited/passionate. **rhap•so•dize**, *v.* (**over**) to praise (sth) extravagantly.

rhe•o•stat ['rɪəstæt] *n.* device for making lights lower by cutting down the flow of electric current gradually.

rhe•sus ['riːsəs] *adj.* **r. monkey** = small monkey, often used in laboratories for scientific research; **r. factor** = Rh factor.

rhet•o•ric ['retərɪk] *n.* art of speaking forcefully and eloquently. **rhe•tor•i•cal** [rɪ'tɒrɪkl] *adj.* referring to rhetoric; **r. question** = question to which you do not expect an answer.

rheu•ma•tism ['ruːmətɪzəm] *n.* disease causing pains in the joints or muscles.

rheu•mat•ic [ruː'mætɪk] *adj.* referring to rheumatism; **r. fever** = serious disease of children and young people where the joints swell. **rheu•mat•ic**, *adj.* referring to or having rheumatism. **rheu•ma•toid ar•thri•tis**, *n.* continuing disease of the joints where they become stiff, swollen and painful.

Rh fac•tor [ ] *n.* substance in the blood (or absent from it) which can affect newborn babies and people having blood transfusions; **Rh positive** = having an Rh factor; **Rh negative** = with no Rh factor.

rhine•stone ['raɪnstəʊn] *n.* imitation colorless precious stone.

rhi•noc•er•os [raɪ'nɒsərəs], *inf.* **rhi•no** ['raɪnəʊ] *n.* (*pl.* **-es, -os**) huge Asiatic or African animal with a thick skin and one or two horns on its head.

rhi•zome ['raɪzəʊm] *n.* thick stem which lies on the ground like a root and produces shoots.

rho•do•den•dron [rəʊdə'dendrən] *n.* large evergreen shrub with clusters of huge colorful flowers.

rhom•bus ['rɒmbəs] *n.* shape with four equal sides but with no right angles. **rhom•boid**. 1. *adj.* shaped like a rhombus/diamond-shaped. 2. *n.* four-sided shape with opposite sides equal in length and no right angles.

rhu•barb ['ruːbɑːb] *n.* garden plant with large poisonous leaves, whose stalks are cooked as a dessert.

rhyme [raɪm] 1. *n.* (a) sameness of sounds between two words (used in poetry). (b) little piece of poetry; **nursery r.** = (often nonsensical) piece of poetry for children. 2. *v.* (**with**) to have the same sound as.

rhythm ['rɪðəm] *n.* regular beat in music/poetry, etc. **rhyth•mic(al)** ['rɪðmɪk(l)] *adj.* with a regular beat. **rhyth•mi•cal•ly**, *adv.* in a rhythmical way.

rib [rɪb] 1. *n.* (a) one of several bones forming a cage across the chest. (b) piece of meat with the rib attached to it; **spare ribs** = cooked pork ribs in a usu. spicy sauce. (c) curved timber whch is part of the structure of a ship; one of the spokes of an umbrella. (d) thicker part in a leaf. (e) thicker line of stitches in knitting. 2. *v. inf.* to tease (s.o.). **rib•bed**, *adj.* with ribs. **rib cage**, *n.* all the ribs in an animal.

rib•ald ['rɪbəld] *adj.* rude (song/joke). **rib•ald•ry**, *n.* rude jokes.

rib•bon ['rɪbn] *n.* long flat thin piece of mate-

æ back, ɑː farm, ɒ top, aɪ pipe, aʊ how, aiə fire, aʊə flower, ɔː bought, ɔɪ toy, e fed, eəhair, eɪ take, ə afraid, əʊ boat, əʊə lower, ɜː word, iː heap, ɪ hit, ɪə hear, uː school, ʊ book, ʌ but, b back, d dog, ð then, dʒ just, f fog, g go, h hand, j yes, k catch, l last, m mix, n nut, ŋ sing, p penny, r round, s some, ʃ short, t too, tʃ chop, θ thing, v voice, w was, z zoo, ʒ treasure

rial for tying or decoration; **typewriter r.** = flat piece of material covered with ink, which is struck by the letters in a typewriter.

ri•bo•fla•vin [raibəu'fleivin] *n.* type of vitamin B.

ri•bo•nu•cle•ic ac•id [ri:bəunju:'kleiik 'æsid] *n.* substance in cells which takes information from the DNA and converts it to enzymes and proteins.

rice [rais] *n.* common tropical cereal, grown in wet ground or water; **brown r.** = rice which still has its outer covering; **wild r.** = plant of North America, which resembles rice; **r. pudding** = dessert made of rice, milk and sugar; **r. paper** = very thin paper which you can eat and which is used in cooking.

rich [ritʃ] 1. *adj.* (**-er, -est**) (a) having a great deal of money. (b) (food) with a lot of cream/fat/eggs, etc. in it. (c) deep and resonant (voice); dark (color). (d) fertile (soil). (e) **r. in** = with many resources. 2. *n.* **the r.** = rich people. **rich•es** ['ritʃiz] *n.* wealth. **rich•ly,** *adv.* splendidly; **which you so r. deserve** = which you deserve very much. **rich•ness,** *n.* wealth; being rich.

Rich•ter scale ['riXtə'skeil] *n.* scale for measuring earthquakes.

rick [rik] 1. *n.* (a) large pile of straw or hay in a field. (b) sprain. 2. *v.* to twist/sprain (ankle, back).

rick•ets ['rikits] *n.* disease of children (caused by lack of vitamins) where bones become bent. **rick•et•y,** *adj.* wobbly (chair).

rick•shaw, ['rikʃɔ:] *n.* light wheeled chair pulled by a man.

ric•o•chet ['rikəʃei] *v.* (**ricocheted** ['rikəʃeid]) to bounce off a surface at an angle.

rid [rid] *v.* (**rid**) to clear away; **to get r. of sth** = to dispose of sth/to throw sth away. **rid•dance,** *n.* **good r.** = I am glad to get rid of it.

-ridden [ridn] *suffix meaning* filled with/affected by.

rid•dle ['ridl] 1. *n.* (a) guessing game where you have to guess the answer to a deliberately puzzling question. (c) large sieve for separating soil from stones. 2. *v.* (a) to put (soil) through a sieve. (b) **to r. with bullets** = to shoot many times. **rid•dled with,** *adj.* full of.

ride [raid] 1. *n.* (a) trip/journey on horseback/on a bicycle/in a car, etc.; *Sl.* **he was taken for a r.** = (i) they tricked him; (ii) they murdered him. (b) a vehicle or device which people ride on or in for fun at a fair or amusement park. 2. *v.* (**rode, has ridden**) (a) to go for a trip on horseback/on a bicycle/in a car, etc. (b) (*of ships*) **to r. at anchor** = to float; **the ships rode out the storm** = they remained at anchor during the storm. **rid•er,** *n.* (a) person who rides. (b) additional clause to a contract.

rid•er•less, *adj.* (horse) with no rider. **ride up,** *v.* (*of dress, etc.*) to move upward through movement of the body. **ri•ding,** *n.* sport of going on horseback; **r. school** = school where you learn to ride a horse. **rid•ing lights,** *n. pl.* lights on a ship at anchor.

ridge [ridʒ] *n.* long narrow raised part. **ridged,** *adj.* with ridges.

rid•i•cule ['ridikju:l] 1. *n.* mocking/laughing at s.o.; **to hold s.o. up to r.** = to laugh at s.o. 2. *v.* to laugh at (s.o./sth). **ri•dic•u•lous,** *adj.* silly/which can be laughed at. **ri•dic•u•lous•ly,** *adv.* in a silly way. **ri•dic•u•lous•ness,** *n.* silliness.

rife [raif] *adj.* common.

rif•fle ['rifl] *v.* to turn quickly (**through** the pages of a book).

riff•raff ['rifræf] *n.* (*no pl.*) worthless ordinary people.

ri•fle ['raifl] 1. *n.* hand gun with a long barrel with spiral grooves inside. 2. *v.* (a) to search and to steal from. (b) to make spiral grooves inside a gun barrel.

rift [rift] *n.* split/crack.

rig [rig] 1. *n.* (a) way in which a ship's sails are arranged. (b) metal construction for drilling for minerals. (c) *inf.* set of clothes. 2. *v.* (**rigged**) (a) to fit out a ship with sails. (b) to arrange a dishonest result. **rig•ging,** *n.* ropes on a ship. **rig up,** *v.* to arrange/to construct (sth) quickly.

right [rait] 1. *adj.* (a) good/honest. (b) correct. (c) **to get on the r. side of s.o.** = to make s.o. favor you; *inf.* **on the r. side of forty** = less than forty years old. (d) **r. angle** = angle of 90°. (e) straight/in order; **is he in his r. mind?** = is he sane? **she's all r. again** = she's better. (f) not left; referring to the hand which most people use for writing. 2. *n.* (a) what is correct/good; **in the r.** = not to be criticized. (b) legal title to sth; **she has no r. to be here** = she should not be here; **civil rights** = legal entitlements of every citizen; **by rights** = if things were done properly. (c) the right-hand side/the right-hand direction; **the r.** = political parties which are conservative. 3. *adj.* (a) **r. on** = straight on. (b) **r. away** = immediately. (c) completely. (d) correctly; **it serves you r.** = you deserved it. (e) to the right-hand side. 4. *v.* to correct; to make (sth) return to its correct position. 5. *inter.* (a) agreed/OK. (b) *inf.* do you understand? **right-an•gled,** *adj.* with a 90° angle. **right•eous** ['raitʃəs] *adj.* virtuous/very good. **right•eous•ly,** *adv.* in a righteous way. **right•eous•ness,** *n.* virtue/goodness. **right•ful,** *adj.* legally correct. **right•ful•ly,** *adv.* in a rightful way. **right-hand,** *adj.* referring to the right hand; **right-hand man** = most important assistant. **right-hand•ed,** *adj.* (person) who uses the right hand for writing/working, etc. **right•ist,** *n.* member of a conservative political group. **right•ly,** *adv.* correctly; **I can't r. say** = I am not very sure. **right-mind•ed,** *adj.* (person) who has correct ideas/who thinks in the way most people think. **right•ness,** *n.* correctness. **right of way,** *n.* (a) right to walk over s.o. else's property. (b) right (of one vehicle) to go first at an intersection. **right•size,** *v.* to reduce a company's workforce to the optimum size in order to reduce costs and maximize efficiency, without excessive downsizing. **right-wing,** *adj.* belonging to the conservative political parties. **right-wing•er,** *n.* person who is on the right politically.

rig•id ['rɪdʒɪd] *adj.* stiff/unbending/inflexible. **rig•id•ly,** *adv.* stiffly. **ri•gid•i•ty** [rɪ-'dʒɪdɪtɪ] *n.* being rigid.

rig•ma•role ['rɪgmərəʊl] *n.* long incoherent speech/meaningless jumble of words.

rig•or, *Brit.* **rig•our** ['rɪgə] *n.* severity (of the law, etc.); harshness (of the climate). **rig•or mor•tis** [-'mɔːtɪs] *n.* stiffening of a body after death. **rig•or•ous,** *adj.* very strict. **rig•or•ous•ly,** *adv.* in a rigorous way.

rile [raɪl] *v. inf.* to annoy.

rill [rɪl] *n.* small stream.

rim [rɪm] *n.* edge of a wheel/of a cup; frame of glasses. **rim•less,** *adj.* (glasses) with no frame. **rimmed,** *adj.* with a rim.

rime [raɪm] *n.* white frost.

rind [raɪnd] *n.* skin on fruit/meat/cheese.

ring [rɪŋ] **1.** *n.* (a) circular piece of metal/wood, etc., with a hole in the center. (b) anything shaped like a circle; *inf.* **to run rings around s.o.** = to do things more efficiently than s.o. (c) group of people (usu. criminals). (d) center of a circus where performances take place; square place where a boxing/wrestling match takes place. (e) sound of a bell. (f) call on the telephone. **2.** *v.* **(rang, has rung)** (a) to make a sound of a bell; *inf.* **it rings a bell** = it reminds me of sth. (b) **my ears are ringing** = there is a sound like that of bells in my ears. (c) (*esp. Brit.*) to telephone; **to r. s.o. up** = to call s.o. on the telephone; **to r. back** = to phone in reply to a phone call; **to r. off** = to stop the telephone call/to put down the receiver. **3.** *v.* **(ringed)** (a) to put a ring on the leg of a wild bird for marking purposes. (b) to mark with a circle. **ring•er,** *n.* (a) person who rings church bells.

(b) *inf.* **dead r.** = person/horse exactly similar to another. **ring•lead•er,** *n.* head of a gang or group/person who organizes a crime. **ring•let,** *n.* long curl (of hair). **ring•mas•ter,** *n.* master of ceremonies in a circus. **ring•side,** *adj.* by the side of a boxing/wrestling ring. **ring•worm,** *n.* disease of the skin which causes round red patches.

rink [rɪŋk] *n.* place where you can roller-skate or ice-skate; surface for skating.

rinse [rɪns] **1.** *n.* (a) putting soapy laundry/soapy dishes/soapy hair through clean water to remove the soap. (b) colored liquid for the hair. **2.** *v.* to put (soapy/dirty things) into clean water to remove the soap/the dirt.

ri•ot ['raɪət] **1.** *n.* (a) noisy, violent disorder among crowds of people; **to run r.** = to become disordered/to get out of control; **to read s.o. the r. act** = to warn s.o. to stop being disorderly. (b) mass (of sounds/colors). (c) very amusing motion picture/play, etc. **2.** *v.* to take part in a riot/to get out of control. **ri•ot•er,** *n.* person who takes part in a riot. **ri•ot•ing,** *n.* riots/outbreaks of civil disorder. **ri•ot•ous,** *adj.* wild/out of control. **ri•ot•ous•ly,** *adv.* in a riotous way. **ri•ot po•lice,** *n.* police specially equipped to deal with rioters.

rip [rɪp] **1.** *n.* tear (in cloth). **2.** *v.* **(ripped)** to tear; *inf.* **to let r.** = to allow sth to go freely. **rip cord,** *n.* cord you pull to make a parachute open. **rip off,** *v.* (a) to tear off. (b) *Sl.* **to rip s.o. off** = to cheat s.o./to make s.o. pay too much. **rip-off,** *n. Sl.* bad deal/thing which costs too much. **rip-roar•ing,** *adj.* wild/noisy (party); great (success). **rip•saw,** *n.* saw with large teeth, for rough cutting.

RIP [ɑːraɪpiː] *short for* Rest in Peace, Requiescat in Pace.

ri•par•i•an [rɪ'peərɪən] *adj.* (*formal*) referring to the banks of a river.

ripe [raɪp] *adj.* **(-er, -est)** ready to eat/to be harvested; **to a r. old age** = until very old; **the time is r. for sth** = it is the right time to do sth. **rip•en,** *v.* to become ripe. **ripe•ness,** *n.* readiness; state of being ripe.

ri•poste [rɪ'pɒst] **1.** *n.* quick, sharp reply. **2.** *v.* to make a quick, sharp reply.

rip•ple ['rɪpl] **1.** *n.* little wave. **2.** *v.* to make little waves.

rise [raɪz] **1.** *n.* (a) movement upward; slope upward. (b) **to give r. to sth** = to start sth. **2.** *v.* **(rose, has risen)** (a) to move upward; to get up;

æ back, ɑː farm, ɒ top, aɪ pipe, aʊ how, aɪə fire, aʊə flower, ɔː bought, ɔɪ toy, e fed, eəhair, eɪ take, ə afraid, əʊ boat, əʊə lower, vː word, iː heap, ɪ hit, ɪə hear, uː school, ʊ book, ʌ but, b back, d dog, ð then, dʒ just, f fog, g go, h hand, j yes, k catch, l last, m mix, n nut, ŋ sing, p penny, r round, s some, ʃ short, t too, tʃ chop, θ thing, v voice, w was, z zoo, ʒ treasure

to get out of bed. (b) (*of a court or legislative body*) to stop meeting. (c) **to r. in revolt/to r. against s.o.** = to riot/to rebel. **ris•er**, *n.* (a) **early r.** = person who gets up early in the morning. (b) vertical board holding up the tread of a staircase. **ris•ing**. 1. *adj.* which is moving upward/which is increasing; **r. genera-tion** = new generation which will follow the present one; **r. forty** = nearly forty years old. 2. *n.* (a) movement upward. (b) rebellion/revolt.

ris•i•ble ['rɪzɪbl] *adj.* laughable.

risk [rɪsk] 1. *n.* possible harm; dangerous chance; **they run the r. of being caught** = they may well be caught. 2. *v.* to chance/to do sth which may possibly cause harm. **risk•i•ly**, *adv.* in a risky way. **risk•i•ness**, *n.* being risky. **risk•y**, *adj.* (**-ier, -iest**) danger-ous/which may cause harm.

ri•sot•to [rɪ'sɒtəʊ] *n.* Italian dish of cooked rice with meat/fish/vegetables in it.

ris•qué ['riːskeɪ] *adj.* slightly indecent.

ris•sole ['rɪsəʊl] *n.* fried ball of meat/fish, etc.

rite [raɪt] *n.* religious ceremony; **last rites** = communion for a s.o. who is dying. **rit•u•al** ['rɪtjʊəl] *adj. & n.* (referring to) a religious cer-emony. **rit•u•al•ly**, *adv.* in a ritual way.

ri•val ['raɪvl] 1. *n. & adj.* (person) who com-petes. 2. *v.* (**rivaled, rivalled**) to compete with s.o.; to be of similar quality. **ri•val•ry**, *n.* competition.

riv•en ['rɪvn] *adj.* (*formal*) split.

riv•er ['rɪvə] *n.* large stream of water which goes into another stream, or into the sea. **riv•er•side**, *adj.* on the banks of a river.

riv•et ['rɪvɪt] 1. *n.* nail which fastens metal plates together. 2. *v.* (a) to fasten metal plates together. (b) to attract s.o.'s attention.

Riv•i•er•a [rɪvɪ'eərə] *n.* beautiful south coast, esp. along the Mediterranean.

riv•u•let ['rɪvjʊlət] *n.* little stream.

Rn *symbol for* radon.

RNA [ɑːen'eɪ] *abbrev. for* ribonucleic acid.

roach [rəʊtʃ] *n.* (a) (*pl.* **roaches, roach**) small freshwater fish. (b) (*pl.* **roaches**) *inf.* cock-roach.

road [rəʊd] *n.* (a) path for cars and other vehi-cles; way of getting somewhere; **the r. to suc-cess** = the path which leads to success; **on the r.** = traveling from place to place (as a sales-man/worker). (b) **roads** = part of the sea near a port where ships can lie at anchor. **road•block**, *n.* barrier put across a road by the police. **road hog**, *n. inf.* dangerous driver who takes up two lanes. **road•house**, *n.* inn, tavern, etc. along a main road. **road•ie**, *n. inf.* person who organizes a traveling musical or theatrical group. **road•kill**, *n.* animal(s) killed on a road by motor vehicles.

road•rage, *n.* aggressive behavior by driv-ers. **road•side**, *n.* by the side of a road. **road•stead**, *n.* part of the sea near a port where ships can lie at anchor. **road•way**, *n.* main surface of a road. **road•works**, *n. pl.* repairs to a road. **road•wor•thi•ness**, *n.* being roadworthy. **road•wor•thy**, *adj.* in a fit state to be driven on a road.

roam [rəʊm] *v.* to wander.

roan [rəʊn] *adj. & n.* (brown horse) with gray hairs in its coat.

roar [rɔː] 1. *n.* loud, deep call; loud shouting. 2. *v.* to make a loud call. **roar•ing**. 1. *adj.* wild (success); **to do a r. business in** = to sell sth rap-idly. 2. *n.* sound of loud, deep calls.

roast [rəʊst] 1. *n.* meat which has been/which will be cooked in an oven. 2. *v.* to cook over a fire/in an oven. 3. *adj.* which has been roasted; **r. beef. roast•ing**, *adj.* (chicken) which is ready to be roasted.

rob [rɒb] *v.* (**robbed**) to steal from s.o. **rob•ber**, *n.* person who steals money from s.o. **rob•ber•y**, *n.* stealing.

robe [rəʊb] *n.* 1. long, loose garment (for men or women), as worn by judges; long garment worn over pajamas or a nightgown. 2. *v.* to dress in a robe.

rob•in ['rɒbɪn] *n.* common small brown bird with a red breast; **round r.** = letter of com-plaint signed by many people.

ro•bot ['rəʊbɒt] *n.* machine which works like a human being; (*in science fiction*) machine which looks a little like a human being and which can act like one. **ro•bot•ics** [rəʊ-'bɒtɪks] *n.* science of electronic robots.

ro•bust [rə'bʌst] *adj.* strong/vigorous. **ro•bust•ly**, *adv.* in a robust way. **ro•bust•ness**, *n.* being robust.

rock [rɒk] 1. *n.* (a) stone/solid part of the earth's surface. (b) large piece of stone; *inf.* **on the rocks** = (i) bankrupt; (ii) (whisky) with ice; **r. plant** = alpine plant. (c) music with a strong rhythm. 2. *v.* to sway from side to side; to make (sth) sway from side to side; *inf.* **don't r. the boat** = don't disturb what has been ar-ranged. **rock bot•tom**, *n.* the lowest point. **rock•er**, *n.* (a) semicircular wooden piece which a rocking chair or rocking horse stands on. (b) rocking chair; *inf.* **off one's r.** = mad. **rock gar•den** (*also* **rockery**) *n.* garden planted around a collection of rocks. **rock•ing**, *adj.* swaying; **rocking horse** = child's wooden horse on rockers; **rocking chair** = chair which rocks backward and forward on rockers. **rock•y**, *adj.* (a) full of rocks. (b) *inf.* wobbly.

rock•et ['rɒkɪt] 1. *n.* (a) type of firework which, when lit, flies up into the sky; spacecraft; type of bomb which is shot through space at an enemy. (b) engine driven by burning gas, which powers a spacecraft or bomb. 2. *v.* to shoot upward very fast. **rock•et•ry**, *n.* (*no pl.*) science of space rockets.

ro•co•co [rə'kəukəu] *adj. & n.* ornate flowery (style of architecture of the 18th century).

rod [rɒd] *n.* (a) long stick. (b) **fishing r.** = long stick with a line attached, used for fishing.

rode [rəud] *v. see* **ride.**

ro•dent ['rəudənt] *n.* animal which chews and gnaws (such as a mouse/rat, etc.).

ro•de•o [rəu'deɪəu] *n.* (*pl.* **-os**) display of skill by cowboys.

roe [rəu] *n.* (a) fish eggs. (b) type of small deer. **roe•buck**, *n.* male roe deer.

roent•gen ['rʌntjən] *adj.* referring to X-rays.

rog•er ['rɒdʒə] *inter. & signal meaning* message received and understood.

rogue [rəug] *adj. & n.* (a) wicked/dishonest person. (b) **r. elephant** = elephant driven out of the herd by the other elephants. **ro•guer•y**, *n.* roguish behavior. **ro•guish**, *adj.* wicked/dishonest.

roist•er•er ['rɔɪstərə] *n.* person who celebrates noisily. **roist•er•ing**, *n.* noisy celebrations.

role [rəul] *n.* part played by s.o. (in a play, motion picture, or real life).

roll [rəul] 1. *n.* (a) thing which has been turned over and over to make a tube; **jelly r.** = cake rolled up with jam in it; **sausage r.** = small pastry with a sausage inside. (b) very small loaf of bread. (c) list of names; **r. of honor** = list of prizewinners/list of soldiers who have died during a war. (d) movement from side to side. (e) rumble (of drums). 2. *v.* (a) to make a tube out of sth flat. (b) to flatten by using a roller. (c) to make (sth) move forward by turning it over and over; *inf.* **rolling in money** = having a great deal of money. (d) to rock from side to side. (e) **to r. one's r's** = when speaking the letter "r", to make the tip of the tongue vibrate. (f) to make a low rumbling noise. (g) *inf.* to rob (s.o.), esp. when he is asleep. **roll•call**, *n.* calling names from a list. **roll•er**, *n.* (a) round object which rolls; **steam r.** = machine for flattening new road surfaces. (b) large wave in the sea. (c) **r. towel** = continuous towel hanging on a horizontal bar. (d) plastic tube used for rolling hair into curls. **Roll•er•blade** ['rəuləbleɪd] *n.* trademark for a type of roller skate. *see* **in-line skate. roll•er coast•er**, *n.* railroad in an amusement park which goes

up and down steep slopes. **roll•er skate**, *n.* shoe or device with wheels which you strap to your foot so as to glide along fast on a surface. **roll•er-skate** *v.* to glide on roller skates. **roll•er-skat•ing**, *n.* sport of going on roller skates. **roll•ing**, *adj.* (countryside) which is a mass of small hills; **r. pin** = wooden roller with handles, for flattening pastry; **r. stock** = passenger cars, engines, etc. used on a railroad. **roll-top**, *adj.* **r. desk** = desk with a cover made of slats of wood which slide upward to open it.

roll•ick•ing ['rɒlɪkɪŋ] *adj.* noisy and jolly.

ro•ly-po•ly ['rəulɪ'pəulɪ] *adj. & n. inf.* fat (person).

ROM [rɒm] *n.* read-only memory computer memory with data programmed into it, which can only be read, but not changed.

Ro•man ['rəumən] *adj.* referring to Rome; **roman** = printing type with straight letters; **R. candle** = type of firework giving a brilliant fountain of light; **R. numerals** = numbers written in the Roman style (I, II, III, IV, etc.). **Ro•man Cath•o•lic**, *adj. & n.* (person) belonging to the Christian church of which the Pope is the head. **Ro•man Cath•ol•i•cism**, *n.* beliefs of the Roman Catholic church.

ro•mance [rə'mæns] 1. *n.* (a) **r. language** = language which has derived from Latin, as French and Italian. (b) love affair. (c) love story. (d) invented story. 2. *v.* to invent/to make up a story. **ro•man•tic** [rə'mæntɪk] *adj.* (*a*) full of mystery and romance. (b) (literary/artistic style) which is very imaginative/based on personal emotions. **ro•man•ti•cal•ly**, *adv.* in a romantic way. **ro•man•ti•cism**, *n.* romantic literary style. **ro•man•ti•cize**, *v.* to turn (sth) into a romantic story.

Ro•man•esque [rəumə'nesk] *adj. & n.* architectural style with round arches and vaults found in Europe in the early Middle Ages.

Ro•ma•ni•an [ruː'meɪnɪən] 1. *adj.* referring to Romania. 2. *n.* (a) person from Romania. (b) language spoken in Romania.

Rom•a•ny ['rəumənɪ] *n.* (a) gypsy. (b) language spoken by gypsies.

romp [rɒmp] 1. *n.* (a) energetic play. (b) easy win. 2. *v.* (a) to play energetically. (b) to win easily. **romp•ers**, *n.* one-piece suit for a baby.

ron•do ['rɒndəu] *n.* (*pl.* **-os**) piece of music where the same theme is repeated several times.

æ back, aː farm, ɒ top, aɪ pipe, aʊ how, aɪe fire, aʊə flower, ɔː bought, ɔɪ toy, e fed, eəhair, eɪ take, ə afraid, əʊ boat, əʊə lower, vː word, iː heap, ɪ hit, ɪə hear, uː school, ʊ book, ʌ but, b back, d dog, ð then, dʒ just, f fog, g go, h hand, j yes, k catch, l last, m mix, n nut, ŋ sing, p penny, r round, s some, ʃ short, t too, tʃ chop, θ thing, v voice, w was, z zoo, ʒ treasure

rood [ru:d] *n.* **r. screen** = screen built across a church, separating the chancel from the nave.

roof [ru:f] 1. *n.* (a) covering over a building. (b) top of the inside of the mouth. (c) top of a car/bus/truck, etc.; **sun r.** = roof of a car which you can open in good weather; **r. rack** = grid fixed to the roof of a car for carrying luggage. 2. *v.* to put a roof on (a building).

rook [ruk] 1. *n.* (a) large black bird of the crow family. (b) (*in chess*) piece shaped like a castle. 2. *v. Sl.* to cheat. **rook•er•y,** *n.* place where rooks nest; colony of penguins/seals.

rook•ie ['rukɪ] *n. inf.* new recruit in the armed forces/in the police.

room [ru:m] 1. *n.* (a) one of the divisions inside a house. (b) space; **to make r. for** = squeeze up to give space for; **there's r. for improvement** = things could be improved. 2. *v.* to live in furnished rooms. **room•ing-house,** *n.* house with furnished rooms to rent. **room•mate,** *n.* person with whom you share a room. **room•y,** *adj.* (**-ier, -iest**) spacious.

roost [ru:st] 1. *n.* perch for a bird; **to rule the r.** = be in charge/be the boss. 2. *v.* to perch. **roost•er,** *n.* male bird (esp. a domestic chicken).

root [ru:t] 1. *n.* (a) part of a plant which goes down into the ground, and which takes nourishment from the soil; part of a hair/a tooth which goes down into the skin; **to take r.** = to start to grow; **to put down roots** = to begin to feel at home in a place. (b) source. (c) (*in language*) word which is a base for other words. (d) **square r.** = number which if multiplied by itself gives the number you have; **cube r.** = number which if multiplied by itself twice gives the number you have. 2. *v.* to make roots; **deeply rooted fear** = fear which is very strongly felt. (b) (**for**) to dig (sth) up/to look for (sth); **to r. for a team** = to cheer a team on. **root beer,** *n.* dark sweet drink, flavored with roots. **root crop,** *n.* crop which is grown for its edible roots (such as carrots, turnips, etc.). **root•less,** *adj.* with no roots. **root•stock,** *n.* plant on which another is grafted. **root up, root out,** *v.* to pull up (a plant) by its roots; to remove (sth) completely.

rope [rəup] 1. *n.* thick string/thick cord; *inf.* **he knows the ropes** = he knows all about it/how to go about doing it. 2. *v.* to tie together with a rope; **to r. s.o. in** = to get s.o. to help/to join; **to r. off** = to stop people going into a place by putting a rope around it. **rop•y,** *adj.* (**-ier, -iest**) forming thick threads, as a liquid.

ro•sa•ry ['rəuzərɪ] *n.* string of beads used by Catholics when saying prayers.

rose [rəuz] 1. *n.* (a) scented flower which grows on a prickly bush. (b) pink color; *inf.* **wearing r. colored glasses** = seeing things as being very

good, when they are not. (c) piece of metal/plastic with many holes in it, which is attached to the spout of a watering can, so that the water comes out in a spray. 2. *v. see* **rise. ro•se•ate** ['rəuzɪət] *adj.* deep pink. **rose•bud,** *n.* flower bud of a rose. **rose win•dow,** *n.* large round decorated window found usu. in the west wall of a church. **rose•wood,** *n.* fragrant hard red wood, used for making furniture. **ros•i•ness,** *n.* being rosy. **ros•y,** *adj.* (**-ier, -iest**) (a) bright pink. (b) very favorable.

ro•sé [rəu'seɪ] *n.* pink wine.

rose•mar•y ['rəuzmərɪ] *n.* common evergreen herb with scented leaves.

ro•sette [rə'set] *n.* ribbon bunched to look like a flower, used as a decoration or as a badge.

ros•in ['rɒzɪn] *n.* solid resin used to rub a violin bow.

ros•ter ['rɒstə] *n.* list of duties which have to be done and the people who have to do them.

ros•trum ['rɒstrəm] *n.* raised stand for a speaker.

rot [rɒt] 1. *n.* (a) decay; **dry r.** = decay in house timbers caused by a fungus. (b) nonsense. 2. *v.* (**rotted**) to decay; to go bad. **rot•ten,** *adj.* decayed; *inf.* **to feel r.** = (i) to feel ill; (ii) to feel ashamed.

ro•ta ['rəutə] *n.* roster.

ro•tate [rəu'teɪt] *v.* to turn around. **ro•ta•ry** ['rəutərɪ] *adj.* which turns/rotates; **r. printing press** = one where the paper passes around large rollers. **ro•ta•tion** [rəu'teɪʃn] *n.* turning/taking turns; **r. of crops** = growing different crops in turn. **ro•ta•to•ry,** *adj.* turning (motion). **ro•tor,** *n.* piece of machinery which rotates; the blades of a helicopter.

rote [rəut] *n.* learning by heart.

ro•tis•ser•ie [rəu'ti:sərɪ] *n.* electric machine for turning meat on a spit in front of heat.

ro•tund [rə'tʌnd] *adj.* round/fat. **ro•tun•da,** *n.* circular building with a dome. **ro•tun•di•ty,** *n.* being rotund.

rou•ble ['ru:bl] *n.* ruble.

rouge [ru:ʒ] *n.* pink cream/powder which you put on your face to give yourself more color. **rouged,** *adj.* wearing rouge.

rough [rʌf] 1. *adj.* (**-er, -est**) (a) not smooth/bumpy/uneven; **to give s.o. a r. time** = treat s.o. badly. (b) unfinished; approximate (translation). 2. *n.* (a) area of long grass on a golf course. (b) unfinished design. 3. *adv.* brutally/harshly. 4. *v.* **to r. out** = to make a rough design; **to r. it** = to live uncomfortably; **to r. s.o. up** = to beat/to attack s.o. **rough•age,** *n.* coarse stuff, such as bran, which you eat to help digestion. **rough and read•y,** *adj.* approximate; not completely finished.

rough-and-tum•ble, *adj.* disorderly and often violent; **rough and tumble life, rough and tumble game. rough•cast,** *n.* covering for the outside of the walls of a house, made of small stones. **rough•en,** *v.* to make/to become rough. **rough•ly,** *adv.* in a rough way. **rough•neck,** *n.* coarse, rowdy person. **rough•ness,** *n.* being rough. **rough•shod,** *adj.* **to ride r. over s.o.'s feelings** = to pay no attention to s.o.'s feelings.

rou•lette [ru:'let] *n.* game of chance where bets are made on the number of a box where a small ball will stop in a rotating wheel; **Russian r.** = game played with a revolver containing a single bullet which is spun around and then fired at the player's head.

round [raund] 1. *adj.* (-er, -est) (a) circular/shaped like a circle. (b) **r. trip** = trip to a destination and back. (c) exact (number). 2. *n.* (a) circle. (b) complete or regular course or route; **r. of golf** = going around all the holes in a golf course. (c) part of a contest/of a boxing match. (d) **r. of drinks** = series of drinks bought by one person; **r. of applause** = burst of clapping. (e) one bullet; one shell. (f) song for several voices, each starting at a different point. 3. *adv.* (a) around. (b) completely; **all year r.** = during the whole year. 4. *prep.* around; approximately. 5. *v.* (a) (*also* **round off**) to make round. (b) to go around (a corner). (c) **to r. up** = to gather together. (d) to make a whole number; **to r. a number up** = to increase it to the nearest whole number above. **round•a•bout,** *adj.* not straight; indirect. **round•ed,** *adj.* with smooth/round corners or edges. **Round•head,** *n.* supporter of Parliament in the English Civil War in the 17th century. **round•house,** *n.* circular building for repairing railroad engines. **round•ly,** *adv.* sharply/critically; totally. **round•up,** *n.* gathering together.

rouse [rauz] *v.* to wake (s.o.) who is sleeping; to get (s.o.) to act. **rous•ing,** *adj.* loud/exciting.

roust•a•bout ['raustəbaut] *n.* laborer on an oil rig.

rout [raut] 1. *n.* complete defeat (of an army). 2. *v.* (a) to defeat completely. (b) to search; **to r. s.o. out** = to pull s.o. out from where he is hidden.

route [ru:t] 1. *n.* way to be followed to get to a destination; **bus r.** = normal way which a bus follows. 2. *v.* to send (s.o.) along a route.

rou•tine [ru:'ti:n] 1. *n.* (a) normal/regular way of doing things; **daily r.** = things which you do every day. (b) instructions which carry out a task as part of a computer program. 2. *adj.* normal/everyday. **rou•tine•ly,** *adv.* (done) as a routine.

roux [ru:] *n.* mixture of fat and flour cooked to make a base for a sauce.

rove [rəuv] *v.* to wander.

row¹ [rəu] 1. *n.* (a) line (of chairs, etc.). (b) short trip in a rowboat. 2. *v.* to make a boat go forward by using oars. **row•boat,** *n.* small boat for rowing. **row•er,** *n.* person who rows. **row•ing,** *n.* making a boat move by the use of oars.

row² [rau] 1. *n.* (a) loud noise. (b) loud argument. 2. *v.* to argue loudly.

row•an ['rəuən] *n.* mountain ash.

row•dy ['raudı] 1. *adj.* making a great deal of noise. 2. *n.* rough person, who makes a lot of noise. **row•di•ly,** *adv.* in a rowdy way. **row•di•ness,** *n.* rowdy behavior.

row•el ['rəuəl] *n.* little wheel with spikes, attached to a spur.

roy•al ['rɔıəl] *adj.* referring to a king or queen; **r. blue** = bright dark blue. **roy•al•ist,** *n.* person who is a political supporter of a king. **roy•al•ly,** *adv.* splendidly/with great pomp. **roy•al•ty,** *n.* (a) state of being royal; members of a king's family. (b) money paid to the author of a book/the owner of land where oil is found, etc., as a percentage of the receipts of sale.

RSVP [ɑːesvi:'pi:] *abbrev. for* répondez s'il vous plaît *meaning* please reply.

RTA ['ɑːtiːeı] *abbrev. for* road traffic accident.

rub [rʌb] *v.* (**rubbed**) (a) to move sth across the surface of sth else. (b) *inf.* **to r. s.o. the wrong way** = to make s.o. irritable. **rub•bing,** *n.* action of rubbing; **r. alcohol** = pure alcohol used as an antiseptic. **rub down,** *v.* to rub (s.o./a horse) vigorously. **rub in,** *v.* to make (a cream) enter the skin by rubbing; *inf.* **don't rub it in** = don't go on talking about my mistake. **rub out,** *v.* to remove or erase (as a pencil mark).

rub•ber ['rʌbə] *n.* (a) elastic material made from the sap of a tree; **r. plant** = type of indoor plant with thick shiny green leaves. (b) **rubbers** = rubber/plastic shoes worn over ordinary shoes to protect them. (c) number of games of bridge. (d) piece of rubber used for removing pencil marks. **rub•ber band,** *n.* thin loop of

---

æ back, ɑː farm, ɒ top, aı pipe, au how, aıə fire, auə flower, ɔː bought, ɔı toy, e fed, eəhair, eı take, ə afraid, əu boat, əuə lower, vː word, iː heap, ı hit, ıə hear, uː school, u book, ʌ but, b back, d dog, ð then, dʒ just, f fog, g go, h hand, j yes, k catch, l last, m mix, n nut, ŋ sing, p penny, r round, s some, ʃ short, t too, tʃ chop, θ thing, v voice, w was, z zoo, ʒ treasure

rubber for holding things together.
rub•ber•ize, *v.* to coat with rubber.
rub•ber•neck, *v. inf.* to stare with curiosity
while straining the neck to do so. **rub•ber
stamp.** 1. *n.* stamp made of rubber, with
words or figures cut on it, which is used for
stamping documents. 2. *v.* to agree to (sth) automatically   without   examining   it.
rub•ber•y, *adj.* flexible and strong like rubber.

rub•bish ['rʌbɪʃ] *n.* (*no pl.*) (a) things which are
to be thrown away; trash. (b) nonsense.
rub•bish•y, *adj.* useless; stupid.

rub•ble ['rʌbl] *n.* small stones/broken bricks,
etc. used in constructing paths, etc.

ru•bel•la [ru:'belə] *n.* (*formal*) German measles.

ru•bi•cund ['ru:bɪkənd] *adj.* (*formal*) red
(face).

ru•bric ['ru:brɪk] *n.* (a) written instruction; direction. (b) written heading to a piece of writing, sometimes in red.

ru•by ['ru:bɪ] 1. *n.* red precious stone. 2. *adj.*
dark red (color).

ruche [ru:ʃ] *n.* cloth gathered into folds.
ruched, *adj.* gathered in folds.

ruck [rʌk] 1. *n.* crease in cloth. 2. *v.* to form
creases.

ruck•sack ['rʌksæk] *n.* bag carried on the back
by a walker, bicyclist, etc.

ruck•us ['rʌkəs] *n. inf.* fight.

ruc•tion ['rʌkʃənz] *n. inf.* argument/angry
scene.

rud•der ['rʌdə] *n.* flat plate at the stern of a
boat/on the tail of an aircraft, used for steering.

rud•dy ['rʌdɪ] *adj.* (**-ier, -iest**) red/fire-colored.

rude [ru:d] *adj.* (**-er, -est**) (a) impolite; obscene.
(b) having coarse manners or behavior. (c)
rough/primitive. **rude•ly**, *adv.* not politely.
rude•ness, *n.* being rude.

ru•di•ments ['ru:dɪmənts] *n.* simple/elemen-
tary facts. **ru•di•men•ta•ry** [ru:dɪ'mentərɪ]
adj. basic; not fully developed.

rue [ru:] 1. *n.* bitter herb. 2. *v.* to regret.
rue•ful, *adj.* sorry/regretful. **rue•ful•ly**,
adv. in a rueful way.

ruff [rʌf] *n.* (a) wide collar of ruffled lace. (b)
bird with a ring of colored feathers around its
neck.

ruf•fi•an ['rʌfɪən] *n.* tough/violent person.

ruf•fle ['rʌfl] 1. *n.* material/lace gathered into a
bunch and used as decoration on clothes/cur-
tains, etc. 2. *v.* to disturb (feathers/water/s.o.'s
hair); *inf.* **ruffled** = flustered.

rug [rʌg] *n.* small carpet.

Rug•by ['rʌgbɪ] *n.* type of football played with

an oval ball, which can be passed from hand
to hand as well as being kicked.

rug•ged ['rʌgɪd] *adj.* (a) rough/uneven. (b)
strict; sturdy. **rug•ged•ly**, *adv.* in a rugged
way. **rug•ged•ness**, *n.* being rugged.

ru•in ['ru:ɪn] 1. *n.* (a) wreck; complete loss of all
your money. (b) **ruins** = remains of collapsed
buildings. 2. *v.* (a) to wreck/to spoil completely. (b) to bring to financial collapse.
ru•in•a•tion [ruɪ'neɪʃn] *n.* act of ruining.
ru•ined, *adj.* in ruins. **ru•in•ous**, *adj.* so expensive as to cause ruin. **ru•in•ous•ly**, *adv.*
extremely (expensive).

rule [ru:l] 1. *n.* (a) general way of conduct; **as a r.**
= generally/usually. (b) strict order of the way
to behave. (c) government. (d) ruler (for measuring, etc.). (e) straight line (in printing). 2. *v.*
(a) to govern/to control. (b) to give an
official/legal decision. (c) to draw a straight
line using a ruler; **ruled paper** = paper with
lines on it. **rul•er**, *n.* (a) person who governs.
(b) strip of wood/plastic with measurements
marked on it, used for drawing straight lines,
measuring, etc. **rul•ing.** 1. *adj.* (party) which
governs. 2. *n.* legal decision. **rule out**, *v.* to
leave (sth) out/not to consider (sth).

rum [rʌm] *n.* alcoholic drink made from the
juice of sugar cane.

rum•ba ['rʌmbə] *n.* Caribbean dance with a
strong rhythm.

rum•ble ['rʌmbl] 1. *n.* (a) low rolling noise. (b)
inf. street fight. 2. *v.* to make a low rolling
noise.

ru•mi•nate ['ru:mɪneɪt] *v.* (a) to chew over
food which has already been swallowed once
(as a cow does). (b) to think over a problem.
ru•mi•nant ['ru:mɪnənt] *adj. & n.* animal
(like a cow) which chews its cud.
ru•mi•na•tion [ru:mɪ'neɪʃn] *n.* deep
thought. **ru•mi•na•tive**, *adj.* thoughtful.

rum•mage ['rʌmɪdʒ] 1. *n.* (a) searching about
for sth. (b) miscellaneous things; **r. sale** = sale
of unwanted objects. 2. *v.* to search about for
sth.

rum•my ['rʌmɪ] *n.* card game where each
player tries to collect sets of similar cards or
several cards in sequence.

ru•mor, *Brit.* **ru•mour** ['ru:mə] *n.* story
passed on from one person to another without
necessarily being true. **ru•mored**, *adj.*
spread by rumor.

rump [rʌmp] *n.* back part of an animal.

rum•ple ['rʌmpl] *v.* to crush/to dishevel.

rum•pus ['rʌmpəs] *n.* (*pl.* **-es**) noisy disturbance; fuss.

run [rʌn] 1. *n.* (a) act of going quickly on foot;
on the r. = running away; **the soldiers broke
into a r.** = started to run; **go for a r.** = to exercise by running; **take a r.** = to go for a short

trip in a car. (b) period; **in the long r.** = eventually. (c) access to; **he has the r. of the house** = he can go anywhere in the house. (d) track for running, skiing, etc. (e) caged area where animals (as dogs or chickens) are kept. (f) point made in baseball. (g) long hole in a stocking. (h) excessive demand; sudden selling of sth. (i) carrying out of a task by a computer. 2. *v.* (**ran, has run**) (a) to go very quickly on foot; to race. (b) to travel (fast). (c) (*of motor, transport*) to work. (d) to amount to. (e) to go in a direction. (f) to direct; **he runs his own business.** (g) **to r. a bath** = to fill a bath (h) (*of liquid*) to flow; **this color won't r.** = will not come out if put in water; **his nose is running** = liquid is coming from his nose (because he has a cold). **run a•cross**, *v.* (a) to cross quickly on foot. (b) to find/to meet by chance. **run a•long**, *v.* to go alongside. **run a•way**, *v.* to escape. **run•a•way.** 1. *n.* person who has escaped. 2. *adj.* escaping from control; **r. horse. run down**, *v.* (a) to go down quickly on foot. (b) (*of clock, machine*) to go slower. (c) to criticize (s.o.). (d) to knock down (with a vehicle). (e) **to be r.-down** = to feel unwell/tired. **run•down.** 1. *adj.* delapidated/not looked after. 2. *n.* summary. **run for**, *v.* to be a candidate for (an office). **run in**, *v.* (a) to work (a new engine) slowly until it works properly. (b) *inf.* to arrest (s.o.). **run in•to**, *v.* to meet (s.o.) by chance. **run•ner**, *n.* (a) person who is running (in a race). (b) shoot of a plant which makes roots where it touches the soil. (c) sharp blade of a skate/a sled. (d) narrow carpet. **run•ner-up**, *n.* (*pl.* **runners-up**) person who comes after the winner in a race. **run•ning.** 1. *adj.* (a) which runs; **r. commentary** = commentary on an action while the action is taking place; **r. total** = total which is carried from one column of figures to the next. (b) used in running a race. (c) **for three days r.** = one after another. 2. *n.* (a) race; **in the r. for** = a candidate for. (b) working. **run off**, *v.* (a) to escape/to flee. (b) **to run off several photocopies** = to make several photocopies. **run-of-the-mill**, *adj.* ordinary. **run on**, *v.* (a) to continue. (b) to use (sth) as a fuel. **run out**, *v.* (*of goods/supplies*) to become used up. **run out of**, *v.* to be short of. **run o•ver**, *v.* (a) to go over (sth) quickly; review. (b) to knock (s.o.) down with a car. **run up**, *v.* (a) to go up quickly on foot. (b) **to run up against sth** = to meet with or find. (c) to sew (sth)

quickly. **run•way**, *n.* track on which aircraft land.

runes [ru:nz] *pl. n.* ancient form of writing, used by early Germans. **ru•nic**, *adj.* referring to runes; magic.

rung [rʌŋ] 1. *n.* one of the bars on a ladder. 2. *v. see* **ring.**

run•nel ['rʌnl] *n.* small stream.

run•ny ['rʌnɪ] *adj.* liquid; **he's got a r. nose** = his nose is running (because he has a cold).

runt ['rʌnt] *n.* small person or animal.

ru•pee [ru:'pi:] *n.* money used in India and other countries.

rup•ture ['rʌptʃə] 1. *n.* (a) break (in negotiations/friendly relations); burst/break (of part of the body). (b) hernia. 2. *v.* (a) to break off (negotiations/friendly relations). (b) to burst through; **he ruptured himself lifting a heavy box** = the strain caused a hernia.

ru•ral ['rʊərəl] *adj.* referring to the countryside.

ruse ['ru:z] *n.* clever trick.

rush [rʌʃ] 1. *n.* (*pl.* **-es**) (a) type of wild grass growing in water. (b) fast movement; **r. hour** = time of day when traffic is heaviest/when trains are full. (c) **rushes** = first prints of a motion picture, before it has been edited. 2. *v.* (a) to go forward fast; **don't r. me** = don't hurry me. (b) to attack suddenly.

rusk [rʌsk] *n.* hard biscuit given to babies to suck.

rus•set ['rʌsɪt] 1. *n.* type of sweet brown apple. 2. *adj. & n.* reddish-brown (color).

Rus•sian ['rʌʃn] 1. *adj.* referring to Russia. 2. *n.* (a) person from Russia. (b) language spoken in Russia.

Russo- ['rʌsəu] *prefix meaning* between Russia and another country.

rust [rʌst] 1. *n.* (a) red substance formed on iron or steel which is left in damp air. (b) red fungus disease of plants. (c) reddish-brown (color). 2. *v.* to get rusty. **rust belt**, *n.* depressed area where heavy industry is in decline. **rust•i•ness**, *n.* being rusty. **rust•less**, *adj.* with no rust. **rust•proof**, *adj.* (metal) which will not rust. **rust•y**, *adj.* (-ier, -iest) (a) covered with rust. (b) not in practice; (person) who lacks practice.

rus•tic ['rʌstɪk] 1. *adj.* rough/of country style. 2. *n.* country/unsophisticated person. **rus•ti•cate**, *v.* to send to live in the country.

rus•tle ['rʌsl] 1. *n.* noise of dry leaves/silk, etc. rubbing together. 2. *v.* (a) to make a soft crackling noise. (b) to steal cattle. **rus•tler**, *n.*

æ back, a: farm, ɒ top, aɪ pipe, aʊ how, aɪə fire, aʊə flower, ɔ: bought, ɔɪ toy, e fed, eəhair, eɪ take, ə afraid, əʊ boat, əʊə lower, ɜ: word, i: heap, ɪ hit, ɪə hear, u: school, ʊ book, ʌ but, b back, d dog, ð then, dʒ just, f fog, g go, h hand, j yes, k catch, l last, m mix, n nut, ŋ sing, p penny, r round, s some, ʃ short, t too, tʃ chop, θ thing, v voice, w was, z zoo, ʒ treasure

cattle thief. **rustle up,** *v. inf.* to get (sth) ready quickly. **rust•ling,** *n.* stealing (of cattle).

rut [rʌt] *n.* (a) long deep track made in soft earth by a wheel; **to get into a r.** = to start to lead a dull life with no excitement or career prospects. (b) period when a male deer is sexually excited. **rut•ted,** *adj.* (path) full of ruts. **rut•ting,** *adj.* (deer) in rut.

ru•ta•ba•ga ['ruːtəbɑːgə] *n.* type of root vegetable like a yellow turnip.

ruth•less ['ruːθləs] *adj.* pitiless/cruel. **ruth•less•ly,** *adv.* cruelly. **ruth•less•ness,** *n.* cruelty.

rye [raɪ] *n.* (a) type of dark brown cereal. (b) type of whisky made from rye. **rye•grass,** *n.* type of grass grown in pastures.

Ss

S *symbol for* sulfur.

Sab•bath ['sæbəθ] *n.* seventh day of the week; religious day of rest; (*for Jews*) Saturday; (*for Christians*) Sunday.

sab•bat•i•cal [sə'bætɪkl] *n. & adj.* (leave) granted to teachers, etc., for study and travel after a period of work.

sa•ble ['seɪbl] *n.* small brown-furred arctic animal; fur from this animal.

sab•o•tage ['sæbətɑːʒ] 1. *n.* malicious/deliberate destruction. 2. *v.* to destroy/to render useless deliberately. **sab•o•teur** [sæbə'tɜ:] *n.* person who commits sabotage.

sa•ber, *Brit.* **sa•bre** ['seɪbə] *n.* sword with curved blade.

sac [sæk] *n.* baglike part of an animal/plant.

sac•cha•rin ['sækərɪn] *n.* extremely sweet substance used as a substitute for sugar. **sac•cha•rine,** *adj.* too sweet/sickly.

sac•er•do•tal [sæsə'dəʊtl] *adj.* referring to priests.

sa•chet ['sæʃeɪ] *n.* small bag (a fragrant substance), used to perfume drawers, closets, etc.

sack [sæk] 1. *n.* (a) plundering (of a town). (b) large bag made of strong rough cloth. (c) *inf.* dismissal; **to get/to be given the s.** = to be dismissed from a job. (d) *inf.* bed. 2. *v.* (a) to plunder. (b) *inf.* to dismiss (s.o.) from a job. **sack•cloth,** *n.* **s. and ashes** = (i) clothes worn at times of penitence; (ii) symbol of repentance. **sack•ful,** *n.* amount held in a sack. **sack•ing,** *n.* coarse material from which sacks are made; old sacks.

sac•ra•ment ['sækrəmənt] *n.* (a) Christian religious ceremony. (b) the consecrated bread (and wine) taken at Communion. **sac•ra•men•tal** [sækrə'mentl] *adj.* referring to sacrament.

sa•cred ['seɪkrəd] *adj.* (a) associated with religion. (b) holy. (c) respected. **sa•cred cow,** *n. inf.* belief/idea which is not to be criticized. **sa•cred•ness,** *n.* being sacred.

sac•ri•fice ['sækrɪfaɪs] 1. *n.* (a) killing of animal/person as an offering to a god. (b) animal killed as an offering to a god. (c) thing given up at personal cost in order to achieve sth else. 2. *v.* (a) to offer (sth) as a sacrifice. (b) to give up/to devote. **sac•ri•fi•cial** [sækrɪ'fɪʃl] *adj.* as a sacrifice.

sac•ri•lege ['sækrɪlɪdʒ] *n.* using sth sacred in a disrespectful way. **sac•ri•le•gious** [sækrɪ'lɪdʒəs] *adj.* referring to sacrilege.

sac•ris•ty ['sækrɪstɪ] *n.* room in a church where vestments/ vessels, etc., are kept. **sac•ris•tan,** *n.* person who looks after a church, esp. the vestments/holy vessels, etc.

sac•ro•sanct ['sækrəʊsæŋkt] *adj.* very sacred/protected by religious respect.

sac•rum ['seɪkrəm] *n.* triangular bone at the base of the spine.

sad [sæd] *adj.* (**sadder, saddest**) unhappy/sorrowful. **sad•den,** *v.* to make unhappy. **sad•ly,** *adv.* unhappily. **sad•ness,** *n.* being sad.

sad•dle ['sædl] 1. *n.* (a) rider's seat on a bicycle/on the back of a horse; **in the s.** = in control. (b) ridge between two mountains. (c) **s. of lamb** = joint of meat from the back of a sheep. 2. *v.* (a) to put a saddle on (a horse, etc.). (b) to burden (s.o.) **with** a task or responsibility. **sad•dle•bag,** *n.* bag attached to a bicycle; one of a pair of bags on a horse. **sad•dler,** *n.* maker of saddles and other equipment for horses. **sad•dler•y,** *n.* shop making/selling saddles.

sa•dism ['seɪdɪzəm] *n.* pleasure derived from being cruel or watching cruelty. **sa•dist** ['seɪdɪst] *n.* person who delights in sadism. **sa•dis•tic** [sə'dɪstɪk] *adj.* referring to sadism. **sa•dis•ti•cal•ly,** *adv.* in a sadistic way.

SAD ['eseɪ'diː] *abbrev. for* seasonal affective disorder.

S.A.E. self-addressed envelope.

sa•fa•ri [sə'fɑːrɪ] *n.* hunting expedition in Africa; **s. park** = park where large wild animals run free, and visitors can look at them from their cars.

æ back, ɑː farm, ɒ top, aɪ pipe, aʊ how, aɪə fire, aʊə flower, ɔː bought, ɔɪ toy, e fed, eəhair, eɪ take, ə afraid, əʊ boat, əʊə lower, ɜː word, iː heap, ɪ hit, ɪə hear, uː school, ʊ book, ʌ but, b back, d dog, ð then, dʒ just, f fog, g go, h hand, j yes, k catch, l last, m mix, n nut, ŋ sing, p penny, r round, s some, ʃ short, t too, tʃ chop, θ thing, v voice, w was, z zoo, ʒ treasure

safe [seɪf] 1. *n.* (a) strong, usu. fireproof, box for valuables. (b) ventilated cupboard for food. 2. *adj.* (**-er, -est**) (a) uninjured. (b) secure/out of danger. (c) certain/to be relied upon. **safe•con•duct**, *n.* paper which allows s.o. to go through enemy territory. **safe-de•pos•it box**, *n.* box (in a bank) in which you can store valuables. **safe•guard** ['seɪfgɑːd] 1. *n.* protection. 2. *v.* to guard/to protect. **safe•ly**, *adv.* without any danger; without being harmed. **safe•ty** ['seɪftɪ] *n.* freedom from danger or risk; **road s.** = care to be taken by pedestrians and drivers; **s. belt** = belt worn in a car/in an aircraft as protection in case of accident; **s. catch** = lock which stops a gun being fired by accident; **s. curtain** = fireproof barrier between the stage and the auditorium in a theater; **s. pin** = type of bent pin whose point is protected by a guard; **s. valve** = valve as in a steam boiler, which lets out excess pressure automatically.

saf•flow•er ['sæflaʊə] *n.* plant which produces an oil used in cooking.

saf•fron ['sæfrən] 1. *n.* orange-colored powder made from crocus flowers, from which coloring and flavoring are obtained. 2. *adj.* orange-colored.

sag [sæg] 1. *n.* bending under weight or pressure. 2. *v.* (**sagged**) to sink/to bend (in the middle) under weight or pressure.

sa•ga ['sɑːgə] *n.* (a) story of heroic achievement or adventure. (b) series of books telling the history of a family.

sa•ga•cious [sə'geɪʃəs] *adj.* (*formal*) wise/shrewd. **sa•ga•cious•ly**, *adv.* wisely. **sa•gac•i•ty** [sə'gæsɪtɪ] *n.* exceptional intelligence/wisdom.

sage [seɪdʒ] 1. *n.* (a) aromatic herb used in cookery; **s. green** = grayish green color. (b) very wise man. 2. *adj.* wise/discreet. **sage•ly**, *adv.* in a wise way.

Sag•it•tar•i•us [sædʒɪ'teərɪəs] *n.* one of the signs of the zodiac, shaped like an archer.

sa•go ['seɪgəʊ] *n.* white powder used as food; **s. palm** = palm tree whose pith yields sago.

said [sed] *v. see* **say.**

sail [seɪl] 1. *n.* (a) piece of canvas/nylon, etc., attached to the mast of a boat to catch the wind. (b) trip in a boat. (c) arm of a windmill which turns with the wind. 2. *v.* (a) to travel on water. (b) to travel in a sailboat; **to s. close to the wind** = to sail nearly against the wind. (c) to control (a sailboat). **sail•boat**, *n.* boat which has sails for propulsion. **sail•cloth**, *n.* canvas for making sails. **sail•ing**. 1. *adj.* (ship) which uses sails. 2. *n.* journey by ship; **easy s.** = straightforward progress with no problems. **sail•or** ['seɪlə] *n.* seaman/person who sails;

good/bad s. = person who is liable/not liable to seasickness.

saint [seɪnt] *n.* (a) (*abbreviated with names to* **St.** [snt]) person recognized by the Christian church as having led an exceptionally holy life, and canonized after death. (b) very good/devoted person. **saint•hood**, *n.* being a saint. **saint•li•ness**, *n.* holiness/piety. **saint•ly**, *adj.* holy.

sake[1] [seɪk] *n.* **for the s. of s.o./sth** = out of consideration for/in the interest of.

sake[2] ['sɑːkɪ] *n.* Japanese rice wine.

sa•laam [sə'lɑːm] 1. *n.* bow made in Eastern countries to greet s.o. 2. *v.* to make a salaam.

sa•la•cious [sə'leɪʃəs] *adj.* erotic/obscene. **sa•la•cious•ly**, *adv.* in a salacious way. **sa•la•cious•ness, salacity** [sə'læsɪtɪ] *n.* being salacious.

sal•ad ['sæləd] *n.* cold dish of various cooked or raw vegetables; cold meat served with a dressing and lettuce; **s. dressing** = mixture of oil/vinegar, etc., used on salad; **fruit s.** = mixture of chopped fresh fruit.

sal•a•man•der ['sæləmændə] *n.* small animal like a lizard.

sa•la•mi [sə'lɑːmɪ] *n.* salty Italian sausage, eaten cold.

sal•a•ry ['sælərɪ] *n.* fixed payment made to an employee at regular intervals. **sal•a•ried**, *adj.* (person) who is paid a salary.

sale [seɪl] *n.* (a) exchange of sth for money; **on/for s.** = ready to be sold. (b) goods sold at reduced/special prices for a short period of time. (c) organized selling of goods; **tag s.** = selling of unwanted household goods. (d) **sales** = money received in a business. **sal•a•ble, saleable**, *adj.* fit for sale. **sales•girl**, *n.* woman in a store who sells goods to customers. **sales•la•dy**, *n.* saleswoman. **sales•man**, *n.* (*pl.* **-men**) (a) person who sells a producer's goods to a store. (b) man in a store who sells goods to customers. **sales•man•ship**, *n.* the art of selling. **sales•per•son**, *n.* person who sells goods in a store. **sales•wom•an**, *n.* (*pl.* **-women**) woman in a store who sells goods to customers.

sa•li•ent ['seɪlɪənt] 1. *n.* projecting part of a fortification/of a line of battle. 2. *adj.* prominent/conspicuous/most important.

sa•line ['seɪlaɪn] *adj.* containing salt. **sa•lin•i•ty** [sə'lɪnɪtɪ] *n.* amount of salt.

sa•li•va [sə'laɪvə] *n.* liquid formed in the mouth to help digestion. **sal•i•var•y**, *adj.* **s. gland** = gland which produces saliva. **sal•i•vate** ['sæliveɪt] *v.* to make saliva. **sal•i•va•tion** [sælɪ'veɪʃn] *n.* act of salivating.

sal•low ['sæləʊ] *adj.* (-er, -est) sickly yellow (complexion).

sal•ly ['sælɪ] 1. *n.* (a) sudden rush (of soldiers) out of a defended position. (b) witticism. 2. *v.* (*also* **sally forth**) to go out.

salm•on ['sæmən] 1. *n.* (*pl.* **salmon**) large pink-fleshed fish. 2. *adj. & n.* orange-pink (color). **salmon trout**, *n.* large sea trout with pink flesh.

Sal•mo•nel•la [sælmə'nelə] *n.* type of bacteria which grows on meat, eggs, and fish, and causes food poisoning.

sa•lon ['sælɒn] *n.* hairdresser's/dressmaker's business; room/building housing a hairdresser's or dressmaker's.

sa•loon [sə'luːn] *n.* (a) large lounge in a ship. (b) public bar.

sal•si•fy ['sælsɪfɪ] *n.* vegetable with a long white root.

salt [sɔːlt] 1. *n.* (a) white substance (sodium chloride) used to season and preserve food; *inf.* **to take sth with a grain of s.** = not to believe sth completely. (b) (*in chemistry*) combination of a metal with an acid; (c) *inf.* **old s.** = experienced sailor. 2. *adj.* containing salt; cured/preserved/seasoned with salt. 3. *v.* to add salt to. **salt a•way**, *v.* to put (sth) aside for the future. **salt•cel•lar**, *n.* small dish or shaker containing salt to be sprinkled on food. **salt-free**, *adj.* without salt. **salt•i•ness, saltness**, *n.* being salty. **salt lick**, *n.* block of salt put in a field for animals to lick. **salt pan**, *n.* enclosure where salt is formed as sea water evaporates. **salt•pe•ter**, *Brit.* **salt•pe•tre** [sɔːlt'piːtə] *n.* potassium nitrate/powder used to make gunpowder. **salt•y**, *adj.* (-ier, -iest) containing salt.

sa•lu•bri•ous [sə'luːbrɪəs] *adj.* (*formal*) healthy. **sa•lu•bri•ty**, *n.* healthiness.

sa•lu•ki [sə'luːkɪ] *n.* breed of hound.

sa•lute [sə'luːt] 1. *n.* gesture expressing respect/homage/recognition. 2. *v.* to give a salute to (s.o.).

sal•u•tar•y ['sæljutərɪ] *adj.* useful/helpful; which has a good effect. **sal•u•ta•tion** [sælju'teɪʃn] *n.* words spoken/written in praise of s.o./to greet s.o.

sal•vage ['sælvɪdʒ] 1. *n.* (a) payment made for saving a ship/its cargo from loss by wreck. (b) objects saved (from a boat/fire, etc.). 2. *v.* to save (from wreck/fire, etc.).

sal•va•tion [sæl'veɪʃn] *n.* saving of the soul from sin; saving of a person from evil.

Sal•va•tion Ar•my, *n.* religious organization run on military lines which specializes in missionary and welfare work among poor people.

salve [sælv] 1. *n.* healing ointment; **lip s.** = ointment which prevents lips cracking in cold weather. 2. *v.* **to s. one's conscience** = to do sth to ease one's conscience.

sal•ver ['sælvə] *n.* large tray (usu. made of silver).

sal•vi•a ['sælvɪə] *n.* common summer garden plant with red or purple flowers.

sal•vo ['sælvəʊ] *n.* (*pl.* -os, -oes) (a) simultaneous firing of several guns in a battle at sea or as a salute. (b) round of applause.

sal vo•la•ti•le [sælvə'lætəlɪ] *n.* smelling-salts.

Sa•mar•i•tan [sə'mærɪtən] *n.* person who helps s.o. in trouble.

same [seɪm] 1. *adj.* identical; unchanging; **it's all the s. to me** = I don't mind. 2. *pron.* the identical thing. 3. *adv. inf.* **all the s./just the s.** = nevertheless. **same•ness**, *n.* (a) being the same. (b) monotony.

sam•o•var ['sæməʊvɑː] *n.* urn used in Russia for boiling water for tea.

sam•pan ['sæmpæn] *n.* small Chinese boat.

sam•phire ['sæmfaɪə] *n.* type of European fern which grows near the sea.

sam•ple ['sɑːmpl] 1. *n.* specimen. 2. *v.* (a) to test/to try (by taking a small amount). (b) to ask a group of people questions to find out a general reaction. **sam•pler**, *n.* decorated tapestry panel (usu. with letters, numbers and simple pictures) made to show skill in sewing stitches.

sam•u•rai ['sæmuraɪ] *n.* medieval Japanese warrior.

san•a•to•ri•um [sænə'tɔːrɪəm] *n.* hospital for the treatment of invalids, esp. people suffering from tuberculosis.

sanc•ti•fy ['sæŋktɪfaɪ] *v.* to consecrate/to make holy. **sanc•ti•fi•ca•tion** [sæŋktɪfɪ'keɪʃn] *n.* making holy. **sanc•ti•mo•ni•ous** [sæŋktɪ'məʊnɪəs] *adj.* pretending to be holy. **sanc•ti•mo•ni•ous•ly**, *adv.* in a sanctimonious way. **sanc•ti•ty** ['sæŋktɪtɪ] *n.* holiness of life/saintliness.

sanc•tion ['sæŋkʃn] 1. *n.* (a) official permission or approval. (b) penalty for breaking a rule; **economic sanctions** = restrictions on trade with a country in order to try to influence its political development. 2. *v.* (a) to approve. (b) to permit.

sanc•tu•ar•y ['sæŋktjʊərɪ] *n.* (a) holy place.

æ back, ɑː farm, ɒ top, aɪ pipe, aʊ how, aɪə fire, aʊə flower, ɔː bought, ɔɪ toy, e fed, eəhair, eɪ take, ə afraid, əʊ boat, əʊə lower, ɜː word, iː heap, ɪ hit, ɪə hear, uː school, ʊ book, ʌ but, b back, d dog, ð then, dʒ just, f fog, g go, h hand, j yes, k catch, l last, m mix, n nut, ŋ sing, p penny, r round, s some, ʃ short, t too, tʃ chop, θ thing, v voice, w was, z zoo, ʒ treasure

(b) part of a church where the high altar is placed. (c) place for the protection of wild animals or birds. (d) refuge.

sanc•tum ['sæŋktəm] *n.* (a) holy place. (b) private room; **inner s.** = most private/secret office.

sand [sænd] 1. *n.* (a) mass of tiny fragments of worn-down rock, etc., found on seashores/river beds/deserts, etc. 2. *v.* (a) (*also* **sand down**) to rub smooth with sandpaper. (b) to spread sand on (icy roads). **sand•bag.** 1. *n.* bag filled with sand and used as a defense/as ballast. 2. *v.* (**-bagged**) (a) to protect (sth) with a wall of sandbags. (b) to knock (s.o.) out by hitting him with a sandbag. **sand•bank,** *n.* ridge of sand, as on a hillside. **sand•blast,** *v.* to clean (the exterior of a building) by directing a powerful jet of sand on to it. **sand•box,** *n.* place with sand where children can play. **sand•er,** *n.* machine/person who sands. **sandpa•per.** 1. *n.* paper with a coating of sand for smoothing. 2. *v.* to rub (sth) smooth with sandpaper. **sand•pi•per,** *n.* small bird with a long bill which lives on beaches. **sands,** *n.pl.* sandy place. **sand•stone,** *n.* rock made of compressed sand. **sand•storm,** *n.* high wind in a desert blowing clouds of sand. **sand•y,** *adj.* like sand; made of sand.

san•dal ['sændl] *n.* light open shoe worn in the summer. **san•dal•wood,** *n.* (a) tropical tree; fragrant wood from this tree. (b) scent from this tree.

sand•wich ['sændwɪtʃ] 1. *n.* (*pl.* **-es**) two slices of bread with meat, cheese or other filling between the slices. 2. *v.* to insert (sth) between two others. **sand•wich board,** *n.* pair of boards worn over the shoulders in the street to advertise sth. **sandwich man,** *n.* man who carries a sandwich board.

sane [seɪn] *adj.* (**-er, -est**) reasonable/not mad. **sane•ly,** *adv.* in a sane way. **san•i•ty** ['sænɪtɪ] *n.* being sane.

sang [sæŋ] *v. see* **sing.**

sang'froid [sɑːŋ'frwɑː] *n.* calmness when in danger.

san•gui•nar•y ['sæŋgwɪnərɪ] *adj.* delighting in bloodshed or killing.

san•guine ['sæŋgwɪn] *adj.* confident/optimistic.

san•i•ta•tion [sænɪ'teɪʃn] *n.* hygiene/conditions affecting health. **san•i•tar•y** ['sænɪtərɪ] *adj.* referring to sanitation/hygiene; **s. napkin** = pad of material worn by women to absorb blood lost during menstruation.

sank [sæŋk] *v. see* **sink.**

San•skrit ['sænzkrɪt] *n.* classical language of India.

sans ser•if ['sænz'serɪf] *n.* typeset character with no serifs.

San•ta Claus ['sæntə'klɔːz] *n.* man dressed in red robes with a long white beard who is believed to bring gifts to children on Christmas Day.

sap [sæp] 1. *n.* (a) juice circulating in plants and trees. (b) (*in warfare*) tunnel dug to get near to the enemy. (c) *inf.* silly person. 2. *v.* (**sapped**) (a) to weaken/to drain away. (b) to undermine/to make insecure by removing foundations.

sap•ling ['sæplɪŋ] *n.* young tree.

sap•phire ['sæfaɪə] 1. *n.* blue precious stone. 2. *adj.* clear blue (color).

sap•ro•phyte ['sæprəʊfaɪt] *n.* fungus which lives on decaying plants. **sap•ro•phyt•ic** [sæprəʊ'fɪtɪk] *adj.* living on decaying plants.

sar•a•band ['særəbænd] *n.* slow Spanish dance.

sar•casm ['sɑːkæzəm] *n.* making sharp unpleasant remarks. **sar•cas•tic** [sɑː'kæstɪk] *adj.* scornful, with sarcasm. **sar•cas•ti•cal•ly,** *adv.* in a sarcastic way.

sar•co•ma [sɑː'kəʊmə] *n.* kind of malignant tumor.

sar•coph•a•gus [sə'kɒfəgəs] *n.* (*pl.* **-gi** [gaɪ]) stone coffin often decorated with sculpture.

sar•dine [sɑː'diːn] *n.* small fish of the herring family; **packed like sardines** = very tightly.

sar•don•ic [sɑː'dɒnɪk] *adj.* scornful/cynical. **sar•don•i•cal•ly,** *adv.* in a sardonic way.

sar•don•yx ['sɑːdɒnɪks] *n.* semiprecious stone, with red layers.

Sar•gas•so Sea [sɑː'gæsəʊ'siː] *n.* area of the Atlantic Ocean, with few currents, covered with drifting weed.

sa•ri ['sɑːrɪ] *n.* long piece of cloth worn by Indian women.

sa•rong [sə'rɒŋ] *n.* cloth worn wrapped round the lower part of the body by S.E. Asian men and women.

sar•sa•pa•ril•la [sɑːspə'rɪlə] *n.* drink made from the root of a tropical American plant.

sar•to•ri•al [sɑː'tɔːrɪəl] *adj.* (*formal*) referring to men's clothes.

sash [sæʃ] *n.* (*pl.* **-es**) (a) ornamental scarf or band, as worn by military officers. (b) wooden frame holding panes of glass. **sash cord,** *n.* rope in a sash window which allows the frames to slide up and down smoothly. **sash win•dow,** *n.* window made of panes of glass set in two frames which slide up and down.

sa•shay [sə'ʃeɪ] *v.* to walk confidently.

sat [sæt] *v. see* **sit.**

Sa•tan ['seɪtən] *n.* the devil. **sa•tan•ic** [sə'tænɪk] *adj.* diabolical/like the devil.

satch•el ['sætʃəl] *n.* small leather/canvas bag, sometimes worn on the shoulders.

sate [seɪt] *v.* (*formal*) to satisfy (s.o.) by giving him too much.

sa•teen [sə'tiːn] *n.* type of fine cotton cloth which looks like satin.

sat•el•lite ['sætəlaɪt] *n.* (a) heavenly body which goes around a planet. (b) artificial body which was launched from and which goes around the earth; **s. broadcast** = radio/TV broadcast which is transmitted via a satellite; **s. dish** = aerial, shaped like a dish, used to capture satellite broadcasts. **satellite state,** *n.* country controlled by a more powerful one. **satellite town,** *n.* small town dependent on a larger town near by.

sa•ti•ate ['seɪʃeɪt] *v.* to satisfy totally/to fill to overflowing. **sa•ti•a•tion,** *n.* act of satiating. **sa•ti•e•ty** [sə'taɪətɪ] *n.* being satiated.

sat•in ['sætɪn] 1. *n.* silk fabric with a glossy surface. 2. *adj.* made of satin. **sat•in•wood,** *n.* type of hard tropical wood. **sat•in•y,** *adj.* smooth and shiny, like satin.

sat•ire ['sætaɪə] *n.* (a) attacking s.o. in speech/writing by making them seem ridiculous. (b) humorously critical piece of writing. **sa•tir•ic, satirical** [sə'tɪrɪkl] *adj.* humorously critical. **sa•tir•i•cal•ly,** *adv.* in a satirical way. **sat•i•rist** ['sætɪrɪst] *n.* writer of satires. **sat•i•rize** ['sætɪraɪz] *v.* to attack (sth) in a more or less amusing way.

sat•is•fac•tion [sætɪs'fækʃn] *n.* (a) payment of debt; compensation (for damage). (b) good feeling; sense of comfort/happiness. **sat•is•fac•to•ry,** *adj.* causing satisfaction; quite good. **sat•is•fac•to•ri•ly,** *adv.* in a satisfactory way. **sat•is•fy** ['sætɪsfaɪ] 1. *v.* (a) to comply with/to fulfill. (b) to show adequate proof. (c) to make (s.o.) content/pleased. (d) to convince/to rid of doubt. **sat•is•fy•ing,** *adj.* which satisfies.

sat•u•rate ['sætʃureɪt] 1. *v.* to make very wet. **sat•u•rat•ed fat,** *n.* fat (such as animal fat) which contains the largest amount of hydrogen possible. **sat•u•ra•tion** [sætʃu'reɪʃn] *n.* complete filling; **s. point** = point at which a substance cannot absorb any more liquid.

Sat•ur•day ['sætədeɪ] *n.* sixth day of the week; day between Friday and Sunday.

sat•ur•na•li•a [sætə'neɪlɪə] *n.* wild orgy.

sat•ur•nine ['sætənaɪn] *adj.* gloomy character.

sa•tyr ['sætə] *n.* classical god living in woods, with a human body, but with legs and ears like a goat's.

sauce [sɔːs] *n.* (a) liquid poured over food. (b) *inf.* impertinence. **sauce•boat,** *n.* vessel in which sauce is served. **sauce•pan,** *n.* deep cooking pot with a long handle. **sau•ci•ly,** *adv. inf.* insolently. **sau•ci•ness,** *n. inf.* being saucy. **sau•cy,** *adj.* (-ier, -iest) *inf.* insolent.

sau•cer ['sɔːsə] *n.* shallow dish placed under a cup; **flying s.** = object shaped like a saucer which people say they have seen in the sky.

Sa•u•di (A•ra•bi•an) ['saudɪ(ə'reɪbɪən)] *adj. n.* (person) from Saudi Arabia.

sau•er•kraut ['sauəkraut] *n.* German dish of pickled cabbage.

sau•na ['sɔːnə] *n.* (a) very hot steam bath. (b) room where you can have a sauna bath.

saun•ter ['sɔːntə] 1. *n.* stroll/leisurely walk. 2. *v.* to walk in a leisurely way/to stroll.

sau•ri•an ['sɔːrɪən] *adj. & n.* (animal) like a lizard.

sau•sage ['sɒsɪdʒ] *n.* tube of edible skin full of minced and seasoned pork or other meat. **sausage roll,** *n.* small piece of sausage cooked in pastry.

sau•té ['səuteɪ] 1. *adj.* fried in a little fat. 2. *v.* (**sautéed**) to fry in a little fat.

sav•age ['sævɪdʒ] 1. *adj.* (a) uncivilized/primitive. (b) fierce/ferocious. 2. *n.* wild/uncivilized human being. 3. *v.* to attack with teeth. **sav•age•ly,** *adv.* in a savage way. **sav•age•ness, savagery,** *n.* being savage.

sa•van•na(h) [sə'vænə] *n.* grassy plain in a tropical country.

sa•vant ['sævɒn] *n.* learned person; **idiot s.** = person of limited intelligence, but with a highly developed skill in a single faculty (such as memorizing numbers).

save [seɪv] 1. *v.* (a) to rescue from misfortune. (b) to keep for future use/to reserve; (*computers*) to keep data in storage after it has been keyboarded. (c) to economize/to not spend. (d) (*in sports*) to prevent opponents from scoring by keeping a ball or puck out of one's goal. (e) to gain (time). (f) to avoid (trouble). 2. *prep. & conj.* except. **sav•er,** *n.* person who saves money. **sav•ing.** 1. *n.* economy. 2. *adj.* redeeming. 3. *prep.* (*old*) except. **sav•ings,** *n.* money saved. **sav•ings bank,** *n.* bank which gives interest on deposits of money.

sav•ior, Brit. sav•iour ['seɪvjə] *n.* person who saves; **our Savior** = Jesus Christ.

sa•vor•y ['seɪvərɪ] *n.* herb used in cooking.

æ back, aː farm, ɒ top, aɪ pipe, aʊ how, aɪə fire, aʊə flower, ɔː bought, ɔɪ toy, e fed, eəhair, eɪ take, ə afraid, əʊ boat, əʊə lower, vː word, iː heap, ɪ hit, ɪə hear, uː school, ʊ book, ʌ but, b back, d dog, ð then, dʒ just, f fog, g go, h hand, j yes, k catch, l last, m mix, n nut, ŋ sing, p penny, r round, s some, ʃ short, t too, tʃ chop, θ thing, v voice, w was, z zoo, ʒ treasure

sa•vor, *Brit.* **savour** ['seɪvə] 1. *n.* characteristic taste. 2. *v.* (a) to appreciate (food and wine). (b) **to s. of** = to suggest. **sa•vor•i•ness**, *Brit.* **sa•vour•i•ness**, *n.* appetizing taste or smell. **sa•vor•y**, *Brit.* **sa•vour•y**, *adj.* (a) appetizing. (b) spicy/not sweet.

sa•voy [sə'vɔɪ] *n.* curly winter cabbage.

saw [sɔː] 1. *n.* (a) steel tool with a blade with a serrated edge, used for cutting wood/metal etc. (b) old saying. 2. *v.* (**sawed; sawn**) (a) to cut (wood, etc.) with a saw. (b) *see also* **see**. **saw•dust**, *n.* powder produced from sawing wood. **saw•fish**, *n.* large sea fish with a nose shaped like a saw. **saw•mill**, *n.* place where wood is sawed mechanically. **saw•yer**, *n.* person who saws wood.

sax [sæks] *n. inf.* saxophone.

sax•i•frage ['sæksɪfreɪdʒ] *n.* low alpine plant with pink flowers.

sax•o•phone ['sæksəfəʊn] *n.* brass musical instrument with keys. **sax•o•phon•ist** [sæk-'sɒfənɪst] *n.* saxophone player.

say [seɪ] 1. *n.* right to decide. 2. *v.* (**said** [sed]) (a) to speak. (b) to give (an opinion); to put an idea into words. (c) to suggest. **say•ing**, *n.* proverb/phrase which is often used.

scab [skæb] *n.* (a) dry rough crust formed over a wound when it is healing. (b) *inf.* workman who refuses to take part in a strike. **scab•by**, *adj.* covered with scabs.

scab•bard ['skæbəd] *n.* sheath/holder for a dagger or sword.

sca•bies ['skeɪbiːz] *n.* (*no pl.*) skin disease which makes you itch.

sca•bi•ous ['skeɪbɪəs] *n.* perennial plant with pincushion-shaped flowers.

scab•rous ['skeɪbrəs] *adj.* (*formal*) with a rough surface.

scaf•fold ['skæfəld] *n.* platform on which executions take place. **scaf•fold•ing**, *n.* structure of poles and planks providing workmen with a platform to stand on while working.

scal•a•wag [skæl'əwæg] *n.* naughty person; rascal.

scald [skɔːld] 1. *n.* burn caused by boiling liquid. 2. *v.* to injure with hot liquid or steam. **scald•ing.** 1. *n.* being burned by a hot liquid. 2. *adj.* very hot.

scale [skeɪl] 1. *n.* (a) thin horny plate protecting the skin of fish and snakes; **s. insect** = insect which sucks sap from plants and covers itself with a scale. (b) hard deposit stuck to a surface. (c) arrangement of musical notes in order. (d) graded system. (e) relative measurements of a small object which are exactly similar to those of a larger object. 2. *v.* (a) to remove scales from. (b) to remove deposit from (teeth). (c) to drop off in thin layers. (d) to climb up/to climb over. (e) **to s. up/down** = to increase/to reduce proportionally. **scale•a•ble**, *adj.* which can be scaled. **scale, scales**, *n.* instrument for weighing. **scal•y**, *adj.* covered with scales.

scal•lion ['skælɪən] *n.* young onion.

scal•lop ['skɒləp] *n.* (a) type of shellfish with a semi-circular ridged shell. (b) ornamental edging of material in small semicircles. **scal•loped**, *adj.* with scallops along the edge.

scal•ly•wag ['skælɪwæg] *n.* scalawag.

scalp [skælp] 1. *n.* skin and hair on the top of the head. 2. *v.* (a) to cut off the scalp of (s.o.). (b) *inf.* to sell tickets at a very high price. **scalp•er**, *n. inf.* person who sells tickets at a very high price.

scal•pel ['skælpl] *n.* small surgical knife.

scam [skæm] *n.* fraud.

scamp [skæmp] 1. *n.* rascal. 2. *v.* to do (sth) in an unsatisfactory way.

scamp•er ['skæmpə] 1. *n.* quick run. 2. *v.* to run quickly.

scam•pi ['skæmpɪ] *n. pl.* large prawns.

scan [skæn] 1. *v.* (**scanned**) (a) to test the rhythm of (a line of poetry); (*of poetry*) to fit a regular rhythm. (b) to look intently all over. (c) to pass a radar beam over (an area); to pass X-rays through part of the body. 2. *n.* action of passing a radar beam or X-ray over an area; **brain s.** = examining the inside of the brain by passing X-rays through the head. **scan•ner**, *n.* machine for carrying out scanning.

scan•dal ['skændl] *n.* (a) unkind gossip. (b) thing that produces a general feeling of anger. **scan•dal•ize**, *v.* to shock. **scan•dal•ized**, *adj.* shocked. **scan•dal•mon•ger**, *n.* person who spreads gossip. **scan•dal•ous**, *adj.* shameful. **scan•dal•ous•ly**, *adv.* terribly.

Scan•di•na•vi•an [skændɪ'neɪvɪən] *n. & adj.* (person) from Scandinavia.

scan•sion ['skænʃn] *n.* art of scanning poetry.

scant [skænt] *adj.* hardly enough. **scant•i•ly**, *adj.* **s. dressed** = with very few clothes on. **scant•i•ness**, *n.* lack; meagerness. **scant•y**, *adj.* (**-ier, -iest**) meager/not sufficient.

scape•goat ['skeɪpgəʊt] *n.* person who carries the blame for s.o. else.

scap•u•la ['skæpjʊlə] *n.* shoulder blade.

scar [skɑː] 1. *n.* mark left after a wound has healed. 2. *v.* (**scarred**) (a) to wound (s.o.) causing a permanent mark. (b) to leave a mark on the mind of.

scar•ab ['skærəb] *n.* carved beetle.

scarce [skeəs] *adj.* (**-er, -est**) insufficient for the demand/hard to find; *inf.* **to make oneself s.** = to disappear/to keep out of the way.

scarce•ly, *adv.* hardly/only just. **scarce•ness, scarcity,** *n.* lack/insufficiency.

scare [skeə] 1. *n.* fright/terror. 2. *v.* (a) to frighten. (b) to be alarmed. **scared,** *adj.* frightened. **scare•crow,** *n.* figure looking like a man set up in a field to frighten off birds. **scare•mon•ger,** *n.* person who likes to alarm others. **scare•mon•ger•ing,** *n.* spreading of alarm. **scar•y,** *adj.* (-ier, -iest) frightening.

scarf [skɑːf] *n.* (*pl.* **scarves**) long strip or square of material worn around the neck to keep you warm or for ornament.

scar•i•fy ['skærıfaı] *v.* to make slits in (sth).

scar•let ['skɑːlət] *adj.* brilliant red color. **scar•let fe•ver,** *n.* (*also* **scarlatina**) infectious disease producing a bright red rash.

scarp [skɑːp] *n.* steep hillside.

Scart, SCART [skɑːt] *n.* electronic plug and socket system, used to carry signals in cables for TV/video, etc.

scath•ing ['skeıðıŋ] *adj.* very critical.

scat•ter ['skætə] 1. *v.* (a) to throw here and there. (b) to go/to run in all directions. **scat•ter•brain,** *n.* forgetful person. **scat•ter•brained,** *adj.* forgetful/careless. **scat•tered,** *adj.* spread out.

scaup [skɔːp] *n.* type of wild duck.

scav•en••ger ['skævındʒə] *n.* (a) animal which feeds on dead animals. (b) person who looks for useful things among things thrown away. **scav•enge,** *v.* to look for useful things among things thrown away.

sce•nar•i•o [sı'nɑːrıəʊ] *n.* (*pl.* -os) written version of a play with details of characters/scenes, etc.

scene [siːn] *n.* (a) subdivision of an act in a play; **behind the scenes** = without being obvious/without many people knowing. (b) place in which events actually occur. (c) view/surroundings. (d) display of temper. (e) *inf.* **it's not my s.** = it doesn't interest me/it is not the sort of thing I usually do. **scen•er•y,** *n.* (a) painted cloth backgrounds and other props used in a theater to make the stage resemble the supposed scene of action. (b) view of the countryside. **sce•nic,** *adj.* referring to scenery; **s. route** = road running through beautiful countryside.

scent [sent] 1. *n.* pleasant smell. (b) characteristic smell; **on the s. of** = following a trail. (c) perfume. (d) sense of smell. 2. *v.* (a) to find out by smelling. (b) to begin to suspect. (c) to make fragrant.

scep•tic ['skeptık] *n.* skeptic.

scep•ter, *Brit.* **scep•tre** ['septə] *n.* gold stick covered with precious stones carried by a king or queen.

sched•ule ['ʃedjuːl, *Am.* 'skedʒuːl] 1. *n.* (a) timetable. (b) program/list of events. (c) plan. (d) appendix to a document. 2. *v.* (a) to list officially. (b) to plan (sth) for a particular time.

scheme [skiːm] 1. *n.* (a) plan/arrangement. (b) plot. 2. *v.* to plot. **sche•mat•ic** [skı'mætık] *adj.* laid out like a diagram. **sche•mat•i•cal•ly,** *adv.* in a schematic way. **schem•er,** *n.* person who plots. **schem•ing,** *adj.* (person) who plots.

scher•zo ['skeətsəʊ] *n.* (*pl.* -os, -zi) lively section of a longer piece of music.

schism ['skızəm] *n.* division of a religious community into factions. **schis•mat•ic** [skız'mætık] *adj.* tending to break away.

schist [ʃıst] *n.* rock which splits into thin layers.

schiz•o•phre•ni•a [skıtsəʊ'friːnıə] *n.* mental illness where thoughts, feelings and actions are all disconnected. **schiz•oid** ['skıtsɔıd] *adj. & n.* (person) suffering from schizophrenia. **schiz•o•phren•ic** [skıtsəʊ'frenık] *adj.* referring to schizophrenia.

schmaltz [ʃmɒlts] *n.* too much sentimentality (in writing/music, etc.).

schnapps [ʃnæps] *n.* colorless German alcohol.

schnit•zel ['ʃnıtzl] *n.* thin flat piece of veal fried in breadcrumbs.

schol•ar ['skɒlə] *n.* (a) person who studies. (b) learned person. (c) student at a school, college or university who has a scholarship. **schol•ar•li•ness,** *n.* being scholarly. **schol•ar•ly,** *adj.* learned/seeking to learn. **schol•ar•ship,** *n.* (a) profound learning. (b) money given to a student to help pay for the cost of studying at a school, college or university. **scho•las•tic** [skɒ'læstık] *adj.* referring to schools or teaching.

school [skuːl] 1. *n.* (a) place for teaching (usu. children); department of a college or university. (b) followers of a philosopher/artist, etc. (c) large group of fish or sea animals. 2. *v.* to teach/to train. **school•book,** *n.* book used in school. **school•boy, schoolgirl,** *n.* child who goes to school. **school•chil•dren,** *n.pl.* children who go to school. **school•ing,** *n.* education at school level. **school•mas•ter,**

æ back, ɑ: farm, ɒ: top, aı pipe, aʊ how, aıə fire, aʊə flower, ɔ: bought, ɔı toy, e fed, eəhair, eı take, ə afraid, əʊ boat, ʊə hear, v: word, i: heap, ı hit, ıə hear, u: school, ʊ book, ʌ but, b back, d dog, ð then, dʒ just, f fog, g go, h hand, j yes, k catch, l last, m mix, n nut, ŋ sing, p penny, r round, s some, ʃ short, t too, tʃ chop, θ thing, v voice, w was, z zoo, ʒ treasure

schoolmistress, *n.* schoolteacher.
school•teach•er, *n.* person who teaches in a school.

schoon•er ['sku:nə] *n.* (a) sailing ship with two or more masts and sails running lengthwise down the ship. (b) tall glass for beer, etc.

sci•at•i•ca [saɪ'ætɪkə] *n.* pain in the back and legs. **sci•at•ic nerve,** *n.* nerve in the hip.

sci•ence ['saɪəns] *n.* (a) knowledge obtained from observation and arranged into a system. (b) study based on observation and experiment (such as chemistry/biology, etc.). **sci•ence fic•tion,** *n.* stories on the subject of space travel/life in the future. **sci•en•tif•ic** [saɪən'tɪfɪk] *adj.* referring to science. **sci•en•tif•i•cal•ly,** *adv.* according to scientific experiment. **sci•en•tist** ['saɪəntɪst] *n.* person who studies science.

scim•i•tar ['sɪmɪtə] *n.* short sword with a curved blade.

scin•til•late ['sɪntɪleɪt] *v.* to sparkle. **scin•til•lat•ing,** *adj.* sparkling. **scin•til•la•tion** [sɪntɪ'leɪʃn] *n.* wit/sparkle.

sci•on ['saɪən] *n.* piece of a plant which is grafted on to another; young member of a noble family.

scis•sors ['sɪzəz] *n.pl.* (**a pair of**) **s.** = instrument for cutting fabric/paper etc. constructed of two blades with handles for thumb and fingers.

scle•ro•sis [sklə'rəʊsɪs] *n.* hardening of soft tissue; **multiple s.** = gradual disease where hardening of tissue causes general paralysis.

scoff [skɒf] *v.* (a) **to s. at** = to make fun of in a nasty way. (b) *inf.* to eat greedily. **scoff•er,** *n.* person who scoffs. **scoffing,** *adj.* mocking. **scoff•ing•ly,** *adv.* mockingly.

scold [skəʊld] *v.* to speak to (s.o.) angrily. **scold•ing,** *n.* rebuke.

sconce ['skɒns] *n.* decorated bracket which holds a light.

scone [skɒn] *n.* small soft cake usu. eaten with cream and jam.

scoop [sku:p] 1. *n.* (a) short-handled shovel/spoon; round spoon for serving ice cream. (b) portion of ice cream, etc. (c) piece of news which is published in one newspaper before any other. 2. *v.* (a) to lift, using a scoop; **to s. out the inside of sth** = to remove the inside of sth with a spoon, etc. (b) **to s. a newspaper** = to print a news item before another paper does.

scoot•er ['sku:tə] *n.* (a) child's two-wheeled vehicle with footboard and a long steering handle, pushed along with one foot. (b) **motor s.** = motorized two-wheel bicycle with a curving shield in front and a platform for the feet. **scoot,** *v. inf.* to go quite fast.

scope [skəʊp] *n.* (a) reach of observation/action. (b) opportunity, as for expression.

scor•bu•tic [skɔ:'bu:tɪk] *adj.* suffering from scurvy.

scorch [skɔ:tʃ] 1. *v.* to burn slightly/to brown; **scorched-earth policy** = tactics in war where all the resources are destroyed before retreating and giving up territory to the enemy. **scorch•er,** *n. inf.* very hot day. **scorch•ing,** *adj.* very hot/which scorches.

score [skɔ:] 1. *n.* (a) scratch/line/mark (in paint, etc.). (b) debt; **to settle old scores** = to finally get even with s.o. (c) number of points made in a game; *inf.* **he knows the s.** = he knows all the facts of the case. (d) piece of music written out showing the parts for each instrument or voice. (e) twenty; **scores of** = many. (f) question/matter. 2. *v.* (a) to scratch. (b) to make a point in a game. (c) to write down the score in a game. (d) to write out (a piece of music) with parts for each instrument or voice. **score•board,** *n.* large board showing the score in a tennis match, etc. **scor•er,** *n.* person who makes a point in a game; person who writes down the scores in a game.

scorn [skɔ:n] 1. *n.* feeling of looking down/disrespect. 2. *v.* to look down on/not respect. **scorn•ful,** *adj.* disrespectful. **scorn•ful•ly,** *adv.* in a scornful way.

Scor•pi•o ['skɔ:pɪəʊ] *n.* one of the signs of the zodiac, shaped like a scorpion.

scor•pi•on ['skɔ:pɪən] *n.* poisonous tropical insect which stings with a long curved tail.

Scot [skɒt] *n.* person from Scotland. **Scots.** 1. *adj.* referring to Scotland. 2. *n.* form of English spoken in Scotland. **Scots•man, Scotswoman,** *n.* (*pl.* **-men, -women**) person from Scotland. **Scot•tish,** *adj.* referring to Scotland; **S. terrier** = type of black or white terrier.

Scotch [skɒtʃ] 1. *adj.* referring to Scotland; (**Scottish** *is preferred in Scotland, but* **Scotch** *is always used in the following*) **S. broth** = soup made with mutton, barley, etc.; **S. mist** = thick mist and rain; **S. terrier** = Scottish terrier; **S. whisky** = whisky made in Scotland. 2. *n.* (a) (*pl.* **-es**) Scotch whisky; a glass of this drink. (b) **S. tape** = trademark for a type of transparent sticky tape. 3. *v.* **to s.** = to try to stop (a rumor).

scot-free [skɒt'fri:] *adj.* **to get off s.** = without being punished.

scoun•drel ['skaʊndrəl] *n.* wicked person.

scour ['skaʊə] *v.* (a) to clean by scrubbing with a hard material. (b) to search everywhere. **scour•er,** *n.* pad of steel wool for cleaning pans.

scourge [skɜ:dʒ] 1. *n.* thing which causes suffering. 2. *v.* to cause suffering.

scout [skaʊt] 1. *n.* (a) person sent out to look

for information. (b) boy who belongs to the Boy Scouts; **the Scouts** = the Boy Scouts. 2. *v.* to reconnoiter; **to s. around for** = to search for. **scout•mas•ter**, *n.* leader of a group of Boy Scouts.

scowl [skaʊl] 1. *n.* angry look made by wrinkling the forehead. 2. *v.* to make a scowl.

scrab•ble ['skræbl] *v.* **to s. (about)** = to scratch wildly with your hands or feet.

scrag [skræg] *n.* lean end of a sheep's neck used to make soup. **scrag•gy** ['skrægɪ] *adj.* (**-ier, -iest**) thin and bony.

scram [skræm] *inter. meaning* go away!

scram•ble ['skræmbl] 1. *n.* (a) act of scrambling (up sth). (b) rush. 2. *v.* (a) to hurry along on hands and knees. (b) to try to get somewhere by pushing. (c) **scrambled eggs** = eggs mixed together and stirred as they are cooked in butter. (d) to mix up (a radio signal/telephone link) so that it cannot be understood without an apparatus for unmixing it. **scram•bler**, *n.* machine for scrambling radio signals.

scrap [skræp] 1. *n.* (a) small piece. (b) waste materials; **scraps** = bits of waste food/waste material; **s. heap** = heap of sth to be thrown away, esp. metal; **s. metal/paper** = waste metal/paper. (c) *inf.* fight. 2. *v.* (**scrapped**) (a) to throw away as waste. (b) to give up (plans). (c) to fight. **scrap•book**, *n.* large book with blank pages for sticking photographs/newspaper cuttings, etc., into. **scrap•py**, *adj.* (**-ier, -iest**) made of bits and pieces.

scrape [skreɪp] 1. *n.* (a) mark made by sth hard being pulled across a surface. (b) awkward situation/trouble. 2. *v.* to scratch with a hard object being pulled across a surface; **s. together** = to collect with difficulty; **s. through** = to get through (an examination, etc.) with difficulty. **scrap•er**, *n.* instrument for scraping. **scrap•ie**, *n.* usu. fatal disease of the nervous system in sheep, caused by an abnormal prion protein in the brain. **scrap•ings**, *n.pl.* pieces which have been scraped off.

scratch [skrætʃ] 1. *n.* (*pl.* **-es**) (a) long slight wound/mark made by a sharp point. (b) sound of a sharp point being pulled across a surface. (c) act of scratching a part of the body which itches. (d) **to start from s.** = to start at the beginning/with no previous preparation; **up to s.** = satisfactory. 2. *adj.* **s. player** = player who starts with no handicap. 3. *v.* (a) to make a long wound/mark with a sharp pointed instrument; **to s. the surface** = to deal with only the first part of the problem and not to get down to the basic details. (b) to make a sound by pulling a sharp point across a surface. (c) to rub with your fingernails (a part of the body which itches). (d) (*of competitor*) to cross one's name off the list of entrants for a race. **scratch•y**, *adj.* which makes a scratching noise.

scrawl [skrɔːl] 1. *n.* bad/careless handwriting. 2. *v.* to write badly/carelessly.

scrawn•y ['skrɔːnɪ] *adj.* (**-ier, -iest**) thin and bony.

scream [skriːm] 1. *n.* (a) loud/piercing cry. (b) **screams of laughter** = loud/piercing laughter. (c) *inf.* very funny thing/person. 2. *v.* (a) to make loud/piercing cries. (b) **s. with laughter** = laugh uproariously. **scream•ing•ly**, *adv.* **s. funny** = extremely funny.

scree [skriː] *n.* loose stones on a mountainside.

screech [skriːtʃ] 1. *n.* (*pl.* **-es**) piercing cry (of an animal). 2. *v.* to make a piercing cry. **screech owl**, *n.* type of owl which screeches.

screed [skriːd] *n.* very long document.

screen [skriːn] 1. *n.* (a) flat surface which protects/divides. (b) thing which acts as protection against draft/fire/noise, etc. (c) flat white surface for projecting movies/slides. (d) device like a large sieve for sifting sand/gravel into varying sizes. 2. *v.* (a) to protect from draft/fire/noise, etc. (b) to show a movie/slides on a screen. (c) to question/to examine (people) to find out if they have a disease/if they have committed a crime. (d) to sift (sand/gravel) into varying sizes. **screen•play**, *n.* scenario of a motion picture. **screen•writ•er**, *n.* person who writes screenplays.

screw [skruː] 1. *n.* (a) metal pin with a groove winding up from the point to the head, so that when twisted it goes into a hard surface. (b) act of turning a screw with a screwdriver. (c) twisting motion. (d) *Sl.* prison guard. 2. *v.* (a) to attach with screws. (b) to attach by twisting. (c) to twist/distort. **screw•ball**, *n. inf.* odd/crazy person. **screw•driv•er**, *n.* tool with a long handle and small flat end which is used for turning screws. **screw-top jar**, *n.* jar with a top which screws on and off. **screw•y**, *adj.* (**-ier, -iest**) *inf.* mad.

scrib•ble ['skrɪbl] 1. *n.* (a) (child's) meaningless marks. (b) bad writing. 2. *v.* (a) to make meaningless marks. (b) to write badly/hurriedly. **scrib•bly**, *adj.* scribbled (writing).

æ back, aː farm, ɒ top, aɪ pipe, aʊ how, aiǝ fire, aʊǝ flower, ɔː bought, ɔɪ toy, e fed, eǝhair, eɪ take, ǝ afraid, ǝʊ boat, ǝʊǝ lower, vː word, iː heap, ɪ hit, ɪǝ hear, uː school, ʊ book, ʌ but, b back, d dog, ð then, dʒ just, f fog, g go, h hand, j yes, k catch, l last, m mix, n nut, ŋ sing, p penny, r round, s some, ʃ short, t too, tʃ chop, θ thing, v voice, w was, z zoo, ʒ treasure

scribe [skraɪb] *n.* (*old*) person who writes copies (of letters/books, etc.) by hand.

scrim•mage ['skrɪmɪdʒ] *n.* wild struggle.

scrimp [skrɪmp] *v.* to use as little as possible (of sth).

scrim•shaw ['skrɪmʃɔ:] *n.* carvings made by sailors on whalebone or ivory.

scrip [skrɪp] *n.* (*no pl.*) new shares issued by a company instead of paying a dividend.

script [skrɪpt] *n.* (a) style of handwriting. (b) thing written by hand/manuscript. (c) written version of words which are spoken in a motion picture/play.

scrip•ture ['skrɪptʃə] *n.* holy writing; the Bible. **scrip•tur•al,** *adj.* referring to scripture.

scroll [skrəʊl] 1. *n.* (a) roll of paper with writing on it. (b) curved shape. 2. *v.* to move text up or down on a computer screen.

scro•tum ['skrəʊtəm] *n.* bag containing the testicles. **scro•tal,** *adj.* referring to the scrotum.

scrounge [skraʊndʒ] *v.* to try to get (sth) from s.o. without paying for it. **scroung•er,** *n.* person who scrounges.

scrub [skrʌb] 1. *n.* (a) (area of land covered by) small bushes. (b) action of cleaning with a stiff brush. 2. *v.* (**scrubbed**) to clean by rubbing with a stiff brush. **scrub brush,** *n.* (*also* **scrubbing brush**) stiff brush with no handle, for scrubbing floors, etc. **scrub•by,** *adj.* (**-ier, -iest**) *inf.* shabby, small and unpleasant.

scruff [skrʌf] *n.* skin at the back of the neck. **scruff•i•ly,** *adv.* in a scruffy way. **scruff•i•ness,** *n.* being scruffy. **scruff•y,** *adj.* (**-ier, -iest**) untidy/dirty.

scrump•tious ['skrʌmʃəs] *adj. inf.* very good to eat or pleasant to look at, etc.

scrunch [skrʌntʃ] *v. inf.* to crush.

scru•ple ['skru:pl] 1. *n.* doubt about whether sth is right which stops you from doing it. 2. *v.* to have scruples about doing sth. **scru•pu•lous** ['skru:pjʊləs] *adj.* very careful. **scru•pu•lous•ly,** *adv.* in a scrupulous way. **scru•pu•lous•ness,** *n.* being scrupulous.

scru•ti•nize ['skru:tɪnaɪz] *v.* to examine very carefully. **scru•ti•ny,** *n.* careful examination/very close look.

scu•ba ['sku:bə] *n.* underwater breathing apparatus.

scud [skʌd] *v.* (**scudded**) (*of clouds*) to rush past.

scuff [skʌf] *v.* to scrape the outside surface/the soles of (shoes) when walking.

scuf•fle ['skʌfl] 1. *n.* small fight. 2. *v.* to fight.

scull [skʌl] 1. *n.* one of two short oars used by a single rower. 2. *v.* to row a boat with two oars.

scul•ler•y ['skʌlərɪ] *n.* (*esp. Brit.*) small room at the back of a kitchen, used for washing up.

sculpt [skʌlpt] *v.* to carve (figures, etc.) out of wood/metal/stone. **sculp•tor** ['skʌlptə] *n.* person who makes figures/artistic constructions out of wood/metal/stone. **sculp•ture** ['skʌlptʃə] 1. *n.* (a) art of sculpting. (b) figure made by a sculptor. 2. *v.* to sculpt.

scum [skʌm] *n.* (a) thick dirty foam layer on the surface of a liquid. (b) people of the worst type; worthless person. **scum•my,** *adj.* covered with scum.

scup•per ['skʌpə] *n.* hole in the side of a ship to let water run off the deck.

scurf [skɜ:f] *n.* dandruff/bits of dead skin in the hair.

scur•ril•ous ['skʌrɪləs] *adj.* very insulting/rude. **scur•ril•ous•ly,** *adv.* in a scurrilous way. **scur•ril•ous•ness, scurrility** [skʌ'rɪlɪtɪ] *n.* being scurrilous.

scur•ry ['skʌrɪ] 1. *n.* fast movement. 2. *v.* to run fast, taking short steps.

scur•vy ['skɜ:vɪ] *n.* disease caused by lack of Vitamin C which is found in fruit and vegetables.

scut [skʌt] *n.* little tail (of a rabbit/deer).

scut•tle ['skʌtl] 1. *n.* type of bucket for keeping coal in the house. 2. *v.* (a) to sink (a ship) intentionally by opening holes in the bottom to allow water to come in. (b) **to s. off** = to run away fast.

scythe [saɪð] 1. *n.* tool with a wide blade on the end of a long handle, used for cutting grass. 2. *v.* to cut (grass) with a scythe.

sea [si:] *n.* (a) area of salt water; *inf.* **at s.** = not understanding what is happening. (b) salt water. (c) waves; **a heavy s.** = very large waves. (d) mass (of faces in a crowd). **sea a•nem•o•ne,** *n.* primitive sea animal which looks like a flower. **sea bird,** *n.* bird which lives by the sea. **sea•board,** *n.* land by the edge of the sea. **sea•borne,** *adj.* (troops, etc.) brought by sea. **sea breeze,** *n.* light wind blowing inland from the sea. **sea•coast,** *n.* land along the edge of the sea. **sea•far•er,** *n.* person who travels/works on the sea. **sea•far•ing,** *adj.* which works/travels on the sea. **sea•food,** *n.* fish and shellfish which can be eaten. **sea front,** *n.* area with buildings, running along the edge of the sea at a resort town. **sea•go•ing,** *adj.* (boat) which is used on the sea. **sea•gull,** *n.* white sea bird. **sea horse,** *n.* small black fish which looks like a horse. **sea legs,** *n.* **he's got his s. legs** = he is used to traveling by sea and isn't seasick. **sea lev•el,** *n.* the level of the sea, taken as a point for measuring altitude. **sea li•on,** *n.* large type of seal. **sea•man,** *n.* (*pl.* **-men**) sailor; person who travels/works on the sea. **sea•man•ship,** *n.* art of sailing a ship. **sea•plane,** *n.* plane with floats which can

land on water. **sea•port,** *n.* port.
sea•scape, *n.* painting of the sea. **sea•shell,**
n. shell of a shellfish which lives in the sea.
sea•shore, *n.* land along the edge of the sea.
sea•sick, *adj.* ill because of the motion of a
ship. **sea•sick•ness,** *n.* being seasick.
sea•side, *n.* land by the side of the sea. **sea
ur•chin,** *n.* type of small spiny sea animal.
sea•ward, *adj.* toward the sea. **sea•ward,
seawards,** *adv.* toward the sea. **sea•weed,**
n. plant which grows in the sea.
sea•wor•thy, *adj.* (boat) which is fit to go to
sea.

seal [siːl] 1. *n.* (a) large animal living mainly in
the sea, with flippers for swimming. (b) piece
of hard red wax with a design stamped on it,
used for showing that a document has been
officially approved or for closing an enve-
lope/package so that it cannot be opened secretly. (c) metal stamp with a design, used for
sealing with wax. (d) tight fit (of a bottle, etc.).
2. *v. (a)* to attach and stamp a piece of hard
wax to show that a document has been
officially approved/to prevent an envelope
being opened. (b) to close (sth) tightly so that
something cannot be opened. (c) to agree on
the terms of (an agreement/bargain).
seal•ant, *n.* substance used for sealing.
seal•ing wax, *n.* hard red wax used for making official seals. **seal off,** *v.* to close off so as
to prevent anyone entering. **seal•skin,** *n.* skin
of a seal.

seam [siːm] *n.* (a) line where two pieces of cloth
are sewn together/where two pieces of metal
are welded together. (b) layer (of coal, etc.).
seam•less, *adj.* (stockings, etc.) with no
seam. **seam•stress** ['semstrəs] *n.* woman
who sews. **seam•y,** *adj.* (-ier, -iest) **s. side of
life** = the unpleasant parts of life.

sé•ance ['seɪɑːns] *n.* meeting where people try
to get in touch with the spirits of dead people.

sear ['sɪə] *v.* to burn severely/to scorch.

search [sɜːtʃ] 1. *n.* (*pl.* -es) trying to find sth; **s.
engine** = Internet service that allows users to
search for specified items; **s. warrant** = official
permit to carry out a search; **s. party** = group
of people sent to look for s.o. 2. *v.* (a) to examine carefully in order to find sth. (b) **to s. for** =
try to find. **search•er,** *n.* person who
searches. **search•ing,** *adj.* very careful (examination). **search•light,** *n.* powerful light
used to try to see things, esp. aircraft, at night.

sea•son ['siːzn] 1. *n.* (a) one of four parts into

which a year is divided. (b) any period of the
year when sth usually takes place. 2. *v.* (a) to
add spices to (food). (b) to dry (wood) until it
is ready to be used. **sea•son•a•ble,** *adj.*
which fits the season. **sea•son•a•bly,** *adv.*
as is usual for the season. **sea•son•al,** *adj.*
which only lasts for a season; (work) for the
(summer) season only; **s. affective disorder
(SAD)** = depressive condition affecting some
people in late autumn/winter, thought to be
caused by lack of sunlight. **sea•soned,** *adj.*
(wood) which has been dried; (traveler) who
has much experience of traveling.
sea•son•ing, *n.* spices which are added to
food.

seat [siːt] 1. *n.* (a) thing you sit on. (b) place (on
a committee/town council, etc.). (c) part of a
chair on which you sit. (d) part of a pair of
trousers which covers the buttocks. (e) **s. of
government** = place where the government is
carried on. (f) way of sitting on a horse. 2. *v.*
(a) to make (s.o.) sit down. (b) to have room
for people to sit down. **seat belt,** *n.* belt worn
in a car/in an aircraft as protection in case of
accident. **seat•ing,** *n.* giving seats to people.

se•ba•ceous [sɪ'beɪʃəs] *adj.* which produces
fat.

se•cant ['siːknt] *n.* line which crosses a curve.

se•cede [sɪ'siːd] *v.* (*formal*) to break away from
a group. **se•ces•sion** [sɪ'seʃn] *n.* act of seced-
ing.

se•clud•ed [sɪ'kluːdɪd] *adj.* (place) which is
quiet/away from crowds. **se•clu•sion** [sɪ-
'kluːʒn] *n.* quiet/solitude.

sec•ond ['sekənd] (*as a number can be written
2nd*) 1. *n.* (a) sixtieth part of a minute; a moment; **s. hand** = long fast-moving hand on a
watch. (b) sixtieth part of a degree. (c) per-
son/thing which comes after the first. (d) person who helps a boxer/wrestler. (e) **seconds** =
articles which are not perfect and are sold
cheaply. (f) second gear. 2. *adj.* (a) coming
next after the first; **s. class** = ordinary railroad
travel, etc., which is not as luxurious or
expensive as first class; **s. in command** =
person directly under the commanding
officer/managing director, etc.; **the s. century**
= period from A.D. 100 to 199. (b) **every s. day**
= every other day/on alternate days. 3. *v.* to
support (a proposal). **sec•ond•ar•y**
['sekəndrɪ] *adj.* (a) second in importance/in
position. (b) **s. school** = school between primary school and a college or university. (c) **s.
colors** = colors made by mixing primary col-

ors. **sec•ond•ar•i•ly,** *adv.* in second place in importance. **sec•ond best,** *adj. & adv.* in second place; not as good as the best. **sec•ond child•hood,** *n.* period in old age when old people seem to act like children. **sec•ond•er,** *n.* person who supports a motion. **second half,** *n.* second section (as of a football game). **sec•ond hand,** *adj. & adv.* not new/used; **I heard it at s. h.** = not from the original source of the news. **sec•ond•ly,** *adv.* in second place. **sec•ond na•ture,** *n.* **it is s. n. to him** = he does it quite naturally. **sec•ond-rate,** *adj.* not of good quality. **sec•ond sight,** *n.* being able to tell what will happen in the future. **sec•ond thoughts,** *n. pl.* **to have s. t. about** = to change one's mind. **sec•ond wind,** *n.* **he got his s. w.** = he could breathe again easily after having lost his breath.

se•cret ['sɪkrət] 1. *adj.* hidden from other people; not known. 2. *n.* thing which is not known/which is kept hidden; **in s.** = without anyone knowing. **se•cre•cy,** ['siːkrəsɪ] *n.* keeping sth secret. **se•cre•tive,** *adj.* liking to keep things secret. **se•cre•tive•ly,** *adv.* in a secretive way. **se•cre•tive•ness,** *n.* being secretive. **se•cret•ly,** *adv.* in secret. **se•cret serv•ice,** *n.* government department which deals in espionage.

sec•re•taire [sekrə'teə] *n.* desk with many little drawers.

sec•re•tar•y ['sekrətərɪ] *n.* (a) person who writes letters/files documents, etc., for s.o. (b) person who deals with correspondence/arranges meetings, etc., in a club/society. (c) official in charge of a government department. (d) official in an embassy; **first s.** = senior official in an embassy. **Sec•re•tar•y Gen•er•al,** *n.* chief administrative officer of an international organization. **sec•re•tar•i•al** [sekrə'teərɪəl] *adj.* referring to a secretary. **sec•re•tar•i•at,** *n.* group of officials who administer a large office.

se•crete [sɪ'kriːt] *v.* (a) to hide. (b) to produce (a liquid). **se•cre•tion** [sɪ'kriːʃn] *n.* liquid produced by an organ/a plant.

sect [sekt] *n.* religious group. **sec•tar•i•an** [sek'teərɪən] *adj.* referring to a religious group.

sec•tion ['sekʃn] *n.* (a) cutting; cutting tissue in an operation. (b) part. (c) picture of sth showing what it is like when cut through. (d) part of sth which, when joined to other parts, goes to make up a whole. **sec•tion•al,** *adj.* (a) (diagram) showing a section through sth. (b) (built) in sections.

sec•tor ['sektə] *n.* (a) section of a circle between two lines drawn from the center to the circum-

ference; section of the surface of a computer disk. (b) **private s.** = part of industry which is privately owned; **public s.** = nationalized industries and the civil service.

sec•u•lar ['sekjʊlə] *adj.* not religious/not connected with religion. **sec•u•lar•ize,** *v.* to make secular.

se•cure [sɪ'kjuːə] 1. *adj.* (a) safe. (b) firmly fixed; **s. job** = where you can't be fired. (c) confident. 2. *v.* (a) to make firm/to fasten. **se•cure•ly,** *adv.* in a secure way. **se•cu•ri•ty,** *n.* (a) safety. (b) protection against criminals/against hardship; **airport s.** = measures to protect aircraft against hijackers. (c) thing given to s.o. who has lent you money and which is returned when the loan is repaid. (d) **securities** = stocks and bonds. **Se•cu•ri•ty Coun•cil,** *n.* ruling body of the United Nations.

se•dan [sɪ'dæn] *n.* covered car which has two or four doors. **se•dan chair,** *n.* (*old*) seat in a box carried on long poles by bearers.

se•date [sɪ'deɪt] 1. *adj.* serious/dignified. 2. *v.* to give (a patient) sedatives. **se•date•ly,** *adv.* in a calm/serious way. **se•date•ness,** *n.* being sedate. **sed•a•tive** ['sedətɪv] *adj. & n.* (medicine) which makes you calm/which makes you go to sleep. **se•da•tion** [sɪ'deɪʃn] *n.* giving medicine to calm a patient or make him go to sleep.

sed•en•tar•y ['sedəntrɪ] *adj.* always sitting down.

sedge [sedʒ] *n.* type of grass which grows in water.

sed•i•ment ['sedɪmənt] *n.* solid which forms at the bottom of a liquid. **sed•i•men•ta•ry** [sedɪ'mentərɪ] *adj.* (rocks) which were formed from mud deposited at the bottom of the sea/rivers, etc. **sed•i•men•ta•tion,** *n.* action of depositing solid particles at the bottom of liquid.

se•di•tion [sə'dɪʃn] *n.* encouraging people to rebel against the government. **se•di•tious,** *adj.* which encourages people to rebel.

se•duce [sɪ'djuːs] *v.* (a) to persuade (s.o.) to do sth which is perhaps wrong. (b) to persuade (s.o.) to have sexual intercourse. **se•duc•er,** *n.* person who seduces. **se•duc•tion** [sɪ'dʌkʃn] *n.* act of seducing. **se•duc•tive** [sɪ'dʌktɪv] *adj.* attractive.

sed•u•lous ['sedjʊləs] *adj.* very careful and persistent. **sed•u•lous•ly,** *adv.* in a sedulous way.

se•dum ['siːdəm] *n.* succulent rock plant.

see [siː] 1. *n.* area over which a bishop rules. 2. *v.* (**saw** [sɔː], **seen**) (a) to sense with your eyes. (b) to accompany; **to s. s.o. home.** (c) to understand. (d) to examine. (e) to make sure (**that**).

(f) to visit/to meet. (g) to go to a performance of (a play/motion picture, etc.). **see•ing**, *n.* action of sensing with the eyes; **s. that** = since. **see through**, *v.* (a) to understand s.o.'s plans to trick you. (b) to work on (sth) until it is finished. **see-through**, *adj.* transparent. **see to**, *v.* to busy yourself about sth; **see to it** = make sure (**that**).

seed [si:d] 1. *n.* (a) part of a plant which appears after the flowers and then can produce a new plant; **to go/to run to s.** = produce flowers and seeds which are not needed; **he's gone to s.** = he's lost energy, power, etc.; deteriorated. (b) tennis player selected as one of the best players in a tournament (before the tournament starts). 2. *v.* (a) to produce seeds. (b) to select (the best players) in a tennis tournament and arrange them so that they do not play each other until the later rounds. **seed•bed**, *n.* special area of fine soil where you can sow seeds. **seed•less**, *adj.* (fruit) with no seeds in it. **seed•ling**, *n.* very young plant. **seed•y**, *adj.* (-ier, -iest) worn-out (clothes); shabby (person).

seek [si:k] *v.* (**sought** [sɔ:t]) (a) to look for. (b) to ask for. **seek•er**, *n.* person who seeks.

seem [si:m] *v.* to appear. **seem•ing**, *adj.* not real, though appearing to be. **seem•ing•ly**, *adj.* apparently. **seem•ly**, *adj.* decent/correct.

seen [si:n] *v. see* **see.**

seep [si:p] *v.* (*of a liquid*) to pass through a crack. **seep•age**, *n.* act of seeping; liquid which has seeped.

seer ['si:ə] *n.* (*old*) person who sees into the future.

seer•suck•er ['sɪəsʌkə] *n.* cotton cloth with a wrinkled surface.

see•saw ['si:sɔ:] 1. *n.* children's toy made of a plank with seats at each end, balanced in the middle, so that when one end goes up the other goes down. 2. *v.* to go up and down.

seethe [si:ð] *v.* (a) to be very angry. (b) to move about like boiling water. **seeth•ing**, *adj.* very angry.

seg•ment ['segmənt] *n.* part of sth (which seems to form a natural division); part of a circle or sphere. **seg•men•ta•tion** [segmən'teɪʃn] *n.* being segmented. **seg•ment•ed** [seg'mentɪd] *adj.* with segments.

seg•re•gate ['segrɪgeɪt] *v.* to divide one group from another. **seg•re•ga•tion** [segrɪ'geɪʃn] *n.* division of one group from another; **racial s.**

= splitting of a population into groups according to race or color.

seine [seɪn] *n.* type of fishing net.

seis•mic ['saɪzmɪk] *adj.* referring to earthquakes. **seis•mo•graph**, *n.* instrument for recording earthquakes. **seis•mo•log•i•cal** [saɪzmə'lɒdʒɪkl] *adj.* referring to seismology. **seis•mol•o•gy** [saɪz'mɒlədʒɪ] *n.* study of earthquakes.

seize [si:z] *v.* (a) to grab/to hold tight. (b) to confiscate/to take by force. **seize up**, *v.* (*of an engine*) to stop working/to become blocked. **sei•zure** ['si:ʒə] *n.* (a) confiscation of goods by the police. (b) stroke/illness caused by lack of blood to the brain.

sel•dom ['seldəm] *adv.* rarely/not often.

se•lect [sɪ'lekt] 1. *v.* to choose. 2. *adj.* (a) of top quality. (b) **s. group** = group which only lets in certain people. **se•lec•tion** [sɪ'lekʃn] *n.* (a) choice. (b) things chosen. **se•lec•tive**, *adj.* which chooses (carefully). **se•lec•tive•ly**, *adv.* in a selective way. **se•lec•tiv•i•ty**, *n.* being able to choose carefully.

self [self] *n.* (*pl.* **selves**) your own person or character. **self-ad•dressed**, *adj.* (envelope) on which you have written your own address. **self-as•ser•tive**, *adj.* (person) who makes others do what he wants. **self-as•sur•ance**, *n.* being self-assured. **self-as•sured**, *adj.* sure you are capable of doing sth. **self-cen•tered**, *adj.* (person) who only thinks of himself. **self-con•fi•dence**, *n.* being self-confident. **self-con•fi•dent**, *adj.* sure you are capable of doing sth. **self-con•scious**, *adj.* embarrassed because you feel you have certain faults. **self-con•scious•ly**, *adv.* with embarrassment. **self-con•scious•ness**, *n.* being self-conscious. **self-con•trol**, *n.* keeping your feelings under control. **self-de•feat•ing**, *adj.* (plan) which works in such a way that it defeats its own purpose. **self-de•fense**, *n.* protecting yourself. **self-de•ni•al**, *n.* refusing to give yourself sth/going without sth which you would like. **self-de•ter•mi•na•tion**, *n.* choosing your own political future. **self-ed•u•cat•ed**, *adj.* (person) who has taught himself everything he knows and who has not been to school. **self-ef•fac•ing**, *adj.* (person) who tries to be inconspicuous/who does not want people to notice him. **self-em•ployed**, *adj.* (person) who works for himself, and is not an employee

---

æ back, a: farm, ɒ: top, aɪ pipe, aʊ how, aɪə fire, aʊə flower, ɔ: bought, ɔɪ toy, e fed, eəhair, eɪ take, ə afraid, əʊ boat, əʊə lower, v: word, i: heap, ɪ hit, ɪə hear, u: school, ʊ book, ʌ but, b back, d dog, ð then, dʒ just, f fog, g go, h hand, j yes, k catch, l last, m mix, n nut, ŋ sing, p penny, r round, s some, ʃ short, t too, tʃ chop, θ thing, v voice, w was, z zoo, ʒ treasure

receiving a salary from s.o. else. **self-es•teem,** *n.* pride in yourself. **self-ev•i•dent,** *adj.* obvious. **self-ex•plan•a•to•ry,** *adj.* obvious/which explains itself. **self-gov•ern•ing,** *adj.* (country) which governs itself. **self-gov•ern•ment,** *n.* control of a country by its own people, not by another country. **self-help,** *n.* improving one's condition by one's own efforts. **self-im•por•tant,** *adj.* (person) who feels he is very important when he really is not. **self-in•dul•gent,** *adj.* (person) who gives himself everything he wants. **self-in•ter•est,** *n.* working for one's own benefit. **self-made man,** *n.* person who has become rich or successful entirely through his own efforts. **self-pit•y,** *n.* pity for yourself. **self-por•trait,** *n.* painting which an artist has made of himself. **self-pos•sessed,** *adj.* calm/not bothered. **self-ris•ing flour,** *n.* flour which contains baking powder to make cakes rise. **self-re•li•ance,** *n.* being self-reliant. **self-re•li•ant,** *adj.* independent/relying only on yourself. **self-re•spect,** *n.* pride in yourself/concern that you have a good character and work well. **self-right•eous,** *adj.* feeling sure that you are doing what is right. **self-rule,** *n.* self-government. **self-sac•ri•fice,** *n.* giving up sth which you would like, so that others may enjoy it. **self-sac•ri•fic•ing,** *adj.* (person) who gives up pleasures, so that others may enjoy them. **self-sat•is•fac•tion,** *n.* being self-satisfied. **self-sat•is•fied,** *adj.* contented with what you have done. **self-seek•ing,** *adj.* (person) who works to his own advantage, at the expense of others. **self-serv•ice,** *n. & adj.* (store, restaurant, gas station, etc.) where you help yourself and pay at a cashier's desk. **self-styled,** *adj.* (person) who has given himself a title. **self-suf•fi•cien•cy,** *n.* being self-sufficient. **self-suf•fi•cient,** *adj.* producing enough food, etc., for all needs. **self-sup•port•ing,** *adj.* providing for one's own needs, with no help from others. **self-taught,** *adj.* (person) who has taught himself a certain skill. **self-willed,** *adj.* obstinate/always wanting to have your own way.

self•ish ['selfɪʃ] *adj.* only interested in yourself/doing sth only for yourself. **self•ish•ly,** *adv.* (done) only for yourself. **self•ish•ness,** *n.* being selfish.

self•less ['selfləs] *adj.* not selfish/thinking only of others.

self•same ['selfseɪm] *adj.* exactly the same.

sell [sel] 1. *n.* act of selling; **hard s.** = forceful selling of a product. 2. *v.* (**sold, has sold**) (a) to give goods to s.o. in exchange for money. (b) *inf.* to betray. **sell date,** *n.* date on a package of food, which is the last date on which the food is guaranteed to be good. **sell•er,** *n.* (a) person who sells. (b) **good s.** = thing that sells well. **sell off,** *v.* to sell (sth) cheaply to get rid of it. **sell out,** *v.* (a) to sell so many things that you have none left. (b) *inf.* to abandon your principles. **sell-out,** *n.* (a) show/play, etc. where all the tickets have been sold. (b) *inf.* abandoning of principles.

sel•vage, selvedge ['selvɪdʒ] *n.* edge of a piece of cloth which does not fray.

se•man•tics [sɪ'mæntɪks] *n.* study of the meaning of language. **se•man•ti•cal•ly,** *adv.* in a way which refers to semantics.

sem•a•phore ['semfɔ:] *n.* way of signaling using two arms (and flags) in different positions for each letter.

sem•blance ['sembləns] *n.* appearance.

se•men ['si:mən] *n.* liquid in which male sperm floats.

se•mes•ter [sə'mestə] *n.* division of an academic year, usu. 15 to 18 weeks.

semi- ['semɪ] *prefix meaning* half. **sem•i•cir•cle,** *n.* half a circle. **sem•i•cir•cu•lar,** *adj.* like a half circle in shape. **sem•i•co•lon,** *n.* punctuation mark (;) showing a pause. **sem•i•con•duc•tor,** *n.* material (such as silicon) which is partly able to conduct electricity. **sem•i•con•scious,** *adj.* half conscious. **sem•i•de•tached,** *adj.* (house) which is joined to another similar house on one side, but is not joined on the other. **sem•i•fi•nal,** *n.* one of two matches in a competition, the winners of which go into the final game. **sem•i•fi•nal•ist,** *n.* team/player in a semifinal. **sem•i•of•fi•cial,** *adj.* not quite official. **sem•i•pre•cious,** *n.* (stone) which is quite valuable, but not in the same class as diamonds/rubies/sapphires, etc. **sem•i•skilled,** *adj.* (worker) who has been trained to a certain level. **sem•i•tone,** *n.* (*in music*) half a tone on the scale.

sem•i•nal ['semɪnl] *adj.* which acts as the starting point for sth new.

sem•i•nar ['semɪnɑː] *n.* meeting of a small group of students with a teacher to have discussions and report on research findings, etc.

sem•i•nar•y ['semɪnərɪ] *n.* college for priests.

Se•mit•ic [sə'mɪtɪk] *adj.* referring to a group of races including Jews and Arabs.

sem•o•li•na [semə'liːnə] *n.* hard crushed wheat, used to make spaghetti and milk puddings.

sen•ate ['senət] *n.* (a) governing or lawmaking group. (b) upper house of the legislature of the

United States, most U.S. states and certain other countries. **sen•a•tor,** *n.* member of a senate.

send [send] *v.* **(sent)** (a) to tell (s.o.) to go somewhere; to make (sth) go from one place to another. (b) to give (s.o.) a sensation; **it sends chills up my spine.** (c) to put out (roots, etc.). (d) *inf.* to make (s.o.) excited. **send a•way,** *v.* (a) to make (s.o./sth) go away. (b) **to s. a. for =** to write asking s.o. to send sth to you. **send back,** *v.* to return (sth). **send•er,** *n.* person who sends. **send for,** *v.* to pass a message to (s.o.) asking them to come. **send off,** *v.* (a) to make (s.o./sth) go off. (b) to mail; **to s. o. for =** send away for. **send-off,** *n.* party to say goodbye to s.o. leaving on a trip, starting a new job, etc. **send out,** *v.* to make (s.o./sth) go out. **send up,** *v.* to make (s.o./sth) go up.

se•nile ['si:naɪl] *adj.* old and mentally weak. **se•nil•i•ty** [sə'nɪlɪtɪ] *n.* being senile.

sen•ior ['si:njə] 1. *adj.* (a) older; **J. Smith S. =** father of J. Smith Junior; **s. citizen =** older person esp. one living on a pension. (b) more important (rank, etc.). 2. *n.* (a) older person. (b) student in his final year of school. **sen•ior•i•ty** [si:nɪ'ɒrɪtɪ] *n.* being senior.

sen•na ['senə] *n.* **s. pods =** dried pods used as a laxative.

sen•sa•tion [sen'seɪʃn] *n.* (a) feeling. (b) (thing/person that causes) great excitement. **sen•sa•tion•al,** *adj.* very exciting. **sen•sa•tion•al•ly,** *adv.* in a sensational way.

sense [sens] 1. *n.* (a) one of the five ways in which you notice sth; **sixth s. =** ability to feel that sth has taken place/will take place, without using any of the five senses. (b) feeling. (c) **senses =** power of reasoning; **to come to one's senses =** become reasonable. (d) meaning; **to make s. =** to have a meaning; **to make s. of =** to understand. (e) reasonableness/good judgment. 2. *v.* to feel. **sense•less,** *adj.* (a) stupid. (b) unconscious. **sense•less•ness,** *n.* stupidity.

sen•si•ble ['sensɪbl] *adj.* (a) reasonable/showing good judgment. (b) (person) who has common sense. (c) **s. walking shoes =** strong, but not fashionable, walking shoes. (d) (*formal*) **s. of =** aware of. **sen•si•bil•i•ty** [sensɪ'bɪlɪtɪ] *n.* being capable of delicate feeling. **sen•si•bly,** *adv.* in a sensible way.

sen•si•tive ['sensɪtɪv] *adj.* (a) able to feel keenly/sharply. (b) (instrument) which mea-

sures very accurately. (c) (substance) which reacts to light, etc. **sen•si•tiv•i•ty** [sensɪ'tɪvɪtɪ], **sen•si•tive•ness,** *n.* being sensitive. **sen•si•tive•ly,** *adv.* in a sensitive way. **sen•si•tize** ['sensɪtaɪz] *v.* to make sensitive (to light, etc.).

sen•sor ['sensə] *n.* apparatus which detects sth by sense of heat/light/smell of smoke, etc. **sen•so•ry,** *adj.* referring to the senses.

sen•su•al ['sensjʊəl] *adj.* referring to pleasures of the body, not of the mind. **sen•su•al•i•ty,** *n.* experience of sensual pleasure. **sen•su•al•ly,** *adv.* in a sensual way.

sen•su•ous ['sensjʊəs] *adj.* which gives pleasure to the senses. **sen•su•ous•ly,** *adv.* in a sensuous way.

sent [sent] *v. see* **send.**

sen•tence ['sentəns] 1. *n.* (a) words put together to form a complete separate statement. (b) decision of a judge which gives the details of punishment. 2. *v.* to condemn (s.o.) to a certain punishment.

sen•ten•tious [sen'tenʃəs] *adj.* too full of moral sense. **sen•ten•tious•ly,** *adv.* in a sententious way.

sen•tient ['senʃnt] *adj.* able to feel.

sen•ti•ment ['sentɪmənt] *n.* (a) show of feeling. (b) **sentiments =** opinions. **sen•ti•men•tal** [sentɪ'mentəl] *adj.* full of emotion/full of feeling. **sen•ti•men•tal•i•ty** [sentɪmən'tælɪtɪ] *n.* playing on the emotions (in literature/music). **sen•ti•men•tal•ly,** *adv.* by feeling.

sen•ti•nel ['sentɪnl] *n.* person or thing that watches or guards.

sen•try ['sentrɪ] *n.* sentinel, esp. a soldier on duty at a gate, etc. who watches and alerts others of danger. **sen•try box,** *n.* wooden shelter for a sentry.

se•pal ['sepəl] *n.* green leaf under the petals of a flower.

sep•a•rate 1. *adj.* ['seprət] detached/not together. 2. *v.* ['sepərert] to detach/to divide. 3. *n.* **separates =** pieces of women's clothing (skirts/blouse/sweater, etc.) which can be worn in different combinations. **sep•a•ra•ble** ['seprəbl] *adj.* which can be separated. **sep•a•rate•ly,** *adv.* in a separate way. **sep•a•ra•tion** [sepə'reɪʃn] *n.* dividing/living apart. **sep•a•ra•tism** ['sepərətɪzəm] *n.* political ideal of separating from a large country. **sep•a•ra•tist,** *adj. &*

n. (person) who wants his region to separate from a large country. **sep•a•ra•tor,** *n.* person/machine that separates.

se•pi•a ['si:pɪə] *n.* brown color.

sep•sis ['sepsɪs] *n.* being septic.

Sep•tem•ber [sep'tembə] *n.* 9th month of the year.

sep•ten•ni•al [sep'tenɪəl] *adj.* for seven years.

sep•tet [sep'tet] *n.* group of seven musicians; piece of music for seven instruments.

sep•tic ['septɪk] *adj.* (wound) which has gone bad/become poisoned; **s. tank** = underground tank near a house for collecting sewage.

sep•ti•ce•mi•a, septicaemia [septɪ'si:mɪə] *n.* poisoning of the blood.

sep•tu•a•ge•nar•i•an [septjuədʒə'neərɪən] *n.* person who is between seventy and seventy-nine years old.

sep•tum ['septəm] *n.* (*pl.* **-ta**) wall between two sections of the body/a plant.

sep•ul•cher, *Brit.* **sep•ul•chre** ['sepəlkə] *n.* tomb. **se•pul•chral** [se'pʌlkrəl] *adj.* referring to a sepulcher; very deep gloomy (voice).

se•quel ['si:kwəl] *n.* (a) continuation of a story, play, etc. (b) result.

se•quence ['si:kwəns] *n.* (a) series of things happening; series of numbers which follow each other. (b) scene in a motion picture. **se•quen•tial,** *adj.* in sequence. **se•quen•tial•ly,** *adv.* in sequence.

se•ques•ter [sɪ'kwestə] *v.* (*formal*) to seclude. **se•ques•trate** ['sekwɪstreɪt] *v.* (*formal*) to confiscate (property). **se•ques•tra•tor,** *n.* person who seizes property on the orders of a court.

se•quin ['si:kwɪn] *n.* small round shiny metal ornament. **se•quined,** *adj.* covered with sequins.

se•quoi•a [sɪ'kwɔɪə] *n.* redwood.

se•ragl•io [se'ræljəʊ] *n.* harem.

ser•aph ['serəf] *n.* (*pl.* **seraphs, seraphim**) highest angel. **se•raph•ic, seraphical,** *adj.* like a seraph.

ser•e•nade [serə'neɪd] 1. *n.* love song. 2. *v.* to sing a love song to (s.o.).

ser•en•dip•i•ty [serən'dɪpɪtɪ] *n.* pleasure which you get from finding things by accident.

se•rene [sə'ri:n] *adj.* calm/not worried. **se•rene•ly,** *adv.* in a serene way. **se•ren•i•ty** [sə'renɪtɪ] *n.* being serene.

serf [sɜ:f] *n.* peasant/slave working on a farm. **serf•dom,** *n.* state of being a serf.

serge [sɜ:dʒ] *n.* type of thick cloth.

ser•geant ['sɑ:dʒənt] *n.* (a) noncommissioned officer in the army/air force/marine corps. (b) police officer below a captain.

se•ri•al ['sɪərɪəl] 1. *adj.* (number) of a series. 2.

n. story/TV play which is told in several installments. **se•ri•al•ize,** *v.* to make (a novel, etc.) into a serial. **se•ri•al mo•nog•a•my,** *n.* practice of having a succession of long-lasting romantic sexual relationships.

se•ri•a•tim [sɪərɪ'ɑ:tɪm] *adv.* in order; in a series.

se•ries ['sɪəri:z] *n.* (*pl.* **series**) (a) group of things which come one after the other in a set order. (b) group of things that go together.

ser•if ['serɪf] *n.* little line added to the end of a stroke in a typeset character.

se•ri•ous ['sɪərɪəs] *adj.* (a) not humorous. (b) important/grave. **se•ri•ous•ly,** *adv.* in a serious way. **se•ri•ous•ness,** *n.* being serious.

ser•mon ['sɜ:mən] *n.* serious speech made in church. **ser•mon•ize,** *v.* to preach to (s.o.).

ser•pent ['sɜ:pənt] *n.* snake. **ser•pen•tine,** *adj.* like a snake; winding.

ser•rat•ed [sə'reɪtɪd] *adj.* toothed (blade); with a zigzag edge. **ser•ra•tion,** *n.* being serrated; serrated edge.

ser•ried ['serɪd] *adj.* **in s. ranks** = in ranks close together.

se•rum ['sɪərəm] *n.* yellow liquid in the blood, which can be injected into s.o.'s body to fight disease.

serve [sɜ:v] 1. *n.* act of serving the ball in tennis. 2. *v.* (a) to provide/to give (food); to put (food) before/at a table in a restaurant, etc.; (*of a recipe*) to make enough food for. (b) to work for. (c) to be useful (**as**). (d) to deal with (a customer). (e) to undergo punishment. (f) to start a game of tennis by hitting the ball first. (g) **it serves you right** = you deserve the punishment you got. (h) to assist a priest (at mass). **serv•ant,** *n.* (a) person who is paid to work in the house. (b) **civil s.** = government employee. **serv•er,** *n.* (a) person who serves at a table. (b) large flat knife for serving food; spoon/fork for serving fish or salad. (c) person who helps a priest (at mass). (d) computer hardware/software that distributes files/databases to other computers on a network.

serv•ice ['sɜ:vɪs] 1. *n.* (a) working for s.o.; **military s.** = period which you spend in the armed forces; **s. charge** = charge added to a bill for sth done; **s. road** = road which runs alongside a major highway, giving access to stores and houses. (b) group of people working together; **civil s.** = all the government employees; **the foreign s.** = people who represent their country abroad; **the services** = the armed forces. (c) providing basic essentials which people require; **bus s.** = regularly passing bus. (d) regular religious ceremony. (e) act of starting a game of tennis by hitting the ball first. (f) set of china for use at meals. (g) repairs to a machine, done on a regular basis; **the car needs a**

s. = examination by the garage; **s. area** = place along a highway where you can stop and buy fuel/get food, etc. 2. *v.* to do any repairs which need doing to (a car, etc.). **serv•ice•a•ble**, *adj.* practical; which will be useful. **serv•ice•man**, *n.* (*pl.* **-men**) member of the armed forces of a country. **serv•ice sta•tion**, *n.* place which sells fuel/oil, etc. **serv•ice•wom•an**, *n.* (*pl.* **-women**) woman member of the armed forces of a country.

ser•vile ['sɜː vail] *adj.* like a slave. **ser•vile•ly**, *adv.* in a servile way. **ser•vil•i•ty** [sɜː'vɪlɪtɪ] *n.* acting like a slave. **ser•vi•tude** ['sɜːvɪtjuːd] *n.* slavery.

servo- ['sɜː vəʊ] *prefix meaning* power-assisted.

ses•a•me ['sesəmiː] *n.* tropical plant whose seeds produce oil or are eaten.

ses•sion ['seʃn] *n.* (a) meeting of a committee/legislative body, etc.; **in s.** = in the process of meeting. (b) meeting to study/to practice.

set [set] 1. *n.* (a) group of things which go together; (*in mathematics*) group of numbers, etc., which are linked. (b) apparatus for sending or receiving radio, television, or other communication. (c) one of the main parts of a tennis match. (d) group of people. (e) scenery on a stage. (f) position/direction. (g) arranging of hair. 2. *v.* (**set**) (a) to put/to place; **to s. the table** = put the knives and forks, etc. on the table. (b) to arrange/to fix (a machine, etc.). (c) to arrange in place. (d) to make (free, etc.). (e) to become solid. (f) (*of sun/stars*) to go down. (g) to write music to go with (a poem, etc.). (h) to place scenery on a stage; to put (the action of a story) in a certain period. (i) to arrange letters in rows for printing. 3. *adj.* (a) fixed/which cannot be changed. (b) ready. **set a•bout**, *v.* to start doing (sth). **set a•side**, *v.* (a) to put to one side/to reject. (b) to keep (for future use). **set back**, *v.* (a) to make late. (b) *inf.* **it s. me back $10** = it cost me $10. **set•back**, *n.* holding back of progress. **set down**, *v.* to write down on paper. **set forth**, *v.* (a) to start a journey. (b) to write out (a list, etc.). **set in**, *v.* to start. **set off**, *v.* (a) to start a journey (b) to light (fireworks); to make (a bomb) explode; to start (a reaction). (c) to show up; make prominent. **set out**, *v.* (a) to put out. (b) to start a journey. **set•ting**, *n.* (a) action of setting. (b) background for a story; frame in which a diamond or other stone is fixed. (c) **place s.** = set of knives/forks/spoons, etc., for one person. **set to**, *v.* to get to work.

set-to, *n. inf.* argument/fight. **set up**, *v.* to build/to establish. **set•up**, *n. inf.* arrangement/organization. **set up•on**, *v.* to attack.

set•tee [se'tiː] *n.* sofa.

set•ter ['setə] *n.* hunting dog trained to point out game by standing still.

set•tle ['setl] 1. *n.* long wooden bench with a back. 2. *v.* (a) to arrange/to agree; to end (a dispute); **to s. up** = pay the bill; **to s. on/for** = to decide on/to choose. (b) (*also* **settle down**) to place yourself in a comfortable position/to rest. (c) to go to live in a new country. (d) (*of sediment*) to fall to the bottom of a liquid; (*of building*) to sink into the ground. (e) to pass money, etc. to s.o. by a formal or legal process. **set•tled**, *adj.* fixed/unchanging. **set•tle•ment**, *n.* (a) payment (of a bill); agreement in a dispute. (b) place where a group of people has settled. (c) settling money, etc., on s.o. (d) (*of building*) act of sinking into the ground. **set•tler**, *n.* person who goes to settle in a new country.

sev•en ['sevn] *n.* number 7. **sev•en•teen**, *n.* number 17. **sev•en•teenth**, **17th**, *adj. & n.* referring to seventeen; **the s. century** = period from 1600 to 1699. **sev•enth**, **7th**, *adj. & n.* referring to seven. **sev•en•ti•eth**, **70th**, *adj. & n.* referring to seventy. **sev•en•ty**, *n.* number 70.

sev•er ['sevə] *v.* to cut off. **sev•er•ance**, *n.* cutting off; **s. pay** = money paid as compensation to s.o. who is losing a job.

sev•er•al ['sevrəl] *adj. & pron.* more than a few, but not very many. **sev•er•al•ly**, *adv.* separately.

se•vere [sə'vɪə] *adj.* (**-er**, **-est**) (a) very strict. (b) very bad (illness, weather, etc.). **se•vere•ly**, *adv.* (a) strictly. (b) badly. **se•ver•i•ty** [sə-'verɪtɪ] *n.* being severe.

sew [səʊ] *v.* (**sewn**) to attach/to mend by using a needle and thread; to make (with a needle and thread). **sew•ing**, *n.* (a) action of attaching/mending with needle and thread. (b) work which s.o. is in the process of sewing. **sew•ing ma•chine**, *n.* machine which sews. **sew up**, *v.* (a) to close (a hole) by sewing. (b) *inf.* to settle (a deal).

sew•er ['suə] *n.* large tube in the ground used for taking away waste and dirty water from houses and other buildings. **sew•age** ['suːɪdʒ] *n.* waste and dirty water. **sew•er•age**, *n.* system of sewers for removing waste and dirty water.

æ **back**, ɑː **farm**, ɒ **top**, aɪ **pipe**, aʊ **how**, aɪə **fire**, aʊə **flower**, ɔː **bought**, ɔɪ **toy**, e **fed**, eə **hair**, eɪ **take**, ə **afraid**, əʊ **boat**, əʊə **lower**, ɜː **word**, iː **heap**, ɪ **hit**, ɪə **hear**, uː **school**, ʊ **book**, ʌ **but**, b **back**, d **dog**, ð **then**, dʒ **just**, f **fog**, g **go**, h **hand**, j **yes**, k **catch**, l **last**, m **mix**, n **nut**, ŋ **sing**, p **penny**, r **round**, s **some**, ʃ **short**, t **too**, tʃ **chop**, θ **thing**, v **voice**, w **was**, z **zoo**, ʒ **treasure**

sex [seks] 1. *n.* (*pl.* **-es**) (a) one of two groups (male and female) into which animals and plants can be divided; **s. appeal** = attractiveness to members of the other sex. (b) **to have s. with s.o.** = to have sexual intercourse. 2. *v.* **to s. chickens** = to tell whether chickens are male or female. **sex•ism**, *n.* bias against one sex. **sex•ist**, *adj. & n.* (person) who is biased against one of the sexes. **sex•less**, *adj.* without sex; not involving sexual feeling. **sex•o•log•i•cal**, *adj.* referring to sexology. **sex•ol•o•gist**, *n.* person who studies sexual behavior. **sex•ol•o•gy** [sek'sɒlədʒi] *n.* study of sexual behavior. **sex•u•al** ['seksjʊəl] *adj.* referring to sex; **s. intercourse** = reproductive act between a male and female. **sex•u•al•i•ty**, *n.* interest in sexual intercourse. **sex•u•al•ly**, *adv.* in a sexual way. **sex•y**, *adj.* sexually attractive.

sex•a•ge•nar•i•an [seksədʒə'neərɪən] *adj. & n.* (person) who is between sixty years and sixty-nine years old.

sex•tant ['sekstənt] *n.* instrument for calculating the position of a ship by referring to the stars.

sex•tet [seks'tet] *n.* (a) group of six musicians playing together. (b) piece of music for six musicians.

sex•ton ['sekstən] *n.* man who works in a church/rings the bells/digs graves, etc.

sh [ʃ] *inter.* used to make silence.

shab•by ['ʃæbɪ] *adj.* (**-ier, -iest**) poor/worn out (clothes); mean (trick). **shab•bi•ly**, *adv.* in a shabby way. **shab•bi•ness**, *n.* being shabby.

shack [ʃæk] 1. *n.* rough wooden hut. 2. *v. Sl.* **to s. up with s.o.** = to go to live with s.o.

shack•le ['ʃækl] 1. *n.* thing which hampers movement; **shackles** = chains (for attaching a prisoner). 2. *v.* to attach (s.o.) with a chain.

shade [ʃeɪd] 1. *n.* (a) dark place which is not in the sunlight. (b) dark part of a picture. (c) cover put on a lamp; blind on a window. (d) type of color; slight difference. (e) little bit. (f) *inf.* **shades** = sunglasses. (g) (*formal*) ghost. 2. *v.* (a) to protect (sth) from sunlight. (b) to make (a picture) darker. (c) (*also* **shade off**) to change from one color to another gradually. **shad•i•ness**, *n.* being shady. **shad•ing**, *n.* action of making shade; making part of a picture darker. **shad•y**, *adj.* (**-ier, -iest**) (a) full of shade. (b) dishonest/disreputable.

shad•ow ['ʃædəʊ] 1. *n.* (a) shade made by an object in light; **five o'clock s.** = dark tint on a man's chin as his beard begins to grow. (b) small amount. (c) person who follows s.o. 2. *v.* to follow (s.o.). **shad•ow•y**, *adj.* vague/indistinct.

shaft [ʃɑːft] *n.* (a) long stick which is the main part of an arrow/a javelin, etc.; long pole in front of a cart to which a horse is attached. (b) ray of light. (c) rod which turns in an engine. (d) pillar. (e) deep hole in the ground; **elevator s.** = hole down the center of a building in which an elevator moves up and down.

shag [ʃæg] *n.* (a) thick tobacco. (b) type of black sea bird.

shag•gy ['ʃægɪ] *adj.* (**-ier, -iest**) with long hair; **s. dog story** = very long story with an unexpectedly silly ending.

shake [ʃeɪk] 1. *n.* (a) act of moving from side to side or up and down. (b) drink made by mixing milk and flavoring. 2. *v.* (**shook** [ʃʊk]; **shaken**) to move from side to side or up and down; **to s. one's head** = to move one's head from side to side to indicate "no". **shake down**, *v.* to cause to settle. **shake•down**, *n.* rough bed. **shak•en**, *adj.* very upset/disturbed. **shake off**, *v.* to get rid of (sth unpleasant). **shak•er**, *n.* person/machine which shakes; container for mixing cocktails. **shake-up**, *n. inf.* total change. **shak•i•ly**, *adv.* in a shaky way. **shak•i•ness**, *n.* being shaky. **shak•y**, *adj.* (**-ier, -iest**) (a) wobbly; trembling. (b) not very reliable.

shale [ʃeɪl] *n.* type of rock which splits into soft thin slices.

shall [ʃæl] *v.* used with **I** *and* **we** *to form future* (*past* **should**) (a) (*suggestion/request*) **s. we sit down?** (b) (*emphasis in the future*) **yes I s.!** (*note: except for* (a) **shall** *is gradually being replaced by* **will**); *see also* **should**.

shal•lot [ʃə'lɒt] *n.* type of small onion which grows in clusters.

shal•low ['ʃæləʊ] 1. *adj.* (**-er, -est**) (a) not deep. (b) superficial (mind). 2. *n.* **shallows** = water which is not deep. **shal•low•ness**, *n.* being shallow.

sham [ʃæm] 1. *adj.* false. 2. *n.* thing which is false. 3. *v.* (**shammed**) to pretend.

sham•ble ['ʃæmbl] *v.* **to s. along** = to wander along dragging your feet.

sham•bles ['ʃæmblz] *n.* disorder/mess.

shame [ʃeɪm] 1. *n.* (a) feeling caused by being guilty/being ashamed. (b) **what a s.** = what a pity/how sad. 2. *v.* **to s. s.o. into** = to make s.o. ashamed so that he does sth. **shame•faced**, *adj.* embarrassed/ashamed. **shame•fac•ed•ly**, *adv.* in embarrassment. **shame•ful**, *adj.* scandalous/disgraceful. **shame•ful•ly**, *adv.* in a shameful way. **shame•less**, *adj.* without shame. **shame•less•ly**, *adv.* in a shameless way.

sham•poo [ʃæm'puː] 1. *n.* liquid soap for washing your hair/a carpet, etc. 2. *v.* to wash (your hair/the carpet, etc.) with a shampoo.

sham•rock [ˈʃæmrɒk] n. small cloverlike plant with leaves which are split into three parts.

shang•hai [ʃæŋˈhaɪ] v. (**shanghaied**) to capture (s.o.) and force them to obey your orders, esp. to force s.o. to join the crew of a ship.

shank [ʃæŋk] n. (a) straight shaft. (b) leg.

shan't [ʃɑːnt] v. contraction of shall not.

shan•ty [ˈʃæntɪ] n. (a) rough wooden hut; **s. town** = group of huts belonging to poor people. (b) chantey.

shape [ʃeɪp] 1. n. (a) form; **the picture is taking s.** = is beginning to look like sth. (b) mold or pattern for forming sth into a shape. (c) condition. 2. v. (a) to form/to make into a shape. (b) **to s. up well** = turn out well. **shape•less**, adj. with no definite shape. **shape•less•ness**, n. being shapeless. **shape•li•ness**, n. being shapely. **shape•ly**, adj. with an attractive shape.

shard [ʃɑːd] n. piece of broken pottery.

share [ˈʃeə] 1. n. (a) part which belongs to someone. (b) contribution which each person makes. (c) one of the parts into which a company's capital is divided. (d) plowshare, the metal blade of a plow. 2. v. (a) to divide up among several people. (b) **to s. sth with s.o.** = to allow s.o. to use sth which you also use. (c) to have/to use (sth) in common. **share•hold•er**, n. person who owns shares in a company. **share•hold•ing**, n. group of shares in a company owned by one person.

shark [ʃɑːk] n. (a) large dangerous fish which can kill a man. (b) inf. crook/swindler.

sharp [ʃɑːp] 1. adj. (-er, -est) (a) with a fine cutting edge. (b) very cutting/harsh. (c) with a very acute angle. (d) bitter. (e) clever/intelligent. (f) with a highly-developed sense. (g) high-pitched (sound). (h) (in music) (note) which is slightly higher than the correct pitch. (i) clear (image). 2. n. note in music which is a semitone higher. 3. adv. (a) acutely. (b) exactly. (c) (in music) higher than the correct pitch. **sharp•en**, v. to make sharp. **sharp•en•er**, n. pencil s. = instrument for sharpening pencils. **sharp•er**, n. (also **sharpie**) person who cheats at cards. **sharp•ly**, adv. (a) acutely. (b) completely. (c) harshly. **sharp•ness**, n. being sharp. **sharp•shoot•er**, n. person who can shoot very accurately. **sharp-wit•ted**, adj. clever.

shat•ter [ˈʃætə] v. to break into little pieces; to upset (s.o.) very badly.

shave [ʃeɪv] 1. n. act of cutting off the hair on your face, legs, etc. with a razor; **close s.** = near miss. 2. v. (a) to cut off the hair on your face, legs, etc. (b) to slice very thin pieces off (sth).

shav•en, adj. (old) shaved. **shav•er**, n. razor; machine for shaving. **shav•ing**, n. (a) act of cutting off hair; **s. cream** = cream which you put on your face before shaving. (b) **shavings** = small thin slices of wood cut off by a plane.

shawl [ʃɔːl] n. large square of warm material for wrapping around your shoulders/your head.

she [ʃiː] (a) pron. referring to a female person. (b) prefix meaning female; **she-wolf.**

sheaf [ʃiːf] n. (pl. **sheaves** [ʃiːvz]) bundle of corn/of papers.

shear [ˈʃɪə] v. (**sheared/shorn** [ʃɔːn]) to cut the wool off (sheep, etc.); to cut (**through** sth). **shear•er**, n. person who cuts the wool off sheep. **shears**, n. cutting tool like large scissors. **shear•wa•ter**, n. type of small dark sea bird.

sheath [ʃiːθ] n. (a) holder (for a knife, etc.). (b) rubber contraceptive. **sheathe** [ʃiːð] v. to put a knife back into its sheath. **sheath knife**, n. (pl. **-knives**) knife kept in a sheath.

sheaves [ʃiːvz] n. see **sheaf.**

shed [ʃed] 1. n. wooden building. 2. v. (**shed**) (a) to lose (leaves); to lose/to take off (clothes). (b) to let flow (blood, tears, light); **to s. light on** = to make clearer.

sheen [ʃiːn] n. brilliant shining surface.

sheep [ʃiːp] n. (pl. **sheep**) farm animal, reared for wool or for meat. **sheep dip**, n. bath of disinfectant into which sheep are put to kill parasites. **sheep•dog**, n. type of dog specially trained for herding sheep. **sheep•ish**, adj. ashamed/embarrassed. **sheep•ish•ly**, adv. with a sheepish air. **sheep•ish•ness**, n. being sheepish. **sheep•shank**, n. knot tied to make a rope shorter. **sheep•skin**, n. skin of a sheep with the wool attached.

sheer [ˈʃɪə] 1. adj. (a) complete/total. (b) very steep. (c) very fine (stockings, etc.). 2. adv. straight up or down. 3. v. to swerve.

sheet [ʃiːt] n. (a) large piece of thin cloth which is put on a bed. (b) large flat piece (of paper/cardboard/plywood, etc.); **s. feed** = device which allows separate sheets of paper to be fed into a printer. **s. lightning** = lightning which appears as a sheet and not as a single flash. (c) rope for attaching a sail. **sheet an•chor**, n. large anchor used if a ship is in difficulties.

æ back, ɑː farm, ɒ top, aɪ pipe, aʊ how, aɪə fire, aʊə flower, ɔː bought, ɔɪ toy, e fed, eəhair, eɪ take, ə afraid, əʊ boat, əʊə lower, ɜː word, iː heap, ɪ hit, ɪə hear, uː school, ʊ book, ʌ but, b back, d dog, ð then, dʒ just, f fog, g go, h hand, j yes, k catch, l last, m mix, n nut, ŋ sing, p penny, r round, s some, ʃ short, t too, tʃ chop, θ thing, v voice, w was, z zoo, ʒ treasure

sheik [ʃeɪk] *n.* Arab leader. **sheik•dom** [ʃeɪkdəm] *n.* country ruled by a sheik.

shel•drake, shelduck [ʃeldreɪk, ʃeldʌk] *n.* type of wild duck.

shelf [ʃelf] *n. (pl.* **shelves** [ʃelvz]) (a) plank attached to a wall/in a cupboard on which things can be put; *inf.* **on the s.** = (i) left behind/forgotten about; (ii) not married (when all your friends are married); **s. life** = length of time food can be kept in a store before it goes bad. (b) narrow ledge of rock.

shell [ʃel] 1. *n.* (a) hard outside of some animals. (b) hard outside of an egg/a nut. (c) exterior of a car/building. (d) metal tube full of explosive fired from a gun. 2. *v.* (a) to take (peas) out of their pods/(a hardboiled egg) out of its shell. (b) to bombard with shells. **shell•fish,** *n. (no pl.)* sea animal with a shell (such as a crab/mussel, etc.). **shell out,** *v. inf.* to pay money. **shell shock,** *n.* illness in soldiers caused by being in battle.

shel•lac [ʃelæk] *n.* resin used to make varnish.

shel•ter [ʃeltə] 1. *n.* place where you can go for protection. 2. *v.* to give (s.o.) protection; to take shelter. **shel•tered,** *adj.* protected from wind/cold/unpleasant happenings.

shelve [ʃelv] 1. *v.* (a) to put off discussing a problem. (b) to slope down. (c) to put (sth) on a shelf. 2. *n. pl. see* **shelf. shelv•ing,** *n.* set of shelves.

she•nan•i•gans [ʃɪˈnænɪgənz] *n. pl. inf.* (a) mischief. (b) dishonest trick.

shep•herd [ʃepəd] 1. *n.* man who looks after sheep; **s.'s pie** = minced meat cooked with mashed potatoes on top. 2. *v.* to guide. **shep•herd•ess,** *n.* woman who looks after sheep.

sher•bet [ʃɜːbət] *n.* frozen dessert made with fruit juice, water and either milk or egg white.

sher•iff [ʃerɪf] *n.* county police officer.

sher•ry [ʃerɪ] *n.* type of strong wine, originally from Spain.

shib•bo•leth [ʃɪbələθ] *n.* slogan/policy formerly considered important.

shield [ʃiːld] 1. *n.* (a) large protective plate carried by riot police/knights in armor, etc. (b) protection against sth dangerous. 2. *v.* to protect.

shift [ʃɪft] 1. *n.* (a) change of place/of direction; **s. key** = key on a typewriter/computer which makes capital letters. (b) group of workers who work for a period and whose place is then taken by another group. (c) loose dress. 2. *v.* (a) to change position/direction; to move. (b) *inf.* **to s. for yourself** = to look after yourself. **shift•i•ness,** *n.* dishonesty. **shift•less,** *adj.* lazy. **shift•y,** *adj.* (-ier, -iest) looking dishonest.

shil•le•lagh [ʃɪˈleɪlɪ] *n.* (*in Ireland*) thick stick.

shil•ling [ʃɪlɪŋ] *n.* currency used in Kenya and some other countries; old British coin worth 12 pence.

shil•ly-shal•ly [ʃɪlɪˈʃælɪ] *v.* to hesitate.

shim•mer [ʃɪmə] 1. *n.* soft quivering light. 2. *v.* to quiver with light.

shin [ʃɪn] 1. *n.* front of the bottom part of your leg. 2. *v.* (**shinned**) **to s. up a tree** = to climb up.

shin•dig, shindy [ʃɪndɪg, ʃɪndɪ] *n. inf.* row/noisy party.

shine [ʃaɪn] 1. *n.* (a) brightness. (b) act of polishing. 2. *v.* (**shone** [ʃɒn]) (a) to glint brightly. (b) to be brilliant. (c) to polish. **shin•ing,** *adj.* brilliant. **shin•y,** *adj.* (-ier, -iest) bright/polished.

shin•gle [ʃɪŋgl] *n.* (a) mass of small stones on a beach. (b) flat piece of wood/slate, etc. nailed on a wall or roof as a covering. (c) **shingles** = disease related to chickenpox causing a painful rash. **shin•gly,** *adj.* covered with small stones.

ship [ʃɪp] 1. *n.* large boat for carrying goods/passengers. 2. *v.* (**shipped**) (a) to put/to take on board a ship. (b) to send (goods), not necessarily on a ship. **ship•build•er,** *n.* person who builds ships. **ship•build•ing,** *n.* building of ships. **ship•mate,** *n.* sailor on the same ship as you. **ship•ment,** *n.* (a) sending of goods. (b) quantity of goods shipped. **ship•own•er,** *n.* person who owns a ship. **ship•per,** *n.* person who sends goods. **ship•ping,** *n.* (a) sending of goods; **s. company** = which specializes in the sending of goods. (b) (group of) ships; **s. lanes** = routes across the sea which are regularly used by ships. **ship•shape,** *adj.* neat/tidy. **ship•wreck,** *n.* wrecking of a ship. **ship•wrecked,** *adj.* (person) involved in a shipwreck. **ship•yard,** *n.* works where ships are built.

shire [ʃaɪə] *n. Brit.* county.

shirk [ʃɜːk] *v.* to try not to do sth/not to work. **shirk•er,** *n.* person who shirks.

shirr [ʃɜː] *v.* (a) to gather (cloth) by running threads through it. (b) to bake (beaten eggs).

shirt [ʃɜːt] *n.* piece of light clothing worn on the top part of the body; *inf.* **keep your s. on!** = keep calm/don't lose your temper or patience. **shirt•sleeves,** *n.* **in one's s.** = not wearing a jacket. **shirt•waist,** *n.* woman's dress where the top part looks like a shirt. **shirt•y,** *adj. inf.* angry.

shish•ke•bab [ʃɪʃkɪbæb] *n.* small pieces of meat and vegetables cooked on a skewer.

shit [ʃɪt] 1. *n.* (*vulgar*) (a) excreta/solid waste matter from the body. (b) *Sl* dirt. (c) *Sl* nonsense. 2. *v.* (*vulgar*) to pass solid waste matter from the body.

shiv•er ['ʃɪvə] 1. *n.* tremble (with cold/fear). 2. *v.* (a) to tremble (with cold/fear/fever). (b) to break into tiny pieces. **shiv•er•y**, *adj.* trembling (esp. with fever).

shoal [ʃəʊl] *n.* (a) (*also* **shoals**) bank of sand under the water. (b) group of fish swimming about.

shock [ʃɒk] 1. *n.* (a) untidy mass (of hair). (b) sudden (unpleasant) surprise. (c) mental/physical collapse (after a blow/a sudden surprise). (d) **electric s.** = sudden painful passing of electric current through the body; **electric s. treatment** = medical treatment of mental illness using electric shocks. (e) great blow; **s. absorbers** = part of a car/aircraft which reduces the effect of bumps. 2. *v.* to give (s.o.) a sudden (unpleasant) surprise. **shock•er**, *n. inf.* shocking person/thing. **shock•head•ed**, *adj.* with a mass of hair. **shock•ing**, *adj.* upsetting/unpleasant. **shock•ing•ly**, *adv.* in a shocking way. **shock jock** *n. inf.* radio disc jockey who is intentionally outrageous. **shock•proof**, *adj.* (watch, etc.) which is not affected by shocks. **shock troops**, *n.* soldiers specially trained to attack violently.

shod [ʃɒd] *adj.* wearing shoes.

shod•dy ['ʃɒdɪ] 1. *n.* poor quality cloth. 2. *adj.* (-ier, -iest) (a) badly made. (b) low/nasty (trick). **shod•di•ly**, *adv.* in a shoddy way. **shod•di•ness**, *n.* bad quality.

shoe [ʃu:] 1. *n.* (a) article of clothing which you wear on your feet both inside and outside the house, not covering your ankles; **in his shoes** = in his place/in the situation he is in. (b) ring of metal nailed under a horse's hoof. (c) **brake shoes** = curved metal blocks which tighten around a wheel. 2. *v.* (**shod/shoed**) to attach metal horseshoes to the hooves of (a horse). **shoe•horn**, *n.* curved piece of plastic/metal which you put into the heel of a shoe to make it easier to put on. **shoe•lace**, *n.* lace for tying up shoes. **shoe•mak•er**, *n.* person who makes and mends shoes. **shoe•shine**, *n.* polishing of shoes. **shoe•string**, *n.* shoelace; on **a s.** = with only a little money. **shoe•tree**, *n.* device which is put in a shoe to help keep its shape.

shone [ʃɒn] *v. see* **shine.**

shoo [ʃu:] 1. *inter. meaning* go away. 2. *v.* **to s. away** = to frighten away (birds/small children, etc.).

shook [ʃʊk] *v. see* **shake.**

shoot [ʃu:t] 1. *n.* (a) new growth on a plant. (b) expedition to kill wild animals with guns; **turkey s.** 2. *v.* (**shot** [ʃɒt]) (a) to fire a bullet from a gun/an arrow from a bow; to kill (s.o./an animal) with a bullet or an arrow. (b) to rush/to go fast; **to s. the rapids** = to race through rapids in a light boat. (c) (*in sports*) to kick or throw a ball, etc.; to score (a goal). (d) to make (a motion picture). **shoot down**, *v.* to make (an aircraft) crash by hitting it with a shell. **shoot•ing**. 1. *n.* action of shooting with a gun; **s. stick** = walking stick with a handle which unfolds to make a seat. 2. *adj.* which goes very fast; **s. star** = meteor. **shoot up**, *v.* to go up fast.

shop [ʃɒp] 1. *n.* (a) store, usu. small, where you can buy goods. (b) workshop/place where goods are made; **closed s.** = works where all the workers have to belong to a single union; **to talk s.** = to talk about your job/about your office. 2. *v.* (**shopped**) to buy things in a store; **to s. around** = to go to various stores and compare prices before buying what you want. **shop•keep•er**, *n.* person who owns or runs a shop. **shop•lift•er**, *n.* person who steals things from a store. **shop•lift•ing**, *n.* stealing from a store. **shop•per**, *n.* person who buys goods from a store. **shop•ping**, *n.* (a) goods which you have bought in a store. (b) action of buying things in a store. **shop•worn**, *adj.* made dirty by being on display in a store. **shop stew•ard**, *n.* elected union representative in a factory/office, etc.

shore [ʃɔ:] 1. *n.* (a) land at the edge of the sea or a lake; beach. (b) prop. 2. *v.* to hold **up** (sth) which might fall down.

shorn [ʃɔ:n] *adj.* cut off; *see also* **shear.**

short [ʃɔ:t] 1. *adj.* (-er, est) (a) not long. (b) not long in time; **in s.** = briefly. (c) not tall. (d) rude. (e) not enough/not as much as is needed (of); **s. weight** = not quite as much in weight as supposed. (f) light/crumbly (pastry). 2. *n.* (a) short motion picture. (b) short-circuit. (c) *pl.* **shorts** = trousers not going below the knee. 3. *adv.* (a) abruptly; **to stop s.** (b) not far enough; **to fall s.** 4. *v.* to short-circuit. **short•age**, *n.* lack. **short•bread**, *n.* thick sweet crumbly biscuit. **short•cake**, *n.* (a) shortbread. (b) dessert made with biscuits or cake with fruit and cream. **short•change**, *v.* to cheat (s.o.). **short-cir•cuit**. 1. *n.* jump of electric current between two points, missing out part of the normal circuit. 2. *v.* (a) to make a short-circuit. (b) to get through difficulties by

---

æ back, a: farm, ɒ: top, aɪ pipe, aʊ how, aɪə fire, aʊə flower, ɔ: bought, ɔɪ toy, e fed, eəhair, eɪ take, ə afraid, əʊ boat, əʊə lower, ɜ: word, i: heap, ɪ hit, ɪə hear, u: school, ʊ book, ʌ but, b back, d dog, ð then, dʒ just, f fog, g go, h hand, j yes, k catch, l last, m mix, n nut, ŋ sing, p penny, r round, s some, ʃ short, t too, tʃ chop, θ thing, v voice, w was, z zoo, ʒ treasure

taking a short cut. **short•com•ing,** *n.* fault/defect. **short•cut,** *n.* way which is shorter than usual; quicker way of reaching your destination. **short•en,** *v.* to make/to become shorter. **short•en•ing,** *n.* lard/cooking fat. **short•fall,** *n.* amount which is missing to make up an expected total. **short•hand,** *n.* way of writing fast by using a system of signs. **short-hand•ed,** *adj.* not having enough workers. **short•horn,** *n.* type of cattle with short horns. **short list,** *n.* list of some of the people who have applied for a job, and who have been chosen to come for an interview. **short-list,** *v.* to make a short list of (candidates) for a job; to put (s.o.'s name) on a short list. **short-lived,** *adj.* which does not last long. **short•ly,** *adv.* (a) soon. (b) abruptly/rudely. **short•ness,** *n.* (a) state of being short. (b) rudeness. **short or•der,** *n.* food cooked on the spot in a restaurant (such as ham and eggs). **short•sight•ed,** *adj.* (a) (person) who can only see near objects. (b) not paying attention to what may happen in the future. **short•sight•ed•ness,** *n.* being shortsighted. **short-sleeved,** *adj.* (shirt, etc.) with short sleeves. **short-staffed,** *adj.* with not enough workers. **short-tem•pered,** *adj.* (person) who easily gets angry. **short-term,** *adj.* not lasting long. **short time,** *n.* shorter working hours than usual. **short wave,** *n.* radio wave about 50 meters long.

shot [ʃɒt] 1. *adj.* (silk) which changes color according to the light. 2. *n.* (a) (*no pl.*) small pellets/bullets fired from a gun. (b) large heavy ball thrown in a competition; **to put the s.** = throw the weight in a competition. (c) act of shooting; the sound of shooting; **like a s.** = very rapidly. (d) person who shoots. (e) *inf.* attempt. (f) *Sl.* injection. (g) *Sl.* small drink of alcohol. (h) *inf.* photograph. *see also* **shoot. shot•gun,** *n.* gun which fires small pellets.

should [ʃud] *v. used to show certain moods.* (a) ought; **they s. have arrived by now** = they ought to have arrived. (b) must; **why s. I be the one to go?** = why must I be the one? (c) **who s. we meet but my aunt** = what a surprise we had when we met my aunt. (d) (*tentative suggestion*) **s. I try again?** (e) (*future after* that) **it is strange that he s. want to go.**

shoul•der ['ʃəuldə] 1. *n.* (a) part of the body at the top of the arm/between the top of the arm and the neck. (b) part of a piece of clothing between the top of the arm and the neck. (c) top part of the front leg of an animal. (d) reinforced side part of a road. 2. *v.* (a) to put on your shoulder. (b) to push with your shoulder. (c) to take on (a burden). **shoulder bag,** *n.* bag which can be carried over the shoulder.

shoul•der blade, *n.* large flat bone in the shoulder.

shout [ʃaut] 1. *n.* loud cry. 2. *v.* to make a loud cry; **to s. s.o. down** = to shout so loudly that s.o. cannot speak.

shove [ʃʌv] 1. *n. inf.* sharp push. 2. *v. inf.* to give a push to. **shove off,** *v. inf.* to go away.

shov•el ['ʃʌvl] 1. *n.* tool with a wide blade and a long handle, used for lifting dirt, snow, etc. 2. *v.* (**shoveled, shovelled**) to lift up with a shovel. **shov•el•ful,** *n.* contents of a shovel. **shov•el•er,** *n.* wild duck with a wide flat beak.

show [ʃəu] 1. *n.* (a) exhibition/display. (b) performance; **s. business** = actors/actresses/producers etc. (considered as a group); the entertainment world. (c) pretense. 2. *v.* (**shown**) (a) to make (sth) seen; to allow s.o. to see (sth); to be seen. (b) to indicate. (c) to point out/to direct. (d) to prove/to demonstrate. **show•case,** *n.* case or box with a glass front or a glass top for putting things on show in a store or museum. **show•down,** *n.* final argument which will solve a crisis. **show•i•ly,** *adv.* in a showy way. **show•i•ness,** *n.* being showy. **show-jump•er,** *n.* horse specially trained for show-jumping. **show-jump•ing,** *n.* riding competition where horses have to jump over different obstacles in a short time. **show•man,** *n.* (*pl.* **-men**) person who puts on shows (such as circuses, etc.); person who is good at presenting things. **show•man•ship,** *n.* art of putting on attractive shows. **show off,** *v.* (a) to display (sth) to great effect. (b) to try to make people look at you by doing sth which will attract their attention. **show-off,** *n. inf.* person who shows off. **show•piece,** *n.* important item in an exhibition. **show•room,** *n.* room where goods are shown to customers. **show up,** *v.* (a) to reveal/to show (s.o.'s/sth's faults). (b) to stand out. (c) *inf.* to arrive. **show•y,** *adj.* (**-ier, -iest**) too bright (colors); too ostentatious.

show•er ['ʃauə] 1. *n.* (a) light fall of rain/small stones, etc. (b) (*also* **showerhead**) spray device in a bathroom for washing your whole body. (c) (*also* **shower bath**) bath taken in a spray of water from above. (d) party where presents are given to a girl about to get married. 2. *v.* (a) (*also* **shower down**) to pour/to fall in a quantity. (b) to wash under a spray. **show•er•proof,** *adj.* (coat) which can protect against light rain. **shower stall,** *n.* separate unit with a shower in it. **show•er•y,** *adj.* with many showers.

shrank [ʃræŋk] *v. see* **shrink.**

shrap•nel ['ʃræpnl] *n.* (*no pl.*) pieces of metal from an exploded shell or bomb, etc.

shred [ʃred] 1. *n.* (a) long strip torn off sth. (b) small piece. 2. *v.* (**shredded**) to tear into long strips; to cut into very thin strips. **shred•der,** *n.* machine for tearing waste paper into long strips; device for cutting vegetables into long thin strips.

shrew [ʃruː] *n.* (a) animal like a mouse with a long nose. (b) unpleasant bad-tempered woman who is always criticizing. **shrew•ish,** *adj.* bad-tempered (woman).

shrewd [ʃruːd] *adj.* (**-er, -est**) clever/wise. **shrewd•ly,** *adv.* in a shrewd way. **shrewd•ness,** *n.* being shrewd.

shriek [ʃriːk] 1. *n.* loud high-pitched cry. 2. *v.* to make a shriek.

shrift [ʃrɪft] *n.* **to get short s.** = to be treated curtly.

shrike [ʃraɪk] *n.* bird which pins insects to spines before eating them.

shrill [ʃrɪl] *adj.* (**-er, -est**) high-pitched. **shril•ly,** *adv.* in a shrill way. **shrill•ness,** *n.* being shrill.

shrimp [ʃrɪmp] *n.* (a) small shellfish with a long tail. (b) *inf.* small person. **shrimp•ing,** *n.* fishing for shrimps.

shrine [ʃraɪn] *n.* tomb/chapel where a saint is buried.

shrink [ʃrɪŋk] 1. *n. Sl.* psychiatrist. 2. *v.* (**shrank; shrunk**) (a) to make smaller; to get smaller. (b) to move back (**from**). **shrink•age,** *n.* action of shrinking; amount by which sth shrinks.

shriv•el ['ʃrɪvl] *v.* (**shriveled, shrivelled**) to make/to become dry and wrinkled.

shroud [ʃraʊd] 1. *n.* (a) long cloth covering a dead body. (b) **shrouds** = ropes from a mast to the sides of a ship. 2. *v.* to cover up.

Shrove Tues•day ['ʃrəʊv'tjuːzdeɪ] *n.* the Tuesday before Lent.

shrub [ʃrʌb] *n.* small bush. **shrub•ber•y,** *n.* planting of shrubs.

shrug [ʃrʌg] 1. *n.* raising the shoulders to show you are not interested. 2. *v.* (**shrugged**) **to s. your shoulders** = to raise your shoulders to show you are not interested. **shrug off,** *v.* to treat (sth) as if it is not a cause of worry.

shrunk [ʃrʌŋk] *v. see* **shrink.**

shrunk•en ['ʃrʌŋkən] *adj.* wrinkled; dried up.

shuck [ʃʌk] 1. *n.* shell/outer covering. 2. *v.* to take the shell off (sth).

shud•der ['ʃʌdə] 1. *n.* tremble of horror. 2. *v.* to tremble with horror.

shuf•fle ['ʃʌfl] *v.* (a) to walk dragging your feet. (b) to mix (playing cards). **shuf•fle**

play, *n.* function on a CD player that randomly selects and plays tracks from any of several loaded CDs.

shun [ʃʌn] *v.* (**shunned**) to avoid.

shunt [ʃʌnt] *v.* to move (a train) into a siding; to move (s.o.) to the side; get out of the way.

shush [ʃʊʃ] *inf. inter.* meaning be quiet.

shut [ʃʌt] *v.* (**shut**) (a) to close. (b) to lock up (sth) so that it cannot escape. (c) to close for business. **shut down,** *v.* to make (a factory) stop working. **shut•down,** *n.* closure of a factory. **shut•eye,** *n. inf.* sleep. **shut in,** *v.* to lock inside; to surround. **shut off,** *v.* to switch off (an engine/the water supply, etc.). **shut out,** *v.* (a) to block. (b) to lock (s.o.) outside. **shut•ter,** *n.* (a) folding wooden/metal cover which covers a window. (b) (*in camera*) part which opens and closes very rapidly to allow the light to go on to the film. **shut•tered,** *adj.* with shutters. **shut up,** *v.* (a) to close. (b) *inf.* to be quiet; to make (s.o.) be quiet.

shut•tle ['ʃʌtl] 1. *n.* part of a loom which carries the thread from side to side; **s. service** = bus/plane which goes backward and forward between two places; **s. diplomacy** = action of a diplomat going backward and forward between two countries to try to make them reach agreement. 2. *v.* to go backward and forward; to send (s.o.) backward and forward. **shut•tle•cock,** *n.* light ball with feathers stuck in it, which is hit in badminton.

shy [ʃaɪ] 1. *adj.* timid/afraid to do sth. 2. *n.* throwing (of a ball). 3. *v.* (a) to throw. (b) (*of horse*) to jump with fear. **shy•ly,** *adv.* timidly. **shy•ness,** *n.* being shy. **shy•ster,** *n. Sl.* dishonest businessman.

SI *abbrev. for* Système International, the international system of units for measuring physical properties, such as weight, speed, heat, etc.

Si•a•mese [saɪə'miːz] *adj.* referring to Siam; **S. twins** = twins born with parts of their bodies joined together; **S. cat** = type of cat with pale fawn fur, dark brown face and blue eyes.

sib•i•lant ['sɪbɪlənt] *adj. & n.* (sound) like a hiss.

sib•ling ['sɪblɪŋ] *n.* brother or sister.

sic [sɪk] *adv.* this (used to indicate a mistake).

sick [sɪk] *adj.* (a) ill/not well; **s. leave** = time off work because of illness. (b) vomiting; feeling ready to vomit. (c) (**of**) showing disgust/dislike. **sick•bay,** *n.* hospital ward (esp. on a ship). **sick•bed,** *n.* bed where a sick person is

---

æ back, aː farm, ɒ: top, aɪ pipe, aʊ how, aie fire, aʊə flower, ɔ: bought, ɔɪ toy, e fed, eəhair, eɪ take, ə afraid, əʊ boat, əʊə lower, vː word, iː heap, ɪ hit, ɪə hear, uː school, ʊ book, ʌ but, b back, d dog, ð then, dʒ just, f fog, g go, h hand, j yes, k catch, l last, m mix, n nut, ŋ sing, p penny, r round, s some, ʃ short, t too, tʃ chop, θ thing, v voice, w was, z zoo, ʒ treasure

lying. **sick•en,** v. to make or become ill. **sick•en•ing,** adj. which makes you sick. **sick•ly,** adj. (-ier, -iest) not well; weak. **sick•ness,** n. (a) illness. (b) feeling of being about to vomit. **sick pay,** n. wages paid to s.o. who is ill and cannot work. **sick•room,** n. room where a sick person is in bed.

sick•le ['sɪkl] n. tool with a semicircular blade, used for cutting corn.

side [saɪd] 1. n. (a) edge; area near the edge; **on the s.** = (i) apart from one's usual job; (ii) dishonestly. (b) one of four parts which (with the top and bottom) make a box, etc.; wall (of a house). (c) part of the body between the hips and the shoulder; **s. by s.** = close together (in a row). (d) surface. (e) slope (of a mountain); surface/part. (f) team. (g) group holding a particular point of view; **to take sides** = to support one party or another in a quarrel. (h) family connection. 2. adj. (a) secondary/less important (road, etc.). (b) at the side (not the front or back). 3. v. **to s. with s.o.** = to support s.o. in an argument. **side•board,** n. piece of dining room furniture with shelves and drawers for holding plates, etc. **side•burns,** n. short whiskers down the side of a person's face. **side•car,** n. small compartment for one passenger attached to the side of a motorcycle. **side ef•fects,** n. secondary and unexpected effects (as of a drug). **side is•sue,** n. secondary problem. **side•kick,** n. inf. companion/helper. **side•light,** n. (a) incidental information. (b) small light, as on the side of a boat. **side•line,** n. (a) business which is extra to your normal work. (b) pl. **sidelines** = lines at the edge of a football field, tennis court, etc. **side•long,** adj. from one side. **side•sad•dle,** adv. (of woman) (to ride) with both legs on the same side of the horse. **side•show,** n. small show in addition to the main show, as at a circus. **side•step,** v. (side-stepped) to avoid. **side•swipe,** v. inf. (of car) to hit another vehicle in passing. **side•track,** v. to attract s.o.'s attention away from the main problem. **side•walk,** n. path at the side of a road, usu. paved. **side•ward, side•wards,** adv. to the side. **side•ways,** adv. to the side; with the side in front. **side•whisk•ers,** n. pl. long whiskers down the side of a person's face. **sid•ing,** n. minor railroad line where trains are kept until needed.

si•de•re•al [saɪ'dɪərɪəl] adj. referring to the stars.

si•dle ['saɪdl] v. to walk sideways, not directly forward.

siege [siːdʒ] n. act of surrounding an enemy town with an army to make it surrender.

si•en•na [sɪ'enə] n. **burnt s.** = reddish-brown color; **raw s.** = yellowish-brown color.

si•es•ta [sɪ'estə] n. afternoon rest.

sieve [sɪv] 1. n. kitchen utensil with very small holes for passing liquid through to hold back lumps/for sorting out large pieces in flour, sugar, etc. 2. v. to pass (a liquid/a powder) through a sieve to sort out large lumps.

sift [sɪft] v. (a) to sieve. (b) to examine carefully. **sift•er,** n. container with small holes in the lid for sprinkling sugar or flour.

sigh [saɪ] 1. n. deep breath, showing sadness/relief, etc. 2. v. to breathe deeply showing sadness, relief, etc.

sight [saɪt] 1. n. (a) one of the five senses, the ability to see. (b) glimpse; act of seeing. (c) range of vision. (d) spectacle; thing which you ought to see. (e) funny/odd thing. (f) part of a gun through which you look to take aim. (g) inf. **a s. more** = a lot more. 2. v. (a) to see for the first time. (b) to aim a gun. **sight•less,** adj. blind. **sight-read,** v. to play written music without having practiced it. **sight•see•ing,** n. visiting the sights of a place. **sight•se•er,** n. tourist/person seeing the sights of a place.

sign [saɪn] 1. n. (a) movement (of hand/head, etc.) which means sth; **s. language** = signs of the hands used by deaf and dumb people to communicate. (b) mark. (c) indication/thing which suggests that sth may happen. (d) trace. (e) board advertising the name of a product, store, service, etc.; plate or board giving information, directions, warning, etc. 2. v. (a) to write your signature at the end of (a letter or on a document, etc.). (b) to make a movement which has a meaning. **sign a•way,** v. to give up possession of (sth) by signing a document. **sign•board,** n. board with a sign. **sign off,** v. to end a letter/a radio broadcast. **sign on,** v. to join the armed services for a period; to start work. **sign•post.** 1. n. post with a sign showing directions to a place. 2. v. to indicate a direction with signs. **sign up,** v. (a) to join the armed services for a period. (b) to volunteer or register for sth.

sig•nal ['sɪgnl] 1. n. (a) movement of the hand/head, etc., which tells s.o. to do sth. (b) lights/mechanical flags, etc., used to announce or warn of sth. (c) sound heard on a radio receiver. 2. adj. (formal) remarkable. 3. v. (signaled, signalled) to make signs to tell s.o. to do sth. **sign•al•er,** n. person who signals. **sig•nal•ly,** adv. (formal) remarkably. **sig•nal•man,** n. (pl. -men) person who controls railroad signals.

sig•na•to•ry ['sɪgnətrɪ] n. person who signs (a treaty, etc.).

sig•na•ture ['sɪgnətʃə] n. (a) name which has

been signed. (b) group of pages of a book (usually 32 or 64) which are folded out of one sheet of paper. (c) **s. tune** = theme song.

sig•net ['sɪgnɪt] *n.* seal (for sealing with wax); **s. ring** = ring worn on the little finger with a design carved on to it to use as a seal.

sig•ni•fy ['sɪgnɪfaɪ] *v.* (a) to mean. (b) to show; make known. (c) to be of importance. **sig•nif•i•cance,** *n.* (a) meaning. (b) importance. **sig•nif•i•cant,** *adj.* which is important/which has a lot of meaning. **sig•nif•i•cant•ly,** *adv.* in a significant way. **sig•ni•fi•ca•tion,** *n.* meaning.

si•lage ['saɪlɪdʒ] *n.* green crops fermented in a silo and used to feed animals.

si•lence ['saɪləns] 1. *n.* (a) lack of noise. (b) not saying anything. 2. *v.* (a) to make (s.o.) stop talking. (b) to stop (sth) making a noise. **si•lenc•er,** *n.* apparatus attached to a gun to stop the noise of it being fired. **si•lent,** *adj.* quiet. **si•lent•ly,** *adv.* in a silent way.

sil•hou•ette [sɪluː'et] 1. *n.* black outline of s.o.'s head or sth in profile. 2. *v.* to stand out in profile.

sil•i•ca ['sɪlɪkə] *n.* mineral compound of silicon. **sil•i•ca gel,** *n.* hard crystals used to keep things dry in humid conditions. **sil•i•cate,** *n.* common silicon compound.

sil•i•con ['sɪlɪkən] *n.* (*element:* Si) common element which is not a metal, and which is usu. found in compounds; **s. chip** = small piece of silicon used in transistors and very small electronic devices.

sil•i•cone ['sɪlɪkəʊn] *n.* chemical substance used in making oils.

sil•i•co•sis [sɪlɪ'kəʊsɪs] *n.* disease of the lungs caused by breathing in dust.

silk [sɪlk] *n.* thread which is produced by a caterpillar; cloth woven from this thread. **silk•en,** *adj.* soft and shiny. **silk•screen pro•cess,** *n.* method of printing by forcing colors through a taut piece of cloth. **silk•worm,** *n.* caterpillar which produces silk. **silk•y,** *adj.* soft and shiny.

sill [sɪl] *n.* ledge beneath a window/a door.

sil•ly ['sɪlɪ] *adj.* (-ier, -iest) stupid/idiotic. **sil•li•ness,** *n.* being silly.

si•lo ['saɪləʊ] *n.* (*pl.* -os) (a) large tower for storing grain/for storing green crops (as food for animals). (b) deep hole in the ground in which rockets are kept.

silt [sɪlt] 1. *n.* fine mud washed down by a river. 2. *v.* **to s. up** = to fill with silt.

sil•ver ['sɪlvə] *n.* (a) (*element:* Ag) precious white metal; **s. jubilee** = 25th anniversary of an important event; **s. wedding** = anniversary of 25 years of marriage. (b) **s. foil** = sheet of thin shiny metal which looks like silver, used for wrapping food in. (c) coins made of white metal. (d) light shining color like silver. **sil•ver birch,** *n.* common northern tree with white bark. **sil•ver•fish,** *n.* small silvery insect found in kitchens, etc. **sil•ver•smith,** *n.* craftsman who makes things in silver. **sil•ver•ware,** *n.* (*no pl.*) articles made of silver. **sil•ver•y,** *adj.* (a) shiny like silver. (b) light ringing (sound).

sim•i•an ['sɪmɪən] *adj.* like a monkey.

sim•i•lar ['sɪmɪlə] *adj.* very alike but not quite the same. **sim•i•lar•ly,** *adv.* in a similar way. **sim•i•lar•i•ty,** *n.* sameness/likeness.

sim•i•le ['sɪmɪlɪ] *n.* comparison using "like" or "as."

sim•mer ['sɪmə] *v.* to boil gently; **to s. down** = to become calmer.

sim•per ['sɪmpə] 1. *n.* silly affected smile. 2. *v.* to say with a simper.

sim•ple ['sɪmpl] *adj.* (-er, -est) (a) not complicated; not difficult. (b) *inf.* not very intelligent. (c) **s. interest** = interest calculated on the original sum without adding each year's interest to the capital. (d) plain/ordinary. **sim•ple•mind•ed,** *adj.* not very intelligent. **sim•ple•ton,** *n.* person who is not very intelligent. **sim•plic•i•ty** [sɪm'plɪsɪtɪ] *n.* being simple. **sim•pli•fi•ca•tion** [sɪmplɪfɪ'keɪʃn] *n.* making simple. **sim•pli•fy** ['sɪmplɪfaɪ] *v.* to make (sth) simple. **sim•ply,** *adv.* (a) without complication. (b) absolutely. (c) purely/only.

sim•u•late ['sɪmjuleɪt] *v.* to pretend. **sim•u•la•tion** [sɪmju'leɪʃn] *n.* pretense. **sim•u•la•tor** ['sɪmjuleɪtə] *n.* machine which allows a learner to experience simulated conditions (as in a car/aircraft, etc.).

si•mul•ta•ne•ous [sɪməl'teɪnɪəs] *adj.* happening at the same time. **si•mul•ta•ne•ous•ly,** *adv.* at the same time.

sin [sɪn] 1. *n.* wicked deed; action which goes against the rules of religion; **to live in s.** = to live together without being married. 2. *v.* (**sinned**) to do sth wicked/wrong. **sin•ful,** *adj.* wicked (person/action). **sin•ner,** *n.* person who has sinned.

since [sɪns] 1. *adv.* from then onward. 2. *prep.*

æ back, ɑ: farm, ɒ: top, aɪ pipe, aʊ how, aɪə fire, aʊə flower, ɔ: bought, ɔɪ toy, e fed, eə hair, eɪ take, ə afraid, əʊ boat, əʊə lower, v: word, i: heap, ɪ hit, ɪə hear, u: school, ʊ book, ʌ but, b back, d dog, ð then, dʒ just, f fog, g go, h hand, j yes, k catch, l last, m mix, n nut, ŋ sing, p penny, r round, s some, ʃ short, t too, tʃ chop, θ thing, v voice, w was, z zoo, ʒ treasure

from a certain time. 3. *conj.* (a) from a certain time. (b) because.

sin•cere [sɪn'sɪə] *adj.* very honest/open. **sin•cere•ly,** *adv.* really/truly; **s. yours** = greeting written at the end of a letter. **sin•cer•i•ty** [sɪn'serɪtɪ] *n.* honesty.

sine [saɪn] *n.* (*in mathematics*) ratio between the length of one of the shorter sides opposite an acute angle to that of the hypotenuse in a right-angled triangle.

si•ne•cure ['saɪnɪkjʊə] *n.* job for which you get paid but which does not involve much work.

si•ne di•e ['sɪneɪdɪeɪ] *adv.* to a later date, which is unspecified.

si•ne qua non ['sɪneɪkwɑːˈnɒn] *n.* condition without which something cannot function.

sin•ew ['sɪnjuː] *n.* strong cord which joins a muscle to a bone. **sin•ew•y,** *adj.* very strong.

sing [sɪŋ] *v.* (**sang, sung**) (a) to make music with your mouth. (b) to make a buzzing noise. **sing•er,** *n.* person who sings. **sing•song,** *adj.* (voice) with a rising and falling tone.

singe ['sɪndʒ] *v.* to burn slightly.

sin•gle ['sɪŋgl] 1. *adj.* (a) alone/one by itself. (b) for one person. (c) unmarried. 2. *n.* (a) **singles** = tennis game played between two people. (b) small phonograph record with only one piece of music on each side. 3. *v.* **to s. out** = to select. **sin•gle-breast•ed,** *adj.* (coat) which does not fold over widely in the front to button. **sin•gle-hand•ed,** *adj.* all by yourself. **sin•gle-mind•ed,** *adj.* thinking only of one aim. **sin•gle-mind•ed•ness,** *n.* being single-minded. **sin•gle•ness,** *n.* (a) being single. (b) **s. of purpose** = having only one aim. **sin•gly,** *adv.* one by one.

sin•gu•lar ['sɪŋgjʊlə] 1. *adj. & n.* referring to one person/thing. 2. *adj.* (a) odd/peculiar. (b) remarkable. **sin•gu•lar•i•ty** [sɪŋgjʊ'lærɪtɪ] *n.* oddness/peculiarity. **sin•gu•lar•ly,** *adv.* (a) strangely. (b) particularly.

sin•is•ter ['sɪnɪstə] *adj.* looking evil; which promises evil.

sink [sɪŋk] 1. *n.* (a) basin for washing as in a kitchen. (b) place where substances pass to be absorbed out of the atmosphere. 2. *v.* (**sank; sunk**) (a) to (cause to) go to the bottom of water/mud, etc. (b) to go down. (c) to make (a well). (d) **to s. your teeth into** = to bite. (e) to invest. **sink•er,** *n.* lead weight used to pull down a fishing line into the water. **sink in,** *v.* to become fixed in the mind.

Sino- ['saɪnəʊ] *prefix meaning* Chinese/between China and another country.

sin•u•ous ['sɪnjʊəs] *adj.* winding. **sin•u•os•i•ty** [sɪnjʊ'ɒsɪtɪ] *n.* (a) being sinuous. (b) bend (in a pipe or road).

si•nus ['saɪnəs] *n.* (*pl.* **-es**) hole in the bones of the head connected with the nose and air passages. **si•nus•i•tis** [saɪnə'saɪtɪs] *n.* infection of the sinuses.

sip [sɪp] 1. *n.* small quantity of liquid. 2. *v.* (**sipped**) to drink taking only a small quantity at a time.

si•phon ['saɪfn] 1. *n.* (a) device for aerating water. (b) bent tube to allow you to take liquid from one container to another placed at a lower level. 2. *v.* (a) to remove (liquid) by using a siphon. (b) to remove (money) from a source illegally.

sir [sɜː] *n.* (a) respectful way of addressing a man (usu. an older or more important man). (b) title given to a knight or baronet. (c) way of addressing a man in a formal letter.

sire ['saɪə] 1. *n.* (a) male horse which is a father. (b) (*old*) **Sire** = way of addressing a king. 2. *v.* (*of a horse*) to be father of.

si•ren ['saɪrən] *n.* loud warning signal which wails.

sir•loin ['sɜːlɔɪn] *n.* best cut of beef from the back of the animal.

si•sal ['saɪsl] *n.* rope made from fibers from a tropical plant.

sis•kin ['sɪskɪn] *n.* small finch.

sis•sy ['sɪsɪ] *n.* weak girlish man/boy.

sis•ter ['sɪstə] 1. *n.* (a) female child whose parents are the same as yours. (b) nun; title given to nuns. 2. *adj.* similar/identical; **s. ship** = ship of the same design. **sis•ter•hood,** *n.* state of being a sister. **sis•ter-in-law,** *n.* (*pl.* **sisters-**) wife of your brother; sister of your husband or wife. **sis•ter•ly,** *adj.* like a sister.

sit [sɪt] *v.* (**sat**) (a) to be seated; to make (s.o.) be seated; to rest in a seated position with your behind on a chair/on the ground, etc.; **to s. for your portrait** = to pose (not necessarily in a seated position). (b) to be in session/to meet. (c) to be a member of. (d) (*of bird*) to sit on her eggs. **sit back,** *v.* to be seated and lean backward. **sit down,** *v.* to take a seat. **sit-down,** *adj.* (a) **sit-down dinner** = meal where you sit at a table. (b) **sit-down strike** = strike where workers do not move from their place of work. **sit-in,** *n.* occupation of a place, as by workers/students, etc. **sit on,** *v.* (a) to be a member of (a committee). (b) *inf.* to delay (a request). **sit•ter,** *n.* person who sits/poses for a painter; **baby-sitter** = person who looks after a child when its parents are out. **sit tight,** *v.* to stay where you are/to refuse to move. **sit•ting,** *n.* act of sitting; session. **sit•ting-room,** *n.* small living room. **sit up,** *v.* (a) to straighten yourself on your chair. (b) to stay up/not to go to bed.

site [saɪt] 1. *n.* (a) place where a building/town is situated. (b) place where an event took place.

(c) Internet location devoted to a particular subject. 2. *v.* to place (a building/town) on a particular piece of land. **sit•u•ate** ['sɪtjʊeɪt] *v.* to place. **sit•u•a•tion** [sɪtjʊ'eɪʃn] *n.* (a) place where a building is. (b) state of affairs. (c) job.

sitz bath ['sɪtsbɑːθ] *n.* small low bath in which a person can sit, but not lie down.

six [sɪks] *n.* number 6; *inf.* **they're all at sixes and sevens** = they're very disorganized/they can't agree. **six•teen,** *n.* number 16. **six•teenth, 16th,** *adj. & n.* referring to sixteen. **sixth, 6th,** *adj. & n.* referring to six. **six•ti•eth, 60th,** *adj. & n.* referring to sixty. **six•ty,** *n.* number 60; **she's in her sixties** = she is aged between 60 and 69.

size [saɪz] 1. *n.* (a) largeness of sth. (b) measurements. (c) type of pastelike glue. 2. *v.* (a) **to s. s.o. up** = to judge s.o.'s capabilities. (b) to cover with glue. **size•a•ble,** *adj.* quite large.

siz•zle ['sɪzl] *v.* to make a hissing sound when frying; *inf.* to be very hot.

skate [skeɪt] 1. *n.* (a) (*pl.* **skate**) large flat fish with white flesh. (b) sharp blade under boots worn for gliding on ice. 2. *v.* to glide on ice wearing skates. **skate•board,** *n.* board with two pairs of wheels which you stand on to glide about. **skat•er,** *n.* person who goes skating.

ske•dad•dle [skɪ'dædl] *v. inf.* to go quickly.

skein [skeɪn] *n.* length of wool loosely wound around and around into a loop.

skel•e•ton ['skelɪtn] *n.* (a) bones inside a body; **s. in the closet** = secret that a family or person is trying to keep hidden. (b) **s. staff** = few staff left to carry on essential work while the others are away. (c) **s. key** = key which will fit any lock in a building. (d) rough outline. **skel•e•tal,** *adj.* like a skeleton.

skep [skep] *n.* straw beehive.

skep•tic ['skeptɪk] *n.* (a) person who doubts the truth of religion. (b) person who always doubts the truth of what he is told. **skep•ti•cal,** *adj.* doubtful/(person) who doubts. **skep•ti•cal•ly,** *adv.* doubtfully/distrustfully. **skep•ti•cism,** *n.* doubt/uncertainty.

sketch [sketʃ] 1. *n.* (*pl.* **-es**) (a) rough drawing. (b) short amusing play. 2. *v.* to make a rough drawing/a rough plan of. **sketch•book,** *n.* book of drawing paper for sketching. **sketch•i•ly,** *adv.* in a sketchy way. **sketch•i•ness,** *n.* being sketchy. **sketch**

map, *n.* roughly drawn map. **sketch pad,** *n.* pad of paper for sketching. **sketch•y,** *adj.* (**-ier, -iest**) rough/incomplete.

skew [skjuː] *adj.* not straight.

skew•bald ['skjuːbɔːld] *adj.* (horse) with patches of white with another color, but not black.

skew•er ['skjʊə] 1. *n.* long thin metal rod for putting through pieces of meat when cooking. 2. *v.* to stick a long metal rod through (sth).

ski [skiː] 1. *n.* long flat narrow piece of wood, etc., which you attach under your boot for moving over snow; **water skis** = similar pieces of wood for gliding over water. 2. *v.* to travel on skis; **to go skiing** = to travel on skis as a sport. **ski boots,** *n. pl.* special boots for skiing. **ski•er,** *n.* person traveling on skis. **ski jump,** *n.* slope with a sudden drop at the bottom to allow a skier to jump high in the air. **ski lift,** *n.* device to take skiers to the top of a slope.

skid [skɪd] 1. *n.* (a) sliding sideways. (b) plank for sliding heavy objects along. 2. *v.* (**skidded**) to slide sideways in a vehicle with the wheels not gripping the surface.

skiff [skɪf] *n.* light sailboat or rowboat.

skill [skɪl] *n.* cleverness/ability to do something. **skill•ful,** *adj.* clever/very able. **skill•ful•ly,** *adv.* in a skillful way. **skilled,** *adj.* having/requiring a particular skill.

skil•let ['skɪlɪt] *n.* frying pan.

skim [skɪm] *v.* (**skimmed**) (a) to remove things floating on the surface of (a liquid). (b) to dash over the surface of sth; **to s. through a book** = to read a book quickly.

skimp [skɪmp] *v.* (a) to do a job badly. (b) not to give enough of; **they s. on food** = they don't spend much money on food. **skimp•y,** *adj.* (**-ier, -iest**) insufficient (meal); tight/short (clothes).

skin [skɪn] 1. *n.* (a) outer surface of an animal's body; **by the s. of their teeth** = only just. (b) outer surface. 2. *v.* (**skinned**) to remove the skin of. **skin-deep,** *adj.* on the surface/superficial. **skin div•er,** *n.* person who goes skin diving. **skin div•ing,** *n.* sport of swimming underwater with breathing apparatus but without special clothing. **skin•flint,** *n.* miser. **skin•ny,** *adj.* (**-ier, -iest**) *inf.* thin. **skin•tight,** *adj.* (clothes) which are close-fitting.

skip [skɪp] 1. *n.* act of skipping. 2. *v.* (**skipped**) (a) to jump over a rope; to run along half hop-ping and half jumping. (b) to miss out (part of a book).

skip•per ['skɪpə] 1. *n.* captain (of a ship/of a team). 2. *v.* to be the captain of (a team).

skirl [skɜːl] *n.* wailing sound made by bagpipes.

skir•mish ['skɜːmɪʃ] *n.* (*pl.* -es) slight battle between opposite sides.

skirt [skɜːt] 1. *n.* piece of woman's clothing covering the lower part of the body from the waist to the knees or ankles. 2. *v.* to go around/to avoid going through or dealing with.

skit [skɪt] *n.* short humorous play/story.

skit•tish ['skɪtɪʃ] *adj.* (*of horse, etc.*) liable to jump about unexpectedly.

skit•tle ['skɪtl] *n.* bottle-shaped wooden object used with a ball in a game.

sku•a ['skjuːə] *n.* type of large sea bird.

skul•dug•ger•y [skʌl'dʌgərɪ] *n. inf.* deceitful or dishonest actions; trickery.

skulk [skʌlk] *v.* (a) to hide away (because you are planning sth wicked). (b) to creep about mysteriously.

skull [skʌl] *n.* bony part of the head. **skull•cap,** *n.* tight-fitting small round hat.

skunk [skʌŋk] *n.* American mammal with black and white fur, which produces a bad smell when frightened or attacked.

sky [skaɪ] *n.* area above the earth which is blue during the day, and where the moon and stars appear at night. **sky-blue,** *adj. & n.* bright light blue (color). **sky di•ver,** *n.* person who jumps from an aircraft, and falls freely for some time before opening his parachute. **sky-high,** *adv.* as high as the sky; very high; **to blow sth sky-high** = to blow sth up with a powerful explosive. **sky•lark.** 1. *n.* small singing bird which sings as it flies upward. 2. *v.* to play; frolic. **sky•light,** *n.* window in a roof or ceiling. **sky•line,** *n.* horizon; shape of buildings silhouetted against the sky. **sky•scrap•er,** *n.* very tall building.

slab [slæb] *n.* thick flat rectangular block.

slack [slæk] 1. *adj.* (-er, -est) (a) not taut/not tight. (b) not busy. (c) lazy/not working well. 2. *n.* (a) looseness; loose part of a rope. (b) very small pieces of coal. (c) **slacks** = trousers. 3. *v.* **to s. (off)** = to be lazy/to do less work. **slack•en,** *v.* (a) to loosen. (b) **to s. off** = to work less. **slack•er,** *n.* person who doesn't work hard. **slack•ly,** *adv.* (a) loosely. (b) lazily. **slack•ness,** *n.* being slack.

slag [slæg] *n.* waste material left after metal has been extracted from ore; **s. heap** = mountain of slag left near a metal works or coalmine.

slain [sleɪn] *v. see* **slay.**

slake [sleɪk] *v.* (a) **to s. your thirst** = to drink to remove your thirst. (b) to mix lime with water.

sla•lom ['slɑːləm] *n.* race in skiing, where you have to ski fast between a series of posts.

slam [slæm] 1. *n.* (a) banging of a door. (b) **grand s.** = winning all the card games in a competition. 2. *v.* (**slammed**) (a) to bang. (b) *inf.* to criticize very unfavorably.

slan•der ['slɑːndə] 1. *n.* untrue thing said about a person which hurts his reputation; crime of saying such things. 2. *v.* to say untrue things about a person. **slan•der•ous,** *adj.* (statement) which is slander.

slang [slæŋ] *n.* words or phrases used by certain groups of people in popular speech which are not used in correct or written language. **slang•y,** *adj. inf.* using slang.

slant [slɑːnt] 1. *n.* (a) slope; **on the s.** = sloping. (b) point of view. 2. *v.* (a) to slope. (b) to show (news or information) in a biased way. **slant•ing,** *adj.* sloping. **slant•wise, slantways,** *adv.* at an angle; on a slope.

slap [slæp] 1. *n.* smack with your hand flat. 2. *v.* **slapped**) (a) to hit with your hand flat. (b) to bring (sth) down flat on to a surface; **to s. down** = criticize sharply. 3. *adv.* **to run s. into the wall** = right into the wall. **slap•dash,** *adj.* careless. **slap•hap•py,** *adj. inf.* happily careless. **slap•stick,** *adj. & n.* rough (comedy) which depends on physical jokes.

slash [slæʃ] 1. *n.* (*pl.* -es) long cut. 2. *v.* (a) to make a long cut. (b) to shorten; to reduce (a price) drastically.

slat [slæt] *n.* thin flat piece of wood. **slat•ted,** *adj.* made of slats.

slate [sleɪt] 1. *n.* (a) dark-gray stone which splits into thin sheets; piece of this stone used as a roof covering or for writing on; **to start a clean s.** = to start again (without any faults held against you). (b) group of candidates in an election. 2. *v. inf.* to criticize severely; censure. **slate gray,** *adj. & n.* very dark blue-gray (color).

slat•tern ['slætən] *n.* dirty woman. **slat•tern•ly,** *adj.* (*of a woman*) dirty.

slaugh•ter ['slɔːtə] 1. *n.* (a) killing of animals for meat. (b) killing of people (in war). 2. *v.* (a) to kill (animals) for meat. (b) to kill (many people) in war. **slaugh•ter•house,** *n.* place where animals are slaughtered.

slave [sleɪv] 1. *n.* person who belongs to and works for s.o. 2. *v.* (*also* **slave away**) to work hard. **slave driv•er,** *n. inf.* employer who makes his workers work very hard. **slav•er•y,** *n.* being a slave; buying and selling slaves. **slav•ish,** *adj.* exact (imitation) without any imagination. **slav•ish•ly,** *adv.* (to obey rules) exactly without exercising any imagination.

slav•er ['sleɪvə] 1. *n.* liquid which dribbles out

of your mouth. 2. *v.* to dribble/to let liquid trickle out of your mouth.

slay [sleɪ] *v. (formal)* (**slew** [sluː], **slain**) to kill.

slea•zy ['sliːzɪ] *adj.* (**-ier, -iest**) *inf.* dirty/disreputable.

sled [sled] 1. *n.* small vehicle with runners for sliding over snow. 2. *v.* **to go sledding** = to play on the snow using a sled.

sledge [sledʒ] *n. & v. see* **sled**. **sledge•ham•mer**, *n.* very large heavy hammer.

sleek [sliːk] 1. *adj.* (**-er, -est**) smooth/shiny; well-kept. 2. *v.* to smooth down (hair) with oil. **sleek•ly**, *adv.* in a sleek way. **sleek•ness**, *n.* being sleek.

sleep [sliːp] 1. *n.* state of resting naturally and unconsciously; **to go/to get to s.** = to start sleeping; **to send s.o. to s.** = to make s.o. go to sleep (from boredom/by hypnosis); **to put to s.** = to kill; **my foot has gone to s.** = has become numb. 2. *v.* (**slept**) (a) to be in a state of natural rest and unconsciousness; **I'll s. on it** = I will make a decision on the problem in the morning; **to s. sth off** = to get rid of the effects of sth by sleeping; **to s. with s.o.** = to have sexual intercourse with s.o. (b) to have enough beds for. **sleep•er**, *n.* (a) person who is asleep. (b) sleeping car. (c) overnight train with sleeping cars. **sleep•i•ly**, *adv.* in a sleepy way. **sleep•i•ness**, *n.* being sleepy. **sleep•ing**. 1. *adj.* asleep. 2. *n.* being asleep; **s. pill** = medicine which makes you go to sleep; **s. car** = railroad car on a train with beds where passengers can sleep; **s. bag** = quilted bag for sleeping in a tent, etc.; **s. sickness** = tropical disease which affects the nervous system. **sleep•less**, *adj.* with no sleep. **sleep•less•ness**, *n.* having no sleep; not able to get to sleep. **sleep•walk**, *v.* to walk about when you are asleep. **sleep•walk•er**, *n.* person who sleepwalks. **sleep•y**, *adj.* (**-ier, -iest**) half asleep; ready to go to sleep.

sleet [sliːt] 1. *n.* mixture of snow and rain. 2. *v.* **it is sleeting** = snow and rain are falling together.

sleeve [sliːv] *n.* (a) part of clothing which covers the arm; **to have sth up your s.** = to have a plan which you are keeping secret. (b) cover for a piece of machinery. (c) square cardboard cover for a phonograph record. **sleeve•less**, *adj.* with no sleeves.

sleigh [sleɪ] *n.* large sled pulled by horses or reindeer, etc.

sleight [slaɪt] *n.* **s. of hand** = quickness of a magician's movements when performing a card trick.

slen•der ['slendə] *adj.* (a) very thin/slim. (b) not strong; not large. **slen•der•ness**, *n.* being slender.

slept [slept] *v. see* **sleep**.

sleuth [sluːθ] *n. inf.* detective.

slew [sluː] *v. see* **slay**.

slice [slaɪs] 1. *n.* (a) thin piece cut off sth. (b) **fish s.** = flat broad knife for serving fish. (c) (*in games*) stroke which makes the ball spin toward the right. 2. *v.* (a) to cut into slices. (b) to cut sharply. (c) to hit a ball so that it spins toward the right. **slic•er**, *n.* machine for slicing meat/bread, etc.

slick [slɪk] 1. *adj.* (**-er, -est**) clever (in a way which tricks people). 2. *n.* **oil s.** = layer of oil which has spilled on the sea from a tanker or oil rig. 3. *v.* **to s. down** = to make (hair) sleek.

slid [slɪd] *v. see* **slide**.

slide [slaɪd] 1. *n.* (a) action of slipping on a smooth surface. (b) slippery surface for sliding, esp. a metal slope for children to slide down. (c) thin glass plate to put under a microscope. (d) plastic transparent photograph which can be projected on a screen. 2. *v.* (**slid** [slɪd]) (a) to move smoothly. (b) **to let things s.** = to allow things to become worse/not to care if things get worse. **slide rule**, *n.* device for calculating, made of a ruler marked with numbers and a central part which slides sideways. **slid•ing scale**, *n.* system of marks/points/taxes, etc., which vary according to a scale.

slight [slaɪt] 1. *adj.* (**-er, -est**) (a) thin/slender (person). (b) not very large; not very important. 2. *n.* insult. 3. *v.* to insult/to be rude to (s.o.). **slight•ing•ly**, *adv.* rudely/insultingly. **slight•ly**, *adv.* not very much.

slim [slɪm] 1. *adj.* (**slimmer, slimmest**) (a) thin/slender/not fat. (b) small. 2. *v.* (**slimmed**) to diet in order to become thin. **slim•mer**, *n.* person who is trying to lose weight. **slim•ness**, *n.* being slim.

slime [slaɪm] *n.* thin mud; dirty, sticky liquid. **slim•i•ness**, *n.* being slimy. **slim•y**, *adj.* (**-ier, -iest**) unpleasantly muddy/slippery/sticky.

sling [slɪŋ] 1. *n.* (a) device for throwing a stone. (b) carrying strap; bandage tied around your neck to hold your wounded arm steady. (c) apparatus made of ropes and pulleys for hoisting and carrying goods. 2. *v.* (**slung**) (a) to throw. (b) to hold up/to hang by a sling.

sling•shot, *n.* catapult/strong elastic band on a forked stick, used for throwing stones.

slink [slɪŋk] *v.* (**slunk**) to creep about furtively. **slink•y,** *adj.* (**-ier, -iest**) smooth (shape); tight, smooth (clothes).

slip [slɪp] 1. *n.* (a) action of sliding by mistake. (b) mistake; **s. of the tongue** = mistake in speaking. (c) **to give s.o. the s.** = to escape from s.o. (d) **pillow s.** = pillowcase. (e) small piece of paper. (f) petticoat. (g) **slips** = long smooth slope on which ships are built. (h) mixture of clay and water which is used in pottery. 2. *v.* (**slipped**) (a) to slide by mistake. (b) to go quietly. (c) (*of machinery*) to miss/not to connect; **slipped disk** = painful state where one of the cushioning disks in the spine has become displaced. **slip•per,** *n.* light comfortable shoe worn indoors. **slip•per•y,** *adj.* (a) so smooth that one can easily slip on it. (b) *inf.* (person) who cannot be trusted. **slip•py,** *adj. inf.* slippery. **slip•shod,** *adj.* badly carried out (work); careless (dress). **slip•stream,** *n.* air blown backward by an aircraft engine; point just behind a fast-moving vehicle. **slip up,** *v. inf.* to make a mistake. **slip-up,** *n. inf.* mistake. **slip•way,** *n.* smooth slope on which ships are built or repaired.

slit [slɪt] 1. *n.* long cut; narrow opening. 2. *v.* (**slit**) to make a slit.

slith•er ['slɪðə] *v.* to slide along, down, or in various directions.

sliv•er ['slɪvə] *n.* thin piece of wood or meat.

slob [slɒb] *n. inf.* sloppy/untidy person. **slob•ber** ['slɒbə] *v.* to dribble saliva from your mouth. **slob•ber•y,** *adj.* covered with saliva.

sloe [sləʊ] *n.* bitter wild fruit like a plum; tree which bears this fruit.

slog [slɒg] 1. *n.* difficult work; difficult walk. 2. *v.* (**slogged**) to work hard at sth difficult. **slog•ger,** *n.* person who works hard.

slo•gan ['sləʊgən] *n.* phrase used in publicity for a product/for a political party, etc.

sloop [slu:p] *n.* type of small ship.

slop [slɒp] *v.* (**slopped**) to spill. **slop•pi•ly,** *adv.* in a sloppy way. **slop•pi•ness,** *n.* being sloppy. **slop•py,** *adj.* (**-ier, -iest**) (a) untidy; badly done (work). (b) stupidly sentimental. **slops,** *n. pl.* (a) waste food given to pigs. (b) liquid refuse.

slope [sləʊp] 1. *n.* slanting surface; angle of a slanting surface; slanting piece of ground. 2. *v.* to slant upward or downward. **slop•ing,** *adj.* (roof, etc.) which slopes.

slosh [slɒʃ] *v.* to splash. **sloshed,** *adj. inf.* drunk.

slot [slɒt] 1. *n.* narrow opening (for putting a coin, mail, etc. into); **s. machine** = vending machine. 2. *v.* (**slotted**) **to s. into** = to fit into (a slot).

sloth [sləʊθ] *n.* (a) (*formal*) laziness. (b) slow-moving South American mammal, like a bear. **sloth•ful,** *adj.* (*formal*) lazy.

slouch [slaʊtʃ] *v.* to stand/to sit in a bad position/with bent shoulders; **to s. along** = to walk along bending forward. **slouch hat,** *n.* hat with a wide brim which can be turned down.

slough 1. *n.* (a) [slʌf] old skin of a snake. (b) [slaʊ] marshy place. 2. *v.* [slʌf] (*of a snake*) to lose (its skin).

slov•en•ly ['slʌvənlɪ] *adj.* untidy; careless (work). **slov•en•li•ness,** *n.* being slovenly.

slow [sləʊ] 1. *adj.* (**-er, -est**) (a) not fast. (b) (*of clock, etc.*) **to be s.** = to show a time which is earlier than the correct time. (c) not quick to learn; *inf.* **to be s. on the uptake** = not to understand quickly. 2. *adv.* not fast; **to go s.** = to advance less quickly. 3. *v.* **to s. down** = to make (sth) go slowly; to go more slowly. **slow•down,** *n.* slowing down (of business activity). **slow•ly,** *adv.* in a slow way. **slow mo•tion,** *n.* (*in motion pictures*) action which appears to take place very slowly because the film speed has been slowed down. **slow•ness,** *n.* being slow. **slow•worm,** *n.* snakelike lizard.

sludge [slʌdʒ] *n.* wet mud; wet refuse.

slug [slʌg] 1. *n.* (a) common garden animal like a snail with no shell. (b) small metal pellet. 2. *v.* (**slugged**) *inf.* to hit (s.o.) a heavy blow. **slug•gard,** *n.* lazy person. **slug•gish,** *adj.* lazy/slow-moving. **slug•gish•ly,** *adv.* in a slow way.

sluice [slu:s] 1. *n.* channel for taking water around a dam. 2. *v.* to wash (sth) with lots of water. **sluice gate,** *n.* gate which allows water to enter the sluice channel.

slum [slʌm] *n.* poor, rundown area of a town. **slum•ming,** *n.* visiting slums; visiting people who you think are of a lower class or less rich than yourself.

slum•ber ['slʌmbə] 1. *n.* gentle sleep. 2. *v.* to sleep gently. **slum•ber•er,** *n.* person who slumbers.

slump [slʌmp] 1. *n.* collapse (of prices); economic collapse (of a country). 2. *v.* (a) to fall suddenly. (b) to sit/to lie clumsily/heavily.

slung [slʌŋ] *v. see* **sling.**

slunk [slʌŋk] *v. see* **slink.**

slur [slɜ:] 1. *n.* (a) insult. (b) slurring of several notes; mark on a musical score to show that notes should be slurred. 2. *v.* (**slurred**) (a) to speak words indistinctly. (b) (*in music*) to play several notes without a break between them.

slurp [slɜ:p] *v. inf.* to drink noisily.

slur•ry ['slʌrɪ] *n.* (*no pl.*) watery mud/cement.

slush [slʌʃ] *n.* (a) half-melted snow. (b) sentimentality. **slush fund,** *n. inf.* money kept for the purposes of bribery. **slush•y,** *adj.* (a) covered with half-melted snow. (b) very sentimental.

slut [slʌt] *n. inf.* dirty, untidy woman. **slut•tish,** *adj.* like a slut.

sly [slaɪ] *adj.* (-er, -est) cunning (person); **on the s.** = without anyone knowing. **sly•ly,** *adv.* in a sly way. **sly•ness,** *n.* being sly.

smack [smæk] 1. *n.* (a) blow with the flat of the hand. (b) loud kiss. (c) slight taste or hint of sth. 2. *v.* (a) to hit (s.o.). (b) **to s. one's lips** = make a loud noise (as if hungry). (c) to smell/to taste; **that smacks of bribery** = it sounds as though bribery is involved. 3. *adv. inf.* straight/directly. **smack•er,** *n. inf.* dollar.

small [smɔːl] 1. *adj.* (-er, -est) (a) not large; little. (b) delicate/soft (voice). (c) not imposing. (d) petty/thinking only of trivial things. 2. *n.* **the s. of the back** = the lower part of the back. 3. *adv.* into little bits. **small hours,** *n.* period after midnight. **small-mind•ed,** *adj.* thinking only of yourself/of trivial things. **small•ness,** *n.* being small. **small•pox,** *n.* dangerous infectious disease causing a rash which leaves marks on the skin. **small talk,** *n.* general conversation about sth unimportant. **small-time,** *adj.* unimportant.

smarm•y ['smɑːmɪ] *adj.* (-ier, -iest) (person) who is unpleasantly smooth. **smarm•i•ness,** *n.* being smarmy.

smart [smɑːt] 1. *n.* sharp pain (from a wound). 2. *v.* to hurt/to feel as if burning. 3. *adj.* (-er, -est) (a) sharp (blow). (b) rapid/efficient. (c) clever. (d) well-dressed/elegant. **smart•en,** *v.* **to s. yourself up** = to make yourself look smart. **smart•ly,** *adv.* in a smart way. **smart•ness,** *n.* being smart.

smash [smæʃ] 1. *n.* (*pl.* -es) (a) crash (of a car). (b) financial collapse. (c) powerful shot (in tennis). 2. *v.* (a) to break (sth) to pieces. (b) to hit sth hard. (c) to hit (a ball) hard. **smash hit,** *n. inf.* play/motion picture, etc., which is very successful. **smash•ing,** *adj. inf.* very good/fantastic.

smat•ter•ing ['smætrɪŋ] *n.* small knowledge (of a language).

smear ['smɪə] 1. *n.* (a) dirty mark; thing which is smeared (esp. a small amount of sth for examining under a microscope). (b) insult; **s. campaign** = campaign to discredit s.o. by spreading gossip about his private life. 2. *v.* (a)

to make dirty marks on sth. (b) to spread (sth greasy).

smell [smel] 1. *n.* (a) one of the five senses, felt through the nose. (b) thing which you can sense through the nose. (c) unpleasant thing which you can sense through the nose. 2. *v.* (**smelled/smelt**) (a) to notice (sth) by the nose. (b) to sniff in order to sense the smell. (c) to give off a smell. **smell•ing salts,** *n. pl.* crystals of a compound of ammonia, which are smelled to cure faintness. **smell•y,** *adj.* (-ier, -iest) which gives off an unpleasant smell.

smelt [smelt] 1. *n.* (*pl.* smelt) small edible fish. 2. *v.* (a) to produce metal by melting ore. (b) *see also* **smell. smelter,** *n.* works where metal is extracted from ore. **smelt•ing,** *n.* production of metal by heating ore with coke and limestone.

smid•gen ['smɪdʒn] *n. inf.* very small amount.

smile [smaɪl] 1. *n.* expression of pleasure with the mouth turned up at the corners. 2. *v.* to make an expression of happiness by turning up the corners of the mouth. **smil•ey,** *n.* symbol of a smile/frown, esp. those sent in electronic mail.

smirk [smɜːk] 1. *n.* unpleasant superior smile. 2. *v.* to give a smirk.

smite [smaɪt] *v.* (**smote, has smitten**) (*formal*) to hit; **smitten with** = liking.

smith [smɪθ] *n.* person who works in metal. **smith•y** ['smɪðɪ] *n.* workshop where a blacksmith works.

smith•er•eens [smɪðə'riːnz] *n.* very small bits.

smit•ten ['smɪtn] *v. see* **smite.**

smock [smɒk] *n.* long loose overall worn over clothes to protect them. **smock•ing,** *n.* embroidery on gathered material.

smog [smɒg] *n.* mixture of fog and exhaust fumes of cars.

smoke [sməʊk] 1. *n.* (a) vapor and gas given off when sth burns. (b) action of smoking a cigarette. 2. *v.* (a) to send out clouds of vapor and gas. (b) to cure (bacon/fish, etc.) by hanging in wood smoke. (c) to suck in smoke from a burning cigarette/pipe, etc. **smoke•less,** *adj.* which makes no smoke. **smok•er,** *n.* (a) person who smokes cigarettes, etc. (b) railroad car where you can smoke. **smoke•screen,** *n.* thick smoke made so that the enemy cannot see; anything which is deliberately used to hide what is going on. **smok•y,** *adj.* (-ier, -iest) full of cigarette smoke.

smol•der, *Brit.* **smoul•der** ['sməʊldə] *v.* to burn slowly.

æ **back,** ɑː **farm,** ɒ **top,** aɪ **pipe,** aʊ **how,** aɪə **fire,** aʊə **flower,** ɔː **bought,** ɔɪ **toy,** e **fed,** eə **hair,** eɪ **take,** ə **afraid,** əʊ **boat,** əʊə **lower,** ɜː **word,** iː **heap,** ɪ **hit,** ɪə **hear,** uː **school,** ʊ **book,** ʌ **but,** b **back,** d **dog,** ð **then,** dʒ **just,** f **fog,** g **go,** h **hand,** j **yes,** k **catch,** l **last,** m **mix,** n **nut,** ŋ **sing,** p **penny,** r **round,** s **some,** ʃ **short,** t **too,** tʃ **chop,** θ **thing,** v **voice,** w **was,** z **zoo,** ʒ **treasure**

smooth [smu:ð] 1. *adj.* (-er, -est) (a) (surface) with no bumps/no roughness. (b) with no bumps/jolts. (c) with no hair. (d) too pleasant (person). 2. *v.* to make smooth; **to s. the way for sth** = to make it easy; **to s. things over** = to settle an argument. **smooth•ly**, *adv.* in a smooth way. **smooth•ness**, *n.* being smooth.

smor•gas•bord ['smɔːgəsbɔːd] *n.* Swedish buffet of many cold dishes.

smote [sməʊt] *v. see* **smite**.

smoth•er ['smʌðə] *v.* (a) to stifle and kill (s.o.). (b) to cover.

smudge [smʌdʒ] 1. *n.* dirty (ink) stain. 2. *v.* to make a mark, such as by rubbing ink which is not dry. **smudg•y**, *adj.* (paper) with a dirty mark on it.

smug [smʌg] *adj.* **(smugger, smuggest)** self-satisfied. **smug•ly**, *adv.* in a way which shows you are pleased with yourself. **smug•ness**, *n.* being smug.

smug•gle ['smʌgl] *v.* to take (goods) past a customs check without declaring them for duty; to take (sth) into or out of a prison without the guards seeing. **smug•gler**, *n.* person who smuggles goods.

smut [smʌt] 1. *n.* (a) small black mark. (b) indecent stories. **smut•ty**, *adj.* (-ier, -iest) indecent.

Sn *symbol for* tin.

snack [snæk] *n.* light meal. **snack•bar**, *n.* restaurant where you can have a light meal, usu. sitting at a counter.

snaf•fle ['snæfl] *n.* horse's bit.

snag [snæg] 1. *n.* (a) obstacle; thing which prevents you from doing sth. (b) sharp point; place where a piece of clothing has been caught on a sharp point. 2. *v.* **(snagged)** to catch and tear (your clothes) on a sharp point.

snail [sneɪl] *n.* common slimy animal with a shell; **at a s.'s pace** = extremely slowly. **snail mail**, *n. inf.* conventional mail system, slow when compared to almost instantaneous electronic mail.

snake [sneɪk] 1. *n.* long, sometimes poisonous, reptile which wriggles along the ground. 2. *v.* to wriggle like a snake.

snap [snæp] 1. *n.* (a) sudden dry noise. (b) **cold s.** = sudden spell of cold weather. (c) type of crisp cracker. (d) snapshot. (e) fastening for clothes, made of two small metal studs which fit into each other. 2. *adj.* (decision) taken hurriedly. 3. *v.* **(snapped)** (a) to try to bite. (b) to speak sharply. (c) to break sharply; to make a dry noise (in breaking). (d) to take a photograph of (s.o.). (e) **to s. up** = to buy quickly. (f) *inf.* **to s. out of it** = to get out of a state of depression. **snap•drag•on**, *n.* antirrhinum. **snap•per**, *n.* type of fish. **snap•pi•ly**, *adv.*

in a snappy way. **snap•py**, *adj.* (-ier, -iest) (a) irritable/short-tempered. (b) *inf.* **make it s.!** = do it quickly. **snap•shot**, *n.* informal photograph taken quickly.

snare ['sneə] 1. *n.* trap for catching animals made with a noose which is pulled tight. 2. *v.* to catch with a snare.

snarl [snɑːl] 1. *n.* (a) angry growl. (b) tangle. 2. *v.* (a) to growl angrily. (b) to make tangled.

snatch [snætʃ] 1. *n.* (*pl.* -es) (a) grabbing sth. (b) short piece (of a song, etc.). 2. *v.* to grab (sth) rapidly.

snaz•zy ['snæzɪ] *adj.* (-ier, -iest) *inf.* smart/in fashion.

sneak [sni:k] 1. *n. inf.* dishonest person. 2. *v.* to creep without being seen. **sneak•ers**, *n. pl.* soft sports shoes with rubber soles. **sneak•ing**, *adj.* secret. **sneak•y**, *adj. inf.* deceitful/not open.

sneer ['snɪə] 1. *n.* sarcastic smile; unpleasant smile. 2. *v.* to give s.o. a sarcastic smile to show contempt; to speak in a contemptuous way.

sneeze [sni:z] 1. *n.* sudden blowing out of air through your mouth and nose because of irritation in your nose. 2. *v.* make a sneeze; *inf.* **it's nothing to s. at** = you should not refuse it/despise it.

snick [snɪk] 1. *n.* small cut (with a knife). 2. *v.* to hit (a ball) a sharp glancing blow. **snick•er** ['snɪkə] 1. *n.* quiet unpleasant laugh. 2. *v.* to laugh quietly in an unpleasant way. **snick•er•ing**, *n.* hidden laughter.

snide [snaɪd] *adj. inf.* unpleasant/envious (remark).

sniff [snɪf] 1. *n.* short intake of air through the nose. 2. *v.* to take in air rapidly through the nose. **sniff•er**, *n.* person who sniffs. **snif•fle**. 1. *n.* slight cold in the head. 2. *v.* to keep on sniffing because of a cold.

snig•ger ['snɪgə] *n. & v. see* **snick•er**.

snip [snɪp] 1. *n.* piece which has been cut off. 2. *v.* **(snipped)** to cut with scissors. **snip•pet**, *n.* little bit (of cloth, etc.).

snipe [snaɪp] 1. *n.* large marsh bird with a long beak. 2. *v.* **to s. at s.o.** = to shoot at s.o. from a hiding place/to make continuous criticism of s.o. **snip•er**, *n.* hidden soldier who shoots at the enemy.

snitch [snɪtʃ] *v. inf.* to steal.

sniv•el ['snɪvl] *v.* **(sniveled, snivelled)** (a) to have a runny nose. (b) to cry and complain.

snob [snɒb] *n.* person who likes people who are of a higher social class than himself; **intellectual s.** = person who looks down on those who are not as well-educated as he feels he is himself. **snob•ber•y, snobbishness**, *n.* being a snob. **snob•bish**, *adj.* referring to a snob.

snood [snu:d] *n.* (old) ornamental bag-shaped

net for holding a woman's hair at the back of the head.

snook•er ['snuːkə] *n.* game like billiards played on a table with twenty-two balls of various colors.

snoop [snuːp] *v.* to creep about investigating sth secretly. **snoop•er,** *n.* person who spies on s.o. secretly.

snoot•y ['snuːtɪ] *adj.* (**-ier, -iest**) *inf.* superior (air/expression). **snoot•i•ly,** *adv.* in a snooty way. **snoot•i•ness,** *n.* being snooty.

snooze [snuːz] 1. *n.* short sleep. 2. *v.* to sleep lightly for a short time.

snore [snɔː] 1. *n.* loud noise in the throat made by breathing air when you are asleep. 2. *v.* to make a snore. **snor•er,** *n.* person who snores.

snor•kel ['snɔːkl] *n.* tube which goes from the mouth or mask of an underwater swimmer to the surface to allow him to breathe in air. **snor•kel•ing,** *n.* to go s. = to go swimming with a snorkel.

snort [snɔːt] 1. *n.* (a) snorting noise. (b) *inf.* small drink. 2. *v.* to make a loud noise blowing air out through the nose.

snot [snɒt] *n. inf.* mucus in the nose.

snout [snaʊt] *n.* nose of an animal (esp. a pig).

snow [snəʊ] 1. *n.* water vapor which freezes and falls in light white flakes. 2. *v.* to fall in flakes of snow; **snowed under** = overwhelmed. **snow•ball.** 1. *n.* ball of snow. 2. *v.* (a) to throw snowballs. (b) to get bigger and bigger. **snow•blind•ness,** *n.* painful lack of sight caused by the brightness of snow. **snow•drift,** *n.* heap of snow which has been piled up by the wind. **snow•drop,** *n.* small spring bulb with little white flowers. **snow•fall,** *n.* amount of snow which has fallen. **snow•flake,** *n.* flake of snow. **snow line,** *n.* point on a high mountain above which there is always snow. **snow•man,** *n.* (*pl.* **-men**) figure of a man made out of snow. **snow•mo•bile** ['snəʊməbiːl] *n.* vehicle with caterpillar tracks specially designed for driving on snow. **snow•plow,** *n.* heavy vehicle with a plow on the front for clearing snow off roads/railroads, etc. **snow•shoes,** *n. pl.* frames shaped like tennis rackets, with a light web, which are tied under the feet for walking on snow. **snow•storm,** *n.* storm which brings snow. **snow-white,** *adj.* pure white. **snow•y,** *adj.* (**-ier, -iest**) covered with snow; white like snow.

snub [snʌb] 1. *n.* insult; insulting refusal to speak to s.o. 2. *v.* (**snubbed**) to insult (s.o.) by refusing to speak to them/by not paying any attention to them. 3. *adj.* s. **nose** = small nose which is turned up at the end.

snuff [snʌf] 1. *n.* powdered tobacco which is sniffed into the nose. 2. *v.* to put out (a candle).

snuf•fle ['snʌfl] 1. *n.* loud sniff. 2. *v.* to sniff noisily.

snug [snʌg] *adj.* (**snugger, snuggest**) warm and comfortable. **snug•gle,** *v.* to curl yourself up to be warm; to curl up close to s.o. for warmth. **snug•ly,** *adv.* in a snug way.

so [səʊ] 1. *adv.* (a) to such an extent. (b) in this way. (c) true/correct; **I think s.** = I think it is true. (d) in the same way. (e) **or s.** = approximately. (f) **and s. on** = and in a similar way; etcetera. 2. *conj.* (a) therefore. (b) **s. that/s. as to** = for the purpose of. **so-and-so,** *n.* (a) somebody (whom you do not want to name). (b) hated person. **so-called,** *adj.* wrongly called. **so-so,** *adj. & adv. inf.* not very well.

soak [səʊk] 1. *n.* being very wet. 2. *v.* to put (sth) in a liquid so as to be completely covered; to get/to make very wet. **soak•ing.** 1. *n.* (action of) being soaked. 2. *adj. & adv.* wet through. **soak up,** *v.* to absorb (a liquid).

soap [səʊp] 1. *n.* material made of oil and fat used for washing. 2. *v.* to wash with soap. **soap•box,** *n.* box on which a speaker stands to talk to a meeting outdoors. **soap op•er•a,** *n.* trite serial story on television. **soap•stone,** *n.* type of soft gray stone which can be easily carved. **soap•suds,** *n. pl.* foam made from soap. **soap•y,** *adj.* full of soap; covered with soap.

soar [sɔː] *v.* (a) to fly high into the air; (*of bird*) to glide without beating its wings. (b) to rise rapidly.

sob [sɒb] 1. *n.* short breath like a hiccup when crying. 2. *v.* (**sobbed**) to weep, taking short breaths like hiccups.

so•ber ['səʊbə] 1. *adj.* (a) not drunk. (b) serious. (c) dark (color). 2. *v.* **to s. up** = to recover from drunkenness. **so•ber•ly,** *adv.* seriously. **so•ber•ness, sobriety** [sə'braɪtɪ] *n.* being sober.

so•bri•quet ['səʊbrɪkeɪ] *n.* nickname.

soc•cer ['sɒkə] *n.* form of football played between two teams of eleven players who can only kick or bounce the ball off a point of the body.

so•cia•ble ['səʊʃəbl] *adj.* friendly/liking the

æ back, ɑː farm, ɒ top, aɪ pipe, aʊ how, aɪə fire, aʊə flower, ɔː bought, ɔɪ toy, e fed, eəhair, eɪ take, ə afraid, əʊ boat, əʊə lower, ɜː word, iː heap, ɪ hit, ɪə hear, uː school, ʊ book, ʌ but, b back, d dog, ð then, dʒ just, f fog, g go, h hand, j yes, k catch, l last, m mix, n nut, ŋ sing, p penny, r round, s some, ʃ short, t too, tʃ chop, θ thing, v voice, w was, z zoo, ʒ treasure

company of other people. **so•cia•bil•i•ty** [səʊʃə'bɪlɪtɪ] *n.* being sociable.

so•cial ['səʊʃl] 1. *adj.* (a) referring to society; **s. science** = study of the problems of society; **s. security** = system of old-age, unemployment, or disability insurance provided by the U.S. government through regular payments made by an employer and employee; **s. services** = state services to help people's problems; **s. worker** = person who works to help families in need. (b) living in groups. 2. *n.* party. **so•cial•ism,** *n.* political system where the state owns and runs the wealth of the country; belief that all property should belong to the state and that every citizen is equal. **so•cial•ist,** *adj. & n.* (person) who believes in socialism; (policies) which follow the principles of socialism. **so•cial•ite,** *n.* person who moves in high society. **so•cial•ize,** *v.* (a) to be friendly with other people (at a party). (b) to organize (a country) along the principles of socialism. **so•cial•ly,** *adv.* in a social way.

so•ci•e•ty [sə'saɪɪtɪ] *n.* (a) way in which people are organized; group of people who live in the same way. (b) group/club/association of people with the same interests. (c) (*also* **high society**) top class of people. **so•ci•ol•o•gy** [səʊsɪ'ɒlədʒɪ] *n.* study of society and how people live in society. **so•ci•o•log•i•cal** [səʊsɪə'lɒdʒɪkl] *adj.* referring to society and the way in which society changes. **so•ci•ol•o•gist** [səʊsɪ'ɒlədʒɪst] *n.* person who studies society and how people live in it.

sock [sɒk] 1. *n.* covering for the foot and lower part of the leg. 2. *v. inf.* to hit.

sock•et ['sɒkɪt] *n.* hole(s) into which sth is fitted; **electric s.** = one which a plug/bulb can be fitted into.

sod [sɒd] *n.* piece of soil with grass growing on it.

so•da ['səʊdə] *n.* compound of sodium; **s. (water)** = water aerated by putting gas into it; **ice cream s.** = sweet drink mixed with ice cream. **so•da foun•tain,** *n.* bar where sweet drinks and ice cream are served.

sod•den ['sɒdn] *adj.* very wet.

so•di•um ['səʊdɪəm] *n.* (*element:* Na) white soft metal, which can catch fire, and is usu. found in combination with other substances.

sod•om•y ['sɒdəmɪ] *n.* anal or oral sexual intercourse, esp. between men.

so•fa ['səʊfə] *n.* long seat with a soft back for several people.

sof•fit ['sɒfɪt] *n.* underside of an arch.

soft [sɒft] *adj.* (-er, -est) (a) not hard; (pencil) which makes wide blurred marks. (b) quiet (voice). (c) not strict. (d) *inf.* stupid. (e) (water) with little calcium in it; (drink) which is not alcoholic; (drugs) which are not addictive.

soft-boiled, *adj.* (egg) which has not been boiled very much. **soft•en** ['sɒfn] *v.* to make/to become soft; **to s. up** = to make weak before attacking or before asking for a favor. **soft•en•er,** *n.* **water s.** = apparatus for making hard water soft. **soft-heart•ed,** *adj.* not strict/too kind. **soft•ly,** *adv.* in a soft way. **soft•ness,** *n.* being soft. **soft soap,** *n. inf.* flattery. **soft•ware,** *n.* computer programs (as opposed to the machines). **soft•wood,** *n.* wood from pine and fir trees.

sog•gy ['sɒgɪ] *adj.* (-ier, -iest) wet and soft. **sog•gi•ness,** *n.* being soggy.

soil [sɔɪl] 1. *n.* earth. 2. *v.* to make dirty.

so•journ ['sʌdʒən] 1. *n.* (*formal*) stay. 2. *v.* (*formal*) to stay.

sol•ace ['sɒləs] *n.* (*formal*) comfort.

so•lar ['səʊlə] *adj.* referring to the sun; **s. energy/s. power** = electricity produced from the radiation of the sun; **s. heating** = heating system run by light from the sun; **s. system** = series of planets orbiting the sun; **s. plexus** = (i) group of nerves behind the bottom of the lungs and the stomach; (ii) *inf.* the lower part of the body where the stomach is. **so•lar•i•um** [sə'leərɪəm] *n.* room where you can enjoy real or artificial sunlight.

sold [səʊld] *v. see* **sell.**

sol•der ['səʊldə] 1. *n.* soft metal used to join metal surfaces together when it is melted. 2. *v.* to join (metal surfaces together) with solder. **sol•der•ing i•ron,** *n.* tool which is heated to apply solder.

sol•dier ['səʊldʒə] 1. *n.* member of the army. 2. *v.* (a) to be on military service. (b) **to s. on** = to continue doing a hard job. **sol•dier•y,** *n.* soldiers.

sole [səʊl] 1. *n.* (a) underside of the foot; bottom part of a shoe. (b) flat sea fish. 2. *v.* to put a new sole on (a shoe). 3. *adj.* (a) only. (b) belonging to one person; **he has the s. right to** = he is the only person allowed to. **sole•ly,** *adv.* only.

sol•e•cism ['sɒlɪsɪzəm] *n.* embarrassing mistake made in speaking.

sol•emn ['sɒləm] *adj.* (a) special and religious (ceremony). (b) very serious. **so•lem•ni•ty** [sə'lemnɪtɪ] *n.* being solemn. **sol•em•ni•za•tion** [sɒləmnaɪ'zeɪʃn] *n.* celebration (of a marriage/of a religious ceremony). **sol•em•nize** ['sɒləmnaɪz] *v.* to celebrate/to perform (a marriage/a religious ceremony). **sol•emn•ly,** *adv.* in a solemn way.

so•le•noid ['sɒlənɔɪd] *n.* coiled wire which produces a magnetic field when an electric current passes through it.

sol-fa [ˌsɒlˈfɑː] *n.* system of indicating tones in music by syllables (*doh-ray-me*, etc.).

so•lic•it [səˈlɪsɪt] *v.* to ask for. **so•lic•i•ta•tion** [səlɪsɪˈteɪʃn] *n.* soliciting. **so•lic•i•tor,** *n.* lawyer who gives advice to people on legal problems. **so•lic•i•tous,** *adj.* worried/anxious about sth. **so•lic•i•tous•ly,** *adv.* in a solicitous way. **so•lic•i•tude,** *n.* anxiety/worry about sth.

sol•id [ˈsɒlɪd] 1. *adj.* (-er, -est) (a) not liquid. (b) not hollow. (c) made all of one material; **for eight hours s.** = without stopping. (d) trustworthy. 2. *n.* (a) solid sustance. (b) three-dimensional shape. **sol•i•dar•i•ty** [sɒlɪˈdærɪtɪ] *n.* common interest with s.o. **so•lid•i•fi•ca•tion** [səlɪdɪfɪˈkeɪʃn] *n.* act of solidifying. **so•lid•i•fy** [səˈlɪdfaɪ] *v.* to (make sth) become solid. **so•lid•i•ty** [səˈlɪdɪtɪ] *n.* being solid. **sol•id•ly,** *adv.* completely. **sol•id-state,** *adj.* (TV set, etc.) which uses transistors and not valves.

so•lil•o•quy [səˈlɪləkwɪ] *n.* speech spoken by a character alone on the stage. **so•lil•o•quize,** *v.* to speak all alone.

sol•i•taire [sɒlɪˈteə] *n.* (a) game for one person, as any of various card games or a game played on a board with balls which have to be jumped from hole to hole removing the intervening balls one at a time. (b) single diamond (in a ring, etc.).

sol•i•tar•y [ˈsɒlɪtrɪ] *adj.* (a) single/sole. (b) lonely; **s. confinement** = imprisonment alone in a cell. **sol•i•tude,** *n.* being alone.

so•lo [ˈsəʊləʊ] 1. *n.* (*pl.* -os, -li) piece of music for one person. 2. *adj. & adv.* carried out by one person. **so•lo•ist,** *n.* musician who plays a solo.

sol•stice [ˈsɒlstɪs] *n.* **summer s.** = period of the longest day (June 21st); **winter s.** = period of the longest night (December 21st).

sol•u•ble [ˈsɒljubl] *adj.* (a) which can be dissolved. (b) (problem) which can be solved. **sol•u•bil•i•ty** [sɒlju'bɪlɪtɪ] *n.* ability to be dissolved/solved. **so•lu•tion** [səˈluːʃn] *n.* (a) liquid in which sth has been dissolved. (b) act of solving a problem; answer to a problem.

solve [sɒlv] *v.* to find the answer to (a problem). **solv•a•ble,** *adj.* which can be solved. **solv•er,** *n.* person who solves a problem.

sol•ven•cy [ˈsɒlvənsɪ] *n.* state of being solvent. **sol•vent.** 1. *adj.* having enough money to pay your debts. 2. *n.* liquid which dissolves another substance.

so•ma•to•tro•pin [səmɑːtəʊˈtrɒfɪn] *n.* growth hormone.

som•ber, *Brit.* **som•bre** [ˈsɒmbə] *adj.* dark and gloomy. **som•ber•ly,** *adv.* in a somber way.

som•bre•ro [səmˈbreərəʊ] *n.* (*pl.* -os) hat with a wide brim worn in South America.

some [sʌm] 1. *adj.* (a) not a particular one. (b) certain; (c) several/a few; a little. (d) *inf.* wonderful; **that was s. party!** 2. *pron.* several out of a group; part of a whole. 3. *adv.* approximately. **some•bod•y** [ˈsʌmbədɪ] *pron.* (a) a particular unknown person. (b) *inf.* important person. **some•how** [ˈsʌmhaʊ] *adv.* in one way or another. **some•one** [ˈsʌmwʌn] *pron.* somebody. **some•place** [ˈsʌmpleɪs] *adv.* somewhere. **some•thing** [ˈsʌmθɪŋ] *pron.* (a) a particular unknown thing. (b) (*replacing a forgotten detail*) **the 4 s. train** = the train which leaves at some time after 4 o'clock. **some•time** [ˈsʌmtaɪm] *adv.* (a) at a particular unknown time. (b) (*old*) formerly. **some•times** [ˈsʌmtaɪmz] *adv.* from time to time/at times. **some•what** [ˈsʌmwɒt] *adv.* rather. **some•where** [ˈsʌmweə] *adv.* at some particular unknown place.

som•er•sault [ˈsʌməsɔːlt] 1. *n.* rolling over, with your head underneath and feet over your head. 2. *v.* to do a somersault/to roll over.

som•nam•bu•lism [sɒmˈnæmbjulɪzəm] *n.* walking in your sleep. **som•nam•bu•list** [sɒmˈnæmbjulɪst] *n.* person who walks when asleep.

som•no•lence [ˈsɒmnələns] *n.* (*formal*) being sleepy/sleepiness. **som•no•lent,** *adj.* sleepy.

son [sʌn] *n.* male child of a parent. **son-in-law** *n.* (*pl.* **sons-in-law**) husband of a daughter.

so•nar [ˈsəʊnɑː] *n.* device for finding underwater objects by using sound waves.

so•na•ta [səˈnɑːtə] *n.* piece of music in three or four movements for one or two instruments.

sonde [sɒnd] *n.* device attached to a balloon, used for taking samples of the atmosphere.

son et lu•mi•ère [sɒneɪluːmɪˈɜː] *n.* sound-and-light show.

song [sɒŋ] *n.* (a) singing. (b) words and music to be sung; **for a s.** = for very little money; *inf.* **he gave us a great s. and dance about it** = a great fuss. **song•bird,** *n.* bird which sings particularly well. **song•ster,** *n.* person or bird that sings.

son•ic [ˈsɒnɪk] *adj.* referring to sound waves; **s.**

æ back, ɑː farm, ɒ top, aɪ pipe, aʊ how, aɪə fire, aʊə flower, ɔː bought, ɔɪ toy, e fed, eə hair, eɪ take, ə afraid, əʊ boat, əʊə lower, ɜː word, iː heap, ɪ hit, ɪə hear, uː school, ʊ book, ʌ but, b back, d dog, ð then, dʒ just, f fog, g go, h hand, j yes, k catch, l last, m mix, n nut, ŋ sing, p penny, r round, s some, ʃ short, t too, tʃ chop, θ thing, v voice, w was, z zoo, ʒ treasure

boom = bang made by an aircraft traveling faster than the speed of sound.

son•net ['sɒnɪt] *n.* poem with fourteen lines.

son•ny ['sʌnɪ] *n. inf.* way of addressing a boy.

so•no•rous ['sɒnərəs] *adj.* which makes a loud ringing noise.

soon [su:n] *adv.* (**-er, -est**) (a) in a very short time; **sooner or later** = at some time to come. (b) **I would as s./sooner stay than go away** = I would rather stay.

soot [sʊt] *n.* black carbon dust which collects in chimneys. **soot•y**, *adj.* (**-ier, -iest**) black; covered with soot.

soothe [su:ð] *v.* to calm. **sooth•ing**, *adj.* which calms. **sooth•ing•ly**, *adv.* in a soothing way.

sooth•say•er ['su:θseɪə] *n.* person who foretells the future.

sop [sɒp] 1. *n.* (a) piece of bread dipped in liquid. (b) sth given as a bribe to make s.o. keep quiet. 2. *v.* (**sopped**) to soak in liquid; to soak up (a liquid). **sop•ping**, *adj.* **s. wet** = soaked. **sop•py**, *adj.* soaked.

so•phis•ti•ca•tion [səfɪstɪ'keɪʃn] *n.* (a) cultured way of life. (b) advanced ideas behind the construction of a machine. **so•phis•ti•cat•ed**, *adj.* (a) cultured. (b) complicated/advanced (machine).

soph•ist•ry ['sɒfɪstrɪ] *n.* clever argument which is probably wrong.

soph•o•more ['sɒfəmɔ:] *n.* second-year student at a school, college, or university.

sop•o•rif•ic [sɒpə'rɪfɪk] *adj. & n.* (medicine) which makes you go to sleep.

so•pran•o [sə'prɑ:nəʊ] *n.* (*pl.* **-os**) high-pitched singing voice; woman or boy with such a voice.

sor•bet ['sɔ:beɪ] *n.* water ice.

sor•cer•y ['sɔ:sərɪ] *n.* witchcraft/magic. **sor•cer•er, sorceress**, *n.* person who makes magic.

sor•did ['sɔ:dɪd] *adj.* unpleasant/dirty. **sor•did•ly**, *adv.* in a sordid way. **sor•did•ness**, *n.* being sordid.

sore [sɔ:] 1. *adj.* (**-er, -est**) (a) painful/which hurts. (b) *inf.* upset/annoyed. 2. *n.* painful spot on the skin. **sore•ly**, *adv.* very much. **sore•ness**, *n.* being sore.

sor•ghum ['sɔ:gəm] *n.* type of grass, used as a cereal.

so•ror•i•ty [sə'rɒrɪtɪ] *n.* student society for women.

sor•rel ['sɒrəl] *n.* (a) common sour-tasting edible plant. (b) (horse which is) a reddish brown color.

sor•row ['sɒrəʊ] *n.* sadness. **sor•row•ful**, *adj.* very sad. **sor•row•ful•ly**, *adv.* in a sorrowful way. **sor•ry**, *adj.* (**-ier, -iest**) (a) regretting

sth. (b) feeling pity/sympathy **for** s.o. (c) pitiful.

sort [sɔ:t] 1. *n.* type/variety; **good s.** = pleasant type of person; *inf.* **s. of tired** = rather tired; **a meal of sorts** = not a very good meal; **out of sorts** = slightly unwell. 2. *v.* to arrange in different groups. **sort•er**, *n.* person who sorts; **mail s.** = person who sorts letters in a post office.

sort•ie ['sɔ:ti:] *n.* sudden attack; bombing raid (by aircraft).

SOS [esəʊ'es] *n.* international code for showing that you are in distress.

souf•flé ['su:fleɪ] *n.* light cooked dish, made from beaten eggs.

sought [sɔ:t] *v. see* **seek. sought after**, *adj.* which people want.

soul [səʊl] *n.* (a) the spirit in a person (as opposed to the body). (b) spirited or animating part. (c) **she is the s. of honor** = a fine example of honor. (d) person. **soul•ful**, *adj.* with a lot of feeling. **soul•ful•ly**, *adv.* in a soulful way. **soul•less**, *adj.* very dull/inhuman. **soul mu•sic**, *n.* popular music played by black musicians, which conveys deep feelings. **soul-search•ing**, *n.* examination of your own motives/conscience.

sound [saʊnd] 1. *n.* (a) noise; **s. wave** = wave in the air which carries sound; **s. barrier** = the speed of sound. (b) stretch of sea water. 2. *v.* (a) to make a noise. (b) **to s. like** = to be similar in sound to (sth). (c) **to s. s.o. out** = to talk to s.o. to test his opinion. (d) to measure the depth of water. 3. *adj.* (**-er, -est**) (a) healthy/not rotten. (b) reasonable/trustworthy. (c) deep (sleep). **sound-and-light show**, *n.* entertainment consisting of sound and lighting effects, shown in the open air at night. **sound ef•fects**, *n. pl.* noises made in a play/motion picture, etc., which imitate real sounds (such as thunder/gunfire, etc.). **sound•ing**, *n.* (a) making of noise; **s. board** = (i) board (as above a pulpit) which reflects sound; (ii) way of spreading ideas. (b) measuring the depth of water. **sound•less**, *adj.* which does not make any noise. **sound•less•ly**, *adv.* not making any noise. **sound•ly**, *adv.* thoroughly/deeply. **sound•ness**, *n.* being sound. **sound off**, *v. inf.* to start talking loudly **about** sth. **sound•proof.** 1. *adj.* made so that sound cannot get through. 2. *v.* to make (a building) soundproof. **sound•track**, *n.* part of a motion picture where the sound is recorded.

soup [su:p] *n.* liquid food usu. eaten at the beginning of a meal; *inf.* **in the s.** = in real trouble. **soup kitch•en**, *n.* place where soup and other food is given to the poor/to victims of a disaster. **soup up,** v. inf. to increase the power of (an engine).

soupçon ['suːpsɒn] n. slight taste; very small amount.

sour ['sauə] 1. adj. (-er, -est) (a) not sweet; sharp-tasting; inf. **s. grapes** = saying unpleasant things because of envy. (b) (milk) which has gone bad. (c) bad-tempered/unpleasant (person). 2. v. to make bad. **sour•ly,** adv. in a bad-tempered way. **sour•ness,** n. being sour. **sour•puss,** n. inf. unpleasant bad-tempered person.

source [sɔːs] n. place of origin/place where something starts or comes from.

souse [saus] v. (a) to soak in water. (b) to pickle (herrings, etc.) in salt water.

south [sauθ] 1. n. one of the points of the compass; (in areas north of the equator) the direction of the sun at midday. 2. adj. of the south. 3. adv. toward the south. **south•bound,** adj. going toward the south. **south•east,** adj., adv. & n. direction between south and east. **south•east•er•ly, southeastern,** adj. referring to the southeast. **south•er•ly** ['sʌðəlɪ] adj. (a) (wind) from the south. (b) **in a s. direction** = toward the south. **south•ern** ['sʌðən] adj. referring to the south. **south•ern•er** ['sʌðənə] n. person who lives in the south. **south•ern•most,** adj. farthest south. **south•paw,** n. inf. (in sports) player/boxer who is left-handed. **south•ward.** 1. adj. toward the south. 2. adv. (also **southwards**) toward the south. **south•west,** adj., adv. & n. direction between south and west. **south•west•er•ly, south•west•ern,** adj. referring to the southwest.

sou•ve•nir [suːvə'nɪə] n. thing which reminds you of a place/an event.

sou'•west•er [sau'westə] n. waterproof hat, worn esp. by sailors.

sov•er•eign ['sɒvrɪn] 1. n. (a) ruler/king or queen. (b) former British gold coin worth one pound sterling. 2. adj. (a) powerful (remedy). (b) self-governing. **sov•er•eign•ty,** n. total power; self-government.

So•vi•et ['səuvɪət] adj. & n. (a) (person) from Russia/the Commonwealth of Independent States (formerly the Soviet Union). (b) council/committee in a Communist country. **So•vi•et Un•ion,** n. former name for government of Russia/the Commonwealth of Independent States.

sow 1. n. [sau] female pig. 2. v. [səu] (**sowed, sown**) to put seed into earth so that it grows. **sow•er** ['səuə] n. person who sows seed.

soy [sɔɪ, 'sɔjə] n. (also **soy bean**) kind of very nutritious tropical bean; **s. sauce** = salty Chinese sauce made from soy beans.

soz•zled ['sɒzld] adj. inf. drunk.

spa [spɑː] n. place where mineral water comes out of the ground naturally and where people go to drink or bathe in the water because of its medicinal properties.

space [speɪs] 1. n. (a) place; empty area between two objects/on a sheet of paper, etc. (b) short period of time; **s. bar** = key on a typewriter/computer which makes a space between letters. (c) (also **outer space**) area beyond the earth's atmosphere. 2. v. **to s. out** = to time (things) at intervals; to place (things) with gaps between them. **space•craft,** n. rocket in which astronauts travel in space. **space•man,** n. (pl. -men) person who travels in space. **space-sav•ing,** adj. (piece of furniture, etc.) which is compact or which folds, and so saves space. **space•ship,** n. rocket in which astronauts travel in space. **space•suit,** n. special clothes worn by spacemen. **spa•cious** ['speɪʃəs] adj. very large/with lots of space. **spa•cious•ness** ['speɪʃəsnəs] n. state of being spacious.

spade [speɪd] n. (a) long-handled tool for digging holes in the ground; **to call a s. a s.** = to say what you think without trying to hide your opinions. (b) **spades** = one of the four suits in a pack of cards. **spade•work,** n. preliminary work.

spa•ghet•ti [spə'getɪ] n. Italian food formed of long strips of pasta.

spam [spæm] v. (**spamming, spammed**) to send an unsolicited electronic mail message, e.g. sales literature, to members of Internet newsgroups.

span [spæn] 1. n. (a) width (of wings/an arch, etc.). (b) arch of a bridge. (c) length of time. 2. v. (**spanned**) to stretch across.

span•drel ['spændrəl] n. wall between adjoining arches.

span•gle ['spæŋgl] n. small piece of bright metal which is sewn on a dress as an ornament. **span•gled,** adj. covered with spangles.

Span•iard ['spænjəd] n. person from Spain.

span•iel ['spænjəl] n. type of dog with large hanging ears.

æ back, ɑː farm, ɒ top, aɪ pipe, au how, aiə fire, auə flower, ɔː bought, ɔɪ toy, e fed, eəhair, eɪ take, ə afraid, əu boat, əuə lower, vː word, iː heap, ɪ hit, ɪə hear, uː school, u book, ʌ but, b back, d dog, ð then, dʒ just, f fog, g go, h hand, j yes, k catch, l last, m mix, n nut, ŋ sing, p penny, r round, s some, ʃ short, t too, tʃ chop, θ thing, v voice, w was, z zoo, ʒ treasure

Span•ish ['spænɪʃ] 1. *adj.* referring to Spain. 2. *n.* language spoken in Spain and Latin America.

spank [spæŋk] *v.* to smack on the behind. **spank•ing.** 1. *adj. inf.* (a) fast (pace). (b) bright new. 2. *n.* series of smacks on the behind.

spar [spɑː] 1. *n.* (a) ship's mast or a wooden beam for holding the sails. (b) type of mineral crystal. 2. *v.* (**sparred**) to practice boxing. **spar•ring part•ner,** *n.* person a boxer spars with.

spare ['speə] 1. *adj.* (a) not used/extra; **s. parts** = replacement parts for a machine; **s. tire** = tire carried to replace one that has a puncture. *inf.* **s. tire** = fold of fat around the waist of a plump person. (b) thin (person/body). 2. *n.* extra thing/replacement. 3. *v.* (a) to do without. (b) to give up; not to need. (c) **to s. s.o.'s life** = not to kill s.o. whom you have defeated; to have mercy on s.o. (d) **he was spared the embarrassment** = it saved him from being embarrassed. **spare ribs,** *n. pl.* cooked pork ribs in a spicy sauce. **spar•ing,** *adj.* **to be s. with** = to economize. **spar•ing•ly,** *adv.* using little.

spark [spɑːk] 1. *n.* little flash of fire/of electricity/of life. 2. *v.* to send out sparks/to make electric sparks. **spark plug,** *n.* (*in a car engine*) device which produces a spark which ignites the mixture of gasoline and air. **spar•kle** ['spɑːkl] 1. *n.* bright shiny light; small spark. 2. *v.* to glitter/to shine brightly; **sparkling wine** = wine which bubbles. **spar•kler,** *n.* type of firework which sends out sparks.

spar•row ['spærəʊ] *n.* common small brown and gray bird. **spar•row•hawk,** *n.* common small European hawk.

sparse [spɑːs] *adj.* (**-er, -est**) not thick; thinly spread. **sparse•ly,** *adv.* with few (things); thinly. **sparse•ness, sparsity,** *n.* being sparse.

spar•tan ['spɑːtən] *adj.* harsh/hard (discipline)/uncomfortable (conditions).

spasm ['spæzəm] *n.* (a) sudden uncontrollable pulling of muscles. (b) sudden fit (of energy, activity, etc.). **spas•mod•ic** [spæz'mɒdɪk] *adj.* coming in spasms/from time to time. **spas•mod•i•cal•ly,** *adv.* from time to time.

spas•tic ['spæstɪk] *adj. & n.* (person) who has suffered from brain damage which causes partial paralysis.

spat [spæt] 1. *n.* (a) small gaiter which just covers the shoe. (b) minor argument. 2. *v.* see **spit.**

spate [speɪt] *n.* sudden rush (of orders, etc.).

spathe [speɪθ] *n.* leaf which encloses a flower.

spa•tial ['speɪʃəl] *adj.* referring to space. **spa•tial•ly,** *adv.* in a spatial way.

spat•ter ['spætə] *v.* to splash with little spots of liquid.

spat•u•la ['spætjʊlə] *n.* wide flat blunt flexible knife.

spawn [spɔːn] 1. *n.* eggs (of a fish/frog, etc.); **mushroom s.** = material like seeds from which mushrooms grow. 2. *v.* to produce eggs.

spay [speɪ] *v.* to make (a female animal) sterile by removing her ovaries.

speak [spiːk] *v.* (**spoke, spoken**) (a) to say words and phrases; **I know him to s. to** = I know him enough to get into conversation with him. (b) to talk in public. (c) to be able to say things in (a foreign language). **speak•er,** *n.* (a) person who speaks. (b) chairman of the U.S. House of Representatives, the British House of Commons, and certain other legislative bodies. (c) loudspeaker. **speak for,** *v.* to plead on s.o.'s behalf. **speak•ing,** *n.* action of talking; **we're not on s. terms** = we have quarreled and don't speak to each other. **speak up,** *v.* (a) to speak louder. (b) **to s. up for** = to support.

spear ['spɪə] 1. *n.* long pointed throwing weapon. 2. *v.* to jab (s.o./sth) with a spear. **spear•head.** 1. *n.* front part of a force of attackers. 2. *v.* to be in the front of an attacking force. **spear•mint,** *n.* common type of mint, often used in chewing gum.

spec [spek] *n. inf.* **to buy on s.** = without being sure of the value/condition.

spe•cial ['speʃəl] 1. *adj.* (a) particular/referring to one particular thing. (b) extraordinary/rare/unusual. 2. *n.* (a) particular edition of a newspaper. (b) particular dish on a menu. (c) article reduced in price. **spe•cial•ist,** *n.* person who has studied sth very deeply. **spe•cial•i•ty** [speʃɪ'ælɪtɪ] *n.* particular interest; subject which you have studied/thing you are known for. **spe•cial•i•za•tion** [speʃəlaɪ'zeɪʃn] *n.* act of specializing; thing you specialize in. **spe•cial•ize** ['speʃəlaɪz] *v.* **to s. in sth** = to study/to produce sth in particular. **spe•cial•ly,** *adv.* particularly; unusually.

spe•cies ['spiːʃɪz] *n.* (*pl* **species**) (a) group of animals/plants which are closely similar, and which can breed together. (b) *inf.* sort. **spe•cie,** *n. pl.* (*formal*) coins.

spec•i•fy ['spesɪfaɪ] *v.* to state clearly what is required. **spe•cif•ic** [spe'sɪfɪk] *adj.* particular/precise (details). **spe•cif•i•cal•ly,** *adv.* particularly. **spec•i•fi•ca•tion** [spesɪfɪ'keɪʃn] *n.* detailed plan/information. **spec•i•fic grav•i•ty,** *n.* density of a substance divided by the density of water.

spec•i•men ['spesɪmən] *n.* (a) sample which is

selected for study or exhibition. (b) sample/example.

spe•cious ['spiːʃəs] *adj.* not really true as it seems. **spe•cious•ly**, *adv.* in a specious way. **spe•cious•ness**, *n.* being specious.

speck [spek] *n.* tiny spot. **speck•le**, *n.* small (usu. brown) spot. **speck•led**, *adj.* covered with speckles.

specs [speks] *n. pl. inf.* eyeglasses.

spec•ta•cle ['spektəkl] *n.* (a) show. (b) eyeglasses. **spec•tac•u•lar** [spek'tækjulə] *adj.* impressive (show/display). **spec•tac•u•lar•ly**, *adv.* in a spectacular way. **spec•ta•tor**, *n.* person who watches a show/a sports event, etc.

spec•ter, *Brit.* **spec•tre** ['spektə] *n.* (a) ghost. (b) fear. **spec•tral**, *adj.* like a ghost.

spec•trum ['spektrəm] *n.* bands of colors varying from red to blue (as seen in a rainbow); range (of ideas, etc.). **spec•trog•ra•phy**, *n.* recording of a spectrum, used to analyze the chemical composition of a substance.

spec•u•late ['spekjuleɪt] *v.* (a) to **s. about** = to make guesses about. (b) to gamble by buying things whose value you hope will rise. **spec•u•la•tion** [spekju'leɪʃn] *n.* (a) guesses made about sth. (b) gambling by buying things whose value you hope will rise. **spec•u•la•tive** ['spekjulətɪv] *adj.* (a) made by guessing. (b) gambling; **s. venture** = one whose outcome is uncertain. **spec•u•la•tor** ['spekjuleɪtə] *n.* person who buys goods in the hope or reselling them again at a profit.

spec•u•lum ['spekjuləm] *n.* (a) reflector in a telescope. (b) tube for inspecting the interior of the body.

sped [sped] *v. see* **speed.**

speech [spiːtʃ] *n.* (*pl.* **-es**) (a) ability to talk. (b) spoken language; **the parts of s.** = different groups of words (nouns/verbs, etc.) which are used in a similar way in language. (c) talk given in public. **speech•i•fy**, *v. inf.* to make long speeches. **speech•less**, *adj.* incapable of saying anything.

speed [spiːd] 1. *n.* (a) quickness of movement. (b) rate of movement. 2. *v.* (**sped** or **speeded**) (a) to go fast. (b) to drive a car faster than the legal speed; to make (progress) go faster. **speed•boat**, *n.* racing motor boat. **speed•i•ly**, *adv.* very fast. **speed•i•ness**, *n.* being speedy. **speed•om•e•ter** [spiː'dɒmɪtə] *n.* dial which shows you how fast you

are driving. **speed up**, *v.* to go faster; to make (sth) go faster. **speed•way**, *n.* racing track for automobiles or motorcycles. **speed•well**, *n.* small wild plant with blue flowers. **speed•y**, *adj.* (**-ier, -iest**) very fast.

spe•le•ol•o•gy [spiːlɪ'ɒlədʒɪ] *n.* climbing down into caves or holes in the ground. **spe•le•o•log•i•cal**, *adj.* referring to speleology. **spe•le•ol•o•gist**, *n.* person who climbs in or explores caves and holes in the ground.

spell [spel] 1. *n.* (a) magic curse; words which may have a magic effect. (b) period of time. 2. *v.* (**spelled/spelt**) (a) to say aloud/to write correctly the letters which form a word; **to s. out** = (i) to write out all the letters of; (ii) to explain very clearly. (b) to mean. **spell•bind•er**, *n.* thing which enchants/attracts and keeps the attention. **spell•bound**, *adj.* bewitched/enchanted. **spell check**, *v.* to check the spelling of text, using a computer program. **spell•er**, *n.* person who spells. **spell•ing**, *n.* way in which a word is spelled; writing words correctly. **spell•ing check•er**, *n.* computer program which checks spelling.

spen•cer ['spensə] *n.* type of sleeved vest worn by women in the 19th century.

spend [spend] *v.* (**spent**) (a) to pay (money) in exchange for sth. (b) to pass (time). (c) **to s. oneself** = to tire oneself out. **spend•er**, *n.* person who spends. **spend•ing**, *n.* action of using money to buy sth. **spend•thrift**, *adj. & n.* (person) who spends money fast.

spent [spent] *adj.* used; **s. fuel** = fuel which has been used in a nuclear reactor; *see also* **spend.**

sperm [spɜːm] *n.* (a) male fluid which fertilizes the eggs of a female. (b) **s. whale** = large whale which provides oil. **sper•ma•cet•i** [spɜːmə-'setɪ] *n.* (*no pl.*) white substance taken from a sperm whale, and used as a base for perfumes. **sper•ma•to•zo•a** [spɜːmətə'zəuə] *n. pl.* sperms. **sper•mi•cid•al**, *adj.* which kills sperm.

spew [spjuː] *v. inf.* **to s. (out)** = to vomit; to pour out.

sphag•num ['sfægnəm] *n.* type of moss.

sphere ['sfɪə] *n.* (a) object which is perfectly round. (b) area (of influence); society. **spher•i•cal** ['sferɪkl] *adj.* shaped like a sphere/perfectly round.

sphinc•ter ['sfɪŋktə] *n.* circular muscle which controls an opening.

æ back, aː farm, ɒ top, aɪ pipe, aʊ how, aɪə fire, aʊə flower, ɔː bought, ɔɪ toy, e fed, eəhair, eɪ take, ə afraid, əʊ boat, əʊə lower, ɜː word, iː heap, ɪ hit, ɪə hear, uː school, ʊ book, ʌ but, b back, d dog, ð then, dʒ just, f fog, g go, h hand, j yes, k catch, l last, m mix, n nut, ŋ sing, p penny, r round, s some, ʃ short, t too, tʃ chop, θ thing, v voice, w was, z zoo, ʒ treasure

sphinx [sfɪŋks] n. (pl. **-es, -ges**) legendary animal in Egypt with the head of a woman and the body of a lion; large stone monument of this animal.

spice [spaɪs] 1. n. (a) flavoring made from seeds/leaves of plants, etc. (b) thing which excites interest. 2. v. to add spices to (a dish). **spic•i•ness**, n. being spicy. **spic•y**, adj. (a) with a lot of spices. (b) rather rude (story).

spick-and-span ['spɪkən'spæn] adj. very clean/tidy.

spi•der ['spaɪdə] n. eight-legged animal, which makes a web and eats flies; **s. plant** = common house plant, with long yellow and green leaves. **spi•der web, spider's web**, n. web made by a spider. **spi•der•y**, adj. thin and scrawling (handwriting).

spiel [spiːl] n. inf. long flow of talk (aimed at persuading).

spig•ot ['spɪgət] n. tap/faucet (in a barrel).

spike [spaɪk] 1. n. (a) long sharp point. (b) **spikes** = sharp points in the soles of sports or running shoes. 2. v. (a) to attach spikes to. (b) to jam (a gun). (c) to cut (another player/runner) with your spikes. **spiked**, adj. covered with spikes. **spik•y**, adj. standing up in sharp points.

spill [spɪl] 1. n. (a) fall. (b) long thin piece of wood for lighting cigarettes/candles, etc. 2. v. (**spilled/spilt**) to pour (liquid) out of a container by mistake. **spill•age**, n. action of spilling; amount of liquid spilt.

spin [spɪn] 1. n. (a) action of turning around and around. (b) short fast trip. 2. v. (**spun**) (a) to turn around and around very fast; to make (a ball) turn as it goes through the air. (b) to twist (raw wool/cotton, etc.) to form a thread. **spin-dri•er**, n. machine for drying laundry by turning it around very fast. **spin-dry**, v. to dry (laundry) in a spin-drier. **spin•ner**, n. person who spins thread. **spin•ner•et** [spɪnə'ret] n. part of the spider which spins the threads to make a web. **spin•ning wheel**, n. apparatus for twisting and winding wool. **spin-off**, n. secondary result; useful by-product. **spin out**, v. inf. to make (sth) last a long time.

spi•na bif•i•da [spaɪnə'bɪfɪdə] n. condition from birth, where the spine is badly formed allowing the membrane covering the spinal cord to protrude.

spin•ach ['spɪnɪtʃ] n. common green-leaved vegetable.

spin•dle ['spɪndl] n. (a) pin used for twisting thread in a spinning machine. (b) central pin around which sth turns.

spin•dly ['spɪndlɪ] adj. (**-ier, -iest**) long, thin and weak.

spin•drift ['spɪndrɪft] n. spray which is blown from breaking waves.

spine [spaɪn] n. (a) backbone. (b) back of a book. (c) prickle (on a cactus/hedgehog, etc.). **spi•nal**, n. referring to the spine; **s. column** = backbone; **s. cord** = group of nerves running down the inside of the spine. **spine•less**, adj. (person) who is weak and indecisive. **spin•y**, adj. covered with prickles.

spin•et [spɪ'net] n. old musical instrument, like a small rectangular harpsichord.

spin•na•ker ['spɪnəkə] n. large balloonlike sail on the front of a racing yacht.

spin•ster ['spɪnstə] n. unmarried woman (usu. middle-aged).

spi•ral ['spaɪərəl] 1. n. (a) thing which is twisted around and around like a spring. (b) thing which turns around and around getting higher or lower all the time. 2. adj. twisted around and around like a spring. 3. v. (**spiraled, spiralled**) to go around and around and rise at the same time. **spi•ral•ly**, adv. in a spiral shape.

spire ['spaɪə] n. pointed construction on top of a church tower.

spir•it ['spɪrɪt] 1. n. (a) soul. (b) ghost; **Holy S.** = the third person of the Christian Trinity. (c) energetic way of doing sth. (d) real meaning (not always expressed in words). (e) **spirits** = strong alcoholic drink (whisky/gin, etc.). 2. v. **to s. away** = to remove as if by magic. **spir•it•ed**, adj. very vigorous. **spir•it•ed•ly**, adv. in a spirited way. **spir•it lev•el**, n. tool for testing if a surface is level using a glass tube containing an airbubble. **spir•it•u•al**. 1. adj. referring to the spirit; dealing with the soul. 2. n. religious song sung by blacks in the southern United States. **spir•it•u•al•ism**, n. belief that you can communicate with the spirits of dead people. **spir•it•u•al•ist**, n. person who tries to communicate with the spirits of dead people. **spir•it•u•al•i•ty**, n. state of being spiritual. **spir•it•u•al•ly**, adv. in a spiritual way. **spir•it•u•ous**, adj. alcoholic.

spit [spɪt] 1. n. (a) long metal rod passed through meat which turns so that the meat is evenly cooked. (b) long thin stretch of land going out into the sea. (c) liquid formed in the mouth; **s. and polish** = excessive cleaning; inf. **he is the dead s. and image of his father** = he looks exactly like his father. 2. v. (a) (**spitted**) to put (meat) on a spit to roast. (b) (**spit, spat**) to send liquid out of the mouth; inf. **he is the spitting image of his father** = he looks exactly like his father. (c) to send sparks out; to rain slightly. **spit•tle** ['spɪtl] n. saliva. **spit•toon** [spɪ'tuːn] n. dish for spitting into.

spite [spaɪt] 1. n. (a) bad feeling against s.o./desire to hurt s.o. (b) **in s. of sth** = without bothering about. 2. *v.* to try to annoy. **spite•ful**, *adj.* full of bad feeling/wishing to hurt s.o. **spite•ful•ly**, *adv.* in a spiteful way. **spite•ful•ness**, *n.* being spiteful.

splash [splæʃ] 1. *n.* (*pl.* **-es**) (a) noisy throwing of liquid; sound of liquid being thrown noisily. (b) mark made by dirty liquid being scattered. (c) bright patch of color. (d) short spurt (of soda water, etc.). (e) sudden show; sudden spending of money. 2. *v.* (a) (*of liquid*) to make a noise while hitting (a solid). (b) to send dirty liquid on to. (c) to display. **splash down**, *v.* (*of space capsule*) to land in the sea. **splash•down**, *n.* landing (of a spacecraft) in the sea. **splash•y**, *adj.* which splashes.

splat•ter ['splætə] *v.* to splash.

splay [spleɪ] 1. *adj.* turned outward. 2. *v.* to slant outward.

spleen [spli:n] *n.* organ near the stomach which keeps the blood in good condition.

splen•did ['splendɪd] *adj.* magnificent/wonderful. **splen•did•ly**, *adv.* wonderfully/extremely well. **splen•dor**, *Brit.* **splen•dour**, *n.* magnificence.

sple•net•ic [splə'netɪk] *adj.* violently angry.

splice [splaɪs] 1. *n.* joint which links two pieces of rope. 2. *v.* to join (two pieces of rope) by twisting the threads together; to join (two pieces of film) together. **splic•er**, *n.* device for joining pieces of film together.

splint [splɪnt] *n.* stiff bar tied to a broken leg, etc., to keep it straight.

splin•ter ['splɪntə] 1. *n.* small pointed piece (of wood/metal); **s. group** = group of people who have separated from a main group. 2. *v.* to split into thin pointed pieces.

split [splɪt] 1. *n.* (a) thin crack; sharp break. (b) **the splits** = gymnastic exercise where you sit on the floor with one leg stretched out in front, and the other behind you. (c) **banana s.** = dessert of bananas, whipped cream, ice cream and nuts. 2. *v.* (**split**) to divide (sth) into parts; to make (sth) divide/crack; *inf.* **my head is splitting** = I have a bad headache. 3. *adj.* which has been cracked; **s. peas** = dried peas broken in half; **in a s. second** = very fast; **to have a s. personality** = to have two ways of behaving which are quite different in varying circumstances. **split-lev•el**, *adj.* (house) having a room or rooms with part of the floor higher than the rest. **split up**, *v.* to divide.

splotch [splɒtʃ] *n.* dirty mark; oddly-shaped spot of color.

splurge [splɜ:dʒ] 1. *n. inf.* spending spree. 2. *v. inf.* to spend money extravagantly.

splut•ter ['splʌtə] *v.* (a) to spit when speaking; to speak rapidly. (b) to sputter (when cooking).

spoil [spɔɪl] 1. *v.* (**spoiled/spoilt**) (a) to ruin/to make bad. (b) to treat (a child) so leniently that it ruins his character. 2. *n. pl.* **spoils** (a) booty, goods taken by soldiers from a defeated enemy. (b) waste material from a mine. **spoil•er**, *n.* decorative panel at the front or back of a car, which is intended to slow the vehicle down. **spoil for**, *v.* to be eager for sth. **spoil•sport**, *n.* person who spoils other people's enjoyment.

spoke [spəʊk] 1. *n.* one of the rods running from the axle of a wheel to the rim. 2. *v. see also* **speak**. **spokeshave**, *n.* tool with a curved blade for smoothing sth round.

spo•ken ['spəʊkn] *v. see* **speak**.

spokes•man, **spokeswoman,** **spokesperson** ['spəʊksmən, -wʊmən, -pɜ:sən] *n.* (*pl.* **-men, -women**) person who speaks on behalf of s.o.

spo•li•a•tion [spəʊlɪ'eɪʃn] *n.* (*formal*) act of plundering.

spon•dee ['spɒndeɪ] *n.* measure (two long syllables) used in Latin poetry.

sponge [spʌndʒ] 1. *n.* (a) soft skeleton of a sea animal/block of synthetic material full of small holes, which soaks up water and is used for washing; **s. bath** = washing a patient in bed, using a sponge; *inf.* **to throw up/in the s.** = to give in/to admit you are beaten. (b) act of washing with a sponge. (c) **s. cake** = light soft cake. 2. *v.* (a) to wash with a sponge. (b) *inf.* **to s. sth from s.o.** = to get by begging or borrowing from s.o. **spong•er**, *n.* person who doesn't work but gets money by begging for or borrowing it from friends. **spon•gy**, *adj.* soft and full of holes.

spon•sor ['spɒnsə] 1. *n.* (a) person who helps s.o. by taking responsibility. (b) person or firm who pays for a television show/sports event, etc., as a form of advertisement. (c) person who pays money to a charity if s.o. else walks, swims, runs, a certain distance, etc. 2. *v.* to be a sponsor; to be responsible for (a bill in a legislative body); to pay for (a television show/a sports event, etc.); (*of godparent*) **to s. a child at baptism** = to promise to help the child to lead a Christian life. **spon•sor•ship**, *n.* action of sponsoring.

spon•ta•ne•ous [spɒn'teɪnɪəs] *adj.* which

æ **back,** a: **farm,** ɒ: **top,** aɪ **pipe,** aʊ **how,** aɪə **fire,** aʊə **flower,** ɔ: **bought,** ɔɪ **toy,** e **fed,** eəhair, eɪ **take,** ə **afraid,** əʊ **boat,** əʊə **lower,** v: **word,** i: **heap,** ɪ **hit,** ɪə **hear,** u: **school,** ʊ **book,** ʌ **but,** b **back,** d **dog,** ð **then,** dʒ **just,** f **fog,** g **go,** h **hand,** j **yes,** k **catch,** l **last,** m **mix,** n **nut,** ŋ **sing,** p **penny,** r **round,** s **some,** ʃ **short,** t **too,** tʃ **chop,** θ **thing,** v **voice,** w **was,** z **zoo,** ʒ **treasure**

happens freely/which is not forced. **spon•ta•ne•ous•ly,** *adv.* in a spontaneous/natural way. **spon•ta•ne•i•ty** [spɒntə-'niɪətɪ] *n.* acting in a natural way.

spoof [spuːf] *n. inf.* hoax/amusing imitation.

spook [spuːk] *n.* ghost. **spook•y,** *adj. inf.* frightening; (place) which is likely to be haunted.

spool [spuːl] *n.* cylinder around which sth is wound.

spoon [spuːn] 1. *n.* eating utensil with a small bowl and a long handle. 2. *v.* **to s. sth up/into** = to lift sth up/to put sth in with a spoon. **spoon•bill,** *n.* large white bird with a spoon-shaped end to its bill. **spoon-feed,** *v.* to give (a baby) food with a spoon; to teach (people) by giving them answers to questions and not allowing them to work by themselves; to provide everything for (s.o.) so that they need do nothing to help themselves. **spoon•ful,** *n.* amount contained in a spoon.

spoon•er•ism ['spuːnərɪzəm] *n.* exchanging letters of words by mistake (**queer old dean** for *dear old queen*).

spoor ['spʊə] *n. (no pl.)* tracks left by an animal.

spo•rad•ic [spə'rædɪk] *adj.* which happens at irregular intervals. **spo•rad•i•cal•ly,** *adv.* in a sporadic way.

spore [spɔː] *n.* plant cell which reproduces without requiring to be fertilized.

spor•ran ['spɒrən] *n.* leather bag worn by Scotsmen in front of the kilt.

sport [spɔːt] 1. *n.* (a) game (such as soccer/hockey/tennis, etc.); **blood sports** = hunting animals as a sport; **sports car** = light fast open car; **sports jacket/sports coat** = man's casual jacket. (b) *inf.* **good s.** = pleasant person always willing to help. (c) animal/plant which is very different from its parents. 2. *v.* to wear. **sport•ing,** *adj.* (person) who plays according to the rules/who is pleasant and willing to help; **s. chance** = a good or fair chance. **spor•tive,** *adj.* playful. **sports•man,** *n. (pl. -men)* (a) person who takes part in a sport. (b) person who plays properly. **sports•man•like,** *adj.* (playing a game) in a proper way/according to the rules; not cheating. **sports•man•ship,** *n.* quality of being a good sportsman/of not cheating. **sports•wear,** *n. (no pl.)* clothes worn to play sports or for casual wear. **sports•wom•an,** *n. (pl. -women)* woman who takes part in a sport. **sport•y,** *adj.* interested in or engaged in sports.

spot [spɒt] 1. *n.* (a) place; **on the s.** = on duty/at your post; **in a s.** = in a difficult position; **to put s.o. on the s.** = in a position where he has to act. (b) pimple. (c) usu. round colored mark. (d) *inf.* small amount. (e) spotlight/bright light

which only shines on one spot. 2. *v.* (**spotted**) (a) to mark with a spot. (b) to notice. **spot check,** *n.* surprise check (on items at random). **spot•less,** *adj.* very clean. **spot•less•ly,** *adj.* **s. clean** = extremely clean. **spot•light.** 1. *n.* bright light which shines on one small area. 2. *v.* to highlight/to draw attention to (sth). **spot•ter,** *n.* person who notes or watches for things. **spot•ty,** *adj.* (-ier, -iest) full of spots.

spouse ['spauz] *n. (formal)* husband or wife.

spout [spaut] 1. *n.* tube for pouring liquid out of a pitcher, etc.; tube for sending waste water/rainwater away from the wall of a building. 2. *v.* (a) to come out in a stream. (b) *inf.* to speak continuously.

sprain [spreɪn] 1. *n.* twist of a joint. 2. *v.* to twist (a joint).

sprang [spræŋ] *v. see* **spring.**

sprat [spræt] *n.* very small herringlike fish.

sprawl [sprɔːl] 1. *n.* irregular spread; **urban s.** = unregulated spread of houses built over what formerly was countryside. 2. *v.* (a) to lie with arms and legs spread out. (b) to spread out in an irregular way.

spray [spreɪ] 1. *n.* (a) branch with flowers on it. (b) liquid in the form of tiny drops/in a mist. (c) sprayer. 2. *v.* to send out liquid in a fine mist. **spray•er,** *n.* machine for spraying. **spray gun,** *n.* tool shaped like a pistol with a small container attached (used for spraying paint/insecticide, etc.).

spread [spred] 1. *n.* (a) wide expanse; width. (b) act of sending out over a wide area. (c) *inf.* feast. (d) soft food of meat/cheese for spreading on bread, crackers, etc. (e) **double-page s.** = text which runs over two facing pages in a book or newspaper. 2. *v.* (**spread**) (a) to send out/to go out over a wide area. (b) to space out over a period of time. (c) to cover with a layer of sth. **spread-ea•gled,** *adj.* lying flat with arms and legs stretched out. **spread•sheet,** *n.* computer printout of tables of figures.

spree [spriː] *n.* happy time; **to go on a spending s.** = to have a happy time spending money.

sprig [sprɪg] *n.* (a) small branch. (b) design of small branches.

spright•ly ['spraɪtlɪ] *adj.* (-ier, -iest) light and vigorous. **spright•li•ness,** *n.* being sprightly.

spring [sprɪŋ] 1. *n.* (a) small stream of water coming out of the ground. (b) season of the year following winter when plants begin to grow and put out leaves. (c) leap in the air. (d) coiled wire which returns to its original shape after being stretched or compressed. (e) bounciness. 2. *v.* (**sprang, has sprung**) (a) to leap/to bounce. (b) to set (sth) off/to make (sth) happen suddenly. (c) to come **from.** (d) **to**

s. a leak = to start taking in water through a crack. **spring•board,** *n.* long flexible board used to give an impetus to a diver or jumper. **spring•bok** ['sprɪŋbɒk] *n.* type of African deer. **spring-clean,** *v.* to clean thoroughly after the winter. **spring fe•ver,** *n.* feeling of excitement at the coming of spring. **spring•i•ness,** *n.* being springy. **spring•like,** *adj.* (weather) which is mild like in spring. **spring tide,** *n.* tide which rises and falls very sharply, and occurs at the new and full moon. **spring•time,** *n.* spring/the season after winter. **spring•y,** *adj.* (-ier, -iest) flexible; (board) which bends; (carpet/grass) which is very soft.

sprin•kle ['sprɪŋkl] *v.* to scatter water/sand, etc. **sprin•kler,** *n.* device for sprinkling; **s. system** = system of automatic fire control which sprinkles water on a fire and is set off by rising heat. **sprin•kling,** *n.* (a) action of scattering water/sand, etc. (b) small quantities.

sprint [sprɪnt] 1. *n.* short fast running race. 2. *v.* to run very fast over a short distance. **sprint•er,** *n.* runner who specializes in sprint races.

sprit [sprɪt] *n.* small spar which goes diagonally across a sail. **sprit•sail,** *n.* sail held by a sprit.

sprite [spraɪt] *n.* fairy.

sprock•et ['sprɒkɪt] *n.* small tooth on a wheel. **sprock•et wheel,** *n.* toothed wheel which connects with a chain.

sprout [spraut] 1. *n.* young shoot of a plant; **Brussels sprouts** = edible shoots from a type of cabbage. 2. *v.* to send out (shoots/horns).

spruce [spru:s] 1. *n.* type of fir tree. 2. *adj.* smart. 3. *v.* **to s. yourself up** = to make yourself neat. **spruce•ly,** *adv.* in a spruce way. **spruce•ness,** *n.* being spruce.

sprung [sprʌŋ] *v. see* **spring.**

spry [spraɪ] *adj.* (old person) who is vigorous and active. **spry•ly,** *adv.* in a spry way. **spry•ness,** *n.* being spry.

spud [spʌd] *n. inf.* potato.

spume [spju:m] *n.* foam (on the sea).

spun [spʌn] *v. see* **spin.**

spunk [spʌŋk] *n. inf.* courage.

spur [spɜ:] 1. *n.* (a) metal point attached to the heels of a rider's boots which pricks a horse to make it go faster; **to win your spurs** = to show for the first time how good you are. (b) low hill running from a higher range of mountains; minor road/railroad line leading off a main one. (c) impetus/stumulus; **on the s. of the moment** = without planning in advance. 2. *v.* **(spurred)** to urge (s.o.) **on.**

spurge ['spɜ:dʒ] *n.* common weed with bitter white sap.

spu•ri•ous ['spjuərɪəs] *adj.* false. **spu•ri•ous•ly,** *adv.* in a spurious way. **spu•ri•ous•ness,** *n.* being spurious.

spurn [spɜ:n] *v.* to reject (an offer) scornfully.

spurt [spɜ:t] 1. *n.* (a) jet of liquid. (b) sudden effort. 2. *v.* (a) **to s. out** = to come out in a jet. (b) to show sudden energy.

sput•ter ['spʌtə] *v.* to spit/to send out sparks or fat.

spu•tum ['spju:təm] *n.* mucus which is spit out of the mouth.

spy [spaɪ] 1. *n.* person who is paid to try to find out what the enemy/a criminal gang/a rival company is planning to do. 2. *v.* to see; **to s. on s.o.** = to try, in secret, to find out what s.o. is doing. **spy•ing,** *n.* trying to find out information about the enemy. **spy out,** *v.* to try to find out (sth) secretly.

squab [skwɒb] *n.* small pigeon.

squab•ble ['skwɒbl] 1. *n.* quarrel/argument. 2. *v.* to argue.

squad [skwɒd] *n.* (a) small group of soldiers; **firing s.** = group of soldiers who shoot s.o. who has been condemned to death. (b) small group of workmen/police; **s. car** = police car on patrol. (c) (sports) team.

squad•ron ['skwɒdrən] *n.* group of soldiers; group of aircraft; group of naval ships.

squal•id ['skwɒlɪd] *adj.* sordid/unpleasant/dirty. **squal•id•ly,** *adv.* in a squalid way. **squal•or,** *n.* dirt; dirty state.

squall [skwɔ:l] 1. *n.* sudden gust of wind. 2. *v.* to cry loudly. **squal•ly,** *adj.* accompanied by gusts of wind.

squan•der ['skwɒndə] *v.* to waste (money/energy).

square ['skweə] 1. *n.* (a) shape with four equal sides and four right angles; *inf.* **we're back to s. one** = we'll have to start planning again from the beginning. (b) open area in a town, surrounded by buildings. (c) instrument for drawing right angles. (d) a number multiplied by itself. 2. *adj.* (a) shaped like a square. (b) **s. corner** = corner with a right angle. (c) fair/straightforward; **s. deal** = honest treatment; **s. meal** = a good filling meal. (d) straight. (e) multiplied by itself; **s. mile** = area of one mile multiplied by one mile; **s. root** =

number which when multiplied by itself produces the number you have. 3. *adv.* (a) in a level/straight way. (b) directly. 4. *v.* (a) to make (a round stone, etc.) square; **squared paper** = paper with squares drawn on it (for making graphs, etc.). (b) to balance (accounts); to pay (s.o.) what is owed; to pay (s.o.) a bribe. (c) to multiply (sth) by itself. (d) to straighten (your shoulders); **to s. off with s.o.** = to prepare to fight. **square•ly,** *adv.* in a straightforward way.

squash [skwɒʃ] 1. *n.* (a) fast game played with rackets in a court with high walls. (b) vegetable like a pumpkin, etc. 2. *v.* (a) to crush. (b) to stop (a revolt) by force; to stop (s.o.) speaking by being rude to them. **squash court,** *n.* court for playing squash. **squash•y,** *adv.* (-ier, -iest) soft and wet.

squat [skwɒt] 1. *n.* action or position of squatting. 2. *v.* (**squatted**) (a) to crouch down, sitting on your heels. (b) to occupy an empty house without the permission of the owner. 3. *adj.* (**squatter, squattest**) short and thick. **squat•ter,** *n.* person who occupies an empty house without the permission of the owner.

squaw [skwɔː] *n.* North American Indian woman.

squawk [skwɔːk] 1. *n.* short harsh cry. 2. *v.* to make short harsh cries.

squeak [skwiːk] 1. *n.* little high-pitched cry (like that of a mouse); high-pitched sound (like a rusty hinge). 2. *v.* to make a squeak. **squeak•y,** *adj.* (gate) which squeaks.

squeal [skwiːl] 1. *n.* long loud high-pitched cry. 2. *v.* to make long loud high-pitched cries.

squeam•ish ['skwiːmɪʃ] *adj.* easily made sick/easily shocked. **squeam•ish•ness,** *n.* being squeamish.

squee•gee ['skwiːdʒiː] *n.* implement for removing water from floors, windows, etc. made of a wad of sponge attached to a hinged plate.

squeeze [skwiːz] 1. *n.* (a) pressure; crushing. (b) **s. of lemon** = few drops of lemon juice. 2. *v.* (a) to crush/to force/to press. (b) to push together; to push to get into/through a small space. **squeez•er,** *n.* device for pressing citrus fruit to get the juice out.

squelch [skweltʃ] 1. *n.* noise made by a wet sticky substance ▪ 2. *v.* to make a wet sucking noise.

squib [skwɪb] *n.* (a) small firework which bangs. (b) short saying or piece of writing, often witty or satirical.

squid [skwɪd] *n.* sea animal like a small octopus.

squig•gle ['skwɪgl] 1. *n.* illegible curly marks/handwriting. 2. *v.* to make squiggles.

squint [skwɪnt] 1. *n.* (a) state where your two

eyes look in different directions. (b) act of squinting. 2. *v.* (a) to have eyes which look in different directions. (b) to half-close your eyes when looking at sth.

squire ['skwaɪə] *n.* (a) (*in England*) gentleman living in the country, often the owner of a large house. (b) male escort for a woman.

squirm [skwɜːm] *v.* to wriggle about; **it makes me s.** = it makes me very embarrassed.

squir•rel ['skwɪrəl] *n.* common small mammal with a large bushy tail, living in trees.

squirt [skwɜːt] 1. *n.* (a) sharp jet of liquid. (b) *inf.* **little s.** = small insignificant person. 2. *v.* to send out a sharp jet of liquid.

squish•y ['skwɪʃɪ] *adj.* soft and squashy.

Sr *symbol for* strontium.

St. [snt; striːt] *short form of* Saint or Street.

stab [stæb] 1. *n.* wound made with a sharp knife; **s. in the back** = attack by s.o. who is thought to be loyal; *inf.* **to have a s. at** = to try to do. 2. *v.* (**stabbed**) to wound with a sharp knife; **to s. s.o. in the back** = to attack s.o. who thinks you are his friend.

sta•ble ['steɪbl] 1. *n.* (a) building for keeping a horse. (b) **stables** = place where horses are kept for breeding/racing, etc. 2. *v.* to keep (a horse) in a stable. 3. *adj.* (**-er, -est**) solid; steady/not wobbly. (b) (*in chemistry*) (compound) which does not change or decompose easily. **sta•bil•i•ty** [stə'bɪlɪtɪ] *n.* steadiness. **sta•bi•li•za•tion** [steɪbɪlaɪ'zeɪʃn] *n.* making stable. **sta•bi•lize** ['steɪbɪlaɪz] *v.* to make steady. **sta•bi•liz•er,** *n.* (a) fin attached to the hull of a ship to prevent rolling. (b) substance added to processed food to keep it in a stable condition. **sta•ble•boy,** *n.* man who looks after horses in a stable. **sta•bly,** *adv.* in a stable way.

stac•ca•to [stə'kɑːtəʊ] *adj. & n.* sharp (noise).

stack [stæk] 1. *n.* (a) heap; *inf.* lots (of). (b) brick structure housing a chimney. (c) inner part of a library where books are kept without being open to the public. 2. *v.* (a) to pile up. (b) (*of aircraft*) to circle around waiting in turn for permission to land at a busy airport.

sta•di•um ['steɪdɪəm] *n.* large building for sports events.

staff [stɑːf] 1. *n.* (a) long thick stick. (b) people working in a school/college/company, etc. (c) officers who help the commander organize a military force; **general s.** = officers who work at headquarters. (d) (*pl.* **staves**) set of five lines on which musical notes are written. 2. *v.* to provide employees for (a company, etc.). **staff•er,** *n.* member of a staff.

stag [stæg] *n.* male deer; **s. party** = party for men only. **stag bee•tle,** *n.* large black beetle with horns.

stage [steɪdʒ] 1. *n.* (a) platform (on which a

play is acted, etc.); **s. directions** = notes in the script of a play showing what the actors have to do; **s. fright** = nervousness before appearing before an audience; **s. whisper** = loud whisper which everyone can hear; **to go on the s.** = to become an actor. (b) period/phase. (c) each of the parts of a rocket. (d) part of a journey. 2. *v.* (a) to put on/to arrange (a performance of a play, etc.). (b) to make/to organize. **stage•coach**, *n.* (*old*) horsedrawn passenger coach which ran regularly along certain routes. **stage•craft**, *n.* art of the theater. **stage•hand**, *n.* person who moves scenery/prepares the stage (in a theater). **stage•man•age**, *v.* to arrange/to organize (a performance); to plan (a trick/a coup). **stage man•ag•er**, *n.* person who organizes a performance of a play/opera, etc. **stag•er**, *n. inf.* **old s.** = old experienced person. **stag•ing**, *n.* putting on (of a play). **stag•y**, *adj.* unreal; looking too much as if being acted on a stage.

stag•fla•tion [stæg'fleɪʃn] *n.* period when the economy stagnates but inflation increases.

stag•ger ['stægə] *v.* (a) to walk unsteadily. (b) to astonish. (c) to arrange things so that they do not coincide exactly. **stag•ger•ing**, *adj.* astonishing. **stag•ger•ing•ly**, *adv.* astonishingly.

stag•nant ['stægnənt] *adj.* (a) (water) which does not flow/which is not pure enough to drink. (b) (business) which does not make increased sales. **stag•nate** [stæg'neɪt] *v.* to stay static; not advance. **stag•na•tion** [stæg-'neɪʃn] *n.* being stagnant.

staid [steɪd] *adj.* serious/not adventurous.

stain [steɪn] 1. *n.* (a) dirty mark which is difficult to remove. (b) liquid used to change the color of wood. 2. *v.* (a) to make a dirty mark on (sth). (b) to change the color of (wood, etc.); **stained glass** = colored glass for windows (esp. in church). **stain•less**, *adj.* without any stain; **s. steel** = steel which contains nickel and chromium so that it does not rust in contact with air or water.

stair ['steə] *n.* (a) step (on a staircase) (b) (**flight of**) **stairs** = series of steps leading from one floor of a building to the next. **stair car•pet**, *n.* long narrow piece of carpet for covering stairs. **stair•case**, *n.* flight of stairs (usu. with a handrail). **stair rod**, *n.* metal rod which keeps a stair carpet in place. **stair•way**, *n.* staircase.

stake [steɪk] 1. *n.* (a) strong pointed stick. (b) money which is gambled; **he has a s. in the company** = he has invested some money in the company, hoping to make a profit; **at s.** = which may be lost. 2. *v.* (a) to put a stick in the ground; **to s. your claim to** = to suggest that you hold the right to own sth. (b) to bet (money, etc.).

sta•lac•tite ['stæləktaɪt] *n.* long point of limestone hanging from the ceiling of a cave, formed by mineral deposits from dripping water.

sta•lag•mite ['stæləgmaɪt] *n.* long point of limestone rising from the floor of a cave formed by mineral deposits from dripping water.

stale [steɪl] *adj.* (**-er, -est**) (a) no longer fresh; (joke) that has been repeated many times. (b) **to grow s.** = to become bored/tired so that you are no longer working well. **stale•mate**, *n.* (a) (*in chess*) position where a player cannot move without being checkmated. (b) situation where neither side will compromise. **stale•ness**, *n.* being stale.

stalk [stɔːk] 1. *n.* (a) thin stem of a plant. (b) small part of the stem which attaches a fruit to the plant. 2. *v.* (a) to try to get close enough to an animal to shoot it. (b) to march along proudly. **stalk•er**, *n.* person who stalks animals.

stall [stɔːl] 1. *n.* (a) compartment for one animal in a stable, etc. (b) **stalls** = seats in church for the choir and clergy. (c) booth or table with goods laid out for sale; small moveable store. 2. *v.* (a) (*of a car engine*) to stop unintentionally. (b) (*of an aircraft*) to go so slowly that it falls suddenly. (c) to put off making a decision.

stal•lion ['stæljən] *n.* male horse, esp. one kept for breeding.

stal•wart ['stɒlwət] 1. *adj.* strong/vigorous/brave. 2. *n.* strong/vigorous/brave person.

sta•men ['steɪmən] *n.* one of the thin spikes in the center of a flower which carry the pollen.

stam•i•na ['stæmɪnə] *n.* ability to do sth for a long time.

stam•mer ['stæmə] 1. *n.* unintentional repetition of sounds when speaking. 2. *v.* to repeat sounds when speaking. **stam•mer•er**, *n.* person who stammers.

stamp [stæmp] 1. *n.* (a) banging your foot on the ground. (b) object for making a mark on sth. (c) device for cutting out a design. (d) small piece of gummed paper for sticking on an envelope/package, etc., to pay for it to be

---

æ **back**, a: **farm**, ɒ: **top**, aɪ **pipe**, aʊ **how**, aɪə **fire**, aʊə **flower**, ɔ: **bought**, ɔɪ **toy**, e **fed**, eə**hair**, eɪ **take**, ə **afraid**, əʊ **boat**, əʊə **lower**, ɜː **word**, iː **heap**, ɪ **hit**, ɪə **hear**, uː **school**, ʊ **book**, ʌ **but**, b **back**, d **dog**, ð **then**, dʒ **just**, f **fog**, g **go**, h **hand**, j **yes**, k **catch**, l **last**, m **mix**, n **nut**, ŋ **sing**, p **penny**, r **round**, s **some**, ʃ **short**, t **too**, tʃ **chop**, θ **thing**, v **voice**, w **was**, z **zoo**, ʒ **treasure**

sent by mail; **s. machine** = machine which sells stamps automatically. (e) any small piece of gummed paper used to show you have made a payment. (f) mark made by a rubber stamp. 2. *v.* (a) to bang your foot hard on the ground. (b) to make a mark on sth. (c) to stick a stamp on (sth); **stamped self-addressed envelope** = envelope with your own name, address and a stamp, which you enclose in a letter so that the person you are writing to can reply. **stamp out,** *v.* to stop/to eradicate.

stam•pede [stæm'pi:d] 1. *n.* mad rush (of animals/people). 2. *v.* to rush madly.

stance [stɑ:ns] *n.* (a) way of standing. (b) attitude/position.

stanch [stɑ:nʃ] *v.* to stop blood flowing.

stan•chion ['stænʃn] *n.* vertical post/bar which holds sth up.

stand [stænd] 1. *n.* (a) position; **to make a s. against** = to resist. (b) support; thing which holds sth up; flat base. (c) arrangement of shelves/posters, etc., at an exhibition. (d) **stands** = series of seats for spectators at a sports event. (e) **witness s.** = place where a witness sits in a law court. (f) **taxi s.** = place where taxis wait. (g) **one-night s.** = stop for a single performance (of a play/by a musical group) before moving to another location the following night. 2. *v.* (**stood**) to be/to place in an upright position. (b) to be on your feet/not be sitting down. (c) to stay/to remain. (d) to bear/to accept. **stand a•side,** *v.* to step to one side. **stand back,** *v.* to step backward; to be behind. **stand by,** *v.* (a) to be ready. (b) to stand at one side without taking part in the action. (c) to support/to be faithful. **stand•by,** *n.* (a) thing which is ready to go into action if necessary. (b) waiting; **he is on s.** = he is waiting to see if he is needed; (*at an airport*) traveler waiting for a ticket to become available because of a cancellation. **stand for,** *v.* (a) to mean. (b) to be in favor of. **stand in for,** *v.* to take s.o.'s place. **stand-in,** *n.* person who takes s.o.'s place. **stand•ing.** 1. *n.* (a) being on your feet; **s. room only** = room for people to stand, not to sit. (b) social position. 2. *adj.* (a) upright/not lying or sitting. (b) permanent; **s. order** = permanent order always in effect; **it is a s. joke** = it is sth we always laugh about. **stand•off•ish,** *adj.* (person) who is cold/who does not make friends. **stand•off•ish•ness,** *n.* unfriendliness. **stand out,** *v.* to be obvious. **stand o•ver,** *v.* to supervise s.o. very closely. **stand•pipe,** *n.* upright pipe connected to the water main in the street, with a tap which allows water to be taken off when the supply to buildings has been cut. **stand•point,** *n.* point of view/position from which you look at a problem.

stand•still, *n.* state of being stopped. **stand to,** *v.* (*in army, etc.*) to be ready to go into action. **stand up,** *v.* (a) to get to your feet. (b) **s. up straight!** = hold yourself straight. (c) **to s. up for sth** = to defend/to support; **to s. up to s.o.** = to fight or confront s.o. bravely; **to s. s.o. up** = to fail to meet s.o. at a rendezvous. **stand-up,** *adj.* **stand-up buffet** = buffet where you eat standing up; **stand-up fight** = real fight where people come to blows.

stand•ard ['stændəd] 1. *n.* (a) model with which sth is compared. (b) excellent quality which is set as a target. (c) large flag. (d) tree/bush grown with a single tall trunk. 2. *adj.* (a) normal/usual; **s. pronunciation** = pronunciation which is generally used by educated speakers. (b) **s. rose** = rose grown with a single tall trunk. (c) which is taken as a measure. **stand•ard•i•za•tion** [stændədaɪ'zeɪʃn] *n.* setting of a standard; making sure that everything conforms to a standard. **stand•ard•ize** ['stændədaɪz] *v.* to make everything conform to a standard.

stank [stæŋk] *v. see* **stink.**

stan•za ['stænzə] *n.* section of a poem made up of a series of lines.

sta•pes ['steɪpɪz] *n.* one of the ossicles in the ear.

staph•y•lo•coc•cus [stæfɪlə'kɒkəs] *n.* (*pl.* **-cocci** [-kɒkaɪ]) type of bacterium which causes food poisoning and infection in the blood.

sta•ple ['steɪpl] 1. *n.* piece of strong bent wire used to hold things in place; small wire clip for attaching papers together by being passed through them and then bent over. 2. *adj.* (a) main product of a country/town, etc. (b) **s. diet** = main part of what you eat. 3. *v.* to attach with a staple. **sta•pler,** *n.* small instrument for stapling.

star [stɑ:] 1. *n.* (a) body in the sky like a very distant sun which shines at night. (b) the sign of the zodiac which marks your birth; *inf.* **thank your lucky stars** = consider yourself very lucky. (c) shape with several regular points. (d) asterisk. (e) actor/actress who is very well known to the public. 3. *v.* (**starred**) (a) to play an important part (**in** a play, motion picture, etc.). (b) to have (a famous actor) playing. (c) to mark with a star. **star•dom,** *n.* being a star in motion pictures, etc. **star•fish,** *n.* sea animal shaped like a star. **star•less,** *adj.* (night) when no stars are visible. **star•let,** *n.* young actress, esp. in motion pictures. **star•light,** *n.* light from the stars. **star•lit,** *adj.* (night) lit by the light of the stars. **star•ry,** *adj.* covered with stars. **star•ry-eyed,** *adj.* wildly hopeful. **Stars and Stripes,** *n.* the flag of the United States.

star•board ['stɑːbəd] *n. & adj.* right side of a ship when facing forward.

starch [stɑːtʃ] 1. *n.* (a) white energy-giving carbohydrate in bread/potatoes/rice, etc. (b) white powder mixed with water to make cloth stiff. 2. *v.* to make (cloth) stiff with starch. **starch•y,** *adj.* (a) full of starch. (b) very formal (manner).

stare ['steə] 1. *n.* fixed look from the eyes. 2. *v.* to look **at** s.o./sth with a fixed gaze; *inf.* **it's staring you in the face** = it is very obvious. **star•ing,** *adj., adv.* with a fixed look.

stark [stɑːk] 1. *adj.* (**-er, -est**) (a) total/pure (nonsense). (b) bare (landscape/details). 2. *adv.* completely (naked); **s. raving mad** = completely mad. **stark•ly,** *adv.* in a stark way. **stark•ness,** *n.* being stark.

star•ling ['stɑːlɪŋ] *n.* common dark bird with a green sheen to its feathers.

start [stɑːt] 1. *n.* (a) beginning; **for a s.** = in the first place. (b) **to give s.o. two meters' s.** = to place them at the beginning of a race two meters in front of you. (c) sudden jump/sudden movement; **by fits and starts** = at odd moments. 2. *v.* (a) to begin. (b) to (cause to) begin to work. (c) to set (sth) going. (d) to jump (in surprise). **start•er,** *n.* (a) person or animal who starts. (b) person who gives the signal for the start of a race. (c) *inf.* first course in a meal. (d) machine which starts a car engine. **start•ing,** *n.* beginning (of a race, etc.); **starting point** = point from which everything begins. **start off, start out,** *v.* to begin to do/to go. **start up,** *v.* to make (an engine, etc.) begin to work.

star•tle ['stɑːtl] *v.* to make (s.o.) jump in surprise. **star•tling,** *adj.* remarkable/surprising.

starve [stɑːv] *v.* to deprive of food; to die from lack of food; *inf.* **I'm starving** = I am very hungry; **starved for** = not having enough of. **star•va•tion** [stɑːˈveɪʃn] *n.* lack of food.

stash [stæʃ] *v. inf.* **to s. away** = to store in a safe place.

state [steɪt] 1. *n.* (a) condition; *inf.* **in a s.** = very angry. (b) government of a nation; **state-owned** = owned by the country/government (not privately owned). (c) independent country. (d) one of the semi-independent parts of a federal country. 2. *adj.* belonging to/run by/given by the government. 3. *v.* to say clearly/to claim. **stat•ed,** *adj.* fixed/regulated. **State De•part•ment,** *n.* section of the U.S. government dealing with foreign

affairs. **state•less,** *adj.* (person) who is not a citizen of any state. **state•li•ness,** *n.* being stately. **state•ly,** *adj.* noble/dignified. **state•ment,** *n.* declaration clearly written or spoken. **state-of-the-art,** *adj.* very advanced technically. **state•room,** *n.* large cabin on a ship. **state•side,** *adj. & adv.* in/to the United States of America. **states•man,** *n.* (*pl.* **-men**) person who is or was a member of a government. **states•man•like,** *adj.* like a statesman. **states•man•ship,** *n.* skill in government of a country.

stat•ic ['stætɪk] 1. *adj.* not moving; **s. electricity** = electricity which stays in one place (in a car/cloth). 2. *n.* electrical interference in the air which disturbs a radio signal. **stat•ics,** *n.pl.* study of physical forces in equilibrium or of motionless bodies.

sta•tion ['steɪʃn] 1. *n.* (a) place where trains stop to pick up and put down passengers; place where buses begin or end their journeys. (b) central building for some sort of service. (c) **radio s./TV s.** = broadcasting headquarters with its own frequency. (d) position in society. (e) **sheep s.** = large sheep farm in Australia. 2. *v.* to place (s.o.) at a spot. **sta•tion•ar•y,** *adj.* not moving. **sta•tion•mas•ter,** *n.* person in charge of a railroad station. **sta•tion wag•on,** *n.* long car with a part at the back for carrying goods.

sta•tion•er ['steɪʃənə] *n.* person who sells stationery. **sta•tion•er•y,** *n.* materials for writing, such as paper/pens/ink.

sta•tis•tic [stəˈtɪstɪk] *n.* fact given in the form of a figure; **statistics** = study of facts given in the form of figures. **sta•tis•ti•cal,** *adj.* referring to statistics. **sta•tis•ti•cal•ly,** *adv.* in a statistical way. **stat•is•ti•cian** [stætɪsˈtɪʃn] *n.* person who studies/analyzes statistics.

stat•ue ['stætjuː] *n.* figure of a person or thing carved in stone/made of metal, etc. **stat•u•ar•y,** *n.* collection of statues. **stat•u•esque** [stætjuˈesk] *adj.* (woman) who is beautiful but large and dignified. **stat•u•ette** [stætjuˈet] *n.* small statue.

stat•ure ['stætʃə] *n.* (a) height. (b) importance.

sta•tus ['steɪtəs] *n.* (*no pl.*) (a) legal position. (b) importance/position in the eyes of other people; **s. symbol** = object which may make other people think more highly of you. **sta•tus quo** ['steɪtəsˈkwəʊ] *n.* state of things as they are at the moment.

æ back, ɑː farm, ɒ top, aɪ pipe, aʊ how, aɪə fire, aʊə flower, ɔː bought, ɔɪ toy, e fed, eə hair, eɪ take, ə afraid, əʊ boat, əʊə lower, vː word, iː heap, ɪ hit, ɪə hear, uː school, ʊ book, ʌ but, b back, d dog, ð then, dʒ just, f fog, g go, h hand, j yes, k catch, l last, m mix, n nut, ŋ sing, p penny, r round, s some, ʃ short, t too, tʃ chop, θ thing, v voice, w was, z zoo, ʒ treasure

stat•ute ['stætjuːt] *n.* law. **stat•u•to•ry** ['stætjʊtrɪ] *adj.* legal; officially imposed.

staunch [stɔːnʃ] 1. *adj.* (-er, -est) firm (friend). 2. *v.* to stop (a flow of blood). **staunch•ly,** *adv.* firmly.

stave [steɪv] 1. *n.* (a) curved piece of wood which forms part of a barrel. (b) set of five lines on which music is written. 2. *v.* (a) **(staved/stove) to s. in** = to batter a hole in a boat/a barrel. (b) **to s. off** = to hold off/to prevent.

stay [steɪ] 1. *n.* (a) time which you spend in a place. (b) **s. of execution** = delay ordered by a governor in carrying out a sentence. (c) strong rope which supports, e.g. a mast on a ship. (d) (*old*) **stays** = corset. 2. *v.* to stop in a place. **stay-at-home,** *n.* person who does not go out much. **stay a•way,** *v.* to keep away. **stay in,** *v.* to stay at home. **stay out,** *v.* not to come home. **stay up,** *v.* to postpone going to bed.

stead [sted] *n.* (a) **it stood him in good s.** = it was very useful to him. (b) **in your s.** = in place of you.

stead•fast ['stedfɑːst] *adj.* firm/constant. **stead•fast•ly,** *adv.* firmly/constantly.

stead•y ['stedɪ] 1. *adj.* (-ier, -iest) (a) firm/not wobbling. (b) continuing regularly. (c) (person) who is not easily upset. 2. *n. inf.* boyfriend/girlfriend with whom you go out regularly. 3. *inter.* be careful. 4. *v.* to make/to keep firm. **Stead•i•cam** ['stedɪkæm] *n.* trademark for a device for steadying a hand-held camera. **stead•i•ly,** *adv.* (a) firmly. (b) regularly/continuously. **stead•i•ness,** *n.* being steady.

steak [steɪk] *n.* (a) thick slice of meat, esp. beef, cut from the best part of the animal. (b) thick slice of fish. **steak•house,** *n.* restaurant serving steak and other grilled food.

steal [stiːl] *v.* **(stole; stolen)** (a) to take (sth which does not belong to you). (b) **to s. a glance at** = to look at quickly and secretly. (c) **to s. a march on s.o.** = to do sth stealthily before s.o. can do it. (d) to creep very quietly (into).

stealth [stelθ] *n.* **by s.** = in a secret way/without anyone knowing. **stealth•i•ly,** *adv.* in a stealthy way. **stealth•i•ness,** *n.* being stealthy. **stealth•y** *adj.* (-ier, -iest) without anyone knowing or seeing.

steam [stiːm] 1. *n.* (a) vapor which comes off hot water/from warm breath; **s. engine** = engine which runs on steam pressure. (b) *inf.* **to let off s.** = (i) to use up your excess energy; (ii) to explode with anger. 2. *v.* (*a*) to cook by steam. (b) to send out steam. (c) to move by steam power. (d) (*of window*) **to s. up** = to be covered by a mist; *inf.* **to get steamed up about**

= to get very annoyed. **steam•boat,** *n.* boat powered by steam. **steam•er,** *n.* (a) large passenger ship (powered by steam). (b) type of pan with holes in the bottom which is placed over boiling water for steaming vegetables, etc. **steam•roll•er,** *n.* vehicle with a very heavy roller for flattening newly laid road surfaces. **steam•ship,** *n.* large passenger ship (powered esp. by steam). **steam•y,** *adj.* full of steam.

ste•a•tite ['stɪətaɪt] *n.* soft gray stone which can be carved.

steed [stiːd] *n.* (*in literature*) horse.

steel [stiːl] 1. *n.* (a) hard flexible metal made from iron and carbon; **s. band** = West Indian band which plays music on steel drums of varying sizes. (b) bar of rough steel for sharpening knives. 2. *v.* **to s. yourself to do sth** = to get up enough courage to do sth. **steel•i•ness,** *n.* being steely. **steel wool,** *n.* very fine steel wire used in wads for cleaning metal. **steel•works,** *n.* factory which produces steel. **steel•y,** *adj.* sharp/hard like steel.

steep [stiːp] 1. *adj.* (-er, -est) (a) which rises or falls sharply. (b) *inf.* excessive. 2. *v.* to soak in a liquid for a long time. **steep•en,** *v.* to become steeper. **steep•ly,** *adv.* (rising) sharply. **steep•ness,** *n.* being steep.

stee•ple ['stiːpl] *n.* church tower with the top rising to a point. **stee•ple•chase,** *n.* race run across open country, over fences, hedges, etc.; race on a track over hurdles. **stee•ple•chas•er,** *n.* person/horse that runs in a steeplechase. **stee•ple•jack,** *n.* person who climbs towers/factory chimneys, etc., to do repairs.

steer ['stɪə] 1. *n.* young bull raised for meat. 2. *v.* to guide/to make (a vehicle) go in a certain direction; **to s. clear of** = to avoid. **steer•age,** *n.* (a) act of steering. (b) cheapest accommodation in a passenger ship. **steer•ing,** *n.* mechanism in a car which steers it; **s. wheel** = wheel which is turned by the driver to alter the direction of a car; **s. column** = metal tube to which the steering wheel is attached; **s. committee** = small committee which does detailed work on the agenda for a large committee meeting. **steers•man,** *n.* (*pl.* -men) man who steers a ship.

ste•le [stiːl] *n.* carved slab of stone, placed upright.

stel•lar ['stelə] *adj.* referring to stars.

stem [stem] 1. *n.* (a) long stalk on which flowers and leaves grow. (b) thin part of a wine glass/of a tobacco pipe. (c) basic part of a word to which endings or prefixes are added. (d) **from s. to stern** = from the bows to the stern of a boat. 2. *v.* **(stemmed)** (a) to result **from.** (b) to stop/to prevent (a flow, etc.).

stench [stentʃ] *n.* strong unpleasant smell.

sten•cil ['stensl] 1. *n.* sheet of cardboard or metal with a pattern cut out of it, so that if it is placed on a surface and color is passed over it, the pattern will appear on the surface; pattern/letters/numbers, etc., which are painted in this way. 2. *v.* (**stenciled, stencilled**) (a) to mark with a stencil. (b) to make using a stencil.

sten gun ['stengʌn] *n.* British small machine gun.

ste•nog•ra•pher [stə'nɒɡrəfə] *n.* person who can take shorthand. **ste•nog•ra•phy** [stə-'nɒɡrəfɪ] *n.* shorthand.

ste•no•sis [sten'əusɪs] *n.* condition where an artery becomes narrow.

sten•to•ri•an [sten'tɔ:rɪən] *adj.* (*formal*) very loud (voice).

step [step] 1. *n.* (a) single movement of the foot when walking/running; distance covered by this movement; **s. by s.** = little by little. (b) sound made by moving a foot forward. (c) regular movement of the feet; **keep in s.** = move at the same pace as everyone else; **out of s.** = not moving at the same pace as everyone else. (d) action. (e) stair (on a staircase); flat rung (on a ladder). 2. *v.* (**stepped**) to make a movement with a foot; **to s. on the brakes** = to push the brake pedal hard. **Step,** *n.* aerobic exercise system that involves repeatedly stepping on and off a specially-designed box. **step in,** *v.* to involve yourself/to interfere. **step•lad•der,** *n.* ladder with flat rungs. **step•ping•stone,** *n.* one of a series of stones in a stream which allow you to cross it. **step up,** *v.* to increase.

step- [step] *prefix* showing a family relationship which is through a parent who has remarried. **step•broth•er,** *n.* male child of your stepfather or stepfather. **step•daugh•ter,** *n.* daughter of your wife/husband by another marriage. **step•fa•ther,** *n.* husband of your mother who is not your father. **step•moth•er,** *n.* wife of your father, who is not your mother. **step•sis•ter,** *n.* female child of your stepfather or stepmother. **step•son,** *n.* son of your wife/husband by another marriage.

steppe [step] *n.* wide grass-covered plain in Russia and Asia.

stereo- ['sterɪəu] *prefix* referring to sth which has two dimensions.

ster•e•o ['sterɪəu] *n. & adj.* (machine) which reproduces sound through two different channels and loudspeakers.

ster•e•o•phon•ic [sterɪəu'fɒnɪk] *adj.* referring to sound which comes from two places at once.

ster•e•o•scope ['sterɪəuskəup] *n.* apparatus which shows a picture which appears to have depth and be three-dimensional. **ster•e•o•scop•ic** [sterɪə'skɒpɪk] *adj.* referring to seeing in three dimensions; **s. vision** = ability to see the same object with both eyes, and so judge distance.

ster•e•o•type ['sterɪətaɪp] *n.* pattern for certain types of person. **ster•e•o•typed,** *adj.* fitting certain patterns.

ster•ile ['steraɪl] *adj.* (a) not capable of bearing fruit/children. (b) so clean that no germs/bacteria can grow. **ste•ril•i•ty** [ste'rɪlɪtɪ] *n.* inability to grow fruit/to produce children or ideas. **ster•i•li•za•tion** [sterɪlaɪ'zeɪʃn] *n.* action of sterilizing. **ster•i•lize** ['sterɪlaɪz] *v.* (a) to make (s.o.) incapable of producing children. (b) to make so clean that bacteria/germs cannot grow. **ster•i•liz•er,** *n.* apparatus for sterilizing.

ster•ling ['stɜ:lɪŋ] 1. *adj.* of a certain standard/of good quality; **s. silver** = silver of a certain high purity. 2. *n.* standard measure of British currency.

stern [stɜ:n] 1. *adj.* (-er, -est) harsh/strict. 2. *n.* rear part of a ship. **stern•ly,** *adv.* in a stern way. **stern•ness,** *n.* being stern. **stern•wheel•er,** *n.* large pleasure ship with a paddle wheel at the stern.

ster•num ['stɜ:nəm] *n.* central bone on the chest. **ster•nal,** *adj.* referring to the sternum.

ste•roid ['stɪərɔɪd] *n.* one of a group of natural substances in plants and animals, including hormones.

ster•to•rous ['stɜ:tərəs] *adj.* making a snoring sound.

stet [stet] *v.* word showing that a correction should not be made.

steth•o•scope ['steθəskəup] *n.* doctor's instrument for listening to a patient's chest.

stet•son ['stetsən] *n.* tall cowboy hat with a wide brim.

ste•ve•dore ['sti:vədɔ:] *n.* person who works at a port, unloading or loading ships.

stew [stju:] 1. *n.* dish of meat and vegetables cooked together for a long time; *inf.* **in a s.** = in an agitated state. 2. *v.* to cook for a long time in liquid. **stewed,** *adj. Sl.* drunk.

æ back, a: farm, ɒ: top, aɪ pipe, aʊ how, aɪə fire, aʊə flower, ɔ: bought, ɔɪ toy, e fed, eəhair, eɪ take, ə afraid, əʊ boat, əʊə lower, ɜ: word, i: heap, ɪ hit, ɪə hear, u: school, ʊ book, ʌ but, b back, d dog, ð then, dʒ just, f fog, ɡ go, h hand, j yes, k catch, l last, m mix, n nut, ŋ sing, p penny, r round, s some, ʃ short, t too, tʃ chop, θ thing, v voice, w was, z zoo, ʒ treasure

stew•ard ['stjʊəd] n. (a) man who serves meals or drinks on a ship/aircraft/in a club. (b) person who organizes a meeting; person who looks after a farm or estate for the owner. (c) **shop s.** = elected union representative. **stew•ard•ess,** n. woman who looks after passengers on a ship or aircraft.

stick [stɪk] 1. n. (a) piece of wood; strong piece of wood with a handle used as a support when walking; **hockey s.** = stick with a curved end, used in playing hockey. (b) long piece. 2. v. **(stuck)** (a) to jab or push (sth sharp) **into** sth. (b) to glue; to attach. (c) to stay close/to keep **(to).** (d) to be fixed/not to be able to move. **stick•er,** n. small piece of paper or plastic which you can stick on a surface as a decoration or advertisement. **stick•i•ly,** adv. in a sticky way. **stick•i•ness,** n. state of being sticky. **stick•ing plas•ter,** n. strip of cloth which can be stuck to the skin to cover a wound. **stick-in-the-mud,** n. inf. person who will not accept new ideas. **stick-on,** adj. (label) which sticks on to a surface. **stick out** v. (a) to push out; to be further out than usual. (b) to be easily seen. **stick up,** v. (a) to put up (a notice, etc.); **s. them up!** = put your hands up (to show you surrender). (b) inf. **to s. up for s.o.** = to defend s.o. **stick•y,** adj. **(-ier, -iest)** (a) covered with glue; which sticks easily. (b) inf. difficult/awkward/unpleasant; **s. wicket** (esp. Brit.) = difficult situation.

stick•le•back ['stɪklbæk] n. common small freshwater fish with spines along its back.

stick•ler ['stɪklə] n. (for) person who attaches great importance to sth.

stiff [stɪf] adj. **(-er, -est)** (a) which cannot be bent or moved easily; (brush) with hard bristles; starched (collar); **bored s.** = very bored. (b) solid/thick (paste). (c) strong (breeze). (d) difficult/hard (examination, penalty). (e) (whisky, etc.) with not much water added. (f) high (price). (g) unfriendly/unsociable. **stiff•en,** v. (a) to become/make stiff. (b) to become cautious/unfriendly. (c) (of wind) to become stronger. (d) to make (resistance) stronger. **stiff•en•er,** n. thing which stiffens. **stiff•ly,** adv. in a stiff way. **stiff-necked,** adj. obstinate. **stiff•ness,** n. being stiff.

sti•fle ['staɪfl] v. (a) to prevent (s.o.) from breathing. (b) to hold back (a yawn, etc.). **stif•ling,** adj. suffocating; extremely hot.

stig•ma ['stɪgmə] n. (a) disgrace; feeling of shame. (b) top of the center of a flower which receives pollen to make seeds. **stig•ma•tize** ['stɪgmətaɪz] v. to give a bad name to (sth).

stile [staɪl] n. steps which allow people, but not animals, to get over a wall or fence.

sti•let•to [stɪ'letəʊ] n. (pl. **-os**) (a) long thin

dagger. (b) **s. heels** = high thin heels on women's shoes.

still [stɪl] 1. n. (a) apparatus for producing alcohol. (b) one picture from a motion-picture film. 2. adj. **(-er, -est)** calm/motionless; **s. life** = picture of flowers or objects, not people or animals. 3. adv. (a) up until this/that moment. (b) even. (c) however. **still•birth,** n. birth of a dead child. **still•born,** adj. (child) which is born dead; (idea) which is never put into practice. **still•ness,** n. calm. **still•room,** n. pantry/storage area in a large house.

stilts [stɪlts] n. pl. poles to raise (sth) above the ground; **pair of stilts** = two poles with foot rests to enable you to walk high in the air. **stilt•ed,** adj. (style of writing) which is very formal/not natural.

stim•u•late ['stɪmjʊleɪt] v. to excite/to encourage; to make more active. **stim•u•lant,** n. drug which makes you more active. **stim•u•la•tion** [stɪmjʊ'leɪʃn] n. being stimulated. **stim•u•lus,** n. (pl. **-li** [-laɪ]) thing that encourages further activity.

sting [stɪŋ] 1. n. (a) tiny needle in the tail of an insect/leaf of a plant which injects poison. (b) wound made by an insect or plant. (c) burning feeling. 2. v. **(stung** [stʌŋ]) (a) to wound with a sting. (b) to have a burning feeling. (c) to hurt (s.o.) so that he reacts. (d) inf. to cheat (s.o.) of money. **sting•ing net•tle,** n. common wild plant which causes a rash. **sting•ray,** n. large flat fish with a sting in its tail.

stin•gy ['stɪndʒɪ] adj. **(-ier, -iest)** inf. mean; not free with money. **stin•gi•ness,** n. meanness.

stink [stɪŋk] 1. n. unpleasant smell; inf. **to create a s.** = to object vigorously. 2. v. **(stank; stunk)** to make an unpleasant smell.

stint [stɪnt] 1. n. (a) amount of time spent doing sth. (b) **without s.** = in large quantities/with no restriction. 2. v. to give in very small amounts.

sti•pend ['staɪpend] n. fixed salary. **sti•pen•di•ar•y** [staɪ'pendjərɪ] adj. person who is paid a stipend.

stip•ple ['stɪpl] v. to color with small dots.

stip•u•late ['stɪpjʊleɪt] v. to insist; to make a condition. **stip•u•la•tion** [stɪpjʊ'leɪʃn] n. condition (in a contract).

stir [stɜː] 1. n. (a) mixing up a liquid. (b) fuss/agitation. 2. v. **(stirred)** (a) to mix up (a liquid). (b) to cause fuss/agitation. (c) to move. **stir•ring,** adj. exciting. **stir up,** v. to cause (trouble).

stir•rup ['stɪrəp] n. metal loop hanging from the saddle into which the rider puts his foot; **s. cup** = drink taken on horseback before setting off on a ride.

stitch [stɪtʃ] 1. n. (pl. **-es**) (a) small loop of cotton or wool made with a needle in sewing or knitting; inf. **I haven't got a s. to wear** = I have no suitable clothes. (b) small loop of thread used by a surgeon to attach a wound together. (c) sharp pain in the side of the body which comes after you have been running; *inf.* **in stitches** = laughing uproariously. 2. *v.* to attach with a needle and thread.

stoat [stəʊt] *n.* small brown flesh-eating animal whose fur turns white in winter.

stock [stɒk] 1. *n.* (a) plant on which other plants are grafted. (b) race/family. (c) handle of a rifle. (d) **stocks** = frame which a boat rests on when being built. (e) **stocks** = wooden frame with holes for the feet, in which criminals were placed. (f) quantity of things for use; quantities of goods for sale; **to take s.** = (i) to count what you have in stock; (ii) to assess a situation. (g) farm animals. (h) liquid made from boiling bones, etc., in water, used as a base for soups and sauces. (i) common scented garden flower. (j) capital invested in a business; **s. market** = buying and selling of shares; **s. exchange** = building in which shares are bought and sold. 2. *v.* (a) to keep (goods) for sale. (b) to provide with goods/animals/plants, etc. 3. *adj.* usual; **s. size** = normal size; **s. argument** = one which is frequently used. **stock•breed•er**, *n.* farmer who specializes in breeding animals. **stock•breed•ing**, *n.* breeding animals. **stock•brok•er**, *n.* agent who buys shares on the stock exchange. **stock•car**, *n.* car adapted for brutal racing. **stock•hold•er**, *n.* owner of stocks in a company. **stock•i•ness**, *n.* being stocky. **stock-in-trade**, *n.* things needed to carry on a business; habitual way of acting. **stock•man**, *n.* (*pl.* **-men**) man who looks after farm animals. **stock•pile**. 1. *n.* supplies kept in reserve (in case of an emergency). 2. *v.* to collect supplies in case of emergency. **stock•pot**, *n.* large pot for making soup. **stock•room**, *n.* room where stocks are kept. **stock-still**, *adv.* without moving. **stock•tak•ing**, *n.* counting of goods in stock at the end of a period. **stock up on**, *v.* to buy supplies for use in the future. **stock•y**, *adj.* (**-ier, -iest**) short and strong (person). **stock•yard**, *n.* place where animals are kept before they are slaughtered or shipped.

stock•ade [stɒˈkeɪd] *n.* strong fence made of thick upright poles.

stock•i•nette, stockinet [stɒkiˈnet] *n.* elastic material.

stock•ing [ˈstɒkɪŋ] *n.* long close-fitting piece of clothing to cover your leg and foot; **in his s. feet** = without his shoes on.

sto•ic [ˈstəʊɪk] *n.* person who accepts problems or pain without complaining. **sto•i•cal,** *adj.* accepting problems or pain without complaining. **sto•i•cal•ly,** *adv.* in a stoical way. **sto•i•cism** [ˈstəʊɪsɪzəm] *n.* being stoical.

stoke [stəʊk] *v.* to put fuel in (a furnace). **stok•er,** *n.* person who stokes a furnace; seaman who looks after the engines.

stole [stəʊl] 1. *n.* wide light scarf worn around the shoulders. 2. *v. see* **steal.**

sto•len [ˈstəʊlən] *v. see* **steal.**

stol•id [ˈstɒlɪd] *adj.* slow and heavy; not excitable. **sto•lid•i•ty** [stɒˈlɪdɪtɪ] *n.* being stolid. **stol•id•ly,** *adv.* in a stolid way.

sto•ma [ˈstəʊmə] *n.* (*pl.* **-ata, -as**) pore in a plant.

stom•ach [ˈstʌmək] 1. *n.* (a) bag inside the body in which food is digested; **s. ache** = pain in the stomach. (b) part of the body lower than the chest. (c) desire. 2. *v.* to put up with/to tolerate.

stomp [stɒmp] *v.* to stamp/to walk with a heavy tread.

stone [stəʊn] 1. *n.* (a) small piece of rock. (b) piece of rock which has been cut for building, etc.; **Stone Age** = prehistoric period when humans made tools out of stone; **precious s.** = rare mineral which is very valuable. (c) hard seed inside some types of fruit. (d) hard piece of mineral which forms inside the body (in the kidneys, etc.) and causes pain. (e) measure of weight (= 14 pounds or 6.35 kilograms). 2. *adv.* completely (deaf); **s. broke** = with no money. 3. *v.* (a) **to s. (s.o.) to death** = to throw stones at (s.o.) and kill him. (b) to take the pits/stones out of (fruit). **stone•chat,** *n.* small dark bird with a red breast. **stone•crop,** *n.* type of plant which grows among stones. **stoned,** *adj. Sl.* (a) drunk. (b) drugged. **stone•ma•son,** *n.* person who cuts and builds with stone. **stone•wall,** *v.* to be uncooperative, as by refusing to answer when questioned. **stone•ware,** *n.* (*no pl.*) pottery made of rough clay and fired at high temperatures. **stone•work,** *n.* walls, etc., made of stone. **ston•i•ly,** *adv.* with no feeling. **ston•y,** *adj.* (**-ier, -iest**) (a) covered with stones. (b) hard; with no feeling. (c) *inf.* **s. broke** = stone broke.

stood [stʊd] *v. see* **stand.**

stooge [stuːdʒ] 1. *n. inf.* (a) person who does

what he is told to do. (b) the stupid one of a pair of comedians. 2. *v.* to act as a stooge.

stook [stʌk] *n.* (*esp. Brit.*) group of sheaves of corn, leaning together.

stool [stuːl] *n.* (a) seat with no back. (b) lump of waste matter passed from the bowels. **stool•pi•geon**, *n.* criminal who helps the police to trap another criminal.

stoop [stuːp] 1. *n.* bending forward. 2. *v.* (a) to bend forward. (b) **he stoops** = he has a permanently bent back. (c) **to s. to do sth** = to allow yourself to do sth which you feel is beneath you.

stop [stɒp] 1. *n.* (a) act of not moving/not doing sth. (b) place where a bus, etc., usually stops to pick up or let out passengers. (c) block which prevents a door, etc., closing. (d) knob on an organ which switches on a different set of pipes; set of pipes on an organ which produce a particular sound; **to pull out all the stops** = to do everything possible. 2. *v.* (**stopped**) (a) to make (sth which is moving) come to a halt; to come to a halt. (b) to make (sth) cease working; to cease working/doing sth. (c) to stay in a place. (d) to block; to fill (a gap). (e) to cut off (supply); to prevent (money) being paid; **to s. a check** = to tell the bank not to pay a check which you have written; **to s. s.o.'s wages** = not to pay s.o. **stop by,** *v. inf.* to visit s.o. for a short time. **stop•cock,** *n.* tap which stops the supply of water. **stop down,** *v.* to make the aperture of a lens smaller. **stop•gap,** *n. & adj.* thing which is used temporarily while waiting for sth more suitable to turn up. **stop off,** *v.* to make a stop on a long journey. **stop o•ver,** *v.* to make an overnight stop on a long journey. **stop•o•ver,** *n.* overnight stop on a long journey. **stop•page,** *n.* action of stopping/blocking. **stop•per,** *n.* piece of glass/cork, etc., which fits the mouth of a jar to close it. **stop•watch,** *n.* watch which can be started and stopped by pressing a button, used for timing races.

store [stɔː] 1. *n.* (a) supply of food, etc., kept for later use; **to set great s. by sth** = think that sth is very important. (b) place where you buy goods. 2. *v.* (a) to keep (sth) for future use. (b) to put (sth) in a warehouse. **stor•age,** *n.* (a) act of keeping/putting in store. (b) memory, the part of a computer where data is stored. **store•house,** *n.* place where things are stored. **store•keep•er,** *n.* person who owns a store. **store•room,** *n.* room where things are stored.

sto•ry, *Brit.* **sto•rey** ['stɔːrɪ] *n.* whole floor in a building. **sto•ried,** *Brit.* **sto•reyed,** *adj.* with several stories.

stork [stɔːk] *n.* large, usu. white, bird with long legs and long beak.

storm [stɔːm] 1. *n.* (a) period of bad weather with wind. (b) **s. of applause** = loud burst of clapping and cheering. (c) sudden violent attack; **s. troops** = soldiers who are specially trained to attack and capture. 2. *v.* (a) to be violently angry. (b) to attack and capture. **storm•y,** *adj.* referring to a storm; like a storm.

sto•ry ['stɔːrɪ] *n.* (a) tale of what has happened. (b) piece of fiction. (c) *inf.* lie. **sto•ry•line,** *n.* plot of a novel/motion picture, etc. **sto•ry•tell•er,** *n.* (a) person who tells a story. (b) *inf.* person who tells lies.

stoup [stuːp] *n.* bowl for holy water in a church.

stout [staut] 1. *adj.* (**-er, -est**) (a) fat. (b) strong/thick (material). (c) brave. 2. *n.* strong dark beer. **stout-heart•ed,** *adj.* brave. **stout•ly,** *adv.* (a) vigorously. (b) solidly/strongly. **stout•ness,** *n.* being stout.

stove [stəuv] *n.* machine for heating or cooking. **stove•pipe,** *n.* metal chimney which carries the smoke from a stove.

stow [stəu] *v.* to put away; to pack. **stow a•way,** *v.* (a) to pack. (b) to travel secretly on a ship/aircraft without paying the fare. **stow•a•way,** *n.* person who stows away.

stra•bis•mus [strə'bɪzməs] *n.* squint.

strad•dle ['strædl] *v.* to stand with legs apart, and your feet on either side of (sth).

strafe [strɑːf] *v.* to attack (sth) by shooting at it from a low-flying plane.

strag•gle ['strægl] *v.* to hang/to walk in an untidy way. **strag•gler,** *n.* person who walks well behind the main group of people. **strag•gling, straggly,** *adj.* which grows untidily.

straight [streɪt] 1. *adj.* (**-er, -est**) (a) not curved; **s. hair** = not curly. (b) honest/frank. (c) simple/not complicated; (whisky, etc.) with nothing added. (d) tidy; not crooked. (e) serious (actor/play); **to keep a s. face** = to stop yourself smiling. (f) *Sl.* not homosexual. 2. *n.* **the s.** = part of a racecorse (usu. near the finish) which is not curved. 3. *adv.* (a) in a straight line. (b) immediately. (c) directly. (d) honestly; *inf.* **to go s.** = to lead an honest life after having been a criminal. **straight•a•way,** *adv.* immediately/at once. **straight•en,** *v.* to make/to become straight. **straight•for•ward,** *adj.* frank/honest. **straight•for•ward•ly,** *adv.* in an honest way. **straight•ness,** *n.* being straight. **straight off,** *adv.* at once. **straight out,** *adv.* directly.

strain [streɪn] 1. *n.* (a) act of pulling tight; tension. (b) hurt caused by pulling a muscle too hard. (c) stress; mental/physical tension. (d) way of speaking. (e) breed. (f) tune. 2. *v.* (a) to pull/to work too hard. (b) to make a great effort (**to**). (c) to put too much stress on (credulity/patience). (d) to pass (a liquid) through a sieve to separate it from solids. **strained,** *adj.* (a) which has been pulled/worked too hard. (b) tense/unfriendly. **strain•er,** *n.* sieve for separating liquids from solids.

straits [streɪts] *n. pl.* (a) narrow piece of sea water between two masses of land. (b) money difficulties. **strait•ened,** *adj.* **in s. circumstances** = not having enough money to live on. **strait•jack•et,** *n.* (a) strong coat whose sleeves are tied behind the back to prevent a mad person from attacking people. (b) thing which prevents you from acting freely. **strait•laced,** *adj.* with very strict ideas about correct moral behavior.

strake [streɪk] *n.* plank which runs along a ship lengthwise.

strand [strænd] **1.** *n.* (a) long piece of hair/thread, etc. (b) (*formal*) shore. **2.** *v.* to leave (your ship) on the shore. **strand•ed,** *adj.* alone and helpless.

strange [streɪnʒ] *adj.* (**-er, -est**) (a) odd/bizarre. (b) which you have never seen/heard before. **strange•ly,** *adv.* oddly/curiously. **strange•ness,** *n.* being strange. **stran•ger,** *n.* person whom you do not know; **you're quite a s.** = I haven't seen you for a long time; **he is a s. to the town** = he does not know it well.

stran•gle [ˈstræŋgl] *v.* to kill (s.o.) by pressing on his throat so that he cannot breath; to crush (initiative/a plan). **stran•gle•hold,** *n.* control which prevents you doing what you want to do. **stran•gler,** *n.* person who strangles. **stran•gu•la•tion** [stræŋgjuˈleɪʃn] *n.* being strangled.

strap [stræp] **1.** *n.* long flat piece of leather or material for attaching sth. **2.** *v.* (**strapped**) (a) to attach with a strap. (b) to hit (s.o.) with a strap. **strap•hang•ing,** *n.* traveling standing in a crowded bus/train, holding onto a strap attached to the roof. **strap•less,** *adj.* with no straps. **strap•ping,** *adj.* big/strong (young man/girl).

stra•ta [ˈstrɑːtə] *n. see* **stra•tum.**

strat•a•gem [ˈstrætədʒəm] *n.* clever plan to trick an enemy.

stra•te•gic, strategical [strəˈtiːdʒɪk(l)] *adj.* referring to strategy; (position) which gives an advantage over the enemy. **stra•te•gi•cal•ly,** *adv.* according to strategy. **strat•e•gist** [ˈstrætədʒɪst] *n.* officer

who plans military attacks. **strat•e•gy** [ˈstrætədʒɪ] *n.* planning of war/of an action.

strat•i•fy [ˈstrætɪfaɪ] *v.* to form layers; to be arranged in layers. **strat•i•fi•ca•tion** [strætɪfɪˈkeɪʃn] *n.* forming layers; arranging in layers.

strat•o•sphere [ˈstrætəsfɪə] *n.* upper layer of the earth's atmosphere.

stra•tum [ˈstrɑːtəm] *n.* (*pl.* **-ta** [-tə], **-ums**) layer (esp. of rock); **social strata** = levels of society.

stra•tus [ˈstrɑːtəs] *n.* **s. clouds** = low flat clouds.

straw [strɔː] *n.* (a) dry stalks of plants like corn. (b) one single dry stalk of a plant; thin plastic tube for sucking liquid; *inf.* **that's the last s.** = that is all I can stand/as much as I can take; **s. vote/poll** = random questioning to test the general opinion of the public/of a group.

straw•ber•ry [ˈstrɔːberɪ] *n.* common red summer fruit growing on low plants; **s. mark** = red mark on the skin, which is present from birth.

stray [streɪ] **1.** *adj. & n.* (animal, etc.) which is wandering away from home. **2.** *adj.* (bullet, etc.) wandering off course. **3.** *v.* to wander.

streak [striːk] **1.** *n.* (a) band/line (of color); flash (of light). (b) quality of character. **2.** *v.* (a) to rush. (b) *inf.* to run about naked in public as a joke. **streak•y,** *adj.* with smudges of color or dirt.

stream [striːm] **1.** *n.* (a) small flow of water; small river. (b) continuous flow. (c) current. **2.** *v.* to flow. **stream•er,** *n.* long thin flag; long paper or ribbon used as a decoration. **stream•ing,** *adj.* act of flowing. **stream•line,** *v.* (a) to design (a car/plane/boat, etc.) so that it can move easily through water or air. (b) to make more efficient; to modernize.

street [striːt] *n.* road in a town, with houses or businesses on each side; **the man in the s.** = the ordinary citizen; **at s. level** = on the same level as the street. **street•car,** *n.* form of public transportation, consisting of vehicles running on rails laid in the street.

strength [streŋθ] *n.* (a) being strong. (b) number of people in a force or group. (c) **on the s. of** = because of. **strength•en,** *v.* to make stronger.

stren•u•ous [ˈstrenjʊəs] *adj.* energetic. **stren•u•ous•ly,** *adv.* vigorously. **stren•u•ous•ness,** *n.* being strenuous.

strep•to•coc•cus [streptəˈkɒkəs] *n.* (*pl.* **-cocci** [-kɒkaɪ]) bacterium which causes infections,

---

æ back, ɑː farm, ɒ top, aɪ pipe, aʊ how, aɪə fire, aʊə flower, ɔː bought, ɔɪ toy, e fed, eəhair, eɪ take, ə afraid, əʊ boat, əʊə lower, ɜː word, iː heap, ɪ hit, ɪə hear, uː school, ʊ book, ʌ but, b back, d dog, ð then, dʒ just, f fog, g go, h hand, j yes, k catch, l last, m mix, n nut, ŋ sing, p penny, r round, s some, ʃ short, t too, tʃ chop, θ thing, v voice, w was, z zoo, ʒ treasure

such as a sore throat. **strep•to•my•cin** [streptə'maɪsɪn] *n.* type of antibiotic.

stress [stres] 1. *n.* (*pl.* **-es**) (a) force; pressure. (b) nervous strain. (c) emphasis. 2. *v.* to emphasize; to put stress on (sth).

stretch [stretʃ] 1. *n.* (*pl.* **-es**) (a) act of being pulled out. (b) act of putting out your arms and legs as far as they will go. (c) long piece (of road); long period (of time); *Sl.* time spent in prison. 2. *v.* (a) to pull out (sth elastic). (b) to pull (sth) out too far. (c) to be able to be pulled out. (d) to put out your arms or legs as far as they will go. (e) to extend for a great distance. (f) to relax (a rule). **stretch•er**, *n.* (a) portable bed with handles at each end for carrying sick people; **s. bearer** = person who lifts one end of a stretcher. (b) thing which stretches.

strew [struː] *v.* (**strewn**) to scatter.

stri•at•ed [straɪ'eɪtɪd] *adj.* marked with parallel furrows. **stri•a•tion**, *n.* furrow/ridge parallel to several others.

strick•en ['strɪkn] *adj.* hit/struck by disease/emotion, etc.

strict [strɪkt] *adj.* (**-er, -est**) (a) exact (meaning). (b) (orders) which must be obeyed. (c) severe/harsh; (person) who insists that rules are obeyed. **strict•ly**, *adv.* in a strict way. **strict•ness**, *n.* being strict. **stric•ture** ['strɪktʃə] *n.* criticism/words of blame.

stride [straɪd] 1. *n.* long step with your legs. 2. *v.* (**strode** [strəʊd]) to take long steps.

stri•dent ['straɪdənt] *adj.* unpleasantly loud harsh high (sound). **stri•den•cy**, *n.* being strident. **stri•dent•ly**, *adv.* in a strident way.

strife [straɪf] *n.* fighting; trouble between people.

strike [straɪk] 1. *n.* (a) stopping of work by workers (because of disagreement with management). (b) **air s.** = rapid attack from the air. (c) **oil s.** = discovery of oil. 2. *v.* (**struck** [strʌk]) (a) to hit. (b) to light (a match); to make (a coin/a medal); to make/to agree (a bargain). (c) **to be struck down with flu** = to have a sudden attack of flu. (d) to make an impression on (s.o.). (e) to discover (oil, etc.). (f) to lower (a flag); to pack up (a tent). (g) to make (a note) sound in music; (*of clock*) to ring (the hour). (h) to go in a certain direction. (i) to stop working because of disagreement or in protest. **strike•bound**, *adj.* closed because of a strike. **strike•break•er**, *n.* worker who continues to work when his colleagues are on strike. **strike off**, *v.* to cross off (a list). **strike out**, *v.* to cross off (a list). **strike ben•e•fit/pay**, *n.* wages paid to striking workers by their union. **strik•er**, *n.* person who goes on strike. **strike up**, *v.* (a) to start playing a piece of music. (b) **to s. up an acquaintance with s.o.** = to start getting to know

s.o. **strik•ing**, *adj.* remarkable. **strik•ing•ly**, *adv.* remarkably.

string [strɪŋ] 1. *n.* (a) thin rope for tying things together; *inf.* **strings** = hidden conditions; *inf.* **to pull strings** = to try to obtain sth through influential friends. (b) series of things tied together. (c) thin wire in a musical instrument; **the strings** = part of an orchestra playing stringed instruments. (d) tough thread (in meat/vegetables). 2. *v.* (**strung** [strʌŋ]) (a) to tie together in a series. (b) to put a string in (a musical instrument). (c) **highly strung** = excitable; very nervous. **string a•long**, *v.* (a) to agree with s.o. (b) to make (s.o.) promises to get him to cooperate. **string bag**, *n.* shopping bag made of a net of knotted string. **string bean**, *n.* type of bean. **string course**, *n.* horizontal line of projecting bricks. **stringed**, *adj.* (musical instrument) with strings. **string out**, *v.* to put (things) in a long line. **string up**, *v.* to hang up with a string; *inf.* to hang (s.o.). **string•y**, *adj.* (meat/vegetables) with tough threads.

strin•gent ['strɪndʒənt] *adj.* strict/severe. **strin•gen•cy**, *n.* being stringent. **strin•gent•ly**, *adv.* in a stringent way.

strip [strɪp] 1. *n.* long narrow piece; **cartoon s./comic s.** = cartoon story made of a series of small drawings side by side. 2. *v.* (**stripped**) (a) to make naked; to take off your clothes. (b) to remove (sth). **strip down**, *v.* to take (an engine) to pieces. **strip•per**, *n.* (a) liquid for removing old paint, wax, etc. (b) person who performs a striptease. **strip•tease**, *n.* entertainment where s.o. takes their clothes off piece by piece.

stripe [straɪp] *n.* (a) long strip of color. (b) strip of colored cloth sewn to a uniform to show a certain rank in the armed forces. **striped**, *adj.* with stripes. **strip•y**, *adj.* covered with many stripes.

strip•ling ['strɪplɪŋ] *n.* very young man.

strive [straɪv] *v.* (**strove** [strəʊv]; **has striven**) to try very hard (**to**).

strobe [strəʊb] *n.* light which flashes on and off very rapidly. **stro•bo•scope**, *n.* device which makes lights flash on and off (on a dance floor).

strode [strəʊd] *v. see* **stride**.

stroke [strəʊk] 1. *n.* (a) gentle touch. (b) line made by a pen/brush, etc. (c) blow. (d) illness/paralysis caused by damage to part of the brain. (e) one movement; **s. of luck** = piece of luck. (f) particular style of swimming. (g) one ring of a bell. (h) rower seated in the stern who gives the time for all the others in a boat. 2. *v.* (a) to run your hands gently over. (b) to set the time for the other rowers in a boat.

stroll [strəul] 1. *n.* short leisurely walk. 2. *v.* to walk slowly along. **stroll•er**, *n.* (a) person who strolls. (b) light carriage for babies.

strong [strɒŋ] 1. *adj.* (-er, -est) (a) powerful. (b) large (in numbers). (c) with a powerful smell/noise, etc.; **s. drink** = alcohol. 2. *adv. inf.* **still going s.** = still working well after a long time. **strong•box**, *n.* small safe for keeping jewels. **strong•hold**, *n.* fortress; place which is difficult to capture. **strong•ly**, *adv.* powerfully. **strong•man**, *n.* powerful/influential man. **strong-mind•ed** *adj.* with clear fixed ideas. **strong point**, *n.* good quality/characteristic. **strong•room**, *n.* room with thick walls and door where money/jewels, etc. are kept. **strong-willed**, *adj.* with a strong character.

stron•ti•um ['strɒntɪəm] *n.* (*element:* Sr) white radioactive metal.

strop [strɒp] 1. *n.* leather strap for sharpening razors. 2. *v.* (**stropped**) to sharpen (a razor) on a strop.

strove [strəuv] *v. see* **strive**.

struck [strʌk] *v. see* **strike**.

struc•ture ['strʌktʃə] 1. *n.* (a) way in which things are put together. (b) building. 2. *v.* to arrange in a certain way. **struc•tur•al**, *adj.* referring to a structure. **struc•tur•al•ly**, *adv.* referring to a structure.

strug•gle ['strʌgl] 1. *n.* bitter/violent fight. 2. *v.* to fight violently.

strum [strʌm] *v.* (**strummed**) to play (a guitar, etc.) in an informal way.

strung [strʌŋ] *v. see* **string**.

strut [strʌt] 1. *n.* (a) bar of wood, metal, etc., which supports sth. (b) strutting way of walking. 2. *v.* (**strutted**) to walk in a proud and important way.

strych•nine ['strɪknin] *n.* bitter poison.

stub [stʌb] 1. *n.* (a) small piece left after sth has been used. (b) piece of paper left after a check or a ticket has been torn out of a book. 2. *v.* (**stubbed**) (a) to hurt (your toe) by hitting it against a rock. (b) to put out (a cigarette) by pressing the stub against sth. **stub•by**, *adj.* short and fat (fingers).

stub•ble ['stʌbl] *n.* (a) short stems left after corn has been cut. (b) short hairs which grow if a man does not shave for several days. **stub•bly**, *adj.* covered with short bristles.

stub•born ['stʌbən] *adj.* obstinate; (person) who will only do what he wants to do; (thing) which will not do what you want it to do. **stub•born•ly**, *adv.* obstinately. **stub•born•ness**, *n.* being stubborn.

stuc•co ['stʌkəu] *n.* plaster put on walls and painted; plaster used to make molded decorations in buildings. **stuc•coed**, *adj.* covered with stucco.

stuck [stʌk] *v. see* **stick**. **stuck-up**, *adj. inf.* thinking very highly of oneself; conceited.

stud [stʌd] *n.* (a) nail head or other metal object sticking out from a surface, often for decoration. (b) type of button with two heads for passing through two holes to fasten a shirt. (c) horses which are kept for breeding; (*also* **stud farm**) farm where horses are kept for breeding; **s. book** = register of pedigree horses, etc. 2. *v.* (**studded**) to cover with nails, etc. **stud•ded**, *adj.* covered (**with** nails/stars, etc.).

stu•dent ['stjuːdənt] *n.* person who is studying at a school/college/university.

stu•di•o ['stjuːdɪəu] *n.* (*pl.* -os) (a) place where artists paint/where photographers take photographs. (b) place where motion pictures/broadcasts/recordings are made. (c) very small apartment, having one room and a bathroom and kitchen area.

stu•di•ous ['stjuːdɪəs] *adj.* (a) showing careful study. (b) careful. **stu•di•ous•ly**, *adv.* carefully. **stu•di•ous•ness**, *n.* being studious.

stud•y ['stʌdɪ] 1. *n.* (a) act of examining sth carefully to learn more about it. (b) room in which s.o. works/studies. (c) piece of music which aims to improve the player's technique; work of art in which new ideas are practiced. 2. *v.* (a) to examine (sth) in detail to learn more about it. (b) to follow a course at a college or university. **stud•ied**, *adj.* done very carefully; done on purpose.

stuff [stʌf] 1. *n.* (a) material of which sth is made. (b) *inf.* equipment/belongings; **that's the s.** = that's it! 2. *v.* (a) to fill (sth) very full. (b) to block (a hole). (c) to fill the skin of (a dead animal) with material to make it look lifelike. (d) to put stuffing into (a chicken, etc.). **stuff•ing**, *n.* (a) seasoned mixture put inside a chicken, etc., before cooking. (b) material used to fill cushions/chair seats, etc.

stuff•y ['stʌfɪ] *adj.* (-ier, -iest) (a) (room) full of bad air from lack of ventilation. (b) prudish; old-fashioned. **stuff•i•ly**, *adv.* in a stuffy way. **stuff•i•ness**, *n.* being stuffy.

stul•ti•fy ['stʌltɪfaɪ] *v.* (*formal*) to make (s.o.) stupid. **stul•ti•fi•ca•tion** [stʌltɪfɪ'keɪʃn] *n.* act of stultifying.

æ back, aː farm, ɒ top, aɪ pipe, aʊ how, aɪə fire, aʊə flower, ɔː bought, ɔɪ toy, e fed, eəhair, eɪ take, ə afraid, əʊ boat, əʊə lower, ɜː word, iː heap, ɪ hit, ɪə hear, uː school, ʊ book, ʌ but, b back, d dog, ð then, dʒ just, f fog, g go, h hand, j yes, k catch, l last, m mix, n nut, ŋ sing, p penny, r round, s some, ʃ short, t too, tʃ chop, θ thing, v voice, w was, z zoo, ʒ treasure

stum•ble ['stʌmbl] 1. *n.* tripping over; awkward step. 2. *v.* (a) to trip over sth; to walk awkwardly. (b) **to s. across** = to find by chance. **stum•bling block**, *n.* thing which prevents you from doing sth.

stump [stʌmp] 1. *n.* (a) short piece left after sth has been finished or cut down. (b) one of the three sticks placed in the ground as a target in cricket. 2. *v.* (a) **to s. along** = to walk along heavily. (b) *inf.* to puzzle. (c) (*in cricket*) to put (a batsman) out by touching the stumps with the ball when he is not in the hitting area. **stump•y**, *adj.* (-ier, -iest) *inf.* short and squat.

stun [stʌn] *v.* (**stunned**) to knock out; to shock completely. **stun•ning**, *adj.* extraordinary/marvelous.

stung [stʌŋ] *v. see* **sting.**

stunk [stʌŋk] *v. see* **stink.**

stunt [stʌnt] 1. *n.* trick; dangerous action done to attract attention. 2. *v.* to shorten/to prevent (sth) from growing. **stunt man**, *n.* person who carries out dangerous actions in motion pictures in place of the star.

stu•pe•fy ['stjuːpɪfaɪ] *v.* (a) to make stupid. (b) to astonish. **stu•pe•fac•tion** [stjupɪ'fækʃn] *n.* astonishment.

stu•pen•dous [stju'pendəs] *adj.* extraordinary/magnificent.

stu•pid ['stjuːpɪd] *adj.* (a) not very intelligent; with no sense. (b) dull; with a dull mind. **stu•pid•i•ty** [stju'pɪdɪ tɪ] *n.* being stupid. **stu•pid•ly**, *adv.* in a stupid way. **stu•por** ['stjuːpə] *n.* being in a daze; being half senseless.

stur•dy ['stɜːdɪ] *adj.* (-ier, -iest) strong and vigorous. **stur•di•ly**, *adv.* in a sturdy way. **stur•di•ness**, *n.* being sturdy.

stur•geon ['stɜːdʒən] *n.* (*pl.* **sturgeon**) large edible fish whose eggs are caviar.

stut•ter ['stʌtə] 1. *n.* speech defect where you stutter. 2. *v.* to repeat the same sounds when speaking.

sty [staɪ] *n.* (a) shed in which a pig lives. (b) (*also* **stye**) infected pimple near the eye.

style [staɪl] 1. *n.* (a) way/manner of doing sth; **in s.** = very grandly. (b) fashion. (c) elegance. 2. *v.* (a) to name. (b) to give a certain style to (hair, etc.). **styl•ish**, *adj.* elegant/fashionable. **styl•ish•ly**, *adv.* in a stylish way. **styl•ish•ness**, *n.* fashion/elegance. **styl•ist**, *n.* person who gives (a) style to sth; **hair s.** = hairdresser. **sty•lis•tic** [staɪ'lɪstɪk] *adj.* referring to style in art. **sty•lis•ti•cal•ly**, *adv.* referring to style in art. **sty•lis•tics**, *n.* study of style of writing. **styl•i•za•tion** [staɪlaɪ'zeɪʃn] *n.* showing sth in a stylized way. **styl•ize**, *v.*

to show (sth) according to a fixed pattern/not in a natural way.

sty•lus ['staɪləs] *n.* needle of a record player.

sty•mie ['staɪmɪ] *v.* to block (a plan).

styp•tic ['stɪptɪk] *adj.* which stops bleeding; **s. pencil** = small stick of white substance (alum) which stops bleeding from cuts.

suave [swɑːv] *adj.* (-er, -est) extremely polite with very smooth manners (but often with an unpleasant character). **suave•ly**, *adv.* in a suave way. **suav•i•ty**, *n.* being suave.

sub [sʌb] 1. *n. inf.* (a) substitute. (b) submarine. 2. *v.* (**subbed**) *inf.* to act as a substitute. 3. *prefix* **sub-** = below/under.

sub•al•tern ['sʌbəltən] *n. & adj.* (person) in a subordinate position.

sub•com•mit•tee ['sʌbkəmɪti] *n.* small committee which is part of a large committee.

sub•con•scious [sʌb'kɒnʃəs] 1. *adj.* (idea/feeling) which you have in your mind without being aware of it. 2. *n.* part of your mind which has subconscious ideas or feelings. **sub•con•scious•ly**, *adv.* in a subconscious way.

sub•con•ti•nent [sʌb'kɒntɪnənt] *n.* mass of land which is part of a continent.

sub•con•tract 1. *n.* [sʌb'kɒntrækt] agreement between a main contractor and another person or company who will do part of the work which the contractor has agreed to do. 2. *v.* [sʌbkən'trækt] to agree with another person or company that they will do part of the work which you have agreed to do. **sub•con•trac•tor**, *n.* person/company who does work for a contractor.

sub•cu•ta•ne•ous [sʌbkju'teɪnɪəs] *adj.* (*formal*) under the skin.

sub•di•vide [sʌbdɪ'vaɪd] *v.* to divide (sth) which has already been divided. **sub•di•vi•sion**, *n.* (a) division of sth into smaller units. (b) land which has been divided up into plots for houses.

sub•due [sʌb'djuː] *v.* (a) to overcome/to conquer. (b) to make quiet; to make less bright. **sub•dued**, *adj.* (a) overcome/beaten. (b) low (light); **s. colors** = (i) dull colors; (ii) pastel shades.

sub•head•ing ['sʌbhedɪŋ] *n.* secondary heading.

sub•hu•man [sʌb'hjuːmən] *adj.* less advanced than a human.

sub•ject 1. *n.* ['sʌbdʒɪkt] (a) person who belongs to a country. (b) (*in grammar*) word which shows the person or thing which does an action. (c) thing which is being discussed. (d) thing which is being studied. 2. *adj.* ['sʌbdʒɪkt] (a) belonging to; under the power of (a state, king, etc.). (b) **s. to** = (i) likely to be ruled by/to suffer from; (ii) depending on. 3. *v.*

[sʌb'dʒekt] (**to**) to make (sth/s.o.) undergo sth unpleasant. **sub•jec•tion** [sʌb'dʒekʃn] *n.* being subjected. **sub•jec•tive** [sʌb'dʒektɪv] *adj.* seen from your own point of view. **sub•jec•tive•ly**, *adv.* in a subjective way. **sub•jec•tiv•i•ty**, *n.* being subjective. **sub•ject mat•ter**, *n.* subject dealt with in a book/TV program.

sub•join [sʌb'dʒɔɪn] *v.* to add (sth) at the end.

sub ju•di•ce [sʌb'dʒuːdɪsɪ] *adv.* being considered in a court of law.

sub•ju•gate ['sʌbdʒʊɡeɪt] *v.* (*formal*) to bring (a country) under your control. **sub•ju•ga•tion** [sʌbdʒʊ'ɡeɪʃn] *n.* act of subjugating.

sub•junc•tive [sʌb'dʒʌŋktɪv] *adj. & n.* (referring to) a form of a verb used to show doubt/desire, etc.

sub•lease [sʌb'liːs] 1. *n.* lease of a building/house/apartment which is already leased. 2. *v.* to sublet.

sub•let [sʌb'let] *v.* (**sublet**) to lease (a building/house/apartment) which you yourself rent.

sub•li•mate. 1. *n.* ['sʌblɪmət] substance formed when a substance is changed from solid to vapor. 2. *v.* ['sʌblɪmeit] (a) to change a substance from solid to vapor. (b) (*formal*) to channel (crude energy/emotion) into an activity which is accepted in society. **sub•li•ma•tion,** *n.* act of sublimating.

sub•lime [sə'blaɪm] *adj.* grand/wonderful; noble; very great. **sub•lime•ly**, *adv.* wonderfully.

sub•lim•i•nal [sʌb'lɪmɪnl] *adj.* below the consciousness of the senses.

sub•ma•chine gun [sʌbmə'ʃiːngʌn] *n.* light machine gun.

sub•ma•rine [sʌbmə'riːn] 1. *adj.* which lives/takes place under the water. 2. *n.* ship which can travel under the water. **sub•ma•rin•er** [sʌb'mærɪnə] *n.* member of the crew of a submarine.

sub•merge [sʌb'mɜːdʒ] *v.* (a) to (make sth) go under the surface of the water. **sub•mer•gence, submersion** [sʌb'mɜːʃn] *n.* being submerged.

sub•mis•sion [sʌb'mɪʃn] *n.* (a) state of giving in/giving way. (b) evidence/document/opinion submitted to s.o. **sub•mis•sive** [sʌb'mɪsɪv] *adj.* meek (person) who gives in easily. **sub•mis•sive•ly**, *adv.* in a submissive way. **sub•mis•sive•ness,** *n.* meekness.

sub•mit, *v.* (a) to give way; to yield. (b) to give (evidence/documents/opinion) for s.o. to examine.

sub•nor•mal [sʌb'nɔːml] *adj.* less than normal; below normal standard.

sub•or•di•nate 1. *adj. & n.* [sə'bɔːdnət] (person) who is under the control of s.o. else; **s. clause** = phrase in a sentence which cannot stand alone, and is dependent on another clause. 2. *v.* [sə'bɔːdɪneɪt] to put (sth) in a less important position; to consider (sth) as less important. **sub•or•di•na•tion** [sʌbɔːdɪ'neɪʃn] *n.* act of subordinating.

sub•orn [sə'bɔːn] *v.* (*formal*) to bribe (s.o.) to commit perjury.

sub•poe•na [sʌb'piːnə] 1. *n.* order to come to a court. 2. *v.* to order (s.o.) to come to a court.

sub•scribe [sʌb'skraɪb] *v.* (a) to give money (to a charity). (b) to pay for a series of issues of a magazine/for a series of tickets to concerts, etc. (c) **to s. to an opinion** = to agree with it. **sub•scrib•er,** *n.* person who subscribes to a charity/to a magazine; person who subscribes to a particular service. **sub•scrip•tion** [sʌb'skrɪpʃn] *n.* (a) money paid to a charity. (b) money paid to a magazine/to a club for a a series of issues/a year's membership.

sub•sec•tion ['sʌbsekʃn] *n.* part of a section.

sub•se•quent ['sʌbsɪkwənt] *adj.* which follows later. **sub•se•quent•ly**, *adv.* later.

sub•ser•vi•ent [səb'sɜːvɪənt] *adj.* weak/always giving in to s.o. **sub•ser•vi•ent•ly**, *adv.* in a subservient way. **sub•ser•vi•ence,** *n.* being subservient.

sub•side [sʌb'saɪd] *v.* (a) to sink down. (b) to become less violent or active. **sub•sid•ence** [sʌb'saɪdəns] *n.* sinking down (of the ground).

sub•sid•i•ar•y [sʌb'sɪdjərɪ] *adj. & n.* (thing) which is less important; **s. (company)** = company which is controlled by another.

sub•si•dy ['sʌbsɪdɪ] *n.* contribution of money. **sub•si•dize** ['sʌbsɪdaɪz] *v.* to help by giving money.

sub•sist [sʌb'sɪst] *v.* to exist (with difficulty). **sub•sist•ence** [sʌb'sɪstəns] *n.* existence; survival with very little money or food; **s. level** = having only just enough to live on.

sub•soil ['sʌbsɔɪl] *n.* layer of soil under the topsoil.

sub•son•ic ['sʌbsɒnɪk] *adj.* (plane) which flies at a speed less than the speed of sound.

sub•stance ['sʌbstəns] *n.* (a) matter/material of which things can be made. (b) basis (of an

---

æ back, ɑː farm, ɒ top, aɪ pipe, aʊ how, aɪə fire, aʊə flower, ɔː bought, ɔɪ toy, e fed, eəhair, eɪ take, ə afraid, əʊ boat, əʊə lower, vː word, iː heap, ɪ hit, ɪə hear, uː school, ʊ book, ʌ but, b back, d dog, ð then, dʒ just, f fog, g go, h hand, j yes, k catch, l last, m mix, n nut, ŋ sing, p penny, r round, s some, ʃ short, t too, tʃ chop, θ thing, v voice, w was, z zoo, ʒ treasure

argument/report). (c) **a man of s.** = a wealthy man. **sub•stan•tial** [sʌb'stænʃl] *adj.* (a) large/important. (b) large/solid. **sub•stan•tial•ly,** *adv.* mostly/mainly. **sub•stan•ti•ate** [sʌb'stænʃıeıt] *v.* to justify; to prove that (sth) is true. **sub•stan•ti•a•tion** [sʌbstænʃı'eıʃn] *n.* act of substantiating.

sub•stand•ard [sʌb'stændəd] *adj.* second-rate; below the normal standard.

sub•stan•tive ['sʌbstəntıv] 1. *adj.* real; existing. 2. *n.* noun.

sub•sta•tion ['sʌbsteıʃn] *n.* small local electricity station.

sub•sti•tute ['sʌbstıtjuːt] 1. *n.* person/thing taking the place of s.o./sth else. 2. *v.* to put (sth/s.o.) in the place of (s.o./sth). **sub•sti•tu•tion** [sʌbstı'tjuːʃn] *n.* act of substituting.

sub•stra•tum [sʌb'strɑːtəm] *n.* (*pl.* **-ta**) a layer, as of earth, that lies under another.

sub•sume [səb'sjuːm] *v.* (*formal*) to include in a certain category.

sub•ten•ant [sʌb'tenənt] *n.* person to whom a building/house/apartment has been sublet. **sub•ten•an•cy,** *n.* act of subletting.

sub•ter•fuge ['sʌbtəfjuːdʒ] *n.* trick; clever plot.

sub•ter•ra•ne•an [sʌbtə'reınıən] *adj.* under the ground.

sub•ti•tle ['sʌbtaıtl] 1. *n.* (a) secondary title on a book. (b) **subtitles** = translation of the dialogue of a foreign motion picture which is shown on the bottom of the screen. 2. *v.* to give a subtitle or subtitles to (sth).

sub•tle ['sʌtl] *adj.* (a) difficult to explain; very delicate (scent). (b) cunning. **sub•tle•ty** ['sʌtltı] *n.* thing which is difficult to explain/to describe. **sub•tly,** *adv.* in a subtle way.

sub•to•tal ['sʌbtəutl] *n.* total of one section of a set of figures.

sub•tract [sʌb'trækt] *v.* to take away (sth from a group). **sub•trac•tion** [sʌb'trækʃn] *n.* act of subtracting.

sub•trop•i•cal [sʌb'trɒpıkl] *adj.* referring to the subtropics. **sub•trop•ics,** *n.* areas of the world between the tropics and the temperate zones.

sub•urb ['sʌbɜːb] *n.* residential area on the outskirts of a city or town; **the suburbs** = area made up of suburbs. **sub•ur•ban** [sə'bɜːbən] *adj.* referring to the suburbs. **sub•ur•bi•a** [sə'bɜːbıə] *n. inf.* the suburbs.

sub•ven•tion [sʌb'venʃn] *n.* subsidy.

sub•ver•sion [sʌb'vɜːʃn] *n.* act of subverting. **sub•ver•sive** [sʌb'vɜːsıv] *adj.* which tries to subvert. **sub•vert** [sʌb'vɜːt] *v.* to try to destroy the authority of (the government).

sub•way ['sʌbweı] *n.* underground railroad system.

sub-ze•ro [sʌb'zıərəu] *adj.* (temperature) below zero degrees.

suc•ceed [sək'siːd] *v.* (a) to follow on; to take the place of. (b) to do well; to do what you have been trying to do. **suc•cess** [sək'ses] *n.* (*pl.* **-es**) (a) doing what you have been trying to do. (b) thing/person who does well. **suc•cess•ful,** *adj.* which succeeds. **suc•cess•ful•ly,** *adv.* in a successful way. **suc•ces•sion** [sək'seʃn] *n.* (a) series. (b) right to take s.o.'s place; act of taking s.o.'s place. **suc•ces•sive** [sək'sesıv] *adj.* one after the other. **suc•ces•sive•ly,** *adv.* one after the other. **suc•ces•sor,** *n.* person who takes s.o.'s place.

suc•cinct [sək'sıŋkt] *adj.* concise/not using many words. **suc•cinct•ly,** *adv.* in a succinct way.

suc•cor, *Brit.* **suc•cour** ['sʌkə] 1. *n.* (*formal*) help. 2. *v.* (*formal*) to help.

suc•cu•lent ['sʌkjulənt] 1. *adj.* juicy/full of juice. 2. *n.* type of plant with thick fleshy leaves and stems (like a cactus).

suc•cumb [sə'kʌm] *v.* (**to**) to give in/to yield; to die (from).

such [sʌtʃ] 1. *adj.* (a) like/similar. (b) so large/so great. (c) of this type. 2. *pron.* thing/person of a certain kind; **s. as it is** = although it is not very good. **such and such, such-and-such,** *pron.* a particular/a certain. **such•like,** *adj. pron.* similar (people/things).

suck [sʌk] 1. *n.* action of drawing in liquid through the mouth. 2. *v.* (a) to pull (liquid) into your mouth. (b) to pull in (sth) by suction. **suck•er,** *n.* (a) shoot which sprouts from an underground stem or root. (b) thing which sticks onto a surface by suction. (c) *inf.* person who is easily tricked. **suck•le,** *v.* to give (a child) milk from the breast. **suck•ling,** *n.* young animal/child still taking milk from its mother. **suck up to,** *v. Sl.* to try to make (s.o.) like you (by giving presents/making compliments, etc.). **suc•tion** ['sʌkʃən] *n.* action of sucking in air/liquid, so that sth will be pulled in/will stick to a surface because of the vacuum created; **s. cup** = small concave pad which will stick to a surface if pressed hard; **s. pump** = pump which sucks up liquid when air is pulled out of it.

su•crose ['suːkrəuz] *n.* sugar found in plants.

sud•den ['sʌdn] *adj.* which happens rapidly/unexpectedly; **all of a s.** = suddenly. **sud•den•ly,** *adv.* rapidly/unexpectedly. **sud•den•ness,** *n.* being rapid/unexpected.

suds [sʌdz] *n. pl.* foam made with soap.

sue [suː] v. to take (s.o.) to court/to start a lawsuit against (s.o.).

suede [sweɪd] n. soft leather with a rough/furry surface.

su•et ['suɪt] n. hard fat from an animal, used in cooking. **su•et•y**, adj. made of suet; like suet.

suf•fer ['sʌfə] v. (a) to feel pain; to be in a difficult situation. (b) to put up with. (c) to undergo. **suf•fer•ance**, n. he is only here on s. = we allow him to be here but we don't really want him. **suf•fer•er**, n. person who suffers. **suf•fer•ing**, n. feeling pain.

suf•fice [sə'faɪs] v. (formal) to be enough. **suf•fi•cien•cy** [sə'fɪʃənsɪ] n. enough supplies. **suf•fi•cient** [sə'fɪʃənt] adj. enough. **suf•fi•cient•ly**, adv. enough.

suf•fix ['sʌfɪks] n. (pl. -es) part added after a word to make another word.

suf•fo•cate ['sʌfəkeɪt] v. to not be able to breathe; to kill/to die by stopping breathing. **suf•fo•ca•tion** [sʌfə'keɪʃn] n. not being able to breathe.

suf•fra•gan ['sʌfrəgən] n. bishop who helps another bishop run a large diocese.

suf•frage ['sʌfrɪdʒ] n. right to vote in elections. **suf•fra•gette**, n. (old) woman who campaigned for the right to vote.

suf•fuse [sə'fjuːz] v. to cover with (color). **suf•fu•sion**, n. act of suffusing.

sug•ar ['ʃugə] 1. n. sweet substance made from the juice of a sugar cane or from sugar beet. 2. v. (a) to put sugar into. (b) to make sth more pleasant or more acceptable. **sug•ar beet**, n. plant with a large root which when crushed gives sugar. **sug•ar cane**, n. tropical plant whose stalks when crushed give sugar and rum. **sug•ar•coat•ed**, adj. covered with a coating of hard sugar. **sug•ar dad•dy**, n. old man who entertains young girls, and gives them presents. **sug•ar•y**, adj. with too much sugar.

sug•gest [sə'dʒest] v. (a) to propose (an idea). (b) to hint/to insinuate. **sug•gest•i•ble**, adj. (person) who can easily be influenced. **sug•ges•tion**, n. proposal. **sug•ges•tive**, adj. (a) which suggests. (b) which gives an impression of indecency. **sug•ges•tive•ly**, adv. in a suggestive way.

su•i•cide ['suɪsaɪd] n. (a) killing yourself; to commit s. = to kill yourself. (b) person who has killed himself. **su•i•cid•al** [suɪ'saɪdl] adj. referring to suicide.

suit [suːt] 1. n. (a) two or three pieces of clothing

made of the same cloth (jacket/vest and trousers or skirt). (b) lawsuit/court case. (c) one of the four groups with the same symbol in a pack of cards; **to follow s.** = to do what s.o. else has done. 2. v. (a) to go together; be appropriate for each other. (b) to be completely acceptable/convenient; **s. yourself** = do what you want. (c) to fit s.o.'s appearance. **suit•a•bil•i•ty** [suːtə'bɪlɪtɪ] n. being suitable. **suit•a•ble** ['suːtəbl] adj. convenient; (thing) which fits. **suit•a•bly**, adv. in a convenient/fitting way. **suit•case**, n. box with a handle for carrying clothes in when you are traveling. **suit•or**, n. person who wants to marry a certain girl.

suite [swiːt] n. (a) series of rooms/pieces of furniture which make a set. (b) group of people accompanying a king, queen or other important person. (c) several short pieces of music which are played together as a group. (d) **en s.** ['ɒn'swiːt] = attached.

sul•fa, Brit. **sul•pha** ['sʌlfə] n. **s. drug** = sulfonamide.

sul•fur, Brit. **sul•phur** ['sʌlfə] n. (element: S) solid substance, usu. found as a yellow powder. **sul•fate**, n. salt formed from sulfuric acid. **sul•fide**, n. combination of sulfur with another substance. **sul•fon•a•mide**, n. drug used against bacteria. **sul•fu•ric ac•id** [sʌl'fjuərɪk'æsɪd] n. very strong acid containing sulfur. **sul•fur•ous** ['sʌlfərəs] adj. like sulfur.

sulk [sʌlk] 1. n. **sulks** = being grumpy/annoyed in silence. 2. v. to show you are annoyed by not saying anything. **sulk•i•ly**, adv. in a sulky way. **sulk•i•ness**, n. being sulky. **sulk•y**, adj. bad-tempered/grumpy.

sul•len ['sʌln] adj. silently angry; unpleasant. **sul•len•ly**, adv. in a sullen way.

sul•ly ['sʌlɪ] v. (formal) to dirty (a reputation).

sul•pha ['sʌlfə] n. Brit. see **sul•fa**.

sul•phur ['sʌlfə] n. Brit. see **sul•fur**.

sul•tan ['sʌltən] n. Muslim prince. **sul•tan•a** [sʌl'tɑːnə] n. (a) wife of a sultan. (b) type of seedless raisin. **sul•tan•ate**, n. country ruled by a sultan.

sul•try ['sʌltrɪ] adj. (-ier, -iest) (a) hot/heavy (weather). (b) attractive in a dark way; passionate. **sul•tri•ness**, n. being sultry.

sum [sʌm] 1. n. (a) total of numbers added together; **the s. total** = the total of several sums added together. (b) quantity of money. (c) arithmetic problem. 2. v. (summed) **to s. up** =

æ back, aː farm, ɒ top, aɪ pipe, aʊ how, aɪə fire, aʊə flower, ɔː bought, ɔɪ toy, e fed, eə hair, eɪ take, ə afraid, əʊ boat, əʊə lower, ɜː word, iː heap, ɪ hit, ɪə hear, uː school, ʊ book, ʌ but, b back, d dog, ð then, dʒ just, f fog, g go, h hand, j yes, k catch, l last, m mix, n nut, ŋ sing, p penny, r round, s some, ʃ short, t too, tʃ chop, θ thing, v voice, w was, z zoo, ʒ treasure

to give a summary/to tell briefly what has happened. **sum•ma•rize** ['sʌmərɑɪz] v. to give a brief account of (sth). **sum•ma•ry.** 1. n. short account of what has happened; short version of sth longer. 2. adj. (a) brief. (b) done quickly without wasting too much time. **sum•mar•i•ly,** adv. quickly. **sum•ma•tion,** n. summary of evidence given by both attorneys at the end of a trial. **sum•ming-up,** n. summarizing statement or summation.

sum•mer ['sʌmə] n. season of the year following spring, when plants begin to make fruit; the warmest season; **s. vacation** = main/longest vacation during a school year; **s. school** = classes held at a school/university/college during the summer vacation. **sum•mer•house,** n. small house in a garden where you can sit in the summer. **sum•mer•time,** n. summer season. **sum•mer•y,** adj. like the summer.

sum•mit ['sʌmɪt] n. (a) top (of a mountain). (b) **s. (meeting)** = meeting of heads of government to discuss international problems. **sum•mit•ry,** n. inf. diplomacy carried on at summit meetings.

sum•mon ['sʌmən] v. (a) to call. (b) **to s. up courage** = to get together courage to do sth. **sum•mons.** 1. n. (a) official demand to go to see s.o. (b) official legal order to appear in court. 2. v. to order (s.o.) to appear in court.

sump [sʌmp] n. pit in which water collects.

sump•tu•ous ['sʌmtʃʊəs] adj. very luxurious/splendid. **sump•tu•ous•ly,** adv. in a sumptuous way.

sun [sʌn] 1. n. (a) very hot body around which the earth revolves and which provides heat and daylight. (b) light from the sun. 2. v. (**sunned**) **to s. yourself** = to sit in the sun. **sun•bathe,** v. to lie in the sun to get your body brown. **sun•beam,** n. ray of sunlight. **sun•burn,** n. painful inflammation of the skin caused by being in the sun for too long. **sun•burned,** adj. made brown or red by the sun. **sun•deck,** n. deck where people can sit in the sun. **sun•di•al,** n. round clock face with a central pointer whose shadow points to the time when the sun shines on it. **sun•down,** n. moment when the sun goes down. **sun•drenched,** adj. (always) very sunny. **sun•flow•er,** n. very large yellow flower on a tall stem; **s. oil** = oil made from its seeds. **sun•glass•es,** n. dark glasses to protect your eyes from the sun. **sun•lamp,** n. lamp which gives off ultraviolet rays like the sun, used to give a suntan indoors. **sun•less,** adj. with no sun. **sun•light,** n. light from the sun. **sun•lit,** adj. lit by the sun. **sun•ni•ly,** adv. in a happy way. **sun•ny,** adj. (-ier, -iest)

full of sunlight; happy (character); inf. **s. side up** = (egg) fried without being turned over. **sun•rise,** n. time at which the sun rises. **sun•roof,** n. part of a roof of a car which slides open. **sun•set,** n. time when the sun goes down behind the horizon; colorful sky as the sun goes down. **sun•shade,** n. light bright-colored umbrella to protect from the sun. **sun•shine,** n. light from the sun. **sun•shine roof,** n. sunroof. **sun•spot,** n. dark spot which appears on the surface of the sun. **sun•stroke,** n. illness caused by being overly exposed to the sun's rays or extreme heat. **sun•tan,** n. brown color of the skin caused by the sun. **sun•tanned,** adj. with a skin made brown by the sun. **sun•up,** n. sunrise.

sun•dae ['sʌndɪ] n. dessert of ice cream, whipped cream, chopped nuts and fruit.

Sun•day ['sʌndɪ] n. last day of the week; day between Saturday and Monday; **S. best** = best clothes; **S. school** = school for teaching religion to children, usu. held on a Sunday.

sun•der ['sʌndə] v. (formal) to split into parts.

sun•dew ['sʌndju:] n. wild plant which catches insects for food.

sun•dry ['sʌndrɪ] 1. adj. various. 2. n. (a) **all and s.** = everyone. (b) **sundries** = various small articles/small items on a list.

sung [sʌŋ] v. see **sing.**

sunk [sʌŋk] adj. ruined/lost; see also **sink.** **sunken,** adj. (a) which is beneath the surface. (b) lower than the surrounding area.

sup [sʌp] 1. n. mouthful of liquid. 2. v. (**supped**) to drink in small mouthfuls.

su•per ['su:pə] 1. adj. inf. wonderful. 2. n. inf. (a) superintendent. (b) extra actor. 3. **super-** prefix meaning more/greater/of better quality.

su•per•a•bun•dance [su:pərə'bʌndəns] n. great abundance; very large quantity. **su•per•a•bun•dant,** adj. very abundant/in very large quantities.

su•per•an•nu•at•ed [su:pə'rænjʊeɪtɪd] adj. too old to work properly; old-fashioned. **su•per•an•nu•a•tion** [su:pərænjʊ'eɪʃn] n. (a) retirement of workers when they reach a certain age. (b) pension paid to s.o. who has retired.

su•perb [su:'pɜ:b] adj. marvelous/wonderful. **su•perb•ly,** adv. wonderfully.

su•per•charged ['su:pətʃɑ:dʒd] adj. (motor/person) with much increased energy. **su•per•charg•er,** n. apparatus on a car engine for increasing the power.

su•per•cil•i•ous [su:pə'sɪlɪəs] adj. looking down on others; considering others as inferior. **su•per•cil•i•ous•ly,** adv. in a supercilious way. **su•per•cil•i•ous•ness,** *n.* being supercilious.

su•per•fi•cial [suːpəˈfɪʃl] *adj.* touching only the top surface; not going deeply beneath the surface. **su•per•fi•ci•al•i•ty** [suːpəfɪʃɪˈælɪtɪ] *n.* being superficial. **su•per•fi•cial•ly,** *adv.* in a superficial way.

su•per•fine [suːpəˈfaɪn] *adj.* very fine.

su•per•flu•ous [suːˈpəːfluəs] *adj.* which is more than is needed. **su•per•flu•i•ty** [suːpəˈfluːɪtɪ] *n.* being superfluous/more than is needed; excess. **su•per•flu•ous•ly,** *adv.* in a superfluous way.

su•per•high•way [suːpəˈhaɪweɪ] *n.* main highway, usu. having more than one line per direction.

su•per•hu•man [suːpəˈhjuːmən] *adj.* more than is normal in human beings.

su•per•im•pose [suːpəɪmˈpəʊz] *v.* to place on top of sth.

su•per•in•tend [suːpərɪnˈtend] *v.* to be in charge. **su•per•in•tend•ent,** *n.* (a) person in charge. (b) senior police officer.

su•pe•ri•or [suːˈpɪərɪə] 1. *adj.* (a) of better quality; of a larger quality. (b) higher in rank. (c) thinking yourself to be better than others. 2. *n.* (a) person of higher rank. (b) leader of a religious community. **su•pe•ri•or•i•ty** [suːpɪərɪˈɒrɪtɪ] *n.* being superior.

su•per•la•tive [suːˈpəːlətɪv] 1. *adj.* of the best quality. 2. *n.* form of an adjective or adverb showing the highest level of comparison. **su•per•la•tive•ly,** *adv.* extremely well.

su•per•man [ˈsuːpəmæn] *n.* (*pl.* **-men**) man who has superhuman strength/power/ability.

su•per•mar•ket [ˈsuːpəmɑːkɪt] *n.* large store selling mainly food, where you serve yourself.

su•per•nat•u•ral [suːpəˈnætʃərəl] *adj. & n.* (things) which happen not in accordance with the laws of nature. **su•per•nat•u•ral•ly,** *adv.* in a supernatural way.

su•per•no•va [ˈsuːpənəʊvə] *n.* large star which explodes and suddenly appears in the sky.

su•per•nu•mer•ar•y [ˈsuːpəˈnjuːmərərɪ] *adj. & n.* (person) who is in addition to the usual number of people.

su•per•phos•phate [suːpəˈfɒsfeɪt] *n.* fertilizer based on phosphates.

su•per•pow•er [ˈsuːpəpaʊə] *n.* extremely powerful country.

su•per•scrip•tion [suːpəˈskrɪpʃn] *n.* words written above sth.

su•per•sede [suːpəˈsiːd] *v.* to take the place of (sth which is older or less efficient).

su•per•son•ic [suːpəˈsɒnɪk] *adj.* faster than the speed of sound.

su•per•sti•tion [suːpəˈstɪʃn] *n.* belief in magic and the supernatural. **su•per•sti•tious** [suːpəˈstɪʃəs] *adj.* believing in magic and the supernatural.

su•per•struc•ture [ˈsuːpəstrʌktʃə] *n.* top structure of a ship; structure built on top of sth else.

su•per•tank•er [ˈsuːpətæŋkə] *n.* very large oil tanker.

su•per•vene [suːpəˈviːn] *v.* to happen as something extra, usu. causing change.

su•per•vise [ˈsuːpəvaɪz] *v.* to watch over work, etc., to see that it is well done. **su•per•vi•sion** [suːpəˈvɪʒn] *n.* act of supervising. **su•per•vi•sor** [ˈsuːpəvaɪzə] *n.* person who supervises. **su•per•vi•so•ry** [suːpəˈvaɪzərɪ] *adj.* as a supervisor.

su•per•wom•an [ˈsuːpəwʊmən] *n.* (*pl.* **-women**) woman who has superhuman strength/power/ability.

su•pine [ˈsuːpaɪn] *adj.* (*formal*) (a) lying flat on your back. (b) uninterested/lazy.

sup•per [ˈsʌpə] *n.* evening meal.

sup•plant [səˈplɑːnt] *v.* to take (s.o.'s) place by cunning maneuvers.

sup•ple [ˈsʌpl] *adj.* flexible/which bends easily. **sup•ple•ness,** *n.* being supple. **sup•ply** [ˈsʌplɪ], **supplely** *adv.* in a supple way.

sup•ple•ment 1. *n.* [ˈsʌplɪmənt] (a) thing which is in addition. (b) addition to a book; magazine which is part of a newspaper. 2. *v.* [ˈsʌplɪment] to add to sth. **sup•ple•men•ta•ry** [sʌplɪˈmentrɪ] *adj.* in addition.

sup•pli•ant [ˈsʌplɪənt] *n.* person who begs for help.

sup•pli•cate [ˈsʌplɪkeɪt] *v.* (*formal*) to beg for sth. **sup•pli•cant,** *n.* person who begs for help. **sup•pli•ca•tion** [sʌplɪˈkeɪʃn] *n.* (*formal*) begging for help.

sup•ply [səˈplaɪ] 1. *n.* (a) providing sth which is needed. (b) stock of sth which has been provided. (c) **supplies** = food, etc., which has been stocked/which is going to be provided. 2. *v.* (a) to provide (sth which is necessary). (b) **to s. s.o. with sth** = to provide sth to s.o. (c) to satisfy. 3. *adv.* [ˈsʌplɪ] *see* **sup•ple. sup•pli•er** [səˈplaɪə] *n.* person/store/country which supplies.

sup•port [səˈpɔːt] 1. *n.* (a) thing which sup-

æ back, ɑː farm, ɒ top, aɪ pipe, aʊ how, aɪə fire, aʊə flower, ɔː bought, ɔɪ toy, e fed, eəhair, eɪ take, ə afraid, əʊ boat, əʊə lower, vː word, iː heap, ɪ hit, ɪə hear, uː school, ʊ book, ʌ but, b back, d dog, ð then, dʒ just, f fog, g go, h hand, j yes, k catch, l last, m mix, n nut, ŋ sing, p penny, r round, s some, ʃ short, t too, tʃ chop, θ thing, v voice, w was, z zoo, ʒ treasure

ports. (b) moral/financial encouragement. 2. *v.* (a) to hold up. (b) to provide/to earn money so that s.o. can live. (c) to encourage/to agree with. **sup•port•er**, *n.* person who encourages a plan/a sports team, etc. **sup•port•ing cast**, *n.* group of actors who play the minor parts in a play.

sup•pose [sə'pəuz] *v.* (a) to assume sth to be correct (even if it is not). (b) to think. (c) what happens if? **sup•pos•ed•ly** [sə'pəuzɪdlɪ] *adv.* as it is assumed. **sup•pos•ing**, *conj.* what happens if? **sup•po•si•tion** [sʌpə'zɪʃn] *n.* thing which is assumed; guess.

sup•pos•i•to•ry [sə'pɒzɪtərɪ] *n.* tablet of medicinal material which is put into the rectum or vagina where it melts.

sup•press [sə'pres] *v.* (a) to crush; to stop (a revolution). (b) to forbid the publication of (sth). (c) to hide (feelings). **sup•pres•sion** [sə'preʃn] *n.* act of suppressing.

sup•pu•rate ['sʌpjureɪt] *v.* (*formal*) to produce pus.

supra- ['su:prə] *prefix.* beyond.

su•pra•na•tion•al [su:prə'næʃnl] *adj.* over/beyond the interests of a single nation or several nations.

su•preme [su'pri:m] *adj.* highest; total (indifference). **su•preme•ly**, *adv.* totally/completely. **su•prem•a•cy** [su'preməsɪ] *n.* highest power.

sur•charge 1. *n.* ['sɜ:tʃɑ:dʒ] extra charge. 2. *v.* [sɜ:'tʃɑ:dʒ] to charge an extra amount.

surd [sɜ:d] *n.* (*in mathematics*) quantity (like a root) which cannot be expressed as a whole number.

sure [ʃɔ:, 'ʃuːə] 1. *adj.* (-er, -est) (a) without any doubt; certain; **for s.** = for certain. (b) reliable. (c) **s. of yourself** = confident. 2. *adv.* certainly. **sure•fire**, *adj. inf.* absolutely certain to work; which cannot fail. **sure•foot•ed**, *adj.* able to walk on slippery rocks/narrow ledges without slipping. **sure•ly**, *adv.* (a) carefully. (b) naturally/of course. **sure•ness**, *n.* being sure. **sur•e•ty**, *n.* (a) person who takes the responsibility that s.o. will do sth. (b) money paid as a guarantee that s.o. will appear in court.

surf [sɜ:f] 1. *n.* line of breaking waves along a shore; foam from breaking waves. 2. *v.* (a) to ride on breaking waves on a board. (b) **to s. the Internet** = to browse through the information on the Internet, usu. with no definite objective. **surf•board**, *n.* board which you stand on to ride on breaking waves. **surf boat**, *n.* light boat for riding on surf. **surf•er**, *n.* person who surfs. **surf•ing, surfriding**, *n.* riding on breaking waves as a sport.

sur•face ['sɜ:fəs] 1. *n.* top layer; outside of sth.

2. *v.* (a) to come up from under/to appear on the top of water, etc. (b) to cover (a road, etc.) with a hard substance. **sur•face mail**, *n.* mail which travels by truck/train/ship, etc., and not by air.

sur•feit ['sɜ:fɪt] 1. *n.* (*formal*) too much. 2. *v.* to feed (s.o.) too much.

surge [sɜ:dʒ] 1. *n.* (a) rising up of water into waves. (b) sudden increase. 2. *v.* (a) to rise up. (b) move (forward) in a mass.

sur•geon ['sɜ:dʒən] *n.* doctor who performs operations. **sur•ger•y**, *n.* treatment of disease or wounds by cutting open part of the body. **sur•gi•cal** ['sɜ:dʒɪkl] *adj.* referring to surgery; **s. gloves** = gloves worn by a surgeon. **sur•gi•cal•ly**, *adv.* in a surgical way.

sur•ly ['sɜ:lɪ] *adj.* (-ier, -iest) grumpy/sullen. **sur•li•ness**, *n.* being surly.

sur•mise [sə'maɪz] 1. *n.* guess/supposition. 2. *v.* to guess.

sur•mount [sɜ:'maunt] *v.* (a) to overcome (an obstacle). (b) to be on top of (sth). **sur•mount•a•ble**, *adj.* which can be surmounted.

sur•name ['sɜ:neɪm] *n.* family name.

sur•pass [sə'pɑːs] *v.* to do better than.

sur•plice ['sɜ:pləs] *n.* long white robe worn by clergy/choirboys.

sur•plus ['sɜ:pləs] *adj. & n.* (*pl.* -es) extra (stock); (material) left over.

sur•prise [sə'praɪz] 1. *n.* shock caused by sth unexpected. 2. *v.* (a) to give (s.o.) a surprise/an unexpected shock. (b) to catch (s.o.) unexpectedly. **sur•pris•ing**, *adj.* astonishing/unusual. **sur•pris•ing•ly**, *adv.* in an unusual way.

sur•re•al•ism [sə'rɪəlɪzəm] *n.* 20th century art movement in which an artist depicts realistic objects in an unreal environment, emphasizing the meaning he sees beyond reality. **sur•re•al•ist**, *adj. & n.* (artist) following the principles of surrealism. **sur•re•al•is•tic**, *adj.* very strange/totally unreal.

sur•ren•der [sə'rendə] 1. *n.* (a) giving in (to an enemy). (b) giving up (of goods); giving up (of an insurance policy); **s. value** = amount of money you will receive if you end an insurance policy before the normal completion date. 2. *v.* (a) to give in (to an enemy). (b) to give up (a ticket/insurance policy, etc.).

sur•rep•ti•tious [sʌrəp'tɪʃəs] *adj.* done in secret. **sur•rep•ti•tious•ly**, *adv.* in secret.

sur•ro•gate ['sʌrəgɪt] *n.* deputy/person who acts in place of s.o.

sur•round [sə'raund] 1. *n.* border; edge. 2. *v.* to be/to come all around (sth). **sur•round•ing**, *adj.* which surrounds. **sur•round•ings**, *n.pl.* area around a place/person.

sur•tax ['sɜːtæks] *n.* extra tax, as on incomes over a certain amount.

sur•veil•lance [sɜː'veɪləns] *n.* strict watch.

sur•vey 1. *n.* ['sɜːveɪ] (a) general view. (b) careful examination of sth. (c) taking measurements of land heights/distances/roads/buildings, etc., to produce accurate plans or maps. 2. *v.* [sə'veɪ] (a) to look at/to talk about (sth) in a general way. (b) to make a survey of sth. (c) to measure (land) in order to produce an accurate plan or map. **sur•vey•or,** *n.* person who surveys land.

sur•vive [sə'vaɪv] *v.* (a) to continue to live (after an accident, etc.). (b) to live longer than (s.o.). **sur•viv•al,** *n.* continuing to live. **sur•vi•vor,** *n.* person who survives.

sus•cep•ti•ble [sə'septɪbl] *adj.* (a) **s. to** = likely to catch (a disease). (b) easily upset. **sus•cep•ti•bil•i•ty** [səseptə'bɪlɪtɪ] *n.* being susceptible.

sus•pect 1. *adj. & n.* ['sʌspekt] (person) who is thought to have committed a crime; (food) which might be poisonous. 2. *v.* [sə'spekt] (a) **to s. s.o. of** = to think that (s.o.) may have committed a crime. (b) to guess/to think.

sus•pend [sə'spend] *v.* (a) to hang; to make (sth) hang in a liquid. (b) to stop (sth) for a time. (c) to take (sth) away as a punishment; to stop (s.o.) from doing sth. **sus•pend•ers,** *n.pl.* (a) elastic straps to hold up stockings or socks. (b) elastic straps worn over the shoulders to hold up trousers. **sus•pense,** *n.* impatient wait for sth to happen or for a decision to be reached. **sus•pen•sion,** *n.* (a) act of suspending; being suspended; **s. bridge** = one which hangs by ropes/chains, etc., from tall towers. (b) system of springs, etc., in a car which attaches the chassis to the axles.

sus•pi•cion [sə'spɪʃn] *n.* (a) feeling that sth is wrong or that s.o. has committed a crime. (b) guess; general feeling. (c) slight hint. **sus•pi•cious,** *adj.* which can be suspected. **sus•pi•cious•ly,** *adv.* (a) in a suspicious way. (b) as if suspecting sth.

sus•tain [sə'steɪn] *v.* (a) to keep (sth) going. (b) to suffer. (c) to support. **sus•tain•a•ble,** *adj.* referring to the use of natural resources in such a way that the environment is preserved, e.g. forestry that replaces each tree felled. **sus•tained,** *adj.* which continues for a long time. **sus•tain•ing,** *adj.* which will support or nourish.

sus•te•nance ['sʌstənəns] *n.* (a) food. (b)

means of s. = way of keeping alive/of keeping strong.

su•ture ['suːtʃə] *n.* thread used for stitching wounds together; stitching (of a wound); stitch made to hold a wound together.

su•ze•rain ['suːzəreɪn] *n.* (*formal*) overlord. **su•ze•rain•ty,** *n.* rule over (a state).

svelte [svelt] *adj.* slim and graceful.

swab [swɒb] 1. *n.* (a) large mop for wiping floors, decks, etc. clear of water. (b) piece of material used for cleaning a wound or for taking samples of infection for analysis. (c) sample of infection taken for analysis. 2. *v.* (**swabbed**) to clean (a floor, deck, etc.) with a swab.

swad•dle ['swɒdl] *v.* (*old*) to wrap (a baby) in pieces of cloth.

swag [swæg] *n. inf.* stolen goods (esp. jewelry/silver, etc.).

swag•ger ['swægə] 1. *n.* proud way of walking. 2. *v.* to walk in a proud way, swinging your body.

swal•low ['swɒləʊ] 1. *n.* (a) mouthful of liquid which you drink in one movement; act of swallowing. (b) common fast-flying bird with long wings and tail. 2. *v.* (a) to make (food/liquid) pass down your throat from your mouth to the stomach. (b) to accept (a story) as true. (c) to make disappear.

swam [swæm] *v. see* **swim.**

swamp [swɒmp] 1. *n.* area of wet soft land. 2. *v.* to fill (a boat) with water; **swamped with** = having so much (work, etc.) that it is impossible to deal with. **swamp•y,** *adj.* (-ier, -iest) wet (land) like a marsh.

swan [swɒn] *n.* large white water bird with a long curved neck. **swan dive,** *n.* dive where the arms are stretched out sideways from the shoulder at the start. **swan song,** *n.* last performance by an artist (esp. a singer); last work by a writer.

swank [swæŋk] 1. *n. inf.* showing off. 2. *v. inf.* to show off; to show that you think a lot of yourself. **swank•y,** *adj. inf.* pretentious; (acting) in a swanking way.

swap, swop [swɒp] 1. *n. inf.* exchange. 2. *v.* (**swapped/swopped**) *inf.* to exchange (sth **for** sth).

sward [swɔːd] *n.* soft grassy surface.

swarm [swɔːm] 1. *n.* large group of insects, etc., flying about together. 2. *v.* (a) to move about in a large group. (b) (**up**) to climb using your hands and feet like a monkey.

æ back, ɑː farm, ɒ top, aɪ pipe, aʊ how, aɪə fire, aʊə flower, ɔː bought, ɔɪ toy, e fed, eəhair, eɪ take, ə afraid, əʊ boat, əʊə lower, ɜː word, iː heap, ɪ hit, ɪə hear, uː school, ʊ book, ʌ but, b back, d dog, ð then, dʒ just, f fog, g go, h hand, j yes, k catch, l last, m mix, n nut, ŋ sing, p penny, r round, s some, ʃ short, t too, tʃ chop, θ thing, v voice, w was, z zoo, ʒ treasure

swarth•y ['swɔːðɪ] *adj.* (**-ier, -iest**) with a dark complexion.

swash•buck•ling ['swɒʃbʌklɪŋ] *adj.* daring; living dangerously.

swas•ti•ka ['swɒstɪkə] *n.* ancient sign, shaped like a cross with each arm bent at right angles.

swat [swɒt] *v.* (**swatted**) to hit and kill (a fly, etc.). **swat•ter**, *n.* (*also* **fly swatter**) flat piece of stiff netting, plastic, etc. on a handle for killing flies and other insects.

swatch [swɒtʃ] *n.* (*pl.* **-es**) small sample of fabric.

swath [swɒθ] *n.* strip cut by a scythe/harvester/mower.

swathe [sweɪð] *v.* to wrap up.

sway [sweɪ] 1. *n.* (a) power. (b) act of swaying. 2. *v.* (a) to (cause to) move from side to side. (b) to influence.

swear ['sweə] *v.* (**swore** [swɔː]; **sworn** [swɔːn]) (a) to promise solemnly. (b) to (make s.o.) take an oath. (c) to curse. (d) **to s. by** = to believe completely or enthusiastically in. **swear word**, *n.* word used as a curse or to show annoyance.

sweat [swet] 1. *n.* drops of liquid which come through your skin when you are hot. 2. *v.* to produce sweat; **we'll have to s. it out** = keep on with it, even if it is unpleasant/difficult. **sweat•band**, *n.* band of fabric worn around your head or wrist to stop sweat trickling down. **sweat•er**, *n.* piece of clothing made of wool, cotton, etc. covering the top part of the body which you usu. pull on over your head. **sweat•shirt**, *n.* loose long-sleeved cotton shirt with no collar or buttons. **sweat shop**, *n.* factory using people who work hard for little money under poor conditions. **sweat•y**, *adj.* damp with sweat.

Swede [swiːd] *n.* person from Sweden. **Swed•ish**. 1. *adj.* referring to Sweden. 2. *n.* language spoken in Sweden.

sweep [swiːp] 1. *n.* (a) act of sweeping (with a brush); act of swinging (a sword or your hand); **to make a clean s.** = to clear sth away completely/to win completely. (b) wide stretch (of water, etc.). (c) person who cleans chimneys. (d) sweepstakes. 2. *v.* (**swept** [swept]) (a) to clean with a brush. (b) to win completely. (c) to clear up (dust/snow, etc.) with a brush. (d) to make a wide movement. (e) to move rapidly; to carry (sth) along rapidly. **sweep•er**, *n.* person/machine that sweeps. **sweep•ing**, *adj.* wide-ranging/far-reaching; **s. statement** = statement which is partly true but too general. **sweep•stakes**, *n.* form of gambling where the holders of the winning tickets take all the money which has been bet.

sweet [swiːt] 1. *adj.* (**-er, -est**) (a) tasting like sugar; not sour; **s. tooth** = liking for sweet things. (b) pleasant; **s. pea** = pea with scented flowers. (c) fresh (air). 2. *n.* small piece of sweet food, made with sugar or chocolate. **sweet•bread**, *n.* pancreas of an animal eaten as food. **sweet corn**, *n.* corn, eaten as food. **sweet•en**, *v.* (a) to make sweet. (b) *inf.* to give (s.o.) a bribe to make sure he is favorable to you. **sweet•en•er**, *n.* (a) thing/material which sweetens. (b) *inf.* bribe. **sweet•en•ing**, *n.* act of making sweet; substance which makes sweet. **sweet•heart**, *n.* darling; boy/girl friend. **sweet•ie**, *n. inf.* (a) sweet. (b) darling. **sweet•ly**, *adv.* in a sweet way. **sweet•meat**, *n.* (*old*) sweet. **sweet•ness**, *n.* being sweet. **sweet po•ta•to**, *n.* yam. **sweet wil•liam**, *n.* type of common scented garden flower.

swell [swel] 1. *n.* (a) rising movement of the sea. (b) increasing loudness. 2. *adj.* fine. 3. *v.* (**swelled/swollen**) (a) to increase. (b) **to s. (up)** = to become larger/to increase in size. (c) **to s. (out)** = to become/to make (sails) fully rounded. **swell•ing**, *n.* part of the body which has swollen.

swel•ter ['sweltə] *v.* to be very hot. **swel•ter•ing**, *adj.* very hot.

swept [swept] *v. see* **sweep**.

swerve [swɜːv] 1. *n.* movement to the side. 2. *v.* to move to one side.

swid•den ['swɪdən] *n.* type of farming, where forest is cut and burned to create space for growing crops.

swift [swɪft] 1. *adj.* (**-er, -est**) fast. 2. *n.* fast-flying bird like a swallow but with shorter wings and tail. **swift•ly**, *adv.* fast. **swift•ness**, *n.* rapidity.

swig [swɪg] 1. *n. inf.* large mouthful of liquid. 2. *v.* (**swigged**) *inf.* to drink in large mouthfuls.

swill [swɪl] 1. *n.* food for pigs. 2. *v. inf.* to drink a lot of alcohol, etc.

swim [swɪm] 1. *n.* act of moving in the water using arms/legs/flippers, etc.; **in the s.** = up to date/knowing what's going on. 2. *v.* (**swam; swum**) (a) to move in water using arms, legs, flippers, etc. (b) to cross (a river, etc.) by swimming. (c) to be covered with liquid. (d) (*of head, room*) to seem to turn. **swim•mer**, *n.* person who swims. **swim•ming**, *n.* action of swimming. **swim•ming•ly**, *adv. inf.* very well. **swim•ming pool**, *n.* pool for swimming. **swim•suit**, *n.* one- or two-piece garment worn for swimming.

swin•dle ['swɪndl] 1. *n.* trick to get money from s.o. 2. *v.* to get money from (s.o.) by a trick. **swin•dler**, *n.* person who swindles s.o.

swine [swaɪn] *n.* (*no pl.*) (a) pig. (b) *inf.* unpleasant person. **swine fe•ver**, *n.* infectious disease of pigs. **swine•herd**, *n.* (*old*) person who looks after pigs.

swing [swɪŋ] 1. *n.* (a) movement from side to side or forward and backward; movement of voters to vote for a certain party. (b) **in full s.** = going very well. (c) seat on the end of two ropes which you can sit on and swing backward and forward. 2. *v.* (**swung** [swʌŋ]) (a) to move from side to side or forward and backward. (b) to make (sth) turn around; to turn around. (c) to move in a rhythmic way with a regular motion. **swing bridge,** *n.* bridge which can be made to turn to allow ships to pass underneath. **swing•er,** *n.* person who is fashionably modern. **swing•ing,** 1. *n.* action of moving backward and forward. 2. *adj.* (a) moving backward and forward. (b) *inf* lively; fashionably modern. **swing•ing door,** *n.* door which is not attached with a catch, and which opens when you push it. **swing-wing,** *adj.* (aircraft) with adjustable wings.

swipe [swaɪp] 1. *n. inf.* sweeping hit/blow. 2. *v.* (a) *inf.* to hit (s.o.) with a sweeping blow. (b) *Sl.* to steal.

swirl [swɜ:l] 1. *n.* whirling/twisting movement. 2. *v.* to move with a whirling/twisting motion.

swish [swɪʃ] 1. *n.* soft rustle (of a dress/of dead leaves); whistle (of a stick). 2. *v.* to make a whistling noise with a whip/stick.

Swiss [swɪs] 1. *adj.* referring to Switzerland. 2. *n.* (*pl.* **Swiss**) person from Switzerland.

switch [swɪtʃ] 1. *n.* (*pl.* **-es**) (a) apparatus for starting or stopping an electric current. (b) sudden change. (c) whip made of a thin stick. (d) tuft of hair at the end of an animal's tail, as a cow. 2. *v.* (a) to send (a train, etc.) in a different direction; to do sth quite different. (b) to hit with a switch. **switch•back,** *n.* road or railroad having many curves. **switch•board,** *n.* central telephone panel where calls can be transferred to different rooms. **switch off,** *v.* to stop an electric current. **switch on,** *v.* to start an electric current flowing. **switch o•ver to,** *v.* to change to sth quite different.

swiv•el ['swɪvl] 1. *n.* joint between two parts which enables either part to turn without the other. 2. *v.* (**swiveled, swivelled**) to turn around; to pivot. **swiv•el chair,** *n.* chair which pivots, so that the seat can turn while the legs stay stationary.

swiz•zle•stick ['swɪzlstɪk] *n.* small stick used to stir an alcoholic drink.

swol•len ['swəʊlən] *adj.* blown up; increased in size; *see also* **swell.**

swoon [swu:n] *v.* to faint.

swoop [swu:p] 1. *n.* coming rapidly down from a height to attack; sudden attack; **at/in one fell s.** = in a sudden move/all at once. 2. *v.* to come down rapidly to attack; to attack suddenly.

swop [swɒp] *n. & v. see* **swap.**

sword [sɔ:d] *n.* weapon with a long sharp blade held by a handle; **to cross swords with** = to get into an argument with. **sword•fish,** *n.* fish with a long pointed upper jaw like a sword. **swords•man,** *n.* (*pl.* **-men**) person who fights well with a sword.

swore [swɔ:] *v. see* **swear.**

sworn [swɔ:n] *adj.* **s. enemies** = total enemies; *see also* **swear.**

swum [swʌm] *v. see* **swim.**

swung [swʌŋ] *v. see* **swing.**

syb•a•rite ['sɪbəraɪt] *n.* person who enjoys luxury. **syb•a•rit•ic** [sɪbə'rɪtɪk] *adj.* very comfortable and luxurious.

syc•a•more ['sɪkəmɔ:] *n.* common deciduous tree with very large leaves.

syc•o•phant ['sɪkəfænt] *n.* person who flatters s.o. in power. **syc•o•phan•tic** [sɪkə-'fæntɪk] *adj.* which flatters excessively.

syl•la•ble ['sɪləbl] *n.* unit of sound which forms a whole word or part of a word. **syl•lab•ic** [sɪ'læbɪk] *adj.* referring to a syllable.

syl•la•bub ['sɪləbʌb] *n.* dessert made of cream whipped with wine.

syl•la•bus ['sɪləbəs] *n.* (*pl.* **-es, -bi**) list of subjects to be studied.

syl•lo•gism ['sɪlədʒɪzəm] *n.* logical reasoning where a conclusion is reached from two statements.

sylph [sɪlf] *n.* thin girl. **sylph•like,** *adj.* very slim.

syl•van ['sɪlvən] *adj.* (*formal*) referring to woods.

sym•bi•o•sis [sɪmbɪ'əʊsɪs] *n.* state where two living organisms live close together and depend on each other to a certain extent. **sym•bi•ot•ic** [sɪmbaɪ'ɒtɪk] *adj.* referring to symbiosis.

sym•bol ['sɪmbl] *n.* sign/letter/picture/object which represents sth/which is a short way of indicating sth. **sym•bol•ic(al)** [sɪm'bɒlɪk(l)] *adj.* which acts as a symbol. **sym•bol•i•cal•ly,** *adv.* used as a symbol. **sym•bol•ism,** *n.* (a) movement in literature and art which used symbols to express emotion, etc. (b) using symbols to express emotion, etc. **sym•bol•ist,** *adj. & n.* (follower) of

---

symbolism. sym•bol•ize ['sɪmbəlaɪz] v. to represent (sth) by a symbol; to be a symbol for (sth).

sym•me•try ['sɪmətrɪ] n. state where two sides of sth are exactly alike. **sym•met•ri•cal** [sɪ'metrɪkl] adj. referring to symmetry.

sym•pa•thy ['sɪmpəθɪ] n. (a) feeling of pity or sorrow for s.o. who has problems. (b) common feeling; sharing ideas. **sym•pa•thet•ic** [simpə'θetɪk] adj. showing sympathy. **sym•pa•thet•i•cal•ly,** adv. in a sympathetic way. **sym•pa•thize,** v. (with) (a) to show sympathy to (s.o. in trouble). (b) to approve; to agree. **sym•pa•thiz•er,** n. person who sympathizes with s.o.'s political views.

sym•pho•ny ['sɪmfənɪ] n. piece of music in several parts for a full orchestra. **sym•phon•ic** [sɪm'fɒnɪk] adj. referring to a symphony.

sym•po•si•um [sɪm'pəʊzɪəm] n. (pl. -ia) organized meeting to discuss a specific subject; collection of articles written on a specific subject.

symp•tom ['sɪmptəm] n. thing which shows visibly that feelings exist/that changes are taking place. **symp•to•mat•ic** [sɪmptə'mætɪk] adj. (of) which shows visibly that changes are taking place or that feelings exist.

syn•a•gogue ['sɪnəgɒg] n. building where Jews worship.

syn•apse ['sɪnæps] n. point in the nervous system where neurons join.

sync [sɪŋk] n. inf. synchronization; **out of s.** = not synchronized.

syn•chro•mesh ['sɪŋkrəmeʃ] n. type of gear system where the gears revolve at the same speeds before being engaged.

syn•chro•nize ['sɪŋkrənaɪz] v. to adjust (watches) to the same time; to arrange (things) so that they happen at the same time. **syn•chro•ni•za•tion** [sɪŋkrənaɪ'zeɪʃn] n. act of synchronizing.

syn•co•pate ['sɪŋkəpeɪt] v. (in music) to stress (a beat) which would not normally be stressed and so change the rhythm. **syn•co•pa•tion** [sɪŋkə'peɪʃn] n. act of syncopating.

syn•co•pe ['sɪŋkəpɪ] n. fainting attack.

syn•di•cal•ism ['sɪndɪkəlɪzm] n. form of socialism, where control is in the hands of the labor unions.

syn•di•cate 1. n. ['sɪndɪkət] group of people or companies working together to make money. 2. v. ['sɪndɪkeɪt] to produce (an article/a cartoon) which is then sold to a series of newspapers. **syn•di•ca•tion** [sindi'keiʃn] n. act of syndicating.

syn•drome ['sɪndrəʊm] n. (a) series of symptoms which show an illness. (b) symptoms which show a general feeling/way of approaching a problem, etc.

syn•er•gy ['sɪnədʒɪ] n. (of two organizations) working together better than working separately.

syn•od ['sɪnəd] n. meeting of religious leaders.

syn•o•nym ['sɪnənɪm] n. word which means the same thing as another word. **syn•on•y•mous** [sɪ'nɒnɪməs] adj. which has the same meaning.

syn•op•sis [sɪ'nɒpsɪs] n. (pl. -ses) summary (of main points made in a book or article).

syn•o•vi•tis ['saɪnəʊ'vaɪtɪs] n. inflammation of the membrane covering a joint.

syn•tax ['sɪntæks] n. grammatical rules for putting words together into sentences. **syn•tac•tic** [sɪn'tæktɪk] adj. referring to syntax.

syn•the•sis ['sɪnθəsɪs] n. (pl. -ses) bringing several parts together to form a whole. **syn•the•size** ['sɪnθəsaɪz] v. to combine (several things) together to make a whole. **syn•the•siz•er,** n. electronic device which can make musical sounds similar to those of different instruments.

syn•thet•ic [sɪn'θetɪk] 1. n. artificial/man-made material. 2. adj. artificial; made in such a way that it looks natural. **syn•thet•i•cal•ly,** adv. in a synthetic way.

syph•i•lis ['sɪfɪlɪs] n. serious disease transmitted by sexual intercourse or inherited. **syph•i•lit•ic,** adj. & n. (person) suffering from syphilis.

Syr•i•an ['sɪrɪən] adj. & n. (person) from Syria;

sy•rin•ga [sɪ'rɪŋgə] n. tall shrub with scented white flowers.

sy•ringe [sɪ'rɪndʒ] 1. n. tube with a piston or rubber bulb so that liquids can be sucked into it then squeezed out, as in giving injections. 2. v. to clean by blowing liquid with a syringe.

syr•up ['sɪrəp] n. thick sweet liquid; thick golden juice from sugar. **syr•up•y,** adj. like syrup; very sweet.

sys•tem ['sɪstəm] n. (a) arrangement of things which work together. (b) way of organizing things to work together. (c) method. (d) body. **sys•tem•at•ic** [sɪstə'mætɪk] adj. orderly/methodical. **sys•tem•at•i•cal•ly,** adv. in a methodical way. **sys•tem•a•tize** ['sɪstəmətaɪz] v. to organize into a system. **sys•tem•ic** [sɪs'temɪk] adj. which affects the whole system. **sys•tems a•nal•y•sis,** n. use of a computer to forecast needs, etc., by analyzing the way in which a system is actually operating. **sys•tems an•a•lyst,** n. person who specializes in systems analysis.

sys•to•le [sɪs'təʊlɪ] n. phase in the heartbeat, when the heart contracts and pumps blood out.

Tt

T, t [tiː] *inf.* **it suits him to a T** = it suits him perfectly; **to dot one's i's and cross one's t's** = to settle the final details (of an agreement)/to be very careful about sth; **T-bone steak** = type of beef steak with a bone shaped like a T in it. **T shirt** = light short-sleeved shirt with no buttons or collar; **T square** = device shaped like a T for drawing right angles.

tab [tæb] *n.* (a) small loop of cloth for hanging up a coat/for pulling open a box. (b) little colored marker attached to cards in an index so that they can be found easily; *inf.* **to pick up the t.** = to pay the bill; **to keep tabs on s.o.** = keep watch on s.o.

tab•ard ['tæbɑːd] *n.* short sleeveless coat worn by knights over their armor.

ta•bas•co [tə'bæskəʊ] *n.* trademark for a hot red sauce.

tab•by (cat) ['tæbi(kæt)] *n.* striped black, brown, and gray cat.

tab•er•nac•le ['tæbənækl] *n.* (a) place of worship. (b) ornamental box for consecrated bread and wine.

ta•ble ['teɪbl] 1. *n.* (a) piece of furniture with a flat top and legs, used for eating at/for working at, etc.; **to set the t.** = to get the table ready for a meal; **to clear the t.** = to remove dirty plates/knives, etc. after a meal; **to turn the tables on s.o.** = to put yourself in a superior position, where before you were in an inferior one. (b) printed list of figures/facts; **multiplication tables** = lists of figures to learn by heart how each number is multiplied. **t. of contents** = list of contents of a book. 2. *v.* to put aside for future consideration; **to t. a proposal.**

ta•ble•cloth, *n.* cloth for covering a table during a meal. **ta•ble•land**, *n.* high flat land.

ta•ble lin•en, *n.* tablecloths/napkins, etc.

ta•ble man•ners, *n. pl.* polite way of eating according to the rules of society.

ta•ble•spoon, *n.* large spoon for serving food at the table. **ta•ble•spoon•ful**, *n.* quantity held in a tablespoon. **ta•ble ten•nis**, *n.* game played on a large table with a net across the center, using small round paddles and a very light white ball.

ta•ble•ware, *n.* knives, forks, spoons, plates, etc.

tab•leau ['tæbləʊ] *n.* (*pl.* **-eaux** [-əʊz], **-eaus**) scene where actors represent a historic occasion, etc., without moving.

ta•ble d'hôte ['tɑːbləʊdəʊt] *n.* menu which has a restricted number of dishes at a reduced price.

tab•let ['tæblət] *n.* (a) small round pill of medicine. (b) flat stone with an inscription on it. (c) bar (of soap/chemical, etc.).

tab•loid ['tæblɔɪd] *n.* popular newspaper with a small page size, usu. with a large number of pictures.

ta•boo [tə'buː] 1. *adj.* forbidden (by religion/by custom). 2. *n.* (religious) custom which forbids sth.

ta•bor ['teɪbɔː] *n.* small drum beaten with the hand.

tab•u•lar ['tæbjʊlə] *adj.* arranged in a table. **tab•u•late** ['tæbjʊleɪt] *v.* to arrange (figures) in a table. **tab•u•la•tion** [tæbjuː'leɪʃn] *n.* arrangement (of figures) in a table. **tab•u•la•tor**, *n.* device on a typewriter/in a computer program which allows the typist to make columns automatically.

tach•o•graph ['tækəɡrɑːf] *n.* machine placed in the cab of a truck which records details of the mileage and time spent on a journey.

tach•y•car•di•a [tækɪ'kɑːdɪə] *n.* rapid heartbeat.

tac•it ['tæsɪt] *adj.* (agreement, etc.) which is understood, but not actually given. **tac•it•ly**, *adv.* (agreement given) without speaking, but nevertheless understood. **tac•i•turn**, *adj.* (person) who does not say much. **tac•i•tur•ni•ty** [tæsɪ'tɜːnɪti] *n.* silence/not saying much.

tack [tæk] 1. *n.* (a) small nail (with a large head); *inf.* **to get down to brass tacks** = to talk real business/to start discussing the real problem. (b) (*in sewing*) light stitch to hold cloth in place

---

æ back, aː farm, ɒː top, aɪ pipe, aʊ how, aie fire, aʊə flower, ɔː bought, ɔɪ toy, e fed, eəhair, eɪ take, ə afraid, əʊ boat, əʊə lower, vː word, iː heap, ɪ hit, ɪə hear, uː school, ʊ book, ʌ but, b back, d dog, ð then, dʒ just, f fog, ɡ go, h hand, j yes, k catch, l last, m mix, n nut, ŋ sing, p penny, r round, s some, ʃ short, t too, tʃ chop, θ thing, v voice, w was, z zoo, ʒ treasure

and which can be taken out later. (c) diagonal movement of a ship so that it is sailing against the wind; **on the wrong t.** = in error. (d) saddle and equipment for riding a horse. 2. *v.* (a) to nail (sth) using tacks; (b) to make a light temporary stitch. (c) to change direction so that you are sailing into the wind; **they were tacking up the river** = they sailed in a zigzag way up the river against the wind. **tack on,** *v.* to add (sth) at the end.

tack•le ['tækl] 1. *n.* (a) equipment. (b) **block and t.** = arrangement of ropes, pulleys and hooks for lifting heavy weights. (c) (*in football, etc.*) grabbing an opposing player so that he falls to the ground and releases the ball. 2. *v.* (a) to grab (s.o./sth); to try to deal with (a problem). (b) (*in football, etc.*) to grab (an opposing player) so that he falls to the ground. **tack•ler,** *n.* person who tackles.

tack•y ['tækɪ] *adj.* (-ier, -iest) sticky. **tack•i•ness,** *n.* being tacky.

tact [tækt] *n.* care in your relationships with people so that you do not offend them. **tact•ful,** *adj.* using tact. **tact•ful•ly,** *adv.* in a tactful way. **tact•less,** *adj.* lacking tact/unintentionally offensive. **tact•less•ly,** *adv.* in a tactless way. **tact•less•ness,** *n.* lack of tact.

tac•tic ['tæktɪk] *n.* (*often pl.*) way of doing sth so as to be at an advantage; way of placing troops/guns, etc., so as to be in a better position than the enemy. **tac•ti•cal,** *adj.* referring to tactics; **t. error** = mistake in planning. **tac•ti•cal•ly,** *adv.* in a tactical way. **tac•ti•cian** [tæk'tɪʃn] *n.* person who is expert at tactics.

tac•tile ['tæktaɪl] *adj.* sensitive to touch; referring to the sense of touch.

tad•pole ['tædpəʊl] *n* baby frog/toad in its first stage after hatching.

taf•fe•ta ['tæfɪtə] *n.* thin shiny stiff cloth.

taff•rail ['tæfreɪl] *n.* guard rail round the stern of a ship.

taf•fy ['tæfɪ] *n.* sticky chewy candy made with sugar and butter.

tag [tæg] 1. *n.* (a) small loop of cloth; metal piece at the end of a shoelace. (b) label. (c) common old saying. (d) children's game where you have to try to touch another child who chases the others in his turn. 2. *v.* (**tagged**) *inf.* **to t. after s.o.** = to stay close to s.o.; **to t. along behind** = to follow closely.

tai•ga ['taɪgæ] *n.* forest in north Siberia.

tail [teɪl] 1. *n.* (a) part of an animal at the rear of its body, usu. sticking out at the back; **to turn t.** = run away. (b) back part of a long coat/of a shirt, etc.; **wearing tails** = wearing evening-dress. (c) back part (of a line of people, etc.); back (of a car). (d) **tails** = reverse side of a coin/the side of a coin without the head of a person, etc., on it. (e) *inf.* detective who is following s.o. closely. 2. *v.* to follow (s.o.) closely.

tail•gate, tail•board, *n.* hinged board at the back of a truck, station wagon, etc., which can be let down to load or unload the contents. **tail coat,** *n.* man's black evening jacket with a long tail at the back. **tail end,** *n.* back part (of a line); last part (of a motion picture, etc.). **tail•less,** *adj.* (animal) with no tail. **tail•light,** *n.* rear light (of a car, etc.). **tail off,** *v.* to die away/to fade away. **tail•pipe,** *n.* exhaust pipe of a motor vehicle or aircraft. **tail•spin,** *n.* dive by an aircraft, where the machine turns around and around. **tail wind,** *n.* wind blowing behind an aircraft, making it go faster.

tai•lor ['teɪlə] 1. *n.* person who makes outer clothes (suits/coats, etc.) usu. for men. 2. *v.* (a) to make clothes which fit. (b) to make (sth) fit particular circumstances. **tai•lor-made,** *adj.* made to fit.

taint [teɪnt] 1. *n.* slight trace of evil/of corruption. 2. *v.* to infect/to corrupt; **tainted food** = food which has become rotten (by touching other rotten food).

take [teɪk] 1. *n.* (a) one scene of a motion picture which has been filmed. (b) money taken in a store/in a business. 2. *v.* (**took; has taken**) (a) to hold/to grasp/to carry. (b) to remove/to steal. (c) to buy/to rent/to occupy; to have a (newspaper) delivered to your house regularly; **to t. a seat** = sit down; **to t. the chair** = to act as chairman (at a meeting). (d) to win (a prize). (e) to be a candidate for (an examination). (f) to eat/to drink (usually); **do you t. sugar in your tea?** (g) to make (a photograph). (h) to accept; **t. it from me** = believe what I say; **t. my advice** = do as I suggest. (i) to need; **it took three men to lift the piano; we took two days/it took us two days to get the work done.** (j) to lead; to go (in a direction); **can you t. me to the station?** = can you drive me to the station? (k) to hold; (*of machine*) to accept/to be able to work with. (l) to do (a certain action); **to t. a walk/a bath/a vacation.** (m) to stand/to put up with. (n) to be successful/to have effect; **the kidney transplant has taken** = has been successful; **the cuttings have taken** = have sprouted roots. **take af•ter,** *v.* to be like (a parent). **take aw•ay,** *v.* (a) to remove. (b) to subtract. **take back,** *v.* (a) to return. (b) **I take it all back** = I withdraw what I said and apologize for having said it. **take down,** *v.* (a) to lower (sth which is hanging). (b) to write down (what s.o. says). (c) to demolish. **take-home pay,** *n.* amount of money you actually receive out of your wages, after tax, etc., has been deducted. **take in,** *v.* (a) to accept/to bring inside. (b) to include. (c) to trick (s.o.). (d) to understand. (e) to make (a skirt, etc.) smaller. **ta•ken with,** adj. inf. attracted by. **take off,** v. (a) to remove (clothes). (b) to fly into the air. (c) inf. to imitate. **take•off,** n. (a) departure (of an aircraft). (b) inf. imitation. **take on,** v. (a) to agree to do (some work). (b) to agree to employ (s.o.). (c) to fight; to play against. **take out,** v. (a) to pull (sth) out. (b) to invite (s.o.) to go out. (c) **to t. o. an insurance policy on** = to start to insure. (d) **to take it out on s.o.** = to make s.o. suffer to help relieve your own feelings. (e) **the heat takes it out of me** = makes me very tired. **take•out,** n. & adj. (place where you can buy) food to take and eat elsewhere. **take o•ver,** v. (a) to buy (a business). (b) **to t. o. from s.o.** = to start to do sth in place of s.o. else. **take•o•ver,** n. buying of a business; **t. bid** = offer to buy a business. **tak•er,** n. person who wants to take or buy sth. **take to,** v. (a) to do sth, usu. to help you out of a bad situation; **he took to the woods** = went into the woods to hide; **she took to drink** = started to drink alcohol regularly. (b) to start to like (s.o.). **take up,** v. (a) to pick up; **they've taken up the carpeting** = removed the carpeting. (b) to occupy (space). (c) to start to do (a sport/a craft). (d) to start to work on (an idea); to start to discuss (a case). (e) to make (a skirt, etc.) shorter. (f) inf. **to take s.o. up on sth** = to accept a suggestion which s.o. has made. **take up with,** v. to become friendly with (s.o.). **tak•ings,** n. pl. money received in a store/in a business.

talc [tælk] n. smooth soft mineral used to make powder to put on the body; powder made from this mineral. **tal•cum pow•der,** n. powder made from talc.

tale [teɪl] n. story; **old wives' t.** = superstitious belief.

tal•ent ['tælənt] n. (a) natural gift/ability. (b) people with natural ability. **t. contest** = contest to find new singers/comedians, etc. **tal•ent•ed,** adj. very gifted.

tal•is•man ['tælɪzmən] n. object kept because it supposedly brings good luck.

talk [tɔːk] 1. n. (a) spoken words; **idle t.** = gossip; **double t.** = saying one thing and thinking the opposite. (b) conversation. (c) lecture/informal speech. 2. v. (a) to speak (a language). inf. **now you're talking** = that's a good idea. (b) to gossip. (c) to give information (usu. unwillingly). **talk•a•tive,** adj. (person) who likes to

chat/to gossip. **talk down,** v. (a) to speak in a condescending way/in an exaggeratedly simple way (**to** s.o.). (b) to give instructions over the radio to a pilot for landing his aircraft when visibility is bad. **talk•er,** n. person who talks. **talk•ing,** n. speech, conversation; **he did all the t.** = the others said nothing. **talk•ing point,** n. thing which supports one side in a disagreement or debate. **talk•ing-to,** n. inf. scolding. **talk into,** v. to **talk s.o. into doing sth** = to persuade. **talk o•ver,** v. **come and talk it over** = come and discuss it. **talk a•round,** v. **I talked him around** = I persuaded him to change his mind; **we just talked around the subject** = we never discussed the main problem.

tall [tɔːl] adj. (-er, -est) (a) high. (b) inf. unbelievable (story); **t. order** = command which is extremely difficult to carry out. **tall•boy,** n. type of tall chest of drawers.

tal•low ['tæləʊ] n. fat from animals, used to make candles.

tal•ly ['tælɪ] 1. n. note/account. 2. v. to agree (**with**).

tal•on ['tælən] n. claw (of a bird).

tam•a•risk ['tæmərɪsk] n. shrub with feathery evergreen leaves, which is often grown near the sea.

tam•bo•rine [tæmbə'riːn] n. small drum with metal pieces loosely attached to the rim, so that they jangle when it is beaten.

tame [teɪm] 1. adj. (-er, -est) (a) (animal) which is not wild/which can be approached by human beings. (b) not very exciting. 2. v. to make (an animal) tame; to make safe. **tame•ness,** n. being tame. **tam•er,** n. person who tames wild animals.

tam-o'-shan•ter [tæmə'ʃæntə] n. flat Scottish cap, like a beret.

tamp [tæmp] v. to press down.

tam•per ['tæmpə] v. **to t. with** = to meddle with.

tam•pon ['tæmpɒn] n. pad of cotton or similar material used to soak up blood.

tan [tæn] 1. n. & adj. brownish yellow (color). 2. n. brown color of the skin after being in the sun. 3. v. (**tanned**) to treat (animal skin) to make leather. (b) to get brown by sitting in the sun. **tan•ner,** n. person who makes animal skins into leather. **tan•ner•y,** n. factory where skins are made into leather.

tan•dem ['tændəm] n. bicycle for two people; **in t.** = in pairs/together.

æ back, ɑː farm, ɒ top, aɪ pipe, aʊ how, aɪə fire, aʊə flower, ɔː bought, ɔɪ toy, e fed, eəhair, eɪ take, ə afraid, əʊ boat, əʊə lower, ɜː word, iː heap, ɪ hit, ɪə hear, uː school, ʊ book, ʌ but, b back, d dog, ð then, dʒ just, f fog, g go, h hand, j yes, k catch, l last, m mix, n nut, ŋ sing, p penny, r round, s some, ʃ short, t too, tʃ chop, θ thing, v voice, w was, z zoo, ʒ treasure

tang [tæŋ] *n.* sharp smell/taste. **tang▪y**, *adj.* with a sharp taste/smell.

tan▪gent ['tændʒənt] *n.* line which touches a curve without cutting through it; **to go off on/at a t.** = to change direction/to follow another line of thought. **tan▪gen▪tial** [tæn-'dʒənʃl] *adj.* referring to a tangent.

tan▪ge▪rine ['tændʒə'riːn] *n.* small orange with soft skin which peels easily.

tan▪gi▪ble ['tændʒəbl] *adj.* which can be touched; real. **tan▪gi▪bil▪i▪ty** [tændʒɪ'brlɪtɪ] *n.* being tangible. **tan▪gi▪bly**, *adv.* in a real/definite way.

tan▪gle ['tæŋgl] 1. *n.* mix of threads/string/ hair; **in a t.** = all mixed up. 2. *v.* to mix (things) together in knots; **to t. with s.o.** = to get into an argument.

tan▪go ['tæŋgəʊ] *n.* (*pl.* **-os**) dance where you glide sideways.

tank [tæŋk] *n.* (a) large (metal) container for liquids. (b) **t. truck** = truck having a tank for carrying gas or liquids. (c) armored vehicle with caterpillar tracks and a powerful gun. **tank▪er**, *n.* (a) special ship for carrying liquids (esp. oil). (b) special truck for carrying gas or liquids. **tank up**, *v. inf.* to drink a lot.

tan▪kard ['tæŋkəd] *n.* large covered mug for drinking beer.

tan▪nin ['tænɪn] *n.* red-brown liquid (found in the bark of trees/in tea) which is used to make leather. **tan▪nic**, *adj.* **t. acid** = tannin.

tan▪sy ['tænzɪ] *n.* herb with yellow flowers.

tan▪ta▪lize ['tæntəlaɪz] *v.* to tease (s.o.) by offering him sth which he can't have. **tan▪ta▪liz▪ing**, *adj.* which tantalizes. **tan▪ta▪liz▪ing▪ly**, *adv.* in a tantalizing way.

tan▪ta▪mount ['tæntəmaʊnt] *adj.* equivalent/equal (**to**).

tan▪trum ['tæntrəm] *n.* attack of uncontrollable bad temper.

tap [tæp] 1. *n.* (a) apparatus with a twisting knob and a valve which, when you turn it, allows liquid to come out of a pipe/container; **t. water** = water which comes from the mains and not from a well; **on t.** = readily available. (b) slight blow; light knock. 2. *v.* (**tapped**) (a) to run liquid out of (a barrel) by fixing a tap; to cut a hole in so that the sap flows out; **to t. a sugar maple.** (b) to attach a secret listening device to (a telephone). (c) to start to exploit (sth new). (d) to hit lightly. **tap dance**, *n.* dance done by beating time to the music with metal-soled shoes. **tap danc▪er**, *n.* dancer who specializes in tap dancing. **tap-danc▪ing**, *n.* dancing with special shoes with metal soles, so that the dancer beats time to the music. **tap▪root**, *n.* main root (of a tree) which goes straight down into the soil.

tape [teɪp] 1. *n.* (a) long thin flat strip (of cloth/plastic, etc.); **adhesive t.** = glued plastic strip for sticking things together, etc.; **insulating t.** = sticky tape for wrapping round electrical connections: **measuring tape** = long strip marked in inches/centimeters, etc. for measuring; **magnetic t.** = sensitive plastic tape for recording. (b) long string held across the finishing line of a race. 2. *v.* (a) to attach with a tape. (b) to record (sth) on magnetic tape. **tape deck**, *n.* apparatus which plays tape and records on tape, but does not have its own amplifier or loudspeakers. **tape meas▪ure**, *n.* long strip of cloth/metal marked in inches/ centimeters, etc., used for measuring. **tape-re▪cord**, *v.* to record (sth) on tape. **tape re▪cord▪er**, *n.* apparatus which records on tape and plays back these tapes. **tape re▪cord▪ing**, *n.* recording done on tape. **tape▪worm**, *n.* long flatworm which lives in the intestines of human beings and other animals.

tap▪er ['teɪpə] 1. *n.* long slender candle, made of a wick covered with a thin layer of wax. 2. *v.* to make (sth) become thinner at the end; (*also* **taper off**) to become thinner at the end.

tap▪es▪try ['tæpɪstrɪ] *n.* thick woven cloth with a picture or design, usu. hung on walls or used to cover chairs.

tap▪i▪o▪ca [tæpɪ'əʊkə] *n.* white starchy powder which comes from a tropical plant and is used to make puddings.

ta▪pir ['teɪpə] *n.* South American animal like a pig with a short trunk.

tap▪pet ['tæpɪt] *n.* small projecting piece which opens or closes a valve by tapping on it.

tar [tɑː] 1. *n.* (a) black oily substance which comes from coal and is used for covering roads. (b) *inf.* sailor. 2. *v.* (**tarred**) to cover with tar; **tarpaper** = thick brown waterproof paper with an inner layer of tar; **to t. and feather s.o.** = to cover s.o. with hot tar and feathers as a punishment; **to be tarred with the same brush** = to have the same weaknesses/to make the same mistakes (as s.o.).

ta▪ran▪tu▪la [tæ'ræntjʊlə] *n.* large mildly poisonous tropical spider.

tar▪dy ['tɑːdɪ] *adj.* (**-ier, -iest**) (*formal*) late. **tar▪di▪ly**, *adv.* late. **tar▪di▪ness**, *n.* being tardy.

tare [teə] *n.* (a) allowance made for the weight of the truck, etc., in calculating transport costs. (b) (*old*) weed.

tar▪get ['tɑːgɪt] *n.* thing which you aim at; **t. practice** = practicing at shooting at a target.

tar▪iff ['tærɪf] *n.* (a) tax to be paid for importing goods; **to lift t. barriers** = to reduce import taxes. (b) list of prices (as of public transportation).

tar•mac ['tɑːmæk] *n.* (a) trademark for a hard surface of a road made of tar mixed with small stones. (b) runway of an airport. **tar•macked**, *adj.* covered with tarmac.

tarn [tɑːn] *n.* small mountain lake.

tar•nish ['tɑːnɪʃ] *v. (of metal)* to become discolored; to ruin (a reputation).

ta•rot ['tærəu] *n.* set of cards designed for use in telling fortunes.

tar•pau•lin [tɑː'pɔːlin] *n.* large waterproof cloth.

tar•ra•gon [ˌærəgən] *n.* common herb used in cooking.

tar•ry ['tærɪ] *v. (old)* to stay behind.

tar•sus ['tɑːsəs] *n.* set of bones in the ankle.

tart [tɑːt] 1. *n.* (a) small pastry shell filled with cooked fruit, vegetables, etc. (b) *Sl.* prostitute. 2. *adj.* (-er, -est) (a) bitter (taste). (b) sharp (answer). 3. *v. inf.* **to t. yourself up** = to dress, esp. in a flashy manner. **tart•ly**, *adv.* sharply. **tart•ness**, *n.* sourness (of taste).

tar•tan ['tɑːtən] *n. & adj.* (cloth) woven into a special pattern for one of the Scottish clans; distinctive pattern in such a cloth.

tar•tar ['tɑːtə] *n.* (a) hard substance which forms on teeth. (b) **cream of t.** = white powder used in cooking and in medicine. (c) *inf.* fierce person. **tar•tar•ic** [tɑː'tærɪk] *adj.* **t. acid** = acid used in cooking.

tar•tar(e) sauce [tɑːtɑː'sɔːs] *n.* mayonnaise containing finely chopped pieces of vegetables.

task [tɑːsk] *n.* (a) work which has to be done. (b) **to take s.o. to t.** = to criticize. **task force**, *n.* special group (esp. of soldiers) chosen to carry out a hard task. **task•mas•ter**, *n.* person who sets a hard task.

tas•sel ['tæsl] *n.* group of threads tied together at one end to form a ball, with the other ends hanging free. **tas•seled**, *adj.* with tassels.

taste [teɪst] 1. *n.* (a) sense by which you can tell differences of flavor between things you eat; **t. buds** = cells on the tongue which enable you to tell differences in flavor. (b) flavor of food or drink. (c) very small quantity (of food/drink); **he's had a t. of prison** = he has been in prison once. (d) liking (for sth); **expensive tastes** = liking for expensive things. (c) **good/bad t.** = ability/inability to judge what is fine/beautiful/refined. 2. *v.* (a) to sense the flavor of (sth). (b) to have a flavor (**of**). (c) to try (sth); to experience (freedom). **taste•ful**, *adj.* showing good taste. **taste•ful•ly**, *adv.* in good taste.

taste•less, *adj.* (a) with no particular flavor. (b) showing bad taste. **taste•less•ly**, *adv.* in a tasteless way. **tast•er**, *n.* person whose job is to taste food to test its quality. **tast•y**, *adj.* (-ier, -iest) with a particular pleasant flavor.

tat•ters ['tætəz] *n.* **in t.** = (i) torn (clothes); (ii) (person) wearing old torn clothes. **tat•tered** ['tætəd] *adj.* torn and old.

tat•ting ['tætɪŋ] *n.* type of lace made by hand.

tat•tle ['tætl] *v. (formal)* to gossip.

tat•too [tə'tuː] 1. *n.* (a) rapid beating (of drums). (b) decoration on skin made by pricking with a needle and putting color into the wound. 2. *v.* to make decorations on s.o.'s skin by pricking it and putting color into the wound.

tat•ty ['tætɪ] *adj.* (-ier, -iest) untidy/shabby.

taught [tɔːt] *v. see* **teach.**

taunt [tɔːnt] 1. *n.* sarcastic jeering. 2. *v.* to jeer at (s.o.) sarcastically.

Tau•rus ['tɔːrəs] *n.* one of the signs of the zodiac, shaped like a bull.

taut [tɔːt] *adj.* stretched tight. **taut•en**, *v.* to make tight; to become tight. **taut•ly**, *adv.* tightly. **taut•ness**, *n.* being taut.

tau•tol•o•gy [tɔː'tɒlədʒɪ] *n.* unnecessary use in a phrase of different words which mean the same thing. **tau•to•log•i•cal**, *adj.* using tautology.

tav•ern ['tævən] *n.* inn/bar.

taw [tɔː] *n.* big fancy marble.

taw•dry ['tɔːdrɪ] *adj.* (-ier, -iest) cheap and in bad taste.

taw•ny ['tɔːnɪ] *adj.* (-ier, -iest) orange brown.

tax [tæks] 1. *n.* (*pl.* -es) (a) money taken by the government from incomes/sales, etc., which pays for government services and its support; **t.-free** = without having to pay any tax. (b) burden; **it's a severe t. on our resources** = it strains our resources. 2. *v.* (a) to put a tax on (sth/s.o.). (b) to strain. (c) *(formal)* **to t. s.o. with** = to accuse s.o. of. **tax•a•ble**, *adj.* which can be taxed. **tax•a•tion** [tæk'seɪʃn] *n.* (a) (system of) imposing taxes. (b) money raised from taxes. **tax•pay•er**, *n.* person who pays taxes. **tax re•turn**, *n.* form to be filled in to report your earnings and allowances to the government.

tax•i ['tæksɪ] 1. *n.* car which can be hired; **t. stand** = place in the street where taxis can wait. 2. *v. (of aircraft)* to go along the ground before take-off or after landing. **tax•i•cab**, *n.* taxi.

æ back, ɑː farm, ɒ top, aɪ pipe, aʊ how, aɪə fire, aʊə flower, ɔ: bought, ɔɪ toy, e fed, eəhair, eɪ take, ə afraid, əʊ boat, əʊə lower, vː word, iː heap, ɪ hit, ɪə hear, uː school, ʊ book, ʌ but, b back, d dog, ð then, dʒ just, f fog, g go, h hand, j yes, k catch, l last, m mix, n nut, ŋ sing, p penny, r round, s some, ʃ short, t too, tʃ chop, θ thing, v voice, w was, z zoo, ʒ treasure

tax•i•me•ter, *n.* machine fitted inside a taxi which shows the price for the journey.

tax•i•der•my ['tæksɪdɜːmɪ] *n.* art of stuffing the skins of dead animals so that they look lifelike. **tax•i•der•mist,** *n.* person who stuffs the skins of dead animals so that they look lifelike.

tax•on•o•my [tæk'sɒnəmɪ] *n.* scientific classification (esp. of plants and animals). **tax•on•o•mist,** *n.* person who specializes in taxonomy.

TB ['ti:'bi:] *abbreviation for* tuberculosis.

tea [ti:] *n.* (a) dried leaves of a tropical plant which are used to make a common drink. (b) drink made by pouring boiling water on to dried leaves of the tea plant. (c) any hot drink made in a similar way; **herb t.** = tea made with the dried flowers or leaves of herbs. (d) *Brit.* afternoon meal; **t. service/t. set** = plates/cups/ saucers, etc., used at tea; **high tea** = large meal eaten in the early evening in the North of England and Scotland. **tea•bag,** *n.* small paper bag full of tea which is put into the pot instead of loose tea. **tea•cad•dy,** *n.* small wooden box or can for holding tea. **tea co•zy,** *n.* cover for putting over a teapot to keep it warm. **tea•cup,** *n.* large cup for tea. **tea par•ty,** *n.* party (held in the afternoon or early evening) when you drink tea, eat cakes, etc. **tea•pot,** *n.* special pot with a handle and spout for making tea in. **tea•room,** *n.* small restaurant which serves mainly tea and light meals. **tea•spoon,** *n.* small spoon for stirring tea. **tea•spoon•ful,** *n.* quantity contained in a teaspoon. **tea•time,** *n.* time when you have tea (about 4 o'clock in the afternoon). **tea tow•el,** *n.* cloth for drying dishes. **tea trol•ley,** *n.* small table on wheels from which you can serve food.

teach [ti:tʃ] *v.* (**taught** [tɔ:t]) to give (s.o.) information; to give lessons (in a school); to show (s.o.) how to do sth; *inf.* **that'll t. him to be so rude** = will punish him for being rude. **teach•a•ble,** *adj.* which can be taught. **teach•er,** *n.* person who teaches. **teach-in,** *n. inf.* informal lengthy period of discussions on a topic. **teach•ing,** *n.* (a) action of giving knowledge/giving lessons; **the t. profession** = teachers as a group. (b) (*also* **teachings**) political or moral ideas/philosophy.

teak [ti:k] *n.* large tropical tree; hard wood of this tree, which does not warp, and is used for making furniture, etc.

teal [ti:l] *n.* (*pl.* **teal**) small type of wild duck.

team [ti:m] 1. *n.* (a) group of people playing together/working together. **t. spirit** = good feeling among those who play or work well together as a team. (b) group of animals working together. 2. *v.* **to t. up with s.o.** = to join s.o. to work together. **team•ster,** *n.* truck driver. **team•work,** *n.* ability to work together as a group; working together as a group.

tear¹ ['tɪə] *n.* drop of water formed in the eyes when you cry; **he burst into tears** = suddenly started to cry; **in tears** = crying. **tear•drop,** *n.* one tear. **tear•ful,** *adj.* sad/crying. **tear•ful•ly,** *adv.* in a tearful way. **tear gas,** *n.* gas which makes you cry, used to control crowds of rioters. **tear•jerk•er,** *n. inf.* motion picture/novel which makes you cry. **tear-stained,** *adj.* (face) with the marks of tears.

tear² ['teə] 1. *n.* (a) hole torn in a piece of cloth; (b) **wear and t.** = normal usage (of a house/car, etc.) which wears sth away. 2. *v.* (**tore** [tɔ:]; **has torn** [tɔ:n]) (a) to make a hole in (sth) by pulling; **torn between** = unable to decide between. (b) to pull to pieces; **to t. into s.o.** = to attack s.o.; **they tore up the road** = dug up the road surface; **to t. oneself away from** = to leave reluctantly. (c) *inf.* to go fast; **to t. down the road** = to drive very fast.

tease [ti:z] 1. *n.* person who annoys/irritates people on purpose. 2. *v.* (a) to annoy (s.o.)/to irritate (s.o.) on purpose. (b) to disentangle threads (with a comb); to brush (cloth) to make it soft. **teas•er,** *n. inf.* problem which is difficult to solve/question which is difficult to answer.

tea•sel ['ti:zl] *n.* tall plant with prickly flower heads.

teat [ti:t] *n.* (a) projection on a cow's udder through which milk passes. (b) rubber cap put on a baby's feeding bottle through which the baby sucks milk.

tech•ni•cal ['teknɪkl] *adj.* (a) referring to a particular industry/trade/profession, etc.; **t. term** = term used by specialists; **t. school** = school where technical skills are taught. (b) referring to a fixed interpretation of the rules; **t. knockout** = where the referee stops the fight because a boxer is too hurt to continue. **tech** [tek] *n. inf.* technician. **tech•ni•cal•ly,** *adv.* (a) in a technical way; (b) strictly speaking. **tech•ni•cal•i•ty** [teknɪ'kælɪtɪ] *n.* (a) technical detail. (b) strict interpretation of rules/of laws. **tech•ni•cian** [tek'nɪʃn] *n.* person who is specialized in industrial or scientific work. **tech•nique** [tek'ni:k] *n.* skilled way of doing sth. **tech•no•crat** ['teknəkræt] *n.* person with particular technical/organizational skills, brought in to run a country/an organization. **tech•no•log•i•cal** [teknə'lɒdʒɪkl] *adj.* referring to technology. **tech•no•log•i•cal•ly,** *adv.* in a technological way. **tech•nol•o•gist,** *n.* specialist in technology. **tech•nol•o•gy** [tek'nɒlədʒɪ] *n.*

knowledge/study of new industrial or scientific skills.

tec•ton•ics [tek'tɒnɪks] *n.* study of the earth's crust and its movements.

ted•dy (bear) ['tedɪ('beə)] *n.* child's toy bear.

te•di•ous ['tiːdɪəs] *adj.* boring. **te•di•ous•ly,** *adv.* in a boring way. **te•di•ous•ness, te-dium** ['tiːdɪəm] *n.* boredom/being boring.

tee [tiː] 1. *n.* (a) spot on a golf course where the ball is placed before you hit it. (b) little peg, on which the golf ball is placed. 2. *v.* **to t. off** = to hit the ball from a tee.

teem [tiːm] *v.* (a) to be full of/covered with sth; (b) *inf.* **it's teeming** = it's pouring (rain).

teens [tiːnz] *n. pl.* age between 13 and 19. **teen•age** ['tiːneɪdʒ] *adj.* adolescent; referring to s.o. aged between 13 and 19. **teen•ag•er,** *n.* person aged between 13 and 19.

tee•ny(-wee•ny) ['tiːnɪ'(wiːnɪ)] *adj. inf.* very small.

tee-shirt ['tiːʃɜːt] *n.* light short-sleeved shirt with no buttons or collar.

tee•ter ['tiːtə] *v.* to wobble. **tee•ter-tot•ter,** *n.* seesaw.

teeth [tiːT] *n. see* **tooth. teethe** [tiːð] *v.* to grow your first teeth. **teeth•ing,** *n.* time when a baby grows its first teeth.

tee•to•tal [tiː'təʊtl] *adj.* (person) who never drinks any alcohol. **tee•to•tal•er,** *n.* person who never drinks any alcohol.

Tef•lon ['teflɒn] *n.* trademark for a non-stick surface, used on frying pans, etc.

tele- ['telɪ] *prefix meaning* over a distance.

tel•e•cast ['telɪkɑːst] *n.* TV broadcast.

tel•e•com•mu•ni•ca•tions [telɪkəmjuːnɪ-'keɪʃnz] *n. pl.* system of passing messages over a great distance (such as telephone/radio, etc.).

tel•e•com•mute ['telɪkɒmjuːt] *v.* to work (for an employer) from home by using communications technology, such as computers, to keep in touch with colleagues, managers, customers, etc.

tel•e•con•fer•ence ['telɪkɒnfərəns] *n.* conference between people located in different places via telephone links.

tel•e•gram ['telɪgræm] *n.* message sent by telegraph.

tel•e•graph ['telɪgrɑːf] 1. *n.* system of sending messages along wires; **t. line** = wire along which telegraph messages are sent; **t. pole** = pole which holds up a telegraph line. 2. *v.* to send (a message) along wires. **te•leg•ra•pher** [tə'legrəfə] *n.* person who

sends messages by telegraph.

tel•e•graph•ese, *n.* abbreviated language used when writing telegrams.

tel•e•graph•ic [telɪ'græfɪk] *adj.* referring to telegraph. **te•leg•ra•phy** [tə'legrəfɪ] *n.* sending messages by telegraph.

tel•ep•a•thy [tə'lepəTɪ] *n.* sending feelings/sympathy/mental images from one person to another without the use of the senses. **tel•e•path•ic** [telɪ'pæTɪk] *adj.* referring to telepathy.

tel•e•phone ['telɪfəʊn] 1. *n.* device/system for speaking to s.o. over a distance usu. using electric current running along wires; **on the t.** = speaking into the telephone; **t. banking** = banking services provided over the telephone; **t. booth** = outdoor booth with a public telephone in it. 2. *v.* to speak to (s.o.) by telephone. **tel•e•phon•ic** [telɪ'fɒnɪk] *adj.* referring to the telephone. **tel•e•phon•ist** [tə'lefənɪst] *n.* person who connects telephone calls at a switchboard. **te•leph•o•ny,** *n.* science of telephones.

tel•e•pho•to lens [telɪ'fəʊtəʊ'lenz] *n.* lens for a camera which gives a large picture of sth which is at a distance.

tel•e•print•er ['telɪprɪntə] *n.* teletypewriter.

tel•e•sales [telɪ'seɪlz] *n.* sales made by telephone.

tel•e•scope ['telɪskəʊp] 1. *n.* tube with a series of lenses for looking at very distant objects; **radio t.** = apparatus which detects radio signals from stars and follows their movements. 2. *v.* to push together, so that one piece slides into another; to crush together. **tel•e•scop•ic** [telɪ'skɒpɪk] *adj.* (a) referring to a telescope. (b) (parts) which slide together like a telescope.

tel•e•type•writ•er [telɪ'taɪpraɪtə] *n.* apparatus like a typewriter which sends out and receives messages by telegraph, and which prints them when they are received.

tel•e•vi•sion [telɪ'vɪʒn] *n.* system for sending pictures by radio waves; **t. (set)** = apparatus for showing pictures sent by radio waves.

tel•e•vise ['telɪvaɪz] *v.* to broadcast (sth) by television. **televised live** = shown direct/not recorded and broadcast later.

tel•ex ['teleks] 1. *n.* (*pl.* **-es**) system of sending messages by teletypewriter; message sent by teletypewriter. 2. *v.* to send a message to (s.o.), using the teletypewriter.

tell [tel] *v.* (**told**) (a) to say. (b) to pass on information. (c) to give instructions (**how to do**

æ back, aː farm, ɒ top, aɪ pipe, aʊ how, aie fire, aʊə flower, ɔː bought, ɔɪ toy, e fed, eəhair, eɪ take, ə afraid, əʊ boat, əʊə lower, vː word, iː heap, ɪ hit, ɪə hear, uː school, ʊ book, ʌ but, b back, d dog, ð then, dʒ just, f fog, g go, h hand, j yes, k catch, l last, m mix, n nut, ŋ sing, p penny, r round, s some, ʃ short, t too, tʃ chop, θ thing, v voice, w was, z zoo, ʒ treasure

sth). (d) to make out (the difference) **between** two things); to notice a quality. (e) to have an effect; **his age told in the end** = finally he lost because he was older than the other competitors. (g) to count (money/votes, etc.); **all told** = altogether. **tell•er** ('telə) n. person who counts votes; clerk in a bank who counts money and pays it out to customers. **tell•ing,** adj. which has an effect. **tell•ing•ly,** adv. in a telling way. **tell off,** v. inf. to reprimand/to criticize (s.o.). **tell on,** v. inf. **to tell on s.o.** = to let out a secret about someone. **tell•tale.** 1. n. person who gives away a secret. 2. adj. (thing) which gives away a secret.

te•mer•i•ty [tə'merɪtɪ] n. audacity; daring to do sth.

temp [temp] 1. n. inf. short for temporary secretary. 2. v. inf. to work as a temp.

tem•per ['tempə] 1. n. (a) usually calm state of mind; **he lost his t.** = he became very angry; **she kept her t.** = she stayed calm and did not get angry. (b) (good/bad) state of mind. (c) fit of anger. (d) hardness of a metal due to beating. 2. v. (a) to harden (steel). (b) to moderate/to make less strong.

tem•per•a ['tempərə] n. type of thick paint which can be diluted with water.

tem•per•a•ment ['temprəmənt] n. state of mind; nature of a person. **tem•per•a•men•tal** [temprə'mentl] adj. (person) likely to change his state of mind frequently; likely to get easily excited or depressed. **tem•per•a•men•tal•ly,** adv. according to a state of mind.

tem•per•ance ['temprəns] n. (a) being moderate/controlled. (b) not drinking alcohol; **t. movement** = group of people who try to persuade others not to drink alcohol.

tem•per•ate ['temprət] adj. (a) moderate/sober (language/habits). (b) (climate) which is neither extremely hot nor cold. **tem•per•a•ture** ['temprətʒə] n. (a) amount of heat measured in degrees. (b) state where the temperature of the body is higher than it should be.

tem•pest ['tempɪst] n. storm. **tem•pes•tu•ous** [tem'pestjuəs] adj. violently stormy/very wild.

tem•plate ['templeɪt] n. thin sheet used as a pattern for cutting pieces of wood/metal, etc., to an exact shape.

tem•ple ['templ] n. (a) flat part of the front of the head on each side of the forehead. (b) building for worship (not usu. Christian or Muslim).

tem•po ['tempəʊ] n. (pl. -os/tempi ['tempi:]) rhythm; beat (of music, etc.).

tem•po•ral ['temprəl] adj. (a) referring to the temple/the flat part of the side of the head

near the forehead. (b) referring to this world/not eternal/not spiritual. (c) referring to time.

tem•po•rar•y ['temprərɪ] adj. which only lasts a short time/which is meant to last a short time. **tem•po•rar•i•ly** ['temprərəlɪ] adv. for a short time. **tem•po•rize,** v. to try to gain time.

tempt [temt] v. (a) to attract (s.o.); to try to persuade (s.o.) to do sth. (b) **I am tempted to accept** = I think I will accept. (c) **to t. fate** = to take a great risk. **temp•ta•tion** [tem'teɪʃn] n. state of being tempted; thing which attracts you. **tempt•er, temptress,** n. person who tempts. **tempt•ing,** adj. attractive.

ten [ten] n. number 10; inf. **t. to one he finds out** = he's very likely to find out.

ten•a•ble ['tenəbl] adj. (theory) which can be held/supported.

te•na•cious [tɪ'neɪʃəs] adj. which holds on to sth tightly; obstinate; determined. **te•na•cious•ly,** adv. in a tenacious way. **te•nac•i•ty** [tə'næsɪtɪ] n. holding to sth too tightly.

ten•ant ['tenənt] n. person who rents a room/apartment/house/land. **ten•an•cy,** n. period during which a tenant rents a property.

tench [tentʃ] n. (pl. **tench**) type of small fish.

tend [tend] v. (a) to look after. (b) to be likely (to do sth). (c) to lean (in a certain direction). **ten•den•cy,** n. being likely to do sth. **ten•den•tious** [ten'denʃəs] adj. (book/article/speech) which puts over a strong point of view which is not generally approved.

tend•er ['tendə] 1. n. (a) boat which brings supplies to a large ship. (b) offer to do work at a certain price. (c) **legal t.** = coins/notes which are legally acceptable when offered in payment. 2. adj. (a) soft/delicate; **t. meat** = which can be chewed/cut easily. (b) **t. plants** = which cannot stand frost; **child of t. years** = very young child. (c) **a t. heart** = very compassionate/very loving. (d) painful; inf. **you've touched him on a t. spot** = you have mentioned sth which he is very touchy about. 3. v. (a) (formal) to offer. (b) (**for**) to offer to do work at a certain price. **ten•der•foot,** n. inexperienced person. **ten•der•heart•ed,** adj. kind. **ten•der•ize,** v. to make (meat) tender. **ten•der•loin** ['tendəlɔːn] n. piece of tender beef or pork from the side of the backbone. **ten•der•ly,** adv. gently; with kindness. **ten•der•ness,** n. being tender.

ten•don ['tendən] n. strong cord of tissue attaching a muscle to a bone.

ten•dril ['tendrəl] n. thin curling part with which a plant clings to a support.

ten•e•ment ['tenəmənt] n. large (often dilapidated) building which is divided into apartments.

ten•et ['tenɪt] *n.* basic principle/belief.

ten•fold ['tenfəʊld] *adv.* ten times as much.

ten•ner ['tenə] *n. inf.* ten-dollar bill.

ten•nis ['tenɪs] *n.* game for two players or two pairs of players who use rackets to hit a ball backward and forward over a net; **t. court** = specially marked ground for playing tennis; **t. elbow** = painful condition of the elbow joint caused by strain.

ten•on ['tenən] *n.* small projection from the end of a piece of wood which fits into a corresponding mortise in another piece to form a joint.

ten•or ['tenə] *n.* (a) man who sings with the highest normal male voice. (b) highest male voice; musical instrument with a high pitch. (c) (*formal*) general meaning or condition.

tense [tens] 1. *n.* form of a verb which shows when the action takes place. 2. *adj.* (**-er, -est**) (a) stretched tight. (b) nervous and anxious. (c) warlike (state between countries). 3. *v.* to make/to become tense. **tense•ly**, *adv.* in a tense way. **tense•ness**, *n.* being tense. **ten•sile** ['tensail] *adj.* referring to tension; **t. strength** = force needed to stretch sth until it breaks. **ten•sion** ['tenʃn] *n.* (a) tightness; being stretched. (b) nervous anxiety. (c) state of aggravation (between countries). (d) electric power; **high-t. wires.**

tent [tent] *n.* small canvas shelter held up by poles and attached to the ground with pegs and ropes; **to pitch a t.** = to put up a tent; **oxygen t.** = cover put up over a sick person's bed to allow oxygen to be pumped in.

ten•ta•cle ['tentəkl] *n.* long arm with suckers (such as that of an octopus).

ten•ta•tive ['tentətɪv] *adj.* uncertain; done as a trial; **t. offer** = made to find out what the response is. **ten•ta•tive•ly**, *adv.* in a tentative way.

ten•ter•hooks ['tentəhuːks] *n. pl.* **on t.** = impatiently waiting/anxious and uncertain.

tenth [tenT], **10th**, *adj. & n.* referring to ten; **the t. century** = period from 900 to 999.

ten•u•ous ['tenjʊəs] *adj.* thin; not strong. **ten•u•ous•ly**, *adv.* in a tenuous way. **ten•u•ous•ness**, *n.* being tenuous.

ten•ure ['tenjə] *n.* (a) right to hold property/to have employment; holding of a property or employment. (b) right to hold a job permanently.

te•pee ['tiːpiː] *n.* cone-shaped tent of North American Indians.

tep•id ['tepɪd] *adj.* slightly warm.

te•qui•la [te'kiːlə] *n.* Mexican alcoholic drink.

ter•a•flop ['terəflɒp] *n.* measure of computer processing speed.

ter•cen•ten•ar•y [tɜːsen'tiːnərɪ] *n.* tricentennial.

term [tɜːm] 1. *n.* (a) length of time; **in the long t./in the short t.** = for a long period from now/for a short period from now. (b) end of a period of time; **she was approaching her t.** = nearly at the end of her pregnancy. (c) part of a school/college/university year. (d) conditions; **to come to terms with** = to accept as inevitable; **they came to terms** = they reached agreement; **terms of payment** = way in which a payment shall be made; **our terms are ninety days** = we allow 90 days' credit. (e) relationship; **on good/bad terms** = having a friendly/unfriendly relationship. (f) particular word. (g) expressing; **in terms of health** = regarding health; **I'm thinking in terms of weekly payments** = my idea is that the payments should be made each week. 2. *v.* to call.

ter•ma•gant ['tɜːməgənt] *n.* noisy woman who bullies people.

ter•min•al ['tɜːmɪnl] 1. *adj.* (a) at the end; **t. shoot** = shoot at the end of a branch. (b) in the last period of life; **t. case** = patient who is soon going to die. 2. *n.* (a) building at an airport where passengers arrive or depart. (b) **bus t.** = building in the center of a town where buses arrive or depart. (c) **electric t.** = one of the connecting points in an electric circuit. (d) apparatus which can be used for putting information into and getting information from a distant computer (to which it is linked by cable). **ter•mi•na•ble**, *adj.* which can be terminated. **ter•mi•nal•ly**, *adv.* in a terminal way; **t. ill** = in the last stages of an illness before death. **ter•mi•nate** ['tɜːmɪneɪt] *v.* to finish/to bring (sth) to an end. **ter•mi•na•tion** [tɜːmɪ'neɪʃn] *n.* bringing to an end.

ter•mi•nol•o•gy [tɜːmɪ'nɒlədʒɪ] *n.* special words or phrases used in a particular science, art or subject. **ter•mi•no•log•i•cal** [tɜːmɪnə'lɒdʒɪkl]] *adj.* referring to terminology.

ter•mi•nus ['tɜːmɪnəs] *n.* (*pl.* **-ni** [-naɪ], **-nuses**) either end of a railroad line.

ter•mite ['tɜːmaɪt] *n.* destructive white insect, rather like an ant, which lives in tropical countries.

æ back, a: farm, ɒ: top, aɪ pipe, aʊ how, aiə fire, aʊə flower, ɔ: bought, ɔɪ toy, e fed, eəhair, eɪ take, ə afraid, əʊ boat, əʊə lower, v: word, i: heap, ɪ hit, ɪə hear, u: school, ʊ book, ʌ but, b back, d dog, ð then, dʒ just, f fog, g go, h hand, j yes, k catch, l last, m mix, n nut, ŋ sing, p penny, r round, s some, ʃ short, t too, tʃ chop, θ thing, v voice, w was, z zoo, ʒ treasure

tern [tɜːn] *n.* white sea bird similar to a gull.

ter•race ['terəs] 1. *n.* (a) flat area which is raised above another area. (b) row of houses built along the top of a sloping area. 2. *v.* to make a flat raised area.

ter•ra•cot•ta [terə'kɒtə] *n.* red clay used to make small statues; statue made of red clay.

ter•ra fir•ma ['terə'fɜːmə] *n.* dry land.

ter•rain [tə'reɪn] *n.* area of country.

ter•ra•pin ['terəpɪn] *n.* type of small American turtle.

ter•rar•i•um [te'reɪrɪəm] *n.* glass box in which plants are grown.

ter•raz•zo [te'rætsəʊ] *n.* polished surface, made of little chips of stone embedded in mortar.

ter•res•tri•al [tə'restrɪəl] *adj.* referring to the earth.

ter•ri•ble ['terɪbl] *adj.* (a) awful/which makes you very frightened. (b) *inf.* very bad. **ter•ri•bly,** *adv.* (a) frighteningly. (b) *inf.* very.

ter•ri•er ['terɪə] *n.* small dog (originally used in hunting).

ter•rif•ic [tə'rɪfɪk] *adj. inf.* (a) extremely great/wonderful. (b) causing fear; awful. **ter•rif•i•cal•ly,** *adv. inf.* wonderfully/greatly/awfully. **ter•ri•fy** ['terɪfaɪ] *v.* to frighten completely. **ter•ri•fy•ing,** *adj.* frightening.

ter•rine [tə'riːn] *n.* type of pâté.

ter•ri•to•ry ['terɪtrɪ] *n.* (a) land which belongs to a country; large stretch of land. (b) area which an animal/bird, etc. considers as its own. (c) area visited by a traveling salesman. **ter•ri•to•ri•al** [terɪ'tɔːrɪəl] *adj.* referring to a territory; **t. waters** = area of sea around a country which that country controls.

ter•ror ['terə] *n.* (a) extreme fear. (b) thing which causes fear. (c) *inf.* naughty/uncontrollable person. **ter•ror•ism,** *n.* policy of using violence in a political cause. **ter•ror•ist,** *adj. & n.* (person) who practices terrorism. **ter•ror•ize,** *v.* to frighten (s.o.) very much. **ter•ror-strick•en, terror-struck,** *adj.* extremely frightened.

ter•ry ['terɪ] *n.* type of cloth where uncut loops stand above the surface.

terse [tɜːs] *adj.* concise/short; using few words. **terse•ly,** *adv.* briefly/concisely. **terse•ness,** *n.* being terse.

ter•ti•ar•y ['tɜːʃərɪ] *adj.* referring to a third stage or period.

tes•sel•lat•ed ['tesəleɪtɪd] *adj.* covered with mosaic.

test [test] 1. *n.* (a) examination to see if sth works well/is reliable/if s.o. is healthy. **t. pilot** = pilot who flies a new aircraft to see if it works well. (b) short written or practical examination to see if s.o. knows information/knows how to do sth; **intelligence t./aptitude t.** = test to show how intelligent/how capable you are; **driving t.** = to see if you can drive a car. (c) **to put sth/s.o. to the t.** = to try sth/s.o. out to see if they can stand up to certain conditions. 2. *v.* (a) to examine (sth) to see if it is working well; to examine (s.o.) to see if he is healthy. (b) to give (s.o.) a short examination. **test case,** *n.* court case where the decision sets a precedent for other similar cases to follow. **test-drive,** *v.* to drive (a new car) before you buy it to see if it works well. **test tube,** *n.* small round-bottomed glass tube used in a laboratory for making chemical tests; **t.-t. baby** = baby born through artificial insemination.

tes•ta•ment ['testəmənt] *n.* (a) **last will and t.** = document written by a person before death to indicate what should happen to his property after he dies. (b) **Old T./New T.** = the two main sections of the Bible. **tes•ta•men•ta•ry,** [testə'mentərɪ] *adj.* referring to a will.

tes•tate ['testeɪt] *adj.* (person who has died) leaving a will. **tes•ta•tor, testatrix** [tes-'teɪtə, -teɪtrɪks] *n.* (*pl.* **-trices** [-trɪsiːz]) man/woman who makes a will.

tes•ti•cle ['testɪkl] *n.* one of two male glands which produce sperm.

tes•ti•fy ['testɪfaɪ] *v.* to give evidence that sth is true. **tes•ti•mo•ni•al** [testɪ'məʊnɪəl] *n.* (a) statement showing what you know of a person's qualities. (b) thing done for a person/given to a person to show appreciation; **t. dinner** = dinner organized to give a present to s.o. **tes•ti•mo•ny** ['testɪmənɪ] *n.* evidence that sth is true.

tes•tis ['testɪs] *n.* (*pl.* **testes** ['testiːz]) (*formal*) testicle.

tes•tos•ter•one [tes'tɒstərəʊn] *n.* male sex hormone.

tes•ty ['testɪ] *adj.* irritable; easily made angry. **tes•ti•ly,** *adv.* irritably/angrily.

tet•a•nus ['tetənəs] *n.* serious disease caused by infection in a wound, which can make esp. the jaw muscles stiffen.

tetch•y ['tetʃɪ] *adj.* (-ier, -iest) bad-tempered. **tetch•i•ly,** *adv.* in a tetchy way.

tête-à-tête [teɪtɑː'tet] *n.* private conversation between two people.

teth•er ['teðə] 1. *n.* rope which attaches an animal to a post; **he's at the end of his t.** = he can't stand any more/he has lost all patience. 2. *v.* to attach (an animal) to a post with a rope.

tet•ra•he•dron [tetrə'hiːdrən] *n.* solid shape with four sides, each of which is a triangle.

Teu•ton•ic [tjuː'tɒnɪk] *adj.* German.

text [tekst] *n.* (a) main written part of a book

(not the notes or pictures, etc.). (b) original words of a speech. (c) quotation from the Bible used as a moral guide. **text•book**, *n.* book which students read for information about the subject they are studying. **tex•tu•al**, *adj.* referring to a text.

tex•tile ['tekstaɪl] *adj. & n.* (referring to) cloth.

tex•ture ['tekstʃə] *n.* quality which can be felt; degree of fineness. **tex•tured**, *adj.* with a certain feel.

than [ðæn, ðən] *conj. & prep. used to introduce the second part of comparisons and clauses;* I have less t. you; there are more t. twenty people in the room; no sooner had we arrived t. the music started.

thank [Tæŋk] *v.* to t. s.o. for = to show gratitude to (s.o.). **thank•ful**, *adj.* showing gratitude; glad because an anxiety has gone. **thank•ful•ly**, *adv.* showing relief that an anxiety has gone. **thank•ful•ness**, *n.* being thankful. **thank•less**, *adj.* (work) for which no one will thank you; difficult/hopeless (task). **thank•less•ly**, *adv.* in a thankless way. **thank•less•ness**, *n.* being thankless. **thanks**, *n.pl.* (a) word which shows you are grateful. (b) thank you; no, t. = no, thank you. (c) t. to = as a result of. **thanks•giv•ing**, *n.* day for giving thanks to God; Thanksgiving = national holiday celebrated in the United States on the 4th Thursday of November and in Canada on the 2nd Monday of October in commemoration of the harvest feast of the Pilgrims. **thank you**, *inter. showing* gratitude (for); t.-y. letter = letter in which you thank s.o. for sth.

that [ðæt] 1. *adj. & pron. (pl.* those [ðəʊz]) *used to indicate* something further away *(as opposed to this)* 2. *pron. linking a subject or object to a verb where is the letter* t. he sent you? 3. *adv. inf.* to such an extent; so much; I knew they were going to be early, but not t. early. 4. *conj. introducing a clause* he knew t. we were late.

thatch [Tætʃ] 1. *n.* reeds/straw, etc., used to make a roof. 2. *v.* to cover (a house) with a roof of reeds/straw, etc. **thatch•er**, *n.* a person who thatches houses.

thaw [Tɔ:] 1. *n.* warm weather (which results in the melting of snow/ice). 2. *v.* (a) to melt; to unfreeze (sth which is frozen). (b) to get less unfriendly/less shy/become friendlier.

the [ðə] *(before a vowel or when stressed* [ði:]). 1. *definite article.* (a) *(referring to a particular* person or thing) the man with t. red nose. (b) *(referring to something in general)* t. Russians are lively people. (c) *(stressed)* it is t. store for furniture. 2. *adv. (in comparisons)* it will be all t. easier = that much easier; the sooner t. better.

the•a•ter, *Brit.* **the•a•tre** ['Tɪətə] *n.* (a) building in which plays are performed. (b) place where motion pictures are shown. (c) art of acting/of producing plays; business of putting on plays. (d) collection of plays. (e) place where important events happen. **the•a•ter•go•er**, *n.* person who goes to the theater. **the•at•ri•cal** [Tɪ'ætrɪkl] *adj.* (a) referring to the theater. (b) very dramatic/not acting naturally. **the•at•ri•cal•ly**, *adv.* in a theatrical way. **the•at•ri•cals**, *n.pl.* amateur t. = performances of a play by amateurs.

thee [ði:] *pron. (old)* you.

theft [Teft] *n.* stealing.

their ['ðeə] *adj.* belonging to them.

theirs ['ðeəz] *pron.* belonging to them; she's a friend of t.

the•ism ['Ti:ɪzəm] *n.* belief that a god exists. **the•ist**, *n.* person who believes that a god exists.

them [ðem] *pron. referring to persons/things which are objects of a verb.* **them•selves** [ðem'selvz] *pron. referring to a plural subject;* all by t. = without any help from anyone else.

theme [Ti:m] *n.* (a) subject (of book/article). (b) main tune in a piece of music; t. song = catchy tune/song played several times in a motion picture or TV serial which makes the audience recognize it. **the•mat•ic** [Tɪ'mætɪk] *adj.* referring to a theme.

then [ðen] 1. *adv.* (a) at that time; t. and there = immediately; now and t. = from time to time. (b) afterward. (c) also/in any case. (d) therefore; the result is. 2. *n.* that time. 3. *adj.* existing at that time; the t. president.

thence [ðens] *adv. (formal)* (a) from that place; from there. (b) so/therefore. **thence•forth**, *adv. (formal)* from that time onward.

the•od•o•lite [Tɪ'ɒdəlaɪt] *n.* device for measuring angles when surveying land.

the•ol•o•gy [Tɪ'ɒlədʒɪ] *n.* study of belief in God; study of God and God's relations with human beings. **the•o•lo•gian** [Tɪə'ləʊdʒɪən] *n.* person who specializes in the study of God/in the interpretation of religion. **the•o•log•i•cal** [Tɪə'lɒdʒɪkl] *adj.* referring to theology; t. college = college where people study to become priests.

æ back, a: farm, ɒ: top, aɪ pipe, aʊ how, aɪə fire, aʊə flower, ɔ: bought, ɔɪ toy, e fed, eəhair, eɪ take, ə afraid, əʊ boat, əʊə lower, v: word, i: heap, ɪ hit, ɪə hear, u: school, ʊ book, ʌ but, b back, d dog, ð then, dʒ just, f fog, g go, h hand, j yes, k catch, l last, m mix, n nut, ŋ sing, p penny, r round, s some, ʃ short, t too, tʃ chop, θ thing, v voice, w was, z zoo, ʒ treasure

the•o•log•i•cal•ly, *adv.* in a theological way.

the•o•rem ['Ti:ərəm] *n.* thing which has to be proved in mathematics.

the•o•ry ['Tɪərɪ] *n.* (a) explanation of sth which has not been proved but which you believe is true. (b) statement of general principles (which may not apply in practice); **in t. it should work** = if you follow general principles. **the•o•ret•i•cal** [Tɪə'retɪkl] *adj.* referring to a theory; not proved in practice. **the•o•ret•i•cal•ly,** *adv.* in theory, but not in practice. **the•o•re•ti•cian, the•o•rist** [Tɪərə'tɪʃn, 'Tɪərɪst] *n.* person who forms (political) theories. **the•o•rize** ['Tɪəraɪz] *v.* to make up a theory about sth.

the•os•o•phy [Tɪ'ɒsəfɪ] *n.* philosophical or religious system which states that the working of God and divine nature can be understood through mystical insight.

ther•a•py ['Terəpɪ] *n.* treatment of illness (esp. without using medicine); **speech t.** = treatment of difficulty in speaking; **occupational t.** = treatment by getting patients to do things; **group t.** = treatment by getting patients together in groups to discuss their problems. **ther•a•peu•tic** [Terə'pju:tɪk] *adj.* which may cure. **ther•a•peu•ti•cal•ly,** *adv.* in a therapeutic way. **ther•a•peu•tics,** *n. pl.* study of curing diseases. **ther•a•pist,** *n.* person who applies therapy.

there ['ðeə] 1. *adv.* in that place/to that place; *inf.* **t. she goes again** = that is her doing it again. 2. *inter. showing various feelings* **t., t., don't cry.** 3. *pron. used as subject of a clause usually with the verb* **to be,** *when the real subject follows the verb* **there's a big car coming up the hill; t. weren't very many people at the meeting; t. appears to be a mistake. there•a•bout(s)** [ðeərə'baut(s)] *adv.* approximately. **there•af•ter** [ðeər'ɑ:ftə] *adv. (formal)* after that. **there•by** [ðeə'baɪ] *adv. (formal)* by doing that. **there•fore** ['ðeəfɔ:] *adv.* consequently; for this reason. **there•up•on** [ðeərə'pɒn] *adv. (formal)* immediately after that.

therm [Tɜ:m] *n.* measure of heat. **ther•mal** 1. *adj.* referring to heat; **t. baths** = baths of natural hot water; **t. underwear** = which keeps you warm; **t. current** = current of warm air/water. 2. *n.* current of warm air.

thermo- ['Tɜ:məu] *adj.* referring to heat.

ther•mo•dy•nam•ics [Tɜ:məudaɪ'næmɪks] *n.* study of heat and its relationship to power.

ther•mom•e•ter [Tɜ:'mɒmɪtə] *n.* instrument for measuring the temperature.

ther•mo•nu•cle•ar [Tɜ:məu'nju:klɪə] *adj.* referring to the high temperature caused by atomic fusion.

ther•mo•plas•tic [Tɜ:mə'plæstɪk] *adj. & n.* (material) which becomes soft when heated and hard when cold.

ther•mos (bot•tle) ['Tɜ:məs'] *n.* former trademark for a type of vacuum bottle.

ther•mo•stat ['Tɜ:məstæt] *n.* instrument which controls the temperature by setting off heating or cooling devices. **ther•mo•stat•ic** [Tɜ:mə'stætɪk] *adj.* referring to a thermostat. **ther•mo•stat•i•cal•ly,** *adv.* (controlled) by a thermostat.

the•sau•rus [Tə'sɔ:rəs] *n.* (*pl.* **-es, -ri**) book with words collected according to their similar meanings, and not in alphabetical order.

these [ði:z] *adj. & pron. see* **this.**

the•sis ['Ti:sɪs] *n.* (*pl.* **-ses** [-si:z] (a) long piece of written research done for a college/university degree. (b) particular point of view.

Thes•pi•an ['Tespɪən] *n.* actor, actress.

thews [Tju:z] *n.pl.* strength.

they [ðeɪ] *pron. subject* (a) *referring to several persons or things* (b) (*referring to people in general*) **t. say it's going to rain.**

thi•a•mine ['Taɪəmi:n] *n.* Vitamin B, found in cereals, liver and pork.

thick [Tɪk] 1. *adj.* (**-er, -est**) (a) fat/not thin/with a large distance between the two surfaces. (b) with a large diameter. (c) dense/packed close together. (d) (liquid) which does not flow easily. (e) (voice) which is not clear. (f) *inf.* **that's a bit t.** = that's very unrealistic; exaggerated. (g) *inf.* stupid; **she's a bit t.** (h) *inf.* very friendly. 2. *n.* (a) center (of a battle). (b) **through t. and thin** = through times of difficulty as well as through easy times. 3. *adv.* in a thick layer; *inf.* **to lay it on t.** = to praise s.o. excessively. **thick•en,** *v.* to make thick/to become thick. **thick•et** ['Tɪkɪt] *n.* small wood of trees and bushes growing close together. **thick•ly,** *adv.* in a thick way. **thick•ness,** *n.* being thick; distance between sides. **thick•set,** *adj.* (a) (hedge) planted with bushes close together. (b) short stocky (person). **thick-skinned,** *adj.* (a) (fruit) with a thick skin. (b) (*of person*) insensitive/not easily hurt.

thief [Ti:f] *n.* (*pl.* **thieves** [Ti:vz]) person who steals. **thieve,** *v.* to steal. **thiev•er•y,** *n.* stealing. **thiev•ing,** *n.* act of stealing. **thiev•ish,** *adj.* like a thief.

thigh [Taɪ] *n.* thick top part of the leg between the knee and the hip.

thim•ble ['Tɪmbl] *n.* small cover worn to protect the end of your finger when sewing. **thim•ble•ful,** *n. inf.* very small quantity (of liquid).

thin [Tɪn] 1. *adj.* (**thinner, thinnest**) not

thick/with only a small distance between the two surfaces. (b) not fat. (c) with a small diameter. (d) not very dense/not close together. (e) very watery (liquid). 2. *adv.* in a thin way. 3. *v.* (**thinned**) (a) to become thin. (b) to make liquid thin. (c) to make less dense; to become less dense. **thin down,** *v.* to reduce; to make (sth) thinner. **thin•ly,** *adv.* in a thin way. **thin•ner,** *n.* substance used to thin paint. **thin•ness,** *n.* being thin. **thin out,** *v.* to remove (seedlings) to give more room to those which are left. **thin-skinned,** *adj.* (a) (fruit) with a thin skin. (b) (*of person*) sensitive/easily hurt.

thine [ðaɪn] *pron.* (*old*) your.

thing [θɪŋ] *n.* (a) object. (b) *inf.* person/animal. (c) **things** = clothes/equipment. (d) item; unspecified subject; object referred to; **it's just one t. after another** = one problem after another; **it's a good t. you came with us** = it's lucky. (e) **first t. in the morning/last t. at night** = as soon as you get up/just before you go to bed. (f) *inf.* **to have a t. about sth** = to like/dislike sth irrationally. (g) *inf.* **he wants to do his own t.** = to do what he really feels like doing. **thing•a•ma•jig, thing•a•ma•bob** *n. inf.* some object/person whose name you have forgotten.

think [θɪŋk] 1. *n.* time when you have thoughts/when you consider plans in your mind; *inf.* **you've got another t. coming** = you'll have to change your ideas, as this idea won't work. 2. *v.* (**thought** [θɔːt]) (a) to use your mind; **to t. aloud** = to speak your thoughts as they come into your mind. (b) to believe; to have as your opinion. (c) to expect. (d) to plan; **to t. again** = to change your mind; *inf.* **t. big!** = consider only large-scale projects. **think•a•ble,** *adj.* which can be thought. **think a•bout,** *v.* (a) to consider (sth) in your mind. (b) to plan (sth). (c) to have an opinion. **think back,** *v.* to remember. **think•er,** *n.* person who thinks; **great t.** = philosopher. **think•ing,** *n.* reasoning; **to my way of t.** = my opinion is. **think of,** *v.* (a) to consider (sth) in your mind. (b) to plan (sth). (c) to remember. (d) to have an opinion; **I told him what I thought of him** = I criticized him; **he thinks highly of his teacher** = has a high opinion of him; **she thinks nothing of working 12 hours a day** = she finds it easy; **think nothing of it** = don't bother to thank me for it; **he thought better of it** = changed his mind. **think out,** *v.* to consider carefully all the details. **think**

o•ver, *v.* to consider (sth) seriously. **think tank,** *n.* group of experts who advise the government on matters of general policy. **think through,** *v.* to consider carefully all the details. **think up,** *v.* to invent.

third, 3rd [θɜːd] *n. & adj.* referring to three; **t. person** = pronoun or part of a verb referring to a person or thing who is being referred to. **the car went up the hill in t.** = in third gear; **the Third World** = countries with no strong connections to the superpowers. **third de•gree,** *n.* hard questioning (by the police). **third par•ty,** *n.* any person who is not one of the two parties involved in a contract; person (usu. s.o. injured in an accident) who is not the driver of the car or the insurance company which insured it. **t. party insurance** = insurance which covers s.o. not named in it; **third-rate,** *adj.* very bad.

thirst [θɜːst] 1. *n.* (a) wanting to drink. (b) desire (**for**). 2. *v.* (*formal*) to desire (**after/for** sth). **thirst•y,** *adj.* (**-ier, -iest**) wanting to drink; **t. work** = hard/hot work which makes you thirsty. **thirst•i•ly,** *adv.* in a thirsty way.

thir•teen [θɜː'tiːn] *n.* number 13; **the t. hundreds** = years between 1300 and 1399. **thir•teenth, 13th,** *adj. & n.* referring to thirteen; **the t. century** = period from 1200 to 1299.

thir•ty ['θɜːtɪ] *n.* number 30; **she's in her thirties** = she is more than thirty years old but less than forty. **thir•ti•eth, 30th,** *adj. & n.* referring to thirty.

this [ðɪs] 1. *adj. & pron.* (*pl.* **these** [ðiːz]) *used to indicate* something near (*as opposed to* **that**). (a) **t. is the book I meant, not that one.** (b) **t. morning/t. evening** = today in the morning/evening. 2. *adv. inf.* to such an extent; **I didn't expect you to be t. late** = so late.

this•tle ['θɪsl] *n.* large prickly weed with purple flowers. **this•tle•down,** *n.* soft white feathery substance attached to thistle seeds.

thith•er ['ðɪðə] *adv.* (*formal*) to that place.

thole [θəʊl] *n.* peg used as oarlock.

thong [θɒŋ] *n.* (a) thin leather strap used for tying. (b) light sandal, held by a strap between the toes.

tho•rax ['θɔːræks] *n.* part of the body between the neck and the abdomen; chest (of an animal/a person); part of an insect's body to which the wings and legs are attached. **tho•rac•ic** [θɔː'ræsɪk] *adj.* referring to a thorax.

æ back, ɑː farm, ɒ top, aɪ pipe, aʊ how, aɪə fire, aʊə flower, ɔː bought, ɔɪ toy, e fed, eəhair, eɪ take, ə afraid, əʊ boat, əʊə lower, ɜː word, iː heap, ɪ hit, ɪə hear, uː school, ʊ book, ʌ but, b back, d dog, ð then, dʒ just, f fog, g go, h hand, j yes, k catch, l last, m mix, n nut, ŋ sing, p penny, r round, s some, ʃ short, t too, tʃ chop, θ thing, v voice, w was, z zoo, ʒ treasure

thorn [Tɔːn] *n.* spike (of a prickly plant); **a t. in one's side** = a constant annoyance. **thorn•y**, *adj.* (-ier, -iest) covered with thorns; (problem) which is difficult to solve.

thor•ough ['TʌrƏ] *adj.* (a) very careful/detailed. (b) complete. **thor•ough•bred**, *adj. & n.* pure-bred (horse). **thor•ough•fare**, *n.* way through which the public can go. **thor•ough•go•ing**, *adj.* complete. **thor•ough•ly**, *adv.* completely/totally. **thor•ough•ness**, *n.* completeness.

those [ðƏuz] *adj. & pron. see* **that**.

thou [ðƏu] *pron.* (*old*) you.

though [ðƏu] 1. *conj.* although; in spite of the fact that; **strange t. it may seem** = although it may seem strange; **as t.** = as if. 2. *adv.* in spite of this.

thought [Tɔːt] 1. *n.* (a) action of thinking; **he was lost in t.** = thinking so hard that you could not attract his attention. (b) considering in your mind; **after much t.** = after considering (the plan) for a long time; **on second t.** = having considered everything a second time. (c) plan. (d) regard. 2. *v. see* **think**. **thoughtful**, *adj.* (a) thinking hard. (b) considerate to other people. (c) showing deep thought. **thought•ful•ly**, *adv.* in a thoughtful way. **thought•ful•ness**, *n.* being thoughtful. **thought•less**, *adj.* without thinking; not thinking about. **thought•less•ly**, *adv.* in a thoughtless way. **thought•less•ness**, *n.* being thoughtless.

thou•sand ['Tauzənd] *n.* number 1000. **thou•sandth, 1000th.** 1. *adj.* referring to thousand. 2. *n.* one of a thousand parts.

thrall [Trɔːl] *n.* (*formal*) **in t.** = in slavery.

thrash [Træʃ] *v.* (a) to beat (with a stick). (b) to beat (another team) decisively. **thrash a•bout**, *v.* to move/to wave your arms and legs violently. **thrash•ing**, *n.* beating. **thrash out**, *v.* to discuss in detail.

thread [Tred] 1. *n.* (a) long thin piece of cotton/silk, etc.; **his life hangs by a t.** = he is very likely to die. (b) **to lose the t. of a conversation** = to miss what the conversation is about. (c) spiral ridge going around a screw/a bolt or inside a nut. 2. *v.* (a) to put a piece of cotton, etc., through the eye of a needle; to pass (a magnetic tape) through a slit. (b) to put (beads, etc.) on a string. (c) **to t. your way through a crowd** = to squeeze through a crowd carefully. **thread•bare**, *adj.* worn out (clothes). **thread•like**, *adj.* long and thin like a thread. **thread•worm**, *n.* long thin worm which lives in human intestines.

threat [Tret] *n.* (a) warning that sth unpleasant will happen or will be done. (b) person/thing which may harm. **threat•en**, *v.* to warn that

sth unpleasant will be done/that some action will be taken. **threat•en•ing•ly**, *adv.* menacingly.

three [Triː] *n.* number 3. **three-di•men•sion•al**, *adj.* (picture) which has depth as well as length and breadth. **three•fold**, *adv.* three times as much. **three-piece**, *adj.* with three parts; (suit) with jacket, trousers and vest; (suite of living room furniture) consisting of a sofa and two armchairs. **three-ply**, *adj.* (wool) with three threads twisted together; (plywood) made of three layers stuck together. **three-quar•ter(s)**, *adj.* referring to three fourths of a whole. **three•score**, *adj.* sixty. **three•some**, *n.* group of three people, esp. three players playing a game.

thren•o•dy ['Trenədɪ] *n.* (*formal*) funeral song.

thresh [Treʃ] *v.* to beat (corn) so that the grain falls out; **threshing machine** = machine which threshes corn automatically. **thresh•er**, *n.* person/machine that threshes.

thresh•old ['Treʃəuld] *n.* (a) bar across the floor of a doorway. (b) edge/beginning of sth. (c) limit; **t. of pain** = point at which pain becomes felt.

threw [Truː] *v. see* **throw**.

thrice [Trais] *adv.* three times.

thrift [Trɪft] *n.* (a) saving (money) by wise use and restricting spending. (b) type of seashore plant with small tufts of pink flowers. **thrift•i•ly**, *adv.* in a thrifty way. **thrift•i•ness**, *n.* being thrifty. **thrift•y**, *adj.* (-ier, -iest) careful with money.

thrill [Trɪl] 1. *n.* (shudder of) excitement. 2. *v.* to give (s.o.) a shudder of excitement; to be excited. **thrill•er**, *n.* exciting novel/motion picture, etc. (usu. about crime). **thrill•ing**, *adj.* very exciting.

thrips [Trɪps] *n.pl.* small insects which live on plants.

thrive [Traiv] *v.* (**thrived/throve** [TrƏuv]) to grow well/to be strong.

throat [TrƏut] *n.* (a) front part of your neck below the chin. (b) pipe running from the back of your mouth down the inside of your neck; **to clear your t.** = to give a short cough; *inf.* **he always ramming his opinions down my t.** = telling me his opinions. **throat•i•ly**, *adv.* in a throaty voice. **throat•y**, *adj.* **t. voice** = low, rough-sounding voice.

throb [Trɒb] 1. *n.* beating (of heart/machine). 2. *v.* (**throbbed**) to beat regularly; to have a regular pain.

throes [TrƏuz] *n.pl.* **death t.** = great suffering just before death; **in the t. of** = in the middle of.

throm•bo•sis [Trɒmˈbəʊsɪs] *n.* clot in a blood vessel, esp. in the heart.

throne [Trəʊn] *n.* ceremonial chair for a king/queen, etc.; **the t.** = the position of king/queen, etc.

throng [Trɒŋ] 1. *n.* great crowd of people. 2. *v.* to crowd together.

throt•tle [ˈTrɒtl] 1. *n.* valve on a pipe which allows variable quantities of steam/gas, etc., to pass into an engine; **to open up the t.** = to make the engine go faster. 2. *v.* to strangle (s.o.) by squeezing the neck, and preventing breathing. **throt•tle back, throttle down,** *v.* to reduce the supply of fuel to an engine, making it go more slowly.

through [Tru:] 1. *prep.* (a) crossing sth on the inside/going in at one side and coming out at the other. (b) during. (c) up to and including; **Monday t. Friday** = from Monday to Friday inclusively. (d) by means of. (e) because of. 2. *adv.* (a) from one side to another. (b) completely/to the finish; **we must see the plan t.** = see that it is completed. 3. *adj.* (a) which goes from one side to the other without stopping; **t. ticket** = ticket for a whole journey, with no stops or changes; **t. traffic** = traffic going through a town without stopping. (b) finished/completed; *inf.* **I'm t. with her** = I've broken off our friendship. **through and through,** *adv.* completely. **through•out** [Tru:ˈaʊt] 1. *prep.* in every part; at all times; from beginning to end. 2. *adv.* everywhere; at all times. **through•way,** *n.* thruway.

throve [Trəʊv] *v. see* **thrive.**

throw [Trəʊ] 1. *n.* (a) sending sth through the air. (b) distance sth is sent through the air; **they live a stone's t. away** = quite close. 2. *v.* **(threw; has thrown)** (a) to send (sth) through the air. (b) to shine (a light) **on; can you t. any light on the problem?** = make the problem clearer. (c) to make (a pot) with clay on a wheel. (d) *inf.* to hold (a party). (e) *inf.* to surprise/to confuse (s.o.). **throw a•way,** *v.* (a) to get rid of (sth) which you no longer need. (b) to waste. **throw•a•way,** *adj.* which can be discarded. **throw•back,** *n.* person/animal showing characteristics of distant ancestors; thing which shows a connection with the past. **throw•er,** *n.* person who throws. **throw in,** *v.* to add. **throw off,** *v.* to get rid of (sth). **throw out,** *v.* (a) to put (sth/s.o.) outside using force. (b) to send out (heat). (c) to reject. **throw o•ver,** *v.* to reject (a lover). **throw**

up, *v.* (a) to send up into the air. (b) to vomit. (c) to give up/to abandon.

thru [Tru:] *prep., adv. & adj. inf.* = **through. thru•way,** *n.* toll highway, usu. having more than one lane per direction.

thrum [TrAm] *v.* **(thrummed)** to make a continuous low-pitched sound.

thrush [TrAʃ] *n.* (a) (*pl.* **-es**) common brown bird with a speckled breast. (b) infectious throat disease caused by the bacterium *candida.*

thrust [TrAst] 1. *n.* (a) push; force which pushes. (b) stab with a sword or dagger. 2. *v.* **(thrust)** (a) to push energetically. (b) **to t. yourself on s.o.** = to force s.o. to accept you as a guest/companion, etc.

thud [TrAd] 1. *n.* dull, heavy noise. 2. *v.* **(thudded)** to make a dull noise.

thug [TAg] *n.* rough/violent person.

thumb [TAm] 1. *n.* (a) short thick finger which is placed apart from the other four fingers on each hand; **he is all thumbs** = he is awkward with his hands; **it's a useful rule of t.** = (i) a useful way of calculating approximately; (ii) a practical way of approaching a problem; **to be under s.o.'s t.** = to be dominated by s.o.; *inf.* **thumbs up (sign)** = gesture to show that everything is all right; *inf.* **thumbs down (sign)** = gesture to show disapproval. (b) part of a glove into which the thumb goes. 2. *v.* (a) **to t. through** = to look through (a book, etc.) quickly using your thumb; **well-thumbed book** = one which has been used often. (b) **to t. a ride** = to get a ride from a passing car by making a sign with your thumb. **thumb•nail,** *n.* nail on a thumb; **t. sketch** = rapid, very small sketch/description. **thumb in•dex,** *n.* series of notches cut in the edges of the pages of a book so that you can easily see where a new letter starts. **thumb-in•dex,** *v.* to give a book a thumb index. **thumb•screw,** *n.* machine for torturing, which squeezes the victim's thumb. **thumb•tack,** *n.* pin with a large flat head for pinning paper to a wall, etc.

thump [TAmp] 1. *n.* (a) dull noise. (b) punch; heavy blow with the fist. 2. *v.* (a) to hit with the fist. (b) to make a dull noise. **thump•ing,** *adj. inf.* very large.

thun•der [ˈTAndə] 1. *n.* (a) rumbling noise in the air caused by lightning; **to steal s.o.'s t.** = to take the credit for sth done by s.o. else/to do sth remarkable so that no one notices what another person has done. (b) loud rumbling noise. 2. *v.* (a) to make a rumbling noise. (b) to

---

æ **back,** a: **farm,** ɒ: **top,** aɪ **pipe,** aʊ **how,** aiə **fire,** aʊə **flower,** ɔ: **bought,** ɔɪ **toy,** e **fed,** eə **hair,** eɪ **take,** ə **afraid,** əʊ **boat,** əʊə **lower,** v: **word,** i: **heap,** ɪ **hit,** ɪə **hear,** u: **school,** ʊ **book,** ʌ **but,** b **back,** d **dog,** ð **then,** dʒ **just,** f **fog,** g **go,** h **hand,** j **yes,** k **catch,** l **last,** m **mix,** n **nut,** ŋ **sing,** p **penny,** r **round,** s **some,** ʃ **short,** t **too,** tʃ **chop,** θ **thing,** v **voice,** w **was,** z **zoo,** ʒ **treasure**

speak loudly. **thun•der•bolt,** *n.* (a) flash of lightning and thunder. (b) sudden (unpleasant) surprise. **thun•der•clap,** *n.* sudden noise of thunder. **thun•der•cloud,** *n.* large black cloud which will bring thunder and lightning. **thun•der•ing,** *adj. inf.* very big/great. **thun•der•ous,** *adj.* very loud (applause). **thun•der•storm,** *n.* rainstorm with thunder and lightning. **thun•der•struck,** *adj.* astonished. **thun•der•y,** *adj.* (weather) when thunder is likely.

Thurs•day ['Tɜːzdeɪ] *n.* fourth day of the week/day between Wednesday and Friday.

thus [ðʌs] *adv.* (*formal*) (a) in this way. (b) and so.

thwack [Twæk] 1. *n.* sound made when hitting sth hard. 2. *v.* to hit (sth) hard.

thwart [Twɔːt] 1. *n.* seat for a rower in a boat. 2. *v.* to prevent (s.o.) doing sth.

thy [ðaɪ] *adj.* (*old*) your. **thy•self,** *pron.* (*old*) yourself.

thyme [taɪm] *n.* common herb used as flavoring.

thy•mus ['Taɪməs] *n.* lymph gland at the base of the neck.

thy•roid (gland) ['Taɪrɔɪd('glænd)] *n.* gland in the neck which influences the growth, etc., of the body. **thy•roi•dec•to•my,** *n.* operation to remove the thyroid.

Ti *symbol for* titanium.

ti•ar•a [tɪ'ɑːrə] *n.* headpiece with jewels, like a small crown.

tib•i•a ['tɪbɪə] *n.* one of the two large bones between the knee and the ankle.

tic [tɪk] *n.* twitch of the muscles which cannot be controlled.

tick [tɪk] 1. *n.* (a) mark on paper to indicate that sth is correct. (b) small insect or similar creature which lives on the skin of birds and animals. (c) small click made by a clock/watch, etc. 2. *v.* (a) to mark with a tick. (b) to make a small clicking noise; *inf.* **what makes s.o. t.** = what is the reason for his behavior. **tick a•way,** *v.* (*of time*) to pass. **tick•er,** *n. inf.* (a) watch. (b) heart. **tick•er tape,** *n.* long paper tape which carries information printed automatically by telegraph. **tick off,** *v.* (a) to mark with a tick. (b) *inf.* to make (s.o.) angry or annoyed.

tick•et ['tɪkɪt] 1. *n.* (a) piece of paper/card allowing you to travel, to go into a theater/cinema, etc.; piece of paper showing a price/information; **parking t.** = piece of paper showing that you have parked illegally and must pay a fine. (b) license held by the captain of a ship or an airplane pilot which shows he is qualified. (c) list of candidates sponsored by a political party. 2. *v.* to stick a ticket on (sth for sale).

tick•ing ['tɪkɪŋ] *n.* thick cloth for covering mattresses, etc.

tick•le ['tɪkl] 1. *n.* irritation which makes you laugh/cough. 2. *v.* (a) to irritate mildly (a part of s.o.'s body) in order to make him laugh; *inf.* **tickled pink** = very pleased and amused. (b) to itch/to be irritated. **tick•lish,** *adj.* (a) (person) who is easily made to laugh by tickling. (b) *inf.* difficult (problem). **tick•ly,** *adj.* irritated so as to make you want to scratch.

tic-tac-toe [tɪktæk'təʊ] *n.* game for two players where each puts an X or a O in one of nine squares in turn, the object being to be the first to make a line of three X's or O's.

tid•bit, *Brit.* **tit•bit** ['tɪdbɪt] *n.* special little piece (of food or information).

tid•dly•winks, *n.* game where small disks have to be flicked into a little cup.

tide [taɪd] 1. *n.* (a) regular rising and falling movement of the sea. (b) movement (of public opinion, etc.); **to swim against the t.** = to go against what most people think. 2. *v.* **to t. s.o. over** = to help him get past a difficult period. **tid•al,** *adj.* referring to the tide; **t. wave** = huge wave in the sea. **tide•mark,** *n.* mark showing the top limit of a tide. **tide•way,** *n.* channel caused by the tide running.

ti•dings ['taɪdɪŋz] *n. pl.* (*formal*) news.

ti•dy ['taɪdɪ] 1. *adj.* (**-ier, -iest**) (a) neat/in good order. (b) *inf.* quite large (sum). 2. *n.* small container for putting things in to keep them tidy. 3. *v.* to make (sth) neat. **ti•di•ly,** *adv.* in a tidy way. **ti•di•ness,** *n.* being tidy. **ti•dy up,** *v.* to make (sth) completely tidy; to remove (a mess).

tie [taɪ] 1. *n.* (a) thing which attaches/which restricts; **the ties of friendship.** (b) band of cloth which is worn knotted around the neck under the shirt collar; **a school t.** = particular tie which shows which school you went to. (c) linking mark in music to show that several notes are to be played as one long note. (d) equal score in a competition/election; **there was a t. for second place** = two people were equal second. 2. *v.* (a) to attach/to fasten; **she's tied to her work** = can never get away from it. (b) to make (a knot). (c) to be equal in a competition. **tie•break•er,** *n.* (*in tennis*) game to decide the winner of a set, played when the score is 6-6. **tie down,** *v.* to attach (to the floor/ground); **to tie s.o. down** = to limit s.o.'s activities. **tie-dyed,** *adj.* (shirt, etc.) which has been tied and then dyed to give a mottled effect. **tie•pin,** *n.* pin for attaching a tie. **tie up,** *v.* (a) to attach/to fasten. (b) to keep motionless; *inf.* **tied up** = busy. (c) to use (money) to purchase sth, so that it is not available for other purposes. **tie-up,** *n.* link/connection.

tier ['tɪə] *n.* one of a series of steps, usu. a row of seats in a theater; **wedding cake with four tiers** = made of four separate cakes placed one on top of the other. **ti•ered,** *adj.* with tiers.

tiff [tɪf] *n.* small argument/quarrel.

ti•ger ['taɪgə] *n.* (a) large striped catlike wild animal; **t. lily** = lily with spotted orange flowers; **paper t.** = thing which seems fierce but is really harmless. (b) country, esp. in East Asia, with a rapidly expanding economy; **t. market** = any of four key Pacific rim markets (Hong Kong/Singapore/Taiwan/South Korea), less important only than Japan. **ti•gress,** *n.* female tiger.

tight [taɪt] 1. *adj.* (-er, -est) (a) which fits (too) closely; (b) closely packed together; (schedule) which allows no spare time. (c) stretched taut. (d) *inf.* (money) which is difficult to get. (e) *inf.* drunk. 2. *adv.* (a) closely/firmly (shut). (b) closely packed. (c) *inf.* **to sit t.** = to stay where you are. **tight•en,** *v.* to make/to become tight; **we must t. our belts** = be prepared to eat less/to spend less. **tight•fis•ted,** *adj. & n.* mean/not generous. **tight•fi•tting,** *adj.* which fits tightly. **tight-lipped,** *adj.* with the mouth firmly closed; (person) who refuses to speak. **tight•ly,** *adv.* in a tight way. **tight•ness,** *n.* being tight. **tight•rope,** *n.* rope stretched between two poles on which s.o. can walk/can perform tricks. **tights,** *n.pl.* close-fitting piece of clothing worn by girls, women, dancers, etc., on the legs and lower part of the body.

tile [taɪl] 1. *n.* flat piece of baked clay used to cover floors/walls/roofs; **carpet tiles** = square pieces of carpet which can be laid on a floor like tiles. 2. *v.* to cover (a roof/a floor/a wall) with tiles. **til•er,** *n.* person who tiles (a roof, etc.).

till [tɪl] 1. *n.* drawer for keeping cash in a store, etc. 2. *v.* to cultivate (land). 3. *prep.* until/up to (the time of). 4. *conj.* to the time when/until.

till•er ['tɪlə] *n.* handle which is attached to a rudder and so steers a boat.

tilt [tɪlt] 1. *n.* (a) slope/slant. (b) **at full t.** = at full speed. 2. *v.* to slope; to place at a slope.

tilth [tɪlθ] *n.* good crumbly soil.

tim•ber ['tɪmbə] *n.* (a) cut wood ready for building. (b) growing trees which could be cut down and used for building. (c) large beam/plank used in building. **tim•bered,** *adj.* (house) made of wooden beams.

tim•bre ['tæmbə] *n.* quality of sound (of voice/musical instrument).

time [taɪm] 1. *n.* (a) existence for a period (such as years/centuries, etc.); **t. alone will tell** = the result will only become apparent later; **to have t. on your hands** = to have a period with nothing to do; **there's no t. to be lost** = we must hurry; **by the t. I got there** = when I got there; **from t. to t./at times** = occasionally; **for the t. being** = temporarily. (f) point expressed in hours and minutes; **Greenwich Mean Time** = internationally accepted correct time system. (g) hour at which sth usually happens; **the train arrived on t.** = at the right time; **we were in t.** = we were early enough. (h) (pleasant/bad) period. (i) one of several occasions. (j) **times** = multiplied by. (k) rhythm. 2. *v.* (a) to choose the right moment. (b) to calculate the time sth takes. **time bomb,** *n.* bomb with a clock attached, which sets off the bomb at a particular moment. **time-hon•ored,** *adj.* (custom) observed for a long time, and therefore respected. **time•keep•er,** *n.* (a) person who times a race. (b) watch or clock. **time-lag,** *n.* delay. **time•less,** *adj.* permanent; untouched by time. **time•less•ness,** *n.* being timeless. **time lim•it,** *n.* period during which sth should be done. **time•li•ness,** *n.* being timely. **time•ly,** *adj.* which happens at the right moment. **time•piece,** *n.* watch or clock. **tim•er,** *n.* (a) person/device which times; **egg t.** = device which times how long an egg boils. (b) device which can be set to start a machine/to stop a light, etc. at a particular time. **time•sav•ing,** *adj.* (device) which saves time. **time•serv•er,** *n.* person who changes his opinions to match those of people in power. **time•shar•ing,** *n.* system where several people buy shares in a property, each one being allowed to use it for a limited period each year. **time-sig•nal,** *n.* accurate radio signal showing the exact time. **time•ta•ble.** 1. *n.* list which shows the times of trains/aircraft/classes in school/appointments. 2. *v.* to draw up a list of times; to appear on a list of times. **time•work,** *n.* work which is paid for at a rate of money by the hour or day. **time zone,** *n.* zone of the earth in which a uniform

---

æ **back,** a: **farm,** ɒ: **top,** aɪ **pipe,** aʊ **how,** aɪə **fire,** aʊə **flower,** ɔ: **bought,** ɔɪ **toy,** e **fed,** eəhair, eɪ **take,** ə **afraid,** əʊ **boat,** əʊə **lower,** v: **word,** i: **heap,** ɪ **hit,** ɪə **hear,** u: **school,** ʊ **book,** ʌ **but,** b **back,** d **dog,** ð **then,** dʒ **just,** f **fog,** g **go,** h **hand,** j **yes,** k **catch,** l **last,** m **mix,** n **nut,** ŋ **sing,** p **penny,** r **round,** s **some,** ʃ **short,** t **too,** tʃ **chop,** θ **thing,** v **voice,** w **was,** z **zoo,** ʒ **treasure**

time is kept. **tim•ing,** *n.* (a) action of recording the time (of a race). (b) controlling the time at which sth happens.

tim•id ['tɪmɪd] *adj.* afraid/frightened. **ti•mid•i•ty** [tɪmɪdɪtɪ] *n.* being timid. **tim•id•ly** ['tɪmɪdlɪ] *adv.* in a timid way. **tim•or•ous** ['tɪmərəs] *adj.* very frightened.

tim•pa•ni ['tɪmpənɪ] *n.pl.* group of kettledrums in an orchestra. **tim•pa•nist,** *n.* person who plays the timpani.

tin [tɪn] 1. *n.* (a) (*element:* Sn) silvery metal. (b) metal covered with a thin layer of tin. (c) (usu. round) metal box for keeping food in; **cookie t.** = tin for keeping cookies in. 2. *v.* to cover with tin. **tin•foil,** *n.* thin metal sheet used esp. to wrap food up. **tin•ny** ['tɪnɪ] *adj.* (-ier, -iest) weak, metallic (sound); (car) which rattles. **tin pan alley,** *n. inf.* area where publishers of popular music have offices. **tin plate** ['tɪnpleɪt] *n.* thin sheet of iron covered with tin. **tin•pot,** *adj. inf.* not of good quality.

tinc•ture ['tɪŋktʃə] *n.* medicine dissolved in alcohol.

tin•der ['tɪndə] *n.* very dry material for starting a fire.

tine [taɪn] *n.* prong of a fork.

tinge [tɪndʒ] 1. *n.* slight color/taste, etc., of sth. 2. *v.* to give a slight color/taste to (sth).

tin•gle ['tɪŋgl] 1. *n.* sharp prickling feeling. 2. *v.* to have a sharp prickling feeling; **tingling with excitement** = very excited.

tin•ker ['tɪŋkə] 1. *n.* mender of pots, pans, etc. who travels from place to place. 2. *v.* **to t. with sth** = to try to make sth work better.

tin•kle ['tɪŋkl] 1. *n.* ringing (like a little bell). 2. *v.* to make a little ringing noise.

tin•ni•tus [tɪ'naɪtəs] *n.* ringing noise in the ears.

tin•sel ['tɪnsl] *n.* thin strips of glittering metal used for decorating Christmas trees, etc.

tint [tɪnt] 1. *n.* slight shade of color. 2. *v.* to give a slight shade of color; **tinted glass** = glass which has a slight shade of brown/blue, etc.

ti•ny ['taɪnɪ] *adj.* (-ier, -iest) very small.

tip [tɪp] 1. *n.* (a) pointed end; **the t. of the iceberg** = small part of sth (usu. unpleasant) which makes you eventually discover the rest. (b) money given to a waiter, etc., to show thanks for his services. (c) piece of helpful information; **racing tips** = suggestions as to which horses are likely to win; **take a t. from me** = take my advice. 2. *v.* (**tipped**) (a) to put a tip on (sth); (b) to make (sth) slope/lean. (c) to pour out/to empty (sth). (d) to give (a waiter, etc.) a small gift of money. (e) to give (s.o.) a piece of helpful information; **to t. s.o. off** = to warn s.o. **tip-off,** *n. inf.* piece of useful information; warning. **tip o•ver,** *v.* to lean and fall over; to

make (sth) lean and fall over. **tip•ster,** *n.* person who gives advice on which horse is likely to win a race. **tip•toe.** 1. *n.* **on t.** = quietly on the tips of your toes. 2. *v.* to walk quietly on the tips of your toes. **tip•top,** *adj. inf.* excellent.

tip•ple ['tɪpl] 1. *n. inf.* drink. 2. *v. inf.* to drink alcohol regularly.

tip•sy [tɪpsɪ] *adj.* (-ier, -iest) *inf.* rather drunk. **tip•si•ly,** *adv.* in a tipsy way. **tip•si•ness,** *n.* being tipsy.

ti•rade [taɪ'reɪd] *n.* long angry speech.

tire [taɪə] 1. *n. Brit.* **tyre.** thick rubber cover around a wheel; **flat t.** = tire with a hole in it through which the air leaks out. 2. *v.* (a) to become/to make weary; to need a rest after physical exercise. (b) (**of**) to lose interest in doing sth. **tired,** *adj.* (a) feeling sleepy/in need of rest. (b) **t. of sth** = bored with sth/having no patience with sth. **tired•ness,** *n.* feeling in need of rest. **tire•less,** *adj.* full of energy/never needing to rest. **tire•less•ly,** *adv.* in a tireless way. **tire•some,** *adj.* annoying/bothering. **tir•ing,** *adj.* which makes you tired.

ti•ro ['taɪrəu] *n.* (*pl.* -os) *see* **ty•ro.**

tis•sue ['tɪʃu:] *n.* (a) group of cells which make up a part of an animal or plant. (b) thin cloth. (c) soft paper handkerchief. (d) **t. of lies** = mass of lies. **tis•sue pa•per,** *n.* thin soft paper used for wrapping delicate objects.

tit [tɪt] *n.* (a) type of common small bird. (b) *Sl.* teat; breast. (c) **t. for tat** = paying back a blow with another blow.

ti•tan ['taɪtn] *n.* very large/strong person. **ti•tan•ic** [taɪ'tænɪk] *adj.* very large.

ti•ta•ni•um [tɪ'teɪnɪəm] *n.* (*element:* Ti) light gray metal.

tit•bit ['tɪtbɪt] *n. Brit. see* **tid•bit.**

tithe [taɪð] *n.* one-tenth part of produce or income paid to the church.

tit•il•late ['tɪtɪleɪt] *v.* to excite. **tit•il•la•tion,** *n.* act of titillating.

tit•i•vate ['tɪtɪveɪt] *v. inf.* **to t. (yourself)** = to make yourself look smart.

ti•tle ['taɪtl] *n.* (a) name of a book/play/motion picture, etc.; **t. page** = page at the beginning of a book, where the title is written in large letters; **t. role** = part in a play/motion picture which gives the name to the play/motion picture. (b) word (usu. put in front of a name) to indicate an honor/a qualification. (c) (*in sports*) position of champion. (d) right to own (property); **t. deed** = paper showing that you are the owner of a property. **ti•tled,** *adj.* with a title (such as Lord, Sir, etc.) to show that you are a nobleman.

tit•mouse ['tɪtmaʊs] *n.* (*pl.* -mice) type of small bird.

ti•trate [taɪ'treɪt] *v.* to analyze the concentration of a chemical solution. **ti•tra•tion** [taɪ'treɪʃn] *n.* act of titrating.

tit•ter ['tɪtə] 1. *n.* little laugh. 2. *v.* to give a little laugh.

tit•tle-tat•tle ['tɪtl'tætl] *n. inf.* gossip.

tit•u•lar ['tɪtjʊlə] *adj.* holding a title but without direct power.

tiz•zy ['tɪzɪ] *n. inf.* bother/nervous state.

TNT ['tiːen'tiː] *abbreviation for* trinitrotoluene, common high explosive.

to [tuː] 1. *prep.* (a) (*showing direction or position*) **he went to France; move to the right.** (b) (*showing time*) **from day to day; it's ten to six** = ten minutes before six o'clock. (c) (*showing person who receives something*) **give it to me.** (d) (*showing relationship*) **is this the key to the box? secretary to the managing director.** (e) concerning; **there's nothing to it** = there's no difficulty in doing it. (f) (*showing ratio*) **they lost by six goals to four; the rate is two dollars to the pound.** (g) (*showing comparison*) **I prefer butter to margarine.** 2. *adv.* (a) **he came to** = he regained consciousness. (b) **pull the door to** = pull it until it is almost shut. 3. (*forming infinitive*) (a) *after verbs* **they came to help us.** (b) *after adjectives* **good to eat.** (c) *after nouns* **he made no attempt to run away.** (d) *when the verb is a subject* **to refuse the invitation would have been rude. to and fro,** *adv.* backward and forward. **-to-be** *suffix showing something in the near future* **a mother-to-be.**

toad [təʊd] *n.* amphibian like a large frog, which lives mostly on land. **toad•stool,** *n.* fungus shaped like a mushroom, but usu. not edible, and sometimes poisonous. **toad•y.** 1. *n.* person who flatters s.o. (in the hope of getting sth in return). 2. *v.* to flatter (s.o.).

toast [təʊst] 1. *n.* (a) slices of bread which have been grilled brown. (b) taking a drink and wishing s.o. success. 2. *v.* (a) to grill (bread, etc.) until it is brown; to warm. (b) to drink and wish s.o. success. **toast•er,** *n.* electric device for toasting bread. **toast•mas•ter,** *n.* person (at a banquet) who calls on people to speak and announces the toasts.

to•bac•co [tə'bækəʊ] *n.* (dried leaves of a) plant used for smoking in cigarettes/cigars and in pipes. **to•bac•co•nist,** *n.* person who sells tobacco/cigarettes, etc.

to•bog•gan [tə'bɒgən] 1. *n.* long sled curved upward at the front. 2. *v.* to slide on a toboggan. **to•bog•gan•ing,** *n.* sport of sliding on a toboggan.

to•by jug ['təʊbɪ 'dʒʌg] *n.* small mug made in the shape of a head.

toc•ca•ta [tɒ'kɑːtə] *n.* piece of music for the organ or piano.

toc•sin ['tɒksɪn] *n.* warning bell.

to•day [tə'deɪ] *adv. & n.* (a) this present day; **a week t.** = in exactly seven days' time. (b) this present time.

tod•dle ['tɒdl] *v.* to walk unsteadily. **tod•dler,** *n.* child who is just learning to walk.

tod•dy ['tɒdɪ] *n.* alcohol and hot water and sugar.

to-do [tə'duː] *n. inf.* excitement/confusion/bother.

toe [təʊ] 1. *n.* (a) one of the five parts like fingers at the end of your foot; **big t./little t.** = the largest/smallest of the five toes; **to be on your toes** = to be ready/prepared. (b) end part of a shoe/a sock. 2. *v.* to touch with the toe; **to t. the line** = to do what you should or are told to do. **toe•hold,** *n.* grip with the toes; small foothold. **toe•nail,** *n.* nail at the end of a toe.

tof•fee ['tɒfɪ] *n.* taffy.

to•ga ['təʊgə] *n.* robe worn by men in ancient Rome.

to•geth•er [tə'geðə] *adv.* (a) in a group/all at the same time; **get t.** = meet. (b) into contact one with another; **stick the pieces t. to•geth•er•ness,** *n.* being together with other people.

togs [tɒgz] *n. pl. inf.* clothes.

tog•gle ['tɒgl] *n.* short piece of wood attached to a coat with string, used in place of a button.

toil [tɔɪl] 1. *n.* hard work. 2. *v.* to work hard.

toi•let ['tɔɪlət] *n.* (a) washing and dressing. (b) bowl with a seat on which you sit to pass waste matter from the body; room with this bowl in it; **t. paper** = soft paper for wiping your anus after getting rid of waste matter; **t. water** = scented water. **toi•let•ries,** *n. pl.* deodorant/soap/perfume, etc., used in cleaning or grooming.

to•ken ['təʊkən] *n.* (a) visible thing which is a mark/sign (of respect, etc.); **by the same t.** = in a similar way; **t. payment** = a small symbolic payment; **t. woman/black** = woman/black person appointed to a position (on a committee, etc.) to placate rights movements. (b) piece of

---

æ back, ɑː farm, ɒ top, aɪ pipe, aʊ how, aɪə fire, aʊə flower, ɔː bought, ɔɪ toy, e fed, eə hair, eɪ take, ə afraid, əʊ boat, əʊə lower, ɜː word, iː heap, ɪ hit, ɪə hear, uː school, ʊ book, ʌ but, b back, d dog, ð then, dʒ just, f fog, g go, h hand, j yes, k catch, l last, m mix, n nut, ŋ sing, p penny, r round, s some, ʃ short, t too, tʃ chop, θ thing, v voice, w was, z zoo, ʒ treasure

paper/card/plastic which is used to replace money.

told [təʊld] v. see **tell**.

tol•er•ate ['tɒləreɪt] v. (a) to suffer (noise, etc.) without complaining. (b) to allow (sth which you do not agree with) to exist. **tol•er•a•ble** ['tɒlərəbl] adj. (a) bearable. (b) fairly good. **tol•er•a•bly**, adv. in a fairly good way. **tol•er•ance**, n. (a) putting up with (unpleasantness, etc.); allowing (sth which you do not agree with) to exist. (b) amount by which a measurement can vary from what is specified on a plan. (c) ability to stand the effect of a drug/a poison. **tol•er•ant**, adj. (person) who tolerates. **tol•er•ant•ly**, adv. in a tolerant way. **tol•er•a•tion** [tɒlə'reɪʃn] n. allowing (sth which you do not agree with) to exist.

toll [təʊl] 1. n. (a) payment for using a road/a bridge/a ferry; **t. bridge** = one where a toll is paid. (b) loss/damage; **death t.** = number of deaths. (c) solemn ringing of a bell. 2. v. to ring (a bell) solemnly as for a funeral. **toll call**, n. long-distance telephone call for which there is a higher charge than for a local call. **toll free**, adv. without having to pay the charge for a long-distance call. **toll•gate**, n. gate across a road where a toll has to be paid. **toll•house**, n. house where the tollkeeper lives. **toll•keep•er**, n. person who takes the toll on a road/bridge, etc.

tom•(cat) ['tɒm(kæt)] n. male cat.

tom•a•hawk ['tɒməhɔːk] n. light North American Indian ax.

to•ma•to [tə'meɪtəʊ] n. (pl. -oes) red fruit growing on annual plants and used in salads; plant which bears tomatoes; **t. sauce** = sauce made with tomatoes.

tomb [tuːm] n. large grave (usu. with an underground vault in which to put a dead person). **tomb•stone**, n. large stone placed on a grave with the name of the dead person written on it.

tom•boy ['tɒmbɔɪ] n. girl who plays rough games like a boy.

tome [təʊm] n. (formal) large book.

tom•fool ['tɒmfuːl] adj. inf. idiotic. **tom•fool•er•y**, n. stupid behavior.

Tom•my gun ['tɒmɪgʌn] n. small machine gun.

to•mor•row [tə'mɒrəʊ] adv. & n. (a) the day which follows today. (b) the future.

tom-tom ['tɒmtɒm] n. small drum beaten with your hands.

ton [tʌn] n. (a) weight equal to 2000 pounds; **metric t.** = 1000 kilograms. (b) space in a ship equivalent to 100 cubic feet. (c) inf. **tons of** = lots. **ton•nage**, n. (a) space in a ship mea-

sured in tons. (b) total number of ships in a navy/belonging to a company, calculated by adding together their individual sizes. **tonne** [tʌn] n. metric ton.

tone [təʊn] 1. n. (a) quality of sound of music/voice. (b) (in music) difference between two notes which have one note between them on the piano. (c) way of speaking/writing which shows a particular emotion. (d) shade of color. (e) strength of the body and muscles. (f) general quality or appearance. 2. v. **to t. (in) with** = to fit in well/to harmonize. **ton•al** ['təʊnl] adj. referring to tone. **to•nal•i•ty** [tə'nælɪtɪ] n. quality of tone (in the colors of a painting/in a piece of music). **tone-deaf**, adj. not able to recognize differences in musical pitch. **tone down**, v. to reduce in intensity; moderate. **tone•less**, adj. with no variation in tone. **ton•er**, n. chemical used in laser printers and photocopiers. **tone up**, v. to make fitter.

tongs [tɒŋz] n. pl. **(pair of) t.** = instrument for picking things up, with small claws on the end of two arms; **sugar t.** = tongs for picking up lumps of sugar.

tongue [tʌŋ] n. (a) long, movable piece of muscular flesh in the mouth, which is used for tasting and speaking; **with t. in cheek** = not really meant seriously; **to hold one's t.** = not to speak; **it's on the tip of my t.** = I will remember it in a moment. (b) piece of movable flesh in an animal's mouth, used as food. (c) language; **mother t.** = first language. (d) loose piece of leather under the laces in a shoe. (e) long, thin flame/piece of land. **tongue-and-groove joint**, n. type of interlocking joint in which a board with a projecting tongue along one edge fits into a corresponding groove along the edge of the next board. **tongue-tied**, adj. so shy as to be unable to say anything. **tongue twist•er**, n. phrase (like **red truck, yellow truck**) which is difficult to say quickly.

ton•ic ['tɒnɪk] 1. adj. (a) referring to a musical tone; **t. solfa** = system of writing the tones in music using syllables (doh-ray-me, etc.). (b) referring to physical strength/well-being. 2. n. (a) note which sets the key to a scale of music. (b) anything (such as medicine) which strengthens the body; **to act as a t. on s.o.** = make s.o. more energetic. (c) **t. (water)** = aerated drink containing quinine.

to•night [tə'naɪt] adv. & n. the night of the present day.

ton•nage ['tʌnɪdʒ] n. see **ton**.

tonne [tʌn] n. see **ton**.

ton•sil ['tɒnsl] n. one of two soft lumps of flesh at the back of your throat. **ton•sil•lec•to•my**, n. operation to remove the tonsils. **ton•sil•li•tis** [tɒnsɪ'laɪtɪs] *n.* painful infection of the tonsils.

ton•sure ['tɒnʃə] *n.* shaving off all or part of the hair of people becoming monks; part of the head which has been shaved. **ton•su•red**, *adj.* with a tonsure.

ton•tine ['tɒntiːn] *n.* type of investment where the survivors each receive more as investors die.

too [tuː] *adv.* (a) more than necessary. (b) as well/also. (c) *inf.* very; **t. bad!** = it's a shame!

took [tʊk] *v. see* **take.**

tool [tuːl] 1. *n.* instrument for doing work (such as hammer/spade, etc.); person used by s.o. else. 2. *v.* to decorate using a tool. **tool up,** *v.* to equip (a factory) with machinery.

toot [tuːt] 1. *n.* short sound made by a horn. 2. *v.* to blow a horn sharply.

tooth [tuːT] *n. (pl.* **teeth** [tiːT]) (a) one of a set of bony structures in the mouth, used by animals for chewing and biting; **milk teeth** = first set of teeth grown by a baby, and replaced by permanent teeth as a child; **false teeth** = set of artificial teeth to replace teeth which have been taken out; **in the teeth of** = running against/into; **long in the t.** = old; **armed to the teeth** = fully armed. (b) part of a saw/of a comb/of a cogwheel shaped like a tooth. **tooth•ache** ['tuːTeɪk] *n.* pain in a tooth. **tooth•brush,** *n.* small brush with a long handle used for cleaning your teeth. **toothed** *adj.* with teeth; **t. wheel** = cogwheel. **tooth•less,** *adj.* with no teeth. **tooth•paste,** *n.* paste used with a toothbrush for cleaning your teeth. **tooth•pick,** *n.* small pointed piece of wood/metal, etc., for pushing between the teeth to remove pieces of food. **tooth•some,** *adj.* good to eat. **tooth•y,** *adj.* showing a lot of teeth.

too•tle ['tuːtl] 1. *n. inf.* little toot, as on a flute. 2. *v. inf.* (a) to make a tootle. (b) to go (**along/off**).

top [tɒp] 1. *n.* (a) highest point; **on t. of everything else** = in addition to everything else. (b) upper surface. (c) roof (of a car). (d) highest/most important place. (e) **big t.** = large circus tent. (f) **at the t. of his voice** = as loud as possible. (g) child's toy which spins when twisted sharply. (h) piece of clothing covering the upper part of the body. 2. *adj.* (a) highest. (b) most important. 3. *v.* (**topped**) (a) to cut the top off. (b) to put sth on top. (c) to go higher than; *inf.* **to t. it all** = in addition to everything

else. **top•coat,** *n.* light overcoat. **top dog,** *n. Sl.* winner. **top dress•ing,** *n.* scattering fertilizer on the surface of the soil; fertilizer to be scattered in this way. **top flight,** *adj. inf.* excellent/of very high quality. **top hat,** *n.* man's tall black hat. **top-heav•y,** *adj.* unstable because the top part is heavier than the bottom. **top•knot,** *n.* small bunch of hair tied on the top of the head. **top•less,** *adj. (of woman)* wearing nothing on the top part of the body. **top-lev•el,** *adj.* (talks) involving important people. **top•most,** *adj.* highest. **top notch,** *adj.* top flight. **top•per,** *n. inf.* top hat. **top•ping,** *n.* cream, sauce, etc., put on the top of food. **top se•cret,** *adj.* very secret. **top•soil,** *n.* layer of good light soil on the surface (of a field, etc.).

to•paz ['təʊpæz] *n.* yellow semi-precious stone.

to•pee, topi ['təʊpɪ] *n.* helmet worn in hot countries (like India) to protect your head from the sun.

to•pi•ar•y ['təʊpjərɪ] *n.* art of cutting bushes into odd shapes for ornament.

top•ic ['tɒpɪk] *n.* subject (for discussion/of a conversation). **top•i•cal,** *adj.* which is of interest at the present time. **top•i•cal•i•ty,** *n.* being topical. **top•i•cal•ly,** *adv.* in a topical way.

to•pog•ra•phy [tə'pɒgrəfɪ] *n.* description of land mentioning rivers, mountains, roads, buildings, etc. **to•pog•ra•pher,** *n.* person who studies topography. **top•o•graph•i•cal** [tɒpə'græfɪkl] *adj.* which describes land.

to•pol•o•gy [tə'pɒlədʒɪ] *n.* study of the properties of geometrical shapes which remain the same even when the shapes change.

top•ple [tɒpl] *v.* to make a government/dictator lose power. **top•ple o•ver** ['tɒpl'əʊvə] *v.* to make (sth) fall down; to fall down.

top•sy-tur•vy ['tɒpsɪ'tɜːvɪ] *adj. & adv.* upside down/in confusion.

toque [təʊk] *n.* round hat (for a woman) with no brim.

tor [tɔː] *n.* rocky hill.

torch [tɔːtʃ] *n. (pl.* **-es**) (a) (*esp. Brit.*) portable electric light which you can hold in your hand. (b) flaming piece of wood. **torch•light,** *n.* light from a flaming torch; **t. parade** = procession of people carrying flaming torches.

tore [tɔː] *v. see* **tear.**

tor•e•a•dor ['tɒrɪədɔː] *n.* Spanish bullfighter.

tor•ment 1. *n.* ['tɔːmənt] extreme pain; **in t.** =

æ back, aː farm, ɒ top, aɪ pipe, aʊ how, aie fire, aʊə flower, ɔ: bought, ɔɪ toy, e fed, eəhair, eɪ take, ə afraid, əʊ boat, əʊə lower, vː word, ɪ heap, ɪ hit, ɪə hear, uː school, ʊ book, ʌ but, b back, d dog, ð then, dʒ just, f fog, g go, h hand, j yes, k catch, l last, m mix, n nut, ŋ sing, p penny, r round, s some, ʃ short, t too, tʃ chop, θ thing, v voice, w was, z zoo, ʒ treasure

in great pain. 2. *v.* [tɔːˈment] to make (s.o.) suffer. **tor•men•tor,** *n.* person who torments.

torn [tɔːn] *v. see* **tear.**

tor•na•do [tɔːˈneɪdəʊ] *n.* (*pl.* **-oes**) violent whirlwind.

tor•pe•do [tɔːˈpiːdəʊ] 1. *n.* (*pl.* **-oes**) self-propelled missile which travels through the water. 2. *v.* to sink (a ship) using a torpedo; to ruin (s.o.'s plans). **tor•pe•do boat,** *n.* small fast naval ship which carries torpedoes.

tor•pid [ˈtɔːpɪd] *adj.* half asleep with heat; dull; sluggish. **tor•por,** *n.* being half asleep/sluggish.

torque [tɔːk] *n.* (a) mechanical force to make sth rotate. (b) prehistoric necklace made of twisted gold or silver.

tor•rent [ˈtɒrənt] *n.* (a) fast rushing stream. (b) fast flow. **tor•ren•tial** [təˈrenʃəl] *adj.* like a torrent.

tor•rid [ˈtɒrɪd] *adj.* (a) very hot. (b) intense (passion).

tor•sion [ˈtɔːʃn] *n.* being twisted; strain caused by twisting.

tor•so [ˈtɔːsəʊ] *n.* (*pl.* **-os, -si**) body (excluding the head, arms and legs).

tort [tɔːt] *n.* act which is the subject of a civil action in court.

tor•til•la [tɔːˈtiːjæ] *n.* type of Spanish omelette, with vegetables.

tor•toise [ˈtɔːtəs] *n.* reptile covered with a hard domed shell, which moves very slowly and can live to a great age. **tor•toise•shell,** *adj.* & *n.* speckled brown material (from the shell of a tortoise) or something like it used for making combs/frames for glasses, etc.; **t. cat** = brown, yellow and black cat; **t. butterfly** = common brown and red butterfly.

tor•tu•ous [ˈtɔːtjuəs] *adj.* which twists and turns. **tor•tu•ous•ly,** *adv.* in a tortuous way.

tor•ture [ˈtɔːtʃə] 1. *n.* pain inflicted on s.o. as a punishment or to make them reveal a secret. 2. *v.* to inflict torture on s.o. **tor•tur•er,** *n.* person who tortures.

To•ry [ˈtɔːrɪ] *adj.* & *n.* (member) of the Conservative party in Great Britain or Canada.

toss [tɒs] 1. *n.* (*pl.* **-es**) (a) action of throwing sth into the air; **t. of a coin** = throwing a coin up to see which side is on top when it comes down; (*in sports*) **to win the t.** = guess correctly which side of the coin comes down on top and so play first. (b) sharp disdainful movement of the head. 2. *v.* (a) to throw (sth) into the air; **to t. a coin** = to throw a coin to see which side is on top when it comes down; **let's t. for it** = the person who guesses right, starts to play first/has first choice. (b) to move (sth) about; to mix (a salad); **she tossed her head** = made a sharp disdainful movement of her head.

toss•up, *n. inf.* **it's a t. which one will win** = you can't tell which one will win.

tot [tɒt] 1. *n.* (a) little child. (b) *inf.* small glass of alcohol. 2. *v.* (**totted**) **to t. up** = to add up.

to•tal [ˈtəʊtl] 1. *adj.* & *n.* complete/whole (amount). 2. *v.* (**totaled, totalled**) to add up (to). **to•tal•i•ty** [təʊˈtælɪtɪ] *n.* whole amount. **to•tal•ize,** *v.* to add up (figures). **to•tal•ly,** *adv.* completely.

to•tal•i•tar•i•an [təʊtælɪˈteərɪən] *adj.* (state) governed by a single party/group which refuses to allow the existence of any opposition.

to•tal•i•za•tor [ˈtəʊtələlaɪzeɪtə] *n.* machine which calculates the amount to be paid to people who bet on a winning horse.

tote [təʊt] 1. *n. inf.* **the t.** = totalizator. 2. *v.* to carry. **tote bag,** *n.* large carrying bag.

to•tem pole [ˈtəʊtəmpəʊl] *n.* tall carved pole on which North American Indians carve figures of gods.

tot•ter [ˈtɒtə] *n.* to walk unsteadily/to wobble. **tot•ter•y,** *adj.* wobbly/likely to fall.

tou•can [ˈtuːkæn] *n.* American tropical bird with a huge colored beak.

touch [tʌtʃ] 1. *n.* (*pl.* **-es**) (a) sense by which you feel sth. (b) way of bringing your fingers into contact with sth; **she's lost her t.** = she isn't as successful/capable as she was. (c) slight tap. (d) slight stroke (of a paintbrush); **to put the finishing touches to sth** = to finish sth off. (e) contact; **to get in t. with/to lose t. with** = to contact/to lose contact with. (f) slight taste/trace. 2. *v.* (a) to feel (with the fingers); to come into contact; **I wouldn't t. it** = I wouldn't have anything to do with it; **don't t. my things** = don't interfere with them/don't move them. (b) **to t. on** = to refer to (a subject). (c) to eat or drink (*usu. negative*); **I don't t. alcohol.** (d) to affect the emotions of (s.o.). (e) to reach the same level as (s.o.). (f) *inf.* to ask (s.o.) **for** a loan. **touch-and-go,** *n.* **it was touch-and-go** = it was doubtful. **touch down,** *v.* (*of plane*) to land. **touch•down,** *n.* (a) landing (of a plane). (b) (*in football*) scoring of six points for having possession of the ball on or behind the opponent's goal. **tou•ché** [ˈtuːʃeɪ] *inter.* *meaning* you have scored a point against me. **touched,** *adj.* (a) grateful/pleased with. (b) slightly mad. **touch•i•ness,** *n.* being susceptible/easily offended. **touch•ing.** 1. *adj.* which affects the emotions. 2. *prep.* concerning/about. **touch off,** *v.* to set off (an explosion, etc.). **touch on,** *v.* to refer to (a question) briefly. **touch pa•per,** *n.* chemically treated paper used as a fuse to light a firework. **touch•screen,** *n.* computer screen which is sensitive to touch, and where a cursor can be positioned by touching the screen.

touch•stone, *n*. thing used as a standard to test other things against. **touch-tone**, *adj*. (of a telephone dialing system) transmitting instructions/information in the form of tones produced by pressing the telephone's buttons. **touch-type**, *v*. to type without looking at the keys on the typewriter. **touch up**, *v*. to add little strokes of paint to improve the appearance of sth. **touch•y**, *adj. inf*. highly susceptible/easily offended.

tough [tʌf] 1. *adj*. (**-er, -est**) (a) hard; difficult to chew/to cut/to break; *inf*. **it's as t. as shoe leather** = extremely tough. (b) strong/hardy. (c) difficult; **to get t. with s.o.** = to deal roughly/harshly with s.o. (d) *inf*. **t. luck!** = hard luck! 2. *n. inf*. rough criminal. **tough•en**, *v*. to make tough; **toughened glass** = specially strengthened glass. **tough•ness**, *n*. being tough.

tou•pee ['tuːpeɪ] *n*. small wig.

tour ['tʊə] 1. *n*. journey which goes around various places and returns to its starting point; **package t.** = one which has been totally organized in advance. 2. *v*. to visit; to go on a tour; **touring company** = theater company which goes from one town to another. **tour•ism**, *n*. business of providing lodging and entertainment for tourists. **tour•ist**, *adj. & n*. person who goes on vacation to visit places; **t. class** = type of seating in an aircraft which is cheaper than first class; **t. trap** = place whch overcharges tourists.

tour de force [tuːrdə'fɔːs] *n*. act showing remarkable skill.

tour•ma•line ['tʊəmɔliːn] *n*. type of semiprecious stone.

tour•na•ment ['tʊənəmənt] *n*. (a) (*old*) contest between groups of knights. (b) sporting competition with many games which eliminate competitors.

tour•ne•dos ['tʊənədəʊ] *n*. piece of fillet steak.

tour•ni•quet ['tʊənɪkeɪ] *n*. tight bandage put around an arm or leg to stop bleeding from a wound.

tou•sle ['taʊzl] *v*. to make (hair) untidy.

tout [taʊt] 1. *n*. person who tries to sell something to people he meets. 2. *v*. (a) to try to persuade people to vote/to buy things, etc. (b) to praise highly; **to t. a new restaurant.**

tow [təʊ] 1. *n*. (a) pulling a car/a ship, etc. behind you; **he had his family in t.** = coming behind him. (b) short, coarse pieces of flax. 2. *v*. to pull (a car/a ship, etc.) which cannot move

by itself. **tow•bar**, *n*. bar fitted to a car, to attach a trailer, etc. **tow-head•ed**, *adj*. with very light, almost white, blond hair. **tow-line, tow-rope**, *n*. rope which attaches a car/a ship, etc. to sth being towed. **tow•path**, *n*. path along the bank of a river/canal (along which horses used to walk to tow barges).

to•ward [tə'wɔːdz] *prep*. (*also* **towards**) (a) in the direction of. (b) to (a person/a country, etc.). (c) as part payment for. (d) near (a time).

tow•el ['taʊəl] 1. *n*. piece of soft absorbent cloth for drying; **to throw in the t.** = to give up/not to continue a contest. 2. *v*. (**toweled, towelled**) to rub dry with a towel. **tow•el•ing**, *n*. soft cloth used for making towels.

tow•er ['taʊə] 1. *n*. tall building; **control t.** = tall airport building containing the control room; **t. of strength** = very strong and sympathetic person. 2. *v*. to rise very high (**above**). **tow•er•ing**, *adj*. (a) very tall. (b) very great (**rage**).

town [taʊn] *n*. place where people live and work, with houses, stores, offices and factories (as opposed to the country); **t. clerk** = administrative official in a town who keeps records and issues licenses. **t. council** = elected committee which runs a town; **t. hall** = offices of the town council; public building used for meetings; **t. planning** = science of planning the development of a town; *inf*. **to go to t. over sth** = to spend a lot of money/time on sth; *inf*. **to paint the t. red** = to have a party; celebrate. **town•ie**, *n. inf*. person who lives in a town. **town house**, *n*. (a) house in a town or city. (b) expensive house in a city for one family. **towns•folk**, *n. pl*. people who live in a town. **town•ship**, *n*. (a) (*in the United States and Canada*) small town and the administrative area around it. (b) (*in South Africa*) area where black people live near a large town. **towns•man, townswoman**, *n*. (*pl*. **-men, -women**) person who lives in a town. **towns•peo•ple**, *n. pl*. people who live in a town.

tox•e•mi•a, *Brit*. **tox•ae•mi•a** [tɒk'siːmɪə] blood poisoning. **tox•ic** ['tɒksɪk] *adj*. poisonous. **tox•ic•i•ty**, *n*. being toxic. **tox•i•col•o•gist** [tɒksɪ'kɒlədʒɪst] *n*. scientist who studies poisons. **tox•i•col•o•gy**, *n*. scientific study of poisons. **tox•in**, *n*. poisonous substance.

æ back, aː farm, ɒ: top, aɪ pipe, aʊ how, aiə fire, aʊə flower, ɔ: bought, ɔɪ toy, e fed, eəhair, eɪ take, ə afraid, əʊ boat, əʊə lower, vː word, iː heap, ɪ hit, ɪə hear, uː school, ʊ book, ʌ but, b back, d dog, ð then, dʒ just, f fog, g go, h hand, j yes, k catch, l last, m mix, n nut, ŋ sing, p penny, r round, s some, ʃ short, t too, tʃ chop, θ thing, v voice, w was, z zoo, ʒ treasure

tox•oph•i•ly [tɒk'sɒfɪlɪ] n. (formal) archery.

toy [tɔɪ] 1. adj. & n. thing which children play with. 2. v. **to t. with** = (i) to eat (food) reluctantly; (ii) to turn over (an idea) in your mind. **toy•shop**, n. shop which sells toys.

trace [treɪs] 1. n. (a) **traces** = set of tracks/footprints left by an animal. (b) small amount; **he's vanished without a t.** = leaving nothing behind to show where he has gone. (c) **traces** = straps by which a horse is attached to a carriage; **to kick over the traces** = to rebel (against authority). 2. v. (a) to follow the tracks left by (sth); to try to find where (s.o./sth) is. (b) to copy (a picture/a map) by placing a piece of thin transparent paper over it and drawing on it. **trace•a•ble,** adj. which can be traced. **trace el•e•ment,** n. chemical element of which a tiny amount is needed by a plant or animal to grow properly. **trac•er,** n. type of bullet/shell which leaves a visible stream of sparks/smoke as it flies. **trac•er•y,** n. delicate stone patterns holding the glass in a church window. **trac•ing,** n. drawing done by tracing; **t. paper** = thin transparent paper for tracing drawings.

tra•che•a [træ'kiːə] n. windpipe. **tra•che•ot•o•my** [trækɪ'ɒtəmɪ] n. operation to make a hole in the windpipe from the outside of the neck.

tra•cho•ma [trə'kəʊmə] n. eye disease caused by a virus.

track ['træk] 1. n. (a) footprints of animal/marks of wheels, etc.; **the police are on the t. of the criminal** = they are following him; **to keep t. of** = to keep an account/to keep oneself informed of; **to lose t. of sth** = not to know where it is any longer; **to make tracks for home** = to set off for home. (b) path; **on the wrong t.** = working wrongly/making a wrong assumption. (c) course for racing; **t. events** = running competitions in an athletics tournament; **t. suit** = type of warm two-piece suit worn by sportsmen when practising; **t. shoes** = running shoes with spikes in the soles; **he has a good t. record** = he has been very successful in the past. (d) line of rails for a train, streetcar, etc.; inf. **to have a one-t. mind** = to think on only one thing/have only one interest. (e) endless belt on which a caterpillar tractor/tank, etc., runs. (f) part of a magnetic tape on which sth can be recorded. (g) set of grooves on a phonograph record, etc. 2. v. to follow (an animal); to follow (a moving subject) with a camera. **track•ball, track•er•ball,** n. device that consists of a small ball mounted on bearings within a socket, which can be freely rotated by the fingers to control a cursor on a computer monitor. **track down,** v. to follow and catch (an animal/a criminal). **track•er,**

n. animal/person who follows tracks. **track•less,** adj. with no paths.

tract [trækt] n. (a) wide stretch of countryside. (b) short (religious or political) pamphlet. (c) system of organs in the body which are linked together.

trac•ta•ble ['træktəbl] adj. which can be tamed/made to do what is necessary. **trac•ta•bil•i•ty** [træktə'bɪlɪtɪ] n. being tractable.

trac•tion ['trækʃn] n. (a) pulling force. (b) pulling (a broken leg, etc.) up with pulleys.

trac•tor ['træktə] n. farm vehicle with large back wheels for pulling a plow, etc.; **t. feed** = paper feed in a printer, where the paper is pulled by sprocket wheels.

trade [treɪd] 1. n. (a) business; buying and selling. (b) people who buy and sell a particular type of goods/who work in a particular industry. (c) job. 2. v. (a) to carry on a business. (b) to exchange (sth **for** sth). **trade in,** v. to exchange an old car, etc., as part payment for a new one. **trade-in,** n. exchange of an old car, etc., for a newer one. **trade•mark,** n. particular name, symbol, etc., which has been officially registered by a manufacturer and which cannot be copied by other manufacturers. **trade name,** n. name, often registered as a trademark, used by a manufacturer to distinguish his products from those of competitors. **trade on,** v. to exploit/to profit from. **trad•er,** n. person who buys and sells. **trades•man,** n. (pl. **-men**) person engaged in a trade. **trades•peo•ple,** n. pl. people engaged in a trade. **trade un•ion,** n. labor union which groups together workers in a particular trade. **trade un•ion•ist,** n. member of a trade union. **trade wind,** n. tropical wind blowing toward the equator. **trad•ing,** n. business.

tra•di•tion [træ'dɪʃn] n. customs/habits/stories which are passed from generation to generation. **tra•di•tion•al,** adj. referring to tradition. **tra•di•tion•al•ist,** n. person who does things in a traditional way. **tra•di•tion•al•ly,** adv. according to tradition.

tra•duce [trə'djuːs] v. (formal) to slander (s.o.).

traf•fic ['træfɪk] 1. n. (a) movement of vehicles, esp. cars/trucks/buses, etc., on the roads; **t. jam** = blockage of traffic on a road; **t. circle** = place where several roads meet and traffic moves in a circle; **air t.** = aircraft flying. (b) illegal international business. 2. v. (**trafficked**) to deal **in** (drugs) illegally. **traf•fic lights,** n. red, green and amber lights which regulate the movement of traffic. **traf•fick•er,** n. person who traffics (in drugs).

trag•e•dy ['trædʒədɪ] *n.* play/motion picture/story with a sad story; unhappy event. **tra•ge•di•an** [trə'dʒiːdɪən] *n.* person who acts in tragedies. **trag•ic**, *adj.* referring to tragedy; very sad. **trag•i•cal•ly**, *adv.* very sadly.

trail [treɪl] 1. *n.* (a) tracks left by an animal. (b) path. (c) thing which stretches a long way behind. 2. *v.* (a) to let (sth) drag behind you. (b) to follow the tracks of (an animal/a person). (c) **trailing plant** = one which hangs or creeps along the ground. **trail•er**, *n.* (a) vehicle pulled behind a car, truck, etc. for transporting goods, etc. (b) van with beds, tables, washing and cooking facilities, etc. which can be towed by a car. (c) short motion picture showing parts of a full-length motion picture as an advertisement.

train [treɪn] 1. *n.* (a) series of cars pulled by a railroad engine. (b) series of events; line of animals carrying goods; retinue (of an important person); **t. of thought** = series of thoughts following one another. (c) long fuse (to light an explosive). (d) part of a dress which hangs down and trails along the ground at the back. 2. *v.* (a) to teach (s.o./an animal) to do sth; to learn how to do sth. (b) to practice (for a sport). (c) to point (a rifle/a telescope) at sth. **train•a•ble**, *adj.* which can be trained. **train•ee** [treɪ'niː] *n.* person who is being taught. **train•er**, *n.* (a) person who trains animals/sportsmen. (b) small aircraft in which you learn to fly. **train•ing**, *n.* action of being taught/of practicing; **in t.** = (i) practicing (for a sport); (ii) fit/in good physical condition.

traipse [treɪps] *v. inf.* to walk about in an aimless, idle way.

trait [treɪ(t)] *n.* particular point of s.o.'s character.

trai•tor ['treɪtə] *n.* person who sides with the enemy/who gives away secrets to the enemy. **trai•tor•ous**, *adj.* like a traitor.

tra•jec•to•ry [trə'dʒektrɪ] *n.* curved course taken by sth which has been thrown through the air.

tram [træm] *n. Brit.* streetcar. **tram•line**, *n. pl. Brit.* system of rails along which a tram runs.

tram•mel ['træml] 1. *n.* (a) (*also* **trammel net**) type of fishing net. (b) thing which prevents you from doing sth. 2. *v.* (**trammeled, trammelled**) (*formal*) to prevent (s.o.) from doing sth.

tramp [træmp] 1. *n.* (a) noise of feet hitting the ground heavily. (b) long energetic walk. (c)

person who has nowhere to live and walks from place to place begging for food or money. 2. *v.* (a) to walk heavily. (b) to trample on (sth); to crush (grapes) by stepping on them to extract the juice. **tramp steam•er**, *n.* cargo boat which goes from port to port, but not on a regular route.

tram•ple ['træmpl] *v.* (**on**) to crush (by walking).

tram•po•line ['træmpəliːn] *n.* frame with a large sheet of elastic material on which you can bounce/perform exercises, etc.

trance [trɑːns] *n.* state when you are not fully conscious, and do not notice what is going on.

tran•quil ['træŋkwɪl] *adj.* calm/peaceful. **tran•quil•li•ty, tranquility** [træŋ'kwɪlɪtɪ] *n.* calm. **tran•quil•ize** ['træŋkwɪlaɪz] *v.* to make (s.o.) calm (by giving drugs). **tran•quil•iz•er**, *n.* drug which makes a person calm. **tran•quil•ly, tranquily** *adv.* in a tranquil way.

trans- [trænz] *prefix meaning* through/across.

trans•act [træn'zækt] *v.* to carry out (a piece of business). **trans•ac•tion**, *n.* piece of business; **cash t.** = piece of business paid for in cash; **transactions** = published report of what takes place at a meeting of a learned/scientific society.

trans•at•lan•tic [trænzət'læntɪk] *adj.* across the Atlantic; from the other side of the Atlantic; involving countries on both sides of the Atlantic.

trans•ceiv•er ['trænzsiːvə] *n.* transmitter and receiver.

trans•cend [træn'send] *v.* to go beyond/further than sth. **tran•scend•ent**, *adj.* which transcends. **tran•scen•den•tal** [trænsən'dentəl] *adj.* which rises above the level of ordinary thought or reasoning.

trans•con•ti•nen•tal [trænzkɒntɪ'nentl] *adj.* across a continent.

tran•scribe [træn'skraɪb] *v.* to write out the text (of sth which is heard); to write out in full (what has been written down in shorthand); to rewrite (a piece of music) for another instrument than the one for which it was originally written. **tran•script** ['trænskrɪpt] *n.* written text of what was said (on the radio/at a trial, etc.). **tran•scrip•tion**, *n.* act of transcribing.

tran•sept ['trænsept] *n.* one of the two branches at right angles to the nave and choir in a cross-shaped church.

trans-fat•ty ac•id [trænz'fætɪ 'æsɪd] *n.* poly-

æ **back**, ɑː **farm**, ɒ: **top**, aɪ **pipe**, aʊ **how**, aɪə **fire**, aʊə **flower**, ɔː **bought**, ɔɪ **toy**, e **fed**, eəhair, eɪ **take**, ə **afraid**, əʊ **boat**, əʊə **lower**, ɜː **word**, iː **heap**, ɪ **hit**, ɪə **hear**, uː **school**, ʊ **book**, ʌ **but**, b **back**, d **dog**, ð **then**, dʒ **just**, f **fog**, g **go**, h **hand**, j **yes**, k **catch**, l **last**, m **mix**, n **nut**, ŋ **sing**, p **penny**, r **round**, s **some**, ʃ **short**, t **too**, tʃ **chop**, θ **thing**, v **voice**, w **was**, z **zoo**, ʒ **treasure**

unsaturated fatty acid, used in manufacturing margarine.

trans•fer 1. *n.* ['trænsfə] (a) movement of sth/s.o. to a new place. (b) design which can be stuck on to a surface. 2. *v.* [træns'fɜː] (**transferred**) to move (sth/s.o.) to another place. **trans•fer•a•ble** [trænz'fɜːrəbl] *adj.* which can be transferred; **not t.** = (ticket) which can only be used by the person to whom it was issued. **trans•fer•ence**, *n.* act of transferring.

trans•fig•ure [trænz'fɪgə] *v.* to change for the better (the appearance of sth/s.o.). **trans•fig•u•ra•tion**, *n.* act of transfiguring.

trans•fix [trænz'fɪks] *v.* to prevent (s.o.) from moving (by giving a shock).

trans•form [trænz'fɔːm] *v.* to change completely. **trans•for•ma•tion** [trænzfə'meɪʃn] *n.* complete change of appearance. **trans•form•er** [trænz'fɔːmə] *n.* apparatus for changing the voltage of an alternating electric current.

trans•fuse [trænz'fjuːz] *v.* to move liquid from one container to another. **trans•fu•sion** [trænz'fjuːʒn] *n.* moving of liquid from one container to another; **blood t.** = giving blood to a sick patient.

trans•gress [trænz'gres] *v.* (*formal*) to go against (a rule). **trans•gres•sion**, *n.* act of transgressing. **trans•gres•sor**, *n.* person who transgresses.

tran•ship [trænz'ʃɪp] *v. see* **trans•ship**.

tran•sience ['trænzɪəns] *n.* state of not being permanent. **tran•sient** ['trænzɪənt] *adj. & n.* which will not last; **transients** = people who stay in a hotel for a short time.

tran•sis•tor [træn'zɪstə] *n.* (a) device made of semi-conductors which can increase an electric current. (b) **t.** (**radio**) = small pocket radio which uses transistors. **tran•sis•tor•ize**, *v.* to put transistors into (sth).

tran•sit ['trænzɪt] 1. *n.* (a) movement of passengers/goods (on the way to another destination). (b) moving of a planet across the face of the sun or other planet. 2. *v.* (*formal*) to go across. **tran•si•tion** [træn'zɪʃn] *n.* movement between one state or condition and another. **tran•si•tion•al**, *adj.* referring to transition.

tran•si•tive ['trænzɪtɪv] *adj.* (verb) which has an object.

tran•si•to•ry ['trænzɪtrɪ] *adj.* which does not last for long.

trans•late [trænz'leɪt] *v.* (a) to put (words) into another language. (b) to move (a bishop) to another see. **trans•lat•a•ble**, *adj.* which can be translated. **trans•la•tion** [trænz'leɪʃn] *n.* text which has been translated; action of translating; **simultaneous t.** = translating directly into another language what a speaker is

saying. **trans•la•tor**, *n.* person who translates.

trans•lit•er•ate [trænz'lɪtəreɪt] *v.* to put (words) into the letters of a different alphabet. **trans•lit•er•a•tion**, *n.* act of transliterating.

trans•lu•cent [trænz'luːsnt] *adj.* which light can pass through, but which you cannot see through. **trans•lu•cence**, *n.* being translucent.

trans•mi•gra•tion [trænzmaɪ'greɪʃn] *n.* moving of a soul from a dead body to a living one.

trans•mit [trænz'mɪt] *v.* (**transmitted**) (a) to pass (from one person to another). (b) to send out by rado/TV. **trans•mis•sion** [trænz'mɪʃn] *n.* (a) passing (of disease) from one person to another. (b) sending out by radio/TV; a radio/TV broadcast. (c) (*in a car*) series of moving parts which pass the power from the engine to the wheels. **trans•mit•ter**, *n.* apparatus for sending out radio/TV signals.

trans•mog•ri•fy [trænz'mɒgrɪfaɪ] *v.* to change (sth) totally, usu. grotesquely.

trans•mute [trænz'mjuːt] *v.* to make (sth) change its shape or substance. **trans•mu•ta•tion**, *n.* act of transmuting.

tran•som ['trænsəm] *n.* (a) cross beam in a window; beam across the top of a door. (b) stern piece of a boat.

trans•par•en•cy [træns'pærənsɪ] *n.* (a) being transparent. (b) photograph which is printed on transparent film so that it can be projected onto a screen. **trans•par•ent**, *adj.* (a) which you can see through. (b) obvious (lie). **trans•par•ent•ly**, *adv.* obviously.

tran•spire [træn'spaɪə] *v.* (a) to happen. (b) to pass moisture through the surface of the skin/of a leaf, etc. **tran•spi•ra•tion** [trænspɪ'reɪʃn] *n.* act of transpiring.

trans•plant 1. *n.* ['trɑːnsplɑːnt] (a) act of taking an organ from one person and grafting it into another's body. (b) plant which is moved to another place to grow. 2. *v.* [træns'plɑːnt] (a) to graft (an organ) into s.o.'s body. (b) to plant (plants) in another place where they will grow permanently.

trans•port 1. *n.* ['trænspɔːt] (a) movement of goods/people; means of moving goods/people; **public t. system** = system of buses/subways/streetcars for moving the public. (b) ship/aircraft which carries goods or soldiers. (c) great emotion. 2. *v.* [træn'spɔːt] (a) to move (goods/people) from one place to another. (b) **transported with joy** = very happy. (c) (*old*) to send (a criminal) to a prison in a colony. **trans•port•a•ble**, *adj.* which can be transported. **trans•por•ta•tion** [trænspɔː'teɪʃn] *n.* (a) movement of goods/people; means of moving goods/people. (b) (*old*) sending of a

criminal to a prison in a colony.
trans•port•er [træn'spɔːtə] *n.* large truck
for carrying large loads; **t. bridge** = platform
which is suspended from a bridge and moves
across a river on cables, carrying cars, etc.

trans•pose [træn'spəʊz] *v.* to make (two
things) change places. **trans•po•si•tion**
[trænspə'zɪʃn] *n.* act of transposing.

trans•ship [træns'ʃɪp] *v.* **(transshipped)** to
move (goods) from one ship/truck/railroad
car to another.

tran•sub•stan•ti•a•tion [trænsʌbstænʃɪ-
'eɪʃn] *n.* belief that the wine and bread become
the blood and body of Christ at the Communion service.

trans•u•ran•ic [trænzju'rænɪk] *adj.* (element)
which has atoms heavier than those of uranium.

trans•verse ['trænzvɜːs] *adj.* which lies across.

trans•ves•tite [trænz'vestaɪt] *n.* person who
wants to wear the clothes of the opposite sex.
trans•ves•tism [trænz'vestɪzəm] *n.* desire to
wear the clothes of the opposite sex.

trap [træp] 1. *n.* (a) device to catch an animal;
plan to catch (s.o.)/to take (s.o.) by surprise;
radar t. = device used by police to catch a motorist who is driving too fast. (b) **t. door** = door
in a floor/in a ceiling. (c) bend in a waste pipe
which is filled with water, and so stops unpleasant smells coming back up the pipe from
a sewer. (d) *Sl.* mouth. 2. *v.* **(trapped)** to catch.
trap•per, *n.* person who catches wild animals for their fur.

tra•peze [træ'piːz] *n.* bar which hangs from
ropes, and which acrobats use in a circus.

tra•pe•zi•um [træ'piːzɪəm] *n.* (a) four-sided
shape, where no two sides are parallel. (b)
Brit. trapezoid. (c) little bone in the wrist.
trap•e•zoid ['træpɪzɔɪd] *n.* (a) four-sided
shape, where two of the sides are parallel. (b)
Brit. trapezium.

trap•pings ['træpɪŋz] *n. pl.* orna-
ments/clothes/decorations which are suitable
for a particular occasion.

trash [træʃ] *n.* things to be thrown away; refuse.
trash can, *n.* container for household trash.
trash•y, *adj.* **(-ier, -iest)** very bad/completely
worthless.

trau•ma ['trɔːmə] *n.* (a) terrible shock/unpleas-
ant experience which affects your mental outlook. (b) injury. **trau•mat•ic** [trɔː'mætɪk]
adj. which gives a terrible and unpleasant
shock. **trau•mat•i•cal•ly,** *adv.* in a trau-
matic way.

trav•el ['trævl] 1. *n.* moving from one country
to another/from one place to another. 2. *v.*
(traveled, travelled) (a) to move from one
country to another/from one place to another.
(b) to be a sales representative (in an area).
trav•el a•gen•cy, *n.* office which arranges
tickets/hotel reservations, etc., for you when
you are making a journey. **trav•el a•gent,**
n. person who runs or works in a travel
agency. **trav•el•er,** *n.* person who is traveling from one place to another; **traveler's
checks** = checks which you can buy at your
bank and which can then be cashed in a foreign country. **trav•e•logue,** *n.* motion picture describing travel.

trav•erse 1. *n.* ['trævɜːs] (a) crossing. (b) thing
which crosses another. (c) (*in mountaineering*)
crossing of a dangerous flat rock face. 2. *v.*
[trə'vɜːs] to cross.

trav•es•ty ['trævəstɪ] 1. *n.* parody; ridiculous
copy/poor imitation. 2. *v.* to imitate (sth) in a
ridiculous way.

trawl [trɔːl] 1. *n.* long net shaped like a bag,
pulled at sea by a trawler. 2. *v.* to fish with a
trawl. **trawl•er,** *n.* fishing boat which uses a
trawl.

tray [treɪ] *n.* (a) flat board for carrying
glasses/cups and saucers, etc. (b) flat open
box/basket for papers (as on a desk).

treach•er•y ['tretʃərɪ] *n.* act of betray-
ing/being a traitor to your friends, etc.
treach•er•ous, *adv.* (a) likely to betray. (b)
dangerous. **treach•er•ous•ly,** *adv.* in a
treacherous way.

trea•cle ['triːkl] *n.* thick dark-brown syrup
produced when sugar is refined. **trea•cly,**
adj. thick and sticky like treacle.

tread [tred] 1. *n.* (a) way of walking. (b) sound
of a footstep. (c) part of a step (on stairs/an escalator) on which you put your foot. (d) surface of a tire marked with a pattern of lines. 2.
v. **(trod** [trod]; **has trodden)** (a) to walk. (b) to
trample on/to crush with your feet; **to t. water**
= to keep afloat in water by moving your legs
up and down. **trea•dle** ['tredl] 1. *n.* foot
pedal which makes a machine turn. 2. *v.* to
push a treadle with the foot. **tread•mill,** *n.*
(a) device turned by people/animals as they
walk around a circular path or inside a large
wheel. (b) dull routine work.

trea•son ['triːzn] *n.* betraying your coun-
try/giving your country's secrets to the enemy.
trea•son•a•ble, *adj.* which can be considered as treason.

æ back, ɑː farm, ɒ top, aɪ pipe, aʊ how, aɪə fire, aʊə flower, ɔː bought, ɔɪ toy, e fed, eəhair, eɪ take, ə
afraid, əʊ boat, əʊə lower, ɜː word, iː heap, ɪ hit, ɪə hear, uː school, ʊ book, ʌ but, b back, d dog, ð then,
dʒ just, f fog, g go, h hand, j yes, k catch, l last, m mix, n nut, ŋ sing, p penny, r round, s some, ʃ short, t
too, tʃ chop, θ thing, v voice, w was, z zoo, ʒ treasure

treas•ure ['treʒə] 1. *n.* (a) store of money/jewels/gold, etc.; **t.-trove** = buried treasure found by accident which then becomes the property of the state; **t. hunt** = game where you follow clues from place to place until you find a prize. (b) thing which is highly valued. 2. *v.* to value (sth) very highly. **treas•ur•er**, *n.* person who looks after the finances of a club, etc. **treas•ur•y**, *n.* (a) place where treasure is kept. (b) government department which deals with the nation's money.

treat [triːt] 1. *n.* special meal/outing, etc., which should give pleasure; **a t. in store** = a special future surprise; **this is my t.** = I am paying the bill. 2. *v.* (a) to deal with; to write about (a subject). (b) **to t. s.o. to** = to give (s.o.) a special meal/outing as a surprise gift. (c) to look after (a sick person) or deal with (a disease). (d) to pass (a substance) through a certain process. (e) (*formal*) to negotiate (**with** an enemy). **treat•ment**, *n.* (a) way of dealing with sth. (b) way of looking after a sick person or dealing with a disease.

trea•tise ['triːtɪz] *n.* long learned piece of writing on a subject.

trea•ty ['triːtɪ] *n.* (a) agreement between two or more countries. (b) any agreement, as between private people.

tre•ble ['trebl] 1. *n.* voice which sings high-pitched notes; high-pitched musical instrument. 2. *adj.* (a) three times as large. (b) high (voice/note); **t. clef** = sign in music showing that the notes are in a high pitch. 3. *v.* to increase by three times. **tre•bly**, *adv.* three times as much.

tree [triː] *n.* (a) large plant with a wooden stem and branches. (b) **family t.** = diagram showing the development of a family over a long period of time. **tree creep•er**, *n.* small bird which creeps up the trunk of trees, looking for insects. **tree•less**, *adj.* with no trees. **tree line**, *n.* line at a certain altitude above which trees do not grow. **treen**, *n.* (*no pl.*) small spoons/rings, etc., made of wood. **tree•top**, *n.* top of a tree.

tre•foil ['triːfɔɪl] *n.* design/leaf shaped in three equal parts like that of a clover.

trek [trek] 1. *n.* long and difficult journey. 2. *v.* (**trekked**) to make a long and difficult journey.

trel•lis ['trelɪs] *n.* (*pl.* **-es**) openwork fence made of thin pieces of wood in a crisscross pattern.

trem•ble ['trembl] 1. *n.* shaking/shuddering. 2. *v.* (a) to shake/to quiver. (b) to be very worried. **trem•bly**, *adj.* shaky/shaking.

tre•men•dous [trɪˈmendəs] *adj.* (a) enormous/very large. (b) wonderful. **tre•men•dous•ly**, *adv.* greatly.

trem•o•lo ['tremələʊ] *n.* (*pl.* **-os**) trembling note in music.

trem•or ['tremə] *n.* shaking; **earth t.** = slight earthquake.

trem•u•lous ['tremjʊləs] *adj.* shaking/quivering.

trench [trentʃ] 1. *n.* (*pl.* **-es**) long narrow ditch in the ground. 2. *v.* to dig a long narrow ditch. **trench coat**, *n.* belted waterproof coat.

trench•ant ['trentʃənt] *adj.* sharp/biting (remark); vigorous (style).

trench•er ['trentʃə] *n.* (*old*) wooden plate for food. **trench•er•man**, *n.* person who eats a lot.

trend [trend] *n.* general tendency. **trend•i•ness**, *n.* being trendy. **trend-set•ter**, *n.* person who sets the fashion. **trend•y**. 1. *adj.* (**-ier, -iest**) *inf.* following fashion; fashionable. 2. *n. inf.* person who follows fashion.

tre•pan, trephine [trɪˈpæn, trɪˈfiːn] 1. *n.* saw for cutting out round pieces of bone. 2. *v.* (**trepanned**) to cut a round piece of bone out of (esp. the skull).

trep•i•da•tion [trepɪˈdeɪʃn] *n.* anxiety.

tres•pass ['trespəs] *v.* (**on**) to go into or onto s.o.'s property without permission. **tres•pass•er**, *n.* person who trespasses.

tres•ses ['tresɪz] *n. pl.* long hair.

tres•tle ['tresl] *n.* support made of a horizontal bar supported by four transverse legs; **t. table** = table with a top resting on a trestle.

tri- [traɪ] *prefix meaning* three.

tri•ad ['traɪæd] *n.* group of three people or things.

tri•al ['traɪəl] *n.* (a) court case to judge a criminal; **to stand t.** = to appear in court. (b) test; **on t.** = being tested to see if it is acceptable; **t. and error** = testing and rejecting various things until you find the one which works.

tri•an•gle ['traɪæŋgl] *n.* (a) geometrical shape with three sides and three angles; **eternal t.** = situation where s.o. is in love with s.o. who is in love with a third person. (b) musical instrument made of a piece of metal bent into the shape of a triangle. **tri•an•gu•lar** [traɪˈæŋgjʊlə] *adj.* shaped like a triangle. **tri•an•gu•la•tion** [traɪæŋgjuˈleɪʃn] *n.* method of measuring land to produce maps.

tribe [traɪb] *n.* (a) group of people ruled by a chief. (b) *inf.* large family/group. **trib•al**, *adj.* referring to a tribe. **trib•al•ism**, *n.* customs and beliefs of tribes. **tribes•man**, *n.* (*pl.* **-men**) member of a tribe.

trib•u•la•tion [trɪbjuˈleɪʃn] *n.* (*formal*) great misery.

tri•bu•nal [traɪˈbjuːnl] *n.* court of justice.

trib•une ['trɪbjuːn] *n.* leader who upholds the rights of the people.

trib•ute ['trɪbjuːt] *n.* (a) money paid to a conqueror by people who have been conquered. (b) words/gifts, etc., to show thanks/praise; **to pay t. to** = to praise. **trib•u•tar•y.** 1. *adj.* (person) who pays tribute. 2. *n.* river which flows into a larger river.

trice [traɪs] *n.* **in a t.** = very rapidly.

tri•cen•ten•ni•al [traɪsɛn'tɛnɪəl] *n.* anniversary of 300 years.

tri•chol•o•gy [trɪk'ɒlədʒɪ] *n.* study of the diseases of the hair. **tri•chol•o•gist,** *n.* person who studies the diseases of the hair.

trick [trɪk] 1. *n.* (a) clever action which can deceive/confuse s.o.; **to play a t. on s.o.** = to deceive/confuse s.o.; *inf.* **tricks of the trade** = clever dealings which are associated with a certain trade; **card tricks/magic tricks** = clever games with cards/with hats, handkerchiefs, etc., to amuse an audience; *inf.* **that should do the t.** = should do what is wanted/should make it work; *inf.* **he doesn't miss a t.** = he is very alert. (b) (*in card games*) points won at the end of a round. 2. *adj.* which deceives; **t. question** = one which is intended to cause s.o. to make a mistake. 3. *v.* to deceive/to confuse; **to t. s.o. into doing sth** = to deceive s.o. so that he does sth which he did not intend to do. **trick•er•y,** *n.* act of deceiving. **trick•i•ness,** *n.* being tricky. **trick•ster,** *n.* person who tricks, esp. s.o. who cheats. **trick•y,** *adj.* **(-ier, -iest)** (a) difficult/awkward. (b) *inf.* sly/deceitful/untrustworthy.

trick•le ['trɪkl] 1. *n.* small flow of water; **t. charger** = device which charges a car battery slowly. 2. *v.* to flow/move in a small quantity. **trick•le-down ef•fect,** *n.* supposed indirect benefit to the poor, claimed by some economists, that results from implementing economic policies that directly benefit the rich, as such policies may boost the economy generally.

tri•col•or ['trɪkələ] *n.* flag with three bands of color, esp. the national flag of France.

tri•cy•cle ['traɪsɪkl] *n.* three-wheeled pedal vehicle like a bicycle with two back wheels.

tri•dent ['traɪdənt] *n.* spear with three prongs.

tried [traɪd] *v. see* **try.**

tri•en•ni•al [traɪ'ɛnɪəl] *adj.* happening every three years.

tri•er ['traɪə] *n.* person who tries.

tri•fle ['traɪfl] 1. *n.* (a) small insignificant thing. (b) small amount. (c) dessert made of

cake/biscuits/jelly/jam/sherry and whipped cream. 2. *v.* **(with)** to play with/not to treat (sth) seriously. **tri•fler,** *n.* person who trifles with s.o./sth. **tri•fling,** *adj.* slight/very small.

trig•ger ['trɪgə] 1. *n.* small metal lever on a gun which you pull to fire it. 2. *v.* **to t. off** = to start (a series of things) happening. **trig•ger-hap•py,** *adj.* ready to shoot/ready to act quickly without thinking.

trig•o•nom•e•try [trɪgə'nɒmɪtrɪ] *n.* science which deals with the relationships between the sides and angles of triangles.

trike [traɪk] *n. inf.* tricycle.

tri•lat•er•al [traɪ'lætrəl] *adj.* with three sides.

tri•lin•gual [traɪ'lɪŋgwəl] *adj.* (person) who can speak three languages.

trill [trɪl] 1. *n.* (a) warbling song (like a bird). (b) (*in music*) two notes rapidly repeated. 2. *v.* to warble/to sing like a bird.

tril•lion ['trɪljən] *n.* (a) one and 12 zeros. (b) *esp. Brit.* one and 18 zeros.

tri•lo•bite ['traɪəbaɪt] *n.* ancient shellfish found in fossils.

tril•o•gy ['trɪlədʒɪ] *n.* novel/play in three separate related parts.

trim [trɪm] 1. *n.* (a) state of fitness or preparedness. (b) cutting (of hair/bush, etc.). (c) decoration (on a car). 2. *adj.* **(trimmer, trimmest)** neat. 3. *v.* **(trimmed)** (a) to cut (sth) so that it is tidy. (b) to cut back; to reduce. (c) to ornament/to decorate. (d) (*on a sailboat*) to put sails into the best position. (e) to change your (political) opinions to fit the current popular trend. **trim•ly,** *adv.* in a trim way. **trim•mer,** *n.* person/device which trims; **hedge t.** = electric cutter for hedges. **trim•ming,** *n.* (a) ornament added to decorate sth; **roast pork with all the trimmings** = with the usual sauces and vegetables. (b) **trimmings** = pieces cut off (a hedge, etc.) when it is being trimmed. **trim•ness,** *n.* being trim.

tri•ma•ran ['traɪməræn] *n.* yacht with three parallel hulls.

tri•ni•tro•tol•u•ene [traɪnaɪtrəʊ'tɒljuiːn] *n.* high explosive/TNT.

trin•i•ty ['trɪnɪtɪ] *n.* (a) group of three. (b) **the T.** = the three persons in the Christian God—the Father, Son and Holy Ghost.

trin•ket ['trɪŋkɪt] *n.* cheap ornament.

tri•o ['triːəʊ] *n.* (*pl.* **-os**) (a) piece of music for three instruments. (b) three musicians; group of three people.

trip [trɪp] 1. *n.* (a) journey; **day t.** = journey lasting one day. (b) switch which activates a motor/light, etc. (c) *Sl.* trance caused by drugs. 2. *v.* (**tripped**) (a) **to t. along** = to go along with light footsteps. (b) to catch your foot so that you stagger and fall. (c) to set off (a switch). (d) *Sl.* to go into a trance induced by drugs. **trip•me•ter,** *n.* dial on a car dashboard which shows how far you go on one particular journey. **trip•per,** *n.* person on a short (usu. one day) trip. **trip up,** *v.* to t. s.o. **up** = (i) to make s.o. fall down; (ii) to force s.o. to make a mistake. **trip•wire,** *n.* wire stretched low above the ground, which, when you touch it, sets off a gun/camera, etc.

tri•par•tite ['traɪ'pɑːtaɪt] *adj.* with three parts; (agreement) between three countries.

tripe [traɪp] *n.* (a) part of a cow's/sheep's stomach used as food. (b) *inf.* worthless speech or writing/nonsense.

tri•ple ['trɪpl] 1. *adj.* made of three parts; three times as big. 2. *v.* to become three times as large; to make (sth) three times as large. **tri•plet,** *n.* (a) (*in music*) three notes played quickly together. (b) one of three children born at the same birth. **tri•plex,** *adj.* with three layers. **trip•li•cate,** *n.* **in t.** = in three copies.

tri•pod ['traɪpɒd] *n.* stand with three legs.

trip•tych ['trɪptɪk] *n.* religious picture formed of three parts, often placed on or above an altar.

trite [traɪt] *adj.* very ordinary/unexciting (remark). **trite•ly,** *adv.* in a trite way. **trite•ness,** *n.* being trite.

tri•umph ['traɪəmf] 1. *n.* (a) great victory. (b) celebration of a victory. 2. *v.* (a) **to t. over s.o.** = to win a victory over s.o. (b) to show that you are very glad that you won a victory. **tri•um•phal** [traɪ'ʌmfl] *adj.* referring to triumph; **t. arch** = archway set up to celebrate a victory. **tri•um•phant,** *adj.* victorious. **tri•um•phant•ly,** *adv.* in victory.

tri•um•vi•rate [traɪ'ʌmvɪrət] *n.* group of three people who rule/manage.

triv•et ['trɪvət] *n.* (a) small three-legged stand for a kettle, pot, etc. over a fire. (b) stand for putting under a hot plate, pot, etc. to protect a table.

triv•i•al ['trɪvɪəl] *adj.* not important; ordinary. **triv•i•a,** *n. pl.* unimportant details. **triv•i•al•i•ty** [trɪvɪ'ælɪtɪ] *n.* being unimportant; unimportant detail. **triv•i•al•ize,** *v.* to make (sth) trivial. **triv•i•al•ly,** *adv.* in a trivial way.

tro•chee ['trəʊkiː] *n.* poetic measure made of one strong beat followed by a weak one. **tro•cha•ic** [trəʊ'keɪɪk] *adj.* referring to trochee.

trod, trodden [trɒd, 'trɒdn] *v. see* tread.

trog•lo•dyte ['trɒglədaɪt] *n.* person who lives in a cave.

troi•ka ['trɔɪkə] *n.* (a) Russian carriage pulled by three horses. (b) three people holding power together (usu.) in Communist countries).

troll [trəʊl] *n.* (*in Scandinavia*) bad-tempered dwarf.

trol•ley ['trɒlɪ] *n.* trolley car. **trol•ley car,** *n.* car which works on electricity taken from overhead wires by contact poles.

trol•lop ['trɒləp] *n.* immoral woman.

trom•bone [trɒm'bəʊn] *n.* brass wind instrument with a sliding tube. **trom•bon•ist,** *n.* person who plays the trombone.

troop [truːp] 1. *n.* (a) group of people. (b) group of Boy Scouts. (c) **troops** = soldiers; **t. ship/t. train** = ship/train which carries soldiers. 2. *v.* to move in a large group. **troop•er,** *n.* (a) cavalry soldier. (b) state police officer.

tro•phy ['trəʊfɪ] *n.* (a) prize given for winning a competition. (b) thing taken from the enemy and kept as a prize.

trop•ic ['trɒpɪk] *n.* (a) **T. of Cancer/of Capricorn** = two imaginary lines running around the earth, parallel to the equator, and about 23° north/south of it. (b) **the tropics** = the hot areas of the world lying between these two imaginary lines. **trop•i•cal,** *adj.* very hot; (plant, etc.) growing in the tropics.

tro•pism ['trɒpɪzəm] *n.* growth of a plant towards or away from sth.

trop•o•sphere ['trɒpəsfɪə] *n.* layer of atmosphere between the surface of the earth and the stratosphere.

trot ['trɒt] 1. *n.* running with short regular steps; **they broke into a t.** = started to run. 2. *v.* (**trotted**) to run with short regular steps; *inf.* **to t. out** = to produce or bring out for display, etc. **trot•ter,** *n.* pig's foot cooked for food.

troth [trəʊθ] *n.* (*old*) promise.

trou•ba•dour ['truːbəduːə] *n.* wandering medieval singer.

trou•ble ['trʌbl] 1. *n.* (a) misfortune. (b) problem/difficult situation; **it's just asking for t.** = that type of behavior will simply cause problems for you; **he's in t. with the police** = has been accused by the police of a crime; **to get s.o. into t.** = (i) to cause s.o. to be accused of doing sth wrong; (ii) to make s.o. pregnant. (c) care which is put into an action. (d) illness; mechanical defect. 2. *v.* (a) to worry (s.o.). (b) to create problems for (s.o.); to bother (s.o.). (c) to bother (**to do sth**). **trou•ble•mak•er,** *n.* person who creates problems/who stirs up unrest. **trou•ble•shoot•er,** *n.* person whose job is to sort out problems. **trou•ble•some,** *adj.* causing trouble. **trou•ble spot,** *n.* area where trouble is likely to occur.

trough [trɒf] *n.* (a) large container for animal food or drink; **horse t./water t.** = container for water for horses to drink. (b) low place; low point between two peaks (on a graph); low-pressure area in the atmosphere; low part of the sea between two waves.

trounce [traʊns] *v.* to beat (s.o.) soundly.

troupe [truːp] *n.* company (of actors/circus clowns, etc.). **troup•er,** *n.* member of a troupe.

trou•sers ['traʊzəz] *n. pl.* **(pair of)** t. = outer clothes which cover the legs and the lower part of the body.

trous•seau ['truːsəʊ] *n.* clothes and linen collected by the bride before her wedding.

trout [traʊt] *n.* (*pl.* **trout**) type of edible freshwater fish.

trove [trəʊv] *adj. see* **treas•ure.**

trow•el ['traʊəl] *n.* (a) small hand spade used in gardening. (b) tool with a flat blade used for spreading mortar between bricks.

troy [trɔɪ] *n.* **t. weight** = system for weighing gold/silver/precious gems.

tru•ant ['truːənt] *adj. & n.* (child) who is absent from school without permission. **tru•an•cy** ['truːənsɪ] *n.* being away from school without permission.

truce [truːs] *n.* period when two armies/enemies, etc., agree to stop fighting temporarily.

truck [trʌk] *n.* (a) large motor vehicle for carrying goods, etc. (b) small hand cart. (c) **to have no t. with** = not to have anything to do with. (d) fruit and vegetables grown for sale in the market. **truck•driv•er, trucker,** *n.* driver of a truck. **truck•ing,** *n.* transport of goods, etc. by truck. **truck•load,** *n.* amount carried in a truck.

truck•le ['trʌkl] *v.* to give in (**to** s.o.) weakly. **truck•le bed,** *n.* (*also* **trundle bed**) low bed which can be pushed under another bed when not in use.

truc•u•lence ['trʌkjʊləns] *n.* being truculent. **truc•u•lent,** *adj.* threatening/fierce; eager to quarrel. **truc•u•lent•ly,** *adv.* in a truculent way.

trudge [trʌdʒ] 1. *n.* tiring walk. 2. *v.* to walk heavily.

true [truː] 1. *adj.* (**-er, -est**) (a) correct. (b) real. (c) correctly adjusted; **t. north** = north toward the north pole, and not the magnetic north. (d) faithful. 2. *adv.* correctly; **to come t.** = to happen as forecast. 3. *n.* **out of t.** = not quite straight/not correctly adjusted. **true-blue,** *adj.* totally loyal. **true•ness,** *n.* being true. **tru•ly,** *adv.* really; **yours t.** = ending of a slightly formal letter.

truf•fle ['trʌfl] *n.* (a) type of round black or white edible fungus found under the earth. (b) soft chocolate-covered candy (usu. flavored with rum, champagne, etc.).

trug [trʌg] *n.* (*esp. Brit.*) long shallow basket for picking flowers.

tru•ism ['truːɪzəm] *n.* saying which is quite obviously true and therefore need not be said.

trump [trʌmp] 1. *n.* (*in card games*) suit which is chosen as being of higher value than the other suits; **t. card** = advantage which is kept ready for use to win an argument. 2. *v.* (a) **to t. a card** = to play a card of the suit which is trumps, and so win. (b) **to t. up** = to invent; **trumped-up charge** = false charge.

trump•er•y ['trʌmpərɪ] *adj.* (*formal*) useless and showy.

trum•pet ['trʌmpɪt] 1. *n.* brass musical instrument with three keys. 2. *v.* (a) to play the trumpet. (b) to make a loud noise. (c) (*of elephant*) to call. **trum•pet•er,** *n.* person who plays the trumpet.

trun•cat•ed [trʌn'keɪtɪd] *adj.* cut off; shortened.

trun•cheon ['trʌnʃn] *n.* short, heavy stick used by police officers.

trun•dle ['trʌndl] *v.* to roll/to push along (sth heavy). **trun•dle bed,** *n. see* **truck•le bed.**

trunk [trʌŋk] *n.* (a) main stem (of a tree); body (of a person). (b) long nose (of an elephant). (c) large box for sending/storing clothes, etc., in. (d) back part of a car (where luggage, etc. can be put). (e) **trunks** = men's shorts for swimming.

truss [trʌs] 1. *n.* (*pl.* **-es**) (a) beam holding up a bridge/a roof. (b) belt to support a hernia. 2. *v.* (a) to support with a truss. (b) to tie up (a chicken) ready for the oven; to tie up (a prisoner).

trust [trʌst] 1. *n.* (a) confidence that sth is correct/is good/will work well, etc.; **to take on t.** = without examining to see if it is all right. (b) hope. (c) responsibility. (d) passing of goods/money to s.o. who will look after it; **t. fund** = money/property, etc. administered by a trustee for the benefit of a person, company, or institution. (e) illegal grouping of business companies to eliminate competition, control prices, etc. 2. *v.* (a) to be sure of (s.o.); to have confidence in (s.o.); *inf.* **t. him to be late** = as usual, he is late. (b) to hope. **trust•ee** [trʌs'tiː]

n. person who has charge of money/property, etc. held in trust for a person/company, or institution. **trust•ee•ship,** *n.* position of trustee. **trust•ful, trust•ing,** *adj.* full of confidence (in s.o.). **trust•ful•ly, trust•ing•ly,** *adv.* in a trustful/trusting way. **trust•wor•thi•ness,** *n.* being trustworthy. **trust•wor•thy,** *adj.* which can be depended upon. **trust•y** ['trʌstɪ] 1. *n.* prisoner who is given certain responsibilities and privileges because he can be trusted. 2. *adj.* (**-ier, -iest**) which can be depended upon.

truth [truːθ] *n.* thing which is true; true story; **to tell s.o. a few home truths** = to tell s.o. what you think of them/to criticize s.o.'s behavior/character. **truth•ful,** *adj.* (person) who always tells the truth. **truth•ful•ly,** *adv.* in a truthful way. **truth•ful•ness,** *n.* being truthful.

try [traɪ] 1. *n.* attempt (to do sth). 2. *v.* (a) to test. (b) to attempt. (c) to judge (a case/a person) in court. **try•ing,** *adj.* difficult to put up with. **try on,** *v.* to put (clothes) on to see if they fit. **try out,** *v.* to test (sth).

try•pan•o•some [trɪ'pænəsəum] *n.* parasite, carried by the tsetse fly, causing sleeping sickness.

tryst [trɪst] *n.* (*old*) lovers' meeting.

tsar [zɑː] *n.* former title of the emperor of Russia.

tset•se ['tsetsɪ] *n.* type of African fly which transmits disease by biting.

tub [tʌb] *n.* (a) round (wooden) container; small, round cardboard or plastic box for ice cream, butter, etc. (b) bathtub. (c) *inf.* old ship. **tub•bi•ness,** *n.* being tubby. **tub•by,** *adj.* (**-ier, -iest**) *inf.* fat.

tu•ba ['tjuːbə] *n.* large bass brass instrument.

tube [tjuːb] *n.* (a) long pipe for carrying liquids or gas; **inner t.** = rubber tube holding air inside a tire. (b) long pipe (in the body); **bronchial tubes** = tubes leading to the lungs. (c) soft pipe with a screw top which contains toothpaste, etc. (d) (*esp. Brit.*) subway. (e) glass bulb in a television set which projects the picture on the screen. **tube•less,** *adj.* (tire) with no inner tube. **tub•ing,** *n.* tubes made of metal/plastic, etc. **tu•bu•lar** ['tjuːbjulə] *adj.* like a tube.

tu•ber ['tjuːbə] *n.* thick piece of root which can be planted to make a new plant grow. **tu•ber•ous,** *adj.* (root) which produces tubers.

tu•ber•cle ['tjuːbəkl] *n.* rounded bump on the skin; scar caused by tuberculosis. **tu•ber•cu•lo•sis** [tjuːbɜːkjuˈləusɪs] *n.* disease of the lungs. **tu•ber•cu•lar** [tjuː-ˈbɜːkjulə] *adj.* suffering from tuberculosis. **tu•ber•cu•lin-test•ed,** *adj.* (milk/cow)

which has been tested to show that it is free from tuberculosis.

tuck [tʌk] 1. *n.* little fold/pleat in a piece of cloth. 2. *v.* (a) to fold (a blanket) around s.o. and push the ends underneath. (b) to fold cloth into little pleats. **tuck in,** *v.* (a) to push the edge of a piece of cloth underneath s.o. to keep them warm. (b) *inf.* (*also* **tuck away**) to eat a large quantity of food. **tuck up,** *v.* **to tuck s.o. up (in bed)** = to push the edge of the bedclothes around (s.o.) to keep them warm.

Tues•day ['tjuːzdeɪ] *n.* second day of the week/day between Monday and Wednesday.

tu•fa ['tjuːfə] *n.* type of porous volcanic rock.

tuft [tʌft] *n.* small bunch of grass/hair, etc. **tuft•ed,** *adj.* with tufts.

tug [tʌg] 1. *n.* (a) sudden pull. (b) tugboat. 2. *v.* (**tugged**) to pull hard. **tug•boat,** *n.* powerful boat used for towing barges/ships. **tug-of-war,** *n.* (a) competition where two teams pull against each other on a strong rope. (b) bitter struggle between opposing forces.

tu•i•tion [tjuːˈɪʃn] *n.* charge for teaching/instruction, as at a private school or college.

tu•lip ['tjuːlɪp] *n.* common spring bulb with brilliant flowers shaped like cups. **tu•lip tree,** *n.* large evergreen tree, with big shiny leaves and large white flowers.

tulle [tjuːl] *n.* thin silk/artificial material like a veil.

tum•ble ['tʌmbl] 1. *n.* fall. 2. *v.* (a) to fall (**down**). (b) to come down in confusion. **tum•ble-down,** *adj.* (house) which is falling down/coming to pieces. **tum•bler,** *n.* round, straight glass for drinking. **tum•ble-dry,** *v.* to put laundry in a machine which dries it with warm air.

tu•mes•cent [tjuːˈmesənt] *adj.* swollen.

tum•my ['tʌmɪ] *n.* *inf.* stomach. **tum•my ache,** *n.* *inf.* pain in the stomach.

tu•mor, *Brit.* **tu•mour** ['tjuːmə] *n.* abnormal growth in or on the body.

tu•mult ['tjuːmʌlt] *n.* loud, excited noise (of a crowd). **tu•mul•tu•ous** [tjuːˈmʌltjuəs] *adj.* noisy/excited.

tu•mu•lus ['tjuːmjuləs] *n.* (*pl.* **-li**) mound of earth covering an ancient tomb.

tun [tʌn] *n.* large barrel (for wine/beer).

tu•na ['tjuːnə] *n.* (*pl.* **tuna**) large sea fish (used for food).

tun•dra ['tʌndrə] *n.* Arctic plain with no trees.

tune [tjuːn] 1. *n.* (a) series of musical notes which make a recognizable melody; **he's changed his t.** = he has changed his way of thinking; *inf.* **to the t. of $100** = at least $100. (b) **in t.** = with the correct musical tone; **in t. with** = harmonizing with/similar to. 2. *v.* (a) to adjust (a musical instrument) so that it has the correct tone. (b) to adjust (an engine) so that it works more efficiently. **tune•ful**, *adj.* full of catchy tunes. **tune in**, *v.* to adjust a radio to a particular station. **tun•er**, *n.* piano t. = person who tunes pianos. **tune up**, *v.* (a) to adjust instruments before playing. (b) to adjust (an engine) so that it works more efficiently. **tun•ing fork**, *n.* metal fork which gives a correct note when it is hit.

tung•sten ['tʌŋstən] *n.* (*element:* W) hard gray metal used to make steel and electric light filaments.

tu•nic ['tjuːnɪk] *n.* (a) loose top garment. (b) (*esp. Brit.*) short jacket worn by soldiers/policemen, etc.

tun•nel ['tʌnl] 1. *n.* long hole in the ground. 2. *v.* (**tunneled, tunnelled**) to make a long passage under the ground.

tur•ban ['tɜːbən] *n.* long piece of cloth wrapped around the head to cover the hair.

tur•bid ['tɜːbɪd] *adj.* muddy (water). **tur•bid•i•ty** [tɜːˈbɪdɪtɪ] *n.* being turbid.

tur•bine ['tɜːbaɪn] *n.* engine driven by the force of water/steam which turns a wheel with blades.

tur•bo-jet ['tɜːbəʊˈdʒet] *n.* jet engine driven by a turbine; aircraft powered by this engine. **tur•bo•prop** ['tɜːbəʊˈprɒp] *n.* jet and propeller engine driven by a turbine; aircraft powered by this engine.

tur•bot ['tɜːbət] *n.* (*pl.* **turbot**) large flat edible sea fish.

tur•bu•lent ['tɜːbjulənt] *adj.* (a) disturbed/violently moving (water/air). (b) likely to riot. **tur•bu•lence**, *n.* disturbance in the air causing an aircraft to rock suddenly; disturbance in water.

turd [tɜːd] *n. Sl.* (*vulgar*) lump of human excreta.

tu•reen [tjuˈriːn] *n.* large bowl for serving soup.

turf [tɜːf] 1. *n.* (a) stretch of grassy area. (b) (*pl.* **turves** [tɜːvz]) piece of grass with soil around its roots which can be planted to form a lawn; (*in Ireland*) block of peat for burning. (c) **the t.** = the world of horse racing. 2. *v.* to make a lawn with turf.

tur•gid ['tɜːdʒɪd] *adj.* swollen; grand-sounding, meaningless (words). **tur•gid•ly**, *adv.* in a turgid way.

Turk [tɜːk] *n.* person from Turkey.

tur•key ['tɜːkɪ] *n.* large domestic bird, often eaten at Thanksgiving and Christmas.

Turk•ish ['tɜːkɪʃ] 1. *adj.* referring to Turkey; **T. bath** = steam bath after which you plunge into cold water. **T. delight** = scented sweet jelly eaten in lumps. 2. *n.* language spoken in Turkey.

tur•mer•ic ['tɜːmərɪk] *n.* yellow spice, used esp. in curries.

tur•moil ['tɜːmɔɪl] *n.* wild disorder.

turn [tɜːn] 1. *n.* (a) circular movement (of a wheel, etc.); **the meat is done to a t.** = properly cooked all through. (b) change of direction/condition; **to take a t. for the better/for the worse** = suddenly to start to get better/worse; **at the t. of the century** = about 1900. (c) sudden attack (of fear, shock, etc.). (d) chance to do sth in order; (*of several people*) **to take (it in) turns to do sth** = to do sth, each person doing it in order. (e) way of speaking/thinking/acting. (f) **to do s.o. a good t.** = to do sth to help them. (g) performance (in a variety show). 2. *v.* (a) to go around; to make (sth) go around in a circle. (b) to change direction; (*of tide*) to start to rise/fall; **his luck turned** = changed. (c) to change (**into** sth else); (*of milk*) to go sour. (d) to aim (a gun). (e) **to t. s.o.'s head** = to make s.o. very proud/vain; **to t. s.o.'s stomach** = to make s.o. feel sick. (f) to shape (a round piece of wood) by carving it on a lathe. (g) to pass a particular point in time; **it's turned seven** = it is past seven o'clock; **he's turned fifty** = he's more than fifty years old. **turn•a•bout**, *n.* act of turning to face in another direction. **turn a•side**, *v.* to move to one side. **turn a•way**, *v.* (a) to move away. (b) to send (s.o.) away. **turn back**, *v.* (a) to turn and go back in the opposite direction. (b) to send (s.o.) back. **turn•coat**, *n.* person who switches from one opinion to another. **turn down**, *v.* (a) to refuse. (b) to reduce. (c) to fold back (a sheet on a bed), so that the pillow is uncovered. **turn•er**, *n.* person who makes chair legs, etc., on a lathe. **turn•e•ry**, *n.* (a) trade of a turner. (b) articles which are turned on a lathe. **turn in**, *v.* (a) to hand back (equipment) to s.o. in authority. (b) *inf.* to go to bed. (c) **to t. oneself in** = to give oneself up to the police. **turn•ing**, *n.* (a) action of moving in a circle/of changing direction. (b) point where sth turns. **turn•ing point**, *n.* important/decisive moment. **turn off**, *v.* (a) to switch off. (b) to change direction away from a straight line. **turn on**, *v.* (a) to switch on. (b) to attack. **turn out**, *v.* (a) to throw (s.o.) out. (b) to produce. (c) to switch off. (d) to happen. (e) to come out (in a crowd); show up. (g) **well turned-out** = well dressed. **turn•out**, *n.*

æ **back**, aː **farm**, ɒ **top**, aɪ **pipe**, aʊ **how**, aɪə **fire**, aʊə **flower**, ɔː **bought**, ɔɪ **toy**, e **fed**, eə **hair**, eɪ **take**, ə **afraid**, əʊ **boat**, aʊə **lower**, ɜː **word**, iː **heap**, ɪ **hit**, ɪə **hear**, uː **school**, ʊ **book**, ʌ **but**, b **back**, d **dog**, ð **then**, dʒ **just**, f **fog**, g **go**, h **hand**, j **yes**, k **catch**, l **last**, m **mix**, n **nut**, ŋ **sing**, p **penny**, r **round**, s **some**, ʃ **short**, t **too**, tʃ **chop**, θ **thing**, v **voice**, w **was**, z **zoo**, ʒ **treasure**

crowd of people who turn out. **turn o•ver,** *v.* (a) to move (the page of a book) so that you can read the next one; **to t. o. a new leaf** = to be better behaved. (b) to think about. (c) to roll over. (d) (*of engine*) to run gently. (e) to have sales of (a certain amount). (f) to hand (a criminal) to the police. **turn•o•ver,** *n.* (a) type of pie made with pastry turned over a filling. (b) change (in staff). (c) amount of sales.

turn•pike, *n.* highway with tolls.

turn•stile, *n.* gate which turns around on a pivot, allowing only one person to go through at a time. **turn•ta•ble,** *n.* (a) flat part of a record player which turns with the record on it. (b) flat turning platform with rails on it, to enable railroad locomotives to go off in a different direction. **turn up,** *v.* (a) to arrive; to be found. (b) to increase. (c) to roll or fold up the bottom of a garment to shorten it. (d) to unfold/unroll (a collar).

tur•nip ['tɜːnɪp] *n.* common vegetable, with a round white root.

tur•pen•tine ['tɜːpəntaɪn] *n.* oil which comes from fir trees, used for removing or thinning paint. **turps** [tɜːps] *n. inf.* turpentine.

tur•pi•tude ['tɜːpɪtjuːd] *n.* (*formal*) wickedness.

tur•quoise ['tɜːkwɔɪz] 1. *n.* green-blue precious stone. 2. *adj.* green-blue (color).

tur•ret ['tʌrɪt] *n.* small tower; small armored construction housing a gun (on a ship/tank,etc.). **tur•ret•ed,** *n.* with turrets.

tur•tle ['tɜːtl] *n.* sea reptile with a hard shell like a tortoise; **to turn t.** = to capsize. **tur•tle•dove,** *n.* type of wild pigeon with a soft, cooing call. **tur•tle•neck,** *n.* sweater with a high, usu. rolled, neck.

turves [tɜːvz] *n. see* turf.

tusk [tʌsk] *n.* long tooth coming far out from the mouth of some animals (such as elephants/walruses, etc.). **tusk•er,** *n. inf.* elephant.

tus•sah [tʌsə] *n.* type of coarse silk from India.

tus•sle ['tʌsl] 1. *n.* fight/argument. 2. *v.* to fight/to struggle.

tus•sock ['tʌsək] *n.* large tuft of grass.

tus•sore ['tʌsə] *n.* tussah.

tu•te•lage ['tjuːtəlɪdʒ] *n.* being responsible for s.o.; training/instruction given to a student.

tu•tor ['tjuːtə] 1. *n.* teacher (who teaches a student, esp. privately). 2. *v.* to act as a tutor to.

tu•to•ri•al [tjuːˈtɔːrɪəl] *n.* discussion meeting between a tutor and a student or small group of students.

tut•ti-frut•ti ['tʊtɪ'frʊtɪ] *n.* ice cream with pieces of preserved fruit in it.

tut-tut [tʌt'tʌt] 1. *n.* sound made to show you disapprove. 2. *v.* (**tut-tutted**) to make disapproving sounds.

tu•tu ['tuːtuː] *n.* girl ballet dancer's short stiff skirt.

tux•e•do [tʌk'siːdəʊ] *n.* (*pl.* -os) man's dinner jacket or an outfit including this jacket.

TV [tiː'viː] *n.* (a) television. (b) television set.

twad•dle ['twɒdl] *n. inf.* silly talk/nonsense.

twain [tweɪn] *n.* (*formal*) two things.

twang [twæŋ] 1. *n.* (a) sound made, such as when a guitar string is pulled and released. (b) **nasal t.** = accent made by speaking through the nose. 2. *v.* to make a twang.

tweak [twiːk] 1. *n.* sharp pull. 2. *v.* to pull suddenly.

tweed [twiːd] *n.* rough woolen cloth made of strands of different colors. **tweeds,** *n. pl.* clothes made of tweed.

tweet [twiːt] 1. *n.* little sound made by a small bird. 2. *v.* to make a little sound like a bird. **tweet•er,** *n.* loudspeaker which reproduces high sounds.

tweez•ers ['twiːzəz] *n. pl.* (**pair of**) t. = small pincers.

twelve [twelv] *n.* number 12. **twelfth** [twelfT] **12th,** *adj. & n.* referring to twelve; **the t. century** = period from 1100 to 1199.

twen•ty ['twentɪ] *n.* number 20; **she's in her twenties** = she is over twenty but under thirty years old. **twen•ti•eth, 20th,** *adj. & n.* referring to twenty; **the t. century** = period from 1900 to 1999.

twerp [twɜːp] *n. Sl.* stupid person.

twice [twaɪs] *adv.* two times; double; **he's t. my age** = two times as old as I am.

twid•dle ['twɪdl] *v.* to turn/to twist with no particular aim; **to t. your thumbs** = holding your hands together, to turn your thumbs around and around as a sign of not having anything to do.

twig [twɪg] *n.* little branch.

twi•light ['twaɪlaɪt] *n.* (period of) weak light between night and sunrise or between sunset and night.

twill [twɪl] *n.* thick cloth woven in diagonal lines.

twin [twɪn] 1. *adj. & n.* (child) born at the same birth as another; **identical twins** = two children born at the same time who look very similar. 2. *adj. & prefix* made of two similar parts. 3. *v.* (**twinned**) (**with**) to join or be combined.

twine [twaɪn] 1. *n.* thick rough string. 2. *v.* to twist around and around.

twinge [twɪndʒ] *n.* short sharp pain; small worry; **t. of guilt.**

twin•kle ['twɪŋkl] 1. *n.* little flicker of light; **with a t. in his eye** = with his eyes shining with amusement. 2. *v.* (a) to glitter. (b) (*of eyes*) to shine (with amusement/wickedness, etc.).

twin•kling, n. little flicker; **in the t. of an eye** = very fast.

twirl [twɜːl] 1. n. (a) spinning movement. (b) spiral shape. 2. v. (a) to spin around. (b) to twist in your fingers.

twirp [twəːp] n. twerp.

twist [twɪst] 1. n. (a) thing which has a twisted shape. (b) curve or turn; **t. in the road. (c)** act of twisting; **a new t. to the story** = an unexpected change. 2. v. (a) to turn around and around. (b) to wind (sth) around sth. (c) to bend in the wrong way; to sprain (an ankle); inf. **to t. s.o.'s arm** = to persuade s.o. to do what you want. (d) to change the meaning of (words). **twist•er,** n. (a) person or thing that twists. (b) whirlwind or tornado. **twist•y,** adj. which twists.

twit [twɪt] 1. n. Sl. silly person. 2. v. (**twitted**) to make fun of (s.o.).

twitch [twɪtʃ] 1. n. (pl. **-es**) sudden jerk/sudden movement. 2. v. to jerk suddenly/to make a sudden movement.

twit•ter ['twɪtə] 1. n. little calls made by birds; **she was all in a t.** = very excited. 2. v. to make little sounds (like birds).

twixt [twɪkst] prep. (old) between.

two [tuː] n. number 2. (a) **one or t.** = a few; **to put t. and t. together** = to come to a conclusion by comparing various facts; **to be of t. minds about sth** = not to be able to decide. **two-bit,** adj. inf. cheap/second-rate. **two-edged,** adj. (a) (knife) with two sharp edges. (b) (remark/action) which has two results (one good, one bad). **two-faced,** adj. deceitful. **two•fold,** adv. twice as much. **two•leg•ged** [tuːˈlegɪd] adj. with two legs. **two•pen•ny** ['tʌpnɪ] adj. costing or having a value of two pennies. **two-piece,** adj. made of two pieces; **t.-p. suit** = suit made of a jacket and skirt/trousers. **two-ply,** adj. made of two threads/two pieces. **two-seat•er,** n. car/aircraft with only two seats. **two•some,** n. two people (playing a game); game for two people. **two•step,** n. dance with smooth steps. **two-stroke,** adj. (engine) with two pistons. **two-time,** v. inf. to be unfaithful (to a girlfriend/boyfriend). **two- tim•er,** n. inf. unfaithful person. **two-tone,** adj. colored with two tones of the same color. **two-way,** adj. going in two directions.

ty•coon [taɪˈkuːn] n. wealthy businessman.

ty•ing ['taɪɪŋ] v. see **tie.**

tyke [taɪk] n. child, esp. a small boy.

tym•pa•num [tɪmˈpɑːnəm] n. (formal) eardrum.

type [taɪp] 1. n. (a) sort/kind. (b) example; **a real conservative t.** = a good example of a conservative. (c) small pieces of metal with letters molded on them, used for printing; collection of pieces of metal for printing. 2. v. to write with a typewriter. **type•cast,** v. (typecast) to give (an actor) the same type of part all the time. **type•script,** n. document typed on a typewriter. **type•set•ter,** n. person who sets manuscripts in type ready for printing. **type•set•ting,** n. action of setting type; type which has been set. **type•writ•er,** n. machine which prints letters on a piece of paper when you press the keys. **type•writ•ten,** adj. (document) which has been written with a typewriter. **typ•ing,** n. (a) action of writing letters with a typewriter; **t. pool** = group of typists who work for several departments in a company; **t. paper** = special paper for typewriters. (b) action of classifying into types; **blood t.** = classification of blood into certain groups. **typ•ist,** n. person whose job is to type letters on a typewriter. **ty•pog•ra•pher,** n. specialist in typography. **ty•po•graph•ic(al)** [taɪpəˈgræfɪk(l)] adj. referring to typography. **ty•pog•ra•phy** [taɪˈpɒgrəfɪ] n. (a) art of arranging material for printing/of designing a printed page. (b) study of the appearance of printed characters.

ty•phoid ['taɪfɔɪd] adj. & n. **t. (fever)** = serious disease caused by infected food or drink.

ty•phoon [taɪˈfuːn] n. tropical storm (in the Far East).

ty•phus ['taɪfəs] n. serious fever, where the virus is carried by lice.

typ•i•cal ['tɪpɪkl] adj. obviously belonging to a particular group; characteristic; **that's t. of him** = that's exactly what he always does. **typ•i•cal•ly,** adv. in a typical way. **typ•i•fy,** v. to be an excellent example of.

ty•po ['taɪpəʊ] n. typesetting mistake.

tyr•an•ny ['tɪrənɪ] n. cruel rule by an undemocratic government/ruler. **ty•ran•ni•cal, tyr•annous** [tɪˈrænɪkl, 'tɪrənəs] adj. cruel. **tyr•an•nize,** v. to rule (s.o.) in a cruel way. **ty•rant** ['taɪrənt] n. cruel, undemocratic ruler.

tyre ['taɪə] n. Brit. see **tire.**

ty•ro, tiro ['taɪrəʊ] n. (pl. **-os**) complete beginner/person with no experience.

Uu

U, u [juː]; **U-turn** = turn made by a car in a road so that it faces in the opposite direction; **to do a U-turn** = change policy completely. **U-boat,** *n.* German submarine.

U *symbol for* uranium.

u•biq•ui•tous [juːˈbɪkwɪtəs] *adj.* (thing) which is/which seems to be everywhere. **u•biq•ui•ty,** *n.* being everywhere.

ud•der [ˈʌdə] *n.* bag producing milk which hangs under the body of a cow or goat.

UFO [juːefˈəu] *n. abbrev. for* unidentified flying object.

ugh [ɜː] *inter. showing a feeling that something is unpleasant.*

ug•ly [ˈʌglɪ] *adj.* (-ier, -iest) (a) not pleasant to look at. (b) dangerous (mood). **ug•li•ness,** *n.* being ugly.

UHF [juːeɪtʃˈef] *abbrev. for* ultrahigh frequency.

UHT [juːeɪtʃˈtiː] *adj. abbrev. for* ultrahigh temperature.

U.K. [juːˈkeɪ] *abbrev. for* United Kingdom.

u•ku•le•le [juːkəˈleɪlɪ] *n.* very small guitar.

ul•cer [ˈʌlsə] *n.* sore on the body. **ul•cer•ate,** *v.* to cover with ulcers; to become covered with ulcers. **ul•cer•a•tion,** *n.* being covered with ulcers; place where an ulcer is. **ul•cer•ous,** *adj.* covered with ulcers.

ul•lage [ˈʌlɪdʒ] *n.* amount of missing liquid which would make a container full.

ul•na [ˈʌlnə] *n.* one of the two bones of the lower arm.

ul•te•ri•or [ʌlˈtɪərɪə] *adj.* hidden/secret; **u. motive** = reason for doing sth. which anticipates the result of the action.

ul•ti•mate [ˈʌltɪmət] *adj.* final. **ul•ti•mate•ly,** *adv.* finally.

ul•ti•ma•tum [ʌltɪˈmeɪtəm] *n.* message sent to an opponent stating that unless demands are met by a certain time, violent action (usu. war or a strike) will start.

ultra- [ˈʌltrə] *prefix meaning* extremely/very. **ul•tra•ma•rine** [ʌltrəməˈriːn] *adj. & n.* (color) of deep sea blue. **ul•tra•mod•ern,** *adj.* extremely modern. **ul•tra•son•ic,** *adj.* (sound waves) which cannot be heard by humans. **ul•tra•sound,** *n.* very high frequency sound wave, used to detect objects in the body or under water. **ul•tra•vi•o•let** [ʌltrə-ˈvaɪələt] *adj.* (light rays) which are beyond the violet of the spectrum and which tan the skin. **ul•tra vi•res,** *adv.* (acting) beyond one's powers.

um•bel [ˈʌmbl] *n.* flower head made of many single flowers on long stalks. **um•bel•lif•er•ous** [ʌmbəˈlɪfərəs] *adj.* (plant) with umbels.

um•ber [ˈʌmbə] *adj. & n.* brown (color) like earth; **burnt u.** = reddish-brown (color).

um•bil•i•cal [ʌmˈbɪlɪkl] *adj.* **u. cord** = tube joining the mother to her baby before birth, and through which nourishment passes.

um•bra [ˈʌmbrə] *n. (formal)* shadow.

um•brage [ˈʌmbrɪdʒ] *n.* **to take u. at** = to feel insulted by.

um•brel•la [ʌmˈbrelə] *n.* round shade of folded cloth which opens on a frame and is held over your head to keep off the rain; **u. organization** = large organization which includes small ones.

um•pire [ˈʌmpaɪə] 1. *n.* person who acts as a judge in tennis/baseball, etc., to see if the game is played according to the rules. 2. *v.* to act as umpire.

ump•teen [ʌmˈtiːn] *adj. & n. inf.* very large number. **ump•teenth,** *adj. inf.* referring to umpteen.

un- [ʌn] *prefix meaning* not; the opposite.

un, 'un [ʌn] *pron. inf.* one.

UN [ˈjuːen] *abbrev. for* United Nations.

un•a•bashed [ʌnəˈbæʃt] *adj.* not ashamed/not timid.

un•a•bat•ed [ʌnəˈbeɪtɪd] *adj.* with no loss of vigor.

un•a•ble [ʌnˈeɪbl] *adj.* not able.

un•a•bridged [ʌnəˈbrɪdʒd] *adj.* (text) which has not been shortened.

un•ac•cept•a•ble [ʌnəkˈseptəbl] *adj.* which cannot be accepted.

un•ac•com•pa•nied [ʌnəˈkʌmpnɪd] *adj.* alone; (singer/instrument) without any accompaniment.

un•ac•count•a•ble [ʌnəˈkauntəbl] *adj.* which cannot be explained. **un•ac•count•a•bly,** *adv.* without explanation. **un•ac•count•ed for,** *adj.* lost, with no explanation for the loss.

un•ac•cus•tomed [ʌnə'kʌstəmd] *adj.* not accustomed.

un•ac•quaint•ed [ʌnə'kweɪntɪd] *adj.* **to be u. with** = not knowing.

un•a•dul•ter•at•ed [ʌnə'dʌltəreɪtɪd] *adj.* pure; with nothing added.

un•af•fect•ed [ʌnə'fektɪd] *adj.* sincere/natural.

un•aid•ed [ʌn'eɪdɪd] *adj.* without help.

un•al•loyed [ʌnə'lɔɪd] *adj.* pure.

un•al•ter•a•ble [ʌn'ɒltrəbl] *adj.* which cannot be altered. **un•al•tered,** *adj.* which has not changed.

un•am•big•u•ous [ʌnæm'bɪgjuəs] *adj.* clear/not ambiguous.

u•nan•i•mous [jʊ'nænɪməs] *adj.* where everyone agrees. **u•nan•i•mous•ly,** *adv.* all agreeing together. **u•na•nim•i•ty** [junə'nɪmɪtɪ] *n.* being unanimous.

un•an•nounced [ʌnə'naʊnst] *adj.* which has not been announced.

un•ap•pe•tiz•ing [ʌn'æpɪtaɪzɪŋ] *adj.* which does not make you want to eat/which takes away your appetite.

un•ap•proach•a•ble [ʌnə'prəʊtʃəbl] *adj.* (person) who is very formal; (place) which cannot be approached easily.

un•armed [ʌn'ɑːmd] *adj.* with no weapons.

un•a•shamed [ʌnə'ʃeɪmd] *adj.* not ashamed.

un•asked [ʌn'ɑːskt] *adj.* without being asked.

un•as•sum•ing [ʌnə'sjuːmɪŋ] *adj.* quiet/modest.

un•at•tached [ʌnə'tætʃt] *adj.* not attached; not married.

un•at•tain•a•ble [ʌnə'teɪnəbl] *adj.* which cannot be reached.

un•at•tend•ed [ʌnə'tendɪd] *adj.* alone; not looked after.

un•at•trac•tive [ʌnə'træktɪv] *adj.* not attractive.

un•au•thor•ized [ʌn'ɔːˈTəraɪzd] *adj.* which is not permitted.

un•a•void•a•ble [ʌnə'vɔɪdəbl] *adj.* which cannot be avoided. **un•a•void•a•bly,** *adv.* in an unavoidable way.

un•a•ware [ʌnə'weə] *adj.* (**of**) not knowing/not aware. **un•a•wares,** *adv.* without noticing; **to catch s.o. u.** = by surprise.

un•bal•anced [ʌn'bælənst] *adj.* erratic/slightly mad.

un•bear•a•ble [ʌn'beərəbl] *adj.* intolerable. **un•bear•a•bly,** *adv.* so much that you cannot bear it.

un•beat•a•ble [ʌn'biːtəbl] *adj.* which cannot be beaten. **un•beat•en,** *adj.* which has not been beaten.

un•be•com•ing [ʌnbɪ'kʌmɪŋ] *adj.* which is not decent.

un•be•known [ʌnbɪ'nəʊn] *adj.* (*also* **unbeknownst**) *inf.* **u. to anyone** = without anyone knowing.

un•be•liev•a•ble [ʌnbɪ'liːvəbl] *adj.* incredible/which you cannot believe. **un•be•liev•a•bly,** *adv.* incredibly/amazingly. **un•be•liev•er,** *n.* person who does not believe in god.

un•bend [ʌn'bend] *v.* (**unbent**) to stop being stiff and start behaving naturally. **un•bend•ing,** *adj.* inflexible/harsh (rule).

un•bi•ased [ʌn'baɪəst] *adj.* impartial/not biased.

un•bid•den [ʌn'bɪdn] *adj.* (*formal*) without having been asked.

un•bleached [ʌn'bliːtʃt] *adj.* (cloth, etc.) which has not been bleached.

un•block [ʌn'blɒk] *v.* to take a blockage away from (sth).

un•blush•ing [ʌn'blʌʃɪŋ] *adj.* showing no shame.

un•bolt [ʌn'bəʊlt] *v.* to pull back the bolt on (a door).

un•born [ʌn'bɔːn] *adj.* not yet born.

un•bos•om [ʌn'bʊzəm] *v.* **to u. oneself to s.o.** = tell all one's private thoughts and troubles.

un•bound•ed [ʌn'baʊndɪd] *adj.* with no limits.

un•break•a•ble [ʌn'breɪkəbl] *adj.* which cannot be broken.

un•bri•dled [ʌn'braɪdld] *adj.* (passion) which is not controlled.

un•bro•ken [ʌn'brəʊkn] *adj.* which has not been broken.

un•bur•den [ʌn'bɜːdn] *v.* **to u. yourself to s.o.** = to tell (s.o.) all your troubles/secrets.

un•but•ton [ʌn'bʌtn] *v.* to undo the buttons on.

un•called-for [ʌn'kɔːldfɔː] *adj.* not necessary; not deserved.

un•can•ny [ʌn'kænɪ] *adj.* mysterious/which seems unnatural.

un•cared-for [ʌn'keədfɔː] *adj.* not looked after.

un•ceas•ing [ʌn'siːsɪŋ] *adj.* ceaseless; without any stopping.

un•cer•e•mo•ni•ous [ʌnserɪ'məʊnɪəs] *adj.* not dignified; not polite.

æ back, ɑː farm, ɒ top, aɪ pipe, aʊ how, aɪə fire, aʊə flower, ɔː bought, ɔɪ toy, e fed, eəhair, eɪ take, ə afraid, əʊ boat, əʊə lower, vː word, iː heap, ɪ hit, ɪə hear, uː school, ʊ book, ʌ but, b back, d dog, ð then, dʒ just, f fog, g go, h hand, j yes, k catch, l last, m mix, n nut, ŋ sing, p penny, r round, s some, ʃ short, t too, tʃ chop, θ thing, v voice, w was, z zoo, ʒ treasure

un•cer•e•mo•ni•ous•ly, *adv*. in an undignified way.

un•cer•tain [ʌn'sɜːtən] *adj*. (a) not certain/not sure. (b) which cannot be forecast. un•cer•tain•ty, *n*. being uncertain; lack of certainty.

un•chal•lenged [ʌn'tʃælənʒd] *adj*. without a challenge; **to let sth pass u.** = to let sth be said or written without questioning it.

un•char•ac•ter•is•tic [ʌnkærəkte'rɪstɪk] *adj*. not in character.

un•char•i•ta•ble [ʌn'tʃærɪtəbl] *adj*. unkind. un•char•i•ta•bly, *adv*. in an uncharitable way.

un•checked [ʌn'tʃekt] *adj*. with no check.

un•chris•tian [ʌn'krɪstʃn] *adj*. not kind/generous, etc.

un•ci•al ['ʌnsiəl] *adj*. & *n*. (rounded) letters used in early medieval manuscripts.

un•civ•i•lized [ʌn'sɪvɪlaɪzd] *adj*. not civilized; barbarous.

un•claimed [ʌn'kleɪmd] *adj*. which has not been claimed.

un•clas•si•fied [ʌn'klæsɪfaɪd] *adj*. not classified/not secret.

un•cle ['ʌŋkl] *n*. brother of your father or mother; husband of your aunt. **Un•cle Sam,** *n. inf*. person symbolizing the United States.

un•clean [ʌn'kliːn] *adj*. dirty.

un•cloud•ed [ʌn'klaʊdɪd] *adj*. not troubled/clear (liquid).

un•clut•tered [ʌn'klʌtəd] *adj*. tidy.

un•coil [ʌn'kɔɪl] *v*. to unwind.

un•com•fort•a•ble [ʌn'kʌmftəbl] *adj*. (a) not comfortable. (b) embarrassed; ill at ease. un•com•fort•a•bly, *adv*. in an uncomfortable way.

un•com•mit•ted [ʌnkə'mɪtɪd] *adj*. with no strong beliefs; (country) which has not decided which group to support; (voter) who has not decided which way to vote.

un•com•mon [ʌn'kɒmən] *adj*. (-er, -est) strange/odd; rare. un•com•mon•ly, *adv*. in an uncommon way; *inf*. very.

un•com•mu•ni•ca•tive [ʌnkə'mjuːnɪkətɪv] *adj*. silent/not talkative.

un•com•pli•men•ta•ry [ʌnkɒmplɪ'mentərɪ] *adj*. rude/not complimentary.

un•com•pro•mis•ing [ʌn'kɒmprəmaɪzɪŋ] *adj*. unwilling to give in or to change ideas.

un•con•cealed [ʌnkən'siːld] *adj*. open; not hidden.

un•con•cerned [ʌnkən'sɜːnd] *adj*. not worried/not bothered.

un•con•di•tion•al [ʌnkən'dɪʃnl] *adj*. without any conditions. un•con•di•tion•al•ly, *adv*. without insisting on conditions.

un•con•nect•ed [ʌnkə'nektɪd] *adj*. with no connection.

un•con•scious [ʌn'kɒnʃəs] 1. *adj*. (a) not conscious. (b) not aware. 2. *n*. **the u.** = deep level of the mind, with thoughts or feelings of which you are not conscious. un•con•scion•a•ble [ʌn'kɒnʃnəbl] *adj. inf*. unreasonable/excessive. un•con•scious•ly, *adv*. in an unconscious way. un•con•scious•ness, *n*. being unconscious.

un•con•sti•tu•tion•al [ʌnkɒnstɪ'tjuːʃnl] *adj*. going against the constitution.

un•con•test•ed [ʌnkən'testɪd] *adj*. (divorce) which is not disputed.

un•con•trol•la•ble [ʌnkən'trəʊləbl] *adj*. which cannot be controlled.

un•con•ven•tion•al [ʌnkən'venʃnl] *adj*. not usual.

un•cooked [ʌn'kʊkt] *adj*. not cooked.

un•co•op•er•a•tive [ʌnkəʊ'ɒpərətɪv] *adj*. not helpful/not cooperative.

un•cork [ʌn'kɔːk] *v*. to take the cork out of (a bottle).

un•cor•rob•o•rat•ed [ʌnkə'rɒbəreɪtɪd] *adj*. (evidence) which has not been confirmed.

un•cou•ple [ʌn'kʌpl] *v*. to detach (things) which are coupled.

un•couth [ʌn'kuːθ] *adj*. rude/badly brought up.

un•cov•er [ʌn'kʌvə] *v*. (a) to take the cover off. (b) to find (sth hidden).

un•crit•i•cal [ʌn'krɪtɪkl] *adj*. (person) who does not think critically.

un•crowned [ʌn'kraʊnd] *adj*. (king) who has not been crowned; (leader) who is like a king.

un•crush•a•ble [ʌn'krʌʃəbl] *adj*. (material) which does not make creases if it is crushed.

unc•tion ['ʌŋkʃn] *n*. putting oil on a person in a religious ceremony. unc•tu•ous ['ʌŋkʃuəs] *adj*. extremely and unpleasantly polite. unc•tu•ous•ly, *adv*. in an unctuous way.

un•cul•ti•vat•ed [ʌn'kʌltɪveɪtɪd] *adj*. (land) which has not been cultivated.

un•cut [ʌn'kʌt] *adj*. which has not been cut; (motion picture) which has not been censored; (book) with pages still joined together at the edges.

un•daunt•ed [ʌn'dɔːntɪd] *adj*. bold/with no fear.

un•de•cid•ed [ʌndɪ'saɪdɪd] *adj*. (person) who has not made up his mind.

un•de•clared [ʌndɪ'kleəd] *adj*. which has not been declared.

un•de•fend•ed [ʌndɪ'fendɪd] *adj*. not defended.

un•de•mand•ing [ʌndɪ'mɑːndɪŋ] *adj*. not difficult.

un•dem•o•crat•ic [ʌndemə'krætɪk] *adj.* not democratic.

un•de•ni•a•ble [ʌndɪ'naɪəbl] *adj.* which cannot be denied/which is quite clearly true.

un•der ['ʌndə] 1. *prep.* (a) in a place which is directly below. (b) less than; **u. an hour** = less than an hour. (c) being ruled/managed/commanded by s.o. (d) because of/according to (terms). (e) in a state of; **u. repair** = being repaired; **u. lock and key** = locked up; **u. treatment** = being treated; **u. control** = controlled. 2. *adv.* in a lower place; **to go u.** = to fail/to go bankrupt; *inf.* **down u.** = in Australia and New Zealand. 3. *adj.* lower/bottom. 4. **under-** *prefix meaning* less important; not enough.

un•der•a•chieve [ʌndərə'tʃiːv] *v.* to do less well than expected. **un•der•a•chiev•er,** *n.* student who does not do as well as expected.

un•der•age [ʌndər'eɪdz] *adj.* younger than the legal age.

un•der•arm ['ʌndərɑːm] *adv. & adj.* (thrown) with the hand kept lower than the shoulder.

un•der•car•riage ['ʌndəkærɪdʒ] *n.* aircraft's wheels and supports.

un•der•charge [ʌndə'tʃɑːdʒ] *v.* to charge less than you should.

un•der•clothes ['ʌndəkləʊðz] *n. pl.* clothes worn next to the skin, under other clothes.

un•der•coat ['ʌndəkəʊt] *n.* first coat of paint.

un•der•cov•er ['ʌndəkʌvə] *adj.* secret; **u. agent** = spy.

un•der•cur•rent ['ʌndəkʌrənt] *n.* (a) current of water under the surface. (b) hidden feelings.

un•der•cut ['ʌndəkʌt] *v.* (**undercut**) to sell more cheaply than (s.o.).

un•der•de•vel•oped [ʌndədɪ'veləpt] *adj.* not developed; not industrially advanced.

un•der•dog ['ʌndədɒg] *n.* person who is weaker/who always loses.

un•der•done ['ʌndədʌn] *adj.* not cooked enough; not too cooked.

un•der•es•ti•mate 1. *n.* [ʌndər'estɪmət] estimate which is less than the real quantity. 2. *v.* [ʌndər'estɪmeɪt] to estimate at less than the real quantity.

un•der•ex•posed [ʌndərɪk'spəʊzd] *adj.* (film) which has not been exposed sufficiently.

un•der•fed [ʌndə'fed] *adj.* with not enough to eat.

un•der•foot [ʌndə'fʊt] *adv.* under the feet/in the way.

un•der•gar•ment ['ʌndəgɑːmənt] *n.* piece of clothing worn next to the skin, under other clothes.

un•der•go [ʌndə'gəʊ] *v.* (**underwent, undergone**) to suffer/to experience.

un•der•grad•u•ate [ʌndə'grædjʊət] *n.* student at a college or university who has not yet received a degree.

un•der•ground 1. *adv.* [ʌndə'graʊnd] (a) under the ground. (b) in hiding. 2. *adj.* ['ʌndəgraʊnd] (a) under the ground. (b) secret; against the ruling authorities. 3. *n.* ['ʌndəgraʊnd] (a) (*esp. Brit.*) subway. (b) secret organization.

un•der•growth ['ʌndəgrəʊθ] *n.* bushes which grow thickly together under trees.

un•der•hand(ed) [ʌndə'hænd(ɪd)] *adj.* cunning; deceitful.

un•der•lay ['ʌndəleɪ] *v. see* **un•der•lie.**

un•der•lie [ʌndə'laɪ] *v.* (**underlay, underlain**) to be underneath; to be the basic cause (of sth). **un•der•ly•ing,** *adj.* basic (cause).

un•der•line ['ʌndəlaɪn] *v.* to write a line under (a word); to emphasize.

un•der•ling ['ʌndəlɪŋ] *n.* person who works for s.o. else.

un•der•manned [ʌndə'mænd] *adj.* with not enough staff.

un•der•mine [ʌndə'maɪn] *v.* to weaken.

un•der•neath [ʌndə'niːθ] 1. *prep.* under/beneath. 2. *adv.* under. 3. *n.* the bottom part.

un•der•nour•ished [ʌndə'nʌrɪʃt] *adj.* not having enough to eat.

un•der•paid [ʌndə'peɪd] *adj.* not paid enough.

un•der•pants ['ʌndəpænts] *n. pl.* men's undergarment for the lower part of the body.

un•der•pass ['ʌndəpɑːs] *n.* (*pl.* -es) place where one road goes under another.

un•der•pin [ʌndə'pɪn] *v.* (**underpinned**) to support. **un•der•pin•ning,** *n.* support.

un•der•priv•i•leged [ʌndə'prɪvɪlɪdʒd] *adj.* not having the same opportunities as other people.

un•der•rate [ʌndə'reɪt] *v.* to value (sth) less than you ought.

un•der•score [ʌndə'skɔː] *v.* to underline.

un•der•sea ['ʌndəsiː] *adj. & adv.* under the sea.

un•der•sec•re•tar•y [ʌndə'sekrətrɪ] *n.* official who is subordinate to a secretary of a government department.

un•der•sell [ʌndə'sel] *v.* (**undersold**) to sell more cheaply than (s.o.).

æ back, ɑː farm, ɒ top, aɪ pipe, aʊ how, aɪə fire, aʊə flower, ɔː bought, ɔɪ toy, e fed, eəhair, eɪ take, ə afraid, əʊ boat, əʊə lower, ɜː word, iː heap, ɪ hit, ɪə hear, uː school, ʊ book, ʌ but, b back, d dog, ð then, dʒ just, f fog, g go, h hand, j yes, k catch, l last, m mix, n nut, ŋ sing, p penny, r round, s some, ʃ short, t too, tʃ chop, θ thing, v voice, w was, z zoo, ʒ treasure

un•der•shirt ['ʌndəʃɜːt] *n.* men's light undergarment for the top half of the body.

un•der•side ['ʌndəsaɪd] *n.* side which is underneath.

un•der•signed ['ʌndəsaɪnd] *n.* **the u.** = people who have signed a letter.

un•der•size(d) ['ʌndəsaɪz(d)] *adj.* smaller than normal.

un•der•slung ['ʌndəslʌŋ] *adj.* (car chassis) which hangs below the axles.

un•der•staffed [ʌndə'stɑːft] *adj.* with not enough staff.

un•der•stand [ʌndə'stænd] *v.* (**understood**) (a) to know; to see the meaning of (sth). (b) to be an expert in (sth). (c) to think/to have an impression. (d) to take sth for granted, even if it is not written or spoken. (e) to know why (sth is done) and accept it. **un•der•stand•a•ble,** *adj.* which can be understood. **un•der•stand•a•bly,** *adv.* in a way which can be understood. **un•der•stand•ing.** 1. *n.* (a) ability to understand. (b) sympathy for another person's problems. (c) private agreement. 2. *adj.* sympathetic.

un•der•state [ʌndə'steɪt] *v.* to make (sth) seem less important than it really is. **un•der•state•ment,** *n.* statement which does not tell the facts forcefully enough.

un•der•stood [ʌndə'stʊd] *v.* see **un•der•stand.**

un•der•stud•y ['ʌndəstʌdɪ] 1. *n.* actor who learns a part in the play so as to be able to act it if the main actor is ill. 2. *v.* to be the understudy of (an actor).

un•der•take [ʌndə'teɪk] *v.* (**undertook, has undertaken**) to promise to do (sth); to accept to do (sth). **un•der•tak•er,** *n.* person who organizes funerals. **un•der•tak•ing,** *n.* (a) business. (b) promise. (c) job; **quite an u.** = very difficult job.

un•der•tone ['ʌndətəun] *n.* (a) quiet voice. (b) hidden feeling.

un•der•tow ['ʌndətəu] *n.* strong current under the surface of water, which flows in a different direction to that on the surface.

un•der•val•ue [ʌndə'væljuː] *v.* to value at less than the true rate.

un•der•wa•ter [ʌndə'wɔːtə] *adj.* below the surface of the water.

un•der•wear ['ʌndəweə] *n.* (*no pl.*) clothes worn next to your skin under other clothes.

un•der•weight [ʌndə'weɪt] *adj.* which weighs less than usual.

un•der•went [ʌndə'went] *v.* see **un•der•go.**

un•der•world ['ʌndəwɜːld] *n.* (a) (*in mythology*) place inhabited by the dead. (b) criminal world; **u. killing** = murder of a criminal by other criminals.

un•der•write [ʌndə'raɪt] *v.* (**underwrote, has underwritten**) to insure (esp. ships); to accept responsibility for (sth). **un•der•writ•er** ['ʌndəraɪtə] *n.* person who insures (esp. ships).

un•de•served [ʌndɪ'zɜːvd] *adj.* not deserved. **un•de•serv•ed•ly** [ʌndɪ'zɜːvɪdlɪ] *adv.* in an undeserved way.

un•de•sir•a•ble [ʌndɪ'zaɪərəbl] 1. *adj.* not wanted; not pleasant. 2. *n.* person who is not wanted/ who is considered a bad influence. **un•de•sir•a•bil•i•ty** [ʌndɪzaɪərə'bɪlɪtɪ] *n.* being undesirable.

un•de•tect•ed [ʌndɪ'tektɪd] *adj.* not noticed. **un•de•tect•a•ble,** *adj.* which cannot be detected.

un•de•terred [ʌndɪ'tɜːd] *adj.* not put off.

un•de•vel•oped [ʌndɪ'veləpt] *adj.* which has not been developed.

un•did [ʌn'dɪd] *v. see* **un•do.**

un•dies ['ʌndɪz] *n. pl. inf.* (women's) underwear.

un•dig•ni•fied [ʌn'dɪgnɪfaɪd] *adj.* not dignified.

un•di•lut•ed [ʌndaɪ'ljuːtɪd] *adj.* without any water added.

un•dis•charged [ʌndɪs'tʃɑːʒd] *adj.* (debt) which has not been paid.

un•dis•tin•guished [ʌndɪs'tɪŋgwɪʃt] *adj.* ordinary.

un•di•vid•ed [ʌndɪ'vaɪdɪd] *adj.* complete/not split.

un•do [ʌn'duː] *v.* (**undid, has undone**) (a) to untie (a knot); to unbutton. (b) to ruin. **un•do•ing,** *n.* ruin. **un•done,** *adj.* (a) unfastened. (b) not complete.

un•doubt•ed [ʌn'dautɪd] *adj.* certain. **un•doubt•ed•ly,** *adv.* certainly.

un•dreamt-of [ʌn'dremtɒv] *adj.* which no one can imagine.

un•dress [ʌn'dres] *v.* to take off (usu. all your) clothes. **un•dressed,** *adj.* not wearing clothes.

un•drink•a•ble [ʌn'drɪŋkəbl] *adj.* (liquid) which is so unpleasant/so polluted that you cannot drink it.

un•due ['ʌndjuː] *adj.* excessive/too much. **un•du•ly** [ʌn'djuːlɪ] *adv.* excessively/too much.

un•du•lant ['ʌndjuːlənt] *adj.* **u. fever** = brucellosis.

un•du•late ['ʌndjuleɪt] *v.* to rise and fall like waves. **un•du•la•tion** [ʌndju'leɪʃn] *n.* rise and fall (of land, etc.).

un•dy•ing [ʌn'daɪɪŋ] *adj.* (emotion) which lasts for ever.

un•earned ['ʌnɜːnd] *adj.* (income) from investments/rents, etc.

un•earth [ʌn'ɜːT] *v.* to dig up; to discover.

un•earth•ly, *adj.* supernatural; *inf.* very early/late (hour).

un•eas•y [ʌn'iːzɪ] *adj.* (-ier, -iest) worried. **un•eas•i•ly,** *adv.* in an uneasy way. **un•eas•i•ness,** *n.* worry/anxiety.

un•eat•a•ble [ʌn'iːtəbl] *adj.* (food) which is so unpleasant that you cannot eat it.

un•ec•o•nom•ic(al) [ʌniːkə'nɒmɪk(l)] *adj.* which is not economic/which does not make a profit.

un•ed•u•cat•ed [ʌn'edjʊkeɪtɪd] *adj.* not educated; (person) who has not been well brought up; (way of speaking) which is not refined.

un•em•ployed [ʌnɪm'plɔɪd] *adj.* without any permanent work; **the u.** = people with no jobs. **un•em•ploy•ment** [ʌnɪm'plɔɪmənt] *n.* lack of jobs; **mass u.** = situation where large numbers of people are out of work.

un•end•ing [ʌn'endɪŋ] *adj.* ceaseless/with no end.

un•en•light•ened [ʌnɪn'laɪtənd] *adj.* lacking knowledge.

un•en•vi•a•ble [ʌn'envɪəbl] *adj.* which no one would envy.

un•e•qual [ʌn'iːkwəl] *adj.* (a) not equal. (b) **u. to** = not good/strong enough for. **un•e•qualed,** *adj.* which has no equal.

un•e•quiv•o•cal [ʌnɪ'kwɪvəkl] *adj.* clear; easily understood; which cannot be misunderstood.

un•err•ing [ʌn'ɜːrɪŋ] *adj.* faultless/making no mistake.

un•eth•i•cal [ʌn'eθɪkl] *adj.* (conduct) which does not follow the usual rules of a profession.

un•e•ven [ʌn'iːvn] *adj.* (a) bumpy/not flat. (b) not always very good. **un•e•ven•ness,** *n.* being uneven.

un•e•vent•ful [ʌnɪ'ventfəl] *adj.* without any particularly exciting incidents.

un•ex•am•pled [ʌnɪg'zɑːmpld] *adj.* extraordinary; of which there is no other example.

un•ex•cep•tion•a•ble [ʌnɪk'sepʃənəbl] *adj.* very satisfactory.

un•ex•cep•tion•al [ʌnɪk'sepʃnəl] *adj.* ordinary.

un•ex•pect•ed [ʌnɪk'spektɪd] *adj.* which was not expected. **un•ex•pect•ed•ly,** *adv.* in an unexpected way.

un•ex•plored [ʌnɪk'splɔːd] *adj.* which has never been explored.

un•ex•posed [ʌnɪk'spəʊzd] *adj.* (film) which has not been used.

un•ex•pur•gat•ed [ʌn'ekspɜːgeɪtɪd] *adj.* (book, etc.) which has not had offensive parts removed.

un•fail•ing [ʌn'feɪlɪŋ] *adj.* which never fails. **un•fail•ing•ly,** *adv.* without fail.

un•fair [ʌn'feə] *adj.* not fair.

un•faith•ful [ʌn'feɪθfəl] *adj.* not faithful (to your husband or wife).

un•fa•mil•iar [ʌnfə'mɪlɪə] *adj.* not familiar.

un•fas•ten [ʌn'fɑːsn] *v.* to undo (sth which is fastened).

un•fath•om•a•ble [ʌn'fæðəməbl] *adj.* (mystery) which cannot be solved.

un•fa•vor•a•ble [ʌn'feɪvrəbl] *adj.* not favorable.

un•feel•ing [ʌn'fiːlɪŋ] *adj.* insensitive; not sympathetic **to** s.o.

un•fet•tered [ʌn'fetəd] *adj.* free.

un•fit [ʌn'fɪt] *adj.* (a) (person) who is not fit/not in good physical condition. (b) not suitable.

un•flag•ging [ʌn'flægɪŋ] *adj.* tireless.

un•flap•pa•ble [ʌn'flæpəbl] *adj.* (person) who is always calm.

un•flinch•ing [ʌn'flɪntʃɪŋ] *adj.* brave. **un•flinch•ing•ly,** *adv.* bravely.

un•fold [ʌn'fəʊld] *v.* (a) to spread out (a newspaper). (b) (*of story*) to become clear/be told.

un•fore•seen [ʌnfɔː'siːn] *adj.* not foreseen/not anticipated.

un•for•get•ta•ble [ʌnfə'getəbl] *adj.* which cannot be forgotten.

un•for•tu•nate [ʌn'fɔːtʃənət] *adj.* (a) unlucky. (b) sad; to be regretted. **un•for•tu•nate•ly,** *adv.* sadly.

un•found•ed [ʌn'faʊndɪd] *adj.* without any basis in truth.

un•freeze [ʌn'friːz] *v.* (**unfroze, unfrozen**) to warm (sth) so that it stops being frozen.

un•fre•quent•ed [ʌnfrɪ'kwentɪd] *adj.* (place) where few people go.

un•friend•ly [ʌn'frendlɪ] *adj.* (-ier, -iest) not like a friend.

un•frock [ʌn'frɒk] *v.* to remove (a priest) from holy orders.

un•furl [ʌn'fɜːl] *v.* to unroll (like a flag).

un•fur•nished [ʌn'fɜːnɪʃt] *adj.* (house) with no furniture in it.

un•gain•ly [ʌn'geɪnlɪ] *adj.* awkward/clumsy (way of walking).

un•gen•tle•man•ly [ʌn'dʒentəmənlɪ] *adj.* (behavior) not like that of a true gentleman.

un•god•ly [ʌn'gɒdlɪ] *adj.* wicked; unpleasant/dreadful. *inf.* very early/late (hour).

æ back, ɑː farm, ɒ top, aɪ pipe, aʊ how, aɪə fire, aʊə flower, ɔː bought, ɔɪ toy, e fed, eə hair, eɪ take, ə afraid, əʊ boat, əʊə lower, ɜː word, iː heap, ɪ hit, ɪə hear, uː school, ʊ book, ʌ but, b back, d dog, ð then, dʒ just, f fog, g go, h hand, j yes, k catch, l last, m mix, n nut, ŋ sing, p penny, r round, s some, ʃ short, t too, tʃ chop, θ thing, v voice, w was, z zoo, ʒ treasure

un•gra•cious [ʌn'greɪʃəs] *adj.* not gracious/not polite.

un•gram•mat•i•cal [ʌngrə'mætɪkl] *adj.* which goes against the rules of grammar.

un•grate•ful [ʌn'greɪtfəl] *adj.* not grateful.

un•guard•ed [ʌn'gɑːdɪd] *adj.* careless; **in an u. moment** = without thinking about the consequences.

un•guent ['ʌŋgʊənt] *n.* (*formal*) ointment.

un•gu•late ['ʌŋgjʊleɪt] *n.* animal with hooves.

un•hap•py [ʌn'hæpɪ] *adj.* (-ier, -iest) sad. **un•hap•pi•ly,** *adv.* sadly/unfortunately. **un•hap•pi•ness,** *n.* being unhappy.

un•harmed [ʌn'hɑːmd] *adj.* safe.

un•health•y [ʌn'helθɪ] *adj.* (-ier, -iest) (a) not healthy. (b) unnatural.

un•heard-of [ʌn'hɜːdɒv] *adj.* strange/odd.

un•heat•ed [ʌn'hiːtɪd] *adj.* which has no heating.

un•help•ful [ʌn'helpfəl] *adj.* not helpful.

un•her•ald•ed [ʌn'herəldɪd] *adj.* not announced/publicized beforehand.

un•hinged [ʌn'hɪndʒd] *adj.* extremely upset/mad.

un•ho•ly [ʌn'həʊlɪ] *adj. inf.* unpleasant.

un•hook [ʌn'hʊk] *v.* to take (sth) off a hook; to unfasten (sth) which is attached with hooks.

un•hoped-for [ʌn'həʊptfɔː] *adj.* unexpected.

un•horse [ʌn'hɔːs] *v.* to make (s.o.) fall off his horse.

un•hurt [ʌn'hɜːt] *adj.* not hurt; safe and sound.

un•hy•gi•en•ic [ʌnhaɪ'dʒiːnɪk] *adj.* dirty/not hygienic.

u•ni•cam•er•al [juːnɪ'kæmərəl] *adj.* having only one legislative chamber, house or branch.

u•ni•corn ['juːnɪkɔːn] *n.* mythical animal like a horse, with one long, straight horn.

un•i•den•ti•fied [ʌnaɪ'dentɪfaɪd] *adj.* which has not been identified; **u. flying object** = mysterious object in the sky which cannot be identified.

u•ni•fi•ca•tion [juːnɪfɪ'keɪʃn] *n.* act of unifying; joining together into one.

u•ni•form ['juːnɪfɔːm] 1. *n.* specially designed clothing worn by all members of a group. 2. *adj.* all the same; never changing. **u•ni•form•i•ty** [juːnɪ'fɒmɪtɪ] *n.* being uniform. **u•ni•form re•source lo•ca•tor,** *n.* standardized address of a site on the Internet. **u•ni•form•ly,** *adv.* in a uniform way.

u•ni•fy ['juːnɪfaɪ] *v.* to join together into one.

u•ni•lat•er•al [juːnɪ'lætərəl] *adj.* on one side only; done by one side only. **u•ni•lat•er•al•ly,** *adv.* (done) by one side only.

un•im•ag•i•na•tive [ʌnɪ'mædʒɪnətɪv] *adj.* lacking flair.

un•im•paired [ʌnɪm'peəd] *adj.* not damaged.

un•im•peach•a•ble [ʌnɪm'piːtʃəbl] *adj.* which can be trusted completely.

un•im•por•tant [ʌnɪm'pɔːtənt] *adj.* not important.

un•in•formed [ʌnɪn'fɔːmd] *adj.* without full knowledge.

un•in•hab•it•a•ble [ʌnɪn'hæbɪtəbl] *adj.* which cannot be lived in. **un•in•hab•it•ed,** *adj.* not lived in.

un•in•hib•it•ed [ʌnɪn'hɪbɪtɪd] *adj.* free; not bound by the customs of society.

un•in•i•ti•at•ed [ʌnɪ'nɪʃɪeɪtɪd] *n.* **the u.** = people who are not experts.

un•in•tel•li•gi•ble [ʌnɪn'telɪdʒəbl] *adj.* which cannot be understood.

un•in•ter•rupt•ed [ʌnɪntə'rʌptɪd] *adj.* with no breaks; continuous.

un•in•vit•ed [ʌnɪn'vaɪtɪd] *adj.* without an invitation. **un•in•vit•ing,** *adj.* not very attractive.

un•ion ['juːnɪən] *n.* (a) being joined together; countries or states which are joined together. (b) (*formal*) marriage. (c) group of people working in the same type of industry joined together for mutual protection; labor union. **un•ion•ist,** *n.* member of a labor union. **un•ion•ize,** *v.* to form a labor union in (a factory/a group of workers). **Un•ion Jack,** *n.* national flag of the United Kingdom.

u•nique [juˈniːk] *adj.* so special that there is nothing similar to it. **u•nique•ly,** *adv.* in a special or unique way.

u•ni•sex ['juːnɪseks] *adj.* which can be used by both men and women.

u•ni•son ['juːnɪsn] *n.* **in u.** = (i) singing the same note all together; (ii) in total agreement.

u•nit ['juːnɪt] *n.* (a) one part (of a larger whole); one cupboard/one set of shelves, etc., which can be matched with others to form a whole. (b) one part (of an army). (c) standard measurement by which sth is counted. (d) number one; single number. **u•ni•tar•y,** *adj.* referring to a unit.

u•nite [juːˈnaɪt] *v.* to join together as a whole. **u•ni•ty** ['juːnɪtɪ] *n.* being one whole.

u•ni•valve ['juːnɪvælv] *n.* animal (such as a snail) with a single shell.

u•ni•verse ['juːnɪvɜːs] *n.* all that exists, including the earth, the planets and the stars. **u•ni•ver•sal** [juːnɪ'vɜːsəl] *adj.* which is everywhere; which affects everyone; **u. joint** = mechanical joint made so that each of two connected rods can move in any direction; **u. suffrage** = situation where all adults have the right to vote. **u•ni•ver•sal•ly,** *adv.* everywhere; by everyone.

u•ni•ver•si•ty [juːnɪ'vɜːsɪtɪ] *n.* place of higher

learning, where degrees are given to successful students, and a wide range of specialized subjects are taught.

un•just [ʌn'dʒʌst] *adj.* not fair. **un•just•ly,** *adv.* in an unjust way.

un•jus•ti•fied [ʌn'dʒʌstɪfaɪd] *adj.* which is not justified.

un•kempt [ʌn'kemt] *adj.* disheveled/untidy.

un•kind [ʌn'kaɪnd] *adj.* (-er, -est) harsh/cruel. **un•kind•ly,** *adv.* in a cruel way.

un•known ['ʌnnəʊn] *adj.* not known.

un•lad•en [ʌn'leɪdn] *adj.* without a load.

un•la•dy•like [ʌn'leɪdɪlaɪk] *adj.* (behavior) which is not like that of a lady.

un•law•ful [ʌn'lɔːfəl] *adj.* against the law.

un•lead•ed [ʌn'ledɪd] *adj.* (gasoline) without lead additives.

un•leash [ʌn'liːʃ] *v.* to unfasten the leash (of a dog); to set free/to set loose.

un•leav•ened [ʌn'levnd] *adj.* (bread) made without yeast.

un•less [ʌn'les] *conj.* (a) if…not. (b) except if.

un•like ['ʌnlaɪk] *adj. & prep.* not similar to; different from; **it is u. him to be rude** = he is not usually rude. **un•like•ly** [ʌn'laɪklɪ] *adj.* improbable; (story) which is probably not true.

un•lim•it•ed [ʌn'lɪmɪtɪd] *adj.* with no limits.

un•lined [ʌn'laɪnd] *adj.* (a) without lines. (b) without a lining.

un•list•ed [ʌn'lɪstɪd] *adj.* not included in a list.

un•load [ʌn'ləʊd] *v.* to remove a load from (a vehicle). **un•load•ed,** *adj.* (gun) with no bullets in it.

un•lock [ʌn'lɒk] *v.* to open (sth) which was locked.

un•looked-for [ʌn'lʌkdfɔː] *adj.* not expected.

un•luck•y [ʌn'lʌkɪ] *adj.* (-ier, -iest) not lucky; bringing bad luck. **un•luck•i•ly,** *adv.* unfortunately.

un•man•age•a•ble [ʌn'mænɪdʒəbl] *adj.* difficult to control.

un•manned [ʌn'mænd] *adj.* without a crew/without any staff.

un•man•ner•ly [ʌn'mænəlɪ] *adj.* with no manners.

un•mar•ried ['ʌnmærɪd] *adj.* not married; **u. mother** = woman who has a child but is not married.

un•mask [ʌn'mɑːsk] *v.* to remove a mask; to show (s.o.) as they really are.

un•matched [ʌn'mætʃt] *adj.* which has no equal.

un•men•tion•a•ble [ʌn'menʃnəbl] *adj.* which you must not talk about because it is so indecent/unpleasant, etc.

un•mis•tak•a•ble [ʌnmɪs'teɪkəbl] *adj.* which is easily recognized/which cannot be mistaken.

un•mit•i•gat•ed [ʌn'mɪtɪgeɪtɪd] *adj.* total/complete.

un•moved [ʌn'muːvd] *adj.* not touched/not affected.

un•mu•si•cal [ʌn'mjuːzɪkl] *adj.* not interested in music; not able to play a musical instrument.

un•named [ʌn'neɪmd] *adj.* (person) who has not been named.

un•nat•u•ral [ʌn'nætʃərəl] *adj.* which is not natural; which does not follow the usual pattern.

un•nec•es•sar•y [ʌn'nesəsərɪ] *adj.* which is not necessary. **un•nec•es•sar•i•ly,** *adv.* uselessly; for no good reason.

un•nerve [ʌn'nɜːv] *v.* to make (s.o.) lose his nerve/his courage.

un•no•ticed [ʌn'nəʊtɪst] *adj.* not noticed; without anyone noticing.

un•num•bered [ʌn'nʌmbəd] *adj.* with no numbers; which cannot be counted.

un•ob•serv•ant [ʌnəb'zɜːvənt] *adj.* not observant; (person) who does not notice things.

un•ob•struct•ed [ʌnəb'strʌktɪd] *adj.* with nothing in the way.

un•ob•tain•a•ble [ʌnəb'teɪnəbl] *adj.* which cannot be obtained.

un•ob•tru•sive [ʌnəb'truːsɪv] *adj.* not obvious; not easily noticed.

un•oc•cu•pied [ʌn'ɒkjupaɪd] *adj.* not occupied; empty.

un•of•fi•cial [ʌnə'fɪʃl] *adj.* not official; (strike) which has not been officially approved by a union. **un•of•fi•cial•ly,** *adv.* in an unofficial way.

un•op•posed [ʌnə'pəʊzd] *adj.* with no opposition.

un•or•tho•dox [ʌn'ɔːTədɒks] *adj.* not usual.

un•pack [ʌn'pæk] *v.* to take (things) out of containers in which they were transported.

un•paid [ʌn'peɪd] *adj.* (person) who is not paid a salary; (bill) which has not been settled.

un•pal•at•a•ble [ʌn'pælətəbl] *adj.* not pleasant to the taste; unpleasant (fact).

un•par•al•leled [ʌn'pærəleld] *adj.* with no parallel or no equal.

un•par•don•a•ble [ʌn'pɑːdnəbl] *adj.* which cannot be excused.

æ back, aː farm, ɒ top, aɪ pipe, aʊ how, aie fire, aʊə flower, ɔː bought, ɔɪ toy, e fed, eəhair, eɪ take, ə afraid, əʊ boat, əʊə lower, vː word, iː heap, ɪ hit, ɪə hear, uː school, ʊ book, ʌ but, b back, d dog, ð then, dʒ just, f fog, g go, h hand, j yes, k catch, l last, m mix, n nut, ŋ sing, p penny, r round, s some, ʃ short, t too, tʃ chop, θ thing, v voice, w was, z zoo, ʒ treasure

un•pa•tri•ot•ic [ˌʌnpætrɪˈɒtɪk] *adj.* not patriotic.

un•per•son [ˈʌnpɜːsən] *n.* person who is treated as if he did not exist (because of opposition to the government).

un•pleas•ant [ʌnˈplezənt] *adj.* not pleasing. **un•pleas•ant•ness**, *n.* argument/disagreement.

un•pop•u•lar [ʌnˈpɒpjʊlə] *adj.* not popular. **un•pop•u•lar•i•ty** [ʌnpɒpjʊˈlærɪtɪ] *n.* being unpopular.

un•prec•e•dent•ed [ʌnˈpresɪdentɪd] *adj.* which has never happened before.

un•prej•u•diced [ʌnˈpredʒʊdɪst] *adj.* fair; not prejudiced.

un•pre•med•i•tat•ed [ʌnprɪˈmedɪteɪtɪd] *adj.* which has not been planned.

un•pre•pared [ʌnprɪˈpeəd] *adj.* not ready.

un•pre•pos•ses•sing [ʌnpriːpəˈzesɪŋ] *adj.* not very attractive.

un•pre•ten•tious [ʌnprɪˈtenʃəs] *adj.* modest/not showing off.

un•prin•ci•pled [ʌnˈprɪnsɪpld] *adj.* without any moral standards.

un•print•a•ble [ʌnˈprɪntəbl] *adj.* (words) so rude that you cannot print them.

un•pro•duc•tive [ʌnprəˈdʌktɪv] *adj.* (discussion) which does not produce any result; (land) which does not produce any crops.

un•pro•fes•sion•al [ʌnprəˈfeʃnəl] *adj.* (conduct) which is not of the sort you would expect from a member of a particular profession.

un•prof•it•a•ble [ʌnˈprɒfɪtəbl] *adj.* which does not make a profit; which is useless.

un•prompt•ed [ʌnˈprɒmptɪd] *adj.* without anyone suggesting it.

un•pro•nounce•a•ble [ʌnprəˈnaʊnsəbl] *adj.* (name) which is difficult to say.

un•pro•voked [ʌnprəˈvəʊkt] *adj.* (action) which was not provoked.

un•qual•i•fied [ʌnˈkwɒlɪfaɪd] *adj.* (a) (person) who does not have the necessary skills, etc. to qualify for a job, position, etc. (b) total/complete (success).

un•ques•tion•a•ble [ʌnˈkwestʃənəbl] *adj.* which is certain/not doubtful. **un•ques•tion•a•bly,** *adv.* certainly. **un•ques•tion•ing,** *adj.* without doubting.

un•quote [ˈʌnkwəʊt] *v.* to indicate the end of a quotation (when speaking).

un•rav•el [ʌnˈrævl] *v.* (**unraveled, unravelled**) to disentangle (sth knotted); to solve (a mystery).

un•read•a•ble [ʌnˈriːdəbl] *adj.* (book) which is so boring that you cannot read it.

un•re•al [ʌnˈriːl] *adj.* not like the real world. **un•re•al•is•tic** [ʌnrɪəˈlɪstɪk] *adj.* impractical/not facing facts.

un•rea•son•a•ble [ʌnˈriːznəbl] *adj.* not reasonable/too large.

un•rec•og•niz•a•ble [ʌnrekəgˈnaɪzəbl] *adj.* which cannot be recognized.

un•reel [ʌnˈriːl] *v.* to undo (sth wound round a reel).

un•re•fined [ʌnrɪˈfaɪnd] *adj.* (sugar/oil) which has not been refined.

un•re•lat•ed [ʌnrɪˈleɪtɪd] *adj.* not related/with no connection.

un•re•lent•ing [ʌnrɪˈlentɪŋ] *adj.* which never stops/weakens.

un•re•li•a•ble [ʌnrɪˈlaɪəbl] *adj.* which cannot be relied on.

un•re•lieved [ʌnrɪˈliːvd] *adj.* not lessened.

un•re•mit•ting [ʌnrɪˈmɪtɪŋ] *adj.* never ceasing.

un•re•quit•ed [ʌnrɪˈkwaɪtɪd] *adj.* (love) which is not returned.

un•re•served [ʌnrɪˈzɜːvd] *adj.* not reserved. **un•re•serv•ed•ly** [ʌnrɪˈzɜːvɪdlɪ] *adv.* definitely.

un•rest [ʌnˈrest] *n.* being restless/dissatisfied; agitation to get political/industrial change.

un•ri•valed, *Brit.* **un•ri•valled** [ʌnˈraɪvəld] *adj.* with no equal.

un•roll [ʌnˈrəʊl] *v.* to undo (sth which is rolled up).

un•ruf•fled [ʌnˈrʌfld] *adj.* calm/not anxious.

un•ru•ly [ʌnˈruːlɪ] *adj.* wild/with no discipline. **un•ru•li•ness,** *n.* wild behavior.

un•safe [ʌnˈseɪf] *adj.* (**-er, -est**) dangerous.

un•said [ʌnˈsed] *adj.* **better left u.** = better not to say it.

un•salt•ed [ʌnˈsɒltɪd] *adj.* (butter, etc.) with no salt.

un•sat•is•fac•to•ry [ʌnsætɪsˈfæktrɪ] *adj.* not satisfactory.

un•sat•is•fied [ʌnˈsætɪsfaɪd] *adj.* not satisfied.

un•sat•u•rat•ed [ʌnˈsætjuːreɪtɪd] *adj.* (fat) which contains little hydrogen, and so can be broken down easily in the body.

un•sa•vor•y, *Brit.* **un•sa•vour•y** [ʌnˈseɪvərɪ] *adj.* unpleasant/disgusting.

un•scathed [ʌnˈskeɪðd] *adj.* not harmed.

un•sched•uled [ʌnˈʃedjuːld] *adj.* not on a schedule.

un•schooled [ʌnˈskuːld] *adj.* not taught; without any experience (**in**).

un•sci•en•tif•ic [ʌnsaɪənˈtɪfɪk] *adj.* not scientific.

un•scram•ble [ʌnˈskræmbl] *v.* to put back in order; to put (a coded message) back into plain language.

un•screw [ʌnˈskruː] *v.* to open by twisting a screw or a screw lid anticlockwise.

un•scru•pu•lous [ʌn'skruːpjuləs] *adj.* not worrying too much about honesty.

un•sealed [ʌn'siːld] *adj.* (envelope, etc.) which has not been sealed.

un•sea•son•a•ble [ʌn'siːzənəbl] *adj.* not usual for the season.

un•seat [ʌn'siːt] *v.* to make (s.o.) fall off a horse; to remove from political office at an election.

un•seem•ly [ʌn'siːmlɪ] *adj.* offensive/rude (behavior).

un•seen [ʌn'siːn] *adj.* not seen/invisible.

un•sel•fish [ʌn'selfɪʃ] *adj.* not selfish/thinking of others before yourself.

un•ser•vice•a•ble [ʌn'səːvɪsəbl] *adj.* not in a good enough state to be used.

un•set•tle [ʌn'setl] *v.* to upset. **un•set•tled,** *adj.* (weather) which changes often.

un•shak•a•ble, unshakeable [ʌn'ʃeɪkəbl] *adj.* solid/firm (belief/faith).

un•sight•ly [ʌn'saɪtlɪ] *adj.* ugly.

un•signed [ʌn'saɪnd] *adj.* not signed.

un•skilled ['ʌnskɪld] *adj.* (worker) who has no particular skill.

un•so•cia•ble [ʌn'səʊʃəbl] *adj.* not friendly; not wishing to make friends.

un•so•lic•it•ed [ʌnsə'lɪsɪtɪd] *adj.* which has not been asked for.

un•solved ['ʌnsɒlvd] *adj.* (problem) which has not been solved.

un•so•phis•ti•cat•ed [ʌnsə'fɪstɪkeɪtɪd] *adj.* simple; not sophisticated.

un•sound ['ʌnsaʊnd] *adj.* (a) **of u. mind** = mad. (b) (reasoning) not based on fact or logic.

un•spar•ing [ʌn'speərɪŋ] *adj.* generous; not reluctant.

un•speak•a•ble [ʌn'spiːkəbl] *adj.* extremely unpleasant.

un•spoiled, unspoilt ['ʌnspɔɪlt] *adj.* (countryside) which has not been spoiled.

un•sta•ble [ʌn'steɪbl] *adj.* (a) not stable; changeable; (government) which is likely to fall at any moment. (b) dangerously mad.

un•stead•y [ʌn'stedɪ] *adj.* not steady; wobbly.

un•stick [ʌn'stɪk] *v.* (**unstuck**) to remove sth which is stuck on; **to come unstuck** = to go badly wrong.

un•stop•pa•ble [ʌn'stɒpəbl] *adj.* which cannot be stopped.

un•suc•cess•ful [ʌnsək'sesfəl] *adj.* not successful.

un•suit•a•ble [ʌn'suːtəbl] *adj.* not suitable.

un•sul•lied [ʌn'sʌlɪd] *adj.* pure.

un•sung [ʌn'sʌŋ] *adj.* (hero) who is not famous.

un•sure [ʌn'ʃʊə] *adj.* not sure; **u. of oneself** = lacking self-confidence.

un•sus•pect•ed [ʌnsəs'pektɪd] *adj.* which is not suspected to exist. **un•sus•pect•ing,** *adj.* (person) who does not realize sth/that a danger is imminent.

un•sweet•ened [ʌn'swiːtənd] *adj.* (food) with no sugar added.

un•swerv•ing [ʌn'swɜːvɪŋ] *adj.* (loyalty) which does not change.

un•sym•pa•thet•ic [ʌnsɪmpə'θetɪk] *adj.* not sympathetic.

un•tan•gle [ʌn'tæŋgl] *v.* to disentangle.

un•tapped [ʌn'tæpt] *adj.* not previously used.

un•ten•a•ble [ʌn'tenəbl] *adj.* (position/theory) which cannot be defended.

un•think•a•ble [ʌn'θɪŋkəbl] *adj.* which cannot be considered or thought of. **un•think•ing** [ʌn'θɪŋkɪŋ] *adj.* done without thinking. **un•thought-of,** *adj.* which no one has thought possible.

un•ti•dy [ʌn'taɪdɪ] *adj.* (**-ier, -iest**) not tidy/in disorder. **un•ti•di•ly,** *adv.* in an untidy way. **un•ti•di•ness,** *n.* being untidy.

un•tie [ʌn'taɪ] *v.* to unfasten (sth which is tied with a knot).

un•til [ʌn'tɪl] *prep. & conj.* up to (a certain time).

un•time•ly [ʌn'taɪmlɪ] *adj.* (a) happening too soon. (b) not suitable.

un•to ['ʌntu] *prep.* (old) to.

un•told [ʌn'təʊld] *adj.* very large; so large that it cannot be counted.

un•touch•a•ble [ʌn'tʌtʃəbl] **1.** *adj.* which cannot be touched. **2.** *n.* person from the lowest caste in India.

un•to•ward [ʌntə'wɔːd] *adj.* unlucky/inconvenient; **nothing u. took place** = everything went off well.

un•trained [ʌn'treɪnd] *adj.* (person) who has had no training.

un•tried [ʌn'traɪd] *adj.* which has not been tested.

un•true [ʌn'truː] *adj.* wrong/not true.

un•trust•wor•thy [ʌn'trʌstwɜːðɪ] *adj.* (person) who cannot be trusted.

un•truth [ʌn'truːθ] *n.* lie. **un•truth•ful,** *adj.* (person) who does not tell the truth; (statement) which is wrong.

un•us•a•ble [ʌn'juːzəbl] *adj.* which cannot be used.

æ back, ɑː farm, ɒ top, aɪ pipe, aʊ how, aɪə fire, aʊə flower, ɔː bought, ɔɪ toy, e fed, eəhair, eɪ take, ə afraid, əʊ boat, əʊə lower, ɜː word, iː heap, ɪ hit, ɪə hear, uː school, ʊ book, ʌ but, b back, d dog, ð then, dʒ just, f fog, g go, h hand, j yes, k catch, l last, m mix, n nut, ŋ sing, p penny, r round, s some, ʃ short, t too, tʃ chop, θ thing, v voice, w was, z zoo, ʒ treasure

un•used adj. (a) [ʌn'juːzd] new/clean; which has not been used. (b) [ʌn'juːsd] not accustomed (**to**).

un•u•su•al [ʌn'juːʒəl] adj. strange/extraordinary. **un•u•su•al•ly**, adv. strangely/extraordinarily.

un•ut•ter•a•ble [ʌnʌ'tərəbl] adj. so terrible that it cannot be expressed.

un•var•nished [ʌn'vɑːnɪʃt] adj. with no varnish; plain/simple (truth).

un•veil [ʌn'veɪl] v. to uncover (a new statue/a new plan, etc.).

un•versed [ʌn'vɜːst] adj. with no experience (**in**).

un•want•ed [ʌn'wɒntɪd] adj. which is not wanted.

un•war•rant•ed [ʌn'wɒrəntɪd] adj. which is not justified.

un•war•y [ʌn'weərɪ] adj. (person) who does not take care.

un•well [ʌn'wel] adj. sick/ill.

un•whole•some [ʌn'həʊlsəm] adj. not healthy/which might harm.

un•wield•y [ʌn'wiːldɪ] adj. large and awkward.

un•will•ing [ʌn'wɪlɪŋ] adj. reluctant; not willing.

un•wind [ʌn'waɪnd] v. (**unwound** [ʌn'waʊnd]) (a) to undo (sth which has been wound). (b) inf. to relax.

un•wise [ʌn'waɪz] adj. rash/imprudent; not wise.

un•wit•ting [ʌn'wɪtɪŋ] adj. not knowing/intending. **un•wit•ting•ly**, adv. without intending to; not intentionally.

un•wont•ed [ʌn'wɒntɪd] adj. not usual.

un•work•a•ble [ʌn'wɜːkəbl] adj. (plan) which will not work in practice.

un•wor•thy [ʌn'wɜːðɪ] adj. (**of**) (a) which does not deserve (sth). (b) not as good as one might expect from (a person).

un•wound [ʌn'waʊnd] v. see **un•wind**.

un•wrap [ʌn'ræp] v. (**unwrapped**) to take the wrapping off (sth).

un•writ•ten [ʌn'rɪtən] adj. **u. law** = custom which has grown up over a period of time but which is not written down.

un•zip [ʌn'zɪp] v. (**unzipped**) to undo a zipper.

up [ʌp] 1. adv. (a) toward a higher place; **hands u.!** = lift your hands into the air to show you surrender. (b) in a higher place; **this side u.** = this side must be on top. (c) toward the north. (d) to a higher level. (e) to the end; completely. (f) not in bed. (g) close to. 2. prep. (a) toward a higher part of (sth). (b) along; toward the source of (a river); **to walk u. and down** = backward and forward. 3. adj. (a) which is going up. (b) which is in a higher position; completely built; **the house is u.** = completely built.

(c) not in bed. (d) finished; **your time is u.** = you have to stop now; **his leave is u.** = he has to go back to the army. (e) inf. **what's u.** = what is the matter? 4. n. **ups and downs** = good and bad periods. 5. v. (**upped**) (a) to raise (prices, etc.). (b) inf. to get up suddenly.

up-and-com•ing [ʌpən'kʌmɪŋ] adj. (person) who looks as though he might succeed. **up-and-up** ['ʌpənʌp] n. **to be on the u.-and-u.** = to be honest/trustworthy. **up•com•ing**, adj. imminent/likely to happen soon. **up for**, prep. ready for; **u. f. sale** = on sale. **up•mar•ket**, adj. aiming at the expensive end of the market. **up to**, prep. (a) as many as. (b) capable enough to do (sth). (c) **it's u. t. you** = it is your responsibility. (d) doing (sth bad). **up-to-date**, adj. & adv. modern/using the most recent information, etc.

up•braid [ʌp'breɪd] v. (formal) to scold.

up•bring•ing ['ʌpbrɪŋɪŋ] n. education; training of a child.

up•date [ʌp'deɪt] v. to revise (sth) so that it is more up-to-date.

up•end [ʌp'end] v. to stand (sth) on its end.

up•grade [ʌp'greɪd] v. to put (s.o.) into a more important job; to improve the quality of (sth).

up•heav•al [ʌp'hiːvəl] n. great change/disturbance.

up•hill [ʌp'hɪl] 1. adj. going upward; difficult. 2. adv. upward.

up•hold [ʌp'həʊld] v. (**upheld**) to support; to say that (a decision) is right.

up•hol•ster [ʌp'həʊlstə] v. to cover (chairs, etc.) with padded seats and covers. **up•hol•ster•er**, n. person who upholsters. **up•hol•ster•y**, n. (a) covering chairs, etc. with padded seats and covers. (b) covers for chairs; padded seats and cushions.

up•keep [ʌp'kiːp] n. (cost of) keeping a house/a car, etc., in good condition.

up•land [ʌp'lənd] n. mountainous area (of a country).

up•lift 1. n. ['ʌplɪft] (a) thing which gives a feeling of happiness or goodness. (b) increase/raising. 2. v. [ʌp'lɪft] to lift up/to raise.

up•load [ʌp'ləʊd] v. to bring information from the Internet into a personal computer.

up•on [ʌ'pɒn] prep. (formal) on; **battle u. battle** = one battle after another.

up•per ['ʌpə] 1. adj. (a) higher. (b) further up. (c) more important; of higher rank; **the u. classes** = the nobility; (in school) **the u. grades** = grades with older pupils; **u. case** = capital (letters); **u. house/chamber** = one of two branches of a legislature, as the U.S. Senate; senate; **to get the u. hand** = begin to win. 2. n. top part of a shoe. **up•per•cut**, n. blow with the fist upward on the chin. **up•per•most.**

1. *adj.* (a) highest. (b) furthest up. (c) most important. 2. *adv.* **what is u. in their minds** = the subject they think about most. **up•pish, up•pi•ty,** *adj. inf.* feeling superior to other people.

up•right ['ʌpraɪt] 1. *adj.* (a) vertical. (b) very honest. 2. *n.* (a) vertical post. (b) piano with the strings and body vertical.

up•ris•ing ['ʌpraɪzɪŋ] *n.* revolt (against authority).

up•roar ['ʌprɔ:] *n.* loud noise/disturbance. **up•roar•i•ous** [ʌp'rɔ:rɪəs] *adj.* noisy.

up•root [ʌp'ru:t] *v.* (a) to dig up (a plant) with its roots. (b) to make (a family) move to a totally new area.

up•set 1. *n.* ['ʌpset] (a) complete change for the worse. (b) great worry/cause of unhappiness. (c) slight illness. 2. *v.* [ʌp'set] (**upset**) (a) to knock over; to fall over. (b) to change completely (for the worse). (c) to make (s.o.) worried/unhappy. (d) to make (s.o.) slightly ill. 3. *adj.* [ʌp'set] (a) very worried/unhappy/anxious. (b) made ill.

up•shot ['ʌpʃɒt] *n.* result.

up•side down ['ʌpsaɪd'daʊn] *adv.* with the top turned to the bottom.

up•stage [ʌp'steɪdʒ] 1. *adv.* at the back of the stage. 2. *v.* (a) to move nearer the front of the stage than (s.o.). (b) to take attention away from (s.o. who feels he ought to have it).

up•stairs [ʌp'steəz] 1. *adv.* toward the upper part of a house. 2. *adj.* on the upper floors of a house. 3. *n.* the upper floors of a house.

up•stand•ing [ʌp'stændɪŋ] *adj.* strong/honest.

up•start [ʌp'stɑ:t] *n.* inexperienced person who has become unexpectedly important.

up•stream [ʌp'stri:m] *adv. & adj.* (moving) toward the source or a river, against the flow of the current.

up•surge ['ʌpsɜ:dʒ] *n.* sudden increase (of emotion).

up•take ['ʌpteɪk] *n.* **slow/quick on the u.** = slow/quick to understand.

up•tight ['ʌptaɪt] *adj. inf.* nervous and annoyed.

up•turn ['ʌptɜ:n] *n.* movement upward (in sales, etc.). **up•turned,** *adj.* (boat, etc.) turned upside down.

up•ward ['ʌpwəd] *adj.* moving toward a higher level. **up•ward, upwards,** *adv.* toward a higher level. **up•wards of,** *prep.* more than.

u•ra•ni•um [jʊ'reɪnɪəm] *n.* (*element:* U) radioactive metal used in producing atomic energy.

ur•ban ['ɜ:bən] *adj.* (a) referring to towns. (b) living in towns. **ur•ban•i•za•tion,** *n.* act of urbanizing. **ur•ban•ize,** *v.* to make (an area) into a town; to make (sth/s.o. from the country) become accustomed to the town.

ur•bane [ɜ:'beɪn] *adj.* very polite. **ur•ban•i•ty** [ə:'bænɪtɪ] *n.* being urbane.

ur•chin ['ɜ:tʃɪn] *n.* dirty little boy; **sea u.** = small sea creature with a round shell covered with spikes.

u•re•a [ju:'ri:ə] *n.* substance produced by the liver and excreted into the urine.

u•re•ter [ju:'ri:tə] *n.* tube taking urine from the kidneys to the bladder.

u•re•thra [ju:'ri:Trə] *n.* tube taking urine from the bladder out of the body.

urge [ɜ:dʒ] 1. *n.* strong desire. 2. *v.* (a) to encourage; to push (s.o.) to do sth. (b) to suggest strongly. **ur•gen•cy** ['ɜ:dʒənsɪ] *n.* being urgent; need for sth to be done quickly; **what's the u.?** = why are you hurrying? **ur•gent,** *adj.* which needs to be done quickly. **ur•gent•ly,** *adv.* quickly/immediately.

u•rine ['jʊərɪn] *n.* liquid waste matter from the body. **u•ri•nal** [jʊə'raɪnəl] *n.* place where men can pass waste liquid from the body; bowl to catch waste liquid passed from the body. **u•ri•nar•y** ['jʊərɪnərɪ] *adj.* referring to urine; **u. tract** = organs which create and excrete urine. **u•ri•nate,** *v.* to pass waste liquid from the body.

URL [ju:ɑ:'el] *abbrev. for* uniform resource locator; standardized address of sites on the Internet.

urn [ɜ:n] *n.* very large vase; **coffee u.** = large metal container with a tap, in which large quantities of coffee can be made.

us [ʌs] *pron. referring to* we.

U.S., U.S.A. ['ju'es, jues'eɪ] *abbreviations for* United States (of America).

use 1. *n.* [ju:s] (a) being used; way in which sth is used. (b) ability to be used. (c) usefulness. 2. *v.* [ju:z] (a) to put to a purpose. (b) to take advantage of (s.o.). (c) *inf.* **I could use a beer** = I would like a beer. (d) [ju:s] to do sth regularly in the past; **she used to smoke. us•a•ble** ['ju:zəbl] *adj.* which can be used. **us•age** ['ju:sɪdʒ] *n.* (a) custom; way of doing things. (b) way of using a word. **used,** *adj.* (a) [ju:zd] not new; which has been put to a purpose. (b) [juːsd] accustomed (**to**). **use•ful** ['juːsfəl] *adj.* which helps; **to make oneself u.** = to do helpful things. **use•ful•ly**, *adv.* in a helpful way. **use•ful•ness**, *n.* being useful. **use•less** ['juːsləs] *adj.* which does not help; *inf.* **she is quite u.** = of no help at all. **use•less•ness**, *n.* being useless. **us•er** ['juːzə] *n.* person who uses. **us•er-friend•ly**, *adj.* (program/machine) which a user finds easy to use. **use up**, *v.* to finish.

ush•er ['ʌʃə] 1. *n.* person who shows people to their seats (in a theater/in a church). 2. *v.* **to u. in** = (i) to bring (s.o.) in; (ii) to be the beginning of. **ush•er•ette** [ʌʃə'ret] *n.* girl who shows people to their seats in a theater.

U.S.S.R. [juːeses'ɑː] *abbreviation for* former Union of Soviet Socialist Republics, now referred to as Russia/the Commonwealth of Independent States.

u•su•al ['juːʒuəl] *adj.* ordinary; which happens often. **u•su•al•ly**, *adv.* mostly/ordinarily.

u•su•rer ['juːzjurə] *n.* person who lends money for high interest. **u•su•ri•ous** [juː'zjuərɪəs] *adj.* excessively high (interest rate). **u•su•ry**, *n.* lending money for high interest.

u•surp [juː'zɜːp] *v.* to take the place of (s.o.). **u•sur•pa•tion** [juːzɜː'peɪʃn] *n.* act of usurping. **u•surp•er**, *n.* person who usurps (a throne).

u•ten•sil [juː'tensl] *n.* tool/pan/knife, etc., used for work in the kitchen.

u•ter•us ['juːtərəs] *n.* part of a female body where an unborn baby is carried. **u•ter•ine** ['juːtəraɪn] *adj.* referring to the uterus.

u•til•i•ty [juː'tɪlɪtɪ] *n.* (a) usefulness; **u. room** = room, esp. in a house, where you put the washing machine/freezer, etc. (b) **utilities** = essential public services (such as electricity/gas/water, etc.). **u•til•i•tar•i•an** [juːtɪlɪ'teərɪən] *adj.* used for a practical purpose, not decoration. **u•til•iz•a•ble** [juːtɪ'laɪzəbl] *adj.* which can be used. **u•ti•li•za•tion** [juːtɪlaɪ'zeɪʃn] *n.* making use of sth. **u•ti•lize** ['juːtɪlaɪz] *v.* to use; to make use of (sth) for profit.

ut•most ['ʌtməust] *adj.* (a) greatest that can be. (b) farthest.

u•to•pi•a [juː'təupɪə] *n.* imaginary perfect world. **u•to•pi•an**, *adj.* very perfect (ideas).

ut•ter ['ʌtə] 1. *adj.* complete/total. 2. *v.* to speak; to make (a sound). **ut•ter•ance**, *n.* thing spoken. **ut•ter•ly**, *adv.* completely. **ut•ter•most**, *adj.* (a) greatest that can be. (b) farthest.

UV ['juː'viː] *abbrev. for* ultraviolet.

u•vu•la ['juːvjulə] *n.* small lump of flesh hanging down at the back of the mouth.

ux•o•ri•ous [ʌk'sɔːrɪəs] *adj.* (man) who is very fond of his wife.

Vv

V,v [viː]. **V-chip** = device fitted to a TV that can block reception of programs that have been classified as unsuitable for children; **V-neck** = neckline shaped like a V; **V sign** = sign made with two fingers raised in the air (usu. meaning victory).

v. ['vɜːsəs] *prep.* against; *see* **ver•sus.**

va•can•cy ['veɪkənsɪ] *n.* (a) being vacant. (b) empty place/room/job. **va•cant,** *adj.* (a) empty/not occupied. (b) (expression) showing no interest/liveliness. **va•cant•ly,** *adv.* with a vacant expression. **va•cate** [və'keɪt] *v.* to leave/to make (sth) empty. **va•ca•tion** [və'keɪʃn] 1. *n.* (a) period of time when a person does not engage in a regular activity, as work or study. (b) act of vacating (an office, etc.). 2. *v.* to go on a vacation.

vac•ci•nate ['væksɪneɪt] *v.* **to v. s.o. against a disease** = to put a vaccine into s.o.. so that his body will react against it and thus protect him from catching the disease. **vac•ci•na•tion** [væksɪ'neɪʃn] *n.* act of vaccinating. **vac•cine** ['væksiːn] *n.* substance which contains the virus of a disease which when injected, gives protection against the disease.

vac•il•late ['væsɪleɪt] *v.* to waver/to hesitate. **vac•il•la•tion** ['væsɪ'leɪʃn] *n.* hesitation/wavering.

vac•u•ous ['vækjʊəs] *adj.* with no meaning/sense; silly/vacant (expression). **va•cu•i•ty** [və'kjuɪtɪ], **vac•u•ous•ness,** *n.* emptiness of meaning/silliness.

vac•u•um ['vækjʊəm] 1. *n.* space from which all matter, including air, has been removed; **vacuum-packed** = (food) packed in a vacuum, so that no air can enter the package. 2. *v. inf.* to clean with a vacuum cleaner. **vac•uum clean•er,** *n.* cleaning machine which sucks up dust. **vac•u•um bot•tle,** *n.* bottle or flask with double walls to keep liquids warm or cold.

vag•a•bond ['vægəbɒnd] *adj. & n.* (person) who wanders about/who has no home.

va•gar•y ['veɪgərɪ] *n.* oddity/strange behavior.

va•gi•na [və'dʒaɪnə] *n.* tube in a female mammal connecting the uterus to the vulva and through which a baby is born. **vag•i•nal,** *adj.* referring to the vagina.

va•grant ['veɪgrənt] *adj. & n.* (tramp/person) who wanders from place to place with no home or work. **va•gran•cy,** *n.* being a vagrant.

vague [veɪg] *adj.* (**-er, -est**) not clear/not precise; **I haven't the vaguest idea** = I have no idea at all. **vague•ly,** *adv.* more or less; in a vague way. **vague•ness,** *n.* being vague.

vain [veɪn] *adj.* (**-er, -est**) (a) useless; meaningless; (b) very proud of one's appearance. (c) **in v.** = without any success/result. **vain•ly,** *adv.* with no success/with no result.

val•ance ['væləns] *n.* short curtain.

vale [veɪl] *n.* valley.

val•e•dic•tion [vælɪ'dɪkʃn] *n.* (*formal*) farewell. **val•e•dic•to•ry,** *adj.* which says farewell.

val•ence, valency ['veɪləns, 'veɪlənsɪ] *n.* (*in chemistry*) power of an atom to combine.

val•en•tine ['væləntaɪn] *n.* (a) person chosen as a loved one on 14th February (St. Valentine's Day). (b) card or gift sent to someone you love on 14th February.

va•le•ri•an [və'lɪərɪən] *n.* type of wild plant with pink flowers.

val•et ['væleɪ, 'vælɪt] *n.* male servant who looks after his master's clothes; **v. service** = cleaning service in a hotel.

val•e•tu•di•nar•i•an [vælɪtjuːdɪ'neərɪən] *n.* person who likes to feel he is an invalid.

val•iant ['vælɪənt] *adj.* brave. **val•iant•ly,** *adv.* bravely.

val•id ['vælɪd] *adj.* (a) which is acceptable because it is true. (b) which can be lawfully used for a time. **val•i•date,** *v.* to make valid. **val•i•da•tion** [vælɪ'deɪʃn] *n.* act of validating. **va•lid•i•ty** [və'lɪdɪtɪ] *n.* (a) legal force. (b) truth.

æ back, ɑː farm, ɒ top, aɪ pipe, aʊ how, aɪə fire, aʊə flower, ɔː bought, ɔɪ toy, e fed, eəhair, eɪ take, ə afraid, əʊ boat, əʊə lower, ɜː word, iː heap, ɪ hit, ɪə hear, uː school, ʊ book, ʌ but, b back, d dog, ð then, dʒ just, f fog, g go, h hand, j yes, k catch, l last, m mix, n nut, ŋ sing, p penny, r round, s some, ʃ short, t too, tʃ chop, θ thing, v voice, w was, z zoo, ʒ treasure

val•ley ['vælɪ] *n.* long stretch of low land through which a river runs.

val•or, *Brit.* **val•our** ['vælə] *n.* bravery.

val•ue ['vælju:] 1. *n.* (a) worth (in money or esteem); **to get v. for one's money** = to get a good bargain. (b) usefulness. (c) **values** = principles/important things in life. 2. *v.* (a) to put a price in money on (an object). (b) to set a high value on (sth). **val•u•a•ble**. 1. *adj.* worth a lot of money; very useful. 2. *n.* **valuables** = objects of great value. **val•u•a•tion** [vælju'eɪʃn] *n.* estimate of the worth of sth; act of estimating the worth of sth. **val•ue-add•ed tax**, *n.* tax imposed on the value of goods or services. **val•ue•less**, *adj.* worthless/with no value.

valve [vælv] *n.* (a) mechanical device which allows air/liquid to pass through in one direction only; **safety v.** = valve which allows gas/steam, etc. to escape if the pressure is too great. (b) flap in a tube in the body which allows air/blood, etc. to circulate in one direction only. (c) part of a brass musical instrument which lengthens the tube. (d) single shell (of a shellfish). **val•vu•lar** ['vælvjulə] *adj.* referring to a valve in the heart.

vamp [væmp] *n.* (a) front part of the upper of a shoe or boot. (b) (*old*) flirtatious woman.

vam•pire ['væmpaɪə] *n.* person who supposedly sucks blood from his victims. **vam•pire bat**, *n.* type of small bat which sucks blood from animals.

van [væn] *n.* covered vehicle for carrying or moving goods, furniture, etc.

van•dal ['vændl] *n.* person who destroys property for the pleasure of destruction. **van•dal•ism**, *n.* meaningless destruction of property. **van•dal•ize**, *v.* to smash (sth) for no reason at all.

vane [veɪn] *n.* one of the blades on a water wheel/pump, etc.

van•guard ['vænɡɑːd] *n.* front part of an army; **in the v.** = in the front (of a movement).

va•nil•la [və'nɪlə] *n.* flavoring made from the seed pods of a tropical plant.

van•ish ['vænɪʃ] *v.* to disappear/to go out of sight; **to v. into thin air** = disappear completely. **van•ish•ing cream**, *n.* scented cream rubbed into the skin to make it soft. **van•ish•ing point**, *n.* point in a drawing where the horizontal lines seem to meet at eye level.

van•i•ty ['vænɪtɪ] *n.* (a) pride/feeling that you are more handsome etc. than you really are; conceit. (b) uselessness. **van•i•ty case**, *n.* small bag for carrying makeup/toiletries, etc. **van•i•ty pub•lish•ing**, *n.* practice of an author paying to have his/her book published.

van•quish ['væŋkwɪʃ] *v.* to defeat.

van•tage point ['vɑːntɪdʒpɔɪnt] *n.* place from which you can see well.

vap•id ['væpɪd] *adj.* dull (conversation). **va•pid•i•ty** [və'pɪdɪtɪ] *n.* dullness.

va•por•ize ['veɪpəraɪz] *v.* to turn into vapor. **va•por•i•za•tion** [veɪpəraɪ'zeɪʃn] *n.* changing into vapor. **va•por•iz•er**, *n.* machine which turns liquids (esp. water) into vapor.

va•por, *Brit.* **va•pour**, *n.* gas form of a liquid, usu. caused by heating; **v. trail** = line of white vapor left in the sky by an aircraft.

var•i•a•bil•i•ty [veərɪə'bɪlɪtɪ] *n.* being variable. **var•i•a•ble** ['veərɪəbl] 1. *adj.* which varies/changes all the time. 2. *n.* thing which varies. **var•i•ance** ['veərɪəns] *n.* **to be at v. with** = to disagree. **var•i•ant**, *adj. & n.* (version/spelling, etc.) which is slightly different. **var•i•a•tion** [veərɪ'eɪʃn] *n.* (a) act of varying. (b) amount by which sth varies. (c) **variations** = pieces of music which repeat the same theme but written in a different fashion.

var•i•cel•la [værɪ'selæ] *n.* chickenpox.

var•i•col•ored ['vɜːrɪkʌləd] *adj.* variegated.

var•i•cose vein ['værɪkəus'veɪn] *n.* swollen vein, esp. in the leg.

var•i•e•gat•ed ['veərɪɡeɪtɪd] *adj.* (plant which is) striped/marked in contrasting colors. **var•i•e•ga•tion** [veərɪ'ɡeɪʃn] *n.* irregular marking in contrasting colors.

va•ri•e•ty [və'raɪətɪ] *n.* (a) being of different sorts; **for a v. of reasons** = for several different reasons. (b) different type (of plant). (c) **v. show** = entertainment which includes several different types of performer (such as singers/magicians/ventriloquists, etc.).

va•ri•e•tal, *adj.* referring to a variety of plant. **var•i•ous** ['veərɪəs] *adj.* different/several. **var•i•ous•ly**, *adv.* in different ways.

var•i•fo•cal [veərɪ'fəukl] *adj. & n.* **v. glasses/varifocals** = glasses with a graduated lens in each frame, allowing the correction of more than one defect of vision with only one lens.

var•nish ['vɑːnɪʃ] 1. *n.* (a) liquid which when painted on sth gives it a shiny surface. (b) shiny surface made by painting with varnish. 2. *v.* (a) to paint with a liquid varnish; to give a shiny surface to sth. (b) to make seem more acceptable, better than it is, etc. in order to fool s.o.; **to v. the truth.**

var•y ['veərɪ] *v.* (a) to make different; to be different; **you ought to v. your diet** = eat different sorts of food. (b) to deviate **from**. **var•ied**, *adj.* of various kinds/different.

vas [væs] *n.* tube in the body.

vas•cu•lar ['væskjulə] *adj.* referring to veins, etc., which carry blood or sap.

vase [vɑːz] *n.* container for cut flowers or for decoration.

vas•ec•to•my [və'sektəmɪ] *n.* operation on a man to cut the tubes through which sperm flows and so to make him sterile.

vas•sal ['væsl] *n.* (a) servant. (b) **v. state** = country which is under the rule of another.

vast [vɑːst] *adj.* very large. **vast•ly,** *adv.* very much. **vast•ness,** *n.* large size.

vat [væt] *n.* large container for liquids (esp. wine).

VAT [væt, viːeɪ'tiː] *abbrev. for* Value-Added Tax, government tax on goods or services.

vaude•ville ['vɔːdəvɪl] *n.* variety show.

vault [vɔːlt] 1. *n.* (a) arched stone ceiling. (b) underground room (for keeping things safe). (c) underground room for burying people. (d) high jump; **pole v.** = leap over a high bar, using a pole to swing you up. 2. *v.* to jump over (sth) by putting one hand on it to steady yourself. **vault•ed,** *adj.* with a stone arch.

vaunt [vɔːnt] *v.* to boast about (sth).

VD ['viː'diː] *abbrev. for* venereal disease.

VDU [viːdiː'juː] *abbrev. for* visual display unit.

veal [viːl] *n.* meat from a calf.

vec•tor ['vektə] *n.* (*in mathematics*) (a) thing which has both direction and size. (b) insect, etc., which carries disease.

veer ['vɪə] *v.* to turn.

veg•e•ta•ble ['vedʒɪtəbl] *adj. & n.* (a) (referring to) plants; **the v. kingdom** = all plant life. (b) plant grown for food, not usu. sweet. (c) person who is more or less incapable of movement or thought. **veg•e•tar•i•an** [vedʒɪ'teərɪən] *adj. & n.* (person) who does not eat meat; (restaurant) which does not serve meat. **veg•e•tar•i•an•ism,** *n.* belief that not eating meat is good for you. **veg•e•tate,** *v.* to live like a vegetable, not moving or doing anything. **veg•e•ta•tion** [vedʒɪ'teɪʃn] *n.* (a) act of vegetating. (b) plants.

ve•he•mence ['vɪəməns] *n.* forceful way (of saying what you think). **ve•he•ment** ['vɪəmənt] *adj.* forceful. **ve•he•ment•ly,** *adv.* in a forceful way.

ve•hi•cle ['vɪəkl] *n.* (a) machine on wheels which travels along the road; rocket which travels in space. (b) **v. for** = means of expressing (sth). **ve•hic•u•lar** [vɪ'ɪkjulə] *adj.* referring to vehicles.

veil [veɪl] 1. *n.* light cloth which can cover a woman's head or face; **to take the v.** = to be-

come a nun. 2. *v.* to cover with a veil; **veiled** = hidden or disguised.

vein [veɪn] *n.* (a) small tube in the body along which blood runs to the heart. (b) thin line on the leaf of a plant. (c) thin layer of a mineral in a rock. (d) mood; **humorous v. veined,** *adj.* covered with veins.

veldt [velt] *n.* grass-covered plain in South Africa.

vel•lum ['veləm] *n.* (a) good quality writing paper. (b) skin of an animal made very thin and used for binding books or writing on.

ve•loc•i•ty [və'lɒsɪtɪ] *n.* speed.

ve•lour [və'luə] *n.* thick, soft cloth with a soft surface like velvet.

ve•lum ['viːləm] *n.* soft membrane. **ve•lar,** *adj.* referring to a soft membrane.

vel•vet ['velvət] *adj. & n.* (a) cloth (made from silk, etc.) with a soft surface of cut threads. (b) soft skin covering a deer's antlers. **vel•vet•een,** *n.* velvet made of cotton. **vel•vet•y,** *adj.* with soft surface like velvet.

ve•nal ['viːnəl] *adj.* (person) who will take a bribe; (act) which is dishonest/which is done for a bribe. **ve•nal•i•ty** [vɪ'nælɪtɪ] *n.* being venal.

ven•det•ta [ven'detə] *n.* private quarrel between families/persons.

vend•ing ['vendɪŋ] *n.* selling; **v. machine** = machine which provides cigarettes/chocolate, etc., when money is put into a slot. **ven•dor** ['vendə] *n.* person who sells.

ve•neer [və'nɪə] 1. *n.* (a) thin layer of expensive wood glued to the surface of ordinary wood. (b) thin layer of politeness/knowledge which covers a person's bad qualities. 2. *v.* to cover (wood) with a veneer.

ven•er•ate ['venəreɪt] *v.* to respect greatly. **ven•er•a•ble,** *adj.* very old and likely to be respected. **ven•er•a•tion** [venə'reɪʃn] *n.* respect.

ve•ne•re•al [və'nɪərɪəl] *adj.* (disease) transmitted during sexual intercourse.

ve•ne•tian blind [və'niːʃn'blaɪnd] *n.* blind to shut out light, made of horizontal strips of plastic/wood, etc., which can be opened or shut or raised and lowered by pulling a string.

venge•ance ['vendʒəns] *n.* harm caused to s.o. in return for harm they have caused you; *inf.* **with a v.** = very strongly.

ve•ni•al ['viːnɪəl] *adj.* slight (mistake); (sin) which can be excused. **ve•ni•al•i•ty** [viːnɪ'ælɪtɪ] *n.* being venial.

ven•i•son ['venɪzn] *n.* meat from a deer.

ven•om ['venəm] *n.* (a) poison (from a snake, etc.). (b) bitter hatred. **ven•om•ous,** *adj.* (a) poisonous. (b) bitterly spiteful.

ve•nous ['viːnəs] *adj.* referring to veins (in the body).

vent [vent] 1. *n.* (a) hole through which air/gas can escape. (b) slit in the back of a coat. (c) **to give v. to** = to let (an emotion) come out. 2. *v.* **he vented his anger on her** = he made her the target of his anger.

ven•ti•late ['ventɪleɪt] *v.* (a) to allow fresh air to come into. (b) to discuss (a question) in the open. **ven•ti•la•tion** [ventɪ'leɪʃn] *n.* bringing in fresh air; **v. shaft** = tube which allows fresh air to go down into a coal mine. **ven•ti•la•tor** ['ventɪleɪtə] *n.* opening which allows fresh air to come in; machine which pumps in fresh air.

ven•tral ['ventrəl] *adj.* (*formal*) referring to the abdomen.

ven•tri•cle ['ventrɪkl] *n.* space in the heart which fills up with blood and then pumps it out into the arteries.

ven•tril•o•quist [ven'trɪləkwɪst] *n.* person who can make his voice appear to come from a puppet. **ven•tril•o•quism,** *n.* act of being a ventriloquist.

ven•ture ['ventʃə] 1. *n.* commercial deal which involves risk. 2. *v.* to dare/to be bold enough to do sth dangerous or risky. **ven•ture•some,** *adj.* (person) who dares to take a risk.

ven•ue ['venju] *n.* agreed place where sth will take place.

ve•ra•cious [və'reɪʃəs] *adj.* truthful. **ve•rac•i•ty** [və'ræsɪtɪ] *n.* truth.

ve•ran•da(h) [və'rændə] *n.* covered terrace along the side of a house with no outside wall.

verb [vɜːb] *n.* part of speech which shows how s.o./sth acts or feels. **ver•bal,** *adj.* (a) referring to a verb. (b) spoken; not written down. **ver•bal•ize,** *v.* to express in words. **ver•bal•ly,** *adv.* in spoken words.

ver•ba•tim [vɜː'beɪtɪm] *adj. & adv.* word for word; in exactly the same words.

ver•be•na [vɜː'biːnə] *n.* type of scented herb, used to make soap or in hot drinks.

ver•bi•age ['vɜːbɪdʒ] *n.* excess, useless words.

ver•bose [vɜː'bəʊs] *adj.* using more words than necessary. **ver•bos•i•ty** [və'bɒsɪtɪ] *n.* being verbose.

ver•dant ['vɜːdənt] *adj.* (*formal*) green (grass).

ver•dict ['vɜːdɪkt] *n.* (a) judgment/decision by a judge or jury. (b) opinion.

ver•di•gris ['vɜːdɪgrɪs] *n.* green discoloring of copper, etc., through contact with the atmosphere over a period of time.

ver•dure ['vɜːdjʊə] *n.* (*formal*) green vegetation.

verge [vɜːdʒ] 1. *n.* edge of sth; **on the v. of** = near to. 2. *v.* **to v. on** = to be near to.

ver•i•fy ['verɪfaɪ] *v.* to check/to see if (a statement) is correct. **ver•i•fi•a•ble** [verɪ'faɪəbl] *adj.* which can be verified. **ver•i•fi•ca•tion** [verifɪ'keɪʃn] *n.* checking that sth is correct.

ver•i•ly ['verɪlɪ] *adv.* (*old*) truly.

ver•i•si•mil•i•tude [verɪs'mɪlɪtjuːd] *n.* appearance of being true/sth having the appearance of being true.

ver•i•ta•ble ['verɪtəbl] *adj.* true/real.

ver•mi•cel•li [vɜːmɪ'selɪ] *n.* type of very thin spaghetti.

ver•mic•u•lite [vɜː'mɪkjuːlaɪt] *n.* grains of silica, used as a growing medium for some types of pot plants.

ver•mi•form [və'mɪfɔːm] *adj.* shaped like a worm.

ver•mil•ion [və'mɪlɪən] *adj. & n.* bright red (color).

ver•min ['vɜːmɪn] *n.* unwanted, disgusting animals, esp. those which are pests, as cockroaches, rats, etc. **ver•min•ous,** *adj.* covered with vermin.

ver•mouth ['vɜːməθ] *n.* type of strong wine flavored with herbs.

ver•nac•u•lar [və'nækjʊlə] *adj. & n.* (referring to) the ordinary spoken language of a country or region.

ver•nal ['vɜːnl] *adj.* (*formal*) referring to the spring.

ve•ron•i•ca [və'rɒnɪkə] *n.* low creeping plant with blue flowers.

ver•ru•ca [və'ruːkə] *n.* wart.

ver•sa•tile ['vɜːsətaɪl] *adj.* (person/machine) able to do various things equally well; (musician) who can play many different instruments. **ver•sa•til•i•ty** [vɜːsə'tɪlɪtɪ] *n.* ability to do various things with equal skill.

verse [vɜːs] *n.* (a) group of lines of poetry which form a part of a poem. (b) poetry; lines of writing with a rhythm and sometimes rhyme. (c) one line of a poem. (d) short (numbered) sentence from the Bible; **to give chapter and v. for sth** = to quote exactly the origin of a statement. **versed,** *adj.* **well v. in** = knowing a lot about/being well skilled in. **ver•si•fi•ca•tion** [vɜːsɪfɪ'keɪʃn] *n.* making of poetry; way in which a poem is written. **ver•si•fy** ['vɜːsɪfaɪ] *v.* to write poetry.

ver•sion ['vɜːʃn] *n.* (a) story of what happened as seen from a particular point of view. (b) translation.

ver•so ['vɜːsəʊ] *n.* left side/back (of a piece of paper/a page of a book, etc.).

ver•sus ['vɜːsəs] *prep.* (*usu. written* **v.**) (*in a civil court case/in sports*) against.

ver•te•bra ['vɜːtɪbrə] n. (pl. -brae [-briː]) one of the bones which form the spine. **ver•te•brate** ['vɜːtɪbrət] adj. & n. (animal) which has a backbone.

ver•tex ['vɜːteks] n. (pl. -texes, -tices [-tɪsiːz]) top; angle at the top of a triangle.

ver•ti•cal ['vɜːtɪkl] 1. adj. upright. 2. n. upright line (in geometry). **ver•ti•cal•ly**, adv. straight up/down.

ver•ti•go ['vɜːtɪgəʊ] n. dizziness caused by heights. **ver•tig•i•nous** [vɜː'tɪdʒɪnəs], adj. which makes one dizzy.

verve [vɜːv] n. enthusiasm/feeling of liveliness.

ver•y ['verɪ] 1. adv. (a) to a high degree; v. **much the same** = almost the same. (b) exactly; **the v. same** = exactly the same. 2. adj. (a) exactly the same. (b) exact; precise; **at the v. beginning** = right at the beginning.

ve•si•cle ['vesɪkl] n. small hollow in the body (usu. filled with liquid). **ve•sic•u•lar** [ve-'sɪkjʊlə] adj. referring to a vesicle.

ves•pers ['vespəz] n. church service in the evening.

ves•sel ['vesl] n. (a) container (for liquid); **blood v.** = tube which carries blood around the body. (b) ship.

vest [vest] n. short, close-fitting sleeveless garment which goes over a shirt and usu. under a jacket. **vest•ed**, adj. v. **interest** = sth which is to s.o.'s advantage, and makes him want to avoid changes, because it is in his interest to keep the present system.

ves•ti•bule ['vestɪbjuːl] n. entrance hall.

ves•tige ['vestɪdʒ] n. trace/remains. **ves•tig•i•al** [ves'tɪdʒəl] adj. which exists as a vestige; v. **tail** = very small tail.

vest•ments ['vestmənts] n. pl. clergyman's robes.

ves•try ['vestrɪ] n. clergyman's room in a church.

vet [vet] 1. n. inf. short for veterinarian. 2. v. (vetted) to examine carefully.

vetch [vetʃ] n. (pl. -es) type of wild pea.

vet•er•an ['vetrən] n. (a) person who has given long service and has much experience. (b) person who has served in the armed forces.

vet•er•i•nar•y ['vetrɪnrɪ] adj. referring to the medical and surgical treatment of animals. **vet•er•i•nar•i•an** [vetərɪ'neərɪən] n. doctor who specializes in veterinary medicine.

ve•to ['viːtəʊ] 1. n. (pl. -oes) power to reject sth. 2. v. to reject.

vex [veks] v. to annoy. **vex•a•tion** [vek'seɪʃn] n. annoyance. **vex•a•tious** [vek'seɪʃəs] adj. annoying; v. **litigation** = legal action brought for no real reason, meant only to annoy. **vexed,** adj. (a) annoyed. (b) (question) which is often discussed but which has not been solved.

VHF [viːeɪtʃ'ef] abbreviation for very high frequency.

vi•a ['vaɪə] prep. (traveling) through.

vi•a•ble ['vaɪəbl] adj. (a) able to work in practice. (b) (of new-born young) sufficiently developed to survive. **vi•a•bil•i•ty** [vaɪə'bɪlɪtɪ] n. being viable.

vi•a•duct ['vaɪədʌkt] n. long bridge carrying a road/railroad over a wide valley.

vi•al ['vaɪəl] n. small glass bottle.

vi•ands ['vaɪəndz] n. pl. (formal) food.

vibes [vaɪbz] n. pl. inf. (a) vibraharp. (b) sensations.

vi•brate [vaɪ'breɪt] v. to shudder/to shake. **vi•bra•harp,** n. (also **vibraphone**) instrument like a xylophone with an amplifier. **vi•bran•cy,** n. being vibrant. **vi•brant** ['vaɪbrənt] adj. full (of energy). **vi•bra•tion** [vaɪ'breɪʃn] n. act of vibrating; rapid movement. **vi•bra•to** [vɪ'brɑːtəʊ] n. (in music) trembling effect. **vi•bra•tor,** n. machine which vibrates. **vi•bra•to•ry,** adj. which vibrates.

vi•bur•num [vaɪ'bɜːnəm] n. common shrub with pink or white flowers.

vic•ar ['vɪkə] n. (a) (in the Church of England) clergyman in charge of a parish. (b) (in the Protestant Episcopal Church) clergyman in charge of a chapel in a parish. (c) (in the Roman Catholic Church) prelate who represents the pope or a bishop. **vic•ar•age** ['vɪkrɪdʒ] n. vicar's house.

vi•car•i•ous [vɪ'keərɪəs] adj. felt through imagining what another person feels; (pleasure) felt because you imagine how s.o. is enjoying sth. **vi•car•i•ous•ly,** adv. in a vicarious way.

vice [vaɪs] n. (a) sexual wickedness/immorality; v. **squad** = police department dealing with prostitution, etc. (b) great wickedness. (c) bad habit. (d) vise.

vice- [vaɪs] prefix meaning deputy; second in rank.

vice-pres•i•dent [vaɪs'prezɪdənt] n. deputy to a president.

vice•roy ['vaɪsrɔɪ] n. person who represents a

king or queen. **vice•re•gal** [vaɪs'riːgl] *adj.* referring to a viceroy.

vice ver•sa [vaɪsə'vɜːsə] *adv.* the other way round.

vi•cin•i•ty [vɪ'sɪnɪtɪ] *n.* area around sth; **in the v. (of)** = near (by); approximately.

vi•cious ['vɪʃəs] *adj.* (a) wicked. (b) **v. circle** = interlocking chain of bad circumstances from which it is impossible to escape. **vi•cious•ly**, *adv.* in a wicked/spiteful way.

vi•cis•si•tude [vɪ'sɪsɪtjuːd] *n.* (*formal*) variation in luck.

vic•tim ['vɪktɪm] *n.* person who suffers an attack/an accident. **vic•tim•i•za•tion** [vɪktɪmaɪ'zeɪʃn] *n.* act of victimizing. **vic•tim•ize** ['vɪktɪmaɪz] *v.* to choose (s.o.) as a victim; to treat s.o. more harshly than others. **vic•tim•ol•o•gy**, *n.* study of the psychological impact of crime on its victims.

vic•tor ['vɪktə] *n.* person who wins (a game/a battle). **Vic•to•ri•an** [vɪk'tɔːrɪən] *adj.* referring to the reign of Queen Victoria of England (1837–1901). **vic•to•ri•ous** [vɪk'tɔːrɪəs] *adj.* (person/general) who has won a game/a battle. **vic•to•ry** ['vɪktrɪ] *n.* win; winning of a battle.

vict•ual ['vɪtl] (*formal*) 1. *n.* **victuals** = food. 2. *v.* to supply (a ship/an army) with food.

vi•cu•na [vɪ'kjuːnə] *n.* soft wool from a South American animal.

vi•de ['vɪdeɪ] *Latin word meaning* see.

vid•e•o ['vɪdɪəʊ] *adj. & n.* (system) which shows pictures on a television screen. **vid•e•o•cas•sette**, *n.* small cassette containing a videotape. **vid•e•o•con•fer•ence**, *n.* conference between people located in different places via video and sound links. **vid•e•o•disk**, *n.* disk which contains recorded sound and pictures. **vid•e•o•re•cord•er**, *n.* machine which records television pictures on tape, so that they can be played back later. **vid•e•o•tape.** 1. *n.* magnetic tape which can record pictures and sound for playing back through a television set. 2. *v.* to record (pictures, etc.) on magnetic tape.

vie [vaɪ] *v.* **to v. with s.o.** = to rival/to try to beat s.o.

view [vjuː] 1. *n.* (a) scene (which you can see from a certain place). (b) sight/action of looking at sth; **on v.** = on show for people to look at. (c) opinion. **I share your v.** = I agree with your opinion; **to take a dim v. of** = to disapprove of. (d) **in v. of** = when you consider. (e) intention/what you hope to do; **with a v. to** = planning to. 2. *v.* (a) to look at (sth)/to consider (a problem). (b) to watch television; **the viewing public** = people who watch television.

view•er, *n.* (a) person who watches television. (b) small device for looking at color slides. **view•find•er**, *n.* small window in a camera which you look through when taking a picture, and which shows the exact picture you are about to take. **view•point**, *n.* way of looking at things/of considering things.

vig•il ['vɪdʒɪl] *n.* keeping awake/on guard all night. **vig•i•lance**, *n.* being watchful/on guard. **vig•i•lant**, *adj.* watchful/on guard. **vig•i•lan•te** [vɪdʒɪ'læntɪ] *n.* person who tries to enforce law and order, esp. when the police find it impossible to do so.

vi•gnette [vɪ'njet] *n.* small sketch.

vig•or, *Brit.* **vig•our** ['vɪgə] *n.* energy. **vig•or•ous**, *adj.* energetic/very active; strong. **vig•or•ous•ly**, *adv.* in a vigorous way.

vile [vaɪl] *adj.* extremely unpleasant/bad. **vile•ly**, *adv.* in a vile way. **vile•ness**, *n.* being vile.

vil•i•fy ['vɪlɪfaɪ] *v.* to say extremely bad things about (s.o.). **vil•i•fi•ca•tion** [vɪlɪfɪ'keɪʃn] *n.* act of vilifying.

vil•la ['vɪlə] *n.* large country (or seaside) house (usu. in a warm country).

vil•lage ['vɪlɪdʒ] *n.* small group of houses (usu. smaller than a town) in the country. **vil•lag•er**, *n.* person who lives in a village.

vil•lain ['vɪlən] *n.* wicked person. **vil•lain•ous**, *adj.* wicked. **vil•lain•y**, *n.* wickedness.

vil•lein ['vɪleɪn] *n.* medieval agricultural laborer.

vim [vɪm] *n. inf.* energy.

vin•ai•grette [vɪneɪ'gret] *n.* (a) small bottle of smelling salts. (b) sauce made of oil and vinegar.

vin•di•cate ['vɪndɪkeɪt] *v.* to justify; to show that (s.o.) was right. **vin•di•ca•tion** [vɪndɪ'keɪʃn] *n.* (**of**) proving that sth was right.

vin•dic•tive [vɪn'dɪktɪv] *adj.* wanting to take revenge; spiteful. **vin•dic•tive•ly**, *adv.* spitefully. **vin•dic•tive•ness**, *n.* spite; desire to take revenge.

vine [vaɪn] *n.* (a) climbing plant which bears grapes. (b) climbing plant.

vin•e•gar ['vɪnɪgə] *n.* liquid made from sour wine/cider, used in cooking and for preserving food. **vin•e•gar•y**, *adj.* (wine, etc.) tasting like vinegar; bad-tempered (person).

vine•yard ['vɪnjəd] *n.* field of vines for producing wine.

vi•no ['viːnəʊ] *n. Sl.* wine, esp. red Italian wine.

vi•nous ['vaɪnəs] *adj.* referring to wine.

vin•tage ['vɪntɪdʒ] *n.* (a) collecting of grapes to make wine; grapes which are collected. (b) fine wine made in a particular year; **v. wine/v.**

port = fine/expensive old wine/port. (c) year of make. (d) of typical high quality.

vint•ner ['vɪntnə] *n.* person who makes or sells wine.

vi•nyl ['vaɪnl] *n.* type of plastic sheet which looks like leather/tiles, etc.

vi•ol ['vaɪəl] *n.* early stringed instrument.

vi•o•la [vaɪ'əʊlə] *n.* (a) small pansylike garden flower. (b) stringed instrument slightly larger than a violin.

vi•o•late ['vaɪəleɪt] *v.* (a) to break/to go against (the law/a treaty). (b) (*formal*) to rape. **vi•o•la•tion** [vaɪə'leɪʃn] *n.* act of violating; **in v. of an agreement** = against the terms of an agreement. **vi•o•la•tor**, *n.* person who violates.

vi•o•lence ['vaɪələns] *n.* (a) force/strength. (b) rough action. **vi•o•lent**, *adj.* (a) strong. (b) rough. **vi•o•lent•ly**, *adv.* strongly; roughly.

vi•o•let ['vaɪələt] *n. & adj.* (a) small wild plant with bluish purple flowers. (b) bluish purple (color).

vi•o•lin [vaɪə'lɪn] *n.* stringed musical instrument played with a bow. **vi•o•lin•ist**, *n.* person who plays the violin. **vi•o•lon•cel•lo** [vaɪələn'tʃeləʊ] *n.* (*pl.* **-os**) (*formal*) cello.

VIP [viːaɪ'piː] *abbreviation for* very important person; **VIP treatment** = being treated like a very important person.

vi•per ['vaɪpə] *n.* adder/poisonous snake.

vi•ra•go [vɪ'rɑːgəʊ] *n.* (*pl.* **-oes, -os**) fierce loud-mouthed woman.

vi•ral ['vaɪrəl] *adj.* referring to a virus.

vir•gin ['vɜːdʒɪn] 1. *n.* (a) person who has never had sexual intercourse. (b) **the V. (Mary)** = the mother of Jesus Christ. 2. *adj.* pure/untouched. **vir•gin•al**, *adj.* pure like a virgin. **vir•gin•als**, *n. pl.* type of 16th century harpsichord. **vir•gin•i•ty** [vɜː'dʒɪnɪtɪ] *n.* being a virgin; **to lose your v.** = to have sexual intercourse for the first time.

vir•gin•i•a creep•er [vɜː'dʒɪnɪə'kriːpə] *n.* common climbing plant which grows on walls, with leaves which turn bright red in autumn.

Vir•go ['vɜːgəʊ] *n.* one of the signs of the zodiac, shaped like a girl.

vir•ile ['vɪraɪl] *adj.* manly; masculine. **vi•ril•i•ty** [vɪ'rɪlɪtɪ] *n.* being virile; strength; manliness.

vi•rol•o•gy [vaɪ'rɒlədʒɪ] *n.* study of viruses. **vi•rol•o•gist**, *n.* scientist who studies viruses.

vir•tu•al ['vɜːtjʊəl] *adj.* almost, if not in fact. **vir•tu•al•ly**, *adv.* almost. **vir•tu•al re•al•i•ty**, *n.* artificial three-dimensional environment, generated by interactive computer software.

vir•tue ['vɜːtjuː] *n.* (a) particular goodness (of character); good quality. (b) special quality. (c) **by v. of** = because of. **vir•tu•ous**, *adj.* very good/very honest. **vir•tu•ous•ly**, *adv.* in a virtuous way.

vir•tu•o•so [vɜːtjʊ'əʊzəʊ] *n.* (*pl.* **-os/-si** [-siː]) person who is skilled in an art, esp. who can play a musical instrument extremely well. **vir•tu•os•i•ty** [vɜːtjʊ'ɒsɪtɪ] *n.* ability to play a musical instrument/sing, etc., extremely well.

vir•u•lence ['vɪrjʊləns] *n.* (*of a disease*) great strength. **vir•u•lent**, *adj.* very bad (attack of disease); very harsh (attack). **vir•u•lent•ly**, *adv.* in a virulent way.

vi•rus ['vaɪrəs] *n.* (*pl.* **-es**) (a) germ which is smaller than bacteria and which causes colds/pneumonia, etc. (b) hidden routine placed in a computer program, which corrupts or destroys files.

vi•sa ['viːzə] *n.* special mark on a passport/special paper allowing you to enter a country; **30-day v.** = visa which allows you to stay in a country for 30 days.

vis-à-vis [viːzə'viː] *prep.* (a) in relation to. (b) compared with.

vis•cer•a ['vɪsərə] *n. pl.* organs inside the body, esp. the intestines. **vis•cer•al**, *adj.* referring to the viscera.

vis•cos•i•ty [vɪs'kɒsɪtɪ] *n.* state of being viscous. **vis•cose** ['vɪskəʊz] *n.* artificial silk material, made from viscous cellulose. **vis•cid, viscous** ['vɪsɪd, 'vɪskəs] *adj.* thick/sticky (liquid).

vis•count ['vaɪkaʊnt] *n.* title of a nobleman below an earl. **vis•count•ess**, *n.* (*pl.* **-es**) wife of a viscount.

vise [vaɪs] *n.* tool with jaws that screw tight to hold sth. **vise•like**, *adj.* tight, as in a vise.

vis•i•ble ['vɪzɪbl] *adj.* which can be seen. **vis•i•bil•i•ty** [vɪzɪ'bɪlɪtɪ] *n.* ability to be seen clearly; **good v.** = ability for things to be seen at long distances because the air is clear. **vis•i•bly**, *adv.* obviously; in a way which can be seen.

vi•sion ['vɪʒn] *n.* (a) ability to see; **field of v.** = range from one side to another over which you can see clearly; **tunnel v.** = very narrow or

---

æ back, ɑː farm, ɒ top, aɪ pipe, aʊ how, aɪə fire, aʊə flower, ɔː bought, ɔɪ toy, e fed, eəhair, eɪ take, ə afraid, əʊ boat, əʊə lower, ɜː word, iː heap, ɪ hit, ɪə hear, uː school, ʊ book, ʌ but, b back, d dog, ð then, dʒ just, f fog, g go, h hand, j yes, k catch, l last, m mix, n nut, ŋ sing, p penny, r round, s some, ʃ short, t too, tʃ chop, θ thing, v voice, w was, z zoo, ʒ treasure

prejudiced way of looking at things; nar-row-mindedness. (b) ability to look and plan ahead. (c) thing which you imagine; **he has visions of himself as president** = he imagines he will be president one day. (d) ghost; strange sight. **vi•sion•ar•y**. 1. *adj.* idealistic/impracticable (plan). 2. *n.* person whose plans are idealistic and impracticable.

vis•it ['vɪzɪt] 1. *n.* short stay; **to pay a v. to** = to go to see (s.o.)/to stay a short time in (a place). 2. *v.* to stay a short time (in a place/with s.o.); **visiting hours** = times when you can visit patients in a hospital; **visiting team** = opposing team who has come to play on the home ground. **vis•it•ant**, *n.* ghost. **vis•it•a•tion** [vɪzɪ'teɪʃn] *n.* (a) trouble which is thought to be sent as a divine punishment. (b) official visit. **vis•i•tor** ['vɪzɪtə] *n.* person who visits.

vi•sor ['vaɪzə] *n.* moveable part of a helmet, which drops down to protect the face; folding shield above the windshield which protects the driver of a car from bright sunshine.

vis•ta ['vɪstə] *n.* wide view.

vis•u•al ['vɪzjʊəl] *adj.* referring to what can be seen; **v. arts** = painting/sculpture, etc. (as opposed to music); **v. aids** = slides/motion pictures used for teaching purposes. **vis•u•al•ize** ['vɪzjʊəlaɪz] *v.* to picture/to see (sth) in your mind. **vis•u•al•ly**, *adv.* in a visual way.

vi•tal ['vaɪtl] *adj.* (a) very important. (b) vigorous/energetic (person). (c) (organs in the body) which are essential to life. **vi•tal•ly**, *adv.* in a very important way. **vi•tal•i•ty** [vaɪ'tælɪtɪ] *n.* great energy. **vi•tal•ize**, *v.* to make (sth) more energetic. **vi•tals**, *n. pl.* important organs in a body. **vi•tal sta•tis•tics**, *n.* (a) official statistics concerning populations, births, deaths, etc. (b) *inf.* measurements of bust, waist and hips of a woman.

vi•ta•min ['vɪtəmɪn] *n.* chemical substance occurring in food which is important for the development or health of the human body.

vi•ti•ate ['vɪʃɪeɪt] *v.* to make bad/to make weak. **vi•ti•a•tion** [vɪʃɪ'eɪʃn] *n.* act of vitiating.

vit•re•ous ['vɪtrɪəs] *adj.* like glass. **vit•ri•fi•ca•tion** [vɪtrɪfɪ'keɪʃn] *n.* act of vitrifying. **vit•ri•fy** ['vɪtrɪfaɪ] *v.* to make into glass; to become like glass.

vit•ri•ol ['vɪtrɪəl] *n.* sulfuric acid. **vit•ri•ol•ic** [vɪtrɪ'ɒlɪk] *adj.* very violent/very rude (attack).

vi•tu•per•a•tion [vɪtjupə'reɪʃn] *n.* (*formal*) abuse; insulting words. **vi•tu•per•a•tive**, *adj.* (*formal*) insulting/abusive.

vi•va vo•ce ['vaɪvə 'vəʊsɪ] *adj.* orally.

vi•va•cious [vɪ'veɪʃəs] *adj.* full of life/full of excitement. **vi•va•cious•ly**, *adv.* in a vivacious

way. **vi•va•cious•ness, vivacity** [vɪ'væsɪtɪ] *n.* being vivacious.

viv•id ['vɪvɪd] *adj.* (a) very bright (light/color). (b) very lifelike (description); very lively (imagination). **viv•id•ly**, *adv.* in a vivid way. **viv•id•ness**, *n.* being vivid.

vi•vip•a•rous [vɪ'vɪpərəs] *adj.* (animal) which produces live young (that is, which does not lay eggs).

viv•i•sec•tion [vɪvɪ'sekʃən] *n.* operating on a live animal for the purpose of scientific research.

vix•en ['vɪksn] *n.* female fox.

viz. [vɪz *or* 'neɪmlɪ] *adv.* namely.

vo•cab•u•lar•y [və'kæbjʊlərɪ] *n.* (a) words used by a person or group of persons. (b) printed list of words.

vo•cal ['vəʊkl] 1. *adj.* (a) referring to the voice; **v. cords** = muscles in the throat which produce sounds. (b) very loud/insistent (opposition). 2. *n. pl.* **vocals** = popular songs performed with a group. **vo•cal•ic** [vəʊ'kælɪk] *adj.* referring to vowels. **vo•cal•ist**, *n.* singer. **vo•cal•ize**, *v.* to make a sound with your voice. **vo•cal•ly**, *adv.* in a loud way.

vo•ca•tion [və'keɪʃn] *n.* job which you feel you have been called to do/for which you have a special talent; **she missed her v.** = she should be in another job for which she is better suited. **vo•ca•tion•al**, *adj.* referring to a vocation; **v. training** = training for a particular job.

vo•cif•er•ate [və'sɪfəreɪt] *v.* (*formal*) to shout protests against sth. **vo•cif•er•ous**, *adj.* loud/shouting. **vo•cif•er•ous•ly**, *adv.* loudly.

vod•ka ['vɒdkə] *n.* colorless alcohol made originally in Russia or Poland.

vogue [vəʊg] *n.* fashion; popularity; **in v.** = fashionable.

voice [vɔɪs] 1. *n.* (a) sounds made by a person speaking or singing; **she's lost her v.** = she can't speak (because of a cold); **in a low v.** = quietly; **don't raise your v.** = don't talk so loudly. (b) right to express an opinion. (c) **active v./passive v.** = forms of a verb which show whether the subject is doing sth or having sth done to it. 2. *v.* to express (an opinion). **voice•less**, *adj.* silent; with no voice. **voice mail**, *n.* electronic answering system that records telephone messages.

void [vɔɪd] 1. *adj.* (a) empty. (b) **null and v.** = not valid. 2. *n.* emptiness. 3. *v.* to empty.

voile [vɔɪl] *n.* very thin cotton or silk material.

vol•a•tile ['vɒlətaɪl] *adj.* (a) (liquid) which can easily change into vapor. (b) (person) who changes his mind/his mood frequently. **vol•a•til•i•ty** [vɒlə'tɪlɪtɪ] *n.* being volatile.

vol-au-vent [vɒləʊ'vɒn] *n.* small pastry case

with a filling of meat, vegetables, or fish inside.

vol•ca•no [vɒl'keɪnəʊ] n. (pl. **-oes, -os**) mountain with a hole on the top through which lava, ash and gas can come. **vol•can•ic** [vɒl-'kænɪk] adj. referring to volcanoes. **vol•can•ol•o•gy** [vɒlkə'nɒlədʒɪ] n. study of volcanoes.

vole [vəʊl] n. small animal, resembling a mouse.

vo•li•tion [və'lɪʃn] n. (formal) wish/will. **of one's own v.** = because one wants to and not because one is told to.

vol•ley ['vɒlɪ] 1. n. (a) series of shots/missiles which are fired/thrown at the same time. (b) (in sports) hitting the ball before it touches the ground. 2. v. (a) to fire several shots/throw several missiles at the same time. (b) (in sports) to hit the ball before it touches the ground. **vol•ley•ball**, n. team game in which a large ball is thrown across a high net, and must not touch the ground.

volt [vɒlt] n. standard unit of electric potential. **volt•age**, n. amount of electric force. **volt•me•ter**, n. instrument for measuring voltage.

volte-face ['vɒlt'fæs] n. sudden unexpected change of opinion.

vol•u•ble ['vɒljʊbl] adj. speaking easily with a lot of words. **vol•u•bil•i•ty** [vɒlju'bɪlɪtɪ] n. use of a lot of words. **vol•u•bly**, adj. with a lot of words.

vol•ume ['vɒljuːm] n. (a) book (esp. one book of a series). (b) space taken up by sth. (c) amount, esp. large. (d) loudness. **vo•lu•mi•nous** [və'ljuːmɪnəs] adj. large; taking up a lot of space.

vol•un•teer [vɒlən'tɪə] 1. n. (a) person who offers to do sth without being told to do it. (b) soldier who has joined the military of his own free will. 2. v. (a) to offer to do sth; to join the armed forces of your own free will. (b) to give (information) without being forced to do so. **vol•un•tar•i•ly**, adv. freely. **vol•un•tar•y** ['vɒləntrɪ] 1. adj. done of your own free will. 2. n. organ v. = solo piece of music played on the organ during or at the beginning or end of a church service.

vo•lup•tu•ous [və'lʌptjʊəs] adj. absorbed in/evoking sensual pleasure. **vo•lup•tu•ar•y**, n. person who enjoys sensual pleasure. **vo•lup•tu•ous•ly**, adv. in a voluptuous way.

vom•it ['vɒmɪt] 1. n. food vomited. 2. v. to

bring up food through your mouth when you are sick.

voo•doo ['vuːduː] n. witchcraft practiced in the West Indies. **voo•doo•ism**, n. belief in voodoo.

vo•ra•cious [və'reɪʃəs] adj. greedy; wanting to eat a lot; v. reader = person who reads a lot. **vo•ra•cious•ly**, adv. greedily. **vo•ra•cious•ness, voracity** [vɒ'ræsɪtɪ] n. being voracious.

vor•tex ['vɔːteks] n. (pl. **-texes, -tices** [-tɪsiːz]) matter which is turning around and around very fast.

vo•ta•ry ['vəʊtrɪ] n. (formal) person who worships/who admires sth fervently.

vote [vəʊt] 1. n. (a) expressing your opinion by marking a paper/by holding up your hand/by speaking. (b) action of voting; **to put sth to the v.** = to ask people to vote on sth. (c) the right to vote in an election/to vote on a proposal; **to give s.o. the v.** 2. v. (a) to express an opinion by marking a paper/by holding up your hand/by speaking. (b) **he was voted on to/off the committee** = he was elected/was not re-elected a member of the committee. **vot•er**, n. person who votes/who has the right to vote.

vo•tive ['vəʊtɪv] adj. (offering) given to fulfill a promise made to a god or to a saint.

vouch [vaʊtʃ] v. to v. for sth = to guarantee sth. **vouch•er**, n. paper which guarantees payment. **vouch•safe** [vaʊtʃ'seɪf] v. (formal) to ensure/to guarantee (that s.o. can do sth).

vow [vaʊ] 1. n. solemn promise (esp. one sworn to God). 2. v. to make a solemn promise.

vow•el ['vaʊəl] n. sound made without using the teeth, tongue or lips; one of the letters (a, e, i, o, u and sometimes y) which represent these sounds.

voy•age ['vɔɪɪdʒ] 1. n. long journey (esp. by water). 2. v. to make a long journey (by water). **voy•ag•er**, n. person who voyages.

vo•yeur [vwɑː'jɜː] n. person who watches people making love.

VR ['viː'ɑː] abbrev. for virtual reality.

vul•can•ize ['vʌlkənaɪz] v. to treat rubber with sulfur so that it is made stronger, harder and more elastic. **vul•can•ite**, n. vulcanized rubber. **vul•can•i•za•tion**, n. process of vulcanizing.

vul•can•ol•o•gy [vʌlkə'nɒlədʒɪ] n. volcanology.

vul•gar ['vʌlgə] adj. (a) rude/indecent. (b) not in good taste. (c) v. fraction = fraction written

---

æ back, ɑː farm, ɒ top, aɪ pipe, aʊ how, aiə fire, aʊə flower, ɔː bought, ɔɪ toy, e fed, eəhair, eɪ take, ə afraid, əʊ boat, əʊə lower, ɜː word, iː heap, ɪ hit, ɪə hear, uː school, ʊ book, ʌ but, b back, d dog, ð then, dʒ just, f fog, g go, h hand, j yes, k catch, l last, m mix, n nut, ŋ sing, p penny, r round, s some, ʃ short, t too, tʃ chop, θ thing, v voice, w was, z zoo, ʒ treasure

as one number above and another below a line. **vul•gar•i•an** [vʌlˈgeərɪən] *n.* vulgar person. **vul•gar•ism,** *n.* rude expression.. **vul•gar•i•ty** [vʌlˈgærɪtɪ] *n.* rudeness; lack of good taste. **vul•gar•i•za•tion,** *n.* making common/popular. **vul•gar•ly,** *adv.* in a rude/indecent way.

vul•ner•a•ble [ˈvʌlnərəbl] *adj.* which can be easily attacked/easily hurt.

vul•ner•a•bil•i•ty [vʌlnərəˈbɪlɪtɪ] *n.* being vulnerable.

vul•pine [ˈvʌlpaɪn] *adj.* referring to foxes.

vul•ture [ˈvʌltʃə] *n.* large tropical bird that eats mainly dead flesh.

vul•va [ˈvʌlvə] *n.* part of female body around the opening of the vagina.

Ww

wack•y ['wækɪ] *adj.* (**-ier, -iest**) *inf.* crazy/silly.

wad [wɒd] 1. *n.* (a) thick piece of soft material. (b) thick pile of banknotes/papers. 2. *v.* (**wadded**) to form/to press into a wad. **wad•ding**, *n.* thick, soft material used for lining, packing or padding.

wad•dle ['wɒdl] 1. *n.* walk swaying from side to side like a duck. 2. *v.* to walk with a waddle.

wade [weɪd] *v.* to walk through deep water or mud; **to w. through** = to find (a book) difficult to read; **to w. into a pile of work** = to start dealing with a pile of work vigorously. **wad•er**, *n.* (a) bird which spends most of its time in shallow water or mud. (b) **waders** = long waterproof boots worn by fishermen.

wa•fer ['weɪfə] *n.* (a) thin sweet cookie eaten with ice cream. (b) thin disk of bread eaten at communion or mass.

waf•fle ['wɒfl] 1. *n.* (a) type of crisp cake cooked in an iron mold and eaten with syrup. (b) ambivalent, unclear speech/writing. 2. *v.* to speak or write in an ambivalent, unclear way. **waf•fle i•ron**, *n.* iron mold used for making waffles.

waft [wɒft] 1. *n.* gentle smell. 2. *v.* to carry (sth) gently through the air.

wag [wæg] 1. *n.* (a) movement from side to side or up and down. (b) *inf.* person who likes making jokes/facetious remarks. 2. *v.* (**wagged**) to move from side to side or up and down. **wag•gish**, *adj.* joking (remark).

wage [weɪdʒ] 1. *n.* (*also* **wages**) weekly payment given for work done; **w. freeze** = period of standstill in wages. 2. *v.* to fight (a war); **to w. war (on** sth) = to fight against sth. **wage earn•er**, *n.* person who works for wages.

wa•ger ['weɪdʒə] 1. *n.* bet/money which you promise to pay if sth you expect to happen does not take place. 2. *v.* to bet.

wag•gle ['wægl] *v.* to move from side to side.

wag•on, *Brit.* **wag•gon** ['wægn] *n.* (a) four-wheeled vehicle pulled by horses and used for carrying heavy loads. (b) *inf.* **to be on** the w. = to drink only non-alcoholic drinks. **wag•on•er**, *n.* person who drives a wagon.

wag•tail ['wægteɪl] *n.* small bird which wags its tail up and down as it walks.

waif [weɪf] *n.* homeless child or animal.

wail [weɪl] 1. *n.* high-pitched sad cry. 2. *v.* to make a high-pitched mournful cry.

wain•scot(ing) ['weɪnzkət(ɪŋ)] *n.* wood paneling covering the lower part of a wall in a house. **wain•scot•ed**, *adj.* with a wainscot.

waist [weɪst] *n.* (a) narrow part of the body between the chest and the hips. (b) narrow part (of a bottle, etc.). **waist•band**, *n.* band of cloth around the waist of a pair of trousers/skirt. **waist•line**, *n.* measurement around the waist.

wait [weɪt] 1. *n.* act of staying until sth happens or s.o. arrives; **to lie in w. for s.o.** = to hide waiting for s.o. to pass by in order to attack him. 2. *v.* (a) (**for**) to stay somewhere until sth happens or s.o./sth arrives. (b) **to w. on s.o.** = to serve food to s.o. at a table, as in a restaurant. **wait•er**, *n.* man who serves food to people in a restaurant; **head w.** = person in charge of other waiters; **dumb w.** = (i) small table (usu. with wheels) for keeping food on; (ii) apparatus for carrying food from one floor to another. **wait•ing room**, *n.* room where travelers wait for their trains/buses, etc./where patients wait to see a doctor, etc. **wait•ing list**, *n.* list of people waiting to see s.o. or do sth. **wait•ress**, *n.* (*pl.* -es) woman who serves food to people in a restaurant. **wait up**, *v.* to stay up/not to go to bed.

waive [weɪv] *v.* to give up (a right/a claim). **waiv•er**, *n.* giving up (of a right/claim).

wake [weɪk] 1. *n.* (a) waves left by a boat, etc., moving through water; **in the w. of** = immediately behind. (b) staying up all night with a dead body before a funeral. 2. *v.* (**waked** or **woke** [wəuk]; **has woken**) to stop (s.o.) sleeping; to stop sleeping. **wake•ful**, *adj.* not at all sleepy/not able to go to sleep. **wak•en**, *v.* to

---

æ back, ɑː farm, ɒ top, aɪ pipe, aʊ how, aɪə fire, aʊə flower, ɔː bought, ɔɪ toy, e fed, eə hair, eɪ take, ə afraid, əʊ boat, əʊə lower, ɜː word, iː heap, ɪ hit, ɪə hear, uː school, ʊ book, ʌ but, b back, d dog, ð then, dʒ just, f fog, g go, h hand, j yes, k catch, l last, m mix, n nut, ŋ sing, p penny, r round, s some, ʃ short, t too, tʃ chop, θ thing, v voice, w was, z zoo, ʒ treasure

stop (s.o.) sleeping. **wake up,** v. (a) to stop sleeping. (b) **to w. u. to** = to realize.

walk [wɔːk] 1. n. (a) journey on foot. (b) way of walking. (c) wide path in a park or garden. (d) **w. of life** = social position or occupation. 2. v. (a) to move along on the feet at a normal speed. (b) to accompany (s.o./an animal) on foot. **walk•er,** n. person who walks, or who is fond of walking. **walk•ie-talk•ie,** n. portable two-way radio-telephone. **walk in,** v. to enter. **walk-in,** adj. (closet) which you can walk into. **walk•ing stick,** n. stick used to rest on when walking; cane. **walk in•to,** v. (a) to enter. (b) to hit by accident. **walk off,** v. (a) to go away; **to walk off with** = (i) to win (a prize) easily; (ii) to steal. (b) **to walk off your dinner** = to go for a walk after a big dinner to help you digest it. **walk on,** v. to continue walking. **walk-on,** n. & adj. (part) in a play where the actor doesn't have to speak. **walk out,** v. (a) to go out. (b) to leave angrily. (c) to go on strike. (d) **to w. o. on s.o.** = to leave s.o. suddenly. **walk•out,** n. strike of workers. **walk o•ver,** v. to walk across; to cross (a room) **to see s.o./to go up to s.o. walk•o•ver,** n. inf. easy victory. **walk up,** v. (a) to climb (on foot). (b) **to w. u. (to s.o.)** = to approach/to go to speak (to s.o.). **walk•way,** n. passage/path where you can walk.

wall [wɔːl] n. structure of brick/stone, etc., forming the side of a room/building, or the boundary of a piece of land; **w. painting** = mural; **to go to the w.** = to be defeated; inf. **he sends me up the w.** = he makes me furious. **walled,** adj. with walls. **wall•eyed,** adj. (person) who squints badly. **wall•flow•er,** n. (a) garden flower with a sweet scent. (b) (at a dance) inf. woman who is not asked to dance and is left sitting alone. **wall in,** v. to surround with walls. **wall•pa•per.** 1. n. decorative paper stuck on the walls of a room. 2. v. to stick paper on the walls of (a room). **Wall Street,** n. major U.S. financial center, in New York City. **wall-to-wall,** adj. (carpet) which covers all the floor space of a room. **wall up,** v. to close/to block with a wall.

wal•la•by ['wɒləbɪ] n. Australian animal like a small kangaroo.

wal•let ['wɒlɪt] n. small leather case used for holding paper money, credit cards, etc. in a pocket.

wal•lop ['wɒləp] 1. n. inf. hard blow. beer. 2. v. inf. to hit hard. **wal•lop•ing,** adj. inf. huge.

wal•low ['wɒləʊ] 1. n. mud hollow where animals can roll. 2. v. (a) (of animals) to roll delightedly around in mud. (b) (of person) to take too much pleasure in.

wal•nut ['wɒlnʌt] n. (a) hard round nut with a

wrinkled shell. (b) tree on which walnuts grow. (c) wood from a walnut tree.

wal•rus ['wɒlrʌs] n. (pl. -es) Arctic animal like a large seal with two long tusks pointing downward; **w. mustache** = mustache whose long ends point downward.

waltz [wɒls] 1. n. (pl. -es) (a) dance in which a man and woman turn around together as they move forward. (b) music suitable for such a dance. 2. v. (a) to dance together. (b) inf. to walk smoothly/happily.

wan [wɒn] adj. pale/looking ill. **wan•ly,** adv. in a wan way. **wan•ness,** n. being wan.

wand [wɒnd] n. (a) slim stick used by magicians. (b) hand-held electronic device that is passed over a printed item, e.g. a bar code, to read the data represented there.

wan•der ['wɒndə] v. (a) to walk about with no special purpose or direction. (b) **to w. off** = to walk away from the correct path. (c) to go away from the subject when talking. (d) to be confused because of illness or old age. **wan•der•er,** n. person who wanders. **wan•der•ings,** n. long random journeys. **wan•der•lust,** n. passion for going off on journeys and adventures.

wane [weɪn] 1. n. **the moon is on the w.** = appears to be getting smaller; **his influence is on the w.** = is diminishing. 2. v. to appear smaller; to decrease.

wan•gle ['wæŋgl] 1. n. inf. trick/thing dishonestly obtained. 2. v. inf. to get (sth) by trickery. **wan•gler,** n. inf. person who gets things by trickery.

want [wɒnt] 1. n. (a) state of being without; **for w. of sth better** = as sth better is not available. (b) desire/wish. (c) **wants** = things needed. 2. v. (a) to wish/to desire/to long for. (b) to need/to require. **want•ed,** adj. (a) desired/needed. (b) searched for by the police, usu. because of a crime. **want•ing,** adj. (a) needing. (b) having very little of sth.

wan•ton ['wɒntn] adj. wild/undisciplined.

war [wɔː] n. (a) fighting carried on between two or more nations; **civil w.** = war between two groups in one country. (b) fight/battle; **w. of words** = bitter argument. **war cry,** n. loud shout given when going into battle; slogan used in a political campaign. **war dance,** n. dance before the start of a battle. **war•fare,** n. fighting a war; type of war. **war•head,** n. explosive top of a missile. **war-horse,** n. (a) heavy, strong horse formerly used for carrying soldiers into battle. (b) old soldier/politician who has seen many battles. **war•like,** adj. liking or ready for war. **war•lord,** n. military leader who rules part of a country. **war•mon•ger,** n. person who wants to start a war. **war paint,** n. bright color put on the face and body before battle to make the enemy afraid. **war•path,** *n. inf.* **to be on the w.** = to be angry and looking for a fight. **war•ring,** *adj.* at war. **war•ship,** *n.* armed fighting ship. **war•time,** *n.* time of war.

war•ble ['wɔːbl] 1. *n.* trembling song (of a bird). 2. *v.* to sing with a trembling note. **war•bler,** *n.* type of bird which sings with a trembling note.

ward [wɔːd] 1. *n.* (a) young person in the care of s.o. other than his parents; **w. of the court** = child who is under the protection of the court. (b) large room in a hospital; section of a hospital. (c) part of a town for election purposes. 2. *v.* **to w. (sth) off** = to keep away. **war•den,** *n.* (a) person in charge of persons, animals, or things. (b) official in charge of a prison.

ward•robe ['wɔːdrəʊb] *n.* (a) large piece of furniture in which clothes may be hung. (b) a person's clothes. (c) costumes in a theater; **w. mistress** = woman in charge of the costumes in a theater.

ward•room [wɔːdrʊm] *n.* general living-room of officers on a warship.

ware ['weə] *n.* (a) *suffix meaning* goods made of a certain material/for a special purpose. (b) *pl.* **wares** = things that have been made and are for sale. **ware•house** ['weəhaʊs] 1. *n.* large building for storing goods. 2. *v.* to store (goods) in a large building. **ware•house•man,** *n.* (*pl.* **-men**) person who works in a warehouse.

warm [wɔːm] 1. *adj.* (**-er, -est**) (a) quite hot/pleasantly hot; (*in a game*) **you're getting w.** = you're near the right answer. (b) kind and friendly (welcome). 2. *n.* being/keeping warm; warm place. 3. *v.* to make hot or hotter; **to w. up to s.o.** = to feel more and more friendly toward s.o. **warm-blood•ed,** *adj.* having warm blood. **warm-heart•ed,** *adj.* friendly and welcoming. **warm•ing pan,** *n.* metal container in which hot coals were put and which was used to warm beds. **warm•ly,** *adv.* in a warm way. **warmth,** *n.* (a) heat/state of being warm. (b) enthusiasm. **warm up,** *v.* (a) to heat/to make warm again; to become warm again. (b) to exercise before a game/a contest.

warn [wɔːn] *v.* to tell of possible danger; to inform (s.o.) in advance; **to w. s.o. off sth** = to advise s.o. not to eat/drink/touch sth. **warn•ing.** 1. *n.* (a) notice of danger. (b) **without w.** = suddenly. 2. *adj.* which tells of danger.

warp [wɔːp] 1. *n.* (a) twisting out of shape of a

piece of wood. (b) threads running lengthwise in a piece of material. (c) heavy rope used for moving boats along. 2. *v.* (a) to twist out of shape. (b) to make (mind/character) evil. (c) (*of boats*) to move by pulling on a rope. **warped,** *adj.* twisted (wood/character).

war•rant ['wɒrənt] 1. *n.* (a) written official paper permitting or certifying sth. (b) **w. officer** = highest non-commissioned officer in the U.S. armed forces. 2. *v.* (a) to guarantee/to promise. (b) to justify/to deserve. **war•ran•ty,** *n.* written guarantee promising that a machine will work, etc.

war•ren ['wɒrn] *n.* land with rabbit burrows.

war•ri•or ['wɒrɪə] *n.* person who fights in a war.

wart [wɔːt] *n.* small, hard, dark lump on the skin; **warts and all** = with all faults known. **wart•hog,** *n.* type of wild African pig.

war•y ['weərɪ] *adj.* (**-ier, -iest**) careful/cautious. **war•i•ly,** *adv.* cautiously/looking around all the time. **war•i•ness** ['weərɪnəs] *n.* being wary.

was [wɒz] *v. see* **be.**

wash [wɒʃ] 1. *n.* (*pl.* **-es**) (a) act of cleaning with water or another liquid; *inf.* **it will all come out in the w.** = it will all be made clear in due course. (b) clothes which are being washed. (c) movement of the sea or water. (d) waves left behind a boat. (e) thin mixture of liquid; **color w.** = thin pale mixture of paint and water. 2. *v.* (a) to clean with water or another liquid. (b) to be able to be washed; *inf.* to be believable. (c) (*of water*) to flow past. (d) to be carried by water. (e) **to be washed overboard** = to be swept off the deck of a ship by a wave. **wash a•way,** *v.* to remove by water. **wash•a•ble,** *adj.* able to be washed. **wash•bowl, wash•ba•sin,** *n.* container, esp. when fixed and having faucets, for holding water for washing the hands and face. **wash•cloth,** *n.* small piece of cloth for washing the face or body. **wash•day,** *n.* day when the clothes are washed. **wash down,** *v.* (a) to clean with a lot of water. (b) **to w. down medicine with a drink of water** = to drink water to help swallow medicine. **wash•down,** *n.* complete wash all over. **wash•er,** *n.* (a) person who washes. (b) steel or rubber ring under a bolt or nut; rubber ring inside a faucet which prevents water escaping when the faucet is turned off. (c) machine for washing. (d) **windshield w.** = attachment on a car which squirts water onto the windshield to clean the glass.

æ back, ɑː farm, ɒ top, aɪ pipe, aʊ how, aɪə fire, aʊə flower, ɔː bought, ɔɪ toy, e fed, eəhair, eɪ take, ə afraid, əʊ boat, aʊə lower, vː word, iː heap, ɪ hit, ɪə hear, uː school, ʊ book, ʌ but, b back, d dog, ð then, dʒ just, f fog, g go, h hand, j yes, k catch, l last, m mix, n nut, ŋ sing, p penny, r round, s some, ʃ short, t too, tʃ chop, θ thing, v voice, w was, z zoo, ʒ treasure

wash•er•wom•an, *n.* (*pl.* **-women**) woman who washes clothes. **wash•ing,** *n.* (a) act of cleaning with water. (b) clothes which are to be washed/which have just been washed. **wash•ing ma•chine,** *n.* machine for washing clothes. **wash•ing-up,** *n.* washing of cups/plates/knives and forks, etc., after a meal. **wash•leath•er,** *n.* piece of soft leather used for cleaning windows. **wash off,** *v.* to clean away with water. **wash out,** *v.* (a) to clean/to be cleaned with water. (b) **washed out** = tired and without energy. **wash•out,** *n. inf.* (a) useless person. (b) thing that has failed. (c) removal of pollutants by the rain. **wash•room,** *n.* room where you can wash your hands and use the toilet. **wash•stand,** *n.* (a) (*old*) table on which a washbowl and jug of water stood in a bedroom. (b) fixed bowl, with faucets, for holding water for washing the hands and face. **wash up,** *v.* (a) to clean with water the cups/plates/knives and forks, etc., used during a meal. (b) to wash yourself. (c) (*of the sea*) to throw (wreckage) onto the shore.

wasp [wɒsp] *n.* striped insect, like a bee, which can sting but which does not make honey; **w. waist** = (woman's) very slim waist. **WASP,** *n.* White Anglo-Saxon Protestant. **wasp•ish,** *adj.* irritable/quick-tempered. **wasp•ish•ly,** *adv.* in a waspish way.

waste [weɪst] 1. *n.* (a) wild/uncultivated land. (b) unnecessary use (of time/money). (c) garbage; refuse; **w. pipe** = pipe which takes dirty water from a sink to the drains. 2. *v.* (a) to use more than necessary/to use badly. **w. not, want not** = don't throw anything away, you may need it later. (b) **to w. away** = to become thin/to lose weight. 3. *adj.* (a) (*of land*) uncultivated/not used for any particular purpose; **to lay w.** = to destroy the crops and houses in an area, esp. in time of war. (b) old and useless; **w. paper basket** = small container where useless papers can be put. **wast•age,** *n.* (a) loss due to waste. (b) amount lost by waste. **waste•ful,** *adj.* extravagant/which wastes a lot. **waste•ful•ly,** *adv.* in an extravagant way. **wast•er,** *n.* person/thing which wastes a lot. **wast•rel,** *n.* person who is useless and idle.

watch [wɒtʃ] 1. *n.* (*pl.* **-es**) (a) act of looking at s.o./sth; close observation. (b) person or group of people who guards or patrols an area. (c) period of duty for sailors on a ship. (d) small clock worn on the arm or carried in a pocket; **digital w.** = watch which shows the time in numbers (10:27) rather than on a circular dial. 2. *v.* (a) to look at/to observe. (b) to be careful. **neighborhood watch,** *n.* group of people in a neighborhood who make sure that people and houses are safe at night. **watch•dog,** *n.* (a) dog which guards a house or other buildings. (b) person/committee which examines public spending/public morals, etc. **watch•er,** *n.* person who watches/observes. **watch•ful,** *adj.* very careful. **watch•ful•ly,** *adv.* very carefully. **watch•ing,** *n.* act of looking/observing. **watch•mak•er,** *n.* person who makes and repairs clocks and watches. **watch•man,** *n.* (*pl.* **-men**) person who guards a building, usu. when it is empty. **watch out,** *v.* to be careful; **to w. o. for** = to be careful to avoid. **watch•tow•er,** *n.* tower from the top of which you can see if the enemy is coming. **watch•word,** *n.* slogan/password.

wa•ter ['wɔːtə] 1. *n.* (a) compound of hydrogen and oxygen; liquid that is in rain/rivers/lakes and the sea; **drinking w.** = water that is safe to drink; **hot w. bottle** = rubber bottle filled with hot water and used to warm a bed or a part of the body; **by w.** = on a boat; **to be under w.** = to be covered by water; **high w./low w.** = high/low tide; **to keep your head above w.** = (i) to swim with your head out of the water; (ii) to be able to keep out of difficulties; **to pass w.** = to urinate. (b) **waters** = the water of a lake, sea, etc.; **to take the waters** = to drink mineral water at a spa. (c) *inf.* **w. on the brain** = illness where liquid forms on the brain, causing mental deficiency. (d) mixture of water with other substances. (e) (*old*) (*of diamonds/precious stones*) brilliance; **of the first w.** = of the finest quality. 2. *v.* (a) to give water to. (b) (**down**) to add water to (wine or spirits); to make (a statement) less forceful. (c) (*of eyes/mouth*) to fill with water. (d) (*of boats*) to take in supplies of drinking water. **wa•te•rbed,** *n.* mattress made of a plastic or rubber bag filled with water. **wa•ter bis•cuit,** *n.* thin hard biscuit eaten with cheese. **wa•ter boat•man,** *n.* insect which skims across the surface of lakes/rivers, etc. **wa•ter•borne,** *adj.* (troops) carried in boats; (disease) carried in water. **water brash,** *n.* bitter liquid which comes up from the stomach into the mouth. **wa•ter buf•fa•lo,** *n.* large Asian animal, with a hump, which is used for farm work. **wa•ter can•non,** *n.* machine for sending strong jets of water (for dispersing rioters, etc.). **wa•ter clos•et,** *n.* room with a toilet. **wa•ter•col•or,** *n.* (a) paint used by artists which is mixed with water, not oil. (b) picture painted in watercolors. **wa•ter•course,** *n.* path of a stream/river. **wa•ter•cress,** *n.* creeping plant grown in water and eaten in salads. **wa•tered,** *adj.* (silk) with wavy markings in it. **wa•ter•fall,** *n.* fall of a river, etc., from a high level over the edge of a cliff.

wa•ter•fowl, *n.pl.* birds which like to live around ponds and lakes (such as ducks/geese, etc.). **wa•ter•front**, *n.* bank of a river/shore of the sea and the buildings along it. **wa•ter hole**, *n.* pond in the desert, where wild animals come to drink. **water ice**, *n.* type of light ice cream made of water and flavoring. **wa•ter•ing**, *n.* (a) act of giving water. (b) **w. down** = dilution (of wine or spirits) by adding water. (c) filling of the eyes with water. **wa•ter•ing can**, *n.* container with a long spout used for giving water to plants, etc. **wa•ter•ing hole**, *n.* *inf.* bar where a group of people often get together. **wa•ter•less**, *adj.* without water. **wa•ter lev•el**, *n.* level of water. **wa•ter lil•y**, *n.* plant with round leaves and big flowers, growing in water. **water line**, *n.* line where the water reaches on the hull of a ship. **wa•ter•logged**, *adj.* very wet/full of water. **Wa•ter•loo**, *n.* *inf.* **to meet one's W.** = to have a disaster/be completely defeated. **wa•ter main**, *n.* principal pipe carrying water underground along a road, and into buildings. **wa•ter•man**, *n.* (*pl.* -men) man who ferries people in a rowing boat. **wa•ter•mark**, *n.* (a) faint design put in paper to show who made it. (b) mark showing where the water reaches or has reached. **wa•ter mead•ow**, *n.* meadow often flooded by a river. **wa•ter•mel•on**, *n.* large juicy fruit with red flesh. **water mill**, *n.* mill driven by the power of water running over a large wheel. **wa•ter pis•tol**, *n.* toy gun which squirts water when the trigger is pressed. **wa•ter po•lo**, *n.* ball game played in water between two teams. **wa•ter pow•er**, *n.* power/energy of running water, used to drive machines. **wa•ter•proof.** 1. *adj.* which will not let water through. 2. *v.* to make (sth) waterproof. **wa•ter rat**, *n.* small mammal living in holes in a river bank. **wa•ter•shed**, *n.* (a) area drained by a river, stream, etc. (b) point where the situation changes permanently. **wa•ter•side**, *n.* bank of a river/lake/sea. **wa•ter-ski•er**, *n.* person who goes in for water-skiing. **wa•ter-ski•ing**, *n.* sport of gliding along the surface of water standing on a pair of skis pulled by a fast boat. **wa•ter sof•ten•er**, *n.* chemical/device for removing the hardness in water. **wa•ter•spout**, *n.* (a) pipe carrying rainwater away from a roof. (b) tornado at sea when the water rises in a high column.

wa•ter sup•ply, *n.* system of pipes/tanks, etc., bringing water to people's homes; amount of water in the system. **wa•ter ta•ble**, *n.* natural level of water below ground. **wa•ter•tight**, *adj.* (a) fitting so tightly that water cannot get in or out. (b) sth so strong that it cannot be defeated, disproved, avoided; **w. argument; w. case.** **wa•ter tow•er**, *n.* tower holding a large tank of water. **wa•ter•way**, *n.* canal or deep river along which boats can easily travel. **wa•ter•weed**, *n.* weed which grows in water. **wa•ter•wheel**, *n.* wheel which is turned by water and so makes a machine work. **wa•ter wings**, *n.* inflatable rings attached to the arms of children learning to swim. **wa•ter•works**, *n.* buildings from which water is piped to houses and factories; **to turn on the w.** = to cry. **wa•ter•y**, *adj.* which has a lot of water.

watt [wɒt] *n.* standard unit of electrical power. **watt•age** ['wɒtɪdʒ] *n.* amount of electricity in watts.

wat•tle ['wɒtl] *n.* (a) woven twigs/laths used to make light walls; **w. and daub** = type of medieval construction consisting of woven strips of wood covered with mud. (b) type of Australian tree. (c) fold of red skin hanging under the throat of some birds (such as turkeys).

wave [weɪv] 1. *n.* (a) ridge on the surface of the sea. (b) up-and-down movement; **a w. of the hand.** (c) ridge on the surface; **permanent w.** = treatment which makes hair wave and curl. (d) sudden feeling; sudden spell (of hot/cold weather). 2. *v.* (a) to move up and down; **to w. to s.o.** = to signal to s.o. with the hand; **to w. s.o. aside** = to dismiss s.o. with a movement of the hand; **to w. s.o. on** = to tell s.o. to go on by a movement of the hand. (b) to have/to make ridges on the surface. **wave band**, *n.* group of wavelengths which are close together. **waved**, *adj.* (*of hair*) treated to look wavy. **wave•length**, *n.* distance between similar points on radio waves; *inf.* **they're not on the same w.** = they do not understand each other at all. **wav•y**, *adj.* (-ier, -iest) which goes up and down.

wa•ver ['weɪvə] *v.* (a) to tremble/to move from side to side. (b) to hesitate. **wa•ver•er**, *n.* person who hesitates. **wa•ver•ing**, *adj.* trembling/hesitant.

wax [wæks] 1. *n.* (a) solid substance made by bees to build the cells of their honeycomb. (b) solid substance similar to this. 2. *v.* (a) to put

---

æ back, aː farm, ɒ top, aɪ pipe, aʊ how, aɪə fire, aʊə flower, ɔː bought, ɔɪ toy, e fed, eəhair, eɪ take, ə afraid, əʊ boat, əʊə lower, vː word, iː heap, ɪ hit, ɪə hear, uː school, ʊ book, ʌ but, b back, d dog, ð then, dʒ just, f fog, g go, h hand, j yes, k catch, l last, m mix, n nut, ŋ sing, p penny, r round, s some, ʃ short, t too, tʃ chop, θ thing, v voice, w was, z zoo, ʒ treasure

polish on (furniture, etc.). (b) (*of the moon*) to grow bigger. **wax•en**, *adj.* pale (like wax). **wax•wing**, *n.* small bird with bright marks on its wings. **wax•works**, *n.* exhibition of wax models of famous people. **wax•y**, *adj.* like wax.

way [weɪ] 1. *n.* (a) road/path; **to make your w. through a crowd** = to push through a crowd; **w. in** = entrance; **w. out** = exit; **by the w.** = incidentally/in passing; **by w. of** = (i) via; (ii) as a method of. (b) right direction/right road; **to go out of your w. to help s.o.** = to make a special effort to help s.o. (c) particular direction; **one-way street** = street where the traffic can only move in one direction. (d) method/means/manner; **she always gets her own w.** = she gets what she wants; **to have a w. with** = know how to amuse and please; **I know all his ways** = I know all the odd little things he does; **w. out of a difficulty** = solution to a problem. (e) distance (from one place to another); **he'll go a long w.** = he will be very successful. (f) space in which s.o. wants to move. (g) state/condition; **in the ordinary w.** = usually; **out of the w.** = unusual; **in many ways** = in lots of aspects/points; **(in) no w.** = not at all. (h) progress/movement forward; **under w.** = moving forward; **to make your w. in the world** = to be successful; **to pay your w.** = to pay for yourself. 2. *adv. inf.* away/far. **way•bill**, *n.* list of goods carried, as on a railroad. **way•far•er**, *n.* (*formal*) traveler. **way•lay** [weɪˈleɪ] *v.* (**waylaid**) to wait for (s.o.) in order to attack/to ambush. **way-out**, *adj. Sl.* strange/unusual. **way•side**, *adj. & n.* (referring to the) side of the road. **way•ward**, *adj.* (child) who wants to do what he wants. **way•ward•ness**, *n.* being difficult/uncontrollable.

WC [ˈdʌbljuˈsiː] *n. short for* water closet.

we [wiː] *pron.* (a) referring to people who are speaking/to the person speaking and others. (b) *inf.* you.

weak [wiːk] *adj.* (**-er, -est**) (a) not strong in body or in character. (b) (*of a liquid*) watery/not strong. (c) not good **at** (a subject). (d) (*in grammar*) (verb) which forms its past tense using a suffix. **weak•en**, *v.* to make/to become weak. **weak-kneed**, *adj.* soft/timid/cowardly. **weak•ling**, *n.* weak person. **weak•ly**. 1. *adj.* not strong. 2. *adv.* not strongly/feebly. **weak-mind•ed**, *adj.* not strong in character. **weak•ness**, *n.* (a) being weak. (b) *inf.* liking (**for**).

weal [wiːl] *n. see* **wheal**.

wealth [welθ] *n.* (a) riches. (b) large amount. **wealth•y**, *adj. & n.* (**-ier, -iest**) very rich (person).

wean [wiːn] *v.* to make (a baby) start to eat solid food after only drinking milk; **to w. s.o. off/away from sth** = to get s.o. to drop a (bad) habit.

weap•on [ˈwepən] *n.* object with which you fight. **weap•on•ry**, *n.* (*no pl.*) weapons.

wear [weə] 1. *n.* (a) act of carrying on your body as a piece of clothing; **normal w. and tear** = normal use. (b) clothes. (c) damage through much use. (d) ability to stand much use. 2. *v.* (**wore** [wɔː]; **has worn** [wɔːn]) (a) to carry on your body as a piece of clothing. (b) to become damaged through much use. (c) to stand up to much use/to last a long time. (d) to have (an expression) or your face. **wear•a•ble**, *adj.* able to be worn. **wear a•way, wear down**, *v.* to disappear/to make (sth) disappear by rubbing or much use. **wear•er**, *n.* person who wears clothes. **wear•ing**, *adj.* tiring. **wear off**, *v.* to disappear gradually; to make (sth) disappear. **wear on**, *v.* (*of time*) to pass. **wear out**, *v.* (a) to become useless through much use; to make (sth) become useless through much use. (b) **to wear yourself out/to be worn out** = to become tired through doing a lot.

wear•y [ˈwɜːrɪ] 1. *adj.* (**-ier, -iest**) very tired/tiring. 2. *v.* to become tired/to make tired. **wear•i•ly**, *adv.* in a tired way. **wear•i•ness**, *n.* tiredness. **wear•i•some**, *adj.* tiring/boring.

wea•sel [ˈwiːzl] *n.* small animal with a long thin body and short legs, which kills and eats rabbits, etc.

weath•er [ˈweðə] 1. *n.* state of the air and atmosphere at a certain time; **in all weathers** = in every sort of instance, good or bad; **under the w.** = miserable/unwell. 2. *v.* (a) (*of sea/frost/wind, etc.*) to wear down (rocks, etc.). (b) to season (planks of wood); to make (wood) suitable for use by leaving it outside for several years. (c) to survive (a storm/crisis). **weath•er-beat•en**, *adj.* (a) marked by the weather. (b) (*of face*) tanned/made brown by the wind, rain and sun. **weath•er bu•reau, weather center**, *n.* office where the weather is forecast. **weath•er•cock**, *n.* weather vane in the shape of a cock. **weath•er fore•cast, weather report**, *n.* description of the weather about to come in the next few hours or days. **weath•er•man**, *n.* (*pl.* **-men**) *inf.* expert who describes the coming weather, usu. on TV or radio. **weath•er•proof**, *adj.* able to keep out the wind and the rain. **weath•er sta•tion**, *n.* place where weather conditions are recorded. **weath•er strip(ping)**, *n.* strip of wood, metal, etc. which is attached to the inside of a window frame to prevent drafts. **weath•er**

vane, *n.* metal pointer on a high building which turns around to show the direction of the wind.

weave [wi:v] 1. *n.* pattern of cloth; way in which cloth has been woven. 2. *v.* (**wove** [wəʊv] or **weaved, has woven** or **wove**) (a) to make cloth by winding threads in and out. (b) to make (sth) by a similar method, using straw, etc. (c) to twist and turn. **weav•er,** *n.* person who weaves. **weav•ing,** *n.* action of making cloth by winding threads in and out.

web [web] *n.* (a) thing that is woven. (b) net spun by spiders. (c) skin between the toes of a water bird, etc. (d) *inf.* **the Web** = the World Wide Web. **webbed,** *adj.* with skin between the toes. **web•bing,** *n.* strong tape used in upholstery. **web•foot•ed,** *adj.* with webbed feet. **web•site,** *n.* group of linked pages on the Internet devoted to a particular subject.

wed [wed] *v.* (**wedded** or **wed**) (a) (*formal*) to marry (s.o.); to become husband and wife. (b) **to be wedded to an idea** = to be firmly attached to an idea. **wed•ding,** *n.* marriage ceremony; **silver/golden w.** = anniversary of 25/50 years of marriage; **w. ring** = ring which is put on the finger during the wedding ceremony. **wed•lock,** *n.* being married.

wedge [wedʒ] 1. *n.* (a) V-shaped piece of wood/metal, used for splitting wood. (b) V-shaped piece, as of pie. 2. *v.* (a) to split with a wedge. (b) to fix firmly with a wedge. (c) to become tightly fixed.

Wednes•day ['wenzdɪ, 'wedənzdeɪ] *n.* third day of the week/day between Tuesday and Thursday.

wee [wi:] 1. *adj.* very small. 2. *n.* (*child's word*) (*also* **wee-wee**) urine. 3. *v.* (*child's word*) (*also* **wee-wee**) to urinate.

weed [wi:d] 1. *n.* (a) plant that you do not want in a garden. (b) **weeds** = black clothes worn by a widow. (c) *inf.* thin, skinny person. (d) *inf.* tobacco; *Sl.* marijuana. 2. *v.* (a) to pull out unwanted plants from. (b) **to w. out** = to remove. **weed-kill•er,** *n.* chemical which kills unwanted plants. **weed•y,** *adj.* (-ier, -iest) (a) covered with weeds. (b) thin and skinny (person).

week [wi:k] *n.* (a) period of seven days. **a w. from now/a w. today** = this day next week; **yesterday w.** = a week ago yesterday. (b) part of a seven day period; **he works a 35-hour w.** = he works 35 hours every week. **week•day,** *n.* any day of the week except Sunday (and sometimes Saturday). **week•end,** *n.* period from Friday evening or Saturday morning until Sunday evening or Monday morning. **week•ly.** 1. *adv. & adj.* once a week. 2. *n.* magazine published once a week.

wee•nie, weeny ['wi:nɪ] *adj. inf.* very small.

weep [wi:p] *v.* (**wept** [wept]) to cry. **weep•ing,** *adj.* (a) crying. (b) (*of tree*) with branches hanging down.

wee•vil ['wi:vl] *n.* type of beetle which eats plants, grain, etc.

weft [weft] *n.* threads going across a length of material.

weigh [weɪ] *v.* (a) to measure how heavy sth is. (b) to have a certain heaviness; **time weighs heavily on his hands** = he has nothing to do. (c) **to w. anchor** = to lift the anchor of a ship in order to sail away. (d) **to w. the pros and cons** = to examine all the arguments for and against. **weigh•bridge,** *n.* large machine for weighing heavy trucks and their goods. **weigh down,** *v.* (a) to press down. (b) to make (s.o.) gloomy. **weigh in,** *v.* (*of boxers/jockeys*) to be weighed before a fight or race. **weigh•ing ma•chine,** *n.* device for weighing.

weight [weɪt] 1. *n.* (a) heaviness (of sth); **to lose/put on w.** = to get thinner/fatter; **to pull your w.** = to do your share. (b) piece of metal used to measure the exact heaviness of sth else. (c) heavy object; **that's a w. off my mind!** = I no longer need to worry about that. (d) importance; *inf.* **to throw your w. about** = to use your authority in an arrogant way. 2. *v.* (a) to attach a weight to (sth). (b) to add (a quantity) to a sum to produce a certain result. **weight•less,** *adj.* with no weight. **weight•less•ness,** *n.* having no weight. **weight•lift•er,** *n.* person who lifts heavy weights as a sport. **weight•lift•ing,** *n.* sport of lifting heavy weights. **weight•y,** *adj.* (-ier, -iest) (a) heavy. (b) important (problem, etc.).

weir ['wɪə] *n.* (a) small dam built across a river to control the flow of water. (b) fence across a lake or river to trap fish.

weird ['wɪəd] *adj.* (-er, -est) strange/odd. **weird•ly,** *adv.* in a strange way. **weird•ness,** *n.* being weird. **weird•o** ['wɪədəʊ] *n.* (*pl.* -os) *inf.* strange/odd person; person who behaves in a strange way.

wel•come ['welkəm] 1. *n.* greeting/reception. 2. *v.* (a) to greet (s.o.) as he arrives. (b) to hear (news) with pleasure. 3. *adj.* (a) pleasing/received with pleasure. (b) (**to**) willingly permit-

ted. (c) *inf.* (*as a reply to* **thank you**) **you're w.** =
it was a pleasure to do it.

weld [weld] 1. *n.* joint made by joining two
pieces of metal together by first heating, then
pressing. 2. *v.* to join (two pieces of metal) together by first heating, then pressing.
weld•er, *n.* person/machine that welds
metal. **weld•ing,** *n.* process of joining two
pieces of metal together; place where two
pieces are welded.

wel•fare ['welfeə] *n.* happiness/comfort/free-
dom from want; **W. State** = state which looks
after the health and well-being of its citizens;
child w. = health and well-being of children.

wel•kin ['welkɪn] *n.* (*old*) sky.

well [wel] 1. *n.* (a) deep hole at the bottom of
which is water or oil. (b) deep hole; space in
the center of a building where the staircase or
elevator is. 2. *v.* **to w. up** = to start to flow. 3.
adv. (**better, best**) (a) in a good way/properly;
to do w. = to prosper; **to go w.** = (i) to be suc-
cessful/to have good results; (ii) to fit/to suit;
to speak w. of = to praise/to say nice things
about. (b) to a large degree; **w. after 7 o'clock**
= a long time after 7 o'clock; **pretty w. all the
family** = almost all the family. (c) lucky/desir-
able; **you may w. be right** = you probably are
right; **all's w. that ends w.** = if the result is fine
then everything is fine; **to wish s.o. w.** = to wish
them good luck. (d) **as w.** = also/too. 4. *adj.*
healthy and in good condition. 5. *inter. starting a sentence and meaning nothing in particular or showing surprise.* **well-ad•vised,** *adj.*
wise. **well-ap•point•ed,** *adj.* luxuriously
furnished. **well-bal•anced,** *adj.* steady/sen-
sible. **well-be•haved,** *adj.* good/having
good manners. **well-be•ing,** *n.* health and
happiness. **well•born,** *adj.* of an aristocratic
family. **well-bred,** *adj.* polite/well-educated.
well-con•nect•ed, *adj.* with influential
friends or family. **well-dis•posed,** *adj.*
kindly. **well-done,** *adj.* (meat) which has
been cooked a long time. **well-earned,** *adj.*
which has been deserved. **well-found•ed,**
adj. (fears) which are justified.
well-groomed, *adj.* clean and tidy (person).
well-ground•ed, *adj.* (fears) which are
justified. **well-heel•ed,** *adj. inf.* rich.
well-in•formed, *adj.* knowing a lot about a
subject. **well-in•ten•tioned,** *adj.* (person)
with good intentions. **well-knit,** *adj.* strong
(body). **well-known,** *adj.* famous/known by
many people. **well-man•nered,** *adj.* po-
lite/with good manners. **well-mean•ing,**
adj. (person) who does sth with good intentions. **well-meant,** *adj.* (action) done with
good intentions. **well-nigh,** *adv.* (*formal*) almost. **well-off,** *adj. inf.* rich. **well-oiled,** *adj.*

Sl. drunk. **well-read,** *adj.* having read many
books and therefore knowing a lot.
well-spo•ken, *adj.* (person) who speaks politely and correctly. **well-timed,** *adj.* which
happens at the right time. **well-to-do,** *adj.*
inf. wealthy. **well-wish•er,** *n.* person who is
friendly toward another. **well-worn,** *adj.*
used a lot.

wel•ling•ton boots, wellingtons, *inf.*
wel•lies ['welɪŋtən'buːts, 'welɪŋtənz, 'welɪz]
n. pl. rubber waterproof boots.

Welsh [welʃ] 1. *adj.* referring to Wales; **W. rare-
bit** = toasted cheese on bread. 2. *n.* (a) *pl.* **the
W.** = the people of Wales. (b) language spoken in Wales. 3. *v.* **to w. on s.o.** = (i) to break a
promise made to s.o.; (ii) to not pay s.o. a
debt, esp. a gambling debt. **Welsh•man,
Welshwoman,** *n.* person from Wales.

welt [welt] *n.* (a) leather edging for attaching
the upper part of a shoe to the sole. (b) strong
edge along a seam. (c) wheal.

wel•ter ['weltə] *n.* confused mass.
wel•ter•weight, *n.* medium weight in boxing between middleweight and lightweight.

wen [wen] *n.* tumor.

wench [wenʃ] *n.* (*pl.* -es) (*old*) young woman.

wend [wend] *v.* **to w. one's way** = to go.

went [went] *v. see* **go.**

wept [wept] *v. see* **weep.**

were [wɜː] *v. see* **be.**

were•wolf ['wɪəwulf] *n.* (*pl.* -wolves) person
who changes into a wolf.

west [west] 1. *n.* (a) one of the points of the
compass, the direction in which the sun sets;
w. wind = wind coming from the west. (b) **the
W.** = the non-communist world. 2. *adv.* toward the west. **west•bound,** *adj.* going toward the west. **west•er•ly,** *adj.* (a) (wind)
from the west. (b) toward the west.
west•ern. 1. *adj.* of the west. 2. *n.* novel/mo-
tion picture about cowboys and Indians in the
western United States. **west•ern•er,** *n.* person who lives in the west.
west•ern•i•za•tion, *n.* act of westernizing.
west•ern•ize, *v.* to make more European or
American. **west•ern•most,** *adj.* furthest
west. **West In•dian,** *n. & adj.* (person) from
the West Indies. **west•ward** 1. *adj.* toward
the west. 2. *adv.* (*also* **westwards**) toward the
west.

wet [wet] 1. *adj.* (**wetter, wettest**) (a) covered or
soaked with water or other liquid; **I'm w.
through/soaking w.** = all my clothes are very
wet; *inf.* **w. blanket** = person who spoils any
fun. (b) rainy. 2. *n.* rain. 3. *v.* (**wetted**) to
dampen with water. **wet•lands,** *n.* marshy
areas which are often covered by water.
wet•ness, *n.* being wet. **wet suit,** *n.* suit

worn by divers which keeps the body warm with a layer of warm water. **wet•ting,** *n.* soaking/getting wet.

weth•er ['weðə] *n.* castrated ram.

whack [wæk] 1. *n.* (a) hard, noisy blow. (b) *inf.* **let's have a w. at it!** = let's try to do it. 2. *v.* to hit hard, making a loud noise. **whack•ing,** *adj. inf.* huge.

whale [weɪl] *n.* (a) huge sea mammal. (b) *inf.* **we had a w. of a time** = we enjoyed ourselves very much. **whale•boat,** *n.* boat used when hunting whales. **whale•bone,** *n.* thin bone taken from the jaws of whales and formerly used in corsets. **whal•er,** *n.* (a) boat used when hunting whales. (b) person who hunts whales. **whal•ing,** *n.* hunting of whales.

wharf [wɔːf] *n.* (*pl.* **wharves** [wɔːvz], **wharfs**) place in a dock where a ship can tie up and load or unload. **wharf•in•ger,** *n.* person who is in charge of a wharf.

what [wɒt] 1. *adj.* (a) that which. (b) (*asking a question*) which? **w. good is this to us?** = what is the use of this? (c) (*showing surprise*) how much/how great/how strange. 2. *pron.* (a) that which; **come w. may** = whatever happens. (b) (*asking a question*) which thing or things; **w. is the German word for table? what's the use of learning Latin?** = why learn Latin? **w. about stopping for lunch now?** = do you think we should stop for lunch now?; **w. did you say?/**(*not polite*) **w.?** = I didn't hear what you said, please say it again; **w. if?** = what will happen if; **he knows what's w.** = he knows what the situation is and what to do. 3. *inter. showing surprise.* **whats-it, what-d'you-call-it,** *n. inf.* thing of which you have forgotten the name for the moment. **what•ev•er** [wɒ'evə] 1. *pron.* anything at all. 2. *adj.* (a) (*strong form of* **what**) (b) **none w.** = none at all. **what for,** *pron.* (a) why. (b) what is the purpose of. (c) *inf.* **to give s.o. what for** = to be angry with s.o. **what•not,** *n.* stand with shelves for small books and ornaments. **what•so•ev•er** [wɒtsəu'evə] *adj. & pron.* (*strong form of* **whatever**) **none w.** = none at all.

wheal [wiːl] *n.* raised mark left on the skin by a blow from a whip or stick.

wheat [wiːt] *n.* cereal plant. **wheat•ear,** *n.* brown bird living in fields. **wheat•en,** *adj.* made of wheat. **wheat germ,** *n.* central part of a grain of wheat. **wheat meal,** *n.* brown flour containing most of the grain. **wheat**

sheaf, *n.* large bundle of stalks of wheat bound together.

whee•dle ['wiːdl] *v.* to ask s.o. for sth in a flattering way.

wheel [wiːl] 1. *n.* (a) circular frame which turns around a central axis (as a support for cars/trains/bicycles, etc.). (b) any similar circular object; **steering w.** = wheel which the driver of a car holds and turns to follow the road; **to take the w.** = to drive; **potter's w.** = horizontal disk on which a potter throws the clay to make pottery. 2. *v.* (a) to push along (sth) that has wheels. (b) **to w. around** = to turn around suddenly. (c) to fly in circles; **seagulls wheeling above the fishing boats.** (d) **to w. and deal** = to be involved in a number of different activities all to one's own advantage. **wheel•bar•row,** *n.* small handcart used by builders and gardeners, which has one wheel in front, and two handles behind. **wheel•base,** *n.* distance between the front and rear axles of a car/truck, etc. **wheel•chair,** *n.* chair on wheels used by people who cannot walk. **wheel•er-deal•er,** *n.* businessman who lives by making deals. **wheel•wright,** *n.* man who makes wheels.

wheeze [wiːz] 1. *n.* noisy breathing. 2. *v.* to breathe noisily and with difficulty. **wheez•i•ly,** *adv.* in a wheezy way. **wheez•i•ness,** *n.* being wheezy. **wheez•y,** *adj.* (person) who wheezes.

whelk [welk] *n.* type of edible sea snail.

whelp [welp] 1. *n.* young of a dog. 2. *v.* to give birth to a young dog.

when [wen] 1. *adv.* (*asking a question*) at what time. 2. *conj.* (a) at the time that. (b) if. **when•ev•er** [we'nevə] *adv.* at any time that.

whence [wens] *adv.* (*formal*) from where.

where ['weə] 1. *adv.* (*asking a question*) in/at/to what place? 2. *adv.* in the place. **where•a•bouts.** 1. *n. pl.* ['weərəbauts] place where s.o./sth is. 2. *adv.* [weərə'bauts] in what place? **where•as** [weər'æz] *conj.* on the other hand/while/in contrast with the fact that. **where•by** [weə'baɪ] *adv.* (*formal*) by which; according to which. **where•fore,** *adv.* (*old*) why? **where•in** [weər'ɪn] *adv.* (*formal*) in which way? **where•up•on** [weərə'pɒn] *conj.* at that point/after that. **wher•ev•er** [weər'evə] *conj.* in every place. **where•with•al,** *n.* (*formal*) necessary money.

wher•ry ['werɪ] *n.* small rowboat.

whet [wet] *v.* (**whetted**) (a) to sharpen (a knife).

æ back, aː farm, ɒ top, aɪ pipe, au how, aie fire, auə flower, ɔː bought, ɔɪ toy, e fed, eəhair, eɪ take, ə afraid, əu boat, əuə lower, vː word, iː heap, ɪ hit, ɪə hear, uː school, u book, ʌ but, b back, d dog, ð then, dʒ just, f fog, g go, h hand, j yes, k catch, l last, m mix, n nut, ŋ sing, p penny, r round, s some, ʃ short, t too, tʃ chop, θ thing, v voice, w was, z zoo, ʒ treasure

(b) **to w. your appetite** = to make you more interested in sth by giving you a little taste of it. **whet•stone,** *n.* stone used to sharpen knives, etc.

wheth•er ['weðə] *conj.* (a) if. (b) either.

whey [weɪ] *n.* liquid left when milk is made into cheese.

which [wɪtʃ] 1. *adj.* what (person/thing). 2. *pron.* (a) (*asking a question*) what person/what thing. (b) (*only used with things not persons*) that/the thing that. **which•ev•er,** *pron. & adj.* (a) anything that. (b) no matter which.

whiff [wɪf] *n.* slight smell.

while [waɪl] 1. *n.* length of time; **quite a w./a good w.** = a fairly long time; **once in a w.** = from time to time. 2. *v.* **to w. away the time** = to make the time pass while you are waiting for something. 3. *conj.* (a) during/as long as. (b) although. (c) whereas/in contrast with. **whilst** [waɪlst] *conj.* while.

whim [wɪm] *n.* sudden wish or desire. **whim•si•cal** ['wɪmzɪkl] *adj.* odd/fanciful. **whim•si•cal•i•ty,** *n.* being whimsical. **whim•sy,** *n.* strange/fanciful idea.

whim•per ['wɪmpə] 1. *n.* sad/weak cry. 2. *v.* (*of small dogs*) to cry weakly.

whine [waɪn] 1. *n.* complaint/moan. 2. *v.* to moan/to complain in a long high voice.

whin•ny ['wɪnɪ] 1. *n.* sound which a horse makes when pleased. 2. *v.* (*of a horse*) to make a neigh.

whip [wɪp] 1. *n.* (a) long, thin piece of leather fixed to a handle and used for hitting animals. (b) **party w.** = member of a legislative body whose job it is to secure votes and assist in formulating party policy. 2. *v.* (**whipped**) (a) to hit with a whip. (b) to beat sharply. (c) to beat (cream, eggs, etc.) until firm. (d) to wind string around (the end of a piece of rope). (e) *inf.* to move quickly; **to w. out a gun** = to pull a gun out quickly. **whip•cord,** *n.* type of corduroy. **whip hand,** *n.* advantage. **whip•lash,** *n.* (a) piece of thin leather which is part of a whip. (b) neck injury, caused by the head moving back suddenly. **whip off,** *v.* to move quickly; to do/remove quickly. **whip•per•snap•per,** *n.* boy/young man who is too sure of himself. **whip•ping,** *n.* beating. **whip a•round,** *v.* to turn around quickly. **whip up,** *v.* to encourage/to make (sth) increase.

whip•pet ['wɪpɪt] *n.* breed of small thin dog trained for racing.

whirl [wɜːl] 1. *n.* (a) rapid turning movement. (b) giddy/dizzy feeling. 2. *v.* (a) to turn around quickly/to spin. (b) to move quickly. **whirl•i•gig,** *n.* something which turns around rapidly (like a top). **whirl•pool,** *n.*

water which turns rapidly around and around. **whirl•wind,** *n.* (a) wind blowing around and around in a circle. (b) confused rush; **w. engagement** = very rapid engagement before marriage.

whir, whirr [wɜː] *n.* noise of sth spinning around quickly. 2. *v.* to make a spinning noise.

whisk [wɪsk] 1. *n.* (a) swift movement. (b) kitchen utensil used for beating eggs/cream, etc. 2. *v.* (a) to move quickly. (b) to beat (eggs/cream) very quickly. **whisk broom,** *n.* small brush with a short handle, for removing lint, etc. from clothes.

whisk•er ['wɪskə] *n.* (a) long stiff hair at the side of an animal's mouth. (b) **whiskers** = mustache and beard on the side of a man's face. **whisk•er•y,** *adj.* covered with whiskers.

whis•key, whisky ['wɪskɪ] *n.* alcoholic drink distilled from grain; glass of this drink.

whis•per ['wɪspə] 1. *n.* (a) quiet sound/words quietly spoken. (b) rumor. 2. *v.* (a) to speak very quietly. (b) to make a very quiet sound.

whist [wɪst] *n.* card game for four people.

whis•tle ['wɪsl] 1. *n.* (a) simple instrument played by blowing; **penny w./tin w.** = cheap metal flute. (b) small pipe which gives a loud shrill noise when blown. (c) musical sound made by almost closing the lips and blowing air through the small hole; **to wet one's w.** = to have a drink. 2. *v.* (a) to blow through the lips and make a musical or shrill sound; *inf.* **you can w. for it** = you will never get it. (b) to make a shrill sound. **whis•tle•stop tour,** *n.* election tour where a candidate stops for a brief period in many different towns.

whit [wɪt] *n.* very small amount; **not a w. more** = nothing more.

white [waɪt] 1. *adj.* (-er, -est) color of snow; **w. Christmas** = Christmas with snow on the ground. 2. *n.* (a) color of snow. (b) person whose skin is not black, brown, yellow or red. (c) light-colored meat (on a chicken); **w. of an egg** = part of the egg which is not yellow. **white ant,** *n.* termite. **white•bait,** *n.* (*pl.* **whitebait**) small young fish eaten fried. **white-col•lar work•er,** *n.* office worker. **white el•e•phant,** *n.* thing which is big and expensive but useless to its owner. **white flag,** *n.* symbol of surrender. **white goods,** *n.* household linen (sheets, pillowcases, etc.); household machines, such as refrigerators and washing machines, which are usually white. **white-haired,** *adj.* with white hair. **white heat,** *n.* very high temperature, when white light is produced by heated metal. **white hot,** *adj.* extremely hot. **White House,** *n.* house of the President of the United States; *inf.* the U.S. government. **white knight,** *n.* person/company which rescues another threatened with a takeover. **white lie,** *n.* innocent lie. **whit•en,** *v.* to make white. **whit•en•er, whitening,** *n.* white liquid for making shoes, etc., white. **white•ness,** *n.* being white. **white•out,** *n.* blinding conditions caused by wind and snow. **white pa•per,** *n.* official government report. **white sale,** *n.* sale of sheets/pillowcases, etc. **white slave,** *n.* woman captured and sent abroad as a prostitute. **white slav•er•y,** *n.* trade in white slaves. **white•wash.** 1. *n.* (a) mixture of water and lime used for painting the walls of houses. (b) attempt to cover up mistakes. 2. *v.* (a) to paint with a mixture of water and lime. (b) to attempt to cover up (mistakes). **white•wood,** *n.* unpainted soft wood, such as pine. **whit•ish,** *adj.* quite white.

whith•er ['wɪðə] *adv.* (*formal*) to which place.

whit•ing ['waɪtɪŋ] *n.* (*pl.* **whiting**) type of small sea fish.

whit•low ['wɪtləʊ] *n.* infected spot near a nail.

Whit•sun ['wɪtsən] *n.* Whitsunday or Whitsuntide. Christian festival on the seventh Sunday after Easter. **Whit•sun•tide,** *n.* the week which begins with Whitsunday, esp. the first three days.

whit•tle ['wɪtl] *v.* (a) to shape (a piece of wood) by cutting off small pieces with a knife. (b) **to w. sth away/down** = to make sth gradually smaller.

whiz [wɪz] *v.* (**whizzed**) to move very fast. **whiz kid,** *n. inf.* brilliant, successful young business person.

who [hu:] *pron.* (a) (*asking a question*) which person/which people? (b) the person/people that. **who•dun•it** [hu:'dʌnɪt] *n. inf.* detective story. **who•ev•er,** *pron.* anyone who/no matter who.

WHO *abbrev. for* World Health Organization.

whoa [wəʊ] *inter. used to tell a horse to stand still.*

whole [həʊl] 1. *adj.* complete; not broken/not damaged; **he ate the w. cake** = he ate all the cake; **he ate the cookie w.** = he put it all in his mouth at once and ate it, without breaking it up. 2. *n.* all; **as a w.** = altogether; **on the w.** = for the most part. **whole•heart•ed,** *adj.* complete/total. **whole•heart•ed•ly,** *adv.* completely/totally. **whole num•ber,** *n.* number which is not a fraction. **whole•sale.** 1. *n.* & *adj.* sale of goods in large quantities to shops which then sell them to people in small quantities. 2. *adj.* in large quantities/on a large scale.

whole•sal•er, *n.* person who buys and sells goods in large quantities. **whole•some,** ['həʊlsəm] *adj.* healthy/good; **w. food** = food that is good for your health. **whole•some•ness,** *n.* being wholesome. **whole•wheat,** *n.* brown flour containing all the grain. **whol•ly,** *adv.* completely/altogether.

whom [hu:m] *pron.* (a) (*formal*) (*object in questions*) which person/which persons. (b) (*object in statements*) the person/persons that.

whoop [wu:p] *n.* loud cry. **whoop•ee** [wu'pi:] *inter. showing excitement*; **to make w.** = to enjoy yourself noisily. **whoop•ing cough** ['hu:pɪŋkɒf] *n.* children's illness which causes coughing and loud noises when the child tries to breathe. **whoops,** *inter. showing surprise.*

whoosh [wu:ʃ] *n.* sound of air blowing past.

whop•per ['wɒpə] *n. inf.* (a) very large thing. (b) very big lie. **whop•ping,** *adj. inf.* very large.

whore ['hɔ:] *n.* (*formal*) prostitute.

whorl [wɜ:l] *n.* coiled/spiral shape.

whose [hu:z] *pron.* (a) (*asking a question*) of who. (b) belonging to who. **who•so•ev•er** [hu:səʊ'evə] *pron.* whoever.

why [waɪ] 1. *adv.* (*asking a question*) for what reason. 2. *n.* the reason. 3. *inter. showing surprise.*

wick [wɪk] *n.* length of string in the middle of a candle/piece of material in an oil lamp which is lit and burns slowly.

wick•ed ['wɪkɪd] *adj.* very bad/very nasty. **wick•ed•ly,** *adv.* in a wicked way. **wick•ed•ness,** *n.* evil; being wicked.

wick•er ['wɪkə] *n.* thin twigs used to make furniture or baskets. **wick•er•work,** *n.* (*no pl.*) objects made of thin twigs woven together.

wick•et ['wɪkɪt] *n.* (a) small door set in or next to a larger one (as in a castle gate or city wall). (b) position on the counter in a post office/bank, etc. (c) (*in cricket*) set of three sticks put in the ground and used as the target; main playing area between two sets of these sticks; *inf.* **a sticky w.** = an awkward/difficult situation. **wick•et-keep•er,** *n.* (*in cricket*) player standing behind the wicket to stop the balls that the batsman does not hit.

wide [waɪd] 1. *adj.* (-er, -est) (a) stretching far from side to side. (b) measurement from side to side. (c) enormous (range). 2. *adv.* (a) greatly/a long way apart/far. (b) **to fall w. of the target** = miss the target. **wide-an•gle,**

æ back, ɑ: farm, ɒ: top, aɪ pipe, aʊ how, aɪə fire, aʊə flower, ɔ: bought, ɔɪ toy, e fed, eəhair, eɪ take, ə afraid, əʊ boat, əʊə lower, v: word, i: heap, ɪ hit, ɪə hear, u: school, ʊ book, ʌ but, b back, d dog, ð then, dʒ just, f fog, g go, h hand, j yes, k catch, l last, m mix, n nut, ŋ sing, p penny, r round, s some, ʃ short, t too, tʃ chop, θ thing, v voice, w was, z zoo, ʒ treasure

adj. (lens) which takes in a wider area than an ordinary lens. **wide a•wake,** *adj.* very much awake/not at all sleepy. **wide•ly,** *adv.* (a) greatly; **w. read** = (i) (book) which many people have read; (ii) (person) who has read many books. **wid•en,** *v.* to make larger/to become wide. **wide-rang•ing,** *adj.* (discussion) which covers a wide field of subjects. **wide•spread,** *adj.* far/over a large area.

widg•eon ['wɪdʒn] *n.* (*pl.* **widgeons** or **widgeon**) type of small wild duck.

wid•ow ['wɪdəʊ] *n.* woman whose husband has died. **wid•owed,** *adj.* (woman) who has become a widow; (man) who has become a widower. **wid•ow•er,** *n.* man whose wife has died. **wid•ow•hood,** *n.* being a widow.

width [wɪdT] *n.* (a) measurement from side to side. (b) piece of material (cut right across a roll).

wield ['wiːld] *v.* (a) to hold (sth), usu. by the handle, and use it. (b) to use/to control (power).

wie•ner ['wiːnə] *n.* frankfurter. **wie•ner schnit•zel,** *n.* veal escalope, fried in breadcrumbs.

wife [waɪf] *n.* (*pl.* **wives**) woman to whom a man is married. **wife•ly,** *adj.* like a wife.

wig [wɪg] *n.* false hair worn on the head.

wig•gle ['wɪgl] *v. inf.* to move slightly up and down or from side to side. **wig•gly,** *adj. inf.* wavy; (line) which goes up and down.

wig•wam ['wɪgwæm] *n.* cone-shaped tent of the North American Indians.

wild [waɪld] 1. *adj.* (**-er, -est**) (a) not tame/free to live naturally. (b) (plant) which is not a garden plant. (c) stormy/rough (sea/wind). (d) savage/angry/fierce (animal); **to be w. with excitement** = to be over-excited; *inf.* **w. about** = very enthusiastic about. (e) rough/uncivilized (country). (f) rash/reckless (plan); badly aimed (shot). 2. *n.* **in the w.** = in country which is uninhabited and where animals can live freely. **wild•cat.** 1. *n.* small wild animal of the cat family. 2. *adj.* risky/reckless; **w. strike** = unofficial strike/strike of workers without the union's permission. **wil•der•ness** ['wɪldənəs] *n.* uncultivated/uninhabited country; desert. **wild•fire,** *n.* **like w.** = very quickly. **wild•fowl,** *n. pl.* wild birds shot for sport (such as ducks and geese). **wild-goose chase,** *n.* hopeless search. **wild•life,** *n.* (*no pl.*) birds/plants/animals living free, untouched by human beings; **w. preserve** = place where wild animals are allowed to run wild. **wild•ly,** *adv.* in a wild way; **w. inaccurate** = completely wrong. **wild•ness,** *n.* being wild.

wil•de•beest ['wɪldɪbɪːst] *n.* large African antelope.

wiles [waɪlz] *n. pl.* clever tricks.

wil•ful ['wɪlful] *adj.* willful.

will [wɪl] 1. *n.* (a) strength of mind and character. (b) wish; **of one's own free w.** = not forced; **at w.** = as you wish. (c) written instructions made by s.o. as to what should happen to his belongings when he dies. 2. *v.* (a) **to w. s.o. to do sth** = to suggest strongly to s.o. else by power of mind. (b) to leave (your belongings) after death to others by writing down your wishes. 3. *v.* (*used with an infinitive*) (a) to wish; **do what you w.** (b) (*polite form of asking someone to do something*) **would you please sit down?/won't you sit down?** (c) (*stressed*) to be certain to happen. 4. *used with verbs forming future tense.* **will•ing,** *adj.* wanting (**to do** sth); eager (to help). **will•ing•ly,** *adv.* eagerly. **will•ing•ness,** *n.* eagerness. **will pow•er,** *n.* strength of will.

will•ful ['wɪlfəl] *adj.* (a) (person) determined to do what he wants. (b) done on purpose; **w. murder** = murder which was planned. **will•ful•ly,** *adv.* intentionally/on purpose.

wil•lies ['wɪlɪz] *n. pl. inf.* **it gives me the w.** = it makes me scared.

will-o'-the-wisp ['wɪləðəwɪsp] *n.* bluish light caused in marshes by burning methane gas.

wil•low ['wɪləʊ] *n.* tree with thin supple branches often found along river banks. **wil•low pat•tern,** *n.* china with a blue and white Chinese design on it. **wil•low•y,** *adj.* tall and slender.

wil•ly-nil•ly [wɪlɪ'nɪlɪ] *adv.* whether you want to or not.

wilt [wɪlt] 1. *n.* disease of plants which makes them droop. 2. *v.* to become weak and droop.

wil•y ['waɪlɪ] *adj.* (**-ier,-iest**) crafty/full of tricks. **wil•i•ness,** *n.* being wily.

wimp [wɪmp] *n.* weak individual.

wim•ple ['wɪmpl] *n.* linen covering worn by nuns over their heads.

win [wɪn] 1. *n.* action of beating s.o. in a competition/game. 2. *v.* (**won** [wʌn]) (a) to defeat s.o. in a contest/race, etc.; to be first in a race/competition. (b) to gain/to get (a prize). **win back,** *v.* to get back/to regain. **win•ner,** *n.* (a) person who has won a race/a prize, etc. (b) *inf.* thing which is (certain to be) successful. **win•ning.** 1. *adj.* (a) which wins. (b) attractive (smile). 2. *n.* (a) victory. (b) **winnings** = money, etc., which has been won at a game of chance. **win o•ver,** *v.* to persuade. **win out,** *v.* to succeed in the end after many difficulties.

wince [wɪns] 1. *n.* movement which shows you feel pain. 2. *v.* to show signs of pain, esp. by moving the face.

winch [wɪnʃ] 1. *n.* (*pl.* **-es**) device which pulls

things up by winding a rope around a drum. 2. *v.* to pull up/to lift by using a winch.

wind¹ [wɪnd] 1. *n.* (a) moving air; **high winds** = very strong winds; **to sail close to the w.** = (i) to sail a boat almost directly into the wind; (ii) to be very near to being dishonest or rude; **to take the w. out of s.o.'s sails** = to spoil s.o.'s plans, usually by doing what he was going to do. (b) breath; **to get your second w.** = to get enough breath again after being tired; to be able to make a second effort. (c) smell/scent, when hunting; **to get w. of** = to hear a rumor about. (d) gas in the stomach. (e) (*also* **wind instruments, wind section**) woodwind instruments in an orchestra. 2. *v.* (a) to make (s.o.) breathless, esp. by hitting him in the chest. (b) to smell/scent when hunting. **wind•bag**, *n. inf.* person who talks too much. **wind•break**, *n.* fence/hedge which protects sth against the wind. **wind•burn**, *n.* inflammation of the skin caused by cold wind. **wind•break•er**, *n.* short jacket, to keep out the wind. **wind•chill fac•tor**, *n.* air temperature including the effect of the wind. **wind•fall**, *n.* (a) fruit which has been blown to the ground from a fruit tree. (b) unexpected good fortune. **wind gauge**, *n.* instrument for measuring the force of the wind. **wind•jam•mer**, *n.* (*old*) large sailing ship. **wind•less**, *adj.* with no wind. **wind•mill**, *n.* mill driven by sails pushed around by the wind. **wind•pipe**, *n.* pipe leading from the nose and mouth to the lungs. **wind•shield**, *n.* glass window in the front of a car/truck, etc. **windsock**, *n.* tube of material at the end of a tall pole, which shows the direction of the wind at an airfield. **wind•surf•er**, *n.* person who does windsurfing. **wind•surf•ing**, *n.* sport of riding on the sea on a surfboard with a sail attached. **wind•swept**, *adj.* blown by strong winds. **wind•ward**, *adj., adv. & n.* (side of a ship) from which the wind blows. **wind•y**, *adj.* (-ier, -iest) (a) having much wind. (b) full of empty talk.

wind² [waɪnd] 1. *n.* bend/twist/turn. 2. *v.* (**wound** [waʊnd]) (a) to turn. (b) to roll up/to roll around. (c) to turn a key of (a watch/clock) until the spring is tight. **wind•ing**. 1. *adj.* turning/twisting. 2. *n.* action of turning/rolling. **wind up**, *v.* (a) to roll up. (b) to tighten a spring on a watch/clockwork toy, etc. (c) to finish; bring to an end. (d) *inf.* **to be wound up** = to be nervous/tense. **wind•lass** ['wɪndləs] *n.* (*pl.* -es) hand winch for pulling sth up by winding a rope around a drum.

win•dow ['wɪndəʊ] *n.* (a) opening in a wall/door, etc., filled with glass; **stained-glass w.** = window made of small pieces of colored glass, found esp. in churches. (b) section of a computer screen reserved for a special purpose. **win•dow box**, *n.* long box for plants kept on an outside window ledge. **win•dow dress•ing**, *n.* (a) displaying goods in an artistic way in a store window. (b) putting on a display to hide the real state of affairs. **window ledge, window sill**, *n.* ledge/flat piece of wood, etc., inside and outside a window. **win•dow•pane**, *n.* single piece of glass, used as part of a whole window. **win•dow shop•ping**, *n.* looking at goods in store windows without buying them.

wine [waɪn] 1. *n.* (a) alcoholic drink made from the juice of grapes; **w. list** = list of wines which are available at a restaurant. (b) alcoholic drink made from the juice of fruit or flowers. 2. *v.* **to w. and dine s.o.** = to take s.o. out for an expensive dinner and drinks. **wine cel•lar**, *n.* cool room underground where wine is kept. **wine•glass**, *n.* glass used for drinking wine. **wine-grow•ing**, *adj.* (district) where vines are grown to produce wine. **wine mer•chant**, *n.* person who sells wines and spirits in a shop. **wine stew•ard**, *n.* person in charge of serving the wines in a restaurant.

wing [wɪŋ] 1. *n.* (a) one of the two limbs which a bird/butterfly, etc., use to fly; **to take s.o. under your w.** = to protect/to look after. (b) one of the two flat projecting parts on an aircraft. (c) side part of a large building which leads off the main part. (d) part of an army which stretches to one side; part of a political party which has a certain tendency. (e) unit of the U.S. air force; **w. commander** = officer in charge of a wing. (f) **wings** = side of the stage in a theater where actors wait before going on stage. (g) **wings** = pilot's badge. (h) (*in hockey/soccer*) forward player on the side of the center. 2. *v.* (a) to fly. (b) to shoot (in the wing/arm). **winged**, *adj.* with wings. **wing•er**, *n. suffix showing* person on the right/left of a political party. **wing•less**, *adj.* having no wings. **wing nut**, *n.* nut with two projecting parts for screwing easily. **wing•span**, *n.* distance from the tip of one wing to the tip of another (of a bird/aircraft, etc.).

æ back, ɑː farm, ɒ top, aɪ pipe, aʊ how, aɪə fire, aʊə flower, ɔː bought, ɔɪ toy, e fed, eə hair, eɪ take, ə afraid, əʊ boat, əʊ lower, vː word, iː heap, ɪ hit, ɪə hear, uː school, ʊ book, ʌ but, b back, d dog, ð then, dʒ just, f fog, g go, h hand, j yes, k catch, l last, m mix, n nut, ŋ sing, p penny, r round, s some, ʃ short, t too, tʃ chop, θ thing, v voice, w was, z zoo, ʒ treasure

wink [wɪŋk] 1. *n.* act of quickly shutting and opening one eye; *inf.* **to have forty winks** = to have a short sleep. 2. *v.* (a) to shut one eye and then quickly open it again. (b) (*of lights/stars*) to shine on and off.

win•now ['wɪnəʊ] *v.* to separate the grain from chaff, by allowing the wind to blow the chaff away.

win•some ['wɪnsəm] *adj.* pleasant/charming.

win•ter ['wɪntə] 1. *n.* coldest season of the year; **w. sports** = sports which are played on snow or ice. 2. *v.* to spend the cold months of the year. **win•try**, *adj.* like winter; unfriendly/cold (smile).

wipe [waɪp] 1. *n.* act of cleaning or drying with a cloth. 2. *v.* to clean/to dry with a cloth. **wipe a•way**, *v.* to clean away. **wipe out**, *v.* (a) to clean and dry the inside of (sth). (b) to kill/to destroy. **wip•er**, *n.* thing that wipes; device on a car which wipes rain away from the windshield; **rear w.** = device for wiping the rain from the rear window of a car.

wire ['waɪə] 1. *n.* (a) thin metal line or thread; **w. netting** = pieces of wire twisted together to make a net; **barbed w.** = wire with sharp pieces of metal twisted in at intervals, used to stop animals or people from getting in or out; **live w.** = (i) wire which carries an electrical current; (ii) person who is full of energy; **telegraph/telephone w.** = wire along which telegraph/telephone messages are sent; *inf.* **we must have our wires crossed** = we must have misunderstood each other; **w. service** = news agency sending news to subscribers by teleprinter; **w. tapping** = listening to other people's telephone conversations with special equipment. (b) *inf.* telegram. 2. *v.* (a) to fasten with wires. (b) to put in wires to carry electricity to (a house). (c) to send a telegram. **wire•less.** 1. *n.* (*esp. Brit.*) radio. 2. *adj.* without wires. **wire•worm**, *n.* type of small insect which attacks plants. **wir•ing**, *n.* system of wires used to carry electricity. **wir•y**, *adj.* (**-ier, -iest**) (a) (*of person*) thin but strong. (b) (*of hair*) stiff and strong, not easily combed.

wis•dom ['wɪzdəm] *n.* intelligence/knowledge/common sense; **w. tooth** = one of four back teeth which grow when you are an adult.

wise [waɪz] *adj.* (**-er, -est**) having intelligence and common sense/knowing a great deal/prudent; **no one will be any the wiser** = no one will know anything about it; **I'm none the wiser** = I know no more than I did before. **wise•crack.** 1. *n.* clever remark. 2. *v.* to make a joke/a wisecrack. **wise guy**, *n.* person who pretends to know more than anyone else. **wise•ly**, *adv.* (a) in a wise way. (b) prudently.

wish [wɪʃ] 1. *n.* (*pl.* **-es**) want/desire. (b) **good wishes** = kind feelings/greetings. 2. *v.* (a) to want/to desire sth which is unlikely to happen. (b) to express a desire or a hope. **wish•bone**, *n.* V-shaped bone in a chicken's breast, which you are supposed to pull with your partner, each having made a wish, the person who holds the larger piece getting his wish. **wish•ful**, *adj.* **w. thinking** = believing sth because you would like it to happen.

wish•y-wash•y ['wɪʃɪwɒʃɪ] *adj.* watery; not strong (color/character, etc.).

wisp [wɪsp] *n.* small strand; little piece. **wisp•y**, *adj.* thin/slight.

wis•te•ri•a, wistaria [wɪ'stɪərɪə, wɪ'steərɪə] *n.* climbing plant with sweet-smelling blue flowers.

wist•ful ['wɪstfəl] *adj.* longing for sth, but sad as there is no hope of getting it. **wist•ful•ly**, *adv.* in a wistful way. **wist•ful•ness**, *n.* being wistful.

wit [wɪt] 1. *n.* (a) (*usu.* **wits**) intelligence; **at your wit's end** = not knowing what to do next; **to keep your wits about you** = to keep calm in a difficult situation and think hard what to do next. (b) ability to say clever/funny things. (c) person who says clever and funny things. 2. *v.* (*old*) **to w.** = namely/that is.

witch [wɪtʃ] *n.* (*pl.* **-es**) woman believed to have evil magic powers. **witch•craft**, *n.* art of magic. **witch doc•tor**, *n.* man in a primitive tribe who appears to cure illnesses by magic. **witch•er•y**, *n.* witchcraft. **witch ha•zel**, *n.* shrub with tiny yellow flowers blooming in early spring. **witch hunt**, *n.* cruel investigation of people who are supposed to be politically unreliable.

with [wɪð, wɪT] *prep.* (a) accompanied by/together/beside. (b) having/possessing. (c) in spite of (faults). (d) using. (e) from/because of. (f) showing (an emotion). (g) (*used after many verbs to show a connection*) **to part w. sth** = to give sth away; **to meet w.** = to have/to experience unexpectedly; **I can do nothing w. him** = I can't change him; **to have nothing to do w.** = to have no connection with; **I'm w. you there!** = (i) I agree with you! (ii) I understand you; *inf.* **to be w. it** = to be fashionable/modern.

with•draw [wɪT'drɔ:] *v.* (**withdrew; withdrawn**) to move back/to take back/to pull back; to take (money) out of a bank account; to retract (sth which has been said). **with•draw•al**, *n.* taking back; removing of money (from a bank account); **w. symptoms** = symptoms shown by s.o. who is trying to stop taking a drug/smoking, etc. **with•drawn**, *adj.* shy; (person) who does not like meeting other people.

with•er ['wɪðə] *v.* (a) (*of plants*) to grow weaker and dry up. (b) to make (sth) grow weaker and dry up; to make (s.o.) feel embarrassed by looking disapprovingly.

with•er•ing, *adj.* scornful/disapproving (look).

with•ers ['wɪðəz] *n. pl.* part of a horse's back just below the neck.

with•hold [wɪT'həuld] *v.* (**withheld**) to keep back/to refuse to give.

with•in [wɪ'ðɪn] *prep.* inside.

with•out [wɪ'ðaut] *prep.* not having/not with; **to go w.** = not to have (sth); **it goes w. saying that** = it hardly needs to be said that.

with•stand [wɪT'stænd] *v.* (**withstood**) to resist/to endure.

withy ['wɪðɪ] *n.* thin willow twig used to tie things together.

wit•ness ['wɪtnəs] 1. *n.* (*pl.* **-es**) (a) person who sees sth happening. (b) **to bear w. to** = to be evidence of. (c) person who witnesses s.o.'s signature. 2. *v.* (a) to see (sth) happen. (b) to sign your name on a legal paper to say that s.o.'s signature is genuine. (c) to give evidence in court. **wit•ness stand,** *n.* place where a witness sits in a law court.

wit•ting•ly ['wɪtɪŋlɪ] *adv.* on purpose/intentionally.

wit•ty ['wɪtɪ] *adj.* (**-ier, -iest**) clever and funny. **wit•ti•cism** ['wɪtɪsɪzəm] *n.* clever/funny remark.

wives [waɪvz] *n. see* **wife.**

wiz•ard ['wɪzəd] *n.* (a) man who is believed to have magic powers. (b) clever person/expert. **wiz•ard•ry,** *n.* being a wizard; cleverness.

wiz•ened ['wɪzənd] *adj.* dried up and wrinkled (face).

woad [wəud] *n.* wild plant with blue flowers, used to make a blue dye.

wob•ble ['wɒbl] 1. *n.* shaking movement. 2. *v.* to shake/to move unsteadily. **wob•bly,** *adj.* unsteady/shaking.

woe [wəu] *n.* sadness/trouble. **woe•be•gone,** *adj.* very sad (look). **woe•ful,** *adj.* full of sadness. **woe•ful•ly,** *adv.* sadly.

woke, woken [wəuk, wəukn] *v. see* **wake.**

wold [wəuld] *n.* (*esp. Brit.*) area of gently rounded hills.

wolf [wulf] 1. *n.* (*pl.* **wolves**) (a) wild animal like a dog, usu. living in a large group in cold northern regions; **pack of wolves** = group of wolves living together; **lone w.** = person who prefers to be alone/who does not associate with other people; **she-wolf** = female wolf; **w. cub** = young wolf; **w. in sheep's clothing** = person who seems inoffensive but really is wicked; **to keep the w. from the door** = to have enough food to live on; **to cry w.** = to raise a false alarm. (b) *inf.* man who chases women. 2. *v.* to eat quickly. **wolf•hound,** *n.* large hunting dog. **wolf•ish,** *adj.* like a wolf.

wol•ver•ine ['wulvəriːn] *n.* dark-furred North American carnivorous mammal.

wom•an ['wumən] *n.* (*pl.* **women** ['wɪmɪn]) (a) female adult human being; **Women's Lib** = movement to give women equal status with men in business, education, society, etc. (b) female. **wom•an•hood,** *n.* state of being a woman. **wom•an•ish,** *adj.* (man) who behaves like a woman. **wom•an•ize,** *v.* to try to seduce women often. **wom•an•iz•er,** *n.* man who womanizes. **wom•an•kind,** *n.* all women. **wom•an•li•ness,** *n.* being womanly. **wom•an•ly,** *adj.* feminine, like a woman. **wom•en•folk,** *n. pl.* all women (in a family, etc.).

womb [wuːm] *n.* uterus.

wom•bat ['wɒmbət] *n.* small Australian animal.

won [wʌn] *v. see* **win.**

won•der ['wʌndə] 1. *n.* (a) amazing thing; **no w.** = it isn't surprising. (b) astonishment/surprise. 2. *v.* (a) to be surprised/to marvel (**at**). (b) to want to know/to ask yourself (why). (c) (*used when asking someone politely to do something*) **I w. if you could open the door. won•der•ful,** *adj.* marvelous/very good/exciting. **won•der•ful•ly,** *adv.* in a wonderful way. **won•der•land,** *n.* marvelous place. **won•der•ment,** *n.* astonishment/wonder. **won•drous,** *adj.* wonderful.

wont [wəunt] *n.* (*formal*) habit; **as is his w.** = as he usually does. **wont•ed,** *adj.* (*formal*) habitual.

won't [wəunt] *v.* will not.

woo [wuː] *v.* to try to attract (a woman) to marry you; to try to get (s.o.) to support you/to vote for you, etc. **woo•er,** *n.* person who woos.

wood [wud] *n.* (a) (*also* **woods**) large group of trees/small forest; **we're not out of the w. yet** = our problems are not over. (b) material that a tree is made of. **wood•bine,** *n.* wild climbing plant. **wood•burn•ing stove,** *n.* stove which is designed to use wood as a fuel. **wood•carv•ing,** *n.* (i) art of sculpture in wood; (ii) wooden sculpture. **wood•chuck,** *n.* North American rodent. **wood•cock,** *n.* small brown bird shot for sport or food. **wood•craft,** *n.* skill at finding your way

---

æ **back,** a: **farm,** ɒ: **top,** aɪ **pipe,** au **how,** aiə **fire,** auə **flower,** ɔ: **bought,** ɔɪ **toy,** e **fed,** eə **hair,** eɪ **take,** ə **afraid,** əu **boat,** əuə **lower,** v: **word,** i: **heap,** ɪ **hit,** ɪə **hear,** u: **school,** u **book,** ʌ **but,** b **back,** d **dog,** ð **then,** dʒ **just,** f **fog,** g **go,** h **hand,** j **yes,** k **catch,** l **last,** m **mix,** n **nut,** ŋ **sing,** p **penny,** r **round,** s **some,** ʃ **short,** t **too,** tʃ **chop,** θ **thing,** v **voice,** w **was,** z **zoo,** ʒ **treasure**

about woods and forests and living in them. **wood•cut**, *n.* print made from a carved wooden plate. **wood•ed**, *adj.* covered in trees. **wood•en**, *adj.* (a) made of wood. (b) stiff/showing no feeling. **wood•en•ly**, *adv.* stiffly. **wood•land**, *n.* land covered in woods. **wood•louse**, *n.* (*pl.* **-lice**) very small animal with a hard shell, which curls up when attacked, and lives in rotten wood, etc. **wood•peck•er**, *n.* bird with a long sharp beak which finds insects under the bark of trees. **wood•pig•eon**, *n.* common European wild pigeon. **wood pulp**, *n.* fragments of wood made into a pulp, used for making paper. **wood•shed**, *n.* small shed/hut used for storing wood. **wood(s)•man**, *n.* (*pl.* **-men**) man who works in woods and forests. **wood•winds**, *n.* wind instruments in an orchestra which are usu. made of wood. **wood•work**, *n.* (a) carpentry. (b) interior wooden parts of a building. **wood•worm**, *n.* small grub which bores holes in wood. **wood•y**, *adj.* (**-ier, -iest**) like wood; made of wood.

woof [wuf] 1. *n.* (a) weft. (b) sound of a dog's bark. 2. *v.* (*of dog*) to bark. **woof•er**, *n.* loudspeaker which reproduces low sounds.

wool [wul] *n.* (a) short, thick hair of a sheep/goat, etc. (b) long threads of twisted hair, used to make clothes/carpets, etc.; cloth woven from hair; **to pull the w. over s.o.'s eyes** = to deceive s.o. (c) material which looks like sheep's wool; **steel w. wool•gath•er•ing**, *n.* daydreaming/not thinking of what you are doing. **wool•en, woollen**, *adj.* made of wool. **wool•ens, wool•lens**, *n. pl.* clothing made of knitted wool. **wool•li•ness**, *n.* being woolly. **wool•ly, wooly**, 1. *adj.* (**-ier, -iest**) (a) made of wool/like wool. (b) vague/not clear. 2. *n. inf.* sweater, etc. made of wool.

wooz•y ['wu:zi] *adj. inf.* dizzy/in a daze.

word [wɜ:d] 1. *n.* (a) unit of speech either spoken or written; **to have words with s.o.** = to quarrel with s.o.; **to have a w. with s.o.** = to have a short talk with s.o.; **in other words** = explaining sth in a different way; **you've taken the words out of my mouth** = you've said what I was going to say; **without a w.** = without speaking; **w. for w.** = exactly as is said or written. (b) message/news; **by w. of mouth** = by spoken message. (c) promise; **to give one's w.** = to promise; **he kept his w.** = he did what he promised to do; **I'll take your w. for it** = I'll believe what you say. (d) **my w.!** *inter. expressing* surprise. 2. *v.* to put in words, either written or spoken. **word•i•ly**, *adv.* in a wordy way. **word•i•ness** *n.* being wordy. **word•ing**, *n.*

choice of words. **word proc•es•sor**, *n.* typewriter with a computer memory and a screen on which the text can be displayed. **word•y**, *adj.* (**-ier, -iest**) *adj.* using too many words.

wore ['wɔ:] *v. see* **wear**.

work [wɜ:k] 1. *n.* (a) mental or physical activity; **to have one's w. cut out** = find it difficult (to do sth). (b) job; **out of w.** = with no job. (c) thing that has been made by s.o. (d) **works** = factory. (e) **road w.** = repairs to a road. (f) **works** = moving parts of a machine; *inf.* **to give s.o. the works** = to give s.o. everything/the full treatment. 2. *v.* (a) to use energy/to make s.o. use energy in carrying out an activity. (b) (*of machine*) to operate/to move. (c) to make (a machine) function. (d) to have a job. (e) to be successful. (f) to embroider/to sew. (g) **to w. one's way** = to move gradually; **he was working himself into a rage** = he was becoming more and more angry. (h) to take coal/copper, etc., from (a mine); **worked out** = (mine) where all the ore has been extracted. **work•a•ble**, *adj.* able to be worked. **work•a•day**, *adj.* plain/ordinary. **work•a•hol•ic**, *n. inf.* person who cannot stop working. **work•book**, *n.* book of excercises to help teach a subject. **worked up**, *adj.* excited/annoyed (**about**). **work•er**, *n.* (a) person who works. (b) member of the working class. (c) type of female bee which works to provide the queen with honey, but which is sterile. **work force**, *n.* all the workers (in a factory). **work•horse**, *n.* person who can work hard. **work•ing**. 1. *adj.* which works; referring to work; **w. class** = people who work with their hands/who earn wages not salaries. 2. *n.* (*usu. pl.* **workings**) (a) place where mineral has been dug. (b) way sth works. **work•man**, *n.* (*pl.* **-men**) man who works with his hands. **work•man•like**, *adj.* skillful/expert. **work•man•ship**, *n.* skill of a good workman. **work off**, *v.* to get rid of (sth) by working. **work on**, *v.* (a) to continue to work. (b) to be busy doing sth. (c) to try to influence/to persuade. **work out**, *v.* (a) to succeed/to do well. (b) to plan (sth) in detail/to find an answer to (sth). (c) (**at**) to amount to (a price). **work•out**, *n.* exercise/practice before an athletic event. **work•room**, *n.* room where work is done. **work•shop**, *n.* place in a small factory or house where things are made. **work sta•tion**, *n.* desk with terminal, monitor, keyboard, etc., where a computer operator works. **work up**, *v.* to develop/to reach slowly.

world [wɜ:ld] *n.* (a) the earth; particular part of the earth; **the Old W.** = Europe, Asia and Africa; **the New W.** = North and South America; **the Third W.** = countries with no strong connections to the superpowers; **W. War** = war in which many countries all over the world take part. (b) people on Earth; everything; **to come into the w.** = to be born; **to be all alone in the w.** = to have no family; **out of this w.** = magnificent; **to think the w. of s.o.** = to think very highly of s.o.; **it will do you the w. of good** = it will help you greatly. (c) people with a particular interest/things which form a particular group. **world-fa•mous,** *adj.* known everywhere. **world•li•ness,** *n.* being worldly/not being idealistic. **world•ly,** *adj.* (a) of the material world. (b) not idealistic. **world•ly-wise,** *adj.* wise about worldly things. **world•wide,** *adj. & adv.* throughout the whole world. **World Wide Web,** *n.* global network of linked hypertext files containing information that can be accessed by an Internet user.

worm [wɜːm] 1. *n.* (a) small, spineless burrowing creature which looks like a very small snake and lives in earth. (b) similar animal which lives in the intestines of animals. (c) woodworm. (d) spiral thread of a screw. 2. *v.* to move slowly like a worm; **to w. yourself into s.o.'s favor** = to make s.o. like you by being especially nice to them; **to w. information out of s.o.** = to get information by asking many persistent questions. **worm•eat•en,** *adj.* which has been eaten by worms. **worm•wood,** *n.* bitter plant.

worn [wɔːn] *adj.* much used; *see also* **wear. worn out,** *adj.* (a) used so much that it is now useless. (b) tired.

wor•ry ['wʌrɪ] 1. *n.* (a) thing which makes you anxious. (b) being anxious. 2. *v.* (a) to be upset/anxious; to make (s.o.) upset/anxious. (b) *(of dogs)* to shake and tear with the teeth. **wor•ried,** *adj.* anxious/troubled. **wor•ri•er,** *n.* person who worries. **wor•ri•some,** *adj.* which makes you worried/anxious.

worse [wɜːs] 1. *adj.* (a) more inferior in quality, condition, etc. (b) in less good health; sicker. 2. *adv.* in a worse way. **wors•en,** *v.* to become or make worse. **worse off,** *adj.* in a worse condition.

wor•ship ['wɜːʃɪp] 1. *n.* (a) praise and honor shown to God. (b) praise and honor shown to s.o./sth. 2. *v.* **(worshipped)** (a) to praise and love (God). (b) to take part in a church service. (c) to praise and love (s.o./sth). **wor•ship•er,** *n.* person who worships; **sun w.** = person who loves sunbathing.

worst [wɜːst] 1. *adj.* very bad/worse than anyone/anything else. 2. *n.* most awful thing. 3. *adv.* very badly/worse than anyone/anything else.

wor•sted ['wustɪd] *n.* fine woolen cloth.

worth [wɜːT] 1. *adj.* (a) having a value/price. (b) useful; giving satisfaction; **it is w. (your) while** = it is worth the effort. (c) having riches/money, etc; **for all you are w.** = as much as possible. 2. *n.* value. **wor•thi•ly,** *adv.* in a worthy way. **wor•thi•ness,** *n.* being worthy. **worth•less,** *adj.* having no worth/no use. **worth•while** ['wɜːTwaɪl] *adj.* which is worth doing. **wor•thy** ['wɜːðɪ] 1. *adj.* **(-ier, -iest)** deserving. 2. *n.* notable person (in a town).

would [wud] *v. see* **will.**

wound [wuːnd] 1. *n.* (a) cut/damage to the skin, usu. received in a fight. (b) hurt to the feelings. 2. *v.* (a) to hurt. (b) to hurt the fellings of (s.o.). (c) [waund] *see also* **wind**[2].

wove, woven [wəuv, 'wəuvn] *v. see* **weave.**

wow [wau] 1. *n. inf.* (a) great success. (b) fluctuation of sound in a record-player. 2. *v. inf. (of a singer, etc.)* to excite (the audience).

wraith [raɪT] *n.* ghost.

wran•gle ['ræŋgl] 1. *n.* argument/dispute. 2. *v.* to argue.

wrap [ræp] 1. *n.* shawl; *inf.* **to keep sth under wraps** = to keep sth a secret. 2. *v.* **(wrapped)** to cover (sth) all around with paper/cloth, etc. **wrap up,** *v.* (a) to cover up completely. (b) to wear warm clothes. (c) **to be wrapped up in your work** = to think only of the work and take no notice of other things. **wrap•per,** *n.* piece of paper used to cover sth. **wrap•ping,** *n.* paper/cardboard/plastic, etc., used to wrap things; **w. paper** = paper used to wrap presents.

wrasse [ræs] *n.* type of sea fish.

wrath [rɒT] *n.* great anger. **wrath•ful,** *adj.* angry.

wreak [riːk] *v.* to carry out/to do (sth violent).

wreath [riːT] *n.* (a) circle of flowers or leaves esp. given at a funeral in memory of the dead person. (b) winding clouds (of smoke/mist). **wreathe** [riːð] *v.* (a) to put a circle of flowers on (s.o./sth). (b) to cover with twisting clouds of smoke/mist.

wreck [rek] 1. *n.* (a) ship which has been sunk/badly damaged on rocks, etc. (b) action of being wrecked. (c) anything which has been damaged and is useless. (d) person who, be-

---

æ **back,** ɑː **farm,** ɒ **top,** aɪ **pipe,** au **how,** aie **fire,** auə **flower,** ɔː **bought,** ɔɪ **toy,** e **fed,** eəhair, eɪ **take,** ə **afraid,** əu **boat,** əuə **lower,** vː **word,** iː **heap,** i **hit,** ɪə **hear,** uː **school,** u **book,** ʌ **but,** b **back,** d **dog,** ð **then,** dʒ **just,** f **fog,** g **go,** h **hand,** j **yes,** k **catch,** l **last,** m **mix,** n **nut,** ŋ **sing,** p **penny,** r **round,** s **some,** ʃ **short,** t **too,** tʃ **chop,** θ **thing,** v **voice,** w **was,** z **zoo,** ʒ **treasure**

cause of illness, can do very little. 2. *v.* to cause severe damage to (sth); to ruin (sth). **wreck•age,** *n.* broken remains of a building/ship, etc., after a disaster. **wreck•er,** *n.* (a) person who destroys a building/plan, etc., on purpose, or tries to make a ship crash on to rocks. (b) person who is employed to destroy old buildings/break up old cars, etc. (c) truck which goes to help cars which have broken down on the road; engine which goes to help a train which has broken down on the track.

wren [ren] *n.* very small brown songbird.

wrench [renʃ] 1. *n.* (*pl.* **-es**) (a) violent twisting movement. (b) tool for turning bolts, nuts, etc. (c) sadness at leaving. 2. *v.* to turn and pull (sth) violently.

wrest [rest] *v.* (*formal*) to twist/to wrench away.

wres•tle ['resl] *v.* (a) to fight with s.o. in a contest by trying to throw him to the ground. (b) to fight/struggle with (a problem). **wres•tler,** *n.* person who wrestles in contests. **wres•tling,** *n.* **w. match** = contest of wrestlers watched by crowds of people.

wretch [retʃ] *n.* (*pl.* **-es**) (a) person who looks poor and miserable. (b) despicable/annoying person. **wretch•ed** ['retʃɪd] *adj.* (a) miserable and poor; **to feel w.** = to feel ill. (b) terrible/annoying. **wretch•ed•ly,** *adv.* miserably. **wretch•ed•ness,** *n.* being wretched.

wrig•gle ['rɪgl] *v.* to twist and turn; **to w. out of** = to get out of (a difficult situation) by trickery.

wring [rɪŋ] *v.* (**wrung**) to twist (sth), esp. to get water out of it; **to w. information from** = to manage to get information with difficulty; **to w. one's hands** = to twist and turn one's hands, showing sadness and emotion. **wring•er,** *n.* machine for squeezing the water out of wet washing. **wring•ing,** *adj.* very (wet).

wrin•kle ['rɪŋkl] 1. *n.* (a) line/fold of the skin. (b) line or crease in cloth. 2. *v.* to make lines/creases in.

wrist [rɪst] *n.* joint between the arm and the hand; **w. watch** = small watch worn on a strap around the wrist. **wrist•let,** *n.* band worn around the wrist.

writ [rɪt] *n.* legal paper ordering s.o. to do/not to do wth. **Holy Writ,** *n.* the Bible.

write [raɪt] *v.* (**wrote** [rəʊt], **has written**) (a) to put down words on paper. (b) to be the author of books/music, etc.. (c) to put a letter in writing and send it to s.o. *inf.* **that's nothing to w. home about** = it's nothing special. **write in,** *v.* (a) to ask for by sending a letter. (b) to vote for a candidate whose name does not appear on the ballot, by writing the name there. **write off,** *v.* to remove (sth) from a written list; to cancel (a debt); to see (sth) as a failure; **the car was written off** = the insurance company considered it a total loss. **write-off,** *n. inf.* total loss. **writ•er,** *n.* person who writes, esp. to earn money. **write up,** *v.* to describe fully in writing. **write-up,** *n. inf.* article in a newspaper. **writ•ing,** *n.* (a) thing that is written; **w. paper** = paper used for writing letters. (b) handwriting. **writ•ings,** *n. pl.* books, etc., written by an author.

writhe [raɪð] *v.* to twist and turn (in agony).

wrong [rɒŋ] 1. *adj.* (a) bad/not right. (b) not right/incorrect. (c) **what's w.?** = what is the matter? **I hope nothing's w.** = I hope nothing bad has happened. 2. *n.* bad/incorrect thing; **to be in the w.** = to have made a mistake. 3. *adv.* badly/incorrectly; **to go w.** = to break down/not to work properly. 4. *v.* to treat (s.o.) unfairly. **wrong•do•er,** *n.* person who has committed a sin/crime. **wrong•do•ing,** *n.* crime/unlawful/evil act. **wrong•ful,** *adj.* unjust/unlawful. **wrong•ful•ly,** *adv.* in a wrongful way. **wrong•head•ed,** *adj.* mistaken but refusing to admit it. **wrong•ly,** *adv.* incorrectly/badly.

wrote [rəʊt] *v. see* **write.**

wrought [rɔːt] *adj.* **w. iron** = hammered, twisted and bent iron used for making decorative gates/balconies, etc.

wrung [rʌŋ] *v. see* **wring.**

wry [raɪ] *adj.* showing dislike by twisting the mouth.

WWW *abbrev. for* World Wide Web.

WYS•I•WYG ['wɪzɪwɪg] what-you-see-is-what-you-get (when the text on a computer screen is exactly the same as the printed output).

Xx

X, x [eks]. **X-ray.** 1. *n.* (a) ray which will pass through solids and is used esp. in hospitals for photographing the inside of the body. (b) photograph taken with X-rays. 2. *v.* to take an X-ray photograph of.

xen•o•phobe ['zenəfəʊb] *n.* person who hates, dislikes, or fears foreigners.

xen•o•pho•bi•a [zenə'fəʊbɪə] *n.* hatred, dislike, or fear of foreigners.

xen•o•pho•bic, *adj.* hating, disliking, or fearing foreigners.

Xe•rox ['zɪərɒks] 1. *n.* (a) (*pl* -es) trademark for a type of photocopier. (b) (*also* **xerox**) photocopy made with this machine. 2. *v.* (*also* **xerox**) to make a photocopy with a Xerox machine.

Xmas ['krɪsməs, 'eksməs] *n. short for* **Christmas.**

xy•lo•phone ['zaɪləfəʊn] *n.* musical instrument consisting of wooden bars of different lengths which make different notes when they are tapped with a hammer.

Yy

yacht [jɒt] *n.* boat used for pleasure and sport; **y. club** = sailing club. **yacht•ing**, *n.* art of sailing a yacht. **yachts•man**, *n.* (*pl.* **-men**) person who sails a yacht.

ya•hoo ['jɑːhuː] *n. inf.* crude boorish person.

yak [jæk] *n.* long-haired ox from Asia. 2. *v. inf.* to talk incessantly.

yam [jæm] *n.* tropical plant with an edible root.

yank [jæŋk] 1. *n. inf.* short sharp pull. 2. *v. inf.* to pull hard and sharply. **Yank, Yank•ee**, *n. inf.* American (esp. from a northern U.S. state).

yap [jæp] 1. *n.* short sharp bark of a dog. 2. *v.* (**yapped**) to make short sharp barks.

yard [jɑːd] *n.* (a) measure of length (= 3 feet or 36 inches or 0.91 meter). (b) piece of wood attached to the mast holding a sail. (c) enclosed space behind a house or other building. (d) enclosed space used for a certain purpose; **train y.** = place where trains are stored or repaired; **Scotland Y.** *inf.* **the Y.** = headquarters of the London Metropolitan Police. **yard•age**, *n.* length in yards or area in square yards. **yard•arm**, *n.* end of the yard holding a sail. **yard•stick**, *n.* standard for measurement.

yarn [jɑːn] 1. *n.* (a) long thread of wool/fiber used in knitting or weaving. (b) *inf.* long story. 2. *v. inf.* to tell stories.

yar•row ['jærəʊ] *n.* wild plant with clusters of small white flowers.

yash•mak ['jæʃmæk] *n.* veil worn by Muslim women in public.

yaw [jɔː] *v.* (*of ship/aircraft*) to go away from the course.

yawl [jɔːl] *n.* type of two-masted sailboat.

yawn [jɔːn] 1. *n.* movement of opening the mouth when tired; **to stifle a y.** = to try to stop yawning. 2. to open the mouth wide when feeling sleepy, and to breathe in and out. **yawn•ing**, *adj.* open wide; **y. hole** = deep wide hole.

yaws [jɔːz] *n. pl.* tropical skin disease.

yd *abbreviation for* yard.

ye [jiː] 1. *pron.* (*old*) you. 2. *article used in false old names* the.

yea [jeɪ] *adv.* (*old*) yes.

year ['jɜː] *n.* (a) period of twelve months starting on January 1st and ending on December 31st; **the New Y.** = the first few days of the year; **to see the New Y. in** = to stay up until midnight on December 31st and celebrate with a party the beginning of the next year; **calendar y.** = year beginning on January 1st

and ending on December 31st; **leap y.** = year with 366 days in it, one more than the normal year. (b) any period of twelve months; **the project took two years; all (the) y. round** = through the whole year; **y. in, y. out** = happening regularly over a long period of time. (c) **his early years** = his childhood; **getting on in years** = quite old; **I haven't seen him for (donkey's) years** = I haven't seen him for a long time. **year•book**, *n.* reference book which comes out each year with up-to-date information. **year•ling**, *n.* one year old animal. **year•ly**, *adj. & adv.* every year; once a year.

yearn [jɜːn] *v.* to long for sth/to want sth. **yearn•ing**, *n.* desire/longing.

yeast [jiːst] *n.* living fungus used to make bread and beer. **yeast•y**, *adj.* like yeast; referring to yeast.

yell [jel] 1. *n.* loud shout. 2. *v.* to shout loudly.

yel•low ['jeləʊ] 1. *n. & adj.* (a) color of the sun/of gold; **y. fever** = type of tropical fever; **y. pages** = section of a telephone directory giving a classified list of businesses. (b) cowardly. 2. *v.* to turn yellow. **yel•low•ham•mer**, *n.* small bird with a yellow breast. **yel•low•ish**, *adj.* rather yellow.

yelp [jelp] 1. *n.* cry of pain. 2. *v.* (*usu. of animals*) to cry out in pain.

yen [jen] *n.* (a) currency of Japan. (b) *inf.* strong desire.

yeo•man ['jəʊmən] *n.* (*pl.* **-men**) (*Brit.*) farmer with his own land; **to do y. service** = work long and hard. **yeo•man•ry**, *n.* (*old*) all yeomen.

yes [jes] *adv. & inter.* expression of agreement. **yes man**, *n.* person who always agrees with a person in authority.

yes•ter•day ['jestədeɪ] *adv. & n.* (a) the day before today; **the day before y.** = two days before today. (b) recent times. **yes•ter•year**, *adv. & n.* (*formal*) times past.

yet [jet] 1. *adv.* (a) up till now/up till this time. (b) in spite of everything. (c) even. 2. *conj.* still/but.

yet•i ['jetɪ] *n.* large animal, like an ape or bear, which is said to exist in the snows of the Himalayas.

yew [juː] *n.* evergreen tree with small cones and poisonous red berries.

Yid•dish ['jɪdɪʃ] *n.* language spoken by European Jews.

yield [jiːld] 1. *n.* crop/product; return on your

investment. 2. *v.* (a) to give/to produce. (b) to produce money. (c) (**to**) to give up/to surrender. (d) to give way when pressed. (e) (**to**) (*of traffic*) to allow other vehicles to pass first.

yo•del ['jəʊdl] *v.* to sing with quick changes from low to high notes. **yo•del•er,** *n.* person who yodels.

yo•ga ['jəʊgə] *n.* system of exercises and meditation practiced by Hindu thinkers, and now popular in western countries.

yo•gurt, yo•ghurt ['jɒgət] *n.* fermented milk often sweetened or flavored.

yo•gi ['jəʊgɪ] *n.* Hindu thinker who practices yoga.

yoke [jəʊk] 1. *n.* (a) piece of wood placed over the neck of a pair of animals when they are used for plowing, etc.; **y. of oxen** = two oxen attached together. (b) part of a dress which covers the shoulders and upper chest. 2. *v.* to join together (with a yoke).

yo•kel ['jəʊkl] *n.* stupid person from the country.

yolk [jəʊk] *n.* yellow part of an egg.

yon, yon•der [jɒn, 'jɒndə] *adj. & adv.* (which is) over there.

yore [jɔː] *n.* (*formal*) **in days of y.** = in the past.

York•shire pud•ding ['jɔːkʃə'pʊdɪŋ] *n.* baked batter eaten with roast beef.

you [juː] *pron.* (a) (*referring to the person/persons to whom we are speaking*). (b) (*referring to anybody/people in general*).

young [jʌŋ] 1. *adj.* (**-er, -est**) not old/recently born. 2. *n.* (a) young animals or birds. (b) young people. **young•ster,** *n.* young person.

your ['jɔː] *adj.* belonging to you. **yours** ['jɔːz] *pron.* belonging to you. **your•self, your•selves** [jɔː'self, jɔː'selvz] *pron. referring to the subject* you.

youth [juːT] *n.* (a) time when you are young. (b) young man. (c) young people; **y. club** = club where young people meet; **y. hostel** = building where young walkers, etc., can spend the night cheaply. **youth•ful,** *adj.* young. **youth•ful•ness,** *n.* being youthful.

yowl [jaʊl] *v.* (*esp. of animals*) to howl/to cry out loudly.

yo-yo ['jəʊjəʊ] *n.* toy made of a circular piece of wood/metal with a groove around the edge, which can be made to run up and down a string.

yuc•ca ['jʌkə] *n.* type of large succulent plant.

yuck•y [jʌkɪ] *adj. inf.* unappealing; distasteful.

Yu•go•slav ['juːgəʊslɑːv] *adj. & n.* (person) from Yugoslavia.

yuk•ky ['jʌkɪ] *adj. inf. see* **yuck•y.**

yule [juːl] *n.* Christmas; **y. log** = log burned at Christmas. **yule•tide,** *n.* the Christmas period.

yum-yum ['jʌmjʌm] *inter. showing* liking for food. **yum•my,** *adj. inf.* nice to eat; tasting good.

Zz

za•ny ['zeɪnɪ] *adj.* (-ier, -iest) *inf.* wildly mad.

zap [zæp] *v.* (**zapped**) *inf.* to hit/kill.

zeal ['ziːl] *n.* keenness/eagerness. **zeal•ous** ['zeləs] *adj.* eager. **zeal•ot** ['zelət] *n.* person who is too enthusiastic about religion or politics.

ze•bra ['zebrə] *n.* African animal similar to a horse, but with a striped coat; **z. crossing** = pedestrian crossing painted with white stripes.

ze•nith ['zenɪT] *n.* (a) point of the sky directly overhead. (b) highest point.

zeph•yr ['zefə] *n.* (*formal*) gentle (often westerly) breeze.

ze•ro ['zɪərəu] *n.* (a) number 0/nothing/nil. (b) temperature on a thermometer corresponding to zero. **zero hour**, *n.* time fixed to start sth important. **zero in on**, *v.* to aim at (sth)/to go straight to (sth). **zero tol•er•ance**, *n.* policy of rigorously enforcing a law/code by punishing very minor infringements in order to deter others.

zest [zest] *n.* (a) enthusiasm/enjoyment. (b) added pleasure/spice. (c) thin piece of orange or lemon peel. **zest•ful**, *adj.* enthusiastic.

zig•zag ['zɪgzæg] 1. *adj. & n.* (line) which turns sharply one way, then the opposite way. 2. *v.* (**zigzagged**) to move in a zigzag.

zilch [zɪltʃ] *n. Sl.* nothing/zero.

zinc [zɪŋk] *n.* (*element:* Zn) hard bright light-colored metal.

zin•ni•a ['zɪnjə] *n.* annual garden plant with bright flowers.

zip [zɪp] 1. *n.* (a) whistling sound made by a bullet as it goes through the air. (b) *inf.* energy. 2. *v.* (**zipped**) (a) to go fast; to whistle by. (b) **to z. up** = to close a zipper on sth. (c) to compress a computer file, by using a zip program, so that it takes up less memory. **zip code**, *n.* system of numbers written on a letter; package; etc. after the address to identify the U.S. postal area to which it is to be delivered. **zip disk**, *n.* computer disk holding compressed files. **zip•per**, *n.* device for closing openings on trousers/dresses, etc., consisting of two rows

of teeth which lock together. **zip•py**, *adj. inf.* quick and lively.

zir•co•ni•um [zɜːˈkəunɪəm] *n.* (*element:* Zr) rare metal used in alloys.

zith•er ['zɪðə] *n.* flat musical instrument played by plucking strings.

Zn *symbol for* zinc.

zo•di•ac ['zəudɪæk] *n.* part of the sky (divided into twelve imaginary sections) through which the sun and planets are supposed to travel during the year; **signs of the z.** = twelve signs named after groups of stars. **zo•di•a•cal** [zəuˈdaɪəkəl] *adj.* referring to the zodiac.

zom•bie ['zɒmbɪ] *n.* (a) (West Indian) dead body which is revived and controlled by witchcraft. (b) *inf.* person who is half-asleep/moving slowly.

zone [zəun] 1. *n.* (a) region/area/part (of a country/town). (b) region of the Earth showing a particular type of climate. 2. *v.* to divide (a town) into parts for planning purposes. **zon•al**, *adj.* of a zone. **zon•ing**, *n.* the splitting up (of a town or area) into zones.

zoo [zuː] *n.* place where wild animals are kept in enclosures and which the public can visit.

zo•ol•o•gy [zuːˈɒlədʒɪ] *n.* study of animals. **zo•o•log•i•cal** [zuːəˈlɒdʒɪkl] *adj.* referring to the study of animals; **z. gardens** = zoo. **zo•ol•o•gist** [zuːˈɒlədʒɪst] *n.* person who studies animals.

zoom [zuːm] 1. *n.* deep buzzing noise made by sth traveling fast. 2. *v.* (a) to make a deep buzzing noise when moving fast. (b) (*of prices, etc.*) to rise suddenly and steeply. (c) **to z. in on sth** = to focus a camera lens so that it makes a distant object appear to come closer. **zoom lens**, *n.* camera lens which allows you to change quickly from distant to close-up shots while still keeping in focus.

zo•on•o•sis [zəuəˈnəusɪs] *n.* disease which can be caught from animals.

zuc•chi•ni [zuˈkiːnɪ] *n.* green squash shaped like a cucumber.

zwie•back ['zwiːbæk] *n.* type of hard crumbly cookie.

Information
Section

SI UNITS

Base and Supplementary SI Units

Physical quantity	SI unit	Symbol
length	meter	m
mass	kilogram	kg
time	second	s
electric current	ampere	A
thermodynamic temperature	kelvin	K
luminous intensity	candela	cd
amount of substance	mole	mol
plane angle (supplementary unit)	radian	rad
solid angle (supplementary unit)	steradian	sr

Derived SI Units with Special Names

Physical quantity	SI unit	Symbol
frequency	hertz	Hz
energy	joule	J
force	newton	N
power	watt	W
pressure	pascal	Pa
electric charge	coulomb	C
electric potential difference	volt	V
electric resistance	ohm	Ω
electric conductance	siemens	S
electric capacitance	farad	F
magnetic flux	weber	Wb
inductance	henry	H
magnetic flux density (magnetic induction)	tesla	T
luminous flux	lumen	lm
illuminance	lux	lx
absorbed dose	gray	Gy
activity	becquerel	Bq
dose equivalent	sievert	Sv

Decimal Multiples and Submultiples used with SI Units

Submultiple	Prefix	Symbol
10^{-1}	deci-	d
10^{-2}	centi-	c
10^{-3}	milli-	m
10^{-6}	micro-	μ
10^{-9}	nano-	n
10^{-12}	pico-	p
10^{-15}	femto-	f
10^{-18}	atto-	a
10^{-21}	zepto-	z
10^{-24}	yocto-	y

Multiple	Prefix	Symbol
10	deca-	da
10^2	hecto-	h
10^3	kilo-	k
10^6	mega-	M
10^9	giga-	G
10^{12}	tera-	T
10^{15}	peta-	P
10^{18}	exa-	E
10^{21}	zetta-	Z
10^{24}	yotta-	Y

Computer Storage Capacity

kilo- $= 2^{10}$ 1 kilobyte = 1,024 bytes
mega- $= 2^{20}$ 1 megabyte = 1,024 kilobytes
giga- $= 2^{30}$ 1 gigabyte = 1,024 megabytes

Note: in all other computing contexts the prefixes retain their usual meanings.

WEIGHTS AND MEASURES

Metric Measures

Length

1 millimeter (mm)		= 0.0394 in.
1 centimeter (cm)	= 10 mm	= 0.3937 in.
1 meter (m)	= 100 cm	= 1.0936 yd.
1 kilometer (km)	= 1,000 m	= 0.6214 mile

Weight

1 milligram (mg)		= 0.0154 grain
1 gram (g)	= 1,000 mg	= 0.0353 oz.
1 kilogram (kg)	= 1,000 g	= 2.2046 lb.

Area

1 cm^2	= 100 mm^2	= 0.1550 sq. in.
1 m^2	= 10,000 cm^2	= 1.1960 sq. yd.
1 are (a)	= 100 m^2	= 119.60 sq. yd.
1 hectare (ha)	= 100 ares	= 2.4711 acres
1 km^2	= 100 hectares	= 0.3861 sq. mi.

Capacity

1 cm^3		= 0.0610 cu. in.
1 dm^3	= 1,000 cm^3	= 0.0351 cu. ft.
1 m^3	= 1,000 dm^3	= 1.3080 cu. yd.
1 liter	= 1 dm^3	= 0.2200 gallons
1 hectoliter	= 100 liters	= 2.7497 bushels

Imperial Measures

Length

1 inch		= 2.54 cm
1 foot (ft.)	= 12 inches	= 0.3048 m
1 yard (yd.)	= 3 feet	= 0.9144 m
1 rod	= 5.5 yards	= 5.0292 m
1 chain	= 22 yards	= 20.117 m
1 furlong	= 220 yards	= 201.17m
1 mile	= 1,760 yards	= 1.6093 km
1 nautical mile	= 6,080 feet	= 1.8532 km

Weight

1 ounce (oz.)	= 437.5 grains	= 28.350 g
1 pound (lb.)	= 16 ounces	= 0.4536 kg
1 stone	= 14 pounds	= 6.3503 kg
1 hundred-weight (cwt.)	= 100 pounds	= 45.359 kg
1 ton	= 20 cwt.	= 2,000 lb.

Area

1 sq. inch		= 6.4516 cm^2
1 sq. foot	= 144 sq. in.	= 0.0929 m^2
1 sq. yard	= 9 sq. ft.	= 0.8361 m^2
1 acre	= 4,840 sq. yd.	= 4,046.9 m^2
1 sq. mile	= 640 acres	= 259.0 hectares

Capacity

1 cu. inch		=16.387 cm^3
1 cu. foot	= 1,728 cu. in.	= 0.0283 m^3
1 cu. yard	= 27 cu. ft.	= 0.7646 m^3
1 pint (pt)	= 4 gills	= 0.5683 liters
1 quart	= 2 pints	= 1.1365 liters
1 gallon	= 8 pints	= 4.5461 liters
1 bushel	= 8 gallons	= 36.369 liters
1 fluid ounce	= 8 fl. drachms	= 28.413 cm^3
1 pint	= 20 fl. oz.	= 568.26 cm^3

American and British Measures

Dry Measures

1 pint	= 0.9689 U.K. pt.	= 0.5506 liter
1 bushel	= 0.9689 U.K. bu.	= 35.238 liters

Liquid Measures

1 fluid ounce	= 1.0408 U.K. fl. oz.	= 0.0296 liter
1 pint (16 oz.)	= 0.8327 U.K. pt.	= 0.4732 liter
1 gallon	= 0.8327 U.K. gal.	= 3.7853 liters

CONVERSION TABLES

Length

centimeters	cm or inches	inches
2.54	1	0.39
5.08	2	0.79
7.62	3	1.18
10.16	4	1.58
12.70	5	1.97
15.24	6	2.36
17.78	7	2.76
20.32	8	3.15
22.86	9	3.54
25.40	10	3.94
50.80	20	7.87
76.20	30	11.81
101.60	40	15.75
127.00	50	19.69
152.40	60	23.62
177.80	70	27.56
203.20	80	31.50
228.60	90	35.43
254.00	100	39.37

kilometers	km or miles	miles
1.61	1	0.62
3.22	2	1.24
4.83	3	1.86
6.44	4	2.49
8.05	5	3.11
9.66	6	3.73
11.27	7	4.35
12.88	8	4.97
14.48	9	5.59
16.09	10	6.21
32.19	20	12.43
48.28	30	18.64
64.37	40	24.86
80.47	50	31.07
96.56	60	37.28
112.65	70	43.50
128.75	80	49.71
144.84	90	55.92
160.93	100	62.14

CONVERSION TABLES (CONTINUED)

Weight

kilograms	kg or pounds	pounds
0.45	1	2.20
0.91	2	4.41
1.36	3	6.61
1.81	4	8.82
2.27	5	11.02
2.72	6	13.23
3.18	7	15.43
3.63	8	17.64
4.08	9	19.84
4.54	10	22.05
9.07	20	44.09
13.61	30	66.14
18.14	40	88.19
22.68	50	110.23
27.22	60	132.28
31.75	70	154.32
36.29	80	176.37
40.82	90	198.41
45.36	100	220.46

Area

hectares	hectares or acres	acres
0.41	1	2.47
0.81	2	4.94
1.21	3	7.41
1.62	4	9.88
2.02	5	12.36
2.43	6	14.83
2.83	7	17.30
3.24	8	19.77
3.64	9	22.24
4.05	10	24.71
8.09	20	49.42
12.14	30	74.13
16.19	40	98.84
20.23	50	123.56
24.28	60	148.27
28.33	70	172.98
32.38	80	197.69
36.42	90	222.40
40.47	100	247.11

CONVERSION TABLES (CONTINUED)

Capacity

liters	liters or gallons	gallons
3.85	1	0.26
7.69	2	0.44
11.54	3	0.78
15.38	4	1.04
19.23	5	1.30
23.08	6	1.56
26.92	7	1.82
30.77	8	2.08
34.61	9	2.34
38.46	10	2.60
76.92	20	5.20
115.38	30	7.80
153.85	40	10.40
192.31	50	13.00
230.77	60	15.60
269.23	70	18.20
307.69	80	20.80
346.15	90	23.40
348.61	100	26.00

Temperature Conversion

To convert a Fahrenheit temperature to Celsius (centigrade), subtract 32, then multiply by 5/9.

To convert a Celsius (centigrade) temperature to Fahrenheit, multiply by 9/5, then add 32.

TABLE OF CHEMICAL ELEMENTS

Element	Symbol	atomic number	atomic weight	Element	Symbol	atomic number	atomic weight
actinium	Ac	89	227*	molybdenum	Mo	42	95.94
aluminum	Al	13	26.982	neodymium	Nd	60	144.24
americium	Am	95	243*	neon	Ne	10	20.179
antimony	Sb	51	112.76	neptunium	Np	93	237.048
argon	Ar	18	39.948	nickel	Ni	28	58.69
arsenic	As	33	74.92	niobium	Nb	41	92.91
astatine	At	85	210	nitrogen	N	7	14.0067
barium	Ba	56	137.327	nobelium	No	102	259*
berkelium	Bk	97	247*	osmium	Os	76	190.23
beryllium	Be	4	9.012	oxygen	O	8	15.9994
bismuth	Bi	83	208.98	palladium	Pd	46	106.42
bohrium	Bh	107	262*	phosphorus	P	15	30.9738
boron	B	5	10.811	platinum	Pt	78	195.08
bromine	Br	35	79.904	plutonium	Pu	94	244*
cadmium	Cd	48	112.411	polonium	Po	84	209*
calcium	Ca	20	40.078	potassium	K	19	39.098
californium	Cf	98	251*	praseodymium	Pr	59	140.91
carbon	C	6	12.011	promethium	Pm	61	145*
cerium	Ce	58	140.115	protactinium	Pa	91	231.036
cesium	Cs	55	132.905	radium	Ra	88	226.025
chlorine	Cl	17	35.453	radon	Rn	86	222*
chromium	Cr	24	51.996	rhenium	Re	75	186.21
cobalt	Co	27	58.933	rhodium	Rh	45	102.91
copper	Cu	29	63.546	rubidium	Rb	37	85.47
curium	Cm	96	247*	ruthenium	Ru	44	101.07
dubnium	Db	105	262*	rutherfordium	Rf	104	261*
dysprosium	Dy	66	162.50	samarium	Sm	62	150.36
einsteinium	Es	99	252*	scandium	Sc	21	44.956.
erbium	Er	68	167.26	seaborgium	Sg	106	263*
europium	Eu	63	151.965	selenium	Se	34	78.96
fermium	Fm	100	257*	silicon	Si	14	28.086
fluorine	F	9	18.9984	silver	Ag	47	107.868
francium	Fr	87	223*	sodium	Na	11	22.9898
gadolinium	Gd	64	157.25	strontium	Sr	38	87.62
gallium	Ga	31	69.723	sulfur	S	16	32.066
germanium	Ge	32	72.61	tantalum	Ta	73	180.948
gold	Au	79	196.967	technetium	Tc	43	99*
hafnium	Hf	72	178.49	tellurium	Te	52	127.60
hassium	Hs	108	265*	terbium	Tb	65	158.925
helium	He	2	4.0026	thallium	Tl	81	204.38
holmium	Ho	67	164.93	thorium	Th	90	232.038
hydrogen	H	1	1.008	thulium	Tm	69	168.934
indium	In	49	114.82	tin	Sn	50	118.71
iodine	I	53	126.904	titanium	Ti	22	47.867
iridium	Ir	77	192.217	tungsten	W	74	183.84
iron	Fe	26	55.845	uranium	U	92	238.03
krypton	Kr	36	83.80	vanadium	V	23	50.94
lanthanum	La	57	138.91	xenon	Xe	54	131.29
lawrencium	Lr	103	262*	ytterbium	Yb	70	173.04
lead	Pb	82	207.19	yttrium	Y	39	88.906
lithium	Li	3	6.941	zinc	Zn	30	65.39
lutetium	Lu	71	174.967	zirconium	Zr	40	91.22
magnesium	Mg	12	24.305				
manganese	Mn	25	54.938				
meitnerium	Mt	109	266*				
mendelevium	Md	101	258*				
mercury	Hg	80	200.59				

* mass number of most stable isotope

Note: elements 110–118 have not been included here as they have not yet been officially named.

THE PERIODIC TABLE

Group	1	2	3	4	5	6	7	8	9	10	11	12	13	14	15	16	17	18	n / Period
	1 H																	2 He	1
	3 Li	4 Be											5 B	6 C	7 N	8 O	9 F	10 Ne	2
	11 Na	12 Mg											13 Al	14 Si	15 P	16 S	17 Cl	18 Ar	3
	19 K	20 Ca	21 Sc	22 Ti	23 V	24 Cr	25 Mn	26 Fe	27 Co	28 Ni	29 Cu	30 Zn	31 Ga	32 Ge	33 As	34 Se	35 Br	36 Kr	4
	37 Rb	38 Sr	39 Y	40 Zr	41 Nb	42 Mo	43 Tc	44 Ru	45 Rh	46 Pd	47 Ag	48 Cd	49 In	50 Sn	51 Sb	52 Te	53 I	54 Xe	5
	55 Cs	56 Ba	57-71 La-Lu	72 Hf	73 Ta	74 W	75 Re	76 Os	77 Ir	78 Pt	79 Au	80 Hg	81 Tl	82 Pb	83 Bi	84 Po	85 At	86 Rn	6
	87 Fr	88 Ra	89-103 Ac-Lr	104 Unq	105 Unp	106 Unh	107 Uns	108 Uno	109 Une	110 Uun	111 Uuu	112 Uub	113 Uut	114 Uuq	115 Uup	116 Uuh	117 Uus	118 Uuo	7

Lanthanoids (6)	57 La	58 Ce	59 Pr	60 Nd	61 Pm	62 Sm	63 Eu	64 Gd	65 Tb	66 Dy	67 Ho	68 Er	69 Tm	70 Yb	71 Lu
Actinoids (7)	89 Ac	90 Th	91 Pa	92 U	93 Np	94 Pu	95 Am	96 Cm	97 Bk	98 Cf	99 Es	100 Fm	101 Md	102 No	103 Lr

Correspondence of recommended group designations to other designations in recent use

	1	2	3	4	5	6	7	8	9	10	11	12	13	14	15	16	17	18
IUPAC Recommendations 1990	1	2	3	4	5	6	7	8	9	10	11	12	13	14	15	16	17	18
Usual European Convention	IA	IIA	IIIA	IVA	VA	VIA	VIIA	VIII (or VIIIA)			IB	IIB	IIIB	IVB	VB	VIB	VIIB	0 (or VIIIB)
Usual US Convention	IA	IIA	IIIB	IVB	VB	VIB	VIIB	VIII (or VIIIB)			IB	IIB	IIIA	IVA	VA	VIA	VIIA	VIIIA (or 0)

SYMBOLS USED IN MATHEMATICS, LOGIC, AND ELECTRONICS

Operation	Symbol	Operation	Symbol
AND operation, conjunction	$\wedge .$	integral, with limits	$\int_a^b dx$
OR operation, disjunction	$\vee +$	elements of vector v	v_i
NOT operation, negation	$' - \sim$	elements of matrix A	a_{ij}
NAND operation	$\mid \triangle$	transpose of matrix A	A^{T}
NOR operation	$\uparrow \triangledown$	inverse of matrix A	A^{-1}
EXOR operation	$\veebar$	equivalence	$\leftrightarrow \equiv$
		biconditional	$\leftrightarrow \equiv$
		conditional	$\rightarrow \Rightarrow$
For set S and/or set T:		general binary operation	$\circ$
		universal quantifier	$\forall$
x is a member of S	$x \in S$	existential quantifier	$\exists$
x is not a member of S	$x \notin S$	union of S and T	$S \cup T$
S is a subset of T	$S \subseteq T$	intersection of S and T	$S \cap T$
S is a proper subset of T	$S \subset T$	Cartesian product of S and T	$S \times T$
complement of S	$S' \sim S \bar{S}$	set of all x for which $p(x)$ is true	$\{x \mid p(x)\}$
relation	R	greater than	$>$
function of x	$f(x)$	greater than or equal to	$\geqslant$
function f from set X to set Y	$f : X \rightarrow Y$	less than	$<$
inverse function	f^{-1}	less than or equal to	$\leqslant$
inverse relation	R^{-1}	approx. equal to	$\cong$
sum, with limits	$\sum_{i=1}^{k}$	not equal to	$\neq$
		infinity	∞

THE SOLAR SYSTEM

	Approximate distance from sun		Diameter	
	millions of miles	*(millions of km)*	*miles*	*(km)*
Sun	—	—	864,950	(1,392,000)
Mercury	36	(58)	3,032	(4,880)
Venus	67	(108)	7,500	(12,100)
Earth	93	(150)	7,908	(12,755)
Mars	141	(228)	4,220	(6,790)
Jupiter	484	(778)	89,000	(143,000)
Saturn	887	(1,427)	75,000	(120,000)
Uranus	1,780	(2,870)	32,560	(52,400)
Neptune	2,794	(4,497)	30,760	(49,500)
Pluto	3,658	(5,900)	1,800	(3,000)

	Rotation period on its axis			Revolution around the sun
	days	*hours*	*minutes*	
Sun	25	09	00	—
Mercury	59	00	00	88.00 days
Venus	243	00	00	224.70 days
Earth	00	23	56	365.25 days
Mars	00	24	37	1.88 years
Jupiter	00	09	50	11.86 years

THE SOLAR SYSTEM (CONTINUED)

	Rotation period on its axis			Revolution around the sun
	days	*hours*	*minutes*	
Saturn	00	10	14	29.45 years
Uranus	00	11	00	84.00 years
Neptune	00	10	00	164.79 years
Pluto	6	09	14	248.50 years

PLANETARY SATELLITES

Planet & satellite*	Year of discovery	Diameter (km)**	Planet & satellite	Year of discovery	Diameter (km)
Earth			Dione	1684	1120
Moon	—	3476	Helene	1980	36 × 32 × 30
Mars			Rhea	1672	1530
			Titan	1655	5150
Phobos	1877	27 × 22 × 19	Hyperion	1848	405 × 260 × 220
Deimos	1877	15 × 12 × 11	Iapetus	1671	1440
Jupiter			Phoebe	1898	230 × 220 × 210
Metis	1979	40	**Uranus**		
Adrastea	1979	25 × 20 × 15	Ophelia	1986	30
Amalthea	1892	270 × 166 × 150	Bianca	1986	42
Thebe	1979	110 × 90	Cressida	1986	62
Io	1610	3660 × 3637 × 3631	Desdemona	1986	54
Europa	1610	3138	Juliet	1986	84
Ganymede	1610	5262	Portia	1986	108
Callisto	1610	4800	Rosalind	1986	54
Himalia	1904	186	Belinda	1986	66
Lysithea	1938	36	Puck	1985	154
Elara	1905	76	Miranda	1948	472
Ananke	1951	30	Ariel	1851	1158
Carme	1938	40	Umbriel	1851	1172
Pasiphae	1908	50	Titania	1787	1580
Sinope	1914	36	Oberon	1787	1524
Saturn			**Neptune**		
Atlas	1980	37 × 34 × 27	Naiad	1989	54
Prometheus	1980	148 × 100 × 68	Thalassa	1989	80
Pandora	1980	110 × 88 × 62	Despina	1989	150
Epimetheus	1978	194 × 190 × 154	Galatea	1989	160
Janus	1978	276 × 220 × 160	Larissa	1989	208 × 178
Mimas	1789	421 × 395 × 385	Proteus	1989	436 × 416 × 402
Enceladus	1789	512 × 495 × 488	Triton	1846	2700
Tethys	1684	1050	Nereid	1949	340
Telesto	1980	34 × 28 × 26	**Pluto**		
Calypso	1980	34 × 22 × 22	Charon	1978	1186

*Only major named satellites are shown.
**For satellites with irregular shapes, measurements along principal axes are given.

THE PLANT KINGDOM (SIMPLIFIED)

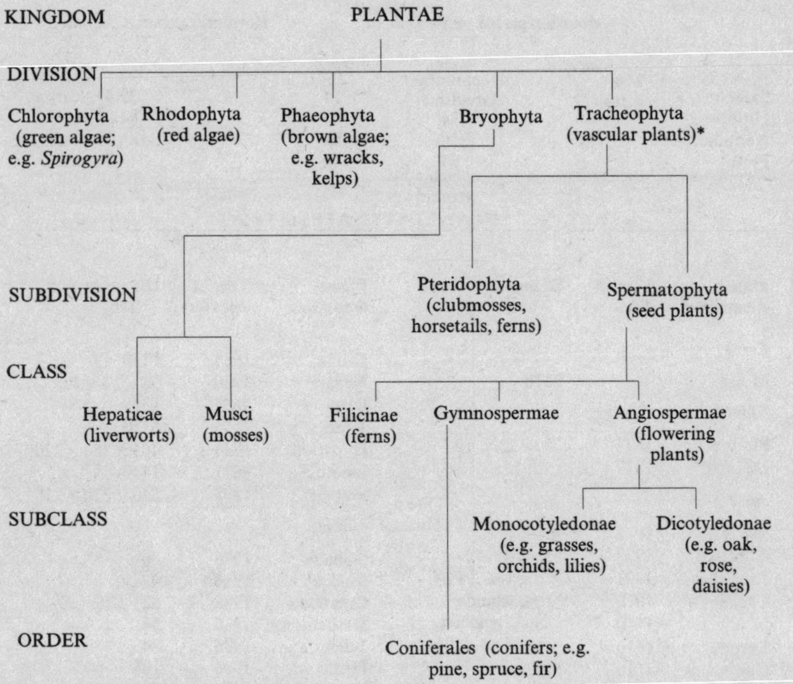

KINGDOM	PLANTAE

DIVISION

Chlorophyta (green algae; e.g. *Spirogyra*) — Rhodophyta (red algae) — Phaeophyta (brown algae; e.g. wracks, kelps) — Bryophyta — Tracheophyta (vascular plants)*

SUBDIVISION

Pteridophyta (clubmosses, horsetails, ferns) — Spermatophyta (seed plants)

CLASS

Hepaticae (liverworts) — Musci (mosses) — Filicinae (ferns) — Gymnospermae — Angiospermae (flowering plants)

SUBCLASS

Monocotyledonae (e.g. grasses, orchids, lilies) — Dicotyledonae (e.g. oak, rose, daisies)

ORDER

Coniferales (conifers; e.g. pine, spruce, fir)

* In some classifications vascular plants are split into three divisions: Lycopsida (clubmosses), Sphenopsida (horsetails), and Pteropsida (ferns, conifers, flowering plants)
Note: fungi are now usually classified as a separate kingdom.

Five-kingdom classification

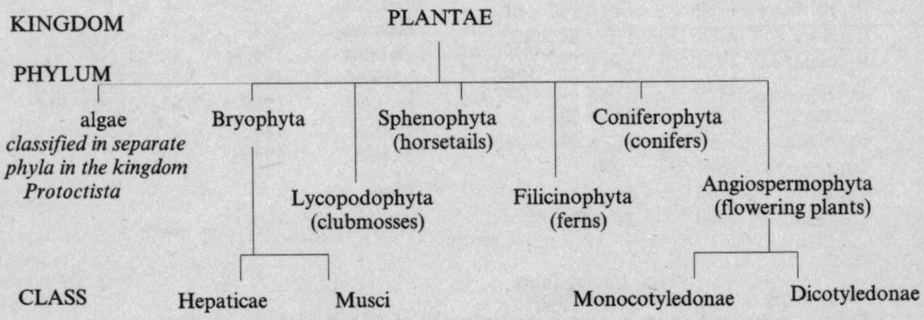

KINGDOM	PLANTAE

PHYLUM

algae *classified in separate phyla in the kingdom Protoctista* — Bryophyta — Lycopodophyta (clubmosses) — Sphenophyta (horsetails) — Filicinophyta (ferns) — Coniferophyta (conifers) — Angiospermophyta (flowering plants)

CLASS

Hepaticae — Musci — Monocotyledonae — Dicotyledonae

THE ANIMAL KINGDOM (SIMPLIFIED)

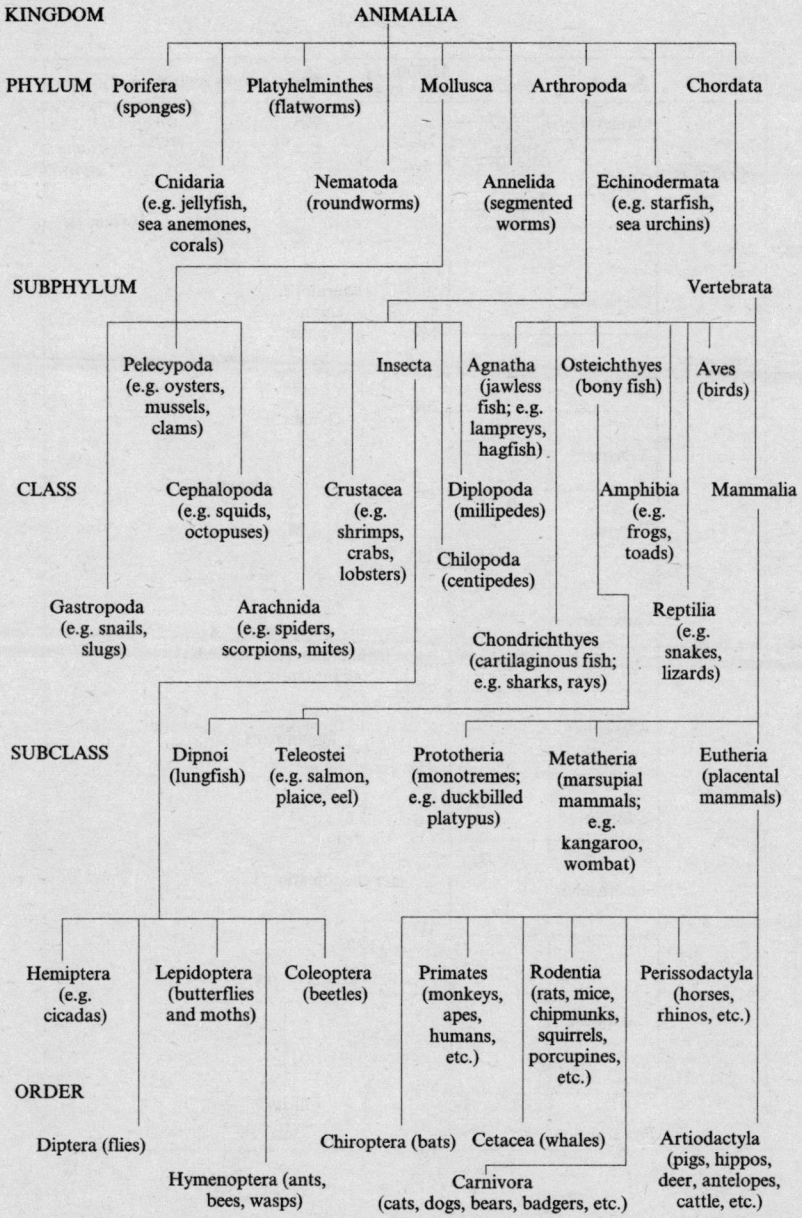

KINGDOM   ANIMALIA

PHYLUM — Porifera (sponges) · Platyhelminthes (flatworms) · Mollusca · Arthropoda · Chordata

Cnidaria (e.g. jellyfish, sea anemones, corals) · Nematoda (roundworms) · Annelida (segmented worms) · Echinodermata (e.g. starfish, sea urchins)

SUBPHYLUM — Vertebrata

Pelecypoda (e.g. oysters, mussels, clams) · Insecta · Agnatha (jawless fish; e.g. lampreys, hagfish) · Osteichthyes (bony fish) · Aves (birds)

CLASS — Cephalopoda (e.g. squids, octopuses) · Crustacea (e.g. shrimps, crabs, lobsters) · Diplopoda (millipedes) · Chilopoda (centipedes) · Amphibia (e.g. frogs, toads) · Mammalia

Gastropoda (e.g. snails, slugs) · Arachnida (e.g. spiders, scorpions, mites) · Chondrichthyes (cartilaginous fish; e.g. sharks, rays) · Reptilia (e.g. snakes, lizards)

SUBCLASS — Dipnoi (lungfish) · Teleostei (e.g. salmon, plaice, eel) · Prototheria (monotremes; e.g. duckbilled platypus) · Metatheria (marsupial mammals; e.g. kangaroo, wombat) · Eutheria (placental mammals)

Hemiptera (e.g. cicadas) · Lepidoptera (butterflies and moths) · Coleoptera (beetles) · Primates (monkeys, apes, humans, etc.) · Rodentia (rats, mice, chipmunks, squirrels, porcupines, etc.) · Perissodactyla (horses, rhinos, etc.)

ORDER — Diptera (flies) · Chiroptera (bats) · Cetacea (whales) · Artiodactyla (pigs, hippos, deer, antelopes, cattle, etc.)

Hymenoptera (ants, bees, wasps) · Carnivora (cats, dogs, bears, badgers, etc.)

GEOLOGICAL TIME SCALE

Era	Period	Epoch	Millions of years ago	Emergence of main animal groups
Cenozoic	Quaternary	Holocene		
		Pleistocene	1.8	*Homo sapiens*
	Tertiary	Pliocene		
		Miocene		
		Oligocene		primates
		Eocene		
		Palaeocene	65	
Mesozoic	Cretaceous		135	birds
	Jurassic		200	
	Triassic		240	mammals
Palaeozoic	Permian		280	
	Carboniferous		370	reptiles
	Devonian		415	amphibians
	Silurian		445	fish
	Ordovician		515	
	Cambrian		590	invertebrates
	Precambrian			

COUNTRIES OF THE WORLD

The Americas

America, United
   States of
Antigua and
   Barbuda
Argentina
Bahamas, The
Barbados
Belize
Bolivia
Brazil
Canada
Chile
Colombia
Costa Rica
Cuba
Dominica
Dominican Republic
Ecuador
El Salvador
Grenada
Guatemala
Guyana
Haiti
Honduras
Jamaica
Mexico
Nicaragua
Panama
Paraguay
Peru
St. Kitts and Nevis
St. Lucia
St. Vincent
Suriname
Trinidad and Tobago
Uruguay
Venezuela

Europe

Albania
Andorra
Austria
Belarus
Belgium
Bosnia and
  Hercegovina
Bulgaria
Croatia
Czech Republic
Denmark
Estonia
Finland
France
Germany
Greece

Hungary
Iceland
Ireland
Italy
Latvia
Liechtenstein
Lithuania
Luxembourg
Macedonia,
   Former Yugoslav
   Republic of
Malta
Moldavia
Monaco
Netherlands, The
Norway
Poland
Portugal
Romania
Russia
San Marino
Slovakia
Slovenia
Spain
Sweden
Switzerland
Ukraine
United Kingdom
Vatican City
Yugoslavia

Asia

Afghanistan
Armenia
Azerbaijan
Bahrain
Bangladesh
Bhutan
Brunei
Cambodia
China
Cyprus
Georgia
India
Indonesia
Iran
Iraq
Israel
Japan
Jordan
Kazakhstan
Kuwait
Kyrgyzstan
Laos
Lebanon

Malaysia
Maldives, The
Mongolia
Myanmar
Nepal
North Korea
Oman
Pakistan
Philippines
Qatar
Saudi Arabia
Singapore
South Korea
Sri Lanka
Syria
Taiwan
Tajikistan
Thailand
Turkey
Turkmenistan
United Arab
   Emirates
Uzbekistan
Vietnam
Yemen

Africa

Algeria
Angola
Benin
Botswana
Burkina-Faso
Burundi
Cameroon
Cape Verde
Central African
   Republic
Chad
Comoros
Congo
Congo, Democratic
   Republic of the
Côte d'Ivoire
Djibouti
Egypt
Equatorial Guinea
Eritrea
Ethiopia
Gabon
Gambia, The
Ghana
Guinea
Guinea-Bissau
Kenya
Lesotho

Liberia
Libya
Madagascar
Malawi
Mali
Mauritania
Mauritius
Morocco
Mozambique
Namibia
Niger
Nigeria
Rwanda
São Tomé and
   Príncipe
Senegal
Seychelles
Sierra Leone
Somalia
South Africa
Sudan, The
Swaziland
Tanzania
Togo
Tunisia
Uganda
Zambia
Zimbabwe

Australasia and Oceania

Australia
Fiji
Kiribati
Marshall Islands
Micronesia,
   Federated States of
Nauru
New Zealand
Palau
Papua New Guinea
Samoa
Solomon Islands
Tonga
Tuvalu
Vanuatu

THE AMERICAN STATES

State	Abbreviation	Capital	State	Abbreviation	Capital
Alabama	AL	Montgomery	New Hampshire	NH	Concord
Alaska	AK	Juneau	New Jersey	NJ	Trenton
Arizona	AZ	Phoenix	New Mexico	NM	Santa Fe
Arkansas	AR	Little Rock	New York	NY	Albany
California	CA	Sacramento	North Carolina	NC	Raleigh
Colorado	CO	Denver	North Dakota	ND	Bismarck
Connecticut	CT	Hartford	Ohio	OH	Columbus
Delaware	DE	Dover	Oklahoma	OK	Oklahoma City
Florida	FL	Tallahassee			
Georgia	GA	Atlanta	Oregon	OR	Salem
Hawaii	HI	Honolulu	Pennsylvania	PA	Harrisburg
Idaho	ID	Boise	Rhode Island	RI	Providence
Illinois	IL	Springfield	South Carolina	SC	Columbia
Indiana	IN	Indianapolis	South Dakota	SD	Pierre
Iowa	IA	Des Moines	Tennessee	TN	Nashville
Kansas	KS	Topeka	Texas	TX	Austin
Kentucky	KY	Frankfort	Utah	UT	Salt Lake City
Louisiana	LA	Baton Rouge			
Maine	ME	Augusta	Vermont	VT	Montpelier
Maryland	MD	Annapolis	Virginia	VA	Richmond
Massachusetts	MA	Boston	Washington	WA	Olympia
Michigan	MI	Lansing	West Virginia	WV	Charleston
Minnesota	MN	St. Paul	Wisconsin	WI	Madison
Mississippi	MS	Jackson	Wyoming	WY	Cheyenne
Missouri	MO	Jefferson City	*District of Columbia	DC	(Washington)
Montana	MT	Helena			
Nebraska	NE	Lincoln			
Nevada	NV	Carson City			

*(Washington, D.C. is the capital of the United States.)

THE CANADIAN PROVINCES

The Provinces

Province	Capital
Alberta	Edmonton
British Columbia	Victoria
Manitoba	Winnipeg
New Brunswick	Fredericton
Newfoundland	St. John's
Nova Scotia	Halifax
Ontario	Toronto
Prince Edward Island	Charlottetown
Quebec	Quebec
Saskatchewan	Regina

The Territories

Territory	Capital
Yukon Territory	Whitehorse
Northwest Territories	Yellowknife

Semiautonomous Region

Nunavut	Iqaluit

THE WORLD'S TEN HIGHEST MOUNTAINS

Peak	Range	Location	Height	
			feet	*meters*
Everest	Himalayas	Nepal-Tibet	29,023	8,846
Godwin Austen (K-2)	Karakoram	Kashmir	28,250	8,611
Kanchenjunga	Himalayas	Nepal-Sikkim	28,208	8,598
Lhotse	Himalayas	Nepal-Tibet	27,890	8,501
Makalu	Himalayas	Tibet-Nepal	27,790	8,470
Dhaulagiri I	Himalayas	Nepal	26,810	8,172
Manaslu	Himalayas	Nepal	26,760	8,156
Cho Oyu	Himalayas	Nepal	26,750	8,153
Nanga Parbat	Himalayas	Kashmir	26,660	8,126
Annapurna I	Himalayas	Nepal	26,504	8,078

THE WORLD'S TEN LONGEST RIVERS

River	*Source*	*Outflow*
Nile	Tributaries of Lake Victoria, Africa	Mediterranean Sea
Amazon	Glacier-fed lakes, Peru	Atlantic Ocean
Mississippi-Missouri Red Rock	Source of Red Rock, Montana	Gulf of Mexico
Yangtze Kiang	Tibetan plateau, China	China Sea
Ob	Altai Mts., Russia	Gulf of Ob
Huang Ho (Yellow)	Eastern part of Kunlan Mts., west China	Gulf of Chihli
Yenisei	Tannu-Ola Mts., western Tuva, Russia	Arctic Ocean
Paraná	Confluence of Paranaiba and Grande Rivers	Rio de la Plata
Irtish	Altai Mts., Russia, Kazakhstan, Mongolia, China	Ob River
Congo	Confluence of Lualab and Luapula Rivers, Democratic Republic of Congo	Atlantic Ocean

THE LARGEST LAKES IN THE WORLD

	Continent	*Area*	
		sq. mi.	*sq. km*
Caspian Sea	Asia	152,239	394,299
Lake Superior	North America	31,820	82,414
Lake Victoria	Africa	26,828	69,485
Aral Sea	Asia	25,659	66,457
Lake Huron	North America	23,010	59,596
Lake Michigan	North America	22,400	58,016
Lake Tanganyika	Africa	12,700	32,893
Lake Baikal	Asia	12,162	31,500
Great Bear Lake	North America	12,000	31,080
Lake Nyasa	Africa	11,600	30,044
Great Slave Lake	North America	11,170	28,930

THE LARGEST OCEANS AND SEAS IN THE WORLD

Name	Area		Average depth		Greatest known depth	
	sq. mi.	*sq. km*	*feet*	*meters*	*feet*	*meters*
Pacific Ocean	64,000,000	165,760,000	13,215	4,028	36,198	11,033
Atlantic Ocean	31,815,000	82,400,000	12,880	3,926	30,246	9,219
Indian Ocean	25,300,000	65,526,700	13,002	3,963	24,460	7,455
Arctic Ocean	5,440,200	14,090,000	3,953	1,205	18,456	5,625
Mediterranean Sea	1,145,100	2,965,800	4,688	1,429	15,197	4,632
Caribbean Sea	1,049,500	2,718,200	8,685	2,647	22,788	6,946
South China Sea	895,400	2,319,000	5,419	1,652	16,456	5,016
Bering Sea	884,900	2,291,900	5,075	1,547	15,659	4,773
Gulf of Mexico	615,000	1,592,800	4,874	1,486	12,425	3,787
Okhotsk Sea	613,800	1,589,700	2,749	838	12,001	3,658

TIME ZONES

The following list gives corresponding times to 12:00 noon, eastern standard time.

Adelaide	2:30 A.M. *	Mexico City	11:00 A.M.
Algiers	6:00 P.M.	Montevideo	2:00 P.M.
Amsterdam	6:00 P.M.	Montreal	12:00 noon
Ankara	7:00 P.M.	Moscow	8:00 P.M.
Athens	7:00 P.M.	Nairobi	8:00 P.M.
Beijing	1:00 A.M. *	New Orleans	11:00 A.M.
Belgrade	6:00 P.M.	New York	12:00 noon
Berlin	6:00 P.M.	Oslo	6:00 P.M.
Bombay	10:30 P.M.	Ottawa	12:00 noon
Brisbane	3:00 A.M. *	Panama	12:00 noon
Brussels	6:00 P.M.	Paris	6:00 P.M.
Bucharest	7:00 P.M.	Perth	1:00 A.M. *
Budapest	6:00 P.M.	Prague	6:00 P.M.
Buenos Aires	2:00 P.M.	Quebec	12:00 noon
Cairo	7:00 P.M.	Rangoon	11:30 P.M.
Calcutta	10:30 P.M.	Rio de Janeiro	2:00 P.M.
Cape Town	7:00 P.M.	St. Louis	11:00 A.M.
Caracas	1:00 P.M.	St. Petersburg	8:00 P.M.
Chicago	11:00 A.M.	San Francisco	9:00 A.M.
Colombo	10:30 P.M.	Santiago	1:00 P.M.
Copenhagen	6:00 P.M.	Singapore	12:30 A.M. *
Delhi	10:30 P.M.	Stockholm	6:00 P.M.
Denver	10:00 A.M.	Sydney	3:00 A.M. *
Dublin	5:00 P.M.	Tehran	8:30 P.M.
Helsinki	7:00 P.M.	Tokyo	2:00 A.M. *
Hobart	3:00 A.M. *	Toronto	12:00 noon
Hong Kong	1:00 A.M. *	Vancouver	9:00 A.M.
Istanbul	7:00 P.M.	Vienna	6:00 P.M.
Jerusalem	7:00 P.M.	Warsaw	6:00 P.M.
Lima	12:00 noon	Wellington	5:00 A.M. *
Lisbon	6:00 P.M.		
London	5:00 P.M.	* Next day	
Los Angeles	9:00 A.M.		
Madrid	6.00 P.M.		

UNITS OF MONEY USED IN VARIOUS COUNTRIES

Argentina	new peso	Kuwait	dinar
Australia	dollar	Lebanon	pound
Austria	schilling	Libya	dinar
Belgium	franc	Malaysia	ringgit
Brazil	real	Malta	lira
Canada	dollar	Mexico	peso
Chile	peso	Netherlands	guilder
China	yuan	New Zealand	dollar
Croatia	kuna	Nigeria	naira
Cuba	peso	Norway	krone
Cyprus	pound	Pakistan	rupee
Czech Republic	koruna	Peru	sol
Denmark	krone	Philippines	peso
Egypt	pound	Poland	zloty
Finland	markka	Portugal	escudo
France	franc	Romania	leu
Georgia	lari	Russia	new rouble
Germany	Deutschmark	Saudi Arabia	riyal
Ghana	cedi	Slovakia	koruna
Greece	drachma	Slovenia	tolar
Hungary	forint	South Africa	rand
India	rupee	Spain	peseta
Iran	rial	Sri Lanka	rupee
Iraq	dinar	Sweden	krona
Ireland	punt (pound)	Switzerland	franc
Israel	shekel	Syria	pound
Italy	lira	Thailand	baht
Jamaica	dollar	Tunisia	dinar
Japan	yen	Turkey	lira
Kenya	shilling	United Kingdom	pound
North and South		United States	dollar
Korea	won	Zambia	kwacha

CLASSIFICATION OF LANGUAGES (SIMPLIFIED)

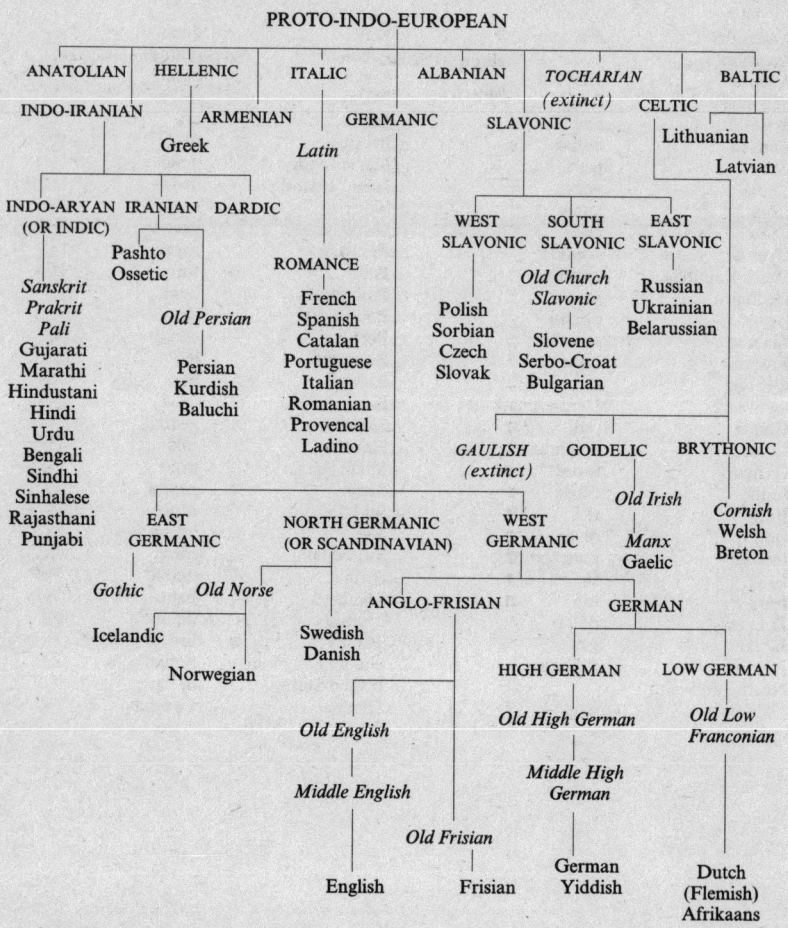

PROTO-INDO-EUROPEAN

ANATOLIAN | HELLENIC | ITALIC | ALBANIAN | *TOCHARIAN (extinct)* | BALTIC

INDO-IRANIAN | ARMENIAN | GERMANIC | SLAVONIC | CELTIC

Greek | *Latin* | Lithuanian | Latvian

INDO-ARYAN (OR INDIC) | IRANIAN | DARDIC

Pashto
Ossetic

WEST SLAVONIC | SOUTH SLAVONIC | EAST SLAVONIC

Old Church Slavonic | Russian
Ukrainian
Belarussian

Sanskrit
Prakrit
Pali
Gujarati
Marathi
Hindustani
Hindi
Urdu
Bengali
Sindhi
Sinhalese
Rajasthani
Punjabi

Old Persian

Persian
Kurdish
Baluchi

ROMANCE

French
Spanish
Catalan
Portuguese
Italian
Romanian
Provencal
Ladino

Polish
Sorbian
Czech
Slovak

Slovene
Serbo-Croat
Bulgarian

GAULISH (extinct) | GOIDELIC | BRYTHONIC

Old Irish | Cornish
Welsh
Breton

EAST GERMANIC | NORTH GERMANIC (OR SCANDINAVIAN) | WEST GERMANIC

Manx
Gaelic

Gothic | *Old Norse*

Icelandic

Norwegian

Swedish
Danish

ANGLO-FRISIAN | GERMAN

HIGH GERMAN | LOW GERMAN

Old English | *Old High German* | *Old Low Franconian*

Middle English | *Middle High German*

Old Frisian

English | Frisian | German
Yiddish | Dutch
(Flemish)
Afrikaans

Italicized languages are no longer spoken

DEVELOPMENT OF THE ROMAN ALPHABET

Phoenician	⟨ ϟ 𐤀 ◁ △ ⋏ Ϥ 𐤀 Ⴄ 𐤆 ⋎ ϟ 𐤄 ϟ ◇ 𐤏 𐤐 Ϙ ϟ W ✝ Ϥ Ϥ ⵉ Ξ 𐤕 Ⲍ
Hebrew	⟨ ϟ ᐱ ◁ ᗱ Ⴤ ⋏ 𐤀 ϟ ϟ ϟ 𐤍 ϟ ϟ ◯ 𐤏 ϟ Ϙ ⟨ W X Ϥ Ϥ ⵉ 𐤕 𐤕
Classical Greek	Α Β Γ Δ Ε Ϝ Η Ι Ι Κ Λ Μ Ν Ο Π Ρ Σ Τ Υ Υ Υ Ξ Ζ
Russian-Cyrillic	А Б Г П Е Ф Г И І К Л М Н О П Р С Т У З
Modern Roman	A B C D E F G H I J K L M N O P Q R S T U V W X Y Z

FOREIGN ALPHABETS

Greek Alphabet			Hebrew Alphabet		German Gothic Alphabet		
Character		*Name*	*Character*	*Name*	*Character*		*Roman Character*
A	α	alpha	א	aleph	𝔄	α	Aa
B	β	beta	ב	beth	𝔅	b	Bb
Γ	γ	gamma	ג	gimel	ℭ	c	Cc
Δ	δ	delta	ד	daleth	𝔇	d	Dd
E	ε	epsilon	ה	he	𝔈	e	Ee
Z	ζ	zeta	ו	vav	𝔉	f	Ff
H	η	eta	ז	zayin	𝔊	g	Gg
Θ	θ	theta	ח	cheth	ℌ	h	Hh
I	ι	iota	ט	teth	ℑ	i	Ii
K	κ	kappa	י	yod	𝔍	j	Jj
Λ	λ	lambda	כ	kaph	𝔎	f	Kk
M	μ	mu	ל	lamed	𝔏	l	Ll
N	ν	nu	מ	mem	𝔐	m	Mm
Ξ	ξ	xi	נ	nun	𝔑	n	Nn
O	ο	omicron	ס	samekh	𝔒	o	Oo
Π	π	pi	ע	ayin	𝔓	p	Pp
P	ρ	rho	פ	pe	𝔔	q	Qq
Σ	σ, ς	sigma	צ	ṣadie	𝔕	r	Rr
T	τ	tau	ק	koph	𝔖	s	Ss
Y	υ	upsilon	ר	resh	𝔗	t	Tt
Φ	φ	phi	ש	shin	𝔘	u	Uu
X	χ	chi	שׂ	śin	𝔙	v	Vv
Ψ	ψ	psi	ת	tav	𝔚	w	Ww
Ω	ω	omega			𝔛	x	Xx
					𝔜	y	Yy
					𝔷	z	Zz

ACCENTS AND DIACRITICAL MARKS

Accent	Name	Example	Accent	Name	Example
´	acute	é	ˇ	háček	č
/	bar	ø	'	hamza	'a
°	bol	å	‒	macron	ō
˘	breve	ŏ	~	tilde	ñ
ʾ	cedilla	ç	¨	umlaut	ü
^	circumflex	ê			
¨	diaeresis	oë			
`	grave	à			

PROOFREADERS' MARKS

Instruction	Textual mark	Marginal Mark
Insert in text the matter indicated in margin	λ or $\wedge$	*New matter followed by* /
Delete	Strike through characters to be deleted	δ
Delete and close up	Strike through characters to be deleted and use linking marks	$\hat{\delta}$
Leave as printed	... under characters to remain	*stet*
Change to italic	__ under characters to be altered	*ital*
Change to even small capitals	= under characters to be altered	*s.c.*
Change to capital letters	≡ under characters to be altered	*caps*
Use capital letters for initial letters and small capitals for rest of words	= under initial letters and = under the rest of the words	*c. & s.c.*
Change to bold type	~~ under characters to be altered	*bold*
Change to lower case	Encircle characters to be altered	*l.c.*
Change to roman type	Encircle characters to be altered	*rom*
Underline word or words	__ under words affected	*underline*
Substitute or insert character(s) under which this mark is placed, in 'superior' position	/ through character or λ where required	γ under character (e.g. $\acute{y}$)
Substitute or insert character(s) over which this mark is placed, in 'inferior' position	/ through character or λ where required	$\wedge$ over character (e.g. $\underset{\wedge}{}$)
Change damaged character(s)	Encircle character(s) to be altered	X
Close up – delete space between characters	$\frown$ linking characters	$\frown$
Insert space	λ	#
Transpose	⊔⊓ between characters or words	*trs*
Move matter to right	⊣ at left side of group to be moved	⊣
Move matter to left	⊢ at right side of group to be moved	⊢
Raise lines	⊤ over lines to be moved ⌴ under lines to be moved	*raise*
Lower lines	⌐ over lines to be moved ⊥ under lines to be moved	*lower*
Correct the vertical alignment	‖	‖
Straighten lines	= through lines to be straightened	=
Begin a new paragraph	⊏ before first word of new paragraph	*n.p.*
No fresh paragraph here	⌇ between paragraphs	*run on*
Insert en (half-em) rule	λ	*en*
Insert one-em rule	λ	*em*

MUSIC

Notes and rests

Note	Rest	American	British
𝅄	▬	double-whole note	breve
o	▬	whole note	semibreve
𝅗𝅥	▬	half note	minim
𝅘𝅥	𝄽 *or* 𝄼	quarter note	crotchet
𝅘𝅥𝅮	𝄿	eighth note	quaver
𝅘𝅥𝅯	𝅀	sixteenth note	semiquaver
𝅘𝅥𝅰	𝅁	thirty-second note	demisemiquaver
𝅘𝅥𝅱	𝅂	sixty-fourth note	hemidemisemiquaver

Clefs

Fixed note	Position of middle C	Clef
		G *or* treble clef
		F *or* bass clef
		C (soprano) clef
		C (alto) clef
		C (tenor) clef

Ornaments and decorations

	acciaccatura		
	upper mordent	played	
	lower mordent	played	
	appoggiatura		
	turn	played	
	inverted turn	played	
	trill or shake		
	tremolo; rapid repetition		

MUSIC (CONTINUED)

Accidentals

♯	sharp; raising note one semitone
𝄪	double sharp; raising note one tone
♭	flat; lowering note one semitone
♭♭	double flat; lowering note one tone
♮	natural; restoring note to normal pitch after sharp or flat

Time signatures

Simple duple

$\frac{2}{2}$ or ¢ — two half-note beats

$\frac{2}{4}$ — two quarter-note beats

$\frac{2}{8}$ — two eighth-note beats

Compound duple

$\frac{6}{4}$ — two dotted half-note beats

$\frac{6}{8}$ — two dotted quarter-note beats

$\frac{6}{16}$ — two dotted eighth-note beats

Simple triple

$\frac{3}{2}$ — three half-note beats

$\frac{3}{4}$ — three quarter-note beats

$\frac{3}{8}$ — three eighth-note beats

Compound triple

$\frac{9}{4}$ — three dotted half-note beats

$\frac{9}{8}$ — three dotted quarter-note beats

$\frac{9}{16}$ — three dotted eighth-note beats

Simple quadruple

$\frac{4}{2}$ — four half-note beats

$\frac{4}{4}$ or ¢ — four quarter-note beats

$\frac{4}{8}$ — four eighth-note beats

Compound quadruple

$\frac{12}{4}$ — four dotted half-note beats

$\frac{12}{8}$ — four dotted quarter-note beats

$\frac{12}{16}$ — four dotted eighth-note beats

Staccato marks and signs of accentuation

mezzo-staccato: shorten note by about $\frac{1}{4}$

staccato: shorten note by about $\frac{1}{2}$

staccatissimo: shorten note by about $\frac{3}{4}$

detached: accented

attack

Irregular rhythms

duplet or couplet

triplet

quadruplet

quintuplet

Dynamics

crescendo

diminuendo

Curved lines

tie or bind; two notes played as one

slur or legato; play smoothly (in one bow on stringed instrument)

Other

repeat preceding section

end of section or piece

pause

8ᵉ — play an octave above notes written

Keys and Key Signatures

Major key	Relative minor key	Key signature (sharp keys)	Key signature (flat keys)
C	A		
G	E		
D	B		
A	F♯		
E	C♯		
B = C♭	G♯		
F♯ = G♭	E♭		
C♯ = D♭	B♭		
A♭	F		
E♭	C		
B♭	G		
F	D		

MUSIC (CONTINUED)

Range of various orchestral instruments

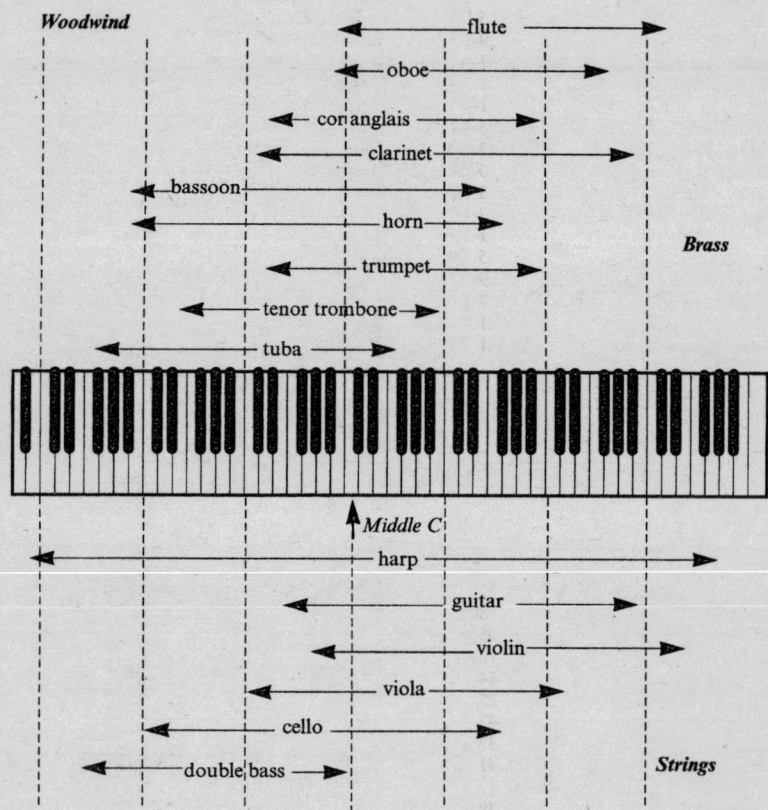

PRESIDENTS OF THE UNITED STATES

Name	Term	Name	Term
George Washington	1789–97	Grover Cleveland	1885–89
John Adams	1797–1801	Benjamin Harrison	1889–93
Thomas Jefferson	1801–09	Grover Cleveland	1893–97
James Madison	1809–17	William McKinley	1897–1901
James Monroe	1817–25	Theodore Roosevelt	1901–09
John Quincy Adams	1825–29	William Howard Taft	1909–13
Andrew Jackson	1829–37	Woodrow Wilson	1913–21
Martin Van Buren	1837–41	Warren Gamaliel Harding	1921–23
William Henry Harrison	1841	Calvin Coolidge	1923–29
John Tyler	1841–45	Herbert Clark Hoover	1929–33
James Knox Polk	1845–49	Franklin Delano Roosevelt	1933–45
Zachary Taylor	1849–50	Harry S. Truman	1945–53
Millard Fillmore	1850–53	Dwight David Eisenhower	1953–61
Franklin Pierce	1853–57	John Fitzgerald Kennedy	1961–63
James Buchanan	1857–61	Lyndon Baines Johnson	1963–69
Abraham Lincoln	1861–65	Richard Milhous Nixon	1969–74
Andrew Johnson	1865–69	Gerald Rudolph Ford	1974–77
Ulysses Simpson Grant	1869–77	James Earl Carter, Jr.	1977–81
Rutherford Hayes	1877–81	Ronald Wilson Reagan	1981–89
James Abram Garfield	1881	George Herbert Walker Bush	1989–93
Chester Alan Arthur	1881–85	William Jefferson Clinton	1993–

VICE PRESIDENTS OF THE UNITED STATES

Name	Term	Name	Term
John Adams	1789–97	Garret A. Hobart	1897–99
Thomas Jefferson	1797–1801	Theodore Roosevelt	1901
Aaron Burr	1801–05	Charles W. Fairbanks	1905–09
George Clinton	1805–12	James S. Sherman	1909–12
Elbridge Gerry	1813–14	Thomas R. Marshall	1913–21
Daniel D. Thompkins	1817–25	Calvin Coolidge	1921–23
John C. Calhoun	1825–32	Charles G. Dawes	1925–29
Martin Van Buren	1833–37	Charles Curtis	1929–33
Richard M. Johnson	1837–41	John Nance Garner	1933–41
John Tyler	1841	Henry Agard Wallace	1941–45
George M. Dallas	1845–49	Harry S. Truman	1945
Millard Fillmore	1849–50	Alben W. Barkley	1949–53
William R. King	1853	Richard Milhous Nixon	1953–61
John C. Breckinridge	1857–61	Lyndon Baines Johnson	1961–63
Hannibal Hamlin	1861–65	Hubert H. Humphrey	1965–69
Andrew Johnson	1865	Spiro T. Agnew	1969–73
Schuyler Colfax	1869–73	Gerald Rudolph Ford	1973–74
Henry Wilson	1873–75	Nelson A. Rockefeller	1974–77
William A. Wheeler	1877–81	Walter F. Mondale	1977–81
Chester Alan Arthur	1881	George Herbert Walker Bush	1981–89
Thomas A. Hendricks	1885	James Danforth Quayle	1989–93
Levi P. Morton	1889–93	Albert Gore, Jr.	1993–
Adlai E. Stevenson	1893–97		

KINGS AND QUEENS OF ENGLAND FROM 1066

The House of Normandy

William I	1066–87
William II	1087–1100
Henry I	1100–35
Stephen	1135–54

The House of Anjou or Plantagenet

Henry II	1154–89
Richard I	1189–99
John	1199–1216
Henry III	1216–72
Edward I	1272–1307
Edward II	1307–27
Edward III	1327–77
Richard II	1377–99

The House of Lancaster
(sub-division of Plantagenet)

Henry IV	1399–1413
Henry V	1413–22
Henry VI	1422–61

The House of York
(sub-division of Plantagenet)

Edward IV	1461–83
Edward V	1483
Richard III	1483–85

The House of Tudor

Henry VII	1485–1509
Henry VIII	1509–47

The House of Tudor (continued)

Edward VI	1547–53
Mary I	1553–58
Elizabeth I	1558–1603

The House of Stuart

James I	1603–25
Charles I	1625–49
The Commonwealth	1649–59
Charles II	1660–85
James II	1685–88
Mary II	1689–94
& William III	1689–1702
Anne	1702–14

The House of Hanover

George I	1714–27
George II	1727–60
George III	1760–1820
George IV	1820–30
William IV	1830–37
Victoria	1837–1901

The House of Saxe–Coburg

Edward VII	1901–10

The House of Windsor

George V	1910–36
Edward VIII	1936
George VI	1936–52
Elizabeth II	1952–

PRIME MINISTERS OF THE U.K.

Name	Term	Name	Term
Robert Walpole	1721–42	Augustus Henry Fitzroy, Duke of Grafton	1768–70
Spencer Compton, Earl of Wilmington	1742–43	Frederick North	1770–82
Henry Pelham	1743–54	Charles Watson-Wentworth, Marquis of Rockingham	1782
Thomas Pelham-Holles, Duke of Newcastle	1754–56	William Petty, Earl of Shelburne	1782–83
William Cavendish, Duke of Devonshire	1756–57	William Henry Cavendish Bentinck, Duke of Portland	1783
Thomas Pelham-Holles, Duke of Newcastle	1757–62	William Pitt (the Younger)	1783–1801
John Stuart, Earl of Bute	1762–63	Henry Addington	1801–04
George Granville	1763–65	William Pitt	1804–06
Charles Watson-Wentworth, Marquis of Rockingham	1765–66	William Wyndham Grenville, Baron Grenville	1806–07
William Pitt, Earl of Chatham	1766–68	William Bentinck, Duke of Portland	1807–09

PRIME MINISTERS OF THE U. K. (CONTINUED)

Name	Term	Name	Term
Spencer Perceval	1809–12	William Ewart Gladstone	1886
Robert Banks Jenkinson, Earl of Liverpool	1812–27	Robert Gascoyne-Cecil, Marquis of Salisbury	1886–92
George Canning	1827	William Ewart Gladstone	1892–94
Frederick John Robinson, Viscount Goderich	1827–28	Archibald Philip Primrose, Earl of Rosebery	1894–95
Arthur Wellesley, Duke of Wellington	1828–30	Robert Gascoyne-Cecil, Marquis of Salisbury	1895–1902
Charles Grey, Earl Grey	1830–34	Arthur James Balfour	1902–05
William Lamb, Viscount Melbourne	1834	Henry Campbell-Bannerman	1905–08
Robert Peel	1834–35	Herbert Henry Asquith	1908–16
William Lamb, Viscount Melbourne	1835–41	David Lloyd George	1916–22
Robert Peel	1841–46	Andrew Bonar Law	1922–23
John Russell	1846–52	Stanley Baldwin	1923–24
Edward George Geoffrey Smith Stanley, Earl of Derby	1852	James Ramsay MacDonald	1924
George Hamilton Gordon, Earl of Aberdeen	1852–55	Stanley Baldwin	1924–29
Henry John Temple, Viscount Palmerston	1855–58	James Ramsay MacDonald	1929–35
Edward Stanley, Earl of Derby	1858–59	Stanley Baldwin	1935–37
Henry Temple, Viscount Palmerston	1859–65	Neville Chamberlain	1937–40
John Russell, Earl Russell	1865–66	Winston Churchill	1940–45
Edward Stanley, Earl of Derby	1866–68	Clement Richard Attlee	1945–51
Benjamin Disraeli	1868	Winston Churchill	1951–55
William Ewart Gladstone	1868–74	Anthony Eden	1955–57
Benjamin Disraeli, Earl of Beaconsfield (ennobled in 1876)	1874–80	Harold Macmillan	1957–63
William Ewart Gladstone	1880–85	Alec Douglas-Home	1963–64
Robert Gascoyne-Cecil, Marquis of Salisbury	1885–86	Harold Wilson	1964–70
		Edward Heath	1970–74
		Harold Wilson	1974–76
		James Callaghan	1976–79
		Margaret Thatcher	1979–90
		John Major	1990–97
		Tony Blair	1997–

PRIME MINISTERS OF CANADA

Name	Term	Name	Term
John A. Macdonald	1867–73	Richard B. Bennett	1930–35
Alexander Mackenzie	1873–78	W. L. Mackenzie King	1935–48
John A. Macdonald	1878–91	Louis Stephen St. Laurent	1948–57
John J. C. Abbott	1891–92	John George Diefenbaker	1957–63
John S. D. Thompson	1892–94	Lester B. Pearson	1963–68
Mackenzie Bowell	1894–96	Pierre Elliott Trudeau	1968–79
Charles Tupper	1896	Joseph Clark	1979–80
Wilfrid Laurier	1896–1911	Pierre Elliott Trudeau	1980–84
Robert L. Borden	1911–20	John Turner	1984
Arthur Meighen	1920–21	Brian Mulroney	1984–93
W. L. Mackenzie King	1921–26	Kim Campbell	1993
Arthur Meighen	1926	Jean Chrétien	1993–
W. L. Mackenzie King	1926–30		

BOOKS OF THE BIBLE

Old Testament

Genesis
Exodus
Leviticus
Numbers
Deuteronomy
Joshua
Judges
Ruth
1 Samuel
2 Samuel
1 Kings
2 Kings
1 Chronicles
2 Chronicles
Ezra
Nehemiah
Esther
Job
Psalms
Proverbs
Ecclesiastes
Song of Solomon
Isaiah
Jeremiah
Lamentations
Ezekiel
Daniel
Hosea
Joel
Amos
Obadiah
Jonah
Micah
Nahum
Habakkuk
Zephaniah
Haggai
Zechariah
Malachi

New Testament

Matthew
Mark
Luke
John
The Acts
Romans
1 Corinthians
2 Corinthians
Galatians
Ephesians
Philippians
Colossians
1 Thessalonians
2 Thessalonians
1 Timothy
2 Timothy
Titus
Philemon
Hebrews
James
1 Peter
2 Peter
1 John
2 John
3 John
Jude
Revelation

Introductory Algebra
for College Students

Introductory Algebra for College Students
Second Edition

Robert Blitzer
Miami-Dade Community College

PRENTICE HALL
Upper Saddle River, New Jersey 07458

Library of Congress Cataloging-in-Publication Data

Blitzer, Robert.
   Introductory algebra for college students   /   Robert Blitzer.—2nd ed.
    p.   cm.
   Includes index.
   ISBN 0-13-275745-1 (Student Edition)
   1. Algebra.   I. Title.
QA152.2.B586 1997   97-15280
512.9—dc21   CIP

Editorial Director: Tim Bozik
Editor-in-Chief: Jerome Grant
Acquisitions Editor: Karin E. Wagner
Editorial Assistant/Supplements Editor: April Thrower/Audra Walsh
Assistant Vice President of Production and Manufacturing: David W. Riccardi
Executive Managing Editor: Linda Mihatov Behrens
Manufacturing Manager: Trudy Pisciotti
Manufacturing Buyer: Alan Fischer
Director of Marketing: John Tweeddale
Marketing Manager: Jolene Howard
Marketing Assistants: Diana Penha, Jennifer Pan
Creative Director: Paula Maylahn
Art Manager: Gus Vibal
Text/Cover Design and Project Management: Elm Street Publishing Services, Inc.
Art Studio: Academy Artworks/Laurel Technical Services
Photo Researcher: Clare Maxwell
Cover image: Jean Metzinger "At the Cycle-Race Track" (Au Velodrome) 1914, oil with sand on canvas, $40\frac{9}{16} \times 38\frac{1}{4}$ in. Solomon R. Guggenheim Museum, New York. Photo by David Heald © The Solomon R. Guggenheim Foundation, New York. FN 76.2553PG18. © 1998 Artists Rights Society (ARS), New York/ADAGP, Paris.

©1998 by Prentice-Hall, Inc.
Simon & Schuster/A Viacom Company
Upper Saddle River, New Jersey 07458

Printed in the United States of America
10 9 8 7 6 5 4 3

ISBN 0-13-275745-1 (Student Edition)

Prentice-Hall International (UK) Limited, *London*
Prentice-Hall of Australia Pty. Limited, *Sydney*
Prentice-Hall Canada Inc., *Toronto*
Prentice-Hall Hispanoamericana, S.A., *Mexico*
Prentice-Hall of India Private Limited, *New Delhi*
Prentice-Hall of Japan, Inc., *Tokyo*
Simon & Schuster Asia Pte. Ltd., *Singapore*
Editora Prentice-Hall do Brasil, Ltda., *Rio de Janeiro*

Contents

CHAPTER 3

Problem Solving   221

CHAPTER 4

Linear Equations and Inequalities in Two Variables   279

CHAPTER 5

Systems of Linear Equations and Inequalities   359

Exponents and Polynomials   415

Factoring Polynomials   495

Rational Expressions   561

Preface

Introductory Algebra for College Students, Second Edition, provides comprehensive, in-depth coverage of the topics required in a one-term course in beginning or introductory algebra. The book is written for college students who have no previous experience in algebra and for those who need a review of basic algebraic concepts. The primary goals of the Second Edition are to help students acquire a solid foundation in the basic skills of algebra and to show how algebra can model and solve authentic real-world problems.

New to the Second Edition

The Second Edition is a significant revision of the First Edition, with increased emphasis on problem solving, graphing, functions, mathematical modeling, technology, discovery approaches, critical thinking, geometry, collaborative learning, and contemporary applications that use real data. The book's changes are based on the recommendations of the *Curriculum and Evaluation Standards for School Mathematics* published by the National Council of Teachers of Mathematics and *Standards for Introductory College Mathematics* published by the American Mathematical Association of Two-Year Colleges. Following are the new features in the Second Edition.

Readability and Level. The chapters have been extensively rewritten to make them more accessible. The Second Edition pays close attention to ensuring that the amount of detail and depth of coverage is appropriate for this level. Every section has been rewritten to contain a better range of simple, intermediate, and challenging examples. Chapter 1 opens with a review of fractions.

Problem Solving. As with the First Edition, the emphasis of the book is on learning to use the language of algebra as a tool for solving problems related to everyday life. Problem-solving steps introduced in Chapter 2 are simply and explicitly described, and used regularly. Chapter 3, devoted entirely to problem solving, has a new opening section on strategies for solving problems. Since students have such difficulty translating word problems, increased emphasis has been placed on translating the words and phrases of verbal models into algebraic equations. The extensive collection of applications promotes the problem-solving theme and demonstrates the usefulness of mathematics to students. Problem-solving strategies in the Second Edition are written specifically for the average student with the appropriate amount of detail and depth of coverage.

Graphing. Chapter 1 contains an introduction to graphing, a topic that is integrated throughout the book. Line, bar, circle, and rectangular coordinate graphs that use real data appear in nearly every section and problem set. Many examples and exercises use graphs to explore relationships between data and to provide ways of visualizing a problem's solution.

Functions and Modeling. Increased emphasis has been placed on the use of formulas and functions that describe interesting and relevant quantitative relations in the real world. Old-fashioned, routine word problems have been replaced by an extensive collection of contemporary applications from a wide range of disciplines, many of which are unique.

Interactive Learning. Discover for yourself exercises encourage students to actively participate in the learning process as they read the book. This new feature encourages students to read with a pen in hand and interact with the text. Through the discovery exercises, they can explore problems in order to better understand them and their solutions.

Technology. The Second Edition offers the option of using graphing utilities, without requiring their use. Graphing utilities are utilized in Using technology boxes to enable students to visualize, discover, and explore procedures for manipulating algebraic expressions and solving equations. Use of graphing utilities is also reinforced in the technology problems appearing in the problem sets for those who want this option. With the book's early introduction to graphing, students can look at the calculator screens in the Using technology boxes and gain an increased understanding of an example's solution even if they are not actually using a graphing utility in the course.

Study Tips. Study tip boxes offer suggestions for problem solving, point out common student errors, and provide informal tips and suggestions. These invaluable hints appear in abundance throughout the book.

Contemporary Fine Art. Algebra and fine art enable us to view the world in new and exciting ways. An extensive collection of contemporary, thought-provoking images selected by the author provides visual commentary to the book's unique collection of contemporary applications. The art adds an aesthetic sense to the book's pages, while visually reminding students of how algebra is connected to the whole spectrum of learning.

New and Reorganized Problem Sets. Problem sets are revised, expanded, and reorganized for easy use in the Second Edition. Problem sets are organized into eight categories:

- *Practice Problems:* These problems give students an opportunity to practice the concepts that have been developed in the section. Many new problems have been added, with attention paid to making sure that the problems are appropriate for the level and graded in difficulty.
- *Application Problems:* Up to 70 percent of the application problems are new to the Second Edition. Included are many relevant, up-to-date applications that will provoke student interest. Many of these problems offer students the opportunity to construct mathematical models from data.

- *True-False Critical Thinking Problems:* Several true-false problems that take students beyond the routine application of basic algebraic concepts are included in nearly every problem set. The true-false format is less intimidating than a more open-ended format, helping students gain confidence in divergent thinking skills.
- *Technology Problems:* These problems, also new to the Second Edition, enable students to use graphing utilities to explore algebraic concepts and relevant mathematical models.
- *Writing in Mathematics:* These exercises are intended to help students communicate their mathematical knowledge by thinking and writing about algebraic topics.
- *Critical Thinking Problems:* This category contains the most challenging exercises in the problem sets. These open-ended problems were written to explore concepts while stimulating student thinking.
- *Group Activity Problems:* These collaborative activities give students the opportunity to work cooperatively as they think and talk about mathematics. There are enough of these problems in each chapter to allow instructors to use collaborative learning as an instructional format quite extensively. It is hoped that many of these problems will result in interesting group discussions.
- *Review Problems:* As with the First Edition, each problem set concludes with three review problems.

Chapter Introductions. Chapter introductions present fine art that is related either to the general idea of the chapter or to an application of algebra contained within the chapter.

Learning Objectives. Learning objectives open every section. The objectives are restated in the margin at their point of use.

New and Revised Enrichment Essays. As with the First Edition, interspersed throughout the book are enrichment essays that germinate from ideas appearing in expository sections. Most of the essays are new to the Second Edition, and stimulating fine art has been added to many.

Expanded Use of Tables. Tables that summarize the procedures discussed in the book, with supporting examples, now appear throughout.

Chapter Projects. Also new to the Second Edition are projects at the end of each chapter that use challenging and interesting applications of mathematics that not only stand alone as ways to stimulate class discussions on a variety of topics, but also cultivate an interest in independent explorations of mathematics on the Worldwide Web. Using the Worldwide Web, with links to many countries, as well as links to art, music, and history, students are encouraged to develop a multicultural, multidisciplinary approach to the study of algebra.

Chapter Tests. New to the Second Edition is a test at the end of each chapter, following the comprehensive collection of chapter review problems. The chapter tests focus on the review problems so that students can see if they are prepared for an actual class test.

Preserved and Expanded from the First Edition

The features described below that helped make the First Edition so popular continue in the Second Edition. However, they have been modified by the book's increased attention to the issue of ensuring that the amount of detail and depth of coverage is appropriate for this level. Modification of these features also reflects the book's increased emphasis on problem solving and modeling with multidisciplinary, relevant applications.

Detailed Step-by-Step Explanations. Illustrative examples are still presented one step at a time. No steps are omitted, and each step is clearly explained. Where applicable, the detailed explanations appearing to the right of each mathematical step have been improved and expanded. A second color has been added to the mathematics to show precisely where this explanation applies.

Example Titles. All examples have titles so that students immediately see the purpose of each example.

Extensive Application to Geometric Problem Solving. Chapter 3 on problem solving contains a section that teaches geometric concepts that are important to a student's understanding of algebra. A discussion of similar triangles has been added to this section. The Second Edition provides more emphasis on problem solving in geometric situations, as well as on geometric models that allow students to visualize algebraic formulas.

Screened Boxes. Screened boxes are used to highlight all important definitions, formulas, and procedures.

Chapter Summaries. Inclusive summaries appear at the conclusion of each chapter, helping students to bring together what they have learned after reading the chapter.

Review Problems. A comprehensive collection of review problems follows the summary at the end of each chapter. (A chapter test, new to the Second Edition, follows this collection of review problems.) In addition, Chapters 3–9 conclude with cumulative review problems. Cumulative review problems covering the entire book appear in the appendix. The appendix has been completely rewritten and reformatted to emphasize the changes throughout the book.

Supplements for the Instructor

Printed Supplements

Instructor's Edition (0-13-860412-6) Consists of the complete student text, with a special Instructor's answer section at the back of the text containing answers to all exercises.

Instructor's Solutions Manual (0-13-860453-3)
- Step-by-step solutions for every even-numbered exercise.
- Step-by-step solutions (even and odd) of the Chapter Review Problems, Chapter Tests, and Cumulative Reviews.

Test Item File (0-13-860420-7)
- 6 tests per chapter, consisting of 20 questions each.
  - 4 free-response tests
  - 2 multiple-choice tests

- 4 final exams
    - 2 free-response tests
    - 2 multiple-choice tests

Media Supplements

TestPro3 Computerized Testing
IBM Single-User (0-13-860552-1)
IBM Online (0-13-897984-7)
MAC (0-13-860560-2)

- Allows instructors to generate tests or drill worksheets from algorithms keyed to the text by chapter, section, and learning objective.
- Instructors select from thousands of test questions and hundreds of algorithms which generate different but equivalent equations.
- A user-friendly expression-building toolbar, editing and graphing capabilities are included.
- Customization toolbars allow for customized headers and layout options which provide instructors with the ability to add or delete workspace or add columns to conserve paper.

Supplements for the Student

Printed Supplements

Student's Solution Manual   (0-13-860594-7)
- Contains complete step-by-step solutions for every odd-numbered exercise
- Contains complete step-by-step solutions for all (even and odd) Chapter Review Problems, Chapter Tests and Cumulative Reviews.

How to Study Math   (ISBN 0-13-020884-1)
- Free booklet which gives developmental math students strategies for preparing for class, studying and taking exams and improving grades.

Life on the Internet: Mathematics   (ISBN 0-13-268616-3)
- Free guide which provides a brief history of the Internet, discusses the use of the Worldwide Web, and describes how to find your way within the Internet and how to find others on it. Contact your local Prentice Hall representative for *Life on the Internet: Mathematics*.

NY Times Themes of the Times
- A free newspaper, created new each year, from Prentice Hall and *The New York Times*
- Interesting and current articles on mathematics
- Invites discussion and writing about mathematics

Media Supplements

MathPro Tutorial Software
IBM Single-User (0-13-860537-8)
IBM Network (0-13-860479-7)
MAC Single-User (0-13-860545-9)
MAC Network (0-13-899170-7)

- Fully networkable Windows-based tutorial package for campus labs or individual use
- Designed to generate practice exercises based on the exercise sets in the text

- Algorithmically driven, providing the student with unlimited practice
- Generates graded and recorded practice problems with optional step-by-step tutorial
- Includes a complete glossary including graphics and cross-references to related words

Videotapes   (0-13-860586-6)
- Instructional tapes in a lecture format featuring worked-out examples and exercises taken from each section of the text.
- Presentation by Professors Michael C. Mayne and (Biff) John D. Pietro of Riverside Community College in Riverside, California.

Review Video   (0-13-901075-0)
- Contains an end-of-chapter summary for every chapter in the text (10 in all).
- Each 5 minute summary highlights the most important features learned in each chapter.
- Excellent preparation for final exams.

Acknowledgments

I wish to express my appreciation to all the reviewers, of both the current and new edition, for their helpful criticisms and suggestions. In particular I would like to thank:

Howard Anderson	*Skagit Valley College*
John Anderson	*Illinois Valley Community College*
Michael H. Andreoli	*Miami Dade Community College— North Campus*
Warren J. Burch	*Brevard Community College*
Alice Burstein	*Middlesex Community College*
Sandra Pryor Clarkson	*Hunter College*
Sally Copeland	*Johnson County Community College*
Robert A. Davies	*Cuyahoga Community College*
Ben Divers, Jr.	*Ferrum College*
Irene Doo	*Austin Community College*
Charles C. Edgar	*Onondaga Community College*
Susan Forman	*Bronx Community College*
Gary Glaze	*Eastern Washington University*
Jay Graening	*University of Arkansas*
Robert B. Hafer	*Brevard Community College*
Mary Lou Hammond	*Spokane Community College*
Donald Herrick	*Northern Illinois University*
Beth Hooper	*Golden West College*
Tracy Hoy	*College of Lake County*
Gary Knippenberg	*Lansing Community College*
Mary Koehler	*Cuyahoga Community College*
Hank Martel	*Broward Community College*
John Robert Martin	*Tarrant County Junior College*
Irwin Metviner	*State University of New York at Old Westbury*
Allen R. Newhart	*Parkersburg Community College*
Peg Pankowski	*Community College of Allegheny County— South Campus*

Nancy Ressler	*Oakton Community College*
Gayle Smith	*Lane Community College*
Dick Spangler	*Tacoma Community College*
Janette Summers	*University of Arkansas*
Robert Thornton	*Loyola University*
Lucy C. Thrower	*Francis Marion College*
Andrew Walker	*North Seattle Community College*

Additional acknowledgments are extended to Professor John (Biff) Pietro and Professor Michael C. Mayne of Riverside Community College, for creating the videotapes for each section of the book; Donna Gerken of Miami-Dade Community College, for writing the chapter projects; Phyllis Barnidge and the mathematicians at Laurel Technical Services, for the Herculean task of solving all the book's problems, preparing the answer section and the solutions manuals, as well as serving as accuracy checker; Amy Mayfield, whose meticulous work as copy editor put me at my syntactical best; Clare Maxwell, photo researcher, for playing detective and pursuing the book's photographs and contemporary art across the globe; Paula Maylahn and Gus Vibal, for contributing to the book's wonderful look; the team of graphic artists at Academy Artworks, whose superb illustrations provide visual support to the verbal portions of the text; Progressive Information Technologies, the book's compositor, for inputting hundreds of pages with hardly an error; and especially, Ingrid Mount of Elm Street Publishing Services, whose talents as supervisor of production resulted in a book that looks even more wonderful than the First Edition.

Most of all I wish to thank Karin Wagner and Tony Palermino. Tony, my developmental editor, contributed invaluable edits and suggestions that resulted in a finished product that is both accessible and up to date. His influence on the Second Edition is extraordinary, with the improved pace in the text and problem sets a result of his remarkable talents. Karin, my editor at Prentice Hall, guided and coordinated every detail of the project, overseeing both text and supplements. From the inclusion of chapter tests to the quality of the videos to the choice of the book's cover art, Karin's influence can be seen. She is the key person in making this book a reality, and I am grateful to have had an editor with her experience and professionalism.

Karin Wagner is a part of the terrific team at Prentice Hall who made this book possible, including her assistant April Thrower and supplements editor Audra Walsh. Editor-in-Chief Jerome Grant urged me onward in my quest to create the first math textbook with an extensive collection of art, always providing support and commitment. Linda Behrens, managing editor, and Alan Fischer, manufacturing buyer, kept an ever-watchful eye on the production process. Jolene Howard, marketing manager, and Jennifer Pan, marketing assistant, I thank for their outstanding sales force and very impressive marketing efforts.

Finally, as I did in the First Edition, I must conclude by extending my heartfelt thanks to the gifted artists who gave me permission to share their exciting works, and, ultimately, their humanity within the pages of this book.

Robert Blitzer

TO THE STUDENT:

How to use *Introductory Algebra for College Students* to find success in this course and become a better problem solver.

Selections of fine art by contemporary artists introduce each chapter. Read the interesting chapter introductions to discover where artists find algebraic inspiration in their works.

CHAPTER 3

Problem Solving

Robert Longo, "Pressure" 1983. Two parts: and charcoal, graphite, and ink on paper. The Museum of Modern Art, New York. Gift of the Louis and Bessie Adler Foundation, Inc., Seymour M. Klein, President. Photograph © 1997. The Museum of Modern Art, New York.

Thinking skills and problem-solving activities are indispensable to every area of our lives. To some extent, we are all problem solvers. The problem solver's work is mostly a tangle of guesswork, analogy, wishful thinking, observing patterns, and frustration. To become a master problem solver may be as inaccessible as acquiring the skills of a virtuoso, but everyone can become a better, more confident problem solver.

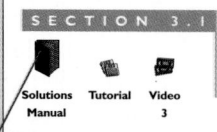

SECTION 3.1

Solutions Manual   **Tutorial**   **Video 3**

Strategies for Solving Problems

Objectives

1 Solve problems using linear equations.
2 Solve problems using critical thinking strategies.

Begin each section by reading the learning objectives. These objectives will help you organize your studies and prepare for class.

Supplement icons appear at the beginning of every section. Ask your instructor how you can gain access to the supplements. Use these supplements to reinforce the topics in the text.

Become a problem solver! Apply the algebra presented in *Introductory Algebra for College Students* to model and solve a wide variety of problems. Many exercises and examples include sourced data, relevant to problems you encounter in real life.

PROBLEM SET 2.3

Practice Problems

Solve and check each equation in Problems 1–34.

1. $3x - 7x + 30 = 10 - 2x$
2. $2x - 8x + 35 = 5 - 3x$
3. $3x + 6 - x = 8 + 3x - 6$
4. $4x - 7 - x = 5 + 4x - 12$
5. $6y + 25 - 4y = 4y - 4 + y + 29$
6. $7y + 26 - 5y = 5y - 2 + y$
7. $3(x - 2) = 12$
8. $3(x + 2) = 6$
9. $-2(y + 3) = -9$
10. $-3(2 - 3y) = 9$
11. $-2(y + 4) + 7 = 3$
12. $3(3x + 5) - 6 = 86$
13. $6x - (3x + 10) = 14$
14. $5x - (2x + 14) = 10$
15. $2(4 - 3x) = 2(2x + 5)$
16. $3(5 - x) = 4(2x + 1)$
17. $3(2y + 3) = -3y - 9$
18. $2(x + 2) = -4x - 2$
19. $3(y + 3) = -2(2y - 1)$
20. $2(5 + 5y) = 3(5 + 3y)$
21. $8(y + 2) = 2(3y + 4)$
22. $3(3x - 1) = 4(3 + 3x)$
23. $3(y + 1) = 7(y - 2) - 3$
24. $5y - 4(y + 9) = 2y - 3$
25. $5(2z - 8) - 2 = 5(z - 3) + 3$
26. $7(3m - 2) + 5 = 6(2m - 1) + 24$
27. $17(x + 3) = 13 + 4(x - 10)$
28. $2(5y + 4) + 19 = 4y - 3(2y + 11)$
29. $6 = -4(1 - x) + 3(x + 1)$
30. $100 = -(x - 1) + 4(x - 6)$
31. $10(y + 4) - 4(y - 2) = 3(y - 1) + 2(y - 3)$
32. $-2(x - 4) - (3x - 2) = -2 - (6x - 2)$
33. $9 - 6(2z + 1) = 3 - 7(z - 1)$
34. $2 - 6(w - 3) = 8 - 5(2w + 1)$

Practice the section's concepts and test your understanding in these exercises.

---

36. In 1990, the average cost of an advertisement during the Super Bowl was $700,000. On the average, this cost has increased by $60,000 each year. Using this model, in what year will the cost of an advertisement during the Super Bowl be $1,480,000? (*Hint:* Let $x = $ the number of years after 1990 when this will occur.)

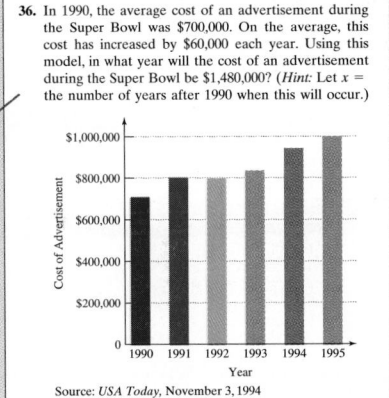

Source: *USA Today*, November 3, 1994

Construct your own mathematical models from data and *experience* how the math you learn in class *applies* to the world around you.

True–False Critical Thinking Problems

55. Which one of the following is true?
   a. The slope-intercept equation verifies the fact that no line can have a y-intercept that is numerically equal to its slope.
   b. A pair of equations must be in slope-intercept form if they represent parallel lines.
   c. The line $3x + 2y = 5$ has slope $-\frac{3}{2}$.
   d. The line $2y = 3x + 7$ has a y-intercept of 7.

56. Which one of the following is true?

   a. Every line in rectangular coordinates has an equation that can be expressed in slope-intercept form.
   b. If an equation in slope-intercept form models some physical situation, then the y-intercept represents rate of change.
   c. The slope-intercept equation verifies the fact that a line's y-intercept is usually an integer.
   d. The lines whose equations are $2x - 4y = 9$ and $\frac{1}{3}x - \frac{2}{3}y = -8$ are parallel.

Gain confidence and develop your critical thinking skills. True/False questions help you become comfortable with section concepts.

Writing in Mathematics

Describe the error in Problems 89–94.

89.
$$7x = 21$$
$$7x - 7 = 21 - 7$$
$$x = 14$$

90.
$$x + 4 = 4x$$
$$x + 4 - 4 = 4x - 4$$
$$x = 3x$$

91.
$$3|x| + 6 = 12$$
$$3|x| + 6 - 6 = 12 - 6$$
$$3|x| = 6$$
$$\frac{3|x|}{3} = \frac{6}{3}$$
$$|x| = 2$$
The equation has only 2 as a solution.

Use the language of algebra as a tool for solving problems. *Communicate* your mathematical knowledge by writing and thinking about algebra "in your own words."

In Problems 100–101 it is not necessary to use a graphing calculator. Instead, you will be asked to interpret what appears on the screen of a graphing calculator, as illustrated in the figures.

100. **a.** Solve: $4x - 5 < 2x + 7$.
    b. In Chapter 4 we will learn how to graph $y = 4x - 5$ and $y = 2x + 7$. These graphs were obtained with a graphing calculator and are shown in the figure. Describe how you can use these graphs to give visual meaning to your algebraic solution in part (a).

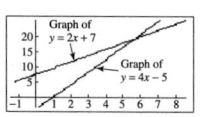

101. **a.** Solve: $3(x - 2) + 4 < 8(x + 1)$.
    b. The graphs of $y = 3(x - 2) + 4$ and $y = 8(x + 1)$ were obtained with a graphing calculator and are shown in the figure. Describe how you can use these graphs to give visual meaning to your algebraic solution in part (a).

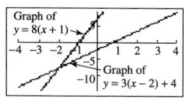

Enhance your understanding— explore algebraic and graphical concepts using a graphing utility.

58. Solve for x: $|x| + 4 = 10$.

59. Use the graph to make up and solve a word problem similar to the one in Problem 49.

The Gender Pay Gap: The Annual Income of Full-Time Workers and the Percentage of the Men's Income Earned by Women

Sources: Beeghley 1989: 239; U.S. Bureau of the Census, *Statistical Abstract* 1993: Table 727.

Challenge yourself! Critical Thinking Problems are designed to really get you thinking.

74. Suppose you are an algebra teacher correcting an examination on solving linear equations. In your group, determine whether the following student solution is correct. If the solution is incorrect, write an explanation for exactly where the error lies.

$$5(x + 3) - 15 = 2x \quad \text{This is the given equation.}$$
$$5x + 15 - 15 = 2x \quad \text{Apply the distributive property.}$$
$$5x = 2x \quad \text{Simplify.}$$
$$5 = 2 \quad \text{Divide both sides by } x.$$

There is no solution because $5 \neq 2$.

75. In your group, describe the best procedure for solving an equation like

$$0.47x + \frac{19}{4} = -0.2 + \frac{2}{5}x.$$

Use this procedure to actually solve the equation. Then compare procedures with other groups working on this problem. Which group devised the most streamlined method?

In the workplace, problems and projects are often solved with a collaborative effort. Group Activity Problems encourage cooperative work in and out of the classroom setting.

96. Evaluate: $\frac{1}{3} - \left(-\frac{1}{4}\right)$.

97. The graph shows health-care expenditures per American for the period from 1960 through 1993.
    a. In what year were health-care expenditures approximately $1800 per person?
    b. What is a reasonable estimate for health-care expenditures in 1975?
    c. Use the graph to predict health-care expenditures in the year 2000. Describe how you arrived at this amount.

98. Simplify: $\frac{2}{3}(3y + 9) + \frac{1}{2}(2y - 6) + 8$.

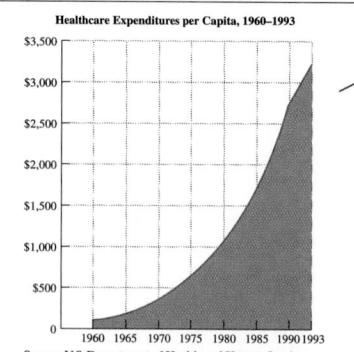

Healthcare Expenditures per Capita, 1960–1993

Source: U.S. Department of Health and Human Services

Review Problems give you the opportunity to connect all of the concepts you have learned and reinforce procedures and problem-solving strategies throughout the course.

Enrich your mathematical experience—these interactive activities encourage your participation in the learning process and demonstrate the usefulness of mathematics.

Discover for yourself

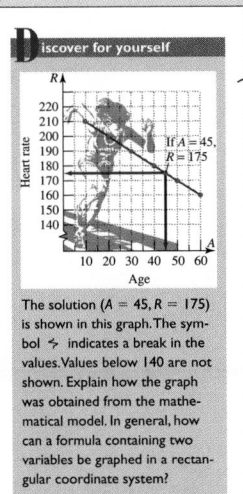

The solution ($A = 45, R = 175$) is shown in this graph. The symbol ⌇ indicates a break in the values. Values below 140 are not shown. Explain how the graph was obtained from the mathematical model. In general, how can a formula containing two variables be graphed in a rectangular coordinate system?

Interact with algebra—explore these problems and interpret their solutions.

Enrichment Essay

Opposites and Solving Equations

Opposites play an important role in solving equations. If we have addition, we subtract; if we have multiplication, we divide. The word *algebra* is from the title of a ninth-century Arabic text and translates as "the science of transposition and opposition." Transposing terms using opposites is precisely what we do when solving equations.

This theme of opposites is found in M. C. Escher's print *Day and Night:* white geese fly over a night view of a town, whereas black geese fly over a sunlit mirror image of the same scene. Notice how the flat checkerboard of the farmland turns into the dual flocks of geese, showing how every three-dimensional scene depicted on a two-dimensional surface must somehow fool the viewer.

Can you think of ideas that have appeared in algebra that are given visual expression in this print?

M.C. Escher (1898–1972) "Day and Night" © 1997 Cordon Art – Baarn – Holland. All rights reserved.

Investigate the use of art, historical information, and interdisciplinary connections in *Enrichment Essays* as a means to express interesting mathematical ideas.

Enhance your preparation

Study tip

Here's a summary of useful strategies for solving problems.

Make a table or a chart.
Look for a pattern.
Solve a similar simpler problem.
Draw a sketch.
Write an equation and solve it.
If a formula applies, use it.
Work backward.
Guess and check.
Use trial and error.
Use common sense.
Look for a "catch" if an answer seems too obvious, or impossible.

Find informal tips and suggestions for problem-solving throughout the text.

Increase your understanding, visualize, discover, explore, and solve problems using a graphing utility.

Using technology

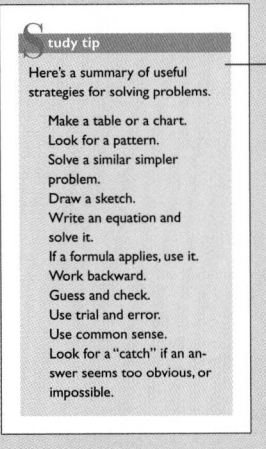

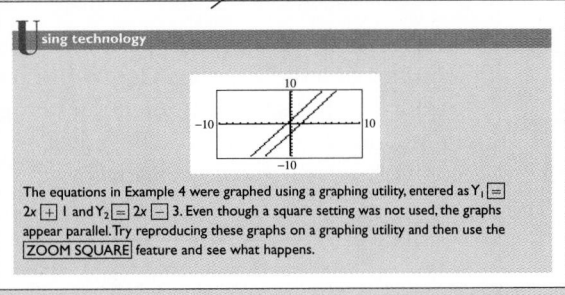

The equations in Example 4 were graphed using a graphing utility, entered as Y₁ $\boxed{=}$ 2x $\boxed{+}$ 1 and Y₂ $\boxed{=}$ 2x $\boxed{-}$ 3. Even though a square setting was not used, the graphs appear parallel. Try reproducing these graphs on a graphing utility and then use the $\boxed{\text{ZOOM SQUARE}}$ feature and see what happens.

HAPTER PROJECT

Designing Word Problems — Writing in Mathematics

One of the best ways to learn how to *solve* a word problem in algebra is to *design* word problems of your own. Creating a word problem makes you very aware of precisely how much information is needed to solve the problem. You must also focus on the best way to present information to a reader and on how much information to give. As you write your problem, you gain skills that will help you solve problems created by others.

You are surrounded by potential word problems in everyday life. Companies offering competing, but very similar, services often spend millions of dollars to present information to consumers about the advantages of their company's pricing plan over that of another; this would include phone companies, online computer services, and airlines, to name just a few. Banks and other financial institutions publish information about rates of return on investments, savings plans, checking accounts, and mortgages. Local, state, and federal agencies publish volumes of statistics cataloging things such as crime rates, public health concerns, and consumer interests. Car dealerships and car manufacturers offer many different payment plans, rebates, and interest rates. Even a quick glance through the mail around your house will undoubtedly show you credit card bills with different interest rates and penalties and utility bills filled with pricing by usage and taxes added by local agencies.

For this project, you will design five different word problems from a variety of sources.

- At least two of the problems should have an accompanying table, graph, or other visual display of information. You may not need to make your own table; many companies already display information to consumers in this fashion.
- At least one of the problems should contain more numerical information than is needed to solve the problem.
- All of the problems should be clearly written and have an exact solution. The solution need not be numerical.
- All of the problems should be distinctly different in style. For example, you should not have more than one problem on telephone company rates.

After you have completed all of your word problems, your instructor will put together a set of problems from the entire class and return them to be analyzed and solved by the class. Discussing and defending your own word problems may give you an entirely new perspective on how you and others analyze these problems in the future.

Try the Chapter Project at the end of each chapter. Engaging explorations challenge your understanding and stimulate class discussion.

Link up to the Worldwide Web and surf the 'Net through the Prentice Hall Website to explore multidisciplinary material that is related to the material you have just computed in the Chapter Project.

- www.prenhall.com/blitzer

U se these text supplements as your resources. Ask your instructor how to obtain these items to complement your learning style.

Instructional videos feature selected worked out examples and exercises from every section of the text. A separate "Graphing Utilities" video and "Review Video" provide further video instruction.

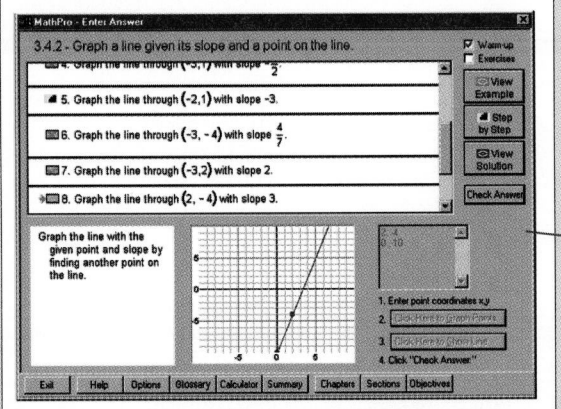

Math Pro Explorer includes explorations as well as algorithmically generated practice exercises. Available in Macintosh and Windows platforms.

A lso available:

To the Student

The process of learning mathematics requires that you do at least three things—read the book, work the problems, and get your questions answered if you are stuck. This book has been written so that you can learn directly from its pages. All concepts are carefully explained, important definitions and procedures are set off in boxes, and worked-out examples that present solutions in a step-by-step manner appear throughout. Study tip boxes offer hints and suggestions, and often point out common errors to avoid. Discovery boxes encourage you to actively participate in the learning process as you read the book. A great deal of attention has been given to show you the vast and unusual applications of algebra in order to make your learning experience both interesting and relevant. As you begin your studies, I would like to offer some specific suggestions for using this book and for being successful in algebra.

- *Read the book.*
  a. Begin with the chapter introduction. Enjoy the art while you obtain a general idea of what the chapter is about.
  b. Move on to the objectives and the introduction to a particular section. The objectives will tell you exactly what you should be able to do once you have completed the section. Each objective is restated in the margin at the point in the section where the objective is taught.
  c. At a slow and deliberate pace, read the section with pen (or pencil) in hand. Move through the illustrative examples with great care. These worked-out examples provide a model for doing the problems in the problem sets. Be sure to read all the hints and suggestions in the Study tip boxes. Your pen is in hand for the Discover for yourself exercises that are intended to encourage you to actively participate in the learning process as you read the book. The Discover for yourself exercises let you explore problems in order to understand them and their solutions better, so be sure not to jump over these valuable discovery experiences in your reading.
  d. Enjoy the Enrichment essays and the contemporary art that is intended to make your reading more interesting and show you how algebra is connected to the whole spectrum of learning.

As you proceed through the reading, do not give up if you do not understand every single word. Things will become clearer as you read on and see how various procedures are applied to specific worked-out examples.

- *Work problems every day and check your answers.* The way to learn mathematics is by *doing* mathematics, which means by *solving problems.* The more problems you work, the better you will become at solving problems which, in turn, will make you a better algebra student.

  a. Work the assigned problems in each problem set. Problem sets are organized into eight categories. Minimally, you should work all odd-numbered problems in the first two categories (Practice Problems and Application Problems), and all three review problems at the end of the problem set. Answers to most odd-numbered problems and all review problems are given in the back of the book. Once you have completed a problem, be sure to check your answer. If you made an error, find out what it was. Ask questions in class about homework problems you don't understand.

  b. Problem sets also include critical thinking problems, technology problems, writing exercises, and group activity learning experiences. Don't panic! You are not expected to work every problem, or even all the odd-numbered problems, in each problem set. This vast collection of problems provides options for your learning style and your instructor's teaching methods. You may be assigned some problems from one or more of these categories. Problems in the critical thinking categories are the most difficult, intended to stimulate your ability to think and reason. Thinking about a particular question, even if you are confused and somewhat frustrated, can eventually lead to new insights.

- *Prepare for chapter exams.* After completing a chapter, study the summary, work assigned problems from the chapter review problems, and work all the problems in the chapter test.

- *Review continuously.* Working review problems lets you remember the algebra you learned for a much longer period of time. Cumulative review problems appear at the end of each chapter, beginning with Chapter 3. The book's appendix contains review problems covering the entire course. By working the appendix problems assigned by your professor, you will be able to bring together the procedures and problem-solving strategies learned throughout the course.

- *Attend all lectures.* No book is intended to be a substitute for the valuable insights and interactions that occur in the classroom. In addition to arriving for a lecture on time and prepared, you might find it helpful to read the section that will be covered in class beforehand so that you have a clear idea of the new material that will be discussed.

- *Use the supplements that come with this book.* A solutions manual that contains worked-out solutions to the book's odd-numbered problems and all review problems, as well as a series of videotapes created for every section of the book, are among the supplements created to help you learn algebra. Ask your instructor what supplements are available and where you can find them.

Algebra is often viewed as the foundation for more advanced mathematics. It is my hope that this book will make algebra accessible, relevant, and an interesting body of knowledge in and of itself.

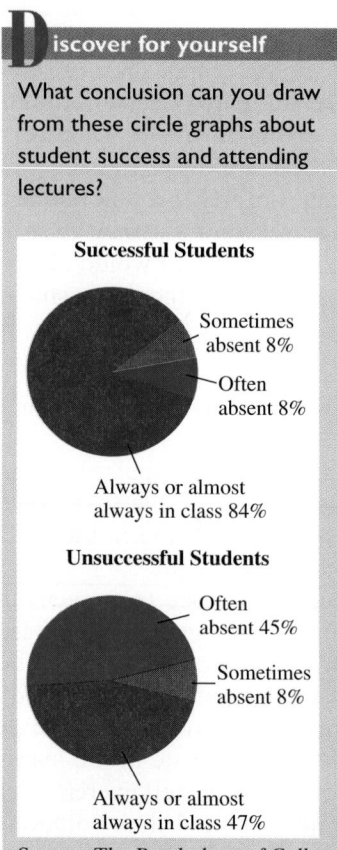

Discover for yourself

What conclusion can you draw from these circle graphs about student success and attending lectures?

Successful Students

Sometimes absent 8%

Often absent 8%

Always or almost always in class 84%

Unsuccessful Students

Often absent 45%

Sometimes absent 8%

Always or almost always in class 47%

Source: *The Psychology of College Success: A Dynamic Approach,* by permission of H. C. Lindgren, 1969

The Real Number System

A lgebra is a problem-solving tool that, like music, expresses its ideas in an abstract, symbolic notation. The wonders of mathematics are not evident to the general population because a special language is required to communicate the logic. This computer-generated image is a visual picture of the equation $f(z) = z^2 + c$. Although the theory of how these compact symbols are transformed into a picture is beyond the comprehension of most people, the resulting visual image is quite interesting. In this chapter, we'll begin to become familiar with algebra's very special language.

Courtesy of Clifford Pickover

> **tudy tip**
>
> Mathematics is based on a few fundamental assumptions from which everything else follows. To understand algebra, a solid foundation is essential. By devoting special attention to the basic skills explained in this chapter, you'll be well on your way to mastering algebra.

SECTION I.I

Solutions Manual **Tutorial** **Video I**

Fractions

Objectives

1 Reduce or simplify fractions.
2 Multiply fractions.
3 Divide fractions.
4 Add and subtract fractions.
5 Change a mixed number to fractional notation.
6 Use fractional notation, decimal notation, and percents.

In this section, we present a brief review of operations with fractions that we will use in algebra.

Fractional Notation

In arithmetic, the numbers that you encounter most frequently are the *natural numbers*

$$1, 2, 3, 4, 5, \ldots$$

the *whole numbers*

$$0, 1, 2, 3, 4, 5, \ldots$$

and *fractions,* such as

$$\frac{5}{8}, \frac{2}{3}, \quad \text{and} \quad \frac{1}{5}.$$

> **tudy tip**
>
> The three dots . . . mean that the pattern of the preceding numbers continues.

In a fraction, the number that is written above the fraction bar is called the *numerator.* The number below the fraction bar is called the *denominator.*

$$\frac{5}{8} \quad \begin{matrix} \leftarrow \text{Numerator} \\ \leftarrow \text{Denominator} \end{matrix}$$

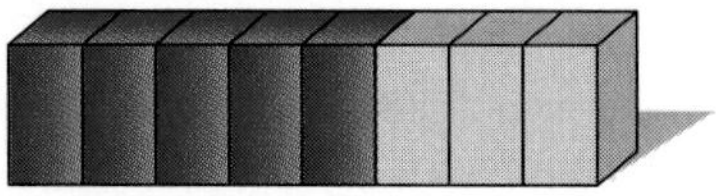

Fractions often refer to parts of a whole. For example, $\frac{5}{8}$ of the solid in Figure 1.1 is shaded. The denominator, 8, tells us how many equal parts the solid is divided into. The numerator, 5, tells us how many equal parts are shaded.

Figure I.I

A geometric model for $\frac{5}{8}$: $\frac{5}{8}$ of the solid is shaded.

Simplifying Fractions

To simplify, or reduce, fractions, we need to factor the numerator and the denominator. To *factor* a number means to write it as a product. For example, 21 can be factored as $7 \cdot 3$. In the statement $7 \cdot 3 = 21$, 7 and 3 are called *factors* and 21 is the *product.*

I Reduce or simplify fractions.

Fractions often refer to parts of a whole. The two parts shown here are the northern and southern hemispheres of the Earth.

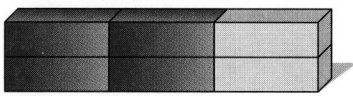

Figure 1.2

4 parts out of 6 ($\frac{4}{6}$) is the same part of the solid as 2 parts out of 3 ($\frac{2}{3}$).

$$7 \cdot 3 = 21$$
$$\uparrow \quad \uparrow \qquad \uparrow$$
Factor Factor Product

Two fractions are *equivalent* if they represent the same value. Writing a fraction as an equivalent fraction with a smaller denominator is called *reducing a fraction.* A fraction is in *reduced form,* or *lowest terms,* when the numerator and denominator have no common factors other than 1.

The model in Figure 1.2 indicates that $\frac{4}{6}$ and $\frac{2}{3}$ are equivalent fractions. We can reduce, or simplify, $\frac{4}{6}$ to $\frac{2}{3}$ by removing a factor of 1 as follows:

$$\frac{4}{6} = \frac{2 \cdot 2}{3 \cdot 2} = \frac{2}{3} \cdot \frac{2}{2} = \frac{2}{3} \cdot 1 = \frac{2}{3}$$

Multiplying a number by 1 gives that same number.

We can speed up this process by dividing the numerator and the denominator of $\frac{4}{6}$ by 2, the *greatest common factor* of 4 and 6.

$$\frac{4}{6} = \frac{2 \cdot \cancel{2}}{3 \cdot \cancel{2}} = \frac{2}{3}$$

Simplifying a fraction

To reduce a fraction to lowest terms, divide both the numerator and the denominator by their greatest common factor.

EXAMPLE 1 **Reducing Fractions**

Reduce each fraction to lowest terms:

a. $\dfrac{6}{8}$ **b.** $\dfrac{45}{27}$ **c.** $\dfrac{11}{25}$ **d.** $\dfrac{11}{33}$

Solution

For each fraction, factor the numerator and denominator. Then divide by the greatest common factor.

a. $\dfrac{6}{8} = \dfrac{\cancel{2} \cdot 3}{\cancel{2} \cdot 4} = \dfrac{3}{4}$ 2 is the greatest common factor of 6 and 8. Divide numerator and denominator by 2.

b. $\dfrac{45}{27} = \dfrac{\cancel{9} \cdot 5}{\cancel{9} \cdot 3} = \dfrac{5}{3}$ 9 is the greatest common factor of 45 and 27. Divide numerator and denominator by 9.

c. Since 11 and 25 share no common factor (other than 1), $\frac{11}{25}$ is already in lowest terms.

d. $\dfrac{11}{33} = \dfrac{\cancel{11} \cdot 1}{\cancel{11} \cdot 3} = \dfrac{1}{3}$ 11 is the greatest common factor of 11 and 33. Divide numerator and denominator by 11.   ■

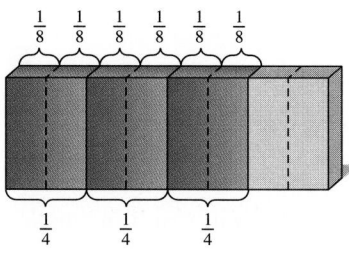

A geometric model showing that $\frac{6}{8} = \frac{3}{4}$

2 Multiply fractions.

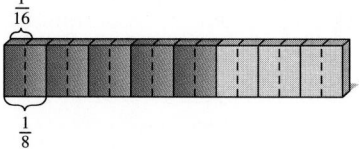

Multiplying Fractions

A geometric picture, or model, is useful in terms of developing a process for multiplying fractions. Begin with a model for $\frac{5}{8}$. The solid is divided into 8 equal parts, 5 of which are shaded. The dashed lines divide each of the 8 parts in half. There are a total of 16 smaller solids. Now let's take half of what we've shaded, or half of $\frac{5}{8}$. We can express this as

$$\frac{1}{2} \cdot \frac{5}{8}.$$

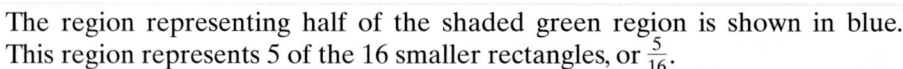

This is half the shaded green region.

The region representing half of the shaded green region is shown in blue. This region represents 5 of the 16 smaller rectangles, or $\frac{5}{16}$.

We can obtain $\frac{5}{16}$ by writing the product of the numerators over the product of the denominators.

$$\frac{1}{2} \cdot \frac{5}{8} = \frac{1 \cdot 5}{2 \cdot 8} = \frac{5}{16} \quad \text{Half of } \frac{5}{8} \text{ is } \frac{5}{16}.$$

Generalizing from this result gives us the following rule.

Multiplying fractions

The product of two or more fractions is the product of their numerators divided by the product of their denominators.

EXAMPLE 2   **Multiplying Fractions**

Multiply:

a. $\dfrac{3}{8} \cdot \dfrac{5}{11}$ **b.** $5 \cdot \dfrac{7}{12}$ **c.** $\dfrac{3}{7} \cdot \dfrac{7}{3}$

Solution

a. $\dfrac{3}{8} \cdot \dfrac{5}{11} = \dfrac{3 \cdot 5}{8 \cdot 11} = \dfrac{15}{88}$ Multiply numerators and denominators.

b. $5 \cdot \dfrac{7}{12} = \dfrac{5}{1} \cdot \dfrac{7}{12} = \dfrac{5 \cdot 7}{1 \cdot 12} = \dfrac{35}{12}$

c. $\dfrac{3}{7} \cdot \dfrac{7}{3} = \dfrac{3 \cdot 7}{7 \cdot 3} = \dfrac{21}{21} = 1$ ■

In Example 2c, we simplify the answer to 1 using the following geometric idea: If we divide a solid into 21 parts and shade all 21 of them, we obtain 1 whole solid. This idea is further modeled in Figure 1.3.

It is usually easier to reduce before multiplying. This will result in smaller numbers. Here's an example.

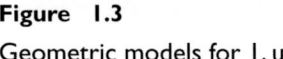

Figure   1.3

Geometric models for 1, using different denominators

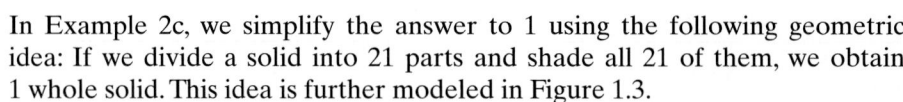

Multiply and then Simplify:

$$\frac{3}{8} \cdot \frac{4}{5} = \frac{3 \cdot 4}{8 \cdot 5} = \frac{12}{40} = \frac{\cancel{4} \cdot 3}{\cancel{4} \cdot 10} = \frac{3}{10}$$

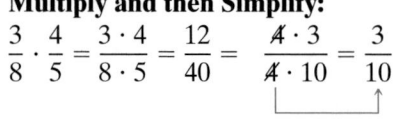

The greatest common factor is 4.

Simplify and then Multiply:

$$\frac{3}{8} \cdot \frac{4}{5} = \frac{3}{\cancel{4} \cdot 2} \cdot \frac{\cancel{4}}{5} = \frac{3}{2 \cdot 5} = \frac{3}{10}$$

Multiplying fractions

1. Factor the numerators and denominators.
2. Divide out the common factors in any numerator and denominator.

3. Take the product of the remaining factors in the numerators divided by the product of the remaining factors in the denominators.

| EXAMPLE 3 | **Simplifying and Then Multiplying Fractions** |

Multiply:

a. $\dfrac{4}{15} \cdot \dfrac{5}{18}$ **b.** $7 \cdot \dfrac{11}{14}$

Solution

a. $\dfrac{4}{15} \cdot \dfrac{5}{18} = \dfrac{2 \cdot 2}{\cancel{5} \cdot 3} \cdot \dfrac{\cancel{5}}{9 \cdot \cancel{2}}$ Factor the numerators and denominators. Divide out the common factors.

$\qquad = \dfrac{2}{3 \cdot 9}$ Multiply the remaining factors.

$\qquad = \dfrac{2}{27}$

b. $7 \cdot \dfrac{11}{14} = \dfrac{\cancel{7}}{1} \cdot \dfrac{11}{\cancel{7} \cdot 2}$ Factor and divide out the common factor.

$\qquad = \dfrac{11}{1 \cdot 2}$ Multiply the remaining factors.

$\qquad = \dfrac{11}{2}$ ■

3 Divide fractions.

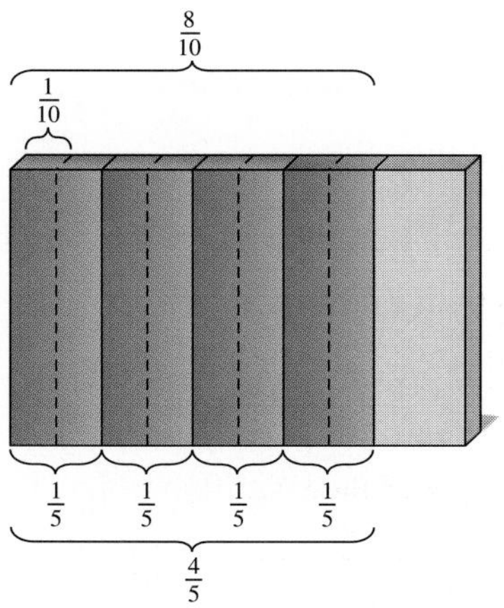

Figure 1.4

There are eight $\frac{1}{10}$'s in $\frac{4}{5}$.

Dividing Fractions

The answer to a division problem is called a *quotient.* A geometric model is useful for developing a process for determining the quotient of two fractions.

Considering the division $\frac{4}{5} \div \frac{1}{10}$. We want to know how many $\frac{1}{10}$'s are in $\frac{4}{5}$. The model in Figure 1.4 indicates that there are eight $\frac{1}{10}$'s in $\frac{4}{5}$. We can obtain the quotient of 8 in the following way.

$$\frac{4}{5} \div \frac{1}{10} = \frac{4}{5} \cdot \frac{10}{1} = \frac{4}{\cancel{5}} \cdot \frac{\cancel{5} \cdot 2}{1} = \frac{4 \cdot 2}{1} = \frac{8}{1} = 8$$

Invert the divisor.

Generalizing from this result gives us the following rule.

Dividing fractions

To find the quotient of two fractions, invert the divisor (the second fraction if written with ÷) and multiply.

| EXAMPLE 4 | **Dividing Fractions** |

Find the indicated quotients:

a. $\dfrac{2}{3} \div \dfrac{7}{15}$ **b.** $\dfrac{3}{4} \div 5$

Solution

a. $\dfrac{2}{3} \div \dfrac{7}{15} = \dfrac{2}{3} \cdot \dfrac{15}{7}$ Invert the divisor and multiply.

$= \dfrac{2}{3} \cdot \dfrac{3 \cdot 5}{7}$ Factor and divide out the common factor.

$= \dfrac{2 \cdot 5}{7}$ Multiply the remaining factors.

$= \dfrac{10}{7}$

b. $\dfrac{3}{4} \div 5 = \dfrac{3}{4} \div \dfrac{5}{1}$ You may work this step mentally.

$= \dfrac{3}{4} \cdot \dfrac{1}{5}$ Invert the divisor and multiply.

$= \dfrac{3 \cdot 1}{4 \cdot 5}$ With no common factors in a numerator and denominator, multiply numerators and denominators.

$= \dfrac{3}{20}$ ■

4 Add and subtract fractions.

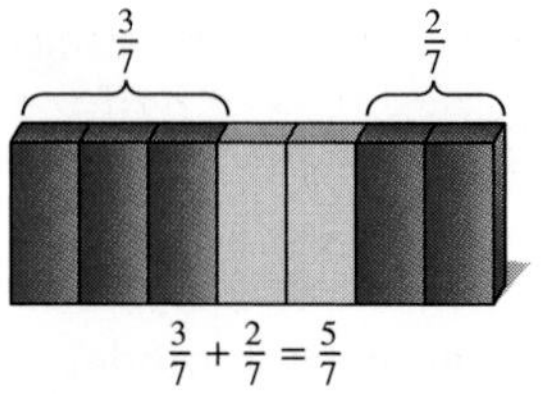

$$\tfrac{3}{7} + \tfrac{2}{7} = \tfrac{5}{7}$$

Figure 1.5

A model for adding fractions with identical denominators

Adding and Subtracting Fractions

The answer to an addition problem is called a *sum*. The answer to a subtraction problem is called a *difference*. We can generalize from the model shown in Figure 1.5 to obtain a procedure for adding or subtracting fractions having the same denominator.

> **Adding and subtracting fractions with identical denominators**
>
> Add or subtract the numerators. Put this result over the common denominator.

EXAMPLE 5 **Adding and Subtracting Fractions with Like Denominators**

Perform the indicated operations:

a. $\dfrac{3}{11} + \dfrac{4}{11}$ **b.** $\dfrac{11}{12} - \dfrac{5}{12}$

Solution

a. $\dfrac{3}{11} + \dfrac{4}{11} = \dfrac{3 + 4}{11}$ Add the numerators. Put this sum over the common denominator.

$= \dfrac{7}{11}$

b. $\dfrac{11}{12} - \dfrac{5}{12} = \dfrac{11 - 5}{12}$ Subtract the numerators. Put this difference over the common denominator.

$$= \frac{6}{12} \qquad \text{Perform the subtraction.}$$

$$= \frac{\cancel{6} \cdot 1}{\cancel{6} \cdot 2} \qquad \text{Now simplify: 6 is the greatest common factor of 6 and 12.}$$

$$= \frac{1}{2} \qquad \text{Divide out the common factor.} \qquad \blacksquare$$

If the fractions to be added or subtracted have different denominators, we must first rewrite them as equivalent fractions with the same denominator. We do this by multiplying fractions by 1, as shown in the next example. Multiplication by 1 does not change the value of a number.

EXAMPLE 6   **Writing an Equivalent Fraction**

Write $\frac{3}{4}$ as an equivalent fraction with a denominator of 16.

Solution

To obtain a denominator of 16, we must multiply the denominator of the given fraction, $\frac{3}{4}$, by 4. So that we do not change the value of the fraction, we also multiply the numerator by 4. Multiplying by $\frac{4}{4} = 1$ does not change the given fraction's value.

$$\frac{3}{4} = \frac{3}{4} \cdot \frac{4}{4} = \frac{3 \cdot 4}{4 \cdot 4} = \frac{12}{16} \qquad \blacksquare$$

Equivalent fractions can be used to add fractions with different denominators, such as $\frac{1}{2}$ and $\frac{1}{3}$. The model in Figure 1.6 indicates that the sum of half the whole figure and one-third of the whole figure results in 5 parts out of 6, or $\frac{5}{6}$, of the figure. We can obtain this result if we build up each fraction to get a denominator of 6.

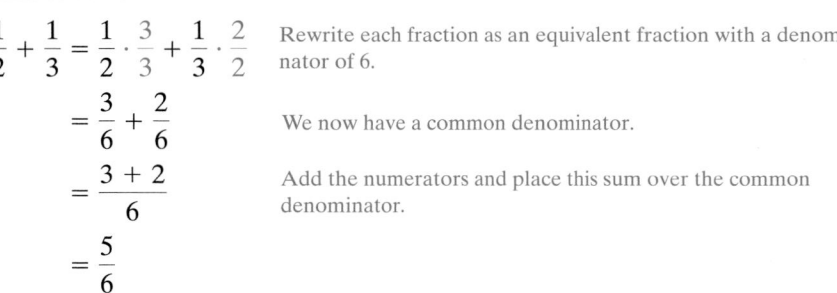

$$\frac{1}{2} + \frac{1}{3} = \frac{1}{2} \cdot \frac{3}{3} + \frac{1}{3} \cdot \frac{2}{2} \qquad \text{Rewrite each fraction as an equivalent fraction with a denominator of 6.}$$

$$= \frac{3}{6} + \frac{2}{6} \qquad \text{We now have a common denominator.}$$

$$= \frac{3 + 2}{6} \qquad \text{Add the numerators and place this sum over the common denominator.}$$

$$= \frac{5}{6}$$

When adding $\frac{1}{2}$ and $\frac{1}{3}$, there are many common denominators that we can use, such as 6, 12, 18, and so on. The given denominators, 2 and 3, divide into all these numbers. However, the denominator 6 is the smallest number that is a multiple of both 2 and 3. Since 6 is the smallest number that 2 and 3 divide into, it is called the *least common denominator (LCD)*.

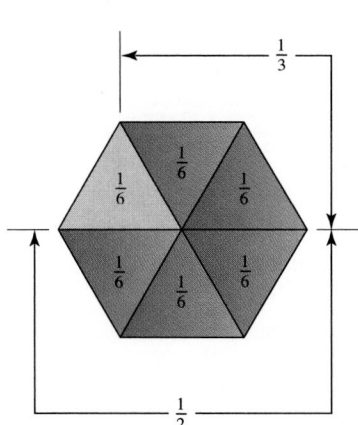

$\frac{3}{4}$ and $\frac{12}{16}$ both represent the same shaded part of the whole square.

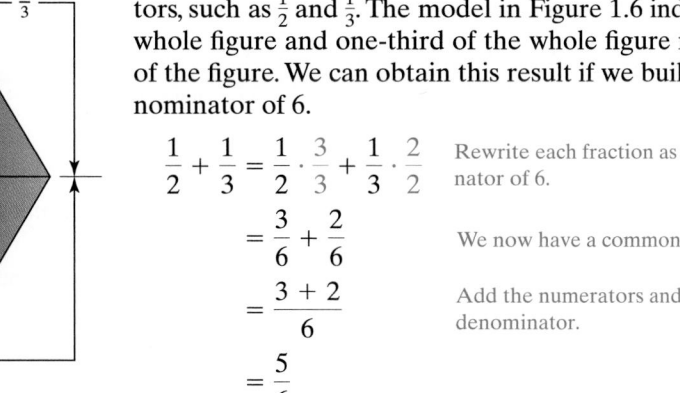

Figure 1.6
$\frac{1}{2} + \frac{1}{3} = \frac{5}{6}$

Adding and subtracting fractions with unlike denominators

1. Rewrite the fractions as equivalent fractions with the least common denominator.
2. Add or subtract the numerators, putting this result over the common denominator.

| EXAMPLE 7 | **Adding and Subtracting Fractions with Unlike Denominators** |

Perform the indicated operations:

$$\textbf{a.}\ \frac{1}{5}+\frac{3}{4} \qquad \textbf{b.}\ \frac{3}{4}-\frac{1}{6} \qquad \textbf{c.}\ \frac{7}{10}-\frac{1}{5}$$

Discover for yourself

Try Example 7a, $\frac{1}{5}+\frac{3}{4}$, using a common denominator of 40. Since both 5 and 4 divide into 40, 40 is a common denominator, although not the *least* common denominator. Describe what happens. What is the advantage of using the least common denominator?

Solution

a. The LCD for the denominators 5 and 4 is 20. By inspection, we can see that 20 is the smallest number divisible by both 5 and 4. We rewrite both fractions as equivalent fractions with the LCD of 20.

$$\frac{1}{5}+\frac{3}{4}=\frac{1}{5}\cdot\frac{4}{4}+\frac{3}{4}\cdot\frac{5}{5}$$ Multiply each fraction by 1. Since $5\cdot4=20$, multiply the first fraction by $\frac{4}{4}$. Since $4\cdot5=20$, multiply the second fraction by $\frac{5}{5}$.

$$=\frac{4}{20}+\frac{15}{20}$$ Perform the multiplications.

$$=\frac{19}{20}$$ Add the numerators and put this sum over the LCD.

b. By inspection, we find that the smallest number that the denominators of 4 and 6 will divide into is 12. Thus, the LCD is 12.

$$\frac{3}{4}-\frac{1}{6}=\frac{3}{4}\cdot\frac{3}{3}-\frac{1}{6}\cdot\frac{2}{2}$$ Rewrite each fraction as an equivalent fraction with a denominator of 12.

$$=\frac{9}{12}-\frac{2}{12}$$ Multiply.

$$=\frac{7}{12}$$ Subtract the numerators and put this difference over the LCD.

c. The smallest number that the denominators of 10 and 5 will divide into is 10. Since the LCD is 10, we only have to rewrite one of the fractions.

$$\frac{7}{10}-\frac{1}{5}=\frac{7}{10}-\frac{1}{5}\cdot\frac{2}{2}$$ Build up the second fraction to a denominator of 10.

$$=\frac{7}{10}-\frac{2}{10}$$ Multiply.

$$=\frac{5}{10}$$ Subtract numerators, putting the difference over the LCD.

$$=\frac{5\cdot1}{5\cdot2}$$ Simplify.

$$=\frac{1}{2}$$ Divide numerator and denominator by 5. ■

5   Change a mixed number to fractional notation.

Mixed Numbers

Consider the number $2\frac{3}{4}$. This number is the sum of a whole number and a fraction; it is called a *mixed number*. The model for the mixed number $2\frac{3}{4}$ in Figure 1.7 indicates that it is equivalent to the fraction $\frac{11}{4}$.

The mixed number $2\frac{3}{4}$ may be changed to a fraction as follows:

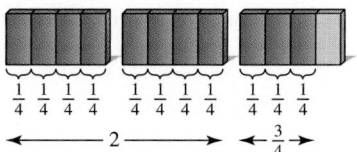

Figure 1.7

$2\frac{3}{4}$ is equivalent to $\frac{11}{4}$.

$$2\frac{3}{4} = 2 + \frac{3}{4} = \frac{2}{1} \cdot \frac{4}{4} + \frac{3}{4} = \frac{8}{4} + \frac{3}{4} = \frac{11}{4}$$

Here's a faster method.

Changing a mixed number to fractional notation

b.
c.
$$2\frac{3}{4} = \frac{11}{4}$$
a.

a. Multiply the denominator of the fraction in the mixed number by the whole number preceding it. $4 \cdot 2 = 8$

b. Add the numerator of the fraction in the mixed number to the product from step a. $8 + 3 = 11$

c. Put the result of step b over the original denominator.

To perform operations with mixed numbers, we often change the mixed numbers to fractions.

EXAMPLE 8   **Operations with Mixed Numbers**

Perform the indicated operations:

a. $3\frac{1}{4} \div \frac{5}{8}$ **b.** $7\frac{2}{3} - 6\frac{1}{2}$

Solution

a. Begin by writing $3\frac{1}{4}$ in fractional notation.

$$3\frac{1}{4} = \frac{4 \cdot 3 + 1}{4} = \frac{13}{4}$$

Now perform the indicated division.

$$3\frac{1}{4} \div \frac{5}{8} = \frac{13}{4} \div \frac{5}{8} \qquad \text{Write } 3\frac{1}{4} \text{ in fractional notation.}$$

$$= \frac{13}{4} \cdot \frac{8}{5} \qquad \text{Invert the divisor and multiply.}$$

$$= \frac{13}{\cancel{4}} \cdot \frac{\cancel{4} \cdot 2}{5} \qquad \text{Factor and divide out the common factor.}$$

$$= \frac{26}{5} \qquad \text{Multiply the remaining factors.}$$

If you want to do so, fractions greater than 1—such as $\frac{26}{5}$—can be changed back to mixed numbers using division.

$$\begin{array}{r} 5 \leftarrow \text{Whole number} \\ \text{Denominator} \rightarrow 5\overline{)26} \leftarrow \text{Numerator} \\ 25 \\ \hline 1 \leftarrow \text{Remainder} \end{array} \qquad \frac{26}{5} = 5\frac{1}{5} \begin{array}{l} \leftarrow \text{Remainder} \\ \leftarrow \text{Denominator} \\ \leftarrow \text{Whole number} \end{array}$$

Having said this, in this book we will leave the result of any computation in fractional form rather than changing it to a mixed number.

b. Begin by writing the given mixed numbers in fractional notation.

$$7\frac{2}{3} = \frac{3 \cdot 7 + 2}{3} = \frac{21 + 2}{3} = \frac{23}{3}$$

$$6\frac{1}{2} = \frac{6 \cdot 2 + 1}{2} = \frac{12 + 1}{2} = \frac{13}{2}$$

Now perform the indicated subtraction.

$$7\frac{2}{3} - 6\frac{1}{2} = \frac{23}{3} - \frac{13}{2} \qquad \text{Write the mixed numbers in fractional notation.}$$

$$= \frac{23}{3} \cdot \frac{2}{2} - \frac{13}{2} \cdot \frac{3}{3} \qquad \text{The LCD is 6. Rewrite each fraction with a denominator of 6.}$$

$$= \frac{46}{6} - \frac{39}{6} \qquad \text{Multiply.}$$

$$= \frac{7}{6} \qquad \text{Subtract the numerators, putting the difference over the LCD.} \qquad \blacksquare$$

6 Use fractional notation, decimal notation, and percents.

Decimal Notation and Percents

Fractions can be represented in decimal notation. As shown in the accompanying place-value chart, this is particularly convenient for fractions with denominators of 10, 100, 1000, and so on. For example,

$$\frac{7}{10} = 0.7$$

$$\frac{3}{100} = 0.03$$

$$\frac{8}{1000} = 0.008$$

Place-Value Chart							
Hundreds	Tens	Ones	Tenths	Hundredths	Thousandths	Ten-Thousandths	Hundred-Thousandths
100	10	1	$\frac{1}{10}$	$\frac{1}{100}$	$\frac{1}{1,000}$	$\frac{1}{10,000}$	$\frac{1}{100,000}$

Fractions with denominators of 100 can also be expressed as percents. The word percent means "per hundred." Thus,

$$\frac{25}{100} = 25\%, \quad \frac{8}{100} = 8\%, \quad \text{and} \quad \frac{500}{100} = 500\%.$$

$$1\% = \frac{1}{100} \quad \text{or} \quad 1\% = 0.01$$

EXAMPLE 9   **Changing Forms**

Write each given fraction, decimal, or percent in its other two notations:

a. $\frac{1}{4}$ **b.** 8%   **c.** 0.16

Solution

a. $\dfrac{1}{4} = \dfrac{1}{4} \cdot \dfrac{25}{25} = \dfrac{25}{100} = 25\%$

and $25\% = 25\,(0.01) = 0.25$

Thus, $\dfrac{1}{4} = 25\% = 0.25$

c. $0.16 = \dfrac{16}{100} = \dfrac{4 \cdot 4}{4 \cdot 25} = \dfrac{4}{25}$

and $0.16 = \dfrac{16}{100} = 16\%$

Thus, $0.16 = \dfrac{4}{25} = 16\%$

b. $8\% = \dfrac{8}{100} = 0.08$

and $8\% = \dfrac{8}{100} = \dfrac{4 \cdot 2}{4 \cdot 25} = \dfrac{2}{25}$

Thus, $8\% = 0.08 = \dfrac{2}{25}$

Fractions can be represented as *terminating* or *repeating decimals*. Shown below are decimal and percent representations for commonly occurring fractions. Notice that the overbar notation indicates repeating digits. You may know many, if not all, of these equivalent notations by heart.

Commonly Occurring Fractions		
Fraction	**Decimal**	**Percent**
$\frac{1}{2}$	0.5	50%
$\frac{1}{3}$	$0.333 \ldots = 0.\overline{3}$	$33\frac{1}{3}\%$
$\frac{2}{3}$	$0.666 \ldots = 0.\overline{6}$	$66\frac{2}{3}\%$
$\frac{1}{4}$	0.25	25%
$\frac{3}{4}$	0.75	75%
$\frac{1}{5}$	0.2	20%
$\frac{2}{5}$	0.4	40%
$\frac{3}{5}$	0.6	60%
$\frac{4}{5}$	0.8	80%
$\frac{1}{8}$	0.125	12.5%
$\frac{3}{8}$	0.375	37.5%
$\frac{5}{8}$	0.625	62.5%
$\frac{7}{8}$	0.875	87.5%

Later in this chapter we will need to find an amount that is a certain percent of a number. As we saw earlier in this section, the word *of* indicates multiplication.

EXAMPLE 10   Using Percents

Find: 14% of 200

Solution

First change 14% to decimal notation.

   $14\% = 0.14$

Now multiply by 200.

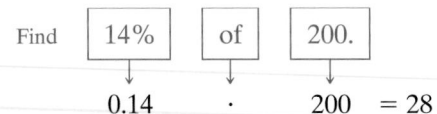

$$0.14 \quad \cdot \quad 200 \quad = 28$$

Thus, 14% of 200 is 28.   ■

P R O B L E M   S E T   1 . 1

Practice Problems

In Problems 1–8, simplify by reducing the fraction to lowest terms.

1. $\frac{10}{15}$ **2.** $\frac{18}{45}$ **3.** $\frac{15}{18}$ **4.** $\frac{16}{64}$

5. $\frac{35}{50}$ **6.** $\frac{40}{64}$ **7.** $\frac{7}{56}$ **8.** $\frac{14}{42}$

In Problems 9–50, perform the indicated operations, and simplify if possible.

9. $\frac{3}{8} \cdot \frac{7}{11}$ **10.** $\frac{5}{8} \cdot \frac{3}{11}$ **11.** $\frac{1}{10} \cdot \frac{5}{12}$ **12.** $\frac{1}{8} \cdot \frac{4}{9}$

13. $\frac{2}{3} \cdot \frac{9}{4}$ **14.** $\frac{5}{4} \cdot \frac{16}{15}$ **15.** $3\frac{2}{5} \cdot 2\frac{7}{8}$ **16.** $2\frac{3}{10} \cdot 4\frac{2}{5}$

17. $\frac{5}{4} \div \frac{3}{8}$ **18.** $\frac{6}{13} \div \frac{3}{26}$ **19.** $\frac{18}{5} \div 2$ **20.** $\frac{12}{7} \div 3$

21. $2\frac{1}{3} \div 1\frac{1}{6}$ **22.** $2\frac{3}{10} \div 1\frac{4}{5}$ **23.** $1\frac{4}{5} \div \frac{3}{20}$ **24.** $20 \div 3\frac{1}{5}$

25. $\frac{2}{11} + \frac{3}{11}$ **26.** $\frac{5}{13} + \frac{2}{13}$ **27.** $\frac{5}{6} - \frac{1}{6}$ **28.** $\frac{7}{12} - \frac{5}{12}$

29. $\frac{7}{12} + \frac{1}{12}$ **30.** $\frac{5}{16} + \frac{5}{16}$ **31.** $\frac{1}{2} + \frac{1}{5}$ **32.** $\frac{1}{3} + \frac{1}{5}$

33. $\frac{3}{4} + \frac{3}{20}$ **34.** $\frac{2}{5} + \frac{2}{15}$ **35.** $\frac{7}{8} + \frac{1}{6}$ **36.** $\frac{5}{8} + \frac{1}{6}$

37. $\frac{17}{25} + \frac{4}{15}$ **38.** $\frac{4}{35} + \frac{18}{25}$ **39.** $\frac{13}{18} - \frac{2}{9}$ **40.** $\frac{13}{15} - \frac{2}{45}$

41. $\frac{4}{3} - \frac{3}{4}$ **42.** $\frac{3}{2} - \frac{2}{3}$ **43.** $\frac{7}{10} - \frac{3}{16}$ **44.** $\frac{9}{10} - \frac{5}{16}$

45. $1\frac{5}{6} + 3\frac{3}{8}$ **46.** $3\frac{1}{3} + 4\frac{2}{9}$ **47.** $6\frac{3}{5} - 3\frac{1}{2}$ **48.** $7\frac{1}{3} - 3\frac{5}{8}$

49. $4\frac{1}{8} - \frac{1}{2} - \frac{3}{4}$ **50.** $2\frac{4}{5} + 3 - \frac{3}{4}$

For Problems 51–58, fill in the missing entries in the columns of the table.

	Fraction	**Decimal**	**Percent**
51.	$\frac{19}{20}$		
52.	$\frac{17}{25}$		
53.		0.35	
54.		0.65	
55.			2%
56.			8%
57.		0.005	
58.		0.008	

59. Find 26% of 400.

60. Find 18% of 300.

Application Problems _____

61. A recipe calls for $\frac{3}{4}$ cup of sugar. How much is needed to make half of the recipe?

62. A recipe calls for $\frac{3}{4}$ teaspoon of salt for each pound of meat. How many teaspoons of salt are needed for $3\frac{1}{2}$ pounds of meat?

63. A $3\frac{3}{4}$-acre lot is to be divided into three equal-size lots. What is the acreage of each lot?

64. A particular shirt requires $\frac{3}{4}$ yard of fabric to be manufactured. How many shirts can be made from 18 yards of the fabric?

65 If you walk $\frac{3}{4}$ mile and then jog $\frac{2}{5}$ mile, what is the total distance covered? How much farther did you walk than jog?

66. A franchise is owned by three people. The first owns $\frac{5}{12}$ of the business and the second owns $\frac{1}{4}$ of the business. What fractional part of the business is owned by the third person?

67. On Wednesday, a person purchased 20 shares of a stock at $38\frac{1}{2}$ per share. On Thursday the stock fell $\frac{1}{4}$ and on Friday it rose $\frac{5}{8}$.

a. What was the value of each share of the stock at the end of the week?

b. What was the value of all 20 shares of stock at the end of the week?

c. What was the total amount of money earned by this investor at the end of the week?

68. One person can mow a lawn in 2 hours and a second person can mow the same lawn in 5 hours. What fractional part of the job can each person accomplish in 1 hour? What fractional part of the job can the two people complete if they work together for an hour?

69. A 15% tip was left on a $60 restaurant bill. How much was the tip?

70. An insurance company pays 80% of doctor bills after a $500 yearly deductible. What will the insurance company pay for $1200 doctor bills for the year?

Shown below is the 1995 tax rate from Schedule X for people whose filing status is single. Use this table to answer Problems 71 and 72.

71. What is the tax if the amount on Form 1040, line 37, is $32,350?

72. What is the tax if the amount on Form 1040, line 37, is $66,550?

Schedule X—Use if your filing status is Single			
If the amount on Form 1040, line 37, is: Over—	But not over—	Enter on Form 1040, line 38	of the amount over—
$0	$23,350	.... 15%	$0
23,350	56,550	$3,502.50 + 28%	23,350
56,550	117,950	12,798.50 + 31%	56,550
117,950	256,500	31,832.50 + 36%	117,950
256,500	....	81,710.50 + 39.6%	256,500

True–False Critical Thinking Problems _____

73. Which one of the following is true?

a. $\frac{1}{2} + \frac{1}{5} = \frac{2}{7}$

b. $\frac{2+6}{2} = \frac{2+6}{2} = 6$

c. $\frac{1}{2} \div 4 = 2$

d. Every fraction has infinitely many equivalent fractions.

74. Which one of the following is true?

a. $\frac{8}{12} = \frac{2 \cdot 4}{2 \cdot 6} = \frac{4}{6}$, and we've reduced $\frac{8}{12}$ to lowest terms.

b. $\frac{1+1}{1+3} = \frac{\not1 + 1}{\not1 + 3} = \frac{1}{3}$

c. When we write $\frac{21}{56} = \frac{3 \cdot 7}{8 \cdot 7} = \frac{3}{8} \cdot \frac{7}{7} = \frac{3}{8} \cdot 1 = \frac{3}{8}$, this shows that reducing a fraction to lowest terms involves removing a factor of 1.

d. In the expression $7 \cdot 3 = 21$, 7 and 3 are called the products and 21 is the factor.

75. Which one of the following is true?
  a. $\frac{17}{74} = \frac{1}{4}$
  b. For every fraction that can be written, a rectangle can be drawn and the fraction represents a part of the whole rectangle.
  c. $\frac{1}{9} + \frac{2}{9} - \frac{1}{5} = \frac{3}{9} - \frac{1}{5} = \frac{2}{4} = \frac{1}{2}$

  d. Canceling produces an equivalent fraction when removing common factors in numerators and denominators. However, canceling does not produce equivalent fractions when removing common numbers from a sum in numerators and denominators.

Writing in Mathematics

Explain how to perform each operation in Problems 76–79.

76. $\frac{5}{6} \cdot \frac{1}{2}$

77. $\frac{5}{6} \div \frac{1}{2}$

78. $\frac{5}{6} + \frac{1}{2}$

79. $\frac{5}{6} - \frac{1}{2}$

80. Discuss one similarity between any two of the solution procedures that you explained in Problems 76–79.

81. Discuss one difference between any two of the solution procedures that you explained in Problems 76–69.

Explain the error (the "fractional disaster") in Problems 82–83.

82. $\frac{1}{2} + \frac{1}{3} = \frac{2}{5}$

83. $\frac{16}{24} = \frac{8+8}{8+16} = \frac{8+8}{8+16} = \frac{8}{16} = \frac{1}{2}$

84. Explain what's wrong with this statement. "If you'd like to save some money, I'll be happy to sell you my

computer system for only $\frac{3}{2}$ of the price that I originally paid for it."

Critical Thinking Problems

85. Evaluate $(\frac{2}{3} + \frac{5}{9}) \div (\frac{1}{4} + \frac{1}{12})$. Begin with the additions in parentheses.

86. At a masquerade party the judges eliminate $\frac{1}{4}$ of the eligible contestants after each half-hour. If 256 contestants were present at the start of the party, how many would still be eligible for a prize after one hour?

87. A team played 70 games and won 60% of the games. If there are 40 games left, how many of these 40 games must they win to ultimately win 70% of all the games they played?

88. Describe two patterns that you notice about the fractions in the following triangular array. Then use these patterns to find the missing numbers in the seventh row.

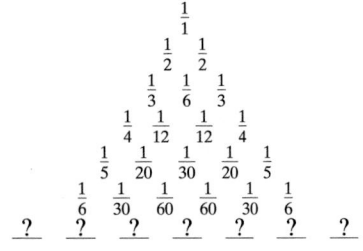

89. You should only cancel when removing common factors in numerators and denominators. You cannot cancel identical digits in the numerator and denominator of a fraction.

$$\frac{17}{74} \ne \frac{1}{4} \quad \text{Incorrect!}$$

However, there are four known cases with two-digit numbers when this "canceling disaster" produces correct results. Here's one of them:

$$\underbrace{\frac{16}{64} = \frac{16 \cdot 1}{16 \cdot 4} = \frac{1}{4}}_{\text{correct}} \quad \text{and} \quad \frac{16}{64} = \frac{1}{4}$$

Use trial and error to discover one of the other three possible cases. (*Hint:* One of the cases uses the digits 1, 5, and 9, and the digit 9 appears in both the numerator and the denominator.)

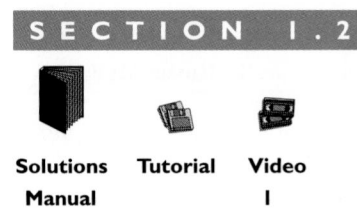

SECTION 1.2

Solutions Manual Tutorial Video I

The Real Numbers

Objectives

1 Use the roster method to write sets of numbers.
2 Define the sets that make up the real numbers.
3 Classify numbers as belonging to one or more sets of the real numbers.
4 Understand and use inequality symbols.
5 Find the opposite (additive inverse) and the absolute value of a real number.

---

1 Use the roster method to write sets of numbers.

Set Notation

In this section, we consider the sets that make up the real numbers. The term *set* appears extensively in mathematics.

> A *set* is a collection of objects. The objects in a set are the *elements* or *members* of the set. A set is *well defined* if it is possible to determine whether or not a given element belongs to it.

The *roster method* of writing a set encloses the elements of the set in braces { }. For example, the set of counting numbers that are less than 6 is written {1, 2, 3, 4, 5}. This set has a limited number of elements and is an example of a *finite* set.

In algebra, letters, called *variables,* are used to represent numbers. Variables are used to express sets in *set-builder notation.* The set {1, 2, 3, 4, 5} can be written using this notation as

$$\{x \mid x \text{ is a counting number between 1 and 5, inclusively}\}$$

which is read "the set of all elements x such that x is a counting number between 1 and 5 inclusively." (The word *inclusively* includes both 1 and 5 as elements of the set.)

EXAMPLE 1 **Representing Sets Using Two Notations**

Represent each of the following sets in roster notation:

a. $\{x \mid x \text{ is an even number between 2, inclusively, and 10, exclusively}\}$
b. $\{x \mid x \text{ is a counting number less than 8}\}$
c. $\{x \mid x \text{ is a counting number greater than 8}\}$

Solution

Table 1.1 represents each set in roster notation. The sets in each row are *equal* because they contain the *same elements.*

TABLE 1.1 Sets in Set-Builder and Roster Notations

Set-Builder Notation	Roster Method
$\{x \mid x$ is an even number between 2, inclusively, and 10, exclusively$\}$	$\{2, 4, 6, 8\}$
$\{x \mid x$ is a counting number less than 8$\}$	$\{1, 2, 3, 4, 5, 6, 7\}$
$\{x \mid x$ is a counting number greater than 8$\}$	$\{9, 10, 11, 12, 13, \ . \ . \ .\}$

Observe that the last set in Table 1.1 contains an unlimited number of elements and is an example of an *infinite set*. The three dots indicate that the pattern continues; the dots are read "and so on." There are infinitely many counting numbers that are greater than 8, so the set $\{9, 10, 11, 12, 13, \ . \ . \ . \}$ also contains the numbers $14, 15, 16,$ and so on.

2 Define the sets that make up the real numbers.

The Set of Real Numbers

We are now in a position to define the various kinds of sets that make up the set of real numbers.

When a child learns to talk, the names of the first few counting numbers are learned almost as soon as the words *mommy, dog,* and *bird.* Counting is followed by words for numbers, which, in turn, are followed by symbolic notation for numbers. It should come as no surprise that the first kinds of numbers children are introduced to are the *natural numbers.* They can find "models" in external reality for these abstractions—one *thing,* two *things,* three *things,* and so on. Our earliest ancestors must have had a parallel experience.

The natural numbers

The set of *natural numbers* or *counting numbers* is the infinite set $\{1, 2, 3, 4, 5, \ . \ . \ .\}$.

Our early mathematical experience with subtraction produced a very strange result. Many of us can remember our first-grade teacher showing us three things, then removing them and saying, "Now what do you see? Nothing." But can we, with conscious awareness, actually visualize nothingness? Where does one find the strange abstraction called zero in a world of physical objects? The ancient Greeks had no conception of nothing, or emptiness, as a number because Aristotle defined number as an accumulation, or "heap." This did not stop the Greeks, or many other cultures, from creating mathematics, although it limited the vision of experts of the day about the nature of numbers and their function in depicting space and time.

When we combine the unusual abstraction called zero with the natural numbers, we obtain the set of *whole numbers.*

The whole numbers

The set of *whole numbers* is the infinite set $\{0, 1, 2, 3, 4, 5, \ . \ . \ .\}$.

Jasper Johns "Figure 2" (1962) en-
caustic and collage on canvas, 51 1/2
× 41 1/2 in. Leo Castelli Gallery
©Jasper Johns/VAGA, New York
1998

Jasper Johns "Figure 5" 1960, encaus-
tic and collage on canvas, 72 × 54 in.
Leo Castelli Gallery ©Jasper
Johns/VAGA, New York 1998

The whole numbers, along with other kinds of numbers, can be represented as points on a *number line,* like the one shown in Figure 1.8.

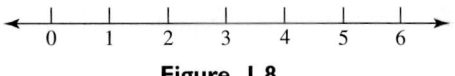

Figure 1.8

The *graph* of a number is a point on the number line. To draw a number
line, choose any point along the line and call it the *origin,* which is labeled 0.
Any point to the right of 0 is labeled 1. The distance between 0 and 1 forms
the unit of measure used to locate other points corresponding to the set of
whole numbers. A consistent distance between two consecutive whole numbers is called a *unit.*

We use numbers to convey the idea of direction as well as magnitude. We
talk about temperatures above or below zero, profit or loss, positive or negative electric charges. Thus, we extend the set of whole numbers to include the
negatives of the natural numbers.

EXAMPLE 2   **Practical Examples of Negative Numbers**

Write a negative number that describes each of the following situations:

a. A debt of $10
b. The shore surrounding the Dead Sea that is 1312 feet below sea level

Solution

a. A debt of $10 can be expressed by the negative number -10 (negative
   ten).
b. The shore surrounding the Dead Sea is 1312 feet below sea level, expressed as -1312 feet. ∎

EXAMPLE 3   **Describing the World with Negative Numbers**

Temperatures sometimes fall below zero. A combination of low temperature and wind makes it feel colder than the actual temperature. The table
shows how cold it feels when low temperatures are combined with different
wind speeds.

Wind (mph)	Temperature (°F)											
	35	**30**	**25**	**20**	**15**	**10**	**5**	**0**	**−5**	**−10**	**−15**	**−20**
5	33	27	21	16	12	7	0	−5	−10	−15	−21	−26
10	22	16	10	3	−3	−9	−15	−22	−27	−34	−40	−46
15	16	9	2	−5	−11	−18	−25	−31	−38	−45	−51	−58
20	12	4	−3	−10	−17	−24	−31	−39	−46	−53	−60	−67
25	8	1	−7	−15	−22	−29	−36	−44	−51	−59	−66	−74

Describe what the number that is circled in the table means in practical terms.

Solution

The circled number indicates that when the temperature is 25° Fahrenheit and the wind is blowing at 20 miles per hour, it feels like it is −3° Fahrenheit (negative three degrees) or 3 degrees below zero. ■

We can use the number line to represent both positive and negative numbers. Numbers to the *left* of 0 are *negative* numbers and numbers to the *right* of 0 are *positive* numbers, as shown in Figure 1.9. Zero is neither positive nor negative. Positive and negative numbers are called *signed numbers*. If we want to describe numbers that may be positive or zero, we use the word *nonnegative*.

0°

−3°

−3° = 3 degrees below zero

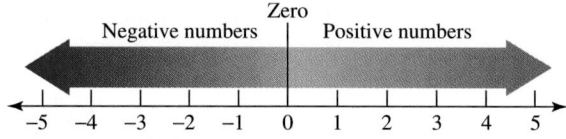

Figure 1.9

The real number line

The negative numbers are represented with a − sign (a negative sign) attached. Although the positive numbers can be represented with a positive sign, +, this sign is usually omitted. Thus, 5 means +5, 7 means +7, 13 means +13, and so on. In short, when no sign of description is attached, the number is assumed to be positive. Since zero is neither positive nor negative, it is always written without a sign of description.

The numbers shown on the number line in Figure 1.9, including the natural numbers, zero, and the negatives of the natural numbers, are part of the set of *integers*.

The integers

The set of *integers* is the infinite set
{. . . , −3, −2, −1, 0, 1, 2, 3, . . .}.

If two integers are added, subtracted, or multiplied, the result is always another integer. This, however, is not always the case with division. For example, 10 divided by 5 is the integer 2, but 5 divided by 10 is $\frac{1}{2}$, and $\frac{1}{2}$ is not an integer. To permit divisions such as $\frac{5}{10}$, we enlarge the set of integers, calling the new collection the *rational numbers*.

The rational numbers

A *rational number* is any number in the form $\frac{a}{b}$, where a and b represent integers, but where b, the integer in the denominator, is not equal to 0. Using set-builder notation, the set of rational numbers is represented by

$$\left\{ \frac{a}{b} \,\middle|\, a \text{ and } b \text{ are integers, } b \neq 0 \right\}.$$

The symbol $\neq$ is read "is not equal to." Thus, $b \neq 0$ means b is not equal to 0.

EXAMPLE 4   **Examples of Rational Numbers**

Explain why each of the following is a rational number.

a. $\frac{3}{4}$ **b.** $-\frac{3}{2}$ **c.** 5   **d.** 0.25   **e.** $-0.\overline{3}$

Solution

a. The fraction $\frac{3}{4}$ is a rational number because it is the quotient of two integers, and the denominator is not 0. The fraction $\frac{3}{4}$ is in the form a/b, where $a = 3$ and $b = 4$.

b. The fraction $-\frac{3}{2}$, which can be thought of as $\frac{-3}{2}$, is a (negative) rational number because it is the quotient (also called a ratio) of two integers. The fraction $\frac{-3}{2}$ is in the form a/b, where $a = -3$ and $b = 2$. (In Section 1.8, we will see that $-\frac{3}{2} = \frac{-3}{2} = \frac{3}{-2}$, so it is possible to consider 3 as the integer in the numerator and -2 as the integer in the denominator.)

c. The integer 5 is a rational number because it can be written as $\frac{5}{1}$ (or as $\frac{10}{2}$, $\frac{15}{3}$, etc.). Observe that every integer can be expressed with a denominator of 1 ($6 = \frac{6}{1}$; $-7 = \frac{-7}{1}$; $0 = \frac{0}{1}$) and that *every integer is a rational number*.

d. The *decimal number* 0.25 is a rational number because it can be expressed as the quotient of two integers: $0.25 = \frac{1}{4}$.

e. The repeating decimal number $-0.\overline{3}$ (meaning $-0.3333 \ldots$) is a rational number because it can be expressed as the quotient of two integers: $-0.\overline{3} = -\frac{1}{3}$. ∎

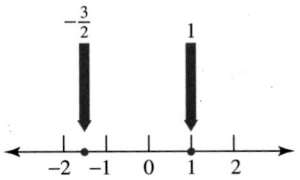

Each real number corresponds to a point on the real number line.

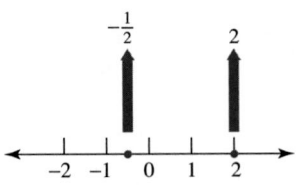

Each point on the real number line corresponds to a real number.

Figure 1.10

Plotting points on a number line

Example 4, containing examples of rational numbers, did not include a number such as $\frac{7}{0}$ because $\frac{7}{0}$ is not a rational number. By the definition of a rational number, the integer in the denominator cannot equal 0.

The rational numbers $-\frac{3}{2}$ and 1 are *graphed* on the number line in Figure 1.10. Also shown are two points that can be represented by the rational numbers $-\frac{1}{2}$ and 2.

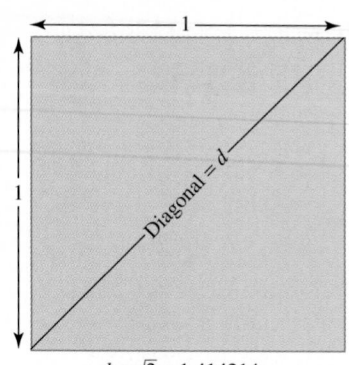

$d = \sqrt{2} \approx 1.414214$

An irrational number cannot be expressed as a fraction using integers. A square with sides each one unit long has a diagonal of length $\sqrt{2}$ ($\sqrt{2} \approx 1.414214$).

The number line also contains points that cannot be represented by rational numbers. The set of rational numbers can be shown to be the set of all repeating or terminating decimals. However, certain numbers when expressed in decimal form do not have a repeating pattern and do not terminate. These numbers are called *irrational.*

An example of an irrational number is $\sqrt{2}$ (the square root of 2). The number $\sqrt{2}$ is a number that can be multiplied by itself to obtain 2. $\sqrt{2}$ is *approximately* equal to 1.414214 because 1.414214 multiplied by itself is 2.0000012378, not 2. There is no decimal that has a repeating pattern or comes to an end that can be multiplied by itself to result in 2.

Notation

The symbol $\approx$ is read "is approximately equal to." Thus, $\sqrt{2} \approx 1.414214$ means $\sqrt{2}$ is approximately equal to 1.414214.

Here are some additional examples of numbers that when expressed as decimals neither have repeating patterns nor terminate. Each of these numbers is described below.

   a. $\sqrt{3}$ **b.** π **c.** $-\sqrt{5}$ **d.** e

a. $\sqrt{3}$ (the square root of 3): $\sqrt{3} \approx 1.732$ because 1.732 multiplied by itself is 2.999824, not precisely 3.
b. π (Greek letter pi) is the distance around a circle (its circumference) divided by the diameter of the circle. π is expressed approximately as 3.1415926535. . . . Notice that this decimal neither terminates nor has a repeating pattern, making π an irrational number.
c. $-\sqrt{5}$ is an irrational number representing the negative of the square root of 5.
d. If \$1 is invested at an interest rate of 100% for 1 year, and the number of times the interest is calculated increases infinitely (calculating the interest every trillionth of a second, every quadrillionth of a second, etc.), the amount of money accumulated at the end of the year would continue getting closer and closer to \$2.718281828459045. . . . Mathematicians represent this irrational number by the symbol e, where e is approximately equal to 2.72 ($e \approx 2.72$).

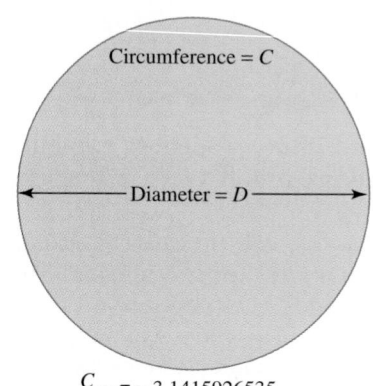

$\frac{C}{D} = \pi \approx 3.1415926535$

Since irrational numbers cannot be represented by decimals that come to an end, mathematicians use symbols such as $\sqrt{2}$, $\sqrt{3}$, π, and e to represent these numbers. However, *not all square roots are irrational.* For example, $\sqrt{25} = 5$ since 5 multiplied by itself is 25. Thus, $\sqrt{25}$ is a natural number, a whole number, an integer, and a rational number ($\sqrt{25} = \frac{5}{1}$).

All numbers that can be represented by points on the number line are called *real numbers.*

Real numbers

The set of *real numbers* is the set of all numbers that can be represented by points on the number line.

ENRICHMENT ESSAY

Pieces of Pi

The nature of the irrational number π has fascinated mathematicians for centuries. Amateur and professional mathematicians have taken up the challenge of calculating π to more and more decimal places.

The most decimal places of an approximation of π that has been calculated is 2,260,321,336 by brothers Gregory and David Chudnovsky, on their homemade supercomputer in New York City in the summer of 1991. If printed on ordinary type, the number would stretch from New York City to Los Angeles.

Pi-Scape is the Chudnovsky brothers' computer-generated image using the first million decimal digits of π, in which each digit is represented as a peak in the image.

What approximation do you obtain for π on a graphing calculator? (Press the $\boxed{\pi}$ key.) Between which two integers should you graph π on the real number line?

Pi-Scape (Reproduced courtesy of David and Gregory Chudnovsky).

Every point on the real number line corresponds to exactly one real number, and every real number corresponds to exactly one point on the real number line.

Since *irrational numbers in decimal form do not repeat or terminate,* and *rational numbers do repeat or terminate in decimal form,* an irrational number such as $\sqrt{2}$ or π cannot be expressed as the quotient of integers. Any real number is either rational or irrational, and we can think of the irrational numbers as real numbers that are not rational.

The irrational numbers

The set of *irrational numbers* is the set of all real numbers that cannot be expressed as the quotient of integers. Using set-builder notation, the set of irrational numbers is represented by

$\{x \mid x \text{ is a real number that is not rational}\}$.

The set of real numbers may be represented by the diagram shown in Figure 1.11. The figure reinforces the fact that every real number is either a rational number or an irrational number.

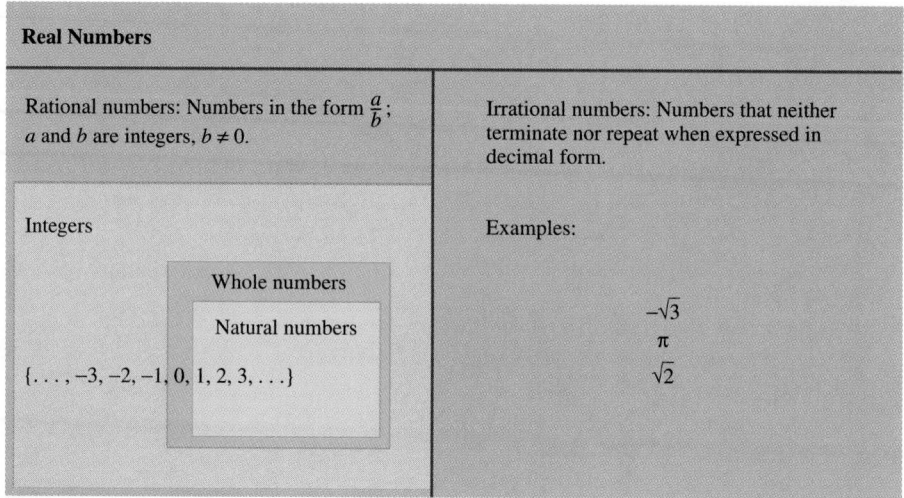

Figure 1.11
The real numbers

3 Classify numbers as belonging to one or more sets of the real numbers.

EXAMPLE 5   Classifying Real Numbers

List the numbers in the set

$$\left\{-7, -\tfrac{3}{4}, 0, 0.\overline{6}, \sqrt{5}, \pi, 6\tfrac{1}{4}, 7.3, \sqrt{81}\right\}$$

that belong to each of the sets of the real numbers:

a. Natural numbers   **d.** Rational numbers
b. Whole numbers   **e.** Irrational numbers
c. Integers   **f.** Real numbers

Solution

a. Natural numbers: The only natural number in the set is $\sqrt{81}$ since $\sqrt{81} = 9$. (9 multiplied by itself is 81.)

b. Whole numbers: The whole numbers consist of the natural numbers and 0. The elements of the set that are whole numbers are 0 and $\sqrt{81}$.

c. Integers: The integers consist of the natural numbers, 0, and the negatives of the natural numbers. The elements of the set that are integers are $\sqrt{81}$, 0, and -7.

d. Rational numbers: All numbers in the set that can be expressed as the quotient of two integers are rational numbers. The rational numbers are $-7 \left(-7 = -\tfrac{7}{1}\right)$, $-\tfrac{3}{4}$, $0 \left(0 = \tfrac{0}{1}\right)$, $0.\overline{6} \left(0.\overline{6} = 0.6666 \ldots = \tfrac{2}{3}\right)$, $6\tfrac{1}{4} \left(6\tfrac{1}{4} = \tfrac{25}{4}\right)$, $7.3 \left(7.3 = 7\tfrac{3}{10} = \tfrac{73}{10}\right)$, and $\sqrt{81} \left(\sqrt{81} = \tfrac{9}{1}\right)$.

e. Irrational numbers: The irrational numbers in the set are $\sqrt{5}$ $\left(\sqrt{5} \approx 2.236\right)$ and π $\left(\pi \approx 3.14\right)$. Both $\sqrt{5}$ and π are only approximately equal to 2.236 and 3.14, respectively. In decimal form, $\sqrt{5}$ and π neither terminate nor have repeating patterns.

f. Real numbers: All the numbers in the set are real numbers.

4 Understand and use
inequality symbols.

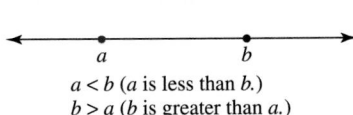

$a < b$ (a is less than b.)
$b > a$ (b is greater than a.)

Ordering Real Numbers

The real number line gives us a way of comparing real numbers. For any two real numbers a and b, a *is less than* b if a is to the left of b on the real number line. The "less than" comparison is shown by the *inequality symbol* $<$. Of course, if a is less than b then, equivalently, b is greater than a, meaning that b lies to the right of a on the number line. The "greater than" comparison is shown by the *inequality symbol* $>$.

EXAMPLE 6 **Ordering Real Numbers Using the Number Line**

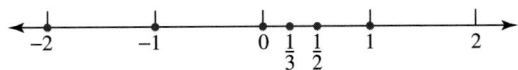

Use the graphs of the numbers shown on this number line to place the correct inequality symbol ($<$ or $>$) in the box.

a. $-2 \ \square \ 0$ **b.** $\frac{1}{3} \ \square \ \frac{1}{2}$ **c.** $-2 \ \square \ 1$

$0 \ \square \ -2$ $\frac{1}{2} \ \square \ \frac{1}{3}$ $1 \ \square \ -2$

Solution

a. From the number line, we see that

$$-2 \text{ is to the left of } 0 \quad \text{so} \quad -2 < 0 \qquad {\scriptstyle -2 \text{ is less than } 0.}$$
$$\text{and} \quad 0 > -2 \qquad {\scriptstyle 0 \text{ is greater than } -2.}$$

The inequality symbol points to the smaller number, which is -2.

b. $\frac{1}{3}$ is to the left of $\frac{1}{2}$ so $\quad \frac{1}{3} < \frac{1}{2} \quad {\scriptstyle \frac{1}{3} \text{ is less than } \frac{1}{2}.}$
$$\text{and} \quad \frac{1}{2} > \frac{1}{3} \quad {\scriptstyle \frac{1}{2} \text{ is greater than } \frac{1}{3}.}$$

Again, the inequality symbol points to the smaller number, which is $\frac{1}{3}$.

c. -2 is to the left of 1 so $\quad -2 < 1 \quad {\scriptstyle -2 \text{ is less than } 1.}$
$$\text{and} \quad 1 > -2 \quad {\scriptstyle 1 \text{ is greater than } -2.}$$

The symbols $<$ and $>$ may be combined with an equal sign, as shown in the table.

Symbols	Meaning	Examples	
$a \leqslant b$	a is less than or equal to b.	$3 \leqslant 7$	Because $3 < 7$
		$7 \leqslant 7$	Because $7 = 7$
$b \geqslant a$	b is greater than or equal to a.	$7 \geqslant 3$	Because $7 > 3$
		$-5 \geqslant -5$	Because $-5 = -5$

When using the symbol ≤ (is less than or equal to), if either the < part or the = part is true, then the inequality ≤ is true. Consequently, $3 \leq 7$ is true because $3 < 7$, and $7 \leq 7$ is true because $7 = 7$. However, it is not true that $9 \leq 7$ because neither $9 < 7$ nor $9 = 7$ is true. The same remarks apply to ≥.

5 Find the opposite (additive inverse) and the absolute value of a real number.

Opposites and Absolute Value

Opposites are pairs of real numbers that are the same distance from, but on opposite sides of, zero on the number line. For example, -3 is the opposite of 3, and 5 is the opposite of -5.

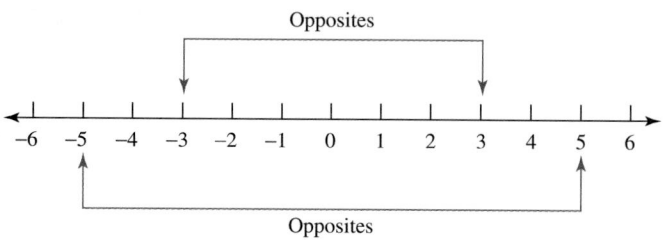

Opposites are also called *additive inverses.*

> **Additive inverse (opposite)**
>
> The *additive inverse* or *opposite* of a real number x is the number that is the same distance from 0 on the number line as x, but on the opposite side of 0. The additive inverse of 0 is 0 itself. Other additive inverses or opposites come in pairs.

The opposite (additive inverse) of a number is indicated by writing a dash in front of the number. Since a dash also indicates that a number is negative, when it is used in front of parentheses or a variable, it should be read as "opposite." For example,

$$-(4) = -4$$
↑
The opposite

The opposite of 4 is negative 4.
The additive inverse of 4 is negative 4.

$$-(0) = 0$$
↑
The opposite

The opposite of 0 is 0.
The additive inverse of 0 is 0.

$$-(-3) = 3$$
↑
The opposite

The opposite of negative 3 is 3.
The additive inverse of negative 3 is 3.

The idea that $-(-3) = 3$ also tells us that $-(-7) = 7$, $-(-\pi) = \pi$, and $-(-\frac{2}{3}) = \frac{2}{3}$ and can be generalized as follows.

The double negative rule

If x represents any real number, then

$$-(-x) = x$$ The opposite or additive inverse of negative x is x.

Opposites (additive inverses) are pairs of numbers that are the same distance from 0 on the number line. The distance between a real number x and 0 on the number line is given a special name, called the *absolute value* of x. Thus, a number and its opposite have the same absolute value.

Absolute value

The *absolute value* of a real number x, denoted by $|x|$, is the distance between the number x and 0 on the number line, and this distance is always taken to be positive.

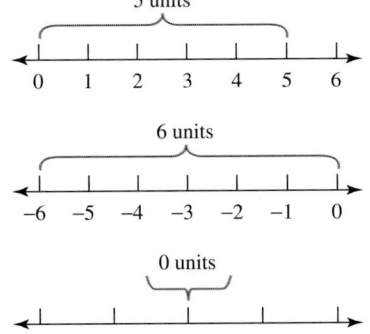

5 units

6 units

0 units

For example,

$|5| = 5$ The absolute value of 5 is 5 because the distance between 5 and 0 on the number line is 5.

$|-6| = 6$ The absolute value of negative 6 is 6 because the distance between -6 and 0 on the number line is 6.

$|0| = 0$ The absolute value of 0 is 0 because 0 is 0 units from 0 on the number line.

Observe that the absolute value of a real number is either positive or zero. Zero is the only real number whose absolute value is 0 ($|0| = 0$). *The absolute value of a real number is never negative.*

EXAMPLE 7   Finding Absolute Values

Simplify by removing the absolute value symbols:

a. $|4|$ **b.** $|-4|$ **c.** $\left|\frac{3}{5}\right|$ **d.** $|-\sqrt{2}|$ **e.** $-|9|$ **f.** $-|-9|$

Solution

a. $|4| = 4$ The absolute value of 4 is 4 because the distance between 4 and 0 is 4.

b. $|-4| = 4$ The absolute value of -4 is 4 because the distance between -4 and 0 is 4. Notice that $|4| = |-4|$. A number and its opposite have the same absolute value.

c. $\left|\frac{3}{5}\right| = \frac{3}{5}$ The absolute value of $\frac{3}{5}$ is $\frac{3}{5}$ because the distance between $\frac{3}{5}$ and 0 is $\frac{3}{5}$.

d. $|-\sqrt{2}| = \sqrt{2}$ The absolute value of $-\sqrt{2}$ is $\sqrt{2}$ because the distance between $-\sqrt{2}$ and 0 is $\sqrt{2}$, or approximately 1.4 units.

e. $-|9| = -(9)$ Use the fact that $|9| = 9$. Bring over the $-$ sign.
    $= -9$ The opposite of 9 is negative 9.

f. $-|-9| = -(9)$ Use the fact that $|-9| = 9$. Bring over the $-$ sign.
    $= -9$ The opposite of 9 is negative 9.

PROBLEM SET 1.2

Practice Problems

Use the roster method to write each set in Problems 1–18.

1. $\{x \mid x$ is a natural number that is less than 4$\}$.

2. $\{x \mid x$ is a natural number that is less than 6$\}$

3. $\{x \mid x$ is a whole number that is less than or equal to 5$\}$

4. $\{x \mid x$ is a whole number that is less than or equal to 4$\}$

5. $\{x \mid x$ is an integer that is greater than $-3\}$

6. $\{x \mid x$ is an integer that is greater than $-4\}$

7. $\{x \mid x$ is an integer that is greater than or equal to $-6\}$

8. $\{x \mid x$ is an integer that is greater than or equal to $-5\}$

9. $\{x \mid x$ is the opposite of $-7\}$

10. $\{x \mid x$ is the opposite of $-9\}$

11. $\{x \mid x$ is the additive inverse of $\frac{3}{4}\}$

12. $\{x \mid x$ is the additive inverse of $\frac{4}{5}\}$

13. $\{x \mid x$ is a whole number but not a natural number$\}$

14. $\{x \mid x$ is its own additive inverse$\}$

15. $\left\{ \frac{a}{b} \,\middle|\, a = 2 \text{ and } b = 2 \text{ or } 3 \right\}$

16. $\left\{ \frac{a}{b} \,\middle|\, a = 4 \text{ and } b = 4 \text{ or } 5 \right\}$

17. $\{x \mid x$ is the irrational number representing the circumference of a circle divided by its diameter$\}$

18. $\{x \mid \sqrt{x}$ is irrational and x is a natural number between 1 and 5, inclusively$\}$

In Problems 19–22, list all numbers from the given set that are **a.** *Natural numbers* **b.** *Whole numbers* **c.** *Integers* **d.** *Rational numbers* **e.** *Irrational numbers* **f.** *Real numbers.*

19. $\{-9, -\frac{4}{5}, 0, 0.25, \sqrt{3}, e, 5\frac{1}{8}, 9.2, \sqrt{100}\}$

20. $\{-11, -\frac{5}{6}, 0, 0.75, \sqrt{5}, \pi, 7\frac{2}{3}, \sqrt{64}\}$

21. $\{-7, -0.\overline{6}, 0, \sqrt{49}, \sqrt{50}\}$

22. $\{-5, -0.\overline{3}, 0, \sqrt{2}, \sqrt{4}\}$

In Problems 23–40, graph each real number as a point on the real number line and then place the correct inequality symbol ($<$ or $>$) between the two numbers.

23. $\frac{1}{2} \,\square\, 2$

24. $4 \,\square\, -3$

25. $3 \,\square\, -\frac{5}{2}$

26. $3 \,\square\, \frac{3}{2}$

27. $-4 \,\square\, -6$

28. $-\frac{5}{2} \,\square\, -\frac{5}{3}$

29. $-2.5 \,\square\, 1.5$

30. $-1.25 \,\square\, -0.5$

31. $-\frac{3}{4} \,\square\, -\frac{5}{4}$

32. $0 \,\square\, -\frac{1}{2}$

33. $-4.5 \,\square\, 3$

34. $-5.5 \,\square\, 2.5$

35. $\sqrt{2} \,\square\, 1.5$

36. $\sqrt{3} \,\square\, 2$

37. $0.3 \,\square\, 0.3$

38. $0.6 \,\square\, 0.\overline{6}$

39. $-\pi \,\square\, -3.5$

40. $-\frac{\pi}{2} \,\square\, -2.3$

Find the opposite (the additive inverse) of the given number in Problems 41–48.

41. 6

42. 3

43. -7

44. -9

45. $\frac{2}{3}$

46. $\frac{1}{2}$

47. $-\sqrt{5}$

48. $-\sqrt{7}$

Find the absolute value of the numbers listed in Problems 49–56.

49. $|6|$

50. $|3|$

51. $|-7|$

52. $|-9|$

53. $\left|\frac{2}{3}\right|$

54. $\left|\frac{1}{2}\right|$

55. $|-\sqrt{13}|$

56. $|-\sqrt{17}|$

Application Problems

Write a positive or negative number that is the opposite of each situation in Problems 57–64. Then tell what the number represents.

57. Meteorology: 20° below zero

58. Navigation: 65 feet above sea level

59. Health: A gain of 8.5 pounds

60. Economics: A loss of $12,500.00

61. Banking: A withdrawal of $3000.00

62. Physics: An automobile decelerating at a rate of 3 meters per second each second.

63. Economics: A budget deficit of 3.7 billion dollars

64. Football: A 14-yard loss

True–False Critical Thinking Problems

65. Which one of the following statements is true?
   a. Every rational number is an integer.
   b. Some whole numbers are not integers.
   c. Some rational numbers are not positive.
   d. Irrational numbers cannot be negative.

66. Which one of the following statements is true?
   a. $\sqrt{36}$ is an irrational number.
   b. Some real numbers are not rational numbers.
   c. Some integers are not rational numbers.
   d. All whole numbers are positive.

67. Which one of the following statements is true?
   a. Zero is not a rational number.
   b. Negative nine is greater than negative two.
   c. 26 is not an element of $\{1, 2, 3, 4, 5, \ldots\}$.
   d. $\{x \mid x$ is a whole number less than $\frac{7}{3}\}$ can be written as $\{0, 1, 2\}$.

68. Which one of the following statements is true?
   a. The number 9,625,189,723,516 is not a natural number.
   b. Negative nine thousand is greater than negative one.
   c. The additive inverse of every real number other than zero is found by changing the sign of the number.

d. $\{x \mid x$ is a whole number greater than $\frac{1}{2}\}$ can be written as $\{1, 2, 3, 4, 5\}$.

69. Which one of the following statements is true?
   a. $\pi = \frac{22}{7}$
   b. The absolute value of -4 is greater than 3.
   c. The absolute value of -3 is greater than the absolute value of -7.
   d. The rational number $-\frac{5}{2}$ is greater than the rational number $-\frac{9}{4}$.

70. Which one of the following statements is true?
   a. The absolute value of -7 is greater than the absolute value of -12.
   b. The absolute value of any real number is always positive.
   c. 18,326 is not an element of $\{1, 2, 3, 4, \ldots\}$.
   d. If we add the absolute values of -7 and -15, we get 22.

71. Which one of the following statements is false?
   a. $|6| = |-6|$
   b. $|-5| < |-6|$
   c. $|0| > |-4|$
   d. $7 > -(-2)$

Technology Problems

In Problems 72–75, use a calculator to find a decimal approximation for each irrational number, correct to three decimal places. Between which two integers should you graph each of these numbers on the real number line?

72. $\sqrt{3}$ **73.** $-\sqrt{12}$ **74.** $1 - \sqrt{2}$ **75.** $2 - 3\sqrt{5}$

76. The ancient Greeks used 22/7 as an estimate for π. Use your calculator to compare decimal approximations, to four decimal places, for 22/7 and π.

Writing in Mathematics

77. When is the additive inverse of a number equal to the absolute value of the number?

78. When is the additive inverse of a number not equal to the absolute value of the number?

79. Give an example of an everyday situation that can be
   a. described using integers but not by using whole numbers.
   b. described using rational numbers but not by using integers.

80. Describe the difference between a rational number and an irrational number.

81. Describe what is meant by the absolute value of a number. Is absolute value always positive?

82. Describe what you think the "perfect" algebra professor should do in class, including those things that would be most helpful to you.

Critical Thinking Problems

Give three examples of numbers that are elements and three that are not elements of each set in Problems 83–86.

83. $\{x \mid x$ is a positive real number but not an integer$\}$

84. $\{x \mid x$ is a real number but not a rational number$\}$

85. $\{x \mid x$ is a rational number but not an integer$\}$

86. $\{x \mid x$ is a real number but not a whole number$\}$

Group Activity Problem

87. As you discovered by working Problems 65–70, selecting a true statement from a list of statements is not
an easy task, but it does cause you to do something
that this book will constantly encourage. Here is the
activity that we encourage in secret code: Read across
the two rows at the top of the next column.

$(20, 18)$ $(-8, -12)$ $(0, 9)$ $(-14, -17)$

$(0, 11)$ $(-17, 9)$ $(-16, 14)$ $(-22, 7)$

Here is the decoder. Use it to find the activity.

First Decoding	Second Decoding			
Use the greater of the two numbers in each pair.	0 = blank space	1 = A	2 = B	3 = C
	4 = D 5 = E	6 = F	7 = G	8 = H
If the greater number is	9 = I 10 = J	11 = K	12 = L	13 = M
negative, then use its absolute	14 = N 15 = O	16 = P	17 = Q	18 = R
value.	19 = S 20 = T	21 = U	22 = V	23 = W
	24 = X 25 = Y	26 = Z		

Review Problems

*From here on, each problem set will contain three review problems. It is essential to review previously covered topics to im-
prove your understanding of the topics and to help you maintain your mastery of the material.*

In Problems 88–90, perform the indicated operations, and simplify if possible.

88. $\frac{1}{4} \div \frac{1}{2}$ **89.** $\frac{3}{4} - \frac{1}{5}$ **90.** $\frac{8}{5} \cdot \frac{11}{12}$

S E C T I O N   I . 3

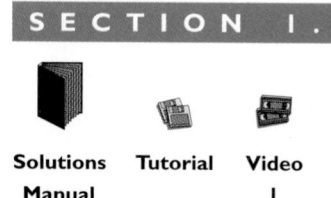

Solutions   Tutorial   Video
Manual   I

Graphing and Ordered Pairs

Objectives

1 Interpret information given by circle graphs.
2 Interpret information given by bar graphs.
3 Interpret information given by line graphs.
4 Plot ordered pairs in the rectangular coordinate system.
5 Find coordinates of points in the rectangular coordinate system.
6 Graph relationships between quantities.

Magazines and newspapers often display information using circle, bar, and
line graphs. In this section, we will discuss how to interpret these graphs and
use them to solve problems. We also introduce graphs that use a coordinate
system, a subject that we will examine in more detail in Chapter 4.

I Interpret information given
by circle graphs.

Problem Solving with Graphs

Circle graphs, also called *pie charts,* display information that often shows
what percent of a whole each item in a group represents. Our first example
shows a circle divided into pieces called *sectors.* The area of each sector is the
respective percentage of the area of the entire circle.

EXAMPLE I   **Displaying Information Using a Circle Graph**

The circle graph in Figure 1.12 shows religious affiliation of people in the
United States in 1992. If the United States population at that time was approximately 255 million, how many people were Roman Catholic?

Religious Affiliation

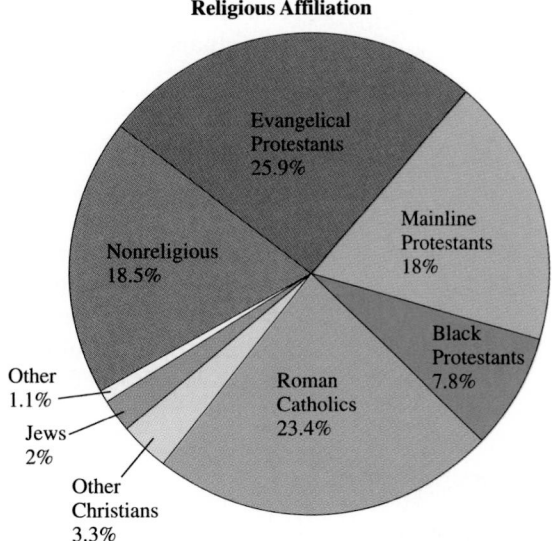

Figure 1.12
Source: *National Survey of Religion and Politics 1992*, University of Akron Survey Research Center

Study tip

To convert from percent form to decimal form, move the decimal point two places to the left. For example,

23.4% = 0.234.

Where NEA money is going in 1995, in millions of dollars

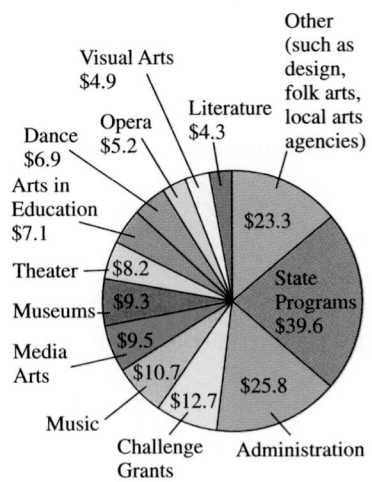

Figure 1.13
Source: NEA

Solution

The circle graph indicates that 23.4% of the population was Roman Catholic. In algebra, we use variables to represent numbers, so let's use the variable R to represent the number of Roman Catholics.

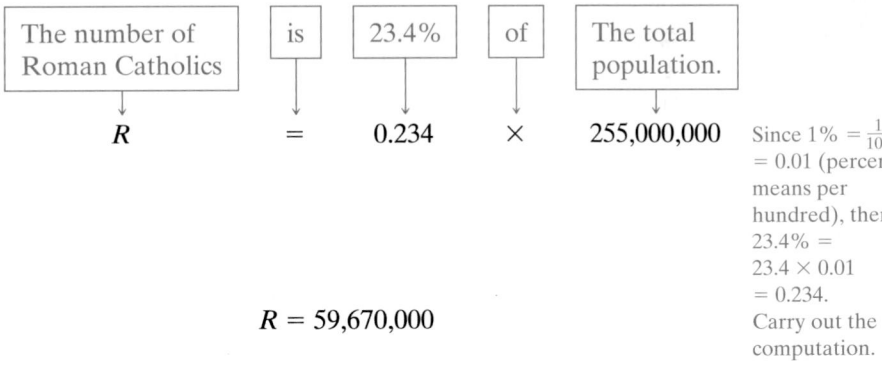

| The number of Roman Catholics | is | 23.4% | of | The total population. |

$$R = 0.234 \times 255{,}000{,}000$$

Since $1\% = \frac{1}{100} = 0.01$ (percent means per hundred), then $23.4\% = 23.4 \times 0.01 = 0.234$. Carry out the computation.

$$R = 59{,}670{,}000$$

In 1992, there were approximately 59,670,000 Roman Catholics in the United States. ■

In our next example, each sector of the circle graph contains a number rather than a percent. The basis for the graph is still to write the number in each category as a percent of the total. Let's see precisely what this involves.

EXAMPLE 2 **Using a Circle Graph**

The circle graph in Figure 1.13 shows where the National Endowment for the Arts (NEA) money went in 1995.

a. What is the meaning of the sum of the amounts in the 13 sectors?
b. What percent of the total budget went to arts in education?

c. How much money did the NEA distribute to organizations and individuals?

Solution

a. The sum of the amounts in the 13 sectors is the total budget for the NEA. This total is $167.5 million. (Verify this figure by carrying out the computation.)

b. The first step in constructing a circle graph is to divide each entry by the total of the entries and express this fraction as a percent. For arts in education, we divide the amount $7.1 million that goes to this category by the total budget $167.5 million, then change the decimal answer to an equivalent percent. We proceed as follows:

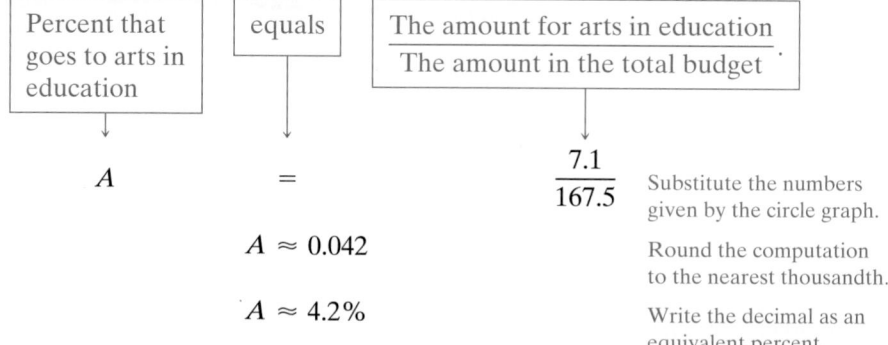

| Percent that goes to arts in education | equals | $\dfrac{\text{The amount for arts in education}}{\text{The amount in the total budget}}$. |

$$A \qquad = \qquad \frac{7.1}{167.5} \qquad \text{Substitute the numbers given by the circle graph.}$$

$$A \approx 0.042 \qquad \text{Round the computation to the nearest thousandth.}$$

$$A \approx 4.2\% \qquad \text{Write the decimal as an equivalent percent.}$$

Approximately 4.2% of the total budget went to arts in education.

c. The circle graph indicates that $25.8 million was used for administrative purposes. The remaining money in the NEA budget was distributed to organizations and individuals.

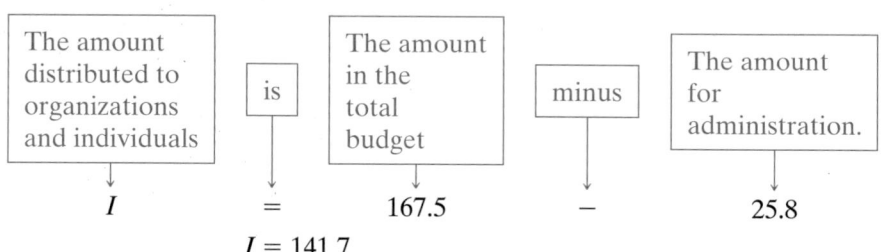

| The amount distributed to organizations and individuals | is | The amount in the total budget | minus | The amount for administration. |

$$I \qquad = \qquad 167.5 \qquad - \qquad 25.8$$

$$I = 141.7$$

In 1995 the NEA appropriated $141.7 million to organizations and individuals. ∎

Study tip

Since approximately 4.2% of the total budget is for arts and education, the sector should be about 4.2% of the area of the circle. The entire circle contains 360°, so the sector for arts and entertainment contains

$$360° \cdot 0.042 \approx 15°.$$

This computation can be done for each item. Once the number of degrees for each category is known, a protractor is used to construct the circle graph.

2 Interpret information given by bar graphs.

Bar Graphs

Bar graphs are convenient for showing comparisons among items. The bars may be either horizontal or vertical, and they are used to show the amount of each item.

EXAMPLE 3   **Using a Bar Graph**

The bar graph in Figure 1.14 shows the percentage of households in the United States in 1995 with various kinds of electronics.

Home Electronics
1995 Percentage of Homes With:

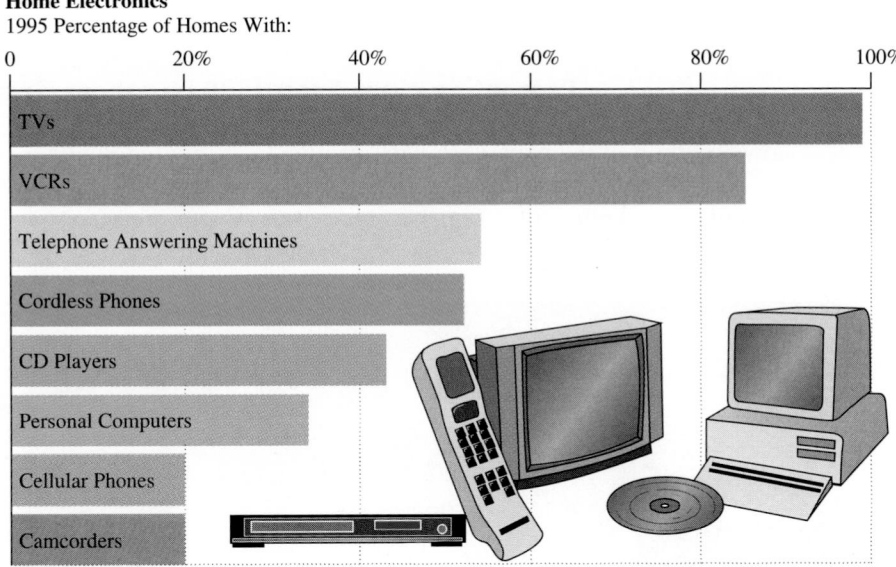

Figure 1.14
Source: EIA

a. Estimate the percentage of 1995 households with CD players.
b. What home electronics are owned by fewer than 40% of American households?

Solution

a. We look at the right edge of the bar representing CD players and then read the percent scale. The bar extends to 40% plus approximately $\frac{1}{4}$ of the distance between the 40% and 60% lines. Since the distance between 40% and 60% is 20%, $\frac{1}{4}$ of 20% is 5%. Thus, 40% + 5%, or 45%, of the 1995 households owned CD players is a reasonable estimate.

b. We locate the 40% mark on the percent scale and then look for bars ending before 40%. There are three such bars, representing personal computers, cellular phones, and camcorders. Thus, fewer than 40% of American households in 1995 owned personal computers, cellular phones, and camcorders. ◼

3 Interpret information given by line graphs.

Line Graphs

Line graphs are often used to illustrate trends over time. Some measure of time, such as months or years, frequently appears on its horizontal axis and amounts are generally listed on the vertical axis. Points are drawn to represent the given information. The graph is formed by connecting the points with line segments.

EXAMPLE 4 **Using a Line Graph**

The line graph in Figure 1.15 illustrates the high school dropout rate for three groups of young Americans. The horizontal axis measures time from

ENRICHMENT ESSAY

Presenting More Than 2000 Numbers Graphically

The following graph of the New York City weather summary for 1980 contains 2200 numbers. The graph organizes a large collection of numbers, makes comparisons between different aspects of the data, and tells a story. Describe specifically how the graph accomplishes each of these things.

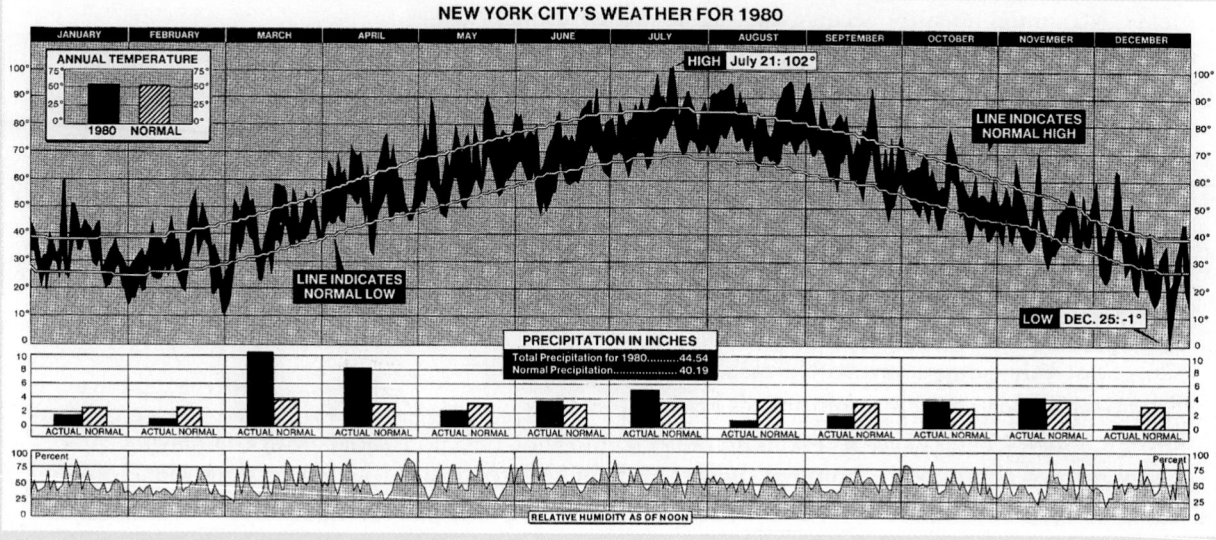

From *The New York Times*, January 11, 1981, p. 32.

Percent of High School Dropouts Among 16- to 24-Year-Olds by Race/Ethnicity, 1972–1992

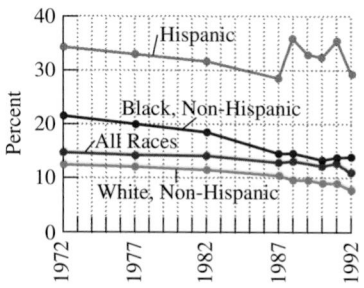

Figure 1.15

Source: National Center for Education Statistics

1972 through 1992. The vertical axis denotes the percent of high school dropouts.

a. In what year was the dropout rate for Hispanics at a minimum? What was the dropout rate for that year?

b. In what year was the dropout rate for black, non-Hispanics approximately 20%?

c. Write one statement describing the trends of the dropout rates of the four groups conveyed by the graph.

Solution

a. The lowest point on the line graph for Hispanics, shown in Figure 1.16, occurs above the number 1987. The corresponding number on the vertical scale, approximately $\frac{4}{5}$ of the distance between 20 and 30, is about 28. The dropout rate for Hispanics was at a minimum in 1987, and the rate for that year was approximately 28%.

b. To find the year the dropout rate was 20%, we locate 20 on the vertical scale and then move right to the line graph for black, non-Hispanics (see Figure 1.17). At that point we move down to the horizontal scale and read the number 1977. Thus, in 1977 the dropout rate for black, non-Hispanics was approximately 20%.

c. Dropout rates for black, non-Hispanics are above those for white, non-Hispanics, and both are lower than those for Hispanics. ■

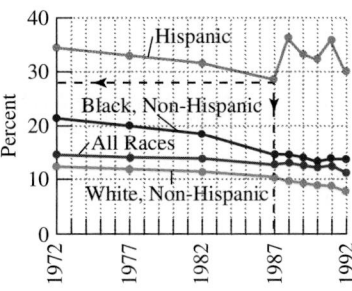

Figure 1.16
Source: National Center for Education Statistics

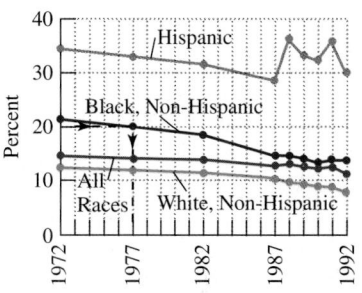

Figure 1.17
Source: National Center for Education Statistics

Points and Ordered Pairs

In Section 1.2 we saw that real numbers can be represented by points on a number line. In a similar way, we can represent pairs of real numbers by points in a plane. The pairs are called *ordered pairs* because the order in which the numbers appear is important. The plane is called the *rectangular,* or *Cartesian, coordinate system,* named for its developer, the French mathematician and philosopher René Descartes (1596–1650).

Points are identified in the rectangular coordinate system in much the same way that any point on the Earth's surface is determined by its latitude and longitude (Figure 1.18). A finer grid system such as the one shown on the right is used in weather prediction.

René Descartes' work advanced several areas of science.

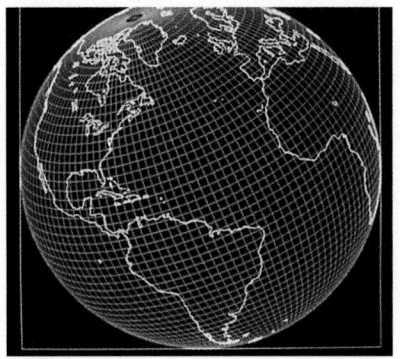

Figure 1.18
Source: National Center for Atmospheric Research/University Corporation for Atmospheric Research/National Science Foundation.

4 Plot ordered pairs in the rectangular coordinate system.

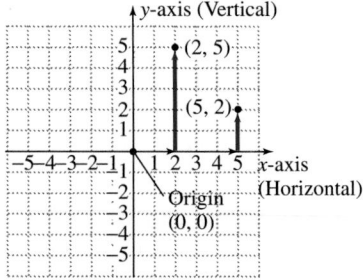

Figure 1.19

Plotting points in the rectangular coordinate system

The Cartesian system, shown in Figure 1.19, is a grid system. To graph pairs of numbers in the system, two perpendicular number lines called *axes* (singular, *axis*) are used. The axes intersect at a point called the *origin*. The horizontal axis is called the *x-axis* and the vertical axis is called the *y-axis*. Arrows on the axes show the positive directions.

Consider the pair (2, 5). The first number, 2, is called the *x-coordinate* and the second number, 5, is called the *y-coordinate*. To *plot* (or locate) (2, 5), we begin at the origin and move horizontally to the 2. Then we move vertically up 5 units, indicating the final location with a dot. The phrase "the point corresponding to the ordered pair (2, 5)" is usually abbreviated "the point (2, 5)."

Notice that we used the phrase *ordered pair*, since *order is important*. To plot (5, 2), we move horizontally 5 units from the origin and then vertically up 2 units. Figure 1.19 shows that (2, 5) and (5, 2) give different points. This is why they are called ordered pairs: The order in which the coordinates appear makes a difference.

The rectangular coordinate system

1. A rectangular coordinate system is formed by placing two number lines at right angles. Each line is called a *coordinate axis*.
2. The horizontal number line is called the *x-axis*.
3. The vertical number line is called the *y-axis*.
4. The intersection of the axes is called the *origin*.
5. The four regions formed by the intersection of the axes are called *quadrants*. These quad-

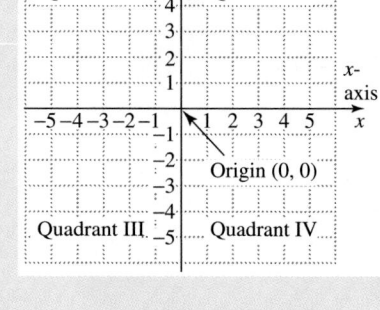

rants are numbered counterclockwise, starting with the upper right. The points located on the axes are not in any quadrant.

EXAMPLE 5 **Plotting Points in a Rectangular Coordinate System**

Plot the ordered pairs: (2, 3), (−2, 3), (−2, −3), (2, −3), (2, 0), (0, 1), (−2, 0), (0, −3), and (0, 0)

Solution

See Figure 1.20. We plot the points in the following way:

(2, 3): 2 units right, 3 units up (in quadrant I)
(−2, 3): 2 units left, 3 units up (in quadrant II)
(−2, −3): 2 units left, 3 units down (in quadrant III)
(2, −3): 2 units right, 3 units down (in quadrant IV)

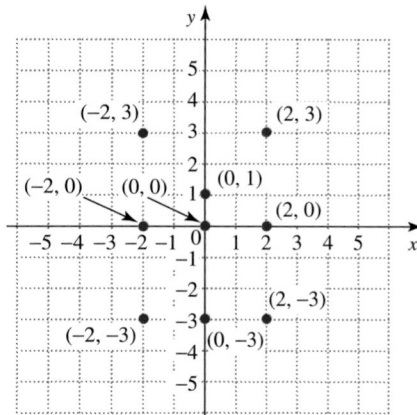

Figure 1.20

$(2, 0)$: 2 units right, 0 units up or down (on the *x*-axis)
$(0, 1)$: 0 units right or left, 1 unit up (on the *y*-axis)
$(-2, 0)$: 2 units left, 0 units up or down (on the *x*-axis)
$(0, -3)$: 0 units right or left, 3 units down (on the *y*-axis)
$(0, 0)$: 0 units right or left, 0 units up or down (at the origin) ■

5 Find coordinates of points in the rectangular coordinate system.

In the rectangular coordinate system, each ordered pair corresponds to exactly one point. Example 6 illustrates that each point in the plane corresponds to exactly one ordered pair.

EXAMPLE 6 **Finding Coordinates of Points**

Determine the coordinates for the points shown in Figure 1.21.

Solution

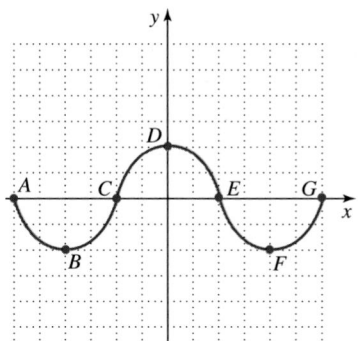

Figure 1.21

Point	Position	Coordinates
A	6 units left, 0 units up or down	$(-6, 0)$
B	4 units left, 2 units down	$(-4, -2)$
C	2 units left, 0 units up or down	$(-2, 0)$
D	0 units right or left, 2 units up	$(0, 2)$
E	2 units right, 0 units up or down	$(2, 0)$
F	4 units right, 2 units down	$(4, -2)$
G	6 units right, 0 units up or down	$(6, 0)$

■

6 Graph relationships between quantities.

The rectangular coordinate system lets us visualize relationships between two quantities, as shown in the next example.

EXAMPLE 7 **An Application of the Rectangular Coordinate System**

An object is thrown directly upward from the ground at a speed of 64 feet per second. The table gives the object's distance above the ground at various times.

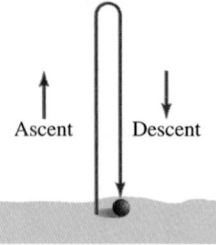

Ascent   Descent

Throwing an object upward
from the ground

Time (seconds)	Distance above Ground (feet)	(Time, Distance) Ordered Pair
0	0	(0, 0)
1	48	(1, 48)
2	64	(2, 64)
3	48	(3, 48)
4	0	(4, 0)

Plot the five ordered pairs. What do they indicate visually?

Solution

Since the values of time and distance are nonnegative, we need only use the portion of the rectangular coordinate system containing the first quadrant. Each (time, distance) ordered pair represents a point, which we can plot using the horizontal axis for time and the vertical axis for distance.

Since the values for distance get as large as 64, it is impractical to count by 1s along the vertical axis. In Figure 1.22 the vertical axis is labeled by counting by 4s (4, 8, 12, 16, etc.) so that we can plot all the pairs listed in the given table.

The five ordered pairs are plotted and labeled in Figure 1.22. The points indicate visually that the object gains height up to 2 seconds and then begins to fall back to the ground. It hits the ground after 4 seconds. ∎

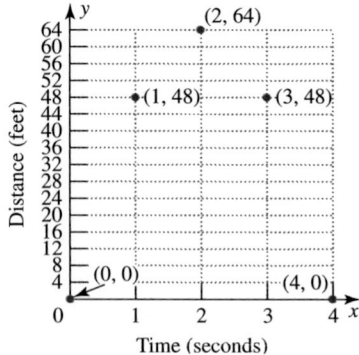

Figure 1.22

Representing an object's height
over time as points

EXAMPLE 8   **An Application of the Rectangular Coordinate System**

A small cruising ship that can hold up to 50 people provides two-day excursions for groups of 34 or more. If the group contains 34 or fewer people, each person pays $60. For larger groups, the cost per person is reduced by $1 for each person in excess of 34. The table shows some possible incomes for the owners of the ship.

Number of People on the Cruise	Number of People Greater Than 34	Cost per Person	Income = Number of People Times Cost per Person
26	0	$60	26 · $60 = $1560
34	0	$60	34 · $60 = $2040
35	1	$60 − $1 = $59	35 · $59 = $2065
40	6	$60 − $6 = $54	40 · $54 = $2160
45	11	$60 − $11 = $49	45 · $49 = $2205

Since the income in the final column of the table is increasing, one of the owners believes that the more people on the cruise—up to the 50 that the boat will hold—the greater the income will be. However, the other owner continues the computations and graphs a number of points in the rectangular system based upon the ordered pairs using data in the second and fourth columns of the preceding table.

Let the x-coordinate be the number of people greater than 34 and let the y-coordinate be income. The graph of these ordered pairs is shown in Figure 1.23. What does this graph indicate in practical terms?

Solution

The graph indicates that the income will increase only up to a point, reach a maximum, and then begin to decrease. This can be verified with some additional computations.

Number of People on the Cruise	x Number of People Greater Than 34	Cost per Person	y Income = Number of People Times Cost per Person
46	12	$60 − $12 = $48	46 · $48 = $2208
47	13	$60 − $13 = $47	47 · $47 = $2209
			↑ Maximum Income
48	14	$60 − $14 = $46	48 · $46 = $2208
49	15	$60 − $15 = $45	49 · $45 = $2205
50	16	$60 − $16 = $44	50 · $44 = $2200

It appears that income will reach a maximum with 47 people on board (13 people in excess of 34). The maximum income is $2209. This is illustrated in Figure 1.24. ■

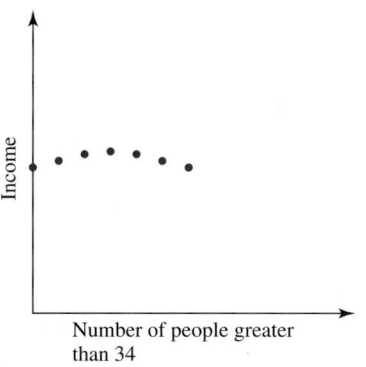

Figure 1.23

Income depends on the number of people on the cruise

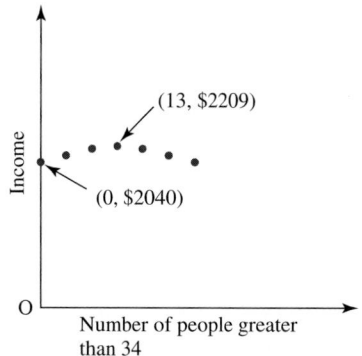

Figure 1.24

Showing the maximum income on a graph

PROBLEM SET 1.3

Practice and Application Problems

1. Use the circle graph to answer the following questions.
    a. If the 1995 world population was approximately 5,720,000,000, how many more people lived in Europe than in North America?
    b. What percent of the 1995 world population did not live in Africa? Describe two methods for obtaining this percent. Which method is faster?
    c. Replace the percents in the seven sectors of the graph using population amounts.
    d. According to the graph, can we say that in 1995 Asia was the most densely populated region in the world? Explain.
    e. According to United Nations estimates, world population will reach 10 billion by 2050. Can we estimate the population of North America in 2050 by using the circle graph and taking 5% of 10 billion? Explain.

Share of U.S. Population
1990 and 2050 (Projected) Percentages

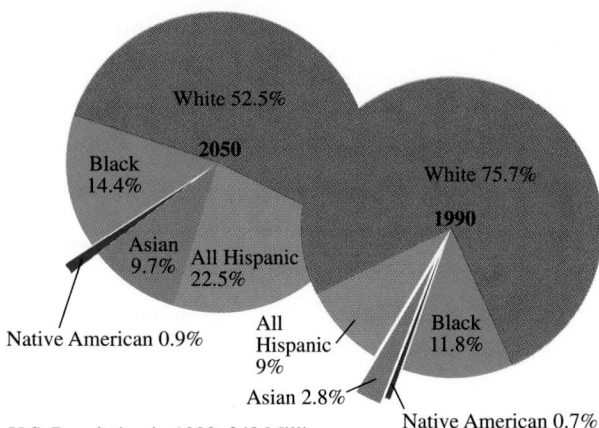

White 52.5%

2050

Black 14.4%

White 75.7%

1990

Asian 9.7%   All Hispanic 22.5%

Native American 0.9%

All Hispanic 9%

Black 11.8%

Asian 2.8%

Native American 0.7%

U.S. Population in 1990: 249 Million
Projected Population for 2050: 392 Million

Source: U.S. Bureau of the Census

Where People Live
Shares of the World Population
1995 Percentages

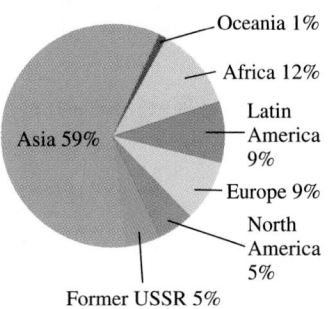

Oceania 1%

Africa 12%

Latin America 9%

Asia 59%

Europe 9%

North America 5%

Former USSR 5%

Source: Population Reference Bureau

2. Use the circle graphs to answer the following questions.
    a. How many more Hispanics will there be in 2050 than 1990?
    b. From the graphs alone (without the 1990 population and the projected 2050 population), is it correct to say that there will be fewer native Americans in 2050 than in 1990? Explain.
    c. Redraw the circle graph for 1990 using population estimates rather than percents.
    d. Write one statement summarizing the information conveyed by the graphs.

3. The circle graph below shows the U.S. population (in millions) in 11 different age groups.

U.S. Population by Age Groups
(in Millions)

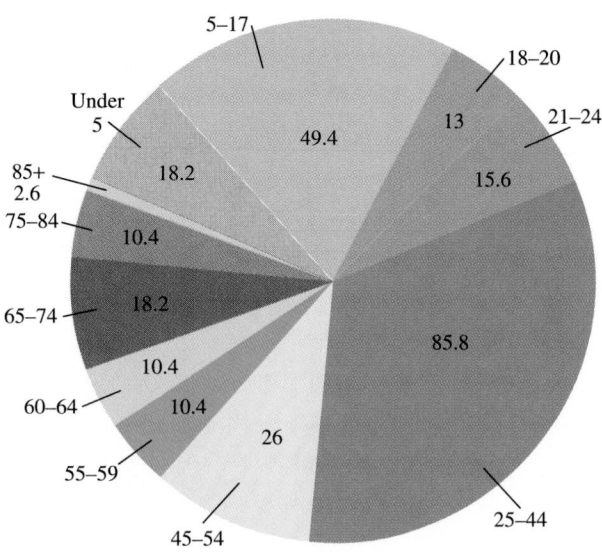

5–17

18–20

Under 5

13

21–24

49.4

15.6

85+ 2.6

18.2

75–84

10.4

85.8

65–74

18.2

10.4

26

60–64

10.4

55–59

25–44

45–54

Source: U.S. Bureau of the Census

a. Find the sum of the numbers in the 11 sectors. What is the meaning of this sum?

b. What percent of the U.S. population is in the 18–20 age group?

c. Use your answer from part (b) to determine the percent of the U.S. population in the 45–54 age group.

4. Suicide rates in the United States in 1970 and 1991 are shown in the bar graph. Use the graph to answer the following questions.

a. Estimate the number of suicides per 100,000 for each age group in 1991.

b. In 1970, which age groups had a suicide rate that exceeded 15 deaths per 100,000 people?

c. Describe one trend that you observe from the graph.

d. What two age groups show the greatest increase in suicide rate from 1970 to 1991?

5. Use the bar graphs to answer the following questions.

a. For what year or years shown in the graphs was the average hospitalization less than 16 days?

b. For what year or years shown in the graphs was the percentage of patients treated as hospital outpatients greater than 3% but less than 10%?

c. Describe one trend that you observe from the graphs.

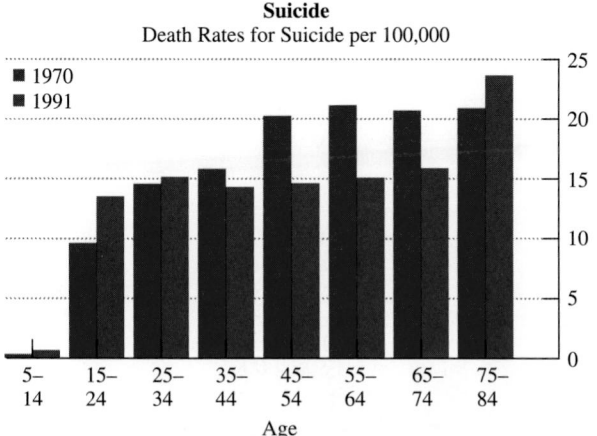

Source: Statistical Abstract of the United States

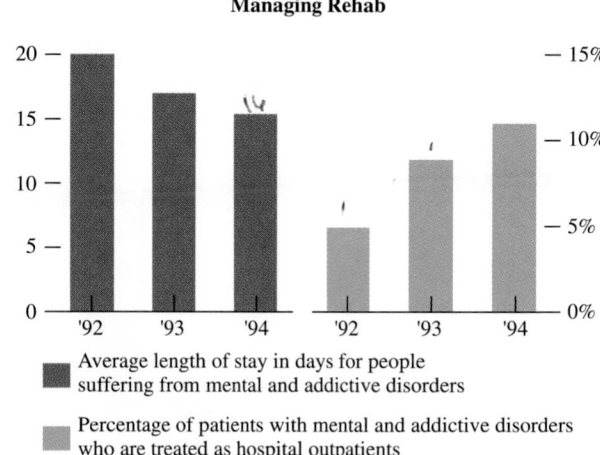

Source: National Association of Psychiatric Health Systems

6. People in developed countries have a longer life expectancy on average than those in the developing world, and women live longer on average than men. The bar graph shows life expectancy figures from 1988 through 1991 for eight countries. Use the graph to answer the following questions.

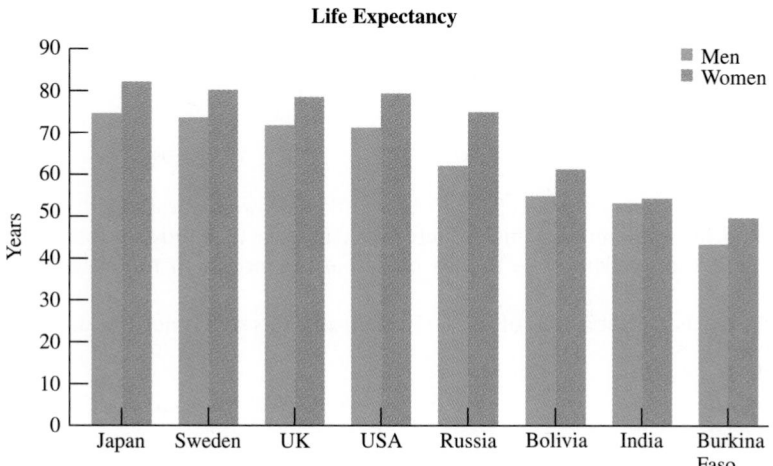

Source: World Health Organization

    a. What countries had a life expectancy for men that exceeds 65 years?

    b. What countries had a life expectancy for women that is less than 60 years?

    c. Estimate the life expectancy for men and women in the United States.

    d. Approximately how much longer do women in Japan live than men?

    e. By observing the graph, is it possible to determine why women live longer than men? Explain.

7. Use the bar graphs to answer the following questions. (*Note:* Gross domestic product is a country's total output of goods and services produced by labor and property.)

    a. The United States spends more on health care than any other country in the world. Is this fact explicitly conveyed by the information in the graphs? Explain.

    b. What is the increase in percentage for the share of U.S. GDP spent on health care from 1960 to 1991?

    c. If we add the four percents in the first graph, we obtain 35.3%. Explain why the sum of these percents does not equal 100%.

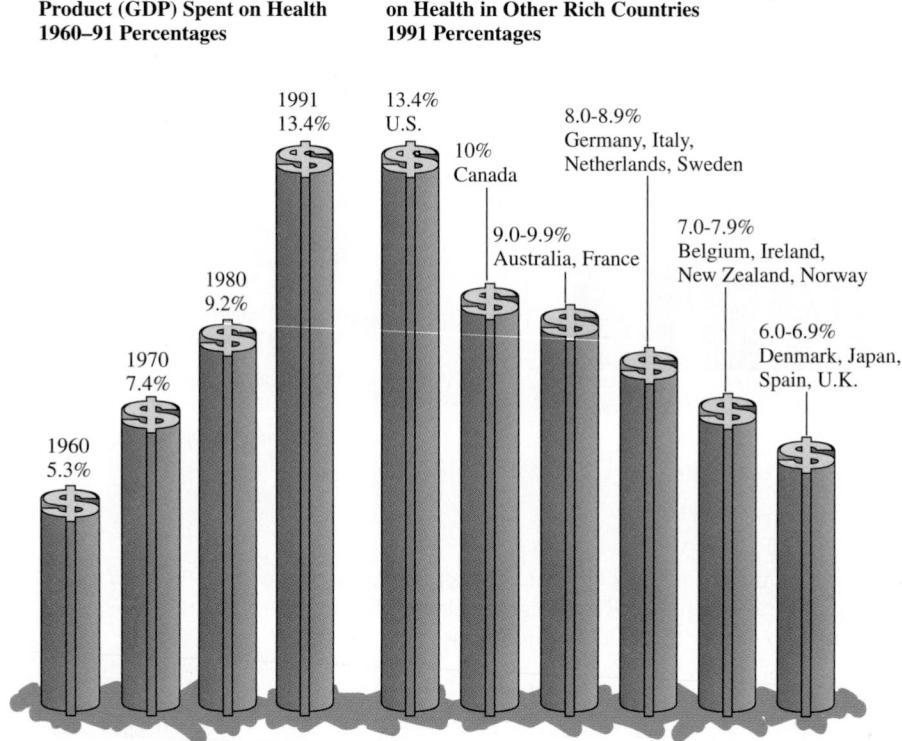

Share of U.S. Gross Domestic Product (GDP) Spent on Health 1960–91 Percentages

Share of Gross Domestic Product (GDP) Spent on Health in Other Rich Countries 1991 Percentages

Source: U.S. National Center for Health Statistics; O.E.C.D.

8. Use the bar graph shown at the top of the next page to answer the following questions.

    a. Do production workers in Germany pay a higher percentage in taxes than those in Italy?

    b. By observing the graph, can we determine the tax bite from the income of top executives in the eight countries? Explain.

    c. If we add the eight percents, we get a total of 131%. Explain why this sum is not 100%.

Tax Bite from the Income of an Average Production Worker: Some International Comparisons, 1991 Percentages

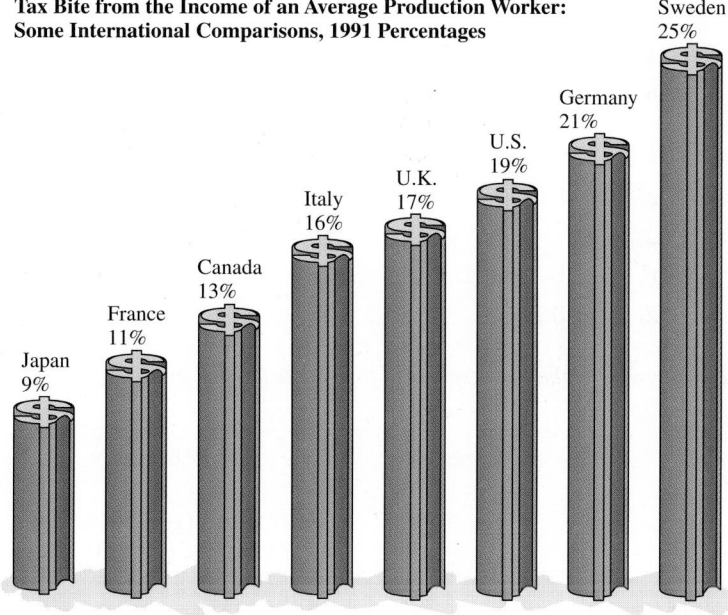

Source: O.E.C.D.

9. The line graph shows the population of the United States from 1970 to 2000 for people under 16 and those 65 and over.
   a. For the period from 1970 to 2000, in what year was the population for people under 16 at a minimum? Estimate the population for that year.
   b. In what year was the population for Americans 65 and over approximately 30 million?

10. The line graph shows the percent of Americans below the poverty level from 1960 to 1992.
    a. In what year was the percent of people under 18 living below the poverty level at a minimum? Estimate the percent for that year.
    b. In what year did approximately 40% of families headed by women live below the poverty level?
    c. Write one statement summarizing the information in the graph.

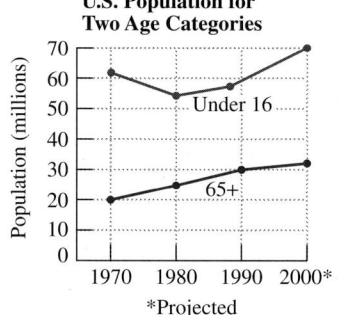

U.S. Population for Two Age Categories

Source: U.S. Bureau of the Census, *Statistical Abstract*

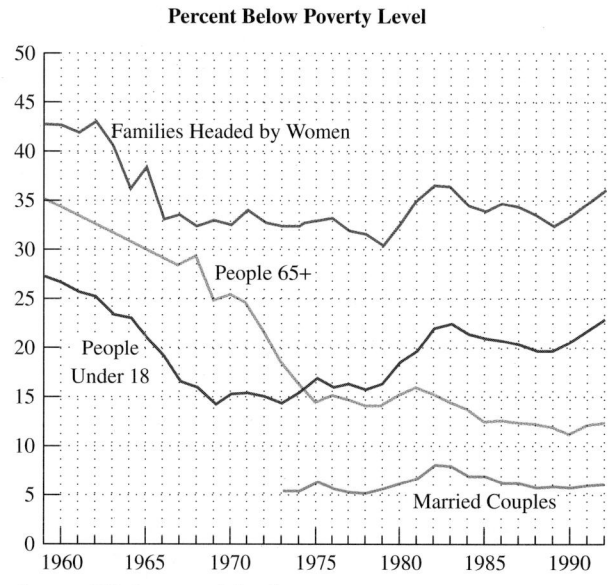

Percent Below Poverty Level

Source: U.S. Bureau of the Census

Plot each ordered pair in Problems 11–18 on a rectangular coordinate system. Indicate in which quadrant each point lies.

11. (3, 4)   **12.** (4, 3)   **13.** (−4, 1)   **14.** (1, −4)

15. (−2, −5)   **16.** (−5, −2)   **17.** (4, −3)   **18.** (−3, 4)

Plot each ordered pair in Problems 19–34 on a rectangular coordinate system.

19. (−3, −3)   **20.** (−5, −5)   **21.** (−2, 0)   **22.** (−5, 0)

23. (0, 2)   **24.** (0, 5)   **25.** (0, −3)   **26.** (0, −5)

27. $\left(\frac{5}{2}, \frac{7}{2}\right)$ **28.** $\left(\frac{7}{2}, \frac{5}{2}\right)$ **29.** $\left(-5, \frac{3}{2}\right)$ **30.** $\left(-\frac{9}{2}, -4\right)$

31. (0, 0)   **32.** $\left(-\frac{5}{2}, 0\right)$ **33.** $\left(0, -\frac{5}{2}\right)$ **34.** $\left(0, \frac{7}{2}\right)$

In Problems 35–42, give the ordered pairs that correspond to the points labeled in the figure.

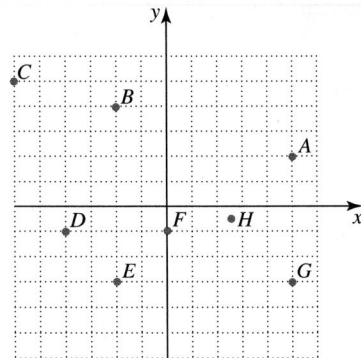

35. A   **36.** B

37. C   **38.** D

39. E   **40.** F

41. G   **42.** H

43. The percent of dentistry degrees awarded to women in the United States from 1970 to 1990 is shown by the graph.
  a. Estimate the ordered pairs that correspond to each of the points in the graph.
  b. Describe the meaning of each of the five ordered pairs.
  c. Is it likely that the trend shown in the graph will continue into the next century? If it does, estimate the year in which 100% of dentistry degrees will be awarded to women.
  d. Graph eight additional points for the years 2000 to 2070 that represent a reasonable continuation for the data.

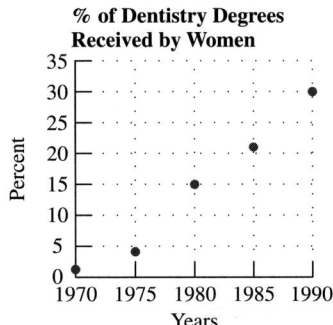

% of Dentistry Degrees Received by Women

Source: U.S. National Center for Education Statistics, *Digest of Education Statistics*, annual in *The American Almanac: Statistical Abstract of the United States*, 1993

44. The graph contrasts costs for a three-bedroom home for electric and solar heating systems over a 40-year period. The cost on the *y*-axis is

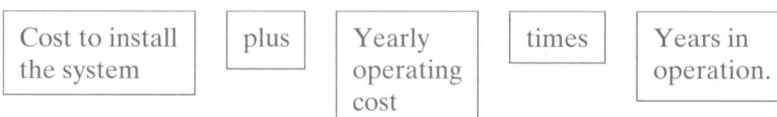

| Cost to install the system | plus | Yearly operating cost | times | Years in operation. |

a. Give the ordered pairs that correspond to points *A* and *B*. What is the meaning of these pairs in terms of installation costs for the two types of heating systems?

b. Estimate the ordered pair corresponding to point *C*. What is the meaning of this point?

c. What do the points in the graph indicate about installation costs and operating costs for the two kinds of systems? How is this information conveyed by the graph?

rings will be sold each month. The graph was prepared by the marketing division of the company.

a. Give the ordered pair that corresponds to point *A*. What does this mean in terms of the price for a pair of earrings and the manufacturer's monthly profit?

b. Repeat the question in part (a) for point *B*.

c. Do the six points indicate that the manufacturer will continue earning more profit for each price increase? Explain.

d. At what price for a pair of earrings will the manufacturer maximize monthly profits. Estimate the maximum monthly profit. How is this information conveyed by the graph?

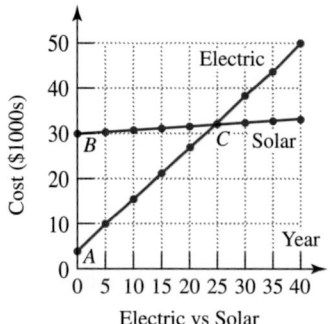

Electric vs Solar

45. A manufacturer can produce a pair of earrings for $3 and sell them for $5. At this price, 4000 pairs of earrings are sold each month. There are plans to raise the price of the earrings, but market research indicates that for each increase in the price, fewer pairs of ear-

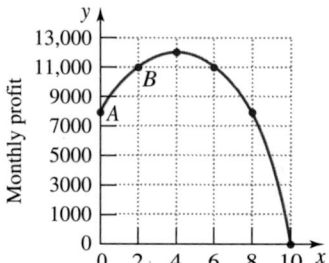

The number of $1 price increases for each pair of earrings

True–False Critical Thinking Problems

46. Which one of the following is true based on the information in the bar graph?
  a. We can expect supplies of bauxite to run out within our lifetime.
  b. Now that supplies of tin are becoming scarcer, the packaging industry is using alternative materials such as glass, plastics, steel, and aluminum.
  c. The mineral that will be depleted in approximately 55 years is copper.
  d. We can expect manganese to be plentiful for at least 200 years.

47. Which one of the following is true based on the information in the line graph?
  a. The number of college graduates with bachelor's degrees exceeded 1 million in 1980.
  b. In 1990, the number of bachelor's degrees awarded to women exceeded the number awarded to men by approximately 60 million.
  c. The year in which $\frac{1}{2}$ million men were awarded bachelor's degrees was 1975.
  d. By 1975, more women were awarded bachelor's degrees than men.

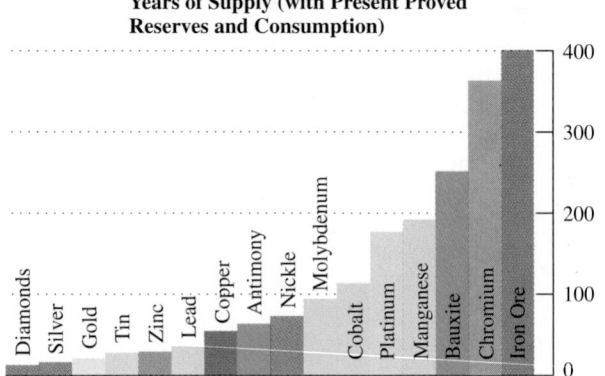

Years of Supply (with Present Proved Reserves and Consumption)

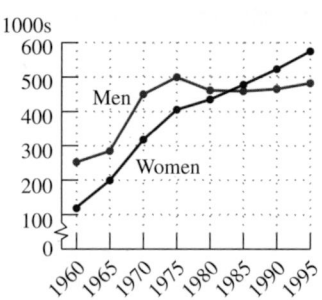

Bachelor Degrees Awarded

Source: U.S. Bureau of the Census, *Statistical Abstract*

Technology Problem

48. Many graphing calculators and computers contain programs that can create circle, bar, and line graphs. Consult a newspaper, magazine, or almanac containing data that you find interesting but is not presented in graphic form. Use a graphing calculator or computer to present the data in the form of one of the graphs discussed in this section.

Writing in Mathematics

49. Describe a circle graph.
50. Describe a bar graph.
51. Describe a line graph.
52. Explain how to plot the ordered pair $(-3, 5)$.

53. Find a graph in a newspaper, magazine, or almanac and describe what the graph illustrates.
54. Explain why $(5, -2)$ and $(-2, 5)$ do not represent the same ordered pair.

55. The population pyramid shows the structure of the American population, in terms of age and sex, in 1995.
  a. Write a true–false question similar to Problems 46–47 in which four statements are given and students are asked to select the one true statement based on the information given in the graph.
  b. Write a question based on the graph in which students are asked to obtain a reasonable estimate. Then answer the question.

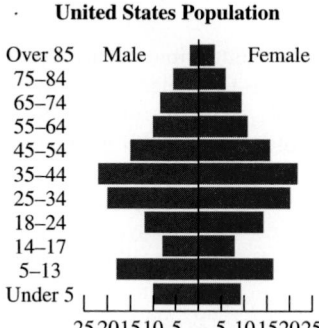

Structure of the United States Population

Over 85 Male Female
75–84
65–74
55–64
45–54
35–44
25–34
18–24
14–17
5–13
Under 5

25 20 15 10 5   5 10 15 20 25
Population in Millions

Critical Thinking Problems _____

56. The circle graphs show how Americans invest their money.

Use the graph to estimate the following amounts.
  a. The amount of money invested in bonds in 1974
  b. The amount of money invested in certificates of deposit in 1984
  c. The amount of money invested in the "other" category in 1994

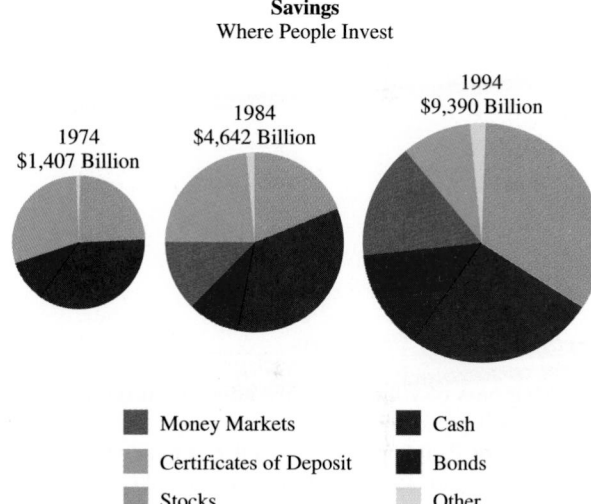

Savings
Where People Invest

1974
$1,407 Billion

1984
$4,642 Billion

1994
$9,390 Billion

■ Money Markets   ■ Cash
■ Certificates of Deposit   ■ Bonds
■ Stocks   ■ Other

Source: *MONEY* Magazine Small Investor Index

57. The line graphs indicate crime rates in the United States.

In 1993, one violent crime occurred every 16 seconds. Based on the graphs, select the option that gives the best reasonable estimate for how often murder, burglary, and motor vehicle theft happened in 1993.

a. Murder:
    A. One every 8 seconds
    B. One every 32 seconds
    C. One every 21 minutes
    D. One every 60 minutes

b. Burglary:
    A. One every 11 seconds
    B. One every 15 seconds
    C. One every 32 seconds
    D. One every 21 minutes

c. Motor Vehicle Theft:
    A. One every 8 seconds
    B. One every 20 seconds
    C. One every minute
    D. One every 20 minutes

Rates

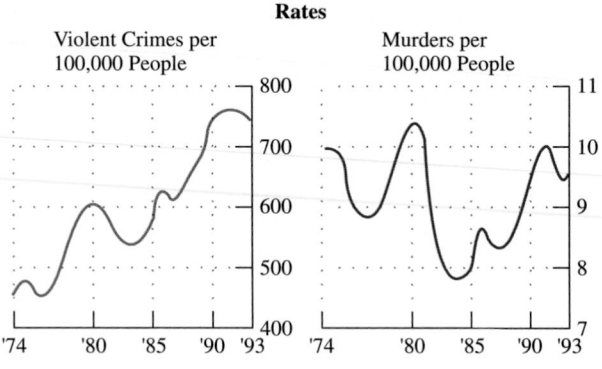

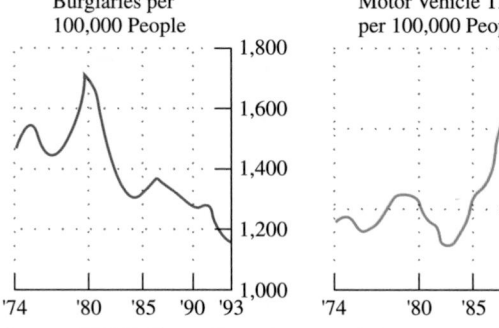

Source: FBI Uniform Crime Report "Crime in the U.S.," U.S. Department of Justice

Group Activity Problems _____

58. Members of your group are advisors to the president of the United States. Select the graph in either Problem 9 or Problem 10. Write a list of policy recommendations that group members would like to make to the president based on the information conveyed by the graph.

59. This question is appropriate for small-group discussion. In Problem 4d you were asked to identify the two age groups with the greatest increase in suicide rate from 1970 to 1991. What explanations can group members give for these increases? Do group participants believe that these trends will continue? Explain.

Review Problems _____

60. Use the roster method to write the set $\{x \mid x$ is a number whose absolute value is 4$\}$.

61. Place the correct symbol ($<, >,$ or $=$) between these two real numbers: $\frac{1}{3} \ \square \ 0.33$.

62. Simplify: $|-5| - |-2|$.

S E C T I O N   1 . 4

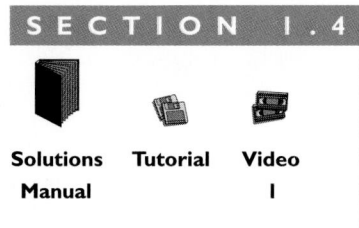

Solutions   Tutorial   Video
Manual   I

Basic Rules of Algebra

Objectives

1 Model reality with algebraic expressions.
2 Evaluate algebraic expressions.
3 Use the commutative properties.
4 Use the associative properties.
5 Use the distributive properties.
6 Simplify algebraic expressions.

In the next chapter, we will study equations and their solutions. The first step in solving an equation is to simplify the expressions that appear on the left and right of the equal sign. In this section, we will study the basic rules of algebra needed to simplify algebraic expressions.

1 Model reality with algebraic expressions.

Modeling Reality with Algebraic Expressions

In algebra we use *variables* to represent numbers. An expression that consists of variables, numbers, and operation signs (addition, subtraction, multiplication, and division) is called an *algebraic expression*. Many algebraic expressions describe some aspect of reality, and we say that they *model* reality.

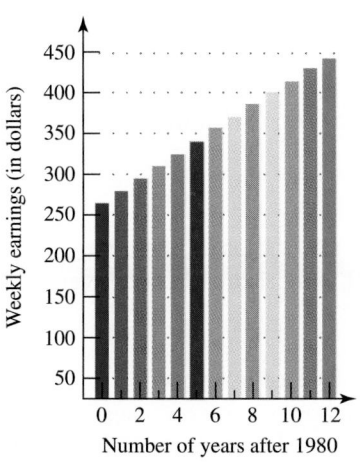

Figure 1.25
Weekly earnings by year

EXAMPLE 1   Describing Reality with an Algebraic Expression

According to the U.S. Bureau of Labor Statistics, workers in the United States earned an average of $270 a week in 1980. This amount has increased steadily by $14.60 each year, shown by the bar graph in Figure 1.25. How much did workers earn 1 year after 1980, 2 years after 1980, 3 years after 1980, 4 years after 1980, and 5 years after 1980? Use the pattern to write an algebraic expression that describes weekly earnings x years after 1980.

Solution

Weekly earnings for the indicated years were organized in Table 1.2.

TABLE 1.2 Average Weekly Earnings in the United States	
Number of Years after 1980	**Average Weekly Earnings**
1	$270 + 1 \cdot \$14.60 = \$270 + \$14.60 = \$284.60$
2	$270 + 2 \cdot \$14.60 = \$270 + \$29.20 = \$299.20$
3	$270 + 3 \cdot \$14.60 = \$270 + \$43.80 = \$313.80$
4	$270 + 4 \cdot \$14.60 = \$270 + \$58.40 = \$328.40$
5	$270 + 5 \cdot \$14.60 = \$270 + \$73.00 = \$343.00$

The pattern in the second column is to take $270 and add the number of years after 1980 times $14.60. Using this pattern, the average weekly earnings x years after 1980 is

1980 earnings	plus	Years after 1980	times	Yearly increase.

$$270 \qquad + \qquad x \qquad \cdot \qquad 14.60$$

Thus, the algebraic expression that describes or models weekly earnings x years after 1980 is

$$270 + x \cdot 14.60.$$ ∎

2 Evaluate algebraic expressions.

Evaluating Algebraic Expressions

We can replace a variable that appears in an algebraic expression by a number. We are *substituting* the number for the variable. The process is called *evaluating the expression.*

EXAMPLE 2   **Evaluating an Algebraic Expression**

Evaluate the expression $270 + x \cdot 14.60$ when $x = 10$. Describe what the answer means in practical terms.

Solution

We substitute 10 for x and carry out the multiplication and addition.

$$270 + x \cdot 14.60 = 270 + 10 \cdot 14.60$$
$$= 270 + 146$$
$$= 416$$

This means that 10 years after 1980, or in 1990, American workers averaged $416 in earnings each week. ∎

Properties of Real Numbers and Algebraic Expressions

We now turn to basic properties or rules that you know from past experiences in working with whole numbers and fractions. These properties will be extended to include all real numbers and algebraic expressions. We will give each property a name so that we can refer to it throughout the study of algebra.

3 Use the commutative properties.

The Commutative Properties

The addition or multiplication of two real numbers can be done in any order. For example, $3 + 5 = 5 + 3$ and $3 \cdot 5 = 5 \cdot 3$. Changing the order does not change the answer of a sum or a product. These facts are called *commutative properties.*

> **The commutative properties**
>
> Let a, b, and c represent real numbers, variables, or algebraic expressions.

> **Commutative property of addition**
>
> $a + b = b + a$
>
> **Commutative property of multiplication**
>
> $ab = ba$

We say that addition and multiplication are commutative operations. You may remember the word *commutative* by thinking of a *commuter* who travels from home to work and then from work to home, traveling the same distance in each direction.

EXAMPLE 3 **Using the Commutative Properties**

Rewrite the algebraic expression $270 + x \cdot 14.60$ using:

a. The commutative property of addition
b. The commutative property of multiplication

Solution

a. $270 + x \cdot 14.60 = x \cdot 14.60 + 270$ Use the commutative property to change the order of the addition.

b. $270 + x \cdot 14.60 = 270 + 14.60 \cdot x$ Use the commutative property to change the order of the multiplication. ∎

The dot representing multiplication is usually omitted between a constant and a variable. Furthermore, it is customary to write the constant first. Thus, the algebraic expression modeling weekly salary would be expressed as

$270 + 14.60x$ or $14.60x + 270$.

These expressions name the same number for all replacements of x and are said to be *equivalent.*

> **Equivalent algebraic expressions**
>
> Two expressions that have the same value for all possible replacements are called *equivalent expressions.*

In the algebraic expression $14.60x + 270$, we refer to $14.60x$ and 270 as *terms.* A term is a number, a variable, or a number multiplied by one or more variables. Terms are separated by addition and subtraction.

The *numerical coefficient* of a term is the number that multiplies the variable. For the term $14.60x$, the numerical coefficient is 14.60 or, equivalently, 14.6.

4 Use the associative properties.

The Associative Properties

A second pair of basic rules of algebra is the associative properties that allow us to change groupings.

The associative properties

Let $a, b,$ and c represent real numbers, variables, or algebraic expressions.

Associative property of addition

$$(a + b) + c = a + (b + c)$$

Associative property of multiplication

$$(ab)c = a(bc)$$

The associative properties can be used to simplify algebraic expressions.

EXAMPLE 4 **Simplifying Using the Associative Property**

Simplify:

a. $3 + (8 + x)$ **b.** $8(4x)$

Solution

a. $3 + (8 + x)$

$\quad = (3 + 8) + x$ Use the associative property of addition to group the first two numbers.

$\quad = 11 + x$ Using the commutative property, the answer can also be expressed as $x + 11$

b. $8(4x)$

$\quad = (8 \cdot 4)x$ Use the associative property of multiplication to group the first two numbers.

$\quad = 32x$ ■

The next example involves the use of both basic properties to simplify an algebraic expression.

EXAMPLE 5 **Using the Commutative and Associative Properties**

Simplify: $7 + (x + 2)$

Solution

$7 + (x + 2)$ This is the given expression.

$= 7 + (2 + x)$ Use the commutative property to change the order of the addition.

$= (7 + 2) + x$ Use the associative property to group the first two numbers.

$= 9 + x$ An equivalent expression is $x + 9$.   ■

5 Use the distributive properties.

The Distributive Properties

The *distributive property* involves both multiplication and addition, showing how to multiply the sum of two numbers by a third number. Consider, for ex-

ENRICHMENT ESSAY

The Associative Property and the English Language

In the English language, phrases can take on many different meanings depending on the way the words are associated. For example,

(man eating) tiger

does not mean the same thing as

man (eating tiger)

Here is another example where regrouping words leads to a different meaning:

(bare facts) person ≠ bare (facts person)

And here's another, where we have to cheat a bit, but which works well in the spoken language:

Walking in the woods with (a bear) behind is not the same as walking in the woods with a (bare behind).

Can you think of nonassociative word triples in certain phrases?

ample, 4(7 + 3), which can be calculated in two ways. One way is to perform the addition within the grouping symbols and then multiply.

$$4(7 + 3) = 4(10) = 40$$

The other way is to *distribute* the multiplication by 4 over the addition by first multiplying each number within the parentheses by 4 and then adding.

$$4(7 + 3) = 4 \cdot 7 + 4 \cdot 3 = 28 + 12 = 40$$

The result in both cases is 40. Thus,

$$4(7 + 3) = 4 \cdot 7 + 4 \cdot 3 \quad \text{Multiplication } \textit{distributes} \text{ over addition.}$$

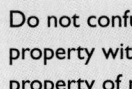

tudy tip

Do not confuse the distributive property with the associative property of multiplication.
Distributive:

$$4(5 + x) = 4 \cdot 5 + 4x$$
$$= 20 + 4x$$

Associative:

$$4(5 \cdot x) = (4 \cdot 5)x$$
$$= 20x$$

The distributive property

Let a, b, and c represent real numbers, variables, or algebraic expressions.

$$a(b + c) = ab + ac$$

Multiplication distributes over addition.

EXAMPLE 6 Modeling a Geometric Situation

A one-story building has floor dimensions represented by $3x$ and $y + 2$ (see Figure 1.26). Find two equivalent algebraic expressions, one with parentheses and one without, that model the area of the floor.

Solution

The floor is a rectangle. The area of a rectangle is its length times its width. Thus, an algebraic expression that models or describes the floor's area is

$$3x(y + 2).$$

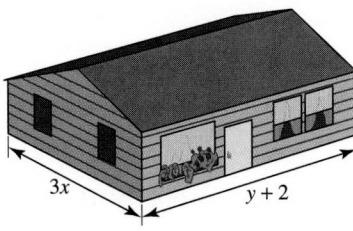

Figure 1.26

A house with floor dimensions $3x$ by $y + 2$

Now let's use the distributive property to obtain an equivalent expression without parentheses.

$$3x(y + 2) = 3xy + 3x \cdot 2 \qquad \text{Use the distributive property.}$$
$$= 3xy + 3 \cdot 2 \cdot x \qquad \text{Use the commutative property of multiplication.}$$
$$= 3xy + 6x \qquad \text{Simplify.}$$

The expressions that model the floor's area $3x(y + 2)$ and $3xy + 6x$ are equivalent. They result in the same area for all replacements of x and y.   ■

It is also true that multiplication distributes over subtraction.

$$a(b - c) = ab - ac$$

EXAMPLE 7   Modeling Optimum Heart Rate

The optimum heart rate is the rate that a person should achieve during exercise for the exercise to be most beneficial. The algebraic expression

$$0.6(220 - a)$$

describes a person's optimum heart rate in beats per minute, where a represents that person's age.

a. Use the distributive property to rewrite the expression without parentheses.
b. Show that the two forms of the expression are equivalent by using each form to determine the optimum heart rate for a 20-year-old runner.

Amanda Borden (USA), 1996 Olympics

Steven E. Sutton/Duomo Photography

Solution

a. $0.6(220 - a) = 0.6(220) - 0.6a \qquad$ Distribute multiplication over subtraction.
$$= 132 - 0.6a \qquad \text{Simplify.}$$

b. Substitute 20 for a in each form of the expression.

Using $0.6(220 - a)$:	**Using $132 - 0.6a$:**
$0.6(220 - 20)$	$132 - 0.6(20)$
$= 0.6(200)$	$= 132 - 12$
$= 120$	$= 120$

Both forms indicate that the optimum heart rate for a 20-year-old runner is 120 beats per minute.   ■

There are a number of other forms of the distributive property. Because multiplication is commutative, the property can be expressed as

$$(b + c)a = ba + ca.$$

The distributive property can also be extended to more than two numbers.

$$a(b + c + d) = ab + ac + ad$$

6 Simplify algebraic expressions.

Simplifying Algebraic Expressions

The algebraic expression $3x + 7x$ contains two terms, namely $3x$ and $7x$. The parts of each term that are multiplied are the *factors* of the term. The factors of the first term are 3 and x. The factors of the second term are 7 and x. These terms are called *like* or *similar* terms because their variable factors are exactly the same. On the other hand, the terms $3x$ and $7y$ have different variable factors and are *unlike terms*.

The distributive property

$$a(b + c) = ab + ac$$

lets us add and subtract like terms. To do this, we will usually apply the property in the form

$$ax + bx = (a + b)x$$

and then combine a and b. For example,

$$3x + 7x = (3 + 7)x = 10x.$$

This process is called *combining like terms*.

| **EXAMPLE 8** | **Combining Like Terms** |

Combine like terms:

a. $4x + 15x$ **b.** $7a - 2a$

Solution

a. $4x + 15x$ These are like terms because $4x$ and $15x$ have identical variable factors.
$\quad = (4 + 15)x$ Apply the distributive property.
$\quad = 19x$ Add within the grouping symbols.

b. $7a - 2a$ These are like terms because $7a$ and $2a$ have identical variable factors.
$\quad = (7 - 2)a$ Apply the distributive property.
$\quad = 5a$ Subtract within the grouping symbols.

As you studied Example 8, did you find that you were able to combine the like terms in your head without writing out all the steps?

Combining like terms mentally

1. Add or subtract the numerical coefficients of the terms.
2. Use the result of step 1 as the numerical coefficient of the terms' variable factor.

When an expression contains three or more terms, use the commutative and associative properties to group like terms. Then combine the like terms.

EXAMPLE 9   Grouping and Combining Like Terms

Simplify:

a. $7x + 5 + 3x + 8$ **b.** $4x + 7y - 2x - 3y$

Solution

a. $7x + 5 + 3x + 8$

$= (7x + 3x) + (5 + 8)$ Rearrange terms and group the like terms using the commutative and associative properties. This step is often done mentally.

$= 10x + 13$ Combine like terms: $7x + 3x = 10x$. Combine constant terms: $5 + 8 = 13$. The constant terms will hereafter be considered like terms.

b. $4x + 7y - 2x - 3y$

$= (4x - 2x) + (7y - 3y)$ Group like terms.

$= 2x + 4y$ Combine like terms by subtracting coefficients and keeping the variable factor. ■

In mathematics, parentheses ( ) are used to show groupings. In simplified form, an algebraic expression contains no grouping symbols and all like terms are combined. We use the distributive property to remove grouping symbols and then combine like terms. Let's illustrate this idea.

EXAMPLE 10   Simplifying an Algebraic Expression

Simplify: $5(3x - 7) - 6x$

iscover for yourself

Substitute 10 for x in both $5(3x - 7) - 6x$ and $9x - 35$. Do you get the same answer in each case? Which form of the expression is easier to work with?

Solution

$5(3x - 7) - 6x$

$= 15x - 35 - 6x$ Use the distributive property to remove the grouping symbols.

$= (15x - 6x) - 35$ Group like terms.

$= 9x - 35$ Combine like terms.

Since $5(3x - 7) - 6x = 9x - 35$, both algebraic expressions have the same value when any real number is substituted for x. ■

Before considering additional examples, let's summarize our work to this point.

Simplifying algebraic expressions

1. Use the distributive property to remove all grouping symbols.
2. Rearrange terms and group like terms using commutative and associative properties. This step may be done mentally.
3. Combine like terms by combining the coefficients of the terms and keeping the same variable factor.

The simplified form of an algebraic expression has the same value when permissible numbers are substituted for the variable(s).

EXAMPLE 11 **Simplifying an Algebraic Expression**

Simplify: $6(2x - 4y) + 10(4x + 3y)$

Solution

$6(2x - 4y) + 10(4x + 3y)$
$= 12x - 24y + 40x + 30y$ Use the distributive property to remove parentheses.
$= (12x + 40x) + (30y - 24y)$ Group like terms.
$= 52x + 6y$ Combine like terms.

Using the commutative property of addition, this simplified form can also be written as $6y + 52x$. ∎

Our final example involves an algebraic expression that models education and income.

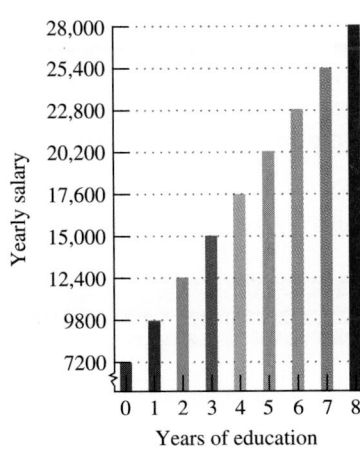

Yearly income based on years of education

EXAMPLE 12 **Simplifying an Applied Expression**

The algebraic expression

$1000(2x + 8) + 300(2x - 2) - 200$

describes approximate yearly income for an American with x years of education.

a. Simplify the expression.
b. Use the simplified expression to predict the yearly income for a person with 0, 1, 2, 3, and 15 years of education.
c. Use the simplified form of the expression to describe the relationship between education and income.

Solution

a. $1000(2x + 8) + 300(2x - 2) - 200$
$= 2000x + 8000 + 600x - 600 - 200$ Use the distributive property to remove parentheses
$= (2000x + 600x) + (8000 - 600 - 200)$ Group like terms.
$= 2600x + 7200$ Combine like terms.

b. To predict the yearly income for a person with 0, 1, 2, 3, and 15 years of education, we substitute each of these numbers for x in the simplified form of the algebraic expression.

$$2600x + 7200$$

$x = 0$:	$x = 1$:	$x = 2$:	$x = 3$:
$2600(0) + 7200$	$2600(1) + 7200$	$2600(2) + 7200$	$2600(3) + 7200$
$= 0 + 7200$	$= 2600 + 7200$	$= 5200 + 7200$	$= 7800 + 7200$
$= 7200$	$= 9800$	$= 12,400$	$= 15,000$

Yearly incomes for people with 0, 1, 2, and 3 years of education are $7200, $9800, $12,400, and $15,000, respectively. Notice that these numbers continue to increase by $2600.

ENRICHMENT ESSAY

Anagrams: Applying Commutative and Associative Properties to Letters of Words and Phrases

When letters of words and phrases are rearranged and regrouped, the new words and phrases do not have the same meaning as they did in their original context. At times, however, commuting and reassociating relates to the meaning of the original phrase in an amusing way.

Original Word or Phrase	An Anagram
Astronomers	Moon-starers
Conversation	Voices rant on
Revolution	To love ruin
Sweetheart	There we sat
Total abstainers	Sit not at ale bars

Finally, for 15 years of education, we substitute 15 for x:

$2600(15) + 7200$
$= 39,000 + 7200$
$= 46,200$

A person with 15 years of education can expect to earn $46,200 yearly.

c. The algebraic expression $2600x + 7200$ indicates that yearly income increases by $2600 for each year of education and a person with no education can expect to earn $7200 yearly. ∎

PROBLEM SET 1.4

Use the commutative property of addition to write an equivalent algebraic expression.

1. $x + 7$
5. $4x + 7y$
2. $x + 13$
6. $7a + 5b$
3. $x + 4y$
7. $4(x + 6)$
4. $3x + y$
8. $5(x + 9)$

In Problems 9–14, use the commutative property of multiplication to write an equivalent algebraic expression.

9. $x \cdot 7$ **10.** $x \cdot 5$ **11.** $6 + xy$ **12.** $5 + ab$ **13.** $4(b + 5)$ **14.** $6(b + 7)$

In Problems 15–18, use the associative property to rewrite each algebraic expression. Once the grouping has been changed, simplify the resulting expression.

15. $7 + (5 + x)$ **16.** $9 + (3 + x)$ **17.** $7(4x)$ **18.** $8(5x)$

In Problems 19–38, use the distributive property to rewrite each expression without parentheses.

19. $3(x + 5)$
23. $\frac{1}{3}(12 + 6r)$
27. $3(x - 2)$
31. $\frac{1}{2}(5x - 12)$
35. $6(x + 3 + 2y)$
20. $4(x + 6)$
24. $\frac{1}{4}(12 + 8r)$
28. $4(x - 5)$
32. $\frac{1}{3}(7x - 21)$
36. $7(2x + 4 + y)$
21. $8(2x + 3)$
25. $5(x + y)$
29. $2(4x - 5)$
33. $(2x + 7)4$
37. $5(3x - 2 + 4y)$
22. $9(2x + 5)$
26. $7(x + y)$
30. $6(3x - 2)$
34. $(5x + 3)6$
38. $4(5x - 3 + 7y)$

In Problems 39–56, simplify each algebraic expression.

39. $7x + 10x$ **40.** $5x + 13x$ **41.** $11a - 3a$ **42.** $14b - 5b$

43. $3 + (x + 11)$

44. $7 + (x + 10)$

45. $5y - 3 + 6y$

46. $8y - 7 + 10y$

47. $2x + 5 + 7x - 4$

48. $7x + 8 + 2x - 3$

49. $11a + 12 - 3a - 2$

50. $13a + 15 - 2a - 11$

51. $5(3x + 2) - 4$

52. $2(5x + 4) - 3$

53. $12 + 5(3x - 2)$

54. $14 + 2(5x - 1)$

55. $7(3a + 2b) + 5(4a - 2b)$

56. $11(6a + 3b) + 4(12a - 5b)$

Application Problems

57. According to the National Education Association, elementary and secondary teachers in the United States earned an average of $16,020 a year in 1980. This amount has increased steadily by $1527 each year. The algebraic expression that describes or models yearly earnings for teachers x years after 1980 is

$16,020 + 1527x$.

a. Evaluate the expression when $x = 8$. Describe what the answer means in practical terms.

b. What was the yearly earnings for teachers in 1991?

c. Rewrite the algebraic expression that models teachers' yearly earnings as an equivalent expression using the commutative property of addition.

58. According to the *Television and Cable Fact Book*, there were 16,424,000 cable television subscribers in the United States in 1980. This number has increased steadily by 3,184,000 subscribers each year. The algebraic expression that describes or models the number of cable subscribers x years after 1980 is

$16,424,000 + 3,184,000x$.

a. Evaluate the expression when $x = 5$. Describe what the answer means in practical terms.

b. How many cable subscribers were there in 1990?

c. Rewrite the algebraic expression that models the number of cable subscribers as an equivalent expression using the commutative property of addition.

59. The equivalent algebraic expressions

$$\frac{DA + D}{24} \quad \text{and} \quad \frac{D(A + 1)}{24}$$

describe the drug dosage for children between the ages of 2 and 13. Within the expression, D stands for an adult dose and A represents the child's age. If an adult dose of ibuprofen is 200 milligrams, what is the proper dose for a 12-year-old child? Use both forms of the expressions to answer the question. Which form is easier to use?

60. The perimeter of a rectangle is the distance around it and can be found by adding 2 times the length and 2 times the width. The picture frame shown here has a length represented by $x + 5$ inches and a width represented by x inches. Write an algebraic expression that models or describes the perimeter of the picture frame. Then simplify the expression.

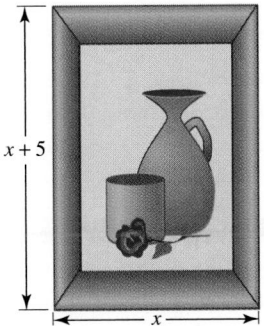

61. The rectangular tennis court shown here has a length represented by $y + 3$ and a width represented by $4x$. Find two equivalent algebraic expressions, one with parentheses and one without, that model the area of the tennis court.

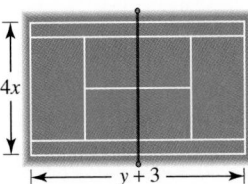

62. The algebraic expression

$2(x + 100) + 0.35x - 20.5$

describes the population of the United States (in millions) x years after 1960.

a. Simplify the expression.

b. Use the simplified expression to find the U.S. population for 1960 ($x = 0$), 1961 ($x = 1$), 1962 ($x = 2$), 1963 ($x = 3$), 1964 ($x = 4$), and 1990 ($x = 30$).

c. Use the simplified form of the expression to complete this statement: In 1960, the population of the United States was _____ million. Since then, the population has steadily increased by approximately _____ million people each year.

True–False Critical Thinking Problems

63. Which one of the following statements is true?
   a. Subtraction is a commutative operation.
   b. $(24 \div 6) \div 2 = 24 \div (6 \div 2)$
   c. $7y + 3y = (7 + 3)y$ for any value of y.
   d. $2x + 5 = 5x + 2$

64. Which one of the following statements is true?
   a. $a + (bc) = (a + b)(a + c)$ In words, addition can be distributed over multiplication.
   b. $4(x + 3) = 4x + 3$
   c. Not every algebraic expression can be simplified.
   d. Like terms contain the same numerical coefficients.

Writing in Mathematics

65. Describe the difference between the commutative and associative properties.

66. Explain what is meant by like terms, and describe how to combine them.

67. What does the distributive property have to do with the following cliche? "You can add apples and apples or pears and pears, but you can't add apples and pears."

68. How do you determine when an algebraic expression has been simplified?

Critical Thinking Problems

The commutative property involves a change in order with no change in the final result. Which of the statements in Problems 69–72 are commutative? Asked in another way, in which of the following statements will the change in order produce no change in the final result?

69. A is the brother of B.
   B is the brother of A.

70. A is taller than B.
   B is taller than A.

71. Put on your left shoe and put on your right shoe.
   Put on your right shoe and put on your left shoe.

72. Get undressed and take a shower.
   Take a shower and get undressed.

73. Give an example of two things that you do that are not commutative.

74. Give an example of two things that you do that are commutative.

75. An operation $*$ is defined by

$a * b = a + b + 3$

In other words, $a * b$ is obtained by first adding a and b and then adding 3 to this result. For example, if $a = 4$ and $b = 6$,

$a * b = 4 + 6 + 3 = 13$

   a. Is the operation $*$ commutative? Asked in another way, is $a * b = b * a$?
   b. Is the operation $*$ associative? That is, is $(a * b) * c = a * (b * c)$?

76. An operation $\oslash$ is defined by "select the first of the two." For example:

$5 \oslash 3 = 5$

$\frac{1}{7} \oslash \frac{1}{2} = \frac{1}{7}$

   a. Is the operation $\oslash$ commutative?
   b. Is the operation $\oslash$ associative?

77. Compare the following calculations.

$3 + 5 \cdot 6 = 3 + 30 = 33$

$3(5 + 6) = 3 \cdot 11 = 33$

Thus, $3 + 5 \cdot 6 = 3(5 + 6)$. Can we generalize from this example and (letting $a = 3$, $b = 5$, and $c = 6$) conclude that $a + bc = a(b + c)$? Explain.

Group Activity Problem

78. Describe the error in the following simplification process.

$3[7 + 5(x - 2)] = 3[7 + 5x - 2]$
$= 3[5x + 5]$
$= 15x + 15$

In your group, discuss some possible errors that might arise when simplifying algebraic expressions. Give examples of these kinds of errors. Then present ways of helping students avoid them.

Review Problems_____

79. Consider the set of numbers

$$\{-23, \tfrac{17}{3}, \tfrac{18}{3}, \tfrac{5\pi}{3}, \sqrt{81}, \sqrt{83}\}.$$

List all numbers from the set that are
a. Natural numbers
b. Whole numbers
c. Integers
d. Rational numbers
e. Irrational numbers
f. Real numbers

80. The bar graph shown here indicates the prison population by race for juveniles and adults in all facilities from 1991 through 1993. What group or groups make up more than 10% but less than 39% of the prison population in the United States?

81. Add: $\tfrac{2}{3} + \tfrac{4}{5}$.

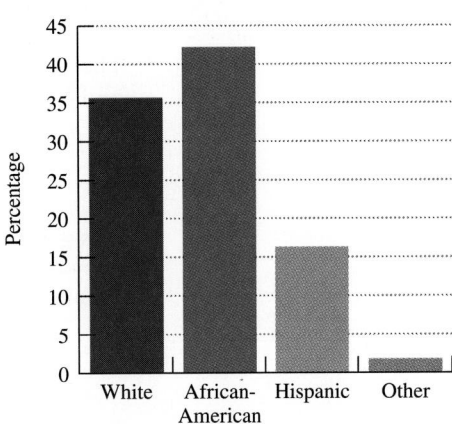

Prison Population by Race

Sources: U.S. Department of Justice, Bureau of Justice Statistics, and Office of Juvenile Justice and Deliquency Prevention

---

SECTION 1.5

Solutions Manual   **Tutorial**   **Video**
                                        1

Addition of Real Numbers

Objectives

1 Add numbers with a number line.
2 Add numbers without a number line.
3 Solve applied problems using a series of additions.
4 Simplify algebraic expressions.
5 Translate algebraic expressions into English.
6 Find sums using the identity and inverse properties.

In this section, we consider the addition of real numbers using a real number line. This will help us find a procedure for adding real numbers.

Adding with a Number Line

1 Add numbers with a number line.

The result of adding two or more numbers is called the *sum* of the numbers. We can use a number line to find $a + b$, the sum of a and b, by the following procedure.

1. Start at a.
2. a. If b is positive, move b units to the right.
   b. If b is negative, move b units to the left.
   c. If b is 0, stay at a.
3. The number where we finish on the number line represents the sum of a and b.

This procedure is illustrated in Table 1.3.

TABLE 1.3 Adding with a Number Line

Example	Finding the Sum on a Number Line	Conclusion
$7 + 4$	Start at 7. Move 4 units to the right. 0 1 2 3 4 5 6 7 8 9 10 11	We finish at 11, so $7 + 4 = 11$
$-7 + (-4)$	Move 4 units to the left. Start at -7. -11 -9 -7 -5 -3 -1	We finish at -11, so $-7 + (-4) = -11$
$7 + (-4)$	Move 4 units to the left. Start at 7. 0 1 2 3 4 5 6 7	We finish at 3, so $7 + (-4) = 3$
$-7 + 4$	Start at -7. Move 4 units to the right. -7 -6 -5 -4 -3 -2 -1 0	We finish at -3, so $-7 + 4 = -3$
$-7 + 0$	Start at -7. Stay at -7. -7 -6 -5 -4 -3 -2 -1 0	We finish at -7, so $-7 + 0 = -7$

2 Add numbers without a number line.

Adding without a Number Line

Using a number line each time we add two numbers can be a bit time consuming. It is more efficient to notice the patterns in Table 1.3 and use these patterns to write a general method for adding signed numbers. From the examples in Table 1.3, we develop the following rules.

Rules for addition of real numbers

Rule

If the numbers have the same sign:

1. Add their absolute values.
2. The sign of the sum is the same as the sign of the two numbers.

Examples

$$7 + 4 = |7| + |4| = 11$$
$$-7 + (-4) = -(|-7| + |-4|)$$
$$= -(7 + 4)$$
$$= -11$$

Rules for addition of real numbers (continued)

If the numbers have different signs:

1. Subtract the smaller absolute value from the larger absolute value.

$$7 + (-4) = +(|7| - |-4|)$$
$$= +(7 - 4)$$
$$= +3 = 3$$

2. The sign of the sum is the same as the sign of the number with the larger absolute value.

$$-7 + 4 = -(|-7| - |4|)$$
$$= -(7 - 4)$$
$$= -3$$

If one number is zero:
The sum is the other number.

$$-7 + 0 = -7$$

Study tip

You can think of gains and losses of money to find sums:

$-7 + (-4) = -11$	A loss of \$7 followed by a loss of \$4 is a net loss of \$11.
$7 + (-4) = 3$	A gain of \$7 followed by a loss of \$4 is a net gain of \$3.
$-7 + 4 = -3$	A loss of \$7 followed by a gain of \$4 is a net loss of \$3.

EXAMPLE 1 **Adding Real Numbers**

Find the sums without using a number line:

a. $-11 + (-15)$ **b.** $-\dfrac{3}{4} + \left(-\dfrac{1}{2}\right)$ **c.** $13 + (-8)$

d. $-13 + 4$ **e.** $-\dfrac{3}{4} + \dfrac{1}{2}$ **f.** $-0.2 + 0.8$

Solution

a. $-11 + (-15) = -(|-11| + |-15|)$ Add the absolute values of the numbers and use their common sign.

$$= -(11 + 15)$$ $|-11| = 11$ and $|-15| = 15$
$$= -26$$

Using a gain-loss interpretation: A loss of 11 followed by a loss of 15 implies a net loss of 26. (You might use this interpretation to work the problem mentally.)

b. $-\dfrac{3}{4} + \left(-\dfrac{1}{2}\right) = -\left(\left|-\dfrac{3}{4}\right| + \left|-\dfrac{1}{2}\right|\right)$ Add the absolute values of the numbers and use their common sign.

$$= -\left(\dfrac{3}{4} + \dfrac{1}{2}\right)$$ $\left|-\tfrac{3}{4}\right| = \tfrac{3}{4}$ and $\left|-\tfrac{1}{2}\right| = \tfrac{1}{2}$

Since we are adding fractions, we need the least common denominator.

Using technology

Try verifying some of the sums shown in Example 1 with a graphing calculator. For example, verify part (a) as follows:

$$-11 + (-15)$$

Keystrokes:

| (–) | 11 | + | (–) | 15 | ENTER |

Verify part (e) as follows:

$$-\dfrac{3}{4} + \dfrac{1}{2}$$

Keystrokes

| (–) | 3 | ÷ | 4 | + | 1 |

| ÷ | 2 | ENTER |

$$= -\left(\frac{3}{4} + \frac{2}{4}\right)$$

The least common denominator is 4, so $\frac{1}{2}$ is expressed as $\frac{2}{4}$.

$$= -\frac{5}{4}$$

The sum of $\frac{3}{4}$ and $\frac{2}{4}$ is found by adding numerators and putting this sum over the common denominator.

c. $13 + (-8)$

$= +(|13| - |-8|)$ Find the difference between the larger and smaller absolute values and use the sign of the number with the larger absolute value: $+13$.

$= +(13 - 8)$ $|13| = 13$ and $|-8| = 8$

$= 5$ The positive sign of description is omitted. A gain of 13 followed by a loss of 8 implies a net gain of 5.

d. $-13 + 4$

$= -(|-13| - |4|)$ Subtract the absolute values, using the sign of the real number with the larger absolute value, -13.

$= -(13 - 4)$ $|-13| = 13$ and $|4| = 4$

$= -9$ A loss of 13 and a gain of 4 implies a net loss of 9.

e. $-\frac{3}{4} + \frac{1}{2}$

$$= -\left(\left|-\frac{3}{4}\right| - \left|\frac{1}{2}\right|\right)$$

Find the difference between the larger and smaller absolute values. Since $\left|-\frac{3}{4}\right| > \left|\frac{1}{2}\right|$, the sum is negative.

$$= -\left(\frac{3}{4} - \frac{1}{2}\right)$$

$\left|-\frac{3}{4}\right| = \frac{3}{4}$ and $\left|\frac{1}{2}\right| = \frac{1}{2}$

$$= -\left(\frac{3}{4} - \frac{2}{4}\right)$$

$\frac{1}{2} = \frac{2}{4}$. You could have started the problem by getting the common denominator first.

$$= -\frac{1}{4}$$

A loss of $\frac{3}{4}$ followed by a gain of $\frac{1}{2}$ (or $\frac{2}{4}$) implies a net loss of $\frac{1}{4}$.

f. $-0.2 + 0.8$

$= +(|0.8| - |-0.2|)$ Use the rule or work the problem mentally using losses and gains.

$= +(0.8 - 0.2)$ $|0.8| = 0.8$ and $|-0.2| = 0.2$

$= 0.6$ A loss of $\frac{2}{10}$ and a gain of $\frac{8}{10}$ implies a net gain of $\frac{6}{10}$. ■

3 Solve applied problems using a series of additions.

Applications

Positive and negative numbers are used in everyday life to represent such things as gains and losses in the stock market, rising and falling temperatures, deposits and withdrawals on bank statements, and ascending and descending motion. Positive and negative numbers are used to solve applied problems involving a series of additions.

The easiest way to add a series of positive and negative numbers is to use the commutative and associative properties. Add all the positive numbers, then add all the negative numbers, and finally add the results. The next example illustrates this idea.

EXAMPLE 2 **An Application of Adding Signed Numbers**

A glider was towed 1000 meters into the air and then let go. It descended 70 meters into a thermal (rising bubble of warm air), which took it up 2100 meters. At this point it dropped 230 meters into a second thermal. Then it rose 1200 meters. What was its altitude at that point?

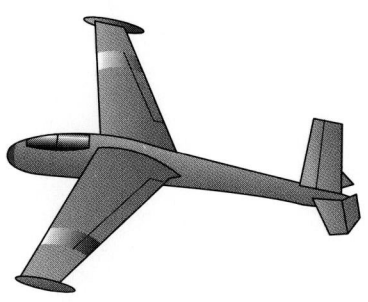

Solution

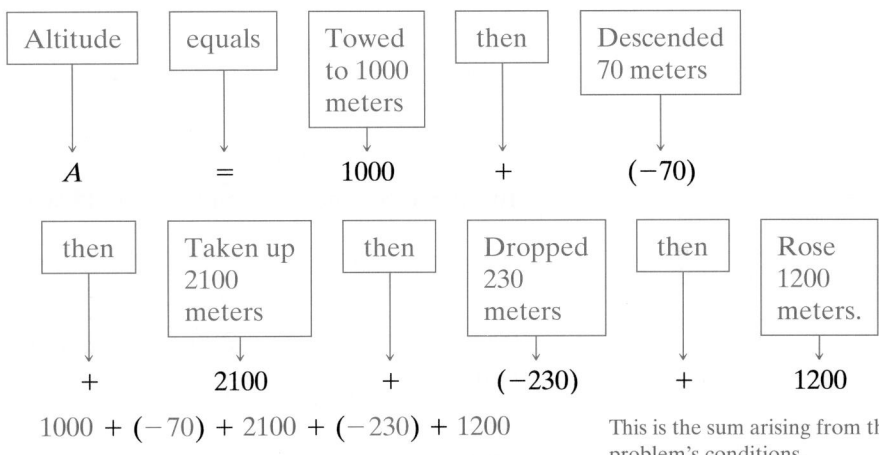

Altitude	equals	Towed to 1000 meters	then	Descended 70 meters
A	=	1000	+	(-70)

then	Taken up 2100 meters	then	Dropped 230 meters	then	Rose 1200 meters.
+	2100	+	(-230)	+	1200

$1000 + (-70) + 2100 + (-230) + 1200$ — This is the sum arising from the problem's conditions.

$= (1000 + 2100 + 1200) + [(-70) + (-230)]$ — Use the commutative and associative properties to group the positive and negative numbers.

$= 4300 + (-300)$ — Add the positive numbers and add the negative numbers.

$= 4000$ — Add the results.

The altitude of the glider is 4000 meters.

iscover for yourself

Try working Example 2 by adding from left to right. You should still obtain 4000 for the sum. What method do you find easier?

EXAMPLE 3 **Moderate Wine Consumption and Health**

Compared with real wine-drinking countries, the United States is practically dry. That may be a reason, scientists say, that our rate of heart disease is higher.

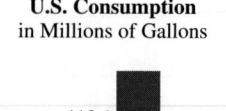

U.S. Consumption
in Millions of Gallons

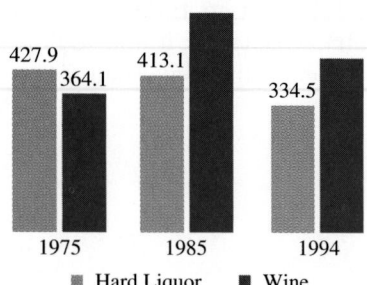

Figure 1.27

Source: Wine Market Council

From 1975 to 1985, U.S. wine consumption increased by 206.7 million gallons (see Figure 1.27). However, from 1985 to 1994, it decreased by 111.2 million gallons. If consumption in 1975 was 364.1 million gallons, what was it in 1994?

Solution

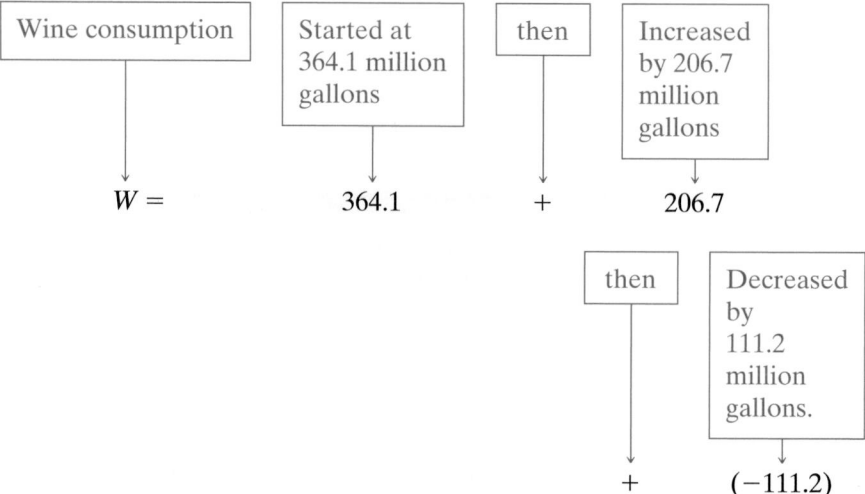

$$364.1 + 206.7 + (-111.2)$$ This is the sum arising from the problem's conditions.
$$= 570.8 + (-111.2)$$ Add the positive numbers.
$$= 459.6$$ Add the positive and negative number.

In 1994, U.S. wine consumption was 459.6 million gallons.   ■

4 Simplify algebraic expressions.

Algebraic Expressions

The rules for adding real numbers can be used to simplify certain algebraic expressions.

EXAMPLE 4   **Simplifying Algebraic Expressions**

Simplify:

a. $-11x + 7x$ **b.** $7y + (-12z) + (-9y) + 15z$
c. $5(2x - 4) + 3(8 - 7x)$

Solution

a. $-11x + 7x$ These are like terms because $-11x$ and $7x$ have identical variable factors.

$$= (-11 + 7)x$$ Apply the distributive property.
$$= -4x$$ Add within the grouping symbols.

b. $7y + (-12z) + (-9y) + 15z$

$= 7y + (-9y) + (-12z) + 15z$ Arrange like terms so that they are next to one another.

$= [7 + (-9)]y + [(-12) + 15]z$ Apply the distributive property.

$= -2y + 3z$ Add within the grouping symbols.

c. $5(2x - 4) + 3(8 - 7x)$

$= 10x - 20 + 24 - 21x$ Use the distributive property to remove the grouping symbols.

$= (10x - 21x) + (-20 + 24)$ Group like terms.

$= -11x + 4$ Combine like terms. We applied the distributive property mentally in the first grouping.

5 Translate algebraic expressions into English.

Translating Algebraic Expressions Involving Sums

There are a number of equivalent ways of translating algebraic expressions containing addition into English. This is illustrated in our next example.

Worldwide Web Users
1995 projected to 1999

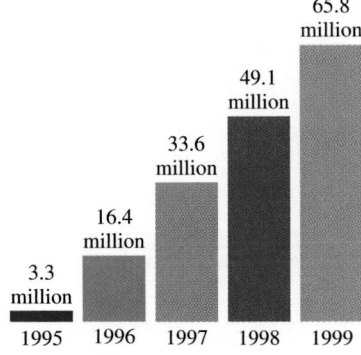

Figure 1.28
Source: IDC/Link

EXAMPLE 5   **The Growth of the Worldwide Web**

The growing popularity of the interconnected computer networks that now spread around the world is due to the ease in which information can be accessed. The Worldwide Web is attractive because users can choose their own paths through the material, browsing through graphic images, sound, and video. Figure 1.28 shows the projected growth of Worldwide Web users from 1995 to 1999.

The projected increase from 1997 to 1998 is 15.5 million users. If x represents the number of users in 1997, translate the algebraic expression $x + 15.5$ into English in as many different ways as possible.

Solution

With the understanding that all numbers are in millions, here are some ways of translating $x + 15.5$. Can you think of others?

$x + 15.5$:   The sum of the number of users in 1997 and 15.5 million

$x + 15.5$:   15.5 million more users than in 1997

$x + 15.5$:   The number of users in 1997 increased by 15.5 million

$x + 15.5$:   The number of users in 1997 plus 15.5 million

$x + 15.5$:   15.5 million users added to the number of Worldwide Web users in 1997

6 Find sums using the identity and inverse properties.

Properties of Addition

In Section 1.4 we discussed the commutative and associative properties of addition. We now add two additional properties to our previous list.

Discover for yourself

Use a number line to show that

$$6 + (-6) = 0.$$

Explain what

$$a + (-a) = 0$$

means in terms of moving along a number line.

Identity and inverse properties of addition

Let a be a real number, a variable, or an algebraic expression.

Property	Examples
Additive Identity Property	$4 + 0 = 4$
$a + 0 = a$	$-3x + 0 = -3x$
	$(5a + b) + 0 = 5a + b$
Additive Inverse Property	
$a + (-a) = 0$	$6 + (-6) = 0$
	$3x + (-3x) = 0$
	$(2y + 1) + [-(2y + 1)] = 0$

PROBLEM SET 1.5

Practice Problems

Find the sums in Problems 1–8 using a number line.

1. $-8 + 3$ **2.** $3 + (-7)$ **3.** $-10 + 2$ **4.** $9 + (-3)$

5. $-6 + 6$ **6.** $9 + (-9)$ **7.** $-4 + (-5)$ **8.** $-3 + (-6)$

Find the sums in Problems 9–42 without the use of a number line. If applicable, use a graphing calculator to verify each sum.

9. $-7 + (-5)$ **10.** $-3 + (-4)$ **11.** $12 + (-8)$ **12.** $13 + (-5)$

13. $6 + (-9)$ **14.** $3 + (-11)$ **15.** $-9 + (+4)$ **16.** $-7 + (+3)$

17. $-0.4 + (-0.9)$ **18.** $-1.5 + (-5.3)$ **19.** $-3.6 + 2.1$ **20.** $-6.3 + 5.2$

21. $-9 + (-9)$ **22.** $-13 + (-13)$ **23.** $9 + (-9)$ **24.** $13 + (-13)$

25. $-\frac{7}{10} + (-\frac{3}{10})$ **26.** $-\frac{7}{8} + (-\frac{1}{8})$ **27.** $\frac{9}{10} + (-\frac{3}{5})$ **28.** $\frac{7}{10} + (-\frac{2}{5})$

29. $-\frac{5}{8} + \frac{3}{4}$ **30.** $-\frac{5}{6} + \frac{1}{3}$ **31.** $-\frac{3}{7} + (-\frac{4}{5})$ **32.** $-\frac{3}{8} + (-\frac{2}{3})$

33. $3\frac{1}{2} + (-4\frac{1}{4})$ **34.** $5\frac{1}{2} + (-6\frac{3}{8})$ **35.** $-8.74 - 8.74$ **36.** $-5.28 + 5.28$

37. $85 + (-15) + (-20) + 12$ **38.** $60 + (-50) + (-30) + 25$

39. $-45 + (-\frac{3}{7}) + 25 + (-\frac{4}{7})$ **40.** $-50 + (-\frac{7}{9}) + 35 + (-\frac{11}{9})$

41. $3.5 + (-45) + (-8.4) + 72$ **42.** $6.4 + (-35) + (-2.6) + 14$

In Problems 43–48, simplify each algebraic expression.

43. $-8x + 5x$ **44.** $-17y + 6y$ **45.** $7x + (-5y) + (-9x) + 2y$

46. $13x + (-9y) + (-11x) + 3y$ **47.** $7(3a - 5) + 6(2 - 9a)$ **48.** $4(2a - 3) + 8(3 - 7a)$

Application Problems

Solve Problems 49–58 by writing a sum of signed numbers and adding.

49. The greatest temperature variation recorded in a day is 100 degrees in Browning, MT on January 23, 1916. The low temperature was $-56°F$. What was the high temperature?

50. In Spearfish, SD, on January 22, 1943, the temperature rose 49 degrees in two minutes. If the initial temperature was $-4°F$, what was the high temperature?

51. The Dead Sea is the lowest elevation on earth, 1312 feet below sea level. What is the elevation of a person standing 712 feet above the Dead Sea?

52. Lake Assal in Africa is 512 feet below sea level. What is the elevation of a person standing 642 feet above Lake Assal?

53. The temperature at 8:00 A.M. was $-7°F$. By noon it had risen 15°F, but by 4:00 P.M. it had fallen 5°F. What was the temperature at 4:00 P.M.?

54. On three successive plays, a football team lost 15 yards, gained 13 yards, and then lost 4 yards. What was the team's total gain or loss for the three plays?

55. A football team started with the football at the 27-yard line, advancing toward the center of the field (the 50-yard line). Four successive plays resulted in a 4-yard gain, a 2-yard loss, an 8-yard gain, and a 12-yard loss. What was the location of the football at the end of the fourth play?

56. A hiking trail has a starting elevation of 6800 feet. Then it falls 400 feet, decreases another 250 feet, and ends with an increase of 125 feet. Determine the trail's final elevation.

57. Stock prices started at $35\frac{1}{2}$ per share, rose $1\frac{1}{2}$ points, fell $\frac{1}{4}$ of a point, and then fell another $\frac{1}{2}$ a point. Determine the final price for the stock.

58. A stock started at $42\frac{1}{2}$ per share, rose $\frac{1}{4}$ of a point, rose another $1\frac{1}{4}$ points, and then fell $1\frac{3}{4}$ points. What was the final price of the stock?

59. In 1970, the average number of persons in a U.S. family was 3.58. Family size then changed as follows:

1975: decrease of 0.19 from 1970
1980: decrease of 0.11 from 1975
1985: decrease of 0.08 from 1980
1990: decrease of 0.06 from 1985

a. What was the average family size in 1990?

b. Use the graph to write a sum of positive and negative numbers representing changes in family size from 1990 through 1994. Your final sum should be 3.19, the average family size for 1994.

60. In 1967, the average score on the mathematics section of the Scholastic Aptitude Test (SAT) was 492. The average score then changed as follows:

1970: decrease of 4 points from 1967
1975: decrease of 16 points from 1970
1980: decrease of 6 points from 1975
1985: increase of 9 points from 1980
1990: increase of 1 point from 1985
1991: decrease of 2 points from 1990
1992: increase of 2 points from 1991
1993: increase of 2 points from 1992
1994: increase of 1 point from 1993

a. What was the average score on the mathematics section of the SAT in 1994?

b. Use the graph to write an estimated sum of positive and negative numbers representing the changes in the verbal SAT scores starting with 1967 and including the years that appear on the horizontal axis. What is a reasonable estimate for the average 1993 verbal score?

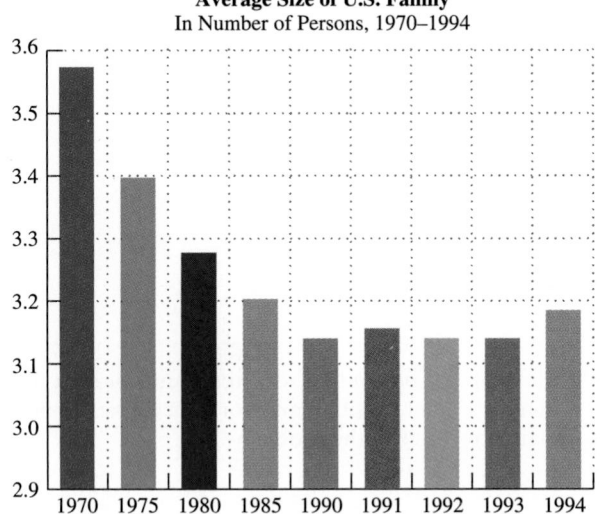

Average Size of U.S. Family
In Number of Persons, 1970–1994

Source: U.S. Bureau of the Census, *Statistical Abstract 1995*

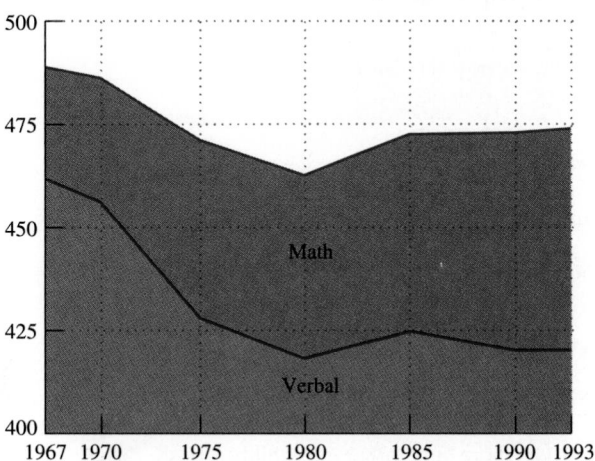

National Results of the Scholastic Aptitude Test (SAT)

61. Shown on the right is a graph relating education, gender, and income. If x represents the yearly income of women with bachelor's degrees, then $x + 18{,}000$ represents the yearly income of men with bachelor's degrees. Translate $x + 18{,}000$ into English in at least five different ways. Use words and phrases such as "sum," "more than," "increased by," "plus," and "added to."

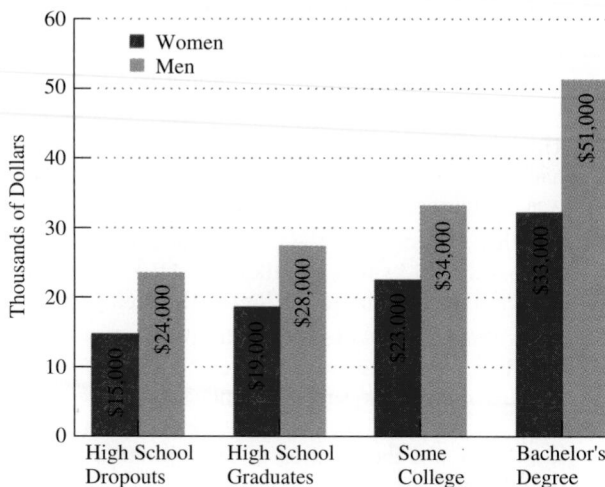

Yearly Income of American Women and Men in Four Education Groups

Source: U.S. Bureau of the Census, *Statistical Abstract* 1993: Table 73

True–False Critical Thinking Problems

62. Which one of the following statements is true?
 a. The sum of a positive number and a negative number is a negative number.
 b. $|-9 + 2| = 9 + 2$
 c. If two numbers are both positive or both negative, then the absolute value of their sum equals the sum of their absolute values.
 d. $\frac{3}{4} + \left(-\frac{3}{5}\right) = -\frac{3}{20}$

63. Which one of the following statements is true?

 a. The sum of a positive number and a negative number is a positive number.
 b. If one number is positive and the other negative, then the absolute value of their sum equals the sum of their absolute values.
 c. $\frac{3}{4} + \left(-\frac{2}{3}\right) = -\frac{1}{12}$
 d. The sum of zero and a negative number is always a negative number.

Technology Problems

In Problems 64–65, use a calculator to estimate each sum to four decimal places.

64. $-\sqrt{2} + \sqrt{5} - \sqrt{7} + \sqrt{3}$

65. $3\sqrt{5} - 2\sqrt{7} - \sqrt{11} + 4\sqrt{3}$

In Problems 66–67, use a calculator so that you can place the correct symbol ($>$ or $<$) in the box.

66. $-\sqrt{6} + 3 \ \square \ -\sqrt{2} - \sqrt{3}$

67. $-2\sqrt{7} - \sqrt{5} \ \square \ -3\sqrt{3} - 2\sqrt{2}$

Writing in Mathematics

68. When adding a positive number and a negative number, explain why the sum can be positive or negative. (Is there any other possibility? If so, discuss this in your answer.)

69. Make up a problem that requires adding at least three numbers, some positive and some negative. Then explain how to solve the problem.

Critical Thinking Problems

In Problems 70–71, find the missing term.

70. $5x + \underline{\quad} + (-11x) + (-6y) = -6x + 2y$

71. $\underline{\quad} + 11x + (-3y) + 3x = 7(2x - 3y)$

72. The perimeter of the rectangle shown here is modeled by the algebraic expression $6x + 8$. If the rectangle's width is 3, write an algebraic expression that describes its length.

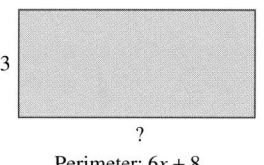

3

?

Perimeter: $6x + 8$

Review Problems

73. Use the roster method to write the set $\{x | x$ is an integer but not a natural number$\}$.

74. Consider the set

$$\{-17, -\tfrac{2}{3}, 0, \overline{3}, \sqrt{5}, \pi, \sqrt{7}, \sqrt{9}, 10\tfrac{1}{7}\}.$$

List all numbers from the set that are
   a. Natural numbers   **b.** Whole numbers
   c. Integers   **d.** Rational numbers
   e. Irrational numbers   **f.** Real numbers

75. The bar graph shows African-Americans as a percent of the U.S. population.
   a. Estimate the percent for 1970.
   b. During what years shown on the horizontal axis were there fewer than 10% African-Americans making up the U.S. population?

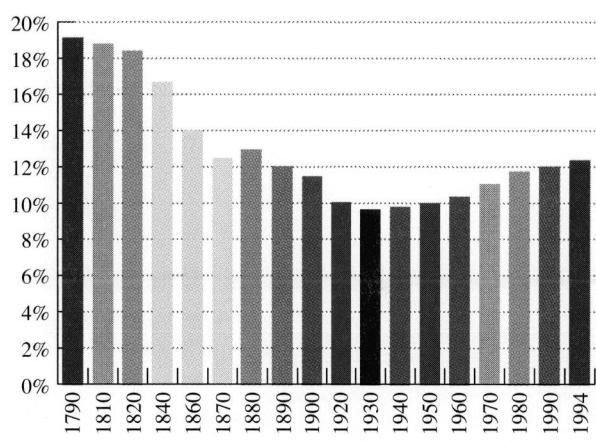

African-Americans as a Percent of U.S. Population, 1790 to 1994

Source: U.S. Bureau of the Census

SECTION 1.6

Solutions Manual   **Tutorial**   **Video**

Subtraction of Real Numbers

Objectives

1 Subtract real numbers.
2 Simplify a series of additions and subtractions.
3 Simplify algebraic expressions.
4 Solve applied problems involving subtraction.
5 Translate algebraic expressions with subtraction into English.

In the last section, we studied ways to add real numbers. In this section, we will define subtraction in terms of addition, using rules for addition to solve subtraction problems.

We can always express a subtraction problem as an equivalent addition problem. For example, we know that

$$8 - 3 = 5.$$

Based on our work in the previous section, we also know that

$$8 + (-3) = 5.$$

This means that

$$8 - 3 = 8 + (-3).$$

To subtract 3 from 8, we add 8 and the opposite (the additive inverse) of 3. Generalizing from this situation, we define subtraction as follows.

1 Subtract real numbers.

Definition of subtraction

For all real numbers a and b,

$$a - b = a + (-b).$$

In words: To subtract b from a, add the opposite of b to a.

This definition gives us a procedure for subtracting real numbers.

Subtracting real numbers

1. Change the subtraction operation to addition.
2. Change the sign of the number being subtracted.
3. Add, using one of the rules for adding numbers with the same signs or different signs.

EXAMPLE 1   **Using the Definition of Subtraction**

Subtract:

a. $7 - 10$ **b.** $5 - (-6)$ **c.** $-9 - (-3)$

Solution

Change $-$ to $+$

a. $7 - 10 = 7 + (-10)$ To subtract a real number, add its opposite.

Opposite of 10

$= -3$ $7 + (-10) = -3$

Change $-$ to $+$

b. $5 - (-6) = 5 + 6$ To subtract a real number, add its opposite.

Opposite of -6

$= 11$ Complete the problem by adding 5 and 6.

Change $-$ to $+$

c. $-9 - (-3) = -9 + 3$ Add the opposite of the number being subtracted.

Opposite of -3

$= -6$ The sum of -9 and 3 is -6.

The definition of subtraction can be applied to real numbers that are not integers.

EXAMPLE 2   **Using the Definition of Subtraction**

Subtract:

a. $-5.2 - (-11.4)$ **b.** $-\dfrac{3}{4} - \dfrac{2}{3}$ **c.** $4\pi - (-9\pi)$

Solution

a. Change $-$ to $+$

$$-5.2 - (-11.4) = -5.2 + 11.4 = 6.2$$

Opposite of -11.4

b. Change $-$ to $+$

$$-\frac{3}{4} - \frac{2}{3} = -\frac{3}{4} + \left(-\frac{2}{3}\right) = -\frac{9}{12} + \left(-\frac{8}{12}\right) = -\frac{17}{12}$$

Opposite of $\frac{2}{3}$

c. Change $-$ to $+$

$$4\pi - (-9\pi) = 4\pi + 9\pi = (4 + 9)\pi = 13\pi$$

Opposite of -9π

This step can be worked mentally.

2 Simplify a series of additions and subtractions.

If a problem contains a series of additions and subtractions:

1. Change all subtractions to additions of opposites.
2. Group and then add all the positive numbers.
3. Group and then add all the negative numbers.
4. Add the results of steps 2 and 3.

EXAMPLE 3   **Simplifying a Series of Additions and Subtractions**

Simplify: $7 - (-5) - 11 - (-6) - 19$.

Solution

$$7 - (-5) - 11 - (-6) - 19$$
$$= 7 + 5 + (-11) + 6 + (-19) \qquad \text{Write subtractions as additions of opposites.}$$
$$= (7 + 5 + 6) + [(-11) + (-19)] \qquad \text{Group the positive and the negative numbers.}$$
$$= 18 + (-30) \qquad \text{Add the positive numbers and add the negative numbers.}$$
$$= -12 \qquad \text{Add the results.}$$

3 Simplify algebraic expressions.

Algebraic Expressions

The procedure for subtracting real numbers can be used to simplify certain algebraic expressions.

EXAMPLE 4   **Simplifying Algebraic Expressions**

Simplify:

a. $-13y - (-15y)$ b. $-11a - 8b - (-2a) + 14b$

Solution

Change − to +

a. $-13y - (-15y) = -13y + 15y$ Use the definition of subtraction.

Opposite of $-15y$

$$= 2y$$ Add like terms mentally.

b. $-11a - 8b - (-2a) + 14b$
$$= -11a + (-8b) + 2a + 14b$$ Write subtractions as additions of opposites.
$$= -11a + 2a + (-8b) + 14b$$ Arrange like terms so that they are next to one another.
$$= -9a + 6b$$ Add like terms mentally.

Using the commutative property of addition, we can write this simplified expression as $6b + (-9a)$ or, more simply, $6b - 9a$.   ■

4 Solve applied problems involving subtraction.

Applications

Subtraction is used to solve problems in which the word "difference" appears.

EXAMPLE 5   **An Application of Subtraction**

Figure 1.29 shows that the peak of Mount Everest is 8848 meters above sea level. The Marianas Trench, on the floor of the Pacific Ocean, is 10,915 meters below sea level. What is the distance from the Marianas Trench to the peak of Mount Everest?

8848 Meters Above Sea Level   Mt. Everest

Sea Level ⊢ 0

10,915 Meters Below Sea Level   ⊢ Marianas Trench

Figure 1.29

The distance from the Marianas Trench to Mt. Everest

Solution

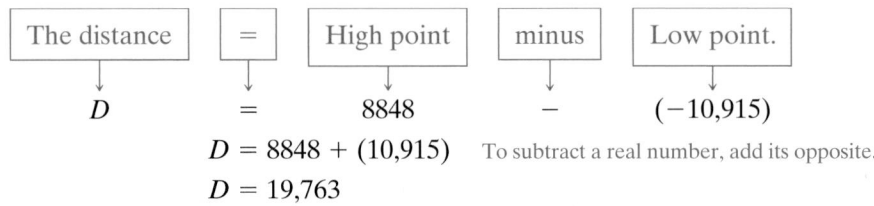

The distance	=	High point	minus	Low point.
D	=	8848	−	$(-10,915)$

$$D = 8848 + (10,915)$$ To subtract a real number, add its opposite.
$$D = 19,763$$

The distance from the Marianas Trench to the peak of Mount Everest is 19,763 meters.   ■
In Example 5, we can also say that the *difference* in elevation between the peak of Mount Everest and the Marianas Trench is 19,763 meters.

> The difference between a and b is translated by the algebraic expression $a - b$.

EXAMPLE 6   **An Application of Subtraction Using the Word Difference**

The high temperature for one day on the surface of Mars is $-25°C$ and the low temperature is $-110°C$. What is the difference between the high and the low temperatures on that day?

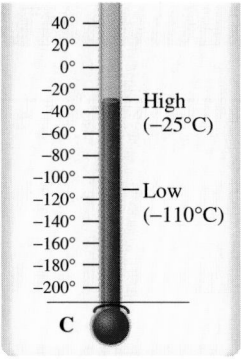

Figure 1.30

5 Translate algebraic expressions with subtraction into English.

Most Popular Spectator Sports in the U.S.

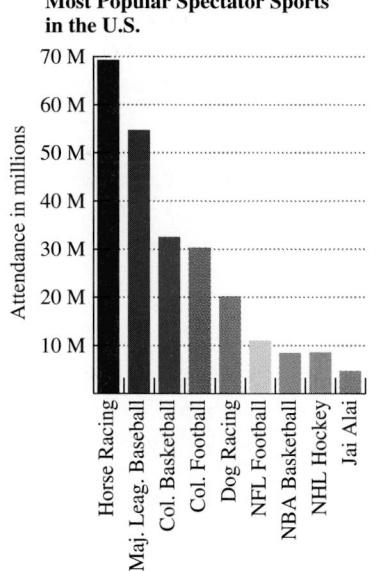

Figure 1.31
Source: U.S. Bureau of the Census

Solution

The difference between the high and low temperatures can be seen in Figure 1.30.

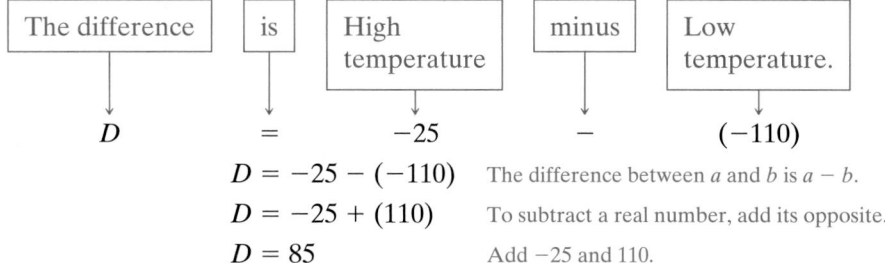

$$D \qquad = \qquad -25 \qquad - \qquad (-110)$$

$D = -25 - (-110)$ The difference between a and b is $a - b$.

$D = -25 + (110)$ To subtract a real number, add its opposite.

$D = 85$ Add -25 and 110.

The difference between the high and low temperatures is 85°C. ■

There are a number of equivalent ways of translating algebraic expressions containing subtraction into English. This is illustrated in Example 7.

EXAMPLE 7   Spectator Sports

America's passion for gambling has overtaken its passion for baseball. The graph in Figure 1.31 shows the top spectator sports in the United States by annual attendance.

The actual numbers for the first two categories in the graph are:

Sport	Spectators	
Horse racing	69,946,000	⎱ The difference is 69,946,000 −
Major league baseball	53,800,000	⎰ 53,800,000 = 16,146,000.

If x represents the number of annual spectators at horse racing, then $x - 16,146,000$ represents the number of annual spectators at major league baseball games. Translate $x - 16,146,000$ into English in as many different ways as possible.

Solution

Here are some possible translations for $x - 16,146,000$. Can you think of others?

• The number of spectators at horse racing minus 16,146,000
• The number of spectators at horse racing decreased by 16,146,000
• The difference between the number of spectators at horse racing and 16,146,000
• 16,146,000 less than the number of spectators at horse racing
• 16,146,000 subtracted from the number of spectators at horse racing ■

tudy tip

Here are two similar English phrases that have very different translations:

    7 less than 10: $10 - 7$

    7 *is* less than 10: $7 < 10$

Think carefully about what is expressed in English before you translate into the language of algebra.

P R O B L E M   S E T   1 . 6

Practice Problems

In Problems 1–44, perform the indicated subtraction. If your course uses graphing calculators, verify each result with the calculator.

1. $13 - 8$

2. $14 - 3$

3. $8 - 15$

4. $9 - 20$

5. $4 - (-10)$

6. $3 - (-17)$

7. $-6 - (-17)$

8. $-4 - (-19)$

9. $-12 - (-3)$

10. $-19 - (-2)$

11. $-11 - 17$

12. $-19 - 21$

13. $\frac{1}{5} - (-\frac{3}{5})$

14. $\frac{1}{7} - (-\frac{3}{7})$

15. $-\frac{4}{5} - (-\frac{1}{5})$

16. $-\frac{4}{9} - (-\frac{1}{9})$

17. $\frac{1}{2} - (-\frac{1}{4})$

18. $\frac{2}{5} - (-\frac{1}{10})$

19. $-4.4 - 9.3$

20. $-5.7 - 6.1$

21. $-7.2 - (-5.1)$

22. $-9.8 - (-3.4)$

23. $3.1 - (-6.03)$

24. $5.2 - (-8.04)$

25. $13 - 2 - (-8)$

26. $14 - 3 - (-7)$

27. $9 - 8 + 3 - 7$

28. $8 - 2 + 5 - 13$

29. $-6 - 2 + 3 - 10$

30. $-9 - 5 + 4 - 17$

31. $-10 - (-5) + 7 - 2$

32. $-6 - (-3) + 8 - 11$

33. $-23 - 11 - (-7) + (-25)$

34. $-19 - 8 - (-6) + (-21)$

35. $-823 - 146 - 50 - (-832)$

36. $-726 - 422 - 921 - (-816)$

37. $1 - \frac{2}{3} - (-\frac{5}{6})$

38. $2 - \frac{3}{4} - (-\frac{7}{8})$

39. $-30 - 14 + 11 - (-9) - (-6) + 17$

40. $-20 - 18 + 11 - (-13) - (-4) + 30$

41. $-0.16 - 5.2 - (-0.87)$

42. $-1.9 - 3 - (-0.26)$

43. $-\frac{3}{4} - \frac{1}{4} - (-\frac{5}{8})$

44. $-\frac{1}{2} - \frac{2}{3} - (-\frac{1}{3})$

In Problems 45–54, simplify each algebraic expression.

45. $-17x - (-23x)$

46. $-25x - (-17x)$

47. $7a - (-15a) + 4a$

48. $4b - (-11b) + 6b$

49. $3 - 4y - (-9) + 6y$

50. $8 - 9y - (-5) + 7y$

51. $-6 - (-7b) + 7b + 5b - (-13)$

52. $-12 - (-6b) + 6b + 4b - (-14)$

53. $-13x - 5y - (-9x) + 7y$

54. $-17x - 6y - (-8y) + 12x$

Application Problems

55. The peak of Mount Whitney is 14,494 feet above sea level. Mount Whitney can be seen directly above Death Valley, which is 282 feet below sea level. How far above Death Valley is the peak of Mount Whitney?

56. Mount Kilimanjaro, the highest point in Africa, is 19,321 feet above sea level. Qattara Depression, Egypt, the lowest point in Africa, is 436 feet below sea level. What is the difference in elevation between these geographic locations?

57. The greatest recorded temperature ranges are around the Siberian "cold pole" in the east of Russia. Temperatures in Verkhoyansk have ranged from $-90°F$ to $98°F$. What is the difference between these high and low temperatures? Express the answer in a sentence using the word *range*.

58. The highest temperature ever recorded in the United States was 134°F in Death Valley, California. The lowest temperature ever recorded was $-79.8°F$ in Prospect Creek, Alaska. What is the difference between these high and low temperatures? Express the answer in a sentence using the word *range*.

59. The following list gives the percentage of adults attending major art activities in the United States in 1992 and 1982. For each event, find the difference between the percentage of people who attended the event in 1992 and the percentage of people who attended the event in 1982. Use the graph below the list to verify each difference.

Activity	1992	1982
Art museums	26.7%	22.1%
Arts and crafts fairs	40.7	39.0
Plays	13.5	11.9
Jazz	10.6	9.6
Ballet	4.7	4.2
Opera	3.3	3.0
Classical music	12.5	13.0
Musicals	17.4	18.6
Historic parks	34.5	39.0

Increases/Decreases in Art-Related Activities in 10-Year Period 1982–1992

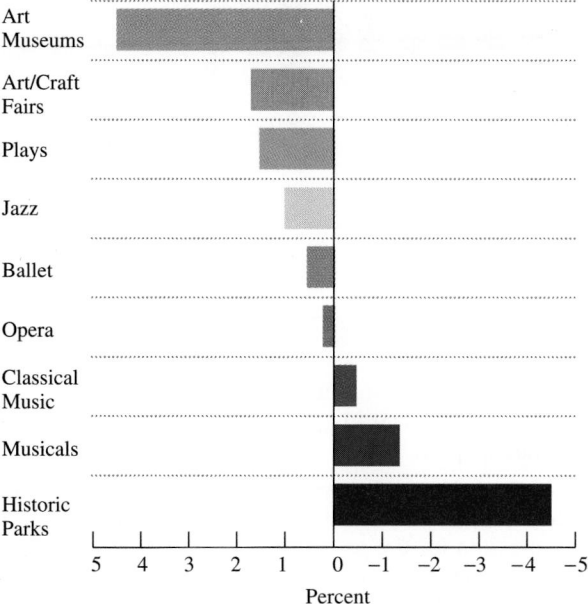

Source: U.S. Bureau of the Census

60. The graph compares the increase or decrease in murder rates for selected U.S. cities in 1994 and 1995. Compute the difference between the percents in the graph for the following cities and then interpret your result. Sample: New York and Seattle

$$-25\% - (-32\%) = -25\% + 32\% = 7\%$$

New York's change in murder rate was 7% more than Seattle's change in murder rate.
   a. New York and Miami
   b. Washington and St. Louis
   c. Boston and Baltimore
   d. Baltimore and New Orleans
   e. Boston and Seattle
   f. New Orleans and Miami

Murder Rates, Selected U.S. Cities Increase/Decrease, by Percent, 1994 vs. 1995

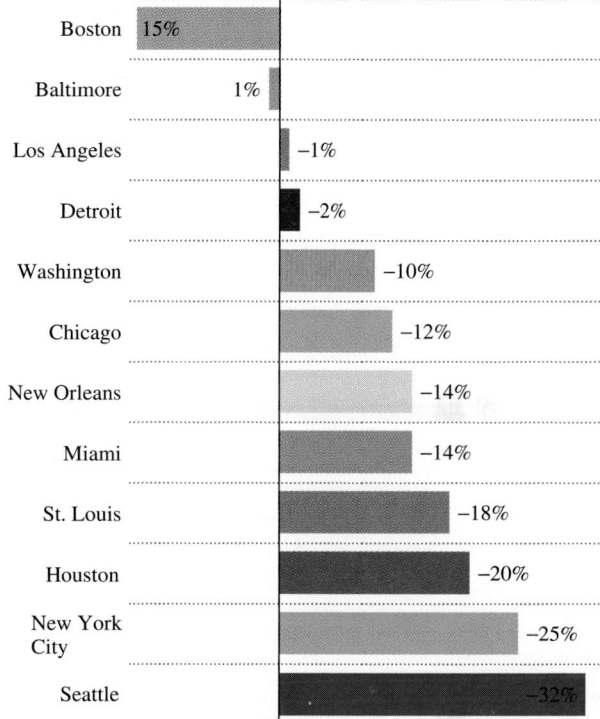

Source: Local Police Departments

61. The table below and graph in the left column on the next page show the percentage of American adults who feel stressed several times each week ("frequently stressed"). If x represents the percentage of people who feel frequently stressed in the 30 to 39 age group, then $x - 8$ represents the percentage of people who feel frequently stressed in the 18 to 29 age group. Translate $x - 8$ into English in at least four different ways. Use words and phrases such as "minus," "decreased by," "difference between," and "less than" in your English translations.

Age	Frequently stressed
18 to 29	29%
30 to 39	37
40 to 49	35
50 to 64	29
65 and older	22

Who Gets Stressed By Age Groups

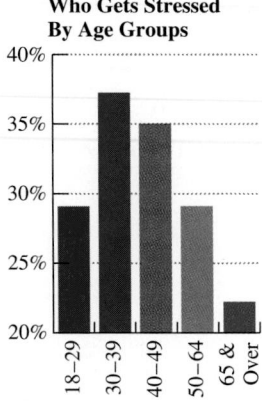

Source: Prevention Index, 1994

The table below and graph on the right indicate America's confidence in its institutions, as measured by a Gallup poll in 1994.

Use the table to answer Problems 62–65.

Institutions	Great deal/ quite a lot	Very little or none
Military	64%	8%
Organized religion	54	16
Police	54	12
Supreme Court	42	17
Presidency	38	27
Medical system	36	26
Television news	35	27
Banks	35	17
Public schools	34	25
Newspapers	29	28
Organized labor	26	31
Big business	26	30
Congress	18	32
Criminal justice system	15	49

Confidence in America's Institutions
Percent Who Have "a Great Deal" of Confidence in Various Institutions

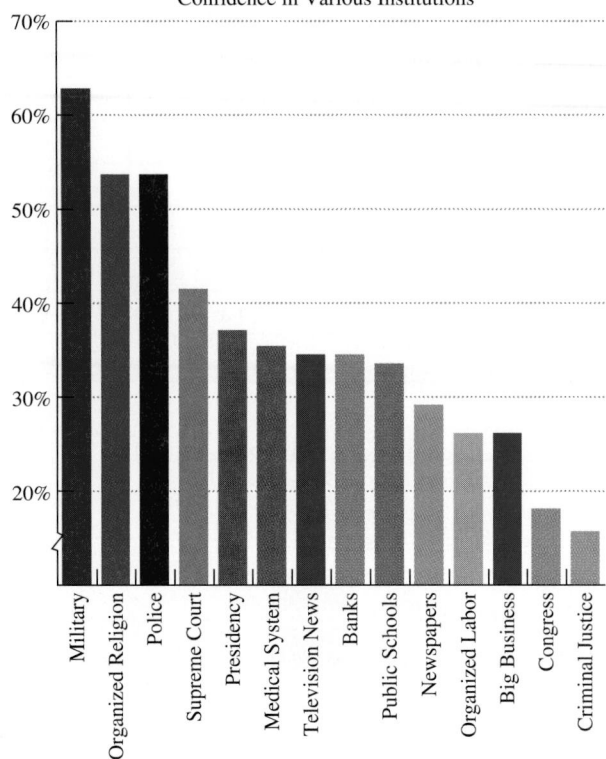

Source: Gallup poll of 1994

62. If a represents the percent who have a great deal of confidence in the military, write an algebraic expression for the percent having a great deal of confidence in newspapers.

63. If b represents the percent who have a great deal of confidence in the medical system, write an algebraic expression for the percent having a great deal of confidence in the criminal justice system.

64. If c represents the percent who have a great deal of confidence in newspapers, write an algebraic expression for the percent having a great deal of confidence in the police.

65. If d represents the percent who have a great deal of confidence in big business, write an algebraic expression for the percent having a great deal of confidence in television news.

66. The figure shows a board that is x feet long with a 3-foot piece cut from it. Write an algebraic expression for the length of the remaining piece.

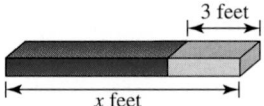

67. The total floor area of a two-story house is 3600 square feet. If the area of the first floor is x square feet, write an algebraic expression for the area of the second floor.

True–False Critical Thinking Problems

68. Which of the following statements is true?
  a. A jar contains 422 marbles. One person estimates that it contains 325 marbles, and a second estimates that it contains 500 marbles. The closer of the two estimates is 325.
  b. If a and b are negative numbers, then $a - b$ is a negative number.
  c. $7 - (-2) = 5$
  d. The result of a subtracted from b is the same as the sum of b and the opposite of a.

69. Which one of the following statements is true?
  a. If two people have had a 10-year relationship in a year represented by x, then their relationship began in a year represented by $10 - x$.
  b. $-6 - (-2) = -8$
  c. The difference between 0 and a negative number is always a positive number.
  d. The difference between two negative numbers is never a positive number.

Technology Problems

Use a calculator to estimate the expressions in Problems 70–71 to four decimal places.

70. $4\sqrt{2} - (-3\sqrt{5}) - (-\sqrt{7}) + \sqrt{3}$

71. $-5\sqrt{3} - (-2\sqrt{11}) - (-\sqrt{17}) + \sqrt{6}$

In Problems 72–73, use a calculator so that you can place the correct symbol ($<$ or $>$) in the box.

72. $-\sqrt{3} + 5 \ \square \ -\sqrt{2} - (-5\frac{1}{4})$

73. $-\sqrt{7} - (-\sqrt{3}) \ \square \ -\sqrt{11} - (-\sqrt{5})$

Writing in Mathematics

74. Explain how to subtract real numbers.

75. Make up a real world problem that involves the difference between a positive and negative number. Then explain how to solve the problem.

Critical Thinking Problems

76. The golden age of Athens culminated in 212 B.C. and the golden age of India culminated in A.D. 500. Determine the number of years that elapsed between these dates. [*Note:* When the calendar was reformed, the number 0 had not been invented. There was no year 0 and the year A.D. 1 followed the year 1 B.C. Calculate the difference between the years in the usual way and then use this added bit of information to modify your answer.]

77. If two people have birth years 1 year apart, what is the smallest and largest possible difference in their birth days?

78. Find the value:
  $-1 + 2 - 3 + 4 - 5 + 6 - \cdots - 99 + 100$.

Group Activity Problem

79. Identify the error in the following solution:

$$\frac{18}{17} - \frac{20}{17} - \frac{15}{17} = \frac{18}{17} - \frac{5}{17} = \frac{13}{17}$$

In your group, list common errors that can occur when adding or subtracting real numbers. Give examples and discuss ways in which these common errors can be avoided.

Review Problems

80. Consider the set

$$\{-123, -\tfrac{3}{9}, 0, 0.45, \sqrt{1}, \sqrt{7}, e, 8\tfrac{1}{5}\}.$$

List all numbers from the set that are
a. Natural numbers   **b.** Whole numbers
c. Integers   **d.** Rational numbers
e. Irrational numbers   **f.** Real numbers

81. The first reading on a thermometer is at 12°F and in three consecutive readings there is an increase of 4°F, a decrease of 17°F, and a decrease of 2°F. What is the temperature of the final reading?

82. Place the correct symbol ($<$, $>$, or $=$) between the two numbers. $-\tfrac{1}{2}$ ☐ $-\tfrac{1}{10}$

S E C T I O N   1 . 7

Solutions   Tutorial   Video
Manual   2

| Multiply real numbers.

Multiplication of Real Numbers

Objectives

1 Multiply real numbers.
2 Use the order of operations.
3 Simplify algebraic expressions.
4 Model reality with algebraic expressions.

In this section, we begin by viewing multiplication as repeated addition. Using this approach and the patterns we find, we will show how to multiply real numbers.

Multiplication of two counting numbers can be described as repeated addition. For example,

$$3 \times 7 = 7 + 7 + 7$$

where 7 is repeated as an addend three times. Since $3 \times 7 = 7 \times 3$, we can think of 3×7 as indicating that 3 is repeated as an addend seven times. Thus,

$$3 \times 7 = 3 + 3 + 3 + 3 + 3 + 3 + 3.$$

Multiplying real numbers is referred to as finding the *product* of the numbers. The numbers being multiplied are called *factors* of the product. For example, the product of 3 and 7 is 21. Furthermore, 3 and 7 are factors of 21.

The product of 3 and 7 can be shown in a number of ways. These include

$$3 \times 7 \qquad 3 \cdot 7 \qquad 3(7) \qquad (3)7 \qquad \text{and} \qquad (3)(7).$$

Rules for multiplying signed numbers can be obtained by representing multiplication as repeated addition. Here are some examples.

Multiplication	Repeated Addition	
$4(-3)$	$(-3) + (-3) + (-3) + (-3) = -12$	Add -3 four times.
$3(-3)$	$(-3) + (-3) + (-3) = -9$	Add -3 three times.
$2(-3)$	$(-3) + (-3) = -6$	Add -3 two times.
$1(-3)$	-3	-3 is used as a factor once.

Observe that if two factors have opposite signs (one factor is positive and the other is negative), the sign of the product is negative.

Multiplying numbers with different signs

The product of two numbers with different signs is a negative number. The multiplication is performed by multiplying the absolute values of the two numbers and giving the answer a negative sign.

EXAMPLE 1 **Multiplying Two Numbers with Opposite Signs**

Find the product:

a. $(-6)(3)$ **b.** $\left(3\frac{1}{5}\right)\left(-\frac{7}{6}\right)$

Solution

a. $(-6)(3) = -(6 \cdot 3)$ The multiplication is performed by multiplying $|-6|$ and $|3|$, or $6 \cdot 3$.

$\qquad\qquad = -18$ Two numbers with opposite signs have a negative product.

b. $\left(3\frac{1}{5}\right)\left(-\frac{7}{6}\right)$

$= -\left(\frac{16}{5} \cdot \frac{7}{6}\right)$ Multiply absolute values and attach a negative sign to the product. Recall that $3\frac{1}{5} = \frac{5 \cdot 3 + 1}{5} = \frac{15 + 1}{5} = \frac{16}{5}$

$= -\left(\frac{2 \cdot 8}{5} \cdot \frac{7}{2 \cdot 3}\right)$ Factor and divide out the common factor.

$= -\left(\frac{8 \cdot 7}{5 \cdot 3}\right)$ Multiply the remaining factors

$= -\frac{56}{15}$

Using technology

You can verify part (b) with a graphing calculator as follows:

(	3	+	1	÷	5	)
×	(	(−)7	÷	6
)	ENTER

What happens if parentheses are not placed around $-\frac{7}{6}$?

Let's consider the product of two negative numbers by looking at the pattern formed when one factor keeps decreasing by 1.

This first number keeps decreasing by 1.

$\rightarrow 4(-3) = -12 \leftarrow$ These products keep increasing by 3.

$3(-3) = -9$
$2(-3) = -6$
$1(-3) = -3$
$\rightarrow 0(-3) = 0 \quad$ increases by 3
$-1(-3) = 3 \quad$ increases by 3
$-2(-3) = 6$
$-3(-3) = 9$

Study tip

The product of 0 and any real number is 0.

$0 \cdot a = a \cdot 0 = 0$

Notice that in each case, by continuing the pattern, the product of two negative numbers results in a positive number. This observation can be generalized as follows.

> **Multiplying two negative numbers**
>
> The product of two negative numbers is a positive number. The multiplication is performed by multiplying the absolute values of the two numbers.

EXAMPLE 2   **Multiplying Two Negative Numbers**

Find the product:

a. $(-9)(-10)$ **b.** $\left(-\dfrac{1}{3}\right)\left(-\dfrac{1}{2}\right)$ **c.** $(-0.03)(-0.2)$

Solution

a. $(-9)(-10)$

$\quad = +(9 \cdot 10)$ Multiply the absolute values: $|-9| = 9$ and $|-10| = 10$. The product of two negative numbers is positive.

$\quad = 90$ There is no need to attach a positive sign since when no sign is attached, a number is assumed to be positive.

b. $\left(-\dfrac{1}{3}\right)\left(-\dfrac{1}{2}\right)$

$\quad = \dfrac{1}{3} \cdot \dfrac{1}{2}$ Multiply the absolute values. The product is positive.

$\quad = \dfrac{1}{6}$ $\frac{1}{3} \cdot \frac{1}{2} = \frac{1 \cdot 1}{3 \cdot 2} = \frac{1}{6}$

c. $(-0.03)(-0.2)$

$\quad = (0.03)(0.2)$ This step is usually omitted.

$\quad = 0.006$ Place the decimal point so that the number of decimal places equals the sum of the decimal places in the two factors.

$\frac{1}{3}$ of $\frac{1}{2} = \frac{1}{3} \cdot \frac{1}{2} = \frac{1}{6}$

We know from our prior work in arithmetic that the product of two positive numbers is positive. We have seen now that the product of two negative numbers is positive. We can tie together these results by saying that two numbers with the same sign have a positive product.

Let's take a moment to summarize the rules for multiplying real numbers.

> **Multiplying real numbers**
>
> **1.** The product of two numbers with the same sign is a positive number. The product of two numbers with different signs is a negative number. The multiplication is performed by multiplying the absolute values of the two numbers and giving the answer the proper sign.
> **2.** The product of 0 and any real number is 0.

Discover for yourself

When multiplying more than two numbers, you can determine whether the product is positive or negative by applying a rule. Use the following to discover the rule:

$\underbrace{(-1)(-1)}_{1}(-1) = 1(-1) = -1$

$\underbrace{(-1)(-1)}_{-1}\underbrace{(-1)(-1)}$

$\quad = (-1)(-1) = 1$

The ability to describe patterns is an important part of mathematics. Take a few minutes to read the Discover for Yourself box that appears on

Enrichment Essay

Multiplying Negative Numbers

Minus times minus equals plus.
The reason for this we need not discuss.
— *W. H. Auden (poet)*

The property $(-a)(-b) = ab$ can be proved in more advanced mathematics courses. However, a stumbling block as students begin studying algebra is "seeing" how the product of two negative numbers can be positive. What do you think of the following explanation?

Good People as Positive; Bad People as Negative

"Imagine a town, where good people are moving in and out," wrote Roy Dubisch (*The Mathematics Teacher*, December 1971), "and bad people are also moving in and out. Obviously a good person is a $+$ and a bad person, $-$. Equally obvious, moving in is $+$ and moving out is $-$. Still further, it is evident that a good person moving into town is a $+$ for the town, a good person leaving town is a $-$; a bad person moving into town is a $-$; and, finally, a bad person leaving town is a $+$." Thus, if ten groups of people containing five bad people per group move out, the town gains $-10(-5) = 50$ points.

Explain how to interpret $-3(4) = -12$ and $-3(-4) = 12$ according to this code.

page 80. Continue adding additional factors of -1 and write a rule for the number of negative factors and the sign of the product. Did you discover the following rule?

Multiplying more than two numbers

Assuming that no number in a product is zero: If a multiplication problem involves an even number of negative factors, the sign of the product is positive. If there is an odd number of negative factors, the sign of the product is negative.

EXAMPLE 3   **Multiplying More Than Two Numbers**

Find the product:

a. $(4)(-1)(3)(-2)(-5)$ **b.** $(-1)(-2)(-2)(3)(-4)$

Solution

a. $(4)(-1)(3)(-2)(-5)$
$= -120$

The product is negative because we have an odd number of negative factors, namely, three and $4 \cdot 1 \cdot 3 \cdot 2 \cdot 5 = 120$.

b. $(-1)(-2)(-2)(3)(-4)$
$= 48$

The product is positive because we have an even number of negative factors, namely, four and $1 \cdot 2 \cdot 2 \cdot 3 \cdot 4 = 48$. ■

2 Use the order of operations.

Order of Operations

In Section 1.4, we pointed out in a Study Tip that the order in which we add, subtract, multiply, and divide is important. There are rules for the order in which operations should be done.

An order of operations agreement

1. Perform all calculations in parentheses, working multiplications before additions and subtractions.
2. Do any multiplications in the order in which they occur, working from left to right.
3. Perform the remaining series of additions and subtractions last.

We will expand on this order in Section 1.9. At this point, we have a systematic procedure for working with problems that contain grouping symbols, multiplications, additions, and subtractions.

EXAMPLE 4   **Using the Order of Operations**

Perform the indicated operations:

a. $(-7)(3) - (-5)(4)$ **b.** $3 - 5(-4 - 2)$

Solution

a. $(-7)(3) - (-5)(4)$ First, find all products, working from left to right.
$= -21 - (-20)$ $(-7)(3) = -21$ and $(-5)(4) = -20$
$= -21 + 20$ Now perform the subtraction by adding an opposite.
$= -1$

b. $3 - 5(-4 - 2)$ Begin work within the parentheses.
$= 3 - 5(-4 + (-2))$ Perform subtraction by adding an opposite.
$= 3 - 5(-6)$ Finish the addition in parentheses. Once grouping symbols are removed, we work the multiplication.
$= 3 - (-30)$ $5(-6) = -30$. Finally, perform the subtraction.
$= 3 + 30$ Add an opposite.
$= 33$ Complete the problem by adding. ■

3 Simplify algebraic expressions.

Algebraic Expressions

In Section 1.4, we discussed the commutative and associative properties of multiplication. We also know that multiplication distributes over addition and subtraction. We now add some additional properties to our previous list. These properties are frequently helpful in simplifying algebraic expressions.

Additional properties of multiplication

Let a be a real number, a variable, or an algebraic expression.

Property	Examples
Multiplicative identity property *(Multiplication property of 1)*	$\sqrt{3} \cdot 1 = \sqrt{3}$

$a \cdot 1 = a$ $1 \cdot \pi = \pi$

$1 \cdot a = a$ $1x = x$

1 is called the *multiplicative* $1(2x + 3) = 2x + 3$
identity.

Multiplication property of -1 $-1 \cdot \sqrt{3} = -\sqrt{3}$

$-1 \cdot a = -a$ $-1\left(-\dfrac{3}{4}\right) = \dfrac{3}{4}$

$a(-1) = -a$ $-1x = -x$

Negative one times a is the
opposite of a. $-(x + 4) = -1(x + 4) = -x - 4$

Multiplication property of 0 $0(-17) = 0$

$a \cdot 0 = 0$ $4\pi \cdot 0 = 0$

$0 \cdot a = 0$ $3x \cdot 0 = 0$

            $0(y + 4) = 0$

In the preceding box, we used three steps to remove the parentheses from $-(x + 4)$. First, we used the multiplication property of -1.

$$-(x + 4) = -1(x + 4)$$

Then we used the distributive property, distributing -1 to each term in parentheses.

$$-1(x + 4) = (-1)x + (-1)4 = -x + (-4) = -x - 4$$

The Study Tip explains a fast way to obtain $-(x + 4) = -x - 4$ in just one step. Here are some examples that illustrate the Study Tip.

$$-(11x + 5) = -11x - 5$$
$$-(11x - 5) = -11x + 5$$
$$-(-11x + 5) = 11x - 5$$
$$-(-11x - 5) = 11x + 5$$

study tip

If a negative sign precedes parentheses, remove parentheses and change signs of all the terms within parentheses.

EXAMPLE 5   **Simplifying Algebraic Expressions**

Simplify:

a. $-2(3x)$ **b.** $6x + x$ **c.** $8a - 9a$
d. $-3(2x - 5)$ **e.** $-(3y - 8)$

iscover for yourself

Verify each simplification in Example 5 by substituting −5 for the variable. The value of the given expression should be the same as the value of the simplified expression. Which expression is easier to evaluate?

Solution

We will show all steps in the solution process. However, you probably are working many of these steps mentally.

a. $-2(3x)$
$$= (-2 \cdot 3)x \quad \text{Use the associative property and group the first two numbers.}$$
$$= -6x \quad \text{Numbers with opposite signs have a negative product.}$$

b. $6x + x$
$$= 6x + 1x \quad \text{Use the multiplication property of 1.}$$
$$= (6 + 1)x \quad \text{Apply the distributive property.}$$
$$= 7x$$

c. $8a - 9a$
$$= (8 - 9)a \quad \text{Apply the distributive property.}$$
$$= -1a$$
$$= -a \quad \text{Apply the multiplication property of } -1.$$

d. $-3(2x - 5)$
$$= -3(2x) - (-3)(5) \quad \text{Apply the distributive property.}$$
$$= -6x - (-15) \quad \text{Multiply.}$$
$$= -6x + 15 \quad \text{Subtraction is the addition of an opposite.}$$

e. $-(3y - 8)$
$$= -3y + 8 \quad \text{Remove parentheses by changing the sign of every term inside the parentheses.}$$

Before turning to applications, let's try one additional example involving simplification.

EXAMPLE 6   **Simplifying Algebraic Expressions**

Simplify:

a. $5(2y - 9) - (9y - 8)$ **b.** $4\left(\dfrac{1}{4}x + \dfrac{1}{4}\right)$

iscover for yourself

Verify each simplification in Example 6 by evaluating the given expression and its simplified form for a negative number of your choice.

Solution

a. $5(2y - 9) - (9y - 8)$
$$= 10y - 45 - 9y + 8 \quad \text{Distribute, and use the rule for a negative sign preceding parentheses.}$$
$$= (10y - 9y) + (-45 + 8) \quad \text{Group like terms.}$$
$$= 1y + (-37) \quad \text{Combine like terms.}$$
$$= y - 37 \quad \text{Use the multiplication property of 1 and the definition of subtraction.}$$

b. $4\left(\dfrac{1}{4}x + \dfrac{1}{4}\right)$

$$= 4\left(\dfrac{1}{4}x\right) + 4\left(\dfrac{1}{4}\right) \quad \text{Use the distributive property.}$$

$$= x + 1 \quad \text{Multiply and simplify. Since } 4(\tfrac{1}{4}x) = 1x, \text{ the 1 is omitted in multiplication because it is the multiplicative identity. However, the 1 that appears in the sum cannot be left out.}$$

4 Model reality with algebraic expressions.

Modeling Reality with Algebraic Expressions

For the remainder of this section, our interest is in algebraic expressions that describe some aspect of reality.

EXAMPLE 7 **Modeling Winning Times in the Olympics**

The winning times for the men's Olympic 200-meter dash and the winners are shown below. The algebraic expression

$$-(0.03x - 20) + 0.78 + 0.00576x$$

approximately models the winning times in the 200-meter dash x years after 1948.

200 Meters	Winning Time (Seconds)	200 Meters	Winning Time (Seconds)
1900 John W.B. Tewksbury, U.S.	22.20	1956 Bobby J. Morrow, U.S.	20.60
1904 Archie Hahn, U.S.	21.60	1960 Livio Berruti, Italy	20.50
1908 Robert Kerr, Canada	22.60	1964 Henry Carr, U.S.	20.30
1912 Ralph C. Craig, U.S.	21.70	1968 Tommie Smith, U.S.	19.80
1920 Allan Woodring, U.S.	22.00	1972 Valery Borzov, USSR	20.00
1924 Jackson V. Scholz, U.S.	21.60	1976 Donald Quarrie, Jamaica	20.23
1928 Percy Williams, Canada	21.80	1980 Pietro Mennea, Italy	20.19
1932 Eddie Tolan, U.S.	21.20	1984 Carl Lewis, U.S.	19.80
1936 Jesse Owens, U.S.	20.70	1988 Joe DeLoach, U.S.	19.75
1948 Melvin Patton, U.S.	21.10	1992 Mike Marsh, U.S.	20.01
1952 Andrew W. Stanfield, U.S.	20.70		

Michael Johnson (USA) heads for gold and a world record in 200m run—1996 Olympic Games, Atlanta, Georgia.

Gary M. Prior/Allsport Photography (USA), Inc.

a. Simplify the model.
b. How well does the model describe Andrew W. Stanfield's winning time?
c. How well does the model describe Mike Marsh's winning time?

Solution

a. $-(0.03x - 20) + 0.78 + 0.00576x$
$= -0.03x + 20 + 0.78 + 0.00576x$ Change signs inside parentheses.
$= (-0.03x + 0.00576x) + (20 + 0.78)$ Group like terms.
$= -0.02424x + 20.78$ Combine like terms.

b. Andrew W. Stanfield won the 200-meter dash in 1952. Since 1952 is 4 years after 1948, evaluate the simplified form of the model for $x = 4$.

$-0.02424x + 20.78$ This is the simplified form of the model from part (a).
$= -0.02424(4) + 20.78$ Substitute 4 for x.
$= -0.09696 + 20.78$ Multiply.
$= 20.68304$ Add.

The evaluation of the algebraic expression indicates a winning time of approximately 20.68 seconds. Since Stanfield's actual time was 20.70 seconds, the model seems to describe reality fairly accurately.

c. Mike Marsh won the event in 1992, 44 years after 1948, so this time we

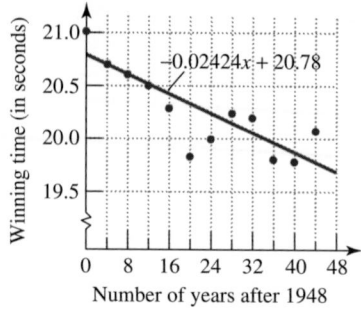

Figure 1.32

Modeling winning times for Olympic athletes in the 200-meter dash

evaluate the algebraic expression for $x = 44$. Using the same procedure as in part (b), we obtain 19.71344, or approximately 19.71 seconds. Since the actual winning time was 20.01 seconds, the model's description of reality is not quite as accurate as it was for part (b). ■

A challenge to applied mathematicians is the creation of models that describe reality relatively accurately over long periods of time. From such models, useful predictions about the future can be made.

Figure 1.32 shows points that represent the year and the winning time for 12 Olympic athletes in the 200-meter dash. In Chapter 4 we will learn how to create visual images of algebraic expressions. The visual image for the expression in Example 7 is shown as a line. In some cases the points fall directly on the line, so the line is an accurate model for the data in these cases. In other cases, the points are fairly distant from the line, indicating less accuracy in modeling real events.

In Example 7, although we were required to simplify it, the algebraic expression was given to us. A more difficult situation in problem solving is to *create* an algebraic expression that models or describes a given situation. For example, suppose you work at a job that pays $9 per hour, but the number of hours that you work varies from week to week. Let us use x to represent the number of hours worked. *Implied* (but not explicitly given) in this situation is that

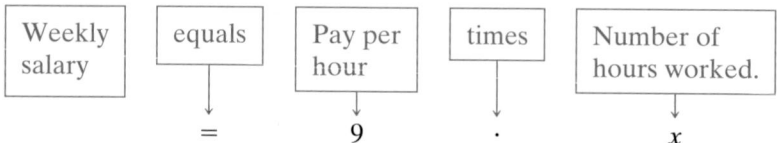

The algebraic expression $9x$ represents the weekly salary. In the product $9x$, the number 9 is a constant and the letter x is a variable. If you work 20 hours in a particular week, we would substitute 20 for x in the expression $9x$. The expression $9x$ would then become $9(20)$ or 180, meaning that the weekly salary is $180 for a 20-hour work week.

One of the difficulties in this situation is that nowhere do we have an explicit English phrase that translates as $9x$. We must use common sense to obtain the product. This is frequently the case when translating real life situations into algebraic expressions.

EXAMPLE 8   **Translating Implied English Phrases**

Translate into an algebraic expression:
a. The value in cents of x dimes
b. The amount of minoxidil (used to treat male pattern baldness) in x milliliters of a solution that is 2% minoxidil
c. The total cost of a meal that comes to x dollars when you leave a 15% tip
d. The amount of weight in an elevator with an elevator operator who weighs 185 pounds and x bags of cement weighing 65 pounds each

Solution

a. The value in cents of *x* dimes is

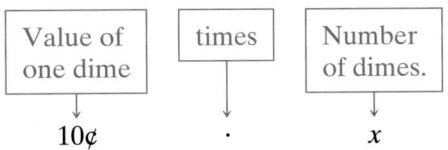

The value in cents of *x* dimes is represented by 10*x*.

b. The amount of minoxidil in *x* milliliters of a 2% solution is

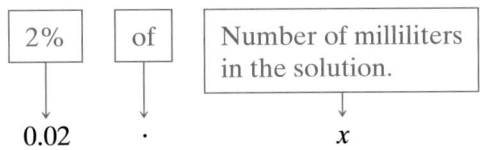

The amount of minoxidil is represented by 0.02*x*. (For example, 12 milliliters of solution contains (0.02)(12) or 0.24 milliliter of minoxidil.)

c. The total cost of a meal that comes to *x* dollars with a 15% tip is

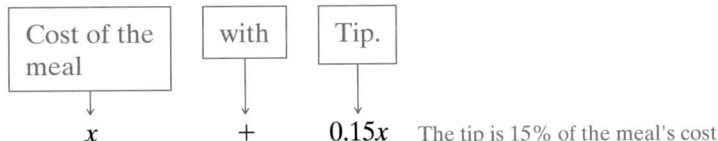

The total cost is represented by *x* + 0.15*x*.

d. The total weight in an elevator with a 185-pound operator and *x* bags of cement weighing 65 pounds each is

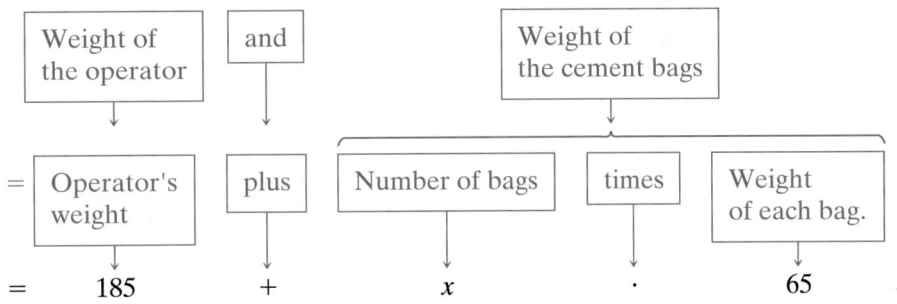

Using the commutative properties, the total weight is represented by the algebraic expression 65*x* + 185. For example, if there are 4 cement bags, the total weight is 65(4) + 185 = 260 + 185, or 445 pounds. ∎

PROBLEM SET 1.7

Practice Problems

Find the product in Problems 1–38. If your course uses graphing calculators, verify each result with your calculator.

1. $6(-9)$

2. $5(-7)$

3. $(-7)(-3)$

4. $(-8)(-5)$

5. $(-2)(6)$

6. $(-3)(10)$

7. $(-13)(-1)$

8. $(-17)(-1)$

9. $0(-5)$

10. $0(-8)$

11. $\frac{1}{2}(-14)$

12. $\frac{1}{3}(-15)$

13. $(-\frac{3}{4})(-20)$

14. $(-\frac{4}{5})(-25)$

15. $-\frac{3}{5} \cdot (-\frac{4}{7})$

16. $-\frac{5}{7} \cdot (-\frac{3}{8})$

17. $-\frac{7}{9} \cdot \frac{2}{3}$

18. $-\frac{5}{11} \cdot \frac{2}{7}$

19. $(\frac{4}{15})(-1\frac{1}{4})$

20. $(\frac{6}{7})(-1\frac{5}{9})$

21. $(-4.1)(0.03)$

22. $(-6.1)(0.02)$

23. $(-3.8)(-2.4)$

24. $(-2.9)(-3.6)$

25. $(3.08)(-0.25)$

26. $(7.05)(-0.75)$

27. $(-5)(-2)(-3)(4)$

28. $(-4)(-3)(-1)(6)$

29. $-2(-3)(-4)(-1)$

30. $-3(-2)(-5)(-1)$

31. $-3(-\frac{1}{6})(-50)$

32. $-55(-\frac{1}{11})(-4)$

33. $(-3)(-1)(-2)(-\frac{1}{2})(-4)$

34. $(-4)(-\frac{1}{2})(3)(-1)(-1)(2)$

35. $-\frac{1}{8}(-24)(-\frac{1}{2})(-6)$

36. $-\frac{2}{11}(-99)(-\frac{1}{3})(2)(-1)$

37. $(-5)(-5)(-5)$

38. $(-4)(-4)(-4)$

Perform the indicated operations in Problems 39–74. If applicable, verify each result with your graphing calculator.

39. $-7 - (-3)(2)$

40. $4(-3) - (-6)$

41. $8(-7) - (-11)$

42. $-5 - (-7)(-10)$

43. $(-6)(4) - (-4)(2)$

44. $(-5)(3) - (-7)(4)$

45. $7(-2)(-5) - (-11)$

46. $8(-3)(-2) - (-19)$

47. $-15 - (-3)(-4)(-2)$

48. $-18 - (-2)(-5)(-6)$

49. $(-4)(2)(-1) - (-5)(3)(-2)$

50. $(-8)(3)(-1) - (-6)(2)(-3)$

51. $-6(-8 - 2)$

52. $-8(-3 - 1)$

53. $6 - 4(2 - 10)$

54. $8 - 3(4 - 11)$

55. $4(2 + 5) - 5(7 + 3)$

56. $5(3 + 7) - 4(2 + 5)$

57. $2(8 - 10) - 3(-6 + 4)$

58. $3(7 - 11) - 4(-8 + 2)$

59. $(4 - 11)(6 - 10)$

60. $(3 - 12)(7 - 9)$

61. $(-3 - 2)(-6 + 10)$

62. $(-10 - 2)(9 - 7)$

63. $(-4 - 6)(-3) + 5$

64. $(-2 - 7)(-4) + 11$

65. $-3(-5) + 7(-1)$

66. $-4(-7) + 8(-3)$

67. $4(3) - 5(-2) + 7(-3)$

68. $7(2) - 6(-3) + 8(-4)$

69. $\frac{1}{2} - (-\frac{1}{2})(\frac{1}{4})$

70. $\frac{1}{3} - (-\frac{1}{3})(\frac{1}{2})$

71. $(-\frac{1}{2})(\frac{1}{6}) - (-\frac{1}{3})(3)$

72. $(-\frac{2}{3})(\frac{1}{4}) - (-\frac{1}{5})(5)$

73. $\frac{2}{3} - 2(\frac{7}{8} - \frac{5}{12})$

74. $\frac{3}{4} - 2(\frac{4}{5} - \frac{9}{8})$

Simplify each algebraic expression in Problems 75–100. Then verify your simplification by substituting −3 for the variable in both the given expression and its simplified form.

75. $-5(2x)$

76. $-6(\frac{1}{2}x)$

77. $-4(-\frac{3}{4}y)$

78. $-5(-\frac{3}{5}y)$

79. $8x + x$

80. $12x + x$

81. $-5x + x$

82. $-6x + x$

83. $6b - 7b$

84. $12b - 13b$

85. $-y + 4y$

86. $-y + 9y$

87. $-4(2x - 3)$

88. $-3(4x - 5)$

89. $-3(-2x + 4)$

90. $-4(-3x + 2)$

91. $-(2y - 5)$

92. $-(3y - 1)$

93. $4(2y - 3) - (7y + 2)$

94. $5(3y - 1) - (14y - 2)$

95. $-5(-2x - 1) - 11x$

96. $-4(-3x - 2) - 13x$

97. $3(\frac{1}{3}x + \frac{1}{3})$

98. $5(\frac{1}{5}x + \frac{1}{5})$

99. $2(-\frac{1}{2}x + \frac{1}{2})$

100. $4(-\frac{1}{4}x + \frac{1}{4})$

Application Problems

Problems 101–108 deal with the spread of the AIDs epidemic among women.

Based on the data obtained from the World Health Organization (WHO), the number of women (in millions) who have contracted AIDS is approximated by the expression

$$1.271x - 1.4$$

where $x = 0$ corresponds to the year 1980, $x = 1$ corresponds to 1981, $x = 2$ to 1982, and so on, up to $x = 12$ corresponding to 1992. Use the given expression to approximate the number of women who have contracted AIDS for the following years.

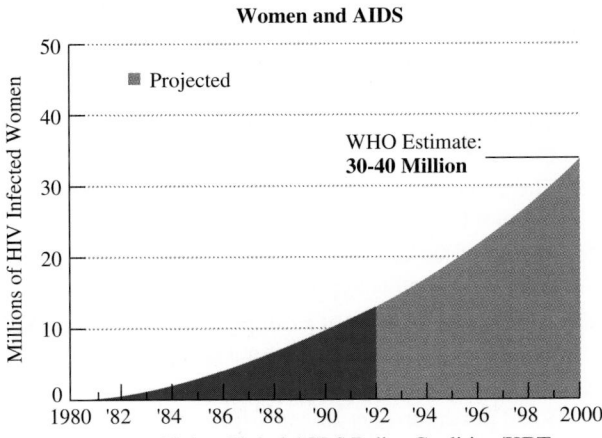

Women and AIDS

Source: Boston Globe, Global AIDS Policy Coalition/KRT

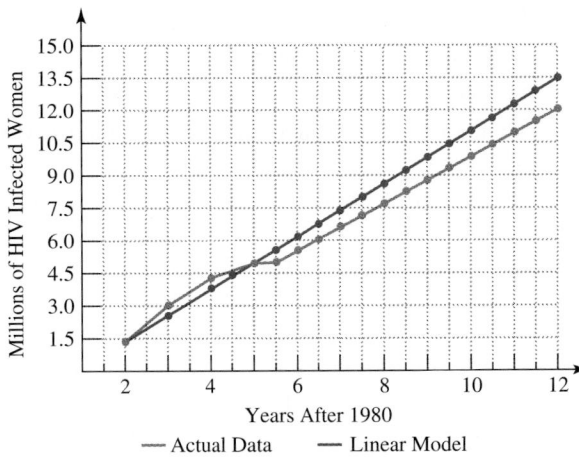

Women and AIDS

101. 1982   **102.** 1984   **103.** 1986

107. The points along the blue line in the right-hand graph were obtained from the expression

$$1.271x - 1.4$$

and the points along the purple line represent the actual number of women who have contracted AIDS. How well does the algebraic expression appear to describe what actually occurred? Explain.

108. Use the algebraic expression

$$1.271x - 1.4$$

to approximate the number of women who contract AIDS for 1996 and 2000. How well does the algebraic expression describe the projected figures given by WHO in the left-hand figure? Explain why the given algebraic expression extended only up to $x = 12$. What conclusion can you draw about using algebra to describe trends over time?

109. The winning times for the women's Olympic 200-meter dash are given in the table in the next column. The algebraic expression

$$-(0.04x - 30) - 5.7 - 0.031x$$

approximately models these winning times x years after 1948.

a. Simplify the algebraic expression.

b. How well does the expression model reality for the winning time in 1980?

104. 1988   **105.** 1990   **106.** 1992

c. How well does the expression model reality for the winning time in 1960?

d. Use the expression to predict the winning time in the year 2000.

Year	Time
1948	24.2
1952	23.7
1956	23.4
1960	24.0
1964	23.0
1968	22.5

Year	Time
1972	22.40
1976	22.37
1980	22.03
1984	21.81
1988	21.34
1992	21.81

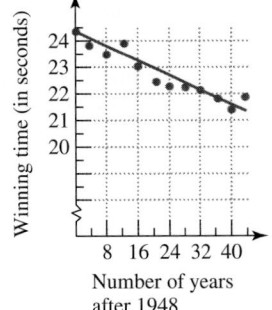

Translate each phrase in Problems 110–131 into an algebraic expression. If you are not sure where to begin, try using the Study Tip on page 87.

110. The value in cents of x nickels

111. The value in cents of x quarters.

112. The amount of acid in x liters of a solution that is 40% acid

113. The amount of tin in x kilograms of a metal that is 70% tin

114. The distance covered by a car traveling at 50 miles per hour for x hours

115. The distance covered by a car traveling at 45 miles per hour for x hours.

116. The total cost of a computer that sells for x dollars plus 8% tax

117. The total cost of a VCR that sells for x dollars plus 12% tax

118. The dollar amount of the discount received for a 30% discount on an item priced at x dollars

119. The dollar amount of the discount received for a 45% discount on an item priced at x dollars

120. The sale price of an item priced at x dollars with a 30% discount

121. The sale price of an item priced at x dollars with a 45% discount

122. The amount of weight in an elevator that is carrying a person who weighs 155 pounds plus x pieces of luggage weighing 40 pounds each

123. The amount of weight in an elevator that is carrying a person who weighs 140 pounds plus x bags of cement weighing 80 pounds each

124. The annual salary of a person who gets paid x dollars per week

125. The annual salary of a person who gets paid x dollars per month

126. The total fee charged at a campground that charges $35 for two adults and $4 for each of x children

127. The total fee charged at a campground that charges $20 per night plus $5 per person for a group of x people

128. The total hourly earnings for an employee earning $5.50 per hour plus 25 cents for each of x units of a product manufactured during the hour

129. The total hourly earnings for a college math lab tutor who helps x students during an hour and is paid $4.50 per hour plus 30¢ for each student helped

130. The next integer that follows any integer represented by x

131. The next odd integer that follows any odd integer represented by x

True–False Critical Thinking Problems

132. Which one of the following statements is true?
    a. Multiplying a negative number by a nonnegative number will always give a negative number.
    b. The product of two negative numbers is always a positive number.
    c. The product of -3 and 4 is 12.
    d. The product of real numbers a and b is not always equal to the product of real numbers b and a.

133. Which one of the following statements is true?
    a. The product of two negative numbers is sometimes a negative number.
    b. Both the addition and the multiplication of two negative numbers results in a positive number.
    c. $\left(-\frac{1}{2}\right)\left(-\frac{1}{2}\right) = \frac{1}{4}$
    d. Reversing the order of the two factors in a product results in a different answer.

134. Which of the following is true?
    a. The term x has no numerical coefficient.
    b. $5 + 3(x - 4) = 8(x - 4) = 8x - 32$
    c. $-x - x = -x + (-x) = 0$
    d. $x - 0.02(x + 200) = 0.98x - 4$

135. Which one of the following is true?
    a. A fast way to deal with a minus sign in front of parentheses is to drop the parentheses and change the sign of every term within the parentheses.
    b. $3 - 3(y - 4)$ simplifies to 0.
    c. If a minus sign appears in front of the parentheses, it is not essential to drop the parentheses as long as the sign of every term inside the parentheses is changed.
    d. If a product contains over one million factors, even if one of the factors is 0, the huge number of factors cannot result in a product that is 0.

Technology Problems

136. Simplify using a calculator:
$0.03(4.7x - 5.9) - 0.07(3.8x - 61)$.

137. The national average family health-care cost (in dollars) between 1980 and 2000 (predicted) is approximated by the algebraic expression

$$382.75x + 1742$$

where $x = 0$ corresponds to 1980, $x = 1$ to 1981, $x = 2$ to 1982, and so on, up to $x = 20$ corresponding

to 2000. Use a graphing calculator to evaluate the expression for $x = 0, 1, 2, 3, \ldots, 20$ and then create a graph similar to the blue line in the figure in Problems 101–108 that represents the data. If you have access to a computer program that generates bar graphs, create such a graph that shows family health-care cost for the 21 years, using a bar to represent the cost for each year.

Writing in Mathematics

138. Describe the differences in the procedures for each of the following computations: $(-8) + (-2)$; $-8 - (-2)$; $-8(-2)$.

Critical Thinking Problems

In Problems 139–140, translate each phrase into an algebraic expression.

139. The cost (in cents) for a phone call lasting x minutes if the company charges 15 cents for the first minute and 5 cents for each additional minute

140. The charge (in cents) for a library book that is overdue for x days if the library charges 40 cents for the first day and 90 cents for each additional day

141. Identifying patterns is one of the most important elements of mathematical research. In general, the sum of two real numbers is not equal to their product; that is, $a + b \neq ab$. However, here are some exceptions:

$$5 + 1\frac{1}{4} = 6\frac{1}{4} \quad \text{and} \quad 5\left(1\frac{1}{4}\right) = 6\frac{1}{4}$$

$$3 + 1\frac{1}{2} = 4\frac{1}{2} \quad \text{and} \quad 3\left(1\frac{1}{2}\right) = 4\frac{1}{2}$$

$$4 + 1\frac{1}{3} = 5\frac{1}{3} \quad \text{and} \quad 4\left(1\frac{1}{3}\right) = 5\frac{1}{3}$$

$$6 + 1\frac{1}{5} = 7\frac{1}{5} \quad \text{and} \quad 6\left(1\frac{1}{5}\right) = 7\frac{1}{5}$$

There is a pattern that governs the behavior of these numbers. What sort of number must you add to a natural number or multiply the natural number by so that the same answer results in addition and multiplication?

Review Problems

142. Consider the set

$$\left\{-\sqrt{25}, -\sqrt{2}, 0, \frac{17}{125}, \frac{\pi}{2}, 1492\right\}.$$

List all numbers from the set that are
  a. Natural numbers
  b. Whole numbers
  c. Integers
  d. Rational numbers
  e. Irrational numbers
  f. Real numbers

143. Use the roster method to write the set: $\{x \mid \sqrt{x}$ is irrational and x is a natural number between 2 and 10, not including 2 and not including 10$\}$.

**Most Popular Pure Breed Dogs
and Number Registered (in thousands)**

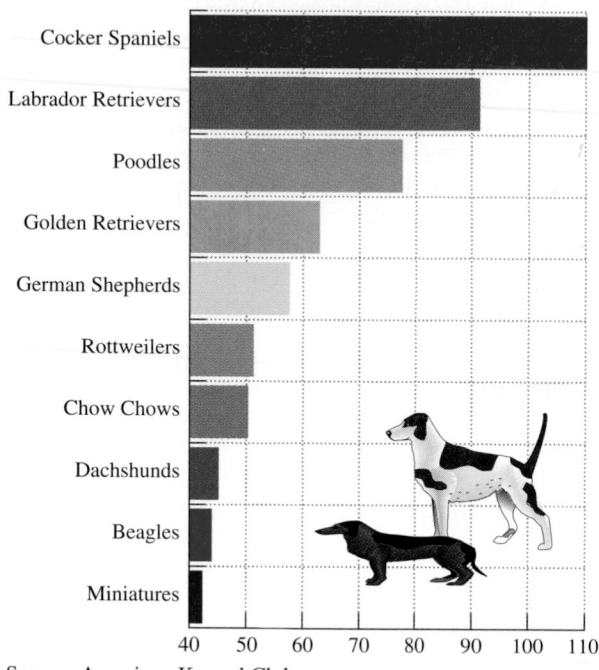

Source: American Kennel Club

144. Thirty-seven percent of U.S. households own at least one dog. The number of the most popular pure breed dogs registered (in thousands) is shown in the graph.
  a. Approximately how many golden retrievers are registered?
  b. What breed has approximately 90,000 dogs registered?

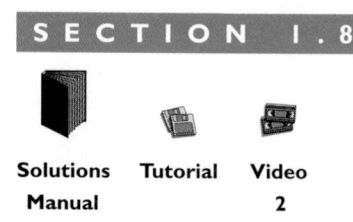

SECTION 1.8

Solutions Manual **Tutorial** **Video 2**

Exponents; Division of Real Numbers

Objectives

1 Evaluate exponential expressions.
2 Divide real numbers.
3 Model reality with division.

In the last section, we developed rules for multiplying real numbers. We will again use these rules by looking at exponents as a shorthand for repeated multiplication. We will also define division in terms of multiplication (just as we defined subtraction in terms of addition), thereby using rules for multiplication to solve division problems. In a sense, this section could be subtitled "Outgrowths of Multiplication."

1 Evaluate exponential expressions.

Natural Number Exponents

In Section 1.7, we saw that multiplication by a positive number represents repeated addition.

Repeated Addition	**Multiplication**
$3 + 3 + 3 + 3$	4×3

Now let's consider repeated multiplication in which the same factor appears several times. For example, the product

$$3 \cdot 3 \cdot 3 \cdot 3$$

The expression x^2 is read "x squared" because the area of a square of side x is given by $A = x^2$. The expression x^3 is read "x cubed" because the volume of a cube of side x is given by $V = x^3$.

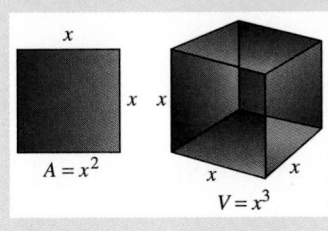

$A = x^2$

$V = x^3$

Using technology

We can verify each part of Example 1 on a graphing calculator as follows:

a. 4^2:

4 $\boxed{x^2}$ $\boxed{\text{ENTER}}$

or 4 $\boxed{\wedge}$ 2 $\boxed{\text{ENTER}}$

b. $(-5)^3$:

$\boxed{(}$ $\boxed{(-)}$ 5 $\boxed{)}$

$\boxed{\wedge}$ 3 $\boxed{\text{ENTER}}$

c. $(-3)^4$:

$\boxed{(}$ $\boxed{(-)}$ 3 $\boxed{)}$

$\boxed{\wedge}$ 4 $\boxed{\text{ENTER}}$

d. 1^6:

1 $\boxed{\wedge}$ 6 $\boxed{\text{ENTER}}$

e. $(-\frac{1}{3})^5$:

$\boxed{(}$ $\boxed{(-)}$ 1 $\boxed{\div}$ 3 $\boxed{)}$

$\boxed{\wedge}$ 5 $\boxed{\text{ENTER}}$

contains four factors of 3. We can express this repeated multiplication in *exponential form*.

Repeated Multiplication	Exponential Form
$3 \cdot 3 \cdot 3 \cdot 3$	3^4

In the exponential form 3^4, the number 4 is the *exponent* and 3 is the *base*. The exponential form 3^4 indicates that we are raising 3 to the *fourth power*. A natural number exponent tells how many times the base is used as a factor. If a number is raised to the first power, the result is that number. For example, $6^1 = 6$ and $(\frac{1}{3})^1 = \frac{1}{3}$. For this reason, exponents of 1 are omitted.

EXAMPLE 1   **Evaluating Exponential Expressions**

Find the value:

a. 4^2 **b.** $(-5)^3$ **c.** $(-3)^4$ **d.** 1^6 **e.** $\left(-\dfrac{1}{3}\right)^5$

Solution

a. $4^2 = 4 \cdot 4$ An exponent of 2 indicates that the base, 4, is used as a factor two times.

$\quad\;\; = 16$

A number raised to the second power is also read as that number *squared*. Thus, $4^2 = 16$ is read as "4 to the second power is 16" or "4 squared is 16."

b. $(-5)^3 = (-5)(-5)(-5)$ The base, -5, is repeated three times in multiplication.

$\quad\quad\;\;\; = -125$ Recall that an odd number of negative factors yields a negative product.

A number raised to the third power is also read as that number *cubed*. Thus, $(-5)^3 = -125$ is read as "the number negative 5 to the third power is negative 125" or "negative 5 cubed is negative 125."

c. $(-3)^4 = (-3)(-3)(-3)(-3)$ An exponent of 4 indicates that the base, -3, is used as a factor four times.

$\quad\quad\;\;\; = 81$ An even number of negative factors yields a positive product.

d. $1^6 = 1 \cdot 1 \cdot 1 \cdot 1 \cdot 1 \cdot 1$ 1 to the sixth power indicates that 1 is used as a factor six times.

$\quad\;\; = 1$ Observe that 1 to any power is 1.

e. $\left(-\dfrac{1}{3}\right)^5 = -\dfrac{1}{3}\left(-\dfrac{1}{3}\right)\left(-\dfrac{1}{3}\right)\left(-\dfrac{1}{3}\right)\left(-\dfrac{1}{3}\right)$ The base, $-\frac{1}{3}$, is used as a factor five times.

$\quad\quad\quad = -\dfrac{1}{243}$ An odd number of negative factors yields a negative product. The product of the absolute values of the numerators $(1 \cdot 1 \cdot 1 \cdot 1 \cdot 1)$ is written over the product of the absolute values of the denominators $(3 \cdot 3 \cdot 3 \cdot 3 \cdot 3 = 243)$. ∎

When working with exponents, it is important to distinguish between expressions such as $(-3)^4$ and -3^4. Observe that

$(-3)^4 = (-3)(-3)(-3)(-3)$ The base is -3. The negative sign is part of the base.
$= 81$ -3 to the fourth power is 81.

while

$-3^4 = -(3 \cdot 3 \cdot 3 \cdot 3)$ The negative sign is not part of the base.
$= -81$ The negative of 3 to the fourth power is -81.

The negative of a number is taken to a power only when the negative sign is inside the parentheses.

Let's take a moment to summarize our discussion of repeated multiplication of the same factor using exponential notation.

If b is a real number and n is a natural number, then

Exponent
↓
$$b^n = \underbrace{b \cdot b \cdot b \cdots \cdot b}$$
↑
Base b appears as a
factor n times

b^n is read "the nth power of b" or "b to the nth power." Thus, the nth power of b is defined as the product of n factors of b. Furthermore, $b^1 = b$ and $0^n = 0$.

Exponents and Algebraic Expressions

EXAMPLE 2 **Simplifying Algebraic Expressions**

Simplify, if possible:

a. $7x^3 + 2x^3$ **b.** $5x^2 + x^2$ **c.** $3x^2 + 4x^3$

Solution

a. $7x^3 + 2x^3$ These are like terms with the same variable factor, namely, x^3.
$= (7 + 2)x^3$ Apply the distributive property.
$= 9x^3$

b. $5x^2 + x^2$
$= 5x^2 + 1x^2$ Use the multiplication property of 1.
$= (5 + 1)x^2$ Apply the distributive property.
$= 6x^2$

c. $3x^2 + 4x^3$ cannot be simplified. The terms $3x^2$ and $4x^3$ are not like terms because they have different variable factors, namely, x^2 and x^3. ∎

Algebraic expressions with exponents frequently appear in descriptions of reality, as Example 3 shows.

ENRICHMENT ESSAY

Modeling and Accuracy

This map shows gravity around the moon based on data gathered by the spacecraft Clementine. Shown are the differences between the gravity distribution given by a mathematical model and observed gravity. The areas in yellow are where the model is correct. Red areas have more gravity than predicted, while green, blue, and purple areas have progressively less than expected.

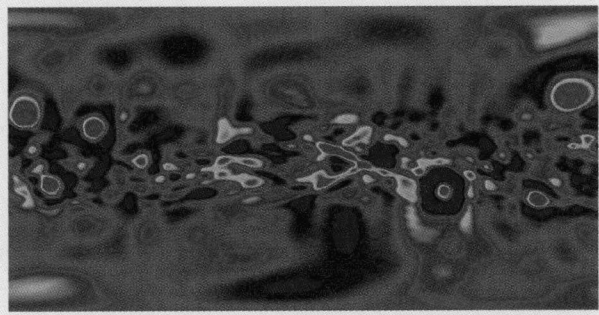

Geosciences Node of the Planetary Data Systems, NASA/Courtesy Jim Alexopoulos

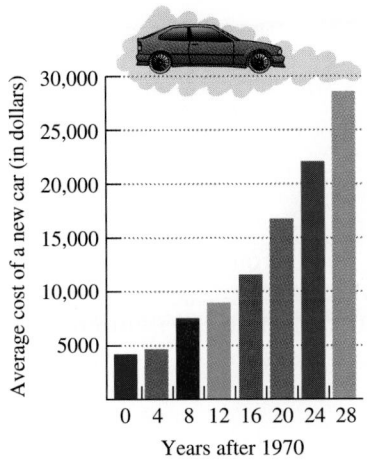

Average cost of a new car

EXAMPLE 3 **Modeling the Cost of a New Car**

The average cost of a new car (in dollars) can be modeled by the expression

$$30.5x^2 + 4192$$

where x represents the number of years after 1970. Evaluate the expression for $x = 30$ and describe what this represents in practical terms.

Solution

$30.5x^2 + 4192$ This is the given expression.

$= 30.5(30)^2 + 4192$ Substitute 30 for x.

$= 30.5(900) + 4192$ Since exponents denote multiplication, which is performed before addition, square 30. $30^2 = 30 \cdot 30 = 900$

$= 27,450 + 4192$ Complete the multiplication.

$= 31,642$ Add.

Since $x = 30$ is 30 years after 1970, or the year 2000, we can conclude (if the model is accurate) that the average cost of a new car will reach \$31,642 by the year 2000. ■

2 Divide real numbers.

Division of Real Numbers

Just as subtraction is defined in terms of addition of an opposite, we can define division in terms of multiplication. For example, we know that

$$\frac{8}{2} = 4 \quad \text{and} \quad 8 \cdot \frac{1}{2} = 4.$$

This means that

$$\frac{8}{2} = 8 \cdot \frac{1}{2}.$$

We call $\frac{1}{2}$ the *reciprocal* of 2. Pairs of numbers (such as 2 and $\frac{1}{2}$) whose

Discover for yourself

The product of any nonzero real number and its reciprocal is I.

$$a \cdot \frac{1}{a} = 1, \quad a \neq 0$$

This property can be illustrated on a graphing calculator using the reciprocal key $\boxed{1/x}$ or $\boxed{x^{-1}}$. To show that $7 \cdot \frac{1}{7} = 1$:

$\boxed{7}\ \boxed{x}\ \boxed{7}\ \boxed{x^{-1}}\ \boxed{\text{ENTER}}$

Try doing this for other values. What happens in the case of 0?

product is 1 are called *reciprocals of each other.* Thus, dividing 8 by 2 is the same as multiplying 8 by $\frac{1}{2}$.

We can generalize this result and say that

$$\frac{a}{b} = a \cdot \frac{1}{b}$$

as long as b is not zero. Thus, to divide a by b, multiply a by the reciprocal of b.

The result of dividing the real number a by the nonzero real number b is called the *quotient* of the numbers. This quotient can be denoted by $a \div b$ or $\frac{a}{b}$.

Because division is defined in terms of multiplication, the same rules hold for the sign of a quotient as for the sign of a product.

Dividing signed numbers: the sign of the quotient

The quotient of two numbers with the same sign is positive, and the quotient of two numbers with different signs is negative.

This gives us a way to divide real numbers without showing division as multiplication by a reciprocal.

Dividing real numbers

1. To divide real numbers with like signs, find the quotient of their absolute values. The quotient is positive.
2. To divide real numbers with different signs, find the quotient of their absolute values. The quotient is negative, so attach a negative sign.
3. Division by zero is undefined.
4. Any nonzero number divided into zero is zero.

Study tip

Multiplication	**Division**	
$(+)(+) = +$	$\dfrac{(+)}{(+)} = +$	Like signs: positive products and quotients
$(-)(-) = +$	$\dfrac{(-)}{(-)} = +$	
$(+)(-) = -$	$\dfrac{(+)}{(-)} = -$	Unlike signs: negative products and quotients
$(-)(+) = -$	$\dfrac{(-)}{(+)} = -$	

study tip

If the quotient of a and b is c,

$$\frac{a}{b} = c$$

then the product of c and b must be a:

$$c \cdot b = a.$$

This gives you a way to check division results.

EXAMPLE 4   **Dividing Real Numbers**

Find the quotient:

a. $\dfrac{8}{-4}$ **b.** $\dfrac{-8}{4}$ **c.** $-45 \div (-3)$ **d.** $-\dfrac{3}{4} \div \left(-\dfrac{5}{9}\right)$

Solution

a. $\dfrac{8}{-4} = -2$ Divide absolute values: $\frac{|8|}{|-4|} = \frac{8}{4} = 2$. With unlike signs, the quotient is negative.

You can check this result by multiplying the quotient, -2, by -4 and obtaining 8.

b. $\dfrac{-8}{4} = -2$ Divide absolute values: $\frac{|-8|}{|4|} = \frac{8}{4} = 2$. With unlike signs, the quotient is negative.

c. $-45 \div (-3) = 15$ Divide absolute values: $45 \div 3 = 15$. With like signs, the quotient is positive.

We can express this as $\frac{-45}{-3} = 15$. You can check this result by multiplying the quotient, 15, by -3 to obtain -45.

d. $-\dfrac{3}{4} \div \left(-\dfrac{5}{9}\right)$

$= \dfrac{3}{4} \div \dfrac{5}{9}$ Divide absolute values. With like signs, the quotient is positive.

$= \dfrac{3}{4} \cdot \dfrac{9}{5}$ Invert the divisor and multiply.

$= \dfrac{27}{20}$

Observe from Example 4 that $\frac{8}{-4} = \frac{-8}{4} = -2$. In addition, $-\frac{8}{4}$ is also equal to -2. In general, we have the following rule.

sing technology

You can verify part (d) on a graphing calculator as follows:

$$-\frac{3}{4} \div \left(-\frac{5}{9}\right)$$

([(−)] 3 [÷] 4) [÷]

([(−)] 5 [÷] 9)

ENTER

For any positive real numbers a and b

$$\frac{-a}{b} = \frac{a}{-b} = -\frac{a}{b}.$$

The form $\frac{a}{-b}$ is used very infrequently.

Notice also that $\frac{-45}{-3} = \frac{45}{3}$. In general, we have the following rule.

For any positive real numbers a and b

$$\frac{-a}{-b} = \frac{a}{b}.$$

Operations with real numbers are summarized in Table 1.4.

TABLE 1.4 Summary of Operations on Real Numbers

Signs of Numbers	Addition	Subtraction	Multiplication	Division
Both Numbers Are Positive	Sum Is Always Positive	Difference May Be Either Positive or Negative	Product Is Always Positive	Quotient Is Always Positive
Examples				
8 and 2	$8 + 2 = 10$	$8 - 2 = 6$	$8 \cdot 2 = 16$	$8 \div 2 = 4$
2 and 8	$2 + 8 = 10$	$2 - 8 = -6$	$2 \cdot 8 = 16$	$2 \div 8 = \frac{1}{4}$
One Number Is Positive and the Other Number Is Negative	Sum May Be Either Positive or Negative	Difference May Be Either Positive or Negative	Product Is Always Negative	Quotient Is Always Negative
Examples				
8 and -2	$8 + (-2) = 6$	$8 - (-2) = 10$	$8(-2) = -16$	$8 \div (-2) = -4$
-8 and 2	$-8 + 2 = -6$	$-8 - 2 = -10$	$-8(2) = -16$	$-8 \div 2 = -4$
Both Numbers Are Negative	Sum Is Always Negative	Difference May Be Either Positive or Negative	Product Is Always Positive	Quotient Is Always Positive
Examples				
-8 and -2	$-8 + (-2) = -10$	$-8 - (-2) = -6$	$-8(-2) = 16$	$-8 \div (-2) = 4$
-2 and -8	$-2 + (-8) = -10$	$-2 - (-8) = 6$	$-2(-8) = 16$	$-2 \div (-8) = \frac{1}{4}$

3 Model reality with division.   **Modeling Reality with Division**

Algebraic expressions that model reality frequently contain division.

EXAMPLE 5   **Modeling Average Cost**

A business that manufactures racing bicycles has weekly fixed costs of $30,000. The average cost per bicycle for the business to manufacture x racing bicycles is modeled by

$$\frac{50x + 30,000}{x}.$$

Find the average cost per bicycle when $x = 1000$, 10,000, and 100,000. What happens to the average cost as the production level increases?

A. Collinelli (Italy) gold medal winner in cycling: Velodrome, 1996 Olympics

William R. Sallaz/Duomo Photography

Solution

When $x = 1000$, the average cost per bicycle is

$$\frac{50x + 30,000}{x} = \frac{50(1000) + 30,000}{1000} = \frac{50,000 + 30,000}{1000} = \frac{80,000}{1000} = \$80.00$$

When $x = 10,000$, the average cost per bicycle is

$$\frac{50x + 30,000}{x} = \frac{50(10,000) + 30,000}{10,000} = \frac{500,000 + 30,000}{10,000}$$

$$= \frac{530,000}{10,000} = \$53.00$$

When $x = 100{,}000$, the average cost per bicycle is

$$\frac{50x + 30{,}000}{x} = \frac{50(100{,}000) + 30{,}000}{100{,}000} = \frac{5{,}000{,}000 + 30{,}000}{100{,}000}$$

$$= \frac{5{,}030{,}000}{100{,}000} = \$50.30$$

As the production level increases, the cost of producing each racing bicycle decreases. This illustrates the difficulty with small businesses. It is nearly impossible to have competitively low prices when production levels are low. ∎

    In Example 5, we were given the algebraic expression that modeled average cost. In our next example, we must create algebraic expressions that describe given situations. We must use common sense to construct an English phrase and then translate that phrase into the special language of algebra.

EXAMPLE 6 Creating Algebraic Models

Translate into an algebraic expression:

a. The weekly salary for a person earning x dollars per year
b. The cost per gallon of gasoline that costs $20 for x gallons
c. The fractional part of a job done by a person who can do a complete job in 4 hours but who works only for x hours (where x is less than 4 hours; $x < 4$)

Solution

a. The weekly salary for a person earning x dollars per year is

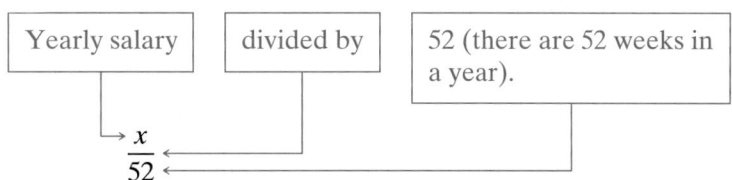

The weekly salary is represented by $\frac{x}{52}$. If you get stuck, replace x by some specific numbers, decide what to do with the numbers, and then generalize to x. For example, the weekly salary for a person earning \$20,000 yearly is $\frac{20{,}000}{52}$, so earning x dollars yearly translates as $\frac{x}{52}$.

b. The cost per gallon of gasoline that comes to \$20 for x gallons is

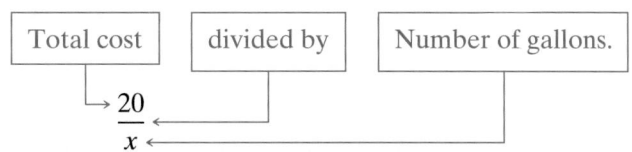

The cost per gallon is represented by $\frac{20}{x}$.

c. We are given that the person can complete the job in 4 hours. In 1 hour, $\frac{1}{4}$ of the job is done; in 2 hours, $\frac{2}{4}$ or $\frac{1}{2}$ the job is done; in 3 hours, $\frac{3}{4}$ of the job is done. Thus, to find the fractional part of the job done by a person who works only for x hours, we divide by 4.

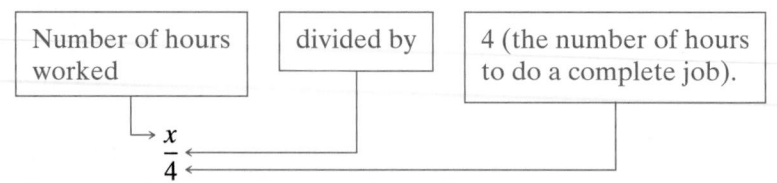

The fractional part of the job done is represented by $\frac{x}{4}$. ∎

PROBLEM SET 1.8

Practice Problems _____

If applicable, verify all numerical results with a graphing calculator.
Find the value of each exponential expression in Problems 1–36.

1. 7^2

2. 9^2

3. 4^3

4. 6^3

5. $(-4)^2$

6. $(-10)^2$

7. $(-4)^3$

8. $(-10)^3$

9. $(-2)^4$

10. $(-1)^4$

11. -2^4

12. -1^4

13. 2^6

14. 3^6

15. $(\frac{2}{3})^2$

16. $(\frac{3}{4})^2$

17. $(-\frac{1}{3})^3$

18. $(-\frac{1}{4})^3$

19. $(-\frac{3}{4})^3$

20. $(-\frac{3}{5})^3$

21. $(-\frac{2}{3})^4$

22. $(-\frac{2}{5})^4$

23. $-(\frac{2}{3})^4$

24. $-(\frac{2}{5})^4$

25. $-(-\frac{1}{2})^3$

26. $-(-\frac{1}{5})^3$

27. $(-1)^{17}$

28. $(-1)^{19}$

29. $-(-1)^{13}$

30. $-(-1)^{11}$

31. $-(-1)^{12}$

32. $-(-1)^{10}$

33. $(-1.2)^3$

34. $(-1.4)^3$

35. $\dfrac{1}{4^3}$

36. $\dfrac{1}{(-5)^3}$

Find the quotient in Problems 37–78, or, if applicable, state that the expression is undefined.

37. $\frac{-12}{4}$

38. $\frac{-40}{5}$

39. $\frac{21}{-3}$

40. $\frac{60}{-6}$

41. $\frac{-90}{-3}$

42. $\frac{-66}{-6}$

43. $\frac{0}{-7}$

44. $\frac{0}{-8}$

45. $\frac{-7}{0}$

46. $\frac{0}{0}$

47. $(-480) \div 24$

48. $(-300) \div 12$

49. $(465) \div (-15)$

50. $(-594) \div (-18)$

51. $\dfrac{-15.9}{0.003}$

52. $\dfrac{-87.5}{0.007}$

53. $\dfrac{-8.25}{-0.05}$

54. $\dfrac{-52.4}{-0.04}$

55. $4.06 \div (-0.7)$

56. $5.22 \div (-0.9)$

57. $-\frac{14}{9} \div \frac{7}{8}$

58. $-\frac{5}{16} \div \frac{25}{8}$

59. $\frac{3}{8} \div (-\frac{3}{4})$

60. $\frac{15}{8} \div (-\frac{3}{8})$

61. $-\frac{4}{3} \div (-\frac{16}{9})$

62. $-\frac{3}{4} \div (-\frac{5}{8})$

63. $0 \div (-\frac{3}{7})$

64. $0 \div (-\frac{4}{9})$

65. $-\frac{3}{7} \div 0$

66. $-\frac{4}{9} \div 0$

67. $-\frac{5}{7} \div (-\frac{5}{7})$

68. $-\frac{3}{4} \div (-\frac{3}{4})$

69. $-\frac{5}{7} \div \frac{5}{7}$

70. $-\frac{3}{4} \div \frac{3}{4}$

71. $6 \div (-\frac{2}{5})$

72. $8 \div (-\frac{2}{9})$

73. $-1\frac{2}{3} \div (-\frac{2}{9})$

74. $-1\frac{1}{2} \div (-\frac{9}{7})$

75. $\frac{7}{12} \div (-7)$

76. $\frac{3}{17} \div (-3)$

77. $(3 - 4\frac{1}{3}) \div (-\frac{2}{3} + \frac{5}{6})$

78. $[3 - (-\frac{5}{4})] \div (-5 + \frac{3}{4})$

Simplify each algebraic expression in Problems 79–92, or explain why the expression cannot be simplified.

79. $6x^2 + 11x^2$

80. $5x^2 + 17x^2$

81. $9x^3 - 4x^3$

82. $13x^3 - 7x^3$

83. $7x^4 + x^4$

84. $13x^4 + x^4$

85. $16x^2 - 17x^2$

86. $19x^2 - 20x^2$

87. $2x^2 + 2x^3$ **88.** $3x^2 + 3x^3$ **89.** $6x^2 - 6x^2$ **90.** $7x^2 - 7x^2$

91. $3x^2 + 4x^3 - 2x^2 - x^3$ **92.** $7x^2 + 11x^3 - 6x^2 - x^3$

Application Problems

93. The algebraic expression

$$3x^2$$

models the weight (in grams) of a human fetus that is x weeks old. The expression is valid up to and including 39 weeks. What is the weight of the fetus after 17 weeks?

94. The algebraic expression

$$10.675x^2 + 1007.775$$

models the value in millions of dollars of private-property loss to fire damage in the United States x years after 1970. Evaluate the expression for $x = 10$ and describe what this represents in practical terms.

95. A lightbulb is accidentally dropped from a building that is 200 feet high. The algebraic expression

$$200 - 16t^2$$

describes the height of the lightbulb in feet above the ground after t seconds. How far above the ground is the lightbulb when it has been falling for 3 seconds?

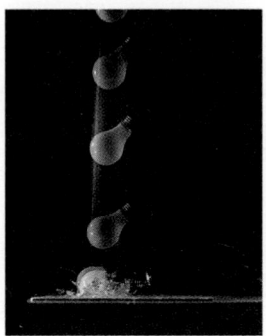

Time lapse image of a
falling lightbulb.
Henry Groskinsky/Peter
Arnold, Inc.

96. If the lightbulb described in Problem 95 is dropped from a 200-foot height on the surface of the moon, its height above the ground after t seconds is modeled by

$$200 - 2.7t^2.$$

How far above the moon's surface is the lightbulb when it has been falling for 3 seconds?

97. The algebraic expression

$$\frac{893.5}{x + 14.2}$$

models the success rate for plaintiffs in personal injury suits x years after 1989. The model measures success rate as a percent and is valid only for 1989 through 1992.

a. Find the percentage of cases that resulted in success for the plaintiff in personal injury cases from 1989 through 1992.

b. What happened to the plaintiff's rate of success over this period?

c. If this model is extended into the future, what is a reasonable estimate for the success rate in the year 2000?

98. A business that manufactures small alarm clocks has weekly fixed costs of $5000. The average cost per clock for the business to manufacture x clocks is modeled by

$$\frac{0.5x + 5000}{x}.$$

a. Find the average cost when $x = 100$, 1000, and 10,000.

b. Like all businesses, the alarm clock manufacturer must make a profit. To do this, each clock must be sold for at least 50¢ more than what it costs to manufacture. Due to competition from a larger company, the clocks can be sold for $1.50 each and no more. Our small manufacturer can only produce 2000 clocks weekly. Does this business have much of a future? Explain.

To find the mean (or average) of a group of numbers, add the numbers and then divide the sum by the number of terms added. Use this concept to answer Problems 99–100.

99. Among 11 countries named in an opinion poll conducted by Roper Starch International in 1993, only

three were regarded as more friendly to the United States than they had been in the early 1980s. The poll results are shown in the graph. Find the mean for the percent of change for the 11 countries. Try describing what this result signifies.

Who Do You Trust?
Percent Who View Various
Nations as Allies, 1982 vs. 1993

*1982 Data for Soviet Union

Source: Roper Starch International

Trends in U.S. Cancer Mortality, 1973–1992

Change in Death Rate (percent)

Source: *SEER Statistics Review, 1973–1992*. NIH Publication No. 96-2789. National Cancer Institute, 1995.

100. Trends in U.S. cancer mortality from 1973 through 1992 are shown in the graph.
    a. Find the mean trend for the following four cancers: skin melanoma, lung (males), ovary, stomach. Try describing what this result signifies.
    b. Describe the overall trend in cancer mortality during the period indicated in the graph.

Model each phrase in Problems 101–108 with an algebraic expression.

101. The cost per orange when x oranges cost $5
102. The cost per grapefruit when x grapefruits cost $7
103. The height (in feet) of a person who is c inches tall
104. The length (in yards) of a jogging trail that is x feet long
105. The average of 12 and x

106. The average of -14 and x
107. The length (in meters) of a line segment that measures x centimeters
108. The length (in meters) of a line segment that measures x kilometers

True–False Critical Thinking Problems _____

109. Which one of the following is true?
    a. Every real number has a reciprocal.
    b. If a is negative, b is positive, and c is positive, then $\dfrac{a-c}{b}$ must be negative.
    c. $0 \div 17$ is undefined.
    d. The quotient of 0 and 0 is 1.

110. Which one of the following is true?
    a. $8 - \dfrac{8}{2} = \dfrac{0}{2}$
    b. If a is negative, b is positive, and c is positive, then $\dfrac{a}{bc}$ must be negative.
    c. Zero cubed is undefined.
    d. Dividing the difference between any real number and itself by a negative number is undefined.

111. Which one of the following is true?
   a. $x^2 + x^2 = x^4$
   b. $x^3 + x^3 = 2x^6$

   c. $(-4)^2$ and -4^2 name the same number.
   d. $(-4)^3$ and -4^3 name the same number.

Technology Problems

112. Use your calculator to attempt to find the quotient of -3 and 0. Describe what happens. Does the same thing occur when finding the quotient of 0 and -3? Explain the difference. Finally, what happens when you enter the quotient of 0 and itself?

113. The model

$$\frac{600{,}000\, p}{100 - p}$$

describes the cost in dollars to dairy farmers to remove p percent of polluting bacteria from a river. Use your calculator to evaluate the expression for $p = 90, 95, 98, 99, 99.9$, and 99.999. Describe what happens to cleanup costs as the percent of pollutants removed from the river increases.

Writing in Mathematics

114. Describe what it means to raise a number to a power. In your description, include a discussion of the difference between -5^2 and $(-5)^2$.

115. Why is $\frac{0}{4}$ equal to 0, but $\frac{4}{0}$ is undefined?

116. If you haven't already, work Problems 95 and 96. Describe what the difference in the two answers represents.

Critical Thinking Problems

Translate each phrase in Problems 117–120 into an algebraic expression.

117. The cost per calculator when all but one of x calculators are sold for $50

118. The fraction of people in a room who are women if there are 40 women and x men in the room

119. The number of campaign workers needed to distrib-

ute x boxes of fliers so that each campaign worker gets $\frac{1}{2}$ of a box

120. The worth of x words if a picture is worth a thousand words

121. A ball is rolling down an inclined plane. The distance that the ball rolls (in meters) at the end of 1, 2, 3, 4, 5, and 6 seconds is indicated in the table of measurements. Write an algebraic expression that models the distance that the ball rolls at the end of t seconds.

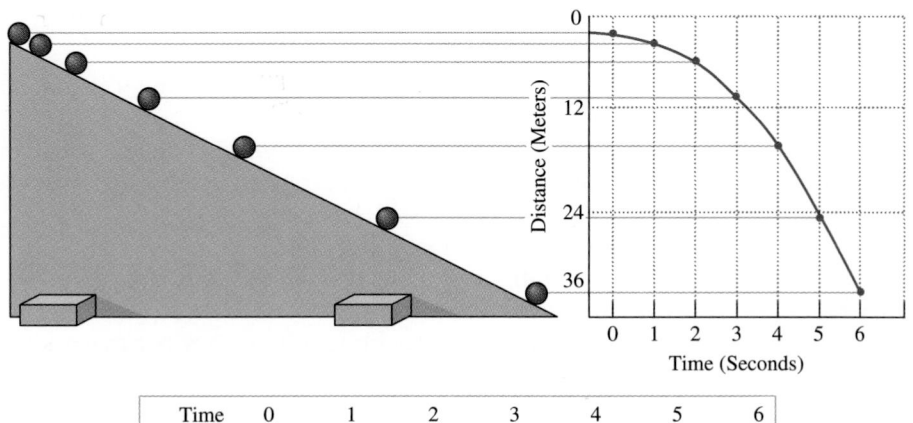

Time	0	1	2	3	4	5	6
Distance	0	1	4	9	16	25	36

Review Problems _____

122. Use the roster method to write the following set.

    $\{x \mid x$ is a whole number less than 6 and a positive number$\}$

123. What is the difference between a temperature of $12°F$ and $-16°F$?

124. Find the product of $\frac{5}{8}$ and $\frac{1}{3}$. Describe how this problem is modeled by the figure.

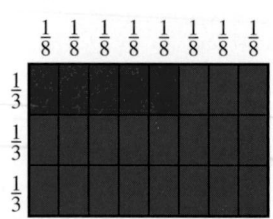

SECTION 1.9

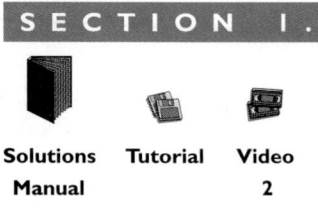

Solutions   Tutorial   Video
Manual   2

Order of Operations; Mathematical Models

Objectives

1 Use the order of operations agreement.
2 Evaluate mathematical models.

In this section, we summarize the agreed-upon order of operations when numerical expressions contain addition, subtraction, multiplication, division, exponents, and grouping symbols. We apply this agreement to *mathematical models*—descriptions of reality that are expressed in a condensed, symbolic style. One aim of algebra is to provide a symbolic description of the world, and in this section we will see how this description fits situations as diverse as the feeling of being underpaid, blood pressure, handicaps for bowlers, human memory, cleanup of toxic chemicals, and a relationship between population and air pollution.

1 Use the order of operations agreement.

Order of Operations

We have seen that to evaluate expressions consistently, we follow an accepted *order of operations*. We agree to perform operations in the following order.

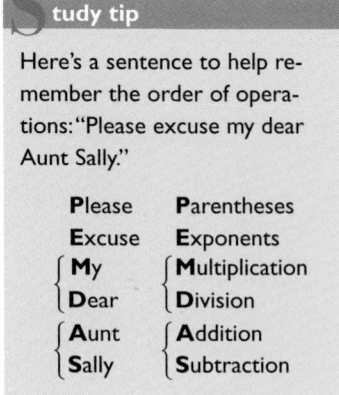

Study tip

Here's a sentence to help remember the order of operations:"Please excuse my dear Aunt Sally."

Please	**Parentheses**
Excuse	**Exponents**
⎰ **My**	⎰ **Multiplication**
⎱ **Dear**	⎱ **Division**
⎰ **Aunt**	⎰ **Addition**
⎱ **Sally**	⎱ **Subtraction**

The order of operations agreement

1. Perform operations above and below any fraction bar, following steps 2 to 5 below.
2. Perform operations inside grouping symbols, following steps 3 to 5. Work from innermost grouping symbols, parentheses ( ), to outermost grouping symbols, brackets [ ].
3. Simplify exponential expressions.
4. Do multiplications or divisions as they occur, working from left to right.
5. Do additions and subtractions as they occur, working from left to right.

Examples 1 through 5 illustrate the order of operations agreement.

EXAMPLE 1 **Using the Order of Operations**

Simplify: $-36 \div 6 \cdot 2$

Solution

$\boxed{-36 \div 6} \cdot 2$ Multiplication and division are performed as they occur from left to right, so start with division, which we have highlighted.

$= -6 \cdot 2$ $\frac{-36}{6} = -6$

$= -12$

EXAMPLE 2 **Using the Order of Operations**

Simplify: $-2 + 7(1 - 5)^3$

Solution

$-2 + 7(1 - 5)^3$ Subtract within the grouping symbols, the parentheses.

$= -2 + 7(-4)^3$ Now consider the exponent.

$= -2 + 7(-64)$ $(-4)^3 = (-4)(-4)(-4) = -64$

$= -2 + (-448)$ Multiply: $7(-64) = -448$

$= -450$

EXAMPLE 3 **Using the Order of Operations**

Simplify: $12 + 3 \cdot 16 \div 4^2 - 2$

Solution

$12 + 3 \cdot 16 \div 4^2 - 2$ With no grouping symbols, work with the exponential expression first.

$= 12 + 3 \cdot 16 \div 16 - 2$ $4^2 = 16$. Now do multiplication and division as they occur from left to right.

$= 12 + 48 \div 16 - 2$ $3 \cdot 16 = 48$. Now do the division.

$= 12 + 3 - 2$ $48 \div 16 = 3$. Finally, do the addition and subtraction from left to right.

$= 15 - 2$ $12 + 3 = 15$

$= 13$

EXAMPLE 4 **Using the Order of Operations**

Simplify: $\frac{1}{2} \cdot 10 + [4(6 \div 3) - 15]$

Solution

$\frac{1}{2} \cdot 10 + [4(6 \div 3) - 15]$

$$= \frac{1}{2} \cdot 10 + [4(2) - 15]$$ Work within the parentheses first: $6 \div 3 = \frac{6}{3} = 2$.

$$= \frac{1}{2} \cdot 10 + [8 - 15]$$ Work within the brackets, performing multiplication before subtraction.

$$= \frac{1}{2} \cdot 10 + [-7]$$ Finish the subtraction within the brackets.

$$= 5 + [-7]$$

$$= -2$$ ■

EXAMPLE 5   **Using the Order of Operations**

Simplify: $\frac{1}{4} - 6(2 + 8) \div \left(-\frac{1}{3}\right)\left(-\frac{1}{9}\right)$

Solution

This problem is a bit tricky, so we'll highlight the steps that we consider as we move through the order of operations.

$$\frac{1}{4} - 6(2 + 8) \div \left(-\frac{1}{3}\right)\left(-\frac{1}{9}\right)$$ Do the operation in the grouping symbols, the parentheses.

$$= \frac{1}{4} - 6(10) \div \left(-\frac{1}{3}\right)\left(-\frac{1}{9}\right)$$ $2 + 8 = 10$. Now do the multiplication and divisions from left to right.

$$= \frac{1}{4} - 60 \div \left(-\frac{1}{3}\right)\left(-\frac{1}{9}\right)$$ $6 \cdot 10 = 60$. Move next to the division, multiplying by a reciprocal.

$$= \frac{1}{4} - (-180)\left(-\frac{1}{9}\right)$$ $60 \div (-\frac{1}{3}) = 60 \cdot (-\frac{3}{1}) = -180$. Move next to the multiplication.

$$= \frac{1}{4} - 20$$ $(-180)(-\frac{1}{9}) = 20$. Finally, do the subtraction.

$$= \frac{1}{4} + (-20)$$ Subtract by adding an opposite.

$$= \frac{1}{4} + \left(\frac{-80}{4}\right)$$ A common denominator is needed, so write -20 as $\frac{-80}{4}$.

$$= \frac{-79}{4}$$ Add by finding $1 + (-80)$, or -79, putting this sum over the common denominator.

The answer can also be expressed as $-\frac{79}{4}$, $-19\frac{3}{4}$, or -19.75.   ■

The order of operations agreement is also used when we simplify algebraic expressions. Grouping symbols are removed from innermost (parentheses) to outermost (brackets).

EXAMPLE 6 **Simplifying an Algebraic Expression**

Simplify: $50x - 5[4x - 3y - 2(-3x - y)]$

Solution

$50x - 5[4x - 3y - 2(-3x - y)]$

$= 50x - 5[4x - 3y + 6x + 2y]$ — First remove the innermost grouping symbols. Use the distributive property: $-2(-3x - y) = -2(-3x) - 2(-y) = 6x + 2y.$

$= 50x - 5[(4x + 6x) + (-3y + 2y)]$ — Although we can remove brackets by distributing -5 to every term, we'll first group like terms inside the brackets.

$= 50x - 5[10x + (-y)]$ — Combine like terms inside the brackets.

$= 50x - 5(10x) + (-5)(-y)$ — Distribute -5 over both terms in the brackets. You could express $10x + (-y)$ as $10x - y$ and then distribute -5 over subtraction.

$= 50x - 50x + 5y$

$= 0 + 5y$ — $50x - 50x = (50 - 50)x = 0x = 0$

$= 5y$ — Use the additive identity property to omit 0 from the sum. ∎

2 Evaluate mathematical models.

Mathematical Models

One aim of algebra is to provide a compact, symbolic description of the world. These descriptions involve the use of *formulas,* statements of equality expressing a relationship among two or more variables. For example, the formula

$$C = \frac{5}{9}(F - 32)$$

is used to express the relationship between Fahrenheit temperature (F) and Celsius temperature (C).

The Formula	What the Formula Tells Us
$C = \dfrac{5}{9}(F - 32)$	If 32 is subtracted from the Fahrenheit temperature $(F - 32)$ and this difference is multiplied by $\frac{5}{9}$, the resulting product, $\frac{5}{9}(F - 32)$, gives the Celsius temperature.

We can use this formula to determine the Celsius temperature given a Fahrenheit temperature such as 77°. Here's how it's done.

$C = \dfrac{5}{9}(F - 32)$ — This is the given formula.

$C = \dfrac{5}{9}(77 - 32)$ — To find the Celsius temperature when the Fahrenheit temperature is 77°, replace F by 77 (*substitute* 77 for F) and solve for C.

Temperature scales

There are three main temperature scales. The Fahrenheit scale is being replaced internationally by the Celsius scale. Scientists use the kelvin scale.

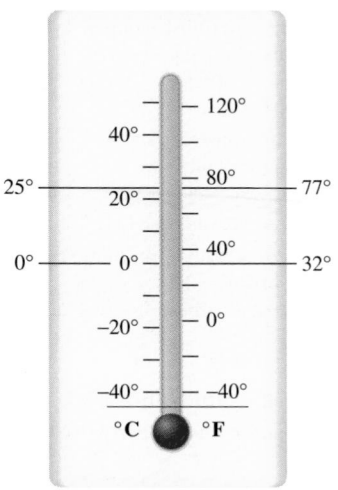

Water's freezing point is 0°C, 32°F, and 273 K.

James Sugar/Black Star

$$C = \frac{5}{9}(45)$$ Within parentheses, $77 - 32 = 45$.

$$C = 25$$ Multiply: $\frac{5}{9} \cdot \frac{\overset{5}{45}}{\underset{1}{1}} = 25$. We have *evaluated* the formula for $F = 77$.

When the Fahrenheit temperature is 77°, the equivalent Celsius temperature is 25°.

Formulas express relationships between quantities and are used in almost all academic disciplines as well as in everyday life. One of the aims of applied mathematics is to find formulas that describe real world phenomena. These formulas are frequently called *mathematical models*.

In our next examples, a mathematical model is given, along with the value of one of the variables in the model. We can use the order of operations to *evaluate* the formula by *substituting* the numerical value for the given variable.

EXAMPLE 7   Altitude and Weightlessness

As the altitude of a space shuttle increases, the weight of an astronaut decreases until a state of weightlessness is reached. The mathematical model

$$W = 125\left(\frac{6400}{6400 + x}\right)^2$$

describes the weight W (in pounds) of a 125-pound astronaut at an altitude of x kilometers above sea level. What is the astronaut's weight at an altitude of 25,600 kilometers?

Solution

$$W = 125\left(\frac{6400}{6400 + x}\right)^2$$ This is the given mathematical model.

$$W = 125\left(\frac{6400}{6400 + 25{,}600}\right)^2$$ Since the altitude is given to be 25,600, substitute 25,600 for x and solve for W.

$$W = 125\left(\frac{6400}{32{,}000}\right)^2$$ Work within parentheses, adding below the fraction bar.

$$W = 125(0.2)^2$$ Divide: $\frac{6400}{32{,}000} = 0.2$ or $\frac{1}{5}$.

$$W = 125(0.04)$$ Evaluate $(0.2)^2$: $(0.2)^2 = (0.2)(0.2) = 0.04$.

$$W = 5$$ Finally, multiply.

At an altitude of 25,600 kilometers, a 125-pound astronaut weighs 5 pounds. ■

EXAMPLE 8   A Person's Actual Pay and the Feeling of Being Underpaid

Research shows that as income rises, people shift from comparing their income to what they need to "get along" to what they require to "get ahead." The mathematical model

$$U = 0.018S^2 - 0.757S + 9.047$$

ENRICHMENT ESSAY

The Three Faces of Algebra

The way in which algebra describes the behavior of variables has evolved through several stages of development. Here's an example of a mathematical model transmitted in the notation of algebra's three styles:

- *The Rhetoric Stage* (in which relationships are written out in sentences): The length of the tibia bone, extending from the ankle to the knee, can be used to calculate a person's height. For adult women, if the tibia's length (in centimeters) is multiplied by 2.53 and then 72.57 is added, the resulting number is the height of the woman, also expressed in centimeters.
- *The Syncoptic Stage* (in which some abbreviations and symbols are used):

A woman's height = (2.53)(length of her tibia bone) + 72.57
- *The Modern Symbolic Stage* (in which a condensed symbolic language replaces all words):

$$h = 2.53t + 72.57$$

Modern notation continues to evolve as mathematicians search for the best methods to communicate concepts symbolically and compactly.

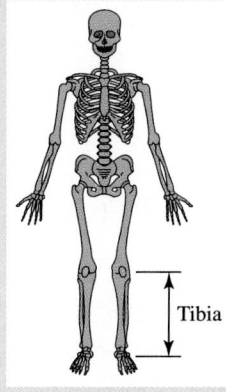

Tibia

---

describes the amount that people feel they are underpaid (U, in thousands of dollars) in terms of their salary S (also expressed in thousands of dollars). If a person earns $40,000 yearly, by how much does that person feel underpaid?

Solution

$U = 0.018S^2 - 0.757S + 9.047$	This is the given mathematical model.
$U = 0.018(40)^2 - 0.757(40) + 9.047$	Since salary S is expressed in *thousands* of dollars, replace S by 40. We are given that the salary is 40 thousand dollars.
$U = 0.018(1600) - 0.757(40) + 9.047$	Evaluate the exponential expression: $40^2 = 1600$
$U = 28.8 - 30.28 + 9.047$	Multiply from left to right: $(0.018)(1600) = 28.8$ and $(0.757)(40) = 30.28$
$U = 28.8 + (-30.28) + 9.047$	Express subtraction as addition of an opposite.
$U = -1.48 + 9.047$	Add from left to right: $28.8 + (-30.28) = -1.48$
$U = 7.567$	Remember that U, the amount one feels underpaid, is in *thousands* of dollars.

Thus, a person earning $40,000 yearly feels underpaid by 7.567 thousand dollars, or by $7567. ∎

PROBLEM SET 1.9

Practice Problems _____

Use the agreed-upon order of operations to find the value of the expressions in Problems 1–56. If applicable, verify each value using a graphing calculator.

1. $-45 \div 5 \cdot 3$

2. $-40 \div 4 \cdot 2$

3. $-3 + 5(1 - 4)^3$

4. $-5 + 3(2 - 6)^3$

5. $16 - 2 \cdot 3 - 25$

6. $15 - 3 \cdot 7 - 4$

7. $-12 \div 3 + 18 \div 9$

8. $26 - 12 \div 4 - 9$

9. $6 + 12 - 12 \div 4$

10. $14 + 8 - 8 \div 2$

11. $14 - 2 \cdot 5 - 20$

12. $16 - 4 \cdot 3 - 25$

13. $(14 - 2) \cdot 5 - 20$

14. $(16 - 4) \cdot 3 - 25$

15. $(-30) \div (-6)(-\frac{1}{3})$

16. $(-40) \div (-12)(-\frac{1}{4})$

17. $\dfrac{10 + 8}{5^2 - 4^2}$

18. $\dfrac{6^2 - 4^2}{2 - (-8)}$

19. $[2(6 - 2)]^2$

20. $[3(4 - 6)]^3$

21. $-8 + 4(3 - 5)^3$

22. $-5 + 3(2 - 2)^3$

23. $36 - 24 \div 2^3 \cdot 3 - 1$

24. $100 - 36 \div 3^2 \cdot 4 - 1$

25. $(15 - 3^3)^2$

26. $(60 - 4^3)^3$

27. $16 - (-3)(-12) \div 9$

28. $7 - (-8)(-11) \div 4$

29. $[7 + 3(2^3 - 1)] \div 21$

30. $[11 - 4(2 - 3^3)] \div 37$

31. $\dfrac{37 + 15 \div (-3)}{16}$

32. $\dfrac{22 + 20 \div (-5)}{9}$

33. $\frac{3}{5}(\frac{2}{3} - \frac{3}{4})$

34. $\frac{7}{25}(\frac{1}{8} - \frac{7}{16})$

35. $4(3 - 6)^2 - 2(3 - 4)$

36. $6(-8 + 10)^2 - 5(7 - 10)$

37. $\dfrac{5(4 - 6)}{2} - \dfrac{27}{-3}$

38. $\dfrac{3(6 - 8)}{2} - \dfrac{12}{-2}$

39. $5 - 5 \div 5 \cdot 5 - 5^2$

40. $7 - 7 \div 7 \cdot 7 - 7^2$

41. $\dfrac{4^2 - 3^2}{(4 - 3)^2}$

42. $\dfrac{5^2 - 4^2}{(5 - 4)^2}$

43. $3(-2)^3 - 5(-2) + 4$

44. $2(-4)^3 - 9(-10) + 3$

45. $[5 + 3(-2)]^7$

46. $[8 + 5(-2)]^5$

47. $\left(\dfrac{3}{2}\right)^2 \div \left(-\dfrac{3}{4}\right)$

48. $\left(\dfrac{4}{5}\right)^2 \div \left(-\dfrac{3}{5}\right)$

49. $6(6 - 7)^3 - 9(3 - 6)^2$

50. $3(4 - 6)^3 - 5(3 - 8)^2$

51. $\dfrac{(-11)(-4) + 2(-7)}{7 - (-3)}$

52. $\dfrac{-5(7 - 2) - 3(4 - 7)}{-13 - (-5)}$

53. $-2^2 + 4[16 \div (3 - 5)]$

54. $-3^2 + 2[20 \div (7 - 11)]$

55. $24 \div \dfrac{3^2}{8 - 5} - (-6)$

56. $30 \div \dfrac{5^2}{7 - 12} - (-9)$

Simplify each algebraic expression in Problems 57–68.

57. $5(x - 3) + 2$

58. $4(y - 2) + 3$

59. $-3[5(x - 3) + 2]$

60. $-5[4(y - 2) + 3]$

61. $3[6 - (y + 1)]$

62. $5[2 - (y + 3)]$

63. $7 - 4[3 - (-4y - 5)]$

64. $6 - 5[8 - (-9y - 3)]$

65. $3[6x - 2y - 4(-5x - y)]$

66. $2[7x - 2y - 5(-4x - y)]$

67. $12x - 4[6x - 8y - (2x - 4y)]$

68. $13x - 5[10x - 7y - (3x - 15y)]$

Application Problems _____

69. Bowlers who average under 200 often have handicaps added to their score. The handicap H of a bowler whose average score is A is often determined using the mathematical model

$$H = 0.8(200 - A).$$

What is the handicap of a person whose average score is 150? What is that bowler's final score for that game?

David Hosted bowling
Damien Stroymeyer/Allsport
Photography (USA), Inc.

70. In the United States, the life expectancy L of a 12- to 16-year-old white male is often determined using the mathematical model

$$L = 60.7 + 0.95(A - 12)$$

where A is the age of the person. What is the life expectancy of a 16-year-old white male according to this formula?

71. In Silicon Valley, California, a government agency orders computer-related companies to contribute to a monetary pool to clean up underground water supplies. (The companies had stored toxic chemicals in leaking underground containers.) The required monetary pool M (in millions of dollars) depends on the percent of the contaminant removed, given by the mathematical model

$$M = \frac{2x}{1 - x}$$

where x is the percentage of the total contaminant removed, expressed as a decimal. Complete the following table.

Percentage of Contaminant Removed	Required Amount of Money in Monetary Pool
50% (Let $x = 0.5$.)	$2 million
60% (Let $x = 0.6$.)	$3 million
70% (Let $x = 0.7$.)	
80%	
90%	
95%	
99%	

What happens to the cost of the cleanup as the desired percent of contaminant removed gets closer and closer to 100%?

72. In 1917, L. L. Thurstone, a pioneer in learning theory, proposed mathematical models to describe the number of successful acts per unit time that a person could accomplish after x practice sessions. Suppose, for a particular person who is learning to type, Thurstone's model is

$$W = \frac{60(x + 1)}{x + 5}$$

where W is the number of words per minute that the person is able to type after x weeks of lessons. How many words per minute can be typed after 10 weeks of lessons? Try substituting larger and larger values for x into the model to determine if there is a limit to how many words this person will eventually be able to type per minute. What is this limit?

73. According to classical economic theory, the demand for a commodity in a free market decreases as the price increases. The model

$$D = \frac{14,400}{x^2 + 10x}$$

describes the number of calculators D that people are willing to purchase per week in a given city at a price of x dollars. How many more people are willing to purchase calculators at a price of $10 than at a price of $15?

74. The Internal Revenue Service approves linear depreciation as one of several methods for depreciating business property. If the original cost of the property is C dollars and it is depreciated linearly (steadily) for N years, its value V at the end of n years is described by

$$V = C\left(1 - \frac{n}{N}\right).$$

Equipment having an original cost of $10,000 is depreciated linearly over 20 years. What will the value of the equipment be at the end of 7 years?

75. The models

$$C = 469x - 1700 \quad \text{and} \quad T = -82x + 1972$$

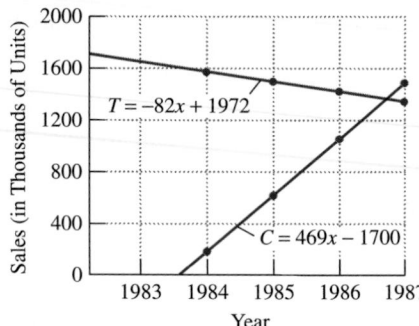

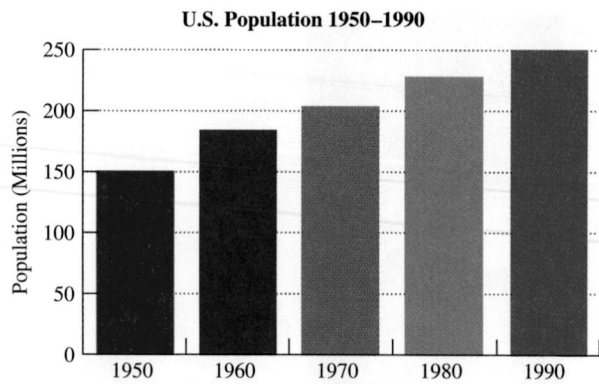

U.S. Population 1950–1990

Data Source: U.S. Bureau of the Census

describe the annual sale (in thousands of units) of compact disc players, C, and turntables, T, where x represents the number of years after 1980. Evaluate each formula for $x = 5, 6$, and 7. What trend do you observe? Describe how this trend is illustrated by the graphs.

76. The models

$$M = 2.89x + 70.64 \quad \text{and} \quad F = 2.75x + 71.48$$

estimate the height (in centimeters) of males, M, and females, F, where $x =$ the length of the humerus (the bone from the elbow to the shoulder), also measured in centimeters. Evaluate each formula for $x = 24$ and describe what your answer represents in practical terms. How might archeologists use these models?

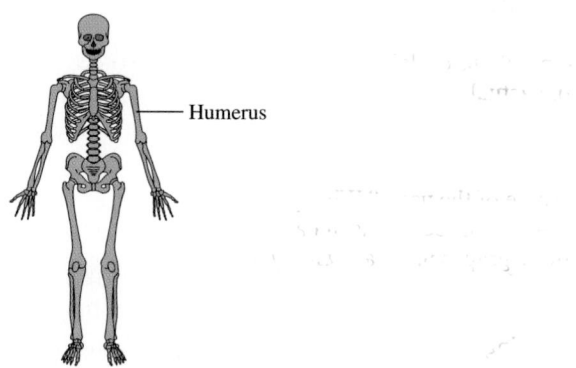

— Humerus

77. The U.S. population from 1950 through 1990 can be approximated by the model

$$y = 0.0002x^3 - 0.02x^2 + 3x + 151$$

where y represents the population (in millions) and x represents the number of years after 1950. Evaluate the model for $x = 0, 10, 20, 30$, and 40. Compare the numbers obtained from the model with the actual numbers in the bar graph. How close does the model come to approximating U.S. population for the present year?

78. The life expectancy of women in the United States can be approximated by the model

$$E = 0.215t + 71.05$$

where E represents life expectancy and t represents the number of years after 1950. Evaluate the model for $t = 0, 10, 20, 30$, and 40. Are the points in the rectangular coordinate system graphed correctly? What does the model predict for the life expectancy of women in the year 2000?

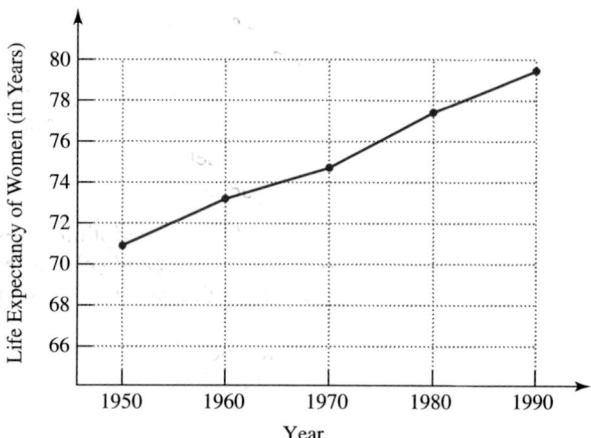

79. A book on dog training published by its author resulted in fixed costs of $5000 and $8 for each book. The average cost per book for the author to publish x books is modeled by

$$C = \frac{8x + 5000}{x}$$

where C is the average cost per book in dollars. Find the average cost per book for printing 100, 200, 300, 400, and 500 books. Are the points representing these solutions shown correctly in the graph? What happens to the average cost per book as the number of books published increases?

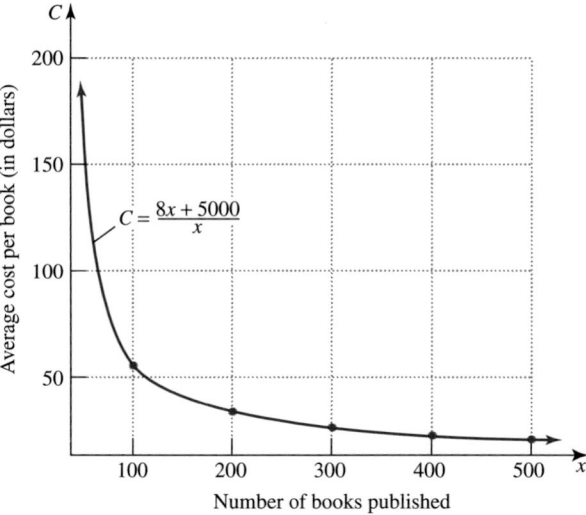

$$C = \frac{8x + 5000}{x}$$

Number of books published

80. The gross national product (GNP) of a country is the total market value of all the goods and services produced by the country during a given time period. The table gives the GNP for the United States during the years 1960, 1970, 1980, and 1990.

Year	1960	1970	1980	1990
U.S. GNP (in billions of $)	515.3	1015.5	2732.0	5524.5

Source: Bureau of Economic Analysis, U.S. Department of Commerce

a. One model for the GNP is given by

GNP $= 110.835t + 312.583$

where t is the number of years after 1960, and the GNP is in billions of dollars. Evaluate this model for $t = 0, 10, 20,$ and 30. How accurate is the model in terms of describing the actual GNP?

b. Repeat part (a) using the model

GNP $= 6.081t^2 - 10.795t + 515.3.$

Does this model provide a better description of reality for some of the years? What years?

c. Graphs of the models for parts (a) and (b) are shown below. The three points in each rectangular system represent the GNP for the years 1960, 1970, and 1980. Explain how these graphs illustrate what you discovered algebraically in parts (a) and (b).

d. Does either of the given models accurately describe the GNP for 1990? How can this be shown if you extend the two graphs to include $t = 30$? What does this tell you about using mathematical models to describe trends over long periods of time?

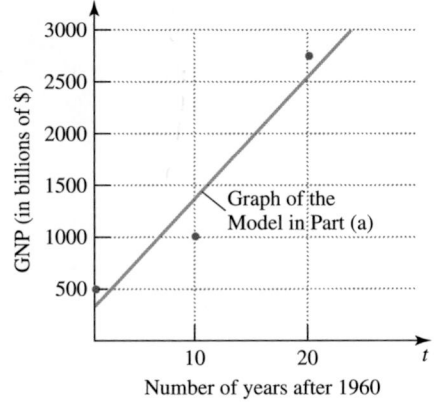

Graph of the Model in Part (a)

Number of years after 1960

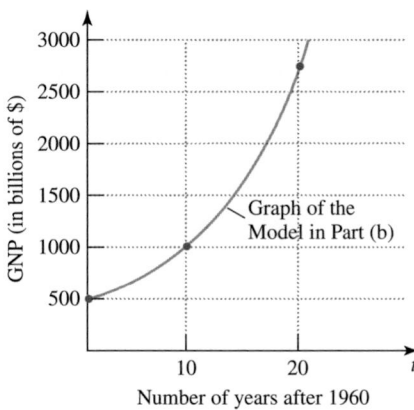

Graph of the Model in Part (b)

Number of years after 1960

True–False Critical Thinking Problems

81. Which one of the following is true?

  a. If x is -3, then the value of $-3x - 9$ is -18.

  b. The algebraic expression $\dfrac{6x + 6}{x + 1}$ cannot have the same value when two different replacements are made for x such as $x = -3$ and $x = 2$.

  c. A miniature version of a space shuttle is an example of a mathematical model.

  d. The value of $\dfrac{|3 - 7| - 2^3}{(-2)(-3)}$ is the fraction that results when $\frac{1}{3}$ is subtracted from $-\frac{1}{3}$.

82. Which one of the following is true?

  a. When x is replaced by -1, $|-x|$ and $-|-x|$ have the same value.

  b. $-2(6 - 4^2)^3 = -2(6 - 16)^3$
$$= -2(-10)^3 = (-20)^3 = -8000$$

  c. Using the mathematical model $C = \frac{5}{9}(F - 32)$, when the Fahrenheit temperature is 95.9°, the equivalent Celsius temperature is 35.5°.

  d. The order of operations for the natural numbers is different from that for rational numbers in decimal form.

Technology Problems

83. The number of marriages and divorces (in millions) in the United States is given in the table.

Number of Marriages and Divorces (Millions)						
Year	**1965**	**1970**	**1975**	**1980**	**1985**	**1990**
x	**Marriages**	1.800	2.158	2.152	2.413	2.425	2.448
y	**Divorces**	0.479	0.708	1.036	1.182	1.187	1.175

Source: National Center for Health Statistics

  a. Can the data be approximately modeled by the formula

$$y = 1.113x - 1.5239$$

where x = the number of marriages and y = the number of divorces in a year? Use your graphing calculator to find y for each of the six values of x in the table. How close do your computations for y come to the actual values in the table?

  b. Graph the six ordered pairs (x, y) in the table in a rectangular coordinate system. You can do this by hand or by using your graphing calculator. (Read the section on drawing scatter plots in your manual.) What do you observe about the six data points?

84. The average annual salary for a major league baseball player t years after 1976 is modeled by

$$S = 74{,}741(1.17)^t$$

where S is annual salary in dollars. Use your calculator to evaluate the model from $t = 0$ to $t = 18$. Using the graph of the actual data that is shown here, how accurate is the model in terms of describing major league baseball salaries?

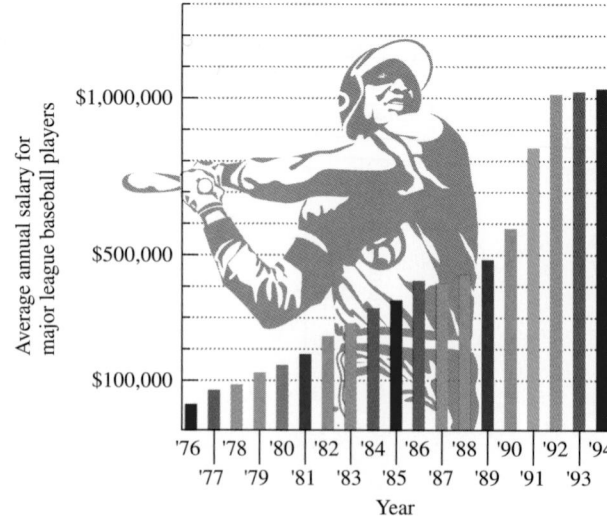

Source: MLBPA

85. Compound interest is calculated by the formula

$$A = P\left(1 + \frac{r}{n}\right)^{nt}$$

where P = principal (the amount invested), r = interest rate (in decimal form), n = number of times interest is compounded per year, t = number of years, and

A = amount in the account after t years. A sum of $5000 ($P$ = 5000) is invested at an interest rate of 7% per year ($r = 0.07$). Use your calculator to find the amount in the account after ten years ($t = 10$) if interest is compounded (a) annually ($n = 1$), (b) semiannually ($n = 2$), (c) quarterly ($n = 4$), (d) monthly ($n = 12$), (e) daily ($n = 365$).

Writing in Mathematics

86. Why is the order of operations agreement needed?

87. At one time algebra used words rather than symbols to convey ideas. What advantages are there to presenting ideas in a compact, symbolic style rather than in a rhetorical, verbal style? Can you think of any disadvantages to the compact, symbolic language of modern algebra?

Critical Thinking Problems

88. Grouping symbols can be inserted into $4 + 3 \cdot 7 - 4$ so that the resulting value is 45. By placing parentheses around the addition we obtain

$$(4 + 3) \cdot 7 - 4 = 7 \cdot 7 - 4 = 49 - 4 = 45.$$

Insert parentheses, *if needed,* in each of the following so that the resulting value is 45.
a. $2 \cdot 3 + 3 \cdot 5$
b. $2 \cdot 5 - \frac{1}{2} \cdot 10 \cdot 9$
c. $4^2 \div \frac{1}{4} - 3 \cdot 5 - 2^2$

89. Given the following formulas

$$Q = ac \qquad M = Q^2 - a^2 \qquad P = \tfrac{1}{3}a^2M$$

find the value of P if $a = -1$ and $c = -2$.

90. Using *only* the symbols $+$, $-$, $\times$, and $\div$ as replacements for the blanks, find the greatest value for the given expression.

$$1 \underline{\quad} 2 \underline{\quad} 3 \underline{\quad} 4 \underline{\quad} 5$$

91. In Problem 90, if parentheses can be used [placing (in a blank and) in a blank], what would be the greatest value?

92. This problem is based upon a math game called Krypto. Using the numbers 2, 4, 9, 14, and 17, show how

$$\underline{\quad} \ \underline{\quad} \ \underline{\quad} \ \underline{\quad} \ \underline{\quad} = 1$$

Each number can be used only once. An exponent can replace one or more of the blanks. Through much trial and error, it can be shown that

$$(9 + 14) \div (2 + 4 + 17) = 1.$$

Many solutions are possible, depending on whether only $+$, $-$, $\times$, $\div$, and parentheses are used or if exponents are brought into the picture.
a. Use 2, 4, 9, 14, and 17, using all five numbers precisely once, to show how $\underline{\quad} \ \underline{\quad} \ \underline{\quad} \ \underline{\quad} \ \underline{\quad}$ equals 1 in a different way.
b. Use each number precisely once to show how $\underline{\quad} \ \underline{\quad} \ \underline{\quad} \ \underline{\quad} \ \underline{\quad}$ equals 2.
c. Use each number precisely once to show how $\underline{\quad} \ \underline{\quad} \ \underline{\quad} \ \underline{\quad} \ \underline{\quad}$ equals 3.

Review Problems_____

93. Find the indicated sum: $\frac{5}{12} + \frac{7}{9}$.

94. Use this weather chart for Antarctica to find a reasonable estimate for the difference in Fahrenheit temperature between June and January.

Weather Chart

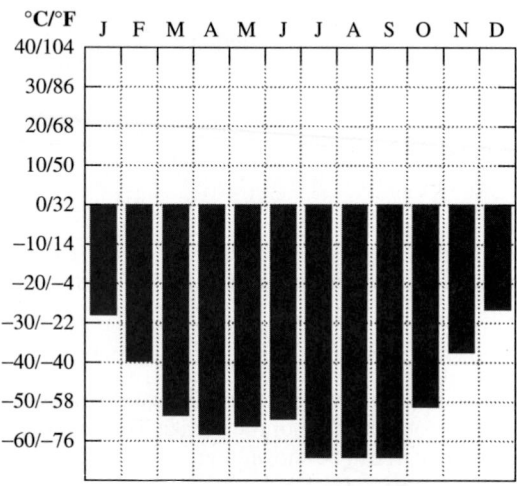

━━ Average Daily Temperature

95. The model

$$P = 2t^2 + 22t + 320$$

describes the number of inmates P (in thousands) in U.S. federal and state prisons t years after 1980. Use the model to predict the number of inmates in the year 2000.

C HAPTER PROJECT

Measures of Fitness

Most people exercise to maintain muscular strength and flexibility and to reduce fat. No matter what style of exercise you choose, doctors and exercise physiologists usually suggest exercising at a certain percentage of your *maximum heart rate,* or MHR. Thus, before beginning any exercise program, you should determine your MHR. Your can use the formula

   $220 - a = $ MHR

where a is your age in years. We saw this formula in Section 1.4, Example 7, as part of determining optimum heart rate. We used the model

   $0.6(220 - a)$

or 60% of the maximum heart rate as the optimal heart rate.

   While 60% may be the *best* rate, your personal goal may range from 50% to 70% of your maximum heart rate, depending on a combination of factors. These factors include your age, gender, previous level of physical activity, and current level of physical fitness. The first three factors are easily recorded, but what is meant by physical fitness? We'll look at two different measures in this project.

   One measure of physical fitness is your *resting heart rate.* Generally speaking, the more fit you are, the lower your resting heart rate. The best time to take this measurement is when you first awaken in the morning, before you get out of bed. Lie on your back with no body parts crossed and take your pulse in your neck or wrist. Use your index and second fingers and count your pulse beat for one full minute to get your resting heart rate.

Another measure of physical fitness is your percentage of bodyfat. You can estimate your bodyfat using the following formulas:

For men: $\text{Bodyfat} = -98.42 + 4.15\,w - 0.082\,b$

For women: $\text{Bodyfat} = -76.76 + 4.15\,w - 0.082\,b$

where, w = waist measurement in inches and b = total body weight in pounds. Then divide your bodyfat by your total weight to get your *bodyfat percentage.*

In this project, you will use this information to analyze data.

1. Using yourself as a source, record the following information on a single sheet of paper to bring to class.

   Age   Gender   Resting Heart rate   Bodyfat Percentage

   In class, collect all of the information and present it in the form of a table that the entire class can use.

2. Divide into groups and prepare the following graphs using the information you have collected.
   a. Age vs. resting heart rate
   b. Age vs. bodyfat percentage
   c. Resting heart rate vs. bodyfat percentage
   d. Graphs for each gender

   Study the data you will be using to determine which style of graph will be most appropriate (circle, bar, or line) and to find the range of values for your scale.

3. For each graph, determine where your source data would be found and use this to determine your personal level of physical fitness. Compare your conclusions from the class data with the following:

Resting Heart Rate	Description
under 48 to 57	High fitness
58 to 62	Above average
63 to 70	Average
71 to 82	Below average
83 or more	Low fitness

Using bodyfat percentages: For men, less than 15% is considered athletic, 25% about average.

For women, less than 22% is considered athletic, 30% about average.

Discussion Questions

1. Did arranging the data in graphical form help in your analysis?
2. What decisions did you need to make when preparing the graphs?
3. Do some types of graphs seem better suited to these data than others?
4. Do you think the graphs would look the same if your survey had included all members of your household?
5. Do you think the two measures of fitness described here accurately reflect your level of fitness?

Worldwide Web Resources

Go to the Prentice Hall website (http://www.prenhall.com/blitzer) to access other locations on the Internet that will allow you to futher explore the concepts presented in this project.

Chapter Review

SUMMARY

1. Fractions

  a. *Simplifying (Reducing) Fractions:* Divide both the numerator and the denominator by their greatest common factor.

  b. *Multiplying Fractions:*

    1. Factor the numerators and denominators.

    2. Divide out the common factors in any numerator and denominator.

    3. Take the product of the remaining factors in the numerators divided by the product of the remaining factors in the denominators.

  c. *Dividing Fractions:* Invert the divisor and multiply.

  d. *Adding and Subtracting Fractions with Identical Denominators:* Add or subtract the numerators. Put this result over the common denominator.

  e. *Adding and Subtracting Fractions with Unlike Denominators:*

    1. Rewrite the fractions as equivalent fractions with the least common denominator.

    2. Add or subtract the numerators, putting this result over the common denominator.

  f. *Changing a Mixed Number to Fractional Notation:*

    1. Multiply the denominator of the fraction in the mixed number by the whole number preceding it.

    2. Add the numerator of the fraction in the mixed number to the product from step 1.

    3. Put the result of step 2 over the original denominator.

2. Sets

  a. A *set* is a collection of objects. The objects in a set are the *elements* or *members* of the set.

  b. Sets are represented by *set-builder notation* and the *roster method*.

3. The Real Numbers

The set of *real numbers* consists of both the set of rational numbers and the set of irrational numbers.

  a. The set of *natural numbers* is $\{1, 2, 3, 4, 5, \ldots\}$.

  b. The set of *whole numbers* is $\{0, 1, 2, 3, 4, 5, \ldots\}$.

  c. The set of *integers* consists of the natural numbers, zero, and the negatives of the natural numbers. This set is $\{\ldots, -3, -2, -1, 0, 1, 2, 3, \ldots\}$.

  d. *Rational numbers* are numbers in the form $\dfrac{a}{b}$, where a and b are integers and b is not zero, represented by $\left\{ \dfrac{a}{b} \,\middle|\, a \text{ and } b \text{ are integers, } b \neq 0 \right\}$.

  e. The *irrational numbers* are real numbers that are not rational, represented by $\{x \mid x$ is a real number that is not rational$\}$. When expressed in decimal form, irrational numbers neither terminate nor repeat. Examples are $\sqrt{2} \approx 1.414$, $\pi \approx 3.14$, $e \approx 2.72$ ($\approx$ means "is approximately equal to").

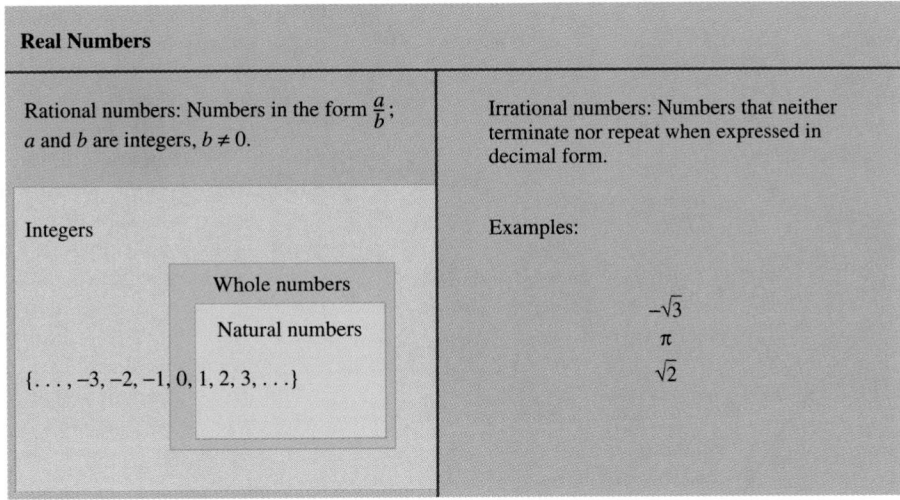

Real Numbers

Rational numbers: Numbers in the form $\frac{a}{b}$; a and b are integers, $b \neq 0$.	Irrational numbers: Numbers that neither terminate nor repeat when expressed in decimal form.
Integers	Examples:
Whole numbers	
Natural numbers	$-\sqrt{3}$
$\{\ldots, -3, -2, -1, 0, 1, 2, 3, \ldots\}$	π
	$\sqrt{2}$

4. **Ordering Real Numbers**

   a.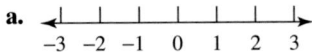

   Corresponding to every real number there is precisely one point on the number line. Corresponding to every point on the real line there is precisely one real number.

   b.

   $a < b$ (a is less than b) means that a is to the left of b on the real number line. Equivalently, $b > a$ (b is greater than a).

   c. Other symbols: $\leq$ means "less than or equal to" and $\geq$ means "greater than or equal to."

5. **Opposites (Additive Inverses) and Absolute Value**

   a. The opposite or additive inverse of a real number x, represented by $-x$, is the number that is the same distance from 0 on the number line as x, but on the opposite side of 0.

   b. The Double Negative Rule: $-(-x) = x$

   c. $|x|$, the absolute value of x, is the (positive) distance between x and 0 on the number line. $|x|$ is never negative.

6. **Graphing**

   a. Circle graphs (pie charts) display information that often shows what percent of a whole each item in a group represents.

   b. Bar graphs show comparisons among items, using horizontal or vertical bars to indicate the amount of each item.

   c. Line graphs use points to represent given information. The graph is formed when line segments are drawn connecting the points.

7. **The Rectangular Coordinate System**

   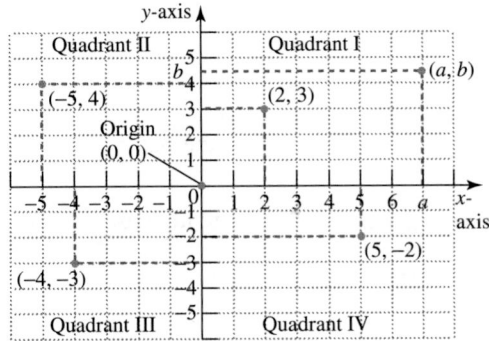

8. **Algebraic Expressions**

   a. An *algebraic expression* is a collection of constants and variables combined using addition, subtraction, multiplication, division, and/or exponents.

   b. *Terms* indicate a product and may contain any number of *factors*. The numerical factor is the numerical coefficient.

   c. *Like terms or similar terms* contain the same variables raised to the same powers. Combine like terms by adding or subtracting numerical coefficients, keeping the same variable factors.

   d. Simplify an algebraic expression by using the distributive property to remove grouping symbols. Then combine like terms.

9. **Basic Rules of Algebra**

   Let a, b, and c represent real numbers, variables, or algebraic expressions.

   a. *Commutative Properties:* $a + b = b + a$; $ab = ba$

   b. *Associative Properties:* $(a + b) + c = a + (b + c)$; $(ab)c = a(bc)$

c. *Distributive Property:*
$a(b + c) = ab + ac; (b + c)a = ba + ca$
d. *Additive Identity Property:* $a + 0 = a$
e. *Additive Inverse Property:* $a + (-a) = 0$
f. *Properties of Multiplication*
　1. Multiplication Property of 1: $a \cdot 1 = a$ and $1 \cdot a = a$
　2. Multiplication Property of -1: $-1 \cdot a = -a$ and $a(-1) = -a$
　3. Multiplication Property of 0: $a \cdot 0 = 0$ and $0 \cdot a = 0$
　4. Reciprocal or Multiplicative Inverse Property: $a \cdot \frac{1}{a} = 1, a \neq 0$
g. *Property for a Negative Sign Preceding Parentheses:*
$-(a - b + c) = -a + b - c.$ Remove parentheses and change signs of all terms within parentheses.

10. Translating Phrases into Algebraic Expressions

English Phrase	Algebraic Expression
The sum of a and b	$a + b$
a minus b	$a - b$
a decreased by b	$a - b$
The difference between a and b	$a - b$
b less than a	$a - b$
b is less than a	$b < a$
The product of a and b	ab
Double a	$2a$
Two-thirds of a	$\frac{2}{3}a$
35% of b	$0.35b$
The quotient of a and b	$\frac{a}{b}$
The additive inverse (opposite) of a	$-a$

11. Operations with Real Numbers
a. *Addition:* The sum of two numbers with the same (like) sign has the same sign as the two numbers and is found by adding their absolute values. If the two numbers have different signs, the sign of the sum is the sign of the original number having the larger absolute value. The sum is found by subtracting the smaller absolute value from the larger ab-

solute value. A gain-loss interpretation can be used to mentally determine the sum.
b. *Subtraction:* $a - b = a + (-b)$. To subtract b from a, add the opposite of b to a.
c. *Multiplication and division:* The product or quotient of two numbers with like signs is positive. The product or quotient of two numbers with different signs is negative. The multiplication or division is performed by multiplying or dividing the absolute values of the two numbers and giving the answer the proper sign. The product of 0 and any real number is 0. Division by 0 is undefined.
d. Assuming no number in a product is 0, a multiplication problem involving an even number of negative factors has a positive product and one with an odd number of negative factors has a negative product.
e. *Exponents:* b^n (b to the nth power) means the product of n factors of b, so that b^2 (b squared) $= b \cdot b$; b^3 (b cubed) $= b \cdot b \cdot b$; $b^4 = b \cdot b \cdot b \cdot b$; and so on. Furthermore, $b^1 = b$.

12. The Order of Operations Agreement
a. Perform operations above and below any fraction bar, following steps (b) through (e).
b. Perform operations inside grouping symbols, innermost grouping symbols first, following steps (c) through (e).
c. Simplify exponential expressions.
d. Do multiplication or division as they occur, working from left to right.
e. Do addition and subtraction as they occur, working from left to right.

13. Evaluating Mathematical Models and Algebraic Expressions
a. A *mathematical model* is a statement of equality expressing a relationship among variables that describe real world phenomena.
b. We can find the value of an expression or one of the variables in a mathematical model by replacing specified variables with given numbers. We then use the order of operations agreement.

REVIEW PROBLEMS

In Problems 1–5, perform the indicated operation, and simplify if possible.

1. $\frac{9}{10} \cdot \frac{18}{7}$　　**2.** $\frac{15}{32} \div 5$　　**3.** $\frac{7}{9} + \frac{5}{12}$　　**4.** $\frac{3}{4} - \frac{2}{15}$　　**5.** $5\frac{3}{4} - 3\frac{5}{8}$

6. Simplify $\frac{20}{36}$. Then use this simplified form to express the fraction in both decimal and percent notations.

Use the roster method to write each set in Problems 7–8.

7. $\{x \mid x$ is a whole number that is less than 6$\}$
8. $\{x \mid x$ is an integer that is greater than $-3\}$
9. Consider the set
$\{-17, -\frac{9}{13}, 0, 0.75, \sqrt{2}, \pi, 5\frac{1}{4}, \sqrt{81}\}.$

List all numbers from the set that are
a. Natural numbers　　**b.** Whole numbers
c. Integers　　**d.** Rational numbers
e. Irrational numbers　　**f.** Real numbers

Place the correct symbol (< , > , or =) between the two numbers in Problems 10–13.

10. 17 ☐ 5

11. $-|-3.2|$ ☐ $-(-3.2)$

12. 0 ☐ $-\frac{1}{3}$

13. $-\frac{1}{4}$ ☐ $-\frac{1}{5}$

14. India's population is approximately 880 million. Use the circle graph to estimate how many more Muslims than Christians there are in India.

Religious Persuasion

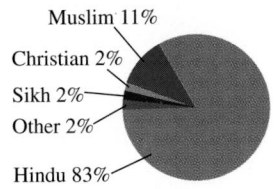

Muslim 11%

Christian 2%

Sikh 2%

Other 2%

Hindu 83%

15. The circle graph below shows the housing units in which Americans live.
  a. Does the sum of the numbers in the four sectors represent the population of the United States? Explain.
  b. What percent of Americans represented in the graph live in mobile homes? Round to the nearest whole percent.
  c. Use your answer from part (b) to obtain a reasonable estimate for the percents in the other three sectors.

Housing Units in Which Americans Live

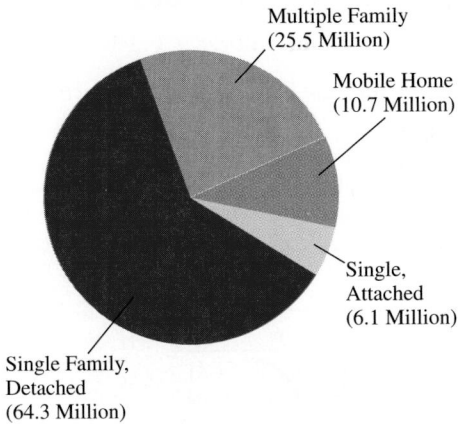

Multiple Family
(25.5 Million)

Mobile Home
(10.7 Million)

Single,
Attached
(6.1 Million)

Single Family,
Detached
(64.3 Million)

Source: U.S. Bureau of the Census

16. The bar graph at the upper right shows the leading causes of death in the United States by percent of total deaths.
  a. Estimate the percent of total deaths caused by heart disease.
  b. What disease causes about 7% of total deaths?
  c. What categories in the graph cause less than 5% of total deaths?

Leading Causes of Death in the U.S.,
by Percent of Total Deaths

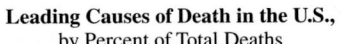

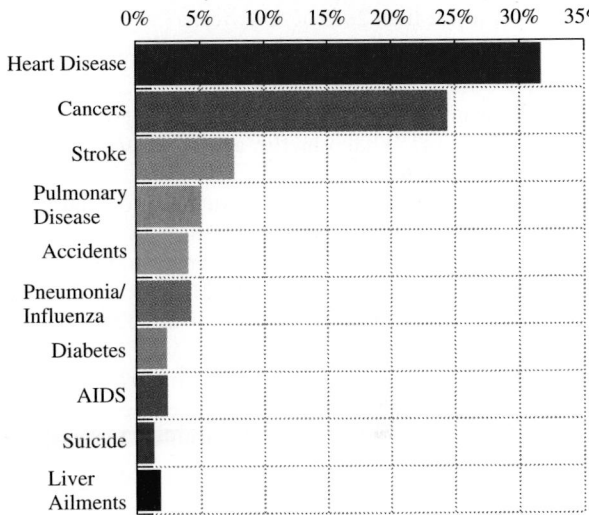

Source: National Safety Council, 1994

17. The bar graph below indicates the percent of Americans who participate in the country's ten most popular sports.

Most Popular Participatory Sports

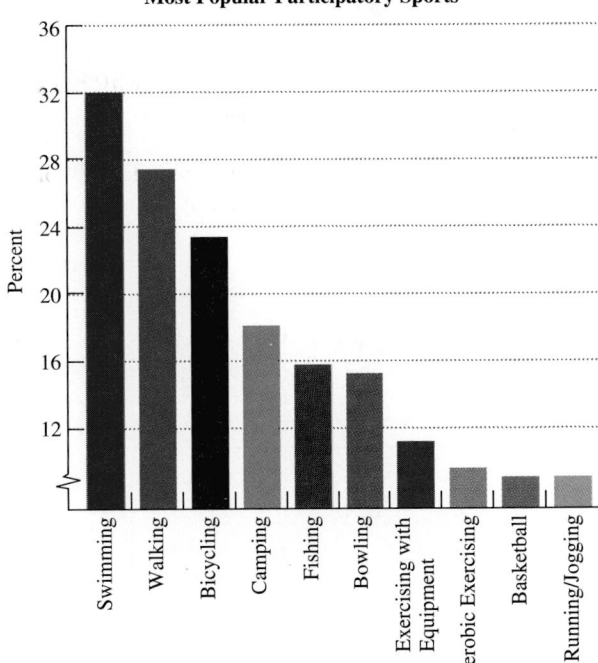

Source: U.S. Bureau of the Census

a. Estimate the percent of people who participate in bicycling.

b. In a group of 400 Americans, approximately how many would you expect to participate in swimming?

c. What sports are participated in by more than 16% but fewer than 28% of Americans?

18. The graphs show America's crime and unemployment rates from 1974 through 1994.

   a. In what year was crime per 1000 population at a maximum? What was the approximate crime rate for that year?

   b. In what years was the crime rate approximately 5.3 per 1000 population?

   c. In what years was the unemployment rate 7%?

   d. What was the crime rate for the year in which the unemployment rate was at a maximum?

   e. What was the crime rate for the year in which the unemployment rate was at a minimum?

   f. Is there a relationship between crime and unemployment as indicated by the graphs? If so, what is the relationship?

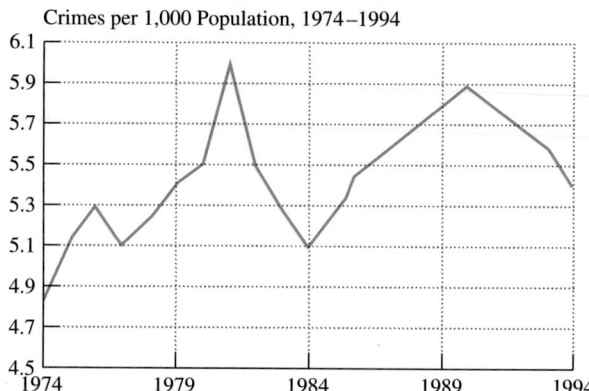

Crime and Unemployment
Is There a Relationship?
Crimes per 1,000 Population, 1974–1994

Unemployment Rate, 1974–1994

Source: FBI

Plot each ordered pair in Problems 19–22 on a rectangular coordinate system. Indicate in which quadrant each point lies.

19. $(1, -5)$

20. $(4, -3)$

21. $\left(\frac{7}{2}, \frac{5}{2}\right)$

22. $(-5, 2)$

23. Give the ordered pairs that correspond to the points labeled in the figure.

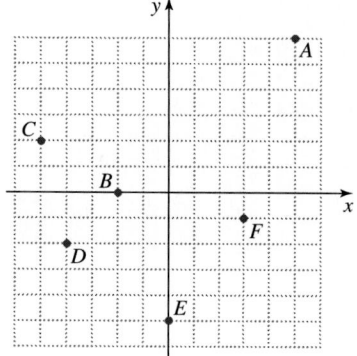

24. Graph the following data as ten ordered pairs in a rectangular coordinate system. What do the points suggest about wine consumption and heart disease?

	x	y	
France	63.5	61.1	Wine consumption in liters per capita
Italy	58.0	94.1	
Switzerland	46.0	106.4	
Australia	15.7	173.0	Deaths per 100,000 due to heart disease
Britain	12.2	199.7	
U.S.A.	8.9	176.0	
Russia	2.7	373.6	
Czech Republic	1.7	283.7	
Japan	1.0	34.7	
Mexico	0.2	36.4	

Source: World Health Organization

25. Use the commutative property of addition to write an expression equivalent to $3x + 5$.

26. The algebraic expression

$$t(1.24) + 313.6$$

models carbon dioxide concentration (in parts per million) t years after 1960. Use the commutative property of multiplication to write an equivalent expression.

In Problems 27–28, use the associative property to rewrite each algebraic expression. Once the grouping has been changed, simplify the resulting expression.

27. $6 + (4 + y)$

28. $-3(5x)$

29. The algebraic expression

$$100(2x + 6) - 41.5x - 25$$

models the average payment in thousands of dollars for automobile accidents x years after 1989. (Source: Insurance Research Council)
a. Simplify the expression.
b. Use the simplified expression to determine the average payment for catastrophic claims in automobile accidents for the years 1989, 1990, and 1991. By how much is the payment increasing each year?

30. The Dead Sea is the lowest elevation on earth, 1312 feet below sea level. If a person is standing 512 feet above the Dead Sea, what is that person's elevation?

31. What is the difference in elevation between a plane flying 26,500 feet above sea level and a submarine traveling 650 feet below sea level?

32. In 1993, 1821 Americans under the age of 21 were killed in alcohol-related car accidents. Changes in the numbers of fatal driving accidents related to alcohol are shown in the table.

Age Group	Fatal Driving Accidents
Under 21	1821
Age 21–34	5400 increase from the under 21 group
Age 35–49	4330 decrease from the age 21–34 group
Age 50–64	1714 decrease from the age 35–49 group
over 65	478

How many of the fatal car accidents in 1993 for the 50–64 age group were alcohol related?

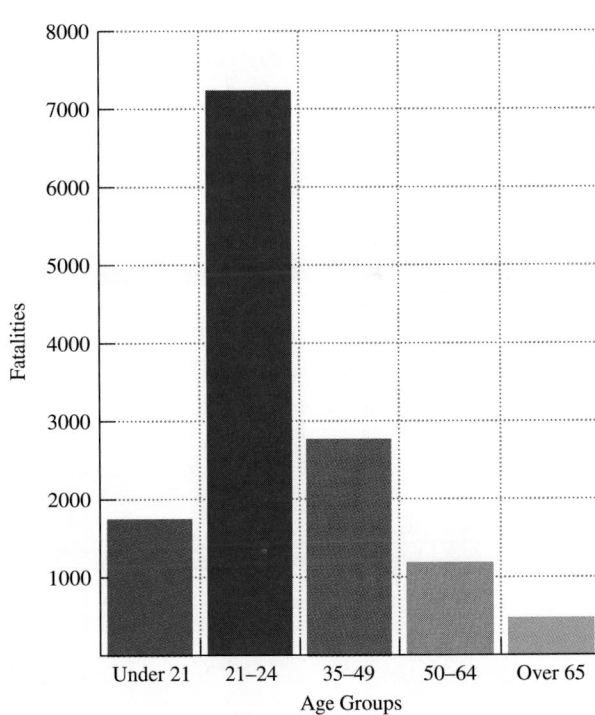

Alcohol Related Fatalities
by Age Groups

Source: National Highway Traffic Safety Administration, 1993

33. The bar graph on page 124 indicates gender changes in professional degrees.
a. If a represents the percentage of M.D. degrees awarded to women in 1970, write an algebraic expression in terms of a that represents the percentage of M.D. degrees awarded to women in 1990.

b. If *b* represents the percentage of degrees in dentistry awarded to men in 1970, write an algebraic expression in terms of *b* that represents the percentage of dentistry degrees awarded to men in 1990.

c. If *c* represents the percentage of law degrees awarded to women in 1970, use multiplication to write an algebraic expression in terms of *c* that represents the percentage of law degrees awarded to men for that same year.

d. If *d* represents the percentage of law degrees awarded to women in 1990, then $d + 16$ represents the percentage of law degrees awarded to men in that same year. Translate $d + 16$ into English in

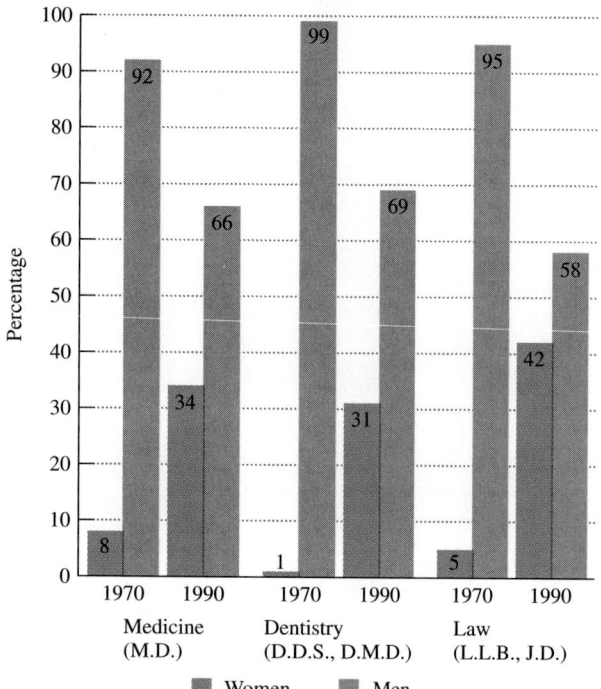

Percentage

Source: U.S. Bureau of the Census, *Statistical Abstract* 1993: Table 294

three different ways, using words and phrases such as "sum," "more," "added to," "plus," and "increased by."

e. If *e* represents the percentage of degrees in dentistry awarded to men in 1990, then $e - 38$ represents the percentage of degrees in dentistry awarded to women in that same year. Translate $e - 38$ into English in three different ways, using words and phrases such as "minus," "decreased by," "difference between," and "less than."

34. The 12 points in the figure represent the average temperature in Fairbanks, Alaska, based on records of the National Weather Service, for each of the 12 months of the year. Use the graph to find a reasonable estimate for each of the following.

a. The difference in temperature between February and May

b. The sum of the temperatures for January and April

c. The mean temperature for January through June (*Hint:* The mean, also known as the arithmetic average, is the sum of the values divided by the total number of values.)

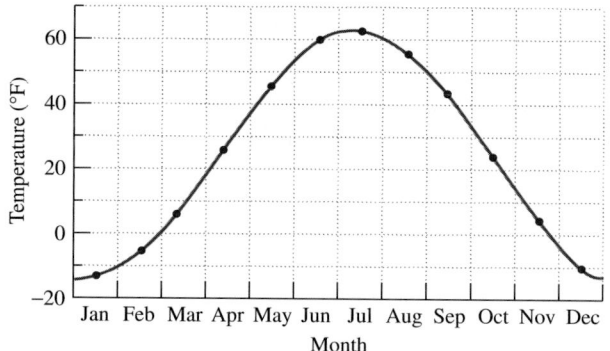

Translate each phrase in Problems 35–42 into an algebraic expression.

35. The value in dollars of *x* five-dollar bills

36. The perimeter of the parallelogram shown in the figure

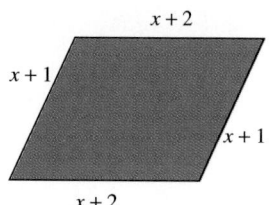

37. The enrollment in public and secondary schools in the United States *x* years after 1985 if it is known that:
   1. The 1985 enrollment was 39.05 million.
   2. Enrollment has increased by approximately 0.45 million each year.

38. The amount of weight in an elevator that is carrying a 150-pound passenger and *x* pieces of luggage weighing 10 pounds each

39. The sale price of an item with a 35% discount

40. The monthly salary for a person earning x dollars per year

41. The length of a rectangle with a width of x inches and an area of 20 square inches

42. The cost per tennis ball when x tennis balls are purchased for $6

Perform the indicated operations in Problems 43–71.

43. $8 + (-11)$

44. $-\frac{3}{4} + \frac{1}{5}$

45. $7 + (-5) + (-13) + 4$

46. $-7.8 + 4.1 + 13 + (-5.2)$

47. $-9 - (-13)$

48. $-7 - (-5) + 11 - 16$

49. $-\frac{3}{5} - \frac{9}{10}$

50. $-7(-12)$

51. $-2.3(4.5)$

52. $\frac{3}{5}\left(-\frac{5}{11}\right)$

53. $5(-3)(-2)(-4)$

54. $-3\left(-\frac{1}{6}\right)(40)$

55. $(-4)^2$

56. $(-2)^5$

57. $\left(-\frac{2}{3}\right)^2$

58. $45 \div (-5)$

59. $-\frac{4}{5} \div \left(-\frac{2}{5}\right)$

60. $\frac{-25}{0.05}$

61. $-40 \div 5 \cdot 2$

62. $-3 + 4(4 - 7)^3$

63. $16 \div 4^2 - 2$

64. $(16 \div 4)^2 - 2$

65. $16 \div (4^2 - 2)$

66. $(-10)(-6) - (-8)(4)$

67. $-8[-4 - 5(-3)]$

68. $\dfrac{6(-10 + 3)}{2(-15) - 9(-3)}$

69. $8^2 - 36 \div 3^2 \cdot 4 - (-7)$

70. $3 + (9 \div 3)^3 - 25 \div 5 \cdot 2 - (4 - 1)^3$

71. $\frac{5}{12} - \frac{11}{12} \div \left(\frac{1}{6} - \frac{3}{8}\right)$

Simplify each algebraic expression in Problems 72–80.

72. $11x + 7y + (-13x) + (-6y)$

73. $-13a - 7b - (-5a) + 13b$

74. $3(x + 5) - 7x$

75. $-6(3x - 4)$

76. $7(2y - 5) - (15y - 2)$

77. $4(-5x - 1) - 3(6x - 1)$

78. $\frac{1}{6}(6x - 6)$

79. $2[7x - 3(2x - 1)]$

80. $[3(x + 5) - 7] - [2(x - 1) + 5]$

81. The model

$$D = -1545.5x + 49,391$$

describes the number of motor vehicle deaths D in the United States x years after 1988. How many deaths were there in 1988, 1989, and 1990? Describe the trend over the three years.

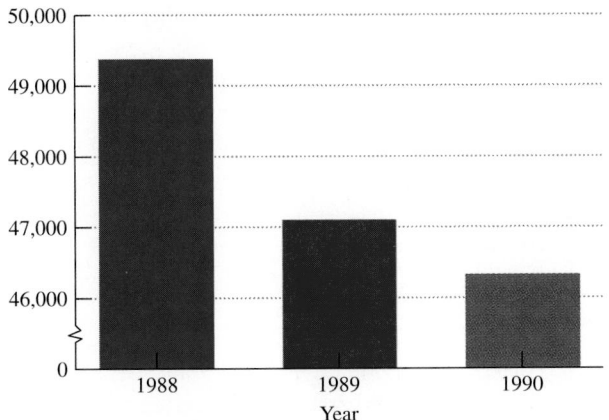

Motor Vehicle Deaths in the United States

Source: National Safety Council

82. The formula

$$t = \sqrt{\frac{h}{16}}$$

describes the time t in seconds that it takes for an object dropped from a height of h feet to reach the ground. If an apple is dropped from a height of 144 feet, how long will it take for it to reach the ground?

James Sugar/Black Star

83. The model

$$D = 9.2t^2 - 46.7t + 480$$

describes the U.S. national debt D in billions t years after 1970. Use the model to find the national debt for 1980 and 1990. The actual numbers are shown in the table. How well does the model describe reality for these two years?

Year	National Debt (in billions of $)
1980	$907.7
1990	$3233.3

84. An equation for the path of the bouncing ball outlined in the figure is

$$y = 12x - x^2.$$

a. Evaluate this model for $x = 3, 4, 5, \ldots, 12$.

b. Use your answers from part (a) to complete the following table. Then graph the 13 ordered pairs in the table in a rectangular coordinate system. How does the resulting graph showing the 13 points compare with the outlined path shown in the figure?

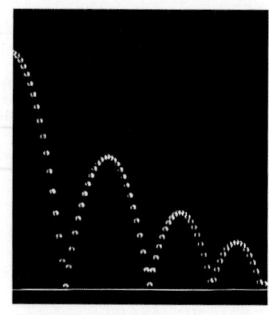

Berenice Abbott/Commerce Graphics Ltd., Inc.

x	0	1	2	3	4	5	6	7	8	9	10	11	12
y	0	11	20										

85. Recently the U.S. population has been growing in a way that can be modeled by

$$P = 1.7t + 230$$

where P is the population in millions t years after 1980.

a. Use this model to determine U.S. population in 1990.

b. Use this model to predict U.S. population in the years 2000, 2010, 2020, 2030, 2040, and 2050.

c. The graph shows high, medium, and low population projections for the United States. Which one of these projections is closest to the projections made by the model given in this problem? Explain.

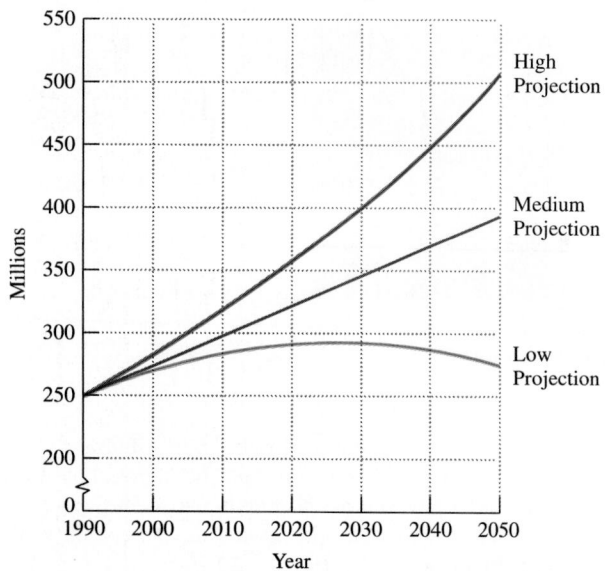

Population Projections of the United States

Source: U.S. Bureau of the Census, *Statistical Abstract* 1993: Table 17

86. The formula

$$T = 3(A - 20)^2 \div 50 + 10$$

describes the average time T in seconds for a person who is A years old to run the 100-yard dash. What is the difference in time between a 40-year-old and a 30-year old runner?

87. The mathematical model

$$N = -45t^4 + 446t^3 - 517t^2 + 2026t + 984$$

approximates the number of new AIDS cases in the United States, where N represents the number of new cases and t denotes the year (with $t = 0$ corresponding to 1982). Substitute $t = 0$, $t = 1$, and $t = 2$ in the formula. Is the bar graph drawn correctly? Then use the model to complete the graph for the years 1985 through 1989. The model applies only if $t \geq 0$ and $t \leq 8$. What happens if $t = 9$ and $t = 10$? Explain why the formula no longer models reality for the years 1990 and 1991.

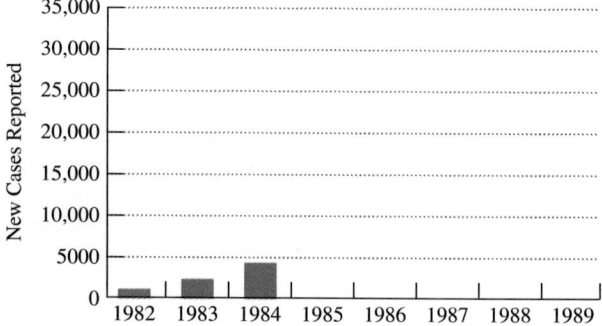

New AIDS Cases 1982–1989

Source: U.S. Centers for Disease Control

CHAPTER 1 TEST

1. Use the roster method to write this set.

$\{x \mid x$ is a negative integer greater than $-6\}$

2. List all the rational numbers in this set.

$\{-7, -\frac{4}{5}, 0, 0.25, \sqrt{3}, \sqrt{4}, \frac{22}{7}, \pi\}$

3. The circle graph shows the ethnic breakdown of America's population in the year 2050. If the projected population for that year is 390 million, how many African-Americans will there be?

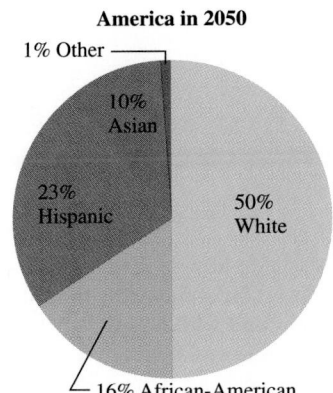

America in 2050

1% Other
10% Asian
23% Hispanic
50% White
16% African-American

Source: U.S. Census Bureau

4. The number of people shopping at home by computer is on the rise. The circle graph shows the 1996 revenues in millions of dollars generated by people making purchases on computer Web sites. What percent of this revenue was spent on computer products?

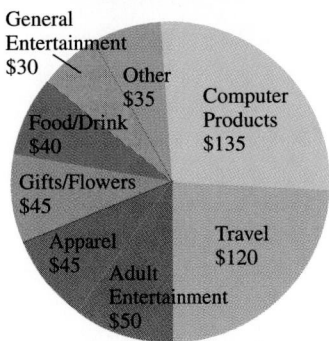

1996 Web Shopping Revenues in Millions of Dollars

General Entertainment $30
Other $35
Computer Products $135
Food/Drink $40
Gifts/Flowers $45
Apparel $45
Adult Entertainment $50
Travel $120

Source: Worldwide Web

5. In 1993, Americans made 425 million visits to unconventional practitioners, such as acupuncturists, chiropractic physicians, and massage therapists. The percent of people with six ailments who visited one or more of these care providers is shown in the graph. List the ailment or ailments for which more than 20% but fewer than 30% of people visited alternative practitioners.

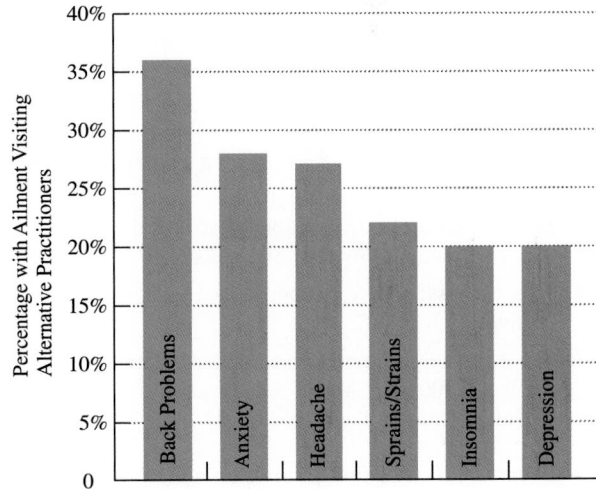

Visits to Alternative Practitioners

Percentage with Ailment Visiting Alternative Practitioners

Back Problems, Anxiety, Headache, Sprains/Strains, Insomnia, Depression

Source: *New England Journal of Medicine*

6. The line graph shows the total number of crimes in the United States from 1973–1993.

   a. In what year did the greatest number of crimes occur? What is a reasonable estimate (to the nearest whole million) of the number of crimes for that year?

   b. In what year were there 12 million crimes?

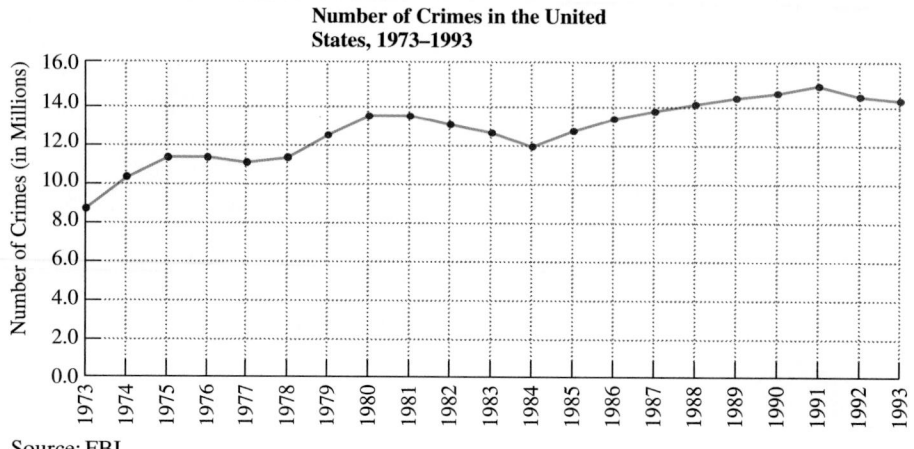

Source: FBI

7. Find the coordinates of point A in the figure.

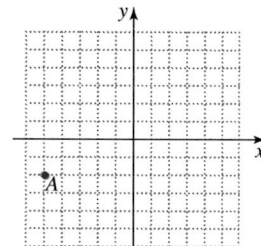

8. Plot the ordered pair $(-4, 3)$ on a rectangular coordinate system.

9. Use the commutative property of addition to rewrite $8x^2 + 7x$ as an equivalent expression.

10. Use the associative property to write an expression equivalent to $x \cdot (5 \cdot y)$.

11. What is the difference in elevation between a plane flying 16,200 feet above sea level and a submarine traveling 830 feet below sea level?

12. There is a simple rule to find how many lights are needed on a Christmas tree. Find the product of the tree's height and width, both expressed in inches, and then triple this number. If h represents the tree's height, in inches, and w its width, also in inches, write an algebraic expression for the number of lights needed.

13. The figure shows a rectangular garden whose length is 1 foot longer than twice the width. Represent the perimeter of this garden in an algebraic expression and then simplify the expression.

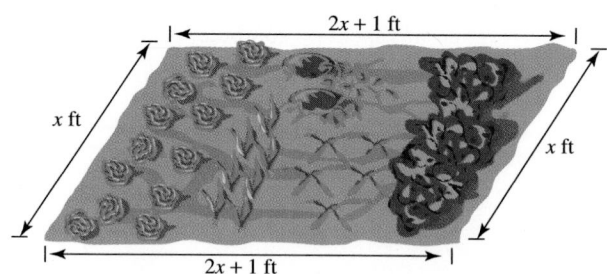

Perform the indicated operation or operations in Problems 14–25.

14. $5.3 - (-9.2)$

15. $-9 + 3 + (-11) + 6$

16. $-\frac{2}{11} + \frac{5}{44}$

17. $7.3 - 10.4$

18. $3(-17)$

19. $\left(-\frac{3}{7}\right)\left(-\frac{7}{15}\right)$

20. $-50 \div 10$

21. $-\frac{5}{9} \div \frac{2}{5}$

22. $-6 - (5 - 12)$

23. $(-3)(4) - (2)(6)$

24. $\dfrac{3(-2) - 2(2)}{-2(8 - 3)}$

25. $(6 - 8)^2(5 - 7)^3$

Simplify each algebraic expression in Problems 26–28.

26. $11x - (7x - 4)$ **27.** $9(-3x - 2) - 4(5x - 3)$ **28.** $6 - 2[3(x + 1) - 5]$

29. The model $S = 91t + 164$ describes the average annual salary S of major league baseball players in thousands of dollars t years after 1984. What was the average annual salary in 1994?

30. The model $C = -3.1t^2 + 51.4t + 4024$ describes the average annual consumption C of cigarettes in the United States by adults 18 and older t years after 1960. What was the average annual consumption in 1970?

Linear Equations and Inequalities in One Variable

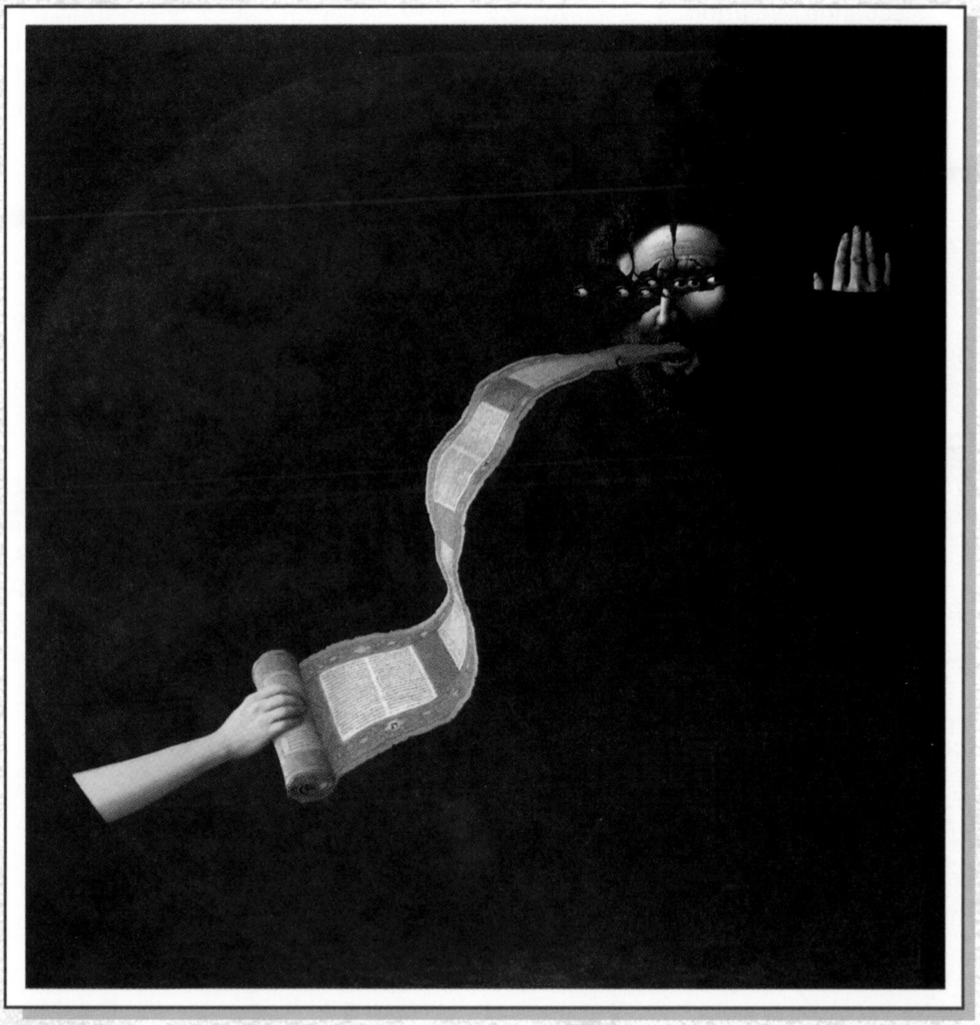

Alfredo Castaneda, "The Vocation of Ezekiel," 1986, oil on canvas, $47\frac{1}{4} \times 47\frac{1}{4}$ in. Mary–Anne Martin/Fine Art, New York

By using techniques for solving equations and a mathematical model that describes the relationship between vocabulary and age, we can make useful predictions about vocabulary based on a person's age. In this chapter we will learn how to solve equations, thereby gaining further insight into the variables that appear in mathematical models.

SECTION 2.1

The Addition Property of Equality

Objectives

1 Check possible solutions to an equation.
2 Identify equivalent equations.
3 Use the addition property to solve equations.
4 Solve applied problems using the addition property.

Solutions Manual   **Tutorial**   **Video 2**

Many equations may be solved using two properties—the addition property of equality and the multiplication property of equality. In this section, we begin solving equations using the addition property, a property that allows us to add the same real number to both sides of an equation without changing the equation's solution.

An *equation* is a statement that two mathematical expressions are equal. The expressions can be either numerical or variable expressions.

Numerical equations may be true or false. The following are examples of numerical equations.

$$5 + 4 = 9 \qquad \text{True}$$
$$6 + 15 = 22 \qquad \text{False}$$
$$7 - 4 = 2 + 1 \qquad \text{True}$$

Algebraic equations contain one or more variables. The following are examples of algebraic equations.

$$x = 8 \qquad x^2 - x - 6 = 0 \qquad 4x + 8y = 16$$
$$x - 7 = 6 \qquad\qquad 3y = 15 \qquad y^2 - 5 = 4y + 7$$
$$5z - 2 = 10 \qquad\qquad 7ab = 9$$

Algebraic equations such as $x - 7 = 6$ are neither true nor false until a number is substituted for the variable. For example, if we replace x with 13, $x - 7 = 6$ becomes $13 - 7 = 6$, which is a true statement. *Solving an equation* is the process of finding the number (or numbers) that makes the algebraic equation a true numerical statement. Such numbers are called *solutions* or *roots* of the equation, and we say that the solutions *satisfy* the equation.

1 Check possible solutions to an equation.

EXAMPLE 1   **Checking Possible Solutions**

Consider the equation $5x - 3 = 17$. Determine whether

a. 3 is a solution.   **b.** 4 is a solution.

Solution

a. $5x - 3 = 17$ This is the given equation.

$5(3) - 3 \overset{?}{=} 17$ Replace the variable x by the possible solution 3. The question mark over the equality sign indicates that we do not know yet whether the two sides are equal.

$15 - 3 \overset{?}{=} 17$ Evaluate the left-hand side, first performing the multiplication.

$12 \neq 17$ 12 is not equal to ($\neq$) 17.

Since the left-hand and the right-hand sides are not the same, we conclude that 3 is not a solution of the given equation.

b. $5x - 3 = 17$ Once again, use the given equation.

$5(4) - 3 \stackrel{?}{=} 17$ Replace the variable x by the possible solution, 4.

$20 - 3 \stackrel{?}{=} 17$ The continued question mark over the equality sign indicates that we are not yet sure whether the two sides are equal.

$17 = 17$ Now that the two sides are equal, remove the question mark.

Since the left-hand and right-hand sides are the same, we conclude that 4 is a solution to the given equation. ∎

We can determine the solution to fairly simple equations by using some common number facts and relationships.

EXAMPLE 2   **Solving Equations by Inspection**

Solve:
a. $x + 3 = 12$
b. $y - 3 = 10$
c. $9z = 45$
d. $\dfrac{m}{10} = 4$

Solution

In each case, translate the variable as "some number."

a. $x + 3 = 12$ can be read as "some number plus 3 equals 12." By inspection, the number is 9. Thus, the equation's solution is 9.

b. $y - 3 = 10$ can be read as "some number minus 3 equals 10." The number must be 13. Thus, the equation's solution is 13.

c. $9z = 45$ translates as "9 times some number is 45." The number is 5, and so the equation's solution is 5.

d. $\dfrac{m}{10} = 4$ translates as "some number divided by 10 equals 4." The number is 40, which is the equation's solution. ∎

As equations become more complicated, solution by inspection becomes more difficult, if not impossible. We shall now consider techniques for solving *linear equations of one variable,* meaning that the equations contain only one variable and this variable has an exponent of 1 (remember that x is x^1).

Definition of linear equation

A *linear equation* in one variable x is an equation that can be written in the standard form

$$ax + b = c$$

where a, b, and c are real numbers with $a \neq 0$.

Examples of linear equations in one variable are

$x + 3 = 12$

$5x - 2 = 8$

2 Identify equivalent equations.

The process of solving a linear equation involves the use of *equivalent equations.*

Equivalent equations are equations that have the same solution.

EXAMPLE 3 **Identifying Equivalent Equations**

a. Are $x - 3 = 12$ and $x = 15$ equivalent equations?
b. Are $3x = 21$ and $x + 1 = 9$ equivalent equations?

Solution

a. Using inspection, the solution to $x - 3 = 12$ is 15, which is also the solution to $x = 15$. Thus, the equations are equivalent.
b. The solution to $3x = 21$ is 7. The solution to $x + 1 = 9$ is 8. Since the equations have different solutions, they are not equivalent. ■

To solve a linear equation, rewrite the equation as a series of simpler equations until you obtain the solution. Your goal is to isolate the variable on one side of the equation. For example, suppose we want to solve the equation

$$x - 8 = 3.$$

To isolate the variable x on the left side, we need to eliminate the term -8 by adding its opposite, 8, to both sides.

$$x - 8 = 3 \qquad \text{This is the given equation.}$$

$$x - 8 + 8 = 3 + 8 \qquad \text{Add 8 to both sides.}$$

$$x + 0 = 11 \qquad \text{Since we added the opposite of } -8, \text{ the sum } -8 + 8 \text{ is 0.}$$

$$x = 11$$

Although it appears that the solution of the original equation is 11, we should verify this by substituting 11 for the variable in the original given equation.

Check

$$x - 8 = 3 \qquad \text{This is the original equation.}$$

$$11 - 8 \overset{?}{=} 3 \qquad \text{Substitute 11 for } x.$$

$$3 = 3 \qquad \text{True}$$

Now we can be sure that the solution is 11.

We solved $x - 8 = 3$ by adding 8 to each side of the equation. This illustrates the *addition property of equality.*

The addition property of equality

The same number or variable term can be added to each side of an equation without changing the solution of the equation. If A, B, and C are real numbers or algebraic expressions, then the equations

$$A = B \quad \text{and} \quad A + C = B + C$$

have the same solution.

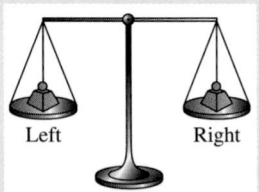
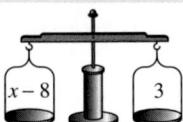
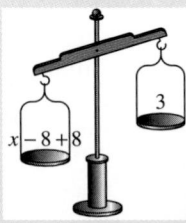
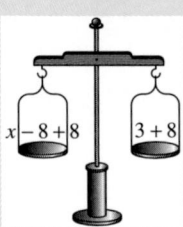

3 Use the addition property to solve equations.

EXAMPLE 4 **Using the Addition Property to Solve an Equation**

Solve and check: $y - 12 = 15$

Solution

Our goal is to isolate the variable. We can do this by remembering that the sum of opposites is 0.

$y - 12 = 15$	This is the given equation.
$y - 12 + 12 = 15 + 12$	The opposite of -12 is 12, so use the addition property of equality and add 12 to both sides.
$y + 0 = 27$	Simplify by using the fact that -12 and 12 are opposites or additive inverses. This step is usually done mentally.
$y = 27$	Simplify using the fact that 0 is the identity of addition.

Check

$y - 12 = 15$	This is the original equation.
$27 - 12 \overset{?}{=} 15$	Substitute 27 for y.
$15 = 15$	True

This true equation indicates that 27 is the solution. ∎

When we use the addition property of equality, we add the same number on both sides of an equation. Since subtraction is the addition of an opposite, the addition property also lets us subtract the same number on both sides of an equation without changing the equation's solution.

EXAMPLE 5 **Subtracting the Same Number from Both Sides**

Solve and check: $z + 1.4 = 2.06$

Solution

$z + 1.4 = 2.06$	This is the given equation.
$z + 1.4 - 1.4 = 2.06 - 1.4$	Subtract 1.4 from both sides. This is equivalent to adding -1.4 to both sides.
$z = 0.66$	Subtracting 1.4 on both sides eliminates 1.4 on the left.

Check

$z + 1.4 = 2.06$	This is the original equation.
$0.66 + 1.4 \overset{?}{=} 2.06$	Substitute 0.66 for z.
$2.06 = 2.06$	True

The solution is 0.66. ∎

When isolating the variable, it can be isolated on either the left or right side of an equation.

EXAMPLE 6 **Isolating the Variable on the Right**

Solve and check: $-\dfrac{1}{2} = x - \dfrac{2}{3}$

The equations $a = b$ and $b = a$ have the same meaning. If you prefer, you can solve

$$-\frac{1}{2} = x - \frac{2}{3}$$

by reversing both sides and solving

$$x - \frac{2}{3} = -\frac{1}{2}.$$

Solution

Since x is on the right side of the equation, we add the opposite of $-\frac{2}{3}$ to both sides.

$$-\frac{1}{2} = x - \frac{2}{3} \qquad \text{This is the given equation.}$$

$$-\frac{1}{2} + \frac{2}{3} = x - \frac{2}{3} + \frac{2}{3} \qquad \text{Add } \tfrac{2}{3} \text{ to both sides, isolating } x \text{ on the right.}$$

$$-\frac{3}{6} + \frac{4}{6} = x \qquad \text{Rewrite fractions as equivalent fractions with a denominator of 6.}$$

$$\frac{1}{6} = x$$

Check

$$-\frac{1}{2} = x - \frac{2}{3} \qquad \text{This is the original equation.}$$

$$-\frac{1}{2} \overset{?}{=} \frac{1}{6} - \frac{2}{3} \qquad \text{Substitute } \tfrac{1}{6} \text{ for } x.$$

$$-\frac{1}{2} \overset{?}{=} \frac{1}{6} - \frac{4}{6} \qquad \text{Rewrite } \tfrac{2}{3} \text{ as } \tfrac{4}{6}.$$

$$-\frac{1}{2} \overset{?}{=} -\frac{3}{6}$$

$$-\frac{1}{2} = -\frac{1}{2} \qquad \text{True}$$

This true equation verifies that $\frac{1}{6}$ is the solution.   ■

EXAMPLE 7   **Solving an Equation by Isolating the Variable**

Solve and check: $7.3 + y = -6.4$

Solution

$$7.3 + y = -6.4 \qquad \text{This is the given equation.}$$

$$7.3 - 7.3 + y = -6.4 - 7.3 \qquad \text{Isolate } y \text{ by subtracting 7.3 on both sides.}$$

$$y = -13.7$$

Take a moment to check this proposed solution in the original equation. You will find that the solution is -13.7.   ■

In Example 8, we combine like terms before using the addition property.

EXAMPLE 8   **Combining Like Terms; Using the Addition Property**

Solve and check: $5y + 3 - 4y - 8 = 6 + 9$

Solution

$$5y + 3 - 4y - 8 = 6 + 9 \qquad \text{This is the given equation.}$$

$$y - 5 = 15 \qquad \text{Combine like terms: } 5y - 4y = y, 3 - 8 = -5, \text{ and } 6 + 9 = 15.$$

$$y - 5 + 5 = 15 + 5 \qquad \text{Add 5 to both sides.}$$

$$y = 20$$

Check

$$5y + 3 - 4y - 8 = 6 + 9 \qquad \text{Be sure to use the original equation and not the simplified form in the second step. (Why?)}$$

$$5(20) + 3 - 4(20) - 8 \overset{?}{=} 6 + 9 \qquad \text{Substitute 20 for } y.$$

$$100 + 3 - 80 - 8 \overset{?}{=} 6 + 9 \qquad \text{Multiply on the left.}$$

$$103 - 88 \overset{?}{=} 6 + 9 \qquad \text{Combine positive and negative numbers on the left.}$$

$$15 = 15$$

This true statement verifies that the solution is 20.   ■

We can use the addition property of equality to add or subtract the same variable term on both sides of an equation without changing the solution. Let's see how this works.

> **EXAMPLE 9**   **Using the Addition Property to Isolate Variable Terms**

Solve and check: $4x = 7 + 3x$

Solution

If variable terms appear on both sides of an equation, our goal is to isolate them on one side. We can do this by subtracting $3x$ on each side.

$$4x = 7 + 3x \qquad \text{This is the given equation.}$$

$$4x - 3x = 7 + 3x - 3x \qquad \text{Isolate the variable on the left by subtracting } 3x \text{ on both sides.}$$

$$x = 7 \qquad \text{Subtracting } 3x \text{ on both sides eliminates } 3x \text{ on the right.}$$

Check

$$4x = 7 + 3x \qquad \text{Use the original equation.}$$

$$4(7) \overset{?}{=} 7 + 3(7) \qquad \text{Substitute 7 for } x.$$

$$28 \overset{?}{=} 7 + 21$$

$$28 = 28 \quad \checkmark \qquad \text{The use of a check } (\checkmark) \text{ is another notation to indicate that we have a true statement and that the proposed solution checks.}$$

The solution is 7.   ■

> **EXAMPLE 10**   **Solving an Equation by Isolating the Variable**

Solve and check: $3y - 9 = 2y + 6$

Solution

Our goal is to isolate variable terms on one side and constant terms on the other side. Let's begin by isolating the variable on the left.

$$3y - 9 = 2y + 6$$ This is the given equation.

$$3y - 2y - 9 = 2y - 2y + 6$$ Isolate the variable terms on the left by subtracting $2y$ on both sides.

$$y - 9 = 6$$

Now we isolate the constant terms on the right by adding 9 on both sides.

$$y - 9 + 9 = 6 + 9$$

$$y = 15$$

Check

$$3y - 9 = 2y + 6$$ Use the original equation.

$$3(15) - 9 \stackrel{?}{=} 2(15) + 6$$ Substitute 15 for y.

$$45 - 9 \stackrel{?}{=} 30 + 6$$

$$36 = 36 \quad \checkmark$$

The solution is 15.   ■

4 Solve applied problems using the addition property.

Applications

Equations frequently appear in the business world. For example, the cost (C) of an item (the price paid by a retailer) plus the markup (M) on that item (the retailer's profit) equals the selling price (S) of the item. The mathematical model is

$$C + M = S$$

and is used in Example 11.

EXAMPLE 11 **Using the Addition Principle to Solve a Business Problem**

The selling price of a computer is $1035.74. If the markup on the computer is $150.66, find the cost to the retailer for the computer.

Solution

$$C + M = S$$ Use the formula that states cost plus markup equals selling price.

$$C + 150.66 = 1035.74$$ Since the selling price is $1035.74 and the markup is $150.66, let $S = 1035.74$ and $M = 150.66$ in the mathematical model.

$$C + 150.66 - 150.66 = 1035.74 - 150.66$$ Subtract 150.66 from both sides.

$$C = 885.08$$

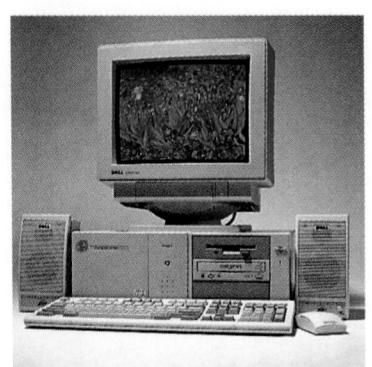

Selling price: $1035.74

Markup: $150.66

Cost to retailer: ?

Weinberg Clark/The Image Bank

The computer cost the dealer $885.08. Notice that in the business world "cost" refers to the dealer's cost and not the cost that a customer pays for an item. The customer's cost is the selling price.   ■

The mathematical model $C + M = S$ contains more than one variable and is sometimes called a *literal equation*.

A *literal equation* is an equation containing more than one variable.

The addition property of equality can be used to solve some literal equations for a specified variable.

EXAMPLE 12   **Solving a Literal Equation for a Specified Variable**

Solve for C: $C + M = S$

Solution

$$C + M = S$$
$$C + M - M = S - M \quad \text{Isolate } C \text{ by subtracting } M \text{ from both sides.}$$
$$C = S - M \quad \text{Simplify.}$$

Our final result, $C = S - M$, tells us that the cost is the selling price minus the markup. ∎

If a mathematical model contains two variables, it is often convenient to express one variable in terms of the other. This is done by isolating one variable on one side of the equation and the other variable on the other side of the equation. We do this in Example 13.

EXAMPLE 13   **Vocabulary and Age**

There is a relationship between a child's vocabulary V and the child's age A (in months) that can be modeled by

$$60A - V = 900.$$

a. Solve the model for V, expressing vocabulary in terms of age.
b. Use the form of the model in part (a) to predict the vocabulary of a child at the age of 15, 20, 30, 40, and 50 months.

Solution

a. One way to solve $60A - V = 900$ for V is to isolate V on the right side and put all the other terms on the left side. We can isolate V on the right by adding V to both sides.

$$60A - V = 900 \quad \text{This is the given model.}$$
$$60A - V + V = 900 + V \quad \text{Add } V \text{ to both sides.}$$
$$60A = 900 + V$$

The variable V can now be isolated by subtracting 900 from both sides.

$$60A - 900 = 900 - 900 + V \quad \text{Subtract 900 from both sides.}$$
$$60A - 900 = V$$

We can reverse the sides of this equation, expressing the model as

$$V = 60A - 900$$

b. We now substitute the given values of A into the form of the model we obtained.

$$V = 60A - 900$$

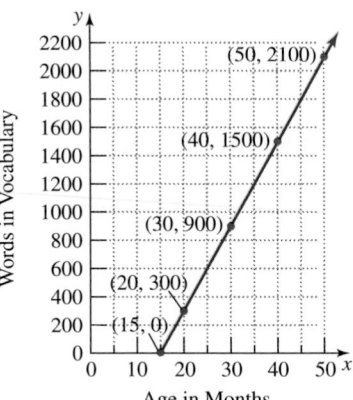

Figure 2.1

Vocabulary and age

$A = 15$	$A = 20$	$A = 30$
$V = 60(15) - 900$	$V = 60(20) - 900$	$V = 60(30) - 900$
$V = 900 - 900$	$V = 1200 - 900$	$V = 1800 - 900$
$V = 0$	$V = 300$	$V = 900$
A typical child at age 15 months has a vocabulary of 0 words.	At age 20 months, the vocabulary is 300 words.	At age 30 months, the vocabulary is 900 words.

$A = 40$	$A = 50$
$V = 60(40) - 900$	$V = 60(50) - 900$
$V = 2400 - 900$	$V = 3000 - 900$
$V = 1500$	$V = 2100$
At age 40 months, the vocabulary is 1500 words.	By 50 months, the child's vocabulary has increased to 2100 words.

Discover for yourself

The line shown in Figure 2.1 is said to be the *graph* of the equation $V = 60A - 900$. Generalize from this situation and explain how to graph an equation that contains two variables.

We can represent the computations from Example 13 in terms of ordered pairs. The first coordinate is the child's age and the second coordinate is the child's vocabulary. The ordered pairs (15, 0), (20, 300), (30, 900), (40, 1500), and (50, 2100) are plotted in Figure 2.1. They are also connected by a straight line. The fact that the line rises from left to right shows that a typical child's vocabulary is steadily increasing with age.

PROBLEM SET 2.1

Practice Problems

Solve each equation in Problems 1–44 using the addition property of equality. Be sure to check your answers.

1. $x - 7 = 13$	**2.** $y - 3 = -17$	**3.** $z + 5 = -12$	**4.** $z + 12 = -14$
5. $-3 = x + 14$	**6.** $-12 = x + 17$	**7.** $-18 = y - 5$	**8.** $-20 = y - 6$
9. $7 + z = 13$	**10.** $18 + z = 11$	**11.** $-3 + y = -17$	**12.** $-5 + y = -19$
13. $x + \frac{1}{3} = \frac{7}{3}$	**14.** $x + \frac{7}{8} = \frac{9}{8}$	**15.** $t + \frac{5}{6} = -\frac{7}{12}$	**16.** $t + \frac{2}{3} = -\frac{7}{6}$
17. $x - \frac{3}{4} = \frac{9}{2}$	**18.** $x - \frac{3}{5} = \frac{7}{10}$	**19.** $-\frac{1}{5} + y = -\frac{3}{4}$	**20.** $-\frac{1}{8} + y = -\frac{1}{4}$
21. $3.2 + x = 7.5$	**22.** $-2.7 + w = -5.3$	**23.** $x + \frac{3}{4} = \frac{9}{2}$	**24.** $r + \frac{3}{5} = -\frac{7}{10}$
25. $5 = -13 + y$	**26.** $-11 = 8 + x$	**27.** $-\frac{3}{5} = -\frac{3}{2} + s$	**28.** $\frac{7}{3} = -\frac{5}{2} + z$
29. $830 + y = 520$	**30.** $-90 + t = -35$	**31.** $r + 3.7 = 8$	**32.** $x + 10.6 = -9$
33. $3\frac{2}{5} + x = 5\frac{2}{5}$	**34.** $-4\frac{2}{3} + y = 6\frac{2}{3}$	**35.** $-3.7 + m = -3.7$	**36.** $y + \frac{7}{11} = \frac{7}{11}$

39. $7 - 5x + 8 + 2x + 4x - 3 = 2 + 3 \cdot 5$

40. $13 - 3r + 2 + 6r - 2r - 2r - 1 = 3 + 2 \cdot 8$

41. $7y + 4 = 6y - 9$ **42.** $4r - 3 = 5 + 3r$

43. $18 - 7x = 12 - 6x$ **44.** $26 - 8s = 20 - 7s$

Application Problems

45. The mathematical model

$$C + M = S$$

describes the relationship among the cost (C), markup (M), and selling price (S) of an item.

  a. If the cost of a television is $325 and the selling price is $650, what is the markup?

  b. Solve the formula for M.

46. If we add the length (L) and the width (W) of a rectangle, we obtain half the perimeter (P), as shown in the figure.

  a. If the perimeter of a rectangle is 60 feet and the length is 20 feet, use the formula to find the width.

  b. Solve the formula for W.

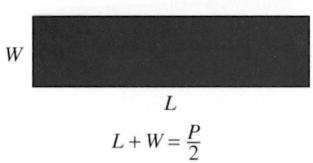

$$W$$

$$L$$

$$L + W = \frac{P}{2}$$

47. The mathematical model

$$F - \frac{9}{5}C = 32$$

describes the relationship between Celsius temperature C and Fahrenheit temperature F.

  a. Solve the model for F, expressing Fahrenheit temperature in terms of Celsius temperature.

  b. Use the form of the model in part (a) to find the Fahrenheit temperature that corresponds to Celsius temperatures of $0°, 5°, 10°, 15°$, and $20°$.

  c. Represent your computations from part (b) in terms of ordered pairs. The first coordinate should be the Celsius temperature, and the second coordinate should be the corresponding Fahrenheit temperature. Graph the ordered pairs in a rectangular coordinate system and connect them. Describe what you observe.

48. The mathematical model

$$H - 0.7E = 3.6$$

describes the relationship between hourly salary H and years of education E.

  a. Solve the model for H, expressing hourly salary in terms of years of education.

  b. Use the form of the model in part (a) to find the hourly salary for people with $0, 1, 2, 6, 12, 14$, and 16 years of education.

  c. Represent your computations from part (b) in terms of ordered pairs. The first coordinate should be years of education, and the second coordinate should be the corresponding hourly salary. Graph the ordered pairs in a rectangular coordinate system and connect them. Describe what you observe.

49. The bar graph indicates that the average salary in major league baseball increased by $68,425 from 1993 to 1994 and then decreased by $115,100 from 1994 to 1995.

  a. If the average salary in 1995 was $1,073,579, what was it in 1993? (*Hint:* Let $x =$ the salary in 1993. Solve the equation $x + 68,425 - 115,100 = 1,073,579$.)

  b. Explain how the equation is a translation of the conditions given in the problem.

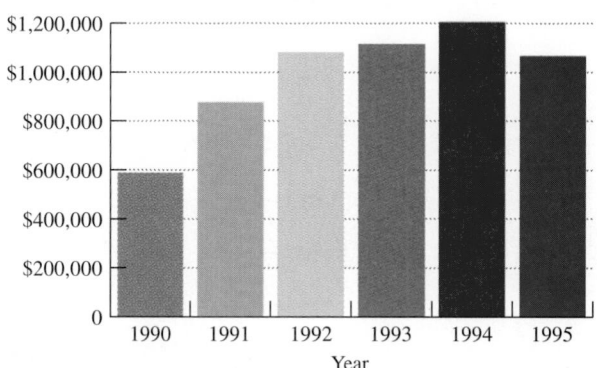

Average Salary in Major League Baseball

Year

Source: NBL

True–False Critical Thinking Problems

50. Which one of the following statements is true?

  a. The equation $x + 2x + 5 = 3x + 7 - 2$ has 1 as a solution. Therefore, the only solution is 1.

  b. If $x + a = b$, then $x = a - b$.

  c. The translation of "eight less than a number (x) gives 15" is $x - 8 = 15$.

  d. Every equation has a solution consisting of one number.

51. Which one of the following statements is true?
  a. If $y - a = -b$, then $y = a + b$.
  b. If $y + 7 = 0$, then $y = 7$.
  c. The solution to $4 - x = -3x$ is -2.
  d. If 7 is added on one side of an equation, then it should be subtracted on the other side.

Technology Problems

52. In 1991, the monthly charge C (in dollars) for residents of Chicago who used w kilowatt-hours of electricity was modeled by

$$C - 0.10819w = 9.06, \quad \text{where} \quad w \leqslant 400$$

Solve the model for C, and then use a graphing calculator to determine the monthly electric bill for customers using 285 and 396 kilowatt-hours of electricity.

53. Use a graphing calculator to help with the computations in solving $17x - 0.12973 = 16x + 4.1$. Use your calculator to check the proposed solution.

Writing in Mathematics

54. Explain how to check a solution of an equation.

55. Explain what is meant by the *solution* of an equation.

56. The equations $x + 2 = 9$ and $x + 2 = -6$ are not equivalent equations. Explain.

57. When solving $x + 5 = 13.2$, we can either add -5 to both sides or subtract 5 from both sides. Why do we have this option?

Critical Thinking Problems

58. Solve for x: $|x| + 4 = 10$.

59. Use the graph to make up and solve a word problem similar to the one in Problem 49.

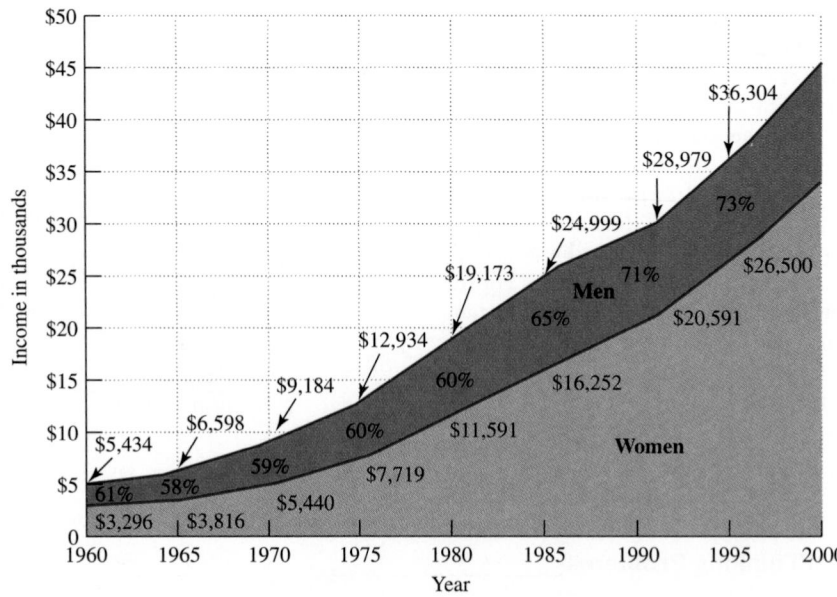

The Gender Pay Gap: The Annual Income of Full-Time Workers and the Percentage of the Men's Income Earned by Women

Sources: Beeghley 1989: 239: U.S. Bureau of the Census, *Statistical Abstract* 1993: Table 727.

60. By checking, determine which of the following are solutions to the equation $3(x + 2) = 3x + 6$.
  a. -4 **b.** 2   **c.** 1/2

d. Select any three additional numbers and check to see whether those numbers are solutions to the equation. What can you conclude about the solution to this equation?

e. Try solving the equation. What happens? What does this mean in terms of the solution to this equation?

f. Try writing an equation that has no solution.

Review Problems

61. Evaluate: $-16 - (50 \div 5^2)$.

62. Simplify: $2(5 - 3y) - (2y - 4)$.

63. The model

$$d = t^2 + 7t$$

describes the distance (d, in miles) that it takes for the shock waves from an explosion to travel from the explosion site in t seconds. How many miles will the shock waves travel in 5 seconds?

SECTION 2.2

Solutions Manual   Tutorial   Video 2

The Multiplication Property of Equality

Objectives

1 Use the multiplication property to solve equations.
2 Use the addition and multiplication properties to solve equations.
3 Solve equations with fractions.
4 Solve applied problems using the multiplication property.

This section introduces the second property for solving equations—the multiplication property of equality. Just as we can add the same real number to both sides of an equation without changing the equation's solution, we can also multiply both sides by any nonzero number and not change the equation's solution.

We now know that adding the same number to both sides of an equation does not change the solution. The same idea is true if we multiply both sides of an equation by any number other than zero. This leads us to state the multiplication property of equality.

1 Use the multiplication property to solve equations.

The multiplication property of equality

Both sides of an equation can be multiplied by the same nonzero number without changing the solution of the equation. Thus, if A, B, and C are real numbers or algebraic expressions, where $C \neq 0$, then the equations

$$A = B \quad \text{and} \quad AC = BC$$

have the same solution.

EXAMPLE 1 **Using the Multiplication Property to Solve an Equation**

Solve for x: $6x = 30$

Solution

Notice that we have $6x$ on the left side, but we would like to have x alone. We can multiply both sides by $\frac{1}{6}$, the multiplicative inverse of 6, since $(\frac{1}{6})(6) = 1$.

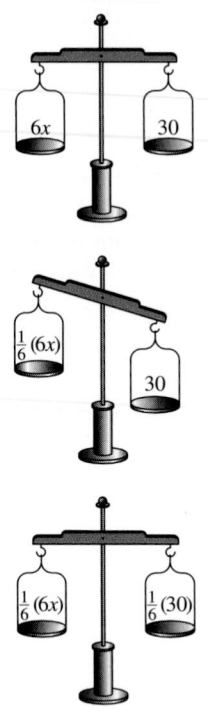

$$6x = 30 \qquad \text{This is the given equation.}$$

$$\frac{1}{6}(6x) = \frac{1}{6}(30) \qquad \text{Use the multiplication property of equality, multiplying both sides by } \tfrac{1}{6}.$$

$$\left(\frac{1}{6} \cdot 6\right)x = \frac{1}{6}(30) \qquad \text{Use the associative property of multiplication to group } \tfrac{1}{6} \text{ and 6. This step is usually done mentally.}$$

$$1x = \frac{1}{6}(30) \qquad \text{This step, using the fact that } \tfrac{1}{6} \text{ and 6 are reciprocals, is usually done mentally.}$$

$$x = 5$$

Check

$$6x = 30 \qquad \text{As always, use the original equation.}$$

$$6 \cdot 5 \overset{?}{=} 30 \qquad \text{Substitute 5 for } x.$$

$$30 = 30 \quad \checkmark$$

The solution is 5. ∎

In Example 1 we multiplied by $\frac{1}{6}$ because $\frac{1}{6}$ is the reciprocal (the multiplicative inverse) of 6. We do not want to multiply both sides by zero because zero is not the reciprocal of any number; nor does it have a reciprocal. In short, we can always multiply both sides of an equation by any number other than zero. The number that we choose will be the reciprocal of the variable's coefficient.

Since division is defined in terms of multiplication, the multiplication property of equality also lets us divide both sides of an equation by the same nonzero number. For example, the equation $6x = 30$ could be solved by dividing both sides by 6 since division by 6 is the same as multiplication by $\frac{1}{6}$. Which approach do you prefer?

$$6x = 30 \qquad\qquad 6x = 30$$

$$\frac{1}{6}(6x) = \frac{1}{6}(30) \qquad \text{or} \qquad \frac{6x}{6} = \frac{30}{6}$$

$$x = 5 \qquad\qquad x = 5$$

It is usually easier to divide when the coefficient of the variable is an integer. On the other hand, it is usually easier to multiply if the coefficient of the variable is a fraction. Let's see what this means in the following examples.

EXAMPLE 2 **Using the Multiplication Property to Divide Both Sides**

Solve for a: $-7a = -77$

Solution

Since we want a alone on the left side, we can multiply both sides by $-\frac{1}{7}$. Remember that $-\frac{1}{7}$ is the reciprocal of -7. Multiplying by $-\frac{1}{7}$ is the same as dividing by -7.

$$-7a = -77 \qquad \text{This is the given equation.}$$

$$\frac{-7a}{-7} = \frac{-77}{-7} \qquad \text{Use the multiplication property to divide both sides by } -7.$$

$$a = 11 \qquad \text{Simplify.}$$

The solution is 11, verified by substituting 11 for a in the original equation. ■

In the next three examples, multiplication produces the solution more rapidly than division.

EXAMPLE 3 **Using the Multiplication Property to Multiply Both Sides**

Solve for m: $\dfrac{m}{5} = -6$

Solution

Remember that $\dfrac{m}{5}$ means $\dfrac{1}{5}m$ since division by 5 is the same as multiplication by $\dfrac{1}{5}$.

$$\frac{m}{5} = -6 \qquad \text{This is the given equation.}$$

$$\frac{1}{5}m = -6 \qquad \text{This step is optional. We can get } m \text{ alone by multiplying both sides by 5, the reciprocal of } \tfrac{1}{5}.$$

$$5 \cdot \frac{1}{5}m = 5 \cdot (-6) \qquad \text{Use the multiplication property of equality.}$$

$$1m = -30 \qquad \text{This step, using the inverse property of multiplication, is usually done mentally.}$$

$$m = -30 \qquad 1m = m \text{ because 1 is the identity of multiplication.}$$

The solution is -30, verified by substituting -30 for m in the original equation. ■

EXAMPLE 4 **Using the Multiplication Property to Multiply Both Sides**

Solve: $\dfrac{3}{4}y = 12$

Solution

To get y alone, multiply both sides by $\tfrac{4}{3}$, the reciprocal of $\tfrac{3}{4}$. Note that $\tfrac{4}{3} \cdot \tfrac{3}{4}y = 1y = y$.

$$\frac{3}{4}y = 12 \qquad \text{This is the given equation.}$$

$$\frac{4}{3}\left(\frac{3}{4}y\right) = \frac{4}{3} \cdot 12 \qquad \text{Multiply both sides by } \tfrac{4}{3}.$$

$$1y = \frac{4}{3} \cdot 12 \quad \text{Use the inverse property of multiplication.}$$

$$y = 16$$

The solution is 16, verified by substituting 16 for y in the original equation. ■

Sometimes when solving an equation we end up with a coefficient of -1 attached to a variable. Since we want the variable rather than its negative, we need to know how to deal with this situation.

Discover for yourself

Use inspection (or multiplication of both sides by -1) to state the solution for $-x = 7$ and $-y = -13$. In general, if $-x = a$, what is the value of x?

In the Discover for Yourself, were you able to find the following principle?

Coefficients of -1

If $-x = a$, then $x = -a$.
Examples:

$$-x = 5 \qquad -x = -4$$
$$x = -5 \qquad x = -(-4)$$
$$x = 4$$

In Example 5, we simplify both sides of the equation before using the multiplication property.

EXAMPLE 5   **Simplifying Sides and Using the Multiplication Property**

Solve: $10 \cdot 4 + 12 = 20y - 4y + 10y$

Solution

$$10 \cdot 4 + 12 = 20y - 4y + 10y \quad \text{This is the given equation.}$$
$$40 + 12 = 16y + 10y \quad \text{Simplify.}$$
$$52 = 26y \quad \text{Continue to apply the order of operations.}$$
$$\frac{52}{26} = \frac{26y}{26} \quad \text{Isolate } y \text{ on the right, dividing both sides by 26.}$$
$$2 = y$$

The solution is 2, verified by substituting 2 for y in the original equation. ■

2 Use the addition and multiplication properties to solve equations.

Solving some equations requires both the addition and multiplication properties of equality. Be sure that you understand the difference between the two properties.

study tip

The *addition property* is used to solve equations of the form $x + a = b$. It is used when a number is *added to or subtracted from* a variable.

$$x + 7 = -5 \qquad\qquad x - 4 = -2$$

$$x + 7 - 7 = -5 - 7 \qquad x - 4 + 4 = -2 + 4$$

$$x = -12 \qquad\qquad\qquad x = 2$$

The *multiplication property* is used to solve equations of the form $ax = b$. It is used when a variable is *multiplied or divided by a number*.

$$7x = 21 \qquad\qquad \frac{x}{2} = 8 \qquad\qquad\qquad \frac{3}{5}x = 12$$

$$\frac{7x}{7} = \frac{21}{7} \qquad 2\left(\frac{x}{2}\right) = 2(8) \qquad \left(\frac{5}{3}\right)\left(\frac{3}{5}x\right) = \left(\frac{5}{3}\right)(12)$$

$$x = 3 \qquad\qquad x = 16 \qquad\qquad\qquad x = 20$$

When an equation does not contain fractions or decimals, we will often use the addition property of equality before the multiplication property of equality. Our overall goal is to isolate the variable with a coefficient of 1 on either the left or right side of the equation.

EXAMPLE 6 **Using Both the Addition and Multiplication Properties**

Solve for x: $\quad 3x + 1 = 7$

Solution

We begin by isolating $3x$ by subtracting 1 from both sides. Then we isolate x by dividing both sides by 3.

Step 1. Use the addition property to isolate the x-term.

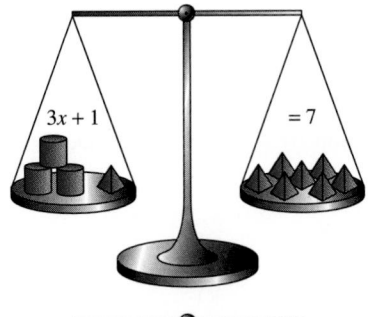

$$3x + 1 = 7 \qquad \text{This is the given equation.}$$

$$3x + 1 - 1 = 7 - 1 \qquad \text{Apply the addition property, subtracting 1 on both sides.}$$

$$3x = 6 \qquad \text{Simplify.}$$

Step 2. Use the multiplication property to isolate x.

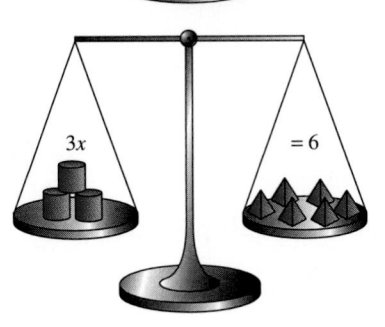

$$\frac{3x}{3} = \frac{6}{3} \qquad \text{Divide both sides by 3.}$$

$$x = 2 \qquad \text{Simplify.}$$

The solution is 2, verified by substituting 2 for x in the original equation. ∎

ENRICHMENT ESSAY

Opposites and Solving Equations

Opposites play an important role in solving equations. If we have addition, we subtract; if we have multiplication, we divide. The word *algebra* is from the title of a ninth-century Arabic text and translates as "the science of transposition and opposition." Transposing terms using opposites is precisely what we do when solving equations.

This theme of opposites is found in M. C. Escher's print *Day and Night:* white geese fly over a night view of a town, whereas black geese fly over a sunlit mirror image of the same scene. Notice how the flat checkerboard of the farmland turns into the dual flocks of geese, showing how every three-dimensional scene depicted on a two-dimensional surface must somehow fool the viewer.

Can you think of ideas that have appeared in algebra that are given visual expression in this print?

M.C. Escher (1898–1972) "Day and Night" © 1997 Cordon Art – Baarn – Holland. All rights reserved.

EXAMPLE 7   **Using Both the Addition and Multiplication Properties**

Solve for y: $-2y - 28 = 4$

Solution

We begin by isolating $-2y$, adding 28 to both sides. Then we isolate y by dividing both sides by -2.

Step 1. Use the addition property to isolate the y-term.

$$-2y - 28 = 4 \qquad \text{This is the given equation.}$$
$$-2y - 28 + 28 = 4 + 28 \qquad \text{Apply the addition property, adding 28 to both sides.}$$
$$-2y = 32 \qquad \text{Simplify.}$$

Step 2. Use the multiplication property to isolate y.

$$\frac{-2y}{-2} = \frac{32}{-2} \qquad \text{Divide both sides by } -2.$$
$$y = -16 \qquad \text{Simplify.}$$

The solution is -16, verified by substituting -16 for y in the original equation. ∎

EXAMPLE 8   **Using Both the Addition and Multiplication Properties**

Solve for x: $3x - 14 = -2x + 6$

Solution

We will use the addition property to collect all terms involving x on the left and all numerical terms on the right. Then we will isolate x by dividing both sides by its numerical coefficient.

Step 1. Use the addition property to isolate the x-term.

$$3x - 14 = -2x + 6 \qquad \text{This is the given equation.}$$
$$3x + 2x - 14 = -2x + 2x + 6 \qquad \text{Add } 2x \text{ to both sides.}$$
$$5x - 14 = 6 \qquad \text{Simplify.}$$
$$5x - 14 + 14 = 6 + 14 \qquad \text{Add 14 to both sides.}$$
$$5x = 20 \qquad \text{Simplify. All terms with } x \text{ are now on the left and numerical terms are on the right.}$$

Step 2. Use the multiplication property to isolate x.

$$\frac{5x}{5} = \frac{20}{5} \qquad \text{Divide both sides by 5.}$$
$$x = 4 \qquad \text{Simplify.}$$

Check

$$3x - 14 = -2x + 6 \qquad \text{Use the original equation.}$$
$$3(4) - 14 \stackrel{?}{=} -2(4) + 6 \qquad \text{Substitute the proposed solution for } x.$$
$$12 - 14 \stackrel{?}{=} -8 + 6$$
$$-2 = -2 \quad \checkmark$$

The solution is 4. ∎

3 Solve equations with fractions.

Clearing Fractions

Equations are easier to solve when they do not contain fractions. Equations involving fractions can be written as equivalent equations by applying the multiplication property of equality. Multiplying every term on both sides of an equation by the *least common multiple (LCM)* of all the denominators in the equation clears the equation of fractions. This idea is illustrated in Example 9.

EXAMPLE 9 **Using the Multiplication Property to Clear Fractions**

Solve: $\dfrac{2}{3}y - \dfrac{1}{2} = \dfrac{3}{4}$

Solution

The equation has denominators 3, 2, and 4. The LCM for these numbers is 12 because 12 is the smallest number that 3, 2, and 4 will divide into with a remainder of zero. If we multiply both sides of the equation by 12, each denominator will divide into 12 and we will obtain an equivalent equation without any denominators other than 1. This will clear the equation of fractions.

Step 1. Clear fractions.

$$\frac{2}{3}y - \frac{1}{2} = \frac{3}{4}$$ This is the given equation.

$$12\left(\frac{2}{3}y - \frac{1}{2}\right) = 12\left(\frac{3}{4}\right)$$ Multiply both sides by 12, the LCM of 3, 2, and 4.

$$12\left(\frac{2}{3}y\right) - 12\left(\frac{1}{2}\right) = 12\left(\frac{3}{4}\right)$$ Use the distributive property on the left.

$$\left(\overset{4}{\frac{\cancel{12}}{1}} \cdot \frac{2}{3}\right)y - \overset{6}{\frac{\cancel{12}}{1}} \cdot \frac{1}{\underset{1}{\cancel{2}}} = \overset{3}{\frac{\cancel{12}}{1}} \cdot \frac{3}{\underset{1}{\cancel{4}}}$$ Multiply fractions.

$$8y - 6 = 9$$ Simplify. The equation is now cleared of fractions.

Step 2. Use the addition and multiplication properties.

$$8y - 6 + 6 = 9 + 6$$ Add 6 to both sides.

$$8y = 15$$ Simplify.

$$\frac{8y}{8} = \frac{15}{8}$$ Divide both sides by 8.

$$y = \frac{15}{8}$$

Check

$$\frac{2}{3}y - \frac{1}{2} = \frac{3}{4}$$ Use the original equation.

$$\frac{2}{3}\left(\frac{15}{8}\right) - \frac{1}{2} \overset{?}{=} \frac{3}{4}$$ Substitute $\frac{15}{8}$ for y.

$$\frac{\cancel{2}}{3} \cdot \frac{3 \cdot 5}{2 \cdot 4} - \frac{1}{2} \overset{?}{=} \frac{3}{4}$$ Divide out common factors in the multiplication.

$$\frac{5}{4} - \frac{1}{2} \overset{?}{=} \frac{3}{4}$$ Complete the multiplication.

$$\frac{5}{4} - \frac{2}{4} \overset{?}{=} \frac{3}{4}$$ Write $\frac{1}{2}$ as an equivalent fraction with a denominator of 4.

$$\frac{3}{4} = \frac{3}{4} \quad \checkmark$$

The solution is $\frac{15}{8}$.   ∎

4 Solve applied problems using the multiplication property.

Applications

The multiplication property can be used to solve certain formulas for an indicated variable.

EXAMPLE 10   **Solving a Mathematical Model for a Specified Variable**

A car that travels constantly at 50 miles per hour is in uniform motion, meaning that the rate of speed of the car does not change. The model for uniform motion is

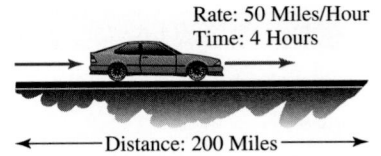

Rate: 50 Miles/Hour
Time: 4 Hours

Distance: 200 Miles

Study tip

$50 \dfrac{\text{miles}}{\text{hour}} \cdot 4 \; \text{hours} = 200 \; \text{miles}$

Observe how the hours "cancel," leaving the answer in terms of miles.

$RT = D$

where R is the uniform rate of speed, T is the traveling time, and D is the distance traveled. For example, traveling at 50 miles per hour for 4 hours means that

$$RT = D \qquad \text{so that} \qquad (50)(4) = 200$$

or 200 miles were traveled. Solve the model for T.

Solution

$RT = D$ This is the given formula. (Rate times time equals the distance.)

$\dfrac{RT}{R} = \dfrac{D}{R}$ Isolate T on the left by dividing both sides by R.

$T = \dfrac{D}{R}$ Simplify.

Thus, $T = \dfrac{D}{R}$. In uniform motion situations, time traveled equals distance covered divided by the uniform rate of speed. ∎

We conclude this section with an applied problem whose solution involves the multiplication property.

EXAMPLE 11   **The Human Body: Relating Body Parts**

The radius is one of two bones that connect the elbow and the wrist. Scientists have found that the length of a woman's radius is approximately one-seventh of her height. If the radius of a woman is 9 inches long, approximately how tall is the woman?

Solution

Let h = the woman's height.

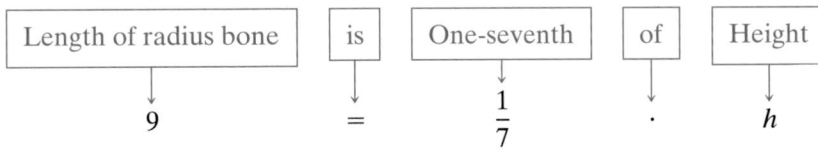

Length of radius bone	is	One-seventh	of	Height
9	=	$\dfrac{1}{7}$	$\cdot$	h

$9 = \dfrac{1}{7} h$ This is the algebraic equation for the given sentence, where the length of the radius is 9 inches.

$7 \cdot 9 = 7 \cdot \dfrac{1}{7} h$ Multiply both sides by 7.

$63 = h$ Simplify.

The woman is approximately 63 inches tall. Since 12 inches = 1 foot, she is 5 feet, 3 inches tall.

Check

$$\dfrac{1}{7} \text{ of height } = \dfrac{1}{7}(63) = 9$$

We are given that the length of the radius bone is 9 inches, so the solution checks. ∎

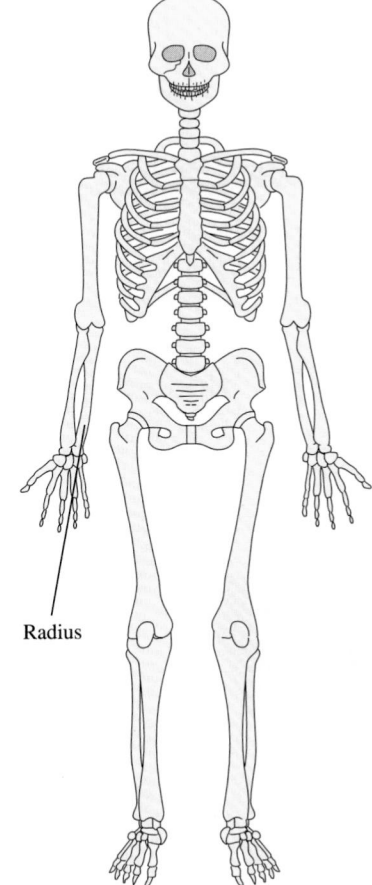

Radius

PROBLEM SET 2.2

Practice Problems

Solve each equation in Problems 1–64. Check your answers either by hand or with a calculator.

1. $5x = 45$
2. $6x = 18$
3. $7b = 56$
4. $4b = 44$

5. $8r = -24$
6. $5s = -25$
7. $-3y = -15$
8. $-9x = -45$

9. $-8m = 2$
10. $-6r = 3$
11. $7y = 0$
12. $-3m = 0$

13. $\dfrac{y}{3} = 4$
14. $\dfrac{x}{5} = 3$
15. $-\dfrac{x}{5} = 11$
16. $-\dfrac{y}{7} = 2$

17. $-\dfrac{x}{5} = -10$
18. $-\dfrac{y}{7} = -1$
19. $\frac{2}{3}y = 8$
20. $\frac{3}{4}x = 12$

21. $-\frac{2}{5}a = \frac{6}{15}$
22. $-\frac{3}{5}b = \frac{9}{5}$
23. $-\frac{7}{2}x = -21$
24. $-\frac{5}{8}x = -25$

25. $-r = 7$
26. $-s = -\frac{1}{3}$
27. $-15 = -y$
28. $\frac{1}{5} = -m$

29. $-4y - 2y = 24$
30. $-5x + 8x = -21$

31. $5y + 3y - 4y = 10 + 2$
32. $4s + 8s - 2s = 20 - 15$
33. $-6 - 2 = 5y + 3y - 10y$

34. $12 - 18 = 12y - 6y - 3y$
35. $3y - 2 = 9$
36. $2r - 3 = 9$

37. $2a + 1 = 7$
38. $5x - 3 = 12$
39. $-2y + 5 = 7$

40. $-3r + 4 = 13$
41. $-2y - 5 = 7$
42. $-3y - 7 = -1$

43. $12 = 4m + 3$
44. $14 = 5y - 21$
45. $0.03x + 21 = 27$

46. $0.05y - 9 = 6$
47. $-x - 3 = 3$
48. $-y - 5 = 5$

49. $-x - \frac{1}{3} = \frac{2}{3}$
50. $-y - \frac{1}{2} = \frac{1}{2}$
51. $6y = 2y - 12$

52. $8r = 3r - 10$
53. $3x = -2x - 15$
54. $2x = -4x + 18$

55. $-5y = -2y - 12$
56. $-7m = -3m - 8$
57. $8y + 4 = 2y - 5$

58. $5a + 6 = 3a - 6$
59. $6x - 5 = x + 5$
60. $6y - 3 = y + 2$

61. $6x + 14 = 2x - 2$
62. $9m + 2 = 6m - 4$
63. $-3y - 1 = 5 - 2y$

64. $-3y - 2 = -5 - 4y$

The equations in Problems 65–78 contain fractions. Solve each equation by first multiplying both sides by the least common multiple of all denominators in the equation. Once the equation is cleared of fractions, continue solving. Check your answers.

65. $\frac{1}{5}y - 4 = -6$
66. $\frac{1}{2}x + 13 = -22$
67. $\frac{2}{3}y - 5 = 7$
68. $\frac{3}{4}w - 9 = -6$

69. $\frac{2}{3}x - \frac{3}{4} = \frac{5}{12}$
70. $\frac{3}{4}x - \frac{2}{3} = \frac{7}{12}$
71. $\frac{1}{2}x + \frac{1}{12} = \frac{3}{8}$
72. $\frac{1}{2}x + \frac{7}{12} = \frac{5}{8}$

73. $\frac{3}{7} - \frac{5}{8}x = \frac{1}{7}$
74. $\frac{2}{7} - \frac{3}{8}x = \frac{4}{7}$
75. $\frac{1}{6}x - \frac{1}{8}x = \frac{1}{12}$
76. $\frac{1}{7}x + \frac{1}{5}x = 1$

77. $\frac{1}{3}x + \frac{2}{5} = \frac{1}{5}x - \frac{2}{5}$
78. $\frac{1}{12}x + \frac{1}{6} = \frac{1}{2}x - \frac{1}{4}$

Application Problems

79. The area A of a parallelogram with base B and height H is given by

$$A = BH.$$

a. Solve the formula for B.
b. If the area of a parallelogram is 40 square inches and the base measures 10 inches, find the measure of the height.

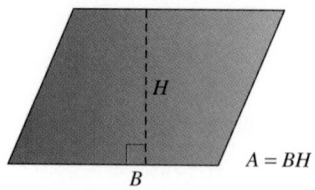

80. Simple yearly interest I on an investment of P dollars (called the principal) at interest rate r is given by

$$I = Pr.$$

a. Solve the formula for P.
b. How much money was invested at an interest rate of 4% ($r = 0.04$) if the yearly interest is $240?

81. The model

$$M = \frac{1}{5} n$$

is used to determine how far you are from a lightning strike in a thunderstorm. In the formula, n represents the number of seconds it takes the sound of thunder to reach you after the flash of lightning, and M is the distance (in miles) that you are from the lightning.

a. If you are 3 miles away from the lightning flash, how long will it take the sound of thunder to reach you?
b. Solve $M = \frac{1}{5} n$ for n.

Randy Wells/
Tony Stone Images

Mach Numbers. The speed of a supersonic aircraft is usually represented by a Mach number, named after Austrian physicist Ernst Mach (1838–1916). The model

$$M = \frac{A}{s}$$

indicates that the speed of an aircraft (A) in miles per hour divided by the speed of sound (s) (approximately 740 miles per hour) results in the Mach number (M). Use the model to determine the speed of the following aircrafts. (*Note:* When an aircraft's speed increases beyond Mach 1, it is said to have broken the sound barrier.)

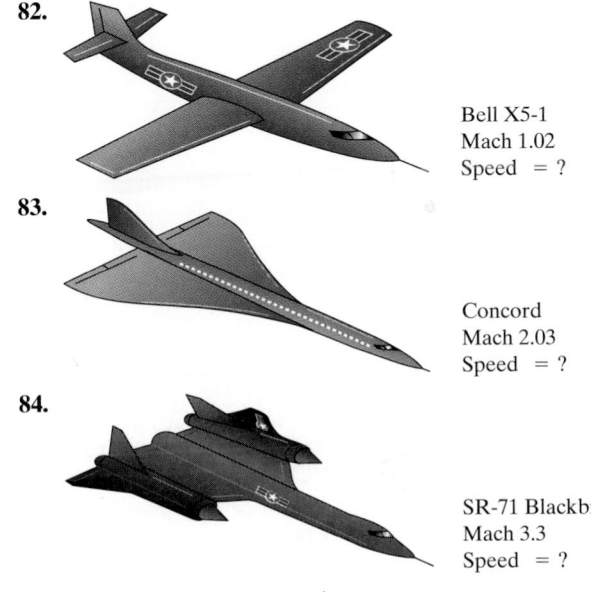

82.

Bell X5-1
Mach 1.02
Speed = ?

83.

Concord
Mach 2.03
Speed = ?

84.

SR-71 Blackbird
Mach 3.3
Speed = ?

85. Solve the formula $M = \dfrac{A}{s}$ for A.

True–False Critical Thinking Problem

86. Which one of the following statements is true?

a. To solve $\dfrac{1}{3} x = 7$, we should divide both sides by 3.

b. The equation $\dfrac{x}{2} = 5$ is equivalent to the equation $x - 10 = 0$.

c. If $-x = 3$, then $x = -\dfrac{1}{3}$.

d. If $RT = D$, then $T = D - R$.

Technology Problems

Solve each equation. Use a calculator to help with the arithmetic. Check your answers using your calculator.

87. $3.7x - 19.46 = -39.74$

88. $-72.93y - 14.6 = 3.7 - 4.98y$

Writing in Mathematics

Describe the error in Problems 89–94.

89.
$$7x = 21$$
$$7x - 7 = 21 - 7$$
$$x = 14$$

90.
$$x + 4 = 4x$$
$$x + 4 - 4 = 4x - 4$$
$$x = 3x$$

91.
$$3|x| + 6 = 12$$
$$3|x| + 6 - 6 = 12 - 6$$
$$3|x| = 6$$
$$\frac{3|x|}{3} = \frac{6}{3}$$
$$|x| = 2$$

The equation has only 2 as a solution.

92.
$$2y - 6y + 24 = 32$$
$$-4y + 24 = 32$$
$$-4y = -8$$
$$y = 2$$

93.
$$0x = 17$$
$$\frac{0x}{0} = \frac{17}{0}$$
$$x = 0$$

94.
$$\frac{x}{\frac{1}{3}} = -12$$
$$3 \cdot \frac{x}{\frac{1}{3}} = 3(-12)$$
$$x = -36$$

Group Activity Problem

95. Study the errors made in Problems 89–94. In your group, list common errors that can arise in solving equations. Give examples of these kinds of errors. Then present ways of helping students to avoid them.

Review Problems

96. Evaluate: $\frac{1}{3} - \left(-\frac{1}{4}\right)$.

97. The graph shows health-care expenditures per American for the period from 1960 through 1993.
a. In what year were health-care expenditures approximately $1800 per person?
b. What is a reasonable estimate for health-care expenditures in 1975?
c. Use the graph to predict health-care expenditures in the year 2000. Describe how you arrived at this amount.

98. Simplify: $\frac{2}{3}(3y + 9) + \frac{1}{2}(2y - 6) + 8$.

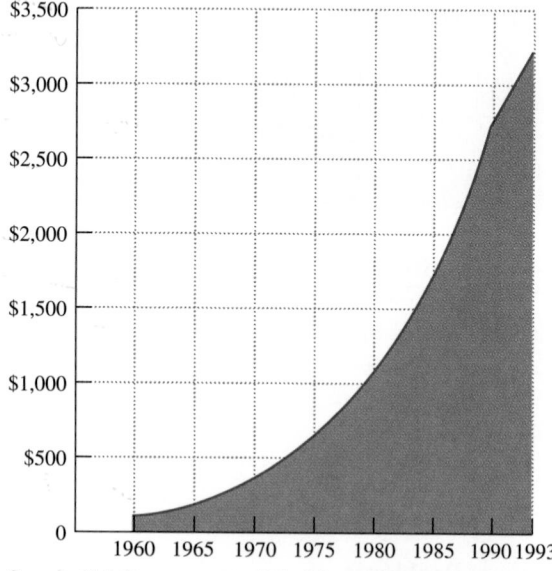

Healthcare Expenditures per Capita, 1960–1993

Source: U.S. Department of Health and Human Services

SECTION 2.3

**Solutions Tutorial Video
Manual 3**

| Solve linear equations.

Solving Linear Equations

Objectives

1 Solve linear equations.
2 Solve linear equations containing fractions and decimals.
3 Solve applied problems involving linear equations.

Simplifying Each Side

When equations do not contain fractions or decimals, we first simplify each side and then solve for the variable. Simplification often means using the distributive property to remove grouping symbols. It also involves combining like terms.

> **EXAMPLE 1** **Simplifying Sides and Then Solving**
>
> Solve: $10x - 6 - 2x + 4 = 5 - 6x - 1$

Solution

Step 1. Simplify each side.

$$10x - 6 - 2x + 4 = 5 - 6x - 1 \qquad \text{This is the given equation.}$$
$$8x - 2 = 4 - 6x \qquad \text{Combine like terms on each side: } 10x - 2x = 8x;$$
$$-6 + 4 = -2; \; 5 - 1 = 4.$$

Step 2. Isolate the variable terms on one side and the constant terms on the other side. We will use the addition property to isolate the x-term on the left, so add $6x$ to both sides.

$$8x - 2 + 6x = 4 - 6x + 6x \qquad \text{Add } 6x \text{ to both sides.}$$
$$14x - 2 = 4 \qquad \text{Simplify.}$$
$$14x - 2 + 2 = 4 + 2 \qquad \text{Add 2 to both sides to collect the numerical terms on the right.}$$
$$14x = 6 \qquad \text{Simplify.}$$

Step 3. Now use the multiplication property to isolate x.

$$\frac{14x}{14} = \frac{6}{14} \qquad \text{Divide both sides by 14.}$$

$$x = \frac{6}{14} = \frac{3}{7}$$

The solution is $\frac{3}{7}$. ∎

> **Discover for yourself**
>
> Checking $\frac{3}{7}$ in Example 1 leads to some fairly involved arithmetic. Here's something else that you can try. Rework the solution process by collecting variable terms on the right and numerical terms on the left. Do this now. Your answer should still be $\frac{3}{7}$, and you've avoided the cumbersome fractions.

> **EXAMPLE 2** **Using the Distributive Property and then Solving**
>
> Solve: $5x = 8(x + 3)$

Solution

Step 1. Simplify each side. For this example, use the distributive property to remove parentheses on the right.

The compact, symbolic notation of algebra enables us to use a clear step-by-step method for solving equations, designed to avoid the confusion shown in Carnwath's painting.

Squeak Carnwath, "Equations" 1981, oil on cotton canvas 96 in. h × 72 in. w.

$5x = 8(x + 3)$ This is the given equation.

$5x = 8x + 24$ Apply the distributive property.

Step 2. Isolate the variable terms on one side and the constant terms on the other side.

$5x - 8x = 8x - 8x + 24$ Subtract $8x$ to get the x-terms on the left.

$-3x = 24$ Simplify.

Step 3. Now use the multiplication property to isolate x.

$$\frac{-3x}{-3} = \frac{24}{-3}$$ Divide both sides by -3.

$x = -8$

Step 4. Check the proposed solution in the original equation.

$5x = 8(x + 3)$ Always use the original equation.

$5(-8) \overset{?}{=} 8(-8 + 3)$ Substitute -8 for x.

$5(-8) \overset{?}{=} 8(-5)$

$-40 = -40$ ✓

The solution is -8.

In our next example, we must both distribute and combine like terms. Then we solve for the variable.

EXAMPLE 3   **Solving a Linear Equation Involving Parentheses**

Solve: $12 - 2y - 3(y + 2) = 2(2y + 3) - y$

Solution

Step 1. Simplify each side.

$12 - 2y - 3(y + 2) = 2(2y + 3) - y$ This is the given equation.

$12 - 2y - 3y - 6 = 4y + 6 - y$ Use the distributive property to multiply and remove parentheses.

$6 - 5y = 3y + 6$ Combine like terms on each side: $12 - 6 = 6; -2y - 3y = -5y;$ $4y - y = 3y.$

Step 2. Isolate the variable terms on one side and the constant terms on the other side.

$6 - 5y - 3y = 3y - 3y + 6$ Subtract $3y$ to get the y-terms on the left.

$6 - 8y = 6$ Simplify.

$6 - 6 - 8y = 6 - 6$ Subtract 6 to get the numerical terms on the right.

$-8y = 0$ Simplify.

Step 3. Use the multiplication property to isolate y.

$$\frac{-8y}{-8} = \frac{0}{-8}$$ Divide both sides by -8.

$y = 0$ Simplify.

Step 4. Check the proposed solution in the original equation.

$$12 - 2y - 3(y + 2) = 2(2y + 3) - y \qquad \text{Use the original equation.}$$
$$12 - 2(0) - 3(0 + 2) \stackrel{?}{=} 2(2 \cdot 0 + 3) - 0 \qquad \text{Substitute 0 for } y.$$
$$12 - 2(0) - 3(2) \stackrel{?}{=} 2(3) - 0$$
$$12 - 0 - 6 \stackrel{?}{=} 6 - 0$$
$$6 = 6 \quad \checkmark$$

The solution is 0.

∎

2 Solve linear equations containing fractions and decimals.

Clearing Fractions and Decimals

In the last section we cleared an equation of fractions by multiplying every term on both sides by the least common denominator. Let's repeat this procedure for a more complicated equation containing fractions.

EXAMPLE 4 **Solving a Linear Equation Involving Fractions**

Solve: $\dfrac{3x}{2} = \dfrac{x}{5} - \dfrac{39}{5}$

Solution

Step 1. Clear fractions. The least common multiple for 2, 5, and 5 is 10. We will multiply both sides by 10.

$$\frac{3x}{2} = \frac{x}{5} - \frac{39}{5} \qquad \text{This is the given equation.}$$

$$10 \cdot \frac{3x}{2} = 10\left(\frac{x}{5} - \frac{39}{5}\right) \qquad \text{Multiply both sides by 10.}$$

$$10 \cdot \frac{3x}{2} = 10 \cdot \frac{x}{5} - 10 \cdot \frac{39}{5} \qquad \begin{array}{l}\text{Use the distributive property. Be sure}\\ \text{to multiply all terms by 10.}\end{array}$$

$$\left(\frac{5 \cdot \cancel{2}}{1} \cdot \frac{3}{\cancel{2}}\right)x = \left(\frac{2 \cdot \cancel{5}}{1} \cdot \frac{1}{\cancel{5}}\right)x - \left(\frac{2 \cdot \cancel{5}}{1} \cdot \frac{39}{\cancel{5}}\right) \qquad \begin{array}{l}\text{Divide out common factors in the}\\ \text{multiplication.}\end{array}$$

$$15x = 2x - 78 \qquad \begin{array}{l}\text{Complete the multiplication. The frac-}\\ \text{tions are now cleared.}\end{array}$$

Step 2. Isolate the variable terms on one side and the constant terms on the other side.

$$15x - 2x = 2x - 2x - 78 \qquad \text{Subtract } 2x \text{ to get the } x\text{-terms on the left.}$$
$$13x = -78 \qquad \text{Simplify.}$$

Step 3. Use the multiplication property to isolate x.

$$\frac{13x}{13} = \frac{-78}{13} \qquad \text{Divide both sides by 13.}$$
$$x = -6 \qquad \text{Simplify.}$$

Step 4. Check the proposed solution in the original equation.

$$\frac{3x}{2} = \frac{x}{5} - \frac{39}{5} \qquad \text{Use the original equation.}$$

$$\frac{3(-6)}{2} \overset{?}{=} \frac{-6}{5} - \frac{39}{5} \qquad \text{Substitute} -6 \text{ for } x.$$

$$\frac{3(\overset{-3}{\cancel{-6}})}{\cancel{2}} \overset{?}{=} \frac{-6}{5} - \frac{39}{5}$$

$$\frac{-9}{1} \overset{?}{=} -\frac{45}{5}$$

$$-9 = -9 \quad \checkmark$$

The solution is -6. ∎

EXAMPLE 5   Solving a Linear Equation Involving Fractions

Solve: $\dfrac{x+3}{6} - \dfrac{x-5}{4} = \dfrac{3}{8}$

Solution

Step 1. Clear fractions. The least common multiple for 6, 4, and 8 is 24. We will multiply both sides by 24.

$$\frac{x+3}{6} - \frac{x-5}{4} = \frac{3}{8} \qquad \text{This is the given equation.}$$

$$24\left(\frac{x+3}{6} - \frac{x-5}{4}\right) = 24\left(\frac{3}{8}\right) \qquad \text{Multiply both sides by 24, the LCM of 6, 4, and 8.}$$

$$24 \cdot \frac{x+3}{6} - 24 \cdot \frac{x-5}{4} = 24 \cdot \frac{3}{8} \qquad \text{Distribute.}$$

$$\frac{\overset{4}{\cancel{24}}}{1} \cdot \frac{x+3}{\underset{1}{\cancel{6}}} - \frac{\overset{6}{\cancel{24}}}{1} \cdot \frac{x-5}{\underset{1}{\cancel{4}}} = \frac{\overset{3}{\cancel{24}}}{1} \cdot \frac{3}{\underset{1}{\cancel{8}}} \qquad \text{Simplify.}$$

$$4(x+3) - 6(x-5) = 3 \cdot 3 \qquad \begin{array}{l}\text{Notice that 4 multiplies the entire expression}\\ x+3 \text{ and parentheses are necessary. The same}\\ \text{is true for 6 and } x-5\end{array}$$

Step 2. Simplify each side.

$$4x + 12 - 6x + 30 = 9 \qquad \text{Distribute.}$$

$$-2x + 42 = 9 \qquad \text{Combine like terms.}$$

Step 3. Isolate the variable terms on one side and the constant terms on the other side.

$$-2x + 42 - 42 = 9 - 42 \qquad \text{Subtract 42 from both sides.}$$

$$-2x = -33 \qquad \text{Simplify.}$$

Step 4. Use the multiplication property to isolate x.

$$\frac{-2x}{-2} = \frac{-33}{-2} \qquad \text{Divide both sides by } -2.$$

$$x = \frac{33}{2}$$

Step 5. Check the proposed solution in the original equation. Since the original equation contains fractions, using $\frac{33}{2}$ leads to fractions over fractions. To make our check easier, we will write $\frac{33}{2}$ as $16\frac{1}{2}$, or 16.5.

$$\frac{x+3}{6} - \frac{x-5}{4} = \frac{3}{8}$$ Use the original equation.

$$\frac{16.5+3}{6} - \frac{16.5-5}{4} \overset{?}{=} \frac{3}{8}$$ Substitute 16.5 for x.

$$\frac{19.5}{6} - \frac{11.5}{4} \overset{?}{=} \frac{3}{8}$$

$$3.25 - 2.875 \overset{?}{=} 0.375$$

$$0.375 = 0.375 \quad \checkmark$$

The solution is 16.5, or $\frac{33}{2}$. ∎

To clear an equation of decimals, keep in mind that in fractional notation decimals have denominators of 10, 100, 1000, and so on. Count the greatest number of decimal places in any term of the equation. If this number is 1, multiply both sides by 10^1, or 10; if this number is 2, multiply both sides by 10^2, or 100; and so on.

EXAMPLE 6 **Clearing Decimals**

Solve: $19.6 - 4.3y = -11.36$

Solution

Step 1. Clear decimals. The greatest number of decimal places in any one term is 2, so multiply both sides by 10^2, or 100.

$$19.6 - 4.3y = -11.36$$ This is the given equation.

$$100(19.6 - 4.3y) = 100(-11.36)$$ Multiply both sides by 100 to clear decimals.

$$100(19.6) - 100(4.3y) = 100(-11.36)$$ Apply the distributive property.

$$1960 - 430y = -1136$$ Simplify. The equation is now cleared of decimals.

Step 2. Isolate the variable terms on one side and the constant terms on the other side.

$$1960 - 1960 - 430y = -1136 - 1960$$ Subtract 1960 from both sides.

$$-430y = -3096$$ Simplify.

Step 3. Use the multiplication property to isolate y.

$$\frac{-430y}{-430} = \frac{-3096}{-430}$$ Divide both sides by -430.

$$y = 7.2$$ Simplify.

The solution is 7.2. We leave the check to you. ∎

Solve Example 6 without clearing the equation of decimals. This is one way to check the proposed solution. Which method do you find easier?

Based on our work in this section, we can summarize the steps involved in the solution of a linear equation. Not all of these steps are necessary in every equation.

Solving a linear equation

1. Multiply on both sides to clear fractions or decimals.
2. Simplify each side. Use the distributive property to remove grouping symbols, and combine like terms.
3. Use the addition property to get all the variable terms on one side and all the constant terms on the other side.
4. Use the multiplication property to isolate the variable, and solve.
5. Check the proposed solution in the original equation.

3 Solve applied problems involving linear equations.

Applications

The Rhind papyrus is a document that dates back to 1650 B.C., and it now serves as our major source of information about ancient Egyptian mathematics. The papyrus was purchased in Egypt in 1858 by the Scottish Egyptologist A. Henry Rhind and was later acquired by the British Museum. Example 7 is one of the 85 problems from the Rhind papyrus.

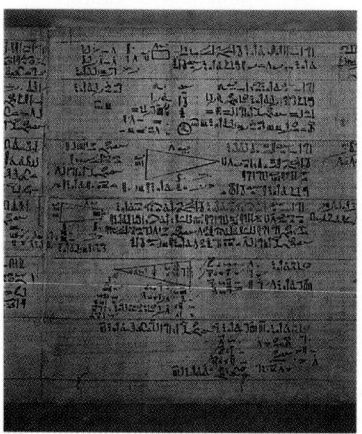

A portion of the Rhind papyrus dating back to ca. 1650 B.C. It is the most extensive mathematical document from ancient Egypt.

Bridgeman/Art Resource

| EXAMPLE 7 | **An Egyptian Word Problem from the Rhind Papyrus** |

"A quantity, its $\frac{2}{3}$, and its $\frac{1}{7}$, added together, become 38. What is the quantity?"

Solution

Let x = the quantity. The English "its $\frac{2}{3}$" means $\frac{2}{3}$ of the quantity, or $\frac{2}{3}x$. We now translate from English into an algebraic equation.

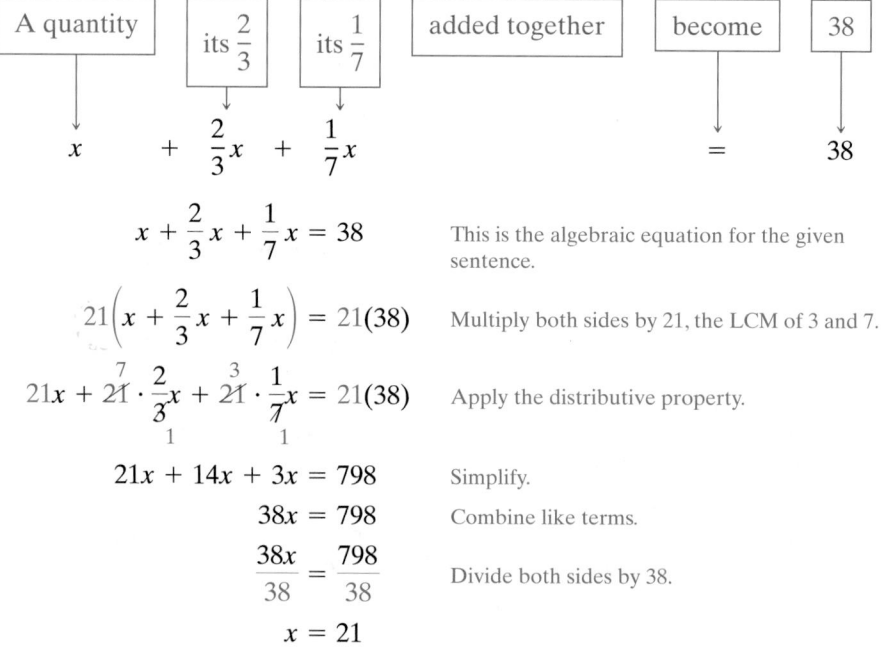

$$x + \frac{2}{3}x + \frac{1}{7}x = 38 \qquad \text{This is the algebraic equation for the given sentence.}$$

$$21\left(x + \frac{2}{3}x + \frac{1}{7}x\right) = 21(38) \qquad \text{Multiply both sides by 21, the LCM of 3 and 7.}$$

$$21x + \overset{7}{\cancel{21}} \cdot \frac{2}{\cancel{3}}x + \overset{3}{\cancel{21}} \cdot \frac{1}{\cancel{7}}x = 21(38) \qquad \text{Apply the distributive property.}$$

$$21x + 14x + 3x = 798 \qquad \text{Simplify.}$$

$$38x = 798 \qquad \text{Combine like terms.}$$

$$\frac{38x}{38} = \frac{798}{38} \qquad \text{Divide both sides by 38.}$$

$$x = 21$$

Check

A quantity (21), its $\frac{2}{3}$ ($\frac{2}{3} \cdot 21 = 14$), and its $\frac{1}{7}$ ($\frac{1}{7} \cdot 21 = 3$), added together (21 + 14 + 3 = 38) do give 38. The quantity is 21. ∎

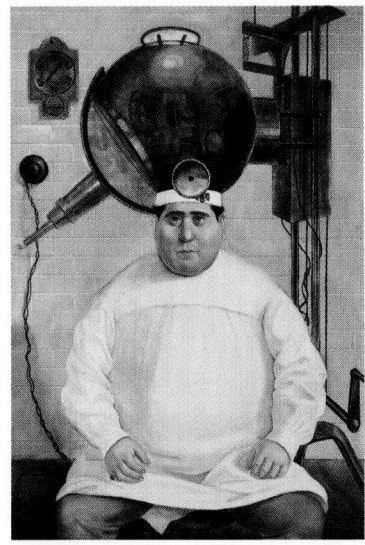

Otto Dix, "Dr. Mayer-Hermann" 1926, oil and tempera on wood, $58\frac{3}{4} \times 39$ in. (149.2 × 99.1 cm). The Museum of Modern Art, New York. Gift of Philip Johnson. Photograph © The Museum of Modern Art, New York. © 1998 Artists Rights Society (ARS), New York/VG Bild–Kunst, Bonn.

U.S. conversion factors for length

12 inches = 1 foot
3 feet = 1 yard
1760 yard = 1 mile
5280 feet = 1 mile

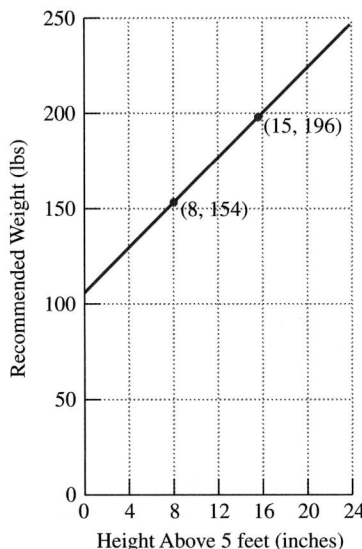

Figure 2.2

EXAMPLE 8 **Modeling Weight and Height**

The mathematical model

$$\frac{W}{2} - 3H = 53$$

describes the recommended weight W in pounds for a male, where H represents the man's height in inches over 5 feet.

a. Solve the model for W.
b. What are the recommended weights for a male 5 feet, 8 inches and for a male 6 feet, 3 inches tall?

Solution

a.

$\dfrac{W}{2} - 3H = 53$	This is the given model.
$2\left(\dfrac{W}{2} - 3H\right) = 2(53)$	Clear fractions. Multiply both sides by 2.
$2 \cdot \dfrac{W}{2} - 2 \cdot 3H = 2(53)$	Apply the distributive property.
$W - 6H = 106$	Simplify.
$W - 6H + 6H = 106 + 6H$	Isolate W by adding $6H$ to both sides.
$W = 106 + 6H$	Simplify.

b. Keep in mind that H represents height in inches above 5 feet. For a 5-foot, 8-inch-tall male, his height is 68 inches. Since 5 feet = 60 inches, he is 8 inches above 5 feet, so $H = 8$.

$W = 106 + 6H$	Use the form of the model from part (a).
$W = 106 + 6(8)$	Substitute 8 for H.
$W = 106 + 48$	
$W = 154$	

The recommended weight for a man whose height is 5 feet, 8 inches is 154 pounds.

We now follow the same procedure for a man whose height is 6 feet, 3 inches. This height exceeds 60 inches by 15 inches, so $H = 15$.

$$W = 106 + 6(15) = 106 + 90 = 196$$

The recommended weight for a man whose height is 6 feet, 3 inches is 196 pounds. ∎

We can represent the computations from Example 8 in terms of ordered pairs. The first coordinate is the man's height above 5 feet (in inches) and the second coordinate is the man's recommended weight. Additional computations indicate that these ordered pairs lie along a straight line, as shown in Figure 2.2. This line is the *graph* of the model $W = 106 + 6H$.

PROBLEM SET 2.3

Practice Problems

Solve and check each equation in Problems 1–34.

1. $3x - 7x + 30 = 10 - 2x$

2. $2x - 8x + 35 = 5 - 3x$

3. $3x + 6 - x = 8 + 3x - 6$

4. $4x - 7 - x = 5 + 4x - 12$

5. $6y + 25 - 4y = 4y - 4 + y + 29$

6. $7y + 26 - 5y = 5y - 2 + y$

7. $3(x - 2) = 12$

8. $3(x + 2) = 6$

9. $-2(y + 3) = -9$

10. $-3(2 - 3y) = 9$

11. $-2(y + 4) + 7 = 3$

12. $3(3x + 5) - 6 = 86$

13. $6x - (3x + 10) = 14$

14. $5x - (2x + 14) = 10$

15. $2(4 - 3x) = 2(2x + 5)$

16. $3(5 - x) = 4(2x + 1)$

17. $3(2y + 3) = -3y - 9$

18. $2(x + 2) = -4x - 2$

19. $3(y + 3) = -2(2y - 1)$

20. $2(5 + 5y) = 3(5 + 3y)$

21. $8(y + 2) = 2(3y + 4)$

22. $3(3x - 1) = 4(3 + 3x)$

23. $3(y + 1) = 7(y - 2) - 3$

24. $5y - 4(y + 9) = 2y - 3$

25. $5(2z - 8) - 2 = 5(z - 3) + 3$

26. $7(3m - 2) + 5 = 6(2m - 1) + 24$

27. $17(x + 3) = 13 + 4(x - 10)$

28. $2(5y + 4) + 19 = 4y - 3(2y + 11)$

29. $6 = -4(1 - x) + 3(x + 1)$

30. $100 = -(x - 1) + 4(x - 6)$

31. $10(y + 4) - 4(y - 2) = 3(y - 1) + 2(y - 3)$

32. $-2(x - 4) - (3x - 2) = -2 - (6x - 2)$

33. $9 - 6(2z + 1) = 3 - 7(z - 1)$

34. $2 - 6(w - 3) = 8 - 5(2w + 1)$

Solve and check each equation in Problems 35–56. Begin your work by clearing fractions or decimals.

35. $\dfrac{x}{3} + \dfrac{x}{2} = \dfrac{5}{6}$

36. $\dfrac{y}{4} - 1 = \dfrac{y}{5}$

37. $20 - \dfrac{z}{3} = \dfrac{z}{2}$

38. $\dfrac{w}{5} - \dfrac{1}{2} = \dfrac{w}{6}$

39. $\dfrac{3x}{4} - 3 = \dfrac{x}{2} + 2$

40. $\dfrac{y}{3} - 1 = -y - \dfrac{1}{2}$

41. $\dfrac{3x}{5} - x = \dfrac{x}{10} - \dfrac{5}{2}$

42. $2y - \dfrac{2y}{7} = \dfrac{y}{2} + \dfrac{17}{2}$

43. $\dfrac{5z - 1}{7} - \dfrac{3z - 2}{5} = 1$

44. $\dfrac{4y - 3}{3} - 6 = \dfrac{3y}{2} - 8$

45. $\dfrac{z - 3}{4} - 1 = \dfrac{z}{2}$

46. $\dfrac{y}{4} = 2 + \dfrac{y - 3}{3}$

47. $\dfrac{2y - 3}{9} + \dfrac{y - 3}{2} = \dfrac{y + 5}{6} - 1$

48. $\dfrac{3z + 4}{3} + \dfrac{z - 2}{15} = \dfrac{z - 2}{5} - 1$

49. $15.2 - 3.4x = 9.76$

50. $17.3 - 2.7x = 10.55$

51. $2.24y - 9.28 = 5.74y + 5.42$

52. $4.8y + 32.5 = 124.8 - 9.4y$

53. $0.2x - 0.5 = 1.2x - 0.6$

54. $1.3x - 1.8 = 2.3x + 5.2$

55. $3.2y - 2.2 = 4.9y + 5.9$

56. $0.5x - 1.9 = 0.6x + 2.8$

Application Problems

57. The equation

$$\frac{c}{2} + 80 = 2F$$

models the relationship between F, the temperature in degrees Fahrenheit, and c, the number of cricket chirps per minute for the snow tree cricket.

a. Solve the model for c.

b. Use the form of the model from part (a) to calculate the number of chirps per minute at temperatures of $40°, 60°, 65°, 70°$, and $80°$ Fahrenheit.

c. Represent your computations from part (b) as ordered pairs. The first coordinate should be the Fahrenheit temperature and the second coordinate should be the number of chirps per minute. Graph the five ordered pairs in a rectangular coordinate system. What do you observe?

58. Solve this problem from the Rhind Papyrus: "A quantity, its $\frac{3}{4}$, and its $\frac{1}{5}$, added together, become 78. What is the quantity?"

True–False Critical Thinking Problems

59. Which one of the following statements is true?
 a. The equation $3(x + 4) = 3(4 + x)$ has precisely one solution.
 b. The equation $2y + 5 = 0$ is equivalent to $2y = 5$.
 c. If $2 - 3y = 11$, then when the solution to the equation is substituted into $y^2 + 2y - 3$, a number results that is neither positive nor negative.
 d. The equation $x + \frac{1}{3} = \frac{1}{2}$ is equivalent to $x + 2 = 3$.

60. Which one of the following statements is true?
 a. $y - (y - 3) = 5y$ is equivalent to $3 = 5y$.
 b. Multiplying both sides of an equation by the same real number will result in an equation that is equivalent to the original equation.
 c. To solve $5x - 8 = 11$, we should first divide both sides by 5 and then add 8 to both sides.
 d. The solution to $3y - 7 = 0$ is $-\frac{7}{3}$.

Technology Problems

Solve Problems 61–67 by using a calculator.

61. $8.05x + 2.03x = 17.06 - 4.3$

62. $8497x + 7947 = -5689x - 8576$

63. $3.7y - 15.1 = 9y - 6.2$

64. $0.003x - 0.1297 = 1.43x + 8.5$

65. $19.25x - 63.1x = 14.9 - 52.04$

66. $0.00794 - 0.00843x = 0.00574x - 0.007325$

67. $-6.1x + 11.03 = 11x + 5.17$

68. Use a calculator to show that $\frac{3}{7}$ satisfies

$$2(5y - 3) - (2y - 4) = 5 - (6y + 1).$$

Writing in Mathematics

69. There is no solution to the equation $4x - 3 = 2(x - 1) + 2x$. Try solving the equation and describe what happens.

70. The equation $4x + 6 = 2(x + 3) + 2x$ is satisfied regardless of what real number is substituted for x. Sub-

stitute a few real numbers and then try solving the equation. Describe what happens.

Critical Thinking Problems

Solve each equation in Problems 71–73.

71. $2(3x + 4) = 3x + 2[3(x - 1) + 2]$

73. $x(x - 5) = 4x(x + 2) - 3(x^2 + x - 7)$

72. $0.25x + 0.35(x - 6000) = 500$

Group Activity Problems

74. Suppose you are an algebra teacher correcting an examination on solving linear equations. In your group, determine whether the following student solution is correct. If the solution is incorrect, write an explanation for exactly where the error lies.

$5(x + 3) - 15 = 2x$	This is the given equation.
$5x + 15 - 15 = 2x$	Apply the distributive property.
$5x = 2x$	Simplify.
$5 = 2$	Divide both sides by x.

There is no solution because $5 \neq 2$.

75. In your group, describe the best procedure for solving an equation like

$$0.47x + \frac{19}{4} = -0.2 + \frac{2}{5}x.$$

Use this procedure to actually solve the equation. Then compare procedures with other groups working on this problem. Which group devised the most streamlined method?

Review Problems

76. Evaluate $\dfrac{10 - 3x}{2}$ if $x = -4$.

77. Simplify: $3(2x - 5) - (x - 4)$.

78. Place $<$ or $>$ in the box to write a true statement: $-10\frac{1}{2}\ \square\ -10\frac{1}{4}$.

S E C T I O N   2 . 4

Solutions   Tutorial   Video
Manual   3

▮ Answer questions about mathematical models.

Mathematical Models

Objectives

1 Answer questions about mathematical models.
2 Solve a mathematical model for a specified variable.

Strategies for solving linear equations can be applied to mathematical models that describe practical situations. In this section we consider a wide variety of formulas that describe situations ranging from exercise and heart rate to the Indianapolis 500. We begin with a model for exercise and heart rate.

EXAMPLE 1   **Exercise and Heart Rate**

Medical researchers have found that the desirable maximum heart rate R (in beats per minute) of a person exercising is given by the mathematical model

$$R = 110 + 3A - 4(A - 27.5)$$

where A is the person's age. If the desirable maximum heart rate is 175 beats per minute, how old is that person?

Solution

$R = 110 + 3A - 4(A - 27.5)$	This is the given equation.
$175 = 110 + 3A - 4(A - 27.5)$	We are given that $R = 175$. We must solve the equation for A.
$175 = 110 + 3A - 4A + 110$	Use the distributive property on the right.
$175 = 220 - A$	Combine like terms.
$175 - 220 = 220 - 220 - A$	Subtract 220 from each side.
$-45 = -A$	Simplify.
$45 = A$	If $-x = a$, then $x = -a$.

The person is 45 years old.   ▮

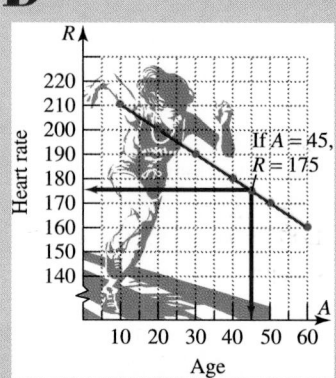

iscover for yourself

The solution $(A = 45, R = 175)$ is shown in this graph. The symbol ⭤ indicates a break in the values. Values below 140 are not shown. Explain how the graph was obtained from the mathematical model. In general, how can a formula containing two variables be graphed in a rectangular coordinate system?

EXAMPLE 2   **Using a Mathematical Model to Predict the Future**

The following list shows the winner of the Indianapolis 500 from 1980 through 1992 and their race speeds (in miles per hour).

1980	Johnny Rutherford	192.256
1981	Bobby Unser	200.546
1982	Gordon Johncock	207.004
1983	Tom Sneva	207.395
1984	Rick Mears	210.029
1985	Danny Sullivan	212.583

Specially built racing cars compete in the Indianapolis 500 by racing 500 miles around the 2.5 mile track.

Duomo Photography

1986	Bobby Rahal	216.828
1987	Al Unser	215.390
1988	Rick Mears	219.198
1989	Emerson Fitipaldi	223.885
1990	Airie Luyendyk	225.301
1991	Rick Mears	224.113
1992	Al Unser, Jr.	232.482

A mathematical model that closely approximates this data is given by

$$y = 2.5x + 198.73$$

where x represents the number of years after 1980 (so $x = 0$ corresponds to 1980 and $x = 12$ corresponds to 1992) and y represents the winning racing speed. Predict the year in which the winning speed will be 248.73 miles per hour.

Solution

$y = 2.5x + 198.73$	Use the given model.
$248.73 = 2.5x + 198.73$	We are given that y (the winning speed) is 248.73 miles per hour. We must solve the equation for x.
$100(248.73) = 100(2.5x + 198.73)$	Clear decimals by multiplying both sides by 100.
$100(248.73) = 100(2.5x) + 100(198.73)$	Apply the distributive property.
$24{,}873 = 250x + 19{,}873$	Simplify. The equation is now cleared of decimals.
$24{,}873 - 19{,}873 = 250x + 19{,}873 - 19{,}873$	Isolate the term with x, subtracting 19,873 from both sides.
$5000 = 250x$	Simplify.
$\dfrac{5000}{250} = \dfrac{250x}{250}$	Isolate x, dividing both sides by 250.
$20 = x$	Simplify.

The model indicates that 20 years after 1980, or in the year 2000, the winning racing speed will be 248.73 miles per hour. ■

Modeling Percents

In Section 1.1 we saw that the word *percent* means "per hundred." One percent means "one per hundred," so

$$1\% = \frac{1}{100} \quad \text{or} \quad 1\% = 0.01$$

We also saw percents in Section 1.3 when we studied circle graphs. The area of each sector in these graphs is a percent of the area of the entire circle.

Percents are useful in comparing two numbers. To compare the number A to the number B using a percent P, the following model is used.

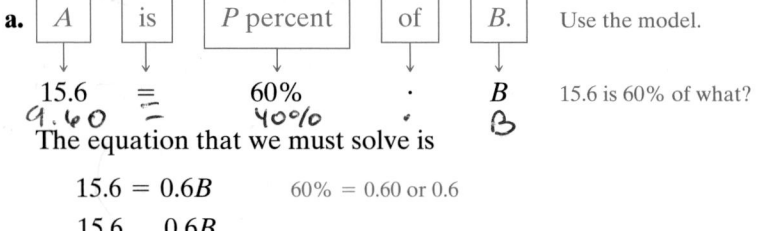

In the model

$$A = PB$$

B = the base number, P = the percent (in decimal form), and A = the number compared to B.

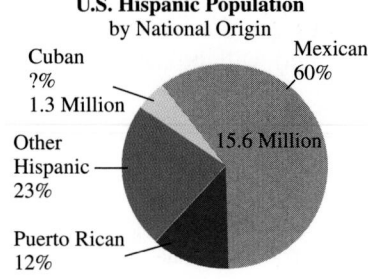

U.S. Hispanic Population by National Origin

Cuban ?%
1.3 Million

Mexican 60%

Other Hispanic 23%

15.6 Million

Puerto Rican 12%

Figure 2.3

Source: U.S. Department of Naturalization and Immigration

EXAMPLE 3   **Using the Percent Model**

Use the percent model to answer the following questions.

a. 15.6 is 60% of what?
b. What is 12% of 26?
c. What percent of 26 is 1.3?

Solution

The circle graph in Figure 2.3 gives meaning to the numbers in this problem.

a.

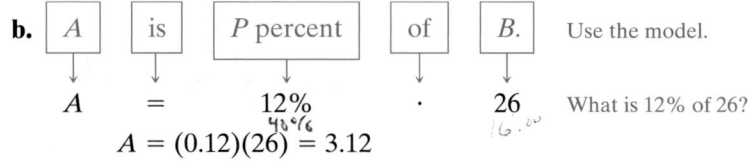

| A | is | P percent | of | B. | Use the model. |

15.6 = 60% · B 15.6 is 60% of what?

The equation that we must solve is

$$15.6 = 0.6B \qquad 60\% = 0.60 \text{ or } 0.6$$

$$\frac{15.6}{0.6} = \frac{0.6B}{0.6} \qquad \text{Divide both sides by 0.6.}$$

$$26 = B$$

Therefore, 15.6 is 60% of 26. The answer is 26. In terms of the circle graph in Figure 2.3, there are 26 million Americans of Hispanic origin in the United States.

b.

| A | is | P percent | of | B. | Use the model. |

A = 12% · 26   What is 12% of 26?

$$A = (0.12)(26) = 3.12$$

Therefore, 3.12 is 12% of 26. The answer is 3.12. In terms of the circle graph in Figure 2.3, there are 3.12 million Puerto Ricans among the 26 million Hispanics.

c. The question "What percent of 26 is 1.3?" can be reworded as "1.3 is what percent of 26?" to fit the wording of the model.

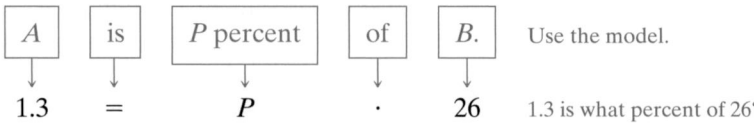

| A | is | P percent | of | B. | Use the model. |

1.3 = P · 26   1.3 is what percent of 26?

The equation that we must solve is

$$1.3 = 26P$$

$$\frac{1.3}{26} = \frac{26P}{26} \quad \text{Divide both sides by 26.}$$

$$0.05 = P \quad \text{Simplify.}$$

We can now change 0.05 to a percent by moving the decimal point two places to the right and adding a percent sign. Since 0.05 = 5%, this means that 5% of 26 is 1.3. The answer is 5%. In terms of the graph in Figure 2.3, there are 1.3 million Cubans among the 26 million Hispanics. ∎

Example 4 represents a basic type of percent problem that can be solved using the percent model.

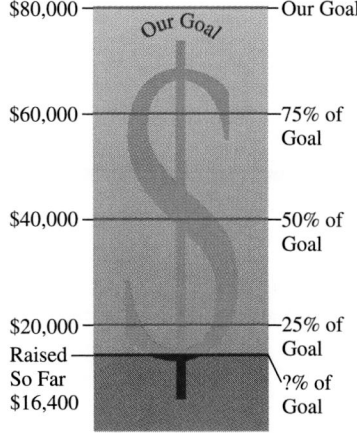

$80,000 ―――――――― Our Goal
            Our Goal

$60,000 ―――――――― 75% of
                    Goal

$40,000 ―――――――― 50% of
                    Goal

$20,000 ―――――――― 25% of
Raised   Goal
So Far
$16,400 ――――――――― ?% of
                    Goal

Raising money for a charity

EXAMPLE 4 **Using the Percent Model**

A charity has raised $16,400, with a goal of raising $80,000. What percent of the goal has been raised?

Solution

The question that we must address is "$16,400 is what percent of $80,000?"

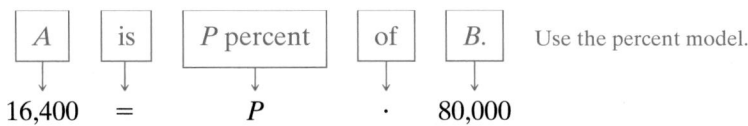

| A | is | P percent | of | B. | Use the percent model. |

$$16,400 \quad = \quad P \quad \cdot \quad 80,000$$

The equation that we must solve is

$$16,400 = 80,000P$$

$$\frac{16,400}{80,000} = \frac{80,000P}{80,000} \quad \text{Divide both sides by 80,000.}$$

$$0.205 = P \quad \text{Simplify.}$$

Since 0.205 = 20.5%, 20.5% of the charity's goal has been raised. ∎

Study tip

There are three basic types of percent problems that can be solved using the percent model.

$A = PB$ A is P percent of B.

Question	Given	Percent Model
A is P percent of what?	A and P	Solve for B.
What is P percent of B?	P and B	Solve for A.
A is what percent of B?	A and B	Solve for P.

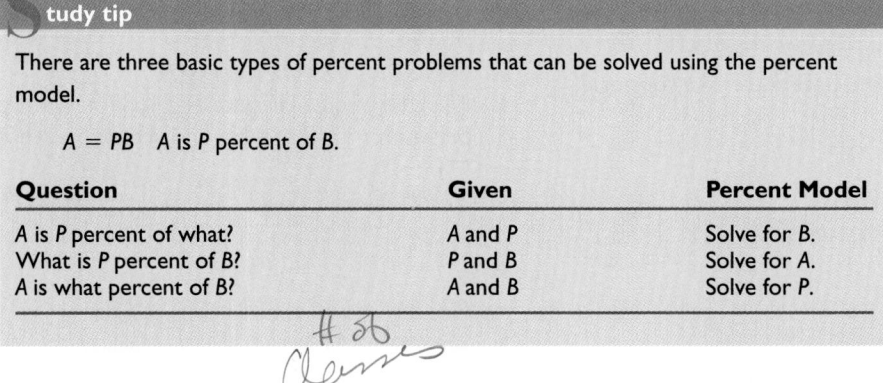

2 Solve a mathematical model for a specified variable.

Solving for a Variable in a Mathematical Model

In Examples 1–4, we obtained information about a variable contained within a mathematical model. Often we are given a mathematical model solved for one variable, and we have to solve the model for a different variable. We will now focus on this procedure. The examples that follow reinforce what we learned about solving equations in the previous section.

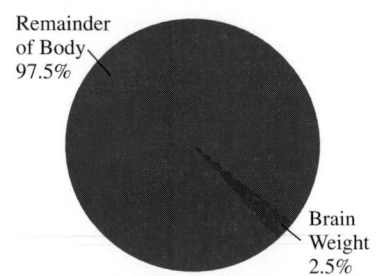

Remainder of Body 97.5%

Brain Weight 2.5%

The human brain's weight as a percent of total body weight

EXAMPLE 5   **Using the Percent Model**

a. Solve for B: $A = PB$

b. Use the result of part (a) to solve this problem: The human brain weighs 2.5% of total body weight. If a person's brain weighs 4.5 pounds, what is that person's body weight?

Solution

a. $A = PB$ | This is the given percent model. We want B alone.

$\dfrac{A}{P} = \dfrac{PB}{P}$ To isolate B, divide both sides of the equation by P.

$\dfrac{A}{P} = B$ Simplify: $\dfrac{PB}{P} = \dfrac{\cancel{P}B}{\cancel{P}} = \dfrac{B}{1} = B$.

b. The question that we must address is "2.5% of what is 4.5?". We are given that $A = 4.5$ and $P = 2.5\% = 0.025$, and we must solve for B. We use the form of the model from part (a).

$$B = \frac{A}{P} = \frac{4.5}{0.025} = 180$$

If the brain weighs 4.5 pounds, the body weight is 180 pounds.   ■

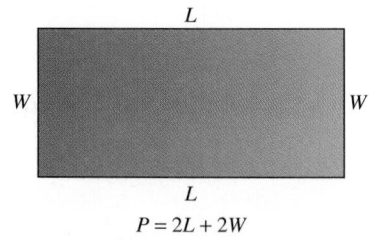

L

W W

L

$P = 2L + 2W$

The perimeter of a rectangle

EXAMPLE 6   **Perimeter of a Rectangle**

The formula

$$P = 2L + 2W$$

describes the perimeter P of a rectangle in terms of its length L and its width W.

a. Solve the formula for L.

b. Use the result of part (a) to determine the length of a rectangle whose perimeter is 48 meters and whose width is 6 meters.

Solution

a. $P = 2L + 2W$ | This is the given formula. We want L alone.

$P - 2W = 2L + 2W - 2W$ Subtract $2W$ from both sides.

$P - 2W = 2L$ Simplify.

$\dfrac{P - 2W}{2} = \dfrac{2L}{2}$ Divide both sides by 2.

$\dfrac{P - 2W}{2} = L$ Simplify.

Therefore, $L = \dfrac{P - 2W}{2}$.

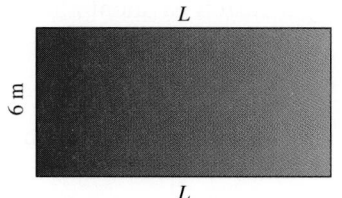

L

6 m

6 m

L

Perimeter: $P = 48$ meters

Width: $W = 6$ meters

Length: $L = ?$

b. $L = \dfrac{P - 2W}{2}$ Use the formula obtained in part (a).

$L = \dfrac{48 - 2(6)}{2}$ Find L when $P = 48$ and $W = 6$.

$L = \dfrac{48 - 12}{2}$

$L = \dfrac{36}{2}$

$L = 18$

The length is 18 meters.

Check

$$P = 2L + 2W = 2(18) + 2(6) = 36 + 12 = 48 \text{ meters}$$

This checks with the conditions given in the problem.   ■

EXAMPLE 7   **Using the Simple Interest Model**

The model $I = Prt$ describes the simple interest, I, on an investment, where P is the principal (the amount invested), r is the rate, and t is the time of the investment in years.

a. Solve the formula for r.
b. Use the result of part (a) to determine the annual simple interest rate if the simple interest is $300, the principal is $3000, and the time is 2 years.

Solution

a. $I = Prt$ | Use the simple interest formula. We want r alone.

$\dfrac{I}{Pt} = \dfrac{Prt}{Pt}$ To isolate r, divide both sides by Pt.

$\dfrac{I}{Pt} = r$ Simplify: $\dfrac{Prt}{Pt} = \dfrac{\cancel{Pr}t}{\cancel{Pt}} = \dfrac{r}{1} = r$.

The formula solved for r is $r = \dfrac{I}{Pt}$.

b. $r = \dfrac{I}{Pt}$ Use the formula from part (a).

$r = \dfrac{300}{3000(2)}$ Substitute the values for I, P, and t.

$r = \dfrac{300}{6000}$

$r = 0.05$ $\frac{300}{6000} = \frac{3}{60} = \frac{1}{20} = 0.05$

$r = 5\%$ Move the decimal point two places to the right and add a % sign.

The rate of interest is 5%.   ■

Discover for yourself

The simple interest for a $3000 investment over 2 years is $300. Can you guess at the simple interest rate for one year?

EXAMPLE 8   A Model for Deferred Payment Buying

The total price of an article purchased on a monthly deferred payment plan is described by the model

$$T = D + pm$$

where T is the total price, D is the down payment, p is the monthly payment, and m is the number of months one pays.

a. Solve the model for p.

b. A stereo system that sells for $3308 on the deferred payment plan was purchased with a down payment of $500 and 36 monthly payments. How much is each monthly payment?

Solution

Total price: $T = \$3308$
Downpayment: $D = \$500$
Number of monthly payments:
$m = 36$
Amount of each monthly payment: $p = ?$

Anthony Meshkinyar/
Tony Stone Images

a. $T = D + pm$ This is the given model. We want p alone.

$T - D = D - D + pm$

$T - D = pm$ Simplify.

$\dfrac{T - D}{m} = \dfrac{pm}{m}$ Now isolate p by dividing both sides by m.

$\dfrac{T - D}{m} = p$ Simplify: $\dfrac{pm}{m} = \dfrac{p\cancel{m}}{\cancel{m}} = \dfrac{p}{1} = p$.

The formula solved for p is $p = \dfrac{T - D}{m}$.

b. $p = \dfrac{T - D}{m}$ Use the formula obtained in part (a).

$p = \dfrac{3308 - 500}{36}$ Substitute the values for $T, D,$ and m.

$p = \dfrac{2808}{36}$ Subtract in the numerator.

$p = 78$ Divide.

Each monthly payment is $78.

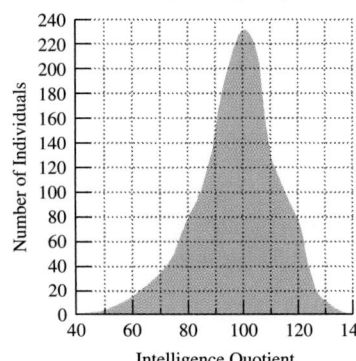

Distribution of IQ in Sample Population

(graph: Number of Individuals vs Intelligence Quotient)

This distribution of adult intelligence quotients (IQs) is from a sample of 2052 people in the United States.

EXAMPLE 9   A Mathematical Model for Intelligence

In psychology, an intelligence quotient, Q, also called IQ, is measured by the model

$$Q = \dfrac{100M}{C}$$

where M = mental age and C = chronological age. Solve the formula for C.

ENRICHMENT ESSAY

Palindromes

Palindromes are words, phrases, numbers, or sentences that read the same forward and backward. Simple examples are the words *Bob, madam, mom, dad,* and *Eve,* as well as the prime numbers 11 and 101. The equality property $a = a$ is a palindrome. The number 121, a palindrome, is also the square of a palindrome $[(11)^2 = 121]$. Furthermore, $11^3 = 1331$ and $11^4 = 14641$ are also palindromic. Also, 22 is a palindrome whose square is palindromic: $22^2 = 484$. Other numbers whose squares are palindromes include 26 and 121.

If 87 is reversed and added to itself, and the process is repeated, after only four steps it becomes a palindrome:

$$87 + 78 = 165 \qquad 165 + 561 = 726$$
$$726 + 627 = 1353 \qquad 1353 + 3531 = 4884$$

Do all numbers eventually become palindromes if this process is followed? This is an unanswered question of mathematics. So far, 196 is the only number less than 10,000 that has not yet produced a palindrome by this process.

A challenge to linguists is to construct palindromic sentences that make sense, such as:

1. Draw, o coward!
2. Dennis sinned.
3. Doc, note, I dissent. A fast never prevents a fatness. I diet on cod.
4. Ma is a nun, as I am.
5. Revolting is error. Resign it, lover.
6. Naomi, did I moan?
7. Al lets Della call Ed Stella.
8. He lived as a devil, eh?

Religious art often looks the same from left to right and right to left to express divine harmony.
James Strachan/Tony Stone Images

Solution

$$Q = \frac{100M}{C} \qquad \text{Use the the given model. We want } C \text{ alone.}$$

$$CQ = C \cdot \frac{100M}{C} \qquad \text{Multiply both sides by } C \text{ to clear the fraction.}$$

$$CQ = 100M \qquad \text{Simplify: } \frac{\cancel{C}}{1} \cdot \frac{100M}{\cancel{C}} = \frac{100M}{1} = 100M. \text{ Reminder: We want } C \text{ alone.}$$

$$\frac{CQ}{Q} = \frac{100M}{Q} \qquad \text{To isolate } C, \text{ divide both sides by } Q.$$

$$C = \frac{100M}{Q} \qquad \text{Simplify: } \frac{CQ}{Q} = \frac{C\cancel{Q}}{\cancel{Q}} = \frac{C}{1} = C.$$

This form of the model can be used to determine a person's chronological age if the person's mental age and IQ are known. ∎

In Chapter 4, we will be discussing graphing. At that time, it will be necessary to solve equations in the form $Ax + By = C$ for y. Example 10 illustrates how to do this.

EXAMPLE 10   **Solving for y**

a. Solve $3x + 2y = 10$ for y.
b. Find the value of y when $x = 4$.

Solution

a. Begin by isolating the term containing the variable y.

$$3x + 2y = 10 \qquad \text{This is the given equation. We want } y \text{ alone.}$$

$$3x - 3x + 2y = 10 - 3x \qquad \text{To isolate the term with } y, \text{ subtract } 3x \text{ from both sides.}$$

$$2y = 10 - 3x \qquad \text{Simplify.}$$

$$\frac{2y}{2} = \frac{10 - 3x}{2} \qquad \text{Now isolate } y \text{ by dividing both sides by 2.}$$

$$y = \frac{10 - 3x}{2} \qquad \text{Equivalently, } y = \frac{1}{2}(10 - 3x). \text{ Using the distributive}$$
$$\text{property, } y = \frac{1}{2} \cdot 10 - \frac{1}{2} \cdot 3x = 5 - \frac{3x}{2}.$$

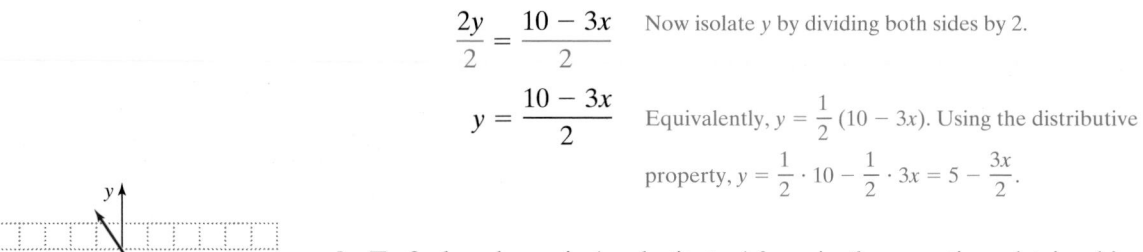

b. To find y when x is 4, substitute 4 for x in the equation obtained in part (a).

$$y = \frac{10 - 3x}{2} \qquad \text{Use the equation we obtained in part (a).}$$

$$y = \frac{10 - 3(4)}{2} \qquad \text{Substitute 4 for } x.$$

$$y = \frac{10 - 12}{2} \qquad \text{Multiply in the numerator.}$$

$$y = \frac{-2}{2} \qquad \text{Subtract in the numerator.}$$

$$y = -1 \qquad \text{Divide.}$$

The graph of $3x + 2y = 10$. The point shows that when $x = 4$, $y = -1$.

We see that when $x = 4$, $y = -1$.   ■

(4, −1)

PROBLEM SET 2.4

Practice and Application Problems

In Massachusetts, speeding fines are determined by the mathematical model

$$y = 10(x - 65) + 50$$

where y is the cost in dollars of the fine if a person is caught driving x miles per hour. In the model, $x \geqslant 65$. Use the model to answer Problems 1–2.

1. If a fine comes to $250, how fast was that person speeding? How is this illustrated in the graph?

2. If a fine comes to $400, how fast was that person speeding? How is this illustrated in the graph?

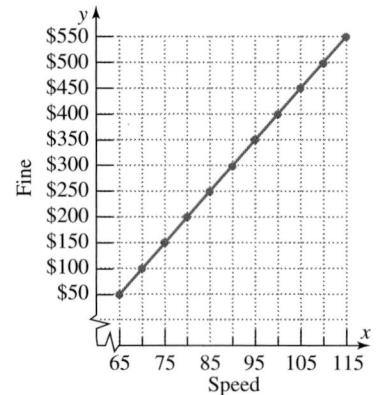

3. The model $E = 0.215t + 71.05$ describes the life expectancy, E (in years), for women t years after 1950.
  a. In what year was life expectancy 73.2 years? How is this illustrated in the graph shown below?
  b. Solve the formula for t.
  c. According to the formula in part (b), in what year will life expectancy be 81.8 years? How can this be illustrated in the graph?

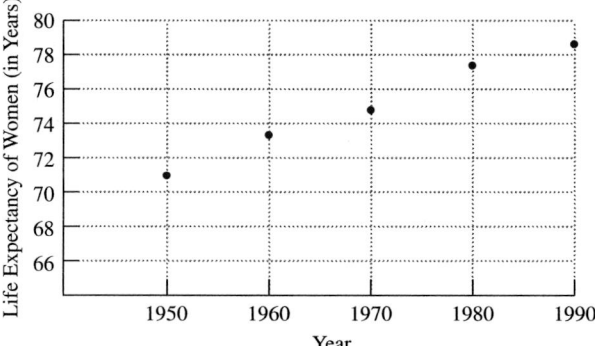

4. There is a relationship between runner injuries in the Boston Marathon and the temperature at the time of the race (*The Boston Globe*, April 20, 1992). The mathematical model

$$p = 0.27t - 8.46$$

describes the percentage of runners injured, p, when the Fahrenheit temperature is t degrees.
  a. In 1985, 12.3% of the runners were injured ($p = 12.3$). What was the temperature at the time of the race?
  b. Solve the formula for t.
  c. In 1989, 10.3% of the runners were injured. Use the formula in part (b) to find the temperature at the time of the race.

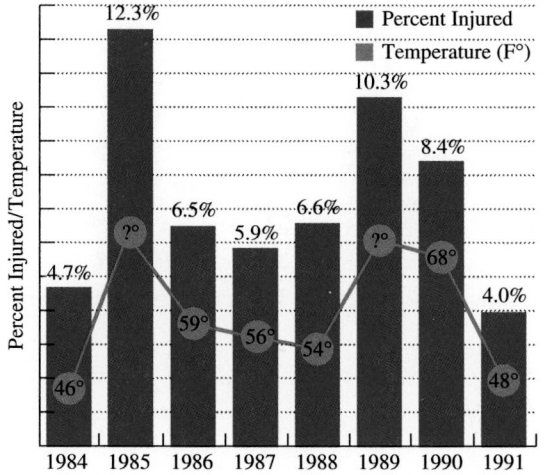

5. The weight W of a car is usually nearly evenly distributed over the area A of contact of each of the four wheels with the ground. If P is the tire pressure in pounds per square inch, then

$$\frac{W}{4A} = P.$$

If the tire pressure in each of the four tires is 28 pounds per square inch and the area of contact for each tire is 24 square inches, what is the weight of the car? Can these numbers apply to the Volkswagen "Beetle" in the illustration? Explain.

Ron Kimball/Ron Kimball Photography

6. The model

$$p = 15 + \frac{15d}{33}$$

describes the pressure of sea water (p, in pounds square foot) at a depth of d feet below the surface. The record depth for breath-held diving, by Francisco Ferreras (Cuba) off Grand Bahama Island, on November 14, 1993, involved pressure of 201 pounds per square foot. To what depth did Ferraras descend on this ill-advised venture? (He was underwater for 2 minutes and 9 seconds!)

Kurt Amsler/Agence Vandystadt/Allsport Photography (USA), Inc.

7. A pilot of a small plane may need a model to judge how high to fly before icing becomes a problem. As dry air moves upward, it cools at a rate of about 1°C for each 11-meter rise, up to 12,000 meters. This situation is represented by the model

$$T = t - \frac{h}{100} \qquad h < 12,000$$

where t is the ground temperature and T is the temperature at height h. If the ground temperature is 30°C, at what height will the air temperature be freezing (0°C)?

8. The amplifier in a stereo system must be powerful enough to produce loud peak volume level (106 decibels) in the speakers. The model

$$P = \frac{V}{180} + \frac{80}{9}$$

describes the relationship between the power P of a loudspeaker (in watts) and the volume V of a room (in cubic feet). If a system produces 40 watts, what should the volume of a room be that will allow the speakers to produce loud peak levels?

$180/9 \times 40$

In Problems 9–20, use the percent model $A = PB$, *which states that* A *is* P *percent of* B.

9. What is 18% of 40? $A = .18 \cdot 40$

10. What is 16% of 90?

11. What percent of 15 is 3?

12. What percent of 90 is 45?

13. What percent of 3 is 15?

14. What percent of 45 is 90?

15. 60% of what number is 3?

16. 75% of what number is 6?

17. If 18% of your yearly salary is spent on entertainment, and one year you spend $2970 on entertainment, what is your salary for that year? $18/500$

18. If 35% of your yearly salary is spent on housing, and one year you spend $11,340 on housing, what is your salary for that year?

19. A charity has raised $7500, with a goal of raising $60,000. What percent of the goal has been raised?

20. A charity has raised $225,000, with a goal of raising $500,000. What percent of the goal has been raised?

In Problems 21–38, solve each formula for the specified variable. Do you recognize the formula? If so, what does it describe?

21. $A = LW$ for L

22. $D = RT$ for R

23. $A = \frac{1}{2}bh$ for b

24. $V = \frac{1}{3}Bh$ for B

25. $Prt = I$ for P

26. $C = 2\pi r$ for r

27. $E = mc^2$ for m

28. $V = \pi r^2 h$ for h

29. $y = mx + b$ for m

30. $P = C + MC$ for M

31. $A = \frac{1}{2}(a + b)$ for a

32. $A = \frac{1}{2}(a + b)$ for b

33. $S = P + Prt$ for r

34. $S = P + Prt$ for t

35. $I = E/R$ for R

36. $A = M/(fgd)$ for d

37. $L = a + (n - 1)d$ for n

38. $L = 2d + \pi(a + r)$ for a

In Problems 39–48, solve each equation for y. *Then find the value of* y *for the given value of* x.

39. $3x + y = 6; x = 2$

40. $2x + 6y = -12; x = -2$

41. $2x = 4y - 6; x = 10$

42. $2x - 5y = -10; x = 0$

43. $2y = 6 - 5x; x = -1$

44. $18 = 3y - x; x = -4$

45. $-3x = 21 - 6y; x = 0$

46. $-18 = -2x - 3y; x = -5$

47. $-12 = -x - 4y; x = -3$

48. $2x + 5y = 10; x = -7$

True–False Critical Thinking Problems

49. Which one of the following statements is true?

   a. No real numbers satisfy the equation $y + 3y = 4y$.

   b. If we solve $A = LW$ for W, we obtain $W = \dfrac{L}{A}$.

   c. Solving $y - x = 7$ for y gives $y = x + 7$.

   d. The final step in solving $x - b = 6x - c$ for x is $x = 6x - c + b$.

50. Which one of the following statements is true?

   a. If $ax + b = 0$, then $x = b/a$.

   b. If $a(x - 2) = b$, then $x = \dfrac{b + 2a}{a}$.

   c. If a car can be rented for $80.00 plus $0.40 cents per mile, then the rental cost C after x miles is described by the model $C = 80 + .40x$.

   d. If $A = \dfrac{1}{2}bh$, then $b = \dfrac{A}{2h}$.

Technology Problem

51. The world record for the mile run has decreased with surprising regularity since 1954.

World Record for the Mile Run

Name (country)	Year	Time
Roger Bannister (Great Britain)	1954	3:59.4
John Landy (Australia)	1954	3:58
Derek Ibbotson (Great Britain)	1957	3:57.2
Herb Elliott (Australia)	1958	3:54.5
Peter Snell (New Zealand)	1962	3:54.4
Peter Snell (New Zealand)	1964	3:54.1
Michel Jazy (France)	1965	3:53.6
Jim Ryun (United States)	1966	3:51.3
Jim Ryun (United States)	1967	3:51.1
Filbert Bayi (Tanzania)	1975	3:50
John Walker (New Zealand)	1975	3:49.4
Sebastian Coe (Great Britain)	1979	3:49.1
Steve Ovett (Great Britain)	1980	3:48.8
Sebastian Coe (Great Britain)	1981	3:48.53
Steve Ovett (Great Britain)	1981	3:48.4
Sebastian Coe (Great Britain)	1981	3:47.33
Steve Cram (Great Britain)	1985	3:46.31
Noureddine Morceli (Algeria)	1993	3:44.39

The mathematical model

$$y = -0.358709x + 256.835$$

describes the projected time for the mile run (y, in seconds) x years after 1900. (Notice how the model provides useful data much outside the range of values contained in the table.) In what year will the mile be run in 3 minutes flat? (*Hint:* Let $y = 180$ seconds and use a calculator to solve for x.)

Writing in Mathematics

52. Explain how the ability to solve linear equations can be used to acquire information about variables contained in mathematical models. Be sure to explain what is meant by a mathematical model.

Critical Thinking Problems

53. The model

$$F = \frac{9}{5}C + 32$$

describes Fahrenheit temperature (F) in terms of Celsius temperature (C), and the model $K = C + 273$ describes temperature on the Kelvin scale (K) in terms of Celsius temperature (C). If normal body temperature is 98.6°F, what is the corresponding temperature on the Kelvin scale?

54. The height (h, in feet) of water in a fountain is described by the model

$$h = -16t^2 + 64t$$

and the velocity (v, in feet per second) of water in the fountain is described by $v = -32t + 64$. Find the time when the water's velocity is 16 feet per second, and then find the water's height at that time.

Review Problems

Use the graph to answer these questions.

55. Estimate the percent of 20-year-old young men who are sexually active.

56. What group has approximately half of its members sexually active?

57. Describe the trend shown by this graph.

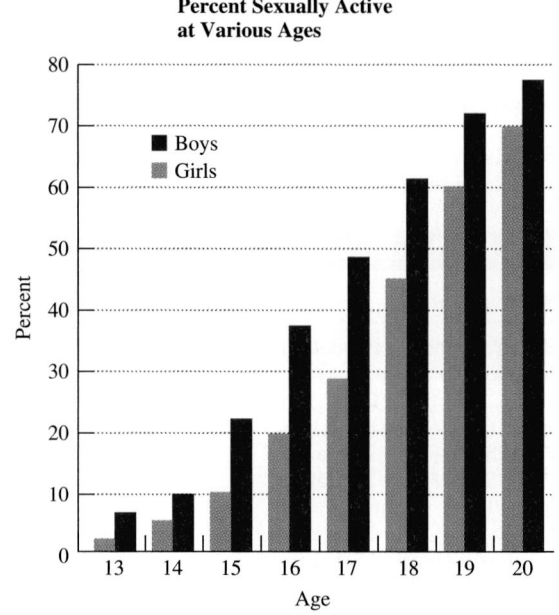

Percent Sexually Active at Various Ages

Source: Alan Guttmacher Institute, 1994

SECTION 2.5

Solutions Manual Tutorial Video 3

An Introduction to Problem Solving

Objective

1 Solve algebraic word problems using linear equations.

The year is 1700 B.C. The place is Egypt. A brief sentence in a 3600-year-old Egyptian papyrus reads, "A quantity and its seventh make 19."

From the time of the pharaohs, people have been intrigued by applying mathematics to situations that are described verbally. Some of these situations are artificial, some intended to amuse, and others may produce potentially useful information. In all cases, skills for solving algebraic word problems form the basis for problem-solving strategies in a wide variety of disciplines. This section presents an approach for solving verbal problems that can be used as a strategy for numerous kinds of problems.

Problem solving is the central theme of algebra. Throughout the previous sections we have touched on some problems that were presented in English. We *translated* from the ordinary language of English into the language of algebraic equations. But to translate, we must understand the English prose and also be familiar with the forms of algebraic language. Here are some general steps we will follow in solving word problems:

Solve algebraic word problems using linear equations.

> **Strategy for solving word problems**
>
> *Step 1.* Read the problem and determine the quantities that are involved. Let *x* (or any variable) represent one of the quantities in the problem.
> *Step 2.* If necessary, write expressions for any other unknown quantities in the problem in terms of *x*.
> *Step 3.* Write an equation in *x* that describes the verbal conditions of the problem.
> *Step 4.* Solve the equation written in step 3 and answer the question in the problem.
> *Step 5.* Check the solution *in the original wording* of the problem, not in the equation obtained from the words.

Take great care with step 1 of the strategy for solving word problems. Reading mathematics is not the same as reading a newspaper. Reading the problem involves slowly working your way through its parts, making notes on what is given, and perhaps rereading the problem a few times. Only at this point should you let *x* represent one of the quantities.

The most difficult step in this process is step 3 since it involves translating verbal conditions into an algebraic equation. In some situations, the conditions are given explicitly. In other instances, the conditions are only implied, making it necessary to use one's knowledge about the type of word problem to generate an English sentence that must then be translated into an equation.

Translations of some commonly used English phrases are listed in Table 2.1.

iscover for yourself

Cover the right column in Table 2.1 with a sheet of paper and try to write the algebraic expression on your own. Then slide the paper down and check your answer. Work through the entire table in this manner.

TABLE 2.1 Algebraic Translations of English Phrases

English Phrase	Algebraic Expression
Addition	
The sum of a number and seven	$x + 7$
Five more than a number	$x + 5$
A number increased by six	$x + 6$
Subtraction	
A number minus four	$x - 4$
A number decreased by five	$x - 5$
A number subtracted from eight	$8 - x$
The difference between a number and six	$x - 6$
The difference between six and a number	$6 - x$
Seven less than a number	$x - 7$
Seven minus a number	$7 - x$
Nine fewer than a number	$x - 9$
Multiplication	
Five times a number	$5x$
The product of three and a number	$3x$
Two-thirds of a number (used with fractions)	$\frac{2}{3}x$
Seventy-five percent of a number (used with decimals)	$0.75x$
Thirteen multiplied by a number	$13x$
A number multiplied by thirteen	$13x$
Twice a number	$2x$
Division	
A number divided by three	$\dfrac{x}{3}$
The quotient of seven and a number	$\dfrac{7}{x}$
The quotient of a number and seven	$\dfrac{x}{7}$
The reciprocal of a number	$\dfrac{1}{x}$
More Than One Operation	
The sum of twice a number and seven	$2x + 7$
Twice the sum of a number and seven	$2(x + 7)$
Three times the sum of one and twice a number	$3(2x + 1)$
Nine subtracted from eight times a number	$8x - 9$
Twenty-five percent of the sum of three times a number and fourteen	$0.25(3x + 14)$
Seven times a number increased by twenty-four	$7x + 24$
Seven times the sum of a number and twenty-four	$7(x + 24)$

EXAMPLE 1   A Word Problem Involving an Unknown Number

Nine subtracted from eight times a number is 39. Find the number.

Solution

Step 1. Read the problem and determine the quantities that are involved. Since we are asked to find a number, let x = the number.
Step 2. There are no other unknown quantities to find.
Step 3. Write an equation in x that describes the verbal conditions of the problem.

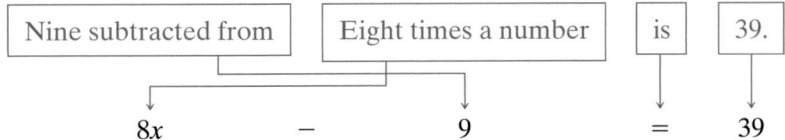

Step 4. Solve the equation and answer the question.

$8x - 9 = 39$ This is the algebraic equation for the given sentence.

$8x = 48$ Add 9 to both sides.

$x = 6$ Divide both sides by 8.

The number is 6.

Step 5. Check the solution in the original wording of the problem.

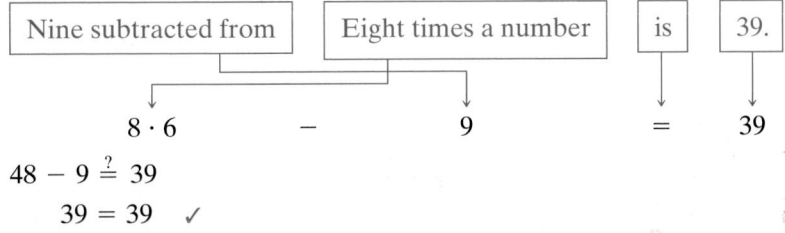

$48 - 9 \overset{?}{=} 39$

$39 = 39$ ✓

This verifies that the number is 6.

Example 2 involves consecutive integers, such as 8, 9, and 10 or 23, 24, and 25. If we let x represent the first integer in a series of consecutive integers, the next integer can be represented by $x + 1$, the third integer by $x + 2$, and so on.

EXAMPLE 2   **A Word Problem Involving Consecutive Integers**

Two pages that face each other in a book have 145 as the sum of their page numbers. What are the page numbers?

Solution

Page numbers on facing pages are consecutive integers.

Step 1. Let x = the smaller page number (or the first integer).
Step 2. Let $x + 1$ = the larger page number (or the next consecutive integer).
Step 3. Write an equation in x that describes the verbal conditions. Since the facing page numbers are consecutive integers and have a sum of 145:

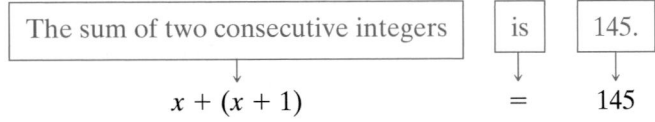

Step 4. Solve the equation and answer the question.

$x + (x + 1) = 145$ This is the algebraic equation for the implied sentence.

$2x + 1 = 145$ Combine like terms.

$2x = 144$ Subtract 1 from both sides.

$x = 72$ Divide both sides by 2.

ENRICHMENT ESSAY

Checking Proposed Solutions

The sentence "Two facing pages have 145 as the sum of their page numbers" makes sense only when the proposed solution, 72 and 73, is substituted into it and it is read from beginning to end. "Two facing pages with numbers of 72 and 73 have 145 as the sum of their page numbers" now becomes a meaningful sentence.

The situation is similar to the letters on the license plates in the accompanying figure. By themselves, each license plate is meaningless. The same is true of the phrases and sentences that make up an algebraic word problem. But when the license plates are read in a continuous manner, much like a word problem with the proposed solution substituted into the wording, the situation takes on meaning and significance.

Why should the proposed solution to a word problem be checked in the original wording of the problem and not in the equation obtained from the words?

Mike Wilkins "Preamble" 1987. Painted metal on vinyl and wood. 96 × 96 in. National Museum of American Art, Washington, DC, USA/Art Resource, NY

Thus,

The smaller page number = x = 72.

The larger page number = $x + 1$ = 72 + 1 = 73.

The page numbers are 72 and 73.

Step 5. Check the solution in the original wording of the problem. The facing pages have a page-number sum of 145.

$$72 + 73 \stackrel{?}{=} 145$$
$$145 = 145 \quad \checkmark$$

This verifies that the page numbers are 72 and 73. ■

Some algebraic word problems involve consecutive odd integers, such as 5, 7, and 9, or consecutive even integers, such as 6, 8, and 10. In both these situations, we must continuously add 2 to move from one integer to the next successive integer in the list.

Table 2.2 should be helpful in solving consecutive integer problems.

TABLE 2.2 Consecutive Integers

English Phrase	Algebraic Expression	Example
Two consecutive integers	$x, x + 1$	$13, 14$
Three consecutive integers	$x, x + 1, x + 2$	$-8, -7, -6$
Two consecutive even integers	$x, x + 2$	$40, 42$
Two consecutive odd integers	$x, x + 2$	$-37, -35$
Three consecutive even integers	$x, x + 2, x + 4$	$30, 32, 34$
Three consecutive odd integers	$x, x + 2, x + 4$	$9, 11, 13$

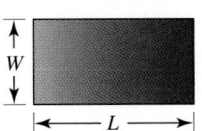

Perimeter $= 2L + 2W$

Example 3 involves both consecutive even integers and the perimeter of a rectangle. The formula $P = 2L + 2W$ describes the perimeter P of a rectangle in terms of its length L and its width W.

EXAMPLE 3   Art and Consecutive Even Integers

Andy Warhol (1928–1987) defined his art entirely on the shallow plane of recognizable images. "If you want to know all about Andy Warhol, just look at the surface of my paintings and there I am," he said. "There's nothing behind it." Warhol's first gallery show, in the fall of 1962, included 32 identical works, each a painting of a Campbell's soup can. Each uniform work has dimensions that are the first and third of three consecutive even integers. Each canvas, with no trace of expressive gesture or individuality, has a perimeter of 72 inches. What are the dimensions of each piece?

Andy Warhol "Campbell's Soup Can" 1962, synthetic polymer paint on canvas, thirty-two works, each 20 × 16 in. (50.8 × 40.6 cm). The Museum of Modern Art, New York. Purchase and partial gift of Irving Blum. Photograph © 1997 The Museum of Modern Art, New York. © 1998 The Andy Warhol Foundation for the Visual Arts/Artists Rights Society (ARS), New York.

Solution

Step 1. Let x = the width of each piece.
Step 2. After x, the next consecutive even integer is $x + 2$. After $x + 2$, the next consecutive even integer is $x + 4$. Since the dimensions are the first and third of three consecutive even integers, let $x + 4$ = the length of each piece.
Step 3. Write an equation in x that describes the verbal conditions. We are given that the perimeter of each piece is 72 inches.

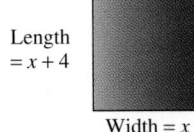

Length $= x + 4$

Width $= x$

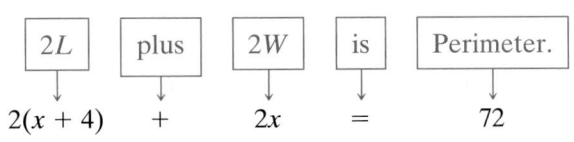

$2L$	plus	$2W$	is	Perimeter.
$2(x + 4)$	$+$	$2x$	$=$	72

The perimeter of a rectangle is the sum of twice its length and twice its width.

Step 4. Solve the equation and answer the question.

$$2(x + 4) + 2x = 72 \quad \text{This is the equation from the formula for a rectangle's perimeter.}$$
$$2x + 8 + 2x = 72 \quad \text{Apply the distributive property.}$$
$$4x + 8 = 72 \quad \text{Combine like terms.}$$
$$4x = 64 \quad \text{Subtract 8 from both sides.}$$
$$x = 16 \quad \text{Divide both sides by 4.}$$

Thus,

The width of each piece $= x = 16$ inches.
The length of each piece $= x + 4 = 16 + 4 = 20$ inches.

The dimensions of each piece are 16 inches by 20 inches.
Step 5. Check. The perimeter of each piece is $2(16) + 2(20) = 72$ inches. This checks with the conditions given in the problem. ∎

Figure 2.4

| EXAMPLE 4 | **Constructing a Ski Ramp** |

A ski ramp is to be built from a 135-foot board. Figure 2.4 indicates that the board must be cut into three pieces. The longest piece is three times the length of the shortest piece, and the middle-sized piece is 35 feet longer than the shortest piece. How long are the pieces?

Solution

Step 1. Let x represent one of the quantities. Notice that the shortest piece is mentioned in both comparisons. We let

$x =$ the length of the shortest piece.

Step 2. Represent the other unknown quantities in terms of x.

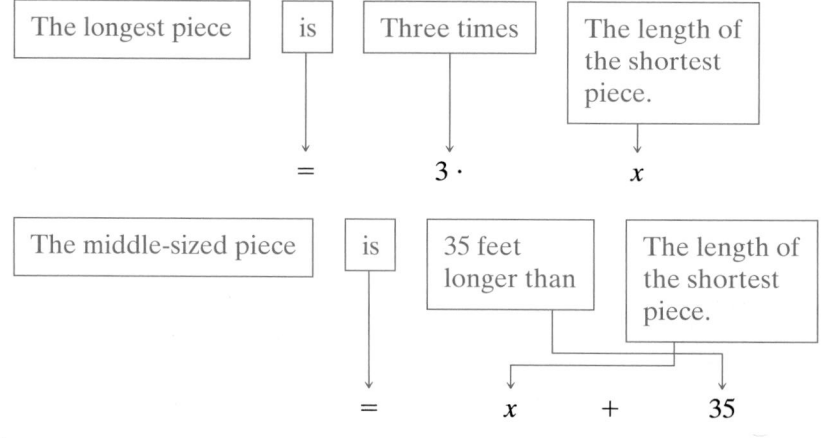

Thus,

$3x =$ the length of the longest piece.
$x + 35 =$ the length of the middle-sized piece.

Step 3. Write an equation in x that describes the conditions.

The sketch in Figure 2.5 enables us to state the conditions.

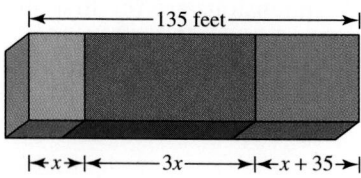

Figure 2.5

The three pieces used to construct a ski ramp

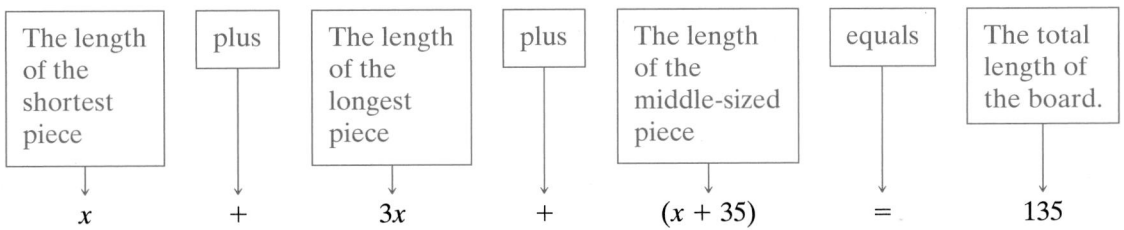

The length of the shortest piece	plus	The length of the longest piece	plus	The length of the middle-sized piece	equals	The total length of the board.
x	$+$	$3x$	$+$	$(x + 35)$	$=$	135

Step 4. Solve the equation and answer the question.

$$x + 3x + (x + 35) = 135 \qquad \text{This is the equation implied by the problem's conditions.}$$
$$5x + 35 = 135 \qquad \text{Combine like terms on the left side.}$$
$$5x = 100 \qquad \text{Subtract 35 from both sides.}$$
$$x = 20 \qquad \text{Divide both sides by 5.}$$

Thus,

The length of the shortest piece $= x = 20$.

The length of the longest piece $= 3x = 3(20) = 60$.

The length of the middle-sized piece $= x + 35 = 20 + 35 = 55$.

The shortest piece is 20 feet long, the longest piece is 60 feet long, and the middle-sized piece is 55 feet long.

Step 5. Check.

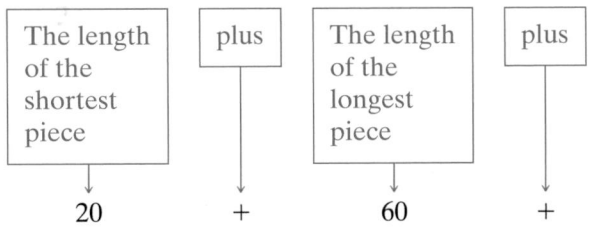

The length of the shortest piece	plus	The length of the longest piece	plus
20	$+$	60	$+$

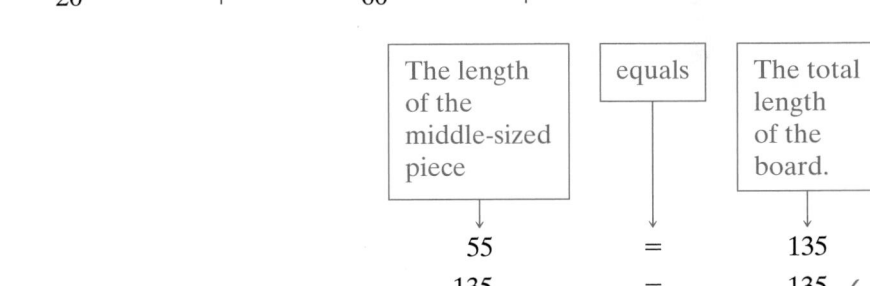

The length of the middle-sized piece	equals	The total length of the board.
55	$=$	135
135	$=$	135 ✓

This verifies that the pieces measure 20 feet, 60 feet, and 55 feet. ■

EXAMPLE 5 Television Sets per 1000 Persons

Few people today doubt the pervasiveness of television's influence in America. A great majority of American households have two or more televisions. Indeed, the number of television sets per 1000 persons in the United States is only 55 fewer than twice that in Great Britain. If the average number of televisions per thousand in the United States and Great Britain is 625, determine the number of televisions in each country for every 1000 persons.

Bill Roseman, *The Champion,* 1964/Epstein/Powell Gallery, New York.

Solution

Step 1. Let *x* represent one of the quantities.

Let x = the number of televisions per 1000 persons in Great Britain.

Step 2. Represent the other quantities in terms of *x*.

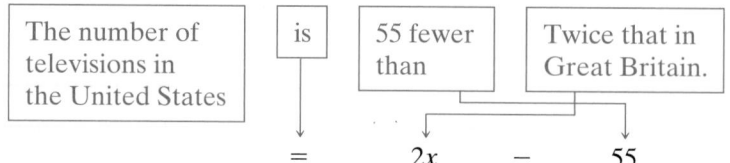

Thus,

Step 3. Write an equation in *x* that describes the conditions.

$2x - 55$ = the number of televisions per 1000 persons in the United States.

The United States and Great Britain average 625 televisions per 1000 persons. The average (or the mean) is the sum of the number of television sets in the two countries divided by 2:

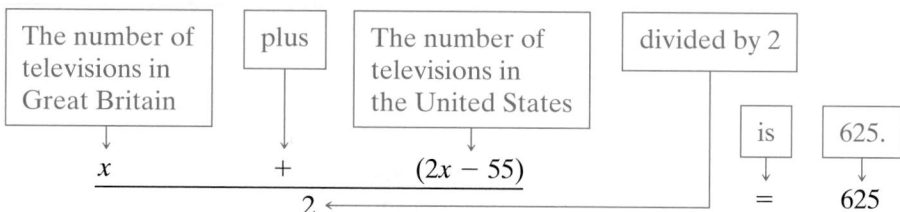

Step 4. Solve the equation and answer the question.

$$\frac{x + (2x - 55)}{2} = 625$$ This is the equation for the given conditions.

$$2\left[\frac{x + (2x - 55)}{2}\right] = 2(625)$$ Clear fractions by multiplying both sides by 2.

$$\frac{2}{1} \cdot \left[\frac{x + (2x - 55)}{2}\right] = 2(625)$$ Observe that 2 cancels in the numerator and denominator on the left. You will probably do this step mentally.

$$x + (2x - 55) = 1250$$ Multiply on the right side.

$$3x - 55 = 1250$$ Combine like terms on the left side.

$$3x = 1305$$ Add 55 to both sides.

$$x = 435$$ Divide both sides by 3.

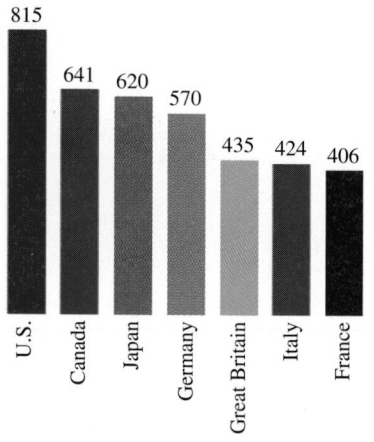

Number of TV Sets per 1000 Persons

Source: Human Development Report 1993

Thus,

The number of television sets per 1000 persons in Great Britain = x = 435.

The number of television sets per 1000 persons in the United States = $2x - 55 = 2(435) - 55 = 870 - 55 = 815$.

There are 435 television sets per 1000 persons in Great Britain and 815 in the United States.

Step 5. Check.

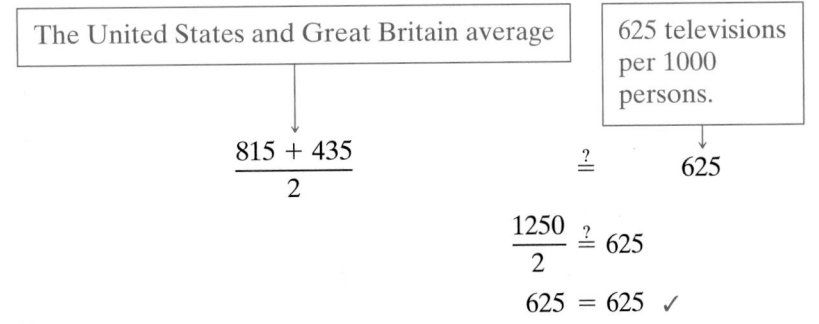

EXAMPLE 6 Problem Solving Using a Circle Graph

The circle graph in Figure 2.6 shows the percentage of people estimated to have the HIV virus in different regions of the world in 1993. If approximately 1 million people in North America have the virus, how many people worldwide were infected in 1993?

Solution

Step 1. Let x represent one of the quantities. (Omit step 2. There is only one unknown.)

Let x = the number of people (in millions) infected worldwide.
We are given that 1 million people in North America have the virus. The circle graph shows this is 8% of those infected worldwide.

Step 3. Write an equation in x that describes the verbal conditions.

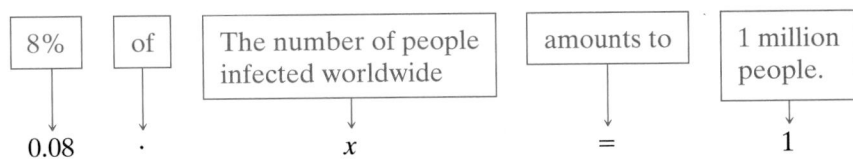

Step 4. Solve the equation and answer the question.

$0.08x = 1$ This is the equation implied by translating the given conditions.

$x = \dfrac{1}{0.08}$ Solve for x by dividing both sides by 0.08. If you prefer you can first multiply both sides by 100 to clear the decimals.

$x = 12.5$

Step 5. Check.

Percentage of People Infected with HIV

Thus, an estimated 12.5 million people worldwide were infected with the HIV virus in 1993.

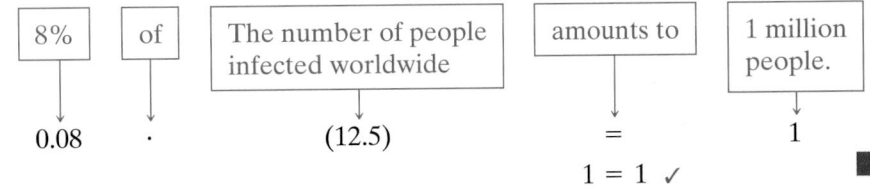

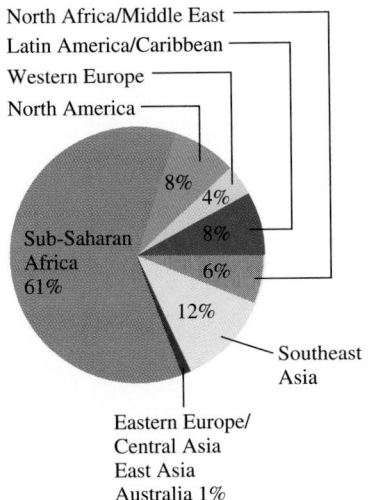

Southeast Asia

Eastern Europe/
Central Asia
East Asia
Australia 1%

Figure 2.6

Source: *Newsweek* (March 23, 1993)

Our five-step strategy for solving word problems can be applied to numerous situations.

EXAMPLE 7 A Price Reduction

After a 35% price reduction, a graphing calculator sold for $81.90. What was the calculator's price before the reduction?

Discover for yourself

Example 7 asks for the calculator's price before reduction. Before solving the problem using algebra, let's consider a few specific values for this price.

Price before Reduction	Reduced Price
	35% Price Reduction
$100	$100 − (0.35)(100)$
$120	$120 − (0.35)(120)$
$140	$140 − (0.35)(140)$
$160	$160 − (0.35)(160)$

Do you see a pattern forming? If the price before reduction is x dollars, use this pattern to write an algebraic expression for the reduced price.

Take a moment to compute the four reduced prices shown above. Since the actual reduced price of the calculator is $81.90, what is a reasonable estimate of its price before the reduction?

Step 1. Let x represent one of the quantities.

Step 2. Represent the other quantities in terms of x.

Solution

Let x = the original price of the calculator prior to the reduction. Another unknown quantity is the reduction. We know that the reduction is 35% of the original price.

Reduction	is	35%	of	The original price.
↓	↓	↓	↓	↓
	$=$	0.35	$\cdot$	x

Thus,

$$0.35x = \text{the reduction.}$$

Step 3. Write an equation in x that describes the conditions.

Implied within this problem is the statement:

Original price	minus	Reduction	equals	Reduced price.
↓	↓	↓	↓	↓
x	$-$	$0.35x$	$=$	81.90

Step 4. Solve the equation and answer the question.

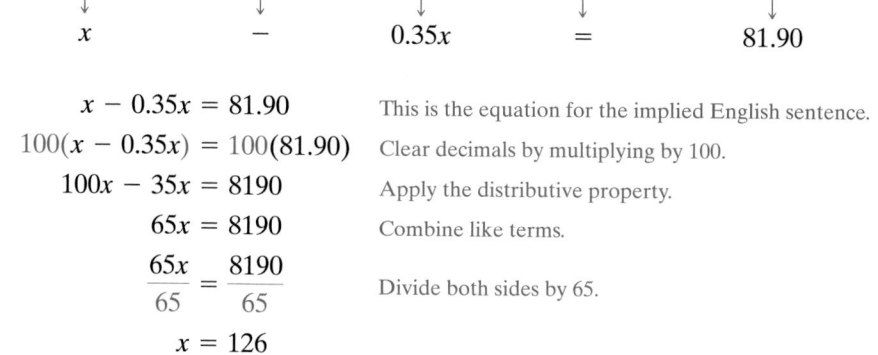

$$x - 0.35x = 81.90 \qquad \text{This is the equation for the implied English sentence.}$$
$$100(x - 0.35x) = 100(81.90) \qquad \text{Clear decimals by multiplying by 100.}$$
$$100x - 35x = 8190 \qquad \text{Apply the distributive property.}$$
$$65x = 8190 \qquad \text{Combine like terms.}$$
$$\frac{65x}{65} = \frac{8190}{65} \qquad \text{Divide both sides by 65.}$$
$$x = 126$$

Step 5. Check.

The graphing calculator's price before the reduction was $126.00.
The reduction is 35% of 126.

$$(0.35)(126) = 44.10$$

The reduced price is the original price minus the reduction.

$$126 − 44.10 = 81.90$$

This checks with the conditions of the problem.   ∎

EXAMPLE 8   Phone Charges

The rate for a particular long distance telephone call is $0.55 for the first
minute and $0.40 for each additional minute. Determine the length of a call
that cost $6.95.

D iscover for yourself

Before solving Example 8 using algebra, let's consider a few specific values for the length
of the long distance call.

Length of Call	Cost
10 minutes	0.55 for first minute + 0.40 for next 9 minutes = 0.55 + 0.40(9)
11 minutes	0.55 for first minute + 0.40 for next 10 minutes = 0.55 + 0.40(10)
12 minutes	0.55 for first minute + 0.40 for next 11 minutes = 0.55 + 0.40(11)
13 minutes	0.55 for first minute + 0.40 for next 12 minutes = 0.55 + 0.40(12)

Do you see a pattern forming? If the length of the call is *x* minutes, use this pattern to
write an algebraic expression for the cost of the call.
    Take a moment to compute the four costs shown in the table above. Since the ac-
tual cost of the long distance call is **$6.95**, what is a reasonable estimate for the length of
the call?

Solution

Step 1. Let *x* represent one of the
quantities.

Step 2. Represent the other
quantities in terms of *x*.

Let x = the length of the long distance call.
Thus,

$$x − 1 = \text{the number of minutes after the first minute.}$$

Implied within this problem is the statement:

Step 3. Write an equation in *x* that describes the conditions.

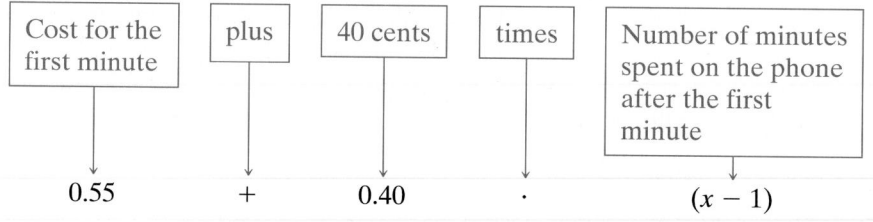

| Cost for the first minute | plus | 40 cents | times | Number of minutes spent on the phone after the first minute |

0.55   +   0.40   ·   (x − 1)

Step 4. Solve the equation and answer the question.

| equals | Total cost of the call. |

=   6.95

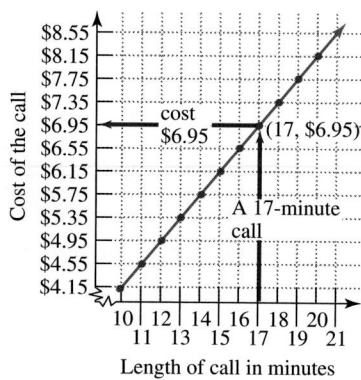

The cost of a 17-minute call

$$0.55 + 0.40(x - 1) = 6.95 \quad \text{This is the equation that models the problem's conditions.}$$

$$55 + 40(x - 1) = 695 \quad \text{Multiply by 100.}$$

$$55 + 40x - 40 = 695 \quad \text{Apply the distributive property.}$$

$$40x + 15 = 695 \quad \text{Combine like terms.}$$

$$40x = 680 \quad \text{Subtract 15 from both sides.}$$

$$x = 17 \quad \text{Divide both sides by 40.}$$

The length of the call was 17 minutes.

Step 5. Check.

Cost for first minute = $0.55.

Cost for each additional minute at $0.40 per minute = ($0.40)(16) = $6.40.

Total cost of the call = $0.55 + $6.40 = $6.95.

This checks with the conditions of the problem.   ■

EXAMPLE 9   **Education and Income**

It is reasonable to assume that increased education provides access to higher-paying jobs. Using variables to represent years of education and income, mathematicians have developed models to show this relationship. A simplified form of one such model indicates that yearly income increases by $2600 for each year of education. It also shows that a person with no education earns $7200 yearly. Using this model, how many years of education are needed to earn $43,600 per year?

iscover for yourself

Before we solve Example 9 using algebra, let's consider what happens to income as the number of years of education increases. Recall that a person with 0 years of education earns $7200 and income increases by $2600 for each additional year of education.

Years of Education	Yearly Income
0	$7200
1	$7200 + 1(2600)
2	($7200 + $2600) + $2600 = 7200 + 2(2600)
3	[$7200 + 2($2600)] + $2600 = 7200 + 3(2600)
4	[$7200 + 3($2600)] + $2600 = 7200 + 4(2600)
5	[$7200 + 4($2600)] + $2600 = 7200 + 5(2600)
6	[$7200 + 5($2600)] + $2600 = 7200 + 6(2600)

Do you see a pattern forming? If the number of years of education is represented by x, use the pattern to write an algebraic expression for the yearly income.

Take a moment to compute the yearly incomes in the second column of the table. Since we are interested in a yearly income of **$43,600**, what is a reasonable estimate for the number of years of education needed to earn this amount?

Solution

Step 1. Let x represent one of the quantities. (With only one unknown, omit step 2.)

Let x = the years of education needed to earn $43,600 per year.
The problem states that yearly income equals $7200 plus $2600 for each year of education. Thus,

Step 3. Write an equation in x that describes the verbal conditions.

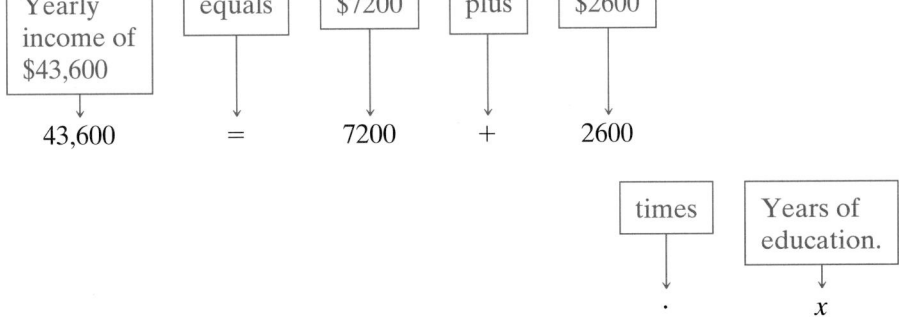

Step 4. Solve the equation and answer the question.

$43,600 = 7200 + 2600x$ This is the equation that translates the verbal conditions of the model.

$36,400 = 2600x$ Isolate the term with the variable on the right by subtracting 7200 from both sides.

$14 = x$ Divide both sides by 2600.

Our solution indicates that 14 years of education are needed to earn $43,600 per year.

Step 5. Check.

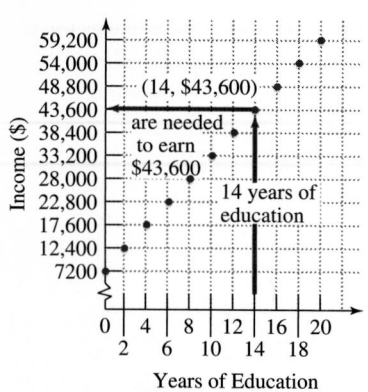

Income for 14 years of education

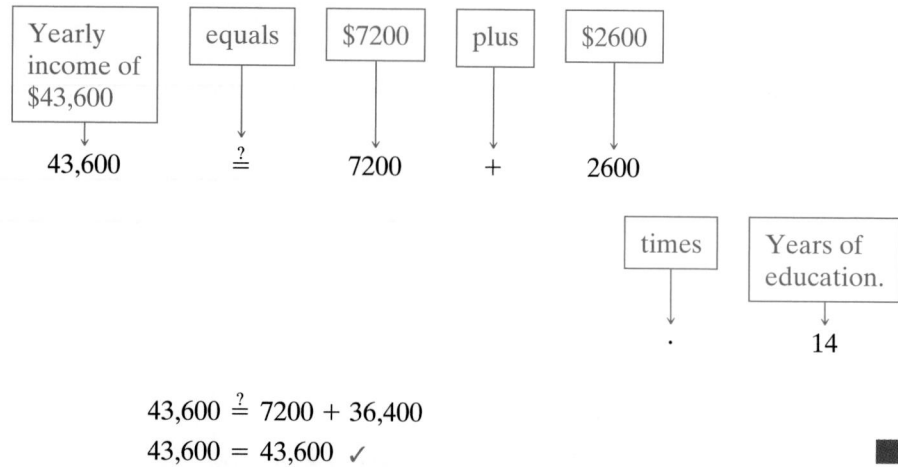

$$43,600 \overset{?}{=} 7200 + 36,400$$
$$43,600 = 43,600 \checkmark$$

■

| EXAMPLE 10 | **The Impact of Gender on Education and Income** |

Numerous variables affect the relationship between education and income. Once again, a simplified form of two such models focuses on the effect of gender. Yearly income for men increases by $1600 each year of education; men with no education earn $6300 yearly. For women, the comparable model involves a $1200 increase for each year of education; women with no education earn $2100 yearly. Using these models, how many years of education must a woman achieve to earn the same yearly salary as a man with 11 years of education?

Solution

Step 1. Let *x* represent one of the quantities. (With only one unknown, omit Step 2.)

Let x = the years of education needed by a woman to earn the same yearly salary as a man with 11 years of education.

Step 3. Write an equation in *x* that describes the verbal conditions.

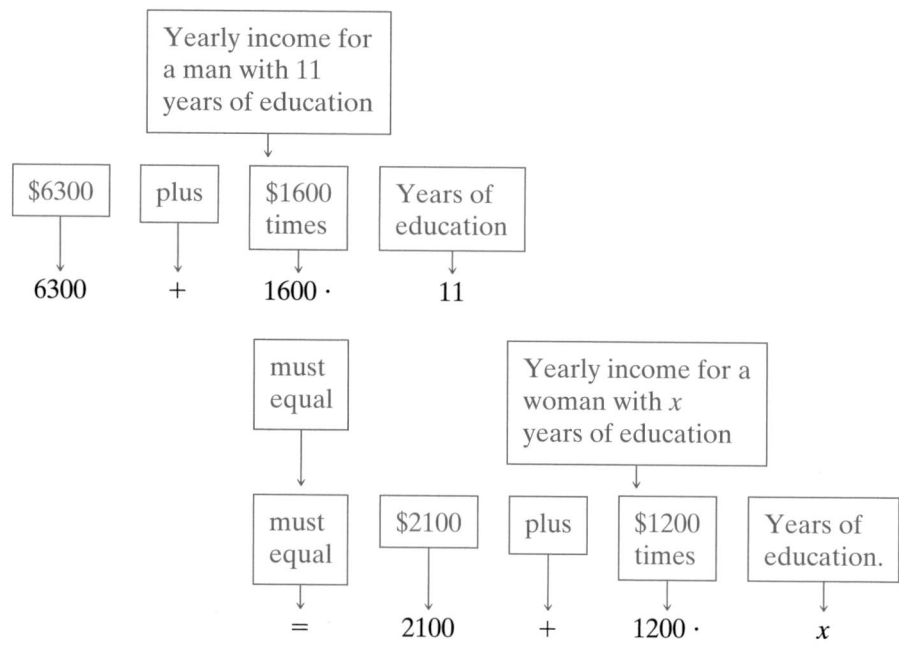

Step 4. Solve the equation and answer the question.

$$6300 + 1600 \cdot 11 = 2100 + 1200x$$

This is the equation that translates the verbal conditions of the models.

$$23{,}900 = 2100 + 1200x$$

Multiply and add on the left.

$$21{,}800 = 1200x$$

Subtract 2100 from both sides.

$$\frac{21{,}800}{1200} = x$$

Divide both sides by 1200.

$$x \approx 18.2$$

Perform the computation. Remember that $\approx$ means "is approximately equal to."

The models show that a woman must achieve approximately 18.2 years of education to earn the same salary as a man with 11 years of education. ∎

D iscover for yourself

Take a few minutes to check the solution to Example 10. Explain how the line graphs shown in Figure 2.7 illustrate the solution.

Years of Education	Predicted Average Personal Wages for Men
0	$6300
1	$7900
2	$9500
3	$11,100
4	$12,700
5	$14,300
6	$15,900
7	$17,500
8	$19,100
9	$20,700
10	$22,300
11	$23,900
12	$25,500
13	$27,100
14	$28,700
15	$30,300
16	$31,900
17	$33,500
18	$35,100
19	$36,700
20	$38,300

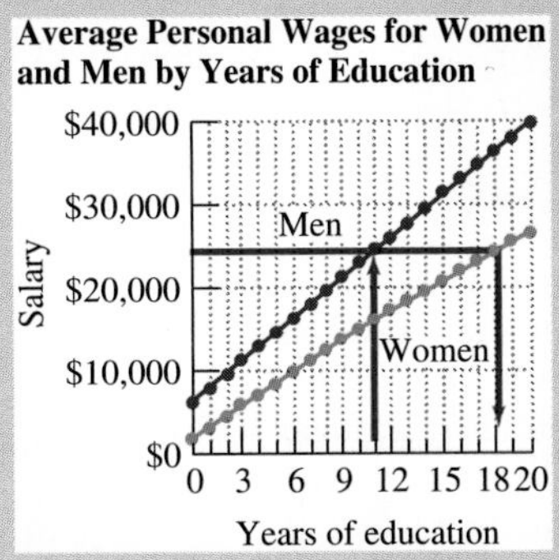

Figure 2.7

Average Personal Wages for Women and Men by Years of Education

Years of Education	Predicted Average Personal Wages for Women
0	$2100
1	$3300
2	$4500
3	$5700
4	$6900
5	$8100
6	$9300
7	$10,500
8	$11,700
9	$12,900
10	$14,100
11	$15,300
12	$16,500
13	$17,700
14	$18,900
15	$20,100
16	$21,300
17	$22,500
18	$23,700
19	$24,900
20	$26,100

PROBLEM SET 2.5

Practice and Application Problems

1. Seven subtracted from five times a number is 123. Find the number.

2. Eight subtracted from six times a number is 184. Find the number.

3. The sum of four and twice some number is 36. Find the number.

4. The sum of five and three times some number is 29. Find the number.

5. Twice the sum of four and some number is 36. Find the number. Describe how this problem differs from Problem 3.

6. Three times the sum of five and some number is 48. Find the number. Describe how this problem differs from Problem 4.

7. The sum of the page numbers on the facing pages of a book is 629. What are the page numbers?

8. The sum of the page numbers on the facing pages of a book is 525. What are the page numbers?

9. The front of the fence shown in the figure is divided into two triangles by a diagonal piece of wood. In each triangle, the sides have lengths that are consecutive integers. The shortest side of the triangle is represented by x meters. If the triangle has a perimeter of 12 meters, how long is the diagonal piece of wood?

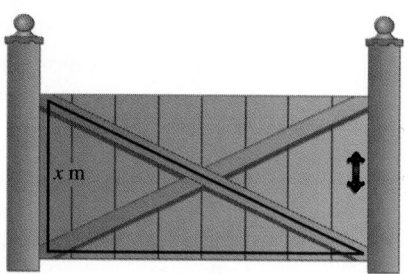

10. The rectangular bathtub shown in the figure is divided into two triangles by the diagonal drawn from lower-left to upper-right. The sides of the outlined triangle have lengths that are consecutive even integers. The shortest side of the triangle is represented by x feet. If the triangle has a perimeter of 24 feet, what are the bathtub's dimensions?

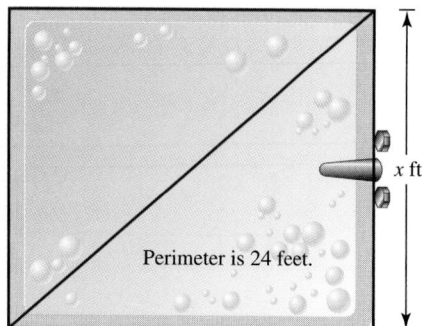

Perimeter is 24 feet.

11. The rectangular playground shown in the figure on the upper right has dimensions that are consecutive even integers. The playground's perimeter is 332 feet. Find the playground's dimensions.

12. The rectangular patio shown in the figure has dimensions that are consecutive odd integers. The patio's perimeter is 48 feet. Find the patio's dimensions.

13. The circle graph shows residence of Asian-Americans. The percents for the Midwest and South sectors are missing from the graph, but it is known that the numbers in the sectors are consecutive odd percents (such as 81% and 83%). Find the percent of Asian-Americans living in the Midwest and the South.

Residence of Asian-Americans

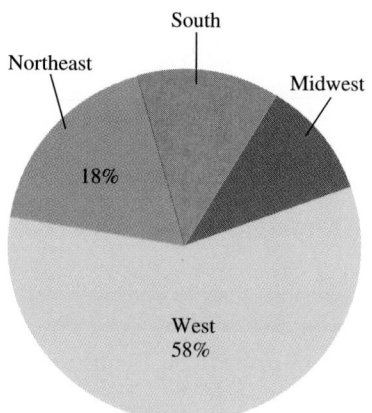

Source: U.S. Bureau of the Census

14. The circle graph shows residence of the total U.S. population. The percents for the Northeast and West are missing from the graph, but it is known that the numbers in the sectors are consecutive percents (such as 80% and 81%). Find the percent of the U.S. population living in the Northeast and the West.

Total U.S. Population

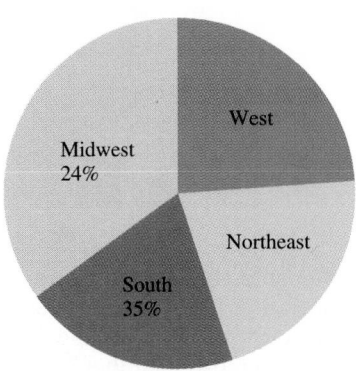

Source: U.S. Bureau of the Census

15. A 64-meter rope is cut into three pieces. The second piece is twice as long as the first. The third piece is 4 meters longer than the first. How long is each piece of rope?

16. A 95-meter wire is cut into three pieces. The second piece is 1 meter shorter than twice as long as the first. The third piece is 4 meters longer than the first. How long is each piece of wire?

In Problems 17–18, information in each table is missing. Use the given conditions to fill in the incomplete data.

17. The number of deaths per year from heart disease exceeds 4 times that from stroke by 140,900. Both diseases combined kill 889,600 Americans each year.

U.S. Causes of Death	
Cause	**Deaths per Year**
Heart disease	
Cancer	530,870
Stroke	
Chronic obstructive pulmonary diseases	101,090
Accidents	88,630
Pneumonia and influenza	81,730
Diabetes	55,110
HIV/AIDS	38,500
Suicide	31,230
Homicide	25,470

Source: Centers for Disease Control, December 31, 1994

18. The loss due to Andrew's wrath exceeded 11 times that of Hugo by $355 million. Together, the two hurricanes caused a loss of $50,695 million.

Costliest Hurricanes in U.S. History			
Year	**Hurricane**	**Area**	**Losses (in millions)**
1992	Andrew	Florida, Louisiana	
1989	Hugo	Georgia to Virginia	
1992	Iniki	Hawaii	$1600
1979	Frederic	Florida to New York	$752
1983	Alicia	Texas	$675
1991	Bob	New Jersey to Maine	$620
1985	Elena	Gulf region	$543
1965	Betsy	Gulf region	$515
1985	Gloria	North Carolina to Maine	$418
1970	Celia	Texas	$309

Source: Insurance Information Institute

19. Many countries are now having second thoughts about nuclear power. The bar graph indicates the number of nuclear reactors no longer in service in 11 selected countries. The number in the United States is four less than twice that of Russia. The number in France is two less than that of Russia. If the three countries have 38 nuclear reactors no longer in service, determine the number of nuclear reactors no longer in service for the United States, Russia, and France. Then use the graph to estimate the number of nuclear reactors not in service for the other eight countries.

20. On the "feelings thermometer" graph shown in the figure, the rating for police is eight less than twice that for gay men and lesbians. The rating for environmentalists is 28 more than that for gay men and lesbians. If the combined ratings for these three groups is 176, find their individual ratings. Which of these ratings do you believe will change in the future? On what basis do you make your predictions?

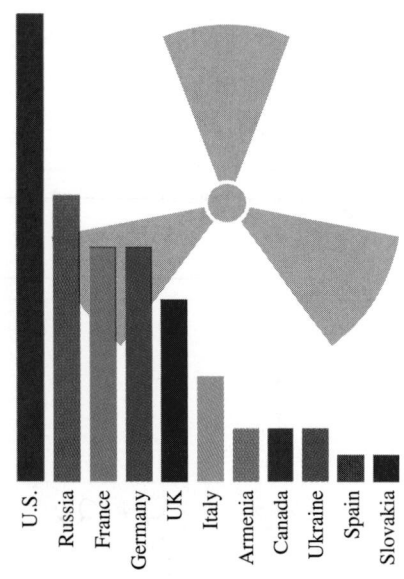

Nuclear Reactors No Longer in Service
1994

Source: *Nuclear News*

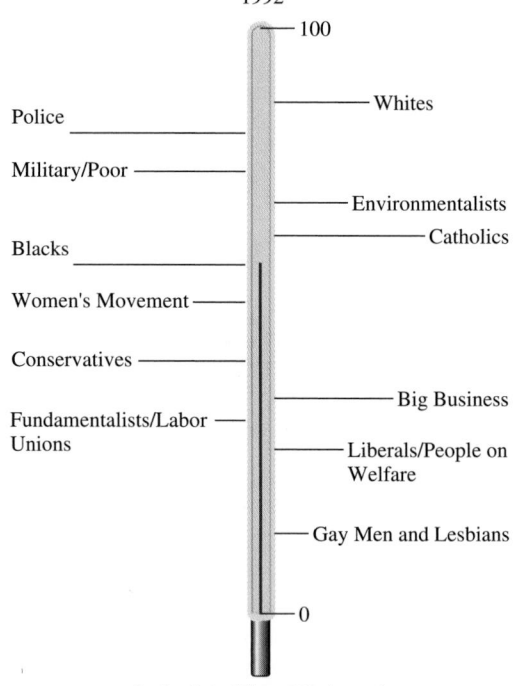

Feelings Thermometer: How Americans View Their Fellow Citizens
1992

Scale: 0 (cold) to 100 (warm)

Source: Mark Hertzog, from American National Election Study 1992, University of Michigan

21. Every year, approximately 1760 Americans suffer spinal cord injuries due to falls. Use the circle graph to determine the number of Americans who suffer spinal cord injuries. Then determine the number of Americans in each of the remaining sectors.

Causes of U.S. Spinal Cord Injuries

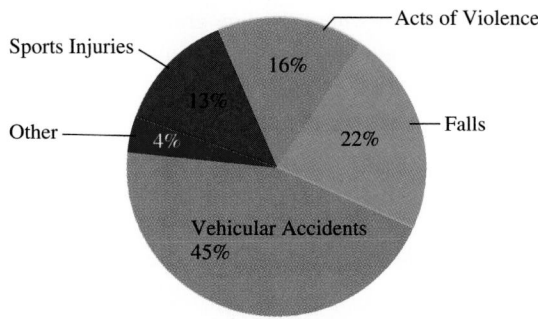

Source: *U.S. News and World Report,* January 24, 1994

22. In 1993, cities received $0.63 billion from state lottery proceeds. Use the circle graph to determine total state lottery proceeds for the year. Then determine the dollar distribution in each of the graph's sectors.

Percent Distribution of 1993 State Lottery Proceeds

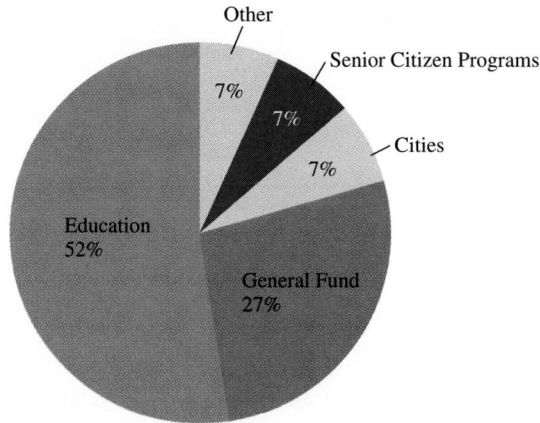

Source: U.S. Bureau of the Census

23. After a 12% price reduction, a car sold for $17,600. What was the car's price before the reduction?

24. After a 20% discount, a VCR cost $320. What was the original price of the VCR?

25. Inclusive of a 6.5% sales tax, a car sold for $17,466. Find the price of the car before the tax was added.

26. Inclusive of 6.5% sales tax, a color television sold for $788.10. Find the price of the television before the tax was added.

27. Markup is the amount added to the dealer's cost of an item to arrive at the selling price of that item. The selling price of a refrigerator is $584. If the markup is 25% of the dealer's cost, what is the dealer's cost of the refrigerator?

28. A calculator costs a dealer $80. Determine the selling price if the markup is 20% of the selling price.

29. After being reduced by two-sevenths of its original price, a sofa sold for $235. What was the sofa's price before the reduction?

30. After being reduced by three-fifths of its original price, a sofa sold for $426. What was the sofa's price before the reduction?

31. The weekday rate for a telephone call is $0.75 for the first minute and $0.60 for each additional minute. Determine the length of a call that cost $12.15.

32. The weekday rate for a telephone call is $0.65 for the first minute and $0.35 for each additional minute. Determine the length of a call that cost $7.30.

33. An advertiser pays workers $45.00 a day plus $0.05 for every advertisement distributed. After a day's work, a person received $82.50. How many advertisements were distributed?

34. A kennel charges a flat fee of $16 plus $12 a day to board an animal. If a bill came to $100, how many days did the animal stay at the kennel?

35. According to a 1995 United Nations report, the increased levels of atmospheric carbon dioxide indicates that global warming is already under way, and the effects could severely damage the world's ecosystems. The graph shows that carbon dioxide concentration accounts for about 55% of the warming. Carbon dioxide concentration of 280 parts per million (ppm) remained fairly constant until 1939. One mathematical model indicates that carbon dioxide has increased by 1.44 ppm for each year after 1939. Using this model, in what year will the concentration reach 366.4 ppm? (*Hint:* Let x = the number of years after 1939 when this will occur.)

Greenhouse Gases
Proportion of Global Warming
Attributed to Various Gases, 1992

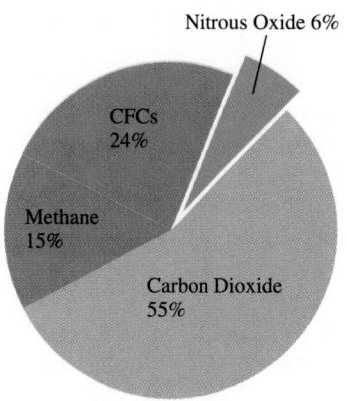

Source: U.S. Office of Technology Assessment

36. In 1990, the average cost of an advertisement during the Super Bowl was $700,000. On the average, this cost has increased by $60,000 each year. Using this model, in what year will the cost of an advertisement during the Super Bowl be $1,480,000? (*Hint:* Let x = the number of years after 1990 when this will occur.)

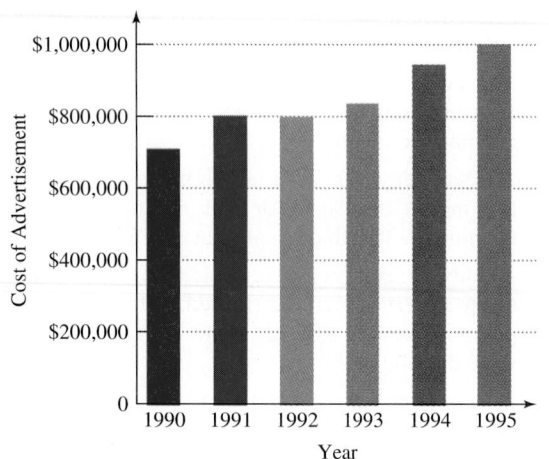

Source: *USA Today*, November 3, 1994

37. Costs for two different kinds of heating systems for a three-bedroom home are given below.

System	Cost to Install	Operating Cost/Year
Solar	$30,000	$150
Electric	$5000	$1100

a. After how many years will the total costs (cost to install plus operating cost/year) for solar heating be $36,000? What will the total costs for electric heating be at that time?

b. After how many years will total costs for solar heating and electric heating be the same? What will be the cost at that time?

c. The line graphs represent costs for both kinds of heating systems over 40 years. Estimate the ordered pair where the line graphs intersect. Explain what this has to do with your answer in part (b).

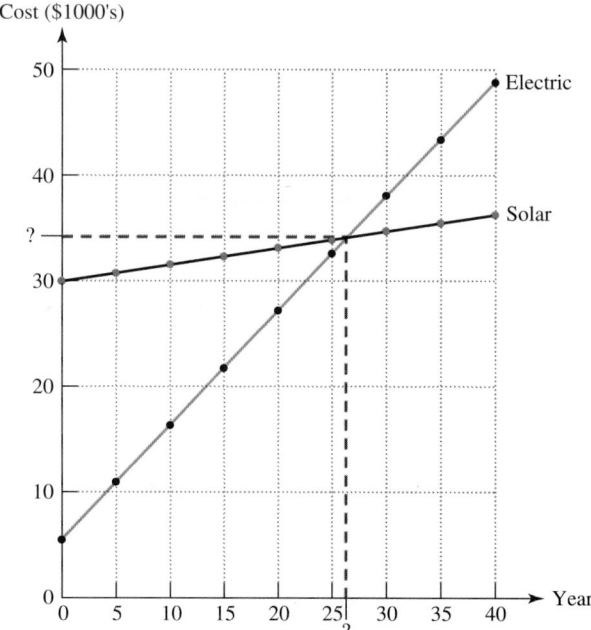

True–False Critical Thinking Problems

38. Which English statement given below is correctly translated into an algebraic equation?
a. Ten pounds less than Bill's weight (x) equals 160 pounds: $10 - x = 160$.
b. Four more than five times a number (x) is one less than six times that number: $5x + 4 = 1 - 6x$.
c. Seven is three more than some number (x): $7 + 3 = x$.
d. None of the above is correctly translated.

39. Which one of the following statements is true?
a. For any value of x, the numbers represented by x and $x + 7$ differ by 7.
b. If two numbers have a sum of 9 and x represents one of the numbers, then the other number is represented by $x - 9$.

c. The only solution for $2 + y = y + 2$ is 7.
d. The solution for $\dfrac{y}{0} = 1$ is 0.

40. Which one of the following statements is true?
a. Three consecutive odd integers should be represented by $x, x + 1$, and $x + 3$.
b. If a realtor gets 8% of the selling price of a house and the house sells for x dollars, then the owner receives $x - 0.08x$ dollars.
c. Every equation has a solution consisting of one number.
d. No number satisfies the following condition: The product of the number and 6 equals the product of the number and 4.

Writing in Mathematics

Translate the information and equations in Problems 41–42 into word problems.

Sample: Let x = a number. $4x + 3 = 23$

Solution: If four times some number is increased by 3, the sum is 23. Find the number.

41. Let $x =$ the length of one piece of a board:
$x + 2x = 78$

42. Let $x =$ the price of a car before a reduction.
$x - 0.09x = 16,289$

43. Use the circle graph to write and then solve an algebraic word problem similar to Example 6 on page 185. Base the problem around the fact that the number of inmates in the federal prison system for drug offenses is 45,384.

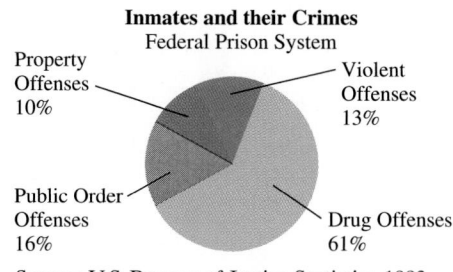

Inmates and their Crimes
Federal Prison System

Property Offenses 10%
Violent Offenses 13%
Public Order Offenses 16%
Drug Offenses 61%

Source: U.S. Bureau of Justice Statistics, 1993

Critical Thinking Problems

44. The St. Lawrence River is 160 kilometers longer than the Rhine River. The Zambezi River is twice as long as the St. Lawrence River. The Amazon River is 320 kilometers shorter than six times the length of the Rhine River. If the Amazon River exceeds the sum of the lengths of the other three rivers by 1440 kilometers, how long is the Zambezi River?

45. In 1978, the number of inhabitants per square mile in the United States was one less than nine times that of Canada, and Australia's number of inhabitants per square mile was two less than that of Canada's. England's population density at that time was nine people less than ten times that of the United States. If the number of people per square mile in England exceeded the sum of the number of people per square mile in the other three countries by 537, find the 1978 population density for the four countries in terms of the inhabitants per square mile.

46. The price of a VCR is reduced by 30%. When the VCR still does not sell, it is reduced by another 40%.

If the price of the VCR after both reductions is $372.40, what was the original price?

47. If you spend $\frac{1}{5}$ of your money and then lose $\frac{1}{3}$ of what you still have left, leaving you with $96, how much money did you originally have?

48. When 6 gallons of gasoline are put into a car's tank, the indicator goes from $\frac{1}{4}$ of a tank to $\frac{5}{8}$. Find the total capacity of the gasoline tank.

49. Sitting on the top of a table are three piles of oranges, with the same number of oranges in each pile. When eight defective oranges are found, two are thrown away and the oranges that remain are divided into two piles of 32 oranges each. How many oranges were in each of the original three piles?

50. Suppose that we agree to pay you 8¢ for every problem in this chapter that you solve correctly and fine you 5¢ for every problem done incorrectly. If at the end of 26 problems we do not owe each other any money, how many problems did you solve correctly?

Group Activity Problem

51. The models for education and income for men and women presented in Example 10 on page 190 do not distinguish among types of jobs. They do not indicate if men and women earn the same salaries with the same job types, or if there are more men in higher-paying jobs. In your group, determine what other variables are not accounted for in these simplified models.

Review Problems

52. Use the bar graph on page 198 to answer these questions.
   a. Estimate the starting salary of accounting majors.
   b. What major can expect a starting salary of approximately $22,000?

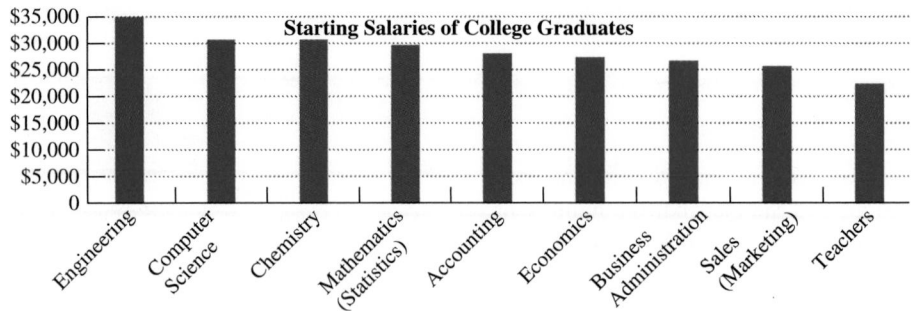

Starting Salaries of College Graduates

Source: U.S. Bureau of the Census, *Statistical Abstract* 1993: Table 246

53. Simplify: $4 - 2(2 - y)$.

54. Solve: $4 - \dfrac{3y}{2} = y - 1$.

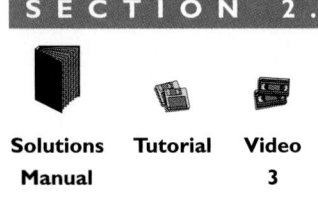

SECTION 2.6

Solutions Manual   Tutorial   Video 3

Solving Linear Inequalities

Objectives

1 Check possible solutions to an inequality.
2 Graph an inequality on a number line.
3 Solve linear inequalities.
4 Solve applied problems that are modeled by linear inequalities.

Solving linear inequalities is similar to solving linear equations. The solutions, however, are quite different. This section presents the steps that are used in solving linear inequalities.

Reviewing Inequality Symbols

Inequalities were introduced in Section 1.2 to *order* the real numbers, that is, to say which of two numbers is the greater. Symbols for inequality are summarized in Table 2.3

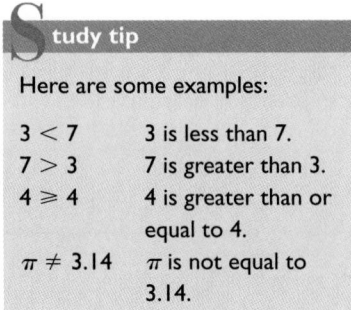

study tip

Here are some examples:

$3 < 7$	3 is less than 7.
$7 > 3$	7 is greater than 3.
$4 \geq 4$	4 is greater than or equal to 4.
$\pi \neq 3.14$	π is not equal to 3.14.

TABLE 2.3 Symbols for Inequality

Symbol	Meaning
$<$	Less than (points to the smaller number)
$>$	Greater than (points to the smaller number)
$\leq$	Less than or equal to
$\geq$	Greater than or equal to
$\neq$	Not equal to

Solutions of Algebraic Inequalities

Check possible solutions to an inequality.

An *algebraic inequality* contains one or more variable terms such as

$$x < 4 \quad \text{or} \quad 2x + 3 \geqslant 5.$$

These are *linear inequalities* in the variable x because the exponent that is implied on x is 1.

Values of x that make an inequality a true statement are called the *solutions* of the inequality.

EXAMPLE 1 **Checking Possible Solution**

Consider the inequality $x < 4$. Determine whether

a. -4 is a solution. **b.** 4 is a solution.

Solution

a. Replace x in $x < 4$ by -4. Since $-4 < 4$ is true, -4 is a solution.
b. Replace x in $x < 4$ by 4. Since $4 < 4$ is false, 4 is not a solution. ■

EXAMPLE 2 **Checking Possible Solutions**

Consider the inequality $2x + 3 \geqslant 5$. Determine whether

a. 1 is a solution. **b.** -1 is a solution.

Solution

a. $2x + 3 \geqslant 5$	This is the given inequality.
$2(1) + 3 \overset{?}{\geqslant} 5$	Replace the variable x by the possible solution 1. The question mark over the inequality symbol indicates that we do not know yet if the statement is true.
$2 + 3 \overset{?}{\geqslant} 5$	Multiply.
$5 \geqslant 5$ ✓	We obtain a true statement.

The true statement in the last step shows that 1 is a solution of $2x + 3 \geqslant 5$.

b. $2x + 3 \geqslant 5$	Once again, use the given inequality.
$2(-1) + 3 \overset{?}{\geqslant} 5$	Replace the variable x by the possible solution -1.
$-2 + 3 \overset{?}{\geqslant} 5$	Multiply.
$1 \geqslant 5$	False

The false statement in the last step shows that -1 is not a solution of $2x + 3 \geqslant 5$. ■

2 **Graph an inequality on a number line.**

Graphs of Inequalities

There are infinitely many solutions to the inequality $x < 3$, namely, all real numbers that are less than 3. Although we cannot list all the solutions, we can make a drawing on a number line that represents these solutions. Such a drawing is called the *graph* of the inequality.

Graphs of linear inequalities are shown on a number line by shading all points representing numbers that are solutions. *Open dots* indicate endpoints that are *not solutions* and *closed dots* indicate endpoints that *are solutions*.

EXAMPLE 3   **Graphing Inequalities**

Graph:

a. $x < 3$ **b.** $x \geq -1$ **c.** $-1 < x \leq 3$

Solution

a. The solutions of $x < 3$ are all real numbers that are less than 3. They are graphed on a number line by shading all points to the left of 3. The open dot at 3 indicates that 3 is not part of the graph, but numbers such as 2.9999 and 2.6 are.

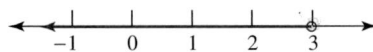

b. The solutions of $x \geq -1$ are all real numbers that are greater than or equal to -1. We shade all points to the right of -1 and the point for -1 itself. The closed dot at -1 shows that -1 is part of the graph.

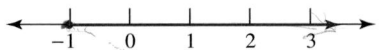

c. The inequality $-1 < x \leq 3$ is read "-1 is less than x *and* x is less than or equal to 3," or "x is greater than -1 *and* less than or equal to 3." The solutions of $-1 < x \leq 3$ are all real numbers between -1 and 3, not including -1 but including 3. In the graph for all real numbers between -1, exclusively, and 3, inclusively, the open dot at -1 indicates that -1 is not part of the graph. The closed dot at 3 shows that 3 belongs to the graph. Shading indicates the other solutions.

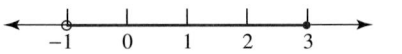   ■

3 Solve linear inequalities.

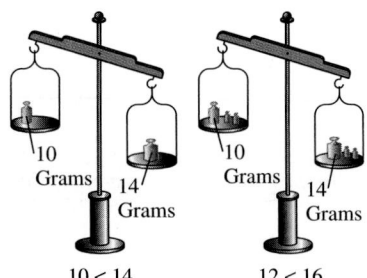

10 < 14   12 < 16

Figure 2.8

Adding 2 to both sides of an inequality.

Solving Inequalities Using the Addition Property

Consider the inequality $10 < 14$. We've modeled this inequality in Figure 2.8 by showing two weights on a scale that weigh 10 and 14 grams. The model shows that if we add 2 to both sides of the inequality, we obtain another true inequality:

$10 + 2 < 14 + 2$ or $12 < 16$

In the same way, we can subtract 2 from both sides and still obtain a true inequality:

$10 - 2 < 14 - 2$ or $8 < 12$

Since subtracting 2 on both sides is the same thing as adding -2, we can generalize these results with the *addition property of inequality*.

Study tip

The addition property of inequality allows us to add or subtract the same number or variable on both sides of an inequality.

The addition property of inequality

Let a, b, and c be real numbers, variables, or algebraic expressions.

If $a < b$, then $a + c < b + c$.
If $a \leq b$, then $a + c \leq b + c$.
If $a > b$, then $a + c > b + c$.
If $a \geq b$, then $a + c \geq b + c$.

Solving an inequality involves finding all values of the variable that make the inequality a true statement. As with linear equations, our goal is to isolate the variable on one side.

EXAMPLE 4 Solving a Linear Inequality

Solve and graph the solution: $x + 3 < 8$

Solution

Our goal is to isolate x. We can do this by using the addition property, subtracting 3 on both sides.

$x + 3 < 8$ This is the given inequality.

$x + 3 - 3 < 8 - 3$ Subtract 3 from both sides.

$x < 5$ Simplify.

The solution to $x + 3 < 8$ consists of all real numbers that are less than 5. The graph is shown in Figure 2.9. ■

In Example 4 we began with $x + 3 < 8$ and wrote $x < 5$ in the final step. However, $x < 5$ is an inequality and is not a solution. The solution is the *set* of all real numbers less than 5. To describe the set of solutions, we use set-builder notation. Thus, the *solution set* of $x + 3 < 8$ is

$\{x \mid x < 5\}$

which we read as "the set of all x such that x is less than 5." Solutions of inequalities should be expressed in set-builder notation.

Study tip

Since an inequality symbol points to the smaller number, $x < 5$ (x is less than 5) may be expressed as $5 > x$ (5 is greater than x).

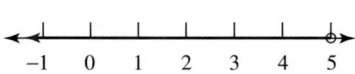

Figure 2.9

Real numbers less than 5

Discover for yourself

Can you check all solutions to Example 4 in the given inequality? Is a partial check possible? Select a real number that is less than 5 and show that it satisfies $x + 3 < 8$.

EXAMPLE 5 Solving a Linear Inequality

Solve and graph the solution set: $4x - 1 \geq 3x - 6$

Solution

Our goal is to isolate the variable terms on one side and the constant terms on the other side, exactly as we did when solving equations. Let's begin by isolating the variable on the left.

$4x - 1 \geq 3x - 6$	This is the given inequality.
$4x - 3x - 1 \geq 3x - 3x - 6$	Isolate the variable on the left by subtracting $3x$ from both sides.
$x - 1 \geq -6$	Simplify.

Now we isolate the constant terms on the right by adding 1 to both sides:

$$x - 1 + 1 \geq -6 + 1$$
$$x \geq -5$$

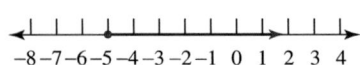

Figure 2.10

Real numbers greater than or equal to -5

The solution set for the given inequality is $\{x \mid x \geq -5\}$, read "the set of all x such that x is greater than or equal to -5." The graph of the solution set is shown in Figure 2.10. ■

Solving Inequalities Using the Multiplication Properties

Consider the inequality $10 < 14$. Table 2.4 shows multiplication and division on both sides by 2 and -2.

TABLE 2.4 Multiplication and Division on Both Sides of $10 < 14$ with Positive and Negative Numbers

	Multiply by 2	Divide by 2	Multiply by -2	Divide by -2
Begin with $10 < 14$	$20 < 28$	$5 < 7$	$-20 > -28$	$-5 > -7$

Observe that the direction of the inequality is reversed in the last two results. In general, when we multiply or divide an inequality by a negative number, the sense, or direction, of the inequality is reversed. Multiplication or division by a positive number preserves the sense of the inequality.

Since dividing by 2 is the same as multiplying by $\frac{1}{2}$ and dividing by -2 is the same as multiplying by $-\frac{1}{2}$, we can generalize the results in Table 2.4 with the *multiplication properties of inequality*.

Study tip

In words, here's what the multiplication properties state:

1. The same positive number can multiply or divide both sides of an inequality.
2. The same negative number can multiply or divide both sides of an inequality, but the direction of the inequality symbol changes.

The multiplication properties of inequality

Let a, b, and c be real numbers, variables, or algebraic expressions.

The Positive Multiplication Property

If $a < b$ and c is positive, then $ac < bc$.

If $a > b$ and c is positive, then $ac > bc$.

The Negative Multiplication Property

If $a < b$ and c is negative, then $ac > bc$.
If $a > b$ and c is negative, then $ac < bc$.

Similar statements hold for $\leq$ and $\geq$.

EXAMPLE 6   Using the Multiplication Properties

Solve and graph the solution set:

a. $\dfrac{1}{3}x < 5$ **b.** $-3y < 21$

Solution

a. $\dfrac{1}{3}x < 5$ This is the given inequality.

$3 \cdot \dfrac{1}{3}x < 3 \cdot 5$ Isolate x by multiplying by 3 on both sides. The symbol $<$ stays the same since we are multiplying by a positive number.

$x < 15$ Simplify.

The solution set is $\{x \mid x < 15\}$. The graph of the solution set is shown in Figure 2.11.

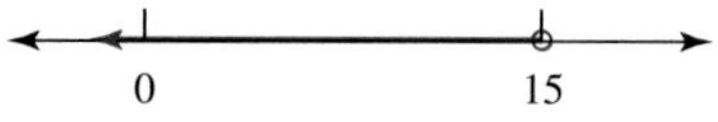

b. $-3y < 21$ This is the given inequality.

$\dfrac{-3y}{-3} > \dfrac{21}{-3}$ Isolate y by dividing by -3 on both sides. The symbol $<$ must be reversed since we are dividing by a negative number.

$y > -7$ Simplify.

The solution set is $\{y \mid y > -7\}$. The graph of the solution set is shown in Figure 2.12. ∎

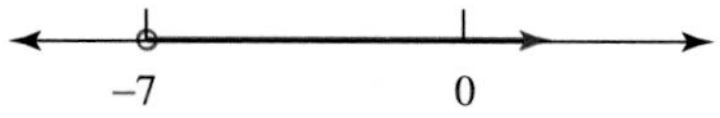

Figure 2.11

Real numbers less than 15

Figure 2.12

Real numbers greater than -7

Using the Addition and Multiplication Properties to Solve Inequalities

Solving some inequalities requires both the addition and multiplication properties of inequality. As with equations, our goal is to isolate the variable with a coefficient of 1 on one side of the inequality. We generally use the addition property before the multiplication properties.

EXAMPLE 7   Solving Inequalities

Solve and graph the solution set:

a. $4x - 7 \geqslant 5$ **b.** $6x - 12 > 8x + 2$

Solution

a. To solve $4x - 7 \geqslant 5$, use the addition property to isolate the x-term.

$4x - 7 \geqslant 5$ This is the given inequality.

$4x - 7 + 7 \geqslant 5 + 7$ Add 7 to both sides with the goal of isolating x on the left.

$4x \geqslant 12$ Simplify.

Now use the positive multiplication property to isolate x.

$\dfrac{4x}{4} \geqslant \dfrac{12}{4}$ Divide both sides by 4.

$x \geqslant 3$ Simplify.

The solution set is $\{x \mid x \geqslant 3\}$. The graph of the solution set is shown in Figure 2.13.

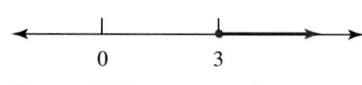

iscover for yourself

As a partial check, select one number from the solution set for each inequality in Examples 7 and 8. Substitute that number into the original inequality. Perform the resulting computations. You should obtain a true statement.

Is it possible to perform a partial check using a number that is not in the solution set? What should happen in this case? Try doing this.

Figure 2.13

Real numbers greater than or equal to 3

b. To solve $6x - 12 > 8x + 2$, use the addition property to isolate the x-term.

$$6x - 12 > 8x + 2 \qquad \text{This is the given inequality.}$$

$$6x - 8x - 12 > 8x - 8x + 2 \qquad \text{Subtract } 8x \text{ on both sides with the goal of isolating } x \text{ on the left.}$$

$$-2x - 12 > 2 \qquad \text{Simplify.}$$

$$-2x - 12 + 12 > 2 + 12 \qquad \text{Add 12 to both sides.}$$

$$-2x > 14 \qquad \text{Simplify.}$$

Now use the negative multiplication property to isolate x.

$$\frac{-2x}{-2} < \frac{14}{-2} \qquad \text{Divide both sides by } -2 \text{ and reverse the sense of the inequality.}$$

$$x < -7 \qquad \text{Simplify.}$$

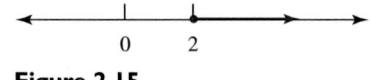

Figure 2.14

Real numbers less than -7

The solution set is $\{x \,|\, x < -7\}$. The graph of the solution set is shown in Figure 2.14. ■

Have you noticed that solving a linear inequality is nearly identical to solving a linear equation? The main difference is that you must remember to reverse the direction of the inequality when multiplying or dividing on both sides by a negative number.

EXAMPLE 8   **Solving Inequalities**

Solve and graph the solution set:

a. $2(x - 3) + 5x \leqslant 8(x - 1)$ **b.** $4 - \dfrac{3y}{2} \geqslant y - 1$

Solution

a. $2(x - 3) + 5x \leqslant 8(x - 1)$ This is the given inequality.

$$2x - 6 + 5x \leqslant 8x - 8 \qquad \text{Use the distributive property to multiply and remove grouping symbols.}$$

$$7x - 6 \leqslant 8x - 8 \qquad \text{Combine like terms.}$$

$$7x - 8x \leqslant -8 + 6 \qquad \text{Subtract } 8x \text{ and add 6 on both sides. This gets } x\text{-terms on the left and numerical terms on the right.}$$

$$-x \leqslant -2 \qquad \text{Simplify.}$$

$$x \geqslant 2 \qquad \text{Multiply (or divide) both sides by } -1 \text{ and reverse the inequality symbol.}$$

Figure 2.15

Real numbers greater than or equal to 2

The solution set is $\{x \,|\, x \geqslant 2\}$. The graph of the solution set is shown in Figure 2.15.

b.

$$4 - \frac{3y}{2} \geqslant y - 1 \qquad \text{This is the given inequality.}$$

$$2\left(4 - \frac{3y}{2}\right) \geqslant 2(y - 1) \qquad \text{Multiply both sides by 2 to clear the inequality of fractions.}$$

$$2 \cdot 4 - 2 \cdot \frac{3y}{2} \geqslant 2y - 2 \qquad \text{Apply the distributive property.}$$

$$8 - 3y \geqslant 2y - 2 \qquad \text{Simplify.}$$

$$-3y - 2y \geqslant -2 - 8 \qquad \text{Subtract } 2y \text{ and subtract 8 on both sides to get } y\text{-terms on the left and numerical terms on the right.}$$

$$-5y \geqslant -10 \qquad \text{Simplify.}$$

$$y \leqslant 2 \qquad \text{Divide both sides by } -5 \text{ and reverse the sense of the inequality.}$$

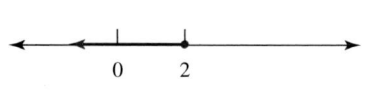

Figure 2.16
Real numbers less than or equal to 2

The solution set is $\{y \mid y \leqslant 2\}$. The graph of the solution set is shown in Figure 2.16. ∎

We are now ready to summarize the steps involved in the solution of a linear inequality.

Solving a linear inequality

1. If the inequality contains fractions, multiply both sides by the least common multiple of all denominators to clear fractions. To clear decimals, multiply both sides by a multiple of 10.
2. Remove any grouping symbols, using the distributive property, and combine like terms.
3. Use the addition property to collect all the variable terms on one side and all the constant terms on the opposite side.
4. Use the multiplication properties to isolate the variable by dividing both sides by its coefficient. If the coefficient is negative, make sure to reverse the sense of the inequality.
5. Express the solution in set-builder notation and graph the solution set on a number line.

---

4 Solve applied problems that are modeled by linear inequalities.

Modeling Using Inequalities

The most difficult part in solving applied problems that are modeled by linear inequalities is translating the verbal conditions. Translations of some commonly used English sentences are listed in Table 2.5. The table is based on the graph in Figure 2.17. The variable x in the table represents the number of days that people were so sick they had to cut down on their usual activities.

Number of Days per Year That People Were So Sick They Had to Cut Down on Their Usual Activities

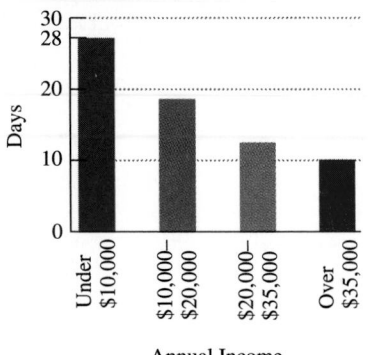

Annual Income

Figure 2.17

Source: U.S. Bureau of the Census, *Statistical Abstract* 1993: Table 199

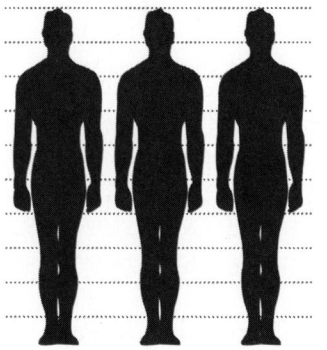

The Average American Guy

According to researchers, "Robert" is 31, 5 feet 9 inches, 172 pounds, watches TV 2567 hours yearly, commutes to work, works 6.1 hours daily, and sleeps 7.7 hours.

TABLE 2.5 Algebraic Translations of English Sentences that Result in Inequalities

English Sentence	Inequality
For all four groups, the number of days is at most 28.	$x \leqslant 28$
The number of days is no more than 28.	$x \leqslant 28$
The number of days does not exceed 28.	$x \leqslant 28$
The number of days is at least 10.	$x \geqslant 10$
The number of days is no less than 10.	$x \geqslant 10$
The number of days is between 10 and 28, inclusively	$10 \leqslant x \leqslant 28$

EXAMPLE 9   An Application: Final Course Grade

To earn an A in a course, a student must have a final average of at least 90%. On the first four examinations, a student has scores of 86%, 88%, 92%, and 84%. If the final examination counts as two examinations, what must this student get on the final to earn an A in the course?

Solution

Let x = the score on the final exam. Since the final counts double, we add x twice to get the average grade.

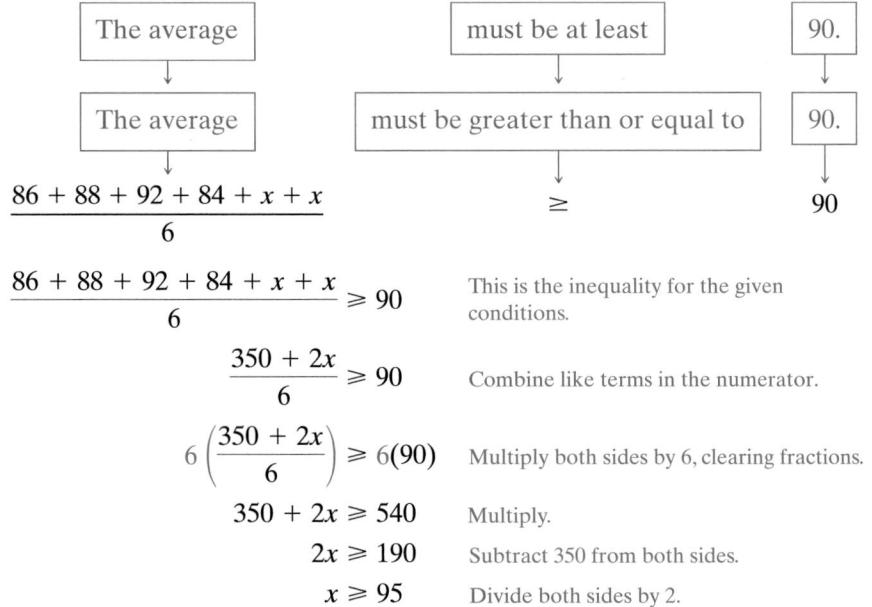

$$\frac{86 + 88 + 92 + 84 + x + x}{6} \geqslant 90 \qquad \text{This is the inequality for the given conditions.}$$

$$\frac{350 + 2x}{6} \geqslant 90 \qquad \text{Combine like terms in the numerator.}$$

$$6\left(\frac{350 + 2x}{6}\right) \geqslant 6(90) \qquad \text{Multiply both sides by 6, clearing fractions.}$$

$$350 + 2x \geqslant 540 \qquad \text{Multiply.}$$

$$2x \geqslant 190 \qquad \text{Subtract 350 from both sides.}$$

$$x \geqslant 95 \qquad \text{Divide both sides by 2.}$$

The student must get at least 95% on the final examination to earn an A in the course. ∎

EXAMPLE 10 **An Application: Elevator Capacity**

An elevator at a construction site has a maximum capacity of 2500 pounds. If the elevator operator weighs 205 pounds and each cement bag weighs 85 pounds, how many bags of cement can be safely lifted on the elevator in one trip?

iscover for yourself

Before we solve Example 10 using algebra, let's consider what happens to the total weight in the elevator as the number of cement bags increases. Recall that the operator weighs 205 pounds and each cement bag weighs 85 pounds.

Operator and Bags of Cement	Weight = Operator's Weight + Weight of the Bags
Operator and 1 bag	Weight = 205 + 1(85) = 290
Operator and 2 bags	Weight = 205 + 2(85) = 375
Operator and 3 bags	Weight = 205 + 3(85) = 460
Operator and 4 bags	Weight = 205 + 4(85) = 545
Operator and 5 bags	Weight = 205 + 5(85) = 630

Do you see a pattern forming? If there are x bags of cement, use the pattern to write an algebraic expression for the total weight in the elevator.

Based on the computations in the right column, what is a reasonable estimate for the number of bags that can be lifted to keep the total weight less than or equal to 2500 pounds?

Solution

Let x = the number of cement bags that can be lifted. The maximum elevator capacity is 2500 pounds.

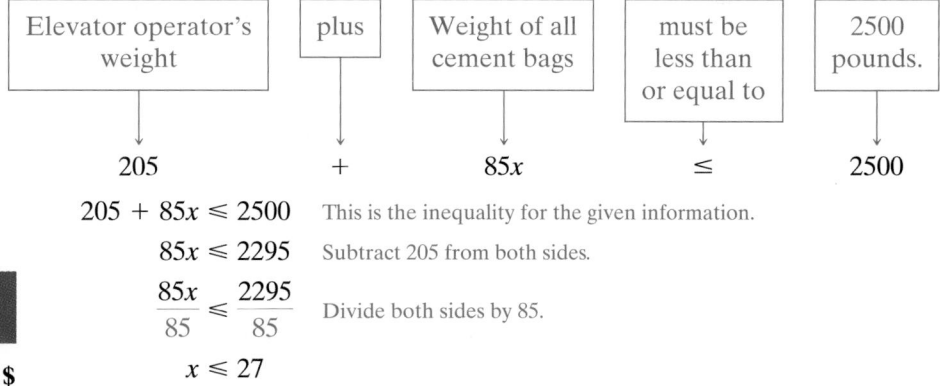

Elevator operator's weight	plus	Weight of all cement bags	must be less than or equal to	2500 pounds.
205	+	$85x$	$\leq$	2500

$205 + 85x \leq 2500$ This is the inequality for the given information.

$85x \leq 2295$ Subtract 205 from both sides.

$\dfrac{85x}{85} \leq \dfrac{2295}{85}$ Divide both sides by 85.

$x \leq 27$

Twenty-seven or fewer bags of cement can be safely lifted on the elevator in one trip. ■

Heating System Total Costs

Year	Solar, $	Gas, $
0	30,000	12,000
5	30,750	15,500
10	31,500	19,000
15	32,250	22,500
20	33,000	26,000
25	33,750	29,500
30	34,500	33,000
35	35,250	36,500
40	36,000	40,000

EXAMPLE 11 **Solar versus Conventional Heating**

For a three-bedroom house, the cost of installing solar heating is $30,000 plus operating costs of $150 per year. Gas heating has a $12,000 installation cost plus operating costs of $700 yearly. The models

$$C_{\text{solar}} = 30,000 + 150x$$
$$C_{\text{gas}} = 12,000 + 700x$$

describe this situation, where x represents the number of years each system is in operation. After how many years is solar heating more economical than gas heating?

Solution

We want to know when (for what x) the total cost of solar heating will be less than the total cost of gas heating.

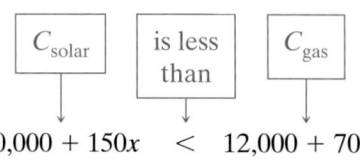

| C_{solar} | is less than | C_{gas} |

$30,000 + 150x \quad < \quad 12,000 + 700x$ Substitute the given algebraic expressions.

$30,000 < 12,000 + 550x$ For variety, isolate variable terms on the right, subtracting $150x$ from both sides.

$18,000 < 550x$ Isolate constants on the left, subtracting $12,000$ from both sides.

$\dfrac{18,000}{550} < x$ Isolate x, dividing both sides by 550.

Since $\dfrac{18,000}{550} \approx 32.7$, when $x > 32.7$ solar heating has a cheaper total cost than gas heating. That is, after approximately 32.7 years, the solar heating system is more economical than the gas heating system. ∎

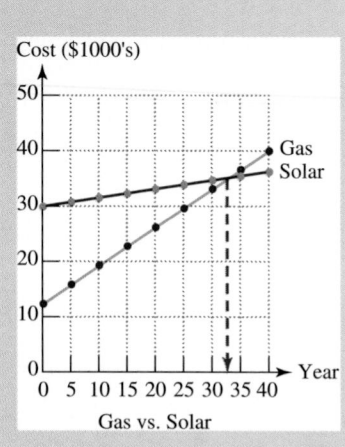

Discover for yourself

Explain how these line graphs illustrate the solution to Example 11.

Cost ($1000's)

Gas
Solar

Year

Gas vs. Solar

PROBLEM SET 2.6

Practice Problems

In Problems 1–4, determine whether each number is a solution of the given equality.

1. $x > -7$
    a. 7   **b.** 0
    c. -7.2

2. $x < -6$
    a. 6   **b.** -13
    c. -6.7

3. $6 - 5y \geqslant 7$
    a. $-\frac{1}{5}$ **b.** 0
    c. -4

4. $-4x + 3 \geqslant 23$
    a. -5 **b.** 0
    c. -9

In Problems 5–16, graph each inequality on a number line.

5. $x > 6$
6. $x > -2$
7. $y < -4$
8. $y < 0$
9. $x \geqslant -3$
10. $x \geqslant -5$
11. $x \leqslant 4$
12. $x \leqslant 7$
13. $-2 < x \leqslant 5$
14. $-3 \leqslant x < 7$
15. $-1 < x < 4$
16. $-7 \leqslant x \leqslant 0$

Describe each graph in Problems 17–22 using set-builder notation.

17.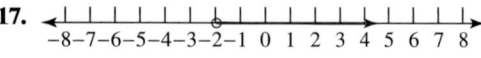

18.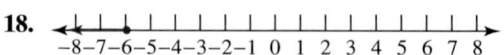

19.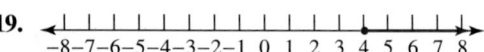

20.

21.

22.

Use the addition property of inequality to solve Problems 23–40. Graph the solution sets.

23. $x - 3 > 2$

24. $x + 1 < 5$

25. $x + 4 \leq 9$

26. $x - 5 \geq 1$

27. $y - 3 < 0$

28. $y + 4 \geq 0$

29. $3x + 4 \leq 2x + 7$

30. $2x + 9 \leq x + 2$

31. $5x - 9 < 4x + 7$

32. $3x - 8 < 2x + 11$

33. $7x - 7 > 6x - 3$

34. $8x - 9 > 7x - 3$

35. $x - \frac{2}{3} > \frac{1}{2}$

36. $x - \frac{1}{3} \geq \frac{5}{6}$

37. $y + \frac{7}{8} \leq \frac{1}{2}$

38. $y + \frac{1}{3} \leq \frac{3}{4}$

39. $-15y + 13 > 13 - 16y$

40. $-12y + 17 > 20 - 13y$

Use the multiplication properties of inequality to solve Problems 41–52. Graph the solution sets.

41. $4x < 20$

42. $6x \geq 18$

43. $3x \geq -15$

44. $7x < -21$

45. $-3x < 15$

46. $-7x > 21$

47. $-3x \geq -15$

48. $-7x \leq -21$

49. $-2y > \frac{1}{5}$

50. $-4y > \frac{4}{7}$

51. $-\frac{1}{3}x < 7$

52. $-\frac{1}{4}x < 8$

Use the addition and multiplication properties to solve Problems 53–80. Graph the solution sets.

53. $2y - 3 > 7$

54. $3z + 2 \leq 14$

55. $3(x - 1) < 9$

56. $4(2y - 1) > 12$

57. $-2x - 3 < 3$

58. $14 - 3y > 5$

59. $3 - 7y \leq 17$

60. $5 - 3z \geq 20$

61. $-x < 4$

62. $-y > -3$

63. $5 - y \leq 1$

64. $3 - x \geq -3$

65. $2y - 5 > -y + 6$

66. $6x - 2 \geq 4x + 6$

67. $2y - 5 < 5y - 11$

68. $4z - 7 > 9z - 2$

69. $3(x + 1) - 5 < 2x + 1$

70. $4(y + 1) + 2 \geq 3y + 6$

71. $8x + 3 > 3(2x + 1) - x + 5$

72. $7(2x - 1) < 9x + 11$

73. $7(y + 4) - 13 < 12 + 13(3 + y)$

74. $7 - 2(y - 4) < 5(1 - 2y)$

75. $\frac{x}{4} - \frac{3}{8} < 2$

76. $\frac{3x}{4} + \frac{1}{2} > 0$

77. $\frac{y}{3} + \frac{y}{4} \geq 1$

78. $\frac{z}{5} - \frac{z}{2} \leq 1$

79. $-0.4y + 2 > -1.2y - 0.4$

80. $-2y - 0.4 \geq 1.2 - 0.4y$

Application Problems

Use the graph to answer Problems 81–86. Let x represent the number of births per 1000 population for women aged 14–44 for the period shown in the graph. Translate each sentence into an inequality.

81. The number of births per 1000 population is at most 125.

82. The number of births per 1000 population is no more than 125.

83. The number of births per 1000 population exceeds 65.

84. The number of births per 1000 population is no less than 66.

85. The number of births per 1000 population is at least 66.

86. The number of births per 1000 population is between 60 and 125.

Births per 1000 Population, U.S. Women Aged 15–44

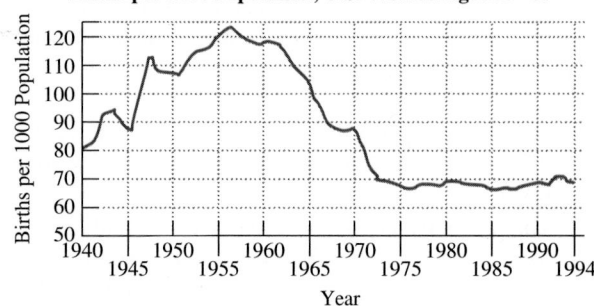

Source: U.S. Bureau of the Census

87. To pass a course, a student must have an average on three examinations of at least 60. If a student scores 44 and 72 on the first two tests, describe the range of scores that this student needs on a third test to pass the course.

88. To earn an A in a course, a student must have an average on three examinations of at least 90. If a student scores 86 and 88 on the first two tests, describe the range of scores that the student needs on the third test to earn an A in the course.

89. An elevator at a construction site has a maximum capacity of 3000 pounds. If the elevator operator weighs 245 pounds and each cement bag weighs 95 pounds, how many bags of cement can be safely lifted on the elevator in one trip?

90. An elevator at a construction site has a maximum capacity of 2800 pounds. If the elevator weighs 265 pounds and each cement bag weighs 65 pounds, how many bags of cement can be safely lifted on the elevator in one trip?

91. The number N of chirps that the cricket *Gryllus pennsylvanicum* makes per minute is given by the model

$$N = 4t - 160$$

where t represents temperature in degrees Fahrenheit. How must the temperature be controlled so that a cricket of this species will chirp no more than 160 times per minute?

92. The pressure p (in pounds per square inch) is related to depth below the surface of the ocean by the model

$$p = \frac{5}{11}d + 15$$

where d is depth below the surface (in feet). At what depths does pressure exceed 60 pounds per square inch?

93. The profit of a company is 40 times the number of customers served less $200. Profits must exceed $12,000 or the company will be sold by the stockholders. What does this mean in terms of the number of customers served by the company?

94. The profit of a company is 70 times the number of customers served less $300. Its profits cannot exceed $35,680 or the company will be nationalized. What does this mean in terms of the number of customers served by the company?

95. For a three-bedroom house, the cost of installing gas heating is $12,000 plus operating costs of $700 per year. Electric heating has a $5000 installation cost plus operating costs of $1100 per year. The models

$$C_{\text{gas}} = 12,000 + 700x$$
$$C_{\text{electric}} = 5000 + 1100x$$

describe this situation, where x represents the number of years each system is in operation.

a. After how many years is gas heating more economical than electric heating?

b. Explain how the line graphs in the figure illustrate the solution to part (a).

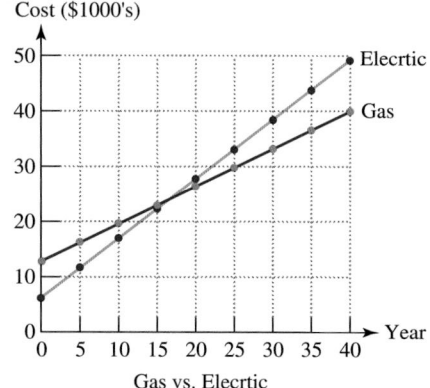

Gas vs. Elecrtic

96. Membership in a fitness club costs $500.00 yearly plus $1.00 for each hour spent working out, described by $C = 500 + x$, where x represents the number of hours spent working out. A competing club charges $440.00 yearly plus $1.75 per hour, with $C = 440 + 1.75x$. How many hours must a person work out yearly to make membership in the first club cheaper than membership in the second club?

True–False Critical Thinking Problems _____

97. Which one of the following statements is true?
a. $-7 < 0 < -3$
b. The inequalities $3y - 2 < y$ and $y < 3y - 2$ have the same solutions.
c. The number -4 is a solution to $-3 < x$.
d. The inequalities $5 < x$ and $x > 5$ have solution sets with identical graphs.

98. Which one of the following statements is true?
  a. The inequality $x - 3 > 0$ is equivalent to $x < 3$.
  b. The statement "x is at most 5" is written $x < 5$.
  c. The inequality $-4x < -20$ is equivalent to $x > -5$.
  d. The statement "the sum of x and 6% of x is at least 80" is written $x + 0.06x \geqslant 80$.

99. Which one of the following statements is true?
  a. The smallest integer satisfying $-2x + 5 \geqslant 13$ is -4.
  b. The inequality $-x/3 > -7$ is equivalent to $x < 21$.
  c. 80 is 8000% of 10.
  d. The inequality $8x > 4x$ has no solution.

Technology Problems

In Problems 100–101 it is not necessary to use a graphing calculator. Instead, you will be asked to interpret what appears on the screen of a graphing calculator, as illustrated in the figures.

100. a. Solve: $4x - 5 < 2x + 7$.
  b. In Chapter 4 we will learn how to graph $y = 4x - 5$ and $y = 2x + 7$. These graphs were obtained with a graphing calculator and are shown in the figure. Describe how you can use these graphs to give visual meaning to your algebraic solution in part (a).

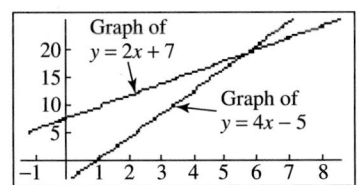

101. a. Solve: $3(x - 2) + 4 < 8(x + 1)$.
  b. The graphs of $y = 3(x - 2) + 4$ and $y = 8(x + 1)$ were obtained with a graphing calculator and are shown in the figure. Describe how you can use these graphs to give visual meaning to your algebraic solution in part (a).

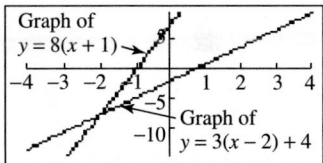

Writing in Mathematics

102. Explain what must be done to solve $2 - \dfrac{y}{3} \geqslant 4$, describing each step in detail.

103. Discuss similarities and differences between solving a linear equation and solving a linear inequality.

104. Let $x =$ the number of unmarried couples living together in the United States from 1960 through 1990. Use the graph on page 212 to write at least six English statements that can be translated into inequalities. Use phrases such as "is at most," "is no more than," "exceeds," "does not exceed," "is less than," "is no less than," "is between," and so on. Then translate each English sentence into an inequality.

Cohabitation in the United States

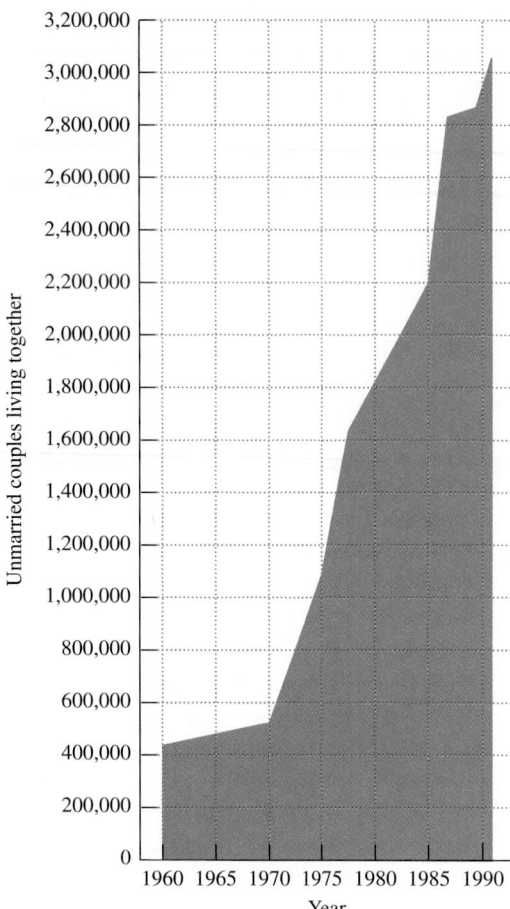

Source: U.S. Bureau of the Census

Critical Thinking Problems

105. Solve: $4x - 4 < 4(x - 5)$. What happens? What does this mean in terms of the solution set for this inequality?

106. Solve: $3(x + 3) \leq 7x - 4x + 10$. What happens? What does this mean in terms of the solution set for this inequality?

107. If $a < 0$, solve $y \leq ax + b$ for x.

108. Graph the solution set for $|x| < 4$ on a number line.

109. Graph the solution set for $|x| > 2$ on a number line.

110. In this section, we did not discuss the meaning of the symbol $\not<$. Why did we leave out this discussion?

111. A salesperson is paid a monthly commission of 30% of all sales over $1000. What monthly sales will generate a commission greater than $700?

112. The sum of three consecutive even integers is greater than or equal to 24 and less than or equal to 36. List all permissible values for the three integers.

113. Eleanor's age is 3 years more than two times Mia's age. The sum of their ages is greater than or equal to 24 years. Which of the following is true?
a. Mia cannot be 8 years old.
b. Eleanor can be 19.
c. Eleanor cannot be 17.
d. Mia can be 6.

Review Problems

114. Evaluate $b^2 - 4ac$ if $a = -1$, $b = -2$, and $c = 3$.

116. Solve: $-\frac{1}{3}(6x - 9) = 23$.

115. Simplify: $2[10 - (y - 1)]$.

C HAPTER PROJECT

Designing Word Problems — Writing in Mathematics

One of the best ways to learn how to *solve* a word problem in algebra is to *design* word problems of your own. Creating a word problem makes you very aware of precisely how much information is needed to solve the problem. You must also focus on the best way to present information to a reader and on how much information to give. As you write your problem, you gain skills that will help you solve problems created by others.

You are surrounded by potential word problems in everyday life. Companies offering competing, but very similar, services often spend millions of dollars to present information to consumers about the advantages of their company's pricing plan over that of another; this would include phone companies, on-line computer services, and airlines, to name just a few. Banks and other financial institutions publish information about rates of return on investments, savings plans, checking accounts, and mortgages. Local, state, and federal agencies publish volumes of statistics cataloging things such as crime rates, public health concerns, and consumer interests. Car dealerships and car manufacturers offer many different payment plans, rebates, and interest rates. Even a quick glance through the mail around your house will undoubtedly show you credit card bills with different interest rates and penalties and utility bills filled with pricing by usage and taxes added by local agencies.

For this project, you will design five different word problems from a variety of sources.

- At least two of the problems should have an accompanying table, graph, or other visual display of information. You may not need to make your own table; many companies already display information to consumers in this fashion.
- At least one of the problems should contain more numerical information than is needed to solve the problem.
- All of the problems should be clearly written and have an exact solution. The solution need not be numerical.
- All of the problems should be distinctly different in style. For example, you should not have more than one problem on telephone company rates.

After you have completed all of your word problems, your instructor will put together a set of problems from the entire class and return them to be analyzed and solved by the class. Discussing and defending your own word problems may give you an entirely new perspective on how you and others analyze these problems in the future.

Worldwide Web Resources

Go to the Prentice Hall website (http://www.prenhall.com/blitzer) to access other locations on the Internet that will allow you to further explore the concepts presented in this project.

Chapter Review

SUMMARY

1. Solving a Linear Equation
  a. If the equation contains fractions, consider multiplying both sides by the least common multiple (LCM) of all denominators. If the equation contains decimals, consider multiplying both sides by a multiple of 10, thereby eliminating the decimals.
  b. Simplify each side.
  c. Use the addition property of equality to collect all variable terms on one side and all the constant terms on the other side.
  d. Use the multiplication principle to isolate the variable, dividing both sides of the equation by the variable's coefficient. This will produce the equation's solution.
  e. Check the proposed solution in the original equation.

2. Mathematical Models and Formulas
  a. The formulas contain two or more variables. If certain values are given for the variables, substitute these values into the model and then solve for the specified variable.

  b. A formula may be solved for a specified variable by using the properties of equality and the procedure for solving linear equations.

3. Solving Word Problems
  Step 1. Read the problem and determine the quantities that are involved. Let x (or any variable) represent one of the quantities in the problem.
  Step 2. If necessary, write expressions for any other unknown quantities in the problem in terms of x.
  Step 3. Write an equation in x that describes the verbal conditions of the problem.
  Step 4. Solve the equation written in step 3 and answer the question in the problem.
  Step 5. Check the solution *in the original wording* of the problem, not in the equation obtained from the words.

4. Examples of Translations from English into Equations

English	Equation
When 9 is subtracted from eight times a number, the result is three times the sum of 1 and twice that number.	$8x - 9 = 3(1 + 2x)$
The sum of three consecutive integers is 24.	$x + (x + 1) + (x + 2) = 24$
The sum of three consecutive odd integers is 21.	$x + (x + 2) + (x + 4) = 21$
7% of what number is 23?	$0.07x = 23$
After a 45% reduction, a television sold for $247.50. What was the price before the reduction (x)?	$x - 0.45x = 247.50$

5. Set-Builder Notation and Graphs

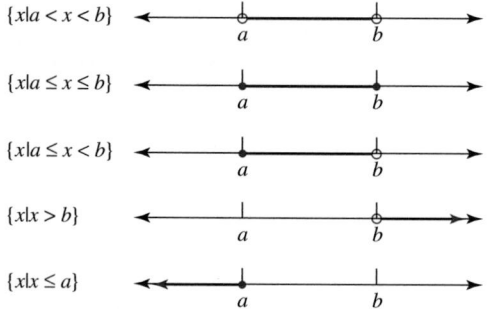

Open dots indicate that the endpoints are not in the solution set. Closed dots indicate that the endpoints are in the solution set.

6. Solving a Linear Inequality. Use the procedure for solving a linear equation. However, when multiplying or dividing both sides by a negative number, reverse the sense of the inequality. Graph the solution set on a number line.

Solve each equation in Problems 1–12.

1. $2y - 5 = 7$

2. $5z + 20 = 3z$

3. $7(y - 4) = y + 2$

4. $1 - 2(6 - y) = 3y + 2$

5. $2(y - 4) + 3(y + 5) = 2y - 2$

6. $2z - 4(5z + 1) = 3z + 17$

7. $\frac{2}{3}x = \frac{1}{6}x + 1$

8. $\frac{1}{2}y - \frac{1}{10} = \frac{1}{5}y + \frac{1}{2}$

9. $0.2y - 0.3 = 0.8y - 0.3$

10. $17.4 - 3.6y = -16.08$

11. $-2(y - 4) - (3y - 2) = -2 - (6y - 2)$

12. $\frac{x}{4} = 2 + \frac{x - 3}{3}$

13. Medical researchers have found that the desirable maximum heart rate R (in beats per minute) of a person exercising is given by the mathematical model

$$R = 110 + 3A - 4(A - 27.5)$$

where A is the person's age. If the desirable maximum heart rate is 190 beats per minute, how old is that person?

14. The model

$$H = 2.2F + 69.1$$

is used by forensic scientists to estimate a man's height H (in centimeters) in terms of the length of the femur (also measured in centimeters).

a. If the height of a man is 179.1 centimeters, what is the length of the femur? How is this illustrated in the graph?

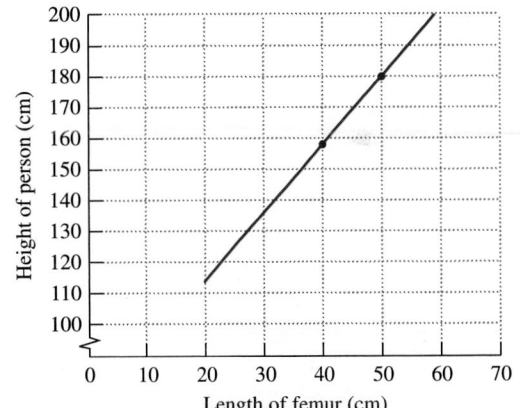

b. Solve the formula for F.

c. Use the result of part (b) to answer this question: If the height of a man is 157.1 centimeters, what is the length of the femur? How is this illustrated in the graph?

In Problems 15–19, use the percent model, A $=$ PB, *which states that* A *is* P *percent of* B.

15. 33.6 is 70% of what?

16. What is 28% of 26?

17. What percent of 60 is 1.2?

18. Solve the percent model for P.

19. Use the form of the percent model in Problem 18 to answer this question: A 40 milliliter solution of acid in water contains 14 milliliters of acid. What percent of the solution is acid?

20. The formula for converting Celsius temperature (C) to Fahrenheit temperature (F) is

$$F = \frac{9}{5}C + 32.$$

a. If the Fahrenheit temperature is 104°, what is the Celsius temperature?

b. Solve the formula for C.

Solve each formula for the specified variable in Problems 21–25.

21. $P = 2L + 2W$ for W

22. $I = Prt$ for P

23. $A = \dfrac{B + C}{2}$ for B

24. $F = f(1 - M)$ for M

25. $P = \dfrac{RT}{V}$ for V

In Problems 26–28, solve each equation for y. Then find the value of y for the given value of x.

26. $2x - y = 14$; $x = 6$

27. $3x - 2y = -6$; $x = -2$

28. $-3 = 3y - 4x$; $x = -\frac{1}{2}$

29. Solve for y: $Ax + By = C$. How can this result be used to solve Problems 26–28?

Write an equation using the information given in Problems 30–43. Then solve the equation. Check your answer in the original wording of the problem.

30. Six times a number, decreased by 20, is four times the number. What is the number?

31. When 8 is added to 60% of a number, the sum is 332. What is the number?

32. The first Super Bowl was played between the Green Bay Packers and the Kansas City Chiefs in 1967. Only once, in 1991, were the winning and losing scores in the Super Bowl consecutive integers. If the sum of the scores was 39, what were the scores?

34. A 51-centimeter board is cut into three pieces. The longest piece is two times the length of the shortest piece, and the middle-sized piece is 3 centimeters longer than the shortest piece. How long are the pieces?

35. A molecule contains 1 more atom of carbon than twice the number of atoms of oxygen and 1 less atom of hydrogen than carbon. If the molecule contains a total of 21 atoms, how many atoms of carbon are there?

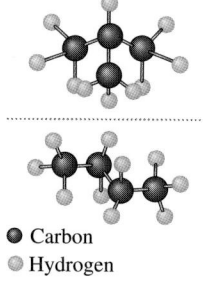

● Carbon
◯ Hydrogen

Tony Stone Images

33. The rectangular gate shown in the figure has dimensions that are consecutive odd integers. The gate's perimeter is 56 feet. Find the gate's dimensions.

36. The graph shows the 26 worst U.S. metropolitan areas in terms of unhealthy air days in 1992. The number of unhealthy air days in Los Angeles exceeds 5 times that of New York by 29 days. If Los Angeles and New York combined have 185 unhealthy air days, determine the number of unhealthy days for the two cities. Then use the graph to obtain a reasonable estimate for the number of unhealthy air days for the metropolitan areas whose numbers are missing from the graph.

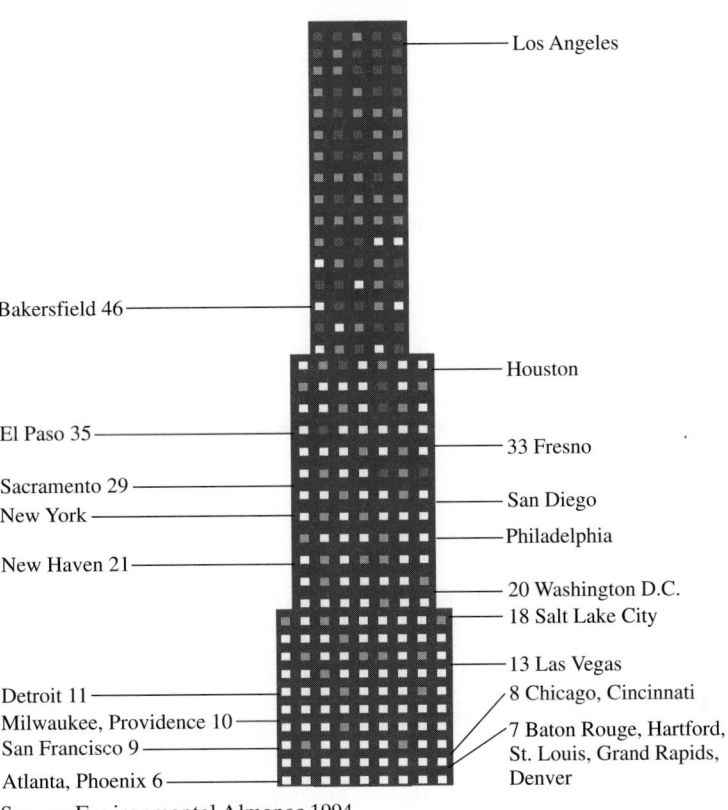

Unhealthy Air Days 1992
26 Worst U.S. Metropolitan Areas

Los Angeles

Bakersfield 46

Houston

El Paso 35

33 Fresno

Sacramento 29

San Diego

New York

Philadelphia

New Haven 21

20 Washington D.C.

18 Salt Lake City

13 Las Vegas

Detroit 11

8 Chicago, Cincinnati

Milwaukee, Providence 10

7 Baton Rouge, Hartford,

San Francisco 9

St. Louis, Grand Rapids,

Atlanta, Phoenix 6

Denver

Source: Environmental Almanac 1994.

37. As of this writing Cuba, the Caribbean's largest island, is the only communist state in the Caribbean. If Cuba's black population is approximately 1.2 million, use the circle graph to estimate the country's population.

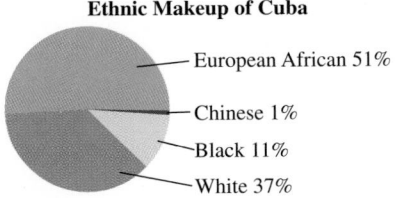

Ethnic Makeup of Cuba

European African 51%

Chinese 1%

Black 11%

White 37%

38. After a 45% price reduction, a VCR sold for $247.50. What was the price before the reduction?

39. To satisfy all recreational needs, a person figures that $32,630 is needed after taxes. If the government takes 35% of this person's income, what must the yearly income be for all recreational needs to be satisfied?

40. A lending library charges $1.25 for the first day and $0.55 for each additional day. If the library charged $10.05 for lending a book, for how many days was that book on loan?

41. Dora, age 18, has this strange thing about dating only older people. She is thinking about dating the math club president who told her, "If I were 10 years older, I would be 5 years younger than twice my present age." Will Dora date the math club president?

42. A study entitled *Performing Arts—The Economic Dilemma* documents the relationship between the number of concerts given yearly by a major orchestra and the attendance per concert. For each additional concert given per year, attendance per concert drops by approximately 8 people. If 50 concerts are given, attendance per concert is 2987 people. How many concerts should be given to ensure an audience of 2627 people at each concert? Explain how this solution is illustrated in the graph.

43. The graph shows that a small business sells $100,000 worth of merchandise during its first year, and increases its sales by a fixed amount each year. How many years will it take to generate annual sales of $525,000?

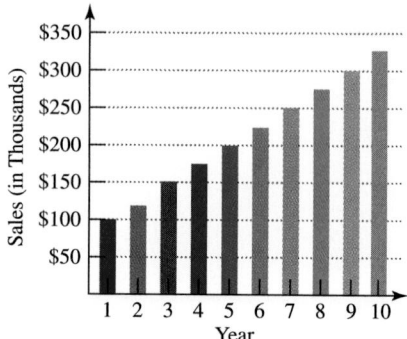

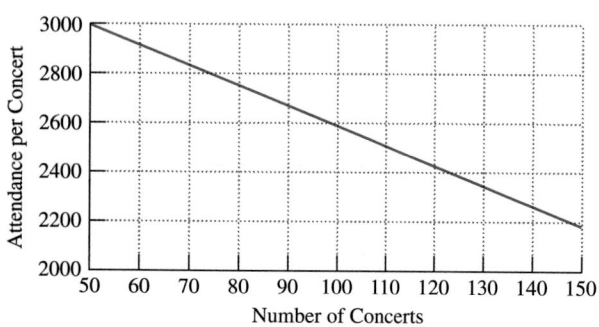

Describe each graph in Problems 44–45 using set-builder notation.

44.

$$-5\ -4\ -3\ -2\ -1\ \ 0\ \ 1\ \ 2\ \ 3\ \ 4\ \ 5$$

45.

$$-5\ -4\ -3\ -2\ -1\ \ 0\ \ 1\ \ 2\ \ 3\ \ 4\ \ 5$$

Solve each inequality in Problems 46–54, and graph the solution set on a number line.

46. $2y - 5 < 3$

47. $3 - 5x \le 18$

48. $4x + 6 < 5x$

49. $9(z - 1) \ge 10(z - 2)$

50. $-3(4 - x) < 4x + 3 + x$

51. $4y - (y - 3) \le -3(2y - 7)$

52. $\dfrac{5y}{4} - \dfrac{1}{4} \le \dfrac{6y}{5} + \dfrac{1}{5}$

53. $1.1y - 0.2 \le 1.0 - 0.4y$

54. $-2x \ge 0$

Use the graph on page 219 and table at the bottom of this page to answer Problems 55–58. Let x represent the number of age discrimination suits filed from 1990 to 1994, in thousands. Translate each sentence into an inequality.

55. The number of age discrimination suits is at least 24.3 thousand.

56. The number of age discrimination suits is at most 33.9 thousand.

57. The number of age discrimination suits is between 24 and 35 thousand.

58. The number of age discrimination suits does not exceed 33.9 thousand.

Year	Suits
1990	24.3
1991	28.3
1992	30.4
1993	30.8
1994	33.9

**Age Discrimination Suits
1990–1994, in Thousands**

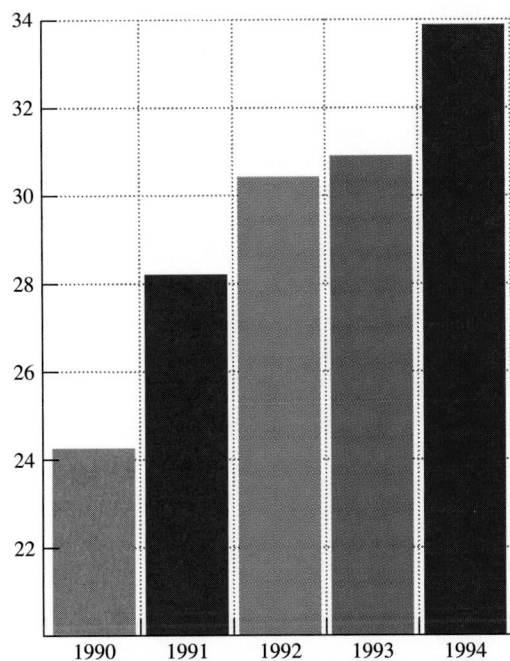

1990 1991 1992 1993 1994

Source: U.S. Equal Opportunity Employment
Commission

59. To pass a course, a student must have an average on three examinations of at least 60. If a student scores 42 and 74 on the first two tests, what is the range of scores that this student needs on the third test to pass the course?

60. The profit of a company is 90 times the number of customers served less $300. If its profits exceed $150,000, the company will be nationalized. What does this mean in terms of the number of customers served by the company?

61. A small powerboat has a maximum capacity of 1000 pounds. The boat's operators weigh 240 and 160 pounds. How many of the operators' small dogs can accompany them safely on one trip if each dog weighs 25 pounds?

62. The graph indicates that the percent of children living with a never-married parent is increasing and will overtake the percent of children living with a divorced parent. The models

$$P_{\text{divorced}} = -0.5x + 42$$
$$P_{\text{never-married}} = 1.1x + 24$$

approximate this situation, where P represents the respective percents and x represents the number of years after 1983. After what year (to the nearest whole year) will the percent of children living with a never-married parent exceed the percent of children living with a divorced parent?

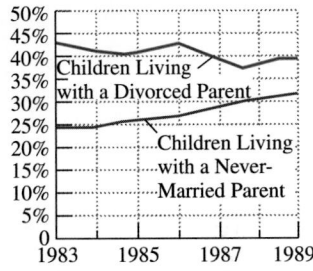

Source: U.S. Bureau of the
Census

C H A P T E R   2   T E S T

Solve each equation.

1. $4x - 15 = 13$

2. $12x + 4 = 7x - 21$

3. $8x - 5(x - 2) = x + 26$

4. $-\frac{3}{4}x = -15$

5. $\frac{x}{10} + \frac{1}{3} = \frac{x}{5} + \frac{1}{2}$

6. $x = 0.97 + 0.03x$

Solve each inequality. Write the answers in set-builder notation and graph the solution set on a number line.

7. $3x - 11 \leq -23$

8. $-5x > 30$

9. $2x + 3 < 4x - 1$

10. $3(x + 4) \geq 5x - 12$

11. $\frac{x}{6} + \frac{1}{8} \leq \frac{x}{2} - \frac{3}{4}$

Solve for the variable indicated.

12. $4x + 3y = 8$, for y

13. $V = \pi r^2 h$, for h

14. $L = \frac{P - 2W}{2}$ for W

15. 13.2 is 60% of what number?

16. What percent of 90 is 12.6?

Solve each problem.

17. The average annual salary S for teachers in the United States is given by the mathematical model

$$S = 1472t + 21,700$$

where t represents the number of years after 1984. How many years after 1984 will teachers be earning $48,196 annually? What year will that be?

18. Six more than twice a number is 34. What is the number?

19. The longest word in Spanish is *superextraordinarisimo,* meaning "extraordinary." The longest words in French and Portuguese mean "anticonstitutionally" and "with the highest degree of unconstitutionality" respectively, with the longer word in Portugese. The number of letters in these French and Portugese words form consecutive odd integers whose sum exceeds the longest word in Spanish by 30 letters. How many letters are there in the longest words in French and Portugese?

20. The bar graph indicates the ten longest rivers in the United States. The Missouri, Mississippi, and Yukon combined have a length of 6860 miles. The Missouri is 560 miles longer than the Yukon and the Mississippi is 1620 miles shorter than twice the length of the Yukon. Find the lengths of the top three longest U.S. rivers.

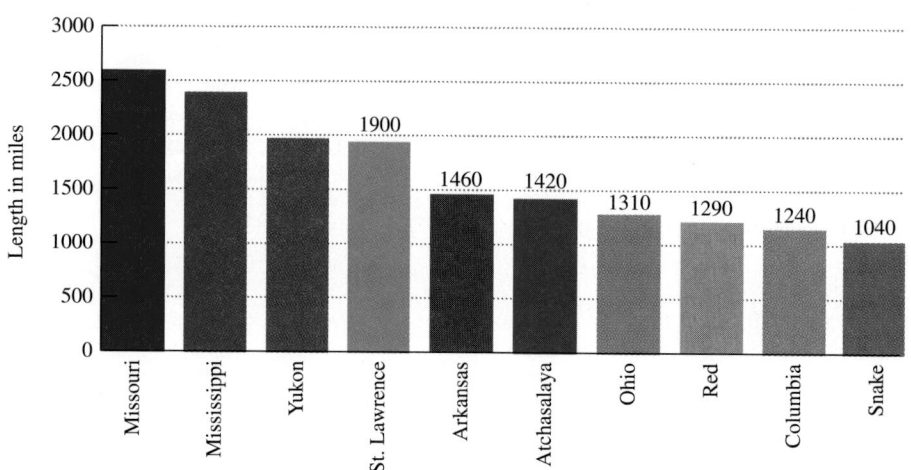

The Ten Longest Rivers in the United States

Source: U.S. Geological Survey

21. After a 35% price reduction, a computer is sold for $1430. What was the price before the reduction?

22. A mathematical model indicates that a person with no education can expect to earn $7200 yearly with annual income increases of $2600 for each year of education. How many years of education are needed to earn $35,800 per year?

23. The circle graph shows living arrangements of people over age 15 in the United States in 1995. If 24 million people lived alone, what was the U.S. population over age 15 in 1995?

24. The model $D = 43t + 381$ describes the U.S. gross federal debt D, in billions of dollars, t years after 1970. For what years from 1970 onward was the debt less than $639 billion?

25. A student has grades on three examinations of 76%, 80%, and 72%. What must the student earn on a fourth examination in order to have an average of at least 80%?

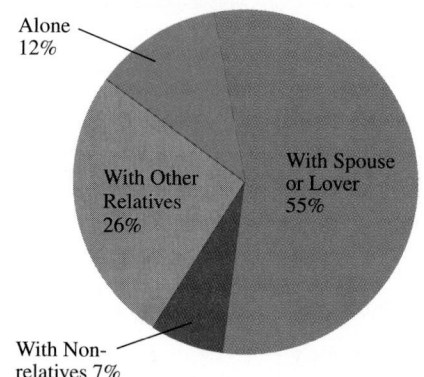

Living Arrangements in the United States, 1995

Alone 12%

With Spouse or Lover 55%

With Other Relatives 26%

With Non-relatives 7%

Source: U.S. Bureau of the Census

Problem Solving

Robert Longo, "Pressure" 1983. Two parts: and charcoal, graphite, and ink on paper. The Museum of Modern Art, New York. Gift of the Louis and Bessie Adler Foundation, Inc., Seymour M. Klein, President. Photograph © 1997. The Museum of Modern Art, New York.

Thinking skills and problem-solving activities are indispensable to every area of our lives. To some extent, we are all problem solvers. The problem solver's work is mostly a tangle of guesswork, analogy, wishful thinking, observing patterns, and frustration. To become a master problem solver may be as inaccessible as acquiring the skills of a virtuoso, but everyone can become a better, more confident problem solver.

Solutions   Tutorial   Video
Manual   3

Strategies for Solving Problems

Objectives

1 Solve problems using linear equations.
2 Solve problems using critical thinking strategies.

Critical thinking and problem solving are essential skills for success in both school and work. In Chapter 2, you learned about problem solving and translating a word problem into an equation. This section develops these strategies in more detail. You will also learn new problem-solving strategies, along with how and when to use them.

As you develop and gain confidence in your problem-solving abilities, you will be well on your way to become a skilled critical thinker who can solve problems in mathematics as well as other disciplines.

1 Solve problems using linear equations.

Study tip

Follow the five steps used to solve problems that appear in the margin.

Solving Problems by Translating Given Conditions into an Equation

Let's begin with the kind of word problems that were introduced in the previous chapter. You may want to take a minute or two to review the strategy for solving these problems on page 177 and the algebraic translation of English phrases on page 178. Remember that the most difficult part of the strategy involves translating the verbal conditions into an algebraic equation.

EXAMPLE 1 | **Finding an Unknown Number: Commas Make a Difference**

The product of 5, and a number decreased by 9, is 310. Find the number.

Solution

Let x = the number, the only unknown in the problem.

Steps 1 and 2. Represent unknown quantities in terms of x.

Step 3. Write an equation in x that describes the verbal conditions.

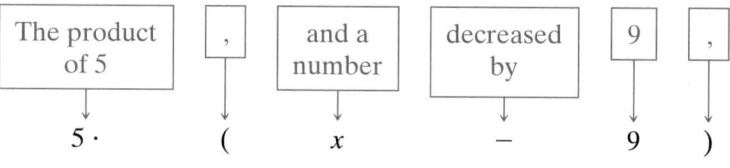

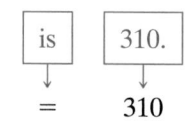

Step 4. Solve the equation and answer the question.

$$5(x - 9) = 310 \quad \text{This is the equation for the given sentence.}$$
$$5x - 45 = 310 \quad \text{Distribute.}$$
$$5x = 355 \quad \text{Add 45 to both sides.}$$
$$x = 71 \quad \text{Divide both sides by 5.}$$

The number is 71.

Step 5. Check.

When 71 is decreased by 9, we obtain $71 - 9 = 62$. The product of 5 and 62 is 310, as stated in the problem. ∎

ENRICHMENT ESSAY

Commas Make a Difference

The Study tip below illustrates that commas can alter the meaning of an algebraic word problem. Misplaced commas also lead to amusing and unexpected results. Some examples:

What's the latest dope?
What's the latest, dope?

Mr. Rogers, the secretary is 2 hours late.
Mr. Rogers, the secretary, is 2 hours late.

The play ended, happily.
The play ended happily.

Population of New York City broken down by age and sex.
Population of New York City, broken down by age and sex.

In the parade will be several hundred children, carrying flags, and many important officials.
In the parade will be several hundred children, carrying flags and many important officials.

Do not break your bread or roll in your soup.
Do not break your bread, or roll in your soup.

Woman, without her man, is nothing.
Woman, without her, man is nothing.

Study tip

When you translate given conditions into an equation, always think about the meaning of the phrases you are translating. For example, changing just the position of a comma can alter the meaning of the problem, leading to a different equation. Consider the translation of "The product of 5 and a number, decreased by 9, is 310." If x = the number, we obtain:

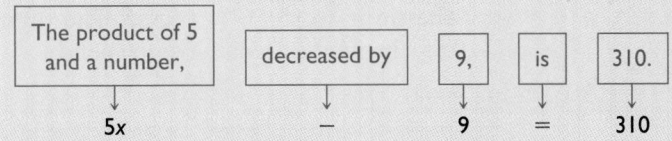

The product of 5 and a number,	decreased by	9,	is	310.
$5x$	$-$	9	$=$	310

Solving the equation gives $x = 63.8$. In this case, the number is 63.8.

Solving Problems by Creating Verbal Models and then Translating into an Equation

Some word problems about an unknown number are fairly routine because the conditions necessary for writing an equation are clearly given. A more difficult situation is when the conditions are only implied. The first step in such a situation is to write an English sentence that clearly identifies the operations involved. This sentence should contain a word such as "is" or "equals." Such a sentence serves as a *verbal model* that is then translated into an equation.

We illustrate how to write verbal models that describe problems in Examples 2–4.

EXAMPLE 2   A Word Problem with Implied Conditions

If you have $19.55 to spend for dinner and plan to leave a 15% tip, what is the maximum-priced dinner you can purchase?

Solution

To have the maximum-priced dinner, you must spend the entire $19.55. This implies that the cost of the meal plus the amount of the tip is $19.55, which serves as our verbal model.

Let

Steps 1 and 2. Represent unknown quantities in terms of x.

$$x = \text{Cost of the meal}$$
$$0.15x = \text{Amount of the tip (15\% of the meal's cost)}$$

Step 3. Write an equation in x that describes the verbal conditions.

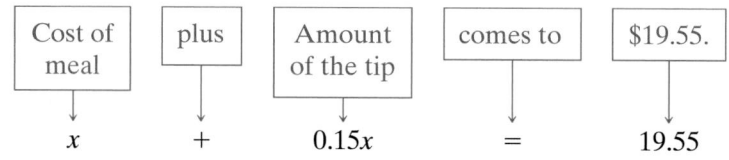

Cost of meal	plus	Amount of the tip	comes to	$19.55.
↓	↓	↓	↓	↓
x	$+$	$0.15x$	$=$	19.55

Step 4. Solve the equation.

$$x + 0.15x = 19.55 \qquad \text{This is the equation for the implied English sentence.}$$
$$100(x + 0.15x) = 100(19.55) \qquad \text{Clear the decimals by multiplying by 100. (This step is optional.)}$$
$$100x + 15x = 1955 \qquad \text{Apply the distributive property.}$$
$$115x = 1955 \qquad \text{Combine like terms.}$$
$$x = 17 \qquad \text{Divide both sides by 115.}$$

The maximum-priced dinner is $17.00.

The tip is $(0.15)(17) = \$2.55$. The dinner plus the tip equals $17 + 2.55 = \$19.55$, the amount you have to spend. ∎

Study tip

Example 2 can be solved by using the inequality $x + 0.15x \leq 19.55$, since the meal plus tip must be less than or equal to $19.55. The solution $x \leq 17$ implies that $17.00 or less can be spent on the meal, so that the maximum-priced dinner is $17.00.

EXAMPLE 3   Modeling U.S. Population

In 1960, the population of the United States was approximately 179.5 million. If the population has been growing by 2.35 million yearly, in what year will the population reach 297 million?

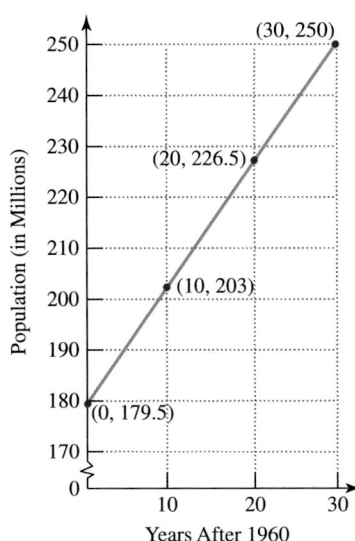

Figure 3.1

U.S. population over time

Steps 1 and 2. Represent unknown quantities in terms of *x*.

Step 3. Write an equation in *x* that describes the verbal conditions.

Step 4. Solve the equation and answer the question.

Step 5. Check.

Discover for yourself

Copy the graph in Figure 3.1 and leave room so that you can extend it to the right. To find the year in which population will reach 297 million, locate 297 on the vertical axis and then move right to the line graph. At that point, move down to the horizontal axis and read the number. This will give you the number of years after 1960 for the 297 million population. Use arithmetic to verify this number.

Solution

Let x = the number of years after 1960 when the population will reach 297 million. Since the population has been growing by 2.35 million people each year and the 1960 population was 179.5 million, we can form the following verbal model.

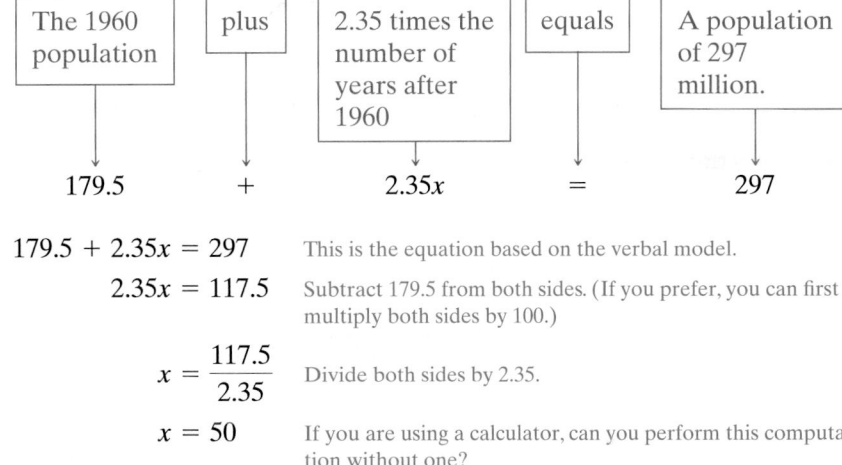

$$179.5 + 2.35x = 297 \quad \text{This is the equation based on the verbal model.}$$

$$2.35x = 117.5 \quad \text{Subtract 179.5 from both sides. (If you prefer, you can first multiply both sides by 100.)}$$

$$x = \frac{117.5}{2.35} \quad \text{Divide both sides by 2.35.}$$

$$x = 50 \quad \text{If you are using a calculator, can you perform this computation without one?}$$

The model predicts that the population of the United States will be 297 million 50 years after 1960, in the year 2010.

Population 50 years after 1960
= 179.5 + 2.35(50)
= 179.5 + 117.5
= 297 (million) ✓

Discover for yourself

Solve Example 4 without introducing a variable and without using algebra.

Steps 1 and 2. Represent unknown quantities in terms of *x*.

EXAMPLE 4   Modeling Height and Weight

An HMO pamphlet contains the following recommended weight model for women: "Give yourself 100 pounds for the first 5 feet plus 5 pounds for every inch over 5 feet tall." Using this model, what height corresponds to an ideal weight of 135 pounds?

Solution

It is certainly possible to let x represent height in inches. However, since the pamphlet emphasizes heights over 5 feet, let's instead let x = height in inches in excess of 5 feet. Since the ideal weight is 100 pounds for a height of 5 feet and 5 pounds is recommended for every inch over 5 feet, we can form the following verbal model.

Step 3. Write an equation in x that describes the verbal conditions.

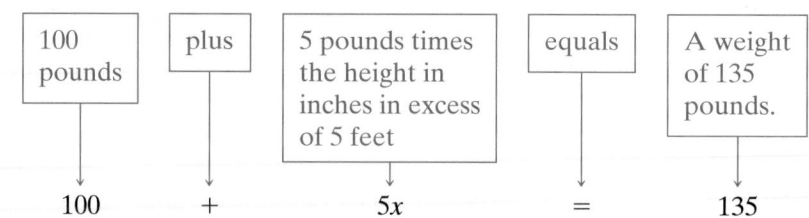

100 pounds	plus	5 pounds times the height in inches in excess of 5 feet	equals	A weight of 135 pounds.
100	+	5x	=	135

Step 4. Solve the equation and answer the question.

$100 + 5x = 135$ This is the equation based on the verbal model.

$5x = 35$ Subtract 100 from each side.

$x = 7$ Divide both sides by 5.

The ideal weight of 135 pounds corresponds to a woman who is 5 feet + 7 inches, or 5 feet, 7 inches tall. This is illustrated in Figure 3.2.

The ideal weight for a 5-foot, 7-inch woman is 100 pounds (for the first 5 feet) plus 5 pounds times 7, for a total of 135 pounds. This is the weight given in the problem. ∎

Step 5. Check.

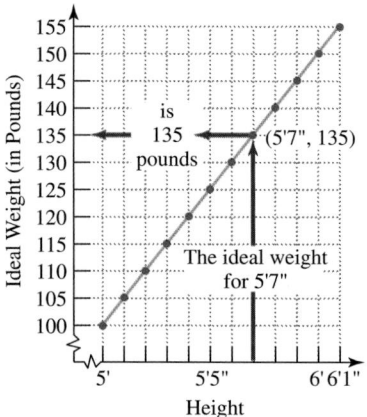

Figure 3.2

Visualizing ideal weight for a height of 5'7"

Steps 1 and 2. Use a variable to represent unknown quantities.

> **S**tudy tip
>
> If two quantities have a sum of T, and x represents one quantity, the other quantity is represented by $T − x$.

Solving Problems by Using Tables to Organize Information

In Section 2.4, we encountered the simple interest model $Prt = I$ (the product of the principal invested and the interest rate and the time of the investment gives the interest). If the time is one year, the model is $Pr = I$. Problems involving this model can frequently be organized by using a table.

EXAMPLE 5   **Solving a Simple Interest Problem**

A person invested $16,000, part at 8% and the remainder at 6%. If the total yearly interest from these investments was $1180, find the amount invested at each rate.

Solution

Let

x = Amount invested at 8%

$16,000 − x$ = Amount invested at 6% (since the total amount invested was $16,000)

	Principal	×	**Rate**	=	**Interest**
8% Investment	x		0.08		$0.08x$
6% Investment	$16,000 − x$		0.06		$0.06(16,000 − x)$

Total yearly interest was $1180.

Step 3. Write an equation in x that describes the verbal conditions.

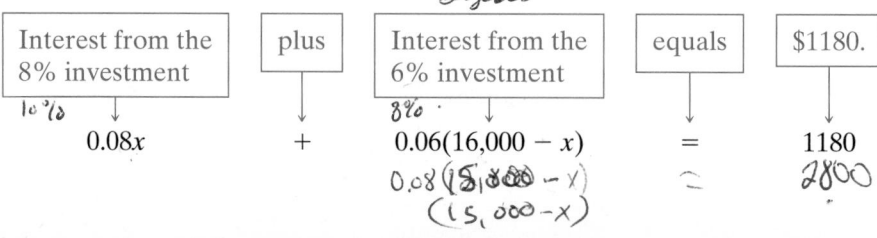

Interest from the 8% investment	plus	Interest from the 6% investment	equals	$1180.
$0.08x$	+	$0.06(16,000 − x)$	=	1180

$0.09 \quad 0.12\,(25,000 - x) = 2410$

Step 4. Solve the equation and answer the question.

$$0.08x + 0.06(16,000 - x) = 1180 \qquad \text{This is the equation implied by the problem's conditions.}$$

$$8x + 6(16,000 - x) = 118,000 \qquad \text{Multiply by 100 to clear the decimals (optional).}$$

$$8x + 96,000 - 6x = 118,000 \qquad \text{Use the distributive property.}$$

$$2x + 96,000 = 118,000 \qquad \text{Combine like terms.}$$

$$2x = 22,000 \qquad \text{Subtract 96,000 from both sides.}$$

$$x = 11,000 \qquad \text{Divide by 2.}$$

Amount invested at 8% $= x = \$11,000$

Amount invested at 6% $= 16,000 - x = 16,000 - 11,000 = \$5000$

Thus, \$11,000 was invested at 8% and \$5000 was invested at 6%.

Step 5. Check.

Annual interest at 8% $= (11,000)(0.08) = \$880$

Annual interest at 6% $= (5000)(0.06) = \$300$

Total yearly interest $= 880 + 300 = \$1180$ ■

Chemists and pharmacists often have to change the concentration of solutions and other mixtures. In these situations, the amount of a particular ingredient in the solution or mixture is expressed as a percent of the total. The basic percent model

$$A = PB \quad (A \text{ is } P \text{ percent of } B)$$

and a table similar to the one in Example 5 are helpful in solving mixture problems.

EXAMPLE 6   A Solution Mixture Problem

A chemist needs to mix an 18% acid solution with a 45% acid solution to obtain a 12-liter mixture consisting of 36% acid. How many liters of each of the acid solutions must be used?

Solution

Steps 1 and 2. Use a variable to represent unknown quantities.

Let $x =$ the number of liters of the 18% acid solution to be used in the mixture. Since the solution contains 12 liters, let $12 - x =$ the number of liters of the 45% acid solution to be used in the mixture. The situation is illustrated in Figure 3.3 at the bottom of page 228.

	Number of Liters	×	Percent of Acid	=	Amount of Acid
18% Acid Solution	x		18% = 0.18		$0.18x$
45% Acid Solution	$12 - x$		45% = 0.45		$0.45(12 - x)$
36% Acid Solution	12		36% = 0.36		$0.36(12)$

Step 3. Write an equation in x that describes the verbal conditions.

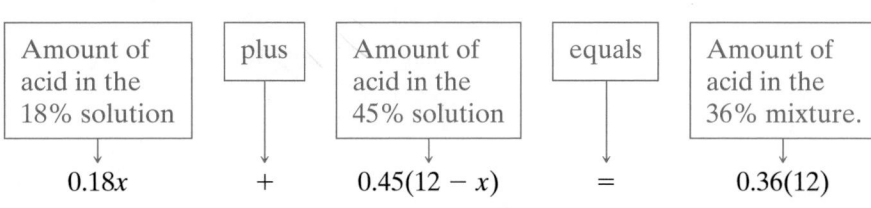

$$0.18x \qquad + \qquad 0.45(12 - x) \qquad = \qquad 0.36(12)$$

Step 4. Solve the equation and answer the question.

$$0.18x + 0.45(12 - x) = 0.36(12)$$ This is the equation implied by the problem's conditions.

$$18x + 45(12 - x) = 36(12)$$ Multiply by 100 to clear the decimals. (Optional.)

$$18x + 540 - 45x = 432$$ Use the distributive property.

$$-27x + 540 = 432$$ Combine like terms.

$$-27x = -108$$ Subtract 540 from both sides.

$$x = 4$$ Divide both sides by -27.

Number of liters of the 18% solution $= x = 4$

Number of liters of the 45% solution $= 12 - x = 12 - 4 = 8$

The chemist should mix 4 liters of the 18% acid solution with 8 liters of the 45% acid solution.

Step 5. Check.

Amount of acid in 18% solution $= 0.18(4) = 0.72$ liter

Amount of acid in 45% solution $= 0.45(8) = \underline{3.6 \text{ liters}}$

Amount of acid in mixture $= 4.32$ liters

This checks because it was originally known that the 12-liter mixture was 36% acid, and 0.36(12) is 4.32 liters of acid. ∎

Examples 5 and 6 are nearly identical. They are both based on mathematical models, the simple interest model and the basic percent model, and they are both solved by organizing information in tables.

Another similar situation involves *uniform motion,* in which an object is moving at a specified rate R for a specified period of time T. The distance that the object travels is modeled by

$$D = RT \quad \text{(Distance equals rate times time)}$$

which is called the *distance formula* or the *uniform motion model.*

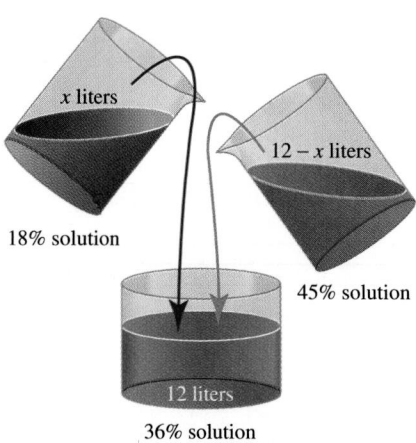

Figure 3.3

Obtaining a 12-liter 36% acid mixture

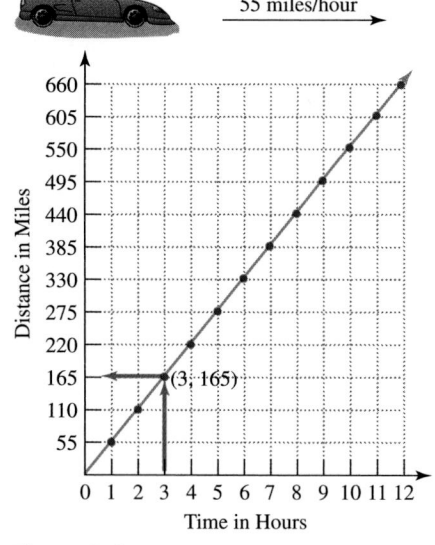

Figure 3.4

Distance for 3 hours of travel

Figure 3.4 at the bottom of page 228, shows the distance traveled by an automobile moving at an average rate of 55 miles per hour for various periods of time. The ordered pair (3, 165) signifies that in 3 hours the car covers 165 miles. This is verified using the uniform motion model

$$D = RT = 55(3) = 165.$$

Example 7 is solved by using the distance formula and organizing information in a table.

EXAMPLE 7   Solving a Uniform Motion Problem

New York City and Washington, D.C., are about 240 miles apart. A car leaves New York City traveling toward Washington, D.C., at 55 miles per hour. At the same time, a bus leaves Washington bound for New York at 45 miles per hour. How long will it take before they meet?

Solution

Let t = the number of hours it takes for the vehicles to meet.

	Rate	×	**Time**	=	**Distance**
Car	55		t		$55t$
Bus	45		t		$45t$

At the moment that the two vehicles meet, the sum of their distances $(55t + 45t)$ is equal to the distance they were originally apart (240 miles), as shown in Figure 3.5.

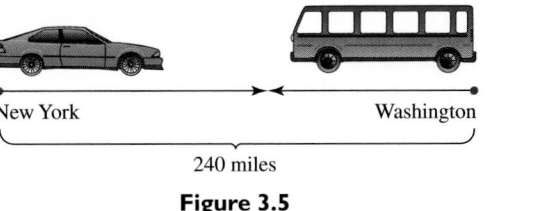

Figure 3.5

When these vehicles meet, the sum of their distances is 240 miles.

Step 3. Write an equation in t that describes the verbal conditions.

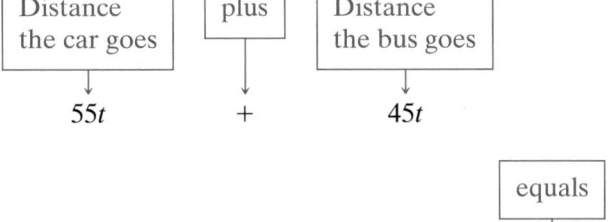

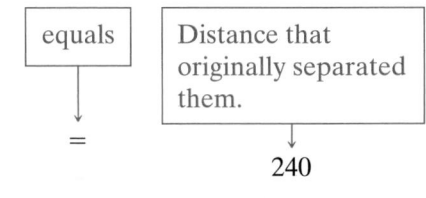

Step 4. Solve the equation and answer the question.

$55t + 45t = 240$ This is the equation implied by the problem's conditions.

$100t = 240$ Combine like terms.

$t = 2.4$ Divide both sides by 100.

The vehicles meet after 2.4 hours (or 2 hours 24 minutes).

S
tudy tip

When using $D = RT$, if rate is given in *miles per hour,* time must be expressed in *hours.* Observe how the units cancel:

$$\left(55 \frac{miles}{hour}\right) \cdot (3 \; hours)$$

$$= 165 \; miles$$

Steps 1 and 2. Use a variable to represent unknown quantities.

Step 5. Check.

During these 2.4 hours, the car travels 55 · 2.4, or 132 miles, while the bus travels 45 · 2.4, or 108 miles. The sum of these distances is 132 + 108, or 240 miles, the distance between New York and Washington. ∎

2 Solve problems using critical thinking strategies.

Solving Problems Using Critical Thinking Strategies

The problems we have considered so far can all be solved by writing an equation. However, if a mathematical problem cannot be solved by translating sentences into equations, we must find a different approach. The following examples show some other strategies that we can use to solve problems.

EXAMPLE 8   **Solving a Problem by Making a Systematic List**

Suppose you are an engineer programming the automatic gate for a 50-cent toll. The gate is programmed for exact change only and will not accept pennies. How many coin combinations must you program the gate to accept?

Solution

The total of the change must always be 50 cents. Let's tackle the problem by making a list, beginning with the coins of larger value and working toward the coins of smaller value. The list is shown in Table 3.1.

TABLE 3.1 Exact Change for 50 Cents; No Pennies

Half-Dollars	Quarters	Dimes	Nickels
1	0	0	0
0	2	0	0
0	1	2	1
0	1	1	3
0	1	0	5
0	0	5	0
0	0	4	2
0	0	3	4
0	0	2	6
0	0	1	8
0	0	0	10

Table 3.1 indicates that there are 11 coin combinations that you must program the gate to accept. ∎

EXAMPLE 9   **Solving a Problem by Looking for a Pattern**

Consider the first four rectangular numbers (2, 6, 12, and 20):

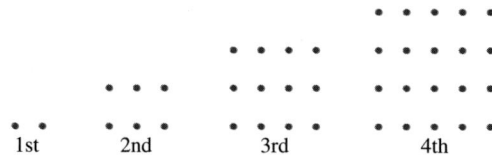

1st   2nd   3rd   4th

Use patterns to complete the following table.

Rectangular Number	1st	2nd	3rd	4th	5th	6th	12th	nth
Number of Dots	2	6	12	20				

Solution

Mathematics involves the study of patterns. As you look at this example, you probably realize that a great deal of thought may be involved to actually determine a possible emerging pattern. A bit more information in the table should be helpful:

1st Rectangular Number	2nd	3rd	4th
$2 = 1 \times 2$	$6 = 2 \times 3$	$12 = 3 \times 4$	$20 = 4 \times 5$

Notice that each rectangular number is expressed as the product of two numbers. The first number is the position of the rectangular number in the list. The second number is one more than the first number. Thus, the fifth rectangular number (fifth in the list) is 5×6, or 30. The sixth rectangular number is $6 \times 7 = 42$. The 12th is $12 \times 13 = 156$. The pattern has emerged, and we see that the nth number is n times $(n + 1)$ or $n(n + 1)$.

1st Rectangular Number	2nd	3rd	4th	5th	6th	12th	nth
2	6	12	20	30	42	156	$n(n + 1)$

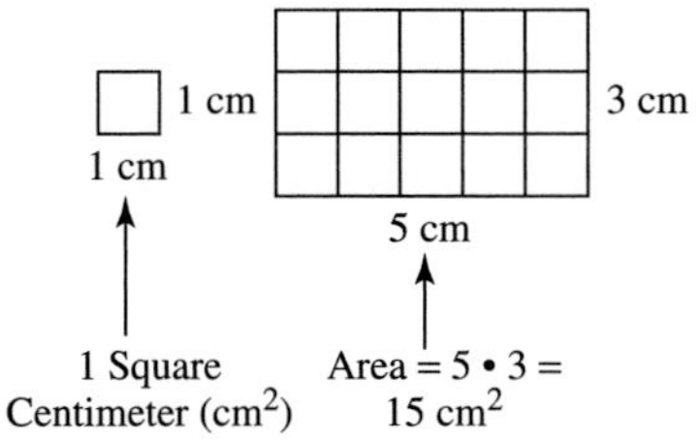

■

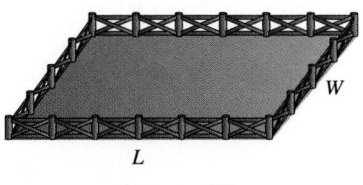

1 cm / 1 cm
1 Square Centimeter (cm²)
3 cm
5 cm
Area $= 5 \cdot 3 = 15$ cm²

Figure 3.6

Measuring area with square units

Example 10 involves both the area and the perimeter of a rectangle. To determine the area of any plane geometric figure, we must find the number of square units in the region bounded by the figure. A square unit of area is a region bounded by a square whose sides are all one unit long. For example, the left-hand side of Figure 3.6 shows a square with sides each 1 centimeter long, called a square centimeter (cm²), that can serve as a unit of area. We can use this unit of area to determine the area of the rectangle on the right-hand side of the figure.

W
L
Area: $A = LW$
Perimeter: $P = 2L + 2W$

Figure 3.7

Area and perimeter of a rectangle

7 yards
1 yard Area $= 7$ yd² Width $= 1$ yard
Length $= 7$ yards

EXAMPLE 10   Solving a Problem by Guessing and Checking

The rectangular corral in Figure 3.7 is to be fenced off with 16 yards of wood planking. What should be the dimensions of the rectangular corral to have the maximum area possible?

Solution

Let's guess at various dimensions for the length and then see what happens to the resulting area. For example, if the length is 7 yards, this means that we have already used 14 yards of planking for the two opposite sides, leaving 2 yards. Thus, the width must be 1 yard and the area of the corral is

$$A = LW = 7 \cdot 1 = 7 \text{ square yards (yd}^2\text{)}.$$

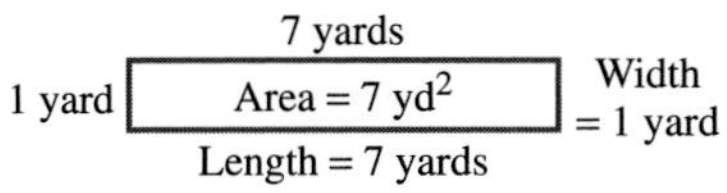

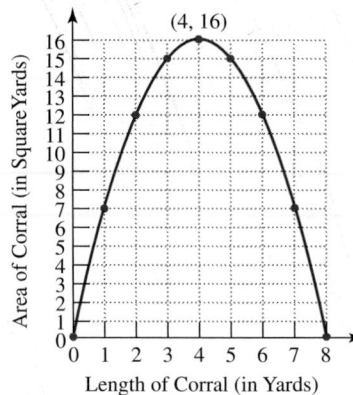

Figure 3.8

Maximizing area

iscover for yourself

Explain how the graph in Figure 3.8 verifies the solution to Example 10. Also explain the geometric significance of the point (8, 0).

Study tip

Here's a summary of useful strategies for solving problems.

Make a table or a chart.
Look for a pattern.
Solve a similar simpler problem.
Draw a sketch.
Write an equation and solve it.
If a formula applies, use it.
Work backward.
Guess and check.
Use trial and error.
Use common sense.
Look for a "catch" if an answer seems too obvious, or impossible.

We can organize our work in a table, with the amount of planking used for the length getting smaller.

Amount of Planking for the Length	Planking Left for the Width	Area = LW	
7	1	7 yd^2	←This area is too small. Guess again.
6	2	12 yd^2	←The area is getting larger. Guess again.
5	3	15 yd^2	←This is better. Guess again.
4	4	16 yd^2	←This might be it.
4.5	3.5	15.75 yd^2	←Now the area is getting smaller.

Try some other combinations for the length and width of the corral. Guessing and checking these possibilities should convince you that the dimensions of the rectangular corral with maximum area (and a perimeter of 16 yards) are 4 yards by 4 yards. In other words, a square corral should be enclosed. ■

EXAMPLE 11   **Solving a Problem by Working Backward and Eliminating Possibilities**

Equally priced legal pads were purchased for $3.21. If it is known that each pad cost more than 50 cents, how many pads were purchased and what did each pad cost?

Solution

Let's begin by working backward from the total $3.21. If 7 pads were purchased at 50¢, the total would be $3.50, which exceeds $3.21. This means that the number of pads purchased must be 6, 5, 4, 3, or 2. (We know that more than one pad was purchased since the example uses the plural, pads.)

Now let's eliminate some of these possibilities. The number of pads purchased must divide evenly into 321.

$$
\begin{array}{r} 160 \\ 2\overline{)321} \\ 320 \\ \hline 1 \end{array}
\qquad
\boxed{\begin{array}{r} 107 \\ 3\overline{)321} \\ 321 \\ \hline 0 \end{array}}
\qquad
\begin{array}{r} 80 \\ 4\overline{)321} \\ 320 \\ \hline 1 \end{array}
\qquad
\begin{array}{r} 64 \\ 5\overline{)321} \\ 320 \\ \hline 1 \end{array}
\qquad
\begin{array}{r} 53 \\ 6\overline{)321} \\ 318 \\ \hline 3 \end{array}
$$

Remainder   Remainder   Remainder   Remainder

These divisions show that 321 is a multiple of 3 and is not a multiple of 2, 4, 5, or 6. Thus, we conclude that 3 pads were purchased. Each pad cost $\dfrac{\$3.21}{3}$ or $1.07. ■

ENRICHMENT ESSAY

Critical Thinking: Is This a Trick Question?

Think about the following questions carefully before answering since each contains some sort of trick.

Sample: Is it legal in Miami for a man to marry his widow's sister?

Answer: Of course, it is not legal. Dead people aren't allowed to marry.

The clue to this question is the phrase "his *widow's* sister." Now that you've been set up, see if you can answer each question without developing mental whiplash. (The answers appear in the answer section.)

1. Can a woman living in San Francisco, California, be buried in Los Angeles?

2. Do they have a fourth of July in England?
3. How many animals of each species did Moses take aboard the ark with him?
4. Some months have 30 days. Some have 31. How many months have 28 days?
5. If you had only one match and entered a log cabin in which there was a candle, a fireplace, and a woodburning stove, which should you light first?
6. Two people played chess. They played five games and each won the same number of games. How?
7. What is the product?

$$(x - a)(x - b)(x - c)(x - d) \cdots (x - y)(x - z)$$

PROBLEM SET 3.1

Practice and Application Problems

1. The product of 7, and a number decreased by 11, is 588. Find the number.

2. The product of 8, and a number decreased by 14, is 296. Find the number.

3. The product of 7 and a number, decreased by 11, is 290. Find the number.

4. The product of 8 and a number, decreased by 14, is 218. Find the number.

5. If you have $32.20 to spend for dinner and plan to leave a 15% tip, what is the maximum-priced dinner you can purchase?

6. If you have $55.20 to spend for dinner and plan to leave a 15% tip, what is the maximum-priced dinner you can purchase?

7. Arnold is selling his house and must sell it at a price that allows him to pay off his mortgage of $111,600. Arnold's realtor receives 7% of the selling price of the house. What should be the selling price?

8. Maria is working with a realtor whose commission is 10% of the selling price of her house. If she wants to get $72,000 to pay off her mortgage, what should be the selling price?

9. An automobile repair shop charged a customer $448, listing $63 for parts and the remainder for labor. If the cost of labor is $35 per hour, how many hours of labor did it take to repair the car?

10. A repair bill on a yacht came to $1603, including $532 for parts and the remainder for labor. If the cost of labor is $63 per hour, how many hours of labor did it take to repair the yacht?

11. The preindustrial carbon dioxide (CO_2) level of concentration was 280 parts per million (ppm). This level remained relatively constant until 1939. After 1939, the level has been increasing by 1.44 ppm yearly. In what year will the level reach 559.36 ppm? (It is estimated that a doubling of the preindustrial level of CO_2 will cause an average global temperature increase of 5.4°F. An increase of 1.8°F in global temperature can cause a one-foot rise in ocean levels.)

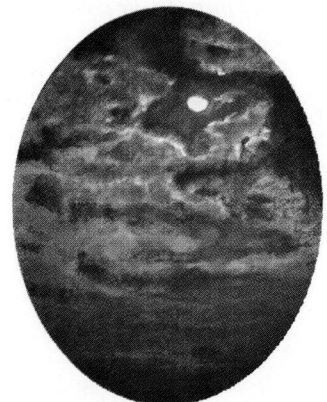

Jordan Massengale, "Heaven Night"

12. In 1980, the average yearly salary for teachers in the United States was $16,116. If the salary is increasing by $1496 per year, in what year will the salary reach $44,540?

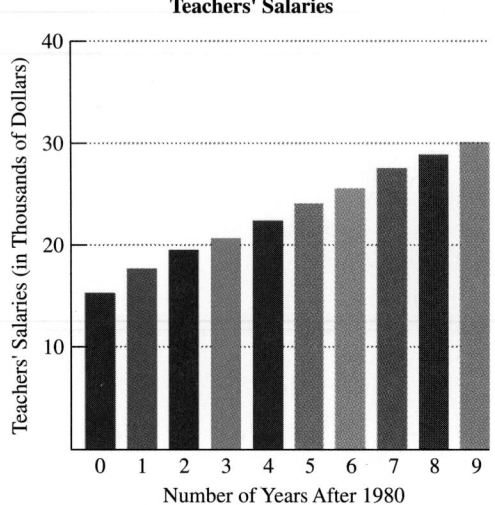

Teachers' Salaries

Source: National Education Association

13. The average weight for female infants at birth is 7 pounds, with a monthly weight gain of 1.5 pounds. After how many months does a baby girl weigh 16 pounds?

14. The average height for men is 34 inches plus half of their father's height in inches. What is the approximate height of a father whose son is 5 feet, 10 inches tall?

15. A person invested $25,000, part at 9% and the remainder at 12% simple interest. If the total yearly interest from these investments was $2550, find the amount invested at each rate.

16. A person invested $18,750, part at 12% and the remainder at 10% simple interest. If the total yearly interest from both investments was $2117, find the amount invested at each rate.

17. Money was invested at 12% and 14% simple interest, with twice as much invested at 12% than at 14%. If the yearly interest from both investments was $256.50, how much was invested at each rate?

18. Money was invested at 8% and 12% simple interest, with $3000 more invested at 8% than at 12%. If the yearly interest from both investments was $760, how much was invested at each rate?

19. A chemist needs to mix a 30% acid solution with a 12% acid solution to obtain a 50-liter mixture consisting of 20% acid. How many liters of each of the acid solutions must be used?

20. A chemist needs to mix a 5% acid solution with a 10% acid solution to obtain a 50-liter mixture consisting of 8% acid. How many liters of each of the acid solutions must be used?

21. Two cities are 315 miles apart. A car leaves one of the cities traveling toward the second city at 50 miles per hour. At the same time, a bus leaves the second city at 55 miles per hour. How long will it take for them to meet?

22. Two cities are 210 kilometers apart. A car leaves one of the cities traveling toward the second city at 60 kilometers per hour. At the same time, a bus leaves the second city bound for the first city at 80 kilometers per hour. How long will it take for them to meet?

23. Two cyclists, one averaging 10 miles per hour and the other 12 miles per hour, start from the same town at the same time. If they travel in opposite directions, after how long will they be 66 miles apart?

24. Two cars start from the same place at the same time. They travel in opposite directions. One averages 62 kilometers per hour, and the other 48 kilometers per hour. After how long will they be 550 kilometers apart?

Looking for a pattern is an important component in solving problems. Find a possible pattern in the number sequences in Problems 25–30 and then use the pattern to determine the three missing numbers in each sequence. (Note: Answers may vary.)

25. 2, 8, 14, 20, _____, _____, _____

26. 1, 3, 6, 10, _____, _____, _____

27. 15, 11, 7, 3, _____, _____, _____

28. 1, 2, 6, 24, 120, _____, _____, _____

29. 3, 4, 7, 11, 18, 29, _____, _____, _____

30. −16, −8, −4, −2, _____, _____, _____

31.
$$1 + 3 = 4$$
$$1 + 3 + 5 = 9$$
$$1 + 3 + 5 + 7 = 16$$
$$1 + 3 + 5 + 7 + 9 = 25$$

As shown here, the sum of the first two odd numbers is 4, the sum of the first 3 odd numbers is 9, the sum of the first four odd numbers is 16, and the sum of the first five odd numbers is 25. Determine a pattern and use this pattern to find the sum of the first 100 odd numbers.

32. How many ways are there of making change for 25 cents using only nickels and dimes?

33. In basketball, 3 points are given for a long shot, 2 points for a field goal, and 1 point for a free throw. In how many ways can 15 points be scored?

34. What number is less than 100, odd, a multiple of 5, divisible by 3, and has a sum of digits that is odd?

35. Three people have telephone area codes whose three digits have the same sum. One of the area codes is 252. None of the area codes contains a digit that is in one of the other area codes. No area code has a first digit of 4. One of the area codes begins with 6. Another area code ends with 1. What is the area code that ends with 1?

Use the number of dots in the first four terms in Problems 36–38 to determine a pattern. Use this pattern to describe how many dots would occur in the tenth term and how many dots would occur in the nth term.

36.

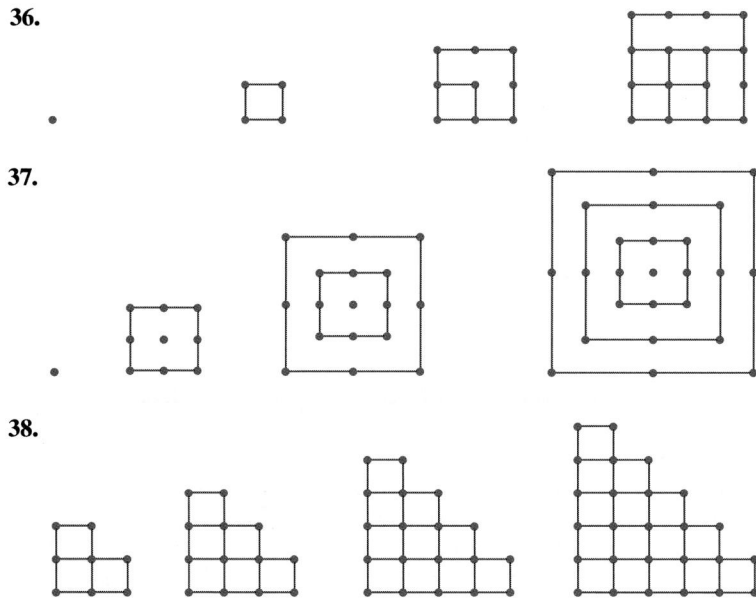

37.

38.

39. Consider the first four triangular numbers (1, 3, 6, and 10):

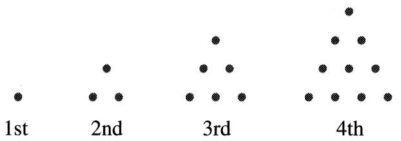

1st	2nd	3rd	4th
1st	2nd	3rd	4th

Use patterns to complete the table:

1st Triangular Number	2nd	3rd	4th	5th	6th	12th	nth
1	3	6	10				

Each row below (Problems 40–46) contains a sequence of numbers. In each row there is a pattern, and consequently a formula, for the number in the nth position. Fill in the missing entries in the table.

	1st Term ($n = 1$)	2nd Term ($n = 2$)	3rd Term ($n = 3$)	4th Term ($n = 4$)	5th Term ($n = 5$)	Formula for the nth Term
40.	2	4	6	8		$2n$
41.	1	3	5			$2n - 1$
42.	3	5				$2n + 1$
43.	5	7	9	11		
44.	1	4	9	16		
45.	2		18			$2n^2$
46.	1	8	27	64	125	

47. Place addition signs in the left side of the equation so that a true statement results.

9 8 7 6 5 4 3 2 1 = 99

48. Use the following clues to find what year the first Super Bowl was played.
   a. No digit is an 8.
   b. The hundreds digit is 3 more than the tens digit.
   c. The sum of the digits is 23.

Problems 49–59 consist of true given statements followed by a conclusion. If the conclusion is true, the argument is valid. *If the conclusion is false or not necessarily true, the argument is* invalid. *Label each argument valid or invalid.*

49. Given: One more than three times some number is 16.
   Conclusion: The number is 5.

50. Given: The first number contains two digits. The second number contains one digit.
   Conclusion: The first number is greater than the second number.

51. Given: Two numbers are both even.
   Conclusion: The numbers differ by two.

52. Given: My number is less than 7. Your number is greater than 3.
   Conclusion: Our numbers cannot be equal.

53. Given: My number is 8. Your number is 10. Fred's number is three greater than mine.
   Conclusion: Fred's number is 1 less than yours.

54. Given: Ana's number is odd. Jose's number is one greater than Ana's number. Jud's number is three less than Jose's number.
   Conclusion: Jud's number is even.

55. Given: Tony's number is divisible by 5. Maria's number is divisible by 3.
   Conclusion: Tony and Maria cannot have the same number.

56. Given: My number is greater than 16 and less than 19. Your number is greater than 12 and less than 20.
   Conclusion: Our numbers could be the same.

57. Given: In a football game, twice the number of points scored by the winning team was 14 less than 3 times the number of points scored by the losing team. The winners won by 4 points.
   Conclusion: The final score of the game was 26 to 22.

58. Given: 50 is divided by $\frac{1}{2}$. 10 is then added.
   Conclusion: The resulting number is 35.

59. Given: Two numbers have a sum of B. One of the numbers is A.
   Conclusion: The other number is $B - A$.

Do not actually solve Problems 60–67. However, as you consider the solution process, determine if you have been given too little numerical information to solve the problem, just the right amount of numerical information to solve the problem, or too much numerical information (meaning that you can solve the problem and not use some of the given numbers).

60. When three times a number is increased by 2, the result is 14. The number is greater than zero. Find the number.

61. The mathematical model

$$GP\% = \frac{\text{Sales} - \text{Overhead}}{\text{Sales}} \times 100$$

describes gross profit percent ($GP\%$) in terms of sales and overhead. Suppose that a company wanted to make a gross profit of 25%. What would be the company's overhead in this situation?

62. The model $I = E/R$ describes current (I) in terms of voltage (E) and resistance (R). Find the voltage necessary to push a 0.5-ampere current through a resistance of 440 ohms.

63. Ada weighs 10 pounds more than Lorna, and Ana weighs 10 pounds more than Ada. Determine each person's weight.

64. An automobile repair shop pays its employees $20 an hour. The cost of labor is $35 an hour. The shop charged a customer $180, listing $40 for parts and the remainder for labor. How many hours did the shop work on the auto?

65. A pair of shoes is on sale at 35% off the original price. If the sale price is $55, what was the original price?

66. A merchant sells ballpoint pens, some for $1.50 each and the rest for $2.00 each. If receipts from a day's sale of pens total $51.00, how many of each kind were sold?

67. A 56-inch board is cut into three pieces. The shortest piece is 16 inches shorter than the middle-sized piece, and the longest piece is 1 foot longer than the middle-sized piece. What is the length of the shortest piece?

Technology Problems

Use a graphing calculator to solve Problems 68–70.

68. There are four different ways to express 96 as the difference of the squares of two natural numbers. Find three of the ways.

69. A prime number is a natural number greater than 1 divisible only by itself and 1. Find the least prime number greater than 720.

70. Find $7^1, 7^2, 7^3, 7^4, \ldots$ through 7^9. In each case write down the units digit or the ones digit of the result. Describe the pattern that you observe. Use this pattern to find the units digit of 7^{100}.

Writing in Mathematics

Write a word problem associated with each of the situations in Problems 71–73. Sample: Let x = a number: $4x + 3 = 23$. Solution: When four times some number is increased by three, the sum is 23. Find the number.

71. Let x = a number: $4x - 5 = 45$

72. Let x = a number: $4(x - 5) = 24$

73. $5x + 10(3x - 1) = 60$ (*Hint:* The problem should involve nickels and dimes.)

74. Translate the phrase "the sum of 6 and a number times 2" into an algebraic expression in two different ways. What further information must be given to determine which translation into algebra is desired? Is English more ambiguous than the language of algebra? Describe additional examples of this ambiguity.

Critical Thinking Problems

Problems 75–79 are trick questions that can be solved without using an equation.

75. How many three-cent stamps are there in a dozen?

76. How much dirt is there in a hole that is 4 feet wide, 6 feet long, and 5 feet deep?

77. A doctor had a brother, but this brother had no brothers. What was the relationship between doctor and brother?

78. What symbol can be placed between 6 and 7 so that the resulting expression is the name of a number that lies between 6 and 7?

79. Rearrange the letters of "new door" to form one word.

Solve Problems 80–83 using linear equations.

80. A new car cost 125% of what it cost 4 years ago. Determine the price 4 years ago of a car now selling for $32,500.

81. A collection of 15 tennis balls consists of some worth $3 each and the remainder worth $4 each. If the value of the 15 tennis balls is $49, how many of each kind of ball are in the collection?

82. If all of Lee's nickels were dimes, he would be 45 cents richer. How many nickels does he have?

83. As he was feeding his horses, a man noticed that a number of ducks had wandered into his stable. The man counted 20 heads and 64 legs on horses and ducks combined. How many of each animal were in the stable?

Group Activity Problem

84. In your group, solve this problem on Farey sequences. A Farey sequence F_n consists of all proper fractions arranged in order of size with denominators of 2 to n. For example, the Farey sequence F_3 contains all proper fractions whose denominators are 2 and 3. These fractions are $\frac{1}{2}, \frac{1}{3}$, and $\frac{2}{3}$. Arranged in order, the sequence is $\frac{1}{3}, \frac{1}{2}, \frac{2}{3}$. The Farey sequence F_4 contains all proper fractions whose denominators are 2, 3, and 4. These fractions are $\frac{1}{2}, \frac{1}{3}, \frac{2}{3}, \frac{1}{4}, \frac{2}{4}$, and $\frac{3}{4}$. Arranged in order, the sequence F_4 is $\frac{1}{4}, \frac{1}{3}, \frac{1}{2}, \frac{2}{3}, \frac{3}{4}$.

a. Write the Farey sequence F_5.
b. Write the Farey sequence F_6.
c. Fill in the following table.

Farey Sequence	A Fraction in the Sequence	Fractions Appearing Before and After This Fraction	Sum of Numerators and Denominators of Fractions in Previous Column
F_3: $\dfrac{1}{3}, \dfrac{1}{2}, \dfrac{2}{3}$	$\dfrac{1}{2}$	$\dfrac{1}{3}, \dfrac{2}{3}$	$\dfrac{1+2}{3+3} = \dfrac{3}{6} = \dfrac{1}{2}$
F_1: $\dfrac{1}{4}, \dfrac{1}{3}, \dfrac{1}{2}, \dfrac{2}{3}, \dfrac{3}{4}$	$\dfrac{2}{3}$	$\dfrac{1}{2}, \dfrac{3}{4}$	$\dfrac{1+3}{2+4} = \dfrac{4}{6} = \dfrac{2}{3}$
F_5:	$\dfrac{1}{4}$		
F_6:	$\dfrac{4}{5}$		

d. Describe the pattern that emerges in the final column of part (c).

e. Use F_3 through F_6 to determine the sum of the pairs of fractions that are equidistant from $\frac{1}{2}$. Describe the general pattern.

Review Problems

85. Solve for y: $5(2 - y) + 3 = 3 + 4(3 - y)$.

86. Solve and graph the solution set on a number line: $2y - (y + 7) < 3(y + 2) - 5$.

87. Solve for s: $P = 2s + b$.

SECTION 3.2

Solutions Manual   Tutorial   Video 4

Ratio and Proportion

Objectives

1 Find ratios.
2 Solve proportions.
3 Solve problems using proportions.

Figure 3.9

Attempts have been made to analyze the relationship between numbers and our reactions to art and architecture. The rectangle in Figure 3.9 is very nearly a *golden rectangle,* discovered by the ancient Greeks and used often in art and architecture. One of the most satisfying of all geometric forms, the ratio of two adjacent sides in the golden rectangle is approximately 1.618 to 1. The Parthenon at Athens fits into the golden rectangle once the triangular pediment is reconstructed.

ENRICHMENT ESSAY

George Seurat and the Golden Rectangle

The French impressionist George-Pierre Seurat (1859–1891) used the golden rectangle in *The Bathers at Asnieres* to create balance and symmetry. There are three golden rectangles shown.

George-Pierre Seurat, *The Bathers at Asnieres.* Reproduced by courtesy of the Trustees, The National Gallery, London.

In this section, we discuss ratios and proportions. Applications range from pleasing visual shapes to calculating taxes and estimating wildlife population.

Find ratios.

Ratios

A ratio compares quantities by division. For example, if a group contains 60 women and 30 men, the ratio of women to men is $\frac{60}{30}$, or 2 to 1. This ratio can be expressed as $2:1$.

> **Ratio**
>
> The **ratio** of the real number a to the real number b ($b \neq 0$) is given by
>
> $$\frac{a}{b}.$$
>
> The ratio of a to b is sometimes written as $a:b$.

EXAMPLE 1   **Finding Ratios**

The bar graph in Figure 3.10 shows the number of divorced people for every thousand married persons. The figure for the year 2000 is a projection. Find the ratio of the number of divorced people for every thousand married persons:

a. For 1995 to 1980.   **b.** For 1975 to 2000.

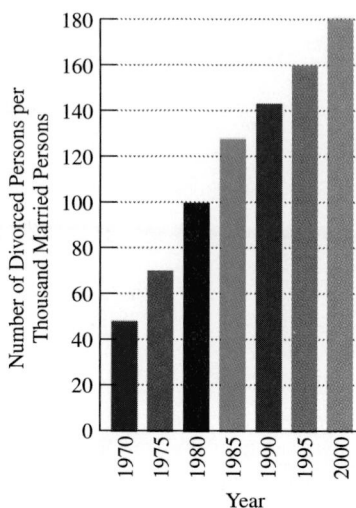

Figure 3.10

Source: U.S. Bureau of the Census
Statistical Abstract 1992; Table 50

Solution

a. The ratio for 1995 to 1980 is

$$\frac{160}{100} = \frac{16}{10} = \frac{8}{5}, \quad \text{or} \quad 8{:}5 \quad (8 \text{ to } 5).$$

Note: When possible, ratios should be expressed in reduced form.

b. An estimate for the number of divorced people in 1975 for every thousand married persons is 68. Using this estimate, the ratio for 1975 to 2000 is

$$\frac{68}{180} = \frac{4 \cdot 17}{4 \cdot 45} = \frac{17}{45}, \quad \text{or} \quad 17{:}45 \quad (17 \text{ to } 45). \qquad \blacksquare$$

Ratios have numerous applications. They are used by environmental analysts (for example, the ratio of hydrocarbons to nitrogen oxide in the air affects the production of smog), stockbrokers (one measure of a stock is the ratio of its selling price to its earnings per share), developers of national parks (plans are affected by benefit-to-cost ratios), attorneys (a sampling of recent cases showed the ratio of monthly child support to a father's yearly income to be 1:40), and so on.

When comparing measurements involving length, area, volume, weight, and time, the same unit of measure should appear in both the numerator and

iscover for yourself

Work Example 2 by calculating the ratio in feet. You should obtain the same answer we found in Example 2. Describe what this ratio means in terms of the actual area and its photograph.

denominator. For example, to find the ratio of 2 feet to 36 inches, we could use two approaches:

$$\frac{2 \text{ feet}}{36 \text{ inches}} = \frac{24 \text{ inches}}{36 \text{ inches}} \qquad\qquad \frac{2 \text{ feet}}{36 \text{ inches}} = \frac{2 \text{ feet}}{3 \text{ feet}}$$

$$= \frac{24}{36} \qquad\qquad\qquad\qquad\qquad = \frac{2}{3} \quad \text{or} \quad 2{:}3$$

$$= \frac{2}{3} \quad \text{or} \quad 2{:}3$$

Notice that we can omit units of measure when the same unit appears in the numerator and denominator of a ratio.

EXAMPLE 2   An Environmental Application

A researcher is taking an aerial photo of an environmentally sensitive area. To provide environmentalists with important information, an area 300 feet long in reality must be $\frac{1}{8}$ inch long on the photograph. Express this ratio in inches to inches.

Solution

$$\frac{300 \text{ feet}}{\frac{1}{8} \text{ inch}}$$ Since 12 inches = 1 foot, 300 feet = (300)(12) inches or 3600 inches.

$$= \frac{3600 \text{ inches}}{\frac{1}{8} \text{ inch}}$$ Replace 300 feet by 3600 inches and omit the units of measurement.

$$= 3600 \div \frac{1}{8}$$ Rewrite the fraction bar as division.

$$= 3600 \cdot \frac{8}{1}$$ Multiply by the reciprocal of the divisor.

$$= \frac{28{,}800}{1}$$

The ratio is 28,800:1 (28,800 to 1).   ∎

EXAMPLE 3   Ratios Comparing Measurements

Find each of the following ratios, using the same unit of measurement in the numerator and denominator:

a. $2\frac{1}{2}$ quarts to $5\frac{1}{4}$ quarts   **b.** 7 meters to 50 centimeters

c. 2 gallons to 3 quarts

Solution

a. $$\frac{2\frac{1}{2} \text{ quarts}}{5\frac{1}{4} \text{ quarts}} = \frac{\frac{5}{2}}{\frac{21}{4}}$$

$$= \frac{5}{2} \cdot \frac{4}{21}$$ Rewrite the division bar as multiplication by multiplying the reciprocal of the divisor.

$$= \frac{10}{21} \quad \text{or} \quad 10{:}21 \qquad \overset{2}{\underset{1}{\frac{5}{2} \cdot \frac{4}{21}}} = \frac{10}{21}$$

b. $\dfrac{7 \text{ meters}}{50 \text{ centimeters}} = \dfrac{700 \text{ centimeters}}{50 \text{ centimeters}}$ 1 meter = 100 centimeters

$\quad\quad\quad\quad = \dfrac{700}{50}$ Divide the numerator and denominator by 10.

$\quad\quad\quad\quad = \dfrac{70}{5}$

$\quad\quad\quad\quad = \dfrac{14}{1}$ or   14:1

c. $\dfrac{2 \text{ gallons}}{3 \text{ quarts}} = \dfrac{8 \text{ quarts}}{3 \text{ quarts}}$ 4 quarts = 1 gallon

$\quad\quad\quad\quad = \dfrac{8}{3}$ or   8:3   ■

Discover for yourself

Ratios in Baseball

Bryan Yablonsky/Duomo
Photography

A baseball player's batting average is the ratio of the number of hits to the number of times at bat. What unusual paradox do you notice about the batting averages for the following players?

Year	Player A	Player B
Year 1	$\dfrac{20}{40} = 0.500$ (1:2)	$\dfrac{90}{200} = 0.450$ (9:20)
Year 2	$\dfrac{60}{200} = 0.300$ (3:10)	$\dfrac{10}{40} = 0.250$ (1:4)
Two-year total	$\dfrac{80}{240} = 0.\overline{3}$ (1:3)	$\dfrac{100}{240} = 0.417$ (5:12)

It is possible to use a ratio to compare two different kinds of measure. The word *per* indicates that we are comparing two different kinds of quantities by division.

For example, if a car is driven 200 miles in 4 hours, the ratio

$$\dfrac{200 \text{ miles}}{4 \text{ hours}} = \dfrac{50}{1} \text{ miles/hour} \quad \text{or} \quad 50 \text{ miles per hour}$$

is the rate traveled in miles per hour. If a ratio compares two different kinds of measure, we frequently call the ratio a *rate*.

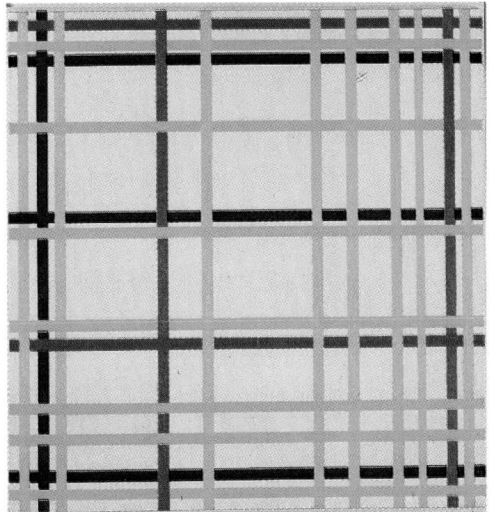

Golden Ratios in Art.
Piet Mondrian, *New York City I,* 1942 (Musée National d'Art Moderne, Centre National d'Art et de Culture Georges Pompidou, courtesy the Mondrian Estate/Holtzman Trust)

Table 3.2 illustrates the use of ratio in comparing two kinds of quantities.

TABLE 3.2 Ratios Comparing Different Measures		
Example	**Ratio**	**Interpretation**
There are eight apples for four people.	$\dfrac{8 \text{ apples}}{4 \text{ people}} = \dfrac{2}{1}$ apples/person	There are two apples per person.
Six cans of juice sell for 70 cents.	$\dfrac{6 \text{ cans}}{70 \text{ cents}} = \dfrac{3}{35}$ cans/cents	Three cans sell for 35 cents.
Oranges are selling for 89 cents per pound.	$\dfrac{89 \text{ cents}}{1 \text{ pound}} = 89$ cents/pound	The rate is 89 cents for one pound.

The third example in Table 3.2 is developed in more detail in Example 4.

EXAMPLE 4 **An Application: Unit Prices**

The unit price of an item is the ratio of the total price to the total units. The word *per* is used to state unit prices. Find the unit price (in dollars per ounce) for a 12-ounce box of cereal that sells for $3.00.

Solution

$$\text{Unit price} = \frac{\text{Total price}}{\text{Total units}}$$ Use the definition of a unit price.

$$= \frac{\$3.00}{12 \text{ ounces}}$$ Substitute the given numbers.

$$= 0.25$$

The unit price for the cereal is $0.25 per ounce.   ■

2 Solve proportions.

Proportions

A *proportion* is a special kind of fractional equation of the form

$$\frac{a}{b} = \frac{c}{d}$$ where $b \neq 0$ and $d \neq 0$.

A proportion states that the ratios a/b and c/d are equal. We read $(a/b) = (c/d)$ as "a is to b as c is to d." The numbers, a, b, c, and d are called the *terms* of the proportion.

We can clear the equation $(a/b = c/d)$ of fractions by multiplying both sides by bd, a common multiple of the denominators.

$$\frac{a}{b} = \frac{c}{d}$$ This is the given proportion.

$$bd \cdot \frac{a}{b} = bd \cdot \frac{c}{d}$$ Multiply both sides by bd ($b \neq 0$ and $d \neq 0$). Then simplify. On the

left: $\frac{bd}{1} \cdot \frac{a}{b} = da = ad$. On the right: $\frac{bd}{1} \cdot \frac{c}{d} = bc$.

$$ad = bc$$

We see that the following principle is true for any proportion.

The cross products principle

The cross products principle for proportions

If $\dfrac{a}{b} = \dfrac{c}{d}$ then $ad = bc$ $b \neq 0$ and $d \neq 0$

The cross products ad and bc are equal.

For example, if $\frac{2}{3} = \frac{6}{9}$, we see that $2 \cdot 9 = 3 \cdot 6$ or $18 = 18$.

In most examples, three of the numbers in a proportion are known and the value of the missing quantity can be found by using the cross products principle. This idea is illustrated in Example 5.

EXAMPLE 5   **Solving Proportions**

Solve each proportion for x:

a. $\dfrac{63}{x} = \dfrac{7}{5}$ **b.** $\dfrac{-8}{3} = \dfrac{32}{x}$

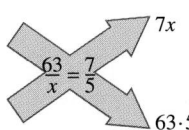

$$\frac{63}{x} = \frac{7}{5}$$

Cross products

Solution

a. $\dfrac{63}{x} = \dfrac{7}{5}$ This is the given proportion.

$63 \cdot 5 = 7x$ Apply the cross products principle, setting the cross products equal.

$315 = 7x$ Multiply.

$45 = x$ Divide both sides by 7.

This means that the ratio of 63 to 45 is the same as the ratio 7 to 5. This can be checked by simplifying $\dfrac{63}{45}$, dividing the numerator and denominator by 9 as follows:

$$\frac{63}{45} = \frac{\cancel{9} \cdot 7}{\cancel{9} \cdot 5} = \frac{7}{5}$$

The solution to the equation is 45.

b. $\dfrac{-8}{3} = \dfrac{32}{x}$ This is the given proportion.

$-8x = 3 \cdot 32$ Apply the cross products principle, setting the cross products equal.

$-8x = 96$ Multiply.

$x = -12$ Divide both sides by -8.

This means that the ratio of 32 to -12 is the same as the ratio of -8 to 3.

$$\frac{32}{-12} = \frac{4 \cdot 8}{-4 \cdot 3} = \frac{8}{-3} = \frac{-8}{3}$$

The solution to the equation is -12. ■

3 Solve problems using proportions.

Modeling Using Proportions

Many practical situations lead to questions that can be answered by using proportions. Here's a procedure for solving applied proportion problems.

> **Solving applied problems using proportions**
> 1. Read the problem and represent the unknown quantity by x (or any letter).
> 2. Set up a proportion by listing the given ratio on one side and the unknown ratio on the other side.
> 3. Drop units and apply the cross products principle.
> 4. Solve for x and answer the question.

EXAMPLE 6 **Applying Proportions: Calculating Taxes**

The tax on a house whose assessed value is $65,000 is $825. Determine the tax on a house with an assessed value of $180,000, assuming the same tax rate.

Solution

Steps 1 and 2. Represent the unknown by x.

Since the tax rate is usually stated in dollars per thousand, we will set up a proportion comparing taxes to assessed value. Let $x =$ the tax on a $180,000 house.

Step 2. Set up a proportion.

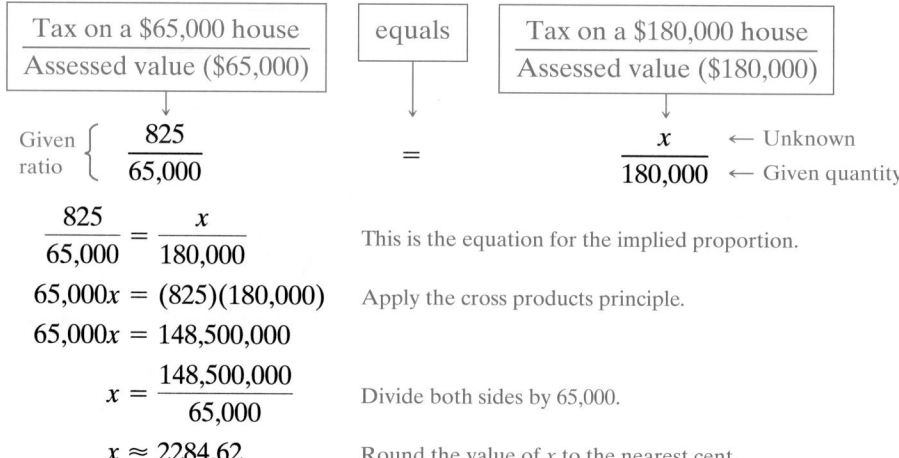

Tax on a $65,000 house	equals	Tax on a $180,000 house
Assessed value ($65,000)		Assessed value ($180,000)

Given ratio $\left\{ \dfrac{825}{65,000} \right.$ $=$ $\dfrac{x}{180,000}$ ← Unknown
← Given quantity

Step 3 and 4. Apply the cross products principle, solve, and answer the question.

$$\frac{825}{65,000} = \frac{x}{180,000}$$ This is the equation for the implied proportion.

$$65,000x = (825)(180,000)$$ Apply the cross products principle.

$$65,000x = 148,500,000$$

$$x = \frac{148,500,000}{65,000}$$ Divide both sides by 65,000.

$$x \approx 2284.62$$ Round the value of x to the nearest cent.

The tax on the $180,000 house is approximately $2284.62. ■

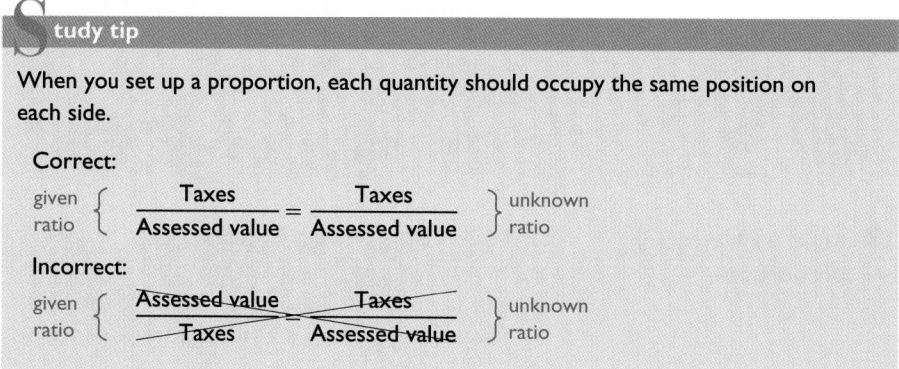

Study tip

When you set up a proportion, each quantity should occupy the same position on each side.

Correct:

given ratio $\left\{ \dfrac{\text{Taxes}}{\text{Assessed value}} = \dfrac{\text{Taxes}}{\text{Assessed value}} \right\}$ unknown ratio

Incorrect:

given ratio $\left\{ \dfrac{\text{Assessed value}}{\text{Taxes}} = \dfrac{\text{Taxes}}{\text{Assessed value}} \right\}$ unknown ratio

Sampling in Nature

The capture-recapture method is used to estimate the size of a wildlife population. Because it is impossible to count each individual animal within a population, wildlife biologists randomly catch and tag a given number of animals. Sometime later they select a second sample of animals and count the number of recaptured tagged animals. The total size of the wildlife population is then estimated using the following proportion.

Initially unknown $(x) \rightarrow$ $\dfrac{\text{Original number of tagged animals}}{\text{Total number of animals in the population}} = \dfrac{\text{Number of recaptured tagged animals}}{\text{Number of animals in second sample}} \Big\}$ Known ratio

EXAMPLE 7 **Applying Proportions: Estimating Wildlife Population**

Wildlife biologists catch, tag, and then release 135 deer back into a wildlife refuge. Two weeks later they select a sample of 140 deer, 30 of which are tagged. Assuming the ratio of tagged deer in the sample holds for all deer in the refuge, approximately how many deer are in the refuge?

(© Frans Lanting, Minden Pictures)

Solution

Step 1. Represent the unknown by x.

We can set up a proportion comparing tagged deer with the total number of deer. Let x = the total number of deer in the refuge.

Step 2. Set up a proportion.

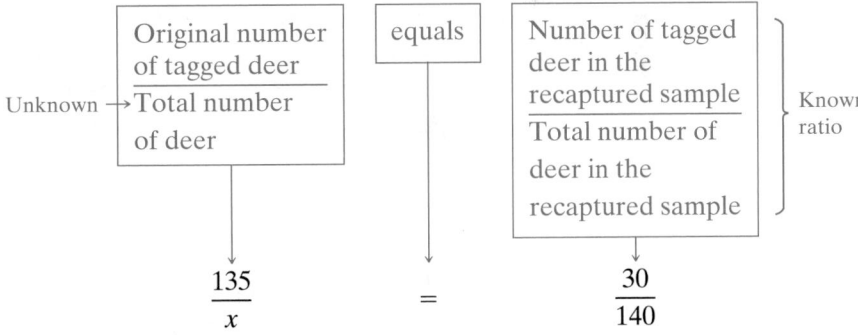

Unknown → $\dfrac{\text{Original number of tagged deer}}{\text{Total number of deer}}$ equals $\dfrac{\text{Number of tagged deer in the recaptured sample}}{\text{Total number of deer in the recaptured sample}}$ } Known ratio

$$\frac{135}{x} = \frac{30}{140}$$

Steps 3 and 4. Apply the cross products principle, solve, and answer the question.

$$\frac{135}{x} = \frac{30}{140}$$ This is the equation for the implied proportion.

$(135)(140) = 30x$ Apply the cross products principle.

$18,900 = 30x$ Multiply.

$630 = x$ Divide both sides by 30.

There are approximately 630 deer in the refuge. ■

ENRICHMENT ESSAY

Saving Whales

The method of Example 7 was used to estimate that the blue whale population is as small as 1000. This led the International Whaling Commission to ban the killing of blue whales to prevent their extinction.

David E. Myers/Tony Stone Images

Inflation

Barton Lidicé Beneš, *Inflated*, 1997. Photo by Karen Furth

Inflation is a sustained rise in the general price level in the economy. The Consumer Price Index (CPI) (also called the Cost-of-Living Index) is used to measure how the price of a fixed amount of goods increases over time. Inflation causes a fixed amount of money to have less buying power in a given year than in previous years.

The following proportion is used to find the change in buying power of a dollar from one year to another:

$$\frac{\text{Price in year } A}{\text{CPI in year } A} = \frac{\text{Price in year } B}{\text{CPI in year } B}$$

Example 8 illustrates exactly how this works.

Year	CPI
1980	82.4
1994	148.2

Source: U.S. Bureau of Labor and Statistics

EXAMPLE 8 **Applying Proportions: The Consumer Price Index**

A condominium was purchased in 1980 for $40,000. Estimate the value of the condominium in 1994 using the Consumer Price Index shown in the table.

Solution

Step 1. Represent the unknown by x.

Let $x =$ the value of the condominium in 1994.

Step 2. Set up a proportion.

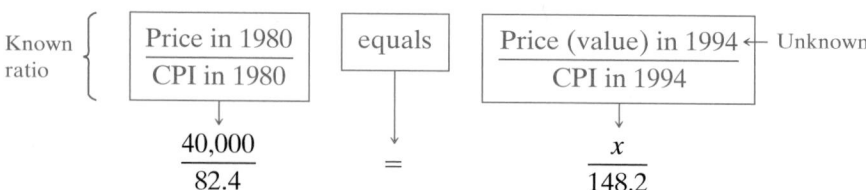

Step 3. Apply the cross products principle, solve, and answer the question.

$$\frac{40,000}{82.4} = \frac{x}{148.2}$$ This is the equation for the implied proportion.

$82.4x = 40,000(148.2)$ Apply the cross products principle.

$82.4x = 5,928,000$ Multiply.

$$x = \frac{5,928,000}{82.4} \qquad \text{Divide both sides by 82.4.}$$

$$x \approx 71,942 \qquad \text{Perform the computation.}$$

The value of the condominium in 1994 is approximately \$71,942. ■

PROBLEM SET 3.2

Practice Problems

Use the same units of measure in the numerator and denominator of Problems 1–12 to express the ratio as a fraction in reduced form.

1. 24 feet to 36 feet

2. 12 quarts to 15 quarts

3. $3\frac{1}{2}$ yards to 5 yards

4. $4\frac{1}{2}$ gallons to 6 gallons

5. 4 inches to 3 feet

6. 2 feet to 4 yards

7. 3 gallons to 2 quarts

8. 5 quarts to 2 pints

9. 30 centimeters to 1 meter

10. 20 millimeters to 5 meters

11. 2000 pounds to 6 tons

12. 20 minutes to 3 hours

Solve each proportion in Problems 13–24.

13. $\dfrac{24}{x} = \dfrac{12}{7}$

14. $\dfrac{56}{y} = \dfrac{8}{7}$

15. $\dfrac{y}{6} = \dfrac{18}{4}$

16. $\dfrac{z}{32} = \dfrac{3}{24}$

17. $\dfrac{y}{3} = -\dfrac{3}{4}$

18. $\dfrac{x}{2} = -\dfrac{1}{5}$

19. $\dfrac{-3}{8} = \dfrac{x}{40}$

20. $\dfrac{-3}{8} = \dfrac{6}{x}$

21. $\dfrac{x-2}{5} = \dfrac{3}{10}$

22. $\dfrac{y+4}{8} = \dfrac{3}{16}$

23. $\dfrac{y+10}{10} = \dfrac{y-2}{4}$

24. $\dfrac{2}{z-5} = \dfrac{3}{z+6}$

(handwritten) $\dfrac{2x-4}{10} = \dfrac{3}{10}$ $2x-4=3$ $\dfrac{2x}{2}=\dfrac{7}{2}$

Application Problems

25. A boy who is 4 feet tall measures 0.6 inch in a photograph. What is the ratio of his actual height to his height in the picture?

26. A woman's forearm is $1\frac{1}{2}$ feet long. In a photograph, her forearm is 1 inch long. What is the ratio of the actual forearm length to the length of the forearm in the picture?

In Problems 27–30, use the graph to find each ratio in lowest (reduced) form.

27. The ratio of newspaper circulation in the United States to that in Germany.

28. The ratio of newspaper circulation in Canada to that in Germany.

29. The ratio of newspaper circulation in Italy and Canada combined to that in Japan.

30. The ratio of newspaper circulation in Germany and the United States combined to that in Canada and Italy combined.

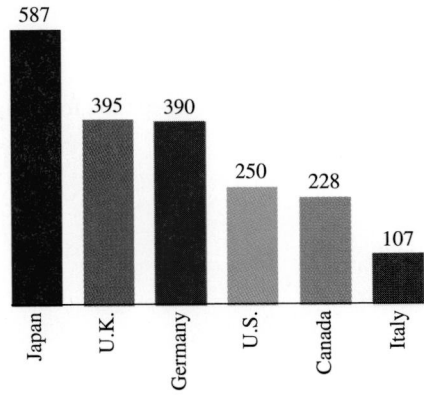

Newspaper Circulation per 1000 Persons 1988–1990

Japan	587
U.K.	395
Germany	390
U.S.	250
Canada	228
Italy	107

Source: Human Development Report 1993

The bar graph shows the amount of money that Americans spent on five forms of entertainment in 1994. Use the graph to obtain a reasonable estimate for each of the ratios in Problems 31–32.

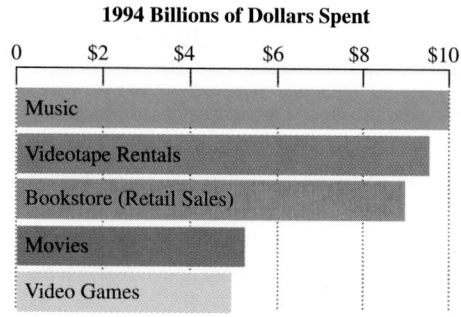

1994 Billions of Dollars Spent

Source: RIAA, VDSA, ABA, MPAA, EIA

31. The amount spent on movies to the amount spent on music.

32. The amount spent on movies to the amount spent on videotape rentals.

The graph compares the length and type of sleep for humans, chimpanzees, and cats. Note the different periods of REM (rapid eye movement) sleep, when dreaming occurs. Use the graph to obtain a reasonable estimate for each of the ratios in Problems 33–36.

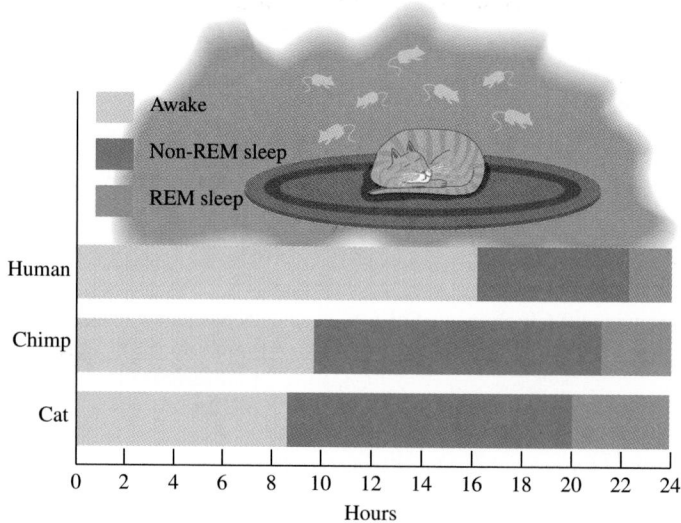

33. Awake time to sleep time for humans.

34. Awake time to sleep time for cats.

35. REM sleep to non-REM sleep time for humans.

36. REM sleep time to non-REM sleep time for chimpanzees.

Use the graph to find a reasonable estimate for each of the ratios in Problems 37–39.

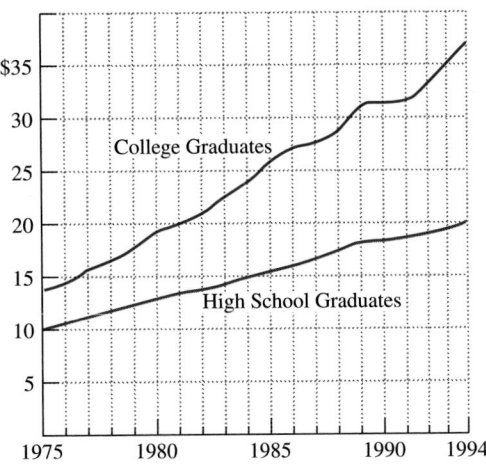

The Earnings Gap
Average Earnings for Workers Age 18 and Older
(in Thousands of Dollars)

College Graduates

High School Graduates

37. Average earnings for college graduates to high school graduates in 1990.

38. Average earnings for high school graduates to college graduates in 1994.

39. What happens to the ratio of earnings for college graduates to high school graduates from 1975 through 1994? Describe what this means in practical terms.

In Problems 40–41, find the unit price for each size of the given product. Then find the size that gives the best buy based on the lowest unit price.

40. *Cereal:* 10-ounce size = $1.85, 16-ounce size = $2.78

41. *Can of fruit:* 20-ounce size = $0.96, 50-ounce size = $2.20

42. The models

$$C_{\text{Gas}} = 12{,}000 + 700x$$
$$C_{\text{Solar}} = 30{,}000 + 150x$$

describe the total cost in dollars for gas and solar heating systems x years since installation. What is the ratio of the total cost for gas heating to the total cost of solar heating 5 years after installation? What happens to this ratio 40 years after installation? What does this mean in practical terms?

43. The models

$$C_{\text{Electric}} = 5000 + 1100x$$
$$C_{\text{Solar}} = 30{,}000 + 150x$$

describe the total cost in dollars for electric and solar heating systems x years since installation. What is the ratio of the total cost for electric heating to the total cost of solar heating 5 years after installation? What happens to this ratio 40 years after installation? What does this mean in practical terms?

Use a proportion to solve Problems 44–49.

44. The maintenance bill for a shopping center containing 180,000 square feet is $45,000. What is the bill for a store in the center that is 4800 square feet?

45. A particular brand of paper weighs 11 pounds per 500 sheets. What is the weight of 3200 sheets?

46. The ratio of monthly child support to a father's yearly income is 1:40. How much should a father earning $38,000 annually pay in monthly child support?

47. A person who weighs 55 kilograms on earth weighs 8.8 kilograms on the moon. Find the moon weight of a person who weighs 90 kilograms on earth.

48. St. Paul Island in Alaska has 12 fur seal rookeries (breeding places). In 1961, to estimate the fur seal pup population in the Gorbath rookery, 4963 fur seal pups were tagged in early August. In late August, a sample of 900 pups was examined and 218 of these were found to have been previously tagged. Estimate the total number of fur seal pups in this rookery.

49. To estimate the number of bass in a lake, wildlife biologists tagged 50 bass and released them in the lake. Later they netted 108 bass and found that 27 of them were tagged. Approximately how many bass are in the lake?

In Problems 50–51, use the values for the Consumer Price Index given on page 248 to estimate the price of the item in the indicated year.

50. The 1994 value of a house purchased for $50,000 in 1980

51. The 1980 price of a theater ticket that cost $60 in 1994

52. The tax on a property with an assessed value of $65,000 is $725. Find the tax on a property with an assessed value of $100,000.

53. The batting average of a baseball player is the ratio of hits made to the number of times the player comes to bat. If a player has a batting average of 0.325, how many hits have been made in 40 times at bat?

54. The front sprocket on a bicycle has 60 teeth, and the rear sprocket has 20 teeth. For mountain biking, an owner needs a 5:1 front:rear ratio. If only one of the sprockets is to be replaced, describe the two ways in which this can be done.

True–False Critical Thinking Problems

55. Which one of the following is true?
   a. The ratio of 3 yards to 4 feet is 3:4.
   b. The ratio of men to women in a class is 4 to 3. There are 30 men. Consequently, there are 40 women.
   c. If $\dfrac{4}{y} = \dfrac{5}{7}$, then $7y = 20$.
   d. If $\dfrac{y-4}{y} = \dfrac{3}{4}$, then $4y - 16 = 3y$.

56. Which one of the following is true?
   a. A statement that two proportions are equal is called a ratio.
   b. The ratio of 1.25 to 2 is equal to the ratio 5:8.
   c. The ratio of a 12-inch plant to a 4-foot plant is 3:1.
   d. If 30 people out of 70 are men, then the ratio of women to men is 40:100.

Technology Problems

Use a calculator to answer Problems 57–58, rounding your answer to two decimal places.

57. Solve: $\dfrac{7.32}{2y-5} = \dfrac{-19.03}{28-5y}$.

58. On a map, 2 centimeters represents 13.47 miles. How many miles does a person plan to travel if the distance on the map is 9.85 centimeters?

Writing in Mathematics

59. Explain the difference between a ratio and a proportion.

60. Explain how to solve a proportion. If possible, illustrate with an example.

61. Use the graph to describe what happens to the ratio of a man's income to that of a woman's income with increasing years of education. How is this trend shown in the graph?

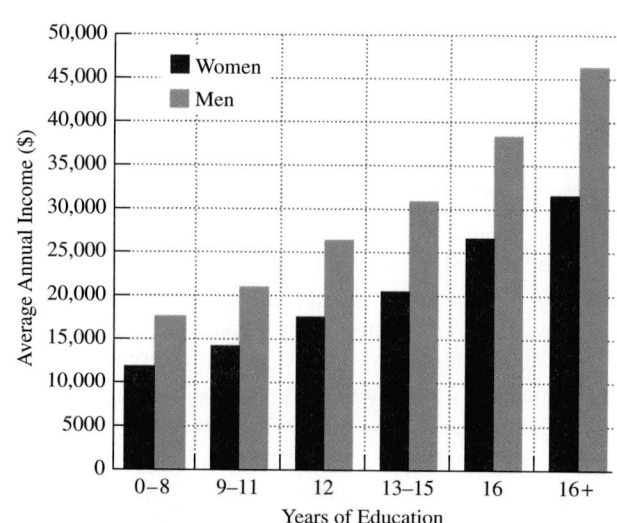

Source: Ries, P., & Stone, A. J. (1992). *The American Woman 1992–93: A Status Report.* New York: Norton.

Critical Thinking Problems

62. My friend is 44 years old. My dog Phideaux is 7 years old. If Phideaux were human, he would be 56. Phideaux thinks my friend is another dog, which makes me wonder: If my friend were a dog, how old would my friend be?

63. Fran builds three boats in 2 days. Martell works half as fast. In how many days will Martell build nine boats?

64. A team has won only 8 out of 20 games so far in the season. How many consecutive games must be won to raise the team's winning record to 60%?

65. Three people form a corporation, investing A dollars, B dollars, and B dollars, respectively. Each person shares in the profits in proportion to the amount invested. What part of a $1000 profit should the first person receive? (Express your answer in terms of A and B.)

Group Activity Problems

66. Each person in your group is to go to the supermarket and find one brand item that is packaged in more than one size. Determine and record the unit price of each size package. Share your results with other people in the group. Describe the pattern that emerges from the group's results.

67. Find examples of art and architecture that use the golden ratio and share the examples with the group.

Review Problems

68. Solve for x: $\frac{1}{2}x + 7 = 13 - \frac{1}{4}x$.

69. Solve and graph the solution set on a number line: $2x - 3 \leq 5$.

70. A 40 milliliter solution of acid in water contains 35% acid. How much acid is in the solution?

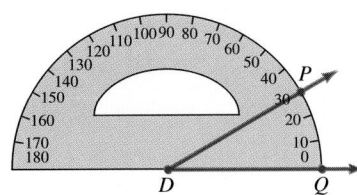

SECTION 3.3

Solutions Manual   **Tutorial**   **Video 4**

Geometry Problems

Objectives

1   Solve problems involving angles.
2   Solve problems involving perimeter, area, and volume.
3   Solve problems involving similar triangles.

In this section we use basic geometric principles to solve problems. These principles were established by Euclid, the Greek mathematician, more than 2000 years ago. They comprise what has come to be called *Euclidean geometry*.

1   Solve problems involving angles.

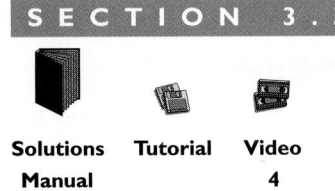

Figure 3.11

Measuring a 30° angle with a protractor

Angles

Figure 3.11 represents a *plane angle* with a protractor placed over it. The two rays DP and DQ have a common endpoint, D, called the *vertex* of the angle. The rays DP and DQ are called the *sides* of the angle. The angle is angle PDQ (denoted $\angle PDQ$) or angle QDP (denoted $\angle QDP$) or simple angle D ($\angle D$). The letter representing the vertex of the angle is the middle letter when three letters are used to name the angle.

The protractor shown in Figure 3.11 indicates that angles are measured in degrees. The measure of an angle is a positive number between 0° and 180°.

Angle pairs that occur often in geometry are given special names.

Complementary and supplementary angles

Name	Definition	Example
Complementary angles	Two angles whose measures have a sum of 90°. Each angle is a *complement* of the other.	
Supplementary angles	Two angles whose measures have a sum of 180°. Each angle is a *supplement* of the other.	

If an angle measures 72°, then its complement measures 18° (90° − 72° = 18°), and its supplement measures 108° (180° − 72° = 108°). Observe that the measure of the complement can be found by subtracting the angle's measure from 90°. The measure of the supplement can be found by subtracting the angle's measure from 180°.

Algebraic expressions for complements and supplements

Measure of an angle: $x°$
Measure of the angle's complement: $90° − x°$
Measure of the angle's supplement: $180° − x°$

EXAMPLE 1   Angle Measures and Complements

Find the measure of an angle if its measure is 40° less than four times the measure of its complement.

Solution

Steps 1 and 2. Use a variable to represent unknown quantities.

Let

$$x = \text{Measure of the angle}$$
$$90 − x = \text{Measure of its complement}$$

Step 3. Write an equation in x that describes the verbal conditions.

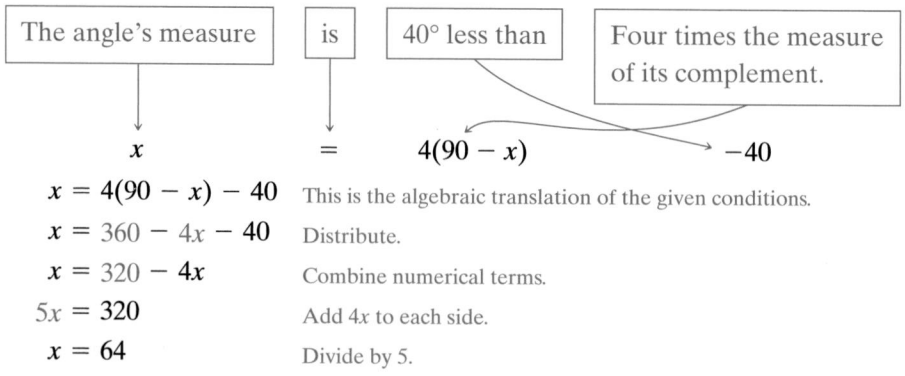

The angle's measure	is	40° less than	Four times the measure of its complement.

$$x \qquad = \qquad 4(90 − x) \qquad −40$$

Step 4. Solve the equation and answer the question.

$x = 4(90 − x) − 40$ This is the algebraic translation of the given conditions.

$x = 360 − 4x − 40$ Distribute.

$x = 320 − 4x$ Combine numerical terms.

$5x = 320$ Add $4x$ to each side.

$x = 64$ Divide by 5.

The angle measures 64°.

Step 5. Check.

The measure of the complement is $90° − 64° = 26°$. Four times the measure of the complement is $4 \cdot 26 = 104°$. The angle's measure ($64°$) is $40°$ less than four times the measure of its complement ($104°$). ∎

Example 2 is based on the fact that the sum of the measures of the three angles in a triangle is $180°$.

EXAMPLE 2   Finding the Measures of a Triangle's Angles

Find the measures of the three angles of a triangle if the second is $8°$ less than three times the first and the third is $1°$ more than seven times the first.

Solution

Steps 1 and 2. Represent unknown quantities in terms of x.

Let

$x = $ Measure of the first angle

$3x − 8 = $ Measure of the second angle ($8°$ less than three times the first)

$7x + 1 = $ Measure of the third angle ($1°$ more than seven times the first)

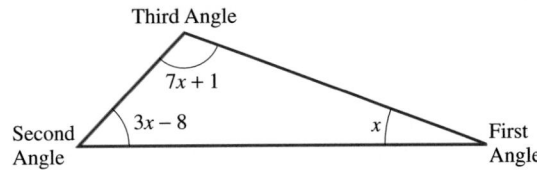

Step 3. Write an equation in x that describes the verbal conditions.

The sum of the measures of the three angles of a triangle is $180°$.

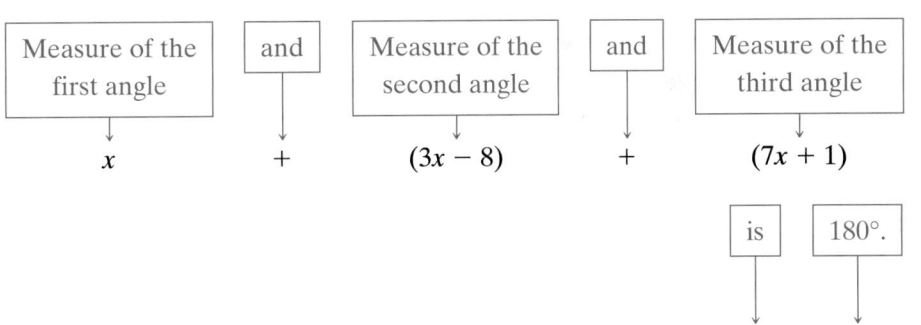

Step 4. Solve the equation and answer the question.

$$x + (3x − 8) + (7x + 1) = 180$$
$$11x − 7 = 180 \quad \text{Combine like terms.}$$
$$11x = 187 \quad \text{Add 7 to both sides.}$$
$$x = 17 \quad \text{Divide both sides by 11.}$$

Measure of the first angle $= x = 17$

Measure of the second angle $= 3x − 8 = 3(17) − 8 = 43$

Measure of the third angle $= 7x + 1 = 7(17) + 1 = 120$

The angles measure $17°$, $43°$, and $120°$.

Step 5. Check.

Take a moment to check these angle measures by showing that they add up to $180°$. ∎

2 Solve problems involving perimeter, area, and volume.

Width:
x

Length: $3x - 5$

Figure 3.12

Perimeter, Area, and Volume

The *perimeter* of a plane geometric figure is the sum of the lengths of its sides. Our next example involves the perimeter of a rectangle, which is given by

$$P = 2L + 2W$$

where L is the rectangle's length and W is the rectangle's width.

EXAMPLE 3 **Finding the Dimensions of a Rectangular Lot**

The length of a rectangular lot is 5 meters shorter than three times its width (see Figure 3.12). If it takes 110 meters of fencing to enclose the lot, what are the lot's dimensions?

Solution

Steps 1 and 2. Represent unknown quantities in terms of x.

Let

$$x = \text{Width of the lot}$$
$$3x - 5 = \text{Length of the lot (5 meters shorter than three times the width)}$$

Since 110 meters of fencing enclose the lot, its perimeter is 110 meters.

Step 3. Write an equation in x that describes the verbal conditions.

Step 4. Solve the equation and answer the question.

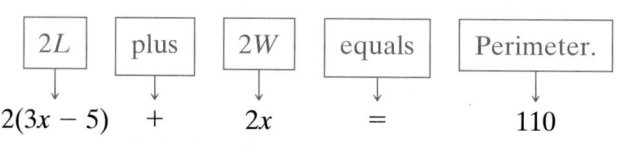

2L	plus	2W	equals	Perimeter.

$$2(3x - 5) \quad + \quad 2x \quad = \quad 110$$

The perimeter of a rectangle is the sum of twice its length and twice its width.

This is the equation from the formula for a rectangle's perimeter.

$$6x - 10 + 2x = 110$$

Apply the distributive property.

$$8x - 10 = 110$$

Combine like terms.

$$8x = 120$$

Add 10 to both sides.

$$x = 15$$

Divide both sides by 8.

Thus:

$$\text{Width} = x = 15$$
$$\text{Length} = 3x - 5 = 3(15) - 5 = 40$$

The dimensions are 15 meters by 40 meters.

Step 5. Check.

The perimeter is $2(15) + 2(40) = 110$.   ■

Formulas for perimeter and area are summarized in Table 3.3. Remember that perimeter is measured in linear units, such as feet or meters, and area is measured in square units, such as square feet (ft^2) or square meters (m^2).

TABLE 3.3 Formulas for Areas and Perimeters of Quadrilaterals and Triangles

Figure	Sketch	Area	Perimeter
Square	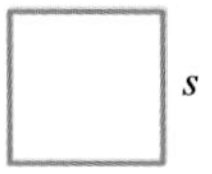	$A = s^2$	$P = 4s$
Rectangle	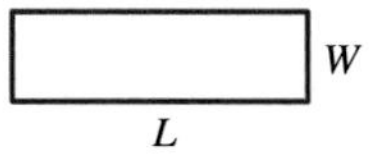	$A = LW$	$P = 2L + 2W$
Parallelogram	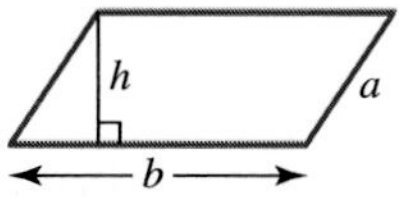	$A = bh$	$P = 2b + 2a$
Trapezoid	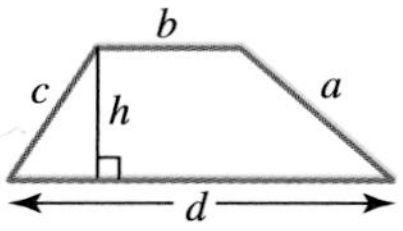	$A = \frac{1}{2}h(d + b)$	$P = a + b + c + d$
Triangle	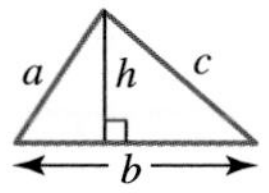	$A = \frac{1}{2}bh$	$P = a + b + c$

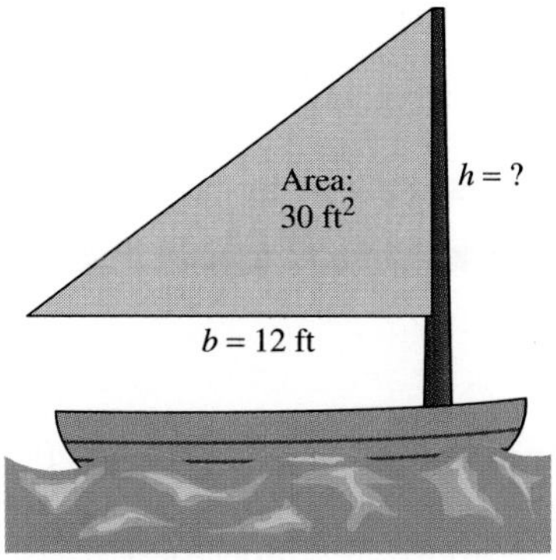

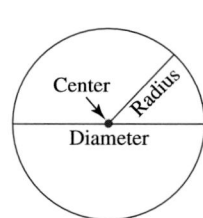

Figure 3.13

Finding the height of a triangular sail

Figure 3.14

EXAMPLE 4 **Using the Formula for the Area of a Triangle**

A sailboat with a triangular sail has an area of 30 square feet and a base that is 12 feet long, as shown in Figure 3.13. Find the height of the sail.

Solution

We begin with the formula for the area of a triangle.

$A = \frac{1}{2}bh$ The area of a triangle is $\frac{1}{2}$ the product of its base and height.

$30 = \frac{1}{2}(12)h$ Substitute 30 for A and 12 for b.

$30 = 6h$ Simplify.

$5 = h$ Divide both sides by 5.

The height of the sail is 5 feet.

Check

The area is $A = \frac{1}{2}bh = \frac{1}{2}(12 \text{ feet})(5 \text{ feet}) = 30 \text{ feet}^2$. ■

Another plane figure that occurs frequently in geometry is the circle. As shown in Figure 3.14, a circle is the set of points in the plane equally distant from a given point, its center. The radius, r, is the line segment from the center to any point on the circle. (For a given circle, all radii have equal measure. Why?) The diameter, d, of a circle is a line segment through the center whose endpoints both lie on the circle. The distance around the circle is its circumference, C.

Formulas for the area and circumference of a circle are given in terms of π and appear in Table 3.4. We have seen that π is an irrational number and is only approximately equal to 3.14.

TABLE 3.4 Formulas for Circles

Circle	Area	Circumference
⊙ *r*	$A = \pi r^2$	$C = 2\pi r$

EXAMPLE 5　**Finding the Area and Circumference of a Circle**

Find the area and circumference of a circle whose diameter measures 20 inches.

Solution

The radius is half the diameter, so $r = \frac{20}{2} = 10$ inches.

$A = \pi r^2$　　　$C = 2\pi r$　　　Use the formulas for area and circumference of a circle.

$A = \pi (10)^2$　　$C = 2\pi (10)$　　Substitute 10 for r.

$A = 100\pi$　　　$C = 20\pi$

The area of the circle is 100π square inches and the circumference is 20π inches. Using the fact that $\pi \approx 3.14$, the area is approximately $100(3.14)$ or 314 square inches and the circumference is approximately $20(3.14)$ or 62.8 inches. ■

　　To find the *volume* of a geometric solid, a cubic unit is used. As shown in Figure 3.15 a cubic unit of measure is a cube whose edges each measure 1 unit of length. For example, a cube with sides each 1 centimeter long can serve as a unit of volume called a cubic centimeter (cm³). The volume of a solid is the number of cubic units that can be contained in the solid.

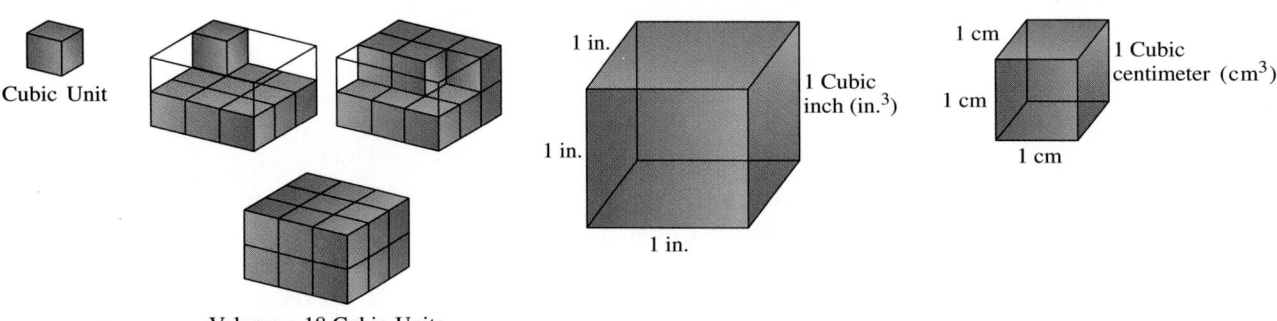

Cubic Unit

1 in.　1 Cubic inch (in.³)　1 in.　1 in.

1 cm　1 Cubic centimeter (cm³)　1 cm　1 cm

Volume = 18 Cubic Units

Figure 3.15

Measuring volume with cubic units

Formulas for volume are summarized in Table 3.5.

TABLE 3.5 Formulas for Volumes of Three-Dimensional Figures

Figure	Sketch	Volume
Rectangular solid		$V = LWH$
Right circular cylinder		$V = \pi r^2 h$
Right circular cone		$V = \dfrac{1}{3}\pi r^2 h$
Sphere		$V = \dfrac{4}{3}\pi r^3$

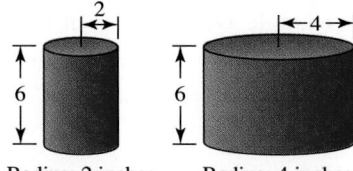

Radius: 2 inches   Radius: 4 inches
Height: 6 inches   Height: 6 inches

Figure 3.16

Doubling a cylinder's radius

EXAMPLE 6   **Finding the Volume of a Cylinder**

A cylinder whose radius is 2 inches and whose height is 6 inches has its radius doubled, as shown in Figure 3.16. How does the volume of the larger cylinder compare to that of the smaller cylinder?

Solution

$$V = \pi r^2 h$$

Use the formula for the volume of a cylinder.

Radius is doubled.

$V_{\text{Smaller}} = \pi(2)^2(6)$ $V_{\text{Larger}} = \pi(4)^2(6)$ Substitute the given values.

$V_{\text{Smaller}} = \pi(4)(6)$ $V_{\text{Larger}} = \pi(16)(6)$

$V_{\text{Smaller}} = 24\pi$ $V_{\text{Larger}} = 96\pi$

The volume of the smaller cylinder is 24π cubic inches and the volume of the larger cylinder is 96π cubic inches. The volume of the larger cylinder is 4 times that of the smaller cylinder $(24\pi(4) = 96\pi)$. ∎

3 Solve problems involving similar triangles.

Similar Triangles

Proportions can be used to solve problems in geometry involving *similar triangles*. Two triangles are said to be similar if their corresponding angles have the same measure and their corresponding sides are proportional. Similar triangles have the same shape, but not necessarily the same size.

ENRICHMENT ESSAY

Euclidean Geometry and Art

Geometric forms play a predominant role in the paintings of Wassily Kandinsky (1886–1944). Triangles, circles, and trapezoids make up the forms in this picture. They are overlaid with large and small forms, some geometric and some free.

See if you can find an example of an artistic work based on the figures in Table 3.3 through 3.5.

Wassily Kandinsky "Unbroken Line"
(Durchgehender Strich) 1923, oil on canvas.
Kunstsammlung Nordrhein-Westfalen, Dusseldorf.
Photo © Walter Klein, Dusseldorf. © VG Bild-Kunst.

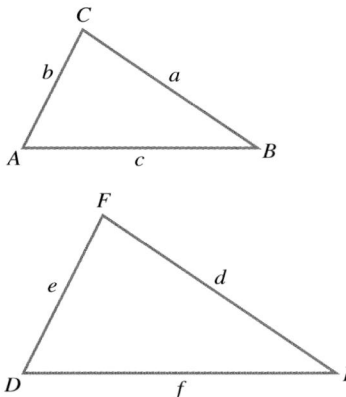

Figure 3.17
Similar triangles have the same shape.

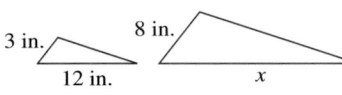

Figure 3.18

study tip

The following proportions can also be used to solve Example 7.

$$\frac{8}{3} = \frac{x}{12} \quad \text{or} \quad \frac{3}{12} = \frac{8}{x}$$

If we are told that triangle ABC is similar to triangle DEF, shown in Figure 3.17, we immediately know that corresponding angles have the same measure. This means that

The measure of $\angle A$ = the measure of $\angle D$
The measure of $\angle C$ = the measure of $\angle F$
The measure of $\angle B$ = the measure of $\angle E$

We also know that the corresponding sides are proportional. This means that

$$\frac{a}{d} = \frac{b}{e} = \frac{c}{f}.$$

EXAMPLE 7   **Using Similar Triangles**

The triangles in Figure 3.18 are similar. Find the length of the side marked with an x.

Solution

Because the triangles are similar, their corresponding sides are proportional. We have

$$\frac{3}{8} = \frac{12}{x}.$$

$3x = 8 \cdot 12$ Apply the cross products principle.

$3x = 96$

$x = 32$ Divide both sides by 3.

The length of the side marked with an x is 32 inches.   ■

There is a fast way of determining if two triangles are similar. This result, which can be proved in a formal geometry course, is useful in solving certain kinds of problems.

Determining similar triangles

Two triangles are similar if two angles of one are equal in measure to two corresponding angles of the other.

EXAMPLE 8 **Problem Solving Using Similar Triangles**

A man who is 6 feet tall is standing 10 feet from the base of a lamp post (see Figure 3.19). The man's shadow has a length of 4 feet. How tall is the post?

Solution

The drawing in Figure 3.20 makes the similarity of the triangles easier to see. The large triangle with the lamp post on the left and the small triangle with the man on the left both contain 90° angles. They also share an angle. Thus, two angles of the large triangle are equal in measure to two angles of the small triangle. This means that the triangles are similar and their corresponding sides are proportional.

If we let $x =$ the height of the lamp post, we have

$$\frac{x}{6} = \frac{14}{4}.$$

$$4x = 6 \cdot 14 \quad \text{Apply the cross products principle.}$$

$$4x = 84$$

$$x = 21 \quad \text{Divide both sides by 4.}$$

The lamp post is 21 feet tall.

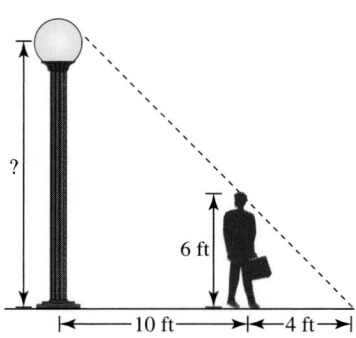

Figure 3.19

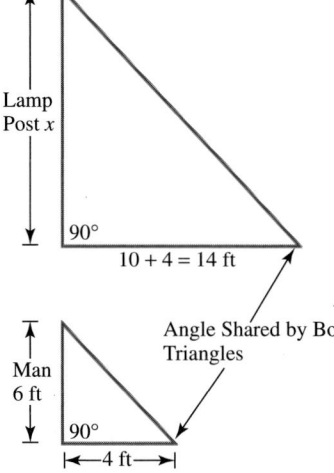

Figure 3.20

P R O B L E M   S E T   3 . 3

Practice and Application Problems_____

Use the information given in Problems 1–6 to find the measure of the angle described.

1. The angle's measure is 60° more than that of its complement.

2. The angle's measure is 78° less than that of its complement.

3. The angle's measure is three times that of its supplement.

4. The angle's measure is 16° more than triple that of its supplement.

5. The measure of the angle's supplement is 10° more than three times that of its complement.

6. The measure of the angle's supplement is 52° more than twice that of its complement.

7. Two angles of a triangle have the same measure and the third angle is 30° greater than the measure of the other two. Find the measure of each angle.

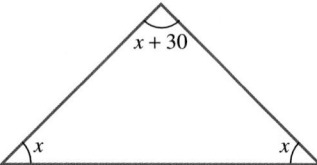

Find the measure of each angle in the triangles in Problems 9–10.

9.

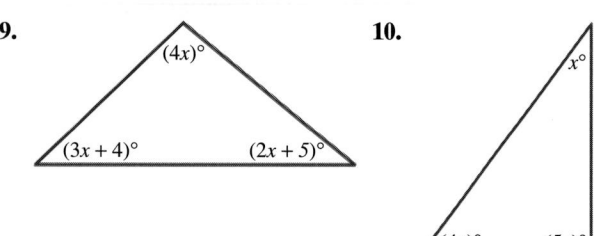

10.

11. One angle of a triangle is twice as large as another. The measure of the third angle is 20° more than that of the smallest angle. Find the measure of each angle.

12. One angle of a triangle is three times as large as another. The measure of the third angle is 30° greater than that of the smallest angle. Find the measure of each angle.

13. A *quadrilateral* is a four-sided figure. If it is known that the sum of the measures of the interior angles of a quadrilateral is 360°, find the measure of each angle in the figure. This particular quadrilateral has both pairs of opposite sides parallel, and is called a *parallelogram*. What do you observe about the opposite angles of a parallelogram?

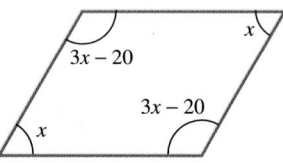

14. A *right triangle* contains one angle measuring 90°. One angle of a right triangle is 18° less than three times the measure of the smallest angle. Find the measure of each angle.

15. The state of Wyoming is almost perfectly rectangular in shape, with a width that is 90 miles less than its

8. One angle of a triangle is three times as large as another. The measure of the third angle is 40° more than that of the smallest angle. Find the measure of each angle.

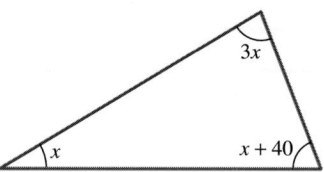

length. If the state has a perimeter of 1280 miles, what are its dimensions?

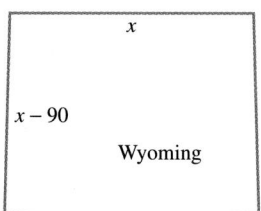

16. The length of a rectangle is 3 meters longer than its width. If the perimeter is 22 meters, what are the rectangles dimensions?

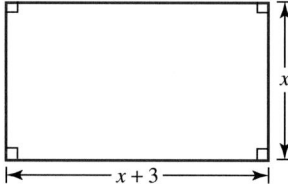

17. The length of the rectangular tennis court at Wimbledon is 6 feet longer than twice the width. If the perimeter is 228 feet, what are the court's dimensions?

18. The length of a rectangular lot is 1 yard less than three times its width. If 90 yards of fencing were purchased to enclose the lot and 12 yards of fencing were not needed, find the lot's dimensions.

19. A piece of copper tubing is to be bent into the shape of a triangle such that one side measures 1 inch less than twice the length of the second side and the third side measures 1 inch more than twice the length of the second side. If the piece of tubing is 30 inches long, find the length of each side of the triangle.

20. A bookcase is to have four shelves, including the top, as shown in the figure. The height of the bookcase is to be 3 feet more than the width, and only 30 feet of lumber is available. What should be the dimensions of the bookcase?

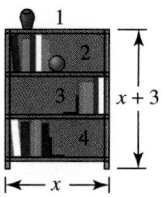

21. The swimming pool in the figure has a width of 25 meters and an area of 1250 square meters. What is the pool's length?

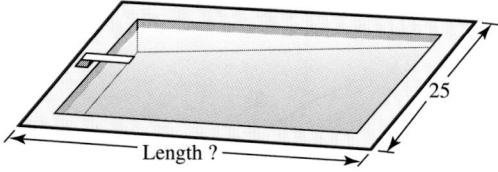

22. The room shown in the figure has a floor with a width of 18 feet. If the area of the floor is 468 square feet, what is the floor's length?

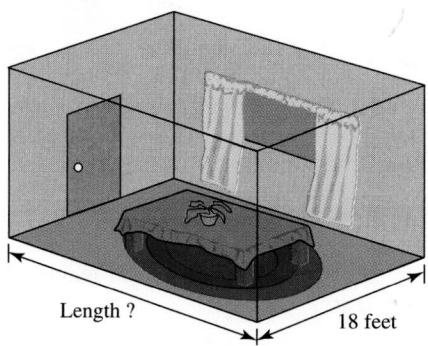

23. As shown in the figure, a sailboat has a triangular sail whose area is 147 square meters. If the sail's base is 21 meters, what is its height?

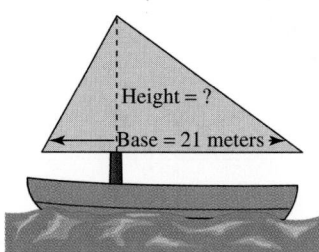

24. A sailboat has a triangular sail whose area is 221 square meters. If the sail's base is 26 meters, what is its height?

25. Find the area and circumference of a circle whose diameter measures 6 inches. Express the answers in terms of π. Then use $\pi \approx 3.14$ to find approximations for the area and circumference.

26. Find the area and circumference of a circle whose diameter measures 12 centimeters. Express the answers in terms of π. Then use $\pi \approx 3.14$ to find approximations for the area and circumference.

27. The circular swimming pool shown in the figure is to be surrounded by a 2-meter-wide walk. The diameter of the pool is 40 meters. Find the area of the walk in terms of π. Then use $\pi \approx 3.14$ to find an approximation for the area.

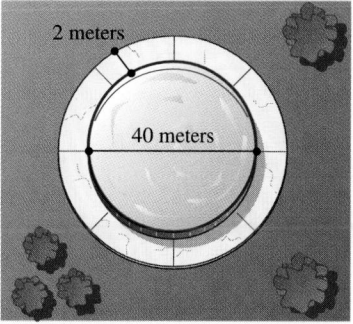

28. Hardwood flooring costs $9.50 per square foot. How much will it cost (to the nearest cent) to cover the dance floor shown in the figure with hardwood flooring?

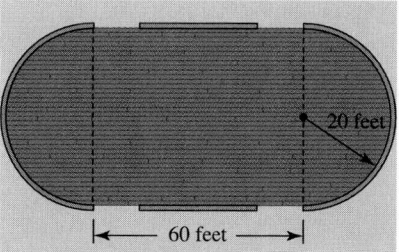

29. A cylinder whose radius is 3 inches and whose height is 4 inches has its radius tripled. How many times greater is the volume of the larger cylinder than the smaller cylinder?

30. A cylinder whose radius is 2 inches and whose height is 3 inches has its radius quadrupled. How many times greater is the volume of the larger cylinder than that of the smaller cylinder?

31. Find the area of a trapezoid with a height of 5 feet and bases that measure 10 feet and 6 feet.

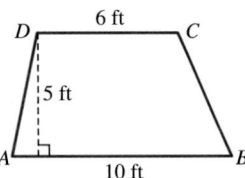

32. A trapezoid has a height of 10 centimeters and a longer base measuring 26 centimeters. If the trapezoid's area is 175 square centimeters, find the length of the shorter base.

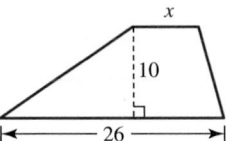

The triangles in Problems 33–36 are similar. Find the length of the side marked with an x.

33.

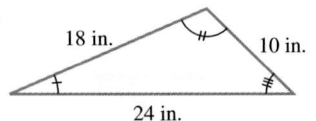

37. A tree casts a shadow 12 feet long. At the same time, a vertical rod 8 feet high casts a shadow of 6 feet long. How tall is the tree?

34.

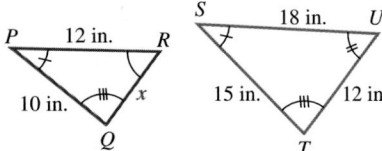

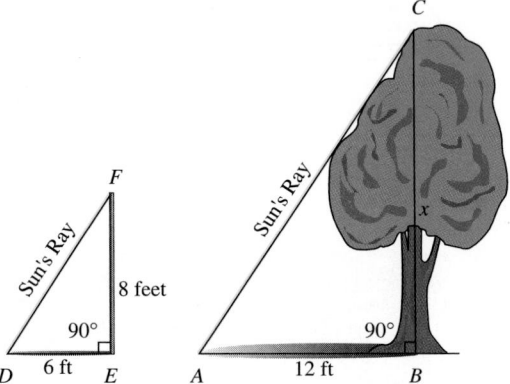

35.

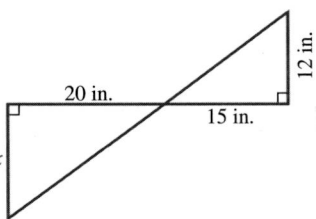

36.

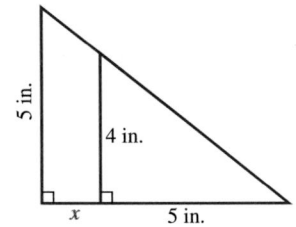

38. A person who is 5 feet tall is standing 80 feet from the base of a tree, and the tree casts an 86 foot shadow. The person's shadow is 6 feet in length. What is the tree's height?

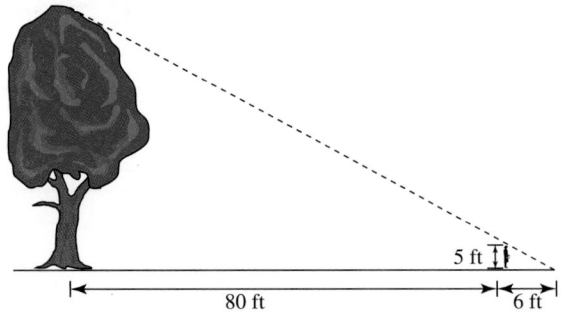

39. Find the measure of the angle of inclination, denoted by $x°$ in the figure, for the road leading to the bridge.

40. If the radius of Earth is 4000 miles, what is its circumference at the equator? (Use $\pi \approx 3.14$)

41. The Pantheon in Rome, built by Agrippa (27 B.C.), was destroyed. It was then rebuilt in the second century by Hadrian. Well preserved today, its dome, the largest built until modern times, is supported only by the walls of concrete it rests upon.
   a. The outside circumference of the cylindrical part of the Pantheon measures 446 feet. Use the formula for the circumference of a circle (with $\pi \approx 3.14$) to approximate the length of the Pantheon's radius.
   b. If the walls of the Pantheon are 4 feet thick, what is the area of its marble floor?
   c. The volume of the cylindrical part of the Pantheon, not including its domed ceiling, is approximately 1,691,455 cubic feet. Approximate the height of its cylindrical part.

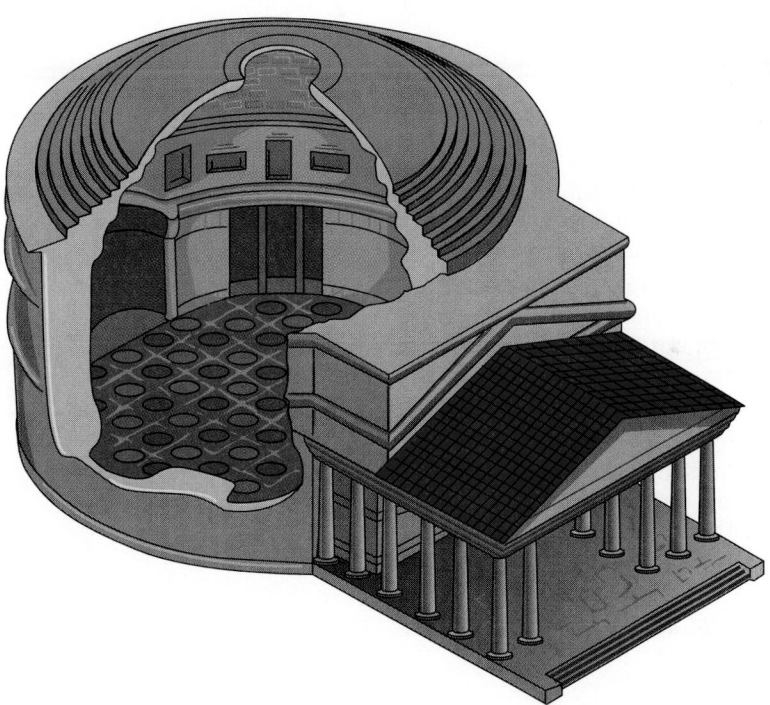

True–False Critical Thinking Problems

42. Which one of the following is true?
   a. If the perimeter of a rectangle is represented by $48x$ and its length by $8x$, then the width in terms of x is $32x$.
   b. It is not possible to have a square whose perimeter is numerically equal to its area.
   c. The difference between the measures of the supplement and the complement of an angle is $90°$.
   d. When the measure of a given angle is added to twice the measure of its complement, the sum is not equal to the measure of its supplement.

43. Which one of the following is true?
  a. It is not possible to have a circle whose circumference is numerically equal to its area.
  b. When the measure of a given angle is added to three times the measure of its complement, the sum equals the sum of the measures of the complement and supplement of the angle.
  c. The complement of an angle that measures less than 90° is an angle that measures more than 90°.
  d. Two complementary angles cannot be equal in measure.

Writing in Mathematics

44. The figure shows a triangle with angle measurements represented in terms of x. Write a word problem associated with this situation.

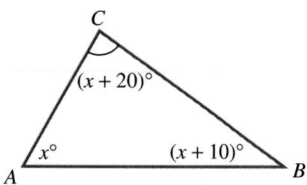

45. If x represents the measure of an angle, write a word problem that can be modeled by the equation $x = (90 - x) - 10$.

Critical Thinking Problems

Problems 46–51 cannot be solved by translating geometric information into equations. They require you to use a drawing, look for patterns, or use some of the other skills discussed earlier in this chapter.

46. A rectangular garden measures 8 yards by 12 yards. A 1-yard-wide sidewalk is to be built around the outside of the garden. Determine the area of the sidewalk.

47. A square piece of cardboard measuring 10 centimeters on a side has a 2 centimeter by 2 centimeter square cut out of each corner. The sides are then folded up to make a box without a lid. What is the volume of the box? (The volume of a box—a rectangular solid—is the product of its length, width, and height.)

48. The dimensions of a packing box are represented by consecutive integers, the first of which is x. Each edge of the box is fastened with masking tape. Write an expression in terms of x, in simplified form, for the total amount of tape needed.

49. Suppose that 40 yards of fencing is to be used to en-

close a rectangular region. What are the dimensions that will provide a region of the greatest possible area?

50. The figure shows a square with four identical equilateral triangles attached. What is the perimeter of the figure in terms of k?

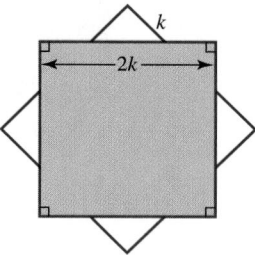

51. Fill in the missing entries in the table. Use the pattern in the table to write a formula for the sum of the angle measures of a polygon of n sides.

Polygon	Number of Sides	Number of Triangles	Sum of the Angle Measures
	4	2	$2 \times 180 = 360$

Problems 52–56 can be solved by modeling geometric information with equations.

52. A 12 inch by 18 inch rectangular picture is to have a frame of uniform width. If the perimeter of the framed picture is 84 inches, determine the width of the frame.

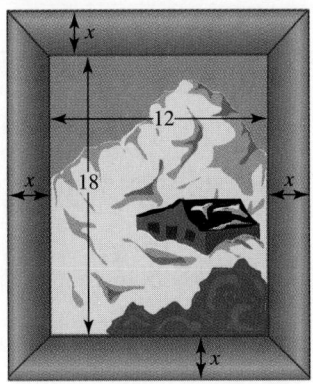

53. The figure shows a rectangle surmounted by an *equilateral triangle* (all three sides have the same length). If the height of the rectangle is 3 meters less than a side of the triangle, and the perimeter of the figure

is 34 meters, determine the length of a side of the triangle.

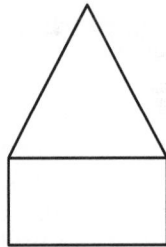

54. The length of a rectangle is 2 feet more than twice the width. If the length of the rectangle is increased by 3 feet and the width is decreased by 1 foot, the perimeter of the resulting rectangle is 38 feet. Find the dimensions of the original rectangle.

55. The figure shows the cross section of a house consisting of a square surmounted by an isosceles triangle. If the combined area of the square and the triangle is 1020 square feet, find the height of the triangle.

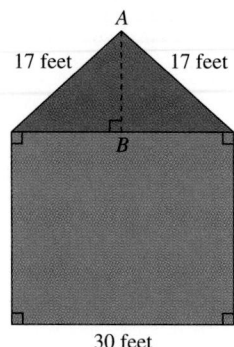

56. The figure shows a large equilateral triangle. Three smaller equilateral triangles are removed from the corners of the larger triangle and a figure of six equal sides (a *regular hexagon*) is formed. The perimeter of the hexagon is 54 decimeters. Find the perimeter of the larger triangle.

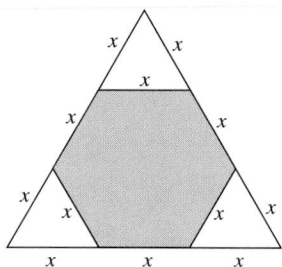

Review Problems

57. Solve for x: $2(x - 7) - 3(x + 4) = 4 - (5x - 2)$.

58. Fourteen is 25% of what?

59. Evaluate: $[3(12 \div 2^2 - 3)^2]^2$.

HAPTER PROJECT

Measures We Live By

In this chapter, we studied problems with angles measured in degrees and problems with length, area, and volume using a variety of measures. Some of the measures described in the problems make sense outside of a strict mathematical definition. For example, a foot can be thought of as approximately the length of one human foot. However, many of the other measures seem distinctly artificial. For example, do miles and quarts or meters and liters remind you of anything in human terms? Probably not.

Have you ever wondered why there are 360 degrees in a circle? Why are there 24 hours in a day or 60 minutes in an hour? When you step on a scale, why is your weight in pounds? Why do you buy milk by the gallon? Discovering how a particular measure came into common usage requires a look at the history of mathematics and sometimes the history of everyday life. Most of the shorter measures we use for length or area came from the measure of different parts of the human body. Ancient Egyptians, Mesopotamians, Greeks, and Romans all had measures based on the width of a finger or the span of a palm. For example, the smallest Roman measure, the width of a finger, was named *uncia,* the Latin word for one-twelfth, which has survived to this day in the form of "inch."

The Babylonians and Assyrians took over the use of 60 as a number base from the Summerians. The ancient Greeks then adopted the Babylonian conventions for some measures, and we have inherited these as angular measures of 360 degrees in a circle, as well as divisions of time in minutes and seconds.

Listed below are various units of measure grouped into four categories: Length or Area, Volume, Time, and Weight or Mass. For this project, you will select a measure and determine how it came into its current usage.

1. Prepare a brief rough draft of your research concerning your measure. Bring this information to class and be prepared to discuss it with other students.
2. After listening to other students describe their research, form a group that shares some common links among measures and pool your research. These groups could be formed along historical lines—

such as Babylonian units of time or Egyptian units of distance—or along cultural lines—such as English units of measure or metric units of measure. You may even wish to use the group categories listed below.

3. Working as a group, prepare a short presentation describing your findings. Show the common link for your information and present your work to the class as a smoothly connected whole.

4. After listening to all of the presentations, use the board to present one master diagram showing the links from our ancient past to our present systems of measures.

Length/Area	Volume	Time	Weight/Mass
statute mile	bushel	month	stone
furlong	quart	day	pound
foot	liter	hour	gram
inch	dram	minute	troy ounce
yard	stere	year	ton
meter	cord	second	grain
acre	gill	week	scruple
rod	firkin	century	dram
nautical mile	gallon (U.S.)		
arc	gallon (Imperial)		
degree	barrel		
cubit			
span			
fathom			
hand			

Worldwide Web Resources

Go to the Prentice Hall website (http://www.prenhall.com/blitzer) to access other locations on the Internet that will allow you to further explore the concepts presented in this project.

Chapter Review

SUMMARY

1. Strategies for Solving Problems

a. Translate given conditions into an equation.

1. Example of Translations from English into Equations

English	Equation
The product of 5, and a number decreased by 9, is 310.	$5(x - 9) = 310$
The product of 5 and a number, decreased by 9, is 310.	$5x - 9 = 310$
A meal and a 15% tip comes to $19.55.	Let x = cost of meal. Then $x + 0.15x = 19.55$.

b. Create verbal models and then translate into an equation.

c. Use tables to organize information.

1. *Simple Interest Problems*

Model:

Principle × Rate = Annual interest ($PR = I$)

Table:

	Principal × Rate = Interest
Investment 1	?
Investment 2	?

Represent the principal invested at each rate in terms of x. Set the sum of the interests from the final column equal to the given number for the yearly interest.

2. *Mixture Problems*

Model: A is P percent of B ($A = PB$).

Set up a table and model an equation based on this verbal model: The amount of a substance in solution 1 plus the amount of a substance in solution 2 equals the amount of the substance in the mixture.

3. Uniform Motion Problems

Model: Rate times time equals distance ($RT = D$)

Table:

	Rate × Time = Distance
Number 1	?
Number 2	?

The algebraic expressions for distance in the final column are used to set up an equation based on the problem's conditions.

d. Use critical thinking skills such as making systematic lists, looking for patterns, guessing and checking, working backward, and eliminating possibilities.

2. Ratio and Proportion

The ratio of a to b is written a/b, $a \div b$, or $a:b$ ($b \neq 0$).

A proportion is a statement in the form $\dfrac{a}{b} = \dfrac{c}{d}$. The cross products principal states that if $\dfrac{a}{b} = \dfrac{c}{d}$ then $ad = bc$ ($b \neq 0$ and $d \neq 0$).

3. Geometry Problems

a. Two complementary angles have measures whose sum is 90°. Supplementary angles have measures whose sum is 180°. If an angle measures $x°$, its complement measures $90° - x°$, and its supplement measures $180° - x°$.

b. The sum of the measures of the three angles of a triangle is 180°.

c. Formulas for perimeter, area, and volume, summarized in Section 3.3, often form the basis for writing algebraic equations and finding the length of a part of a geometric figure.

d. Similar triangles have corresponding angles with the same measure and corresponding sides that are proportional. Two triangles are similar if two angles of one are equal in measure to two corresponding angles of the other.

REVIEW PROBLEMS

1. The product of 4, and a number decreased by 8, is 24. Find the number.

2. The product of 4 and a number, decreased by 8, is 24. Find the number.

3. If you have $21.25 to spend for dinner and plan to leave a 25% tip, what is the maximum-priced dinner you can purchase?

4. After a 5% gain in weight, a woman weighs 126 pounds. What was her original weight?

5. Acid rain attacks lakes, rivers, forests, and buildings. The main components of acid rain are sulphur dioxide and nitrogen oxides, which are released by burning oil, coal, and gas. The graph shows the top ten producers of sulphur dioxide emissions. The United States produces 3 million tons more than 3 times that of Germany and China produces 2 million tons more than twice that of Germany. Together the three countries produce 41 million tons of sulphur dioxide. Find the number of millions of tons produced by each of the three countries.

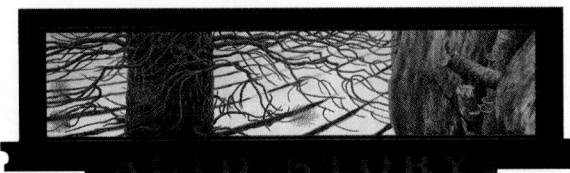

Neil Jenney, United States, b. 1945– , "Acid Story" 1983–84, oil on wood, $34\frac{1}{2}$ x 114 inches–87.6 x 289.6 cm. Los Angeles County Museum of Art, Gift of Steve Martin. Copyright © 1997 Museum Associates, Los Angeles County Museum. All rights reserved.

Top Ten Producers Sulphur Dioxide Emissions
(Million Tons)

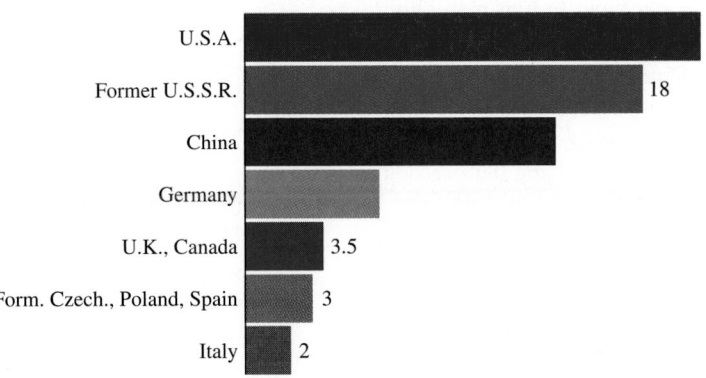

Sources: UNEP; OECD; UN Economic Commission for Europe.

6. In 1960, the population of the United States was approximately 179.5 million. If the population is growing by 2.35 million yearly, in what year will the population reach 320.5 million?

7. Two different groups of union employees have their salaries described in the table.

	Starting Salary	**Yearly Increase**
Group A	$30,000	$1500
Group B	$21,000	$2000

  a. Which group will be making the most money after ten yearly increases? How much will that be?

  b. Can the salaries of group *B* ever catch up with group *A*? If so, after how many yearly increases will this occur?

8. Answer the question in the following *Peanuts* cartoon strip. (*Note:* You may not use the answer given in the cartoon!)

PEANUTS reprinted by permission of United Features Syndicate, Inc.

9. A person invested $1000, part at 8% and the remainder at 10% simple interest. If the total yearly interest from these investments was $94, find the amount invested at each rate.

10. Money was invested at 8% and 9% simple interest. The amount invested at 9% was $100 more than twice the amount invested at 8%. If the yearly interest from both investments was $1910, how much was invested at each rate?

11. A person needs to mix a 75% saltwater solution with a 50% saltwater solution to obtain a 10 gallon mixture that is 60% salt water. How many gallons of each of the solutions must be used?

12. A school board plans to merge two schools into one school of 1000 students in which 42% of the students will be African-American. One of the schools has a 10% African-American student body and the other has a 90% African-American student body. What is the student population in each of the two schools?

13. Two trains start simultaneously from the same place. Train A travels north at 60 miles per hour and train B travels south at 80 miles per hour. In how many hours will they be 400 miles apart?

14. How many ways are there of making change for 15 cents using only pennies, nickels, and dimes?

15. A geometric sequence is a sequence in which each term after the first is obtained by multiplying the preceding term by a nonzero constant. Find the missing term in the following geometric sequence: $9, -6, 4, \underline{\hspace{1cm}}, \frac{16}{9}$.

16. If $A = 7$ and $B = 5$, then $C = \frac{49}{5}$. If $A = 8$ and $B = 2$, then $C = 32$. What is a possible formula for finding C in terms of A and B?

17. The numbers in the squares have been added to obtain the numbers between the squares.

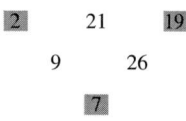

What numbers should be put in the squares below?

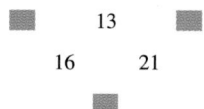

18. Find the digit represented by each different letter in the problem at the right.

$$\begin{array}{r} ABC \\ ABC \\ + \ ABC \\ \hline BBB \end{array}$$

19. What row in the table contains the square of an integer and the cube of a different integer?

a.	9	25	27	125
b.	52	64	75	81
c.	36	216	292	381
d.	320	450	566	678

20. Simplify the following expression.
$(99 - 9)(99 - 19)(99 - 29) \cdots (99 - 199)$.

21. Twelve toothpicks are arranged as shown in the figure. Form five squares by moving three toothpicks.

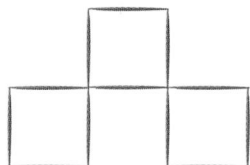

Use the same units of measure in the numerator and denominator to express the ratios in Problems 22–23 as fractions in reduced form.

22. 6 inches to 4 feet

23. 10 centimeters to 3 meters

24. A group of 40 people contains two dozen men. What is the ratio of women to men for this group?

25. The bar graph indicates countries where ten or more languages have become extinct. Use the graph to find each of the following ratios.
   a. The number of extinct languages in Brazil to that of the United States.
   b. The number of extinct languages in Australia and India combined to that of Colombia.

Countries Where 10 or More Languages Have Become Extinct (Number of Languages)

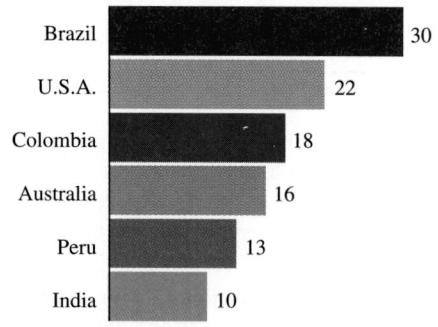

Source: Grimes

26. Find the unit price of an 18-ounce box of cereal that sells for $3.96.

Solve the proportions in Problems 27–28.

27. $\dfrac{3}{x} = \dfrac{15}{25}$

28. $\dfrac{-3}{8} = \dfrac{x}{64}$

29. If a school board determines that there should be 3 teachers for every 50 students, how many teachers are needed for an enrollment of 5400 students?

30. To determine the number of trout in a lake, a conservationist catches 112 trout, tags them, and returns them to the lake. Later, 82 trout are caught, and 32 of them are found to be tagged. How many trout are in the lake?

31. A house was purchased in 1970 for $20,000. Estimate the value of the house in 1994, using the CPI in the table.

Year	Consumer Price Index
1970	38.8
1994	148.2

Source: U.S. Bureau of Labor and Statistics

32. The measure of the complement of an angle is 10° less than three times the measure of the angle. Find the measure of the angle and its complement.

33. The measure of the supplement of an angle is 45° less than four times the measure of the angle. Find the measure of the angle and its supplement.

34. Find the measure of each angle of the triangle shown in the figure.

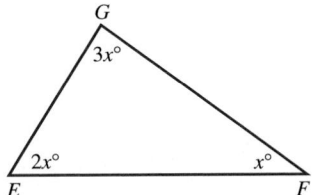

35. In triangle ABC, the measure of angle B is 11° more than seven times the measure of angle A. The measure of angle C is five times that of angle A. Find the measures of the angles.

36. Use the figure to find the value of x and then find the length of each side if the marked angles have equal measures and the sides opposite them are equal in length.

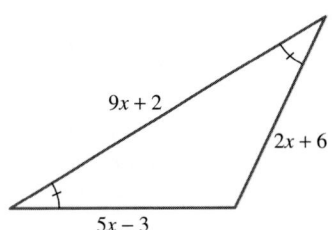

37. The length of a rectangular football field is 14 meters more than twice the width. If the perimeter is 346 meters, find the field's dimensions.

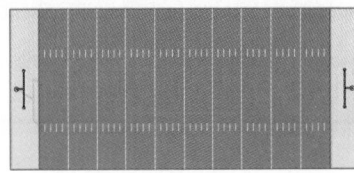

38. The three sides of a triangle have measures that are consecutive odd integers. What are the lengths of the sides if the perimeter is 87 yards?

39. A bookcase is to be constructed as shown in the figure. The length is to be 3 times the height. If 60 feet of lumber is available for the entire unit, find the length and height of the bookcase.

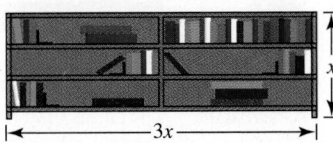

40. A sailboat has a triangular sail with an area of 42 square feet and a base that measures 14 feet. Find the height of the sail.

41. Find the area and circumference of a circle with a diameter of 10 meters. Express the answers in terms of π. Then use $\pi \approx 3.14$ to find approximations for the area and circumference.

42. The area of a trapezoid is 36 square yards. The length of one base is 7 yards and the height is 6 yards. Find the length of the other base.

43. A cylinder has a radius of 3 feet and a height of 5 feet. A larger cylinder has a radius of 6 feet and a height of 10 feet. Find the ratio of the volume of the smaller cylinder to that of the larger cylinder.

44. A sphere with radius r has a volume given by the formula

$$V = \frac{4}{3}\pi r^3.$$

A sphere whose radius measures 3 centimeters has its radius doubled to 6 centimeters. How many times greater is the volume of the larger sphere than that of the smaller sphere?

45. The triangles shown in the figure are similar. Find the length of the side marked with an x.

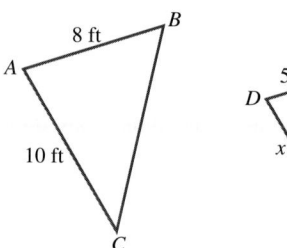
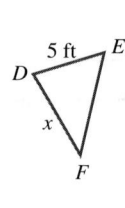

46. A pole casts a shadow 15 feet at the same time that an 8-foot rod casts a shadow of 24 feet. How high is the pole?

CHAPTER 3 TEST

1. A physical therapist's salary is $33,600, which is a 5% increase over the previous year's salary. What was the previous salary?

2. As of 1996, more than a half-million Americans had been stricken by AIDS. Among men, the caseload for Blacks exceeded that for Hispanics by 63,770, and the caseload for Whites was 2188 fewer than triple that for Hispanics. For these three groups, a total of 460,622 men had AIDS. Find the number diagnosed with the virus in each group.

Number of AIDS Cases Diagnosed through June 1996

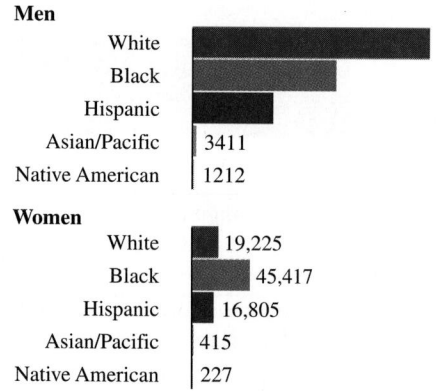

3. In 1993, the average weekly earning for workers in the United States was $462. If this amount is increasing by $15 yearly, find the year when the average weekly salary will reach $807.

4. A person invested $6000, part at 9% and the remainder at 6%. If the total yearly interest from the investments was $480, find the amount invested at each rate.

5. A chemist needs to mix a 50% acid solution with an 80% acid solution to obtain a 100 liter mixture that is 68% acid. How many liters of each of the acid solutions must be used?

6. Two cars that are 400 miles apart are traveling directly toward each other on the same road. One is averaging 45 miles per hour and the other, 35 miles per hour. How long will it take before they meet?

7. Express 45 as the difference of two squares.

8. The figure shows a number of small triangles in the interior of larger triangles. Although it is not shown, there are 144 small triangles contained within the interior when the base measures 12. Write an algebraic expression for the number of small triangles in the interior when the base measures n.

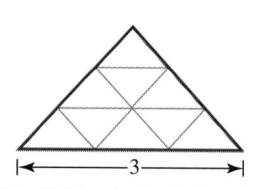
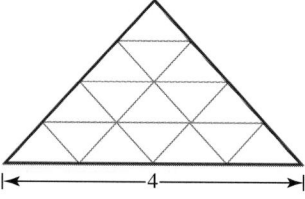

(a) 9 Triangles in the Interior   (b) 16 Triangles in the Interior

9. Find the missing number: 1, 2, 6, 24, 120, _____.

10. Find the ratio of 3 inches to 5 feet. Express the answer as a fraction in reduced form.

11. Find the unit price (in dollars per ounce) for an 18-ounce box of cereal that sells for $6.66.

12. Solve the proportion for x:

$$\frac{-7}{5} = \frac{91}{x}.$$

13. Park rangers catch, tag, and release 200 deer back into a wildlife refuge. Two weeks later they catch a sample of 150 deer, of which 5 are tagged. Assuming that the ratio of tagged deer in the sample holds for all deer in the refuge, how many deer are there in the park?

14. If a water bill is charged at a rate of $1.87 for every 1000 gallons of water used, what is the bill if 20,000 gallons are used?

15. How many degrees are there in an angle that measures 16° more than the measure of its complement?

16. Find the measure of each angle of the triangle in the figure.

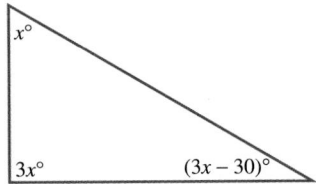

17. The circular dartboards in the figure come in two sizes with radii of 9 inches and 12 inches. How much larger is the area of the larger-sized dartboard? Express your answer in terms of π.

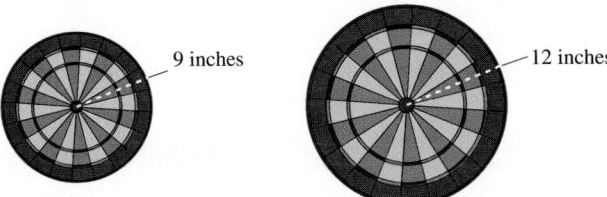

18. The height of the bookcase in the figure is 3 feet longer than the length of a shelf. If 18 feet of lumber is available for the entire unit, find the length and height of the unit.

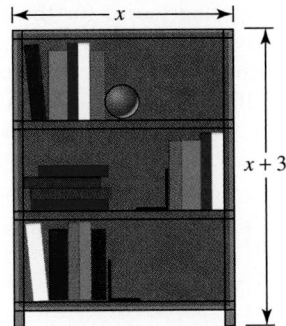

19. A sailboat has a triangular sail with an area of 56 square feet and a base that measures 8 feet. Find the height of the sail.

20. The triangles in the figure are similar. Find the length of the side marked with an x.

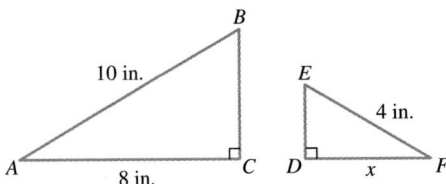

CUMULATIVE REVIEW PROBLEMS (CHAPTERS 1–3)

1. The algebraic expression $330 + 1700E$ describes the earnings in dollars for American women living in the Northeast who have E years of education. Rewrite the expression using the commutative property of addition.

2. The rectangular field shown in the figure is to be constructed with 1200 feet of fencing. The field will be a corral for two horses and so has a divider down the middle as shown. The field's area is given by the formula

$$A = W(600 - 1.5W)$$

where the area is expressed in square feet. What is the area of the corral if the width W is 200 feet?

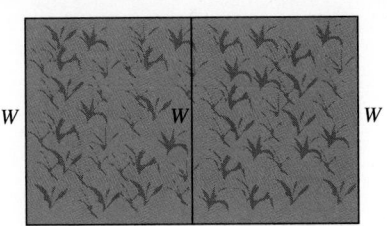

3. Perform the indicated operations:

$$\frac{-9(3 - 6)}{(-12)(3) + (-3 - 5)(8 - 4)}.$$

4. On February 8, the temperature in Manhattan at 10 P.M. was −4°F. By 3 A.M. the next day, the temperature had fallen 11°, but by noon the temperature increased by 21°. What was the temperature at noon?

5. Winning and losing scores for the Super Bowl from 1992 through 1994 are shown in the graph. Write a reasonable estimate for the final scores for each of these years. If you'd like, consult a sports reference book to see how close your estimates are to the actual final scores.

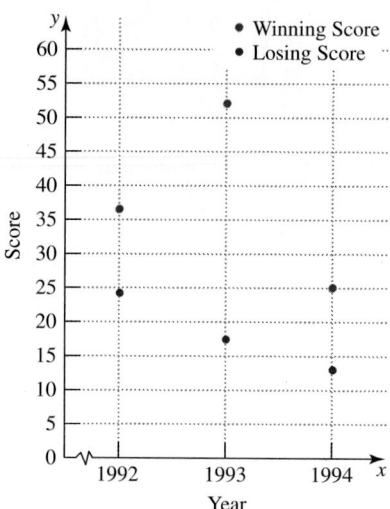

6. Given $\{-3, -\frac{1}{2}, \frac{1}{7}, 0, 8, 9.\overline{3}, \sqrt{25}, \sqrt{29}\}$, list the numbers in this set that also belong to the set of:
   a. Natural numbers **b.** Whole numbers
   c. Integers **d.** Rational numbers
   e. Irrational numbers **e.** Real numbers

7. The graph shows the decline in the number of inpatients in U.S. public mental hospitals since the late 1950s.
   a. Estimate the years in which the inpatient population was 300,000.
   b. What is a reasonable estimate of the year in which the inpatient population was at a maximum? Estimate the population for that year.

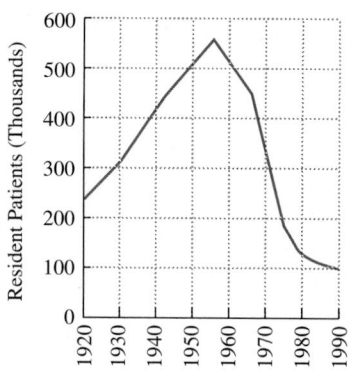

Source: American Psychiatric Association

8. Solve: $\frac{1}{5}y + \frac{2}{3}y = y + \frac{1}{15}$.

9. Two pages that face each other in a book have 385 as the sum of their page numbers. What are the page numbers?

10. A toll to a bridge costs 50¢. Commuters have the option of purchasing a monthly coupon book for $10. With this purchase, the toll is reduced to 10¢. How many times must the toll be used in a month to make the total costs with and without the coupon book the same?

11. After a 25% weight loss, a person weighed 135 pounds. What was the weight before the loss?

12. Solve: $10(2x - 1) = 8(2x + 1) + 14$.

13. Solve and then graph the solution set on a number line: $-4y + 7 \le 15$.

14. In 1992, there were five times as many vehicles per kilometer of paved road as there were in 1953. In particular, the number of vehicles per kilometer in Colombia is 20 less than twice that in Belgium, and the number in Brazil is 3 times that in Belgium. If the sum of the number of vehicles per kilometer in the three countries is 520, determine the number for each of the countries. Then use the graph to obtain a reasonable estimate for the countries shown.

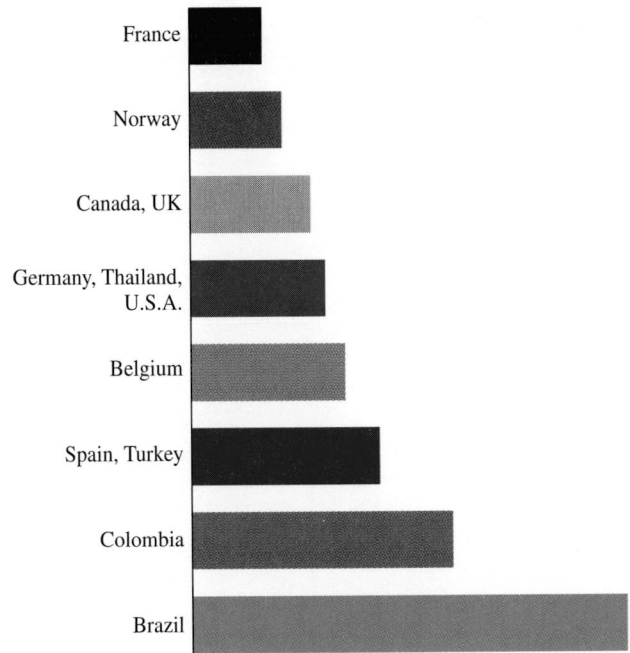

Congestion: Number of Vehicles per Kilometer of Paved Road 1992
(1 Kilometer = 0.62 Miles)

France
Norway
Canada, UK
Germany, Thailand, U.S.A.
Belgium
Spain, Turkey
Colombia
Brazil

Sources: CIA; International Road Federation

15. Simplify: $4(2x - 1) - 3(x - 11) - 2(-4x - 5)$.

16. The five data points in the graph show the relationship between the average number of hours per day that men sleep and their death rate.
   a. What are the coordinates of point A? Describe what these coordinates mean in practical terms.
   b. Write a brief description of the pattern indicated by the five data points.

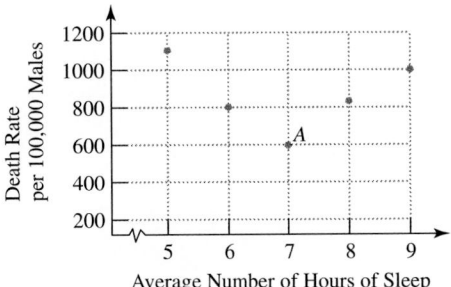

17. Find the height of the lamp post in the figure.

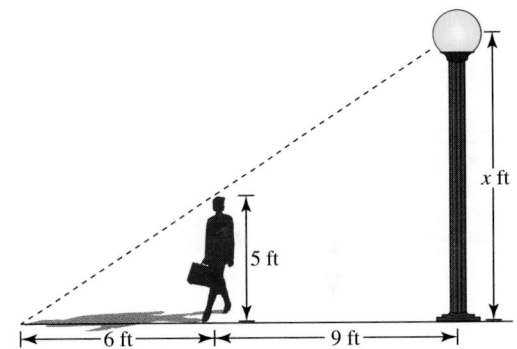

18. Solve the proportion: $\dfrac{x}{21} = \dfrac{5}{20}$.

19. If nine compact disks cost $135, find the cost of five compact disks.

20. The length of a rectangular parking lot is 10 yards less than twice the width. If the perimeter is 400 yards, find the lot's dimensions.

21. The graph shows the percent of groups targeted by hate crimes in Maine over a three-year period (1993–1995). If 170 of the hate crimes targeted blacks, how many hate crimes were there in Maine during this period? Use the graph to determine the number of crimes against the groups in the remaining three sectors.

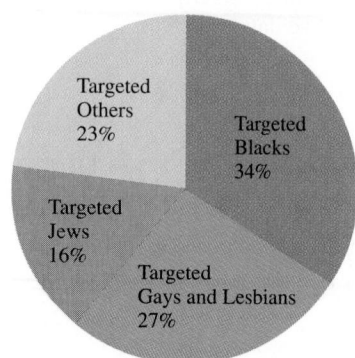

Targeted Others 23%

Targeted Blacks 34%

Targeted Jews 16%

Targeted Gays and Lesbians 27%

Source: Maine attorney general's office

22. Complete the pattern:

$$3^2 + 4^2 = 5^2$$
$$10^2 + 11^2 + 12^2 = 13^2 + \underline{\quad}$$
$$21^2 + 22^2 + 23^2 + \underline{\quad} = \underline{\quad}$$

23. If $2x > 23$, x is even, and $9x < 865$, which one of the following is not possible?
   a. $x = 96$ **b.** $x < 50$ **c.** $x > 23$ **d.** $x > 100$

24. The world record for weight lifting was set in 1984 by the Russian athlete Alexander Gunyashev. In theory, a gorilla could lift 775 pounds more than what Gunyashev lifted to break the world record. If the sum of what Gunyashev lifted and what a gorilla could lift is five less than the solution of $3x - 17 = 8443$, how many pounds did Gunyashev lift?

25. The difference between the measure of an angle and the measure of its complement is 16°. Find the measure of the angle.

26. How many sheets of paper, weighing 2 grams each, can be put in an envelope weighing 4 grams if the total weight must not exceed 29 grams?

27. Part of $15,000 is invested at 8% simple interest and the rest at 6% simple interest for 1 year. If the total interest is $1100, how much is invested at each rate?

28. Two runners start at the same point and run in opposite directions. One runs at 6 miles per hour and the other runs at 8 miles per hour. In how many hours will they be 21 miles apart?

29. If x, y, and z can each represent 2, 3, 6, or 12, select appropriate values so that $x \div y \div z = 2$. Each number should be used only once.

30. Solve for m: $A = \dfrac{m + n}{2}$.

4

Linear Equations and Inequalities in Two Variables

Nancy Fried "Cradling Her Sorrow" 1989, terra cotta, $10 \times 12\frac{1}{4} \times 7\frac{1}{4}$ in. Courtesy of the artist and DC Moore Gallery, New York.

Mathematicians use data points that appear to lie along a line to model the monsters of malignancy. Using data from numerous countries for daily fat intake and deaths per 100,000 population from breast cancer, the model $D = 0.2F - 1$ was derived. In the formula, F represents daily fat intake in grams and D represents deaths per 100,000 people from breast cancer. Our focus in this chapter is on models such as $D = 0.2F - 1$, called linear equations in two variables, whose graphs are straight lines.

Although this linear formula models reality, it cannot begin to convey how deeply cancer intrudes into the ordinary course of our lives. One woman in ten in the United States will be afflicted with breast cancer; 40,000 will die of the disease this year.

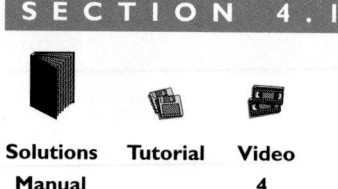

SECTION 4.1

Solutions   Tutorial   Video
Manual   4

Graphing Linear Equations and Linear Functions

Objectives

1 Determine if an ordered pair is a solution to a linear equation in two variables.
2 Graph a linear equation.
3 Use function notation.

In this section, we use ordered pairs that satisfy an equation to graph the equation in a rectangular coordinate system. We also introduce a notation for a concept that is extremely important in higher mathematics: *functions*.

1 Determine if an ordered pair is a solution to a linear equation in two variables.

iscover for yourself

Write six ordered pairs whose sum is 10. Equivalently, find six ordered pairs satisfying $x + y = 10$. Graph the ordered pairs in a rectangular coordinate system. What figure do these points suggest about the graph of the equation $x + y = 10$?

Solutions of Equations

Consider the equation $x + y = 10$. We can translate this equation into words by saying that the sum of two numbers, x and y, must be 10. Many pairs of numbers fit this description, such as $x = 1$ and $y = 9$, or $x = 3$ and $y = 7$. The phrase "$x = 1$ and $y = 9$" is abbreviated using the ordered pair $(1, 9)$. Similarly, the phrase "$x = 3$ and $y = 7$" is abbreviated by the ordered pair $(3, 7)$. Both $(1, 9)$ and $(3, 7)$ are *solutions* of the equation $x + y = 10$ and are said to *satisfy* the equation. Since there are infinitely many pairs of numbers that have a sum of 10, the equation $x + y = 10$ has infinitely many solutions.

The equation $x + y = 10$ is an example of a *linear equation in two variables*.

Linear equation in two variables

A *linear equation in two variables* is an equation that can be put in the form

$$Ax + By = C$$

where A, B, and C are real numbers and A and B are not both zero. A *solution* of the equation is written as the *ordered pair* (x, y), ordered in the sense that the value of x is always written first.

EXAMPLE 1   Deciding Whether an Ordered Pair Satisfies an Equation

Is $(3, 2)$ a solution to the equation $2r + 3s = 12$?

Solution

$$2r + 3s = 12 \qquad \text{This is the given linear equation in two variables.}$$

$$2(3) + 3(2) \overset{?}{=} 12 \qquad \text{To decide if } (3, 2) \text{ is a solution, replace } r \text{ by 3 and } s \text{ by 2. The ordered pair, in alphabetical order, is } (r, s).$$

$$6 + 6 \overset{?}{=} 12$$

$$12 = 12 \qquad \text{True}$$

This true statement indicates that $(3, 2)$ is a solution to $2r + 3s = 12$ and is said to satisfy the equation. ■

EXAMPLE 2   Deciding Whether an Ordered Pair Satisfies an Equation

Is $(-2, -7)$ a solution to the equation $x + 5y = 33$?

Solution

$$x + 5y = 33 \qquad \text{This is the given linear equation in two variables.}$$
$$-2 + 5(-7) \overset{?}{=} 33 \qquad \text{To decide if } (-2, -7) \text{ is a solution, replace } x \text{ by } -2 \text{ and } y \text{ by } -7.$$
$$-2 + (-35) \overset{?}{=} 33$$
$$-37 = 33 \qquad \text{False}$$

This false statement indicates that $(-2, -7)$ is *not* a solution to $x + 5y = 33$. The ordered pair $(-2, -7)$ does *not* satisfy the equation. ∎

EXAMPLE 3   Verifying Solutions to a Linear Equation

Show that the ordered pairs $(3, 5)$, $(0, -1)$, and $(-2, -5)$ are solutions of $y = 2x - 1$.

Solution

We substitute, replacing x with the first coordinate and y with the second coordinate of each pair.

Checking $(3, 5)$:

$$y = 2x - 1$$
$$5 \overset{?}{=} 2(3) - 1$$
$$5 \overset{?}{=} 6 - 1$$
$$5 = 5 \quad \text{True}$$

$(3, 5)$ is a solution.

Checking $(0, -1)$:

$$y = 2x - 1$$
$$-1 \overset{?}{=} 2(0) - 1$$
$$-1 \overset{?}{=} 0 - 1$$
$$-1 = -1 \quad \text{True}$$

$(0, -1)$ is a solution.

Checking $(-2, -5)$:

$$y = 2x - 1$$
$$-5 \overset{?}{=} 2(-2) - 1$$
$$-5 \overset{?}{=} -4 - 1$$
$$-5 = -5 \quad \text{True}$$

$(-2, -5)$ is a solution.

Since all three substitutions result in true statements, the ordered pairs $(3, 5)$, $(0, -1)$, and $(-2, -5)$ are all solutions. ∎

Take a moment to study the graph of $y = 2x - 1$, shown in the Discover for Yourself box. Identify the points along the line that correspond to the ordered pairs $(-1, -3)$, $(\frac{1}{2}, 0)$, and $(1, 1)$. The pairs $(-1, -3)$, $(\frac{1}{2}, 0)$, and $(1, 1)$ are also solutions to $y = 2x - 1$. Just as there are infinitely many points along the line, the equation $y = 2x - 1$ has infinitely many solutions.

Graphing Linear Equations in the Form $y = mx + b$

We have seen that solutions of a linear equation in two variables can be represented by points in a rectangular coordinate system. The set of all such points is called the *graph* of the equation. Let's see how we can obtain such a graph.

EXAMPLE 4   Graphing a Linear Equation

Graph the linear equation: $y = 3x$

Discover for yourself

The points corresponding to the three ordered pairs in Example 3 that satisfy $y = 2x - 1$ are plotted and connected in the graph. What do you observe?

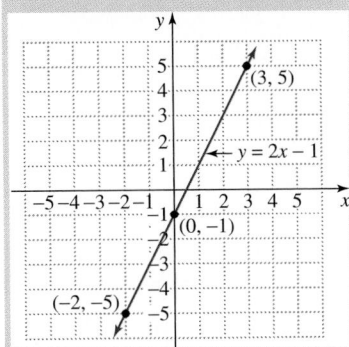

Study tip

All linear equations in two variables have infinitely many solutions.

2 Graph a linear equation.

Solution

We begin by finding several ordered pairs that are solutions to the equation. (Since there are infinitely many solutions, we cannot list them all.) To find some solutions to the equation, we choose a value for x, the first coordinate, and then find the corresponding value for y by substitution.

If $x = 2$,	then $y = 3 \cdot 2 = 6$;	thus, $(2, 6)$ is a solution.
If $x = 1$,	then $y = 3 \cdot 1 = 3$;	thus, $(1, 3)$ is a solution.
If $x = 0$,	then $y = 3 \cdot 0 = 0$;	thus, $(0, 0)$ is a solution.
If $x = -1$,	then $y = 3(-1) = -3$;	thus, $(-1, -3)$ is a solution.
If $x = -2$,	then $y = 3(-2) = -6$;	thus, $(-2, -6)$ is a solution.

We can list these results in a *table of values*.

x	$y = 3x$	(x, y)
2	6	$(2, 6)$
1	3	$(1, 3)$
0	0	$(0, 0)$
-1	-3	$(-1, -3)$
-2	-6	$(-2, -6)$

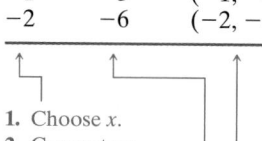

1. Choose x.
2. Compute y.
3. Form the pair (x, y).
4. Plot the points.

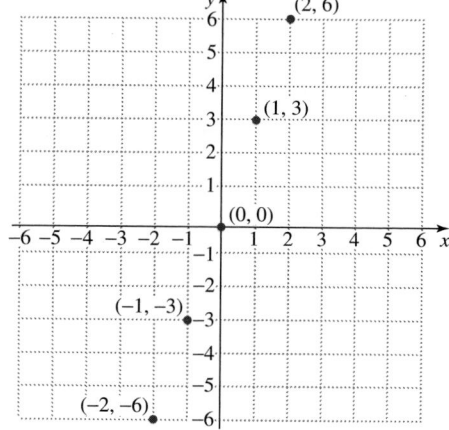

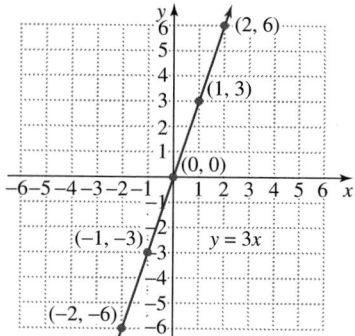

Figure 4.1

The graph of $y = 3x$

Finally, find a pattern for the plotted points and draw a curve through them. In this case, the points lie along a straight line. The graph of $y = 3x$ is shown in Figure 4.1.   ■

The point-plotting method of graphing $y = mx + b$

1. Make a table of values showing three or four ordered pairs that are solutions to the equation.
2. Plot these points on a rectangular coordinate system.
3. Since the graph of $y = mx + b$ is a straight line, connect the points with a line.

EXAMPLE 5   **Graphing a Linear Equation**

Graph the linear equation $y = 3x - 2$ and compare the graph with that of $y = 3x$, shown in Figure 4.1.

Solution

To compare the two graphs, we graph $y = 3x - 2$ using the same choices for x. The table of values, along with a list of the ordered pairs that satisfy $y = 3x$, and the graph of $y = 3x - 2$ are shown below.

x	$y = 3x - 2$	(x, y)	Solutions to $y = 3x$
2	$y = 3 \cdot 2 - 2 = 6 - 2 = 4$	$(2, 4)$	$(2, 6)$
1	$y = 3 \cdot 1 - 2 = 3 - 2 = 1$	$(1, 1)$	$(1, 3)$
0	$y = 3 \cdot 0 - 2 = 0 - 2 = -2$	$(0, -2)$	$(0, 0)$
−1	$y = 3(-1) - 2 = -3 - 2 = -5$	$(-1, -5)$	$(-1, -3)$
−2	$y = 3(-2) - 2 = -6 - 2 = -8$	$(-2, -8)$	$(-2, -6)$

$(-2, -8)$ is not shown on the graph. Why?

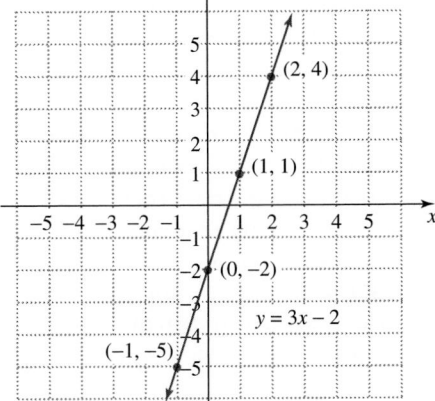

The graph of $y = 3x - 2$ looks exactly like the graph of $y = 3x$, but shifted 2 units down. Instead of crossing the y-axis at $(0, 0)$, the graph now crosses the y-axis at $(0, -2)$. ∎

EXAMPLE 6 **Graphing a Linear Equation**

Graph the linear equation: $y = \dfrac{2}{3}x + 1$

Solution

Make a table of values showing four ordered-pair solutions. We choose multiples of 3 for x so that the y-coordinates are not fractions.

x	$y = \frac{2}{3}x + 1$	(x, y)
−6	$y = \frac{2}{3}(-6) + 1 = -4 + 1 = -3$	$(-6, -3)$
−3	$y = \frac{2}{3}(-3) + 1 = -2 + 1 = -1$	$(-3, -1)$
0	$y = \frac{2}{3} \cdot 0 + 1 = 0 + 1 = 1$	$(0, 1)$
3	$y = \frac{2}{3} \cdot 3 + 1 = 2 + 1 = 3$	$(3, 3)$

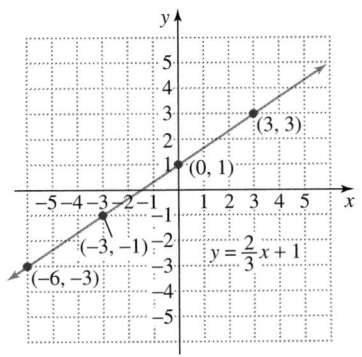

Figure 4.2

The graph of $y = \frac{2}{3}x + 1$

We now plot the four points and complete the graph by drawing a line through them. The graph of $y = \frac{2}{3}x + 1$ is shown in Figure 4.2. ∎

3 Use function notation.

Linear Equations in the Form $y = mx + b$ as Functions

The equation $y = 1700x + 330$ models the yearly salary (y, in dollars) for American women living in the Northeast who have x years of education. The graph of $y = 1700x + 330$, shown in Figure 4.3, indicates that as the number

ENRICHMENT ESSAY

Modeling with Linear Equations

The points in the figure show the relationship between average fat intake and death from breast cancer. Since both variables are positive, only the first quadrant of the rectangular coordinate system is shown.

The ordered pair for the United States, approximately (150, 22), means that when fat intake averages 150 grams per day, there are 22 deaths per 100,000 people from breast cancer. Mathematicians use these points to write a linear equation in two variables describing a line that passes very near to all of the points. This line is called the *line of best fit* and is used to predict the number of deaths from breast cancer in other countries based on a knowledge of fat intake.

Source: From "Diet and Cancer" by Leonard A. Cohen, Copyright © 1987 by Scientific American, Inc. All rights reserved.

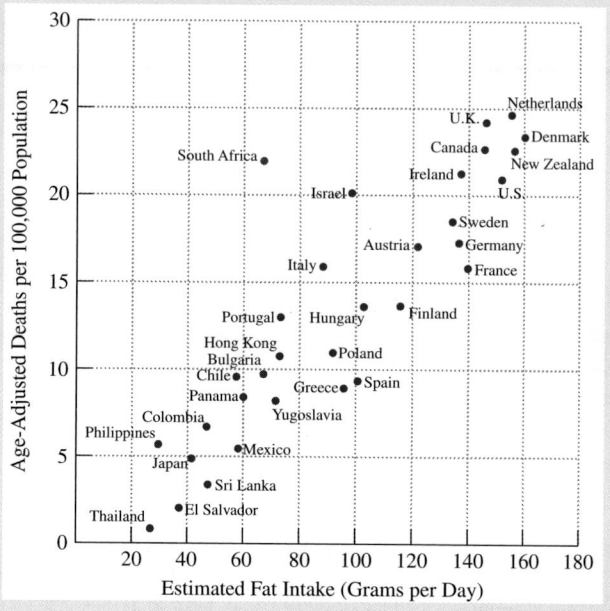

Figure 4.3

The graph of $y = 1700x + 330$

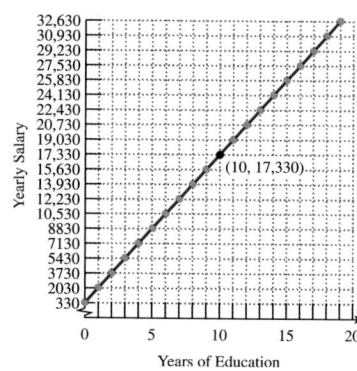

of years of education increases, so does yearly salary. For each level of education x, we obtain one value for yearly salary y. Under these circumstances, the model defines salary as a *function* of education. The variable y is a function of x.

The concept of function is so important in mathematics that a special notation has been developed to express it.

Function notation

If an equation in two variables (x and y) yields precisely one value of y for each value of x, we say that y is a function of x. The notation $y = f(x)$ indicates that the variable y is a function of x. The notation $f(x)$ is read "f of x" or "f at x."

For example, the model for salary

$$y = 1700x + 330$$

can be expressed in function notation.

$$f(x) = 1700x + 330$$ We read this as "f of x is equal to $1700x + 330$."

If, say, x equals 10 (meaning a woman has 10 years of education), we can find the corresponding value of y (yearly salary) using the equation $f(x) = 1700x + 330$.

$$f(x) = 1700x + 330 \qquad f \text{ of } x \text{ equals } 1700x + 330.$$
$$f(10) = 1700(10) + 330 \qquad \text{To find } f(10), \text{ or } f \text{ of } 10, \text{ replace } x \text{ by } 10.$$
$$f(10) = 17{,}000 + 330$$
$$f(10) = 17{,}330 \qquad \text{Thus, } f \text{ of } 10 \text{ is equal to } 17{,}330.$$

The process of finding $f(x)$ for a given value of x is called *evaluating the function*. When we find $f(10)$—that is, f of 10—we are evaluating the function at 10. By saying that $f(10) = 17{,}330$, we mean that if $x = 10$, then $y = 17{,}330$. Thus, a woman in the Northeast with 10 years of education is predicted to earn \$17,330 yearly. The point $(10, 17{,}330)$ is shown on the graph of the function in Figure 4.3.

Table 4.1 compares our previous notation with the new notation of functions.

TABLE 4.1 Function Notation

$y = mx + b$ Notation	$f(x) = mx + b$ Notation
The notation $f(x)$ is another way of writing y in a function.	
$y = 1700x + 330$	$f(x) = 1700x + 330$
If $x = 10$, $\qquad y = 1700(10) + 330 = 17{,}330$	$f(10) = 1700(10) + 330 = 17{,}330$ f of 10 equals 17,330.

We'll have more to say about functions in Section 4.3. For now, you can think of function notation as another way to express a relationship between two variables. When the variables are x and y, we must first isolate y if we want to use this new notation. As shown in Table 4.1, once y is isolated, we can replace y with $f(x)$.

EXAMPLE 7   Using Function Notation

a. Solve the equation $x + 2y = -4$ for y.
b. Write the equation in function notation.
c. Make a table of values and graph the function.

Solution

a. First isolate the y-term.

$$x + 2y = -4 \qquad \text{This is the given linear equation in two variables.}$$

$$2y = -x - 4 \qquad \text{To begin isolating the } y\text{-term, subtract } x \text{ from both sides.}$$

$$y = \frac{-x - 4}{2} \qquad \text{Now isolate } y \text{ by dividing both sides by 2.}$$

$$y = -\frac{1}{2}x - 2 \qquad \frac{-x - 4}{2} = \frac{1}{2}(-x - 4) = -\frac{1}{2}x - 2, \text{ using the distributive property. We have expressed the equation in the form } y = mx + b.$$

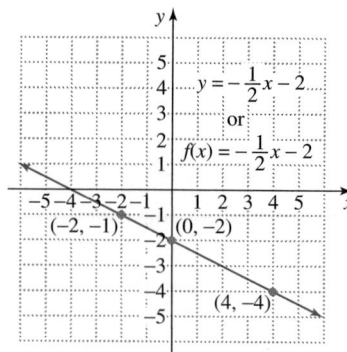

Figure 4.4
The graph of $y = -\frac{1}{2}x - 2$ or $f(x) = -\frac{1}{2}x - 2$

Rene Magritte "Golconde" 1953.
Menil Collection, Houston, TX,
U.S.A./Giraudon/Art Resource, NY.
©1998 C. Herscovici, Brussels/Artists
Rights Society (ARS), New York.

b. We can now write the equation in function notation by replacing y with $f(x)$.

$$y = -\frac{1}{2}x - 2 \qquad \text{This is our equation from part (a).}$$

$$f(x) = -\frac{1}{2}x - 2 \qquad \text{Replace } y \text{ with } f(x). \text{ Thus, } f \text{ of } x \text{ equals } -\frac{1}{2}x - 2.$$

c. We present our table of values using both our former notation and function notation. Choose values of x that are multiples of 2 so that the y-values are not fractions.

x	Equation $y = -\frac{1}{2}x - 2$	Function Notation $f(x) = -\frac{1}{2}x - 2$	(x, y)
-2	$y = -\frac{1}{2}(-2) - 2 = -1$	$f(-2) = -\frac{1}{2}(-2) - 2 = -1$	$(-2, -1)$
0	$y = -\frac{1}{2}(0) - 2 = -2$	$f(0) = -\frac{1}{2}(0) - 2 = -2$	$(0, -2)$
4	$y = -\frac{1}{2}(4) - 2 = -4$	$f(4) = -\frac{1}{2}(4) - 2 = -4$	$(4, -4)$

To graph $y = -\frac{1}{2}x - 2$, expressed as $f(x) = -\frac{1}{2}x - 2$ in function notation, we plot the three points and draw a line through them. The graph is shown in Figure 4.4. ∎

The mathematical models containing two variables that we saw throughout Chapters 1 through 3 can be expressed in the new notation of functions.

EXAMPLE 8   **Modeling U.S. Population**

The population of the United States was 179.5 million in 1960 and has been growing by approximately 2.35 million people per year. The linear function

$$f(x) = 2.35x + 179.5$$

models this population growth, where x represents the number of years after 1960 and $f(x)$ describes the U.S. population in millions. Use the function to find $f(0), f(10), f(20),$ and $f(30)$. Describe what these results mean.

Solution

Our goal is to find $f(x)$ (or y) when $x = 0, x = 10, x = 20,$ and $x = 30$.

x	$f(x) = 2.35x + 179.5$	Description
0	$f(0) = 2.35(0) + 179.5$ $= 0 + 179.5$ $= 179.5$	0 years after 1960, or in 1960 itself, U.S. population was approximately 179.5 million.
10	$f(10) = 2.35(10) + 179.5$ $= 23.5 + 179.5$ $= 203$	10 years after 1960, or in 1970, U.S. population was approximately 203 million.
20	$f(20) = 2.35(20) + 179.5$ $= 47 + 179.5$ $= 226.5$	20 years after 1960, or in 1980, U.S. population was approximately 226.5 million.
30	$f(30) = 2.35(30) + 179.5$ $= 70.5 + 179.5$ $= 250$	30 years after 1960, or in 1990, U.S. population was approximately 250 million.

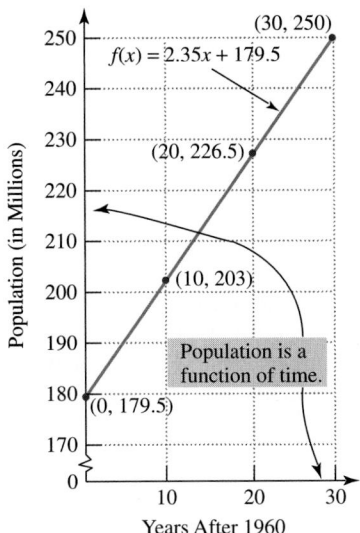

Figure 4.5

The graph. of $f(x) = 2.35x + 179.5$

We can use these results to graph the linear function. Since $f(0) = 179.5$, $f(10) = 203$, $f(20) = 226.5$, and $f(30) = 250$, we see that $(0, 179.5)$, $(10, 203)$, $(20, 226.5)$, and $(30, 250)$ are ordered-pair solutions of the equation $y = 2.35x + 179.5$. Choosing an appropriate scale along the axes, we plot the four points and complete the graph by drawing a line through them (see Figure 4.5). ∎

Using technology

Texas Instruments Inc., Dallas, Texas

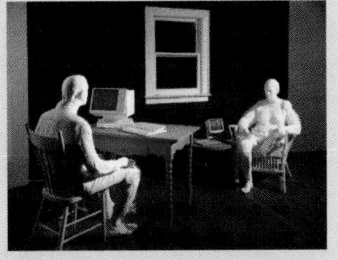

George Segal "Machine of the Year" 1983, plaster, wood, plastic and mixed media, 96 × 144 × 96 inches. Courtesy Sidney Janis Gallery, New York. © George Segal/Licensed by VAGA, New York 1998.

Graphing calculators or graphing software are referred to as *graphing utilities* or *graphers*. The point-plotting method is used by all graphing utilities. A graphing utility displays only a portion of the rectangular coordinate system, called a *viewing rectangle* or a *viewing window*. The viewing rectangle is determined by six values: the minimum x-value (Xmin), the maximum x-value (Xmax), the x-scale (Xscl), the minimum y-value (Ymin), the maximum y-value (Ymax), and the y-scale (Yscl). By entering these six values into a graphing utility, you set the *range* of the viewing rectangle, which is the boundary of the screen.

The standard viewing rectangle for many graphing utilities is shown in the accompanying figure.

Range
Xmin = −10
Xmax = 10
Xscl = 1
Ymin = −10
Ymax = 10
Yscl = 1

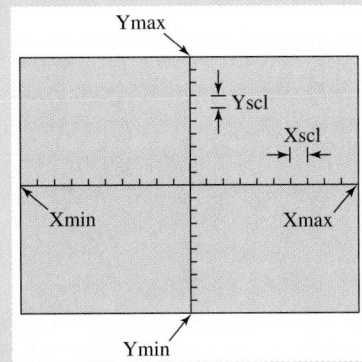

This viewing rectangle can be described as [−10, 10] by [−10, 10] and in general is described as [Xmin, Xmax] by [Ymin, Ymax].

Graphing an Equation in x and y. Using a Graphing Utility

1. If necessary, solve the equation for y in terms of x.
2. Enter the equation into the graphing utility.
3. Use the standard viewing rectangle or set the range to determine a viewing rectangle that will show a complete picture of the equation's graph.
4. Start the graphing utility.

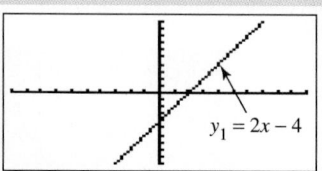

Figure 4.6 shows the graph of $y = 2x - 4$, entered as $Y_1 \boxed{=} 2X - 4$ on many graphing utilities. The viewing rectangle is $[-10, 10]$ by $[-10, 10]$. What do you observe about the spacing of the horizontal and vertical tick marks on the axes?

Figure 4.6
The graph of $Y_1 \boxed{=} 2X - 4$.

Problems for a Graphing Utility

Use a graphing utility to graph each equation in a standard viewing rectangle.

1. $y = 2x + 4$ **2.** $y = -3x + 6$ **3.** $y = \frac{1}{2}x$

4. $y = -\frac{1}{3}x$ **5.** $\frac{1}{4}x + y = -2$ **6.** $-\frac{1}{3}x + y = -6$

The $\boxed{\text{TRACE}}$ feature of a graphing utility enables you to find the coordinates of points along a graph. A blinking cursor appears on the graph displaying its x- and y-coordinates. As the cursor is moved along the graph, the coordinates change. Use the $\boxed{\text{TRACE}}$ feature of a graphing utility to approximate the coordinates of the points where the following graphs cross the x- and y-axes.

7. $y = 2x - 5$ **8.** $y = -2x + 5$

P R O B L E M   S E T   4 . I

Practice Problems

For the linear equations in two variables in Problems 1–12, tell which of the given ordered pairs are solutions.

1. $y = 3x$ (2, 3)   (3, 2)   (−4, −12)

2. $y = 4x$ (3, 12)   (12, 3)   (−5, −20)

3. $y = -4x$ (−5, −20)   (0, 0)   (9, −36)

4. $y = -3x$ (−5, 15)   (0, 0)   (7, −21)

5. $y = 2x + 6$ (0, 6)   (−3, 0)   (2,−2)

6. $y = 8 - 4x$ (8, 0)   (16,−2)   (3, −4)

7. $3x + 5y = 15$ (−5, 6)   (0, 5)   (10, −3)

8. $2x - 5y = 0$ (−2, 0)   (−10, 6)   (5, 0)

9. $x + 3y = 0$ (0, 0) $(1, \frac{1}{3})$ $(2, -\frac{2}{3})$

10. $4x - y = 0$ (1, 4)   (−2, −8)   (−3, 12)

11. $x - 4 = 0$ (4, 7)   (3, 4)   (0, −4)

12. $y + 2 = 0$ (0, 2)   (2, 0)   (0, −2)

Write each equation in Problems 13–48 in function notation. If necessary, solve for y and then replace y by f(x). Then make a table of values showing three or four ordered pairs that are solutions to the equation. Finally, graph the equation (or the function) on a rectangular coordinate system.

13. $y = x$ **14.** $y = -x$ **15.** $y = 2x$ **16.** $y = 4x$

17. $y = -2x$ **18.** $y = -4x$ **19.** $y = \frac{1}{2}x$ **20.** $y = \frac{1}{3}x$

21. $y = -\frac{2}{3}x$ **22.** $y = -\frac{3}{4}x$ **23.** $y = x + 2$ **24.** $y = x - 2$

25. $y = x - 3$ **26.** $y = x + 1$ **27.** $y = 2x + 1$ **28.** $y = 3x - 1$

29. $y = \frac{1}{3}x + 1$ **30.** $y = \frac{1}{2}x - 1$ **31.** $x + y = -1$ **32.** $x + y = -2$

33. $y = \frac{3}{2}x - 1$ **34.** $y = \frac{3}{5}x - 2$ **35.** $y = -\frac{5}{2}x - 1$ **36.** $y = -\frac{5}{3}x + 1$

37. $y = \frac{1}{2}x - 3$ **38.** $y = \frac{3}{2}x - 4$ **39.** $2x + y = 1$ **40.** $3x + y = 1$

41. $y = x + \frac{1}{2}$ **42.** $y = x - \frac{2}{3}$ **43.** $x + 2y = -2$ **44.** $x + 2y = 4$

45. $6x - 3y = 6$ **46.** $4x - 8y = 8$ **47.** $6y + 2x = -6$ **48.** $4y + 2x = -8$

Application Problems

49. In 1980, the average teacher's salary in the United States was \$16,116 and has been increasing by approximately \$1496 per year. The linear function $f(x) = 1496x + 16{,}116$ models this, where x represents the number of years after 1980 and $f(x)$ describes the average yearly salary. Use the function to find $f(0)$, $f(5)$, and $f(10)$. Describe what these results mean. Identify each of your computations as an appropriate point on the graph.

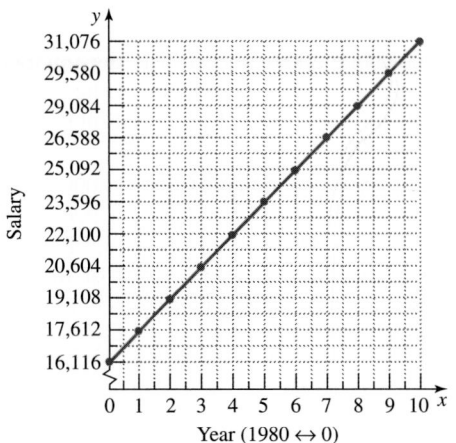

50. On the average, infant girls weigh 7 pounds at birth and gain 1.5 pounds each month for the first six months. The linear function $f(x) = 1.5x + 7$ models this, where x represents the infant's age in months ($x \le 6$) and $f(x)$ describes the baby's weight in pounds. Use the function to find $f(0)$, $f(2)$, $f(4)$, and $f(6)$. Describe what these results mean. Identify each of your computations as an appropriate point on the graph.

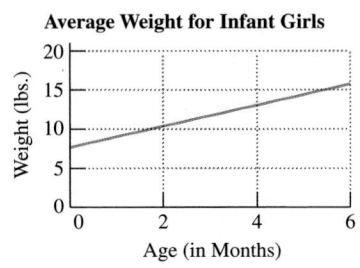

Average Weight for Infant Girls

51. If one side of a square measures x linear units, the perimeter of the square is given by $f(x) = 4x$. Find and interpret $f(2)$, $f(5)$, and $f(100)$, assuming that all measures are in meters. What values of x should we exclude when evaluating this function in the sense that these values produce results that are not geometrically meaningful?

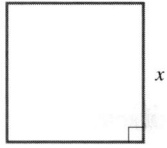

52. A triangle with all sides equal in measure is called an *equilateral triangle*. If one side of an equilateral triangle measures x linear units, the perimeter of the triangle is given by $f(x) = 3x$. Find and interpret $f(2)$, $f(5)$, and $f(100)$, assuming that all measures are in meters. What values of x produce results that are not geometrically meaningful and that we should exclude when evaluating the function?

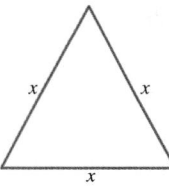

53. The mathematical model $M = \frac{1}{5}t$ can be used to calculate how far away lightning is during a thunderstorm. The variable M represents the distance, in miles, that the lightning is from a person who hears the sound of thunder t seconds after the lightning has been sighted.
a. Complete the table.

t	0	1	5	10	15	20
M						

b. Use the table to graph the model, graphing values of t along the x-axis and values of M along the y-axis.

54. The mathematical model $F = \frac{9}{5}C + 32$ can be used to change a Celsius temperature (C) to a Fahrenheit temperature (F).
a. Complete the table.

C	0	5	10	15	20
F					

b. Use the table to graph $F = \frac{9}{5}C + 32$, graphing values of C along the x-axis and values of F along the y-axis.

55. A business that manufactures racing bicycles has weekly fixed costs of $30,000 plus a cost of $50 to manufacture each racing bicycle. The total weekly costs for the business is the sum of their fixed costs plus the costs that vary depending on how many bicycles are manufactured. The function $f(x) = 30,000 + 50x$ models total weekly costs, where x represents the number of racing bicycles manufactured and $f(x)$ describes weekly costs in dollars.
a. Complete the table.

x	$f(x) = 30,000 + 50x$	(x, y)
0		
10		
100		
1000		

b. Use the table to graph the total cost model. (*Hint:* Let each unit along the y-axis represent $10,000.)

56. An online computer service provider charges $10 per month plus $3 for each hour of use. The function $f(x) = 10 + 3x$ models total monthly costs, where x represents the number of hours that a customer is online and $f(x)$ describes monthly costs in dollars.
a. Complete the table.

x	$f(x) = 10 + 3x$	(x, y)
0		
5		
10		
15		
20		

b. Use the table to graph the total monthly cost function.

57. A building purchased for $60,000 is depreciated by $5000 each year. The equation that models this is $y = 60,000 - 5000x$, where x is the number of years from 0 to 12, and y is the value of the building. Graph this equation. (*Hint:* Let each unit on the y-axis represent $10,000.)

58. An automobile purchased for $21,000 is depreciated by $3000 each year. The equation that models this is $y = 21,000 - 3000x$, where x is the number of years from 0 to 7, and y is the value of the automobile. Graph this equation. (*Hint:* Let each unit on the y-axis represent $3000.)

True–False Critical Thinking Problems

59. Which one of the following is true?
a. The graph of $y = 3x + 1$ looks exactly like the graph of $y = 2x$, but shifted up 1 unit.
b. The graph of any equation in the form $y = mx + b$ passes through the point $(0, b)$.
c. The ordered pair $(3, 4)$ satisfies the equation $2y - 3x = -6$.
d. If $(2, 5)$ satisfies an equation, then $(5, 2)$ also satisfies the equation.

60. Which one of the following is true?
a. The graph of $y = 2x - 1$ looks exactly like the graph of $y = 2x + 1$, but shifted down 2 units.
b. If $f(x) = -2x - 5$, then $f(-1) = -7$.
c. Every line that is graphed in the rectangular coordinate system crosses the x-axis at exactly one point.
d. The equations $y = -\frac{1}{2}x + 3$ and $x + 2y = 3$ are equivalent.

Technology Problems

61. Graph $y = x$ by hand. Then use a graphing utility to graph $y = x$. Observe that the graph generated by the graphing utility does not look like the one that you drew by hand. This is because the tick marks on the x-axis are slightly farther apart than those on the y-axis, creating some distortion in the graph. Although the

graph of $y = x$ should make a 45° angle with the x-axis, the distortion creates a graph that does not appear to form this 45° angle. To create the same distance between tick marks on both axes, press the ZOOM SQUARE feature on your graphing utility. Now observe what happens to the graph of $y = x$.

62. Use a graphing utility to graph any six of the linear equations in Problems 13–48 that you have already graphed by hand. Use an appropriate range setting and the $\boxed{\text{ZOOM SQUARE}}$ feature to make the graph look exactly like the one you drew by hand. Then use the utility's $\boxed{\text{TRACE}}$ feature to identify the x- and y-values that you listed in your table of values.

In Problems 63–65, graph both equations on the same screen. What do you observe? What algebraic rule is illustrated?

63. $y = 2x - 1$
$y = -1 + 2x$

64. $y = 3(\frac{1}{2}x)$
$y = (3 \cdot \frac{1}{2})x$

65. $y = 2 + (x + 3)$
$y = (2 + x) + 3$

Writing in Mathematics

66. How many points are needed to graph a line? How many points should actually be used? Explain.

67. The function $f(x) = 5.5x - 220$ approximates the weight ($f(x)$, in pounds) for a man who is x inches tall.

Describe the process needed to find $f(72)$. Carry out this process and describe what your answer represents. Why do you think this process is called evaluating the function?

Critical Thinking Problems

68. The linear function $f(x) = 1.44x + 280$ models the carbon dioxide concentration (in parts per million) x years after 1939. Find and interpret $f(21), f(26), f(31), f(36)$, and $f(41)$. Based on the bar graph, how well does the linear function model reality for the five years represented in the graph?

69. Complete the following table of values for $y = x^2 - 1$. Plot the points on a rectangular coordinate system and draw the graph.

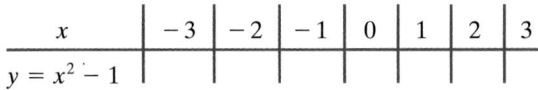

x	-3	-2	-1	0	1	2	3
$y = x^2 - 1$							

CO_2 Concentration 1960–1980

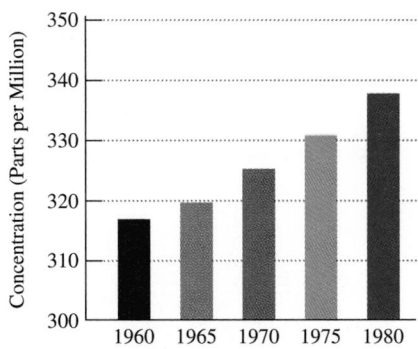

Data Source: *World Resources 1992–1993*
A Report by the World Resources Institute
Dr. Allen L. Hammond, Ed Oxford
University Press, 1992.

Review Problems

70. Solve: $2(x - 8) = 3(x - 4) - 5x$.

71. Solve: $2(x + 6) \leq 4x - 2$.

72. Solve: $\dfrac{12}{x} = \dfrac{5}{2}$.

S E C T I O N   4 . 2

Solutions Manual **Tutorial** **Video 4**

More on Graphing Linear Equations

Objectives

1 Graph a linear equation in two variables using intercepts.
2 Graph horizontal or vertical lines.
3 Solve problems involving linear equations in two variables.

Although equations such as $3x - 2y = 6$ can be rewritten in the form $y = mx + b$ and then graphed as we saw in the previous section, there is another way to graph linear equations of the form $Ax + By = C$. We will consider two important points on many graphs: the *intercepts*.

Graph a linear equation in two variables using intercepts.

Graphing Using Intercepts

We have seen that the graph of every linear equation in two variables $(Ax + By = C)$ is a straight line. Since two points determine a line, we really need only find two ordered pairs that are solutions to the equation to draw the graph. However, it is more accurate to find three ordered pairs that satisfy the equation, in case there was an error calculating one of the points.

EXAMPLE 1 Graphing a Linear Equation

Graph the linear equation: $3x - 2y = 6$

Solution

For many linear equations, two ordered pairs that satisfy the equation can be found by first letting $x = 0$ and then letting $y = 0$. That is:

If $x = 0$: $3x - 2y = 6$ If $y = 0$: $3x - 2y = 6$

$3(0) - 2y = 6$ $3x - 2(0) = 6$

$-2y = 6$ $3x = 6$

$y = -3$ $x = 2$

$(0, -3)$ is a solution. $(2, 0)$ is a solution.

As a check, get a third ordered pair by assigning any value to x and solving for y, or vice versa.

If $x = 4$: $3x - 2y = 6$

$3(4) - 2y = 6$

$12 - 2y = 6$

$-2y = -6$

$y = 3$

$(4, 3)$ is a solution.

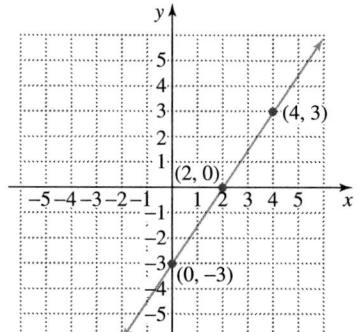

Figure 4.7

The graph of $3x - 2y = 6$

Now plot the three ordered pairs $(0, -3)$, $(2, 0)$, and $(4, 3)$. Draw a line that passes through them. This line, shown in Figure 4.7, is the graph of $3x - 2y = 6$. ■

In Figure 4.7, the graph crosses the x-axis at 2 and we say that 2 is the *x-intercept* of the line. The graph crosses the y-axis at -3 and we say that -3 is the *y-intercept* of the line. These observations are reinforced in Table 4.2.

TABLE 4.2 Ordered Pairs and Intercepts

Ordered Pair	Intercept	Observation
$(2, 0)$	x-intercept $= 2$	The graph crosses the x-axis at 2. If the x-intercept is a, then $(a, 0)$ lies on the graph.
$(0, -3)$	y-intercept $= -3$	The graph crosses the y-axis at -3. If the y-intercept is b, then $(0, b)$ lies on the graph.

Graphing $Ax + By = C$ using intercepts ($C \neq 0$)

1. Find the x-intercept by letting $y = 0$ and solving the given equation for x. This will give the x-coordinate of the point where the graph crosses the x-axis.
2. Find the y-intercept by letting $x = 0$ and solving the given equation for y. This will give the y-coordinate of the point where the graph crosses the y-axis.
3. Find a third checkpoint.
4. Draw a line that passes through these points.

EXAMPLE 2   **Graphing a Linear Equation by Using Intercepts**

Graph the linear equation: $2x - y = 4$

Solution

Find the x-intercept by letting $y = 0$ in the equation.

$$2x - y = 4$$
$$2x - 0 = 4$$
$$2x = 4$$
$$x = 2$$

The x-intercept is 2, so (2, 0) satisfies the equation.
    Find the y-intercept by letting $x = 0$ in the equation.

$$2x - y = 4$$
$$2(0) - y = 4$$
$$-y = 4$$
$$y = -4$$

The y-intercept is -4, so $(0, -4)$ satisfies the equation.
    Checkpoint: Let $x = 1$, then

$$2x - y = 4$$
$$2(1) - y = 4$$
$$-y = 2$$
$$y = -2$$

$(1, -2)$ satisfies the equation. The graph of $2x - y = 4$ is shown in Figure 4.8. ∎

Based on your work in the Discover for Yourself box, we can generalize and obtain the following observation.

> If A and B are real numbers, the graph of the linear equation $Ax + By = 0$ passes through the origin (0, 0).

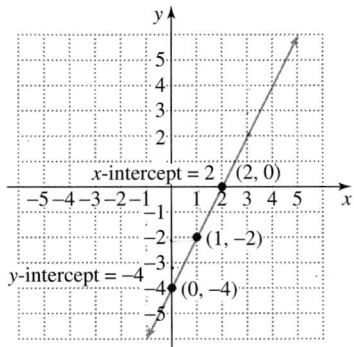

Figure 4.8
The graph of $2x - y = 4$

2 Graph horizontal or vertical lines.

Equations of Lines Parallel to the Coordinate Axes

EXAMPLE 3   Graphing a Linear Equation in the Form $x = a$

Graph the linear equation: $x = 5$

Solution

The equation $x = 5$ can be written as $1x + 0y = 5$, so it does fit the form of a linear equation ($Ax + By = C$). All the ordered pairs that are solutions to $x = 5$ have an x-value of 5, where any value can be used for y. Three such ordered pairs are $(5, -2)$, $(5, 0)$, and $(5, 3)$. Drawing a line that passes through these points gives the vertical line shown in Figure 4.9. ∎

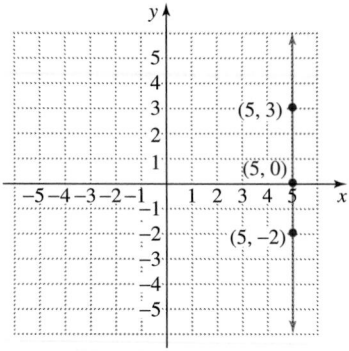

Figure 4.9

The graph of $x = 5$

By generalizing from Example 3, we obtain the following result:

> The graph of the linear equation $x = a$ is a vertical line parallel to the y-axis that intersects the x-axis at a. In particular, the graph of $x = 0$ is the y-axis.

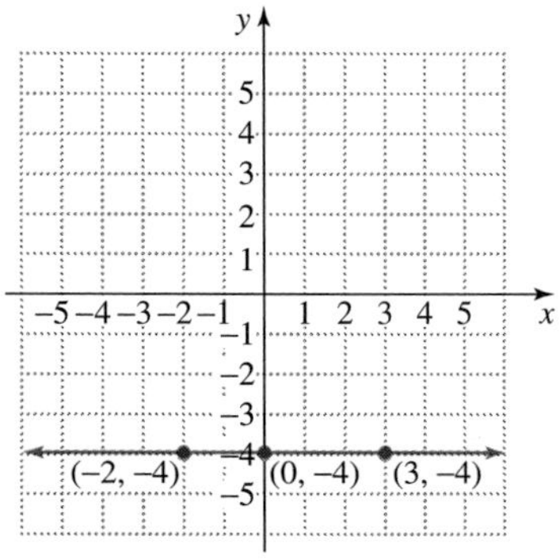

EXAMPLE 4   Graphing a Linear Equation in the Form $y = b$

Graph the linear equation: $y + 4 = 0$

Solution

The equation $y + 4 = 0$ can be written as $y = -4$ or as $0x + 1y = -4$, fitting the form of a linear equation. Using the form $y = -4$, all the ordered pair solutions have a y-value of -4, where any value can be used for x. Three such ordered pairs are $(-2, -4)$, $(0, -4)$, and $(3, -4)$. Drawing a line that passes through these points gives the horizontal line shown in Figure 4.10. ∎

Figure 4.10

The graph of $y + 4 = 0$

By generalizing from Example 4, we obtain the following result:

> The graph of the linear equation $y = b$ is the horizontal line parallel to the x-axis that intersects the y-axis at b. In particular, the graph of $y = 0$ is the x-axis.

Table 4.3 summarizes the techniques we have considered for graphing linear equations.

TABLE 4.3 Graphing Linear Equations

Equation	Graphing Technique	Example	
$Ax + By = C$	Find the x- and y-intercepts. To find the x-intercept, let $y = 0$ and solve for x. To find the y-intercept, let $x = 0$ and solve for y. Choose a third checkpoint	$4x + 3y = 12$ $x = 0:\quad 3y = 12$ $\qquad\qquad y = 4$ $y = 0:\quad 4x = 12$ $\qquad\qquad x = 3$ $x = 2:\quad 8 + 3y = 12$ $\qquad\qquad 3y = 4$ $\qquad\qquad y = \frac{4}{3}$	
$Ax + By = 0$	The graph passes through the origin. Find two other points by selecting values for x and solving for y, or vice versa.	$x + 2y = 0$ $x = 2:\quad 2 + 2y = 0$ $\qquad\qquad 2y = -2$ $\qquad\qquad y = -1$ $y = 1:\quad x + 2(1) = 0$ $\qquad\qquad x = -2$	
$x = a$	Draw a line parallel to the y-axis that intersects the x-axis at a.	$x = -1$	
$y = b$	Draw a line parallel to the x-axis that intersects the y-axis at b.	$y = 5$	

3 Solve problems involving linear equations in two variables.

Graphs and Problem Solving

Some problem-solving situations have verbal conditions that translate into a linear equation in two variables. The graph of the resulting equation gives a visual representation of the problem's conditions.

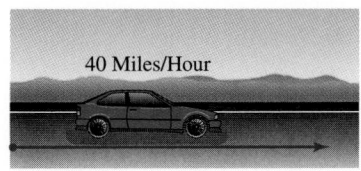

40 Miles/Hour

Distance traveled is a function of time.

EXAMPLE 5 Graphing a Model for Uniform Motion

A car travels at a speed of 40 miles per hour for t hours. The distance that the car travels in t hours is given by the model $d = 40t$.

a. Use the mathematical model to estimate the distance covered in 1 hour, 2 hours, 2.5 hours, and 4 hours.

b. Graph the model with values of t along the x-axis and values of d along the y-axis.

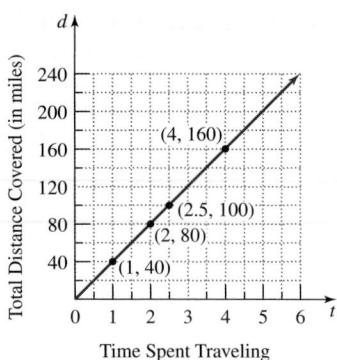

Figure 4.11

The graph of $d = 40t$

Solution

a. To find the distance covered in 1, 2, 2.5, and 4 hours, we substitute these values for t into the linear equation in two variables, and then calculate d.

$$d = 40t$$

If $t = 1$:	$d = 40(1) = 40$;	Distance in 1 hour is 40 miles.
If $t = 2$:	$d = 40(2) = 80$;	Distance in 2 hours is 80 miles.
If $t = 2.5$:	$d = 40(2.5) = 100$;	Distance in $2\frac{1}{2}$ hours is 100 miles.
If $t = 4$:	$d = 40(4) = 160$;	Distance in 4 hours is 160 miles.

b. We can use the values computed in part (a) as ordered pairs satisfying $d = 40t$. We plot the four points corresponding to $(1, 40)$, $(2, 80)$, $(2.5, 100)$, and $(4, 160)$. We complete the graph of $d = 40t$ by drawing a line through them, as shown in Figure 4.11. ∎

EXAMPLE 6 **Graphing a Model for Weekly Salary**

The salary (S) received by a salesperson is $400 per week plus a 5% commission on all sales (x).

a. Write an equation that models the salary S in terms of sales x.
b. Graph the model.
c. Use the graph to determine the weekly salary for sales of $12,000.
d. Use the graph to determine the sales needed to generate a weekly salary of $1300.

Solution

a. We obtain our equation by translating each phrase in the given verbal conditions.

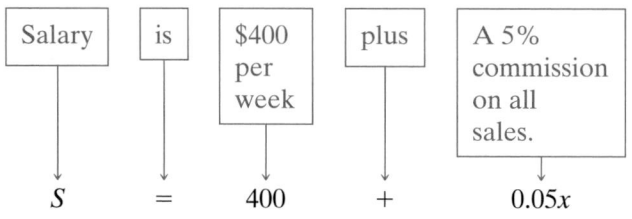

5% of all sales translates as $0.05x$.

The equation that models weekly salary is

$$S = 400 + 0.05x.$$

b. We make a table of values by selecting some convenient choices for x.

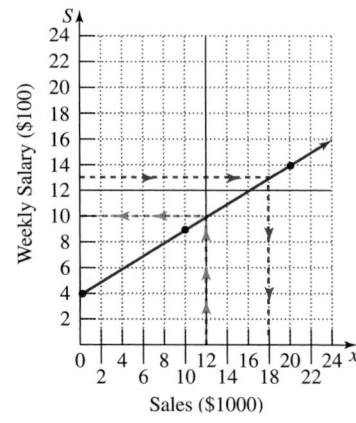

Figure 4.12

The graph of $S = 400 + 0.05x$

x (sales)	S (Salary) $= 400 + 0.05x$	(x, S)
0	$S = 400 + 0.05(0) = 400$	$(0, 400)$
10,000	$S = 400 + 0.05(10,000) = 900$	$(10,000, 900)$
20,000	$S = 400 + 0.05(20,000) = 1400$	$(20,000, 1400)$

The graph is shown in Figure 4.12 at the bottom of page 296. To keep the numbers smaller, sales are represented in thousands of dollars and salary is shown in hundreds of dollars.

c. To determine the weekly salary for $12,000 worth of sales:
   1. Locate $12,000 (12) on the horizontal sales axis.
   2. Draw a vertical line (shown in green in Figure 4.12) until it intersects the graph.
   3. Draw a horizontal line across to the weekly salary axis.
   The green horizontal line intersects the salary axis at 10. This indicates that weekly salary is $1000 for sales of $12,000.

Check

$$S = 400 + 0.05x \qquad \text{Use the equation modeling salary.}$$
$$= 400 + 0.05(12,000) \qquad \text{Substitute 12,000 for } x, \text{ weekly sales.}$$
$$= 400 + 600 \qquad \text{The model verifies that the weekly salary is \$1000 for sales}$$
$$= 1000 \qquad \text{of \$12,000.}$$

d. To determine the sales needed to generate a weekly salary of $1300:
   1. Locate $1300 (13) on the vertical weekly salary axis.
   2. Draw a horizontal line (shown in blue in Figure 4.12) until it intersects the graph.
   3. Draw a vertical line down to the sales axis.

The blue vertical line intersects the sales axis at 18. This indicates that sales needed to generate a weekly salary of $1300 amount to $18,000. Try checking this using the equation $S = 400 + 0.05x$. ∎

PROBLEM SET 4.2

Practice Problems

Graph each linear equation in Problems 1–34.

1. $x - y = 3$ **2.** $x + y = 4$ **3.** $3x = 4y - 12$ **4.** $2x = 5y - 10$

5. $7x - 2y = 14$ **6.** $5x + 3y = 15$ **7.** $2x - y = 0$ **8.** $3x + y = 0$

9. $y = -3x$ **10.** $y = -5x$ **11.** $y = 3x + 1$ **12.** $y = 2x - 1$

13. $x = 4$ **14.** $x = 5$ **15.** $x = -2$ **16.** $x = -3$

17. $x - 6 = 0$ **18.** $x + 4 = 0$ **19.** $y = 5$ **20.** $y = 4$

21. $y = -3$ **22.** $y = -2$ **23.** $y + 6 = 0$ **24.** $y + 1 = 0$

25. $x = 0$ **26.** $y = 0$ **27.** $3y = 9$ **28.** $5y = 20$

29. $-3x - 2y = 6$ **30.** $-10x - 30y = 45$ **31.** $20x - 240 = -60y$

32. $10x - 300 = -40y$ **33.** $\frac{1}{3}x + \frac{1}{4}y = 12$ **34.** $\frac{2}{3}y - \frac{1}{5}x = -60$

Application Problems

35. *Calorie Expenditure as a Function of Time Jogging.* A person who jogs slowly can expect to expend 300 calories per hour. The number of calories C expended after t hours is given by the model $C = 300t$.
   a. Use the formula to determine the number of calo-

ries expended in 1 hour, 2 hours, 2.5 hours, and 4 hours.
   b. Graph the model with values of t along the x-axis and values of C along the y-axis.

36. *Simple Interest as a Function of the Amount Invested.* The annual simple interest I on an amount of money P in an account that pays 4% simple interest is given by the model $I = 0.04P$.
  a. Use the formula to determine the simple interest on investments of $1000, $7500, and $10,000.
  b. Graph the model with values of P along the x-axis and values of I along the y-axis.

37. *The Cost of Renting a Truck as a Function of Miles Driven.* A truck rental company charges $50 per day plus $2 per mile.
  a. Write an equation that models the daily cost C for renting the truck if x miles are to be driven.
  b. Graph the model with values of x along the horizontal axis and values of C along the vertical axis.
  c. Use the graph to determine the cost of renting the truck for one day and driving 12 miles. Check your result by using the formula.

38. *Annual Cost of a Fitness Club as a Function of Time Spent at the Club.* A fitness club has an annual membership fee of $100 plus $1.50 for each hour spent at the club.

  a. Write an equation that models the annual cost C for the club if x hours are spent for the year at the club.
  b. Graph the model with values of x along the horizontal axis and values of C along the vertical axis.
  c. Use the graph to determine (or estimate) the number of hours spent working out at the club if the annual cost is $193. Check your result by using the formula.

39. *The Number of U.S. Physicians as a Function of Time.* According to the American Medical Association, there were 577 thousand physicians in the United States in 1985. This number has been increasing steadily by approximately $\frac{69}{5}$ thousand physicians each year.
  a. Write an equation that models the number of physicians (y, in thousands) x years after 1985.
  b. Use the equation to estimate the number of physicians in 1990 and 1995.
  c. Graph the model.
  d. Use the graph to estimate the number of physicians in 1987. Check this result by using the formula.

True–False Critical Thinking Problems

40. Which one of the following is true?
  a. The y-intercept for the graph of $x + 2y = 4$ is 4.
  b. The graph of $x = -4$ is a horizontal line.
  c. As long as A, B, and C are not zero, the graph of $Ax + By = C$ always has two different intercepts.
  d. The equation of the x-axis is $x = 0$.

41. Which one of the following is true?
  a. Intercepts must always be integers.
  b. A line cannot have two different intercepts that have the same numerical value.
  c. An x-intercept can never fall on the y-axis.
  d. The graph of $x + 1,000,000 = 0$ is a vertical line.

Technology Problems

42. A truck rental agency charges $39.95 per day plus 45¢ per mile. The total daily cost y of driving x miles is given by $y = 39.95 + 0.45x$.
  a. Use a graphing utility to graph the model with the following range settings:

  Xmin = 0, Xmax = 400, Xscl = 50,

  Ymin = 0, Ymax = 250, Yscl = 50.

  b. Use the $\boxed{\text{TRACE}}$ feature to approximate the cost of driving 206 miles. (For more precision, consult your manual and use the $\boxed{\text{ZOOM}}$ feature to magnify the appropriate part of the graph.)

43. A salesperson receives a salary of $300 weekly plus

4% commission on all sales.
  a. Write a linear model that describes weekly salary (y) in terms of sales (x).
  b. Use a graphing utility to graph the model in part (a). Use the following settings:

  Xmin = 0, Xmax = 10,000, Xscl = 1000,

  Ymin = 200, Ymax = 600, Yscl = 50.

  c. Use the $\boxed{\text{TRACE}}$ feature to approximate the weekly salary for sales of $4500. (For more precision, consult your manual and use the $\boxed{\text{ZOOM}}$ feature to magnify the appropriate part of the graph.)

Writing in Mathematics

44. Explain what intercepts are. How are intercepts used in graphing an equation such as $2x - 3y = 6$?

45. When graphing a linear equation in two variables using intercepts, why is a third point used?

46. Explain why the y-values can be any number for the equation $x = 5$. How is this shown in the graph of the equation?

Critical Thinking Problems _____

47. The perimeter of the larger rectangle in the figure is 58 meters.
  a. Write a linear equation in two variables that reflects this condition. Then write the equation in the form $Ax + By = C$.
  b. Graph the equation from part (a). Then use the graph to find y if $x = 4.5$ meters. What are the dimensions of the larger rectangle if $x = 4.5$ meters?

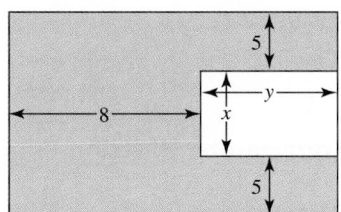

48. The figure represents a trapezoid drawn inside a square. The trapezoid shares one side with the square whose length is designated by x.

  a. If the perimeter of the trapezoid is 84 feet, write a linear equation in two variables that reflects this condition. Then write the equation in the form $Ax + By = C$.
  b. Graph the equation from part (a). Use the graph to find x if $y = 7$ feet. What are the measures of the trapezoid's parallel sides when $y = 7$ feet?

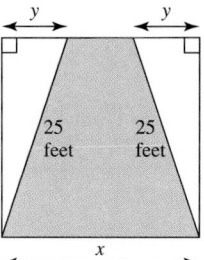

Review Problems _____

49. Solve for y: $3(y - 2) + y = y - 7$.
50. Find the measure of each angle in the triangle shown in the figure.

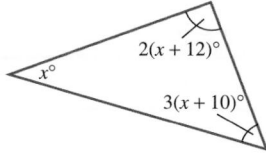

51. A house and a lot are appraised at $112,200. If the house is worth five times the value of the lot, how much is the lot worth?

S E C T I O N 4 . 3	**Graphing Other Types of Equations and Functions**

Solutions Manual   **Tutorial**   **Video 4**

Objectives

1 Graph equations that are not linear.
2 Use function notation to evaluate functions.
3 Graph functions.
4 Interpret information given by a function's graph.

In this section we study equations and functions whose graphs are not straight lines.

1 Graph equations that are not linear.

Equations Whose Graphs Are Not Lines

We have seen that the graph of an equation involving two variables (usually x and y) is the set of all points whose coordinates are solutions of the equation. Up to this point we have concentrated on graphing linear equations in two variables. The resulting graphs are lines. The graph of every equation is not a straight line. However, equations can still be graphed by plotting a number of points whose coordinates satisfy the equation.

The point-plotting method of sketching a graph

1. If possible, rewrite the equation by expressing y in terms of x.
2. Make a table of values showing several ordered pairs.
3. Plot these ordered pairs on a rectangular coordinate system.
4. If the points do not lie along a line, connect them with a smooth curve.

EXAMPLE 1   Graphing an Equation by Plotting Points

Graph the equation: $y = x^2 + 2$

Solution

Since y is expressed in terms of x, we make a table of values showing several ordered pairs.

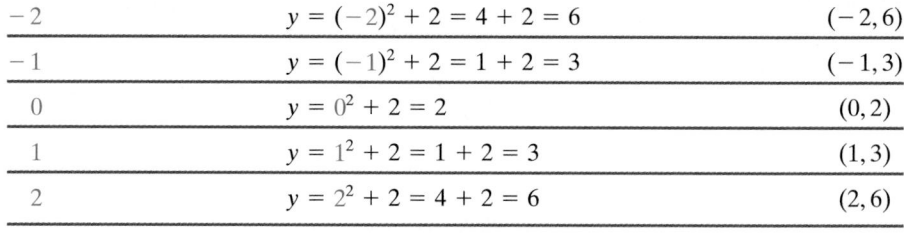

x	$y = x^2 + 2$	(x, y)
-2	$y = (-2)^2 + 2 = 4 + 2 = 6$	$(-2, 6)$
-1	$y = (-1)^2 + 2 = 1 + 2 = 3$	$(-1, 3)$
0	$y = 0^2 + 2 = 2$	$(0, 2)$
1	$y = 1^2 + 2 = 1 + 2 = 3$	$(1, 3)$
2	$y = 2^2 + 2 = 4 + 2 = 6$	$(2, 6)$

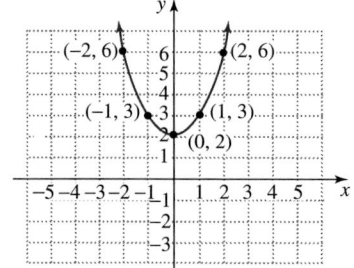

Figure 4.13

The graph of $y = x^2 + 2$

Now we plot these five ordered pairs on a rectangular coordinate system. Since they do not lie along a line, we connect them with a smooth curve. The graph is shown in Figure 4.13. In later courses, you will learn about a graph's shape by applying techniques other than connecting points.   ∎

2 Use function notation to evaluate functions.

Using Function Notation

In Section 4.1, we introduced function notation, replacing y with $f(x)$. We can use this notation on the equation of Example 1. Replacing y in $y = x^2 + 2$ by $f(x)$, we obtain

$$f(x) = x^2 + 2.$$

We read this formula as "f of x equals x squared plus 2." Table 4.4 compares the two notations.

TABLE 4.4 A Comparison Between Notations

"y Equals" Notation	"f(x) Equals" Notation
$y = x^2 + 2$	$f(x) = x^2 + 2$
$(-1, 3)$ is a solution.	$f(-1) = 3$ f of -1 equals 3.
$(2, 6)$ satisfies the equation.	$f(2) = 6$ f of 2 equals 6.
If $x = 2$, then $y = 6$.	$f(2) = 6$ f of 2 equals 6.

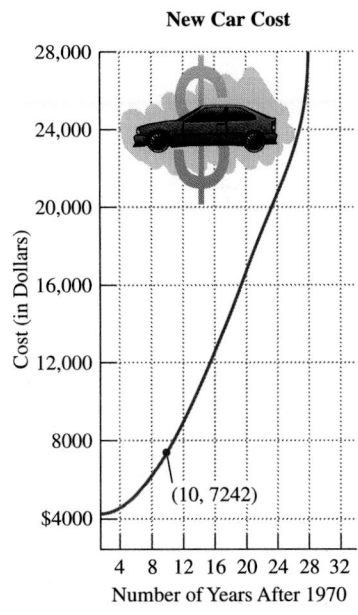

New Car Cost

(10, 7242)

Cost (in Dollars)

Number of Years After 1970

Figure 4.14

The graph of $f(x) = 30.5x^2 + 4192$

Source: Commerce Department

3 Graph functions.

Evaluating Functions

In Chapter 1, we evaluated mathematical models by substituting a numerical value for a variable in the model's formula. We do the same thing with functions. To find $f(x)$ for a particular value of x, we need only replace x by that value. This forms the basis of our next example.

EXAMPLE 2 **Evaluating a Function**

The average cost of a new car is a function of time, approximated by the model

$$f(x) = 30.5x^2 + 4192.$$

The function measures the car's cost in dollars and x represents the number of years after 1970. Find and interpret $f(10)$.

Solution

$$f(x) = 30.5x^2 + 4192 \qquad \text{This is the given function.}$$
$$f(10) = 30.5(10)^2 + 4192 \qquad \text{To find } f \text{ of } 10, \text{ replace } x \text{ with } 10.$$
$$= 30.5(100) + 4192$$
$$= 3050 + 4192$$
$$f(10) = 7242 \qquad \text{We have evaluated the function for } x = 10. f \text{ of } 10 \text{ is } 7242.$$

Since $f(10) = 7242$, this means that 10 years after 1970 (that is, in 1980), the average cost of a new car was approximately $7242. The ordered pair (10, 7242) is a point on the graph of the function, shown in Figure 4.14. ∎

Modeling with Functions

Many functions describe real world phenomenon.

Gerard Fritz/Tony Stone
Images

EXAMPLE 3 **Summer's Air Pollution as a Function of the Time of Day**

Although the level of air pollution varies from day to day and from hour to hour, during the summer the level of air pollution is a function of the time of the day. The function

$$f(x) = 0.1x^2 - 0.4x + 0.6$$

describes the level of air pollution (in parts per million [ppm]) where x corresponds to the number of hours after 9 A.M.

a. Construct a table of values using integers from 0 to 5 for x, and graph the function from 0 to 5.
b. Researchers have determined that a level of 0.3 ppm of pollutants in the air can be hazardous to your health. Based on the graph, at what time of day should runners exercise to avoid unsafe air?

Solution

a. Begin by constructing a table of values.

Since $f(0) = 0.6$, zero hours after 9 A.M., or at 9 A.M. itself, air pollution is 0.6 ppm.

Since $f(3) = 0.3$, three hours after 9 A.M., or at noon, air pollution is 0.3 ppm.

x	$f(x) = 0.1x^2 - 0.4x + 0.6$	(x, y)
0	$f(0) = 0.1(0)^2 - 0.4(0) + 0.6$ $= 0.6$	$(0, 0.6)$
1	$f(1) = 0.1(1)^2 - 0.4(1) + 0.6$ $= 0.3$	$(1, 0.3)$
2	$f(2) = 0.1(2)^2 - 0.4(2) + 0.6$ $= 0.2$	$(2, 0.2)$
3	$f(3) = 0.1(3)^2 - 0.4(3) + 0.6$ $= 0.3$	$(3, 0.3)$
4	$f(4) = 0.1(4)^2 - 0.4(4) + 0.6$ $= 0.6$	$(4, 0.6)$
5	$f(5) = 0.1(5)^2 - 0.4(5) + 0.6$ $= 1.1$	$(5, 1.1)$

We plot the points representing the six ordered pairs in our table of values and connect them with a smooth curve. The graph is shown in Figure 4.15.

tudy tip

Letters other than f can be used to name functions. For example, the function in Example 3 could be named g, so that

$$g(x) = 0.1x^2 - 0.4x + 0.6.$$

Commonly used letters are $f, g,$ and h.

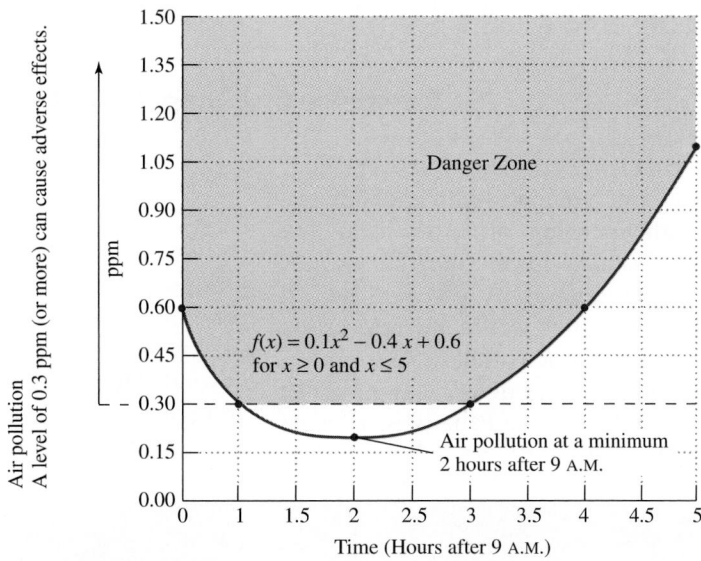

Figure 4.15

Air pollution as a function of time

b. The graph in Figure 4.15 indicates that the level of air pollution decreases to a minimum 2 hours after 9 A.M. (at 11 A.M.) and then increases above safe levels. Thus a runner should exercise sometime between 1 and 3 hours after 9 A.M. (between 10 A.M. and noon), with 11 A.M. being the ideal time of day to run. ■

4 Interpret information given by a function's graph.

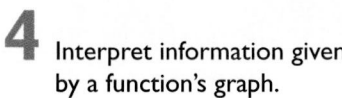

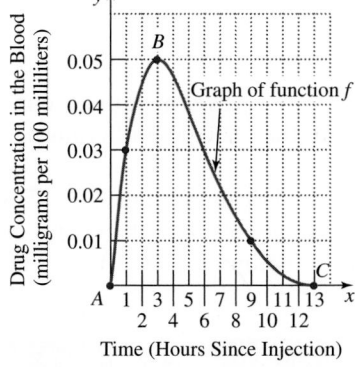

Figure 4.16

Concentration of a drug as a function of time

EXAMPLE 4 **Modeling Drug Concentration as a Function of Time**

When a person receives a drug injected into a muscle, the concentration of the drug in the blood (measured in milligrams per 100 milliliters) is a function of the time elapsed since the injection (measured in hours). Let

$$x = \text{hours since the injection}$$
$$f(x) = \text{drug concentration at time } x$$

Although we are not given an equation for this function, its graph is shown in Figure 4.16. Use the graph, referring to points A, B, and C, to find and interpret:

a. $f(0)$ **b.** $f(3)$ **c.** $f(13)$

Solution

The problem is solved by determining the coordinates for points A, B, and C.

a. To find $f(0)$, we must find the value of y when $x = 0$. Refer to point A in Figure 4.18. The coordinates of A are $(0, 0)$. Thus, $f(0) = 0$. This means that at the beginning ($x = 0$), no drug was in the blood ($y = 0$).

b. To find $f(3)$, refer to point B. The coordinates of B are $(3, 0.05)$. Thus, $f(3) = 0.05$. Now let's see what this means. Once the drug is injected into

ENRICHMENT ESSAY

Descartes: One Step Beyond

Descartes' rectangular coordinate system connected every algebraic equation with a geometric figure. Some mathematicians are now using the computer to carry his idea one step further. A new challenge is to use computers to represent logical ideas as visual images that would be interesting and informative to nonmathematicians.

Math Design (Figure 4.17) by nuclear physicist and computer artist Melvin L. Prueitt is a visual representation of the equation

$$z = \frac{xy^2}{x^2 + y^2}.$$

In Figure 4.18, Dr. Prueitt took the equation that produced *Math Design* but used the computer to generate a different viewpoint, enhancing the visual representation with color. Moving one step beyond Descartes, the union of mathematician and computer has produced an art medium of exciting promise.

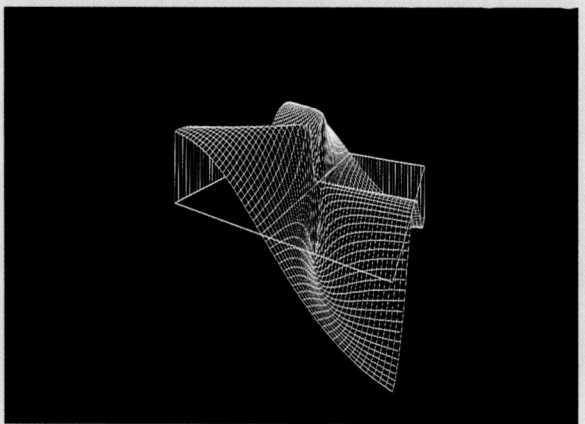

Figure 4.17

Melvin L. Prueitt, Los Alamos National Laboratory

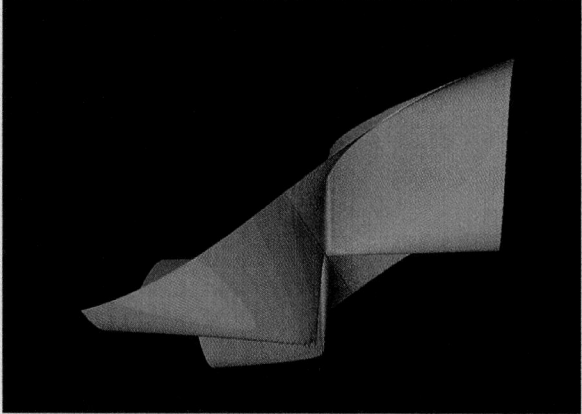

Figure 4.18

Melvin L. Prueitt, Los Alamos National Laboratory

the muscle, the drug spreads into the blood and reaches a maximum concentration at 3 hours ($x = 3$). The concentration then is 0.05 milligram per 100 milliliters.

   c. To find $f(13)$, refer to point C in Figure 4.16 at the bottom of page 303. The coordinates of C are $(13, 0)$. Thus, $f(13) = 0$. This means that at the end of 13 hours ($x = 13$), there is no longer any drug in the blood ($y = 0$). ∎

PROBLEM SET 4.3

Practice Problems _____

In Problems 1–14, fill in the table of values and then sketch the graph of the function.

1. $y = x^2$

x	$y = x^2$	(x, y)
-3		
-2		
-1		
0		
1		
2		
3		

2. $y = x^2 - 1$

x	$y = x^2 - 1$	(x, y)
-3		
-2		
-1		
0		
1		
2		
3		

3. $f(x) = x^2 - 5$

x	$f(x) = x^2 - 5$	(x, y)
-3		
-2		
-1		
0		
1		
2		
3		

4. $f(x) = x^2 + 3$

x	$f(x) = x^2 + 3$	(x, y)
-3		
-2		
-1		
0		
1		
2		
3		

5. $y = -x^2$

x	$y = -x^2$	(x, y)
-3		
-2		
-1		
0		
1		
2		
3		

6. $y = -x^2 + 2$

x	$y = -x^2 + 2$	(x, y)
-3		
-2		
-1		
0		
1		
2		
3		

7. $f(x) = x^2 + x - 6$

x	$f(x) = x^2 + x - 6$	(x, y)
-2		
-1		
0		
1		
2		
3		

8. $f(x) = x^2 + 2x + 1$

x	$f(x) = x^2 + 2x + 1$	(x, y)
-3		
-2		
-1		
0		
1		
2		

9. $y = x^2 - x - 2$

x	$y = x^2 - x - 2$	(x, y)
-2		
-1		
0		
1		
2		
3		

10. $y = x^2 - 2x$

x	$y = x^2 - 2x$	(x, y)
-1		
0		
1		
2		
3		

11. $f(x) = x^3$

x	$f(x) = x^3$	(x, y)
-2		
-1		
0		
1		
2		

12. $f(x) = x^3 - 4$

x	$f(x) = x^3 - 4$	(x, y)
-2	-12	
-1	-5	
0	-4	
1	-3	
2	4	

13. $f(x) = \sqrt{x}$

x	$f(x) = \sqrt{x}$	(x, y)
0		
1		
4		
9		
16		

14. $f(x) = |x|$

x	$f(x) = |x|$	(x, y)
-4		
-3		
-2		
-1		
0		
1		
2		
3		
4		

Application Problems

15. According to the Recording Industry Association of America, the number of CDs sold in the United States is a function of time, approximated by the model

$$f(x) = \frac{11}{3}x^2 + \frac{94}{3}x + 23.$$

The number of CDs sold is expressed in millions and x represents the number of years after 1985. Find and interpret $f(10)$. Then use the circle graph to estimate the number of jazz CDs sold in 1995.

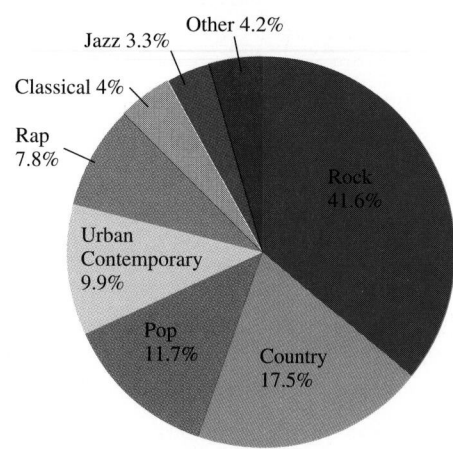

Recording Sales

Source: 1995 figures, RIAA

16. According to the U.S. Bureau of Justice, the number of inmates in federal and state prisons in the United States is a function of time, approximated by the model $f(x) = 2x^2 + 22x + 320$. In this function, the number of inmates is measured in thousands and x represents years after 1980. Find and interpret $f(0)$, $f(10)$, and $f(15)$. Use the function to predict the number of inmates in the year 2000.

17. A baseball is tossed straight up into the air. Let

$x = $ the number of seconds that have passed since the ball was thrown

$f(x) = $ the ball's height above the ground (in feet) after x seconds

The figure at the top of the next column shows the graph of this function: Use the graph to find and interpret:

a. $f(0)$ **b.** $f(1)$ **c.** $f(2)$ **d.** $f(3)$ **e.** $f(4)$

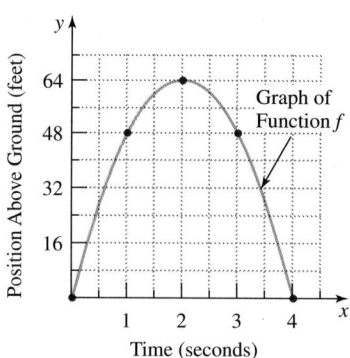

18. The figure shows the average age of an American woman at the time of her first marriage as a function of time. Let

$x = $ the number of years after 1970

$f(x) = $ the average age of an American woman at the time of her first marriage in year x

Use the graph to estimate and interpret:
a. $f(10)$ **b.** $f(15)$ **c.** $f(20)$
d. Describe the trend shown by the function's graph.

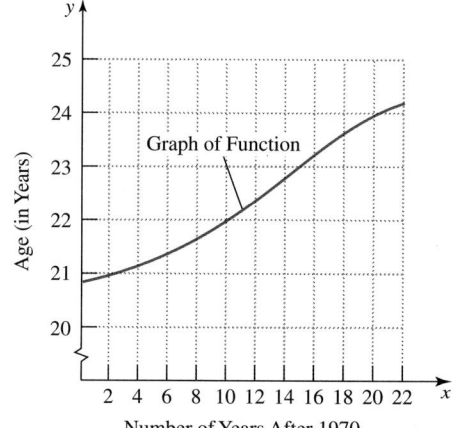

Source: U.S. Bureau of the Census

19. *Birds in Flight.* Based on a study by Vance Tucker (*Scientific American,* May, 1969), the power expenditure of parakeets in flight is a function of their flying speed, approximated by

$$f(x) = 0.67x^2 - 27.74x + 387.$$

Find $f(12)$, $f(20)$, and $f(30)$, filling in the missing y-coordinates in the graph. (A calculator would be helpful, although you should be able to perform the computations by hand.) Describe what each of these ordered pairs means. According to the graph, approximately what flying speed results in the least amount of power expenditure for parakeets? Verify this estimate by evaluating the function at values slightly less than and slightly more than this flying speed.

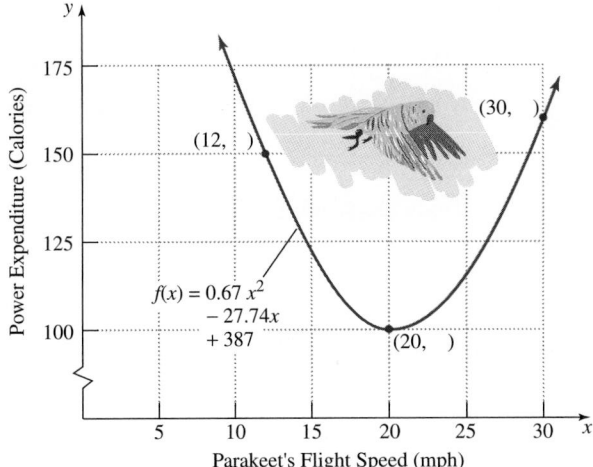

Parakeet's Flight Speed (mph)

20. The opposition to an electric current offered by some components is called resistance, measured in units called ohms. Resistors are specifically placed in a circuit to add resistance. As shown in the figure, a fixed 8-ohm resistor is connected in parallel with a variable resistor whose resistance is x ohms. The total or combined resistance in the circuit is given by the function

$$f(x) = \frac{8x}{x + 8}.$$

True–False Critical Thinking Problem _____

21. As a manufacturer raises prices, the number of units of a product that customers are willing to purchase decreases, so if prices are too high there will be a decline in income for the manufacturer. The graph shows the weekly income of a roller skate manufacturer as a function of the skate's price. The graph is based on the equation $f(x) = 360x - 2x^2$, where x is the price and $f(x)$ is the weekly income in thousands of dollars. Which one of the following is true?
  a. Regardless of the price of the skates, the manufacturer will always generate some weekly income.
  b. If the skates are priced at $90 per pair, the manufacturer will receive the maximum weekly income $16,500.
  c. Two different prices for the skates will result in a weekly income of $10,000.

A graph of this function, obtained with a graphing utility, is shown below the circuit.

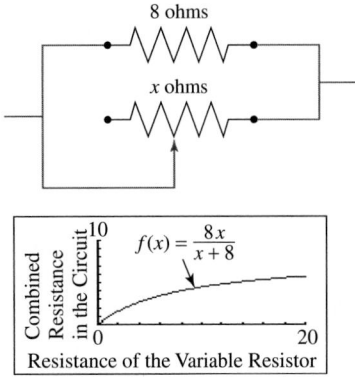

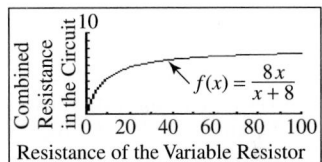

Resistance of the Variable Resistor

  a. Find and interpret $f(2)$, $f(4)$, and $f(16)$. Locate the three points along the function's graph corresponding to these values.
  b. Find $f(100)$ and $f(1000)$. If you have a calculator, find $f(1,000,000)$. Use these results to complete this sentence: No matter how large the variable resistance x, the combined resistance in the circuit is never greater than _____ ohms.
  c. Explain how the sentence that you completed in part (b) is illustrated by the following graph.

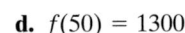

Resistance of the Variable Resistor

  d. $f(50) = 1300$

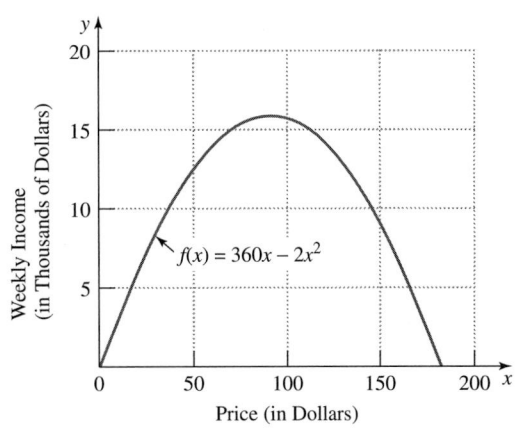

Price (in Dollars)

Technology Problems

22. According to the Department of Health and Human Services, the life expectancy of a child in the United States as a function of time is approximated by the model

$$f(x) = \frac{x + 66.94}{0.01x + 1}.$$

In this function, x represents the number of years after 1950. Use a calculator to find $f(0)$, $f(10)$, $f(20)$, $f(30)$, and $f(40)$, rounding each result to the nearest whole number. Describe what each computation represents in practical terms. Then present the information described by the five ordered pairs in a bar graph.

23. *Automobile Efficiency as a Function of Time.* The function $f(x) = 0.0075x^2 - 0.2676x + 14.8$ models automobile fuel efficiency as a function of time with

$$x = \text{years after 1940}$$

$$f(x) = \text{average number of miles per gallon}$$

Use a graphing utility to graph the function, entering the function as

$$Y_1 \boxed{=} .0075 \boxed{\times} \boxed{\wedge} 2 \boxed{-} .2676 \boxed{\times} \boxed{+} 14.8.$$

Use the following range settings:

$$\text{Xmin} = 0, \quad \text{Xmax} = 40, \text{Xscl} = 1,$$

$$\text{Ymin} = 10, \text{Ymax} = 20, \text{Yscl} = 1$$

Describe what the resulting graph shows about fuel efficiency and time. Use the utility's $\boxed{\text{TRACE}}$ feature to trace along the curve and estimate when fuel efficiency for automobiles was at its worst. What was the average number of miles per gallon in that year?

Dennis Kitchen/Tony Stone Images

24. Use a graphing utility to reproduce the graphs shown in Figures 4.14 and 4.15 on pages 301 and 303. Use the $\boxed{\text{TRACE}}$ feature to trace along each curve and verify the coordinates given in the respective figures.

25. Use a graphing utility to verify the graphs in Problems 1 through 14 that you drew by hand. Use the $\boxed{\text{TRACE}}$ feature to trace along each curve and verify the values you generated in the table of coordinates.

Writing in Mathematics

26. Researchers at Yale University have suggested that levels of passion and commitment are functions of time. Based on the shapes of the following graphs, which do you think depicts passion and which represents commitment? Explain how you arrived at your answer.

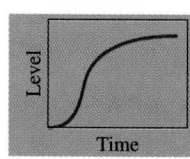 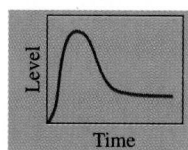

27. *Population Growth.* In a report entitled *Resources and Man,* the U.S. National Academy of Sciences con-

Paul Chesley/Tony Stone Images

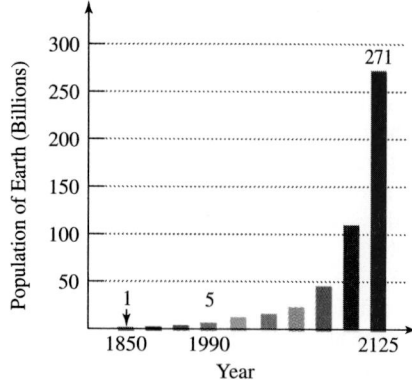

cluded that a world population of 10 billion "is close to (if not above) the maximum that an intensely managed world might hope to support with some degree of comfort and individual choice." The graph on the right represents world population as a function of time. Write a paragraph describing population growth based on the graph, including an estimate of when a population of 10 billion will be reached.

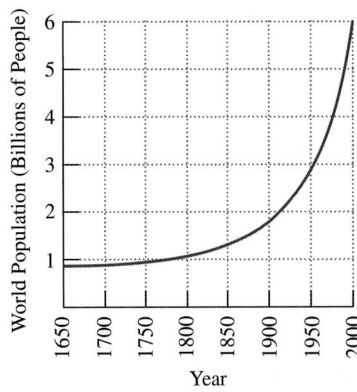

Critical Thinking Problem

28. A photographic light meter is used to measure the brightness of a shining flashlight on a wall. The intensity of brightness measured by the light meter is a function of the flashlight's distance from the wall, shown by the graph. As the distance from the light to the wall doubles, by what fraction does the light intensity decrease?

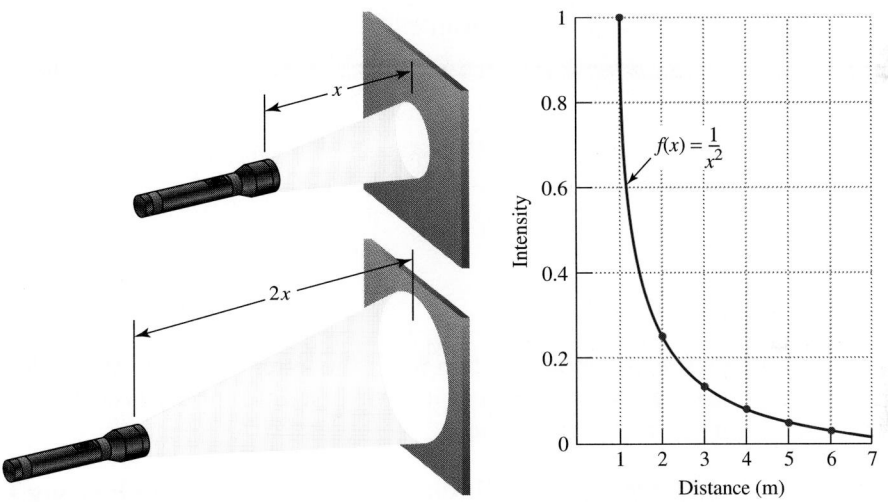

Review Problems

29. A student has grades of 96, 82, and 91 on three tests. Describe the scores that can be obtained on the fourth test so that the student's average on the four tests will be an A (at least 90).

30. A 36-inch board is cut into two pieces. One piece is twice as long as the other. How long are the pieces?

31. Two small planes leave an airport at the same time and fly in opposite directions. If one plane's speed is 150 miles per hour and the other plane's speed is 250 miles per hour, in how many hours will they be 800 miles apart?

S E C T I O N   4 . 4

Solutions Manual   Tutorial   Video 4

Slope

Objectives

1 Calculate a line's slope.
2 Calculate rate of change over time.
3 Graph a line given its slope and a point on the line.
4 Use slope to show that lines are parallel.

Figure 4.19 shows a traffic sign that indicates a slope, warning the driver that a steep downgrade lies ahead. *Slope* refers to the steepness of a line, and in this section we study the idea of steepness from a mathematical perspective.

Calculate a line's slope.

Slope and the Steepness of a Line

Mathematicians have developed a useful measure of the steepness of a line, called the *slope* of the line. Slope compares the vertical change (the *rise*) to the horizontal change (the *run*) encountered when moving from one fixed point to another along the line. To calculate the slope of a line, mathematicians use a ratio comparing the change in y (the rise) to the change in x (the run).

Figure 4.19

Definition of slope

The *slope* of the line through the distinct points (x_1, y_1) and (x_2, y_2) is

$$\frac{\text{Change in } y}{\text{Change in } x} = \frac{\text{Rise}}{\text{Run}} = \frac{y_2 - y_1}{x_2 - x_1}$$

where $x_2 - x_1 \neq 0$.

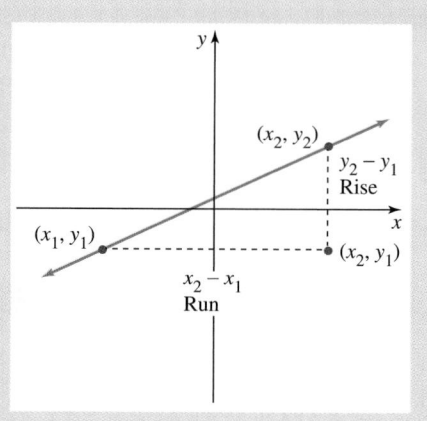

It is common notation to let the letter m represent the slope of a line. The letter m is used because it is the first letter of the French verb *monter*, meaning to rise or to ascend.

EXAMPLE 1   Finding the Slope of a Line Passing Through Two Points

Find the slope of the line connecting the points whose coordinates are $(1, 2)$ and $(4, 6)$.

Solution

See Figure 4.20. We can let $(x_1, y_1) = (1, 2)$ and $(x_2, y_2) = (4, 6)$. Then

$$m = \frac{y_2 - y_1}{x_2 - x_1} = \frac{6 - 2}{4 - 1} = \frac{4}{3} \qquad \text{Slope is the ratio of vertical change to horizontal change.}$$

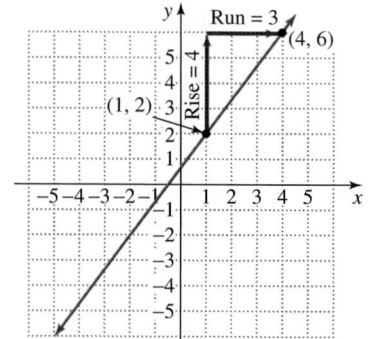

Figure 4.20

A line with slope $\frac{4}{3}$

The slope is $\frac{4}{3}$. For every vertical change (rise) of 4 units, there is a corresponding horizontal change (run) of 3 units. For any two points on the same line, the ratio of the change in y to the corresponding change in x is always $\frac{4}{3}$. A line that slants upward to the right has a positive slope.

If we let $(x_1, y_1) = (4, 6)$ and $(x_2, y_2) = (1, 2)$, we obtain

$$m = \frac{y_2 - y_1}{x_2 - x_1} = \frac{2 - 6}{1 - 4} = \frac{-4}{-3} = \frac{4}{3} \qquad \text{It makes no difference which of the points is considered } (x_1, y_1).$$

E

ENRICHMENT ESSAY

Slope as Pitch

Rather than slope, roofers and builders refer to the *pitch* of a roof as a measure of steepness.

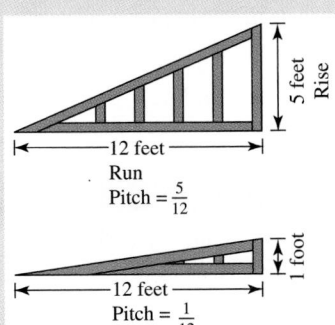

Cross sections of roof gables: pitch (or slope) is rise/run.

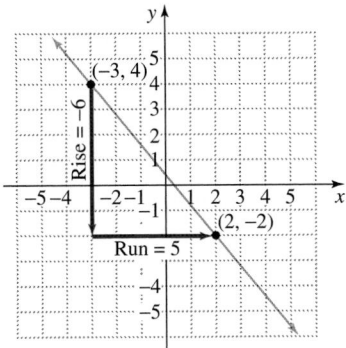

Figure 4.21

A line with slope $-\frac{6}{5}$

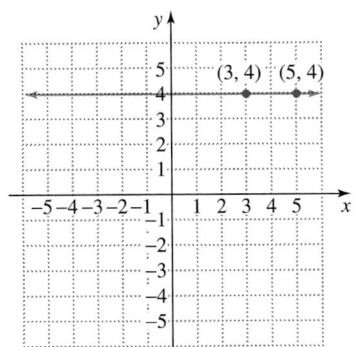

Figure 4.22

which is still the same as our previous result. However, we cannot subtract in one order $(y_1 - y_2)$ in the numerator and then in another $(x_2 - x_1)$ in the denominator. The slope is *not* equal to $\dfrac{6 - 2}{1 - 4}$.

Study tip

When computing slope, subtract y- and x-coordinates in the same order.

Discover for yourself

Two other points along the line in Figure 4.20 are $(-2, -2)$ and $(-5, -6)$. Use these points to compute the slope of the line. Is your answer the same as the value computed in Example 1? What can you conclude?

Based on your work in the Discover for Yourself box, were you able to make the important observation in the Study Tip box?

Study tip

The slope of a line does not depend on which two particular points on the line are used in the calculation.

EXAMPLE 2 Finding the Slope of a Line Passing Through Two Points

Find the slope of the line connecting the points whose coordinates are $(-3, 4)$ and $(2, -2)$.

Solution

See Figure 4.21. We can let $(x_1, y_1) = (-3, 4)$ and $(x_2, y_2) = (2, -2)$. Then

$$m = \frac{y_2 - y_1}{x_2 - x_1} = \frac{-2 - 4}{2 - (-3)} = \frac{-6}{5} = -\frac{6}{5}$$ Slope is the ratio of vertical change to horizontal change.

The slope is $-\frac{6}{5}$. For every vertical change of -6 units (6 units down), there is a corresponding horizontal change of 5 units. The slope is a negative number, indicating that the line slants downward (falls) from left to right.

EXAMPLE 3 Slope and Horizontal Lines

Find the slope of the horizontal line connecting the points $(5, 4)$ and $(3, 4)$.

Solution

By letting $(x_1, y_1) = (5, 4)$ and $(x_2, y_2) = (3, 4)$, we obtain

$$m = \frac{y_2 - y_1}{x_2 - x_1} = \frac{4 - 4}{3 - 5} = \frac{0}{-2} = 0$$ Slope is the ratio of the change in y to the corresponding change in x.

See Figure 4.22. All horizontal lines neither increase nor decrease from left to right. Thus, *the slope of any horizontal line is 0.*

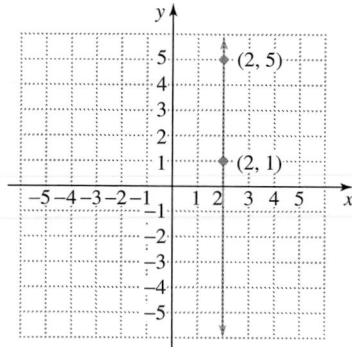

Figure 4.23

| EXAMPLE 4 | **Slope and Vertical Lines** |

Find the slope of the vertical line connecting the points (2, 5) and (2, 1).

Solution

By letting $(x_1, y_1) = (2, 5)$ and $(x_2, y_2) = (2, 1)$, we obtain

$$m = \frac{y_2 - y_1}{x_2 - x_1} = \frac{1 - 5}{2 - 2} = \frac{-4}{0} \text{ (undefined)}.$$

Since division by 0 is not defined, the slope of this line is not defined. Figure 4.23 shows that the line is a vertical line. In general, *the slope of any vertical line is undefined.* ∎

Table 4.5 summarizes the four possibilities for the slope of a line.

TABLE 4.5 Possibilities for a Line's Slope

Positive Slope	Negative Slope	Zero Slope	Undefined Slope
$m > 0$	$m < 0$	$m = 0$	m is undefined.
Line rises from left to right.	Line falls from left to right.	Line is horizontal.	Line is vertical.

2 Calculate rate of change over time.

Slope as the Average Rate of Change

Slope is defined as the ratio of a change in y to a corresponding change in x. In applied situations, slope can be thought of as the average rate of change in y per unit of change in x, where the value of y depends on the value of x. Example 5 illustrates this idea.

| EXAMPLE 5 | **Slope as the Average Rate of Change** |

Figure 4.24 on page 313 shows the graph of the population of Los Angeles from 1930 through 1990. The graph is based on the table beside it. The line that is shown is the line that best models (or fits) the data, called the *regression line*. Find the slope of the regression line passing through the points for the years 1930 and 1990. Describe what the slope represents.

Solution

Using the coordinates in Figure 4.24, we obtain

$$m = \frac{3,485,398 - 1,238,048}{1990 - 1930}$$ In this situation, slope is the change in population divided by the change in time.

$$= \frac{2,247,350}{60}$$ These numbers are shown by the vertical rise line and the horizontal run line in Figure 4.24.

$$\approx 37,456$$ This is the average change in y per unit change in x.

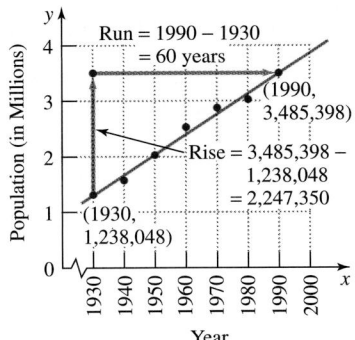

Year	Population of Los Angeles
1930	1,238,048
1940	1,504,277
1950	1,970,358
1960	2,479,015
1970	2,816,061
1980	2,966,850
1990	3,485,398

Figure 4.24

The slope indicates that between 1930 and 1990, the population of Los Angeles was increasing by approximately 37,456 people each year. The rate of change of population is about 37,456 people per year. ■

The concept of slope as average rate of change can be applied to data presented in line and bar graphs.

ENRICHMENT ESSAY

Slope and Acoustic Loudspeakers

The figure below shows the relationship between the volume of a room and the power needed to achieve a peak volume level of 106 decibels for a pair of acoustic loudspeakers. Three different kinds of rooms—dead, average, and live—require different power to achieve loud peak volume levels, as shown by the different slopes for the three lines. The graph indicates that the larger the volume of the room, the more power needed, although more power is needed in a dead room than an average room no matter what the volume.

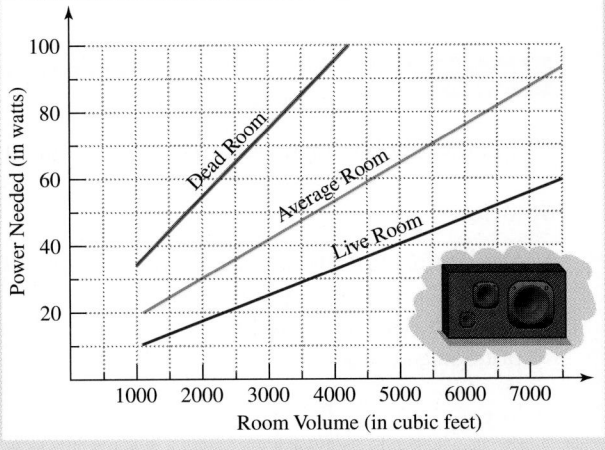

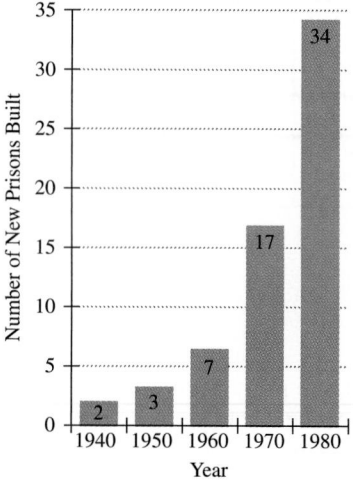

Number of New Women's Prisons in the United States per Decade, 1940–1980

Figure 4.25
Source: Chesney-Lind, Meda (1993), *Sentencing Women to Prison: Equality Without Justice,* paper presented at the Seventh National Roundtable on Women in Prison, American University, Washington, D.C., June 17–20, 1993.

EXAMPLE 6   **Slope as the Average Rate of Change**

The bar graph in Figure 4.25 shows the number of new women's prisons in the United States per decade, from 1940 through 1980. Find:

a. The average rate of change in the number of new women's prisons from 1960 through 1970.

b. The average rate of change in the number of new women's prisons from 1970 through 1980.

Solution

We can represent each bar by an ordered pair, as follows:

bar for 1960:   (1960, 7)
bar for 1970:   (1970, 17)
bar for 1980:   (1980, 34)

a. The average rate of change from 1960 through 1970 is found by using the slope formula.

$$\text{Average rate of change} = \frac{y_2 - y_1}{x_2 - x_1} = \frac{17 - 7}{1970 - 1960} = \frac{10}{10} = 1$$

The result, 1, indicates that on the average the number of new women's prisons increased by 1 each year from 1960 through 1970.

b. The average rate of change from 1970 through 1980 is found by again using the slope formula.

$$\text{Average rate of change} = \frac{y_2 - y_1}{x_2 - x_1} = \frac{34 - 17}{1980 - 1970} = \frac{17}{10} = 1.7$$

The result, 1.7, indicates that on the average the number of new women's prisons increased by 1.7 each year from 1970 through 1980. ■

3 Graph a line given its slope and a point on the line.

Graphing a Line Using Its y-Intercept and Slope

We can use the *y*-intercept of a line and its slope to determine the graph of the line. Let's see how this is done.

EXAMPLE 7   **Using the y-Intercept and Slope to Graph a Line**

Graph the line having a *y*-intercept of − 3 and a slope of 4.

Solution

1. We begin by representing the *y*-intercept of − 3, (see Figure 4.26(a)) the point (0, − 3), on a graph.

2. A second point on the line is determined by the slope, which should be expressed as a fraction.

$$\text{Slope} = \frac{4}{1} = \frac{\text{Rise}}{\text{Run}}$$

Since the slope is positive, we determine the second point by moving up and to the right. Start at $(0, -3)$ and move 4 units up (a rise of 4) and 1 unit to the right (a run of 1). We obtain a second point on the graph, as shown in Figure 4.26(b).

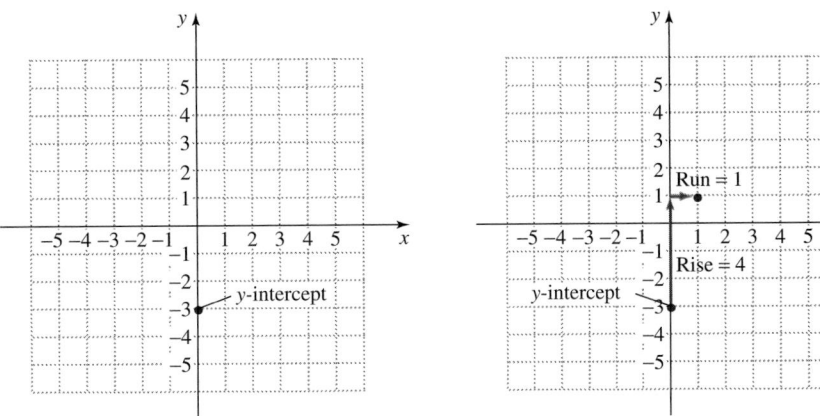

Figure 4.26

a. The y-intercept is -3.

b. The slope is $\frac{4}{1}$.

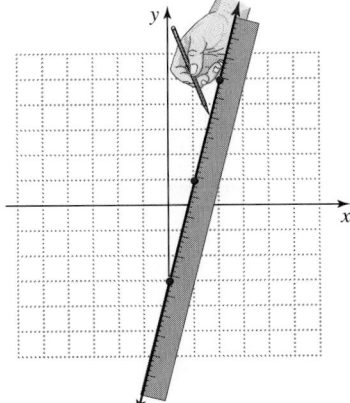

Figure 4.27

Using y-intercept -3 and slope 4 to graph a line

The coordinates of the second point are $(1, 1)$. We can obtain these coordinates by adding numbers to the coordinates of the point $(0, -3)$, representing the y-intercept.

$$\text{Second point} = (0 + 1, -3 + 4) = (1, 1)$$

We add 1 to the x-coordinate because 1 is the change in x. We add 4 to the y-coordinate because 4 is the change in y.

3. Use a straightedge to draw a line through $(0, -3)$ and $(1, 1)$. The graph of the line with a y-intercept of -3 and slope 4 is shown in Figure 4.27. ∎

We follow a similar procedure when a line has a slope that is negative. First we plot the y-intercept on the y-axis. The second point is found by moving down and to the right.

EXAMPLE 8 **Using the y-Intercept and Slope to Graph a Line**

Graph the line having a y-intercept of 2 and a slope of $-\frac{2}{3}$.

Solution

1. We begin by representing the y-intercept of 2 (see Figure 4.28 on page 316). The point $(0, 2)$ is on the graph.
2. A second point on the line is determined by the slope.

$$\text{Slope} = \frac{-2}{3} = \frac{\text{Rise}}{\text{Run}}$$ Notice that when the "rise" is negative, it is actually a "fall."

Since the slope is negative, we find the second point by moving down and to the right. Start at $(0, 2)$ and move 2 units down (a rise of -2) and 3 units to the right (a run of 3). We obtain a second point on the graph, as shown in Figure 4.28.

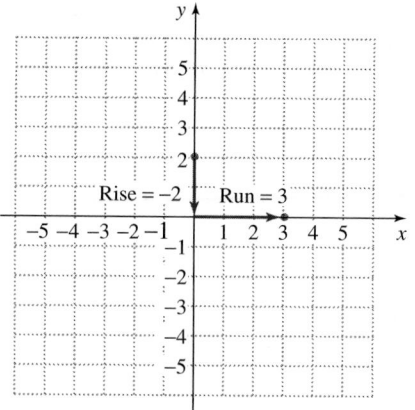

Figure 4.28

The y-intercept is 2 and the slope is $-\frac{2}{3}$.

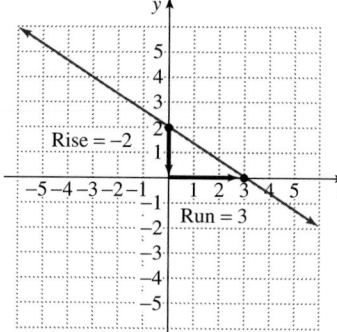

Figure 4.29

Using y-intercept 2 and slope $-\frac{2}{3}$ to graph a line

The coordinates of the second point are (3, 0). We can obtain these coordinates by adding numbers to the coordinates of the point (0, 2), representing the y-intercept.

$$\text{Second point} = (0 + 3, 2 - 2) = (3, 0)$$

We add 3 to the x-coordinate because 3 is the change in x. We add -2 to the y-coordinate because -2 is the change in y.

3. Use a straightedge to draw a line through (0, 2) and (3, 0). The graph of the line with a y-intercept of 2 and slope $-\frac{2}{3}$ is shown in Figure 4.29. ■

iscover for yourself

Obtain a second point in Example 8 by writing the slope as $\frac{2}{-3}$, moving up 2 units and to the left 3 units. What do you observe once you graph the line?

In summary, here's a step-by-step procedure for using a line's y-intercept and slope to obtain its graph.

Graphing a line using slope and y-intercept

1. Plot the y-intercept on the y-axis.
2. Use the slope to find a second point on the graph.
   a. If the slope is positive and in the form $\frac{p}{q}$, find a second point by moving up p units and to the right q units. The rise is p and the run is q.
   b. If the slope is negative and in the form $-\frac{p}{q}$, find a second point by moving down p units and to the right q units. The rise is a fall of p units and the run is q.
3. Use a straightedge to draw a line through the two points. Draw arrowheads at the ends of the line to show that the line continues indefinitely in both directions.

4 Use slope to show that lines are parallel.

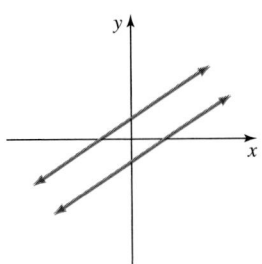

Figure 4.30

Parallel lines have the same slope.

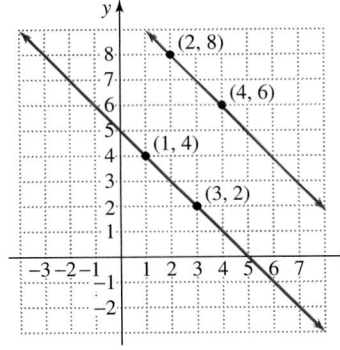

Figure 4.31

Using slope to show that lines are parallel

Slope of Parallel Lines

Lines that do not intersect are called parallel. Figure 4.30 shows that if two lines do not intersect, then the steepness (or slope) of the lines must be the same. Since two parallel lines must have the same steepness, then the following must be true.

1. If two lines are parallel, then they have the same slope.
2. If two distinct lines have the same slope, then they are parallel.

EXAMPLE 9 **Using Slope to Show That Lines are Parallel**

Show that the line passing through (1, 4) and (3, 2) is parallel to the line passing through (2, 8) and (4, 6).

Solution

The situation is illustrated in Figure 4.31. The lines certainly look like they are parallel. Let's use equal slopes to confirm this fact. For each line, we compute the ratio of the difference in y-coordinates to the difference in x-coordinates. (Be sure to subtract the coordinates in the same order.)

Slope of the line through (1, 4) and (3, 2) is

$$\frac{4-2}{1-3} = \frac{2}{-2} = -1.$$

Slope of the line through (2, 8) and (4, 6) is

$$\frac{8-6}{2-4} = \frac{2}{-2} = -1.$$

With equal slopes, the lines are parallel. ∎

PROBLEM SET 4.4

Practice Problems

Find the slope of the line connecting the points with the coordinates in Problems 1–20. Indicate whether the line through the pair of points rises, falls, is horizontal, or is vertical.

1. (2, 6), (3, 5)

2. (4, 2), (3, 4)

3. (4, 7), (8, 10)

4. (2, 1), (3, 4)

5. (−2, 1), (2, 2)

6. (−1, 3), (2, 4)

7. (4, −2), (3, −2)

8. (4, −1), (3, −1)

9. (−2, 4), (−1, −1)

10. (6, −4), (4, −2)

11. (5, 3), (5, −2)

12. (3, −4), (3, 5)

13. (5, −2), (1, 0)

14. (−1, 2), (−3, −7)

15. (2, 0), (0, 8)

16. (3, 0), (0, −9)

17. (5, 1), (−2, 1)

18. (−2, 3), (1, 3)

19. (−1, 2), (−1, 3)

20. (−2, −3), (−2, 1)

Use the coordinates of the indicated points to find the slope of each of the lines in Problems 21–28.

21.

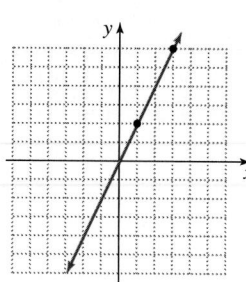

22.

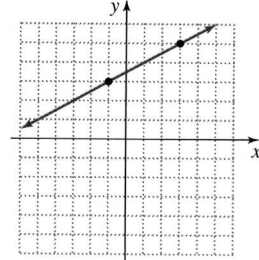

23.

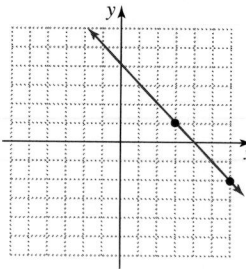

24.

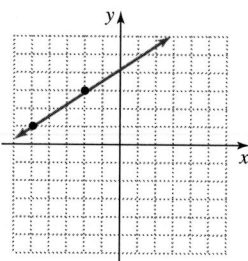

25.

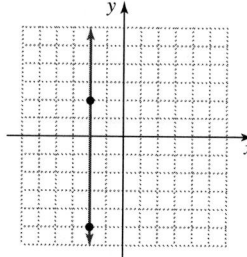

26.

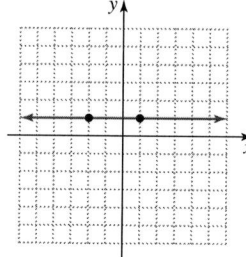

27.

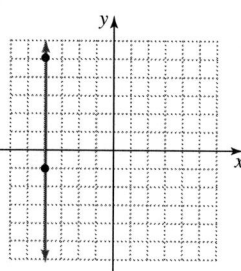

28.

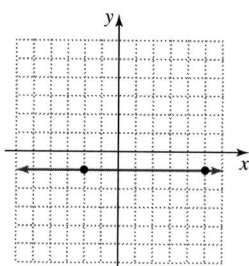

29. Graph the line that has an *x*-intercept of 6 and a *y*-intercept of -2. Determine the slope of this line.

30. Graph the line that has an *x*-intercept of 4 and a *y*-intercept of -1. Determine the slope of this line.

In Problems 31–32, match the lines in the figure with the appropriate slope.

31. **a.** $m = 0$
 b. $m = \frac{1}{3}$
 c. $m = \frac{1}{5}$

32. **a.** $m = -\frac{7}{5}$
 b. m is undefined.
 c. $m = -\frac{2}{5}$

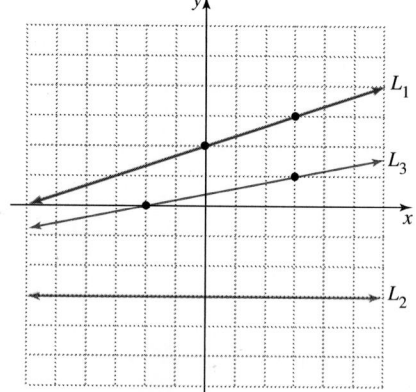

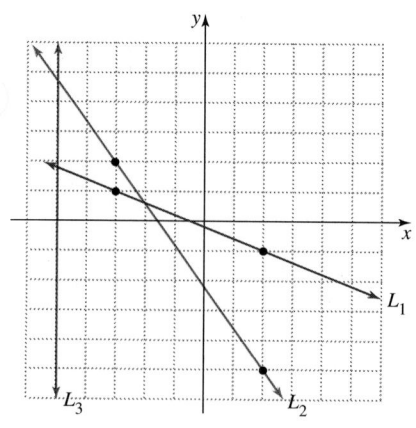

Graph each line in Problems 33–52 using the given conditions.

33. y-intercept $= 4$ and slope $= 3(= \frac{3}{1})$

34. y-intercept $= 2$ and slope $= 3(= \frac{3}{1})$

35. y-intercept $= -1$ and slope $= \frac{1}{2}$

36. y-intercept $= -2$ and slope $= \frac{1}{3}$

37. y-intercept $= 1$ and slope $= -\frac{1}{2}$

38. y-intercept $= 3$ and slope $= -\frac{1}{3}$

39. y-intercept $= -3$ and slope $= -\frac{2}{3}$

40. y-intercept $= -4$ and slope $= -\frac{2}{5}$

41. y-intercept $= 0$ and slope $= \frac{5}{3}$

42. y-intercept $= 0$ and slope $= \frac{5}{4}$

43. y-intercept $= 0$ and slope $= -4$

44. y-intercept $= 0$ and slope $= -3$

45. x-intercept $= 2$ and slope $= \frac{2}{3}$

46. x-intercept $= 1$ and slope $= \frac{3}{4}$

47. x-intercept $= 1$ and slope $= -\frac{3}{4}$

48. x-intercept $= 3$ and slope $= -\frac{2}{3}$

49. y-intercept $= -3$ and slope $= 0$

50. y-intercept $= -5$ and slope $= 0$

51. x-intercept $= 3$ and slope is undefined

52. x-intercept $= 2$ and slope is undefined

53. Show that the line passing through $(0, -3)$ and $(-1, -5)$ is parallel to the line passing through $(1, 3)$ and $(-2, -3)$.

54. Show that the line passing through $(-2, 3)$ and $(6, -5)$ is parallel to the line passing through $(0, 10)$ and $(10, 0)$.

55. Show that the points whose coordinates are $(-3, -3)$, $(2, -5)$, $(5, -1)$, and $(0, 1)$ are the vertices of a four-sided figure whose opposite sides are parallel. (Such a figure is called a *parallelogram*.)

56. Show that the points whose coordinates are $(-3, 6)$, $(2, -3)$, $(11, 2)$, and $(6, 11)$ are the vertices of a four-sided figure whose opposite sides are parallel.

Application Problems

57. The pitch of a roof refers to its slope. What is the pitch of the roof shown in the figure?

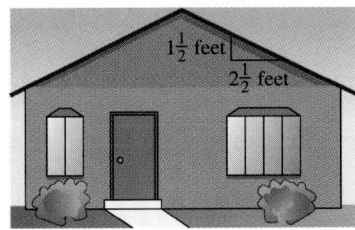

58. The pitch (slope) of the roof shown in the figure is $\frac{1}{5}$. What is the measurement indicated by x?

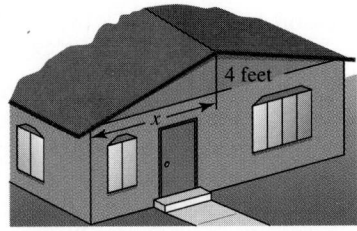

59. The term *grade* is used to describe the inclination of a road. A 7% grade means that for every horizontal distance of 100 feet, the road rises or drops 7 feet. A road rises 50 feet vertically over a horizontal distance of 625 feet. Find the grade of the road.

60. A highway that is descending has a 6% grade, which means that its slope is $-\frac{6}{100}$. If a car has descended a distance of 800 feet, what is its change in horizontal distance?

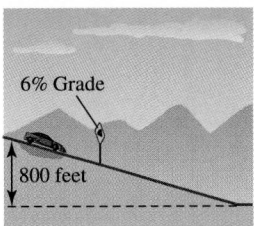

61. The graph on page 320 shows the life expectancy in years for U.S. women whose year of birth is indicated on the x-axis. Find the slope of the line passing through the points whose coordinates are shown on the graph. Describe what the slope represents.

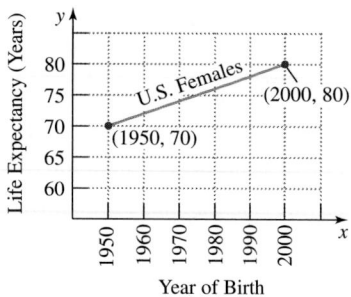

Year of Birth

Find the slope of the line, using the points for the years 1987 and 1991. Describe what the slope represents.

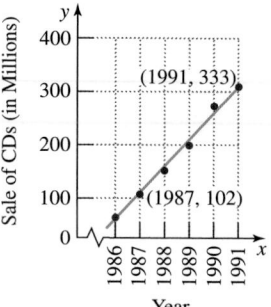

Year

62. The graph on the right shows the sales of CDs in millions in the United States from 1986 through 1991. The line that is shown is the line that best models the data.

The graph shown below indicates the percentage of U.S. teenagers who smoked cigarettes daily for the four indicated years. Use the information provided by the graph to answer Problems 63–64.

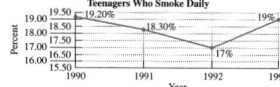

through points *A* and *B*, through points *B* and *C*, and through points *C* and *D*. In each case, describe what the slope represents.

63. Find the average rate of change in the percentage of teenagers who smoked daily from 1990 through 1992. Why is the slope negative? What does this mean in practical terms.

64. Find the average rate of change in the percentage of teenagers who smoked daily from 1991 through 1993. Why is the slope positive? What does this mean in practical terms?

65. The graph on the right shows annual Social Security benefits for persons retiring at ages 62 through 70 in the year 2005 or later. Compute the slope of the line

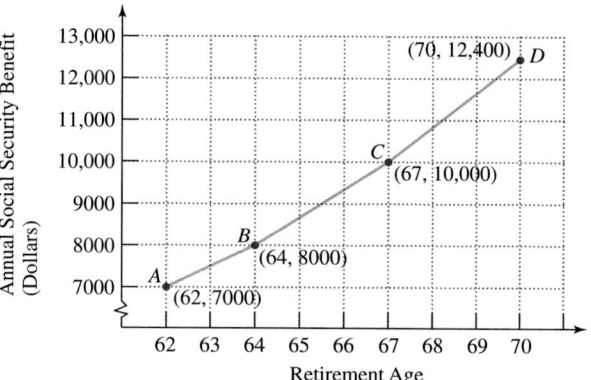

Retirement Age

The graph shown below indicates the average salary of major league baseball players for six years since 1967. Use the information provided in the graph to answer Problems 66–67.

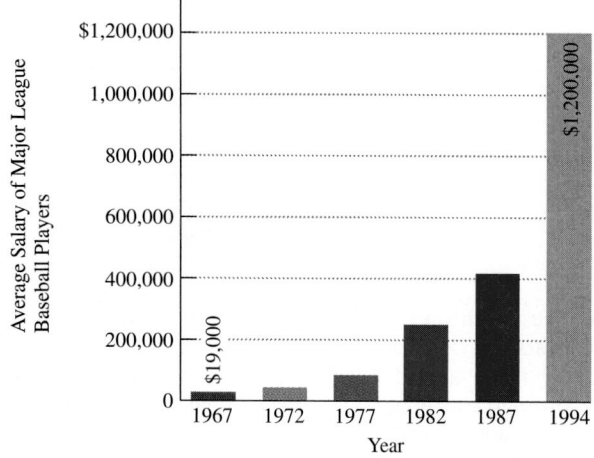

Year

66. Find a reasonable estimate for the average yearly rate of change in the salaries between 1982 and 1987.

67. Find a reasonable estimate for the average yearly rate of change in the salaries between 1987 and 1994. What do the slopes computed in this problem and Problem 66 indicate about the change in salaries from 1982 to 1994?

True–False Critical Thinking Problems _____

68. Which one of the following is true?
  a. In the figure shown below, the slope of line L_2 is greater than the slope of line L_1.
  b. Two different lines cannot have the same slope.
  c. Every line has a number associated with it called the slope.
  d. Slope can be negative.

69. Which one of the following is true?
  a. Slope is run divided by rise.
  b. The line through $(2, 2)$ and the origin has slope 1.
  c. A line with slope 3 can be parallel to a line with slope -3.
  d. The line through $(3, 1)$ and $(3, -5)$ has zero slope.

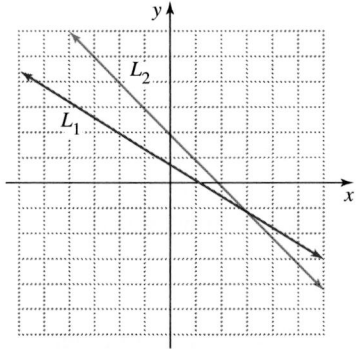

Technology Problem _____

70. Consult the manual that comes with your graphing utility to find out how to use the DRAWLINE format to draw a line given two points. Use this capability to draw the four lines in Figures 4.20 through 4.23 on pages 311 to 312.

Writing in Mathematics _____

71. Explain how to find the slope of a line.

72. Explain how to graph a line when the slope of the line and a fixed point on the line are known. Illustrate your explanation with an example.

Critical Thinking Problem _____

73. Three points are collinear if they all lie on the same line. Graph the following points: $(3, 1)$, $(6, 3)$, and $(9, 5)$. Do they appear to be collinear? Repeat this process for the points $(0, -1)$, $(4, -16)$, and $(-2, 7)$. Now for the hard part: See if you can determine how to use slope to decide if three points are collinear. State a test for collinearity using slope.

Group Activity Problem _____

74. Have each member of the group graph one of the following linear equations, using two points along each line to determine its slope.

$$y = 2x + 4; \quad y = 3x + 6; \quad y = \tfrac{1}{2}x;$$
$$y = -3x + 1; \quad y = -2x + 3; \quad y = -\tfrac{1}{3}x - 1$$

After the computations, have each member of the group report the value for the slope of the line. Use the emerging pattern based on the group's computations to state a relationship between the equation and the line's slope. How can the slope be determined immediately?

Review Problems

75. The triangles shown are similar. Find the length x.

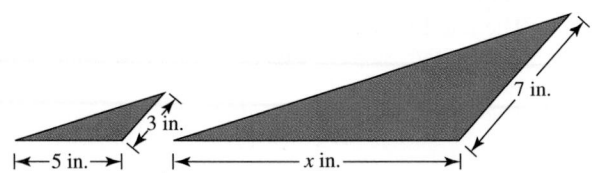

76. Five percent of what number is 36?

77. The number of personal computers in U.S. homes has been increasing by approximately 2 million each year. In 1996, there were 7.98 million personal computers. In what year will this number reach approximately 35.98 million?

S E C T I O N   4 . 5

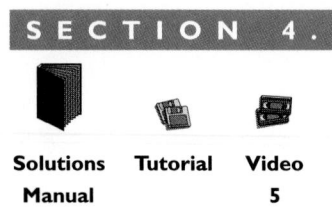

Solutions   Tutorial   Video
Manual   5

The Slope-Intercept Equation of a Line

Objectives

1 Find a line's slope and y-intercept from its equation.
2 Graph lines in slope-intercept form.
3 Write the slope-intercept equation of a mathematical model.

In Section 4.1, we studied equations in the form $y = mx + b$ and found ordered pairs satisfying these equations. In this section, we will learn how to find a line's slope and y-intercept from its equation. This will help us to graph equations in the form $y = mx + b$ fairly rapidly.

1 Find a line's slope and y-intercept from its equation.

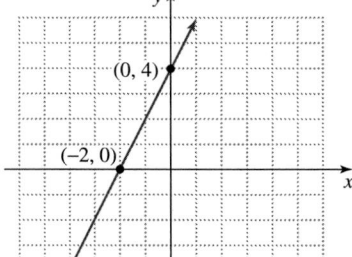

Figure 4.32
The graph of $y = 2x + 4$

Slope-Intercept Form

Let's begin with an example to show how easy it is to find a line's slope and y-intercept from its equation.

Figure 4.32 shows the graph of $y = 2x + 4$. Verify that the x-intercept is -2 by setting y equal to 0 and solving for x. Similarly, verify that the y-intercept is 4 by setting x equal to 0 and solving for y.

Now that we have two points on the line, we can calculate the slope of the graph of $y = 2x + 4$.

$$\text{Slope} = \frac{\text{Change in } y}{\text{Change in } x}$$

$$= \frac{4 - 0}{0 - (-2)} = \frac{4}{2} = 2$$

We see that the slope of the line is 2, the same as the coefficient of x in the equation $y = 2x + 4$. The y-intercept is 4, the same as the constant in the equation $y = 2x + 4$.

$$y = \boxed{2}\,x + \boxed{4}$$
$$\quad\quad\uparrow\quad\quad\uparrow$$
$$\quad\text{Slope}\quad y\text{ -Intercept}$$

It is not merely a coincidence that the x-coefficient is the line's slope and the constant term is the y-intercept. Let's find the general equation of a line with slope m and y-intercept b. Since the y-intercept is b, the point $(0, b)$ lies on the line. Let (x, y) be any other point on the line. This is shown in Figure 4.33. We now apply the formula for slope.

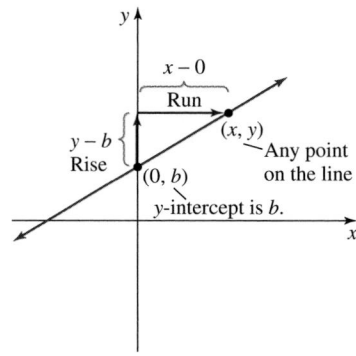

Figure 4.33

A line with slope m and y-intercept b

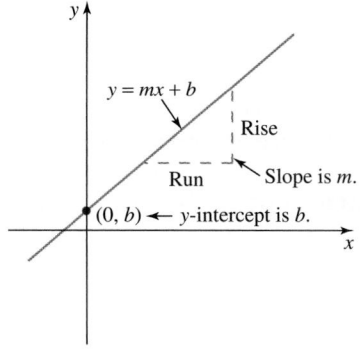

$$\frac{y - b}{x - 0} = m \qquad \frac{\text{Rise}}{\text{Run}} = \text{Slope}$$

$$\frac{y - b}{x} = m$$

$$x\left(\frac{y - b}{x}\right) = mx \qquad \text{Clear fractions by multiplying both sides by } x.$$

$$y - b = mx \qquad \text{Notice that } x \text{ cancels in the numerator and denominator.}$$

$$y = mx + b \qquad \text{Add } b \text{ to both sides.}$$

We have established the following result.

> **The slope-intercept form of the equation of a line**
>
> If a linear equation is written in the form
>
> $$y = mx + b$$
>
> where m and b are constants, then the slope of the line is m and the y-intercept is b.

EXAMPLE 1 **Finding a Line's Slope and y-Intercept from Its Equation**

Find the slope and the y-intercept of the line:

a. $y = 2x - 4$ **b.** $y = \frac{1}{2}x + 2$ **c.** $5x + y = 4$

Solution

a. We write $y = 2x - 4$ as $y = 2x + (-4)$. The slope is the x-coefficient and the y-intercept is the constant term.

$$y = 2x + (-4)$$

The slope is 2. The y-intercept is -4.

b. The equation is in the form $y = mx + b$, so we can read the slope and the y-intercept.

$$y = \frac{1}{2}x + 2$$

The slope is $\frac{1}{2}$. The y-intercept is 2.

c. We rewrite the equation in the form $y = mx + b$ by solving for y.

$$5x + y = 4$$

$$y = -5x + 4 \qquad \text{Subtract } 5x \text{ on both sides.}$$

The slope is -5. The y-intercept is 4.

In Example 1c, we began with the equation $5x + y = 4$. This is the form $Ax + By = C$, the familiar form for a linear equation in two variables. We then wrote the equations in the form $y = mx + b$ to determine the slope and y-intercept. The form $Ax + By = C$ is called the *standard form* of the equation of a line.

> **The standard form of the equation of a line**
>
> If A, B, and C are real numbers with A and B both not zero, then
>
> $$Ax + By = C$$
>
> is called the *standard form* of the equation of a line.

2 Graph lines in slope-intercept form.

Graphing and Slope-Intercept Form

In Section 4.4, we learned how to graph a line using its slope and y-intercept. Now that we can find a line's slope and y-intercept from an equation, we can sketch this equation using only two points. One point is the y-intercept and the other is obtained from the slope.

EXAMPLE 2   **Using the Slope and y-Intercept to Graph a Line**

Use the slope and y-intercept to graph $y = \frac{1}{2}x + 2$.

Solution

The equation is in slope-intercept form.

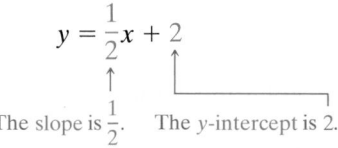

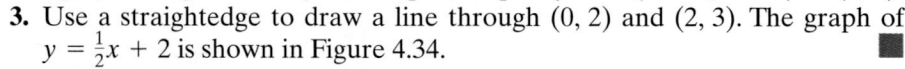

The slope is $\frac{1}{2}$.   The y-intercept is 2.

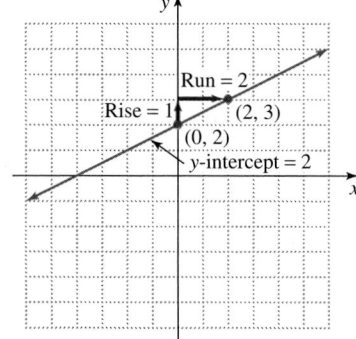

Figure 4.34

The graph of $y = \frac{1}{2}x + 2$

1. Graph the line by first plotting 2, the y-intercept. This gives the point $(0, 2)$.
2. Now, using a slope of $\frac{1}{2}$,

$$m = \frac{1}{2} = \frac{\text{Rise}}{\text{Run}}$$

locate a second point on the line by moving 1 unit up and 2 units to the right, starting from the y-intercept. This puts you at $(0 + 2, 2 + 1)$ or $(2, 3)$.
3. Use a straightedge to draw a line through $(0, 2)$ and $(2, 3)$. The graph of $y = \frac{1}{2}x + 2$ is shown in Figure 4.34. ■

EXAMPLE 3   **Finding an Equation of a Line**

Write the slope-intercept equation of the line with slope $-\frac{2}{3}$ and y-intercept 4. Then graph the line.

Solution

We begin with the line's equation. Use the slope-intercept equation, substituting $-\frac{2}{3}$ for m and 4 for b.

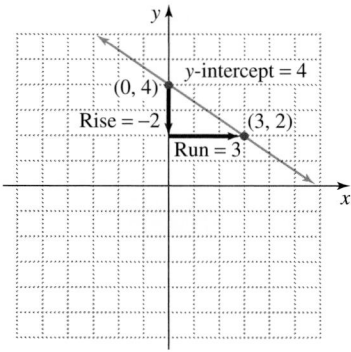

Figure 4.35

The graph of $y = -\frac{2}{3}x + 4$

$$y = mx + b$$

$$y = -\frac{2}{3}x + 4$$

Now we use the y-intercept and slope to graph the line, using our three-step procedure:

1. Plot the point $(0, 4)$ corresponding to the y-intercept of 4.
2. Since the slope is $-\frac{2}{3}$, move 2 units down (a rise of -2) and 3 units to the right (a run of 3). This gives a second point, namely $(3, 2)$.
3. Draw a line through $(0, 4)$ and $(3, 2)$. This gives the graph of the line, shown in Figure 4.35. ■

In Section 4.4, we saw that parallel lines have the same slope. We now know how to quickly graph lines in slope-intercept form. Our next example illustrates the fact that lines with the same slope but different y-intercepts are parallel.

EXAMPLE 4 Lines That Have the Same Slope

On the same set of axes, graph the lines of the equations $2x - y = -1$ and $y = 2x - 3$.

Solution

Let's express the first equation in $y = mx + b$ form.

$$2x - y = -1 \qquad \text{This is the first given equation.}$$
$$-y = -2x - 1 \qquad \text{Subtract } 2x \text{ from both sides.}$$
$$y = 2x + 1 \qquad \text{Multiply both sides by } -1.$$

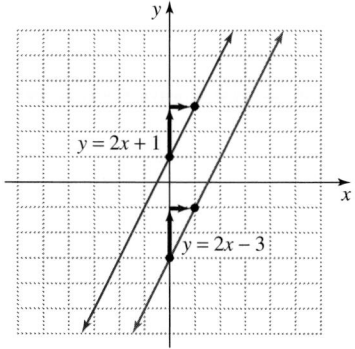

Figure 4.36

Graph of parallel lines

For the line $y = 2x + 1$, the y-intercept is 1 and the slope $m = 2$. For the line

$$y = 2x - 3$$

the y-intercept is -3 and the slope is also $m = 2$. The graphs in Figure 4.36 show that these lines with the same slope are parallel. ■

Using technology

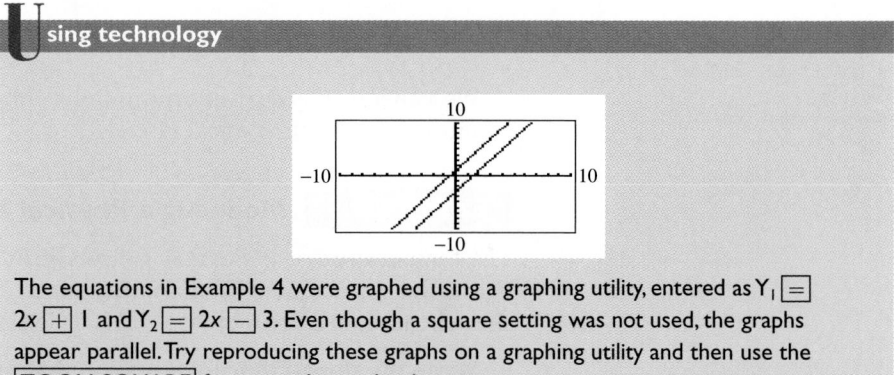

The equations in Example 4 were graphed using a graphing utility, entered as $Y_1 \boxed{=}$ $2x \boxed{+} 1$ and $Y_2 \boxed{=} 2x \boxed{-} 3$. Even though a square setting was not used, the graphs appear parallel. Try reproducing these graphs on a graphing utility and then use the $\boxed{\text{ZOOM SQUARE}}$ feature and see what happens.

3 Write the slope-intercept equation of a mathematical model.

Modeling with the Slope-Intercept Equation

If an equation in slope-intercept form models some physical situation, then the slope and y-intercept have physical interpretations. For the equation $y = mx + b$, the y-intercept b tells us what is happening to y when x is 0. If x

represents time, the y-intercept describes the value of y at the beginning, or when time equals 0. The slope represents the rate of change in y per unit change in x.

These ideas are illustrated in Table 4.6.

TABLE 4.6 Interpreting Slope and y-Intercept

Linear Model	What the Model Describes	Interpretation
$C = 1.44t + 280$ ↑ ↑ Slope y-intercept $= 1.44$ $= 280$	Carbon dioxide concentration (in ppm) t years after 1939	At the onset (in 1939), carbon dioxide concentration was 280 ppm and increased by 1.44 ppm each year.
$N = 3.657t + 14.784$ ↑ ↑ Slope y-intercept $= 3.657$ $= 14.784$	The number of cable television subscribers in the United States (in millions) t years after 1980 *(Source: Television and Cable Fact Book)*	At the beginning (in 1980), there were 14.784 million subscribers, and that number increased by 3.657 million people each year.
$p = -6.9A + 40.3$ ↑ ↑ Slope y-intercept $= -6.9$ $= 40.3$	The percentage of men injured in the Boston Marathon by age group A: 0: under 20 3: 40–49 1: 20–29 4: 50–59 2: 30–39 *(Source: The Boston Globe, April 20, 1992)*	For the first age group (men under 20), 40.3% were injured. The percentage injured decreased by 6.9% for each subsequent group.

We can use physical interpretations for slope and y-intercept to find an equation for a mathematical model.

EXAMPLE 5 **Modeling a Physical Problem**

The temperature, y, in degrees Celsius, inside the earth is a function of depth below the surface, x, in kilometers. At the surface, the temperature is 20° Celsius. The temperature increases by 10° Celsius for each kilometer of depth.

a. Write the slope-intercept equation that models this situation.
b. Find the temperature at 30 kilometers below the surface.

Inside the Earth

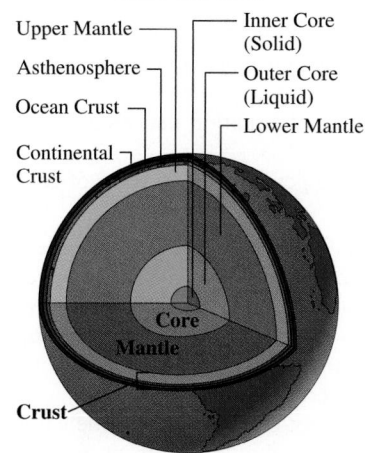

Upper Mantle — Inner Core (Solid)

Asthenosphere — Outer Core (Liquid)

Ocean Crust — Lower Mantle

Continental Crust —

Core

Mantle

Crust

The Earth's interior consists of three layers—the crust on the surface, the mantle underneath and the core at the center. The upper mantle reaches down to a depth of about 435 miles (261 km), below which lies the lower mantle and the core.

Solution

a. $y = mx + b$

This is the slope-intercept equation. y (temperature) is a function of x (depth).

Temperature ↑   depth

$y = mx + 20$

Since the temperature at the surface is 20°, the y-intercept is 20. (When x, depth, is 0, then y, temperature, is 20.)

$y = 10x + 20$

Since the temperature changes by 10° for each kilometer of depth, m (the rate of change) is 10.

We may want to change variables and let T represent temperature and d depth. Using these letters, the model can be written

$$T = 10d + 20 \qquad \text{In function notation, we can write } T(d) = 10d + 20.$$

b. To find the temperature at 30 kilometers, substitute 30 for d.

$T = 10d + 20$ This is our model from part (a).
$= 10(30) + 20$ Substitute 30 for d.
$= 300 + 20$
$= 320$ Equivalently (in function notation) $T(30) = 320$.

At a depth of 30 kilometers, the temperature inside the earth is 320° Celsius. ■

PROBLEM SET 4.5

Practice Problems

Find the slope and the y-intercept for the line described by each of the equations in Problems 1–20.

1. $y = 3x - 4$

2. $y = 4x - 2$

3. $y = -\frac{1}{2}x + 5$

4. $y = -\frac{3}{4}x + 6$

5. $y = \frac{3}{4}x$

6. $y = -\frac{3}{5}x$

7. $y = -5 - 7x$

8. $y = -9 - 6x$

9. $-5x + y = 7$

10. $-9x + y = 5$

11. $x + y = 6$

12. $x + y = 8$

13. $y = 2$

14. $y + 3 = 7$

15. $8x + 4y = 8$

16. $6x + 3y = 12$

17. $3x - 2y = 6$

18. $8x - 4y = 12$

19. $x - y = 0$

20. $y - x = 0$

Write the slope-intercept equation for each of the lines described in Problems 21–28.

21. Slope 6; y-intercept 5

22. Slope -4; y-intercept 3

23. Slope -4; y-intercept -2

24. Slope -5; y-intercept -6

25. Slope $\frac{1}{2}$; y-intercept -3

26. Slope $\frac{1}{2}$; y-intercept -4

27. Slope $-\frac{3}{5}$; y-intercept -4

28. Slope $-\frac{7}{5}$; y-intercept -2

Use the y-intercept and the slope to graph each line described by the equations in Problems 29–44.

29. $y = 2x + 3$

30. $y = 2x + 1$

31. $y = -2x + 4$

32. $-y = -2x + 5$

33. $y = \frac{1}{2}x + 3$

34. $y = \frac{1}{2}x + 2$

35. $y = \frac{2}{3}x - 4$

36. $y = \frac{3}{4}x - 5$

37. $y = -\frac{3}{4}x + 4$

38. $y = -\frac{2}{3}x + 5$

39. $y = -\frac{3}{2}x - 1$

40. $y = -\frac{4}{3}x - 2$

41. $y = 3x$

42. $y = -4x$

43. $y = -\frac{5}{3}x$

44. $y = -\frac{4}{3}x$

In Problems 45–48, graph the lines of the given equations on the same set of axes. In each case, the lines should be parallel. (Why?)

45. $y = 3x + 1$
$y = 3x - 3$

46. $y = -\frac{1}{2}x + 2$
$y = -\frac{1}{2}x - 1$

47. $4x - y = 2$
$y = 4x + 2$

48. $\quad y = \frac{1}{3}x$
$x - 3y = 12$

Application Problems

49. According to Dealerscope Merchandising, the model $S = -82t + 1972$ describes the number of turntables sold each year (S, in thousands of units) t years after 1980. What is the y-intercept for this model? Describe what the y-intercept represents in terms of the variables in the model. What is the slope and what does this number mean?

50. The model $p = -\frac{1}{2}d + 100$ describes the percentage (p) of lost hikers found by search and rescue teams whose members walk parallel to one another through the area to be searched. The separation distance (d) between searchers is expressed in feet. What is the y-intercept for this model? What does the y-intercept mean in practical terms about the searchers? What is the slope and what does this number mean? What happens to the percentage of lost hikers found with each 20-foot increase in distance between members of the search and rescue team?

51. The pressure (y, in atmospheres) in the sea is a function of depth below the surface (x, measured in feet). At the surface, the depth is 1 atmosphere. The pressure increases by $\frac{1}{33}$ of an atmosphere for every 1 foot increase in depth.
   a. Write the slope-intercept equation that models this situation. (Once you've written the equation, replace y (pressure) with p and replace x (depth) with d.)
   b. Find the pressure at a depth of 99 feet.

52. A simplified form of a mathematical model relating years of education (x) and income (y, measured in dollars) states that with no education a person can expect to earn $7200 yearly. Earnings increase by $2600 for each year of education.
   a. Write the slope-intercept equation that models this situation.
   b. Find the earnings for a person with 16 years of education.

53. Maximum annual Social Security benefit at retirement (y) is a function of your current age (x). The younger you are, the greater your annual maximum benefit will be. In particular, a 20-year-old can expect maximum benefits of $20,151 yearly. This amount decreases by $185 for every year of increase in age.
   a. Write the slope-intercept equation that models this situation. The variable x should represent ages 20 and older.
   b. Find the maximum annual Social Security benefit for a person who is now 35.

54. In 1980, 38% of men in the United States smoked cigarettes. This percent has decreased by 0.42% each year.
   a. Let x represent the number of years after 1980 and let y represent the percent of men in the United States who smoke cigarettes. Write the slope-intercept equation that models the given data.
   b. Use your model to predict the percent of men in the United States who will be smoking cigarettes in the year 2010.

True–False Critical Thinking Problems

55. Which one of the following is true?
   a. The slope-intercept equation verifies the fact that no line can have a y-intercept that is numerically equal to its slope.
   b. A pair of equations must be in slope-intercept form if they represent parallel lines.
   c. The line $3x + 2y = 5$ has slope $-\frac{3}{2}$.
   d. The line $2y = 3x + 7$ has a y-intercept of 7.

56. Which one of the following is true?
   a. Every line in rectangular coordinates has an equation that can be expressed in slope-intercept form.
   b. If an equation in slope-intercept form models some physical situation, then the y-intercept represents rate of change.
   c. The slope-intercept equation verifies the fact that a line's y-intercept is usually an integer.
   d. The lines whose equations are $2x - 4y = 9$ and $\frac{1}{3}x - \frac{2}{3}y = -8$ are parallel.

Technology Problems

57. Use a graphing utility to verify the graphs that you drew by hand in Problems 29–44.

58. If the product of the slopes of two lines is -1, then the lines are perpendicular. Use a graphing utility to graph $y = 2x - 3$ and $y = -\frac{1}{2}x + 1$ in the same viewing rectangle. Start with a standard range setting. Do the lines appear to be perpendicular? Now set the $\boxed{\text{ZOOM}}$ feature to the square setting. Describe what happens.

59. Graph the model $T = 10d + 20$ (or $y = 10x + 20$) described in Example 5 using the following range settings:

   Xmin = 0, Xmax = 60, Xscl = 10,

   Ymin = 0, Ymax = 700, Yscl = 10

   Now use the $\boxed{\text{TRACE}}$ feature to trace along the curve and verify that at a depth of 30 kilometers, the temperature inside the Earth is 320° Celsius.

Writing in Mathematics

60. Suppose you are looking at the graphs of two linear equations and the lines appear to be parallel, but you are not sure if they really are. If each equation is in the form $Ax + By = C$, explain how to use the equations to decide if their graphs are parallel lines.

Critical Thinking Problems

61. Reread Problem 49. What would you estimate to be the slope for a similar model that describes the number of CD players (rather than turntables) sold each year t years after 1980? Describe how you arrived at this estimate.

If the product of the slopes of two lines is -1, then the lines are perpendicular. In Problems 62–65, determine whether the pairs of equations represent perpendicular lines.

62. $y = 3x + 2$
$y = -\frac{1}{3}x$

63. $y = 5x + 2$
$y = \frac{1}{5}x$

64. $y = 2x + 1$
$x + 2y = -6$

65. $y = 2x - 3$
$x + 2y = 1$

66. The graph indicates that lower fertility rates (the number of births per woman) are correlated with the percent of the population using contraceptives. A line that best fits the data is shown. Estimate the y-intercept and the slope of this line. Then write the line's slope-intercept equation. Use the equation to find the number of births per woman if 90% of the population used contraceptives.

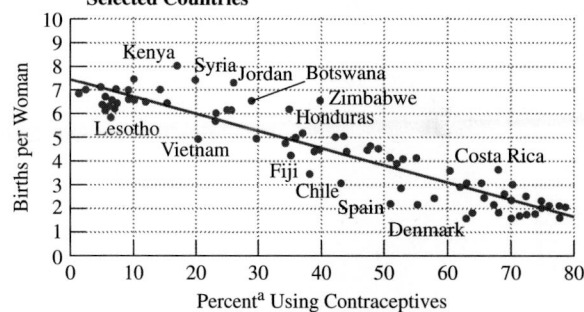

Contraceptive Prevalence and Births per Woman, Selected Countries

Percent of married women of child bearing age.

Source: Peter J. Donaldson and Amy Ong Tsui. "International Family Planning Movement," *Population Bulletin 45,* November 1990, Population Reference Bureau, Inc.

Group Activity Problem

67. This activity is appropriate for six people. Two people can work out part (c), two can concentrate on part (d), and two can work out part (e). The group should begin by reading the problem and work on parts (a) and (b) together.

Heating Systems. The total cost for three different kinds of heating systems for a three-bedroom home is given by the following models.

Solar system:	$C = 150x + 30,000$
Gas system:	$C = 700x + 12,000$
Electric system:	$C = 1100x + 5000$

In each model, C is measured in dollars and x represents the number of years the system has been in operation.

a. For each model, give the y-intercept and slope, describing what these values mean.

b. What does the y-intercept for the solar model indicate about why solar heating is rarely used?

c. Graph the lines described by the gas and electric models in the same rectangular coordinate system. The lines should intersect at approximately (17, 24,000). What does this point of intersection represent? Compare the models to the left and right of the intersection point. Describe what you observe in terms of costs of gas and electricity.

d. Repeat part (c) for the solar and gas models.

e. Repeat part (c) for the solar and electric models.

Review Problems

68. The length of the soccer field shown is 33 yards less than twice the width. If the perimeter of the field is 378 yards, find its dimensions.

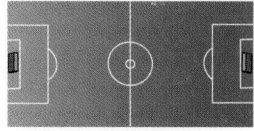

69. Solve for x: $-3x + 7 \leq -38$.

70. Find the altitude of the balloon shown in the figure.

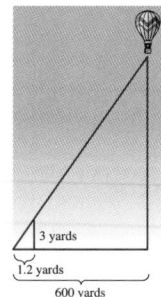

3 yards

1.2 yards

600 yards

The Point-Slope Equation of a Line

Objectives

1 Write equations of a line.
2 Write linear equations that model data and make predictions.

Solutions   Tutorial   Video
Manual   5

Leonard Koscianski "Wednesday Evening" 1988, oil on canvas, 60 × 40 in. Photo courtesy Phyllis Kind Gallery, New York and Chicago.

The line serves as a basis for describing many of our activities. We assume the presence of a line when we see a *line* of trees, or a *row* of houses, even when the line is not actually visible. We follow a *line* of reasoning and the *direction* of an argument. If there is an interruption in a conversation, we attempt to *bridge* the gap. Even our perception of time (past, present, and future) is linear. Descartes' rectangular system is based on intersecting *lines.*

Since the line forms the basis of our thinking and our perception of time, it should come as no surprise that mathematicians are interested in linear relationships, graphing lines, and writing equations for lines. In this section, we turn our attention to writing an equation of a line using the line's slope and any one point through which the line passes.

Point-Slope Form

Another useful form of the equation of a line is the point-slope form. As shown in Figure 4.37 the line contains the fixed point (x_1, y_1), and (x, y) is any other point on the line. Let m represent the slope of the line. Then

$$\frac{y - y_1}{x - x_1} = m \qquad \frac{\text{Change in } y \text{ (rise)}}{\text{Change in } x \text{ (run)}} = m, \text{ by the definition of slope.}$$

$$(x - x_1)\left(\frac{y - y_1}{x - x_1}\right) = m(x - x_1) \qquad \text{Clear fractions by multiplying both sides by } x - x_1.$$

$$y - y_1 = m(x - x_1).$$

This last equation is called *point-slope form* of the equation of a line.

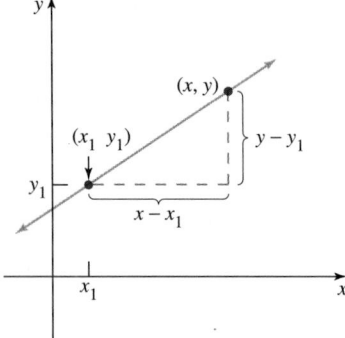

Figure 4.37

A line passing through (x_1, y_1) with slope m

> **The point-slope form of the equation of a line**
>
> The equation of the line through (x_1, y_1) with slope m is
>
> $$y - y_1 = m(x - x_1).$$

Write equations of a line.

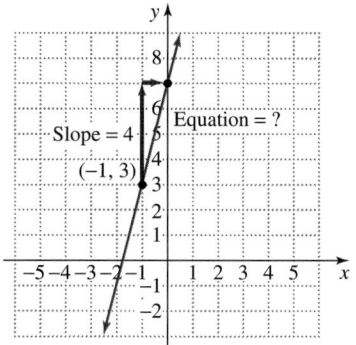

A line with slope 4 passing
through (− 1, 3)

Using the Point-Slope Form to Write a Line's Equation

If we know the slope of a line and a point through which the line passes, the point-slope form is the equation that we should use. Once we have obtained this equation, it is customary to solve for y and write the equation in slope-intercept form. Examples 1 and 2 illustrate these ideas.

EXAMPLE 1   **Writing the Point-Slope Form and the Slope-Intercept Form**

Write the point-slope form and the slope-intercept form of the equation of the line with slope 4 that passes through the point $(-1, 3)$.

Solution

Step 1. First write the point-slope form of the line's equation.

$$y - y_1 = m(x - x_1)$$ Begin with the point-slope form since we are given the point $(-1, 3)$ and slope 4.

$$y - 3 = 4[x - (-1)]$$ $(x_1, y_1) = (-1, 3)$, so substitute -1 for x_1, 3 for y_1, and 4 for m.

$$y - 3 = 4(x + 1)$$ This is the point-slope form.

Step 2. Solve for y and write the line's equation in slope-intercept form $(y = mx + b)$.

$$y - 3 = 4x + 4$$ Apply the distributive property.

$$y = 4x + 7$$ Add 3 to both sides.

The slope-intercept form $(y = mx + b)$ is $y = 4x + 7$. ∎

EXAMPLE 2   **Writing the Point-Slope Form and the Slope-Intercept Form**

Write the point-slope form and the slope-intercept form of the line passing through $(3, 2)$ and $(-3, -6)$.

Solution

To use the point-slope form, we need to find the slope. The slope is the change in the y-coordinates divided by the corresponding change in the x-coordinates.

$$m = \frac{2 - (-6)}{3 - (-3)} = \frac{2 + 6}{3 + 3} = \frac{8}{6} = \frac{4}{3}$$

Now we follow the two steps used in Example 1. In step 1, we write the point-slope equation. In step 2, we use the point-slope equation to write the slope-intercept equation.

Step 1. Write the point-slope form of the line's equation. We can take either fixed point to be (x_1, y_1). Let us use $(x_1, y_1) = (3, 2)$. Then

$$y - y_1 = m(x - x_1)$$ Begin with the point-slope form. $(x_1, y_1) = (3, 2)$ and $m = \frac{4}{3}$.

$$y - 2 = \frac{4}{3}(x - 3)$$ This is the point-slope form of the line.

Step 2. Solve for y and write the line's equation in slope-intercept form $(y = mx + b)$.

Writing an equation of the line
through two points

Discover for yourself

Work Example 2 again, using $(-3, -6)$ instead of $(3, 2)$ as the fixed point (x_1, y_1) on the line. Is the slope-intercept form of the equation the same or different from the one we obtained using $(3, 2)$? Write a statement that generalizes this situation.

$$y - 2 = \frac{4}{3}x - 4 \qquad \text{Use the distributive property.}$$

$$y = \frac{4}{3}x - 2 \qquad \text{Add 2 to both sides.}$$

The slope-intercept form is $y = \frac{4}{3}x - 2$.

Check

We can check this result by showing that the coordinates of the other point, $(-3, -6)$, satisfy the equation:

$$y = \frac{4}{3}x - 2 \qquad \text{This is the slope-intercept equation.}$$

$$-6 \stackrel{?}{=} \frac{4}{3}(-3) - 2 \qquad \text{To see if } (-3, -6) \text{ satisfies the equation, let } x = -3 \text{ and } y = -6.$$

$$-6 \stackrel{?}{=} -4 - 2$$

$$-6 = -6 \quad \checkmark \qquad \text{This true statement indicates that } (-3, -6) \text{ satisfies the equation and that we have written the slope-intercept form correctly.} \quad \blacksquare$$

Study tip

From Examples 1 and 2, we eventually write a line's equation in slope-intercept form. But where do we start our work?

Starting with $y = mx + b$	Starting with $y - y_1 = m(x - x_1)$
Begin with the slope-intercept form if you know: 1. The slope of the line and the y-intercept	Begin with the point-slope form if you know: 1. The slope of the line and a point on the line or 2. Two points on the line

The major forms for equations of lines and methods for graphing them are summarized in Table 4.7.

TABLE 4.7 Summary of Equations of Lines and Graphing Techniques

Form	Example	How to Graph the Example
Slope-Intercept Form $y = mx + b$ m = slope b = y-intercept	$y = -\frac{3}{4}x + 1$ $-\frac{3}{4}$ = Slope 1 = y-intercept	Use the y-intercept and slope. 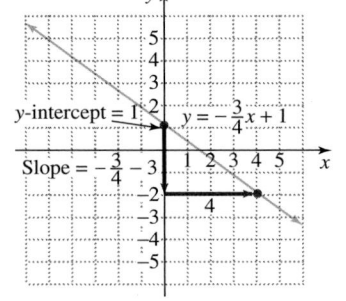

Form	Example	How to Graph the Example
Standard Form $Ax + By = C$	$2x - 4y = 8$ x-intercept $(y = 0)$: $2x = 8$ $x = 4$ y-intercept $(x = 0)$: $-4y = 8$ $y = -2$	Use the intercepts.
Point-Slope Form $y - y_1 = m(x - x_1)$ $m = $ slope $(x_1, y_1) = $ point on the line	$y - 2 = \dfrac{3}{2}(x - 1)$ Slope $= \dfrac{3}{2}$ Point on the line $= (1, 2)$	Use the point on the line and the slope.
Horizontal Line Parallel to the x-Axis $y = b$	$y = 5$	Draw a line parallel to the x-axis with y-intercept $= 5$
Vertical Line Parallel to the y-Axis $x = b$	$x = -2$	Draw a line parallel to the y-axis with x-intercept $= -2$.

2 Write linear equations that model data and make predictions.

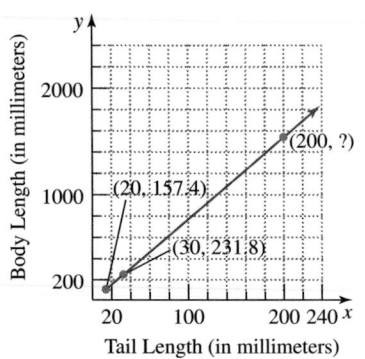

Figure 4.38

A linear relationship between a snake's tail length and body lengths

James Carmichael/The Image Bank

Modeling with the Point-Slope Equation

An important aspect of applied mathematics involves using equations to predict the behavior of variables. Example 3 shows how equations of lines can be useful to biologists.

EXAMPLE 3 **Applying the Slope-Intercept Equation**

A biologist takes the following measurements on the tail and body length of two snakes of the same species.

	Snake 1	Snake 2
x (Tail Length in Millimeters)	20.0	30.0
y (Body Length in Millimeters)	157.4	231.8

The graph in Figure 4.38 indicates that the data points representing a snake's tail and body length fall along a straight line. Thus, there is a linear relationship between a snake's body length and its tail length. Write the slope-intercept equation of the line on which these measurements fall. Then predict the body length of a snake of this species whose tail length is 200 millimeters.

Solution

This example is identical to Example 2 on page 331. The only difference is that we are now working with data points that have meaning in an applied situation. We will write the point-slope equation and then use this equation to write the slope-intercept equation. We start by finding the slope of the line in Figure 4.38.

$$m = \frac{231.8 - 157.4}{30 - 20} = \frac{74.4}{10} = 7.44 \qquad \text{Find the slope by taking the change in } y \text{ divided by the change in } x.$$

Now we write the point-slope form of the line's equation. We can take either ordered pair [that is, either (20.0, 157.4) or (30.0, 231.8)] to be (x_1, y_1). Using the smaller numbers, we let $(x_1, y_1) = (20.0, 157.4)$. Then

$$y - y_1 = m(x - x_1) \qquad \text{Begin with the point-slope form.}$$
$$y - 157.4 = 7.44(x - 20) \qquad \text{Substitute: } x_1 = 20, y_1 = 157.4, \text{ and } m = 7.44.$$

Next, we solve for y and write the line's equation in slope-intercept form ($y = mx + b$).

$$y - 157.4 = 7.44x - 148.8 \qquad \text{Apply the distributive property. Our goal is to solve for } y.$$
$$y = 7.44x + 8.6 \qquad \text{Add 157.4 to both sides.}$$

The equation $y = 7.44x + 8.6$ is the slope-intercept form. To predict the body length (y) of a snake whose tail is 200 millimeters long (x), substitute 200 for x in the equation.

$$y = 7.44x + 8.6 \qquad \text{Slope-intercept form } (y = mx + b)$$
$$= 7.44(200) + 8.6 \qquad \text{Let } x = 200.$$
$$= 1488 + 8.6$$
$$= 1496.6$$

A snake whose tail length is 200 millimeters will have a body length of 1496.6 millimeters.

We can summarize these results in function notation. Since body length, y, is a function of tail length, x, we can write

$$f(x) = 7.44x + 8.6.$$

If the tail length is 200 millimeters, the body length of the snake is

$$f(200) = 7.44(200) + 8.6 = 1496.6 \text{ millimeters.}$$ ∎

PROBLEM SET 4.6

Practice Problems

Write the point-slope form of the line satisfying each of the conditions in Problems 1–28. Then use the point-slope form of the equation to write the slope-intercept form of the equation.

1. Slope = 2, passing through (3, 5)

2. Slope = 4, passing through (1, 3)

3. Slope = 6, passing through (−2, 5)

4. Slope = 8, passing through (4, −1)

5. Slope = −3, passing through (−2, −3)

6. Slope = −5, passing through (−4, −2)

7. Slope = −4, passing through (−4, 0)

8. Slope = −2, passing through (0, −3)

9. Slope = −1, passing through $\left(-\frac{1}{2}, -2\right)$

10. Slope = −1, passing through $\left(-4, -\frac{1}{4}\right)$

11. Slope = $\frac{1}{2}$, passing through the origin

12. Slope = $\frac{1}{3}$, passing through the origin

13. Slope = $-\frac{2}{3}$, passing through (6, −2)

14. Slope = $-\frac{3}{5}$, passing through (10, −4)

15. Passing through (1, 2) and (5, 10)

16. Passing through (3, 5) and (8, 15)

17. Passing through (−3, 0) and (0, 3)

18. Passing through (−2, 0) and (0, 2)

19. Passing through (−3, −1) and (2, 4)

20. Passing through (−2, −4) and (1, −1)

21. Passing through (−3, −2) and (3, 6)

22. Passing through (−3, 6) and (3, −2)

23. Passing through (−3, −1) and (4, −1)

24. Passing through (−2, −5) and (6, −5)

25. Passing through (2, 4) with x-intercept = −2

26. Passing through (1, −3) with x-intercept = −1

27. x-intercept = $-\frac{1}{2}$ and y-intercept = 4

28. x-intercept = 4 and y-intercept = −2

Application Problems

In Problems 29–32, the two data points that are given fall along a straight line. For each problem:

a. Find the slope of this line.

b. Use either ordered pair and write the point-slope equation of the line.

c. Use the point-slope equation to write the slope-intercept form of the equation.

d. Use the slope-intercept equation to answer the given question.

29. The table shows two measurements for age and blood pressure, variables that have a linear relationship.

	Person 1	Person 2
x (Age)	10	30
y (Blood Pressure)	115	125

This linear relationship means that (10, 115) and (30, 125) are points that lie along a line. Do parts (a) through (c) listed above, and then answer the question in part (d).

d. What blood pressure does the model predict for an 80-year-old person?

30. The table shows two measurements for years a person smoked and percent of lung damage, variables that have a linear relationship.

	Person 1	Person 2
x (Years a Person Smoked)	9	31
y (Percentage of Lung Damage)	17	54

This linear relationship means that (9, 17) and (31, 54) are points that lie along a line. Do parts (a) through (c) listed above, and then answer the question in part (d).

d. What percentage of lung damage does the model predict for a person who has smoked 40 years?

31. The data in the table are from an article in the *Journal of Environmental Health* (May–June 1965, Volume 27, Number 6, pages 883–897). Radioactive wastes seeping into the Columbia River have exposed citizens of eight Oregon counties and the city of Portland to radioactive contamination. The value of *x* is an index formulated by the author that measures the proximity of the residents to the contamination. The values of *y* in the table are for Sherman and Columbia counties, respectively.

	County 1	County 2
x (Proximity of Residents to Radioactive Wastes)	1.3	6.4
y (Number of Cancer Deaths per 100,000 Residents)	114	178

The variables in this table have a linear relationship, meaning that (1.3, 114) and (6.4, 178) are points that lie along a line. Do parts (a) through (c) listed above, and then answer the question in part (d).

d. What is the predicted number of cancer deaths per 100,000 residents for Portland, with an index of 11.6?

32. The death rate from lung cancer increased steadily from 1980 through 1990. The variables shown below have a linear relationship.

x (Number of Years after 1980)	0	10
y (Lung Cancer Death Rate per 100,000 Americans)	43.2	48

This linear relationship means that (0, 43.2) and (10, 48) are points that lie along a line. Do parts (a) through (c) listed above, and then answer the question in part (d).

d. What death rate from lung cancer does the model predict for the year 2000?

True–False Critical Thinking Problems

33. Which one of the following is true?
   a. If a line has undefined shape, then it has no equation.
   b. The line whose equation is $y - 3 = 7(x + 2)$ passes through $(-3, 2)$.
   c. The point-slope form will not work for the line through the points $(2, -5)$ and $(2, 6)$.
   d. The slope of the line whose equation is $3x + y = 7$ is 3.

34. Which of the following is true?
   a. The point-slope form for the equation of a line is $y - y_1 = mx + b$.
   b. The lines whose equations are $y = x$ and $y = -x$ both pass through the origin and are perpendicular.
   c. A line with no slope and one with zero slope cannot be perpendicular.
   d. The line whose equation is $y = 5x$ has no y-intercept.

35. Which one of the following is true?
   a. The slope-intercept form of the equation of the line through (1, 4) with slope 2 is $y = 2x + 4$.
   b. The vertical line described by $x = 3$ has no y-intercept.
   c. The line described by $2y = 5x + 3$ has a slope of 5 and a y-intercept of 3.
   d. More than one line can be drawn with a y-intercept $= 3$ and a slope $= \frac{1}{2}$.

36. Which one of the following is true?
   a. The effect of increasing the coefficients of x on the graph of $y = mx + b$ is to increase the y-intercept.
   b. The line whose equation is
$$\frac{x}{3} + \frac{y}{4} = 1$$
   has an x-intercept of 3 and a y-intercept of 4.
   c. If the slope-intercept form of the line through (0, 1) and (4, 9) is written, then (3, 7) is not a point on the line because it does not satisfy the equation.
   d. Since vertical lines have no slope, the equation of a vertical line cannot be written in standard form.

Technology Problems

37. Use a graphing utility to graph $y = 1.75x - 2$. Select the best viewing rectangle possible by experimenting with the range settings to show that the line's slope is $\frac{7}{4}$. Also find a viewing rectangle that makes it impossible to tell that the line's slope is $\frac{7}{4}$.

38. Use a graphing utility to graph the model $y = 7.44x + 8.6$ (discussed in Example 3), which describes a snake's body length (y, in millimeters) as a function of its tail length (x, in millimeters). Experiment with various range settings so that you can use the $\boxed{\text{TRACE}}$ feature to confirm that a snake whose tail length is 200 millimeters will have a body length of approximately 1497 millimeters.

39. Use a graphing utility to graph the slope-intercept equation that you wrote in part (c) for Problems 29–32. Then select an appropriate range setting and use the $\boxed{\text{TRACE}}$ feature to graphically show your solution to part (d) of each problem.

40. The model $y = 0.625x - 50.5$ describes the number of transactions at automated teller machines (y, in billions) in the year 19 _x_ , where x represents the last two digits of the year.

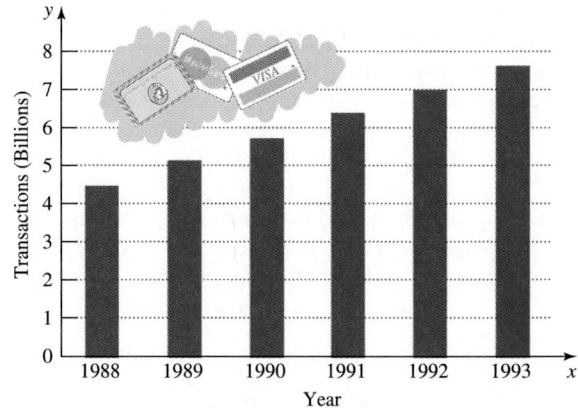

Source: *New York Times,* October 23, 1994

Graph the model with the following range settings:

Xmin = 80, Xmax = 99, Xscl = 1,

Ymin = 0, Ymax = 20, Yscl = 2

Then use the $\boxed{\text{TRACE}}$ feature to predict the number of transactions at automated teller machines in 1999. Change the range settings so that you can make predictions for the first decade of the 21st century. Then make one such prediction.

Writing in Mathematics

41. How do you select which graphing method to use when graphing a linear equation in two variables—intercepts, or slope and y-intercept?

42. Two forms of lines studied in this chapter are the slope-intercept form ($y = mx + b$) and the point-slope form $[y - y_1 = m(x - x_1)]$. Explain which of these forms works best for:
  a. Graphing the line represented by an equation.
  b. Writing the equation of a line passing through a given point with a given slope.

Critical Thinking Problems

43. Write an equation of the line passing through $(-3, 2)$ and parallel to the line whose equation is $y = 2x + 1$. Express the equation in point-slope form and slope-intercept form.

44. If two lines are perpendicular, then the product of their slopes is -1. Use this fact to write an equation of the line passing through $(-9, 3)$ and perpendicular to the line whose equation is $3x + y = 5$. Express the equation in point-slope form and slope-intercept form.

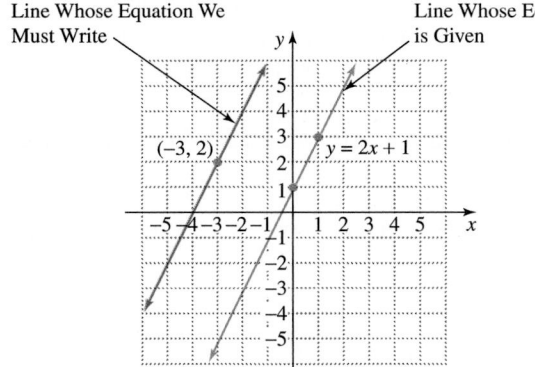

Group Activity Problem

45. "To use mathematical principles to devise a grand theory, one must simplify. In doing so, mathematicians can forget that their mathematical model is not the real world. Reality is infinitely complex and impossible to capture completely in a model."
—John Allen Paulos (mathematics professor at Temple University)

a. In your group, find two examples of mathematical models discussed up to this point in the book that appear to simplify the complexities of reality. In what specific ways do these models fail to work in the real world? What complexities do they ignore?

b. In your group, find two examples of mathematical models discussed up to this point in the book that appear to accurately describe the relationship among variables. Explain how you selected these models.

c. What conclusions can you draw about modeling reality based on the formulas that the group selected from the book in parts (a) and (b)?

Review Problems

46. Solve and graph the solution set on a number line: $4 - 3(x - 5) < -2x$.

47. If the area of a triangle is 54 square centimeters and the base is 12 centimeters, then what is the height?

48. The measure of the smallest angle of a triangle is one-half the measure of the second largest angle and one-third the measure of the largest angle. Find the measure of each of the triangle's angles.

SECTION 4.7

Solutions Manual   Tutorial   Video 5

Graphing Linear Inequalities in Two Variables

Objectives

1 Determine whether ordered pairs are solutions of linear inequalities.
2 Graph a linear inequality.

In Chapter 2, we followed our discussion of equations in one variable ($3x + 4 = 7$) with inequalities containing one variable ($3x + 4 > 7$). In this section, we continue the same pattern, moving from linear equations in two variables ($2x + 3y = 6$) to linear inequalities in two variables ($2x + 3y > 6$).

1 Determine whether ordered pairs are solutions of linear inequalities.

Linear Inequalities in Two Variables

A linear inequality in two variables (x and y) is an inequality that can be written in one of the following forms:

$$Ax + By > C \quad \text{or} \quad Ax + By \geqslant C$$
$$Ax + By < C \qquad\qquad Ax + By \leqslant C$$

where A, B, and C are real numbers, and A and B are not both zero. Examples of linear inequalities are $2x - 3y \geqslant 6, x - y < 4, x \geqslant 3$, and $y < -2$.

An ordered pair (x_1, y_1) is a *solution* to an inequality in two variables if the inequality is true when x_1 is substituted for x and y_1 is substituted for y. Under these conditions, we say that (x_1, y_1) *satisfies* the inequality.

EXAMPLE I **Deciding Whether Ordered Pairs Are Solutions of Inequalities**

Determine whether each of the following ordered pairs satisfies the inequality $2x - 3y \geqslant 6$.

a. $(0, 0)$ **b.** $(3, -1)$

Solution

a. To determine whether $(0, 0)$ is a solution to the inequality, we replace x by 0 and y by 0 in the inequality.

$$2x - 3y \geqslant 6 \qquad \text{This is the given inequality.}$$
$$2(0) - 3(0) \overset{?}{\geqslant} 6 \qquad \text{Replace } x \text{ by } 0 \text{ and } y \text{ by } 0.$$
$$0 \geqslant 6 \qquad \text{A false statement results.}$$

Because $0 \geqslant 6$ is false, the ordered pair $(0, 0)$ does not satisfy the inequality $2x - 3y \geqslant 6$.

b. Does $(3, -1)$ satisfy the inequality?

$$2x - 3y \geqslant 6 \qquad \text{This is the given inequality.}$$
$$2(3) - 3(-1) \overset{?}{\geqslant} 6 \qquad \text{Replace } x \text{ by } 3 \text{ and } y \text{ by } -1.$$
$$6 - (-3) \overset{?}{\geqslant} 6$$
$$9 \geqslant 6 \qquad \text{A true statement results.}$$

Because $9 \geqslant 6$ is true, the ordered pair $(3, -1)$ satisfies the inequality $2x - 3y \geqslant 6$. ∎

2 Graph a linear inequality.

The Graph of a Linear Inequality in Two Variables

The graph of a linear inequality in two variables is the collection of all points in the rectangular coordinate system whose ordered pairs satisfy the inequality. The graph consists of an *entire region* rather than a line. The boundary for this region is found by replacing the inequality symbol with an equal sign and graphing the resulting equation. Let's see exactly what this means.

EXAMPLE 2	**Using a Line and a Test Point to Graph an Inequality**

Graph the inequality: $2x - 3y \geqslant 6$

Solution

The boundary for the graph is the graph of $2x - 3y = 6$, found by replacing $\geqslant$ with $=$. To graph $2x - 3y = 6$ by using intercepts, we begin with the x-intercept. We set $y = 0$, and solve for x.

$$2x - 3(0) = 6$$
$$2x = 6$$
$$x = 3 \qquad \text{The } x\text{-intercept is 3.}$$

For the y-intercept, we set $x = 0$ and solve for y.

$$2(0) - 3y = 6$$
$$-3y = 6$$
$$y = -2 \qquad \text{The } y\text{-intercept is 2.}$$

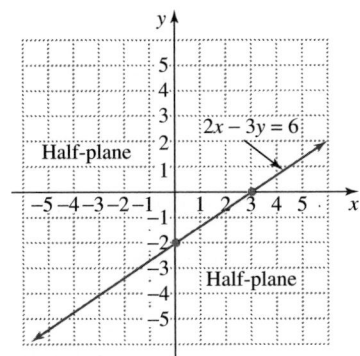

Figure 4.39

The graph of $2x - 3y = 6$

The graph is shown in Figure 4.39.

A *half-plane* is formed on either side of a straight line that divides the plane in two. The graph of $2x - 3y \geqslant 6$ is one of these half-planes and the boundary line. To find which half-plane is included in the graph, test a point from either half-plane that is *not* on the boundary line.

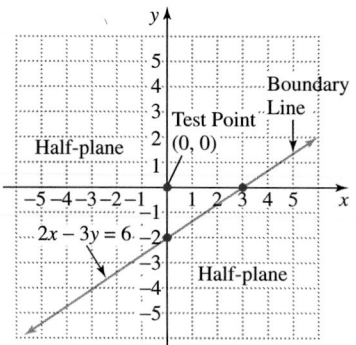

Figure 4.40

Figure 4.40 indicates that a convenient point to test is the origin $(0, 0)$.

$$2x - 3y \geqslant 6 \qquad \text{This is the given inequality.}$$

$$2(0) - 3(0) \overset{?}{\geqslant} 6 \qquad \text{Test the origin by substituting 0 for } x \text{ and } y.$$

$$0 \geqslant 6 \qquad \text{False}$$

Since $(0, 0)$ results in a false statement, it is not a solution. Thus, all the points in this half-plane do not satisfy the inequality. In other words, the graph includes the half-plane that does not contain $(0, 0)$. The graph of $2x - 3y \geqslant 6$ is the line of $2x - 3y = 6$ and the half-plane below the line, shown in Figure 4.41. ∎

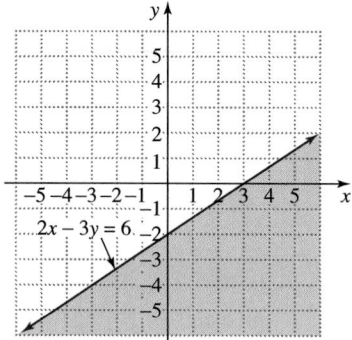

Figure 4.41

The graph of $2x - 3y \geqslant 6$

Discover for yourself

Every point in the shaded region of Figure 4.41 satisfies $2x - 3y > 6$. Take any two points in the region and verify this. (Furthermore, every point on the line satisfies $2x - 3y = 6$.)

Suppose we wanted to graph $2x - 3y > 6$. First, notice that equality is not included when we use the symbol $>$. This means that the line whose equation is $2x - 3y = 6$ is not part of the graph of $2x - 3y > 6$. Thus, the boundary line dividing the half-plane is not included in the graph. This is shown by representing the boundary line as a *dashed line,* as in Figure 4.42.

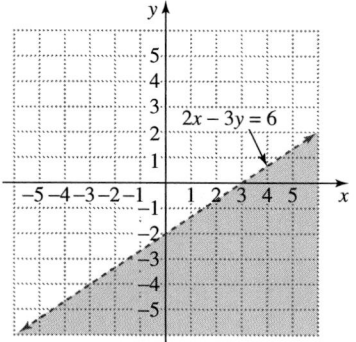

Figure 4.42

The graph of $2x - 3y > 6$

Study tip

Graphing a Linear Inequality in Two Variables

1. The boundary line dividing the half-planes is a solution of the inequality when the symbols $\leqslant$ and $\geqslant$ appear. This is indicated by drawing the boundary line as a solid line.
2. The boundary line dividing the half-planes is not a solution of the inequality when the symbols $>$ and $<$ appear. This is indicated by drawing the boundary line as a dashed line.
3. If a test point in a half-plane satisfies an inequality, then all points in that half-plane also satisfy the inequality.
4. If a test point in one half-plane does not satisfy the inequality, then all points in the other half-plane do satisfy the inequality.

Before considering another example, let's summarize the procedure for graphing a linear inequality in two variables:

Graphing a linear inequality $Ax + By > C$, $Ax + By \geq C$, $Ax + By < C$, $Ax + By \leq C$

1. Draw the graph of the boundary line, which is the graph of $Ax + By = C$. Use the x- and y-intercepts. Draw a solid boundary line if the order relation is $\geq$ or $\leq$. Draw a dashed boundary line if the order relation is $>$ or $<$.
2. Choose a test point in one of the half-planes that is not on the line. Substitute the coordinates of the test point into the inequality. If a true statement results, shade the half-plane containing this test point. If a false statement results, shade the half-plane not containing this test point.

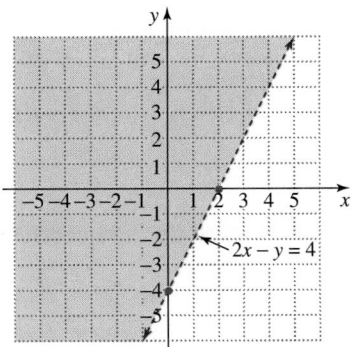

Figure 4.43

The graph of $2x - y < 4$

EXAMPLE 3 **Graphing a Linear Inequality**

Graph the inequality: $2x - y < 4$

Solution

The graph of the corresponding equation

$$2x - y = 4$$

is the line in Figure 4.43. (Verify that the x-intercept is 2 and the y-intercept is -4.) The graph is indicated by a dashed line since equality is not included in $2x - y < 4$. To find which half-plane is the graph, test a point from either half-plane. The origin $(0, 0)$, is easiest.

$$2x - y < 4 \quad \text{This is the given inequality.}$$
$$2(0) - 0 \stackrel{?}{<} 4 \quad \text{Test the origin by substituting 0 for } x \text{ and } y.$$
$$0 < 4 \quad \text{True}$$

This true statement indicates that $(0, 0)$ is a solution to the inequality. The graph is the half-plane including $(0, 0)$, which is the half-plane above the line in Figure 4.43. All points in that half-plane have coordinates satisfying $2x - y < 4$. ∎

Inequalities can have boundary lines that are vertical or horizontal.

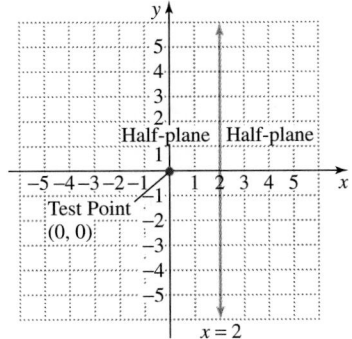

Figure 4.44

The graph of $x = 2$

EXAMPLE 4 **Graphing a Linear Inequality with a Vertical Boundary Line**

Graph the inequality: $x \geq 2$

Solution

We graph $x = 2$ as a solid line to show that all points on the line are solutions. The line of $x = 2$ is a vertical line parallel to the y-axis, whose x-intercept is 2 (see Figure 4.44). Now we use $(0, 0)$ as a test point.

$$x \geq 2 \quad \text{This is the given inequality.}$$
$$x + 0y \geq 2 \quad \text{We write the inequality in this form so you can see how we substitute } (0, 0), \text{ the test point.}$$
$$0 + 0 \cdot 0 \stackrel{?}{\geq} 2 \quad \text{Test } (0, 0) \text{ by substituting 0 for } x \text{ and } y.$$
$$0 \geq 2 \quad \text{False}$$

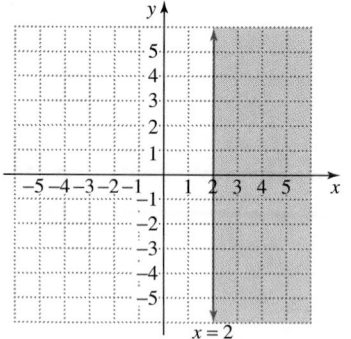

Figure 4.45

The graph of $x \geqslant 2$

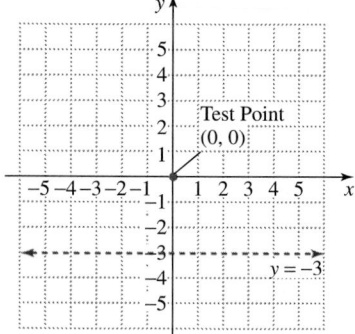

Figure 4.46

The graph of $y = -3$

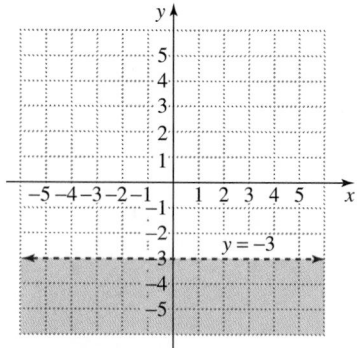

Figure 4.47

The graph of $y \leqslant -3$

This false statement indicates that $(0, 0)$ is not a solution. We shade the half-plane that does not contain the origin, which is the half-plane to the right of the vertical boundary line. The graph of $x \geqslant 2$ is shown in Figure 4.45. The solution consists of all ordered pairs whose first coordinates are greater than or equal to 2. ∎

EXAMPLE 5 **A Linear Inequality with a Horizontal Boundary Line**

Graph the inequality: $y < -3$

Solution

The graph of $y = -3$ is a horizontal line parallel to the x-axis, whose y-intercept is -3. We graph $y = -3$ as a dashed line to show that all points on the line are not solutions of $y < -3$ (see Figure 4.46). Again, we use $(0, 0)$ as a test point.

$$y < -3 \qquad \text{This is the given inequality.}$$

$$0x + y < -3 \qquad \text{Write the inequality in this form so the substitution of the test point can be seen.}$$

$$0 \cdot 0 + 0 \overset{?}{<} -3 \qquad \text{Test } (0, 0) \text{ by substituting } 0 \text{ for } x \text{ and } y.$$

$$0 < -3 \qquad \text{False}$$

This false statement indicates that $(0, 0)$ is not a solution. We shade the half-plane that does not contain the origin, which is the half-plane below the horizontal line $y = -3$. The graph of $y < -3$ is shown in Figure 4.47. The solution consists of all ordered pairs whose second coordinates are less than -3. ∎

> **Study tip**
>
> When a boundary line is vertical, $x > a$ is the half-plane to the right of the line and $x < a$ is the half-plane to the left of the line. When a boundary line is horizontal, $y > b$ is the half-plane above the line and $y < b$ is the half-plane below the line.
>
>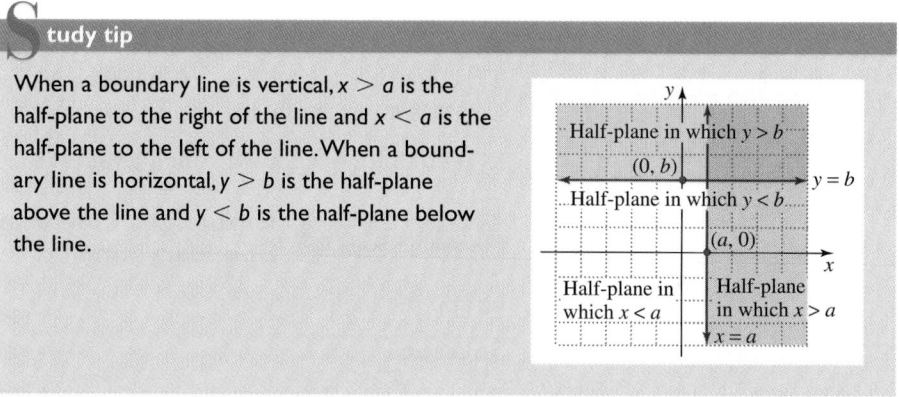

Graphing Inequalities Without Using Test Points

If an inequality is in slope-intercept form, such as $y < x + 3$, it is not necessary to use a test point to obtain the graph. Take a moment to verify this by working the Discover for Yourself box.

Discover for yourself

Figure 4.48 shows the graph of $y = x + 3$. Use a test point to identify the half-plane correspond-ing to $y < x + 3$. Use a test point to identify the half-plane corresponding to $y > x + 3$. General-ize from this situation and complete this state-ment: If the line $y = mx + b$ is graphed, then $y < mx + b$ is the half-plane _____ the line and $y > mx + b$ is the half-plane _____ the line.

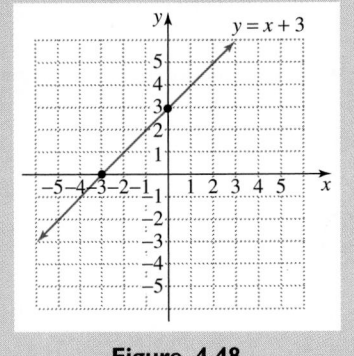

Figure 4.48

Table 4.8 summarizes how to graph inequalities in slope-intercept form. Were you able to state the descriptions in the first and third row of the table when you worked the Discover for Yourself box?

TABLE 4.8 Graphing Inequalities in Slope-Intercept Form

Inequality	Description of the Graph
$y < mx + b$	Half-plane *below* the line $y = mx + b$
$y \leq mx + b$	Half-plane *on* and *below* the line $y = mx + b$
$y > mx + b$	Half-plane *above* the line $y = mx + b$
$y \geq mx + b$	Half-plane *on* and *above* the line $y = mx + b$

Study tip

The results in Table 4.8 are easy to remember. If $y < mx + b$, the solutions contain all y-values less than the boundary values, so the graph lies below the boundary line. If $y > mx + b$, the solu-tions contain all y-values greater than the bound-ary values, so the graph lies above the boundary line.

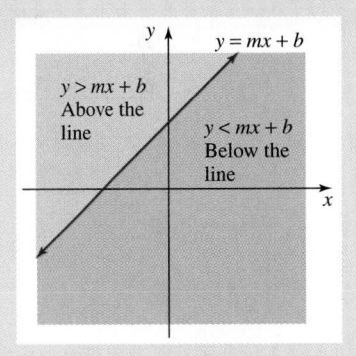

EXAMPLE 6   Graphing an Inequality in Slope-Intercept Form

Graph the inequality: $y < 2x - 1$

Solution

Graph the boundary line by graphing $y = 2x - 1$.

$$y = 2x + (-1)$$

$$\underbrace{\text{Slope} = \frac{2}{1} = \frac{\text{Rise}}{\text{Run}}}_{} \quad \underbrace{y\text{-intercept} = -1}_{}$$

Figure 4.49

The graph of $y < 2x - 1$

$y = 2x - 1$

Since we are graphing $y < 2x - 1$, the solution is the half-plane lying *below* the line. The graph is shown in Figure 4.49 at the bottom of page 343. ■

PROBLEM SET 4.7

Practice Problems

Determine which of the ordered pairs following each inequality in Problems 1–8 satisfy that inequality.

1. $x + y > 4$:　$(2, 2), (3, 2), (-3, 8)$

2. $2x - y < 3$:　$(0, 0), (3, 0), (-4, -15)$

3. $2x + y \geq 5$:　$(4, 0), (1, 3), (0, 0)$

4. $3x - 5y \geq -12$:　$(2, -3), (2, 8), (0, 0)$

5. $y \geq -2x + 4$:　$(4, 0), (1, 3), (-2, -4)$

6. $y \leq -x + 5$:　$(5, 0), (0, 5), (8, -4)$

7. $y > -2x + 1$:　$(2, 3), (0, 0), (0, 5)$

8. $x < -y - 2$:　$(-1, -1), (0, 0), (4, -5)$

Graph each inequality in Problems 9–36.

9. $x + y \geq 4$

10. $x + y \geq 5$

11. $x - y < 3$

12. $x - y < 4$

13. $2x + y > 4$

14. $x + 2y > 6$

15. $x - 3y \leq 6$

16. $3x - y \leq -6$

17. $3x - 2y \leq 6$

18. $x - 3y \geq 3$

19. $4x + 3y > 12$

20. $5x + 10y > 20$

21. $5x - y < -10$

22. $3x - 4y < -12$

23. $2x - \frac{1}{2}y \geq 2$

24. $3x - \frac{2}{3}y \leq 3$

25. $x + y \leq 0$

26. $2x + y \geq 0$

27. $x \geq 3$

28. $x \leq 2$

29. $x > -4$

30. $x < -5$

31. $y \leq 2$

32. $y \geq 4$

33. $y > -1$

34. $y < -3$

35. $x \geq 0$

36. $y \leq 0$

Graph each inequality in Problems 37–54.

37. $y \geq x + 1$

38. $y \geq x + 2$

39. $y < -x + 4$

40. $y < -x + 3$

41. $y < 2x + 3$

42. $y > 3x - 1$

43. $y \geq 3x - 2$

44. $y \leq 2x - 3$

45. $y > \frac{1}{2}x + 2$

46. $y > \frac{1}{3}x - 2$

47. $y < \frac{3}{4}x - 3$

48. $y < \frac{2}{3}x + 1$

49. $y > 2x$

50. $y < 4x$

51. $y \leq \frac{5}{4}x$

52. $y \geq \frac{4}{5}x$

53. $y > -\frac{2}{3}x + 1$

54. $y < -\frac{1}{3}x - 2$

Match each inequality in Problems 55–60 with its graph. [The graphs are labeled (a)–(f).]

a.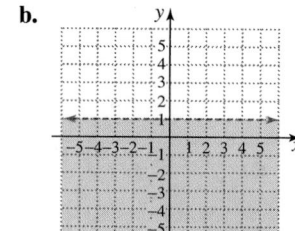

b.

c.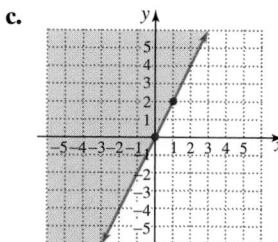

d.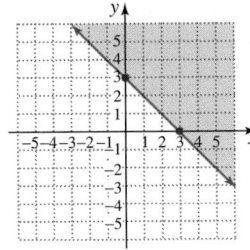

e.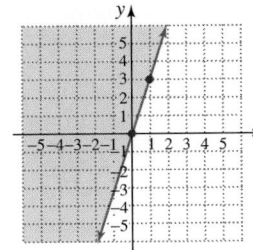

f.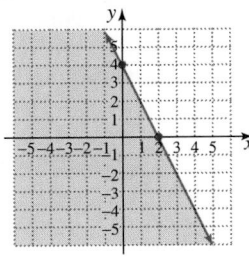

55. $2x + y \leqslant 4$

58. $x < 1$

56. $x + y \geqslant 3$

59. $y \geqslant 3x$

57. $y < 1$

60. $y \geqslant 2x$

Application Problems

61. A meal is to consist of fish and salad. Each serving of fish contain 75 calories and each serving of salad contains 50 calories.
   a. Express the number of calories in x servings of fish.
   b. Express the number of calories in y servings of salad.
   c. Suppose that the combined number of calories from x servings of fish and y servings of salad must exceed 300 calories. Express this condition as a linear inequality in x and y.
   d. Graph the linear inequality of part (c). (Remember that $x \geqslant 0$ and $y \geqslant 0$.)
   e. Give two ordered pairs that satisfy the inequality and describe what they mean in the context of this problem.

62. A student works at two part-time jobs, one paying $8 an hour and the other paying $12 a hour.
   a. Express the amount earned at the job paying $8 an hour when the student works for x hours.
   b. Express the amount earned at the job paying $12 an hour when the student works for y hours.
   c. The student wants to earn at least $48 a week. Express this condition as a linear inequality in x and y.
   d. Graph the linear inequality of part (c). (Remember that $x \geqslant 0$ and $y \geqslant 0$.)
   e. Give two ordered pairs that satisfy the inequality and describe what they mean in the context of this problem.

True–False Critical Thinking Problems

63. Which one of the following is true?
   a. The ordered pair $(0, -3)$ satisfies $y > 2x - 3$.
   b. The graph of $x < y + 1$ is the half-plane below the boundary line $x = y + 1$.
   c. In graphing $y \geqslant 4x$, a dashed boundary line is used.
   d. The graph of $x < 4$ is the half-plane to the left of the vertical line described by $x = 4$.

64. Which one of the following is true?
   a. The ordered pair $(2, -3)$ satisfies $3x - 2y > 12$.
   b. The graph of $y \geqslant 4$ is the half-plane above the horizontal line described by $y = 4$.
   c. The graph of $y > x + 7$ is the half-plane above the boundary line $y = x + 7$.
   d. The graph of $x = 4$ is a single point on the x-axis.

Technology Problems

Graphing utilities have a SHADE *feature that enables you to shade regions in the plane, thereby graphing inequalities in two variables. For example, the graph of $y \geqslant 3x - 7$, obtained on a graphing utility, is shown below.*

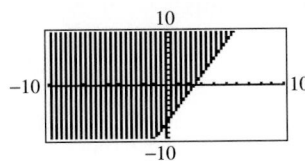

(Note: Many graphing utilities will not draw excluded lines as dashed lines, so you still must have an understanding of what the solution does and does not include.) See the shade instructions in your manual and use your graphing utility to graph each of the inequalities in Problems 65–68.

65. $y \leqslant -3x + 4$ **66.** $y \geqslant x - 2$ **67.** $y \geqslant \frac{1}{2}x + 4$ **68.** $y \leqslant -\frac{1}{2}x + 4$

69. Use a graphing utility to graph $y = 2(2x + 1) - 3x$ in a standard viewing rectangle.

   a. Use the ⃞TRACE feature to find the *x*-intercept.

   b. Solve the equation: $2(2x + 1) - 3x = 0$. What do you observe about the equation's solution and the *x*-intercept of $y = 2(2x + 1) - 3x$? Explain your observation.

   c. Use the graph generated by the graphing utility to solve $2(2x + 1) - 3x > 0$.

   d. Use the graph generated by the graphing utility to solve $2(2x + 1) - 3x < 0$.

70. a. Solve for *y* and use a graphing utility to sketch the graph of $2y + x = 4$.

   b. Your graph in part (a) should appear as shown below. Use the graph to find the solution set for $-\frac{1}{2}x + 2 \geqslant 0$.

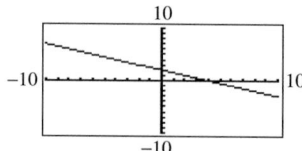

Writing in Mathematics

71. Describe the graph of a linear inequality in two variables.

72. How does one decide whether to use a solid line or a dashed line in graphing a linear inequality in two variables?

73. What is a test point? How is a test point used to graph a linear inequality in two variables?

74. Compare the graphs of $3x - y > 6$ and $3x - 2y \leqslant 6$. Discuss similarities and differences between the graphs.

75. Write a paragraph explaining how to graph $2x - 3y \leqslant 6$.

Critical Thinking Problems

76. Translate the following conditions into a linear inequality in two variables. Then graph the inequality.

Five times the x-coordinate minus ten times the y-coordinate is at most 20.

Write an inequality that represents each graph in Problems 77–78.

77.

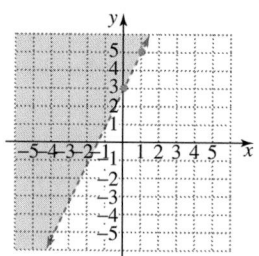

78.

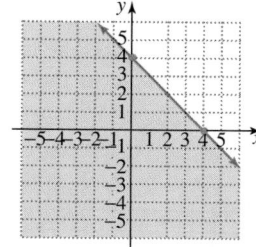

79. Graph $xy \leqslant 0$. Try using a number of different test points.

Review Problems

80. Multiply: $-\frac{7}{8}\left(-\frac{4}{15}\right)$.

81. Simplify: $-10 + 16 \div 2(-4)$.

82. Graph on a number line: $-2 \leqslant x < 4$.

CHAPTER PROJECT

Interpreting Graphs

Each graph in this chapter suggests a story, just as a painting may suggest a story. Whether we look at a graph on a graphing calculator or on a piece of paper sketched by hand, we are seeing a picture of the relationship between two quantities. For example, in the graph in Figure 4.50, if the horizontal axis is labeled in units of time, the graph is showing that something increases over time, stays the same for a while, then decreases as more time passes. If the vertical axis were also labeled, we could be more specific in our interpretation.

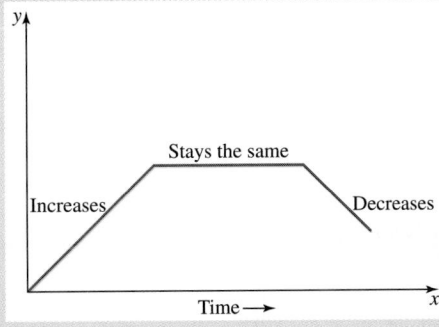

Figure 4.50

Reading a graph to discover information is an important skill. There are many ways to create a graph using computers or graphing calculators, but only a human observer has the ability to look at an abstract collection of line segments or curves and interpret that information. How any particular graph is interpreted depends on the quantities being graphed. In the graph in Figure 4.51, if the horizontal axis is labeled as time and the vertical axis is labeled as the temperature of a pizza, we can interpret the graph as showing the relationship between time and temperature as a pizza is cooked and then eaten.

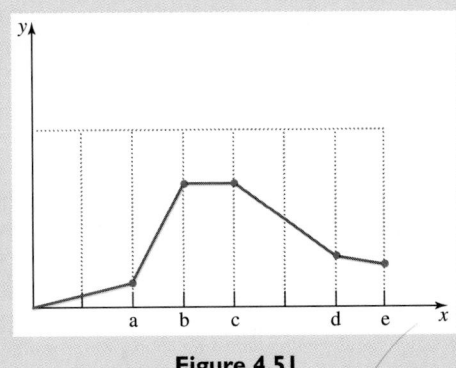

Figure 4.51

0–a: The frozen pizza is sitting on the counter as the oven is preheated. (The pizza warms slightly as it sits on the counter.)

a–b: The pizza is placed in the oven and its temperature gradually rises to match the temperature of the oven.

b–c: The pizza is still in the oven, cooking now at the oven temperature.

c–d: The pizza comes out of the oven and you start to eat. (The pizza cools as you eat.)

d–e: The pizza cools to room temperature (if you haven't eaten it all).

If we keep the same graph but label the axes as heart rate or pulse vs. time, we may be looking at a graph describing a morning jog.

0–a: You wake up and get dressed to go jogging.

a–b: You begin to jog, starting out slowly to warm up, gradually increasing your pace.

b–c: You reach your usual pace and jog for a bit at this rate.

c–d: You gradually slow down and return to your house to do a few stretches and cool down.

d–e: You shower and get dressed.

For this project you will be creating your own graphs and interpreting the graphs of others. You will not be using your algebra skills or technology to *create* these graphs; however, you should try to make them as precise as possible so they may be analyzed mathematically after you have completed them. Keep in mind you may also use negative numbers.

1. Sketch a graph of a personal experience that involved love, anger, sadness, or any other emotion you choose. Remember to clearly label your axes with the two quantities you are comparing. For example, the horizontal axis may be labeled *time* and the vertical axis *love*. Pool together all of the graphs from the members of your class and study the graphs to see if there are any similarities in the graphs for a particular emotion or for all emotions.

2. Sketch a graph of something that occurs in cycles. This could be an action that can be observed in nature, such as rising and falling tides, or a pattern that is more personal, such as your daily routine for work or school. Include at least three complete cycles.

3. Working in a group, sketch at least two graphs that relate different quantities but describe the same activity. For example, if you graph a period of time during which you are waiting for an important phone call, one graph could be time vs. anxiety level, the other time vs. pulse rate. Compare and analyze the graphs you obtain.

4. Working in groups, make a graphical model of a book, TV show, movie, or play. Begin with a loose idea of what you will be modeling, such as characters or plot. All members of the group should prepare a graph comparing *different* quantities. Compare the graphs and analyze how they all reflect your common experience. Decide if someone outside your group would be able to interpret them.

5. After the class has had time to prepare and analyze a number of graphs, discuss the limitations you found when trying to present information in graphical form. What were the advantages and disadvantages of presenting information with graphs? Choose at least one graph and try to write a set of algebraic equations to match it. Do the equations give you any different information?

Worldwide Web Resources

Go to the Prentice Hall website (http://www.prenhall.com/blitzer) to access other locations on the Internet that will allow you to further explore the concepts presented in this project.

Chapter Review

SUMMARY

1. Linear Equations in Two Variables: $Ax + By = C$ (A and B Not Both Zero)

The ordered pair (x_1, y_1) is a solution if the equation $Ax + By = C$ is true when x_1 is substituted for x and y_1 is substituted for y. We say then that (x_1, y_1) satisfies the equation.

2. Graphing a Linear Equation in Two Variables

  a. To graph $Ax + By = C$, where $C \neq 0$, find the x-intercept (let $y = 0$; solve for x), find the y-intercept (let $x = 0$; solve for y), find a third checkpoint, and draw a line that passes through these points.

  b. To graph $Ax + By = 0$, use the origin and any two other points (any two ordered pairs satisfying the equation), drawing a line that passes through these points.

  c. The graph of $x = a$ is a vertical line parallel to the y-axis that intersects the x-axis at a. The graph of $x = 0$ is the y-axis.

  d. The graph of $y = b$ is a horizontal line parallel to the x-axis that intersects the y-axis at b. The graph of $y = 0$ is the x-axis.

3. Graphs of Equations; Functions

  a. The graph of an equation involving two variables (usually x and y) is the set of all points whose coordinates are solutions of the equation.

  b. y is a function of x if for every value of x there is determined at most one value of y.

  c. *Function notation:* The notation $y = f(x)$ indicates that the variable y is a function of x. The notation $f(x)$ is read "f of x."

4. Slope

  a. Slope is designated by m and refers to the steepness of a line.

  b. The slope of a line between two points (x_1, y_1) and (x_2, y_2) is

$$m = \frac{\text{Rise}}{\text{Run}} = \frac{\text{Horizontal change}}{\text{Vertical change}} = \frac{y_2 - y_1}{x_2 - x_1} \qquad x_2 - x_1 \neq 0.$$

  c. The slope of any horizontal line is zero.

  d. Any vertical line has undefined slope.

  e. Lines with negative slope are decreasing (falling) from left to right.

  f. Lines with positive slope are increasing (rising) from left to right.

  g. If two lines are parallel, they have the same slope. If two distinct lines have the same slope, they are parallel.

5. Equations of Lines

  a. *Slope-intercept form:* $y = mx + b$
  m is the line's slope and b is its y-intercept.

  b. *Standard form:* $Ax + By = C$

  c. *Point-slope form:* $y - y_1 = m(x - x_1)$
  m is the line's slope and (x_1, y_1) is a fixed point on the line.

  d. *Horizontal line parallel to the x-axis:* $y = b$

  e. *Vertical line parallel to the y-axis:* $x = a$

6. Linear Inequalities in Two Variables (x and y)

  a. A linear inequality in two variables can be written in the form $Ax + By > C$, or $Ax + By \geq C$, or $Ax + By < C$, or $Ax + By \leq C$ (A and B not both zero).

  b. An ordered pair (x_1, y_1) is a solution of an inequality if the inequality is true when x_1 is substituted for x and y_1 is substituted for y. Then (x_1, y_1) satisfies the inequality.

  c. To graph a linear inequality, draw the graph of $Ax + By = C$, the boundary line, using a solid line for $\geq$ and $\leq$ and a dashed line for $>$ and $<$. Then choose a test point in one of the half-planes, making sure the test point is not on the line. Substitute the coordinates of the test point into the inequality. If a true statement results, shade the half-plane containing this test point. If a false statement results, shade the half-plane not containing this test point.

  d. The graph of $x > a$ is the half-plane to the right of $x = a$ (a vertical line). The graph of $x < a$ is the half-plane to the left of $x = a$.

  e. The graph of $y > b$ is the half-plane above $y = b$ (a horizontal line). The graph of $y < b$ is the half-plane below $y = b$.

  f. To graph a linear inequality in the form $y > mx + b$, $y < mx + b$, $y \geq mx + b$, or $y \leq mx + b$, graph $y = mx + b$, the boundary line, using the y-intercept (b) and the slope (m). Then $y > mx + b$ is the half-plane above the line and $y < mx + b$ is the half-plane below the line.

REVIEW PROBLEMS

1. Which of the following ordered pairs are solutions of $3x - y = 12$?

$$(0, -12), (0, 4), (-1, 15), (-2, -18)$$

2. Complete the table of values on the next page for $y = -\frac{1}{2}x + 1$ and use the five ordered pairs that you calculate to graph the linear equation.

x	$y = -\frac{1}{2}x + 1$	(x, y)
-4		
-2		
0		
2		
4		

3. a. Solve the equation $x - 2y = 4$ for y.
   b. Write the equation in function notation.
   c. Graph the function.

4. The function $f(x) = 2.35x + 179.5$ models the population $(f(x)$, in millions) of the United States x years after 1960. Find and interpret $f(20)$.

5. Henry Schultz, an economist, formulated a price-demand function for sugar in the United States using the demand function $f(x) = -2.26x + 70.62$. In this function, x is the wholesale price (in cents) of one pound of sugar and $f(x)$ is the quantity (in millions) of one-pound bags of sugar purchased yearly at price x.

a. Find and interpret $f(10), f(20), f(50),$ and $f(100)$. (A calculator might be useful, but it is not a necessity.)
b. What appears to be happening to the demand for sugar as the price increases? In general, what is the relationship between the price of any product and the demand for that product?
c. Graph the linear function $f(x) = -2.26x + 70.62$ for $x \geqslant 10$ and $x \leqslant 100$ using the four ordered pairs computed in part (a). Choose a suitable scale on the vertical axis. How does the graph visually show the relationship between price and demand?
d. If you are using a graphing utility as part of this course, use your graphing utility to verify your graph in part (c).

6. A car travels at a speed of 30 miles per hour for t hours. The distance that the car travels in t hours is given by the model $d = 30t$.
a. Use the mathematical model to estimate the distance covered in 1 hour, 2 hours, 2.5 hours, and 4 hours.
b. Graph the model with values of t along the x-axis and values of d along the y-axis.

Graph each linear equation in Problems 7–12.

7. $2x + y = 4$

8. $3x - 2y = 12$

9. $3x = 6 - 2y$

10. $3x - y = 0$

11. $x = 3$

12. $2y = -10$

13. The salary (S) received by a salesperson is $200 per week plus a 10% commission of all sales (x).
   a. Write an equation that models the weekly salary S in terms of sales x.
   b. Find the salary for weekly sales of $0, $10,000, $20,000, and $30,000. Use these computations to graph the model that you wrote in part (a).
   c. Use your graph to estimate the weekly salary for sales of $6000.
   d. Use your graph to estimate the sales needed to generate a weekly salary of $1700.

14. A car rental company charges $30 per day plus $0.25 per mile.
   a. Write an equation that models the daily cost (C) for renting the car if x miles are to be driven.
   b. Find the daily rental cost for driving 100 miles, 200 miles, 300 miles, 400 miles, and 500 miles. Use these computations to graph the model that you wrote in part (a).
   c. Use the graph to estimate the rental charge for driving 350 miles per day.
   d. Use the graph to estimate the number of miles driven if the daily rental cost is $100.

In Problems 15–16, fill in the table of values and then graph the function.

15. $y = x^2 - 2$

x	$y = x^2 - 2$	(x, y)
-3		
-2		
-1		
0		
1		
2		
3		

16. $f(x) = x^2 + 2x + 1$

x	$f(x) = x^2 + 2x + 1$	(x, y)
-3		
-2		
-1		
0		
1		
2		

17. The function $f(x) = 2x^2 + 22x + 320$ models the number of inmates in federal and state prisons in the United States ($f(x)$, in thousands) x years after 1980.
  a. Find and interpret $f(5)$.
  b. Use the function to predict the number of inmates in the year 2010.

18. The function $f(x) = -0.0013x^3 + 0.078x^2 - 1.43x + 18.1$ models the percent of families below the poverty level x years after 1960. Find and interpret $f(10)$.

19. The linear function $f(x) = 4.98x - 41.34$ describes the percentage of American adults doing volunteer work as a function of their educational level (x). Find and interpret $f(10)$, $f(12)$, $f(14)$, and $f(16)$. Again, a calculator might be helpful, but is not a necessity. Once these computations have been performed, describe how well the function models the real world data shown in the table.

x (Years of Education)	10	12	14	16
y (Percentage Doing Volunteer Work)	8.3%	18.8%	28.1%	38.4%

Data Source: U.S. Bureau of Labor

20. The graph at the top of the next column indicates the Fahrenheit temperature x hours after noon.
  a. At what time did the minimum temperature occur? What is the minimum temperature?
  b. At what time did the maximum temperature occur? What is the maximum temperature?
  c. What are the x-intercepts? In terms of time and temperature, interpret the meaning of these intercepts.
  d. What is the y-intercept? What does this mean in terms of time and temperature?
  e. If the function is represented by f, use the graph to find $f(8) - f(7)$. What does this number mean in terms of time and temperature?

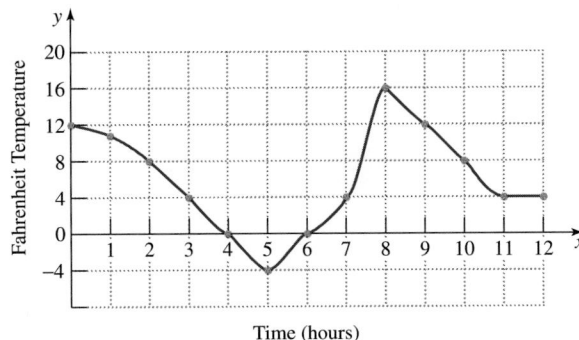

Time (hours)

21. The figure below shows the average age of the U.S. population. Let

$$x = \text{the number of years after 1980}$$

$$f(x) = \text{the average age of the U.S. population in year } x$$

Use the graph to estimate and interpret:
  a. $f(10)$ **b.** $f(50)$ **c.** $f(80)$
  d. Describe the trend shown by the function's graph.

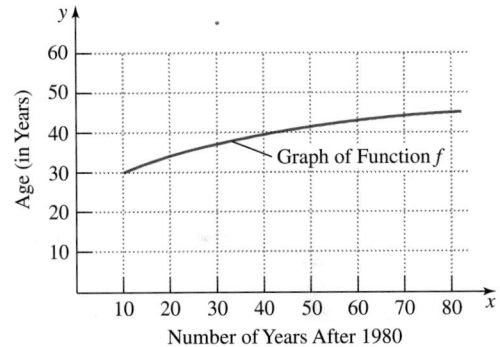

Number of Years After 1980

Source: U.S. Bureau of the Census

In Problems 22–25, find the slope of the line connecting the points with the given coordinates. Indicate whether the line through the pair of points rises, falls, is horizontal, or is vertical.

22. $(3, 2), (5, 1)$ **23.** $(-1, -2), (-3, -4)$ **24.** $(-3, \frac{1}{4}), (6, \frac{1}{4})$ **25.** $(-2, 5), (-2, 10)$

26. Use the coordinates of the indicated points to find the slope of the line in the figure.

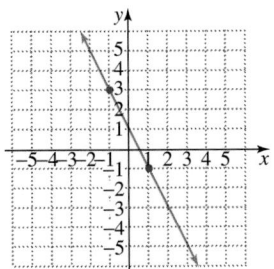

27. The pitch (slope) of the roof shown in the figure is $\frac{1}{6}$. What is the measurement indicated by x?

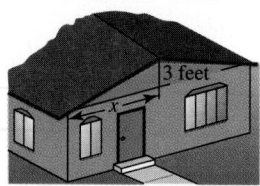

28. The graph shows the average salary of public school teachers in the United States from 1985 through 1995. Find the slope of the line, using the points for the years 1988 and 1995. Describe what the slope represents.

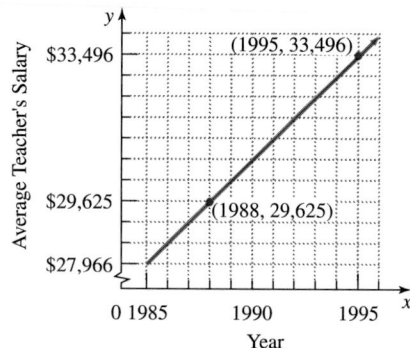

Year

29. The graph is based on a study of the percentage of professional works completed in each age of life by 738 men who lived to be at least 79. Use the graph to answer the following questions.

a. At approximately what age did productivity peak for men in all disciplines?

b. For men in the arts, estimate the average rate of change in the percentage of works completed from age 20 to age 30.

c. Repeat part (b) for men in the sciences from age 60 to age 70. Why is the slope negative? What does this mean in terms of professional productivity?

d. Identify a line segment in the graph with a slope that is approximately 0. Describe what this means in terms of age, discipline, and professional productivity.

e. For what discipline did professional output remain strong from age 60 to age 70?

f. What line segment shown in the graph has a negative slope whose absolute value is greater than that of any of the other negative slopes? What is a reasonable estimate for the slope of this line segment? Describe what this means in terms of age, discipline, and professional productivity.

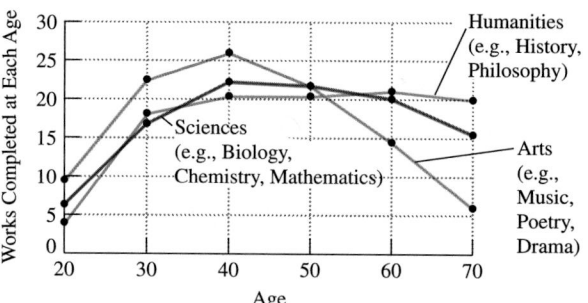

Source: Dennis, W. (1966). "Creative productivity between the ages of 20 and 80 years." *Journal of Gerontology*, 21, 1–8

Find the slope and the y-intercept for the line described by each equation in Problems 30–32.

30. $y = 5x - 7$

31. $y = -8 - 9x$

32. $2x + 3y = -6$

Write the slope-intercept equation for each line in Problems 33–34.

33. Slope -5; y-intercept 3

34. Slope $-\frac{1}{2}$; y-intercept -2

In Problems 35–36, use the graph to write the slope-intercept equation of the line.

35.

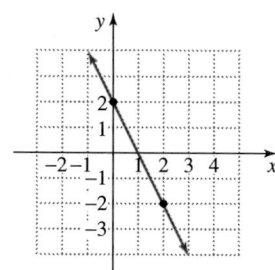

36.

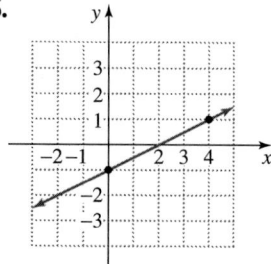

Use the y-intercept and the slope to graph the line described by the equations in Problems 37–39.

37. $y = 2x - 4$

38. $y = -\frac{2}{3}x + 5$

39. $y = \frac{3}{4}x - 2$

40. Graph the lines of the given equations on the same set of axes.

$$y = -\frac{1}{3}x + 4$$
$$y = -\frac{1}{3}x - 1$$

Why are the lines parallel?

41. The model $y = 3.657x + 14.784$ describes the number of cable television subscribers (y, in millions) x years after 1980.

a. What is the y-intercept for this model? Describe what the y-intercept represents in terms of the variables in the model.

b. What is the slope for this model? What does this number mean?

42. In 1960 the United States generated 87.1 million tons of solid waste. This amount has increased by approximately 3.14 million tons each year.

a. Let x represent the number of years since 1960 and let y represent millions of tons of solid waste generated. Write the slope-intercept equation that models this situation.

b. How many million tons of solid waste will the United States generate in the year 2000?

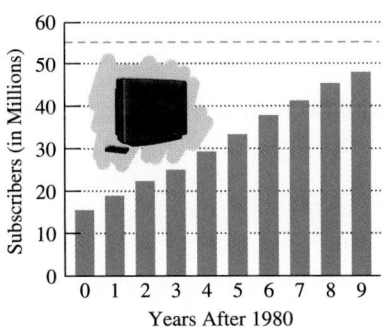

Source: *Television and Cable Fact Book*

Write the point-slope form of the line satisfying the conditions in Problems 43–45. Then use the point-slope form of the equation to write the slope-intercept form.

43. Slope $= 6$, passing through $(-4, 7)$

44. Passing through $(3, 4)$ and $(2, 1)$

45. Passing through $(-2, -3)$ and $(4, -1)$

46. A physiologist interested in predicting adult height from child height recorded the data shown in the table.

	Person 1	Person 2
x (Height in Inches of a 2-Year-Old Child)	31	38
y (Height in Inches of Same Person as an Adult)	61	75

The variables x and y have a linear relationship, meaning that $(31, 61)$ and $(38, 75)$ are points that lie along a line.

a. Find the slope of this line.

b. Use either ordered pair and write the point-slope equation of the line.

c. Use the point-slope equation to write the slope-intercept form of the equation.

d. Use the equation in part (c) to answer this question. What adult height does the model predict for a 2-year-old child whose height is 36 inches?

47. Which of the following ordered pairs are solutions of $3x - 4y > 7$?

$$(0, 0), (-2, -1), (-2, -5), (-3, 4), (3, -6)$$

Graph each inequality in Problems 48–55.

48. $x - 2y > 6$

49. $4x - 6y \leq 12$

50. $x + 2y \leq 0$

51. $y > 3x + 2$

52. $y \leq \frac{1}{3}x + 2$

53. $y < -\frac{1}{2}x$

54. $x < 4$

55. $y \geq -2$

CHAPTER 4 TEST

1. Solve $x + 2y = 6$ for y and write the equation in function notation.

2. The function $f(x) = 0.43x + 30.86$ models the number of married women in the United States in the civilian work force, $f(x)$, in millions, where x represents the number of years after 1990. Find and interpret $f(7)$.

Graph each linear equation in the rectangular coordinate system.

4. $4x - 2y = -8$ **5.** $2y = -6$

6. A car that is purchased for $12,000 has a loss in value of $1250 per year. Write an equation that models the value, V, of the car after x years.

7. The graph of the model in Problem 6 is shown in the accompanying figure. Use the graph to determine the car's value after 4 years.

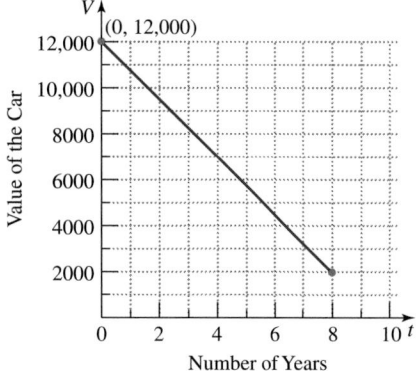

8. Fill in the table of values and then sketch the graph of the function $f(x) = 2 - x^2$.

x	$f(x) = 2 - x^2$	(x, y)
-3		
-2		
-1		
0		
1		
2		
3		

9. A ball is thrown directly upward from a height of 10 meters. The figure at the top of the next column shows the height of the ball, with

x = the number of seconds the ball is in motion

$f(x)$ = the ball's height, in meters, above the ground

3. The function $f(x) = 0.002x^2 + 0.41x + 7.34$ models the percent of the population in the United States that graduated from college, where x represents the number of years after 1960. Find and interpret $f(30)$.

a. After how long did the ball reach its maximum height above the ground? What is its maximum height?

b. Find and interpret $f(4.5)$.

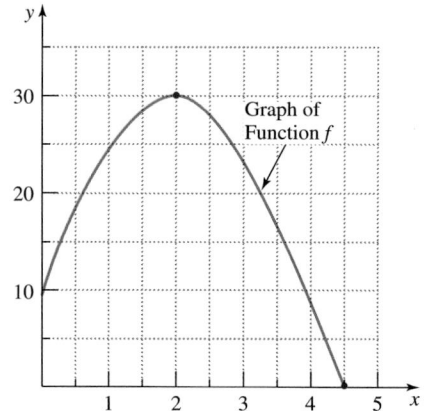

10. Find the slope of the line connecting the points $(-3, 4)$ and $(-5, -2)$.

11. Use the coordinates of the indicated points to find the slope of the line in the figure shown.

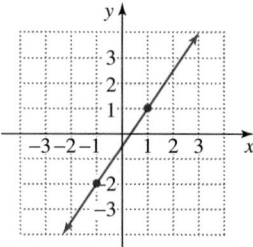

12. Find the slope and y-intercept for the line whose equation is $3x + 2y = 8$.

Graph each linear equation in the rectangular coordinate system.

13. $y = \frac{2}{3}x - 1$

14. $y = -2x + 3$

15. Write the slope-intercept equation for the line with slope -6 and y-intercept 4.

16. The model $y = 89x + 3231$ describes the population y, in thousands, of Arizona x years after 1985.

a. What is the y-intercept for this model? Describe what this number represents in terms of the variables in the model.

b. What is the slope for this model? What does this number mean in terms of Arizona's population?

Write the point-slope form of the line satisfying the following conditions. Then use the point-slope form of the equation to write the slope-intercept form.

17. Slope $= \frac{1}{2}$, passing through $(-2, 3)$

18. Passing through $(1, -2)$ and $(3, -8)$

Graph each linear inequality in the rectangular coordinate system.

19. $2x - y \geq 4$

20. $y < 2x - 2$

CUMULATIVE REVIEW PROBLEMS (CHAPTERS 1–4)

1. Perform the indicated operations: $\dfrac{5(-3) - 3(-4)}{5(-10) + 2}$.

2. Solve: $3(y + 1) + 11 = 16 + 5y$.

3. Solve: $\frac{1}{4}y + \frac{2}{3}y = \frac{1}{6}$.

4. Solve and graph the solution set on a number line:

$$-7(2y + 1) > 4(3 - y) + 1.$$

5. After a 35% price reduction, a VCR sold for $185.25. What was the price before the reduction?

6. The model $y = 4.5x - 46.7$ estimates the stopping distance (y, in feet) for a vehicle traveling at x miles per hour, where $x \geq 10$ and $x \leq 60$. If the stopping distance is 133.3 feet, how fast was the vehicle traveling?

7. Shopping by computer is projected to generate $6.6 billion dollars in revenues by the year 2000. Use the circle graph to determine the revenue amount for adult entertainment.

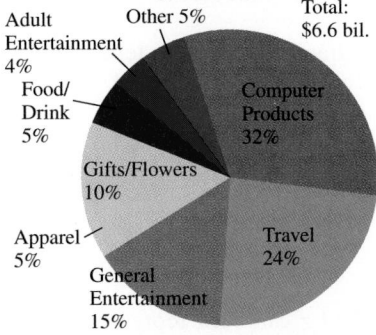

Projected Web Shopping Revenues by Sector/ Industry, Year 2000

Total: $6.6 bil.

Adult Entertainment 4%
Other 5%
Food/ Drink 5%
Computer Products 32%
Gifts/Flowers 10%
Apparel 5%
Travel 24%
General Entertainment 15%

Source: *U.S. News and World Report*

8. Fertility has declined throughout the industrialized world and is highest in Africa. The average number of children per woman in Africa is four greater than that in Europe. The average number of children per woman in Latin America is double that in Europe. If these average numbers are combined, the sum is 12. Find the average number of children per woman in Europe, Africa, and Latin America. Use the graph to estimate the numbers, to the nearest tenth, for the Middle East, Asia, the Caribbean, the United States, Canada, and the world.

Fertility Rates

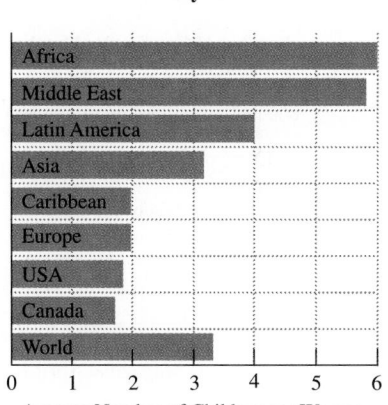

Average Number of Children per Woman

9. Find the height of the tree shown in the figure.

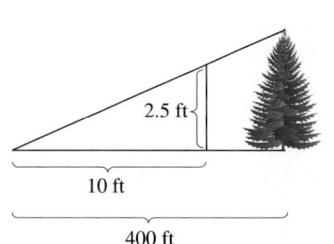

2.5 ft

10 ft

400 ft

10. A plumber charged a customer $228, listing $18 for parts and the remainder for labor. If the cost of the labor is $35 per hour, how many hours did the plumber work?

11. In 1963, U.S. athlete Robert Hayes broke a world record during a 100-yard sprint. His average running speed was 29 miles per hour less than the average running speed of a cheetah. The sum of their average running speeds exceeds the solution of $3x + 5 = 242$ by 4. At what speed did Robert Hayes run when he broke the world record?

12. Solve the proportion: $\dfrac{135}{6} = \dfrac{360}{x}$.

13. Find the measure of an angle if the sum of the measures of its supplement and its complement is 114°.

14. The function $f(x) = 9.2x^2 - 46.7x + 480$ describes the national debt ($f(x)$, in billions of dollars) x years after 1970. Find $f(10)$ and describe what this means.

15. Use the slope and y-intercept to graph the line whose equation is $y = -3x + 2$.

16. Since the U.S. military's "don't ask, don't tell" policy went into effect in 1993, the number of dismissals of gay service members has gone down, but so has the military population. Use the graph to find a reasonable estimate for the ratio of dismissals to total active troops for the years 1989 and 1994. What conclusion can you draw about the "don't ask, don't tell" policy?

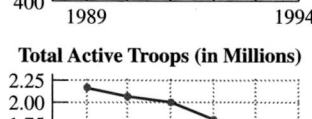

Number of Gay Service Members Discharged

Total Active Troops (in Millions)

Source: *Time Magazine*, April 10, 1995

17. A square and an equilateral triangle have the same perimeter. If each side of the triangle is 6 decimeters longer than each side of the square, find the length of each side of the triangle.

18. The mathematical model $T = \frac{1}{4}C + 37$ reflects the ability of crickets to indicate the temperature. In the model, C represents the number of cricket chirps per minute and T represents the temperature in degrees Fahrenheit.
    a. Complete the table.

C	0	4	8	12	16
T					

   b. Use the table to graph $T = \frac{1}{4}C + 37$, graphing values of C along the x-axis and values of T along the y-axis.

19. Solve for L: $P = 2L + 2W$.

20. Write the point-slope form of the line passing through $(1, 3)$ and $(3, 5)$. Then use the point-slope form of the equation to write the slope-intercept form and the standard form.

21. Graph: $3x - 4y > 12$.

22. The graph shows the average amount that each person paid in taxes in the United States from 1960 through 1993.
    a. What is a reasonable estimate for per capita income tax in 1985?
    b. In what year was per capita income tax approximately $1500?
    c. What is unusual about the way the numbers on the horizontal axis appear? How might this create a false impression in terms of identifying the year in which per capita income tax increased most rapidly?

Per Capita Income Tax, 1960–1993

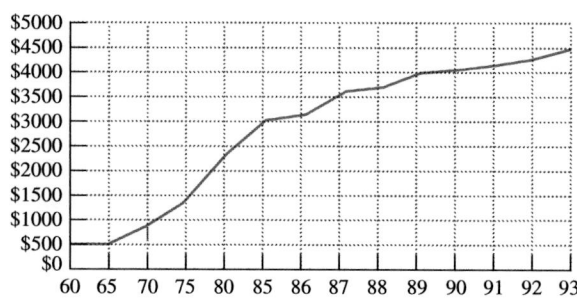

Source: Internal Revenue Service

23. Write a fraction in lowest terms that represents the part of the figure that is shaded.

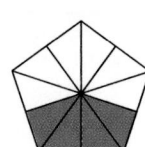

24. If x, y, and z can each represent 2, 3, 6, or 12, select values of x, y, and z such that $\dfrac{xy}{z} = 4$. Each number should be used only once.

25. The area of a triangular lot is 150 square yards. If the height is 20 yards, find the base of the lot.

26. Graph $y = x^2 + 2x + 2$ by first completing the table of values.

x	$y = x^2 + 2x + 2$	(x, y)
-3		
-2		
-1		
0		
1		
2		

27. The graph indicates the decrease in the number of hectares of the tropical forests of the world from 1980 through 1992 (1 hectare = 10,000 square meters). Find the slope of the line through the points (1980, 1080) and (1992, 1006). Describe what your computation means in terms of the average rate of change in the forest area from 1980 through 1992.

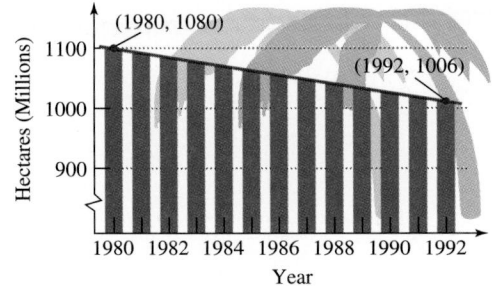

28. Two people leave by car from the same point of departure and travel uniformly in opposite directions. If one car travels at 40 miles per hour and the other car at 60 miles per hour, in how many hours will the cars be 350 miles apart?

29. Use the circle graph to estimate, to the nearest whole percent, the percent of incoming freshmen who anticipate majoring in business.

Anticipated Majors of Incoming Freshmen

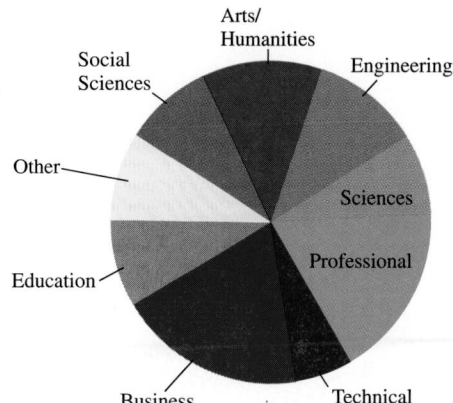

30. Find the next number in each group of numbers.
  a. 6, 10, 15, 21, 28, ___?___
  b. 1, 4, 9, 16, 25, ___?___

Systems of Linear Equations and Inequalities

Mathematical models often have thousands of equations, sometimes a million variables. Problems ranging from scheduling airline flights to controlling traffic flow to routing phone calls over the nation's communication network often require solutions in a matter of moments. AT&T's domestic long distance network involves 800,000 variables. Meteorologists modeling atmospheric conditions surrounding a hurricane must solve huge systems rapidly and efficiently. The difference between a two-hour warning and a two-day warning is a life-and-death issue for thousands of people in the path of one of nature's most destructive forces.

Before dealing with systems containing 800,000 variables, we will turn our attention to systems of two equations in two variables. The three methods that we consider in this chapter for solving such systems provide the foundation for solving far more complex systems with far more variables.

Roger Brown "Tropical Storm" 1972, oil on canvas, 72 × 48 in. Photo courtesy Phyllis Kind Gallery, New York and Chicago.

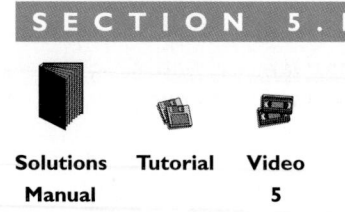

Solutions   Tutorial   Video
Manual   5

SECTION 5.1

Solving Systems of Linear Equations by Graphing

Objectives

1 Determine whether an ordered pair is a solution to a system of equations.
2 Solve a system of two equations in two variables by graphing.
3 Use graphing to identify systems that have no solution and systems with infinitely many solutions.

---

1 Determine whether an ordered pair is a solution to a system of equations.

Descartes' analytic geometry connected every linear equation in two variables with a geometric picture, namely, a line. In this section, we will see what two linear equations in two variables have in common by finding the point of intersection for two lines.

We have seen that the graph of a linear equation in two variables is a straight line. Points along the line represent ordered pairs that are solutions of the equation. We now turn our attention to a *system* of two equations in two variables. The following are examples of such systems.

$$\begin{cases} 2x + y = 8 \\ x - y = 2 \end{cases} \quad \begin{cases} y = x + 1 \\ y = 3x - 1 \end{cases} \quad \begin{cases} x = 5 \\ 2x - y = 4 \end{cases}$$

> A *solution* of a system of two equations in two variables is an ordered pair (a, b) that satisfies both equations in the system.

EXAMPLE 1   Checking Solutions of a System of Linear Equations

Consider the following system of linear equations.

$$3x + 2y = 6 \qquad \text{Equation 1}$$
$$3x - 4y = 24 \qquad \text{Equation 2}$$

Is either of the given ordered pairs a solution to this system of linear equations?

a. $(0, 3)$ **b.** $(4, -3)$

Solution

a. To decide whether $(0, 3)$ is a solution of the system, we substitute the coordinates into each equation.

$$3x + 2y = 6 \qquad \text{Equation 1}$$
$$3(0) + 2(3) \overset{?}{=} 6 \qquad \text{Is } (0, 3) \text{ a solution? Let } x = 0 \text{ and } y = 3.$$
$$6 = 6 \qquad \text{This true statement shows that } (0, 3) \text{ is a solution of Equation 1.}$$

$$3x - 4y = 24 \qquad \text{Equation 2}$$
$$3(0) - 4(3) \overset{?}{=} 24 \qquad \text{Is } (0, 3) \text{ a solution? Let } x = 0 \text{ and } y = 3.$$
$$-12 \neq 24 \qquad \text{This false statement shows that } (0, 3) \text{ is not a solution of Equation 2.}$$

Since the ordered pair $(0, 3)$ fails to satisfy *both* equations, it is not a solution of the given system of linear equations.

b. To decide whether $(4, -3)$ is a solution of the system, we substitute the coordinates into each equation.

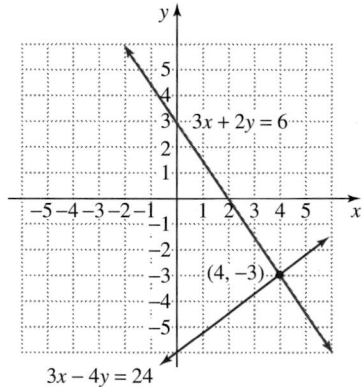

Figure 5.1

The solution to a system of equations

$$3x + 2y = 6 \quad \text{Equation 1}$$

$$3(4) + 2(-3) \overset{?}{=} 6 \quad \text{Is } (4, -3) \text{ a solution? Let } x = 4 \text{ and } y = -3.$$

$$12 + (-6) \overset{?}{=} 6$$

$$6 = 6 \quad \text{This true statement shows that } (4, -3) \text{ is a solution of Equation 1.}$$

$$3x - 4y = 24 \quad \text{Equation 2}$$

$$3(4) - 4(-3) \overset{?}{=} 24 \quad \text{Is } (4, -3) \text{ a solution? Let } x = 4 \text{ and } y = -3.$$

$$12 - (-12) \overset{?}{=} 24$$

$$24 = 24 \quad \text{This true statement shows } (4, -3) \text{ is a solution of Equation 2.}$$

Since the ordered pair $(4, -3)$ satisfies both equations, it is a solution of the given system of linear equations.

In Figure 5.1, the lines representing the two equations are graphed. Note that the solution, the ordered pair $(4, -3)$, is the intersection point of the two lines. ■

Our work in Example 1 brings forth the following very important idea.

> The solution to a system of two equations in two variables corresponds to the point(s) of intersection of their graphs.

2 Solve a system of two equations in two variables by graphing.

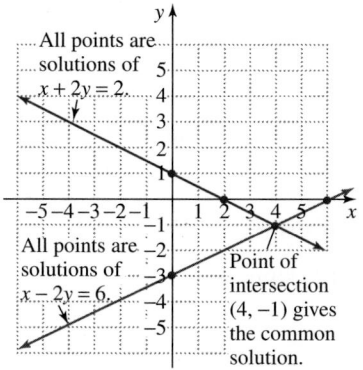

Figure 5.2

Visualizing a system's solution

EXAMPLE 2 **Solving a System by Graphing**

Solve the system by graphing both equations on the same axes:

$$x + 2y = 2$$
$$x - 2y = 6$$

Solution

$$x + 2y = 2 \quad x\text{-intercept } (y = 0): x = 2$$
$$y\text{-intercept } (x = 0): 2y = 2$$
$$y = 1$$

$$x - 2y = 6 \quad x\text{-intercept } (y = 0): x = 6$$
$$y\text{-intercept } (x = 0): -2y = 6$$
$$y = -3$$

The graphs of the equations are shown in Figure 5.2. We can see that they intersect at $(4, -1)$. Let us take a moment to check $(4, -1)$ in both equations.

Substitute into Equation 1: **Substitute into Equation 2:**

$$x + 2y = 2 \qquad\qquad x - 2y = 6$$
$$4 + 2(-1) \overset{?}{=} 2 \qquad 4 - 2(-1) \overset{?}{=} 6$$
$$4 + (-2) \overset{?}{=} 2 \qquad 4 - (-2) \overset{?}{=} 6$$
$$2 = 2 \checkmark \qquad\qquad 6 = 6 \checkmark$$

Because *both* equations are satisfied, $(4, -1)$ is the solution of the system. ■

We can generalize the procedure of Example 2, obtaining a step-by-step method for solving a linear system by graphing.

Must two lines intersect at exactly one point? Sketch two lines that have less than one intersection point. Now sketch two lines that have more than one intersection point. What does this say about each of these systems?

Solving systems of two linear equations in two variables (*x* and *y*) by graphing

1. Graph the first equation.
2. Graph the second equation on the same axes.
3. If the lines representing the two graphs intersect at a point, determine the coordinates of this point of intersection. The ordered pair is the solution to the system.
4. Check the solution in both equations.

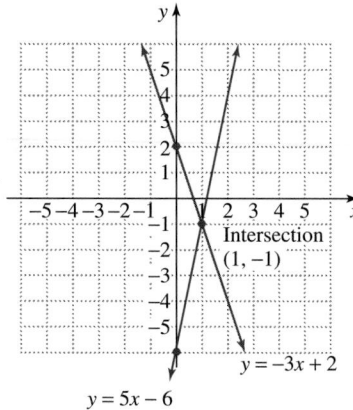

Figure 5.3

A system whose solution is $(1, -1)$

EXAMPLE 3   **Solving a System by Graphing**

Solve the system by graphing both equations on the same axes:

$$y = -3x + 2$$
$$y = 5x - 6$$

Solution

Since each equation is in the form $y = mx + b$, we can use the *y*-intercept (b) and the slope (m) to graph the lines.

$y = -3x + 2$ *y*-intercept $= 2$ and slope $= -\frac{3}{1}$
$y = 5x - 6$ *y*-intercept $= -6$ and slope $= \frac{5}{1}$

The graphs of the equations are shown in Figure 5.3. The lines intersect at $(1, -1)$. Check this solution in each equation.

Substitute into Equation 1:	**Substitute into Equation 2:**
$y = -3x + 2$	$y = 5x - 6$
$-1 \overset{?}{=} -3(1) + 2$	$-1 \overset{?}{=} 5(1) - 6$
$-1 = -1$ ✓	$-1 = -1$ ✓

Since $(1, -1)$ satisfies both equations, the solution to the system is $(1, -1)$. ∎

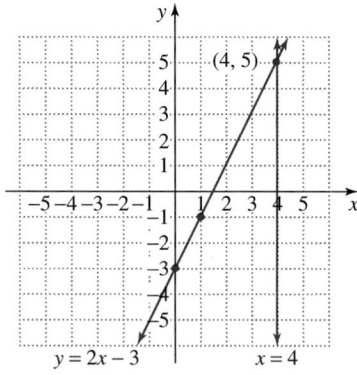

Figure 5.4

A system whose solution is $(4, 5)$

EXAMPLE 4   **Solving a System by Graphing**

Solve the system by graphing both equations on the same axes:

$$y = 2x - 3$$
$$x = 4$$

Solution

The graphs of the equations are shown in Figure 5.4. There, $y = 2x - 3$ is graphed by using *y*-intercept $= -3$ and slope $= \frac{2}{1}$. The graph of $x = 4$ is a vertical line parallel to the *y*-axis with *x*-intercept $= 4$.

The intersection occurs at $(4, 5)$ and this ordered pair can be shown to satisfy both equations in the system. The solution is $(4, 5)$. ∎

Use a method other than graphing to show that (4, 5) is the solution to Example 4.

3 Use graphing to identify systems that have no solution and systems with infinitely many solutions.

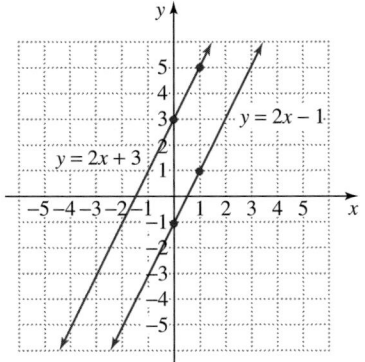

Figure 5.5

The graphs of a system with no solution

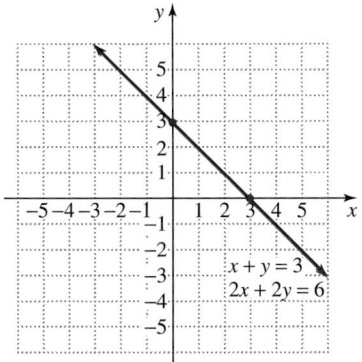

Figure 5.6

A system with infinitely many solutions

Discover for yourself

1. Use Figure 5.6 to find two points along the line. Show that both points are solutions to the system in Example 6.
2. Multiply both sides of the first equation in Example 6 by 2. What do you observe?

Inconsistent and Dependent Systems

In some systems the graphs of the two equations do not intersect because the lines are parallel.

EXAMPLE 5 A System of Linear Equations with No Solution

Solve the system by graphing both equations on the same axes:

$$y = 2x - 1$$
$$y = 2x + 3$$

Solution

The graphs of the equations are shown in Figure 5.5. Since $y = 2x - 1$ and $y = 2x + 3$ represent lines with y-intercepts of -1 and 3, respectively, but with the same slope, 2, the lines are parallel and do not intersect. The system has no ordered pair as a solution because the lines representing the equations in the system do not intersect. ∎

As we saw in Example 5, some systems have no solution; that is, there is no ordered pair that satisfies both equations. A linear system with no ordered pair satisfying both equations is called an *inconsistent system*.

Inconsistent systems

Linear systems with no solution are called *inconsistent systems*.

In some systems, the graphs of the two equations are the same line. All points on one line lie on the second line, and so all ordered pairs satisfying one equation in the system also satisfy the other equation in the system. Thus, the system has an infinite number of solutions.

EXAMPLE 6 A System of Linear Equations with Infinitely Many Solutions

Solve the system by graphing both equations on the same axes:

$$x + y = 3$$
$$2x + 2y = 6$$

Solution

As shown in Figure 5.6, the graphs of these two equations are the same line. (Both lines have x-intercept $= 3$ and y-intercept $= 3$.) The lines are said to coincide. Thus, the two equations have the same solutions. Any ordered pair that is a solution to one is a solution to the other, and, consequently, a solution to the system. The system has an infinite number of solutions, namely, all points that are solutions of either line. ∎

In the Discover for Yourself box, did you observe that by multiplying both sides of $x + y = 3$ by 2, you obtained $2x + 2y = 6$? This is the second equation in Example 6. Because $x + y = 3$ and $2x + 2y = 6$ are different forms of the same equation, these equations are called *dependent equations*.

Dependent systems

Linear systems whose graphs coincide have infinitely many solutions. All ordered pairs that satisfy either equation are solutions of the system. The equations in the system are called *dependent*.

We can now summarize the possibilities that can occur when solving a linear system involving two equations in two variables.

Study tip

In each of the three cases shown in the box, we can comment about the slopes and y-intercepts of the two equations in the system.

Case 1. Slopes are not equal.

Case 2. Slopes are equal, but y-intercepts are not equal.

Case 3. Slopes are equal and y-intercepts are equal.

Possibilities that can occur when two linear equations in two variables are graphed

1. The graphs intersect at one point. This ordered pair is the system's solution.

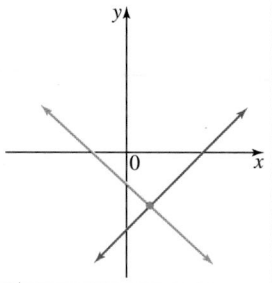

2. The graphs are parallel lines and the system has no solution. The system is inconsistent.

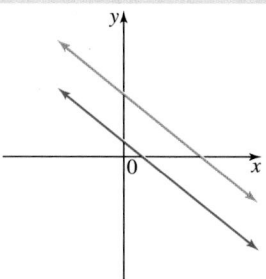

3. The graphs are the same line. The system equations has infinitely many solutions. The are dependent since the graphs are the same.

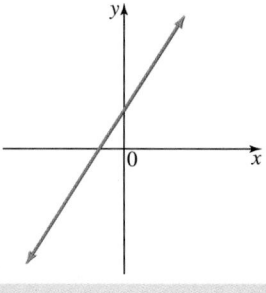

ENRICHMENT ESSAY

Dizzying Effects

Overwhelmed by intersecting lines? They may take on a new appeal if you focus on the nonintersecting curves in Bridget Riley's work. It illustrates the impact of our mental categories upon perception. The curves aren't moving, regardless of what your eyes tell you!

Bridget Riley "Cataract III" 1967 emulsion PVA on linen, 221.9×222.9 cm. British Council Collection. © Bridget Riley.

PROBLEM SET 5.1

Practice Problems

Decide whether the given ordered pair is the solution of the system in Problems 1–12.

1. $(2, 3)$
$x + 3y = 11$
$x - 5y = -13$

2. $(-3, 5)$
$9x + 7y = 8$
$8x - 9y = -69$

3. $(-3, -1)$
$5x - 11y = -4$
$6x - 8y = -10$

4. $(-2, 6)$
$7x + 3y = 4$
$8x + 7y = 26$

5. $(2, 5)$
$2x + 3y = 17$
$x + 4y = 16$

6. $(3, -1)$
$2x - y = 7$
$3x = 6$

7. $\left(\frac{1}{3}, 1\right)$
$6x - 9y = -7$
$9x + 5y = 8$

8. $\left(\frac{1}{3}, \frac{1}{2}\right)$
$15x + 4y = 7$
$6x + 14y = 9$

9. $(8, 5)$
$5x - 4y = 20$
$3y = 2x + 1$

10. $(5, -2)$
$4x - 3y = 26$
$x = 15 - 5y$

11. $(0, 5)$
$\frac{3}{5}x + \frac{2}{5}y = 2$
$y = 5$

12. $(1, 2)$
$\frac{1}{4}x - \frac{1}{2}y = -\frac{3}{4}$
$x = 1$

Solve each system in Problems 13–46 by graphing both equations on the same axes. If the system is inconsistent or the equations are dependent, state that.

13. $x + y = 6$
$x - y = 2$

14. $x + y = 2$
$x - y = 4$

15. $x + y = 1$
$y - x = 3$

16. $x + y = 4$
$y - x = 4$

17. $3x + y = 3$
$6x + 2y = 12$

18. $3x - y = 3$
$-x + y = -3$

19. $2x - 3y = 6$
$4x + 3y = 12$

20. $x + 2y = 2$
$x - y = 2$

21. $x + y = 5$
$-x - y = -6$

22. $x + y = 5$
$2x + 2y = 12$

23. $x - y = 2$
$3x - 3y = -6$

24. $2x + y = 4$
$-4x - 2y = -8$

25. $4x + y = 4$
$3x - y = 3$

26. $5x - y = 10$
$2x + y = 4$

27. $x + y = 4$
$x = -2$

28. $x + y = 6$
$y = -3$

29. $x = -3$
$y = 5$

30. $x = -2$
$y = 4$

31. $y = x + 5$
$y = -x + 3$

32. $y = x + 1$
$y = 3x - 1$

33. $y = 2x$
$y = -x + 6$

34. $y = -2x + 3$
$y = -x + 1$

35. $y = 3x - 4$
$y = -2x + 1$

36. $y = 2x + 1$
$y = -2x - 3$

37. $y = 2x - 1$
  $y = 2x + 1$

38. $y = 3x - 1$
  $y = 3x + 2$

39. $x - y = 0$
  $2x = 2y$

40. $2x - y = 0$
  $y = 2x$

41. $y = 2x - 1$
  $x - 2y = -4$

42. $y = -2x - 4$
  $4x - 2y = 8$

43. $y = \frac{1}{2}x - 1$
  $x - y = -1$

44. $y = \frac{1}{3}x + 2$
  $x + 3y = 0$

45. $x = 2$
  $x = -1$

46. $y = 3$
  $y = -2$

Application Problems

47. An artist has fixed costs of $20. The cost of producing each ceramic piece is $4, and the pieces sell for $9. Thus,

Cost for artist = Fixed cost + 4
  × Number of units produced

$$y = 20 + 4x$$

Revenue for artist = 9 × Number of units sold

$$y = 9x$$

The graphs of $y = 20 + 4x$ and $y = 9x$ are shown in the figure below. Answer the following questions about these graphs.

a. The artist breaks even when revenue from sales is equal to production cost. How many pieces must the artist sell to break even? How is this indicated by the graphs?

b. The artist makes a profit when the revenue from sales exceeds production cost. For what values of x does this occur?

c. What is the artist's loss if only two ceramic pieces are produced and sold?

d. What is the artist's profit if ten ceramic pieces are produced and sold?

48. An important economic application involving intersecting lines arises in connection with *the law of supply and demand.* As the price of an item increases, the demand for that item decreases. As the price of an item increases, the manufacturers are willing to supply more units of that item, so supply increases.

The figure below shows supply and demand lines for raincoats. The *x*-axis represents the number of raincoats (in hundreds). The *y*-axis represents the price per raincoat.

a. At what price per raincoat does supply equal demand?

b. When $x > 30$, does demand exceed supply or does supply exceed demand?

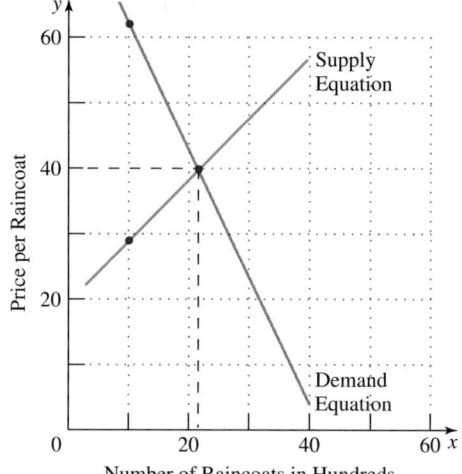

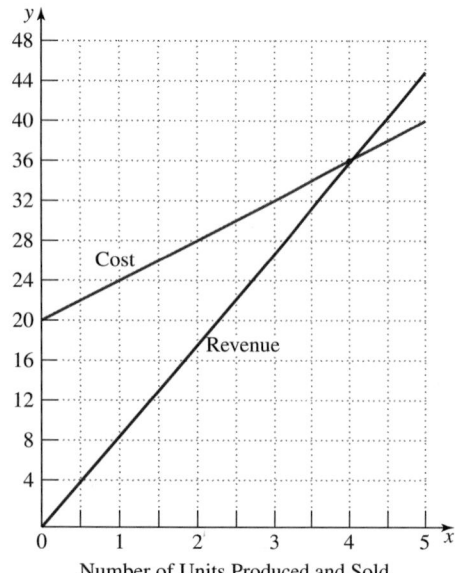

Number of Units Produced and Sold

True–False Critical Thinking Problems

49. Which one of the following statements is true?

a. The ordered pair $(2, 3)$ satisfies the system

$$3x - y = 3$$
$$-6x + 2y = -6$$

so $(2, 3)$ is the solution.

b. A system of two linear equations cannot have exactly two ordered-pair solutions.

c. The system

$$y = 3x - 1$$
$$y = -3x - 1$$

is an inconsistent system.

d. The ordered pair $(1, 4)$ is a solution to the system

$$2x + y = 6$$
$$x - y = 3$$

50. Which one of the following statements is true?

a. There is one ordered pair that satisfies the system

$$y = 3x + 5$$
$$y = 3x + 1$$

b. The ordered pair $(\frac{1}{5}, 10)$ is not a solution of the system

$$10x + 12y = 18$$
$$15x - 8y = -77$$

c. There is only one ordered pair that satisfies the system

$$y = 3x - 17$$
$$y = 3x + 5$$

d. If a system of linear equations has one solution, that solution cannot be $(0, 0)$.

51. Which one of the following statements is true?

a. If a system has graphs with equal slopes, the system must be inconsistent.

b. If a system has graphs with equal y-intercepts, the system must have infinitely many solutions.

c. If a system has two points that are solutions, then the graphs of the system's equations have equal slopes and equal y-intercepts.

d. It is possible for a system with one solution to have graphs with equal slopes.

Technology Problems

Use a graphing utility to solve the systems in Problems 52–55. After entering the two equations (one as y_1 and the other as y_2; if necessary, first solve the equation for y) and graphing them, use the $\boxed{\text{TRACE}}$ *and* $\boxed{\text{ZOOM}}$ *features to find the coordinates of the intersection point. Many graphing utilities have a special intersection feature that displays the coordinates of the intersection point once the equations are graphed; consult your manual.*

52. $y = 2x + 2$
$\quad\ y = -2x + 6$

53. $y = -x + 5$
$\quad\ y = x - 7$

54. $x + 2y = 2$
$\quad\ x - y = 2$

55. $2x - 3y = 6$
$\quad\ 4x + 3y = 12$

You can use a graphing utility (or graph by hand) to solve a linear equation such as $3x - 5 = 10 - 2x$. By graphing each side, namely $y_1 = 3x - 5$ and $y_2 = 10 - 2x$, the equation's solution corresponds to the value of x where the lines intersect. Using the $\boxed{\text{TRACE}}$ *or intersection feature of a graphing utility, the solution to $3x - 5 = 10 - 2x$ is 3, shown in the graph. Use this method to solve the equations in Problems 56–59. Check the solution by direct substitution.*

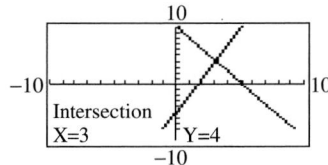

56. $2x - 4 = 3x - 9$

57. $2x - 3 - 5x = 13 + 4x - 2$

58. $3(x - 4) = 2(x - 8) + 5x$

59. $2x + 5 = 12 - 6x + 3(2x + 3)$

Writing in Mathematics

60. Explain how to decide if a given ordered pair is a solution to a system of two equations in two variables.

61. Explain how to use graphing to solve a system of two linear equations in two variables.

62. Why can't a system of two linear equations in two variables have only two or three ordered-pair solutions?

63. Describe the three possible outcomes that can occur when using graphing to solve two linear equations in two variables.

64. Describe the relationship between the slopes of two lines and the number of points of intersection.

Critical Thinking Problems

65. Graph $y = x^2$ and $y = x + 2$ on the same axes. Find two ordered pairs that satisfy the system. Check that your answers satisfy both equations in the system.

66. The solution to the following system is $(-1, 8)$. Find A and B.

$$Ax - y = -6$$
$$3x + By = 5$$

67. Write a system of linear equations whose solution is $(5, 1)$. How many different systems are possible? Explain.

68. Write a system of equations with one solution, a system of equations with no solution, and a system of equations with infinitely many solutions. Explain how you were able to think of these systems.

Group Activity Problems

69. Each member of the group should use graphing to solve the following system:

$$2x + 3y = -1$$
$$5x + 4y = 7$$

Have the group come together to present the solution. What weaknesses do the group members notice about the graphing method?

70. Create a system of linear equations and graph it. Label the intersection point, but do not write the equations of the lines on your graph. Give your graph to another member of the group, asking that person to provide the missing equations for the two lines. What conclusion can you draw?

Review Problems

71. Simplify: $3(y - 4) - (y + 7) - 2(3y - 6)$.

72. Solve for y: $6y - 2(y + 4) - 2y = -4(y - 1)$.

73. If five people produce 13 kilograms of garbage in 1 day, how many kilograms of garbage are produced in 1 day in a city of 700,000 people?

SECTION 5.2

Solutions Manual   Tutorial   Video 5

Solving Systems of Linear Equations by the Addition (Elimination) Method

Objectives

1 Solve linear systems using the addition (elimination) method.
2 Use the addition method to identify inconsistent and dependent systems.

In the previous section, we deliberately chose systems of equations that had solutions consisting of integers. It is not difficult to see that two lines intersect at, say, $(-1, 3)$. But what if the point of intersection is $(-1\frac{14}{17}, 2\frac{5}{39})$? It would be most difficult to look at intersecting lines and determine that at the intersection point x is $-1\frac{14}{17}$ and y is $2\frac{5}{39}$. Consequently, in this section, we turn to a method of solving linear systems that does not depend on looking at graphs of equations. The method, called the *addition, or elimination, method,* is used to identify solutions that can only be suggested by intersecting graphs.

The addition property of equality lets us add the same number to both sides of an equation. Let's apply this idea to a linear system.

1 Solve linear systems using the addition (elimination) method.

$$x + y = 4 \quad \text{Equation 1}$$
$$x - y = 6 \quad \text{Equation 2}$$

According to Equation 2, $x - y$ and 6 are the same number. This means that we can add $x - y$ to the left side of Equation 1 and 6 to the right side. In other words, we can add the two left sides and the two right sides of Equations 1 and 2.

$$x + y = 4 \qquad \text{Equation 1}$$
$$\underline{x - y = 6} \qquad \text{Equation 2}$$
$$2x + 0y = 10 \qquad \text{Add } x - y \text{ to the left side of Equation 1. Add 6 to the right side of Equation 1.}$$

When we add the two equations, the variable y is eliminated. This is because the coefficients of y are opposites, differing only in sign. By adding equations and eliminating y, we obtain a single equation in one variable, x. This is why the use of the extended addition property for solving linear systems is called the *addition* or *elimination* method. As shown in Example 1, our goal is to *add* the equations and *eliminate* one of the variables.

EXAMPLE 1 **Using the Addition (Elimination) Method to Solve a System**

Solve the system:

$$x + y = 4 \qquad \text{Equation 1}$$
$$x - y = 6 \qquad \text{Equation 2}$$

Solution

The coefficients of y differ only in sign. Therefore, by adding the two equations, we can eliminate y.

$$x + y = 4$$
$$\underline{x - y = 6}$$
$$\text{Add:} \quad 2x \quad = 10$$

Now y is eliminated and we can solve $2x = 10$ for x.

$$2x = 10$$
$$x = 5 \qquad \text{Divide both sides by 2.}$$

This result, $x = 5$, gives the value of the x-coordinate of the solution of the system. To find the y-coordinate, we back-substitute 5 for x in either one of the two original equations.

$$x + y = 4 \qquad \text{Equation 1}$$
$$5 + y = 4 \qquad \text{Back-substitute 5 for } x.$$
$$y = -1 \qquad \text{Then subtract 5 from both sides.}$$

The solution to the system is $(5, -1)$. In Figure 5.7, we see that $(5, -1)$ is the intersection point for the graphs of the equations in the system. Furthermore, the solution $(5, -1)$ can be checked by substituting 5 for x and -1 for y in both equations.

Study tip

Back-substitute means that we work backward. After solving for one of the variables, substitute that value back into *either one* of the given equations. Then solve for the other variable.

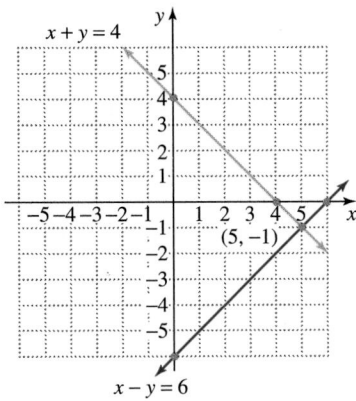

Figure 5.7

A system whose solution is $(5, -1)$

Substitute into Equation 1:

$$x + y = 4$$
$$5 + (-1) \stackrel{?}{=} 4$$
$$4 = 4 \quad \checkmark$$

Substitute into Equation 2:

$$x - y = 6$$
$$5 - (-1) \stackrel{?}{=} 6$$
$$5 + (+1) \stackrel{?}{=} 6$$
$$6 = 6 \quad \checkmark$$

The ordered pair $(5, -1)$ satisfies both equations of the system, so the solution is $(5, -1)$. ∎

The crucial part of the addition (elimination) method is *eliminating* one of the variables by *adding* left- and right-hand sides of the two equations. But we can only eliminate one of the variables if the coefficients of x (or y) are opposites of each other. We may have to work with one or both equations separately before we can add them to eliminate a variable. Let's see precisely what this means.

EXAMPLE 2 Using the Addition (Elimination) Method

Solve the system:

$$3x - y = 11 \quad \text{Equation 1}$$
$$2x + 5y = 13 \quad \text{Equation 2}$$

Solution

Adding the equations as they stand results in $5x + 4y = 24$, and we have not eliminated a variable. Only if the coefficients of x (or y) are opposites of each other will a variable be eliminated.

For this system, we can obtain coefficients of y that differ only in sign by multiplying the first equation by 5.

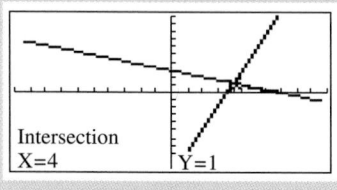
$$3x - y = 11 \quad \xrightarrow{\text{Multiply by 5.}} \quad 15x - 5y = 55$$
$$2x + 5y = 13 \quad \xrightarrow{\text{No change}} \quad \underline{2x + 5y = 13}$$
$$17x + 0y = 68 \quad \text{Now add the left and right sides.}$$
$$17x = 68$$
$$x = 4$$

Now we can back-substitute 4 for x in either of the original equations.

$$2x + 5y = 13 \quad \text{Equation 2}$$
$$2(4) + 5y = 13 \quad \text{Back-substitute 4 for } x.$$
$$8 + 5y = 13$$
$$5y = 5$$
$$y = 1$$

Therefore, the solution is $(4, 1)$. Check to see that it satisfies both of the original equations. ∎

Before considering additional examples, let's summarize the steps for solving two equations in two variables by the addition (elimination) method.

> **Solving linear systems by the addition (elimination) method**
> 1. Write each equation of the system in the form $Ax + By = C$.
> 2. If necessary, multiply one or both equations by appropriate numbers so that the sum of the coefficients of x or y is zero.
> 3. Add the equations in step 2. The sum is an equation in one variable.
> 4. Solve the equation from step 3.
> 5. Back-substitute the value obtained in step 4 into either of the original equations and solve for the other variable.
> 6. Write the solution as an ordered pair and check the solution in both of the original equations.

EXAMPLE 3 Using the Addition (Elimination) Method

Solve the system:

$$2x - 3y = 16 \quad \text{Equation 1}$$
$$3x + 4y = 7 \quad \text{Equation 2}$$

tudy tip

A solution of a linear system is an ordered *pair* of numbers. Once you have the value of one variable, don't forget to back-substitute and solve for the other variable.

Solution

We can obtain coefficients of y that will have a sum of zero by multiplying Equation 1 by 4 and Equation 2 by 3.

$$
\begin{array}{llll}
2x - 3y = 16 & \xrightarrow{\text{Multiply by 4.}} & & 8x - 12y = 64 \\
3x + 4y = 7 & \xrightarrow{\text{Multiply by 3.}} & & \underline{9x + 12y = 21} \\
& & \text{Add:} & 17x = 85 \\
& & & x = 5
\end{array}
$$

We can now back-substitute 5 for x in either original equation.

$$
\begin{array}{ll}
3x + 4y = 7 & \text{Equation 2} \\
3(5) + 4y = 7 & \text{Back-substitute 5 for } x. \\
15 + 4y = 7 & \\
4y = -8 & \\
y = -2 &
\end{array}
$$

The solution is $(5, -2)$. Check to see that it satisfies both of the original equations.

NOTE: We could also eliminate y by obtaining x-coefficients whose sum is zero.

$$
\begin{array}{llll}
2x - 3y = 16 & \xrightarrow{\text{Multiply by 3.}} & & 6x - 9y = 48 \\
3x + 4y = 7 & \xrightarrow{\text{Multiply by } -2.} & & \underline{-6x - 8y = -14} \\
& & \text{Add:} & -17y = 34 \\
& & & y = -2
\end{array}
$$

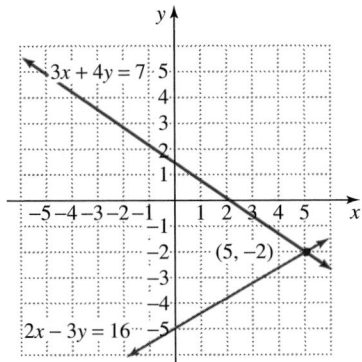

Figure 5.8

A system whose solution is $(5, -2)$

Back-substituting -2 for y in either original equation results in the same solution as above. The solution is illustrated in Figure 5.8. ∎

EXAMPLE 4   **Using the Addition (Elimination) Method**

Solve the system:

$$2x = 7y - 17 \quad \text{Equation 1}$$
$$3x + 5y = 17 \quad \text{Equation 2}$$

Solution

We rearrange the terms in Equation 1 so that it is written in the form $Ax + By = C$.

$$2x = 7y - 17 \quad \text{Subtract } 7y \text{ from both sides of Equation 1.}$$
$$2x - 7y = -17$$

Our system can now be written as

$$2x - 7y = -17$$
$$3x + 5y = 17$$

Like terms are now aligned in columns. We can eliminate x by multiplying Equation 1 by 3 and Equation 2 by -2.

$$
\begin{array}{ll}
2x - 7y = -17 & \xrightarrow{\text{Multiply by 3.}} \\
3x + 5y = 17 & \xrightarrow{\text{Multiply by } -2.}
\end{array}
\qquad
\begin{array}{l}
6x - 21y = -51 \\
\underline{-6x - 10y = -34} \\
{-31y = -85} \\
 y = \dfrac{85}{31}
\end{array}
$$

Add:

Back-substitution of this value into either original equation of the system results in cumbersome arithmetic. Another option is to go back to the equations and this time eliminate y instead of x. We can eliminate y by multiplying Equation 1 by 5 and Equation 2 by 7.

$$
\begin{array}{ll}
2x - 7y = -17 & \xrightarrow{\text{Multiply by 5.}} \\
3x + 5y = 17 & \xrightarrow{\text{Multiply by 7.}}
\end{array}
\qquad
\begin{array}{l}
10x - 35y = -85 \\
\underline{21x + 35y = 119} \\
31x = 34
\end{array}
$$

Add:

The solution to this system is $\left(\frac{34}{31}, \frac{85}{31}\right)$.

$$x = \dfrac{34}{31}$$

2 Use the addition method to identify inconsistent and dependent systems.

The Addition Method with Inconsistent and Dependent Systems

Recall that an inconsistent system has no solution. The graphs of the equations are parallel lines with no point of intersection. Example 5 shows that when the addition (elimination) method is used, an inconsistent system will result in a false statement.

EXAMPLE 5   **Using the Addition (Elimination) Method on an Inconsistent System**

Solve the system:

$$6x - 2y = -2 \quad \text{Equation 1}$$
$$3x - y = 4 \quad \text{Equation 2}$$

ENRICHMENT ESSAY

Intersecting Lines and Art

Intersecting lines provide the geometric meaning for the solution of a linear system of equations. They also play an important role in the paintings of Wassily Kandinsky (1866–1944). Circles and intersecting lines are the dominant form in *Composition VIII*. Find another example of intersecting lines in art or architecture.

Wassily Kandinksy "Composition 8", July 1923, oil on canvas, $55\frac{1}{8} \times 79\frac{1}{8}$ (140 × 201 cm). Solomon R. Guggenheim Museum, New York. Photo by David Heald © The Solomon R. Guggenheim Foundation, NY. FN 37.262.

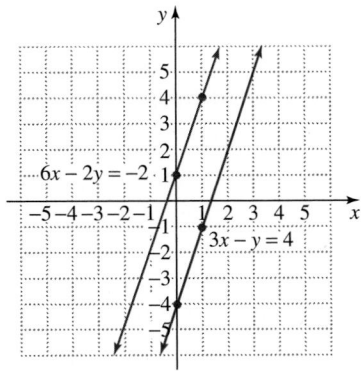

Figure 5.9

A system with no solution

iscover for yourself

Solve each equation in Example 5 for y. What is the slope and y-intercept of each line? What does this mean?

Discover for yourself

Write the given equations in Example 6 in slope-intercept form. What do you observe?

Solution

We can eliminate x by multiplying Equation 2 by -2.

$$
\begin{array}{ll}
6x - 2y = -2 & \xrightarrow{\text{No change}} & 6x - 2y = -2 \\
3x - y = 4 & \xrightarrow{\text{Multiply by } -2.} & -6x + 2y = -8 \\
& \text{Add:} & \overline{0 = -10}
\end{array}
$$

The false statement $0 = -10$ shows that there is no solution to this inconsistent system. Said in another way, there are no values of x and y for which $0 = -10$. The graphs of the equations, shown in Figure 5.9, are parallel lines and visually demonstrate that the system has no solution. ∎

The addition (elimination) method with inconsistent systems

Whenever both variables have been eliminated and the resulting statement is false, the system is inconsistent and has no solution.

Recall that a system with dependent equations has infinitely many solutions. The graphs of the equations are lines that coincide, with infinitely many points of intersection. Example 6 shows that when the addition (elimination) method is used, dependent equations result in a true statement, such as $0 = 0$.

EXAMPLE 6 **Using the Addition (Elimination) Method on a Dependent System**

Solve the system:

$$
\begin{array}{ll}
2x = y + 3 & \text{Equation 1} \\
2y = 4x - 6 & \text{Equation 2}
\end{array}
$$

Solution

First write both equations in the form $Ax + By = C$.

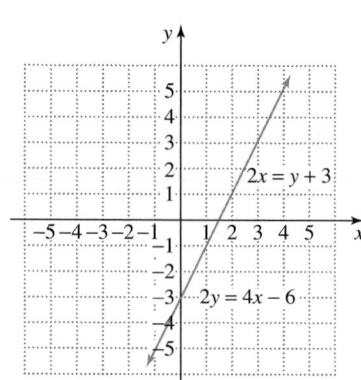

Figure 5.10

The graphs of the given equations coincide.

Equation 1:

$$2x = y + 3$$
$$2x - y = 3 \quad \text{Subtract } y \text{ from both sides.}$$

Equation 2:

$$2y = 4x - 6$$
$$-4x + 2y = -6 \quad \text{Subtract } 4x \text{ from both sides.}$$

Our system can now be written as

$$2x - y = 3 \quad \text{Equation 1}$$
$$-4x + 2y = -6 \quad \text{Equation 2}$$

We can eliminate y by multiplying Equation 1 by 2.

$$2x - y = 3 \quad \xrightarrow{\text{Multiply by 2.}} \quad 4x - 2y = 6$$
$$-4x + 2y = -6 \quad \xrightarrow{\text{No change}} \quad \underline{-4x + 2y = -6}$$
$$\text{Add:} \qquad\qquad 0 = 0$$

Both variables have been eliminated and the resulting statement, $0 = 0$, is true for all values of x and y. This identity indicates that the equations are dependent. The system has infinitely many solutions. Any ordered pair that satisfies the first equation also satisfies the second equation (see Figure 5.10). ■

The addition (elimination) method with dependent systems

Whenever both variables have been eliminated and the resulting statement is true, the system is dependent and has infinitely many solutions.

Intersecting lines and the repetition of simple forms play a role in modern architecture.

Ken Biggs/Tony Stone Images

We can now summarize the possibilities that can occur when solving a linear system involving two equations in two variables by the addition (elimination) method.

Possibilities that can occur when two linear equations in two variables are solved by the addition (elimination) method

1. The result of the method is a statement such as $x = 6$ and $y = -5$. The graphs of the equations of the system are lines that intersect.

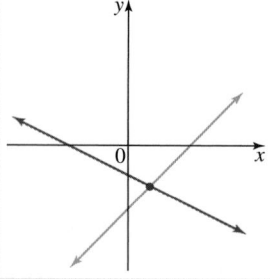

2. The result of the method is a false statement, such as $0 = 2$. The system is inconsistent, having no solution. The graphs of the equations of the system are parallel lines.

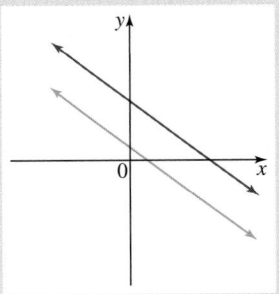

3. The result of the method is a true statement, such as $0 = 0$. The system has infinitely many solutions. The equations are dependent, and their graphs are the same line.

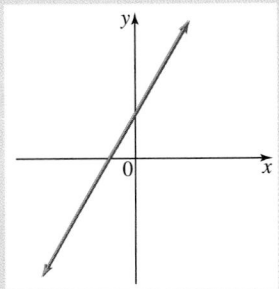

PROBLEM SET 5.2

Practice Problems

Solve each system in Problems 1–42 by the addition (elimination) method. Where applicable, state that the system is inconsistent or contains dependent equations.

1. $x + y = 1$
$x - y = 3$

2. $x + y = 6$
$x - y = -2$

3. $2x + 3y = 6$
$2x - 3y = 6$

4. $3x + 2y = 14$
$3x - 2y = 10$

5. $x + 2y = 7$
$-x + 3y = 18$

6. $2x + y = -2$
$-2x - 3y = -6$

7. $5x - y = 9$
$-5x + 2y = -8$

8. $7x - 4y = 13$
$-7x + 6y = -11$

9. $x + 2y = 2$
$-4x + 3y = 25$

10. $2x - y = -7$
$3x + 2y = 0$

11. $2x - 7y = 2$
$3x + y = -20$

12. $5x + 2y = -7$
$x + 3y = 9$

13. $x + 5y = -1$
$2x + 7y = 1$

14. $2x + y = 1$
$6x + 5y = 13$

15. $4x + 3y = 15$
$2x - 5y = 1$

16. $3x - 7y = 13$
$6x + 5y = 7$

17. $3x - y = 1$
$3x - y = 2$

18. $4x - 9y = -2$
$-4x + 9y = -2$

19. $3x - 4y = 11$
$2x + 3y = -4$

20. $2x + 3y = -16$
$5x - 10y = 30$

21. $3x + 2y = -1$
$-2x + 7y = 9$

22. $5x + 3y = 27$
$7x - 2y = 13$

23. $x + 3y = 2$
$3x + 9y = 6$

24. $4x - 2y = 2$
$2x - y = 1$

25. $3x = 2y + 7$
$5x = 2y + 13$

26. $9x = 25 + y$
$2y = 4 - 9x$

27. $2x = 3y - 4$
$-6x + 12y = 6$

28. $5x = 4y - 8$
$3x + 7y = 14$

29. $7x - 3y = 4$
$-14x + 6y = -7$

30. $2x - y = 1$
$y = 2x + 5$

31. $2x - y = 3$
$4x + 4y = -1$

32. $3x - y = 22$
$4x + 5y = -21$

33. $4x = 5 + 2y$
$2x + 3y = 4$

34. $3x = 4y + 1$
$4x + 3y = 1$

35. $4x - 8y = 36$
$3x - 6y = 27$

36. $x = 5 - 3y$
$2x + 6y = 10$

37. $2x + 4y = 5$
$3x + 6y = 6$

38. $2x + 3y = 8$
$4x + 6y = 12$

39. $5x + y = 2$
$3x + y = 1$

40. $2x - 5y = -1$
$2x - y = 1$

41. $2x + 2y = -2 - 4y$
$3x + y = 7y + 27$

42. $2y - 8 = -2x - 8x$
$8x - 3y = 31 + y$

If a system contains fractions as coefficients, multiply each equation by the least common multiple of all denominators of all the fractions appearing in the equation. This will clear the equation of fractions. Once equations have integers as coefficients, use the addition (elimination) method. Use this procedure to solve the systems in Problems 43–48.

43. $x + y = 11$
$\frac{1}{5}x + \frac{1}{7}y = 1$

44. $x - y = -3$
$\frac{1}{9}x - \frac{1}{7}y = -1$

45. $\frac{3}{5}x + \frac{4}{5}y = 1$
$\frac{1}{4}x - \frac{3}{8}y = -1$

46. $\frac{1}{3}x + y = 3$
$\frac{1}{2}x - \frac{1}{4}y = 1$

47. $\frac{4}{5}x - y = -1$
$\frac{2}{5}x + y = 1$

48. $\frac{1}{3}x - \frac{1}{2}y = \frac{2}{3}$
$\frac{2}{3}x + y = \frac{4}{3}$

Application Problems

49. The perimeter of the playing field for American football is 1040 feet. Thus, if L represents the length and W the width, $2L + 2W = 1040$. The length exceeds the width by 200 feet, so that $L = W + 200$. Find the dimensions of the playing field by solving this system using the addition (elimination) method.

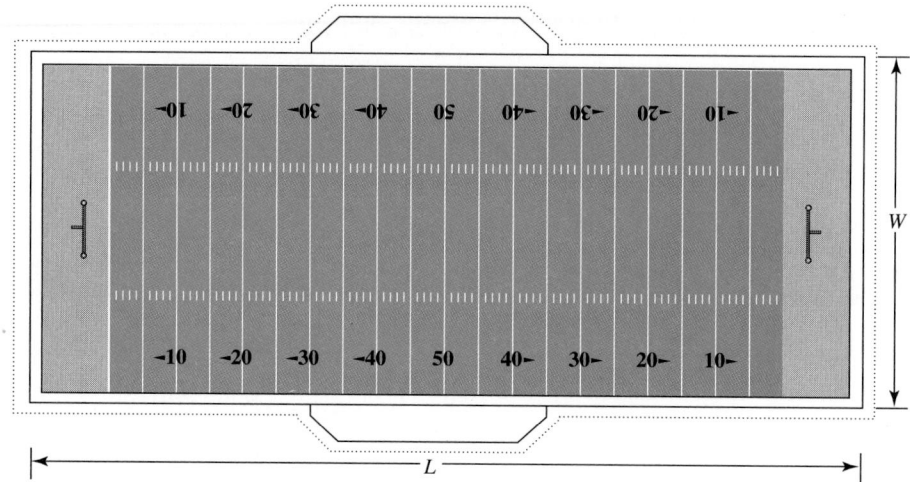

50. Let x and y represent the measures of two angles. The two angles are supplementary, meaning the sum of their measures is 180°. Thus, $x + y = 180$. One angle is 30° less than twice the other. Thus, $y = 2x - 30$. Find the measures of the two angles by solving this system using the addition (elimination) method.

True–False Critical Thinking Problems

51. Which one of the following statements is true?
   a. To eliminate x by addition (elimination) in the system

$$5x - 3y = 7$$
$$4x + 9y = 11$$

   we multiply the first equation by 4 and the second equation by 5.
   b. The equations $x + y = 3$ and $-2x - 2y = -6$ are inconsistent.
   c. The system

$$y = x - 1$$
$$x = y + 1$$

   has infinitely many solutions.

   d. If $A, B, C, D, E,$ and F are consecutive integers, the system

$$Ax + By = C$$
$$Dx + Ey = F$$

   will never have $(-1, 2)$ as a solution.

52. Which one of the following statements is true?
   a. Both $(0, 5)$ and $(6, -1)$ satisfy the system

$$x + y = 5$$
$$2x = 10 - 2y$$

b. Once x is eliminated by the addition (elimination) method, y cannot be eliminated by using the original equations of the system.

c. The equations $x + 2y = 15$ and $x - 2y = 45$ are inconsistent.

d. If $Ax + 2y = 2$ and $2x + By = 10$ have graphs that intersect at $(2, -2)$, then $A = -3$ and $B = 3$.

Technology Problems

53. Use a graphing utility to check your solution to any four of the systems you solved in Problems 1–42.

54. Many graphing utilities will solve systems of equations. Usually, this is found under the $\boxed{\text{SIMULT}}$ (simultaneous equations) feature. Generally, you will enter

Number $= \boxed{2}$

(for two equations in two variables), followed by the coefficient of x, y, and the right-hand constant for each equation, respectively. By pressing $\boxed{\text{SOLVE}}$, the values of x and y are printed on the screen. Consult your manual for specifics, and then use this feature to check solutions to the systems you solved in Problems 1–42.

Writing in Mathematics

55. Explain the addition (elimination) method for solving a system of two linear equations in two variables.

56. When using the addition (elimination) method for solving a system of two linear equations in two variables, an equation such as $0 = -10$ is obtained. Explain what this means. What does it mean to obtain an equation such as $0 = 0$?

57. In Example 5 on page 373, we verified the solution by using graphing. Take a moment to look back at the Discover for Yourself box in the margin. Explain why we suggested writing each equation in slope-intercept form rather than using the equations as given.

Critical Thinking Problem

58. In subsequent algebra courses, you will be studying systems of three equations in three variables, such as

$$x + 2y - 3z = 9$$
$$2x - y + 2z = -8$$
$$-x + 3y - 4z = 15$$

Solve this system by taking two different pairs of equations and eliminating the same variable from each pair. Then solve the resulting system of two equations in two variables to find the value of one of the variables. Back-substitution will be necessary to find the value for the other variables.

Group Activity Problems

59. The addition (elimination) method can be used to show that the solution of the system of equations

$$Ax + By = C$$
$$Dx + Ey = F$$

is given by

$$x = \frac{CE - FB}{AE - BD} \quad \text{and} \quad y = \frac{?}{AE - BD}.$$

a. Have each member of the group take the formula for x and use it to check one of the equations that was solved in Problems 1–42. One group member should verify the value of x in Example 4 on page 372.

b. Using Example 4 on page 372, have members of the group experiment with the missing numerator for y in the formula given above, filling in an expression so that 85 in the numerator for y (the value of the y-numerator in Example 4) is obtained. Check the group's conjectured formula by

seeing if it gives the correct value for y in the systems considered in part (a).

c. Try verifying the formula given for x by using the addition method. This is fairly difficult, so you will want to work on this as a group. Since your goal is to eliminate y, try multiplying the first given equation by E and the second by $-B$. Then add equations. If your group gets stuck, ask your instructor for assistance.

d. For the formulas for x and y to give specific values, the expression in the denominator $(AE - BD)$ cannot be zero. (Why not?) What happens if the expression is zero? The group should consider this possibility by experimenting with the formulas for x and y in Examples 5 and 6 on pages 372 and 373. What conclusions can the group draw?

60. Even if you are not using a graphing utility in this course, group members should read Problem 54. What this means, of course, is that linear systems can be solved simply by pressing the correct key sequence on a graphing utility! In light of this fact, what do the members of the group believe is the role of technology in learning algebra? In particular, should this entire chapter be rewritten with a concentration instead on how to get the solution to a linear system using a graphing utility? Or should graphing utilities not be permitted at all? Should they be used to check results only after algebraic skills have been mastered? In your group, discuss and debate these issues. Ask faculty teaching this course for their opinions. Are they in agreement with each other about the role of technology in the course?

Review Problems

61. Substitute 2, 3, 6, or 12 for $x, y,$ and z in each equation to make it true. Use each number you select only once in each part of this problem.
  a. $x + y - z = 9$
  b. $x \div y + z = 5$
  c. $xy \div z = 4$

62. The sum of the measures of the complement and supplement of an angle is 196°. Find the measure of the angle.

63. Solve for y: $6(y - 5) - 9y < -4y - 5(2y - 5)$.

SECTION 5.3

Solutions Manual

Tutorial

Video 6

| Solve linear systems by the substitution method.

Solving Systems of Linear Equations by the Substitution Method

Objectives

1 Solve linear systems by the substitution method.
2 Use the substitution method to identify inconsistent and dependent systems.

A second algebraic method for solving systems of linear equations that does not involve looking at intersecting graphs is called the *substitution method*. All systems that can be solved by the substitution method can also be solved by the addition (elimination) method. You may wonder why you need to consider this new method. The answer is that for certain systems the substitution method is a bit faster. An example is the system

$$y = -x - 3 \quad \text{Equation 1}$$
$$7x + 2y = 4 \quad \text{Equation 2}$$

where Equation 1 has y expressed in terms of x. The addition (elimination) method would require rewriting an equation and then multiplying. Using substitution, since y *equals* $-x - 3$, we can simply replace y with $-x - 3$ in Equation 2, immediately eliminating a variable. Like the addition (elimination) method, the goal of the substitution method is to reduce a system of two equations in two variables to one equation in one variable. Example 1 illustrates the steps of the substitution method.

study tip

These boxes may help you to see how we substitute.

EXAMPLE 1   **Solving a System of Linear Equations by Substitution**

Solve the system:

$$y = -x - 3 \quad \text{Equation 1}$$
$$7x + 2y = 4 \quad \text{Equation 2}$$

Solution

Since Equation 1 states that y is $-x - 3$, we can replace y in Equation 2 with $-x - 3$. That is, we *substitute* $-x - 3$ from Equation 1 for y in Equation 2. This is what it looks like.

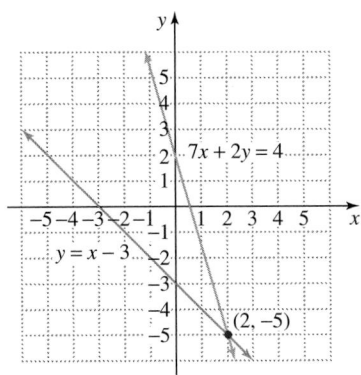

Figure 5.11

A system whose solution is
$(2, -5)$

Discover for yourself

Solve Example 1 by the addition (elimination) method. Begin by writing Equation 1 as $x + y = -3$, adding x to each side. Do you still obtain the same solution? Which method do you find easier?

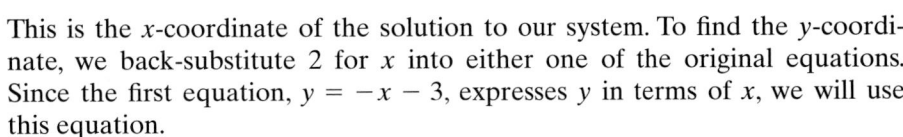

$$7x + 2y = 4 \qquad \text{Equation 2}$$
$$7x + 2(-x - 3) = 4 \qquad \text{Replace } y \text{ with } -x - 3 \text{ since Equation 1 states that } y = -x - 3.$$
$$7x - 2x - 6 = 4 \qquad \text{Solve this equation for } x. \text{ Use the distributive property.}$$
$$5x - 6 = 4 \qquad \text{Combine like terms.}$$
$$5x = 10 \qquad \text{Add 6 to both sides.}$$
$$x = 2 \qquad \text{Divide both sides by 5.}$$

This is the x-coordinate of the solution to our system. To find the y-coordinate, we back-substitute 2 for x into either one of the original equations. Since the first equation, $y = -x - 3$, expresses y in terms of x, we will use this equation.

$$y = -x - 3 \qquad \text{Equation 1}$$
$$y = -2 - 3 \qquad \text{Since } x = 2, \text{ substitute 2 for } x.$$
$$y = -5$$

The solution to the system is $(2, -5)$, shown in Figure 5.11. Check to see that the solution satisfies both of the original equations. ∎

Observe that both the addition (elimination) and substitution methods involve elimination of one of the variables. With the substitution method, the variable is eliminated by substitution rather than addition.

Before considering additional examples, let's summarize the steps used in the substitution method.

> **Solving linear systems of two equations in two variables (x and y) by the substitution method**
>
> 1. Solve one equation for x in terms of y or y in terms of x, if necessary.
> 2. Substitute this expression for that variable into the other equation.
> 3. Solve the resulting equation in one variable.
> 4. Back-substitute the solution from step 3 into the equation in step 1 to find the value of the other variable.
> 5. Check the solution in both of the given equations.

EXAMPLE 2   **Solving a System of Linear Equations by Substitution**

Solve the system:

$$3x - 2y = -5 \qquad \text{Equation 1}$$
$$4x + y = 8 \qquad \text{Equation 2}$$

Solution

Step 1. We must solve one equation for x in terms of y or y in terms of x. *Always solve for the variable that has a coefficient of 1 or -1.* Thus, we will solve for y in Equation 2.

$$4x + y = 8 \qquad \text{Equation 2}$$
$$y = 8 - 4x \qquad \text{Solve for } y \text{ by subtracting } 4x \text{ from both sides.}$$

Step 2. Substitute $8 - 4x$ for y in Equation 1.

$$3x - 2y = -5 \quad \text{Equation 1}$$
$$3x - 2(8 - 4x) = -5 \quad \text{Substitute } 8 - 4x \text{ for } y \text{ since } y = 8 - 4x.$$

 tudy tip

Be sure to use parentheses when you substitute $8 - 4x$ for y.

Step 3. Solve the resulting equation in one variable.

$$3x - 2(8 - 4x) = -5$$
$$3x - 16 + 8x = -5 \quad \text{Apply the distributive property.}$$
$$11x - 16 = -5 \quad \text{Combine like terms.}$$
$$11x = 11 \quad \text{Add 16 to both sides.}$$
$$x = 1 \quad \text{Divide both sides by 11.}$$

Step 4. Find the value of y.

$$y = 8 - 4x \quad \text{Use this form of Equation 2, where } y \text{ is expressed in terms of } x.$$
$$y = 8 - 4(1) \quad \text{Back-substitute 1 for } x \text{ since } x = 1.$$
$$y = 4$$

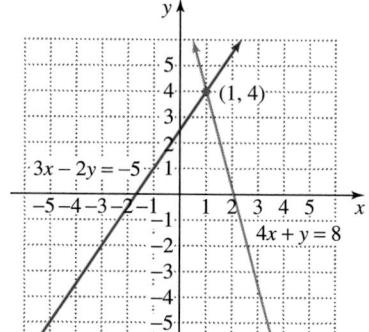

Figure 5.12

A system whose solution is (1, 4)

Step 5. The solution to the system is $(1, 4)$, shown in Figure 5.12. Check to see that it satisfies both of the original equations. ■

Comparing the Three Solution Methods

The substitution method works particularly well when one of the original equations has y expressed in terms of x (or vice versa) or when an equation has a variable with a coefficient of 1 or -1. The variable with this coefficient is the one we should solve for. If the system has neither characteristic, use the addition (elimination) method rather than the substitution method.

 tudy tip

With increased practice, it becomes easier to select the best method for solving a particular linear system.

The following summary compares the graphing, addition (elimination), and substitution methods for solving linear systems of equations.

Method	Advantages	Example	Disadvantages
Graphing	You can see the solutions.	$2x + y = 6$ $x - 2y = 8$ Solution: $(4, -2)$	If the solution does not involve integers or is too large to be seen on the graph, it's impossible to tell exactly what the solutions are.
Addition (Elimination)	Gives exact solutions. Easy to use if no variable has a coefficient of 1 or -1.	$2x + 3y = -8$ $5x + 4y = -34$ Multiply by 5 and -2, respectively: $10x + 15y = -40$ $\underline{-10x - 8y = \quad 68}$ Add: $\quad 7y = 28$ $\qquad y = 4$ Then back-substitute. Solution: $(-10, 4)$	Solutions cannot be seen.
Substitution	Gives exact solutions. Easy to use if a variable is on one side by itself.	$y = 3x - 1$ $3x - 2y = -4$ Substitute $3x - 1$ for y: $3x - 2(3x - 1) = -4$ Solve for x: $\quad x = 2$ Back-substitute: $y = 3(2) - 1 = 5$ Solution: $(2, 5)$	Solutions cannot be seen.

2 Use the substitution method to identify inconsistent and dependent systems.

The Substitution Method with Inconsistent and Dependent Systems

As with the addition (elimination) method, if the substitution method results in a false statement, the linear system is inconsistent and has no solution. If the result is a true statement, like $0 = 0$, the linear system is dependent and has infinitely many solutions.

EXAMPLE 3 Using the Substitution Method on an Inconsistent System

Solve the system:

$$y + 1 = 5(x + 1) \quad \text{Equation 1}$$
$$y = 5x - 1 \quad \text{Equation 2}$$

ENRICHMENT ESSAY

Analytic Cubism

The lines of Descartes' coordinate system reflect the logical order of linear equations and their graphs. The underlying rational order of Descartes' plane also appeared in a style of art called analytical cubism (1907–1912). The straight lines, a narrow range of color, and a kind of slicing of the figure into geometric shapes suggest that beyond the casual way in which we view the world lies a rational order like the order of mathematics. Shown here is *The Table* by French cubist Georges Braque (1882–1963). As one views the painting, the world of appearance becomes analyzable into a world of patterns open to endless explorations and adjustment.

Georges Braque, The Table, 1928. Oil and sand on canvas, $70\frac{3}{4} \times 28\frac{3}{4}$ in. The Museum of Modern Art, New York. Acquired through the Lillie P. Eliss Bequest. © 1998 ARS, New York/ADAGP, Paris.

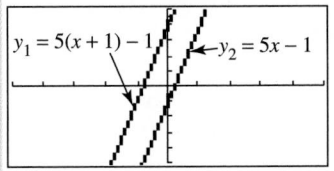
Solution

$$y + 1 = 5(x + 1) \quad \text{Equation 1}$$
$$(5x - 1) + 1 = 5(x + 1) \quad \text{Replace } y \text{ with } 5x - 1 \text{ since } y = 5x - 1 \text{ in Equation 2.}$$
$$5x = 5x + 5 \quad \text{Simplify and apply the distributive property. Then subtract } 5x \text{ from both sides.}$$
$$0 = 5 \quad \text{There are no values of } x \text{ and } y \text{ for which } 0 = 5.$$

This false statement indicates that the system is inconsistent and has no solution. ∎

EXAMPLE 4 **Using the Substitution Method on a Dependent System**

Solve the system:

$$9x - 3y = 12 \quad \text{Equation 1}$$
$$y = 3x - 4 \quad \text{Equation 2}$$

Solution

$$9x - 3y = 12 \quad \text{Equation 1}$$
$$9x - 3(3x - 4) = 12 \quad \text{Replace } y \text{ with } 3x - 4 \text{ since } y = 3x - 4 \text{ in Equation 2.}$$
$$9x - 9x + 12 = 12 \quad \text{Apply the distributive property.}$$
$$12 = 12 \quad \text{This statement is true for all values of } x \text{ and } y.$$

This true statement indicates that the system contains dependent equations and has infinitely many solutions. ∎

PROBLEM SET 5.3

Practice Problems _____

Solve the systems in Problems 1–30 by the substitution method. Where applicable, state that the system is inconsistent or contains dependent equations. Check your solution algebraically or with a graphing utility.

1. $x + y = 4$
     $y = 3x$

2. $x + y = 6$
     $y = 2x$

3. $x + 3y = 8$
     $y = 2x - 9$

4. $2x - 3y = -13$
     $y = 2x + 7$

5. $x = 9 - 2y$
     $x + 2y = 13$

6. $x = 2y + 2$
     $2x + 3y = 11$

7. $2(x - 1) - y = -3$
     $y = 2x + 3$

8. $x + 2y = -12$
     $y = 20 - 2x$

9. $x + 3y = 5$
     $4x + 5y = 13$

10. $x + 2y = 5$
     $2x - y = -15$

11. $2x - y = -5$
     $x + 5y = 14$

12. $2x + 3y = 11$
     $x - 4y = 0$

13. $21x - 35 = 7y$
     $y = 3x - 5$

14. $x + y - 1 = 2(y - x)$
     $y = 3x - 1$

15. $x - y = 11$
     $x - 6y = -9$

16. $x + y = 9$
     $8x - y = -18$

17. $2x - y = 3$
     $5x - 2y = 10$

18. $-x + 3y = 10$
     $2x + 8y = -6$

19. $x + 8y = 6$
     $2x + 4y = -3$

20. $-4x + y = -11$
     $2x - 3y = 5$

21. $x = 4y - 2$
     $x = 6y + 8$

22. $x = 3y + 7$
     $x = 2y - 1$

23. $y = 2x - 8$
     $y = 3x - 13$

24. $y = -3x - 1$
     $y = -4x + 2$

25. $5x + 2y = 0$
     $x - 3y = 0$

26. $4x + 3y = 0$
     $2x - y = 0$

27. $6x + 2y = 7$
     $y = 2 - 3x$

28. $2x - 4y = -6$
     $x = 2y$

29. $2x + 5y = -4$
  $3x - y = 11$

30. $2x + 5y = 1$
  $-x + 6y = 8$

Solve each system in Problems 31–50 by either the addition (elimination) method or the substitution method. Explain why you selected one method over the other. Check your solution algebraically or with a graphing utility.

31. $2x + 3y = 2$
  $x - 3y = -6$

32. $2x - 3y = -7$
  $5x + y = -9$

33. $x + y = 1$
  $3x - y = 3$

34. $2x - 3y = 2$
  $4x + 3y = 22$

35. $3x + 2y = -3$
  $2x - 5y = 17$

36. $2x - 7y = 17$
  $4x - 5y = 25$

37. $3x - 2y = 6$
  $y = 3$

38. $2x + 3y = 7$
  $x = 2$

39. $3x + 7y = -10$
  $x + 2 = 0$

40. $4x + 13y = 6$
  $x - 2 = 0$

41. $3x - 2y = 8$
  $x = -2y$

42. $2x - y = 10$
  $y = 3x$

43. $4x + y = -12$
  $-3x - y = 10$

44. $2x - y = 7$
  $5x + y = -7$

45. $3(1 - 2x) - 2(3y + 4) = 1$
  $3(x - 1) - 2y = -5$

46. $2(3x - 4) + 5y = -7$
  $3(x + 1) - 5(y + 2) = 1$

47. $y = 3x - 1$
  $-12x + 4y = -3$

48. $y = 2x - 7$
  $3y - 6x = 10$

49. $3x - 4y = 19$
  $7x + 18y = 17$

50. $4x + 3y = 2$
  $5x - 7y = -19$

Application Problems

51. The perimeter of the playing field for Canadian football is 1294 feet. Thus, if L represents the length and W the width, $2L + 2W = 1294$. The length exceeds the width by 253 feet, so that $L = W + 253$. Find the dimensions of the playing field by solving this system using the substitution method.

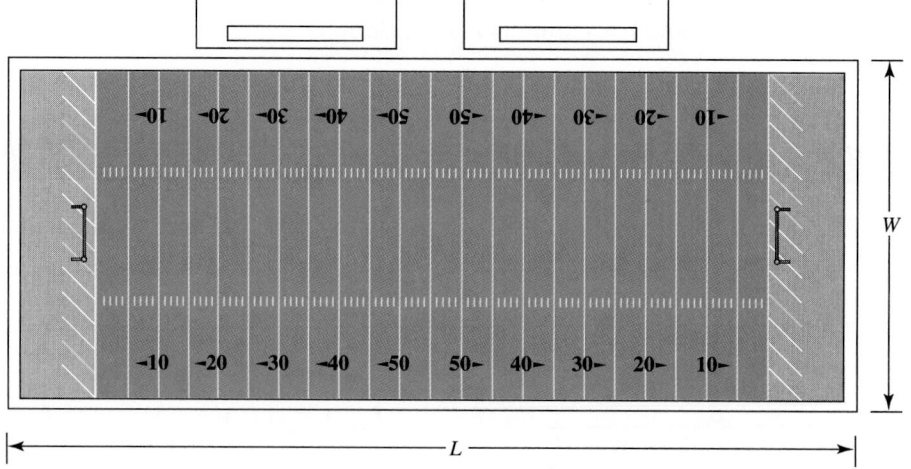

52. Let x and y represent the measures of two angles. The two angles are complementary, meaning the sum of their measures is 90°. Thus, $x + y = 90$. One angle is 42° less than twice the other. Thus, $y = 2x - 42$. Find the measures of the two angles by solving this system using the substitution method.

53. The mathematical model $7x + 8y = 14{,}066$ describes the relationship between the annual number of deaths from motor vehicle accidents in the United States (y, in deaths per hundred thousand) in year x, where $x \geq 1965$. Similarly, the model $x + 10y = 2120$ describes the relationship between deaths from gunfire in the United States (y, in deaths per hundred thousand) in year x, again for $x \geq 1965$.

a. Use the substitution method to solve the system for x, rounding the answer to the nearest year. Describe what this means in practical terms.

b. Back-substitute the rounded value for x in either equation. Find the value of y, rounded to the nearest tenth. What does this indicate in practical terms?

c. Write each of the given models in slope-intercept form. What is the slope for each equation? What do these numbers indicate about the rate of change in

deaths from motor vehicle accidents and gunfire since 1965?

True–False Critical Thinking Problems

54. Which one of the following statements is true?
    a. The following solution is correct.
      Solve by substitution:

$$4x + y = 5$$
$$7x + 3y = 10$$

    Solution:

$$y = 5 - 4x \quad \text{Solve the first equation for } y.$$

$$4x + (5 - 4x) = 5 \quad \text{Substitute } 5 - 4x \text{ for } y.$$
$$4x + 5 - 4x = 5$$
$$5 = 5$$

    The system has infinitely many solutions.
    b. It is impossible to solve some systems by substitution.
    c. Solving an inconsistent system by substitution will result in a true statement.
    d. Solving the system

$$x = 2y - 2$$
$$2x - 2y = 1$$

    by substitution results in $2y - 4 = 1$.

55. Which one of the following statements is true?
    a. The line passing through the intersection of the graphs of $x + y = 4$ and $x - y = 0$ with slope $= 3$ has an equation given by $y - 2 = 3(x - 2)$.
    b. Substitution is a more efficient method than addition (elimination).
    c. To solve the system

$$2x - y = 5$$
$$3x + 4y = 7$$

    by substitution, we replace y in the second equation by $5 - 2x$.
    d. The system

$$3x - 2y = y$$
$$2x + y = 3x$$

    does not have infinitely many solutions.

Technology Problem

56. The model $0.03x + y = 20.86$ describes the relationship between the record time (y, in seconds) for men in the 200-meter run, where x is the number of years after 1948. The parallel model for women is

$0.06x + y = 24.07$. Use the substitution method, with the help of a calculator or graphing utility, to determine in what year the time for men and women will be the same.

Writing in Mathematics

57. In solving a system such as

$$2x - 7y = -17$$
$$3x + 5y = 17$$

explain why we might select the addition (elimination) method rather than the substitution method.

58. In solving a system such as

$$3x - 2y = -5$$
$$4x + y = 8$$

suppose we decide to use the substitution method. Discuss the four possible ways in which we can begin the solution process. Which way is easiest? Why?

Critical Thinking Problem

59. If $x = 3 - y - z$, $2x + y - z = -6$, and $3x - y + z = 11$, find the values for $x, y,$ and z.

Group Activity Problem

60. a. In solving

$$3x + 5y = 26$$
$$y = 2x$$

by substitution, a student found that $x = 2$. At that point the student asserted that the system's solution is $x = 2$. What is the error?

b. In solving

$$y = 4 - x$$
$$2x + 2y = 8$$

by substitution, a student obtained $0 = 0$, giving the solution as $(0, 0)$. What is the error?

c. In your group, discuss other common errors that can occur in solving linear systems by any of the three methods discussed in this chapter. Give specific examples of these kinds of errors. What suggestions can group members offer for avoiding these errors?

Review Problems

61. Graph: $2x - 3y < 6$.

62. Write the point-slope form and the slope-intercept form for the equation of a line passing through $(-1, 6)$ with slope -4.

63. Two investments produce annual simple interest income of $270. The amount invested at 9% is $800 more than the amount invested at 7.5%. How much is invested at each rate?

SECTION 5.4

Solutions Manual   Tutorial   Video 6

I Solve word problems that result in systems of linear equations.

Problem Solving Using Systems of Equations

Objective

I Solve word problems that result in systems of linear equations.

When we solved word problems earlier, we had to translate them into algebraic equations. In a similar way, we will now have two critical sentences, each of which must be translated into a linear equation containing two variables. Here are some general steps we will follow in solving these verbal problems.

> **Strategy for solving word problems that result in a system of linear equations**
>
> 1. Carefully work your way through the problem until you can let x and y (or any variables) represent the unknown quantities.
> 2. Write a system of linear equations (in x and y) that describes the verbal conditions of the problem.
> 3. Solve the system written in step 2 using the method of addition (elimination) or substitution, and answer the problem's question.
> 4. Check the answers *in the original wording* of the problem, not in the system of equations.

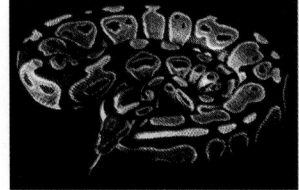
Ron Watts/Black Star

EXAMPLE 1   **The World's Longest Snakes**

The royal python and the anaconda are the world's longest snakes. The maximum length for each of these snakes is implied by the following description.

Three royal pythons and two anacondas measure 161 feet. The royal python's length increased by triple the anaconda's length is 119 feet. Find the maximum length for each of these snakes.

Solution

Step 1. Use variables to represent unknowns.

Let

x = Royal python's length

y = Anaconda's length

Step 2. Write a system describing the problem's conditions.

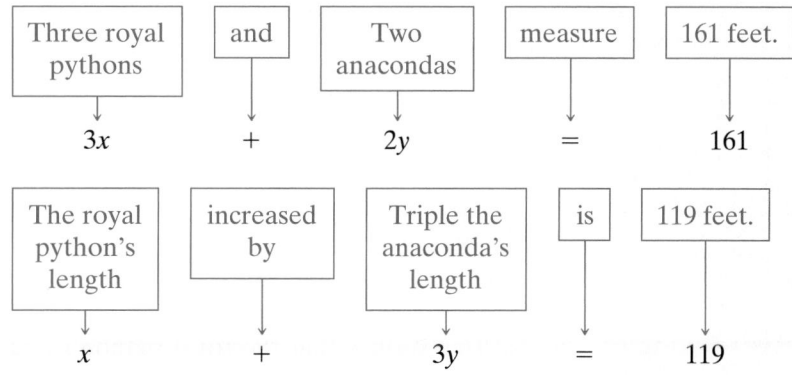

Step 3. Solve the system and answer the problem's question.

The system

$3x + 2y = 161$ Equation 1

$x + 3y = 119$ Equation 2

can be solved by addition or substitution. We'll use addition, multiplying Equation 2 by -3 to eliminate x.

$$3x + 2y = 161 \xrightarrow{\text{No change}} 3x + 2y = 161$$
$$x + 3y = 119 \xrightarrow{\text{Multiply by } -3.} -3x - 9y = -357$$
$$\text{Add:} \quad \overline{-7y = -196}$$
$$y = 28$$

We now use back-substitution to find the value of x.

$x + 3y = 119$ Equation 2

$x + 3(28) = 119$ Back-substitute 28 for y.

$x + 84 = 119$ Multiply.

$x = 35$ Subtract 84 from both sides.

Since x represents the royal python's length and y the anaconda's length, the royal python is 35 feet long and the anaconda is 28 feet long.

Step 4. Check the answers in the original wording of the problem.

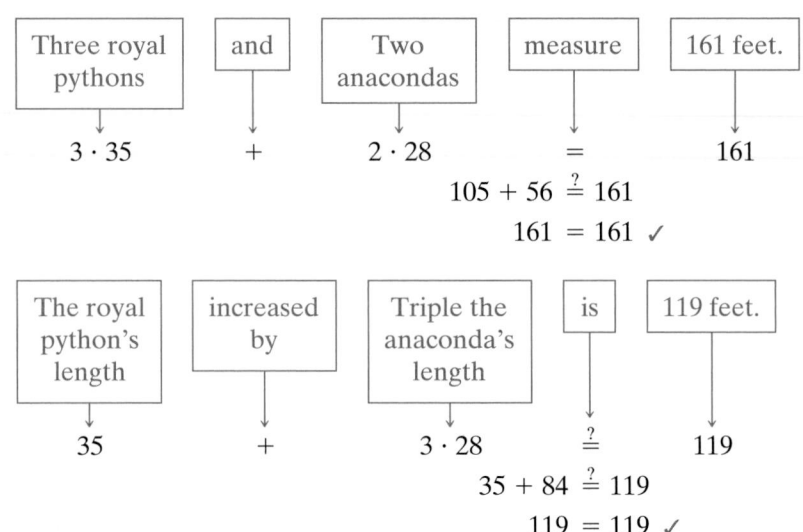

$$105 + 56 \stackrel{?}{=} 161$$
$$161 = 161 \checkmark$$

$$35 + 84 \stackrel{?}{=} 119$$
$$119 = 119 \checkmark$$

This verifies that the royal python's and the anaconda's lengths are 35 feet and 28 feet, respectively. ∎

In Examples 2 and 3, information is given about the content (or cost) of a group of items. We must determine the content or cost for each individual item.

Alexander Apostol "Corazon" Heart, 1989, toned gelatin silver print. Courtesy of Throckmorton Fine Art, Inc., New York.

Step 1. Use variables to represent unknown quantities.

EXAMPLE 2 Cholesterol and Heart Disease

The verdict is in: After years of research, the nation's health experts agree that high cholesterol in the blood is a major contributor to heart disease. Cholesterol intake should be limited to 300 mg or less each day. Fast foods provide a cholesterol carnival. Two Burger King Whoppers and three Egg McMuffins from McDonalds contain 920 mg of cholesterol. One Whopper and one Egg McMuffin exceed the suggested daily cholesterol intake by 36 mg. Determine the cholesterol content in each item.

Solution

Let

x = Cholesterol content of one Whopper

y = Cholesterol content of one Egg McMuffin

Step 2. Write a system of equations describing the problem's conditions.

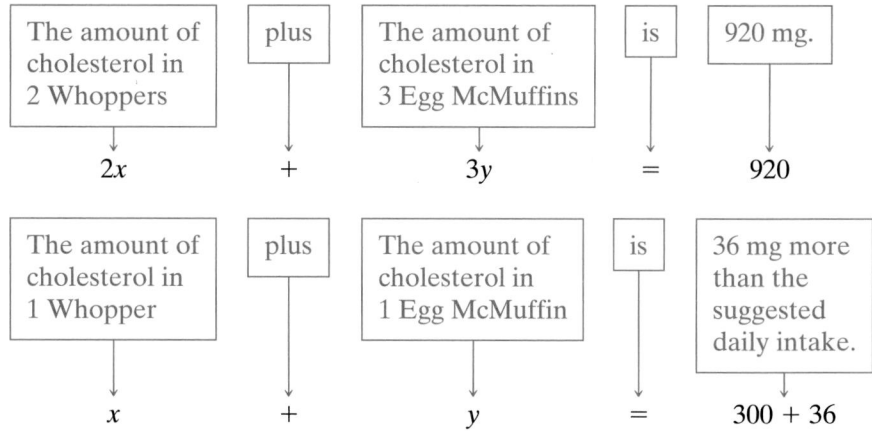

The amount of cholesterol in 2 Whoppers	plus	The amount of cholesterol in 3 Egg McMuffins	is	920 mg.
$2x$	$+$	$3y$	$=$	920

The amount of cholesterol in 1 Whopper	plus	The amount of cholesterol in 1 Egg McMuffin	is	36 mg more than the suggested daily intake.
x	$+$	y	$=$	$300 + 36$

Step 3. Solve the system and answer the problem's question.

The system

$$2x + 3y = 920 \quad \text{Equation 1}$$
$$x + y = 336 \quad \text{Equation 2}$$

can be solved by substitution or addition. We'll use addition, multiplying the second equation by -2 to eliminate x.

$$2x + 3y = 920 \quad \xrightarrow{\text{No change}} \quad 2x + 3y = 920$$
$$x + y = 336 \quad \xrightarrow{\text{Multiply by } -2.} \quad \underline{-2x - 2y = -672}$$
$$\text{Add:} \qquad y = 248$$

We now find the value of x by back-substituting 248 for y in either of the system's equations.

$$x + y = 336 \quad \text{Equation 2.}$$
$$x + 248 = 336 \quad \text{Back-substitute 248 for } y.$$
$$x = 88 \quad \text{Subtract 248 from both sides.}$$

Since $x = 88$ and $y = 248$, this means that a Whopper contains 88 mg of cholesterol, and an Egg McMuffin contains 248 mg of cholesterol.

Step 4. Check the answers in the original wording of the problem.

Two Whoppers and 3 Egg McMuffins contain $2(88) + 3(248) = 920$ mg, which checks with the given conditions. Furthermore, one Whopper and one Egg McMuffin contain $88 + 248 = 336$ mg, which does exceed the daily suggested intake of 300 mg by 36 mg. ∎

EXAMPLE 3 **Quantities and Costs**

A nursery offers orange and grapefruit trees for sale in two packages. One package consists of three orange trees and four grapefruit trees for $22. The other option is a package of four orange trees and six grapefruit trees for $31. Find the cost of each tree.

Step 1. Use variables to represent unknown quantities.

Solution

Let

$$x = \text{Cost of one orange tree}$$
$$y = \text{Cost of one grapefruit tree}$$

Step 2. Write a system of equations describing the problem's conditions.

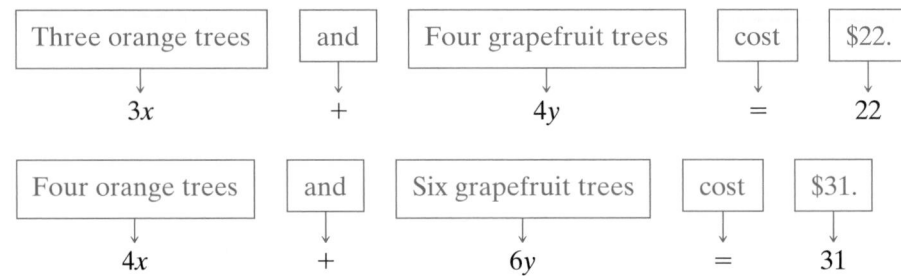

Three orange trees	and	Four grapefruit trees	cost	$22.
$3x$	$+$	$4y$	$=$	22

Four orange trees	and	Six grapefruit trees	cost	$31.
$4x$	$+$	$6y$	$=$	31

Step 3. Solve the system and answer the problem's question.

The system

$$3x + 4y = 22 \quad \text{Equation 1}$$
$$4x + 6y = 31 \quad \text{Equation 2}$$

can be solved by addition. We will eliminate x.

$$3x + 4y = 22 \quad \xrightarrow{\text{Multiply by 4.}}$$
$$4x + 6y = 31 \quad \xrightarrow{\text{Multiply by } -3.}$$

$$\begin{aligned} 12x + 16y &= 88 \\ -12x - 18y &= -93 \\ \hline -2y &= -5 \end{aligned}$$

Add:

$$y = \frac{-5}{-2} = 2.5$$

We now find the value of x by back-substituting 2.5 for y in either of the system's equations.

$$3x + 4y = 22 \quad \text{Equation 1}$$
$$3x + 4(2.5) = 22 \quad \text{Back-substitute 2.5 for } y.$$
$$3x + 10 = 22$$
$$3x = 12 \quad \text{Subtract 10 from both sides.}$$
$$x = 4 \quad \text{Divide both sides by 3.}$$

Since $x = 4$ and $y = 2.5$, each orange tree costs \$4.00 and each grapefruit tree costs \$2.50.

Step 4. Check the answers in the original wording of the problem.

We leave the check to you. ■

Geometry Problems

In some situations, writing a system of equations depends on having a knowledge of geometric equations or relationships. This idea is illustrated in Examples 4 and 5.

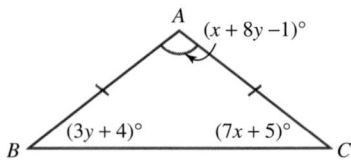

Figure 5.13

EXAMPLE 4 **The Angles of an Isosceles Triangle**

In the isosceles triangle shown in Figure 5.13, $AB = AC$. Find the measure of each angle in the triangle.

Step 1. Use variables to represent unknown quantities.

Step 2. Write a system of equations describing the problem's conditions.

Solution

We can omit step 1 because Figure 5.13 uses variables to represent the unknown angle measures.

To write a system of equations, there are two things we must know. First, the sum of the measures of the angles of a triangle is 180°.

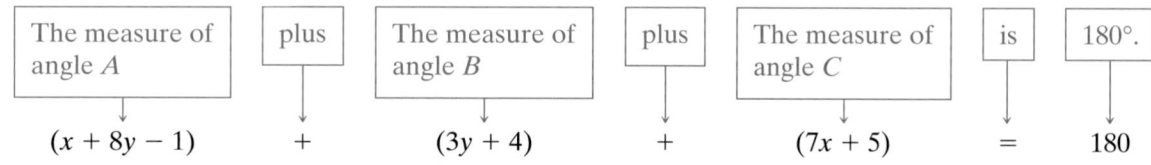

| The measure of angle A | plus | The measure of angle B | plus | The measure of angle C | is | 180°. |

$$(x + 8y - 1) \quad + \quad (3y + 4) \quad + \quad (7x + 5) \quad = \quad 180$$

Also, in an isosceles triangle, angles opposite the sides that have equal measure also have equal measure.

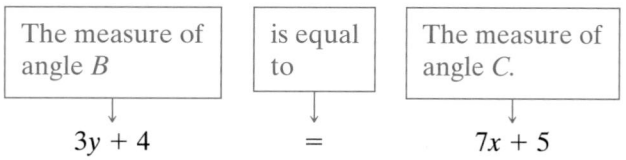

| The measure of angle B | is equal to | The measure of angle C. |

$$3y + 4 \qquad = \qquad 7x + 5$$

Step 3. Solve the system and answer the problem's question.

The resulting system is

$$x + 8y - 1 + 3y + 4 + 7x + 5 = 180 \qquad \text{Equation 1}$$
$$3y + 4 = 7x + 5 \qquad \text{Equation 2}$$

Writing each equation in the form $Ax + By = C$ results in a simplified system.

$$8x + 11y = 172 \qquad \text{Take a moment to verify that this step is correct.}$$
$$-7x + 3y = 1$$

We solve by addition to eliminate x.

$$8x + 11y = 172 \quad \xrightarrow{\text{Multiply by 7.}} \quad 56x + 77y = 1204$$
$$-7x + 3y = 1 \quad \xrightarrow{\text{Multiply by 8.}} \quad \underline{-56x + 24y = 8}$$
$$\text{Add:} \qquad 101y = 1212$$
$$y = 12$$

We now find the value of x by back-substituting 12 for y in either of the system's equations.

$$-7x + 3y = 1 \qquad \text{Equation 2}$$
$$-7x + 3(12) = 1 \qquad \text{Back-substitute 12 for } y.$$
$$-7x + 36 = 1$$
$$-7x = -35 \qquad \text{Subtract 36 from both sides.}$$
$$x = 5 \qquad \text{Divide both sides by } -7.$$

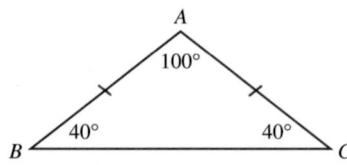

$$m\angle A = x + 8y - 1 = 5 + 8(12) - 1 = 5 + 96 - 1 = 100°$$
$$m\angle B = 3y + 4 = 3(12) + 4 = 36 + 4 = 40°$$
$$m\angle C = 7x + 5 = 7(5) + 5 = 35 + 5 = 40°$$

The angles measure 100°, 40°, and 40°.

Step 4. Check the answers in the original wording of the problem.

The sum of the measures of the angles is 180°: $100 + 40 + 40 = 180$. Furthermore, angles B and C have equal measure. Both measure 40°.   ■

EXAMPLE 5   A Standard Badminton Court

The perimeter of a badminton court is 128 feet. After a game of badminton, a player's coach estimates that the athlete has run a total of 444 feet, which is equivalent to six times the court's length plus nine times its width. What are the dimensions of a standard badminton court?

Solution

Step 1. Use variables to represent unknown quantities.

As shown in Figure 5.14 in the margin on page 393, L represents the court's length and W represents its width.

Step 2. Write a system of equations describing the problem's conditions.

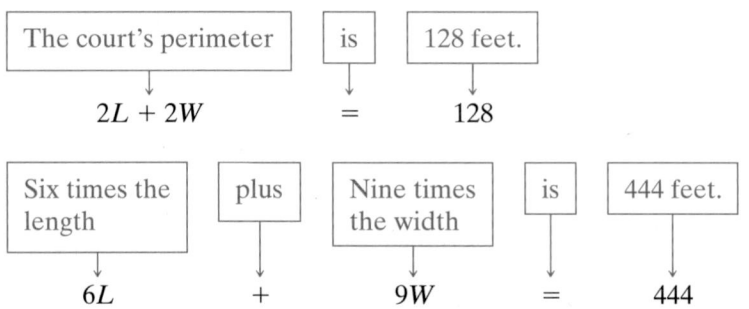

Step 3. Solve the system and answer the problem's question.

The system

$$2L + 2W = 128 \quad \text{Equation 1}$$
$$6L + 9W = 444 \quad \text{Equation 2}$$

can be solved by addition. We'll eliminate L by multiplying both sides of equation 1 by -3.

$$2L + 2W = 128 \quad \xrightarrow{\text{Multiply by } -3.} \quad -6L - 6W = -384$$
$$6L + 9W = 444 \quad \xrightarrow{\text{No change}} \quad \underline{6L + 9W = \quad 444}$$
$$\text{Add:} \qquad 3W = 60$$
$$W = 20$$

We now find the value of L by back-substituting 20 for W in either of the system's equations.

$$2L + 2W = 128 \quad \text{Equation 1}$$
$$2L + 2(20) = 128 \quad \text{Back-substitute 20 for } W.$$
$$2L + 40 = 128 \quad \text{Multiply.}$$
$$2L = 88 \quad \text{Subtract 40 from both sides.}$$
$$L = 44 \quad \text{Divide both sides by 2.}$$

Step 4. Check the answers in the original wording of the problem.

A badminton court measures 20 feet by 44 feet. We leave the check to you.   ■

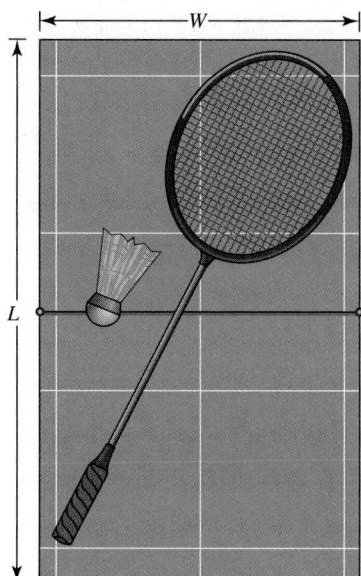

Figure 5.14

A badminton court

In some situations, writing a system of equations requires knowing a formula that models the variables under consideration. We have seen how the formula

$RT = D$ (rate times time equals distance)

models uniform motion situations. Some uniform motion problems involve airplanes that fly with or against the wind, or boats that move with or against the current. These problems contain two unknowns—the speed of the plane in still air and the speed of the wind, or the speed of the boat in still water and the speed of the current. These situations are summarized in the box.

Uniform motion involving two unknown speeds

A Plane Flying With or Against the Wind

$x =$ Plane's speed in still air

$y =$ Wind's speed

$x + y =$ Plane's speed moving with the wind (the wind is called the tailwind)

$x - y =$ Plane's speed moving against the wind (the wind is called the headwind)

A Boat Moving With or Against the Current

$x =$ Boat's speed in still water

$y =$ Current's speed

$x + y =$ Boat's speed moving with the current (the boat is moving downstream)

$x - y =$ Boat's speed moving against the current (the boat is moving upstream)

EXAMPLE 6 **A Uniform Motion Problem Involving Two Unknown Speeds**

When an airplane flies with the wind, it can travel 3500 kilometers in 5 hours. When the same airplane flies in the opposite direction, against the wind, it takes 7 hours to fly the same distance. Find the speed of the plane in still air and the speed of the wind.

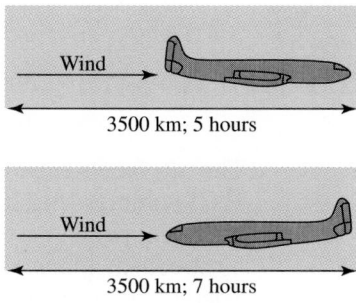

Solution

Step 1. Use variables to represent unknown quantities.

Let

$x =$ Speed of plane in still air

$y =$ Speed of wind

Recall that $RT = D$ (the rate, or speed, multiplied by time equals distance).

	R	**×**	**T**	**=**	**D**
Trip with the Wind	$x + y$		5		$5(x + y)$
Trip Against the Wind	$x - y$		7		$7(x - y)$

Step 2. Write a system of equations describing the problem's conditions.

The distance of the trip with the wind	is	3500 kilometers.
$5(x + y)$	$=$	3500

The distance of the trip against the wind	is	3500 kilometers.
$7(x - y)$	$=$	3500

Our system is

$5(x + y) = 3500$ Equation 1

$7(x - y) = 3500$ Equation 2

Step 3. Solve the system and answer the problem's question.

Using the distributive property, we obtain

$5x + 5y = 3500$

$7x - 7y = 3500$

We will solve by addition, eliminating y.

$5x + 5y = 3500$ → Multiply by 7. → $35x + 35y = 24{,}500$

$7x - 7y = 3500$ → Multiply by 5. → $\underline{35x - 35y = 17{,}500}$

Add: $70x \qquad = 42{,}000$

$x = 600$

$5x + 5y = 3500$ Equation 1

$5(600) + 5y = 3500$ Back-substitute 600 for x.

$3000 + 5y = 3500$

$5y = 500$ Subtract 3000 from both sides.

$y = 100$ Divide both sides by 5.

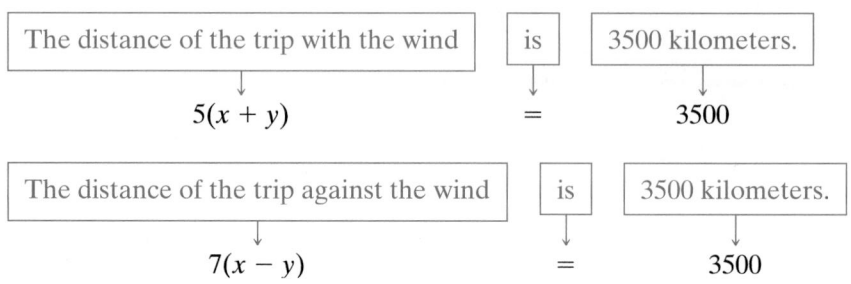

3000

2000

1000

500

0 km/h

1975 Concorde

1965 DC-8/63

1955 Comet 4

1945 Constellation

1935 DC-3

1925 Fokker

Passenger aircrafts and their maximum speeds

The airplane's speed is 600 kilometers per hour and the speed of the wind is 100 kilometers per hour. (The graph shown in the margin puts this answer in historical perspective.)

Step 4. Check the answers in the original wording of the problem.

Speed of plane with the wind $= 600 + 100$ or 700 kilometers per hour.

Speed of plane against the wind $= 600 - 100$ or 500 kilometers per hour.

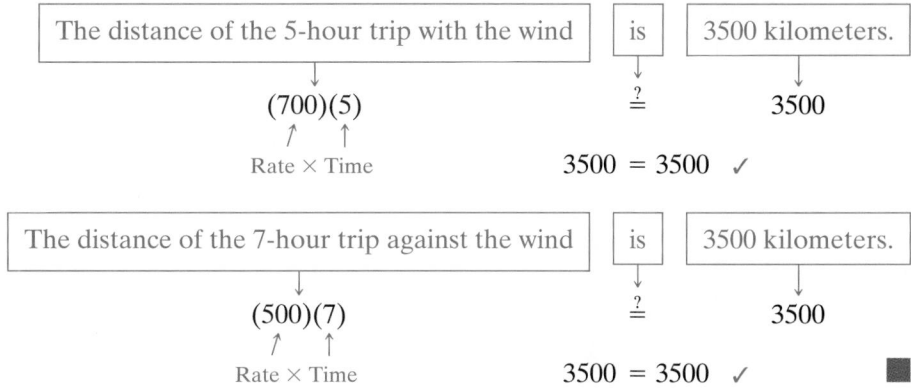

| The distance of the 5-hour trip with the wind | is | 3500 kilometers. |

$$(700)(5)$$

Rate × Time

$$\overset{?}{=}$$

3500

$$3500 = 3500 \checkmark$$

| The distance of the 7-hour trip against the wind | is | 3500 kilometers. |

$$(500)(7)$$

Rate × Time

$$\overset{?}{=}$$

3500

$$3500 = 3500 \checkmark$$ ■

PROBLEM SET 5.4

Practice and Application Problems

1. In 1995, Sweden and Norway had more women members of parliament (MPs) than any other democratic countries. Combined, the two countries had 206 women in parliaments. Taking double the number of women MPs in Sweden and adding this to triple the number of women MPs in Norway results in 477.
   a. How many women MPs are there in each country?
   b. The total MPs in Sweden is 349 and in Norway the number is 165. What percent (to the nearest whole percent) of the total MPs are women for each of the two countries?

World Parliaments in 1995 with Most Women Members

	Country	Women MPs	Total MPs	% Women
1	Sweden		349	
2	Norway		165	
3	Denmark	60	179	34
4	Finland	67	200	34
5	Netherlands	47	150	31
6	Seychelles	9	33	27
7	Germany	177	672	26
8	Mozambique	63	250	25
9	South Africa	100	400	25
10	Iceland	15	63	24

2. Simon Rose, author of *One FM Essential Film Guide* (1993) surveyed feature films released from 1983

through 1993, listing the most common names of movie characters. The list is shown here, but the number of characters with the names Jack and John is omitted. Combined, there were 230 movie characters with these names. Taking triple the number of Jack characters and subtracting double the number of John characters gives 16 less than triple the number of George characters. How many movie characters had the names Jack and John from 1983 through 1993?

Most Common Names of Movie Characters

	Name	Characters
1	Jack	
2	John	
3	Frank	87
4	Harry	72
5	David	63
6	George	62
7	Michael	59
7	Tom	59
9	Mary	54
10	Paul	53

3. The bar graph at the top of the next page shows where people over 65 in the United States live. A total of 23% of elderly men live either alone or with relatives. The sum of double the percent of men who live alone and triple the percent who live with relatives exceeds the percent of U.S. women over 65 who live with their spouse by 13%. What percent of elderly men live alone and what percent live with relatives?

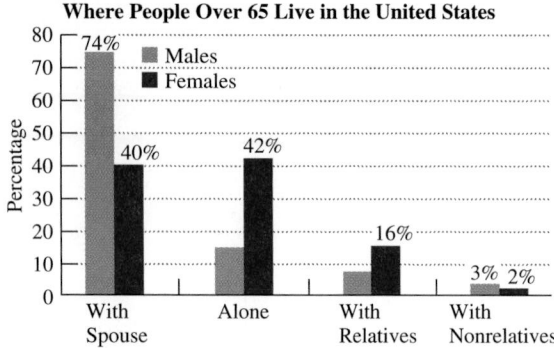

Where People Over 65 Live in the United States

Source: U.S. Bureau of the Census *Statistical Abstract 1993:* Table 71.

4. The bar graph below is based on surveys of double-income families and the percent of men and women in these families who said they had the greater responsibility for various areas of the housework. In the category of paying bills, a total of 98% of this responsibility was taken on by either women or men. (One can surmise that in 2% of the families, this responsibility was equally shared.) The difference between the percent of women and the percent of men with the greater responsibility for paying bills was 28%. Find the percent of women and the percent of men who said they had the greater responsibility for paying bills.

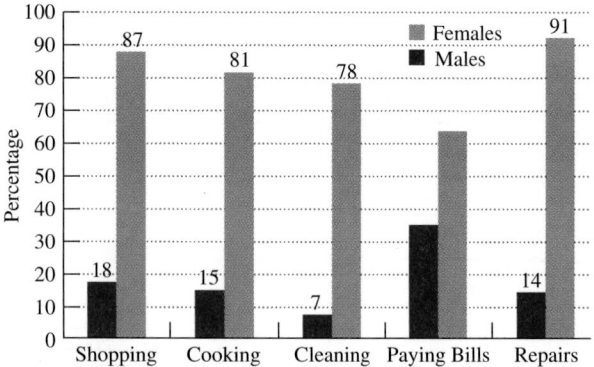

Source: Galinsky et al. 1993.

5. Cholesterol intake should be limited to 300 mg or less each day. One serving of scrambled eggs from Mc-Donalds and one Double Beef Whopper from Burger King exceed this intake by 241 mg. Two servings of scrambled eggs and three Double Beef Whoppers provide 1257 mg of cholesterol. Determine the cholesterol content in each item.

6. Two McDonald's Quarter Pounders and three Burger King Whoppers with cheese contain 520 mg of cholesterol. Three Quarter Pounders and one Whopper with

cheese exceed the suggested daily cholesterol intake of 300 mg by 53 mg. Determine the cholesterol content in each item.

Claes Oldenburg Two Cheeseburgers, with Everything (Dual Hamburgers), 1962. Burlap soaked in plaster, painted with enamel $7 \times 14\frac{3}{4} \times 8\frac{5}{8}$ in. Collection, The Museum of Modern Art, New York. Philip Johnson Fund. Photograph ©1997 The Museum of Modern Art, New York.

7. Nutritional information for macaroni and broccoli is given in the table. How many servings of each would it take to get exactly 14 grams of protein and 48 grams of carbohydrates?

	Macaroni	Broccoli
Protein (grams/serving)	3	2
Carbohydrates (grams/serving)	16	4

8. The calorie-nutrient information for an apple and an avocado is given in the table. How many of each should be eaten to get exactly 1000 calories and 100 grams of carbohydrates?

	One Apple	One Avocado
Calories	100	350
Carbohydrates (grams)	24	14

9. In a clothing store, all sweaters are sold at one fixed price and all shirts are sold at another fixed price. If one sweater and three shirts cost $42, while three sweaters and two shirts cost $56, find the price of one sweater and one shirt.

10. A restaurant purchased eight tablecloths and five napkins for $106. A week later, a tablecloth and six napkins were bought for $24. Find the cost of one tablecloth and one napkin, assuming the same prices for both purchases.

11. In the isosceles triangle shown in the figure, $AB = AC$. Find the measure of each angle in the triangle.

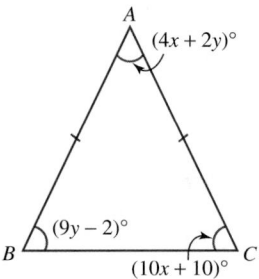

12. Find x and y in the figure, and then find the measure of each of the three angles.
(*Hint:* Here are two relationships needed to write this system of equations:
a. Angles A and B are supplementary, so the sum of their measures is $180°$.
b. Angles B and C are also supplementary.)

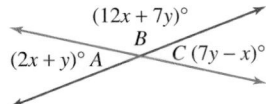

13. Find the measure of each angle in the parallelogram shown in the figure if it is known that consecutive angles of a parallelogram are supplementary and opposite angles of a parallelogram are equal in measure.

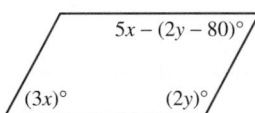

14. In the figure, lines L_1 and L_2 are parallel. Line L_3 is a transversal, passing through the parallel lines. If two lines are parallel, the interior angles on the same side of the transversal (angles A and B) are supplementary. If two lines are parallel, the corresponding angles (angles in the same corresponding positions, angles A and C) are equal in measure. Use these geometric statements to find the measures of angles A, B, and C.

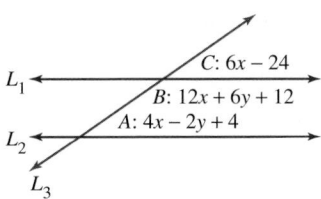

15. The perimeter of a tennis court is 228 feet. After a round of tennis, a player's coach estimates that the athlete has run a total of 690 feet, which is equivalent

to 7 times the court's length plus four times its width. What are the dimensions of a standard tennis court?

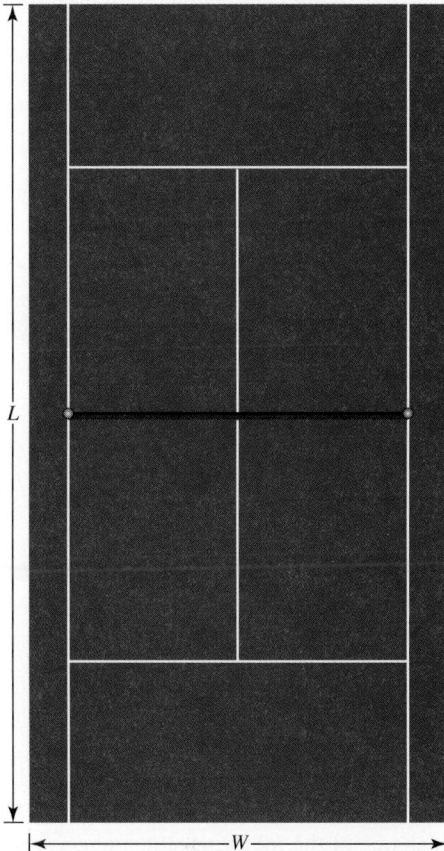

16. The perimeter of a rectangle is 20 meters. If the length is increased by four times the width, the sum is 19 meters. What are the dimensions of the rectangle? What is its area?

17. The perimeter of a rectangle is 32 meters. If the length is increased by four times the width, the sum is 31 meters. What are the dimensions of the rectangle? What is its area?

18. When a crew rows with the current, it travels 16 miles in 2 hours. Against the current, the crew rows 8 miles in 2 hours. Find the rate of rowing in still water and the rate of the current.

19. When a boat travels upstream (against the current), it takes 2 hours to travel 12 kilometers. The return trip downstream (with the current) takes 1 hour. Find the speed of the boat in still water and the rate of the current.

20. A swimmer takes 2 hours to swim 10 miles with the current. If the return trip against the current takes four times as long, what is the rate of the current?

21. A hawk can fly 300 miles in 8 hours with the wind. Flying against the wind, the hawk covers only one- third of the distance in 7 hours. What is the rate of the wind?

A business that manufactures and sells a product has cost and revenue equations that form a system. The break-even point is the number of products that must be manufactured and sold so that the cost of making the product equals the revenue brought in from the sale of the product. This information forms the basis of Problems 22–27.

22. A company that manufactures and sells small tables has fixed costs of $250 daily. Each table costs $100 to manufacture. Explain why the linear equation $y = 250 + 100x$ gives the total cost of manufacturing x tables daily.

Manufacturing Cost: $100
Selling Price: $125
Daily Operating Costs: $250

23. The tables are sold at $125 each. Write an equation for y that describes the revenue generated from selling x tables each day.

24. Write a system of equations for cost and revenue using the two equations in Problems 22 and 23. Then solve the system.

25. The value of x from Problem 24 represents the number of tables needed to break even. How many tables must the company sell each day to break even? At that point, how much has the company spent and how much has it taken in?

26. Describe how the graph below, generated by a graphing utility, shows the results from Problems 22–25.

27. Looking at the graph, write a statement about the company's daily profit and loss if $x < 10$ and $x > 10$.

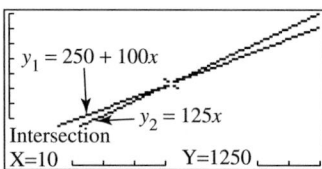

True–False Critical Thinking Problem

28. Which one of the following statements is true?

a. A cash register contains $24.35 in dimes and quarters. There are 134 coins in all. If x represents the number of dimes and y represents the number of quarters, the system that models this situation is

$$x + y = 134$$
$$0.10x + 0.25y = 24.35$$

b. A company purchases six large delivery vans and three small ones. One of the company's stores receives three of the large vans and one small one for a total cost of $122,000. The company's other store receives the remaining vans for a total cost of $148,000. If x represents the cost of a large van and y represents the cost of a small van, the system that models this situation is

$$3x + y = 122,000$$
$$6x + 3y = 148,000$$

c. Three times the tens digit plus two times the units' digit of a two-digit number is 24. The number is seven less than four times its units digit. If t represents the tens' digit and u the units' digit, the system that models this situation is

$$3t + 2u = 24$$
$$tu = 4u - 7$$

d. When a crew rows with the current, it travels 18 miles in 2 hours. Against the current, the crew rows 10 miles in 2 hours. If x represents the rate of the boat in still water and y represents the rate of the current, the system that models this situation is

$$2(x - y) = 18$$
$$2(x + y) = 10$$

Technology Problem

29. Select any two problems that you solved from Problems 1–21. Use a graphing utility to graph the system of equations that you wrote for that problem. Then use the ⬚TRACE⬚ or intersection feature to show the point on the graphs that corresponds to the problem's solution.

Writing in Mathematics

30. Describe the conditions in a problem that enable it to be solved using a system of linear equations.

31. Write a word problem that can be solved by translating to a system of linear equations. Then solve the problem.

Critical Thinking Problems

32. In Lewis Carroll's *Through the Looking Glass,* the following dialogue takes place:

> **Tweedledum (to Tweedledee):** *The sum of your weight and twice mine is 361 pounds.*
> **Tweedledee (to Tweedledum):** *Contrawise, the sum of your weight and twice mine is 362 pounds.*

Find the weight of the two enantiomorphs.

The characters are what geometers called enantiomorphs, mirror-image forms of each other. Illustration by Sir John Tenniel. Courtesy of Lilly Library, Indiana University.

33. The perimeter of the larger rectangle in the figure shown below is 58 meters. The combined lengths of the three sides of the smaller rectangle, excluding the side that it shares with a portion of the side of the larger rectangle, is 17.5 meters. Find x and y.

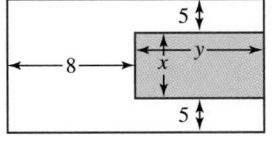

34. The perimeter of parallelogram $ABCD$ in the figure is 50 meters. The perimeter of trapezoid $AECD$ is 39 meters. Using the fact that opposite sides of a parallelogram have equal measures, find AE, EB, and DC.

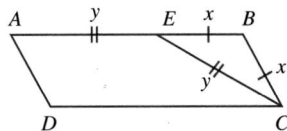

35. One apartment is directly above a second apartment. The resident living downstairs calls his neighbor living above him and states, "If one of you is willing to come downstairs, we'll have the same number of people in both apartments." The upstairs' resident responds, "We're all too tired to move. Why don't one of you come up here? Then we will have twice as many people up here as you've got down there." How many people are in each apartment?

36. Tourist: "How many birds and lions do you have in your zoo?" Zookeeper: "There are 30 heads and 100 feet." Tourist: "I can't tell from that." Zookeeper: "Oh, yes, you can!" Can you?

37. A boat in distress was sighted from a Coast Guard station located at $(-1, 0)$ on a line with slope $\frac{2}{3}$. The same boat was spotted on a line with slope $-\frac{2}{3}$ from another Coast Guard station located at $(14, -2)$. Find the coordinates of the boat in distress.

Review Problems

38. Graph: $4x - 2y > 8$.

39. A wallet contains $800 in $20 and $10 bills. If there are 32 more tens than twenties, how many $20 bills are there?

40. If $f(x) = x^2 - x - 2$, what is $f(-1)$?

SECTION 5.5

Solutions Manual   Tutorial   Video 6

Solving Systems of Inequalities

Objective

I Graph the solution for a system of linear inequalities.

In Section 4.7, we graphed linear inequalities in two variables, such as $2x - y < 4$. We now turn our attention to solving systems of inequalities, such as

$$2x - y < 4$$
$$x + y \geqslant -1$$

A *system of linear inequalities* consists of two or more inequalities. The *solution* of a system of linear inequalities contains all ordered pairs that make all inequalities of the system true. Sometimes these systems represent physical situations in which two or more constraints are imposed, as we shall see in some of the applied problems.

The steps we use to solve a system of linear inequalities are shown in the box.

I Graph the solution for a system of linear inequalities.

Solving systems of linear inequalities

1. Graph each inequality in the system on the same coordinate axes.
2. The solution of the system is shown graphically by the region where the graphs overlap. Indicate this region by using dark shading on the intersection of the graphs.
3. Verify the solution by selecting a test point from the region shaded in step 2. The coordinates of the test point must satisfy each inequality in the system.

EXAMPLE I   **Solving a System of Linear Inequalities**

Graph the solution of the system:

$$y \geqslant x + 1$$
$$x \geqslant 2$$

Solution

We begin by graphing $y \geqslant x + 1$, and we graph $y = x + 1$ as a solid line. The form of the equation is $y = mx + b$, so $b = 1$ (y-intercept $= 1$) and $m = 1 \left(\text{slope} = \dfrac{1}{1} = \dfrac{\text{Rise}}{\text{Run}} \right)$. The graph of $y \geqslant x + 1$ includes the line of $y = x + 1$ and the half-plane above this line, shown in Figure 5.15 on page 401.

Now we graph $x \geqslant 2$ on the same coordinate axes. The graph of $x = 2$ is a line parallel to the y-axis with x-intercept $= 2$. Since $x \geqslant 2$, the half-plane to the right of $x = 2$ is included. The solution of the system is shown as the blue shaded region in Figure 5.16, the intersection of the two graphs. The solution of the system is shown again in Figure 5.17. The region, including portions of the graphs of both lines, contains points whose coordinates satisfy both $y \geqslant x + 1$ and $x \geqslant 2$. ∎

Discover for yourself

Select two points from the region in Figure 5.17. Show that each point satisfies both $y \geqslant x + 1$ and $x \geqslant 2$. Now select a point that lies on the part of $y = x + 1$ shown in Figure 5.17 and verify that this point satisfies both inequalities of the system.

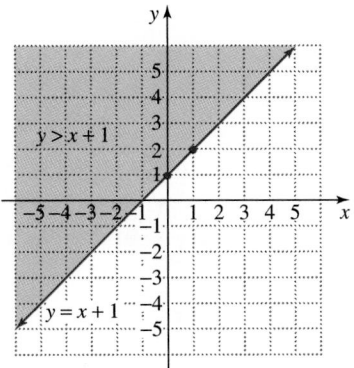

Figure 5.15

The graph of $y \geqslant x + 1$

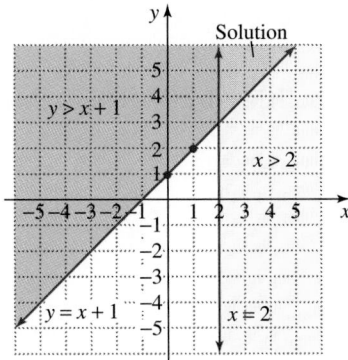

Figure 5.16

Adding the graph of $x \geqslant 2$

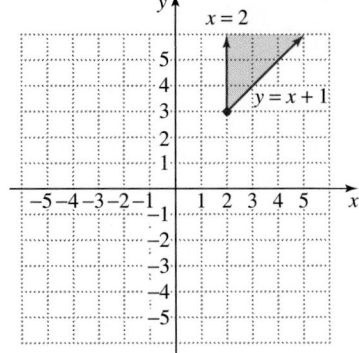

Figure 5.17

The graph of $y \geqslant x + 1$ and $x \geqslant 2$

EXAMPLE 2 Solving a System of Linear Inequalities

Graph the solution of the system:

$$2x - y < 4$$
$$x + y \geqslant -1$$

iscover for yourself

Select two points from the region in Figure 5.20. Show that each point satisfies both of the system's inequalities. Now select a point along the solid line in Figure 5.20 and show that it satisfies both of the system's inequalities.

Solution

We begin by graphing $2x - y < 4$, and we graph $2x - y = 4$ as a dashed line. (If $x = 0$, $y = -4$, and if $y = 0$, then $x = 2$. The x-intercept is 2 and the y-intercept is -4.) Since $(0, 0)$ makes the inequality true, we shade the half-plane containing $(0, 0)$, shown in dark blue in Figure 5.18 at the bottom of the page.

Now we graph $x + y \geqslant -1$ on the same coordinate axes, graphing $x + y = -1$ as a solid line. (If $x = 0$, then $y = -1$, and if $y = 0$, then $x = -1$. The x-intercept and y-intercept are both -1.) Since $(0, 0)$ makes the inequality true, we shade the half-plane containing $(0, 0)$. The solution of the system is shown graphically by the intersection (the overlap) of the two half-planes, shown in Figure 5.19 as the light blue shaded region. The solution of the system is shown again in Figure 5.20.

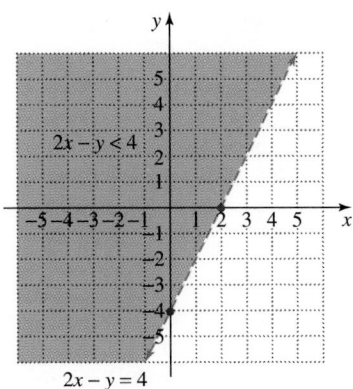

Figure 5.18

The graph of $2x - y < 4$

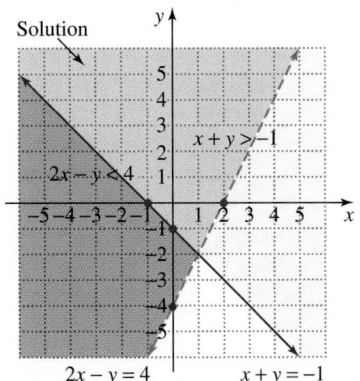

Figure 5.19

Adding the graph of $x + y \geqslant -1$

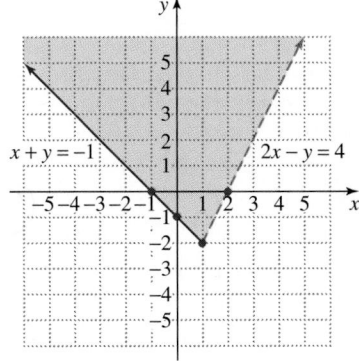

Figure 5.20

The graph of $2x - y < 4$ and $x + y \geqslant -1$

ENRICHMENT ESSAY

Inequalities and Aerobic Exercise

The target zone for aerobic exercise is given by the following system of inequalities in which a represents one's age and p is one's pulse rate.

$$10 \leq a \leq 70$$
$$p \geq -\frac{2}{3}a + 150$$
$$p \leq -a + 190$$

The graph of this target zone is shown in the figure. As you find your age, the shaded region indicates upper and lower limits for your pulse rate when engaging in aerobic exercise. Why do pulse rates in the target zone decrease with age?

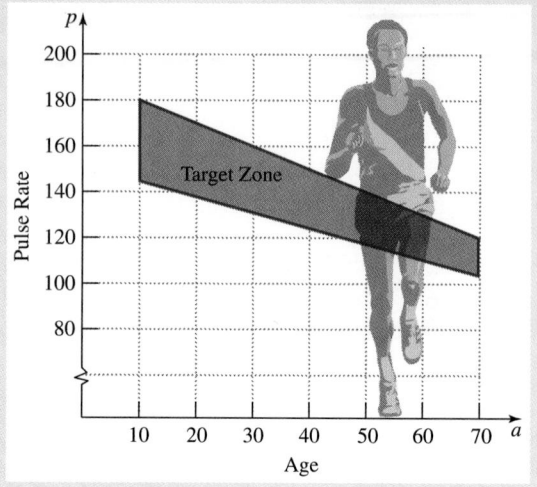

PROBLEM SET 5.5

Practice Problems

Graph the solution for each system of linear inequalities in Problems 1–36.

1. $x + y \leq 4$
    $x - y \leq 1$

2. $x + y \geq 3$
    $x - y \leq 2$

3. $2x - 4y \leq 8$
    $x + y \geq -1$

4. $4x + 3y \leq 12$
    $x - 2y \leq 4$

5. $x + 3y \leq 6$
    $x - 2y \leq 4$

6. $2x + y \leq 4$
    $2x - y \leq 6$

7. $x - 4y \leq 4$
    $x \geq 2y$

8. $3x + 2y \leq 6$
    $x - y \geq 4$

9. $2x + y \leq 4$
    $x + 2 \geq y$

10. $y \leq 2x - 1$
    $y \geq 2x - 3$

11. $y \leq 2x + 2$
    $y \geq 2x + 1$

12. $y \leq 2x - 3$
    $y \geq -x + 2$

13. $y > 2x - 3$
    $y < 2x + 1$

14. $y < -2x + 3$
    $y > -2x$

15. $x - 2y > 4$
    $2x + y \geq 6$

16. $3x + y < 6$
    $x + 2y \geq 2$

17. $x \geq 3$
    $y \geq 3$

18. $x \leq 3$
    $y \geq 2$

19. $x \geq 2$
    $y < 3$

20. $x \geq -1$
    $y < -2$

21. $x + y < 1$
    $x + y > 4$

22. $x - y < 1$
    $x - y > 3$

23. $x > 0$
    $y \leq 0$

24. $x \leq 0$
    $y > 0$

25. $2x + y \geq 6$
    $y \leq -2x - 4$

26. $3x + y \geq 6$
    $y \leq -3x - 2$

27. $y \geq 2x + 1$
    $y \leq 5$

28. $y \geq \frac{1}{2}x + 2$
    $y \leq 3$

29. $x + y \leq 5$
    $x \geq 0$
    $y \geq 0$

30. $2x + y \leq 4$
    $x \geq 0$
    $y \geq 0$

31. $4x - 3y > 12$
    $x \geq 0$
    $y \leq 0$

32. $2x - 6y > 12$
    $x \leq 0$
    $y \geq 0$

33. $0 \leq x \leq 3$
    $0 \leq y \leq 3$

34. $0 \leq x \leq 5$
    $0 \leq y \leq 5$

35. $x - y \leq 4$
    $x + 2y \leq 4$
    $x \geq 0$

36. $x - y \leq 3$
    $2x + y \leq 4$
    $y \geq 0$

Application Problems

37. The graph shows the percent of married couples using contraceptives in developing regions of the world from 1960 through 1990. Write a system of inequalities in *y* estimating:
   a. The percent of married couples in Latin America using contraception for $x \geq 1975$ and $x \leq 1990$.
   b. The percent of married couples in East Asia using contraception for $x \geq 1970$ and $x \leq 1985$.

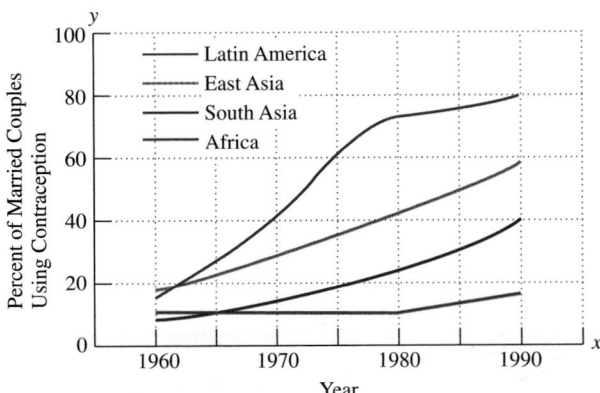

Source: Thomas Merrick, *U.S. Population Assistance. A Continued Priority for the 1990s?* (Population Reference Bureau, Washington, D.C., April 1990). p. 16.

38. The calorie/nutrient information for a banana and a bowl of bran cereal is given in the table. Suppose that a person's breakfast consists of these two foods, with *x* representing the number of bananas and *y* the number of bowls of bran cereal.
   a. The calorie content of the breakfast is not to exceed 500 calories. Thus, $100x + 125y \leq 500$. Graph this inequality.
   b. The carbohydrate content of the breakfast must be at least 120 grams. Thus, $20x + 40y \geq 120$. Graph this inequality in the same rectangular coordinate system as part (a).
   c. Breakfast is to consist of both foods, with fractional parts of either a banana or a bowl of cereal permitted. Select two points from the region that you graphed in part (b). These two points are part of the solution of the inequality's system. Describe what these two points mean in terms of the number of bananas and the number of bowls of cereal that will make up the breakfast.

	One Banana	One Bowl of Bran Cereal
Calories	100	125
Carbohydrates (grams)	20	40

True–False Critical Thinking Problems

39. Which one of the following statements is true?
   a. The system of inequalities shown by the graph in the figure on the right is $x \leq 3$ and $y \geq 2$.
   b. The graph of the system

   $$x + y > 5$$
   $$x - y < 0$$

   is the region containing the point $(0, 6)$.
   c. The graph of the system

   $$y > 2x - 4$$
   $$y > 2x + 4$$

   is the region between two parallel lines.
   d. There are no solutions to the system.

   $$y \geq 4x + 3$$
   $$y \leq 4x + 3$$

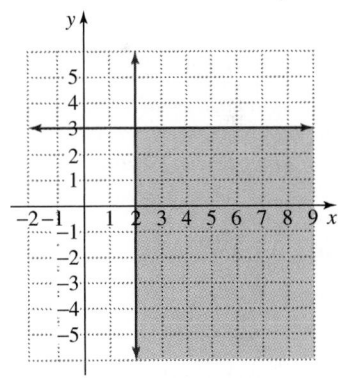

40. Which one of the following statements is true?
   a. The system of inequalities shown by the graph in the first figure on the next page is $3x - y \leq 6$ and $x \geq -1$.
   b. The ordered pair $(2, 5)$ is a solution to the system.

   $$2x > 4$$
   $$y \leq 5$$

c. The graph of the system

$$y < x + 3$$
$$y > x - 2$$

is the region between two parallel lines.

d. The ordered pair $(4, -3)$ is a solution to the system.

$$2x + 3y < 6$$
$$y > 2x - 1$$

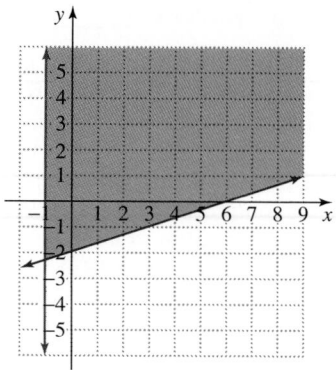

Writing in Mathematics

41. Explain how to solve systems of linear inequalities.

42. Describe the conditions that will result in a system of two linear inequalities having no solution. Give an example of such a system.

43. Describe the conditions that will result in a system of two linear inequalities having all points in the rectangular coordinate system as a solution. Give an example of such a system.

Critical Thinking Problems

Linear programming is a technique used in business, social science, and the military as a method for finding the best, or optimal, solution to problems. The quantity to be optimized is expressed in the form $Ax + By$ and is subject to a number of constraints, represented by a system of inequalities. The inequality system can be graphed using the techniques discussed in this section. The solution to the problem occurs at one of the corner points of the graphed region. Here's a specific example. Read the example and then work Problems 44–49 in order.

Robert Yager/Tony Stone Images

Bottled water and medical supplies are to be shipped to victims of an earthquake by plane. Each container of bottled water serves 10 people and each medical kit aids 6 people. However, the planes are bound by the following constraints: They can carry no more than 80,000 pounds and a total volume that does not exceed 6000 cubic feet. The bottled water weighs 20 pounds per container and is 1 cubic foot. The medical kits each weigh 10 pounds and also measure 1 cubic foot. The problem: How many bottles of water and how many medical kits should be sent on each plane to maximize the number of earthquake victims who can be helped?
Begin by letting

$x =$ The number of bottles of water

$y =$ The number of medical kits

44. Each bottle of water serves 10 people and each kit aids 6 people. Fill in the missing portion of the following translation, and write an expression in the form $Ax + By$ for the number of people who can be helped.

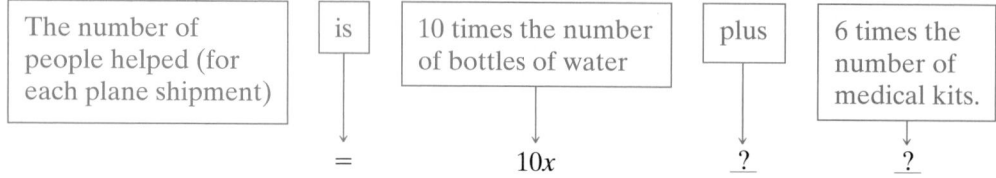

45. One constraint is that each plane can carry no more than 80,000 pounds. Fill in the missing portions of the following translation, and write an inequality that models the pound-limit constraint.

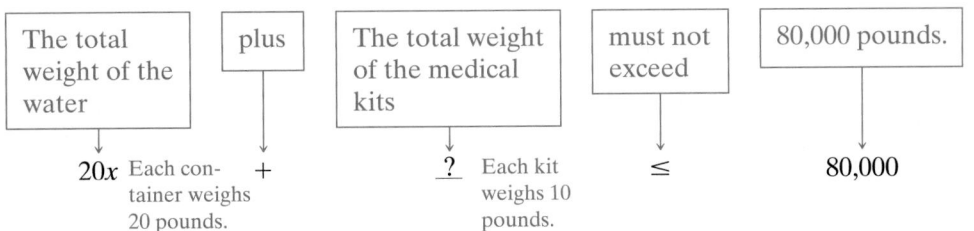

| The total weight of the water | plus | The total weight of the medical kits | must not exceed | 80,000 pounds. |

$20x$ Each container weighs 20 pounds. $\quad + \quad$? Each kit weighs 10 pounds. $\quad \leq \quad$ 80,000

46. A second constraint is that each plane can carry a total volume that does not exceed 6000 cubic feet. Fill in the missing portions of the following translation, and write an inequality that models the volume-limit constraint.

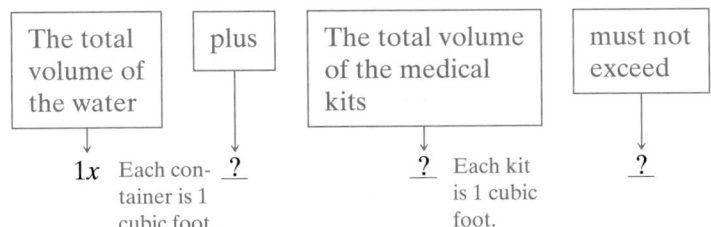

| The total volume of the water | plus | The total volume of the medical kits | must not exceed | 6000 cubic feet. |

$1x$ Each container is 1 cubic foot. ? $\quad$? Each kit is 1 cubic foot. $\quad$? $\quad$?

47. The graph of the system of inequalities representing the pound and volume constraints is shown here. Since x and y represent the number of bottles of water and medical kits, respectively, only the first quadrant is shown. Take a moment to verify that the system is drawn correctly, verifying the intercepts and the intersection point.

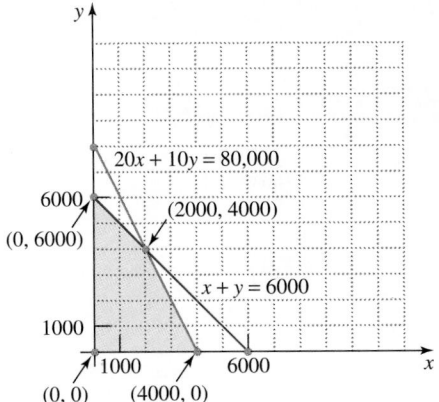

$20x + 10y = 80,000$
(2000, 4000)
$x + y = 6000$
6000
(0, 6000)
1000
(0, 0)
(4000, 0)
1000
6000

48. Remember that we want to maximize the expression $10x + 6y$, the number of people who can be helped. Linear programming theory states that this expression can be maximized at a corner point of the graphed re-

gion of constraints. Fill in the missing portions of the following table.

Number of People Who Can Be Helped	Corner Point of the Graphed Region	Evaluating the Number of People Who Can Be Helped, Using the Corner Point
$10x + 6y$	$(0, 0)$	$10(0) + 6(0) = 0$
$10x + 6y$	$(4000, 0)$	$10(4000) + 6(0) = $?
$10x + 6y$	$(2000, 4000)$	?
$10x + 6y$	$(0, 6000)$	?

49. Look at the table in Problem 48. What is the maximum value for $10x + 6y$? What is the value of x and what is the value of y that gives the maximum? Use this information to fill in the missing portions of the following sentence: In practical terms, the maximum number of earthquake victims who can be helped with each plane shipment is _____. This can be accomplished by sending _____ water containers and _____ medical kits per plane.

Review Problems _____

50. Graph $y = x^2 - 1$ by filling in the table of coordinates and then sketching the graph of the function.

x	-2	-1	0	1	2
y					

51. Write the point-slope form, the slope-intercept form, and the standard form of the line passing through $(-5, -2)$ and $(-1, 6)$.

52. Perform the indicated operations:

$$-5 + [(-11 + 3) - (-1 - 9)].$$

CHAPTER PROJECT

Magic Squares

Interesting lines may form many patterns as they cross a plane. When we look at the precise square grid of tile on a bathroom floor or the seemingly random bits of sharp-edged stone in a mosaic, we are also seeing the intersecting lines between the hard surfaces. One way to produce an interesting pattern of intersecting lines is by connecting the numbers in a *magic square*. The lines thus created are called *magic lines*.

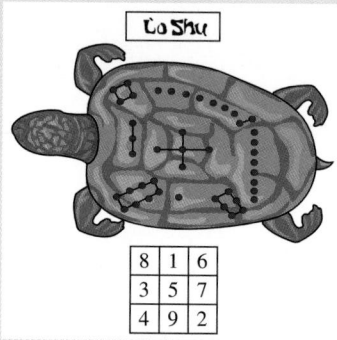

Figure 5.21

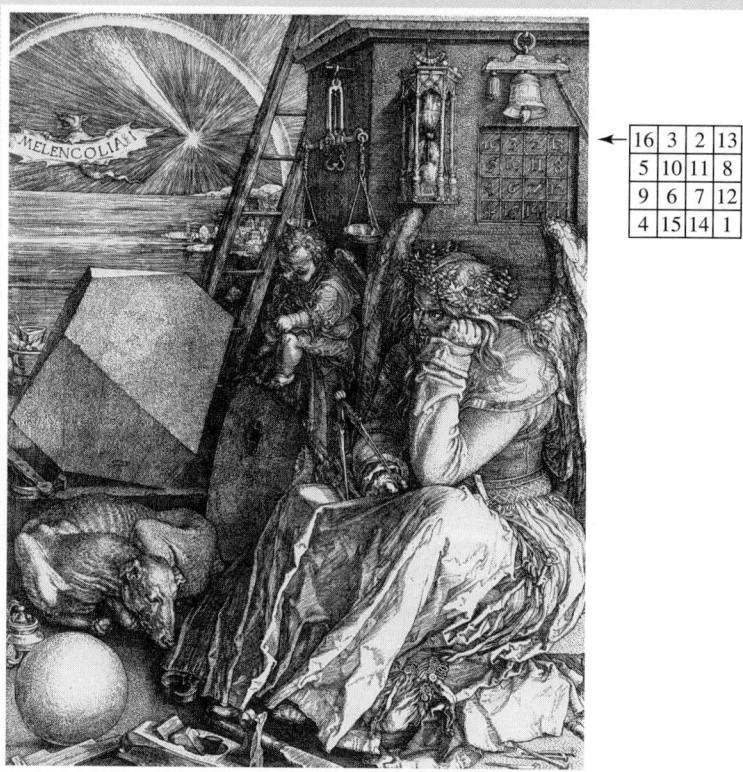

Figure 5.22
Albrecht Dürer, "Melancholia." Foto Marburg/Art Resource, N Y.

Magic squares are an array of numbers in a grid such that the sum of the numbers in each row, each column, and the two diagonals is the same for a particular square. For example, in Figure 5.21, the sum of the numbers in each row, each column, and the two diagonals is 15. The squares are described by how many rows and columns they contain. Thus, we have 3 × 3 squares, 4 × 4 squares, 11 × 11 squares, and so on.

Magic squares have been studied for thousands of years, with the earliest known reference from 2200 B.C. in the Chinese legend of Lo Shu, where a 3 × 3 square was said to be inscribed on the back of a turtle. (See Figure 5.21.) Another famous magic square is found in Albrecht Duer's engraving of *Melancholia*. (See Figure 5.22.) You can see the 4 × 4 magic square in the upper-right-hand corner of the engraving. Notice that the date of the engraving, 1514, is given in the last row.

If you place a small dot in the center of each square in a magic square and connect those dots together in numerical order, you obtain the magic lines. (See Figure 5.23.) If you erase the underlying numbers and color in the spaces between the lines, you can create many interesting patterns. (See Figure 5.24) Every magic square will yield a collection of magic lines. Using different shadings, you can also create patterns from the intersecting lines.

Magic squares can be created from a preexisting square in several ways by exchanging rows and columns. For example, compare the magic square in Figure 5.25 to the one in *Melancholia*.

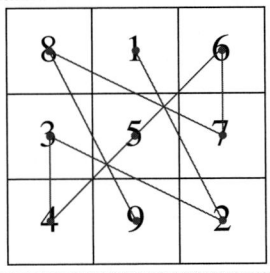

Figure 5.23

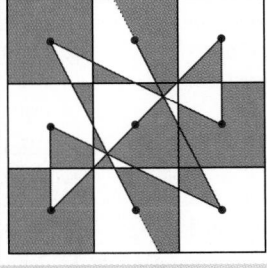

Figure 5.24

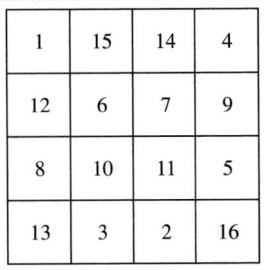

1	15	14	4
12	6	7	9
8	10	11	5
13	3	2	16

Figure 5.25

For this project, you will work in groups and experiment with magic squares.

1. Prepare a collection of magic squares for other groups to use in their work. You may wish to experiment with moving entire rows and columns to different positions in the square, or try exchanging rows and columns to see if you can obtain new magic squares from the ones presented here. The resources listed below will also lead to listings of hundreds of magic squares on the Worldwide Web. Present to the class the largest magic square you were able to find.

2. Using the magic squares prepared for the class, create the magic lines for each square. Study the lines you see in each square and look for patterns. For example, do the lines resemble each other on the left and right side of the square? Using colors or simple black-and-white shadings, fill in between the lines to create designs. Duplicate the most interesting designs and use them to "tile" a plane and present these artistic creations to the class.

3. Using the magic squares prepared for the class, create the magic lines for each square and then place these lines on the rectangular coordinate plane to obtain algebraic equations for the lines. You may wish to use a large piece of graph paper and your calculator to help with accuracy of your equations. Examine the equations you obtain and the intersection points of the lines. Do you find any similarities in the equations? Are the intersection points found in places you might have predicted? Present at least one complete set of magic lines and equations to the class and discuss your findings.

4. Prepare a report for the class on the history of magic squares. Your report should include the legend of Lo Shu, the work of Albrecht Düer, and Thomas Jefferson's fascination with magic squares. You may wish to include information on the "magical" significance of the numbers as well.

Worldwide Web Resources

Go to the Prentice Hall website (http://www.prenhall.com/blitzer) to access other locations on the Internet that will allow you to further explore the concepts presented in this project.

Chapter Review

SUMMARY

1. Solving Systems of Linear Equations by Graphing
  a. Graph the first equation.
  b. Graph the second equation on the same set of axes.
  c. If the lines representing the two graphs intersect at a point, determine the coordinates of this point of intersection. The ordered pair is the solution to the system.
  d. Check the solution in both equations.
  e. If the graphs are parallel lines, the system has no solution. The system is inconsistent.
  f. If the graphs are the same line, the system has infinitely many solutions. The equations are dependent.

2. Solving Systems of Linear Equations by Addition
  a. Write each equation of the system in the form $Ax + By = C$.
  b. If necessary, multiply one or both equations by appropriate numbers so that the sum of the coefficients of x or y is zero.
  c. Add the equations from part (b). The sum is an equation in one variable.
  d. Solve the equation from part (c).
  e. Back-substitute the value obtained from part (d) into either of the given equations and solve for the other variable.
  f. Write the solution as an ordered pair and check the solution in both of the original equations.
  g. If adding the equations results in a false statement, such as $0 = 2$, the inconsistent system has no solution.
  h. If adding the equations results in a true statement, such as $0 = 0$, the system has infinitely many solutions, and the equations are dependent.

3. Solving Systems of Linear Equations by Substitution
  Use this method when one of the original equations contains x in terms of y or y in terms of x, or possibly when an equation has a variable with a coefficient of 1 or -1.
  a. Solve one equation for x in terms of y or y in terms of x. (Solve for a variable whose coefficient is 1 or -1. This step is unnecessary if one of the original equations is in this form.)
  b. Substitute this expression for that variable into the other equation.
  c. Solve the resulting equation in one variable.
  d. Back-substitute the solution for part (c) into the equation in part (a) to find the value of the other variable.

e. Write the solution as an ordered pair and check the solution in both of the given equations.
  f. If part (c) results in a false statement, such as $0 = 2$, the inconsistent system has no solution.
  g. If part (c) results in a true statement, such as $3 = 3$, the system has infinitely many solutions, and the equations are dependent.

4. Problem Solving Using Systems of Equations
  a. Read the problem and let x and y (or any other variables) represent the quantities that are unknown.
  b. Write a system of linear equations in x and y that describes the verbal conditions of the problem.
  c. Solve the system by using the addition (elimination) or substitution method and answer the problem's question.
  d. Check the answer in the original wording of the problem, not in the system of equations obtained from the words.

5. Hints for Solving Problems by Using Systems of Equations
  a. *Geometry problems:* Perimeter of a rectangle = $2L + 2W$. The sum of the measures of a triangle's angles is $180°$. If lines are parallel, alternate interior angles formed with a transversal have equal measures. Supplementary angles have a sum of measures of $180°$.
  b. *Motion problems with wind or current:* Let $x =$ speed without wind or current and $y =$ speed of wind or current. Then $x + y =$ speed with the wind or current and $x - y =$ speed against the wind or current. In uniform motion situations: Rate × Time = Distance.

6. Solving Linear Inequalities
  a. Graph each inequality in the system on the same coordinate axes.
  b. The solution of the system is shown graphically by the region where the graphs overlap. Indicate this region by using dark shading on the intersection of the graphs.
  c. Verify the solution by selecting a test point from the region shaded in part (b). The coordinates of the test point must satisfy each inequality in the system.

REVIEW PROBLEMS

In Problems 1–2, decide whether the ordered pair is a solution of the system.

1. $(1, -5)$
   $4x - y = 9$
   $2x + 3y = -13$

2. $(-5, 2)$
   $2x + 3y = -4$
   $x - 4y = -10$

Solve each system in Problems 3–10 by graphing both equations on the same axes. If the system is inconsistent or the equations are dependent, so indicate. If applicable, use a graphing utility with TRACE *or intersection features to verify your result.*

3. $x + y = 2$
   $x - y = 6$

4. $2x - 3y = 12$
   $-2x + y = -8$

5. $y = \frac{1}{2}x$
   $y = 2x - 3$

6. $3x + 2y = 6$
   $3x - 2y = 6$

7. $y = 4x$
   $y = 4x - 2$

8. $2x - 4y = 8$
   $x = 2y + 4$

9. $x - y = 4$
   $x = -2$

10. $x = -3$
   $y = 6$

Solve each system in Problems 11–20 by the addition (elimination) method. Where applicable, state that the system is inconsistent or contains dependent equations. If applicable, use a graphing utility to verify your solution.

11. $x + y = 6$
   $2x + y = 8$

12. $3x - 4y = 1$
   $12x - y = -11$

13. $3x - 7y = 13$
   $6x + 5y = 7$

14. $8x - 4y = 16$
   $4x + 5y = 22$

15. $5x - 2y = 8$
   $3x - 5y = 1$

16. $x = 2y$
   $2x + 6y = 5$

17. $4(x + 3) = 3y + 7$
   $2(y - 5) = x + 5$

18. $2x + y = 5$
   $2x + y = 7$

19. $3x - 4y = -1$
   $-6x + 8y = 2$

20. $2x + 7y = 0$
   $7x + 2y = 0$

Solve each system in Problems 21–30 by the substitution method. Where applicable, state that the system is inconsistent or contains dependent equations. If applicable, use a graphing utility to verify your solution.

21. $x = -3y$
   $3y + x = -1$

22. $x + y = 3$
   $3x + 2y = 9$

23. $x + 3y = -4$
   $3x + 2y = 3$

24. $y + 1 = 3x$
   $8x - 1 = 4y$

25. $3x - 2y = -4$
   $x = -2$

26. $y = 39 - 3x$
   $y = 2x - 61$

27. $3x + 4y = 6$
   $y - 6x = 6$

28. $2x - y = 4$
   $x = y + 1$

29. $4x + y = 5$
   $12x = 15 - 3y$

30. $4x - y = -3$
   $y = 4x$

Solve each system in Problems 31–34 by the method of your choice.

31. $3x + 4y = -8$
   $2x + 3y = -5$

32. $6x + 8y = 39$
   $y = 2x - 2$

33. $x + 2y = 7$
   $2x + y = 8$

34. $y = 2x - 3$
   $y = -2x - 1$

Solve Problems 35–44 by translating the given conditions into a system of linear equations. Solve the system by either the addition (elimination) or substitution method, checking answers in the original wording of the problems.

35. The gorilla and orangutan are the heaviest of the world's apes. Two gorillas and three orangutans weigh 1465 pounds. A gorilla's weight increased by twice an orangutan's weight is 815 pounds. Find the weight for each of these primates.

36. Studies indicate that men have more extramarital affairs than women. The graph shows that over a lifetime, 32.5% of men and women have extramarital affairs, although the difference between the percent of men and women having affairs is 9.9%. Find the percent of men and the percent of women who have extramarital affairs over a lifetime.

Infidelity, Lifetime:

Gender

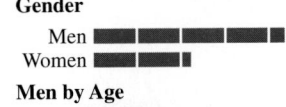

Men by Age

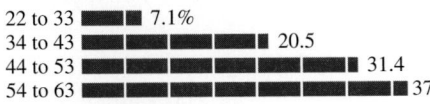

22 to 33   7.1%
34 to 43   20.5
44 to 53   31.4
54 to 63   37

Women by Age

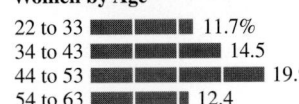

22 to 33   11.7%
34 to 43   14.5
44 to 53   19.9
54 to 63   12.4

Source: National Opinion Research Center, 1994 Survey

37. Nutritional information for an 8-ounce glass of grape juice and an 8-ounce glass of apple juice is given in the table. How many glasses of each should a person drink daily to get exactly 735 calories and 186 grams of carbohydrates?

	8-Ounce Glass of Grape Juice	8-Ounce Glass of Apple Juice
Calories	165	120
Carbohydrates (grams)	42	30

38. If eight pens and six pads cost $3.90 and three of the same pens and two of the same pads cost $1.40, find the cost of one pen.

39. A company with two stores buys seven full-size cars and five compact cars. The first store purchases 3 full-size cars and 2 small cars for a total cost of $108,000. The second store purchases the remaining cars for a total cost of $149,000. What is the cost of each kind of car?

40. In the isosceles triangle shown in the figure, angle A and angle B have equal measures. Find the measure of each angle in the triangle.

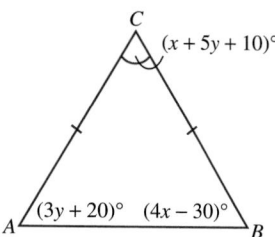

41. In the figure, lines L_1 and L_2 are parallel. Line L_3 is a transversal, passing through the parallel lines. Use alternate interior angles that have equal measures and the two supplementary angles with measures of $(8x + 5)°$ and $(10y + 5)°$ to find x and y. Then find the measures of the three angles designated by $(8x + 5)°$, $(10y + 5)°$, and $(3x + 10)°$.

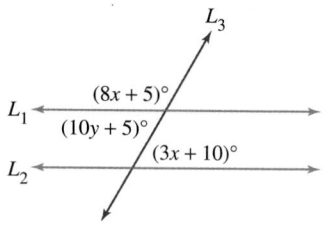

42. The perimeter of a table tennis top is 28 feet. The difference between 4 times the length and 3 times the width is 21 feet. Find the dimensions.

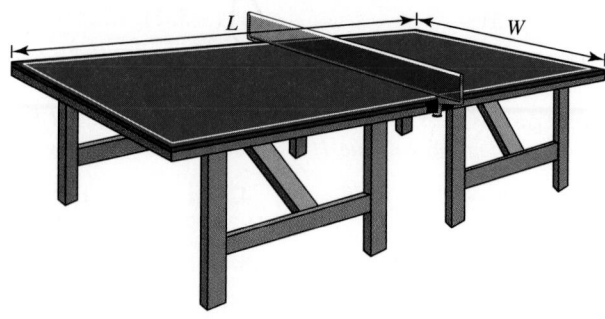

43. A rectangular garden has a perimeter of 24 yards. Fencing across the length cost $3 per yard and along the width $2 per yard. The total cost of the fencing is $62. Find the length and width of the rectangle.

44. When an airplane flies with the wind, it can travel 1080 miles in 6 hours. When the same airplane flies against the wind, it can travel 360 miles in 3 hours. Find the speed of the plane in still air and the speed of the wind.

45. A person with a computer decides to publish a newsletter for stamp collectors. The fixed costs are $400.00. The cost of printing each newsletter is $0.85, and the newsletter sells for $1.25 per copy. Thus:

Expenses = Fixed costs + 85 cents
        × Number of newsletters

$$y = 400 + 0.85x$$

Income = 1.25 × Number of newsletters

$$y = 1.25x$$

The graphs of $y = 400 + 0.85x$ and $y = 1.25x$ are shown in the figure. Answer the questions on the next page by referring back to these graphs.

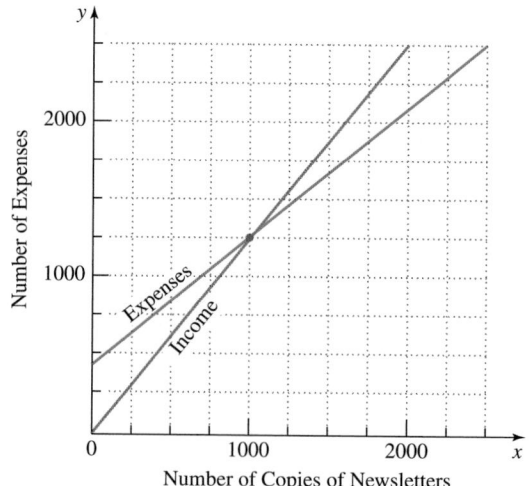

a. How many newsletters must be produced and sold to break even (where income equals expenses)? How is this indicated by the graphs?

b. A profit is achieved when income exceeds expenses. For what values of x does this occur?

c. What is the loss if only 400 newsletters are produced and sold?

d. What is the profit if 2000 newsletters are produced and sold?

Graph the solution for each system of linear inequalities in Problems 46–51.

46. $2x + y < 6$
$y - 2x < 6$

47. $2x + 3y \le 6$
$y > 3x$

48. $y < 2x - 2$
$x > 3$

49. $y \ge 5x - 4$
$y \le 5x + 1$

50. $x < 6$
$y \ge -1$

51. $2x + 3y \ge 6$
$3x - y \le 3$

CHAPTER 5 TEST

1. Determine whether the given ordered pair is a solution of the system of equations.
$(3, -\frac{3}{2})$: $x = 2y + 6$
$3x - 2y = 12$

2. Solve by graphing:
$2x + y = 6$
$x - 2y = 8$

In Problems 3–5, solve using the addition method.

3. $2x + y = 2$
$4x - y = -8$

4. $2x + 3y = 1$
$3x + 2y = -6$

5. $4x - 5y = 9$
$5x - 2y = 24$

In Problems 6–8, solve using the substitution method.

6. $3x - 5y = 2$
$y = 32 - 3x$

7. $2x - 7y = -3$
$x = 3y$

8. $y = 3x - 9$
$y = 3x + 8$

9. As shown in the table, World War II and the Vietnam Conflict were America's costliest wars. In current dollars, the two wars combined cost $500 billion and the difference between their cost was $120 billion. What was the cost of each of these wars in current dollars?

America's Costliest Wars, in Descending Order

War	Original Costs in Current Dollars
World War II	
Vietnam Conflict	
Korean Conflict	$50.0B
Persian Gulf War	$36.4B
World War I	$32.7B
Civil War: Union	$2.3B
Civil War: Confederacy	$1.0B
Spanish-American War	$270.0M
American Revolution	$100.0–$140.0M
War of 1812	$89.0M
Mexican War	$82.0M

10. At a sale in a clothing store, all sweaters are sold at one fixed price and all shirts are sold at another fixed price. If one sweater and three shirts cost $32, while two sweaters and four shirts cost $52, find the price of one sweater and one shirt.

11. Nutritional information for macaroni and broccoli is given in the table. How many servings of each would it take to get exactly 13 grams of protein and 56 grams of carbohydrates?

	Macaroni	**Broccoli**
Protein (grams/serving)	3	2
Carbohydrates (grams/serving)	16	4

12. In the figure shown of an isosceles triangle, angle A and angle B have equal measures. Find the measure of each angle in the triangle.

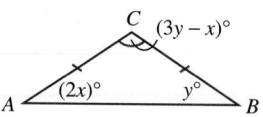

13. Traveling downstream with the current, it takes a motorboat 2 hours to cover a distance of 48 miles. When the motorboat returns upstream against the current, it takes 3 hours to cover the same distance. Find the speed of the motorboat in still water and the speed of the current.

Graph the solution for each system of linear inequalities in Problems 14–15.

14. $y \geq 2x - 4$
$y < 2x + 1$

15. $2x - 3y \leq 6$
$x \geq 3$

CUMULATIVE REVIEW PROBLEMS (CHAPTERS 1–5)

1. Simplify by combining like terms:

$6(3y - 2) - (y - 14) - 2(8y + 7)$.

2. Perform the indicated operations:

$-14 - [18 - (6 - 10)]$.

3. Use the graph to write the slope-intercept equation of the line.

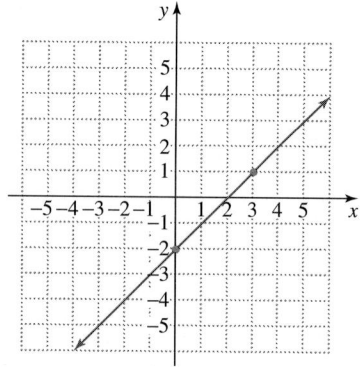

4. Solve: $3y + 2y - 7(y + 1) = -3(y + 4)$.

5. The Recommended Daily Allowance (RDA) of ascorbic acid is 45 milligrams and the RDA for niacin is 14 milligrams. If health bar A contains 15 milligrams of ascorbic acid and 2 milligrams of niacin per ounce and health bar B contains 10 milligrams of ascorbic acid and 4 milligrams of niacin per ounce, how many ounces of each must you consume to have exactly the RDA for ascorbic acid and niacin?

6. Solve for t: $A = p + prt$.

7. A river that contains 20 parts of DDT per million at the beginning of a study has this concentration decreasing each year, as shown in the figure. If a safe concentration for swimming is 4 parts of DDT per million, after how many years will the river be safe for swimming?

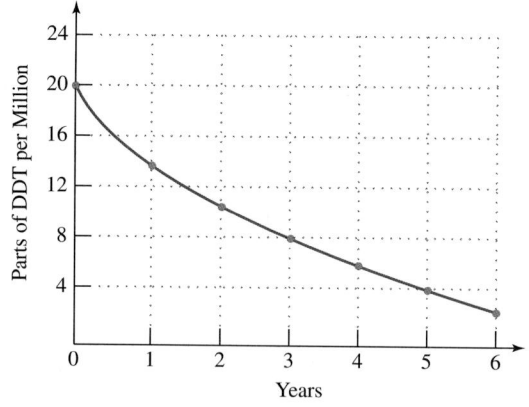

8. Let a, b, c, and d each represent a different nonzero one-digit number. If both a and b are odd, c and d are even, $a > 2$, $b < 8$, $a < c < d$, and $c < d < b$, then what is the value of d?

9. A square and an equilateral triangle have the same perimeter. If each side of the triangle is 10 centimeters less than twice a side of the square, find the length of each side of the triangle.

10. Find values of t (tens digit) and u (units digit) so that the four numbers below have a sum of 161.

$$t5 + 37 + 51 + 4u = 161$$

11. Graph: $6x - 3y = 12$.

12. Use slope and the y-intercept to graph: $y = \frac{1}{2}x - 2$.

13. Graph: $y \geq 3x - 1$.

14. Solve the system:

$$3x - 4y = 8$$
$$4x + 5y = -10$$

15. Using four categories, America's religious preference in 1995 is shown in the circle graph. If the number of Jewish people in the United States at that time was 5.1 million, estimate the 1995 population of the United States. Use this figure to determine the number of people in the remaining three sectors of the graph.

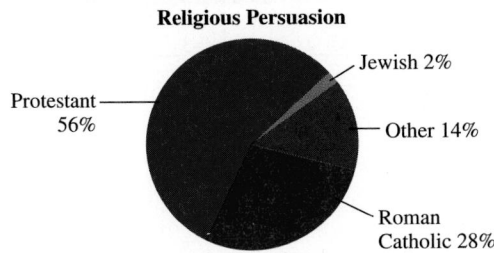

Religious Persuasion

Jewish 2%

Protestant 56%

Other 14%

Roman Catholic 28%

16. The function $f(x) = -0.05x^2 + 2x + 1$ describes the concentration ($f(x)$, in parts per million) of a drug in the bloodstream x hours after it was administered. Find and interpret $f(2)$.

17. Graph: $2x - y < 0$.

18. Write a fraction in lowest terms that represents the shaded portion of the figure.

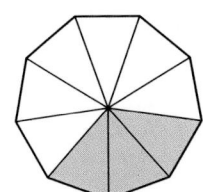

19. Solve and graph the solution on a number line:

$$3(y + 1) \leq 5(2y - 4) + 2.$$

20. The figure represents the average lifespan in the 1990s for four categories of Americans. The lifespan for white men is 8.2 years more than for black men. If the average lifespan for the two groups is 68.6 years, find the life expectancy for each group. Then use the figure to obtain a reasonable estimate of the lifespan for white women and black women.

| White Men | White Women | Black Men | Black Women |

21. The bar graph shows Michigan's budget deficit/surplus from 1990 through 1994. Estimate the difference in the amount between Michigan's 1994 budget surplus and its 1991 deficit.

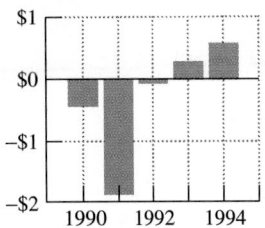

Budget Deficit/Surplus (in Billions)

$1
$0
–$1
–$2
1990   1992   1994

Source: *Time Magazine*

22. The triangles shown in the figure are similar. Find the length of line segment DF.

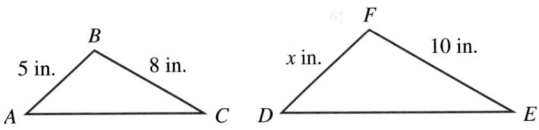

5 in.   *B*   8 in.   *F*   10 in.
A   *C*   *D* x in.   *E*

23. Solve the system:

$$2x - 3y = 9$$
$$y - 4x = -8$$

24. When twice a number is increased by 15, the result is 9 more than the number. Find the number.

25. Graph $y = -x^2 + 4x - 3$ by filling in the table of coordinates and then sketching the graph of the function.

x	-1	0	1	2	3	4
y						

26. Graph $y < -3$ in a rectangular coordinate system.

27. The bar graph shows the percentage of the labor force that is female in ten selected countries. If x represents this percentage, list the countries that satisfy the inequality $40 < x < 50$.

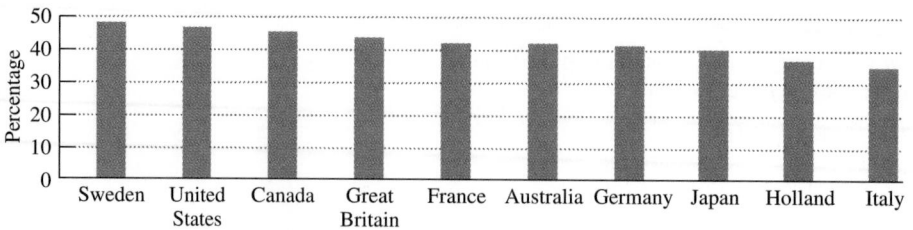

Source: U.S. Bureau of the Census, *Statistical Abstract 1993:* Table 1402

28. The circle graphs compare class attendance of successful and unsuccessful students. Write one sentence that summarizes the information conveyed by the graphs.

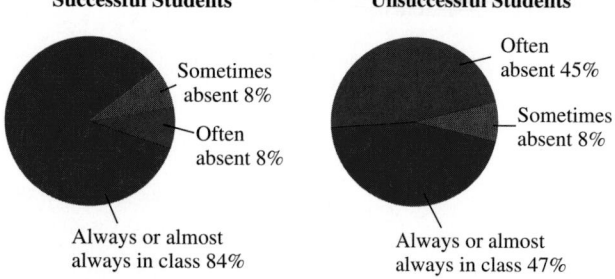

Source: *The Psychology of College Success: A Dynamic Approach,* by permission of H. C. Lindgren, 1969

29. The line graph shows the steady climb in the number of deaths of American men, in thousands, due to prostate cancer. Estimate the slope of the line connecting the years 1988 and 1996, and describe what your computation means using the phrase "rate of change."

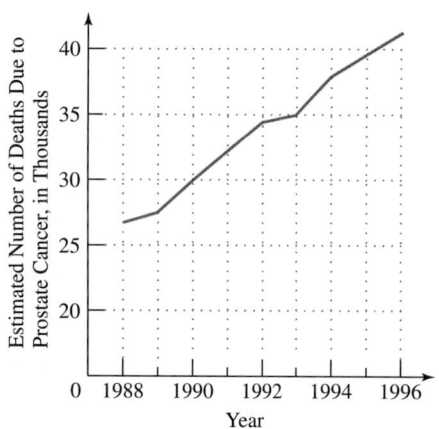

Source: American Cancer Society

30. Can the graphing utility-generated screen be the solution for the system

$$2x + y = -5$$
$$x + y = 2?$$

Explain.

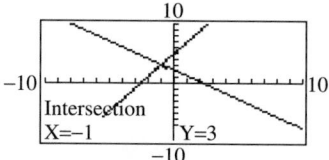

Exponents and Polynomials

6

George Tooker, American, born 1920. "Farewell" 1966, egg tempera on gessoed masonite, 61 × 60.1 cm. p. 967.76. Hood Museum of Art. Dartmouth College, Hanover, New Hampshire; gift of Pennington Haile, Class of 1924.

Mathematicians have modeled the number of deaths per year per thousand people as a function of age. The formula contains a special kind of algebraic expression called a *polynomial*. Polynomials play a fundamental role in the study of algebra and are related to algebraic expressions in much the same way that integers are related to real numbers. Much of what we do in algebra involves operations with polynomials, which forms the basis of this chapter.

SECTION 6.1

Solutions Tutorial Video
Manual   6

Adding and Subtracting Polynomials

Objectives

1 Identify polynomials.
2 Determine the degree of a polynomial.
3 Write a polynomial in standard form.
4 Add and subtract polynomials.
5 Evaluate a polynomial function.
6 Graph a polynomial function.

Many mathematical models involve a finite sum of terms in which all variables have whole number exponents and no variables appear in the denominators. For example, biologists use the model

$$y = 14x^3 - 17x^2 - 16x + 34$$

to describe the number of eggs (y) in a female moth as a function of her abdominal width (x, in millimeters).

Mathematical models are used to study the common cold, which is caused by a rhinovirus. The virus enters our bodies, multiplies, and begins to die at a certain point. After x days of invasion by the viral particles, there are y billion particles in our bodies, where

$$y = -\frac{3}{4}x^4 + 3x^3 + 5.$$

The model enables mathematicians to determine the day on which there is a maximum number of viral particles (and, consequently, the day we feel sickest).

Both of these examples involve formulas called *polynomials*. Polynomial models are used in such diverse areas as science, business, medicine, psychology, and sociology. This section begins by presenting the basic vocabulary of polynomials. We then use our knowledge of combining similar terms to find sums and differences of polynomials.

George Tooker "The Subway" 1950, egg tempera on composition board. Sight: $18\frac{1}{8} \times 36\frac{1}{8}$ in. (46×91.8 cm). Frame: 26×44 in. (66×111.8 cm). Collection of Whitney Museum of America Art. Purchase, with funds from the Juliana Force Purchase Award. 50.23. Photography copyright © 1997: Whitney Museum of American Art. Photo by Geoffrey Clements.

The Vocabulary of Polynomials

In Chapter 1, a *term* was defined as an expression containing a constant or the product of a constant and one or more variables. The number preceding the variable in a term is called the numerical *coefficient* of that term. For example,

Identify polynomials.

   $5x^3$ *is a term whose coefficient is 5.*
   $-8xy$ *is a term whose coefficient is* -8*.*
   -4 *is a term, often called a constant term.*

A *polynomial* is defined as a single term or the sum of two or more terms containing variables with whole number exponents. Thus,

$$7x^3 + (-9x^2) + 13x + (-6)$$

is a polynomial containing four terms. Since addition of a negative expression implies subtraction, this polynomial is written as

$$7x^3 - 9x^2 + 13x - 6.$$

Observe that 7 is the coefficient of x^3, -9 is the coefficient of x^2, 13 is the coefficient of x, and -6 is the constant term. Since a polynomial is an algebraic sum, the coefficients take on the signs between the terms.

It is customary to write polynomials in the order of descending powers of the variables. This is called *standard form*. Thus, we write

$$x^3 - 5x^2 + 7x + 3 \quad \text{rather than} \quad -5x^2 + 7x + 3 + x^3.$$

In standard form, the constant term is written last.

A polynomial with exactly one term is called a *monomial*. A *binomial* is a polynomial that has exactly two terms, and a *trinomial* is a polynomial that has exactly three terms.

EXAMPLE 1	Polynomials That Are Monomials, Binomials, and Trinomials

Give examples of three polynomials that are monomials, three that are binomials, and three that are trinomials.

Solution

These examples are shown in the following table.

Monomials (One Term)	Binomials (Two Terms)	Trinomials (Three Terms)
$4x$	$4x - 17$	$3x^2 - 5x + 2$
$-6x^3$	$-6x^3 + 9x$	$9x^3 + 7x^2 - 1$
5	$17x^2 + 5$	$-x^5 + 2x^2 + 4$

■

2 Determine the degree of a polynomial.

In this section we will restrict our discussion to polynomials containing only one variable. Each term of a polynomial in x is of the form ax^n. The *degree* of ax^n is n. For example, $7x^5$ is a monomial of degree 5.

Degree of a monomial

If $a \neq 0$, the degree of the monomial ax^n is n. The degree of a nonzero constant is 0. The constant 0 has no defined degree.

The degree of a polynomial is determined by considering the degree of each of its terms.

Degree of a polynomial

The *degree of a polynomial* is the highest degree of all the terms of the polynomial.

For example, $4x^2 + 3x$ is a binomial of degree 2 because the degree of the first term is 2, and the degree of the other term is less than 2. Also, $7x^5 - 2x^2 + 4$ is a trinomial of degree 5 because the degree of the first term is 5, and the degrees of the other terms are less than 5.

Table 6.1 summarizes the vocabulary associated with polynomials.

		TABLE 6.1 The Vocabulary of Polynomials			
Polynomial	**Terms of the Polynomial**	**Degree of Each Term**	**Degree of the Polynomial**	**Also Called**	
7	7	Degree 0	0	Monomial	
$4x^3$	$4x^3$	Degree 3	3	Monomial	
$7x^2 + \frac{3}{4}$	$7x^2$	Degree 2	2	Binomial	
	$\frac{3}{4}$	Degree 0			
$5x^4 - 7x^2$	$5x^4$	Degree 4	4	Binomial	
	$-7x^2$	Degree 2			
$9x^8 - 4x^2 + 3$	$9x^8$	Degree 8	8	Trinomial	
	$-4x^2$	Degree 2			
	3	Degree 0			
$6x^4 - 3x^3 + 2x - 5$	$6x^4$	Degree 4	4	No special name	
	$-3x^3$	Degree 3			
	$2x$	Degree 1			
	-5	Degree 0			

3 Write a polynomial in standard form.

Notice that when a polynomial is written in standard form—with the term having the largest exponent on the variable first, followed by the next largest, and so on—the degree of the polynomial is the number corresponding to the exponent of the leading term.

EXAMPLE 2 **Writing a Polynomial in Standard Form**

Write in standard form:

$$7x^2 - 9x^6 + 5x^4 + 3$$

Solution

$$-9x^6 + 5x^4 + 7x^2 + 3$$

In descending powers, the terms are written from the highest degree to the lowest degree from left to right. The degree of the polynomial is 6. ■

4 Add and subtract polynomials.

Adding and Subtracting Polynomials

As we know from our work in Chapter 1, we cannot combine terms in the polynomial $3x^2 + 7x - 5$. Only like terms containing exactly the same variables to the same powers may be combined. For example, $2x^3$ and $-10x^3$ are like terms because each has x raised to the power 3. These like terms can be combined mentally by combining the coefficients of the terms $(2 - 10 = -8)$ and keeping the same variable factor:

$$2x^3 - 10x^3 = -8x^3.$$

The following examples rely on combining like terms.

EXAMPLE 3 **Adding Polynomials Horizontally**

Add: $-9x^3 + 7x^2 - 5x + 3$ and $13x^3 + 2x^2 - 8x - 6$

Solution

The like terms are $-9x^3$ and $13x^3$, containing the same variable to the same power (x^3), as well as $7x^2$ and $2x^2$ (both contain x^2), $-5x$ and $-8x$ (both contain x) and the constant terms 3 and -6. We begin by grouping these pairs of like terms.

$$(-9x^3 + 7x^2 - 5x + 3) + (13x^3 + 2x^2 - 8x - 6)$$
$$= (-9x^3 + 13x^3) + (7x^2 + 2x^2)$$
$$\quad + (-5x - 8x) + (3 - 6)$$

Use the commutative and associative properties to rearrange terms, grouping like terms.

$$= 4x^3 + 9x^2 - 13x - 3$$

Combine like terms by combining coefficients and keeping the same variable factor. ∎

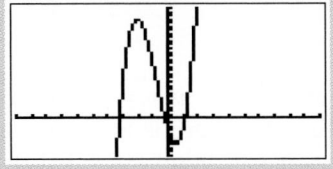
EXAMPLE 4   **Adding Polynomials Vertically**

Add: $-9x^3 + 7x^2 - 5x + 3$ and $13x^3 + 2x^2 - 8x - 6$

Solution

$$
\begin{array}{cccc}
-9x^3 & 7x^2 & -5x & 3 \\
\underline{13x^3} & \underline{2x^2} & \underline{-8x} & \underline{-6} \\
4x^3 & 9x^2 & -13x & -3
\end{array}
$$

We consider each term separately and write like terms in columns.

Add, column by column.

Now add the four sums together:

$$4x^3 + 9x^2 + (-13x) + (-3) = 4x^3 + 9x^2 - 13x - 3$$

This is the same answer found in Example 3. ∎

In Chapter 1, subtraction of real numbers was defined by

$$a - b = a + (-b).$$

For example,

$$8 - 3 = 8 + (-3) = 5 \quad \text{and} \quad -9 - (-4) = -9 + (+4) = -5.$$

We follow a similar method for the subtraction of polynomials.

To subtract two polynomials, change the sign of every term of the second polynomial. Add this result to the first polynomial.

EXAMPLE 5   **Subtracting Polynomials**

Subtract: $(7x^2 + 3x - 4) - (4x^2 - 6x - 7)$

Solution

$$(7x^2 + 3x - 4) - (4x^2 - 6x - 7)$$
$$= (7x^2 + 3x - 4) + (-4x^2 + 6x + 7)$$

Change the sign of each term of the second polynomial and add the two polynomials.

$$= (7x^2 - 4x^2) + (3x + 6x) + (-4 + 7)$$ Group like terms.
$$= 3x^2 + 9x + 3$$ Combine like terms. ∎

tudy tip

Be careful of the order in Example 6. For example, subtracting 2 from 5 is equivalent to 5 − 2. In general, subtracting B from A becomes A − B. The order of the resulting problem is not the same as the order in English.

EXAMPLE 6   **Subtracting Polynomials**

Subtract $2x^3 - 6x^2 - 3x + 9$ from $7x^3 - 8x^2 + 9x - 6$.

Solution

$$(7x^3 - 8x^2 + 9x - 6) - (2x^3 - 6x^2 - 3x + 9)$$
$$= (7x^3 - 8x^2 + 9x - 6) + (-2x^3 + 6x^2 + 3x - 9)$$ Change the sign of each term of the second polynomial and add the two polynomials.

$$= (7x^3 - 2x^3) + (-8x^2 + 6x^2)$$
$$+ (9x + 3x) + (-6 - 9)$$ Group like terms.
$$= 5x^3 + (-2x^2) + 12x + (-15)$$ Combine like terms.
$$= 5x^3 - 2x^2 + 12x - 15$$ ∎

Subtraction can also be performed in vertical columns.

EXAMPLE 7   **Subtracting Polynomials Vertically**

Use the method of subtracting by columns to find:

$$(12y^3 - 9y^2 - 11y - 3) - (4y^3 - 5y + 8).$$

Solution

Arrange like terms in columns.

$$\begin{array}{r} 12y^3 - 9y^2 - 11y - 3 \\ -(4y^3 \quad\quad - 5y + 8) \end{array}$$ Leave space for the missing term.

Change the sign of each term in the second row, and combine like terms.

$$\begin{array}{r} 12y^3 - 9y^2 - 11y - \ 3 \\ + \ -4y^3 \quad\quad + \ 5y - \ 8 \\ \hline 8y^3 - 9y^2 - \ 6y - 11 \end{array}$$ Change the sign of each term.
   Combine like terms.   ∎

Either the horizontal or the vertical method may be used for adding and subtracting polynomials. You may reach the point where you perform these operations mentally by adding or subtracting the coefficients of like terms.

5 Evaluate a polynomial function.

Polynomial Functions

In Section 4.3, we learned that an equation in x and y, such as $y = x + 6$, defines y as a function of x, because for every value of x there is at most one value for y. Replacing y with $f(x)$ gives $f(x) = x + 6$, which indicates that the variable y is a function of x. For example, we saw that the equation

$$y = 0.1x^2 - 0.4x + 0.6$$

represents a function that models the level of pollution during a summer day. Thus, we used $f(x)$ instead of y and wrote

$$f(x) = 0.1x^2 - 0.4x + 0.6.$$

For each value of x, the number of hours after 9 A.M., the value of $f(x)$ describes the level of air pollution. Thus, at $x = 3$ (noon), the level of pollution is

$$f(3) = 0.1(3)^2 - 0.4(3) + 0.6$$

or 0.3 parts per million.

Polynomials often appear in functions that describe real world situations, such as the one in the next example.

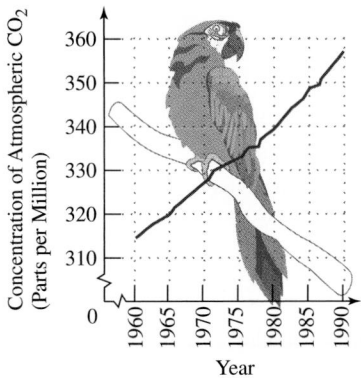

| **EXAMPLE 8** | **Polynomial Functions: An Environmental Application** |

In South America and Africa, trees are being cut at the rate of 30 acres a minute, day and night. An area of forest nearly twice as large as New York state is destroyed every year. This alarming rate of destruction of tropical rain forests is a major factor in the overall upward trend in atmospheric concentration of carbon dioxide (CO_2). A short-term polynomial model for the years from 1985 through 1987 is

$$f(x) = 36x^4 - 142x^3 + 175x^2 - 67x + 340$$

where x denotes the year ($x = 0$ represents April 1985) and $f(x)$ approximates CO_2 concentration (in parts per million). Find and interpret $f(2)$.

Solution

$f(x) = 36x^4 - 142x^3 + 175x^2 - 67x + 340$	This is the given polynomial model.
$f(2) = 36(2)^4 - 142(2)^3 + 175(2)^2 - 67(2) + 340$	To find $f(2)$ (f of 2), substitute 2 for x.
$= 36(16) - 142(8) + 175(4) - 67(2) + 340$	Evaluate exponential expressions.
$= 576 - 1136 + 700 - 134 + 340$	Perform multiplication from left to right.
$= 346$	Perform subtraction and addition from left to right.

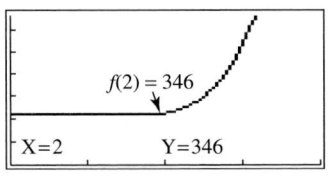

Figure 6.1

We see that $f(2) = 346$ (f of 2 equals 346.) This means that 2 years after April 1985, or in April 1987, CO_2 concentration is modeled at 346 parts per million. The solution is shown in Figure 6.1, obtained with a graphing utility. The polynomial formula given in this problem applies only from 1985 through 1987; after that time its predictions, shown by the rapidly increasing graph, are larger than the actual recorded atmospheric levels of CO_2 concentration. ■

6 Graph a polynomial function.

A function whose formula is given by a polynomial, like the one in Example 8, is called a *polynomial function*. Notice that we evaluated the polynomial function by replacing the variable in the function by the number 2. We then followed the rules for the order of operations. If we evaluate a polynomial function for several values of the independent variable, we can use the point-plotting method to graph the function. This forms the basis of our next example.

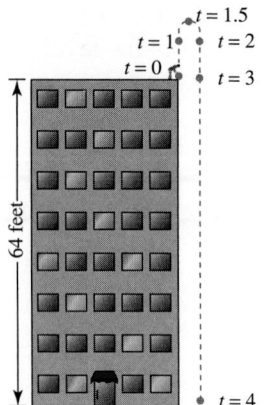

64 feet

Throwing a ball upward from a 64-foot building

EXAMPLE 9 **Using Point-Plotting to Graph a Polynomial Function**

A ball is thrown directly upward from the top of a 64-foot building with a speed of 48 feet/second. The height of the ball above the ground is a function of the time (t, in seconds) that the ball is in flight, and is given by the polynomial function

$$f(t) = -16t^2 + 48t + 64.$$

Find and interpret $f(0)$, $f(1)$, $f(1.5)$, $f(2)$, $f(3)$, and $f(4)$. Use these values to graph the function.

Solution

$f(t) = -16t^2 + 48t + 64$ This is the given polynomial function.

$f(0) = -16(0)^2 + 48(0) + 64$ To find $f(0)$, replace t with 0.
$\quad = 64$ At $t = 0$, the ball is 64 feet above ground. This indicates that the ball is thrown from the top of the 64-foot building.

$f(1) = -16(1)^2 + 48(1) + 64$ To find $f(1)$, replace t with 1.
$\quad = -16 + 48 + 64$
$\quad = 96$ After 1 second, the ball's height is 96 feet.

$f(1.5) = -16(1.5)^2 + 48(1.5) + 64$ To find $f(1.5)$, replace t with 1.5.
$\quad = -16(2.25) + 48(1.5) + 64$
$\quad = -36 + 72 + 64$
$\quad = 100$ After 1.5 seconds, the ball is 100 feet above the ground.

Take a moment to show that $f(2) = 96$ and $f(3) = 64$. Interpret your calculations.

$f(4) = -16(4)^2 + 48(4) + 64$ Finally, to find $f(4)$, replace t with 4.
$\quad = -16(16) + 48(4) + 64$
$\quad = -256 + 192 + 64$
$\quad = 0$ After 4 seconds, the ball's height is 0 feet. This means that the ball is on the ground after 4 seconds.

Now that we have evaluated the polynomial function for six values of t, we can use the six resulting ordered pairs to graph the function, as shown in Figure 6.3 on page 423. It appears that the ball's maximum height occurs at 1.5 seconds and that at 1.5 seconds it is 100 feet above the ground. Since neither time nor distance is negative, our graph is shown only in the first quadrant.

ENRICHMENT ESSAY

Polynomials and the Death Rate

The polynomial model

$$y = 0.036x^2 - 2.8x + 58.14$$

approximates the number of deaths per year per thousand people (y) for people who are x years old, where x lies between age 40 and age 60, inclusively. In the model, death rate is a function of age, so we can write

$$f(x) = 0.036x^2 - 2.8x + 58.14.$$

The graph of

$$y = 0.036x^2 - 2.8x + 58.14$$

is shown in Figure 6.2. The two points shown on the graph indicate that approximately 4 people per 1000 who are 40 years old die annually and that approximately 20 people per 1000 who are 60 years old die annually.

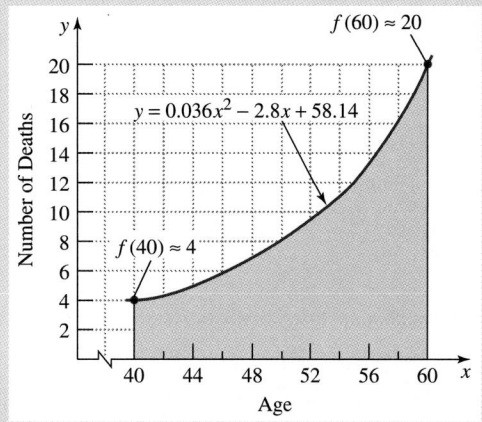

Figure 6.2
Death rate (per 1000 at age x)

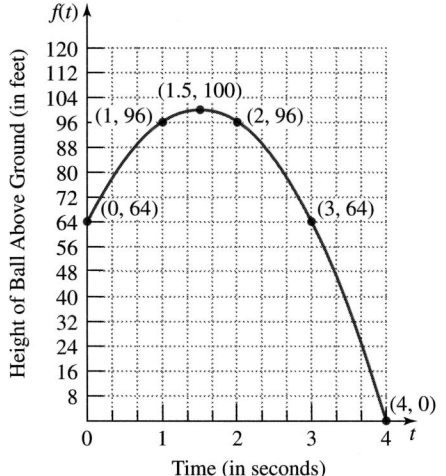

t	$f(t) = -16t^2 + 48t + 64$	**Ordered Pair**
0	$f(0) = 64$	$(0, 64)$
1	$f(1) = 96$	$(1, 96)$
1.5	$f(1.5) = 100$	$(1.5, 100)$
2	$f(2) = 96$	$(2, 96)$
3	$f(3) = 64$	$(3, 64)$
4	$f(4) = 0$	$(4, 0)$

Figure 6.3
Height of a ball as a function of time

iscover for yourself

Convince yourself that the ball reaches its maximum height after 1.5 seconds by evaluating the function at values to the left and right of 1.5, such as 1.4 and 1.6.

PROBLEM SET 6.1

Practice Problems

Identify each polynomial in Problems 1–14 as a monomial, binomial, or trinomial. Give the degree of the polynomial.

1. $3x + 7$
2. -4
3. -9
4. $5x - 2$

5. $x^3 - 2x$
6. $x^5 - 7x$
7. $x^2 - 3x + 4$
8. $x^2 - 9x + 2$

9. $3y^{17}$
10. $-9y^{23}$
11. $7y^2 - 9y^4 + 5$
12. $3y^2 - 14y^5 + 6$

13. $4x - 10x$
14. $6x^2 + 2x^2$

Write each polynomial in Problems 15–22 in standard form and give the degree of the polynomial.

15. $5x - 10x^2$
16. $3x^2 + 9x^3$
17. $3x + 4x^5 - 3x^2 - 2$
18. $4x + 5x^3 - 7x^2 + 11$

19. $3 - 3y^4$
20. $4 - 5y^7$
21. 13
22. -5

Perform the indicated operations in Problems 23–60. If applicable, use a graphing utility to check some of your answers.

23. $(5x + 7) + (-8x + 3)$
24. $(7x - 3) + (-9x + 11)$

25. $(3x^2 + 7x - 9) + (7x^2 + 8x - 2)$
26. $(8x^2 + 5x - 3) + (12x^2 + 7x - 14)$

27. $(5x^2 - 3x) + (2x^2 - x)$
28. $(-2x^2 + x) + (4x^2 + 7x)$

29. $(3x^2 - 7x + 10) + (x^2 + 6x + 8)$
30. $(-5x^2 + 7x + 4) + (2x^2 + x + 3)$

31. $(4y^3 + 7y - 5) + (10y^2 - 6y + 3)$
32. $(2y^3 + 3y + 10) + (3y^2 + 5y - 22)$

33. $(2x^2 - 6x + 7) + (3x^3 - 3x)$
34. $(4x^3 + 5x + 13) + (-4x^2 + 22)$

35. $(4y^2 + 8y + 11) + (-2y^3 + 5y + 2)$
36. $(7y^3 + 5y - 1) + (2y^2 - 6y + 3)$

37. $(-2y^6 + 3y^4 - y^2) + (-y^6 + 5y^4 + 2y^2)$
38. $(7r^4 + 5r^2 + 2r) + (-18r^4 - 5r^2 - r)$

39. $(\frac{1}{2}x^3 + \frac{2}{3}x^2 - \frac{5}{8}x + 3) + (-\frac{3}{4}x^3 - \frac{3}{8}x - 11)$
40. $(\frac{2}{3}x^6 - \frac{1}{5}x^4 + \frac{1}{2}x^2 + 3) + (-\frac{2}{5}x^6 - \frac{1}{4}x^4 - \frac{3}{4}x^2 - 14)$

41. $(0.03x^5 - 0.1x^3 + x + 0.03) + (-0.02x^5 + x^4 - 0.7x + 0.3)$

42. $(0.06x^5 - 0.2x^3 + x + 0.05) + (-0.04x^5 + 2x^4 - 0.8x + 0.5)$

43. $(x - 8) - (3x + 2)$
44. $(x - 2) - (7x + 9)$
45. $(x^2 - 5x - 3) - (6x^2 + 4x + 9)$

46. $(3x^2 - 8x - 2) - (11x^2 + 5x + 4)$

47. $(x^2 - 5x) - (6x^2 - 4x)$
48. $(3x^2 - 2x) - (5x^2 - 6x)$

49. $(x^2 - 8x - 9) - (5x^2 - 4x - 3)$
50. $(x^2 - 5x + 3) - (x^2 - 6x - 8)$

51. $(y - 8) - (3y - 2)$
52. $(y - 2) - (7y - 9)$

53. $(6y^3 + 2y^2 - y - 11) - (y^2 - 8y + 9)$
54. $(5y^3 + y^2 - 3y - 8) - (y^2 - 8y + 11)$

55. $(7n^3 - n^7 - 8) - (6n^3 - n^2 - 10)$
56. $(2n^2 - n^7 - 6) - (2n^3 - n^7 - 8)$

57. $(y^6 - y^3) - (y^2 - y)$
58. $(y^5 - y^3) - (y^4 - y^2)$

59. $(7x^4 + 4x^2 + 5x) - (-19x^4 - 5x^2 - x)$
60. $(-3x^6 + 3x^4 - x^2) - (-x^6 + 2x^4 + 2x^2)$

Add or subtract the polynomials as indicated in Problems 61–88.

61. Add:
$5y^3 - 7y^2$
$6y^3 + 4y^2$

62. Add:
$13x^4 - x^2$
$7x^4 + 2x^2$

63. Add:
$3x^2 - 7x + 4$
$-5x^2 + 6x - 3$

64. Add:
$7x^2 - 5x - 6$
$-9x^2 + 4x + 6$

65. Add:
$\frac{1}{4}x^4 - \frac{2}{3}x^3 - 5$
$-\frac{1}{2}x^4 + \frac{1}{5}x^3 + 4.7$

66. Add:
$\frac{1}{3}x^9 - \frac{1}{5}x^5 - 2.7$
$-\frac{3}{4}x^9 + \frac{2}{3}x^5 + 1$

67. Add:
$y^3 + 5y^2 - 7y - 3$
$-2y^3 + 3y^2 + 4y - 11$

68. Add:
$y^3 + y^2 - 7y + 9$
$-y^3 - 6y^2 - 8y + 11$

69. Add:
$4x^3 - 6x^2 + 5x - 7$
$-9x^3 \qquad - 4x + 3$

70. Add:
$-4y^3 + 6y^2 - 8y + 11$
$2y^3 \qquad + 9y - 3$

71. Add:
$7x^4 - 3x^3 + x^2$
$x^3 - x^2 + 4x - 2$

72. Add:
$7y^5 - 3y^3 + y^2$
$2y^3 - y^2 - 4y - 3$

73. Add:
$$7x^2 - 9x + 3$$
$$4x^2 + 11x - 2$$
$$-3x^2 + 5x - 6$$

74. Add:
$$7y^2 - 11y - 6$$
$$8y^2 + 3y + 4$$
$$-9y^2 - 5y + 2$$

75. Subtract:
$$7x + 1$$
$$-(3x - 5)$$

76. Subtract:
$$4x + 2$$
$$-(3x - 5)$$

77. Subtract:
$$7x^2 - 3$$
$$-(-3x^2 + 4)$$

78. Subtract:
$$9y^2 - 6$$
$$-(-5y^2 + 2)$$

79. Subtract:
$$7y^2 - 5y + 2$$
$$-(11y^2 + 2y - 3)$$

80. Subtract:
$$3x^5 - 5x^3 + 6$$
$$-(7x^5 + 4x^3 - 2)$$

81. Subtract:
$$7x^3 + 5x^2 - 3$$
$$-(-2x^3 - 6x^2 + 5)$$

82. Subtract:
$$3y^4 - 4y^2 + 7$$
$$-(-5y^4 - 6y^2 - 13)$$

83. Subtract:
$$5y^3 + 6y^2 - 3y + 10$$
$$-(6y^3 - 2y^2 - 4y - 4)$$

84. Subtract:
$$4y^3 + 5y^2 + 7y + 11$$
$$-(-5y^3 + 6y^2 - 9y - 3)$$

85. Subtract:
$$7x^4 - 3x^3 + 2x^2$$
$$-(\quad - x^3 - x^2 + x - 2)$$

86. Subtract:
$$5y^6 - 3y^3 - 2y^2$$
$$-(\quad - y^3 - y^2 - y - 1)$$

87. Subtract:
$$4y^3 - \tfrac{1}{2}y^2 + \tfrac{3}{8}y + 1$$
$$-(\tfrac{9}{2}y^3 + \tfrac{1}{4}y^2 - y + \tfrac{3}{4})$$

88. Subtract:
$$5x^3 - \tfrac{1}{4}x^2 + \tfrac{5}{8}x + 2$$
$$-(\tfrac{5}{2}x^3 + \tfrac{1}{2}x^2 - \tfrac{1}{8}x + \tfrac{3}{2})$$

Application Problems

89. The number of eggs in a female moth is a function of her abdominal width (x, in millimeters), given by the polynomial function $f(x) = 14x^3 - 17x^2 - 16x + 34$. Find and interpret $f(2)$.

90. A room is filled with people. Each person in the room shakes hands with everyone else. The total number of hand shakes is a function of the number of people in the room (x) given by the polynomial function $f(x) = \tfrac{1}{2}x^2 - \tfrac{1}{2}x$. Find and interpret $f(90)$.

91. Shown below are the sum of the squares of the first n natural numbers.

If $n = 1$: $1^2 = 1$
If $n = 2$: $1^2 + 2^2 = 5$
If $n = 3$: $1^2 + 2^2 + 3^2 = 14$
If $n = 4$: $1^2 + 2^2 + 3^2 + 4^2 = 30$
If $n = 5$: $1^2 + 2^2 + 3^2 + 4^2 + 5^2 = 55$
If $n = 6$: $1^2 + 2^2 + 3^2 + 4^2 + 5^2 + 6^2 = 91$

The polynomial function $f(n) = \tfrac{1}{3}n^3 + \tfrac{1}{2}n^2 + \tfrac{1}{6}n$ can be used to model these sums. Show that this is the case by finding $f(1), f(2), f(3), f(4), f(5)$, and $f(6)$. Then use the function to find the sum of the squares of the first 10 natural numbers.

92. A polynomial function can be used to estimate the number of pounds of waste produced each day by every American. The model is $f(x) = 0.0001x^3 - 0.0043x^2 + 0.089x + 2.66$, where x denotes the number of years after 1960 and $f(x)$ describes the number of pounds of waste. Find $f(10)$ and interpret the result. Which bar in the graph represents $f(10)$?

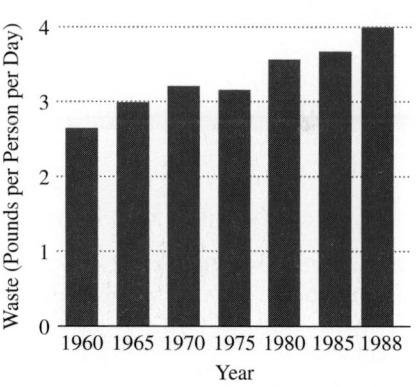

Waste Production 1960–1988

Waste (Pounds per Person per Day) vs. Year (1960, 1965, 1970, 1975, 1980, 1985, 1988)

Data Source: U.S. Environmental Protection Agency

93. An arrow is shot directly upward from ground level with a speed of 128 feet per second. The height of the arrow above the ground is a function of the time (t, in seconds) that the arrow is in flight, modeled by the polynomial function $f(t) = -16t^2 + 128t$.
a. Fill in the following table and then use the ordered pairs in the last column to graph the function. Then use your graph to answer parts (b) and (c).

t	$f(t) = -16t^2 + 128t$	Ordered Pair
0		
2		
4		
6		
8		

b. When does the arrow hit the ground?
c. Based on the values in the table and your resulting graph, when does the arrow appear to reach its

maximum height above the ground? What is the arrow's maximum height? Try convincing yourself that this is, indeed, the maximum height by evaluating the function for decimal values of t just to the left and right of the value of t that appears to result in the maximum height.

94. The concentration of a particular medication in the body, measured in parts per million, is a function of the number of hours t after the medication is administered, modeled by the polynomial function $f(t) = -0.05t^2 + 2t + 2$. Use the graph of the function shown to determine the maximum concentration of the medication.

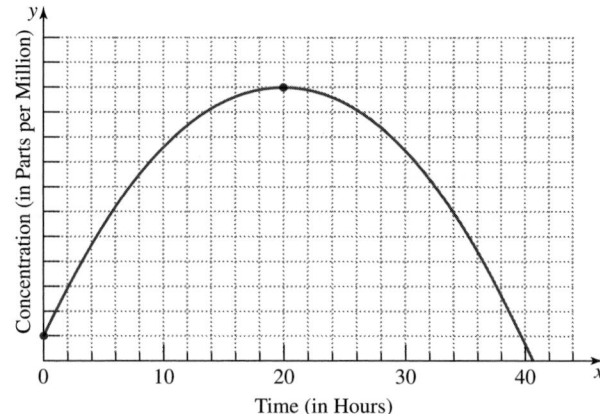

95. Find the polynomial representing the sum of the areas of the regions.

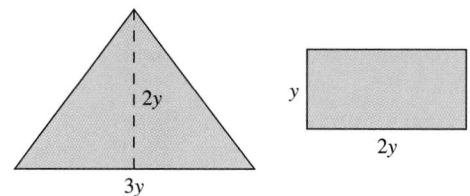

True–False Critical Thinking Problems

96. Which one of the following is true?
a. In the polynomial $3x^2 - 5x + 13$, the coefficient of x is 5.
b. The degree of $3x^2 - 7x + 9x^3 + 5$ is 2.
c. $\dfrac{1}{5x^2} + \dfrac{1}{3x}$ is a binomial.
d. $(2x^2 - 8x + 6) - (x^2 - 3x + 5) = x^2 - 5x + 1$ for any value of x.

97. Which one of the following is true?
a. The degree of 4^3 is 3.
b. In the polynomial $3x^2 + x - 5$, x has no coefficient.
c. $3x^2 - 7x + \sqrt{5}$ is a polynomial of degree 2.
d. $(x^2 - 5x) - (x^2 - 4x) = -9x$ for any value of x.

Technology Problem

98. The common cold is caused by a rhinovirus. The polynomial function $f(x) = -0.75x^4 + 3x^3 + 5$ models the number of viral particles ($f(x)$, in billions) after x days of viral invasion.
a. Use a graphing utility to graph the function. Enter the function as

$$y_1 = \boxed{(-)}.75x \boxed{\land} 4 \boxed{+} 3x \boxed{\land} 3 \boxed{+} 5$$

with the following range setting:

Xmin $= 0$, Xmax $= 5$, Xscl $= 1$,
Ymin $= 0$, Ymax $= 30$, Yscl $= 1$.

b. Use the $\boxed{\text{TRACE}}$ feature or the maximum function (f Max) feature, which gives the peak point on the graph (consult your manual), to find after how many days (to the nearest whole day) the number of viral particles is at a maximum and consequently when we feel the sickest.
c. By when should we feel completely better?

Writing in Mathematics

99. Explain why $4x^2 + \dfrac{9}{x} - 13$ contains three terms but is not a trinomial.

100. Explain how to add polynomials.

101. Explain why it is not possible to add two polynomials of degree 3 and get a polynomial of degree 4.

Critical Thinking Problems

102. The number of people (C) who catch a cold t weeks after January 1 is $C = t^3 - 3t^2 + 5t$ and the number of people (R) who recover t weeks after January 1 is $R = \frac{1}{3}t^3 - t^2 + t$. Write a polynomial, in terms of t, for the number of people who are still ill with a cold t weeks after January 1.

103. Write a polynomial for the surface area of this rectangular solid.

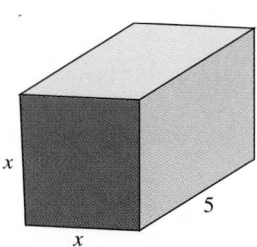

104. What polynomial must be subtracted from $5x^2 - 2x + 1$ so that the difference is $8x^2 - x + 3$?

Review Problems

105. Evaluate: $(-3)^4$.

106. Solve and graph the solution set on a number line: $3(x - 2) \leq 9(x + 2)$.

107. Solve the system by graphing:

$$2x - y = 6$$
$$x + 2y = -2$$

| S E C T I O N 6 . 2 | Multiplying Polynomials |

Solutions Manual   **Tutorial**   **Video 6**

Multiplying Polynomials

Objectives

1 Use properties of exponents.
2 Multiply monomials.
3 Multiply a monomial and a polynomial.
4 Multiply binomials.
5 Multiply two polynomials.

Multiplication of polynomials uses the distributive, associative, and commutative properties and the properties of exponents. We begin with some basic rules for exponents.

1 Use properties of exponents.

Properties of Exponents: Product and Power Rules

To multiply polynomials, we need to be familiar with three basic properties of exponents.

Multiplying Powers with the Same Base. We have seen that exponents are used to indicate repeated multiplication. The exponential expression x^4, where x is the base and 4 is the exponent, indicates that x occurs as a factor four times. Thus,

$$x^4 = x \cdot x \cdot x \cdot x.$$

Discover for yourself

Consider the product of two monomials with the same base.

$$\overbrace{x^4}^{\text{4 factors}} \cdot \overbrace{x^3}^{\text{3 factors}} = \underbrace{(x \cdot x \cdot x \cdot x) \cdot (x \cdot x \cdot x)}_{\text{7 factors of } x}$$

Write the product in terms of x to a power. How can you obtain this power using the given exponents 4 and 3? Repeat this process for $2^7 \cdot 2^5$. How many factors of 2 are there? How can this be expressed in terms of 2 to a power? When multiplying exponential expressions with the same base, what is a fast method for determining the exponent of the product?

In the Discover for Yourself box, were you able to observe that the exponent of the product is the sum of the exponents? This is called the *product rule* for multiplying exponential expressions with the same base.

Product rule for exponents

If x is any real number, and m and n are natural numbers, then

$$x^m \cdot x^n = x^{m+n}.$$

When multiplying exponential expressions with the same base, add the exponents. Use this sum as the exponent of the common base.

EXAMPLE I   **Multiplying Monomials by Using the Product Rule**

Find the indicated products:

a. $y^7 \cdot y^9$ **b.** $(3x^4)(-2x)$ **c.** $(4x^3)^2$
d. $x^3 \cdot y^5$ **e.** $y^7 + y^9$ **f.** $y^3 \cdot y^2 \cdot y^5$

Solution

a. $y^7 \cdot y^9 = y^{7+9} = y^{16}$ Apply the product rule for exponents, retaining the common base and adding exponents.

b. $(3x^4)(-2x) = 3(-2)(x^4 \cdot x^1)$ Use the commutative and associative properties to rearrange factors.

$$= -6x^{4+1}$$ Apply the product rule for exponents. Retain the common base and add exponents.

$$= -6x^5$$

c. $(4x^3)^2 = (4x^3)(4x^3)$

$$= (4 \cdot 4)(x^3 \cdot x^3)$$

$$= 16x^{3+3}$$ Apply the product rule.

$$= 16x^6$$

d. $x^3 \cdot y^5$ cannot be simplified because the bases (x and y) are not the same.

tudy tip

Don't confuse adding and multiplying monomials.

Addition:

$$5x^4 + 6x^4 = 11x^4$$

Multiplication:

$$(5x^4)(6x^4) = (5 \cdot 6)(x^4 \cdot x^4)$$
$$= 30x^{4+4}$$
$$= 30x^8$$

e. The product rule does not apply to $y^7 + y^9$ because the expression is a sum, not a product.

f. We can extend the product rule to cover three or more factors with the same base by adding the exponents on all the factors.

$$y^3 \cdot y^2 \cdot y^5 = y^{3+2+5} = y^{10}$$ ∎

iscover for yourself

Complete the multiplication shown by multiplying the coefficients and adding the exponents. How can you obtain this answer immediately without having to show $2x^4$ repeated three times?

Raising Products and Powers to a Power. If an expression within parentheses is raised to a power, the inside expression is the base. For example,

$$(2x^4)^3 = (2x^4)(2x^4)(2x^4).$$

In the Discover for Yourself box, were you able to find that you could simplify $(2x^4)^3$ by raising each factor within parentheses to the power 3?

$$(2x^4)^3 = 2^3(x^4)^3$$

Also, since $(x^4)^3 = x^4 \cdot x^4 \cdot x^4 = x^{12}$, were you able to discover that when a power is raised to a power, you can multiply the exponents?

$$(x^4)^3 = x^{4 \cdot 3} = x^{12}$$

Raising products and powers to a power

If x and y are nonzero real numbers, and m and n are natural numbers, then:

1. $(xy)^m = x^m y^m$

When a product is raised to a power, raise each factor in the product to the power.

2. $(x^m)^n = x^{mn}$

When an exponential expression is raised to a power, multiply the exponents. Place the product of the exponents on the base and remove the parentheses.

EXAMPLE 2 **Using the Power Rules**

Simplify:

a. $(2^3)^5$ **b.** $(x^6)^4$ **c.** $(5y)^3$ **d.** $(-2y^4)^5$

Solution

a. $(2^3)^5 = 2^{3 \cdot 5}$ Multiplying exponents: $(x^m)^n = x^{mn}$ **b.** $(x^6)^4 = x^{6 \cdot 4}$
$\qquad = 2^{15}$ $\qquad\qquad\qquad\qquad\qquad\qquad\qquad\qquad\qquad\qquad = x^{24}$

c. $(5y)^3 = 5^3 \cdot y^3$ $\qquad\qquad\qquad$ Raise each factor to the third power.
$\qquad\quad = 125y^3$ $\qquad\qquad\qquad\quad$ $5^3 = 5 \cdot 5 \cdot 5 = 125$

d. $(-2y^4)^5 = (-2)^5(y^4)^5$ $\quad$ Raise each factor to the fifth power.
$\qquad\qquad = (-2)^5 y^{4 \cdot 5}$ $\quad$ $(x^m)^n = x^{mn}$
$\qquad\qquad = -32y^{20}$ ∎

The properties of exponents discussed up to this point are summarized in Table 6.2.

TABLE 6.2 **Properties of Exponents (m, n Natural Numbers)**	
Property	**Example**
1. $x^m \cdot x^n = x^{m+n}$	$x^5 \cdot x^6 = x^{5+6} = x^{11}$
2. $(xy)^n = x^n y^n$	$(4x)^3 = 4^3 x^3 = 64x^3$
3. $(x^m)^n = x^{mn}$	$(x^5)^6 = x^{5 \cdot 6} = x^{30}$

Multiplying Polynomials

Now that we have developed three properties of exponents, we are ready to turn to polynomial multiplication. We break our work into four general cases.

2 Multiply monomials.

Case 1. Multiplying Monomials. We have already considered these types of problems. As shown below, after some practice you will probably do most of the work in your head, writing only the answer.

EXAMPLE 3   **Multiplying Monomials Mentally**

Multiply: **a.** $(2x)(4x^2)$ **b.** $(-8x^6)(5x^3)$

Solution

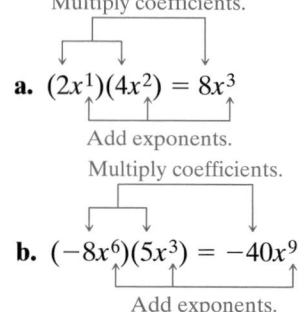

a. $(2x^1)(4x^2) = 8x^3$

b. $(-8x^6)(5x^3) = -40x^9$

3 Multiply a monomial and a polynomial.

Case 2. Multiplying a Monomial and a Polynomial Other Than a Monomial. The distributive property is used to multiply a polynomial by a monomial:

$$a(b + c) = ab + ac.$$

Once the monomial factor is distributed, we can then use the product rule for exponents. Let's see exactly what this means.

EXAMPLE 4   **Multiplying a Monomial and a Binomial**

Multiply: **a.** $2x$ and $x + 4$ **b.** $3x^2(7x + 5)$

Solution

a. $2x(x + 4) = 2x \cdot x + 2x \cdot 4$ Use the distributive property.

$\qquad\qquad\quad = 2 \cdot 1x^{1+1} + 2 \cdot 4x$ To multiply the monomials, multiply coefficients and add exponents.

$\qquad\qquad\quad = 2x^2 + 8x$

b. $3x^2(7x + 5) = (3x^2)(7x) + (3x^2)(5)$ Use the distributive property.

$\qquad\qquad = 3 \cdot 7x^{2+1} + 3 \cdot 5x^2$ To multiply the monomials, multiply coefficients and add exponents.

$\qquad\qquad = 21x^3 + 15x^2$

Study tip

This figure will help you visualize polynomial multiplication.

Area of large rectangle

$\qquad = 2x(x + 4)$

Sum of areas of smaller rectangles

$\qquad = 2x^2 + 8x$

Conclusion:

$\qquad 2x(x + 4) = 2x^2 + 8x$

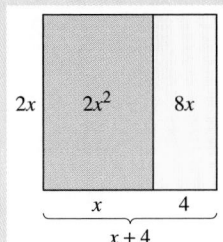

Multiplying a monomial and a polynomial

To multiply a monomial and a polynomial, multiply each term of the polynomial by the monomial.

EXAMPLE 5   **Multiplying a Monomial and a Trinomial**

Multiply: $-4y^3(6y^5 - 3y^4 + 2)$

Solution

$-4y^3(6y^5 - 3y^4 + 2)$

$= (-4y^3)(6y^5) + (-4y^3)(-3y^4) + (-4y^3)(2)$ Use the distributive property.

$= (-4)(6)y^{3+5} + (-4)(-3)y^{3+4} + (-4)(2)y^3$ To multiply the monomials, multiply coefficients and add exponents.

$= -24y^8 + 12y^7 - 8y^3$ How much of this process can you work mentally?

In Examples 6 and 7, we multiply a polynomial and a monomial by using the distributive property as follows:

$(b + c)a = ba + ca.$

EXAMPLE 6   **Multiplying a Binomial and a Monomial**

Multiply: $(x + 3)x$

Solution

$$\overset{\frown}{(x+3)}x = x \cdot x + 3 \cdot x \qquad \text{Use the distributive property.}$$

$$= (1 \cdot 1)x^{1+1} + 3x \qquad \text{To multiply the monomials, multiply coefficients and add exponents.}$$

$$= x^2 + 3x$$

EXAMPLE 7   **Multiplying a Polynomial and a Monomial**

Multiply: $(x^3 + 2x^2 - 4x + 3)(-2x)$

Solution

$$(x^3 + 2x^2 - 4x + 3)(-2x)$$

$$= x^3(-2x) + 2x^2(-2x) + (-4x)(-2x) + 3(-2x) \qquad \text{Use the distributive property.}$$

$$= (1)(-2)x^{3+1} + (2)(-2)x^{2+1} + (-4)(-2)x^{1+1} + (3)(-2)x \qquad \text{To multiply monomials, multiply coefficients and add exponents.}$$

$$= -2x^4 - 4x^3 + 8x^2 - 6x$$

4 Multiply binomials.

Case 3. Multiplying Two Binomials. We now turn to finding an equivalent expression for the product of two binomials, such as

$$(x + 3)(x + 2).$$

To multiply binomials, we want to rewrite the product as two products of a binomial and a monomial, since we know how to perform this multiplication. We will use the distributive property to rewrite $(x + 3)(x + 2)$. Example 8 shows how this is done.

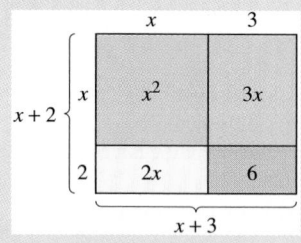
EXAMPLE 8   **Multiplying Binomials**

Multiply: **a.** $x + 3$ and $x + 2$ **b.** $(3x + 7)(2x - 4)$

Solution

a. $(x + 3)(x + 2) = (x + 3)x + (x + 3)2$ Use the distributive property.

$$= x \cdot x + 3 \cdot x + x \cdot 2 + 3 \cdot 2 \qquad \text{Distribute again:}$$

$$\overset{\frown}{(x+3)}\boxed{x}$$

$$= x^2 + 3x + 2x + 6 \qquad \text{Multiply the monomials.}$$

$$= x^2 + 5x + 6 \qquad \text{Combine like terms.}$$

b. $(3x + 7)(2x - 4) = (3x + 7)2x + (3x + 7)(-4)$ Use the distributive property.

$$= 3x(2x) + 7(2x) + 3x(-4) + 7(-4) \qquad \text{Distribute again.}$$

$$= 6x^2 + 14x - 12x - 28 \qquad \text{Multiply the monomials.}$$

$$= 6x^2 + 2x - 28 \qquad \text{Combine like terms.}$$

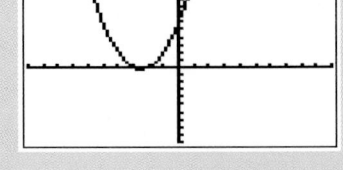
5 Multiply two polynomials.

Case 4. Other Kinds of Polynomial Products. We turn now to the product of a binomial and a trinomial. In this case, we again use the distributive property repeatedly.

EXAMPLE 9 **Multiplying a Binomial and Trinomial**

Multiply: $(2x + 3)(x^2 + 4x + 5)$

Solution

$$(2x + 3)(x^2 + 4x + 5)$$
$$= (2x + 3)x^2 + (2x + 3)4x + (2x + 3)5 \quad \text{Use the distributive property, multiplying each term of the trinomial by the binomial.}$$
$$= 2x^3 + 3x^2 + 8x^2 + 12x + 10x + 15 \quad \text{Distribute again.}$$
$$= 2x^3 + 11x^2 + 22x + 15 \quad \text{Combine like terms.}$$

If you look back at Examples 8 and 9, you may notice a pattern in polynomial multiplication when neither factor is a monomial.

Multiplying polynomials

Multiply two polynomials by multiplying each term of one polynomial by each term of the other polynomial. Then add the like terms in the products.

Try using this rule to solve Examples 8 and 9.

Another method for multiplying polynomials, particularly useful when at least one of the polynomials has three or more terms, involves a vertical format similar to that used for multiplying whole numbers.

| EXAMPLE 10 | **Multiplying Polynomials Using a Vertical Format** |

Multiply: $(2x^2 - 3x)(5x^3 - 4x^2 + 7x)$

Solution

To use the vertical format, it is most convenient to write the polynomial with the greatest number of terms in the top row.

$$5x^3 - 4x^2 + 7x$$
$$\underline{2x^2 - 3x}$$

We now multiply each term in the top polynomial by the last term in the bottom polynomial.

$$5x^3 - 4x^2 + 7x$$
$$\underline{2x^2 - 3x}$$
$$\overline{-15x^4 + 12x^3 - 21x^2} \leftarrow -3x(5x^3 - 4x^2 + 7x)$$

Then we multiply each term in the top polynomial by $2x^2$, the first term in the bottom polynomial. Like terms are placed in columns because the final step involves adding them.

$$5x^3 - 4x^2 + 7x$$
$$\underline{2x^2 - 3x}$$
$$-15x^4 + 12x^3 - 21x^2 \leftarrow -3x(5x^3 - 4x^2 + 7x)$$
$$\underline{10x^5 - 8x^4 + 14x^3} \qquad \leftarrow 2x^2(5x^3 - 4x^2 + 7x)$$
$$10x^5 - 23x^4 + 26x^3 - 21x^2$$

Add like terms, which are lined up in columns. ■

PROBLEM SET 6.2

Practice Problems

Find each product of the monomials in Problems 1–20.

1. $2^2 \cdot 2^3$ **2.** $3^3 \cdot 3^2$ **3.** $(-3)(-3)^3$ **4.** $(-2)^3(-2)$

5. $x^3 \cdot x^7$ **6.** $y^5 \cdot y^6$ **7.** $r \cdot r^8$ **8.** $z^7 \cdot z$

9. $(2x^2)(4x^3)$ **10.** $(3y^5)(6y^4)$ **11.** $(2y)(y^{13})$ **12.** $(3r)(r^{16})$

13. $(-7y)(3y^7)$ **14.** $(-5x)(6x^4)$ **15.** $(-2x^3)(-3x^2)$ **16.** $(-4x^2)(-2x^4)$

17. $x^3 \cdot x^2 \cdot x$ **18.** $y^4 \cdot y^3 \cdot y$ **19.** $(2x^2)(-3x)(8x^4)$ **20.** $(3x^3)(-2x)(5x^6)$

Use properties of exponents to simplify Problems 21–42.

21. $(2^2)^3$ **22.** $(3^2)^3$ **23.** $(x^3)^4$ **24.** $(y^4)^2$

25. $(r^8)^{12}$ **26.** $(r^{12})^5$ **27.** $(5x)^2$ **28.** $(2y)^3$

29. $(-2y)^3$ **30.** $(-3x)^3$ **31.** $(-4x)^2$ **32.** $(-5x)^4$

33. $(2x^2)^2$ **34.** $(3x^2)^2$ **35.** $(4y^2)^3$ **36.** $(5y^2)^3$

37. $(-3y^4)^3$ **38.** $(-4y^5)^3$ **39.** $(-2x^7)^5$ **40.** $(-2x^{11})^7$

41. $(4x)(2x^2) + (4x^2)(3x)$ **42.** $(2x^7)(7x^2) - (6x^3)(5x^2)$

Find each product of the monomial and the polynomial in Problems 43–76.

43. $x(x - 3)$ **44.** $x(x - 7)$ **45.** $-x(x + 4)$ **46.** $-y(5 - y)$

47. $2x(x - 6)$ **48.** $3y(y - 5)$ **49.** $-4y(3y + 5)$ **50.** $-5y(6y + 7)$

51. $4x^2(x - 2)$ **52.** $5y^2(y + 6)$ **53.** $2x^2(x^2 + 3x)$ **54.** $4y^2(y^2 + 2y)$

55. $-5x^2(x^2 - x)$ **56.** $-6x^2(2x^2 + x)$ **57.** $-y^3(3y^2 - 5)$ **58.** $-y^3(4y^2 - 5)$

59. $3x(6x^2 - 5x)$ **60.** $4y(5y - 2y^2)$ **61.** $(4x - 3)5x$ **62.** $(7y - 2)y$

63. $(3x^3 - 4x^2)(-2x)$ **64.** $(4y^3 - 5y^2)(-3y)$ **65.** $x(3x^3 - 2x + 5)$ **66.** $y(5y^3 - 4y + 2)$

67. $-y(-3y^2 - 2y - 4)$ **68.** $-z(5z^2 + 6z - 25)$ **69.** $x^2(3x^4 - 5x - 3)$ **70.** $y^3(-5y^3 - 7y + 3)$

71. $2x^2(3x^2 - 4x + 7)$ **72.** $4y^2(5y^2 - 6y + 3)$ **73.** $(x^2 + 5x - 3)(-2x)$ **74.** $(y^3 - 2y + 2)(-4y)$

75. $-3x^2(-4x^2 + x - 5)$ **76.** $-6y^2(3y^2 - 2y - 7)$

Use the distributive property to find each product in Problems 77–106.

77. $(x + 3)(x + 5)$ **78.** $(x + 4)(x + 6)$ **79.** $(x + 11)(x + 9)$ **80.** $(x + 12)(x + 8)$

81. $(2x + 1)(x + 4)$ **82.** $(2x + 5)(x + 3)$ **83.** $(x + 7)(9x + 10)$ **84.** $(x + 6)(8x + 11)$

85. $(x + 3)(x - 5)$ **86.** $(x + 4)(x - 6)$ **87.** $(x - 11)(x + 9)$ **88.** $(x - 12)(x + 8)$

89. $(2x - 5)(x + 4)$ **90.** $(3x - 4)(x + 5)$ **91.** $(y - 13)(3y - 4)$ **92.** $(y - 14)(5y - 6)$

93. $(3y - 2)(5y - 4)$ **94.** $(4y - 3)(2y - 1)$ **95.** $(2x + 3)(2x - 3)$ **96.** $(4y + 1)(4y - 1)$

97. $(y + 1)(y^2 + 2y + 3)$ **98.** $(x + 2)(x^2 + x + 5)$ **99.** $(y - 3)(y^2 - 3y + 4)$ **100.** $(y - 2)(y^2 - 4y + 3)$

101. $(2a - 3)(a^2 - 3a + 5)$ **102.** $(2a - 1)(a^2 - 4a + 3)$

103. $(z - 4)(-2z^2 - 3z + 2)$ **104.** $(z - 5)(-3z^2 - z + 3)$

105. $(2y - 5)(-2y^2 + 4y - 3)$ **106.** $(2y - 1)(-y^2 - 3y - 4)$

Use a vertical format to find each product in Problems 107–118.

107. $x^2 - 5x + 3$
$\underline{x + 8}$

108. $x^2 - 7x + 9$
$\underline{x + 4}$

109. $x^2 - 3x + 9$
$\underline{2x - 3}$

110. $y^2 - 5y + 3$
$\underline{4y - 5}$

111. $2x^3 + x^2 + 2x + 3$
$\underline{x + 4}$

112. $3y^3 + 2y^2 + y + 4$
$\underline{y + 3}$

113. $4z^3 - 2z^2 + 5z - 4$
$\underline{3z - 2}$

114. $5z^3 - 3z^2 + 4z - 3$
$\underline{2z - 4}$

115. $7x^3 - 5x^2 + 6x$
$\underline{3x^2 - 4x}$

116. $9y^3 - 7y^2 + 5y$
$\underline{-3y^2 + 5y}$

117. $2y^5 - 3y^3 + y^2 - 2y + 3$
$\underline{2y - 1}$

118. $n^4 - n^3 + n^2 - n + 1$
$\underline{2n + 3}$

Application Problems

119. Find a trinomial for the area of the rectangular rug shown below whose sides are $x + 5$ feet and $2x - 3$ feet.

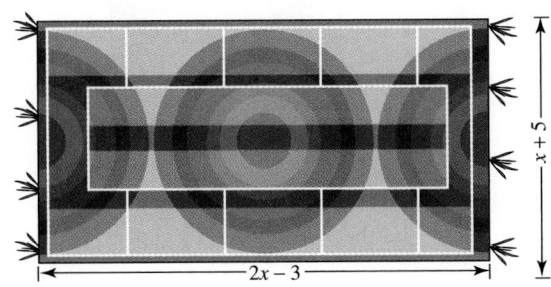

120. The base of a triangular sail is $4x$ feet and its height is $3x + 10$ feet. Write a binomial in terms of x for the area of the sail.

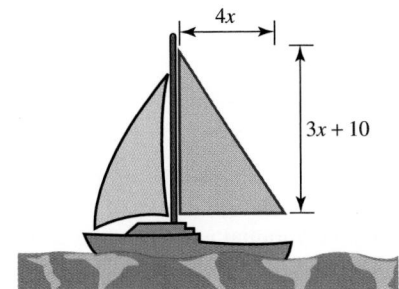

121. Express the area of the rectangle shown in the figure in two different ways.

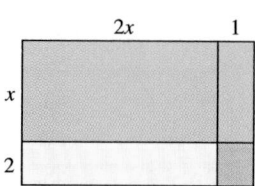

True–False Critical Thinking Problems

122. Which one of the following is true?
  a. $4x^3 \cdot 3x^4 = 12x^{12}$
  b. $5x^2 \cdot 4x^6 = 9x^8$
  c. $(y - 1)(y^2 + y + 1) = y^3 - 1$
  d. Some polynomial multiplications can only be performed by using a vertical format.

123. Which one of the following is true?
  a. $4x^3 + 5x^4 = 9x^7$
  b. $(5y^2)^3(2y - 1) = 250y^7 - 125y^6$
  c. $(x + 5)^3 = x^3 + 125$
  d. $(x - 9)(x - 2) = x^2 - 11x - 18$

Technology Problems

124. Use a graphing utility to verify that $(x - 1)(x + 4) = x^2 + 3x - 4$.

125. Find the product of $x + 1$ and $x - 3$. Use a graphing utility to verify your result.

Writing in Mathematics

126. Explain the difference between solving these two problems:

$$2x^2 + 3x^2 \quad \text{and} \quad (2x^2)(3x^2).$$

127. Explain why $-3^2 = -9$, while $(-3)^2 = 9$.

128. Discuss situations in which a vertical format, rather than a horizontal format, is useful for multiplying polynomials.

129. Explain why $(x + 3)^2$ is not equal to $x^2 + 3^2$.

Critical Thinking Problems

130. The figure shows the area of the four smaller rectangles. Find an expression for the length and width of the large rectangle that contains the four smaller rectangles.

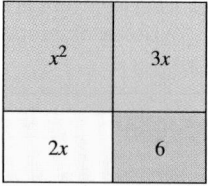

rounded by a border, and each side of the larger square containing the painting and the border is represented by $x + 4$. Write a polynomial in descending powers of x representing the area of the border.

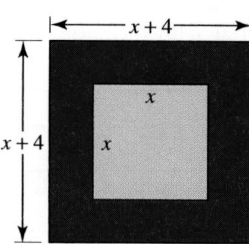

131. Simplify: $(3x + 4)(2x - 1) - (2x + 1)(x - 2)$.

132. One side of a rectangle is represented by $x + 3$ and the adjacent side is the next consecutive odd integer. Write a polynomial in descending powers of x representing the area of the rectangle.

133. This year, Warbucks is five times as old as Annie. If x represents Annie's present age, write a polynomial in descending powers of x representing the product of their ages 6 years from now.

134. The figure on the right shows a square painting whose sides are represented by x. The painting is sur-

135. Find each of the products in parts (a)–(c).
  a. $(x - 1)(x + 1)$
  b. $(x - 1)(x^2 + x + 1)$
  c. $(x - 1)(x^3 + x^2 + x + 1)$
  d. Using the pattern found in parts (a)–(c), find $(x - 1)(x^4 + x^3 + x^2 + x + 1)$ without actually multiplying.

136. Find the missing factor.

$$(\underline{\quad\quad})(-\tfrac{1}{4}xy^3) = 2x^5y^3$$

Review Problems

137. Solve the system:

$$3x + 5y = 9$$
$$4x + 3y = 1$$

138. Graph: $5x - 4y \geq -20$.

139. The denominator of a fraction is two less than three times the numerator. If the sum of the numerator and denominator is 79, what is the fraction?

SECTION 6.3

Solutions
Manual

Tutorial

Video
7

Special Products; Modeling with Polynomials

Objectives

1 Multiply binomials using the FOIL method.
2 Multiply the sum and difference of two terms mentally.
3 Find the square of a binomial mentally.
4 Model geometric situations with polynomials.

In the previous section, we considered the distributive property as a way to multiply polynomials. In this section, we use the distributive property to develop patterns for multiplying certain binomials mentally.

 Multiply binomials using the FOIL method.

Multiplying Two Binomials

The product of two binomials occurs quite frequently in algebra. The product can be found using a method called *FOIL,* which is based on the distributive property. For example, we can find the product of the binomials $3x + 2$ and $4x + 5$ as follows:

$$
\begin{aligned}
(3x + 2)(4x + 5) &= (3x + 2)4x + (3x + 2)5 \\
&= 3x(4x) + 2(4x) + 3x(5) + 2(5) \\
&= 12x^2 + 8x + 15x + 10 \\
&= 12x^2 + 15x + 8x + 10
\end{aligned}
$$

Before combining like terms, let's consider the origin of each of the four terms in the sum.

Origin of	Terms of $(3x + 2)(4x + 5)$	Result of Multiplying Terms	
$12x^2$	$(3x + 2)(4x + 5)$	$(3x)(4x) = 12x^2$	First terms
$15x$	$(3x + 2)(4x + 5)$	$(3x)(5) = 15x$	Outside terms
$8x$	$(3x + 2)(4x + 5)$	$(2)(4x) = 8x$	Inside terms
10	$(3x + 2)(4x + 5)$	$(2)(5) = 10$	Last terms

The product is obtained by adding these four results.

$$
\begin{aligned}
(3x + 2)(4x + 5) &= 12x^2 + 15x + 8x + 10 \\
&= 12x^2 + 23x + 10
\end{aligned}
$$

We see, then, that two binomials can be quickly multiplied by using the FOIL method, in which F represents the product of the *first* terms in each binomial, O represents the product of the *outside* or outermost terms, I represents the product of the two *inside* or innermost terms, and L represents the product of the *last* or *second* terms in each binomial.

$$(3x + 2)(4x + 5) = 12x^2 + 15x + 8x + 10$$
$$= 12x^2 + 23x + 10$$

The FOIL Method

Consider $(3x + 2)(4x + 5)$.

F	**1.** Multiply *first* terms of each binomial.

$$(3x + 2)(4x + 5) \qquad \text{Product: } (3x)(4x) = 12x^2$$

O	**2.** Multiply *outside* terms of each binomial.

$$(3x + 2)(4x + 5) \qquad \text{Product: } (3x)(5) = 15x$$

I	**3.** Multiply *inside* terms of each binomial.

$$(3x + 2)(4x + 5) \qquad \text{Product: } (2)(4x) = 8x$$

L	**4.** Multiply *last* terms of each binomial.

$$(3x + 2)(4x + 5) \qquad \text{Product: } (2)(5) = 10$$

The product of two binomials is the sum of these four products.

$$(3x + 2)(4x + 5) = (3x)(4x) + (3x)(5) + (2)(4x) + (2)(5)$$
$$= 12x^2 + 15x + 8x + 10$$
$$= 12x^2 + 23x + 10 \qquad \text{Combine like terms.}$$

EXAMPLE 1 **Using the FOIL Method**

Multiply: $3x + 4$ and $5x - 3$

SECTION 6.3 SPECIAL PRODUCTS; MODELING WITH POLYNOMIALS **439**

Solution

Study tip

In summary, here's the pattern for FOIL multiplication used in Examples 1 and 2.

$$(A + B)(C + D)$$

F: First terms $= (3x + 4)(5x - 3) = (3x)(5x) = 15x^2$

O: Outside terms $= (3x + 4)(5x - 3) = (3x)(-3) = -9x$

I: Inside terms $= (3x + 4)(5x - 3) = (4)(5x) = 20x$

L: Last terms $= (3x + 4)(5x - 3) = (4)(-3) = -12$

$$(3x + 4)(5x - 3) = 15x^2 - 9x + 20x - 12$$
$$= 15x^2 + 11x - 12 \quad \text{Combine like terms.}$$

EXAMPLE 2 Using the FOIL Method

Use the FOIL method to find each product:

a. $(4y - 7)(3y - 5)$ **c.** $(3a^2 + 4)(a^2 + 2)$
b. $(x^3 - 4)(x^3 + 6)$ **d.** $(2 - 5x)(3 - 4x^3)$

Solution

a. $(4y - 7)(3y - 5) = (4y)(3y) + (4y)(-5) + (-7)(3y) + (-7)(-5)$
$= 12y^2 - 20y - 21y + 35$
$= 12y^2 - 41y + 35 \quad \text{Combine like terms.}$

b. $(x^3 - 4)(x^3 + 6) = (x^3)(x^3) + (x^3)(6) + (-4)(x^3) + (-4)(6)$
$= x^6 + 6x^3 - 4x^3 - 24$
$= x^6 + 2x^3 - 24 \quad \text{Combine like terms.}$

c. $(3a^2 + 4)(a^2 + 2) = (3a^2)(a^2) + (3a^2)(2) + (4)(a^2) + (4)(2)$
$= 3a^4 + 6a^2 + 4a^2 + 8$
$= 3a^4 + 10a^2 + 8 \quad \text{Combine like terms.}$

d. $(2 - 5x)(3 - 4x^3) = (2)(3) + 2(-4x^3) + (-5x)(3) + (-5x)(-4x^3)$
$= 6 - 8x^3 - 15x + 20x^4$
$= 6 - 15x - 8x^3 + 20x^4 \quad$ Since the given binomials are in *ascending* powers of x, we've expressed the product in that form.

The outside and inside products in the FOIL method are often like terms, and these can be combined mentally. Thus, the product of two binomials can be found by immediately writing the answer.

iscover for yourself

Consider the trinomial

$x^2 + ? x + 6.$

If the last term is obtained from the product of 2 and 3, what is the middle term? What is the middle term if the last term is obtained from the product of -1 and -6? What is the relationship between the factors of the last term and the coefficient of the middle term?

2 Multiply the sum and difference of two terms mentally.

| EXAMPLE 3 | **Multiplying Binomials Mentally** |

Use the FOIL method to find each product mentally:

a. $(x + 7)(x + 3)$ **b.** $(3x - 1)(x + 4)$ **c.** $(y + 7)(y - 7)$

Solution

a. $(x + 7)(x + 3) = x^2 + 10x + 21$ Combine like terms mentally: $3x + 7x = 10x$.

b. $(3x - 1)(x + 4) = 3x^2 + 11x - 4$ Combine like terms mentally: $12x - x = 11x$.

c. $(y + 7)(y - 7) = y^2 - 49$ Combine like terms mentally: $-7y + 7y = 0$. ∎

We have seen that the FOIL method makes binomial multiplication fairly easy. We now turn our attention to two rules that are even easier than the FOIL method for certain binomial products.

Multiplying the Sum and Difference of Two Terms

A product that occurs quite frequently in algebra is one that involves the sum and difference of the same two terms, such as

$(x + 5)(x - 5).$

We will use the FOIL method to compute such a product, look for a pattern, and then develop a rule that will instantly give us the answer.

---

iscover for yourself

What do you observe about the outside and inside products in each of the following multiplications?

a. $(x + 5)(x - 5) = x^2 - 5x + 5x - 25$
$\qquad\qquad\qquad\ = x^2 - 25$

b. $(7x - 3)(7x + 3) = 49x^2 + 21x - 21x - 9$
$\qquad\qquad\qquad\qquad = 49x^2 - 9$

c. $(x^3 + \frac{1}{2})(x^3 - \frac{1}{2}) = x^6 - \frac{1}{2}x^3 + \frac{1}{2}x^3 - \frac{1}{4}$
$\qquad\qquad\qquad\qquad = x^6 - \frac{1}{4}$

In the Discover for Yourself box, did you notice that in each case, when multiplying sums and differences of the same two terms, the outside and inside products have a sum of 0 and cancel? This implies the following rule.

tudy tip

The rule in the box is called the *difference-of-squares formula* because the expression on the right is the difference of two squares.

Product of the sum and difference of two terms

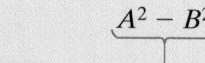

| The product of the sum and the difference of the same two terms | is | The square of the first term minus the square of the second term. |

EXAMPLE 4 **Finding the Product of the Sum and Difference of Two Terms**

Find each product by using the preceding rule:

a. $(4y + 3)(4y - 3)$ **b.** $(3x - 7)(3x + 7)$ **c.** $(5a^4 + 6)(5a^4 - 6)$

Solution

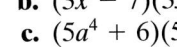

| First term squared | − | Second term squared | = | Answer |

a. $(4y + 3)(4y - 3) = (4y)^2 \quad - 3^2 \quad = 16y^2 - 9$
b. $(3x - 7)(3x + 7) = (3x)^2 \quad - 7^2 \quad = 9x^2 - 49$
c. $(5a^4 + 6)(5a^4 - 6) = (5a^4)^2 \quad - 6^2 \quad = 25a^8 - 36$

To find the product of the sum and difference of two terms:

1. Square the first term.
2. Square the second term.
3. Subtract the result of step 2 from the result of step 1.

3 Find the square of a binomial mentally.

The Square of a Binomial

To compute $(A + B)^2$, the square of a binomial sum, we can again turn to the FOIL method. Since squaring binomials occurs so frequently in algebra, we will begin with the FOIL method, look for a pattern, and then develop a rule that will instantly give us the answer.

Discover for yourself

Describe as many patterns as you can in each of the following multiplications:

a. $(x + 7)^2 = (x + 7)(x + 7)$
$\qquad\qquad = x^2 + 7x + 7x + 49$
$\qquad\qquad = x^2 + 14x + 49$

b. $(2y + 3)^2 = (2y + 3)(2y + 3)$
$\qquad\qquad = 4y^2 + 6y + 6y + 9$
$\qquad\qquad = 4y^2 + 12y + 9$

c. $(7x - 5)^2 = (7x - 5)(7x - 5)$
$\qquad\qquad = 49x^2 - 35x - 35x + 25$
$\qquad\qquad = 49x^2 - 70x + 25$

In the Discover for Yourself, how many of the following patterns did you observe?

1. The outside and inside products are the same and are "doubled" in the final answer.

2. The first and last products are squares.

These patterns imply the following rules.

Squaring binomials

The Square of a Binomial Sum

$$(A + B)^2 = A^2 + 2AB + B^2$$
$$= (\text{First term})^2 + 2 \cdot \text{Product of the terms} + (\text{Last term})^2$$

The Square of a Binomial Difference

$$(A - B)^2 = A^2 - 2AB + B^2$$
$$= (\text{First term})^2 - 2 \cdot \text{Product of the terms} + (\text{Last term})^2$$

---

 tudy tip

This figure will help you visualize the square of a binomial sum.
Area of large rectangle

$$= (A + B)(A + B)$$
$$= (A + B)^2$$

Sum of areas of four smaller rectangles

$$= A^2 + AB + AB + B^2$$
$$= A^2 + 2AB + B^2$$

Conclusion:

$$(A + B)^2 = A^2 + 2AB + B^2$$

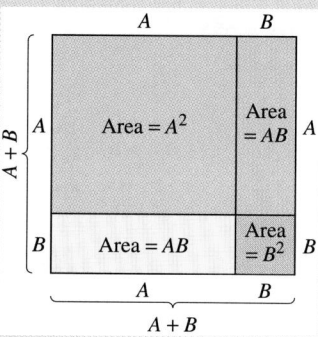

---

 tudy tip

Caution! The square of a sum is *not* the sum of the squares.

$$(A + B)^2 \neq A^2 + B^2$$

↑

The middle term $2AB$ is missing.

$$(x + 3)^2 \neq x^2 + 9$$

Show that $(x + 3)^2$ and $x^2 + 9$ are not equal by substituting 5 for x in each expression and simplifying.

EXAMPLE 5   **Squaring Binomials**

Square the binomials using the preceding rules:

a. $(x + 3)^2$ **b.** $(3x + 7)^2$ **c.** $(x - 4)^2$ **d.** $(5y - 6)^2$

Solution

We square parts (a) and (b) using the pattern for the square of a binomial sum.

	(First Term)^2	+	2 · Product of the Terms	+	(Last Term)^2	
a. $(x + 3)^2 =$	x^2	+	$2 \cdot x \cdot 3$	+	3^2	$= x^2 + 6x + 9$
b. $(3x + 7)^2 =$	$(3x)^2$	+	$2(3x)(7)$	+	7^2	$= 9x^2 + 42x + 49$

We square parts (c) and (d) using the pattern for the square of a binomial difference.

	(First Term)^2	$-$	2 · Product of the Terms	$+$	(Last Term)^2	
c. $(x - 4)^2 =$	x^2	$-$	$2 \cdot x \cdot 4$	$+$	4^2	$= x^2 - 8x + 16$
d. $(5y - 6)^2 =$	$(5y)^2$	$-$	$2(5y)(6)$	$+$	6^2	$= 25y^2 - 60y + 36$

■

Using technology

We can use a graphing utility to show that the square of a sum is not the sum of the squares.

$$(x + 1)^2 \neq x^2 + 1$$

The graphs of $y_1 = (x + 1)^2$ and $y_2 = x^2 + 1$, shown in the figure, clearly are not the same.

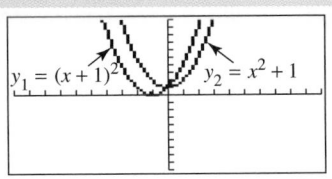

The box below summarizes the FOIL method and the two special products.

FOIL and special products

Let A and B be real numbers, variables, or algebraic expressions.

FOIL	**Example**
$$\begin{array}{cccc} \text{F} & \text{O} & \text{I} & \text{L} \end{array}$$ $(A + B)(C + D) = AC + AD + BC + BD$	$\begin{array}{cccc} \text{F} & \text{O} & \text{I} & \text{L} \end{array}$ $(2x + 3)(4x + 5) = (2x)(4x) + (2x)(5) + (3)(4x) + (3)(5)$ $= 8x^2 + 10x + 12x + 15$ $= 8x^2 + 22x + 15$
Sum and Difference of Two terms	**Example**
$(A + B)(A - B) = A^2 - B^2$	$(2x + 3)(2x - 3) = (2x)^2 - 3^2$ $= 4x^2 - 9$
Square of a Binomial	**Example**
$(A + B)^2 = A^2 + 2AB + B^2$	$(2x + 3)^2 = (2x)^2 + 2(2x)(3) + 3^2$ $= 4x^2 + 12x + 9$
$(A - B)^2 = A^2 - 2AB + B^2$	$(2x - 3)^2 = (2x)^2 - 2(2x)(3) + 3^2$ $= 4x^2 - 12x + 9$

4 Model geometric situations with polynomials.

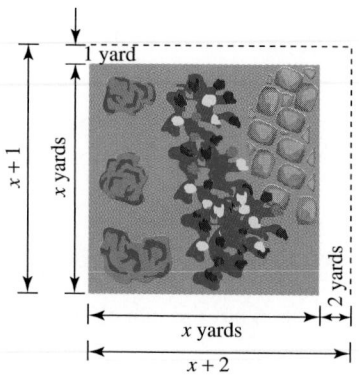

Figure 6.4

Expanding a square garden

x	$f(x) = x^2 + 3x + 2$
0	$f(0) = 0^2 + 3(0) + 2 = 2$
1	$f(1) = 1^2 + 3(1) + 2 = 6$
2	$f(2) = 2^2 + 3(2) + 2 = 12$
3	$f(3) = 3^2 + 3(3) + 2 = 20$
4	$f(4) = 4^2 + 3(4) + 2 = 30$
5	$f(5) = 5^2 + 3(5) + 2 = 42$
6	$f(6) = 6^2 + 3(6) + 2 = 56$
7	$f(7) = 7^2 + 3(7) + 2 = 72$
8	$f(8) = 8^2 + 3(8) + 2 = 90$

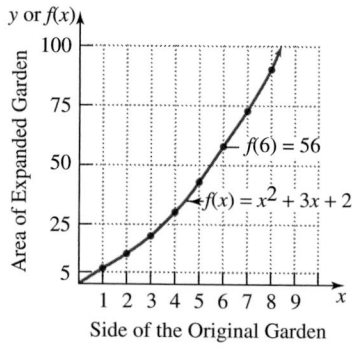

Figure 6.5

Graph of the function

Modeling with Polynomials

Geometric situations can often be modeled by polynomial functions.

EXAMPLE 6   **Modeling with Polynomials**

The square garden shown in Figure 6.4 is to be expanded so that one side is increased by 2 yards and an adjacent side is increased by 1 yard.

a. Find a polynomial that describes the area of the larger garden.
b. Write the expression in part (a) as a polynomial function, calling the function f.
c. Find and interpret $f(6)$.

Solution

a. We begin with a polynomial that models the area of the larger garden.

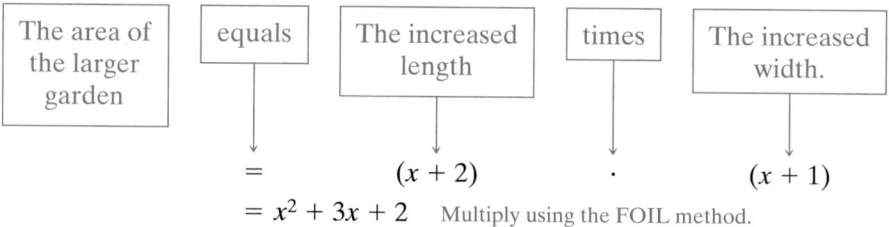

$$= (x + 2) \cdot (x + 1)$$
$$= x^2 + 3x + 2 \quad \text{Multiply using the FOIL method.}$$

b. The area of the larger garden is a function of x, the measure of each side of the original garden. Thus, we can write our trinomial in part (a) in function notation.

$$f(x) = x^2 + 3x + 2$$

c. Now we must find $f(6)$.

$$f(x) = x^2 + 3x + 2 \quad \text{This is the function from part (b).}$$
$$f(6) = 6^2 + 3(6) + 2 \quad \text{To find } f(6), \text{replace } x \text{ with 6.}$$
$$= 36 + 18 + 2$$
$$= 56 \quad \text{f of 6 equals 56.}$$

Since $f(6) = 56$, this means that if the original garden measures 6 yards on a side, the area of the expanded, larger garden will be 56 square yards. This solution is shown on the graph of the function in Figure 6.5. Why have we only shown the portion of the graph in the first quadrant? ∎

Discover for yourself

Use a graphing utility to verify the hand-drawn graph in Figure 6.5. Trace along the curve and show that (6, 56) is a point on the graph. Trace along the curve and find another point on the graph. What is the meaning of the second point in terms of the size of the original garden and the area of the expanded garden?

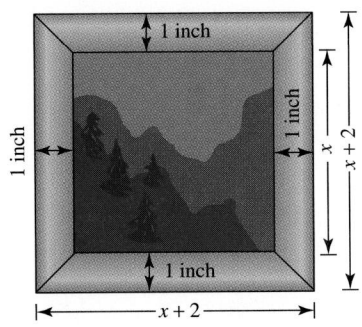

Figure 6.6

A square painting surrounded by a frame

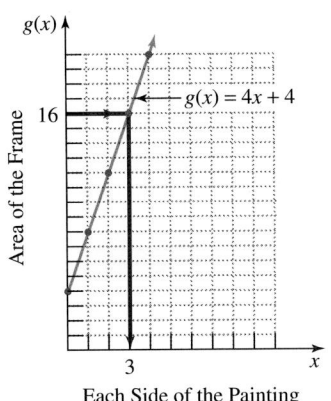

Figure 6.7

Why is the graph only shown in the first quadrant?

EXAMPLE 7 **Modeling with Polynomials**

The square painting shown in Figure 6.6 is surrounded by a frame that uniformly measures 1 inch wide.

a. Find a polynomial that describes the area of the frame.
b. Write the expression in part (a) as a function, calling the function g.
c. Graph the function.
d. Use the graph to answer this question: If the area of the frame is 16 square inches, how long is each side of the square painting?

Solution

a. We begin with a polynomial that models the area of the frame.

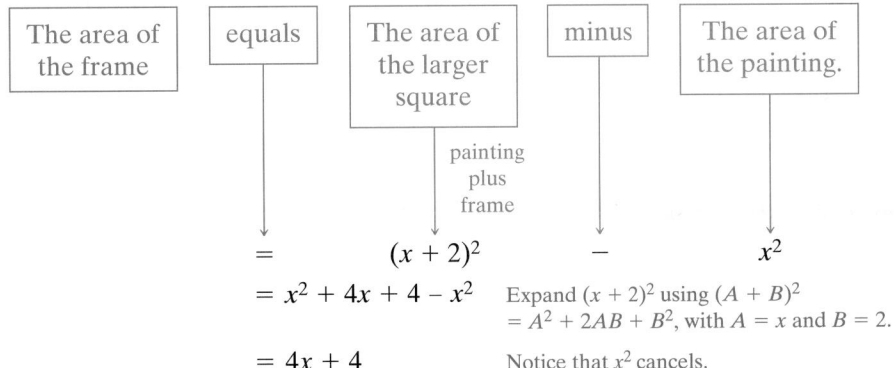

$$= x^2 + 4x + 4 - x^2 \quad \text{Expand } (x+2)^2 \text{ using } (A+B)^2$$
$$= A^2 + 2AB + B^2, \text{ with } A = x \text{ and } B = 2.$$

$$= 4x + 4 \qquad \text{Notice that } x^2 \text{ cancels.}$$

b. The area of the frame is a function of x, the measure of each side of the painting. Thus, we can write our expression in part (a) in function notation.

$$g(x) = 4x + 4$$

c. The function is a linear function with slope and y-intercept both equal to 4. The graph is shown in Figure 6.7.

d. The area of the frame is 16 square inches. Find 16 on the area axis (the y-axis). As shown in Figure 6.7, draw a horizontal line until it intersects the graph. From this point, draw a vertical line down to the x-axis. We see that $x = 3$. This means that if the area of the frame is 16 square inches, each side of the square painting is 3 inches. How can you verify this result? ■

PROBLEM SET 6.3

Practice Problems

Use FOIL to find the product in Problems 1–32.

1. $(x + 3)(x + 5)$ **2.** $(x + 7)(x + 2)$ **3.** $(y - 5)(y + 3)$ **4.** $(y - 1)(y + 2)$

5. $(2b - 1)(b + 2)$ **6.** $(2a - 5)(a + 3)$ **7.** $(2x - 3)(x + 1)$ **8.** $(3y - 5)(y + 4)$

9. $(2y - 3)(5y + 3)$ **10.** $(2x - 5)(7x + 2)$ **11.** $(3y - 7)(4y - 5)$ **12.** $(4z - 5)(7z - 4)$

13. $(x^2 - 5)(x^2 - 3)$ **14.** $(y^2 + 4)(y^2 - 3)$ **15.** $(3y^3 + 2)(y^3 + 4)$ **16.** $(5x^4 - 4)(x^4 - 3)$

17. $(3y^6 - 5)(2y^6 - 2)$ **18.** $(4y^8 - 3)(2y^8 - 5)$ **19.** $(x^2 - 3)(x + 2)$ **20.** $(y^2 - 1)(y + 1)$

21. $(4 + 5y)(5 - 4y)$ **22.** $(8 + 3y)(2 - y)$ **23.** $(-3 + 2y)(4 + y)$ **24.** $(-5 + 6x)(2 - x)$

25. $(-3 + r)(-5 - 2r)$ **26.** $(-6 - 5y)(1 - 4y)$ **27.** $(6x^{10} - 4)(3x^{10} + 7)$ **28.** $(5x^{10} - 7)(4x^{10} + 11)$

29. $(x + 5)(x^2 - 3)$ **30.** $(x - 3)(x^2 + 7)$ **31.** $(2x^2 - 3)(4x^3 + 1)$ **32.** $(3x^3 - 5)(7x^2 + 4)$

In Problems 33–50, multiply by using the rule for finding the product of the sum and difference of two terms.

33. $(x + 3)(x - 3)$ **34.** $(y + 5)(y - 5)$ **35.** $(3x + 2)(3x - 2)$ **36.** $(2x + 5)(2x - 5)$

37. $(3r - 4)(3r + 4)$ **38.** $(5z - 2)(5z + 2)$ **39.** $(3 + r)(3 - r)$ **40.** $(4 + s)(4 - s)$

41. $(5 - 7x)(5 + 7x)$ **42.** $(4 - 3y)(4 + 3y)$ **43.** $(2x + \frac{1}{2})(2x - \frac{1}{2})$ **44.** $(3y + \frac{1}{3})(3y - \frac{1}{3})$

45. $(y^2 + 1)(y^2 - 1)$ **46.** $(y^2 + 2)(y^2 - 2)$ **47.** $(r^3 + 2)(r^3 - 2)$ **48.** $(m^3 + 4)(m^3 - 4)$

49. $(1 - y^4)(1 + y^4)$ **50.** $(2 - s^5)(2 + s^5)$

In Problems 51–66, multiply by using the rule for the square of a binomial.

51. $(x + 2)^2$ **52.** $(y + 5)^2$ **53.** $(y - 3)^2$ **54.** $(x - 4)^2$

55. $(2x^2 + 3)^2$ **56.** $(3y^2 + 2)^2$ **57.** $(4x^2 - 1)^2$ **58.** $(5y^2 - 3)^2$

59. $(2x + \frac{1}{2})^2$ **60.** $(3y + \frac{1}{3})^2$ **61.** $(4y - \frac{1}{4})^2$ **62.** $(2y - \frac{1}{2})^2$

63. $(7 - 2x)^2$ **64.** $(9 - 5x)^2$ **65.** $(7 - 12y^3)^2$ **66.** $(9 - 11y^3)^2$

In Problems 67–80, multiply by the method of your choice.

67. $(-3x - 7)(x + 5)$ **68.** $(x^7 - x^2)(x^7 + x^2)$ **69.** $(2x - 5)^2$

70. $(3a + 0.4)^2$ **71.** $(3x + 11)(3x - 11)$ **72.** $(7x^3 + 1)(x^3 - 5)$

73. $(7m^4 + m^2)(m^2 + m)$ **74.** $(x - 5x^3)^2$ **75.** $(y - 5)(y^2 + 5y + 25)$

76. $(2x^4 + 3)(2x^4 - 3)$ **77.** $(\frac{4}{5} - 2x^3)(\frac{4}{5} + 2x^3)$ **78.** $3x^2(5x^3 - 4x^2 - x)$

79. $(4x^2 - 11)(2x^2 + 3)$ **80.** $(\frac{1}{4}x^2 + 12)(\frac{3}{4}x^2 - 8)$

Find the area in Problems 81–84, writing the answer as a polynomial in descending powers of x.

81.
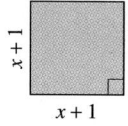
$x + 1$

82.
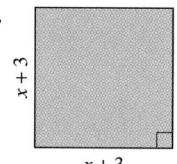
$x + 3$

83.
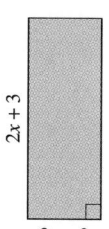
$2x - 3$

84.
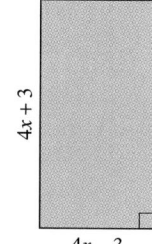
$4x - 3$

85. If x represents an integer, write a polynomial in descending powers of x representing the sum of the squares of two consecutive integers.

86. If x represents an integer, write a polynomial in descending powers of x representing the sum of the squares of two consecutive odd integers.

87. Add the areas of the four rectangular regions shown in the figure. What special product is represented by this sum?

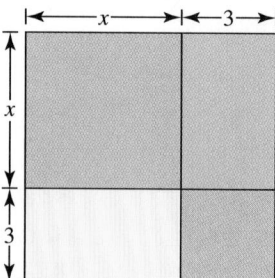

Application Problems

88. The square garden shown in the figure is to be expanded so that both sides are increased by 2 yards.
  a. Find a polynomial that describes the area of the larger garden.
  b. Write the expression in part (a) as a polynomial function, calling the function f.
  c. Find and interpret $f(5)$.

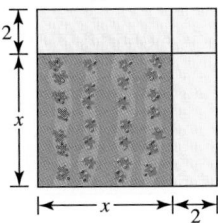

89. A square painting is surrounded by a frame that uniformly measures 2 inches wide.
  a. Make a sketch of this situation similar to Figure 6.6 on page 445. If each side of the square painting is represented by x inches, find a polynomial that describes the area of the frame.
  b. Write the expression in part (a) as a function, calling the function g.
  c. Graph the function in the first quadrant.
  d. Use your graph to answer this question: If the area of the frame is 24 square inches, how long is each side of the square painting?

90. A 3-foot by 3-foot sandbox is placed on a square lawn x feet on a side. Find a polynomial expression for the remaining area. Write the polynomial expression as a function f, and describe the practical meaning of $f(100)$.

91. The number of desks in one row is $5d + 3$. Write a polynomial that models the number of desks in a room of $4d - 2$ rows if they are arranged in a rectangular array. Write the polynomial expression as a function f, and then describe the practical meaning of $f(7)$.

In Problems 92–95, find a polynomial function (call it f) that models the area of the shaded region of each figure. Then find and interpret f(3).

92.

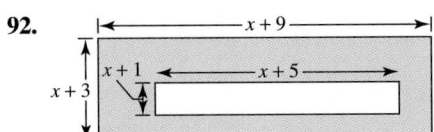

93.

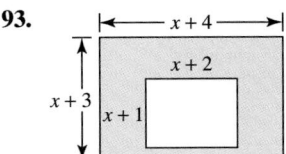

94.

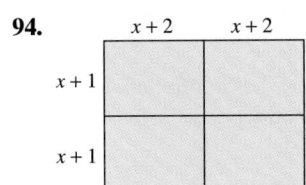

95.

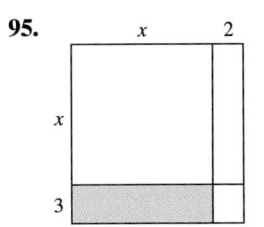

True–False Critical Thinking Problems

96. Which one of the following is true?
  a. $(3 + 4)^2 = 3^2 + 4^2$
  b. $(2y + 7)^2 = 4y^2 + 28y + 49$
  c. $(3x^2 + 2)(3x^2 - 2) = 9x^2 - 4$
  d. $(x - 5)^2 = x^2 - 5x + 25$

97. Which one of the following is true?
  a. $(40 + 1)(40 - 1) = (40)^2 - 1^2 = 1599$
  b. $(2x + 3)^2 = 4x^2 + 9$
  c. $(y + 8)^2 - y^2 = 64$
  d. The FOIL method is useful for adding binomials.

Technology Problems

98. Show that each of the following expressions are not equal by graphing the left side (call the left side y_1) and the right side (call the right side y_2) on your graphing utility.
  a. $(x - 1)^2 \neq x^2 - 1$
  b. $(x + 3)^2 \neq x^2 + 9$
  c. $(x + 2)^2 \neq x^2 + 2x + 4$

99. Correct the right side for each expression in Problem 98 so that the two sides of the resulting equation are, indeed, equal. Then use your graphing utility to graph both sides, showing that the two graphs are identical.

100. Use a graphing utility to graph the following polynomial functions on the same screen:

$$y_1 = x^2$$
$$y_2 = (x + 2)^2$$
$$y_3 = (x - 3)^2$$

What do you observe? Use the word "shift" in your description. Does your observation apply if the exponent is changed from 2 to 3?

Writing in Mathematics

101. Explain how to multiply two binomials using the FOIL method.

102. Explain the difference between simplifying the expressions $(2x + 3) + (2x + 3)$ and $(2x + 3)^2$.

103. Explain how to square a binomial.

Critical Thinking Problems

104. Multiply and simplify: $(5x + 3)(5x - 3) - (3x + 2)(3x - 2)$.

105. Multiply and simplify: $(2x + 3)^2 - (7 - 2x)^2$.

106. Expand: $(x + 1)^4$.

107. Use the figure to write a polynomial in descending powers of x representing the area of the region inside the right triangle and outside the square.

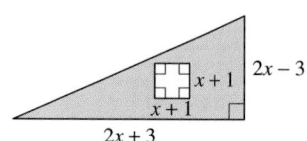

108. Use the figure to write a polynomial in descending powers of x representing the area of the region inside the triangle and outside the square.

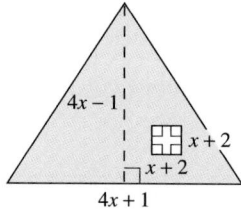

Problems 109–110 involve descriptions of trinomials in the form $ax^2 + bx + c$.

109. The x^2 coefficient is 1 and the last term is $5 \cdot 3$. Find the middle term.

110. The x^2 coefficient is 1 and the last term is $-11 \cdot 2$. Find the middle term.

111. Two binomial factors are multiplied using the FOIL method. The product is $x^2 - 7x + 10$. What are the binomial factors?

112. What two binomials must be multiplied using the FOIL method to give a product of $x^2 - 8x - 20$?

Group Activity Problems

Polynomials and number tricks

Here's a number puzzle that can be verified using polynomial operations.

   Take a number. Add 1. Square the result. Subtract the product of the original number times two more than the original number. The answer will always be 1.

Verification

   Take a number: x.

   Add one: $x + 1$

   Square the result: $(x + 1)^2$

   Subtract the product of the original number times two more than the original number: $(x + 1)^2 - x(x + 2)$

Using polynomial operations:

$$(x + 1)^2 - x(x + 2) = x^2 + 2x + 1 - x^2 - 2x = 1$$

The answer is 1, regardless of what number is originally chosen!

Verify the puzzles in Problems 113–114 by using polynomial operations.

113. Take a number. Add 2. Square the sum. Add 25 to this result. Subtract the product of the original number times four more than the original number. Add 6 to the difference. The result is always 35.

114. Take a number and multiply it by five more than the number. Subtract from this the product of seven more than the original number and two less than the original number. Multiply the total by 5 and subtract 50. The result is always 20.

115. With the other members of your group, write and then verify a puzzle similar to the one in Problem 113 or Problem 114.

Review Problems _____

116. Graph: $y = -\frac{1}{2}x + 3$.

117. Insert either $>$, $<$, or $=$ in the box to make the statement true: $|-5| \;\square\; |-8|$.

118. Solve: $7 - 2x + 5x = -2(4 - 3x)$.

S E C T I O N   6 . 4

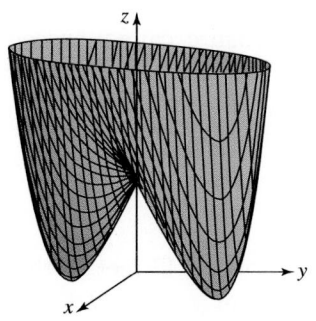

Solutions Manual   **Tutorial**   **Video 7**

Polynomials in two variables have three-dimensional graphs. Shown here is the graph of $z = x^4 + y^4 - 4xy + 1$.

I Evaluate a polynomial in several variables.

Polynomials in Several Variables

Objectives

1 Evaluate a polynomial in several variables.
2 Identify coefficients and degrees.
3 Add and subtract polynomials in several variables.
4 Multiply polynomials in several variables.

Up to this point in the chapter, our focus has been on polynomials that have only one variable. However, a polynomial can contain two or more variables. Here are some examples:

$$x^4 + y^4 - 4xy + 1 \qquad 7a^2 - 5b^2 \qquad 6a^2bc - 4abc^2 + 3b - 2c$$

We call a polynomial containing two or more variables a *polynomial in several variables*. These polynomials can be evaluated, added, subtracted, and multiplied just like polynomials that contain only one variable.

Discover for yourself

Can you use the skills that you have learned for working with polynomials in one variable to evaluate and perform operations with polynomials in several variables without any new instruction? See if this is possible by turning directly to Problem Set 6.4 on page 453 and see how many problems you can successfully solve before having to read all or part of this section.

Evaluating Polynomials

To evaluate a polynomial in several variables,

1. Substitute the given values for each of the variables.
2. Perform the resulting computation using the agreed-upon order of operations.

Discover for yourself

Use a calculator to verify the computation in Example 1.

EXAMPLE 1 Evaluating a Polynomial in Two Variables

Evaluate: $7x^3y + xy^2 - 4xy + 5$, when $x = -4$ and $y = 3$

Solution

We begin by substituting -4 for x and 3 for y.

$7x^3y + xy^2 - 4xy + 5$	This is the given polynomial.
$= 7(-4)^3(3) + (-4)(3)^2 - 4(-4)(3) + 5$	Replace x with -4 and y with 3.
$= 7(-64)(3) + (-4)(9) - 4(-4)(3) + 5$	Evaluate exponential terms.
$= -1344 + (-36) - (-48) + 5$	Perform the indicated multiplications.
$= -1344 + (-36) + 48 + 5$	Rewrite the subtraction as addition of an inverse.
$= -1327$	Add from left to right.

Geometric situations can often be modeled by polynomials in two variables.

EXAMPLE 2 Modeling with Polynomials

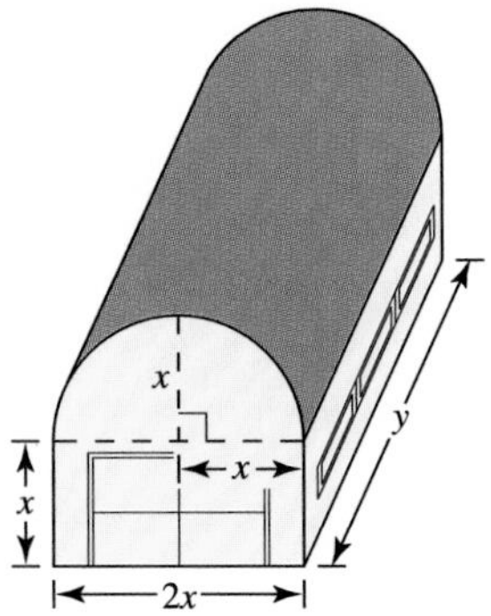

Figure 6.8

A storage building

The storage building shown in Figure 6.8 has a volume given by the polynomial

$$2x^2y + \frac{1}{2}\pi x^2y.$$

A small business requires at least 18,000 cubic feet of storage space and is considering having a building installed just like the one shown in the figure. However, zoning regulations require that:

1. The building's total height, represented by $2x$ in the figure, cannot exceed 26 feet.
2. The building's length, represented by y in the figure, cannot exceed 27 feet.

Should the business construct the storage building?

Solution

Since $2x$ cannot exceed 26 feet, the largest possibility for x is 13 feet. With a maximum length of 27 feet, the largest possible value of y is 27 feet. The greatest possible volume for the storage building is found by evaluating the polynomial for $x = 13$, $y = 27$, and $\pi \approx 3.14$.

$$\begin{aligned} 2x^2y + \frac{1}{2}\pi x^2y &\approx 2(13)^2(27) + \frac{1}{2}(3.14)(13)^2(27) \\ &= 2(169)(27) + \frac{1}{2}(3.14)(169)(27) \\ &= 9126 + 7163.91 \\ &= 16{,}289.91 \end{aligned}$$

The maximum volume that zoning will permit for the storage shed is approximately 16,290 cubic feet. Since, as stated, the business requires at least 18,000 cubic feet, they should not construct the storage building.

2 Identify coefficients and degrees.

The Vocabulary of Polynomials in Several Variables

In Chapter 1, a *term* was defined as an expression containing a constant or the product of a constant and one or more variables. This definition applies nicely to polynomials in several variables. As with polynomials in one variable, the number preceding the variable(s) in a term is the numerical *coefficient* of that term. The *degree* of a term is the *sum of the exponents* of the variables. Just like a polynomial in one variable, the *degree of a polynomial* in several variables is the highest degree of all the terms of the polynomial.

EXAMPLE 3   **Using the Vocabulary of Polynomials**

Determine the coefficient, the degree of each term, and the degree of the polynomial:

$$7x^2y^4 - 17x^3y^2z + 5xy - 6x^2 + 13.$$

Solution

Term	Coefficient	Degree of Term (Sum of the Exponents of the Variables)
$7x^2y^4$	7	$2 + 4 = 6$
$-17x^3y^2z$	-17	$3 + 2 + 1 = 6$
$5xy$	5	$1 + 1 = 2$
$-6x^2$	-6	2
13	13	0

The degree of the polynomial is the highest degree of all its terms, which is 6. ∎

3 Add and subtract polynomials in several variables.

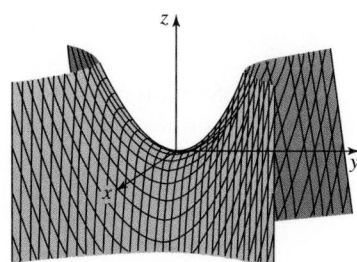

A three-dimensional graph of a polynomial in several variables

Adding and Subtracting Polynomials in Several Variables

Only like terms with the same variables to the same power may be combined. For example, $2x^3y^2$ and $-10x^3y^2$ are like terms because each has x to the power 3 and y to the power 2. These like terms can be combined mentally by combining the coefficients of the terms $(2 - 10 = -8)$ and keeping the same variable factors.

$$2x^3y^2 - 10x^3y^2 = -8x^3y^2$$

The following example relies on combining like terms.

EXAMPLE 4   **Adding and Subtracting Polynomials**

a. Add: $(7xy^2 - 4x^2y - 7xy + 3) + (6xy^2 - 2x^2y + 8xy - 9)$
b. Subtract: $(5a^3 - 9a^2b + 3ab^2 - 4) - (3a^3 - 6a^2b - 2ab^2 + 3)$

Solution

a. $(7xy^2 - 4x^2y - 7xy + 3)$
$\quad + (6xy^2 - 2x^2y + 8xy - 9)$
$= (7xy^2 + 6xy^2) + (-4x^2y - 2x^2y)$
$\quad + (-7xy + 8xy) + (3 - 9)$ Group like terms.
$= 13xy^2 - 6x^2y + xy - 6$ Combine like terms by combining coefficients and keeping the same variable factors.

b. $(5a^3 - 9a^2b + 3ab^2 - 4)$
$\quad - (3a^3 - 6a^2b - 2ab^2 + 3)$
$= (5a^3 - 9a^2b + 3ab^2 - 4)$
$\quad + (-3a^3 + 6a^2b + 2ab^2 - 3)$ Change the sign of each term in the second polynomial and add the two polynomials.

$= (5a^3 - 3a^3) + (-9a^2b + 6a^2b)$
$\quad + (3ab^2 + 2ab^2) + (-4 - 3)$ Group like terms.
$= 2a^3 - 3a^2b + 5ab^2 - 7$ Combine like terms by combining coefficients and keeping the same variable factors.   ■

4 Multiply polynomials in several variables.

Multiplying Polynomials in Several Variables

The product of monomials forms the basis of polynomial multiplication. As with monomials in one variable, multiplication can be done mentally by multiplying coefficients and adding exponents.

EXAMPLE 5   **Multiplying Monomials**

Multiply:

a. $(3xy^2)(4x^3y)$ **b.** $(-8a^7b^3c)(-5a^4bc^7)$

Solution

Multiply coefficients.

a. $(3x^1y^2)(4x^3y^1) = 12x^4y^3$

Add exponents.

b. $(-8a^7b^3c)(-5a^4bc^7) = (-8)(-5)a^{7+4}b^{3+1}c^{1+7}$ Multiply coefficients and add exponents.

$= 40a^{11}b^4c^8$ ■

FOIL multiplication and the special products studied in Section 6.3 can be used to multiply polynomials in several variables. If a product cannot be found by one of these methods, we can always multiply each term of one polynomial factor by every term of the other polynomial factor. As with polynomials in one variable, columns can be used.

EXAMPLE 6   **Multiplying Polynomials**

Multiply:

a. $3x^2y(4x^3y^2 - 6x^2y + 2)$ **b.** $(x + 4y)(3x - 5y)$
c. $(5x + 3y)^2$ **d.** $(7x^2y - y^3)^2$
e. $(4a^2b + 3b)(4a^2b - 3b)$ **f.** $(ab + 4b)(6a^2b - 8ab + 5b)$

iscover for yourself

Before reading the solution, decide which multiplication method works best for each part of Example 6. Why did you select that method?

iscover for yourself

The solution of this problem is based on skills that you have already practiced. Try covering up the solution and work each part of this example on your own. After finding the product in each part, compare your work with what appears on the right.

Solution

a. $3x^2y(4x^3y^2 - 6x^2y + 2)$

$= (3x^2y)(4x^3y^2) + (3x^2y)(-6x^2y) + (3x^2y)(2)$ Use the distributive property.

$= 12x^5y^3 - 18x^4y^2 + 6x^2y$ To multiply monomials, multiply coefficients and add exponents.

b. $(x + 4y)(3x - 5y)$ Multiply these binomials using the FOIL method.

$\quad\quad\quad F \quad\quad\quad O \quad\quad\quad I \quad\quad\quad L$

$= (x)(3x) + (x)(-5y) + (4y)(3x) + (4y)(-5y)$

$= 3x^2 - 5xy + 12xy - 20y^2$

$= 3x^2 + 7xy - 20y^2$ Combine like terms.

$(A + B)^2 = A^2 + 2 \cdot A \cdot B + B^2$

c. $(5x + 3y)^2 = (5x)^2 + 2(5x)(3y) + (3y)^2$

$= 25x^2 + 30xy + 9y^2$

$(A - B)^2 = A^2 - 2 \cdot A \cdot B + B^2$

d. $(7x^2y - y^3)^2 = (7x^2y)^2 - 2(7x^2y)(y^3) + (y^3)^2$

$= 49x^4y^2 - 14x^2y^4 + y^6$

$(A + B)(A - B) = A^2 - B^2$

e. $(4a^2b + 3b)(4a^2b - 3b) = (4a^2b)^2 - (3b)^2$

$= 16a^4b^2 - 9b^2$

f.

$$6a^2b - 8ab + 5b$$
$$ab + 4b$$
$$\overline{}$$
$$24a^2b^2 - 32ab^2 + 20b^2 \leftarrow 4b(6a^2b - 8ab + 5b)$$
$$6a^3b^2 - 8a^2b^2 + 5ab^2 \quad\quad \leftarrow ab(6a^2b - 8ab + 5b)$$
$$\overline{6a^3b^2 + 16a^2b^2 - 27ab^2 + 20b^2}$$

Add like terms, which are lined up in columns.

PROBLEM SET 6.4

Practice Problems

Evaluate each polynomial in Problems 1–4 using $x = 4$ and $y = -3$.

1. $x^2 + 2xy - y^2$ 　　　 **2.** $2x^2 - xy + y^2$ 　　　 **3.** $4xy^3 + x^2y^2 - 3y + 6$ 　　　 **4.** $3xy^3 + x^2y^2 - 5y + 11$

Evaluate each polynomial in Problems 5–8 using $x = -1$, $y = 3$, and $z = -2$.

5. $yz - 2xy + 4xz$ 　　　 **6.** $xy^2z - 4z$ 　　　 **7.** $x^3y + 4x^2yz - 3xyz^2$ 　　　 **8.** $2x^3y - x^2yz + 3xyz^2$

In Problems 9–12, identify the coefficient and the degree of each term of the polynomial. What is the degree of the polynomial?

9. $x^3y^2 - 5x^2y^7 + 6y^2 - 3$ 　　　 **10.** $12x^4y - 5x^3y^7 - x^2 - \pi$ 　　　 **11.** $4x^2yz - 5xyz + 12z^3$ 　　　 **12.** $6xy^2z - 7xyz + 14y^3$

Add or subtract as indicated in Problems 13–24.

13. $(5x^2y - 3xy) + (2x^2y - xy)$ 　　　　　　　　 **14.** $(-2x^2y + xy) + (4x^2y + 7xy)$

15. $(4y^2z + 8yz + 11) + (-2y^2z + 5yz + 2)$ 　　　 **16.** $(7a^4b^2 - 5a^2b^2 + 3ab) + (-18a^4b^2 - 6a^2b^2 - ab)$

17. $(x^3 + 7xy - 5y^2) - (6x^3 - xy + 4y^2)$ 　　　 **18.** $(x^4 - 7xy - 5y^3) - (6x^4 - 3xy + 4y^3)$

19. $(3a^4b^2 + 5a^3b - 3b) - (2a^4b^2 - 3a^3b - 4b + 6a)$

20. $(5x^4y^2 + 6x^3y - 7y) - (3x^4y^2 - 5x^3y - 6y + 8x)$

21. Add:

$$5x^2y^2 - 4xy^2 + 6y^2$$
$$-8x^2y^2 + 5xy^2 - y^2$$

22. Add:

$$7a^2b^2 - 5ab^2 + 6b^2$$
$$-10a^2b^2 + 6ab^2 + 6b^2$$

23. Subtract:

$$3a^2b^4 - 5ab^2 + 7ab$$
$$-(-5a^2b^4 - 8ab^2 - ab)$$

24. Subtract:

$$13x^2y^4 - 17xy^2 + xy$$
$$-(-7x^2y^4 - 8xy^2 - xy)$$

25. Subtract $11a - 5b$ from the sum of $7a + 13b$ and $-26a + 19b$.

26. Subtract $23x - 5y$ from the sum of $6x + 15y$ and $x - 19y$.

Find the indicated products in Problems 27–66.

27. $(6x^2y)(3xy)$

28. $(4a^2b)(5ab)$

29. $(-7x^3y^4)(2x^2y^5)$

30. $(6x^4y^5)(-10x^7y^{11})$

31. $(-7a^{11}b^4c)(12a^3bc^5)$

32. $(-15a^{13}b^4c)(5a^7b^6c)$

33. $5xy(2x + 3y)$

34. $4xy(5x - 2y)$

35. $3ab^2(6a^2b^3 + 5ab)$

36. $15ab^2(4a^2b^3 + 7ab)$

37. $-4y^2z(3y^3z^5 - 14y^2z + 1)$

38. $-5y^2z\,(7y^3z^5 + 20y^2z - 1)$

39. $(x + 5y)(7x + 3y)$

40. $(x + 9y)(6x + 7y)$

41. $(a - 3b)(2a + 7b)$

42. $(3a - b)(2a + 14b)$

43. $(xy + 8)(xy - 7)$

44. $(xy - 12)(xy + 11)$

45. $(3ab - 1)(5ab + 2)$

46. $(7a^2b + 1)(2a^2b - 3)$

47. $(7a + 5b)^2$

48. $(9a + 7b)^2$

49. $(x^2y^2 - 3)^2$

50. $(a^2b^2 - 5)^2$

51. $(x^2 + y^2z^2)^2$

52. $(x^4 + y^2z^2)^2$

53. $(x^2 + yz)(x^2 - yz)$

54. $(xy + z^2)(xy - z^2)$

55. $(x - y)(x^2 + xy + y^2)$

56. $(x + y)(x^2 - xy + y^2)$

57. $(a^2 - b^2)(a + b)$

58. $(a^2 + b^2)(a - b)$

59. $(m - n^3)(2m^3 + n)$

60. $(m + n^3)(3m^3 - n)$

61. $(r^2 - s)(r^2 + s)$

62. $(r - s^2)(r + s^2)$

63. $(xy + ab)(xy - ab)$

64. $(xy + ab^2)(xy - ab^2)$

65. $(x^2 + 1)(x^4y + x^2 + 1)$

66. $(x^2 - 3)(x^4y + 2x^2 - 1)$

Application Problems

67. The construction industry uses a polynomial model in two variables to determine the number of board feet N that can be manufactured from a tree with a diameter of x inches and a length of y feet. The model, called the Doyle log formula, is given by $N = \dfrac{x^2y - 8xy + 16y}{4}$. A building contractor estimates that 800 board feet of lumber is needed for a job. The lumber company has just milled a fresh load of timber from 20 trees that averaged 10 inches in diameter and 16 feet in length. Is this enough to complete the job? If not, what is a reasonable estimate of the number of additional trees that must be milled to meet the job's requirements?

Neil Jenney (American, b. 1945) "Melt Down Morning" 1975, oil on panel, $25\frac{3}{8} \times 112\frac{1}{2}$ in. Philadelphia Museum of Art: Purchased: The Samuel S. White III and Vera White Collection (by exchange) and funds contributed by the Daniel W. Dietrich Foundation in honor of Mrs. H. Gates Lloyd.

68. A sum of money P (the principal) is invested at interest rate r (in decimal form) compounded annually. After t years the total amount of money accumulated A is modeled by the polynomial $A = P(1 + r)^t$. Find the accumulated amount in an account after 3 years if \$20,000 is invested at an interest rate of 6% ($r = 0.06$).

69. The surface area of a right circular cylinder whose height is h and whose base radius is r is given by $2\pi rh + 2\pi r^2$. Find the surface area of a soda can that has a height of 4 inches and a radius of 2 inches. Use 3.14 as an approximation for π.

70. A solid region has a boundary that is a cylinder of radius r and height h, capped on each end by a half-sphere. The region's volume is given by the polynomial $\pi r^2 h + \frac{4}{3}\pi r^3 h$. Find the volume if the height is 4 inches and the radius is 3 inches. Use 3.14 as an approximation for π.

In Problems 71–76, find a polynomial that models the area of each figure. Write each polynomial as the sum or difference of terms.

71.

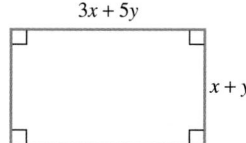

$3x + 5y$

$x + y$

72.

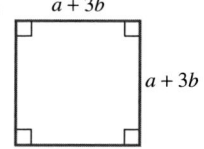

$a + 3b$

$a + 3b$

73.

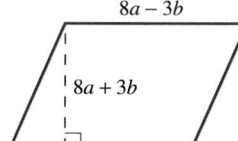

$8a - 3b$

$8a + 3b$

74.

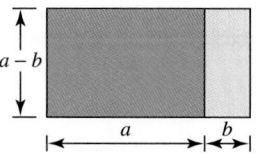

$a - b$

a b

75.

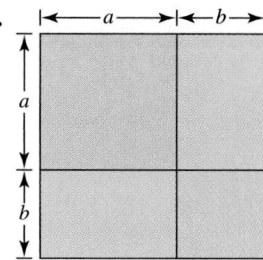

$\mapsto a \mapsto b \mapsto$

a

b

76.

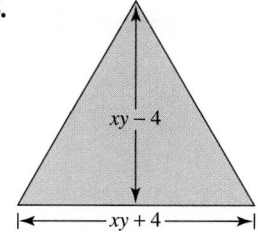

$xy - 4$

$xy + 4$

True–False Critical Thinking Problems

77. Which one of the following is true?
   a. The degree of $5x^{24} - 3x^{16}y^9 - 7xy^2 + 6$ is 24.
   b. In the polynomial $4x^2y + x^3y^2 + 3x^2y^3 + 7y$, the term x^3y^2 has degree 5 and no numerical coefficient.
   c. $(2x + 3 - 5y)(2x + 3 + 5y) =$ $4x^2 + 12x + 9 - 25y^2$
   d. $(6x^2y - 7xy - 4) - (6x^2y + 7xy - 4) = 0$

78. Which one of the following is true?
   a. A polynomial in three variables cannot have a degree less than 3.
   b. The degree of $4^3x^5y^6$ is $3 + 5 + 6 = 14$.
   c. $(x^3y - 5xy) - (x^3y - 4xy) = -9xy$
   d. $(-3x^2y^3z)(5xyz^{50}) = -15x^3y^4z^{51}$

Technology Problems

Equations that define z *in terms of* x *and* y *result in three-dimensional graphs, such as the one shown here. Use a graphing utility capable of graphing in three dimensions to graph each equation in Problems 79–81. (Such equations are also called functions in two variables.)*

79. $z = x^2 + y^2 - 2x + 6y + 14$

80. $z = y^2 - x^2$

81. $z = \dfrac{x^3y - y^3x}{390}$

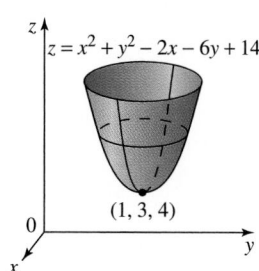

$z = x^2 + y^2 - 2x - 6y + 14$

$(1, 3, 4)$

Writing in Mathematics

82. In Problem 67, the number of board feet that can be manufactured from a tree is a function of both its diameter and its length. In Problem 68, the amount that $20,000 can grow to is a function of both the time of the investment and the interest rate. In Problem 70, the volume of the region is a function of both its radius and its height. Describe another example of a variable in an applied situation that depends on two or more other variables. Use the word *function* in your description.

83. The equation $z = 6 - 3x - 2y$ results in a plane, a portion of which is shown here. Explain how to find z when $x = 1$ and $y = 1$. Now find z and try to explain how this result can be seen on the graph.

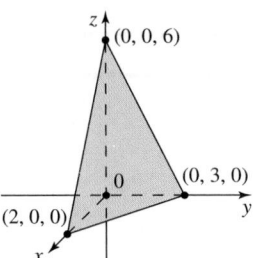

Critical Thinking Problems

In Problems 84–91, find a polynomial that models the shaded area of each figure. Write each polynomial as the sum or difference of terms. Express the polynomial in terms of π where appropriate.

84.

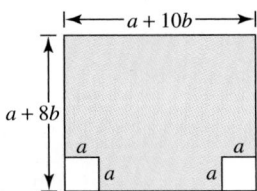

85.

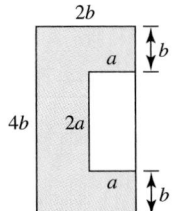

86.

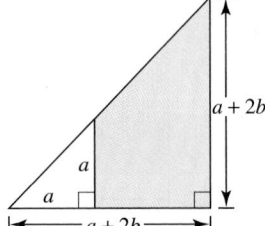

87.

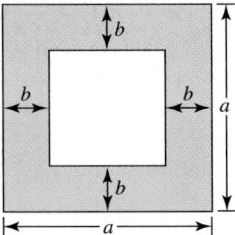

88.

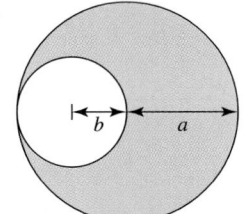

89.

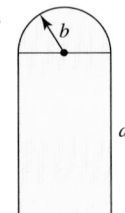

90.

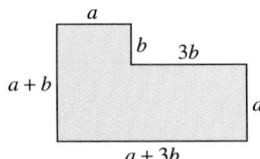

91.

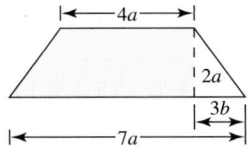

92. Explain how to obtain the formula for the volume of the storage building shown in Figure 6.8 on page 450 using the formulas for the volume of a rectangular solid and a cylinder.

Review Problems

93. Solve the system:

$$y = 5 - x$$
$$4x + 5y = 22$$

94. Solve for h: $A = \pi r^2 + 2\pi rh$.

95. Solve: $\frac{1}{3}x + \frac{2}{3} = \frac{1}{4}x - \frac{3}{4}$.

SECTION 6.5

Solutions Manual **Tutorial** **Video 7**

Dividing Polynomials

Objectives

1 Use the quotient rule to divide monomials.
2 Evaluate expressions containing zero exponents.
3 Simplify powers of quotients.
4 Divide monomials mentally.
5 Divide a polynomial by a monomial.

Paul Klee "Drawn One" (Gezeichneter) 1935, oil and watercolor on undercoated gauze stretched over cardboard, 30.5×27.5 cm. Kunstsammlung Nordrhein-Westfalen, Dusseldorf. Photo © Walter Klein, Dusseldorf. © VG Bild-Kunst.

In this section, we consider division of polynomials. We begin with division of monomials, moving on to the division of a polynomial with more than one term by a monomial. We begin our work by introducing three new exponential properties.

Additional Properties of Exponents

To divide polynomials, we need to develop some additional properties of exponents.

Dividing Powers with the Same Base.

Discover for yourself

Consider the quotient of two monomials with the same base:

$$\frac{x^7}{x^3} = \frac{\overbrace{x \cdot x \cdot x \cdot x \cdot x \cdot x \cdot x}^{7 \text{ factors of } x}}{\underbrace{x \cdot x \cdot x}_{3 \text{ factors of } x}}$$

Now cancel pairs of factors in the numerator and denominator. How many factors of x are left? Write this quotient in terms of x to a power. How can you obtain this power using the given exponents 7 and 3? Repeat this process for

$$\frac{2^{15}}{2^6}.$$

How many factors of 2 are left after canceling? How can this be expressed in terms of 2 to a power? When dividing exponential expressions with the same base, what is a fast method for determining the exponent of the quotient?

In the Discover for Yourself box, were you able to observe that the exponent of the quotient can be obtained by subtracting exponents? This is called the *quotient rule* for dividing exponential expressions with the same nonzero base.

I Use the quotient rule to divide monomials.

Quotient rule for exponents

If x is any nonzero real number, and m and n are natural numbers, then

$$\frac{x^m}{x^n} = x^{m-n}.$$

When dividing exponential expressions with the same nonzero base, subtract the exponent in the denominator from the exponent in the numerator. Use this difference as the exponent of the common base.

EXAMPLE I   Dividing Monomials by Using the Quotient Rule

Find the indicated quotients:

a. $\dfrac{x^{13}}{x^3}$ **b.** $\dfrac{25x^8}{5x^6}$ **c.** $\dfrac{10y^{13}}{-2y^4}$

Solution

a. $\dfrac{x^{13}}{x^3} = x^{13-3} = x^{10}$ **b.** $\dfrac{25x^8}{5x^6} = \dfrac{25}{5} \cdot \dfrac{x^8}{x^6} = 5x^{8-6} = 5x^2$

c. $\dfrac{10y^{13}}{-2y^4} = \dfrac{10}{-2} \cdot \dfrac{y^{13}}{y^4} = -5y^{13-4} = -5y^9$ ∎

2 Evaluate expressions containing zero exponents.

Zero as an Exponent. Let's consider the quotient rule when exponents in the numerator and denominator are equal. For example,

$$\frac{7^5}{7^5} = \frac{7 \cdot 7 \cdot 7 \cdot 7 \cdot 7}{7 \cdot 7 \cdot 7 \cdot 7 \cdot 7} = 1$$

In the Discover for Yourself box, were you able to discover that since

$$\frac{7^5}{7^5} = 1 \quad \text{and} \quad \frac{7^5}{7^5} = 7^{5-5} = 7^0$$

this means that 7^0 should equal 1? This forms the basis for defining a *zero exponent.*

Zero exponent

If x is any nonzero real number,

$$x^0 = 1.$$

EXAMPLE 2   Using Zero Exponents

Evaluate (find the numerical value for):

a. 9^0 **b.** $(-9)^0$ **c.** -9^0 **d.** $5x^0, \ x \neq 0$ **e.** $(5x)^0, \ x \neq 0$

Solution

a. $9^0 = 1$ **b.** $(-9)^0 = 1$ **c.** $-9^0 = -1(9^0) = -1(1) = -1$
d. $5x^0 = 5 \cdot 1 = 5$ **e.** $(5x)^0 = 1$ ∎

3 Simplify powers of quotients.

Raising a Quotient to a Power. We have seen that when a product is raised to a power, we raise every factor in the product to the power:

$$(xy)^m = x^m y^m$$

There is a similar property for raising a quotient to a power.

Power rule for powers of quotients

If x and y are nonzero real numbers, and m is a natural number, then

$$\left(\frac{x}{y}\right)^m = \frac{x^m}{y^m}.$$

When a quotient is raised to a power, raise the numerator to the power and divide by the denominator to the power.

EXAMPLE 3 **Using the Power Rules for Quotients**

Simplify:

a. $\left(\dfrac{x}{4}\right)^2$ **b.** $\left(\dfrac{x^2}{5}\right)^3$ **c.** $\left(\dfrac{-3x^4}{2}\right)^5$

Solution

a. $\left(\dfrac{x}{4}\right)^2 = \dfrac{x^2}{4^2} = \dfrac{x^2}{16}$ Square the numerator and the denominator.

b. $\left(\dfrac{x^2}{5}\right)^3 = \dfrac{(x^2)^3}{5^3} = \dfrac{x^6}{125}$ Cube the numerator and the denominator.

c. $\left(\dfrac{-3x^4}{2}\right)^5 = \dfrac{(-3x^4)^5}{2^5} = \dfrac{(-3)^5(x^4)^5}{2^5} = \dfrac{-243x^{20}}{32}$ ∎

Division of Polynomials

Now that we have developed these additional properties of exponents, we are ready to turn to polynomial division. We break our work into three general cases, the last of which we will study in Section 6.6.

4 Divide monomials mentally.

Case 1. Quotient of Monomials. We have already considered this type of problem, handled by the quotient rule for exponents. As shown below, after some practice you will probably do most of the work in your head, writing only the answer.

EXAMPLE 4 **Dividing Monomials Mentally**

Divide: $\dfrac{-16x^{14}}{8x^2}$

Solution

Divide coefficients.

$$\frac{-16x^{14}}{8x^2} = \frac{-16}{8}x^{14-2} = -2x^{12}$$

Subtract exponents.

5 Divide a polynomial by a monomial.

Case 2. Quotient of a Polynomial and a Monomial. When dividing a monomial into a polynomial, we use the reverse form of the rule for adding two fractions with a common denominator. In particular, since,

$$\frac{3}{7} + \frac{2}{7} = \frac{3+2}{7}$$

it is also true that

$$\frac{3+2}{7} = \frac{3}{7} + \frac{2}{7}.$$

Here are two examples:

$$\begin{array}{ll} \text{dividend} \rightarrow \\ \text{divisor} \rightarrow \end{array} \quad \frac{12x^3 + 6x^2}{2x} = \frac{12x^3}{2x} + \frac{6x^2}{2x} = 6x^2 + 3x \quad \leftarrow \text{quotient}$$

$$\begin{array}{ll} \text{dividend} \rightarrow \\ \text{divisor} \rightarrow \end{array} \quad \frac{x^4 - x}{x} = \frac{x^4}{x} - \frac{x}{x} = x^3 - 1 \quad \leftarrow \text{quotient}$$

Notice that we divide each term of the polynomial by the monomial.

> **Dividing a polynomial by a monomial**
>
> Divide each term of the polynomial by the monomial.

study tip

Try to avoid this common error:

Incorrect:

$$\frac{x^4 - x}{x} = x^4 - 1$$

Correct:

$$\frac{x^4 - x}{x} = \frac{x^4}{x} - \frac{x}{x}$$

Don't leave out the 1.

$$= x^{4-1} - x^{1-1}$$
$$= x^3 - x^0$$
$$= x^3 - 1$$

EXAMPLE 5   Dividing a Polynomial by a Monomial

Find the quotient: $(-12x^8 + 4x^6 - 8x^3) \div 4x^2$

Solution

$$\frac{-12x^8 + 4x^6 - 8x^3}{4x^2}$$ Rewrite the division in a vertical format.

$$= \frac{-12x^8}{4x^2} + \frac{4x^6}{4x^2} - \frac{8x^3}{4x^2}$$ Divide each term of the polynomial by the monomial.

$$= \frac{-12}{4}x^{8-2} + \frac{4}{4}x^{6-2} - \frac{8}{4}x^{3-2}$$ Divide coefficients and subtract exponents.

$$= -3x^6 + x^4 - 2x$$ Simplify.

Check

Just as $\frac{8}{2} = 4$ can be checked by multiplying 2 and 4 and obtaining 8,

$$\frac{-12x^8 + 4x^6 - 8x^3}{4x^2} = -3x^6 + x^4 - 2x$$

can be checked by multiplying $4x^2$ and $-3x^6 + x^4 - 2x$ and obtaining $-12x^8 + 4x^6 - 8x^3$. The product of the *divisor* ($4x^2$) and the *quotient* ($-3x^6 + x^4 - 2x$) should equal the *dividend* ($-12x^8 + 4x^6 - 8x^3$). That is,

$$4x^2(-3x^6 + x^4 - 2x) = -12x^8 + 4x^6 - 8x^3.$$ ∎

sing technology

As with all polynomial operations, we can use a graphing utility to check division problems. To check Example 5, graph

$$y_1 = \frac{-12x^8 + 4x^6 - 8x^3}{4x^2} \quad \text{and} \quad y_2 = -3x^6 + x^4 - 2x$$

on the same screen, as shown below. Both graphs appear to be identical, so we may reason that

$$\frac{-12x^8 + 4x^6 - 8x^3}{4x^2} = -3x^6 + x^4 - 2x.$$

There is, however, a slight difference in the graphs, shown if we use the TRACE feature.

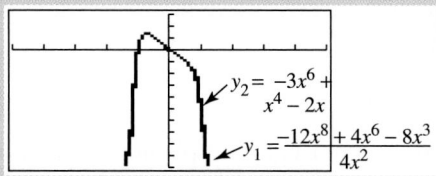

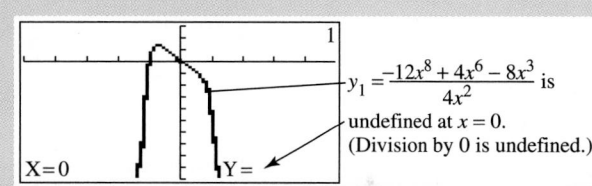

$y_1 = \frac{-12x^8 + 4x^6 - 8x^3}{4x^2}$ is undefined at $x = 0$. (Division by 0 is undefined.)

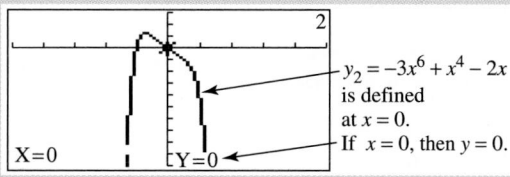

$y_2 = -3x^6 + x^4 - 2x$ is defined at $x = 0$. If $x = 0$, then $y = 0$.

Notice that the fractional expression is not defined for $x = 0$. To make note of this observation brought forth by the technology, we can more precisely write

$$\frac{-12x^8 + 4x^6 - 8x^3}{4x^2} = -3x^6 + x^4 - 2x \quad \text{if} \quad x \neq 0.$$

In our next example, termwise division results in a term with a zero exponent.

EXAMPLE 6 Dividing a Polynomial by a Monomial

Divide: $-9x^4 + 16x^5 + 8x^3$ by $2x^3$

Solution

$$\frac{16x^5 - 9x^4 + 8x^3}{2x^3}$$ Write the polynomial in descending powers before dividing.

$$= \frac{16x^5}{2x^3} - \frac{9x^4}{2x^3} + \frac{8x^3}{2x^3}$$ Divide each term by $2x^3$.

$$= \frac{16}{2}x^{5-3} - \frac{9}{2}x^{4-3} + \frac{8}{2}x^{3-3}$$ Divide coefficients and subtract exponents. Many people will immediately write the last term as 4.

$$= 8x^2 - \frac{9}{2}x + 4x^0$$

$$= 8x^2 - \frac{9}{2}x + 4$$ $x^0 = 1$, so $4x^0 = 4 \cdot 1 = 4$.

Check

Multiply the quotient by the divisor.

$$2x^3\left(8x^2 - \frac{9}{2}x + 4\right) = 16x^5 - 9x^4 + 8x^3$$ Multiply coefficients and add exponents.

Since this multiplication gives the dividend, the quotient is correct. ∎

Study tip

Rather than subtracting exponents for division that results in a zero exponent, you might prefer to cancel.

$$\frac{8x^3}{2x^3} = 4x^{3-3} = 4x^0 = 4$$ Subtract exponents.

$$\frac{8x^3}{2x^3} = 4$$ Cancel.

Dividing a polynomial by a monomial is accomplished by dividing each term by the monomial. The same procedure applies to polynomials in several variables.

EXAMPLE 7   **Dividing Polynomials in Two Variables**

Divide: $(15x^5y^4 - 3x^3y^2 + 9x^2y) \div 3x^2y$

Solution

$$\frac{15x^5y^4 - 3x^3y^2 + 9x^2y}{3x^2y}$$

$$= \frac{15x^5y^4}{3x^2y} - \frac{3x^3y^2}{3x^2y} + \frac{9x^2y}{3x^2y}$$ Divide each term of the polynomial by the monomial.

$$= \frac{15}{3}x^{5-2}y^{4-1} - \frac{3}{3}x^{3-2}y^{2-1} + \frac{9}{3}x^{2-2}y^{1-1}$$ Divide coefficients and subtract exponents.

$$= 5x^3y^3 - xy + 3$$ Simplify.

Check

Multiply the quotient by the divisor.

$$3x^2y(5x^3y^3 - xy + 3)$$
$$= (3x^2y)(5x^3y^3) + (3x^2y)(-xy) + (3x^2y)(3)$$ Apply the distributive property.
$$= 3 \cdot 5x^{2+3}y^{1+3} + 3(-1)x^{2+1}y^{1+1} + 3(3)x^2y$$ Multiply coefficients and add exponents.
$$= 15x^5y^4 - 3x^3y^2 + 9x^2y$$ Simplify.

Since this multiplication gives the dividend, the quotient is correct. ∎

P R O B L E M   S E T   6 . 5

Practice Problems

Find the quotients in Problems 1–12. Throughout the problem set, assume that all variables represent nonzero real numbers.

1. $\dfrac{x^5}{x^2}$ **2.** $\dfrac{x^7}{x^4}$ **3.** $\dfrac{z^{13}}{z^5}$ **4.** $\dfrac{z^{19}}{z^6}$ **5.** $\dfrac{30y^{10}}{10y^5}$ **6.** $\dfrac{45y^{12}}{15y^4}$

7. $\dfrac{-8x^{22}}{4x^2}$ **8.** $\dfrac{-15x^{40}}{3x^4}$ **9.** $\dfrac{-9a^8}{18a^5}$ **10.** $\dfrac{-15a^{13}}{45a^9}$ **11.** $\dfrac{7x^{17}}{5x^5}$ **12.** $\dfrac{9x^{19}}{7x^{11}}$

Evaluate each exponential expression in Problems 13–24.

13. 7^0 **14.** 6^0 **15.** -3^0 **16.** -8^0 **17.** $(-3)^0$ **18.** $(-8)^0$

19. $4x^0$ **20.** $8x^0$ **21.** $(4x)^0$ **22.** $(8x)^0$ **23.** $-5^0 + (-5)^0$ **24.** $-6^0 + (-6)^0$

In Problems 25–32, simplify using the rule for powers of quotients.

25. $\left(\dfrac{x}{3}\right)^2$ **26.** $\left(\dfrac{y}{5}\right)^2$ **27.** $\left(\dfrac{x^2}{4}\right)^3$ **28.** $\left(\dfrac{x^2}{3}\right)^3$ **29.** $\left(\dfrac{2x^3}{5}\right)^2$ **30.** $\left(\dfrac{3x^4}{7}\right)^2$

31. $\left(\dfrac{-3a^3}{4}\right)^3$ **32.** $\left(\dfrac{-2a^4}{5}\right)^3$

Find the quotients in Problems 33–58. Check your answers algebraically (the product of the divisor and quotient should equal the dividend) or by using a graphing utility.

33. $\dfrac{6x^4 + 2x^3}{2}$ **34.** $\dfrac{10x^4 + 5x^3}{5}$ **35.** $\dfrac{6x^4 - 2x^3}{2x}$ **36.** $\dfrac{10x^4 - 5x^3}{5x}$

37. $\dfrac{y^5 - 3y^2 + y}{y}$ **38.** $\dfrac{y^6 - 2y^3 + y}{y}$ **39.** $\dfrac{15x^3 - 24x^2}{-3x}$ **40.** $\dfrac{20x^3 - 10x^2}{-5x}$

41. $\dfrac{18x^5 + 6x^4 + 9x^3}{3x^2}$ **42.** $\dfrac{18x^5 + 24x^4 + 12x^3}{6x^2}$ **43.** $\dfrac{12x^4 - 8x^3 + 40x^2}{4x}$ **44.** $\dfrac{49x^4 - 14x^3 + 70x^2}{-7x}$

45. $(4x^2 - 6x) \div x$ **46.** $(16y^2 - 8y) \div y$ **47.** $\dfrac{30z^3 + 10z^2}{-5z}$ **48.** $\dfrac{12y^4 - 42y^2}{-4y}$

49. $\dfrac{8x^3 + 3x^2 - 2x}{2x}$ **50.** $\dfrac{9x^3 + 12x^2 - 3x}{3x}$ **51.** $\dfrac{25x^7 - 15x^5 - 5x^4}{5x^3}$ **52.** $\dfrac{49x^7 - 28x^5 - 7x^4}{7x^3}$

53. $\dfrac{18x^7 - 9x^6 + 20x^5 - 10x^4}{-2x^4}$ **54.** $\dfrac{25x^8 - 50x^7 + 3x^6 - 40x^5}{-5x^5}$

55. $\dfrac{12x^2y^2 + 6x^2y - 15xy^2}{3xy}$ **56.** $\dfrac{18a^3b^2 - 9a^2b - 27ab^2}{9ab}$

57. $\dfrac{20x^7y^4 - 15x^3y^2 - 10x^2y}{-5x^2y}$ **58.** $\dfrac{8x^6y^3 - 12x^8y^2 - 4x^{14}y^6}{-4x^6y^2}$

True–False Critical Thinking Problems

59. Which one of the following is true?
   a. $x^{10} \div x^2 = x^5$ for all nonzero real numbers x.
   b. $\dfrac{12x^3 - 6x}{2x} = 6x^2 - 6x$
   c. $\dfrac{x^2 + x}{x} = x$
   d. If a polynomial in x of degree 6 is divided by a monomial in x of degree 2, the degree of the quotient is 4.

60. Which one of the following is true?
   a. $0^0 = 1$
   b. $\dfrac{4x^2y^2 - 2xy}{2xy} = 4x^2y^2 - 1$
   c. $\dfrac{6x^{3a} - 3x^{2a}}{-3x^a} = x^a - 2x^{2a}$
   d. Not every problem involving a polynomial divided by a monomial can be checked by multiplying the quotient by the divisor.

Technology Problems _____

61. Use a graphing utility to show that $\dfrac{6x - 7}{3} = 2x - \dfrac{7}{3}$.

62. Here are some common errors that can occur when dividing polynomials. Show that each result is incorrect by using your graphing utility to graph each side separately. The resulting graphs should be different.

a. $\dfrac{x + 2}{2} \neq x + 1$

b. $\dfrac{x^2 + 2x}{x} \neq x^2 + 2$

c. $\dfrac{x + 2}{x} \neq 3$

d. $\dfrac{x^6}{x^2} \neq x^3$

63. Correct the right side for each expression in Problem 62 so that the two sides of the resulting equation are, indeed, equal. Then use your graphing utility to graph both sides, showing that the two graphs are identical.

64. Consider the following division problem:

$$\dfrac{2x^3 + x}{x} = 2x^2 + 1.$$

a. Graph $y_1 = \dfrac{2x^3 + x}{x}$ and $y_2 = 2x^2 + 1$ on the same screen. Both graphs should appear to be identical, but are they?

b. Graph only y_1 by deselecting the equation for y_2. (Consult your manual on how to do this.) Use the $\boxed{\text{TRACE}}$ feature to trace along the curve until you get to $x = 0$. What do you observe and what does this mean?

c. Repeat part (b), but this time graph only y_2 by deselecting y_1.

d. To be more precise, we should write

$$\dfrac{2x^3 + x}{x} = 2x^2 + 1 \quad \text{if} \quad x \neq 0.$$

Explain how this is illustrated by your work in this problem.

Writing in Mathematics _____

65. Explain how to divide a polynomial by a monomial.

66. Are the expressions

$$\dfrac{12x^2 + 6x}{3x} \quad \text{and} \quad 4x + 2$$

equal for every value of x? Explain.

Critical Thinking Problems _____

Simplify each numerator in Problems 67–68, and then divide.

67. $\dfrac{6y^3(3y - 1) + 5y^2(6y - 3)}{3y}$

68. $\dfrac{(y + 2)^2 + (y - 2)^2}{2y}$

69. What polynomial, when divided by $3x^2$, yields the trinomial $6x^6 - 9x^4 + 12x^2$ as a quotient?

70. The area of a rectangle is $x^5 + 3x^4 - x^3$ square meters. If the length is x^2 meters, find a trinomial that represents the width.

In Problems 71–73, find the missing coefficient(s) and exponent designated by question marks.

71. $\dfrac{8x^4 + 4x^3 + 10x^2}{?x^?} = 2x^2 + x + \dfrac{5}{2}$

72. $\dfrac{?x^8 - ?x^6}{3x^?} = 3x^5 - 4x^3$

73. $\dfrac{3x^{14} - 6x^{12} - ?x^7}{?x^?} = -x^7 + 2x^5 + 3$

Review Problems _____

74. Solve the system: $\begin{aligned} 2x + y &= 11 \\ x &= 18 - 3y \end{aligned}$

75. Graph $2x - 3y > 6$ in a rectangular coordinate system.

76. Solve for W: $R = \dfrac{L + 3W}{2}$.

Solutions Tutorial Video
Manual   **7**

Dividing Polynomials by Binomials

Objective

 Divide a polynomial by a binomial.

In the last section, we mentioned that our work with polynomial division would be divided into three general cases. We now turn to the third case, division of a polynomial by a binomial. The process is similar to the method of long division with whole numbers.

Discover for yourself

Divide 3983 by 26 without the use of a calculator. Describe the process of the division using the four steps—*divide, multiply, subtract,* and *bring down.* What do you observe about this process? When does it come to an end?

Divide a polynomial by a binomial.

Example 1 shows that the four steps used to divide whole numbers—*divide, multiply, subtract, bring down* the next term—form the basis for dividing a polynomial by a binomial.

EXAMPLE 1 **Dividing a Polynomial by a Binomial**

Divide: $x^2 + 10x + 21$ by $x + 3$

Solution

The steps shown below illustrate how polynomial division is very similar to numerical division.

$$x + 3\overline{)x^2 + 10x + 21}$$

Arrange the terms of the dividend ($x^2 + 10x + 21$) and the divisor ($x + 3$) in descending powers of x.

$$\begin{array}{r} x \\ x + 3\overline{)x^2 + 10x + 21} \end{array}$$

Divide x^2 (the first term in the dividend) by x (the first term in the divisor). $\dfrac{x^2}{x} = x$. Align like terms.

$$\begin{array}{r} x \\ x + 3\overline{)x^2 + 10x + 21} \\ x^2 + 3x \end{array}$$

times   equals

Multiply each term in the divisor ($x + 3$) by x, aligning under like terms in the dividend.

$$\begin{array}{r} x \\ x + 3\overline{)x^2 + 10x + 21} \\ \underline{x^2 + 3x} \\ 7x \end{array}$$

Subtract $x^2 + 3x$ from $x^2 + 10x$ by changing the sign of each term in the lower expression and adding.

$$\begin{array}{r} x \\ x + 3\overline{)x^2 + 10x + 21} \\ \underline{x^2 + 3x} \downarrow \\ 7x + 21 \end{array}$$

Bring down 21 from the original dividend and add algebraically to form a new dividend.

$$\begin{array}{r} x + 7 \\ x + 3\overline{)x^2 + 10x + 21} \\ \underline{x^2 + 3x} \downarrow \\ 7x + 21 \end{array}$$

Find the second term of the quotient. *Divide* the first term of $7x + 21$ by x, the first term of the divisor. $\dfrac{7x}{x} = 7$

times

$$
\begin{array}{r}
x + 7 \\
x + 3\overline{)x^2 + 10x + 21} \\
\underline{x^2 + 3x} \quad \downarrow \\
7x + 21 \\
\underline{7x + 21} \\
0
\end{array}
$$

equals

Multiply the divisor $(x + 3)$ by 7, aligning under like terms in the new dividend. Then *subtract* to obtain the remainder of 0.

Since the remainder is 0, we say that $x + 3$ is a *divisor* or a *factor* of $x^2 + 10x + 21$.

Answer

$$
(x^2 + 10x + 21) \div (x + 3) = x + 7
$$

$\uparrow$ Dividend $\uparrow$ Divisor $\uparrow$ Quotient

Check

We can check our division by observing that

$$
\underbrace{(x + 3)}_{}\underbrace{(x + 7)}_{} = \underbrace{x^2 + 10x + 21}_{}
$$

(Divisor)(Quotient) =   Dividend

Using technology

The graphs of $y_1 = \dfrac{x^2 + 10x + 21}{x + 3}$ and $y_2 = x + 7$ are identical if $x \neq -3$, as shown in the figures.

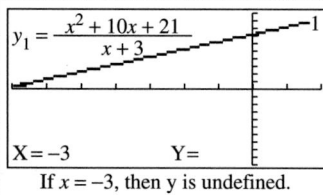

$y_1 = \dfrac{x^2 + 10x + 21}{x + 3}$

X = −3   Y =

If $x = -3$, then y is undefined.

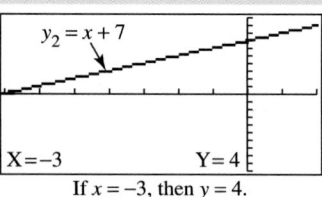

$y_2 = x + 7$

X = −3   Y = 4

If $x = -3$, then $y = 4$.

Because both graphs are nearly the same, we can conclude that

$$
\dfrac{x^2 + 10x + 21}{x + 3} = x + 7 \quad \text{if} \quad x \neq -3.
$$

Why is -3 excluded as a permissible value in y_1?

Before considering other examples, let's summarize the general procedure for dividing one polynomial by another.

Long division of polynomials

1. *Arrange the terms* of both the dividend and the divisor in descending powers.
2. *Divide* the first term in the dividend by the first term in the divisor. The result will be the first term of the quotient.
3. *Multiply* every term in the divisor by the first term in the quotient. Write the resulting product beneath the dividend with similar terms under each other.
4. *Subtract* the product from the dividend.
5. *Bring down* the next term in the original dividend and write it next to the remainder to form a new dividend.
6. Use this new expression as the dividend and repeat this process until the degree of the remainder is smaller than the degree of the divisor.

Pablo Picasso (1881-1973) "Portrait of d'Ambroise Vollard", Museo Pushkin. Scala/Art Resource, NY © 1998 Estate of Pablo Picasso/ Artists Rights Society (ARS), New York.

EXAMPLE 2 **Dividing a Polynomial by a Binomial**

Divide: $7x - 9 - 4x^2 + 4x^3$ by $2x - 1$

Solution

$$2x - 1 \overline{)4x^3 - 4x^2 + 7x - 9}$$
Arrange terms in the dividend and divisor in descending powers of x.

$$\begin{array}{r} 2x^2 \\ 2x - 1 \overline{)4x^3 - 4x^2 + 7x - 9} \end{array}$$
Divide: $\dfrac{4x^3}{2x} = 2x^2$

times
$$\begin{array}{r} 2x^2 \\ 2x - 1 \overline{)4x^3 - 4x^2 + 7x - 9} \\ 4x^3 - 2x^2 \end{array}$$
equals
Multiply: $2x^2(2x - 1) = 4x^3 - 2x^2$

$$\begin{array}{r} 2x^2 \\ 2x - 1 \overline{)4x^3 - 4x^2 + 7x - 9} \\ \ominus 4x^3 \oplus 2x^2 \\ \hline - 2x^2 \end{array}$$
Subtract: $4x^3 - 4x^2 - (4x^3 - 2x^2)$
$= 4x^3 - 4x^2 - 4x^3 + 2x^2$
$= -2x^2$

$$\begin{array}{r} 2x^2 \\ 2x - 1 \overline{)4x^3 - 4x^2 + 7x - 9} \\ 4x^3 - 2x^2 \downarrow \\ \hline - 2x^2 + 7x \end{array}$$
Bring down $7x$. The new dividend is $-2x^2 + 7x$.

$$\begin{array}{r} 2x^2 - x \\ 2x - 1 \overline{)4x^3 - 4x^2 + 7x - 9} \\ 4x^3 - 2x^2 \\ \hline - 2x^2 + 7x \end{array}$$
Divide: $\dfrac{-2x^2}{2x} = -x$

times
$$\begin{array}{r} 2x^2 - x \\ 2x - 1 \overline{)4x^3 - 4x^2 + 7x - 9} \\ 4x^3 - 2x^2 \\ \hline - 2x^2 + 7x \\ - 2x^2 + x \end{array}$$
equals
Multiply: $-x(2x - 1) = -2x^2 + x$

$$\begin{array}{r} 2x^2 - x \\ 2x - 1\overline{)4x^3 - 4x^2 + 7x - 9} \\ \underline{4x^3 - 2x^2} \\ -2x^2 + 7x \\ \underline{\oplus 2x^2 \ominus x} \\ 6x \end{array}$$

Subtract: $-2x^2 + 7x - (-2x^2 + x)$
$= -2x^2 + 7x + 2x^2 - x$
$= 6x$

$$\begin{array}{r} 2x^2 - x \\ 2x - 1\overline{)4x^3 - 4x^2 + 7x - 9} \\ \underline{4x^3 - 2x^2} \\ -2x^2 + 7x \\ \underline{-2x^2 + x} \\ 6x - 9 \end{array}$$

Bring down: -9. The new dividend is $6x - 9$.

$$\begin{array}{r} 2x^2 - x + 3 \\ 2x - 1\overline{)4x^3 - 4x^2 + 7x - 9} \\ \underline{4x^3 - 2x^2} \\ -2x^2 + 7x \\ \underline{-2x^2 + x} \\ 6x - 9 \end{array}$$

Divide: $\dfrac{6x}{2x} = 3$

times

$$\begin{array}{r} 2x^2 - x + 3 \\ 2x - 1\overline{)4x^3 - 4x^2 + 7x - 9} \\ \underline{4x^3 - 2x^2} \\ -2x^2 + 7x \\ \underline{-2x^2 + x} \\ 6x - 9 \\ 6x - 3 \end{array}$$

Multiply: $3(2x - 1) = 6x - 3$

equals

$$\begin{array}{r} 2x^2 - x + 3 \\ 2x - 1\overline{)4x^3 - 4x^2 + 7x - 9} \\ \underline{4x^3 - 2x^2} \\ -2x^2 + 7x \\ \underline{-2x^2 + x} \\ 6x - 9 \\ \underline{\ominus 6x \oplus 3} \\ -6 \end{array}$$

Subtract: $6x - 9 - (6x - 3)$
$= 6x - 9 - 6x + 3 = -6$

The remainder is -6.

Using technology

Try checking our answer using a graphing utility.

Answer

$$\frac{4x^3 - 4x^2 + 7x - 9}{2x - 1} = 2x^2 - x + 3 + \frac{-6}{2x - 1} \quad \text{or} \quad 2x^2 - x + 3 - \frac{6}{2x - 1}$$

Notice that the remainder is written as a fraction with $2x - 1$ as the denominator. The quotient is not a polynomial because of the remainder.

Check

We can check the answer to a division problem having a remainder in the same way we check division of whole numbers.

$$\overset{2}{\underset{\text{Divisor} \rightarrow}{}} \;\; \overset{\leftarrow \; \substack{\text{Partial} \\ \text{quotient}}}{4\overline{)11}} \; \leftarrow \text{Dividend}$$

$$\frac{8}{3} \; \leftarrow \text{Remainder}$$

Check:

$(\text{Divisor})\left(\substack{\text{Partial} \\ \text{quotient}}\right) + \text{Remainder} \overset{?}{=} \text{Dividend}$

$$4(2) + 3 \overset{?}{=} 11$$
$$11 = 11 \quad \checkmark$$

Let's use this pattern to check our result.

$$\overset{2x^2 - \; x + 3}{\underset{\text{Divisor} \rightarrow 2x - 1)}{}} \overline{4x^3 - 4x^2 + 7x - 9} \;\; \leftarrow \text{Partial quotient}$$
$$\text{Divisor} \rightarrow 2x - 1\overline{)4x^3 - 4x^2 + 7x - 9} \;\; \leftarrow \text{Dividend}$$
$$\vdots$$
$$-6 \leftarrow \text{Remainder}$$

Is

$(\text{Divisor})(\text{Partial quotient}) + \text{Remainder} \overset{?}{=} \text{Dividend}$

$\begin{array}{l} 2x^2 - x + 3 \\ \underline{2x - 1} \\ -1(2x^2 - x + 3) \longrightarrow -2x^2 + x - 3 \\ 2x(2x^2 - x + 3) \rightarrow 4x^3 - 2x^2 + 6x \\ \hline 4x^3 - 4x^2 + 7x - 3 \end{array}$

$$(2x - 1)(2x^2 - x + 3) + (-6) \overset{?}{=} 4x^3 - 4x^2 + 7x - 9$$
$$4x^3 - 4x^2 + 7x - 3 - 6 \overset{?}{=} 4x^3 - 4x^2 + 7x - 9$$
$$4x^3 - 4x^2 + 7x - 9 = 4x^3 - 4x^2 + 7x - 9 \;\; \checkmark$$

∎

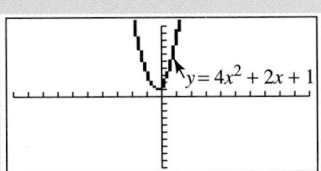
EXAMPLE 3 **Dividing a Polynomial with Missing Terms**

Divide: $8x^3 - 1$ by $2x - 1$

Solution

Because there are no x^2 or x terms in the dividend, we use 0 as the coefficient for these terms. Thus,

$$8x^3 - 1 = 8x^3 + 0x^2 + 0x - 1.$$

$$\overset{4x^2}{2x - 1)\overline{8x^3 + 0x^2 + 0x - 1}}$$
$$\underline{8x^3 - 4x^2}$$
$$4x^2 + 0x$$

Divide $\left(\dfrac{8x^3}{2x} = 4x^2\right)$, multiply, subtract, and bring down the next term. The new dividend is $4x^2 + 0x$.

$$\overset{4x^2 + 2x}{2x - 1)\overline{8x^3 + 0x^2 + 0x - 1}}$$
$$\underline{8x^3 - 4x^2}$$
$$4x^2 + 0x$$
$$\underline{4x^2 - 2x}$$
$$2x - 1$$

Divide $\left(\dfrac{4x^2}{2x} = 2x\right)$, multiply $[2x(2x - 1) = 4x^2 - 2x]$, subtract, and bring down the next term. The new dividend is $2x - 1$.

$$\overset{4x^2 + 2x + 1}{2x - 1)\overline{8x^3 - 0x^2 + 0x - 1}}$$
$$\underline{8x^3 - 4x^2}$$
$$4x^2 + 0x$$
$$\underline{4x^2 - 2x}$$
$$2x - 1$$
$$\underline{2x - 1}$$
$$0$$

Divide $\left(\dfrac{2x}{2x} = 1\right)$, multiply $[1(2x - 1) = 2x - 1]$, and subtract. The remainder is 0.

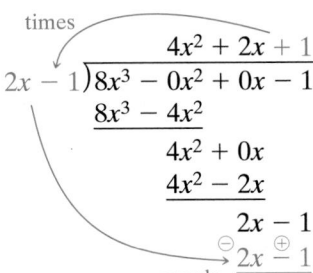

Answer

$$\frac{8x^3 - 1}{2x - 1} = 4x^2 + 2x + 1$$

Check

Check by multiplying $2x - 1$ and $4x^2 + 2x + 1$. This product should be $4x^2 + 2x + 1$. ■

P R O B L E M   S E T   6 . 6

Practice Problems

In Problems 1–37, divide. Verify your result algebraically or by using a graphing utility.

1. $\dfrac{x^2 + 6x + 8}{x + 2}$

2. $\dfrac{x^2 + 7x + 10}{x + 5}$

3. $\dfrac{2x^2 + x - 10}{x - 2}$

4. $\dfrac{2x^2 + 13x + 15}{x + 5}$

5. $\dfrac{x^2 - 5x + 6}{x - 3}$

6. $\dfrac{x^2 - 2x - 24}{x + 4}$

7. $\dfrac{2y^2 + 5y + 2}{y + 2}$

8. $\dfrac{2y^2 - 13y + 21}{y - 3}$

9. $\dfrac{x^2 - 5x + 8}{x - 3}$

10. $\dfrac{x^2 + 7x - 8}{x + 3}$

11. $\dfrac{5y + 10 + y^2}{y + 2}$

12. $\dfrac{-8y + y^2 - 9}{y - 3}$

13. $\dfrac{x^3 - 6x^2 + 7x - 2}{x - 1}$

14. $\dfrac{x^3 + 3x^2 + 5x + 3}{x + 1}$

15. $\dfrac{12y^2 - 20y + 3}{2y - 3}$

16. $\dfrac{4y^2 - 8y - 5}{2y + 1}$

17. $\dfrac{4a^2 + 4a - 3}{2a - 1}$

18. $\dfrac{2b^2 - 9b - 5}{2b + 1}$

19. $\dfrac{3y - y^2 + 2y^3 + 2}{2y + 1}$

20. $\dfrac{9y + 18 - 11y^2 + 12y^3}{4y + 3}$

21. $\dfrac{2x^2 - 9x + 8}{2x + 3}$

22. $\dfrac{4y^2 + 8y + 3}{2y - 1}$

23. $\dfrac{x^3 + 4x - 3}{x - 2}$

24. $\dfrac{x^3 + 2x^2 - 3}{x - 2}$

25. $\dfrac{4y^3 + 8y^2 + 5y + 9}{2y + 3}$

26. $\dfrac{2y^3 - y^2 + 3y + 2}{2y + 1}$

27. $\dfrac{6y^3 - 5y^2 + 5}{3y + 2}$

28. $\dfrac{4y^3 - y - 5}{2y + 3}$

29. $\dfrac{27x^3 - 1}{3x - 1}$

30. $\dfrac{8x^3 + 27}{2x + 3}$

31. $\dfrac{81 - 12y^3 + 54y^2 + y^4 - 108y}{y - 3}$

32. $\dfrac{8y^3 + y^4 + 16 + 32y + 24y^2}{y + 2}$

33. $\dfrac{4y^2 + 6y}{2y - 1}$

34. $\dfrac{10x^2 - 3x}{x + 3}$

35. $\dfrac{y^4 - 2y^2 + 5}{y - 1}$

36. $\dfrac{y^4 + 2y^3 + 2y^2 - y - 1}{y^2 + 1}$

37. $\dfrac{y^4 - 4y^3 + 5y^2 - 3y + 2}{y^2 + 3}$

Application Problems

38. A rectangle with length $2x - 1$ inches has an area of $2x^2 + 5x - 3$ square inches. Write a binomial that represents its width.

Width = ?

Area = $2x^2 + 5x - 3$ square inches

Length = $2x - 1$ inches

39. If the distance traveled is $x^3 + 3x^2 + 5x + 3$ miles and the rate is $x + 1$ miles per hour, write a trinomial for the time traveled.

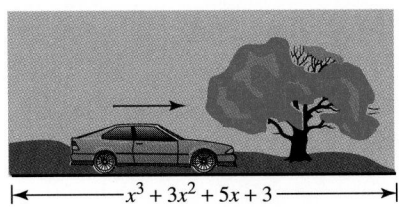

$\xleftarrow{\hspace{1.5cm}} x^3 + 3x^2 + 5x + 3 \xrightarrow{\hspace{1.5cm}}$
Speed $= x + 1$ miles per hour

40. Two people are 25 years old and 20 years old. In x years from now, their ages can be represented by $x + 25$ and $x + 20$.

a. Use long division to find $\dfrac{x + 25}{x + 20}$, the ratio of the older person's age in x years to the younger person's age in x years.

b. Complete the following table.

x	0	5	10	25	50	75
$\dfrac{x + 25}{x + 20}$						

c. Describe what is happening to the ratio $\dfrac{x + 25}{x + 20}$ as x increases. How can this be verified using the result of the long division in part (a)?

True–False Critical Thinking Problems

41. Which one of the following is true?
a. If $4x^2 + 25x - 3$ is divided by $4x + 1$, the remainder is 9.
b. If polynomial division results in a remainder of zero, then the product of the divisor and the quotient is the dividend.
c. The degree of a polynomial is the highest power of the term that appears in the first position.
d. When a polynomial is divided by a binomial, the division process stops when the last term of the dividend is brought down.

42. Which one of the following is true?
a. By looking at the first term of the following quotient, you can immediately see that the division problem has been performed incorrectly:

$$\frac{6x^3 + 14x^2 + 10x + 3}{3x + 1} = 3x^2 + 4x + 2 + \frac{1}{3x + 1}$$

b. The graph of the quotient of $x^2 + 7x + 10$ and $x + 5$ cannot be a straight line because of the fact that x is squared.
c. If a polynomial is divided by a binomial of degree 2, such as $x^2 + 1$, a remainder of 0 cannot be obtained.
d. Since $\dfrac{x^2 - x - 6}{x - 3}$ results in a quotient of $x + 2$, the algebraic expressions $\dfrac{x^2 - x - 6}{x - 3}$ and $x + 2$ are equal for all values of x.

Technology Problems

43. Use a graphing utility to compare the graphs of the following functions.

$$y_1 = \frac{x^2 + 4x + 3}{x + 1}$$

$$y_2 = x + 3$$

a. Do the graphs appear to be the same?
b. Trace along each of the graphs until you reach $x = -1$. What do you observe?
c. For what value of x do $\dfrac{x^2 + 4x + 3}{x + 1}$ and $x + 3$ not represent the same number?

44. Repeat Problem 43 using

$$y_1 = \frac{x^3 + 8}{x + 2}$$

$$y_2 = x^2 - 2x + 4$$

For this problem, explore what happens at $x = -2$ as you trace along the graphs.

Use a graphing utility to determine whether the divisions in Problems 45–48 have been performed correctly. Graph each side of the given equation in the same viewing rectangle. The graphs should be the same. If they are not, correct the expression on the right side by using polynomial division. Then use your graphing utility to show that the division has been performed correctly.

45. $\dfrac{2x^2 + 9x - 35}{x + 7} = 2x - 5$

46. $\dfrac{2x^3 - x^2 + 3x + 2}{2x + 1} = x^2 - x + 4$

47. $\dfrac{6x^3 + 14x^2 + 10x + 3}{3x + 1} = 2x^2 + 4x + 2 + \dfrac{1}{3x + 1}$

48. $\dfrac{4x^3 + 3x^2 - 4x + 1}{x^2 + 1} = 4x + 3 - \dfrac{8x + 4}{x^2 + 1}$

Writing in Mathematics

49. After dividing a polynomial by a binomial, explain how to check the result of the long division process.

50. When dividing a polynomial by a binomial, explain when to stop dividing.

51. When dividing a binomial into a polynomial with missing terms, explain the advantage of writing the missing terms with zero coefficients.

Critical Thinking Problems

52. Simplify the numerator and then divide:

$$\dfrac{(x - 2)^2 + x^2(x - 2) + 5x - 2}{x - 1}.$$

53. When a certain polynomial is divided by $2x + 4$, the quotient is

$$x - 3 + \dfrac{17}{2x + 4}.$$

What is the polynomial?

54. Find the number k such that when $16x^2 - 2x + k$ is divided by $2x - 1$, the remainder is 0.

55. Describe the pattern that you observe in the following quotients and remainders.

$$\dfrac{x^3 - 1}{x + 1} = x^2 - x + 1 - \dfrac{2}{x + 1}$$

$$\dfrac{x^5 - 1}{x + 1} = x^4 - x^3 + x^2 - x + 1 - \dfrac{2}{x + 1}$$

Use this pattern to find $\dfrac{x^7 - 1}{x + 1}$. Verify your result by dividing.

Review Problems

56. Solve the system:

$$x = 3 - 5y$$
$$x - 2y = 10$$

57. Two cars leave from the same destination traveling in opposite directions. One car travels at a uniform rate of 52 miles per hour, and the other travels at a uniform rate of 58 miles per hour. In how many hours will they be 385 miles apart?

58. Graph: $y \geq -2x + 3$.

S E C T I O N   6 . 7

Solutions Manual   Tutorial   Video 7

Negative Exponents and Scientific Notation

Objectives

1 Evaluate expressions containing negative exponents.
2 Divide polynomials where the quotient contains negative exponents.
3 Simplify exponential expressions.
4 Write a number in scientific notation.
5 Perform computations in scientific notation.

Many mathematical descriptions of reality require the use of exponents. Furthermore, our world frequently manifests itself in relatively large and relatively small numbers that are conveniently expressed in *scientific notation,* which uses exponents. In this section, we extend the properties of positive integral exponents discussed throughout the chapter to include negative exponents. We will also express large and small numbers in scientific notation and use exponential properties to perform computations with scientific notation.

Evaluate expressions containing negative exponents.

Negative Integers as Exponents

Let us now consider the quotient rule when the exponent in the numerator is less than the exponent in the denominator. We perform each of the following three divisions by first using cancellation and then by subtracting exponents. In the final column we equate the two results to obtain the conclusion. Assume that all variables do not equal zero.

Using Cancellation	**Subtracting Exponents**	**Conclusion**
$\dfrac{7^2}{7^5} = \dfrac{7 \cdot 7}{7 \cdot 7 \cdot 7 \cdot 7 \cdot 7} = \dfrac{1}{7^3}$	$\dfrac{7^2}{7^5} = 7^{2-5} = 7^{-3}$	$7^{-3} = \dfrac{1}{7^3}$
$\dfrac{x}{x^5} = \dfrac{x}{x \cdot x \cdot x \cdot x \cdot x} = \dfrac{1}{x^4}$	$\dfrac{x}{x^5} = x^{1-5} = x^{-4}$	$x^{-4} = \dfrac{1}{x^4}$
$\dfrac{y^3}{y^8} = \dfrac{y \cdot y \cdot y}{y \cdot y \cdot y \cdot y \cdot y \cdot y \cdot y \cdot y} = \dfrac{1}{y^5}$	$\dfrac{y^3}{y^8} = y^{3-8} = y^{-5}$	$y^{-5} = \dfrac{1}{y^5}$

In the Discover for Yourself box, were you able to define negative integers as exponents as shown in the following box?

> **Definition of a negative integer as an exponent**
>
> If x is any nonzero real number and n is any integer, then
>
> $$x^{-n} = \frac{1}{x^n}.$$

EXAMPLE 1 **Using Negative Exponents**

Evaluate:

a. 7^{-2} **b.** 4^{-3} **c.** $2^{-1} - 4^{-1}$ **d.** $\dfrac{1}{2^{-3}}$ **e.** $\left(\dfrac{3}{4}\right)^{-2}$

Solution

a. $7^{-2} = \dfrac{1}{7^2} = \dfrac{1}{49}$

b. $4^{-3} = \dfrac{1}{4^3} = \dfrac{1}{64}$

c. $2^{-1} - 4^{-1} = \dfrac{1}{2^1} - \dfrac{1}{4^1} = \dfrac{2}{4} - \dfrac{1}{4} = \dfrac{1}{4}$

d. $\dfrac{1}{2^{-3}} = \dfrac{1}{\dfrac{1}{2^3}} = 1 \div \dfrac{1}{2^3} = 1 \cdot \dfrac{2^3}{1} = 8$

e. $\left(\dfrac{3}{4}\right)^{-2} = \dfrac{1}{\left(\dfrac{3}{4}\right)^2} = \dfrac{1}{\dfrac{9}{16}} = 1 \div \dfrac{9}{16} = 1 \cdot \dfrac{16}{9} = \dfrac{16}{9}$ ∎

Discover for yourself

In part (d) of Example 1, notice that

$$\dfrac{1}{2^{-3}} = 2^3.$$

Show that

$$\dfrac{1}{3^{-2}} = 3^2 \quad \text{and} \quad \dfrac{1}{4^{-5}} = 4^5.$$

In general, write an equivalent expression for $\dfrac{1}{x^{-n}}$.

In the Discover for Yourself box, were you able to discover the following generalization?

$$\dfrac{1}{x^{-n}} = x^n$$

Combining this observation with the previous definition of a negative exponent gives us the following important results.

If $x \neq 0$,

$$x^{-n} = \dfrac{1}{x^n} \quad \text{and} \quad \dfrac{1}{x^{-n}} = x^n$$

These results can be used to move the factors in a fraction between the numerator and the denominator if we change the sign of the exponents.

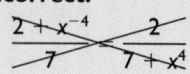

EXAMPLE 2   Using Negative Exponents

Rewrite with positive exponents only:

a. $\dfrac{4^{-3}}{5^{-2}}$ **b.** $\dfrac{1}{4x^{-3}}$ **c.** $\dfrac{2x^{-4}}{7}$ **d.** $\dfrac{x^{-5}}{y^{-1}}$

Solution

a. $\dfrac{4^{-3}}{5^{-2}} = \dfrac{5^2}{4^3} = \dfrac{25}{64}$

b. $\dfrac{1}{4x^{-3}} = \dfrac{x^3}{4}$

c. $\dfrac{2x^{-4}}{7} \searrow \dfrac{2}{7x^4}$

d. $\dfrac{x^{-5}}{y^{-1}} \bowtie \dfrac{y^1}{x^5} = \dfrac{y}{x^5}$ ■

2 Divide polynomials where the quotient contains negative exponents.

Let's see how negative exponents can emerge when dividing polynomials. First we'll look at an example involving the division of monomials. Remember that when dividing with the same base, we subtract exponents.

$$\frac{x^m}{x^n} = x^{m-n}$$

EXAMPLE 3 **Dividing Monomials by Using the Quotient Rule**

Find the indicated quotients, and write the quotient with positive exponents. All variables represent nonzero real numbers.

a. $\dfrac{x^4}{x^9}$ **b.** $\dfrac{25x^6}{5x^8}$ **c.** $\dfrac{10y^7}{-2y^{10}}$

Solution

a. $\dfrac{x^4}{x^9} = x^{4-9} = x^{-5} = \dfrac{1}{x^5}$

b. $\dfrac{25x^6}{5x^8} = \dfrac{25}{5} \cdot \dfrac{x^6}{x^8} = 5x^{6-8} = 5x^{-2} = \dfrac{5}{x^2}$

c. $\dfrac{10y^7}{-2y^{10}} = \dfrac{10}{-2} \cdot \dfrac{y^7}{y^{10}} = -5y^{7-10} = -5y^{-3} = -\dfrac{5}{y^3}$

None of these answers is a monomial because the variable in the quotient appears in the denominator. Polynomials must contain *whole number exponents* on its variables. Thus, the quotient of two monomials need not be a monomial. ■

Study tip

You can work Example 3 mentally by:

1. Dividing coefficients.
2. Subtracting exponents.
3. Moving factors with negative exponents to the denominator.

Try it!

Although the sum, difference, and product of two polynomials are always polynomials, the quotient of polynomials may result in an algebraic expression that does not contain whole number exponents on its variables. Consequently, as illustrated in our next example, the quotient of polynomials may not be a polynomial.

EXAMPLE 4   **Dividing a Polynomial by a Monomial**

Divide: $13x^4 - 9x^3 + 15x$ by $3x^2$

Solution

$$\frac{13x^4 - 9x^3 + 15x}{3x^2}$$ Write the division in a vertical format.

$$= \frac{13x^4}{3x^2} - \frac{9x^3}{3x^2} + \frac{15x}{3x^2}$$ Divide each term by $3x^2$.

$$= \frac{13}{3}x^{4-2} - \frac{9}{3}x^{3-2} + \frac{15}{3}x^{1-2}$$ Divide coefficients and subtract exponents.

$$= \frac{13}{3}x^2 - 3x + 5x^{-1}$$ Simplify.

$$= \frac{13}{3}x^2 - 3x + \frac{5}{x}$$ $x^{-n} = \frac{1}{x^n}$, so $x^{-1} = \frac{1}{x^1} = \frac{1}{x}$

Check

Multiply.

$$3x^2\left(\frac{13}{3}x^2 - 3x + \frac{5}{x}\right) = 3x^2\left(\frac{13}{3}x^2\right) + 3x^2(-3x) + 3x^2\left(\frac{5}{x}\right)$$

$$= 13x^4 - 9x^3 + 15x$$

Since the multiplication gives the dividend, the quotient is correct. ■

3 Simplify exponential expressions.

Simplifying Exponential Expressions

The rules of exponents that we studied in Sections 6.2 and 6.5 can be extended to cover negative integers. We have already done this for the quotient rule. Exponential properties are used to *simplify* algebraic expressions containing powers. An expression containing exponents is simplified when no parentheses appear, when each base occurs only once, and when no negative exponents appear. This gives us a procedure for simplifying expressions that requires a combination of the earlier definitions and properties.

Simplifying exponential expressions

1. If necessary, remove parentheses by using   **Example**

   $$(xy)^m = x^m y^m \quad \text{or} \quad \left(\frac{x}{y}\right)^m = \frac{x^m}{y^m}.$$ $(xy)^3 = x^3 y^3$

2. If necessary, simplify powers to powers by using

   $$(x^m)^n = x^{mn}.$$ $(x^4)^3 = x^{4\cdot3} = x^{12}$

3. If necessary, be sure that each base appears only once, by using

   $$x^m \cdot x^n = x^{m+n} \quad \text{or} \quad \frac{x^m}{x^n} = x^{m-n}.$$ $x^4 \cdot x^3 = x^{4+3} = x^7$

4. If necessary, rewrite exponential expressions with zero powers as 1 ($x^0 = 1$). Furthermore, write the answer with positive exponents by using

$$x^{-n} = \frac{1}{x^n} \quad \text{or} \quad \frac{1}{x^{-n}} = x^n.$$

$$\frac{x^5}{x^8} = x^{-3} = \frac{1}{x^3}$$

The following examples show how to simplify exponential expressions. In each example, assume that the variable in the denominator is not equal to zero.

EXAMPLE 5 **Simplifying an Exponential Expression**

Simplify: $x^{-9} \cdot x^4$

Solution

$$
\begin{aligned}
x^{-9} \cdot x^4 &= x^{-9+4} \quad && x^m \cdot x^n = x^{m+n} \\
&= x^{-5} \quad && \text{The base } x \text{ now appears only once.} \\
&= \frac{1}{x^5} \quad && x^{-n} = \frac{1}{x^n}
\end{aligned}
$$

EXAMPLE 6 **Simplifying an Exponential Expression**

Simplify: $\dfrac{(5x^3)^2}{x^{10}}$

Solution

$$
\begin{aligned}
\frac{(5x^3)^2}{x^{10}} &= \frac{5^2(x^3)^2}{x^{10}} \quad && \text{Remove parentheses around } 5x^3. \text{ Since } (xy)^m = x^m y^m, \text{ raise 5 and} \\
& && x^3 \text{ to the second power.} \\
&= \frac{25x^6}{x^{10}} \quad && \text{Simplify } (x^3)^2 \text{ by using } (x^m)^n = x^{mn}. \text{ Thus, } (x^3)^2 = x^{3 \cdot 2} = x^6. \\
&= 25x^{6-10} \quad && \frac{x^m}{x^n} = x^{m-n}, \text{ so subtract exponents.} \\
&= 25x^{-4} \quad && \text{The base } x \text{ now appears only once.} \\
&= \frac{25}{x^4} \quad && x^{-n} = \frac{1}{x^n}
\end{aligned}
$$

EXAMPLE 7 **Simplifying an Exponential Expression**

Simplify: $\left(\dfrac{x^5}{x^2}\right)^{-3}$

Solution

Method 1. Remove parentheses first by raising the numerator and denominator to the -3 power.

Can you find a third method for solving Example 7? Start with the second line of the solution in Method 1.

$$\left(\frac{x^5}{x^2}\right)^{-3} = \frac{(x^5)^{-3}}{(x^2)^{-3}}$$ $\left(\dfrac{x}{y}\right)^m = \dfrac{x^m}{y^m}$, so raise numerator and denominator to the -3 power.

$$= \frac{x^{-15}}{x^{-6}}$$ $(x^m)^n = x^{mn}$, so multiply exponents.

$$= x^{-15-(-6)}$$ $\dfrac{x^m}{x^n} = x^{m-n}$. The exponent in the denominator is subtracted from the exponent in the numerator.

$$= x^{-9}$$ The base x now appears only once.

$$= \frac{1}{x^9}$$ $x^{-n} = \dfrac{1}{x^n}$

Method 2. First perform the division within the parentheses.

$$\left(\frac{x^5}{x^2}\right)^{-3} = (x^{5-2})^{-3}$$ $\dfrac{x^m}{x^n} = x^{m-n}$

$$= (x^3)^{-3}$$ The base x now appears only once.

$$= x^{-9}$$ $(x^m)^n = x^{mn}$

$$= \frac{1}{x^9}$$ $x^{-n} = \dfrac{1}{x^n}$

Which method do you prefer?

4 Write a number in scientific notation.

Scientific Notation

Many branches of science and engineering work with very large and very small numbers. For example, the number of miles that light travels in 1 year is 5,865,696,000,000. Even worse, a beta ray particle has a mass of

0.000 000 000 000 000 000 000 000 000 91 gram.

The large number of zeros in these numbers make them difficult to read, write, or say. *Scientific notation* gives a compact manner for displaying and saying these numbers.

A scientific notation numeral appears as the product of two factors. The first factor is a number greater than or equal to 1 but less than 10. The second factor is base 10 raised to a power.

For example, in scientific notation, the number of miles light travels in 1 year is

5.865696 $\times$ 10^{12} miles.

Scientific notation uses $\times$ instead of a dot for multiplication.

Charles Henry Demuth "The Figure 5 in Gold" 1928, oil on composition board, H. 36 in. W. 29$\frac{3}{4}$ in. (91.4 × 75.6 cm) Signed (lower left): C.D. Inscribed (bottom center): W.C.W. (William Carlos Williams). The Metropolitan Museum of Art, Alfred Stieglitz Collection, 1949. (49.59.1) Photograph © 1996 The Metropolitan Museum of Art.

Exponents and Time		
1 tetrasecond	10^{12} s	31,689 years
1 gigasecond	10^9 s	31.7 years
1 megasecond	10^6 s	11.6 days
1 kilosecond	10^3 s	16.67 minutes

| EXAMPLE 8 | **Examples of Scientific Notation**

a. A jumbo jet weighs about 3.75×10^5 kilograms.

$$3.75 \times 10^5 = 3.75 \times 100{,}000 = 3.75000. = 375{,}000 \text{ kilograms}$$

5 places

| Decimal point | moves | 5 places to the right. |

b. Each day the earth is covered with 2.6×10^7 pounds of dust.

$$2.6 \times 10^7 = 2.6 \times 10{,}000{,}000 = 2.6000000. = 26{,}000{,}000 \text{ pounds}$$

7 places

| Decimal point | moves | 7 places to the right. |

c. A house spider weighs 1×10^{-4} kilogram.

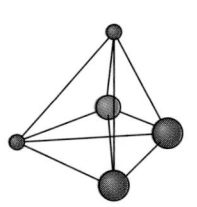

House Spider *(Tegenaria gigantea)*

$$1 \times 10^{-4} = 1 \times \frac{1}{10^4} = 1 \times \frac{1}{10{,}000} = 1 \times 0.000\,1 = 0.0001. = 0.000\,1 \text{ kilogram}$$

4 places

| Decimal point | moves | 4 places to the left. |

d. The length of a blood protein molecule is 6.8×10^{-6} millimeter.

$$6.8 \times 10^{-6} = 6.8 \times \frac{1}{10^6} = 6.8 \times \frac{1}{1{,}000{,}000} = 6.8 \times 0.000\,001 = 0.000\,006. 8$$

6 places

$$= 0.000\,006\,8 \text{ millimeter}$$

| Decimal point | moves | 6 places to the left. | ∎

Observe that when multiplying by 10 to a power, we move the decimal point the same number of places as the exponent of 10. If the exponent is *positive,* we move the decimal point in the first factor to the *right.* If the exponent is *negative,* we move the decimal point in the first factor to the *left.* For example,

$3.4 \times 10^3 = 3.400. = 3400$ Decimal point is moved 3 places to the right.

$3.4 \times 10^5 = 3.40000. = 340{,}000$ Decimal point is moved 5 places to the right.

$3.4 \times 10^{-2} = .03.4 = 0.034$ Decimal point is moved 2 places to the left.

$3.4 \times 10^{-4} = .0003.4 = 0.000\,34$ Decimal point is moved 4 places to the left.

The following procedure can be used to change from decimal notation to scientific notation.

Powers of Ten and Metric Prefixes		
Metric Prefixes	**Symbol**	**Power of 10**
tera-	(T)	$= 10^{12}$
giga-	(G)	$= 10^9$
mega-	(M)	$= 10^6$
kilo-	(k)	$= 10^3$
hecto-	(h)	$= 10^2$
deca-	(da)	$= 10^1$
deci-	(d)	$= 10^{-1}$
centi-	(c)	$= 10^{-2}$
milli	(m)	$= 10^{-3}$
micro-	(μ)	$= 10^{-6}$
nano-	(n)	$= 10^{-9}$
pico-	(p)	$= 10^{-12}$

Writing a number in scientific notation.

Write the number as the product of two factors.

$$a \times 10^n$$

The first factor, a, is a number greater than or equal to 1 and less than 10. n is an integer.

1. *First factor: (a)* Move the decimal point in the original number to the right of the first nonzero digit to obtain a number greater than or equal to 1 and less than 10.
2. *Second factor: (10^n)* Count the number of places you moved the decimal point. This is the absolute value of n. If the original number is 10 or greater, then n is positive. If the original number is less than 1, then n is negative. If the original number is between 1 and 10, then the decimal point does not have to be moved, so $n = 0$.

EXAMPLE 9   **Writing a Number Greater Than 10 in Scientific Notation**

Write in scientific notation: 72,500,000

Solution

$72,500,000 = 7.25 \times 10^n$ Move the decimal point in 72,500,000 to the right of 7, the first nonzero digit. The second factor involves a power of 10. Since the original number is greater than 10, the power of 10 is positive.

$72,500,000 = 7.25 \times 10^7$ In changing 72,500,000 to 7.25, the decimal was moved seven places, so $n = 7$.

We know that $72,500,000 = 7.25 \times 10^7$ is correct because if the decimal point in 7.25 is moved seven places to the right, the resulting numeral is 72,500,000. ∎

EXAMPLE 10   **Writing a Number Less Than 1 in Scientific Notation**

Write in scientific notation: 0.000 308

Solution

$0.000\ 308 = 3.08 \times 10^{-n}$ Move the decimal point in 0.000 308 to the right of 3, the first nonzero digit. The second factor involves a power of 10. Since the original number is less than 1, the power of 10 is negative.

$0.000\ 308 = 3.08 \times 10^{-4}$ In changing 0.000 308 to 3.08, the decimal was moved four places, so $n = 4$.

We know that 3.08×10^{-4} is correct because if the decimal point in 3.08 is moved four places to the left, the resulting numeral is 0.000 308. ∎

Using technology

You can change the mode setting on a graphing calculator so that numbers are displayed in scientific notation. (Consult your manual.) Once you're in the scientific notation mode, simply enter a number and then press ENTER.

Number	**ENTER**	**Display**
72,500,000	ENTER	7.25E7
.000308	ENTER	3.08E − 4
8.937	ENTER	8.937E0

EXAMPLE 11 **Writing a Number That Lies Between 1 and 10 in Scientific Notation**

Write in scientific notation: 8.937

Solution

$$8.937 = 8.937 \times 10^n \qquad \text{The first factor is 8.937, a number between 1 and 10.}$$

$$8.937 = 8.937 \times 10^0 \qquad \text{Since the decimal point was not moved, } n = 0.$$

We know that 8.937×10^0 is correct because $8.937 \times 10^0 = 8.937 \times 1 = 8.937$, the original numeral. ∎

5 Perform computations in scientific notation.

Computations with Scientific Notation

Since numbers in scientific notation are exponential expressions with base 10, multiplication and division can be performed by using special cases of three exponential properties.

$$10^m \cdot 10^n = 10^{m+n} \qquad \frac{10^m}{10^n} = 10^{m-n} \qquad (10^m)^n = 10^{mn}$$

EXAMPLE 12 **Computations with Scientific Notation**

Perform the indicated computations, writing the answers in scientific notation:

a. $(4 \times 10^5)(2 \times 10^9)$ **b.** $\dfrac{1.2 \times 10^6}{4.8 \times 10^{-3}}$ **c.** $(5 \times 10^{-4})^3$

Solution

a. $(4 \times 10^5)(2 \times 10^9) = 4 \cdot 2 \cdot 10^5 \cdot 10^9$ Regroup factors.
$$= 8 \times 10^{5+9} \qquad 10^m \cdot 10^n = 10^{m+n}$$
$$= 8 \times 10^{14}$$

b. $\dfrac{1.2 \times 10^6}{4.8 \times 10^{-3}} = \dfrac{1.2}{4.8} \times \dfrac{10^6}{10^{-3}}$
$$= 0.25 \times 10^{6-(-3)} \qquad \frac{10^m}{10^n} = 10^{m-n}$$
$$= 0.25 \times 10^9 \qquad \text{Since 0.25 is not between 1 and 10, it must be written in scientific notation.}$$
$$= 2.5 \times 10^{-1} \times 10^9 \qquad 0.25 = 2.5 \times 10^{-1}$$
$$= 2.5 \times 10^{-1+9} \qquad 10^m \cdot 10^n = 10^{m+n}$$
$$= 2.5 \times 10^8$$

c. $(5 \times 10^{-4})^3 = 5^3 \times (10^{-4})^3$ $(xy)^m = x^m y^m$. Cube each factor in parentheses.
$$= 5^3 \times 10^{-12} \qquad (10^m)^n = 10^{mn}$$
$$= 125 \times 10^{-12} \qquad \text{125 must be expressed in scientific notation.}$$
$$= 1.25 \times 10^2 \times 10^{-12} \qquad 125 = 1.25 \times 10^2$$
$$= 1.25 \times 10^{2+(-12)} \qquad 10^m \cdot 10^n = 10^{m+n}$$
$$= 1.25 \times 10^{-10}$$ ∎

Using technology

Even if you do not set your graphing calculator to a scientific notation mode, your calculator automatically switches to scientific notation when displaying large or small numbers that exceed the display range. Try multiplying

$$79{,}000 \times 3{,}400{,}000{,}000.$$

The display shows

2.686E14

so that the product is

2.686×10^{14}.

If you set your calculator to the scientific notation mode, answers to all computations are displayed in scientific notation even if they do not exceed the display range.

ENRICHMENT ESSAY

Earthquakes and Exponents

The earthquake that ripped through northern California on October 17, 1989, measured 7.1 on the Richter scale, killed more than 60 people, and injured more than 2400. Shown here is San Fran-cisco's Marina district, where shock waves tossed houses off their foundations and into the street.

The Richter scale is misleading because it is not actually a 1 to 8, but rather a 1 to 10 million scale. Each level indicates a tenfold increase in magnitude from the previous level, making a 7.0 earthquake a million times greater than a 1.0 quake.

Below is a translation of the Richter scale.

David Weintraub/Photo Researchers, Inc.

Richter Number (R)	Increase in Magnitude (10^{R-1})
1	$10^{1-1} = 10^0 = 1$
2	$10^{2-1} = 10^1 = 10$
3	$10^{3-1} = 10^2 = 100$
4	$10^{4-1} = 10^3 = 1000$
5	$10^{5-1} = 10^4 = 10,000$
6	$10^{6-1} = 10^5 = 100,000$
7	$10^{7-1} = 10^6 = 1,000,000$
8	$10^{8-1} = 10^7 = 10,000,000$

PROBLEM SET 6.7

Practice Problems

Evaluate each exponential expression in Problems 1–18.

1. 5^{-2} **2.** 4^{-2} **3.** 5^{-3} **4.** 4^{-4} **5.** $\dfrac{1}{3^{-2}}$ **6.** $\dfrac{1}{4^{-3}}$

7. $2^{-1} + 3^{-1}$ **8.** $3^{-1} - 6^{-1}$ **9.** $\left(\dfrac{1}{4}\right)^{-2}$ **10.** $\left(\dfrac{1}{5}\right)^{-2}$

11. -4^{-2} **12.** -5^{-2} **13.** $(-4)^{-2}$ **14.** $(-5)^{-2}$

15. $\dfrac{2^{-3}}{8^{-2}}$ **16.** $\dfrac{4^{-3}}{2^{-8}}$ **17.** $\dfrac{3}{(-5)^{-3}}$ **18.** $\dfrac{4}{(-3)^{-3}}$

In Problems 19–36, find the quotients and write them with positive exponents.

19. $\dfrac{x^3}{x^9}$ **20.** $\dfrac{y^5}{y^{12}}$ **21.** $\dfrac{z^5}{z^{13}}$ **22.** $\dfrac{w^6}{w^{19}}$ **23.** $\dfrac{30y^5}{10y^{10}}$ **24.** $\dfrac{45y^4}{15y^{12}}$

25. $\dfrac{-8x^3}{2x^7}$ **26.** $\dfrac{-15x^4}{3x^9}$ **27.** $\dfrac{-9a^5}{27a^8}$ **28.** $\dfrac{-15a^8}{45a^{13}}$ **29.** $\dfrac{7w^5}{5w^{13}}$ **30.** $\dfrac{7w^8}{9w^{14}}$

31. $\dfrac{15a^5b^3}{5a^2b^7}$ **32.** $\dfrac{20x^2y^3}{10xy^4}$ **33.** $\dfrac{-20x^4y^7}{4x^2y^{13}}$ **34.** $\dfrac{-30a^3b^8}{2a^2b^{11}}$ **35.** $\dfrac{-20xy^3z^4}{60x^4yz^{11}}$ **36.** $\dfrac{-18a^3bc^5}{90a^2b^8c^{13}}$

In Problems 37–48, find the quotients and write them with positive exponents.

37. $\dfrac{6x^4 - 8x^3 + 20x}{2x^2}$ **38.** $\dfrac{20x^4 - 12x^3 + 40x}{4x^2}$ **39.** $\dfrac{8y^4 - 20y^3 - 10y^2 + 8y - 6}{2y}$

40. $\dfrac{27z^4 - 9z^3 + 30z^2 - 18z - 12}{3z}$

41. $\dfrac{x^6 - x^4 + 2x^3 - 5x^2 + 9x}{x^3}$

42. $\dfrac{6y^6 - y^4 + y^3 - 7y^2 + 10y}{y^3}$

43. $\dfrac{8x^8 - 12x^4 - 16x^3 + 20x}{4x^4}$

44. $\dfrac{50x^8 - 15x^4 - 25x^3 + 40x}{5x^4}$

45. $\dfrac{9x^2y^2 + 3x^2y - 6x^3y^2}{3x^2y^3}$

46. $\dfrac{6x^5y^4 - 15x^4y^5 + 9y^6 - 12x^2y}{3x^2y^5}$

47. $\dfrac{4a^4b - 12a^6b^2 + 8a^8b^6}{-4a^4b}$

48. $\dfrac{12ab^4 - 16a^2b^6 + 20a^6b^8}{-4a^2b^7}$

Simplify each exponential expression in Problems 49–84, writing the answer with positive exponents only. Assume that variables in denominators do not equal zero.

49. $x^{-8} \cdot x^3$

50. $x^{-11} \cdot x^5$

51. $(4x^{-5})(2x^2)$

52. $(5x^{-7})(3x^3)$

53. $\dfrac{z^3}{(z^4)^2}$

54. $\dfrac{z^5}{(z^3)^2}$

55. $\dfrac{z^{-3}}{(z^4)^2}$

56. $\dfrac{z^{-5}}{(z^3)^2}$

57. $\dfrac{(4x^3)^2}{x^8}$

58. $\dfrac{(5x^3)^2}{x^7}$

59. $\dfrac{(6a^4)^3}{a^{-5}}$

60. $\dfrac{(4b^5)^3}{b^{-4}}$

61. $\left(\dfrac{y^4}{y^2}\right)^{-3}$

62. $\left(\dfrac{y^6}{y^2}\right)^{-3}$

63. $\left(\dfrac{4x^5}{2x^2}\right)^{-4}$

64. $\left(\dfrac{6x^7}{2x^2}\right)^{-4}$

65. $(-2z^{-1})^{-2}$

66. $(-3z^{-2})^{-2}$

67. $\dfrac{2x^5 \cdot 3x^7}{15x^6}$

68. $\dfrac{3z^3 \cdot 5z^4}{20z^{14}}$

69. $(x^3)^5 x^{-7}$

70. $(x^4)^3 x^{-5}$

71. $(2y^3)^4 y^{-6}$

72. $(3y^4)^3 y^{-7}$

73. $\dfrac{(y^3)^4}{(y^2)^7}$

74. $\dfrac{(y^2)^5}{(y^3)^4}$

75. $(a^4b^5)^{-3}$

76. $(x^5y^3)^{-4}$

77. $(a^{-2}b^{-6})^{-4}$

78. $(a^{-7}b^{-2})^{-5}$

79. $(a^3b^{-4}c^{-5})(a^{-2}b^{-4}c^9)$

80. $(x^{-5}y^7z^{-3})(x^9y^{-2}z^{10})$

81. $\left(\dfrac{x^2}{y^3}\right)^{-2}$

82. $\left(\dfrac{x^3}{y^2}\right)^{-4}$

83. $\left(\dfrac{2m^2}{3n^4}\right)^{-3}$

84. $\left(\dfrac{3r^4}{2s^2}\right)^{-3}$

Write each number in Problems 85–96 in standard decimal notation without the use of exponents.

85. 2.7×10^2

86. 4.75×10^3

87. 9.12×10^5

88. 8.14×10^4

89. 3.4×10^0

90. 9.115×10^0

91. 7.9×10^{-1}

92. 8.6×10^{-1}

93. 2.15×10^{-2}

94. 3.14×10^{-2}

95. 7.86×10^{-4}

96. 4.63×10^{-5}

Write each number in Problems 97–112 in scientific notation.

97. 32,400

98. 327,000

99. 220,000,000

100. 370,000,000,000

101. 713

102. 623

103. 6751

104. 9832

105. 0.0027

106. 0.000 83

107. 0.000 020 2

108. 0.000 001 03

109. 0.005

110. 0.006

111. 3.141 59

112. 2.718 28

Perform the indicated computations in Problems 113–132, writing the answer in both scientific notation and standard decimal notation without the use of exponents.

113. $(2 \times 10^3)(3 \times 10^2)$

114. $(3 \times 10^4)(3 \times 10^2)$

115. $(2 \times 10^5)(8 \times 10^3)$

116. $(4 \times 10^3)(5 \times 10^4)$

117. $\dfrac{12 \times 10^6}{4 \times 10^2}$

118. $\dfrac{20 \times 10^{20}}{10 \times 10^{10}}$

119. $\dfrac{15 \times 10^4}{5 \times 10^{-2}}$

120. $\dfrac{18 \times 10^2}{9 \times 10^{-3}}$

121. $\dfrac{15 \times 10^{-4}}{5 \times 10^2}$

122. $\dfrac{18 \times 10^{-2}}{9 \times 10^3}$

123. $\dfrac{180 \times 10^6}{2 \times 10^3}$

124. $\dfrac{180 \times 10^8}{2 \times 10^4}$

125. $\dfrac{3 \times 10^4}{12 \times 10^{-3}}$

126. $\dfrac{5 \times 10^2}{20 \times 10^{-3}}$

127. $(5 \times 10^2)^3$

128. $(4 \times 10^3)^2$

129. $(3 \times 10^{-2})^4$

130. $(2 \times 10^{-3})^5$

131. $(4 \times 10^6)^{-1}$

132. $(5 \times 10^4)^{-1}$

Application Problems

Write the number in Problems 133–136 in standard decimal notation.

133. The distance from Earth to the sun is approximately 9.29×10^7 miles.

134. The average life span of a human is 2×10^9 seconds.

135. The shortest wavelength of visible light is approximately 4×10^{-5} centimeter.

136. The human thyroid contains approximately 2.822×10^{-4} ounce of iodine.

Write the numbers in Problems 137–144 in scientific notation.

137. Dancer Fred Astaire insured his legs for $650,000.

138. Warren G. Harding, the U.S. president with the largest feet, wore a size 14 shoe.

139. Polygamist King Mongut of Siam (the king upon whom the musical *The King and I* was based) had 9230 wives.

140. In 1975, the French consumed 124,500,000 bottles of wine.

141. The area of an atom of silver is

0.000 000 000 000 000 7 square centimeter.

142. The average diameter of a human red blood cell is 0.000 007 5 meter.

143. The probability of being dealt a royal flush in poker is 0.000 001 54.

144. The mass of an oxygen molecule is

0.000 000 000 000 000 000 531 milligram.

145. A human brain contains 3×10^{10} neurons and a gorilla brain contains 7.5×10^9 neurons. How many times as many neurons are in the brain of a human as in the brain of a gorilla?

146. If the sun is approximately 9.3×10^7 miles from Earth and light travels 1.86×10^5 miles per second, approximately how many seconds does it take the light of the sun to reach Earth? How many minutes does it take?

147. There are approximately 2×10^4 runners in the New York City Marathon. Each runner runs a distance of 42 kilometers (26 miles).
  a. Write the total distance (in kilometers) covered by all 20,000 runners in scientific notation.
  b. The circumference of the Earth is approximately 4×10^4 kilometers. Use your answer from part (a) to find approximately how many times the marathon runners could circle the Earth as a relay.
  c. The runners in the marathon take an average of 4 hours to finish the race. Write the total time for all 2×10^4 runners to complete the race in scientific notation. Your answer will be expressed in hours.
  d. This part of the problem involves some critical thinking. Convert your answer in part (c) from hours to years. (Round your answer to the nearest tenth of a year.)
  e. Use your work in this problem to complete the following statement: The New York City Marathon run as a relay would circle the Earth _____ times and take more than _____ years to complete.

148. The mass of the Earth is 6×10^{27} grams and the mass of a hydrogen atom is 1.66×10^{-24} gram. If the Earth were made up exclusively of hydrogen atoms, how many hydrogen atoms would it contain?

The graph shows the projected growth of Medicare spending through the year 2005. Use the graph to answer Problems 149–150.

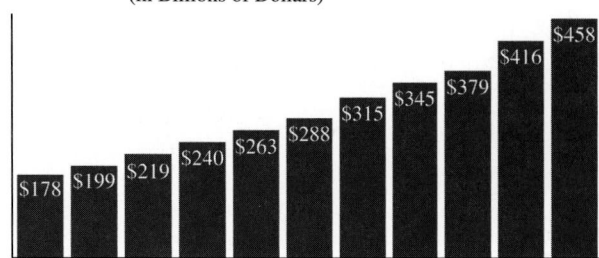

Projected Growth of Medicare Spending
(in Billions of Dollars)

$178 $199 $219 $240 $263 $288 $315 $345 $379 $416 $458

1995 1996 1997 1998 1999 2000 2001 2002 2003 2004 2005
Source: Congressional Budget Office, April 1995

149. Express the Medicare spending for each of the eleven years in scientific notation.

150. Find the difference in Medicare spending between the year 2005 and 1995. Express the answer in scientific notation.

True–False Critical Thinking Problems

151. Which one of the following is true?
  a. $4^{-2} < 4^{-3}$
  b. $5^{-2} > 2^{-5}$
  c. $(-2)^4 = 2^{-4}$
  d. $5^2 \cdot 5^{-2} > 2^5 \cdot 2^{-5}$

152. Which one of the following is true?
  a. $3^5 \cdot 5^{-3} > 5^3 \cdot 3^{-5}$
  b. $(-1)^4 < 1^{-4}$
  c. $6^{-2} < 7^{-2}$
  d. $-2^4 = (-2)^4$

153. Which one of the following is true?
  a. $\dfrac{x^3}{x^7} = \dfrac{1}{x^4}$ for any nonzero real number x.
  b. $2^5 \cdot 2^{-8} = 4^{-3}$ or $\dfrac{1}{64}$
  c. $\dfrac{x^{12}}{x^{-4}} = x^{-3}$ or $\dfrac{1}{x^3}$ for any nonzero real number x.
  d. $(2y)^{-5} = \dfrac{2}{y^5}$ for any nonzero real number y.

154. Which one of the following is true?
  a. $\dfrac{3^{-2}}{3^{-1}} = 3$
  b. $10^{-2} = 0.001$
  c. $0.000\,076 = 7.6 \times 10^{-5}$
  d. $\dfrac{x^7}{x^{-4}} = x^3$ for any nonzero real number x.

155. Which one of the following is true?
  a. $35 \times 10^7 = 3.5 \times 10^6$
  b. $(3 \times 10^{-9})^2 = 6 \times 10^{-18}$
  c. $(3 \times 10^{-5})(2 \times 10^3) = 6 \times 10^{-15}$
  d. $\dfrac{8 \times 10^{-9}}{4 \times 10^{-5}} = 2 \times 10^{-4}$

156. Which one of the following is true?
  a. $\dfrac{(3 \times 10^4)(1.4 \times 10^8)}{(2.1 \times 10^3)} = 2 \times 10^4$
  b. $(9 \times 10^6)(2.1 \times 10^7) = 1.89 \times 10^{14}$
  c. If $\dfrac{10^{16}}{10^n} = 10^2$, then $n = 8$.
  d. If $10^n \times 10^n = 10^{16}$, then $n = 4$.

Technology Problems

157. Use a graphing calculator to check your answers to Problems 1–18.

158. Use the scientific notation mode of your graphing calculator to check your answers to Problems 97–112.

159. Use a graphing calculator to check your answers to Problems 113–132 by:
  a. Entering the given computation in scientific notation.
  b. Setting the calculator's mode to scientific notation and finding the answer to the computation in this notation.

Writing in Mathematics

160. Explain what a negative exponent indicates.

161. Explain how to tell if an exponential expression containing a negative base is positive or negative.

Critical Thinking Problems

162. At a Delta House party, Dean Wormer discretely ate $4^{-2} + 2^{-4}$ of a chocolate cake. Bluto, the craziest party animal of all the Deltas, immediately wolfed down the remainder of the cake. What fractional part of the cake did Bluto devour?

163. The mad Dr. Frankenstein has gathered enough bits and pieces (so to speak) for $2^{-1} + 2^{-2}$ of his creature-to-be. What percentage of his creature must still be obtained?

164. If $x = (((2^2)^2)^2)^2$ and $y = 2^{2^{2^2}}$, find $\dfrac{x}{y}$, expressing the quotient in the form 2^n, where n is an integer.

Review Problems

165. A town has a population of 4000 people. If the population increases by 200 people per year, how long will it be before the population reaches 9400?

166. Solve and graph the solution set on a number line: $6(3 - x) < 2x + 12$.

167. Multiply $5x - 2$ and $2x^2 + 3x - 4$.

CHAPTER PROJECT

Chaos

We have seen many examples in this chapter of how polynomials may be used to help us model and understand real world phenomena. For this project, we will investigate a slightly different looking polynomial equation, called the *logistic equation*.

$$X_{\text{NEW}} = kX_{\text{OLD}}(1 - X_{\text{OLD}})$$

This equation serves as a model for population growth. For example, we may be modeling the number of fish in a pond over a number of years. We would expect the population of fish to rise and fall through the years, possibly affected by how much food is in the pond, how many predators will feed on the fish, or how fast the fish reproduce, among other factors. The k in our equation is a constant reflecting many of these factors and will differ depending on the population we are studying.

Another key point of our model is that the current number of fish in the pond will certainly affect how many fish are in the pond next year. This means we need to know the current population (X_{OLD}) to predict the next years' population (X_{NEW}). Our model also requires that we express the population as a number between 0 and 1. We can think of this as a percent, where 0 represents extinction and 1 represents the largest possible population (100%).

As an illustration, let's use $k = 2$ and let our initial population be 0.1; that is, the pond has 10% of the theoretical maximum number of fish in our first year. If our pond could only hold 200 fish, then we are beginning with a population of 20. We will use subscripts to indicate each year, and our equation is

$$X_{n+1} = k X_n (1 - X_n)$$

where n is the year. Time 0 is our population at the beginning of the year, $X_0 = 0.1$, and we may find the population at the end of one year, X_1.

$$X_1 = k X_0(1 - X_0) = 2(0.1)(1 - 0.1) = 2(0.1)(0.9) = 0.18$$

This tells us that at the end of year 1, our population of fish stands at 18% of the maximum population our pond could hold. So for our 200-fish maximum, we now have 36 fish. For year 2, X_2,

$$X_2 = k X_1(1 - X_1) = 2(0.18)(1 - 0.18) = 2(0.18)(0.82) = 0.2952 \approx 0.295$$

Thus, at the end of year 2, our population of fish would be at 29.5% of its theoretical maximum.
Use this information to complete the problems in this project.

1. Using your calculator, continue this procedure up to the 10th year, rounding each value to the nearest thousandth. What conclusions can you draw about the population of fish in the pond?
2. Repeat these calculations using $k = 2.8$ and an initial population of 0.1, continuing the procedure until the 10th year, rounding each value to the nearest thousandth. What do you observe about this population compared to the population in Problem 1?
3. Repeat these calculations using $k = 3.2$ and an initial population of 0.1, continuing the procedure until the 25th year, rounding values to the nearest hundred-thousandth when needed. How would you interpret these results in terms of the population of the pond?
4. Repeat these calculations using $k = 4$ and an initial population of 0.2, continuing the procedure until the 25th year, rounding values to the nearest hundred-thousandth when needed. Compare your results in this problem with the results in Problem 2. Which population appears to have a predictable behavior?

The results we observe in Problems 1 through 4 depend quite strongly on the value of k that was chosen. When k is less than 1, no matter what starting point we choose, we will eventually end up at zero.

When k is between 1 and 3, we see a different type of behavior, and for k greater than 3 but less than 3.44 yet another pattern emerges. As k changes from 3.45 up to 4, we see an increasingly different look at population size, until, somewhere within this range, we see wildly fluctuating populations, with no apparent pattern at all. At the end, we say the population, or the system, has become *chaotic*.

5. Another way to display the results of our calculations is in graphical form. Number the x-axis from 0 to 25 and the y-axis from 0 to a decimal large enough to allow for the answers you have obtained. Graph each of the points and connect them with straight lines. What patterns can you see emerging in Problems 1 through 4?

Chaos in mathematics does not have the same meaning as chaos in everyday life. You probably think of chaotic behavior as random and meaningless, but mathematical chaos is far from that. In mathematics, as well as in physics, biology, and many other disciplines where chaos is studied, chaotic behavior only *appears* random. Equations such as the ones we have seen here may take many different forms, as do the graphical representations of the equations.

Worldwide Web Resources

Go to the Prentice Hall website (http://www.prenhall.com/blitzer) to access other locations on the Internet that will allow you to further explore the concepts presented in this project.

Chapter Review

SUMMARY

1. The Vocabulary of Polynomials
   a. A *polynomial* is a single term or the sum of two or more terms containing whole number exponents on its variables.
   b. Polynomials involving one variable are in *standard form* when they are written in descending powers of the variable.
   c. A polynomial with one term is a *monomial,* with two terms a *binomial,* and with three terms a *trinomial.*
   d. The degree of a polynomial involving one variable is the greatest exponent of any of its terms.
   e. For a polynomial in several variables, the degree of a term is the sum of the exponents of the variables. The degree of the polynomial is the highest degree of all the terms of the polynomial.

   f. Polynomial functions contain formulas that are polynomials.

2. Sums and Differences of Polynomials
   a. Polynomials are added by combining like terms.
   b. Polynomials are subtracted by changing the sign of every term of the second polynomial and adding this result to the first polynomial.
   c. Polynomials can be added or subtracted by using a horizontal or vertical format.

3. Multiplying Polynomials
   a. Use $x^m \cdot x^n = x^{m+n}$ to multiply monomials.
   b. Use the distributive property and $x^m \cdot x^n = x^{m+n}$ to find the product of a monomial and a polynomial other than a monomial.
   c. When multiplying two polynomials, neither of which is a monomial, multiply each term of one

polynomial by each term of the other polynomial. Then add the like terms in the product.

d. Use the FOIL method to multiply two binomials. (*First* terms multiplied, *Outside* terms multiplied, *Inside* terms multiplied, *Last* terms multiplied.)

e. *The product of the sum and difference of two terms:* $(A + B)(A - B) = A^2 - B^2$. The product is the first term squared minus the second term squared.

f. *The square of a binomial sum:* $(A + B)^2 = A^2 + 2AB + B^2$. Write the sum of the first term squared, twice the product of the first and last terms, and the last term squared. For the square of a binomial difference, use $(A - B)^2 = A^2 - 2AB + B^2$.

4. Dividing Polynomials

a. Use $\dfrac{x^m}{x^n} = x^{m-n}$. to divide monomials.

b. To divide a polynomial containing more than one term by a monomial, divide each term of the polynomial by the monomial. Then use

$$\frac{x^m}{x^n} = x^{m-n}.$$

c. To divide a polynomial by a binomial, arrange terms in the dividend and the divisor in descending powers of the variable. Use 0 as the coefficient for missing terms. Then follow the four steps used to

divide whole numbers—divide, multiply, subtract, and bring down the next term. The division is completed when the degree of the polynomial obtained by subtraction is less than that of the divisor.

5. Integer Exponents: Definitions

a. $x^1 = x$

b. x^n means x is repeated n times as a factor, where $n = 2, 3, 4, 5,$ and so on.

c. $x^0 = 1$, where $x \neq 0$.

d. $x^{-n} = \dfrac{1}{x^n}$ and $\dfrac{1}{x^{-n}} = x^n$, where $x \neq 0$.

6. Properties of Exponents

a. $x^m \cdot x^n = x^{m+n}$

b. $(x^m)^n = x^{mn}$

c. $(xy)^m = x^m y^m$

d. $\dfrac{x^m}{x^n} = x^{m-n}$

e. $\left(\dfrac{x}{y}\right)^m = \dfrac{x^m}{y^m}$

7. Scientific Notation

a. A scientific notation numeral appears as the product of two factors. The first factor is a number greater than or equal to 1 but less than 10. The second factor is base 10 raised to a power.

b. Multiplication and division in scientific notation can be accomplished using

$$10^m \cdot 10^n = 10^{m+n} \quad \text{and} \quad \frac{10^m}{10^n} = 10^{m-n}.$$

REVIEW PROBLEMS

Identify each polynomial in Problems 1–3 as a monomial, binomial, or trinomial. Give the degree of the polynomial.

1. $7x^4 + 9x$

2. $3x + 5x^2 - 2$

3. $16x$

4. The average number of automobile accidents per day in the United States involving drivers of age x is modeled by the polynomial function $f(x) = 0.4x^2 - 40x + 1039$. Find and interpret $f(20)$.

5. A diver jumps from a diving board 32 feet above the water with an initial speed of 16 feet per second. The height of the diver above the water is a function of the time (t, in seconds) that the diver is in the air, modeled by the polynomial function $f(t) = -16t^2 + 16t + 32$.

a. Find and interpret $f(0), f(0.5), f(1), f(1.5),$ and $f(2)$.

b. Use the values from part (a) to graph the function from $t = 0$ to $t = 2$.

c. When does it appear that the diver reaches a maximum height? What is the maximum height?

d. After how many seconds does the diver hit the water? How is this shown by the graph?

e. If your course involves the use of a graphing utility, use it to verify your graph.

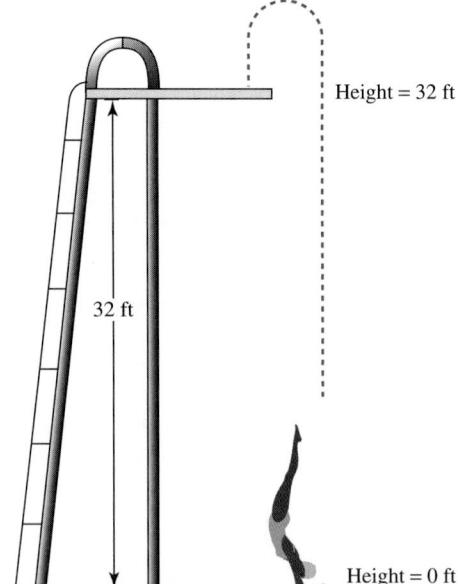
Height = 32 ft

32 ft

Height = 0 ft

Perform the indicated operations in Problems 6–10.

6. $(-6x^3 + 7x^2 - 9x + 3) + (14x^3 + 3x^2 - 11x - 7)$

7. $(-7a^2 + 4 + 9a^3) + (-13 - 8a^3 + 3a^2)$

8. $(5y^2 - y - 8) - (-6y^2 + 3y - 4)$

9. $(13x^4 - 8x^3 + 2x^2) - (5x^4 - 3x^3 + 2x^2 - 6)$

10. Subtract $x^4 + 7x^2 - 11x$ from $-13x^4 - 6x^2 + 5x$.

Add or subtract as indicated in Problems 11–13.

11. Add.

$$7y^4 - 6y^3 + 4y^2 - 4y$$
$$\underline{\ y^3 - \ y^2 + 3y - 4}$$

12. Subtract.

$$7x^2 - 9x + 2$$
$$\underline{-(4x^2 - 2x - 7)}$$

13. Subtract.

$$5x^3 - 6x^2 - \ 9x + 14$$
$$\underline{-(-5x^3 + 3x^2 - 11x + \ \ 3)}$$

Find each product in Problems 14–22.

14. $7x(3x - 9)$

15. $-5x^3(4x^2 - 11x)$

16. $3y^2(-7y^2 + 3y - 6)$

17. $-2y^5(8y^3 - 4y^2 - 10y + 6)$

18. $(x + 3)(x^2 - 5x + 2)$

19. $(3y - 2)(4y^2 + 3y - 5)$

20. $(x - 6)(x + 2)$

21. $(3y - 5)(2y + 1)$

22. $(4x^3 - 2x^2)(x^2 - 3)$

Use a vertical format to find each product in Problems 23–24.

23. $y^2 - 4y + 7$
$$\underline{\ 3y - 5}$$

24. $4x^3 - 2x^2 - 6x - 1$
$$\underline{\ 2x + 3}$$

Find each product in Problems 25–29.

25. $(3x^3 - 2)(x^3 + 4)$

26. $(x + 3)^2$

27. $(3y - 4)^2$

28. $(4x + 5)(4x - 5)$

29. $(2z + 9)(2z - 9)$

30. The parking garage shown in the figure measures 20 yards by 30 yards. The length and the width are to be increased by a fixed amount.
  a. Find a polynomial that describes the area of the expanded garage.
  b. Write the trinomial in part (a) as a polynomial function, calling the function *f*.
  c. Find and interpret $f(5)$.

31. The figure shows a painting whose width is represented by *x*. The length of the painting is 8 inches less than twice its width. The painting is surrounded by a frame that is 4 inches wide.
  a. Write a polynomial that describes the area of the frame.
  b. Write the expression in part (a) as a function, calling the function *g*.
  c. Graph the function in the first quadrant. Take care with the way that you scale the *y*-axis.

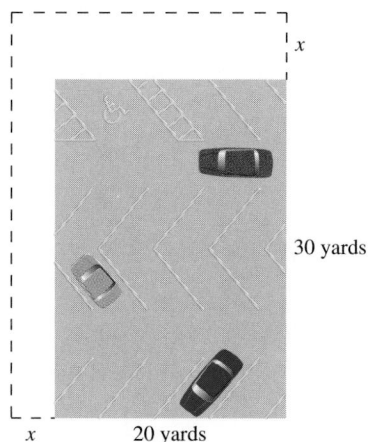

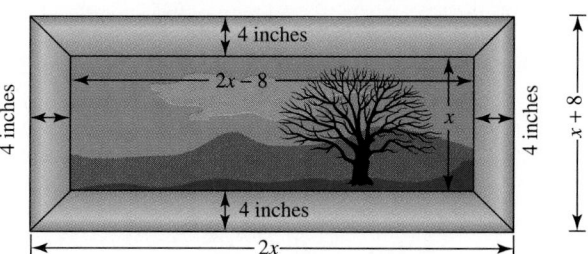

In Problems 32–33, find a polynomial function f that represents the area of the shaded region. Use multiplication to simplify each function. If all units are given in centimeters, find and interpret f(6).

32.

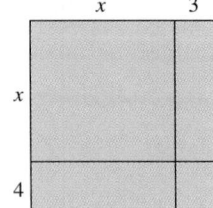

33.

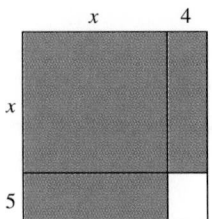

Problems 34–46 involve polynomials in several variables.

34. Evaluate $3 - 4xy + 2y^2 - 5xy^3 + x^8$ when $x = -1$ and $y = 2$.

35. The space shuttle has an external tank for the fuel needed by the main engines for the launch. After eight minutes into the flight, the fuel is gone and the tank is released. As shown in the figure on the right, the tank is a cylinder of radius r and height h, capped on each end by a half-sphere. The tank's radius is 4 meters and its height exceeds the radius by 17 meters. Find the tank's volume, using the formula $V = \pi r^2 h + \frac{4}{3}\pi r^3$ and 3.14 as an approximation for π.

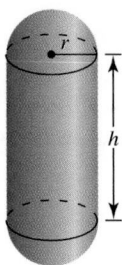

36. What is the coefficient and the degree of each term of the polynomial $4x^2y + 9x^3y^2 - 17x^4 - 12$? What is the degree of the polynomial?

Perform the indicated operations in Problems 37–46.

37. $(7a^2 - 8ab + b^2) + (-8a^2 - 9ab - 4b^2)$

38. $(13x^3y^2 - 5x^2y - 9x^2) -$
$(-11x^3y^2 - 6x^2y + 3x^2 - 4)$

39. $(-7x^2y^3)(5x^4y^6)$

40. $5ab^2(3a^2b^3 - 4ab)$

41. $(x + 7y)(3x - 5y)$

42. $(4xy - 3)(9xy - 1)$

43. $(3x - 5y)^2$

44. $(3a^4 + 2b^3)^2$

45. $(7x + 4y)(7x - 4y)$

46. $(a - b)(a^2 + ab + b^2)$

In Problems 47–55, divide. Check your result algebraically or by using a graphing utility.

47. $\dfrac{-15y^8}{3y^2}$

48. $\dfrac{18y^4 - 12y^2 + 36y}{6y}$

49. $(30x^8 - 25x^7 + 3x^6 - 40x^5) \div (-5x^5)$

50. $\dfrac{2z^3 - 6z^2 + 5z}{2z^2}$

51. $\dfrac{20x^7 - 8x^6 - 16x^4 + 12x^2 - 2}{4x^5}$

52. $\dfrac{27x^3y - 9x^2y - 18xy^2}{3xy}$

53. $\dfrac{2x^2 + 3x - 14}{x - 2}$

54. $\dfrac{2y^3 - 5y^2 + 7y + 5}{2y + 1}$

55. $\dfrac{z^3 - 2z^2 - 33z - 7}{z - 7}$

Simplify Problems 56–70. Write each answer with positive exponents. All variables represent nonzero real numbers.

56. $(3y^6)(-2y^4)$

57. $(3x^3)^4$

58. $4(2y^5)^3$

59. $(2x)(4x)^2 + 15x^3$

60. $\dfrac{x^3}{x^9}$

61. $\dfrac{30y^6}{5y^8}$

62. $(5y^{-7})(6y^2)$

63. $\dfrac{x^4 \cdot x^{-2}}{x^{-6}}$

64. $\dfrac{(3y^3)^4}{y^{10}}$

65. $\dfrac{y^{-7}}{(y^4)^3}$

66. $\left(\dfrac{x^7}{x^4}\right)^{-4}$

67. $\dfrac{(y^3)^4 y^{-3}}{(y^{-2})^4}$

68. $(2x^2 y^{-3})^{-4}$

69. $(4x^{-2} y^3)(-3x^4 y^{-6})$

70. $\left(\dfrac{a^3}{b^2}\right)^{-4}$

Write Problems 71–77 without exponents.

71. 2.3×10^4

72. 1.76×10^{-3}

73. 9.84×10^{-1}

74. 7^{-2}

75. $2^{-1} + 4^{-1}$

76. $(2^3)^{-2}$

77. $\dfrac{5^{-5}}{5^{-3}}$

Write each number in Problems 78–83 in scientific notation.

78. 73,900,000

79. 0.000 089 4

80. 0.000 972 5

81. 0.38

82. 8.639

83. 37,000

Perform the indicated computations in Problems 84–86, writing the answers in scientific notation and standard decimal notation.

84. $(6 \times 10^{-3})(1.5 \times 10^6)$

85. $\dfrac{2 \times 10^2}{4 \times 10^{-3}}$

86. $(4 \times 10^{-2})^2$

87. A microsecond is 10^{-6} second and a nanosecond is 10^{-9} second. How many nanoseconds make a microsecond?

88. The neocortex of the human brain contains 3×10^{10} neurons and the neocortex of a cat contains 6.5×10^7 neurons. How many times as many neurons are there in a human brain as there are in the brain of a cat?

89. The world's population is approximately 5.4×10^9 people. Current projections double this population in 40 years. Write the population 40 years from now in scientific notation.

90. The mass of the Earth is 6×10^{27} grams and a gram is 1.1×10^{-6} ton. What is the Earth's mass in tons?

CHAPTER 6 TEST

1. Classify the polynomial as a monomial, binomial, or trinomial. Give the degree of the polynomial.

$$9x + 6x^2 - 4$$

Perform the indicated operations in Problems 2–14.

2. $(7x^3 + 3x^2 - 5x - 11) + (6x^3 - 2x^2 + 4x - 13)$

3. $(9x^3 - 6x^2 - 11x - 4) - (4x^3 - 8x^2 - 13x + 5)$

4. $-6x^2(8x^2 - 7x - 4)$

5. $(3x - 5)(2x^2 + 4x - 3)$

6. $(3y + 7)(2y - 9)$

7. $(5x - 3)^2$

8. $(4x^3 - 2)(5x^2 - 1)$

9. $(3x + 4y)^2$

10. $(7x + 11)(7x - 11)$

11. $\dfrac{12x^9}{-3x^5}$

12. $\dfrac{15x^4 - 10x^3 + 25x^2}{5x}$

13. $\dfrac{20x^4 - 8x^3 + 12x^2 - 4}{4x^3}$

14. $\dfrac{2x^3 - 3x^2 + 4x + 4}{2x + 1}$

In Problems 15–21, simplify. Write each answer with positive exponents. All variables represent nonzero real numbers.

15. $(-7x^3)(5x^8)$

16. $(-3x^2)^3$

17. $\dfrac{20x^3}{5x^8}$

18. $(-7x^{-8})(3x^2)$

19. $\dfrac{(2x^3)^4}{x^8}$

20. $(3x^3)^2(-2x^3)^5$

21. $\left(\dfrac{x^{11}}{x^5}\right)^{-3}$

Write Problems 22–25 without exponents.

22. 4^{-3}

23. 3.7×10^{-4}

24. $(3^2)^{-2}$

25. $\dfrac{2^{-5}}{2^{-3}}$

26. Write 7,600,000,000,000 in scientific notation.

Perform the indicated operations in Problems 27–28 and write the answer in scientific notation.

27. $\dfrac{3.5 \times 10^4}{1.4 \times 10^{-13}}$

28. $(3.4 \times 10^6)(5 \times 10^{13})$

29. Write a polynomial in descending powers of x that represents the area of the shaded region in the figure.

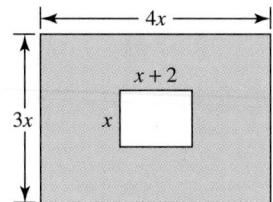

30. Write a polynomial in descending powers of x that represents the area of the figure.

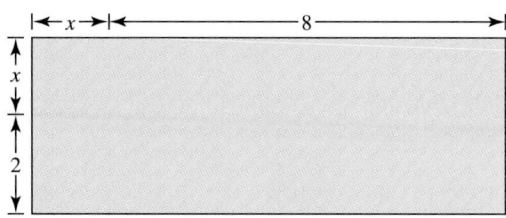

CUMULATIVE REVIEW PROBLEMS (CHAPTERS 1–6)

1. Solve: $2(x + 3) + 2x = x + 4$.

2. In 1994, the federal government spent \$13 billion on its drug-control budget. Use the circle graph to determine what percent of the budget was spent on prosecution, enforcement. Round your answer to the nearest whole percent.

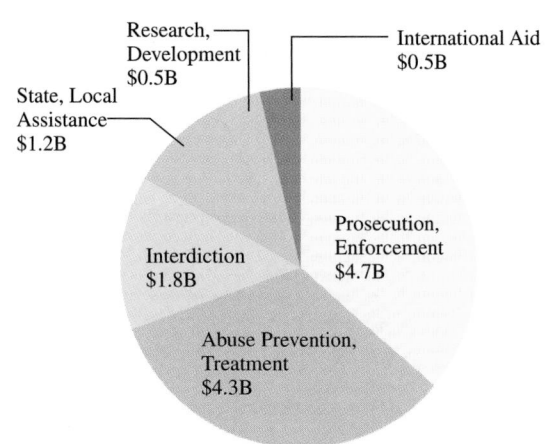

1994 Drug–Control Budget

Research, Development \$0.5B

International Aid \$0.5B

State, Local Assistance \$1.2B

Interdiction \$1.8B

Prosecution, Enforcement \$4.7B

Abuse Prevention, Treatment \$4.3B

Source: Office of Management and Budget

3. Find the solution set: $3 - \frac{1}{4}x \leq 2 + \frac{3}{8}x$.

4. Graph: $5x - 2y = -10$.

5. Graph: $y \geq -\frac{2}{5}x + 2$.

6. Solve the system:

$$3x - 6y = 1$$
$$x = 2y + 3$$

7. The model $f(x) = 0.00011x^4 - 0.013x^3 + 0.44x^2 - 3.6x + 87$ describes $f(x)$, the fertility rate in the United States (in terms of the number of live births per 1000 women of childbearing age) x years after 1930. Find and interpret $f(10)$. Describe how this result is shown in the graph. If applicable, use your graphing utility to graph the function corresponding to the period shown by the bar graph.

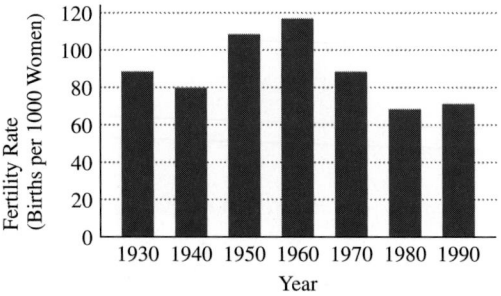

U.S. Fertility Rate 1930–1990

Fertility Rate (Births per 1000 Women)

Year

Data Source: U.S. Bureau of the Census

8. Solve by graphing:

$$x + y = -1$$
$$-2x + y = 5$$

9. The average taxpayer works for 30 years and earns approximately $30,000 per year, paying $405,000 in taxes to the federal government over the 30 years. The graph shows the programs that take the largest amounts of this $405,000. The amount spent on defense is $9000 more than five times that spent on education, and the amount spent on welfare is $6300 less than that spent on education. If defense, education, and welfare combined take a tax bite of $103,500, determine the amount paid in taxes on each of the three categories. Then use the graph to estimate the amount the average taxpayer spends on the other three categories over 30 years.

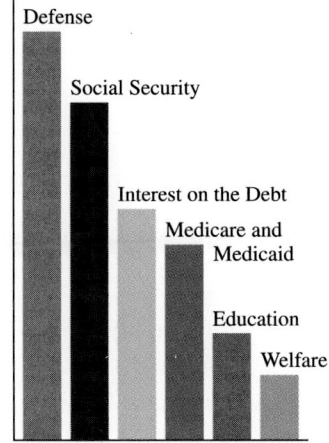

10. The number of serious crimes in the United States ($f(x)$, measured in millions) can be modeled by the linear function $f(x) = 0.25x + 12.75$, where x represents the number of years after 1987. What is the slope and y-intercept for this model? Describe what both numbers represent in practical terms.

Number of Serious Crimes
(in Millions)

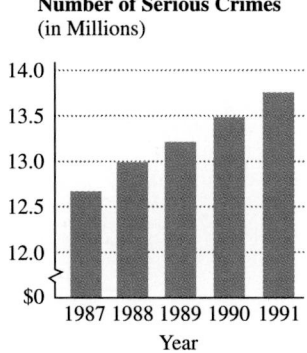

11. Rounding to the nearest foot, the length of a basketball court is 7 feet less than twice the width. If the perimeter is 280 feet, find the length and the width. (Note: In reality, the length is 5 inches longer and the width is 2 inches longer than the numbers that you will find.)

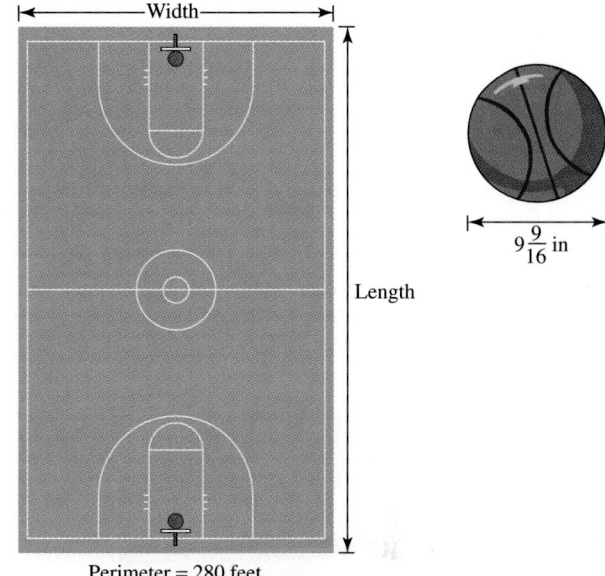

Perimeter = 280 feet

12. Write the point-slope form of the line passing through $(-1, 3)$ and $(-3, 5)$. Then use the point-slope equation to write the slope-intercept form of the line's equation.

13. Find an estimate for the slope of the line segment shown in the figure. Interpret the slope in practical terms using the phrase "rate of change."

Per Pupil Spending in America's Public Schools

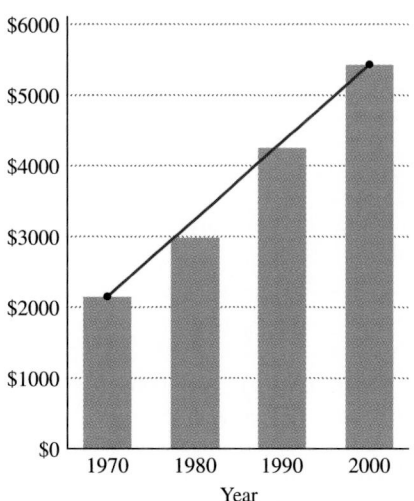

14. Perform the indicated operation:
$$\left(\frac{2}{3} + \frac{6}{11}\right) - \left(-\frac{1}{4} + \frac{5}{12}\right).$$

15. Find the quotient: $\dfrac{x^3 + 3x^2 + 5x + 3}{x + 1}$.

16. Solve: $0.3x - 4 = 0.1(x + 10)$.

17. Subtract $9x^5 + 3x^3 - 7x - 9$ from $9x^5 - 3x^3 + 2x - 7$.

18. Two people located 72 miles apart start riding bicycles at the same time, riding directly toward each other on the same road. If they bike at 13 miles per hour and 11 miles per hour, respectively, in how many hours will they meet?

19. The volume of a box is the product of its length, width, and height. Find a function f that models the volume of the box shown in the figure. If x is given in inches, find and interpret $f(4)$.

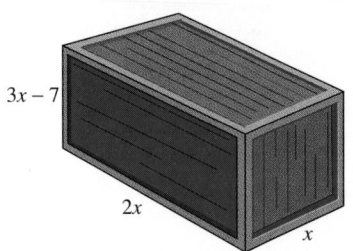

20. Find the product: $(3x - 2)(4x^2 - 5x + 1)$.

21. If a 20-pound bag of fertilizer covers 5000 square feet, how many pounds are needed to cover an area of 26,000 square feet? How many bags of fertilizer are needed?

22. A piece of board 70 centimeters long is cut into three pieces. The longest piece is twice the length of the middle-sized piece, and the shortest piece is 10 centimeters shorter than the middle-sized piece. How long are the pieces?

23. Solve the system:

$$3x + 2y = 10$$
$$4x - 3y = -15$$

24. Graph the solution for the following system of inequalities:

$$2x + 5y \leqslant 10$$
$$x - y \geqslant 4$$

25. The function $f(x) = -0.000625x^2 + 0.025x + 0.501$ describes the percentage of women ages 20–34 in the labor force x years after 1970. Find and interpret $f(10)$. How is this shown in the graph at the top of the next column? What trend does the graph show for this age group of women in the workplace? If applicable, verify the graph with a graphing utility.

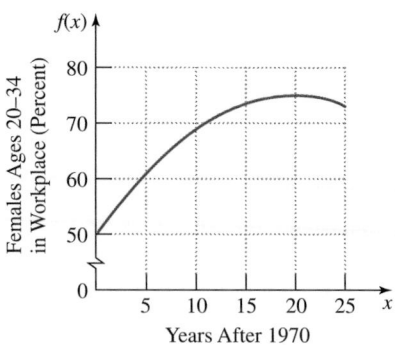

Years After 1970

26. Use the graph to write the slope-intercept equation of the line.

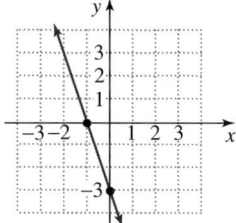

27. Simplify: $\dfrac{(8 - 10)^3 - (-4)^2}{2 + 8(2) \div 4}$.

28. If x, y, and z can each equal 2, 3, 6, or 12, select values such that $x \div y - z = 3$. Each number should be used only once.

29. When a boat travels with the current, it takes 1 hour to travel 16 miles. It takes the boat 8 hours to return the same distance against the current. Find the speed of the boat in still water and the speed of the current.

30. Suppose that three darts are thrown at the board shown in the figure. If each dart hits the board, how many different scores are possible?

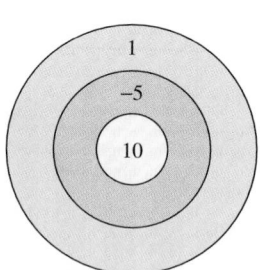

Factoring Polynomials

Rosamond W. Purcell "Its How You Play The Game"
1992. © Rosamond W. Purcell, all rights reserved.
Courtesy of the artist.

F actoring a polynomial means finding an equivalent expression that is a product. The ability to rewrite a polynomial sum or difference in terms of multiplication often provides a condensed, more manageable way of working with the polynomial. Factoring is part of the foundation for solving certain kinds of equations and working with algebraic fractions. Like other algebraic skills, factoring provides information about variables contained in mathematical models, further refining our understanding of reality by describing and predicting the behavior of variables.

S E C T I O N   7 . 1

Solutions Manual   **Tutorial**   **Video 8**

Factoring Polynomials with Common Factors

Objectives

1 Factor monomials.
2 Factor out the greatest common factor of a polynomial.
3 Factor by grouping.

Factoring is the process of writing a number or polynomial in terms of multiplication. It is one of the most useful tools in algebra, necessary for working with algebraic fractions and useful for solving many equations. In this section, our discussion is limited to factoring polynomials with common factors.

 Factor monomials.

Factoring Monomials

Factoring a monomial means finding two monomials whose product gives the original monomial. For example, $30x^2$ can be factored in a number of different ways, such as,

$$30x^2 = (5x)(6x) \qquad \text{The factors are } 5x \text{ and } 6x.$$
$$30x^2 = (15x)(2x) \qquad \text{The factors are } 15x \text{ and } 2x.$$
$$30x^2 = (10x^2)(3) \qquad \text{The factors are } 10x^2 \text{ and } 3.$$
$$30x^2 = (-6x)(-5x) \qquad \text{The factors are } -6x \text{ and } -5x.$$

Observe that each part of the factorization is called a *factor* of the given monomial.

Discover for yourself

Write three more ways of factoring the monomial $30x^2$.

2 Factor out the greatest common factor of a polynomial.

Factoring Out the Greatest Common Factor

We use the distributive property to multiply a monomial and a polynomial of two or more terms. When we factor, we reverse this process, expressing the polynomial as a product.

Multiplication	**Factoring**
$a(b + c) = ab + ac$	$ab + ac = a(b + c)$

Here is a specific example:

Multiplication	**Factoring**
$5x(2x + 3)$	$10x^2 + 15x$
$= 5x \cdot 2x + 5x \cdot 3$	$= 5x \cdot 2x + 5x \cdot 3$
$= 10x^2 + 15x$	$= 5x(2x + 3)$

Factoring is multiplying reversed.

Roger Brown, "Land of Lincoln" 1978, oil on canvas, 72 × 84 in. Photo courtesy Phyllis Kind Gallery, New York and Chicago.

In the process of finding an equivalent expression for $10x^2 + 15x$ that is a product, we used the fact that $5x$ is a factor of both $10x^2$ and $15x$. The factoring on the right shows that $5x$ is a *common factor* for all the terms of the binomial $10x^2 + 15x$.

When we factor a polynomial with two or more terms, we first try to find a factor that is common to all the terms. Sometimes there may not be a common factor other than 1. When common factors other than 1 do exist, we look for the one with the largest possible coefficient and the largest possible exponent. This factor is the *greatest common factor* of the polynomial, abbreviated GCF.

EXAMPLE 1 **Factoring Out the Greatest Common Monomial Factor**

Factor out the greatest common monomial factor: $5x^2 + 30$

Solution

The GCF of $5x^2$ and 30 is 5.

$$5x^2 + 30 = 5 \cdot x^2 + 5 \cdot 6 \qquad \text{Factor each monomial.}$$
$$= 5(x^2 + 6) \qquad \text{Factor out the GCF, 5.}$$

Since factoring reverses the process of multiplication, all factoring results can be checked by multiplying.

$$5(x^2 + 6) = 5 \cdot x^2 + 5 \cdot 6 = 5x^2 + 30$$

The factoring is correct because multiplication gives us the original polynomial. ■

EXAMPLE 2 **Factoring Out the Greatest Common Monomial Factor**

Factor: $18x^3 + 27x^2$

Solution

The greatest common factor for 18 and 27 is 9. The smallest power of x that appears in all the terms is x^2, and this is the largest power of x common to x^3 and x^2. (This becomes more obvious by writing x^3 as $x^2 \cdot x$.) Thus, x^2 is the greatest variable factor for $18x^3$ and $27x^2$, and the GCF of $18x^3$ and $27x^2$ is $9x^2$. We are now ready to factor the polynomial.

$$18x^3 + 27x^2 = 9x^2 \cdot 2x + 9x^2 \cdot 3 \qquad \text{Factor each monomial.}$$
$$= 9x^2(2x + 3) \qquad \text{Factor out the GCF, } 9x^2.$$

We can check this factorization by multiplying $9x^2$ and $2x + 3$, obtaining the original polynomial as the answer. ■

Before considering other examples, let's summarize the procedure we used in Examples 1 and 2.

Factoring a polynomial as the product of a monomial and another polynomial

1. Find the GCF of all the terms. The variable part of the GCF will contain the smallest power of a variable that appears in all terms of the polynomial.
2. Rewrite each term of the polynomial as the product of the GCF and another monomial.
3. Factor out the GCF and write the polynomial in factored form.

EXAMPLE 3 **Factoring Out the Greatest Common Monomial Factor**

Factor: $16y^5 - 12y^4 + 4y^3$

Solution

Using inspection, we see that 4 is the largest number that is a common factor for 16, -12, and 4. Since each term contains y raised to a different power, the GCF has a variable factor of y^3, the *smallest power* that appears in all the terms. The GCF is $4y^3$. We are now ready to factor the polynomial.

$$16y^5 - 12y^4 + 4y^3$$
$$= 4y^3 \cdot 4y^2 - 4y^3 \cdot 3y + 4y^3 \cdot 1 \qquad \text{Factor each monomial.}$$
$$= 4y^3(4y^2 - 3y + 1) \qquad\qquad \text{Factor out } 4y^3, \text{ the GCF.}$$

EXAMPLE 4   **Factoring Out a Negative Common Monomial Factor**

Factor: $-3y^2 + 15y - 6$

Solution

We can factor the polynomial in two ways, using 3 or -3 as the GCF.

Method 1. The GCF is 3.

$$-3y^2 + 15y - 6 = 3(-y^2) + 3(5y) + 3(-2)$$
$$= 3(-y^2 + 5y - 2)$$

Method 2. The GCF is -3.

$$-3y^2 + 15y - 6 = -3(y^2) - 3(-5y) - 3(2)$$
$$= -3(y^2 - 5y + 2)$$

EXAMPLE 5   **Factoring a Polynomial in Two Variables**

Factor: $27x^5y^3 - 9x^4y^4 + 81x^3y^2$

Solution

The greatest common factor for 27, -9, and 81 is 9. Since each term contains an x raised to a power, the GCF has a factor of x^3, the smallest power that appears in all the terms. Similarly, the GCF has a factor of y^2, since 2 is the smallest power of y in all the terms. Thus, the GCF is $9x^3y^2$. We factor as follows:

$$27x^5y^3 - 9x^4y^4 + 81x^3y^2$$
$$= 9x^3y^2 \cdot 3x^2y - 9x^3y^2 \cdot xy^2 + 9x^3y^2 \cdot 9 \qquad \text{Factor each monomial.}$$
$$= 9x^3y^2(3x^2y - xy^2 + 9) \qquad\qquad\qquad \text{Factor out } 9x^3y^2, \text{ the GCF.}$$

Check this factorization by multiplying.

3 Factor by grouping.

Factoring by Grouping

There are cases when the GCF of a polynomial is a binomial. For example, the polynomial

$$x^2(x - 5) + 7(x - 5)$$

has the common binomial factor $(x - 5)$. Factoring out this common factor results in

$$x^2(x - 5) + 7(x - 5) = (x - 5)x^2 + (x - 5)7$$
$$= (x - 5)(x^2 + 7) \qquad \text{Factor out the common factor, } (x - 5).$$

ENRICHMENT ESSAY

Factors: Friendly Numbers

The Greek mathematician Pythagoras regarded two numbers as *friendly* if each was the sum of the other's factors, excluding the numbers themselves. The Greeks knew of only one such pair, 220 and 284. Factors of 220 have a sum of 284:

$$1 + 2 + 4 + 5 + 10 + 11 + 20 + 22 + 44 + 55 + 110 = 284$$

and factors of 284 have a sum of 220:

$$1 + 2 + 4 + 71 + 142 = 220.$$

In 1636, the French mathematician Pierre de Fermat discovered a second pair of friendly numbers, 17,296 and 18,416. By the middle of the nineteenth century, the number of known pairs of friendly numbers exceeded 60. Incredibly, the second-lowest pair of all had gone undiscovered. In 1867, a 16-year-old Italian, Nicolo Paganini demonstrated that 1184 and 1210 are friendly.

There are unanswered questions associated with friendly numbers. All known friendly pairs consist of either two odd or two even numbers. Are pairs consisting of an odd and an even number possible? Why are all the odd friendly numbers multiples of 3?

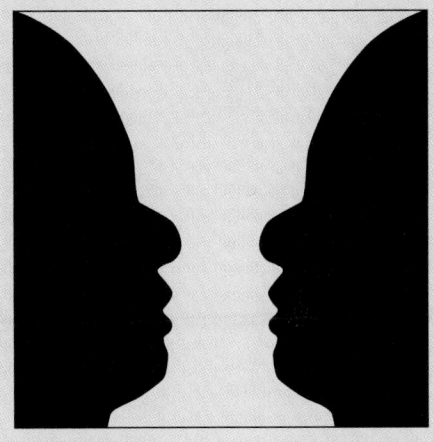

EXAMPLE 6   **Factoring Out Common Binomial Factors**

Factor:

a. $3x^2(5x - 1) - 4(5x - 1)$ **b.** $7x(5x - 3) + (5x - 3)$

Solution

a. Each term of the polynomial has a binomial factor of $(5x - 1)$.

$3x^2(5x - 1) - 4(5x - 1)$
$= (5x - 1)(3x^2 - 4)$ Factor $(5x - 1)$ out of each term.

b. $7x(5x - 3) + (5x - 3)$
$= 7x(5x - 3) + 1(5x - 3)$ The binomial factor of $(5x - 3)$ is common to each term.

$= (5x - 3)(7x + 1)$ When $(5x - 3)$ is factored from itself, we are left with 1.

Study tip

In Example 6b, don't forget the term 1 in the final factorization. We express $5x - 3$ as $1(5x - 3)$ so that we can factor out the GCF $(5x - 3)$.

In Example 6, the polynomials are grouped in such a way that the common binomial factor is obvious. When polynomial expressions contain four (or more) terms, we must do the grouping as well as the factoring. This procedure is explained in the next example.

EXAMPLE 7   **Factoring by Grouping**

Factor: $x^3 - 3x^2 + 2x - 6$

Solution

There is no factor other than 1 common to all terms. However, we can factor $x^3 - 3x^2$ and $2x - 6$ separately:

$$x^3 - 3x^2 = x^2(x - 3) \qquad 2x - 6 = 2(x - 3)$$

We now see that $x^3 - 3x^2$ and $2x - 6$ share a common binomial factor of $x - 3$. We factor out that common factor to obtain a factorization of the original polynomial.

$$x^3 - 3x^2 + 2x - 6$$
$$= (x^3 - 3x^2) + (2x - 6) \quad \text{Group the terms with common factors.}$$
$$= x^2(x - 3) + 2(x - 3) \quad \text{Factor from each group.}$$
$$= (x - 3)(x^2 + 2) \quad \text{Factor out the common binomial factor.}$$

Multiply $(x - 3)$ and $(x^2 + 2)$ using the FOIL method to verify that these are the correct factors. ■

Discover for yourself

Group Example 7 as

$$(x^3 + 2x) + (-3x^2 - 6).$$

Use this grouping to factor the polynomial. Do you get the same answer as the one in Example 7? Explain.

Factoring by grouping

1. Group terms that have a common monomial factor. There will usually be two groups. Sometimes the terms must be rearranged.
2. Factor out the common monomial factor from each group.
3. Factor out the remaining binomial factor (if one exists).

EXAMPLE 8   Factoring by Grouping

Factor: $15x^5 - 12 + 9x^2 - 20x^3$

Solution

The key to factoring by grouping is to look for terms with common factors. Let's see what happens if we factor the first two terms and then the last two terms separately.

$$15x^5 - 12 = 3(x^5 - 4) \qquad 9x^2 - 20x^3 = x^2(9 - 20x)$$

The problem with this grouping is that $15x^5 - 12$ and $9x^2 - 20x^3$ do not share a common factor, so further factorization is impossible. We need to try another grouping.

Let's try grouping the two terms with the highest powers of x, $15x^5 - 20x^3$, since they share a common factor of $5x^3$. Then we'll group the other two terms.

$$15x^5 - 20x^3 = 5x^3(3x^2 - 4) \qquad 9x^2 - 12 = 3(3x^2 - 4)$$

This grouping is more successful because $15x^5 - 20x^3$ and $9x^2 - 12$ share a common binomial factor of $(3x^2 - 4)$. We can factor out that common factor to obtain a factorization of the original polynomial.

$$15x^5 - 12 + 9x^2 - 20x^3$$
$$= (15x^5 - 20x^3) + (9x^2 - 12) \quad \text{Rearrange terms and group the terms with common factors.}$$
$$= 5x^3(3x^2 - 4) + 3(3x^2 - 4) \quad \text{Factor from each group.}$$
$$= (3x^2 - 4)(5x^3 + 3) \quad \text{Factor out the common binomial factor.}$$

Discover for yourself

Try Example 8 using this grouping:

$$(15x^5 + 9x^2) + (-20x^3 - 12).$$

Should you factor 4 or -4 from the second grouping? Try it both ways if necessary, but remember that you want a common binomial factor. Is your final factorization the same as Example 8?

Multiply $(3x^2 - 4)$ and $(5x^3 + 3)$ using the FOIL method to verify that these are the correct factors. ∎

PROBLEM SET 7.1

Practice Problems

In Problems 1–6, find three factorizations for each monomial.

1. $8x^3$ **2.** $20x^4$ **3.** $-12x^5$ **4.** $-15x^6$ **5.** $36x^4$ **6.** $27x^5$

Factor each expression in Problems 7–48 by factoring out the greatest common monomial factor. (Some of the expressions have no common factor other than 1.)

7. $5x + 5$ **8.** $7y + 7$ **9.** $3z - 3$ **10.** $6y - 6$

11. $8x + 16$ **12.** $3y + 12$ **13.** $25x - 10$ **14.** $14x - 7$

15. $y^2 + y$ **16.** $b^2 - b$ **17.** $18x^2 - 24$ **18.** $7y^3 + 21$

19. $25y^2 - 13y$ **20.** $30x^3 - 11x$ **21.** $36x^3 + 24x^2$ **22.** $6x^3 + 2x^2$

23. $27y^6 + 9y^4$ **24.** $15x^7 + 5x^5$ **25.** $8x^2 - 4x^4$ **26.** $11x^2 - 93$

27. $12x^2 - 13y^3$ **28.** $12x^3 - 17y^2$ **29.** $12y^2 + 16y - 8$ **30.** $15x^2 - 3x + 9$

31. $100 + 75y - 50y^2$ **32.** $42x^3 - 21x^2 + 7$ **33.** $9y^4 + 18y^3 + 6y^2$ **34.** $32x^5 - 2x^3 + 6x$

35. $100y^5 - 50y^3 + 100y^2$ **36.** $26x^6 + 13x^5 - 39x^3$ **37.** $10x - 20x^2 + 5x^3$ **38.** $6y^2 - 4y^3 + 2y^4$

39. $-2y^2 - 3y^3 + 6y^5$ **40.** $-7y^3 + 3y^4 - 2y^5$

41. $6x^3y^2 + 9xy$ **42.** $16x^5y^3 - 32xy$ **43.** $30x^3y^2 - 10x^3y + 20x^2y$

44. $27x^5y^2 - 18x^2y^3 + 45x^2y$ **45.** $16a^5b^3 - 48a^4b^4 + 8a^3b^2 - 56a^3b^3$

46. $12a^4b^3 - 15a^3b^3 - 3a^2b + 6a^2b^2$ **47.** $54a^2b^3c - 6a^2b^2c^2 + 12abc$

48. $20a^3b^2c - 4a^2b^2c + 12abc^2$

Factor each polynomial in Problems 49–60 first by using a positive sign on the greatest common factor and then by using a negative sign on the GCF.

49. $-2x^2 + 8x - 10$ **50.** $-4x^2 - 12x + 16$ **51.** $3a - 15$ **52.** $-5x + 15$

53. $-4x + 12x^2$ **54.** $-2x + 6x^2$ **55.** $-y^3 + 7y^2$ **56.** $-3x^4 + 6x^3$

57. $y^2 + y$ **58.** $-2y^2 - 10y$ **59.** $3 - x$ **60.** $7 - y$

Factor each expression in Problems 61–72 by factoring out the greatest common binomial factor.

61. $x(x + 5) + 3(x + 5)$ **62.** $x(2x + 1) + 4(2x + 1)$ **63.** $7x(x - 3) - 4(x - 3)$

64. $2x(x - 6) - 7(x - 6)$ **65.** $3x(2x + 5) + 2x + 5$ **66.** $4x(3x + 1) + 3x + 1$

67. $x^2(x + 7) + 2(x + 7)$ **68.** $3x^2(2x + 1) - 5(2x + 1)$ **69.** $4x^2(3x^3 + 2) - 7(3x^3 + 2)$

70. $5x^2(3x^3 - 4) - 3(3x^3 - 4)$ **71.** $y^2(y + 7) + y + 7$ **72.** $y^2(y - 7) + y - 7$

Factor Problems 73–84 by grouping.

73. $x^3 - 3x^2 + 2x - 6$ **74.** $x^3 + 2x^2 - 4x - 8$ **75.** $3x^3 + 6x^2 + 2x + 4$

76. $x^3 + 2x^2 + x + 2$ **77.** $x^3 + 5x^2 + x + 5$ **78.** $8y^3 - 12y^2 + 6y - 9$

79. $10y^3 - 25y^2 + 4y - 10$ **80.** $2y^3 + 12y^2 - 5y - 30$ **81.** $y^3 + 8y^2 - 3y - 24$

82. $12x^5 + 20x^2 - 21x^3 - 35$ **83.** $8y^5 + 12y^2 - 10y^3 - 15$ **84.** $2y^3 + 6y^2 + y + 3$

Application Problems

85. A rectangular painting with a width of x inches has an area of $44x + x^2$ square inches. Find a binomial that represents the length.

Area $= 44x + x^2$

86. The surface area of a right circular cylinder is given by the polynomial $2\pi rh + 2\pi r^2$, where h is the height and r is the radius of the base. Rewrite the polynomial by factoring out its greatest common factor.

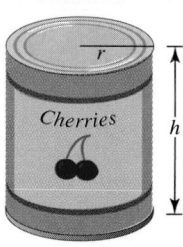

87. The amount after t years when a principal of P dollars is invested at simple interest rate r is given by $P + Prt$. Rewrite the expression by factoring out the greatest common factor.

88. Find the length of the rectangle in the figure.

Area $= x^2 + 3x + 6x + 18$

True–False Critical Thinking Problems

89. Which one of the following is true?
  a. Since a monomial contains one term, it follows that a monomial can be factored in precisely one way.
  b. The GCF for $8x^3 - 16x^2$ is $8x$.
  c. The integers 10 and 31 have no GCF.
  d. $-4x^2 + 12x$ can be factored as $-4x(x - 3)$.

90. Which one of the following is true?
  a. If all terms of a polynomial contain the same letter raised to different powers, the exponent on the variable that you will factor out is the highest power that appears in all the terms.
  b. Since the GCF of $9x^3 + 6x^2 + 3x$ is $3x$, it is not necessary to write 1 when $3x$ is factored from the last term.

  c. The area of the shaded region in the figure is $\pi b^2 - \frac{1}{2}bh = b(\pi b - \frac{1}{2}h)$.

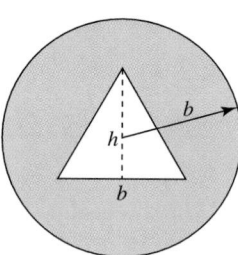

  d. Different groupings of the terms in a polynomial can result in a different factoring for the polynomial.

Technology Problems

In Problems 91–94, use a graphing utility to graph the function on the left side and the function on the right side in the same viewing rectangle. Are the graphs identical? If so, this means that the polynomial on the left side has been correctly factored. If not, factor the polynomial correctly and then use your graphing utility to verify the factorization.

91. $x^2 - 2x + 5x - 10 = (x - 2)(x - 5)$

92. $x^3 - 2x^2 + x - 2 = (x - 2)(x^2 + 1)$

93. $-3x - 6 = -3(x - 2)$

94. $x^5 + 2x^2 - x^3 - 2 = (x^3 - 2)(x^2 + 1)$

Writing in Mathematics

95. Describe what happens if you factor $4x$ rather than the greatest common factor $4x^2$ from $8x^3 - 12x^2$.

96. Explain how to check the result of a factoring problem.

97. Write a polynomial containing two terms that can be factored by factoring out the GCF. Explain how you constructed this polynomial.

98. Write a polynomial containing four terms that can be factored by grouping. Explain how you constructed this polynomial.

99. Write a sentence that uses the word *factor* as a noun. Then write a sentence that uses the word *factor* as a verb.

Critical Thinking Problems

100. Factor: $2x^2 + 4x + 6 + x^2 + 2x + 3$.

Write an expression for the shaded area in each figure in Problems 101–103, and then factor each expression.

101.

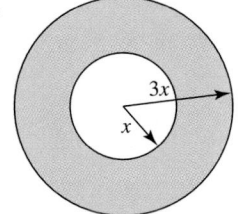

102.

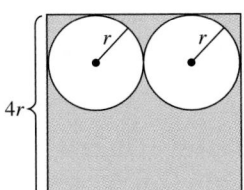

103.

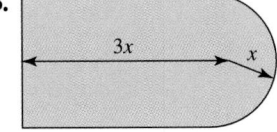

Group Activity Problem

104. a. Can every polynomial containing four terms be factored by grouping? Group members should attempt to answer this question by writing some four-term polynomials at random and attempt factoring by grouping.

   b. In your group, devise a method for creating four-term polynomials that can be factored by group-

ing. After some experimentation, group members should describe the method.

   c. Divide the group in half. Half the group should create four-term polynomials that can be factored by grouping. Then give these polynomials to the members in the other half of the group to factor.

Review Problems

105. A person invested money at 6% and 8% simple interest, investing $350 more at 6% than at 8%. If the annual interest income on the two investments is $147, how much was invested at each rate?

106. Solve the system by graphing:

$$2x - y = -4$$
$$x - 3y = 3$$

107. Write the point-slope form of a line passing through $(-7, 2)$ and $(-4, 5)$. Then use the point-slope equation to write the slope-intercept equation.

S E C T I O N   7 . 2

Solutions   Tutorial   Video
Manual   8

Factor trinomials of the
form $x^2 + bx + c$.

Factoring Trinomials Whose Leading Coefficient is 1

Objective

1 Factor trinomials of the form $x^2 + bx + c$.

In this section we concentrate on factoring trinomials in the form $x^2 + bx + c$, whose leading coefficient is 1. In the next section, we will study factoring methods for $ax^2 + bx + c$, where a is not equal to 1.

In Section 6.3, we used the FOIL method to multiply two binomials. The product was often a trinomial. Below are some examples.

Factored Form	F	O	I	L	Trinomial Form

$$(x + 3)(x + 4) = x^2 + 4x + 3x + 12 = x^2 + 7x + 12$$
$$(x - 3)(x - 4) = x^2 - 4x - 3x + 12 = x^2 - 7x + 12$$
$$(x + 3)(x - 5) = x^2 - 5x + 3x - 15 = x^2 - 2x - 15$$

Observe that each trinomial is of the form $x^2 + bx + c$, where the coefficient of the squared term is 1. Our goal in this section is to start with the trinomial form and, assuming that it is factorable, return to the factored form.

Let's start by multiplying $(x + 3)(x + 4)$ using the FOIL method to obtain $x^2 + 7x + 12$.

$$(x + 3)(x + 4) = x^2 + 7x + 12$$

Now, there are several important observations that we can make:

1. The first term of $x^2 + 7x + 12$ is the product $x \cdot x = x^2$.
2. The coefficient of the middle term $7x$ is the sum $3 + 4 = 7$.
3. The last term 12 is the product $3 \cdot 4 = 12$.

Using these results involving the sum and product of 3 and 4, we can generalize a procedure for factoring $x^2 + bx + c$.

> **Factoring $x^2 + bx + c$**
>
> **1.** List all pairs of integers whose product is c.
> **2.** Choose the pair m and n whose sum is $m + n = b$.
> **3.** The factorization of $x^2 + bx + c$ is
>
> $$x^2 + bx + c = (x + m)(x + n).$$
>
> **4.** If there are no such integers m and n such that $m + n = b$, the trinomial cannot be factored and is called *prime*.

Factoring $x^2 + bx + c$ Where c is Positive

EXAMPLE 1 **Factoring a Trinomial with All Terms Positive**

Factor: $x^2 + 6x + 8$

Using technology

A graphing utility can be used to check factorizations. For example, graph

$$y_1 = x^2 + 6x + 8$$

and

$$y_2 = (x + 4)(x + 2)$$

on the same screen, as shown below. The graphs are identical, so we can conclude that

$$x^2 + 6x + 8$$
$$= (x + 4)(x + 2).$$

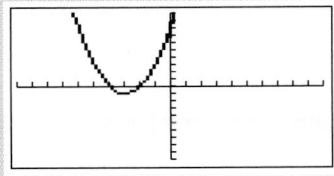

Solution

$$x^2 + 6x + 8 = (x + m)(x + n) \quad \begin{array}{l} m = ? \\ n = ? \end{array}$$

To find the factors, we must find two integers m and n whose product is 8 and whose sum is 6. We try all positive and negative integers whose product is 8.

Pairs of Factors of 8	Sums of Factors
(8)(1)	$8 + 1 = 9$
(4)(2)	$4 + 2 = 6$ ←
(−8)(−1)	$-8 + (-1) = -9$
(−4)(−2)	$-4 + (-2) = -6$

The factors whose sum is 6 are 4 and 2.

From the list, we see that 4 and 2 are the required integers. Since the sum is 6, we need not list $(-8)(-1)$ or $(-4)(-2)$. When all signs are positive, only positive integers are needed. Thus,

$$x^2 + 6x + 8 = (x + 4)(x + 2).$$

We can verify this result by multiplying the right side using the FOIL method to obtain the original trinomial. Because of the commutative property, we can also say that

$$x^2 + 6x + 8 = (x + 2)(x + 4). \qquad ■$$

Study tip

It is possible to construct geometric models for factorizations so that you can see the factoring. For example,

here's a model for $x^2 + 3x + 2$.　　　　Now here's a model for $(x + 1)(x + 2)$.

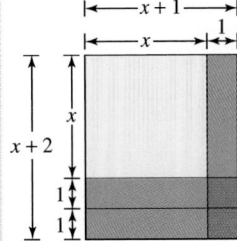

The pieces in both models are the same, so
$$x^2 + 3x + 2$$
$$= (x + 1)(x + 2).$$

EXAMPLE 2	**Factoring a Trinomial with a Negative Middle Term**

Factor: $y^2 - 10y + 24$

Solution

$$y^2 - 10y + 24 = (y + m)(y + n) \quad \begin{matrix} m = ? \\ n = ? \end{matrix}$$

To find the factors, we must find two integers m and n whose product is 24 and whose sum is -10.

Pairs of Factors of 24	Sums of Factors
(8)(3)	$8 + 3 = 11$
(−8)(−3)	$-8 + (-3) = -11$
(6)(4)	$6 + 4 = 10$
(−6)(−4)	$-6 + (-4) = -10$
(24)(1)	$24 + 1 = 25$
(−24)(−1)	$-24 + (-1) = -25$

The factors whose sum is -10 are -6 and -4.

From the list, we see that -6 and -4 are the required integers. Thus,

$$y^2 - 10y + 24 = (y - 6)(y - 4)$$

Verify this result using the FOIL method.   ■

Factoring $x^2 + bx + c$ Where c is Negative

EXAMPLE 3	**Factoring a Trinomial with a Negative Constant Term**

Factor: $y^2 + 2y - 35$

Solution

$$y^2 + 2y - 35 = (y + m)(y + n) \quad \begin{matrix} m = ? \\ n = ? \end{matrix}$$

To find the factors, we must find two integers m and n whose product is -35 and whose sum is 2. Since c is negative, we consider only factors that have opposite signs.

Pairs of Factors of −35	Sums of Factors
(−1)(35)	$-1 + 35 = 34$
(1)(−35)	$1 + (-35) = -34$
(−7)(5)	$-7 + 5 = -2$
(7)(−5)	$7 + (-5) = 2$

The factors whose sum is 2 are 7 and -5.

Thus,

$$y^2 + 2y - 35 = (y + 7)(y - 5).$$ ■

EXAMPLE 4 **Factoring a Trinomial with Two Negative Terms**

Factor: $t^2 - 2t - 99$.

Solution

$$t^2 - 2t - 99 = (t + m)(t + n) \quad \begin{array}{l} m = ? \\ n = ? \end{array}$$

To find the factors, we must find two integers m and n whose product is -99 and whose sum is -2.

Pairs of Factors of -99	Sums of Factors
$(-1)(99)$	$-1 + 99 = 98$
$(1)(-99)$	$1 + (-99) = -98$
$(-11)(9)$	$-11 + 9 = -2$ ← The factors whose
$(11)(-9)$	$11 + (-9) = 2$ sum is -2 are
$(-3)(33)$	$-3 + 33 = 30$ -11 and 9.
$(3)(-33)$	$3 + (-33) = -30$

Thus,

$$t^2 - 2t - 99 = (t - 11)(t + 9).$$ ∎

D **iscover for yourself**

Look at the two factorizations that appear in the Study Tip. What is the relationship between the number with the larger absolute value in the factors and the coefficient of the middle term in the given polynomial?

Let's summarize what we have learned so far about factoring trinomials in the form $x^2 + bx + c$.

Factoring $x^2 + bx + c$

1. Find two integers m and n whose product is c and whose sum is b. If $mn = c$ and $m + n = b$, then

$$x^2 + bx + c = (x + m)(x + n) \quad \text{or} \quad (x + n)(x + m).$$

2. If $b > 0$ and $c > 0$, m and n must be positive.
3. If $b < 0$ and $c > 0$, m and n must be negative.
4. If $c < 0$, m and n must have opposite signs.

Prime Polynomials

Not all trinomials are factorable using integer factors. A polynomial that is not factorable using integers is called a *prime polynomial.*

EXAMPLE 5 **A Trinomial That Cannot Be Factored**

Factor: $x^2 + x - 5$

Solution

$$x^2 + x - 5 = (x + m)(x + n)$$

To find the factors, we must find two integers m and n whose product is -5 and whose sum is 1.

Pairs of Factors of -5	Sum of Factors
$(1)(-5)$	$1 + (-5) = -4$
$(-1)(5)$	$-1 + 5 = 4$

Since no pair has a sum of 1, $x^2 + x - 5$ cannot be factored using only integer factors. This trinomial is a *prime polynomial*. ∎

Factoring Completely

If it is possible, we should first factor out a common monomial factor from a polynomial and then factor the resulting trinomial by the methods in this section. A polynomial is *factored completely* when it is written as the product of prime polynomials.

EXAMPLE 6 **Factoring a Trinomial with a GCF**

Factor completely: $3x^2 - 18x + 15$

Solution

The trinomial has a common monomial factor of 3. We begin by factoring 3 out of each term.

$$\begin{aligned} 3x^2 - 18x + 15 &= 3(x^2 - 6x + 5) && \text{Factor out 3, the GCF.} \\ &= 3(x + m)(x + n) && \text{Find two integers } m \text{ and } n \text{ whose product is 5} \\ & && \text{and whose sum is } -6. \\ &= 3(x - 5)(x - 1) && \text{The integers are } -5 \text{ and } -1. \end{aligned}$$ ∎

EXAMPLE 7 **Factoring a Trinomial with a GCF**

Factor completely: $3y^3 - 15y^2 - 42y$

Solution

The trinomial has a common monomial factor of $3y$. We begin by factoring $3y$ out of each term.

$$\begin{aligned} 3y^3 - 15y^2 - 42y &= 3y(y^2 - 5y - 14) && \text{Factor out } 3y, \text{ the GCF.} \\ &= 3y(y + m)(y + n) && \text{Find two integers } m \text{ and } n \text{ whose product} \\ & && \text{is } -14 \text{ and whose sum is } -5. \\ &= 3y(y - 7)(y + 2) && \text{The integers are } -7 \text{ and 2.} \end{aligned}$$ ∎

Discover for yourself

Write two trinomials that are prime. Explain how you obtained these trinomials and also explain why they cannot be factored.

Using technology

Check Example 7 using a graphing utility. Graph

$$y_1 = 3x^3 - 15x^2 - 42x$$

and

$$y_2 = 3x(x - 7)(x + 2)$$

on the same screen. Identical graphs result, so

$$3x^3 - 15x^2 - 42x$$
$$= 3x(x - 7)(x + 2)$$

(Because polynomial functions have smooth, continuous graphs, we experimented with the range setting so that the graph would not be cut off. We used

Xmin = −10, Xmax = 10, Xscl = 1, Ymin = −250, Ymax = 100, Yscl = 20.)

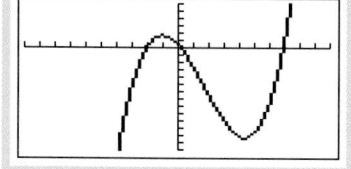

Factoring Polynomials in Several Variables

The method for factoring trinomials whose leading coefficient is 1 can be applied to trinomials in two or more variables, such as $a^2 + 3ab - 18b^2$.

EXAMPLE 8 Factoring a Trinomial in Two Variables

Factor: $a^2 + 3ab - 18b^2$

Solution

We must include the variable b with the factors. The form of the factorization is

$$a^2 + 3ab - 18b^2 = (a + mb)(a + nb).$$

Now we must find two integers m and n whose product is -18 and whose sum is 3. The integers are 6 and -3. Thus,

$$a^2 + 3ab - 18b^2 = (a + 6b)(a - 3b).$$ ■

PROBLEM SET 7.2

Practice Problems _____

Find the missing factor in Problems 1–12. Then check your answer by multiplying the factors using the FOIL method.

1. $x^2 + 3x + 2 = (x + 2)(\quad)$ **2.** $x^2 + 5x + 6 = (x + 3)(\quad)$ **3.** $y^2 + y - 6 = (y + 3)(\quad)$
4. $y^2 - y - 2 = (y + 1)(\quad)$ **5.** $x^2 + x - 12 = (x - 3)(\quad)$ **6.** $x^2 - 2x - 35 = (x - 7)(\quad)$
7. $y^2 - 5y + 4 = (y - 1)(\quad)$ **8.** $y^2 - 3y + 2 = (y - 2)(\quad)$ **9.** $y^2 - 2y - 3 = (y + 1)(\quad)$
10. $y^2 + y - 2 = (y + 2)(\quad)$ **11.** $r^2 - 6r + 8 = (r - 2)(\quad)$ **12.** $r^2 - 21r + 54 = (r - 3)(\quad)$

Factor the trinomials in Problems 13–56, or state that the trinomial is prime. Check your factorization using FOIL multiplication or with a graphing utility.

13. $x^2 + 5x + 6$ **14.** $x^2 + 8x + 15$ **15.** $r^2 + 13r + 12$ **16.** $r^2 + 8r + 12$
17. $x^2 + 9x + 8$ **18.** $x^2 + 5x + 6$ **19.** $y^2 - 2y - 15$ **20.** $y^2 - 4y - 5$
21. $x^2 - 5x - 6$ **22.** $x^2 - 8x + 15$ **23.** $y^2 - 14y + 45$ **24.** $y^2 - 14y + 49$
25. $r^2 + 12r + 27$ **26.** $r^2 - 6r + 8$ **27.** $n^2 - 11n - 42$ **28.** $n^2 + 9n - 70$
29. $y^2 - 9y - 36$ **30.** $y^2 - y - 90$ **31.** $x^2 + 10x - 75$ **32.** $x^2 + 21x - 100$
33. $x^2 - 8x + 32$ **34.** $x^2 - 9x + 81$ **35.** $y^2 + 30y + 200$ **36.** $y^2 - 10y - 200$
37. $x^2 - 6x + 8$ **38.** $x^2 - 2x - 8$ **39.** $r^2 + 17r + 16$ **40.** $r^2 - 15r - 16$
41. $m^2 - 15m + 36$ **42.** $m^2 - 21m + 54$ **43.** $y^2 + y - 56$ **44.** $y^2 - 7y - 44$
45. $r^2 + 4r + 12$ **46.** $r^2 + 4r + 5$ **47.** $y^2 - 4y - 21$ **48.** $y^2 + 16y + 39$
49. $x^2 + 8x - 105$ **50.** $x^2 - 22x + 72$ **51.** $r^2 + 27r + 72$ **52.** $y^2 - 29y + 100$
53. $a^2 + 5ab + 6b^2$ **54.** $a^2 + 9ab + 8b^2$ **55.** $x^2 + 5xy - 24y^2$ **56.** $x^2 + 4xy - 21y^2$

Factor Problems 57–84 completely.

57. $3x^2 + 15x + 18$

58. $20x^2 + 100x + 40$

59. $4y^2 - 4y - 8$

60. $3y^2 + 3y - 18$

61. $10x^2 - 40x - 600$

62. $2x^2 + 10x - 48$

63. $3x^2 - 33x + 54$

64. $2x^2 - 14x + 24$

65. $2r^3 + 6r^2 + 4r$

66. $2r^3 - 14^2 + 24r$

67. $4x^3 + 12x^2 - 72x$

68. $3x^3 - 15x^2 + 18x$

69. $2r^3 + 8r^2 - 64r$

70. $3r^3 - 9r^2 - 54r$

71. $y^4 + 2y^3 - 80y^2$

72. $y^4 - 12y^3 + 35y^2$

73. $x^4 - 3x^3 - 10x^2$

74. $x^4 - 22x^3 + 120x^2$

75. $2w^4 - 26w^3 - 96w^2$

76. $3w^4 + 54w^3 + 135w^2$

77. $-2x^2 + 14x - 24$

78. $-4x^2 - 12x + 16$

79. $-x^3 - 11x^2 + 42x$

80. $-x^3 + 3x^2 + 18x$

81. $2x^2 - 10xy - 28y^2$

82. $3x^2 - 18xy + 24y^2$

83. $x^3 + 8x^2y + 15xy^2$

84. $x^3 - 4x^2y + 4xy^2$

Application Problems

85. A rectangular deck has an area represented by $x^2 + 3x - 10$ square meters and a length represented by $x + 5$ meters. Find a binomial that represents the width.

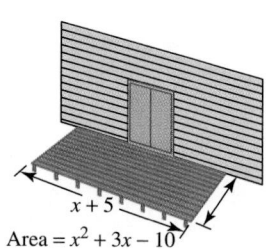

$x + 5$

Area $= x^2 + 3x - 10$

86. What are the dimensions of the solid shown in the figure if the factors of the volume are the dimensions?

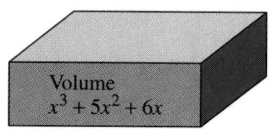

Volume
$x^3 + 5x^2 + 6x$

True–False Critical Thinking Problems

87. Which one of the following is true?
  a. A factor of $x^2 - 8x - 9$ is $x + 9$.
  b. A factor of $x^2 - 10x + 9$ is $x - 1$.
  c. A factor of $x^2 + x + 1$ is $x + 1$.
  d. $y^2 + 1 = (y + 1)(y + 1)$

88. Which one of the following is true?
  a. A factor of $x^2 + x + 20$ is $x + 5$.
  b. A trinomial can never have two identical factors.
  c. A factor of $y^2 + 5y - 24$ is $y - 3$.
  d. $x^2 + 4 = (x + 2)(x + 2)$

89. Which factoring solution is correct?
  a. $y^2 - 3y - 2 = (y \quad)(y \quad)$
    $= (y \quad 2)(y \quad 1)$
    $= (y - 2)(y - 1)$
  b. $y^2 - 3y - 2 = y^2 - 2y - y - 2$
    $= y(y - 2) - 1(y - 1)$
    $= (y - 2)(y - 1)$
  c. $y^2 - 3y - 2 = y^2 - y - 2y - 2$
    $= y(y - 1) - 2(y - 1)$
    $= (y - 1)(y - 2)$
  d. None of these are correct.

Technology Problems

In Problems 90–93, use a graphing utility to graph the function on the left side and the function on the right side in the same viewing rectangle. Are the graphs identical? If so, this means that the polynomial on the left side has been correctly factored. If not, factor the trinomial correctly and then use your graphing utility to verify the factorization.

90. $x^2 - 5x + 6 = (x - 2)(x - 3)$

91. $2x^2 + 2x - 12 = 2(x - 3)(x + 2)$

92. $x^3 - 6x^2 + 8x = x(x - 4)(x - 2)$

93. $x^3 - x^2 - 2x = x(x - 1)(x + 2)$

Writing in Mathematics

94. What helpful suggestions can you give for factoring $x^2 - 5x + 6$ using the FOIL method?

95. In factoring $x^2 + bx + c$, describe how the last terms in each factor are related to b and c.

Without actually factoring and without multiplying the given factors, explain why the factorizations in Problems 96–97 cannot be correct.

96. $x^2 + 46x + 513 = (x - 27)(x - 19)$

97. $x^3 + x^2 - 20x = x^2(x - 4)(x + 5)$

Critical Thinking Problems

98. A box with no top is to be made from an 8-inch by 6-inch piece of metal by cutting identical squares from each corner and turning up the sides (see the figure). The volume of the box is modeled by the polynomial $4x^3 - 28x^2 + 48x$. Factor the polynomial completely. Then use the factored form to explain how the model was obtained.

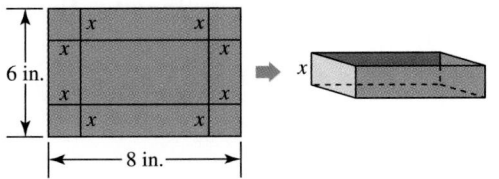

99. If the area of the large rectangle in the figure is represented by $x^2 + 7x + 12$, what is the area of the shaded region?

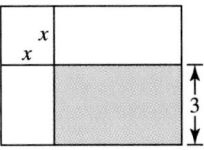

100. Draw a geometric model for factoring $x^2 + 4x + 3$ similar to the one shown in the Study Tip on page 505.

Find all integers b or c in Problems 101–103 so that the trinomial can be factored.

101. $x^2 + bx + 15$

102. $y^2 + by + 10$

103. $x^2 + 4x + c$

Factor the polynomials in Problems 104–105.

104. $x^{2a} + 20x^a + 99$

105. $x^2 - \frac{10}{3}x - \frac{8}{3}$

Review Problems

106. The U.S. population in 1960 was 179.5 million. If the population is increasing at 2.35 million per year, in what year will the population reach 282.9 million?

107. Multiply using the FOIL method: $(4y + 1)(2y - 3)$.

108. Multiply using the FOIL method: $(3x + 4)(3x + 1)$.

SECTION 7.3

Solutions Manual

Tutorial

Video 8

Factoring Trinomials Whose Leading Coefficient is Not I

Objectives

1 Factor trinomials by trial and error.
2 Factor trinomials by grouping.

In this section, we concentrate on factoring a trinomial whose leading coefficient is not 1. Examples of trinomials of the form $ax^2 + bx + c$, with $a \neq 1$, are

$$9x^2 + 15x + 4 \quad a = 9, b = 15, c = 4$$
$$2x^2 + 17x + 35 \quad a = 2, b = 17, c = 35$$

Factor trinomials by trial and error.

Factoring by the Trial-and-Error Method

The process of factoring these trinomials is similar to that discussed in the previous section, but it involves more trial and error. For example, to factor $9x^2 + 15x + 4$, we proceed by steps.

Step 1. We must find two factors such that the product of the two first terms is $9x^2$. The possibilities include

$$9x^2 + 15x + 4 \overset{?}{=} (9x + ?)(x + ?)$$
$$9x^2 + 15x + 4 \overset{?}{=} (3x + ?)(3x + ?)$$

Step 2. The product of the last two terms in each factor must be 4. Since the middle term, $15x$, is positive, the factors of 4 must be positive. Possible pairs of factors of 4 are 4 and 1 or 2 and 2.

Step 3. We first write the factors of 4 with the factors $9x$ and x. Then we write the factors of 4 with the factors $3x$ and $3x$. Determine the middle term of each product using the FOIL method.

Factors of 4	Possible Factors of $9x^2 + 15x + 4$	Sum of Outside and Inside Terms (should equal $15x$)	
4, 1	$(9x + 4)(x + 1)$	$9x + 4x = 13x$	
1, 4	$(9x + 1)(x + 4)$	$36x + x = 37x$	
2, 2	$(9x + 2)(x + 2)$	$18x + 2x = 20x$	
4, 1	$(3x + 4)(3x + 1)$	$3x + 12x = 15x$	This is the required middle term.
2, 2	$(3x + 2)(3x + 2)$	$6x + 6x = 12x$	

Since $(3x + 4)(3x + 1)$ gives the correct middle term,

$$9x^2 + 15x + 4 = (3x + 4)(3x + 1) \quad \text{or} \quad (3x + 1)(3x + 4).$$

Factoring $ax^2 + bx + c$ using trial and error

The general pattern of the factorization is

$$\overset{\lceil \text{Factors of } a \rceil}{\underset{\lfloor \text{Factors of } c \rfloor}{ax^2 + bx + c = (\Box x + \Box)(\Box x + \Box).}}$$

1. Find all the factors of the first term ax^2.
2. Find all the factors of the last term c.
3. Combine the factors in such a way that using the FOIL method gives the sum of the outside and inside products as bx.

This factoring technique uses FOIL backward and can involve quite a bit of trial and error.

EXAMPLE 1   Factoring a Trinomial by Trial and Error

Factor: $3x^2 - 20x + 28$

Solution

Step 1. We must find two factors such that the product of the first two terms is $3x^2$. There is only one possibility.

$$3x^2 - 20x + 28 = (3x \quad)(x \quad)$$

Step 2. The product of the last two terms in each factor must be 28. Since the middle term, $-20x$, is negative, both factors of 28 must be negative. Possibilities include

$$(-1)(-28) \quad (-2)(-14) \quad \text{and} \quad (-4)(-7)$$

Step 3. The sum of the outside and inside products of the correct factorization must equal $-20x$, the middle term of $3x^2 - 20x + 28$.

Possible Factors of $3x^2 - 20x + 28$	Sum of Outside and Inside Products (Should Equal $-20x$)	
$(3x - 1)(x - 28)$	$-84x - \quad x = -85x$	
$(3x - 28)(x - 1)$	$-3x - 28x = -31x$	
$(3x - 2)(x - 14)$	$-42x - \quad 2x = -44x$	
$(3x - 14)(x - 2)$	$-6x - 14x = -20x$	This is the required middle term.

Since we have found the correct factorization, it is not necessary to list other possible factors, but for the sake of completeness, they are $(3x - 4)(x - 7)$ and $(3x - 7)(x - 4)$. Therefore, the correct factorization is

$$3x^2 - 20x + 28 = (3x - 14)(x - 2) \quad \text{or} \quad (x - 2)(3x - 14). \quad \blacksquare$$

Factoring $ax^2 + bx + c$ involves finding possible factors that give the correct first term (ax^2) and the correct last term (c). Select factors whose outside and inside products have a sum of bx. With practice, you will find that it is not necessary to list all the possible factors of the trinomial. As you practice factoring, you will learn how to eliminate factors and use other shortcuts to find the correct factorization faster.

EXAMPLE 2   Factoring a Trinomial by Trial and Error

Factor: $8y^2 - 10y - 3$

Solution

Step 1. We must find two factors such that the product of the first two terms is $8y^2$. The possibilities include $(8y)(y)$ and $(4y)(2y)$.

$$8y^2 - 10y - 3 \stackrel{?}{=} (8y \quad)(y \quad)$$
$$8y^2 - 10y - 3 \stackrel{?}{=} (4y \quad)(2y \quad)$$

Step 2. The product of the last two terms in each factor must be -3. The possibilities include $(1)(-3)$ and $(-1)(3)$.

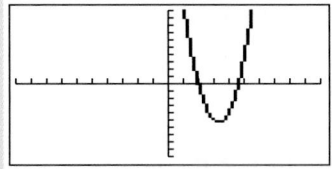

Step 3. List the possible factors, selecting the factorization that has a sum of outside and inside products equal to $-10y$, the middle term of $8y^2 - 10y - 3$.

Possible Factors of $8y^2 - 10y - 3$	Sum of Outside and Inside Products (Should Equal $-10y$)	
$(8y + 1)(y - 3)$	$-24y + y = -23y$	
$(8y - 3)(y + 1)$	$8y - 3y = 5y$	
$(8y - 1)(y + 3)$	$24y - y = 23y$	
$(8y + 3)(y - 1)$	$-8y + 3y = -5y$	
$(4y + 1)(2y - 3)$	$-12y + 2y = -10y$	This is the required middle term.
$(4y - 3)(2y + 1)$	$4y - 6y = -2y$	
$(4y - 1)(2y + 3)$	$12y - 2y = 10y$	
$(4y + 3)(2y - 1)$	$-4y + 6y = 2y$	

Thus,

$$8y^2 - 10y - 3 = (4y + 1)(2y - 3) \quad \text{or} \quad (2y - 3)(4y + 1).$$

We can check the factors using FOIL multiplication.

$$(4y + 1)(2y - 3) = 8y^2 - 12y + 2y - 3 = 8y^2 - 10y - 3$$

The trial-and-error method that we have been using can be applied to trinomials in two or more variables, such as $2x^2 - 7xy + 3y^2$.

EXAMPLE 3 **Factoring a Trinomial in Two Variables**

Factor: $2x^2 - 7xy + 3y^2$

Solution

Step 1. We must find two factors such that the product of the first two terms is $2x^2$. The only possibilities are $2x$ and x.

$$2x^2 - 7xy + 3y^2 = (2x \quad)(x \quad)$$

Step 2. The product of the last two terms in each factor must be $3y^2$. The possibilities include $(y)(3y)$ and $(-y)(-3y)$.

Step 3. List the possible factors, selecting the factorization that has a sum of outside and inside products equal to $-7xy$, the middle term of $2x^2 - 7xy + 3y^2$.

Possible Factors of $2x^2 - 7xy + 3y^2$	Sum of Outside and Inside Products (Should Equal $-7xy$)	
$(2x + 3y)(x + y)$	$2xy + 3xy = 5xy$	
$(2x + y)(x + 3y)$	$6xy + xy = 7xy$	
$(2x - 3y)(x - y)$	$-2xy - 3xy = -5xy$	
$(2x - y)(x - 3y)$	$-6xy - xy = -7xy$	This is the required middle term.

Thus,

$$2x^2 - 7xy + 3y^2 = (2x - y)(x - 3y).$$

Use FOIL multiplication to check these factors.

2 Factor trinomials by grouping.

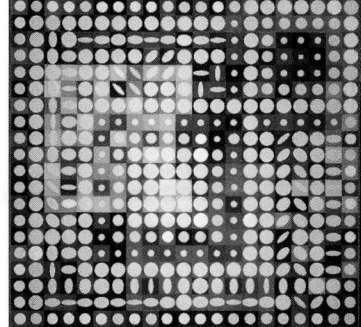

Victor Vasarely, "Orion" 1956–1962, paper on paper mounted on wood, $82\frac{1}{2} \times 78\frac{3}{4}$ in. Hirshhorn Museum and Sculpture Garden, Smithsonian Institution, Gift of Joseph H. Hirshhorn, 1966. Photo by Lee Stalsworth. ©1998 Artists Rights Society (ARS), New York/ADAGP, Paris.

Factoring by the Grouping Method

Factoring a trinomial can involve quite a bit of trial and error. It is possible to use factoring by grouping. Factoring $ax^2 + bx + c$ by grouping depends on finding two numbers p and q for which $p + q = b$ and then factoring $ax^2 + px + qx + c$ using grouping. An understanding of how to find these numbers can come from looking again at our factorization in Example 2.

$$8y^2 - 10y - 3 = (2y - 3)(4y + 1)$$

If we multiply using FOIL on the right, we obtain

$$(2y - 3)(4y + 1) = 8y^2 + 2y - 12y - 3.$$

In this case, the desired numbers p and q are $p = 2$ and $q = -12$. These numbers are factors of ac, or -24, and have a sum of b, namely -10. Expressing the middle term $-10y$ in terms of these numbers enables us to factor by grouping as follows:

$$
\begin{aligned}
&8y^2 - 10y - 3 \\
&= 8y^2 + (2y - 12y) - 3 && \text{Rewrite } -10y \text{ as } 2y - 12y. \\
&= (8y^2 + 2y) + (-12y - 3) && \text{Group terms.} \\
&= 2y(4y + 1) - 3(4y + 1) && \text{Factor from each group.} \\
&= (4y + 1)(2y - 3) && \text{Factor out the common binomial factor.}
\end{aligned}
$$

As we obtained in Example 2,

$$8y^2 - 10y - 3 = (4y + 1)(2y - 3).$$

Generalizing from this example, here's how to factor a trinomial by grouping.

Factoring $ax^2 + bx + c$ Using Grouping $(a \neq 1)$

1. Multiply the leading coefficient a and the constant c.
2. Find the factors of ac whose sum is b.
3. Rewrite the middle term (bx) as a sum or difference using the factors from step 2.
4. Factor by grouping.

EXAMPLE 4   **Factoring a Trinomial by Grouping**

Factor: $5x^2 - 11x - 12$

Solution

Step 1. We first multiply the leading coefficient and the constant.

$$5(-12) = -60$$

Step 2. Now we find factors of -60 whose sum is the coefficient of the middle term, -11.

Factors of -60	Sum of These Factors (Should be -11)	
$1, -60$	-59	
$-1, 60$	59	
$2, -30$	-28	
$-2, 30$	28	
$3, -20$	-17	
$-3, 20$	17	
$4, -15$	-11	This is the desired sum, so we can stop listing pairs of factors.

Step 3. Now we express the middle term of $5x^2 - 11x - 12$ as a sum or difference using the factors from step 2.

$$-11x = -15x + 4x \quad \text{We're using the factors } -15 \text{ and } 4.$$

Step 4. Finally, we factor by grouping.

$$
\begin{aligned}
5x^2 - 11x - 12 &= 5x^2 - 15x + 4x - 12 && \text{Substitute } -15x + 4x \text{ for } -11x. \\
&= (5x^2 - 15x) + (4x - 12) && \text{Group terms.} \\
&= 5x(x - 3) + 4(x - 3) && \text{Factor from each group.} \\
&= (x - 3)(5x + 4) && \text{Factor out the common binomial factor.}
\end{aligned}
$$

Thus,

$$5x^2 - 11x - 12 = (x - 3)(5x + 4). \qquad \blacksquare$$

Discover for yourself

In step 2 we discovered that the desired numbers were 4 and -15, and we wrote $-11x$ as $-15x + 4x$. What happens if we write $-11x$ as $4x - 15x$? Use factoring by grouping on

$$5x^2 - 11x - 12$$
$$= 5x^2 + 4x - 15x - 12.$$

Is your answer the same as the factorization in Example 4? Explain.

Comparing the Two Methods

Have you noticed that both methods for factoring trinomials involve a certain amount of trial and error? Let's try a factorization using both methods.

EXAMPLE 5   **Factoring a Trinomial Using the Two Methods**

Factor: $12x^2 + 7x - 12$

Solution

Method 1. Trial and Error
Step 1. The factors of $12x^2$ are $(12x)(x)$, $(6x)(2x)$, and $(4x)(3x)$.

$$12x^2 + 7x - 12 \stackrel{?}{=} (12x \qquad)(x \qquad)$$
$$12x^2 + 7x - 12 \stackrel{?}{=} (6x \qquad)(2x \qquad)$$
$$12x^2 + 7x - 12 \stackrel{?}{=} (4x \qquad)(3x \qquad)$$

Study tips

Here are some suggestions for reducing the list of possible factors for $ax^2 + bx + c$.

1. If b is relatively small, avoid the larger factors of a.
2. If c is positive, the signs in both binomial factors must match the sign of b.
3. If the trinomial has no common factor, no binomial factor can have a common factor.
4. Reversing the signs in the binomial factors reverses the sign of bx, the middle term.

Which of these tips apply to the partial list of possible factors for $12x^2 + 7x - 12$ shown in the table?

Using technology

Graphing

$$y_1 = 12x^2 + 7x - 12$$

and

$$y_2 = (4x - 3)(3x + 4)$$

results in the same graph, so

$$12x^2 + 7x - 12$$
$$= (4x - 3)(3x + 4).$$

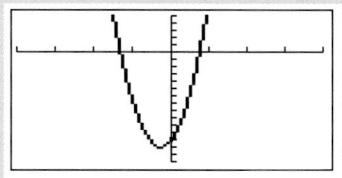

Study tip

In Example 6, be sure you don't leave out the greatest common factor y^2 in the final factorization.

$$y^2(5y + 7)(3y + 1)$$

Step 2. The product of the last two terms in each factor must be -12. Possible factors include $(12)(-1)$, $(-12)(1)$, $(6)(-2)$, $(-6)(2)$, $(4)(-3)$, and $(-4)(3)$.

Step 3. The sum of the outside and inside products of the correct factorization must equal $7x$, the middle term of $12x^2 + 7x - 12$.

Some Possible Factors of $12x^2 + 7x - 12$	Sum of Outside and Inside Products (Should Equal $7x$)	
$(12x - 1)(x + 12)$	$144x - x = 143x$	
$(4x + 2)(3x - 6)$	$-24x + 6x = -18x$	
$(4x + 3)(3x - 4)$	$-16x + 9x = -7x$	
$(4x - 3)(3x + 4)$	$16x - 9x = 7x$	This is the required middle term.

Thus,

$$12x^2 + 7x - 12 = (4x - 3)(3x + 4) \quad \text{or} \quad (3x + 4)(4x - 3).$$

Method 2. Grouping

Rewrite $7x$ in terms of two numbers: factors of ac $[(12)(-12) = -144]$ whose sum is b ($b = 7$). The numbers are 16 and -9, so $7x = 16x - 9x$.

$$
\begin{aligned}
12x^2 &+ 7x - 12 \\
&= 12x^2 + (16x - 9x) - 12 &&\text{Rewrite the middle term.} \\
&= (12x^2 + 16x) + (-9x - 12) &&\text{Group terms.} \\
&= 4x(3x + 4) - 3(3x + 4) &&\text{Factor from each group.} \\
&= (3x + 4)(4x - 3) &&\text{Factor out the common binomial factor.}
\end{aligned}
$$

Thus,

$$12x^2 + 7x - 12 = (3x + 4)(4x - 3) \quad \text{or} \quad (4x - 3)(3x + 4). \qquad \blacksquare$$

Factoring Completely

If each term of a trinomial has a common factor, always begin your work by factoring out the greatest common factor. After doing this, you should attempt to factor the remaining trinomial by one of the methods presented in this section.

EXAMPLE 6   **Factoring a Trinomial with a Common Factor**

Factor completely: $15y^4 + 26y^3 + 7y^2$

Solution

We will first factor out a common monomial factor from the polynomial and then factor the resulting trinomial by the methods of this section. The GCF of each term is y^2.

$$
\begin{aligned}
15y^4 + 26y^3 + 7y^2 &= y^2(15y^2 + 26y + 7) &&\text{Factor out the GCF.} \\
&= y^2(5y + 7)(3y + 1) &&\text{Factor } 15y^2 + 26y + 7 \text{ using trial and error or grouping.}
\end{aligned}
$$

Thus,

$$15y^4 + 26y^3 + 7y^2 = y^2(5y + 7)(3y + 1) \quad \text{or} \quad y^2(3y + 1)(5y + 7). \qquad \blacksquare$$

| EXAMPLE 7 | **Factoring a Trinomial with a Negative Leading Coefficient** |

Factor: $-3x^2 + 4x - 1$

Solution

When a trinomial has a negative leading coefficient, begin by factoring out -1.

$$-3x^2 + 4x - 1 = (-1)(3x^2 - 4x + 1) \quad \text{Factor out } -1.$$
$$= -(3x - 1)(x - 1) \quad \text{Factor the trinomial by trial and error or grouping.}$$

Thus,

$$-3x^2 + 4x - 1 = -(3x - 1)(x - 1) \quad \text{or} \quad -(x - 1)(3x - 1). \quad \blacksquare$$

PROBLEM SET 7.3

Practice Problems

Find the missing factor in Problems 1–12.

1. $5x^2 + 6x + 1 = (5x + 1)(\quad)$

2. $2x^2 + 19x + 35 = (2x + 5)(\quad)$

3. $5y^2 + 29y - 6 = (y + 6)(\quad)$

4. $10y^2 + 17y - 63 = (2y + 7)(\quad)$

5. $24r^2 - 22r - 35 = (6r + 5)(\quad)$

6. $54r^2 - 33r - 35 = (9r + 5)(\quad)$

7. $6y^2 - 31y + 5 = (y - 5)(\quad)$

8. $6y^2 + 7y - 20 = (2y + 5)(\quad)$

9. $7y^2 - 40y - 63 = (y - 7)(\quad)$

10. $11y^2 + 40y + 21 = (y + 3)(\quad)$

11. $15m^2 + 7m - 22 = (m - 1)(\quad)$

12. $6m^2 - 43m + 55 = (2m - 11)(\quad)$

Use the method of your choice to factor the trinomials in Problems 13–76, or state that the trinomial is prime. Check your factorization using FOIL multiplication or with a graphing utility.

13. $2x^2 + 7x + 3$

14. $3x^2 + 7x + 2$

15. $2x^2 + 17x + 35$

16. $2x^2 + 19x + 35$

17. $2y^2 - 17y + 30$

18. $5y^2 - 13y + 6$

19. $4x^2 - 11x + 7$

20. $5x^2 - 8x + 3$

21. $5y^2 - 12y + 6$

22. $3x^2 - 11x + 6$

23. $3x^2 - x - 2$

24. $2x^2 + 5x - 3$

25. $3y^2 + y - 10$

26. $3y^2 - 17y + 10$

27. $3r^2 - 25r - 28$

28. $3r^2 - 2r - 5$

29. $6y^2 - 11y + 4$

30. $6y^2 - 17y + 12$

31. $8t^2 + 33t + 4$

32. $6t^2 + 41t + 55$

33. $5x^2 + 33x - 14$

34. $3x^2 + 22x - 16$

35. $14y^2 + 15y - 9$

36. $6y^2 + 7y - 24$

37. $25r^2 - 30r + 9$

38. $9r^2 + 12r + 4$

39. $6x^2 - 7x + 3$

40. $9x^2 + 3x + 2$

41. $10y^2 + 43y - 9$

42. $16y^2 - 46y + 15$

43. $8r^2 - 38r - 21$

44. $8r^2 - 59r + 21$

45. $15y^2 - y - 2$

46. $15y^2 + 13y - 2$

47. $8m^2 - 2m - 1$

48. $8m^2 - 22m + 5$

49. $35z^2 + 43z - 10$

50. $35z^2 - 39z + 10$

51. $9y^2 - 9y + 2$

52. $9y^2 + 5y - 4$

53. $20x^2 - 41x + 20$

54. $10x^2 - 23x + 12$

55. $-4x^2 - x + 3$

56. $-3x^2 - 2x + 8$

57. $-4y^2 + 5y + 6$

58. $-10y^2 + y + 24$

59. $2 + 7y + 6y^2$

60. $10 + 19y + 6y^2$

61. $38 - 67x + 15x^2$

62. $-34 - 79x + 15x^2$

63. $2x^2 + 3xy + y^2$

64. $3x^2 + 4xy + y^2$

65. $15x^2 + 11xy - 14y^2$

66. $15x^2 - 31xy + 10y^2$

67. $2x^2 - 9xy + 9y^2$

68. $3x^2 + 5xy - 2y^2$

69. $2x^2 + 7xy + 5y^2$

70. $4x^2 - 11xy + 6y^2$

71. $6a^2 - 5ab - 6b^2$

72. $6a^2 - 7ab - 5b^2$

73. $3a^2 - ab - 14b^2$

74. $3a^2 + 19ab - 14b^2$

75. $12r^2 - 25rs + 12s^2$

76. $12r^2 + 7rs - 12s^2$

Factor Problems 77–97 completely by first factoring out a greatest common factor.

77. $18x^2 + 48x + 32$ **78.** $24x^2 - 50x + 24$ **79.** $4y^2 + 2y - 30$ **80.** $36y^2 + 6y - 12$

81. $9r^2 + 33r - 60$ **82.** $16r^2 - 16r - 12$ **83.** $2y^3 - 3y^2 - 5y$ **84.** $6y^3 + 5y^2 + y$

85. $9r^3 - 39r^2 + 12r$ **86.** $10r^3 + 12r^2 + 2r$ **87.** $14m^3 + 94m^2 - 28m$ **88.** $10m^3 - 44m^2 + 16m$

89. $15x^4 - 39x^3 + 18x^2$ **90.** $24x^4 + 10x^3 - 4x^2$ **91.** $10x^5 - 17x^4 + 3x^3$ **92.** $15x^5 - 2x^4 - x^3$

93. $36x^2 + 54xy - 70y^2$ **94.** $12a^2b - 46ab^2 + 14b^3$ **95.** $12a^2b - 34ab^2 + 14b^3$

96. $-32x^2y^4 + 20xy^4 + 12y^4$ **97.** $-15a^2b^2 + 7ab^2 + 4b^2$

Application Problem

98. A person standing close to the edge of a 24-foot rooftop throws a ball upward with an initial speed of 40 feet per second, as illustrated in the figure. The height of the ball above the ground is a function of the time (t, in seconds) that the ball is in flight, given by the polynomial function $f(t) = -16t^2 + 40t + 24$.

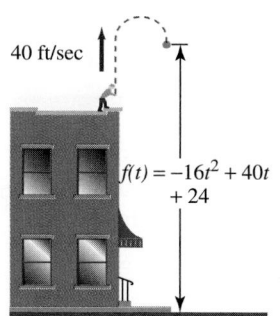

40 ft/sec

$f(t) = -16t^2 + 40t + 24$

  a. Factor the trinomial $-16t^2 + 40t + 24$ by first factoring out the greatest common factor and then factoring the remaining trinomial.

  b. Suppose we want to know how long it takes for the ball to hit the ground. This occurs when $f(t) = -16t^2 + 40t + 24 = 0$. Use the factored form of $f(t)$ to determine what happens to $f(t)$ at $t = 3$. Describe what this means in terms of the height of the ball. How is this illustrated in the graph?

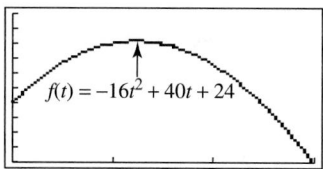

$f(t) = -16t^2 + 40t + 24$

  c. If a polynomial is factored and one of the factors has a value of zero when evaluated for a specific value of the variable, then what is the value of the polynomial?

True–False Critical Thinking Problems

99. Which one of the following is true?
  a. Once a GCF is factored from $18y^2 - 6y + 6$, the remaining trinomial factor is prime.
  b. A factor of $12x^2 - 13x + 3$ is $4x + 3$.
  c. A factor of $4y^2 - 11y - 3$ is $y + 3$.
  d. The trinomial $3x^2 + 2x + 1$ has relatively small coefficients and therefore can be factored.

100. Which one of the following is true?
  a. A trinomial whose leading coefficient is not 1 can never have two identical factors.
  b. A factor of $x^2y + 2xy - 15y$ is $x - 3$.
  c. $6x^2 + 35x - 6$ is a prime trinomial.
  d. Since $4x^2 + 1 = 4x^2 + 0x + 1$, then a factor of $4x^2 + 1$ is $2x + 1$.

Technology Problems

In Problems 101–104, use a graphing utility to graph the function on the left side and the function on the right side in the same viewing rectangle. Are the graphs identical? If so, this means that the polynomial on the left side has been correctly factored. If not, factor the trinomial correctly and then use your graphing utility to verify the factorization.

101. $2x^2 + 5x + 3 = (2x + 3)(x + 1)$

102. $8x^2 + 13x - 6 = (2x - 3)(4x + 2)$

103. $18x^3 - 21x^2 - 9x = 3x(2x - 3)(3x + 1)$

104. $8x^3 + 8x^2 - 6x = 2x(2x + 1)(2x - 3)$

Writing in Mathematics

105. Why is it a good idea to factor out the GCF first and then use other methods of factoring? Use $3x^2 - 18x + 15$ as an example. Discuss what happens if one first uses trial and error FOIL rather than first factoring out the GCF.

106. In factoring $3x^2 - 10x - 8$, a student lists $(3x - 2)(x + 4)$ as a possible factorization. Use FOIL multiplication to determine if this factorization is correct. If it is not correct, describe how the correct factorization can quickly be obtained using these factors.

107. Explain why $2x - 10$ cannot be one of the factors in the correct factorization of $6x^2 - 19x + 10$.

Critical Thinking Problems

Factor the trinomials in Problems 108–110.

108. $3x^{10} - 4x^5 - 15$

109. $2x^{2n} - 7x^n - 4$

110. $12x^{2n} - x^n y^n - 20y^{2n}$

Find all integers b in Problems 111–112 such that the trinomial can be factored.

111. $3x^2 + bx + 2$

112. $2x^2 + bx + 3$

Simplify Problems 113–114, and then factor the resulting trinomial.

113. $3(x + 2)^2 - (x + 2) - 4$

114. $5(y + 1)^2 - 16(y + 1) + 3$

Group Activity Problem

115. Copy the figure and cut out the six pieces. Working in groups, use the pieces to create a geometric model for the factorization $2x^2 + 3x + 1 = (2x + 1)(x + 1)$ by forming a large rectangle using all the pieces. Then use appropriate figures to create a geometric model for factoring $3x^2 + 7x + 2$. Finally, group members should create a geometric model for the factorization of their choice.

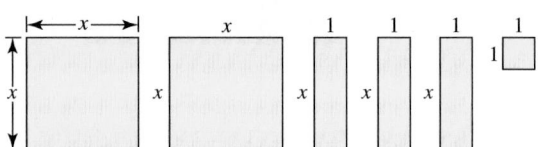

Review Problems

116. Multiply: $(9x + 7)(9x - 7)$.

117. Multiply: $(5x - 6)^2$.

118. Multiply: $(x + 2)(x^2 - 2x + 4)$.

S E C T I O N   7 . 4

Solutions Manual   Tutorial   Video 8

Factoring Special Forms

Objectives

1 Factor the difference of two squares.
2 Factor perfect square trinomials.
3 Factor the sum and difference of two cubes.

In Section 6.3, we considered two special binomial products:

Product of the Sum and Difference of Two Terms	Square of a Binomial
$(A + B)(A - B) = A^2 - B^2$	$(A + B)^2 = A^2 + 2AB + B^2$

Since factoring is the reverse of multiplication, these products can be considered as factorization of special forms. For example,

$$A^2 - B^2 = (A + B)(A - B)$$

gives us a factorization for the difference of two squares. In this section, we study four special factorizations based on polynomial products.

I Factor the difference of two squares.

The Difference of Two Squares

The formula

$$A^2 - B^2 = (A + B)(A - B)$$

gives us a method for factoring the *difference of two squares*.

H. C. Westermann "Memorial to the Idea of Man If He Was An Idea" 1958, pine, bottle caps, metal, glass, enamel, and toys. Open: $75\frac{1}{4} \times 39\frac{1}{2} \times 20\frac{1}{2}$ in. $(191.1 \times 100.3 \times 52.1$ cm). Collection Museum of Contemporary Art, Chicago. Gift of Susan and Lewis Manilow. Photo © MCA, Chicago. © Estate of H. C. Westermann/Licensed by VAGA, New York 1998.

The difference of two squares

If A and B are real numbers, variables, or algebraic expressions, then

$$A^2 - B^2 = (A + B)(A - B).$$

In words: The difference of the squares of two terms factors as the product of a sum and the difference of those terms.

Study tip

It is possible to construct a geometric model so that you can see the factoring for the difference of two squares.

Shaded Area: $A^2 - B^2$

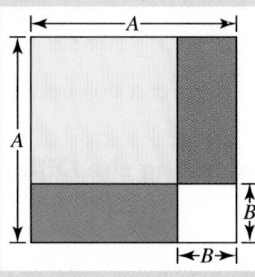

Shaded Area: $(A + B)(A - B)$

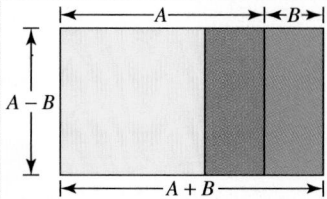

The shaded areas are the same, so $A^2 - B^2 = (A + B)(A - B)$.

For a polynomial to be a perfect square, the coefficient of a term must be the square of an integer and the variable must be raised to an even power. Here are some examples.

Original Polynomial Written as the Difference of Two Squares	Factored Form
$x^2 - 4 = x^2 - 2^2$ $\quad\quad\quad\uparrow\quad\uparrow$ $\quad\quad\quad A^2 - B^2$	$(x + 2)(x - 2)$ $\uparrow\quad\uparrow\quad\uparrow\quad\uparrow$ $(A + B)(A - B)$
$4x^2 - 25 = (2x)^2 - 5^2$ $\quad\quad\quad\quad\uparrow\quad\quad\uparrow$ $\quad\quad\quad\quad A^2 - B^2$	$(2x + 5)(2x - 5)$ $\uparrow\quad\uparrow\quad\uparrow$ $(A + B)(A - B)$
$9 - 16x^4 = 3^2 - (4x^2)^2$ $\quad\uparrow\quad\quad\quad\uparrow$ $\quad A^2 - B^2$	$(3 + 4x^2)(3 - 4x^2)$ $\uparrow\quad\uparrow\quad\uparrow\quad\uparrow$ $(A + B)(A - B)$

EXAMPLE 1 Factoring the Difference of Two Squares

Factor:

a. $x^2 - 64$ **b.** $1 - y^2$ **c.** $x^2 - 5$ **d.** $y^6 - 9$

Solution

a. $x^2 - 64 = x^2 - 8^2$ Write the polynomial as the difference of two squares.
$\quad\quad\quad\quad = (x + 8)(x - 8)$ The factors are the sum and difference of the squared terms.

b. $1 - y^2 = 1^2 - y^2$ Write the polynomial as the difference of two squares.
$\quad\quad\quad = (1 + y)(1 - y)$ The factors are the sum and difference of the squared terms.

c. $x^2 - 5$ is prime. Because 5 is not the square of an integer, $x^2 - 5$ cannot be expressed as the difference of squares of integers and is nonfactorable using integers.

d. To factor $y^6 - 9$, begin by observing that y^6 has an even power. Recall that to raise a power to a power, we multiply the exponents. This means that we can write y^6 as $(y^3)^2$. This enables us to express the polynomial as the difference of squares. Then we can factor.

$\quad\quad y^6 - 9 = (y^3)^2 - 3^2$ Write the polynomial as the difference of two squares.
$\quad\quad\quad\quad = (y^3 + 3)(y^3 - 3)$ The factors are the sum and difference of the squared terms.

Each of these factorizations can be checked by multiplication. ∎

EXAMPLE 2 Factoring the Difference of Two Squares

Factor:

a. $81x^2 - 49$ **b.** $9 - 16x^{10}$ **c.** $(x + 1)^2 - 25$

Solution

a. To factor $81x^2 - 49$, we must express each term as the square of some monomial. Recall that to raise a product to a power, we raise each factor to the power. This means that we can write $81x^2$ as $(9x)^2$ since $(9x)^2 = 9^2x^2$ or $81x^2$.

$$81x^2 - 49 = (9x)^2 - 7^2 = (9x + 7)(9x - 7)$$
$$\quad\quad\quad\quad\quad\uparrow\quad\quad\uparrow\quad\quad\uparrow\quad\uparrow\quad\uparrow\quad\uparrow$$
$$\quad\quad\quad\quad\quad A^2\ -\ B^2\quad (A\ +\ B)\ (A\ -\ B)$$

b. $9 - 16x^{10} = (3)^2 - (4x^5)^2 = (3 + 4x^5)(3 - 4x^5)$
$$\quad\quad\quad\quad\quad\uparrow\quad\quad\uparrow\quad\quad\uparrow\quad\uparrow\quad\uparrow\quad\uparrow$$
$$\quad\quad\quad\quad\quad A^2\ -\ B^2\quad (A\ +\ B)\ (A\ -\ B)$$

c. $(x + 1)^2 - 25 = (x + 1)^2 - 5^2 = [(x + 1) + 5][(x + 1) - 5]$
$$\quad\quad\quad\quad\quad\quad\uparrow\quad\quad\quad\uparrow\quad\quad\uparrow\quad\quad\uparrow\quad\uparrow\quad\quad\uparrow$$
$$\quad\quad\quad\quad\quad\quad A^2\ -\ B^2\quad\ [A\ +\ B]\ [A\ -\ B]$$
$$= (x + 6)(x - 4)$$

Factoring Completely

If it is possible, be sure to first factor out a common monomial factor from a polynomial.

EXAMPLE 3 **Factoring Completely**

Factor completely:

a. $12x^3 - 3x$ **b.** $80 - 125x^2$

Solution

a. $12x^3 - 3x = 3x(4x^2 - 1)$ Factor out $3x$, the GCF.

$= 3x[(2x)^2 - 1^2]$ Express the second factor as the difference of two squares.

$= 3x(2x + 1)(2x - 1)$ The factors are the sum and difference of the squared terms.

b. $80 - 125x^2 = 5(16 - 25x^2)$ Factor out 5, the GCF.

$= 5[4^2 - (5x)^2]$ Express the second factor as the difference of two squares.

$= 5(4 + 5x)(4 - 5x)$ The factors are the sum and difference of the squared terms.

Repeated Factorization

We have seen that a polynomial is factored completely when it is written as the product of prime polynomials. To be sure that you have factored completely, you should check to see whether the factors in the initial factorization might themselves be factorable. This forms the basis of our next example.

EXAMPLE 4 **A Repeated Factorization**

Factor completely: $x^4 - 81$

Solution

$x^4 - 81 = (x^2)^2 - 9^2$ Express as the difference of two squares.

$= (x^2 + 9)(x^2 - 9)$ The factors are the sum and difference of the squared terms.

$= (x^2 + 9)(x^2 - 3^2)$ The factor $x^2 - 9$ is the difference of two squares and can be factored.

$= (x^2 + 9)(x + 3)(x - 3)$ The factors of $x^2 - 9$ are the sum and difference of the squared terms.

Study tip

Factoring $x^4 - 81$ as

$(x^2 + 9)(x^2 - 9)$

is not a complete factorization. The second factor $x^2 - 9$ is itself a difference of two squares and can be factored.

tudy tip

The sum of two squares

$$A^2 + B^2$$

with no common factor other than 1 is a prime polynomial.

In factoring $x^4 - 81$, we noticed that one of the factors, $x^2 - 9$, could be further factored, and so the factorization $(x^2 + 9)(x^2 - 9)$ did not factor the original polynomial *completely*. However, we did not attempt to further factor $x^2 + 9$, the *sum of two squares*. Using FOIL multiplication, we can show that $x^2 + 9$ cannot be further factored.

$$(x + 3)(x - 3) = x^2 - 9$$
$$(x - 3)(x - 3) = x^2 - 6x + 9$$
$$(x + 3)(x + 3) = x^2 + 6x + 9$$

Thus, $x^2 + 9$ is a *prime polynomial*.

2 Factor perfect square trinomials.

Perfect Square Trinomials

We just observed that

$$(A + B)(A + B) = A^2 + 2AB + B^2.$$

By reversing the two sides of this equality and writing $(A + B)(A + B)$ as $(A + B)^2$, we obtain

$$A^2 + 2AB + B^2 = (A + B)^2.$$

Because the trinomial $A^2 + 2AB + B^2$ is the square of $A + B$, it is called a *perfect square trinomial.*

tudy tip

It is possible to construct a geometric model so that you can see the factoring for a perfect square trinomial.

Area: $(A + B)^2$ Sum of areas: $A^2 + 2AB + B^2$

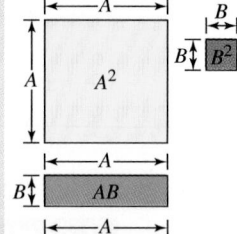

Conclusion: $A^2 + 2AB + B^2 = (A + B)^2$

Although $A^2 + 2AB + B^2$ can be factored using either of the methods discussed in the previous section, if we can recognize a perfect square trinomial, we can immediately factor by inspection.

Identifying and factoring a perfect square trinomial

$$\underbrace{A^2 + 2AB + B^2}_{\substack{\text{Perfect square} \\ \text{trinomial}}} = \underbrace{(A + B)^2}_{\substack{\text{Factored} \\ \text{form}}}$$

1. In a perfect square trinomial, the first term (A^2) and the last term (B^2) are perfect squares and the middle term ($2AB$) is always twice the product of A and B.
2. $A^2 + 2AB + B^2$ is factored as $(A + B)^2$, the square of the sum of A and B.

EXAMPLE 5 **Identifying Perfect Square Trinomials**

Which one of the following is a perfect square trinomial?

a. $x^2 + 10x + 13$　　**b.** $x^2 + 10x + 25$　　**c.** $x^2 + 5x + 25$

Solution

a. $x^2 + 10x + 13$ is not a perfect square trinomial because the last term, 13, is not a perfect square.
b. $x^2 + 10x + 25$ is a perfect square trinomial because the first and last terms are perfect squares ($A^2 = x^2$ and $B^2 = 25$, so $A = x$ and $B = 5$), and the middle term ($10x$) is twice the product of A and B. That is, $2AB = 2 \cdot x \cdot 5 = 10x$, the middle term. This means that we can immediately factor $x^2 + 10x + 25$ as $(A + B)^2$ or $(x + 5)^2$.
c. $x^2 + 5x + 25$ is not a perfect square trinomial. Although it has two perfect square terms ($A^2 = x^2$ and $B^2 = 25$), the middle term, $5x$, is not twice the product of A and B. ∎

Just as $x^2 + 10x + 25$ is a perfect square trinomial, $x^2 - 10x + 25$ is also a perfect square trinomial. Both trinomials are squares of binomials.

$$x^2 + 10x + 25 = (x + 5)^2 \quad \text{and} \quad x^2 - 10x + 25 = (x - 5)^2.$$

Perfect square trinomials thus come in two forms: one in which the middle term is positive and other in which the middle term is negative.

tudy tip

$x^2 + 10x + 25$
$= x^2 + 2 \cdot x \cdot 5 + 5^2$
$\quad \uparrow \quad\quad \uparrow \; \uparrow \quad \uparrow$
$\quad A^2 + 2 \;\; A \;\; B + B^2$

Perfect square trinomials

Let A and B be real numbers, variables, or algebraic expressions.

1. $A^2 + 2AB + B^2 = (A + B)^2$

Same sign

2. $A^2 - 2AB + B^2 = (A - B)^2$

Same sign

EXAMPLE 6   **Factoring Perfect Square Trinomials**

Factor:

a. $x^2 + 6x + 9$ **b.** $x^2 - 16x + 64$ **c.** $25x^2 - 60x + 36$

Solution

a. $x^2 + 6x + 9 = x^2 + 2 \cdot x \cdot 3 + 3^2 = (x + 3)^2$ The middle term has a positive sign.

$$A^2 + 2 \quad A \quad B + B^2 = (A + B)^2$$

b. $x^2 - 16x + 64 = x^2 - 2 \cdot x \cdot 8 + 8^2 = (x - 8)^2$ The middle term has a negative sign.

$$A^2 - 2 \quad A \quad B + B^2 = (A - B)^2$$

c. We suspect that $25x^2 - 60x + 36$ is a perfect square trinomial because $25x^2 = (5x)^2$ and $36 = 6^2$. The middle term can be expressed as twice the product of $5x$ and 6.

$$25x^2 - 60x + 36 = (5x)^2 - 2 \cdot 5x \cdot 6 + 6^2 = (5x - 6)^2$$

$$A^2 - 2 \quad A \quad B + B^2 = (A - B)^2$$

EXAMPLE 7   **Factoring Completely**

Factor completely: $5x^3 - 30x^2 + 45x$

Solution

$5x^3 - 30x^2 + 45x$
$= 5x(x^2 - 6x + 9)$ Factor out $5x$, the GCF.
$= 5x(x^2 - 2 \cdot x \cdot 3 + 3^2)$ The trinomial is written in the form $A^2 - 2AB + B^2$, where $A = x$ and $B = 3$. You may do this step mentally.
$= 5x(x - 3)^2$ Write the factored form $(A - B)^2$.

Perfect square trinomials can contain two or more variables.

EXAMPLE 8   **Factoring a Perfect Square Trinomial in Two Variables**

Factor: $16x^2 + 40xy + 25y^2$

Solution

Since $16x^2 = (4x)^2$, $25y^2 = (5y)^2$, and $40xy$ is twice the product of $4x$ and $5y$, we have a perfect square trinomial.

$$16x^2 + 40xy + 25y^2 = (4x)^2 + 2 \cdot 4x \cdot 5y + (5y)^2 = (4x + 5y)^2$$

$$A^2 + 2 \quad A \quad B + B^2 = (A + B)^2$$

3 Factor the sum and difference of two cubes.

The Sum and Difference of Two Cubes

The polynomial $x^3 + 27$ can be expressed as $x^3 + 3^3$. We can factor $x^3 + 27$, the sum of two cubes, by multiplying two polynomials. Consider the product of $x + 3$ and $x^2 - 3x + 9$.

$$x^2 - 3x + 9$$
$$\underline{\; x + \; 3}$$
$$3x^2 - 9x + 27 \quad \leftarrow 3(x^2 - 3x + 9)$$
$$\underline{x^3 - 3x^2 + 9x \quad \leftarrow x(x^2 - 3x + 9)}$$
$$x^3 + 27$$

Thus,

$$x^3 + 27 = (x + 3)(x^2 - 3x + 9)$$

Factoring reverses the direction of multiplication.

$$\text{or} \quad x^3 + 3^3 = (x + 3)(x^2 - x \cdot 3 + 3^2)$$

In general: $A^3 + B^3 = (A + B)(A^2 - AB + B^2)$

There are factoring formulas for $A^3 + B^3$, the sum of two cubes, as well as for $A^3 - B^3$, the difference of two cubes. The patterns for these two special forms are given below. Notice the signs of the terms in the factorizations.

The sum and difference of two cubes

Let A and B be real numbers, variables, or algebraic expressions.

1. Factoring the Sum of Two Cubes

Like signs

$$A^3 + B^3 = (A + B)(A^2 - AB + B^2)$$

Unlike signs

2. Factoring the Difference of Two Cubes

Like signs

$$A^3 - B^3 = (A - B)(A^2 + AB + B^2)$$

Unlike signs

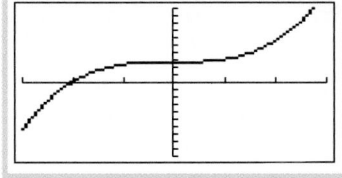

EXAMPLE 9   **Factoring Sums and Differences of Two Cubes**

Factor:

a. $x^3 + 8$ **b.** $27 - y^3$ **c.** $64y^3 + 125$

Solution

a. $x^3 + 8 = x^3 + 2^3 = (x + 2)(x^2 - x \cdot 2 + 2^2) = (x + 2)(x^2 - 2x + 4)$
$$A^3 + B^3 = (A + B)(A^2 - AB + B^2)$$

b. $27 - y^3 = 3^3 - y^3 = (3 - y)(3^2 + 3y + y^2) = (3 - y)(9 + 3y + y^2)$
$$A^3 - B^3 = (A - B)(A^2 + AB + B^2)$$

ENRICHMENT ESSAY

Human Calculators

During the 1860s, 11-year-old Jacques Inaudi toured Europe and the United States, demonstrating an extraordinary ability to mentally manipulate numbers. A typical performance involved completing five complex calculations in only 10 minutes. (On the one occasion that Inaudi attended a Shakespearean play, he noted only the number of words that each actor spoke and the number of entrances and exits each made.)

Calculating geniuses have not been able to explain their gifts. When confronted with numerical calculations, they possess exceptional memories and demonstrate remarkably rapid recall. They use their arithmetical ability to carry out complicated calculations without pen or paper and remember the results for use in future problems.

Born in 1887, Srinivasa Ramanujan was an Indian mathematician with extraordinary abilities in mentally manipulating both numbers and formulas. Once, when a colleague visited, the colleague remarked that his taxicab had the number 1729, a very dull number.

Ramanujan instantly replied that it was in fact very interesting—it was the smallest number expressible as the sum of two cubes in two and only two different ways:

$$1729 = 12^3 + 1^3 = 10^3 + 9^3$$

Most calculating geniuses have been left-handed, related perhaps to the fact that left-handed people rely more on the right hemisphere of the brain, which controls spatial judgment, intuition, and artistic ability.

Corbis–Bettmann

c. $64y^3 + 125 = (4y)^3 + 5^3 = (4y + 5)[(4y)^2 - (4y)(5) + 5^2]$

$$A^3 + B^3 = (A + B)(A^2 - AB + B^2)$$

$$= (4y + 5)(16y^2 - 20y + 25)$$

The special forms factored in this section are summarized in Table 7.1.

TABLE 7.1 Special Factorization

Name	Formula	Example
Difference of two squares	$A^2 - B^2 = (A + B)(A - B)$	$64x^2 - 9 = (8x)^2 - 3^2 = (8x + 3)(8x - 3)$
Perfect square trinomials	$A^2 + 2AB + B^2 = (A + B)^2$	$x^2 - 14x + 49 = x^2 - 2 \cdot x \cdot 7 + 7^2 = (x - 7)^2$
	$A^2 - 2AB + B^2 = (A - B)^2$	
Sum of two cubes	$A^3 + B^3 = (A + B)(A^2 - AB + B^2)$	$x^3 + 1 = x^3 + 1^3 = (x + 1)(x^2 - x \cdot 1 + 1^2)$
		$= (x + 1)(x^2 - x + 1)$
Difference of two cubes	$A^3 - B^3 = (A - B)(A^2 + AB + B^2)$	$y^3 - 216 = y^3 - 6^3 = (y - 6)(y^2 + y \cdot 6 + 6^2)$
		$= (y - 6)(y^2 + 6y + 36)$

PROBLEM SET 7.4

Practice Problems

Factor Problems 1–50 completely, or state that the polynomial is prime. Check your factorization by multiplication or with a graphing utility.

1. $x^2 - 25$ **2.** $y^2 - 16$ **3.** $y^2 - 1$ **4.** $x^2 - 9$ **5.** $4x^2 - 1$

6. $9x^2 - 25$ **7.** $x^2 - 7$ **8.** $x^2 - 13$ **9.** $9y^2 - 4$ **10.** $4y^2 - 9$

11. $9x^2 + 4$ **12.** $4y^2 + 9$ **13.** $1 - 49x^2$ **14.** $1 - 64x^2$ **15.** $25a^2 - 16b^2$

16. $144a^2 - 25b^2$ **17.** $x^2 + 9$ **18.** $x^2 + 25$ **19.** $16z^2 - y^2$ **20.** $81z^2 - y^2$

21. $9 - 121a^2$ **22.** $16 - 25a^2$ **23.** $(x + 1)^2 - 16$ **24.** $(x + 1)^2 - 36$ **25.** $(2x + 3)^2 - 49$

26. $(3x + 2)^2 - 64$ **27.** $(3x - 1)^2 - 64$ **28.** $(3x - 1)^2 - 49$ **29.** $25 - (x + 3)^2$ **30.** $49 - (x + 5)^2$

31. $2y^2 - 18$ **32.** $5y^2 - 45$ **33.** $2x^3 - 72x$ **34.** $81x^3 - 49x$ **35.** $50 - 2y^2$

36. $72 - 2y^2$ **37.** $8y^3 - 2y$ **38.** $12y^3 - 48y$ **39.** $2x^3 - 2x$ **40.** $36x - 49x^3$

41. $x^4 - 16$ **42.** $x^4 - 1$ **43.** $16y^4 - 81$ **44.** $16y^4 - 1$ **45.** $1 - y^4$

46. $81 - y^4$ **47.** $x^8 - 1$ **48.** $1 - x^8$ **49.** $16a^4 - b^4$ **50.** $1 - x^4y^4$

In Problems 51–84, factor any perfect square trinomials, or state that the trinomial is prime. Check as in Problems 1–50.

51. $x^2 + 2x + 1$ **52.** $x^2 + 4x + 4$ **53.** $x^2 - 14x + 49$ **54.** $x^2 - 10x + 25$

55. $x^2 - 2x + 1$ **56.** $x^2 - 22x + 121$ **57.** $x^2 + 24x + 144$ **58.** $x^2 + 26x + 169$

59. $4y^2 + 4y + 1$ **60.** $25y^2 + 10y + 1$ **61.** $9r^2 - 6r + 1$ **62.** $64r^2 - 16r + 1$

63. $16t^2 + 1 + 8t$ **64.** $4t^2 + 25 - 20t$ **65.** $9b^2 - 42b + 49$ **66.** $4b^2 - 28b + 49$

67. $x^2 - 10x + 100$ **68.** $y^2 - 17y + 49$ **69.** $12k^2 - 12k + 3$ **70.** $18k^2 + 24k + 8$

71. $9x^3 + 6x^2 + x$ **72.** $25x^3 - 10x^2 + x$ **73.** $2y^2 - 4y + 2$ **74.** $2y^2 - 40y + 200$

75. $2y^3 + 28y^2 + 98y$ **76.** $50y^3 + 20y^2 + 2y$ **77.** $25x^2 + 20xy + 4y^2$ **78.** $64x^2 + 16xy + y^2$

79. $a^2 - 6ab + 9b^2$ **80.** $p^2 - 14pq + 49q^2$ **81.** $4a^2 - 12ab + 9b^2$ **82.** $81a^2 - 18ab + b^2$

83. $32x^2 + 80xy + 50y^2$ **84.** $36x^2 + 96xy + 64y^2$

Factor in Problems 85–102 using the formula for the sum or difference of two cubes. Check as in Problems 1–50.

85. $x^3 + 27$ **86.** $x^3 + 64$ **87.** $x^3 - 64$ **88.** $x^3 - 27$

89. $8y^3 - 1$ **90.** $27y^3 - 1$ **91.** $64x^3 + 125$ **92.** $8x^3 + 27$

93. $2x^4 + 16x$ **94.** $2x^4 + 54x$ **95.** $27y^4 - 8y$ **96.** $64x - x^4$

97. $54 - 16y^3$ **98.** $128 - 250y^3$ **99.** $64x^3 + 27y^3$ **100.** $8x^3 + 27y^3$

101. $125x^3 - 64y^3$ **102.** $125x^3 - y^3$

True–False Critical Thinking Problems

103. Which one of the following is true?
   a. The polynomial $x^2 + 25x + 16$ is a perfect square trinomial.
   b. $x^2 + 4$ can be factored as $(x + 2)^2$.
   c. $x^9 - 1 = (x^3 + 1)(x^3 - 1)$
   d. When $2x^2 - 18$ is factored completely, there are three distinct factors.

104. Which one of the following is true?
   a. Since $x^2 - 25 = (x + 5)(x - 5)$, then $x^2 + 25 = (x - 5)(x + 5)$.
   b. All perfect square trinomials are squares of binomials.
   c. Any polynomial that is the sum of two squares is prime.
   d. The polynomial $16x^2 + 20x + 25$ is a perfect square trinomial.

Technology Problems

In Problems 105–108, use a graphing utility to graph the function on the left side and the function on the right side in the same viewing rectangle. Are the graphs identical? If so, this means that the polynomial on the left side has been correctly factored. If not, factor the polynomial correctly and then use your graphing utility to verify the factorization.

105. $4x^2 - 9 = (4x + 3)(4x - 3)$

106. $x^2 - 6x + 9 = (x - 3)^2$

107. $4x^2 - 4x + 1 = (4x - 1)^2$

108. $x^3 - 1 = (x - 1)(x^2 - x + 1)$

Writing in Mathematics

109. Describe how to recognize a perfect square trinomial.

110. Explain why $x^2 - 1$ is factorable but $x^2 + 1$ is not.

Critical Thinking Problems

In Problems 111–114 express the area of each shaded region as a polynomial that is factored completely.

111.

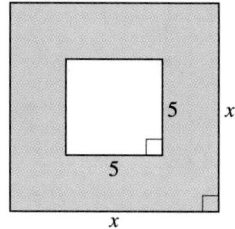

112.

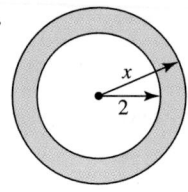

113.

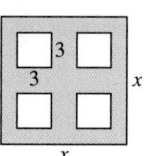

114.

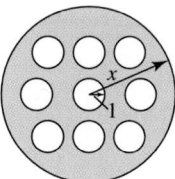

Compute Problems 115–118 without raising any number to a power. For example,

$$100^2 - 99^2 = (100 + 99)(100 - 99) = (199)(1) = 199.$$

115. $1000^2 - 999^2$

116. $100^2 - 90^2$

117. $1000^2 - 990^2$

118. $80^2 - 70^2$

Find all integers k *in Problems 119–120 such that the trinomial is a perfect square trinomial.*

119. $9x^2 + kx + 1$

120. $64x^2 - 16x + k$

Use the factorizations

$$x^2 - 1 = (x - 1)(x + 1)$$
$$x^3 - 1 = (x - 1)(x^2 + x + 1)$$
$$x^4 - 1 = (x - 1)(x^3 + x^2 + x + 1)$$

to factor Problems 121–122 by using the emerging pattern. Check your result by multiplication or with a graphing utility.

121. $x^5 - 1$

122. $x^7 - 1$

Group Activity Problems

123. Members of the group should begin by expressing as many of the first 21 whole numbers as possible as the difference between two squares. For example, $0 = 0^2 - 0^2$; $1 = 1^2 - 0^2$; $3 = 2^2 - 1^2$; and so on. If n is a whole number, see if group members can come up with a formula in terms of n for the numbers that cannot be written as the difference of two squares.

124. Here's a "proof" that $2 = 0$. Group members should study this proof and see if they can find the fallacy in the argument. (*Hint:* There is an algebraic error in one of the steps.)

$a = b$	Suppose that a and b are any equal real numbers.
$a^2 = b^2$	Square both sides of the equation.
$a^2 - b^2 = 0$	Subtract b^2 from both sides.
$2(a^2 - b^2) = 2 \cdot 0$	Multiply both sides by 2.
$2(a^2 - b^2) = 0$	On the right side, $2 \cdot 0 = 0$.
$2(a + b)(a - b) = 0$	Factor $a^2 - b^2$.
$2(a + b) = 0$	Divide both sides by $a - b$.
$2 = 0$	Divide both sides by $a + b$.

Review Problems

125. Simplify: $\left(\dfrac{3x^2}{2}\right)^4$.

126. Solve and graph the solution on a number line: $6 - 2x > 4x - 12$.

127. Solve: $2x + 5 = 12 - 6x + 3(2x + 3)$.

SECTION 7.5

Solutions Manual Tutorial Video 8

1 Recognize the appropriate method for factoring a polynomial.

A General Factoring Strategy

Objectives

1 Recognize the appropriate method for factoring a polynomial.
2 Factor polynomials using two or more factoring techniques.

It is important to practice factoring a wide variety of polynomials so that you can quickly select the appropriate technique. The polynomial is factored completely when all its polynomial factors, except possibly the monomial factors, are prime. Because of the commutative property, the order of the factors does not matter.

The box outlines the methods of factoring covered in this chapter.

> **Study tip**
>
> Get into the habit of checking your factorization either by multiplying or by using a graphing utility.

> **Factoring a polynomial over the integers**
>
> **1.** Is there a common factor? If so, factor out the GCF.
> **2.** Is the polynomial a binomial? If so, can it be factored by one of the following special forms?
>
> Difference of two squares: $A^2 - B^2 = (A + B)(A - B)$
> Sum of two cubes: $A^3 + B^3 = (A + B)(A^2 - AB + B^2)$
> Difference of two cubes: $A^3 - B^3 = (A - B)(A^2 + AB + B^2)$
>
> **3.** Is the polynomial a trinomial? If it is not a perfect square trinomial, use trial and error or grouping as discussed in Section 7.3. If it is a perfect square trinomial, use one of the following special forms:
>
> $$A^2 + 2AB + B^2 = (A + B)^2$$
> $$A^2 - 2AB + B^2 = (A - B)^2$$
>
> **4.** Does the polynomial contain four or more terms? If so, try factoring by grouping.

2 Factor polynomials using two or more factoring techniques.

The following examples and those in the problem set are similar to the previous factoring problems. Although these polynomials may be factored using any of the techniques we have studied in this chapter, they must be factored using at least two of the techniques.

> **EXAMPLE 1** **Factoring a Polynomial**

Factor: $4x^4 - 16x^2$

Solution

We first look for a common factor. Since $4x^2$ is common to both terms, we factor it out.

$$4x^4 - 16x^2 = 4x^2(x^2 - 4) \quad \text{Factor out the GCF.}$$

Now we consider the factor $x^2 - 4$. Since it is a binomial, we look to see if it is one of the special forms. Since x^2 and 4 are perfect squares, $x^2 - 4$ (or $x^2 - 2^2$) is the difference of two squares.

$$4x^4 - 16x^2 = 4x^2(x + 2)(x - 2) \quad \text{Factor the difference of two squares.}$$

We have now factored completely because no factor with more than one term can be factored further. We check by multiplication or with a graphing utility.

$$4x^2(x + 2)(x - 2) = 4x^2(x^2 - 4) = 4x^4 - 16x^2$$

Using technology

Graphing

$$y_1 = 4x^4 - 16x^2$$

and

$$y_2 = 4x^2(x + 2)(x - 2)$$

results in the same graph, so

$$4x^4 - 16x^2 = 4x^2(x + 2)(x - 2).$$

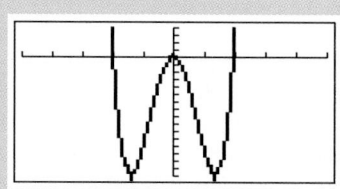

EXAMPLE 2 **Factoring a Polynomial**

Factor: $3x^2 - 6x - 45$

Solution

We begin by looking for a common factor. Since 3 is common to all terms, we factor it out.

$$3x^2 - 6x - 45 = 3(x^2 - 2x - 15) \quad \text{Factor out the GCF.}$$

The factor $x^2 - 2x - 15$ has three terms, but it is not a perfect square trinomial. We factor it using trial and error.

$$\begin{aligned} 3x^2 - 6x - 45 &= 3(x^2 - 2x - 15) \\ &= 3(x - 5)(x + 3) \quad \text{Factor the remaining trinomial.} \end{aligned}$$

We check by multiplication or with a graphing utility.

$$3(x - 5)(x + 3) = 3(x^2 - 2x - 15) = 3x^2 - 6x - 45$$

FOIL

Using technology

Graphing

$$y_1 = 3x^2 - 6x - 45$$

and

$$y_2 = 3(x - 5)(x + 3)$$

results in the same graph, so

$$3x^2 - 6x - 45$$
$$= 3(x - 5)(x + 3).$$

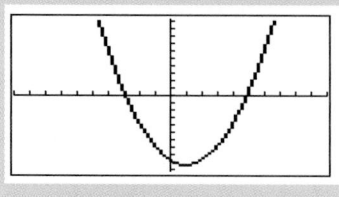

$[-10, 10] \times [-50, 50]$
$\text{Yscl} = 5$

EXAMPLE 3 **Factoring a Polynomial**

Factor: $-10y^2 + 7y + 6$

Solution

Since we usually factor trinomials with positive leading coefficients, we will first factor out -1.

$$-10y^2 + 7y + 6 = -1(10y^2 - 7y - 6) \quad \text{Factor out } -1.$$
$$= -(5y - 6)(2y + 1) \quad \text{Factor the remaining trinomial.}$$

Check this factorization using either multiplication or a graphing utility. ■

U **sing technology**

Graphing

$$y_1 = -10x^2 + 7x + 6$$

and

$$y_2 = -(5x - 6)(2x + 1)$$

results in the same graph, so

$$-10x^2 + 7x + 6 = -(5x - 6)(2x + 1).$$

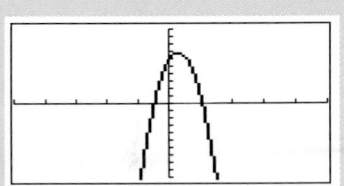

EXAMPLE 4 **Factoring a Polynomial**

Factor: $4x^4 - 64$

Solution

As with all problems in factoring, we begin by looking for a common factor, which in this case is 4.

$$4x^4 - 64 = 4(x^4 - 16) \quad \text{Factor out the GCF.}$$

We now consider the factor $x^4 - 16$. This binomial can be expressed as $(x^2)^2 - 4^2$, so it can be factored as the difference of two squares.

$$4x^4 - 64 = 4(x^4 - 16)$$
$$= 4(x^2 - 4)(x^2 + 4) \quad \begin{array}{l} x^4 - 16 = (x^2)^2 - 4^2, \text{ so factor using the difference of two squares.} \end{array}$$

We note that $(x^2 - 4)$ is also the difference of two squares, so we continue factoring.

$$4x^4 - 16 = 4(x + 2)(x - 2)(x^2 + 4) \quad \begin{array}{l} \text{Factor } x^2 - 4 \text{ as the difference of two squares.} \end{array}$$

We have now factored completely. No factor with more than one term can be factored further. As always, we check by multiplication or with a graphing utility.

$$4(x + 2)(x - 2)(x^2 + 4) = 4(x^2 - 4)(x^2 + 4) = 4(x^4 - 16) = 4x^4 - 64$$

■

U **sing technology**

Graphing

$$y_1 = 4x^4 - 64$$

and

$$y_2 = 4(x + 2)(x - 2)(x^2 + 4)$$

results in the same graph, so

$$4x^4 - 64$$
$$= 4(x + 2)(x - 2)(x^2 + 4).$$

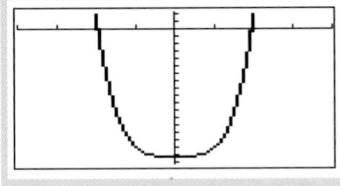

⊔sing technology

If you are having trouble finding a range setting that does not cut off your graph, finding the y-intercept (by setting $x = 0$) is helpful. In Example 4, the function

$$y = 4x^4 - 64$$

has a y-intercept of

$$y = 4(0)^4 - 64 = -64$$

so it's probably a good idea to take the y-axis down to -64 or slightly lower. The y-intercept led us to the following range setting:

Xmin = -4, Xmax = 4, Xscl = 1, Ymin = -68, Ymax = 8, Yscl = 4.

There is not necessarily a "best" setting, but remember that polynomial functions have graphs that are smooth, continuous curves, so this should be evident with the final range setting that you choose.

EXAMPLE 5   **Factoring a Polynomial**

Factor: $x^3 - 5x^2 - 4x + 20$

Solution

Other than 1, there is no common factor. Since there are four terms, we try factoring by grouping.

$$
\begin{aligned}
x^3 - 5x^2 &- 4x + 20 \\
&= (x^3 - 5x^2) + (-4x + 20) && \text{Group the terms with common factors.} \\
&= x^2(x - 5) - 4(x - 5) && \text{Factor from each group.} \\
&= (x - 5)(x^2 - 4) && \text{Factor out the common binomial factor, } (x - 5). \\
&= (x - 5)(x + 2)(x - 2) && \text{Factor completely by factoring } x^2 - 4 \text{ as the difference of two squares.}
\end{aligned}
$$

We have factored completely because no factor with more than one term can be factored further.

Check

$$
(x - 5)(x + 2)(x - 2) = (x - 5)(x^2 - 4) = \overset{F}{x^3} \overset{O}{- 4x} \overset{I}{- 5x^2} \overset{L}{+ 20}
$$
$$
= x^3 - 5x^2 - 4x + 20
$$

■

⊔sing technology

Graphing

$$y_1 = x^3 - 5x^2 - 4x + 20$$

and

$$y_2 = (x - 5)(x + 2)(x - 2)$$

results in the same graph, so

$$x^3 - 5x^2 - 4x + 20$$
$$= (x - 5)(x + 2)(x - 2).$$

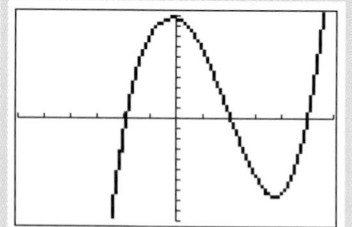

EXAMPLE 6   **Factoring a Polynomial**

Factor: $2x^3 - 24x^2 + 72x$

Solution

We begin by factoring out $2x$, the common factor.

$$2x^3 - 24x^2 + 72x = 2x(x^2 - 12x + 36) \qquad \text{Factor out the GCF.}$$

The factor $x^2 - 12x + 36$ has three terms. The first term (x^2) and the last term (36 or 6^2) are perfect squares. The middle term is twice the product of x and 6, and so we have a perfect square trinomial. We will factor using $A^2 - 2AB + B^2 = (A - B)^2$.

$$2x^3 - 24x^2 + 72x = 2x(x^2 - 12x + 36)$$
$$= 2x(x^2 - 2 \cdot x \cdot 6 + 6^2)$$

The second factor
is a perfect
square trinomial.

$$\uparrow \quad \uparrow \uparrow \uparrow \quad \uparrow$$
$$A^2 - 2 \; A \; B + B^2$$
$$= 2x(x - 6)^2 \qquad A^2 - 2AB + B^2 = (A - B)^2$$

Check this factorization using multiplication or a graphing utility.

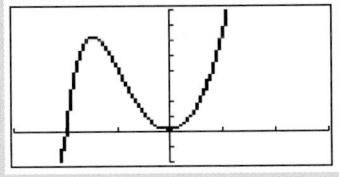
EXAMPLE 7 Factoring a Polynomial

Factor: $3x^5 + 24x^2$

Solution

We begin by factoring out $3x^2$, the common factor.

$$3x^5 + 24x^2 = 3x^2(x^3 + 8) \qquad \text{Factor out the GCF.}$$

Now we consider the factor $x^3 + 8$. Since it is a binomial, we look to see if it is one of the special forms. Since x^3 and 8 are perfect cubes ($8 = 2^3$), $x^3 + 8$ (or $x^3 + 2^3$) is the sum of two cubes.

$$3x^5 + 24x^2 = 3x^2(x^3 + 2^3) \qquad\qquad \text{Express } x^3 + 8 \text{ as}$$
$$\uparrow \quad \uparrow \qquad\qquad \text{the sum of two cubes.}$$
$$A^3 + B^3$$
$$= 3x^2(x + 2)(x^2 - 2x + 4) \qquad \text{Factor the sum of two cubes.}$$
$$\uparrow \quad \uparrow \uparrow \qquad \uparrow \qquad \uparrow$$
$$(A \; + \; B) \, (A^2 - AB + B^2)$$

Check by multiplication or with a graphing utility.

Polynomials in Several Variables

We can apply our factoring strategy to polynomials in two or more variables. The only difference in this situation is that the check of the factorization must be performed using multiplication.

EXAMPLE 8 Factoring a Polynomial in Two Variables

Factor: $5x^3y^4 + 20x^3y^3 - 105x^3y^2$

Solution

We begin by factoring out the greatest common factor. Factors of 5, x^3 (the smallest x power) and y^2 (the smallest y power) are common to the three terms, so the GCF is $5x^3y^2$.

$$5x^3y^4 + 20x^3y^3 - 105x^3y^2 = 5x^3y^2(y^2 + 4y - 21) \qquad \text{Factor out the GCF.}$$
$$= 5x^3y^2(y + 7)(y - 3) \qquad \text{Factor the remaining trinomial.}$$

EXAMPLE 9 Factoring a Polynomial in Two Variables

Factor: $18x^3 + 48x^2y + 32xy^2$

Solution

There is a common factor of $2x$, so we begin by factoring out this GCF.

$$18x^3 + 48x^2y + 32xy^2 = 2x(9x^2 + 24xy + 16y^2) \qquad \text{Factor out the GCF.}$$

The factor $9x^2 + 24xy + 16y^2$ has three terms. The first term, $9x^2$ or $(3x)^2$, and the last term, $16y^2$ or $(4y)^2$, are perfect squares. The middle term is twice the product of $3x$ and $4y$, and so we have a perfect square trinomial. We will factor using $A^2 + 2AB + B^2 = (A + B)^2$.

$$
\begin{aligned}
18x^3 + 48x^2y + 32xy^2 &= 2x(9x^2 + 24xy + 16y^2) \\
&= 2x[\underset{\uparrow}{(3x)^2} + \underset{\uparrow\,\uparrow}{2 \cdot 3x} \cdot \underset{\uparrow}{4y} + \underset{\uparrow}{(4y)^2}] \qquad \text{The second factor is a} \\
&\qquad\quad\; A^2 \;+\; 2\;\; A \;\; B \;+\; B^2 \qquad\qquad \text{perfect square trinomial.} \\
&= 2x(3x + 4y)^2 \qquad\qquad\qquad A^2 + 2AB + B^2 = (A + B)^2 \quad \blacksquare
\end{aligned}
$$

EXAMPLE 10   Factoring a Polynomial in Two Variables

Factor: $32x^4y - 2y^5$

Solution

We begin by looking for a common factor. The GCF is $2y$, so we factor it out.

$$32x^4y - 2y^5 = 2y(16x^4 - y^4) \qquad \text{Factor out the GCF.}$$

The factor $16x^4 - y^4$ is a binomial that can be expressed as $(4x^2)^2 - (y^2)^2$ and factored as the difference of two squares.

$$
\begin{aligned}
32x^4y - 2y^5 &= 2y[\underset{\uparrow}{(4x^2)^2} - \underset{\uparrow}{(y^2)^2}] \qquad\quad \text{Express } 16x^4 - y^4 \text{ as the} \\
&\qquad\quad\; A^2 \;\;-\;\; B^2 \qquad\qquad\qquad \text{difference of two squares.} \\
&= 2y\underset{\uparrow}{(4x^2} + \underset{\uparrow}{y^2)}\underset{\uparrow}{(4x^2} - \underset{\uparrow}{y^2)} \qquad A^2 - B^2 = (A + B)(A - B) \\
&\qquad\; A \;+\; B \quad\;\; A \;-\; B
\end{aligned}
$$

The last factor, $4x^2 - y^2$, can be factored further. It too is a difference of two squares, namely $(2x)^2 - y^2$. Thus,

$$32x^4y - 2y^5 = 2y(4x^2 + y^2)(2x + y)(2x - y). \qquad \blacksquare$$

Discover for yourself

Use multiplication to verify the factorizations in Examples 8–10. Then try evaluating the given polynomial and its factorization for $x = 1$ and $y = 2$. What do you observe? Which method, multiplication or evaluation, provides a more complete check of the factorization? Explain.

PROBLEM SET 7.5

Practice Problems

In Problems 1–64, factor completely, or state that the polynomial is prime. Check factorizations using multiplication or a graphing utility.

1. $3x^3 - 3x$

2. $5x^3 - 45x$

3. $3x^3 + 3x$

4. $5x^3 + 45x$

5. $4x^2 - 4x - 24$

6. $6x^2 - 18x - 60$

7. $2x^4 - 162$

8. $7x^4 - 7$

9. $x^3 + 2x^2 - 9x - 18$

10. $x^3 + 3x^2 - 25x - 75$

11. $3x^3 - 30x^2 + 75x$

12. $5x^3 - 20x^2 + 20x$

13. $2x^5 + 54x^2$

14. $2x^5 + 128x^2$

15. $6x^2 + 8x$

16. $21x^2 - 35x$

17. $2y^2 - 2y - 112$

18. $6x^2 - 6x - 12$

19. $7y^4 + 14y^3 + 7y^2$

20. $2y^4 + 28y^3 + 98y^2$

21. $y^2 + 8y - 16$

22. $y^2 - 18y - 81$

23. $16y^2 - 4y - 2$

24. $32y^2 + 4y - 6$

25. $r^2 - 25r$

26. $3r^2 - 27r$

27. $4w^2 + 8w - 5$

28. $35w^2 - 2w - 1$

29. $x^3 - 4x$

30. $9x^3 - 9x$

31. $x^2 + 64$

32. $y^2 + 36$

33. $9y^2 + 13y + 4$

34. $20y^2 + 12y + 1$

35. $y^3 + 2y^2 - 4y - 8$

36. $y^3 + 2y^2 - y - 2$

37. $9y^2 + 24y + 16$

38. $9y^2 + 6y + 1$

39. $5y^3 - 45y^2 + 70y$

40. $14y^3 + 7y^2 - 10y$

41. $y^5 - 81y$

42. $y^5 - 16y$

43. $20a^4 - 45a^2$

44. $48a^4 - 3a^2$

45. $12y^2 - 11y + 2$

46. $21x^2 - 25x - 4$

47. $9y^2 - 64$

48. $100y^2 - 49$

49. $9y^2 + 64$

50. $100y^2 + 49$

51. $2y^3 + 3y^2 - 50y - 75$

52. $12y^3 + 16y^2 - 3y - 4$

53. $-6x^2 - x + 1$

54. $-8x^2 + 10x + 3$

55. $2r^3 + 30r^2 - 68r$

56. $3r^3 - 27r^2 - 210r$

57. $8x^5 - 2x^3$

58. $y^9 - y^5$

59. $3x^2 + 243$

60. $27x^2 + 75$

61. $x^4 + 8x$

62. $x^4 + 27x$

63. $2y^5 - 2y^2$

64. $2y^5 - 128y^2$

Problems 65–94 contain polynomials in several variables. Factor each polynomial completely and check using multiplication.

65. $6x^2 + 8xy$

66. $21x^2 - 35xy$

67. $xy - 7x + 3y - 21$

68. $xy - 5x + 2y - 10$

69. $x^2 - 3xy - 4y^2$

70. $x^2 - 4xy - 12y^2$

71. $72a^3b^2 + 12a^2 - 24a^4b^2$

72. $24a^4b + 60a^3b^2 + 150a^2b^3$

73. $3a^2 + 27ab + 54b^2$

74. $3a^2 + 15ab + 18b^2$

75. $48x^4y - 3x^2y$

76. $16a^3b^2 - 4ab^2$

77. $6a^2b + ab - 2b$

78. $16a^2 - 32ab + 12b^2$

79. $7x^5y - 7xy^5$

80. $3x^4y^2 - 3x^2y^2$

81. $24a^2b + 6a^3b - 45a^4b$

82. $18x^3y + 57x^2y^2 + 30xy^3$

83. $2bx^2 + 44bx + 242b$

84. $3xz^2 - 72xz + 432x$

85. $15a^2 + 11ab - 14b^2$

86. $25a^2 + 25ab + 6b^2$

87. $36x^3y - 62x^2y^2 + 12xy^3$

88. $10a^4b^2 - 15a^3b^3 - 25a^2b^4$

89. $a^2y - b^2y - a^2x + b^2x$

90. $bx^2 - 4b + ax^2 - 4a$

91. $9ax^3 + 15ax^2 - 14ax$

92. $4ay^3 - 12ay^2 + 9ay$

93. $81x^4y - y^5$

94. $1 - 16a^{12}b^{12}$

Application Problems

95. The building shown in the figure has a height represented by x feet. The building's base is a square and its volume is $x^3 - 60x^2 + 900x$ cubic feet. Express the building's dimensions in terms of x.

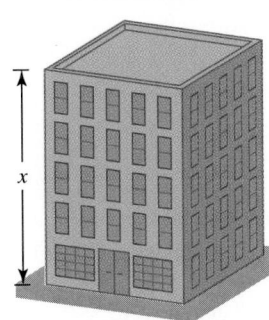

96. Express the area of the shaded ring shown in the figure in terms of π. Then factor this expression completely.

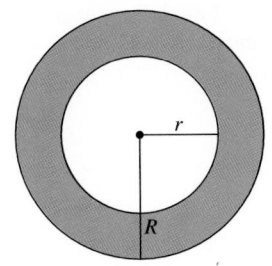

97. A rock is dropped from the top of a 256-foot cliff. The height of the rock above the water after t seconds is modeled by the polynomial $-16t^2 + 256$. Factor this expression completely. Use the factored form of the expression to find when the height of the rock above the water is 0 feet. Asked in an equivalent way, how long will it take the rock to hit the water?

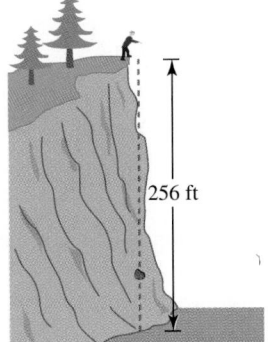

256 ft

True–False Critical Thinking Problems

98. Which one of the following is true?
   a. $x^2 - 9 = (x - 3)^2$ for any real number x.
   b. The polynomial $4x^2 + 100$ is the sum of two squares and therefore cannot be factored.
   c. If the general factoring strategy is used to factor a polynomial, at least two factorizations are necessary before the given polynomial is factored completely.
   d. Once a common monomial factor is removed from $3xy^3 + 9xy^2 + 21xy$, the remaining trinomial factor cannot be factored further.

99. Which one of the following is true?
   a. The polynomial $x^2y^2 + 7xy + 12$ cannot be factored due to the fact that there are two variables in the first term.

   b. A partial check to see if a polynomial has been factored correctly can be performed by evaluating both the polynomial and its factorization for a few values of the variable. If the factorization is correct, the polynomial and its factored form will have the same value for any replacement(s) of the variable.
   c. Once a GCF has been factored out of a polynomial, if the remaining factor is a trinomial whose coefficient is 1, further factorization is always possible.
   d. To factor by grouping, the terms in a polynomial must always be rearranged.

Technology Problems

In Problems 100–104, use a graphing utility to graph the function on the left side and the function on the right side in the same viewing rectangle. Are the graphs identical? If so, this means that the polynomial on the left side has been correctly factored. If not, factor the polynomial correctly and then use your graphing utility to verify the factorization.

100. $4x^2 - 12x + 9 = (4x - 3)^2$

101. $3x^3 - 12x^2 - 15x = 3x(x + 5)(x - 1)$

102. $6x^2 + 10x - 4 = 2(3x - 1)(x + 2)$

103. $x^4 - 16 = (x^2 + 4)(x + 2)(x - 2)$

104. $2x^3 + 10x^2 - 2x - 10 = 2(x + 5)(x^2 + 1)$

Writing in Mathematics

105. Describe a strategy that can be used to factor polynomials.

106. Explain what it means to completely factor a polynomial.

107. Explain why $9 - 6x + x^2$ can be factored as either $(3 - x)^2$ or $(x - 3)^2$.

Critical Thinking Problems

Factor the polynomials in Problems 108–113 completely.

108. $3x^5 - 21x^3 - 54x$

109. $5y^5 - 5y^4 - 20y^3 + 20y^2$

110. $x^2(x + 3) - x(x + 3) - 6(x + 3)$

111. $(x + 5)^2 - 20(x + 5) + 100$

112. $3x^{2n} - 27y^{2n}$

113. Suppose that a polynomial in x is of degree 20. At most, how many factors can this polynomial have? Explain your answer.

Review Problems

114. Graph the solution set in a rectangular coordinate system: $5x - 2y > 10$.

115. Solve the system:

$$x = 13 - 3y$$
$$x + y = 5$$

116. The second angle of a triangle measures three times that of the first angle's measure. The third angle measures 30° more than the first. Find the measure of each angle.

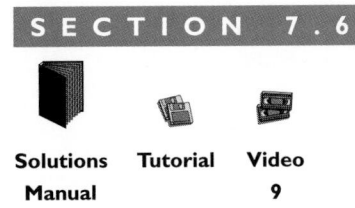

SECTION 7.6

Solutions   Tutorial   Video
Manual   9

Solving Quadratic Equations by Factoring

Objectives

1   Solve quadratic equations by factoring.
2   Solve problems using quadratic models.

In this section, we apply factoring techniques to answer questions about variables contained in mathematical models. To do this, we need to study equations in which the variable is raised to the second power, such as $x^2 - 7x + 10 = 0$.

A quadratic equation contains a variable with an exponent of 2, but no higher power. A *quadratic equation in x* is frequently written in the *standard form* $ax^2 + bx + c = 0$, where a, b, and c are real numbers and $a \neq 0$. (If we allowed a to equal 0, the equation would not be quadratic. The resulting equation, $bx + c = 0$, would be a linear equation.)

> **Quadratic equation in x in standard form**
>
> $$ax^2 + bx + c = 0 \quad a \neq 0$$

A quadratic equation is in standard form if the polynomial is in descending powers and equal to zero. A number of quadratic equations written in standard form are listed below.

Quadratic Equation	Standard Form: $ax^2 + bx + c = 0$	Values of a, b, and c
$5x - 6 = -x^2$	Add x^2 to both sides. $\longrightarrow$ $x^2 + 5x - 6 = 0$	$a = 1, b = 5, c = -6$
$2x^2 = -4x + 3$	Add $4x - 3$ to both sides. $\longrightarrow$ $2x^2 + 4x - 3 = 0$	$a = 2, b = 4, c = -3$
$x^2 = 8x$	Subtract $8x$ from both sides. $\longrightarrow$ $x^2 - 8x = 0$	$a = 1, b = -8, c = 0$
$x^2 = 4$	Subtract 4 from both sides. $\longrightarrow$ $\begin{matrix} x^2 - 4 = 0 \\ x^2 + 0x - 4 = 0 \end{matrix}$	$a = 1, b = 0, c = -4$

■ Solve quadratic equations by factoring.

If the trinomial $ax^2 + bx + c$ can be factored, then $ax^2 + bx + c = 0$ can be solved by using the *zero-product principle*.

> **The zero-product principle**
>
> Let A and B be real numbers, variables, or algebraic expressions. If $AB = 0$, then $A = 0$ or $B = 0$ or A and B are both 0. In words, this says that if a product is zero, at least one of the factors is equal to zero.

EXAMPLE 1   Using the Zero-Product Principle

Solve the equation: $(3x - 1)(x + 2) = 0$

Solution

The product $(3x - 1)(x + 2)$ is equal to zero. By the zero-product principle, the only way that this product can be zero is if at least one of the factors is zero. Thus,

$$3x - 1 = 0 \quad \text{or} \quad x + 2 = 0.$$
$$3x = 1 \quad \text{or} \quad x = -2 \quad \text{Solve each equation for } x.$$
$$x = \tfrac{1}{3} \quad \text{or} \quad x = -2$$

Since each linear equation has a solution, the original equation given above, $(3x - 1)(x + 2) = 0$, has two solutions, $\frac{1}{3}$ and -2.

Check

To check these solutions, we substitute each one separately in the original equation.

For $x = \frac{1}{3}$:

$$(3x - 1)(x + 2) = 0$$
$$(3 \cdot \tfrac{1}{3} - 1)(\tfrac{1}{3} + 2) \stackrel{?}{=} 0$$
$$(1 - 1)(\tfrac{1}{3} + 2) \stackrel{?}{=} 0$$
$$(0)(2\tfrac{1}{3}) \stackrel{?}{=} 0$$
$$0 = 0 \quad \checkmark \quad \text{True}$$

For $x = -2$:

$$(3x - 1)(x + 2) = 0$$
$$[3(-2) - 1](-2 + 2) \stackrel{?}{=} 0$$
$$(-7)(0) \stackrel{?}{=} 0$$
$$0 = 0 \quad \checkmark \quad \text{True}$$

The solutions are $\frac{1}{3}$ and -2.   ∎

In Example 1, the given equation was in factored form. In our next example, we must first do the factoring.

EXAMPLE 2   Using the Zero-Product Principle

Solve: $x^2 - 7x + 10 = 0$

Solution

Notice that the variable is squared and that there are no like terms that can be combined. So, we begin by factoring the polynomial. Then we use the zero-product principle.

$$x^2 - 7x + 10 = 0 \quad \text{This is the given quadratic equation.}$$
$$(x - 5)(x - 2) = 0 \quad \text{Factor on the left.}$$
$$x - 5 = 0 \quad \text{or} \quad x - 2 = 0 \quad \text{Set each factor equal to 0, using the zero-product principle.}$$
$$x = 5 \quad \text{or} \quad x = 2 \quad \text{Solve the two resulting equations.}$$

Check

For $x = 5$:

$$x^2 - 7x + 10 = 0$$
$$5^2 - 7 \cdot 5 + 10 \stackrel{?}{=} 0$$

For $x = 2$:

$$x^2 - 7x + 10 = 0$$
$$2^2 - 7 \cdot 2 + 10 \stackrel{?}{=} 0$$

Using technology

A graphing utility can be used to solve a quadratic equation. To solve Example 2, graph the quadratic function

$$y = x^2 - 7x + 10,$$

as shown below. Observe that the graph crosses the x-axis at 2 and 5. Thus, 2 and 5 are the x-intercepts. It is also the case that 2 and 5 are the solutions to

$$x^2 - 7x + 10 = 0.$$

Can you explain why this is so?

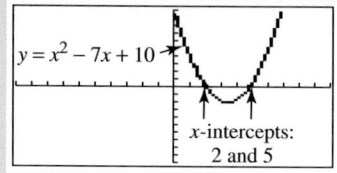

$y = x^2 - 7x + 10$

x-intercepts: 2 and 5

$$25 - 35 + 10 \overset{?}{=} 0 \qquad\qquad 4 - 14 + 10 \overset{?}{=} 0$$
$$-10 + 10 \overset{?}{=} 0 \qquad\qquad -10 + 10 \overset{?}{=} 0$$
$$0 = 0 \quad \checkmark \quad \text{True} \qquad\qquad 0 = 0 \quad \checkmark \quad \text{True}$$

The solutions are 5 and 2. ■

Let's summarize the steps involved in solving a quadratic equation by factoring.

Solving a quadratic equation by factoring

1. If necessary, write the equation in the form $ax^2 + bx + c = 0$, setting one side equal to 0.
2. Factor.
3. Apply the zero-product principle, setting each factor equal to 0.
4. Solve the equations in step 3.
5. Check the solutions in the original equation.

EXAMPLE 3 **Using the Zero-Product Principle**

Solve: $x^2 - 2x = 35$

Solution

To use the zero-product principle, we must have two factors equal to zero. We want 0 on one side of the equation. This can be accomplished by subtracting 35 on both sides, writing the quadratic equation in standard form.

$$x^2 - 2x = 35 \qquad \text{This is the given equation.}$$
$$x^2 - 2x - 35 = 0 \qquad \text{Subtract 35 from both sides.}$$
$$(x - 7)(x + 5) = 0 \qquad \text{Factor.}$$
$$x - 7 = 0 \quad \text{or} \quad x + 5 = 0 \qquad \text{Apply the zero-product principle.}$$
$$x = 7 \quad \text{or} \qquad x = -5 \quad \text{Solve the two resulting equations.}$$

Check the solutions in the *original* equation.

For 7:   **For -5:**

$$x^2 - 2x = 35 \qquad\qquad x^2 - 2x = 35$$
$$7^2 - 2 \cdot 7 \overset{?}{=} 35 \qquad\qquad (-5)^2 - 2(-5) \overset{?}{=} 35$$
$$49 - 14 \overset{?}{=} 35 \qquad\qquad 25 + 10 \overset{?}{=} 35$$
$$35 = 35 \quad \checkmark \quad \text{True} \qquad\qquad 35 = 35 \quad \checkmark \quad \text{True}$$

The solutions are 7 and -5. ■

sing technology

The graphs of all quadratic functions

$$f(x) = ax^2 + bx + c \quad \text{or}$$
$$y = ax^2 + bx + c$$

are shaped as shown in the figure.

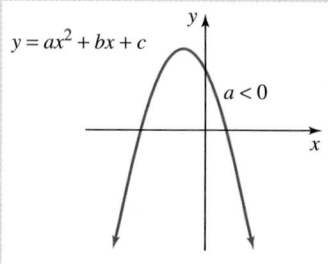

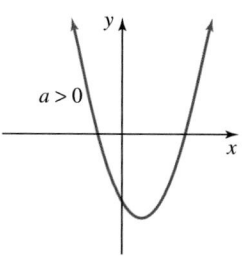

The x-intercepts for the graph can be found by replacing y (or $f(x)$) with 0 and solving for x. This results in

$$ax^2 + bx + c = 0.$$

sing technology

The graph of the quadratic function

$$y = x^2 - 2x - 35$$

is shown at the right. The x-intercepts, -5 and 7, are the solutions to

$$x^2 - 2x - 35 = 0.$$

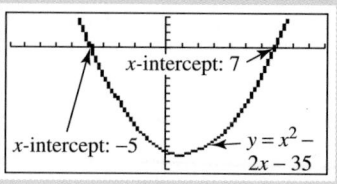

We can summarize the result found in the Using Technology box as follows.

> The x-intercepts of the graph of $y = ax^2 + bx + c$ are the solutions of the quadratic equation $ax^2 + bx + c = 0$.

EXAMPLE 4   **Solving a Quadratic Equation by Factoring**

Solve: $3x^2 = 2x$

Solution

$3x^2 = 2x$		This is the given equation.
$3x^2 - 2x = 0$		Write the equation in standard form, subtracting $2x$ from both sides.
$x(3x - 2) = 0$		Factor the left side.
$x = 0$ or $3x - 2 = 0$		Apply the zero-product principle.
$x = 0$ or $3x = 2$		Solve the resulting two equations.
$x = 0$ or $x = \frac{2}{3}$		

Check these values in the original equation and verify that the solutions are 0 and $\frac{2}{3}$. ∎

sing technology

The graph of the quadratic function $y = 3x^2 - 2x$ is shown in the figure.

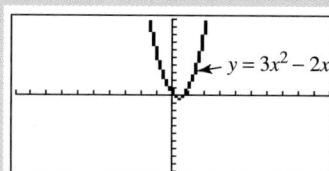

In Example 4, we found that the solutions of $3x^2 - 2x = 0$ are 0 and $\frac{2}{3}$. Although it's somewhat obvious from the graph that 0 is an x-intercept, it's difficult to see that the other x-intercept is $\frac{2}{3}$. Since the greater x-intercept appears to be between 0 and 1, use the ZOOM and TRACE features to focus on this portion of the graph.

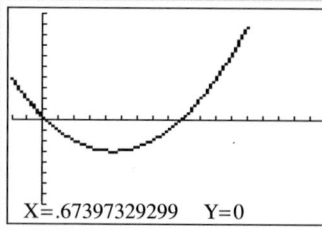

Now you can see that there is an x-intercept at approximately 0.674, or approximately $\frac{2}{3}$.

tudy tip

Avoid dividing both sides of $3x^2 = 2x$ by x. You will obtain $3x = 2$ and, consequently, $x = \frac{2}{3}$. The other solution, 0, is lost. We can divide both sides of an equation by any *nonzero* real number. If x is zero, we lose the second solution.

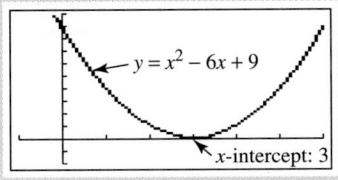

sing technology

The graph of $y = x^2 - 6x + 9$ is shown below. Notice that there is only one x-intercept, namely 3, verifying that the solution of

$$x^2 - 6x + 9 = 0$$

is 3.

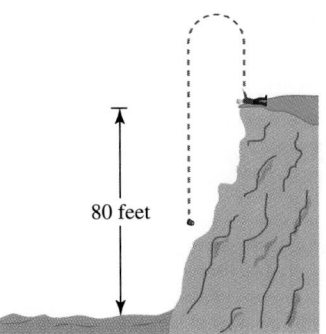

EXAMPLE 5   **A Quadratic Equation with a Repeated Solution**

Solve: $x^2 - 6x + 24 = 15$

Solution

$x^2 - 6x + 24 = 15$	This is the given equation.
$x^2 - 6x + 9 = 0$	Write the equation in standard form, subtracting 15 from both sides.
$(x - 3)^2 = 0$	Factor.
$x - 3 = 0$	Set the factor equal to 0.
$x = 3$	Solve the resulting equation.

Although we can think of the left side of this equation as

$$(x - 3)(x - 3) = 0$$

so

$$x - 3 = 0 \quad \text{or} \quad x - 3 = 0$$

the two factors are the same. Thus, the only solution of the equation is 3. Checking this value in the original equation, we see that the solution is 3. ∎

2 Solve problems using quadratic models.

Using Mathematical Models

Factoring techniques can be used to answer questions about variables contained in mathematical models.

EXAMPLE 6   **Modeling Motion**

A person lying close to the edge of an 80-foot cliff throws a rock upward with an initial speed of 64 feet per second, as shown in Figure 7.1. After t seconds, the height $f(t)$ (in feet) of the rock above the water is described by the quadratic model

$$f(t) = -16t^2 + 64t + 80.$$

How long will it take for the rock to reach the water?

Solution

$f(t) = -16t^2 + 64t + 80$	This is the given function.
$0 = -16t^2 + 64t + 80$	When the rock reaches the water, its height above the water is 0 feet, so substitute 0 for $f(t)$.
$0 = -16(t^2 - 4t - 5)$	Factor out -16, the GCF.
$0 = -16(t - 5)(t + 1)$	Factor the trinomial.
$t - 5 = 0 \quad \text{or} \quad t + 1 = 0$	Set each variable factor equal to 0.
$t = 5 \quad \text{or} \quad t = -1$	Solve the resulting two equations.

Since we begin timing the motion of the rock at $t = 0$, we reject -1 as a meaningful solution. Thus, $t = 5$, meaning that it takes 5 seconds for the rock to reach the water.

Figure 7.1

Throwing a rock directly upward from an 80-foot cliff

80 feet

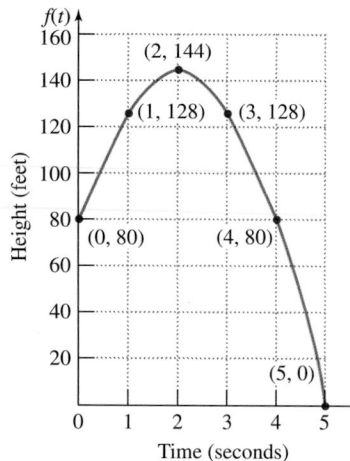

Figure 7.2

The graph of
$f(t) = -16t^2 + 64t + 80$

A better understanding of the solution comes from making a graph of $f(t) = -16t^2 + 64t + 80$. Integer values of t and the corresponding values of $f(t)$ are shown in the table of values.

Time t	Height $f(t) = -16t^2 + 64t + 80$	Ordered Pair
0	$f(0) = -16(0)^2 + 64(0) + 80 = 80$	$(0, 80)$
1	$f(1) = -16(1)^2 + 64(1) + 80 = 128$	$(1, 128)$
2	$f(2) = -16(2)^2 + 64(2) + 80 = 144$	$(2, 144)$
3	$f(3) = -16(3)^2 + 64(3) + 80 = 128$	$(3, 128)$
4	$f(4) = -16(4)^2 + 64(4) + 80 = 80$	$(4, 80)$
5	$f(5) = -16(5)^2 + 64(5) + 80 = 0$	$(5, 0)$

In Figure 7.2, the ordered pairs from the table are plotted and points are connected with a smooth curve, representing the graph of $f(t) = -16t^2 + 64t + 80$. The graph indicates that $f(0) = 80$. That's the situation just before the rock is thrown upward from the 80-foot cliff. The graph shows that the rock reaches its highest point after 2 seconds (144 feet above the water), and then begins to fall. The rock hits the water at $t = 5$ seconds. ∎

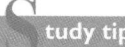 **tudy tip**

In Example 6, notice that when we had

$$-16(t - 5)(t + 1) = 0$$

we did not set -16 equal to 0 since -16 is *not* equal to 0.

We use the zero-product principle to set *variable factors* equal to 0 because they are the only factors that can possibly be 0.

Creating Mathematical Models

In Example 6, we were given the function that modeled the rock's position over time. A more difficult situation is to use a problem's condition to create a mathematical model. By setting this model equal to a value specified in the problem, we wind up with an equation to solve. In the problems that follow, these equations will be quadratic.

In Examples 7–9, we use our five-step problem-solving strategy and methods for solving quadratic equations to solve each problem.

EXAMPLE 7   **Teachers as Victims of Crimes**

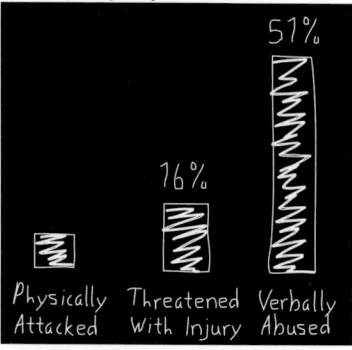

Teachers as Victims of Crimes

Percentage of teachers in U.S. who say they have been:

Figure 7.3

Source: Carnegie Foundation

The bar graph in Figure 7.3 shows the percentage of teachers in the United States who say they have been verbally abused, threatened with injury, or physically attacked. The percentage who say they have been physically attacked is missing from the graph, but this much is known about the number when it is expressed as a percent: The product of the number increased by 1 percent and the number decreased by 2 percent is 40 percent. What percentage of teachers in the United States say they have been physically attacked?

Steps 1 and 2. Represent unknown quantities in terms of x.

Step 3. Write an equation that describes the conditions.

Step 4. Solve the equation and answer the question.

Step 5. Check.

Solution

Let x = the percentage of teachers who say they have been physically attacked.

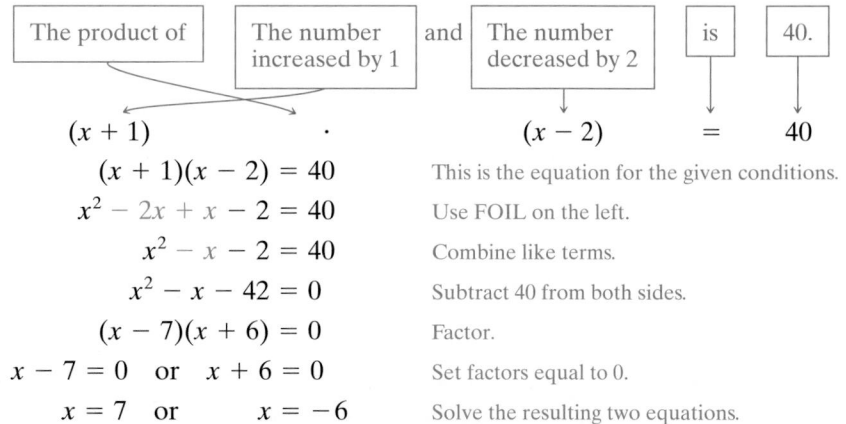

$$(x + 1) \qquad \cdot \qquad (x - 2) \qquad = \qquad 40$$

$(x + 1)(x - 2) = 40$ This is the equation for the given conditions.

$x^2 - 2x + x - 2 = 40$ Use FOIL on the left.

$x^2 - x - 2 = 40$ Combine like terms.

$x^2 - x - 42 = 0$ Subtract 40 from both sides.

$(x - 7)(x + 6) = 0$ Factor.

$x - 7 = 0$ or $x + 6 = 0$ Set factors equal to 0.

$x = 7$ or $x = -6$ Solve the resulting two equations.

Since a negative percent of teachers could not be physically attacked, we reject -6 as a meaningful solution. It appears that 7% of teachers in the United States say they have been physically attacked.

The product of this number increased by 1% (giving 8%) and the number decreased by 2% (giving 5%) is $8 \cdot 5$, or 40%, as specified by the problem's conditions. ■

We have seen that geometric situations can often be modeled by polynomial functions. In Example 8 we set such a function equal to a particular value.

EXAMPLE 8   **A Problem Involving the Area of a Rectangle**

An architect is allowed no more than 15 square meters to add a small bedroom on to a house. Because of the room's design in relationship to the existing structure, the width of its rectangular floor must be 7 meters less than two times the length. Find the precise length and width of the rectangular floor that the architect is permitted.

Steps 1 and 2. Represent unknown quantities in terms of x.

Solution

Let

     x = Length of the floor

$2x - 7$ = Width of the floor (The width is 7 meters less than 2 times the length.)

The function that models this situation is based on the fact that the area of a rectangle is the product of its length and its width. Calling the function f, we have

$$f(x) = x(2x - 7).$$

Since we want an area of 15 square meters, we set the function equal to 15.

$$f(x) = x(2x - 7) = 15.$$

ENRICHMENT ESSAY

Problems of Translation

Solving many word problems involves translating verbal conditions into algebraic equations. To translate, we must understand the English prose and also be familiar with the forms of algebraic language. Literal translations often do not work: for example, 8 less than some number translates as $x - 8$ and not as $8 - x$.

Literal translations from one language to another, with no understanding of idioms or syntax, can lead to bizarre results. An extraordinary book, called *The New Guide of the Conversation in Portuguese and English,* appeared in Paris in 1815. The author took his familiar language, Portuguese, translated it into French, a language of which he had only a rudimentary grasp, and then via literal translation from a French–English dictionary, translated the French into English, a language of which he had not the slightest knowledge. Here are some excerpts:

"Idiotisms of Going Fishing"
    "That pond it seems me many multiplied of fishes. Let us amuse rather to the fishing. . . . I do like it too much. . . . Here, there is a wand and some hooks. . . . Silence! there is a superb perch. Give me quick the rod. Ah! there it is. It is a lamprey. . . . You mistake you, it is a frog."

"Familiar Phrases"
    "I shall not tell you than two words."
    "Let us prick go us more fast."
    "There is some foggy. It is light moon's."
    "He suffer from the vomitory."

What should some of these translations be?

Step 3. Write an equation that describes the conditions.

Chances are you will immediately begin by writing an equation.

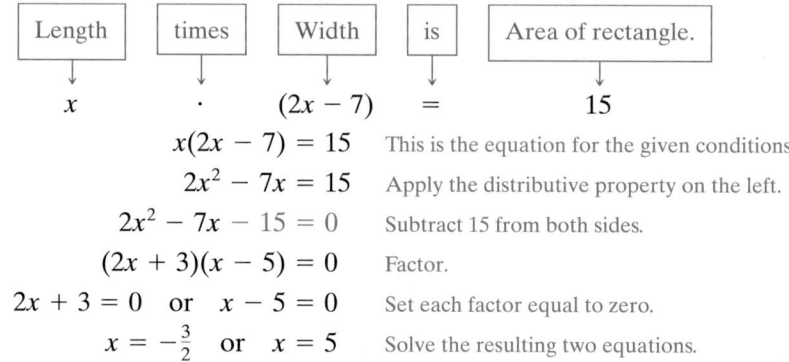

Length	times	Width	is	Area of rectangle.
↓	↓	↓	↓	↓
x	$\cdot$	$(2x - 7)$	$=$	15

Step 4. Solve the equation and answer the question.

$x(2x - 7) = 15$ This is the equation for the given conditions.

$2x^2 - 7x = 15$ Apply the distributive property on the left.

$2x^2 - 7x - 15 = 0$ Subtract 15 from both sides.

$(2x + 3)(x - 5) = 0$ Factor.

$2x + 3 = 0$ or $x - 5 = 0$ Set each factor equal to zero.

$x = -\frac{3}{2}$ or $x = 5$ Solve the resulting two equations.

Step 5. Check.

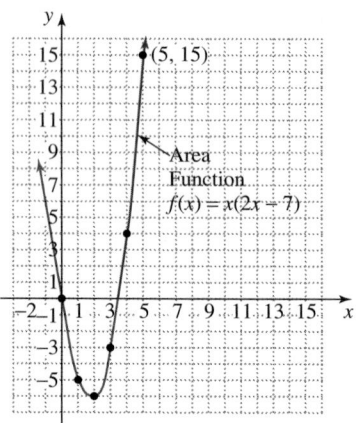

Figure 7.4

Visualizing an area of 15 square meters with a length of 5 meters

Since a rectangle cannot have negative length, we discard the solution $-\frac{3}{2}$. Then 5 meters is the length of the floor and $2x - 7 = 2(5) - 7 = 3$ meters is the width. The area is $3 \cdot 5 = 15$ square meters, as specified in the problem.

The solution to this problem is visually displayed in Figure 7.4. The figure shows the graph of the function that models the bedroom's area. Values along the x-axis represent the bedroom's length and values along the y-axis represent its area. The portion of the graph that is red is the part that is geometrically significant since length and area must both be positive. The point (5, 15) illustrates that with a floor length of 5 meters, the room's area is 15 square meters, the maximum that the architect is allowed. ■

Modeling geometric situations often depends on knowing formulas needed to solve a problem. In Example 8 we needed to know the formula for the area of a rectangle. Example 9 relies on a knowledge of the Pythagorean Theorem.

The Pythagorean theorem

In any right triangle, the square of the longest side (the *hypotenuse*) is equal to the sum of the squares of the other two sides (the *legs*):

$$c^2 = a^2 + b^2$$

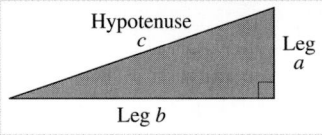

EXAMPLE 9 **A Problem Involving the Pythagorean Theorem**

At point C the ship in Figure 7.5 is 26 miles from lower Manhattan. Cruising west to point B and then north to Manhattan (point A) is a 34-mile trip. If the distance from point C to point B is greater than the distance from point B to Manhattan, how far is it from point C to point B?

Discover for yourself

The problem asks for the distance from C to B. Before solving the problem using algebra, let's consider a few specific values for this distance.

The sum of these distances is 34 miles.

Distance from **C** to **B**	Distance from **B** to **A**
20 miles	$34 - 20 = 14$ miles
21 miles	$34 - 21 = 13$ miles
22 miles	$34 - 22 = 12$ miles
23 miles	$34 - 23 = 11$ miles

Do you see a pattern forming? If x represents the length of leg CB, use this pattern to write an algebraic expression in terms of x for leg BA.

Take a moment to try the Pythagorean Theorem for some of the numbers in the table. Remembering that the hypotenuse of the right triangle formed in Figure 7.5 is 26 miles, if the numbers in the first row are the actual distances, then the sum of the squares of 20 and 14 must give the square of 26. Is $20^2 + 14^2 = 26^2$? Try a few other values in the table. Can you guess at the unknown distances in Figure 7.5? Test to see if the three resulting numbers satisfy the Pythagorean Theorem.

Solution

Steps 1 and 2. Represent unknown quantities in terms of x.

Let

$\quad x = $ the distance from C to B

Since $CB + BA = 34$ miles, then

$\quad 34 - x = $ the distance from B to A

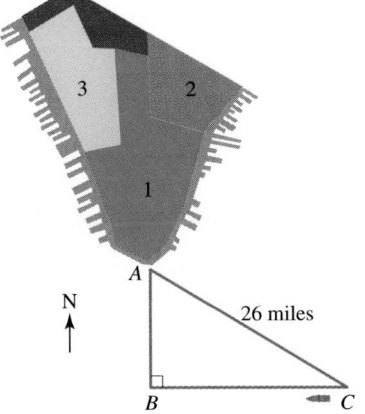

Figure 7.5

Cruising to Manhattan

Step 3. Write an equation that describes the conditions.

The lengths of the legs of the right triangle are x and $34 - x$. The hypotenuse has length 26 miles. These three lengths satisfy the Pythagorean Theorem.

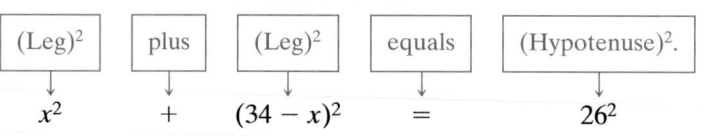

$$x^2 \qquad + \qquad (34 - x)^2 \qquad = \qquad 26^2$$

Step 4. Solve the equation and answer the question.

$$x^2 + (34 - x)^2 = 26^2 \qquad \text{This is the equation arising from the Pythagorean Theorem.}$$

$$x^2 + 1156 - 68x + x^2 = 676 \qquad \text{Square the binomial and square 26.}$$

$$2x^2 - 68x + 1156 = 676 \qquad \text{Combine like terms and write the left side in descending powers of } x.$$

$$2x^2 - 68x + 480 = 0 \qquad \text{Subtract 676 on both sides to get 0 on one side.}$$

$$2(x^2 - 34x + 240) = 0 \qquad \text{Factor out the GCF.}$$

$$2(x - 24)(x - 10) = 0 \qquad \text{Factor the trinomial.}$$

$$x - 24 = 0 \quad \text{or} \quad x - 10 = 0 \qquad \text{Set each variable factor equal to 0.}$$

$$x = 24 \quad \text{or} \quad x = 10 \qquad \text{Solve the resulting two equations.}$$

There appear to be two possibilities:

$$CB = x = 24 \text{ miles} \qquad \text{or} \qquad CB = x = 10 \text{ miles}$$

$$BA = 34 - x = 34 - 24 \qquad\qquad BA = 34 - x = 34 - 10$$
$$= 10 \text{ miles} \qquad\qquad\qquad = 24 \text{ miles}$$

We discard the second possibility because we were told that CB is the greater distance. Thus, the distance from point C to point B is 24 miles.

Step 5. Check.

CB (24 miles), BA (10 miles), and the length of the hypotenuse (26 miles) should satisfy the Pythagorean Theorem. Complete the check by showing that $24^2 + 10^2 = 26^2$. ■

PROBLEM SET 7.6

Practice Problems

Solve the equations in Problems 1–64. Check each solution by substitution or using a graphing utility and identifying x-intercepts.

1. $(x - 2)(x + 3) = 0$ **2.** $(y - 3)(y + 7) = 0$ **3.** $(3x + 4)(2x - 1) = 0$ **4.** $(2y + 5)(y - 3) = 0$

5. $(2y - 1)(4y + 1) = 0$ **6.** $(3x - 7)(3x + 1) = 0$ **7.** $(2y + 7)(3y - 1) = 0$ **8.** $(9x - 4)(3x + 1) = 0$

9. $(z - 2)(3z + 7) = 0$ **10.** $(z - 5)(4z + 9) = 0$ **11.** $(4w - 9)(2w + 5) = 0$ **12.** $(5w - 2)(3w + 1) = 0$

13. $x^2 + 8x + 15 = 0$ **14.** $x^2 + 5x + 6 = 0$ **15.** $y^2 - 2y - 15 = 0$ **16.** $y^2 + y - 42 = 0$

17. $m^2 - 4m = 21$ **18.** $m^2 + 7m = 18$ **19.** $z^2 + 9z = -8$ **20.** $z^2 - 11z = -10$

21. $y^2 + 4y = 0$ **22.** $y^2 - 6y = 0$ **23.** $x^2 - 5x = 0$ **24.** $x^2 + 3x = 0$

25. $x^2 = 4x$ **26.** $x^2 = 8x$ **27.** $2x^2 = 5x$ **28.** $3x^2 = 5x$

29. $3x^2 = -5x$ **30.** $2x^2 = -3x$ **31.** $x^2 + 4x + 4 = 0$ **32.** $x^2 + 6x + 9 = 0$

33. $x^2 - 12x = 36$ **34.** $x^2 - 14x = 49$ **35.** $4x^2 - 12x = 9$ **36.** $9x^2 - 30x = 25$

37. $2x^2 = 7x + 4$ **38.** $3x^2 = x + 4$ **39.** $5x^2 + x = 18$ **40.** $3x^2 - 4x = 15$

41. $x(6x + 23) + 7 = 0$ **42.** $x(6x + 13) + 6 = 0$ **43.** $3s^2 + 4s = -1$ **44.** $7s^2 + 15s = -2$

45. $4x(x + 1) = 15$ **46.** $3x(3x + 2) = 8$ **47.** $12r^2 + 31r + 20 = 0$ **48.** $35r^2 + 34r + 8 = 0$

49. $12s^2 + 28s - 24 = 0$ **50.** $20s^2 - 25s + 5 = 0$ **51.** $w^2 - 5w = 18 + 2w$ **52.** $3w^2 + 8w = 15 + 12w$

53. $z(z + 8) = 16(z - 1)$ **54.** $z(9 + z) = 4(5 + 2z)$ **55.** $16x^2 - 49 = 0$ **56.** $4x^2 - 25 = 0$

57. $(y - 3)(y + 8) = -30$ **58.** $(y - 1)(y + 4) = 14$ **59.** $(z + 1)(2z + 5) = -1$ **60.** $(z + 5)(3z - 2) = -14$

61. $4y^2 + 20y + 25 = 0$ **62.** $4y^2 + 44y + 121 = 0$ **63.** $64w^2 - 48w + 9 = 0$ **64.** $25w^2 - 80w + 64 = 0$

Application Problems

65. A projectile is fired straight upward from the ground with a velocity of 128 feet per second. Its height ($f(t)$, in feet) above the ground after t seconds is described by the model $f(t) = -16t^2 + 128t$.

   a. How long will it take the projectile to hit the ground?

   b. Complete the following table of values.

Time t	Height $f(t) = -16t^2 + 128t$
0	
1	
2	
3	
4	
5	
6	
7	
8	

   c. Graph $f(t) = -16t^2 + 128t$ using the ordered pairs from the table, connecting points with a smooth curve.

   d. As you look at the graph, describe when the projectile reaches its maximum height. What is the maximum height?

   e. How is your solution to part (a) shown in the graph?

66. The function $f(x) = 2x^2 + 22x + 320$ models the number of inmates ($f(x)$ in thousands) in federal and state prisons x years after 1980.

   a. In what year was the prison population 480 thousand?

   b. The graph of $y = 2x^2 + 22x + 320$ was obtained with a graphing utility, using the following range setting:

   Xmin = 0, Xmax = 15, Xscl = 1,
   Ymin = 0, Ymax = 1000, Yscl = 100

The graph is shown below. Identify the ordered pair on the function's graph corresponding to your solution in part (a).

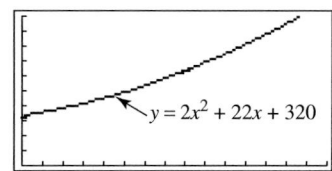
$y = 2x^2 + 22x + 320$

67. The crocodile, an endangered species, is the subject of a protection program. The mathematical model $P = 3500 + 475t - 10t^2$ describes the crocodile population (P) after t years of the protection program, where $0 < t \le 20$.

   a. How long will the program have to be continued to bring the population up to 7250?

   b. The graph of the crocodile population as a function of time is shown here. Identify the ordered pair on the function's graph corresponding to your solution in part (a).

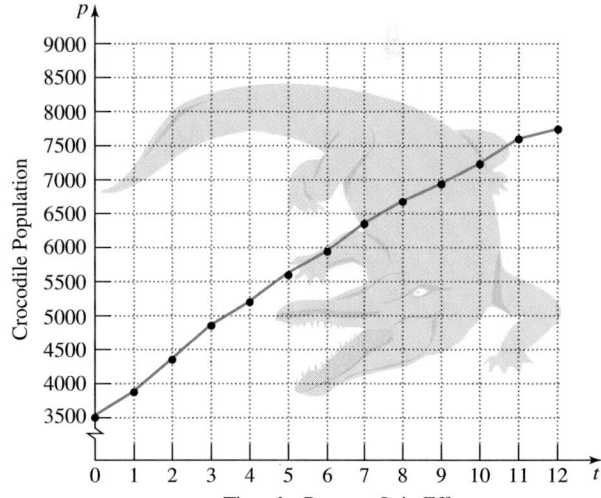
Time the Program Is in Effect

68. The formula

$$N = \frac{t^2 - t}{2}$$

describes the number of football games (N) that must be played in a league with t teams if each team is to play every other team once. If a league has 36 games scheduled, how many teams belong to the league, assuming that each team plays every other team once?

69. The formula

$$S = \frac{n^2 + n}{2}$$

gives the sum (S) of the first n natural numbers. How many consecutive natural numbers beginning with 1 will have a sum of 91?

70. Work injuries caused 6083 deaths in 1992, or approximately 17 deaths each day. The occupations with the highest rate of fatalities per 100,000 workers are shown in the bar graph. The number is missing for the bar representing truck drivers, but this much is known: The product of the number and the number decreased by 23 is 140. How many fatalities per 100,000 workers were there for truck drivers in 1992?

Most Dangerous Jobs

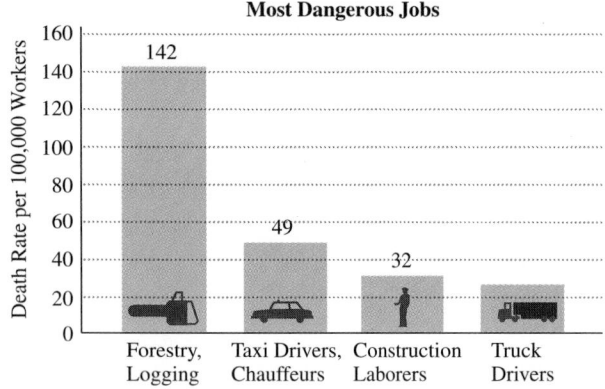

Source: Bureau of Labor Statistics

71. The bar graph shows the number of years it took for four inventions to be found in at least 50% of U.S. households. Find this number for VCRs if the sum of 13 and the square of this number results in 14 times the number. Eliminate any possible solution that is not consistent with the way the information is presented in the graph.

Accepting New Technology
(Number of Years It Took These Inventions to be Found in at Least 50% of U.S. Households)

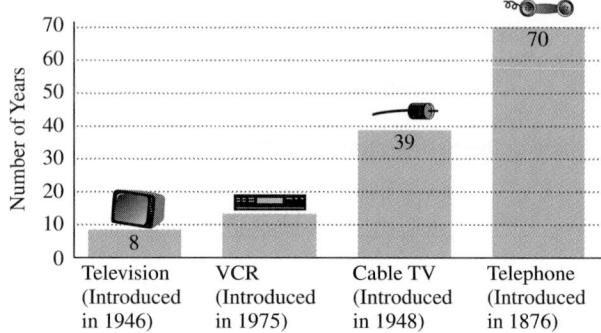

Source: Technologic Partners

72. The product of the page numbers on two facing pages of a book is 156. Find the page numbers.

73. The product of the page numbers on two facing pages of a book is 110. Find the page numbers.

74. The length of a rectangular garden is 5 feet greater than the width. The area of the rectangle is 300 square feet. Find the length and the width.

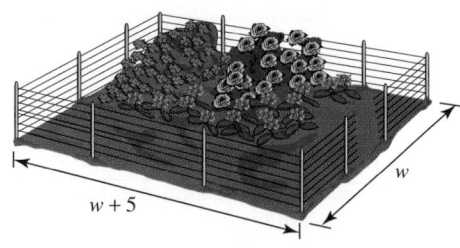

75. A rectangular parking lot has a length that is 3 yards greater than the width. The area of the rectangle is 180 square yards. Find the length and the width.

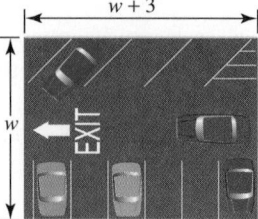

76. Surveyors are working in a rectangular lot. The longer sides of the rectangle are each 11 meters longer than the distance between them. The area of the lot is 80 square meters. Find the length of the lot and the distance between the surveyors.

77. The length of a rectangular rug is 5 feet more than the width. The area of the rug is 10 more than the perimeter. What are the rug's dimensions?

78. Great white sharks have triangular teeth with a height that is 1 centimeter longer than the base. If the area of one tooth is 15 square centimeters, find its height and base.

79. Each end of a glass prism is a triangle with a height that is 1 inch shorter than twice the base. If the area of the triangle is 60 square inches, how long are the base and height?

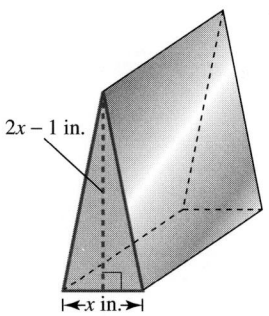

80. Carpet is being purchased for two rooms with square floors. One room's floor is 3 yards wider than the other. If 65 square yards of carpet are needed for both rooms, what are the dimensions of each room's floor?

81. A vacant rectangular lot with an area of 378 square meters is being turned into a community vegetable garden. The garden itself is to measure 15 meters by 12 meters. A path of uniform width is to surround the garden, as shown in the top figure on the right.
   a. Find a polynomial that models the area of the entire vacant lot, namely, the garden and the path combined.

b. Write the expression in part (a) as a polynomial function, calling the function f.

c. Since the area of the vacant lot is 378 square meters, set the function in part (b) equal to 378 and find x, the width of the path surrounding the garden.

d. Graph the function in part (b) either by hand or with a graphing utility. Find the point on the graph that illustrates your solution in part (c).

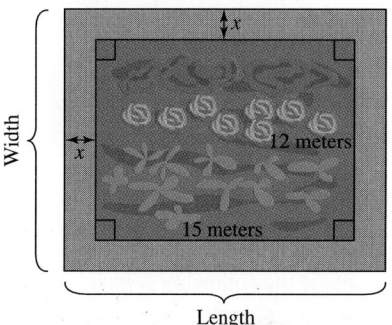

82. One side of a rectangular stage measures 15 meters. The diagonal has a length that is 1 meter more than twice the length of the other side. What are the lengths of the sides?

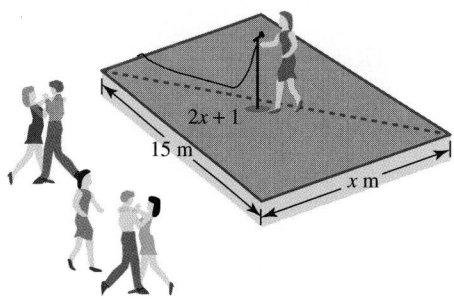

83. The width of a rectangular carpet is 7 meters shorter than the length, and the diagonal is 1 meter longer than the length. What are the carpet's dimensions?

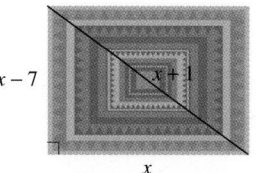

84. At point C the ship shown in the figure is 13 miles from shore. Cruising north to point B and then west to point A is a 17-mile trip. If the distance from point C to point B is greater than the distance from point B to shore, how far is it from point C to point B?

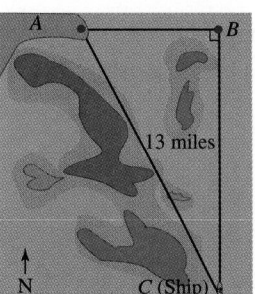

85. A rectangular lake has a perimeter of 34 feet and a diagonal length of 13 feet. What are the lake's dimensions?

True–False Critical Thinking Problems

86. Which one of the following is true?
  a. If $(x + 3)(x - 4) = 2$, then $x + 3 = 0$ or $x - 4 = 0$.
  b. The solutions to the equation $4(x - 5)(x + 3) = 0$ are $4, 5$, and -3.
  c. Equations solved by factoring always have two different solutions.
  d. Both 0 and $-\pi$ are solutions to the equation $x(x + \pi) = 0$.

87. Which one of the following is true?
  a. Both 1 and -3 are solutions to the equation $(x - 1)(2x + 6) = 0$.
  b. Equations solved by factoring never have more than two solutions.
  c. The zero-product principle states that if $ab = 0$, then $a = 0$.

d. If x^2 appears as a term in an equation, then the equation is a quadratic equation.

88. Which one of the following is true?
  a. If $2x(x^2 + 25) = 0$, then

$$2x = 0 \quad \text{or} \quad x^2 + 25 = 0$$
$$x = 0 \qquad\qquad x = 5 \quad \text{or} \quad x = -5$$

  b. If -4 is a solution to $7y^2 + (2k - 5)y - 20 = 0$, then k must equal 14.
  c. If $(x + 5)(2x - 4) = 6$, then

$$x + 5 = 6 \quad \text{or} \quad 2x - 4 = 6$$
$$x = 1 \quad \text{or} \qquad x = 5$$

  d. None of the above is true.

Technology Problems

89. Consider the polynomial equation $x^3 + 2x^2 - 5x - 6 = 0$. The solutions of the equation can be found by identifying the x-intercepts of the graph of $y = x^3 + 2x^2 - 5x - 6$. Use your graphing utility to graph the third-order polynomial function and solve the given equation. Check the solutions by direct substitution.

90. Repeat Problem 89 for the equation $x^4 + x^3 - 4x^2 - 4x = 0$.

91. Most graphing calculators will give the solutions to quadratic equations. Generally, this can be done using the polynomial equation feature. The order of a quadratic equation is 2, so often you will need to enter order $= 2$. With the equation in standard form, enter the coefficients of x^2, x, and the constant, often de-

noted by $a_2 = $, $a_1 = $, and $a_0 = $. After entering these three numbers, press $\boxed{\text{SOLVE}}$. The solutions should be displayed on the screen. Consult your manual and use this feature to check the solutions for some of the equations that you solved in Problems 1–64.

92. Use the polynomial equation feature described in Problem 91 to solve the equations in Problems 89 and 90. In Problem 89 the order is 3, and in Problem 90 the order is 4. Simply enter the coefficients and the constant term, press $\boxed{\text{ENTER}}$, and the solutions will be displayed.

93. Use a graphing utility to graph the functions in Problems 67–69. Then use the $\boxed{\text{TRACE}}$ feature to identify the point on the function's graph corresponding to the problem's solution.

Writing in Mathematics

94. Explain the difference between a linear equation and a quadratic equation.

95. Explain how to solve a factorable quadratic equation. What is the role of the zero-product principle in the solution process?

96. Explain why the zero-product principle cannot be used to solve a linear equation.

Critical Thinking Problems

97. Solve: $x^3 + 3x^2 - 10x = 0$.

98. Solve for x: $3^{x^2 - 9x + 20} = 1$.

99. Solve for x: $(x^2 - 5x + 5)^3 = 1$.

100. Identify the x-intercepts and the y-intercept for the graph of the function $y = x^2 - 4x - 5$, shown in the figure.

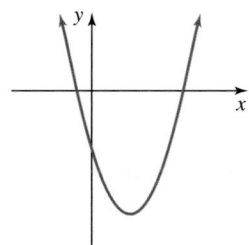

101. The length of a rectangle is 3 feet more than the width. If both the length and width are increased by 2 feet, the area of the new rectangle is 54 square feet. What are the dimensions of the original rectangle?

102. The box shown in the figure has a length that is 1 meter more than its width, and a height of 2 meters. If the volume of the box is 24 cubic meters, what are the dimensions of the rectangular base? ($V = LWH$)

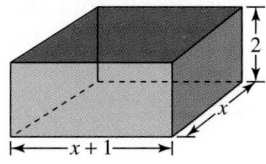

103. The area of the entire trapezoid in the figure is 30 square inches. What is the shaded triangle's area?

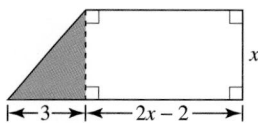

104. A rectangular piece of cardboard has a length that measures 6 inches more than its width. A 2-inch square is cut out of each corner, and the sides are turned up to make a box with no top. The volume of the box is 110 cubic inches. What are the dimensions of the cardboard?

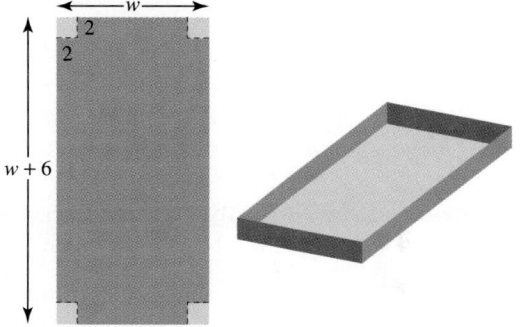

105. A square-shaped vacant lot is being turned into a community vegetable garden. A path 2 yards wide is to run along one end of the lot, and the remaining 63 square yards will be used for the vegetable garden. What are the lot's dimensions?

Group Activity Problem

106. The false statements in Problems 86–88 contain common errors that can arise in solving quadratic equations. In your group, list some of these errors and then suggest strategies for avoiding them.

Review Problems

107. Graph: $y > -\frac{2}{3}x + 1$.

108. Simplify, writing the answer with positive exponents only:

$$\left(\frac{8x^4}{4x^7}\right)^{-2}$$

109. Divide: $3y^3 - 11y^2 + 25y - 25$ by $3y - 5$.

CHAPTER PROJECT

Pythagoras: Philosophy, Mathematics, and Music

The Pythagorean Theorem studied in this chapter is named for the mathematician and philosopher Pythagroras of Samos (6th century, B.C.). Pythagoras, along with Thales of Miletus, is considered to be one of the first mathematicians in the sense of the word today. Veering away from seeing mathematics as a strictly computational tool used for things such as taxes or calculating volumes and areas, these men began developing the field as a theoretical and logical structure. Much of Pythagoras's work, including the theorem that bears his name, survives in the first two books of Euclid's *Elements,* a work devoted to geometry.

The modern form of the Pythagorean Theorem is not the presentation seen by the ancient Greeks. The Greeks had none of the algebraic symbolism we use today. For them, the Pythagorean Theorem was literally a result about squares. The theorem stated that if you constructed a square with sides equal to the length of the hypotenuse of a right triangle, and if you also constructed similar squares for each of the legs, then the *area* of the square on the hypotenuse would equal the sum of the areas of the other two squares (see Figure 7-6).

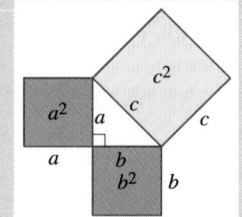

Figure 7.6

Pythagoras founded a school for the study of philosophy, mathematics, and natural science that became a secret order devoted to the study of whole numbers and their relationship to all aspects of life. Many of the concepts studied by the ancient Pythagorean brotherhood remain to this day in the form of the mathematical discipline of number theory and the mystical study of numerology. In Pythagorean philosophy, understanding numbers was thought to be the key to understanding the universe, both physical and spiritual.

Pythagoreans were also credited with revealing the links between music and numbers by analyzing the relationships between musical scales and tones and whole number ratios. Pythagoras observed the connection between the length of a tightly stretched string and the tone it produced when plucked. If two strings are stretched with the same degree of tension and one is exactly half the length of the other, the shorter string gives off a tone that is exactly one octave higher than the longer string.

1. Create your own one-stringed instrument to test this observation. Stretch a wire or string taut between two points, such as screws or nails, over a flat surface or hollow box used as a sounding board. Mark the half-way point on the surface. Pluck the string or draw a bow across it, and listen to the tone. Now press your finger to the middle of the string and pluck on either side to hear the tone. You should hear the same tone, but an octave higher in pitch. Close your eyes and repeat this procedure, this time placing your finger along the string at random points and discovering where the middle is by listening for the tone.

Another ratio discovered by Pythagoras and said to be harmonious to the ear is found by dividing a string into a ratio of 2:3. Plucking the larger two-thirds of the string produces a tone called "the chord of triumph."

2. Use your instrument to discover this sound. Pluck the full string and then close your eyes and move your finger along the string, stopping to pluck and listen, until you think you have found a "harmonious" tone. How close did you come to the two-thirds length determined by Pythagoras?

If we continually divide each two-thirds length by two-thirds again, we will create a series of higher tones until eventually, after the seventh division, we repeat the cycle, but slightly sharper. After the twelfth division almost the original note sounds again, with a slight flattening. The twelve notes thus discovered can be seen on a piano's scale with seven white and five black keys.

The Pythagoreans observed that the materials used made no difference in the relationship of the sounds—the importance was in the *numbers*. If the same ratios were used, the same harmonies were produced. We can create the same set of harmonies by using a taut wire, hollow tubes like those found in wind chimes or pipes, or tall glasses filled with water to the appropriate levels. The sacred lyre of Apollo was said to have seven strings corresponding to the seven tones of the descending musical scale: E-D-C-B-A-G-F and back to E.

3. Working in groups, create a musical instrument based on the ratios of Pythagoras. Start with any length and keep taking two-thirds of the length as described above. For example, if your first string is 90 inches long, the next will be 60 inches, the next 40 inches, and so on. After you have completed this process seven times to obtain the seven tones you want, you will find that the smallest length will give you a very high pitch. To bring the sounds back together within an octave, take the smallest length you have measured and multiply it by eight, take the next two shortest lengths and multiply by four, and then take the next two lengths and multiply by two. The remaining lengths may stay the same. Remember: anything producing these tones will suffice; you are not restricted to stringed creations.

4. The harmonious relationships described by the Pythagoreans are for *Western* musical scales. Harmony, to the Pythagoreans, was not simply a pleasant sound to the ear, but a reflection of the proper order of things—a sign that *numbers* of the universe were in harmonious accord. Many other cultures have developed their own musical scales and harmonies that sound quite pleasing to them. Research and report on some of the other musical scales found around the world and the harmonies created.

Worldwide Web Resources

Go to the Prentice Hall website (http://www.prenhall.com/blitzer) to access other locations on the Internet that will allow you to futher explore the concepts presented in this project.

Chapter Review

SUMMARY

1. **Factoring a Polynomial as the Product of a Monomial and Another Polynomial**
   a. Find the GCF of all the terms. The variable part of the GCF will contain the lowest power of a variable that appears in all terms of the polynomial.
   b. Rewrite each term of the polynomial as the product of the GCF and another monomial.
   c. Factor out the GCF and write the polynomial in factored form.

2. **Factoring by Grouping**
   a. Group terms that have a common monomial factor. There will usually be two groups. Sometimes the terms must be rearranged.
   b. Factor out the common monomial factor from each group.
   c. Factor out the remaining binomial factor (if one exists).

3. **Factoring $x^2 + bx + c$**
   a. List all pairs of integers whose product is c.

b. Choose the pair m and n whose sum is $m + n = b$.

c. The factorization of $x^2 + bx + c$ is $(x + m)(x + n)$.

d. If there are no such integers m and n such that $m + n = b$, the trinomial cannot be factored and is called prime.

4. Factoring $ax^2 + bx + c$, where $a \neq 1$

Use trial and error or factoring by grouping.

Method 1: Trial and Error

a. Find all the factors of the first term ax^2.

b. Find all the factors of the last term c.

c. Combine the factors in such a way that using the FOIL method gives the sum of the outside and inside products as bx.

Method 2: Grouping

a. Multiply the leading coefficient a and the constant c.

b. Find the factors of ac whose sum is b.

c. Rewrite the middle term (bx) as a sum or difference using the factors from part (b).

d. Factor by grouping.

5. Special Factorizations

a. *Difference of two squares:*

$$A^2 - B^2 = (A + B)(A - B)$$

b. *Perfect square trinomials:*

$$A^2 + 2AB + B^2 = (A + B)^2$$
$$A^2 - 2AB + B^2 = (A - B)^2$$

c. *Sum of two cubes:*

$$A^3 + B^3 = (A + B)(A^2 - AB + B^2)$$

d. *Difference of two cubes:*

$$A^3 - B^3 = (A - B)(A^2 + AB + B^2)$$

6. Factoring a Polynomial over the Integers

a. Is there a common factor? If so, factor out the GCF.

b. Is the polynomial a binomial? If so, can it be factored by one of the following special forms?

Difference of two squares: $A^2 - B^2 = (A + B)(A - B)$

Sum of two cubes:
$$A^3 + B^3$$
$$= (A + B)(A^2 - AB + B^2)$$

Difference of two cubes:
$$A^3 - B^3$$
$$= (A - B)(A^2 + AB + B^2)$$

c. Is the polynomial a trinomial? If it is not a perfect square trinomial, use trial and error or grouping. (See item 4 above.) If it is a perfect square trinomial, use one of the following special forms:

$$A^2 + 2AB + B^2 = (A + B)^2$$
$$A^2 - 2AB + B^2 = (A - B)^2$$

d. Does the polynomial contain four or more terms? If so, try factoring by grouping.

7. Quadratic Equations

a. Standard form of a quadratic equation in one variable: $ax^2 + bx + c = 0$, where $a \neq 0$.

b. Some quadratic equations can be solved by using factoring. Factor $ax^2 + bx + c$, set each factor equal to 0 (using the zero-product principle), and solve the resulting equations.

REVIEW PROBLEMS

Factor Problems 1–50 completely, or state that the polynomial is prime.

1. $9y^2 - 18y$

2. $x^2 - 11x + 28$

3. $y^3 - 8y^2 + 7y$

4. $10r^2 + 9r + 2$

5. $15z^2 - z - 2$

6. $x^2 - 144$

7. $64 - y^2$

8. $9r^2 + 6r + 1$

9. $20a^7 - 36a^3$

10. $8x^5 + 6x^2 - 20x^3 - 15$

11. $x^3 - 3x^2 - 9x + 27$

12. $12y^2 + 11y - 5$

13. $16x^2 - 40x + 25$

14. $r^2 + 16$

15. $2x^3 + 19x^2 + 35x$

16. $3x^3 - 30x^2 + 75x$

17. $10z^2 + 37z + 7$

18. $3x^5 - 24x^2$

19. $4y^4 - 36y^2$

20. $36y^2 - 59y - 7$

21. $5x^2 + 20x - 105$

22. $9r^2 + 8r - 3$

23. $10x^5 - 44x^4 + 16x^3$

24. $40x^2 + 17x - 12$

25. $486z^2 - 24$

26. $48r^2 - 120r + 75$

27. $3y^4 - 9y^3 - 30y^2$

28. $100y^2 - 49$

29. $256x^4 - 1$

30. $9x^5 - 18x^4$

31. $3w^2 + w - 5$

32. $64y^2 - 144y + 81$

33. $x^2 + x + 1$

34. $x^4 - 16$

35. $y^3 - 8$

36. $x^3 + 64$

37. $-10y^2 + 31y - 15$

38. $6x^2 + 11x - 10$

39. $3x^4 - 12x^2$

40. $3r^4 + 12r^2$

41. $56y^3 - 70y^2 + 21y$

42. $a^2 + 4a + 16$

43. $s^2 - s - 90$

44. $x^2 - 6x - 27$

45. $8y^2 - 14y - 5$

46. $25x^2 + 25x + 6$

47. $p^4 + 125p$

48. $32y^3 + 32y^2 + 6y$

49. $16x^5 - 25x^7$

50. $2y^2 - 16y + 32$

Problems 51–68 contain polynomials in several variables. Factor each polynomial completely, or state that the polynomial is prime.

51. $12x^4y^3 - 9x^3y^2 + 15x^2y$

52. $x^2 - 2xy - 35y^2$

53. $a^2b^2 + ab - 12$

54. $15x^2 - 11xy + 2y^2$

55. $x^2 + 7x + xy + 7y$

56. $9a^2 + 24ab + 16b^2$

57. $4x^2 - 20xy + 25y^2$

58. $20a^7b^2 - 36a^3b^4$

59. $4x^2 - 20x + 2xy - 10y$

60. $2x^4y - 2x^2y$

61. $39a^2b - 52a + 13ab^4$

62. $100y^2 - 49z^2$

63. $9x^5y^2 - 18x^4y^5$

64. $x^2 + xy + y^2$

65. $a^2q + a^2z - p^2q - p^2z$

66. $x^2y^2 - 16x^2 - 4y^2 + 64$

67. $3x^4y^2 - 12x^2y^4$

68. $125x^3 - 8y^3$

Solve the equations in Problems 69–74.

69. $y^2 + 5y = 14$

70. $x(x - 4) = 32$

71. $8w^2 - 37w + 20 = 0$

72. $2x^2 + 15x = 8$

73. $5x^2 + 20x = 0$

74. $3x^2 = -21x - 30$

In Problems 75–77, write a polynomial that models the area of the shaded region. Then factor the polynomial completely.

75.

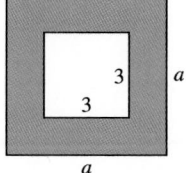

76.

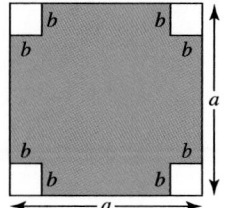

77.

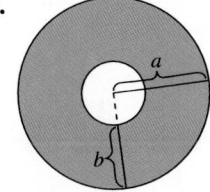

78. Using the formula for the volume of a sphere, the volume of rubber in the hollow racquetball shown in the figure is given by $\frac{4}{3}\pi a^3 - \frac{4}{3}\pi b^3$. Factor this expression completely.

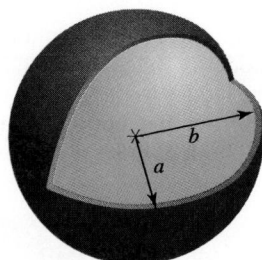

79. The diving board on the right is 32 feet above the water. The model $f(t) = -16t^2 + 16t + 32$ describes the diver's height ($f(t)$, in feet) at any time t (in seconds).
   a. After how many seconds will the diver hit the water?
   b. Complete the table of values.

Time t	Height $f(t) = -16t^2 + 16t + 32$
0	
$\frac{1}{2}$	
1	
$1\frac{1}{2}$	
2	

   c. Graph $f(t) = -16t^2 + 16t + 32$ using the ordered pairs from the table, connecting points with a smooth curve.
   d. As you look at the graph, describe when the diver reaches a maximum height. What is the maximum height?
   e. How is your solution to part (a) shown in the graph?

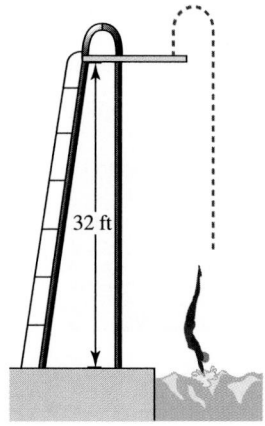

32 ft

80. The model

$$t = \frac{n^2 - n}{2}$$

describes the maximum number of truck routes, t, needed to provide service to n cities, where no three cities lie on a straight line. If a company can handle a maximum of 21 truck routes each day, how many cities can be serviced?

81. The bar graph shows the number of robbery victims per 1000 persons. However, the scale is missing from the vertical axis, so the actual numbers are unknown. If the rate per 1000 persons for African-Americans is increased by two and then decreased by 6, the product of these two numbers is 180. Find the robbery victimization rate for African-Americans and then use the graph to obtain a reasonable estimate for the other two groups.

Crime Victims: Robbery

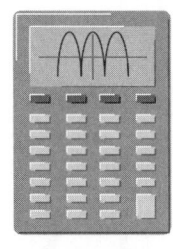

82. The length of a rectangular calculator exceeds the width by 5 centimeters. If the calculator's area is 84 square centimeters, what are its dimensions?

83. The square region shown here has a garden and a 3-meter wide path at one end. If the garden has an area of 88 square meters, what are the dimensions of the square region?

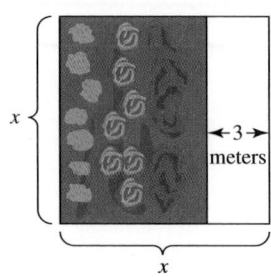

84. The height of a sail is 4 meters longer than the base. If the triangular sail has an area of 30 square meters, find the base and the height.

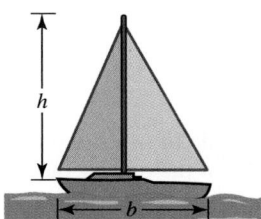

85. A ladder is leaning against a building. As shown in the figure, the ladder is 10 feet long, and the distance from the top of the ladder to the ground is 2 feet more than the distance from the bottom of the ladder to the building. Find both of these distances.

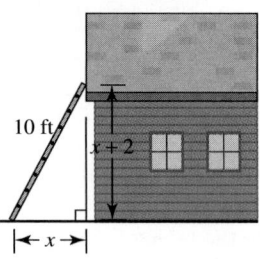

C H A P T E R   7   T E S T

In Problems 1–21, factor completely, or state that the polynomial is prime.

1. $x^2 - 9x + 18$

2. $x^2 - 14x + 49$

3. $15y^4 - 35y^3 + 10y^2$

4. $x^3 + 2x^2 + 3x + 6$

5. $x^2 - 9x$

6. $x^3 + 6x^2 - 7x$

7. $14x^2 + 64x - 30$

8. $25x^2 - 9$

9. $x^3 + 8$

10. $x^2 - 4x - 21$

11. $x^2 + 4$

12. $6y^3 + 9y^2 + 3y$

13. $4y^2 - 36$

14. $16x^2 + 48x + 36$

15. $2x^4 - 32$

16. $36x^2 - 84x + 49$

17. $7x^2 - 50x + 7$

18. $x^4 + 2x^3 - 5x - 10$

19. $12y^3 - 12y^2 - 45y$

20. $y^3 - 125$

21. $5x^2 - 5xy - 30y^2$

Solve the equations in Problems 22–24.

22. $x^2 + 2x - 24 = 0$

23. $3x^2 - 5x = 2$

24. $x(x - 6) = 16$

25. Write a polynomial that models the area of the shaded region in the figure. Then factor the polynomial.

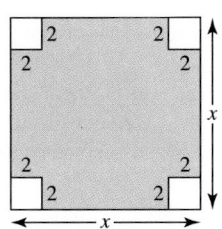

26. The model $f(t) = -5t^2 + 29t + 6$ describes the height ($f(t)$, in feet) of a tennis ball after t seconds that is thrown directly upward from a height of 6 feet. After how many seconds will the ball hit the ground?

27. The length of a rectangle exceeds twice the width by 3 yards. If the area is 90 square yards, find the rectangle's length and width.

CUMULATIVE REVIEW PROBLEMS (CHAPTERS 1–7)

1. Given $\{-3, -2, \frac{1}{7}, 0, 1, 9, 11.3, \sqrt{7}, 8\pi\}$, list the numbers in this set that belong to the set of:

    a. Natural numbers   **b.** Whole numbers

    c. Integers   **d.** Rational numbers

    e. Irrational numbers   **f.** Real numbers

2. Simplify: $6[5 + 2(3 - 8) - 3]$.

3. Solve: $4(x - 2) = 2(x - 4) + 3x$.

4. Solve: $\dfrac{x}{2} - 1 = \dfrac{x}{3} + 1$.

5. Find the measures of the angles of a triangle whose two base angles have equal measure and whose third angle is 10° less than three times the measure of a base angle.

6. Graph: $5x + 6y > -30$.

7. Solve the system:

$$5x + 2y = 14$$
$$y = 2x - 11$$

8. If 4 pens and 7 pads cost \$6.40, and 19 of the same pens and 2 of the same pads cost \$5.40, find the price of each.

9. Find the quotient: $\dfrac{6x^5 - 3x^4 + 9x^2 + 27}{-3x}$.

10. Simplify: $\left(\dfrac{4y^{-1}}{2y^{-3}}\right)^3$.

11. The median age of Roman Catholic nuns in the United States is 65 years. The circle graph shows the percent of American nuns in three age groups. If there are 15,040 nuns in the 50-years-and-under category,

how many Roman Catholic nuns are there in the United States? How many nuns are there in the other two age categories?

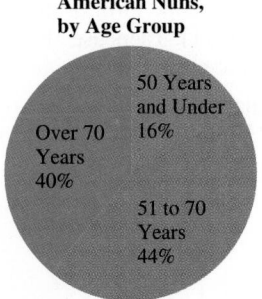

American Nuns, by Age Group

Source: *The Los Angeles Times*

12. Solve: $y(5y + 17) = 12$.

13. Solve: $5 - 5x > 2(5 - x) + 1$.

14. The polynomial function

$$f(x) = 0.025x^3 - 0.7x^2 + 4.43x + 16.77$$

models the percent of 18- to 25-year-olds in the United States who used hallucinogens x years after 1974. Find and interpret $f(10)$.

15. The graph on the next page compares U.S. physician salaries in four specialties to salaries in four other professions. The annual salary of a surgeon is \$18,600 more than six times that of a teacher. If teachers and surgeons have a combined annual salary of \$258,000, find the salary for each of the two professions. Then use the graph to obtain a reasonable estimate for the salaries of the profession whose numbers are not shown above the bars.

Annual Salaries for Eight Professions in the United States

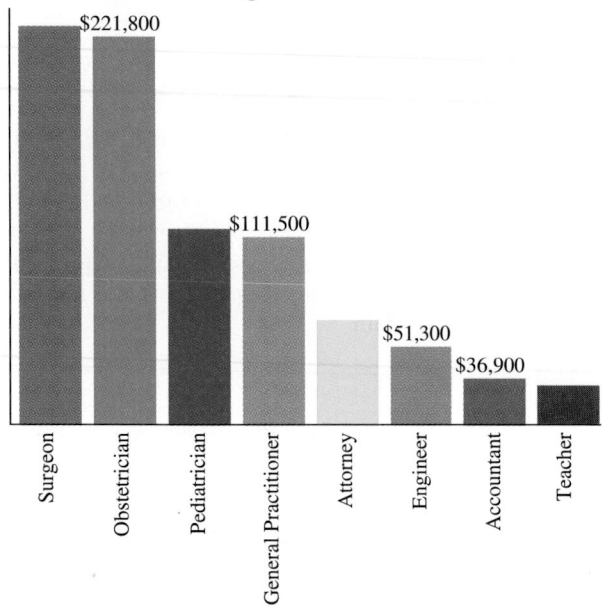

Source: American Medical Association, American Federation of Teachers

16. Write the point-slope form of the line passing through $(2, -4)$ and $(3, 1)$. Then use the point-slope form of the equation to write the slope-intercept equation.

17. A rectangular garden has a length that exceeds the width by 1 meter. Both length and width are to be increased by 1 meter.

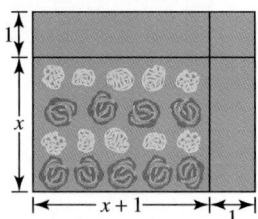

   a. Find a trinomial that describes the area of the larger garden.
   b. Write the expression in part (a) as a polynomial function, calling the function f.
   c. Find and interpret $f(8)$.

18. Graph: $y < -\frac{2}{5}x + 2$.

19. Solve the system:

$$2x + 3y = 5$$
$$3x - 2y = -4$$

20. Find the quotient: $\dfrac{6x^3 + 5x^2 - 34x + 13}{3x - 5}$.

21. The sum of three consecutive integers is 48. Find the integers.

22. Find the digits to replace x and y to make the problem correct.

$$\begin{array}{r} 1y \\ x\overline{)133} \end{array}$$

23. Factor: $3x^2 + 11x + 6$.

24. A projectile is fired straight upward from the ground with a velocity of 64 feet per second. Its height $(f(t)$, in feet) above the ground after t seconds is described by the model $f(t) = -16t^2 + 64t$.
   a. How long will it take the projectile to hit the ground?
   b. Complete the table of values.

Time t	Height $f(t) = -16t^2 + 64t$
0	
1	
2	
3	
4	

   c. Graph $f(t) = -16t^2 + 64t$ using the ordered pairs from the table, connecting points with a smooth curve.
   d. As you look at the graph, describe when the projectile reaches its maximum height. What is the maximum height?
   e. How is your solution to part (a) shown in the graph?

25. Factor completely: $y^5 - 16y$.

26. The length of a rectangle is 2 feet greater than its width. If the rectangle's area is 24 square feet, find its dimensions.

27. A dinner for six people cost $160, including a 7% tax. What was the dinner's cost before tax?

28. Subtract: $\frac{4}{5} - \frac{9}{8}$.

29. Solve for B: $A = \dfrac{B + C}{2}$.

30. A vending machine accepts nickels, dimes, and quarters, requiring exact change for any purchase. How many ways can a person with five nickels, three dimes, and two quarters make a 45-cent purchase from the machine?

Rational Expressions

Red Grooms "Looking Along Broadway Towards Grace Church" 1981, alkyd paint, gator board, celastic, wood, wax foamcore, $71 \times 63\frac{3}{4} \times 28\frac{3}{4}$ in. ($181 \times 162 \times 73$ cm)/Photo courtesy of Marlborough Gallery, NY. © 1998 Red Grooms/Artists Rights Society (ARS), New York.

What are the environmental consequences from increased traffic brought in by a new commercial development in an already congested area? The answer is provided by the mathematical model

$$P = \frac{TEC}{16}$$

in which

P = pollutants from idling cars
T = number of trips to the development
E = emission average
C = correction factor

This model contains a fraction with variables, called a *rational expression*. Rational expressions describe phenomena as diverse as the dose of drugs prescribed for children, when to buy a new car, and the cost of removing pollutants from the atmosphere. Since one aim of algebra is a compact, symbolic description of reality, the time has come to move beyond the rational numbers of ordinary arithmetic into the realm of algebraic fractions.

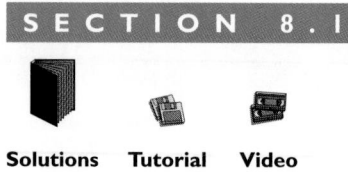

SECTION   8.1

Solutions   Tutorial   Video
Manual   9

Rational Expressions, Rational Functions, and Their Simplification

Objectives

1 Find where a rational expression is undefined.
2 Evalaute rational functions and interpret the result.
3 Simplify rational expressions.

---

1 Find where a rational expression is undefined.

Rational Expressions

We have already learned that a rational number is the quotient of two integers. In a similar way, a *rational expression* is the quotient of two polynomials. Some examples are

$$\frac{x - 2}{4}, \quad \frac{4}{x - 2}, \quad \frac{x}{x^2 - 1}, \quad \text{and} \quad \frac{x^2 + 1}{x^2 + 2x - 3}.$$

Since rational expressions indicate division and division by zero is not defined, we must avoid denominators that are 0. If a variable is replaced by a number that results in a denominator of 0, the rational expression is undefined. For example, in the rational expression

$$\frac{4}{x - 2}$$

when x is replaced by 2, the denominator is 0 and the expression is undefined.

If $x = 2$: $\dfrac{4}{x - 2} = \dfrac{4}{2 - 2} = \dfrac{4}{0}$ ← undefined

Notice that if x is replaced by a number other than 2, such as 1, the expression is defined because the denominator is nonzero.

If $x = 1$: $\dfrac{4}{x - 2} = \dfrac{4}{1 - 2} = \dfrac{4}{-1} = -4$

Thus, only 2 must be excluded as a replacement for x in the rational expression

$$\frac{4}{x - 2}.$$

Excluding values from rational expressions

If a variable in a rational expression is replaced by a number that causes the denominator to be 0, that number must be excluded as a replacement for the variable. The rational expression is undefined at any value that produces a denominator of 0.

EXAMPLE 1 **Finding Values That Result in Undefined Rational Expressions**

Find all the numbers for which the rational expression is undefined:

a. $\dfrac{6x + 12}{7x - 28}$ **b.** $\dfrac{2x + 6}{x^2 + 3x - 10}$ **c.** $\dfrac{x - 2}{4}$

Solution

To determine the values that make each rational expression undefined, we set the denominator equal to 0 and solve.

iscover for yourself

Use a graphing utility to graph

$$y = \dfrac{6x + 12}{7x - 28}$$

and the equations corresponding to parts (b) and (c) of Example 1. What happens as you approach or reach the value(s) excluded from the expression? (Use the $\boxed{\text{TRACE}}$ feature.) What happens if no number is excluded from the expression?

a. We cannot use any values that make the denominator equal to 0, although the numerator may be any real number.

$$7x - 28 = 0 \quad \text{Set the denominator equal to 0.}$$
$$7x = 28 \quad \text{Solve this equation.}$$
$$x = 4$$

Since 4 will make the denominator zero, the rational expression is undefined for 4.

b. Again, we exclude from the rational expression the numbers that make the denominator zero.

$$x^2 + 3x - 10 = 0 \quad \text{Set the denominator equal to 0.}$$
$$(x + 5)(x - 2) = 0 \quad \text{Solve the quadratic equation.}$$
$$x + 5 = 0 \quad \text{or} \quad x - 2 = 0$$
$$x = -5 \text{ or} \quad x = 2$$

Check

For $x = -5$:

$$\dfrac{2x + 6}{x^2 + 3x - 10} = \dfrac{2(-5) + 6}{(-5)^2 + 3(-5) - 10}$$
$$= \dfrac{-10 + 6}{25 - 15 - 10}$$
$$= \dfrac{-4}{0}$$

which is undefined.
Thus,

For $x = 2$:

$$\dfrac{2x + 6}{x^2 + 3x - 10} = \dfrac{2 \cdot 2 + 6}{2^2 + 3 \cdot 2 - 10}$$
$$= \dfrac{4 + 6}{4 + 6 - 10}$$
$$= \dfrac{10}{0}$$

which is undefined.

$$\dfrac{2x + 6}{x^2 + 3x - 10}$$

is undefined for -5 and for 2.

c. Because the denominator of $\dfrac{x - 2}{4}$ is not zero for any value of x, the rational expression is defined for all real numbers. It is not necessary to exclude any values for x. ∎

2 Evaluate rational functions and interpret the result.

Rational Functions

Throughout this book we have seen examples of functions defined by equations. If a function's equation is defined by a rational expression, it is called a *rational function*. Examples of rational functions include

$$f(x) = \frac{4}{x - 2}, \quad g(x) = \frac{x}{x^2 - 1}, \quad \text{and} \quad y = \frac{2x + 6}{x^2 + 3x - 10}.$$

For each of these functions, we must exclude value(s) that make the polynomial in the denominator 0.

| EXAMPLE 2 | **An Application: Rational Expressions and Functions** |

The function

$$f(x) = \frac{4x}{100 - x}$$

describes the cost ($f(x)$, in thousands of dollars) of removing pollutants from a stream as a function of eliminating x percent of the stream's pollutants. Find and interpret:

a. $f(80)$ **b.** $f(95)$ **c.** $f(99)$

Natalie Fobes/Tony Stone Images

Solution

a. To find $f(80)$ (read "f of 80"), we find the value of the rational expression

$$\frac{4x}{100 - x}$$

by substituting 80 for x.

$$f(x) = \frac{4x}{100 - x} \qquad \text{This is the given function.}$$

$$f(80) = \frac{4(80)}{100 - 80} \qquad \text{Substitute 80 for } x.$$

$$= \frac{320}{20}$$

$$= 16$$

Thus, $f(80) = 16$ (f of 80 is 16). Since the cost is given in thousands of dollars, the cost to remove 80% of the pollutants from the stream is $16,000.

b. To find $f(95)$, we substitute 95 for x.

$$f(x) = \frac{4x}{100 - x} \qquad \text{This is the given function.}$$

$$f(95) = \frac{4(95)}{100 - 95} \qquad \text{Substitute 95 for } x.$$

$$= \frac{380}{5}$$

$$= 76$$

Since $f(95) = 76$ (f of 95 is 76), the cost to remove 95% of the pollutants from the stream is $76,000.

c. To find $f(99)$, we substitute 99 for x.

$$f(x) = \frac{4x}{100 - x} \qquad \text{This is the given function.}$$

$$f(99) = \frac{4(99)}{100 - 99} \qquad \text{Substitute 99 for } x.$$

$$= \frac{396}{1}$$

$$= 396$$

Since $f(99) = 396$ (f of 99 is 396), the cost of removing 99% of the pollutants from the stream is \$396,000.

Observe that as x approaches 100%, the cost of removing pollutants becomes extremely expensive. In fact, since

$$f(x) = \frac{4x}{100 - x}$$

we can see that the denominator is 0 if $x = 100$. The number 100 causes the function's equation to be undefined. In terms of cost, this indicates that no amount of money will be enough to remove all pollutants from the stream. ■

EXAMPLE 3 **Graphing a Rational Function**

Graph: $f(x) = \dfrac{4x}{100 - x}$

Solution

This is the rational function discussed in Example 2. We begin by making a table of values that satisfy the function. Since the function describes the cost in terms of removing x percent of a stream's pollutants, only positive values of x are included.

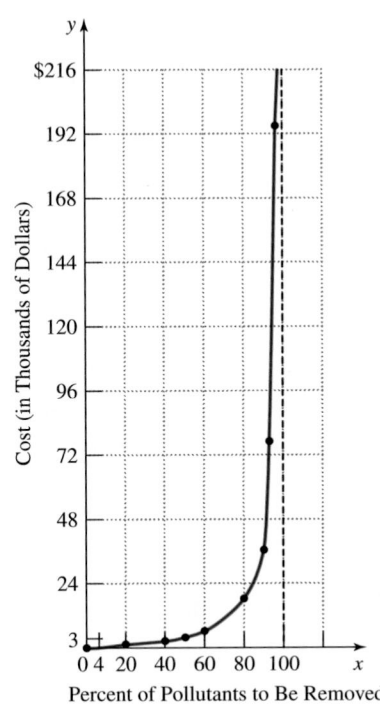

Figure 8.1

Cost as a function of the percent of pollutants removed from a stream

x	$f(x) = \dfrac{4x}{100 - x}$	**Ordered Pair**
0	$f(0) = \dfrac{4 \cdot 0}{100 - 0} = 0$	$(0, 0)$
20	$f(20) = \dfrac{4 \cdot 20}{100 - 20} = 1$	$(20, 1)$
40	$f(40) = \dfrac{4 \cdot 40}{100 - 40} = 2\dfrac{2}{3}$	$\left(40, 2\dfrac{2}{3}\right)$
50	$f(50) = \dfrac{4 \cdot 50}{100 - 50} = 4$	$(50, 4)$
60	$f(60) = \dfrac{4 \cdot 60}{100 - 60} = 6$	$(60, 6)$
80	$f(80) = \dfrac{4 \cdot 80}{100 - 80} = 16$	$(80, 16)$
90	$f(90) = \dfrac{4 \cdot 90}{100 - 90} = 36$	$(90, 36)$

95	$f(95) = \dfrac{4 \cdot 95}{100 - 95} = 76$	$(95, 76)$
98	$f(98) = \dfrac{4 \cdot 98}{100 - 98} = 196$	$(98, 196)$
99	$f(99) = \dfrac{4 \cdot 99}{100 - 99} = 396$	$(99, 396)$
100	$f(100) = \dfrac{4 \cdot 100}{100 - 100} = \dfrac{400}{0}$	Undefined

The graph of

$$f(x) = \frac{4x}{100 - x}$$

is shown in Figure 8.1. Notice that as x approaches 100%, the values of $f(x)$ continue growing larger. These increasingly greater numbers show how expensive it is to remove a large percent of the pollutants. The graph approaches but never touches the dashed vertical line drawn through $x = 100$. Turn back to page 565 and verify these observations. ■

3 Simplify rational expressions.

Harvey Quaytman (American, born 1937) "Full Day, Pompeii" 1991, acrylic and rust on canvas, 28 × 28 in. Courtesy McKee Gallery, New York. Photo credit: Sarah Wells.

Simplifying Rational Expressions

All rational numbers can be thought of as rational expressions. For example,

$$\frac{18}{30} = \frac{18x^0}{30x^0}$$

where $18x^0$ and $30x^0$ are polynomials of degree 0. Consequently, we can use our knowledge about rational numbers to gain insight into rational expressions. For example, we can reduce $\frac{18}{30}$ to lowest terms by factoring the numerator and the denominator. We obtain

$$\frac{18}{30} = \frac{3 \cdot 6}{5 \cdot 6} = \frac{3}{5}.$$

This simplification procedure uses the *fundamental rule of rational numbers*.

Fundamental rule of rational numbers

Let $a, b,$ and c represent real numbers such that $b \neq 0$ and $c \neq 0$. Then

$$\frac{ac}{bc} = \frac{a}{b} \quad \text{and} \quad \frac{a}{b} = \frac{ac}{bc}.$$

The numerator and denominator of a rational number can be divided or multiplied by the same nonzero number without changing the value of the rational number.

Extending this rule to rational expressions enables us to divide out, or cancel, any factors that are common to both the numerator and denominator. Thus, reducing the rational expression to lowest terms can be done as follows.

> **Reducing rational expressions to lowest terms**
>
> **1.** Factor the numerator and denominator completely.
> **2.** Divide both the numerator and denominator by the common factors.

This procedure for *reducing* rational expressions to lowest terms is also called *simplifying* rational expressions and is illustrated in the following examples.

EXAMPLE 4 **Simplifying a Rational Expression**

Simplify: $\dfrac{15x^2}{20x}$

Solution

$$\frac{15x^2}{20x} = \frac{5 \cdot 3 \cdot x \cdot x}{5 \cdot 4 \cdot x}$$ Factor the numerator and denominator. Observe that $x \neq 0$.

$$= \frac{\cancel{5} \cdot 3 \cdot \cancel{x} \cdot x}{\cancel{5} \cdot 4 \cdot \cancel{x}}$$ Divide by the common factors.

$$= \frac{3x}{4}, \quad x \neq 0$$

∎

$\mathcal{S}$**tudy tip**

Simplifying a rational expression can change the numbers that make it undefined. The expression

$$\frac{15x^2}{20x}$$

is undefined for $x = 0$. However, the simplified form

$$\frac{3x}{4}$$

is defined for all real numbers. Thus, to equate

$$\frac{15x^2}{20x} \quad \text{and} \quad \frac{3x}{4}$$

we must restrict the values for x in the simplified expression to exclude 0.

$\mathcal{S}$**tudy tip**

Example 4 can also be solved by using the rules for dividing monomials. Divide the coefficients and subtract exponents:

$$\frac{15x^2}{20x} = \frac{15}{20}x^{2-1} = \frac{3}{4}x = \frac{3x}{4}$$

We can use a graphing utility to verify that a rational expression has been simplified correctly by graphing both the original and simplified expressions on the same screen. The graphs of

$$y_1 = \frac{15x^2}{20x} \quad \text{and} \quad y_2 = \frac{3x}{4}$$

are shown below, using the $\boxed{\text{TRACE}}$ feature to explore what happens at $x = 0$. Notice that y_1 is undefined at $x = 0$ and y_2 is defined at $x = 0$ (when $x = 0, y = 0$). See the Study Tip box under Example 4.

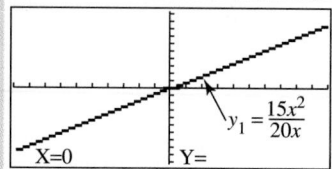
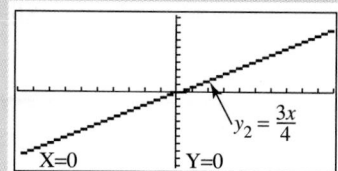

The graphs of

$$y_1 = \frac{x^3 + x^2}{x + 1}$$

and

$$y_2 = x^2$$

are identical if $x \neq -1$.

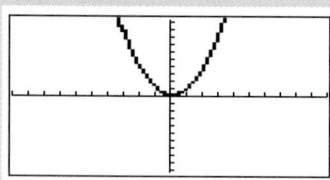

Because both graphs are nearly the same, we can conclude that

$$\frac{x^3 + x^2}{x + 1} = x^2, \quad x \neq -1.$$

Use your utility's $\boxed{\text{TRACE}}$ feature to show that

$$y_1 = \frac{x^3 + x^2}{x + 1}$$

is undefined for $x = -1$. Then use your graphing utility to verify Examples 5a and 5c.

EXAMPLE 5 **Simplifying Rational Expressions**

Simplify: **a.** $\dfrac{5x + 35}{20x}$ **b.** $\dfrac{x^3 + x^2}{x + 1}$ **c.** $\dfrac{x^2 + 6x + 5}{x^2 - 25}$

Solution

a. $\dfrac{5x + 35}{20x} = \dfrac{5(x + 7)}{5 \cdot 4x}$ Factor the numerator and denominator. Observe that $x \neq 0$.

$$= \frac{\overset{1}{\cancel{5}}(x + 7)}{\underset{1}{\cancel{5}} \cdot 4x}$$ Divide out the common factor of 5.

$$= \frac{x + 7}{4x}$$

b. $\dfrac{x^3 + x^2}{x + 1} = \dfrac{x^2(x + 1)}{x + 1}$ Factor the numerator. Observe that $x \neq -1$.

$$= \frac{x^2\overset{1}{\cancel{(x + 1)}}}{\underset{1}{\cancel{x + 1}}}$$ Divide out the common factor of $x + 1$.

$$= x^2, \quad x \neq -1$$ Denominators of 1 need not be written because $\frac{a}{1} = a$.

c. $\dfrac{x^2 + 6x + 5}{x^2 - 25} = \dfrac{(x + 5)(x + 1)}{(x + 5)(x - 5)}$ Factor the numerator and denominator. Observe that $x \neq -5$ and $x \neq 5$.

$$= \frac{\overset{1}{\cancel{(x + 5)}}(x + 1)}{\underset{1}{\cancel{(x + 5)}}(x - 5)}$$ Divide out the common factor of $x + 5$.

$$= \frac{x + 1}{x - 5}, \quad x \neq -5 \text{ and } x \neq 5$$

EXAMPLE 6 **Simplifying and Graphing a Rational Function**

Graph: $y = \dfrac{x^2 - 9}{x - 3}$

Solution

$$y = \frac{x^2 - 9}{x - 3}$$ This is the given function. Since 3 makes the denominator 0, the function is undefined for $x = 3$.

$$= \frac{(x + 3)(x - 3)}{x - 3}$$ Factor.

$$= \frac{(x + 3)\overset{1}{\cancel{(x - 3)}}}{\underset{1}{\cancel{x - 3}}}$$ Divide by $x - 3$, the common factor.

$$= x + 3$$ Keep in mind that $x \neq 3$.

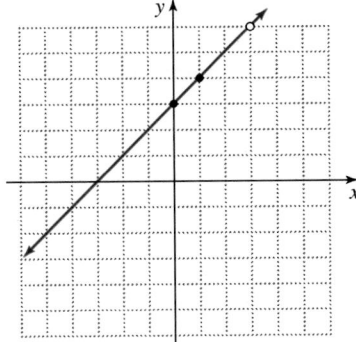

Figure 8.2

The graph of $y = \dfrac{x^2 - 9}{x - 3}$,

showing that $x = 3$ is excluded

The graph of

$$y = \frac{x^2 - 9}{x - 3}$$

is the same as the graph of $y = x + 3$ with $x \neq 3$. The graph of $y = x + 3$, $x \neq 3$, is a line with y-intercept 3 and slope 1, shown in Figure 8.2. The open dot above 3 excludes this value from the graph. ■

Factors That Are Opposites

So far, our work has focused on canceling identical factors in the numerator and denominator of rational expressions. Let's now see what to do if factors in the numerator and denominator are opposites.

Joseph Stella "The Voice of the City of New York Interpreted: The Sky-scrapers" 1920–22, oil and tempera on canvas, $99\frac{3}{4}$ × 54 in. Collection of The Newark Museum. The Newark Museum, Newark, New Jersey, U.S.A./Art Resource, NY

EXAMPLE 7 **The Quotient of Polynomials That Differ Only in Sign**

Simplify: $\dfrac{x - a}{a - x}$

Solution

One approach to reducing the rational expression involves factoring -1 from the numerator.

$$\frac{x - a}{a - x} = \frac{-1(-x + a)}{a - x}$$ Factor -1 from the numerator. Observe that $x \neq a$.

$$= \frac{-1(a - x)}{a - x}$$ In the numerator, $-x + a = a - x$.

$$= \frac{-1\overset{1}{\cancel{(a - x)}}}{\underset{1}{\cancel{a - x}}}$$ Divide by the common factor.

$$= -\frac{1}{1} = -1$$

Example 7 suggests the following useful property.

The quotient of two polynomials that have opposite signs and are additive inverses is -1.

Let's use this property in our next example.

EXAMPLE 8 **Simplifying an Algebraic Fraction**

Reduce: $\dfrac{4x^2 - 25}{15 - 6x}$

Solution

$$\frac{4x^2 - 25}{15 - 6x} = \frac{(2x + 5)(2x - 5)}{3(5 - 2x)}$$ Factor.

$$= \frac{(2x + 5)\overset{(-1)}{\cancel{(2x - 5)}}}{3\underset{1}{\cancel{(5 - 2x)}}}$$ Two polynomials that have opposite signs and are additive inverses have a quotient of -1. Since $5 - 2x \neq 0$, then $x \neq \frac{5}{2}$.

$$= -\frac{2x + 5}{3}, \quad x \neq \frac{5}{2}$$

or

$$\frac{-2x - 5}{3}$$ $-\dfrac{a}{b} = \dfrac{-a}{b}$

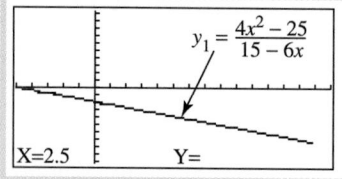

ENRICHMENT ESSAY

Zero

To find numbers for which a rational expression is undefined, we use the fact that 0 is the only real number that can never be used as a divisor in a division. In many ways, zero is a creator of problems! It requires special attention throughout algebra.

1. 0 is the only real number that is neither positive nor negative.
2. 0 is the only number that must be one of the factors if it is the product of two numbers. (If $AB = 0$, then $A = 0$ or $B = 0$.)
3. 0 is the only number that doesn't affect the sum as an addend or the difference when used as a subtrahend. (That is, $a + 0 = a$ and $a - 0 = a$.)

Although we take 0 for granted as a number, the ancient Greeks had no conception of nothing, or emptiness, as a number. Zero is the only number that doesn't have a symbol in most ancient notation systems, including the numeration systems of the Romans, Egyptians, Greeks, Babylonians, and Chinese.

Having said this, you should be aware that 0 is not necessarily "nothing." For example, 0°F does not mean no heat. A line whose slope is 0 does not mean that the line has no slope.

Where does one find the strange abstraction called zero in a world of physical objects? Mathematician and author Lewis Carroll, in *Alice's Adventures in Wonderland,* deals with this idea in an episode where Alice is physically shrinking:

"'It might end, you know,' said Alice to herself, 'in my going out altogether, like a candle. I wonder what I should be like then?' And she tried to fancy what the flame of a candle looks like after the candle is blown out, for she could not remember having seen such a thing."

Finally, 0 is the only number that is frequently incorrectly called a letter of the alphabet. Its name is "zero"—not "oh."

Can you describe a real world example that can be modeled by zero?

Alfredo Castañeda "To Grow" signed and dated 1986, oil on canvas, $31\frac{1}{2} \times 31\frac{1}{2}$ in. (80×80 cm). Mary-Anne Martin/Fine Art, New York

PROBLEM SET 8.1

Practice Problems

List all numbers (if any) for which each rational expression in Problems 1–18 is undefined. If applicable, use a graphing utility to verify that these values are excluded.

1. $\dfrac{7}{2x}$

2. $\dfrac{8}{3x}$

3. $\dfrac{x}{x - 7}$

4. $\dfrac{y}{y + 5}$

5. $\dfrac{5y^2}{5y - 15}$

6. $\dfrac{7y^2}{-6y + 18}$

7. $\dfrac{x + 4}{(x + 7)(x - 3)}$

8. $\dfrac{x + 14}{(x - 8)(x + 6)}$

9. $\dfrac{13z}{(3z - 15)(z + 2)}$

10. $\dfrac{17z}{(z - 1)(2z + 6)}$

11. $\dfrac{x + 5}{x^2 + x - 12}$

12. $\dfrac{7x - 14}{x^2 - 9x + 20}$

13. $\dfrac{y+3}{4y^2+y-3}$ **14.** $\dfrac{y+8}{6y^2-y-2}$ **15.** $\dfrac{7x}{x^2+4}$ **16.** $\dfrac{9x}{x^2+100}$

17. $\dfrac{y^2-16}{8}$ **18.** $\dfrac{y^2-25}{23}$

Simplify each rational expression in Problems 19–66, if possible. If applicable, use a graphing utility to verify the simplification.

19. $\dfrac{14x^2}{7x}$ **20.** $\dfrac{9x^3}{6x}$ **21.** $\dfrac{60x^4}{10x^6}$ **22.** $\dfrac{76x^5}{16x^8}$

23. $\dfrac{5x-15}{25}$ **24.** $\dfrac{7x+21}{49}$ **25.** $\dfrac{-2x+8}{-4x}$ **26.** $\dfrac{-3x+9}{-6x}$

27. $\dfrac{3}{3x-9}$ **28.** $\dfrac{12}{6x-18}$ **29.** $\dfrac{-15}{3x-5}$ **30.** $\dfrac{-21}{7x-14}$

31. $\dfrac{3y+9}{y+3}$ **32.** $\dfrac{5y-10}{y-2}$ **33.** $\dfrac{x+5}{x^2-25}$ **34.** $\dfrac{x+4}{x^2-16}$

35. $\dfrac{2y-10}{3y-6}$ **36.** $\dfrac{6y+18}{11y+33}$ **37.** $\dfrac{s+1}{s^2-2s-3}$ **38.** $\dfrac{s+2}{s^2-s-6}$

39. $\dfrac{4b-8}{b^2-4b+4}$ **40.** $\dfrac{c^2-12c+23}{4c-24}$ **41.** $\dfrac{y^2-3y+2}{y^2+7y-18}$ **42.** $\dfrac{y^2+5y+4}{y^2-4y-5}$

43. $\dfrac{2y^2-7y+3}{2y^2-5y+2}$ **44.** $\dfrac{3b^2+4b-4}{6b^2-b-2}$ **45.** $\dfrac{2x+3}{2x-5}$ **46.** $\dfrac{x-4}{4x-1}$

47. $\dfrac{x^2+5x+2x+10}{x^2-25}$ **48.** $\dfrac{y^3-2y^2+y-2}{y-2}$ **49.** $\dfrac{x^3+5x^2-6x}{x^3-x}$ **50.** $\dfrac{x^3+2x^2-3x}{2x^3+2x^2-4x}$

51. $\dfrac{2y^8+y^7}{2y^6+y^5}$ **52.** $\dfrac{x}{x+1}$ **53.** $\dfrac{x-5}{5-x}$ **54.** $\dfrac{3-y}{y-3}$

55. $\dfrac{2x-2}{1-x}$ **56.** $\dfrac{a^2-4}{2-a}$ **57.** $\dfrac{-2x-8}{x^2-16}$ **58.** $\dfrac{9y+3}{-6y^2-2y}$

59. $\dfrac{4-6y}{3y^2-2y}$ **60.** $\dfrac{y^2-3y}{6-2y}$ **61.** $\dfrac{9-x^2}{x^2-x-6}$ **62.** $\dfrac{1-y^2}{y^2+y-2}$

63. $\dfrac{y^2-9y+18}{y^3-27}$ **64.** $\dfrac{y^3-8}{y^2+2y-8}$ **65.** $\dfrac{b^2-b-12}{4-b}$ **66.** $\dfrac{3-b}{b^2-7b+12}$

Graph each rational function in Problems 67–70 by first simplifying the rational expression in the function's formula. Use an open dot above the value of x that is excluded from the function. If applicable, verify your hand-drawn graph using a graphing utility.

67. $y=\dfrac{x^2-25}{x-5}$ **68.** $y=\dfrac{x^2-16}{x+4}$ **69.** $f(x)=\dfrac{9x-18}{3x-6}$ **70.** $f(x)=\dfrac{10x+40}{5x+20}$

The rational expressions in Problems 71–82 involve several variables. Simplify (reduce) each expression. Partially check your simplification by using a value for each variable and evaluating the given expression and the simplification. If you obtain differing results, then you have made an error in the simplification.

71. $\dfrac{10x^3y}{5xy^2}$ **72.** $\dfrac{12x^5y^6}{30x^3y}$ **73.** $\dfrac{7x+2y}{14x+4y}$ **74.** $\dfrac{ab-2a}{3b-6}$

75. $\dfrac{x^2-4y^2}{x+2y}$ **76.** $\dfrac{xy(x^2+y)}{x^2y^2}$ **77.** $\dfrac{6a^2}{2a(a-3b)}$ **78.** $\dfrac{x^2+2xy-3y^2}{2x^2+5xy-3y^2}$

79. $\dfrac{x^2+3xy-10y^2}{3x^2-7xy+2y^2}$ **80.** $\dfrac{16a^2-25b^2}{4a^2+3ab-10b^2}$ **81.** $\dfrac{6a^2-11ab+4b^2}{9a^2-16b^2}$ **82.** $\dfrac{x^2y-x^2}{x^3-x^3y}$

Application Problems

83. The function

$$f(x) = \frac{130x}{100 - x}$$

describes the cost ($f(x)$ in millions of dollars) to inoculate x percent of the population against a particular strain of flu.

a. Find and interpret $f(40), f(80)$, and $f(90)$.
b. For what value of x is the function undefined?
c. What happens to the cost as x approaches 100%? How can you interpret this observation?
d. Complete the following table of values, rounding values of $f(x)$ to the nearest whole number.

x	0	10	20	40	50	60	70	80	90	95	99	100
$f(x)$												Undefined

e. Use the table of values from part (d) to graph

$$f(x) = \frac{130x}{100 - x}.$$

f. Discuss the behavior of the graph as x approaches 100%.

84. A bicycle manufacturing business has determined that the average cost per bicycle of producing x bicycles is given by the rational function

$$f(x) = \frac{100x + 100,000}{x}.$$

a. Find and interpret $f(500)$, $f(1000)$, $f(2000)$, $f(10,000)$, $f(20,000)$, $f(50,000)$, $f(100,000)$, and $f(1,000,000)$.

b. What appears to be happening to the cost of producing a bicycle with increasingly higher production levels? What problem might this pose for small businesses?
c. Is there any production level (that is, any value of x) that will lower the cost of producing a bicycle to $100?
d. Use the values obtained in part (a) to graph the function in the first quadrant for $x \geqslant 500$. What does the shape of the graph reveal about production level and cost?
e. If applicable, check your hand-drawn graph in part (d) using a graphing utility.

85. An architect is constructing a house whose cross section up to the roof is in the shape of a rectangle with an area of 2500 square feet. As shown in the figure, the width of the rectangle is represented by x. A rational function that models the perimeter of the rectangle is given by

$$f(x) = \frac{5000}{x} + 2x.$$

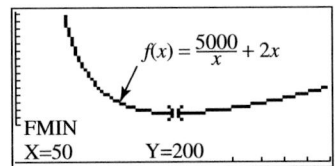

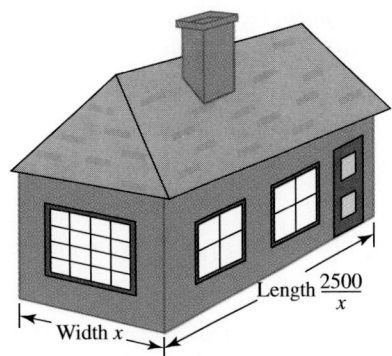

A minimum perimeter will reduce construction costs for the house. Shown on the left is the graph of the perimeter function obtained with a graphing utility. Use the graph to find the minimum perimeter. What are the dimensions of the rectangle with the least possible perimeter? What is the shape of the cross section that results in the minimum perimeter?

True–False Critical Thinking Problems

86. Which one of the following is true?

a. $\dfrac{x+5}{x} = 5$

b. $\dfrac{x^2+3}{3} = x^2 + 1$

c. $\dfrac{3x+9}{3x+13} = \dfrac{9}{13}$

d. The expression $\dfrac{-3y-6}{y+2}$ reduces to the consecutive integer that follows -4.

87. Which one of the following is true?

a. We cannot replace x by -3 or 5 in the rational expression $\dfrac{x+3}{x-5}$.

b. $\dfrac{x^2-36}{x-6} = x - 6$,   if $x \neq 6$

c. $\dfrac{7x}{7} = x$,   for any real number x

d. $\dfrac{x-3}{x+3} = -1$,   if $x \neq -3$

Technology Problems

In Problems 88–90, use a graphing utility to determine if the rational expression has been correctly simplified by graphing the original and simplified expressions on the same screen. If the simplification is wrong, correct it and then verify your answer using the graphing utility.

88. $\dfrac{3x+15}{x+5} = 3$, $x \neq -5$

89. $\dfrac{2x^2-x-1}{x-1} = 2x^2 - 1$, $x \neq 1$

90. $\dfrac{x^2-x}{x} = x^2 - 1$, $x \neq 0$

91. Use a graphing utility to verify the graph of Example 3 on page 565. $\boxed{\text{TRACE}}$ along the graph as x approaches 100. What do you observe?

Writing in Mathematics

92. Describe the difference between a polynomial and a rational expression.

93. Explain how to simplify a rational expression (write it in lowest terms).

94. Determine the numerator that will make this statement true. Describe how you obtained your answer.

$$\dfrac{\boxed{}}{x+3} = x - 1$$

Critical Thinking Problems

What happens to the value of the rational expressions in Problems 95–102 as x becomes very large? If applicable, use a graphing utility to verify your observation.

95. $\dfrac{1}{x+4}$

96. $\dfrac{1}{x-3}$

97. $\dfrac{2x}{x-1}$

98. $\dfrac{3x}{x-1}$

99. $\dfrac{x+2}{x^2}$

100. $\dfrac{x+3}{x^3}$

101. $\dfrac{x}{x^2-1}$

102. $\dfrac{x}{x^2-2}$

Use the expression $x^2 + 7x + 12$ as part of your answer in Problems 103–105.

103. Write a rational expression that can be simplified.

104. Write a rational expression that cannot be simplified.

105. Write a rational expression that is undefined when $x = -4$.

106. In general.

$$\dfrac{a+c}{b+c} \neq \dfrac{a}{b}.$$

For example,

$$\dfrac{2+5}{4+5} \neq \dfrac{2}{4} \quad \text{or} \quad \dfrac{7}{9} \neq \dfrac{1}{2}.$$

However, there are some special cases in which

$$\dfrac{a+c}{b+c} \quad \text{and} \quad \dfrac{a}{b}$$

are equal. See if you can discover values for a, b, c, all nonzero, for which

$$\frac{a + c}{b + c} = \frac{a}{b}$$

Is there a relationship between the variables that makes these expressions equal?

107. The following unusual cancellations are true:

$$\frac{19}{95} = \frac{1\!\!\!/9}{9\!\!\!/5} = \frac{1}{5} \quad \text{and} \quad \frac{16}{64} = \frac{1\!\!\!/6}{6\!\!\!/4} = \frac{1}{4}$$

Can you find other two-digit numbers having similar relationships?

Group Activity Problem

108. Study some of the errors in the false statements of Problems 86–87. In your group, list common errors

that can occur when simplifying rational expressions. Then discuss strategies for avoiding these errors.

Review Problems

109. What percent of 68 is 17?

110. Solve the system:

$$2x - 5y = -2$$
$$3x + 4y = 20$$

111. Perform the indicated operation with the numbers in scientific notation, and then write the answer without exponents.

$$\frac{8.5 \times 10^{-3}}{1.7 \times 10^{-7}}$$

SECTION 8.2

Solutions Manual **Tutorial** **Video 9**

Multiplying and Dividing Rational Expressions

Objectives

1 Multiply rational expressions.
2 Divide rational expressions.

In the preceding section, we saw that reducing rational expressions to lowest terms is identical to reducing rational numbers to lowest terms. In this section, we will see that we can multiply and divide rational expressions in the same way that we multiply and divide rational numbers.

1 Multiply rational expressions.

Multiplying Rational Expressions

In arithmetic, we know that the product of two rational numbers equals the product of their numerators divided by the product of their denominators. Symbolically, this says that

$$\frac{a}{b} \cdot \frac{c}{d} = \frac{ac}{bd}, \quad b \neq 0, d \neq 0.$$

In a similar manner, the product of two rational expressions is the product of their numerators over the product of their denominators.

Multiplying rational expressions

If P, Q, R, and S are polynomials, where $Q \neq 0$ and $S \neq 0$, then

$$\frac{P}{Q} \cdot \frac{R}{S} = \frac{PR}{QS}.$$

EXAMPLE 1 **Multiplying Rational Expressions**

Multiply: $\dfrac{7}{x+3} \cdot \dfrac{x-2}{5}$

Solution

$$\dfrac{7}{x+3} \cdot \dfrac{x-2}{5} = \dfrac{7(x-2)}{(x+3)5} \qquad \text{Multiply numerators. Multiply denominators. } (x \ne -3)$$

$$= \dfrac{7x-14}{5x+15}$$ ∎

The product of two rational expressions can frequently be simplified by factoring all numerators and denominators, dividing out common factors in the numerator and denominator. For example, to find the product of $\frac{3}{5}$ and $\frac{10}{21}$, we can proceed as follows.

$$\dfrac{3}{5} \cdot \dfrac{10}{21} = \dfrac{3}{5} \cdot \dfrac{5 \cdot 2}{7 \cdot 3} \qquad \text{Factor.}$$

$$= \dfrac{3 \cdot 5 \cdot 2}{5 \cdot 7 \cdot 3} \qquad \text{Multiply numerators. Multiply denominators.}$$

$$= \dfrac{\overset{1}{3} \cdot \overset{1}{\cancel{5}} \cdot 2}{\underset{1}{\cancel{5}} \cdot 7 \cdot \underset{1}{\cancel{3}}} \qquad \text{Divide both numerator and denominator by common factors.}$$

$$= \dfrac{2}{7} \qquad \text{Multiply remaining factors in the numerator and do the same in the denominator.}$$

This example gives us a step-by-step procedure for multiplying rational expressions.

Multiplying rational expressions

1. Factor all numerators and denominators completely.
2. Divide both the numerator and denominator by common factors.
3. Multiply the remaining factors in the numerator and multiply the remaining factors in the denominator.

EXAMPLE 2 **Multiplying Rational Expressions**

Multiply and simplify:

a. $\dfrac{x-3}{x+5} \cdot \dfrac{10x+50}{4x-12}$ b. $\dfrac{x-7}{x-1} \cdot \dfrac{2x^2-2}{3x-21}$

Solution

a. $\dfrac{x-3}{x+5} \cdot \dfrac{10x+50}{4x-12}$

$= \dfrac{x-3}{x+5} \cdot \dfrac{10(x+5)}{4(x-3)}$ Factor. ($x \neq -5$ and $x \neq 3$)

$= \dfrac{(x-3)10(x+5)}{(x+5)4(x-3)}$ Multiply numerators and denominators.

$= \dfrac{\overset{1}{\cancel{(x-3)}}\,2 \cdot 5\overset{1}{\cancel{(x+5)}}}{\underset{1}{\cancel{(x+5)}}\,2 \cdot 2\underset{1}{\cancel{(x-3)}}}$ Divide both numerator and denominator by common factors.

$= \dfrac{5}{2}$ Multiply the remaining factors in the numerator and denominator.

b. $\dfrac{x-7}{x-1} \cdot \dfrac{2x^2-2}{3x-21}$

$= \dfrac{x-7}{x-1} \cdot \dfrac{2(x^2-1)}{3(x-7)}$ Factor out the GCF. ($x \neq 1$ and $x \neq 7$)

$= \dfrac{x-7}{x-1} \cdot \dfrac{2(x+1)(x-1)}{3(x-7)}$ Factor completely.

$= \dfrac{(x-7)2(x+1)(x-1)}{(x-1)3(x-7)}$ Multiply numerators and denominators.

$= \dfrac{\overset{1}{\cancel{(x-7)}}\,2(x+1)\overset{1}{\cancel{(x-1)}}}{\underset{1}{\cancel{(x-1)}}3\underset{1}{\cancel{(x-7)}}}$ Divide both numerator and denominator by common factors.

$= \dfrac{2(x+1)}{3}$ or $\dfrac{2x+2}{3}$ Multiply the remaining factors in the numerator and denominator. ∎

Using technology

The graphs of

$$y_1 = \frac{x-7}{x-1} \cdot \frac{2x^2-2}{3x-21} \quad \text{and} \quad y_2 = \frac{2(x+1)}{3}$$

are identical if $x \neq 1$ and $x \neq 7$, so that

$$\frac{x-7}{x-1} \cdot \frac{2x^2-2}{3x-21} = \frac{2(x+1)}{3}.$$

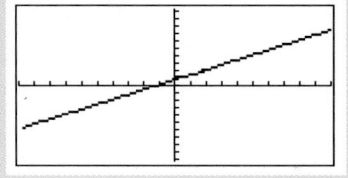

Since

$$-\frac{a}{b} = \frac{-a}{b} = \frac{a}{-b}$$

the product in Example 3

$$-\frac{2+y}{y-1}$$

can be expressed in a number of equivalent ways. Distributing -1 throughout the numerator, we can write

$$\frac{-2-y}{y-1}.$$

Distributing -1 throughout the denominator, we can write

$$\frac{2+y}{-y+1} \quad \text{or} \quad \frac{2+y}{1-y}.$$

2 Divide rational expressions.

EXAMPLE 3 Multiplying Rational Expressions

Find the product of $\dfrac{4-y^2}{y^2+3y-4}$ and $\dfrac{y^2+7y+12}{y^2+y-6}$.

Solution

$$\frac{4-y^2}{y^2+3y-4} \cdot \frac{y^2+7y+12}{y^2+y-6}$$

$$= \frac{(2+y)(2-y)}{(y+4)(y-1)} \cdot \frac{(y+3)(y+4)}{(y+3)(y-2)}$$

Factor. Notice that $y \neq -4$, $y \neq 1$, $y \neq -3$, and $y \neq 2$.

$$= \frac{(2+y)(2-y)(y+3)(y+4)}{(y+4)(y-1)(y+3)(y-2)}$$

Multiply numerators and denominators.

$$= \frac{(2+y)\overset{-1}{\cancel{(2-y)}}\overset{1}{\cancel{(y+3)}}\overset{1}{\cancel{(y+4)}}}{\underset{1}{\cancel{(y+4)}}(y-1)\underset{1}{\cancel{(y+3)}}\underset{1}{\cancel{(y-2)}}}$$

Divide both numerator and denominator by common factors. Observe that

$$\frac{2-y}{y-2} = -1$$

since the polynomials have opposite signs.

$$= -\frac{2+y}{y-1}$$

Multiply the remaining factors in the numerator and denominator. ∎

Dividing Rational Expressions

In arithmetic, we know that the quotient of two rational numbers is found by multiplying the first number by the reciprocal of the second. Symbolically, we have

$$\frac{a}{b} \div \frac{c}{d} = \frac{a}{b} \cdot \frac{d}{c}, \quad b \neq 0, d \neq 0, c \neq 0$$

For example, to find the quotient of $\frac{3}{5}$ and $\frac{15}{11}$, we proceed as follows:

$$\frac{3}{5} \div \frac{15}{11} = \frac{3}{5} \cdot \frac{11}{15}$$

Multiply by the reciprocal of the divisor. The reciprocal of $\frac{15}{11}$ is $\frac{11}{15}$.

$$= \frac{3}{5} \cdot \frac{11}{5 \cdot 3}$$

Factor.

$$= \frac{3 \cdot 11}{5 \cdot 5 \cdot 3}$$

Multiply numerators and denominators.

$$= \frac{\overset{1}{\cancel{3}} \cdot 11}{5 \cdot 5 \cdot \underset{1}{\cancel{3}}}$$

Divide both numerator and denominator by common factors.

$$= \frac{11}{25}$$

Multiply remaining factors in the numerator and do the same in the denominator.

In a similar manner, the quotient of two rational expressions is the product of the first expression and the reciprocal of the second.

Dividing rational expressions

If P, Q, R, and S are polynomials, where $Q \neq 0, S \neq 0$, and $R \neq 0$, then

$$\frac{P}{Q} \div \frac{R}{S} = \frac{P}{Q} \cdot \frac{S}{R} = \frac{PS}{QR}.$$

Table 8.1 shows the reciprocals of various rational expressions, found by inverting the rational expression.

TABLE 8.1 Reciprocals of Rational Expressions

Rational Expression	Reciprocal
$\dfrac{x}{x + 1}$	$\dfrac{x + 1}{x}$
$y^2 + 2y - 35$	$\dfrac{1}{y^2 + 2y - 35}$
$\dfrac{5}{x}$	$\dfrac{x}{5}$
$\dfrac{y^2 + 9y + 14}{y^2 - 3y - 10}$	$\dfrac{y^2 - 3y - 10}{y^2 + 9y + 14}$

The following examples show the division of rational expressions by multiplying by the reciprocal of the rational expression after the division symbol.

EXAMPLE 4   **Dividing Rational Expressions**

Divide: **a.** $\dfrac{x}{7} \div \dfrac{6}{y}$ **b.** $(x + 5) \div \dfrac{x - 2}{x + 9}$

Solution

a. $\dfrac{x}{7} \div \dfrac{6}{y} = \dfrac{x}{7} \cdot \dfrac{y}{6}$ Multiply the reciprocal of the divisor.

$\qquad = \dfrac{xy}{42}$ Multiply the factors in the numerator and denominator.

b. $(x + 5) \div \dfrac{x - 2}{x + 9} = \dfrac{x + 5}{1} \cdot \dfrac{x + 9}{x - 2}$ Multiply by the reciprocal of the divisor.

$\qquad = \dfrac{(x + 5)(x + 9)}{x - 2}$ Multiply the factors in the numerator and denominator. We need not carry out the multiplication in the numerator. ∎

EXAMPLE 5   **Dividing Rational Expressions**

Divide and simplify:

a. $\dfrac{x^2 + 3x}{x + 1} \div \dfrac{x}{x + 1}$ **b.** $\dfrac{a^2 + 7a + 12}{a^2 + 9} \div 7a^2 + 21a$

c. $\dfrac{x^2 - 2x - 8}{x^2 - 9} \div \dfrac{x - 4}{x + 3}$

Solution

a. $\dfrac{x^2 + 3x}{x + 1} \div \dfrac{x}{x + 1} = \dfrac{x^2 + 3x}{x + 1} \cdot \dfrac{x + 1}{x}$ Multiply by the reciprocal of the divisor.

$= \dfrac{x(x + 3)(x + 1)}{(x + 1)x}$ Factor and multiply. What values of x are not permissible?

$= \dfrac{\overset{1}{\cancel{x}}(x + 3)\overset{1}{\cancel{(x + 1)}}}{\underset{1}{\cancel{(x + 1)}}\underset{1}{\cancel{x}}}$ Simplify.

$= \dfrac{x + 3}{1} = x + 3$ Multiply the remaining factors in the numerator and denominator.

b. $\dfrac{a^2 + 7a + 12}{a^2 + 9} \div \dfrac{7a^2 + 21a}{1}$ It is helpful to write the divisor with a denominator of 1.

$= \dfrac{a^2 + 7a + 12}{a^2 + 9} \cdot \dfrac{1}{7a^2 + 21a}$ Multiply by the reciprocal of the divisor.

$= \dfrac{(a + 4)(a + 3)}{(a^2 + 9)7a(a + 3)}$ Factor and multiply. What values of a are not permissible?

$= \dfrac{(a + 4)\overset{1}{\cancel{(a + 3)}}}{(a^2 + 9)7a\underset{1}{\cancel{(a + 3)}}}$ Simplify.

$= \dfrac{a + 4}{7a(a^2 + 9)}$ Multiply the remaining factors in the numerator and denominator.

c. $\dfrac{x^2 - 2x - 8}{x^2 - 9} \div \dfrac{x - 4}{x + 3} = \dfrac{x^2 - 2x - 8}{x^2 - 9} \cdot \dfrac{x + 3}{x - 4}$ Multiply by the reciprocal of the divisor.

$= \dfrac{(x - 4)(x + 2)(x + 3)}{(x + 3)(x - 3)(x - 4)}$ Factor and multiply. What values of x are not permissible?

$= \dfrac{\overset{1}{\cancel{(x - 4)}}(x + 2)\overset{1}{\cancel{(x + 3)}}}{\underset{1}{\cancel{(x + 3)}}(x - 3)\underset{1}{\cancel{(x - 4)}}}$ Simplify.

$= \dfrac{x + 2}{x - 3}$ Multiply the remaining factors in the numerator and denominator. ∎

In the next example, the division of rational expressions is expressed using the fraction bar. In this case, the rules for dividing fractions still apply and we still invert the divisor and multiply.

EXAMPLE 6 **Division of Rational Expressions Shown with Fraction Bars**

Perform the indicated operations:

a. $\dfrac{\dfrac{x^2 + 7}{3}}{5}$ **b.** $\dfrac{\dfrac{3x}{7}}{x}$ **c.** $\dfrac{\dfrac{y}{y - 5}}{\dfrac{5}{5 - y}}$

Solution

a. $\dfrac{\dfrac{x^2 + 7}{3}}{5} = \dfrac{x^2 + 7}{3} \div \dfrac{5}{1}$ Rewrite using $\div$. This step is optional.

$\qquad = \dfrac{x^2 + 7}{3} \cdot \dfrac{1}{5}$ Multiply by the reciprocal of the divisor.

$\qquad = \dfrac{x^2 + 7}{15}$ Multiply the numerators and denominators.

b. $\dfrac{\dfrac{3x}{7}}{x} = \dfrac{3x}{7} \div \dfrac{x}{1}$ Rewrite using $\div$. Again, this is optional.

$\qquad = \dfrac{3x}{7} \cdot \dfrac{1}{x}$ Multiply by the reciprocal of the divisor.

$\qquad = \dfrac{\overset{1}{\cancel{3x}} \cdot 1}{7\underset{1}{\cancel{x}}}$ Multiply and simplify. $(x \ne 0)$

$\qquad = \dfrac{3}{7}$ Multiply the remaining factors in the numerator and denominator.

c. $\dfrac{\dfrac{y}{y - 5}}{\dfrac{5}{5 - y}} = \dfrac{y}{y - 5} \div \dfrac{5}{5 - y}$ Rewrite using $\div$.

$\qquad = \dfrac{y}{y - 5} \cdot \dfrac{5 - y}{5}$ Multiply by the reciprocal of the divisor.

$\qquad = \dfrac{y\overset{-1}{\cancel{(5 - y)}}}{\underset{1}{\cancel{(y - 5)}}5}$ Multiply and simplify. $(y \ne 5)$

$\qquad = -\dfrac{y}{5}$ Multiply the remaining factors in the numerator and denominator.

PROBLEM SET 8.2

Practice Problems _____

Multiply as indicated in Problems 1–30. Express each answer in simplified form. In each case, state value(s) of the variables that are not permissible. If applicable, use a graphing utility to verify your answer.

1. $\dfrac{5}{x + 2} \cdot \dfrac{x - 3}{7}$ **2.** $\dfrac{7}{x - 1} \cdot \dfrac{x + 4}{15}$ **3.** $\dfrac{3x}{7} \cdot \dfrac{x + 1}{x - 2}$ **4.** $\dfrac{5x}{3} \cdot \dfrac{x - 1}{x + 5}$

5. $\dfrac{x}{2} \cdot \dfrac{4}{x + 1}$ **6.** $\dfrac{x}{3} \cdot \dfrac{6}{x - 1}$ **7.** $\dfrac{3}{x} \cdot \dfrac{2x}{9}$ **8.** $\dfrac{7}{2x} \cdot \dfrac{4x}{21}$

9. $\dfrac{x - 2}{3x + 9} \cdot \dfrac{2x + 6}{2x - 4}$ **10.** $\dfrac{6y + 9}{3y - 15} \cdot \dfrac{y - 5}{4y + 6}$ **11.** $\dfrac{y - 5}{y + 2} \cdot \dfrac{6y - 8}{2y + 4}$ **12.** $\dfrac{3y + 27}{y - 7} \cdot \dfrac{y + 4}{2y + 18}$

13. $\dfrac{4y + 30}{y^2 - 3y} \cdot \dfrac{y - 3}{2y + 15}$ **14.** $\dfrac{4y + 2}{3y - 4} \cdot \dfrac{3y - 4}{y^2 - 9y - 5}$ **15.** $\dfrac{r^2 - 9}{r^2} \cdot \dfrac{r^2 - 3r}{r^2 + r - 12}$ **16.** $\dfrac{r^2 - 4}{r^2 - 4r + 4} \cdot \dfrac{2r - 4}{r^2 - 4}$

17. $\dfrac{y^2 - 7y - 30}{y^2 - 6y - 40} \cdot \dfrac{2y^2 + 5y + 2}{2y^2 + 7y + 3}$

18. $\dfrac{3y^2 + 17y + 10}{3y^2 - 22y - 16} \cdot \dfrac{y^2 - 4y - 32}{y^2 - 8y - 48}$

19. $(y^2 - 9)\left(\dfrac{4}{y - 3}\right)$

20. $(y^2 - 49)\left(\dfrac{y + 4}{y - 7}\right)$

21. $\dfrac{x^2 - 2x + 4}{x^2 - 4} \cdot \dfrac{(x + 2)^3}{2x + 4}$

22. $\dfrac{y - 1}{y^2 + 2y + 1} \cdot \dfrac{y^2 - 1}{(y - 1)^2}$

23. $\dfrac{x^2 - x - 6}{3x - 9} \cdot \dfrac{x^2 - 9}{x^2 + 6x + 9}$

24. $\dfrac{x^2 - 4}{x^2 + 3x + 2} \cdot \dfrac{x^2 - 2x - 3}{2x + 4}$

25. $\dfrac{y^2 + 10y + 25}{y - 4} \cdot \dfrac{y^2 - y - 12}{y + 5} \cdot \dfrac{1}{y + 3}$

26. $\dfrac{y^2 + y - 12}{y^2 + y - 30} \cdot \dfrac{y^2 + 5y + 6}{y^2 - 2y - 3} \cdot \dfrac{y^2 + 7y + 6}{y + 3}$

27. $\dfrac{(x - 2)^3}{(x - 1)^3} \cdot \dfrac{x^2 - 2x + 1}{x^2 - 4x + 4}$

28. $\dfrac{(x + 4)^3}{(x + 2)^3} \cdot \dfrac{x^2 + 4x + 4}{x^2 + 8x + 16}$

29. $\dfrac{25 - y^2}{y^2 - 2y - 35} \cdot \dfrac{y^2 - 8y - 20}{y^2 - 3y - 10}$

30. $\dfrac{y^3 - 3y^2}{y^2 - 4} \cdot \dfrac{2 - y}{y^3 - 2y^2 - 3y}$

Divide as indicated in Problems 31–60. Express each answer in simplified form. If applicable, use a graphing utility to verify your answer.

31. $\dfrac{x}{7} \div \dfrac{5}{3}$

32. $\dfrac{x}{3} \div \dfrac{3}{8}$

33. $\dfrac{3}{x} \div \dfrac{12}{x}$

34. $\dfrac{x}{5} \div \dfrac{20}{x}$

35. $\dfrac{15}{x} \div \dfrac{3}{2x}$

36. $\dfrac{9}{x} \div \dfrac{3}{4x}$

37. $\dfrac{2}{x + 1} \div \dfrac{3}{x - 1}$

38. $\dfrac{3}{x + 2} \div \dfrac{4}{x - 2}$

39. $\dfrac{x}{y^2} \div \dfrac{x^4}{y^3}$

40. $\dfrac{x^3}{y^2} \div \dfrac{x^5}{y^3}$

41. $\dfrac{x + 3}{x - 4} \div \dfrac{x - 3}{x + 4}$

42. $\dfrac{x + 5}{x - 3} \div \dfrac{x - 5}{x + 6}$

43. $\dfrac{x + 1}{3} \div \dfrac{3x + 3}{7}$

44. $\dfrac{x + 5}{7} \div \dfrac{4x + 20}{9}$

45. $\dfrac{7}{x - 5} \div \dfrac{28}{3x - 15}$

46. $\dfrac{4}{x - 6} \div \dfrac{40}{7x - 42}$

47. $\dfrac{x^2 - 4}{x} \div \dfrac{x + 2}{x - 2}$

48. $\dfrac{x^2 - 4}{x - 2} \div \dfrac{x + 2}{4x - 8}$

49. $(y^2 - 16) \div \dfrac{y^2 + 3y - 4}{y^2 + 4}$

50. $(y^2 + 4y - 5) \div \dfrac{y^2 - 25}{y + 7}$

51. $\dfrac{y^2 - y}{15} \div \dfrac{y - 1}{5}$

52. $\dfrac{y^2 - 2y}{15} \div \dfrac{y - 2}{5}$

53. $\dfrac{x^2 + 2x + 1}{6x^2} \div \dfrac{x + 1}{12x^3}$

54. $\dfrac{2y^2 - 13y + 15}{6y^2 + 5y - 21} \div \dfrac{y^2 - 6y + 5}{3y^2 + 4y - 7}$

55. $\dfrac{y^3 + y}{y^2 - y} \div \dfrac{y^3 - y^2}{y^2 - 2y + 1}$

56. $\dfrac{3y^2 - 12}{y^2 + 4y + 4} \div \dfrac{y^3 - 2y^2}{y^2 + 2y}$

57. $\dfrac{m^2 + 5m + 4}{m^2 + 12m + 32} \div \dfrac{m^2 - 12m + 35}{m^2 + 3m - 40}$

58. $\dfrac{m^2 + 4m - 21}{m^2 + 3m - 28} \div \dfrac{m^2 + 14m + 48}{m^2 + 4m - 32}$

59. $\dfrac{2y^2 - 128}{y^2 + 16y + 64} \div \dfrac{y^2 - 6y - 16}{3y^2 + 30y + 48}$

60. $\dfrac{3y + 12}{y^2 + 3y} \div \dfrac{12 - y - y^2}{9y - y^3}$

Problems 61–76 show the division of rational expressions with fraction bars. Divide as indicated, expressing each answer in simplified form.

61. $\dfrac{\dfrac{x^2 + 5}{3}}{7}$

62. $\dfrac{\dfrac{x^2 + 1}{7}}{5}$

63. $\dfrac{\dfrac{7x}{9}}{x}$

64. $\dfrac{\dfrac{11x}{15}}{x}$

65. $\dfrac{\dfrac{x^3}{6}}{\dfrac{x}{3}}$

66. $\dfrac{\dfrac{y^4}{12}}{\dfrac{y}{6}}$

67. $\dfrac{\dfrac{3x + 12}{4}}{\dfrac{x + 4}{2}}$

68. $\dfrac{\dfrac{3x^2 + 6x + 3}{5x}}{\dfrac{9x + 9}{10x^2}}$

69. $\dfrac{\dfrac{x}{y-7}}{\dfrac{4}{7-y}}$

70. $\dfrac{\dfrac{x}{y-3}}{\dfrac{12}{3-y}}$

71. $\dfrac{\dfrac{x^2-9x+18}{x^2-9}}{\dfrac{2x^3-11x^2-6x}{2x^2+x}}$

72. $\dfrac{\dfrac{5y^2+34y-7}{2y^2+3y-2}}{\dfrac{y^3+5y^2-14y}{y^3-4y}}$

73. $\dfrac{\left(\dfrac{7x}{3}\right)^2}{\left(\dfrac{7x}{2}\right)^3}$

74. $\dfrac{\left(\dfrac{x}{2y}\right)^3}{\left(\dfrac{2x}{y}\right)^2}$

75. $\dfrac{\dfrac{4}{x^2-3x-28}}{\dfrac{2}{x-7}}$

76. $\dfrac{\dfrac{y-5}{y+3}}{\dfrac{2}{y^2+5y+6}}$

The rational expressions in Problems 77–89 involve several variables. Multiply or divide as indicated.

77. $\dfrac{3x}{y^2}\cdot\dfrac{y}{12x^3}$

78. $\dfrac{3ab^2}{2}\cdot\dfrac{6}{a^2b^3}$

79. $\dfrac{x^2-y^2}{x}\cdot\dfrac{x^2+xy}{x+y}$

80. $\dfrac{a^2+2ab+b^2}{a^2-2ab+b^2}\cdot\dfrac{4a-4b}{3a+3b}$

81. $\dfrac{a^2-b^2}{a+b}\cdot\dfrac{a+2b}{2a^2-ab-b^2}$

82. $\dfrac{1}{7a^2b}\div\dfrac{1}{21a^3b}$

83. $\dfrac{12x^2}{4yz}\div\dfrac{3x^2}{yz}$

84. $\dfrac{2x+2y}{3}\div\dfrac{x^2-y^2}{x-y}$

85. $\dfrac{4a+4b}{ab^2}\div\dfrac{3a+3b}{a^2b}$

86. $\dfrac{a^2-b^2}{8a^2-16ab+8b^2}\cdot\dfrac{4a-4b}{a+b}$

87. $\dfrac{4x^2-y^2}{x^2+4xy+4y^2}\div\dfrac{4x-2y}{3x+6y}$

88. $\dfrac{ab-b^2}{a^2+2a+1}\div\dfrac{2a^2+ab-3b^2}{2a^2+5ab+3b^2}$

89. $\dfrac{a^2-4b^2}{a^2+3ab+2b^2}\div\dfrac{a^2-4ab+4b^2}{a+b}$

True–False Critical Thinking Problems

90. Which one of the following is true?
  a. $5\div x=\frac{1}{5}\cdot x$ for any nonzero number x.
  b. $\dfrac{4}{x}\div\dfrac{x-2}{x}=\dfrac{4}{x-2}$ if $x\neq 0$ and $x\neq 2$.
  c. $\dfrac{x-5}{6}\cdot\dfrac{3}{5-x}=\dfrac{1}{2}$ for any value of x except 5.
  d. When a rational expression is reduced to lowest terms, its value decreases.

91. Which one of the following is true?
  a. The quotient of two rational expressions can be found by dividing their numerators and dividing their denominators.
  b. $\dfrac{y^2+y-2}{3y^2+9y+6}\div(y-1)=\dfrac{1}{3y+1}$
  c. $\dfrac{y}{5}\div 5=\dfrac{y}{25}$ for any real number y.
  d. One-half divided by five is five-halves.

Technology Problems

In Problems 92–94, use a graphing utility to determine if the multiplication or division has been performed correctly by graphing the expressions on both sides on the same screen. If the answer is wrong, correct it and then verify your correction using the graphing utility.

92. $\dfrac{3-x}{3+x}\cdot\dfrac{x+3}{x-3}=1,\qquad x\neq -3\ \text{ and }\ x\neq 3$

94. $\dfrac{x^2-9}{x+4}\div\dfrac{x-3}{x+4}=x-3$

93. $\dfrac{x^3-25x}{x^2-3x-10}\cdot\dfrac{x+2}{x}=x+5,\qquad x\neq -2,\quad x\neq 0,$
  and $x\neq 5$

Writing in Mathematics

95. When considering the division problem

$$\dfrac{P}{Q}\div\dfrac{R}{S}$$

where P, Q, R, and S are polynomials, we say that $Q\neq 0$ and $S\neq 0$, and then include the additional restriction that $R\neq 0$. Explain why the additional restriction $R\neq 0$ is included.

96. Explain the procedure for multiplying and dividing rational expressions.

Critical Thinking Problems _____

97. Find the missing factors: $\dfrac{\boxed{}}{\boxed{}} \cdot \dfrac{3x - 12}{2x} = \dfrac{3}{2}.$

98. Find the missing factors: $-\dfrac{1}{2x - 3} \div \dfrac{\boxed{}}{\boxed{}} = \dfrac{1}{3}.$

99. Find the quotient of the area of the trapezoid and the area of the rectangle shown in the figure.

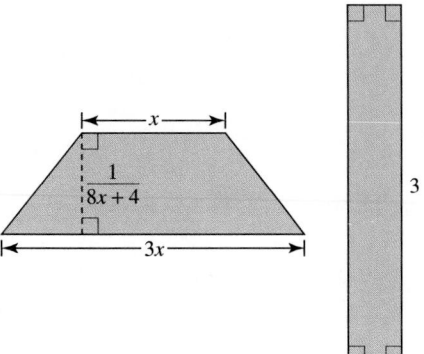

100. Express as a simplified fraction the value of the following product containing 199 factors:

$$\left(1 - \frac{1}{2}\right)\left(1 - \frac{1}{3}\right)\left(1 - \frac{1}{4}\right)\left(1 - \frac{1}{5}\right)\cdots\left(1 - \frac{1}{200}\right).$$

Review Problems _____

101. Simplify: $\dfrac{(3x^{-3})^4}{9x^5}.$

102. Solve: $2x + 3 < 3(x - 5).$

103. Solve for y: $y(2y + 9) = 5.$

S E C T I O N   8 . 3

Solutions Manual   Tutorial   Video 9

Adding and Subtracting Rational Expressions with the Same Denominator

Objectives

1 Add and subtract rational expressions with the same denominators.
2 Add and subtract rational expressions whose denominators are additive inverses.

Like multiplication and division, addition and subtraction of rational expressions are similar to the addition and subtraction of rational numbers. In this section, we once again draw on our experience from arithmetic to add and subtract rational expressions having the same denominator.

1 Add and subtract rational expressions with the same denominators.

Addition and Subtraction When Denominators Are the Same

To add rational numbers having the same denominators, such as $\frac{2}{9}$ and $\frac{4}{9}$, we add the numerators and place the sum over the common denominator.

$$\frac{2}{9} + \frac{4}{9} = \frac{2 + 4}{9} = \frac{6}{9}$$

This sum can be simplified by dividing the numerator and denominator by 3.

$$\frac{6}{9} = \frac{\overset{1}{\cancel{3}} \cdot 2}{\underset{1}{\cancel{3}} \cdot 3} = \frac{2}{3}$$

We can add or subtract rational expressions having the same denominators in an identical manner.

Adding or subtracting rational expressions with the same (like) denominators.

1. Add or subtract the numerators.
2. Place the result over the common denominator.
3. If possible, simplify the answer by reducing it to lowest terms.

EXAMPLE 1 **Adding Rational Expressions with Like Denominators**

Add: $\dfrac{2x-1}{3} + \dfrac{x+4}{3}$

Solution

$$\frac{2x-1}{3} + \frac{x+4}{3} = \frac{2x-1+x+4}{3}$$ Add numerators. Place this sum over the common denominator.

$$= \frac{3x+3}{3}$$ Combine like terms.

$$= \frac{\overset{1}{\cancel{3}}(x+1)}{\underset{1}{\cancel{3}}}$$ Factor and simplify.

$$= x+1$$

Using technology

The graphs of

$$y_1 = \frac{2x-1}{3} + \frac{x+4}{3} \quad \text{and} \quad y_2 = x+1$$

are identical, so that

$$\frac{2x-1}{3} + \frac{x+4}{3} = x+1.$$

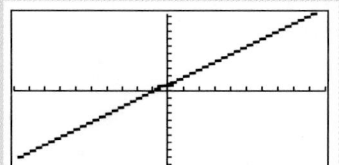

EXAMPLE 2   **Adding Rational Expressions with Like Denominators**

Add: $\dfrac{x^2}{x^2 - 9} + \dfrac{9 - 6x}{x^2 - 9}$

Solution

$$\dfrac{x^2}{x^2 - 9} + \dfrac{9 - 6x}{x^2 - 9} = \dfrac{x^2 + 9 - 6x}{x^2 - 9}$$ Add numerators. Place this sum over the common denominator.

$$= \dfrac{x^2 - 6x + 9}{x^2 - 9}$$ Write the numerator in descending powers of x.

$$= \dfrac{(x - 3)\overset{1}{\cancel{(x - 3)}}}{(x + 3)\underset{1}{\cancel{(x - 3)}}}$$ Factor and simplify. What values of x are not permitted?

$$= \dfrac{x - 3}{x + 3}$$ ∎

In Example 3, we subtract rational expressions with the same denominators by subtracting the numerators and placing the result over the common denominator.

EXAMPLE 3   **Subtracting Rational Expressions with Like Denominators**

Subtract: **a.** $\dfrac{2x + 3}{x + 1} - \dfrac{x}{x + 1}$ **b.** $\dfrac{5x + 1}{x^2 - 9} - \dfrac{4x - 2}{x^2 - 9}$

Solution

a. $\dfrac{2x + 3}{x + 1} - \dfrac{x}{x + 1} = \dfrac{2x + 3 - x}{x + 1}$ Subtract numerators and keep the same denominator.

$$= \dfrac{x + 3}{x + 1}$$ Combine like terms.

b. $\dfrac{5x + 1}{x^2 - 9} - \dfrac{4x - 2}{x^2 - 9} = \dfrac{5x + 1 - (4x - 2)}{x^2 - 9}$ Subtract numerators and include parentheses to indicate that both terms are subtracted. Place this difference over the common denominator.

$$= \dfrac{5x + 1 - 4x + 2}{x^2 - 9}$$ Remove parentheses and then change the sign of each term.

$$= \dfrac{x + 3}{x^2 - 9}$$ Combine like terms.

$$= \dfrac{\overset{1}{\cancel{x + 3}}}{\underset{1}{\cancel{(x + 3)}}(x - 3)}$$ Factor and simplify. $(x \neq -3 \text{ and } x \neq 3)$

$$= \dfrac{1}{x - 3}$$ ∎

EXAMPLE 4 **Adding and Subtracting Rational Expressions**

Perform the indicated operations:

$$\frac{y^2 - 4}{y + 2} + \frac{2(y^2 - 9)}{y + 2} - \frac{3(y^2 - 5)}{y + 2}$$

Solution

$$\frac{y^2 - 4}{y + 2} + \frac{2(y^2 - 9)}{y + 2} - \frac{3(y^2 - 5)}{y + 2}$$

$$= \frac{y^2 - 4 + 2(y^2 - 9) - 3(y^2 - 5)}{y + 2}$$ Combine numerators. Place this result over the common denominator. ($y \neq -2$)

$$= \frac{y^2 - 4 + 2y^2 - 18 - 3y^2 + 15}{y + 2}$$

$$= \frac{-7}{y + 2}$$ Combine like terms. Note that $y^2 + 2y^2 - 3y^2 = 0$. ■

2 Add and subtract rational expressions whose denominators are additive inverses.

Addition and Subtraction When Denominators Are Additive Inverses

Example 5 differs from the previous examples. The two factors in the denominators are opposites of each other.

EXAMPLE 5 **Adding Rational Expressions with Additive Inverse Denominators**

Add: $\dfrac{y^2}{y - 5} + \dfrac{4y + 5}{5 - y}$

Solution

We note that $y - 5$ and $5 - y$ are additive inverses or opposites. With denominators that are additive inverses, we can multiply the numerator and denominator of either rational expression by -1 and immediately obtain a common denominator.

$$\frac{y^2}{y - 5} + \frac{4y + 5}{5 - y} \cdot \frac{-1}{-1} = \frac{y^2}{y - 5} + \frac{-4y - 5}{y - 5}$$

$$= \frac{y^2 - 4y - 5}{y - 5}$$ Add numerators. Put this sum over the common denominator.

$$= \frac{\overset{1}{\cancel{(y - 5)}}(y + 1)}{\underset{1}{\cancel{y - 5}}}$$ Factor and simplify. ($y \neq 5$)

$$= y + 1$$ ■

> **Adding and subtracting rational expressions when denominators are additive inverses**
>
> When one denominator is the additive inverse of the other, first multiply either rational expression by $\frac{-1}{-1}$ to obtain a common denominator.

EXAMPLE 6 **Subtracting Rational Expressions with Additive Inverse Denominators**

Subtract: $\dfrac{5x - x^2}{x^2 - 4x - 3} - \dfrac{3x - x^2}{3 + 4x - x^2}$

Solution

We note that $x^2 - 4x - 3$ and $3 + 4x - x^2$ are opposites. We multiply the second algebraic fraction by $\frac{-1}{-1}$.

$$\dfrac{(3x - x^2)}{(3 + 4x - x^2)} \cdot \dfrac{(-1)}{(-1)} = \dfrac{-3x + x^2}{-3 - 4x + x^2}$$ Multiply by $\frac{-1}{-1}$ and distribute -1 to the numerator and denominator.

$$= \dfrac{x^2 - 3x}{x^2 - 4x - 3}$$ Write the numerator and denominator in descending powers of x.

We now return to the original subtraction problem.

$$\dfrac{5x - x^2}{x^2 - 4x - 3} - \dfrac{3x - x^2}{3 + 4x - x^2}$$

$$= \dfrac{5x - x^2}{x^2 - 4x - 3} - \dfrac{x^2 - 3x}{x^2 - 4x - 3}$$ Replace the second fraction by the form obtained through multiplication by $\frac{-1}{-1}$.

$$= \dfrac{5x - x^2 - (x^2 - 3x)}{x^2 - 4x - 3}$$ Subtract numerators. Place this difference over the common denominator. Don't forget parentheses!

$$= \dfrac{5x - x^2 - x^2 + 3x}{x^2 - 4x - 3}$$ Distribute -1 throughout the parentheses.

$$= \dfrac{-2x^2 + 8x}{x^2 - 4x - 3}$$ Combine like terms in the numerator.

Although the numerator can be factored, further simplification is not possible. ■

PROBLEM SET 8.3

Practice Problems _____

Add or subtract as indicated in Problems 1–36. Express each answer in lowest terms. If applicable, use a graphing utility to verify your answer.

1. $\dfrac{4x}{9} + \dfrac{2x}{9}$

2. $\dfrac{7y}{12} + \dfrac{y}{12}$

3. $\dfrac{5}{x} + \dfrac{3}{x}$

4. $\dfrac{11r}{12} + \dfrac{7r}{12}$

5. $\dfrac{7}{9x} + \dfrac{5}{9x}$

6. $\dfrac{x}{7} + \dfrac{1}{7}$

7. $\dfrac{m}{5} + \dfrac{2m}{5}$

8. $\dfrac{1}{x + 3} + \dfrac{5}{x + 3}$

9. $\dfrac{7}{4 - y} + \dfrac{3}{4 - y}$

10. $\dfrac{4y + 1}{6y + 5} + \dfrac{8y + 9}{6y + 5}$

11. $\dfrac{3x + 2}{3x + 4} + \dfrac{3x + 6}{3x + 4}$

12. $\dfrac{y^2 + 7y}{y^2 - 5y} + \dfrac{y^2 - 4y}{y^2 - 5y}$

13. $\dfrac{y^2 - 2y}{y^2 + 3y} + \dfrac{y^2 + y}{y^2 + 3y}$

14. $\dfrac{4y - 1}{5y^2} + \dfrac{3y + 1}{5y^2}$

15. $\dfrac{y + 2}{6y^3} + \dfrac{3y - 2}{6y^3}$

16. $\dfrac{x^2 - 2}{x^2 + x - 2} + \dfrac{2x - x^2}{x^2 + x - 2}$

17. $\dfrac{y^2 + 9y}{4y^2 - 11y - 3} + \dfrac{3y - 5y^2}{4y^2 - 11y - 3}$

18. $\dfrac{y^2 - 4y}{y^2 - y - 6} + \dfrac{4y - 4}{y^2 - y - 6}$

19. $\dfrac{y}{2y + 7} - \dfrac{2}{2y + 7}$

20. $\dfrac{3y}{5y - 4} - \dfrac{4}{5y - 4}$

21. $\dfrac{x}{x - 1} - \dfrac{1}{x - 1}$

22. $\dfrac{4y}{4y - 3} - \dfrac{3}{4y - 3}$

23. $\dfrac{2y + 1}{3y - 7} - \dfrac{y + 8}{3y - 7}$

24. $\dfrac{14y}{7y + 2} - \dfrac{7y - 2}{7y + 2}$

25. $\dfrac{2y + 3}{3y - 6} - \dfrac{3 - y}{3y - 6}$

26. $\dfrac{3y + 1}{4y - 2} - \dfrac{y + 1}{4y - 2}$

27. $\dfrac{y^3 - 3}{2y^4} - \dfrac{7y^3 - 3}{2y^4}$

28. $\dfrac{3y^2 - 1}{3y^3} - \dfrac{6y^2 - 1}{3y^3}$

29. $\dfrac{y^2 + 3y}{y^2 + y - 12} - \dfrac{y^2 - 12}{y^2 + y - 12}$

30. $\dfrac{2y^2}{2y^2 + 5y - 3} - \dfrac{y}{2y^2 + 5y - 3}$

31. $\dfrac{16r^2 + 3}{16r^2 + 16r + 3} - \dfrac{3 - 4r}{16r^2 + 16r + 3}$

32. $\dfrac{6r^2 + r}{6r^2 - r - 2} - \dfrac{2r^2 - r}{6r^2 - r - 2}$

33. $\dfrac{9x}{10} - \dfrac{7x}{10} + \dfrac{3x}{10}$

34. $\dfrac{6}{15x} + \dfrac{11}{15x} - \dfrac{2}{15x}$

35. $\dfrac{6y^2 + y}{2y^2 - 9y + 9} - \dfrac{2y + 9}{2y^2 - 9y + 9} - \dfrac{4y - 3}{2y^2 - 9y + 9}$

36. $\dfrac{3y^2 - 2}{3y^2 + 10y - 8} - \dfrac{y + 10}{3y^2 + 10y - 8} - \dfrac{y^2 - 6y}{3y^2 + 10y - 8}$

Add or subtract as indicated in Problems 37–52. In all cases, denominators are additive inverses of one another and you will first have to multiply a rational expression by $\frac{-1}{-1}$.

37. $\dfrac{2y + 7}{y - 6} + \dfrac{3y}{6 - y}$

38. $\dfrac{2y + 5}{y - 2} + \dfrac{y + 5}{2 - y}$

39. $\dfrac{5x - 2}{3x - 4} + \dfrac{2x - 3}{4 - 3x}$

40. $\dfrac{9x - 1}{7x - 3} + \dfrac{6x - 2}{3 - 7x}$

41. $\dfrac{y^2}{y - 2} + \dfrac{4}{2 - y}$

42. $\dfrac{x^2}{x - 3} + \dfrac{9}{3 - x}$

43. $\dfrac{b - 3}{b^2 - 25} + \dfrac{b - 3}{25 - b^2}$

44. $\dfrac{s - 7}{s^2 - 16} + \dfrac{7 - s}{16 - s^2}$

45. $\dfrac{y}{y - 1} - \dfrac{1}{1 - y}$

46. $\dfrac{3}{x - 1} - \dfrac{3}{1 - x}$

47. $\dfrac{3 - a}{a - 7} - \dfrac{2a - 5}{7 - a}$

48. $\dfrac{4 - a}{a - 9} - \dfrac{3a - 8}{9 - a}$

49. $\dfrac{z - 2}{z^2 - 25} - \dfrac{z - 2}{25 - z^2}$

50. $\dfrac{z - 8}{z^2 - 16} - \dfrac{z - 8}{16 - z^2}$

51. $\dfrac{3(m - 2)}{2m - 3} + \dfrac{3(m - 1)}{3 - 2m} + \dfrac{5(2m + 1)}{2m - 3}$

52. $\dfrac{m + 3}{4m - 5} + \dfrac{2(3m - 1)}{4m - 5} + \dfrac{2m - 1}{5 - 4m}$

The rational expressions in Problems 53–62 involve several variables. Add or subtract as indicated.

53. $\dfrac{2x - y}{3} + \dfrac{x + 4y}{3}$

54. $\dfrac{5x}{x + 2y} + \dfrac{10y}{x + 2y}$

55. $\dfrac{27x + 18y}{(3x - 2y)(3x + 4y)(3x + 2y)} - \dfrac{18x + 24y}{(3x - 2y)(3x + 4y)(3x + 2y)}$

56. $\dfrac{b}{ac + ad - bc - bd} - \dfrac{a}{ac + ad - bc - bd}$

57. $\dfrac{2(x - 2y)}{(x + 2y)(x + y)(x - 2y)} + \dfrac{4(x + 2y)}{(x + 2y)(x + y)(x - 2y)} - \dfrac{3(x + y)}{(x + 2y)(x + y)(x - 2y)}$

58. $\dfrac{a}{a - b} + \dfrac{b}{b - a}$

59. $\dfrac{2a - b}{a - b} + \dfrac{a - 2b}{b - a}$

60. $\dfrac{a + b}{a - b} + \dfrac{a}{a - b} + \dfrac{b}{b - a} + \dfrac{a - b}{b - a}$

61. $\dfrac{a + b}{a^2 - b^2} + \dfrac{a - b}{a^2 - b^2} - \dfrac{2a}{a^2 - b^2}$

62. $\dfrac{a - 3b}{2(b - a)} + \dfrac{a + b}{2(a - b)} - \dfrac{2a - 2b}{2(a - b)}$

True–False Critical Thinking Problems

63. Which one of the following is true?

  a. The sum of two rational expressions with the same denominator can be found by adding numerators, adding denominators, and then simplifying.

  b. $\dfrac{4}{b} - \dfrac{2}{-b} = -\dfrac{2}{b}$

  c. When the operations of

$$\frac{2y+1}{y-7} + \frac{3y+1}{y-7} - \frac{5y+2}{y-7}$$

  are performed, the numerator of the resulting algebraic fraction is 0, and consequently the value of the fraction is zero.

  d. The difference of two rational expressions with the same denominator can always be reduced to lowest terms.

64. Which one of the following is true?

  a. If $x \neq 0$, $\dfrac{3}{x} + 1 = \dfrac{4}{x}$.

  b. When adding rational expressions whose denominators are opposites of each other, first multiply either rational expression by -1.

  c. $\dfrac{7}{4-y} - \dfrac{3}{4-y} = -\dfrac{1}{y}$

  d. When subtracting

$$\frac{3(y-2)}{y(y-2)} \quad \text{from} \quad \frac{9y}{y(y-2)}$$

  it is not incorrect to express the answer as

$$\frac{6(y+1)}{y(y-2)}$$

  even though no simplification is possible.

Technology Problems

In Problems 65–67, use a graphing utility to determine if the subtraction has been performed correctly by graphing the expressions on both sides on the same screen. If the answer is wrong, correct it and then verify your correction using the graphing utility.

65. $\dfrac{3x+6}{2} - \dfrac{x}{2} = x + 3$

66. $\dfrac{x^2+4x+3}{x+2} - \dfrac{5x+9}{x+2} = x - 2, \quad x \neq -2$

67. $\dfrac{x^2-13}{x+4} - \dfrac{3}{x+4} = x + 4, \quad x \neq -4$

Writing in Mathematics

68. Describe the similarities between the following problems:

$$\frac{3}{8} + \frac{2}{8} \quad \text{and} \quad \frac{x}{x^2-1} + \frac{1}{x^2-1}.$$

69. Explain how to add and subtract rational expressions with the same denominator. Include illustrative examples.

Critical Thinking Problems

70. Perform the indicated operations:

$$\frac{(y+1)(2y-1)}{(y-2)(y-3)} + \frac{(y+2)(y-1)}{(y-2)(y-3)} - \frac{(y+5)(2y+1)}{(3-y)(2-y)}.$$

71. One rectangle has length and width represented by

$$\frac{2x}{x+1} \quad \text{and} \quad \frac{3}{x+1} \text{ meters.}$$

A second rectangle has length and width represented by

$$\frac{x}{x+1} \quad \text{and} \quad \frac{2}{x+1} \text{ meters.}$$

Express the difference between the perimeter of the first and second rectangle as a simplified rational expression in terms of x.

SECTION 8.4 ADDING AND SUBTRACTING RATIONAL EXPRESSIONS WITH DIFFERENT DENOMINATORS   **591**

In Problems 72–76, find the missing expression.

72. $\dfrac{2x}{x + 3} + \dfrac{\boxed{}}{x + 3} = \dfrac{4x + 1}{x + 3}$

73. $\dfrac{3x}{x + 2} - \dfrac{\boxed{}}{x + 2} = \dfrac{6 - 17x}{x + 2}$

74. $\dfrac{6}{x - 2} + \dfrac{\boxed{}}{2 - x} = \dfrac{13}{x - 2}$

75. $\dfrac{a^2}{a - 4} - \dfrac{\boxed{}}{a - 4} = a + 3$

76. $\dfrac{3x}{x - 5} + \dfrac{\boxed{}}{5 - x} = \dfrac{7x + 1}{x - 5}$

Review Problems

77. Factor completely: $81y^4 - 1$.

78. Two planes leave an airport at noon. One flies east at 550 miles per hour, and the other flies west at 475 miles per hour. At what time will they be 2050 miles apart?

79. Divide: $\dfrac{3x^3 + 2x^2 - 26x - 15}{x + 3}$.

Solutions Manual

Tutorial

Video 9

Adding and Subtracting Rational Expressions with Different Denominators

Objectives

1 Find the least common multiple for a group of polynomials.

2 Add or subtract rational expressions with different denominators.

In this section, we continue drawing on our experience from arithmetic to add and subtract rational expressions that have different denominators.

As we have done throughout this chapter, let's see if we can gain insight into adding rational expressions with different denominators by looking closely at what we do when adding fractions with unlike denominators. As we reviewed in Section 1.1, to add fractions like $\frac{1}{2}$ and $\frac{2}{3}$, we must first rewrite them with the same denominator. We look for the smallest number that contains both 2 and 3 as factors. This number, 6, is the *least common multiple* or *LCM,* of 2 and 3. Since 6 is the smallest number divisible by both 2 and 3, it is then used as the *least common denominator,* or *LCD.*

$$\frac{1}{2} + \frac{2}{3} = \frac{1}{2} \cdot \frac{3}{3} + \frac{2}{3} \cdot \frac{2}{2} \qquad \text{The LCM of 2 and 3 is 6. Rewrite each fraction in terms of the denominator 6.}$$

$$= \frac{3}{6} + \frac{4}{6}$$

$$= \frac{7}{6} \qquad \text{Add the numerators, putting this sum over the LCM.}$$

1 Find the least common multiple for a group of polynomials.

Our experience from arithmetic emphasizes that to add (or subtract) fractions with unlike denominators, we must rewrite each fraction as an equivalent fraction using the least common multiple of the denominators. Since the denominators of rational expressions consist of polynomials, the question becomes: How do we determine the least common multiple for a group of polynomials?

The least common multiple for a group of polynomials

1. The least common multiple for a group of polynomials is the polynomial of lowest degree that all polynomials divide into evenly.
2. To find the LCM for two or more polynomials:
   a. Factor each polynomial completely.
   b. List all the different factors of the polynomials.
   c. For each factor, determine the greatest number of times it appears in any polynomial.
   d. Form the product of each different factor taken the greatest number of times that it occurs in any polynomial. This product is the LCM.

EXAMPLE 1   Finding Least Common Multiples

Find the LCM of each of the following polynomials:

a. $15, 24$ **b.** $x - 3, x + 3$ **c.** $8x, 4x^2$ **d.** $5y^2 + 15y, y^2 + 6y + 9$

Solution

We must factor each expression. The LCM should include each factor the greatest number of times that it occurs in any factorization.

a. We factor each number.

$$15 = 5 \cdot 3$$
$$24 = 8 \cdot 3 = 2^3 \cdot 3$$

The different factors are 5, 3, and 2. Using the greatest number of times each factor appears in any factorization, the LCM $= 5 \cdot 3 \cdot 2^3 = 120$.

b. These polynomials are prime, but if we wish, we can write $x - 3 = 1(x - 3)$ and $x + 3 = 1(x + 3)$. The different factors are $1, x - 3$, and $x + 3$, so the LCM $= 1(x - 3)(x + 3)$ or $(x - 3)(x + 3)$.

c. These two polynomials factor as follows:

$$8x = 2^3 \cdot x$$
$$4x^2 = 2^2 \cdot x^2$$

The different factors are 2 and x. Using the highest power of these factors in any factorization, the LCM $= 2^3 \cdot x^2 = 8x^2$. This means that $8x^2$ is the polynomial of lowest degree that $8x$ and $4x^2$ will divide into evenly. To add, for example,

$$\frac{5}{8x} + \frac{3}{4x^2}$$

we would rewrite each fraction with the common denominator $8x^2$.

d. These two polynomials factor as follows:

$$5y^2 + 15y = 5y(y + 3)$$
$$y^2 + 6y + 9 = (y + 3)^2$$

The different factors are $5, y$, and $y + 3$. Using the highest powers of these factors, the LCM $= 5y(y + 3)^2$. ■

2 Add or subtract rational expressions with different denominators.

Al Held "B/WX" 1968, acrylic on canvas, 114 × 114 in. Albright-Knox Art Gallery, Buffalo, New York, Gift of Seymour H. Know, 1969. (© 1998 Al Held/Licensed by VAGA, New York, NY.

Adding or Subtracting Rational Expressions with Different Denominators

To add or subtract rational expressions having different denominators, we must rewrite each fraction so that they have the same denominator.

> **The least common denominator (LCD)**
>
> The like denominator used to add or subtract rational expressions having different denominators is the least common multiple of the original denominators. This like denominator is called the *least common denominator* of the rational expressions.

To combine rational expressions with different denominators, each fraction must be expressed in terms of the LCD. This involves multiplying the numerator and denominator of each fraction by the factors required to form the LCD.

EXAMPLE 2 **Adding Rational Expressions with Unlike Denominators**

Add: $\dfrac{7}{6x^2} + \dfrac{2}{9x}$

Solution

Since the LCD is the least common multiple of $6x^2$ and $9x$, we begin by factoring these expressions.

$$6x^2 = 3 \cdot 2x^2 \quad \text{and} \quad 9x = 3^2 x$$

The LCD has factors of 3, 2, and x. Using the highest powers of these factors, the least common multiple of $6x^2$ and $9x$ is

$$3^2 \cdot 2x^2 = 18x^2.$$

We now must express each fraction with a denominator of $18x^2$. Working first with $\dfrac{7}{6x^2}$, we multiply the numerator and denominator by 3.

$$\frac{7}{6x^2} \cdot \frac{3}{3} = \frac{21}{18x^2} \qquad \text{3 is the factor required to obtain the LCD.}$$

Because $\frac{3}{3} = 1$, multiplication of $\dfrac{7}{6x^2}$ by the multiplicative identity does not change the value of the fraction.

Now we must express $\dfrac{2}{9x}$ in terms of the LCD, $18x^2$. We multiply the numerator and denominator by $2x$.

$$\frac{2}{9x} \cdot \frac{2x}{2x} = \frac{4x}{18x^2} \qquad \frac{2x}{2x} \text{ is the multiplicative identity.}$$

At this point we are ready to add the fractions. In summary, this is how it looks:

$$\frac{7}{6x^2} + \frac{2}{9x}$$
The LCD is $18x^2$.

$$= \frac{7}{6x^2} \cdot \frac{3}{3} + \frac{2}{9x} \cdot \frac{2x}{2x}$$
Rewrite the fractions using the LCD. Multiply the numerator and denominator by the factors required to form the LCD.

$$= \frac{21}{18x^2} + \frac{4x}{18x^2}$$

$$= \frac{21 + 4x}{18x^2}$$
Add the numerators, placing the resulting expression over the LCD.

Before considering additional examples, let's summarize the steps involved in adding or subtracting fractions with different denominators.

> **Adding or subtracting rational expressions with different (unlike) denominators**
>
> 1. Find the LCD of the denominators.
> 2. Multiply the numerator and denominator in each fraction by the factors required to obtain the LCD.
> 3. Add or subtract the numerators, placing the resulting expression over the LCD.
> 4. If necessary, simplify the resulting rational expression.

EXAMPLE 3 **Adding Rational Expressions with Unlike Denominators**

Add: $\dfrac{3}{x + 1} + \dfrac{5}{x - 1}$

Solution

The only factors of the denominators are $(x + 1)$ and $(x - 1)$. Therefore, the LCD is $(x + 1)(x - 1)$.

$$\frac{3}{x + 1} + \frac{5}{x - 1}$$

$$= \frac{3(x - 1)}{(x + 1)(x - 1)} + \frac{5(x + 1)}{(x + 1)(x - 1)}$$
Rewrite each rational expression with the LCD. Multiply the numerator and denominator by the factors required to form the LCD.

$$= \frac{3(x - 1) + 5(x + 1)}{(x + 1)(x - 1)}$$
Add the numerators, putting this sum over the LCD.

$$= \frac{3x - 3 + 5x + 5}{(x + 1)(x - 1)}$$
Apply the distributive property.

$$= \frac{8x + 2}{(x + 1)(x - 1)}$$
Combine like terms.

Discover for yourself

Factor 2 from the numerator of the answer in Example 3. Can you simplify any further? Explain. Why is the answer expressed with the numerator as a sum rather than in factored form?

EXAMPLE 4 **Subtracting Rational Expressions with Unlike Denominators**

Subtract: $\dfrac{y+2}{4y+16} - \dfrac{2}{y^2+4y}$

Solution

We must first find the LCD, and we begin by factoring the denominators.

$$4y + 16 = 4(y+4)$$
$$y^2 + 4y = y(y+4)$$

The LCD is $4y(y+4)$, the product of the different factors. Then,

$$\frac{y+2}{4y+16} - \frac{2}{y^2+4y}$$

$$= \frac{y+2}{4(y+4)} - \frac{2}{y(y+4)}$$ Factor denominators. The LCD is $4y(y+4)$.

$$= \frac{(y+2)y}{4y(y+4)} - \frac{2\cdot4}{4y(y+4)}$$ Rewrite the fractions using the LCD, multiplying the numerator and denominator of the first fraction by y and the second by 4.

$$= \frac{(y+2)y - 2\cdot4}{4y(y+4)}$$ Subtract the numerators, placing the difference over the LCD.

$$= \frac{y^2 + 2y - 8}{4y(y+4)}$$

$$= \frac{\overset{1}{\cancel{(y+4)}}(y-2)}{4y\underset{1}{\cancel{(y+4)}}}$$ Factor the numerator and simplify ($y \neq 0$ and $y \neq -4$).

$$= \frac{y-2}{4y}$$ ∎

In some situations, after factoring to find the LCD, a factor in one denominator is the opposite of a factor in the other denominator. When this happens, we can use the same technique for adding rational expressions with opposite denominators.

> **Adding and subtracting algebraic fractions when denominators contain opposite factors**
>
> When one denominator contains the opposite factor of the other, first multiply either algebraic fraction by $\frac{-1}{-1}$.

EXAMPLE 5 **Adding Rational Expressions with Opposite Factors in the Denominators**

Add: $\dfrac{x^2-2}{2x^2-x-3} + \dfrac{x-2}{3-2x}$

iscover for yourself

In Example 5, the denominators can be factored as follows:

$2x^2 - x - 3 =$
$(2x - 3)(x + 1)$
$3 - 2x = -1(2x - 3)$

Using these factorizations, what is the LCD? Solve Example 5 by obtaining this LCD in each fraction. Then combine the fractions. How does your solution compare with the one shown on the right?

Solution

We must first find the LCD, and we begin by factoring the denominators.

$$2x^2 - x - 3 = (2x - 3)(x + 1)$$
$$3 - 2x = 1(3 - 2x)$$

We observe that $3 - 2x$ is the opposite of $2x - 3$, so we multiply the second fraction by $\frac{-1}{-1}$. This will result in $2x - 3$ in the denominator.

$$\frac{x^2 - 2}{2x^2 - x - 3} + \frac{x - 2}{3 - 2x}$$

$$= \frac{x^2 - 2}{(2x - 3)(x + 1)} + \frac{(x - 2)}{(3 - 2x)} \cdot \frac{-1}{-1}$$ Factor the first denominator.
Multiply the second fraction by $\frac{-1}{-1}$.

$$= \frac{x^2 - 2}{(2x - 3)(x + 1)} + \frac{-x + 2}{-3 + 2x}$$ Apply the distributive property.

$$= \frac{x^2 - 2}{(2x - 3)(x + 1)} + \frac{2 - x}{2x - 3}$$ Use the commutative property.
The LCD is $(2x - 3)(x + 1)$.

$$= \frac{x^2 - 2}{(2x - 3)(x + 1)} + \frac{(2 - x)(x + 1)}{(2x - 3)(x + 1)}$$ Rewrite the fractions using the LCD. This involves multiplying the numerator and denominator of the second fraction by $x + 1$.

$$= \frac{x^2 - 2 + (2 - x)(x + 1)}{(2x - 3)(x + 1)}$$ Add the numerators, putting this sum over the LCD.

$$= \frac{x^2 - 2 + 2x + 2 - x^2 - x}{(2x - 3)(x + 1)}$$ Use the FOIL method for the binomial term in the numerator.

$$= \frac{x}{(2x - 3)(x + 1)}$$ Combine like terms in the numerator. ($x \neq \frac{3}{2}$ and $x \neq -1$)

EXAMPLE 6 **Combining Rational Expressions with Unlike Denominators**

Perform the indicated operations: $\dfrac{t + 2}{4t} - \dfrac{3t - 1}{6t^2} + 1$

Solution

$$4t = 2^2 t \quad \text{and} \quad 6t^2 = 3 \cdot 2t^2$$

The LCD is the least common multiple of $4t$ and $6t^2$ and 1. The LCD is the product of each factor the greatest number of times it occurs in any factorization. Thus, LCD $= 2^2 \cdot 3t^2$ or $12t^2$.

$$\frac{t + 2}{4t} - \frac{3t - 1}{6t^2} + \frac{1}{1}$$ The LCD is $12t^2$. We have expressed 1 as $\frac{1}{1}$.

$$= \frac{(t + 2)}{4t} \cdot \frac{3t}{3t} - \frac{(3t - 1)}{6t^2} \cdot \frac{2}{2} + \frac{1}{1} \cdot \frac{12t^2}{12t^2}$$ Rewrite the fractions using the LCD. Multiply the numerator and denominator by the factors needed to form the LCD.

$$= \frac{(t + 2)3t}{12t^2} - \frac{(3t - 1) \cdot 2}{12t^2} + \frac{12t^2}{12t^2}$$ This optional step expresses each denominator as $12t^2$

$$= \frac{(t + 2)3t - (3t - 1)2 + 12t^2}{12t^2}$$

Combine the numerators, writing this expression over the LCD.

$$= \frac{3t^2 + 6t - 6t + 2 + 12t^2}{12t^2}$$

Apply the distributive property.

$$= \frac{15t^2 + 2}{12t^2}$$

Combine like terms in the numerator. $(t \neq 0)$ ■

PROBLEM SET 8.4

Practice Problems

Find the least common multiple of the monomials and polynomials in Problems 1–24.

1. $12, 10$

2. $10, 25, 35$

3. $3x, x^3$

4. $4t^2, 6t$

5. $15x^2, 24x^5$

6. $25r^3, 35r^5$

7. $100y, 120y$

8. $4y, 15y$

9. $15x^2, 6x^5$

10. $15x^4, 24x^6$

11. $y - 3, y + 1$

12. $w - 5, w + 7$

13. $x, 7(x + 2)$

14. $y, 5(y - 3)$

15. $18x^2, 27x(x - 5)$

16. $24y^2, 18y(y - 1)$

17. $x + 3, x^2 - 9$

18. $y - 5, y^2 - 25$

19. $y^2 - 4, y(y + 2)$

20. $x^2 - 100, x(x - 10)$

21. $y^2 - 25, y^2 - 10y + 25$

22. $y^2 - 16, y^2 - 8y + 16$

23. $2x^2 + 7x - 4, x^2 + 2x - 8$

24. $3x^2 + 14x - 5, 3x^2 + 11x - 4$

Perform the indicated operations in Problems 25–76, expressing each answer in lowest terms.

25. $\dfrac{3}{x} + \dfrac{5}{x^2}$

26. $\dfrac{4}{x} + \dfrac{8}{x^2}$

27. $\dfrac{2}{9w} - \dfrac{11}{6w}$

28. $\dfrac{5}{6w} - \dfrac{7}{8w}$

29. $\dfrac{x - 1}{6} - \dfrac{x + 2}{3}$

30. $\dfrac{x + 3}{2} - \dfrac{x + 5}{4}$

31. $\dfrac{2}{x - 1} + \dfrac{3}{x + 2}$

32. $\dfrac{3}{y - 2} + \dfrac{3}{y + 2}$

33. $\dfrac{2}{r + 5} + \dfrac{3}{4r}$

34. $\dfrac{3}{r + 1} + \dfrac{2}{3r}$

35. $\dfrac{4y - 9}{3y} - \dfrac{3y - 8}{4y}$

36. $\dfrac{3y - 2}{4y} - \dfrac{3y + 1}{6y}$

37. $\dfrac{5a + 3}{2a^2} - \dfrac{3a - 4}{a}$

38. $\dfrac{4a + 2}{3a} - \dfrac{5a - 3}{a^2}$

39. $\dfrac{7}{x + 5} - \dfrac{4}{x - 5}$

40. $\dfrac{2r}{r - 1} - \dfrac{3r}{r + 1}$

41. $\dfrac{2z}{z^2 - 16} + \dfrac{z}{z - 4}$

42. $\dfrac{4z}{z^2 - 25} + \dfrac{z}{z + 5}$

43. $\dfrac{5y}{y^2 - 9} - \dfrac{4}{y + 3}$

44. $\dfrac{8y}{y^2 - 16} - \dfrac{5}{y + 4}$

45. $\dfrac{7}{y - 1} - \dfrac{3}{(y - 1)^2}$

46. $\dfrac{5}{y + 3} - \dfrac{2}{(y + 3)^2}$

47. $\dfrac{3r}{4r - 20} + \dfrac{9r}{6r - 30}$

48. $\dfrac{4r}{5r - 10} + \dfrac{3r}{10r - 20}$

49. $\dfrac{y + 4}{y} - \dfrac{y}{y + 4}$

50. $\dfrac{y}{y - 5} - \dfrac{y - 5}{y}$

51. $\dfrac{z}{z^2 + 2z + 1} + \dfrac{4}{z^2 + 5z + 4}$

52. $\dfrac{7w}{w^2 + w - 2} - \dfrac{3}{w^2 - 4w + 3}$

53. $\dfrac{y - 5}{y + 3} + \dfrac{y + 3}{y - 5}$

54. $\dfrac{w - 7}{w + 4} + \dfrac{w + 4}{w - 7}$

55. $\dfrac{5}{2y^2 - 2y} - \dfrac{3}{2y - 2}$

56. $\dfrac{7}{5y^2 - 5y} - \dfrac{2}{5y - 5}$

57. $\dfrac{4r + 3}{r^2 - 9} - \dfrac{r + 1}{r - 3}$

58. $\dfrac{2r - 1}{r + 6} - \dfrac{6 - 5r}{r^2 - 36}$

59. $\dfrac{y^2 - 39}{y^2 + 3y - 10} - \dfrac{y - 7}{y - 2}$

60. $\dfrac{y^2 - 6}{y^2 + 9y + 18} - \dfrac{y - 4}{y + 6}$

61. $\dfrac{w^2 - 11}{3w^2 + 5w - 2} - \dfrac{w - 5}{3w - 1}$

62. $\dfrac{w^2 - 2}{2w^2 + 3w + 1} - \dfrac{w - 3}{2w + 1}$

63. $4 + \dfrac{1}{x - 3}$

64. $7 + \dfrac{1}{x - 5}$

65. $3 - \dfrac{3y}{y + 1}$

66. $7 - \dfrac{4y}{y + 5}$

67. $\dfrac{9x + 3}{x^2 - x - 6} + \dfrac{x}{3 - x}$

68. $\dfrac{x^2 + 9x}{x^2 - 2x - 3} + \dfrac{5}{3 - x}$

69. $\dfrac{y + 3}{5y^2} - \dfrac{y - 5}{15y}$

70. $\dfrac{y - 7}{3y^2} - \dfrac{y - 2}{12y}$

71. $\dfrac{x + 1}{4x^2 + 4x - 15} - \dfrac{4x + 5}{8x^2 - 10x - 3}$

72. $\dfrac{3x - 4}{2x^2 - 3x - 5} - \dfrac{4x + 3}{3x^2 + 5x + 2}$

73. $\dfrac{4x}{x^2 - 1} - \dfrac{2}{x} - \dfrac{2}{x + 1}$

74. $\dfrac{x + 6}{x^2 - 4} - \dfrac{x + 3}{x + 2} + \dfrac{x - 3}{x - 2}$

75. $\dfrac{7}{3x^2} + \dfrac{4}{x^2} - \dfrac{10}{7x}$

76. $\dfrac{4}{x} + \dfrac{7}{5x^2} - \dfrac{10}{3x}$

The rational expressions in Problems 77–88 involve several variables. Add or subtract as indicated.

77. $\dfrac{2}{x} + \dfrac{3}{y}$

78. $\dfrac{5x}{4y} + \dfrac{11}{6xy}$

79. $\dfrac{5}{4x^2y} - \dfrac{2}{5xy^2}$

80. $\dfrac{a - 1}{a} + \dfrac{b + 1}{b}$

81. $\dfrac{x + 2}{y} + \dfrac{y - 2}{x}$

82. $\dfrac{7}{2x} - \dfrac{2}{3x^2} - \dfrac{5}{9xy}$

83. $\dfrac{y}{xy - x^2} - \dfrac{x}{y^2 - xy}$

84. $\dfrac{x^2}{xy^2 + y^3} + \dfrac{2x}{xy + y^2} + \dfrac{1}{x + y}$

85. $\dfrac{1}{a - b} - \dfrac{a}{a^2 - ab} + \dfrac{a^2}{a^3 - a^2b}$

86. $\dfrac{1}{x + y} - \dfrac{1}{x - y} + \dfrac{2x}{x^2 - y^2}$

87. $\dfrac{a}{b} - \dfrac{c}{d}$

88. $\dfrac{a}{b} + \dfrac{c}{d}$

Application Problems

89. Express the perimeter of the rectangle shown as a single rational expression.

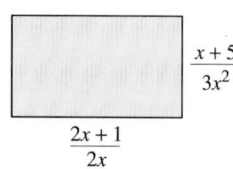

$\dfrac{x + 5}{3x^2}$

$\dfrac{2x + 1}{2x}$

90. After two people work together for t hours on a job, the fractional parts of the job done by each of the people is $\dfrac{t}{5}$ and $\dfrac{t}{4}$. What fractional part of the job has been completed?

91. Doctors use the model

$$C = \dfrac{DA}{A + 12}$$

to determine the dose of a drug prescribed for children. In this formula, C = child's dose, A = child's age, and D = adult dose. What is the difference in the child's dose for a 7-year-old child and a 3-year-old child? Express the answer as a single rational expression in terms of D. Then describe what your answer means in terms of the variables in the model.

True–False Critical Thinking Problems

92. Which one of the following is true?
   a. $a - \dfrac{1}{5} = \dfrac{4}{5}a$
   b. The LCD for $\dfrac{1}{y}$ and $\dfrac{2y}{y - 1}$ is $y^2 - 1$.
   c. The LCM for $2^5 \cdot 3$ and $2^4 \cdot 3^2$ is $2^4 \cdot 3$.
   d. If we rewrite $\dfrac{3}{2x}$ as an equivalent rational expression with a denominator of $10x^3$, the numerator and denominator should be multiplied by $5x^2$.

93. Which one of the following is true?
   a. If the numerator and denominator of a rational expression have the same polynomial added to them, the original rational expression is unchanged.
   b. $\dfrac{2y + 3}{y + 7} - \dfrac{y - 5}{y + 7} = \dfrac{2y + 3 - y - 5}{y + 7} = \dfrac{y - 2}{y + 7}$
   c. The least common multiple for $y^2 + 4$ and $y + 4$ is $y^2 + 4$.
   d. The LCD for $\dfrac{1}{y - 3}$ and $\dfrac{1}{y + 3}$ is $y^2 - 9$.

94. Which one of the following is true?
   a. Since $y^2 - 8y + 16 = (y - 4)(y - 4)$ and $y^2 - 6y + 8 = (y - 2)(y - 4)$, the LCM of $y^2 - 8y + 16$ and $y^2 - 6y + 8$ is $(y - 4)(y - 2)$.
   b. Since the LCM of x and 3 is $3x$, then
$$\dfrac{1}{x} + \dfrac{1}{3} = 3x\left(\dfrac{1}{x} + \dfrac{1}{3}\right) = x + 3$$
   c. $\dfrac{2}{y} + 1 = \dfrac{2 + y}{y}$, if $y \neq 0$
   d. $\dfrac{5}{y} + 1 = \dfrac{6}{y}$, if $y \neq 0$

Technology Problems _____

In Problems 95–96, use a graphing utility to determine if the addition has been performed correctly by graphing the expressions on both sides on the same screen. If the answer is wrong, correct it and then verify your correction using the graphing utility.

95. $\dfrac{x}{5} + \dfrac{1}{3} = \dfrac{3x+1}{15}$

96. $\dfrac{2x}{x^2-9} + \dfrac{1}{3-x} = -\dfrac{1}{x+3}$

Writing in Mathematics _____

97. Why do you think most students find adding rational expressions more difficult than multiplying them? Describe the different procedures needed to solve the following problems:

  a. $\dfrac{1}{x} \cdot 5$ **b.** $\dfrac{1}{x} + 5$

98. When is the least common multiple of two polynomials equal to their product?

99. Explain how to express $\dfrac{y}{y-3}$ as an equivalent rational expression having $y^2 - 4y + 3$ as the denominator.

Critical Thinking Problems _____

100. Perform the indicated operations: $\dfrac{y^2+5y+4}{y^2+2y-3} \cdot \dfrac{y^2+y-6}{y^2+2y-3} - \dfrac{2}{y-1}$

In Problems 101–102, find the missing rational expression.

101. $\dfrac{2}{x-1} + \boxed{} = \dfrac{2x^2+3x-1}{x^2(x-1)}$

102. $\dfrac{4}{x-2} - \boxed{} = \dfrac{2x+8}{(x-2)(x+1)}$

103. A painter paints $\dfrac{1}{x}$ of a wall in the morning and $\dfrac{1}{(x+3)}$ of the wall in the afternoon.

Express the fractional part of the wall that is still left to paint as a rational expression in x.

Review Problems _____

104. Perform the indicated operation: $(3y+5)(2y-7)$.

105. Graph: $3x - y < 3$.

106. Write an equation in the form $y = mx + b$ for the line passing through $(-3, -4)$ and $(1, 0)$.

S E C T I O N 8 . 5

Solutions **Tutorial** **Video**
Manual   **9**

Complex Fractions

Objectives

1 Simplify a complex fraction by adding or subtracting.
2 Simplify a complex fraction by multiplying by 1.

A *complex fraction* is a rational expression whose numerator and/or denominator contains fractions. Examples of complex fractions include

$$\dfrac{\dfrac{1}{2} - \dfrac{1}{3}}{\dfrac{5}{8}}, \quad \dfrac{1 + \dfrac{1}{x}}{1 - \dfrac{1}{x}}, \text{ and } \dfrac{\dfrac{5}{4y} - \dfrac{3}{8}}{\dfrac{3}{2y} + \dfrac{3}{4y^2}}.$$

Alfredo Castañeda "Enajenado"
1967, oil on canvas 90 × 70.5 cm.
Mary-Anne Martin/Fine Art, New York
and Galeria GAM, Mexico City

Simplify a complex fraction
by adding or subtracting.

In this section, we study two methods for simplifying these fractions.

Simplifying a Complex Fraction by Adding or Subtracting (Method 1)

The first method for simplifying complex fractions uses the skills you already have for adding, subtracting, multiplying, and dividing algebraic fractions.

Method 1 for simplifying complex fractions

1. If necessary, add or subtract the fractions in the numerator.
2. If necessary, add or subtract the fractions in the denominator.
3. Divide by multiplying the numerator by the reciprocal of the denominator.

The following examples illustrate the use of this first method.

EXAMPLE 1 **Simplifying a Complex Fraction by Method 1**

Simplify the complex fraction: $\dfrac{\dfrac{1}{2} - \dfrac{1}{3}}{\dfrac{5}{8}}$

Solution

$\dfrac{\dfrac{1}{2} - \dfrac{1}{3}}{\dfrac{5}{8}} = \dfrac{\dfrac{3}{6} - \dfrac{2}{6}}{\dfrac{5}{8}}$ Perform the subtraction in the numerator of the complex fraction. The LCD is 6.

$= \dfrac{\dfrac{1}{6}}{\dfrac{5}{8}}$ Simplify the numerator.

$= \dfrac{1}{6} \div \dfrac{5}{8}$ The main fraction bar is rewritten as ÷.

$= \dfrac{1}{6} \cdot \dfrac{8}{5}$ Multiply by the reciprocal of the divisor.

$= \dfrac{1}{\overset{}{6}} \cdot \dfrac{\overset{4}{8}}{5}$ Simplify.
$\phantom{= \dfrac{1}{6} \cdot } {}_{3}$

$= \dfrac{4}{15}$ Multiply the numerators and denominators.

iscover for yourself

Try working Example 2 on your own.

1. Write $1 + \dfrac{1}{x}$ as a single fraction.

2. Write $1 - \dfrac{1}{x}$ as a single fraction.

3. Divide the result of step 1 by the result of step 2. (Invert and multiply.)

4. Simplify.

Now read the solution on the right and compare it with your solution.

EXAMPLE 2 **Simplifying a Complex Fraction by Method 1**

Simplify the complex fraction: $\dfrac{1 + \dfrac{1}{x}}{1 - \dfrac{1}{x}}$

Solution

$$\frac{1 + \dfrac{1}{x}}{1 - \dfrac{1}{x}} = \frac{\dfrac{x}{x} + \dfrac{1}{x}}{\dfrac{x}{x} - \dfrac{1}{x}}$$

The numerator and denominator are simplified by performing the addition and subtraction. The LCD is x.

$$= \frac{\dfrac{x + 1}{x}}{\dfrac{x - 1}{x}}$$

Perform the addition in the numerator and the subtraction in the denominator.

$$= \frac{x + 1}{x} \div \frac{x - 1}{x}$$

Rewrite the main fraction bar as $\div$.

$$= \frac{x + 1}{x} \cdot \frac{x}{x - 1}$$

Multiply by the reciprocal of the divisor.

$$= \frac{(x + 1)\overset{1}{x}}{\underset{1}{x}(x - 1)}$$

Multiply the numerators. Multiply the denominators. Cancel identical factors.

$$= \frac{x + 1}{x - 1}$$

Multiply the remaining factors in the numerator and denominator.

iscover for yourself

Verify the simplification in Example 2 by graphing

$$y_1 = \frac{1 + \dfrac{1}{x}}{1 - \dfrac{1}{x}} \quad \text{and} \quad y_2 = \frac{x + 1}{x - 1}$$

on the same screen. The graphs should look the same.

iscover for yourself

As you did with Examples 1 and 2, try working Example 3 on your own before studying the solution on the next page.

1. Write $\dfrac{5}{4y} - \dfrac{3}{8}$ as a single fraction.

2. Write $\dfrac{3}{2y} + \dfrac{3}{4y^2}$ as a single fraction.

3. Divide the result of step 1 by the result of step 2.

EXAMPLE 3 **Simplifying a Complex Fraction by Method 1**

Simplify the complex fraction: $\dfrac{\dfrac{5}{4y} - \dfrac{3}{8}}{\dfrac{3}{2y} + \dfrac{3}{4y^2}}$

Solution

$$\frac{\dfrac{5}{4y} - \dfrac{3}{8}}{\dfrac{3}{2y} + \dfrac{3}{4y^2}} = \frac{\dfrac{5}{4y} \cdot \dfrac{2}{2} - \dfrac{3}{8} \cdot \dfrac{y}{y}}{\dfrac{3}{2y} \cdot \dfrac{2y}{2y} + \dfrac{3}{4y^2}}$$
$\Bigg\} \;\leftarrow\;$ Rewrite fractions in terms of the LCD, $8y$.

$\Bigg\} \;\leftarrow\;$ Rewrite the first fraction in terms of the LCD, $4y^2$.

$$= \frac{\dfrac{10}{8y} - \dfrac{3y}{8y}}{\dfrac{6y}{4y^2} + \dfrac{3}{4y^2}}$$
Perform the indicated multiplications.

$$= \frac{\dfrac{10 - 3y}{8y}}{\dfrac{6y + 3}{4y^2}}$$
$\Bigg\} \;\leftarrow\;$ Subtract in the numerator.

$\Bigg\} \;\leftarrow\;$ Add in the denominator.

$$= \frac{10 - 3y}{8y} \div \frac{6y + 3}{4y^2}$$
Rewrite the main fraction bar as $\div$.

$$= \frac{10 - 3y}{8y} \cdot \frac{4y^2}{6y + 3}$$
Multiply by the reciprocal of the divisor.

$$= \frac{(10 - 3y) \cdot \cancel{4}y\cdot y}{2 \cdot \cancel{4}y \cdot 3(2y + 1)}$$
Multiply the numerator and denominators.
Simplify.

$$= \frac{y(10 - 3y)}{6(2y + 1)} \quad \text{or} \quad \frac{10y - 3y^2}{12y + 6}$$
∎

2 Simplify a complex fraction by multiplying by 1.

Simplifying a Complex Fraction by Multiplying by 1 (Method 2)

We now turn to a second method for simplifying complex fractions. This method uses 1, the identity of multiplication. We will multiply the numerator and denominator of the complex fraction by the LCD of all expressions within the fraction. Since we are multiplying by a form of 1, we will obtain an equivalent complex fraction that does not contain fractions in its numerator or denominator.

Method 2 for simplifying complex fractions

1. Find the LCD of all expressions within the complex fraction.
2. Multiply the numerator and denominator of the complex fraction by this LCD.
3. If possible, simplify the resulting expression.

Method 2 is illustrated in the following examples. Since Examples 4 through 6 are the same as Examples 1 through 3, compare the methods of solution to see if there is one method that you prefer.

EXAMPLE 4 **Simplifying a Complex Fraction by Method 2**

Simplify the complex fraction: $\dfrac{\frac{1}{2} - \frac{1}{3}}{\frac{5}{8}}$

Solution

(Compare this solution with Example 1.)

$$\frac{\frac{1}{2} - \frac{1}{3}}{\frac{5}{8}} = \frac{\left(\frac{1}{2} - \frac{1}{3}\right)}{\frac{5}{8}} \cdot \frac{24}{24}$$

The LCD of 2, 3, and 8 is 24. Multiply the numerator and denominator by 24, the LCD of the denominators. Since $\frac{24}{24} = 1$, we are not changing the complex fraction.

$$= \frac{\frac{1}{2} \cdot 24 - \frac{1}{3} \cdot 24}{\frac{5}{8} \cdot 24}$$

Use the distributive property. Be sure to distribute 24 to every term.

$$= \frac{12 - 8}{15}$$

Multiply. The complex fraction is now simplified.

$$= \frac{4}{15}$$

■

EXAMPLE 5 **Simplifying a Complex Fraction by Method 2**

Simplify the complex fraction: $\dfrac{1 + \frac{1}{x}}{1 - \frac{1}{x}}$

Solution

(Compare this solution with Example 2.)

$$\frac{1 + \frac{1}{x}}{1 - \frac{1}{x}} = \frac{\left(1 + \frac{1}{x}\right)}{\left(1 - \frac{1}{x}\right)} \cdot \frac{x}{x}$$

The LCD of the denominators is x. Multiply the numerator and denominator by x. Since $\frac{x}{x} = 1$, we are not changing the complex fraction.

$$= \frac{1 \cdot x + \frac{1}{x} \cdot x}{1 \cdot x - \frac{1}{x} \cdot x}$$

Use the distributive property. Be sure to distribute x to every term.

$$= \frac{x + 1}{x - 1}$$

Multiply. The complex fraction is now simplified.

■

EXAMPLE 6 **Simplifying a Complex Fraction by Method 2**

Simplify the complex fraction: $\dfrac{\frac{5}{4y} - \frac{3}{8}}{\frac{3}{2y} + \frac{3}{4y^2}}$

Solution

(Compare this solution with Example 3.) The denominators within the complex fraction are $4y, 8, 2y,$ and $4y^2$. Their LCD is $8y^2$, so we multiply by $\dfrac{8y^2}{8y^2}$.

$$\frac{\dfrac{5}{4y} - \dfrac{3}{8}}{\dfrac{3}{2y} + \dfrac{3}{4y^2}} = \frac{\left(\dfrac{5}{4y} - \dfrac{3}{8}\right)}{\left(\dfrac{3}{2y} + \dfrac{3}{4y^2}\right)} \cdot \frac{8y^2}{8y^2}$$

Multiply the numerator and denominator by $8y^2$, the LCD of the denominators.

$$= \frac{\dfrac{5}{4y} \cdot \dfrac{8y^2}{1} - \dfrac{3}{8} \cdot \dfrac{8y^2}{1}}{\dfrac{3}{2y} \cdot \dfrac{8y^2}{1} + \dfrac{3}{4y^2} \cdot \dfrac{8y^2}{1}}$$

Be sure to distribute $8y^2$ to every term in the numerator and denominator.

$$= \frac{\dfrac{5}{4\cancel{y}} \cdot \dfrac{4 \cdot 2\cancel{y}y}{1} - \dfrac{3}{8} \cdot \dfrac{8y^2}{1}}{\dfrac{3}{2\cancel{y}} \cdot \dfrac{2 \cdot 4\cancel{y}y}{1} + \dfrac{3}{4y^2} \cdot \dfrac{4 \cdot 2y^2}{1}}$$

Cancel identical factors in the numerator and denominator of each term.

$$= \frac{10y - 3y^2}{12y + 6}$$

Multiply the remaining factors in the numerator and denominator of each term.

PROBLEM SET 8.5

Practice Problems

Simplify each of the complex fractions in Problems 1–34 by either method discussed in this section. If applicable, use a graphing utility to verify your simplifications.

1. $\dfrac{\dfrac{1}{2} + \dfrac{1}{4}}{\dfrac{1}{2} + \dfrac{1}{3}}$

2. $\dfrac{\dfrac{1}{3} + \dfrac{1}{4}}{\dfrac{1}{3} + \dfrac{1}{6}}$

3. $\dfrac{3 + \dfrac{1}{2}}{4 - \dfrac{1}{4}}$

4. $\dfrac{1 + \dfrac{3}{5}}{2 - \dfrac{1}{4}}$

5. $\dfrac{\dfrac{2}{5} - \dfrac{1}{3}}{\dfrac{2}{3} - \dfrac{3}{4}}$

6. $\dfrac{\dfrac{3}{5} - \dfrac{2}{3}}{\dfrac{2}{3} - \dfrac{5}{6}}$

7. $\dfrac{\dfrac{3}{4} - x}{\dfrac{3}{4} + x}$

8. $\dfrac{\dfrac{2}{3} - x}{\dfrac{2}{3} + x}$

9. $\dfrac{5 - \dfrac{2}{x}}{3 + \dfrac{1}{x}}$

10. $\dfrac{4 + \dfrac{2}{y}}{1 - \dfrac{3}{y}}$

11. $\dfrac{2 + \dfrac{3}{y}}{1 - \dfrac{7}{y}}$

12. $\dfrac{4 - \dfrac{7}{y}}{3 - \dfrac{2}{y}}$

13. $\dfrac{\dfrac{1}{y} - \dfrac{3}{2}}{\dfrac{1}{y} + \dfrac{3}{4}}$

14. $\dfrac{\dfrac{1}{y} - \dfrac{3}{4}}{\dfrac{1}{y} + \dfrac{2}{3}}$

15. $\dfrac{\dfrac{x}{5} - \dfrac{5}{x}}{\dfrac{1}{5} + \dfrac{1}{x}}$

16. $\dfrac{\dfrac{3}{x} + \dfrac{x}{3}}{\dfrac{x}{3} - \dfrac{3}{x}}$

17. $\dfrac{1 + \dfrac{1}{x}}{1 - \dfrac{1}{x^2}}$

18. $\dfrac{\dfrac{1}{x^2} - 1}{\dfrac{1}{x} + 1}$

19. $\dfrac{\dfrac{1}{7} - \dfrac{1}{y}}{\dfrac{7 - y}{7}}$

20. $\dfrac{\dfrac{1}{9} - \dfrac{1}{y}}{\dfrac{9 - y}{9}}$

21. $\dfrac{\dfrac{12}{y^2} - \dfrac{3}{y}}{\dfrac{15}{y} - \dfrac{9}{y^2}}$

22. $\dfrac{\dfrac{2}{r} + \dfrac{5}{3}}{\dfrac{3}{r} - \dfrac{3}{r^2}}$

23. $\dfrac{\dfrac{1}{w} + \dfrac{2}{w^2}}{\dfrac{2}{w} + 1}$

24. $\dfrac{\dfrac{2}{w} - \dfrac{3}{w^2}}{2 - \dfrac{3}{w}}$

25. $\dfrac{\dfrac{9}{5} + \dfrac{4}{5s}}{\dfrac{4}{s^2} + \dfrac{9}{5}}$

26. $\dfrac{\frac{2}{s^2}-\frac{5}{s}}{\frac{2}{3s}-\frac{5}{3}}$

27. $\dfrac{\frac{7}{x^3}+\frac{11}{x^2}}{\frac{7}{x^4}+\frac{11}{x^3}}$

28. $\dfrac{\frac{7}{x^2}-\frac{2}{x}}{\frac{7}{x^3}-\frac{2}{x^2}}$

29. $\dfrac{\frac{7}{6x^3}-\frac{5}{12x}}{\frac{7}{2x}+\frac{3}{2x^3}}$

30. $\dfrac{\frac{3}{5b^4}-\frac{1}{10b}}{\frac{7}{3b^2}+\frac{9}{15b}}$

31. $\dfrac{x-5+\frac{3}{x}}{x-7+\frac{2}{x}}$

32. $\dfrac{x+9-\frac{7}{x}}{x-6+\frac{4}{x}}$

33. $\dfrac{\frac{1}{y+2}}{1+\frac{1}{y+2}}$

34. $\dfrac{\frac{1}{y-2}}{1-\frac{1}{y-2}}$

35. Simplify

$$\frac{\frac{1}{x}+\frac{1}{x^2}+\frac{1}{x^3}}{\frac{1}{x^4}+\frac{1}{x^5}+\frac{1}{x^6}}.$$

Then evaluate the given expression and the simplified expression for $x = 1, 2, 3, 4$, and 5.

The complex fractions in Problems 36–53 involve several variables. Simplify each fraction by either method discussed in this section.

36. $\dfrac{\frac{2}{a}+\frac{7}{b}}{12}$

37. $\dfrac{\frac{4}{a}-\frac{8}{b}}{2}$

38. $\dfrac{a+\frac{1}{b}}{\frac{a}{b}}$

39. $\dfrac{a-\frac{a}{b}}{\frac{1+a}{b}}$

40. $\dfrac{\frac{a}{b}-\frac{b}{a}}{\frac{a+b}{a}}$

41. $\dfrac{1}{\frac{1}{a}+b}$

42. $\dfrac{\frac{x^2}{y}-y}{\frac{y^2}{x}-x}$

43. $\dfrac{\frac{1}{x}+\frac{1}{y}}{\frac{1}{xy}}$

44. $\dfrac{\frac{1}{x}+\frac{1}{y}}{\frac{1}{x}}$

45. $\dfrac{\frac{x}{y}+\frac{1}{x}}{\frac{y}{x}+\frac{1}{x}}$

46. $\dfrac{\frac{x}{9y^3}+\frac{4}{9y^2}}{\frac{5}{9y}-\frac{1}{6y^3}}$

47. $\dfrac{\frac{a}{10b^3}-\frac{3}{5b}}{\frac{a}{10b}+\frac{3}{b^4}}$

48. $\dfrac{\frac{3}{ab^2}+\frac{2}{a^2b}}{\frac{1}{a^2b}+\frac{2}{ab^3}}$

49. $\dfrac{\frac{2}{x^3y}+\frac{5}{xy^4}}{\frac{5}{x^3y}-\frac{3}{xy}}$

50. $\dfrac{5+\frac{3}{a^2b}}{\frac{a+3}{a^3b}}$

51. $\dfrac{7-\frac{2}{xy^3}}{\frac{x+2}{x^2y}}$

52. $\dfrac{1+\frac{x}{y-x}}{\frac{x}{x+y}-1}$

53. $\dfrac{\frac{3}{x+y}-\frac{3}{x-y}}{\frac{5}{x^2-y^2}}$

Application Problems

54. If two electrical resistors with resistances R_1 and R_2 are connected in parallel (see the figure), then the total resistance in the circuit is given by the complex fraction

$$\frac{1}{\frac{1}{R_1}+\frac{1}{R_2}}.$$

Simplify this complex fraction. Then find the total resistance if $R_1 = 10$ ohms and $R_2 = 20$ ohms.

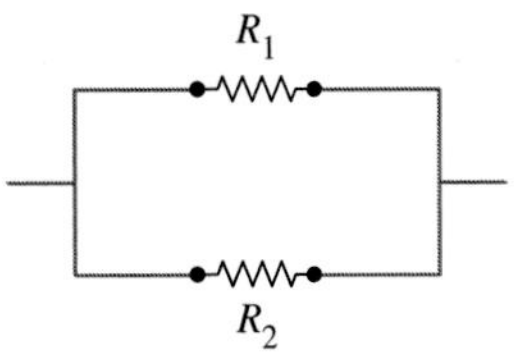

55. The average speed on a round-trip having a one-way distance d is

$$\frac{2d}{\dfrac{d}{r_1} + \dfrac{d}{r_2}}$$

where r_1 and r_2 are the rates on the outgoing and return trips, respectively. Simplify the complex fraction. Then find the average speed for a person who drives from home to work at 30 miles per hour and returns on the same route averaging 20 miles per hour. (Explain why the answer is not 25 miles per hour.)

True–False Critical Thinking Problems

56. Which one of the following is true?
  a. To simplify the complex fraction

$$\frac{\dfrac{1}{2} + \dfrac{x}{3}}{\dfrac{x}{4}}$$

  multiply the numerator and denominator by $12 + x$.

  b. Some complex fractions cannot be simplified by both methods discussed in this section.

  c. $1 + \dfrac{1}{1 + \frac{1}{2}} = \dfrac{5}{3}$

  d. $\dfrac{\dfrac{1}{x} + \dfrac{1}{4}}{\dfrac{1}{x} - \dfrac{1}{4}} = \dfrac{x - 4}{x + 4}$

57. Which one of the following is true?
  a. The fraction $\dfrac{31{,}729{,}546}{72{,}578{,}112}$ is a complex fraction.

  b. $\dfrac{y - \frac{1}{2}}{y + \frac{3}{4}} = \dfrac{4y - 2}{4y + 3}$ for any value of y except $-\dfrac{3}{4}$.

  c. $\dfrac{\frac{1}{4} - \frac{1}{3}}{\frac{1}{3} + \frac{1}{6}} = \dfrac{1}{12} \div \dfrac{3}{6} = \dfrac{1}{6}$

  d. To simplify the complex fraction

$$\frac{1 + \dfrac{2}{x}}{\dfrac{2}{x} + 5}$$

  we should multiply the numerator and denominator by $10 + x$.

Technology Problems

In Problems 58–59, use a graphing utility to determine if the simplification is correct by graphing the expressions on both sides on the same screen. If the answer is wrong, correct it and then verify your corrected simplification using the graphing utility.

58. $\dfrac{\dfrac{9x}{20} - \dfrac{5}{4x}}{\dfrac{3}{10} - \dfrac{1}{2x}} = \dfrac{3x - 5}{2}$

59. $\dfrac{1 + \dfrac{1}{x}}{1 - \dfrac{1}{x}} = \dfrac{x + 1}{x - 1}$

Writing in Mathematics

60. Which method do you prefer for simplifying complex fractions? Why?

Critical Thinking Problems

61. Simplify each complex fraction. Then perform the subtraction.

$$\frac{1 + \dfrac{1}{y} - \dfrac{6}{y^2}}{1 - \dfrac{5}{y} + \dfrac{6}{y^2}} - \frac{1 - \dfrac{1}{y}}{1 - \dfrac{2}{y} - \dfrac{3}{y^2}}$$

62. Simplify the following expressions:

$$1 + \frac{1}{1 + 1} \qquad 1 + \frac{1}{1 + \dfrac{1}{1 + 1}} \qquad 1 + \frac{1}{1 + \dfrac{1}{1 + \dfrac{1}{1 + 1}}}$$

Using the pattern, write the next three fractions that occur in this series.

Review Problems_____

63. Subtract $3x^2 - 7x - 5$ from $x^2 - 4x + 9$.

64. An object thrown upward from the ground with an initial velocity of 32 feet per second has its height (h, in feet) above the ground after t seconds given by the mathematical model $h = -16t^2 + 32t$. After how many seconds will the object reach a height of 16 feet?

65. For $f(x) = 4x - 3$, find $f(-2) + 3f(4)$.

SECTION 8.6

Solutions Manual **Tutorial** **Video 10**

Solving Rational Equations

Objectives

1 Solve rational equations.
2 Solve problems using rational models.

1 Solve rational equations.

Now that we have learned how to add, subtract, multiply, and divide rational expressions, we are ready to solve rational equations. A *rational*, or *fractional*, *equation* is an equation containing one or more rational expressions. Here are some examples.

$$\frac{x}{4} = \frac{1}{4} + \frac{x}{6}, \quad \frac{5}{2x} - \frac{17}{18} = -\frac{1}{3x}, \quad \frac{3}{2y - 2} + \frac{1}{2} = \frac{2}{y - 1}$$

In Chapter 2, we worked with equations like the first one in this list in which denominators in all terms consisted of constants. Our first example reviews the solution procedure.

Using technology

We can use a graphing utility to verify the solution to Example 1. Graph each side of the equation, namely,

$$y_1 = \frac{x}{4}$$

$$y_2 = \frac{1}{4} + \frac{x}{6}$$

Trace along the lines or use the utility's intersection feature. The solution, as shown below, is the first coordinate of the point of intersection. Thus, the solution is **3**.

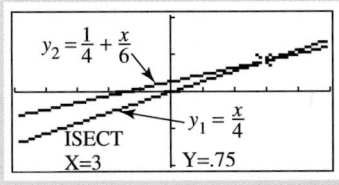

EXAMPLE 1 **Solving a Rational Equation**

Solve: $\dfrac{x}{4} = \dfrac{1}{4} + \dfrac{x}{6}$

Solution

The LCD of 4, 4, and 6 is 12. To clear the equation of fractions, we multiply both sides by 12.

$$\frac{x}{4} = \frac{1}{4} + \frac{x}{6}$$
This is the given equation.

$$12\left(\frac{x}{4}\right) = 12\left(\frac{1}{4} + \frac{x}{6}\right)$$
Multiply both sides by 12, the LCD of all the fractions in the equation.

$$12 \cdot \frac{x}{4} = 12 \cdot \frac{1}{4} + 12 \cdot \frac{x}{6}$$
Apply the distributive property.

$$3x = 3 + 2x$$
Simplify: $\dfrac{\overset{3}{\cancel{12}}}{1} \cdot \dfrac{x}{4} = 3x; \overset{3}{\cancel{12}} \cdot \dfrac{1}{4} = 3; \overset{2}{\cancel{12}} \cdot \dfrac{x}{6} = 2x.$

$$x = 3$$
Subtract $2x$ from both sides.

Check

$$\frac{x}{4} = \frac{1}{4} + \frac{x}{6}$$ This is the original equation.

$$\frac{3}{4} \overset{?}{=} \frac{1}{4} + \frac{3}{6}$$ Substitute 3, the proposed solution, for x.

$$\frac{3}{4} \overset{?}{=} \frac{1}{4} + \frac{1}{2}$$

$$\frac{3}{4} \overset{?}{=} \frac{1}{4} + \frac{2}{4}$$

$$\frac{3}{4} = \frac{3}{4} \quad \checkmark$$

This verifies that the solution is 3.   ∎

Solving rational equations

1. Clear the equation of fractions by multiplying both sides by the LCD of all rational expressions in the equation.
2. Solve the resulting equation.
3. Check all proposed solutions in the original equation.

EXAMPLE 2   **Solving a Rational Equation**

Solve: $\dfrac{5}{2x} - \dfrac{17}{18} = -\dfrac{1}{3x}$

Solution

The LCD of $2x$, 18, and $3x$ is $18x$. Since the multiplication property of equality does not allow multiplying both sides of an equation by 0, we will multiply both sides by $18x$ with the restriction that $x \neq 0$.

$$\frac{5}{2x} - \frac{17}{18} = -\frac{1}{3x}$$ This is the given equation.

$$18x\left(\frac{5}{2x} - \frac{17}{18}\right) = 18x\left(-\frac{1}{3x}\right)$$ Multiply both sides by $18x$, the LCD of the fractions.

$$18x \cdot \frac{5}{2x} - 18x \cdot \frac{17}{18} = 18x\left(-\frac{1}{3x}\right)$$ Multiply to remove parentheses on the left.

$$\frac{2 \cdot 9x}{1} \cdot \frac{5}{2x} - \frac{18x}{1} \cdot \frac{17}{18} = 3 \cdot 6x\left(-\frac{1}{3x}\right)$$ Simplify. This step will probably be worked mentally.

$$45 - 17x = -6$$ Multiply the remaining factors in the numerators and denominators.

$$-17x = -51$$ Subtract 45 from both sides.

$$x = 3$$ Divide both sides by -17.

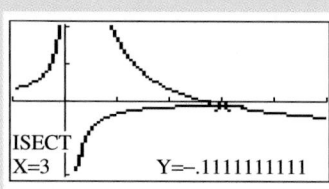

Check

$$\frac{5}{2x} - \frac{17}{18} = -\frac{1}{3x}$$ This is the original equation.

$$\frac{5}{2 \cdot 3} - \frac{17}{18} \overset{?}{=} -\frac{1}{3 \cdot 3}$$ Substitute 3, the proposed solution, for x.

$$\frac{5}{6} - \frac{17}{18} \overset{?}{=} -\frac{1}{9}$$

$$\frac{15}{18} - \frac{17}{18} \overset{?}{=} -\frac{1}{9}$$

$$-\frac{2}{18} \overset{?}{=} -\frac{1}{9}$$

$$-\frac{1}{9} = -\frac{1}{9} \quad \checkmark$$

The solution is 3. ∎

EXAMPLE 3   **Solving a Rational Equation**

Solve: $\dfrac{3}{2y - 2} + \dfrac{1}{2} = \dfrac{2}{y - 1}$

Solution

By factoring $2y - 2$ as $2(y - 1)$, the LCD of the rational expressions is $2(y - 1)$. We multiply both sides of the equation by $2(y - 1)$ with the restriction that $y \neq 1$.

$$\frac{3}{2(y - 1)} + \frac{1}{2} = \frac{2}{y - 1}$$ This is the given equation with the first denominator factored.

$$2(y - 1) \left[\frac{3}{2(y - 1)} + \frac{1}{2} \right] = 2(y - 1) \cdot \frac{2}{y - 1}$$ Multiply both sides by $2(y - 1)$, the LCD, where $y \neq 1$.

$$2(y - 1) \cdot \frac{3}{2(y - 1)} + 2(y - 1) \cdot \frac{1}{2} = 2(y - 1) \cdot \frac{2}{y - 1}$$ Multiply to remove brackets on the left.

$$\overset{1}{\cancel{2(y - 1)}} \cdot \frac{3}{\underset{1}{\cancel{2(y - 1)}}} + \overset{1}{2}(y - 1) \cdot \frac{1}{\underset{1}{2}} = 2\overset{1}{\cancel{(y - 1)}} \frac{2}{\underset{1}{\cancel{y - 1}}}$$ Simplify.

$$3 + (y - 1) = 4$$ Multiply the remaining factors in the numerators and denominators.

$$y + 2 = 4$$ Combine like terms.

$$y = 2$$ Subtract 2 from both sides.

Verify that 2 is the solution by substituting this value into the original equation and obtaining a true statement. The solution 2 does not interfere with the restriction that $y \neq 1$. ■

When solving an equation containing variables in a denominator, any value of a variable that makes any denominator equal zero is not a solution to the equation. This idea is illustrated in Example 4.

EXAMPLE 4   **A Rational Equation with No Solution**

Solve: $\dfrac{3}{y+2} + \dfrac{2}{y-2} = \dfrac{8}{y^2-4}$

Solution

Since $y^2 - 4 = (y+2)(y-2)$, the LCD of the rational expressions is $(y+2)(y-2)$. We will multiply both sides of the equation by $(y+2)(y-2)$. Since multiplication of both sides by 0 is not permitted, the restriction is that $y \neq -2$ and $y \neq 2$.

$$\frac{3}{y+2} + \frac{2}{y-2} = \frac{8}{(y+2)(y-2)}$$

This is the given equation with the last denominator factored.

$$(y+2)(y-2)\left[\frac{3}{y+2} + \frac{2}{y-2}\right] = (y+2)(y-2)\cdot\frac{8}{(y+2)(y-2)}$$

Multiply both sides by $(y+2)(y-2)$.

$$(y+2)(y-2)\cdot\frac{3}{y+2} + (y+2)(y-2)\cdot\frac{2}{y-2} = (y+2)(y-2)\cdot\frac{8}{(y+2)(y-2)}$$

Multiply to remove brackets on the left and simplify.

$$3(y-2) + 2(y+2) = 8$$

Multiply the remaining factors in the numerators and denominators.

$$3y - 6 + 2y + 4 = 8$$ Multiply to remove parentheses.
$$5y - 2 = 8$$ Combine like terms.
$$5y = 10$$ Add 2 to both sides.
$$y = 2$$ Divide both sides by 5.

The proposed solution, 2, is *not* a solution because of the restriction $y \neq 2$. If we substitute 2 for y in the original equation, we obtain undefined terms.

$$\frac{3}{y+2} + \frac{2}{y-2} = \frac{8}{y^2-4}$$ This is the original equation.
$$\frac{3}{2+2} + \frac{2}{2-2} \overset{?}{=} \frac{8}{2^2-4}$$ Substitute 2 for y.
$$\frac{3}{4} + \frac{2}{0} \overset{?}{=} \frac{8}{0}$$

The terms $\frac{2}{0}$ and $\frac{8}{0}$ are undefined. Thus, there is *no solution* to this equation. ■

Using technology

Verify that the equation in Example 4 has no solution. Use your graphing utility to graph

$$y_1 = \frac{3}{x+2} + \frac{2}{x-2}$$

and

$$y_2 = \frac{8}{x^2-4}.$$

By zooming in on various parts of the curves, you will see that they do not intersect.

tudy tip

Reject any proposed solution that causes any denominator in a rational equation to equal 0.

EXAMPLE 5   **A Rational Equation with Two Solutions**

Solve: $x + \dfrac{1}{x} = \dfrac{5}{2}$

Solution

$$x + \dfrac{1}{x} = \dfrac{5}{2}$$ This is the given equation.

$$2x \left(x + \dfrac{1}{x} \right) = 2x \left(\dfrac{5}{2} \right)$$ Multiply both sides by the LCD, $2x$, where $x \neq 0$.

$$2x \cdot x + 2x \cdot \dfrac{1}{x} = 2x \cdot \dfrac{5}{2}$$ Multiply to remove parentheses.

$$2x^2 + 2 = 5x$$ Simplify. Since this equation is quadratic, set the right side to 0.

$$2x^2 - 5x + 2 = 0$$ Subtract $5x$ from both sides.

$$(2x - 1)(x - 2) = 0$$ Factor on the left.

$$2x - 1 = 0 \quad \text{or} \quad x - 2 = 0$$ Set each factor equal to 0, using the zero-product principle.

$$2x = 1 \qquad\qquad x = 2$$ Solve the two resulting equations.

$$x = \dfrac{1}{2}$$

The proposed solutions, $\frac{1}{2}$ and 2, are not part of the restriction that $x \neq 0$. Neither makes a denominator in the original equation equal to zero. Thus, the solutions are $\frac{1}{2}$ and 2. ∎

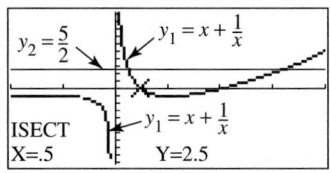

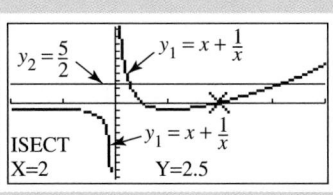

sing technology

The graphs of

$$y_1 = x + \dfrac{1}{x}$$

and

$$y_2 = \dfrac{5}{2}$$

have two intersection points. The first coordinates of these points are $\frac{1}{2}$ and 2, verifying that the solutions of

$$x + \dfrac{1}{x} = \dfrac{5}{2}$$

are $\frac{1}{2}$ and 2.

tudy tip

It is important to distinguish between adding and subtracting rational expressions and solving rational equations. We *simplify* sums and differences of terms. On the other hand, we *solve* equations. This is shown in the following two problems, both with an LCD of $3x$.

Adding Rational Expressions
Simplify:

$$\dfrac{5}{3x} + \dfrac{3}{x}$$

$$= \dfrac{5}{3x} + \dfrac{3}{x} \cdot \dfrac{3}{3}$$

$$= \dfrac{5}{3x} + \dfrac{9}{3x}$$

$$= \dfrac{5 + 9}{3x} = \dfrac{14}{3x}$$

Solving Rational Equations
Solve:

$$\dfrac{5}{3x} + \dfrac{3}{x} = 1$$

$$3x \left(\dfrac{5}{3x} + \dfrac{3}{x} \right) = 3x \cdot 1$$

$$3x \cdot \dfrac{5}{3x} + 3x \cdot \dfrac{3}{x} = 3x$$

$$5 + 9 = 3x$$

$$14 = 3x$$

$$\dfrac{14}{3} = x$$

2 Solve problems using rational models.

Katherina Fritsch "Rat-King" (Rattenkonig) 1993, polyester resin, height: 2.8 m; diameter: 13 m. Courtesy Dia Center for the Arts, NY. Photo Credit: Bill Jacobsen. ©1998 Artist Rights Society (ARS), New York/VG Bild-Kunst, Bonn.

Rational Models

A rational model is a mathematical model containing one or more rational expressions. Techniques for solving rational equations can be used to answer questions about variables contained in rational models.

EXAMPLE 6   Using a Rational Model

A particular rat given n trials in a maze can run through the maze in t minutes, where

$$t = 6 + \frac{20}{n + 2}.$$

How many trials are needed so that the rat can run through the maze in exactly 8 minutes?

Solution

We let $t = 8$, obtaining

$$6 + \frac{20}{n + 2} = 8.$$

We now solve for n.

$$(n + 2)\left(6 + \frac{20}{n + 2}\right) = 8(n + 2) \qquad \text{Multiply by the LCM of the denominators.} \quad n \neq -2$$

$$6(n + 2) + 20 = 8(n + 2) \qquad \text{Apply the distributive property and simplify.}$$

$$6n + 12 + 20 = 8n + 16 \qquad \text{Solve the resulting equation.}$$

$$6n + 32 = 8n + 16$$

$$-2n = -16$$

$$n = 8$$

Eight previous trials are necessary so that the rat can run through the maze in 8 minutes. Verify this result by substituting 8 for n in the rational model. You should find that $t = 8$. ∎

In Example 6 we were given the model that described the rat's time through the maze. A more difficult situation is to use a problem's conditions to create a mathematical model.

In Examples 7–9, we use our five-step problem-solving strategy and methods for solving rational equations to solve each problem.

EXAMPLE 7   The Big Business of Sports

The average value of a professional team in the National Football League exceeds the average value of a team in the National Hockey League by $92 million. If the average value of a professional football team is divided by the average value of a professional hockey team, the partial quotient is 2 and the remainder is 31. Find the average value of a team in each of these leagues.

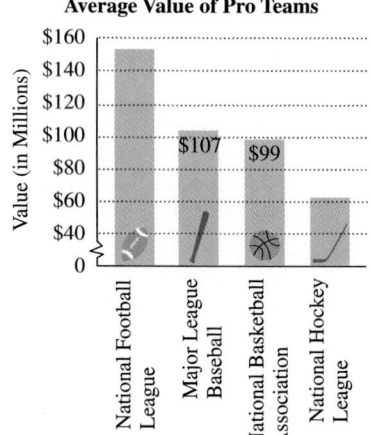

Average Value of Pro Teams

Source: Based on *Financial World* statistics

Steps 1 and 2. Represent unknown quantities in terms of x.

Solution

Let

$$x = \text{the average value of a hockey team (in millions of dollars)}$$
$$x + 92 = \text{the average value of a football team (in millions of dollars)}$$

Step 3. Write an equation that describes the problem's conditions.

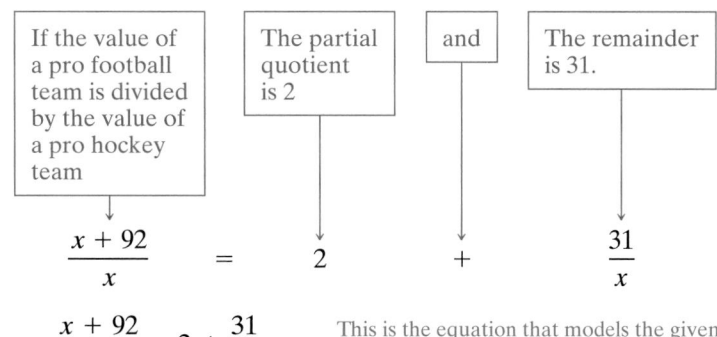

If the value of a pro football team is divided by the value of a pro hockey team	The partial quotient is 2	and	The remainder is 31.
$\dfrac{x + 92}{x}$	$= \quad 2$	$+$	$\dfrac{31}{x}$

Step 4. Solve the equation and answer the question.

$$\frac{x + 92}{x} = 2 + \frac{31}{x} \qquad \text{This is the equation that models the given conditions. Notice that the remainder is written over the divisor.}$$

$$x\left(\frac{x + 92}{x}\right) = x\left(2 + \frac{31}{x}\right) \qquad \text{Multiply both sides by } x, \text{ the LCD.}$$

$$x + 92 = 2x + 31 \qquad \text{Multiply on the left. Distribute on the right.}$$

$$61 = x \qquad \text{Solve the equation.}$$

Thus, the values are $x = 61$ and $x + 92 = 61 + 92 = 153$. The average value of a team in the National Hockey League is $61 million and the average value of a team in the National Football League is $153 million.

Step 5. Check.

When 153 is divided by 61, we do obtain a partial quotient of 2 and a remainder of 31.

```
          2    ← Partial quotient
   61)153
       122
        31    ← Remainder
```

■

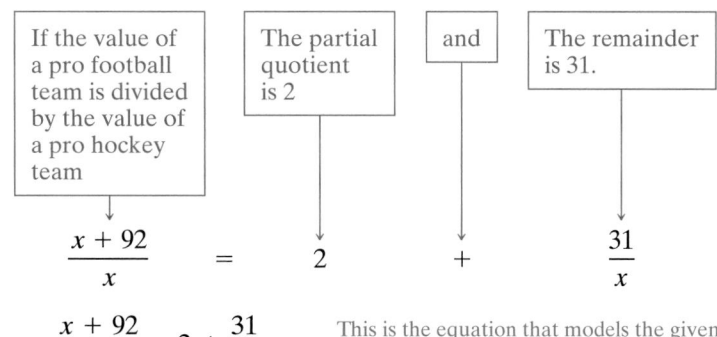

In Chapter 3, we considered a number of strategies for solving problems, including the use of tables to organize information. Uniform motion problems, in which an object is moving at a specified rate for a given period of time, are often solved by this strategy. Modeling these problems is based on the formula $RT = D$ (rate of travel multiplied by time traveled equals the distance traveled). Rational expressions appear in uniform motion problems when the conditions of the problem focus on the time traveled. By solving $RT = D$ for T, we obtain the following.

Max Ernst "Untitled" (formerly, l'avionne meutriere—The Murderous Airplane) 1920 ca. Collage: cut printed and photographic reproductions with pencil on photographic reproduction mounted on paperboard. $2\frac{5}{16} \times 5\frac{5}{8}$ in. (7.4 × 14.61 cm) Access: CA 5602. Photographer: Paul Hester, Houston. The Menil Collection, Houston. © 1998 Artists Rights Society (ARS), New York/ADAGP, Paris.

$$T = \frac{D}{R}$$

$$\text{Time traveled} = \frac{\text{Distance traveled}}{\text{Rate of travel}}$$

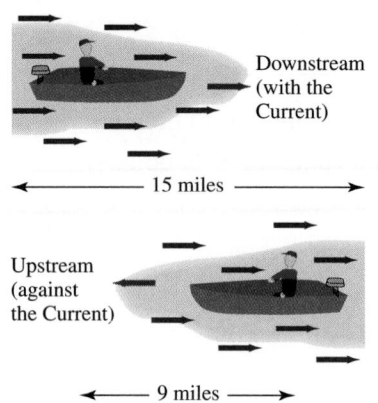

Downstream (with the Current)

←— 15 miles —→

Upstream (against the Current)

←— 9 miles —→

Steps 1 and 2. Represent unknown quantities in terms of x.

Step 3. Write an equation that describes the problem's conditions.

EXAMPLE 8   **Modeling Uniform Motion**

A boat that can travel 8 miles per hour in still water can travel 15 miles with the water's current in the same time that it can travel 9 miles against the water's current. What is the rate of the water's current?

Solution

Let

$$x = \text{Rate of the current}$$
$$8 + x = \text{Rate of the boat with the current}$$
$$8 - x = \text{Rate of the boat against the current}$$

By reading the problem again, we discover that the crucial idea is that the time spent going 15 miles with the current equals the time spent going 9 miles against the current. This information is summarized in the following table.

	D	R	$T = \dfrac{D}{R}$
With the Current	15	$8 + x$	$\dfrac{15}{8 + x}$
Against the Current	9	$8 - x$	$\dfrac{9}{8 - x}$

Times are equal.

We are now ready to write an equation that describes the problem's conditions.

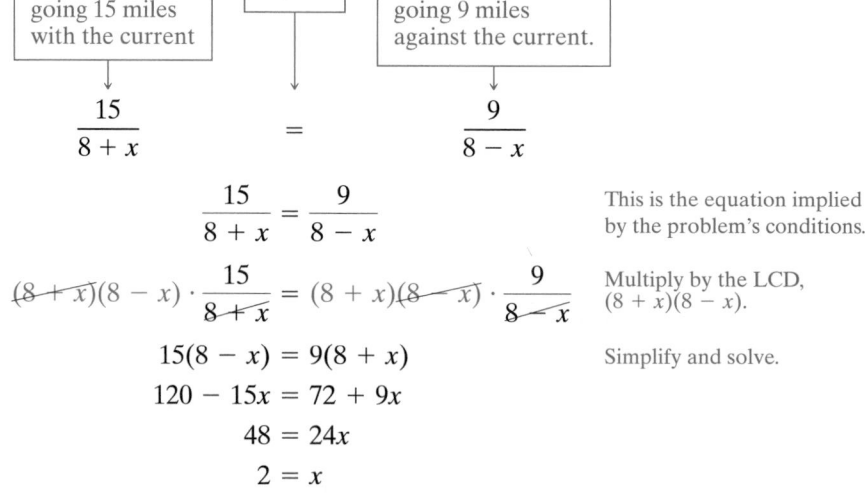

The time spent going 15 miles with the current	equals	The time spent going 9 miles against the current.
$\dfrac{15}{8 + x}$	$=$	$\dfrac{9}{8 - x}$

Step 4. Solve the equation and answer the question.

$$\frac{15}{8 + x} = \frac{9}{8 - x} \qquad \text{This is the equation implied by the problem's conditions.}$$

$$(8 + x)(8 - x) \cdot \frac{15}{8 + x} = (8 + x)(8 - x) \cdot \frac{9}{8 - x} \qquad \text{Multiply by the LCD, } (8 + x)(8 - x).$$

$$15(8 - x) = 9(8 + x) \qquad \text{Simplify and solve.}$$
$$120 - 15x = 72 + 9x$$
$$48 = 24x$$
$$2 = x$$

The current is moving at 2 miles per hour.

Step 5. Check.

Since the boat travels 8 miles per hour in still water, it travels 10 miles per hour with the current and 6 miles per hour against the current.

Time required to travel 15 miles with the current $= \frac{15}{10} = 1\frac{1}{2}$ hours.

Time required to travel 9 miles against the current $= \frac{9}{6} = 1\frac{1}{2}$ hours.

These times are the same, which checks with the original verbal conditions of the problem. ∎

Problems about work and work rates are similar to uniform motion problems. Problems involving work can be solved using our strategy for organizing information in tables.

Suppose that a person can do a job in 5 hours. In 1 hour, one-fifth of the job is completed. In 2 hours, two-fifths of the job is completed. In 3 hours, the fractional part of the job done is three-fifths. In t hours, the fractional part of the job completed is $t/5$.

Problems involving work usually have two people working together to complete a job. The amount of time it takes each person to do the job working alone is frequently known, and the question deals with how long it will take both people working together to do the job.

EXAMPLE 9 Modeling Work

A painter can paint a wall in 20 minutes. Working alone, the painter's apprentice can paint the same wall in 30 minutes. How long will it take them to paint the wall together?

Solution

Steps 1 and 2. Represent unknown quantities in terms of t.

Let t = the number of minutes to paint the wall together.

	Fractional Part of Job Completed in 1 Minute	Time Working Together	Fractional Part of Job Completed in t Minutes
Painter	$\dfrac{1}{20}$	t	$\dfrac{t}{20}$
Apprentice	$\dfrac{1}{30}$	t	$\dfrac{t}{30}$

Step 3. Write an equation that describes the problem's conditions.

Fractional part of the job done by the painter	plus	Fractional part of the job done by the apprentice	equals	One whole job.
$\dfrac{t}{20}$	$+$	$\dfrac{t}{30}$	$=$	1

Step 4. Solve the equation and answer the question.

$$\frac{t}{20} + \frac{t}{30} = 1 \qquad \text{This is the equation implied by the problem's conditions.}$$

$$60\left(\frac{t}{20} + \frac{t}{30}\right) = 60 \cdot 1 \qquad \text{Multiply by 60, the LCD.}$$

$$60 \cdot \frac{t}{20} + 60 \cdot \frac{t}{30} = 60 \qquad \text{Multiply to remove parentheses.}$$

$$3t + 2t = 60 \qquad \text{Simplify.}$$

$$5t = 60 \qquad \text{Combine like terms.}$$

$$t = 12 \qquad \text{Divide both sides by 5.}$$

Working together, they can paint the wall in 12 minutes.

Step 5. Check.

In 12 minutes, the painter can complete $\frac{12}{20}$ or $\frac{3}{5}$ of the job. In 12 minutes, the apprentice can complete $\frac{12}{30}$ or $\frac{2}{5}$ of the job.

$$\frac{3}{5} + \frac{2}{5} = 1$$

which represents the completion of the entire job, or one whole job. ■

---

study tip

Let

$\quad a =$ the time it takes person A to do a job working alone

$\quad b =$ the time it takes person B to do the same job working alone

If t represents the time it takes for A and B to complete the entire job working together, then the situation can be modeled by the rational equation

$$\frac{t}{a} + \frac{t}{b} = 1.$$

PROBLEM SET 8.6

Practice Problems

Find the solution for each equation in Problems 1–38. If applicable, verify your solution using a graphing utility.

1. $\dfrac{x}{3} = \dfrac{x}{2} - 2$

2. $\dfrac{x}{5} = \dfrac{x}{6} + 1$

3. $\dfrac{x}{9} - \dfrac{3}{5} = \dfrac{2}{3}$

4. $\dfrac{3x}{5} = x + 6$

5. $2 - \dfrac{8}{x} = 6$

6. $1 - \dfrac{9}{x} = 4$

7. $\dfrac{2}{3} - \dfrac{5}{6} = \dfrac{1}{y}$

8. $\dfrac{1}{8} - \dfrac{3}{5} = \dfrac{1}{y}$

9. $\dfrac{4}{y} + \dfrac{1}{2} = \dfrac{5}{y}$

10. $\dfrac{5}{y} + \dfrac{1}{3} = \dfrac{6}{y}$

11. $\dfrac{2}{y} + 3 = \dfrac{5}{2y} + \dfrac{13}{4}$

12. $\dfrac{7}{2y} - \dfrac{5}{3y} = \dfrac{22}{3}$

13. $\dfrac{1}{z - 1} + 5 = \dfrac{11}{z - 1}$

14. $\dfrac{3}{z + 4} - 7 = \dfrac{-4}{z + 4}$

15. $\dfrac{8y}{y + 1} = 4 - \dfrac{8}{y + 1}$

16. $\dfrac{2}{y - 2} = \dfrac{y}{y - 2} - 2$

17. $\dfrac{4}{r^2 - 4} + \dfrac{2}{r - 2} = \dfrac{1}{r + 2}$

18. $\dfrac{12}{r^2 - 4} - \dfrac{3}{r - 2} = \dfrac{5}{r + 2}$

19. $\dfrac{2}{y + 1} - \dfrac{1}{y - 1} = \dfrac{2y}{y^2 - 1}$

20. $\dfrac{3}{2y + 1} + \dfrac{3}{2y - 1} = \dfrac{8y}{4y^2 - 1}$

21. $\dfrac{4}{y - 3} - \dfrac{2}{y - 2} = \dfrac{7 - y}{y^2 - 5y + 6}$

22. $\dfrac{4}{y - 1} - \dfrac{7}{y + 3} = \dfrac{y + 3}{y^2 + 2y - 3}$

23. $\dfrac{5}{2x + 6} - \dfrac{1}{x + 3} = \dfrac{1}{x + 1}$

24. $\dfrac{3}{2x + 4} - \dfrac{1}{3x + 1} = \dfrac{1}{x + 2}$

25. $\dfrac{3y}{y - 4} - 5 = \dfrac{12}{y - 4}$

26. $\dfrac{10}{y + 2} = 3 - \dfrac{5y}{y + 2}$

27. $\dfrac{4}{w} - \dfrac{w}{2} = \dfrac{7}{2}$

28. $\dfrac{4}{3w} - \dfrac{1}{3} = w$

29. $\dfrac{5}{3y - 8} = \dfrac{y}{y + 2}$

30. $\dfrac{3}{y - 1} = \dfrac{2y}{y + 4}$

31. $\dfrac{3}{z - 1} + \dfrac{8}{z} = 3$

32. $\dfrac{2}{z - 2} + \dfrac{4}{z} = 2$

33. $\dfrac{2}{y - 2} + \dfrac{y}{y + 2} = \dfrac{y + 6}{y^2 - 4}$

34. $\dfrac{y}{y+4} - 2 = \dfrac{11}{y^2 - 16}$

35. $x + \dfrac{6}{x} = -5$

36. $x + \dfrac{3}{x} = \dfrac{12}{x}$

37. $\dfrac{1}{x} + \dfrac{1}{x-3} = \dfrac{x-2}{x-3}$

38. $\dfrac{1}{x-1} + \dfrac{2}{x} = \dfrac{x}{x-1}$

Application Problems

39. An insect colony that initially contains 100 insects has a population after t hours described by

$$P = \frac{500(1 + 3t)}{5 + t}.$$

How long will it take for the population to increase to 1000 insects?

40. In t years from 1990, the population (P, in thousands) of a community will be

$$P = 20 - \frac{4}{t + 1}.$$

When will the population be 19,000?

41. If x prey are available per unit area, a predator will consume

$$\frac{0.8x}{1 + 0.03x} \text{ prey daily}$$

How should the prey per unit area be controlled if wildlife managers want a predator to consume 20 prey daily?

42. An electrician uses a bridge circuit to locate a ground in an underground cable several miles long. The following formula gives the distance to the ground, d.

$$d = \frac{R_2 L}{R_1 + R_2}$$

If $d = 1000$ feet, $R_1 = 750$ ohms, and $L = 4000$ feet, find R_2 (in ohms).

43. A large tax preparation business holds training sessions for new tax preparers just prior to the busy season. The model

$$Q = \frac{PV}{P - V}$$

describes the number of new tax preparers needed (Q) in terms of the number of people who use the business (P, in thousands) and last year's volume (V, in millions). If 85 new preparers are needed and 80,000 people use the business, what was last year's volume?

44. When the ownership of a business is transferred, auditors are interested in the "taxable measure" of the business. The model

$$M = \frac{P(C + L)}{T}$$

describes the taxable measure (M) in terms of taxable personal property (P), cash (C), liabilities assumed (L), and total considerations (T). At the sale of a business, \$55,000 worth of taxable property changed hands. The buyer paid \$65,000 in cash, assumed \$23,500 in liabilities, and gave the seller \$45,000 in capital stock. The taxable measure of the business was \$22,000. Determine the total consideration for the transaction.

45. The number of emergency room drug-abuse-related incidents in the United States in 1993 is represented in the graph. The number of cocaine incidents exceeds the number of marijuana/hashish incidents by 94,151. If the number of cocaine incidents is divided by the number of marijuana/hashish incidents, the partial quotient is 4 and the remainder is 6653. Find the number of drug-abuse-related incidents for cocaine and for marijuana/hashish.

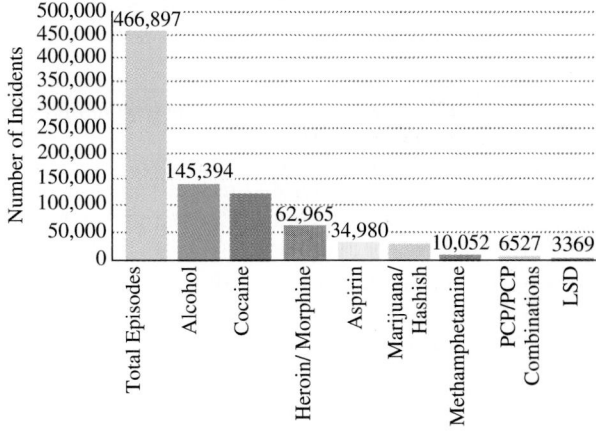

U.S. Emergency Room Drug-Abuse-Related Incidents, 1993

Source: U.S. Department of Health and Human Services, National Institute on Drug Abuse; Drug Abuse Warning Network

46. The annual spending on prescription drugs per person, by country, is shown in the graph. The spending in Germany exceeds that of Britain by \$227. If the spending on pharmaceuticals per person in Germany is divided by the corresponding number in Britain, the partial quotient is 3 and the remainder is 31. How much is spent annually on prescription drugs per person in Britain and Germany? The situation is illustrated in the graph at the top of the next page.

Profile: Spending on Prescription Drugs
(Annual Spending on Pharmaceuticals per Person, by Country)

Annual Spending in Dollars

- $350
- $300
- $250
- $200
- $150
- $100
- $50
- 0

Britain   Japan   U.S.   Canada   France   Germany

$189 $210 $241 $256

Source: Pharmaceutical Manufacturers Association

47. The denominator of a fraction is 5 more than its numerator. If 1 is added to the numerator and 2 is added to the denominator, the result is $\frac{1}{3}$. Find the original fraction.

48. What number must be added to both the numerator and denominator of $\frac{7}{3}$ to obtain $\frac{5}{3}$?

49. The sum of a number and its reciprocal is $\frac{25}{12}$. What is the number?

50. The sum of a number and its reciprocal is $\frac{37}{6}$. What is the number?

51. A boat that can travel 18 miles per hour in still water can travel 33 miles with the current in the same time that it can travel 21 miles against the current. What is the speed of the current?

52. A plane that can travel 225 miles per hour in still air can travel 300 miles with the wind in the same time that it can travel 210 miles against the wind. What is the speed of the wind?

53. A tourist drove 90 miles along a scenic highway and then took a 5 mile walk along a hiking trail. The driving rate was nine times the rate of speed while walking. The total time for driving and hiking was 3 hours. Find the tourist's rate along the hiking trail.

54. An athlete walked a distance of 2 miles on a treadmill. Doubling the treadmill speed, the athlete ran for another 2 miles. The total time for treadmill walking and running was 1 hour. Find the athlete's walking and running speeds.

55. If one person can do a job in 55 hours and a second person can do the same job in 66 hours, how long will it take to complete the job if they work together?

56. If one person can do a job in 14 hours and a second person can do the same job in 35 hours, how long will it take to complete the job if they work together?

57. A hot tub can be filled by one pipe in 15 minutes and by a second pipe in 10 minutes. How long will it take using both pipes to fill the hot tub?

58. A pool can be filled by one pipe in 4 hours and by a second pipe in 6 hours. How long will it take using both pipes to fill the pool?

In baseball, a player's batting average is the total number of hits divided by the total number of times at bat. Use this information to answer Problems 59–60.

59. A player has 12 hits after 40 times at bat. How many additional consecutive times must the player hit the ball to achieve a batting average of 0.440?

60. A player has eight hits after 50 times at bat. How many additional consecutive times must the player hit the ball to achieve a batting average of 0.250?

61. The area of the second rectangle subtracted from the area of the first rectangle is identical to the area of the third rectangle. Find the dimensions of each rectangle.

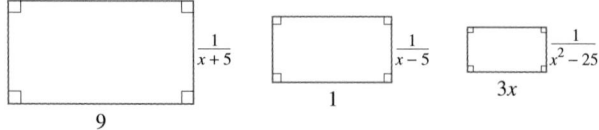

62. A person purchased 18 pounds of fruit consisting of apples and pears, paying $2.40 for the apples and $9 for the pears. The price per pound of the pears was 3 times that of the apples. How many pounds of each fruit were purchased? (*Hint:* Let x = the number of pounds of apples purchased. Then $18 - x$ = the number of pounds of pears purchased.)

True–False Critical Thinking Problems _____

63. Which one of the following is true?
  a. To solve the equation

$$\frac{1}{y} + \frac{1}{y-3} = \frac{y-2}{y-3}$$

we must first add the rational expressions on the left side.

  b. The equation $\dfrac{y+7}{2y-6} = \dfrac{5}{y-3} - 1$ has no solution.

c. $\dfrac{1}{x} + \dfrac{1}{6}$ can be simplified by multiplying by $6x$, so the expression simplifies to $6 + x$.

d. The equation $\dfrac{1}{y-2} - 1 = \dfrac{y}{2y-4}$ has one solution.

64. Which one of the following is true?

a. When both sides of

$$\frac{3+2}{x-4} = \frac{5}{x-4}$$

are multiplied by $x - 4$, we obtain $3 + 2 = 5$ or $5 = 5$. Therefore, all real numbers are solutions of the original equation.

b. The equation $\dfrac{5}{y-2} + \dfrac{10}{y+2} = 7$ has one solution.

c. The best way to subtract $\dfrac{4}{y} - \dfrac{2}{y+1}$ is to multiply by $y(y+1)$.

d. Zero is a solution of

$$\frac{y}{y^2 + y - 2} + \frac{y}{y^2 - 1} = \frac{y}{y^2 + 3y + 2}.$$

65. Which one of the following is true?

a. If a distance of 40 miles is covered at a rate of x miles per hour, then the time required to travel the 40 miles is represented by $\frac{x}{40}$.

b. If Seurat can paint a dotted mural in t days and he works at a uniform rate, then in 6 days he paints

$$\frac{1}{t+6}$$ of the mural.

c. If $\dfrac{1}{x}$ is one less than $\dfrac{3}{x+7}$, then

$$\frac{1}{x} - 1 = \frac{3}{x+7}$$

d. If x represents a nonzero number, then one-third its reciprocal is represented by $\dfrac{1}{3x}$.

Technology Problems

Use a graphing utility to find the solution in Problems 66–69. Graph each side of the equation on the same screen. The solution is the first coordinate of the point(s) of intersection. Check by direct substitution.

66. $\dfrac{x}{2} + \dfrac{x}{4} = 6$ **67.** $\dfrac{50}{x} = 2x$ **68.** $\dfrac{4}{x+2} - \dfrac{1}{x} = \dfrac{1}{x}$ **69.** $\dfrac{2}{x+2} = \dfrac{1}{x^2-4} + 1$

A commuter drove to work a distance of 40 miles and then returned again on the same highway. The average rate on the return trip was 30 miles per hour faster than the average rate on the outgoing trip. Use this information to answer Problems 70–73.

70. Let $x =$ the average rate on the outgoing trip. Write an expression for the average rate on the return trip.

71. Write a function that models the total time on the round trip by completing the missing portions of the function.

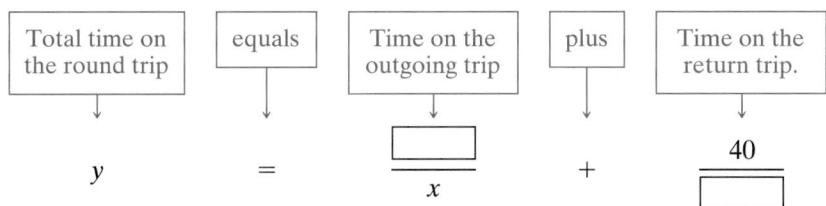

72. Use a graphing utility to graph the function that you wrote in Problem 71. Graph the function for x between 0 and 60, since it seems unlikely that an average outgoing rate exceeds 60 miles per hour with a return rate that is 30 miles per hour faster. In particular, use the following range setting:

Xmin $= 0$, Xmax $= 60$, Xscl $= 3$,
Ymin $= 0$, Ymax $= 10$, Yscl $= 1$

What does the graph indicate about the time for the round trip with increasing rates?

73. Suppose that the commuter would like to complete the round trip in 2 hours. Use the [TRACE] feature of your graphing utility to trace along the curve until $y = 2$, remembering that y represents total time on the round trip. What is the value of x when $y = 2$? Use this value to complete the following sentence: The commuter must average _____ miles per hour on the outgoing trip to complete the round trip in ___ hours.

Writing in Mathematics

74. Describe similarities and differences between the procedures needed to solve the following problems:

Add: $\dfrac{2}{x} + \dfrac{3}{4}$

Solve for x: $\dfrac{2}{x} + \dfrac{3}{4} = 1$

Critical Thinking Problems

75. Solve: $\dfrac{1}{y^2 + 3y + 2} + \dfrac{1}{y - 1} = \dfrac{2}{y^2 - 1}$.

76. Consider the equation $\dfrac{c}{x^2} = \dfrac{c}{x^2} + \dfrac{1}{x}$. Is there a value for c that will result in a solution for this equation? If so, what is the value? If not, describe why the equation cannot have a solution regardless of how c is chosen.

77. A car travels for 125 miles at a uniform speed. If the speed is increased by 5 miles per hour, the trip would take 1 hour less time. What is the car's speed?

78. Two investments have interest rates that differ by 1%. An investment for 1 year at the lower rate earns $175. The same principal amount invested for a year at the higher rate earns $200. What are the two interest rates?

79. On an examination, a student answered 20 of the first 30 problems correctly. After the first 30 problems, the student answered all of the remaining questions correctly, receiving a grade of 75% on the test. How many questions were on the test?

80. The sum of two positive numbers is equal to the sum of their reciprocals. Find the product of the numbers.

Review Problems

81. If 28.4 grams of a particular cereal contains 110 calories, how many calories are there in 42.6 grams of the cereal?

82. Find the slope of the line passing through $(5, -2)$ and $(3, 8)$.

83. Factor completely: $2x^3 + 8x^2 - 42x$.

S E C T I O N   8 . 7

Solutions   Tutorial   Video
Manual   10

1 Solve rational models for a specified variable.

Modeling with Rational Expressions

Objectives

1 Solve rational models for a specified variable.
2 Solve problems about variation.

Solving Rational Models for a Specified Variable

In Section 8.6, we considered the following problem: A particular rat given n trials in a maze can run through the maze in t minutes, where

$$t = 6 + \frac{20}{n + 2}.$$

How can the number of previous trials be controlled so that the rat can run through the maze in exactly 8 minutes?

We solved the problem by substituting 8 for t in the mathematical model and solving for n. The disadvantage of this method is that each time we are given a value for t, we must solve for n. A more efficient approach would be to solve the formula for n in terms of t. This forms the basis of Example 1.

EXAMPLE 1 **Solving a Formula for a Specified Variable**

Solve for n: $t = 6 + \dfrac{20}{n + 2}$

Solution

$$t = 6 + \frac{20}{n + 2}$$ This is the given formula.

$$(n + 2)t = (n + 2)\left[6 + \frac{20}{n + 2}\right]$$ Multiply both sides by the LCD, $n + 2$.

$$(n + 2)t = (n + 2)6 + \cancel{(n + 2)}\left(\frac{20}{\cancel{n + 2}}\right)$$ Multiply to remove brackets on the right and simplify.

$$nt + 2t = 6n + 12 + 20$$ Multiply to remove parentheses.

$$nt + 2t = 6n + 32$$ Combine numerical terms.

Since we must solve for n, we will isolate all terms with n on the left and all other terms on the right.

$$nt - 6n + 2t = 32$$ Subtract $6n$ from both sides.

$$nt - 6n = 32 - 2t$$ Subtract $2t$ from both sides.

$$n(t - 6) = 32 - 2t$$ Use the distributive property (factoring) on the left.

$$\frac{n(t - 6)}{t - 6} = \frac{32 - 2t}{t - 6}$$ Solve for n by dividing both sides by $t - 6$. ($t \neq 6$)

$$n = \frac{32 - 2t}{t - 6}$$ Simplify.

In this form, we can easily control the number of previous trials (n) for a desired time through the maze. If we want the rat to run through the maze in 7 seconds, $t = 7$ and

$$n = \frac{32 - 2t}{t - 6} = \frac{32 - 2(7)}{7 - 6} = \frac{32 - 14}{1} = 18.$$

Thus, 18 previous trials are necessary for a time of 7 seconds to be achieved. ■

In the 1860s, Mathew Brady, along with a team of 20 photographers, shot comprehensive coverage of the Civil War. These clear, sharp pictures, such as the one in the margin on the next page, required precision camera focus and were the first to capture the grim realities of war.

A camera lens has a characteristic measurement f, called its focal length. When an object is in focus, its distance from the lens (p) and the distance from the lens to the film (q) (see Figure 8.3) satisfy the model

$$\frac{1}{p} + \frac{1}{q} = \frac{1}{f}.$$

In Example 2, we use our equation-solving techniques to solve this model for f.

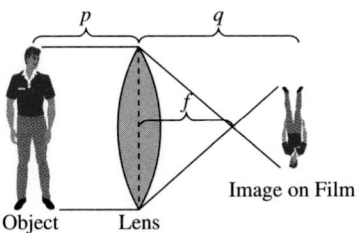

Figure 8.3

ENRICHMENT ESSAY

A Rational Expression Describing When to Buy a New Car

A mathematical model has been devised that tells people how many years they should drive their present car before buying a new one. If y represents this number of years, the formula is

$$y = \frac{GMC}{(G - M)DP}$$

in which

G = New car's mileage (in miles per gallon)

M = Your present car's mileage

C = Cost (in dollars) of the new car

D = Number of miles you drive each year

P = Price of gasoline per gallon

- How many years should you drive your old car before purchasing a new car if the new car gets 40 miles per gallon, your present car gets 10 miles per gallon, the cost of the new car is $20,000, you drive 12,000 miles per year, and the cost of gasoline is $1.40 per gallon?
- Under what conditions does the model yield unrealistic values for y?

Death of a soldier in the Civil War

Corbis-Bettmann

EXAMPLE 2   **The Mathematical Model for a Camera Lens**

Solve: $\dfrac{1}{p} + \dfrac{1}{q} = \dfrac{1}{f}$ for f

Solution

$$\frac{1}{p} + \frac{1}{q} = \frac{1}{f}$$

This is the given model.

$$pqf\left(\frac{1}{p} + \frac{1}{q}\right) = pqf\left(\frac{1}{f}\right)$$

Multiply both sides by the LCD, pqf.

$$pqf \cdot \frac{1}{p} + pqf \cdot \frac{1}{q} = pqf \cdot \frac{1}{f}$$

Multiply to remove parentheses and simplify.

$$qf + pf = pq$$

We now have all terms with f, the letter we are solving for, on the left. Isolate f by factoring it out.

$$(q + p)f = pq$$

Factor out f.

$$f = \frac{pq}{q + p}$$

Divide both sides by $q + p$.

2 Solve problems about variation.

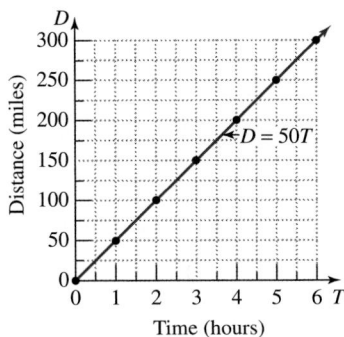

Figure 8.4

Modeling with Variation

Direct Variation. Suppose that a car is traveling at an average rate of 50 miles per hour. Because $D = RT$, the distance covered by the car in T hours is $D = 50T$. Thus,

In 1 hour, the car travels 50 miles.	$D = 50 \cdot 1$
In 2 hours, the car travels 100 miles.	$D = 50 \cdot 2$
In 3 hours, the car travels 150 miles.	$D = 50 \cdot 3$

Possible values for T and D are given in the following table of values. The graph of $D = 50T$ is shown in Figure 8.4.

T (hours)	1	2	3	4	5	6
$D = 50T$ (miles)	50	100	150	200	250	300

As the formula $D = 50T$ illustrates, the distance covered by the car is a constant multiple of time. When the time is doubled, the distance is doubled; when the time is tripled, the distance is tripled; and so on. Because of this, the distance is said to *vary directly* as the time. The *equation of variation* is $D = 50T$.

Generalizing, we obtain the following statement.

> **Direct variation**
>
> If a situation is modeled by an equation in the form
>
> $y = kx$
>
> where k is a constant, we say that *y varies directly as x*. We also say that *y is proportional to x*. The number k is called the *constant of variation* or the *constant of proportionality*.

If we know one pair of values that vary directly, then we can find k, the constant of variation. Once k is known, we can write the equation of variation and use it to determine other values.

EXAMPLE 3 Finding a Constant of Variation

An object's weight on the moon (M) varies directly as its weight on Earth (E). An object that weighs 17.6 kilograms on the moon has a weight of 110 kilograms on Earth. Find the constant of variation, and write the equation of variation.

Solution

$M = kE$	Translate "Moon weight varies directly as Earth weight" into an equation.
$17.6 = k \cdot 110$	Find k. We are given that $M = 17.6$ and $E = 110$.
$\dfrac{17.6}{110} = k$	Solve for k, dividing both sides by 110.
$0.16 = k$	Perform the division.

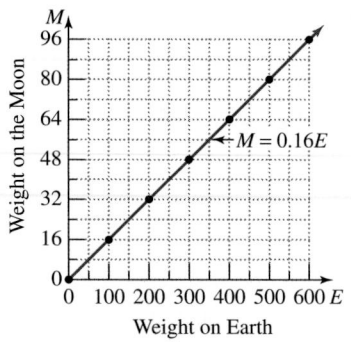

Weight on the moon is a function of weight on Earth, modeled by the direct variation equation $M = 0.16E$.

Thus, the equation of variation is $M = 0.16E$.

In Example 4, once k is known, we can find other weights. For example, the weight on the moon of an object that weighs 180 kilograms on Earth is

$$M = 0.16E = 0.16(180) = 28.8 \text{ kilograms.}$$

Notice that the direct variation equation $y = kx$ is a linear function. If $k > 0$, then the slope of the line is positive. Consequently, as x increases, y also increases. On the other hand, if $k < 0$, then the slope of $y = kx$ is negative. For $k < 0$, the line represented by $y = kx$ goes down from left to right, so that as x increases, y decreases.

In Example 4, we find the constant of variation and use it to solve a variation problem.

EXAMPLE 4 **Solving a Direct Variation Problem**

The cost C of an airplane ticket varies directly as the number of miles M in the trip. A 3000-mile trip costs \$400. What is the cost of a 450-mile trip?

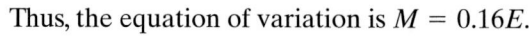
Discover for yourself

Try solving Example 4 using a proportion. Can you see why $y = kx$ also translates as y is proportional to x?

Solution

$C = kM$ — Translate "Cost varies directly as miles" into an equation.

$400 = k \cdot 3000$ — Find k. We are given that a 3000-mile trip costs \$400, so $C = 400$ and $M = 3000$.

$\dfrac{400}{3000} = k$, or $k = \dfrac{2}{15}$ — Solve for k, dividing both sides by 3000.

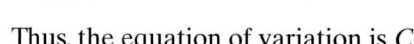

Thus, the equation of variation is $C = \frac{2}{15}M$.
To find the cost of a 450-mile trip, we substitute 450 for M.

$C = \dfrac{2}{15}M$ — This is the equation of variation.

$= \dfrac{2}{15}(450)$ — Substitute 450 for M.

$= 60$ — $\overset{30}{\underset{1}{\frac{2}{15}}}(450) = 60$

Cost of a ticket is a function of a trip's mileage, modeled by the direct variation equation $C = \frac{2}{15}M$.

The cost of a 450-mile trip is \$60.

Inverse Variation. Suppose you plan to make a 200-mile trip by car. The time it takes is a function of your speed, modeled by the formula

$$T = \dfrac{200}{R}$$ — Since $RT = D$, then $T = \dfrac{D}{R}$ and $D = 200$.

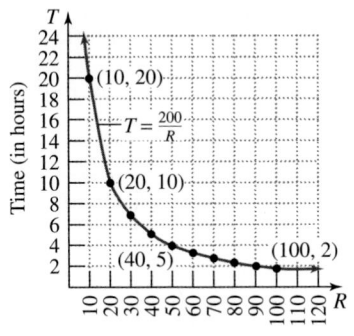

Figure 8.5

A trip's time is a function of one's speed, modeled by the inverse variation equation

$$T = \frac{200}{R}.$$

Possible values of R and T are given in the following table of values.

R (miles/hour)	10	20	40	50	100
$T = \dfrac{200}{R}$ (hours)	20	10	5	4	2

The graph of $T = \dfrac{200}{R}$ is shown in Figure 8.5. Notice that as your rate increases, the trip's time decreases. Time is said to *vary inversely* as rate, and the equation of variation is $T = \dfrac{200}{R}$.

Generalizing, we obtain the following statement.

Inverse variation

If a situation is modeled by an equation in the form

$$y = \frac{k}{x}$$

where k is a constant, we say that y *varies inversely* as x. We also say that y *is inversely proportional to x*. The number k is called the *constant of variation* or the *constant of proportionality*.

We will use the same procedure to solve inverse variation problems as we did in solving direct variation problems. After translating into an equation, we will find the value of k, substitute this value back into the equation, and then answer the given question. This is illustrated in Example 5.

EXAMPLE 5   **Solving an Inverse Variation Problem**

The number of pens sold (N) varies inversely as the price per pen (p). If 4000 pens are sold at a price of $1.50 each, predict the number of pens that will be sold at a price of $1.20 each.

Solution

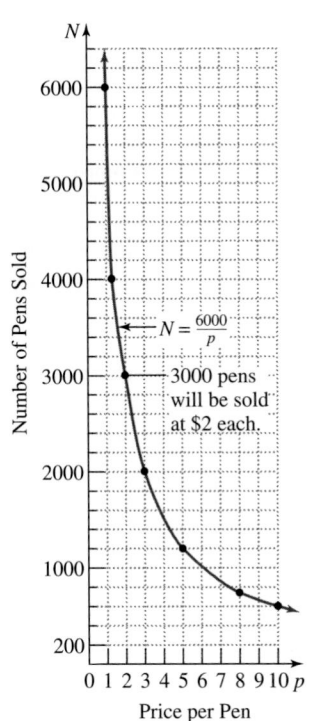

Figure 8.6

As price increases, the demand for the number of pens decreases.

$$N = \frac{k}{p}$$
Translate "Number (N) varies inversely as price (p)" into an equation.

$$4000 = \frac{k}{1.5}$$
Find k. Because 4000 pens are sold at $1.50, when $p = 1.5$, $N = 4000$.

$$1.5(4000) = \cancel{1.5}\left(\frac{k}{\cancel{1.5}}\right)$$
Multiply both sides by 1.5, the LCD.

$$6000 = k$$
Multiply. The constant of variation is 6000.

$$N = \frac{6000}{p}$$
Substitute the value for k into the original equation. This is the equation of variation.

$$N = \frac{6000}{1.2}$$
Find N when $p = 1.2$.

$$= 5000$$

Thus, 5000 pens will be sold at $1.20 each. ∎

The graph of the inverse variation equation $N = \dfrac{6000}{p}$ from Example 5 is shown on page 625 in Figure 8.6. A table of values for N and p, shown below, was used to obtain the graph.

p	0	1	2	3	5	8	10
$N = \dfrac{6000}{p}$	$\dfrac{6000}{0}$, undefined	$\dfrac{6000}{1} = 6000$	$\dfrac{6000}{2} = 3000$	$\dfrac{6000}{3} = 2000$	$\dfrac{6000}{5} = 1200$	$\dfrac{6000}{8} = 750$	$\dfrac{6000}{10} = 600$
Ordered Pair (N, p)	None	$(1, 6000)$	$(2, 3000)$	$(3, 2000)$	$(5, 1200)$	$(8, 750)$	$(10, 600)$

Turn back to the graph in Figure 8.6 and observe its shape. The graph shows that as the price per pen increases, the number of pens sold decreases quite rapidly. The number of pens sold is a function of the price per pen. For each meaningful price per pen, there is exactly one corresponding value that indicates the number of pens sold.

PROBLEM SET 8.7

Practice and Application Problems

1. The cost (C, in thousands of dollars) of eliminating x percent of pollutants from a stream is given by

$$C = \frac{4x}{100 - x}$$

Solve for x, and then find the percent of pollutants that can be eliminated at a cost of $16,000.

2. The formula

$$W = \frac{10x}{150 - x}$$

describes the number of weeks (W) it takes to raise x percent of a campaign's financial goal. Solve for x, and then find the percent of the campaign's financial goal that can be raised in 5 weeks.

3. In t years from 1990, the population of a community will be

$$P = 30 - \frac{9}{t + 1}$$

where P is expressed in thousands. Solve for t. Then determine when the community will have a population of 29,000.

4. To restore the population of tule elk at Point Reyes, California, 50 elk are introduced into a wildlife preserve. The tule elk population (P) after t years is described by the model

$$P = \frac{250(3t + 5)}{t + 25}.$$

a. How many years will it take for the population to increase to 125 tule elk?

b. Solve the formula for t in terms of P.

5. The mathematical model

$$B = \frac{F}{S - V}$$

describes the number of units that a company must manufacture and sell (B) to break even (experience neither profit nor loss), where F is the company's fixed costs, S is the selling price for each unit, and V is the cost to manufacture each unit (the variable costs per unit).

a. Solve the formula for S.

b. Find the selling price per unit for the company to break even if the fixed costs are $20,000, the variable costs per unit are $60, and the company plans to make and sell 100 units.

6. The mathematical model

$$S = \frac{C}{1 - r}$$

describes the selling price of a product (S) in terms of C and r, where C is the cost of the product, and r is the markup rate.

a. Solve the formula for r.

b. What is the markup rate on a product costing $140 and selling for $200?

7. The opposition to an electric current offered by some components is called resistance, measured in units called ohms. Resistors are specifically placed in a circuit to add resistance. As shown in the figure, if R_1 and R_2 are resistors in a parallel circuit, and R is the total resistance in the circuit, then they are related by the mathematical model

$$\frac{1}{R} = \frac{1}{R_1} + \frac{1}{R_2}.$$

a. If the total resistance in the circuit is 4 ohms and the resistance of R_1 is 12 ohms, what is the resistance of R_2?

b. Solve the formula for R.

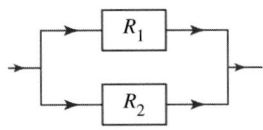

8. The total length F of a concave mirror is described by the model

$$\frac{1}{F} = \frac{1}{a} + \frac{1}{b}$$

where a is the distance of the object from the mirror and b is the distance of the image from the mirror. Solve the formula for F.

9. The formula

$$P = \frac{DN}{N + 2}$$

describes the pitch diameter of a gear (P), where D is the outside diameter of the gear and N is the number of teeth in the gear. Solve the formula for N.

10. The formula

$$p = \frac{2st}{D}$$

describes the safe internal unit pressure (p) of a pipe of thickness t, diameter D, and unit tensile stress, s. Solve the formula for s.

11. The amount A accumulated on an investment of P dollars at an interest rate r for t years is $A = P + Prt$. Solve the formula for P.

12. The gravitational attraction F between two objects of masses m_1 and m_2 is

$$F = \frac{km_1m_2}{d^2}$$

where k is a constant and d is the distance between the two objects. Solve the formula for m_1.

In Problems 13–30, solve for the specified variable. If you recognize the given formula, describe the variables that are being modeled.

13. $A = \dfrac{1}{2}bh$, for h

14. $A = \dfrac{1}{2}h(a + b)$, for a

15. $s = \dfrac{1}{2}at^2$, for a

16. $V = \dfrac{1}{3}\pi r^2h$, for h

17. $F = \dfrac{mv^2}{r}$, for r

18. $\dfrac{t}{a} + \dfrac{t}{b} = 1$, for t

19. $\dfrac{P_1V_2}{T_1} = \dfrac{P_2V_2}{T_2}$, for T_2

20. $H = \dfrac{KA(T_1 - T_2)}{L}$, for T_2

21. $S = \dfrac{a}{1 - r}$, for r

22. $I = \dfrac{2V}{R + 2r}$, for R

23. $f = \dfrac{f_1 f_2}{f_1 + f_2}$, for f_2

24. $S = \dfrac{a_1 - a_n r}{1 - r}$, for a_1

25. $V = \dfrac{4}{3}\pi r^3$, for r^3

26. $V = \dfrac{1}{3}\pi r^2h$, for r^2

27. $A = \dfrac{rs}{r + s}$, for s

28. $A = \dfrac{r - s}{r + s}$, for s

29. $\dfrac{b}{y} = 1 + c$, for y

30. $\dfrac{my}{n} + \dfrac{ny}{m} = 1$, for y

31. A person's weekly pay (P) varies directly as the number of hours worked (H). For 25 hours of work, the weekly pay is \$425.

a. Find the constant of variation, and write the equation of variation that models this situation.

b. Use the equation of variation to find the weekly pay for 40 hours of work.

c. Graph the equation of variation in the first quadrant, with values of H (from 0 to 40) along the x-axis and values of P along the y-axis.

32. The weight (W) of an aluminum canoe varies directly as its length (L). A 6-foot canoe weighs 75 pounds.

a. Find the constant of variation, and write the equation of variation that models this situation.

b. Use the equation of variation to find the weight of a 16-foot canoe.

c. Graph the equation of variation in the first quadrant, with values of L (from 0 to 18) along the x-axis and values of W along the y-axis.

33. The amount of an electric bill A varies directly as the amount of electricity E used. If the bill for 1800 kilowatts of electricity is $126, what is the bill for 2600 kilowatts of electricity?

34. The Mach number is a measurement of speed named after the man who suggested it, Ernst Mach (1838–1916). The speed of an aircraft (S) varies directly as its Mach number (M). Shown below are two old airplanes. Use the figures for the Messerschmitt to write the equation of variation. Then use the equation to determine the Spitfire's speed.

Messerschmitt Me 262
Speed (S) = 555 miles per hour
Mach number (M) = 0.75

Spitfire
Mach number (M) = 0.47
Speed (S) = ?

35. The table of values at the top of the next column shows the values for the current, I, in an electric circuit and the resistance, R, of the circuit.

I (in amperes)	0.5	1.0	1.5	2.0	2.5	3.0	4.0	5.0
R (in ohms)	12	6.0	4.0	3.0	2.4	2.0	1.5	1.2

a. Graph the ordered pairs in the table of values, with values of I along the x-axis and values of R along the y-axis. Connect the eight points with a smooth curve.

b. Does current vary directly or inversely as resistance? Use your graph and explain how you arrived at your answer.

c. Write an equation of variation for I and R, using one of the ordered pairs in the table to find the constant of variation. Then use your variation equation to verify the other seven ordered pairs in the table.

36. If air is pumped into a tire, the pressure (P) required varies inversely as the volume (V) of the air. The pressure is 30 pounds per square inch when the volume is 140 cubic inches. What is the pressure when the volume is 100 cubic inches?

37. For a constant area, the length of a rectangle varies inversely as the width. The length of a rectangle is 27 yards when the width is 8 yards. Find the length of a rectangle with the same area if the width is 12 yards.

38. The time required to accomplish a task varies inversely as the number of people working on the task. It takes 6 hours for 20 people to put a new roof on a porch. How long would it take 30 people to do the job?

True–False Critical Thinking Problems

39. Which one of the following is true?
  a. Solving $I = p + prt$ for p gives $p = I - prt$.
  b. To solve $nt - 6n = 32 - 2t$ for n, we must first factor on the left side.
  c. It seems reasonable that the demand for a product varies directly as the price of the product.
  d. It seems reasonable that the weight of an iguana varies inversely as its length.

40. Which one of the following is true?

  a. The formula $a = \dfrac{1 - a}{b}$, solved for b, is $b = \dfrac{1 - a}{a}$.
  b. If $y = \dfrac{x + y}{b}$, then solved for y, $y = yb - x$.
  c. It seems reasonable that the annual benefit from Social Security varies inversely as one's age.
  d. Any inverse variation problem can be solved by turning it into a direct variation problem and then inverting the order of the solution process.

Technology Problems

41. Use a graphing utility to graph the direct variation equation of Example 4 on page 624. Then TRACE along the curve and illustrate the solution to the question given in the example.

42. Use a graphing utility to graph the inverse variation equation of Example 5 on page 625. Then TRACE along the curve and illustrate the solution to the question given in the example.

43. Use a graphing utility to graph the direct variation equation that you obtained in Problem 33. Then TRACE along the line and illustrate the solution to the problem.

44. Use a graphing utility to graph the inverse variation equation that you obtained in Problem 36. Then TRACE along the curve and illustrate the solution to the problem.

Writing in Mathematics

45. Describe the similarities and differences between solving $\frac{x}{3} + \frac{x}{5} = 1$ and $\frac{x}{a} + \frac{x}{b} = 1$ for x.

46. Psychologists have developed mathematical models to predict the percent of correct responses as a function of the number of trials of a particular task. One such model, called a learning curve, is

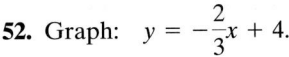

$$P = \frac{0.9n - 0.4}{0.9n + 0.1}$$

where P is the percent of correct responses after n trials. The model is developed so that P is expressed in decimal form. Explain why someone might want to solve this model for n.

Critical Thinking Problems

47. What is the slope of the line that you graphed in Problem 31 part (c)? Describe what this means in terms of each additional hour worked.

48. What is the slope of the line that you graphed in Problem 32 part (c)? Describe what this means in terms of each additional foot of the canoe's length.

49. The cephalic index is used by anthropologists to study differences among races of human beings. The index varies directly as the width of the head and inversely as the length of the head. If the cephalic index is 75 for a width of 6 inches and a length of 8 inches, find the index for a head width of 7 inches and a length of 10 inches.

Review Problems

50. Factor: $25x^2 - 81$.

51. Solve: $x^2 - 12x + 36 = 0$.

52. Graph: $y = -\frac{2}{3}x + 4$.

CHAPTER PROJECT

The Proportions of Nature

In this project, you will use your knowledge of proportions to experiment with proportions found in nature. For example, one popular way to terrorize audiences watching a fantasy or science fiction film is to depict familiar creatures in unfamiliar proportions. This can be accomplished by "growing" small creatures such as ants to great size, by "shrinking" humans so that microscopic creatures loom over them, or by "growing" humans to giant size. Using some basic equations of variation, we can make some guesses about how realistic these horrors would be.

Some of the most basic relationships in nature involve comparisons between length (L), surface area (S), and volume (V). Writing these relationships as variations, and inserting k and k' as constants of proportionality, we have

$$S = kL^2 \quad and \quad V = k'L^3$$

Let's begin by looking at a well-known "giant" in the world of fantasy.

1. In the classic book *Gulliver's Travels* by Jonathan Swift, Gulliver finds himself transported to the land of Lilliput, where his "stature exceeded theirs in the proportion of twelve to one." How many of the Lilliputians would be counted as "equivalent" to Gulliver? If Gulliver was twelve times your height, how tall would he be? Write down the amount of food you consume in one typical dinner and use that to determine what Gulliver would need for an equivalent meal. Be careful how you choose your proportions, and justify your answer.

Now let's see how realistic those giant ants would be. The strength of a muscle varies directly with its cross-sectional area, but the force of gravity acts on a body proportional to its mass and thus, usually, proportional to its volume. When the volume of a body increases, the stress of the force of gravity increases.

If we think of the legs of an animal as columns that support its weight, we can easily see why heavier animals require thicker and shorter legs in proportion to their body. To begin our investigation, let's think of a small-scale model of a bridge made out of light wood. If the bridge were made much larger, the same light wood would no longer support the weight—the bridge would sag or collapse.

2. Use three small pieces of a light material, such as balsa wood or plastic, as legs to support a small, square box filled with sand, dried beans, or some other easily obtained material. Make at least three more models, gradually increasing the height of your model and adjusting the other measurements to remain proportional. Try to discover at what point the legs will no longer support the box. If you work in a group, have other members of the group use different materials for the legs or legs of different cross-sectional area, then shift the box from one set to another. How does the choice of legs affect the weight supported?

3. Working with a group and using resources in the library or on the Worldwide Web, select an insect to scale up to the same height as a human. Using proportions, give estimates of what its weight would be at the scaled-up height. Using your best estimates for the measurements of the insect, explain how the force of gravity would affect it at the new size. Construct the largest model you can of the insect, scaling up its volume and assuming its density remains constant. What is the largest insect that exists of the type you have selected?

Proportions may also be used to relate motion. In the case of a human walking, the maximum possible walking speed is proportional to the square root of the product of the acceleration due to gravity and the length of an adult leg from the hip to the sole of the foot. We write this proportion as

$$v = k \sqrt{gl}$$

where v is the maximum walking speed, $g = 32$ feet per second^2, l is measured in feet and k is the constant of proportionality. For the next two problems, use this proportion and your calculator to obtain the best estimates.

4. On a treadmill, determine at what point you feel comfortable changing from a walking speed to a running speed. Start out at a comfortable walking pace and gradually increase the treadmill's speed until you start running. Use the relationship above to determine what your *maximum* walking speed should be in theory. How did your actual maximum speed compare? (Most people change from walking to running at a slightly lower speed than the maximum.)

5. Use the class data from Problem 3 to determine a range of values for changing from walking to running. Compare the speeds from people who have a similar range of leg length. Do they all change from walking to running at about the same speed? Compare the high end of this range to the speed attained by participants in a walking race. If you can actually watch a walking race, notice the movement of the hips of the participants. This movement lowers the body's center of gravity by a small amount when the stride is at its vertical point, which enables the person to walk at a much faster pace than would ordinarily be possible. (This information comes from a field of study combining biology and mechanical engineering known as *biomechanics*.)

Worldwide Web Resources

Go to the Prentice Hall website (http://www.prenhall.com/blitzer) to access other locations on the Internet that will allow you to further explore the concepts presented in this project.

Chapter Review

SUMMARY

1. Rational Expressions and Functions

  a. A rational expression is the quotient of two polynomials.

  b. A rational expression is undefined at any value that produces a denominator of 0.

  c. A rational function is one whose equation is defined by a rational expression. For rational functions, exclude value(s) that make the polynomial in the denominator of its equation 0.

2. Reducing Rational Expressions to Lowest Terms (Simplifying Rational Expressions)

  a. Factor the numerator and denominator completely.

  b. Divide both the numerator and denominator by the common factors.

  c. The quotient of two polynomials that have opposite signs and are additive inverses is -1.

3. Multiplying Rational Expressions

  a. Factor all numerators and denominators completely.

  b. Divide both the numerator and denominator by common factors.

  c. Multiply the remaining factors in the numerator and multiply remaining factors in the denominator.

4. Dividing Rational Expressions

The quotient of two rational expressions is the product of the first rational expression and the reciprocal of the second rational expression, the divisor.

5. Adding and Subtracting Rational Expressions

  a. To add or subtract rational expressions with the same denominators, add or subtract the numerators and place the result over the common denominator. If possible, simplify the resulting rational expression.

  b. To add or subtract rational expressions whose denominators are additive inverses, first multiply either rational expression by $\frac{-1}{-1}$. Then combine, using part (a).

  c. To add or subtract rational expressions that have different denominators:

    1. Find the LCD, the product of all different factors from each denominator, with each factor raised to the highest power occurring in any denominator.

    2. Multiply the numerator and denominator in each fraction by the factors required to obtain the LCD.

    3. Add or subtract numerators, placing the resulting expression over the LCD.

    4. If necessary, simplify the resulting rational expression.

6. Complex Fractions

  a. A complex fraction is a rational expression whose numerator and/or denominator contains one or more fractions.

  b. To simplify a complex fraction, use one of the following methods.

    Method 1. As necessary, add or subtract fractions in the numerator and denominator of the complex fraction. Then find the quotient by multiplying the numerator by the reciprocal of the denominator.

    Method 2. Multiply the numerator and the denominator of the complex fraction by the LCD of all expressions within the fraction. Then simplify the resulting expression.

7. Solving Rational Equations

  a. A rational equation contains one or more rational expressions.

  b. To solve, clear the equation of fractions by multiplying both sides by the LCD of all rational expressions in the equation. Solve the resulting equation. Any value of a variable that makes any denominator of the original equation equal 0 is not a solution.

8. Rational Models

  a. A rational model is a mathematical model containing one or more rational expressions.

  b. To solve a mathematical model for a specified variable, use the method for solving rational equations.

  c. To model uniform motion problems, since $RT = D$, then $T = D/R$. Find two rational expressions for time and then use the verbal conditions of the problem to write an equation.

  d. Work problems can be modeled using $\dfrac{t}{a} + \dfrac{t}{b} = 1$, where $a =$ the time it takes A to do the job alone, $b =$ the time it takes B to do the job alone, and $t =$ the time it takes A and B working together to complete the job.

9. Variation

  a.

English Statement	Equation
y varies directly as x. y is proportional to x.	$y = kx$
y varies inversely as x. y is inversely proportional to x.	$y = \dfrac{k}{x}$

b. To solve a variation problem,
   1. Translate from an English statement into an equation.
   2. Find the value of k, the variation constant.

3. Substitute the value for k into the equation in step 1.
4. Use the equation from step 3 to answer the given question.

REVIEW PROBLEMS

List all numbers (if any) for which each rational expression in Problems 1–4 is undefined. If applicable, use a graphing utility to verify that these values are excluded.

1. $\dfrac{5x}{6x - 24}$

2. $\dfrac{x + 3}{(x - 2)(x + 5)}$

3. $\dfrac{x^2 + 3}{x^2 - 3x + 2}$

4. $\dfrac{5}{x^2 + 1}$

5. The function

$$f(x) = \dfrac{80{,}000x}{100 - x}$$

describes the cost of removing x percent of pollutants from the stack emission of a utility company that burns coal to generate electricity.
a. Find and interpret $f(20), f(50), f(90)$, and $f(98)$.

b. For what value of x is the function undefined?
c. What happens to the cost as x approaches 100%? How can you interpret this observation?

6. Graph

$$f(x) = \dfrac{80{,}000x}{100 - x}$$

by first completing the table of coordinates.

x	0	10	20	50	60	80	90	98	99	100
$f(x)$										Undefined

Simplify (reduce) each rational expression in Problems 7–12. If applicable, use a graphing utility to verify the simplification.

7. $\dfrac{16x^2}{12x}$

8. $\dfrac{x^3 + 2x^2}{x + 2}$

9. $\dfrac{x^2 + 3x - 18}{x^2 - 36}$

10. $\dfrac{x^2 - 4x - 5}{x^2 + 8x + 7}$

11. $\dfrac{y^2 + 2y}{y^2 + 4y + 4}$

12. $\dfrac{3a^2 - 5a - 2}{4 - a^2}$

13. Graph $y = \dfrac{x^2 - 4}{x - 2}$ by first simplifying the rational expression in the function's formula. Use an open dot above the value of x that is excluded from the function. If applicable, verify your graph using a graphing utility.

Multiply each rational expression in Problems 14–17.

14. $\dfrac{5y + 5}{6} \cdot \dfrac{3y}{y^2 + y}$

15. $\dfrac{x^2 + 6x + 9}{x^2 - 4} \cdot \dfrac{x + 3}{x - 2}$

16. $\dfrac{2y^2 + y - 3}{4y^2 - 9} \cdot \dfrac{3y + 3}{5y - 5y^2}$

17. $\dfrac{x^2 + x - 6}{x^2 + 6x + 9} \cdot \dfrac{x + 2}{x - 3} \cdot \dfrac{x^2 - 7x + 12}{x^2 - x - 2}$

Divide each rational expression in Problems 18–21.

18. $\dfrac{y^2 + y - 2}{10} \div \dfrac{2y + 4}{5}$

19. $\dfrac{6y + 2}{y^2 - 1} \div \dfrac{3y^2 + y}{y - 1}$

20. $\dfrac{y^2 - 5y - 24}{2y^2 - 2y - 24} \div \dfrac{y^2 - 10y + 16}{4y^2 + 4y - 24}$

21. $\dfrac{z^2 - 10z + 21}{7 - z} \div (z + 3)$

Perform the indicated operations in Problems 22–25.

22. $\dfrac{12x - 5}{3x - 1} + \dfrac{1}{3x - 1}$

23. $\dfrac{3y^2 + 2y}{y - 1} - \dfrac{10y - 5}{y - 1}$

24. $\dfrac{2y - 1}{y^2 + 5y - 6} - \dfrac{2y - 7}{y^2 + 5y - 6}$

25. $\dfrac{2x + 7}{x^2 - 9} - \dfrac{x - 4}{x^2 - 9}$

Find the least common multiple of each polynomial in Problems 26–28.

26. $9x^3, 12x$

27. $8y^2(y - 1)^2, 10y^3(y - 1)$

28. $x^2 + 4x + 3, x^2 + 10x + 21$

Perform the indicated operations in Problems 29–36.

29. $\dfrac{3}{10y^2} + \dfrac{7}{25y}$

30. $\dfrac{6y}{y^2 - 4} - \dfrac{3}{y + 2}$

31. $\dfrac{2}{3x} + \dfrac{5}{x + 1}$

32. $\dfrac{2y}{y^2 + 2y + 1} + \dfrac{y}{y^2 - 1}$

33. $\dfrac{4z}{z^2 + 6z + 5} - \dfrac{3}{z^2 + 5z + 4}$

34. $\dfrac{y}{y - 2} - \dfrac{y - 4}{2 - y}$

35. $\dfrac{4y - 1}{2y^2 + 5y - 3} - \dfrac{y + 3}{6y^2 + y - 2}$

36. $\dfrac{x + 1}{5x} + 2$

Simplify each complex fraction in Problems 37–40.

37. $\dfrac{\dfrac{1}{x}}{1 - \dfrac{1}{x}}$

38. $\dfrac{\dfrac{1}{x} - \dfrac{1}{2}}{\dfrac{1}{3} - \dfrac{x}{6}}$

39. $\dfrac{3 + \dfrac{12}{y}}{1 - \dfrac{16}{y^2}}$

40. $\dfrac{\dfrac{3}{5x^3} - \dfrac{1}{10x}}{\dfrac{3}{10x} + \dfrac{1}{x^2}}$

The rational expressions in Problems 41–51 involve several variables. Perform the indicated operations.

41. (Simplify) $\dfrac{2xy + 2xz}{3x^2y + 3x^2z}$

42. (Simplify) $\dfrac{8a^2 + 2a^2b^2}{b^2 + 4b + 4}$

43. $\dfrac{a^2 - 2ab + b^2}{a^2 - b^2} \cdot \dfrac{a^2 + ab}{3a^2b^2 - 3ab^3}$

44. $\dfrac{x^2 - y^2}{x - y} \div \dfrac{xy + x^2}{x + y}$

45. $\dfrac{4a^2 - 16b^2}{9} \div \dfrac{(a + 2b)^2}{12}$

46. $\dfrac{1}{4a} + \dfrac{6}{ab}$

47. $\dfrac{5}{3ab} - \dfrac{4}{a^2}$

48. $\dfrac{x + y}{y} - \dfrac{x - y}{x}$

49. $\dfrac{a - b}{ab} - \dfrac{c - b}{bc}$

50. $\dfrac{a + \dfrac{1}{b}}{b^2}$

51. $\dfrac{\dfrac{a}{3b} - \dfrac{1}{2}}{\dfrac{4}{3b} - \dfrac{2}{a}}$

Solve each equation in Problems 52–57.

52. $\dfrac{2}{x} = \dfrac{2}{3} + \dfrac{x}{6}$

53. $\dfrac{13}{y - 1} - 3 = \dfrac{1}{y - 1}$

54. $\dfrac{3}{4x} - \dfrac{1}{x} = \dfrac{1}{4}$

55. $\dfrac{5}{y + 2} + \dfrac{y}{y + 6} = \dfrac{24}{y^2 + 8y + 12}$

56. $3 - \dfrac{6}{y} = y + 8$

57. $4 - \dfrac{y}{y + 5} = \dfrac{5}{y + 5}$

58. In t years from 1990, the population of a community will be

$$P = 30 - \dfrac{9}{t + 1}$$

where P is expressed in thousands. When will the community have a population of 27 thousand?

59. A company that manufactures small canoes has determined that the average cost per canoe of producing x canoes is given by the rational function

$$f(x) = \dfrac{20x + 20,000}{x}.$$

a. Find the average cost per canoe when $x = 100$, 1000, and 10,000.

b. What appears to be happening to the cost of producing a canoe with increasingly higher production levels?

c. How many canoes must be produced to bring the average cost for producing a canoe down to $20.20?

60. In Silicon Valley, California, a government agency ordered computer-related companies to contribute to a monetary pool to clean up underground water supplies. (The companies had stored toxic chemicals in leaking underground containers.) The cost (C, in tens of thousands of dollars) for removing x percent of the contaminants is modeled by

$$C = \dfrac{200x}{100 - x}.$$

Solve for x, and then find the percent of contaminants that can be removed at a cost of $3,000,000. (*Hint:* Since C is measured in tens of thousands of dollars, $C = 300$.)

61. The dose of drugs for children can be modeled by

$$C = \frac{DA}{A + 12}$$

where C = child's dose, A = child's age, and D = adult dose. If a child takes 80 milligrams of Ibuprofen when the usual adult dose is 200 milligrams, what is the child's age?

62. Solve for A: $C = \frac{DA}{A + 12}$.

63. Solve for a: $\frac{1}{a} + \frac{1}{b} = \frac{1}{c}$.

64. The formula

$$t = \frac{A - P}{Pr}$$

describes the amount (A) that an investment (P) is worth after t years of simple interest at interest rate r. Solve the formula for P.

65. The denominator of a fraction is six more than the numerator. If 3 is added to both the numerator and denominator, the result is $\frac{2}{5}$. Find the original fraction.

66. The bar graph shows the number of African-American officials elected since the passage of the Voting Rights Act in 1965. The number of elected officials in 1993 exceeded the number in 1970 by 6515. If the number for 1993 is divided by the number for 1970, the partial quotient is 5 and the remainder is 639. Find the number of African-American officials elected in 1970 and 1993.

Growth of African-American Elected Officials

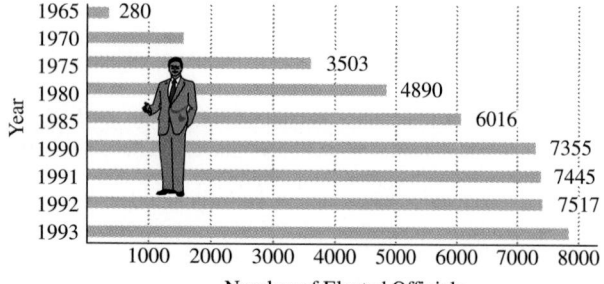

67. The current of a river is moving at 3 miles per hour. A boat can travel 11 miles with the river's current in the same time that it can travel 9 miles against the current. What is the speed of the boat in still water?

68. A painter can paint a fence around a house in 6 hours. Working alone, the painter's apprentice can paint the same fence in 12 hours. How many hours would it take them to do the job if they worked together?

69. One pipe can fill a hot tub in 8 minutes, a second can fill it in 12 minutes, and a third can fill it in 24 minutes. If the tub is empty, how long will it take all three pipes together to fill the hot tub?

70. A person's weekly pay (P) varies directly as the number of hours worked (H). For 15 hours of work, the weekly pay is $210.
  a. Find the constant of variation, and write the equation of variation that models this situation.
  b. Use the equation of variation to find the weekly pay for 40 hours of work.
  c. Graph the equation of variation in the first quadrant, with values of H (from 0 to 40) along the x-axis and values of P along the y-axis. What is the slope of the line? Describe what this means in terms of each additional hour worked.

71. An electric bill varies directly as the amount of electricity used. The bill for 1400 kilowatts of electricity is $98. What is the bill for 2200 kilowatts of electricity?

72. The current I flowing in an electrical circuit varies inversely as the resistance R in the circuit. When $R = 4$ ohms, then $I = 24$ amperes. What is the current I when the resistance is 6 ohms?

CHAPTER 8 TEST

1. List all numbers for which

$$\frac{x + 7}{x^2 + 5x - 36}$$

is undefined.

Simplify each rational expression in Problems 2–3.

2. $\dfrac{x^2 + 2x - 3}{x^2 - 3x + 2}$

3. $\dfrac{4y^2 - 20y}{y^2 - 4y - 5}$

In Problems 4–17, perform the indicated operations, and simplify if possible.

4. $\dfrac{x^2 - 16}{10} \cdot \dfrac{5}{x + 4}$

5. $\dfrac{y^2 - 7y + 12}{y^2 - 4y} \cdot \dfrac{y^2}{y^2 - 9}$

6. $\dfrac{2x + 8}{x - 3} \div \dfrac{x^2 + 5x + 4}{x^2 - 9}$

7. $\dfrac{5y + 5}{(y - 3)^2} \div \dfrac{y^2 - 1}{y - 3}$

8. $\dfrac{2y^2 + 5}{y + 3} + \dfrac{6y - 5}{y + 3}$

9. $\dfrac{y^2 - 2y + 3}{y^2 + 7y + 12} - \dfrac{y^2 - 4y - 5}{y^2 + 7y + 12}$

10. $\dfrac{x}{x + 3} + \dfrac{5}{x - 3}$

11. $\dfrac{2}{y^2 - 4y + 3} + \dfrac{6}{y^2 + y - 2}$

12. $\dfrac{4}{y - 3} + \dfrac{y + 5}{3 - y}$

13. $6 - \dfrac{3}{x - 3}$

14. $\dfrac{2y + 3}{y^2 - 7y + 12} - \dfrac{2}{y - 3}$

15. $\dfrac{8y}{y^2 - 16} - \dfrac{4}{y - 4}$

16. $\dfrac{(x - y)^2}{x + y} \div \dfrac{x^2 - xy}{3x + 3y}$

17. $\dfrac{a + 4b}{4b} - \dfrac{a + 2b}{2a}$

In Problems 18–19, simplify each complex fraction.

18. $\dfrac{5 + \dfrac{5}{x}}{2 + \dfrac{1}{x}}$

19. $\dfrac{\dfrac{1}{x} - \dfrac{1}{y}}{\dfrac{1}{x}}$

In Problems 20–22, solve each rational expression.

20. $\dfrac{5}{y} + \dfrac{2}{3} = 2 - \dfrac{2}{y} - \dfrac{1}{6}$

21. $\dfrac{3}{y + 5} - 1 = \dfrac{4 - y}{2y + 10}$

22. $\dfrac{2}{x - 1} = \dfrac{3}{x^2 - 1} + 1$

23. The formula

$$\dfrac{1}{t} = \dfrac{1}{a} + \dfrac{1}{b}$$

gives the total time (t) required for two workers working together to complete a job, if the workers' individual times are a and b. Solve the formula for t.

24. The formula

$$P = \dfrac{A}{1 + r}$$

describes the principal (P) that must be invested for one year at interest rate r (expressed as a decimal) to accumulate A dollars. If $12,000 is invested for one year, what must the interest rate be to have $12,840 in the account after one year? Express the interest rate in both decimal and percent notations.

25. According to the U.S. Fish and Wildlife Service, the number of endangered species of birds in the United States is 15 less than twice the number of endangered species of mammals. If the number of endangered species of birds is divided by the number of endangered species of mammals, the partial quotient is 1 and the remainder is 21. Find the number of endangered species of birds and mammals in the United States.

26. One pipe can fill a hot tub in 20 minutes and a second pipe can fill it in 30 minutes. If the hot tub is empty, how long will it take both pipes to fill it?

27. The pressure of water on an object below the surface varies directly as its distance below the surface. If a submarine experiences a pressure of 25 pounds per square inch 60 feet below the surface, how much pressure will it experience 330 feet below the surface?

28. The amount of current flowing in an electrical circuit varies inversely as the resistance in the circuit. When the resistance in a particular circuit is 5 ohms, the current is 42 amperes. What is the current when the resistance is 4 ohms?

CUMULATIVE REVIEW PROBLEMS (CHAPTERS 1–8)

1. Name the property illustrated by each equation.
   a. $8 + (7 + 3) = (8 + 7) + 3$
   b. $-3(5 + 9) = (-3) \cdot 5 + (-3) \cdot 9$
   c. $5(3 + 4) = 5(4 + 3)$

2. Solve and graph the solution set on a number line: $2x + 3 < 3(x - 5)$.

3. Seven subtracted from six times a number is 175. Find the number.

4. Graph: $3x - 4y < 12$.

5. The coldest city in the United States is International Falls, Minnesota, and the warmest city is Key West, Florida. The average temperature in Key West (in degrees Fahrenheit) is 6° more than twice that of International Falls. If the average yearly temperatures of the two cities are averaged, the resulting temperature is 57°. Find the average yearly temperatures for America's coldest and warmest cities.

6. Factor completely: $3x^2 - 15x - 42$.

7. A circle whose radius is 3 inches has its radius doubled. How does the area of the larger circle compare to that of the smaller circle?

8. The length of a rectangular floor is 1 yard more than 3 times the width. If the area of the floor is 14 square yards, find the length and width.

9. Factor completely: $2x^3 - 20x^2 + 50x$.

10. Find the quotient: $\dfrac{x^2 + 2x - 12}{x - 3}$.

11. Simplify: $\left(\dfrac{4x^5}{2x^2}\right)^3$.

12. Solve the system:
$$5x + 2y = -1$$
$$2x - 5y = 1$$

13. The function $f(x) = -0.17x^3 + 6.8x^2 + 536x$ models the number of limes produced, $f(x)$, on an acre with x lime trees. Find and interpret $f(10)$.

14. Write the point-slope equation of the line passing through $(1, -5)$ and $(-2, 10)$. Then use the point-slope equation to write the slope-intercept form of the line.

15. A model rocket is propelled into the air at an initial speed of 80 feet per second. The height of the rocket above the ground is a function of the time (t, in seconds) that the rocket is in flight, given by the polynomial function $f(t) = -16t^2 + 80t$. Find and interpret $f(0)$, $f(1)$, $f(2)$, $f(2.5)$, $f(3)$, $f(4)$, and $f(5)$. Use these values and point-plotting to graph the function.

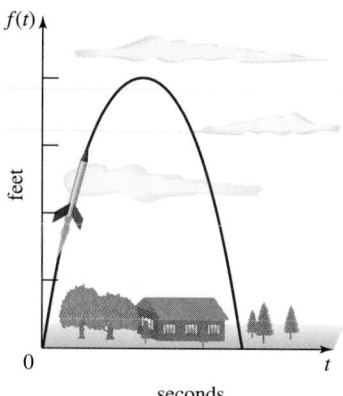

16. The graph reflects fear of crime in ten selected countries. The percentage of people feeling unsafe in their neighborhoods after dark in the United States exceeds twice that of Sweden by 14%. In the two countries combined, 54.5% of the public feel unsafe walking in their neighborhood after dark. Find the exact percent for Sweden and the United States. Then use the graph to obtain a reasonable estimate for the percent for the remaining eight countries.

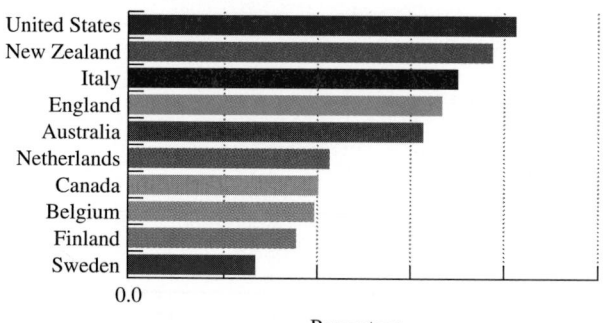

Percentage of the Public Feeling Unsafe when Walking in Their Own Area after Dark

Source: Van Dijk, Jan J. M. (November 1992), *Criminal Victimisation in the Industrialized World*, pp. 10, 24, 33, 57, The Netherlands: Ministry of Justice

17. Until 1991, the lives of South Africa's ethnic groups were controlled by apartheid, the system of racial segregation imposed by the white minority. The white minority's population is 5.32 million. Use the circle graph to determine South Africa's total population. Then determine the population for each of the groups in the other three sectors.

South Africa's Ethnic Makeup

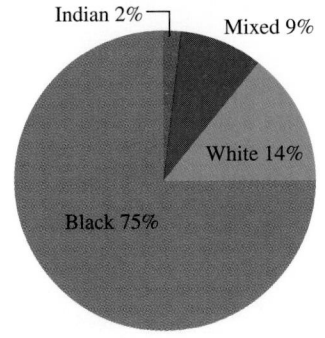

Indian 2%
Mixed 9%
White 14%
Black 75%

18. A sailboat with a triangular sail has an area of 33 square feet and a base that is 11 feet long. Find the height of the sail.

19. Solve: $2 - 3(x - 2) = 5(x + 5) - 1$.

20. Solve by graphing:

$$2x + y = 4$$
$$x + y = 2$$

21. If five cassettes and two compact discs cost $65, and three cassettes and four compact discs cost $81, find the price of each.

22. The hypotenuse of a right triangle is 1 meter longer than twice the shorter leg. The longer leg exceeds the shorter leg by 7 meters. Find the lengths of the sides of the triangle.

23. Solve: $x + \dfrac{12}{x} = -7$.

24. Subtract: $\dfrac{y}{y^2 + 5y + 6} - \dfrac{2}{y^2 + 3y + 2}$.

25. The square lawn shown in the figure at the top on the right is to be expanded so that each side is increased by the same amount, represented by x.
  a. Write a trinomial that describes the area of the expanded lawn.
  b. Write the expression in part (a) as a polynomial function, calling the function f.
  c. Find and interpret $f(5)$.

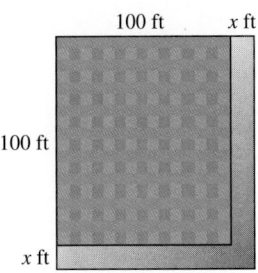

100 ft x ft

100 ft

x ft

26. A boat can travel 240 miles with a current of 5 miles per hour in the same time that it can travel 160 miles against the current. Find the rate of the boat in still water.

27. A simplified form of an income model for American men indicates that yearly income increases by $1600 for each year of education, with a zero-education income of $6300 yearly. Using this model, how many years of education are needed to earn $25,500 per year?

28. Perform the indicated operations with the numbers in scientific notation, and then write the answer in decimal notation.

$$\frac{9 \times 10^{-4}}{3 \times 10^{-6}}$$

29. To earn an A in a course, a student must have a final average of at least 90%. On the first four exams, a student has scores of 80%, 96%, 88%, and 92%. What must the student get on the fifth exam to earn an A in the course?

30. A condominium was purchased in 1980 for $26,000. Using the consumer price index, estimate its value (to the nearest dollar) in 1994.

Year	Consumer Price Index
1980	82.4
1994	148.2

9

Roots and Radicals

Jean Metzinger "At the Cycle Race-Track" (Au Velodrome) 1914, oil with sand on canvas, $40\frac{9}{16} \times 38\frac{1}{4}$ in. Solomon R. Guggenheim Museum, New York. Photo by David Heald © The Solomon R. Guggenheim Foundation, New York. FN 76.2553 PG18. ©1998 Artists Rights Society (ARS), New York/ADAGP, Paris.

What is the maximum velocity that a racing cyclist can turn a corner without tipping over? The answer is provided by the mathematical model $v = 4\sqrt{r}$, where v is the maximum velocity in miles per hour and r is the radius of the corner, in feet.

Mathematical models containing roots describe phenomena as diverse as the evaporation that takes place on the surface of a large body of water, the plant species on the Galápagos chain of islands, a wild animal's territorial area, and Einstein's concept of relative time. In this chapter we study roots and radicals, further expanding our mathematical description of the physical world.

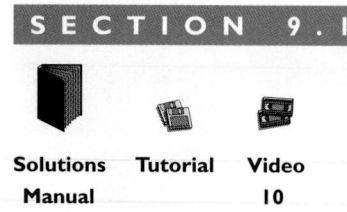

Solutions   Tutorial   Video
Manual   10

Finding Roots

Objectives

1 Find square roots of numbers.
2 Evaluate expressions containing square roots.
3 Use a calculator to find decimal approximations for irrational square roots.
4 Find higher roots of numbers.

| Find square roots of numbers.

In this introductory section, we develop a notation that takes us from a number raised to a power back to the number itself. Squaring and cubing numbers are reversed by taking their square roots and cube roots. We also look at applied mathematical models that contain these roots.

From our earlier work with exponents, we are aware that

$$5^2 = 25 \quad \text{and} \quad (-5)^2 = 25. \qquad \text{The square of both 5 and } -5 \text{ is 25.}$$

We now consider the reverse problem: What number(s) must we square to obtain 25? Since the square of 5 is 25, we say that 5 is a *square root* of 25. Since the square of -5 is also 25, we say that -5 is a *square root* of 25. The square roots of 25 are 5 and -5 since the square of both is 25.

Notice that every positive number has two square roots, one positive and one negative. The positive square root of 36 is 6 because $6^2 = 36$. The negative square root of 36 is -6 because $(-6)^2 = 36$. Finding the square root of a number requires finding another number that when multiplied by itself results in the first number.

> ### Definition of square root
>
> If $b^2 = a$, then b is called a *square root* of a (a is a nonnegative real number and b is a real number).

EXAMPLE I   **Finding Square Roots of Numbers**

Find all square roots: **a.** 64   **b.** 0   **c.** $\frac{9}{16}$ **d.** -4

Solution

a. There are two numbers that can be multiplied by themselves to obtain 64. Consequently, 64 has two square roots.

| Positive square root of $64 = 8$ | Check: $8^2 = 64$ |
| Negative square root of $64 = -8$ | Check: $(-8)^2 = 64$ |

b. There is only one number that can be multiplied by itself to obtain 0, namely, 0. Consequently, 0 has only one square root, the number 0.

c. There are two numbers that can be multiplied by themselves to obtain $\frac{9}{16}$.

| Positive square root of $\frac{9}{16} = \frac{3}{4}$ | Check: $(\frac{3}{4})^2 = \frac{9}{16}$ |
| Negative square root of $\frac{9}{16} = -\frac{3}{4}$ | Check: $(-\frac{3}{4})^2 = \frac{9}{16}$ |

d. There is no real number that can be multiplied by itself to obtain -4. This means that -4 has no square root within the real number system.

2 Evaluate expressions containing square roots.

Radicals

The positive square root of a number, also called the *principal square root,* is written with the radical sign, $\sqrt{}$. For example, the positive or principal square root of 36 is 6, written $\sqrt{36} = 6$. The negative square root of a number is written with the symbol $-\sqrt{}$. For example, the negative square root of 36 is -6, written $-\sqrt{36} = -6$. The number under the radical sign, in this case 36, is called the *radicand.* The entire symbol $\sqrt{36}$ is called a *radical.*

EXAMPLE 2 **Evaluating Expressions Containing Radicals**

Evaluate:

a. $\sqrt{100}$ **b.** $-\sqrt{49}$ **c.** $\sqrt{\dfrac{1}{4}}$ **d.** $\sqrt{9 + 16}$ **e.** $\sqrt{9} + \sqrt{16}$

Solution

a. $\sqrt{100} = 10$
The positive square root of 100 is 10.
Check: $10^2 = 100$.

b. $-\sqrt{49} = -7$
The negative square root of 49 is -7.
Check: $(-7)^2 = 49$.

c. $\sqrt{\dfrac{1}{4}} = \dfrac{1}{2}$
The positive square root of $\frac{1}{4}$ is $\frac{1}{2}$.
Check: $(\frac{1}{2})^2 = \frac{1}{4}$.

d. $\sqrt{9 + 16} = \sqrt{25}$
$\qquad\qquad\quad = 5$
First simplify the expression under the radical sign. Then take the positive square root of 25, which is 5.

e. $\sqrt{9} + \sqrt{16} = 3 + 4$ $\quad \sqrt{9} = 3$ because $3^2 = 9$.
$\qquad\qquad\qquad = 7$ $\qquad \sqrt{16} = 4$ because $4^2 = 16$.

EXAMPLE 3 **An Application: A Mathematical Model Containing a Radical**

The amount of evaporation, in inches per day, of a large body of water can be modeled by the formula

$$E = \frac{w}{20\sqrt{a}}$$

where $\quad a =$ surface area of the water in square miles
$\qquad\quad w =$ average wind speed of the air over the water, in miles per hour
$\qquad\quad E =$ evaporation, in inches per day

Determine the evaporation on a lake whose surface area is 9 square miles on a day when the wind speed over the water is 10 miles per hour. (See Figure 9.1.)

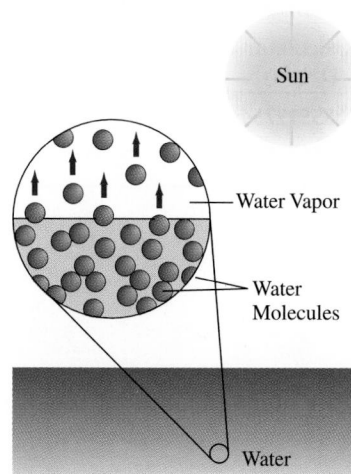

Figure 9.1

Evaporation occurs when the sun's heat causes the lake's water molecules to gain enough energy to escape from the lake.

Solution

$$E = \frac{w}{20\sqrt{a}} \qquad \text{This is the given formula.}$$

$$E = \frac{10}{20\sqrt{9}} \qquad \begin{array}{l}\text{Substitute the given values:}\\ w \text{ (wind speed)} = 10 \text{ miles per hour}\\ a \text{ (area)} = 9 \text{ square miles.}\end{array}$$

$$E = \frac{10}{20 \cdot 3} \qquad \sqrt{9} = 3 \text{ because } 3^2 = 9.$$

$$= \frac{1}{6} \qquad \frac{\overset{1}{\cancel{10}}}{20 \cdot 3} = \frac{1}{6}$$

The evaporation is $\frac{1}{6}$ of an inch on that day. ■

3 Use a calculator to find decimal approximations for irrational square roots.

Irrational Numbers

All numbers considered so far have rational square roots and are called *perfect squares*. For example, $\sqrt{121} = 11$, so 121 is a perfect square. A number that is not a perfect square has a square root that is not a rational number. For example, the numbers $\sqrt{2}, \sqrt{3}, \sqrt{5}, \sqrt{6}$, and $\sqrt{7}$ are not rational numbers and cannot be written as the ratio of two integers. However, $\sqrt{2}, \sqrt{3}, \sqrt{5}, \sqrt{6}$, and $\sqrt{7}$ correspond to points on the number line and represent irrational numbers.

> If a is a positive number that is not a perfect square, then $\sqrt{a}$ is an irrational number.

In applied situations, we frequently need decimal approximations for square roots. On graphing calculators the key that accomplishes this is labeled $\sqrt{}$. Table 9.1 indicates the keystrokes for finding decimal approximations of square roots.

TABLE 9.1 Decimal Approximations of Some Square Roots

Square Root	Keystrokes	Calculator Display	Rounded Answer
$\sqrt{13}$	$\boxed{\sqrt{}}$ $\boxed{13}$ $\boxed{\text{ENTER}}$	3.60555127546	3.606
$-\sqrt{14}$	$\boxed{(-)}$ $\boxed{\sqrt{}}$ $\boxed{14}$ $\boxed{\text{ENTER}}$	-3.74165738677	-3.742

We can use our graphing calculator to obtain a table of values for the *square root function*

$$f(x) = \sqrt{x} \quad \text{or} \quad y = \sqrt{x}.$$

x	0	1	2	3	4	5	6	7	8	9
$y = \sqrt{x}$	0	1	1.4	1.7	2	2.2	2.4	2.6	2.8	3

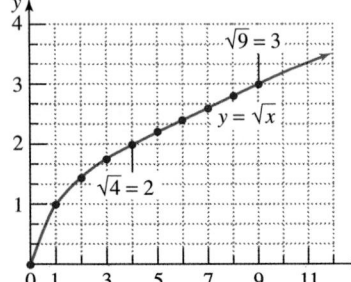

Figure 9.2

The graph of $y = \sqrt{x}$

Plotting the 10 points and connecting them with a smooth curve gives the graph of the square root function $y = \sqrt{x}$, shown in Figure 9.2.

Our graph in Figure 9.2 indicates that only real numbers greater than or equal to zero have real number square roots. Notice, for example, that there is no graph shown above -1 on the x-axis. This is because there is no real number that can be squared to get -1.

> The square of a real number can never be negative. Thus, if a is a negative number, then $\sqrt{a}$ is not a real number.

For example, $\sqrt{25} = 5$ and $-\sqrt{25} = -5$, but $\sqrt{-25}$ is not a real number.

Karen Furth

4 Find higher roots of numbers.

EXAMPLE 4 An Application: A Mathematical Model Containing Radicals

The annual rate of return (r) on an investment of P dollars that grows to A dollars over a 2-year time period is given by the model

$$r = \frac{\sqrt{A} - \sqrt{P}}{\sqrt{P}}.$$

If a collector of hard-to-find Broadway cast albums spent \$50 on the cast album of *Greenwillow* (Anthony Perkins' only musical), selling the album 2 years later for \$65, what was the annual rate of return (to the nearest whole percent)?

Solution

$$r = \frac{\sqrt{A} - \sqrt{P}}{\sqrt{P}}$$ This is the given formula.

$$= \frac{\sqrt{65} - \sqrt{50}}{\sqrt{50}}$$ We are given that $A = 65$ and $P = 50$.

$$\approx 0.14018$$ Use a calculator to obtain a decimal approximation.

$$r \approx 14\%$$

The annual rate of return is approximately 14%.

Roots Greater Than Square Roots

Finding the square root of a number reverses the process of squaring a number. In a similar way, finding the cube root of a number reverses the process of cubing a number. For example, $2^3 = 8$, and so the cube root of 8 is 2. The notation that we use is $\sqrt[3]{8} = 2$.

Table 9.2 shows how various roots reverse raising numbers to powers.

TABLE 9.2 Reversing *n*th Powers with *n*th Roots			
	Powers	**Roots**	**Vocabulary**
Cube Roots	$4^3 = 64$	$\sqrt[3]{64} = 4$	3 is the index
	$(-2)^3 = -8$	$\sqrt[3]{-8} = -2$	of the radical.
	$5^3 = 125$	$\sqrt[3]{125} = 5$	
Fourth Roots	$1^4 = 1$	$\sqrt[4]{1} = 1$	Index = 4
	$3^4 = 81$	$\sqrt[4]{81} = 3$	
Fifth Roots	$2^5 = 32$	$\sqrt[5]{32} = 2$	Index = 5
nth Roots	$b^n = a$	$\sqrt[n]{a} = b$	Index = *n*

EXAMPLE 5   **Finding Higher Roots**

Find the root:

a. $\sqrt[3]{27}$ **b.** $\sqrt[3]{-1}$ **c.** $\sqrt[4]{16}$ **d.** $-\sqrt[4]{16}$ **e.** $\sqrt[4]{-16}$

f. $\sqrt[5]{-32}$

U sing technology

Consult your graphing calculator manual for the location of the root ($\sqrt[x]{\ }$) key. Then verify each part of Example 5.
Example 5a: $\sqrt[3]{27}$

3 $\boxed{\sqrt[x]{\ }}$ 27 $\boxed{\text{ENTER}}$

Solution

a. $\sqrt[3]{27} = 3$ Find a number that when cubed gives 27. The cube root of 27 is 3 because $3^3 = 27$.

b. $\sqrt[3]{-1} = -1$ Find a number that when cubed gives -1. The cube root of -1 is -1 because $(-1)^3 = -1$.

c. $\sqrt[4]{16} = 2$ Find a number that when raised to the fourth power gives 16. There are two numbers: $2^4 = 16$ and $(-2)^4 = 16$. The symbol $\sqrt[4]{\ }$ calls for the *positive* fourth root.

d. $-\sqrt[4]{16} = -2$ Find a number that when raised to the fourth power gives 16. Both $2^4 = 16$ and $(-2)^4 = 16$. The symbol $-\sqrt[4]{\ }$ calls for the *negative* fourth root.

e. $\sqrt[4]{-16}$ is not a real number.   Find a number that when raised to the fourth power gives -16. No real number equals $\sqrt[4]{-16}$ because any real number raised to the fourth power cannot result in a negative number.

f. $\sqrt[5]{-32} = -2$ Find a real number that when raised to the fifth power gives -32. The fifth root of -32 is -2 because $(-2)^5 = -32$. ∎

PROBLEM SET 9.1

Practice Problems _____

Find all square roots of each number in Problems 1–8.

1. 36   **2.** 81   **3.** 144   **4.** 121   **5.** $\frac{9}{16}$ **6.** $\frac{25}{4}$ **7.** $\frac{49}{100}$ **8.** $\frac{1}{900}$

Evaluate each expression in Problems 9–32, if possible.

9. $\sqrt{36}$ **10.** $\sqrt{144}$ **11.** $-\sqrt{36}$ **12.** $-\sqrt{144}$ **13.** $\sqrt{-36}$

14. $\sqrt{-144}$ **15.** $\sqrt{\frac{1}{25}}$ **16.** $\sqrt{\frac{1}{81}}$ **17.** $\sqrt{\frac{49}{25}}$ **18.** $\sqrt{\frac{36}{81}}$

19. $-\sqrt{\frac{1}{9}}$ **20.** $-\sqrt{\frac{1}{144}}$ **21.** $-\sqrt{\frac{49}{100}}$ **22.** $-\sqrt{\frac{64}{121}}$

23. $\sqrt{0.04}$ **24.** $\sqrt{0.64}$ **25.** $\sqrt{33-8}$ **26.** $\sqrt{51+13}$ **27.** $\sqrt{2\cdot32}$

28. $\sqrt{\frac{75}{3}}$ **29.** $\sqrt{144+25}$ **30.** $\sqrt{25-16}$ **31.** $\sqrt{144}+\sqrt{25}$ **32.** $\sqrt{25}-\sqrt{16}$

Indicate whether each square root in Problems 33–54 is a rational number, an irrational number, or not a real number. Give the exact value for each rational number. If the number is irrational, use a calculator to give a decimal approximation, rounded to the nearest thousandth.

33. $\sqrt{\frac{1}{225}}$ **34.** $\sqrt{0.09}$ **35.** $\sqrt{15}$ **36.** $\sqrt{32}$

37. $\sqrt{400}$ **38.** $\sqrt{900}$ **39.** $-\sqrt{225}$ **40.** $-\sqrt{144}$

41. $\sqrt{-1}$ **42.** $-\sqrt{65}$ **43.** $-\sqrt{83}$ **44.** $\sqrt{-4}$

45. $\sqrt{573}$ **46.** $\sqrt{632}$ **47.** $-\sqrt{1369}$ **48.** $-\sqrt{2304}$

49. $\dfrac{9+\sqrt{144}}{3}$ **50.** $\dfrac{7+\sqrt{289}}{12}$ **51.** $\dfrac{12+\sqrt{45}}{2}$

52. $\dfrac{-3+\sqrt{32.2}}{5}$ **53.** $\dfrac{12+\sqrt{-45}}{2}$ **54.** $\dfrac{-3+\sqrt{-32.3}}{5}$

Find the roots or indicate that the root is not a real number in Problems 55–78.

55. $\sqrt[4]{1}$ **56.** $\sqrt[5]{1}$ **57.** $\sqrt[3]{64}$ **58.** $\sqrt[3]{27}$ **59.** $\sqrt[3]{-27}$

60. $\sqrt[3]{-64}$ **61.** $\sqrt[3]{125}$ **62.** $\sqrt[3]{216}$ **63.** $\sqrt[4]{16}$ **64.** $\sqrt[4]{81}$

65. $-\sqrt[4]{81}$ **66.** $-\sqrt[4]{16}$ **67.** $\sqrt[4]{-81}$ **68.** $\sqrt[4]{-16}$ **69.** $\sqrt[4]{256}$

70. $\sqrt[4]{625}$ **71.** $\sqrt[5]{-32}$ **72.** $\sqrt[5]{-243}$ **73.** $\sqrt[3]{\sqrt[3]{64}}$ **74.** $\sqrt[3]{-\sqrt[3]{1}}$

75. $\sqrt[3]{\frac{8}{27}}$ **76.** $\sqrt[3]{\frac{64}{125}}$ **77.** $\sqrt[3]{\frac{-1}{64}}$ **78.** $\sqrt[3]{\frac{-1}{216}}$

79. Graph $y=\sqrt{x-1}$ by filling in the table of values, plotting the resulting five points, and connecting them with a smooth curve.

x	1	2	5	10	17
$y=\sqrt{x-1}$					

   a. For what values of x is $y=\sqrt{x-1}$ defined? How is this shown by your graph?

   b. If applicable, use a graphing utility to verify your hand-drawn graph.

80. Graph $y=\sqrt{x+2}$ by filling in the table of values in the next column, plotting the resulting five points, and connecting them with a smooth curve.

x	-2	-1	2	7	14
$y=\sqrt{x+2}$					

a. For what values of x is $y=\sqrt{x+2}$ defined? How is this shown by your graph?

b. If you also graphed the function in Problem 79, describe one similarity and one difference between the graphs of $y=\sqrt{x-1}$ and $y=\sqrt{x+2}$.

c. If applicable, use a graphing utility to verify your hand-drawn graph.

Application Problems

81. Racing cyclists use the model $v=4\sqrt{r}$ to determine the maximum velocity (v, in miles per hour) to turn a corner of radius r feet without tipping over. What is the maximum velocity that a cyclist should travel around a corner of radius 9 feet without tipping over?

82. Police use the model $v=4.9\sqrt{L}$ to estimate the speed of a car (v, in miles per hour) based on the length (L, in feet) of its skid marks on dry pavement. What is a reasonable estimate for a car's speed if skid marks measure 225 feet?

83. The approximate time (t, in seconds) that it takes an object to fall a distance (d, in feet) under the influence of gravity is given by the mathematical model $t=\sqrt{\dfrac{d}{16}}$. Find the time it takes an object to fall 144 feet.

84. The velocity (v, in feet per second) of an object dropped from a tall building after falling d feet is given by $v=\sqrt{64d}$. What is the velocity of an object that has fallen 100 feet?

85. The formula $H = (10.45 + \sqrt{100W} - W)(33 - t)$ describes the rate of heat loss (H, measured in kilocalories per square meter per hour) when the air temperature is t degrees Celsius and the wind speed is W meters per second. When H is 200 kilocalories per square meter per hour, exposed flesh will freeze in 1 minute. Will this occur when the wind is blowing at 4 meters per second and the temperature is 0°C?

86. A bamboo plant has its height (h, in inches) given by $h = 3\sqrt{t} - 0.23t$, where t is measured in weeks after the plant comes through the soil. What is the height of the bamboo 9 weeks after breaking through the soil?

True–False Critical Thinking Problems

87. Which one of the following is true?

a. $\sqrt{9} + \sqrt{16} = \sqrt{25}$

b. $\dfrac{\sqrt{64}}{2} = \sqrt{32}$

c. $\sqrt[3]{-27}$ is not a real number.

d. $\sqrt{\dfrac{1}{4}} + \sqrt{\dfrac{1}{9}} = \sqrt{\dfrac{25}{36}}$

88. Which one of the following is true?

a. $\sqrt{-144} = -12$

b. $\sqrt{9} \cdot \sqrt{9} = 3$

c. Every real number has two square roots, the positive or principal square root, and the negative square root, written $-\sqrt{}$.

d. $\sqrt{2^6}$ and 2^3 are not equal.

Technology Problems

When an airplane is x feet high, the distance (d, in miles) that can be seen on a clear day from the plane to the horizon is $d = 1.22\sqrt{x}$. Use a calculator to determine how far one can see to the horizon in a plane flying at the altitudes given in Problems 89–90. Round answers to the nearest hundredth.

89. 25,000 feet

90. 30,000 feet

Use the following information to answer Problems 91–92. The annual rate of return (r) on an investment of P dollars that grows to A dollars over a 2-year time period is given by

$$r = \frac{\sqrt{A} - \sqrt{P}}{\sqrt{P}}.$$

91. Find the annual rate of return on an $800 investment in stocks that 2 years later are worth $900.

92. Find the annual rate of return on a $500 investment in stocks that 2 years later are worth $800.

93. Use a graphing utility to graph $y_1 = \sqrt{x + 4}$, $y_2 = \sqrt{x}$, and $y_3 = \sqrt{x - 3}$ in the same viewing rectangle. Use the following range setting:

Xmin $= -5$, Xmax $= 10$, Xscl $= 1$,
Ymin $= 0$, Ymax $= 6$, Yscl $= 1$

Describe one similarity and one difference that you observe among the graphs. Use the word "shift" in your response.

94. Use a graphing utility to graph $y_1 = \sqrt{x} + 4$, $y_2 = \sqrt{x}$, and $y_3 = \sqrt{x} - 3$ in the same viewing rectangle. Use the following range setting:

Xmin $= -1$, Xmax $= 10$, Xscl $= 1$,
Ymin $= -10$, Ymax $= 10$, Yscl $= 1$

Describe one similarity and one difference that you observe among the graphs.

95. The maximum velocity for a cyclist to turn a corner without tipping over is given by the model $v = 4\sqrt{r}$, where $r = $ the radius of the corner in feet and $v = $ the maximum velocity in miles per hour. Use a graphing utility to graph the function $(y = 4\sqrt{x})$ with the following range setting:

Xmin $= 0$, Xmax $= 100$, Xscl $= 10$,
Ymin $= 0$, Ymax $= 40$, Yscl $= 1$

Then $\boxed{\text{TRACE}}$ along the curve to determine the maximum velocity for a radius of 50 feet.

In Problems 96–99, use a graphing utility to determine if the given equation is true for all values of x resulting in a real number square root. Do this by graphing the functions on both sides of the equation on the same screen.

96. $\sqrt{x + 4} = \sqrt{x} + 2$ **97.** $\sqrt{4x} = 2\sqrt{x}$ **98.** $\sqrt{x - 4} = \sqrt{x} - 2$ **99.** $\sqrt{\dfrac{x}{4}} = \dfrac{\sqrt{x}}{2}$

100. Write a statement summarizing the results in Problems 96–99.

Writing in Mathematics

101. Pulse rate (P) in beats per minute is a function of height (h, in inches) given by $P = \dfrac{600}{\sqrt{h}}$. Actually, P is *approximately* equal to $\dfrac{600}{\sqrt{h}}$ $\left(P \approx \dfrac{600}{\sqrt{h}}\right)$, so that

pulse rate can be more than just a function of height. What other factors can you think of that are not taken into account by the given mathematical model?

102. Write a word problem using the formula described below. Then solve the problem.

Users	Description	The Formula
Hikers, mountain climbers	The distance that can be seen to the horizon from a given height	$d = \sqrt{1.5h}$ h = height of the observer, in feet d = distance the observer can see, in miles

103. Why is it that the square root of a negative number is not a real number?

Critical Thinking Problems

104. Simplify: $\sqrt{\sqrt{16}} - \sqrt[3]{\sqrt{64}}$.

105. Between what two consecutive integers is $-\sqrt{47}$?

106. If $x \uparrow y$ means x^y and $x \downarrow y$ means $\sqrt[y]{x}$, find the value of $[(4 \uparrow 4) \downarrow 2] \uparrow 3$.

Review Problems

107. Graph: $4x - 5y = 20$.

108. Divide: $\dfrac{1}{x^2 - 17x + 30} \div \dfrac{1}{x^2 + 7x - 18}$.

109. Solve and graph the solution on a number line: $2(x - 3) > 4x + 10$.

SECTION 9 . 2

Solutions Manual   **Tutorial**   **Video 10**

Multiplying and Dividing Radicals

Objectives

1 Multiply radicals.
2 Simplify radicals using the product rule.
3 Simplify radicals that involve quotients.
4 Divide radicals.

In this section, two rules for multiplying and dividing radicals are presented.

The Product Rule for Radicals

A rule for multiplying radicals can be generalized by comparing $\sqrt{25} \cdot \sqrt{4}$ and $\sqrt{25 \cdot 4}$. Notice that

$$\sqrt{25} \cdot \sqrt{4} = 5 \cdot 2 = 10 \quad \text{and} \quad \sqrt{25 \cdot 4} = \sqrt{100} = 10.$$

Since we obtain 10 in both situations, the original radical expressions must be equal. That is,

$$\sqrt{25} \cdot \sqrt{4} = \sqrt{25 \cdot 4}.$$

This result is a special case of the *product rule for radicals* that can be generalized as follows.

> ### The product rule for radicals
>
> If x and y represent nonnegative real numbers, then
>
> $$\sqrt{x} \cdot \sqrt{y} = \sqrt{xy}.$$
>
> The square root of a product is the product of the square roots.

| Multiply radicals.

EXAMPLE I   **Using the Product Rule to Multiply Square Roots**

Use the product rule for radicals to find each product.

a. $\sqrt{2} \cdot \sqrt{5}$ **b.** $\sqrt{7x} \cdot \sqrt{11y}$ **c.** $\sqrt{7} \cdot \sqrt{7}$ **d.** $\sqrt{\dfrac{2}{5}} \cdot \sqrt{\dfrac{3}{7}}$

Solution

a. $\sqrt{2} \cdot \sqrt{5} = \sqrt{2 \cdot 5} = \sqrt{10}$

b. $\sqrt{7x} \cdot \sqrt{11y} = \sqrt{7x \cdot 11y} = \sqrt{77xy}$ Assuming $x \geq 0$ and $y \geq 0$.

c. $\sqrt{7} \cdot \sqrt{7} = \sqrt{7 \cdot 7} = \sqrt{49} = 7$ Equivalently: $(\sqrt{7})^2 = 7$.

d. $\sqrt{\dfrac{2}{5}} \cdot \sqrt{\dfrac{3}{7}} = \sqrt{\dfrac{2}{5} \cdot \dfrac{3}{7}} = \sqrt{\dfrac{6}{35}}$ ∎

2 Simplify radicals using the product rule.

Simplifying Radicals

The product rule for radicals can be used to simplify radical expressions. Simplified square root expressions contain no factors that are perfect squares under the radical sign. Simplification of radicals involves the use of the product rule in the form

$$\sqrt{xy} = \sqrt{x}\sqrt{y}.$$

We can use the product rule to simplify a radicand that is not a perfect square but has a perfect square factor, such as $\sqrt{18}$. The largest perfect square factor of 18 is 9, so we write 18 as $9 \cdot 2$.

$$\sqrt{18} = \sqrt{9 \cdot 2} = \sqrt{9}\sqrt{2} = 3\sqrt{2}$$

Thus, $\sqrt{18} = 3\sqrt{2}$. Because 2 has no perfect square factor other than 1, the expression $3\sqrt{2}$ is the simplified form of $\sqrt{18}$.

> **∫tudy tip**
>
> When simplifying square root expressions, always look for the largest perfect square factor possible. The following factorization is not useful
>
> $$\sqrt{18} = \sqrt{6 \cdot 3} = \sqrt{6}\sqrt{3}$$
>
> because 6 and 3 are not perfect squares.

EXAMPLE 2   **Using the Product Rule to Simplify Square Roots**

Simplify: **a.** $\sqrt{75}$ **b.** $\sqrt{500t}$ **c.** $\sqrt{17}$

Solution

a. $\sqrt{75} = \sqrt{25 \cdot 3}$ 25 is the largest perfect square that is a factor of 75.

$\qquad = \sqrt{25}\sqrt{3}$ $\sqrt{xy} = \sqrt{x}\sqrt{y}$

$\qquad = 5\sqrt{3}$ $\sqrt{25} = 5$

b. $\sqrt{500t} = \sqrt{100 \cdot 5t}$ 100 is the largest perfect square factor of 500.

$\qquad = \sqrt{100}\sqrt{5t}$ $\sqrt{xy} = \sqrt{x}\sqrt{y}$

$\qquad = 10\sqrt{5t}$ $\sqrt{100} = 10$

c. $\sqrt{17}$ has no perfect square factors (other than 1), which means $\sqrt{17}$ cannot be simplified. ■

Simplifying and Multiplying

When multiplying radicals with constant radicands, if possible you should first attempt to simplify the radicals and then multiply. If you multiply first and then attempt to simplify, rather large numbers whose perfect square factors are not obvious may result. (Note the larger numbers in the column on the right in the Study Tip.)

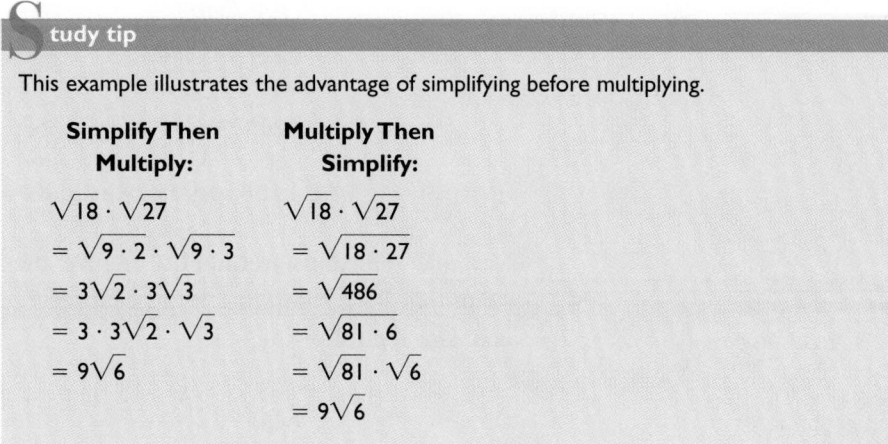

We use the following procedure to multiply radicals.

Multiplying radicals

1. If possible, simplify the radicals.
2. Multiply the radicals using $\sqrt{x}\sqrt{y} = \sqrt{xy}$.
3. If possible, simplify again after multiplying.

EXAMPLE 3   **Simplifying and Then Multiplying Square Roots**

Multiply: $\sqrt{12} \cdot \sqrt{32}$

Solution

$$\sqrt{12} \cdot \sqrt{32} = \sqrt{4 \cdot 3} \cdot \sqrt{16 \cdot 2} \qquad \text{4 is the largest perfect square factor of 12, and 16 is the largest perfect square factor of 32.}$$

$$= 2\sqrt{3} \cdot 4\sqrt{2} \qquad \text{Simplify each radical.}$$

$$= 2 \cdot 4\sqrt{3}\sqrt{2} \qquad \text{Rearrange factors. This step is usually done mentally.}$$

$$= 8\sqrt{6} \qquad \text{Multiply the radicals' coefficients and the radicals.}$$

■

EXAMPLE 4 **Simplifying and Then Multiplying Square Roots**

Multiply: $\sqrt{80a} \cdot \sqrt{15b}$

Solution

$$\sqrt{80a} \cdot \sqrt{15b} = \sqrt{16 \cdot 5a} \cdot \sqrt{15b} \qquad \text{The largest perfect square factor of 80 is 16.}$$

$$= 4\sqrt{5a} \cdot \sqrt{15b} \qquad \text{Simplify the first radical.}$$

$$= 4\sqrt{5 \cdot 15ab} \qquad \sqrt{x}\sqrt{y} = \sqrt{xy}$$

$$= 4\sqrt{75ab} \qquad \text{Now simplify } \sqrt{75}.$$

$$= 4\sqrt{25 \cdot 3ab} \qquad \text{The largest perfect square factor of 75 is 25.}$$

$$= 4 \cdot 5\sqrt{3ab} \qquad \text{Simplify.}$$

$$= 20\sqrt{3ab} \qquad \text{Multiply.}$$

■

Simplifying and Multiplying Radicals with Variable Factors

Variable radicands frequently involve the square root of $x^2 \colon \sqrt{x^2}$. It may seem that $\sqrt{x^2}$ simplifies as x because $x \cdot x = x^2$. However, consider the following: If

$$x = 4 \quad \text{then} \quad \sqrt{x^2} = \sqrt{4^2} = \sqrt{16} = 4 = x.$$

If

$$x = -4 \quad \text{then} \quad \sqrt{x^2} = \sqrt{(-4)^2} = \sqrt{16} = 4 = |x|. \text{ For } x = -4, \\ |x| = |-4| = 4.$$

Without knowing whether x is positive, negative, or zero, we cannot say that $\sqrt{x^2}$ is x.

The square root of x^2

If x is a real number, then

$$\sqrt{x^2} = |x|.$$

If x is a *nonnegative* real number, then

$$\sqrt{x^2} = x.$$

In the remainder of this chapter, we will assume that variables under radical signs represent nonnegative real numbers, and so $\sqrt{x^2} = x$.

ENRICHMENT ESSAY

Radicals in Nature

Nature's creations include a variety of intricate mathematical designs, including that of the seashell, the chambered nautilus. Every radius forms a right angle with the line segments along the curve and each of these line segments has a value of 1. The Pythagorean Theorem enables us to calculate the measure of each hypotenuse. (Take a few minutes to verify the Pythagorean Theorem for each of the triangles shown.) The nautilus builds its shell in stages, each stage consisting of the addition of a chamber to the already existing shell. At every stage of its growth, the shape of the chambered nautilus shell remains the same.

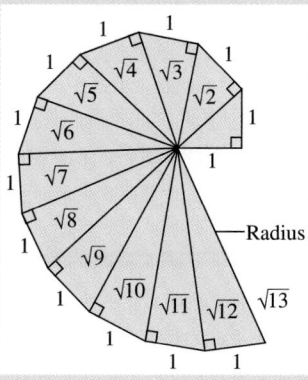

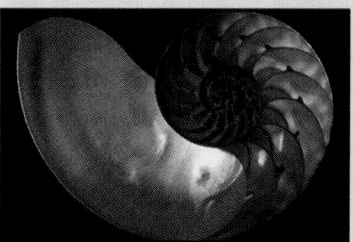

Thomas Taylor/Photo Researchers, Inc.

EXAMPLE 5   **Simplifying Square Roots with Variables in the Radicand**

Simplify: $\sqrt{72x^2}$ (assume that $x \geq 0$)

Solution

$$\sqrt{72x^2} = \sqrt{36 \cdot 2x^2}$$ 36 is the largest perfect square factor of 72.

$$= \sqrt{36}\sqrt{2}\sqrt{x^2}$$ $\sqrt{xyz} = \sqrt{x}\sqrt{y}\sqrt{z}$—the product rule can be extended to three or more factors.

$$= 6\sqrt{2}x \quad \text{or} \quad 6x\sqrt{2}$$ $\sqrt{36} = 6$ and $\sqrt{x^2} = x$ if $x \geq 0$.   ■

To simplify square roots when the radicand contains x to an even power, we can use the following rule.

Simplifying the square root of a radicand containing a variable raised to an even power

$$\sqrt{x^{2n}} = x^n$$

The square root of a variable raised to an even power equals the variable raised to one-half that power.

Just as $\sqrt{25} = 5$ because $5^2 = 25$, so $\sqrt{x^{2n}} = x^n$ because $(x^n)^2 = x^{n \cdot 2} = x^{2n}$. Examples of this rule include

$\sqrt{x^4} = x^2$ In each case, take half of the power that appears in the radicand.

$\sqrt{x^6} = x^3$

$\sqrt{x^{22}} = x^{11}$.

To simplify square roots when the radicand contains x to an odd power, we factor the radicand so that one factor has an even power and the other factor has a power of 1. For example,

$\sqrt{x^5} = \sqrt{x^4 \cdot x}$ x^4 is the largest perfect square factor of x^5.

$\quad\quad = \sqrt{x^4}\sqrt{x}$

$\quad\quad = x^2\sqrt{x}$ $\sqrt{x^4} = x^{\frac{4}{2}} = x^2$.

EXAMPLE 6   **Simplifying a Radical Involving an Odd Power**

Simplify: $\sqrt{48x^{11}}$

Solution

$\sqrt{48x^{11}} = \sqrt{16x^{10} \cdot 3x}$ 16 is the largest perfect square factor of 48; x^{10} is the largest perfect square factor of x^{11}.

$\quad\quad = \sqrt{16}\sqrt{x^{10}}\sqrt{3x}$

$\quad\quad = 4x^5\sqrt{3x}$ Simplify. ∎

EXAMPLE 7   **Multiplying and Simplifying Radicals**

Multiply: $\sqrt{10x^4}\sqrt{5x^3}$

Solution

$\sqrt{10x^4}\sqrt{5x^3} = \sqrt{(10x^4)(5x^3)}$ The square root of a product is the product of the square roots. We'll multiply variable factors and simplify later.

$\quad\quad = \sqrt{50x^7}$ Multiply under the radical.

$\quad\quad = \sqrt{25x^6 \cdot 2x}$ The perfect square factors are 25 and x^6.

$\quad\quad = \sqrt{25}\sqrt{x^6}\sqrt{2x}$ This step can be worked mentally.

$\quad\quad = 5x^3\sqrt{2x}$ Simplify. ∎

The Quotient Rule for Radicals

A rule for dividing radicals can be generalized by comparing

$\sqrt{\dfrac{64}{4}}$ and $\dfrac{\sqrt{64}}{\sqrt{4}}$.

Note that

$\sqrt{\dfrac{64}{4}} = \sqrt{16} = 4$ and $\dfrac{\sqrt{64}}{\sqrt{4}} = \dfrac{8}{2} = 4$.

Since we obtain 4 in both situations, the original radical expressions must be equal:

$$\sqrt{\frac{64}{4}} = \frac{\sqrt{64}}{\sqrt{4}}.$$

This result is a special case of the *quotient rule for radicals* that can be generalized as follows.

> **The quotient rule for radicals**
>
> If x and y represent nonnegative real numbers and $y \neq 0$, then
>
> $$\frac{\sqrt{x}}{\sqrt{y}} = \sqrt{\frac{x}{y}} \quad \text{and} \quad \sqrt{\frac{x}{y}} = \frac{\sqrt{x}}{\sqrt{y}}.$$
>
> The square root of a quotient is the quotient of the square roots.

3 Simplify radicals that involve quotients.

EXAMPLE 8 **Using the Quotient Rule to Simplify Square Roots**

Simplify: **a.** $\sqrt{\dfrac{100}{9}}$ **b.** $\sqrt{\dfrac{3}{25}}$ **c.** $\sqrt{\dfrac{23}{x^6}}$ $x > 0$

Solution

a. $\sqrt{\dfrac{100}{9}} = \dfrac{\sqrt{100}}{\sqrt{9}}$ $\quad \sqrt{\dfrac{x}{y}} = \dfrac{\sqrt{x}}{\sqrt{y}}$

$= \dfrac{10}{3}$ $\quad \sqrt{100} = 10$ and $\sqrt{9} = 3$

b. $\sqrt{\dfrac{3}{25}} = \dfrac{\sqrt{3}}{\sqrt{25}}$ $\quad \sqrt{\dfrac{x}{y}} = \dfrac{\sqrt{x}}{\sqrt{y}}$

$= \dfrac{\sqrt{3}}{5}$ $\quad \sqrt{25} = 5$

c. $\sqrt{\dfrac{23}{x^6}} = \dfrac{\sqrt{23}}{\sqrt{x^6}}$ $\quad \sqrt{\dfrac{x}{y}} = \dfrac{\sqrt{x}}{\sqrt{y}}$

$= \dfrac{\sqrt{23}}{x^3}$ $\quad \sqrt{x^6} = x^3$ Remember that the square root of any even power of x is x with half the original exponent. ∎

4 Divide radicals.

EXAMPLE 9 **Using the Quotient Rule to Divide Square Roots**

Find the quotient: **a.** $\dfrac{\sqrt{75}}{\sqrt{3}}$ **b.** $\dfrac{30\sqrt{10}}{5\sqrt{2}}$ **c.** $\dfrac{\sqrt{48x^5}}{\sqrt{3x}}$

Solution

a. $\dfrac{\sqrt{75}}{\sqrt{3}} = \sqrt{\dfrac{75}{3}}$ $\quad \dfrac{\sqrt{x}}{\sqrt{y}} = \sqrt{\dfrac{x}{y}}$

$= \sqrt{25}$

$= 5$

654 CHAPTER 9 ROOTS AND RADICALS

b. $\dfrac{30\sqrt{10}}{5\sqrt{2}} = \dfrac{30}{5} \cdot \sqrt{\dfrac{10}{2}}$ $\dfrac{\sqrt{x}}{\sqrt{y}} = \sqrt{\dfrac{x}{y}}$

$\qquad\qquad = 6\sqrt{5}$

c. $\dfrac{\sqrt{48x^5}}{\sqrt{3x}} = \sqrt{\dfrac{48x^5}{3x}}$ $\dfrac{\sqrt{x}}{\sqrt{y}} = \sqrt{\dfrac{x}{y}}$

$\qquad\qquad = \sqrt{16x^4}$ $\dfrac{x^5}{x} = x^{5-1} = x^4$

$\qquad\qquad = 4x^2$ $\sqrt{16} = 4 \text{ and } \sqrt{x^4} = x^2$ ■

The Product and Quotient Rules for Other Roots

The product and quotient rules apply to cube roots, fourth roots, and all higher roots.

> **Properties of radicals: product and quotient rules**
>
> For all real numbers, where the indicated roots represent real numbers,
>
> $$\sqrt[n]{x} \cdot \sqrt[n]{y} = \sqrt[n]{xy} \quad \text{and} \quad \dfrac{\sqrt[n]{x}}{\sqrt[n]{y}} = \sqrt[n]{\dfrac{x}{y}} \quad y \neq 0.$$

EXAMPLE 10 **Simplifying, Multiplying, and Dividing Higher Roots**

Simplify: **a.** $\sqrt[3]{24}$ **b.** $\sqrt[4]{8} \cdot \sqrt[4]{4}$ **c.** $\sqrt[4]{\dfrac{81}{16}}$

Solution

a. $\sqrt[3]{24} = \sqrt[3]{8 \cdot 3}$ Find the largest *perfect cube* that is a factor of 24. $\sqrt[3]{8} = 2$, so 8 is a perfect cube and is the largest perfect cube factor of 24.

$\qquad = \sqrt[3]{8} \cdot \sqrt[3]{3}$ $\sqrt[n]{xy} = \sqrt[n]{x}\sqrt[n]{y}$

$\qquad = 2\sqrt[3]{3}$

b. $\sqrt[4]{8} \cdot \sqrt[4]{4} = \sqrt[4]{8 \cdot 4}$ $\sqrt[n]{x} \cdot \sqrt[n]{y} = \sqrt[n]{xy}$

$\qquad\qquad = \sqrt[4]{32}$ Find the largest *perfect fourth root* that is a factor of 32.

$\qquad\qquad = \sqrt[4]{16 \cdot 2}$ $\sqrt[4]{16} = 2$, so 16 is a perfect fourth root and is the largest perfect fourth root that is a factor of 32.

$\qquad\qquad = \sqrt[4]{16} \cdot \sqrt[4]{2}$ $\sqrt[n]{xy} = \sqrt[n]{x} \cdot \sqrt[n]{y}$

$\qquad\qquad = 2\sqrt[4]{2}$

c. $\sqrt[4]{\dfrac{81}{16}} = \dfrac{\sqrt[4]{81}}{\sqrt[4]{16}}$ $\sqrt[n]{\dfrac{x}{y}} = \dfrac{\sqrt[n]{x}}{\sqrt[n]{y}}$

$\qquad\qquad = \dfrac{3}{2}$ $\sqrt[4]{81} = 3 \text{ because } 3^4 = 81 \text{ and } \sqrt[4]{16} = 2 \text{ because } 2^4 = 16.$ ■

PROBLEM SET 9.2

Practice Problems _____

Assume in this problem set that all variables represent nonnegative real numbers and that the variables in the denominators are not zero.

Use the product rule to simplify Problems 1–52.

1. $\sqrt{7} \cdot \sqrt{6}$ **2.** $\sqrt{19} \cdot \sqrt{3}$ **3.** $\sqrt{6} \cdot \sqrt{6}$ **4.** $\sqrt{5} \cdot \sqrt{5}$ **5.** $\sqrt{3} \cdot \sqrt{5y}$

6. $\sqrt{5} \cdot \sqrt{7y}$ **7.** $\sqrt{3x} \cdot \sqrt{6y}$ **8.** $\sqrt{5a} \cdot \sqrt{10b}$ **9.** $\sqrt{\frac{1}{2}} \cdot \sqrt{\frac{5}{7}}$ **10.** $\sqrt{\frac{2}{7}} \cdot \sqrt{\frac{3}{5}}$

11. $\sqrt{50}$ **12.** $\sqrt{27}$ **13.** $\sqrt{45}$ **14.** $\sqrt{125}$ **15.** $\sqrt{80x}$

16. $\sqrt{48x}$ **17.** $\sqrt{600xy}$ **18.** $\sqrt{180xy}$ **19.** $2\sqrt{27}$ **20.** $6\sqrt{20}$

21. $7\sqrt{8a}$ **22.** $6\sqrt{20b}$ **23.** $\sqrt{27} \cdot \sqrt{18}$ **24.** $\sqrt{48} \cdot \sqrt{45}$ **25.** $\sqrt{15} \cdot \sqrt{21x}$

26. $\sqrt{30} \cdot \sqrt{20x}$ **27.** $\sqrt{72a} \cdot \sqrt{50b}$ **28.** $\sqrt{8a} \cdot \sqrt{98b}$ **29.** $\sqrt{3} \cdot \sqrt{6} \cdot \sqrt{18}$ **30.** $\sqrt{3} \cdot \sqrt{4} \cdot \sqrt{12}$

31. $\sqrt{y^3}$ **32.** $\sqrt{z^5}$ **33.** $\sqrt{50x^2}$ **34.** $\sqrt{12y^2}$ **35.** $\sqrt{80x^4}$

36. $\sqrt{20y^6}$ **37.** $\sqrt{72x^5}$ **38.** $\sqrt{500y^7}$ **39.** $\sqrt{12x^{11}}$ **40.** $\sqrt{300x^{13}}$

41. $\sqrt{90p^{23}}$ **42.** $\sqrt{104m^{19}}$ **43.** $\sqrt{2x^2} \cdot \sqrt{6x}$ **44.** $\sqrt{6x} \cdot \sqrt{3x^2}$ **45.** $\sqrt{2y^3} \cdot \sqrt{10y}$

46. $\sqrt{10y^2} \cdot \sqrt{5y^4}$ **47.** $\sqrt{15r^2} \cdot \sqrt{5r^6}$ **48.** $\sqrt{4r^5} \cdot \sqrt{2r^7}$ **49.** $\sqrt{x^2y} \cdot \sqrt{xy^5}$ **50.** $\sqrt{ab} \cdot \sqrt{a^3b^2}$

51. $\sqrt{50xy} \cdot \sqrt{4x^2y^4}$ **52.** $\sqrt{5x^2y^3} \cdot \sqrt{10xy^2}$

Use the quotient rule and, if necessary, the product rule to simplify Problems 53–76.

53. $\sqrt{\dfrac{49}{16}}$ **54.** $\sqrt{\dfrac{121}{9}}$ **55.** $\sqrt{\dfrac{35}{4}}$ **56.** $\sqrt{\dfrac{11}{100}}$ **57.** $\sqrt{\dfrac{7}{x^4}}$

58. $\sqrt{\dfrac{13}{y^6}}$ **59.** $\sqrt{\dfrac{72}{x^6}}$ **60.** $\sqrt{\dfrac{300}{y^4}}$ **61.** $\dfrac{\sqrt{54}}{\sqrt{6}}$ **62.** $\dfrac{\sqrt{75}}{\sqrt{3}}$

63. $\dfrac{\sqrt{72}}{\sqrt{8}}$ **64.** $\dfrac{\sqrt{48}}{\sqrt{3}}$ **65.** $\dfrac{15\sqrt{10}}{3\sqrt{2}}$ **66.** $\dfrac{24\sqrt{20}}{8\sqrt{10}}$ **67.** $\dfrac{30\sqrt{50}}{10\sqrt{5}}$

68. $\dfrac{39\sqrt{10}}{13\sqrt{5}}$ **69.** $\sqrt{\dfrac{28y}{81}}$ **70.** $\sqrt{\dfrac{288x}{25}}$ **71.** $\dfrac{\sqrt{96y^5}}{\sqrt{8y}}$ **72.** $\dfrac{\sqrt{75x^3}}{\sqrt{3x}}$

73. $\dfrac{\sqrt{8x^7}}{\sqrt{2x}}$ **74.** $\dfrac{\sqrt{27x^9}}{\sqrt{3x}}$ **75.** $\dfrac{\sqrt{24y^7}}{\sqrt{6}}$ **76.** $\dfrac{\sqrt{12y^5}}{\sqrt{3}}$

Simplify the radical expressions in Problems 77–94.

77. $\sqrt[3]{32}$ **78.** $\sqrt[3]{40}$ **79.** $\sqrt[3]{128}$ **80.** $\sqrt[3]{150}$

81. $\sqrt[4]{80}$ **82.** $\sqrt[4]{243}$ **83.** $\sqrt[3]{4} \cdot \sqrt[3]{2}$ **84.** $\sqrt[3]{3} \cdot \sqrt[3]{9}$

85. $\sqrt[3]{9} \cdot \sqrt[3]{6}$ **86.** $\sqrt[3]{12} \cdot \sqrt[4]{4}$ **87.** $\sqrt[5]{16} \cdot \sqrt[5]{4}$ **88.** $\sqrt[4]{4} \cdot \sqrt[4]{8}$

89. $\sqrt[3]{\dfrac{27}{8}}$ **90.** $\sqrt[4]{\dfrac{81}{10,000}}$ **91.** $\sqrt[4]{\dfrac{225}{81}}$ **92.** $\sqrt[3]{\dfrac{125}{16}}$

93. $\sqrt[3]{\dfrac{3}{8}}$ **94.** $\sqrt[4]{\dfrac{4}{81}}$

Application Problems

95. What is the area of a rectangle whose length is $13\sqrt{2}$ feet and whose width is $5\sqrt{6}$ feet?

96. What is the area of a triangle whose base is $4\sqrt{5}$ meters and whose height is $7\sqrt{10}$ meters?

97. The height (h) of an equilateral triangle whose sides each measure s is given by the formula

$$h = \frac{s}{2}\sqrt{3}.$$

What is the height of the triangle if each side is $\sqrt{18}$ feet?

98. If a rock is dropped from a building h feet high, the number of seconds t that it takes to reach the ground is given by the mathematical model $t = \sqrt{\dfrac{h}{16}}$. How long will it take a rock to hit the ground if it is dropped from the top of a building 100 feet high?

True–False Critical Thinking Problems

99. Which one of the following is true?
   a. $\sqrt{20} = 4\sqrt{5}$
   b. If $y \geq 0$, $\sqrt{y^9} = y^3$.
   c. $\sqrt{2x}\sqrt{6y} = 2\sqrt{3xy}$ if x and y are nonnegative real numbers.
   d. $\sqrt{2} \cdot \sqrt{8} = 16$

100. Which one of the following is true?
   a. $\frac{25}{4} = \frac{5}{2}$
   b. $\sqrt{5} \cdot \sqrt{4} = 2\sqrt{5}$
   c. $\sqrt{10^8} = 10^6$
   d. $\dfrac{\sqrt{72}}{\sqrt{8}} = \sqrt{3}$

Technology Problems

101. Use a calculator to provide numerical support for some of the problems that you worked in this problem set from 1–68 that do not contain variables. In each case, find a decimal approximation for the given problem. Then find a decimal approximation for your simplified answer. The results should be the same.

102. Show that $\sqrt{x^3} = x\sqrt{x}$ by graphing $y_1 = \sqrt{x^3}$ and $y_2 = x\sqrt{x}$ in the same viewing rectangle for $x \geq 0$.

In Problems 103–106, determine if each simplification is correct by graphing the function on each side of the given equality with your graphing utility. The graphs should be the same. If they are not, correct the right side of the equation and then use your graphing utility to verify the result.

103. $\sqrt{x^4} = x^2 \ (x \geq 0)$
104. $\sqrt{x^9} = x^3 \ (x \geq 0)$
105. $\sqrt{18x^2} = 9\sqrt{2}x \ (x \geq 0)$
106. $\sqrt{x^2} = |x|$ (Consult your manual for the location of the absolute value key.)

Writing in Mathematics

107. Explain why $\sqrt{50x^3}$ is not simplified.

108. Why must x and y represent nonnegative numbers when we write $\sqrt{x}\sqrt{y} = \sqrt{xy}$? Is it necessary to use this restriction in the case of $\sqrt[3]{x}\sqrt[3]{y} = \sqrt[3]{xy}$? Explain.

Critical Thinking Problems

109. Simplify: $\sqrt{x^{12n}}$.
110. Simplify $\sqrt{64}$, $\sqrt{640}$, $\sqrt{6400}$, $\sqrt{64{,}000}$, and $\sqrt{640{,}000}$. What pattern do you observe?

111. Simplify: $\sqrt{3a^3bc^6} \cdot \sqrt{6a^4b^5c^6}$.

Fill in the missing coefficients and exponents to make a true statement in Problems 112–113.

112. $\sqrt{\Box x^{\Box}} = 5x^7$
113. $\sqrt{2a^{\Box}b^5} \cdot \sqrt{\Box a^3 b^{\Box}} = 4a^7b^6\sqrt{a}$

Review Problems

114. Solve the system:
$$4x + 3y = 18$$
$$5x - 9y = 48$$

115. Perform the indicated operations:
$$\frac{2x+1}{6x+12} + \frac{x+1}{x^2+2x} - \frac{1}{6}.$$

116. The height of a triangle is 3 centimeters less than the base, and the area is 35 square centimeters. Find the base and the height.

SECTION 9.3

Solutions Tutorial Video
Manual 10

Operations with Radicals

Objectives

1 Add and subtract radicals.
2 Multiply radicals using the distributive property.
3 Multiply radicals using the FOIL method.
4 Multiply conjugates.

In this section, we focus our attention on adding, subtracting, and multiplying radicals. Adding and subtracting radicals is similar to adding and subtracting like terms of polynomials. Multiplication of certain radicals also resembles polynomial multiplication.

1 Add and subtract radicals.

Adding and Subtracting Like Radicals

In our earlier work with polynomials, we used the distributive property to combine like terms. For example,

$$7x^2 + 6x^2 = (7 + 6)x^2 \quad \text{Apply the distributive property.}$$
$$= 13x^2 \quad \text{Simplify.}$$

In the same way, we can combine radical (square root) expressions if they have the same radicand. Thus,

$$7\sqrt{11} + 6\sqrt{11} = (7 + 6)\sqrt{11} \quad \text{Apply the distributive property.}$$
$$= 13\sqrt{11} \quad \text{Simplify.}$$

Only *like radicals* that contain *square roots of the same number* such as $7\sqrt{11}$ and $6\sqrt{11}$ can be combined using the distributive property.

EXAMPLE 1 **Adding and Subtracting Like Radicals**

Add or subtract as indicated:

a. $7\sqrt{2} + 5\sqrt{2}$ **b.** $2\sqrt{5x} - 6\sqrt{5x}$ **c.** $3\sqrt{7} + 9\sqrt{7} - \sqrt{7}$
d. $5\sqrt{11} + 4\sqrt{3}$

Solution

a. $7\sqrt{2} + 5\sqrt{2} = (7 + 5)\sqrt{2}$ Apply the distributive property.
$$= 12\sqrt{2} \quad \text{Simplify.}$$
b. $2\sqrt{5x} - 6\sqrt{5x} = (2 - 6)\sqrt{5x}$ Apply the distributive property.
$$= -4\sqrt{5x} \quad \text{Simplify.}$$
c. $3\sqrt{7} + 9\sqrt{7} - \sqrt{7} = 3\sqrt{7} + 9\sqrt{7} - 1\sqrt{7}$ Write $\sqrt{7}$ as $1\sqrt{7}$.
$$= (3 + 9 - 1)\sqrt{7} \quad \text{Apply the distributive property.}$$
$$= 11\sqrt{7} \quad \text{Simplify.}$$
d. $5\sqrt{11} + 4\sqrt{3}$ does not involve the addition of like radicals and cannot be simplified. ■

We can also use the distributive property to combine radicals with roots greater than square roots as long as the terms being combined contain the *same root* of the *same number*. This means that we can combine $4\sqrt[3]{7}$ and $5\sqrt[3]{7}$ since both terms involve the cube root of 7. Thus,

$$4\sqrt[3]{7} + 5\sqrt[3]{7} = (4 + 5)\sqrt[3]{7} \qquad \text{Apply the distributive property.}$$
$$= 9\sqrt[3]{7} \qquad \text{Simplify.}$$

EXAMPLE 2 **Combining Radicals with Roots Greater Than Square Roots**

Add or subtract as indicated:

a. $7\sqrt[3]{5} + 8\sqrt[3]{5}$ **b.** $2\sqrt[4]{7} - 3\sqrt[4]{7}$

Solution

a. $7\sqrt[3]{5} + 8\sqrt[3]{5} = (7 + 8)\sqrt[3]{5}$ Apply the distributive property.
$$= 15\sqrt[3]{5} \qquad \text{Simplify.}$$
b. $2\sqrt[4]{7} - 3\sqrt[4]{7} = (2 - 3)\sqrt[4]{7}$ Apply the distributive property.
$$= -1\sqrt[4]{7} \qquad \text{Simplify.}$$
$$= -\sqrt[4]{7}$$

Simplifying and Combining Radicals

At first glance, many radicals might not appear to be like radicals. In some cases, simplification may let us add or subtract. For example, to combine $\sqrt{2}$ and $\sqrt{8}$, we can write $\sqrt{8}$ as $\sqrt{4 \cdot 2}$ since 4 is a perfect square factor of 8. We obtain

$$\sqrt{2} + \sqrt{8} = \sqrt{2} + \sqrt{4 \cdot 2} \qquad \text{Simplify } \sqrt{8}.$$
$$= 1\sqrt{2} + 2\sqrt{2} \qquad \sqrt{4 \cdot 2} = \sqrt{4} \cdot \sqrt{2} = 2\sqrt{2}$$
$$= (1 + 2)\sqrt{2} \qquad \text{Apply the distributive property.}$$
$$= 3\sqrt{2} \qquad \text{Simplify.}$$

You will find that the time-consuming part of adding and subtracting radicals involves simplifying terms. Once you have done this, the distributive property enables you to immediately combine the like radicals.

Adding and subtracting radicals

   1. Where possible, simplify the terms with radicals.
   2. Where possible, combine like radicals.

EXAMPLE 3 **Combining Radicals That First Require Simplification**

Add or subtract as indicated:

a. $7\sqrt{3} + \sqrt{12}$ **b.** $4\sqrt{50x} - 6\sqrt{32x}$ **c.** $\dfrac{3}{7}\sqrt{20} - \dfrac{2}{3}\sqrt{80}$

d. $5\sqrt[3]{16} - 11\sqrt[3]{2}$

Solution

a. $7\sqrt{3} + \sqrt{12}$

$= 7\sqrt{3} + \sqrt{4 \cdot 3}$

Split 12 into two factors such that one is a perfect square.
$\sqrt{4 \cdot 3} = \sqrt{4}\sqrt{3} = 2\sqrt{3}$

$= 7\sqrt{3} + 2\sqrt{3}$

$= (7 + 2)\sqrt{3}$

Apply the distributive property. You will find that this step is usually done mentally.

$= 9\sqrt{3}$

Simplify.

b. $4\sqrt{50x} - 6\sqrt{32x}$

$= 4\sqrt{25 \cdot 2x} - 6\sqrt{16 \cdot 2x}$

25 is the largest perfect square factor of 50 and 16 is the largest perfect factor of 32.
$\sqrt{25 \cdot 2} = \sqrt{25}\sqrt{2} = 5\sqrt{2}$ and
$\sqrt{16 \cdot 2} = \sqrt{16}\sqrt{2} = 4\sqrt{2}$

$= 4 \cdot 5\sqrt{2x} - 6 \cdot 4\sqrt{2x}$

$= 20\sqrt{2x} - 24\sqrt{2x}$

Multiply.

$= (20 - 24)\sqrt{2x}$

Apply the distributive property.

$= -4\sqrt{2x}$

Simplify.

c. $\dfrac{3}{7}\sqrt{20} - \dfrac{2}{3}\sqrt{80} = \dfrac{3}{7}\sqrt{4 \cdot 5} - \dfrac{2}{3}\sqrt{16 \cdot 5}$

Perfect square factors of 20 and 80 are 4 and 16, respectively.

$= \dfrac{3}{7} \cdot 2\sqrt{5} - \dfrac{2}{3} \cdot 4\sqrt{5}$

$\sqrt{4 \cdot 5} = \sqrt{4}\sqrt{5} = 2\sqrt{5}$ and
$\sqrt{16 \cdot 5} = \sqrt{16}\sqrt{5} = 4\sqrt{5}$

$= \dfrac{6}{7}\sqrt{5} - \dfrac{8}{3}\sqrt{5}$

$\dfrac{3}{7} \cdot 2 = \dfrac{6}{7}$ and $\dfrac{2}{3} \cdot 4 = \dfrac{8}{3}$

$= \left(\dfrac{6}{7} - \dfrac{8}{3}\right)\sqrt{5}$

Apply the distributive property.

$= \left(\dfrac{18}{21} - \dfrac{56}{21}\right)\sqrt{5}$

Write $\dfrac{6}{7}$ and $\dfrac{8}{3}$ with an LCD of 21.

$= -\dfrac{38}{21}\sqrt{5}$

d. $5\sqrt[3]{16} - 11\sqrt[3]{2}$

$= 5\sqrt[3]{8 \cdot 2} - 11\sqrt[3]{2}$

Since $\sqrt[3]{8} = 2$, 8 is the largest perfect cube that is a factor of 16.
$\sqrt[3]{8 \cdot 2} = \sqrt[3]{8}\sqrt[3]{2} = 2\sqrt[3]{2}$

$= 5 \cdot 2\sqrt[3]{2} - 11\sqrt[3]{2}$

$= 10\sqrt[3]{2} - 11\sqrt[3]{2}$

Multiply.

$= (10 - 11)\sqrt[3]{2}$

Apply the distributive property.

$= -1\sqrt[3]{2}$ or $-\sqrt[3]{2}$

Simplify. ■

2 Multiply radicals using the distributive property.

Multiplying Radicals Using the Distributive Property

Radical expressions with more than one term are multiplied in much the same way that polynomials with more than one term are multiplied. We begin with three examples that utilize the distributive property.

EXAMPLE 4 **Using the Distributive Property to Multiply Radicals**

Multiply: $\sqrt{3}(\sqrt{7} + \sqrt{3})$

Solution

$$\sqrt{3}(\sqrt{7} + \sqrt{3}) = \sqrt{3} \cdot \sqrt{7} + \sqrt{3} \cdot \sqrt{3} \qquad \text{Apply the distributive property.}$$
$$= \sqrt{21} + \sqrt{9} \qquad\qquad \sqrt{x}\,\sqrt{y} = \sqrt{xy}$$
$$= \sqrt{21} + 3 \qquad\qquad\quad \sqrt{9} = 3$$

EXAMPLE 5 **Using the Distributive Property to Multiply Radicals**

Multiply: $4\sqrt{2}(7\sqrt{3} - 2\sqrt{5})$

Solution

$$4\sqrt{2}(7\sqrt{3} - 2\sqrt{5})$$
$$= 4\sqrt{2} \cdot 7\sqrt{3} - 4\sqrt{2} \cdot 2\sqrt{5} \qquad \text{Apply the distributive property.}$$
$$= 4 \cdot 7\sqrt{2}\sqrt{3} - 4 \cdot 2\sqrt{2}\sqrt{5} \qquad \text{Use the commutative property to rearrange factors.}$$
$$= 28\sqrt{6} - 8\sqrt{10} \qquad\qquad \text{Multiply. You may find that you can work the first two steps in your head, immediately writing this answer.}$$

3 Multiply radicals using the FOIL method.

Multiplying Radicals Using the FOIL Method

The product of the sum of radicals, such as $(\sqrt{3} + \sqrt{5})(\sqrt{3} + 4\sqrt{5})$, can be found in the same way that we multiply polynomials such as $(x + 1)(x + 4)$. The pattern of multiplication applied to these binomial expressions containing radicals is the FOIL method. Let's consider some examples to see how this works.

EXAMPLE 6 **Using the FOIL Method to Multiply Radical Expressions**

Find the product: $(\sqrt{3} + \sqrt{5})(\sqrt{3} + 4\sqrt{5})$

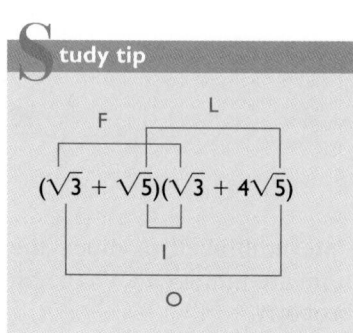

study tip

Solution

$$(\sqrt{3} + \sqrt{5})(\sqrt{3} + 4\sqrt{5})$$
$$\overset{\text{F}}{}\quad\overset{\text{O}}{}\quad\overset{\text{I}}{}\quad\overset{\text{L}}{}$$
$$= \sqrt{3} \cdot \sqrt{3} + \sqrt{3}(4\sqrt{5}) + \sqrt{5} \cdot \sqrt{3} + \sqrt{5}(4\sqrt{5})$$
$$= \sqrt{9} + 4\sqrt{15} + \sqrt{15} + 4\sqrt{25} \qquad \text{Multiply.}$$
$$= 3 + 4\sqrt{15} + \sqrt{15} + 4 \cdot 5 \qquad \text{You may immediately write this step since } \sqrt{3} \cdot \sqrt{3} = \sqrt{9} = 3 \text{ and } \sqrt{5} \cdot \sqrt{5} = \sqrt{25} = 5.$$
$$= 3 + 4\sqrt{15} + \sqrt{15} + 20 \qquad \text{Multiply.}$$
$$= 23 + 5\sqrt{15} \qquad\qquad \text{Combine terms. Notice that } 4\sqrt{15} + 1\sqrt{15} = (4 + 1)\sqrt{15} = 5\sqrt{15}.$$

| EXAMPLE 7 | **Using the FOIL Method to Multiply Radical Expressions** |

Multiply: $(\sqrt{7} + 3)(2\sqrt{11} - 5)$

Solution

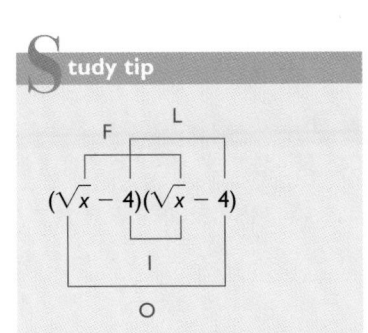

$$(\sqrt{7} + 3)(2\sqrt{11} - 5)$$

$$\overset{F}{} \quad \overset{O}{} \quad \overset{I}{} \quad \overset{L}{}$$

$$= \sqrt{7} \cdot 2\sqrt{11} + \sqrt{7}(-5) + 3 \cdot 2\sqrt{11} + 3(-5)$$

$$= 2\sqrt{77} - 5\sqrt{7} + 6\sqrt{11} - 15 \qquad \text{Multiply. With no like radicals, no terms may be combined.} \ \blacksquare$$

| EXAMPLE 8 | **Using the FOIL Method to Square a Radical Expression** |

Expand and simplify: $(\sqrt{x} - 4)^2$

Solution

$$(\sqrt{x} - 4)^2 = (\sqrt{x} - 4)(\sqrt{x} - 4) \qquad \text{Squaring } \sqrt{x} - 4 \text{ means to multiply } \sqrt{x} - 4 \text{ by itself.}$$

$$\overset{F}{} \quad \overset{O}{} \quad \overset{I}{} \quad \overset{L}{}$$

$$= \sqrt{x} \cdot \sqrt{x} - 4\sqrt{x} - 4\sqrt{x} + 16 \qquad \text{Multiply using FOIL.}$$

$$= x - 8\sqrt{x} + 16 \qquad \sqrt{x} \cdot \sqrt{x} = \sqrt{x^2} = x \text{ and}$$

$$\qquad\qquad -4\sqrt{x} - 4\sqrt{x} = (-4 - 4)\sqrt{x}$$

$$\qquad\qquad = -8\sqrt{x} \ \blacksquare$$

> **Study tip**
>
> Example 8 can be solved using $(A - B)^2$, the formula for squaring binomials:
>
> $$(A - B)^2 = \quad A^2 \quad - 2 \quad A \quad B + B^2$$
>
> $$(\sqrt{x} - 4)^2 = (\sqrt{x})^2 - 2 \cdot \sqrt{x} \cdot 4 + 4^2$$
>
> $$= x \qquad - 8\sqrt{x} \qquad + 16$$

4 Multiply conjugates.

Multiplying Conjugates

Expressions such as $\sqrt{a} + \sqrt{b}$ and $\sqrt{a} - \sqrt{b}$, differing only in the sign between the radicals, are called *conjugates*. For example, $\sqrt{5} + \sqrt{3}$ and $\sqrt{5} - \sqrt{3}$ are conjugates. As we will see in the next section, conjugates are useful in simplifying some quotients. We can multiply conjugates by using the special product that results in the difference of two squares.

$$(A + B)(A - B) = A^2 - B^2$$

Multiply the expressions in Examples 9 and 10 by using the FOIL method.

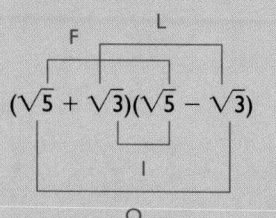

$(\sqrt{5} + \sqrt{3})(\sqrt{5} - \sqrt{3})$

The answer should be 2. What is the advantage of using the rule for the product of two conjugates?

EXAMPLE 9   **Multiplying Conjugates**

Multiply: $(\sqrt{5} + \sqrt{3})(\sqrt{5} - \sqrt{3})$

Solution

$(A + \quad B) \quad (A - \quad B) = \quad A^2 \quad - \quad B^2$

$(\sqrt{5} + \sqrt{3})(\sqrt{5} - \sqrt{3}) = (\sqrt{5})^2 - (\sqrt{3})^2$

$= 5 - 3$
$= 2$

The product of the sum and difference of the same two terms is the difference of their squares.
$(\sqrt{5})^2 = \sqrt{5}\sqrt{5} = \sqrt{25} = 5$
$(\sqrt{3})^2 = \sqrt{3}\sqrt{3} = \sqrt{9} = 3$

EXAMPLE 10   **Multiplying Conjugates**

Multiply: $(2\sqrt{3y} + 4\sqrt{7})(2\sqrt{3y} - 4\sqrt{7})$

Solution

$(A \quad + \quad B) \quad (A \quad - \quad B) = \quad A^2 \quad - \quad B^2$

$(2\sqrt{3y} + 4\sqrt{7})(2\sqrt{3y} - 4\sqrt{7}) = (2\sqrt{3y})^2 - (4\sqrt{7})^2$
$= 4 \cdot 3y - 16 \cdot 7$

$= 12y - 112$

$(2\sqrt{3y})^2 = (2\sqrt{3y})(2\sqrt{3y}) =$
$4\sqrt{9y^2} = 4 \cdot 3y$ and
$(4\sqrt{7})^2 = (4\sqrt{7})(4\sqrt{7}) =$
$16\sqrt{49} = 16 \cdot 7$
Multiply.

PROBLEM SET 9.3

Practice Problems _____

In Problems 1–50, simplify (if necessary) and add or subtract terms whenever possible. All variables represent nonnegative real numbers.

1. $7\sqrt{3} + 6\sqrt{3}$

2. $8\sqrt{5} + 11\sqrt{5}$

3. $4\sqrt{13} - 6\sqrt{13}$

4. $6\sqrt{17} - 8\sqrt{17}$

5. $\sqrt{5} + \sqrt{5}$

6. $\sqrt{3} + \sqrt{3}$

7. $\sqrt{13x} + 2\sqrt{13x}$

8. $4\sqrt{19x} + \sqrt{19x}$

9. $-4\sqrt{11y} - 8\sqrt{11y}$

10. $-4\sqrt{3y} - 8\sqrt{3y}$

11. $5\sqrt{6p} - \sqrt{6p}$

12. $8\sqrt{11p} - \sqrt{11p}$

13. $4\sqrt{2} - 5\sqrt{2} + 8\sqrt{2}$

14. $6\sqrt{3} + 8\sqrt{3} - 16\sqrt{3}$

15. $\sqrt{3} - 6\sqrt{7} - 12\sqrt{3}$

16. $9\sqrt{17} + 5\sqrt{2} - 13\sqrt{17} + \sqrt{2}$

17. $6\sqrt[3]{4} - 5\sqrt[3]{4}$

18. $7\sqrt[4]{11} - 6\sqrt[4]{11}$

19. $\sqrt{2} + \sqrt[3]{2}$

20. $\sqrt[3]{5} + \sqrt{2}$

21. $\sqrt[4]{5} + \sqrt[3]{6} + 8\sqrt[4]{5} - 2\sqrt[3]{6}$

22. $\sqrt[4]{7} + \sqrt[3]{11} + 9\sqrt[4]{7} - 2\sqrt[3]{11}$

23. $\sqrt{8} + 3\sqrt{2}$

24. $\sqrt{20} + 6\sqrt{5}$

25. $6\sqrt{3} - \sqrt{27}$

26. $8\sqrt{5} - \sqrt{80}$

27. $\sqrt{50a} + \sqrt{18a}$

28. $\sqrt{28a} + \sqrt{63a}$

29. $3\sqrt{18b} - 5\sqrt{50b}$

30. $4\sqrt{12b} - 2\sqrt{75b}$

31. $\frac{1}{4}\sqrt{12} - \frac{1}{2}\sqrt{48}$

32. $\frac{1}{5}\sqrt{300} - \frac{2}{3}\sqrt{27}$

33. $3\sqrt{75} + 2\sqrt{12} - 2\sqrt{48}$

34. $2\sqrt{72} + 3\sqrt{50} - \sqrt{128}$

35. $6\sqrt{7} + 2\sqrt{28} - 3\sqrt{63}$

36. $4\sqrt{3} - 2\sqrt{27} + 9\sqrt{75}$

37. $\frac{1}{6}\sqrt{72} - \frac{3}{8}\sqrt{8} + \frac{1}{5}\sqrt{50}$

38. $\frac{3}{4}\sqrt{24} - \frac{1}{3}\sqrt{54} - \frac{3}{5}\sqrt{150}$

39. $3\sqrt{54} - 2\sqrt{20} + 4\sqrt{45} - \sqrt{24}$

40. $4\sqrt{8} - \sqrt{128} + 2\sqrt{48} + 3\sqrt{18}$

41. $\frac{1}{4}\sqrt{2x} + \frac{2}{3}\sqrt{8x}$

42. $\frac{1}{2}\sqrt{7x} - \frac{1}{3}\sqrt{28x}$

43. $\frac{\sqrt{45}}{4} - \sqrt{80} + \frac{\sqrt{20}}{3}$

44. $\frac{2}{3}\sqrt{18} - \frac{\sqrt{50}}{2} + \frac{3}{5}\sqrt{8}$

45. $\sqrt[3]{81} + \sqrt[3]{24}$

46. $\sqrt[3]{32} + \sqrt[3]{4}$

47. $5\sqrt[3]{54b} + 2\sqrt[3]{16b}$

48. $2\sqrt[3]{24b} + 5\sqrt[3]{81b}$

49. $5\sqrt[3]{16} - 2\sqrt[3]{54}$

50. $3\sqrt[3]{128} - 2\sqrt[3]{150}$

Find the products in Problems 51–102.

51. $\sqrt{2}(\sqrt{3} + 4)$ **52.** $\sqrt{3}(\sqrt{5} + 6)$ **53.** $\sqrt{7}(\sqrt{6} - 5)$ **54.** $\sqrt{11}(\sqrt{3} - 4)$

55. $\sqrt{5x}(\sqrt{3} + \sqrt{7})$ **56.** $\sqrt{6x}(\sqrt{5} + \sqrt{11})$ **57.** $\sqrt{2}(\sqrt{5} - \sqrt{2})$ **58.** $\sqrt{5}(\sqrt{11} - \sqrt{5})$

59. $\sqrt{3}(5\sqrt{2} + \sqrt{3})$ **60.** $\sqrt{6}(5\sqrt{7} - \sqrt{6})$ **61.** $\sqrt{3}(4\sqrt{3} + \sqrt{5})$ **62.** $\sqrt{7}(3\sqrt{7} + \sqrt{3})$

63. $5\sqrt{3}(4\sqrt{2} + 6\sqrt{5})$ **64.** $6\sqrt{2}(7\sqrt{3} + 5\sqrt{7})$ **65.** $3\sqrt{10a}(6\sqrt{2a} - 4\sqrt{5b})$

66. $7\sqrt{10a}(5\sqrt{2a} - 2\sqrt{5a})$ **67.** $(\sqrt{5} + 2)(\sqrt{5} + 3)$ **68.** $(\sqrt{7} + 4)(\sqrt{7} + 5)$

69. $(\sqrt{2x} + 6)(\sqrt{2x} - 5)$ **70.** $(\sqrt{3y} + 7)(\sqrt{3y} - 4)$ **71.** $(\sqrt{2} + 1)(\sqrt{3} - 6)$

72. $(\sqrt{5} + 3)(\sqrt{2} - 8)$ **73.** $(\sqrt{3} + \sqrt{a})(\sqrt{3} + 2\sqrt{a})$ **74.** $(\sqrt{5} + \sqrt{b})(\sqrt{5} + 4\sqrt{b})$

75. $(2\sqrt{7} + 3)(4\sqrt{7} - 5)$ **76.** $(3\sqrt{5} + 2)(4\sqrt{5} - 8)$ **77.** $(\sqrt{5} + \sqrt{2})(\sqrt{5} + 3\sqrt{2})$

78. $(\sqrt{3} + \sqrt{7})(\sqrt{3} + 4\sqrt{7})$ **79.** $(\sqrt{a} + \sqrt{b})(\sqrt{a} + 3\sqrt{b})$ **80.** $(\sqrt{a} + \sqrt{b})(\sqrt{a} + 4\sqrt{b})$

81. $(4\sqrt{3} + 7\sqrt{2})(5\sqrt{3} - 6\sqrt{2})$ **82.** $(7\sqrt{3} + 4\sqrt{2})(6\sqrt{3} - 2\sqrt{2})$

83. $(\sqrt{5} + \sqrt{3})^2$ **84.** $(\sqrt{3} + \sqrt{2})^2$ **85.** $(\sqrt{3} - 1)^2$ **86.** $(\sqrt{5} - 4)^2$

87. $(2\sqrt{3} - 4\sqrt{7})^2$ **88.** $(5\sqrt{2} - 3\sqrt{5})^2$ **89.** $(\sqrt{a} + \sqrt{3})^2$ **90.** $(\sqrt{a} + \sqrt{7})^2$

91. $(\sqrt{y} - \sqrt{10})^2$ **92.** $(\sqrt{y} - \sqrt{6})^2$ **93.** $(4 + \sqrt{7})(4 - \sqrt{7})$ **94.** $(5 + \sqrt{11})(5 - \sqrt{11})$

95. $(\sqrt{13} + \sqrt{5})(\sqrt{13} - \sqrt{5})$ **96.** $(\sqrt{7} + \sqrt{3})(\sqrt{7} - \sqrt{3})$ **97.** $(2\sqrt{3} - 7)(2\sqrt{3} + 7)$

98. $(5\sqrt{2} - 4)(5\sqrt{2} + 4)$ **99.** $(2\sqrt{3} + \sqrt{5})(2\sqrt{3} - \sqrt{5})$ **100.** $(4\sqrt{5} + \sqrt{2})(4\sqrt{5} - \sqrt{2})$

101. $(3\sqrt{7} - 2\sqrt{3})(3\sqrt{7} + 2\sqrt{3})$ **102.** $(4\sqrt{6} - 5\sqrt{2})(4\sqrt{6} + 5\sqrt{2})$

Application Problems

103. If the length of a rectangle is $3\sqrt{75}$ meters and the width is $4\sqrt{18}$ meters, what is the rectangle's perimeter?

104. What is the perimeter of a triangle whose sides measure $8\sqrt{8}$ feet, $4\sqrt{32}$ feet, and $9\sqrt{50}$ feet?

There is a formula for adding $\sqrt{a}$ and $\sqrt{b}$. The formula is $\sqrt{a} + \sqrt{b} = \sqrt{(a + b) + 2\sqrt{ab}}$. Use this formula to add the radicals in Problems 105–106. Then work the problem again by the methods discussed in this section. Which method do you prefer? Why?

105. $\sqrt{2} + \sqrt{8}$ **106.** $\sqrt{5} + \sqrt{20}$

In Problems 107–108, write expressions for the perimeter and area of the rectangle. Then simplify these expressions. Assume that all linear measures are given in centimeters.

107.

$5\sqrt{2} + 3$

$2\sqrt{3} - 2$

108.

$7\sqrt{3} + 4$

$2\sqrt{3} - 2$

True–False Critical Thinking Problems

109. Which of the following is true?
  a. $\sqrt{16} + \sqrt{9} = 5$
  b. $7\sqrt[3]{3} - 4\sqrt{3} = 3\sqrt[3]{3}$
  c. $\sqrt{5} + 6\sqrt{5} = 7\sqrt{10}$
  d. None of the above is true.

110. Which of the following is true?
  a. $4\sqrt{3} + 5\sqrt{3} = 9\sqrt{6}$
  b. $\sqrt{2} + \sqrt{8} = 10$
  c. $2\sqrt{5}$ and $\sqrt{5}$ are examples of like radical expressions.
  d. None of the above is true.

111. Which one of the following is true?

a. $2(4\sqrt{5}) = 8\sqrt{20}$
b. $(\sqrt{5} + \sqrt{3})^2 = 5 + 3$
c. $(\sqrt{5} - \sqrt{3})^2 = 8 - 2\sqrt{15}$
d. To add like radicals, add their coefficients and square the common radical.

112. Which one of the following is true?
  a. $(\sqrt{7} + \sqrt{3})(\sqrt{14} - \sqrt{3}) = $
    $\sqrt{42} - 3 + 7\sqrt{2} - \sqrt{21}$
  b. $5(2\sqrt{7}) = 10\sqrt{35}$
  c. $(\sqrt{3} + 8)^2 = 3 + 64$
  d. The conjugate of $\sqrt{3} + 5$ is $\sqrt{3} - 5^2$.

Technology Problems

We can add and subtract expressions containing variable radicands using the methods discussed in this section. For example,

$$\sqrt{25x} + \sqrt{36x} = \sqrt{25}\sqrt{x} + \sqrt{36}\sqrt{x} = 5\sqrt{x} + 6\sqrt{x} = 11\sqrt{x}.$$

In Problems 113–115, determine if each simplification is correct by graphing the function on each side of the given equality with your graphing utility. The graphs should be the same. If they are not, use the method illustrated above to correct the right side of the equation. Then use your graphing utility to verify the result.

113. $\sqrt{4x} + \sqrt{9x} = 5\sqrt{x}$ **114.** $\sqrt{16x} - \sqrt{9x} = \sqrt{7x}$

115. $5\sqrt{x-2} - 6\sqrt{x-2} = -\sqrt{x-2}$

We can multiply expressions containing variable radicands using the methods discussed in this section. For example,

$$\overset{\text{F}\quad\text{O}\quad\text{I}\quad\text{L}}{(\sqrt{x} + 2)(\sqrt{x} + 3) = \sqrt{x}\cdot\sqrt{x} + 3\sqrt{x} + 2\sqrt{x} + 2\cdot 3} = x + 5\sqrt{x} + 6.$$

In Problems 116–119, determine if each multiplication is performed correctly by graphing the function on each side of the given equality with your graphing utility. The graphs should be the same. If they are not, use the method illustrated above or the distributive property to correct the right side of the equation. Then use your graphing utility to verify the result.

116. $(\sqrt{x} + 2)(\sqrt{x} - 1) = x + \sqrt{x} - 2$ **117.** $(\sqrt{x} - 1)(\sqrt{x} - 1) = x + 1$

118. $(\sqrt{x} + 2)(\sqrt{x} - 2) = x^2 - 4$ **119.** $\sqrt{x}(2\sqrt{x} + 1) = 2x + \sqrt{x}$

Writing in Mathematics

120. Explain what is meant by like radicals.

121. If only like radicals can be added, why is it that $4\sqrt{3} + 2\sqrt{48}$ can be simplified?

122. Describe how to perform the addition of several radicals.

123. Describe what is meant by the conjugate of a binomial expression. What happens when the binomial expression is multiplied by its conjugate? Give an example.

124. Explain why $(\sqrt{a} + \sqrt{b})(\sqrt{a} - \sqrt{b}) = a - b$.

Critical Thinking Problems

125. Simplify: $\sqrt{5}\cdot\sqrt{15} + 6\sqrt{3}$.

126. Simplify: $6\sqrt{18x^3} - 2x\sqrt{48x}$.

127. Multiply: $(\sqrt[3]{4} + 1)(\sqrt[3]{2} - 3)$.

128. Fill in the box to make the statement true: $(5 + \sqrt{\Box})(5 - \sqrt{\Box}) = 22$.

129. Multiply: $(4\sqrt{3x} + \sqrt{2y})(4\sqrt{3x} - \sqrt{2y})$.

Review Problems

130. Factor completely: $64y^3 - y$.

131. Multiply and simplify: $(3y - 2)(4y - 3) - (2y - 5)^2$.

132. Graph: $y = -\frac{1}{4}x + 3$.

SECTION 9.4

Solutions Manual   Tutorial   Video 10

Rationalizing Denominators; Simplified Radical Form

Objectives

1 Rationalize denominators that contain one term.

2 Rationalize denominators that contain two terms.

Much of our work throughout this chapter is often categorized as *simplifying radicals*. For example, $\sqrt{5}\cdot\sqrt{3}$ written as $\sqrt{15}$, a single radical, is in simplified radical form. When we combine like radicals, such as $3\sqrt{7} + 5\sqrt{7}$, the sum $8\sqrt{7}$ is also said to be in simplified radical form.

In this section, we look at the characteristics of simplified radical form, with emphasis placed on a new characteristic. In simplified form, a radical expression does not contain roots in any denominator. Consequently,

$$\frac{15}{\sqrt{6}} \quad \text{and} \quad \frac{7}{\sqrt{3}+5}$$

are *not* in simplified radical form. This, of course, raises the main question of the section: How do we get rid of the radicals in the denominator without changing the value of the original radical expression? The process of doing this is called *rationalizing the denominator*.

Rationalizing Denominators That Contain One Term

When a number contains an irrational square root in the denominator, such as $\frac{\sqrt{5}}{\sqrt{2}}$, we can rationalize the denominator by multiplying both the numerator and denominator by the smallest factor that results in a perfect square in the denominator. If we multiply the numerator and denominator of $\frac{\sqrt{5}}{\sqrt{2}}$ by $\sqrt{2}$, we obtain $\sqrt{2}\cdot\sqrt{2}$ or $\sqrt{4}$ or 2 in the denominator, thereby eliminating the irrational number in the denominator. We proceed as follows:

$$\frac{\sqrt{5}}{\sqrt{2}} = \frac{\sqrt{5}}{\sqrt{2}}\cdot\frac{\sqrt{2}}{\sqrt{2}}$$

Multiply the numerator and denominator by $\sqrt{2}$. Since $\frac{\sqrt{2}}{\sqrt{2}}=1$, we are multiplying by the identity and not changing the value of $\frac{\sqrt{5}}{\sqrt{2}}$.

$$= \frac{\sqrt{10}}{\sqrt{4}}$$

$\sqrt{5}\sqrt{2}=\sqrt{5\cdot2}=\sqrt{10}$ and $\sqrt{2}\sqrt{2}=\sqrt{4}$

$$= \frac{\sqrt{10}}{2}$$

$\sqrt{4}=2$. This step can be written immediately, eliminating the previous step.

This means that

$$\frac{\sqrt{5}}{\sqrt{2}} = \frac{\sqrt{10}}{2}.$$

This example illustrates the general procedure for rationalizing denominators containing an irrational square root.

> **Rationalizing denominators that contain an irrational square root**
>
> Multiply the numerator and denominator by the smallest factor that results in a perfect square radicand in the denominator.

EXAMPLE 1 **Rationalizing Denominators**

Rationalize the denominator: **a.** $\frac{15}{\sqrt{6}}$ **b.** $\sqrt{\frac{3}{5}}$ **c.** $\sqrt{\frac{7}{x}}$

Rationalize denominators that contain one term.

Solution

a. If we multiply numerator and denominator by $\sqrt{6}$, the denominator becomes $\sqrt{6} \cdot \sqrt{6} = \sqrt{36} = 6$. Therefore, we multiply by 1, choosing $\dfrac{\sqrt{6}}{\sqrt{6}}$ for 1.

$$\frac{15}{\sqrt{6}} = \frac{15}{\sqrt{6}} \cdot \frac{\sqrt{6}}{\sqrt{6}}$$ Multiply the numerator and denominator by $\sqrt{6}$ to remove the irrational number in the denominator.

$$= \frac{15\sqrt{6}}{6}$$ $\sqrt{6} \cdot \sqrt{6} = \sqrt{36} = 6$

$$= \frac{5\sqrt{6}}{2}$$ Simplify, dividing numerator and denominator by 3.

b. $$\sqrt{\frac{3}{5}} = \frac{\sqrt{3}}{\sqrt{5}}$$ The square root of a quotient is the quotient of the square roots.

$$= \frac{\sqrt{3}}{\sqrt{5}} \cdot \frac{\sqrt{5}}{\sqrt{5}}$$ Since $\sqrt{5}$ is the smallest factor that will produce a perfect square in the denominator, multiply by 1, choosing $\dfrac{\sqrt{5}}{\sqrt{5}}$ for 1.

$$= \frac{\sqrt{15}}{5}$$ $\sqrt{5} \cdot \sqrt{5} = \sqrt{25} = 5$

c. $$\sqrt{\frac{7}{x}} = \frac{\sqrt{7}}{\sqrt{x}}$$ The square root of a quotient is the quotient of the square roots.

$$= \frac{\sqrt{7}}{\sqrt{x}} \cdot \frac{\sqrt{x}}{\sqrt{x}}$$ Multiply by 1, choosing $\dfrac{\sqrt{x}}{\sqrt{x}}$ for 1, and rationalize the denominator.

$$= \frac{\sqrt{7x}}{x}$$ $\sqrt{x} \cdot \sqrt{x} = \sqrt{x^2} = x$ (where $x > 0$) ∎

It is a good idea to simplify a radical expression before attempting to rationalize the denominator.

EXAMPLE 2   **Simplifying and Then Rationalizing Denominators**

Rationalize the denominator: **a.** $\dfrac{12}{\sqrt{8}}$ **b.** $\sqrt{\dfrac{7a}{75}}$ **c.** $\sqrt{\dfrac{x^2}{5}}$

Solution

a. We begin by simplifying $\sqrt{8}$.

$$\frac{12}{\sqrt{8}} = \frac{12}{\sqrt{4 \cdot 2}}$$ 4 is the largest perfect square factor of 8.

$$= \frac{12}{2\sqrt{2}}$$ $\sqrt{4 \cdot 2} = \sqrt{4}\sqrt{2} = 2\sqrt{2}$

$$= \frac{6}{\sqrt{2}}$$ Reduce to lowest terms, dividing the numerator and denominator by 2.

$$= \frac{6}{\sqrt{2}} \cdot \frac{\sqrt{2}}{\sqrt{2}}$$ Rationalize the denominator.

$$= \frac{6\sqrt{2}}{2}$$ $\sqrt{2}\sqrt{2} = \sqrt{4} = 2$

$$= 3\sqrt{2}$$ Simplify.

b. $\sqrt{\dfrac{7a}{75}} = \dfrac{\sqrt{7a}}{\sqrt{75}}$ The square root of a quotient is the quotient of the square roots.

$$= \frac{\sqrt{7a}}{\sqrt{25 \cdot 3}}$$ Simplify the denominator. 25 is the largest perfect square factor of 75.

$$= \frac{\sqrt{7a}}{5\sqrt{3}}$$

$$= \frac{\sqrt{7a}}{5\sqrt{3}} \cdot \frac{\sqrt{3}}{\sqrt{3}}$$ Rationalize the denominator, choosing $\dfrac{\sqrt{3}}{\sqrt{3}}$ for 1.

$$= \frac{\sqrt{21a}}{5 \cdot 3}$$ $\sqrt{3} \cdot \sqrt{3} = \sqrt{9} = \sqrt{3}$

$$= \frac{\sqrt{21a}}{15}$$

c. $\sqrt{\dfrac{x^2}{5}} = \dfrac{\sqrt{x^2}}{\sqrt{5}}$ The square root of a quotient is the quotient of the square roots.

$$= \frac{x}{\sqrt{5}}$$ Assuming that $x \geq 0$, $\sqrt{x^2} = x$.

$$= \frac{x}{\sqrt{5}} \cdot \frac{\sqrt{5}}{\sqrt{5}}$$ Rationalize the denominator, choosing $\dfrac{\sqrt{5}}{\sqrt{5}}$ for 1.

$$= \frac{x\sqrt{5}}{5} \quad \text{or} \quad \frac{\sqrt{5}x}{5}$$ ∎

Study tip

You cannot simplify

$$\frac{\sqrt{21a}}{15}$$

by dividing numerator and denominator by 3. Although 3 is a factor of 15, it is *not* a factor of $\sqrt{21a}$. (The factor is $\sqrt{3}$.) Thus, the answer in Example 2b *cannot* be written as

$$\frac{\sqrt{7a}}{5}.$$

---

2 Rationalize denominators that contain two terms.

Using Conjugates to Rationalize Denominators

In the previous section, we saw that the product of *conjugates* such as $\sqrt{a} + \sqrt{b}$ and $\sqrt{a} - \sqrt{b}$ resulted in a rational number. Multiplying these radical expressions, we now obtain:

$$(\sqrt{a} + \sqrt{b})(\sqrt{a} - \sqrt{b}) = (\sqrt{a})^2 - (\sqrt{b})^2 = a - b.$$

This observation gives us a procedure for rationalizing the denominator in

expressions such as $\dfrac{7}{\sqrt{3} + 5}$. The radical in the denominator can be elimi-

nated by multiplying both the numerator and denominator by $\sqrt{3} - 5$, the conjugate of $\sqrt{3} + 5$. This forms the basis of our next example.

EXAMPLE 3   **Rationalizing a Denominator Using Conjugates**

Rationalize the denominator: $\dfrac{7}{\sqrt{3} + 5}$

ENRICHMENT ESSAY

PEANUTS reprinted by permission of United Feature Syndicate, Inc.

Bird appears to be working steps mentally. Fill in the missing steps that provide the details in going from

$$\frac{7\sqrt{2 \cdot 2 \cdot 3}}{6} \quad \text{to} \quad \frac{7}{3}\sqrt{3}.$$

tudy tip

The answer to Example 3 can be written in a number of equivalent ways. Since

$$\frac{a}{-b} = -\frac{a}{b}$$

the negative sign can be written in front of the number.

$$\frac{7(\sqrt{3} - 5)}{-22} = -\frac{7(\sqrt{3} - 5)}{22}$$

You can also attach the negative sign to the numerator and distribute -7 throughout the parentheses.

$$\frac{-7\sqrt{3} + 35}{22}$$

Solution

$$\frac{7}{\sqrt{3} + 5} = \frac{7}{\sqrt{3} + 5} \cdot \left(\frac{\sqrt{3} - 5}{\sqrt{3} - 5}\right)$$

Multiply the numerator and denominator by the conjugate of the denominator.

$$= \frac{7(\sqrt{3} - 5)}{(\sqrt{3})^2 - 5^2}$$

$(A + B)(A - B) = A^2 - B^2$

$$= \frac{7(\sqrt{3} - 5)}{3 - 25}$$

$(\sqrt{3})^2 = \sqrt{3} \cdot \sqrt{3} = \sqrt{9} = 3$

$$= \frac{7(\sqrt{3} - 5)}{-22}$$

Based on Example 3, we can generalize the following procedure.

Rationalizing denominators that contain two terms with one or more square roots

To rationalize the denominator of an expression containing a binomial denominator with one or more square roots, multiply the numerator and denominator by the conjugate of the denominator.

EXAMPLE 4 **Using Conjugates to Rationalize a Denominator**

Rationalize the denominator: $\dfrac{6}{5 - \sqrt{3}}$

Solution

We multiply the numerator and denominator by the conjugate of the denominator, which is $5 + \sqrt{3}$.

$$\frac{6}{5 - \sqrt{3}} = \frac{6}{5 - \sqrt{3}} \cdot \frac{5 + \sqrt{3}}{5 + \sqrt{3}}$$

Multiply by 1.

$$= \frac{6(5 + \sqrt{3})}{5^2 - (\sqrt{3})^2}$$

$(A - B)(A + B) = A^2 - B^2$

$$= \frac{6(5 + \sqrt{3})}{25 - 3}$$

$(\sqrt{3})^2 = \sqrt{9} = 3$

$$= \frac{6(5 + \sqrt{3})}{22}$$

The denominator is now rationalized. The numerator and denominator have a common factor of 2.

$$= \frac{\overset{1}{\cancel{2}} \cdot 3(5 + \sqrt{3})}{\underset{1}{\cancel{2}} \cdot 11}$$

Divide out the common factor of 2. This step is usually done mentally.

$$= \frac{3(5 + \sqrt{3})}{11} \quad \text{or} \quad \frac{15 + 3\sqrt{3}}{11} \qquad \blacksquare$$

EXAMPLE 5   **Using Conjugates to Rationalize a Denominator**

Rationalize the denominator: $\dfrac{4 + \sqrt{3}}{\sqrt{6} - \sqrt{2}}$

Solution

Multiply the numerator and denominator by the conjugate of the denominator, which is $\sqrt{6} + \sqrt{2}$.

$$\frac{4 + \sqrt{3}}{\sqrt{6} - \sqrt{2}} = \left(\frac{4 + \sqrt{3}}{\sqrt{6} - \sqrt{2}}\right) \cdot \frac{\sqrt{6} + \sqrt{2}}{\sqrt{6} + \sqrt{2}}$$

Multiply by 1.

$$= \frac{4\sqrt{6} + 4\sqrt{2} + \sqrt{18} + \sqrt{6}}{(\sqrt{6})^2 - (\sqrt{2})^2}$$

Use the FOIL method in the numerator. In the denominator, $(A - B)(A + B) = A^2 - B^2$.

$$= \frac{5\sqrt{6} + 4\sqrt{2} + 3\sqrt{2}}{6 - 2}$$

In the numerator, combine $4\sqrt{6} + \sqrt{6} = 5\sqrt{6}$ and simplify $\sqrt{18} = \sqrt{9 \cdot 2} = 3\sqrt{2}$.

$$= \frac{5\sqrt{6} + 7\sqrt{2}}{4}$$

In the numerator, $4\sqrt{2} + 3\sqrt{2} = 7\sqrt{2}$. $\qquad \blacksquare$

Simplifying Radicals

Our work throughout this chapter has involved adding, subtracting, multiplying, and dividing radicals, as well as rationalizing denominators. Those operations result in radical expressions that are in *simplified form*. Table 9.3 outlines the conditions for simplified radical form. Observe that the examples review what we have learned up to this point.

Table 9.3 contains nothing that is new. However, be aware that directions such as "add the radicals" or "rationalize the denominator" can be replaced by the catchall phrase "simplify."

TABLE 9.3 Conditions for Simplified Radical Form

Characteristic of Simplified Form	Examples
There are no perfect square factors under the square root sign, no perfect cube factors under the cube root sign, and so on.	$\sqrt{49} = 7$ $\sqrt{20} = \sqrt{4 \cdot 5} = \sqrt{4}\sqrt{5} = 2\sqrt{5}$ $\sqrt[3]{16} = \sqrt[3]{8 \cdot 2} = \sqrt[3]{8}\sqrt[3]{2} = 2\sqrt[3]{2}$ $\sqrt{\dfrac{9}{25}} = \dfrac{3}{5}$
Products and quotients are written as a single radical.	$\sqrt{7} \cdot \sqrt{3} = \sqrt{21}$ $\dfrac{\sqrt{15}}{\sqrt{3}} = \sqrt{\dfrac{15}{3}} = \sqrt{5}$ $\sqrt[3]{2} \cdot \sqrt[3]{5} = \sqrt[3]{10}$
Like radicals are combined.	$2\sqrt{3} + 7\sqrt{3} = 9\sqrt{3}$ $\sqrt{8} + \sqrt{2} = \sqrt{4 \cdot 2} + \sqrt{2} = 2\sqrt{2} + \sqrt{2} = 3\sqrt{2}$ But: $2\sqrt{5} + 4\sqrt{3}$ cannot be simplified.
Fractions do not appear under the radical sign.	$\sqrt{\dfrac{3}{4}} = \dfrac{\sqrt{3}}{\sqrt{4}} = \dfrac{\sqrt{3}}{2}$ $\sqrt[3]{\dfrac{5}{64}} = \dfrac{\sqrt[3]{5}}{\sqrt[3]{64}} = \dfrac{\sqrt[3]{5}}{4}$
Radicals do not appear in denominators. Any denominator containing a radical should be rationalized.	$\dfrac{2}{\sqrt{3}} = \dfrac{2}{\sqrt{3}} \cdot \dfrac{\sqrt{3}}{\sqrt{3}} = \dfrac{2\sqrt{3}}{3}$ $\sqrt{\dfrac{5}{2}} = \dfrac{\sqrt{5}}{\sqrt{2}} = \dfrac{\sqrt{5}}{\sqrt{2}} \cdot \dfrac{\sqrt{2}}{\sqrt{2}} = \dfrac{\sqrt{10}}{2}$ $\dfrac{3}{\sqrt{2}+1} = \dfrac{3}{\sqrt{2}+1} \cdot \dfrac{\sqrt{2}-1}{\sqrt{2}-1} = \dfrac{3(\sqrt{2}-1)}{2-1} = 3(\sqrt{2}-1)$

PROBLEM SET 9.4

Practice Problems

Rationalize each denominator in Problems 1–34. If applicable, provide numerical support to problems that do not contain variables by obtaining a decimal approximation for the given number and its simplified form using a calculator.

1. $\dfrac{2}{\sqrt{3}}$
2. $\dfrac{5}{\sqrt{6}}$
3. $\dfrac{21}{\sqrt{7}}$
4. $\dfrac{30}{\sqrt{5}}$
5. $\sqrt{\dfrac{2}{5}}$
6. $\sqrt{\dfrac{5}{7}}$

7. $\sqrt{\dfrac{7}{3}}$
8. $\sqrt{\dfrac{5}{2}}$
9. $\sqrt{\dfrac{11}{x}}$
10. $\sqrt{\dfrac{6}{x}}$
11. $\sqrt{\dfrac{x}{y}}$
12. $\sqrt{\dfrac{a}{b}}$

13. $\dfrac{12}{\sqrt{32}}$
14. $\dfrac{15}{\sqrt{50}}$
15. $\dfrac{15}{\sqrt{12}}$
16. $\dfrac{13}{\sqrt{40}}$
17. $\sqrt{\dfrac{5}{18}}$
18. $\sqrt{\dfrac{7}{12}}$

19. $\sqrt{\dfrac{20}{3}}$
20. $\sqrt{\dfrac{32}{5}}$
21. $\sqrt{\dfrac{a}{32}}$
22. $\sqrt{\dfrac{b}{40}}$
23. $\sqrt{\dfrac{x^2}{11}}$
24. $\sqrt{\dfrac{x^2}{15}}$

25. $\dfrac{\sqrt{7x}}{\sqrt{8}}$
26. $\dfrac{\sqrt{3y}}{\sqrt{125}}$
27. $\sqrt{\dfrac{7a}{12}}$
28. $\sqrt{\dfrac{11b}{18}}$
29. $\sqrt{\dfrac{45}{x}}$
30. $\sqrt{\dfrac{27}{x}}$

31. $\sqrt{\dfrac{27}{a^3}}$
32. $\sqrt{\dfrac{45}{b^3}}$
33. $\dfrac{\sqrt{50a^2}}{\sqrt{12a^3}}$
34. $\dfrac{\sqrt{27b^2}}{\sqrt{3b^3}}$

Rationalize each denominator in Problems 35–56. If applicable, use a calculator to provide numerical support for your answer.

35. $\dfrac{5}{\sqrt{3}-1}$ **36.** $\dfrac{7}{\sqrt{5}-2}$ **37.** $\dfrac{15}{\sqrt{7}+2}$ **38.** $\dfrac{16}{\sqrt{11}+3}$ **39.** $\dfrac{18}{3-\sqrt{3}}$ **40.** $\dfrac{40}{5-\sqrt{5}}$

41. $\dfrac{\sqrt{2}}{\sqrt{2}+1}$ **42.** $\dfrac{\sqrt{3}}{\sqrt{3}-1}$ **43.** $\dfrac{\sqrt{12}}{\sqrt{3}-1}$ **44.** $\dfrac{\sqrt{18}}{\sqrt{2}+1}$ **45.** $\dfrac{3\sqrt{2}}{\sqrt{10}+2}$ **46.** $\dfrac{2\sqrt{3}}{\sqrt{3}+5}$

47. $\dfrac{\sqrt{3}+1}{\sqrt{2}-1}$ **48.** $\dfrac{\sqrt{2}+3}{\sqrt{2}+1}$ **49.** $\dfrac{\sqrt{2}-2}{2-\sqrt{3}}$ **50.** $\dfrac{\sqrt{2}+3}{\sqrt{3}-1}$ **51.** $\dfrac{2\sqrt{3}+1}{\sqrt{6}-\sqrt{3}}$ **52.** $\dfrac{2\sqrt{5}+1}{\sqrt{2}+5}$

53. $\dfrac{\sqrt{5}+\sqrt{6}}{\sqrt{5}+\sqrt{3}}$ **54.** $\dfrac{\sqrt{3}-\sqrt{2}}{\sqrt{3}+\sqrt{2}}$ **55.** $\dfrac{\sqrt{5}+\sqrt{2}}{\sqrt{5}-\sqrt{2}}$ **56.** $\dfrac{\sqrt{5}+\sqrt{3}}{\sqrt{5}-\sqrt{3}}$

Simplify each radical expression in Problems 57–70. If applicable, use a calculator to provide numerical support for your answer.

57. $\sqrt{56}$ **58.** $\sqrt{63}$ **59.** $\sqrt[4]{32}$ **60.** $\sqrt[3]{81}$

61. $8\sqrt{27}-3\sqrt{12}$ **62.** $5\sqrt{24}-2\sqrt{54}+3\sqrt{20}$ **63.** $7\sqrt{15}-2\sqrt{5}\cdot\sqrt{3}$

64. $8\sqrt{35}-6\sqrt{5}\sqrt{7}$ **65.** $\dfrac{9}{\sqrt{18}}$ **66.** $\dfrac{8}{\sqrt{28}}$

67. $(2\sqrt{5}+\sqrt{3})(\sqrt{2}+\sqrt{7})$ **68.** $(4\sqrt{3}-\sqrt{2})(\sqrt{5}+\sqrt{6})$

69. $\dfrac{\sqrt{6}+1}{\sqrt{2}-4}$ **70.** $\dfrac{\sqrt{2}+\sqrt{3}}{\sqrt{7}-\sqrt{2}}$

Application Problems

71. The early Greeks believed that the most pleasing of all rectangles were golden rectangles whose ratio of width to height (see figure) is

$$\frac{w}{h}=\frac{2}{\sqrt{5}-1}.$$

Rationalize the denominator for this ratio and then use a calculator to approximate the answer correct to the nearest hundredth. The United Nations Building in New York, shown in the figure, was designed as three golden rectangles, like three Greek Parthenons stacked upon each other. Like the harmony that the Greeks found in the golden rectangle, the design of the United Nations Building was appropriate to its mission of promoting world harmony.

Jon Riley/Tony Stone Images

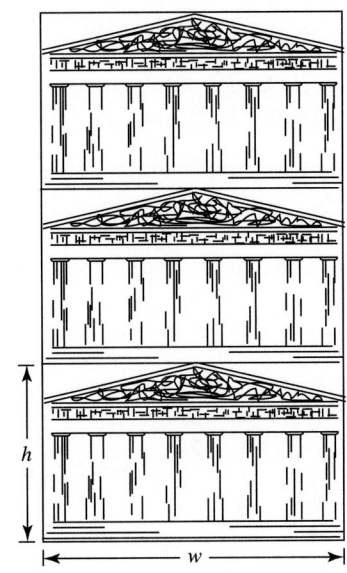

72. The period (p) of a pendulum is the time it takes for it to swing from one side to the other and back. The value of p in seconds is modeled by the formula

$$p = 2\pi \sqrt{\frac{L}{32}},$$

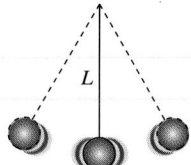

where L is the length of the pendulum in feet. Find the period for a pendulum of length 9 feet. Use 3.14 for π and give the answer as a simplified radical. Then use a calculator to approximate the period correct to the nearest hundredth.

True–False Critical Thinking Problems

73. Which one of the following is true?

a. $\dfrac{4 + 8\sqrt{3}}{4} = 1 + 8\sqrt{3}$

b. $\dfrac{3\sqrt{x}}{x\sqrt{6}} = \dfrac{\sqrt{6x}}{2x}$ for $x > 0$

c. Conjugates are used to rationalize the denominator of $\dfrac{2 - \sqrt{5}}{\sqrt{3}}$.

d. $\sqrt{3} + \sqrt{27}$ is in simplified form.

74. Which one of the following is true?

a. $\dfrac{7}{\sqrt{2} - 7}$ and $\dfrac{-7\sqrt{2} - 49}{47}$ have the same decimal approximations when a calculator is used.

b. $\dfrac{6 + 12\sqrt{5}}{6} = 1 + 12\sqrt{5}$

c. Radical expressions in simplified form require less space to write than before they are simplified.

d. The expression $\dfrac{\sqrt{7}}{13}$ contains a fraction and consequently is not in simplified form.

Technology Problems

In Problems 75–78, determine if each simplification is correct by graphing the function on each side of the equality with your graphing utility. Shown in the same viewing rectangle, the graphs should be the same. If they are not, correct the right side of the equation. Then use your graphing utility to verify the result.

75. $\sqrt{2} \cdot \sqrt{2x} = 4\sqrt{x}$

76. $\dfrac{2}{\sqrt{x}} = \dfrac{2\sqrt{x}}{x}$

77. $\dfrac{x}{\sqrt{2} - 1} = (\sqrt{2} - 1)x$

78. $\sqrt{8x} + \sqrt{2x} = 5\sqrt{2x}$

Writing in Mathematics

79. When a radical expression has its denominator rationalized, we change the denominator so that it no longer contains a radical. Doesn't this change the value of the radical expression? Explain.

80. Suppose that you do not have a calculator and wish to obtain a decimal approximation for $\dfrac{5}{\sqrt{7}}$. From a table of square roots, you know that $\sqrt{7} \approx 2.6458$. Describe the advantage of rationalizing the denominator to obtain a decimal approximation for $\dfrac{5}{\sqrt{7}}$.

81. Square the real number $\dfrac{2}{\sqrt{3}}$. Observe that the radical is eliminated from the denominator. Explain whether this process is equivalent to rationalizing the denominator.

Critical Thinking Problems

82. Simplify: $\sqrt{2} + \sqrt{\frac{1}{2}}$.

83. Find the exact value of: $\sqrt{13 + \sqrt{2} + \dfrac{7}{3 + \sqrt{2}}}$.

84. Fill in the box to make the statement true: $\dfrac{4}{2 + \sqrt{\square}} = 8 - 4\sqrt{3}$.

Denominators with roots higher than square roots can also be rationalized. For example, to rationalize the denominator of

$$\frac{2}{\sqrt[3]{4}}$$

we must produce a perfect cube radicand in the denominator. This can be obtained by multiplying by 1 in the form $\dfrac{\sqrt[3]{2}}{\sqrt[3]{2}}$ *since* $\sqrt[3]{4} \cdot \sqrt[3]{2} = \sqrt[3]{8} = 2$. *Rationalize the denominators in Problems 85–90.*

85. $\dfrac{2}{\sqrt[3]{4}}$ $\left(\text{Multiply by } \dfrac{\sqrt[3]{2}}{\sqrt[3]{2}}.\right)$

86. $\dfrac{\sqrt[3]{7}}{\sqrt[3]{9}}$ $\left(\text{Multiply by } \dfrac{\sqrt[3]{3}}{\sqrt[3]{3}}.\right)$

87. $\dfrac{1}{\sqrt[3]{3}}$

88. $\dfrac{6}{\sqrt[3]{25}}$

89. $\dfrac{1}{\sqrt[4]{2}}$

90. $\dfrac{1}{\sqrt[5]{2}}$

Review Problems

91. Multiply and simplify: $\dfrac{x^2 - 6x + 9}{12} \cdot \dfrac{3}{x^2 - 9}$.

92. Solve: $\dfrac{1}{y - 1} + \dfrac{1}{y + 1} = \dfrac{3y - 2}{y^2 - 1}$.

93. Simplify: $(2x^2)^{-3}$.

S E C T I O N   9 . 5

Solutions Manual   **Tutorial**   **Video**

‖

Equations Containing Radicals

Objectives

1 Solve radical equations.
2 Solve problems using radical models.

In this section, we study equations with variables in the radicand, called *radical equations*. The following are examples of radical equations.

$$\sqrt{3x + 4} = 8, \quad 2\sqrt{y} = \sqrt{3y + 9}, \quad \text{and} \quad \sqrt{2y - 1} + 2 = y$$

Our goal is to establish a process for finding all numbers that when substituted into the equation cause the left and right sides to be equal. The equations that we will study all contain square roots.

❚ Solve radical equations.

Solving Radical Equations

Mathematics is filled with examples where one operation undoes another operation. Changes brought about by addition can be reversed by subtraction; multiplication is undone by division. In a similar way, if we take the square root of a nonnegative number, the number can be restored by squaring this result. For example, if we start with 9, $\sqrt{9} = 3$ and $3^2 = 9$. In general,

$$(\sqrt{x})^2 = x \quad \text{for } x \geqslant 0.$$

Thus, for nonnegative radicands,

$$(\sqrt{x + 1})^2 = x + 1, \quad (\sqrt{2x - 1})^2 = 2x - 1, \quad (\sqrt{3y + 5})^2 = 3y + 5.$$

The addition and multiplication properties of equality are not sufficient to solve equations containing radicals such as $\sqrt{x + 1} = 9$. We can, however, eliminate the radical sign, "undoing the square root," by squaring both sides of the equation.

$$\sqrt{x+1}=9$$
$$(\sqrt{x+1})^2=9^2 \quad \text{Square both sides.}$$
$$x+1=81 \quad (\sqrt{x+1})^2=x+1$$
$$x=80 \quad \text{Subtract 1 from both sides.}$$

At this point, 80 can be shown to satisfy the original equation.

$$\sqrt{x+1}=9$$
$$\sqrt{80+1}\overset{?}{=}9 \quad \text{Substitute 80 for } x.$$
$$\sqrt{81}\overset{?}{=}9$$
$$9=9 \quad \checkmark \quad \text{This true statement shows that 80 is the solution.}$$

There is, however, a problem with squaring both sides of an equation. At times, this process can change a false statement into a true statement. For example, take the false statement $5=-5$ and square both sides.

$$5=-5 \quad \text{This statement is false.}$$
$$5^2=(-5)^2 \quad \text{Square both sides.}$$
$$25=25 \quad \text{This statement is true.}$$

Furthermore, squaring both sides of an equation can result in a new equation that has more solutions than the original equation. Consider, for example, the equation $x=5$.

$$x=5$$
$$x^2=5^2 \quad \text{Square both sides.}$$
$$x^2=25 \quad 5^2=25$$
$$x=5 \quad \text{or} \quad x=-5 \quad \text{Both 5 and } -5 \text{ when squared give 25.}$$

Notice that $x=5$ has only one solution, yet $x^2=25$ has two solutions.

The squaring property of equality is used to solve equations containing square roots.

Squaring property of equality: If $a=b$, then $a^2=b^2$

The square root radicals in an equation can be eliminated by squaring both sides of the equation. When both sides are squared, all solutions of the original equation are among the solutions of the squared equation, but not every solution necessarily satisfies the original equation. Whenever both sides of an equation are squared, all potential solutions must be checked in the original equation.

EXAMPLE I   Using the Squaring Property of Equality

Solve: $\sqrt{3x+4}=8$

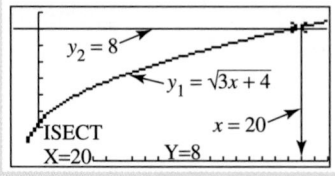

ENRICHMENT ESSAY

Radicals and Relativistic Time

According to Einstein's theory of relativity, if one system is moving rapidly with respect to another system, time passes more slowly in the moving system as observed from Earth.

The model

$$R_a = R_f \sqrt{1 - \left(\frac{v}{c}\right)^2}$$

compares the aging rate of an astronaut (R_a) to the aging rate of a friend on earth (R_f), where v is the astronaut's speed and c is the speed of light. As the astronaut's speed approaches the speed of light, we can substitute c for v in the formula:

$$R_a = R_f \sqrt{1 - \left(\frac{v}{c}\right)^2} \quad \text{Let } v = c.$$
$$= R_f \sqrt{1 - 1^2}$$
$$= R_f \sqrt{0} = 0$$

If the astronaut were to travel at the speed of light, $R_a = 0$, meaning that the astronaut would not age as observed from Earth!

Even more bizarre is Einstein's picture of what happens as a traveler's speed closes in on the velocity of light. Space becomes so thin external to the astronaut that at the speed of light, space would flatten in a way where the rear moves around to the front! In this compressed space, if you were to look forward, you would be confronted with the fact that the back of your head would be the only thing visible.

The absurd image of "back becoming front" at the speed of light is captured by the Belgian surrealist René Magritte (1898–1967) in his painting *The Glasshouse* (1939).

Rene Magritte, "The Glasshouse" 1939. Bridgeman, Art Resource, New York/© 1995 C. Herscovici, Brussels/ARS, New York.

Solution

$$\sqrt{3x + 4} = 8 \qquad \text{This is the original equation.}$$

$$(\sqrt{3x + 4})^2 = 8^2 \qquad \text{Eliminate the radical by squaring both sides with the squaring property of equality.}$$

$$3x + 4 = 64 \qquad (\sqrt{3x + 4})^2 = 3x + 4$$

$$3x = 60 \qquad \text{Subtract 4 from both sides.}$$

$$x = 20 \qquad \text{Divide both sides by 3.}$$

Check

$$\sqrt{3x + 4} = 8 \qquad \text{This is the original equation.}$$

$$\sqrt{3 \cdot 20 + 4} \overset{?}{=} 8 \qquad \text{Substitute 20, the possible solution, for } x.$$

$$\sqrt{64} \overset{?}{=} 8$$

$$8 = 8 \quad \checkmark \qquad \text{This true statement indicates that 20 is the solution.}$$

The solution is 20.

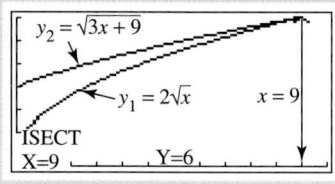

EXAMPLE 2 **Using the Squaring Property of Equality**

Solve: $2\sqrt{y} = \sqrt{3y + 9}$

Solution

$2\sqrt{y} = \sqrt{3y + 9}$	This is the original equation.
$(2\sqrt{y})^2 = (\sqrt{3y + 9})^2$	Eliminate the radicals by squaring both sides.
$2^2(\sqrt{y})^2 = (\sqrt{3y + 9})^2$	On the left: $(ab)^2 = a^2b^2$
	The square of a product is the product of their squares.
$4y = 3y + 9$	$(\sqrt{y})^2 = y$ and $(\sqrt{3y + 9})^2 = 3y + 9$
$y = 9$	Subtract $3y$ from both sides.

Check

$2\sqrt{y} = \sqrt{3y + 9}$	This is the original equation.
$2\sqrt{9} \stackrel{?}{=} \sqrt{3 \cdot 9 + 9}$	Substitute 9, the possible solution, for y.
$2(3) \stackrel{?}{=} \sqrt{36}$	$\sqrt{9} = 3$ and $\sqrt{3 \cdot 9 + 9} = \sqrt{27 + 9} = \sqrt{36}$
$6 = 6$ ✓	This true statement indicates that 9 is the solution.

The solution is 9. ∎

EXAMPLE 3 **A Radical Equation with No Solution**

Solve: $\sqrt{x} = -5$

Discover for yourself

The original equation states that the square root of some number is -5. What number has a square root that is negative? What does this mean about the solution to this equation?

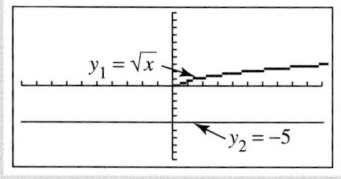

Solution

$\sqrt{x} = -5$	This is the original equation. Since $\sqrt{x}$ represents the nonnegative square root of x, you may realize that this equation has no solution.
$(\sqrt{x})^2 = (-5)^2$	Square both sides.
$x = 25$	

Check

$\sqrt{x} = -5$	This is the original equation.
$\sqrt{25} \stackrel{?}{=} -5$	Substitute 25, the possible solution, for x.
$5 = -5$	This false statement indicates that 25 is not a solution and is said to be *extraneous*.

The equation has no solution. ∎

The examples we have considered so far illustrate the general method for solving equations with radicals that are square roots. Before turning to additional problems, let's summarize the method.

Solving equations containing square roots

1. If necessary, arrange terms so that one radical is isolated on one side of the equation.
2. Square both sides.
3. Combine like terms on each side of the equation.
4. If there is still a term containing a square root, repeat steps 1 through 3.
5. Solve the equation.
6. Substitute all potential solutions into the original equation.

EXAMPLE 4 **A Radical Equation That Becomes Quadratic**

Solve: $\sqrt{2y - 1} + 2 = y$

Discover for yourself

Try squaring both sides of the equation before isolating $\sqrt{2y - 1}$ on the left:

$$(\sqrt{2y - 1} + 2)^2 = y^2$$

Use the FOIL method to square the left side. Describe what happens.

Using technology

Although the equation

$$\sqrt{2x - 1} + 2 = x$$

(equivalently:

$$\sqrt{2y - 1} + 2 = y)$$

initially appears to have two solutions based on our algebraic approach, the graphs of

$$y_1 = \sqrt{2x - 1} + 2$$

and

$$y_2 = x$$

intersect only once. The number of intersections is the number of solutions of the equation. As shown in Example 4, the solution is 5.

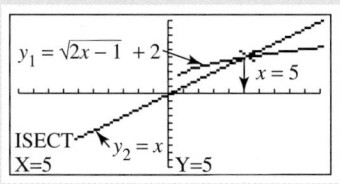

Solution

In the Discover for Yourself, did you observe that squaring both sides before isolating $\sqrt{2y - 1}$ on the left results in an equation that is more complicated and still has a radical? For this reason, we first isolate the radical term and then square both sides.

$\sqrt{2y - 1} + 2 = y$	This is the original equation.
$\sqrt{2y - 1} = y - 2$	Get the radical alone by subtracting 2 from both sides.
$(\sqrt{2y - 1})^2 = (y - 2)^2$	Square both sides to eliminate the radical.
$2y - 1 = (y - 2)(y - 2)$	$(\sqrt{2y - 1})^2 = 2y - 1$
$2y - 1 = y^2 - 4y + 4$	Use the FOIL method or the special product for $(A - B)^2$ on the right. The resulting equation is quadratic.
$0 = y^2 - 6y + 5$	Set the quadratic equation equal to 0 by subtracting $2y$ and adding 1 to both sides.
$0 = (y - 1)(y - 5)$	Factor.
$y - 1 = 0$ or $y - 5 = 0$	Set each factor equal to 0.
$y = 1 \qquad\qquad y = 5$	Solve the resulting equations.

Complete the solution process by substituting the proposed solutions into the original equation.

Check

For $y = 1$	**For $y = 5$**
$\sqrt{2y - 1} + 2 = y$	$\sqrt{2y - 1} + 2 = y$
$\sqrt{2(1) - 1} + 2 \overset{?}{=} 1$	$\sqrt{2(5) - 1} + 2 \overset{?}{=} 5$
$\sqrt{1} + 2 \overset{?}{=} 1$	$\sqrt{9} + 2 \overset{?}{=} 5$
$3 \neq 1$	$3 + 2 \overset{?}{=} 5$
	$5 = 5 \checkmark$

Thus, 1 is an extraneous solution. The solution is 5. ■

2 Solve problems using radical models.

At times, mathematical models do not describe the physical world with total accuracy.

Marisol "Women and Dog" 1964, Wood, plaster, synthetic polymer, taxi-dermed dog head and miscellaneous items. Installed: $72\frac{1}{4} \times 73 \times 30\frac{15}{16}$ in. ($183.5 \times 185.4 \times 78.6$ cm). Purchase, with funds from the Friends of the Whitney Museum of American Art. 64.17a-g. Collection of Whitney Museum of American Art, New York. Photography by: Robert E. Mates, Inc. © 1998 Marisol Escobar/Licensed by VAGA, New York, NY.

Radical Models

A radical model is a mathematical model containing one or more radicals. Techniques for solving radical equations can be used to answer questions about variables contained in radical models.

EXAMPLE 5 **Radical Models and IQ**

The formula $N = 2\sqrt{Q} - 9$ is used by psychologists to determine the number of nonsense syllables (N) a subject with an IQ of Q can repeat. A subject repeats 13 nonsense syllables. What is that person's IQ?

Solution

$N = 2\sqrt{Q} - 9$	This is the given mathematical model.
$13 = 2\sqrt{Q} - 9$	Since 13 syllables are repeated, $N = 13$. We must solve for Q.
$22 = 2\sqrt{Q}$	To isolate the term with the radical, add 9 to both sides.
$11 = \sqrt{Q}$	Since all terms are divisible by 2, divide both sides by 2.
$(11)^2 = (\sqrt{Q})^2$	Square both sides.
$121 = Q$	$11^2 = 121$ and $(\sqrt{Q})^2 = Q$

121 can be shown to satisfy $13 = 2\sqrt{Q} - 9$. The subject who repeats 13 nonsense syllables has an IQ of 121. ■

PROBLEM SET 9.5

Practice Problems _____

Solve the radical equations in Problems 1–42. Check proposed solutions by direct substitution and, if applicable, with a graphing utility.

1. $\sqrt{x} = 4$ **2.** $\sqrt{x} = 9$ **3.** $\sqrt{x} = 5$ **4.** $\sqrt{x} = 3$ **5.** $\sqrt{x + 4} = 2$

6. $\sqrt{x - 2} = 5$ **7.** $\sqrt{x - 4} = 11$ **8.** $\sqrt{x + 6} = 8$ **9.** $\sqrt{3y - 2} = 4$ **10.** $\sqrt{5y - 1} = 8$

11. $\sqrt{3x + 5} = 2$ **12.** $\sqrt{5x - 2} = 6$ **13.** $3\sqrt{z} = \sqrt{8z + 16}$ **14.** $3\sqrt{y} = \sqrt{5y - 1}$

15. $\sqrt{2y - 3} = 2\sqrt{3y - 2}$ **16.** $\sqrt{7y + 4} = 3\sqrt{y - 2}$ **17.** $\sqrt{2y - 3} = -5$ **18.** $\sqrt{3y - 8} = -4$

19. $\sqrt{3y + 4} - 2 = 3$ **20.** $\sqrt{5y - 4} - 2 = 4$ **21.** $\sqrt{6x - 8} - 3 = 1$ **22.** $\sqrt{2y + 1} + 5 = 2$

23. $3\sqrt{y - 1} = \sqrt{3y + 3}$ **24.** $\sqrt{5y + 9} = 2\sqrt{3y + 4}$ **25.** $\sqrt{y + 3} = y - 3$ **26.** $\sqrt{y + 10} = y - 2$

27. $\sqrt{2x + 13} = x + 7$ **28.** $\sqrt{6y + 1} = y - 1$ **29.** $\sqrt{y^2 + 5} = y + 1$ **30.** $\sqrt{y^2 - 2} = y - 1$

31. $\sqrt{3y + 3} + 5 = y$ **32.** $\sqrt{y + 1} - 1 = y$ **33.** $\sqrt{3z + 7} - z = 3$ **34.** $\sqrt{1 - 8y} - y = 4$

35. $\sqrt{3y + 10} = y + 4$ **36.** $\sqrt{y - 3} = y - 9$ **37.** $\sqrt{4z^2 + 3z - 2} - 2z = 0$

38. $\sqrt{16z^2 + 2z + 2} - 4z = 0$ **39.** $\sqrt{3y^2 + 6y + 4} - 2 = 0$ **40.** $\sqrt{2y^2 + 6y + 9} - 3 = 0$

41. $3\sqrt{y} + 5 = 2$ **42.** $3\sqrt{y} + 8 = 5$

Application Problems

43. Out of a group of 50,000 births, the number of people (N) surviving to age x is given by the formula $N = 5000\sqrt{100 - x}$. To what age will 40,000 people in the group survive?

44. The number of addresses (N) that a London taxi driver can correctly locate after t weeks of school is described by $N = 300\sqrt{t} - 10$. How many weeks of schooling are necessary to locate 1790 addresses correctly?

45. Police use the formula $s = 30\sqrt{\dfrac{a}{p}}$ to estimate the speed (s) at which a car traveled at the time of an accident, where a is the length (in feet) of the skid marks made by the car in the accident. A police car traveling at 30 miles per hour simulates the conditions of the accident. In the model, p is the length of the skid marks made by the police test car. A car traveling at 90 miles per hour was in an accident that was simulated by a test car. If the length of the skid marks left by the police test car was 100 feet, what was the length of the skid marks left at the time of the accident?

46. The time (t, in seconds) for a free-falling object to fall d feet is described by the mathematical model $t = \sqrt{\dfrac{d}{16}}$. If a worker accidentally drops a hammer from a building and it hits the ground after 4 seconds, from what height was the hammer dropped?

47. The figure at the top of the next column shows a grandfather clock whose pendulum length is L feet. The time (T, in seconds) it takes the pendulum of the clock to swing through one complete cycle is described by

$$T = \frac{11}{7}\sqrt{\frac{L}{2}}.$$

Determine how long the pendulum must be for one complete cycle to take 2 seconds.

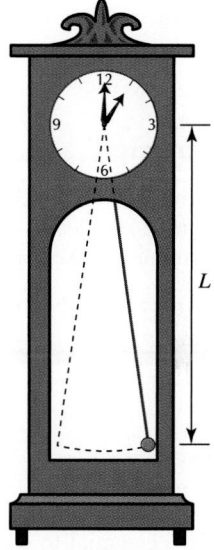

48. The distance d in kilometers that one can see to the horizon from an altitude of h meters is described by the mathematical model $d = 3.5\sqrt{h}$. A plane flying at an altitude of 8 kilometers loses altitude so that the pilot can see a distance of 200 kilometers to the horizon. How much altitude did the plane lose?

49. Two tractors are removing a tree stump from the ground. If two forces A and B pull at right angles to each other, the size of the resulting force is given by the model $R = \sqrt{A^2 + B^2}$. Tractor A exerts 300 pounds of force. If the resulting force is 500 pounds, how much force is tractor B exerting in the removal of the stump?

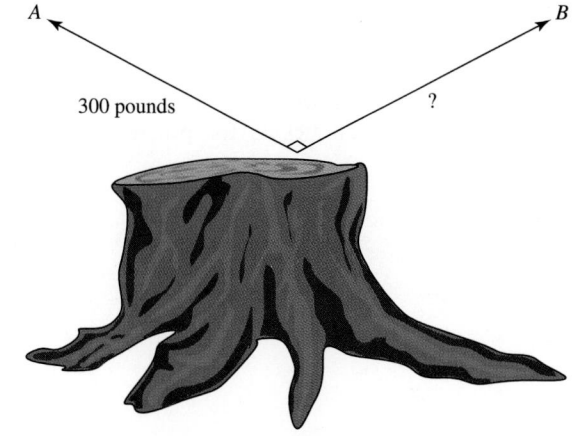

True–False Critical Thinking Problems

50. Which one of the following is true?
   a. The equation $y^2 = 25$ has the same solution as the equation $y = 5$. _____
   b. The equation $\sqrt{x^2 + 2x} = -1$ has no real number solution.
   c. The first step in solving $\sqrt{x} + 3 = 4$ is to take the square root of each side.
   d. When an extraneous root is substituted into an equation with radicals, a denominator of zero results.

51. Which one of the following is true?
   a. When both sides of $5\sqrt{x} = x + 2$ are squared, the resulting equation is $5x^2 = x^2 + 4$.
   b. The first step in solving an equation with square roots is to square both sides.
   c. Any equation in the form $\sqrt{x} = a$, where a is a negative number, has no real number solution.
   d. If an equation with square roots has two possible solutions and one of the possible solutions does not check, the other possible solution will definitely satisfy the equation.

Technology Problems

52. Solving the problem $\sqrt{2x - 3} = x - 3$ algebraically gives the solutions $x = 2$ and $x = 6$. Use a graphing utility to determine whether either of these solutions is extraneous. Describe how you drew your conclusion from the graphs.

Use a graphing utility to solve the equations in Problems 53–57. Check by direct substitution.

53. $\sqrt{2x + 2} = \sqrt{3x - 5}$

54. $\sqrt{x} + 3 = 5$

55. $\sqrt{x^2 + 3} = x + 1$

56. $4\sqrt{x} = x + 3$

57. $\sqrt{x} + 4 = 2$

Writing in Mathematics

58. Explain why $\sqrt{x + 3} = -5$ has no solution.

59. Explain why it is essential to check all potential solutions in the original equation when the squaring property of equality is used to solve an equation with square roots.

Critical Thinking Problems

Solve the equations in Problems 60–61. You will need to square both sides of the equation twice.

60. $\sqrt{x} + 2 = \sqrt{x + 8}$

61. $\sqrt{x - 8} = 5 - \sqrt{x + 7}$

62. The square root of the sum of two consecutive integers is one less than the smaller integer. Find the integers.

63. If $w = 2$, find $x, y,$ and z if $y = \sqrt{x - 2} + 2, z = \sqrt{y - 2} + 2,$ and $w = \sqrt{z - 2} + 2$.

Review Problems

64. A total of $9000 was invested for 1 year, part at 6% and the remainder at 4% simple interest. At the end of the year the investments earned $500 in interest. How much was invested at each rate?

65. Producers of *Elephant!,* a musical version of *The Elephant Man,* are a bit worried about their basic concept and decide to sell tickets for previews at cut-rate prices. If four orchestra and two mezzanine seats sell for $22, while two orchestra and three mezzanine seats sell for $16, what is the price of an orchestra seat?

66. Solve by graphing:
$$2x + y = -4$$
$$x + y = -3$$

SECTION 9.6

Solutions   Tutorial   Video
Manual   II

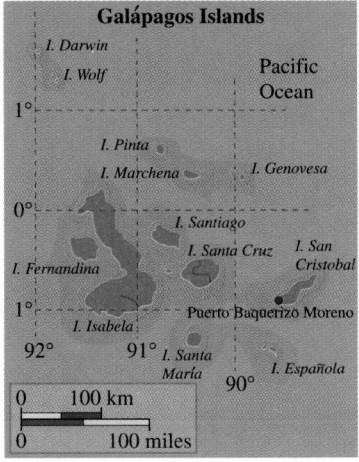

Fractional Exponents

Objectives

1 Evaluate expressions with fractional exponents.
2 Solve problems using models with fractional exponents.

The rate of increase of pollution in a river after t years is described by the mathematical model $R = \frac{1}{4}(t^{1/4} + 3)t^{-3/4}$. The number of plant species S on the various islands of the Galápagos chain of islands is $S = 28.6A^{1/3}$, where A is the area of the island in square miles. Just as descriptions of reality involve the use of integral exponents and roots, fractional exponents frequently come into play as we attempt a more inclusive picture of the world. But what do these fractional exponents mean? How can we interpret the information that is described by these formulas? In this section, we turn our attention to fractional exponents and their relationship to roots of real numbers.

All of the exponents that we considered in Chapter 6 were integers. We know, for example, that

$$7^2 = 7 \cdot 7 = 49, \quad 7^{-2} = \frac{1}{7^2} = \frac{1}{49}, \quad \text{and} \quad 7^0 = 1.$$

It is also possible to give meaning to an expression such as $7^{1/2}$ containing a fractional (rational) exponent. We can define $7^{1/2}$ by comparing the expression with $\sqrt{7}$ and applying the following exponential property.

$(x^m)^n = x^{mn}$ When an exponential expression is raised to a power, multiply exponents and use this new exponent on the base in the exponential expression once parentheses have been removed.

Here is what happens when we square $7^{1/2}$ and $\sqrt{7}$:

$$(7^{1/2})^2 = 7^{(1/2)\cdot 2} \quad (\sqrt{7})^2 = \sqrt{7}\sqrt{7}$$
$$= 7^1 \qquad\qquad = \sqrt{49}$$
$$= 7 \qquad\qquad\quad = 7$$

Since both expressions simplify to 7, it would make sense to define $7^{1/2}$ as $\sqrt{7}$. Generalizing, we obtain the following definition.

$$x^{1/2} = \sqrt{x} \quad \text{for } x \geqslant 0$$

Now work the Discover for Yourself box in the margin. See if you can discover the definition of $x^{1/3}$.

In the Discover for Yourself box, did you obtain $\sqrt[3]{x}$ for the definition of $x^{1/3}$? We can generalize these ideas in the following definitions.

Definitions of fractional exponents

For any nonnegative number x and any index n:

$$x^{1/n} = \sqrt[n]{x}.$$

Furthermore,

$$x^{-1/n} = \frac{1}{x^{1/n}} = \frac{1}{\sqrt[n]{x}}.$$

Evaluate expressions with fractional exponents.

| **EXAMPLE 1**   **Using the Definition of $x^{1/n}$** |

Simplify:

a. $64^{1/2}$ **b.** $\left(\dfrac{1}{25}\right)^{1/2}$ **c.** $8^{1/3}$ **d.** $-16^{1/4}$ **e.** $64^{-1/3}$

Solution

a. $64^{1/2} = \sqrt{64} = 8$

b. $\left(\dfrac{1}{25}\right)^{1/2} = \sqrt{\dfrac{1}{25}} = \dfrac{1}{5}$

c. $8^{1/3} = \sqrt[3]{8} = 2$

d. $-16^{1/4} = -(\sqrt[4]{16})$ Careful! The base of the exponent is 16, and the negative sign is not affected by the exponent.

$= -2$ $\sqrt[4]{16} = 2$

e. $64^{-1/3} = \dfrac{1}{64^{1/3}}$ $x^{-1/n} = \dfrac{1}{x^{1/n}}$

$= \dfrac{1}{\sqrt[3]{64}}$

$= \dfrac{1}{4}$ $\sqrt[3]{64} = 4$ because $4^3 = 64$.

Using technology

Here are the graphing calculator keystroke sequences for Example 1.

a. $64^{1/2}$: $\boxed{\sqrt{}}$ 64 $\boxed{\text{ENTER}}$ or 64 $\boxed{\wedge}$ $\boxed{(}$ 1 $\boxed{\div}$ 2 $\boxed{)}$ $\boxed{\text{ENTER}}$

b. $(\frac{1}{25})^{1/2}$: $\boxed{\sqrt{}}$ $\boxed{(}$ 1 $\boxed{\div}$ 25 $\boxed{)}$ $\boxed{\text{ENTER}}$ or $\boxed{(}$ 1 $\boxed{\div}$ 25 $\boxed{)}$ $\boxed{\wedge}$ $\boxed{(}$ 1 $\boxed{\div}$ 2 $\boxed{)}$ $\boxed{\text{ENTER}}$

c. $8^{1/3}$: 8 $\boxed{\wedge}$ $\boxed{(}$ 1 $\boxed{\div}$ 3 $\boxed{)}$ $\boxed{\text{ENTER}}$

d. $-16^{1/4}$: $\boxed{(-)}$ 16 $\boxed{\wedge}$ $\boxed{(}$ 1 $\boxed{\div}$ 4 $\boxed{)}$ $\boxed{\text{ENTER}}$

e. $64^{-1/3}$: 64 $\boxed{\wedge}$ $\boxed{(}$ $\boxed{(-)}$ 1 $\boxed{\div}$ 3 $\boxed{)}$ $\boxed{\text{ENTER}}$

1. Try entering part a as

64 $\boxed{\wedge}$ 1 $\boxed{\div}$ 2 $\boxed{\text{ENTER}}$

omitting parentheses. Explain the number in the calculator's display.

2. What's wrong with entering part (d) as follows?

$\boxed{(}$ $\boxed{(-)}$ 16 $\boxed{)}$ $\boxed{\wedge}$ $\boxed{(}$ 1 $\boxed{\div}$ 4 $\boxed{)}$ $\boxed{\text{ENTER}}$

In Example 1, each fractional exponent has a numerator of 1. Let's see what happens if the numerator is some other integer. Consider, for example, $8^{2/3}$:

$8^{2/3} = (8^{1/3})^2$ $x^{mn} = (x^m)^n$

$= (\sqrt[3]{8})^2$ $x^{1/3} = \sqrt[3]{x}$

$= 2^2$ $\sqrt[3]{8} = 2$

$= 4$

Since multiplication is commutative, we could write $8^{2/3}$ as $(8^2)^{1/3}$:

$$8^{2/3} = (8^2)^{1/3} \qquad x^{mn} = (x^m)^n$$
$$= 64^{1/3}$$
$$= \sqrt[3]{64} \qquad x^{1/3} = \sqrt[3]{x}$$
$$= 4$$

Thus, $8^{2/3}$ can be evaluated using either method. That is,

$$8^{2/3} = (\sqrt[3]{8})^2 = \sqrt[3]{8^2}.$$

Taking the root first is often preferable because smaller numbers are involved. By generalizing from this example, we can further define fractional exponents.

Definitions of fractional exponents

If x is a positive number and m and n are integers with $n > 0$,

$$x^{m/n} = (\sqrt[n]{x})^m = \sqrt[n]{x^m}.$$

The exponent m/n consists of two parts: the denominator n is the root and the numerator m is the exponent. Furthermore:

$$x^{-m/n} = \frac{1}{x^{m/n}}.$$

EXAMPLE 2 **Using the Definition of $x^{m/n}$**

Simplify: **a.** $27^{2/3}$ **b.** $9^{3/2}$ **c.** $-32^{4/5}$ **d.** $81^{-3/4}$

Solution

a. $27^{2/3} = (\sqrt[3]{27})^2$ $27^{2/3} = (27^{1/3})^2 = (\sqrt[3]{27})^2$
                   More directly: $x^{m/n} = (\sqrt[n]{x})^m$

$\qquad\quad = 3^2$ $\sqrt[3]{27} = 3$
$\qquad\quad = 9$

b. $9^{3/2} = (\sqrt{9})^3$ $x^{m/n} = (\sqrt[n]{x})^m$
                  The denominator of $\frac{3}{2}$ is the root and the numerator is the exponent.

$\qquad\quad = 3^3$ $\sqrt{9} = 3$
$\qquad\quad = 27$

c. $-32^{4/5} = -(\sqrt[5]{32})^4$ The negative sign is not affected by the exponent. The denominator of $\frac{4}{5}$ is the root and the numerator is the exponent.

$\qquad\qquad = -(2)^4$ $\sqrt[5]{32} = 2$ because $2^5 = 32$.
$\qquad\qquad = -16$

d. $81^{-3/4} = \dfrac{1}{81^{3/4}}$ $x^{-m/n} = \dfrac{1}{x^{m/n}}$

$\qquad\quad = \dfrac{1}{(\sqrt[4]{81})^3}$ The denominator of $\frac{3}{4}$ is the root and the numerator is the exponent.

$\qquad\quad = \dfrac{1}{3^3}$ $\sqrt[4]{81} = 3$ because $3^4 = 81$.

$\qquad\quad = \dfrac{1}{27}$

Using technology

Here are the graphing calculator keystroke sequences for Example 2 using the exponential key $\boxed{\wedge}$.

a. $27^{2/3}$: $\quad 27 \boxed{\wedge} \boxed{(} \boxed{2} \boxed{\div} \boxed{3} \boxed{)} \boxed{\text{ENTER}}$

b. $9^{3/2}$: $\quad 9 \boxed{\wedge} \boxed{(} \boxed{3} \boxed{\div} \boxed{2} \boxed{)} \boxed{\text{ENTER}}$

c. $-32^{4/5}$: $\quad \boxed{(-)} 32 \boxed{\wedge} \boxed{(} \boxed{4} \boxed{\div} \boxed{5} \boxed{)} \boxed{\text{ENTER}}$

d. $81^{-3/4}$: $\quad 81 \boxed{\wedge} \boxed{(} \boxed{(-)} \boxed{3} \boxed{\div} \boxed{4} \boxed{)} \boxed{\text{ENTER}}$

Use these sequences to verify the answers in Example 2. In which part does the calculator not provide an exact value? How can you show that this approximation is correct?

---

2 Solve problems using models with fractional exponents.

Giant Galápagos tortoise, Galapagos Island, Ecuador

James Martin/Tony Stone Images

Modeling with Fractional Exponents

Techniques for evaluating expressions with fractional exponents can be applied to mathematical models.

EXAMPLE 3 **Plant Species in the Galápagos Islands**

The Galápagos Islands are a volcanic archipelago lying 600 miles west of Ecuador. They are famed for their extraordinary wildlife, which includes a rare flightless cormorant, marine iguanas, and giant tortoises weighing more than 600 pounds. It was here that naturalist Charles Darwin began to formulate his theory of evolution. Darwin made an enormous collection of the islands' plant species. The model $S = 28.6A^{1/3}$ describes the number of plant species (S) on the various islands of the Galápagos chain as a function of the area (A) of a particular island, where A is expressed in square miles. How many species of plants are there on a Galápagos Island whose area is 125 square miles?

Solution

$S = 28.6A^{1/3}$ This is the given formula.

$S = 28.6(125)^{1/3}$ We are told that the area is 125 square miles, so we substitute 125 for A.

$S = 28.6(5)$ $125^{1/3} = \sqrt[3]{125} = 5$

$S = 143$ Multiply.

Thus, there are 143 species of plants on a Galápagos Island whose area is 125 square miles. ∎

PROBLEM SET 9.6

Practice Problems

Simplify Problems 1–46 by first writing the expression in radical form. If applicable, use a calculator to verify your answer.

1. $49^{1/2}$ **2.** $100^{1/2}$ **3.** $121^{1/2}$ **4.** $25^{1/2}$ **5.** $100^{-1/2}$ **6.** $49^{-1/2}$

7. $16^{-1/2}$ **8.** $144^{-1/2}$ **9.** $27^{1/3}$ **10.** $64^{1/3}$ **11.** $125^{-1/3}$ **12.** $27^{-1/3}$

13. $-125^{1/3}$ **14.** $-27^{1/3}$ **15.** $16^{1/4}$ **16.** $81^{1/4}$ **17.** $\left(\frac{27}{64}\right)^{1/3}$ **18.** $\left(\frac{64}{125}\right)^{1/3}$

19. $32^{-1/5}$ **20.** $243^{-1/5}$ **21.** $-32^{1/5}$ **22.** $-243^{1/5}$ **23.** $81^{3/2}$ **24.** $25^{3/2}$

25. $125^{2/3}$ **26.** $1000^{2/3}$ **27.** $9^{3/2}$ **28.** $16^{3/2}$ **29.** $(-32)^{3/5}$ **30.** $(-27)^{2/3}$

31. $16^{-3/4}$ **32.** $625^{-3/4}$ **33.** $81^{-5/4}$ **34.** $32^{-4/5}$ **35.** $8^{-2/3}$ **36.** $625^{-5/4}$

37. $\left(\frac{4}{25}\right)^{-1/2}$ **38.** $\left(\frac{8}{27}\right)^{-1/3}$ **39.** $\left(\frac{8}{125}\right)^{-1/3}$ **40.** $\left(\frac{9}{100}\right)^{-1/2}$ **41.** $(-8)^{-2/3}$ **42.** $(-64)^{-2/3}$

43. $27^{2/3} + 16^{3/4}$ **44.** $4^{5/2} - 8^{2/3}$ **45.** $25^{3/2} \cdot 81^{1/4}$ **46.** $16^{-3/4} \cdot 16^{3/2}$

Application Problems

47. The maximum velocity (v, in miles per hour) that an automobile can travel around a curve with a radius of r feet without skidding is described by the model

$$v = \left(\frac{5r}{2}\right)^{1/2}.$$

If the curve has a radius of 250 feet, find the maximum velocity a car can travel around it without skidding.

48. The model

$$v = \left(\frac{p}{0.015}\right)^{1/3}$$

describes the wind speed (v, in miles per hour) needed to produce p watts of power from a windmill. How fast must the wind be blowing to produce 120 watts of power?

49. The function $f(t) = 1000t^{5/4} + 14{,}000$ describes the average pollution ($f(t)$, in particles of pollution per cubic centimeter) t years after 1970 in most cities if pollution controls are not put into force. Find and interpret $f(81)$.

50. The rate of increase of pollution in a river after t years is described by the formula $R = \frac{1}{4}(t^{1/4} + 3)t^{-3/4}$. Find the rate of increase (in units of pollution per year) after 16 years.

Smog smothers New York.

Gerard Fritz/Tony Stone Images

True–False Critical Thinking Problems

51. Which one of the following is true?
  a. $2^{1/2} \cdot 2^{1/2} = 4^{1/2}$ **b.** $8^{-1/2} = \frac{1}{4}$
  c. $25^{-1/2} = -5$ **d.** $-3^{-2} = \frac{1}{9}$

52. Which one of the following is true?
  a. $2^{1/2} \cdot 2^{3/2} = \left(\frac{1}{4}\right)^{-1}$ **b.** $16^{-1/4} = -2$
  c. The result of $81^{1/4} \cdot 125^{1/3}$ is not an integer.
  d. $-8^{1/3}$ and $(-8)^{1/3}$ do not result in the same answer.

Technology Problems

53. The territorial area A of an animal in the wild is defined to be the area of the region to which the animal confines its movements. Territorial area (T, in square miles) is a function of an animal's body weight (W, in pounds) approximated by the model

$$T = W^{1.41} = W^{\frac{141}{100}} = {}^{100}\sqrt{W^{141}}.$$

  a. Use a calculator to fill in the table of values, rounding T to the nearest whole square mile.

W	0	25	50	150	200	250	300
$T = W^{1.41}$							

  b. Use the table of values to graph $T = W^{1.41}$. What does the shape of the graph indicate about the relationship between body weight and territorial area?

  c. Verify your hand-drawn graph by using a graphing utility to graph the function.

54. If A is the surface area of a cube and V is its volume, then $A = 6V^{2/3}$.

   a. Graph the equation relating a cube's surface area and volume using a graphing utility ($y = 6x^{2/3}$) and the following range setting:

$$\text{Xmin} = 0, \text{Xmax} = 30, \text{Xscl} = 3,$$
$$\text{Ymin} = 0, \text{Ymax} = 60, \text{Yscl} = 3$$

   b. $\boxed{\text{TRACE}}$ along the curve and verify the numbers in the figure shown on the right. In particular, show that a cube whose volume is 27 cubic units has a surface area of 54 square units.

   c. $\boxed{\text{TRACE}}$ along the curve and find the surface area of a cube whose volume is 15 cubic units.

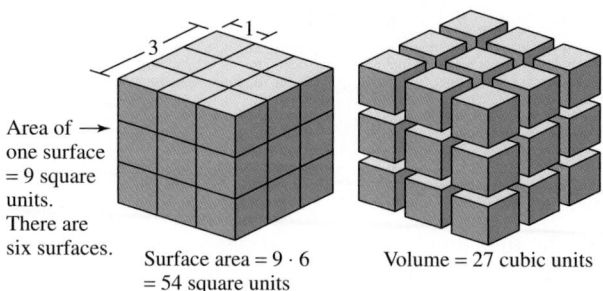

Area of → one surface = 9 square units. There are six surfaces.

Surface area = 9 · 6 = 54 square units

Volume = 27 cubic units

Writing in Mathematics

55. Explain why $x^{1/n}$ is negative when n is odd and x is negative. What happens if n is even and x is negative? Why?

56. In simplifying $36^{3/2}$, is it better to use $x^{m/n} = \sqrt[n]{x^m}$ or $x^{m/n} = (\sqrt[n]{x})^m$? Explain.

Critical Thinking Problems

Without using a calculator, simplify Problems 57–58 completely.

57. $25^{1/4} \cdot 25^{-3/4}$

58. $\dfrac{3^{-1} \cdot 3^{1/2}}{3^{-3/2}}$

Review Problems

59. The number of inches (N) that human hair grows varies directly as the time (t, in months). Hair will grow 6 inches in 12 months. How long will it grow in 20 months?

60. Write the point-slope equation of the line through (6, 8) and (7, 11). Then use the point-slope equation to write the slope-intercept equation.

61. The length of a rectangle is 3 meters longer than twice the width. If the area of the rectangle is 44 square meters, find the length and the width.

C HAPTER PROJECT

The Golden Mean

In Problem 71 in Problem Set 9.4, we introduced a figure called a golden rectangle. The ratio of the sides of the golden rectangle, which we found by rationalizing the denominator, is $\dfrac{1 + \sqrt{5}}{2}$: 1. The number $\dfrac{1 + \sqrt{5}}{2}$, or approximately 1.618, is called the *golden mean*. It is symbolized by the Greek letter Φ, to honor the ancient Greek sculptor Phidias, who used it to proportion his designs. Like π, Φ is a number that seems to arise naturally out of the world around us. In this project, you will discover that Φ seems to appear whenever we see things growing or unfolding in simple steps.

1. Create a sequence of about 20 numbers by following these steps: Write down any pair of numbers. Add those numbers together to get the third number in your sequence. Add the second and third numbers to get the fourth number in the sequence, and continue to create new numbers by adding the two previous numbers together. Using your calculator, find the ratio between each pair of numbers by dividing the larger number by the smaller number. What do you observe?

2. Using your calculator, enter any value except zero and take its reciprocal. Add one. Then take its reciprocal. Add one. Repeat this pattern until the display on your calculator does not change very much. What value do you observe?

3. Using your calculator, enter any number greater than -1. Add one to this number, then take the square root. Add one again, and take the square root. Continue this pattern until the display on your calculator doesn't change very much. What value do you observe?

In Problems 4 and 6, you will discover that Φ has some interesting properties not found with any other number.

4. Show that $\Phi + 1 = \Phi \cdot \Phi$.

5. Discuss how the property in Problem 4 relates to the procedure you followed in Problem 3.

6. Show that $\Phi = \dfrac{1}{\Phi} + 1$.

7. Discuss how the property in Problem 6 relates to the procedure you followed in Problem 2.

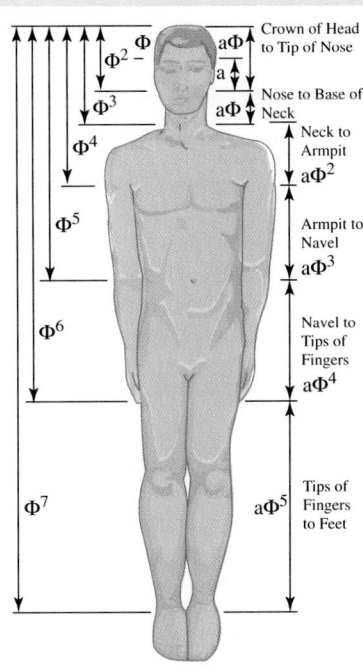

The golden mean also shows up in the work of many Renaissance artists in the proportion of the human body. In fact, the same proportions show up over and over again by artists in all ages. Moreover, the measurements of many people, on the average, are found to have ratios involving the golden mean.

8. Many artists take the following ratios to be $\Phi:1$. Use measurements from each member of the class to determine the average value for the class. How does the class average compare to the artistic ideal?
   a. The ratio from (navel to feet) to (navel to top of head)
   b. The ratio from (elbow to wrist) to (wrist to tips of fingers)

9. In Figure 9.3, we see the "ideal" proportions for the human body used by many artists. The starting point of the comparisons is the distance from the top of the eye to the tip of the nose measured vertically. The vertical measure above the top of the eye and vertical measure from the tip of the nose to the base of the neck will both be approximately Φ times the first measurement. In fact, the body may be divided into seven sections of Φ. Select a painting or sculpture that you find aesthetically appealing and measure the seven sections shown in the figure. How close do your measurements come to the ideal proportions using Φ?

Figure 9.3

Worldwide Web Resources

Go to the Prentice Hall website (http://www.prenhall.com/blitzer) to access other locations on the Internet that will allow you to further explore the concepts presented in this project.

Chapter Review

SUMMARY

1. Basic Ideas Involving Radicals

  a. If a is positive, $\sqrt{a}$ represents the positive square root of a, and $-\sqrt{a}$ represents the negative square root of a. $\sqrt{0} = 0$. The radicand is a.

  b. If a is negative, $\sqrt{a}$ is not a real number.

  c. If a is positive and n is an integer greater than 1, $\sqrt[n]{a} = b$ means that $b^n = a$. Thus, $\sqrt[5]{32} = 2$ because $2^5 = 32$.

2. Multiplying and Dividing Radicals

  a. *The product rule for radicals:*

$$\sqrt{x}\sqrt{y} = \sqrt{xy} \quad \text{and} \quad \sqrt{xy} = \sqrt{x}\sqrt{y}$$

$$\text{for } x \geq 0 \text{ and } y \geq 0$$

  b. *The quotient rule for radicals:*

$$\frac{\sqrt{x}}{\sqrt{y}} = \sqrt{\frac{x}{y}} \quad \text{and} \quad \sqrt{\frac{x}{y}} = \frac{\sqrt{x}}{\sqrt{y}}$$

$$\text{for } x \geq 0 \text{ and } y > 0$$

  c. *Simplifying square roots:*

    1. $\sqrt{x^{2n}} = x^n$

    2. If the radicand contains an odd power, factor the radicand so that one factor has an even power and the other has a power of 1.

  d. In general, if all roots are real numbers,

$$\sqrt[n]{x}\sqrt[n]{y} = \sqrt[n]{xy} \quad \text{and} \quad \frac{\sqrt[n]{x}}{\sqrt[n]{y}} = \sqrt[n]{\frac{x}{y}} \quad (y \neq 0)$$

3. Adding and Subtracting Radicals

  a. Like radicals contain square roots of the same number (or cube roots of the same number). The distributive property is used to add and subtract like radicals.

  b. To add and subtract radicals, simplify (if necessary) and then combine like radicals using the distributive property.

4. Using the Distributive Property and FOIL to Multiply Radicals

  a. The distributive property is used to perform multiplication when a radical expression is in the form $\sqrt{x}(\sqrt{y} + \sqrt{z})$, $x \geq 0, y \geq 0, z \geq 0$.

$$\sqrt{x}(\sqrt{y} + \sqrt{z}) = \sqrt{x}\sqrt{y} + \sqrt{x}\sqrt{z} = \sqrt{xy} + \sqrt{xz}$$

  b. The FOIL method is used to perform multiplication when a radical expression is in the form $(\sqrt{x} + \sqrt{y})(\sqrt{z} + \sqrt{w})$, where all variables are nonnegative.

$$(\sqrt{x} + \sqrt{y})(\sqrt{z} + \sqrt{w})$$

$$\begin{array}{cccc} \text{F} & \text{O} & \text{I} & \text{L} \end{array}$$
$$= \sqrt{x}\sqrt{z} + \sqrt{x}\sqrt{w} + \sqrt{y}\sqrt{z} + \sqrt{y}\sqrt{w}$$
$$= \sqrt{xz} + \sqrt{xw} + \sqrt{yz} + \sqrt{yw}$$

  c. In the case of conjugates:

$$(\sqrt{x} + \sqrt{y})(\sqrt{x} - \sqrt{y})$$
$$= (\sqrt{x})^2 - (\sqrt{y})^2 = x - y \quad x \geq 0, y \geq 0$$

5. Rationalizing Denominators

  a. Rationalizing the denominator refers to eliminating the radical in the denominator of a radical expression without changing the value of the expression.

  b. If the radical expression contains one term in the denominator that involves a square root, multiply the numerator and denominator by the smallest factor that results in a perfect square radicand in the denominator.

  c. If the radical expression contains two terms in the denominator with one or more square roots, multiply the numerator and denominator by a binomial containing the same terms but whose second term has the opposite sign (the conjugate).

6. Solving Equations with Radicals (Square Roots)

  a. If necessary, arrange terms so that one radical is isolated on one side of the equation.

  b. Square both sides.

  c. Combine like terms on each side of the equation.

  d. If there is still a term containing a square root, repeat steps a through c.

  e. Solve the equation.

  f. Substitute all potential solutions into the original equation.

7. Fractional Exponents

  a. For $x \geq 0$; $\quad x^{1/2} = \sqrt{x}, x^{1/3} = \sqrt[3]{x}, x^{1/4} = \sqrt[4]{x}$, and, in general, $x^{1/n} = \sqrt[n]{x}$.

  b. For $x > 0$: $\quad x^{-1/n} = \dfrac{1}{x^{1/n}} = \dfrac{1}{\sqrt[n]{x}}$.

  c. If $x \geq 0$ and m and n are integers, with $n > 0$:

$$x^{m/n} = (\sqrt[n]{x})^m = \sqrt[n]{x^m}.$$

    When x is fairly large, the first form (in which the root is taken first) is often preferable. The denominator of the fractional exponent is the root and the numerator is the exponent.

  d. For $x > 0$ and m and n integers, with $n > 0$,

$$x^{-m/n} = \frac{1}{x^{m/n}} = \frac{1}{(\sqrt[n]{x})^m} = \frac{1}{\sqrt[n]{x^m}}.$$

REVIEW PROBLEMS

Find all square roots in Problems 1–2.

1. 64

2. $\frac{9}{25}$

Find the roots in Problems 3–8, or indicate that the root is not a real number.

3. $\sqrt{121}$

4. $-\sqrt{121}$

5. $\sqrt{-121}$

6. $\sqrt[3]{\frac{8}{125}}$

7. $\sqrt[5]{-32}$

8. $-\sqrt[4]{81}$

Indicate whether each square root in Problems 9–12 is a rational number, an irrational number, or not a real number. Give the exact value for each rational number. If the number is irrational, use a calculator to give a decimal approximation, rounded to the nearest thousandth.

9. $\sqrt{\frac{8}{50}}$

10. $\sqrt{1.21}$

11. $\sqrt{75}$

12. $\sqrt{-4}$

Simplify each expression in Problems 13–19 by using the product rule.

13. $\sqrt{300}$

14. $6\sqrt{20}$

15. $\sqrt{3}\sqrt{12}$

16. $\sqrt{24a}\sqrt{6b}$

17. $\sqrt{48}\sqrt{32}$

18. $\sqrt[3]{81}$

19. $\sqrt[4]{8} \cdot \sqrt[4]{10}$

Simplify each expression in Problems 20–24 by using the quotient rule and, if necessary, the product rule.

20. $\sqrt{\frac{121}{4}}$

21. $\sqrt{\frac{7y}{25}}$

22. $\frac{6\sqrt{200}}{3\sqrt{2}}$

23. $\sqrt{\frac{5}{2}} \cdot \sqrt{\frac{3}{8}}$

24. $\sqrt[3]{\frac{7}{64}}$

Simplify each expression in Problems 25–30. Assume that all variables represent positive real numbers.

25. $\sqrt{63x^2}$

26. $\sqrt{48y^3}$

27. $\sqrt{10x^3}\sqrt{8x^2}$

28. $\sqrt{\frac{7}{y^4}}$

29. $\sqrt{75x^9}$

30. $\sqrt{300x^{23}}$

Simplify (if necessary) Problems 31–36, and add or subtract terms where possible.

31. $7\sqrt{5} + 13\sqrt{5}$

32. $\sqrt{50b} + \sqrt{8b}$

33. $\frac{5}{6}\sqrt{72} - \frac{3}{4}\sqrt{48}$

34. $2\sqrt{18} + 3\sqrt{27} - \sqrt{12}$

35. $\sqrt[4]{7} + 3\sqrt[3]{5} - 2\sqrt[4]{7} - \sqrt[3]{5}$

36. $4\sqrt[3]{16a} + 5\sqrt[3]{2a}$

Find the products in Problems 37–44.

37. $\sqrt{10}(\sqrt{5} + \sqrt{6})$

38. $\sqrt{3a}(7\sqrt{2} + 4\sqrt{3})$

39. $7\sqrt{10}(6\sqrt{2} - 3\sqrt{5})$

40. $(\sqrt{2} + \sqrt{7})(\sqrt{2} + 4\sqrt{7})$

41. $(3\sqrt{6} - 2\sqrt{5})(4\sqrt{6} + \sqrt{10})$

42. $(5\sqrt{x} - 3)^2$

43. $(\sqrt{11} - \sqrt{7})(\sqrt{11} + \sqrt{7})$

44. $(2\sqrt{3} + 7\sqrt{2})(2\sqrt{3} - 7\sqrt{2})$

Simplify Problems 45–54 by rationalizing the denominator.

45. $\frac{30}{\sqrt{5}}$

46. $\frac{13}{\sqrt{50}}$

47. $\frac{7\sqrt{2}}{\sqrt{6}}$

48. $\sqrt{\frac{2}{3}}$

49. $\sqrt{\frac{17}{x}}$

50. $\sqrt{\frac{5x^2}{8}}$

51. $\frac{11}{\sqrt{5} + 2}$

52. $\frac{21}{4 - \sqrt{3}}$

53. $\frac{12}{\sqrt{5} + \sqrt{3}}$

54. $\frac{\sqrt{3} + 2}{\sqrt{6} - \sqrt{3}}$

Find the solution for each equation in Problems 55–61.

55. $\sqrt{2y + 3} = 5$

56. $3\sqrt{x} = \sqrt{6x + 15}$

57. $3\sqrt{z + 3} = \sqrt{2z + 13}$

58. $\sqrt{5x + 1} = x + 1$

59. $\sqrt{y + 1} + 5 = y$

60. $y = \sqrt{y^2 + 4y + 4}$

61. $\sqrt{x - 2} + 5 = 1$

Simplify Problems 62–67.

62. $16^{1/2}$

63. $25^{-1/2}$

64. $125^{1/3}$

65. $27^{-1/3}$

66. $64^{2/3}$

67. $27^{-4/3}$

68. Two divers start to dive at the same time, one from a cliff 128 feet above the water, and the other from a cliff 32 feet above the water. Use the formula

$$t = \sqrt{\frac{2s}{g}}$$

where s represents the number of feet above the water, t represents the time of the dive in seconds, and g represents the acceleration due to gravity, to find how much longer it will take the diver on the higher cliff to hit the water. The acceleration of gravity is 32 feet per second every second ($g = 32$). Express the answer in radical form and then find a decimal approximation correct to the nearest tenth.

Philip H. Coblentz/Tony Stone Images

69. The period (T, in seconds) of a pendulum (the time required for the pendulum to make one complete swing back and forth) is a function of its length (L, in feet) modeled by

$$T = 2\pi\sqrt{\frac{L}{32}}.$$

Find the period of the pendulum if its length is 8 feet. Use 3.14 as an approximation for π.

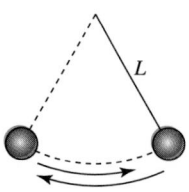

70. The compound interest rate (r) that is paid when one borrows P dollars and pays A dollars at the end of a 2-year period is described by

$$r = \sqrt{\frac{A}{P}} - 1.$$

What is the rate if $100 is borrowed and the amount paid at the end of 2 years is $144?

71. If the length of a rectangle is $4\sqrt{20}$ meters and the width is $2\sqrt{8}$ meters, what is the perimeter and the area of the rectangle? Express both in simplified radical form.

72. The model $S = 28.6A^{1/3}$ describes the number of plant species (S) on the various islands of the Galápagos chain as a function of the area (A) of a particular island, where A is expressed in square miles. Approximately how many species of plants are there on a Galápagos Island whose area is 8 square miles?

73. The formula $v = 2\sqrt{6L}$ is used by police to estimate the speed of a car (v, in miles per hour) based on the length of its skid marks (L, in feet) on dry pavement. How far will a car skid at a speed of 50 miles per hour?

74. Use the formula in Problem 68 (with $g = 32$) to answer this question. A rock is dropped from a bridge, taking 3 seconds to hit the water. How far above the water is the bridge?

75. Use a calculator to answer this question. The average annual rate of growth (r) for a population that grows from P_0 to P_n in n years is modeled by the formula

$$r = \left(\frac{P_n}{P_0}\right)^{1/n} - 1.$$

Find the average annual rate of growth for the United States, whose population grew from 226.5 million in 1980 to 246.7 million in 1990.

CHAPTER 9 TEST

Assume that all variables represent positive real numbers.

1. Find all square roots of 49.

In Problems 2–3, find the roots.

2. $-\sqrt{64}$ **3.** $\sqrt[3]{64}$

Simplify Problems 4–10.

4. $\sqrt{48}$ **5.** $\sqrt{72x^3}$ **6.** $\sqrt{x^{29}}$ **7.** $\sqrt{\dfrac{25}{x^2}}$

8. $\sqrt[3]{\dfrac{5}{8}}$ **9.** $\sqrt{\dfrac{75}{27}}$ **10.** $\sqrt{\dfrac{64x^4}{2x^2}}$

In Problems 11–13, multiply and simplify.

11. $\sqrt{10}\sqrt{5}$ **12.** $\sqrt{6x}\sqrt{6y}$ **13.** $\sqrt{10x^2}\sqrt{2x^3}$

Perform the indicated operations in Problems 14–19.

14. $\sqrt{24} + 3\sqrt{54}$ **15.** $7\sqrt{8} - 2\sqrt{32}$ **16.** $(2\sqrt{2} + 5)(3\sqrt{2} + 4)$
17. $(\sqrt{6} + 2)(\sqrt{6} - 2)$ **18.** $(3 - \sqrt{7})^2$ **19.** $(3\sqrt{x} + 2)^2$

In Problems 20–21, rationalize the denominator.

20. $\dfrac{4}{\sqrt{5}}$ **21.** $\dfrac{5}{4 + \sqrt{3}}$

Solve the equations in Problems 22–23.

22. $5\sqrt{3x - 2} - 3 = 7$ **23.** $\sqrt{2x - 1} = x - 2$

Simplify Problems 24–25.

24. $9^{-1/2}$ **25.** $8^{2/3}$

26. Find the perimeter of the rectangle shown in the figure in simplified radical form.

$\sqrt{45}$

$\sqrt{80}$

27. The approximate time (t, in seconds) that it takes an object to fall d feet under the influence of gravity is given by the mathematical model

$$t = \sqrt{\dfrac{d}{16}}$$

How many feet will a free-falling skydiver fall in 3 seconds?

C U M U L A T I V E   R E V I E W   P R O B L E M S   (C H A P T E R S   1 – 9)

1. The polynomial function $f(x) = -7.7x^3 + 52.7x^2 - 93.4x + 2151$ models the number ($f(x)$ in thousands) of military personnel on active duty in the United States x years after 1985. Find and interpret $f(0)$.

2. The figure shows a portion of the graph of $y = \sqrt{x}$. Explain how the graph could be used to obtain reasonable estimates for $\sqrt{1.5}$ and $\sqrt{4.4}$.

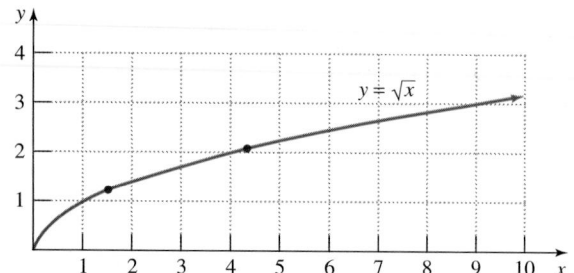

3. The length of a rectangle is 2 meters greater than twice its width. If the perimeter is 40 meters, find the dimensions.

4. Solve: $8(5z - 7) - 4z = 9(4z - 6) - 3$.

5. a. Solve for y: $2x + 3y = 7$.
   b. Find the value of y when $x = -4$.

6. Two pages that face each other in a book have 933 as the sum of their page numbers. What are their page numbers?

7. Find the quotient:
   $(6x^3 - 19x^2 + 16x - 4) \div (x - 2)$.

8. Multiply: $(2x - 3)(4x^2 + 6x + 9)$.

9. Solve: $2x^2 + 5x = 12$.

10. Factor completely: $x^2 - 18x + 77$.

11. Solve and graph the solution on a number line:
   $1 - \dfrac{3x}{2} \leq x - 4$.

12. Graph: $5x + 3y \leq -15$.

13. Solve the system:
   $$8x - 5y = -4$$
   $$2x + 15y = -66$$

14. Park rangers catch, tag, and then release 318 deer back into a state park. Two weeks later, they select a sample of 168 deer, 56 of which are tagged. Assuming the ratio of tagged deer in the sample holds for all deer in the park, approximately how many deer are in the park?

15. Solve by graphing:
   $$y = x + 1$$
   $$y = 2x - 1$$

16. A car travels at a uniform speed of 45 miles per hour for t hours. The distance that the car travels in t hours is given by the model $d = 45t$.

a. Use the mathematical model to estimate the distance covered in 1 hour, 2 hours, 3 hours, and 4 hours.
   b. Graph the model with values of t along the x-axis and values of d along the y-axis.

17. The graph shows the growing cost of Medicaid spending (in billions of dollars). Find the average yearly rate of change in spending between 1995 and 2005 (projected).

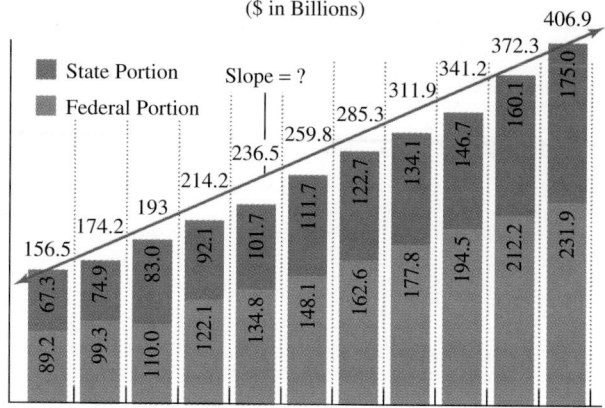

Projected Growth of Medicaid Spending
(\$ in Billions)

Source: CBO March 1995 Baseline

18. Simplify: $\dfrac{8x^3}{-4x^7}$.

19. Multiply: $(4x + 5)^2$.

20. Factor completely: $x^3 - 25x$.

21. The sum of the squares of two consecutive integers is 9 more than eight times the smaller integer. Find the integers.

22. The formula
   $$D = \frac{n(n - 3)}{2}$$
   describes the number of diagonals (D) of a polygon with n sides. What is the number of sides for a polygon with five diagonals?

23. Subtract, and simplify if possible:
   $$\frac{3y}{y^2 + y - 2} - \frac{2}{y + 2}.$$

24. Divide: $\dfrac{5x^2 - 6x + 1}{x^2 - 1} \div \dfrac{16x^2 - 9}{4x^2 + 7x + 3}$.

25. Solve: $\dfrac{15}{x} - 4 = \dfrac{6}{x} + 3$.

26. Simplify the complex fraction: $\dfrac{1 - \dfrac{1}{x^2}}{1 - \dfrac{1}{x}}$.

27. Figures for Switzerland and the United States are missing in the table. The Gross Domestic Product (GDP) is the value of all the goods and services produced annually within a country divided by the country's population. The GDP of Switzerland is $10,007 less than twice that of the United States. Both GDPs combined total $59,350. Use this information to fill in the missing figures in the table.

The 10 Richest Countries in the World

Country	GDP per Capita (US$)
1 Switzerland	
2 Luxembourg	35,260
3 Japan	28,217
4 Sweden	26,784
5 Bermuda	26,600
6 Denmark	25,927
7 Norway	25,805
8 Iceland	23,667
9 US	
10 Finland	22,977

28. Simplify: $6\sqrt{75} - 4\sqrt{12}$.

29. Rationalize the denominator: $\dfrac{5}{6 + \sqrt{11}}$.

30. Solve: $x = \sqrt{x - 2} + 4$.

Quadratic Equations and Functions

John Chamberlain "Nanoweap" 1969, painted and chromium–plated steel, 54 × 63 in. (137.1 × 160 cm) 74–129 DJ. Photographer: Hickey–Robertson, Houston. The Menil Collection, Houston. © 1998 John Chamberlain/Artists Rights Society (ARS), New York

The mathematical model $N = 0.4x^2 - 36x + 1000$ approximates the number of accidents per 50 million miles (N) for a driver who is x years old. How can we determine the age of a driver predicted to have 312 accidents per 50 million miles driven? What is the age of a driver predicted to have the least number of accidents?

We can answer these questions by developing a method of solving all quadratic equations, regardless of whether they are factorable. The physical world presents us with a variety of actions and events described by quadratic functions in the form $y = ax^2 + bx + c$. The formula that we will develop in this chapter for solving quadratic equations and the techniques for graphing quadratic functions will enable us to gain insight into the physical events modeled by these functions. These applications reiterate the major theme of this book: The world is astonishingly mathematical and, indeed, π is in the sky.

SECTION   10.1

Solutions   Tutorial   Video
Manual   11

Solving Quadratic Equations by the Square Root Property

Objectives

1 Solve quadratic equations using the square root property.
2 Solve equations in the form $(x + d)^2 = e$.
3 Solve applied problems using the square root property.

In this section, we consider quadratic equations ($ax^2 + bx + c = 0$) in which the coefficient b is equal to zero. These equations also can be written in the form $ax^2 + 0x + c = 0$, or $ax^2 + c = 0$. Such an equation can be solved by a method other than factoring, called the *square root property of equations*.

Recall that a quadratic equation is an equation that can be written in the form

$$ax^2 + bx + c = 0$$

where a, b, and c are real numbers and $a \neq 0$. In Chapter 7, we solved quadratic equations by factoring, using the *zero-product principle:* If the product of two factors is zero, then at least one of the two factors is zero.

For example, let's solve $x^2 - 9 = 0$. Since $x^2 - 9 = 0$ can be written as $x^2 + 0x - 9 = 0$, the equation is, indeed, quadratic with $a = 1$, $b = 0$, and $c = -9$.

Using technology

The graph of $y = x^2 - 9$ has x-intercepts at -3 and 3, the solutions of $x^2 - 9 = 0$.

x-intercept $= -3$ x-intercept $= 3$

$x^2 - 9 = 0$	This is the original equation.
$(x + 3)(x - 3) = 0$	Factor $x^2 - 9$ as the difference between squares.
$x + 3 = 0$ or $x - 3 = 0$	Apply the zero-product principle, setting each factor equal to 0.
$x = -3$ or $x = 3$	Solve the resulting equations.

The solutions to $x^2 - 9 = 0$ are -3 and 3.

There is a second method for solving $x^2 - 9 = 0$. Begin by adding 9 to both sides of the equation, obtaining $x^2 = 9$. Inspection shows that there are two solutions: $x = 3$ or $x = -3$, the two square roots of 9.

This second method, taking the square roots of both sides of $x^2 = 9$, can be presented as follows:

$x^2 - 9 = 0$	This is the original equation.
$x^2 = 9$	Add 9 to both sides.
$x = \sqrt{9}$ or $x = -\sqrt{9}$	Include both the positive and negative square roots of 9.
$x = 3$ or $x = -3$	

It is the *square root property of equations* that allows us to take the square roots of both sides of an equation.

1 Solve quadratic equations using the square root property.

The square root property of equations

If $x^2 = d$ (where $d > 0$), then $x = \sqrt{d}$ or $x = -\sqrt{d}$.

It is common to use the shorthand notation $x = \pm\sqrt{d}$ to indicate that $x = \sqrt{d}$ or $x = -\sqrt{d}$. Although we usually read $x = \pm\sqrt{d}$ as "x equals plus or minus the square root of d," we actually mean that x is the positive square root of d or the negative square root of d.

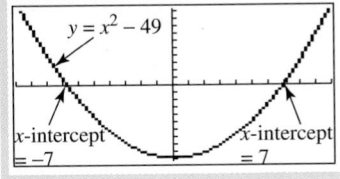
EXAMPLE 1   Applying the Square Root Property

Solve: **a.** $x^2 = 49$ **b.** $4y^2 + 3 = 103$

Solution

a. $x^2 = 49$ This is the original equation.

    $x = \sqrt{49}$ or $x = -\sqrt{49}$ Apply the square root property. You can also write: $x = \pm\sqrt{49}$.

    $x = 7$ or $x = -7$

Each solution is checked by substituting into the original equation, verifying that the solutions are 7 and -7.

b. To solve $4y^2 + 3 = 103$, we isolate y^2 on one side of the equation and then apply the square root property.

    $4y^2 + 3 = 103$ We want to isolate y^2.

       $4y^2 = 100$ Subtract 3 from both sides.

         $y^2 = 25$ Divide both sides by 4.

    $y = \sqrt{25}$ or $y = -\sqrt{25}$ Apply the square root property.

    $y = 5$ or $y = -5$ Equivalently, $y = \pm\sqrt{25} = \pm5$.

Check each solution by substituting into the original equation, verifying that the solutions are 5 and -5. ■

In our next example, the square root property will result in solutions that are irrational numbers. When possible, radicals will be written in simplified form.

EXAMPLE 2   Irrational Solutions by the Square Root Property

Solve: **a.** $3x^2 - 2 = 2(x^2 + 3)$ **b.** $2y^2 - 5 = 0$

Solution

a. $3x^2 - 2 = 2(x^2 + 3)$ This is the original equation.

    $3x^2 - 2 = 2x^2 + 6$ Remove parentheses by using the distributive property. We will isolate x^2 on the left.

        $3x^2 = 2x^2 + 8$ Add 2 to both sides.

          $x^2 = 8$ Subtract $2x^2$ from both sides.

    $x = \sqrt{8}$ or $x = -\sqrt{8}$ Apply the square root property.

    $x = 2\sqrt{2}$ or $x = -2\sqrt{2}$ Simplify $\sqrt{8}$ by using $\sqrt{8} = \sqrt{4 \cdot 2} = \sqrt{4}\sqrt{2} = 2\sqrt{2}$.

Both solutions check. (Try checking at least one of them.) The solutions are $2\sqrt{2}$ and $-2\sqrt{2}$.

b. $2y^2 - 5 = 0$ This is the original equation.

       $2y^2 = 5$ Add 5 to both sides.

        $y^2 = \dfrac{5}{2}$ Divide both sides by 2.

$$y = \sqrt{\frac{5}{2}} \quad \text{or} \quad y = -\sqrt{\frac{5}{2}}$$

Apply the square root property.

$$y = \frac{\sqrt{5}}{\sqrt{2}} \quad \text{or} \quad y = -\frac{\sqrt{5}}{\sqrt{2}}$$

$\sqrt{\frac{x}{y}} = \frac{\sqrt{x}}{\sqrt{y}}$. With radicals in the denominators, we must rationalize the denominator.

$$y = \frac{\sqrt{5}}{\sqrt{2}} \cdot \frac{\sqrt{2}}{\sqrt{2}} \quad \text{or} \quad y = -\frac{\sqrt{5}}{\sqrt{2}} \cdot \frac{\sqrt{2}}{\sqrt{2}}$$

Multiply the numerator and denominator by $\sqrt{2}$.

$$y = \frac{\sqrt{10}}{2} \quad \text{or} \quad y = -\frac{\sqrt{10}}{2}$$

Multiply numerators.
Multiply denominators.

The solutions are $\dfrac{\sqrt{10}}{2}$ and $\dfrac{-\sqrt{10}}{2}$. ∎

2 Solve equations in the form $(x + d)^2 = e$.

Quadratic Equations in the Form $(x + d)^2 = e$

The square root property can be used to solve equations such as $(x - 5)^2 = 16$, where the exponent 2 appears with two terms.

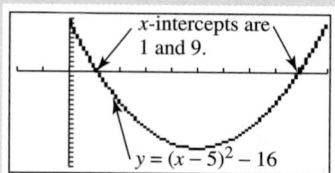
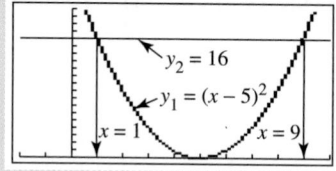
EXAMPLE 3 **Applying the Square Root Property**

Solve: $(x - 5)^2 = 16$

Solution

$(x - 5)^2 = 16$ This is the original equation.

$x - 5 = \sqrt{16}$ or $x - 5 = -\sqrt{16}$ If $x^2 = d$, then $x = \pm\sqrt{d}$. Use $x - 5$ instead of x and $d = 16$.

$x - 5 = 4$ or $x - 5 = -4$ $\sqrt{16} = 4$

$x = 9$ or $x = 1$ Solve the equations, adding 5 to both sides.

Check each solution by substituting into the original equation, verifying that the solutions are 9 and 1. ∎

EXAMPLE 4 **Applying the Square Root Property**

Solve: $(x - 1)^2 = 5$

Solution

$(x - 1)^2 = 5$ This is the original equation.

$x - 1 = \sqrt{5}$ or $x - 1 = -\sqrt{5}$ Apply the square root property.

$x = 1 + \sqrt{5}$ or $x = 1 - \sqrt{5}$ Solve the equations, adding 1 to both sides.

Check

For $x = 1 + \sqrt{5}$:   **For $x = 1 - \sqrt{5}$:**

$(x - 1)^2 = 5$ $(x - 1)^2 = 5$

$(1 + \sqrt{5} - 1)^2 \overset{?}{=} 5$ $(1 - \sqrt{5} - 1)^2 \overset{?}{=} 5$

$(\sqrt{5})^2 \overset{?}{=} 5$ $(\sqrt{5})^2 \overset{?}{=} 5$

$5 = 5$ ✓ $5 = 5$ ✓

The solutions are $1 + \sqrt{5}$ and $1 - \sqrt{5}$, expressed in abbreviated notation as $1 \pm \sqrt{5}$. ∎

3

Solve applied problems using the square root property.

Mathematical Models and the Square Root Property

The square root property can be used to gain information about variables in mathematical models, as illustrated by Example 5.

EXAMPLE 5 An Application: The Weight of a Human Fetus

The weight of a human fetus is given by the model $W = 3t^2$, where W is the weight in grams and t is the time in weeks, $0 \le t \le 39$. After how many weeks does the fetus weigh 300 grams?

Solution

$W = 3t^2$	This is the given formula.
$300 = 3t^2$	The answer to the question (After how many weeks does the fetus weigh 300 grams?) can be found by letting $W = 300$ and solving for t.
$100 = t^2$	Divide both sides by 3.
$t = \sqrt{100}$ or $t = -\sqrt{100}$	Apply the square root property.
$t = 10$ or $t = -10$	The negative root is rejected since it does not apply to measuring time.

The fetus weighs 300 grams after 10 weeks. ∎

In Example 5 we were given the model that described the weight of the human fetus as a function of time. A more difficult situation is to use a problem's conditions to create a mathematical model. In Example 6 we use the Pythagorean Theorem to model the given conditions.

EXAMPLE 6 An Application: The Pythagorean Theorem

A baseball diamond has the shape of a square with 90-foot sides, as shown in Figure 10.1. What is the distance from home plate to second base?

Solution

In Figure 10.1, the hypotenuse of the right triangle having 90 foot sides is designated by x. Since two sides of a right triangle are known and one side is unknown, we can apply the Pythagorean Theorem. In a right triangle,

The sum of the squares of the legs	equals	The square of the hypotenuse.
$90^2 + 90^2$	$=$	x^2

$$90^2 + 90^2 = x^2$$ This is the equation implied by the Pythagorean Theorem.

$$8100 + 8100 = x^2$$

$$16,200 = x^2$$

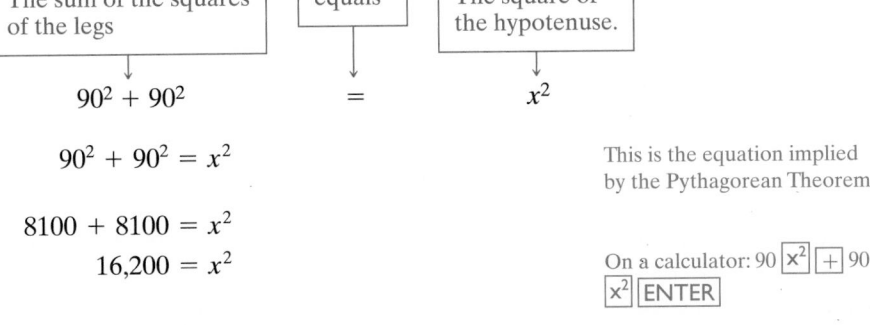

On a calculator: 90 $\boxed{x^2}$ $\boxed{+}$ 90 $\boxed{x^2}$ $\boxed{\text{ENTER}}$

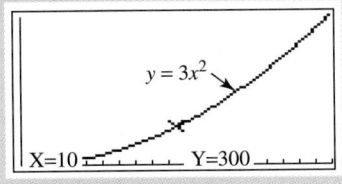
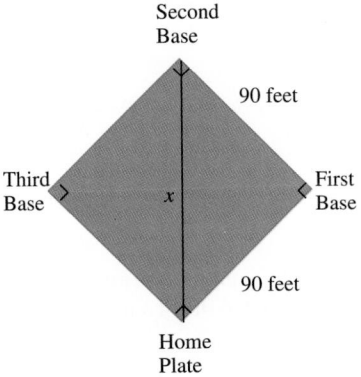

Figure 10.1

The square shape of a baseball diamond

$x = \sqrt{16{,}200}$ or $x = -\sqrt{16{,}200}$ Apply the square root property. The negative root is rejected since it does not apply to measuring the side of a triangle.

$x = 90\sqrt{2}$ $\sqrt{16{,}200} = \sqrt{8100 \cdot 2} =$ $\sqrt{8100}\sqrt{2} = 90\sqrt{2}$

The distance from home plate to second base is $90\sqrt{2}$ feet, which is approximately equal to 127.3 feet. (On a calculator 90 $\boxed{\sqrt{\ }}$ 2 $\boxed{\text{ENTER}}$.) ■

PROBLEM SET 10.1

Practice Problems

Solve the equations in Problems 1–36 by using the square root property. When possible, express the radicals in simplified form. If applicable, verify solutions using a graphing utility.

1. $x^2 = 36$
2. $x^2 = 100$
3. $y^2 = 81$
4. $y^2 = 121$
5. $x^2 = 7$
6. $x^2 = 13$
7. $x^2 = 50$
8. $x^2 = 27$
9. $5y^2 = 20$
10. $3y^2 = 75$
11. $4y^2 = 49$
12. $16y^2 = 25$
13. $y^2 - 2y = 2(3 - y)$
14. $2x^2 - 35 = (x + 3)(x - 3)$
15. $2z^2 + 2z - 5 = z(z + 2) - 3$
16. $3z^2 - 5z + 11 = z(2z - 5) + 21$
17. $11t^2 - 23 = 4t^2 + 33$
18. $5t^2 - 21 = 2(2t^2 + 3)$
19. $3y^2 - 2 = 0$
20. $3y^2 - 5 = 0$
21. $5m^2 - 7 = 0$
22. $-3m^2 + 8 = 0$
23. $(y - 3)^2 = 16$
24. $(y + 2)^2 = 25$
25. $(x + 5)^2 = 121$
26. $(x - 6)^2 = 144$
27. $(2x + 1)^2 = 64$
28. $(2y + 6)^2 = 49$
29. $(b + 3)^2 = 5$
30. $(b - 2)^2 = 11$
31. $(y - 2)^2 = 32$
32. $(y + 3)^2 = 28$
33. $(3x - 1)^2 = 12$
34. $(5x - 4)^2 = 12$
35. $(6w + 2)^2 = 27$
36. $(8w - 3)^2 = 20$

Application Problems

The weight of a human fetus is given by the formula $W = 3t^2$, where W is the weight in grams and t is the time in weeks, $0 \leq t \leq 39$. Use this information to answer Problems 37–38.

37. After how many weeks does the fetus weigh 108 grams?

38. After how many weeks does the fetus weigh 192 grams?

The model $d = \frac{3}{50} v^2$ describes the braking distance d (in feet) for a car traveling at v miles per hour. Use this information to answer Problems 39–40.

39. How fast was the car traveling if the braking distance is 150 feet?

40. How fast was the car traveling if the braking distance is 96 feet?

41. The model $A = P(1 + r)^2$ describes the amount of money (A) in an account after 2 years when P dollars is invested at interest rate r compounded annually. At what interest rate will $100 grow to $121 in 2 years?

42. The distance (d, in feet) that an object falls in t seconds is given by $d = 16t^2$. How long will it take a rock to reach the ground if it is dropped from an airplane whose altitude is 6400 feet?

43. The area of a circle is 49π square meters. Find the radius and the circumference of the circle.

44. The area of a circle is 144π square centimeters. Find the radius and the circumference of the circle.

45. The model $v = 1.2 - 2000r^2$ describes the velocity (v, in centimeters per second) of blood flowing in an arterial capillary whose radius is r centimeters. If the speed of blood in an arterial capillary is 0.7 centimeter per second, find the radius of the capillary to the nearest hundredth of a centimeter.

46. The model $p = 0.003v^2$ describes the pressure (in pounds per square foot) when wind is blowing at v miles per hour. What wind velocity will produce a pressure of 67.5 pounds per square foot?

47. As shown in the figure on page 701, a softball diamond has a square shape with 60-foot sides. Find the

distance from home plate to second base, expressing the answer in simplified radical form.

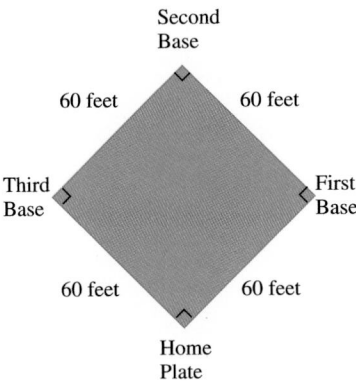

48. As shown in the figure, a proposed road is to be built from A to C. Determine the length of the proposed road, expressing the answer in simplified radical form.

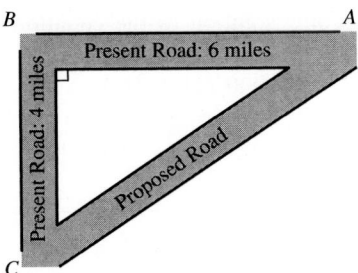

49. An empty rectangular plot is 40 meters long and 30 meters wide. How many meters does a person save by walking diagonally across the plot instead of walking the plot's length and width?

50. A balloon rises at the rate of 12 feet per minute when the wind is blowing horizontally at 9 feet per minute. After 2 minutes, how far from the starting point, in a direct line, is the balloon?

51. Use the figure to find the length of the line segment connecting the points $(1, 2)$ and $(5, 5)$.

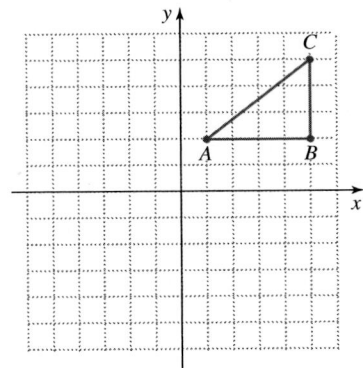

52. Use the figure to find the length of the line segment connecting the points $(-3, -5)$ and $(6, 7)$.

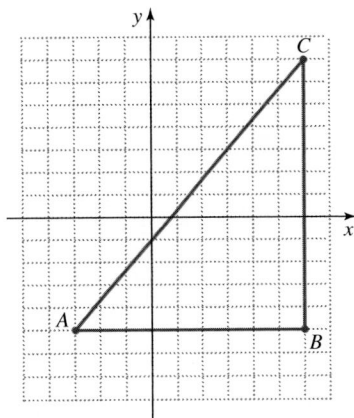

53. The lumber industry uses a formula to determine the number of board feet (N) that can be manufactured from a tree with a diameter of x inches and a length of y feet, described by the Doyle log model

$$N = \left(\frac{x - 4}{4}\right)^2 y.$$

John Mead/Science Photo Library/Photo Researchers, Inc.

Determine the diameter (x) for an 18-foot tree ($y = 18$) if we are required to obtain 162 board feet of lumber ($N = 162$).

54. One square is 3 feet shorter on each side than a larger square. If the smaller square has an area of 9 square feet, what is the length of the side of the larger square?

55. One square is 2 meters shorter on each side than a larger square. If the smaller square has an area of 16 square meters, what is the length of the side of the larger square?

56. A square flower bed is to be enlarged by adding 2 meters on each side. If the larger square has an area of 144 square meters, what is the length of the original square?

57. A square flower bed is to be enlarged by adding 3 feet on each side. If the larger square has an area of 169 square feet, what is the length of the original square?

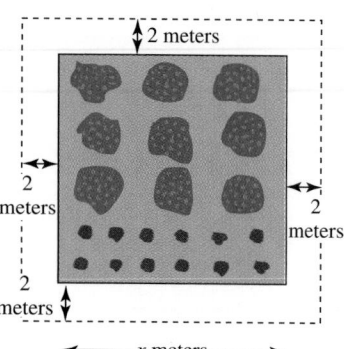

2 meters

2 meters

2 meters

2 meters

← *x* meters →

True–False Critical Thinking Problems

58. Which one of the following is true?
  a. The equation $(x + 5)^2 = 8$ is equivalent to $x + 5 = 2\sqrt{2}$.
  b. The equation $x^2 = 0$ has no solution.
  c. The equation $x^2 = -1$ has no solutions that are real numbers.
  d. The solutions for $3x^2 - 5 = 0$ are $\frac{-\sqrt{5}}{3}$ and $\frac{\sqrt{5}}{3}$.

59. Which one of the following is true?
  a. The solutions for $x^2 + 25 = 0$ are -5 and 5.
  b. The only solution to the equation $(x + 7)^2 = 0$ is -7.
  c. The equation $(x + 3)^2 = 75$ is equivalent to $x + 3 = 5\sqrt{3}$.
  d. The solutions for $5x^2 - 7 = 0$ are $\frac{-\sqrt{7}}{5}$ and $\frac{\sqrt{7}}{5}$.

Technology Problems

60. Solve $4 - (x + 1)^2 = 0$ by using a graphing utility to graph $y = 4 - (x + 1)^2$ and finding the x-intercepts. Check the solutions by direct substitution into the given equation.

61. Solve $(x - 1)^2 - 9$ by using a graphing utility to graph $y = (x - 1)^2 - 9$ and finding the x-intercepts. Check the solutions by direct substitution into the given equation.

62. The distance (d, in feet) that an object falls in t seconds is given by $d = 16t^2$.
  a. Use a graphing utility to graph the model, graphing $y_1 = 16x^2$ using the following range setting:

Xmin = 0, Xmax = 5, Xscl = 1,
Ymin = 0, Ymax = 400, Yscl = 1

  b. TRACE along the curve and determine how long it will take a rock to hit the water if it is dropped from a 100-foot-high bridge.
  c. Verify part (b) algebraically by substituting 100 for d and solving the given model for t.

63. Use a graphing utility to graph the model in Problem 45 or 46. Select an appropriate range setting. Then TRACE along the curve and geometrically illustrate the problem's solution.

Writing in Mathematics

64. Describe the procedure for solving a quadratic equation by the square root property. Use $(x - 1)^2 = 16$ as an example as you describe the procedure.

Critical Thinking Problems

65. Solve for x: $ax^2 - b = 0$ ($a > 0$ and $b > 0$). Express answers in simplified radical form.

66. Factor the left side and solve: $x^2 + 6x + 9 = 25$.

67. Solve for r: $A = p(1 + r)^2$. Assume that r is positive, so take only the positive square root.

Review Problems

68. Factor completely: $6x^2 + 26x + 24$.

69. Perform the indicated operation and simplify:

$$\frac{x}{x^2 + 11x + 30} - \frac{5}{x^2 + 9x + 20}.$$

70. Describe the difference between $-\sqrt{9}$ and $\sqrt{-9}$. Why is one of these expressions a real number, whereas the other is not?

Solutions Manual **Tutorial** **Video**
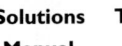

Complete the square of a binomial.

SECTION 10.2

Solving Quadratic Equations by Completing the Square

Objectives

1 Complete the square of a binomial.
2 Solve quadratic equations by completing the square.

In the last section, we solved equations such as

$$(x - 1)^2 = 2.$$

Using the square root property, this equation has two solutions, namely, $1 + \sqrt{2}$ and $1 - \sqrt{2}$. However, how would we solve this equation if it appeared in the form $ax^2 + bx + c = 0$, the standard form of a quadratic equation? Let's take a minute to rewrite the equation in this form.

$(x - 1)^2 = 2$ This is the original equation.

$x^2 - 2x + 1 = 2$ Square the left side.

$x^2 - 2x - 1 = 0$ Set the equation equal to 0, subtracting 2 from both sides.

The problem with $x^2 - 2x - 1 = 0$ is that the left side of the equation is not factorable, and so we cannot use the zero-product principle.

Our goal, then, is to write $x^2 - 2x - 1 = 0$ in the form $(x - 1)^2 = 2$ so that we can solve the equation using the square root property. Any quadratic equation, factorable or not, can be written in the form $(x + d)^2 = e$.

> The process of changing a quadratic equation in standard form
>
> $$ax^2 + bx + c = 0$$
>
> to an equivalent equation in the form $(x + d)^2 = e$ is called *completing the square.*

Richard Anuszkiewicz "Iridescence" 1965, acrylic on canvas, 60 × 60 in. Signed: Anuszkiewicz/1965. Albright–Knox Art Gallery, Buffalo, New York. Gift of Seymour H. Knox, 1966. © Richard Anuszkiewicz/ Licensed by VAGA, New York 1998.

To understand this process, let's take a moment to consider some trinomials that can be rewritten in the form $(x + d)^2$.

$$x^2 + 6x + 9 = (x + 3)^2$$
$$x^2 + 8x + 16 = (x + 4)^2$$
$$x^2 - 10x + 25 = (x - 5)^2$$
$$x^2 - 12x + 36 = (x - 6)^2$$

In each case, the coefficient of x^2 is 1. Furthermore, there is an important relationship between the coefficient of x and the constant term. Taking half the coefficient of x and squaring this result gives the constant term.

Trinomial That Can Be Written as $(x + d)^2$:	Take Half the Coefficient of x and Square This Result:
$x^2 + 6x + 9$	$\frac{1}{2} \cdot 6 = 3$ and $3^2 = 9$
$x^2 + 8x + 16$	$\frac{1}{2} \cdot 8 = 4$ and $4^2 = 16$
$x^2 - 10x + 25$	$\frac{1}{2}(-10) = -5$ and $(-5)^2 = 25$
$x^2 - 12x + 36$	$\frac{1}{2}(-12) = -6$ and $(-6)^2 = 36$

These observations provide us with a method for constructing trinomials in the form $(x + d)^2$, or perfect square trinomials. If we are given $x^2 + bx$, we can construct a perfect square trinomial by *adding the square of half the coefficient of x.* Let's see exactly what this means.

EXAMPLE 1 **Constructing a Trinomial in the Form $(x + d)^2$**

What term should be added to the expression $x^2 + 8x$ so that it becomes a perfect square trinomial?

Solution

In the expression $x^2 + 8x$, the coefficient of x is 8. We take half of 8 and square this result.

$$\frac{1}{2} \cdot 8 = 4 \quad \text{and} \quad 4^2 = 16$$

Thus, we add 16 to $x^2 + 8x$, and a perfect square trinomial will result.

$$x^2 + 8x + 16 = (x + 4)^2 \qquad ■$$

Study tip

The procedure in Example 1 can be modeled geometrically. The area of the accompanying figure is

$x^2 + 8x$.

Area: $x^2 + 8x$

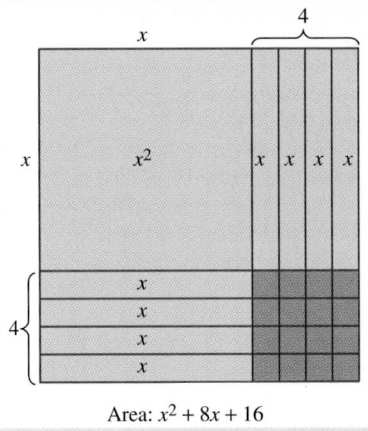

Area: $x^2 + 8x + 16$

S tudy tip (continued)

We add a square to the bottom-right corner whose dimensions are 4 by 4 and whose area is 16 square units.
This new and larger completed square has sides of length $x + 4$ and area given by

$$(x + 4)^2 = x^2 + 8x + 16.$$

EXAMPLE 2 **Constructing Perfect Square Trinomials**

Write the term that must be added to each of the following expressions to make it a perfect square trinomial.

a. $x^2 - 14x$　　**b.** $x^2 + 5x$

Solution

a. In the expression $x^2 - 14x$, the coefficient of x is -14. We take half of -14 and square this result.

$$\frac{1}{2}(-14) = -7 \quad \text{and} \quad (-7)^2 = 49$$

Thus, we add 49 to $x^2 - 14x$ to make it a perfect square trinomial.

$$x^2 - 14x + 49 = (x - 7)^2$$

b. In the expression $x^2 + 5x$, the coefficient of x is 5. We take half of 5 and square this result.

$$\frac{1}{2} \cdot 5 = \frac{5}{2} \quad \text{and} \quad \left(\frac{5}{2}\right)^2 = \frac{25}{4}$$

Thus, we add $\frac{25}{4}$ to $x^2 + 5x$ to make it a perfect square trinomial.

$$x^2 + 5x + \frac{25}{4} = \left(x + \frac{5}{2}\right)^2$$

Completing the square

If $x^2 + bx$ is a binomial, then by adding $\left(\dfrac{b}{2}\right)^2$, which is the square of half the coefficient of x, a perfect square trinomial will result. That is,

$$x^2 + bx + \left(\frac{b}{2}\right)^2 = \left(x + \frac{b}{2}\right)^2.$$

2 Solve quadratic equations by completing the square.

Solving Quadratic Equations by Completing the Square

Completing the square can be used to solve quadratic equations. As you rewrite a quadratic equation in an equivalent form, it is important to preserve the equality. Whatever constant term you add to one side of the equation to complete the square, be certain to add the same constant to the other side of the equation. These ideas are illustrated in the following examples.

EXAMPLE 3 **Solving Quadratic Equations by Completing the Square**

Solve by completing the square:

a. $x^2 + 8x = -15$ **b.** $x^2 - 6x + 2 = 0$

Solution

Discover for yourself

Try to solve the equations in Example 3 by factoring. Which equation can be solved by factoring and which one cannot? Which equation has rational solutions and which one has irrational solutions?

Write a statement about the kinds of real solutions a quadratic equation can have, and relate this statement to whether or not the equation can be solved by factoring.

a. To complete the square on the binomial $x^2 + 8x$, we take half of 8, which is 4, and square 4, giving 16. We add 16 to both sides of the equation. This makes the left side a perfect square trinomial.

$$x^2 + 8x = -15$$ This is the given equation.

$$x^2 + 8x + 16 = -15 + 16$$ Add 16 to both sides to complete the square.

$$(x + 4)^2 = 1$$ Factor and simplify.

$$x + 4 = 1 \quad \text{or} \quad x + 4 = -1$$ Apply the square root property.

$$x = -3 \quad \text{or} \quad x = -5$$ Solve the equations.

The solutions are -3 and 5.

b. To solve $x^2 - 6x + 2 = 0$ by completing the square, we first subtract 2 from both sides. This is done to isolate the binomial $x^2 - 6x$ so that we can complete the square.

$$x^2 - 6x + 2 = 0$$ This is the original equation.

$$x^2 - 6x = -2$$ Subtract 2 from both sides.

$$x^2 - 6x + 9 = -2 + 9$$ Complete the square. Take half the coefficient of x and square this result: $\frac{1}{2}(-6) = -3$ and $(-3)^2 = 9$. Notice that 9 is added to both sides.

$$(x - 3)^2 = 7$$ Factor and simplify.

$$x - 3 = \sqrt{7} \quad \text{or} \quad x - 3 = -\sqrt{7}$$ Apply the square root property.

$$x = 3 + \sqrt{7} \quad \text{or} \quad x = 3 - \sqrt{7}$$ Solve the equations, adding 3 to both sides.

The solutions are $3 + \sqrt{7}$ and $3 - \sqrt{7}$, expressed in abbreviated notation as $3 \pm \sqrt{7}$. ∎

If the coefficient of the squared variable in a quadratic equation is not 1, we divide both sides of the equation by this coefficient. The squared variable will then have a coefficient of 1 and we can complete the square.

EXAMPLE 4 **Completing the Square: Leading Coefficient Is Not 1**

Solve by completing the square: $2x^2 + 3x = 2$

Solution

$$2x^2 + 3x = 2$$ This is the original equation.

$$x^2 + \frac{3}{2}x = 1$$ Divide both sides by 2 so that the leading coefficient is 1.

$$x^2 + \frac{3}{2}x + \frac{9}{16} = 1 + \frac{9}{16}$$ Complete the square, adding the square of half the coefficient of x to both sides: $\frac{1}{2} \cdot \frac{3}{2} = \frac{3}{4}$ and $\left(\frac{3}{4}\right)^2 = \frac{9}{16}$. Thus, $\frac{9}{16}$ is added to both sides.

$$\left(x + \frac{3}{4}\right)^2 = \frac{25}{16}$$ Factor and simplify. On the right: $1 + \frac{9}{16} = \frac{16}{16} + \frac{9}{16} = \frac{25}{16}$.

$$x + \frac{3}{4} = \sqrt{\frac{25}{16}} \quad \text{or} \quad x + \frac{3}{4} = -\sqrt{\frac{25}{16}}$$ Apply the square root property.

$$x + \frac{3}{4} = \frac{5}{4} \quad \text{or} \quad x + \frac{3}{4} = -\frac{5}{4}$$ $\sqrt{\frac{25}{16}} = \frac{\sqrt{25}}{\sqrt{16}} = \frac{5}{4}$

$$x = \frac{2}{4} \quad \text{or} \quad x = -\frac{8}{4}$$ Solve the equations, subtracting $\frac{3}{4}$ from both sides.

$$x = \frac{1}{2} \quad \text{or} \quad x = -2$$ Simplify.

The solutions are $\frac{1}{2}$ and -2. ■

Quadratic equations with irrational solutions cannot be solved by factoring. However, all quadratic equations can be solved by completing the square using the following steps.

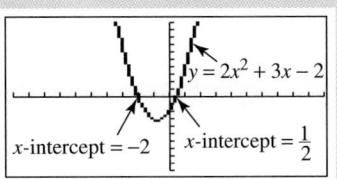

Solving a quadratic equation by completing the square

1. If necessary, write the equation $ax^2 + bx + c = 0$ so that the variable terms are isolated on one side, obtaining $ax^2 + bx = -c$.
2. If the coefficient of x^2 is not 1, divide both sides of the equation by the coefficient of x^2.
3. Add the square of half the coefficient of the x term to both sides of the equation.
4. Factor, writing the perfect square trinomial as the square of a binomial.
5. Apply the square root property and solve.

EXAMPLE 5   Solving a Quadratic Equation by Completing the Square

Solve by completing the square: $2x^2 + 5x - 4 = 0$

Solution

$$2x^2 + 5x - 4 = 0$$ This is the original equation.

$$2x^2 + 5x = 4$$ Isolate variable terms, adding 4 to both sides.

$$x^2 + \frac{5}{2}x = 2$$ Divide both sides by 2 so that the coefficient of x^2 is 1.

$$x^2 + \frac{5}{2}x + \frac{25}{16} = 2 + \frac{25}{16}$$ Complete the square. Since $\frac{1}{2}\left(\frac{5}{2}\right) = \frac{5}{4}$ and $\left(\frac{5}{4}\right)^2 = \frac{25}{16}$, add $\frac{25}{16}$ to both sides.

$$\left(x + \frac{5}{4}\right)^2 = \frac{57}{16}$$ Factor and simplify. On the right: $2 + \frac{25}{16} = \frac{32}{16} + \frac{25}{16} = \frac{57}{16}$.

$$x + \frac{5}{4} = \sqrt{\frac{57}{16}} \quad \text{or} \quad x + \frac{5}{4} = -\sqrt{\frac{57}{16}}$$ Apply the square root property.

$$x + \frac{5}{4} = \frac{\sqrt{57}}{4} \quad \text{or} \quad x + \frac{5}{4} = -\frac{\sqrt{57}}{4}$$ $\sqrt{\frac{57}{16}} = \frac{\sqrt{57}}{\sqrt{16}} = \frac{\sqrt{57}}{4}$

$$x = -\frac{5}{4} + \frac{\sqrt{57}}{4} \quad \text{or} \quad x = -\frac{5}{4} - \frac{\sqrt{57}}{4}$$ Solve the equations, subtracting $\frac{5}{4}$ from both sides.

$$x = \frac{-5 + \sqrt{57}}{4} \quad \text{or} \quad x = \frac{-5 - \sqrt{57}}{4}$$ Express solutions with a common denominator.

The solutions are $\dfrac{-5 \pm \sqrt{57}}{4}$.

Using technology

Obtain a decimal approximation for each solution:

$$\frac{-5 + \sqrt{57}}{4} \approx 0.6$$

$$\frac{-5 - \sqrt{57}}{4} \approx -3.1$$

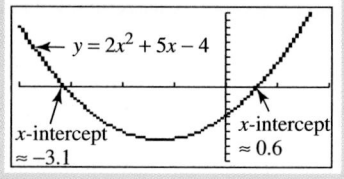

The x-intercepts of $y = 2x^2 + 5x - 4$ verify these solutions.

PROBLEM SET 10.2

Practice Problems

Determine the constant that should be added to Problems 1–12 to make the expression a perfect square trinomial.

1. $x^2 + 12x$ **2.** $x^2 + 16x$ **3.** $x^2 - 10x$ **4.** $x^2 - 14x$ **5.** $y^2 + 3y$ **6.** $y^2 + 5y$

7. $y^2 - 7y$ **8.** $y^2 - 9y$ **9.** $x^2 - \frac{2}{3}x$ **10.** $x^2 + \frac{4}{5}x$ **11.** $y^2 - \frac{1}{3}y$ **12.** $y^2 - \frac{1}{4}y$

Solve each quadratic equation in Problems 13–38 by completing the square. If applicable, verify your solutions with a graphing utility.

13. $x^2 + 6x = 7$ **14.** $x^2 + 6x = -8$ **15.** $x^2 - 2x = 2$ **16.** $x^2 + 4x = 12$

17. $y^2 - 6y - 11 = 0$ **18.** $y^2 - 2y - 5 = 0$ **19.** $r^2 + 4r + 1 = 0$ **20.** $r^2 + 6r - 5 = 0$

21. $x^2 + 3x - 1 = 0$ **22.** $x^2 - 3x - 5 = 0$ **23.** $y^2 = 7y - 3$ **24.** $y^2 = 5y - 3$

25. $2z^2 - 7z + 3 = 0$
26. $2z^2 + 5z - 3 = 0$
27. $3y^2 = 3 + 8y$
28. $3y^2 = 2 - 5y$
29. $4y^2 - 4y - 1 = 0$
30. $2y^2 - 4y - 1 = 0$
31. $3z^2 - 2z - 2 = 0$
32. $3z^2 - 5z - 10 = 0$
33. $2t^2 = 3 - 10t$
34. $2t^2 = -1 - 5t$
35. $6y - y^2 = 4$
36. $4 - y^2 = 2y$
37. $z(3z - 2) = 6$
38. $2z(z - 1) = 3$

Application Problem

39. The process of completing the square can be modeled geometrically. What binomial modeled on the right is about to have a term added so that it becomes a perfect square? What is added to complete the square?

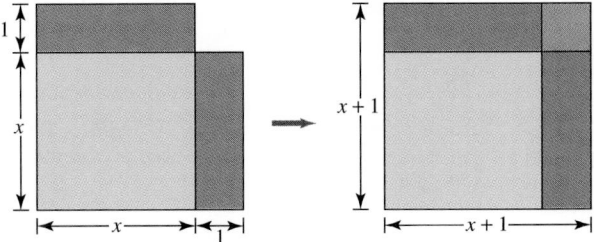

True–False Critical Thinking Problems

40. Which one of the following is true?
  a. Completing the square is a method for finding the area and perimeter of a square.
  b. The trinomial $x^2 - 3x + 9$ is a perfect square trinomial.
  c. Some quadratic equations cannot be solved by completing the square.
  d. In completing the square for $x^2 - 7x = 5$, we should add $\frac{49}{4}$ to both sides.

41. Which of the following is true?
  a. The trinomial $x^2 + \frac{3}{4}x + \frac{9}{16}$ is a perfect square trinomial.
  b. Although not every quadratic equation can be solved by completing the square, they can all be solved using factoring.

  c. The solutions for $x^2 - 8x = -8$ are $4 \pm 2\sqrt{2}$.
  d. If a quadratic equation has solutions that are rational numbers, we know that the equation must have been solved using factoring.

42. Which one of the following is true?
  a. All quadratic equations with irrational solutions have solutions that are opposites or additive inverses of each other.
  b. There are no real solutions to the equation $x^2 + 14x + 49 = -6$.
  c. Only one value of b will make $x^2 + bx + 49$ a perfect square trinomial.
  d. Dividing both sides of a quadratic equation by the coefficient of x^2 is an effective way to avoid fractions when completing the square.

Writing in Mathematics

43. Describe the steps involved in solving a quadratic equation by completing the square. Use $x^2 - 2x - 5 = 0$, or any quadratic equation of your choice, as an example as you clearly describe each step.

44. Describe how to determine what number should be added to the expression $x^2 - 9x$ so that it becomes a perfect square trinomial. What perfect square trinomial is obtained?

45. Describe the error in the following solution process, in which $4x^2 + 6x - 1 = 0$ is solved by completing the square.

$4x^2 + 6x - 1 = 0$ This is the original equation.

$4x^2 + 6x = 1$	Add 1 to both sides.
$4x^2 + 6x + 9 = 1 + 9$	Since $\frac{1}{2} \cdot 6 = 3$ and $3^2 = 9$, add 9 to both sides.
$(2x + 3)^2 = 10$	Factor the resulting perfect square trinomial.
$2x + 3 = \pm \sqrt{10}$	Apply the square root property.
$2x = -3 \pm \sqrt{10}$	Subtract 3 from both sides.
$x = \dfrac{-3 \pm \sqrt{10}}{2}$	Divide both sides by 2.

Critical Thinking Problems

46. Write a perfect square trinomial that has a term of $-20x$.

47. Solve by completing the square: $x^2 + x + c = 0$.

48. Solve by completing the square: $x^2 + bx + c = 0$.

Review Problems

49. Solve: $\sqrt{2x + 3} = 2x - 3$.

50. Simplify: $\dfrac{2x + 3}{x^2 - 7x + 12} - \dfrac{2}{x - 3}$.

51. Solve: $4(2x - 3) + 4 = 9x + 2$.

S E C T I O N   1 0 . 3

Solutions   Tutorial   Video
Manual   II

The Quadratic Formula

Objectives

1 Solve quadratic equations using the quadratic formula.
2 Determine the most efficient technique to use when solving a quadratic equation.
3 Solve problems using the quadratic formula.

The method of completing the square is really a means to an end. The end is a compact formula that can be used to solve every quadratic equation. In this section, we derive and use this formula, called the *quadratic formula*.

Deriving the Quadratic Formula

Discover for yourself

Before studying the derivation in Table 10.1, determine the constant that should be added to

$$x^2 + \frac{b}{a}x$$

to make the expression a perfect square trinomial. Write this perfect square trinomial in factored form.

Mathematicians often like to generalize a procedure to arrive at a formula. Since completing the square is a method that can be used to solve all quadratic equations, let's apply this method to the general quadratic equation in standard form, $ax^2 + bx + c = 0$. Assume that $a > 0$. In the derivation shown in Table 10.1 on the facing page, we also show a particular quadratic equation $3x^2 - 2x - 4 = 0$ to specifically illustrate what we are doing.

A similar derivation gives us the same formula in the last step when a is negative. The formula is called the *quadratic formula* and indicates that the two solutions of

$$ax^2 + bx + c = 0$$

are

$$x = \frac{-b + \sqrt{b^2 - 4ac}}{2a} \quad \text{and} \quad x = \frac{-b - \sqrt{b^2 - 4ac}}{2a}.$$

1 Solve quadratic equations using the quadratic formula.

Solving Equations Using the Quadratic Formula

Here's a step-by-step method for using the quadratic formula.

Study tip

Memorize the quadratic formula. In words: "x equals negative b, plus or minus the square root of b squared minus 4ac, all divided by 2a." Be sure to extend the fraction bar all the way across. The *entire quantity*

$$-b \pm \sqrt{b^2 - 4ac}$$

is divided by 2a.

Solving a quadratic equation by the quadratic formula

1. If necessary, write the quadratic equation in standard form, $ax^2 + bx + c = 0$. Determine the numerical values for a, b, and c.

2. Substitute the values for a, b, and c in the quadratic formula

$$x = \frac{-b \pm \sqrt{b^2 - 4ac}}{2a}.$$

3. Evaluate the formula and obtain the quadratic equation's solutions.

M. C. Escher (1898–1972) "Rind."
© 1997 Cordon Art – Baarn –
Holland. All rights reserved.

TABLE 10.1 Deriving the Quadratic Formula

Standard Form of a Quadratic Equation	Comment	A Specific Example
$ax^2 + bx + c = 0, a > 0$	This is the given equation.	$3x^2 - 2x - 4 = 0$
$x^2 + \dfrac{b}{a}x + \dfrac{c}{a} = 0$	Divide both sides by the coefficient of x^2.	$x^2 - \dfrac{2}{3}x - \dfrac{4}{3} = 0$
$x^2 + \dfrac{b}{a}x = -\dfrac{c}{a}$	Isolate the binomial by adding $-\dfrac{c}{a}$ on both sides.	$x^2 - \dfrac{2}{3}x = \dfrac{4}{3}$
$x^2 + \dfrac{b}{a}x + \dfrac{b^2}{4a^2} = -\dfrac{c}{a} + \dfrac{b^2}{4a^2}$	Complete the square: $\dfrac{1}{2} \cdot \dfrac{b}{a} = \dfrac{b}{2a}$ and $\left(\dfrac{b}{2a}\right)^2 = \dfrac{b^2}{4a^2}$. Add the square of half the coefficient of x to both sides.	$x^2 - \dfrac{2}{3}x + \dfrac{1}{9} = \dfrac{4}{3} + \dfrac{1}{9}$
$\left(x + \dfrac{b}{2a}\right)^2 = -\dfrac{c}{a} \cdot \dfrac{4a}{4a} + \dfrac{b^2}{4a^2}$	Factor on the left and obtain a common denominator on the right.	$\left(x - \dfrac{1}{3}\right)^2 = \dfrac{4}{3} \cdot \dfrac{3}{3} + \dfrac{1}{9}$
$\left(x + \dfrac{b}{2a}\right)^2 = \dfrac{-4ac + b^2}{4a^2}$	Add fractions on the right.	$\left(x - \dfrac{1}{3}\right)^2 = \dfrac{12 + 1}{9}$
$\left(x + \dfrac{b}{2a}\right)^2 = \dfrac{b^2 - 4ac}{4a^2}$		$\left(x - \dfrac{1}{3}\right)^2 = \dfrac{13}{9}$
$x + \dfrac{b}{2a} = \pm\sqrt{\dfrac{b^2 - 4ac}{4a^2}}$	Apply the square root method.	$x - \dfrac{1}{3} = \pm\sqrt{\dfrac{13}{9}}$
$x + \dfrac{b}{2a} = \pm\dfrac{\sqrt{b^2 - 4ac}}{2a}$	Take the square root of the quotient, simplifying the denominator.	$x - \dfrac{1}{3} = \pm\dfrac{\sqrt{13}}{3}$
$x = \dfrac{-b}{2a} \pm \dfrac{\sqrt{b^2 - 4ac}}{2a}$	Solve for x by subtracting $\dfrac{b}{2a}$ from both sides.	$x = \dfrac{1}{3} \pm \dfrac{\sqrt{13}}{3}$
$x = \dfrac{-b \pm \sqrt{b^2 - 4ac}}{2a}$	Combine fractions on the right.	$x = \dfrac{1 \pm \sqrt{13}}{3}$

EXAMPLE 1 Solving a Quadratic Equation Using the Quadratic Formula

Solve using the quadratic formula: $2x^2 + 9x - 5 = 0$

Solution

To use the formula, we must first identify a, b, and c.

$$2x^2 + 9x - 5 = 0$$
$$\updownarrow \quad \updownarrow \quad \updownarrow$$
$$ax^2 + bx + c = 0$$

We see that $a = 2$, $b = 9$, and $c = -5$. Substituting these values into the quadratic formula and simplifying gives the equation's solutions.

sing technology

The graph of $y = 2x^2 + 9x - 5$ has x-intercepts at -5 and $\frac{1}{2}$. This verifies that -5 and $\frac{1}{2}$ are the solutions for $2x^2 + 9x - 5 = 0$.

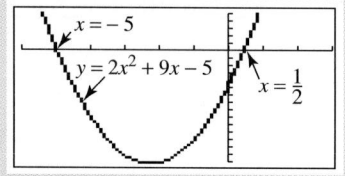

$$x = \frac{-b \pm \sqrt{b^2 - 4ac}}{2a}$$ Use the quadratic formula.

$$x = \frac{-9 \pm \sqrt{9^2 - 4(2)(-5)}}{2(2)}$$ Let $a = 2$, $b = 9$, and $c = -5$.

$$x = \frac{-9 \pm \sqrt{81 + 40}}{4}$$

$$x = \frac{-9 \pm \sqrt{121}}{4}$$

$$x = \frac{-9 \pm 11}{4}$$

$$x = \frac{-9 + 11}{4} \quad \text{or} \quad x = \frac{-9 - 11}{4}$$

$$x = \frac{2}{4} = \frac{1}{2} \quad \text{or} \quad x = \frac{-20}{4} = -5$$

The solutions are $\frac{1}{2}$ and -5.

■

---

tudy tip

In Example 1, the solutions to $2x^2 + 9x - 5 = 0$ are rational numbers. This means that the equation could have been solved by factoring. Notice that the reason the solutions are rational is that $b^2 - 4ac$, the expression under the radical, is 121, a perfect square.

EXAMPLE 2   **Solving a Quadratic Equation Using the Quadratic Formula**

Solve using the quadratic formula: $x^2 = 2x + 16$

Solution

The quadratic equation must be in standard form to determine the values of a, b, and c.

$x^2 = 2x + 16$ This is the given equation.

$x^2 - 2x - 16 = 0$ Subtract $2x$ and 16 on both sides to
                        write the equation in standard form.
$a = 1 \ b = -2 \ c = -16$

Now we can see that $a = 1$, $b = -2$, and $c = -16$. Substituting these values into the quadratic formula and simplifying gives the equation's solutions.

$$x = \frac{-b \pm \sqrt{b^2 - 4ac}}{2a}$$ Use the quadratic formula.

$$x = \frac{-(-2) \pm \sqrt{(-2)^2 - 4(1)(-16)}}{2(1)}$$ Let $a = 1$, $b = -2$, and $c = -16$.

$$x = \frac{2 \pm \sqrt{4 + 64}}{2}$$ Simplify.

$$x = \frac{2 \pm \sqrt{68}}{2}$$ Both solutions, $\frac{2 + \sqrt{68}}{2}$ and $\frac{2 - \sqrt{68}}{2}$, can be simplified.

$$x = \frac{2 \pm 2\sqrt{17}}{2}$$ Simplify $\sqrt{68}$ using $\sqrt{68} = \sqrt{4 \cdot 17} = \sqrt{4}\sqrt{17} = 2\sqrt{17}$.

---

sing technology

You can approximate the solutions by first using your calculator to approximate the square root of $b^2 - 4ac$.

$$\boxed{\sqrt{}}\;\boxed{(}\;\boxed{(}\;\boxed{(-)}\;\boxed{2}\;\boxed{)}\;\boxed{\wedge}\;2$$
$$\boxed{-}\;4\;\boxed{\times}\;1\;\boxed{\times}\;\boxed{(-)}\;16\;\boxed{)}$$
$$\boxed{\text{ENTER}}$$

The display is 8.24621125124. Storing this result and using the recall key, you can find decimal approximations for the two solutions.

$$x \approx \frac{2 + 8.24621125124}{2}$$

$$\approx 5.123$$

$$x \approx \frac{2 - 8.24621125124}{2}$$

$$\approx -3.123$$

Study tip

In Example 2, the solutions to $x^2 - 2x - 16 = 0$ are irrational numbers. This means that the equation could not have been solved by factoring. Notice that the reason the solutions are irrational is that $b^2 - 4ac$, the expression under the radical, is 68, which is not a perfect square.

Discover for yourself

If $b^2 - 4ac = 0$, we have

$$x = \frac{-b \pm \sqrt{b^2 - 4ac}}{2a}$$

$$= \frac{-b \pm \sqrt{0}}{2a} = \frac{-b}{2a}$$

Describe the number of answers and the kinds of solutions (rational or irrational) there will be if this occurs.

We can further simplify these answers by factoring 2 from each term in the numerator:

$$x = \frac{2(1 \pm \sqrt{17})}{2}$$

$$x = \frac{\cancel{2}(1 \pm \sqrt{17})}{\cancel{2}} \qquad \text{Cancel identical factors in the numerator and denominator.}$$

The solutions are $1 + \sqrt{17}$ and $1 - \sqrt{17}$, or $1 \pm \sqrt{17}$. ■

There are quadratic equations where $b^2 - 4ac$ is zero, as shown in our next example.

EXAMPLE 3   **A Quadratic Equation with Only One Solution**

Solve: $x^2 - 6x + 9 = 0$

Solution

One solution method is factoring. Since $x^2 - 6x + 9 = 0$ can be factored to obtain $(x - 3)^2 = 0$, we can use the zero-product principle to get $x = 3$.
A second method is the quadratic formula.

$$\underset{\substack{\uparrow \\ a=1}}{x^2} \underset{\substack{\uparrow \\ b=-6}}{-6x} \underset{\substack{\uparrow \\ c=9}}{+9} = 0 \qquad \text{The original equation. In standard form, we see that } a = 1, b = -6, \text{ and } c = 9.$$

$$x = \frac{-b \pm \sqrt{b^2 - 4ac}}{2a} \qquad \text{Use the quadratic formula.}$$

$$x = \frac{-(-6) \pm \sqrt{(-6)^2 - 4(1)(9)}}{2(1)} \qquad \text{Let } a = 1, b = -6, \text{ and } c = 9.$$

$$x = \frac{6 \pm \sqrt{36 - 36}}{2} \qquad \text{Simplify.}$$

$$x = \frac{6 \pm \sqrt{0}}{2}$$

$$x = \frac{6}{2} = 3 \qquad \sqrt{0} = 0$$

By either method, the quadratic equation has only one solution. The solution is 3. ■

Study tip

When $b^2 - 4ac$ is zero, a quadratic equation has one rational number solution.

Discover for yourself

What can you say about the solutions to a quadratic equation if $b^2 - 4ac$ is negative? Do you have any guesses about what answers such as

$$5 + \sqrt{-4} \quad \text{and} \quad 5 - \sqrt{-4}$$

might mean? What is $\sqrt{-4}$? Can you think of any real number that when squared would result in -4?

2 Determine the most efficient technique to use when solving a quadratic equation.

Which Method to Use

Although all quadratic equations can be solved by the quadratic formula, if an equation is in the form $x^2 = d$, such as $x^2 = 5$ or $(2y + 3)^2 = 8$, it is faster to use the square root property, taking the square root of both sides.

If the equation is not in the form $x^2 = d$, write the quadratic equation in standard form $(ax^2 + bx + c = 0)$. Try to solve the equation by the factoring method.

If $ax^2 + bx + c$ cannot be factored, then solve the quadratic equation by the quadratic formula.

The method of completing the square is useful in more advanced algebra courses, but since we used it to derive the quadratic formula, we no longer need it for solving quadratic equations.

These observations are summarized in Table 10.2.

TABLE 10.2 Determining the Most Efficient Technique to Use When Solving a Quadratic Equation

Description and Form of the Quadratic Equation	Most Efficient Solution Method	Example
$ax^2 + c = 0$ The quadratic equation has no linear (x) term.	Solving for x^2 and using the square root property	$4x^2 - 7 = 0$ $$4x^2 = 7$$ $$x^2 = \frac{7}{4}$$ $$x = \pm\frac{\sqrt{7}}{2}$$
$(x + d)^2 = e$	The square root property	$(x + 4)^2 = 5$ $$x + 4 = \pm\sqrt{5}$$ $$x = -4 \pm \sqrt{5}$$
$ax^2 + bx + c = 0$ and $ax^2 + bx + c$ can be obviously factored.	Factoring and the zero-product principle	$3x^2 + 5x - 2 = 0$ $(3x - 1)(x + 2) = 0$ $$3x - 1 = 0 \quad \text{or} \quad x + 2 = 0$$ $$x = \frac{1}{3} \quad \text{or} \quad x = -2$$
$ax^2 + bx + c = 0$ and $ax^2 + bx + c$ cannot be factored or the factoring is too difficult.	The quadratic formula: $$x = \frac{-b \pm \sqrt{b^2 - 4ac}}{2a}$$	$x^2 - 2x - 6 = 0$ $$x = \frac{2 \pm \sqrt{4 - 4(1)(-6)}}{2(1)}$$ $$x = \frac{2 \pm \sqrt{28}}{2} = \frac{2 \pm \sqrt{4}\sqrt{7}}{2}$$ $$x = \frac{2 \pm 2\sqrt{7}}{2} = \frac{2(1 \pm \sqrt{7})}{2}$$ $$x = 1 \pm \sqrt{7}$$

3 Solve problems using the quadratic formula.

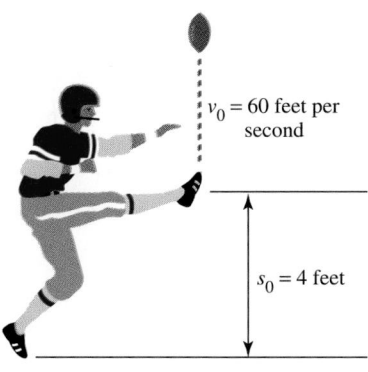

Figure 10.2

Quadratic Models

A quadratic model is a mathematical model containing an expression in the form $ax^2 + bx + c$. The quadratic formula can be used to answer questions about variables contained in quadratic models.

EXAMPLE 4 **A Quadratic Model Describing Motion and Position**

When an object is given an initial velocity of v_0 feet per second from an altitude of s_0 feet, its position s above the ground after t seconds is given by the mathematical model $s = -16t^2 + v_0 t + s_0$. As shown in Figure 10.2, a football is kicked straight up from a height of 4 feet with an initial velocity of 60 feet per second. How long will it take the football to hit the ground?

Solution

$$s = -16t^2 + v_0 t + s_0$$ This is the given formula.

$$0 = -16t^2 + 60t + 4$$ Substitute the values:
$s_0 = $ Initial altitude $= 4$
$v_0 = $ Initial velocity $= 60$
 $s = $ Position above the ground $= 0$, since we want to know when the ball will hit the ground.

$$16t^2 - 60t - 4 = 0$$ Multiply by -1. We must solve for t.

$$\frac{16t^2}{4} - \frac{60t}{4} - \frac{4}{4} = \frac{0}{4}$$ Divide both sides by 4. This will keep the numbers smaller.

$$4t^2 - 15t - 1 = 0$$ Simplify.
$a = 4 \quad b = -15 \quad c = -1$

$$t = \frac{-b \pm \sqrt{b^2 - 4ac}}{2a}$$ Since $4t^2 - 15t - 1$ is prime, use the quadratic formula.

$$= \frac{-(-15) \pm \sqrt{(-15)^2 - 4(4)(-1)}}{2(4)}$$ Let $a = 4, b = -15$, and $c = -1$.

$$t = \frac{15 \pm \sqrt{241}}{8}$$ Simplify. No further simplification is possible.

Since

$$\frac{15 - \sqrt{241}}{8}$$

is negative ($\sqrt{241} \approx 15.5$), it cannot represent the time it takes for the football to reach the ground. It takes the ball

$$\frac{15 + \sqrt{241}}{8} \text{ seconds (approximately 3.8 seconds)}$$

to hit the ground.

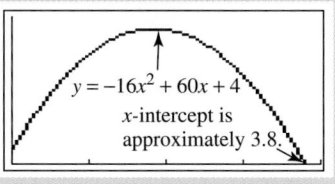

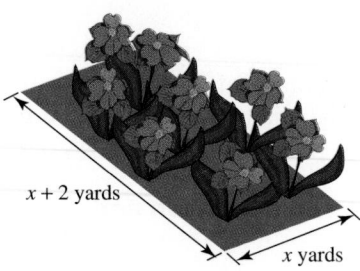

Figure 10.3

A rectangular garden

In Example 4 we were given the model that described the football's position as a function of time. As we have seen throughout the book, a more difficult situation is to use a problem's conditions to create a mathematical model.

In Example 5, we use our five-step problem-solving strategy and the quadratic formula to solve the problem.

EXAMPLE 5 **A Geometric Application**

The length of a rectangular flower bed is 2 yards longer than the width. If the area is 10 square yards, what are the exact values of the length and width of the flower bed? (See Figure 10.3.)

Solution

Steps 1 and 2. Represent unknown quantities in terms of x.

Let

$$x = \text{Width of the rectangle}$$
$$x + 2 = \text{Length of the rectangle}$$

Step 3. Write an equation that describes the problem's conditions.

Product of length and width	equals	Area of rectangle.
↓	↓	↓
$x(x + 2)$	$=$	10

Step 4. Solve the equation and answer the question.

$x(x + 2) = 10$ This is the equation implied by the formula for area.

$\underset{\substack{\uparrow \\ a=1}}{x^2} + \underset{\substack{\uparrow \\ b=2}}{2x} - \underset{\substack{\uparrow \\ c=-10}}{10} = 0$ Write the equation in standard form. Then $a = 1$, $b = 2$, and $c = -10$.

$x = \dfrac{-b \pm \sqrt{b^2 - 4ac}}{2a}$ Since $x^2 + 2x - 10$ is prime, use the quadratic formula.

$x = \dfrac{-2 \pm \sqrt{2^2 - 4(1)(-10)}}{2(1)}$ Substitute for a, b, and c.

$x = \dfrac{-2 \pm \sqrt{44}}{2}$ Simplify.

$x = \dfrac{-2 \pm 2\sqrt{11}}{2}$ $\sqrt{44} = \sqrt{4 \cdot 11} = 2\sqrt{11}$

$x = \dfrac{2(-1 \pm \sqrt{11})}{2}$ Factor 2 from the numerator.

$x = -1 \pm \sqrt{11}$ Divide the numerator and denominator by 2.

Since $-1 - \sqrt{11}$ is a negative number, it cannot be the width of the rectangle. If $x = -1 + \sqrt{11}$, then the rectangle's length is

$$x + 2 = (-1 + \sqrt{11}) + 2 = 1 + \sqrt{11}.$$

The width is $-1 + \sqrt{11}$ yards (approximately 2.3 yards) and the length is $1 + \sqrt{11}$ yards (approximately 4.3 yards).

Step 5. Check.

The area is the product of length and width:

$$(-1 + \sqrt{11})(1 + \sqrt{11}) = \overset{F}{-1} \overset{O}{- \sqrt{11}} \overset{I}{+ \sqrt{11}} \overset{L}{+ 11} = 10$$

as given in the conditions of the problem. ■

Study tip

As you know, when you cancel identical factors in the numerator and denominator, you are actually removing a factor of 1. Here are the details for Example 5.

$$\frac{-2 \pm 2\sqrt{11}}{2} = \frac{2(-1 \pm \sqrt{11})}{2 \cdot 1} = \frac{2}{2} \cdot \frac{-1 \pm \sqrt{11}}{1} = 1 \cdot \frac{-1 \pm \sqrt{11}}{1} = -1 \pm \sqrt{11}$$

This is usually abbreviated as follows:

$$\frac{-2 \pm 2\sqrt{11}}{2} = \frac{\overset{1}{\cancel{2}}(-1 \pm \sqrt{11})}{\underset{1}{\cancel{2}}} = -1 \pm \sqrt{11}.$$

You cannot cancel identical terms in the numerator and denominator.

INCORRECT

$$\frac{\cancel{-2} \pm 2\sqrt{11}}{\cancel{2}} = -1 \pm 2\sqrt{11} \qquad \frac{-2 \pm 2\cancel{\sqrt{11}}}{2} = -2 \pm \sqrt{11}$$

When in doubt, be sure to factor before you cancel.

PROBLEM SET 10.3

Practice Problems _____

Solve the equations in Problems 1–24 by using the quadratic formula. If applicable, verify solutions with a graphing utility.

1. $x^2 + 8x + 15 = 0$ **2.** $x^2 + 8x + 12 = 0$ **3.** $x^2 + 5x + 3 = 0$ **4.** $x^2 + 5x + 2 = 0$

5. $x^2 + 4x - 6 = 0$ **6.** $x^2 + 2x - 4 = 0$ **7.** $x^2 + 4x - 7 = 0$ **8.** $x^2 + 4x + 1 = 0$

9. $x^2 - 3x - 18 = 0$ **10.** $x^2 - 3x - 10 = 0$ **11.** $6x^2 - 5x - 6 = 0$ **12.** $9x^2 - 12x - 5 = 0$

13. $x^2 - 2x - 10 = 0$ **14.** $x^2 + 6x - 10 = 0$ **15.** $x^2 - x = 14$ **16.** $x^2 - 5x = 10$

17. $6y^2 + 6y + 1 = 0$ **18.** $3y^2 - 5y + 1 = 0$ **19.** $4x^2 - 12x + 9 = 0$ **20.** $9x^2 + 6x + 1 = 0$

21. $y^2 = 2(y + 1)$ **22.** $2(y^2 + 2y) = -1$ **23.** $\dfrac{y^2}{4} + \dfrac{3y}{2} + 1 = 0$ **24.** $y^2 - \dfrac{2y}{3} = \dfrac{2}{9}$

Use the method of your choice to solve the quadratic equations in Problems 25–54.

25. $2x^2 - x = 1$ **26.** $3x^2 - 4x = 4$ **27.** $5x^2 + 2 = 11x$ **28.** $5x^2 = 6 - 13x$

29. $y^2 = 20$ **30.** $y^2 = 125$ **31.** $x^2 - 2x = 1$ **32.** $2x^2 + 3x = 1$

33. $(2w + 3)(w + 4) = 1$ **34.** $(2w - 5)(w + 1) = 2$ **35.** $(3r - 4)^2 = 16$ **36.** $(2r + 7)^2 = 25$

37. $3y^2 - 12y + 12 = 0$ **38.** $9 - 6y + y^2 = 0$ **39.** $4w^2 - 16 = 0$ **40.** $3w^2 - 27 = 0$

41. $\frac{3}{4}y^2 - \frac{5}{2}y - 2 = 0$ **42.** $\dfrac{y^2}{3} - \dfrac{3}{2} = \dfrac{y}{2}$ **43.** $10x^2 - 11x + 2 = 0$ **44.** $5x^2 + x - 1 = 0$

45. $\dfrac{y^2}{2} - 2y + \dfrac{3}{4} = 0$ **46.** $y^2 - \frac{1}{2}y - \frac{1}{5} = 0$ **47.** $(3x - 2)^2 = 10$

48. $(4x - 1)^2 = 15$ **49.** $y^2 + 14y + 49 = 0$ **50.** $4y^2 - 4y + 1 = 0$

51. $x^2 + 9x = 0$ **52.** $x^2 - 6x = 0$ **53.** $(x - 2)^2 - 49 = 0$

54. $(3x + 1)^2 - 25 = 0$

Application Problems

55. The formula $N = 0.4x^2 - 36x + 1000$ approximates the number of accidents per 50 million miles (N) for a driver who is x years old, for drivers between ages 16 and 74. What is the age of a driver predicted to have 312 accidents per 50 million miles driven? Round your answer to the nearest whole number.

56. The formula $N = 0.036x^2 - 2.8x + 58.14$ approximately models the number of deaths per year per thousand people (N) for people who are x years old, where $40 \leqslant x \leqslant 60$. Find, to the nearest whole number, the age at which 12 people per 1000 die annually.

For Problems 57–69, find the solution as an exact value in simplified radical form. Then give an approximate answer, rounding to the nearest tenth.

When an object is given an initial velocity of v_0 feet per second from an altitude of s_0 feet, its position s above the ground after t seconds is given by the mathematical model $s = -16t^2 + v_0t + s_0$. Use this formula to answer Problems 57–58.

57. Standing on a platform 50 feet high, a person accidentally fires a gun straight into the air. If the bullet left the gun with a velocity of 100 feet per second, how long will it take for the bullet to hit the ground?

58. A ball is thrown upward from the roof of an 80-foot-tall building with a velocity of 32 feet per second. How long does it take for the ball to hit the ground?

59. The length of a rectangle is 3 meters longer than the width. If the area is 36 square meters, find the dimensions of the rectangle.

60. The length of a rectangle is 2 centimeters longer than the width. If the area is 10 square centimeters, find the dimensions of the rectangle.

61. The base of a triangle is 1 inch less than twice the height. If the area of the triangle is 9 square inches, find the base and height.

62. The base of a triangle is 4 meters longer than the height. If the area of the triangle is 8 square meters, find the base and height.

63. The hypotenuse of a right triangle is 6 millimeters long. One leg is 1 millimeter longer than the other. Find the lengths of the legs.

64. The hypotenuse of a right triangle is 4 meters long. One leg is 1 meter longer than the other. Find the lengths of the legs.

65. The height of the bridge arch shown in the figure is modeled by $h = -0.05x^2 + 27$, where x is the distance in feet from the center of the arch. How far to the right of the center is the height 22 feet?

66. A company manufactures and sells cells for solar collectors. They find that they can sell x cells per day at a price of $100 - 0.05x$ dollars per cell, where $250 \leqslant x \leqslant 800$. How many cells must be sold each day to generate a daily revenue of $37,500? What is the price per cell? (*Hint:* Revenue generated for the company is the product of the number of cells and the price per cell.)

67. The area of the shaded region in the figure is 150 square centimeters. Find the dimensions of the large and small rectangles.

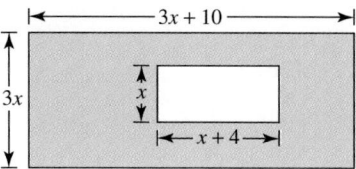

68. It took a boat 20 minutes longer to go 6 miles up a river (against the current) than it did for the return trip with the current. If the current moves at 2 miles per hour, find the speed of the boat in still water.

69. Working together, two people can paint a house in 2 days. Working alone, one person takes a day longer than the other to paint the house. How long does it take each person to paint, working alone?

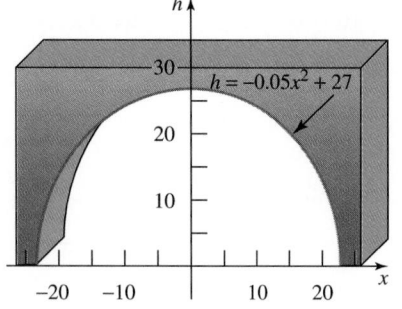

True–False Critical Thinking Problems

70. Which one of the following is true?
  a. When using the quadratic formula to solve the equation $x^2 - x + 3 = 0$, we have $a = 1, b = -x$, and $c = 3$.
  b. The quadratic formula can be expressed as
  $$x = -b \pm \frac{\sqrt{b^2 - 4ac}}{2a}.$$
  c. Completing the square is used to derive the quadratic formula.
  d. If $b^2 - 4ac = 0$, then a quadratic equation has two distinct real numbers as solutions.

71. Which one of the following is true?
  a. For the quadratic equation $-2x^2 + 3x = 0$, we have $a = -2, b = 3$, and $c = 0$.
  b. If a quadratic equation cannot be solved by factoring, it is necessary to use completing the square.
  c. If $a = 2, b = -6$, and $c = 0$, then the quadratic equation with those coefficients has two solutions that are irrational numbers.
  d. If $x^2 - 3x - 5 = 0$, then $x = \dfrac{-3 \pm \sqrt{9 + 20}}{2}$.

Technology Problems

72. a. Try solving $x^2 - 2x + 2 = 0$ using the quadratic formula. Since the square root of a negative number is not a real number, what can you conclude about the number of real solutions to $x^2 - 2x + 2 = 0$?
  b. Use a graphing utility to graph $y = x^2 - 2x + 2$. How can you tell from the graph that the quadratic equation $x^2 - 2x + 2 = 0$ has no real solutions?

73. Safety research uses the model $d = 0.044v^2 + 1.1v$ to estimate the least number of feet (d) in which a car can be stopped at various speeds (v, in miles per hour). If it took a car 550 feet to stop, estimate the car's speed at the moment the brakes were applied.

Writing in Mathematics

74. Without going into specific details for each step, describe how the quadratic formula is derived. Explain why the formula is useful.

75. Describe what technique you would use to solve each of the following quadratic equations and tell why you would choose this particular method.
  a. $2x^2 + 7x - 4 = 0$
  b. $3x^2 + 8x - 1 = 0$
  c. $(2x - 8)^2 = 81$

76. The radicand of the quadratic formula, $b^2 - 4ac$, can be used to determine whether $ax^2 + bx + c = 0$ has solutions that are rational, irrational, or not real numbers. Explain how this works. Is it possible to determine the kinds of answers that one will obtain to a quadratic equation without actually solving the equation? Explain.

Critical Thinking Problems

77. Solve: $\dfrac{1}{x^2} + 3 = \dfrac{6}{x}$.

78. Solve: $\sqrt{2y + 3} = y - 1$.

The quadratic formula tells us that the solutions to $ax^2 + bx + c = 0$ are

$$\frac{-b + \sqrt{b^2 - 4ac}}{2a} \quad \text{and} \quad \frac{-b - \sqrt{b^2 - 4ac}}{2a}.$$

Use this information in Problems 79–80.

79. Show that the sum of the solutions is $-\dfrac{b}{a}$.

80. Show that the product of the solutions is $\dfrac{c}{a}$.

Solve the equations in Problems 81–82 using the quadratic formula.

81. $x^2 + 2\sqrt{3}x - 9 = 0$

82. $x^2 - 4\sqrt{2}x - 2 = 0$

83. As shown in the figure, a rectangular plot measuring 8 meters by 10 meters is to be made smaller so that the area is diminished to 47 square meters. What is the value of x that will result in the reduced area?

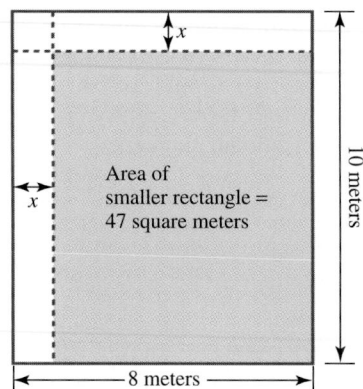

84. A rectangular vegetable garden is 5 feet wide and 9 feet long. The garden is to be surrounded by a tile border of uniform width. If there are 40 square feet of tile for the border, how wide should it be?

85. A photo editor has a 12.5-inch by 8.4-inch picture of a cat in a field of grass. The editor wishes to obtain a print that has half the area of the original photo and focuses on the cat. If the same amount is cut off from all the edges of the photo, how much of the grass section should be cropped from all its edges?

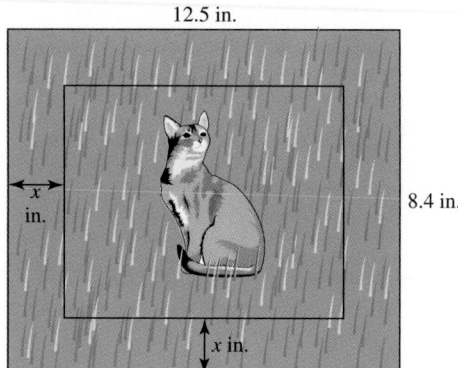

Review Problems _____

86. Solve: $7(y - 2) = 10 - 2(y + 3)$.

87. Solve: $\dfrac{7}{y + 2} + \dfrac{2}{y + 3} = \dfrac{1}{y^2 + 5y + 6}$.

88. Graph: $x - 2y > 2$.

S E C T I O N   1 0 . 4

Solutions   **Tutorial**   **Video**
Manual   **11**

Complex Numbers as Solutions of Quadratic Equations

Objectives

1 Write the square root of a negative number in terms of i.
2 Solve quadratic equations with complex solutions.

| Write the square root of a negative number in terms of i.

Imaginary and Complex Numbers

Throughout this chapter, we have avoided quadratic equations that have no real numbers as solutions. A fairly simple example is the equation

$$x^2 = -1.$$

Since -1 is a negative number and the square of a real number cannot be negative, there is no real number solution for this equation. There is no real number whose square is -1.

To solve quadratic equations such as $x^2 = -1$, we need to define a new set of numbers. This set is based on the number i having the following properties.

Yves Tanguy "Imaginary Numbers" 1954. Fundacion Coleccion Thyssen–Bornemisza, Madrid, Spain. Nimatallah/Art Resource, NY. © 1998 Estate of Yves Tanguy/Artists Rights Society (ARS), New York.

The number i

The number i is defined to be the square root of -1. Thus

$$i = \sqrt{-1} \quad \text{and} \quad i^2 = -1.$$

The number is called the *imaginary unit.*

Observe that i is not a real number since there is no real number whose square is -1. However, we can now express numbers such as $\sqrt{-4}$, $\sqrt{-7}$, and $\sqrt{-8}$ in terms of i.

EXAMPLE 1   Simplifying Square Roots of Negative Numbers

Write as a multiple of i: **a.** $\sqrt{-4}$ **b.** $\sqrt{-7}$ **c.** $\sqrt{-8}$

Solution

The solution is based on a generalization of the product rule for radicals, namely, $\sqrt{xy} = \sqrt{x}\sqrt{y}$.

a. $\sqrt{-4} = \sqrt{-1 \cdot 4} = \sqrt{-1}\sqrt{4} = i \cdot 2 = 2i$

We can check that $\sqrt{-4} = 2i$ by squaring $2i$ and obtaining -4. By extending the properties of exponents to include the newly defined number i, we obtain

$$(2i)^2 = 2^2 i^2 \qquad \text{Square each factor.}$$
$$= 4i^2$$
$$= 4(-1) \quad \text{By definition, } i^2 = -1.$$
$$= -4$$

Since $(2i)^2 = -4$, this verifies that $\sqrt{-4} = 2i$.

b. $\sqrt{-7} = \sqrt{-1 \cdot 7} = \sqrt{-1}\sqrt{7} = i\sqrt{7}$

c. $\sqrt{-8} = \sqrt{-1 \cdot 8} = \sqrt{-1}\sqrt{8} = i\sqrt{4 \cdot 2} = i2\sqrt{2} = 2i\sqrt{2}$ ∎

The numbers in Example 1 are all *imaginary numbers.*

Definition of an imaginary number

An imaginary number is a number that can be written in the form $a + bi$, where a and b are real numbers, and $b \neq 0$.

Here are some examples of imaginary numbers:

$$2i, 5 + 7i, \sqrt{3} - 9i, \text{ and } \pi + i\sqrt{7}.$$

Notice that in the first example, $a = 0$. If we permit b to be 0, we combine the imaginary and real numbers to form the set of *complex numbers.*

Definition of a complex number

A complex number is any number that can be put in the form $a + bi$, where a and b are real numbers and $i = \sqrt{-1}$.

study tip

It is easy to confuse $\sqrt{7}i$ with $\sqrt{7i}$, where the i in the latter case is under the radical. To avoid this confusion, we will write $i\sqrt{7}$, so that it is clear that i is not under the radical.

study tip

The real number a can be expressed as $a + 0i$, so every real number is a complex number. However, not every complex number is real. Complex numbers such as $2i$ or $5 + 3i$ are not real numbers.

2
Solve quadratic equations with complex solutions.

Solving Quadratic Equations with Complex Solutions

The equation $x^2 = -25$ has no real solutions, but it does have complex solutions.

$$x^2 = -25 \qquad \text{No real number squared results in a negative number.}$$
$$x = \pm\sqrt{-25} \qquad \text{Apply the square root property.}$$
$$x = \pm 5i \qquad \sqrt{-25} = \sqrt{25(-1)} = \sqrt{25}\sqrt{-1} = 5i$$

The solutions are $5i$ and $-5i$. The next examples involve quadratic equations that have no real solutions but do have complex solutions.

EXAMPLE 2 **Solving a Quadratic Equation Using the Square Root Property**

Solve: $(x + 4)^2 = -36$

Solution

$$(x + 4)^2 = -36 \qquad \text{This is the given equation.}$$
$$x + 4 = \sqrt{-36} \quad \text{or} \quad x + 4 = -\sqrt{-36} \qquad \begin{array}{l}\text{Apply the square root property.}\\ \text{Equivalently, } x + 4 = \pm\sqrt{-36}.\end{array}$$
$$x + 4 = 6i \quad \text{or} \quad x + 4 = -6i \qquad \sqrt{-36} = \sqrt{36(-1)} = 6i$$
$$x = -4 + 6i \quad \text{or} \quad x = -4 - 6i \qquad \begin{array}{l}\text{Solve the equations by subtracting}\\ \text{4 from both sides.}\end{array}$$

Check

Let's check $-4 + 6i$:

$$(x + 4)^2 = -36 \qquad \text{This is the given equation.}$$
$$(-4 + 6i + 4)^2 \overset{?}{=} -36 \qquad \text{Replace } x \text{ by } -4 + 6i.$$
$$(6i)^2 \overset{?}{=} -36 \qquad \text{Simplify.}$$
$$36i^2 \overset{?}{=} -36 \qquad (6i)^2 = 6^2 i^2 = 36i^2$$
$$36(-1) \overset{?}{=} -36 \qquad \text{Replace } i^2 \text{ with } -1.$$
$$-36 = -36 \quad \checkmark \qquad \text{This true statement indicates that } -4 + 6i \text{ is a solution.}$$

In a similar manner, we can check $-4 - 6i$ (do this), verifying that the solutions are $-4 + 6i$ and $-4 - 6i$.   ■

EXAMPLE 3 **Solving a Quadratic Equation Using the Quadratic Formula**

Solve: $x^2 - 2x + 2 = 0$

Solution

$$x^2 - 2x + 2 = 0$$

$$a = 1 \quad b = -2 \quad c = 2$$

Since $x^2 - 2x + 2$ is prime, we will use the quadratic formula.

$$x = \frac{-b \pm \sqrt{b^2 - 4ac}}{2a}$$

Use the quadratic formula with $a = 1, b = -2$, and $c = 2$.

$$x = \frac{-(-2) \pm \sqrt{(-2)^2 - 4(1)(2)}}{2(1)}$$

$$x = \frac{2 \pm \sqrt{4 - 8}}{2}$$

Simplify.

$$x = \frac{2 \pm \sqrt{-4}}{2}$$

The negative number under the radical indicates that the solutions are not real numbers.

$$x = \frac{2 \pm 2i}{2}$$

$\sqrt{-4} = \sqrt{4(-1)} = 2i$

$$x = \frac{2(1 \pm i)}{2}$$

Factor 2 in the numerator.

$$x = 1 \pm i$$

Divide the numerator and denominator by 2.

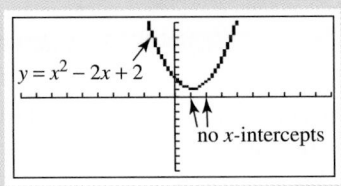

Using technology

The graph of $y = x^2 - 2x + 2$ has no x-intercepts, so $x^2 - 2x + 2 = 0$ has no real solutions. However, the equation does have complex solutions.

$y = x^2 - 2x + 2$

no x-intercepts

The solutions are $1 + i$ and $1 - i$.

P R O B L E M   S E T   1 0 . 4

Practice Problems _____

Write each number in Problems 1–8 as a multiple of i.

1. $\sqrt{-16}$ **2.** $\sqrt{-49}$ **3.** $\sqrt{-20}$ **4.** $\sqrt{-75}$

5. $\sqrt{-45}$ **6.** $\sqrt{-28}$ **7.** $\sqrt{-150}$ **8.** $\sqrt{-700}$

Solve each quadratic equation in Problems 9–16 using the square root property, expressing complex solutions in $a + bi$ form.

9. $(x - 3)^2 = -9$ **10.** $(x - 5)^2 = -36$ **11.** $(x + 7)^2 = -64$ **12.** $(x + 12)^2 = -100$

13. $(y - 2)^2 = -7$ **14.** $(y - 1)^2 = -13$ **15.** $(z + 3)^2 = -18$ **16.** $(z + 4)^2 = -48$

Solve each quadratic equation in Problems 17–28 using the quadratic formula, expressing complex solutions in $a + bi$ form. If applicable, use a graphing utility to confirm that the equations have no real solutions.

17. $x^2 + 4x + 5 = 0$ **18.** $x^2 + 2x + 2 = 0$ **19.** $x^2 - 6x + 13 = 0$

20. $x^2 - 6x + 10 = 0$ **21.** $x^2 - 12x + 40 = 0$ **22.** $x^2 - 4x + 29 = 0$

23. $x^2 = 10x - 27$ **24.** $x^2 = 4x - 7$ **25.** $5y^2 = 2y - 3$

26. $6y^2 = -2y - 1$ **27.** $5y^2 - y = y^2 + y - 5$ **28.** $6y^2 - y - 11 = 2y^2 - 14$

Application Problems

29. The model $y = -x^2 + 2x + 27$ describes the height (y, in meters) of a diver (after x seconds) who jumps from a cliff that is 27 meters above the water. Will the diver ever reach a height of 29 meters? Answer the question by solving the equation $-x^2 + 2x + 27 = 29$. If the equation has no real solutions, the diver will never reach the indicated height. Explain why.

30. The model $P = -5I^2 + 80I$ describes the power P of an 80-volt generator subject to a current I of electricity given in amperes. Can there ever be enough current to generate 340 volts of power?

True–False Critical Thinking Problems

31. Which one of the following is true?
   a. If $3 + 5i$ is a solution to a quadratic equation, the other solution is $-3 + 5i$.
   b. $2 - i$ is a solution of $x^2 - 4x + 5 = 0$.
   c. Some real numbers are not complex numbers.
   d. $\sqrt{-6} = 6i$

32. Which one of the following is true?
   a. $-\sqrt{-9} = -(-3) = 3$
   b. The complex number $a + 0i$ is the real number a.
   c. $2 + \sqrt{-4} = 2 - 2i$
   d. $\dfrac{2 \pm 4i}{2} = 1 \pm 4i$

Technology Problems

33. Reread Problem 29. Use your graphing utility to illustrate the answer to the problem's question by graphing $y_1 = -x^2 + 2x + 27$ and $y_2 = 29$ in the same viewing rectangle. Use the following range setting:

   $\text{Xmin} = 0, \text{Xmax} = 8, \text{Xscl} = 1,$

   $\text{Ymin} = 0, \text{Ymax} = 30, \text{Yscl} = 1$

Explain how the two graphs answer the question in Problem 29.

34. Use the method of Problem 33 and a graphing utility to obtain two graphs that answer the question in Problem 30.

Writing in Mathematics

35. Explain why the square root of a negative number cannot be a real number.

Critical Thinking Problems

36. Show that $1 + i$ is a solution to $x^2 - 2x + 2 = 0$ by substituting $1 + i$ for x. You should obtain $(1 + i)^2 - 2(1 + i) + 2$. Square $1 + i$ as you would a binomial. Distribute -2 as indicated. Then simplify the resulting expression by combining like terms and replacing i^2 by -1. You should obtain 0. Use this procedure to show that $1 - i$ is the equation's other solution.

37. Solve: $3x(x + 3) = (x + 2)^2 - 10$.

38. Prove that there is no real number such that when twice the number is subtracted from its square, the difference is -5.

Review Problems

39. How many liters of an 8% alcohol solution must be added to 32 liters of a 28% alcohol solution to result in a mixture that is 12% alcohol?

40. A rental car is available at $39.00 per day and $0.25 per mile. If a car is rented for 3 days at a total cost of $187.00, how many miles was the car driven?

41. Multiply and simplify: $(2\sqrt{3} + \sqrt{2})(2\sqrt{3} - 5\sqrt{2})$.

SECTION 10.5

Solutions   Tutorial   Video
Manual   12

Quadratic Functions and Their Graphs

Objectives

1 Graph a parabola.
2 Solve applied problems based on graphing parabolas.

▌ Graph a parabola.

In Section 7.6 and throughout this chapter, we have focused on the relation-ship between the *quadratic equation*

$$ax^2 + bx + c = 0$$

and the *quadratic function*

$$y = ax^2 + bx + c \quad \text{equivalently:} \quad f(x) = ax^2 + bx + c$$

Using a graphing utility, we have established the following useful relationship.

The x-intercepts of the graph of $y = ax^2 + bx + c$ are the real solutions to $ax^2 + bx + c = 0$.

Using technology

The solutions for
$x^2 + x - 12 = 0$ are -4 and 3.
These are the x-intercepts of the
quadratic function
$y = x^2 + x - 12$.

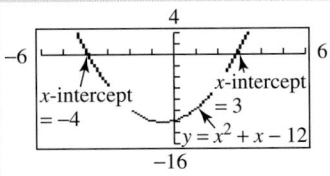

Discover for yourself

Use a graphing utility to graph the following quadratic functions:

$$y_1 = x^2 + 2x - 1$$

$$y_2 = x^2 - 2x - 8$$

$$y_3 = -x^2 - x + 2$$

$$y_4 = -\frac{1}{2}x^2 - x + 1$$

What general description can you use for the shape of the four graphs? How can you tell from the equation whether the graph opens upward or downward?

The graph of the quadratic function $y = ax^2 + bx + c$ is called a *parabola*. We have seen that parabolas are shaped like a cup, as shown in Figure 10.4. If the coefficient of x^2 (a in $ax^2 + bx + c$) is positive, the parabola opens

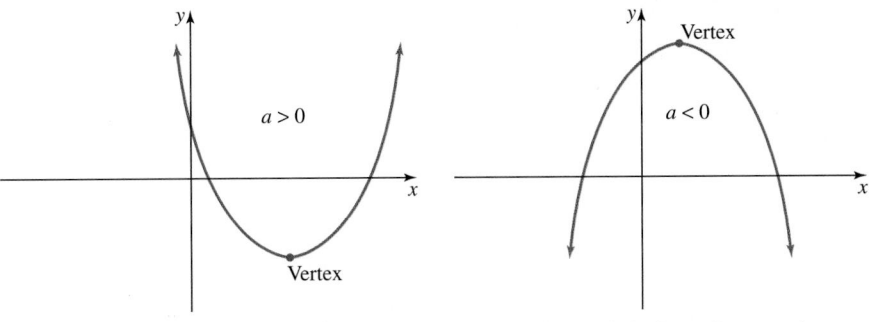

(a) Parabola Opens Upward   (a) Parabola Opens Downward

Figure 10.4
The graphs of $y = ax^2 + bx + c$ for $a > 0$ and $a < 0$

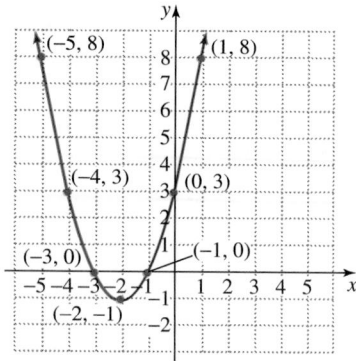

Figure 10.5

The graph of $y = x^2 + 4x + 3$

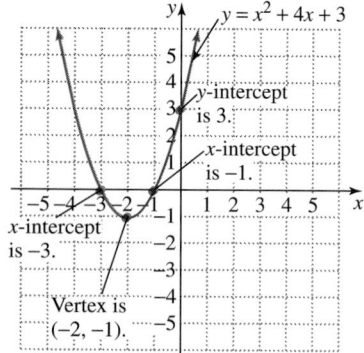

Figure 10.6

Useful points in graphing a parabola

upward. When the coefficient of x^2 is negative, the graph opens downward. The *vertex* (or turning point) of the parabola is the lowest point on the graph when it opens upward and the highest point on the graph when it opens downward.

As early as Section 4.3, we began graphing quadratic functions. We used a partial table of values and the point-plotting method, connecting the points with a smooth curve. We review this procedure in Example 1.

EXAMPLE 1   **Graphing a Parabola**

Graph: $y = x^2 + 4x + 3$

Solution

We first make a table of values.

x	$y = x^2 + 4x + 3$	(x, y)
-5	$y = (-5)^2 + 4(-5) + 3 = 8$	$(-5, 8)$
-4	$y = (-4)^2 + 4(-4) + 3 = 3$	$(-4, 3)$
-3	$y = (-3)^2 + 4(-3) + 3 = 0$	$(-3, 0)$
-2	$y = (-2)^2 + 4(-2) + 3 = -1$	$(-2, -1)$
-1	$y = (-1)^2 + 4(-1) + 3 = 0$	$(-1, 0)$
0	$y = (0)^2 + 4(0) + 3 = 3$	$(0, 3)$
1	$y = (1)^2 + 4(1) + 3 = 8$	$(1, 8)$

Then we plot the points and connect them with a smooth curve. The graph of $y = x^2 + 4x + 3$ is shown in Figure 10.5. ∎

As suggested by the graph in Figure 10.5, there are a number of important points to locate when graphing a quadratic function. These points are labeled in Figure 10.6. They are the x-intercepts (although not every parabola has two x-intercepts), the y-intercept, and the vertex. Let's see how we can determine these points.

1. *The x-intercepts:* When a graph crosses the x-axis, values of y equal zero. Thus, the x-intercepts can be found by replacing y with 0 in the quadratic function. For the function $y = x^2 + 4x + 3$ in Example 1, we must solve $0 = x^2 + 4x + 3$.

$y = x^2 + 4x + 3$	This is the given quadratic function.
$0 = x^2 + 4x + 3$	Find the x-intercepts, replacing y with 0.
$0 = (x + 3)(x + 1)$	Use factoring to solve the resulting quadratic equation.
$x + 3 = 0$ or $x + 1 = 0$	Apply the zero-product principle, setting each factor equal to 0.
$x = -3$ or $x = -1$	The x-intercepts are -3 and -1. The parabola passes through $(-3, 0)$ and $(-1, 0)$.

2. *The y-intercept:* When a graph crosses the y-axis, the value of x equals zero. Thus, the y-intercept can be found by replacing x with 0 in the quadratic function. For the function $y = x^2 + 4x + 3$ in Example 1, we find the y-intercept as follows.

$y = x^2 + 4x + 3$ This is the given quadratic function.

$y = 0^2 + 4 \cdot 0 + 3$ Find the y-intercept, replacing x with 0.

$y = 3$ The y-intercept is 3. The parabola passes through $(0, 3)$.

3. *The vertex:* By studying Figure 10.6, did you discover that the x-coordinate of the vertex is midway between the two x-intercepts? Consequently, it is half their sum.

$x = \frac{1}{2}[-3 + (-1)]$ Half the sum of the x-intercepts, namely, -3 and -1, is the x-coordinate of the vertex.

$x = \frac{1}{2}(-4)$

$x = -2$

$y = x^2 + 4x + 3$ Find the y-coordinate of the vertex by substituting the x-value in the quadratic function.

$y = (-2)^2 + 4(-2) + 3$ From above, the x-coordinate of the vertex is -2.

$y = 4 + (-8) + 3$

$y = -1$ The y-coordinate of the vertex is -1.

The vertex is $(-2, -1)$.

Finding a Parabola's Vertex

Now let's generalize from the procedure that we used to find the x-coordinate of the vertex for $y = x^2 + 4x + 3$. Since the x-coordinate is midway between the two x-intercepts, first we find the x-intercepts of the graph of the function $y = ax^2 + bx + c$.

$y = ax^2 + bx + c$ This is the quadratic function.

$0 = ax^2 + bx + c$ Find x-intercepts, replacing y with 0.

$x = \dfrac{-b \pm \sqrt{b^2 - 4ac}}{2a}$ These solutions to the quadratic equation are given by the quadratic formula.

Now we are ready to find the x-coordinate of the vertex.

$x = \dfrac{1}{2}\left(\dfrac{-b + \sqrt{b^2 - 4ac}}{2a} + \dfrac{-b - \sqrt{b^2 - 4ac}}{2a}\right)$ The x-coordinate of the vertex is half the sum of the x-intercepts.

$x = \dfrac{1}{2}\left(\dfrac{-b + \sqrt{b^2 - 4ac} - b - \sqrt{b^2 - 4ac}}{2a}\right)$ Add the numerators, placing this sum over the common denominator.

$x = \dfrac{1}{2}\left(-\dfrac{2b}{2a}\right)$ Add like terms in the numerator.

$x = \dfrac{1}{2}\left(-\dfrac{b}{a}\right)$ Simplify.

$x = -\dfrac{b}{2a}$ The x-coordinate of the vertex is $-\frac{b}{2a}$.

Not every parabola has two x-intercepts, and some have no x-intercept. However, the x-coordinate of the vertex is $-\dfrac{b}{2a}$ even when the graph does not have x-intercepts.

Finding a parabola's vertex

Consider the parabola defined by the quadratic function $y = ax^2 + bx + c$.

1. The x-coordinate of the vertex is $-\dfrac{b}{2a}$.

2. The y-coordinate of the vertex is found by substituting $-\dfrac{b}{2a}$ for x in the quadratic function and solving for y.

Graphing Parabolas

Before considering some examples, let's summarize what we have learned up to this point.

Graphing the quadratic function $y = ax^2 + bx + c$, whose graph is called a parabola

1. Find any x-intercepts by replacing y with 0.
2. Find the y-intercept by replacing x with 0.
3. Find the vertex. The x-coordinate of the vertex is $-\dfrac{b}{2a}$. The y-coordinate is found by substituting $-\dfrac{b}{2a}$ for x in the quadratic function.
4. Plot the intercepts and the vertex.
5. If needed, find and plot additional ordered pairs located near the vertex and intercepts, connecting points with a smooth curve.

Study tip

Try to visualize what the parabola looks like before working these five steps. Keep in mind that the parabola is cupped upward if $a > 0$ and downward if $a < 0$.

EXAMPLE 2   **Using Intercepts and the Vertex to Graph a Parabola**

Graph: $y = x^2 - 2x - 3$

Solution

Since a, the leading coefficient, is 1, this positive value tells us that the parabola is cupped upward.

Step 1. Find the x-intercepts. Replace y with 0.

$$y = x^2 - 2x - 3 \qquad \text{This is the given quadratic function.}$$
$$0 = x^2 - 2x - 3 \qquad \text{Replace } y \text{ with 0.}$$
$$0 = (x - 3)(x + 1) \qquad \text{Factor.}$$

$$x - 3 = 0 \quad \text{or} \quad x + 1 = 0 \qquad \text{Apply the zero-product principle, setting each factor equal to 0.}$$

$$x = 3 \qquad\qquad x = -1 \qquad \text{The } x\text{-intercepts are 3 and } -1.$$

The parabola passes through $(3, 0)$ and $(-1, 0)$.

Step 2. Find the y-intercept. Replace x with 0.

$$y = x^2 - 2x - 3 \qquad \text{This is the given quadratic function.}$$

$$y = 0^2 - 2 \cdot 0 - 3 \qquad \text{Replace } x \text{ with 0.}$$

$$y = -3 \qquad\qquad \text{The } y\text{-intercept is } -3.$$

The parabola passes through $(0, -3)$.

Step 3. Find the vertex.

$$y = x^2 - 2x - 3 \qquad \text{This is the given function, with } a = 1, b = -2, \text{ and } c = -3.$$
$$\quad\uparrow\qquad\uparrow\qquad\nwarrow$$
$$a = 1 \quad b = -2 \quad c = -3$$

The x-coordinate of the vertex is

$$x = -\frac{b}{2a} = -\frac{(-2)}{2(1)} = \frac{2}{2} = 1.$$

Substitute 1 for x into the function's equation to find the y-coordinate of the vertex.

$$y = x^2 - 2x - 3 = 1^2 - 2 \cdot 1 - 3 = 1 - 2 - 3 = -4$$

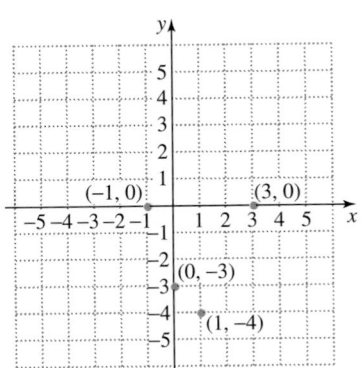

The vertex is $(1, -4)$.

Figure 10.7

Useful points in graphing $y = x^2 - 2x - 3$

Step 4. Plot the intercepts and vertex. The intercepts and vertex are shown in Figure 10.7.

Step 5. Find additional ordered pairs. Let's find two additional points located near the x-intercepts by letting $x = -2$ and $x = 4$.

x	$y = x^2 - 2x - 3$	(x, y)
-2	$y = (-2)^2 - 2(-2) - 3 = 5$	$(-2, 5)$
4	$y = 4^2 - 2 \cdot 4 - 3 = 5$	$(4, 5)$

We add the points $(-2, 5)$ and $(4, 5)$ to those in Figure 10.7 and connect all points with a smooth curve. The parabola, the graph of $y = x^2 - 2x - 3$, is shown in Figure 10.8. Because the parabola opens upward, the vertex is a minimum point. ∎

In Section 4.1, we introduced function notation, replacing y with $f(x)$. The quadratic function in our next example is written in "$f(x)$ equals" notation.

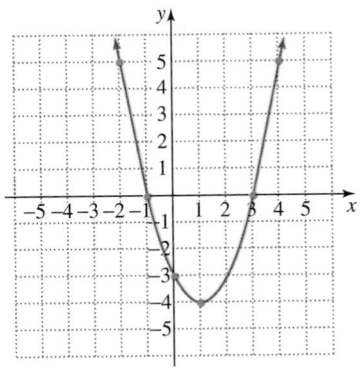

Figure 10.8

The graph of $y = x^2 - 2x - 3$

EXAMPLE 3   A Parabola That Opens Downward

Graph: $f(x) = -x^2 + 4x - 1$

Solution

Since a, the leading coefficient, is -1, this negative value tells us that the parabola opens downward and has the usual cuplike shape.

Step 1. Find the x-intercepts. Instead of replacing y with 0, we replace $f(x)$ with 0.

$$f(x) = -x^2 + 4x - 1 \quad \text{This is the given quadratic function.}$$

$$0 = -x^2 + 4x - 1 \quad \text{Replace } f(x) \text{ with 0.}$$

$$0 = x^2 - 4x + 1 \quad \text{Multiply both sides by } -1.$$

$$x = \frac{4 \pm \sqrt{16 - 4}}{2} \quad \text{Since } x^2 - 4x + 1 \text{ is prime, solve by using } x = \frac{-b \pm \sqrt{b^2 - 4ac}}{2a} \text{ where } a = 1, b = -4, \text{ and } c = 1.$$

$$x = \frac{4 \pm \sqrt{12}}{2} \quad \text{Simplify.}$$

$$x = \frac{4 \pm 2\sqrt{3}}{2} \quad \sqrt{12} = \sqrt{4 \cdot 3} = \sqrt{4}\sqrt{3} = 2\sqrt{3}$$

$$x = \frac{2(2 \pm \sqrt{3})}{2} \quad \text{Factor 2 from the numerator.}$$

$$x = 2 \pm \sqrt{3} \quad \text{Divide the numerator and denominator by 2.}$$

Since $\sqrt{3} \approx 1.7$, the x-intercepts are approximately 3.7 $(2 + \sqrt{3})$ and 0.3 $(2 - \sqrt{3})$. The parabola passes (approximately) through $(3.7, 0)$ and $(0.3, 0)$.

Step 2. Find the y-intercept. Replace x with 0.

$$f(x) = -x^2 + 4x - 1 \quad \text{This is the given quadratic function.}$$

$$f(0) = -0^2 + 4 \cdot 0 - 1 = -1$$

The y-intercept is -1. The parabola passes through $(0, -1)$.

Step 3. Find the vertex.

$$y = -x^2 + 4x - 1 \quad \text{This is the given function, with } a = -1, b = 4, \text{ and } c = -1.$$

$$\begin{array}{ccc} \uparrow & \uparrow & \nwarrow \\ a = -1 & b = 4 & c = -1 \end{array}$$

The x-coordinate of the vertex is

$$x = -\frac{b}{2a} = -\frac{4}{2(-1)} = 2.$$

Substitute 2 for x into $f(x) = -x^2 + 4x - 1$, the function's equation, to find the y-coordinate of the vertex.

$$f(2) = -2^2 + 4 \cdot 2 - 1 = -4 + 8 - 1 = 3$$

The vertex is $(2, 3)$.

Step 4. Plot the intercepts and vertex. The intercepts and vertex are shown in Figure 10.9.

Step 5. Find additional ordered pairs. Let's find four additional points located near the x-intercepts by letting $x = -1, x = 1, x = 3,$ and $x = 4$.

x	$f(x) = -x^2 + 4x - 1$	(x, y)
-1	$f(-1) = -(-1)^2 + 4(-1) - 1 = -6$	$(-1, -6)$
1	$f(1) = -1^2 + 4 \cdot 1 - 1 = 2$	$(1, 2)$
3	$f(3) = -3^2 + 4 \cdot 3 - 1 = 2$	$(3, 2)$
4	$f(4) = -4^2 + 4 \cdot 4 - 1 = -1$	$(4, -1)$

We add the points $(-1, -6), (1, 2), (3, 2),$ and $(4, -1)$ to those in Figure 10.9 and connect all points with a smooth curve. The parabola, the graph of

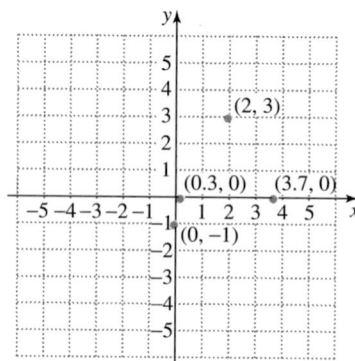

Figure 10.9

Useful points in graphing $f(x) = -x^2 + 4x - 1$

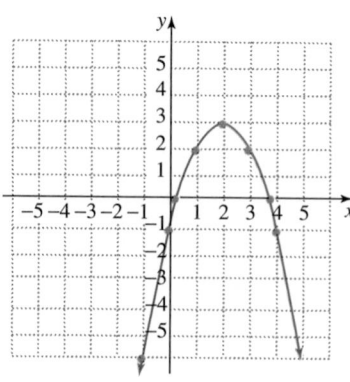

Figure 10.10

The graph of $f(x) = -x^2 + 4x - 1$

$f(x) = -x^2 + 4x - 1$, is shown in Figure 10.10. Because the parabola opens downward, the vertex is a maximum point. ■

Our next example involves graphing a parabola with no x-intercepts.

Discover for yourself

Use a graphing utility to verify all of the hand-drawn graphs in the examples of this section. TRACE along the parabolas and verify the intercepts and the vertex.

EXAMPLE 4 Graphing a Parabola Having No x-Intercepts

Graph: $y = -x^2 + 6x - 10$

Solution

Since $a = -1$, with $a < 0$, the parabola will open downward.

Step 1. Find the x-intercepts. Set $y = 0$.

$$y = -x^2 + 6x - 10$$

$$0 = -x^2 + 6x - 10$$

$$0 = x^2 - 6x + 10 \quad \text{Multiply both sides by } -1. \text{ This step is optional.}$$

$a = 1 \quad b = -6 \quad c = 10$

$$x = \frac{6 \pm \sqrt{36 - 40}}{2} \quad \text{Use } x = \frac{-b \pm \sqrt{b^2 - 4ac}}{2a} \text{ with } a = 1, b = -6, \text{ and } c = 10.$$

$$x = \frac{6 \pm \sqrt{-4}}{2}$$

$$x = \frac{6 \pm 2i}{2} \quad \sqrt{-4} = \sqrt{4(-1)} = 2i$$

$$x = \frac{2(3 \pm i)}{2} = 3 \pm i$$

Study tip

The graph of $y = ax^2 + bx + c$ has no x-intercepts when $ax^2 + bx + c = 0$ has complex solutions that are not real numbers.

The two complex solutions $3 + i$ and $3 - i$ are not real numbers. Since the equation $-x^2 + 6x - 10 = 0$ (or, equivalently, $x^2 - 6x + 10 = 0$) has no real numbers as solutions, the graph of $y = -x^2 + 6x - 10$ has no x-intercepts.

Step 2. Find the y-intercept. Set $x = 0$.

$$y = -0^2 + 6 \cdot 0 - 10 = -10$$

The y-intercept is -10. The graph passes through $(0, -10)$.

Step 3. Find the vertex.

$$y = -x^2 + 6x - 10 \quad \text{This is the given function, with } a = -1, b = 6, \text{ and } c = -10.$$

$a = -1 \quad b = 6 \quad c = -10$

The x-coordinate of the vertex is

$$x = -\frac{b}{2a} = -\frac{6}{2(-1)} = -\frac{6}{-2} = -(-3) = 3.$$

Substitute 3 for x into the function's equation to find the y-coordinate of the vertex.

$$y = -x^2 + 6x - 10 = -3^2 + 6 \cdot 3 - 10 = -9 + 18 - 10 = -1$$

The vertex is $(3, -1)$.

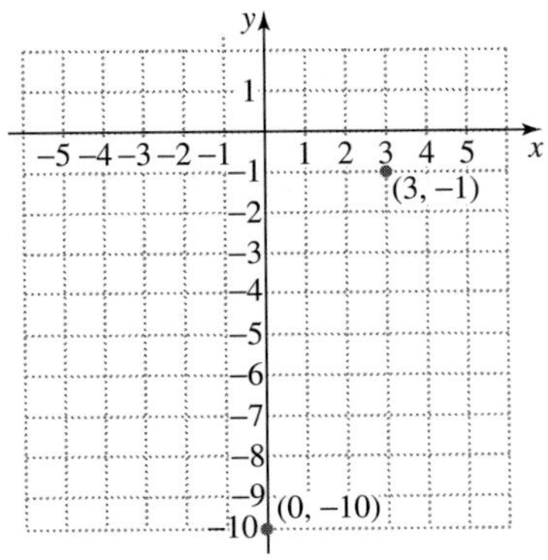

Figure 10.11
Two points on the parabola $y = -x^2 + 6x - 10$

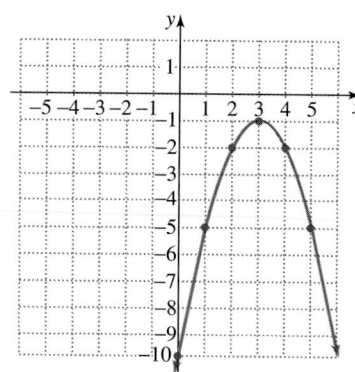

Figure 10.12

The graph of
$y = -x^2 + 6x - 10$

Step 4. Plot the intercepts and vertex. The vertex is a maximum point on the graph since the graph opens downward (see Figure 10.11 on the previous page).

Step 5. Find additional ordered pairs. We will find additional points by letting

x	$y = -x^2 + 6x - 10$	(x, y)
1	$y = -1^2 + 6 \cdot 1 - 10 = -5$	$(1, -5)$
2	$y = -2^2 + 6 \cdot 2 - 10 = -2$	$(2, -2)$
4	$y = -4^2 + 6 \cdot 4 - 10 = -2$	$(4, -2)$
5	$y = -5^2 + 6 \cdot 5 - 10 = -5$	$(5, -5)$

$x = 1, x = 2, x = 4$, and $x = 5$.

We add the points $(1, -5)$, $(2, -2)$, $(4, -2)$, and $(5, -5)$ to those in Figure 10.11 and connect all points with a smooth curve. The parabola, the graph of $y = -x^2 + 6x - 10$, with no x-intercepts, is shown in Figure 10.12. ∎

Study tip

The radicand in the quadratic formula, $b^2 - 4ac$, indicates the number of real solutions to $ax^2 + bx + c = 0$. If the radicand is positive, there are two real solutions. If it is zero, there is only one real solution. If it is negative, there are no real solutions. Since the real solutions appear as x-intercepts, the radicand $b^2 - 4ac$ indicates how many x-intercepts there are for the parabola $y = ax^2 + bx + c$.

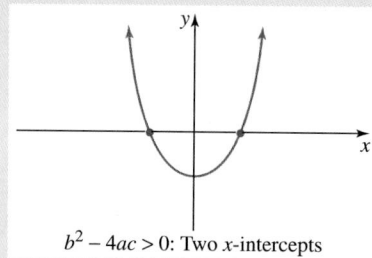

$b^2 - 4ac > 0$: Two x-intercepts

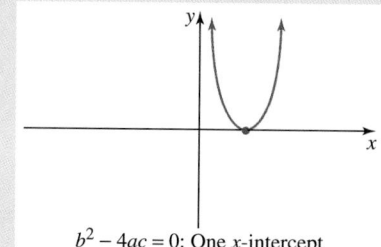

$b^2 - 4ac = 0$: One x-intercept

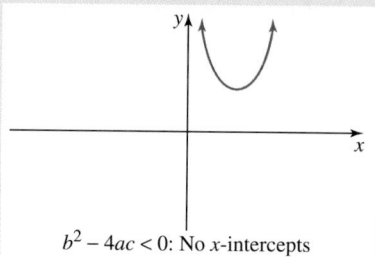

$b^2 - 4ac < 0$: No x-intercepts

---

2 Solve applied problems based on graphing parabolas.

Quadratic Models

The physical world presents us with a variety of actions and events described by quadratic models that can be written in the form $y = ax^2 + bx + c$ or $f(x) = ax^2 + bx + c$. The resulting parabola can be used to gain insight into the physical event.

EXAMPLE 5 **Modeling an Object's Parabolic Path**

An object is thrown directly upward from the ground with an initial velocity of 128 feet per second. Its distance above the ground after x seconds is described by the model

$$y = -16x^2 + 128x$$

where x is measured in feet. Graph the model and explain the physical meaning of the vertex and the greater x-intercept.

Solution

Step 1. Find the x-intercepts. Set $y = 0$.

$$0 = -16x^2 + 128x$$
$$0 = -16x(x - 8)$$
$$-16x = 0 \quad \text{or} \quad x - 8 = 0$$
$$x = 0 \qquad\qquad x = 8$$

The x-intercepts are 0 and 8. The parabola passes through $(0, 0)$ and $(8, 0)$.

Step 2. Find the y-intercept. Set $x = 0$.

$$y = -16x^2 + 128x = -16 \cdot 0^2 + 128 \cdot 0 = 0$$

The y-intercept is 0 and, as noted in step 1, the parabola passes through $(0, 0)$.

Step 3. Find the vertex. Because $y = -16x^2 + 128x$, $a = -16$ and $b = 128$.

$$x = -\frac{b}{2a} = -\frac{128}{2(-16)} = \frac{-128}{-32} = 4$$
$$y = -16 \cdot 4^2 + 128 \cdot 4 = -256 + 512 = 256$$

The vertex is $(4, 256)$. Since a is negative ($a = -16$), the parabola opens downward and the vertex is a maximum point.

Step 4. The graph is shown in Figure 10.13.

Because the model involves time and distance, two positive variables, only the portion of the parabola in quadrant I is shown. The vertex indicates that the object reaches a maximum height of 256 feet after 4 seconds. The second x-intercept, $(8, 0)$, tells us that the object strikes the ground after 8 seconds. ∎

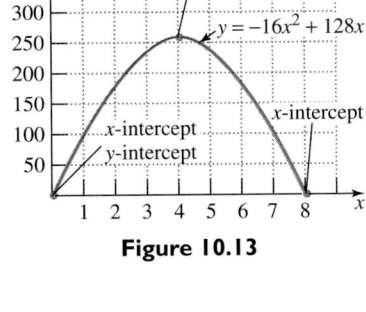

Figure 10.13

EXAMPLE 6   **Car Accidents as a Function of Age**

The model $f(x) = 0.4x^2 - 36x + 1000$ describes the number of accidents $f(x)$ per 50 million miles driven as a function of a driver's age x, in years, where $16 \leq x \leq 74$. The graph of the resulting parabola is shown in Figure 10.14. Find the coordinates of the vertex and describe what this represents in practical terms.

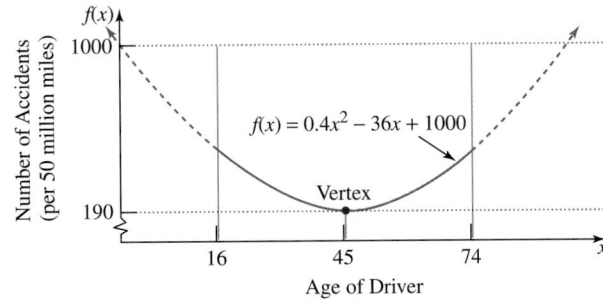

Figure 10.14

Giacomo Balla "Speeding Automobile" 1912, oil on wood, $21\frac{7}{8} \times 27\frac{1}{8}$ in. (55.6 × 68.9 cm). The Museum of Modern Art, New York. Purchase. Photograph © 1997 The Museum of Modern Art, New York. © Giacomo Balla

Solution

Since $f(x) = 0.4x^2 - 36x + 1000$, a (the coefficient of x^2) is 0.4 and b (the coefficient of x) is -36. The x-coordinate of the vertex is

$$x = -\frac{b}{2a} = -\frac{(-36)}{2(0.4)} = \frac{36}{0.8} = 45.$$

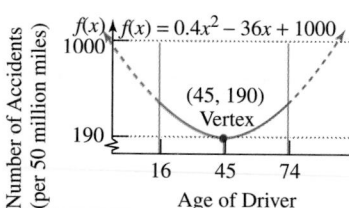

Figure 10.15

We substitute 45 for x into $f(x) = 0.4x^2 - 36x + 1000$, the function's equation, to find the y-coordinate of the vertex.

$$f(45) = 0.4(45)^2 - 36(45) + 1000$$
$$= 0.4(2025) - 36(45) + 1000 = 810 - 1620 + 1000 = 190$$

The vertex, labeled in Figure 10.15, is (45, 190). In practical terms, this indicates that 45-year-olds have the least number of accidents, 190 per 50 million miles driven. Drivers both younger and older than 45 have more. ∎

PROBLEM SET 10.5

Practice Problems

Use intercepts, the vertex, and a few additional points located near the vertex and intercepts to graph the parabola represented by each quadratic function in Problems 1–26. If applicable, use a graphing utility to verify your hand-drawn graph.

1. $y = x^2 + 6x + 5$ **2.** $y = x^2 + x - 6$ **3.** $f(x) = x^2 + 4x + 3$ **4.** $f(x) = x^2 - 2x - 8$

5. $y = x^2 + x$ **6.** $y = x^2 + 4x$ **7.** $f(x) = x^2 - 4$ **8.** $f(x) = x^2 - 1$

9. $y = -x^2 - 1$ **10.** $y = -x^2 - 3$ **11.** $y = -x^2 + 4x - 3$ **12.** $y = -x^2 + 2x + 1$

13. $f(x) = -2x^2 + 16x - 30$ **14.** $f(x) = -3x^2 + 6x - 2$ **15.** $y = x^2 + 4x + 4$ **16.** $y = x^2 + 2x + 1$

17. $g(x) = x^2 - 4x + 6$ **18.** $g(x) = x^2 - 4x + 10$ **19.** $y = -x^2 - 6x - 7$ **20.** $y = -x^2 - 2x + 3$

21. $f(x) = -2x^2 + 4x$ **22.** $f(x) = -x^2 + 4x$ **23.** $y = -x^2 + 4x - 1$ **24.** $y = -x^2 - 4x - 2$

25. $h(x) = 2x^2 + 8x + 1$ **26.** $h(x) = x^2 - 2x + 3$

27. Match each description with the appropriate numbered graph.
   a. The equation that corresponds to this function has no real numbers as solutions.
   b. The equation that corresponds to this function has two real numbers as solutions.
   c. This parabola is based on the quadratic function $y = ax^2 + bx + c$ in which $a > 0$.

1.
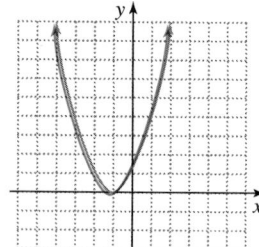

2.
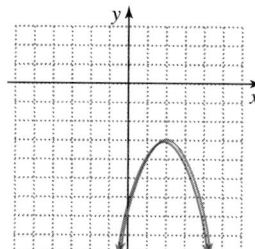

3.
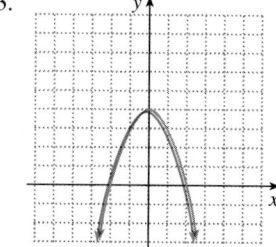

28. Match each description with the appropriate numbered graph.
   a. The equation that corresponds to this function has no real numbers as solutions.
   b. The equation that corresponds to this function has two real numbers that are not integers as solutions.
   c. This parabola is based on the quadratic function $y = ax^2 + bx + c$ in which $a < 0$.

1.
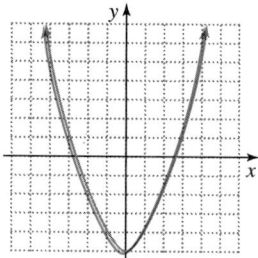

2.
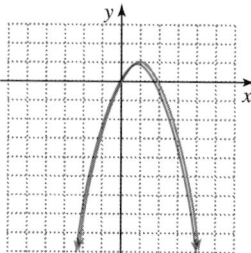

3.
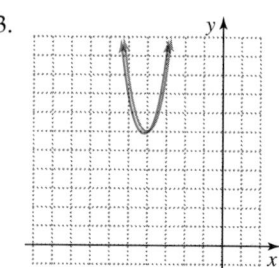

Application Problems

29. The model $f(x) = -0.02x^2 + x + 1$ describes the number of inches $(f(x))$ that a young redwood tree grows per year as a function of annual rainfall $(x$, in inches). The graph of the resulting parabola is shown below. Find the coordinates of the vertex and describe what this represents in practical terms.

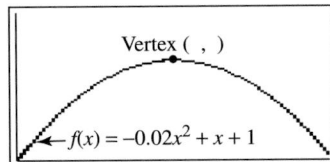

Vertex (,)

$f(x) = -0.02x^2 + x + 1$

30. One would think that the more avocado trees planted per acre, the higher the yield of avocados. However, this is not the case since beyond a certain number of trees per acre, they tend to crowd one another and the yield drops. The model $f(x) = -0.01x^2 + 0.8x$ describes the yield $(f(x)$, in bushels of avocados per tree) as a function of the number of trees per acre (x). The graph of the resulting parabola is shown below. Find the coordinates of the vertex and describe what this represents in practical terms.

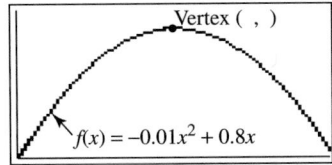

Vertex (,)

$f(x) = -0.01x^2 + 0.8x$

31. There is a relationship between the amount of one's income, $(x$, annual income in thousands of dollars) and the percent of this income (P) that one contributes to charities. This relationship is modeled by the quadratic function $P = 0.0014x^2 - 0.1529x + 5.855$, where $5 \leq x \leq 100$. What annual income corresponds to the minimum percent given to charity? What is this minimum percent?

32. The quadratic function $f(x) = -x^2 + 40x$ describes the number of cases of flu $(f(x))$ in the student body

of a small college reported x days after the outbreak of the epidemic.

a. How long does it take before no students have the flu? Answer the question by replacing $f(x)$ by 0 in the given model, and solve the resulting quadratic equation for x.

b. How many days after the outbreak is the number of cases at a maximum? Answer this question by finding $-\dfrac{b}{2a}$.

c. What is the maximum number of people who become ill? Answer this question by substituting the value for x that you found in part (b) into the function, and find the corresponding value for $f(x)$.

d. Use your work in parts (a)–(c) to graph the function, showing values of $f(x)$ along the y-axis.

33. A person standing close to the edge of an 80-foot building throws a ball upward with an initial speed of 64 feet per second. The height of the ball above the ground $(h$, in feet) is a function of time $(t$, in seconds), modeled by the quadratic function $h = -16t^2 + 64t + 80$.

a. How long does it take the ball to reach the ground? Answer the question by replacing h with 0 in the given model, and solve the resulting quadratic equation for t.

b. Replace t with 0 in the given function. What is the resulting value of h? Describe what this means in practical terms.

c. After how many seconds will the ball reach its maximum height? Answer this question by finding $-\dfrac{b}{2a}$.

d. What is the ball's maximum height? Answer the question by substituting the value for t that you found in part (c) into the function, and find the corresponding value for h.

e. Use your work in parts (a)–(d) to graph the function with values of t along the x-axis and values of h along the y-axis.

True–False Critical Thinking Problems

34. Which one of the following is true?

a. The x-coordinate of the vertex of the parabola whose equation is $y = ax^2 + bx + c$ is $\dfrac{b}{2a}$.

b. If a parabola has only one x-intercept, then the x-intercept is also the vertex.

c. There is no relationship between the graph of $y = ax^2 + bx + c$ and the number of real solutions to the quadratic equation $ax^2 + bx + c = 0$.

d. If $y = 4x^2 - 40x + 4$, then the vertex is the highest point on the graph.

35. Which one of the following is true?

a. If $-\dfrac{b}{2a} > 0$, then the graph of $y = ax^2 + bx + c$ opens upward.

b. Some quadratic functions graph as parabolas that have no y-intercept.

c. The highest point on the graph of the equation $y = -\frac{4}{3}x^2 + 8x - 11$ is $(3, 1)$.

d. If $ax^2 + bx + c = 0$ has no real numbers as solutions, then the graph of $y = ax^2 + bx + c$ intersects the x-axis only once.

36. An object projected directly upward from the ground with an initial velocity of 96 feet per second has its distance above the ground after t seconds described by the model $d = -16t^2 + 96t$, where d is measured in feet. The figure shows the graph of the model. Which one of the following is true?

a. The object strikes the ground after 7 seconds.

b. Without labels along the d- (or y-) axis, the maximum height reached by the object cannot be determined.

c. The maximum height reached by the object is 144 feet.

d. The height reached by the object after 1 second is the same as the height reached by the object after 4 seconds.

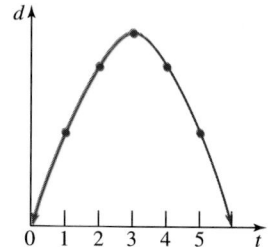

37. The daily profit (y, in dollars) from the production of x units of a product per day is given by the model $y = -x^2 + 500x - 52,500$. The figure shows the graph of the model. Which one of the following is true?

a. If the company produces 200 units of the product, the profit is $8500.

b. Without labels along the y-axis, the number of products that should be produced to maximize profit cannot be determined.

c. It would be profitable for the company to produce more than 500 units of the product on a daily basis.

d. The maximum profit attainable can be calculated by substituting 250 for x in the given quadratic function.

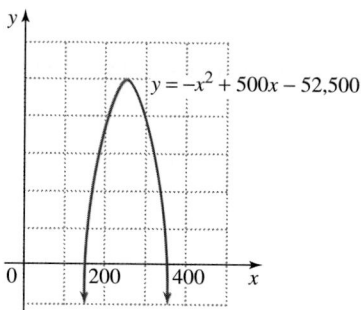

Technology Problems

38. The function $y = -0.053x^2 + 1.17x + 35.6$ models the average number of gallons of alcohol (y) consumed by each adult in the United States x years after 1970. Use a graphing utility to graph the function with the following range setting:

Xmin = 0, Xmax = 20, Xscl = 1,
Ymin = 0, Ymax = 43, Yscl = 1

TRACE along the curve or use your utility's maximum value feature to approximate the coordinates of the parabola's vertex. Describe what this represents in practical terms.

39. The function $y = 0.011x^2 - 0.097x + 4.1$ models the number of people in the United States (y, in millions) holding more than one job x years after 1970. Use a graphing utility to graph the function with the following range setting:

Xmin = 0, Xmax = 20, Xscl = 1,
Ymin = 3, Ymax = 6, Yscl = 1

TRACE along the curve or use your utility's minimum value feature to approximate the coordinates of the parabola's vertex. Describe what this represents in practical terms.

40. Use a graphing utility to graph $y = x^2 - 2$, $y = x^2$, and $y = x^2 + 1$ in the same viewing rectangle. Describe similarities and differences among the three parabolas.

41. Use a graphing utility to graph $y = (x - 2)^2$, $y = x^2$, and $y = (x + 1)^2$ in the same viewing rectangle. Describe similarities and differences among the three parabolas.

42. Use a graphing utility to graph $y = -2x^2$, $y = -\frac{1}{2}x^2$, $y = x^2$, $y = 2x^2$, and $y = \frac{1}{2}x^2$. Describe similarities and differences among the parabolas.

Writing in Mathematics

43. Explain how to decide whether a parabola opens upward or downward.

44. A parabola that opens downward has its vertex at $(1, 5)$. Describe as much information as possible that can be determined by this knowledge. Include in your discussion the number of x-intercepts (if any) for the parabola.

45. Discuss a method for graphing $y = ax^2 + bx + c$, illustrating with $y = x^2 + x - 6$.

46. Describe the relationship between the graph of the equation $y = ax^2 + bx + c$ and the number of real solutions to $ax^2 + bx + c = 0$.

47. A company that sells x units of a product generates an income (I, in dollars) which is a function of x, described by $I = -\frac{1}{2}x^2 + 100x$. Describe how to determine the number of units that must be sold so that the company can maximize its income. How can the maximum income be determined?

Critical Thinking Problems

48. Graph $y = -x$ and $y = -x^2 + 2x$ in the same coordinate plane and label the points of intersection of the line and the parabola.

49. Graph $y = 2x^2 - 8$ and $y = -2x^2 + 8$ in the same coordinate plane and label the points of intersection of the two parabolas.

50. The parabola shown in the figure has x-intercepts at 3 and 7, a y-intercept at -21, and a vertex at $(5, 4)$. Write the equation for this parabola.

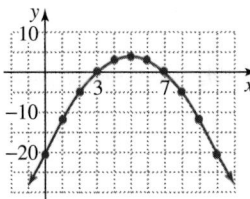

In Problems 51–53, the value of a in $y = ax^2 + bx + c$ and the vertex of the parabola are given. How many x-intercepts does the parabola have? Explain how you arrived at this number.

51. $a = -2$; vertex at $(4, 8)$

52. $a = 1$; vertex at $(2, 0)$

53. $a = 3$; vertex at $(3, 1)$

Group Activity Problem

54. The figure shows a plane region bounded by the x-axis and the y-axis, $y = x^2 + 2$ and $x = 3$. Find the area of the plane region. (*Hint:* You may not be able to find the exact area, but see if group members can devise a method that will approximate the region's area. There is no single correct approach to this problem, so be as creative as possible and see what the group can come up with.)

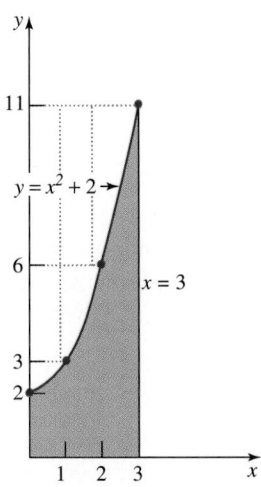

Review Problems

55. Write 0.00397 in scientific notation.

56. Graph: $y = \frac{2}{3}x - 4$.

57. Solve for y: $3x - 4y = 8$.

C HAPTER PROJECT

The Mandelbrot Set

In Example 3 of Section 10.4, we saw that the graph of a quadratic equation with complex number solutions will have no x-intercepts. There is no way to locate the number $1 + i$ on a real number line; thus, there is no way to use it as an x-coordinate. In general, we cannot have a point in the xy-plane with a nonreal complex number for a coordinate. However, we can display complex numbers on what is called the *complex plane*. In this project, you will discover the intricacies of the complex plane and the beauty of one of its applications, the Mandelbrot set.

By definition, a complex number is a number that can be written in the form $a + bi$, where a and b are real. We can use the two parts, a and b, of a complex number to graph the number if we use the y-axis to locate the b numbers and the x-axis to locate the a numbers. In this case, we will call the x-axis the *real axis* and the y-axis the *imaginary axis*. Thus, we would graph the complex number $3 - 2i$ as if we were graphing the point $(3, -2)$. (See Figure 10.16.)

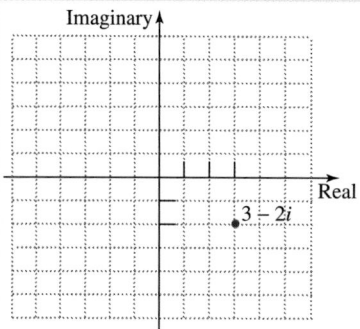

Figure 10.16

We can also find the distance between two complex numbers by using the distance formula. For example, the distance between the origin of our complex plane, $0 + 0i$, and the number $3 - 2i$ is found by evaluating

$$\sqrt{(3)^2 + (-2)^2} = \sqrt{9 + 4} = \sqrt{13}$$

One of the most interesting and beautiful applications of numbers in the complex plane is a creation called the *Mandelbrot set*. You may have seen pictures of the Mandelbrot set, such as the one displayed on the next page. The colors you see in the pictures are assigned by studying numbers in the complex plane and their distances from the origin.

The equation used for the Mandelbrot set is similar to the one we studied in the Chapter 6 project. It is an iterated equation, so we find new values by using the previous values.

$$z_{n+1} = z_n^2 + c$$

In this equation, z is a complex number and c is a constant that is also a complex number. For the Mandelbrot set we will always begin with $z_0 = 0 + 0i$, and c will be a complex number corresponding to some location in the complex plane. As an example, let's begin by choosing $c = 0.37 + 0.4i$. We have

$$z_1 = (0 + 0i)^2 + (0.37 + 0.4i) = 0.37 + 0.4i$$

To find the next value, we put $0.37 + 0.4i$ back into our equation.

$$z_2 = (0.37 + 0.4i)^2 + (0.37 + 0.4i)$$
$$= 0.1369 + 0.296i + 0.16i^2 + 0.37 + 0.4i$$
$$= 0.1369 + 0.296i - 0.16 + 0.37 + 0.4i$$
$$= 0.3469 + 0.696i$$

To find z_3, we put back our value for z_2.

$$z_3 = (0.3469 + 0.696i)^2 + (0.37 + 0.4i)$$

1. Using your calculator, find values for z_3 to z_{12}. Round off each time to the nearest thousandth and record your results in a table.

Each constant, c, that we choose corresponds to a point in the complex plane that we can color. We decide what color to use for a particular point by observing what happens in the equation above. Each time we find a new z_n, we compute the distance from z_n to the origin. If the distance is greater than 2, we will *not* color the point corresponding to c.

2. Using your calculator, compute the distances for each z in Problem 1. Round your answers to the nearest thousandth. Should you color the point at $(0.37, 0.4)$?

In Problem 2, we were able to make a decision about coloring our point after only 12 iterations. Suppose it required 200 iterations before the distance from the point to the origin was greater than 2. Would you have given up?

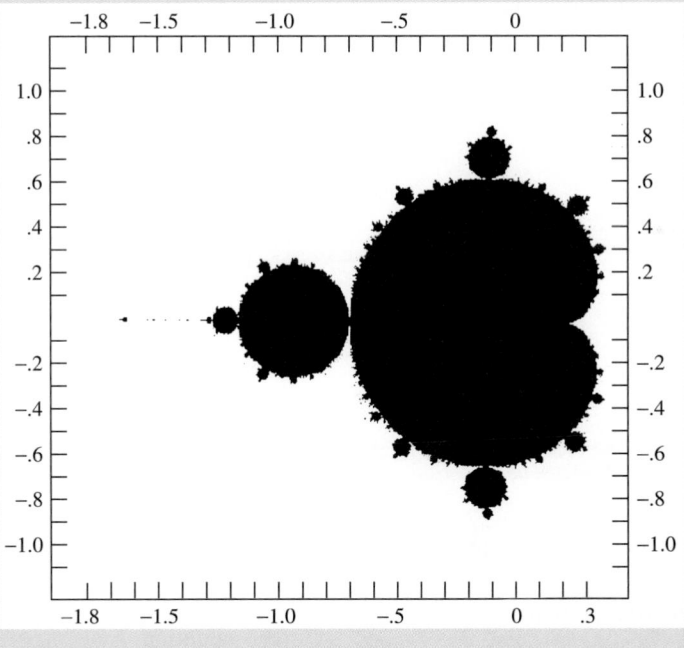

Figure 10.17

The picture in Figure 10.17 is a Mandelbrot set created by coloring a point black if the distance from the origin is less than 2 and leaving the point white if the distance is greater than 2. The number of calculations required to create this relatively simple black-and-white picture goes well beyond what any one person would care to compute; thus it was created on a computer. In creating such a picture on a computer, we must tell the computer when to stop calculating z's and to make a decision about the color. We could say something like "if the distance from the origin is less than 2 after 100 iterations, stop and color the point black." The more iterations we allow, the more accurate the picture and the "fuzzier" the edges of the Mandelbrot set in the picture.

3. Divide the class into groups and have each group select a portion of the Mandelbrot set in Figure 10.17 to study. Each group member should look close to the edge of the Mandelbrot set in the region selected and estimate coordinates for one c. Using only 10 iterations and the estimated coordinates, determine whether the point is or is not in the Mandelbrot set. Consider the point to be in the Mandelbrot set if the distance from the origin is always less than 2 for any of your z's.

4. For the class, how many points were determined to be in the Mandelbrot set? Do you notice any patterns in the distances for any of the points in the class? Do any of the points seem to have a pattern of repetition similar to the patterns observed in the project for Chapter 6?

Color pictures of the Mandelbrot set can be created when we assign different colors to each point based on *how many* iterations it takes until the distance of a z is greater than 2. We might tell the computer, "color the point red if it only takes 12 iterations, color the point green if it takes 20 iterations," and so on. The artistry in the Mandelbrot set comes from making such decisions about the colors to be used.

The complexity and beauty of the Mandelbrot set is revealed only as we inspect the edges of the set at closer and closer magnification. As we look at each small piece on the edge at close range, we begin to see details that are surprisingly rich. The beauty of these pictures has made the Mandelbrot set one of the most studied of all mathematical objects—entire books have been devoted to simply displaying pieces of this set under different colors and magnifications.

Worldwide Web Resources

Go to the Prentice Hall website (http://www.prenhall.com/blitzer) to access other locations on the Internet that will allow you to further explore the concepts presented in this project.

Chapter Review

SUMMARY

1. Quadratic Equations
A quadratic equation is an equation that can be written in the form $ax^2 + bx + c = 0, a \neq 0$.

2. The Square Root Property of Equations
If $x^2 = d$, then $x = \pm\sqrt{d}$. If $(x + d)^2 = e$, then $x + d = \pm\sqrt{e}$.

3. Solving a Quadratic Equation by Completing the Square
  a. If the equation is given in standard form $(ax^2 + bx + c = 0)$, isolate variable terms on one side, obtaining $ax^2 + bx = -c$.

  b. If the coefficient of x^2 is not 1, divide both sides of the equation by the coefficient of x^2.

  c. Complete the square by adding the square of half the coefficient of the x term to both sides of the equation.

  d. Factor, writing the resulting perfect square trinomial as the square of a binomial.

  e. Apply the square root property and solve.

4. Solving a Quadratic Equation by the Quadratic Formula

The formula is derived by completing the square. If $ax^2 + bx + c = 0$, then $x = \dfrac{-b \pm \sqrt{b^2 - 4ac}}{2a}$.

5. Determining Which Method to Use When Solving a Quadratic Equation

a. If the equation is in the form $x^2 = d$, solve by the square root property.

b. If the equation is not in the form $x^2 = d$, write it in standard form ($ax^2 + bx + c = 0$).

  1. If $ax^2 + bx + c$ is factorable, solve the equation by factoring. Set each factor equal to zero and solve.

  2. If $ax^2 + bx + c$ is prime, solve the equation by the quadratic formula.

6. Complex Numbers

A complex number is of the form $a + bi$, where a and b are real numbers and $i = \sqrt{-1}$. (Since $i = \sqrt{-1}$, then $i^2 = -1$.)

7. Solving Quadratic Equations with Complex Solutions

a. Equations in the form $x^2 = d$, where $d < 0$, have no real solutions, but do have complex solutions. These solutions can be found by using the square root property.

b. Quadratic equations in the form $ax^2 + bx + c = 0$, where $b^2 - 4ac < 0$, have no real solutions, but do have complex solutions. These solutions can be found by using the quadratic formula.

8. Quadratic Functions and Their Graphs

a. The graph of the quadratic function $y = ax^2 + bx + c$ is called a parabola, shaped like a cup. If $a > 0$, the parabola opens upward, and if $a < 0$, the graph opens downward. The turning point of the graph is the vertex.

b. Graph $y = ax^2 + bx + c$ by finding any x-intercepts (replace y with 0), the y-intercept (replace x with 0), the vertex, and additional points near the vertex and intercepts. The x-coordinate of the vertex is $-\dfrac{b}{2a}$. The y-coordinate is found by substituting $-\dfrac{b}{2a}$ for x in the quadratic function and solving for y.

c. The vertex of $y = ax^2 + bx + c$ is a minimum point when $a > 0$ and a maximum point when $a < 0$.

REVIEW PROBLEMS

Solve each equation in Problems 1–7 using the square root property. When possible, express radicals in simplified form.

1. $x^2 = 64$
    2. $y^2 = 17$
    3. $r^2 = 75$
    4. $(y - 3)^2 = 9$

5. $(x + 4)^2 = 5$
    6. $(2x - 7)^2 = 25$
    7. $(3x - 4)^2 = 18$

8. Find the length of the diagonal of a rectangle, represented by x in the figure, whose dimensions are 12 inches by 8 inches. Express x in simplified radical form. Then find a decimal approximation to two decimal places.

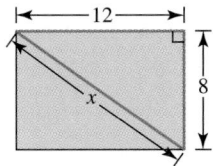

9. As shown in the figure, a 15-foot ladder is 3 feet from the wall of a building. How far up the wall does the ladder reach? Express the answer in simplified radical form and then find a decimal approximation to two decimal places.

10. The weight of a human fetus is given by the model $W = 3t^2$, where W is the weight in grams and t is the time in weeks, $0 \leqslant t \leqslant 39$. After how many weeks does the fetus weigh 675 grams?

11. The figure indicates that the quadratic function

$$y = \frac{1}{9000} x^2 + 5$$

can be used to model the suspension cables on the Golden Gate Bridge connecting San Francisco and Marin County, California. The road lies directly on the

x-axis. How far to the right of the center of the bridge are the cables 45 feet high?

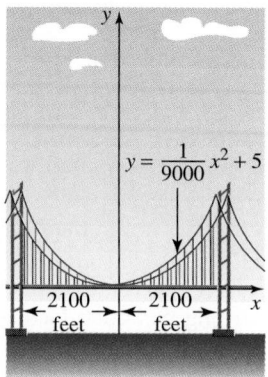

Solve Problems 12–14 by completing the square.

12. $x^2 - 12x + 27 = 0$

13. $x^2 - 6x + 4 = 0$

14. $3x^2 - 12x + 11 = 0$

Solve Problems 15–17 using the quadratic formula.

15. $2x^2 + 5x - 3 = 0$

16. $3x^2 + 5 = 9x$

17. $4y^2 + 2y - 1 = 0$

Use the method of your choice to solve each quadratic equation in Problems 18–22.

18. $2x^2 - 11x + 5 = 0$

19. $(3x + 5)(x - 3) = 5$

20. $3x^2 - 7x + 1 = 0$

21. $x^2 - 9 = 0$

22. $(x - 3)^2 - 25 = 0$

In Problems 23–25, find the solution as an exact value in simplified radical form. Then give an approximate answer, rounding to the nearest tenth.

23. An arrow shot upward from an 80-foot-tall cliff with an initial speed of 48 feet per second has its position above ground level after t seconds given by the mathematical model $s = -16t^2 + 48t + 80$. How long will it take for the arrow to hit the ground?

24. The width of a rectangle is 2 meters shorter than the length. If the area is 16 square meters, find the rectangle's dimensions.

25. One leg of a right triangle is 2 feet longer than the other leg. The hypotenuse is 6 feet long. What are the lengths of the legs of the triangle?

26. The quadratic model $S = -17t^2 + 45t + 2570$ approximates the number of suicides by firearms in the United States for women, where t represents the number of years after 1985. In what year were there 2370 female suicides by firearms?

Write each number in Problems 27–29 as a multiple of i.

27. $\sqrt{-81}$

28. $\sqrt{-48}$

29. $\sqrt{-17}$

Find the complex solutions of each quadratic equation in Problems 30–35.

30. $(x - 4)^2 = -49$

31. $(7y + 1)^2 = -27$

32. $x^2 - 4x + 13 = 0$

33. $x^2 + 4 = 3x$

34. $3y^2 - y + 2 = 0$

35. $2y^2 = 3y - 5$

36. The personnel manager of a roller skate company knows that the company's weekly revenue is a function of the price of each pair of skates, modeled by $R = -2x^2 + 36x$, where x represents the dollar price of a pair of skates and R represents weekly revenue in tens of thousands of dollars. A job applicant promises the personnel manager an advertising campaign guaranteed to generate $190,000 in weekly revenue. Substitute 19 for R in the given model, and use the quadratic formula to solve for x. What kinds of answers do you get? Based on these answers, explain whether or not the applicant will be hired in the advertising department.

Use intercepts, the vertex, and a few additional points located near the vertex and intercepts to graph the parabolas represented by each quadratic equation in Problems 37–42.

37. $y = x^2 + 4x - 5$ **38.** $y = -x^2 + 6x - 9$ **39.** $y = x^2 - 6x + 7$

40. $y = -x^2 + 4x$ **41.** $y = x^2 - 4x + 10$ **42.** $y = -x^2 - 3$

43. An object projected directly upward from the ground with an initial velocity of 160 feet per second has its distance (d, in feet) above the ground after t seconds described by the model $d = -16t^2 + 160t$.

   a. How long does it take the object to reach the ground? Answer the question by replacing d with 0 in the given model, and solve the resulting quadratic equation for t.

   b. After how many seconds will the object reach its maximum height? Answer this question by finding $-\dfrac{b}{2a}$.

   c. What is the object's maximum height? Answer the question by substituting the value for t that you found in part (b) into the function, and find the corresponding value for d.

   d. Use your work in parts (a)–(c) to graph the function with values of t along the x-axis and values of d

along the y-axis. If applicable, use a graphing utility to verify your hand-drawn graph.

44. The model $f(x) = -0.02x^2 + 0.16x + 3.95$ describes the number of secretaries ($f(x)$ in millions) in the United States x years after 1983. The graph of the resulting parabola is shown below. Find the coordinates of the vertex and describe what this represents in practical terms. What explanations can you offer for the trend shown by the graph?

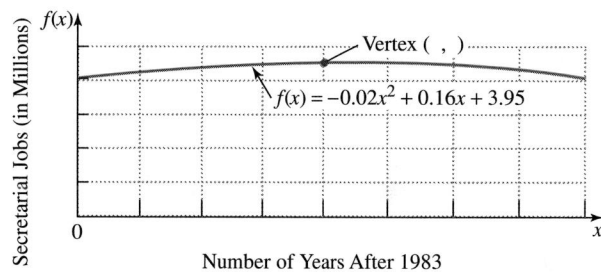

CHAPTER 10 TEST

In Problems 1–10, solve each equation.

1. $9x^2 = 54$ **2.** $3x^2 + 5x = 0$ **3.** $3x^2 + 5x + 1 = 0$

4. $(x - 2)^2 = 5$ **5.** $x(x - 2) = 1$ **6.** $9x^2 - 6x = 2$

7. $8x^2 = 6x - 1$ **8.** $(2x + 1)^2 = 36$ **9.** $3x(x - 2) + 1 = 0$

10. $x^2 - 2x = -5$

11. Solve by completing the square: $x^2 + 4x - 3 = 0$.

In Problems 12–13, express each radical in terms of i.

12. $\sqrt{-121}$ **13.** $-\sqrt{-75}$

In Problems 14–16, find the complex solutions.

14. $x^2 + 36 = 0$ **15.** $(x - 5)^2 = -25$ **16.** $x^2 - 4x + 7 = 0$

Graph the parabolas whose equations are given in Problems 17–18.

17. $y = x^2 - 2x - 8$ **18.** $y = -2x^2 + 16x - 24$

19. To find the distance across a lake, a surveyor inserts poles and P and Q, measuring the respective distances to point R, as shown in the figure. Use the surveyor's measurements given in the figure to find the distance PQ across the lake in simplified radical form.

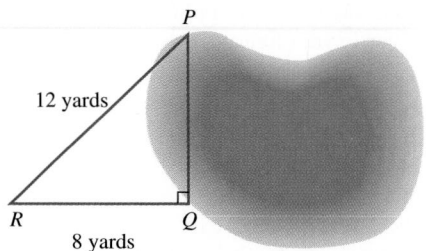

20. For what value of x will the large rectangle in the figure have an area of 72 square inches?

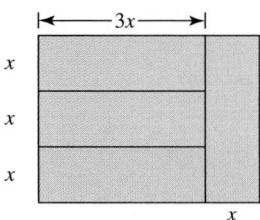

21. The number of diagonals (d) in an n-sided plane figure is given by the formula

$$d = \frac{n^2 - 3n}{2}.$$

If a plane figure has 14 diagonals, use the formula to determine how many sides it has.

(A collection of review problems covering the entire book can be found in the appendix.)

Appendix

Review Problems Covering the Entire Book

If your course included the use of graphing utilities, use your grapher to verify as many of your answers as possible.

Solving Equations and Inequalities

Systematic procedures for solving certain equations and inequalities are an important component of algebra. Problems 1–20 give you the opportunity to review these procedures. Solve each problem, expressing irrational solutions in simplified form and imaginary solutions in the form a + bi.

1. $2(x - 3) + 5x = 8(x - 1)$

2. $\dfrac{2x}{3} + \dfrac{1}{5} = 1 + \dfrac{3x}{5} - \dfrac{1}{3}$

3. $0.4(x + 20) + 0.5x = 13.4$

4. $-2(y - 5) + 10 = -3(y + 2) + y$

5. $-3(2x - 4) > 2(6x - 12)$ (Graph the solution set on a number line.)

6. $\dfrac{-3}{8} = \dfrac{x}{40}$

7. $x^2 + 3x = 18$

8. $6x^2 + 13x + 6 = 0$

9. $\dfrac{3}{y + 5} - 1 = \dfrac{4 - y}{2y + 10}$

10. $\dfrac{2x}{x^2 - 4} + \dfrac{1}{x - 2} = \dfrac{2}{x + 2}$

11. $x + \dfrac{6}{x} = -5$

12. $x - 5 = \sqrt{x + 7}$

13. $(x - 2)^2 = 20$

14. $3 + x(x + 2) = 18$

15. $3x^2 - 6x + 2 = 0$

16. $x^2 + 2x + 2 = 0$

17. $\begin{aligned} y &= 2x - 3 \\ x + 2y &= 9 \end{aligned}$

18. $\begin{aligned} 3x + 2y &= -2 \\ -4x + 5y &= 18 \end{aligned}$

19. $\begin{aligned} 3x - y &= 4 \\ -9x + 3y &= -12 \end{aligned}$

20. Solve for t: $\dfrac{t}{a} + \dfrac{t}{b} = 1.$

Graphs and Graphing

Throughout the book we considered problems solved with bar, line, and circle graphs. We also studied graphing in the rectangular (Cartesian) coordinate system. Problems 21–43 focus on problem solving with graphs.

21. The circle graph indicates where people in the United States lived in 1996. If the population at that time was approximately 263 million, how many people lived in central cities?

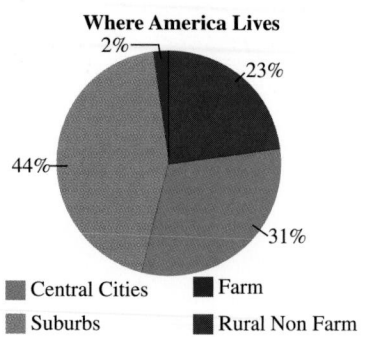

Where America Lives

- Central Cities
- Suburbs
- Farm
- Rural Non Farm

22. The bar graph depicts the number of American women in state and federal prisons over a 34-year period.

a. Estimate the number of women in prisons in 1986.

b. Find a reasonable estimate in the difference in the number of women in prisons between 1994 and 1960.

c. In what years was the number of women prisoners no more than 30,000 and no less than 20,000?

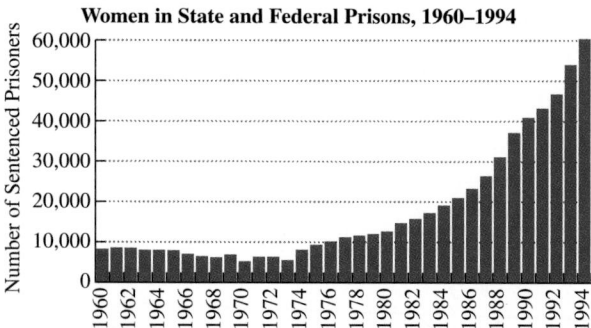

Women in State and Federal Prisons, 1960–1994

Source: U.S. Department of Justice, Bureau of Justice Statistics (1994), *Sourcebook of Criminal Justice Statistics, 1993,* p. 600; U.S. Department of Justice, Bureau of Justice Statistics (August 1995), *Prisoners in 1994,* p. 5, Table 5.

23. The line graph illustrates the murder rate in the United States over a 24-year period.

a. In what years was the murder rate at a minimum? What was the murder rate for those years?

b. In what year was the murder rate at a maximum? What is a reasonable estimate of the murder rate for that year?

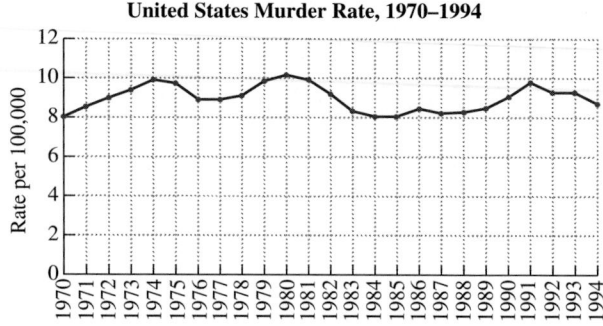

United States Murder Rate, 1970–1994

Source: U.S. Department of Justice, Federal Bureau of Investigation. Data provided by the Criminal Justice Information Services Division (preliminary data for 1994).

24. A small airline has determined that with each $10 decrease in fare, 25 passengers will choose to fly with them over their competitors. The ordered pairs shown in the graph represent the number of $10 price decreases and the airline's profit. Is it true that the more $10 decreases the airline allows, the greater will be its profit? If this is not the case, write a statement about how many $10 decreases will result in a maximum profit, and what will happen after that.

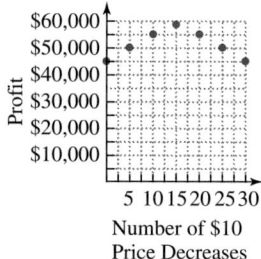

Number of $10 Price Decreases

25. The graph at the top of the next page shows the federal budget deficits for the United States. Use the graph to determine the following.

a. The mean (the average) budget deficit for 1996 and 1997.

b. The difference in the budget deficit between 1996 and 1976.

c. How many times greater is the projected deficit in 1998 than the deficit for Nixon's first year in office?

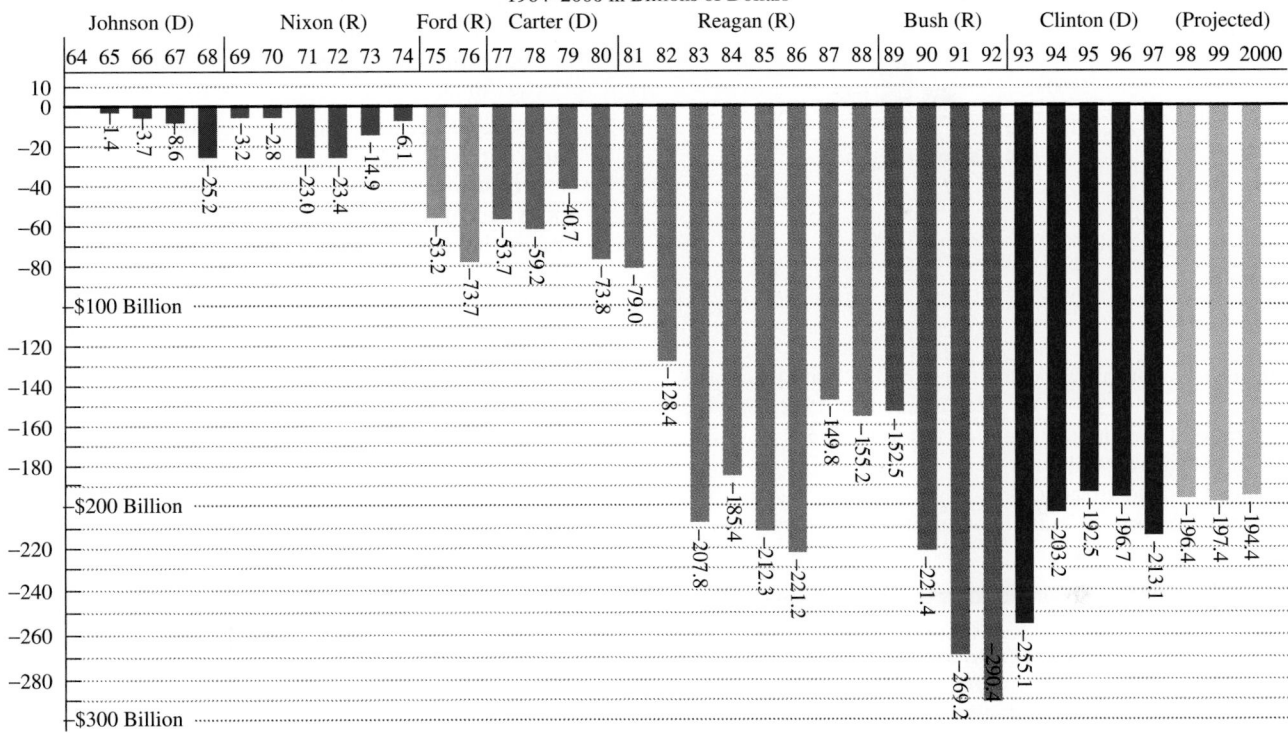

Federal Budget Deficits
1964–2000 in Billions of Dollars

Source: Based on A Citizen's Guide to the Budget. Budget of the United States Government Fiscal Year 1996

26. The circle graph shows the ethnic makeup of the United States in 1995. If there are 10.52 million Americans in the "other" sector, what is the total population? Use this figure to determine the population in each of the other two sectors.

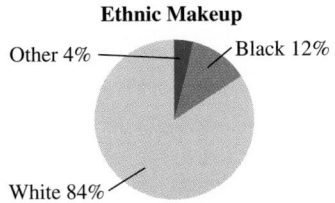

Ethnic Makeup

Other 4%
Black 12%
White 84%

27. The bar graph on the right indicates international rates of incarceration for 17 selected countries from 1992 through 1993. The incarceration rate in the United States (per 100,000 people) is 91 more than 4 times that of Canada. The rate in Spain is 26 less than that of Canada. The three countries combined incarcerate 761 people per 100,000. Determine the rate for each of these countries and then use the graph to estimate the rates for the other 14 countries.

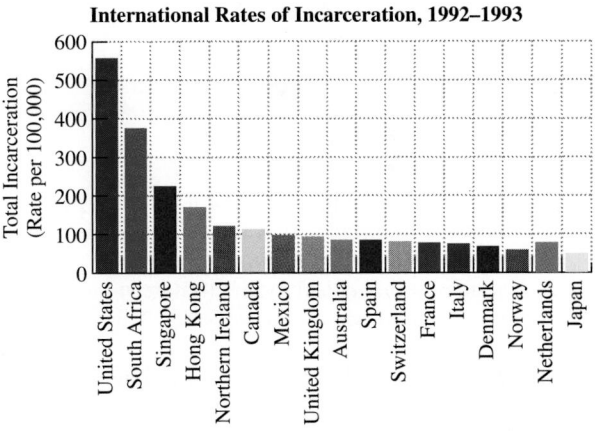

International Rates of Incarceration, 1992–1993

Total Incarceration (Rate per 100,000)

Sources: Mauer, Marc (September 1994), *Americans Behind Bars: The International Use of Incarceration, 1992–1993* (Washington D.C.: The Sentencing Project); Austin, James (January 1994), *An Overview of Incarceration Trends in the United States and Their Impact on Crime* (San Francisco: The National Council on Crime and Delinquency).

28. a. In 1985, the net interest on the federal debt was approximately $100 billion. If the interest is growing by $10 billion yearly, in what year will the interest on the federal debt reach $320 billion?

b. Based on the actual data shown in the bar graph at the top of page 748, how well does the description in part (a) model reality?

**Net Interest on the
Federal Debt**

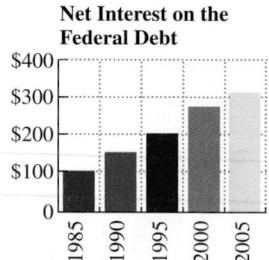

Source: Fiscal Year 1996
Budget of the U.S. Government CBO 1995

29. The bar graph indicates the amount that Americans spent on five forms of entertainment in 1992. Find the ratio of the amount spent on the following:
  a. Music to gambling.
  b. Music to attractions.
  c. Gambling to music, books, attractions, and movies combined.

**Amount Americans Spent on Five
Forms of Entertainment, 1992**

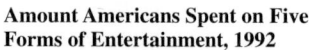
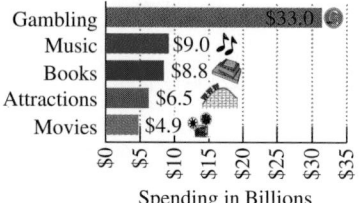

Spending in Billions

Source: MRCI

30. A car travels at a uniform speed of 35 miles per hour for t hours. The distance that the car travels in t hours is given by the model $d = 35t$.
  a. Use the mathematical model to determine the distance covered in 1 hour, 2 hours, 3 hours, and 4 hours.
  b. Graph the model with values of t along the x-axis and values of d along the y-axis.

31. The salary (S) received by a salesperson is $500 per week plus a 4% commission on all sales (x).
  a. Write an equation that models the salary (S) in terms of sales (x).
  b. Make a table of values by selecting some convenient choices for x, and find the corresponding value for S. Use the table to graph the model.
  c. Use the graph to estimate the weekly salary for sales of $1000. Verify this estimate by substituting 1000 for x in the equation that models the salary.

32. The function $f(x) = 0.3x^2 + 2.2x + 5.3$ models the number of cellular phone subscribers ($f(x)$, in millions) in the United States x years after 1990.

  a. Construct a table of values using integers from 0 to 5 for x, and graph the function from 0 to 5.
  b. Describe what the shape of the graph indicates about the number of cellular phone subscribers over time.

33. For several decades, the rate of economic growth in the United States reduced the poverty rate. From a historical low of 11.1% in 1973, the poverty rate has increased to approximately 14.5% in 1995. The graph shows the number of Americans below the poverty line from 1960 through 1992.
  a. Find the average rate of change in the number of millions of whites below the poverty level from 1960 to 1970. Why is the slope negative? What does this mean in practical terms?
  b. Estimate the average rate of change in the number of millions of blacks below the poverty level from 1980 to 1990. Why is the slope positive? What does this mean in practical terms?
  c. What is misleading about the scale on the horizontal axis?

**Millions of People below the Poverty
Line**

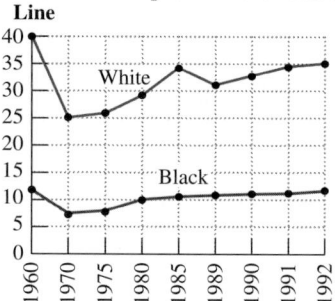

34. One plumbing service charges $35 for a service call and $40 per hour for labor. A second service charges $45 for a service call and $40 per hour for labor. The graphs representing the total price for each of these services are shown here.
  a. Explain why the graphs of the total price models result in parallel lines.
  b. Suppose that a person asks you how many hours of labor must be put in so that the total price for a service call for both companies is the same. Use the graphs to respond to the question.

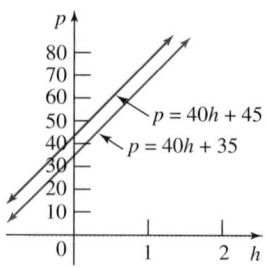

Graph Problems 35–41.

35. $y + 3 = 0$ **36.** $3x - 2y = 6$ **37.** $y = -\frac{2}{3}x + 1$ **38.** $5x + 2y < -10$ **39.** $y > -2x + 3$

40. $y = x^3 - x$ Begin by filling in the table of values.

x	-2	-1	0	1	2
y					

41. $y = x^2 - 2x - 8$ Use intercepts, the vertex, and a few additional points located near the vertex and intercepts.

42. Solve by graphing both equations on the same axes:

$$2x + y = 6$$
$$-2x + y = 2.$$

43. Graph the solution for the following system of linear inequalities:

$$2x + y < 4$$
$$x > 2.$$

Mathematical Models

Describing the world compactly and symbolically using formulas is one of the most important aspects of algebra. Problems 44–63 concentrate on mathematical models.

44. The total price of an article purchased on a monthly deferred payment plan is described by the model $T = D + pm$, where T is the total price, D is the down payment, p is the monthly payment, and m is the number of months one pays.
a. Solve the model for p.
b. A computer has a total price of $1512, was purchased with a down payment of $600 and 16 monthly payments. How much is each monthly payment?

45. The optimum heart rate that a person should achieve during exercise for the exercise to be most beneficial is modeled by $r = 0.6(220 - a)$, where a represents a person's age and r represents that person's optimum heart rate in beats per minute. If the optimum heart rate is 120 beats per minute, how old is that person?

46. Mathematicians have developed a model correlating education and income. A simplified form of one such model for American women indicates that yearly income increases by $1200 for each year of education and that a woman with no education can expect to earn $6300 yearly. Using this model, how many years of education are needed to earn $19,500 yearly?

47. The function $f(x) = 68.9x^2 + 1165.3x + 31,676$ models the yearly number of cases $f(x)$ commenced by the U.S. Court of Appeals x years after 1984. Find and interpret $f(10)$.

48. The linear model $A = 0.445x + 14.7$ describes the atmospheric pressure (A, in pounds per square inch) x feet below the surface of the ocean.
a. What is the y-intercept for this model? Describe what this means in terms of atmospheric pressure at sea level.

b. What is the slope for the model? Describe what this means in terms of the variables modeled in the given formula.
c. The pressure at 30,000 feet below sea level can be compared to having the weight of an elephant pressed against each square inch of your body. What is the pressure at this depth?

49. The table shows two measurements for the height and the corresponding ideal weight of adult women.

x (Height, in Inches)	62	66
y (Weight, in Pounds)	111	130

a. The line on which these data points lie is shown in the graph at the top of page 750. Find the slope of this line.
b. Use either ordered pair and write the point-slope equation of the line on which these data points lie.
c. Use the point-slope form of the equation to write the slope-intercept form of the equation.
d. Use the slope-intercept form of the equation to predict the ideal weights for women who are 64 and 72 inches tall, respectively.

e. The actual ideal weights for women whose heights are 64 and 72 inches are 123 pounds and 158 pounds. How well did your formula in part (d) model this data? Describe how the difference between actual data values and the values predicted by your model are shown in the graph.

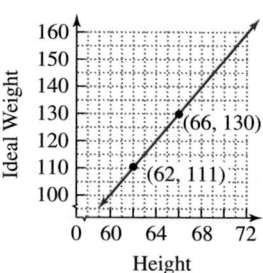

50. The function $f(x) = 0.1x^2 - 3x + 22$ describes the distance ($f(x)$, in feet) needed for an airplane to land when its initial landing speed is x feet per second. Find and interpret $f(90)$. Will there be a problem if 550 feet of runway is available? Explain.

51. A swimming pool is 16 meters by 20 meters. The pool is surrounded by a sidewalk whose width is x meters.
   a. Find a polynomial that models or describes the area of the pool and path combined.
   b. Write the expression in part (a) as a polynomial function, calling the function f.
   c. Find and interpret $f(1)$.

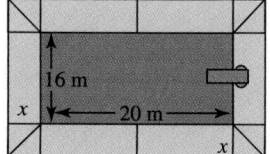

52. The function $f(x) = 2x^2 + 22x + 320$ models the number of inmates, ($f(x)$, in thousands) in federal and state prisons x years after 1980.
   a. In what year was the prison population 524 thousand?
   b. The graph of $y = 2x^2 + 22x + 320$ was obtained with a graphing utility, using the following range setting:

   $$\text{Xmin} = 0, \text{Xmax} = 15, \quad \text{Xscl} = 1,$$
   $$\text{Ymin} = 0, \text{Ymax} = 1000, \text{Yscl} = 100.$$

   The graph is shown below. Identify the ordered pair on the function's graph corresponding to your solution in part (a).

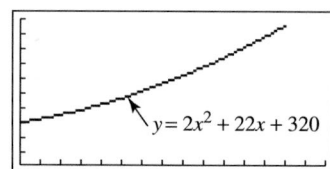

53. The function

   $$f(x) = \frac{20x}{100 - x}$$

   describes the cost ($f(x)$, in thousands of dollars) to eliminate x percent of pollutants from a lake.
   a. Find and interpret $f(20), f(80)$, and $f(90)$.
   b. For what value of x is the function undefined?
   c. What happens to the cost as x approaches 100%? How can you interpret this observation?
   d. Complete the table of values and graph the function.

x	0	10	20	30	40	50	60	70	80	90	95	98	99
$f(x)$													

54. The current (I, in amperes) flowing in an electrical circuit varies inversely as the resistance (R, in ohms) in the circuit. When the resistance of an electric percolator is 22 ohms, it draws 5 amperes of current. How much current is needed when the resistance is 10 ohms?

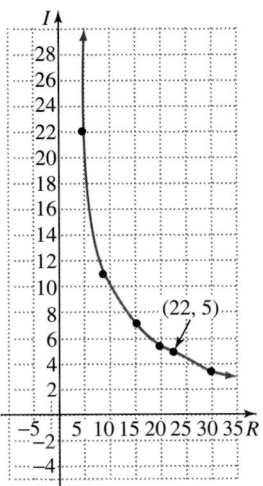

55. The formula

$$v = \sqrt{\frac{Fr}{100}}$$

models the maximum velocity (v, in feet per second) at which a car can safely round a turn of radius r feet, where F is the force the road exerts on the car. The force a road can exert on the tires of a particular car is 2000 pounds. What is the maximum velocity at which this car can safely round a turn of radius 320 feet?

56. The model $S = 28.6A^{1/3}$ describes the number of plant species (S) on the various islands of the Galápagos chain as a function of the area (A, in square miles) of a particular island. Approximately how many species of plants are there on a Galápagos Island whose area is 27 square miles?

57. The distance d between the two points (x_1, y_1) and (x_2, y_2) in a coordinate plane is modeled by the formula $d = \sqrt{(x_2 - x_1)^2 + (y_2 - y_1)^2}$. Use the formula to find the distance between the points (-1, -5) and (2, -2). Express the answer in simplified radical form. Then find a decimal approximation for the distance correct to two decimal places.

58. The formula

$$d^2 = \frac{4050}{I}$$

models the illumination produced by a light source as a function of the distance from the source. In the formula, d is the distance from the source (in feet) and I

is the amount of illumination in foot-candles. How far from the source is the illumination equal to 162 foot-candles?

59. In a softball tournament, a homerun was hit. The figure shows the path of the ball as the graph of the model $f(x) = -0.004x^2 + x + 4$, where x represents the number of feet the ball has traveled from the plate and $f(x)$ represents the height of the ball. Find the coordinates of the parabola's vertex and describe what this represents in the context of the problem.

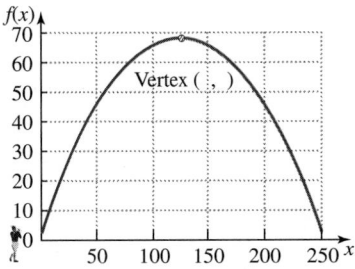

60. In Silicon Valley, California, a government agency ordered computer-related companies to contribute to a monetary pool for the cleanup of underground water supplies that the companies had contaminated with toxic chemicals. The required monetary pool (M, in millions of dollars) depended on the percent of the contaminants removed, given by the mathematical model

$$M = \frac{2x}{1 - x}$$

where x is the percent of the total contamination removed, expressed as a decimal. If the companies pool $3 million ($M = 3$), what percent of the contaminants can be removed?

61. The formula

$$D = \frac{n(n - 3)}{2}$$

describes the number of diagonals (D) for an n-sided polygon. Find the number of sides for a polygon with five diagonals.

62. In t years from 1995, the population (P, in thousands) of a community is described by

$$P = 30 - \frac{9}{t + 1}.$$

When will the community have a population of 27,000?

63. When a ball is thrown vertically upward, its height (h, in feet) above the ground after t seconds is described by the mathematical model $h = -16t^2 + 96t + 80$. At what time is the ball 128 feet above the ground?

Factoring Skills

Factoring is a skill needed when working with rational expressions and solving certain quadratic equations. Factor Problems 64–74 completely, or state that the polynomial is prime.

64. $4x^2 - 13x + 3$

65. $4x^2 - 49$

66. $4x^2 - 20x + 25$

67. $x^3 + 3x^2 - x - 3$

68. $3x^2 - 75$

69. $2x^2 + 8x - 42$

70. $-6x^2 + 7x - 2$

71. $x^5 - 16x$

72. $6x^2 - 3x + 2$

73. $x^3 - 10x^2 + 25x$

74. $x^3 - 8$

The polynomials in Problems 75–78 contain several variables. Factor each polynomial completely.

75. $14x^2y^3 - 10x^2y^2 + 4xy^2$

76. $x^2 + 4xy - 21y^2$

77. $6x^2 - 13xy - 28y^2$

78. $16x^2 - 40xy + 25y^2$

Algebra's Simplifications

The word "simplify" in algebra has a variety of meanings ranging from performing indicated operations, removing grouping symbols and combining like terms, rewriting exponential expressions with positive exponents, reducing rational expressions to lowest terms, and rationalizing denominators. Simplify in Problems 79–112.

79. $24 \div 8 \cdot 3 + 28 \div (-7)$

80. $\dfrac{11 - (-9) + 6(10 - 4)}{2 + 3 \cdot 4}$

81. $-21 - 16 - 3(2 - 8)$

82. $-(-3y + 2) - 4(6 - 5y) - 3y - 7$

83. $(4x^2 - 3x + 2) - (5x^2 - 7x - 6)$

84. $(15x^2y^3 - 7x^2y - 8x^2) - (-9x^2y^3 - 6x^2y + 5x^2 - 3)$

85. $(x - 2)(3x + 7)$

86. $(7x + 4y)(3x - 5y)$

87. $(3x - 5)^2 - (2x - 3)(4x + 5)$

88. $(4y - 3)(5y^2 + 6y - 2)$

89. $(x + y)(x^2 - xy + y^2)$

90. $\dfrac{-8x^6 + 12x^4 - 4x^2}{4x^2}$

91. $\dfrac{20x^4y^3 - 5x^3y^2}{-10x^2y}$

92. $\dfrac{6x^2 + 5x - 6}{2x + 3}$

93. $\dfrac{(4x^3)^2}{x^9}$

94. $\left(\dfrac{x^4}{x^7}\right)^{-3}$

95. $\dfrac{3x^2 - 8x + 5}{4x^2 - 5x + 1}$

96. $\dfrac{y^2 - y - 12}{y^2 - 16} \cdot \dfrac{2y^2 + 7y - 4}{y^2 - 4y - 21}$

97. $\dfrac{15 - 3y}{y + 6} \div (y^2 - 9y + 20)$

98. $\dfrac{x + 6}{x - 2} + \dfrac{2x + 1}{x + 3}$

99. $\dfrac{x}{x^2 + 2x - 3} - \dfrac{x}{x^2 - 5x + 4}$

100. $\dfrac{\dfrac{1}{x} - 2}{4 - \dfrac{1}{x}}$

101. $\sqrt{50x^{11}}$

102. $3\sqrt{20b} + 2\sqrt{45b}$

103. $2\sqrt[3]{16} - 3\sqrt[3]{2}$

104. $\sqrt{3x} \cdot \sqrt{6x}$

105. $\sqrt{5}(\sqrt{2} + 3\sqrt{7})$

106. $(\sqrt{2} + 3\sqrt{6})(\sqrt{2} - \sqrt{6})$

107. $(2 + \sqrt{5})^2$

108. $\dfrac{2}{\sqrt{3b}}$

109. $\dfrac{6}{\sqrt[3]{4}}$

110. $\dfrac{\sqrt{5}}{\sqrt{5} + \sqrt{6}}$

111. $\dfrac{11}{\sqrt{5} - 3}$

112. $8^{2/3}$

A Potpourri of Skills

Problems 113–121 give you the opportunity to review a number of course objectives presented throughout the book.

113. List all numbers from the given set that are:
   a. Natural numbers   **b.** Whole numbers
   c. Integers   **d.** Rational numbers
   e. Irrational numbers   **f.** Real numbers

$$\{-14, -\pi, 0, 0.45, \sqrt{3}, \sqrt{-4}, 6, 7\tfrac{1}{5}, \sqrt{169}\}$$

114. Evaluate $x^3 - 3x^3y + 2y - 5$ when $x = -3$ and $y = -4$.

Identify the property illustrated by Problems 115–117.

115. $8 + (9 + 5) = 8 + (5 + 9)$

116. $(13 \cdot 7) \cdot 3 = 13 \cdot (7 \cdot 3)$

117. $-5\left(-\tfrac{1}{5}\right) = 1$

118. If x represents a number, translate the following statement into an algebraic expression and simplify: Six times the number, added to four times the sum of the number and 5.

119. a. Solve for y: $3x + 2y = 5$.
   b. Find the value of y when $x = -1$.

Problem Solving by Writing an Equation

Problem solving is the central theme of algebra. Some problems can be solved by translating given or implied conditions into linear equations, linear inequalities, quadratic equations, or systems of equations. Use this technique and the five-step strategy for solving problems discussed throughout the book to solve Problems 122–153.

122. Seven subtracted from five times a number is 208. Find the number.

123. Two pages that face each other in a book have 1097 as the sum of their page numbers. What are the page numbers?

124. An 87-inch board is cut into three pieces. The longest piece is 10 inches longer than twice the shortest piece and the middle-sized piece is 17 inches longer than the shortest piece. How long are the pieces?

125. Most of the world's very tall buildings are in the United States, where the skyscraper was first conceived. The height of the World Trade Center in New York is 790 feet less than twice that of New York's Empire State Building. If the mean (average) height of the two buildings is 980 feet, determine the height of each building.

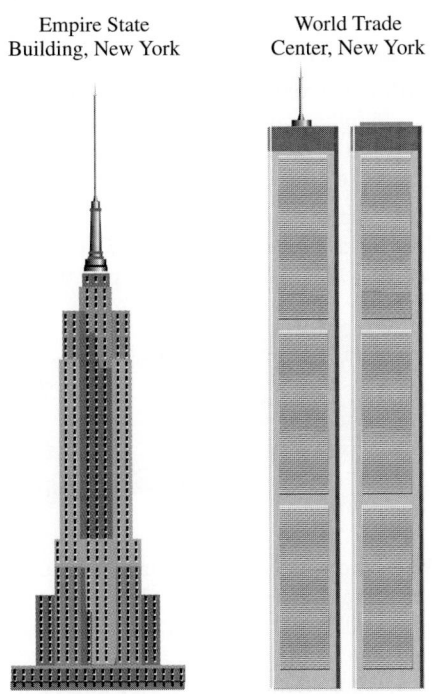

Empire State
Building, New York

World Trade
Center, New York

126. After a 20% price reduction, a VCR sold for $124. What was the price before the reduction?

120. Write the point-slope form of the line passing through $(-2, 6)$ and $(3, -4)$. Then use the point-slope form of the equation to write the slope-intercept form.

121. Write $\sqrt{-75}$ as a multiple of i.

127. A landscape architect charged a customer $971, listing $350 for plants and the remainder for labor. If the architect charged $23 per hour, how many hours did the architect work?

128. A university with 176 people on the faculty wants to maintain a student-to-faculty ratio of 23:2. How many students should they enroll to maintain that ratio?

129. To earn a B in a course, a student must have a final average of at least 80%. On the first three examinations, a student has scores of 76%, 74%, and 78%. What must the student earn on the fourth examination to earn a B in the course?

130. A coupon book for a bridge costs $21 per month. The toll for the bridge is normally $2.50, but is reduced to $1 for people who have purchased the coupon book.
   a. After how many monthly trips across the bridge is the coupon book more economical than paying the full cost of the toll?
   b. Explain how the graphs illustrate the solution to this problem.

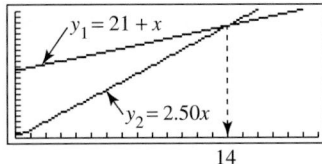

131. The unit price of an item is the ratio of the total price to the total units. What is the unit price (in dollars per ounce) for a 14-ounce box of cereal that sells for $2.24?

132. Park rangers catch, tag, and then release 25 deer back into a state park. Two weeks later, they select a sample of 36 deer, 4 of which are tagged. Assuming the ratio of tagged deer in the sample holds for all deer in the park, approximately how many deer are in the park?

133. A person who is 5 feet tall casts a shadow of 8 feet. At the same time, a building casts a shadow that is 72 feet long. Determine the height of the building.

134. a. The perimeter of a soccer field is 300 yards. If the length is 50 yards longer than the width, what are the field's dimensions?
b. If the length of the field is represented by 5 inches, what is the ratio of the represented length to the actual length?

135. A sailboat's sail has an area of 120 square feet and a base that is 15 feet long. Find the height of the sail.

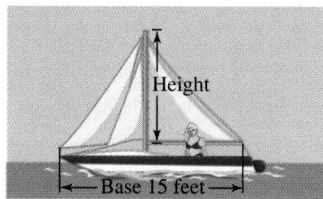

136. A circular garden measures 10 meters across. Answer each of the following questions, first expressing your answer in terms of π, and then using 3.14 for π to obtain a decimal approximation for the answer.
a. How many meters of fencing is needed to completely enclose the garden?
b. How many square meters of sod is needed to completely cover the garden's interior with grass?

137. A cylinder whose radius is 2 decimeters and whose height is 4 decimeters has its radius tripled. How does the volume of the larger cylinder compare to that of the smaller cylinder?

138. Nutritional information for a medium-size apple and a medium-size avocado is given in the table. How many of each should a person eat daily to get exactly 1044 calories and 100 grams of carbohydrates?

	One Apple	**One Avocado**
Calories	96	378
Carbohydrates (grams)	24	14

139. If 10 pens and 12 pads cost $42, and 5 of the same pens and 10 of the same pads cost $29, find the cost of a pen and a pad.

140. Connecticut is the richest state in the United States and Mississippi is the poorest. The average income per person in Connecticut is $1678 less than twice that of Mississippi.
a. If the average income per person for Connecticut is divided by the average income per person for Mississippi, the partial quotient is 1 and the remainder is $13,216. Find the average income for each state.
b. The median income of U.S. citizens in 1993 was approximately $18,177. By how much does the income in Connecticut exceed this figure? What percent (to the nearest whole percent) higher than the U.S. average is the income for Connecticut?
c. Write a statement about how the income per person in Mississippi compares to the median U.S. income.

141. The sum of a number and its reciprocal is 4. Find the number(s).

142. Find the measure of each angle in the figure.

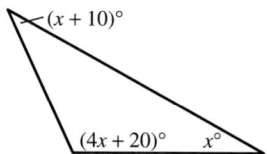

143. The length of a rectangle is 1 meter more than twice the width. If the rectangle's area is 36 square meters, find its dimensions.

144. Earth is approximately 1.5×10^8 kilometers from the sun. If light travels 3×10^5 kilometers per second, how long does it take sunlight to reach Earth? (The time is the quotient of the distance and the rate.)

145. As shown in the figure, a brick wall is 20 feet high. How far away from the base will a 24-foot ladder be located when its top is at the top of the wall?

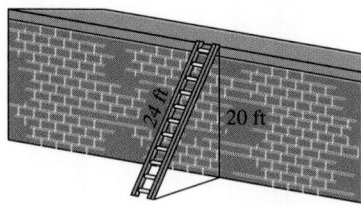

146. The approach speed of an airplane varies directly as its landing speed. An airplane with an approach speed of 90 miles per hour has a landing speed of 75 miles per hour. What is the approach speed of an airplane whose landing speed is 80 miles per hour?

147. According to the Office of National Drug Control Policy, in 1994 two-fifths of the money that college students spent on illegal drugs was spent on marijuana. If $430 million was spent on marijuana, how much did college students spend on illegal drugs in 1994?

148. A person invested $4000, part at 5% and the remainder at 9%. If the total yearly interest from these investments was $311, find the amount invested at each rate.

149. Two boats started at the same time from the same port. One traveled due east at 13 miles per hour, and the other traveled due west at 19 miles per hour. In how many hours will the boats be 232 miles apart?

150. A chemist needs to mix an 80% acid solution with a 65% acid solution to obtain a 10-gallon mixture that is 75% acid. How many gallons of each of the solutions must be used?

151. A painter can paint a house in 4 days. Working alone, the painter's assistant can paint the same house in 12 days. How many days would it take them to paint the house if they worked together?

152. When a boat travels with the current, it takes 2 hours to travel 48 miles. It takes the boat 3 hours to travel the same distance against the current. Find the speed of the boat in still water and the speed of the current.

153. Plane A flies 50 miles per hour faster than plane B. Plane A can fly 500 miles in the same amount of time that plane B flies 400 miles. Find the speed of each plane.

Critical Thinking

Problems 122–153 can be solved by translating conditions into equations or inequalities. However, there are other strategies that can be used to solve problems, including looking for a pattern, eliminating possibilities, making a systematic list, working backward, using a drawing, or guessing at an answer and checking the guess against the conditions of the problem. Use one or more of these strategies to solve Problems 154–165.

154. Study the examples.

$$1 + 2 + 3 = 6 = 4 \cdot \frac{3}{2}$$
$$1 + 2 + 3 + 4 + 5 = 15 = 6 \cdot \frac{5}{2}$$
$$1 + 2 + 3 + 4 + 5 + 6 + 7 + 8 = 36 = 9 \cdot \frac{8}{2}$$
$$1 + 2 + 3 + 4 + 5 + 6 + 7 + 8 + 9 + 10 = 55 = 11 \cdot \frac{10}{2}$$

Use the emerging pattern to find:

$$1 + 2 + 3 + 4 + 5 + \cdots + 68 + 69 + 70 = ?$$
$$1 + 2 + 3 + 4 + 5 + \cdots + (n - 2) + (n - 1) + n = ?$$

155. Suppose that w, x, y, and z represent natural numbers. Furthermore, x is greater than w, y is one less than z, and z is four more than x. What is the relationship between w and z?

156. Use the numbers 2, 4, 8, and 10, each number at most once in every part of this problem, to make each statement true.
  a. $x + y - z = 6$
  b. $ab - c = 22$
  c. $r \div s + w = 13$

157. Which one of the following is true?
  a. My number is 2 more than her number. Her number is 7 more than his number. Therefore, his number is 5 less than my number.
  b. Your number is 3 more than her number. My number is 2 less than her number. Therefore, our numbers are both even.
  c. My number is greater than A's number. B's number is less than my number. C's number is equal to A's number. Therefore, my number is greater than C's number.
  d. My number exceeds your number by 7. My number is divisible by 7. Therefore, your number is not divisible by 7.

158. Fill in all missing entries in the table.

	First Term $n = 1$	Second Term $n = 2$	Third Term $n = 3$	Fourth Term $n = 4$	Fifth Term $n = 5$	Rule for nth Term
a.	1	3	5			$2n - 1$
b.	5					$3(n + 1) - 1$
c.	1	4	9	16	25	
d.	0	3	8	15		
e.	1	8	27		125	

159. How many different-sized squares can be made by connecting dots in the array?

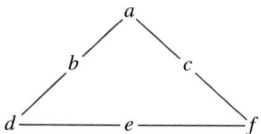

160. Use each of the numbers $-3, -2, -1, 1, 2,$ and 3 only once so that the sum of the numbers on each side of the triangle is 2.

161. Find a two-digit odd number that is divisible by both 3 and 5, and whose digit sum is an odd number.

162. How many ways can you make change for a quarter using only pennies, nickels, and dimes?

163. Cylindrical aluminum cans that are 12 inches tall are used to build a pyramid 120 inches tall. The pyramid's base consists of a single row of cans and each can in the row above it rests on two cans below it. How many cylindrical cans does it take to build the pyramid?

164. Inside a square piece of paper is drawn the largest possible circle. The circle is cut out and the leftover scraps of paper are discarded. Inside the circle, the largest possible square is drawn, cut out, and leftover scraps are discarded. What fractional part of the original square remains?

165. A box is constructed of 64 cubes. Two striped paths are painted on the cube. How many small cubes have no paint on them?

Answers to Selected Exercises

Chapter 1

PROBLEM SET 1.1

1. $\frac{2}{3}$ **3.** $\frac{5}{6}$ **5.** $\frac{7}{10}$ **7.** $\frac{1}{8}$ **9.** $\frac{21}{88}$ **11.** $\frac{1}{24}$ **13.** $\frac{3}{2}$ **15.** $9\frac{31}{40}$ **17.** $\frac{10}{3}$ **19.** $\frac{9}{5}$ **21.** 2 **23.** 12 **25.** $\frac{5}{11}$ **27.** $\frac{2}{3}$ **29.** $\frac{2}{3}$

31. $\frac{7}{10}$ **33.** $\frac{9}{10}$ **35.** $1\frac{1}{24}$ **37.** $\frac{71}{75}$ **39.** $\frac{1}{2}$ **41.** $\frac{7}{12}$ **43.** $\frac{41}{80}$ **45.** $5\frac{5}{24}$ **47.** $3\frac{1}{10}$ **49.** $2\frac{7}{8}$

	Fraction	Decimal	Percent
51.		0.95	95%
53.	$\frac{7}{20}$		35%
55.	$\frac{1}{50}$	0.02	
57.	$\frac{1}{200}$		0.5%

59. 104 **61.** $\frac{3}{8}$ cup   **63.** $1\frac{1}{4}$ acres   **65.** $1\frac{3}{20}$ miles; $\frac{7}{20}$ mile   **67. a.** $\$38\frac{7}{8}$ **b.** $\$777.50$ **c.** $\$7.50$ **69.** $\$9$ **71.** $\$6022.50$

73. d   **75.** d   **85.** $\frac{11}{3}$ **87.** 35 **89.** $\frac{1\cancel{0}}{\cancel{2}5} = \frac{1}{5}$

PROBLEM SET 1.2

1. $\{1, 2, 3\}$ **3.** $\{0, 1, 2, 3, 4, 5\}$ **5.** $\{-2, -1, 0, 1, ...\}$ **7.** $\{-6, -5, -4, -3, ...\}$ **9.** $\{7\}$ **11.** $\left\{-\frac{3}{4}\right\}$ **13.** $\{0\}$ **15.** $\left\{\frac{2}{3}, 1\right\}$

17. $\{\pi\}$ **19. a.** $\{\sqrt{100}\}$ **b.** $\{0, \sqrt{100}\}$ **c.** $\{-9, 0, \sqrt{100}\}$ **d.** $\left\{-9, -\frac{4}{5}, 0, 0.25, 5\frac{1}{8}, 9.2, \sqrt{100}\right\}$ **e.** $\{\sqrt{3}, e\}$

f. $\left\{-9, -\frac{4}{5}, 0, 0.25, \sqrt{3}, e, 5\frac{1}{8}, 9.2, \sqrt{100}\right\}$ **21. a.** $\{\sqrt{49}\}$ **b.** $\{0, \sqrt{49}\}$ **c.** $\{-7, 0, \sqrt{49}\}$ **d.** $\{-7, -0.\overline{6}, 0, \sqrt{49}\}$ **e.** $\{\sqrt{50}\}$

f. $\{-7, -0.\overline{6}, 0, \sqrt{49}, \sqrt{50}\}$

23. <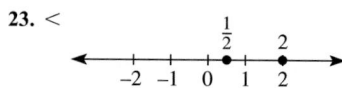

25.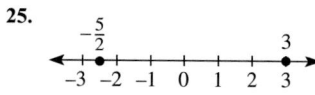

27. >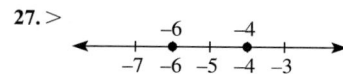

29. <   −2.5   1.5

31. >

33. <   −4.5   3

35. < $\sqrt{2}$

37. > $0.\overline{3}$

39. >   −π

41. −6   **43.** 7   **45.** $-\dfrac{2}{3}$ **47.** $\sqrt{5}$ **49.** 6   **51.** 7   **53.** $\dfrac{2}{3}$ **55.** $\sqrt{13}$ **57.** 20   **59.** −8.5   **61.** 3000   **63.** 3.7   **65.** c   **67.** d
69. b   **71.** c   **73.** −3.464, −4 and −3   **75.** −4.708, −5 and −4

Review Problems

88. $\dfrac{1}{2}$ **89.** $\dfrac{11}{20}$ **90.** $\dfrac{22}{15}$

PROBLEM SET 1.3

1. a. 228,800,000   **b.** 88%   **c.** **Population in Millions**   **d.** No   **e.** No

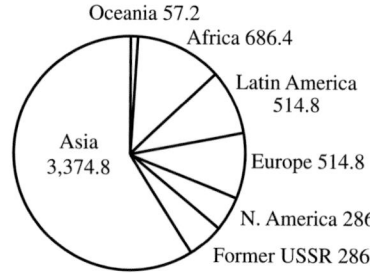

Oceania 57.2
Africa 686.4
Latin America 514.8
Asia 3,374.8
Europe 514.8
N. America 286
Former USSR 286

3. a. 260 million   **b.** 5%   **c.** 10%   **5. a.** 1994   **b.** 1992, 1993   **c.** In the hospital for shorter periods of time; greater percentage are being treated as outpatients, as time goes on.   **7. a.** No   **b.** 8.1%   **c.** Each is independent for each year.   **9. a.** 1980; 55,000,000   **b.** 1990
11. Quadrant I   **13.** Quadrant II   **15.** Quadrant III   **17.** Quadrant IV

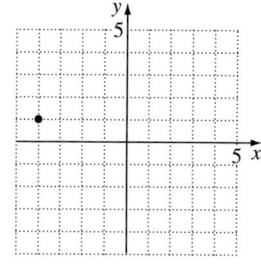

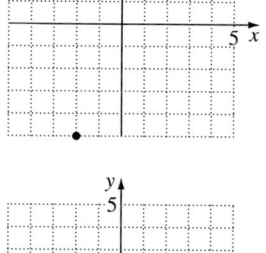

19.

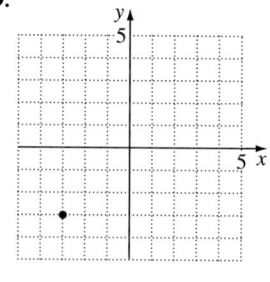

21.

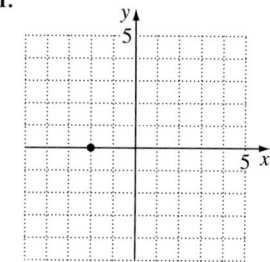

23.

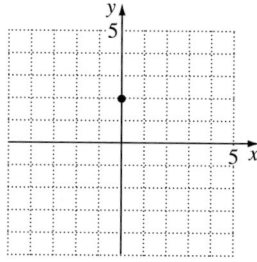

25.

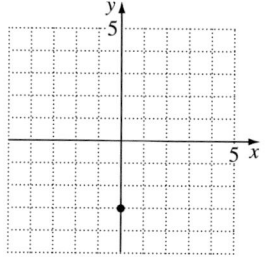

27. 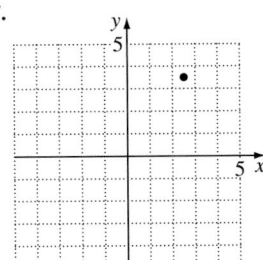   **29.** 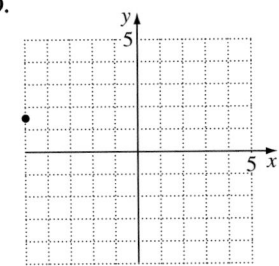   **31.** 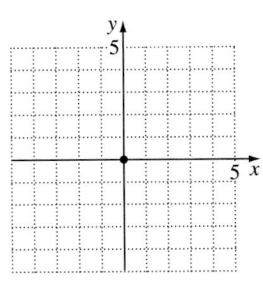   **33.**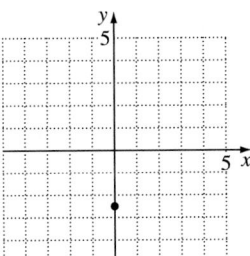

35. (5, 2)   **37.** (−6, 5)   **39.** (−2, −3)   **41.** (5, −3)   **43. a.** (1970, 1.5%), (1975, 4%), (1980, 15%), (1985, 21%), (1990, 30%)
b. In each year (*x*-value) the percent of total degrees given in dentistry (*y*-value) were given to women
c. No; it is unlikely that the trend will continue.
d. Answers may vary. **45. a.** *A*(0, 8000); if the price is not increased, the manufacturer will make $8000.
b. *B*(2, 11,000); if the price is increased by $2.00, the manufacturer will make $11,000.
c. No; the profit peaks at a $4 increase and then declines.
d. $9; $12,000; the highest point is (4, 12,000).   **47.** c   **57. a.** C   **b.** A   **c.** B
59. Group project

Review Problems

60. {−4, 4}   **61.** >   **62.** 3

PROBLEM SET 1.4

1. $7 + x$ **3.** $4y + x$ **5.** $7y + 4x$ **7.** $4(6 + x)$ **9.** $7 \cdot x$ **11.** $6 + yx$ **13.** $(b + 5) \cdot 4$ **15.** $(7 + 5) + x = 12 + x$
17. $(7 \cdot 4)x = 28x$ **19.** $3x + 15$ **21.** $16x + 24$ **23.** $4 + 2r$ **25.** $5x + 5y$ **27.** $3x − 6$ **29.** $8x − 10$ **31.** $\frac{5}{2}x − 6$ **33.** $8x + 28$
35. $6x + 18 + 12y$ **37.** $15x − 10 + 20y$ **39.** $17x$ **41.** $8a$ **43.** $14 + x$ **45.** $11y − 3$ **47.** $9x + 1$ **49.** $8a + 10$ **51.** $15x + 6$
53. $15x + 2$ **55.** $41a + 4b$ **57. a.** $28,236   **b.** $32,817   **c.** $1527x + 16,020$ **59.** $108.\overline{3}$ mg   **61.** $4x(y + 3); 4xy + 12x$
63. c   **69.** Commutative   **71.** Commutative   **73.** Answers may vary.   **75. a.** Yes   **b.** Yes   **77.** No

Review Problems

79. a. $\left\{\frac{18}{3}, \sqrt{81}\right\}$ **b.** $\left\{\frac{18}{3}, \sqrt{81}\right\}$ **c.** $\left\{-23, \frac{18}{3}, \sqrt{81}\right\}$ **d.** $\left\{-23, \frac{17}{3}, \frac{18}{3}, \sqrt{81}\right\}$ **e.** $\left\{\frac{5\pi}{3}, \sqrt{83}\right\}$ **f.** $\left\{-23, \frac{17}{3}, \frac{18}{3}, \frac{5\pi}{3}, \sqrt{81}, \sqrt{83}\right\}$
80. White and Hispanic   **81.** $\frac{22}{15}$

PROBLEM SET 1.5

1. $−5$ **3.** $−8$ **5.** 0 **7.** $−9$ **9.** $−12$ **11.** 4 **13.** $−3$ **15.** $−5$ **17.** $−1.3$ **19.** $−1.5$ **21.** $−18$ **23.** 0 **25.** $−1$
27. $\frac{3}{10}$ **29.** $\frac{1}{8}$ **31.** $−\frac{43}{35}$ **33.** $−\frac{3}{4}$ **35.** $−17.48$ **37.** 62 **39.** $−21$ **41.** 22.1 **43.** $−3x$ **45.** $−2x − 3y$ **47.** $−33a − 23$
49. $44°F$ **51.** 600 feet below sea level.   **53.** $3°F$ **55.** 25-yard line   **57.** $36\frac{1}{4}$ per share   **59. a.** 3.14
b. $3.14 + 0.02 + (−0.02) + 0 + 0.05 = 3.19$
61. The sum of *x* and 18,000; 18,000 more than *x*; *x* increased by 18,000; *x* plus 18,000; 18,000 added to *x*
63. d   **65.** 5.0283   **67.** >   **71.** $−18y$

Review Problems

73. {..., −3, −2, −1, 0}   **74. a.** $\{\sqrt{9}\}$ **b.** $\{0, \sqrt{9}\}$ **c.** $\{-17, 0, \sqrt{9}\}$ **d.** $\left\{-17, -\frac{2}{3}, 0.\overline{3}, \sqrt{9}, 10\frac{1}{7}\right\}$ **e.** $\{\sqrt{5}, \pi, \sqrt{7}\}$
f. $\left\{-17, -\frac{2}{3}, 0, \overline{3}, \sqrt{5}, \pi, \sqrt{7}, \sqrt{9}, 10\frac{1}{7}\right\}$ **75. a.** 11%   **b.** 1930 to 1940

PROBLEM SET 1.6

1. 5 **3.** −7 **5.** 14 **7.** 11 **9.** −9 **11.** −28 **13.** $\frac{4}{5}$ **15.** $-\frac{3}{5}$ **17.** $\frac{3}{4}$ **19.** −13.7 **21.** −2.1 **23.** 9.13 **25.** 19 **27.** −3 **29.** −15 **31.** 0 **33.** −52 **35.** −187 **37.** $1\frac{1}{6}$ **39.** −1 **41.** −4.49 **43.** $-\frac{3}{8}$ **45.** 6x **47.** 26a **49.** 12 + 2y **51.** 7 + 19b **53.** −4x + 2y **55.** 14,776 feet **57.** 188°F **59.** 4.6%; 1.7%; 1.6%; 1.0%; 0.5%; 0.3%; −0.5%, −1.2%, −4.5% **61.** x minus 8%; x decreased by 8%; the difference between x and 8%; 8% less than x **63.** b − 21% **65.** d + 9% **67.** 3600 − x square feet **69.** c **71.** 4.5456 **73.** > **77.** 1 day

Review Problems

80. a. $\{\sqrt{1}\}$ **b.** $\{0, \sqrt{1}\}$ **c.** $\{-123, 0, \sqrt{1}\}$ **d.** $\left\{-123, -\frac{3}{9}, 0, 0.45, \sqrt{1}, 8\frac{1}{5}\right\}$ **e.** $\{\sqrt{7}, e\}$
f. $\left\{-123, -\frac{3}{9}, 0, 0.45, \sqrt{1}, \sqrt{7}, e, 8\frac{1}{5}\right\}$ **81.** −3°F **82.** <

PROBLEM SET 1.7

1. −54 **3.** 21 **5.** −12 **7.** 13 **9.** 0 **11.** −7 **13.** 15 **15.** $\frac{12}{35}$ **17.** $-\frac{14}{27}$ **19.** $-\frac{1}{3}$ **21.** −0.123 **23.** 9.12 **25.** −0.77 **27.** −120 **29.** 24 **31.** −25 **33.** −12 **35.** 9 **37.** −125 **39.** −1 **41.** −45 **43.** −16 **45.** 81 **47.** 9 **49.** −22 **51.** 60 **53.** 38 **55.** −22 **57.** 2 **59.** 28 **61.** −20 **63.** 35 **65.** 8 **67.** 1 **69.** $\frac{5}{8}$ **71.** $\frac{11}{12}$ **73.** $-\frac{1}{4}$ **75.** −10x **77.** 3y **79.** 9x **81.** −4x **83.** −b **85.** 3y **87.** −8x+12 **89.** 6x − 12 **91.** −2y + 5 **93.** y − 14 **95.** 5 − x **97.** x + 1 **99.** −x + 1 **101.** 1.142 million **103.** 6.226 million **105.** 11.31 million **107.** Answers may vary. **109. a.** −0.071x + 24.3 **b.** Very well **c.** Fairly well **d.** 20.608 seconds **111.** 25x cents **113.** 0.70x kilograms **115.** 45x miles **117.** 1.12x dollars **119.** 0.45x dollars **121.** 0.55x dollars **123.** 140 + 80x pounds **125.** 12x dollars **127.** 20 + 5x dollars **129.** 4.50 + 0.30x dollars **131.** x + 2 **133.** c **135.** a **137.** **139.** 10 + 5x cents **141.** $b = \frac{a}{a-1}$, where a is a natural number

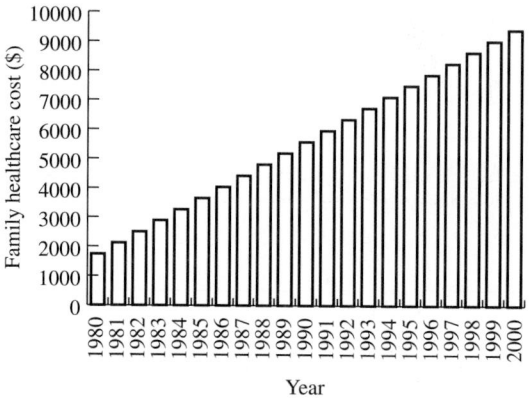

National Average

Year

Review Problems

142. a. {1492} **b.** {0, 1492} **c.** $\{-\sqrt{25}, 0, 1492\}$ **d.** $\left\{-\sqrt{25}, 0, \frac{17}{125}, 1492\right\}$ **e.** $\left\{-\sqrt{2}, \frac{\pi}{2}\right\}$ **f.** $\left\{-\sqrt{25}, -\sqrt{2}, 0, \frac{17}{125}, \frac{\pi}{2}, 1492\right\}$
143. $\{\sqrt{3}, \sqrt{5}, \sqrt{6}, \sqrt{7}, \sqrt{8}\}$ **144. a.** 62,000 **b.** Labrador Retrievers

PROBLEM SET 1.8

1. 49 **3.** 64 **5.** 16 **7.** −64 **9.** 16 **11.** −16 **13.** 64 **15.** $\frac{4}{9}$ **17.** $-\frac{1}{27}$ **19.** $-\frac{27}{64}$ **21.** $\frac{16}{81}$ **23.** $-\frac{16}{81}$ **25.** $\frac{1}{8}$ **27.** −1 **29.** 1 **31.** −1 **33.** −1.728 **35.** $\frac{1}{64}$ **37.** −3 **39.** −7 **41.** 30 **43.** 0 **45.** Undefined **47.** −20 **49.** −31 **51.** −5300 **53.** 165 **55.** −5.8 **57.** $-\frac{16}{9}$ or $-1\frac{7}{9}$ **59.** $-\frac{1}{2}$ **61.** $\frac{3}{4}$ **63.** 0 **65.** Undefined **67.** 1 **69.** −1 **71.** −15 **73.** $\frac{15}{2}$ or $7\frac{1}{2}$

75. $-\dfrac{1}{12}$ **77.** -8 **79.** $17x^2$ **81.** $5x^3$ **83.** $8x^4$ **85.** $-x^2$ **87.** Cannot be simplified.   **89.** 0   **91.** $x^2 + 3x^3$ **93.** 867 grams
95. 56 feet   **97. a.** 62.9%; 58.8%; 55.2%; 51.9%   **b.** Decreased   **c.** 35.5%   **99.** -6.1% **101.** $\dfrac{5}{x}$ dollars   **103.** $\dfrac{c}{12}$ feet   **105.** $\dfrac{12 + x}{2}$
107. $\dfrac{x}{100}$ meters   **109.** b   **111.** d   **113.** \$5,400,000; \$11,400,000; \$29,400,000; \$59,400,000; \$599,400,000; \$59,999,400,000; cost soars upward
117. $\dfrac{50}{x - 1}$ dollars   **119.** $2x$ workers   **121.** t^2 meters

Review Problems

122. $\{1, 2, 3, 4, 5\}$ **123.** $28°F$ **124.** $\dfrac{5}{24}$

PROBLEM SET 1.9

1. -27 **3.** -138 **5.** -15 **7.** -2 **9.** 15   **11.** -16 **13.** 40   **15.** $-\dfrac{5}{3}$ **17.** 2   **19.** 64   **21.** -40 **23.** 26   **25.** 144
27. 12   **29.** $\dfrac{4}{3}$ or $1\dfrac{1}{3}$ **31.** 2   **33.** $-\dfrac{1}{20}$ **35.** 38   **37.** 4   **39.** -25 **41.** 7   **43.** -10 **45.** -1 **47.** -3 **49.** -87 **51.** 3
53. -36 **55.** 14   **57.** $5x - 13$ **59.** $-15x + 39$ **61.** $15 - 3y$ **63.** $-25 - 16y$ **65.** $78x + 6y$ **67.** $-4x + 16y$ **69.** 40; 190
71. Increases rapidly   **73.** 34 people   **75.** $C = 645, 1114, 1583; T = 1562, 1480, 1398$; sales of compact discs are increasing; sales of turntables
are decreasing.   **77.** 151 million; 179.2 million; 204.6 million; 228.4 million; 251.8 million; very close
79. \$58; \$33; \$24.67; \$20.50; \$18; yes; decreases   **81.** d   **83. a.** Very close

b.

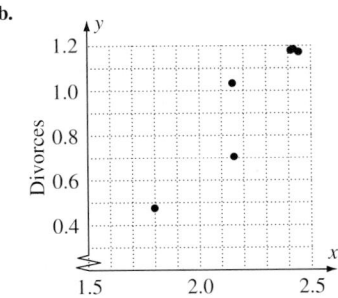

As the number of marriages increase, number of divorces increase   **85. a.** \$9835.76   **b.** \$9948.94
c. \$10,007.99   **d.** \$10,048.31   **e.** \$10,068.09   **89.** $P = 1$ **91.** $1 \div 2 + 3(4 \times 5) = 60\dfrac{1}{2}$

Review Problems

93. $\dfrac{43}{36}$ **94.** $-48°F$ **95.** 1560 thousand

CHAPTER 1 REVIEW

1. $\dfrac{81}{35}$ **2.** $\dfrac{3}{32}$ **3.** $\dfrac{43}{36}$ **4.** $\dfrac{37}{60}$ **5.** $\dfrac{17}{8}$ or $2\dfrac{1}{8}$ **6.** $\dfrac{5}{9}$; $0.\overline{5}$; 55.56%   **7.** $\{0, 1, 2, 3, 4, 5\}$ **8.** $\{-2, -1, 0, 1, 2, ...\}$ **9. a.** $\{\sqrt{81}\}$
b. $\{0, \sqrt{81}\}$ **c.** $\{-17, 0, \sqrt{81}\}$ **d.** $\left\{-17, -\dfrac{9}{13}, 0, 0.75, 5\dfrac{1}{4}, \sqrt{81}\right\}$ **e.** $\{\sqrt{2}, \pi\}$ **f.** $\left\{-17, -\dfrac{9}{13}, 0, 0.75, \sqrt{2}, \pi, 5\dfrac{1}{4}, \sqrt{81}\right\}$
10. $>$ **11.** $<$ **12.** $>$ **13.** $<$ **14.** 79.2 million   **15. a.** No   **b.** 10%   **c.** Multiple family = 24%; single family, detached = 60%;
single, attached = 6%   **16. a.** 32%   **b.** Stroke   **c.** Accidents, pneumonia/influenza, diabetes, AIDS, suicide, and liver ailments
17. a. 23%   **b.** 128   **c.** Walking, bicycling, camping   **18. a.** 1981; 6 crimes   **b.** 1976, 1978, 1983, 1985
c. 1974, 1977, 1981, 1986, 1991, 1992   **d.** 5 crimes   **e.** 5.7 crimes   **f.** When unemployment is down, crime is up.

19. Quadrant IV

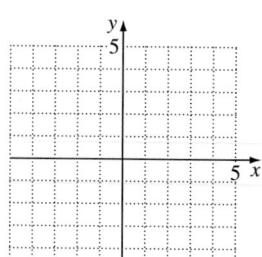

20. Quadrant IV

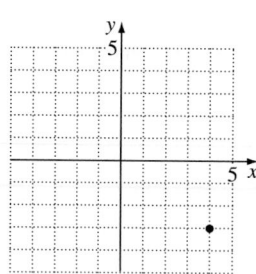

21. Quadrant I

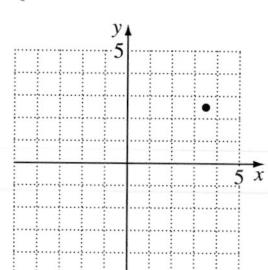

22. Quadrant II

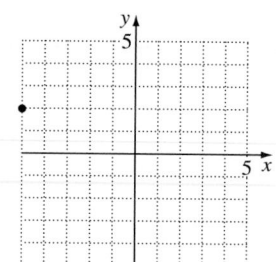

23. $A(5, 6)$; $B(-2, 0)$; $C(-5, 2)$; $D(-4, -2)$; $E(0, -5)$; $F(3, -1)$

24.

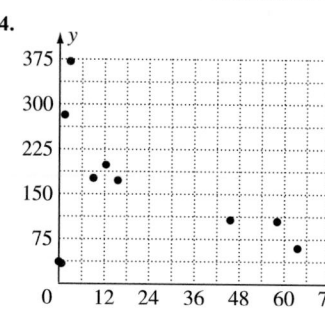

Except for two outliers, as wine consumption increases, deaths due to heart disease decreases.
25. $5 + 3x$ **26.** $1.24t + 313.6$
27. $(6 + 4) + y = 10 + y$
28. $(-3 \cdot 5) = -15x$ **29. a.** $158.5x + 575$
b. \$575 thousand; \$733.5 thousand;
\$892 thousand; \$158.5 thousand
30. 800 feet below sea level   **31.** 27,150 feet
32. 1177   **33. a.** $a + 26$ **b.** $b - 30$
c. $19c$ **d.** The sum of d and 16; 16 more than d; 16 added to d **e.** e minus 38;

e decreased by 38; 38 less than e **34. a.** 50°F   **b.** 14°F   **c.** 20°F   **35.** $5x$ **36.** $4x + 6$ **37.** $39.05 + 0.45x$ **38.** $150 + 10x$
39. $0.65x$ **40.** $\frac{x}{12}$ **41.** $\frac{20}{x}$ **42.** $\frac{6}{x}$ **43.** -3 **44.** $-\frac{11}{20}$ **45.** -7 **46.** 4.1 **47.** 4 **48.** -7 **49.** $-\frac{3}{2}$ or $-1\frac{1}{2}$ **50.** 84
51. -10.35 **52.** $-\frac{3}{11}$ **53.** -120 **54.** 20 **55.** 16 **56.** -32 **57.** $\frac{4}{9}$ **58.** -9 **59.** 2 **60.** -500 **61.** -16 **62.** -111
63. -1 **64.** 14 **65.** $\frac{8}{7}$ or $1\frac{1}{7}$ **66.** 92 **67.** -88 **68.** 14 **69.** 55 **70.** -7 **71.** $\frac{289}{60}$ **72.** $-2x + y$ **73.** $-8a + 6b$
74. $-4x + 15$ **75.** $-18x + 24$ **76.** $-y - 33$ **77.** $-38x - 1$ **78.** $x - 1$ **79.** $2x + 6$ **80.** $x + 5$ **81.** 49,391; 47,845.5; 46,300;
decreasing   **82.** 3 seconds   **83.** \$933 billion; \$3226 billion; very close
84. a.

x	0	1	2	3	4	5	6	7	8	9	10	11	12
y	0	11	20	27	32	35	36	35	32	27	20	11	0

b.

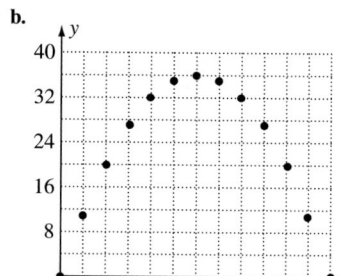

Very similar
85. a. 247 million
b. 264 million; 281 million; 298 million;
315 million; 332 million; 349 million
c. Medium projection
86. 18 seconds

87. No, the bars for 1983 and 1984 in the text are low.

Aids Cases

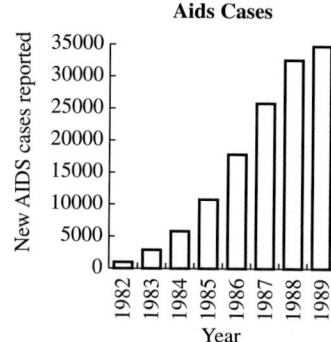

CHAPTER I TEST

1. $\{-5, -4, -3, -2, -1\}$ **2.** $-7, -\frac{4}{5}, 0, 0.25, \sqrt{4}, \frac{22}{7}$ **3.** 62.4 million   **4.** 27%   **5.** Anxiety, Headache, Sprains/strains

6. a. 1991, 15 million crimes   **b.** 1984   **7.** $(-5, -2)$ **8.**

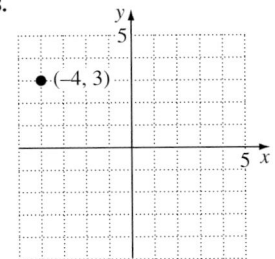

9. $7x + 8x^2$ **10.** $(x \cdot 5) \cdot y$

11. 17,030 feet   **12.** $3hw$ **13.** $6x + 2$ **14.** 14.5   **15.** -11 **16.** $-\dfrac{3}{44}$ **17.** -3.1 **18.** -51 **19.** $\dfrac{1}{5}$ **20.** -5 **21.** $-\dfrac{25}{18}$

22. 1   **23.** -24 **24.** 1   **25.** -32 **26.** $4x + 4$ **27.** $-47x - 6$ **28.** $-6x + 10$ **29.** \$1074 thousand   **30.** 4228 cigarettes

Chapter 2

PROBLEM SET 2.1

1. 20   **3.** -17 **5.** -17 **7.** -13 **9.** 6   **11.** -14 **13.** 2   **15.** $-\dfrac{17}{12}$ **17.** $\dfrac{21}{4}$ **19.** $-\dfrac{11}{20}$ **21.** 4.3   **23.** $\dfrac{15}{4}$ **25.** 18

27. $\dfrac{9}{10}$ **29.** -310 **31.** 4.3   **33.** 2   **35.** 0   **37.** 11   **39.** 5   **41.** -13 **43.** 6   **45. a.** \$325   **b.** $M = S - C$

47. a. $F = 32 + \dfrac{9}{5}C$ **b.** 32°F, 41°F, 50°F, 59°F, 68°F

c. (0, 32), (5, 41), (10, 50), (15, 59), (20, 68)

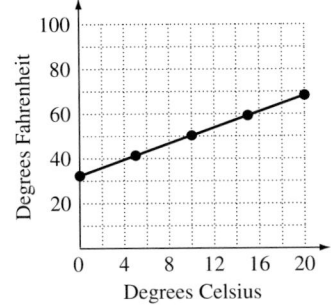

Linear relationship

49. a. \$1,120,254   **b.** Salary in 1993 plus increase minus decrease equals salary in 1995.   **51.** c   **53.** 4.22973

Review Problems

61. -18 **62.** $-8y + 14$ **63.** 60 miles

PROBLEM SET 2.2

1. 9   **3.** 8   **5.** -3 **7.** 5   **9.** $-\dfrac{1}{4}$ **11.** 0   **13.** 12   **15.** -55 **17.** 50   **19.** 12   **21.** -1 **23.** 6   **25.** -7 **27.** 15   **29.** -4

31. 3   **33.** 4   **35.** $\dfrac{11}{3}$ **37.** 3   **39.** -1 **41.** -6 **43.** $\dfrac{9}{4}$ **45.** 200   **47.** -6 **49.** -1 **51.** -3 **53.** -3 **55.** 4   **57.** $-\dfrac{3}{2}$

59. 2   **61.** -4 **63.** -6 **65.** -10 **67.** 18   **69.** $\dfrac{7}{4}$ **71.** $\dfrac{7}{12}$ **73.** $\dfrac{16}{35}$ **75.** 2   **77.** -6 **79. a.** $B = \dfrac{A}{H}$ **b.** 4 in.   **81. a.** 15 sec

b. $n = 5M$ **83.** 1502.2 mi/hr   **85.** $A = sM$ **87.** $x \approx -5.4811$

Review Problems

96. $\dfrac{7}{12}$ **97. a.** 1985   **b.** \$650   **c.** Possible answer: \$6000   **98.** $3y + 11$

PROBLEM SET 2.3

1. 10   **3.** 4   **5.** $\varnothing$ **7.** 6   **9.** $\frac{3}{2}$ **11.** -2 **13.** 8   **15.** $-\frac{1}{5}$ **17.** -2 **19.** -1 **21.** -4 **23.** 5   **25.** 6   **27.** -6 **29.** 1

31. -57 **33.** $-\frac{7}{5}$ **35.** 1   **37.** 24   **39.** 20   **41.** 5   **43.** $\frac{13}{2}$ **45.** -7 **47.** 3   **49.** 1.6   **51.** -4.2 **53.** $\frac{1}{10}$ **55.** -4.765

57. a. $c = 4F - 160$ **b.** 0, 80, 100, 120, 160   **c.** (40, 0), (60, 80), (65, 100), (70, 120), (80, 160)   **59.** c   **61.** 1.265873

63. -1.679245

65. 0.846978

67. 0.342690

71. $\frac{10}{3}$ **73.** $-\frac{21}{10}$

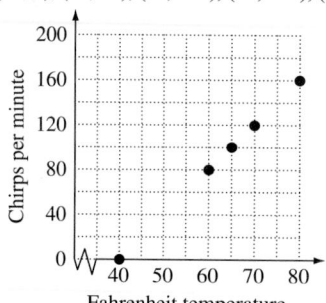

Linear relationship

Review Problems

76. 11   **77.** $5x - 11$ **78.** $<$

PROBLEM SET 2.4

1. 85 mi/hr   **3. a.** 1960   **b.** $t = \dfrac{E - 71.05}{0.215}$ **c.** 2000   **5.** 2688 lb   **7.** 3000 meters   **9.** 7.2   **11.** 20%   **13.** 500%   **15.** 5

17. $16,500   **19.** 12.5%   **21.** $L = \dfrac{A}{W}$ **23.** $b = \dfrac{2A}{h}$ **25.** $P = \dfrac{I}{rt}$ **27.** $m = \dfrac{E}{c^2}$ **29.** $m = \dfrac{y - b}{x}$ **31.** $a = 2A - b$

33. $r = \dfrac{S - P}{Pt}$ or $\dfrac{S}{Pt} - \dfrac{1}{t}$ **35.** $R = \dfrac{E}{I}$ **37.** $n = \dfrac{L + d - a}{d}$ or $\dfrac{L - a}{d} + 1$ **39.** $y = 6 - 3x; y = 0$ **41.** $\dfrac{x + 3}{2} = y; y = \dfrac{13}{2}$

43. $y = \dfrac{6 - 5x}{2}; y = \dfrac{11}{2}$ **45.** $\dfrac{x + 7}{2} = y; y = \dfrac{7}{2}$ **47.** $\dfrac{-12 + x}{-4} = y; y = \dfrac{15}{4}$ **49.** c   **51.** During the year 2114   **53.** 310 K

Review Problems

55. 77%   **56.** 17-year-old boys   **57.** As boys and girls get older, a larger percent is sexually active.

PROBLEM SET 2.5

1. 26   **3.** 16   **5.** 14   **7.** 314 and 315   **9.** 5 m   **11.** 82 ft by 84 ft   **13.** 11% and 13%   **15.** 15 m, 30 m, and 19 m
17. 739,860 and 149,740   **19.** 18, 11, and 9; Germany, 9; UK, 7; Italy, 4; Armenia, Canada, Ukraine, 2; Spain and Slovakia, 1
21. 8000; 1280; 1040; 320; 3600   **23.** $20,000   **25.** $16,400   **27.** $467.20   **29.** $329   **31.** 20 minutes   **33.** 750 advertisements
35. 1999   **37. a.** 40 years; $49,000   **b.** 26.3 years; $33,945   **c.** (26.3, 33,945)   **39.** a   **45.** Canada: 7 inhabitants per square mile;
United States: 62 inhabitants per square mile; Australia: 5 inhabitants per square mile; England: 611 inhabitants per square mile   **47.** $180
49. 22 oranges

Review Problems

52. a. $27,500   **b.** Teachers   **53.** $2y$ **54.** $y = 2$

P R O B L E M   S E T   2 . 6

1. a. Yes   **b.** Yes   **c.** No   **3. a.** Yes   **b.** No   **c.** Yes

5. $x > 6$

7. $y < -4$

9. $x \geq -3$

11. $x \leq 4$

13. $-2 < x \leq 5$

15. $-1 < x < 4$

17. $x > -2$ **19.** $x \geq 4$ **21.** $x \geq 3$

23. $\{x|x > 5\}$

25. $\{x|x \leq 5\}$

27. $\{y|y < 3\}$

29. $\{x|x \leq 3\}$

31. $\{x|x < 16\}$

33. $\{x|x > 4\}$

35. $\left\{x\middle|x > \dfrac{7}{6}\right\}$

37. $\left\{y\middle|y \leq -\dfrac{3}{8}\right\}$

39. $\{y|-\infty < y < \infty\}$

41. $\{x|x < 5\}$

43. $\{x|x \geq -5\}$

45. $\{x|x > -5\}$

47. $\{x|x \leq 5\}$

49. $\left\{y\middle|y < -\dfrac{1}{10}\right\}$

51. $\{x|x > -21\}$

53. $\{y|y > 5\}$

55. $\{x|x < 4\}$

57. $\{x|x > -3\}$

59. $\{y|y \geq -2\}$

61. $\{x|x > -4\}$

63. $\{y|y \geq 4\}$

65. $\left\{y\middle|y > \dfrac{11}{3}\right\}$

67. $\{y|y > 2\}$

69. $\{x|x < 3\}$

71. $\left\{x\middle|x > \dfrac{5}{3}\right\}$

73. $\{y|y > -6\}$

75. $\left\{x\middle|x < \dfrac{19}{2}\right\}$

77. $\left\{y\middle|y \geq \dfrac{12}{7}\right\}$

79. $\{y|y > -3\}$

81. $\{x|x \leq 125\}$ **83.** $\{x|x > 65\}$ **85.** $\{x|x \geq 66\}$ **87.** at least 64   **89.** 29 or less

91. no more than 80°F   **93.** The company must have more than 305 customers.   **95. a.** 17.5 years   **b.** The lines cross at 17.5 years.

97. D   **99.** B   **101. a.** $\{x|x > -2\}$ **b.** $x = -2$ is the x-coordinate where the two lines meet   **105.** No solution   **107.** $\left\{x\middle|x \leq \dfrac{y - b}{a}\right\}$

109. $|x| > 2$ **111.** monthly sales greater than \$3333.33   **113.** b

Review Problems

114. 16   **115.** $22 - 2y$ **116.** $x = -10$

CHAPTER 2 REVIEW

1. 6   **2.** -10 **3.** 5   **4.** -13 **5.** -3 **6.** -1 **7.** 2   **8.** 2   **9.** 0   **10.** 9.3   **11.** -10 **12.** -12 **13.** 30   **14. a.** 50 cm
b. $\dfrac{H - 69.1}{2.2} = F$ **c.** 40 cm   **15.** 48   **16.** 7.28   **17.** 2%   **18.** $P = \dfrac{A}{B}$ **19.** 35%   **20. a.** 40°C   **b.** $C = \dfrac{5}{9}(F - 32)$
21. $W = \dfrac{P - 2L}{2}$ **22.** $P = \dfrac{I}{rt}$ **23.** $B = 2A - C$ **24.** $M = \dfrac{f - F}{f}$ or $1 - \dfrac{F}{f}$ **25.** $V = \dfrac{RT}{P}$ **26.** $y = 2x - 14; y = -2$
27. $y = \dfrac{6 + 3x}{2}; y = 0$ **28.** $y = \dfrac{4x - 3}{3}; y = -\dfrac{5}{3}$ **29.** $y = \dfrac{C - Ax}{B}$ **30.** 10   **31.** 540   **32.** 19 and 20   **33.** 13 ft by 15 ft
34. 12 cm, 15 cm, and 24 cm   **35.** 9   **36.** 26 and 159; Houston, 40; San Diego, 27; Philadelphia, 24   **37.** 10.91 million   **38.** $450
39. $50,200   **40.** 17 days   **41.** No   **42.** 95   **43.** 17   **44.** $\{x|x > 4\}$ **45.** $\{x|x \le -3\}$
46. $\{y|y < 4\}$ **47.** $\{x|x \ge -3\}$ **48.** $\{x|x > 6\}$ **49.** $\{z|z \le 11\}$

50. $\left\{x\middle|x > -\dfrac{15}{2}\right\}$ **51.** $\{y|y \le 2\}$ **52.** $\{y|y \le 9\}$ **53.** $\{y|y \le 0.8\}$

54. $\{x|x \le 0\}$ **55.** $x \ge 24.3$ **56.** $x \le 33.9$ **57.** $24 < x < 35$ **58.** $x \le 33.9$ **59.** at least 64
60. greater than 1670   **61.** at most 24   **62.** 1994

CHAPTER 2 TEST

1. $x = 7$ **2.** $x = -5$ **3.** $x = 8$ **4.** $x = 20$ **5.** $x = -\dfrac{5}{3}$ **6.** $x = 1$ **7.** $\{x|x \le -4\}$;

8. $\{x|x < -6\}$ **9.** $\{x|x > 2\}$ **10.** $\{x|x \le 12\}$ **11.** $\left\{x\middle|x \ge \dfrac{21}{8}\right\}$

12. $y = \dfrac{8 - 4x}{3}$ **13.** $h = \dfrac{V}{\pi r^2}$ **14.** $W = \dfrac{P - 2L}{2}$ **15.** 22   **16.** 14%   **17.** 8 years, 2002   **18.** 14
19. French, 25 letters; Portugese, 27 letters   **20.** Yukon, 1980 miles; Mississippi, 2340 miles; Missouri, 2540 miles   **21.** $2200   **22.** 11 years
23. 200 million   **24.** 1970 to 1975   **25.** 92% or more

Chapter 3

PROBLEM SET 3.1

1. 95   **3.** 43   **5.** $28   **7.** $120,000   **9.** 11 hours   **11.** 2133   **13.** After 6 months   **15.** $15,000 at 9% and $10,000 at 12%
17. $675 at 14%, $1350 at 12%   **19.** $22\dfrac{2}{9}$ liters at 30%, $27\dfrac{7}{9}$ liters at 12%   **21.** 3 hours   **23.** 3 hours   **25.** Add 6 repeatedly: 26, 32, 38
27. Subtract 4 repeatedly: $-1, -5, -9$ **29.** Add the two previous numbers to obtain the next number in the sequence: 47, 76, 123
31. $100^2 = 10,000$ **33.** 27 ways   **35.** 711 or 171   **37.** 73; $8n - 7$ **39.** 15; 21; 78; $\dfrac{n(n + 1)}{2}$ **41.** 7; 9   **43.** 13; $2n + 3$ **45.** 8; 32; 50
47. $9 + 8 + 7 + 65 + 4 + 3 + 2 + 1 = 99$ **49.** Valid   **51.** Invalid   **53.** Invalid   **55.** Invalid   **57.** Valid   **59.** Valid
61. Too little information   **63.** Too little information   **65.** Just the right amount of information   **67.** Just the right amount of information
69. 727   **71–73.** Answers may vary   **75.** 12   **77.** Brother and sister   **79.** one word   **81.** eleven $3 balls, four $4 balls
83. 8 ducks, 12 horses

Review Problems

85. $\{-3\}$ **86.** $\{y \mid y > -4\}$ $-6 \ -5 \ -4 \ -3 \ -2$ **87.** $s = \dfrac{P - b}{2}$

P R O B L E M   S E T   3 . 2

1. $\dfrac{2}{3}$ **3.** $\dfrac{7}{10}$ **5.** $\dfrac{1}{9}$ **7.** 6   **9.** $\dfrac{3}{10}$ **11.** $\dfrac{1}{6}$ **13.** $\{14\}$ **15.** $\{27\}$ **17.** $\left\{-\dfrac{9}{4}\right\}$ **19.** $\{-15\}$ **21.** $\left\{\dfrac{7}{2}\right\}$ **23.** $\{10\}$ **25.** 80 or 80 : 1

27. $\dfrac{25}{39}$ **29.** $\dfrac{335}{587}$ **31.** $\dfrac{5.3}{10}$ **33.** 2 : 1   **35.** 1 : 3   **37.** $\dfrac{31}{17}$ **39.** The ratio increases.   **41.** \$0.048/oz.; \$0.044/oz; 50-ounce size

43. $\dfrac{14}{41}, \dfrac{49}{36}$ dollars   **45.** 70.4 pounds   **47.** 14.4 kg   **49.** 200   **51.** \$33.36   **53.** 13 hits   **55.** D   **57.** -75.21 **63.** 12 days   **65.** $\dfrac{1000A}{A + 2B}$

Review Problems

68. 8   **69.** $\{x \mid x \le 4\}$ $0 \ 1 \ 2 \ 3 \ 4$ **70.** 14 ml

---

P R O B L E M   S E T   3 . 3

1. 75°   **3.** 135°   **5.** 50°   **7.** 50°, 50°, 80°   **9.** 19; 76°; 61°; 43°   **11.** 40°, 80°, and 60°   **13.** 2 angles are 50°, 2 angles are 130°; opposite interior angles are equal.   **15.** 365 miles by 275 miles   **17.** 36 feet by 78 feet   **19.** 6 inches, 11 inches, and 13 inches

21. 50 meters   **23.** 14 m   **25.** $A = 9\pi$ sq in. ≈ 28.26 sq in.; $C = 6\pi" \approx 18.84"$ **27.** 84π m$^2 \approx 1256$ sq m   **29.** 9 times

31. 40 square feet   **33.** 5 in.   **35.** 16 in.   **37.** 16 feet   **39.** 35°   **41. a.** 71 feet   **b.** 4489π sq ft $\approx 14,095.5$ sq ft   **c.** 120 feet   **43.** b

47. 72 cubic cm   **49.** 10 yd $\times$ 10 yd   **51.** 5, 3, 540; 6, 4, 720; $(n - 2)180$ **53.** 8 meters   **55.** 8 ft

Review Problems

57. $x = 8$ **58.** $x = 56$ **59.** 0

C H A P T E R   3   R E V I E W

1. 14   **2.** 8   **3.** \$17   **4.** 120 pounds   **5.** U.S.: 21 million tons; China: 14 million tons; Germany: 6 million tons   **6.** 2020
7. a. Group A, \$45,000   **b.** 18 years   **8.** 7 ounces   **9.** \$300 at 8%, \$700 at 10%   **10.** \$7311.54 at 8%; \$14,723.08 at 9%
11. 4 gallons of 75% salt solution, 6 gallons of 50% salt solution   **12.** 600 students at school with 10% African American; 400 students at school
with 90% African American   **13.** $2\dfrac{6}{7}$ hours   **14.** 6 ways   **15.** $-\dfrac{8}{3}$ **16.** $C = \dfrac{A^2}{B}$ **17.** 4, 9, 12   **18.** $A = B = C = 0$ **19.** Row A   **20.** 0

21.
from
to

where the 4 smaller squares combine to form a fifth, larger square   **22.** $\dfrac{1}{8}$ or 1 : 8   **23.** $\dfrac{1}{30}$ or 1 : 30

24. $\dfrac{2}{3}$ or 2 : 3   **25. a.** $\dfrac{15}{11}$ **b.** $\dfrac{13}{9}$ **26.** 22¢ per ounce   **27.** $x = 5$ **28.** $x = -24$ **29.** 324 teachers

30. 287 trout   **31.** $x = \$76,391.75$ **32.** angle, 25°; complement, 65°   **33.** angle, 45°; supplement, 135°

34. 30°, 60°, 90°   **35.** 13°; 102°;65°   **36.** $x = 3$; 29, 12, 12   **37.** 53 m $\times$ 120 m   **38.** 27 yards, 29 yards, and 31 yards   **39.** 4 feet high by 12 feet wide   **40.** 6 feet   **41.** $A = 25\pi$ m$^2 \approx 78.5$ m^2; $C = 10\pi$ m ≈ 31.4 m;   **42.** 5 yards   **43.** $\dfrac{1}{8}$ **44.** 8 times larger   **45.** $6\dfrac{1}{4}$ feet   **46.** 5 feet

---

C H A P T E R   3   T E S T

1. \$32,000   **2.** 79,808 Hispanics, 143,578 Blacks, 237,236 Whites   **3.** 2016   **4.** \$4000 at 9% and \$2000 at 6%   **5.** 40 liters of the 50% acid solution and 60 liters of the 80% acid solution   **6.** 5 hours   **7.** $9^2 - 6^2 = 45$ **8.** n^2 **9.** 720   **10.** $\dfrac{1}{20}$ **11.** \$0.37 per ounce

12. $x = -65$ **13.** 6000 deer   **14.** \$37.40   **15.** 53°   **16.** 30°, 90°, 60°   **17.** 63π square inches   **18.** length is 2 feet; height is 5 feet
19. 14 feet   **20.** 3.2 inches

CUMULATIVE REVIEW PROBLEMS (CHAPTERS 1–3)

1. $1700E + 330$ **2.** 30,000 sq ft   **3.** $-\dfrac{27}{68}$ **4.** 6°F   **5.** Possible answers: 1992: 37 to 24; 1993: 52 to 17; 1994: 25 to 13   **6. a.** $\{8, \sqrt{25}\}$

b. $\{0, 8, \sqrt{25}\}$ **c.** $\{-3, 0, 8, \sqrt{25}\}$ **d.** $\{-3, -\frac{1}{2}, \frac{1}{7}, 0, 8, 9.3\,25\}$ **e.** $\{\sqrt{29}\}$ **f.** $\{-3, -\frac{1}{2}, \frac{1}{7}, 0, 8, 9.\overline{3}, \sqrt{25}, \sqrt{29}\}$

7. Possible answers: **a.** 1929, 1971   **b.** 1956; 550,000   **8.** $-\dfrac{1}{2}$ **9.** Pages 192 and 193   **10.** 25 trips   **11.** 180 pounds   **12.** $x = 8$

13. $y \geq -2$

14. Colombia: 160, Belgium: 90, Brazil: 270 vehicles per km; France: 40, Norway: 50, Canada, UK: 70, Germany, Thailand, USA: 80, Spain, Turkey: 110 vehicles/km

15. $13x + 39$ **16. a.** $(7, 600)$ **b.** Answers may vary.   **17.** 12.5 feet   **18.** $x = \dfrac{21}{4}$ **19.** $75

20. 70 yds × 130 yds   **21.** 500 hate crimes overall; 115 hate crimes targeted at others; 80 hate crimes targeted at Jews; 135 hate crimes targeted at gays and lesbians   **22.** 14^2; 24^2; $25^2 + 26^2 + 27^2$ **23.** d   **24.** 1020 pounds   **25.** 53°   **26.** 12 sheets or less   **27.** $10,000 at 8% and $5,000 at 6%   **28.** 1.5 hours   **29.** $12 \div 2 \div 3 = 2$ **30.** $m = 2A - n$

Chapter 4

PROBLEM SET 4.1

1. $(-4, -12)$ **3.** $(0, 0), (9, -36)$ **5.** $(0, 6), (-3, 0)$ **7.** $(-5, 6), (10, -3)$ **9.** $(0, 0), \left(2, -\dfrac{2}{3}\right)$ **11.** $(4, 7)$

13. $f(x) = x$ **15.** $f(x) = 2x$ **17.** $f(x) = -2x$ **19.** $f(x) = \dfrac{1}{2}x$

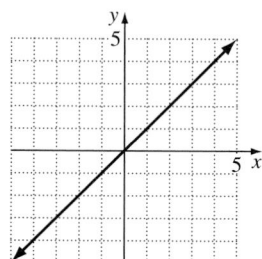   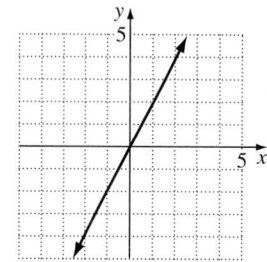   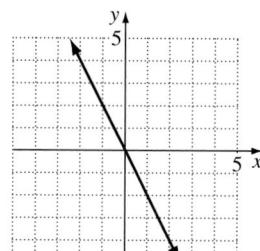   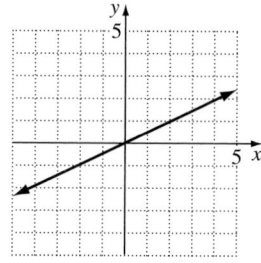

21. $f(x) = -\dfrac{2}{3}x$ **23.** $f(x) = x + 2$ **25.** $f(x) = x - 3$ **27.** $f(x) = 2x + 1$

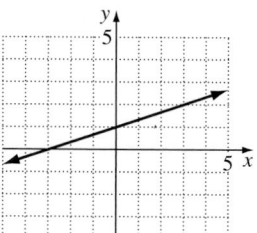   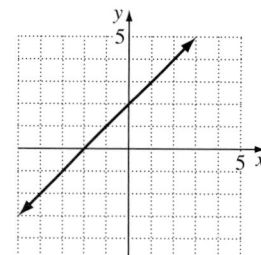   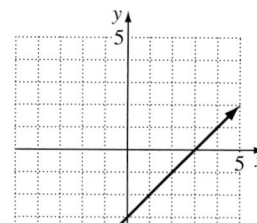   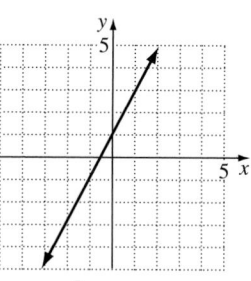

29. $f(x) = \dfrac{1}{3}x + 1$ **31.** $f(x) = -x - 1$ **33.** $y = \dfrac{3}{2}x - 1$ **35.** $f(x) = -\dfrac{5}{2}x - 1$

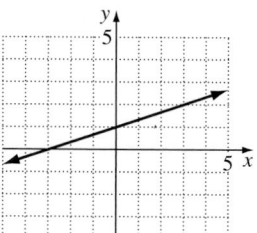   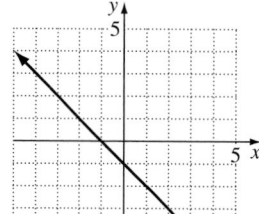   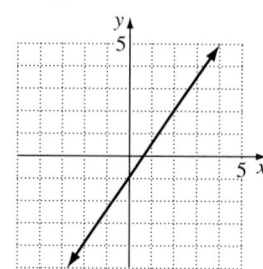   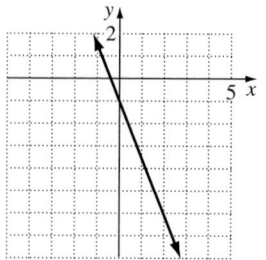

37. $f(x) = \frac{1}{2}x - 3$

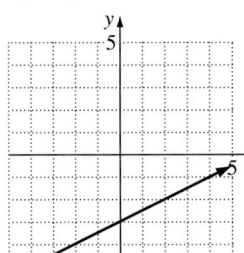

39. $f(x) = -2x + 1$

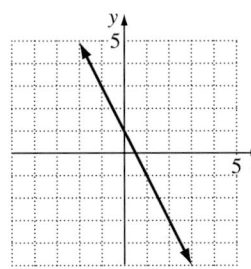

41. $f(x) = x + \frac{1}{2}$

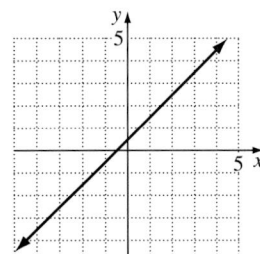

43. $f(x) = -\frac{1}{2}x - 1$

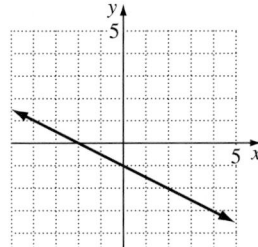

45. $f(x) = 2x - 2$

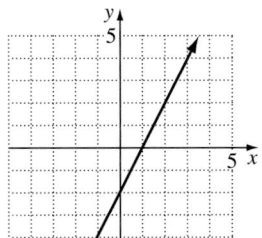

47. $f(x) = -\frac{1}{3}x - 1$

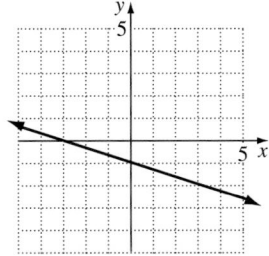

49. 16,116; 23,596; 31,076; In 1980, 1985, and 1990, the average yearly salary was $16,116, $23,596, and $31,076, respectively.

51. 8; 20; 400; A square measuring 2 m, 5 m, and 100 m on a side has a perimeter of 8 m, 20 m, and 400 m, respectively. $x \le 0$ are meaningless because length is a positive measure.

53. a. $0, \frac{1}{5}, 1, 2, 3, 4$ **b.** $M = \frac{1}{5}t$ **55. a.** $(0, 30,000), (10, 30,500), (100,35,000), (1000, 80,000)$

b.

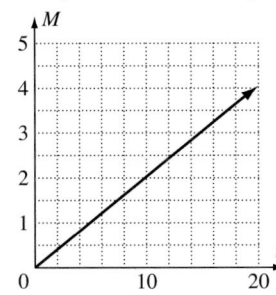

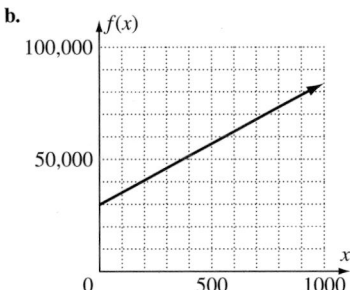

57. $y = 60,000 - 5000x$,   **59.** b
    $0 \le x \le 12$

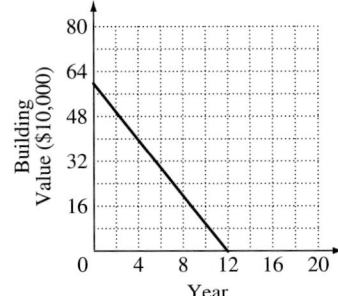

61.

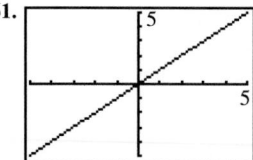 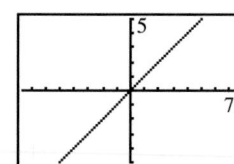

63. $y = 2x - 1$, $y = -1 + 2x$; commutative property of addition

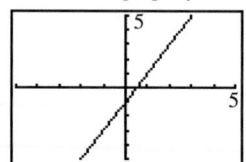

65. $y = 2 + (x + 3)$, $y = (2 + x) + 3$ associative property of addition

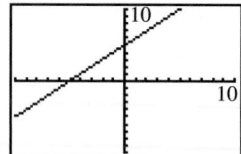

67. Answers may vary.   **69.** $8, 3, 0, -1, 0, 3, 8$

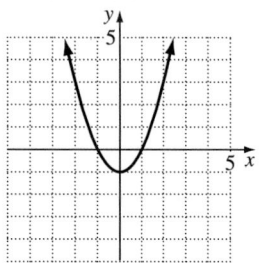

Review Problems

70. 1 **71.** $x \geq 7$ **72.** $x = \dfrac{24}{5}$ or $4\dfrac{4}{5}$

PROBLEM SET 4.2

1. $x - y = 3$

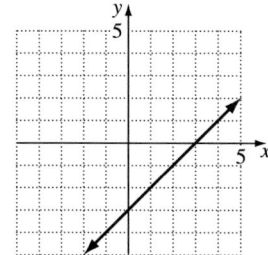

3. $3x = 4y - 12$

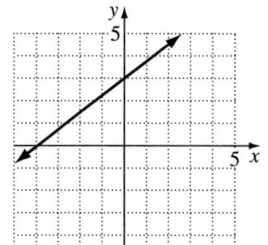

5. $7x - 2y = 14$

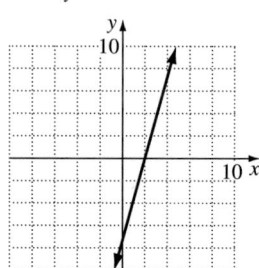

7. $2x - y = 0$

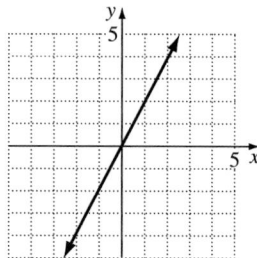

9. $y = -3x$

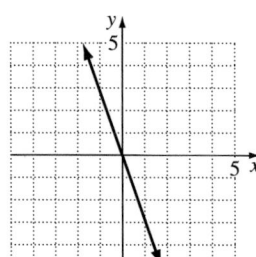

11. $y = 3x + 1$

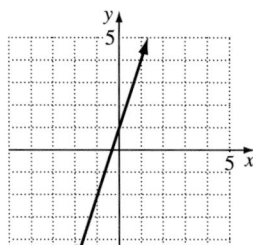

13. $x = 4$

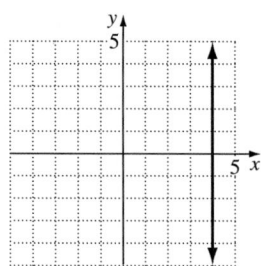

15. $x = -2$

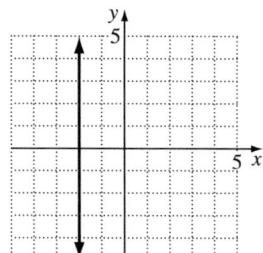

17. $x - 6 = 0$

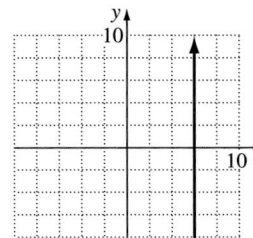

19. $y = 5$

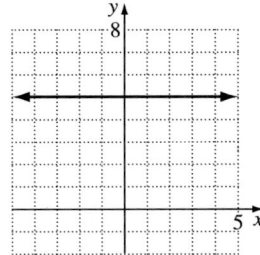

21. $y = -3$

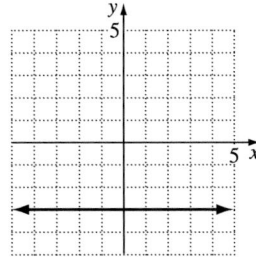

23. $y + 6 = 0$

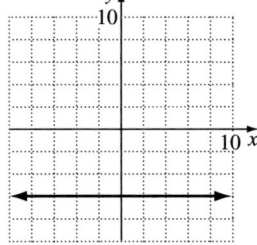

25. $x = 0$

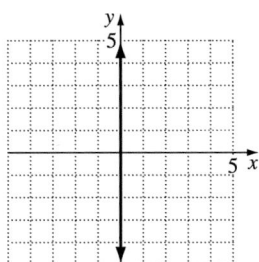

27. $3y = 9$

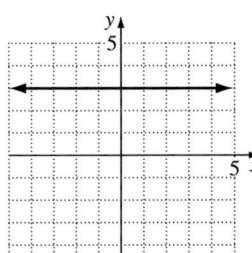

29. $-3x - 2y = 6$

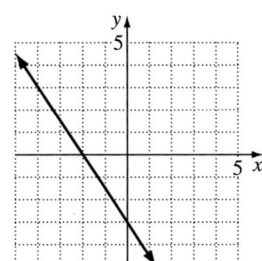

31. $20x - 240 = -60y$

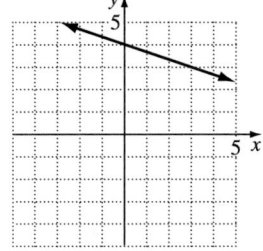

33. $\frac{1}{3}x + \frac{1}{4}y = 12$

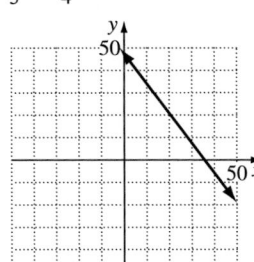

35. a. 300 cal, 600 cal, 750 cal, 1200 cal

b.

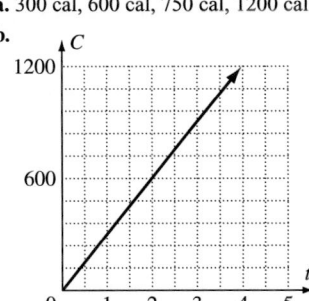

37. a. $C = 50 + 2x$

b.

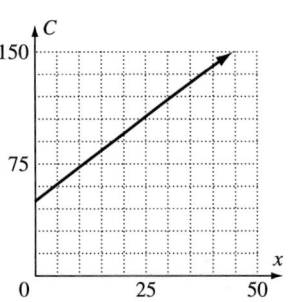

c. $74

39. a. $y = 577 + \frac{69}{5}x$

b. 646 thousand and 715 thousand

c.

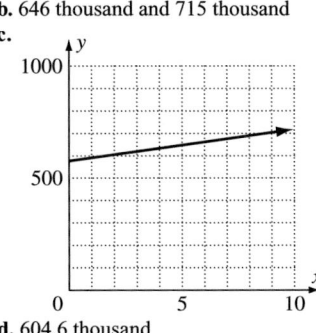

d. 604.6 thousand

41. d   **43. a.** $y = 300 + 0.04x$

b.

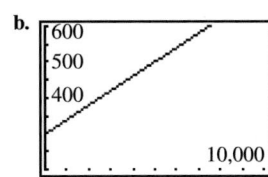

45. Answers may vary.

47. a. $x + y = 11$

b.

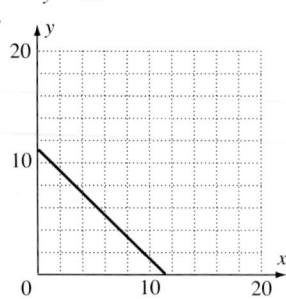

$y = 6.5$; 14.5 m by 14.5 m

Review Problems

49. $-\dfrac{1}{3}$ **50.** 21°, 66°, and 93°   **51.** $18,700

PROBLEM SET 4.3

1. $(-3, 9), (-2, 4), (-1, 1), (0, 0),$
$(1, 1), (2, 4), (3, 9)$

3. $(-3, 4), (-2, -1), (-1, -4),$
$(0, -5), (1, -4), (2, -1), (3, 4)$

5. $(-3, -9), (-2, -4), (-1, -1),$
$(0, 0), (1, -1), (2, -4), (3, -9)$

7. $(-2, -4), (-1, -6), (0, -6),$
$(1, -4), (2, 0), (3, 6)$

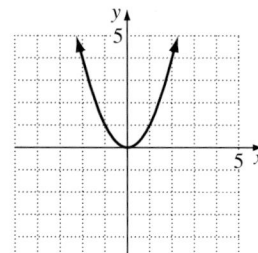
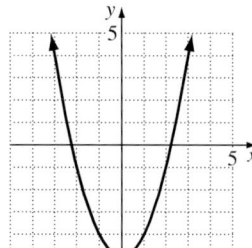
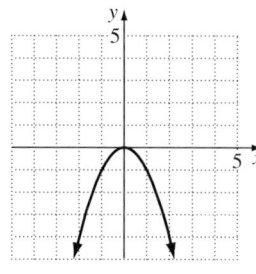
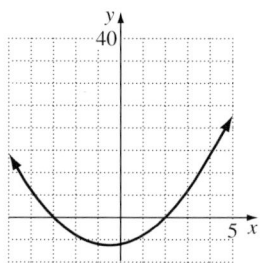

9. $(-2, 4), (-1, 0), (0, -2),$
$(1, -2), (2, 0), (3, 4)$

11. $(-2, -8), (-1, -1), (0, 0),$
$(1, 1), (2, 8)$

13. $(0, 0), (1, 1), (4, 2), (9, 3),$
$(16, 4)$

15. $f(10) = 703$; In 1995,
703 million CDs sold.
23.199 million

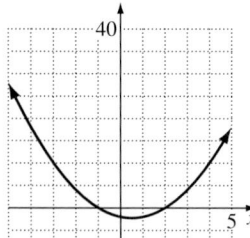
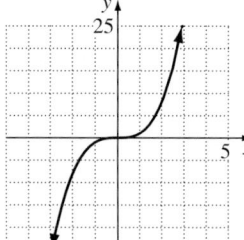
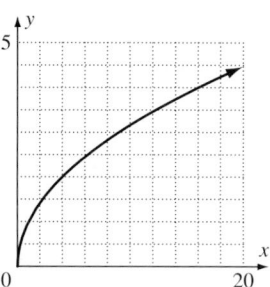

17. a. 0   **b.** 48   **c.** 64   **d.** 48   **e.** 0   **19.** $(12, 150.6), (20, 100.2), (30, 157.8)$; 20 mph   **21.** c

23. $f(x) = 0.0075x^2 - 0.2676x + 14.8$; later part of 1957; 12.4 miles per gallon   **25.** Verify graphs   **27.** Answers may vary.

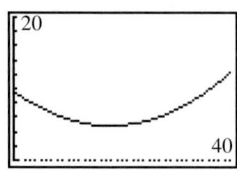

Review Problems

29. $x \geq 91$ **30.** 12 inches and 24 inches   **31.** 2 hours

PROBLEM SET 4.4

1. -1; falls   **3.** $\frac{3}{4}$; rises   **5.** $\frac{1}{4}$; rises   **7.** 0; horizontal   **9.** -5; falls   **11.** Undefined; vertical   **13.** $-\frac{1}{2}$; falls   **15.** -4, falls

17. 0; horizontal   **19.** Undefined; vertical   **21.** 2   **23.** -1 **25.** Undefined   **27.** Undefined

29. $\frac{1}{3}$ **31. a.** L_2 **b.** L_1 **c.** L_3

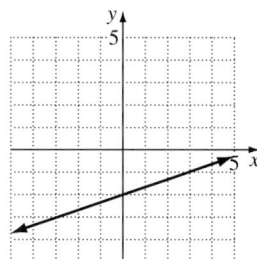

33.   **35.**   **37.** 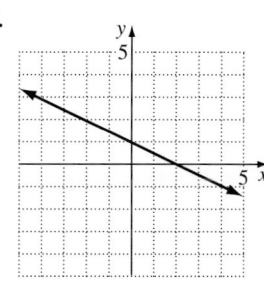   **39.**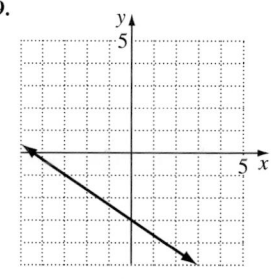

41. 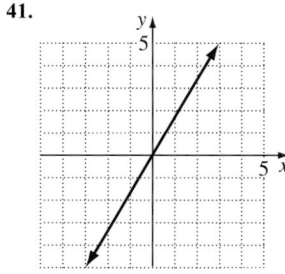   **43.** 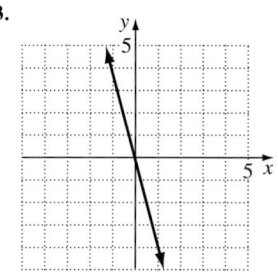   **45.** 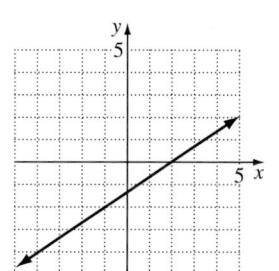   **47.**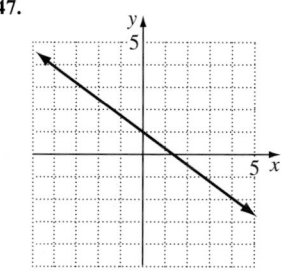

49. 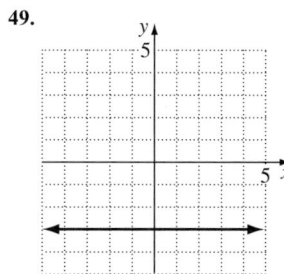   **51.**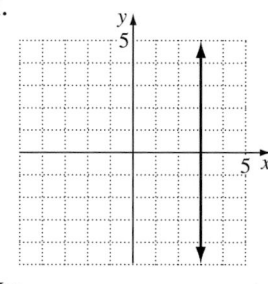

53. Parallel   **55.** The slopes of the opposite sides are equal. Since the opposite sides are parallel, the figure is a parallelogram.

57. $\frac{3}{5}$ **59.** 8% grade   **61.** $\frac{1}{5}$ **63.** -1.1%; percent is decreasing.

65. $m_{AB} = \$500$; $m_{BC} = \$666.67$; $m_{CD} = \$800$ **67.** \$111,429

69. b   **71.** Answers may vary.

73. 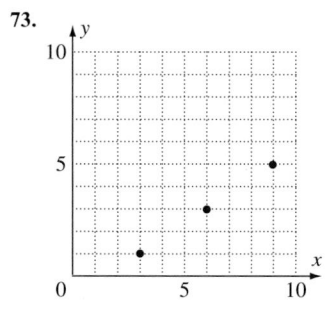   Yes; 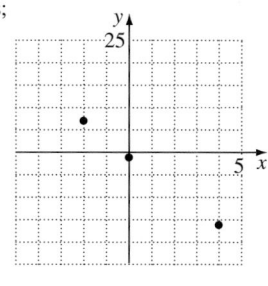   No; If the slopes between each set of two points are equal, then the points are collinear.

Review Problems

75. $11\frac{2}{3}$ in.   **76.** 720   **77.** 2010

PROBLEM SET 4.5

1. $3; -4$ **3.** $-\frac{1}{2}; 5$ **5.** $\frac{3}{4}; 0$ **7.** $-7; -5$ **9.** $5; 7$ **11.** $-1; 6$ **13.** $0; 2$ **15.** $-2; 2$ **17.** $\frac{3}{2}; -3$ **19.** $1; 0$ **21.** $y = 6x + 5$

23. $y = -4x - 2$ **25.** $y = \frac{1}{2}x - 3$ **27.** $y = -\frac{3}{5}x - 4$

29. $y = 2x + 3$ **31.** $y = -2x + 4$ **33.** $y = \frac{1}{2}x + 3$ **35.** $y = \frac{2}{3}x - 4$

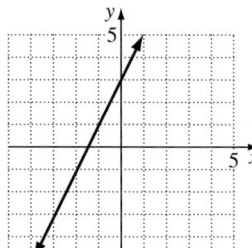   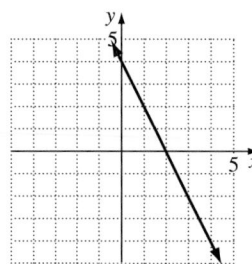   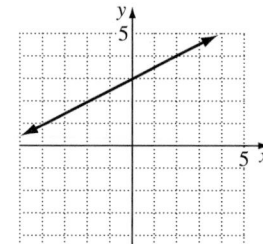   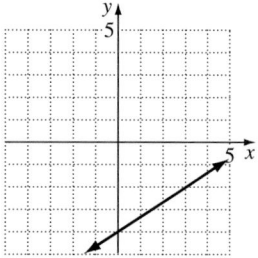

37. $y = -\frac{3}{4}x + 4$ **39.** $y = -\frac{3}{2}x - 1$ **41.** $y = 3x$ **43.** $y = -\frac{5}{3}x$

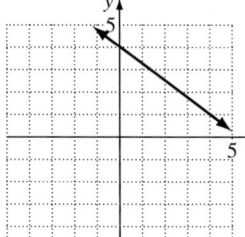   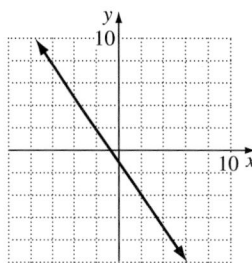   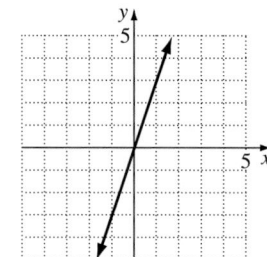   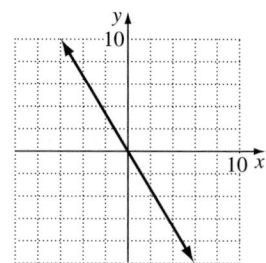

45. $y = 3x + 1; y = 3x - 3$; same slope   **47.** $4x - y = 2$ or $y = 4x - 2; y = 4x + 2$; same slope

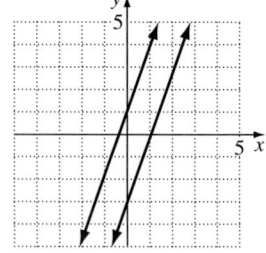   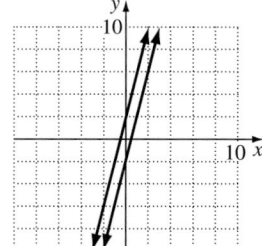

49. 1972; in 1980, 1972 thousand turntables were sold; -82; The average number of turntables sold decreases by 82 thousand each year.

51. a. $p = \frac{1}{33}d + 1$ **b.** 4 atmospheres   **53. a.** $y = -185x + 20{,}151$ **b.** $17,376   **55.** c   **57.** Verify graphs.

59. $T = 10d + 20$

61. Positive slope; number of turntables sold is decreasing because the number of CD players sold is increasing.

63. No   **65.** Yes   **67.** Group Activity

Review Problems

68. 74 yards by 115 yards   **69.** $x \geq 15$ **70.** 1500 yards

PROBLEM SET 4.6

1. $y - 5 = 2(x - 3)$; $y = 2x - 1$ **3.** $y - 5 = 6(x + 2)$; $y = 6x + 17$ **5.** $y + 3 = -3(x + 2)$; $y = -3x - 9$ **7.** $y = -4(x + 4)$; $y = -4x - 16$

9. $y + 2 = -1\left(x + \frac{1}{2}\right)$; $y = -x - \frac{5}{2}$ **11.** $y - 0 = \frac{1}{2}(x - 0)$; $y = \frac{1}{2}x$ **13.** $y + 2 = -\frac{2}{3}(x - 6)$; $y = -\frac{2}{3}x + 2$ **15.** $y - 2 = 2(x - 1)$ or

$y - 10 = 2(x - 5)$; $y = 2x$ **17.** $y - 0 = 1(x + 3)$ or $y - 3 = 1(x - 0)$; $y = x + 3$ **19.** $y + 1 = 1(x + 3)$ or $y - 4 = 1(x - 2)$; $y = x + 2$

21. $y + 2 = \frac{4}{3}(x + 3)$ or $y - 6 = \frac{4}{3}(x - 3)$; $y = \frac{4}{3}x + 2$ **23.** $y + 1 = 0(x + 3)$ or $y + 1 = 0(x - 4)$; $y = -1$

25. $y - 4 = 1(x - 2)$ or $y = x + 2$ **27.** $y - 0 = 8\left(x + \frac{1}{2}\right)$ or $y - 4 = 8(x - 0)$; $y = 8x + 4$ **29. a.** $\frac{1}{2}$ **b.** $y - 115 = \frac{1}{2}(x - 10)$ or

$y - 125 = \frac{1}{2}(x - 30)$ **c.** $y = \frac{1}{2}x + 110$ **d.** Blood pressure $= 150$ **31. a.** $\frac{64}{5.1}$ **b.** $y - 114 = \frac{64}{5.1}(x - 1.3)$ or $y - 178 = \frac{64}{5.1}(x - 6.4)$

c. $y = \frac{64}{5.1}x + \frac{498.2}{5.1}$ **d.** About 243 per 100,000   **33.** c   **35.** b   **37.** $y = 1.75x - 2$

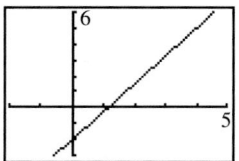

39. Verify graphs.   **41.** Answers may vary.   **43.** $y - 2 = 2(x + 3)$; $y = 2x + 8$ **45.** Group Activity

Review Problems

46. $x > 19$ 17 18 19 20 21   **47.** 9 cm   **48.** $30°$, $60°$, and $90°$

PROBLEM SET 4.7

1. $(3, 2)$; $(-3, 8)$ **3.** $(4, 0)$; $(1, 3)$ **5.** $(4, 0)$; $(1, 3)$ **7.** $(2, 3)$; $(0, 5)$

9. $x + y \geq 4$ **11.** $x - y < 3$ **13.** $2x + y > 4$ **15.** $x - 3y \leq 6$

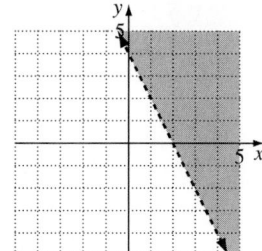 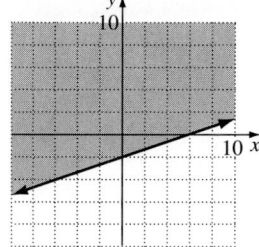

17. $3x - 2y \leq 6$ **19.** $4x + 3y > 12$ **21.** $5x - y < -10$ **23.** $2x - \frac{1}{2}y \geq 2$

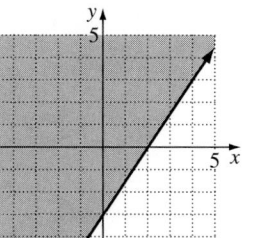 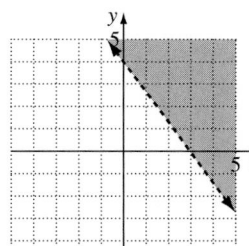 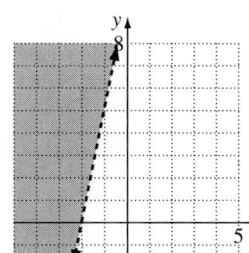 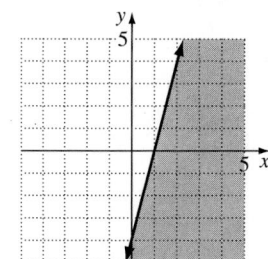

25. $x + y \leq 0$

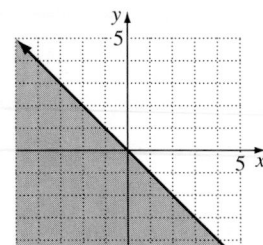

27. $x \geq 3$

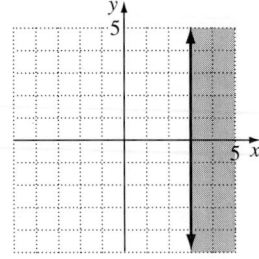

29. $x > -4$

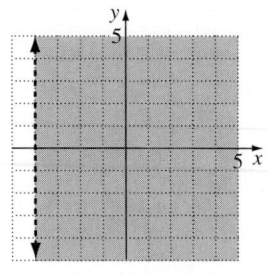

31. $y \leq 2$

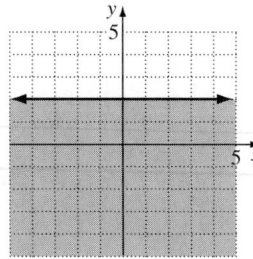

33. $y > -1$

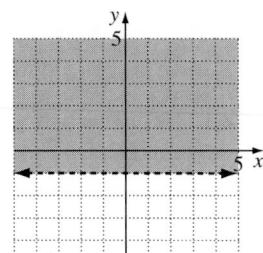

35. $x \geq 0$

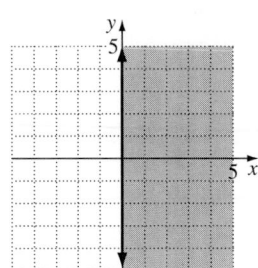

37. $y \geq x + 1$

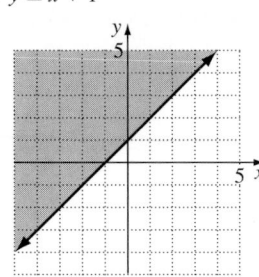

39. $y < -x + 4$

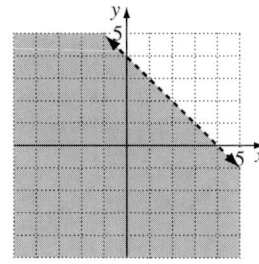

41. $y < 2x + 3$

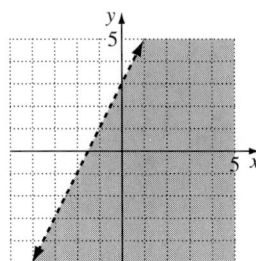

43. $y \geq 3x - 2$

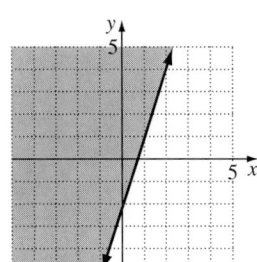

45. $y > \frac{1}{2}x + 2$

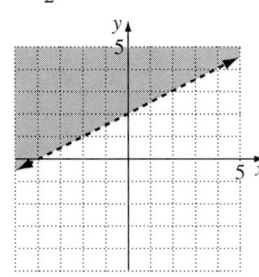

47. $y < \frac{3}{4}x - 3$

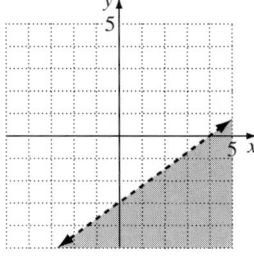

49. $y > 2x$

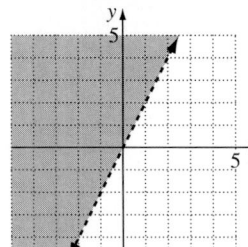

51. $y \leq \frac{5}{4}x$

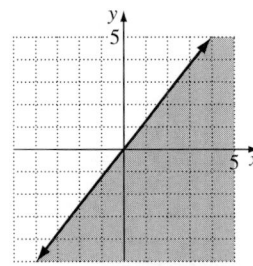

53. $y > -\frac{2}{3}x + 1$

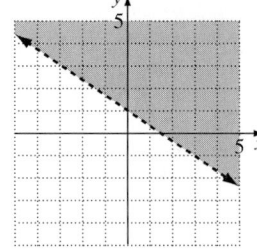

55. f   **57.** b   **59.** e

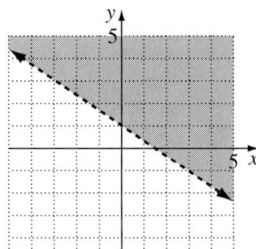

61. a. $75x$ **b.** $50y$ **c.** $75x + 50y > 300$ **d.**

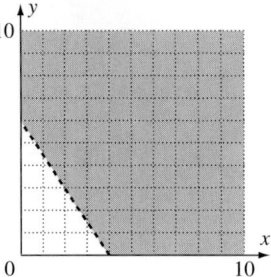

e. Answers may vary.   **63.** d

65. $y \leq -3x + 4$

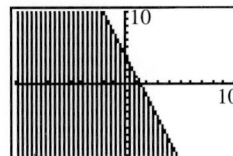

67. $y \geq \frac{1}{2}x + 4$

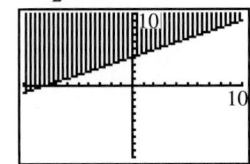

69. a. $x = -2$ **b.** $x = -2$; equal   **c.** $x > -2$ **d.** $x < -2$

71–75. Answers may vary.

77. $y > 2x + 3$

79. $xy \leq 0$

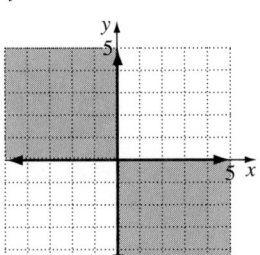

Review Problems

80. $\frac{7}{30}$ **81.** -42 **82.** $-2 \leq x < 4$

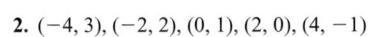

CHAPTER 4 REVIEW PROBLEMS

1. $(0, -12), (-2, -18)$ **2.** $(-4, 3), (-2, 2), (0, 1), (2, 0), (4, -1)$ **3. a.** $y = \frac{1}{2}x - 2$ **b.** $f(x) = \frac{1}{2}x - 2$

c.

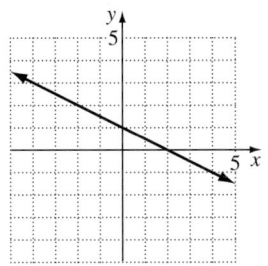

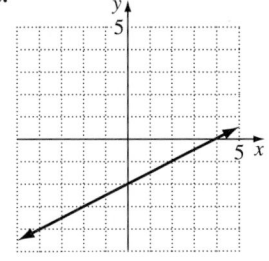

4. In 1980, the world population was 226.5 million.   **5. a.** 48.02, 25.42, −42.38, −155.38; if a bag of sugar is priced at 10¢, 20¢, 50¢, and $1.00, the quantity of bags purchased yearly is 48.02 million, 25.42 million, 0, and 0, respectively.   **b.** As price goes up, demand goes down.

c. $f(x) = -2.26x + 70.62$; negative slope   **d.** Verify graph.   **6. a.** 30 miles, 60 miles, 75 miles, 120 miles   **b.**

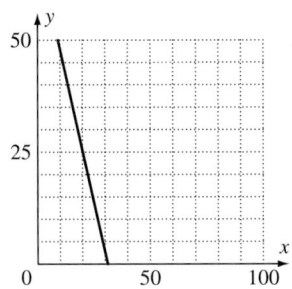

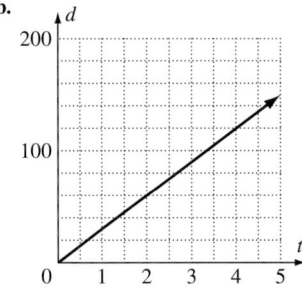

7. $2x + y = 4$

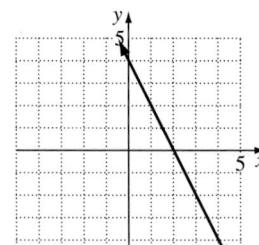

8. $3x - 2y = 12$

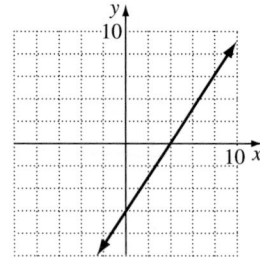

9. $3x = 6 - 2y$

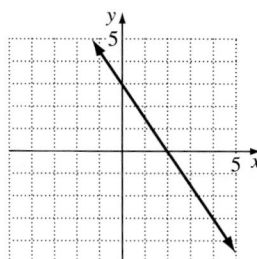

10. $3x - y = 0$

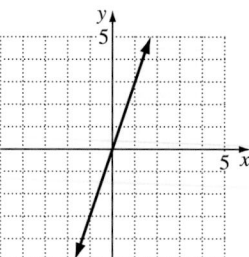

11. $x = 3$

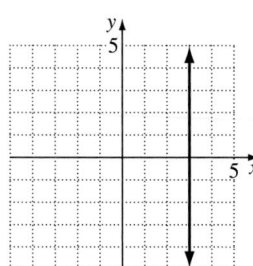

12. $2y = -10$

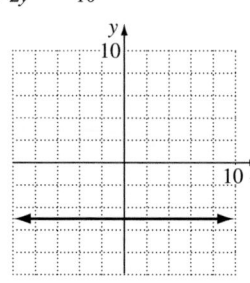

13. a. $S = 0.10x + 200$
b. \$200, \$1200, \$2200, \$3200

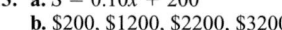
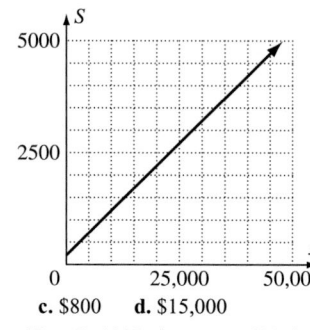

c. \$800   **d.** \$15,000

14. a. $C = 0.25x + 30$
b. \$55, \$80, \$105, \$130, \$155

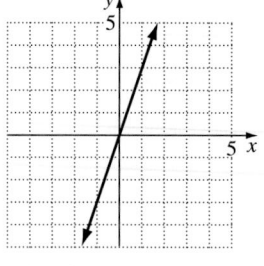
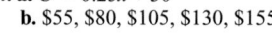
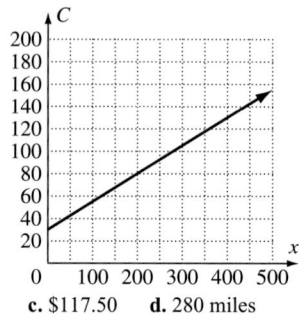

c. \$117.50   **d.** 280 miles

15. $(-3, 7), (-2, 2), (-1, -1),$
$(0, -2), (1, -1), (2, 2), (3, 7)$

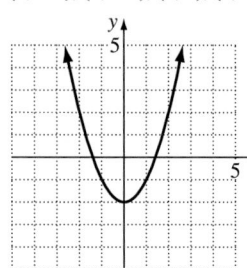

16. $(-3, 4), (-2, 1), (-1, 0), (0, 1),$
$(1, 4), (2, 9)$

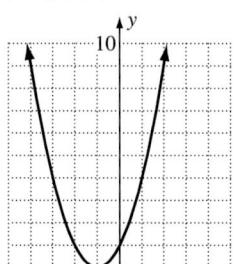

17. a. In 1985, there were 480 thousand inmates.
b. 2780 thousand   **18.** 10.3; in 1970, 10.3% of families were below poverty level.   **19.** 8.46%, 18.42%, 28.38%, 38.34%; The percentage of people with 10 yrs, 12 yrs, 14 yrs, and 16 yrs of education that do volunteer work is 8.46, 18.42, 28.38, and 38.34, respectively. It models the real-world data very well.   **20. a.** 5 P.M.; $-4°$F
b. 8 P.M.; $16°$F
c. 4 and 6   **d.** 12   **e.** Between 7 P.M. and 8 P.M., the temperature rose $16° - 4° = 12°$.   **21. a.** In 1990, the average age is 30 yrs.
b. In 2030, the average age will be 42 yrs.   **c.** In 2060, the average age will be 45 yrs.   **d.** As time passes, the average age increases.
22. $-\frac{1}{2}$; falls   **23.** 1; rises   **24.** 0; horizontal

25. Undefined; vertical   **26.** -2 **27.** 18 feet   **28.** 553; each year, the average salary increases by \$553   **29. a.** 40 years   **b.** 1.4
c. -0.4; productivity is declining   **d.** Between ages 40 and 50, productivity in the humanities is approximately constant.   **e.** Humanities
f. Age 60–70 in teh arts; -0.9 **30.** 5; -7 **31.** -9; -8 **32.** $-\frac{2}{3}$; -2 **33.** $y = -5x + 3$ **34.** $y = -\frac{1}{2}x - 2$ **35.** $y = -2x + 2$
36. $y = \frac{1}{2}x - 1$

37. $y = 2x - 4$

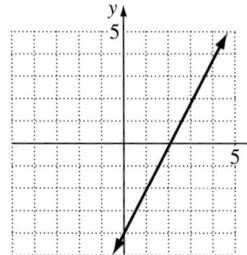

38. $y = -\frac{2}{3}x + 5$

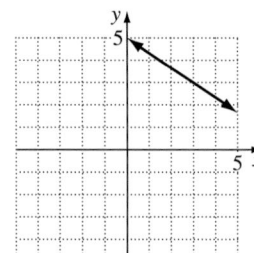

39. $y = \frac{3}{4}x - 2$

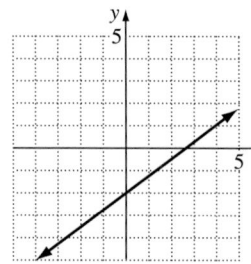

40. $y = -\frac{1}{3}x + 4$; $y = -\frac{1}{3}x - 1$
same slope

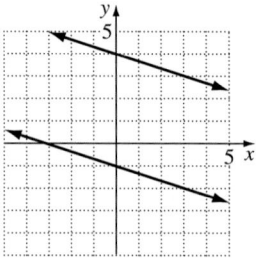

41. a. 14.784; In 1980, there were 14.784 million subscribers.   **b.** 3.657; Each year after 1980, the average number of subscribers increases by 3.657 million.   **42. a.** $y = 3.14x + 87.1$ **b.** 212.7 million tons   **43.** $y - 7 = 6(x + 4)$; $y = 6x + 31$
44. $y - 4 = 3(x - 3)$ or $y - 1 = 3(x - 2)$; $y = 3x - 5$ **45.** $y + 3 = \frac{1}{3}(x + 2)$ or $y + 1 = \frac{1}{3}(x - 4)$; $y = \frac{1}{3}x - \frac{7}{3}$

46. a. 2   **b.** $y - 61 = 2(x - 31)$ or $y - 75 = 2(x - 38)$ **c.** $y = 2x - 1$ **d.** 71 in. or 5 ft 11 in.   **47.** $(-2, -5); (3, -6)$
48. $x - 2y > 6$ **49.** $4x - 6y \leq 12$ **50.** $x + 2y \leq 0$ **51.** $y > 3x + 2$

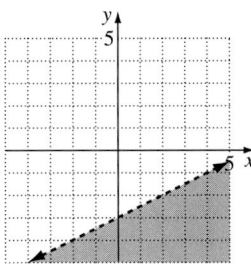   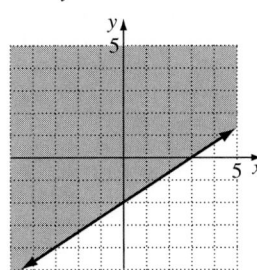   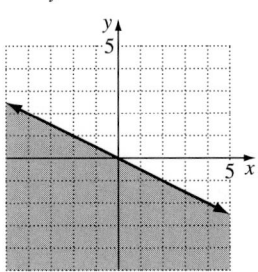   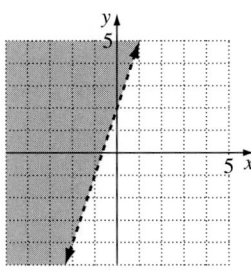

52. $y \leq \dfrac{1}{3}x + 2$ **53.** $y < -\dfrac{1}{2}x$ **54.** $x < 4$ **55.** $y \geq -2$

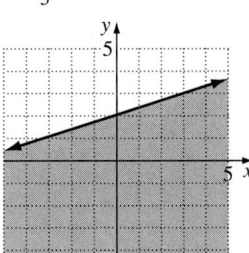   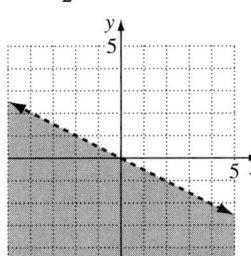   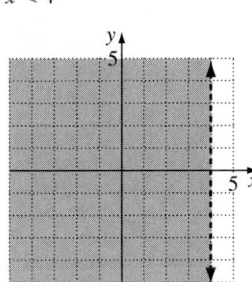   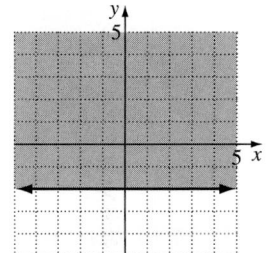

CHAPTER 4 TEST

1. $f(x) = -\dfrac{1}{2}x + 3$ **2.** $f(7) = 33.87$. There were 33.87 million married women in the U.S. in the civilian work froce in 1997.   **3.** $f(30) = 21.44$. 21.44% of the U.S. population graduated from college in 1990.   **4.**   **5.**

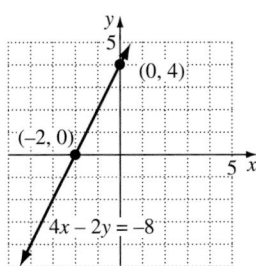   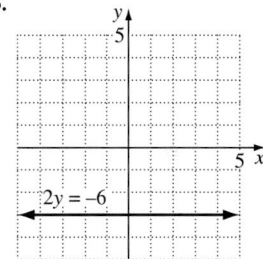

6. $V = 12{,}000 - 1250x$ **7.** \$7000   **8.** $(-3, -7), (-2, -2), (-1, 1), (0, 2), (1, 1), (2, -2), (3, -7)$

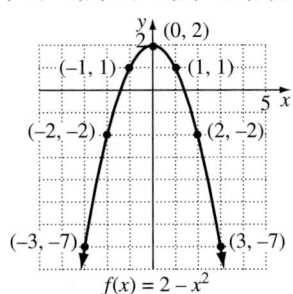

9. a. 30 meters, 2 seconds   **b.** $f(4.5) = 0$. The ball is at ground   level.   **10.** $m = 3$ **11.** $m = \dfrac{3}{2}$ **12.** Slope is $-\dfrac{3}{2}$ and y-intercept is 4.

13.

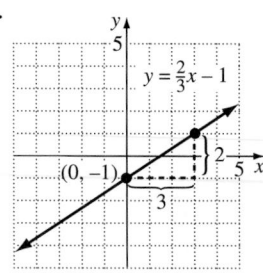

$y = \frac{2}{3}x - 1$

$(0, -1)$

14.

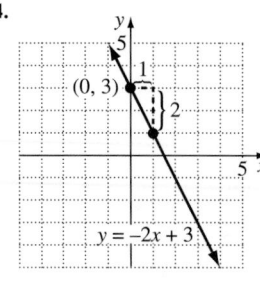

$(0, 3)$

$y = -2x + 3$

15. $y = -6x + 4$ **16. a.** y-intercept is 3231; the population of Arizona, in thousands, in 1985   **b.** Slope is 89; the population increase, in thousands, each year after 1985 of Arizona

17. $y - 3 = \frac{1}{2}(x + 2)$, $y = \frac{1}{2}x + 4$

18. $y + 2 = -3(x - 1)$ or $y + 8 = -3(x - 3)$, $y = -3x + 1$

19.

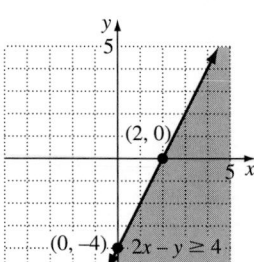

$(2, 0)$

$(0, -4)$ $2x - y \geq 4$

20.

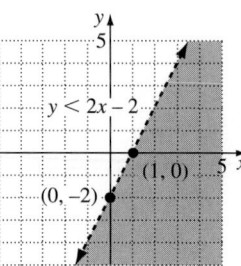

$y < 2x - 2$

$(1, 0)$

$(0, -2)$

CUMULATIVE REVIEW PROBLEMS (CHAPTERS 1-4)

1. $\frac{1}{16}$ **2.** -1 **3.** $\frac{2}{11}$ **4.** $\{y \mid y < -2\}$

(number line: $-5 \quad -4 \quad -3 \quad -2 \quad -1$)

5. $285   **6.** 40 mph   **7.** $0.264 billion

8. 2 in Europe; 6 in Africa; 4 in Latin America; answers may vary.   **9.** 100 feet   **10.** 6 hours   **11.** 27 miles per hour   **12.** 16   **13.** 78°

14. 933; in 1980, the national debt was $933 billion.   **15.**

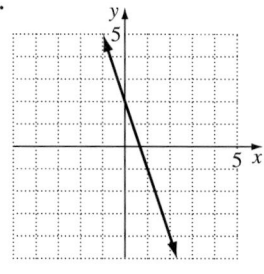

16. Possible answer: 1989: $\frac{1000}{2.15 \text{ million}}$; 1994: $\frac{600}{1.6 \text{ million}}$

17. 24 decimeters   **18. a.** 37, 38, 39, 40, 41   **b.**

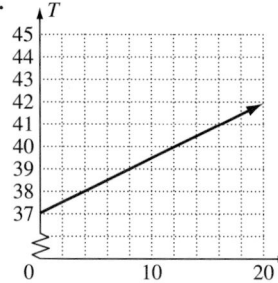

19. $L = \frac{P - 2W}{2}$ or $\frac{P}{2} - W$

20. $y - 3 = 1(x - 1)$ or $y - 5 = 1(x - 3)$; $y = x + 2$

21. $3x - 4y > 12$

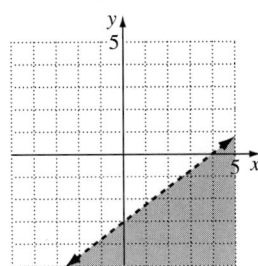

22. a. $3000   **b.** 1976   **c.** They are not evenly spaced from 1960–1985, the space between the marks represent 5 years, whereas from 1986–1993, each space represents one year.   **23.** $\frac{2}{5}$

24. $x = 12, y = 2, z = 6$ **25.** 15 yards   **26.** $(-3, 5), (-2, 2), (-1, 1), (0, 2), (1, 5), (2, 10)$

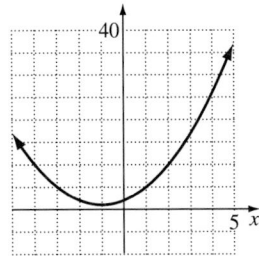

27. -6.2; For each year from 1980 to 1992, the average number of hectares of the tropical forests is decreasing by 6.2 hectares.   **28.** 3.5 hours
29. Possible answer: 18%   **30. a.** 36   **b.** 36

Chapter 5

PROBLEM SET 5.1

1. Solution   **3.** Solution   **5.** Not a solution   **7.** Solution   **9.** Not a solution   **11.** Solution   **13.** $(4, 2)$ **15.** $(-1, 2)$
17. $\varnothing$; inconsistent   **19.** $(3, 0)$ **21.** $\varnothing$; inconsistent   **23.** $\varnothing$; inconsistent   **25.** $(1, 0)$ **27.** $(-2, 6)$ **29.** $(-3, 5)$ **31.** $(-1, 4)$
33. $(2, 4)$ **35.** $(1, -1)$ **37.** $\varnothing$; inconsistent   **39.** Infinite; dependent   **41.** $(2, 3)$ **43.** $(-4, -3)$ **45.** $\varnothing$; inconsistent   **47. a.** 4 pieces
b. $x > 4$ **c.** $10   **d.** $30   **49.** b   **51.** c   **53.** $(6, -1)$ **55.** $(3, 0)$ **57.** $(-2, 3)$ **59.** $(8, 21)$ **61–63.** Answers may vary.
65. $(-1, 1), (2, 4)$ **67.** Possible answer: $y = x - 4$; $y = 1$; infinitely many   **69.** Group project

Review Problems

71. $-4y - 7$ **72.** 2   **73.** 1,820,000 kilograms

PROBLEM SET 5.2

1. $(2, -1)$ **3.** $(3, 0)$ **5.** $(-3, 5)$ **7.** $(2, 1)$ **9.** $(-4, 3)$ **11.** $(-6, -2)$ **13.** $(4, -1)$ **15.** $(3, 1)$ **17.** $\varnothing$; inconsistent   **19.** $(1, -2)$
21. $(-1, 1)$ **23.** Dependent; $x + 3y = 2$ **25.** $(3, 1)$ **27.** $(-5, -2)$ **29.** $\varnothing$; inconsistent   **31.** $\left(\frac{11}{12}, -\frac{7}{6}\right)$ **33.** $\left(\frac{23}{16}, \frac{3}{8}\right)$
35. Dependent; $x - 2y = 9$ **37.** $\varnothing$; inconsistent   **39.** $\left(\frac{1}{2}, -\frac{1}{2}\right)$ **41.** $(5, -2)$ **43.** $(-10, 21)$ **45.** $(-1, 2)$ **47.** $(0, 1)$
49. Length = 360 feet; width = 160 feet   **51.** c   **53.** Check for students   **55–57.** Answers may vary.   **59.** Group project

Review Problems

61. Answers may vary. Samples given.   **a.** $12 + 3 - 6 = 9$ **b.** $12 \div 6 + 3 = 5$ **c.** $(2)(12) \div 6 = 4$ **62.** $37°$ **63.** $\{y \mid y < 5\}$

PROBLEM SET 5.3

1. $(1, 3)$ **3.** $(5, 1)$ **5.** $\varnothing$; inconsistent   **7.** $\varnothing$; inconsistent   **9.** $(2, 1)$ **11.** $(-1, 3)$ **13.** Dependent; $y = 3x - 5$ **15.** $(15, 4)$
17. $(4, 5)$ **19.** $\left(-4, \frac{5}{4}\right)$ **21.** $(-22, -5)$ **23.** $(5, 2)$ **25.** $(0, 0)$ **27.** $\varnothing$; inconsistent   **29.** $(3, -2)$ **31.** $\left(-\frac{4}{3}, \frac{14}{9}\right)$ **33.** $(1, 0)$
35. $(1, -3)$ **37.** $(4, 3)$ **39.** $\left(-2, -\frac{4}{7}\right)$ **41.** $(2, -1)$ **43.** $(-2, -4)$ **45.** $\left(-\frac{4}{5}, -\frac{1}{5}\right)$ **47.** $\varnothing$; inconsistent   **49.** $(5, -1)$
51. Length = 450 feet; width = 197 feet   **53. a.** 1995   **b.** 12.5 per hundred thousand

c. $y = -\frac{7}{8}x + \frac{7033}{4}$; $y = -\frac{1}{10}x + 212$; slope $= -\frac{7}{8}, -\frac{1}{10}$ **55.** a   **57.** Answers may vary.   **59.** $x = 1, y = -3, z = 5$

Review Problems

61. $2x - 3y < 6$ **62.** $y - 6 = -4(x + 1)$; $y = -4x + 2$ **63.** $1200 at 7.5%; $2000 at 9%

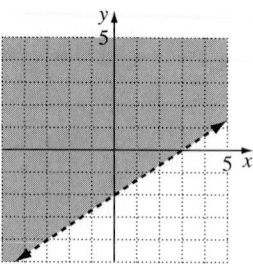

P R O B L E M   S E T   5 . 4

1. a. 141 in Sweden; 65 in Norway   **b.** Sweden has 40%; Norway has 39%   **3.** 16%; 7%   **5.** Eggs have 366 mg; Whopper has 175 mg
7. 2 servings of macaroni; 4 servings of broccoli   **9.** Cost of one sweater, $12; cost of one shirt, $10   **11.** 40°, 70° and 70°
13. 60°, 120°, 60°   **15.** Length = 78 feet; width = 36 feet   **17.** Length = 11 m; width = 5 m; area = 55 sq m
19. Speed of the boat in still water; 9 km/h; speed of current, 3 km/h   **21.** Speed of wind, about 11.6 miles per hour   **23.** $y = 125x$
25. 10; $1250   **7.** Loses money if $x < 10$; profit if $x > 10$ **29.** Check solution   **31.** Answers may vary.   **33.** $x = 4.5, y = 6.5$
35. 7 people upstairs; 5 people downstairs   **37.** (5, 4)

Review Problems

38. $4x - 2y > 8$ **39.** 16   **40.** 0

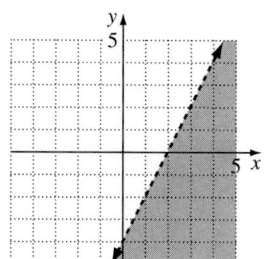

P R O B L E M   S E T   5 . 5

1. $x + y \le 4$; $x - y \le 1$ **3.** $2x - 4y \le 8$; $x + y \ge -1$ **5.** $x + 3y \le 6$; $x - 2y \le 4$ **7.** $x - 4y \le 4$; $x \ge 2y$

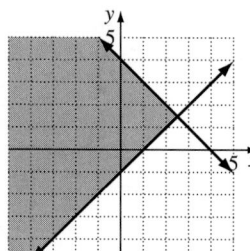   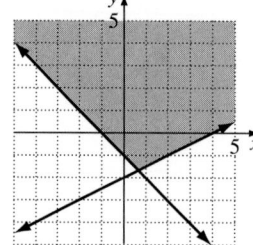   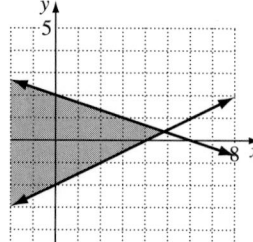   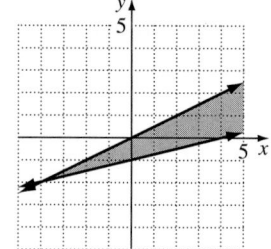

9. $2x + y \leq 4$; $x + 2 \geq y$

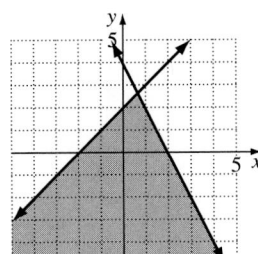

11. $y \leq 2x + 2$; $y \geq 2x + 1$

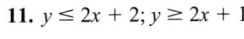
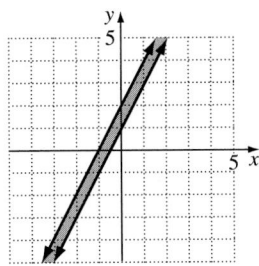

13. $y > 2x - 3$; $y < 2x + 1$

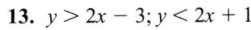
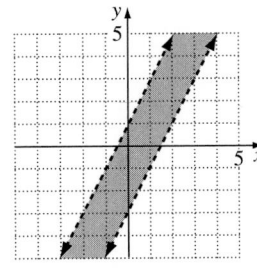

15. $x - 2y > 4$; $2x + y \geq 6$

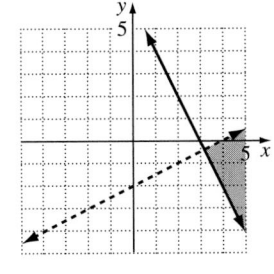

17. $x \geq 3$; $y \geq 3$

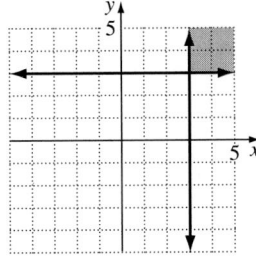

19. $x \geq 2$; $y < 3$

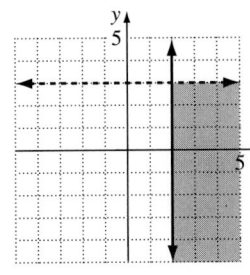

21. $x + y < 1$; $x + y > 4$; no solution

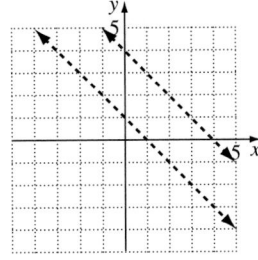

23. $x > 0$; $y \leq 0$

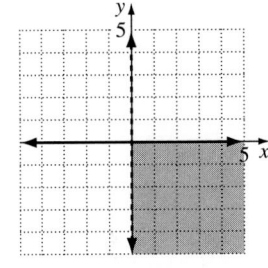

25. $2x + y \geq 6$; $y \leq -2x - 4$; no solution

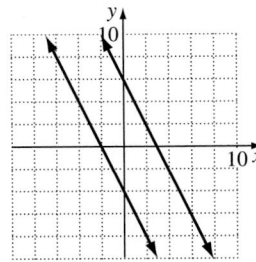

27. $y \geq 2x + 1$; $y \leq 5$

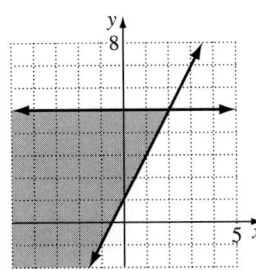

29. $x + y \leq 5$; $x \geq 0$; $y \geq 0$

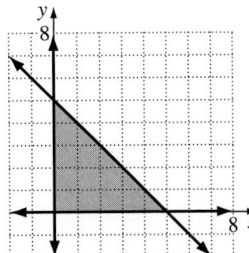

31. $4x - 3y > 12$; $x \geq 0$; $y \leq 0$

33. $0 \leq x \leq 3$; $0 \leq y \leq 3$

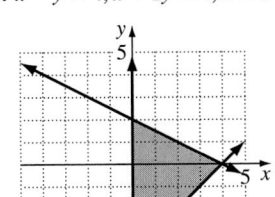
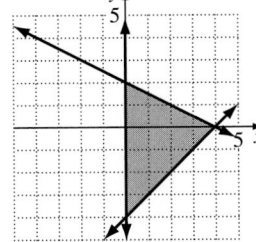

35. $x - y \leq 4$; $x + 2y \leq 4$; $x \geq 0$

37. **a.** $y \geq 60$ and $y \leq 80$ ($60 \leq y \leq 80$)
b. $y \geq 30$ and $y \leq 50$ ($30 \leq y \leq 50$)

39. b   **41.–43.** Answers may vary.   **45.** $20x + 10y \leq 80,000$ **47.** Verify   **49.** 44,000; (2000, 4000); 44,000, 2000, 4000

Review Problems

50. $y = x^2 - 1$

x	-2	-1	0	1	2
y	3	0	-1	0	3

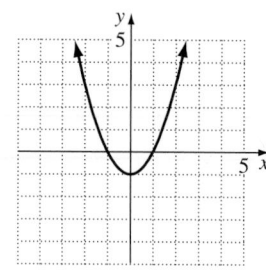

51. $y + 2 = 2(x + 5)$ or $y - 6 = 2(x + 1)$; $y = 2x + 8$; $2x - y = -8$ **52.** -3

CHAPTER 5 REVIEW PROBLEMS

1. Solution   **2.** Not a solution   **3.** $(6, 0)$ **4.** $(3, -2)$ **5.** $(2, 1)$ **6.** $(2, 0)$ **7.** $\varnothing$, inconsistent   **8.** Dependent; $2x - 4y = 8$

9. $(-2, -6)$ **10.** $(-3, 6)$ **11.** $(2, 4)$ **12.** $(-1, -1)$ **13.** $(2, -1)$ **14.** $(3, 2)$ **15.** $(2, 1)$ **16.** $\left(1, \frac{1}{2}\right)$ **17.** $(7, 11)$

18. $\varnothing$, inconsistent   **19.** Dependent; $3x - 4y = -1$ **20.** $(0, 0)$ **21.** $\varnothing$, inconsistent   **22.** $\{(3, 0)\}$ **23.** $\left(\frac{17}{7}, -\frac{15}{7}\right)$ **24.** $\left(\frac{3}{4}, \frac{5}{4}\right)$

25. $(-2, -1)$ **26.** $(20, -21)$ **27.** $\left(-\frac{2}{3}, 2\right)$ **28.** $(3, 2)$ **29.** Dependent; $4x + y = 5$ **30.** $\varnothing$, inconsistent   **31.** $\{(-4, 1)\}$

32. $\left\{\left(\frac{5}{2}, 3\right)\right\}$ **33.** $\{(3, 2)\}$ **34.** $\left\{\left(\frac{1}{2}, -2\right)\right\}$ **35.** Gorilla weighs 485 lbs, orangutan weighs 165 lbs   **36.** 11.3% of women; 21.2% of men

37. 3 glasses of grape juice; 2 glasses of apple juice   **38.** Cost of one pen, $0.30   **39.** Full-size car costs $26,000; compact car costs $15,000
40. 50°, 50°, 80°   **41.** 125°, 55°, 55°   **42.** Width = 5 feet; length = 9 feet   **43.** Length, 7 yards; width, 5 yards
44. Speed of plane in still air, 150 mph; speed of wind, 30 mph   **45. a.** 1000 copies   **b.** $x > 1000$ **c.** $240   **d.** $400
46. $2x + y < 6$; $y - 2x < 6$ **47.** $2x + 3y \leq 6$; $y > 3x$ **48.** $y < 2x - 2$; $x > 3$ **49.** $y \geq 5x - 4$; $y \leq 5x + 1$

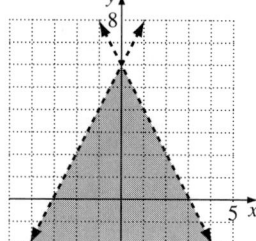   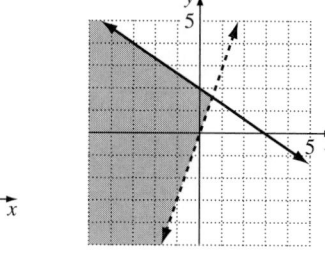   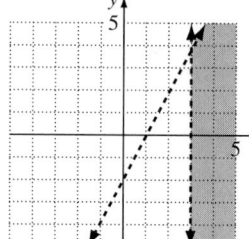   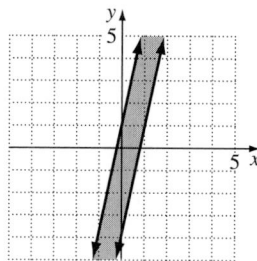

50. $x < 6$; $y \geq -1$ **51.** $2x + 3y \geq 6$; $3x - y \leq 3$

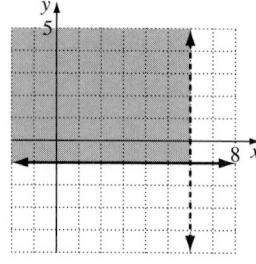   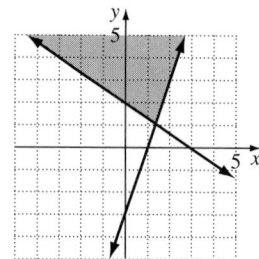

CHAPTER 5 TEST

1. Yes   **2.** $(4, -2)$ **3.** $(-1, 4)$ **4.** $(-4, 3)$ **5.** $(6, 3)$ **6.** $(9, 5)$ **7.** $(9, 3)$ **8.** $\varnothing$ **9.** World War II cost $310 billion and the Vietnam Conflict cost $190 billion.   **10.** A sweater cost $14 and a shirt cost $6.   **11.** Three servings of macaroni and two servings of broccoli.
12. Angle $A = 40°$, Angle $B = 40°$, Angle $C = 100°$ **13.** The speed of the motorboat is 20 MPH and the speed of the current is 4 MPH.

14.

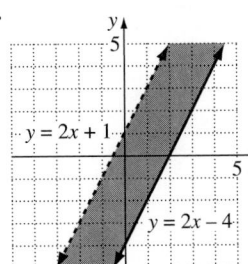

15.

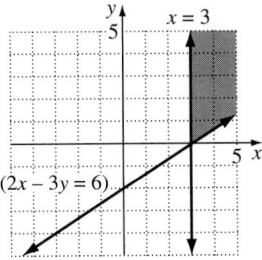

C U M U L A T I V E   R E V I E W   P R O B L E M S   (C H A P T E R S   1 – 5)

1. $y - 12$ **2.** -36 **3.** $y = x - 2$ **4.** -5 **5.** 1 oz of A, 3 oz of B   **6.** $\dfrac{A - p}{pr} = t$ or $t = \dfrac{A}{pr} - \dfrac{1}{r}$ **7.** 5 years   **8.** $d = 6$

9. 20 centimeters   **10.** $t = 2; u = 8$

11. $6x - 3y = 12$ **12.** $y = \dfrac{1}{2}x - 2; m = \dfrac{1}{2}, b = -2$ **13.** $y \geq 3x - 1$

14. $\{(0, -2)\}$
15. 1995 population of U.S. is 255 million;

Protestant = 142.8 million;
Roman Catholic
    = 71.4 million;
Other = 35.7 million
16. 4.8

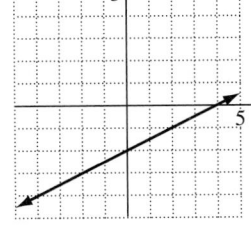

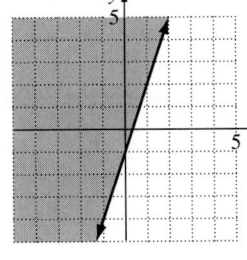

17. $2x - y < 0$ **18.** $\dfrac{1}{3}$ **19.** $\{y \mid y \geq 3\}$

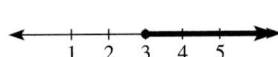

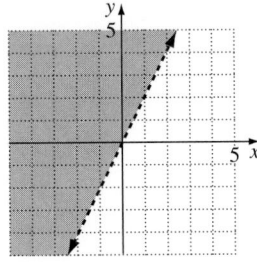

20. Black men = 64.5 yrs; white men = 72.7 yrs; answers may vary   **21.** 2.3 billion dollars   **22.** 6.25 in.   **23.** $\left(\dfrac{3}{2}, -2\right)$ **24.** -6

25. $-8, -3, 0, 1, 0, -3$ **26.** $y < -3$

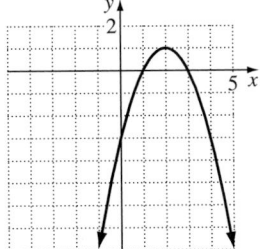

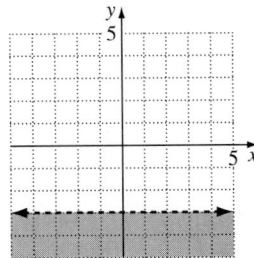

27. Sweden, U.S., Canada, Great Britain, France, Australia, Germany   **28.** Answers may vary.   **29.** 1750 per year   **30.** No

Chapter 6

PROBLEM SET 6.1

1. Binomial; 1   **3.** Monomial; zero   **5.** Binomial; 3   **7.** Trinomial; 2   **9.** Monomial; 17   **11.** Trinomial; 4   **13.** Binomial; 1
15. $-10x^2 + 5x$; 2   **17.** $4x^5 - 3x^2 + 3x - 2$; 5   **19.** $-3y^4 + 3$; 4   **21.** 13; 0   **23.** $-3x + 10$ **25.** $10x^2 + 15x - 11$ **27.** $7x^2 - 4x$
29. $4x^2 - x + 18$ **31.** $4y^3 + 10y^2 + y - 2$ **33.** $3x^3 + 2x^2 - 9x + 7$ **35.** $-2y^3 + 4y^2 + 13y + 13$ **37.** $-3y^6 + 8y^4 + y^2$
39. $-\frac{1}{4}x^3 + \frac{2}{3}x^2 - x - 8$ **41.** $0.01x^5 + x^4 - 0.1x^3 + 0.3x + 0.33$ **43.** $-2x - 10$ **45.** $-5x^2 - 9x - 12$ **47.** $-5x^2 - x$
49. $-4x^2 - 4x - 6$ **51.** $-2y - 6$ **53.** $6y^3 + y^2 + 7y - 20$ **55.** $-n^7 + n^3 + n^2 + 2$ **57.** $y^6 - y^3 - y^2 + y$ **59.** $26x^4 + 9x^2 + 6x$
61. $11y^3 - 3y^2$ **63.** $-2x^2 - x + 1$ **65.** $-\frac{1}{4}x^4 - \frac{7}{15}x^3 - 0.3$ **67.** $-y^3 + 8y^2 - 3y - 14$ **69.** $-5x^3 - 6x^2 + x - 4$
71. $7x^4 - 2x^3 + 4x - 2$ **73.** $8x^2 + 7x - 5$ **75.** $4x + 6$ **77.** $10x^2 - 7$ **79.** $-4y^2 - 7y + 5$ **81.** $9x^3 + 11x^2 - 8$
83. $-y^3 + 8y^2 + y + 14$ **85.** $7x^4 - 2x^3 + 3x^2 - x + 2$ **87.** $-\frac{1}{2}y^3 - \frac{3}{4}y^2 + \frac{11}{8}y + \frac{1}{4}$ **89.** 46 eggs   **91.** $f(10) = 385$
93. a. (0, 0), (2, 192), (4, 256), (6,192), (8, 0)   **b.** 8 seconds   **c.** 4 seconds; 256 feet   **95.** $5y^2$ **97.** c   **99–101.** Answers may vary.   **103.** $2x^2 + 20x$

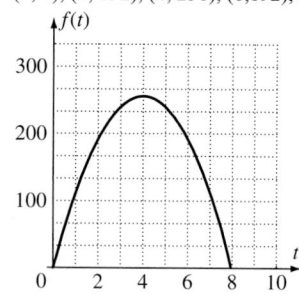

Review Problems

105. 81   **106.** $x \geq -4$ **107.** (2, –2)

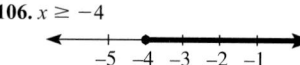

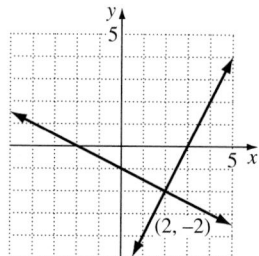

PROBLEM SET 6.2

1. 32   **3.** 81   **5.** x^{10} **7.** r^9 **9.** $8x^5$ **11.** $2y^{14}$ **13.** $-21y^8$ **15.** $6x^5$ **17.** x^6 **19.** $-48x^7$ **21.** 64   **23.** x^{12} **25.** r^{96}
27. $25x^2$ **29.** $-8y^3$ **31.** $16x^2$ **33.** $4x^4$ **35.** $64y^6$ **37.** $-27y^{12}$ **39.** $-32x^{35}$ **41.** $20x^3$ **43.** $x^2 - 3x$ **45.** $-x^2 - 4x$
47. $2x^2 - 12x$ **49.** $-12y^2 - 20y$ **51.** $4x^3 - 8x^2$ **53.** $2x^4 + 6x^3$ **55.** $-5x^4 + 5x^3$ **57.** $-3y^5 + 5y^3$ **59.** $18x^3 - 15x^2$
61. $20x^2 - 15x$ **63.** $-6x^4 + 8x^3$ **65.** $3x^4 - 2x^2 + 5x$ **67.** $3y^3 + 2y^2 + 4y$ **69.** $3x^6 - 5x^3 - 3x^2$ **71.** $6x^4 - 8x^3 + 14x^2$
73. $-2x^3 - 10x^2 + 6x$ **75.** $12x^4 - 3x^3 + 15x^2$ **77.** $x^2 + 8x + 15$ **79.** $x^2 + 20x + 99$ **81.** $2x^2 + 9x + 4$ **83.** $9x^2 + 73x + 70$
85. $x^2 - 2x - 15$ **87.** $x^2 - 2x - 99$ **89.** $2x^2 + 3x - 20$ **91.** $3y^2 - 43y + 52$ **93.** $15y^2 - 22y + 8$ **95.** $4x^2 - 9$
97. $y^3 + 3y^2 + 5y + 3$ **99.** $y^3 - 6y^2 + 13y - 12$ **101.** $2a^3 - 9a^2 + 19a - 15$ **103.** $-2z^3 + 5z^2 + 14z - 8$
105. $-4y^3 + 18y^2 - 26y + 15$ **107.** $x^3 + 3x^2 - 37x + 24$ **109.** $2x^3 - 9x^2 + 27x - 27$ **111.** $2x^4 + 9x^3 + 6x^2 + 11x + 12$
113. $12z^4 - 14z^3 + 19z^2 - 22z + 8$ **115.** $21x^5 - 43x^4 + 38x^3 - 24x^2$ **117.** $4y^6 - 2y^5 - 6y^4 + 5y^3 - 5y^2 + 8y - 3$
119. $2x^2 + 7x - 15$

121. $(2x + 1)(x + 2) = 2x^2 + x + 4x + 2 = 2x^2 + 5x + 2$ **123.** b   **125.** $x^2 - 2x - 3$

127-129. Answers may vary.   **131.** $8x^2 + 8x - 2$ **133.** $5x^2 + 36x + 36$ **135.** $x^2 - 1; x^3 - 1; x^4 - 1; x^5 - 1$

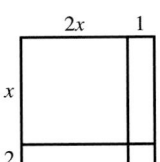

Review Problems

137. $(-2, 3)$ **138.** $5x - 4y \geq -20$ **139.** $\dfrac{81/4}{235/4}$ or $\dfrac{81}{235}$

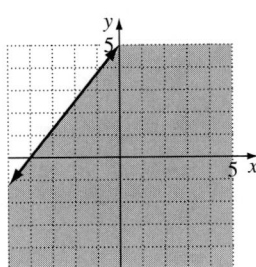

PROBLEM SET 6.3

1. $x^2 + 8x + 15$ **3.** $y^2 - 2y - 15$ **5.** $2b^2 + 3b - 2$ **7.** $2x^2 - x - 3$ **9.** $10y^2 - 9y - 9$ **11.** $12y^2 - 43y + 35$ **13.** $x^4 - 8x^2 + 15$

15. $3y^6 + 14y^3 + 8$ **17.** $6y^{12} - 16y^6 + 10$ **19.** $x^3 + 2x^2 - 3x - 6$ **21.** $20 + 9y - 20y^2$ **23.** $-12 + 5y + 2y^2$ **25.** $15 + r - 2r^2$

27. $18x^{20} + 30x^{10} - 28$ **29.** $x^3 + 5x^2 - 3x - 15$ **31.** $8x^5 - 12x^3 + 2x^2 - 3$ **33.** $x^2 - 9$ **35.** $9x^2 - 4$ **37.** $9r^2 - 16$ **39.** $9 - r^2$

41. $25 - 49x^2$ **43.** $4x^2 - \dfrac{1}{4}$ **45.** $y^4 - 1$ **47.** $r^6 - 4$ **49.** $1 - y^8$ **51.** $x^2 + 4x + 4$ **53.** $y^2 - 6y + 9$ **55.** $4x^4 + 12x^2 + 9$

57. $16x^4 - 8x^2 + 1$ **59.** $4x^2 + 2x + \dfrac{1}{4}$ **61.** $16y^2 - 2y + \dfrac{1}{16}$ **63.** $49 - 28x + 4x^2$ **65.** $49 - 168y^3 + 144y^6$ **67.** $-3x^2 - 22x - 35$

69. $4x^2 - 20x + 25$ **71.** $9x^2 - 121$ **73.** $7m^6 + 7m^5 + m^4 + m^3$ **75.** $y^3 - 125$ **77.** $\dfrac{16}{25} - 4x^6$ **79.** $8x^4 - 10x^2 - 33$ **81.** $x^2 + 2x + 1$

83. $4x^2 - 9$ **85.** $2x^2 + 2x + 1$ **87.** $(x + 3)^2$

89. a. $8x + 16$ square inches   **b.** $g(x) = 8x + 16$ **c.**   **d.** 1 inch   **91.** $f(d) = 20d^2 + 2d - 6$; 988 desks

93. $f(x) = 4x + 10$; 22   **95.** $f(x) = 3x$; 9   **97.** a

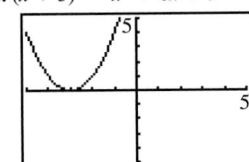

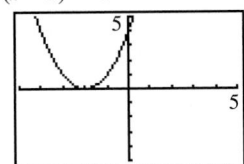

99. a. $(x - 1)^2 = x^2 - 2x + 1$ **b.** $(x + 3)^2 = x^2 + 6x + 9$ **c.** $(x + 2)^2 = x^2 + 4x + 4$

101–103. Answers may vary.   **105.** $40x - 40$ **107.** $x^2 - 2x - \dfrac{11}{2}$ **109.** $8x$ **111.** $(x - 5)(x - 2)$

113. $(x + 2)^2 + 25 - x(x + 4) + 6 = 35; x^2 + 4x + 4 + 25 - x^2 - 4x + 6 = 35; 35 = 35$ **115.** Group problem

Review Problems

116. $y = -\frac{1}{2}x + 3$ **117.** $<$ **118.** $-\frac{7}{5}$

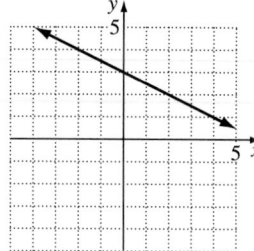

P R O B L E M   S E T   6 . 4

1. -17 **3.** -273 **5.** 8 **7.** 9 **9.** $1, -5, 6, -3; 5, 9, 2, 0$; degree $= 9$ **11.** $4, -5, 12; 4, 3, 3$; degree $= 4$ **13.** $7x^2y - 4xy$
15. $2y^2z + 13yz + 13$ **17.** $-5x^3 + 8xy - 9y^2$ **19.** $a^4b^2 + 8a^3b + b - 6a$ **21.** $-3x^2y^2 + xy^2 + 5y^2$ **23.** $8a^2b^4 + 3ab^2 + 8ab$
25. $-30a + 37b$ **27.** $18x^3y^2$ **29.** $-14x^5y^9$ **31.** $-84a^{14}b^5c^6$ **33.** $10x^2y + 15xy^2$ **35.** $18a^3b^5 + 15a^2b^3$
37. $-12y^5z^6 + 56y^4z^2 - 4y^2z$ **39.** $7x^2 + 38xy + 15y^2$ **41.** $2a^2 + ab - 21b^2$ **43.** $x^2y^2 + xy - 56$ **45.** $15a^2b^2 + ab - 2$
47. $49a^2 + 70ab + 25b^2$ **49.** $x^4y^4 - 6x^2y^2 + 9$ **51.** $x^4 + 2x^2y^2z^2 + y^4z^4$ **53.** $x^4 - y^2z^2$ **55.** $x^3 - y^3$ **57.** $a^3 + a^2b - ab^2 - b^3$
59. $2m^4 + mn - 2m^3n^3 - n^4$ **61.** $r^4 - s^2$ **63.** $x^2y^2 - a^2b^2$ **65.** $x^6y + x^4 + 2x^2 + x^4y + 1$ **67.** 2880 board feet; yes
69. 75.36 square inches   **71.** $3x^2 + 8xy + 5y^2$ **73.** $64a^2 - 9b^2$ **75.** $a^2 + 2ab + b^2$ **77.** c

79. $z = x^2 + y^2 - 2x - 6y + 14$ **81.** $z = \dfrac{x^3y - y^3x}{390}$

83. Answers may vary.

85. $8b^2 - 2a^2$ **87.** $4ab - 4b^2$

89. $2ab + \frac{1}{2}\pi b^2$

91. $11a^2 - 3ab$

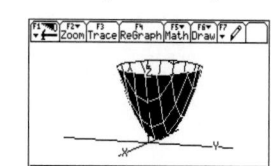
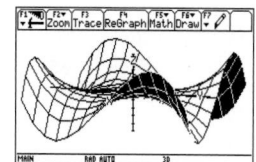

Review Problems

93. $(3, 2)$ **94.** $\dfrac{A - \pi r^2}{2\pi r} = h$ **95.** $x = -17$

P R O B L E M   S E T   6 . 5

1. x^3 **3.** z^8 **5.** $3y^5$ **7.** $-2x^{20}$ **9.** $-\dfrac{a^3}{2}$ **11.** $\dfrac{7}{5}x^{12}$ **13.** 1 **15.** -1 **17.** 1 **19.** 4 **21.** 1 **23.** 0 **25.** $\dfrac{x^2}{9}$ **27.** $\dfrac{x^6}{64}$
29. $\dfrac{4x^6}{25}$ **31.** $-\dfrac{27a^9}{64}$ **33.** $3x^4 + x^3$ **35.** $3x^3 - x^2$ **37.** $y^4 - 3y + 1$ **39.** $-5x^2 + 8x$ **41.** $6x^3 + 2x^2 + 3x$ **43.** $3x^3 - 2x^2 + 10x$
45. $4x - 6$ **47.** $-6z^2 - 2z$ **49.** $4x^2 + \dfrac{3}{2}x - 1$ **51.** $5x^4 - 3x^2 - x$ **53.** $-9x^3 + \dfrac{9}{2}x^2 - 10x + 5$ **55.** $4xy + 2x - 5y$
57. $-4x^5y^3 + 3xy + 2$ **59.** d

61.
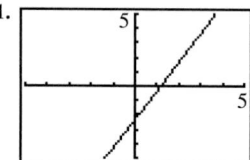

63.a. $\dfrac{x}{2} + 1$
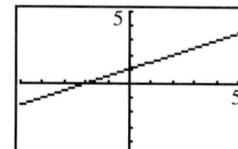

b. $x + 2$
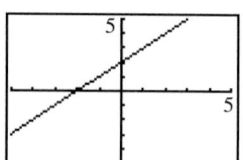

c. $1 + \dfrac{2}{x}$

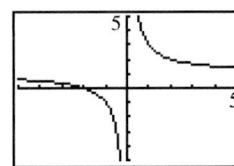

d. x^4

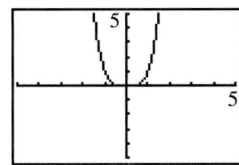

65. Answers may vary.   **67.** $6y^3 + 8y^2 - 5y$ **69.** $18x^8 - 27x^6 + 36x^4$ **71.** 4, 2   **73.** 9, -3, 7

Review Problems

74. $(3, 5)$ **75.** $2x - 3y > 6$ **76.** $\dfrac{2R - L}{3} = W$

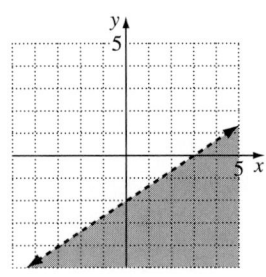

P R O B L E M   S E T   6 . 6

1. $x + 4$ **3.** $2x + 5$ **5.** $x - 2$ **7.** $2y + 1$ **9.** $x - 2 + \dfrac{2}{x-3}$ **11.** $y + 3 + \dfrac{4}{y+2}$ **13.** $x^2 - 5x + 2$ **15.** $6y - 1$ **17.** $2a + 3$

19. $y^2 - y + 2$ **21.** $x - 6 + \dfrac{26}{2x+3}$ **23.** $x^2 + 2x + 8 + \dfrac{13}{x-2}$ **25.** $2y^2 + y + 1 + \dfrac{6}{2y+3}$ **27.** $2y^2 - 3y + 2 + \dfrac{1}{3y+2}$

29. $9x^2 + 3x + 1$ **31.** $y^3 - 9y^2 + 27y - 27$ **33.** $2y + 4 + \dfrac{4}{2y-1}$ **35.** $y^3 + y^2 - y - 1 + \dfrac{4}{y-1}$ **37.** $y^2 - 4y + 2 + \dfrac{9y-4}{y^2+3}$

39. $x^2 + 2x + 3$ hours   **41.** b   **43. a.** Yes

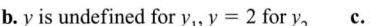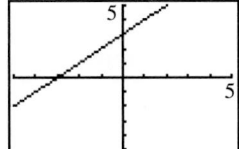

b. y is undefined for y_1, $y = 2$ for y_2 **c.** $x = -1$

45. $2x - 5$ **47.** $2x^2 + 4x + 2 + \dfrac{1}{3x+1}$ **49–51.** Answers may vary.   **53.** $2x^2 - 2x + 5$

55. Answers may vary. $\dfrac{x^7 - 1}{x + 1} = x^6 - x^5 + x^4 - x^3 + x^2 - x + 1 - \dfrac{2}{x+1}$

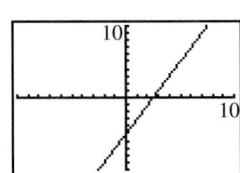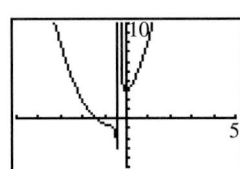

Review Problems

56. $(8, -1)$ **57.** 3.5 hours   **58.** $y \geq -2x + 3$

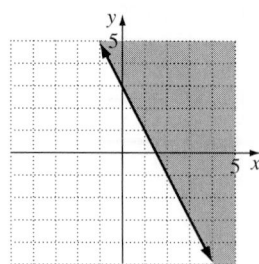

P R O B L E M   S E T   6 . 7

1. $\dfrac{1}{25}$ **3.** $\dfrac{1}{125}$ **5.** 9   **7.** $\dfrac{5}{6}$ **9.** 16   **11.** $-\dfrac{1}{16}$ **13.** $\dfrac{1}{16}$ **15.** 8   **17.** -375 **19.** $\dfrac{1}{x^6}$ **21.** $\dfrac{1}{z^8}$ **23.** $\dfrac{3}{y^5}$ **25.** $-\dfrac{4}{x^4}$ **27.** $-\dfrac{1}{3a^3}$

29. $\dfrac{7}{5w^8}$ **31.** $\dfrac{3a^3}{b^4}$ **33.** $\dfrac{-5x^2}{y^6}$ **35.** $-\dfrac{y^3}{3x^3z^7}$ **37.** $3x^2 - 4x + \dfrac{10}{x}$ **39.** $4y^3 - 10y^2 - 5y + 4 - \dfrac{3}{y}$ **41.** $x^3 - x + 2 - \dfrac{5}{x} + \dfrac{9}{x^2}$

43. $2x^4 - 3 - \dfrac{4}{x} + \dfrac{5}{x^3}$ **45.** $\dfrac{3}{y} + \dfrac{1}{y^2} - \dfrac{2x}{y}$ **47.** $-1 + 3a^2b - 2a^4b^5$ **49.** $\dfrac{1}{x^5}$ **51.** $\dfrac{8}{x^3}$ **53.** $\dfrac{1}{z^5}$ **55.** $\dfrac{1}{z^{11}}$ **57.** $\dfrac{16}{x^{y6}}$ **59.** $216a^{17}$

61. $\dfrac{1}{y^6}$ **63.** $\dfrac{1}{16x^{12}}$ **65.** $\dfrac{z^2y}{4}$ **67.** $\dfrac{2x^6}{5}$ **69.** x^8 **71.** $16y^6$ **73.** $\dfrac{1}{y^2}$ **75.** $\dfrac{1}{a^{12}b^{15}}$ **77.** a^8b^{24} **79.** $\dfrac{ac^4}{b^8}$ **81.** $\dfrac{6}{x^4}$ **83.** $\dfrac{27n^{12}}{8m^6}$

85. 270   **87.** 912,000   **89.** 3.4   **91.** 0.79   **93.** 0.0215   **95.** 0.000786   **97.** 3.24×10^4 **99.** 2.2×10^8 **101.** 7.13×10^2

103. 6.751×10^3 **105.** 2.7×10^{-3} **107.** 2.02×10^{-5} **109.** 5×10^{-3} **111.** 3.14159×10^0 **113.** 6×10^5; 600,000

115. 1.6×10^9; 1,600,000,000   **117.** 30,000   **119.** 3,000,000   **121.** 0.000 003   **123.** 90,000   **125.** 2,500,000   **127.** 125,000,000

129. 0.000 000 81   **131.** 0.000 000 25   **133.** 92,900,000   **135.** 0.00004   **137.** 6.5×10^5 **139.** 9.230×10^3 **141.** 7×10^{-16}

143. 1.54×10^{-6} **145.** 4   **147. a.** 8.4×10^5 km   **b.** 21 times   **c.** 8×10^4 hours   **d.** 9.1 years   **e.** 21, 9

149.

Year	Projected Spending ($)
1995	1.78×10^{11}
1996	1.99×10^{11}
1997	2.19×10^{11}
1998	2.40×10^{11}
1999	2.63×10^{11}
2000	2.88×10^{11}

Year	Projected Spending ($)
2001	3.15×10^{11}
2002	3.45×10^{11}
2003	3.79×10^{11}
2004	4.16×10^{11}
2005	4.58×10^{11}

151. b   **153.** a   **155.** d
157–159. Verify results
161. Answers may vary.   **163.** 25%

Review Problems

165. 27 years   **166.** $x > \dfrac{3}{4}$ **167.** $10x^3 + 11x^2 - 26x + 8$

C H A P T E R   6   R E V I E W   P R O B L E M S

1. Binomial; 4   **2.** Trinomial; 2   **3.** Monomial; 1
4. $f(20) = 399$; The average number of accidents per day in the U.S. involving drivers age 20 is 399.

5. a. 32, 36, 32, 20, 0   **b.**

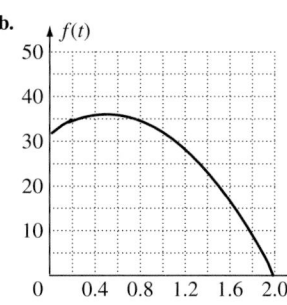

c. 0.5 seconds; 36 feet   **d.** 2 seconds; (2, 0)   **e.** Verify
6. $8x^3 + 10x^2 - 20x - 4$ **7.** $a^3 - 4a^2 - 9$
8. $11y^2 - 4y - 4$ **9.** $8x^4 - 5x^3 + 6$ **10.** $-14x^4 - 13x^2 + 16x$
11. $7y^4 - 5y^3 + 3y^2 - y - 4$ **12.** $3x^2 - 7x + 9$ **13.** $10x^3 - 9x^2 + 2x + 11$
14. $21x^2 - 63x$ **15.** $-20x^5 + 55x^4$ **16.** $-21y^4 + 9y^3 - 18y^2$
17. $-16y^8 + 8y^7 + 20y^6 - 12y^5$ **18.** $x^3 - 2x^2 - 13x + 6$
19. $12y^3 + y^2 - 21y + 10$ **20.** $x^2 - 4x - 12$ **21.** $6y^2 - 7y - 5$
22. $4x^5 - 2x^4 - 12x^3 + 6x^2$ **23.** $3y^3 - 17y^2 + 41y - 35$
24. $8x^4 + 8x^3 - 18x^2 - 20x - 3$ **25.** $3x^6 + 10x^3 - 8$
26. $x^2 + 6x + 9$ **27.** $9y^2 - 24y + 16$ **28.** $16x^2 - 25$ **29.** $4z^2 - 81$
30. a. $x^2 + 50x + 600$ square yards   **b.** $f(x) = x^2 + 50x + 600$

c. 875 square yards   **31. a.** $24x$ square inches   **b.** $g(x) = 24x$

c.

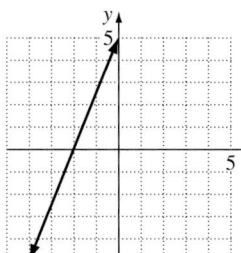

32. $x^2 + 7x + 12$; 90 sq cm   **33.** $x^2 + 9x$; 90 sq cm   **34.** -20
35. 1323 cubic meters   **36.** 4, 9, -17, -12; 3, 5, 4, 0; degree = 5   **37.** $-a^2 - 17ab - 3b^2$
38. $24x^3y^2 + x^2y - 12x^2 + 4$ **39.** $-35x^6y^9$ **40.** $15a^3b^5 - 20a^2b^3$ **41.** $3x^2 + 16xy - 35y^2$
42. $36x^2y^2 - 31xy + 3$ **43.** $9x^2 - 30xy + 25y^2$ **44.** $9a^8 + 12a^4b^3 + 4b^6$ **45.** $49x^2 - 16y^2$
46. $a^3 - b^3$ **47.** $-5y^6$ **48.** $3y^3 - 2y + 6$ **49.** $-6x^3 + 5x^2 - \frac{3}{5}x + 8$ **50.** $z - 3 + \frac{5}{2z}$
51. $5x^2 - 2x - \frac{4}{x} + \frac{3}{x^3} - \frac{1}{2x^5}$ **52.** $9x^2 - 3x - 6y$ **53.** $2x + 7$ **54.** $y^2 - 3y + 5$
55. $z^2 + 5z + 2 + \frac{7}{z - 7}$ **56.** $-6y^{10}$ **57.** $81x^{12}$ **58.** $32y^{15}$ **59.** $47x^3$ **60.** $\frac{1}{x^6}$ **61.** $\frac{6}{y^2}$
62. $\frac{30}{y^5}$ **63.** x^8 **64.** $81y^2$ **65.** $\frac{1}{x^{19}}$ **66.** $\frac{1}{x^{12}}$ **67.** y^{17} **68.** $\frac{y^{12}}{16x^8}$ **69.** $-\frac{12x^2}{y^3}$ **70.** $\frac{b^8}{a^{12}}$
71. 23,000   **72.** 0.00176   **73.** 0.984   **74.** $\frac{1}{49}$ **75.** $\frac{3}{4}$ **76.** $\frac{1}{64}$ **77.** $\frac{1}{25}$ **78.** 7.39×10^7 **79.** 8.94×10^{-5} **80.** 9.725×10^{-4}
81. 3.8×10^{-1} **82.** 8.639×10^0 **83.** 3.7×10^4 **84.** $9 \times 10^3 = 9000$ **85.** 5.0×10^4; 50,000   **86.** 1.6×10^{-3}; 0.0016   **87.** 1000
88. 461.5   **89.** 1.08×10^{10} **90.** 5.4545×10^{33} tons

CHAPTER 6 TEST

1. Trinomial of degree two   **2.** $13x^3 + x^2 - x - 24$ **3.** $5x^3 + 2x^2 + 2x - 9$ **4.** $-48x^4 + 42x^3 + 24x^2$ **5.** $6x^3 + 2x^2 - 29x + 15$
6. $6y^2 - 13y - 63$ **7.** $25x^2 - 30x + 9$ **8.** $20x^5 - 4x^3 - 10x^2 + 2$ **9.** $9x^2 + 24xy + 16y^2$ **10.** $49x^2 - 121$ **11.** $-4x^4$
12. $3x^3 - 2x^2 + 5x$ **13.** $5x - 2 + \frac{3}{x} - \frac{1}{x^3}$ **14.** $x^2 - 2x + 3 + \frac{1}{2x + 1}$ **15.** $-35x^{11}$ **16.** $-27x^6$ **17.** $\frac{4}{x^5}$ **18.** $-\frac{21}{x^6}$ **19.** $16x^4$
20. $-288x^{21}$ **21.** $\frac{1}{x^{18}}$ **22.** $\frac{1}{64}$ **23.** 0.00037   **24.** $\frac{1}{81}$ **25.** $\frac{1}{4}$ **26.** 7.6×10^{12} **27.** 2.5×10^{17} **28.** 1.7×10^{20} **29.** $11x^2 - 2x$
30. $x^2 + 10x + 16$

CUMULATIVE REVIEW PROBLEMS (CHAPTERS 1–6)

1. $x = -\frac{2}{3}$ **2.** 36%   **3.** $\left\{ x \mid x \geq \frac{8}{5} \right\}$ **4.** $5x - 2y = -10$ **5.** $y \geq -\frac{2}{5}x + 2$

6. Inconsistent; $\varnothing$
7. $f(10) = 83.1$; in 1940, 83.1 live births per 1000 women.

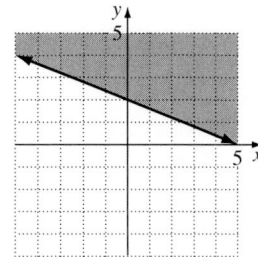

8. (−2, 1)

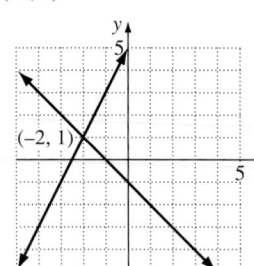

(−2, 1)

9. Education = $14,400; defense = $81,000; welfare = $8100; Social Security ≈ $70,000; interest on debt ≈ $40,000; Medicare and Medicaid ≈ $35,000   **10.** 0.25; 12.75

11. width = 49 feet; length = 91 feet   **12.** $y - 3 = -1(x + 1)$ or $y - 5 = -1(x + 3)$; $y = -x + 2$

13. $106.67 per year   **14.** $\frac{23}{22}$ or $1\frac{1}{22}$ **15.** $x^2 + 2x + 3$ **16.** $x = 25$ **17.** $-6x^3 + 9x + 2$

18. 3 hours   **19.** $f(x) = 6x^3 - 14x^2$ cubic in.; 160 cubic in.   **20.** $12x^3 - 23x^2 + 13x - 2$

21. 104 pounds; 6 bags   **22.** 10 cm, 20 cm, and 40 cm   **23.** (0, 5)   **24.** $2x + 5y \leq 10$; $x - y \geq 4$

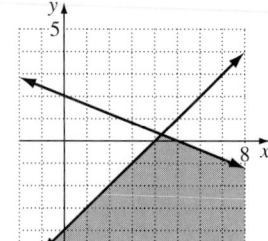

25. $f(10) = 0.6885$; 68.85% of women ages 20–34 were in the workplace in 1980.   **26.** $y = -3x - 3$
27. −4   **28.** $x = 12$, $y = 2$, $z = 3$ **29.** Speed of boat in still water, 9 mph; speed of current, 7 mph   **30.** 10

Chapter 7

PROBLEM SET 7.1

1. Possible answers: $2x \cdot 4x^2$; $x \cdot 8x^2$; $2x \cdot 2x \cdot 2x$ **3.** Possible answers: $-3x^3 \cdot 4x^2$; $-x \cdot 12x^4$; $-2x^2 \cdot 6x^3$
5. Possible answers: $x \cdot 36x^3$; $2x^2 \cdot 18x^2$; $6x^2 \cdot 6x^2$ **7.** $5(x + 1)$ **9.** $3(z - 1)$ **11.** $8(x + 2)$ **13.** $5(5x - 2)$ **15.** $y(y + 1)$
17. $6(3x^2 - 4)$ **19.** $y(25y - 13)$ **21.** $12x^2(3x + 2)$ **23.** $9y^4(3y^2 + 1)$ **25.** $4x^2(2 - x^2)$ **27.** $1(12x^2 - 13y^3)$ **29.** $4(3y^2 + 4y - 2)$
31. $25(4 + 3y - 2y^2)$ **33.** $3y^2(3y^2 + 6y + 2)$ **35.** $50y^2(2y^3 - y + 2)$ **37.** $5x(2 - 4x + x^2)$ **39.** $y^2(-2 - 3y + 6y^3)$ **41.** $3xy(2x^2y + 3)$
43. $10x^2y(3xy - x + 2)$ **45.** $8a^3b^2(2a^2b - 6ab^2 + 1 - 7b)$ **47.** $6abc(9ab^2 - abc + 2)$ **49.** $2(-x^2 + 4x - 5)$; $-2(x^2 - 4x + 5)$
51. $3(a - 5)$; $-3(-a + 5)$ **53.** $4x(-1 + 3x)$; $-4x(1 - 3x)$ **55.** $y^2(-y + 7)$; $-y^2(y - 7)$ **57.** $y(y + 1)$; $-y(-y - 1)$
59. $1(3 - x)$; $-1(-3 + x)$ **61.** $(x + 5)(x + 3)$ **63.** $(7x - 4)(x - 3)$ **65.** $(3x + 1)(2x + 5)$ **67.** $(x^2 + 2)(x + 7)$ **69.** $(4x^2 - 7)(3x^3 + 2)$
71. $(y^2 + 1)(y + 7)$ **73.** $(x^2 + 2)(x - 3)$ **75.** $(3x^2 + 2)(x + 2)$ **77.** $(x^2 + 1)(x + 5)$ **79.** $(5y^2 + 2)(2y - 5)$ **81.** $(y^2 - 3)(y + 8)$
83. $(4y^2 - 5)(2y^3 + 3)$ **85.** $(44 + x)$ in.   **87.** $P(1 + rt)$ **89.** d
91. Correct factorization: **93.** Correct factorization: **95–99.** Answers may vary.   **101.** $8\pi x^2$ **103.** $\frac{1}{2}x^2(12 + \pi)$
$(x + 5)(x - 2)$ $-3(x + 2)$

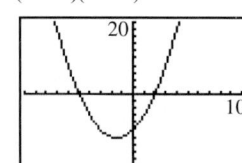   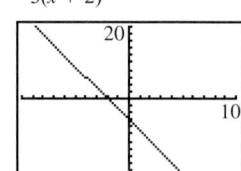

Review Problems

105. $1250 at 6%; $900 at 8%   **106.** (−3, −2)   **107.** $y - 2 = x + 7$ or $y - 5 = x + 4$; $y = x + 9$

PROBLEM SET 7.2

1. $x + 1$ **3.** $y - 2$ **5.** $x + 4$ **7.** $y - 4$ **9.** $y - 3$ **11.** $r - 4$ **13.** $(x + 2)(x + 3)$ **15.** $(r + 1)(r + 12)$ **17.** $(x + 1)(x + 8)$
19. $(y + 3)(y - 5)$ **21.** $(x - 6)(x + 1)$ **23.** $(y - 5)(y - 9)$ **25.** $(r + 3)(r + 9)$ **27.** $(n + 3)(n - 14)$ **29.** $(y + 3)(y - 12)$
31. $(x + 15)(x - 5)$ **33.** Prime   **35.** $(y + 10)(y + 20)$ **37.** $(x - 2)(x - 4)$ **39.** $(r + 1)(r + 16)$ **41.** $(m - 3)(m - 12)$
43. $(y - 7)(y + 8)$ **45.** Prime   **47.** $(y - 7)(y + 3)$ **49.** $(x + 15)(x - 7)$ **51.** $(r + 3)(r + 24)$ **53.** $(a + 2b)(a + 3b)$
55. $(x - 3y)(x + 8y)$ **57.** $3(x + 2)(x + 3)$ **59.** $4(y + 1)(y - 2)$ **61.** $10(x + 6)(x - 10)$ **63.** $3(x - 2)(x - 9)$ **65.** $2r(r + 1)(r + 2)$
67. $4x(x + 6)(x - 3)$ **69.** $2r(r + 8)(r - 4)$ **71.** $y^2(y + 10)(y - 8)$ **73.** $x^2(x - 5)(x + 2)$ **75.** $2w^2(w - 16)(w + 3)$

77. $-2(x-3)(x-4)$ **79.** $-x(x-3)(x+14)$ **81.** $2(x+2y)(x-7y)$ **83.** $x(x+3y)(x+5y)$ **85.** $x-2$ **87.** b   **89.** d
91. $2(x-2)(x+3)$ **93.** $x(x+1)(x-2)$

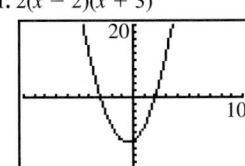   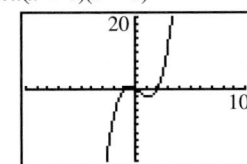

95–97. Answers may vary.   **99.** 12   **101.** 8, 16, -8, -16 **103.** 3 and 4   **105.** $\left(x+\dfrac{2}{3}\right)(x-4)$

Review Problems

106. 2004   **107.** $8y^2-10y-3$ **108.** $9x^2+15x+4$

PROBLEM SET 7.3

1. $x+1$ **3.** $5y-1$ **5.** $4r-7$ **7.** $6y-1$ **9.** $7y+9$ **11.** $15m+22$ **13.** $(2x+1)(x+3)$ **15.** $(2x+7)(x+5)$
17. $(2y-5)(y-6)$ **19.** $(x-1)(4x-7)$ **21.** Prime   **23.** $(3x+2)(x-1)$ **25.** $(3y-5)(y+2)$ **27.** $(3r-28)(r+1)$
29. $(2y-1)(3y-4)$ **31.** $(8t+1)(t+4)$ **33.** $(5x-2)(x+7)$ **35.** $(7y-3)(2y+3)$ **37.** $(5r-3)^2$ **39.** Prime
41. $(5y-1)(2y+9)$ **43.** $(4r-21)(2r+1)$ **45.** $(5y-2)(3y+1)$ **47.** $(4m+1)(2m-1)$ **49.** $(7z+10)(5z-1)$
51. $(3y-2)(3y-1)$ **53.** $(4x-5)(5x-4)$ **55.** $-(4x-3)(x+1)$ **57.** $-(4y+3)(y-2)$ **59.** $(2+3y)(1+2y)$
61. $(2-3x)(19-5x)$ **63.** $(2x+y)(x+y)$ **65.** $(3x-2y)(5x+7y)$ **67.** $(x-3y)(2x-3y)$ **69.** $(x+y)(2x+5y)$
71. $(2a-3b)(3a+2b)$ **73.** $(a+2b)(3a-7b)$ **75.** $(3r-4s)(4r-3s)$ **77.** $2(3x+4)^2$ **79.** $2(2y-5)(y+3)$ **81.** $3(3r-4)(r+5)$
83. $y(2y-5)(y+1)$ **85.** $3r(r-4)(3r-1)$ **87.** $2m(m+7)(7m-2)$ **89.** $3x^2(5x-3)(x-2)$
91. $x^3(5x-1)(2x-3)$ **93.** $2(3x+7y)(6x-5y)$ **95.** $2b(2a-b)(3a-7b)$ **97.** $-b^2(3a+1)(5a-4)$ **99.** a
101. $(2x+3)(x+1)$ **103.** $3x(2x-3)(3x+1)$ **105–107.** Answers may vary.   **109.** $(2x^n+1)(x^n-4)$
111. $b=5$, $b=7$, $b=-5$, $b=-7$ **113.** $(3x+2)(x+3)$
115. Answers may vary.

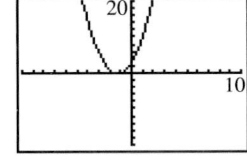   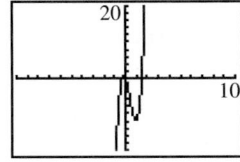

Review Problems

116. $81x^2-49$ **117.** $25x^2-60x+36$ **118.** x^3+8

PROBLEM SET 7.4

1. $(x+5)(x-5)$ **3.** $(y+1)(y-1)$ **5.** $(2x+1)(2x-1)$ **7.** Prime   **9.** $(3y+2)(3y-2)$ **11.** Prime   **13.** $(1+7x)(1-7x)$
15. $(5a-4b)(5a+4b)$ **17.** Prime   **19.** $(4z+y)(4z-y)$ **21.** $(3+11a)(3-11a)$ **23.** $(x+5)(x-3)$ **25.** $4(x+5)(x-2)$
27. $3(3x+7)(x-3)$ **29.** $(2-x)(8+x)$ **31.** $2(y+3)(y-3)$ **33.** $2x(x-6)(x+6)$ **35.** $2(5-y)(5+y)$ **37.** $2y(2y-1)(2y+1)$
39. $2x(x+1)(x-1)$ **41.** $(x^2+4)(x-2)(x+2)$ **43.** $(4y^2+9)(2y-3)(2y+3)$ **45.** $(1+y^2)(1+y)(1-y)$
47. $(x^4+1)(x^2+1)(x-1)(x+1)$ **49.** $(4a^2+b^2)(2a-b)(2a+b)$ **51.** $(x+1)^2$ **53.** $(x-7)^2$ **55.** $(x-1)^2$ **57.** $(x+12)^2$
59. $(2y+1)^2$ **61.** $(3r-1)^2$ **63.** $(4t+1)^2$ **65.** $(3b-7)^2$ **67.** Prime   **69.** $3(2k-1)^2$ **71.** $x(3x+1)^2$ **73.** $2(y-1)^2$
75. $2(y+7)^2$ **77.** $(5x+2y)^2$ **79.** $(a-3b)^2$ **81.** $(2a-3b)^2$ **83.** $2(4x+5y)^2$ **85.** $(x+3)(x^2-3x+9)$ **87.** $(x-4)(x^2+4x+16)$
89. $(2y-1)(4y^2+2y+1)$ **91.** $(4x+5)(16x^2-20x+25)$ **93.** $2x(x+2)(x^2-2x+4)$ **95.** $y(3y-2)(9y^2+6y+4)$
97. $2(3-2y)(9+6y+4y^2)$ **99.** $(4x+3y)(16x^2-12xy+9y^2)$ **101.** $(5x-4y)(25x^2+20xy+16y^2)$ **103.** d

105. $(2x - 3)(2x + 3)$ **107.** $(2x - 1)^2$

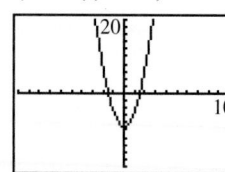   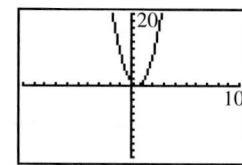

109. Answers may vary.   **111.** $(x - 5)(x + 5)$ **113.** $(x - 6y)(x + 6y)$ **115.** 1999   **117.** 19,900   **119.** $k = 6$
121. $(x - 1)(x^4 + x^3 + x^2 + x + 1)$ **123.** Answers may vary.

Review Problems

125. $\dfrac{81x^8}{16}$ **126.** $3 < x$ **127.** $x = 8$

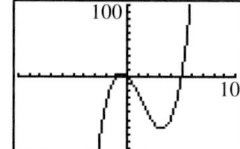

PROBLEM SET 7.5

1. $3x(x - 1)(x + 1)$ **3.** $3x(x^2 + 1)$ **5.** $4(x - 3)(x + 2)$ **7.** $2(x^2 + 9)(x - 3)(x + 3)$ **9.** $(x - 3)(x + 3)(x + 2)$ **11.** $3x(x - 5)^2$
13. $2x^2(x + 3)(x^2 - 3x + 9)$ **15.** $2x(3x + 4)$ **17.** $2(y + 7)(y - 8)$ **19.** $7y^2(y + 1)^2$ **21.** Prime   **23.** $2(2y - 1)(4y + 1)$ **25.** $r(r - 25)$
27. $(2w + 5)(2w - 1)$ **29.** $x(x + 2)(x - 2)$ **31.** Prime   **33.** $(9y + 4)(y + 1)$ **35.** $(y - 2)(y + 2)^2$ **37.** $(3y + 4)^2$
39. $5y(y - 2)(y - 7)$ **41.** $y(y^2 + 9)(y - 3)(y + 3)$ **43.** $5a^2(2a - 3)(2a + 3)$ **45.** $(3y - 2)(4y - 1)$ **47.** $(3y - 8)(3y + 8)$
49. Prime   **51.** $(y - 5)(y + 5)(2y + 3)$ **53.** $-(3x - 1)(2x + 1)$ **55.** $2r(r + 17)(r - 2)$ **57.** $2x^3(2x - 1)(2x + 1)$ **59.** $3(x^2 + 81)$
61. $x(x + 2)(x^2 - 2x + 4)$ **63.** $2y^2(y - 1)(y^2 + y + 1)$ **65.** $2x(3x + 4y)$ **67.** $(x + 3)(y - 7)$ **69.** $(x - 4y)(x + y)$
71. $12a^2(6ab^2 + 1 - 2a^2b^2)$ **73.** $(a + 6b)(3a + 9b)$ **75.** $3x^2y(4x + 1)(4x - 1)$ **77.** $b(3a + 2)(2a - 1)$ **79.** $7xy(x^2 + y^2)(x - y)(x + y)$
81. $3a^2b(2 + 3a)(4 - 5a)$ **83.** $2b(x + 11)^2$ **85.** $(3a - 2b)(5a + 7b)$ **87.** $2xy(2x - 3y)(9x - 2y)$ **89.** $(y - x)(a - b)(a + b)$
91. $ax(3x + 7)(3x - 2)$ **93.** $y(9x^2 + y^2)(3x + y)(3x - y)$ **95.** x ft by $(x - 30)$ ft by $(x - 30)$ ft   **97.** $-16(t + 4)(t - 4)$; 4 seconds   **99.** b
101. $3x(x - 5)(x + 1)$ **103.** $(x^2 + 4)(x - 2)(x + 2)$ **105–107.** Answers may vary.   **109.** $(y - 1)(y + 1)(y - 2)$

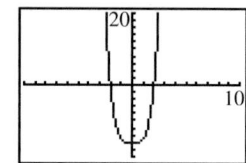

111. $(x - 5)^2$ **113.** Answers may vary.

Review Problems

114. $y < \dfrac{5}{2}x - 5$ **115.** $(1, 4)$ **116.** $30°$, $60°$, and $90°$

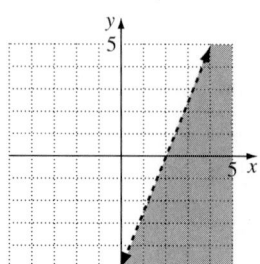

PROBLEM SET 7.6

1. $-3, 2$ **3.** $-\dfrac{4}{3}, \dfrac{1}{2}$ **5.** $-\dfrac{1}{4}, \dfrac{1}{2}$ **7.** $-\dfrac{7}{2}, \dfrac{1}{3}$ **9.** $-\dfrac{7}{3}, 2$ **11.** $-\dfrac{5}{2}, \dfrac{9}{4}$ **13.** $-5, -3$ **15.** $-3, 5$ **17.** $-3, 7$ **19.** $-8, -1$
21. $-4, 0$ **23.** $0, 5$ **25.** $0, 4$ **27.** $0, \dfrac{9}{2}$ **29.** $0, -\dfrac{5}{3}$ **31.** -2 **33.** Prime   **35.** Prime   **37.** $-\dfrac{1}{2}, 4$ **39.** $-2, \dfrac{9}{5}$ **41.** $-\dfrac{7}{2}, -\dfrac{1}{3}$

43. $-1, -\frac{1}{3}$ **45.** $-\frac{5}{2}, \frac{3}{2}$ **47.** $-\frac{4}{3}, -\frac{5}{4}$ **49.** $-3, \frac{2}{3}$ **51.** $-2, 9$ **53.** 4 **55.** $-\frac{7}{4}, \frac{7}{4}$ **57.** $-3, -2$ **59.** $-2, -\frac{3}{2}$ **61.** $-\frac{5}{2}$

63. $\frac{3}{8}$ **65. a.** 8 seconds   **b.** 0, 112, 192, 240, 256, 240, 192, 112, 0   **c.**

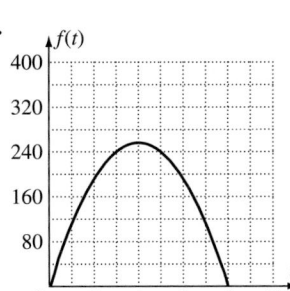

d. 4 seconds; 256 ft
e. (8, 0) is a point on the graph.
67. a. 10 years   **b.** (10, 7250)
69. 13 numbers   **71.** 13 years
73. Pages 10 and 11
75. Width = 12 yds;
length = 15 yds
77. 4 ft by 9 ft
79. Base = 8 in.; height = 15 in.

81. a. $4x^2 + 54x + 180$ **b.** $f(x) = 4x^2 + 54x + 180$ **c.** 3 m
d.

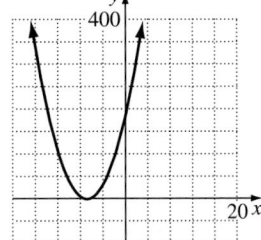

83. 12 m and 5 m   **85.** 12 ft $\times$ 5 ft   **87.** a
89. $-3, -1, 2$

91–93. Students should verify results.   **95.** Answers may vary.   **97.** $-5, 0, 2$ **99.** 1, 4   **101.** Width, 4 feet; length, 7 feet
103. 6 square inches   **105.** 7 yds by 9 yds

Review Problems

107. $y > -\frac{2}{3}x + 1$ **108.** $\frac{x^6}{4}$ **109.** $y^2 - 2y + 5$

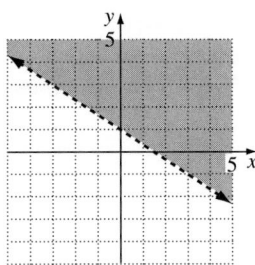

CHAPTER 7 REVIEW

1. $9y(y - 2)$ **2.** $(x - 4)(x - 7)$ **3.** $y(y - 7)(y - 1)$ **4.** $(5r + 2)(2r + 1)$ **5.** $(5z - 2)(3z + 1)$ **6.** $(x + 12)(x - 12)$
7. $(8 - y)(8 + y)$ **8.** $(3r + 1)^2$ **9.** $4a^3(5a^4 - 9)$ **10.** $(2x^2 - 5)(4x^3 + 3)$ **11.** $(x + 3)(x - 3)^2$ **12.** $(4y + 5)(3y - 1)$
13. $(4x - 5)^2$ **14.** Prime   **15.** $x(2x + 5)(x + 7)$ **16.** $3x(x - 5)^2$ **17.** $(5z + 1)(2z + 7)$ **18.** $3x^2(x - 2)(x^2 + 2x + 4)$
19. $4y^2(y - 3)(y + 3)$ **20.** $(9y + 1)(4y - 7)$ **21.** $5(x + 7)(x - 3)$ **22.** Prime   **23.** $2x^3(5x - 2)(x - 4)$ **24.** $(5x + 4)(8x - 3)$
25. $6(9z - 2)(9z + 2)$ **26.** $3(4r - 5)^2$ **27.** $3y^2(y - 5)(y + 2)$ **28.** $(10y - 7)(10y + 7)$ **29.** $(4x - 1)(4x + 1)(16x^2 + 1)$
30. $9x^4(x - 2)$ **31.** Prime   **32.** $(8y - 9)^2$ **33.** Prime   **34.** $(x - 2)(x + 2)(x^2 + 4)$ **35.** $(y - 2)(y^2 + 2y + 4)$ **36.** $(x + 4)(x^2 - 4x + 16)$
37. $-(5y - 3)(2y - 5)$ **38.** $(2x + 5)(3x - 2)$ **39.** $3x^2(x - 2)(x + 2)$ **40.** $3r^2(r^2 + 4)$ **41.** $7y(2y - 1)(4y - 3)$ **42.** Prime
43. $(x - 10)(s + 9)$ **44.** $(x - 9)(x + 3)$ **45.** Prime   **46.** $(5x + 2)(5x + 3)$ **47.** $p(p + 5)(p^2 - 5p + 25)$ **48.** $2y(4y + 1)(4y + 3)$
49. $x^5(4 + 5x)(4 - 5x)$ **50.** $2(y - 4)^2$ **51.** $3x^2y(4x^2y^2 - 3xy + 5)$ **52.** $(x + 5y)(x - 7y)$ **53.** $(ab + 4)(ab - 3)$ **54.** $(3x - y)(5x - 2y)$
55. $(x + y)(x + 7)$ **56.** $(3a + 4b)^2$ **57.** $(2x - 5y)^2$ **58.** $4a^3b^2(5a^4 - 9b^2)$ **59.** $2(2x + y)(x - 5)$ **60.** $2x^2y(x + 1)(x - 1)$
61. $13a(3ab - 4 + b^4)$ **62.** $(10y + 7z)(10y - 7z)$ **63.** $9x^4y^2(x - 2y^3)$ **64.** Prime   **65.** $(a - p)(a + p)(q + z)$
66. $(x - 2)(x + 2)(y - 4)(y + 4)$ **67.** $3x^2y^2(x - 2y)(x + 2y)$ **68.** $(5x - 2)(25x^2 + 10xy + 4y^2)$ **69.** $-7, 2$ **70.** $-4, 8$ **71.** $\frac{5}{8}, 4$

72. $\frac{1}{2}, -8$ **73.** $0, -4$ **74.** $-5, -2$ **75.** $a^2 - 3^2 = (a + 3)(a - 3)$ **76.** $a^2 - 4b^2 = (a + 2b)(a - 2b)$

77. $\pi a^2 - \pi(a - b)^2 = \pi b(2a - b)$ **78.** $\frac{4}{3}\pi(a - b)(a^2 + 2ab + b^2)$ **79. a.** 2 seconds   **b.** 32, 36, 32, 20, 0

c.

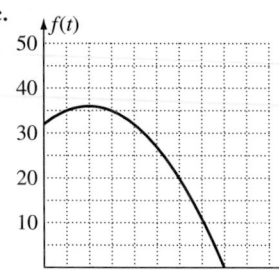

d. 36 ft, $\frac{1}{2}$ sec   **e.** $(2, 0)$ is a point on the graph   **80.** 7 cities   **81.** 16, 11, 5

82. $w = 7$ cm, $l = 12$ cm   **83.** 11 m by 11 m   **84.** Base = 6 m, height = 10 m

85. 6 ft and 8 ft

CHAPTER 7 TEST

1. $(x - 3)(x - 6)$ **2.** $(x - 7)^2$ **3.** $5y^2(3y - 1)(y - 2)$ **4.** $(x^2 + 3)(x + 2)$ **5.** $x(x - 9)$ **6.** $x(x + 7)(x - 1)$ **7.** $2(x + 5)(7x - 3)$
8. $(5x - 3)(5x + 3)$ **9.** $(x + 2)(x^2 - 2x + 4)$ **10.** $(x + 3)(x - 7)$ **11.** Prime   **12.** $3y(y + 1)(2y + 1)$ **13.** $4(y + 3)(y - 3)$
14. $4(2x + 3)^2$ **15.** $2(x^2 + 4)(x + 2)(x - 2)$ **16.** $(6x - 7)^2$ **17.** $(7x - 1)(x - 7)$ **18.** $(x^3 - 5)(x + 2)$ **19.** $3y(2y + 3)(2y - 5)$
20. $(y - 5)(y^2 + 5y + 25)$ **21.** $5(x + 2y)(x - 3y)$ **22.** $-6, 4$ **23.** $-\frac{1}{3}, 2$ **24.** $-2, 8$ **25.** $(x - 4)(x + 4)$ **26.** 6 seconds

27. Width = 6 yd, length = 15 yd

CUMULATIVE REVIEW PROBLEMS (CHAPTERS 1–7)

1. a. $\{1, 9\}$ **b.** $\{0, 1, 9\}$ **c.** $\{-3, -2, 0, 1, 9\}$ **d.** $\left\{-3, -2, \frac{1}{7}, 0, 1, 9, 11.3\right\}$ **e.** $\{\sqrt{7}, 8\pi\}$ **f.** $\left\{-3, -2, \frac{1}{7}, 0, 1, 9, 11.3, \sqrt{7}, 8\pi\right\}$ **2.** -48

3. $x = 0$ **4.** $x = 12$ **5.** 38°, 38° and 104°

6.

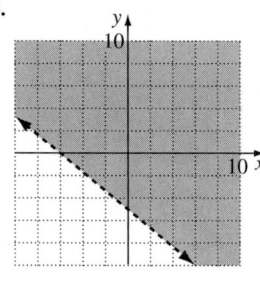

7. $(4, -3)$ **8.** Cost of pen, $0.20; cost of pad, $0.80   **9.** $-2x^4 + x^3 - 3x - \frac{9}{x}$ **10.** $8y^6$

11. 94,000 total number of nuns; over 70 years = 37,600 nuns; 51 to 70 years = 41,360 nuns

12. $-4, \frac{3}{5}$ **13.** $\{x \mid x < -2\}$ **14.** $f(10) = 16.07$; Approximately 16.07% of 18–25 yr olds used hallucinogens in 1984.   **15.** teachers = $34,200; surgeon = $223,800; ped = $115,000; Att. = $62,000
16. $y - 1 = 5(x - 3)$ or $y + 4 = 5(x - 2)$; $y = 5x - 14$
17. a. $x^2 + 3x + 2$ **b.** $f(x) = x^2 + 3x + 2$ **c.** $f(8) = 90$; when the width of the original garden is 8 m, the area of the new garden is 90 m^2

18. $y < -\frac{2}{5}x + 2$

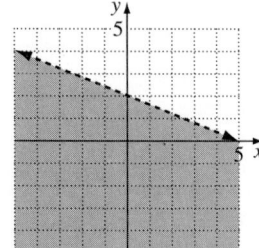

19. $\left(-\frac{2}{13}, \frac{23}{13}\right)$ **20.** $2x^2 + 5x - 3 - \frac{2}{3x - 5}$ **21.** 15, 16, and 17   **22.** $x = 7$ and $y = 9$
23. $(3x + 2)(x + 3)$ **24. a.** 4 seconds   **b.** 0, 48, 64, 48, 0
c.   **d.** 2 seconds; 64 ft   **e.** $(4, 0)$ is a point on the graph.

f(t) graph

25. $y(y^2 + 4)(y - 2)(y + 2)$ **26.** Width = 4 ft, length = 6 ft
27. $149.53   **28.** $-\frac{13}{40}$ **29.** $B = 2A - C$ **30.** 5 ways

PROBLEM SET 8.1

1. $x = 0$ **3.** $x = 7$ **5.** $y = 3$ **7.** $x = -7$ or $x = 3$ **9.** $z = 5$ or $z = -2$ **11.** $x = -4$ or $x = 3$ **13.** $y = \frac{3}{4}$ or $y = -1$

15. No values of x for which the expression is undefined.   **17.** No values of y for which the expression is undefined.   **19.** $2x$ **21.** $\dfrac{6}{x^2}$

23. $\dfrac{x-3}{5}$ **25.** $\dfrac{x-4}{2x}$ **27.** $\dfrac{1}{x-3}$ **29.** Not reducible   **31.** 3   **33.** $\dfrac{1}{x-5}$ **35.** $\dfrac{2(y-5)}{3(y-2)}$ **37.** $\dfrac{1}{s-3}$ **39.** $\dfrac{4}{b-2}$ **41.** $\dfrac{y-1}{y+9}$

43. $\dfrac{y-3}{y-2}$ **45.** Irreducible   **47.** $\dfrac{x+2}{x-5}$ **49.** $\dfrac{x+6}{x+1}$ **51.** y^2 **53.** -1 **55.** -2 **57.** $\dfrac{2}{4-x}$ **59.** $-\dfrac{2}{y}$ **61.** $-\dfrac{3+x}{x+2}$

63. $\dfrac{y-6}{y^2+3y+9}$ **65.** $-b-3$

67. $y = x + 5\ (x \neq 5)$ **69.** $f(x) = 3\ (x \neq 2)$ **71.** $\dfrac{2x^2}{y}$ **73.** $\dfrac{1}{2}$ **75.** $x - 2y$ **77.** $\dfrac{3a}{a-3b}$ **79.** $\dfrac{x+5y}{3x-y}$ **81.** $\dfrac{2a-b}{3a+4b}$

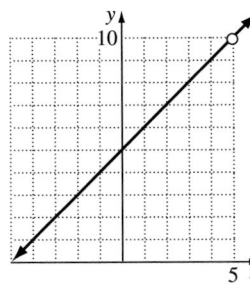   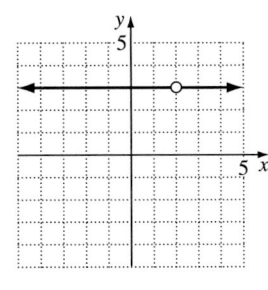

83. a. $86.67 =$ the cost in millions of dollars to inoculate 40% of the population; $520 =$ the cost to inoculate 80% of the population; $1170 =$ cost to inoculate 90% of the population   **b.** $x = 100$ **c.** The cost becomes infinitely large as x approaches 100%.

d.

x	0	10	20	40	50	60	70	80	90	95	99	100
y	0	14	33	87	130	195	303	520	1170	2470	12,870	undefined

e.

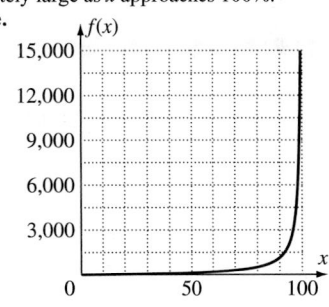

f. The values of the cost increase rapidly as the values of x (% inoculated) approach 100.   **85.** 200 square feet; 50 by 50; square   **87.** c

89. $2x + 1$

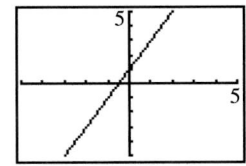

91. $f(x)$ goes to infinity.   **93.** Answers may vary.   **95.** 0   **97.** 2   **99.** 0   **101.** 0

103. Answers may vary.   **105.** Possible answer: $\dfrac{x^2+7x+12}{x+4}$ **107.** $\dfrac{26}{65} = \dfrac{2}{5}, \dfrac{49}{98} = \dfrac{4}{8}$

Review Problems

109. 25%   **110.** $\{(4, 2)\}$ **111.** 50,000

PROBLEM SET 8.2

1. $\dfrac{5(x-3)}{7(x+2)}\ (x \neq -2)$ **3.** $\dfrac{3x^2+3x}{7x-14}\ (x \neq 2)$ **5.** $\dfrac{2x}{x+1}\ (x \neq -1)$ **7.** $\dfrac{2}{3}\ (x \neq 0)$ **9.** $\dfrac{1}{3}\ (x \neq -3, 2)$ **11.** $\dfrac{3y^2-19y+20}{y^2+4y+4}\ (y \neq -2)$

13. $\dfrac{2}{y}\left(y \neq 0, 3, -\dfrac{15}{2}\right)$ **15.** $\dfrac{(r-3)(r+3)}{r(r+4)}\ (r \neq 0, 3, -4)$ **17.** $\dfrac{y+2}{y+4}\left(y \neq -4, 10, -\dfrac{1}{2}, -3\right)$ **19.** $4(y+3)(y \neq 3)$

21. $\dfrac{(x^2-2x+4)(x+2)}{2(x-2)}\ (x \neq -2, 2)$ **23.** $\dfrac{(x+2)(x-3)}{3(x+3)}\ (x \neq -3, 3)$ **25.** $y + 5\ (y \neq -3, 4, -5)$ **27.** $\dfrac{x-2}{x-1}\ (x \neq 1, 2)$ **29.** $-\dfrac{y-10}{y-7}$

31. $\dfrac{3x}{35}$ **33.** $\dfrac{1}{4}\ (x \neq 0)$ **35.** $10\ (x \neq 0)$ **37.** $\dfrac{2x-2}{3x+3}\ (x \neq -1)$ **39.** $\dfrac{y}{x^3}\ (x \neq 0, y \neq 0)$ **41.** $\dfrac{x^2+7x+12}{x^2-7x+12}\ (x \neq 4, 3)$ **43.** $\dfrac{7}{9}\ (x \neq -1)$

45. $\dfrac{3}{4}\ (x \neq 5)$ **47.** $\dfrac{x^2-4x+4}{x}\ (x \neq 0, -2)$ **49.** $\dfrac{(y-4)(y^2+4)}{y-1}\ (y \neq -4, 1)$ **51.** $\dfrac{y}{3}\ (y \neq 1)$ **53.** $2x(x+1)\ (x \neq 0, -1)$

55. $\frac{y^2+1}{y^2}$ $(y \neq 0, 1)$ **57.** $\frac{m+1}{m-7}$ $(m \neq -4, -8, 7, 5)$ **59.** 6 $(y \neq -2, -8, 8)$ **61.** $\frac{x^2+5}{21}$ **63.** $\frac{7}{9}$ $(x \neq 0)$ **65.** $\frac{x^2}{2}$ $(x \neq 0)$

67. $\frac{3}{2}$ $(x \neq -4)$ **69.** $-\frac{x}{4}$ $(y \neq 7)$ **71.** $\frac{1}{x+3}\left(x \neq 3, -3, 0, -\frac{1}{2}, 6\right)$ **73.** $\frac{8}{63x}$ $(x \neq 0)$ **75.** $\frac{2}{x+4}$ $(x \neq -4, 7)$ **77.** $\frac{1}{4x^2y}$ $(x \neq 0, y \neq 0)$

79. $(x+y)(x-y)$ $(x \neq 0, x \neq -y)$ **81.** $\frac{a+2b}{2a+b}\left(a \neq -b, a \neq -\frac{b}{2}, a \neq b\right)$ **83.** 1 $(x \neq 0, y \neq 0, z \neq 0)$ **85.** $\frac{4a}{3b}$ $(a \neq 0, b \neq 0, a \neq -b)$

87. $\frac{3(2x+y)}{2(x+2y)}\left(x \neq -2y, x \neq \frac{y}{2}\right)$ **89.** $\frac{1}{a-2b}$ $(a \neq -2b, a \neq -b, a \neq 2b)$ **91.** c

93. Correct   **95.** Answers may vary.   **97.** $x, x-4$ **99.** $\frac{7x}{6}$

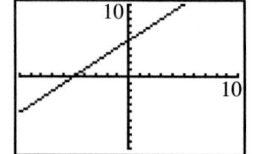

Review Problems

101. $\frac{9}{x^{17}}$ **102.** $x > 18$ **103.** $\frac{1}{2}, -5$

P R O B L E M   S E T   8 . 3

1. $\frac{2x}{3}$ **3.** $\frac{8}{x}$ **5.** $\frac{4}{3x}$ **7.** $\frac{3m}{5}$ **9.** $\frac{10}{4-y}$ **11.** 2   **13.** $\frac{2y-1}{y+3}$ **15.** $\frac{2}{3y^2}$ **17.** $-\frac{4y}{4y+1}$ **19.** $\frac{y-2}{2y+7}$ **21.** 1   **23.** $\frac{y-7}{3y-7}$

25. $\frac{y}{y-2}$ **27.** $-\frac{3}{y}$ **29.** $\frac{3}{y-3}$ **31.** $\frac{4r}{4r+3}$ **33.** $\frac{x}{2}$ **35.** $\frac{3y+2}{y-3}$ **37.** $\frac{7-y}{y-6}$ **39.** $\frac{3x+1}{3x-4}$ **41.** $y+2$ **43.** 0

45. $\frac{y+1}{y-1}$ **47.** $\frac{a-2}{a-7}$ **49.** $\frac{2(z-2)}{z^2-25}$ **51.** $\frac{2(5m+1)}{2m-3}$ **53.** $x+y$ **55.** $\frac{3}{(3x+4y)(3x+2y)}$ **57.** $\frac{3x+y}{(x+2y)(x+y)(x-2y)}$ **59.** $\frac{a+b}{a-b}$

61. 0   **63.** c

65. Correct   **67.** $x-4$ $(x \neq -4)$

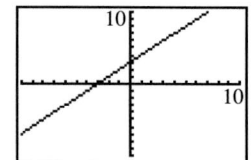   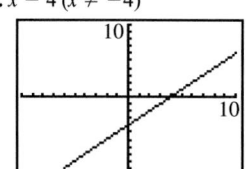

69. Answers may vary.   **71.** 2   **73.** $20x-6$ **75.** $a+12$

Review Problems

77. $(3y-1)(3y+1)(9y^2+1)$ **78.** 2:00 P.M.   **79.** $3x^2 - 7x - 5$

P R O B L E M   S E T   8 . 4

1. 60   **3.** $3x^3$ **5.** $120x^5$ **7.** $600y$ **9.** $30x^5$ **11.** $(y-3)(y+1) = y^2 - 2y - 3$ **13.** $7x(x+2)$ **15.** $54x^2(x-5)$ **17.** $x^2 - 9$

19. $y(y^2 - 4)$ **21.** $(y+5)(y-5)^2$ **23.** $(2x-1)(x-2)(x+4)$ **25.** $\frac{3x+5}{x^2}$ **27.** $-\frac{29}{18w}$ **29.** $-\frac{x+5}{6}$ **31.** $\frac{5x+1}{(x-1)(x+2)}$

33. $\frac{11r+15}{4r(r+5)}$ **35.** $\frac{7y-12}{12y}$ **37.** $\frac{-6a^2+13a+3}{2a^2}$ **39.** $\frac{3x-55}{(x+5)(x-5)}$ **41.** $\frac{z(z+6)}{(z+4)(z-4)}$ **43.** $\frac{y+12}{(y-3)(y+3)}$ **45.** $\frac{7y-10}{(y-1)^2}$

47. $\frac{9r}{4(r-5)}$ **49.** $\frac{8(y+2)}{y(y+4)}$ **51.** $\frac{z^2+8z+4}{(z+1)^2(z+4)}$ **53.** $\frac{2(y^2-2y+17)}{(y+3)(y-5)}$ **55.** $\frac{5-3y}{2y(y-1)}$ **57.** $\frac{-r^2}{(r+3)(r-3)}$ **59.** $\frac{2}{y+5}$ **61.** $\frac{1}{w+2}$

63. $\frac{4x-11}{x-3}$ **65.** $\frac{3}{y+1}$ **67.** $\frac{-x^2+7x+3}{(x-3)(x+2)}$ **69.** $\frac{(-y+9)(y+1)}{15y^2}$ **71.** $\frac{-4x^2-25x-24}{(2x+5)(2x-3)(4x+1)}$ **73.** $\frac{2}{x(x-1)}$ **75.** $\frac{-30x+133}{21x^2}$

77. $\frac{2y+3x}{xy}$ **79.** $\frac{25y-8x}{20x^2y^2}$ **81.** $\frac{x^2+2x+y^2-2y}{xy}$ **83.** $\frac{y+x}{xy}$ **85.** $\frac{1}{a-b}$ **87.** $\frac{ad-cb}{bd}$ **89.** $\frac{6x^2+5x+10}{3x^2}$ **91.** $\frac{16D}{95}$ **93.** d

95. $\dfrac{3x + 5}{15}$

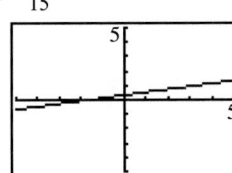

97–99. Answers may vary.   **101.** $\dfrac{3}{x^2}$ **103.** $\dfrac{x^2 + x - 3}{x(x + 3)}$

Review Problems

104. $6y^2 - 11y - 35$ **105.** $3x - y < 3$ **106.** $y = x - 1$

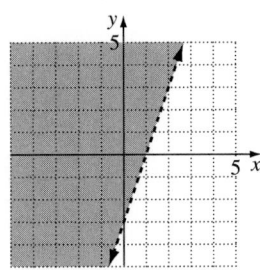

P R O B L E M   S E T   8 . 5

1. $\dfrac{9}{10}$ **3.** $\dfrac{14}{15}$ **5.** $-\dfrac{4}{5}$ **7.** $\dfrac{3 - 4x}{3 + 4x}$ **9.** $\dfrac{5x - 2}{3x + 1}$ **11.** $\dfrac{2y + 3}{y - 7}$ **13.** $\dfrac{2(2 - 3y)}{4 + 3y}$ **15.** $x - 5$ **17.** $\dfrac{x}{x - 1}$ **19.** $-\dfrac{1}{y}$ **21.** $\dfrac{4 - y}{5y - 3}$

23. $\dfrac{1}{w}$ **25.** $\dfrac{s(9s + 4)}{9s^2 + 20}$ **27.** x **29.** $\dfrac{14 - 5x^2}{6(7x^2 + 3)}$ **31.** $\dfrac{x^2 - 5x + 3}{x^2 - 7x + 2}$ **33.** $\dfrac{1}{y + 3}$ **35.** x^3; 1; 8; 27; 64; 125   **37.** $\dfrac{2(b - 2a)}{ab}$

39. $\dfrac{a(b - 1)}{1 + a}$ **41.** $\dfrac{a}{1 + ab}$ **43.** $y + x$ **45.** $\dfrac{x^2 + y}{y(1 + y)}$ **47.** $\dfrac{b(a - 6b^2)}{ab^3 + 30}$ **49.** $\dfrac{2y^3 + 5x^2}{y^3(5 - 3x^2)}$ **51.** $\dfrac{x(7xy^3 - 2)}{y^2(x + 2)}$ **53.** $-\dfrac{6y}{5}$

55. $\dfrac{2r_1 r_2}{r_1 + r_2}$; 24 miles per hour; the answer is not 25 miles per hour, which would be $\dfrac{r_1 + r_2}{2}$, but it is the total distance divided by the total time.

57. b   **59.** Correct   **61.** $\dfrac{5y + 3}{(y - 3)(y + 1)}$

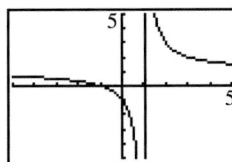

Review Problems

63. $-2x^2 + 3x + 14$ **64.** 1 second   **65.** 28

P R O B L E M   S E T   8 . 6

1. 12   **3.** $\dfrac{57}{5}$ **5.** -2 **7.** -6 **9.** 2   **11.** -2 **13.** 3   **15.** $\varnothing$ **17.** -10 **19.** -3 **21.** $\varnothing$ **23.** 3   **25.** $\varnothing$ **27.** $-8, 1$

29. $-\dfrac{2}{3}, 5$ **31.** $\dfrac{2}{3}, 4$ **33.** -1 **35.** $-3, -2$ **37.** 1   **39.** 9 hours   **41.** 100 prey per unit area

43. Last year's volume, approximately 84.91 thousands = 84,910   **45.** Marijuana/hashish = 29,166; cocaine = 123,317

47. $\dfrac{2}{7}$ **49.** $\dfrac{3}{4}$ or $\dfrac{4}{3}$ **51.** 4 miles per hour   **53.** 5 miles per hour   **55.** 30 hours   **57.** 6 minutes   **59.** 10 additional consecutive times

61. 9 by $\frac{1}{15}$; 1 by $\frac{1}{5}$; 30 by 75   **63.** b   **65.** d   **67.** $x = \pm 5$ **69.** $x = 1$

71. $y = \frac{40}{x} + \frac{40}{x + 30}$ **73.** 30; 2   **75.** -3 **77.** Car's speed is 20 miles per hour   **79.** 40

Review Problems

81. 165 calories   **82.** -5 **83.** $2x(x + 7)(x - 3)$

PROBLEM SET 8.7

1. $x = \frac{100C}{4 + C}$; 80%   **3.** $t = \frac{P - 21}{30 - P}$; 1998   **5. a.** $S = V + \frac{F}{B}$ **b.** \$260   **7. a.** 6 ohms   **b.** $R = \frac{R_1 R_2}{R_1 + R_2}$ **9.** $N = \frac{2P}{D - P}$

11. $P = \frac{A}{1 + rt}$ **13.** $h = \frac{2A}{b}$ **15.** $a = \frac{2s}{t^2}$ **17.** $r = \frac{mv^2}{F}$ **19.** $T_2 = \frac{T_1 P_2 V_2}{P_1 V_1}$ **21.** $r = 1 - \frac{a}{S}$ **23.** $f_2 = -\frac{ff_1}{f - f_1}$ **25.** $r^3 = \frac{3V}{4\pi}$

27. $s = \frac{Ar}{r - A}$ **29.** $y = \frac{b}{1 + c}$ **31. a.** $k = 17$; $P = 17H$ **b.** \$680   **c.**   **33.** \$182

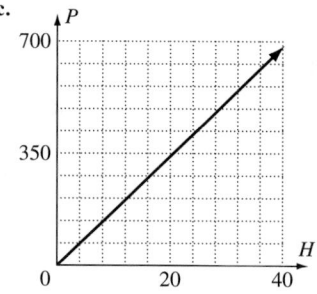

35. a.   **b.** Inversely   **c.** $R = \frac{6}{I}$ **37.** 18 yards   **39.** b

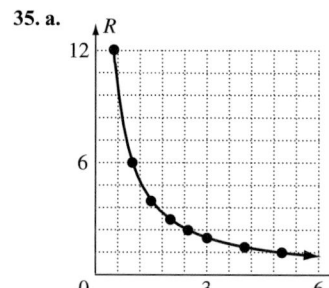

41.   **43.**   **45.** Answers may vary   **47.** 17; \$17 more   **49.** 70

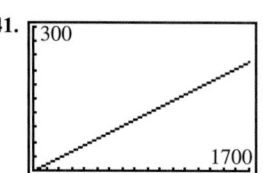   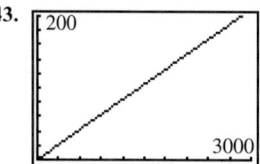

Review Problems

50. $(5x + 9)(5x - 9)$ **51.** $x = 6$ **52.** $y = -\frac{2}{3}x + 4$

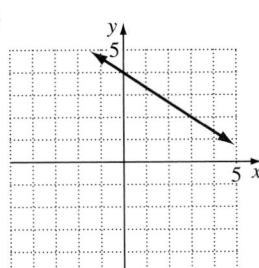

C H A P T E R   8   R E V I E W

1. 4   **2.** 2, -5 **3.** 2, 1   **4.** $\varnothing$ **5. a.** $f(20) = \$20,000; f(50) = \$80,000; f(90) = \$720,000; f(98) = \$3,920,000$ **b.** $x = 100$
c. The cost increases rapidly as x approaches 100%.
The difficulty of removing the pollutants increases greatly as higher levels of purity are demanded.

6.

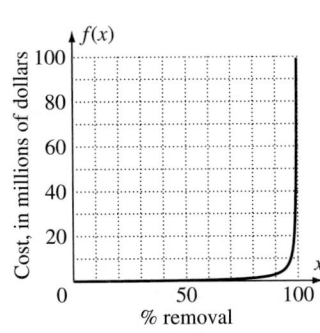

7. $\frac{4x}{3}$ **8.** x^2 **9.** $\frac{x - 3}{x - 6}$ **13.** $y = x + 2 \ (x \neq 2)$

10. $\frac{x - 5}{x + 7}$ **11.** $\frac{y}{y + 2}$

12. $-\frac{3a + 1}{a + 2}$

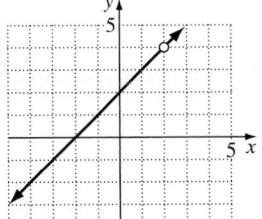

14. $\frac{5}{2}$ **15.** $\frac{(x + 3)^3}{(x + 2)(x - 2)^2}$ **16.** $-\frac{3(y + 1)}{5y(2y - 3)}$ **17.** $\frac{(x + 2)(x - 4)}{(x + 3)(x + 1)}$ **18.** $\frac{y - 1}{4}$ **19.** $\frac{2}{y(y + 1)}$ **20.** $\frac{2(y + 3)}{y - 4}$ **21.** $\frac{3 - z}{3 + z}$

22. 4   **23.** $3y - 5$ **24.** $\frac{6}{(y + 6)(y - 1)}$ **25.** $\frac{x + 11}{(x - 3)(x + 3)}$ **26.** $36x^3$ **27.** $40y^3(y - 1)^2$

28. $(x + 1)(x + 3)(x + 7)$ **29.** $\frac{15 + 14y}{50y^2}$ **30.** $\frac{3}{y - 2}$ **31.** $\frac{17x + 2}{3x(x + 1)}$ **32.** $\frac{y(3y - 1)}{(y + 1)^2(y - 1)}$ **33.** $\frac{4z^2 + 13z - 15}{(z + 1)(z + 4)(z + 5)}$ **34.** 2

35. $\frac{11y^2 - y - 11}{(2y - 1)(y + 3)(3y + 2)}$ **36.** $\frac{11x + 1}{5x}$ **37.** $\frac{x}{x - 1}$ **38.** $\frac{3}{x}$ **39.** $\frac{3y}{y - 4}$ **40.** $\frac{6 - x^2}{x(3x + 10)}$ **41.** $\frac{2}{3x}$ **42.** $\frac{2a^2(4 + b^2)}{(b + 2)(b + 2)}$

43. $\frac{1}{3b^2}$ **44.** $\frac{x + y}{x}$ **45.** $\frac{16(a - 2b)}{3(a + 2b)}$ **46.** $\frac{b + 24}{4ab}$ **47.** $\frac{5a - 12b}{3a^2b}$ **48.** $\frac{x^2 + y^2}{xy}$ **49.** $\frac{-bc + ab}{abc}$ **50.** $\frac{ab + 1}{b^3}$ **51.** $\frac{a}{4}$

52. $-6, 2$ **53.** 5   **54.** -1 **55.** -1 **56.** $-2, -3$ **57.** $\varnothing$ **58.** 1992   **59. a.** $\$220; \$40; \$22$ **b.** Cost decreases, approaching $20

c. 100,000   **60.** $x = \frac{100C}{200 + C}$; 60%   **61.** 8 yrs old   **62.** $A = \frac{-12C}{C - D}$ **63.** $a = \frac{bc}{b - c}$ **64.** $P = \frac{A}{1 + rT}$ **65.** $\frac{1}{7}$ **66.** 1970 was 1469;

1993 was 7984   **67.** 30 miles/hr   **68.** 4 hours   **69.** 4 minutes   **70. a.** $k = 14; P = 14H$ **b.** $560

c. slope = 14; $14 more   **71.** $154   **72.** 16 amperes

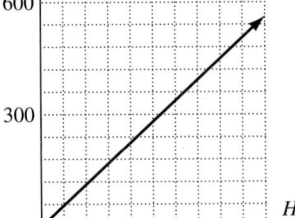

C H A P T E R   8   T E S T

1. $-9, 4$ **2.** $\dfrac{x + 3}{x - 2}$ **3.** $\dfrac{4y}{y + 1}$ **4.** $\dfrac{x - 4}{2}$ **5.** $\dfrac{y}{y + 3}$ **6.** $\dfrac{2(x + 3)}{x + 1}$ **7.** $\dfrac{5}{(y - 3)(y - 1)}$ **8.** $2y$ **9.** $\dfrac{2}{y + 3}$ **10.** $\dfrac{x^2 + 2x + 15}{(x - 3)(x - 3)}$

11. $\dfrac{2(4y - 7)}{(y - 3)(y - 1)(y + 2)}$ **12.** $-\dfrac{y + 1}{y - 3}$ **13.** $\dfrac{3(2x - 7)}{x - 3}$ **14.** $\dfrac{11}{(y - 3)(y - 4)}$ **15.** $\dfrac{4}{y + 4}$ **16.** $\dfrac{3(x + y)}{x}$ **17.** $\dfrac{a^2 + 2ab - 4b^2}{4ab}$

18. $\dfrac{5(x + 1)}{2x + 1}$ **19.** $\dfrac{y - x}{y}$ **20.** $y = 6$ **21.** $y = -8$ **22.** $x = 0$ or $x = 2$ **23.** $t = \dfrac{ab}{a + b}$ **24.** $r = 0.07 = 7\%$ **25.** Mammals: 36, birds: 57   **26.** 12 minutes   **27.** 137.5 psi   **28.** 52.5 amperes

C U M U L A T I V E   R E V I E W   P R O B L E M S   (C H A P T E R S   1 – 8)

1. a. Associative property of addition   **b.** Distributive property   **c.** Commutative property of addition

2. $x > 18$ **3.** $x = 30\frac{1}{3}$ **4.** $3x - 4y < 12$

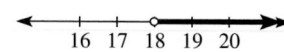

5. Coldest city is 36°F and warmest city is 78°F   **6.** $3(x - 7)(x + 2)$
7. Multiplied by 4   **8.** Width = 2 yards; length = 7 yards   **9.** $2x(x - 5)^2$
10. $x + 5 + \dfrac{3}{x - 3}$ **11.** $8x^9$ **12.** $\left(-\dfrac{3}{29}, -\dfrac{7}{29}\right)$

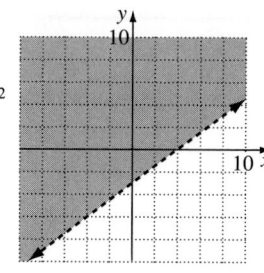

13. $f(10) = 5870$; an acre of 10 trees produces 5870 limes.
14. $y + 5 = -5(x - 1)$ or $y - 10 = -5(x + 2)$; $y = -5x$

15. The height of the rocket above the ground after 0 sec, 1 sec, 2 sec, 3 sec, 4 sec, 5 sec is 0 ft, 64 ft, 96 ft, 96 ft, 64 ft, 0ft, respectively.

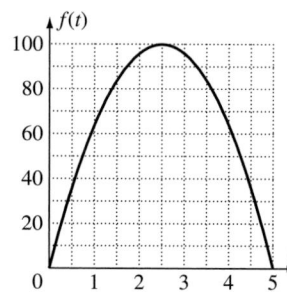

16. Sweden = 13.5%, America = 41%, New Zealand = 38.2%, Italy = 35.1%, England = 33%, Australia = 31.1%, Netherlands = 21.1%, Canada = 20%, Belgium = 19.6%, Finland = 17.9%
17. 38 million; black = 28.5 million; Indian = 0.76 million; mixed = 3.42 million   **18.** 6 feet
19. $x = -2$

20. $(2, 0)$

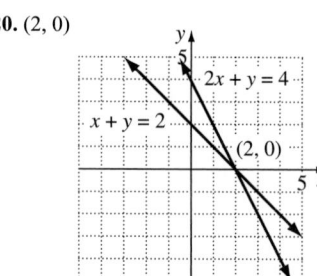

21. Cassette, $7 each; compact disc, $15 each   **22.** 8 meters, 15 meters, and 17 meters
23. $-3, -4$ **24.** $\dfrac{y - 3}{(y + 1)(y + 3)}$ **25. a.** $x^2 + 200x + 10{,}000$
b. $f(x) = x^2 + 200x + 10{,}000$ **c.** If the lawn is increased by 5 feet on each side, the area of the expanded lawn is 11,025 square feet   **26.** 25 miles per hour   **27.** 12 years   **28.** 300
29. 94% or better   **30.** $46,762

P R O B L E M   S E T   9 . 1

1. 6 and -6 **3.** 12 and -12 **5.** $\dfrac{3}{4}$ and $-\dfrac{3}{4}$ **7.** $\dfrac{7}{10}$ and $-\dfrac{7}{10}$ **9.** 6   **11.** -6 **13.** Not a real number   **15.** $\dfrac{1}{5}$ **17.** $\dfrac{7}{5}$ **19.** $-\dfrac{1}{3}$

21. $-\dfrac{7}{10}$ **23.** 0.2   **25.** 5   **27.** 8   **29.** 13   **31.** 17   **33.** $\dfrac{1}{15}$, rational   **35.** 3.873, irrational   **37.** 20, rational   **39.** -15, rational
41. Not a real number   **43.** -9.110, irrational   **45.** 23.937, irrational   **47.** -37, rational   **49.** 7, rational   **51.** 9.354, irrational

53. Not a real number   **55.** 1   **57.** 4   **59.** -3 **61.** 5   **63.** 2   **65.** -3 **67.** Not a real number   **69.** 4   **71.** -2 **73.** 2   **75.** $\frac{2}{3}$

77. $-\frac{1}{4}$ **79.** 0, 1, 2, 3, 4   **a.** $x \geq 1$ **b.** Verify graph.   **81.** 12 miles per hour   **83.** 3 seconds

85. Will freeze in 1 minute or less, yes   **87.** d   **89.** 192.90 miles   **91.** 0.061

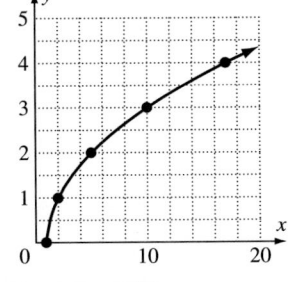

93.
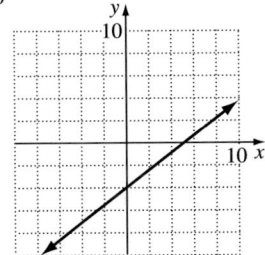

Possible answer: They have the same
shape, but different x- and y-intercepts.

95.
$v \approx 28.2843$ miles per hour

97. Yes   **99.** Yes   **101–103.** Answers may vary.   **105.** -7 and -6

Review Problems

107. $4x - 5y = 20$

108. $\dfrac{x+9}{x-15}, (x \neq 2, 15)$ **109.** $x < -8$

P R O B L E M   S E T   9 . 2

1. $\sqrt{42}$ **3.** 6   **5.** $\sqrt{15y}$ **7.** $3\sqrt{2xy}$ **9.** $\sqrt{\dfrac{5}{14}}$ **11.** $5\sqrt{2}$ **13.** $3\sqrt{5}$ **15.** $4\sqrt{5x}$ **17.** $10\sqrt{6xy}$ **19.** $6\sqrt{3}$ **21.** $14\sqrt{2a}$

23. $9\sqrt{6}$ **25.** $3\sqrt{35x}$ **27.** $60\sqrt{ab}$ **29.** 18   **31.** $y\sqrt{y}$ **33.** $5x\sqrt{2}$ **35.** $4x^2\sqrt{5}$ **37.** $6x^2\sqrt{2x}$ **39.** $2x^5\sqrt{3x}$ **41.** $3p^{11}\sqrt{10p}$

43. $2x\sqrt{3x}$ **45.** $2y^2\sqrt{5}$ **47.** $5r^4\sqrt{3}$ **49.** $xy^3\sqrt{x}$ **51.** $10xy^2\sqrt{2xy}$ **53.** $\dfrac{7}{4}$ **55.** $\dfrac{\sqrt{35}}{2}$ **57.** $\dfrac{\sqrt{7}}{x^2}$ **59.** $\dfrac{6\sqrt{2}}{x^3}$ **61.** 3   **63.** 3

65. $5\sqrt{5}$ **67.** $3\sqrt{10}$ **69.** $\dfrac{2\sqrt{7y}}{9}$ **71.** $2y^2\sqrt{3}$ **73.** $2x^3$ **75.** $2y^3\sqrt{y}$ **77.** $2\sqrt[3]{4}$ **79.** $4\sqrt[3]{2}$ **81.** $2\sqrt[4]{5}$ **83.** 2   **85.** $3\sqrt[3]{2}$

87. $2\sqrt[5]{2}$ **89.** $\dfrac{3}{2}$ **91.** $\dfrac{\sqrt[4]{225}}{3}$ **93.** $\dfrac{\sqrt[3]{3}}{2}$ **95.** $130\sqrt{3}$ square feet   **97.** $\dfrac{3}{2}\sqrt{6}$ feet   **99.** c   **101.** Students should verify solutions.

103. $\sqrt{x^4} = x^2$ **105.** $\sqrt{18x^2} = 3x\sqrt{2}$ **107.** Answers may vary.   **109.** x^{6n}

111. $3a^3b^3c^6\sqrt{2a}$ **113.** 12, 8, 7

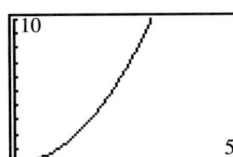

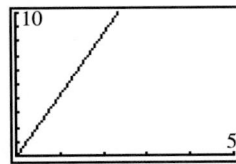

Review Problems

114. $(6, -2)$ **115.** $\dfrac{x^2 + 5x + 6}{6x(x + 2)}, (x \neq -2, 0)$ **116.** base, 10 cm; height, 7 cm

PROBLEM SET 9.3

1. $13\sqrt{3}$ **3.** $-2\sqrt{13}$ **5.** $2\sqrt{5}$ **7.** $3\sqrt{13x}$ **9.** $-12\sqrt{11y}$ **11.** $4\sqrt{6p}$ **13.** $7\sqrt{2}$ **15.** $-6\sqrt{7} - 11\sqrt{3}$ **17.** $\sqrt[3]{4}$

19. Cannot be simplified.   **21.** $9\sqrt[4]{5} - \sqrt[3]{6}$ **23.** $5\sqrt{2}$ **25.** $3\sqrt{3}$ **27.** $8\sqrt{2a}$ **29.** $-16\sqrt{2b}$ **31.** $-\dfrac{3}{2}\sqrt{3}$ **33.** $11\sqrt{3}$ **35.** $\sqrt{7}$

37. $\dfrac{5}{4}\sqrt{2}$ **39.** $7\sqrt{6} + 8\sqrt{5}$ **41.** $\dfrac{19}{12}\sqrt{2x}$ **43.** $-\dfrac{31}{12}\sqrt{5}$ **45.** $5\sqrt[3]{3}$ **47.** $19\sqrt[3]{2b}$ **49.** $4\sqrt[3]{2}$ **51.** $\sqrt{6} + 4\sqrt{2}$ **53.** $\sqrt{42} - 5\sqrt{7}$

55. $\sqrt{15x} + \sqrt{35x}$ **57.** $\sqrt{10} - 2$ **59.** $5\sqrt{6} + 3$ **61.** $12 + \sqrt{15}$ **63.** $20\sqrt{6} + 30\sqrt{15}$ **65.** $36a\sqrt{5} - 60\sqrt{2b}$ **67.** $11 + 5\sqrt{5}$

69. $2x + \sqrt{2x} - 30$ **71.** $6 - 6\sqrt{2} + \sqrt{3} - 6$ **73.** $3 + \sqrt{3a} + 2a$ **75.** $41 + 2\sqrt{7}$ **77.** $11 + 4\sqrt{10}$ **79.** $a + 4\sqrt{ab} + 3b$

81. $-24 + 11\sqrt{6}$ **83.** $8 + 2\sqrt{15}$ **85.** $4 - 2\sqrt{3}$ **87.** $124 - 16\sqrt{21}$ **89.** $a + 2\sqrt{3a} + 3$ **91.** $y - 2\sqrt{10y} + 10$ **93.** 9   **95.** 8

97. -37 **99.** 7   **101.** 51   **103.** $30\sqrt{3} + 24\sqrt{2}$ meters   **105.** $3\sqrt{2}$ **107.** $10\sqrt{2} + 4\sqrt{3} + 2$ cm; $10\sqrt{6} - 10\sqrt{2} + 6\sqrt{3} - 6$ cm^2

109. d   **111.** c

113. $\sqrt{4x} + \sqrt{9x} = 5\sqrt{x}$

115. $5\sqrt{x - 2} - 6\sqrt{x - 2} = -\sqrt{x - 2}$ **117.** $(\sqrt{x} - 1)(\sqrt{x} - 1) = x - 2\sqrt{x} + 1$

119. $\sqrt{x}(2\sqrt{x} + 1) = 2x + \sqrt{x}$

121–123. Answers may vary.   **125.** $11\sqrt{3}$ **127.** $-1 - 3\sqrt[3]{4} + \sqrt[3]{2}$ **129.** $48x - 2y$

Review Problems

130. $y(8y + 1)(8y - 1)$ **131.** $8y^2 + 3y - 19$ **132.** $y = -\dfrac{1}{4}x + 3$

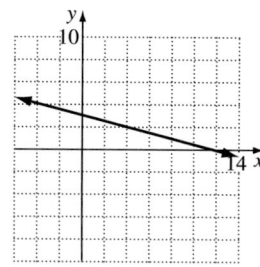

PROBLEM SET 9.4

1. $\dfrac{2\sqrt{3}}{3}$ **3.** $3\sqrt{7}$ **5.** $\dfrac{\sqrt{10}}{5}$ **7.** $\dfrac{\sqrt{21}}{3}$ **9.** $\dfrac{\sqrt{11x}}{x}$ **11.** $\dfrac{\sqrt{xy}}{y}$ **13.** $\dfrac{3\sqrt{2}}{2}$ **15.** $\dfrac{5\sqrt{3}}{2}$ **17.** $\dfrac{\sqrt{10}}{6}$ **19.** $\dfrac{2\sqrt{15}}{3}$ **21.** $\dfrac{\sqrt{2a}}{8}$

23. $\dfrac{x\sqrt{11}}{11}$ **25.** $\dfrac{\sqrt{14x}}{4}$ **27.** $\dfrac{\sqrt{21a}}{6}$ **29.** $\dfrac{3\sqrt{5x}}{x}$ **31.** $\dfrac{3\sqrt{3a}}{a^2}$ **33.** $\dfrac{5\sqrt{6a}}{6a}$ **35.** $\dfrac{5(\sqrt{3} + 1)}{2}$ **37.** $5(\sqrt{7} - 2)$ **39.** $3(\sqrt{3} + 3)$

41. $2 - \sqrt{2}$ **43.** $3 + \sqrt{3}$ **45.** $\sqrt{5} - \sqrt{2}$ **47.** $\sqrt{6} + \sqrt{3} + \sqrt{2} + 1$ **49.** $-4 + 2\sqrt{2} - 2\sqrt{3} + \sqrt{6}$ **51.** $\dfrac{6 + 6\sqrt{2} + \sqrt{3} + \sqrt{6}}{3}$

53. $\dfrac{5 - \sqrt{15} + \sqrt{30} - 3\sqrt{2}}{2}$ **55.** $\dfrac{7 + 2\sqrt{10}}{3}$ **57.** $2\sqrt{14}$ **59.** $2\sqrt[4]{2}$ **61.** $18\sqrt{3}$ **63.** $5\sqrt{15}$ **65.** $\dfrac{3\sqrt{2}}{2}$

67. $2\sqrt{10} + 2\sqrt{35} + \sqrt{6} + \sqrt{21}$ **69.** $-\dfrac{4 + \sqrt{2} + 2\sqrt{3} + 4\sqrt{6}}{}$

71. $\dfrac{w}{h} = \dfrac{\sqrt{5} + 1}{2} \approx 1.62$ **73.** b   **75.** $\sqrt{2} \cdot \sqrt{2x} = 2\sqrt{x}$ **77.** $\dfrac{x}{\sqrt{2} - 1} = (\sqrt{2} + 1)x$

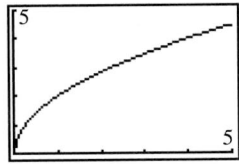

79–81. Answers may vary.   **83.** 4   **85.** $\sqrt[3]{2}$ **87.** $\dfrac{\sqrt[3]{9}}{3}$ **89.** $\dfrac{\sqrt[4]{8}}{2}$

Review Problems

91. $\dfrac{x-3}{4(x+3)}, (x \neq 3, -3)$ **92.** 2   **93.** $\dfrac{1}{8x^6}, x \neq 0$

PROBLEM SET 9.5

1. 16   **3.** 25   **5.** 0   **7.** 125   **9.** 6   **11.** $-\dfrac{1}{3}$ **13.** 16   **15.** $\dfrac{1}{2}$ **17.** $\varnothing$ **19.** 7   **21.** 4   **23.** 2   **25.** 6   **27.** -6 **29.** 2

31. 11   **33.** $-1, -2$ **35.** 12   **37.** $\dfrac{2}{3}$ **39.** $-2, 0$ **41.** $\varnothing$ **43.** 36 years   **45.** 900 feet   **47.** 3.24 feet   **49.** 400 pounds   **51.** c

53.
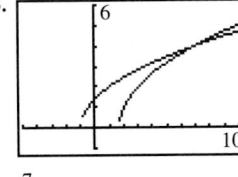
7

55.
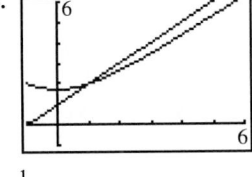
1

57.
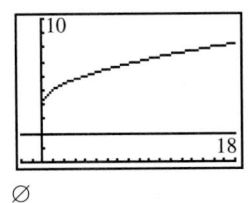
$\varnothing$

59. Answers may vary.   **61.** 9   **63.** $z = 2, y = 2, x = 2$

Review Problems

64. $7000 at 6%, $2000 at 4%   **65.** $4.25   **66.** $(-1, -2)$

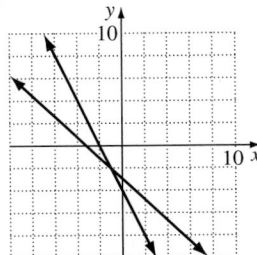

PROBLEM SET 9.6

1. 7   **3.** 11   **5.** $\dfrac{1}{10}$ **7.** $\dfrac{1}{4}$ **9.** 3   **11.** $\dfrac{1}{5}$ **13.** -5 **15.** 2   **17.** $\dfrac{3}{4}$ **19.** $\dfrac{1}{2}$ **21.** -2 **23.** 729   **25.** 25   **27.** 27   **29.** -8

31. $\dfrac{1}{8}$ **33.** $\dfrac{1}{243}$ **35.** $\dfrac{1}{4}$ **37.** $\dfrac{5}{2}$ **39.** $\dfrac{5}{2}$ **41.** $\dfrac{1}{4}$ **43.** 17   **45.** 375   **47.** 25 miles per hour

49. $f(81) = 257{,}000$; In 2051, 81 years after 1970, the average pollution will be 257,000 particles per cubic cm.   **51.** a

53. a. 0, 94, 249, 1170, 1756, 2405, 3110   **b.**

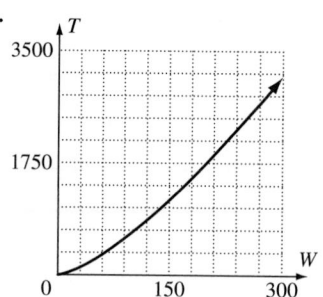

As weight increases, area increases

c. Verify graph   **55.** Answers may vary.   **57.** $\frac{1}{5}$

Review Problems

59. 10 inches   **60.** $y - 8 = 3(x - 6)$ or $y - 11 = 3(x - 7)$; $y = 3x - 10$ **61.** width, 4 meters; length, 11 meters

CHAPTER 9 REVIEW

1. -8 **2.** $-\frac{3}{5}$ **3.** 11   **4.** -11 **5.** Not a real number   **6.** $\frac{2}{5}$ **7.** -2 **8.** -3 **9.** $\frac{2}{5}$, rational   **10.** 1.1, rational

11. 8.660, irrational   **12.** Not a real number   **13.** $10\sqrt{3}$ **14.** $12\sqrt{5}$ **15.** 6   **16.** $12\sqrt{ab}$ **17.** $16\sqrt{6}$ **18.** $3\sqrt[3]{3}$ **19.** $2\sqrt[4]{5}$

20. $\frac{11}{2}$ **21.** $\frac{\sqrt{7y}}{5}$ **22.** 20   **23.** $\frac{\sqrt{15}}{4}$ **24.** $\frac{\sqrt[3]{7}}{4}$ **25.** $3x\sqrt{7}$ **26.** $4y\sqrt{3y}$ **27.** $4x^2\sqrt{5x}$ **28.** $\frac{\sqrt{7}}{y^2}$ **29.** $5x^4\sqrt{3x}$

30. $10x^{11}\sqrt{3x}$ **31.** $20\sqrt{5}$ **32.** $7\sqrt{2b}$ **33.** $5\sqrt{2} - 3\sqrt{3}$ **34.** $6\sqrt{2} + 7\sqrt{3}$ **35.** $-\sqrt[4]{7} + 2\sqrt[3]{5}$ **36.** $13\sqrt[3]{2a}$ **37.** $5\sqrt{2} + 2\sqrt{15}$

38. $7\sqrt{6a} + 12\sqrt{a}$ **39.** $84\sqrt{5} - 105\sqrt{2}$ **40.** $30 + 5\sqrt{14}$ **41.** $72 + 6\sqrt{15} - 8\sqrt{30} - 10\sqrt{2}$ **42.** $25x - 30\sqrt{x} + 9$ **43.** 4

44. -86 **45.** $6\sqrt{5}$ **46.** $\frac{13\sqrt{2}}{10}$ **47.** $\frac{7\sqrt{3}}{3}$ **48.** $\frac{\sqrt{6}}{3}$ **49.** $\frac{\sqrt{17x}}{x}$ **50.** $\frac{x\sqrt{10}}{4}$ **51.** $11(-2 + \sqrt{5})$ **52.** $\frac{21(4 + \sqrt{3})}{13}$

53. $6(\sqrt{5} - \sqrt{3})$ **54.** $\frac{3 + 2\sqrt{3} + 2\sqrt{6} + 3\sqrt{2}}{3}$ **55.** 11   **56.** 5   **57.** -2 **58.** 0, 3   **59.** 8   **60.** $\varnothing$ **61.** $\varnothing$ **62.** 4

63. $\frac{1}{5}$ **64.** 5   **65.** $\frac{1}{3}$ **66.** 16   **67.** $\frac{1}{81}$ **68.** $\sqrt{2} \approx 1.4$ seconds   **69.** 3.14 seconds   **70.** 0.20   **71.** $8(2\sqrt{5} + \sqrt{2})$ meters;

$32\sqrt{10}$ square meters   **72.** 57 species   **73.** 104.2 feet   **74.** 144 feet   **75.** Approximately 0.86% increase per year

CHAPTER 9 TEST

1. 7, -7 **2.** -8 **3.** 4   **4.** $4\sqrt{3}$ **5.** $6x\sqrt{2x}$ **6.** $x^{14}\sqrt{x}$ **7.** $\frac{5}{x}$ **8.** $\frac{\sqrt[3]{5}}{2}$ **9.** $\frac{5}{3}$ **10.** $4x\sqrt{2}$ **11.** $5\sqrt{2}$ **12.** $6\sqrt{xy}$

13. $2x^2\sqrt{5x}$ **14.** $11\sqrt{6}$ **15.** $6\sqrt{2}$ **16.** $32 + 23\sqrt{2}$ **17.** 2   **18.** $16 - 6\sqrt{7}$ **19.** $9x + 12\sqrt{x} + 4$ **20.** $\frac{4\sqrt{5}}{5}$ **21.** $\frac{5(4 - \sqrt{3})}{13}$

22. 2   **23.** 5   **24.** $\frac{1}{3}$ **25.** 4   **26.** $14\sqrt{5}$ **27.** 144 feet

CUMULATIVE REVIEW PROBLEMS (CHAPTERS 1–9)

1. $f(0) = 2151$; In 1985, there were 2,151,000 military personnel   **2.** $\sqrt{1.5} \approx 1.22$; $\sqrt{4.4} \approx 2.10$ **3.** width, 6 meters; length, 14 meters   **4.** $\varnothing$
5. a. $y = -\frac{2}{3}x + \frac{7}{3}$ **b.** $y = 5$ **6.** 466 and 467   **7.** $6x^2 - 7x + 2$ **8.** $8x^3 - 27$ **9.** $\frac{3}{2}$, -4 **10.** $(x - 7)(x - 11)$

11. $\{x|x \geq 2\}$

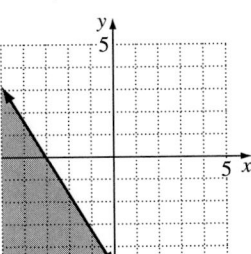

12. $5x + 3y \leq -15$

13. $(-3, -4)$ **14.** 954 deer   **15.** $(2, 3)$

16. a. 45, 90, 135, 180 mi   **b.** $d = 45t$

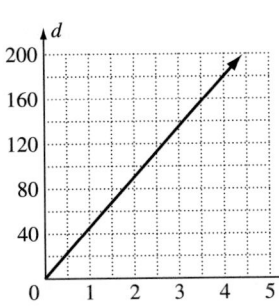

17. \$25.04 billion increase each year   **18.** $-\dfrac{2}{x^4}$

19. $16x^2 + 40x + 25$ **20.** $x(x + 5)(x - 5)$

21. 4 and 5 or -1 and 0   **22.** 5   **23.** $\dfrac{1}{y - 1}$ **24.** $\dfrac{5x - 1}{4x - 3}$

25. $\dfrac{9}{7}$ **26.** $\dfrac{x + 1}{x}$ **27.** \$23,119 for U.S., \$36,231 for Switzerland   **28.** $22\sqrt{3}$ **29.** $\dfrac{6 - \sqrt{11}}{5}$ **30.** 6

Chapter 10

PROBLEM SET 10.1

1. $-6, 6$ **3.** $-9, 9$ **5.** $-\sqrt{7}, \sqrt{7}$ **7.** $-5\sqrt{2}, 5\sqrt{2}$ **9.** $-2, 2$ **11.** $-\dfrac{7}{2}, \dfrac{7}{2}$ **13.** $-\sqrt{6}, \sqrt{6}$ **15.** $-\sqrt{2}, \sqrt{2}$

17. $-2\sqrt{2}, 2\sqrt{2}$ **19.** $-\dfrac{\sqrt{6}}{3}, \dfrac{\sqrt{6}}{3}$ **21.** $-\dfrac{\sqrt{35}}{5}, \dfrac{\sqrt{35}}{5}$ **23.** $-1, 7$ **25.** $-16, 6$ **27.** $-\dfrac{9}{2}, \dfrac{7}{2}$ **29.** $\sqrt{5} - 3, -\sqrt{5} - 3$

31. $2 - 4\sqrt{2}, 2 + 4\sqrt{2}$ **33.** $\dfrac{1}{3} - \dfrac{2\sqrt{3}}{3}, \dfrac{1}{3} + \dfrac{2\sqrt{3}}{3}$ **35.** $-\dfrac{1}{3} - \dfrac{\sqrt{3}}{2}, -\dfrac{1}{3} + \dfrac{\sqrt{3}}{2}$ **37.** 6 weeks   **39.** 50 miles per hour   **41.** 0.10; 10%

43. radius, 7 meters; circumference, 14π meters   **45.** 0.02 cm, rounded   **47.** $60\sqrt{2}$ feet   **49.** 20 meters   **51.** 5   **53.** 16 feet

55. 6 meters   **57.** 7 feet   **59.** b   **61.**

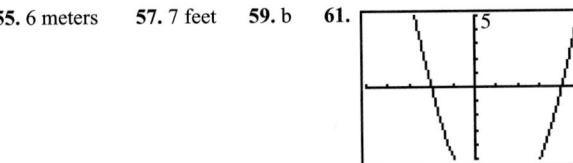

$-2, 4$

63. Verify answers.   **65.** $-\dfrac{\sqrt{ab}}{a}, \dfrac{\sqrt{ab}}{a}$ **67.** $r = \sqrt{\dfrac{A}{p}} - 1$

Review Problems

68. $2(3x + 4)(x + 3)$ **69.** $\dfrac{x - 6}{(x + 6)(x + 2)}$ **70.** $-\sqrt{9} = -3$; $\sqrt{-9}$ is not a real number because the square of two real numbers is always positive.

PROBLEM SET 10.2

1. 36   **3.** 25   **5.** $\dfrac{9}{4}$ **7.** $\dfrac{49}{4}$ **9.** $\dfrac{1}{9}$ **11.** $\dfrac{1}{36}$ **13.** $-7, 1$ **15.** $1 + \sqrt{3}, 1 - \sqrt{3}$ **17.** $3 + 2\sqrt{5}, 3 - 2\sqrt{5}$

19. $-2 + \sqrt{3}, -2 - \sqrt{3}$ **21.** $-\frac{3}{2} - \frac{\sqrt{13}}{2}, -\frac{3}{2} + \frac{\sqrt{13}}{2}$ **23.** $\frac{7}{2} - \frac{\sqrt{37}}{2}, \frac{7}{2} + \frac{\sqrt{37}}{2}$ **25.** $\frac{1}{2}, 3$ **27.** $-\frac{1}{3}, 3$ **29.** $\frac{1}{2} + \frac{\sqrt{2}}{2}, \frac{1}{2} - \frac{\sqrt{2}}{2}$

31. $\frac{1}{3} - \frac{\sqrt{7}}{3}, \frac{1}{3} + \frac{\sqrt{7}}{3}$ **33.** $-\frac{5}{2} - \frac{\sqrt{31}}{2}, -\frac{5}{2} + \frac{\sqrt{31}}{2}$ **35.** $3 - \sqrt{5}, 3 + \sqrt{5}$ **37.** $\frac{1}{3} - \frac{\sqrt{19}}{3}, \frac{1}{3} + \frac{\sqrt{19}}{3}$ **39.** $x^2 + 2x; 1$ **41.** c

43–45. Answers may vary.   **47.** $-\frac{1}{2} - \frac{\sqrt{1 - 4c}}{2}, -\frac{1}{2} + \frac{\sqrt{1 - 4c}}{2}$

Review Problems

49. $\frac{1}{2}, 3$ **50.** $\frac{11}{(x - 3)(x - 4)}$ **51.** $x = -10$

PROBLEM SET 10.3

1. $-5, -3$ **3.** $\frac{-5 - \sqrt{13}}{2}, \frac{-5 + \sqrt{13}}{2}$ **5.** $-2 - \sqrt{10}, -2 + \sqrt{10}$ **7.** $-2 - \sqrt{11}, -2 + \sqrt{11}$ **9.** $-3, 6$ **11.** $-\frac{2}{3}, \frac{3}{2}$

13. $1 - \sqrt{11}, 1 + \sqrt{11}$ **15.** $\frac{1 - \sqrt{57}}{2}, \frac{1 + \sqrt{57}}{2}$ **17.** $\frac{-3 - \sqrt{3}}{6}, \frac{-3 + \sqrt{3}}{6}$ **19.** $\frac{3}{2}$ **21.** $1 - \sqrt{3}, 1 + \sqrt{3}$

23. $-3 - \sqrt{5}, -3 + \sqrt{5}$ **25.** $-\frac{1}{2}, 1$ **27.** $\frac{1}{5}, 2$ **29.** $-2\sqrt{5}, 2\sqrt{5}$ **31.** $1 - \sqrt{2}, 1 + \sqrt{2}$ **33.** $\frac{-11 - \sqrt{33}}{4}, \frac{-11 + \sqrt{33}}{4}$

35. $0, \frac{8}{3}$ **37.** 2   **39.** $-2, 2$ **41.** $-\frac{2}{3}, 4$ **43.** $\frac{11 - \sqrt{41}}{20}, \frac{11 + \sqrt{41}}{20}$ **45.** $2 - \frac{\sqrt{10}}{2}, 2 + \frac{\sqrt{10}}{2}$

47. $\frac{2 - \sqrt{10}}{3}, \frac{2 + \sqrt{10}}{3}$ **49.** -7 **51.** $-9, 0$ **53.** $-5, 9$ **55.** 28 years or 62 years   **57.** $\frac{25 + 5\sqrt{33}}{8}$ seconds ≈ 6.7 seconds

59. length, $\frac{3 + \sqrt{153}}{2} \approx 7.7$ meters; width, $\frac{-3 + \sqrt{153}}{2} \approx 4.7$ meters   **61.** $h = \frac{1 + \sqrt{145}}{4}; b = \frac{-1 + \sqrt{145}}{2}; h \approx 3.3$ inches, $b \approx 5.5$ inches

63. $\frac{-1 + \sqrt{71}}{2}$ mm ≈ 3.7 mm and $\frac{1 + \sqrt{71}}{2} \approx 4.7$ mm   **65.** 10 feet   **67.** 9 cm by 19 cm; 3 cm by 7 cm

69. $\frac{3 + \sqrt{17}}{2}$ days ≈ 3.6 days and $\frac{5 + \sqrt{17}}{2}$ days ≈ 4.6 days   **71.** a   **73.** 100 miles per hour   **75.** Answers may vary.

77. $\frac{3 - \sqrt{6}}{3}, \frac{3 + \sqrt{6}}{3}$ **79.** $\frac{-b + \sqrt{b^2 - 4ac}}{2a} + \frac{-b - \sqrt{b^2 - 4ac}}{2a} = \frac{-2b}{2a} = -\frac{b}{a}$ **81.** $-3\sqrt{3}, \sqrt{3}$ **83.** $9 - 4\sqrt{3}$ meters ≈ 2.1 meters

85. 1.46 in.

Review Problems

86. 2   **87.** $-\frac{8}{3}$ **88.** $x - 2y > 2$

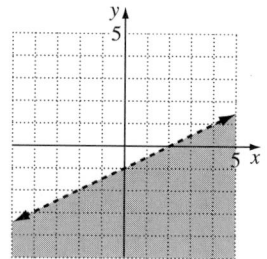

PROBLEM SET 10.4

1. $4i$ **3.** $2i\sqrt{5}$ **5.** $3i\sqrt{5}$ **7.** $5i\sqrt{6}$ **9.** $3 - 3i, 3 + 3i$ **11.** $-7 - 8i, -7 + 8i$ **13.** $2 - i\sqrt{7}, 2 + i\sqrt{7}$

15. $-3 - 3i\sqrt{2}, -3 + 3i\sqrt{2}$ **17.** $-2 - i, -2 + i$ **19.** $3 - 2i, 3 + 2i$ **21.** $6 - 2i, 6 + 2i$ **23.** $5 - i\sqrt{2}, 5 + i\sqrt{2}$

25. $\frac{1}{5} - \frac{i\sqrt{14}}{5}, \frac{1}{5} + \frac{i\sqrt{14}}{4}$ **27.** $\frac{1}{4} - \frac{i\sqrt{19}}{4}, \frac{1}{4} + \frac{i\sqrt{19}}{4}$ **29.** No; there are no real solutions.   **31.** b

33.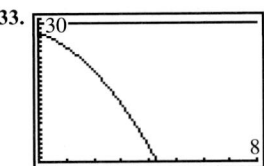

They do not intersect.

35. Answers may vary. **37.** $-\dfrac{5}{4} - \dfrac{i\sqrt{23}}{4}, -\dfrac{5}{4} + \dfrac{i\sqrt{23}}{4}$

Review Problems

39. 128 liters of 8% alcohol solution **40.** 280 miles **41.** $2 - 8\sqrt{6}$

PROBLEM SET 10.5

1. $y = x^2 + 6x + 5$

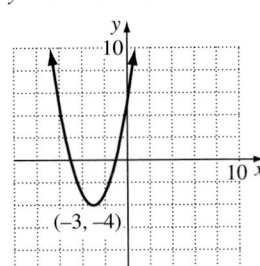

$(-3, -4)$

3. $f(x) = x^2 + 4x + 3$

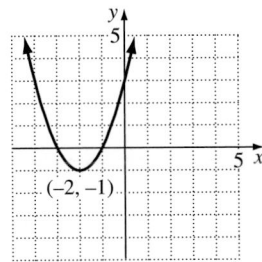

$(-2, -1)$

5. $y = x^2 + x$

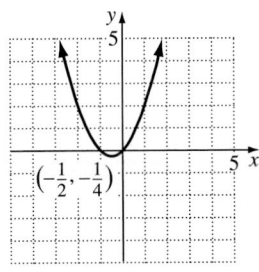

$\left(-\frac{1}{2}, -\frac{1}{4}\right)$

7. $f(x) = x^2 - 4$

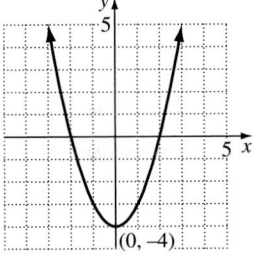

$(0, -4)$

9. $y = -x^2 - 1$

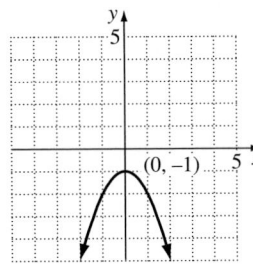

$(0, -1)$

11. $y = -x^2 + 4x - 3$

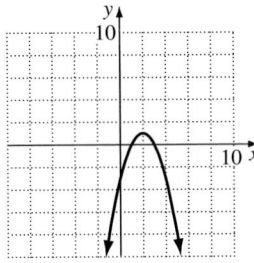

13. $f(x) = -2x^2 + 16x - 30$

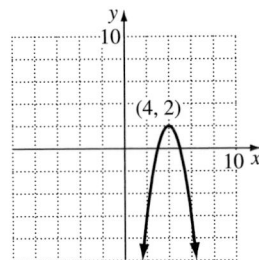

$(4, 2)$

15. $y = x^2 + 4x + 4$

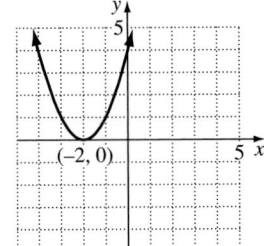

$(-2, 0)$

17. $g(x) = x^2 - 4x + 6$

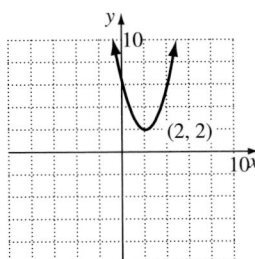

$(2, 2)$

19. $y = -x^2 - 6x - 7$

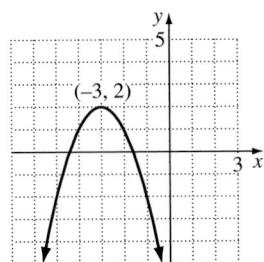

$(-3, 2)$

21. $f(x) = -2x^2 + 4x$

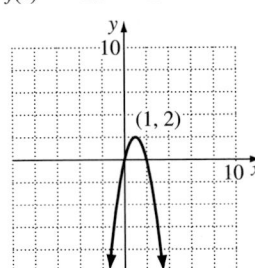

$(1, 2)$

23. $y = -x^2 + 4x - 1$

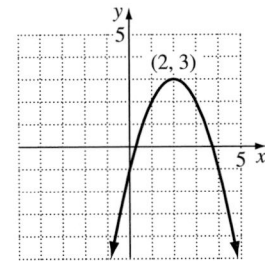

$(2, 3)$

25. $h(x) = 2x^2 + 8x + 1$

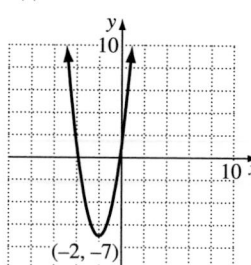

$(-2, -7)$

27. a. 2   **b.** 3   **c.** 1   **29.** (25, 13.5); In a year with 25 in. of rainfall, the tree grows 13.5 inches.
31. $54,610; 1.68%

33. a. 5 seconds   **b.** 80; in 0 seconds, or before the person throws the ball, it is at a height of 80 ft.   **c.** 2 seconds   **d.** 144 feet
e.

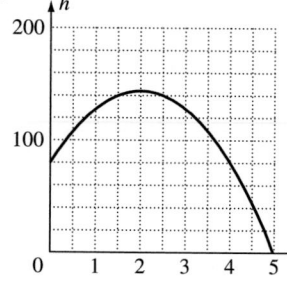

35. c   **37.** d

39. $y = 0.011x^2 - 0.097x + 4.1$

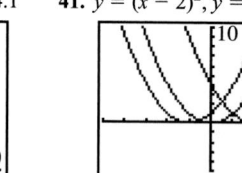

(4.47, 3.89); in mid 1974,
about 3.89 million people
held more than one job.
51. 2   **53.** 0

41. $y = (x - 2)^2, y = x^2, y = (x + 1)^2$

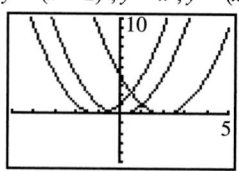

They all have the same shape, but
a different y-intercept and vertex.

43–47. Answers may vary.   **49.** $y = 2x^2 - 8$ and $y = -2x^2 + 8$

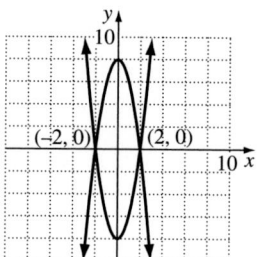

$(-2, 0)$ $(2, 0)$

Review Problems

55. 3.97×10^{-3} **56.** $y = \frac{2}{3}x - 4$ **57.** $y = \frac{3}{4}x - 2$

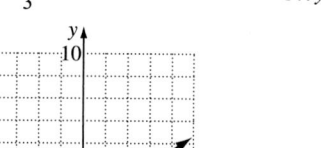

CHAPTER 10 REVIEW

1. ±8   **2.** $\pm\sqrt{17}$ **3.** $\pm 5\sqrt{3}$ **4.** 0, 6   **5.** $-4 - \sqrt{5}, -4 + \sqrt{5}$ **6.** 1, 6   **7.** $\frac{4}{3} - \sqrt{2}, \frac{4}{3} + \sqrt{2}$

8. $4\sqrt{13}$ in.; 14.42 in.   **9.** $6\sqrt{6}$ ft; 14.70 ft   **10.** 15 weeks   **11.** 600 feet   **12.** 3, 9   **13.** $3 - \sqrt{5}, 3 + \sqrt{5}$

14. $2 - \frac{\sqrt{3}}{3}, 2 + \frac{\sqrt{3}}{3}$ **15.** $-3, \frac{1}{2}$ **16.** $\frac{9 - \sqrt{21}}{6}, \frac{9 + \sqrt{21}}{6}$ **17.** $\frac{-1 - \sqrt{5}}{4}, \frac{-1 + \sqrt{5}}{4}$ **18.** $\frac{1}{2}, 5$ **19.** $-2, \frac{10}{3}$

20. $\dfrac{7 - \sqrt{37}}{6}, \dfrac{7 + \sqrt{37}}{6}$ **21.** $-3, 3$ **22.** $-2, 8$ **23.** $\dfrac{3 + \sqrt{29}}{2}$ seconds ≈ 4.2 seconds   **24.** $l = 1 + \sqrt{17}, w = -1 + \sqrt{17}$;

$l \approx 5.1, w \approx 3.1$ **25.** $-1 + \sqrt{17}$ feet and $1 + \sqrt{17}$ feet; 3.1 feet and 5.1 feet   **26.** 1990   **27.** $9i$

28. $4i\sqrt{3}$ **29.** $i\sqrt{17}$ **30.** $4 - 7i; 4 + 7i$ **31.** $-\dfrac{1}{7} - \dfrac{3}{7}i\sqrt{3}, -\dfrac{1}{7} + \dfrac{3}{7}i\sqrt{3}$ **32.** $2 - 3i, 2 + 3i$ **33.** $\dfrac{3}{2} - \dfrac{\sqrt{7}}{2}i, \dfrac{3}{2} + \dfrac{\sqrt{7}}{2}i$

34. $\dfrac{1}{6} - \dfrac{\sqrt{23}}{6}i, \dfrac{1}{6} + \dfrac{\sqrt{23}}{6}i$ **35.** $\dfrac{3}{4} - \dfrac{\sqrt{31}}{4}i, \dfrac{3}{4} + \dfrac{\sqrt{31}}{4}i$ **36.** $0.54 or $17.46 per pair; could be hired

37. $y = x^2 + 4x - 5$ **38.** $y = -x^2 + 6x - 9$ **39.** $y = x^2 - 6x + 7$ **40.** $y = -x^2 + 4x$

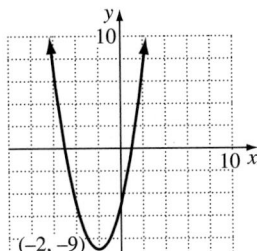   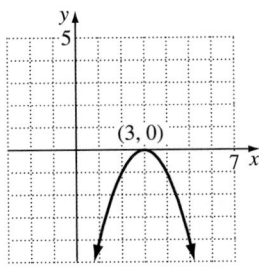   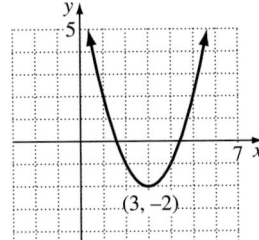   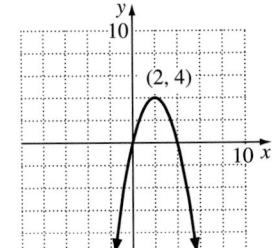

41. $y = x^2 - 4x + 10$ **42.** $y = -x^2 - 3$ **43. a.** 10 seconds   **b.** 5 seconds   **c.** 400 feet

d.

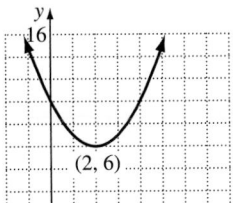   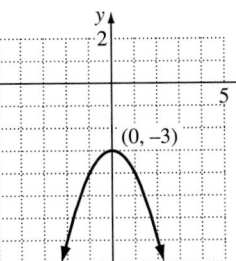   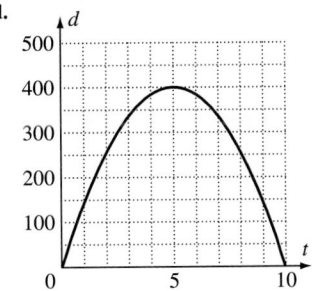

44. (4, 4.27); in 1987, there were 4.27 million secretaries.

CHAPTER 10 TEST

1. $-\sqrt{6}, \sqrt{6}$ **2.** $-\dfrac{5}{3}, 0$ **3.** $\dfrac{-5 - \sqrt{13}}{6}, \dfrac{-5 + \sqrt{13}}{6}$ **4.** $2 - \sqrt{5}, 2 + \sqrt{5}$ **5.** $1 - \sqrt{2}, 1 + \sqrt{2}$ **6.** $\dfrac{1 - \sqrt{3}}{3}, \dfrac{1 + \sqrt{3}}{3}$

7. $\dfrac{1}{4}, \dfrac{1}{2}$ **8.** $-\dfrac{7}{2}, \dfrac{5}{2}$ **9.** $\dfrac{3 - \sqrt{6}}{3}, \dfrac{3 + \sqrt{6}}{3}$ **10.** $1 - 2i, 1 + 2i$ **11.** $-2 - \sqrt{7}, -2 + \sqrt{7}$ **12.** $11i$ **13.** $-5i\sqrt{3}$

14. $-6i, 6i$ **15.** $5 - 5i, 5 + 5i$ **16.** $2 - i\sqrt{3}, 2 + i\sqrt{3}$

17. $y = x^2 - 2x - 8$ **18.** $y = -2x^2 + 16x - 24$ **19.** $PQ = 4\sqrt{5}$ yards   **20.** $\sqrt{6}$ inches   **21.** 7 sides

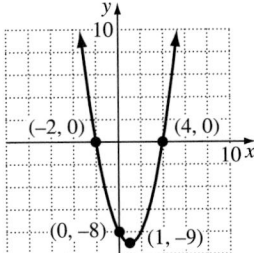   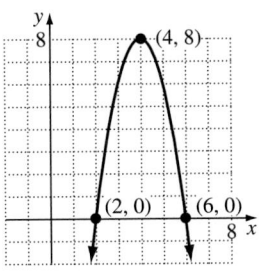

Appendix

1. 2   **2.** 7   **3.** 6   **4.** $\varnothing$ **5.** $\{x|x<2\}$ 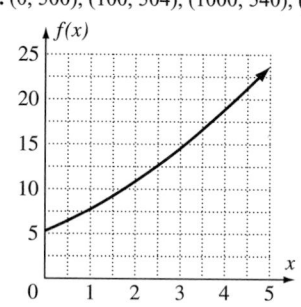   **6.** -15 **7.** $-6,3$ **8.** $-1\frac{1}{2}, -\frac{2}{3}$

9. -8 **10.** -6 **11.** $-2,-3$ **12.** 9   **13.** $2-2\sqrt{5}, 2+2\sqrt{5}$ **14.** $-5,3$ **15.** $1-\dfrac{\sqrt{3}}{3}, 1+\dfrac{\sqrt{3}}{3}$ **16.** $-1-i, -1+i\}$

17. $(3,3)$ **18.** $(-2,2)$ **19.** All real values of x where $3x-4y=4$ **20.** $t=\dfrac{ab}{a+b}$ **21.** 81.53 million   **22.a.** 23,000   **b.** 52,000
c. 1985, 1986, 1987   **23.a.** 1970, 1984, 1985; 8 per 100,000   **b.** 1980; 10.2 per 100,000   **24.** No; 15 \$10 decreases will result in a maximum
profit, then profit goes down.   **25.a.** $-\$204.9$ billion   **b.** $-\$123$ billion   **c.** 61.375 times   **26.** 263 million; black, 31.56 million;
white, 220.92 million   **27.** Canada, 116; U.S., 555; Spain, 90; S. Africa, 369; Singapore, 229; Hong Kong, 179; N. Ireland, 126; Mexico, 97; U.K.,
93; Australia, 91; Switzerland, 85; France, 84; Italy, 80; Denmark, 66; Norway, 59; Netherlands, 49; Japan, 36   **28. a.** 2007   **b.** Fairly close

29.a. $\dfrac{3}{11}$ **b.** $\dfrac{9}{6.5}$ **c.** $\dfrac{33}{29.2}$ **30.a.** 35 miles, 70 miles, 105 miles, 140 miles

b.
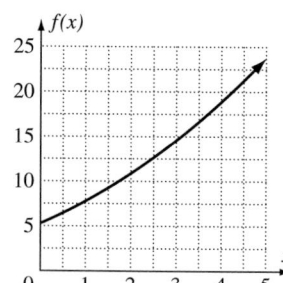

31. a. $S=0.04x+500$ **b.** $(0, 500), (100, 504), (1000, 540), (10,000, 900)$ **c.** \$540

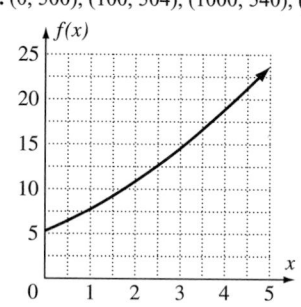

32. a. $(0, 5.3), (1, 7.8), (2, 10.9), (3, 14.6), (4, 18.9), (5, 23.8)$ **b.** As time goes by, the number increases.

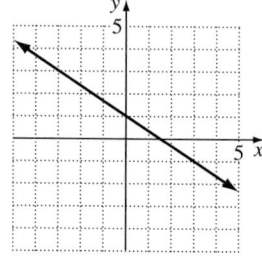

33. a. -1.5, number is decreasing   **b.** Number is increasing
c. Consistent spacing is not used between years.   **34. a.** Slope is the same.
b. Never   **35.** $y+3=0$ **36.** $3x-2y=6$

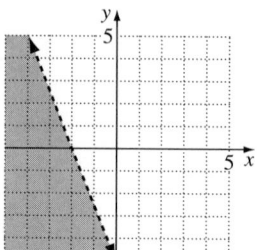

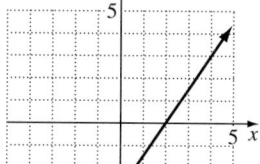

37. $y=-\dfrac{2}{3}x+1$ **38.** $5x+2y<-10$ **39.** $y>-2x+3$

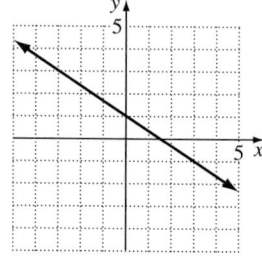

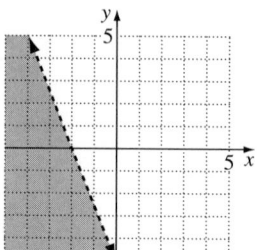

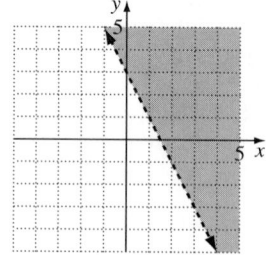

40. $y = x^3 - x$; $-6, 0, 0, 0, 6$

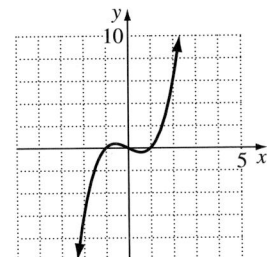

41. $y = x^2 - 2x - 8$

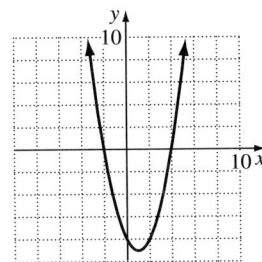

42. $(1, 4)$

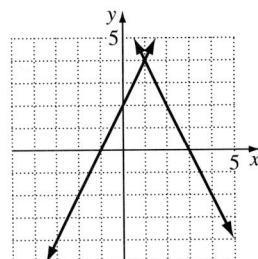

43. $2x + y < 4, x > 2$

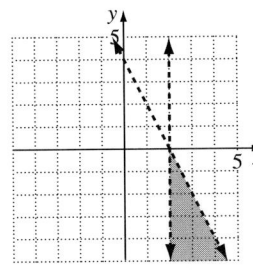

44. a. $p = \dfrac{T - D}{m}$ **b.** $57 **45.** 20 years **46.** 11 years **47.** 50, 219; in 1994, there were 50,219 cases commenced. **48. a.** 14.7; the atmospheric pressure at the surface is 14.7 pounds per square inch. **b.** 0.445; the atmospheric pressure increases at 0.445 pound per square inch for each increase of 1 foot below the surface. **c.** 13,364.7 pounds per square inch **49. a.** 4.75
b. $y - 111 = 4.75(x - 62)$ or $y - 130 = 4.75(x - 66)$ **c.** $y = 4.75x - 183.5$
d. 120.5 lbs, 158.5 lbs
e. reasonably close **50.** 562; if a plane is landing at 90 feet per second, it will need 562 feet of runway; yes, the runway needs to be at least 562 feet. **51. a.** $4x^2 + 72x + 320$
b. $f(x) = 4x^2 + 72x + 320$ **c.** 396; the total area is 396 square meters with a sidewalk 1 meter wide. **52. a.** 1986 **b.** (6, 524) **53. a.** 5; it costs $5000 to remove 20%. 80; it costs $80,000 to remove 80%. 180; it costs $180,000 to remove 90%. **b.** $x = 100$ **c.** Goes to infinity; impossible to remove 100% of pollutants. **d.**

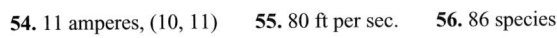

54. 11 amperes, (10, 11) **55.** 80 ft per sec. **56.** 86 species
57. $3\sqrt{2} \approx 4.24$ **58.** 5 feet **59.** (125, 66.5); when the ball has traveled 125 feet from the plate, it is 66.5 feet high **60.** 60%
61. Number of sides, 5 **62.** 1997 **63.** $3 + \sqrt{6}$ seconds or $3 - \sqrt{6}$ second; 5.4 seconds or 0.6 second **64.** $(4x - 1)(x - 3)$
65. $(2x - 7)(2x + 7)$ **66.** $(2x - 5)^2$ **67.** $(x - 1)(x + 1)(x + 3)$ **68.** $3(x - 5)(x + 5)$
69. $2(x + 7)(x - 3)$ **70.** $-(3x - 2)(2x - 1)$ **71.** $x(x^2 + 4)(x + 2)(x - 2)$ **72.** Prime
73. $x(x - 5)^2$ **74.** $(x - 2)(x^2 + 2x + 4)$ **75.** $2xy^2(7xy - 5x + 2)$
76. $(x + 7y)(x - 3y)$ **77.** $(3x + 4y)(2x - 7y)$ **78.** $(4x - 5y)^2$ **79.** 5
80. 4 **81.** -19 **82.** $20y - 33$ **83.** $-x^2 + 4x + 8$ **84.** $24x^2y^3 - x^2y - 13x^2 + 3$
85. $3x^2 + x - 14$ **86.** $21x^2 - 23xy - 20y^2$ **87.** $x^2 - 28x + 40$ **88.** $20y^3 + 9y^2 - 26y + 6$ **89.** $x^3 + y^3$ **90.** $-2x^4 + 3x^2 - 1$
91. $-2x^2y^2 + \dfrac{xy}{2}$ **92.** $3x - 2$ **93.** $\dfrac{16}{x^3}$ **94.** x^9 **95.** $\dfrac{3x - 5}{4x - 1}$ **96.** $\dfrac{2y - 1}{y - 7}$ **97.** $\dfrac{-3}{(y + 6)(y - 4)}$ **98.** $\dfrac{3x^2 + 6x + 16}{(x - 2)(x + 3)}$
99. $\dfrac{-7x}{(x + 3)(x - 1)(x - 4)}$ **100.** $\dfrac{1 - 2x}{4x - 1}$ **101.** $5x^5\sqrt{2x}$ **102.** $12\sqrt{5b}$ **103.** $\sqrt[3]{2}$ **104.** $3x\sqrt{2}$ **105.** $\sqrt{10} + 3\sqrt{35}$
106. $-16 + 4\sqrt{3}$ **107.** $9 + 4\sqrt{5}$ **108.** $\dfrac{2\sqrt{3b}}{3b}$ **109.** $3\sqrt[3]{2}$ **110.** $-5 + \sqrt{30}$ **111.** $\dfrac{11\sqrt{5} + 33}{-4}$ **112.** 4 **113. a.** 6, 169
b. $0, 6, \sqrt{169}$ **c.** $-14, 0, 6, \sqrt{169}$ **d.** $-14, 0, 0.45, 6, 7\frac{1}{5}, \sqrt{169}$ **e.** $-\pi, \sqrt{3}$ **f.** $-14, -\pi, 0, 0.45, \sqrt{3}, 6, 7\frac{1}{5}, \sqrt{169}$
114. -364 **115.** Commutative Property of Addition **116.** Associative Property of Multiplication **117.** Multiplicative Inverse Property
118. $10x + 20$ **119. a.** $y = -\dfrac{3}{2}x + \dfrac{5}{2}$ **b.** $y = 4$ **120.** $y - 6 = -2(x + 2)$ or $y + 4 = -2(x - 3)$; $y = -2x + 2$ **121.** $5i\sqrt{3}$ **122.** 43
123. 548 and 549 **124.** The pieces are 15 in., 32 in., and 40 in. **125.** $916\frac{2}{3}$ ft and $1043\frac{1}{3}$ ft **126.** $155 **127.** 27 hours
128. 2024 students **129.** 92% or better **130. a.** After 14 trips **b.** The lines intersect at $x = 14$. **131.** $0.16 per oz
132. 225 deer **133.** 45 feet **134. a.** 50 feet by 100 feet **b.** 20 feet to 1 inch **135.** 16 feet **136. a.** $10\pi \approx 31.4$ meters
b. $25\pi \approx 78.5$ square meters **137.** 9 times larger **138.** 3 apples and 2 avocados **139.** Cost of pen, $1.80; cost of pad, $2
140. a. Mississippi is $14,894; Connecticut is $28,110. **b.** $9933; 55% **c.** 18% below **141.** $2 + \sqrt{3}$ or $2 - \sqrt{3}$; 3.7 or 0.3
142. 25°, 35°, 120° **143.** width, 4 meters; length, 9 meters **144.** 500 sec **145.** 13.3 feet **146.** 96 miles/hr **147.** $1075 million
148. $1225 at 5%, $2775 at 9% **149.** 7.25 hours **150.** $6\frac{2}{3}$ gallons of 80%, $3\frac{1}{3}$ gallons of 65% **151.** 3 days **152.** Speed of boat in still water, 20 miles per hour; rate of current, 4 miles per hour **153.** Rate of plane A, 250 miles per hour; rate of B, 200 miles per hour **154.** 2485; $\dfrac{n^2 + n}{2}$
155. $z > w + 4$ **156. a.** $x = 10, y = 4, z = 8$ **b.** $a = 4, b = 8, c = 10$ **c.** $r = 10, s = 2, w = 8$ **157.** c **158. a.** 1, 3, 5, 7, 9, $2n - 1$
b. 5, 8, 11, 14, 17, $3(n + 1) - 1$ **c.** 1, 4, 9, 16, 25, n^2 **d.** 0, 3, 8, 15, 24, $n^2 - 1$ **e.** 1, 8, 27, 64, 125, n^3 **159.** five
160. $a = 2, b = -3, c = -1, d = 3, e = -2, f = 1$ **161.** 45 **162.** 12 ways **163.** 55 cans **164.** $\dfrac{1}{2}$ **165.** 40 cubes

Index

Definitions, Rules, and Formulas

The Real Numbers

Natural Numbers: $\{1, 2, 3, \ldots\}$
Whole Numbers: $\{0, 1, 2, 3, \ldots\}$
Integers: $\{\ldots, -3, -2, -1, 0, 1, 2, 3, \ldots\}$
Rational Numbers: $\{\frac{a}{b} \mid a$ and b are integers, $b \neq 0\}$
Irrational Numbers: $\{x \mid x$ is real and not rational$\}$

Basic Rules of Algebra

Commutative: $a + b = b + a$; $ab = ba$
Associative: $(a + b) + c = a + (b + c)$;
$(ab)c = a(bc)$
Distributive: $a(b + c) = ab + ac$;
$a(b - c) = ab - ac$
Identity: $a + 0 = a$; $a \cdot 1 = a$
Inverse: $a + (-a) = 0$; $a \cdot \frac{1}{a} = 1 \ (a \neq 0)$
Multiplication Properties: $(-1)a = -a$;
$(-1)(-a) = a$; $a \cdot 0 = 0$; $(-a)(b) = (a)(-b) = -ab$;
$(-a)(-b) = ab$

Order of Operations

1. Perform operations above and below any fraction bar, following steps (2) through (5).

2. Perform operations inside grouping symbols, innermost grouping symbols first, following steps (3) through (5).

3. Simplify exponential expressions.

4. Do multiplication or division as they occur, working from left to right.

5. Do addition and subtraction as they occur, working from left to right.

Set-Builder Notation and Graphs

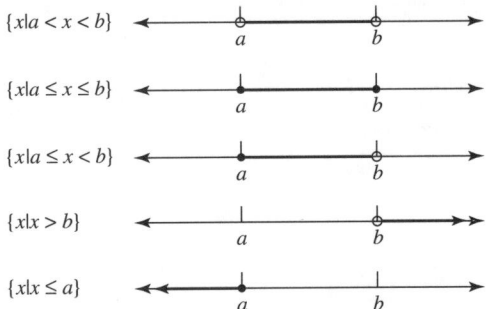

$\{x \mid a < x < b\}$

$\{x \mid a \leq x \leq b\}$

$\{x \mid a \leq x < b\}$

$\{x \mid x > b\}$

$\{x \mid x \leq a\}$

Slope Formula

$$\text{slope } (m) = \frac{\text{change in } y}{\text{change in } x} = \frac{y_2 - y_1}{x_2 - x_1} \quad (x_1 \neq x_2)$$

Equations of Lines

1. *Slope-intercept form:* $y = mx + b$
   m is the line's slope and b is its y-intercept.

2. *Standard form:* $Ax + By = C$

3. *Point-slope form:* $y - y_1 = m(x - x_1)$
   m is the line's slope and (x_1, y_1) is a fixed point on the line.

4. *Horizontal line parallel to the x-axis:* $y = b$

5. *Vertical line parallel to the y-axis:* $x = a$

Linear Function

$$f(x) = mx + b$$

Graph is a line with slope m.

Properties of Exponents

1. $x^m \cdot x^n = x^{m+n}$
2. $(x^m)^n = x^{mn}$
3. $(xy)^m = x^m y^m$
4. $\dfrac{x^m}{x^n} = x^{m-n}$
5. $\left(\dfrac{x}{y}\right)^m = \dfrac{x^m}{y^m}$
6. $x^0 = 1$, where $x \neq 0$
7. $x^{-n} = \dfrac{1}{x^n}$ and $\dfrac{1}{x^{-n}} = x^n$, where $x \neq 0$

Special Factorizations

1. *Difference of two squares:*
$$A^2 - B^2 = (A + B)(A - B)$$
2. *Perfect square trinomials:*
$$A^2 + 2AB + B^2 = (A + B)^2$$
$$A^2 - 2AB + B^2 = (A - B)^2$$
3. *Sum of two cubes:*
$$A^3 + B^3 = (A + B)(A^2 - AB + B^2)$$
4. *Difference of two cubes:*
$$A^3 - B^3 = (A - B)(A^2 + AB + B^2)$$

Variation

English Statement	Equation
y varies directly as x. y is proportional to x.	$y = kx$
y varies inversely as x. y is inversely proportional to x.	$y = \dfrac{k}{x}$

Properties of Radicals

1. $\sqrt[n]{x}\,\sqrt[n]{y} = \sqrt[n]{xy}$
2. $\dfrac{\sqrt[n]{x}}{\sqrt[n]{y}} = \sqrt[n]{\dfrac{x}{y}}$ $(y \neq 0)$

Triangles

1. The sum of the measures of the interior angles of a triangle is $180°$.
2. Similar triangles have corresponding angles with the same measure and corresponding sides that are proportional. Two triangles are similar if two angles of one are equal in measure to two corresponding angles of the other.

Fractional Exponents

1. $x^{1/n} = \sqrt[n]{x}$
2. $x^{m/n} = (\sqrt[n]{x})^m = \sqrt[n]{x^m}$
3. $x^{-m/n} = \dfrac{1}{x^{m/n}} = \dfrac{1}{(\sqrt[n]{x})^m} = \dfrac{1}{\sqrt[n]{x^m}}$

The Quadratic Formula

If $ax^2 + bx + c = 0$ and $a \neq 0$,

then $x = \dfrac{-b \pm \sqrt{b^2 - 4ac}}{2a}$.

Quadratic Functions and Their Graphs

1. The graph of the quadratic function $y = ax^2 + bx + c$ is called a parabola, shaped like a cup. If $a > 0$, the parabola opens upward, and if $a < 0$, the graph opens downward. The turning point of the graph is the vertex.
2. Graph $y = ax^2 + bx + c$ by finding any x-intercepts (replace y with 0), the y-intercept (replace x with 0), the vertex, and additional points near the vertex and intercepts. The x-coordinate of the vertex is $-\dfrac{b}{2a}$. The y-coordinate is found by substituting $-\dfrac{b}{2a}$ for x in the quadratic function and solving for y.
3. The vertex of $y = ax^2 + bx + c$ is a minimum point when $a > 0$ and a maximum point when $a < 0$.

Imaginary and Complex Numbers

1. $i = \sqrt{-1}$ and $i^2 = -1$
2. An imaginary number is any number in the form $a + bi$, where $b \neq 0$. If b is permitted to be 0, $a + bi$ is called a complex number.

3. The Pythagorean Theorem

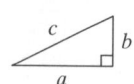

In any right triangle with hypotenuse of length c and legs of length a and b, $c^2 = a^2 + b^2$.